MW01039649

EDITORIAL BOARD

UNIVERSITY CASEBOOK SERIES®

FINANCIAL REGULATION: LAW AND POLICY

MICHAEL S. BARR
The Roy F. and Jean Humphrey Proffitt Professor of Law
University of Michigan Law School
Professor of Public Policy
Gerald R. Ford School of Public Policy

HOWELL E. JACKSON
James S. Reid, Jr., Professor of Law
Harvard Law School

MARGARET E. TAHYAR
Partner
Davis Polk & Wardwell LLP
Bruce W. Nichols Lecturer in Law
Harvard Law School

The publisher is not engaged in rendering legal or other professional advice, and this publication is not a substitute for the advice of an attorney. If you require legal or other expert advice, you should seek the services of a competent attorney or other professional.

444 Cedar Street, Suite 700
St. Paul, MN 55101
1-877-888-1330

Printed in the United States of America

IS
78-1-63459-295-6

For Hannah, Avital, Dani, and Etai,
who keep me focused on what matters.

For WHJ, WD, and KBK,
who introduced me to the law many years ago.

For my beloved husband, Ben,
and our three sons, Christiaan, Julian, and Adam,
in the hope that their generation will do better than ours with the tangled legacies of Hamilton, Jefferson, and Jackson.

[I]t is one of the properties of Banks to increase the active capital of a country. . . . The money of one individual, while he is waiting for an opportunity to employ it by being either deposited in the Bank for safe keeping, or invested in its Stock, is in a condition to administer to the wants of others, without being put out of his own reach. . . . This yields an extra profit, arising from what is paid for the use of his money by others, when he could not himself make use of it, and keeps the money itself in a state of incessant activity. . . . This additional employment given to money, and the faculty of a bank to lend and circulate a greater sum than the amount of its stock in coin, are all to the purposes of trade and industry, an absolute increase of capital. . . . And thus by contributing to enlarge the mass of industrious and commercial enterprise, banks become nurseries of national wealth. . . .

Alexander Hamilton, Report on a National Bank (1790)

I sincerely believe, with you, that banking establishments are more dangerous than standing armies; and that the principle of spending money to be paid by posterity, under the name of funding, is but swindling futurity on a large scale. . . . Bank-paper must be suppressed, and the circulating medium must be restored to the nation to whom it belongs.

Letters from Thomas Jefferson to John Taylor (1816) and John Wayles Epps (1813)

It is to be regretted that the rich and powerful too often bend the acts of government to their selfish purposes. Distinctions in society will always exist under every just government. Equality of talents, of education, or of wealth cannot be produced by human institutions. . . . [B]ut when the laws undertake to add to these natural and just advantages artificial distinctions, to grant titles, gratuities, and exclusive privileges, to make the rich richer and the potent more powerful, the humble members of society—the farmers, mechanics, and laborers—who have neither the time nor the means of securing like favors to themselves, have a right to complain of the injustice of their Government. There are no necessary evils in government. Its evils exist only in its abuses. If it would confine itself to equal protection, and, as Heaven does its rains, shower its favors alike on the high and the low, the rich and the poor, it would be an unqualified blessing. In the Act before me there seems to be a wide and unnecessary departure from these just principles.

Andrew Jackson, Veto Message Regarding the Reauthorization of the Second Bank of the United States (1832)

AUTHOR BIOGRAPHIES

Michael S. Barr

Michael S. Barr is the Roy F. and Jean Humphrey Proffitt Professor of Law at the University of Michigan Law School, Professor of Public Policy at the Gerald R. Ford School of Public Policy, Faculty Director of the Center on Finance, Law, and Policy at the University of Michigan, and a nonresident Senior Fellow at the Center for American Progress and at the Brookings Institution. He served under President Obama from 2009–2010 as the U.S. Department of the Treasury's Assistant Secretary for Financial Institutions, and was a key architect of the Dodd-Frank Wall Street Reform and Consumer Protection Act of 2010. In the Clinton Administration, Barr served as Special Advisor to President William J. Clinton, Deputy Assistant Secretary of the Treasury for Community Development Policy, Special Assistant to the Treasury Secretary, and Special Advisor and Counselor on the Policy Planning Staff at the State Department. During the 1993 October Term, he was a law clerk for Associate Justice David H. Souter. Additional information on Professor Barr's activities is available at http://www.law.umich.edu/FacultyBio/Pages/FacultyBio.aspx?FacID=msbarr.

Howell E. Jackson

Howell E. Jackson is the James S. Reid, Jr., Professor of Law at Harvard Law School. Since joining the Harvard faculty in 1989, he has authored numerous scholarly articles and other publications on financial regulation. He has also advised government officials on regulatory policy in the United States and around the world. Jackson is the founding editor of the SSRN Regulation of Financial Institutions eJournal and a member of the academic advisory panel for the Cambridge University Press financial and corporate law series. Since 2005, Jackson has been a trustee of CREF and affiliated TIAA-CREF mutual funds. He occasionally serves as consultant or expert witness in public enforcement actions and private litigation against financial services firms. During the 1983 October Term, he was a law clerk for Associate Justice Thurgood Marshall. Additional information on Professor Jackson's activities is available at http://hls.harvard.edu/faculty/directory/10423/Jackson.

Margaret E. Tahyar

Margaret E. Tahyar is a partner in the Financial Institutions Group at Davis Polk & Wardwell LLP. Since joining Davis Polk in 1989, she has advised financial institutions on a wide range of regulatory reform, enforcement, and transactions. In addition to her full-time law practice, Tahyar teaches part-time at Harvard Law School (Bruce W. Nichols Lecturer in Law 2015 & 2016) and has also taught as an adjunct at Columbia Law School. She writes and speaks frequently and is recognized as a leading lawyer in the area of financial regulation (band 1 in Chambers and National Law Journal's Outstanding Women Lawyers 2015). After becoming a partner in 1997, she spent 12 years in Europe, first in London and then in Paris. During the 1988 October Term, she was a law clerk for Associate Justice Thurgood Marshall. Additional information on Ms. Tahyar's activities is available at http://www.davispolk.com/lawyers/margaret-tahyar/.

PREFACE

This textbook approaches the teaching of financial regulation in an entirely new way, as is appropriate in the aftermath of the most systemic financial crisis in the last 70 years, which was followed by a major shift in regulatory design. We analyze and compare the market and regulatory architecture of the entire U.S. financial sector as it exists today, from banks, insurance companies, and broker-dealers, to asset managers, complex financial conglomerates, and government-sponsored enterprises. We explore a range of financial activities, from consumer finance and investment to payment systems, securitization, short-term wholesale funding, money markets, and derivatives. We examine a range of regulatory techniques, including supervision, enforcement, and rule-writing, as well as crisis-fighting tools such as resolution and the lender of last resort. We also note the cross-border implications of U.S. rules, and compare, where appropriate, the U.S. financial regulatory framework and policy choices to those in other places around the globe, especially the European Union.

This textbook is different in another way. We have designed each chapter to be a modular, teachable unit. Each professor can easily construct a syllabus that matches his or her own interests, credit-hours, and perspectives. We have also prepared an internet supplement with additional materials, which will be made available to both professors and students. It is available at https://h2o.law.harvard.edu/playlists/27055. The internet supplement, to which we intend to add materials from time to time, will contain case studies and practice-oriented problem sets that are geared towards experiential learning, as well as further primary materials and secondary sources that may be of interest to professors as they make choices about which portions of financial regulation to emphasize in their classes and syllabi.

Our goal is to give students the tools to understand how American history and political economy have shaped the regulatory perimeter, how different policy choices have been made at different times across different parts of the financial sector, and how these choices—whether crisis-driven, accidental, or made in the constant dialectic among legislators, regulators, markets, technological change, the users of financial services and the broader public—matter a great deal in shaping not only financial stability, but also how the financial sector supports the economy and society. Students should come away from the book with both technical skills, and with the situational awareness to understand the theoretical, historical, political, and policy context of key regulatory challenges in the financial sector. Both the technical and policy level skills are essential to be an outstanding lawyer, regulator, or policy-maker in today's world.

The regulation of the financial sector has, for many hundreds of years, been at the center of the cross cutting interests of money, private enterprise, and sovereign power. From European kings' grants of bank monopolies to finance their wars, to struggles in the early American republic between federal and state power over banks and insurance, to the regulatory paradigm shifts of the New Deal, and the recent Financial Crisis, financial regulation has always been the focus of passionate public debate. Many of the most vocal voices have been stakeholders who benefited from the status quo as well as those who looked to profit from its overthrow. There is no reason why today's debates over financial regulation should be any less ardently contested than stakeholder battles of centuries past. Indeed, to a considerable degree, yesterday's debates are still with us. It took decades before the history of the Great Depression was understood, and how the lessons from it should be applied today is still hotly debated. It is hardly surprising that no consensus has yet emerged on either the causes of, or the appropriate regulatory responses to, the Financial Crisis.

Each of your three co-authors comes to the writing of this book with different experiences and points of view. Our goal in this textbook is to set forth, as fairly as we can, the multiple sides of policies, debates, and choices as they existed in history and present them so that professors and students can draw their own lessons and reach their own conclusions. We have not written this book to advance our own views or policy preferences, and each of us can point to excerpts or statements in the book with which we disagree, sometimes strongly, but which are presented here to challenge the reader at home and to promote discussions in the classroom. While many of the topics covered in this book involve events or transactions in which one or more of the authors participated in a professional or official capacity, the materials in this book are drawn solely from public sources and do not contain any confidential, nonpublic information from the consulting, government, or legal practice of the authors. The textbook reflects the work of the three co-authors and does not reflect the views of any university, law firm, or other entity with which any co-author is affiliated.

Financial markets, and thus financial regulations, are always changing, whether it be at the legislative, regulatory or judicial level. The new presidential administration in 2017 is likely to lead to further change. The cut-off date for the printed book is December 31, 2015, with just a few exceptions. Those looking for materials covering later events should consult the internet supplement. Teaching is also a collaborative process, especially in an area with as many policy debates and rapid changes as in financial regulation today, and we invite professors, practitioners, and students who have used the book to help us improve it. Please send any comments, corrections of errors, compliments or complaints to textbook@davispolk.com. We welcome your input and suggestions.

MSB
HEJ
MET

March 31, 2016

ACKNOWLEDGEMENTS

We are deeply grateful to all of those who have helped us with the immense project of writing this book. Many professors, regulators, and attorneys in private practice have taken time from their busy schedules to guest lecture in our courses, field our incessant questions, and comment upon draft chapters within their areas of expertise. We owe particular thanks to William Birdthistle, Tom Brown, Chris Brummer, Derek Bush, Norm Champ, Linda Chatman Thomsen, Peter Conti-Brown, Luigi De Ghenghi, John L. Douglas, James Fanto, Michael Flynn, Stavros Gadinis, Jeffrey Gordon, Randall D. Guynn, Anna Harrington, E. Ashley Harris, Robert Hockett, Kathryn Judge, Wulf Kaal, Michael Krimminger, Arthur Laby, Kyoko Takahashi Lin, Ronald Mann, Patricia McCoy, Mary Miller, Niamh Moloney, Patricia Mosser, Annette L. Nazareth, William Novak, Saule Omarova, Christopher M. Paridon, Morgan Ricks, Joerg Riegel, Mark Roe, Gabriel D. Rosenberg, Hal S. Scott, Daniel Schwarcz, Steven Schwarcz, Michael Wiseman, Pierre-Hugues Verdier, and Yesha Yadav. We have also benefited greatly from the scholarship, past and ongoing, of our many colleagues in the study of financial regulation, on whose work we have heavily and gratefully drawn.

In many ways, this book is the gift of former students to future students. Classroom discussions over many years have shaped the structure of the book and the contents of its chapters. Student and summer associate research papers have informed and enriched the text in many places. We are particularly grateful to our Fall 2015 students in Professor Barr's Financial Regulation course at University of Michigan Law School and Professor Jackson and Professor Tahyar's Regulation of Financial Institutions course at Harvard Law School, to whom an early (and much longer) version of this book was taught on a test basis and from whom we learned a great deal about what worked and what didn't. We received many constructive suggestions that helped us sharpen and shorten the work.

We are also deeply indebted to the many research assistants at the University of Michigan and Harvard Law Schools and the associates, summer associates, and paralegals in the Davis Polk & Wardwell LLP Financial Institutions Group who gave of their time and talents to the project. The very long list of students and Davis Polk personnel who collaborated in creating this text include Valian Afshar, Christianah Akinbamidele, Lindsey Anderson, David Angel, Lori Arakaki, Amelia Bailey, Michael Bendetson, Jordan Boyd, Steven A. Byeff, Sijia Cai, Danny Chami, Samuel Chang, Kimberly N. Chehardy, Jung Eun (Claire) Choi, Christopher Crawford, Lauren Dansey, Nuveen Dhingra, Amy Dreisger, Scott D. Farbish, Jaryn S. Fields, Kate FitzGerald, Michael Formichelli, Ciara Foster, Rachel Garber, Ryan Garber, Joseph Gerstel, Talia Gillis, Ledina Gocaj, Reuben Grinberg, Roohi Gupte, Samuel Han, Joanna Howard, Shinyoung Hwang, Benjamin Johnson, Derek B. Johnson, Andrew Kang, Craig D. Kennedy, Rafeeq Khazin, Meghan E. King, Polly Klyce Pennoyer,

Jessica Kraft, Nicholas Kypriotakis, Kirill Lebedev, Chris Lee, Nancy Lee, Paul Lee, Jason Levin, Ilana Lieberman, Chris MacColl, Joan Martinez, Charlie McDonald, Paul E. Means, Michael Morelli, William P. Morrison, Emma Notis-McConarty, Sanjana V. Nafday, Nick Ognibene, Trisha Parikh, James Y. Park, Neil Patel, Victoria Peng, Alec Puig, Sofia Riffaud, Noel Ripberger, Hanna L. Robinson, Melanie Rosin, Marcel Rosner, Andrew B. Samuel, Elizabeth C. Schauber, Dana E. Seesel, Sam Scarritt-Selman, Shannon Seiferth, Madison Sharko, John Shoettle, Russell Spivak, Josh Strazanac, Gita Subramaniam, Cannelle Trouillot, Danielle Unterschutz, Alexandre-Philippe Vinel (former student from Columbia Law School), Stephen Vnuk, Lyla Wasz-Piper, Ming Wang, Danielle Weinberg, Daniel Wertman, Michael Zhuoran Xu, Claire Yi, Jeong Min Yun, Jeffrey Zhang, and Jeffrey Zink.

Among the many who helped us, we would especially call out Kelley L. O'Mara, an associate at Davis Polk, as well as Jeremy Kress and Elizabeth Benton, the current and former Assistant Executive Directors of the Center on Finance, Law and Policy at the University of Michigan, each of whom worked to coordinate our efforts and mold the drafts into publishable form. Finally, we must call out the extraordinarily sharp eyes and formatting genius of Anne Ulanov, as well as our gratitude to Lauren Schmale Estacio for her insightful copy editing.

Of course, all views expressed and errors are the sole responsibility of the co-authors and we invite you to send any comments, corrections or improvements to textbook@davispolk.com. We are conscious that improvements can be made and we invite future students and readers to do so.

SUMMARY OF CONTENTS

TABLE OF CONTENTS

UNIVERSITY CASEBOOK SERIES®

FINANCIAL REGULATION: LAW AND POLICY

PART I

INTRODUCTION TO FINANCIAL REGULATION

CHAPTER 1.1

FINANCE TODAY

CONTENTS

I. INTRODUCTION

The financial sector is undeniably essential to everyday life, yet few really understand what it is, how it works, or how regulating it intersects with its risks. If you were to ask random people on the street to describe the financial sector and its purpose, you might get a different answer from each of them. Since the devastation of the Financial Crisis, it is more important than ever to have the information and understanding necessary to participate in the ongoing debate about the role of the financial sector in our lives. Participating in that debate means understanding how the financial sector is regulated and how different policy choices can mitigate or heighten the risks inherent in the system. The Financial Crisis that unfolded in the United States and globally beginning in 2007 crushed the real economy and cost countless people their jobs, homes, and businesses. The aftermath has been a period of slow growth in the global economy. The crisis focused attention on the myriad ways that risks and problems in the financial sector can hurt the economy.

The financial sector can also help people do all kinds of things. You use financial intermediaries to store your money, to receive income, and to pay your bills. You use financial intermediaries to borrow money to purchase everyday items like clothes, to make bigger purchases, such as an appliance, a car, or a house, or to cover the cost of tuition. You rely on the financial sector to save for emergencies, or long-term, for a down payment on a home and retirement. You use financial intermediaries to protect against unforeseen future events like a car accident, health problems, or an untimely death. Almost everything you do in your economic life involves a financial intermediary, either directly or indirectly. Of course, businesses also need credit, equity, insurance, and secure payment systems, among other things, to open their doors, to grow, and to create jobs.

The terminology used to discuss the financial sector is muddled by common misusage. Take the word "bank" for example. Every day, the media refers to many types of different institutions, such as the infamous Lehman Brothers, a now defunct broker-dealer, as a "bank," when in fact Lehman Brothers was not regulated as a bank at all. In this book, we will use the word "bank" to mean any entity that accepts insured deposits, not firms like Lehman Brothers nor non-bank affiliates within a financial conglomerate. Within excerpts and sometimes due to context, it may be given a broader meaning. Our most common extension of the word "bank" will be to elide it together with other insured depository institutions such as thrifts, industrial loan companies, and credit unions.

Many of the terms and concepts in this book, even in this introductory Chapter, may be entirely new to you. We do not assume you have any background with the material. The book has a glossary, and we invite you to look at the online materials as well. They can be accessed at https://h2o.law.harvard.edu/playlists/27055.

Since the Financial Crisis, there have been fundamental changes to the way in which the financial sector is regulated, driven by the passage in the United States of the Dodd-Frank Wall Street Reform and Consumer Protection Act of 2010 (Dodd-Frank Act), by changes in financial regulation in other major countries, and by globally coordinated reforms, such as those on capital rules. The Dodd-Frank Act and other post-Financial Crisis reforms have built upon the existing regulatory architecture, not replaced it, so it is necessary to understand both. The Dodd-Frank Act's key reforms include the regulation of systemically important financial firms regardless of their corporate form, new tools to deal with the failure of systemically important financial firms, stronger oversight of financial conglomerates, regulation of derivatives and shadow banking markets, stronger underwriting standards for mortgages, securitization reforms, stronger investor protections, and stronger consumer protections under the new Consumer Financial Protection Bureau (CFPB). Internationally, regulators are harmonizing standards on capital, derivatives, and cross-border resolution, among other matters. Together, these reforms speak to many of the regulatory weaknesses that contributed to the Financial Crisis.

At the same time, controversy remains over the regulatory paradigm shift unleashed by the Dodd-Frank Act and its many pages of regulations. Some of this controversy relates back to older debates. Many commentators point out that there still is unfinished business, especially in the regulation of mortgages and their secondary markets, in wholesale funding markets, in the architecture of the regulatory framework, in accountability, market infrastructure, and in many other areas. Others argue that the post-Financial Crisis reforms went too far already and are contributing to slower growth and more volatile markets. In the meantime, technological and market changes, as they always do, require us to ask whether older regulatory policy choices that might have been sensible when made are now misaligned with their purpose in light of new risks and opportunities. You will explore these and other debates in this book.

Finance and financial regulation continue to evolve at a rapid pace, and new problems in the financial system have continued to become apparent in recent years. As you will see, the financial system is not risk-free today, nor has it ever been. Some risks can be mitigated by an improved regulatory, supervisory, and enforcement system, and some are inherent in the nature of finance. Some see financial regulation as a losing race against financial and technological innovation. Others see financial regulation as creating barriers to entry and innovation and protecting the status quo of existing players. There is a bit of truth in each point of view here. The financial regulation and architecture we have today is the result of principled and differing views about the appropriate nature of regulation, turf battles among congressional committees and regulatory agencies, politics, lobbying and inter-sectoral wars in the private sector, and happenstance, personality, technology, and the long shadow of history. As William Faulkner once wrote, "The past is never dead. It's not even past." WILLIAM FAULKNER, REQUIEM FOR A NUN 73 (2013).

This book will help you figure out what the financial sector is and how it is regulated. We aim to provide you with the context—the situational awareness—you need to understand the financial field, and to be an outstanding lawyer, policy-maker, or participant in it. In Part I, we provide you with the necessary background to contextualize the rest of the book. It will help you to understand finance, the building blocks of regulation, and the history of the financial sector in the United States. In Part II, we look at prudential regulation, focusing on the commercial bank with insured deposits, as well as three other types of insured depository institutions: the thrift, the industrial loan company (ILC), and the credit union. In Part III, we explore the regulation of insurance. In Part IV, we look at the regulation of securities and capital markets and the structure of investment banks, more properly called broker-dealers. In Part V, we analyze consumer protection. In Part VI, we delve into the regulation of large, complex financial conglomerates. In Part VII, we explore the world of payments systems, including new developments such as Apple Pay and Bitcoin. In Part VIII, we analyze the role of regulatory supervision as well as a firm's internal compliance and corporate governance. In Part IX, we explain government backstops such as deposit insurance and the resolution of failed firms, and we examine how the policy-makers are working to mitigate the problem typically dubbed "too big to fail." In Part X, we examine mutual funds and other pooled investment vehicles. In Part XI, we look at the regulation of derivatives and rates markets. In Part XII, we look at shadow banking, including securitization, the government-sponsored enterprises (GSEs), such as the Federal National Mortgage Association (Fannie Mae) and the Federal Home Loan Mortgage Corporation

(Freddie Mac), money market mutual funds (MMFs), and wholesale funding markets, including repo (repurchase) markets so crucial to shadow banking.

In this Chapter, we first explore the functions of finance, and we take a look at the theory of financial intermediation. We then examine the key participants and markets in the U.S. financial system, and we discuss key types of financial intermediaries—entities that channel funds from lenders to borrowers. As you will see, a diverse array of financial intermediaries, not just banks, perform distinct, but oftentimes overlapping, functions in today's financial sector. Our discussion here generally follows the order of the book, giving you a preview of many of the types of firms and markets you will encounter.

II. THE FUNCTIONS OF FINANCE

A. THE ROLE OF THE FINANCIAL SYSTEM

Consider the following description of finance and the role that it plays in society:

> At its broadest level, finance is the science of goal architecture—of the structuring of the economic arrangements necessary to achieve a set of goals and of the stewardship of the assets needed for that achievement. The goals may be those of households, small businesses, corporations, civic institutions, governments, and of society itself. Once an objective has been specified—such as payment for a college education, a couple's comfortable retirement, the opening of a new restaurant, the addition of a new wing on a hospital, the creation of a social security system, or a trip to the moon—the parties involved need the right financial tools, and often expert guidance, to help achieve the goal. In this sense, finance is analogous to engineering.

ROBERT J. SHILLER, FINANCE AND THE GOOD SOCIETY 6–7 (2012).

Professors Robert Merton and Zvi Bodie identify six basic functions that the financial system serves. *See* ROBERT C. MERTON & ZVI BODIE, *A Conceptual Framework for Analyzing the Financial Environment, in* THE GLOBAL FINANCIAL SYSTEM 3,5 (Dwight B. Crane et al. eds., 1995). They are:

- ***Clearing and Settling Payments.*** The financial system enables payments to be exchanged for goods and services. Checking accounts, debit cards, and credit cards all serve as examples of services that financial intermediaries provide to fulfill a clearing and settling function.
- ***Pooling Resources and Subdividing Shares.*** The financial system allows individual investors to aggregate their wealth into larger pools of capital and make that wealth available for firms to use to run their business. When a firm seeks a large loan, it would likely be difficult to procure the funds from a single lender. The financial system enables resources from various investors to be pooled. The financial system facilitates diversification of investments by allowing a firm to obtain a loan from the pooled resources of multiple investors. Likewise, an individual investor may want to make an investment but have

insufficient capital to fund the entire project. Through financial intermediaries, the investor can diversify by investing in a variety of projects.

- ***Transferring Economic Resources.*** The financial system can enable economic resources to be transferred through time. Individuals can smooth their consumption by borrowing now against better times in the future (for example, through student loans), while others can save now for future times (for example, through retirement savings). Furthermore, firms can raise the capital they need from investments across geographies and industries and from individual investors and firms, enabling capital to be put to its most efficient use.
- ***Managing Risk.*** The financial system allows individuals and businesses to pool and share risk. For example, mutual funds might control risk by requiring investments to be diversified. Or, the financial intermediary might bear a risk on behalf of an investor, as in the case of an insurance company that sells protection against loss of life or assets. In addition to bearing risk, financial intermediaries may be in a better position than consumers to evaluate the riskiness of an investment.
- ***Generating and Providing Information.*** Information can help facilitate informed decision-making for businesses looking to exchange financial assets or investors considering making an investment. Businesses and individuals alike might consider information, such as interest rates, when deciding whether to make an investment or obtain a loan. The financial system allows information to be disseminated more efficiently by sharing and reusing information. This information flow, in turn, can reduce costs, for example, investors' costs to observe the activities of the borrower to ensure that funds are being used properly, called monitoring costs.
- ***Dealing with Incentive Problems.*** Incentive problems arise when one party to a transaction has access to information that the other party does not have, or when two parties have a principal-agent relationship. In such a scenario, problems with moral hazard, information asymmetries, and adverse selection can arise. The financial system can mitigate some of these incentive problems by reducing monitoring costs and increasing transparency.

These basic functions can be described in a variety of ways. *See, e.g.*, Gary Gorton & Andrew Winton, *Financial Intermediation* 4–26 (Nat'l Bureau of Econ. Research, Working Paper No. 8928, 2002) (describing the main functions as monitoring, signaling, smoothing, providing liquidity, and improving capital allocation); STUART I. GREENBAUM & ANJAN V. THAKOR, *The Nature and Variety of Financial Intermediation, in* CONTEMPORARY FINANCIAL INTERMEDIATION 23, 24, 38, 43–45 (Stuart I. Greenbaum et al. eds., 2015) (discussing asset transformation, insurance, and brokerage). Keep these basic functions in mind as we explore how the various types of financial intermediaries carry out these functions. Think about how the regulatory landscape shapes the ways in which different types of financial intermediaries fulfill these functions.

Financial intermediation may be thought of as falling into two ideal types, direct finance and indirect finance. Direct finance means an investor or creditor providing funding to a company or person and being exposed directly to gains or losses from the direct relationship. Even direct finance usually involves a financial intermediary, such as a broker, to facilitate the saver's investment. HAL S. SCOTT & ANNA GELPERN, INTERNATIONAL FINANCE 88–96 (19th ed. 2012). Financial intermediaries use their expertise, scale economies in screening and monitoring, and better access to information to match providers of financial capital with users. Recently, new forms of direct finance, such as crowdfunding and peer-to-peer lending, have begun to develop as small businesses, non-profits, individuals, and startups have turned to internet-based platforms to generate investment from individuals. By contrast, financial intermediaries engaging in indirect finance stand between providers and users of capital. Consider the example of a bank into which savers make short-term deposits and the bank transforms these deposits into longer-term loans to borrowers.

B. FINANCIAL INTERMEDIATION

Both direct and indirect finance involve asset transformation—*e.g.*, the pooling of resources from many smaller investors to create a new, larger asset, such as a loan—and maturity transformation—*e.g.*, the conversion of liquid short-term assets (deposits) into illiquid long-term assets (loans). Financial intermediaries engage in asset and maturity transformation so that both suppliers of capital (savers) and users of capital (borrowers) can have access to the financial instrument that best meets their needs. A liquid asset is cash or an asset that may readily be converted into cash without losing value. Liquid assets provide the firm or households with ready access to cash when it is needed. It is not desirable, however, for firms and households to hold only liquid assets. Longer-term assets might provide higher returns and stability over time. Financial intermediaries can transform assets across a number of different attributes: from liquid to illiquid forms, from short- to long-term maturity, from less to more risky forms (or the reverse). Asset transformation can help allocate capital to its highest and best uses. For instance, consumers can smooth their consumption over time by stowing money away for future use and withdrawing it when needed. To save excess money, a consumer can deposit it in a bank, essentially lending those funds to the bank. The bank will pay the consumer interest on the deposit, while the bank in turn transforms the consumer's deposit into a loan to a business. By bundling the funds received from multiple depositors, the bank can create bigger loans. Asset transformation thus involves pooling resources, subdividing shares, and transferring economic resources.

Financial intermediaries help savers manage risks by diversifying their assets. For example, a depositor can lend funds to a bank, and the bank can pool those funds with those of other depositors to invest in a broad range of assets. Financial intermediaries provide a range of insurance functions. For example, banks help provide insurance against shocks, such as a spike in expenses, by providing liquidity—immediate access to one's savings. ILONKA RUHLE, WHY BANKS? 201 (Manfred Nitsch et al. eds., 1997). Insurance companies, for instance, serve an explicit role in bearing risks against uncertainties in a consumer's future, such as death, disability, or property loss. Like other financial intermediaries, insurance companies pay out obligations from a portfolio of assets, thus bearing the risks from changes in the asset values of those portfolios, rather than the consumer bearing such risk. Richard W. Kopke & Richard E. Randall, Fed. Reserve Bank of Boston, *Insurance Companies as Financial Intermediaries: Risk and Return*, 35 Conference Series 19 (1991).

Many theories explaining the function of banks focus on the role of banks as lenders. Professor Douglas Diamond focuses on how banks enable resources to be pooled. If a large loan is needed, it follows that a single borrower will often need to obtain that loan from a variety of sources. As the number of lenders to a single borrower grows, however, each individual has less incentive to monitor the borrower because his share of the total loan is reduced. Individual lenders may either duplicate monitoring costs or free ride off the monitoring of other lenders—both of which would be inefficient outcomes. In such a situation with many lenders, banks step in because the task of monitoring the borrower can be more efficiently delegated to the bank. *See* Douglas Diamond, *Financial Intermediation and Delegated Monitoring*, 51 REV. ECON. STUD. 393 (1984). Diversification also plays a role. The bank is incentivized to diversify its portfolio because that reduces the probability that it will fail to pay its own lenders (*i.e.*, depositors) in the case of default of the borrowers. *Id.* at 402. Professors John Boyd and Edward Prescott posit that financial intermediaries help overcome asymmetrical information, which occurs when one agent (the borrower) has private information that the other does not have. Financial intermediaries invest in evaluating projects to reduce such asymmetries. John H. Boyd & Edward C. Prescott, *Financial-Intermediary Coalitions*, 38 J. ECON. THEORY 211 (1986).

For Diamond and Professor Philip Dybvig, maturity transformation is a key reason why banks exist. Maturity transformation enables banks to offer a liquid asset (a deposit) to savers while providing a long-term loan to borrowers. Maturity transformation fails when all depositors demand liquidity at the same time, a concept that we will return to later in our discussion of bank runs in Chapter 2.4. Douglas Diamond & Philip Dybvig, *Bank Runs, Deposit Insurance, and Liquidity*, 91 J. POL. ECON. 401 (1983).

Financial intermediaries also facilitate the clearing and settling of payments. Intermediaries act as a clearinghouse so that an exchange of payment does not need to occur simultaneously and in one place. Scott Freeman, *The Payments System, Liquidity, and Rediscounting*, 86 AM. ECON. REV. 1126 (1996).

Finally, liquidity provision is key to financial intermediation. Unlike many theories, which focus on the asset-side (lending) role of banks, Professors Gary Gorton and George Pennacchi focus on the creation of the financial intermediary's liabilities. Their key insight is the need for bank debt to be information insensitive—*i.e.*, have value that is not dependent on information known only to informed investors—so that uninformed agents can invest in the debt. Gary Gorton & George Pennacchi, *Financial Intermediaries and Liquidity Creation*, 45 J. FIN. 49 (1990). Demand deposits are an example of how liquidity is created in the Gorton and Pennacchi model. Demand deposits are thought of as information insensitive because private information generally does not need to be known about the value of the asset; they are thought of as safe and riskless. This information insensitivity makes demand deposits liquid, because they can be traded without fear that the other party has secret information about the value of the debt. *Id.* at 60–62. Bank runs have had devastating economic costs at many points in U.S. history, and protecting against such runs has been a principal aim of regulatory policy. Issuance of instruments similar to demand deposits, for example, repos issued by broker-dealers, played a key role in the Financial Crisis, as we will see at several points in this book. Professors Charles Calomiris and Charles Kahn, however, argue that demand debt also helps to discipline banks. If enough depositors demand their debt, the bank will be forced to sell its assets quickly and at a deep discount, often referred to as a fire sale. The threat of fire sales or the failure of the bank will therefore serve as a check on bank behavior, they theorize. Charles Calomiris & Charles Kahn, *The Role of Demandable Debt in Structuring Optimal Banking Arrangements*, 81 AMER. ECON. REV. 497 (1991).

Asset and maturity transformation create risks for financial intermediaries. Policy makers have developed different tools to try to contain these risks. For example, banks are required to fund themselves with at least a certain level of capital—equity that can act as a cushion in case of losses on its assets. Banks are also required to hold cash or liquid assets in the form of reserves that be used to pay off creditors quickly. Bank deposits are insured so that depositors do not have an incentive to run on the bank in the event of concern about the bank's health. As you read about banks, insurance companies, securities firms, and other parts of the financial system, ask yourself which of these kind of tools, or other regulatory techniques, are applied or should be applied in different contexts. To what extent are functionally similar institutions, products, or services regulated similarly?

III. FINANCIAL SERVICES IN THE UNITED STATES

A. OVERVIEW

The U.S. financial system is large, varied, complex, and interconnected. As of the end of 2015, U.S. gross domestic product was about $18 trillion. According to the U.S. Commerce Department's Bureau of Economic Analysis, financial services represented 7% of U.S. gross domestic product, or more than $1.25 trillion, and employed six million people. The U.S. financial sector intermediated more than $85 trillion in assets in 2014. *See* FED. RESERVE BD., FINANCIAL ACCOUNTS OF THE UNITED STATES (2015).

The part of the financial system that you are probably most familiar with is the insured depository sector. This sector, including banks, thrifts, and credit unions, however, has shrunk from more than 40% of the financial system in 1980 to about 20% in 2014, while other sectors, such as mutual funds, have grown. Figure 1.1-1 shows the market share of different segments of U.S. financial services that we will discuss shortly.

Figure 1.1-1 Proportion of Total Financial Assets Held by Financial Intermediaries

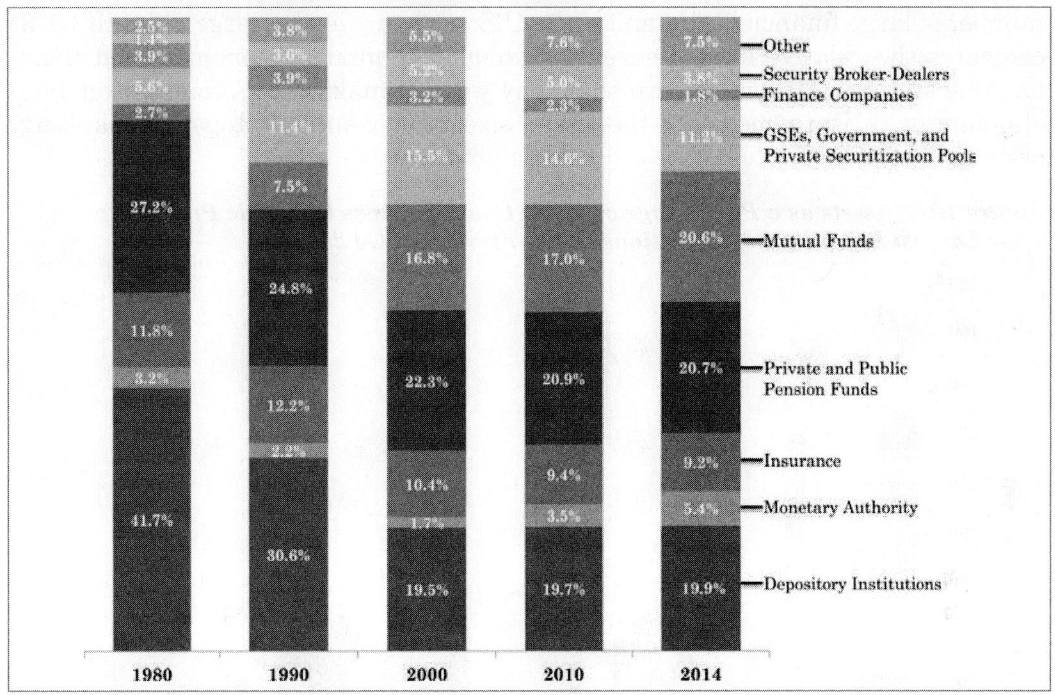

Source: Fed. Reserve Bd., Financial Accounts of the United States (2015).

To give you a sense of the largest participants in the banking, securities, and insurance markets, Figure 1.1-2 shows the biggest U.S. financial conglomerates and insurance companies by asset size.

Figure 1.1-2 Largest U.S. Financial Conglomerates and Insurers (as of Q4 2015) ($ billions)

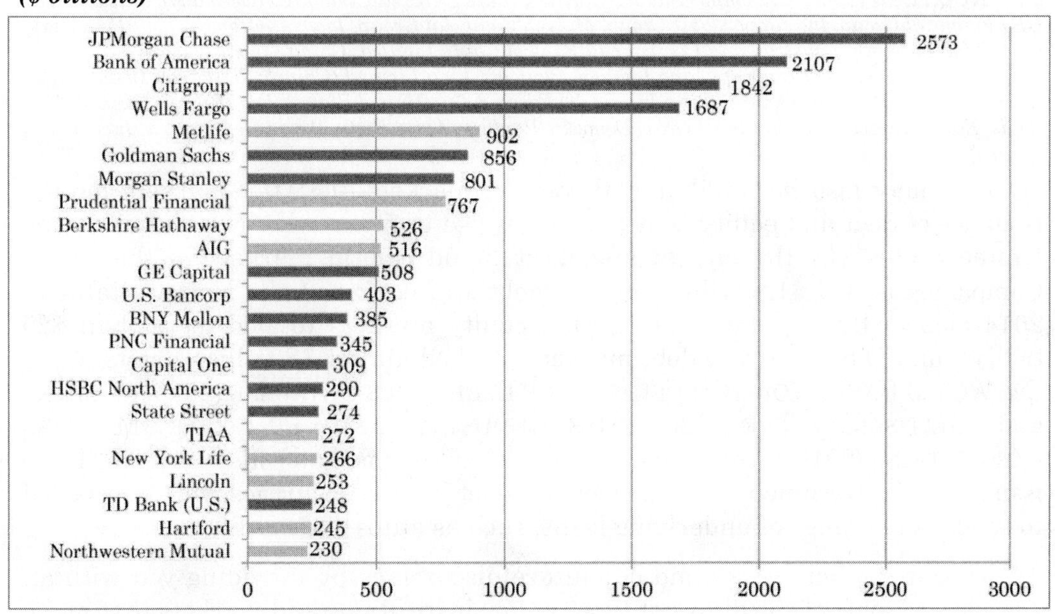

Source: FSOC, Annual Report 69 (2015).

Even though the U.S. financial system is large and the United States has a number of large financial companies, the U.S. economy is also large. Figure 1.1-3 compares the relative size of several developed countries' economies and their banking sectors. Although there are many ways of making this comparison, one standard way is to measure the asset size of a country's top four banking organizations relative to its gross domestic product.

Figure 1.1-3 Assets as a Percentage of Home Country Gross Domestic Product for Four Largest Banking Organizations in Country (as of Q4 2014)

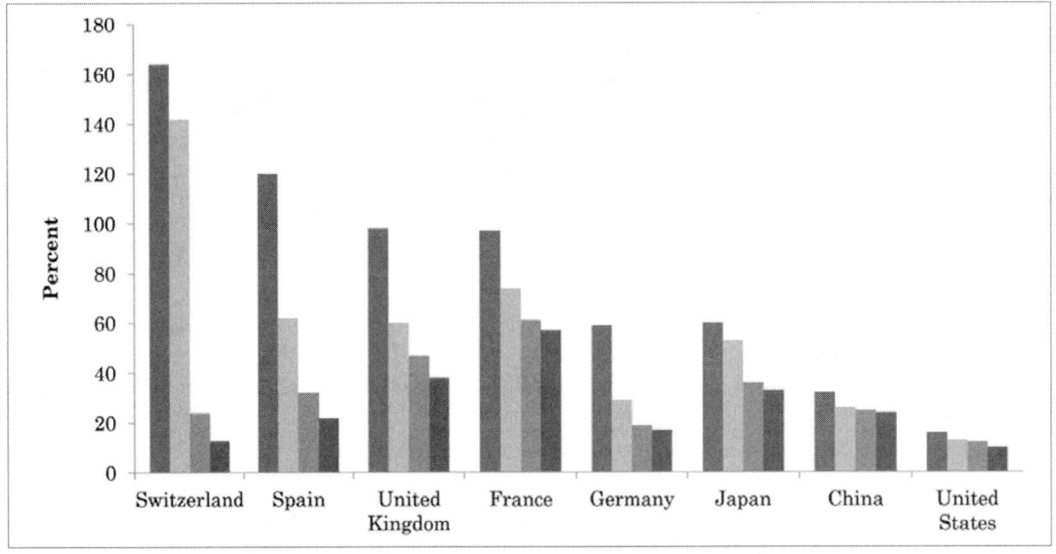

Sources: 2014 Annual Reports of UBS Group AG, Credit Suisse Group AG, Zurcher Kantonalbank, Julius Baer Group Ltd. (Switzerland); Banco Santander, S.A., Banco Bilbao Vizcaya Argentaria, S.A., CaixaBank, S.A., Bankia S.A. (Spain); BNP Paribas, S.A., Credit Agricole, S.A., Societe Generale, Groupe BPCE (France); HSBC Holdings plc, Barclays PLC, Royal Bank of Scotland Group, Lloyds Banking Group plc (UK); Deutsche Bank AG, Commerzbank AG, KfW Group, UniCredit Bank AG (Germany); Mitsubishi UFJ Financial Group, Inc., Japan Post Group, Mizuho Financial Group, Inc., Sumitomo Mitsui Financial Group, Inc. (Japan); Industrial and Commercial Bank of China Limited, China Construction Bank Corporation, Agricultural Bank of China Limited, Bank of China Limited (China); JPMorgan Chase & Co., Bank of America Corporation, Citigroup Inc., Wells Fargo & Co. (United States); Fed. Reserve Bank of St. Louis, Econ. Research, Current Price Gross Domestic Product; World Bank, World Development Indicators.

You may also be familiar with capital markets—*i.e.*, the markets for the issuance of debt and equity that companies use to finance their operations. The United States has the largest and most liquid capital markets in the world. Companies issued $1.8 trillion in new debt and equity in the United States in 2014 alone. By the end of 2014, U.S. equity markets totaled more than $25 trillion, and U.S. corporate debt markets reached almost $8 trillion outstanding. *See* WORLD BANK, WORLD FEDERATION OF EXCHANGES DATABASE (2016) (equities) and STATISTICS, THE SECURITIES INDUSTRY AND FINANCIAL MARKETS ASSOCIATION (2016) (corporate debt). Capital markets also involve large issuances of government debt, as well as asset-backed securities, which are used to fund a wide range of underlying loans, such as autos and credit cards.

In this section, we ground our future discussions by providing you with an overview of some of the different types of key institutions and markets that make up our financial system. These institutions include banks, insurance companies, and securities firms, as well as complex financial conglomerates that own such businesses, asset managers and the funds they manage, including pensions and mutual funds, and GSEs, such as Fannie Mae and Freddie Mac. We also look at a range of financial markets, from consumer finance to derivatives, securitization, and wholesale funding. Our goal is to provide you with a heightened awareness of the financial system working all around you.

A recurring theme throughout this book is the interplay between function, form, and regulation. Financial products, services and institutions bump up against, cross, and help change legal and jurisdictional lines. Products with a similar function but a different legal form may be regulated quite differently. Banking, securities, and insurance firms, products, and services can often serve similar purposes but are governed by differing legal principles, regulatory bodies, congressional committee oversight, and other factors. Similarly, there are often fine lines between the type of products that might be considered financial in nature and those offered by, say, a technology or communications company regulated by quite different rules. The difficulty of line-drawing in the financial sector leads to opportunities for regulatory arbitrage—or efforts to get around regulation by re-characterizing a financial product or service—as well as gaps, weaknesses, or redundancies in financial regulation. The Financial Stability Oversight Council (FSOC), created by the Dodd-Frank Act, is designed to reduce opportunities for arbitrage, but its authorities are constrained in a variety of ways.

The history of the financial sector is replete with examples of how market forces and technological change have eroded boundaries between different types of financial institutions, as you will see in Chapter 1.2. As statutes that were put in place during an earlier era and that reflect earlier stakeholder battles were pushed into obsolescence by market forces and technological change, financial intermediaries have looked for ways to avoid regulation or to change the rules through regulation, legislation, or the courts. Those who benefited from the current system fought back with the same tools. Think, by analogy, to Uber. Stakeholder battles and regulatory arbitrage, which can sometimes serve innovation and sometimes lead to enhanced systemic risk and abuse, are as old as the financial sector itself. Consider the potential for both benefits or problems along these lines as you read the following sections examining different parts of the financial system.

B. INSURED DEPOSITORY INSTITUTIONS

In Part II of the book, we explore prudential regulation, with a particular focus on insured depository institutions, a term which includes any entity that accepts deposits covered by deposit insurance. The term is often shortened to the acronym IDI. The most widely recognized type of IDI is a bank, often referred to as a chartered commercial bank. Thrifts, ILCs, and credit unions are also IDIs. While a handful of U.S. banks are extremely large, the United States also has a thriving regional banking sector and a diverse array of community banks and credit unions around the country. There are more than 6,000 banks and thrifts in the United States, and more than 6,000 credit unions. FDIC, INSTITUTION DIRECTORY (2016); *see* NAT'L CREDIT UNION ADMIN., INDUSTRY AT A GLANCE (2015).

Retail banks (and other depositories) offer customers a range of products, such as checking accounts and residential mortgages. A bank in its simplest form functions in the following way. Customers deposit money into their checking or savings accounts at the bank. Since the establishment of deposit insurance in the wake of the Great Depression, retail deposits are insured (up to a cap) by premiums paid by insured banks and thrifts to a government agency—the Federal Deposit Insurance Corporation (FDIC). These deposits function as short-term loans to the bank. The bank maintains a percentage of the deposits it receives as cash on hand to pay customers who want to withdraw funds from their checking accounts; this fraction is referred to as reserves. The bank then uses the remainder of the deposited money (and other borrowings) to fund the long-term loans it offers, such as 30-year residential mortgages. The disparity between short-term funding and long-term lending is referred to as maturity mismatch. The system where only a fraction of deposits are kept in cash at the bank is referred to as the fractional reserve system. The problems arising from fractional reserves and maturity mismatch motivate many of the regulations governing IDIs.

Banks, of course, also serve businesses, as well as other banks and financial institutions. Banks offer business loans, and they serve as custodians for financial assets. They clear transactions between other financial institutions, and they perform myriad other critical payments and transaction processing functions that smooth the flow of finance. Commercial banks have traditionally been distinguished from other types of depository institutions by their role in the payments system and the transmission of monetary policy.

As you will see in Chapter 2.1, banks and other depositories are defined by their charters. A charter accords an institution with particular privileges and responsibilities. For example, IDIs can raise funds by offering deposit accounts with federal insurance.

Another way to define banks is based on the services they provide—that is, the transformation of liquid liabilities (demand deposits) into illiquid assets (loans). One shortcoming of such a services-based definition can be seen from the entry of other types of financial intermediaries into traditional bank functions, eroding many of the distinctions between commercial banks and other types of financial institutions. Many non-banks perform functions that are similar to those performed by banks. Money market mutual funds (MMFs), for instance, have characteristics similar to demand deposits, including liquidity and the opportunity to earn a return on an investment. On the lending side, a variety of non-bank financial institutions, such as commercial lending companies and insurance companies enable companies to raise capital. As you will see, functionally similar activities are often regulated differently depending on what type of institution offers the service.

C. INSURANCE COMPANIES

In Part III of this book, we explore insurance regulation. There are over 6,000 insurance companies in the United States. *See* NAIC, 2014 INSURANCE DEPARTMENT RESOURCES, VOL. 1, 35–37 (2015). While there are many different types of insurance, two of the largest categories are property/casualty and life insurance. Although these two types of insurance address different risks, all insurance companies specialize in spreading risk as contingent liability intermediaries. Consider for a moment the economic function of insurance: spreading the risk of an adverse event across a group of individuals or firms. In exchange for payments from insurance policyholders, typically known as premiums, insurance companies commit themselves to make contingent payments back to those policyholders in the event that some specified adverse event happens in the future, such as when an automobile is damaged, a house burns down, or a person dies. An insurance company's commitments are probabilistic. Not all policyholders will suffer the event against which they purchase insurance; indeed, the entire business model of insurance companies typically requires that the vast majority of policyholders do not make claims on their policy in any particular time period. With the help of actuaries, the amount of an insurance company's commitments can be predicted, often with considerable accuracy, but the obligations are not fixed in the same way that a bank deposit with a fixed rate of interest is fixed. Insurance companies typically invest policy premiums in a portfolio of assets. The distinguishing characteristic of an insurance company's balance sheet is the presence of future policy claims as the firm's principal liabilities.

Insurance is primarily regulated by the states, although, you will see, the federal role is large or even dominant in specialized sectors, such as health and pensions. The federal role has increased significantly after passage of the Dodd-Frank Act and ongoing developments in international capital reforms, especially with respect to large, internationally active insurance firms.

In many functional ways, insurance companies and banks are similar. Both provide financial intermediation; banks take deposits and turn them into loans, whereas insurance companies take premiums and use that money to invest or provide loans. Both hold fractional reserves; banks hold a fraction of deposits in cash to meet withdrawals and similarly insurance companies only hold a percentage of their assets in liquid form to satisfy claim requests while attempting to match longer-term liabilities with longer-term assets. Both mitigate risk; banks take liquid deposits and turn them into diversified gains for the consumer, and insurance companies take premiums and turn them into future assurances. Both require the trust of customers and therefore are highly regulated with the goal of ensuring that such trust is warranted.

Like banks, insurance firms and their affiliates can also be engaged in complicated and sometimes risky transactions. During the Financial Crisis, for example, the insurance conglomerate AIG faced failure when it was required to post additional collateral on the credit default swaps (CDSs) it sold through its financial subsidiary AIG Financial Products. Before the Financial Crisis, the sale of over-the-counter (OTC) derivatives such as CDSs was almost completely unregulated, and AIG had not been required to hold capital to mitigate against losses in the event of massive defaults. The federal government ended up providing AIG with over $182 billion in financial support by the end of the Financial Crisis. FCIC, FINANCIAL CRISIS INQUIRY REPORT 350 (2011). In part in response to AIG's near failure and an understandably strong reaction to the federal support of AIG, the architects of the Dodd-Frank Act wanted to provide a mechanism to bring large, complex financial firms under the ambit of Federal Reserve Board supervision, even if the firm was not organized as a bank or its holding company. Under § 113 of the Dodd-Frank Act, the FSOC is now empowered to designate non-bank financial companies for Federal Reserve Board supervision. 12 U.S.C. § 5323. The FSOC has since designated AIG and two other insurance conglomerates, Prudential and MetLife, for Federal Reserve Board supervision. MetLife is fighting its designation in federal court and won at the district court level. An appeal is likely. Other insurance conglomerates have come under Federal Reserve Board supervision because of the Dodd-Frank Act's changes to holding company regulation. The Act also created the Federal Insurance Office (FIO) to provide the federal government with greater information on the insurance sector and to negotiate certain international agreements regarding insurance. International capital reforms are moving towards an international system of capital rules for insurance, as they had previously done for banking.

D. SECURITIES FIRMS

In Part IV of the book we explore securities markets. Broker-dealers, often called investment banks, play important roles in those markets. Investment banks are financial intermediaries that seek to connect those looking for funding with those looking to invest. They provide a variety of services that include but are not limited to underwriting, brokering, and dealing securities. Investment banks do not take deposits—at least not in the form of insured deposits—but as you will see, they can fund themselves by borrowing in wholesale markets with other instruments that are functionally similar.

Underwriting refers to the process by which investment banks facilitate a corporation's sale of its securities. Brokering is when an investment bank buys and sells securities as an agent on behalf of a customer, and dealing is when an investment bank buys and sells securities using its own funds.

Investment banks are not regulated as banks, but instead are regulated by the Securities and Exchange Commission (SEC) as broker-dealers. During the Financial Crisis, many of the oldest household names in investment banking disappeared or were incorporated into bank holding companies (BHCs). Lehman Brothers went into bankruptcy, Merrill Lynch was acquired by Bank of America, and Bear Stearns was acquired by JP Morgan Chase. Morgan Stanley and Goldman Sachs converted into bank holding companies during the Financial Crisis with the result that they were able to convey a sense of safety, as they were brought under the supervision of the Federal Reserve Board. At the same time, the Federal Reserve Board provided their broker-dealer subsidiaries access to the Federal Reserve's liquidity—the short-term funding that a central bank supplies to banks as a lender of last resort. Post-Financial Crisis, there are few standalone investment banks left, namely Lazard, Jefferies, and a handful of others. Those that do remain are more specialized in advising. Today, the largest investment banks or broker-dealers are part of bank holding companies, such as JP Morgan Chase, Citigroup, and Bank of America. As noted above with respect to insurance companies, the FSOC has the authority to designate broker-dealers for supervision by the Federal Reserve Board even if they are not part of a bank holding company.

In addition to examining the structural and prudential issues affecting securities markets, Part IV also explores the duties of care owed by brokers, dealers, and investment advisors to their clients under the Securities Act of 1933, the Securities Exchange Act of 1934, and the Investment Advisers Act of 1940 (1940 Act). At the end of 2014, there were approximately 4,300 securities broker-dealers registered with the SEC, holding a total of $4.5 trillion in assets. FSOC, 2015 ANNUAL REPORT 67 (2015). The sector is concentrated with about 60% of broker-dealer assets held by the top ten firms. In addition, there are about 11,500 registered investment advisers, with $67 trillion in assets under management, on behalf of 30 million retail and institutional clients. The top 1% of firms manage about 55% of assets under management. INV. ADVISER ASS'N, 2015 EVOLUTION REVOLUTION 3 (2015).

E. CONSUMER FINANCE

The financial sector is also critical for households, and in Part V of the book, we examine consumer finance. Consumer financial services and products include credit cards, auto loans, student loans, mortgages, money transfers, and other products and services that individuals use every day. As you can see from Figure 1.1-4, student debt has been growing rapidly for the last decade and now eclipses credit card debt and auto loans in total amounts outstanding.

Figure 1.1-4 Consumer Credit

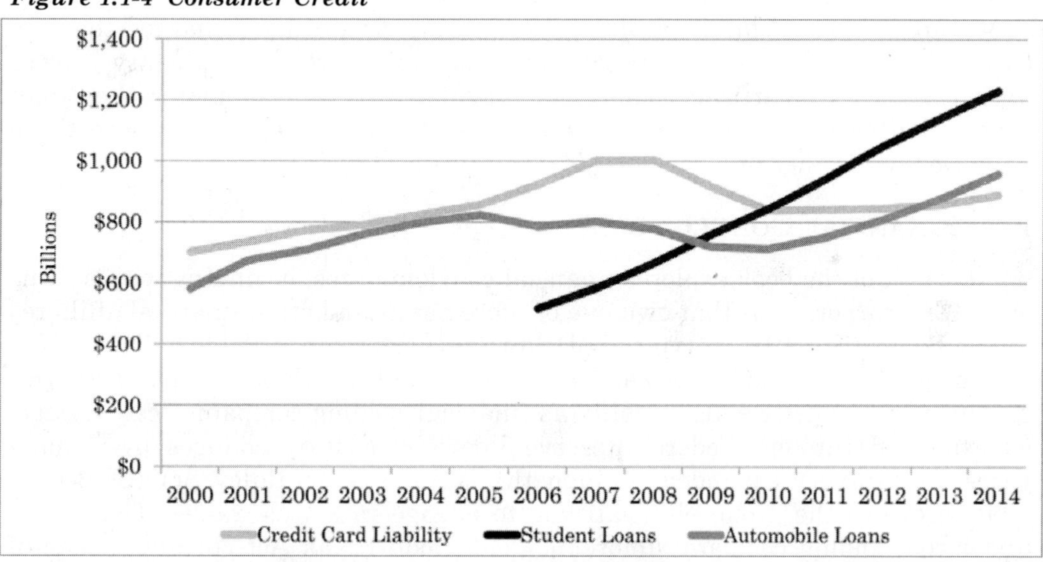

Source: Fed. Reserve Bd., Financial Accounts of the United States (2015).

Before the Dodd-Frank Act, federal financial consumer protection regulation was fragmented among many different agencies, which complicated rule-writing, supervision, and enforcement. This fragmentation also allowed banks to choose the least restrictive consumer protection rules available and non-bank financial institutions to avoid federal supervision altogether. Federal agencies, concerned mostly with the safety and soundness of the institutions within their purview, did not focus on protecting consumers and, in some cases, preempted state consumer protection laws without adequately replacing these important safeguards. Michael S. Barr, *The Financial Crisis and the Path of Reform*, 29 YALE J. ON REG. 91, 106 (2012).

The Dodd-Frank Act replaced much of this fragmented federal system with a single, dedicated regulatory agency, the CFPB. Armed with expanded authority to prohibit unfair, deceptive, and abusive practices, and with a congressional mission to "ensure that . . . consumer protection laws and regulations are comprehensive, fair, and vigorously enforced," H.R. REP. NO. 111-517, at 874 (2010), the newly established CFPB has taken a number of steps to reform consumer credit and mortgage markets. The consolidation of supervision, enforcement, and rule-making authorities in the CFPB may improve feedback in the rulemaking process, as well as general regulatory quality. The CFPB is charged with balancing consumer protection, financial access, and innovation, and with collaborating more closely with state attorneys general. Finally, consumer advocates hope that the CFPB will serve as an innovator in its own right, introducing more efficient supervisory methods for non-bank firms, such as risk-based examinations, and incorporating into its rule-making approach insights on consumer decision-making derived from behavioral economics. Supporters of the CFPB take the view that this new generation of consumer protection regulation may not only promote competition among banks and non-bank institutions on the basis of price and quality, but also may empower consumers to make their own choices and find the most suitable financial products, even when providers have incentives to hide true costs. Barr, *The Financial Crisis and the Path of Reform*, at 107. Critics have charged that the CFPB lacks sufficient accountability, has excessive discretionary power unchecked by a bipartisan commission, regulates by enforcement rather than supervision or rulemaking, and has exceeded its mandate. We explore these controversies further in Part V of this book.

F. FINANCIAL CONGLOMERATES

Part VI of the book explores financial conglomerates, beginning with a focus on BHCs—corporations that own one or more banks and other financial affiliates in one group. The BHC is typically Delaware-chartered and publicly listed. The vast majority of banks are owned by a BHC. The breadth of financial activities in which those BHCs which qualify as financial holding companies can engage, as expanded through Federal Reserve Board regulatory changes over many years, and further expanded through the Gramm-Leach-Bliley Act (GLBA) in 1999, provides the group with latitude to engage in a wide range of activities under the holding company umbrella. The Dodd-Frank Act curtailed some of these authorities through § 619 (the Volcker Rule) and other measures. The Act also moved supervision of savings and loan holding companies from the now-defunct Office of Thrift Supervision (OTS) to the Federal Reserve Board.

As of the end of 2014, there were 1,034 BHCs in the United States with greater than $500 million in assets; these BHCs have aggregate assets of $18.1 trillion. FSOC, 2015 ANNUAL REPORT 57 (2015). During the Financial Crisis, crisis-driven mergers increased concentration at the top among the largest BHCs and the remaining two large stand-alone investment banks, Goldman Sachs and Morgan Stanley, became BHCs themselves. The four largest BHCs—JP Morgan Chase, Bank of America, Citigroup, and Wells Fargo—accounted for more than 45% of all assets held by BHCs at the end of 2014. *See* FED. RESERVE SYS., NAT'L INFO. CTR.

As noted above, in addition to bolstering regulation of BHCs and limiting their activities through the Volcker Rule, the Dodd-Frank Act authorized FSOC to designate non-bank financial firms for systemic-risk supervision by the Federal Reserve Board. We discuss these new authorities in Chapter 6.2. To date, GE Capital, AIG, MetLife, and Prudential have been so designated. As you saw in Figure 1.1-2, these firms are among the largest financial conglomerates in the United States. Problems of the regulatory perimeter (explored in Chapter 1.4) are pervasive in financial regulation, and the new designation authority is an innovative, and controversial, approach to addressing the boundary between the regulation of banking and shadow banking. Since large financial conglomerates operate transnationally, Part VI ends with a chapter that explores the regulation of foreign banks that enter the U.S. and the regulation of U.S. banking organizations that enter foreign markets.

G. PAYMENT SYSTEMS

Part VII of the book explores payment systems. A payment system is a set of instruments, procedures, and rules for the transfer of value among system participants. *See* BANK FOR INT'L SETTLEMENTS, COMM. ON PAYMENT AND SETTLEMENT SYS., A GLOSSARY OF TERMS USED IN PAYMENTS AND SETTLEMENT SYSTEMS 38 (2003). In plainer terms, payments systems permit you to pay for goods or services. Ultimately, when you make a payment at a store, for example, the payment is translated through a series of transactions into a set of debits and credits at banks in accounts they hold at their regional Federal Reserve Banks. Payments are the essential plumbing of the financial system. Technology, rules, and, most importantly, trust undergird the payment system. Despite the importance of payment systems, until recently, little attention has been paid to how they work and how to make them work better.

Chapter 7.1 examines the U.S. payment systems and explores the different legal frameworks—state, federal, and self-regulatory—applicable to each one. It starts with a focus on retail, or consumer-facing, payment methods, including cash, checking, credit cards, debit cards, and remittance transfers. As you will discover, the consumer protection rules for various kinds of payments products vary dramatically from one another, even among the pieces of plastic you carry around in your wallet. We examine the ways in which the payments system affects low- and moderate-income households, including the unbanked and underbanked. The Chapter concludes with an examination of interbank funds transfers, *i.e.*, the transfers of value between banks.

Chapter 7.2 explores critical issues in payments systems, including rapidly-developing alternative payment protocols. The Chapter first examines approaches for controlling risks involved in interbank payment and settlement. The Chapter looks at controversies around interchange fee regulation, including antitrust litigation, as well as the Durbin Amendment (included in the Dodd-Frank Act), which caps interchange fees, and ongoing fights between merchants and the banking sector over fees, fraud prevention and liability, and the future of the payments system. The Chapter concludes with a discussion of Venmo, Apple Pay, and similar mobile apps that are designed to enhance the consumer experience. While easier to use than many of the older technologies such as the plastic in your wallet, these products, as you will learn, still ride the old rails of the existing payment system. Some other new protocols, based on the same underlying blockchain and distributed ledger technology used by Bitcoin, are designed to create new rails for payments. These new technologies could make payments faster and cheaper, but incumbent providers are fighting back, and regulators are worried about everything from money laundering and terrorist financing to privacy and cyber security.

H. ASSET MANAGERS

In Part X (skipping over, for purposes of this introductory chapter, our discussion of supervision in Part VIII and the resolution of failed firms and the lender of last resort in Part IX), the book explores mutual funds, hedge funds, and other private funds. The U.S. asset management sector comprises $40 trillion in financial assets under management as of 2014 and plays a central role in capital formation and credit intermediation. BlackRock is the largest U.S. asset manager, with over $4.7 trillion in assets under management as of 2015. BLACKROCK, WORLDWIDE LEADER IN ASSET AND RISK MANAGEMENT 1 (Aug. 2015). Unlike banks, asset managers do not hold these assets on their balance sheets; rather, they act as agents for their clients. OFR, 2014 ANNUAL REPORT 72 (2014). Asset managers include independent asset management companies, such as BlackRock, asset managers that are part of BHCs, pension fund asset managers, and asset managers that are part of insurance companies.

There are four primary types of funds that these firms manage: mutual funds and MMFs, hedge funds and private equity funds, collective investment funds, and privately managed separate accounts, through which asset managers invest the assets of institutional investors, insurance companies, sovereign wealth funds, and wealthy individuals.

The largest segment of the asset management business consists of publicly registered investment companies, colloquially known as mutual funds. U.S. investment companies held over $18 trillion in assets on behalf of more than 90 million U.S. retail investors. INV. CO. INST., 2015 INVESTMENT COMPANY FACTBOOK 8, 33 (2015). In the United States, there are four main types of public funds: open-end mutual funds, closed-end funds, exchange-traded funds (ETFs), and unit investment trusts. Mutual funds are the most common form of public fund. As of 2014, mutual funds had about $16 trillion in assets. *Id.* at 29. The sector is concentrated. The top five mutual fund complexes manage 49% of U.S. mutual fund assets and the top 25 mutual fund complexes manage 74% of U.S. mutual fund assets. OFR, ASSET MANAGEMENT AND FINANCIAL STABILITY 3 (2013). Ten firms have more than $1 trillion in assets under management, nine of which have U.S.-based managers. *Id.*

Mutual funds referred to as open-end funds allow investors to buy shares in the fund and redeem (or sell) them back to the fund. Through the sale of shares, mutual funds raise capital to invest in the market. Investors then share in the returns from the mutual fund's investment portfolio. Shareholders are endowed with voting rights and, in principle, have the authority to elect directors and approve material changes to the fund's contract with its investment adviser.

A mutual fund is formed when a sponsor organizes the necessary capital and investors to launch the fund. This sponsor often also serves as the fund's investment advisor and charges the fund a management fee for its services. A mutual fund must register with the SEC as an investment company under the 1940 Act. Mutual funds offer investors diversification, liquidity, and the benefit of the investment adviser's expertise. We defer our discussion of MMFs, a special type of mutual fund that seeks to provide a financial substitute for demand deposits, to Part XII of the book.

Unlike mutual funds that are registered with and highly regulated by the SEC, hedge funds were, until recently, largely unregulated. In fact, they were largely defined by their exemption from the 1940 Act registration. The Dodd-Frank Act now requires hedge fund advisers to register with the SEC, but imposes little direct substantive regulation on them.

As described by the President's Working Group on Financial Markets,

> The term "hedge fund" is commonly used to describe a variety of different types of investment vehicles that share some common characteristics. . . . [T]he term encompasses any pooled investment vehicle that is privately organized, administered by professional investment managers, and not widely available to the public. The primary investors in hedge funds are wealthy individuals and institutional investors

THE PRESIDENT'S WORKING GRP. ON FIN. MARKETS, HEDGE FUNDS, LEVERAGE, AND THE LESSONS OF LONG-TERM CAPITAL MANAGEMENT 1 (1999).

In a speech before the Managed Funds Association in 2013, SEC Chair Mary Jo White described some of the regulatory changes occurring for hedge funds:

> There is little doubt that hedge funds have entered a new era of transparency and public openness—a transformation that I believe will benefit investors, the public and regulators. . . . The Dodd-Frank Act, as you know, required most advisers to hedge funds and other private funds to register with the SEC, resulting in public reporting of basic information regarding business operations and regulation. . . . [I]n addition, the Dodd-Frank Act directed the SEC to collect information, on a confidential basis, from private fund advisers regarding the risk-profiles of their funds.

Mary Jo White, Chair, SEC, Managed Funds Ass'n Outlook 2013 Conference: Hedge Funds—A New Era of Transparency and Openness (Oct. 18, 2013).

Since the Financial Crisis, the hedge fund sector has continued to rebound and in 2013 assets grew to an estimated $2.6 trillion. FSOC, 2014 ANNUAL REPORT 85 (2014). With the passage of the Jumpstart Our Business Startups Act (JOBS Act) in 2012, which among other things eased restrictions on marketing, the profile of hedge fund investors is likely to change, with more individual investors participating.

A private equity firm acquires portfolio companies it perceives as undervalued or ripe for improvement. After increasing the value of a company, the private equity firm looks to sell it at a profit. As with hedge funds, private equity firms were structured to avoid regulation under the Investment Advisers Act and registration under the 1940 Act. Now, under the Dodd-Frank Act, advisers to private equity firms also must register with the SEC, but do not face broker-dealer regulation. Private equity has approximately $2 trillion in assets under management as of 2013. FSOC, 2014 ANNUAL REPORT, at 84.

Pension funds, another type of pooled vehicle, held $16 trillion in assets as of 2013. *Id.* at 83. There are two main categories of pension plans: defined contribution plans, under which an employer and employee make contributions to a fund but the employer does not promise any particular retirement benefit, and defined benefit plans, under which employers promise a certain level of benefit payment upon retirement. Defined contribution plans have grown faster than defined benefit plans for many years. At the end of 2014, defined contribution plans held an estimated $6.8 trillion in assets. INV. CO. INST., 2015 INVESTMENT COMPANY FACTBOOK 137 (2015). Defined benefit plan assets totaled about $3.8 trillion as of 2014. *Id.* In many cases, employer-promised pension benefits represent a significant portion of a firm's long-term liabilities. Accordingly, federal law mandates that firms maintain a separate pension trust. Some defined benefit plans, however, lack sufficient funding to meet their promised benefits. The total unfunded liabilities of defined benefit plans were $3.1 trillion at the end of 2014. *Id.* at 138. Underfunding is most pronounced in state and local government pension plans, as exemplified by the public debate over government obligations in the city of Detroit's bankruptcy case, which concluded in 2014.

I. DERIVATIVES

Derivatives, explored in Part XI of the book, are financial products whose value is derived from other assets. There are many different types of derivatives that we will explore in greater depth later in the book. Derivatives include forwards, futures, options, and swaps. A futures contract is an agreement, traded on an exchange, to buy or sell something at a future date for a predetermined price. For example, a farmer might buy the right to sell his grain for a certain price in six months in order to lock in that price. A forward contract is the same agreement, individually negotiated. An option contract is an agreement that one party has the right to either sell or buy something in the future, but without the obligation to do so. Swaps permit parties to exchange one flow of payments for another, such as trading a fixed rate for a floating rate, or U.S. dollars for Japanese yen.

Derivatives may be traded either through central exchanges, such as the Chicago Mercantile Exchange, or over-the-counter (OTC), that is, bilaterally through derivatives dealers. In the years before the Financial Crisis, the market in OTC derivatives reached a notional amount of nearly $700 trillion. While derivatives are used by individual companies to reduce risk, in some respects, parts of the derivatives market increased systemic risk in the lead up to the Financial Crisis. Credit derivatives, which were designed to diffuse risk, instead concentrated it among large banks, investment banks, and other institutions, such as AIG. Derivatives increased firms' counterparty credit exposures and aggravated the effect of any particular firm's failure on the financial system as a whole. Synthetic securitization (with embedded derivatives) magnified failures in the real securitization market. *See* Michael S. Barr, *The Financial Crisis and the Path of Reform*, 29 YALE J. ON REG. 91, 103–04 (2012).

In the wake of the Financial Crisis, derivatives market regulation has been fundamentally changed. The Dodd-Frank Act attempts to reduce risk concentration and market opacity by promoting central clearing and exchange trading, and by strengthening supervision of market participants. Central clearing is encouraged by a combination of requirements and incentives. Standardized derivatives must be centrally cleared and traded either on designated exchanges or through swap execution facilities. All other derivatives are subjected to new reporting requirements and higher capital and margin requirements, which will encourage greater standardization and use of central clearing. Proponents of these measures expect them also to reduce costs by improving price transparency and competition and to reduce risks by preventing the buildup of counterparty risks, although, as you will see, there is a debate as to whether the risks have simply been transferred to the central clearinghouses. The Dodd-Frank Act also provides for prudential regulation of and capital requirements on dealers and other major participants in the OTC derivatives markets. Derivative clearing organizations, which assume counterparty risk for centrally cleared trades, are regulated for capital, margin, conflicts, ownership, and other matters. *See id.* at 104.

J. SHADOW BANKING

Shadow banking has different meanings for different people. It is neither completely a set of entities nor completely a set of activities. According to a highly respected Federal Reserve Board staff report, shadow banking is "a web of specialized financial institutions that channel funding from savers to investors through a range of securitization and secured funding techniques." TOBIAS ADRIAN & ADAM B. ASHCRAFT, FED. RES. BANK OF N.Y., SHADOW BANKING: A REVIEW OF THE LITERATURE 2 (2012). Some use the term market-based financing to refer to these activities.

Shadow banking can broadly be thought of as asset and maturity transformation by entities that are not regulated as banks. Many shadow banking activities rely on short term liabilities to fund illiquid, long-term assets, which means that shadow banking activities are prone to the same kind of runs that used to bedevil banks before deposit insurance. The Financial Crisis has made it abundantly clear that maturity mismatch outside of commercial banks is particularly problematic because, unlike traditional banks, non-bank financial intermediaries do not have the same government backstop of central bank liquidity or deposit insurance that traditional banks have. Shadow banking activities instead rely on private sector liquidity, but these activities may transfer risk from shadow banking activities to other financial institutions. Poorly regulated shadow banking activities may undermine the stability of the financial system.

Some institutions that engage in shadow banking activities are traditional banks and BHCs, investment banks and insurance companies, all of which are highly, if differently, regulated. Some, like hedge funds and private equity funds, however, are more lightly regulated. For shadow banking it is probably better to think in terms of activities rather than institutions. The activities, although diverse, are tightly interconnected with many parts of the financial sector and often share the characteristic that the activity involves short-term funding that may be subject to runs, but does not, unlike bank deposits, benefit from deposit insurance. While the precise definition is still subject to much debate, we think that, at a minimum, shadow banking includes any short-term wholesale borrowing activity, such as repos (widely used as a funding mechanism by investment banks), MMFs, securitization liabilities, short-term wholesale funding, and commercial paper. The figure below, created by the Financial Crisis Inquiry Commission (FCIC), largely follows this definition. You will see variants, however, as we proceed through the book given the unsettled nature of what is thought of as shadow banking.

Figure 1.1-5 Traditional and Shadow Banking Systems

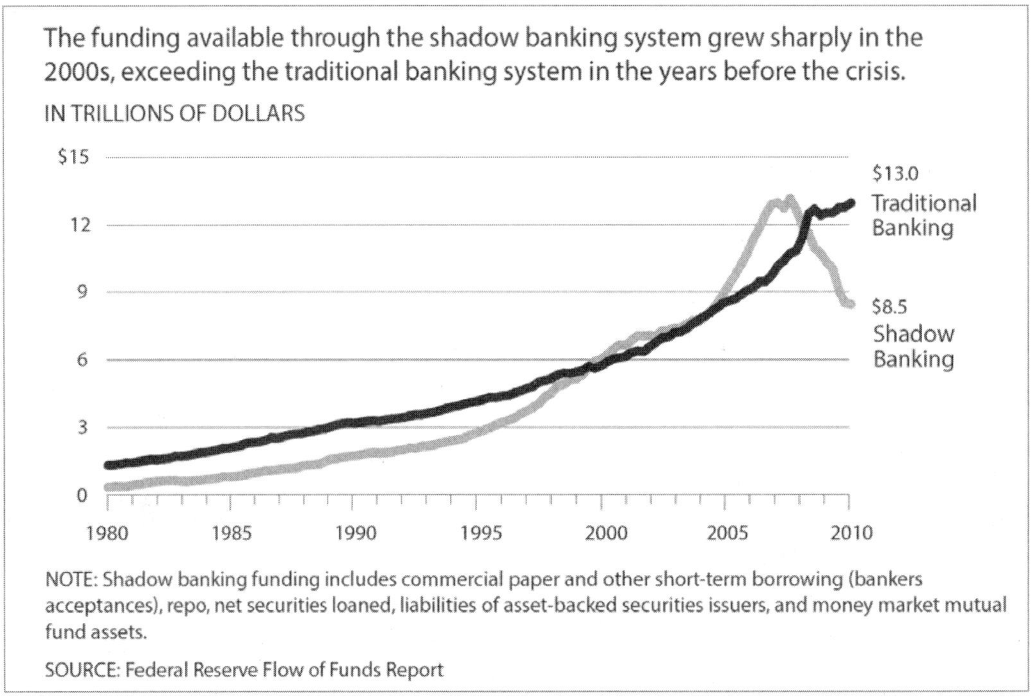

Source: FCIC, Financial Crisis Inquiry Report 32 (2011).

As Figure 1.1-5 shows, the shadow-banking sector grew substantially since the 1980s, and surpassed the size of the banking sector in the years leading up to the Financial Crisis. We explore a few key aspects of this market in this section.

1. Securitization

Since the Financial Crisis, securitization has become popularly associated with toxic mortgages and misleading credit ratings. Although assuredly an important part of the picture, the following excerpt from the FCIC report also explains many of the benefits of securitization:

> Private securitizations, or structured finance securities, had two key benefits to investors: *pooling* and *tranching*. If many loans were pooled into one security, a few defaults would have minimal impact. Structured finance securities could also be sliced up and sold in portions—known as tranches—which let buyers customize their payments. Risk-averse investors would buy tranches that paid off first in the event of default, but had lower yields. Return-oriented

> investors bought riskier tranches with higher yields. Bankers often compared it to a waterfall; holders of the senior tranches—at the top of the waterfall—were paid before the major junior tranches. And if payment came in below expectations, those at the bottom would be the first to be left high and dry.
>
> Securitization was designed to benefit lenders, investment bankers, and investors. Lenders earned fees for originating and selling loans. Investment banks earned fees for issuing mortgage-backed securities. These securities fetched a higher price than if the underlying loans were sold individually, because the securities were customized to the investors' needs, were more diversified, and could be easily traded. Purchasers of the safer tranches got a higher rate of return than ultra-safe Treasury notes without much extra risk—at least in theory.

FCIC, THE FINANCIAL CRISIS INQUIRY REPORT 43 (2011).

Figure 1.1-6 provides a visual representation of securitization. The originator makes the loan to the borrower, and then sells the loan to a securitization sponsor, which puts the loan into a special purpose vehicle (SPV). The SPV divides interests into different risk levels, or tranches. Investors can then purchase interests in the tranches depending on their risk tolerance.

Figure 1.1-6 The Securitization Process

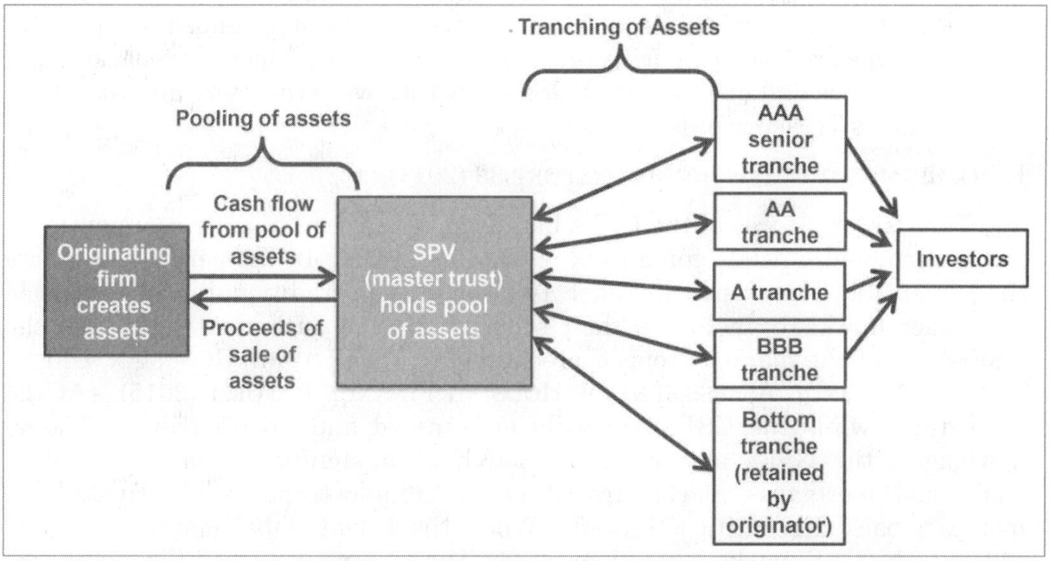

Source: Gary Gorton & Andrew Metrick, Regulating the Shadow Banking System, Brookings Papers on Econ. Activity 261, 271 (2010).

Many financial intermediaries are engaged in securitization. For non-bank financial intermediaries, it is a means to offer bank-like loans without the burden of bank regulation. The originate-to-distribute model, however, is also widely used by banks and BHCs. Under this model, loans are originated with the intention that they will be moved into a securitization vehicle and sold to investors. Securitization is not a new phenomenon, but the 2000s saw a marked increase in the securitization of household debt and mortgages, in part because of the ability of securitization sponsors to borrow cheaply in the wholesale funding markets. In the wake of the Financial Crisis, new regulations under the Dodd-Frank Act and changes in accounting standards have increased the capital requirements for securitization and required that sponsors keep a residual portion of the risk from the securitization to have skin in the game, although regulations exempt broad categories of mortgages from this rule.

2. Fannie Mae and Freddie Mac

Many of you have probably heard of Fannie Mae and Freddie Mac. These two GSEs are privately owned and managed but have some peculiar privileges. The following excerpt from the FCIC Report provides a brief introduction to Fannie Mae's and Freddie Mac's role before the crisis:

> Fannie [Mae] and Freddie [Mac] had dual missions, both public and private: support the mortgage market and maximize returns for shareholders. They did not originate mortgages; they purchased them—from banks, thrifts and mortgage companies—and either held them in their portfolios or securitized and guaranteed them. Congress granted both enterprises special privileges, such as exemptions from state and local taxes and a $2.25 billion line of credit each from the Treasury. . . . Fannie [Mae] and Freddie [Mac] could borrow at rates almost as low as the Treasury paid. Federal laws allowed banks, thrifts, and investment funds to invest in GSE securities with relatively favorable capital requirements and without limits. . . . Such privileges led investors and creditors to believe that the government implicitly guaranteed the GSEs' mortgage-backed securities and debt and that GSE securities were therefore almost as safe as Treasury bills.

FCIC, FINANCIAL CRISIS INQUIRY REPORT 39 (2011).

The risk exposures of the GSEs had been of concern to many commentators and government officials going back to the late 1990s. In the period just before the Financial Crisis, private-label issuers of non-traditional and subprime mortgages markedly increased their securitization of such mortgages, and the GSE share of the market dropped precipitously. *See* LAURIE GOODMAN, URBAN INST., A REALISTIC ASSESSMENT OF HOUSING FINANCE REFORM (2015). At the same time, while the GSEs primarily guaranteed and invested in traditional mortgages, the GSEs also began to purchase a significant amount of non-traditional mortgages and to invest in the senior tranches of private-label mortgage-backed securities (MBSs). When the private-label market began to collapse, the GSE market share increased. These steps increased the significant risks to which the GSEs were already exposed, which were compounded when house prices declined, defaults increased, job losses mounted, and losses spread from non-traditional and subprime mortgages to traditional mortgages that had generally been considered safe.

With the collapse of the housing markets, in the fall of 2008, Fannie Mae and Freddie Mac were placed in conservatorship, where they remain to this day. Taxpayers, through the Treasury, provided nearly $190 billion in support to the two GSEs in the form of preferred stock to avoid widespread housing market dislocation and broader financial contagion. In the aftermath of the Financial Crisis, the two GSEs, along with the Federal Housing Administration (FHA), became responsible for funding nearly the entire mortgage market. As of 2015, the GSEs have paid Treasury dividends of about $230 billion on that taxpayer investment. FHFA, QUARTERLY PERFORMANCE REPORT OF THE HOUSING GSES: FIRST QUARTER 2015 6 (2015). As you will see in Chapter 12.2, it was not politically possible to deal with the future of the GSEs at the time of the Dodd-Frank Act, so the debate over the future of these GSEs, and the private mortgage market, remains.

3. Money Market Mutual Funds

MMFs, discussed in Chapter 12.3, were formed and grew in the 1970s in response to then-existing restrictions on the ability of banks to offer competitive interest rates on demand deposits. These regulatory price controls on bank deposits were a problem in the inflationary 1970s. Functionally, MMFs offer consumers many of the same conveniences as demand deposits: the shares are redeemable on short notice, consumers can write checks on their accounts, and the shares maintain a fixed net asset value of $1 per share.

Refer back to Figure 1. As you can see, the share of assets held in MMFs grew in the lead-up to the Financial Crisis. At their peak in 2008, assets of MMFs were valued at $3.8 trillion. The growth of MMFs is directly correlated to the growth of the repo and commercial paper markets. MMFs needed safe, high quality investments to pay the high interest rates investors came to expect, and the commercial paper and repo markets met these requirements. MMFs were able to earn higher returns than on bank deposits, and financial institutions and other businesses were able to fund themselves cheaply. During the Financial Crisis, however, there was a run on MMFs following the demise of Lehman Brothers. The run was stemmed only by a government guarantee of the entire MMF sector. We explore regulation of the MMF sector in Chapter 12.3.

4. Wholesale Funding

We examine wholesale funding in Chapter 12.4, the final chapter of the book. In particular, we look at how financial intermediaries have funded themselves through commercial paper, repo and securities lending, prime brokerage balances, and derivatives. The system of wholesale funding was in many ways a key accelerant to the Financial Crisis, and regulators both in the United States and globally are still struggling to develop a coherent framework to reduce systemic risks in this system.

Commercial paper is unsecured short-term corporate debt issued by both financial institutions and commercial corporations to finance their operations. Commercial paper is also used by SPVs set up by investment banks and banks to fund pools of particular loans and securities, referred to as asset-backed commercial paper (ABCP).

Wholesale funding from commercial paper grew rapidly alongside the growth of MMFs. This market provided a means for MMFs to invest with relative safety and to earn stable returns. Commercial paper helped depository institutions augment their funding sources beyond deposits, and permitted investment banks to fund themselves in the absence of deposit taking. As of December 2013, there was nearly $1 trillion in outstanding commercial paper. FSOC, 2015 ANNUAL REPORT, at 54. Figure 1.1-7 shows the amount of commercial paper outstanding from 2001 to 2010. As you can see, between 2007 and 2008, the amount of commercial paper peaked at over $2 trillion.

Figure 1.1-7 Commercial Paper

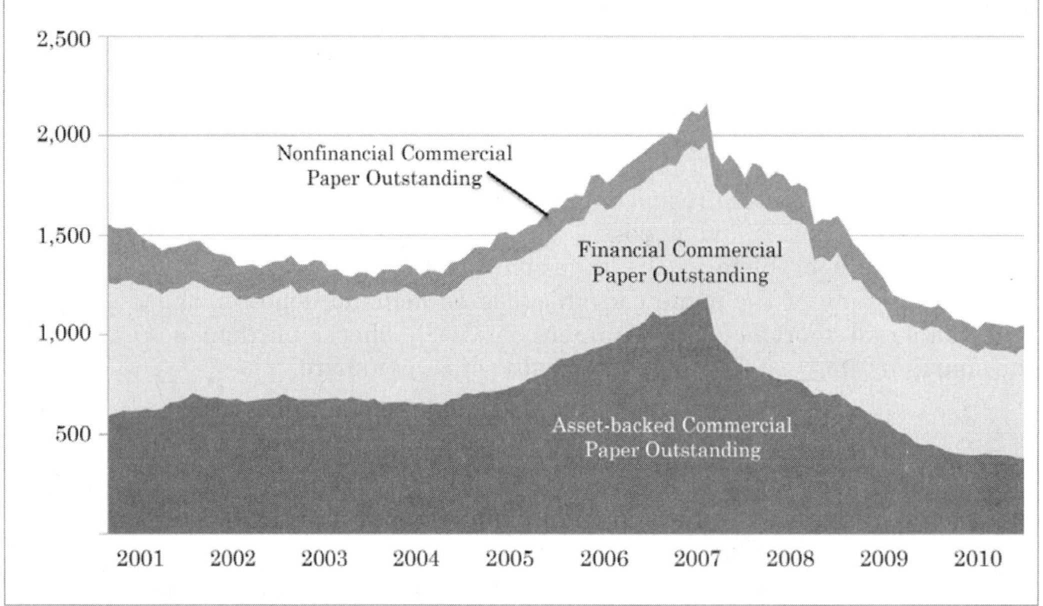

Source: FSOC, 2015 Annual Report 54 (2015).

ABCP issuance, which was over half of the total commercial paper issuance in 2007, plummeted as the Financial Crisis began and has continued to shrink since then.

A repo agreement, like commercial paper, functions as a short-term loan. A repo is structured as a temporary sale of collateral with an agreement to purchase it back at a higher price at a later date, usually the next day. The higher repurchase price functions like interest. The repo market is a way for those with excess cash to earn a return with what they view as safe assets, and those with borrowing needs to obtain funding at relatively low cost. If the borrower fails to repurchase the collateral, the counterparty can sell it, and the collateral is typically highly liquid. In addition to bilateral repo arrangements, JP Morgan and Bank of New York Mellon offer tri-party repo services, under which their banks clear repo transactions for the borrower and lender. The clearing banks insulate the repo parties from settlement risks posed by each other, but expose the parties to risk from the clearing banks themselves. In the process, the clearing banks are exposed to risks from the clearing transactions and from the intraday credit the clearing banks provide to repo counterparties.

Repos are highly liquid, secured, and exempt from the automatic stay in bankruptcy; repo transactions are thus valued as functional substitutes for bank deposits. Professors Gorton and Metrick explain how repo agreements provided investors with bank-like services. Gary Gorton & Andrew Metrick, *Regulating the Shadow Banking System*, BROOKINGS PAPERS ON ECON. ACTIVITY 261, 276–77

(2010). Despite these advantages, repos present real risks. Repo counterparties can refuse to roll over the transactions, cutting off liquidity for banks or broker-dealers. Repo collateral can become difficult to sell in a crisis, leading to fire sales. During the Financial Crisis, there was a devastating run on repos, much like the bank runs in the Great Depression.

As seen in Figure 1.1-8, the value of the repo market peaked during the Financial Crisis and has declined since. This trend is attributable in part to a decreasing reliance on short-term funding as well as "deleveraging by financial institutions in anticipation of enhanced capital regulations." FSOC, 2014 ANNUAL REPORT 59 (2014).

Figure 1.1-8 Value of the Repo Market

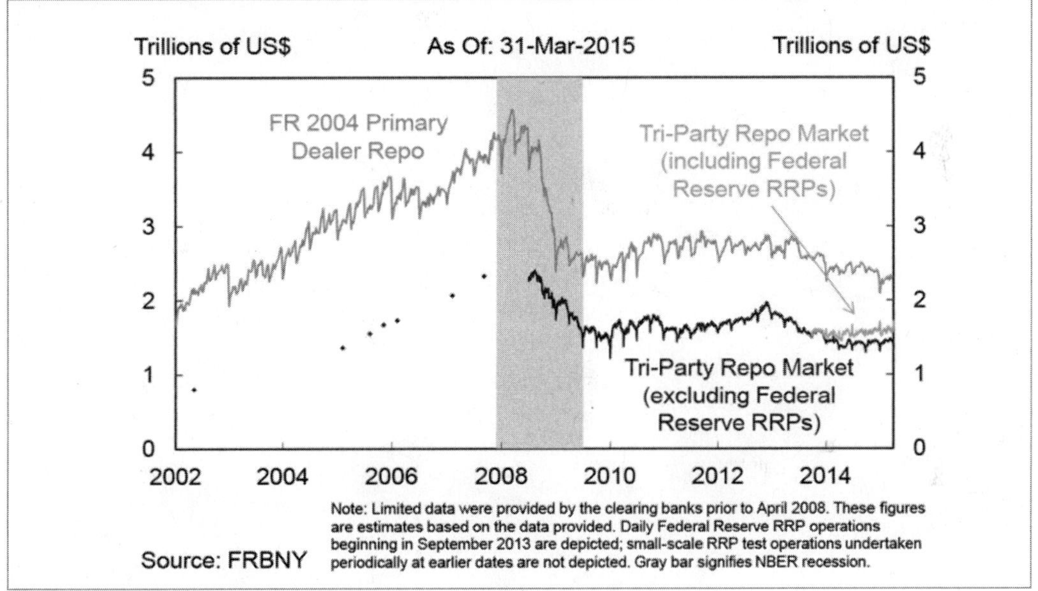

Source: FSOC, 2015 Annual Report 54 (2015).

This Chapter has provided you with an overview of the institutions and markets we will explore throughout this book. In the next chapter, we ground your understanding of the financial sector by exploring its historical evolution. We also introduce you to contending visions of the Financial Crisis.

CHAPTER 1.2

THE HISTORY OF U.S. FINANCIAL REGULATION: A THEMATIC OVERVIEW

CONTENTS

I. INTRODUCTION

In this Chapter, we explore more than 200 years of U.S. financial markets, from the creation of the First Bank of the United States to the Financial Crisis and the Dodd-Frank Act. This Chapter provides historical context to help you understand current financial regulatory debates. While generally organized chronologically, sections of the Chapter occasionally stretch forward in time to capture broader historical themes. This Chapter is an overview; we will delve deeper into selected topics later in the book. The Chapter concludes with contending visions of the Financial Crisis, a debate that shapes views about ongoing efforts to reform the financial system.

A number of themes recur throughout this Chapter and the remainder of the book. Indeed, many present-day controversies in financial regulation are rooted in earlier debates. As you delve into the history of financial regulation, pay particular attention to recurring jurisdictional battles between federal and state regulators, among federal regulators themselves, and competition between agricultural, financial, and commercial interests. Notice how different parts of the financial system, such as banking, securities, and insurance, have at times been at war with one another and at other times have combined forces or created new organizational forms or financial products. Note how financial regulations have ebbed after financial crises and flowed back as memories of those crises faded. How are these themes relevant in today's financial markets? What other common themes do you notice throughout our country's financial history? For an outstanding synthesis of U.S. financial history, see the comprehensive four volume work by Jerry Markham. JERRY W. MARKHAM, A FINANCIAL HISTORY OF THE UNITED STATES 1–4 (Routledge 2011).

II. THE FIRST AND SECOND BANKS OF THE UNITED STATES (1790–1863)

The formative years of the U.S. financial system were marked by tremendous political and legal uncertainty. The creation of the First Bank of the United States, the nation's first central bank, as well as its successor, the Second Bank of the United States, spurred fierce debates about federalism and the constitutionality of federal involvement in banking. The highly contentious battle for the First and Second Banks foreshadowed equally combative debates about dual banking and the Federal Reserve System. Indeed, finance has *always* involved political debates about the role of government.

A. THE FIRST BANK OF THE UNITED STATES

Shortly after declaring its independence in 1776, the United States became mired in financial distress. The Revolutionary War left the young federal government struggling to cope with significant war debts, and many of the states were similarly indebted and at risk of default. President George Washington described the bleak fiscal picture of the United States: "Not then organised as a nation, or known as a people upon the earth – we had no preparation – Money, the nerve of War, was wanting. The Sword was to be forged on the Anvil of necessity: the treasury to be created from nothing." George Washington,

Undelivered First Inaugural Address: Fragments, 30 April 1789, THE RECTORS AND VISITORS OF THE UNIVERSITY OF VIRGINIA, NATIONAL ARCHIVES.

In 1790, Alexander Hamilton, the first Secretary of the Treasury, proposed the creation of a central bank as part of a plan to restore the fiscal health of the nation. A student of European history, Hamilton argued that a central bank would help the fledgling United States grow by issuing currency in the form of banknotes, extending credit to facilitate commercial transactions, and acting as the fiscal agent for the federal government. Hamilton was well aware that the growth of the British Empire was facilitated by the Bank of England, established in 1694 to act as the government's banker and debt-manager, and realized that a central bank would play an important role in the attempt to create a strong, independent nation-state. Soon, a bill to charter the First Bank was introduced in Congress, where it was fiercely contested, as described in the following excerpt.

Richard H. Timberlake, Jr., Monetary Policy in the United States, An Intellectual and Institutional History

7–8 (1993)

The bill for chartering the First Bank provoked a controversy in Congress that was concentrated in the House of Representatives. One Congressman . . . noted that a geographical line separated those who were for the bank from those who were against it. All representatives to the "eastward" were for it and all to the "southward" were against it, almost without exception. The principal spokesman for the group against the bank was James Madison of Virginia. . . .

Madison's chief arguments were not economic but political and legal. They focused on the constitutionality of such a bank and the possible conflict between the states' interests and the federal interest. A national bank issuing notes on a national basis "would directly interfere with the rights of states to prohibit as well as to establish Banks, and [it would also interfere with] the circulation of [state] bank notes." . . . The right of Congress to establish a bank, he stated, was a logical precedent for Congress to incorporate any other business. . . .

The proponents of the bank rested their case on the powers given in the Constitution that enabled Congress to borrow money and to lay and collect taxes. Especially important was the aid the bank would furnish in making quick credit available to the Treasury in time of emergency. "If we have not the power to establish [the bank]," said Fisher Ames of Massachusetts, "our social compact is incomplete, we want the means of self-preservation."

Congress approved the First Bank in 1791, but its passage did not quell the constitutional concerns of many of the nation's leaders, most notably pro-agrarian Thomas Jefferson, then the Secretary of State. Jefferson argued that the Constitution did not authorize Congress to establish the central bank, as proposed by Hamilton, and endorsed by most Federalists. *See* Thomas Jefferson, Opinion on the Constitutionality of a National Bank (Feb. 15, 1791). Despite relentless opposition from Jefferson and other anti-Federalists, President George Washington signed the bill, and the First Bank opened in Philadelphia later that year. The federal government owned a 20% interest in the First Bank, with the remaining shares held by private investors. The First Bank performed a wide array of services for both the government and its citizens.

> The First Bank acted as the federal government's fiscal agent, collecting tax revenues, securing the government's funds, making loans to the government, transferring government deposits through the bank's branch network, and paying the government's bills. . . . Besides its activities on behalf of the government, the Bank of the United States also accepted deposits from the public and made loans to private citizens and businesses. . . .
>
> Unlike modern central banks, the Bank of the United States did not officially set monetary policy. Nor did it regulate other banks. Nonetheless, its prominence as one of the largest corporations in America and its branches' broad geographic position in the emerging American economy allowed it to conduct a rudimentary monetary policy. The bank's notes, backed by substantial gold reserves, gave the country what passed for a more stable national currency. By managing its lending policies and the flow of funds through its accounts, the bank could—and did—alter the supply of money and credit in the economy and hence the level of interest rates charged to borrowers.

FED. RESERVE BANK OF PHILA., THE FIRST BANK OF THE UNITED STATES: A CHAPTER IN THE HISTORY OF CENTRAL BANKING 5–8 (2009)

When the time came to renew the First Bank's charter in 1811, however, the supporters of the First Bank could not marshal sufficient votes. By that time, the anti-Federalists, led by President James Madison, were in control. In addition, the owners of state-chartered banks, which had proliferated during the prosperous decades of the First Bank's existence, feared competition from the First Bank. Congress declined to reauthorize the First Bank by one vote. Alejandro Komai & Gary Richardson, *A History of Financial Regulation in the United States from the Beginning Until Today: 1789 to 2011* 2 (Nat'l Bureau of Econ. Research, Working Paper No. 17443, 2011).

B. THE SECOND BANK OF THE UNITED STATES

Shortly after the failure to renew the First Bank's charter, the War of 1812 plunged the country back into economic turmoil. The federal government racked up heavy debts to finance the war, state banks issued their own banknotes, triggering runaway inflation, and, to top it all off, the British burned the Capitol, White House, Treasury, and other major public buildings in Washington, D.C. Financial panic ensued—the first of many such panics in the 19th Century. Faced with these challenges, Madison reconsidered his original opposition to a central bank. In 1816, with Madison's support, Congress chartered the Second Bank for a term of 20 years.

Not surprisingly, many anti-Federalists and owners of state banks opposed the Second Bank. Fourteen states passed legislation that aimed to prevent the Second Bank from collecting the states' debts. Six other states tried to tax the branches of the Second Bank located within the state borders. The Second Bank fought back. In *McCulloch v. Maryland*, the Supreme Court ruled that the creation of the Second Bank was within Congress's implied powers and that a state tax against the Second Bank violated the Constitution because "the power to tax involves the power to destroy." 17 U.S. 316, 431 (1819). This decision prevented states from imposing restrictive regulations on the Second Bank. Jerry W. Markham, *Banking Regulation: Its History and Future*, 4 N.C. BANKING INST. 221, 225 (2000).

The Second Bank, like state-chartered banks, had the power to issue banknotes, which holders could redeem for gold or silver coin, known as specie, and for government bonds. Banknotes circulated as the currency of the time, what we would call cash today. The Second Bank accepted state banknotes as payments for obligations to the Treasury. Soon, a large proportion of outstanding state banknotes became concentrated on the books of the Second Bank.

In 1819, a financial crisis erupted when the Second Bank presented state banknotes to Western and Southern state banks for conversion into specie, which the Treasury intended to use to pay off the $4 million debt it issued to complete the Louisiana Purchase. Unable to honor the Second Bank's request for so much specie, the state banks foreclosed on outstanding mortgages and suspended convertibility of their banknotes. Depositors and holders of banknotes panicked, precipitating a series of runs and bank failures. MURRAY N. ROTHBARD, THE PANIC OF 1819: REACTIONS AND POLICIES 17–18 (Ludwig von Mises Inst. 2007). The public largely blamed the Panic of 1819 on the Second Bank because of its demands for specie from the state banks. The Second Bank was also the target of public hostility when it foreclosed on large swathes of real estate following the panic. *See* RALPH C.H. CATTERALL, THE SECOND BANK OF THE UNITED STATES 84 (2010).

In 1823, the appointment of Nicholas Biddle as President of the Second Bank restored some of its prominence. Under Biddle, the Second Bank aggressively pursued expansion. By 1830, the Second Bank had established 25 branches around the United States, conducted one-fifth of all banking, and was quite profitable. Jerry W. Markham, *Banking Regulation: Its History and Future*, 4 N.C. BANKING INST. 221, 225 (2000).

C. JACKSON'S WAR AGAINST THE SECOND BANK

In the early 1830s, the Second Bank became the focal point of a major political battle that surpassed the intensity of the original Federalist vs. anti-Federalist fight over the First Bank. President Andrew Jackson and Kentucky Senator Henry Clay were the principal antagonists. Jackson saw the Second Bank as a "monster" that was corrupt and subversive to U.S. democracy. This view was grounded in Jackson's deeply-rooted suspicion of elites, his long-time commitment to maintaining local state sovereignty, and his misgivings about specially chartered corporations. Conversely, Clay, Jackson's long-time political rival, saw the Second Bank as an important American institution. *See id.* In addition, Clay was a member of the Whig party, which was founded by individuals united in their commitment to a strong national financial policy, including the financing of internal improvements that to some extent echoed Hamilton's ambitious proposals.

With the Second Bank's 20-year charter close to expiring, Clay introduced legislation to re-charter it in 1832. Both the House and the Senate passed the re-chartering bill, but Jackson vetoed it. In his veto message, Jackson heavily criticized the Second Bank:

> [S]ome of the powers and privileges possessed by the existing bank are unauthorized by the Constitution, subversive of the rights of the States, and dangerous to the liberties of the people. . . . I sincerely regret that in the act before me I can perceive none of th[e] modifications of the bank charter which are necessary, in my opinion, to make it compatible with justice, with sound policy, or with the Constitution of our country. . . .

Andrew Jackson, President, United States of America, Veto Message Regarding the Bank of the United States (July 10, 1832). Jackson pushed for the sale of the government's stake in the Second Bank, a Congressional investigation into the security of public funds held by the bank, and empowerment of the states to tax the Bank's local branches.

Jackson's message reverberated throughout the nation, weakening the Second Bank's credit and depressing its stock price. The House rejected a proposal to sell the government's stock in the Second Bank and declared that the bank's deposits were safe. In 1833, in defiance of Congress, Jackson ordered the government's deposits removed from the Second Bank and placed in state banks. Although the government's deposits were never actually withdrawn from the Second Bank, Jackson's criticisms of the bank significantly weakened it. RALPH C.H. CATTERALL, THE SECOND BANK OF THE UNITED STATES 286–89 (2010).

D. THE FREE BANKING ERA

The Second Bank's charter expired in 1836, officially marking the death a proto-lender of last resort in the United States for the next 70 years. Jackson had won his war against federal involvement in the U.S. financial system. For the next three decades, the states provided the sole legal framework for banking and there was no banking system or banking regulation operating under federal law. State regulation succeeded in many areas of the country, but ultimately, local control of banking proved to be insufficient. J. WILLARD HURST, A LEGAL HISTORY OF MONEY IN THE UNITED STATES 1774–1970 (1971). This was the era of "wildcat" banks located in remote areas to avoid redemption of banknotes for specie; "shinplasters," banknotes of dubious quality; and "carpetbaggers" who came from the Northeast to the West and South to redeem banknotes. *See* MICHAEL O'MALLEY, FACE VALUE: THE ENTWINED HISTORIES OF MONEY & RACE IN AMERICA 84–85 (2012) (describing etymology of the term carpetbagger). Banknotes traded at a discount from par, reflecting the market's perception of the credit quality of the bank that issued the notes, as well as the ease or difficulty of converting the notes to specie or government bonds. In the wake of the Second Bank's closing, a series of financial panics occurred, with a major crisis in 1837 and another significant one 20 years later. When the panics arose, there were widespread bank runs. Depositors fled and fire sales of banknotes to pay off depositors further depressed values and reinforced bank runs.

As you will see in Chapter 2.1, during this period, new banks were created in most states through a charter of incorporation granted by a special act of the state legislature. This system led to Jacksonian accusations of special privilege, public-private collusion, and even corruption. The counter-reaction involved a turn to general incorporation that ushered in the era of "free banking." Rather than a special act of the state legislature, most states permitted chartering via a general law, with review by a state banking authority.

---

1. ***The Competing Visions of Hamilton and Jefferson.*** The fights over the First and Second Banks were power struggles between the federal government and states over control of the financial sector, between emerging commercial interests in the port cities and the more rural and slaveholding portions of the country. The theme of big versus small continues today. A biographer of Hamilton has suggested that, in the end, the Hamiltonian vision won:

> If Jefferson enunciated the more ample view of political democracy, Hamilton possessed the finer sense of economic opportunity. He was the messenger from a future that we now inhabit. We have democracy and reside in the bustling world of trade, industry, stock markets, and banks that Hamilton envisioned. (Hamilton's staunch abolitionism formed an integral feature of this economic vision.) He has also emerged as the uncontested visionary in anticipating the shape and powers of the federal government. At a time when Jefferson and Madison celebrated legislative power as the purest expression of the popular will, Hamilton argued for a dynamic executive branch and an independent judiciary, along with a professional military, a central bank, and an advanced financial system. Today, we are indisputably the heirs to an advanced financial system. Today, we are indisputably the heirs to Hamilton's America, and to repudiate his legacy is, in many ways, to repudiate the modern world.

RON CHERNOW, ALEXANDER HAMILTON 6 (Penguin Books 2004). In what ways did Hamilton's vision contrast with Jefferson's? How are Hamilton's and Jefferson's philosophies reflected in today's debates about financial regulation?

III. THE RISE OF NATIONAL BANKS (1863–1914)

In April 1861, long-festering political differences over slavery and states' rights sparked the first shots of the Civil War. Once again, the federal government in Washington had to figure out how to pay for a war. Congress passed a series of statutes that authorized the Treasury to issue notes as collateral for loans. When those acts proved insufficient to finance the war, Congress passed the National Banking Acts of 1863 and 1864. Under those laws, investors could apply for a national charter and the owners of a state-chartered bank could convert to a national charter. If granted the charter, the bank was required to buy U.S. government bonds in an amount equal to one-third of its capital. By creating a new class of national banks and requiring them to purchase government bonds, President Abraham Lincoln's Treasury raised money to fund the war against the Confederacy.

The national banking system, however, was more than just a financing arm for the government's war effort. It marked the federal government's return to banking after three decades of exclusive state control. In this section, we explore the most important features of the banking system during this era: the creation of a national currency, the dual banking system, the importance of single-branch banks, known as unit banks, and the role of interbank deposits in the reserve structure. As you read, note how rapidly the federal role in finance grew but also how resilient the states and state-chartered banks were in retaining power at the state level and protecting the market position of small country banks.

A. UNIFORM NATIONAL CURRENCY

From the demise of the Second Bank until 1865, state banks issued currency in the form of banknotes with no oversight by the federal government. These banknotes were redeemable for specie only at the bank from which they were issued. Notes were passed from one person to another and yet another before being returned to the bank. Often, the holder of a banknote could transfer the note to another individual or non-issuing bank only at a steep discount. The acquirer of the note would insist on such a discount because of uncertainty as to whether the issuing bank would ultimately honor the note. *See* S. REP. No. 582, at 14 (1910); *see also* BRAY HAMMOND, BANKS AND POLITICS IN AMERICA: FROM THE REVOLUTION TO THE CIVIL WAR 702-03 (1991); HOWARD BODENHORN, STATE BANKING IN EARLY AMERICA: A NEW ECONOMIC HISTORY 40–41 (2001).

The National Banking Acts addressed this problem by creating a uniform national currency. National banks were authorized to issue national banknotes—*i.e.*, standardized paper money with identical engraving on one side and the issuing bank's name printed on the reverse. The federal government limited note circulation by requiring national banks to hold a reserve against their notes invested in an equivalent amount of U.S. government bonds. The creation of national banknotes was a major victory for the federal government's control of the money supply and authority over the monetary system. The National Banking Acts provided the U.S. financial system with a "paper currency that was uniform in appearance and value, difficult to counterfeit, . . . enabled the government and the public to use the same money . . . [, and] permitted the government to use bank credit, to have bank accounts, to draw bank checks, and to accept them." BRAY HAMMOND, BANKS AND POLITICS IN AMERICA: FROM THE REVOLUTION TO THE CIVIL WAR 734 (1991).

B. THE DUAL BANKING SYSTEM

Recall that after the downfall of the Second Bank, only the states had the power to charter and regulate banks. In a major change, following the National Banking Acts, new or existing banks could choose to operate under either federal or state jurisdiction according to their choice of charter. The dual banking system was born. Under the dual banking system, chartering authority was shared between the states and the federal government. National banks were chartered and supervised by the Office of the Comptroller of the Currency (OCC).

The Acts established a system for granting national charters to existing state banks, at their election, and enabled these new national banks to act as depositories for the federal Treasury. *See id* at 731.

Initially, the Acts did little to change state banks. Key proponents of the National Banking Acts, including Treasury Secretary Salmon P. Chase, expected the Acts to induce state banks to convert to national banks. In reality, however, few did. National banking proponents decided that, if the state banks would not re-charter of their own volition, then the federal government would drive state banks out of business through the imposition of a prohibitive tax on banknotes. Over short but bitter opposition from the state banks, Congress enacted a 10% tax on state banknotes in 1865. This punitive tax was upheld in *Veazie Bank v. Fenno*, 75 U.S. 533 (1869). Almost immediately, state banks began to re-charter as national banks. The number of state banks fell drastically between 1864 and 1869. Emmette S. Redford, *Dual Banking: A Case Study in Federalism*, 31 LAW & CONTEMP. PROBS. 749, 755–56 (1966).

Nonetheless, the state bank system survived. State banks, in a move that we would today call regulatory arbitrage, deployed a paper check system that bequeathed us the one we still use today. They could conduct banking business through checks and deposit balances and avoid issuing banknotes altogether. To spur this resurgence in state banking, state regulators and lawmakers loosened capital and activity restrictions on state banks and cut fees that banks paid for examinations. The states' efforts worked. By 1895, the number of state banks again eclipsed the number of national banks, and state banks have outnumbered national banks ever since. *See id.* at 756.

C. UNIT BANKS AND CORRESPONDENT BANKING

During the 19th Century, many states limited or prohibited branching, even within the state, leading to a system of unit banks or one office banks. In a time when transportation by horse or rail and communications by mail led to many different regional and local economies, there was a limited push for branching and states jealously guarded their rights to keep banks chartered in other states from entering. Concerns about out-of-state banks were part of broader hostility towards out-of-state corporations generally during this period. The creation of national banks during the Civil War had little effect on intrastate and interstate branching since an early Comptroller interpreted the National Bank Act to prohibit branching by national banks. It is now widely accepted by historians that the system of unit banks contributed to the series of banking panics suffered by the United States in 1819, 1837, 1857, 1873, 1884, 1893, 1901, 1907, and during the Great Depression. *See* Charles W. Calomiris & Gary Gorton, *The Origins of Banking Panics: Models, Facts and Regulations in Financial Markets and Financial Crises*, *in* FINANCIAL MARKETS AND FINANCIAL CRISES (1991); EUGENE N. WHITE, THE REGULATION AND REFORM OF THE AMERICAN BANKING SYSTEM, 1900-1929 (1983).

By the last quarter of the 19th Century, the problems stemming from the decentralized, undiversified condition of the U.S. banking system were well-known, and multiple solutions were debated by Congress and the banking sector. *See* ELMUS WICKER, THE GREAT DEBATE ON BANKING REFORM: NELSON ALDRICH AND THE ORIGINS OF THE FED (2005). The political power of state bankers was too strong for interstate branching to be a solution. Despite the widespread expectations of many bankers during the 1920s that branching would soon be permitted, small bank interests convinced the Supreme Court to overturn the Comptroller's decision to permit national banks to branch within the same city of their head office. *See* First National Bank in St. Louis v. Missouri, 263 U.S. 640 (1924). The original McFadden Act of 1927 allowed national banks to operate branches to the same extent as state banks were permitted to branch under state law. Some states, such as New York, permitted state banks (and, indirectly, national banks) to operate branches in the same city as their headquarters. Many states, however, continued to require unit banks. No states permitted interstate branching. *See* EUGENE N. WHITE, THE REGULATION AND REFORM OF THE AMERICAN BANKING SYSTEM, 1900-1929 (1983).

The dominance of unit banks in the banking system at a time of rapid geographic expansion in the economy created challenges for parties conducting business across vast distances, especially between the city and the country. Imagine, for instance, a New York City-based buyer who purchased goods from a country-based vendor while on a business trip and paid by check. That check would be drawn down on the buyer's bank in New York, but the vendor would deposit the check in its own country bank. Settlement would require the shipment of coin from the New York City bank to the country bank.

To avoid the inefficiencies of shipping specie, country banks began to hold deposit accounts with city banks, which would adjust balances on their books to settle transactions. In the previous example, the country bank would have a deposit account with the New York City bank. When the check was deposited by the vendor, the country bank would increase the vendor's deposit balance (an increase in the country bank's liabilities), while instructing the New York City bank to increase its own deposit balance (an offsetting increase in the country bank's assets) and decrease the buyer's deposit balance.

This practice of settling transactions by adjusting interbank deposits is referred to as correspondent banking, where the correspondent, the city bank, would adjust the balances of the respondent, the country bank, to settle transactions. Correspondent banking became common, in part, because unit banks dominated the banking system. Indeed, if city banks had been able to establish branches in the country, they might have settled transactions by updating the accounts in their own books. By the early 20th Century, there was a web of correspondent banking relationships. Banks were increasingly interconnected to each other through a network of interbank deposits. Clearinghouse systems, such as the New York Clearinghouse, developed to clear checks on a multilateral basis. They also acted as a private lender of last resort.

D. INTERBANK DEPOSITS IN THE RESERVE STRUCTURE

Thousands of small, rural banks serving communities across the American heartland held undiversified portfolios of primarily agricultural loans. These rural banks were connected to larger city banks through reserve requirements. The National Banking Act required national banks to hold reserves—*i.e.*, a percentage of high quality, liquid assets that can be sold to pay off customer deposits if they are redeemed. National banks could hold a portion of their reserves in the form of interbank deposits. These interbank deposits contributed to the growth of correspondent banking. Country banks tended to hold reserves in the form of interbank deposits with banks in reserve cities (cities with populations greater than 50,000). Reserve city banks, in turn, tended to hold reserves in the form of interbank deposits with banks in central reserve cities (namely New York, Chicago, and St. Louis), with most of these reserves flowing to New York where interest rates were highest. New York banks, in turn, lent these reserves to the stock market, in many cases to traders engaged in speculation. As a result, the reserve system was structured in a pyramid wherein much of the banking system's reserves were concentrated in central reserve city banks.

This system was inherently fragile. Each autumn, country banks called in their balances from reserve banks to finance crop movements, which in turn required reserve banks to call in reserves from New York, leading New York banks to call in margin loans extended to the stock market. Credit tightened across the economy simultaneously. Banking panics frequently resulted when seasonal liquidity demands from country banks coincided with high volatility in stock markets. *See* ROGER LOWENSTEIN, AMERICA'S BANK: THE EPIC STRUGGLE TO CREATE THE FEDERAL RESERVE 14–15 (2015); *see also* JOHN H. WOOD, CENTRAL BANKING IN A DEMOCRACY: THE FEDERAL RESERVE AND ITS ALTERNATIVES 57 (Routledge 2015); Michael D. Bordo, *The Lender of Last Resort: Alternative Views and Historical Experience*, FED. RESERVE BANK OF RICHMOND ECON. REV. 18 (1990); Jeffrey Miron, *Financial Panics, the Seasonality of the Nominal Interest Rate, and the Founding of the Fed*, 76 AM. ECON. REV. 125, 129–30 (1986). Indeed, bank panics repeatedly struck the United States. You will learn about the most prominent panic in the next section. A key feature of this period was the absence of both deposit insurance, and of a central bank to provide liquidity to the financial system in the event of a panic.

---

1. ***Divergence in Banking and Insurance Regulation.*** The National Banking Acts and the development of the national banking system in the decades following the Civil War reflected a federalization of banking regulation. In contrast, insurance regulation in this era was, and has continued to be, dominated by the states. After the passage of the National Banking Acts, the insurance sector sought to pass a federal insurance law similar in scope. These efforts failed, and the insurance sector turned to the courts for relief. In the landmark case of *Paul v. Virginia*, 75 U.S. 168 (1869), the Supreme Court ruled that insurance lay outside of Congress's Commerce Clause powers, and thus states had free rein to develop a state-based system of insurance regulation. When the Supreme Court in 1944 called into question its holding in *Paul*, Congress passed the McCarran-Ferguson Act of 1945, which provides that the business of insurance is subject to state regulation, unless Congress provides to the contrary. The states have established a regulatory structure, and powerful political forces support such structures in ways that have important implications for U.S. insurance regulation today. We discuss the history of insurance regulation in Chapter 3.1.

IV. THE CREATION OF THE FEDERAL RESERVE SYSTEM (1907–1933)

Since the demise of the Second Bank, the United States had changed from an agricultural economy to a developing industrial economy. Unlike all other developed nations at the time, however, the United States had not established a lender of last resort. The Federal Reserve System evolved over time. The Panic of 1907 created a strong impetus for reform, and after long and contentious debates, Congress enacted the Federal Reserve Act in 1913. As you will see, the hybrid structure of the Federal Reserve System involved compromises between competing factions, echoing the earlier debates around the First and Second Banks. These compromises were revisited in the wake of the Federal Reserve's failures in the Great Depression, resulting in significant reforms enacted in 1935. As you read this material, consider the extent to which debates at the time of the Federal Reserve System's founding remain relevant more than a century later.

A. THE PANIC OF 1907

The Panic of 1907, even more so than the string of panics that had preceded it, demonstrated that the U.S. financial system was inherently fragile. The panic began among trust companies that were not regulated as banks but made loans and offered demand deposits.

Jon R. Moen & Ellis W. Tallman, The Panic of 1907

Fed. Reserve History (Dec. 4, 2015)

The Panic of 1907 was the first worldwide financial crisis of the twentieth century. It transformed a recession into a contraction surpassed in severity only by the Great Depression. . . .

The central role of New York City trust companies distinguishes the Panic of 1907 from earlier panics. Trust companies were state-chartered intermediaries that competed with banks for deposits. . . . [T]hey held a low percentage of cash reserves relative to deposits, around 5 percent, compared with 25 percent for national banks. Because trust-company deposit accounts were demandable in cash, trusts were just as susceptible to runs on deposits as were banks. . . .

[T]rusts were large and important to the financial system. Trust companies loaned large sums directly in New York equity markets, including New York Stock Exchange [(NYSE)] brokers. Trusts did not require collateral for these loans, which had to be repaid by the end of the business day. Brokers used these loans to purchase securities for themselves or their clients and then used these securities as collateral for a call loan—an overnight loan that facilitated stock purchases—from a nationally chartered bank. The proceeds of the call loan were used to pay back the initial loan from the trust company. Trusts were a necessary part of this process, because the law prohibited nationally chartered commercial banks from making uncollateralized loans or guaranteeing the payment of checks written by brokers on accounts without sufficient funds. The extra liquidity provided by trusts supported new daily transactions on the floor of the exchange. Runs on trust company deposits, however, short-circuited their role as the initial liquidity provider to the stock market. . . .

The parallels between the crises in 1907 and 2008 are striking. During 2007–09, the financial crisis was centered on investment banks, institutions without direct access to the Federal Reserve System. In 1907, widespread depositor withdrawals occurred at New

York City trust companies—intermediaries outside the New York Clearing House, the effective lender of last resort. In effect, both financial crises started outside the large banks serving as payments centers. Yet the crises created havoc within markets and among banks that were central to the payments system. Both crises challenged the existing mechanisms used to alleviate crises.

The trust companies in 1907 were like the shadow banks in the financial crisis of 2007–09. Short-term lending during the recent crisis came largely from some shadow banks (hedge funds and money market mutual funds) to fund other shadow banks (investment banks). As key liquidity providers for repurchase agreements, these shadow banks were the "depositors" providing funds for overnight lending to allow investment banks to finance the asset-backed security market, just as uncollateralized loans (overdrafts) by trust companies allowed brokers to purchase stock. Both the trusts and the shadow banks faced runs by their depositors and had to withdraw lending in short-term credit markets.

Consider the events that precipitated the Panic of 1907, as described in the following excerpt:

> Outwardly the cause for the disturbance in the banking system was the widespread rumor that one of the old banks had suffered serious losses through the collapse of a curb brokerage house, and that it was in a dangerous condition. . . . The clamor of depositors for their money would not of itself have thrown the banking system into confusion, nor brought about suspension of payments. These results were due more largely to the action taken by banks in various sections of the country than to the conduct of individual depositors. Fearing a run, the banks made every effort to hold all the cash they had, and at the same time tried to add to their stock of money by calling in their deposits with other banks, notably funds in the hands of agents in reserve and central reserve cities. Their action tended to intensify public distrust, and to call forth a general demand for cash from depositors. The outcome was the panic. The banks naturally could not meet the universal demand for money, and in a short time currency began to disappear from circulation.

LUDWIG BENDIX, THE ALDRICH PLAN IN THE LIGHT OF MODERN BANKING 23 (1912).

In the midst of the panic, J. Pierpont Morgan, namesake of the firm J.P. Morgan, stepped in and personally pledged his own money to prop up the banking system. Simultaneously, Morgan brought in other bankers and institutions to do the same. In a famous finale to this rescue, Morgan gathered the other financiers in his lavish library and held them there until they agreed to provide the funds necessary to stave off collapse. The Treasury also contributed tens of millions of dollars, but Morgan received the lion's share of credit for saving the day. Morgan's involvement quite understandably raised concerns about leaving the fate of the burgeoning financial system in the hands of one private individual. *See* RON CHERNOW, THE HOUSE OF MORGAN 126–28 (1990); *see also* PETER CONTI-BROWN, THE POWER AND INDEPENDENCE OF THE FEDERAL RESERVE 17 (2016); *see also* GARY B. GORTON, MISUNDERSTANDING FINANCIAL CRISES 142–43 (2012).

After the Panic of 1907, many supported reforms that could reduce the banking system's susceptibility to panics as a result of seasonal demands. Consensus for reform did not, however, coalesce in favor of creating a central bank until years afterwards. The period between 1907 and 1913 was marked by vigorous debate. Proponents of decentralized local government, reprising the local power ideals of Jeffersonian and Jacksonian democracy, set themselves against proponents of a strong national government modeled more closely on the Hamiltonian tradition. Before the creation of a single national currency, members of the camp in favor of decentralized local government, led by William Jennings Bryan, favored reforms that would expand the U.S. monetary supply by allowing banks to issue private currency backed not by specie or government securities but by the assets they held, such as loans and discounted notes. Members of the opposing camp, including a German émigré banker named Paul Warburg and, later, Senator Nelson Aldrich, favored the creation of a central bank. Warburg arrived in New York in 1902 and, reared in the efficiently synchronized world of German banking, acutely perceived with an outsider's eye the flaws in the banking system that myopic Americans had missed:

> Warburg stressed that a central bank was a requisite for developing deeper, more liquid credit markets. Even in a second tongue, Warburg waxed poetic over the centralized credit systems of Europe, where "the credit of the whole nation—that is, the farmer, merchant and manufacturer . . . becomes available as a means of exchange." Warburg wanted Americans to see that their system was weakened by its lack of unity. He vividly compared its banks to the infantry in a disorganized platoon. "Instead of sending an army," he admonished, "we send each soldier to fight alone."

LOWENSTEIN, AMERICA'S BANK: THE EPIC STRUGGLE TO CREATE THE FEDERAL RESERVE 55–56 (2015).

In the wake of the Panic of 1907, Congress established a commission to study the banking systems of Europe and the United States. Eventually, Aldrich and a small number of others who went on to lead the central banking movement held a secret summit on Jekyll Island in 1910, developing a plan, which came to be called the Aldrich Plan, setting out their vision for a U.S. central bank. The Aldrich Plan remained a closely guarded secret, however, even as the Jekyll Island group began to unfold their designs in the face of intense opposition to the idea of a central bank. *See id.* at 107–23.

The election of progressive Democrat Woodrow Wilson in 1912 sparked new impetus for reform. Fearing political repercussions from rural voters reflexively opposed to concentrated financial power in any form, however, Wilson avoided publicly supporting the establishment of a central bank during his 1912 presidential campaign but privately signaled he would be receptive. *Id.*; *see also* CONTI-BROWN, THE POWER AND INDEPENDENCE OF THE FEDERAL RESERVE; ALLAN H. MELTZER, A HISTORY OF THE FEDERAL RESERVE (2002); JOHN H. WOOD, CENTRAL BANKING IN A DEMOCRACY: THE FEDERAL RESERVE AND ITS ALTERNATIVES (2015); RICHARD H. TIMBERLAKE, THE ORIGINS OF CENTRAL BANKING IN THE UNITED STATES 6 (1978).

As President, Wilson favored a strong, publicly run central bank based in Washington. Large banks favored a privately run system based on the Bank of England and British clearinghouse model, while those in the Jeffersonian tradition wanted to disperse power away from Washington. Ultimately, Congress enacted a compromise. Then-representative Carter Glass, a Democrat from Virginia, favored a decentralized system of private reserve banks. In a compromise that became the Federal Reserve Act, Wilson accepted a hybrid public-private structure with a publicly appointed Board of Governors based in Washington that supervised 12 privately owned Federal Reserve Banks, each corresponding to a geographically apportioned district. A version of this compromise still exists today. This uneasy balance between decentralized authority focused on local interests and intermittent crises requiring central action in Washington continues to define the Federal Reserve System, though it resulted in especially deleterious friction in the Federal Reserve Board's early decades. *See* CONTI-BROWN, THE POWER AND INDEPENDENCE OF THE FEDERAL RESERVE.

B. FUNCTIONS OF THE FEDERAL RESERVE SYSTEM

The Federal Reserve Act addressed two major deficiencies in the banking system that the Panic of 1907 exposed: the lack of an elastic currency supply, and the absence of a lender of last resort.

During panics, banks faced with a shortage of cash had no way to expand the money supply. Issuing more national banknotes to serve as an emergency currency was not an option because banknotes had to be backed by a corresponding value of Treasury bonds. Additional national banknotes could therefore only be issued through an increase in Treasury bonds deposited with the Comptroller of Currency. In times of panic, that was not an option because banks did not have enough money to purchase more Treasury bonds, let alone pay their depositors. In essence, national banknotes were not an elastic currency because their volume could not expand with rising need during a crisis.

The Federal Reserve Act solved this problem by creating Federal Reserve notes, legal tender whose supply the Federal Reserve System could increase or decrease as needed. The Federal Reserve Banks were authorized to discount short-term commercial and agricultural paper for their member banks against the proceeds of which Federal Reserve notes could be issued and put in circulation. Then, as the discounted paper was paid off, the Federal Reserve notes would be withdrawn from circulation. In this way, the Federal Reserve could control the amount of Federal Reserve notes in circulation and, thus, the elasticity of the money supply.

As the Panic of 1907 demonstrated, the U.S. banking system lacked an adequate lender of last resort that could provide discretionary liquidity to banks in times of crisis. As you will learn in Chapter 9.1, the Federal Reserve Act allowed the Federal Reserve System to serve as a lender of last resort by replenishing member banks' reserves when banks experienced liquidity shortfalls and could not obtain funds elsewhere. When the banking system was unstable, Federal Reserve Banks could now stand ready to inject funds into fundamentally solvent banks experiencing temporary liquidity problems. By doing so, the Federal Reserve System could help these banks avoid forced asset sales to meet their obligations and also discourage depositors from running on a bank due to concerns over a bank's liquidity. Aldrich and his allies hoped that this lender of last resort function would mitigate the risk of bank failure and contagion.

The concept of the lender of last resort dates back to 1797, when it was first suggested by Sir Francis Baring that the Bank of England should be the "dernier resort." SIR FRANCIS BARING, OBSERVATIONS ON THE ESTABLISHMENT OF THE BANK OF ENGLAND AND ON THE PAPER CIRCULATION OF THE COUNTRY 22 (Augustus M. Kelley ed., 1967). In reality, however, the Bank of England did not consistently provide liquidity in times of crisis, nor did it embrace its role as lender of last resort until the mid-19th Century. Thomas M. Humphrey & Robert E. Keleher, *The Lender of Last Resort: A Historical Perspective*, 4 CATO J. 275, 299–300 (1984).

The Bank of England was persuaded to adopt the role of lender of last resort by Walter Bagehot. *Id.* at 291–305. Bagehot argued that, in times of panic, the Bank of England should lend freely in accordance with two rules. First, the loans should only be made at high rates of interest, known as penalty rates. Second, the Bank of England should make loans against all collateral that was considered good, commonly pledged, and easily convertible during ordinary times, so as not to exacerbate the panic. WALTER BAGEHOT, LOMBARD STREET: A DESCRIPTION OF THE MONEY MARKET, ch. 7 ¶¶ 57–60 (Henry S. King & Co. 1873).

C. THE EARLY FEDERAL RESERVE SYSTEM

The Federal Reserve System started operations in November 1914, just after the beginning of World War I. Contending with a more or less constant power struggle between the regional Federal Reserve Banks and the Board in Washington, the Federal Reserve System, by tightening credit during the Stock Market Crash of 1929, worsened the Great Depression and contributed to the failure of many banks between 1929 and 1933. *See* LIAQUAT AHAMED, LORDS OF FINANCE: THE BANKERS WHO BROKE THE WORLD 501–02 (2009); *see also* MILTON FRIEDMAN & ANNA J. SCHWARTZ, THE GREAT CONTRACTION, 1929-1933 (1969) and BEN S. BERNANKE, ESSAYS ON THE GREAT DEPRESSION (2000).

Twenty years after the passage of the Federal Reserve Act, the Banking Act of 1935 altered the Federal Reserve System's structure and governance. The act was the brainchild of Marriner S. Eccles, special assistant to the Secretary of the Treasury. *See* CONTI-BROWN, THE POWER AND INDEPENDENCE OF THE FEDERAL RESERVE. Eccles's goal was to make the Washington-based Federal Reserve Board the true center of national banking policy and to abolish the Reserve Banks, which were dominated by regional banking interests. Whereas in 1913, limiting federal power was a principal concern, in 1935, Eccles's principal focus was increasing the power of the Washington-based Federal Reserve Board. *Id; see also* ROGER LOWENSTEIN, AMERICA'S BANK: THE EPIC STRUGGLE TO CREATE THE FEDERAL RESERVE (2015). Eccles's vision was partially embodied in the Banking Act of 1935. The act strengthened the Federal Reserve Board and prevented the Federal Reserve Banks from undermining a national interest rate and monetary policy; the Federal Reserve Banks, however, were permitted to participate in the Federal Open Market Committee (FOMC), through which the Federal Reserve System sets monetary policy. According to one account, the

Federal Reserve System was transformed from "private banks running a private banking policy with public benefits to a public central bank in the modern sense of the word." CONTI-BROWN, THE POWER AND INDEPENDENCE OF THE FEDERAL RESERVE 31.

---

1. ***The Federal Reserve Board's Evolving Role.*** The Federal Reserve Board's role in financial regulation has continued to expand. For instance, in the Bank Holding Company Act of 1956 (BHCA), Congress gave the Federal Reserve Board supervisory and regulatory power over bank holding companies (BHCs). We will discuss BHCs in Chapter 6.1. Twenty years later, amidst high inflation and unemployment, Congress charged the Federal Reserve Board with pursuing the goals of "maximum employment, stable prices, and moderate long-term interest rates." 12 U.S.C. § 225a (1977). After the Financial Crisis, Congress put the Federal Reserve Board in charge of supervising financial companies that are deemed systemically important. *See, e.g.*, Dodd-Frank Act § 113.

The Federal Reserve Board's power, however, remains controversial, and many critics want the Federal Reserve Board weakened or even abolished. Critics allege that the Federal Reserve Board is secretive and undemocratic, and they argue that the Federal Reserve Board's response to the Financial Crisis exceeded its statutory powers. *See, e.g.*, RON PAUL, END THE FED (Grand Central 2009); *see also* MURRAY N. ROTHBARD, THE CASE AGAINST THE FED (Ludwig von Mises Inst. 2011). You will learn about the Federal Reserve Board in Chapter 9.1.

V. THE NEW DEAL AND ITS LEGACY (1933–1960S)

Following the end of World War I and into the 1920s, the United States enjoyed unprecedented prosperity. Some 20 million shareholders took advantage of post-war prosperity and invested in the stock market, fueling its spectacular growth. This growth, combined with a flow of loose credit, fueled risky and speculative activities. Groups of wealthy investors traded large pools of stocks to manipulate prices and enjoy speculative windfalls. Commercial banks used depositors' funds, which at the time were uninsured, to make speculative loans. Small investors acquired stock beyond their means from brokers who required only a small down payment, or margin, while loaning the remaining price of the stock. Fueling the fire, securities regulation was either vastly inadequate or nonexistent. Although many states attempted to regulate the securities markets at a local level through Blue Sky laws, brokers and dealers found it easy to evade this state regulation.

When stock prices began to decline in September 1929, brokers started demanding repayment of their loans. Many investors lacked sufficient cash to satisfy their obligations, and they resorted to selling their stock. These fire sales further depressed prices, creating a vicious cycle that soon collapsed, bringing the country's financial system to disaster. On October 24, 1929, dubbed Black Thursday, a selling frenzy resulted in record one-day stock market losses that totaled $9 billion. The following Tuesday, October 29, the market traded 16 million shares, and by November stocks shed some $26 billion in value. The losses did not end there:

> Between September 1, 1929, and July 1, 1932, the value of all stocks listed on the [NYSE] shrank from a total of nearly $90 billion to just under $16 billion—a loss of 83 percent. In a comparable period, bonds listed on the [NYSE] declined from a value of $49 billion to $31 billion. . . . Nor did these figures, staggering as they were, fully gauge the extent of the 1929-1932 stock market crash. During the post-World War I decade, approximately $50 billion of new securities were sold in the United States. Approximately half or $25 billion would prove near or totally valueless. Leading "blue chip" securities, including General Electric, Sears, Roebuck, and U.S. Steel common stock, would lose over 90 percent of their value between selected dates in 1929 and 1932.

JOEL SELIGMAN, THE TRANSFORMATION OF WALL STREET: A HISTORY OF THE SECURITIES AND EXCHANGE COMMISSION AND MODERN CORPORATE FINANCE 1–2 (2d ed. 1995).

Soon, the banking system was also thrust into widespread financial panic. There had also been spectacular growth in the number of banks in the 1920s, with almost 30,000 banks in the United States, many of them one branch country banks, existing at the time of the 1929 Stock Market Crash. Indeed, 82% of the bank failures in the 1920s were of small country banks, most of them unit banks. The first wave of bank failures in the early 1930s was seen as weeding out poorly managed and thinly capitalized banks. Fearful of losing their savings, in the era before deposit insurance, many customers withdrew deposits in smaller banks, and bank runs precipitated waves of failures. The market crash in 1929 led to the Great Depression, the longest economic downturn in U.S. history. By 1932, nearly one-quarter of all Americans were unemployed. *See Subcommittee on S. Resolutions 84 and 239 (The Pecora Committee)*, U.S. S. HISTORICAL OFFICE, A HISTORY OF NOTABLE SENATE INVESTIGATIONS 1; *see also* HELEN M. BURNS, THE AMERICAN BANKING COMMUNITY AND NEW DEAL BANKING REFORMS, 1933-35 (1974).

Against the backdrop of the Great Depression, President Franklin D. Roosevelt swept into office on a platform calling for a "new deal for the American People." *Roosevelt's Nomination Address, 1932 (July 2, 1932), in* 1 THE PUBLIC PAPERS AND ADDRESSES OF FRANKLIN D. ROOSEVELT 647, 647 (1938). In the first year of the Roosevelt Administration, new securities and banking laws transformed the federal government's role in the U.S. financial sector. The New Deal also contained a wide range of economic reforms, from the creation of Social Security insurance, jobs programs, and labor rights to housing and agricultural policies.

A. ENHANCING TRANSPARENCY IN SECURITIES MARKETS AND SEPARATING BANKING FROM SECURITIES

In response to the stock market crash, the Senate Committee on Banking conducted an investigation into manipulative and abusive practices in the offering, underwriting, and trading of securities. The investigation, very ably conducted by Ferdinand Pecora, is known to this day as the Pecora hearings and is widely credited with influencing the shape of the New Deal era securities laws reforms. Two important consequences followed from the Pecora hearings: the federal government entered the field of securities regulation for the first time and commercial bank and investment bank activities were separated.

1. The Securities Act of 1933 and the Exchange Act of 1934

Testimony at the Pecora hearings revealed serious deficiencies in the disclosure of information to investors. According to many witnesses, underwriters had marketed securities to the public without revealing critical information about the offering, the prospects of the issuer, the fees earned by the underwriter, or affiliations between the underwriter and the issuer. On March 29, 1933, just three weeks after his inauguration, Roosevelt sent a message to Congress asking for a new law that would "put the burden of telling the whole truth on the seller" of securities. ARTHUR MEIER SCHLESINGER, THE COMING OF THE NEW DEAL, 1933–1935 441 (Houghton Mifflin Co. 2003). Later that year, Roosevelt signed the Securities Act of 1933 (the 1933 Act), which sought to protect the investing public by requiring full and fair disclosures for securities sold in interstate and foreign commerce and through the mails. The 1933 Act established a federal system for the registration of new issues of securities and required the registration statement to contain specified information about the security, the issuer, and the underwriters.

The Pecora hearings also exposed abusive practices in the secondary market for securities. In response, Congress enacted the Securities Exchange Act of 1934 (the 1934 Act), which required all stock exchanges to register with the federal government and all publicly-traded companies to comply with disclosure requirements. The 1934 Act created the SEC to administer the federal securities laws. You will learn more about the Pecora Commission and federal securities laws in Chapter 4.1.

2. The Banking Act of 1933

A series of events in 1933 breathed life into Senator Glass's post-stock market crash efforts to enact banking reform. The most important events were the Banking Panic of 1933, the election of Roosevelt, the switch of the Congress from Republican to Democratic, and the testimony of witnesses under the questioning of Pecora revealing many abuses to the public. Working with Republican Senator Henry Steagall of Alabama, Glass pushed reform through the Congress. As ultimately passed, the Glass-Steagall Act provisions of the Banking Act of 1933 (Glass-Steagall Act) forced the separation of commercial banks from investment banks by (1) prohibiting a broker-dealer from taking deposits from the public, (2) prohibiting member banks in the Federal Reserve System from being affiliated with an investment bank (an entity that was principally engaged in underwriting and dealing in corporate debt and equity), (3) prohibiting a member bank from investing in most equity and in non-investment grade securities, which we call high yield or junk bonds today, and (4) prohibiting employee interlocks. Member banks were still permitted to underwrite and deal in government debt and to invest in both government debt and highly rated corporate bonds, subject to limits. Why do you think that is?

As we will explore in Chapter 6.1, beginning in the 1960s and accelerating in the 1980s and 1990s, as the value of the bank charter began to decline with the growth of money market mutual funds (MMFs) and the increasing use of the bond markets by blue chip borrowers, the commercial banking sector began to push back against the Glass-Steagall Act limits on affiliations. By 1999, the Act was partly repealed in the Gramm-Leach-Bliley Act (GLBA) to permit affiliations among commercial banks, investment banks, and insurance firms. Since the Financial Crisis, some have called for a return to Glass-Steagall Act restrictions. We will explore the pros and cons of a neo-Glass Steagall Act era in Chapter 6.1.

B. STABILIZING THE BANKING SYSTEM THROUGH DEPOSIT INSURANCE

The Banking Panic of 1933 represented the near-complete collapse of the U.S. banking system. The governors of virtually all states declared bank holidays, meaning that banks were closed. It was an event that those who lived through it never forgot. It confronted Roosevelt during his very first hours in office when New York State, which had resisted closing its banks, informed the new president that New York banks would close. One of Roosevelt's first acts was to declare a nationwide bank holiday.

In the aftermath of the bank runs, policy-makers concluded that they needed a more robust mechanism to preserve the public's confidence: explicit deposit insurance. Roughly three months after ordering the bank holiday, Roosevelt signed legislation establishing the nation's first federal deposit insurance system. The Banking Act of 1933 created federal deposit insurance, to be administered by the newly-established FDIC. As initially enacted, the FDIC provided up to $2,500 in insurance for each depositor through an insurance fund backed by assessments on participating banks. We will discuss the Banking Crisis of 1933 and the creation of federal deposit insurance in Chapter 2.4. For now, it is fair to say that the creation of the first effective system of deposit insurance fundamentally altered the behavior of depositors so that banking panics became so rare as to become forgotten. Until the Financial Crisis, that is.

---

1. ***New Deal Era Homeowner Assistance.*** The U.S. economy experienced an unprecedented foreclosure crisis during the Great Depression. In response, the Roosevelt Administration created a government-sponsored corporation to refinance home mortgages in default to prevent further foreclosures:

> In 1933, when a larger share of all homes—one percent of every housing unit in the country—went into foreclosure than any other time in American history, President Roosevelt and Congress worked together to establish the Home Owners' Loan Corporation. The [Home Owners' Loan Corporation] was authorized to issue new loans to replace the existing liens of homeowners in default. Instead of a short-term, interest-only loan, the [Home Owners' Loan Corporation] loans were fully amortizing over 15 years. In addition, the [Home Owners' Loan Corporation] was far more patient with borrowers than the banks could have been, and delinquent loans received

individualized attention, including debt counseling, family meetings, and budgeting help.

Michael S. Barr, *Strengthening Our Economy: Foreclosure Prevention and Neighborhood Preservation*, Testimony Before the S. Comm. on Banking, Hous., & Urban Affairs (Jan. 31, 2008). Decades later, during the Financial Crisis, the Obama Administration adopted the Home Affordable Modification Program, which offered incentive payments to investors, lenders, servicers, and homeowners for successful mortgage modifications, as well as several other initiatives designed to provide relief for at-risk borrowers. Many critics argued that the Obama Administration's homeowner-relief programs were too modest. *See, e.g.*, DAVID WOOLNER, TIME TO BRING BACK THE HOME OWNERS LOAN CORPORATION? (Roosevelt Inst. 2010). Consider why policy options as ambitious as the Home Owners' Loan Corporation might or might not have been politically possible or practically feasible during the Financial Crisis.

2. ***The New Deal's Legacy.*** Many later pieces of legislation reflected the regulatory philosophy of the New Deal. In 1935, for instance, Congress passed the Public Utility Holding Company Act, also known as the Wheeler-Rayburn Act, a trust-busting initiative designed to facilitate the regulation of electric utilities. In 1939, Congress adopted the Trust Indenture Act, which contained mandatory provisions in trust indentures and was designed to protect small investors in bond issuances from private restructuring by large majority bondholders. In 1940, Congress sought to crack down on asset managers who had fleeced their retail customers out of millions of dollars during the lead-up to the stock market crash. The Investment Company Act of 1940 (1940 Act) required companies engaged in the investment business to register with the SEC and disclose information to investors. The 1940 Act further provided that an investment company must have a board of directors to represent shareholders, and it prohibited or regulated potentially abusive transactions and interrelationships. We will explore the 1940 Act in Chapter 10.1.

As noted above, in 1956, the BHCA gave the Federal Reserve Board supervisory power over any group or company that controlled two or more banks. The BHCA also prohibited an out-of-state BHC from entering a new state unless state laws so permitted, which virtually no state laws did. We will discuss the history of the BHCA in detail in Chapter 6.1.

Federal laws governing consumer regulation began to be passed only in the 1960s, quite late in the more than 200-year history of financial regulation in the United States. Like banking, securities, and insurance regulation before them, consumer protection had largely been left to state law, in this case state tort and contract laws. The echoes of the New Deal regulatory philosophy continued to be heard throughout the 1960s and 1970s with respect to housing and consumer protection. These consumer reforms reflected the New Deal's focus on the economic needs of individuals, but were also infused with the ethos of the Civil Rights movement and President Lyndon Johnson's Great Society. For instance, the Fair Housing Act of 1968 and the Equal Credit Opportunity Act of 1974 forbade discrimination in housing and lending, respectively. The Community Reinvestment Act of 1977 (CRA) required banks to help meet the credit needs of low- and moderate-income communities, consistent with safe and sound banking practices. Consumer protection laws such as the Truth in Lending Act of 1968, the Fair Credit Billing Act of 1974, and the Fair Credit Reporting Act of 1970 required new disclosures and protected borrowers from predatory practices. Professor Cass Sunstein has called this era of broad regulatory change in consumer protection, civil rights, workers' rights, anti-poverty programs, and environmental protection the "rights revolution." CASS SUNSTEIN, AFTER THE RIGHTS REVOLUTION: RECONCEIVING THE REGULATORY STATE (1993); *see also* David Vogel, *The New Social Regulation in Historical and Comparative Perspective, in* REGULATION IN PERSPECTIVE: HISTORICAL ESSAYS (Thomas McGraw ed., 1981). In 1968, Congress reorganized Fannie Mae as a government-sponsored enterprise (GSE) to provide access to affordable housing finance. We will further discuss consumer protection in Part V and the government's role in housing finance in Chapter 12.2.

VI. A TREND TOWARDS DEREGULATION (1970S–2000S)

By the 1970s, with the Great Depression receding from memory, and a new era of increased globalization beginning, the country's New Deal-era emphasis on government regulation of financial markets gradually gave way to greater confidence in free markets. President Ronald Reagan and British Prime Minister Margaret Thatcher were elected on platforms of limited government and unencumbered capitalism. Milton Friedman and other scholars from the Chicago school of economics championed free markets. Influenced by the political thought of the Reagan-Thatcher era, as well as changing markets and technology, policy-makers began to view some of the New Deal constraints as obsolete and inefficient. Underpinned by these philosophies, a spirit of deregulation and liberalization permeated the United States starting in the 1970s. At one extreme, Alan Greenspan, the Chairman of the Federal Reserve Board from 1987 to 2006, was famously uninterested in bank regulation and heavily influenced by Ayn Rand's libertarian thinking.

In the financial sector, the deregulatory movement was not absolute and, indeed, not as strong as in many other sectors. Nonetheless, the deregulatory movement liberalized restrictions on financial institutions, particularly those engaged in shadow banking activities, including affiliates of banks within BHCs. At the same time, market innovations, technological changes, the Organization of the Petroleum Exporting Countries oil price shock, and sharp increases in interest rates as a result of inflation shook traditional banking from the competitive protections that the New Deal philosophy had offered. This increased competition on the traditional model of deposit-funded banks intensified with the rise of MMFs, securitization, investment banks and other non-bank financial institutions, and market-based funding through commercial paper, repo, securities lending, and derivatives. Facing business model pressure, the value of the commercial bank and thrift charters declined, and Congress stepped in to deregulate financial markets and open up competition.

A. DEREGULATION OF DEPOSITORY INSTITUTIONS

The economy of the 1970s was characterized by stagflation—stagnant growth combined with inflation—and high interest rates. In the face of these challenging macroeconomic conditions, policy-makers became increasingly convinced that some New Deal-era restrictions on depository institutions had become outdated. Regulation Q, implementing a provision of the Banking Act of 1933, prohibited banks and thrifts from paying interest on demand deposits and restricted interest rates they could pay on time and savings deposits. As interest rates rose in the 1970s, depositors began moving their money from banks and thrifts into alternative investments that offered higher interest rates, such as MMFs. Thrifts faced an additional problem as market interest rates rose because the bulk of their assets were 30-year fixed-rate mortgages and the income they produced was usually insufficient to offset the rise in the cost of attracting deposits. Furthermore, rising rates caused the market value of these long-term assets to decline; if they were sold, the thrift would have to record a loss.

Banks and thrifts lost billions in deposits to MMFs, which grew from $9.5 billion in assets in 1978 to more than $236 billion by the end of 1982. *See* DAVID L. MASON, FROM BUILDINGS AND LOANS TO BAIL-OUTS: A HISTORY OF THE AMERICAN SAVINGS AND LOAN INDUSTRY, 1831–1995 214 (2004). Even though the term had not yet been invented, shadow banking was on the rise. Faced with these developments, Congress enacted legislation to deregulate depository institutions.

> The Depository Institutions Deregulation and Monetary Control Act of 1980 (DIDMCA) phased out deposit interest-rate ceilings, broadened the powers of thrift institutions, and raised the deposit insurance limit from $40,000 to $100,000. Two years later . . . the Garn-St Germain Depository Institutions Act of 1982 (Garn-St Germain Act) authorized money market deposit accounts for banks and thrifts . . . and increased the authority of thrifts to invest in commercial loans to strengthen the institutions' viability over the long term. In the case of national banks, Garn-St Germain Act removed statutory restrictions on real estate lending. With respect to commercial mortgage markets, this legislation set the stage for a rapid expansion of lending and an increase in competition between thrifts and banks. . . .

1 FDIC, HISTORY OF THE EIGHTIES—LESSONS FOR THE FUTURE 10, 176 (1997).

These deregulatory initiatives attempted to modernize regulation of depository institutions and deal with rising interest rates as well as new competition from MMFs, but within a few years it was clear that they helped create a foundation for instability. Attempts to strengthen the banking system by permitting interstate branching did not get enough votes to pass. Many depository institutions that received expanded powers remained highly dependent on a local or regional economy. While the elimination of interest rate ceilings allowed depository institutions to attract deposits by offering higher rates, it squeezed profitability as it forced them to pay more interest on deposits, while they continued to rely on long-term fixed rate assets to generate income in a rising rate environment. The broader scope of activities authorized allowed these institutions, many of which had recently been unsophisticated thrifts focusing on local mortgage lending, to tie up more of their funds in riskier loans, such as commercial real estate, making their assets more susceptible to cyclical fluctuations in the real estate market. When regional booms turned into busts, depository institutions failed in record numbers as they were squeezed on both sides of their balance sheets. Between 1984 and 1995, more commercial banks closed or received FDIC assistance than in any period since the Great Depression. Even more devastating was the widespread collapse of the thrift sector, now known as the Savings & Loans Crisis. Between 1986 and 1995, more than 1,000 thrifts with total assets of over $500 billion failed. *See* Timothy Curry & Lynn Shibut, *The Cost of the Savings and Loan Crisis: Truth and Consequences*, 13 FDIC BANKING REV. 26, 33 (2000). As these crises illustrated, deregulation sometimes brought unintended and devastating consequences.

B. LOOSENING OF GEOGRAPHIC RESTRICTIONS

Recall that in the early years of the U.S. banking system, bank owners expanded geographically primarily through the establishment of new units rather than through additional branches of existing banks. Eventually, most states came to adopt laws restricting intrastate branching, and the federal McFadden Act of 1927 prohibited interstate branching entirely.

Starting in the 1970s, however, these geographic restrictions began to loosen. First, states liberalized their policies on intrastate branching. States began to allow BHCs to convert subsidiary banks that they acquired into branches of a single bank, whereas previously these subsidiaries had been treated by regulators as stand-alone banks. Eventually, some states permitted state-wide *de novo* branching, whereby banks could open new branches anywhere within state borders. Second, states began to permit bank acquisitions by out-of-state BHCs, under the provision in the BHCA that allowed interstate acquisitions when authorized by state law. Third, the Garn-St Germain Act permitted interstate acquisitions of failed banks and thrifts without regard to state laws. Many states entered regional or national reciprocal compacts whereby banks in their state could be bought by banks in any other state in the compact. These compacts effectively facilitated interstate expansion by BHCs. Finally, the passage of the Riegle-Neal Interstate Banking and Branching Efficiency Act in 1994 (Riegle-Neal Act) overturned the McFadden Act's prohibition on interstate branching and permitted BHCs to acquire banks in any other state. *See* Randall S. Kroszner & Philip E. Straphan, *What Drives Deregulation? Economics and Politics of the Relaxation of Bank Branching Restrictions*, 5–7 (Nat'l Bureau of Econ. Research, Working Paper No. 6637, 1998). The last vestiges of geographic restrictions were eliminated in the Dodd-Frank Act of 2010.

The end of most interstate banking barriers and the gradual erosion of the Glass-Steagall Act barriers set off a wave of banking mergers and acquisitions among superregionals and money center banks, leading to the creation of both large regional banks and the megabanks we now refer to as global systemically important banks or systemically important financial institutions (SIFIs). Today, the vast majority of national and state banks are owned by holding companies that are regulated by the Federal Reserve Board as BHCs. The largest banks with nationwide operations tend to be national banks and regional or smaller banks tend to be state-chartered banks. Consolidation has reduced the number of federally insured banks and thrifts from 17,901 in 1984 to 7,357 in 2011. FDIC, COMMUNITY BANKING STUDY, I-II (2012).

The Financial Crisis precipitated another wave of mega-mergers as failing firms were acquired by stronger firms, resulting in a greater concentration in U.S. banking than had been seen before. The top five SIFIs now control more than 50% of commercial banking assets, renewing concerns about the concentration of economic power in a few large financial firms. For a discussion of post-Financial Crisis concerns about the concentration of economic and financial power as well as attempts to break up the largest financial conglomerates, see Chapter 6.2.

C. RE-REGULATION OF BANKS AND THRIFTS

The deregulatory trend of the 1970s through the 2000s, although robust and unmistakable, was far from absolute. In fact, there were many instances during this era in which policy-makers tightened restrictions on banks and thrifts. Congress passed the International Lending Supervision Act of 1983 after several developing countries warned that they might not be able make debt payments. The Act imposed restrictions and disclosure requirements on the foreign lending practices of domestic banks. In addition, the Act, for the first time, required the federal banking agencies to set minimum capital adequacy standards for banks. *See* 12 U.S.C. § 3907; *see also* Nicholas K. Martitsch, *The International Lending Supervision Act of 1983: A First Step Toward Responsible Foreign Lending*, 42 WASH. & LEE L. REV. 193, 194–95 (1985). We will discuss capital regulation in Chapters 2.5, 2.6, and 2.7.

In response to the Savings & Loan Crisis, Congress passed the Financial Institutions Reform, Recovery, and Enforcement Act of 1989, which tightened lending restrictions on thrifts and raised thrift capital requirements to make them commensurate with banks. Two years later, Congress enacted the Federal Deposit Insurance Corporation Improvement Act, which recapitalized the FDIC's insurance fund, increased the FDIC's assessments on insured banks, and strengthened enforcement, supervisory, and examination standards for such banks. Also in 1991, Congress passed new restrictions on foreign banks operating in the United States in response to the failure of Bank of Credit and Commerce International (BCCI), a foreign bank that conducted its U.S. operations secretly through shell companies and nominees. BCCI engaged in money laundering and swindled U.S. customers out of millions of dollars before authorities finally caught on. In response, Congress enacted the Foreign Bank Supervision Enhancement Act of 1991 (FBSEA), which increased the Federal Reserve Board's authority over foreign banks operating in the United States. You will learn about the BCCI scandal and FBSEA in Chapter 6.3.

D. THE EROSION OF THE GLASS-STEAGALL ACT

Over time, BHCs began lobbying Congress to loosen the Glass-Steagall Act's separation of commercial and investment banking. Facing increasingly intense competition from MMFs and other financial instruments that blurred the lines between depositories and securities firms, the banking sector argued that the Glass-Steagall Act restrictions were becoming obsolete. *See* Robert S. Plotkin, *What Meaning Does Glass-Steagall Have for Today's Financial World?*, 95

BANKING L.J. 404, 404–05 (1978). It will not surprise you to know that the investment banks fought hard to keep the commercial banking sector out of their competitive turf. The regulatory, legislative, and court fights appear to involve highly technical lawyers' battles over the meaning of defined terms such as, "the business of banking," "closely related to banking," and "security." Yet, the fight was, in essence, a fight over who would win most from the changing market, the commercial banking sector or investment banking sector.

During the 1980s and 1990s, the barriers enacted by the Glass-Steagall Act eroded through changing regulatory interpretations. As the value of the bank charter declined in tandem with the growth of the capital markets (which displaced commercial lending), the Federal Reserve Board and the OCC adopted interpretations of the Glass-Steagall Act that increasingly permitted the affiliates or subsidiaries of commercial banks to engage in a wider range of securities activities.

With many of the Glass-Steagall Act's restrictions liberalized, Congress passed the GLBA in 1999, repealing the affiliate restrictions of the Glass-Steagall Act. The GLBA eliminated not only the Glass-Steagall Act's restrictions on affiliations between commercial banks and investment banks, but also the long-standing bar on affiliations between insurance firms and banks. In the wake of the Financial Crisis, as you will see, some have argued that the loosening of these restraints brought down the financial system. *See e.g.*, *Frontline: Interview with Joseph Stiglitz* (PBS television broadcast, Oct. 20, 2009). Others contend that these changes had little to do with the problems at the heart of the crisis. *See, e.g.*, Mark A. Calabria, *Did Deregulation Cause the Financial Crisis?*, CATO POL'Y REP. 1, 6–8 (2009). You will learn about contending visions of the GLBA and the Glass-Steagall Act in Chapter 6.1.

E. SECURITIZATION AND THE NEW MODELS OF INTERMEDIATION

In the age-old, traditional model of financial intermediation, banks took deposits and used the funds to make loans, keeping these loans as assets on their balance sheet and generating income through interest payments on those loans. Beginning in the 1970s, however, banks began to securitize their assets. Legislation, including the Tax Reform Act of 1986, facilitated the creation of the securitization market. Under the securitization model, rather than keeping the loans on their balance sheet, banks sold their loans to legally separate entities called special purpose vehicles, or SPVs. These SPVs aggregated and packaged numerous loans and issued securities backed by the underlying loan assets. The securities became known as asset-backed securities (ABSs).

The first widely-used securitization products were agency ABSs, so named because they were used by federal agencies and GSEs, such as the Government National Mortgage Association (Ginnie Mae), Fannie Mae, and Freddie Mac, to pool government-backed or GSE-backed mortgage loans and facilitate the flow of credit. Eventually, these securitization structures spurred the creation of a non-agency securitization market, first in jumbo mortgages that were too large to meet the size limits of the agencies, and then in the rapid growth of the subprime mortgage market in the lead up to the Financial Crisis. Nicola Cetorelli & Stavros Peristiani, *The Role of Banks in Asset Securitization*, 18 FED. RESERVE

BANK N.Y. ECON. POL'Y REV. 47, 61 (2012). You will learn about securitization in Chapter 12.1 and the GSEs in Chapter 12.2.

Shadow banking activities grew in other ways as well over the decades. Investment banks, and banks themselves, could turn to commercial paper markets for funding, helping to give rise to large non-bank financial institutions. It turned out that asset-backed vehicles could be funded as well in the wholesale markets by issuing commercial paper. The securitization process also fueled the growth of secured intermediation transactions, such as repurchase agreements and securities lending, that could be used to fund non-bank as well as banking institutions. Investment banks also offered prime brokerage services to clients, such as hedge funds, and these hedge funds left large cash deposits at the investment banks, akin to retail deposits at depository institutions but without deposit insurance or the Federal Reserve Board as a lender of last resort. These innovative financing arrangements spurred the growth of non-bank intermediaries and shadow banking activities. We discuss market-based financing in Chapter 12.4.

F. THE COMMODITY FUTURES MODERNIZATION ACT

As you will learn in Chapter 11.1, derivatives are a broad category of financial contracts whose value is derived from the value of an underlying asset, security, commodity, rate, or index. While derivatives have been around for centuries, in the 1990s, the financial sector developed a wide range of new derivative instruments. Derivative contracts such as futures are traded on regulated exchanges, while other instruments, known as swaps, are traded privately among large derivative dealers in the over-the-counter (OTC) market. In 1998, a large hedge fund, Long Term Capital Management, blew up when its interest rate contracts went bad, and a panic was stemmed only when the Federal Reserve Bank of New York stepped in to force a bail-in by the largest BHCs. With the rise of OTC derivatives, a fierce political debate developed over how these rapidly developing instruments should be regulated. Brooksley Born, Chairman of the CFTC, argued for CFTC jurisdiction to rein in OTC markets, while the Federal Reserve Board's Alan Greenspan, Treasury Secretary Robert Rubin, and SEC Chairman Arthur Levitt opposed it.

The bitter fight was temporarily settled when Congress enacted the Commodity Futures Modernization Act of 2000, which codified an exemption from CFTC oversight and permitted OTC trading of swaps. The market exploded in size, and a new form of derivative, the credit default swap, was invented and took off. Credit default swaps permitted investors to hedge their exposure to firms and parts of the market or to speculate, as well. The unchecked rise of derivatives played a key role in exacerbating the Financial Crisis. *The Role of Derivatives in the Financial Crisis: Hearing Before the Fin. Crisis Inquiry Comm'n*, 111th Cong. 18 (2010) (statement of Michael Greenberger, Professor, Univ. of Maryland School of Law); *see also* MARK JICKLING, CONG. RESEARCH SERV., R40173, CAUSES OF THE FINANCIAL CRISIS 6 (2009).

VII. THE FINANCIAL CRISIS AND ITS AFTERMATH

A. THE FINANCIAL CRISIS

Mortgage companies, banks, and securities firms began securitizing mortgages in the 1970s and 1980s. (Portions of this section are adapted from MICHAEL S. BARR, CHANGING FINANCE (forthcoming).) Investors believed that mortgage-backed securities (MBSs) were safer than individual mortgages because they diversified the risk of nonpayment across many loans. Credit rating agencies, hired by the sponsors of the securitizations, increased investors' confidence by awarding AAA ratings to many tranches, or investment layers, of MBSs, signaling that the risk of default was low. Securitization thus made mortgages more appealing to investors, and lenders could more easily sell their loans.

In the 1990s, mortgage lenders—a term which includes both bank and non-bank lenders—began expanding into the subprime market. Lenders made credit available to borrowers with low credit scores, high debt, or difficult-to-document income. In some cases, lenders encouraged borrowers to accept loans with complicated or misleading terms that they did not understand, with the lure of low down payment requirements and low initial monthly payments, but with high interest rates after the teaser period, and prepayment penalties. This subprime market exploded in the early 2000s, as did the Alt A market, in which lenders offered no-doc loans to middle income borrowers stretching beyond their means in fast-growing housing markets. Between 2001 and 2006, lenders issued more than $13.4 trillion in subprime mortgages, and total mortgage debt in the United States nearly doubled. *See* FCIC, THE FINANCIAL CRISIS INQUIRY REPORT 83 (2011).

Rising home prices helped feed the financial system's rapid growth and hide declining mortgage underwriting standards. The lack of transparency in the securitization process made it difficult for investors to monitor the quality of mortgage loans comprising MBSs. Originators and securitizers were not willing to police themselves, and credit rating agencies increasingly rated as AAA MBSs and collateralized debt obligations that were based on increasingly weaker underlying mortgage credits. New financial products and rapidly growing markets overwhelmed or blinded traders, firms, and private sector gatekeepers and swamped those parts of the system that were supposed to mitigate risk. At the same time, the political environment in Washington strongly encouraged homeownership with many members of Congress, on both sides of the aisle, actively encouraging Fannie Mae and Freddie Mac to also lower their underwriting standards for mortgage pools that the agencies would securitize and guarantee. Moreover, many of the mortgage lenders were regulated only at a state level and no regulator had any systemic responsibilities. The failure to act on the risks was endemic among the private and public sectors.

As financial institutions became increasingly exposed to more mortgage-related assets, they also became increasingly leveraged. That is, investment and commercial banks funded themselves with more debt relative to equity, leaving slim buffers to absorb losses. The increase in leverage was partially hidden because leverage was also growing off balance sheet, in special investment vehicles and conduits that were funded with slivers of equity. By 2006, large banks had off-balance sheet exposures equal to 85% of their on-balance sheet assets. *See* Sebnem Kalemli-Ozcan et al., *Leverage Across Firms, Banks, and Countries*, 88 J. INT'L ECON. 284, 287 (2012).

Financial institutions were also becoming increasingly reliant on sources of funding that were short-term and vulnerable to run. As we will discuss in Chapter 12.4, these short-term funding sources, including commercial paper, repurchase, or repo, and securities lending agreements, were an attractive source of cheap funding but exposed firms to liquidity risks. If investors became concerned about the health of the dealer or bank or the quality of the securities posted as collateral, the short terms of the loans allowed investors quickly to limit their exposure by lending for even shorter terms, demanding more or better collateral, or refusing to lend altogether. In essence, all of the same conditions as an old fashioned bank run were created but in the wholesale markets.

At the same time, large financial institutions were becoming increasingly interconnected through derivatives. As we will cover in Part XI, derivatives are financial contracts that derive their value from the value of an underlying asset, security, commodity, rate, or index. By the mid-2000s, derivatives trading among financial firms reached historic levels but took place almost entirely in the OTC market where neither regulators nor counterparties could fully see it. Market participants were largely in the dark about just how big the market was, how much derivative-related exposure each firm had, and to whom those firms were exposed.

Amidst this extraordinary expansion of risk in the financial sector, housing prices started to flatten and then decline in the mid-2000s. Many homeowners who had relied on rising prices to refinance could no longer do so. As home prices dropped, many homeowners fell behind and eventually defaulted on their mortgages. Mounting job losses reinforced the trend. Before long, nearly 1 in 10 mortgage loans was seriously delinquent. FCIC, THE FINANCIAL CRISIS INQUIRY REPORT 215–16 (2011).

The dramatic drop in housing prices and rising defaults were calamitous for financial markets. Credit rating agencies downgraded many MBSs, and financial institutions were forced to recognize billions of dollars of losses on mortgage-related assets. Explicit or implicit promises to back special purpose vehicles brought the risks of such activities back onto the balance sheet. The implosion in the value of mortgage-backed assets made it more difficult for the institutions that held these assets to fund themselves. Lenders in the repo market and purchasers of commercial paper became worried that, because of the declining value of mortgage assets, institutions would be unable to repay their loans. In order to protect themselves against this risk, lenders began to demand more and better collateral, to lend for shorter and shorter periods, and to charge higher interest rates. Or they cut off funding altogether.

Beginning in August 2007, when the Federal Reserve System first recognized that a lack of liquidity was adversely affecting the markets, it attempted to inject additional liquidity into the market and encouraged banks to make greater use of the discount window. Kathryn Judge, *The First Year: The Role of a Modern Lender of Last Resort* 11, 19 (Columbia Law and Economics,

Working Paper No. 519, 2016). Conditions had not improved by January 2008, prompting the FOMC to lower the federal funds rate to 3%. *Id.* 35–36. This marked the first time in four years that the Federal Reserve reduced interest rates, but it was too late. When it appeared these moves would not be enough to calm the markets, the Federal Reserve created new mechanisms through which it could lend money to banks and inject liquidity directly into non-bank institutions. As we will discuss in Chapter 9.1 not since the Great Depression, had the Federal Reserve System lent directly to non-bank financial institutions.

Despite the Federal Reserve System's efforts, credit markets continued to tighten, squeezing firms that relied heavily on short-term funding. By March 2008, Bear Stearns, a large broker-dealer with $395 billion in assets, was on the brink of collapse. The Federal Reserve brokered an emergency sale of Bear Stearns to JPMorgan Chase with a nearly $30 billion Federal Reserve backstop.

In September 2008, Lehman Brothers filed for bankruptcy, setting off a cataclysmic cascade. Lehman Brothers's counterparties suffered huge losses. Repo markets shut down. Investors in MMFs began to run. Unsure of which firms were solvent and which were not, and how counterparties were connected through derivative contracts, firms became completely unwilling to lend. Financial institutions that were previously viewed as healthy found themselves unable to borrow. We will discuss Lehman Brothers's bankruptcy and its calamitous results in detail in Chapter 9.3.

Contagion spread in shadow banking activities and spilled into more regulated parts of financial markets. Within two days of Lehman Brothers's failure, Merrill Lynch had sold itself to Bank of America, and the Federal Reserve had backstopped insurance conglomerate AIG with an $85 billion emergency loan. Later that week, the two largest remaining independent investment banks, Morgan Stanley and Goldman Sachs, converted into BHCs and, at the same time, the Federal Reserve Board granted their broker-dealer subsidiaries access to the Federal Reserve's discount window. Washington Mutual Bank, then the nation's largest thrift, failed and went into FDIC receivership, from which it was sold to JP Morgan. After a rescue offered by Citigroup was scuttled, Wachovia Bank merged with Wells Fargo. These unprecedented events led to what the Financial Crisis Inquiry Commission (FCIC) deemed "the worst market disruption in postwar American history and an extraordinary rush to the safest possible investments." FCIC, THE FINANCIAL CRISIS INQUIRY REPORT 353 (2011).

The Federal Reserve System, FDIC, and Treasury undertook massive market interventions to stem the panic. Throughout the fall of 2008, the Federal Reserve continued creating programs to inject liquidity into the financial system and increase credit availability. In a novel reading of its legal authority, the FDIC guaranteed the senior debt of all FDIC-insured institutions and their holding companies, as well as previously uninsured deposits in non-interest-bearing deposit transaction accounts. In another unusual and risky move, the Treasury temporarily guaranteed the net-asset-value of eligible MMFs to slow the run on those funds. The government went to extraordinary lengths to save Fannie Mae and Freddie Mac, the GSEs that provide vital liquidity to the housing markets, as you will learn in Chapter 12.2. Congress authorized the Treasury to spend up to $700 billion under the Troubled Asset Relief Program

(TARP), which the Treasury used to inject capital directly into financial institutions and automakers. In the end, the Treasury disbursed $431.1 billion of TARP funds. U.S. DEP'T OF TREASURY, TARP TRACKER (Jul. 2, 2015).

The U.S. government's interventions during the Financial Crisis were unprecedented in scope. The Congressional Oversight Panel, charged with overseeing TARP, calculated that, at its peak, the federal government guaranteed or insured $4.4 trillion in financial assets. *See* CONG. OVERSIGHT PANEL, 64–832, THE FINAL REPORT OF THE CONG. OVERSIGHT PANEL, 51 (2011). This figure includes the size of the MMF market when the Treasury enacted its MMF guarantee, the amount of senior debt and uninsured deposits guaranteed by the FDIC, and the government's exposure to Citigroup and Bank of America through loss guarantees implemented by the Treasury. *Id.* at n. 211. We will discuss many of the U.S. government's support programs in Chapter 9.1. The U.S. government was not alone. Governments and central banks around the world took drastic actions to keep credit markets running.

Eventually, U.S. financial markets calmed and the real economy began to rebound, but not before millions of people lost their jobs, their homes, their businesses, and their savings. The unemployment rate more than doubled to 10%. Four million Americans lost their homes to foreclosure, and housing prices dropped 32% from their peak. In total, the Financial Crisis wiped out more than $17 trillion in U.S. household net worth, as Figure 1.2-1 demonstrates:

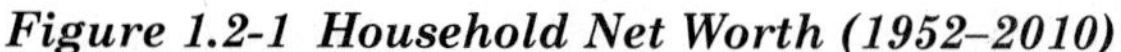

Figure 1.2-1 Household Net Worth (1952–2010)

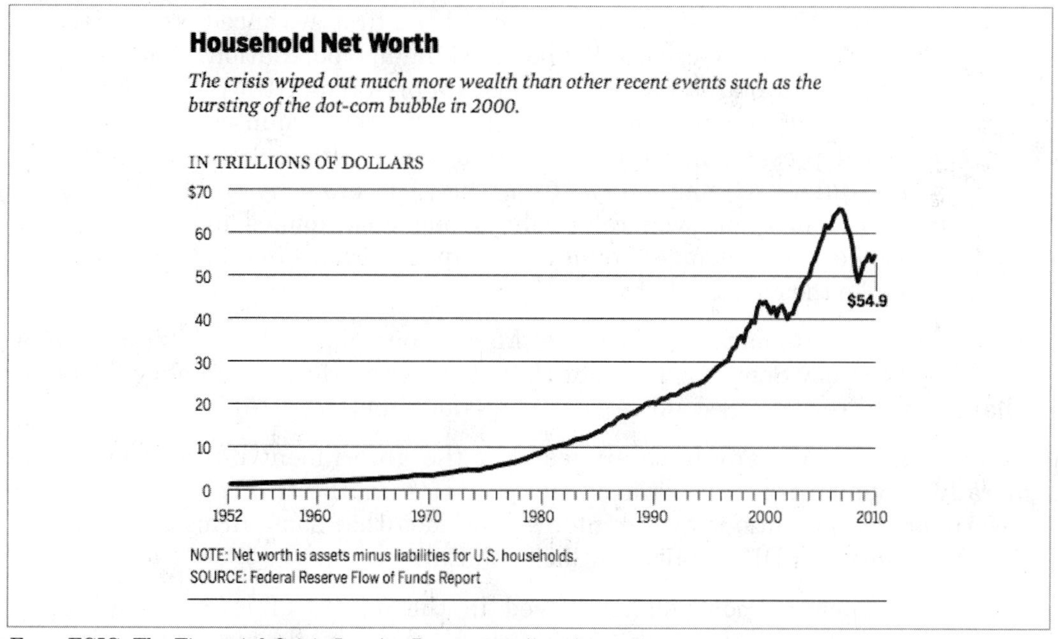

From FCIC, The Financial Crisis Inquiry Report 392 (2011).

---

1. ***Should the Government Have Intervened?*** What would have happened if the government had not stepped in to save the U.S. financial system? Many people have argued that the effects of the Financial Crisis would have been even more extreme. Professor Alan Blinder and Moody's Analytics Chief Economist

Mark Zandi calculated that, without the government's responses, gross domestic product would have declined by 14% rather than 4% and 17 million jobs would have been lost, instead of about half that number. *See* Alan S. Blinder & Mark Zandi, *The Financial Crisis: Lessons for the Next One*, CENTER ON BUDGET AND POL'Y PRIORITIES (Oct. 15, 2015).

Jason Furman, the Chairman of the Council of Economic Advisers, has argued that the government's response helped to prevent another Great Depression:

> A big challenge in assessing the impact of economic policy is to choose the right counterfactual. I will argue that the Great Depression is a reasonable counterfactual for the outcome of the financial crisis that began in 2007. The shocks that initiated the recent financial crisis were, in many dimensions, larger than the shocks that precipitated the Great Depression. Another reasonable counterfactual is the experience of other advanced economies in the wake of the financial crisis. By either benchmark, the recovery in the United States has been relatively strong.
>
> In each case, the shocks to the economy were severe, but different choices led to different outcomes. The United States' policy response . . . combined with the resilience of our private sector and coordination with our international partners to stave off a second Great Depression. Unemployment peaked at 10 percent and then achieved nearly the fastest decline we have seen in the postwar records. The United States was one of the first advanced economies to return to its pre-crisis GDP per working-age population. And even today, the euro area has not reached its pre-crisis GDP per working-age population and some peripheral European countries are still facing depression-like economic conditions. Although our economy today differs in many ways from the U.S. economy in the 1930s, Europe today—or even relatively stronger economies like Japan—those adverse outcomes could have happened here too had we failed to make the choices that we did.

Jason Furman, Remarks Before the Macroeconomic Advisers' 25th Annual Washington Policy Seminar, It Could Have Happened Here: The Policy Response That Helped Prevent a Second Great Depression (Sept. 9, 2015).

At the same time, many have argued that the government interventions were morally repugnant and rewarded bad practices in the financial sector. The government interventions also reinforced the idea that some firms were "too big to fail." As former FDIC Chairman Sheila C. Bair stated:

> The dilemma policymakers faced in the failure of large, complex financial institutions resembles classic hostage drama, where the imperative of saving lives in the short run comes at the expense of encouraging more hostage-taking in the future. And so it is with the largest U.S. banks and other financial companies, which have every incentive to render themselves so large, so complex, and so opaque that no policymaker would dare risk letting them fail in a crisis. With the benefit of this implicit safety net, these institutions are

> insulated from the normal discipline of the marketplace that applies to smaller banks and practically every other private company.

Sheila C. Bair, Remarks before the 47th Annual Conference on Bank Structure and Competition, We Must Resolve to End Too Big to Fail (May 5, 2011).

Amid these contrasting views, some commentators have adopted an intermediate position that supports the government's decisions to intervene, but argues that the interventions could have been more appropriately tailored. These commentators contend, for instance, that the government should have channeled more TARP funding to help mortgage borrowers rather than financial institutions and that the government took on more loss exposure than it needed to when it facilitated JPMorgan Chase's acquisition of Bear Stearns. *See, e.g.*, Charles Calomiris, *Principles That Should Have Guided TARP*, Testimony Before the Cong. Oversight Panel (Nov. 19, 2009).

B. THE DODD-FRANK ACT

On July 21, 2010, President Barack Obama signed into law the Dodd-Frank Act. The bill was passed by Congress largely on party-line votes: no House Republicans and only four Senate Republicans voted for its passage. Many have viewed the Dodd-Frank Act as the most sweeping reform of the financial system since the Great Depression, ushering in comprehensive reform in key areas: creating the authority to regulate large financial conglomerates that pose a threat to financial stability, without regard to their corporate form; enacting a resolution authority to wind down large financial conglomerates in the event of a crisis; restricting risky activities and beefing up banking supervision; requiring central clearing and exchange trading of standardized derivatives, and capital, margin, and transparency throughout the market; improving investor protections; and establishing the CFPB to focus on consumer financial protection. We will discuss these reforms, as well as coordinated reforms adopted by international policy-makers, throughout the remainder of this book. It is critical to keep in mind, however, that the sweeping changes wrought by the Dodd-Frank Act did not fundamentally change the underlying infrastructure—*i.e.*, the alphabet soup of financial regulatory agencies with which the United States is uniquely blessed. Lawyers who wish to master their craft, no matter what point of view you take about the meaning of the history or the policy debates, must fully understand both the pre-Dodd-Frank Act infrastructure as well as the post Dodd-Frank Act era.

C. CONTENDING VISIONS OF THE FINANCIAL CRISIS

Years after the Financial Crisis, there is still significant disagreement as to its root causes. Some observers blame excessively risky behavior by private institutions and the GSEs, some blame the decline in underwriting standards in mortgages, others fault failed regulatory policies, and still others attribute the Financial Crisis to a combination of public and private sector shortcomings. In this section, we examine several contending visions of the Financial Crisis. As you read, consider for yourself what you believe to be the primary causes of the Financial Crisis.

The FCIC, which Congress created in 2009 to examine the causes of the Financial Crisis, concluded that a wide range of factors contributed to the crisis. In the following excerpt, the FCIC majority opinion discusses the role that the mortgage market played in causing the Financial Crisis.

FCIC, Conclusions of the Financial Crisis Inquiry Commission

The Financial Crisis Inquiry Report, xxiii–xxiv (2011)

We conclude that collapsing mortgage-lending standards and the mortgage-securitization pipeline lit and spread the flame of contagion and crisis. . . . Many mortgage lenders set the bar so low that lenders simply took eager borrowers' qualifications on faith, often with a willful disregard for a borrower's ability to repay. Nearly one-quarter of all mortgages made in the first half of 2005 were interest-only loans. During the same year, 68% of "option ARM" loans originated by Countrywide and Washington Mutual had low- or no-documentation requirements. . . .

While many of these mortgages were kept on banks' books, the bigger money came from global investors who clamored to put their cash into newly created mortgage-related securities. It appeared to financial institutions, investors, and regulators alike that risk had been conquered: the investors held highly rated securities they thought were sure to perform; the banks thought they had taken the riskiest loans off their books; and regulators saw firms making profits and borrowing costs reduced. But each step in the mortgage securitization pipeline depended on the next step to keep demand going. From the speculators who flipped houses to the mortgage brokers who scouted the loans, to the lenders who issued the mortgages, to the financial firms that created the mortgage-backed securities . . . no one in this pipeline of toxic mortgages had enough skin in the game. They all believed they could off-load their risks on a moment's notice to the next person in line. They were wrong. When borrowers stopped making mortgage payments, the losses—amplified by derivatives—rushed through the pipeline. As it turned out, these losses were concentrated in a set of systemically important financial institutions.

Others argue that U.S. government housing policy created incentives that caused market participants to create and spread risk. Peter Wallison—an FCIC commissioner who dissented from the FCIC's final report—blamed the government's housing policies for the Financial Crisis in the following excerpt. You will learn more about U.S. government housing policy in Chapter 12.2.

Peter J. Wallison, Government Housing Policy and the Financial Crisis

30 CATO J., 397, 399–400 (2010)

[T]here is an alternative explanation for the [F]inancial [C]risis, and it focuses on the U.S. government's housing policies under both the Clinton and second Bush administrations. Beginning in the early 1990s—in order to enable more Americans to buy homes—the government began to press housing lenders such as banks and . . . Fannie Mae and Freddie Mac to reduce the requirements for a mortgage so that more Americans would be able to buy homes. The first step in this direction was Congress's enactment in 1992, near the end of the first Bush administration, of an affordable housing "mission" for Fannie Mae and Freddie Mac. . . .

At around the same time in the early 1990s, the regulations under the [CRA] were amended to increase their influence on bank mortgage lending. The CRA had been adopted in 1977, and initially required that banks make efforts to increase mortgage lending in all the communities they serve, not just the communities where middle income or well-to-do families lived. The enforcement mechanism was the withholding of regulatory approval for mergers, expansions, or other matters if a bank had not shown that it was working to achieve the CRA's goals. In 1995, however, the rules were tightened, so that banks had to show that they had actually made the required loans, not that they were simply trying to do so. The change had a profound effect.

Other scholars argue that it was neither government housing policies nor risky mortgages themselves that caused the Financial Crisis, but rather the concentration of mortgage risk in the largest financial institutions. Professors Viral Acharya and Matthew Richardson explain this view in the following excerpt.

Viral Acharya & Matthew Richardson, Causes of the Financial Crisis

21 CRITICAL REV. 195, 196–97 (2009)

There is no shortage of proximate causes of the [F]inancial [C]risis. There were mortgages granted to people with little ability to pay them back, and mortgages designed to systemically default or refinance in just a few years, depending on the path of house prices. There was the securitization of these mortgages, which allowed credit markets to grow rapidly, but at the cost of some lenders having little "skin in the game"—contributing to the deterioration in loan quality. . . . Finally, opaquely structured securitized mortgages were rubber-stamped as "AAA" by rating agencies due to modeling failures and, possibly, conflicts of interest, as the rating agencies may have been more interested in generating fees than doing careful risk assessment.

Somewhat surprisingly, however, these are not the ultimate reasons for the collapse of the financial system. If bad mortgages sold to investors hoodwinked by AAA ratings were all there was to it, those investors would have absorbed their losses and the financial system would have moved forward. The crash would have been no different, in principle, than the bursting of the tech bubble in 2000.

In our view, what made the current crisis so much worse than the crash of 2000 was the behavior of many of the large, complex financial institutions (LCFIs)—the universal banks, investment banks, insurance companies, and (in rare cases) even hedge funds—that dominate the financial industry. These LCFIs ignored their own business model of securitization and chose not to transfer the credit risk to other investors

The legitimate and worthy purpose of securitization is to spread risk. It does so by removing large concentrations of risk from the balance sheet of financial institutions, and placing small concentrations into the hands of large numbers of investors. But especially from 2003 to 2007, the main purpose of securitization was not to share risks with investors, but to make an end run around capital-adequacy regulations. The net result was to keep the risk concentrated in the financial institutions—and, indeed, to keep the risk at a greatly magnified level, because of the overleveraging that it allowed.

Many observers contend that extreme leverage created the conditions for the Financial Crisis. In the following excerpt, Professors Anat Admati and Martin Hellwig discuss the role that leverage played in the crisis and delve into the post-crisis debate over new leverage requirements, which we explore in Chapter 2.7.

Anat Admati & Martin Hellwig, The Bankers' New Clothes: What's Wrong with Banking and What to Do About It

4–5 (2013)

Excessive borrowing by banks was . . . a major factor in the crisis of 2007–2008. Bankers themselves sometimes admit this. Nevertheless, the banking industry fights aggressively against tighter restrictions on bank borrowing. The constant refrain is that too much tightening of such restrictions would harm economic growth.

For example, in 2009, when negotiations about a new international agreement on banking regulation were getting under way, Josef Ackermann, then the CEO of Deutsche Bank, asserted in an interview that tighter restrictions on bank borrowing "would restrict [banks'] ability to provide loans to the rest of the economy. This reduces growth and has negative effects for all."

This is a typical bugbear, suggesting that we must make a choice between economic growth and financial stability and that we cannot have both. After all, who would be in favor of a regulation that "reduces growth and has negative effects for all"?

Mr. Ackermann acknowledged that tighter restrictions on banks' borrowing "might increase bank safety," but he insisted that this would come at the expense of growth. He said, nothing, however, about how continued financial instability and turmoil would affect growth.

The sharpest economic downturn since the Great Depression of the early 1930s occurred in the last quarter of 2008, and it was a direct result of the worldwide financial crisis that affected numerous banks and other financial institutions. The unprecedented decline in output in 2009 and the resulting loss of output have been valued in the trillions of dollars. The crisis has caused significant suffering for many. In light of these effects, warnings that greater financial stability would come at the expense of growth sound hollow. Warnings that bank lending would suffer also sounds hollow. In 2008 and 2009, banks that were vulnerable because they had too much debt cut back sharply on their lending. The severe credit crunch was caused by banks' having too much debt hanging over them.

Some scholars attribute the Financial Crisis to the *type* of leverage that financial institutions took on—short-term funding. Professor Gary Gorton argues that broker-dealers' over-reliance on short-term funding, in the form of commercial paper, repo, securities financing transactions, and prime brokerage deposits, made them susceptible to runs. You will learn about short-term funding in Chapter 12.4.

Gary Gorton, Misunderstanding Financial Crises: Why We Don't See Them Coming

32–33 (2012)

A financial crisis can be understood most clearly if there is an observable, widespread bank run, as in the pre-Federal Reserve period in the United States. Then, a financial crisis was a more or less simultaneous run on all the banks in the banking system, with bank liability holders demanding cash. In the pre-Civil War Era in the United States this occurred with private banknotes, starting as early as the Panic of 1819, and then with demand deposits starting with the Panic of 1857 and continuing through the Great Depression. These panics were publicly observable: crowds of people lines up at their banks. They were *systemic* because *all* banks face runs.

Once a central bank exists, crises are more complicated. But at root crises are the same: sudden large demands for cash from financial institutions in exchange for short-term debt obligations. The commonality of crises is one of the points that the Panic of 2007–8 should have made clear—the crisis mechanism was the same. In the Panic of 2007–8, it was sale and repurchase agreements (repo), commercial paper, and prime broker balances that were run on. This panic was not observable to most people because it involved wholesale markets where firms ran on other firms.

A defining feature of a run is that a large number of consumers or firms act at more or less the same time, making such large-scale demands for cash that the banking system cannot meet their demands for legal tender. In this sense, the banking system is insolvent; it cannot honor contractual debt obligations. Then banks either suspend convertibility—they simply do not pay out cash—or they are bailed out by the government or the central bank. In the Panic 2007–8 firms tried to sell assets to raise the cash that was needed to repay repo depositors. But in doing so they just drove asset prices down, and eventually the Federal Reserve [Board] had to buy the assets, and the U.S. Congress passed the Emergency Economic Stabilization Act of 2008, which included an allocation of $700 billion dollars for [TARP] to bail out firms. The alternative would have been to cash in all debts and obligations for the entire banking system—to liquidate the banking system. That alternative has never (intentionally) been chosen.

Two points are worth emphasizing and repeating. The first is the scale of the [F]inancial [C]risis. Typically, a large part of the banking system is involved—many or most banks. This is why these crises are called "systemic." Second, the event is one in which bank liability holders demand cash, rather than holding the bank debt. A large amount of short-term bank debt is turned in for cash at the same time. The scale of the cash demands is so large that banks cannot meet the cash demands. People who were on trading floors at investment banks and other financial firms in August 2007 through 2008 understand the scale of the event. In that case, the panic did not involve depository institutions or the checking accounts of households but the short-term debt issued to firms and institutions depositing in the old investment banks in the form of repurchase agreements or asset-backed commercial paper.

Some commenters attribute the Financial Crisis to improper regulation. Professor Eric Gerding, for example, contends that policy choices—such as bankruptcy exemptions for swaps and repos and the repeal of Regulation Q—fueled a "shadow banking bubble" that exacerbated the crisis. ERIC F. GERDING, LAW, BUBBLES, AND FINANCIAL REGULATION 395 (2014). Others argue, by contrast, that the Financial Crisis was caused by too much regulation. After retiring from his positions as Chairman and CEO of BB&T Corporation, John Allison criticized the FDIC, the SEC, and the Federal Reserve Board for policies that he contends contributed to the Financial Crisis. Allison asserts that FDIC deposit insurance reduced depositors' incentives to monitor banks' activities and thereby allowed banks to raise funds to finance high-risk loan portfolios. *See* JOHN A. ALLISON, THE FINANCIAL CRISIS AND THE FREE MARKET CURE 39–41 (2013). Allison further contends that the SEC, concerned that banks were managing their earnings, forced banks to apply a rigid, mathematical formula for calculating loan loss reserves, which led to banks substantially reducing their reserves. *See id.* at 152. In the following excerpt, Allison alleges that the Federal Reserve System's monetary policy was the primary cause of the Financial Crisis.

John A. Allison, The Financial Crisis and the Free Market Cure

17, 26–27 (2013)

In a simple (but fundamental) sense, the only way there could have been a bubble in the residential real estate market was if the Federal Reserve [System] created too much money. It would have been mathematically impossible for a misinvestment of this scale to have happened without the monetary policies of the [Federal Reserve System]. . . .

The most destructive decisions that [the Federal Reserve System] made took place during the period 2000-2003. During this time, the Federal Reserve [System] created a structure of negative real interest rates. Financial investors could borrow at 2 percent, and inflation was 3 percent. . . . This creates a huge psychological and economic incentive to borrow. . . . The message was clear: make as many loans as possible. It was particularly tempting to finance the residential market, where houses were appreciating at 5 percent or better. The borrower would almost certainly be able to pay you back because his interest rate would be below the inflation rate. How could the bank or the borrower lose?

Some commenters, including Professor Arthur Wilmarth in the following excerpt, identified the erosion of the Glass-Steagall Act as a trigger of the Financial Crisis.

Arthur Wilmarth, The Dark Side of Universal Banking: Financial Conglomerates and the Origins of the Subprime Financial Crisis

41 CONN L. REV. 963, 973–74, 994–96 (2009)

In November 1999, Congress enacted the [GLBA], which . . . authorized universal banking. . . . [O]pponents of GLBA argued that the new universal banks permitted by GLBA were likely to generate financial risks . . . similar to those that occurred during the 1920s. Opponents warned that a removal of [Glass-Steagall Act's] constraints might ultimately cause a financial crisis similar in magnitude to the Great Depression. . . .

Consolidation and convergence among financial conglomerates after 1990 produced a significant increase in systemic risk in both U.S. and global financial markets. By 2007 . . . sixteen large complex financial institutions—including the four largest securities firms (Bear Stearns, Goldman, Lehman, Merrill and Morgan Stanley), and seven major foreign universal banks (Credit Suisse, Deutsche, Barclays, RBS, HSBC, BNP Paribas and Societe Generale)—collectively dominated the markets for debt and equity securities, syndicated loans, securitizations, structured-finance products and OTC derivatives. . . .

One study concluded that, between 2001 and 2004, an increased involvement by large U.S. banks in investment banking, securitization, and sales of loans, derivatives and other assets produced a significant rise in the overall risk of those banks. . . . Other studies determined that consolidation and conglomeration in the U.S. and European banking industries generated higher levels of systemic risk on both sides of the Atlantic. In particular, analysts found that growing convergence among the activities of banks, securities firms and insurance companies since the early 1990s intensified the risk that losses in one sector of the financial services industry would spill over into other sectors and produce a systemic financial crisis.

Others have argued that it was not the size of the financial conglomerates, but rather their corporate culture, that caused the Financial Crisis. Steve Eisman, a money manager portrayed by Steve Carell in the film "The Big Short," made such an argument.

Steve Eisman, Don't Break Up the Banks. They're Not Our Real Problem.

N.Y. TIMES (Feb. 6, 2016)

More than eight years after the financial crisis, many people say that the large banks still pose a threat to the economy and should be broken up. Such a view captures the justifiable anger many Americans still feel toward the large banks. But I don't agree. Breaking up the banks would ignore the significant progress made by regulators to reduce the risks posed by these institutions, and it wouldn't address what I believe is the central problem with the economy today. First, let's analyze why the financial crisis occurred. If I could sum up the catastrophe in one word, it would be "leverage." . . .

The explosion in leverage occurred for several reasons, but one underappreciated factor has to do with psychology and corporate culture. An entire generation of Wall Street executives came of age in the 1990s and 2000s. Their incomes started to rise after the recession of the early 1990s, going up in virtually a straight line until the financial crisis. Each year they made more, and each year the balance sheets of their respective firms grew. The system fed on itself. Unfortunately, Wall Street mistook leverage for genius.

Finally, some scholars see in the Financial Crisis the cycles of history, with financial innovations replicating in new forms the risks that had existed in prior eras as well. In the following excerpt, Professor Michael Barr explains his views on the Financial Crisis, which encapsulate several of the themes we have explored in this section.

Michael S. Barr, The Financial Crisis and the Path of Reform

29 YALE J. ON REG. 91, 93–95 (2012)

At many turns in history, financial innovations have supported economic advances; however, without carefully balanced rules governing the financial sector, these same innovations can also inflict economic damage. One modern example is securitization—the process of bundling large numbers of individual assets, such as mortgages or commercial debt, into larger securities. Securitization can help to diversify the range of capital sources available to supply credit in a wide variety of markets, increasing the supply and lowering the cost of credit. Nonetheless, securitization, without appropriate transparency and rules, can also widen the gap in incentives facing borrowers, lenders and investors, creating the potential for low-quality lending. Similarly, derivative contracts can permit commercial firms to hedge against interest-rate or commodity price risks, enabling them to focus on their core missions, and credit derivatives can assist financial institutions to provide more capital to businesses and families by reducing the risk of credit losses. At the same time, however, derivatives also allow market actors to take positions that magnify losses, heighten risk concentration in the financial system, and raise the vulnerability of interconnected financial firms to cascading liquidity and counterparty credit problems.

Innovations give rise to cycles of regulatory trial and error as market participants seek to balance benefits and risks appropriately. New products develop slowly while market participants are unsure of their value or their risks. As they develop, however, excitement and enthusiasm can overwhelm normal management systems. Participants assume too soon that they really "know how the products work"; shortly thereafter, the new products are applied widely without thought to new (and often riskier) contexts, and flood the market. The cycle turns when this excess and lack of understanding are exposed. Overall, the economy benefits from this cycle if the downsides to the broader economy are mitigated through well-designed regulatory safeguards. The strongest financial markets have regulatory structures that best balance incentives for innovation and competition, on the one hand, and protections from abuse and excessive risk taking, on the other.

For many years, the U.S. financial system successfully maintained this difficult balance. The U.S. financial industry often surpassed its competitors in other major developed economies in innovation and productivity growth. While housing was highly subsidized, the financial system was generally good at directing investment toward the companies and industries that offered the highest returns. Regulatory checks and balances helped create a remarkably long period of relative economic stability, which, in turn, gave rise to extraordinary national wealth. Regulation also provided investors and consumers with strong protections. The system endured crises and recessions, to be sure, including the costly bank and thrift failures of the late 1980s and early 1990s, but these shocks did not threaten the foundations of the financial system.

Over time, those great strengths were undermined: the system found itself outgrown and outmaneuvered by the institutions and markets it was responsible for regulating and constraining, and the carefully designed mix of protections eroded with the development of new products and markets for which those protections had not been designed.

The years leading up to the recent crisis saw the growth of large, short-funded, and substantially interconnected financial firms. Entities performing the same market functions as banks escaped meaningful regulation on the basis of their corporate form, and banks were able to move activities, liabilities, and assets off their balance sheet and outside the reach of more stringent regulation. The "shadow banking" system allowed financial institutions to engage in maturity transformation with too little transparency, capital, or oversight. Derivatives were traded in the shadows with insufficient capital to back the trades; transactions that were designed to disperse risk instead concentrated it. "Repo" markets became riskier as collateral shifted from Treasuries to asset-backed securities. The lack of transparency in securitization hid the growing gap in incentives facing different players in the system and muted the accountability of those who made loans, sold loans, or packaged loans into complex instruments for sale to investors. Synthetic products multiplied risks in the securitization system. These shadow banking markets allowed huge amounts of risk to move outside the more regulated parts of the banking system to places where it was easier to increase leverage.

The financial sector, under the guise of innovation, piled risk upon ill-considered risk. Financial innovations outpaced the capacity of managers, directors, regulators, rating agencies, and the market as a whole to understand and respond. Rapid growth in key markets hid misaligned incentives and underlying risk. Capital buffers were increasingly inadequate throughout the financial system, as both market participants and regulators failed to account for new risks appropriately. The apparent short-term rewards in new financial products and rapidly growing markets overwhelmed or blinded private-sector gatekeepers, swamping those parts of the system designed to mitigate risk. Consumer and investor protections were weakened and households took on risks that they often did not fully understand and could ill-afford.

Rising prices of homes and other assets helped to feed the financial system's rapid growth and to hide the underlying problems in the origination and securitization of loans. When home prices peaked and then began to decline in 2006, fault lines were revealed.

It is our hope that by the end of this book you will have developed a firm grounding in financial regulation, law, and policy in order to form your own opinions about the lessons to be learned from this history and the Financial Crisis.

CHAPTER 1.3

REGULATORY FRAMEWORKS

CONTENTS

I. INTRODUCTION

In Chapters 1.1 and 1.2, we provided an overview of the U.S. financial sector and a brief history of its regulation. In this Chapter, we turn to the goals of financial regulation and its organizational structure, sometimes called architecture, both domestically and internationally. We focus first on the different reasons for why there is a need for financial regulation and the multiple goals such regulation is meant to achieve. We then turn to domestic structures, beginning with a discussion of alternative approaches and then moving onto the framework of financial regulation in the United States, challenges to this framework, and organizational issues in the post-Dodd-Frank Act era. Finally, we focus on the international architecture of financial regulation, which plays an increasingly important role in establishing and enforcing global standards for financial regulation.

II. THE MULTIPLE GOALS OF FINANCIAL REGULATION

Financial institutions provide a variety of specialized services to the public and society. The nature of those services, it is generally assumed, warrants a degree of regulatory control and oversight substantially more intrusive and expensive than the legal rules governing other business enterprises. The validity and robustness of this assumption warrant special attention. The vast majority of the legal rules covered in this book rest, either explicitly or implicitly, on the notion that financial intermediaries and financial services are special. In some areas, the institutions are thought to be special because they are indispensable for effecting governmental programs such as monetary policy. See Chapter 1.2 for a discussion of the Federal Reserve System. Financial institutions are also critical for the efficient allocation of economic resources and the smooth operation of payment systems. In light of these essential functions of financial institutions, a principal justification for regulation in the field concerns the tendency of financial intermediaries to take excessive risks if the government does not intervene in some way. Even with respect to risk-taking, however, there are various strains of justification for governmental intervention.

A. PROTECTION OF PUBLIC CLAIMANTS

1. Collective Solution to Transaction Costs That Impede Self-Help

A common explanation for risk regulation of financial intermediaries proceeds on the assumption that public claimants in financial intermediaries, which include depositors, insurance policy-holders, and mutual fund shareholders, need some degree of protection from risk-taking by such intermediaries. At a minimum, claimants want to know the degree of risk associated with particular investments before they transfer their resources to an intermediary, and ideally also a sense of how those risks compare with the risks associated with other comparable investments. Equally important, once an investment is made, investors want assurances that the risk profile of their intermediary does not change in a way that disadvantages them. Because their individual investments are small and the business of financial intermediation is complex, public investors by themselves lack the expertise and incentives to demand appropriate information about the risk profile of financial intermediaries, to decipher that information, or to monitor later behavior on the part of an intermediary. The government, according to this line of reasoning, has a critical role to play in regulating and supervising the riskiness of financial intermediaries. In this view, much of our regulatory structure can be understood as a collective best guess regarding the form and content of advanced disclosure of institutional risk-taking that most investors would demand before making an investment, as well as a continuing set of restrictions on institutional risk-taking reflecting a tradeoff between risk and return that most of the investing public would demand from financial intermediaries if the public had the time and expertise to police intermediaries directly.

2. Absolute Protection of Terms of Investment

A second justification for risk regulation in financial intermediaries proceeds from a desire to offer complete or near-complete safety for members of the public who invest in financial intermediaries. People who make deposits in banks or purchase insurance contracts expect, or should expect, to have those investments honored according to their literal terms. It is assumed that these investors do not want or expect any degree of variation in return on their investments. Governmental regulation of intermediary operations ensures that the obligations of financial intermediaries are, in fact, honored according to their terms. Government insurance programs, such as those the FDIC operates for depository institutions, also achieve this goal for insured depositors. By protecting terms of investment, programs such as deposit insurance also help to ensure the smooth operation of the payment system for various financial products.

B. ELIMINATION OF EXTERNALITIES FROM THE FAILURE OF INTERMEDIARIES

Other justifications for risk regulation of financial intermediaries focus on possible externalities from risk-taking in financial intermediaries. These justifications proceed on the assumption that public investors may willingly and knowingly place their funds in high-risk intermediaries, presumably in return for the expectation of higher returns. Regulatory justifications that arise out of concerns over externalities are not directly concerned with the losses that a failed intermediary might impose on individuals who have invested funds in an intermediary, but rather with the costs that the intermediary's failure might impose on other members of society.

1. The Internalization of Social Losses

The fiscal ramifications of financial intermediary failures are one sort of externality. The premise here is that the public fisc pays at least partially for intermediary failures, either through underfunded guarantee programs like the now-defunct Federal Savings and Loan Insurance Fund or general welfare programs that support individuals who lose resources through intermediary mismanagement. To contain these public costs, the argument runs, the government must constrain risk-taking by intermediaries.

2. Systemic Costs of Failures

Another form of externality are systemic costs from financial failure, which are costs that are transmitted from failed institutions onto other unrelated participants in the economy. Irrational bank runs are perhaps the most common example of systemic costs, but there are other illustrations, including problems in clearing systems, disruption of capital underwriting, and unexpected contractions of the money supply. Because those injured by systemic costs have no easy way to prevent individual institutions from taking excessive risks and causing uncompensated losses to third parties, the government has another role in regulating financial institutions.

C. OTHER CONSIDERATIONS

While economic considerations often predominate in the regulation of financial institutions, other factors also contribute to legal systems in this field.

1. Redistributive Policies and Other Equitable Norms

Though not inherent in the nature of financial intermediation, redistribution policies and other equitable norms are often factored into financial regulation. Policies of this sort are most apparent in the insurance field, where regulatory systems often restrict the kinds of classifications insurance companies can employ. In the United States, for example, many states prohibit women from being charged lower automobile insurance premiums on the grounds that gender distinctions perpetuate illegitimate stereotypes. Similarly, usury rules prohibit charging interest rates above certain levels. Legal requirements of this sort are not intended to preserve the solvency of financial intermediaries; indeed, at the margin, they probably impair solvency. Rather, their purpose is to achieve various cross-subsidies through the financial system, typically advancing redistributive or other equitable norms.

2. Adjunct to Law Enforcement

As you will see in *United States v. Hom*, 45 F. Supp. 3d 1175 (N.D. Cal. 2014) in Chapter 1.4, sometimes financial regulations aim to advance other social policies, including the prevention of crime, the reduction of corruption, and the prevention of terrorist activities.

3. Political Economy

A final set of justifications for regulation of financial intermediaries are considerations of political economy. The prevention of monopolies is, for example, a goal of many political systems, and antitrust norms are often built into financial regulatory systems. Political factors lead to other structural constraints on financial services. It is, for example, not uncommon for countries to prohibit foreign participation in certain sectors of financial services, and barriers to internal expansion of financial units also exist. In the United States, for example, the federal government for many years restricted the interstate expansion of banks. The justification for these structural restraints is, again, not to improve the performance of financial intermediaries, but rather to ensure that financial services comport with some broader political vision of appropriate financial structures.

Throughout this text, one of the questions to which we regularly return is how do these justifications for regulation differ across sectors of financial services? The economic functions of financial intermediaries are often quite similar. Do the different kinds of public claimants, from securities investors to bank depositors, face the same informational barriers and collective action problems? Or, are some kinds of claimants, such as insurance policy holders, better equipped to look out for themselves than other public claimants? Do all sectors of financial services present the same risks of systemic problems and other negative externalities? Or, could our economy withstand the collapse of a portion of one sector, such as the mutual fund sector, more easily than some other sector, such as commercial banking? What about non-economic considerations? Are they generally applicable to financial services, or do some sectors thereof have better or more appropriate mechanisms for advancing broader social goals?

III. THE STRUCTURE OF FINANCIAL REGULATION

A. ALTERNATIVE APPROACHES

A recurring theme throughout this book is the interplay between function, form, and regulation. Financial regulation can be organized in many different ways. One common approach is to build financial regulation around sectors of financial services, with bank regulators overseeing banks, insurance regulators supervising insurance companies, and securities regulators taking responsibility for the securities sector. This sectoral approach is familiar and intuitive. There are, however, many other possibilities for organizing supervisory bodies. Consolidated supervision is another common approach, with all sectors brought under the control of a single entity, often designated a financial services authority. This approach exists in Japan, South Korea, and Sweden, among other places.

Another strategy is to organize regulatory responsibilities by regulatory objective. An example of this approach can be seen in Australia, where the Australian Securities & Investments Commission is responsible for overseeing market conduct whereas the Australian Prudential Regulation Authority handles prudential oversight. This regulatory structure is sometimes called a twin peaks approach, with the market conduct authority dealing with issues of consumer and investor protection and the prudential authority safeguarding the solvency of financial firms. *See* Michael W. Taylor, *Twin Peaks: A Regulatory Structure for the New Century*, 20 CTR. FOR THE STUDY OF FIN. INNOVATION 1 (Dec. 1995). In some variants of regulation by objective, a third peak is added to address issues of financial stability, sometimes referred to as macro-prudential regulation.

Yet another approach to organizing financial supervision is functional regulation, whereby regulatory requirements extend to specific financial functions wherever those functions happen to take place. The extension of credit or payment services would be examples of financial functions. In a system of functional regulation, any entity—regardless of organizational form—that extends credit or offers payment services would be subject to the same regulatory requirements. The responsibility for supervising each financial function could be assigned to one or more regulatory bodies. An alternative approach would be to regulate based on different kinds of risk, *e.g.*, "bank insurance fund risk, systemic risk, and risk of unfairness." Heidi Schooner, *Regulating Risk Not Function*, 66 U. CIN. L. REV. 441, 443 (1998). Professor Schooner has argued that functional regulation is inferior to risk-based regulation because the latter provides "greater flexibility in achieving regulatory goals in an environment in which the character of entities and products continues to evolve." *Id.* at 487.

The following excerpt explores some of the advantages and disadvantages of several of these alternative approaches.

Howell E. Jackson, Learning from Eddy: A Meditation Upon Organizational Reform of Financial Supervision

Perspectives in Company Law and Financial Regulation (Michel Tison et al. eds. 2009)

In modern debates over regulatory reform, the issue is typically framed in terms of a question of the degree to which and the manner in which traditional sectoral agencies should be consolidated into a smaller number of regulatory bodies. There are two basic approaches to consolidation. The first and simpler approach is to combine two or more sectors of the financial services industry under a consolidated regulatory body, such as the British Financial Services Authority [in the years leading up to the Financial Crisis].

Alternatively, existing agencies can be reconstituted into new and specialized organizational units designed to advance specific regulatory objectives, like ensuring the fairness and transparency of interactions between financial firms and their customers (sometimes called market conduct) or safeguarding the safety and soundness of financial institutions (often denominated prudential supervision). Adopting terminology coined by Michael Taylor, this second approach is often labeled a "twin peak" or "multi-peaked" model, depending on how many different regulatory objectives are specified and assigned to separate agencies. . . .

Within policy circles, the debates over the reform of financial regulatory systems have been well-rehearsed at this point, and the basic trade-offs are fairly well understood. The combination of single-sector agencies offers the promise of greater efficiency and efficacy, as consolidated agencies enjoy economies of both scale and scope. The advantages are, it is argued, capable of simultaneously improving the quality and lowering the cost of financial supervision, while also benefitting regulated firms by offering a single point of supervisory contact and eliminating sources of regulatory duplication and inconsistency. The on-going consolidation of the financial services industry is often cited as further justification for the combination of supervisory functions, as an integrated regulatory supervisor is said to be better equipped to oversee conglomerates that offer a full spectrum of financial products and manage their own risks on an organization-wide basis. The growing dominance of financial conglomerates in global markets also raises the costs of single-sector supervision, as consolidated firms are thought to be more capable of exploiting opportunities for regulatory arbitrage—that is, instances in which different regulators establish different substantive rules to deal with functionally similar products or activities—which single-sector agencies have difficulty identifying and correcting. Relatedly, consolidated agencies are thought to be better equipped to identifying regulatory gaps, that is, pockets of economic activity that fall outside the remit of traditional financial sectors, with hedge funds and perhaps sub-prime mortgage lending activities and securitization activities being prominent examples in recent times.

The case against regulatory consolidation is also multi-faceted. To begin with, there is the absence of irrefutable evidence that consolidated agencies are any more efficient than their single sector predecessors, at least in terms of total regulatory costs. More substantively, critics of consolidated supervisory argue that the goals of supervision differ across industry sectors and that a combination of regulatory functions may actually dilute the quality of supervision by imposing a standardized model of oversight on all sectors of the industry. Combined oversight may also diminish market discipline as government guarantees traditionally limited to certain sectors, like banking, may be assumed to extend more broadly in a country where all sectors have a common supervisory agency. In addition, there is concern that regulatory consolidation produces a governmental monopoly, less likely to respond to changing market conditions and potentially more prone to wholesale regulatory capture or at least a supervisory posture tilted in favor of large conglomerates at the expense of smaller more specialized firms.

Regulation by objective, the third multi-peaked model of regulatory organization, is a bit of a hybrid approach and thus shares some of the advantages and disadvantages of the two other models. By reducing the number of supervisory units, regulation by objective offers potential efficiency advantages over traditional sectoral regulation, and it also addresses concerns of regulatory arbitrage as functionally similar products and services are under the jurisdiction of the same supervisory body. But, like fully consolidated oversight, regulation by objective risks imposing one-size-fits-everyone rules, which discount unique characteristics of traditional sectors and subsectors. Moreover, multi-peaked models generate new problems of coordination, duplication and gaps, as the lines between functions such as market conduct, prudential regulation, and market stability are not clear, and many regulatory structures, like disclosure or even capital requirements, advance all three objectives. With regard to concerns over governmental monopolies and supervisory rigidity, multi-peaked models again constitute an intermediate case, less centralized than fully consolidated operations but less attuned to sectoral differences than traditional sectoral oversight.

Another much discussed dimension of regulatory consolidation is the appropriate supervisory role of central banks. Often times, reorganization entails the movement of bank supervision away from the central bank, as happened in the UK when the supervisory powers of the Bank of England were transferred to the new Financial Services Authority in the late 1990's. Less frequently, but occasionally, the central bank itself becomes the consolidated regulator, thereby expanding its jurisdiction as a result of reorganization. Finally, in certain multi-peaked models . . . the central bank may itself be designated the "peak" responsible for market stability. The often voiced concern about [limiting the responsibilities of central banks] is the possibility that moving direct supervisory oversight out of a central bank diminishes the bank's ability to effect appropriate monetary policy and maintain financial stability. [Supervisory responsibilities can, however, detract from a central bank's ability to focus on its primary task of overseeing monetary policy.]

Like many important issues of public policy, the debates over regulatory reorganization rests on numerous, conflicting claims regarding the consequences of various kinds of reforms. Seldom do policy analysts have unambiguous empirical evidence to validate their intuitions. . . .

In March 2008, just as the Financial Crisis was starting to unfold, the Treasury Department of President George W. Bush released a comprehensive proposal for regulatory reform, including a multi-step plan for modernizing financial regulation in the United States. U.S. DEP'T OF THE TREAS., BLUEPRINT FOR A MODERNIZED FINANCIAL REGULATORY STRUCTURE (Mar. 2008). In terms of combinations, the Treasury recommended in the relatively near future the merger of the SEC and CFTC, as well as the consolidation of banking supervisory bodies, including its proposed merger of the Office of Thrift Supervision (OTS) with the OCC, and also its more obliquely proposed combination of the divided FDIC and Federal Reserve Board oversight of state banks. Over the longer run, the Bush Administration's proposal envisioned the creation of multi-peaked objective-oriented agencies, focusing on prudential regulation, market conduct, and market stability, an objective centered on minimizing systemic risks. As the Bush Treasury Department also envisioned the creation of two smaller regulatory units, one for oversight of corporate issuers and the other to contain government guarantee funds, the proposal's long-term recommendations might best be labeled a "Three Peak, Two Foothill" model of regulation.

The onslaught of the Financial Crisis interrupted serious public debate over the Bush Administration's recommendations, and by January 2009, the Obama Administration had taken office. Within six months, Obama's Treasury Department developed its own plan for financial reform, including significant proposals for organizational reform. *See* U.S. DEP'T OF THE TREAS., FINANCIAL REGULATORY REFORM: A NEW FOUNDATION: REBUILDING FINANCIAL SUPERVISION AND REGULATION (June 2009). These recommendations heavily influenced the organizational changes adopted in the Dodd-Frank Act and the structure of financial regulation in the United States. As you read about the post-Dodd-Frank Act structure of financial regulation, consider the extent to which it deviates from or adheres to the recommendations of the Bush Treasury Department.

B. PRINCIPAL REGULATORY AGENCIES

The following excerpt from a report of the Government Accountability Office (GAO) offers an overview of the structure of financial regulation in the United States today and introduces the principal regulatory agencies that we will be exploring throughout this book.

GAO, Financial Regulatory Reform: Financial Crisis Losses and Potential Impacts of the Dodd-Frank Act

GAO-13-180 (Jan. 2013)

The financial regulatory framework in the United States was built over more than a century, largely in response to crises and significant market developments. As a result, the regulatory system is complex and fragmented.[1] While the Dodd-Frank Act has brought additional changes, including the creation of new regulatory entities and the consolidation of some regulatory responsibilities that had been shared by multiple agencies, the U.S. financial regulatory structure largely remains the same. It is a complex system of multiple federal and state regulators, as well as self-regulatory organizations, that operates largely along functional lines. The U.S. regulatory system is described as "functional" in that financial products or activities are generally regulated according to their function, no matter who offers the product or participates in the activity.

Banking Regulators

In the banking industry, the specific regulatory configuration depends on the type of charter the banking institution chooses. Depository institution charter types include:

- commercial banks, which originally focused on the banking needs of businesses but over time have broadened their services;
- thrifts, which include savings banks, savings associations, and savings and loans and were originally created to serve the needs—particularly the mortgage needs—of those not served by commercial banks; and
- credit unions, which are member-owned cooperatives run by member-elected boards with an historical emphasis on serving people of modest means.

These charters may be obtained at the state or federal level. State regulators charter institutions and participate in their oversight, but all institutions that have federal deposit insurance have a federal prudential regulator. The federal prudential regulators—which generally may issue regulations and take enforcement actions against industry participants within their jurisdiction—are identified in table 1. The [Dodd-Frank Act] eliminated the [OTS] and transferred its regulatory responsibilities to OCC, the Federal Reserve [Board], and FDIC.[2] To achieve their safety and soundness goals,

---

[1] For a more detailed discussion of the evolution of the U.S. financial regulatory framework before the enactment of the Dodd-Frank Act, see GAO, Financial Regulation: A Framework for Crafting and Assessing Proposals to Modernize the Outdated U.S. Financial Regulatory System, GAO-09-216 (Washington, D.C.: Jan. 8, 2009).

[2] OTS chartered and supervised federally chartered savings institutions and savings and loan holding companies [SLHCs]. Rule-making authority previously vested in OTS was transferred to OCC for savings associations and to the Federal Reserve [Board] for [SLHCs]. Other authorities were transferred to OCC, FDIC, and the Federal Reserve [Board]. 12 U.S.C. § 5412.

bank regulators establish capital requirements, conduct onsite examinations and off-site monitoring to assess a bank's financial condition, and monitor compliance with banking laws. Regulators also issue regulations, take enforcement actions, and close banks they determine to be insolvent. [The National Credit Union Administration (NCUA) is the independent federal agency that regulates charters and supervises federal credit unions.]

Table 1: Federal Prudential Regulators and Their Basic Functions

Agency	Basic function
Office of the Comptroller of the Currency	Charters and supervises national banks and federal thrifts.
Board of Governors of the Federal Reserve System	Supervises state-chartered banks that opt to be members of the Federal Reserve System, bank holding companies, thrift holding companies and the nondepository institution subsidiaries of those institutions, and nonbank financial companies designated by the Financial Stability Oversight Council.
Federal Deposit Insurance Corporation	Supervises FDIC-insured state-chartered banks that are not members of the Federal Reserve System, as well as federally insured state savings banks and thrifts; insures the deposits of all banks and thrifts that are approved for federal deposit insurance; and resolves all failed insured banks and thrifts and has been given the authority to resolve large bank holding companies and nonbank financial companies that are subject to supervision by the Board of Governors of the Federal Reserve System.
National Credit Union Administration	Charters and supervises federally chartered credit unions and insures savings in federal and most state-chartered credit unions.

Sources: OCC, Federal Reserve Board, FDIC, and NCUA.

Holding companies that own or control a bank or thrift are subject to supervision by the Federal Reserve [Board]. The Bank Holding Company Act of 1956 [(BHCA)] and the Home Owners' Loan Act [(HOLA)] set forth the regulatory frameworks for bank holding companies [(BHCs)] and [SLHCs], respectively.[3] Before the Dodd-Frank Act, [SLHCs] had been subject to supervision by OTS and a different set of regulatory requirements from those of [BHCs]. The Dodd-Frank Act made the Federal Reserve [Board] the regulator of [SLHCs] and amended the [HOLA] and the [BHCA] to create certain similar requirements for both [BHCs] and [SLHCs].[4] The Dodd-Frank Act also grants new authorities to [the Financial Oversight Council (FSOC)] to designate nonbank financial companies for supervision by the Federal Reserve [Board]. [Note that while federally chartered depository institutions are regulated only at the federal level, state chartered banks and thrifts experience two levels of prudential regulation, both state and federal.]

Securities and Futures Regulation

The securities and futures markets are regulated under a combination of self-regulation (subject to oversight by the appropriate federal regulator) and direct oversight by SEC and CFTC, respectively.[5] SEC regulates the securities markets, including participants such as securities exchanges, broker-dealers, investment companies, and investment advisers. SEC's mission is to protect investors; maintain fair, orderly, and efficient markets; and facilitate capital formation. In the securities industry, certain self-regulatory organizations [SROs]—including the securities exchanges and the Financial Industry Regulatory Authority [FINRA]—have responsibility for overseeing the securities markets and their members; establishing the standards under which their members conduct business; monitoring business conduct; and bringing disciplinary actions against members for violating applicable federal statutes, SEC's rules, and their own rules.

[3] Pub. L. No. 84-511, 70 Stat. 133 (1956) and Pub. L. No. 73-43, 48 Stat. 128 (1933). [BHCs] are companies that own or control a bank, as defined in the [BHCA]. [SLHCs] are companies that own or control [a savings and loan association].

[4] For a more detailed discussion of the regulatory framework for [BHCs] and [SLHCs], see GAO, Bank Holding Company Act: Characteristics and Regulation of Exempt Institutions and the Implications of Removing the Exemptions, GAO-12-160 (Washington, D.C.: Jan. 19, 2012).

[5] Certain securities activities also are overseen by state government entities.

CFTC is the primary regulator of futures markets, including futures exchanges and intermediaries, such as futures commission merchants.[6] CFTC's mission is to protect market users and the public from fraud, manipulation, abusive practices, and systemic risk related to derivatives that are subject to the Commodity Exchange Act, and to foster open, competitive, and financially sound futures markets. Like SEC, CFTC oversees the registration of intermediaries and relies on [SROs], including the futures exchanges and the National Futures Association [(NFA)], to establish and enforce rules governing member behavior.

In addition, Title VII of the Dodd-Frank Act expands regulatory responsibilities for CFTC and SEC by establishing a new regulatory framework for swaps. The act authorizes CFTC to regulate "swaps" and SEC to regulate "security-based swaps" with the goals of reducing risk, increasing transparency, and promoting market integrity in the financial system.[7]

Consumer Financial Protection Bureau

The Dodd-Frank Act established CFPB as an independent bureau within the Federal Reserve System and provided it with rule-making, enforcement, supervisory, and other powers over many consumer financial products and services and many of the entities that sell them.[8]

Certain consumer financial protection functions from seven existing federal agencies were transferred to CFPB.[9] Consumer financial products and services over which CFPB has primary authority include deposit taking, mortgages, credit cards and other extensions of credit, loan servicing, debt collection, and others. CFPB is authorized to supervise certain nonbank financial companies and large banks and credit unions with over $10 billion in assets and their affiliates for consumer protection purposes. CFPB does not have authority over most insurance activities or most activities conducted by firms regulated by SEC or CFTC.

Federal Housing Finance Agency

The Housing and Economic Recovery Act of 2008 (HERA) created FHFA to oversee the government-sponsored enterprises (GSE): Fannie Mae, Freddie Mac, and the Federal Home Loan Banks [(FHLBs)].[10] Fannie Mae and Freddie Mac were created by Congress as private, federally chartered companies to provide, among other things, liquidity to home mortgage markets by purchasing mortgage loans, thus enabling lenders to make additional loans. The system of 12 [FHLBs] provides funding to support housing finance and economic development. Until enactment of HERA, Fannie Mae and Freddie Mac had been overseen since 1992 by the Office of Federal Housing Enterprise Oversight (OFHEO), an agency within the Department of Housing and Urban Development (HUD),

---

[6] Futures commission merchants are individuals, associations, partnerships, corporations, and trusts that solicit or accept orders for the purchase or sale of any commodity for future delivery on or subject to the rules of any exchange and that accept payment from or extend credit to those whose orders are accepted. Firms and individuals who trade futures with the public or give advice about futures trading must be registered with the [NFA], the industry wide self-regulatory organization for the U.S. futures industry.

[7] A swap is a type of derivative that involves an ongoing exchange of one or more assets, liabilities, or payments for a specified period. Financial and nonfinancial firms use swaps and other over-the-counter derivatives to hedge risk, or speculate, or for other purposes. Swaps include interest rate swaps, commodity-based swaps, and broad-based credit default swaps. Security-based swaps include single-name and narrow-based credit default swaps and equity-based swaps. For the purposes of this report, we use "swaps" to refer to both "swaps" and "security-based swaps."

[8] 12 U.S.C. §§ 5481–5603.

[9] These agencies included the Federal Reserve [Board], FDIC, the Federal Trade Commission, the Department of Housing and Urban Development, the [NCUA], OCC, and OTS.

[10] Pub. L. No. 110-289, 122 Stat. 2654 (2008).

and the [FHLBs] were subject to supervision by the Federal Housing Finance Board (FHFB), an independent regulatory agency.[11] In July 2008, HERA created [Federal Housing Finance Agency (FHFA)] to establish more effective and more consistent oversight of the three housing GSEs.[12] Given their precarious financial condition, Fannie Mae and Freddie Mac were placed in conservatorship in September 2008, with FHFA serving as the conservator under powers provided in HERA.

Federal Insurance Office

While insurance activities are primarily regulated at the state level, the Dodd-Frank Act created the Federal Insurance Office [(FIO)] within Treasury to monitor issues related to regulation of the insurance industry.[13] The [FIO] is not a regulator or supervisor, and its responsibilities include identifying issues or gaps in the regulation of insurers that could contribute to a systemic crisis in the insurance industry or the U.S. financial system.

Financial Stability Oversight Council and Office of Financial Research

The Dodd-Frank Act established FSOC to identify risks to the financial stability of the United States, promote market discipline, and respond to emerging threats to the stability of the U.S. financial system. The Dodd- Frank Act also established [the Office of Financial Research (OFR)] within Treasury to serve FSOC and its member agencies by improving the quality, transparency, and accessibility of financial data and information; conducting and sponsoring research related to financial stability; and promoting best practices in risk management.[14] FSOC's membership consists of the Secretary of the Treasury, who chairs the council, and the heads of CFPB, CFTC, FDIC, the Federal Reserve [Board], FHFA, [NCUA], OCC, SEC, the directors of OFR and [FIO], representatives from state-level financial regulators, and an independent member with insurance experience.

---

1. ***Roots of Regulatory Structure in Past Financial and Political Crises.*** As explored in Chapter 1.2, which reviewed the history of financial regulation in the United States, major components of our regulatory structure can be traced to specific historical events: the OCC to the Civil War; the Federal Reserve Board to the financial panics of 1907 and earlier; the FDIC and SEC to New Deal reforms adopted in the midst of the Great Depression; and the CFPB and FSOC to the Financial Crisis. Also important to the understanding of the structure of financial regulation in this country is the continuing importance of state authorities, most prominently in the field of insurance but also to significant degrees in banking, securities regulation, and consumer protection. Classifying the structure of U.S. financial regulation is difficult, because it has evolved into something of a hybrid system. The basic sectoral components are still apparent, but one also can see elements of a twin peak model in the CFPB's responsibilities

---

[11] OFHEO regulated Fannie Mae and Freddie Mac on matters of safety and soundness, while HUD regulated their mission-related activities. FHFB served as the safety and soundness and mission regulator of the [FHLBs].

[12] With respect to Fannie Mae and Freddie Mac, the law gave FHFA such new regulatory authorities as the power to regulate the retained mortgage portfolios, to set more stringent capital standards, and to place a failing entity in receivership. In addition, the law provides FHFA with funding outside the annual appropriations process. The law also combined the regulatory authorities for all the housing GSEs that were previously distributed among OFHEO, FHFB, and HUD. 31 U.S.C. § 313.

[13] 31 U.S.C. § 313.

[14] 12 U.S.C. §§ 5321–5333. For additional information on FSOC and OFR, see GAO, *Financial Stability: New Council and Research Office Should Strengthen the Accountability and Transparency of Their Decisions*, GAO-12-886 (Washington, D.C.: Sept. 11, 2012).

over certain areas of market oversight and the FSOC's responsibilities with respect to systemic risks. The GAO excerpt begins, however, by characterizing the U.S. system as operating "largely along functional lines." In what sense does the U.S. system regulate entities according to the financial function they perform, such as the extension of credit or the provision of payment services?

2. ***What's In and What's Out.*** The GAO report excerpted above gives what might be considered the canonical account of financial regulatory structure in the United States. That view, however, omits some significant areas of legal rules governing financial activities. For example, the account does not mention the quite extensive federal regulation of employer-based retirement plans and other fringe benefits under Employee Retirement Income Security Act of 1974 (ERISA) or the now nearly comprehensive federal involvement of health insurance under Medicare, Medicaid, and the Patient Protection and Affordable Care Act of 2010 (ACA, also known as Obamacare). In addition, anti-money laundering laws, largely administered by the Treasury, are not mentioned in the GAO report but impose important restrictions on the movement of financial resources. Furthermore, a wide range of state laws, from fiduciary duties to a host of consumer protection laws, play a major role in policing consumer financial matters. The actual structure of financial regulation in the United States is therefore a good deal more complicated than the GAO's summary might suggest.

3. ***Quack Legislation or Constructive Interventions?*** Whether financial and political crises produce sound regulatory policies is a question upon which academic experts differ. Professor Roberta Romano of Yale Law School has written extensively and derisively on what she calls quack legislation, which arises out of crises. In contrast, Professor John Coffee has argued that crises allow our political processes to overcome the power of special interests and that, in ordinary times, legislative reforms are less likely to serve the public interest. *Compare* Roberta Romano, *Further Assessment of the Iron Law of Financial Regulation: A Postscript to Regulating in the Dark*, in SYSTEMIC RISK, INSTITUTIONAL DESIGN AND THE REGULATION OF FINANCIAL MARKETS (A. Anand, ed.) (Oxford Univ. Press forthcoming), *with* John C. Coffee, *The Political Economy of Dodd-Frank: Why Financial Reform Tends to Be Frustrated and Systemic Risk Perpetuated*, 97 CORNELL L. REV. 1019 (2012). Which is a more accurate interpretation?

As you saw in Chapter 1.2, throughout U.S. history, the structure of financial regulation has been a hotly contested political issue. The creation of the First and Second Banks of the United States generated serious political backlashes in the early 19th Century, culminating in President Andrew Jackson's veto message in 1832. Passions were equally strong surrounding the creation of the Federal Reserve Board in the early 20th Century, as well as the introduction of the New Deal agencies a few decades later. In the 2000s, the most prominent example of financial regulatory reform, the Dodd-Frank Act, raises blood pressure in certain circles, as the following case demonstrates.

State Nat'l Bank of Big Spring v. Lew

958 F.Supp.2d 127 (D.D.C. 2013)

■ HUVELLE, J.

Plaintiffs State National Bank of Big Spring ("SNB" or the "Bank"), the 60 Plus Association ("60 Plus"), the Competitive Enterprise Institute ("CEI") (collectively the "Private Plaintiffs") . . . have sued to challenge the constitutionality of Titles I . . . of the Dodd-Frank Wall Street Reform and Consumer Protection Act, Pub. L. No. 111-203 (July 21, 2010) (the "Dodd-Frank Act"). . . . Defendants, who include more than a dozen [of] federal government officials and entities, have filed a motion to dismiss pursuant to Fed. R. Civ. P. 12(b)(1) on the grounds that plaintiffs lack Article III standing, or, in the alternative, that their claims are not ripe for review. . . .

BACKGROUND

On July 21, 2010, Congress enacted the Dodd-Frank Act as "a direct and comprehensive response to the financial crisis that nearly crippled the U.S. economy beginning in 2008." S. Rep. No. 111-176, at 2 (2010). The purpose of the Act was to "promote the financial stability of the United States . . . through multiple measures designed to improve accountability, resiliency, and transparency in the financial system[.]" *Id.* Those measures included "establishing an early warning system to detect and address emerging threats to financial stability and the economy, enhancing consumer and investor protections, strengthening the supervision of large complex financial organizations . . . ." *Id.* The Act "creat[ed] several new governmental entities, eliminate[ed] others, and transferr[ed] regulatory authority among the agencies."

Specifically, in Count III, the Private Plaintiffs challenge the constitutionality of Title I on separation-of-powers grounds, alleging that the FSOC "has sweeping and unprecedented discretion to choose which nonbank financial companies to designate as 'systematically important'" and that such "powers and discretion are not limited by any meaningful statutory directives."...

Defendants have moved to dismiss the complaint on the grounds that plaintiffs lack Article III standing to pursue their claims, or, in the alternative, that their claims are not ripe. This is an unusual case, as plaintiffs have not faced any adverse rulings nor has agency action been directed at them. Most significantly, no enforcement action—"the paradigm of direct governmental authority"—has been taken against plaintiffs. *FEC v. NRA Political Victory Fund*, 6 F.3d 821, 824 (D.C. Cir. 1993). As a result, plaintiffs' standing is more difficult to parse here than in the typical case. . . . Furthermore . . . none of the plaintiffs is subject to regulation under Titles I. . . . Nonetheless, plaintiffs maintain that they have standing to pursue their Title I . . . claims, based, respectively, on their status as competitors and as creditors of the regulated entities.

ANALYSIS

I. LEGAL STANDARDS

Plaintiffs bear the burden of establishing that the Court has jurisdiction over their claims. *See Steel Co. v. Citizens for a Better Env't*, 523 U.S. 83, 140 (1998). . . . "For each claim, if constitutional and prudential standing can be shown for at least one plaintiff, [the court] need not consider the standing of the other plaintiffs to raise that claim." *Mountain States Legal Found. v. Glickman*, 92 F.3d 1228, 1232 (D.C. Cir. 1996). . . .

I. TITLE I: FINANCIAL STABILITY OVERSIGHT COUNCIL ("FSOC")

A. The Statutory Provision

Title I of the Dodd-Frank Act established the FSOC. *See* 12 U.S.C. § 5321. The purposes of the Council are

> to identify risks to the financial stability of the United States that could arise from the material financial distress or failure, or ongoing activities, of large, interconnected [BHCs] or nonbank financial companies, or that could arise outside the financial services marketplace; to promote market discipline, by eliminating expectations on the part of shareholders, creditors, and counterparties of such companies that the Government will shield them from losses in the event of failure; and to respond to emerging threats to the stability of the United States financial system.

12 U.S.C. § 5322(a)(1). The Council has ten voting members: the Secretary of the Treasury, who serves as the Council Chairperson; the Chairman of the Federal Reserve Board; the Comptroller of the Currency; the Director of the CFPB; the Chairperson of the [SEC]; the Chairperson of the [FDIC]; the [CFTC]; the Director of the [FHFA]; the Chairman of the [NCUA] Board; and an independent member with insurance expertise appointed by the President with the advice and consent of the Senate. *See* 12 U.S.C. § 5321(b)(1). The Council also includes five nonvoting members. *See id.* § 5321(b)(3).

Title I authorizes the Council, upon a two-thirds vote of its voting members, including the affirmative vote of the Treasury Secretary, to designate certain "nonbank financial companies" as "systematically important financial institutions" or SIFIs.[15] 12 U.S.C. §§ 5323(a)(1), (b)(1), 5365, 5366. SIFI designation is based on consideration of eleven enumerated factors leading to a determination that "material financial distress at the U.S. nonbank financial company, or the nature, scope, size, scale, concentration, interconnectedness, or mix of the activities of the U.S. nonbank financial company, could pose a threat to the financial stability of the United States." 12 U.S.C. § 5323(a)(1). *See id.* (a)(2), (b)(2). If an entity is designated as a SIFI, it "will be subject to supervision by the Federal Reserve Board and more stringent government regulation in the form of prudential standards and early remediation requirements established by the Board." (*See id.*) Before designating any company as a SIFI, the Council must give written notice to the company of the proposed determination. *See* 12 U.S.C. § 5323(e)(1). The company is entitled to a hearing at which it may contest the proposed determination. *See id.* § 5323(e)(2). Additionally, once the Council makes a final decision to designate a company as a SIFI, that company may seek judicial review of the determination, and a court will determine whether the decision was arbitrary and capricious. *See id.* § 5323(h). There is no provision for third-party challenges to SIFI designation under Title I.

On April 11, 2012, following a notice-and-comment period, the Council published a "final rule and interpretive guidance . . . describ[ing] the manner in which the Council intends to apply the statutory standards and considerations, and the processes and procedures that the Council intends to follow, in making determinations under § 113 of the Dodd-Frank Act." Authority to Require Supervision and Regulation of Certain Nonbank Financial Companies, 77 FED. REG. 21637 (Apr. 11, 2012). On June 3, 2013, while this motion was pending, the Council voted to make proposed determinations regarding a set of nonbank financial companies but did not release the names of the designated companies. Those companies then had thirty days to request a hearing before a final determination would be made. American International Group, Inc. ("AIG"), Prudential Financial Inc., and the GE Capital Unit of General Electric have confirmed that they are among the designated companies. AIG and GE Capital have chosen not to contest their designations, but Prudential has announced that it will appeal. . . .

---

[15] A "nonbank financial company" is defined as a company "predominately engaged in financial activities," other than [BHCs] and certain other entities. 12 U.S.C. § 5311(a)(4). The term "systematically important financial institution" does not actually appear in the Dodd-Frank Act, but because it has come into common parlance (*see* Def. Mot. at 3 n.2), and the parties have used the term throughout their briefs, the Court will do so as well.

The Bank claims to have standing to challenge the creation and operation of the FSOC as a violation of the Constitution's separation of powers. The Bank is not a regulated party under Title I and so, while "standing is not precluded, it is . . . substantially more difficult to establish" under these circumstances. *Ass'n of Private Sector Colleges v. Duncan*, 681 F.3d 427 at 458 (D.C. Cir. 2012). The Bank's theory of standing relies on an allegation of "competitor injury" arising out of the "illegal structuring of a competitive environment." *Shays v. Fed. Election Com'n*, 414 F.3d 76, 85 (D.C. Cir. 2005). The D.C. Circuit has "recogniz[ed] that economic actors 'suffer [an] injury in fact when agencies lift regulatory restrictions on their competitors or otherwise allow increased competition against them." *Sherley v. Sebelius*, 610 F.3d 69, 72 (D.C. Cir. 2010) (quoting *La. Energy & Power Auth. v. FERC*, 141 F.3d 364, 367 (D.C. Cir. 1998)). . . .

Importantly, however, the plaintiff must allege that it is "a direct and current competitor whose bottom line may be adversely affected by the challenged government action." *New World Radio, Inc. v. FCC*, 294 F.3d 164, 170 (D.C. Cir. 2002). A plaintiff's "'chain of events' injury is too remote to confer standing" where the plaintiff has not stated a "concrete, economic interest that has been perceptibly damaged" by the agency action. *Id.* at 172 (internal quotation marks and citation omitted) (emphasis in the original). *See also KERM, Inc. v. FCC*, 353 F.3d 57, 60-61 (D.C. Cir. 2004) ("party must make a concrete showing that it is in fact likely to suffer financial injury as a result of the challenged action") (emphasis added). The Supreme Court has likewise made clear that there are limits to the competitor standing doctrine. For instance, in *Already, LLC v. Nike, Inc.*, 133 S.Ct. 721 (2013), the Court rejected plaintiff's "boundless theory of standing," remarking, "[t]aken to its logical conclusion, [plaintiff's] theory seems to be that a market participant is injured for Article III purposes whenever a competitor benefits from something allegedly unlawful—whether a trademark, the awarding of a contract, a landlord-tenant arrangement, or so on." *Id.* at 731.

The Bank relies on just such a "boundless theory." *Id.* The assumption underlying the Bank's assertion of injury is that the FSOC's designation of GE Capital as a SIFI will confer a competitive advantage on GE and a corresponding disadvantage on the Bank. The Bank alleges that GE Capital is its direct competitor in the market to raise capital and in the market to sell consumer loans, and that GE will benefit from a cost-of-capital advantage that "will place SNB at a competitive disadvantage in each" market.

In support of the Bank's allegation that GE is a direct and current competitor in the consumer loan market, Chairman and former President of SNB Jim Purcell asserts in a recent declaration that "approximately 37% of the Bank's outstanding loans are agricultural loans" and "[a]ccording to publicly available information, GE Capital and its subsidiaries offer numerous loans in the agricultural sector, including in markets that are served by the Bank." . . .

While these assertions lend some plausibility to the Bank's allegation that GE is a "direct and current" competitor at least in the agricultural loan business, the Bank relies on conjecture to argue that the SIFI designation will benefit GE and harm the Bank. The Bank speculates that the designation will cause investors to flock to the designees because they will be perceived as safer investments due to the possibility of government backing. Of course, SIFI designation does not, in fact, mean that the federal government is "backing" the SIFI or that the government will not allow the company to fail. Instead, it means that the SIFI will be subject to more stringent regulation and government oversight. *See* 12 U.S.C. § 5323(a)(1), (b)(1), 5365(c)(I). But whether SIFI designation will mean anything else is simply unknown at this early stage.

The ambiguous consequences of SIFI designation are underscored by David Price, the very source cited by the Bank:

> The precise implications of being designated as a SIFI are not known yet because the new regulatory regime has not yet been defined. . . . On the plus

> side, SIFI designation may confer benefits on a company by reducing its cost of capital. Creditors may believe that enhanced supervision lowers an institution's credit risk. . . . The extent of this benefit to creditors, if any, is not clear at this point however. . . . So far, institutions appear to believe that they would be worse off as SIFIs. In public comments filed with FSOC and in public statements, large nonbanks and their trade associations have argued that they should not be considered systematically important. . . . The institutions' concerns about the regulatory regime for SIFIs may be heightened by a fear that the as-yet-unwritten rules will turn out to be

David A. Price, "Sifting for SIFIs," Region Focus, Federal Reserve Bank of Richmond (2011).

Indeed, one of the proposed SIFIs, Prudential Financial, is appealing its designation, which indicates that at least one nonbank perceives the designation more as a detriment than a benefit. On the other hand, GE Capital has declined to appeal, because it "is already supervised by the [Federal Reserve Board] and as a result has strong liquidity and capital." Since the SIFIs themselves are far from unanimous as to the consequences of being designated, it is difficult to prophesize that the designation confers a clear benefit on them, much less a corresponding disadvantage on non-SIFI institutions like SNB. *See Already, Inc.*, 133 S.Ct. at 731. In short, the Bank has not come close to a "concrete showing that it is in fact likely to suffer financial injury as a result of the challenged action." *KERM, Inc. v. FCC*, 353 F.3d 57, 60-61 (D.C. Cir. 2004) (emphasis in original).

---

1. ***Challenges to Other Titles.*** In addition to the plaintiffs' challenge to the FSOC's designation powers under Title I of the Dodd-Frank Act, the case also featured challenges to other Titles. For example, in Count I, the plaintiffs challenged Title X "on the grounds that it violates the separation of powers by delegat[ing] effectively unbounded power to the CFPB, and coupl[ing] that power with provisions insulating the CFPB against meaningful checks by the Legislative, Executive, and Judicial Branches." State National Bank of Big Spring v. Lew, 958 F. Supp. 2d 127, 132 (D.D.C. 2013) (citation omitted) (internal quotation marks omitted). Specifically, the plaintiffs alleged several "financial injuries" caused by the "unconstitutional formation and operation of the [CFPB]." *Id.* at 149. Among these alleged injuries was the cost of compliance required to "keep abreast of developments under the Dodd-Frank Act," including "$230,000 ... in 2012, including over $2,500 to send a representative to 'Compliance School' that offered classes on, *among other things*, CFPB regulations." *Id.* at 151 (emphasis in original) (internal quotation marks omitted). Another alleged injury was the plaintiffs' forced exit from the consumer mortgage business in order to avoid potential enforcement actions under the CFPB's authority to police unfair, deceptive or abusive acts. *Id.* at 150. The court rejected the plaintiffs' challenge to Title X, characterizing the alleged injuries as "self-inflicted" and based on "fears of hypothetical future harm." *See id.* at 153, 162. The plaintiffs also challenged Title II in Counts IV, V, and VI, alleging that its creation of the Orderly Liquidation Authority (OLA) allows the sudden, secretive, and unchecked liquidation of financial companies, violates the due process clause of the Fifth Amendment, and violates the constitutional requirement of uniformity in bankruptcy. *See id.* at 132. The plaintiffs alleged injuries due to, among other things, abridgment of "the federal bankruptcy laws' guarantee of equal treatment of similarly situated creditors"

because the OLA permits differential treatment of creditors in certain situations. *See id.* at 141–42. The court also rejected the plaintiffs' challenge to Title II, characterizing the alleged injuries as "too conjectural and remote" and "depend[ent] upon a chain of potential but far from inevitable developments." *See id.* at 142, 146. In a later decision, the Court of Appeals for the District of Columbia Circuit upheld the District Court's dismissal of the plaintiff's challenges to FSOC and Title II's OLA, but reinstated the plaintiffs' claims with respect to the CFPB. *See* State National Bank of Big Spring v. Lew, 765 F.3d 48 (D.C. Cir. 2015). We will explore the various substantive issues underlying this case in later chapters, but for now note the frequency with which issues of financial regulation present issues of constitutional dimensions in the United States, as well as the intensity of the political passions engendered by such regulation.

C. ORGANIZATIONAL DESIGN AFTER THE DODD-FRANK ACT

This section introduces some specific issues in organizational design with ongoing importance. Ask yourself which of them seem to be the most important, and why. How would you prioritize a list of reforms? To what extent are these reforms driven by the need to address political perceptions?

---

1. ***Variation in Legal Structure of Regulatory Agencies.*** While it is common to discuss financial regulatory agencies as a group of similarly constituted bodies, there are actually considerable differences in the legal structure of each agency. Some regulatory agencies depend on annual appropriations from Congress, whereas others have the authority to raise funds from regulated firms or finance their resources from other activities, for example, insurance premiums from banks for the FDIC and monetary policy transactions for the Federal Reserve Board. Financial regulators generally operate under a number of background legal structures, such as the Administrative Procedure Act (APA) and Freedom of Information Act, but the application of these background rules is not uniform. For example, regulatory review by the Office of Management and Budget's Office of Information and Regulatory Affairs does not extend to most financial regulators. In an article focusing on the structure of the CFPB, Professor Adam Levitin explores how "the CFPB and other federal agencies share several key oversight devices: APA rulemaking, APA adjudication, congressional oversight, simple Congressional majority override of rulemakings under the Congressional Review Act, and moral suasion by the administration." Adam J. Levitin, *The Consumer Financial Protection Bureau: An Introduction*, 32 REV. BANKING & FIN. L. 321, 342 (2012-2013).

Figure 1.3-1 Comparison of Oversight of CFPB and Other Agencies

	EPA	FDIC	FRB	FTC	OCC	SEC	SSA	CFPB
APA Rulemaking	YES	YES	YES	YES	YES	YES	YES	YES
APA Adjudication	YES	YES	YES	YES	YES	YES	YES	YES
Budget Subject to Appropriations	YES			YES		YES	YES	
Budget Capped								YES
OIRA Review of Economically Significant Regulations	YES						YES	
OIRA SBREFA Review	YES							YES
Statutory Cost-Benefit Analysis for Certain Regulations				YES		YES		YES
FSOC Veto								YES
Annual GAO Audit								YES
Term in Office <5 Years	YES							
5-member Commission		YES	YES	YES		YES		
Bipartisan Representation Requirement		YES		YES				
Presidential Removal without Cause	YES				?			
Congressional Oversight	YES	YES	YES	YES	YES	YES	YES	YES
Congressional Review Act Override of Rulemakings	YES	YES	YES	YES	YES	YES	YES	YES
Moral Suasion by Administration	YES	YES	?	YES	YES	YES	YES	YES

Source: Adam J. Levitin, The Consumer Financial Protection Bureau: An Introduction, Consumer Financial Protection Bureau, 32 Rev. of Bank. & Fin. L., 343 (2012-2013).

Notice that there are many differences among the financial regulators, both old and new. For instance, while the FDIC, the Federal Reserve Board, and the SEC are all led by multi-member boards or commissions, the CFPB and the OCC, launched nearly 150 years apart, are both led by a single director. The Federal Reserve Board is nonpartisan in nature, while the SEC and CFTC's commissions are by design divided along partisan lines. The FDIC board includes members that represent other agencies' interests. Further, the SEC and CFTC must manage a budget subject to appropriations, while the Federal Reserve Board, FDIC, OCC, and CFPB do not. Only the SEC and the CFPB are subject to an explicit statutory cost-benefit analysis requirement, while the other regulators face no such mandate. What kinds of incentives do these different structural features create? How can the more harmful incentives be countered adequately and the more beneficial incentives be better harnessed? Is there a particular combination of structural features that is superior, or do structural choices depend on the particular agency, historical factors, and areas of regulation, involving tradeoffs among values? *See, e.g.*, Kirti Datla & Richard L. Revesz, *Deconstructing Independent Agencies (and Executive Agencies)*, 98 CORNELL L. REV. 769 (2013).

2. ***The Contested Role of the Federal Reserve Board in U.S. Supervision.*** The Federal Reserve Board has substantial supervisory powers compared to many other central banks and is also relatively independent from political control. The Federal Reserve Board also does not depend on Congress for annual appropriations. The Federal Reserve Board's political independence has long been a topic of much debate. *See, e.g.*, DONALD KOHN, HUTCHINS CTR. ON FISCAL & MONETARY POL'Y AT BROOKINGS, FEDERAL RESERVE INDEPENDENCE IN THE AFTERMATH OF THE FINANCIAL CRISIS: SHOULD WE BE WORRIED? 3–5 (2014) (tracing the evolution of views on Federal Reserve Board independence over the past few decades).

For instance, some have argued that the Federal Reserve Board's independence is undemocratic because monetary policy affects the well-being of all Americans, yet such policy is designed and implemented by a politically insulated Board of Governors. *See, e.g.*, Mark Weisbrot, *Answer to the People, Not Greedy Elites*, THE GUARDIAN (Feb. 15, 2010). Others have argued against the Federal Reserve Board's independence by pointing out that it has failed to achieve its mandate of low inflation and economic stability. *See, e.g.*, George Selgin et al., *Has the Fed Been a Failure?*, 34 J. MACROECONOMICS 569, 570–74, 575–79 (2012). Defenders of Federal Reserve Board independence have responded by pointing out that "less independence is correlated with higher inflation," Kohn, *Federal Reserve Independence*, at 1, and that monetary policy operates with time lags that are longer than political election cycles. *See* Ben S. Bernanke, Chairman, Bd. of Governors of the Fed. Reserve Sys., Speech at the Institute for Monetary and Economic Studies International Conference: Central Bank Independence, Transparency, and Accountability (May 25, 2010). The Federal Reserve Board itself has undertaken reforms to address the perception that it is beholden to the financial institutions it regulates, even as it is relatively unchecked by Congress. In a shift of power from the Federal Reserve Bank of New York to the Federal Reserve Board headquarters in Washington, D.C., a small committee headed by Federal Reserve Board Governor Daniel Tarullo has taken on the responsibility to oversee Wall Street banks. *See* Jon Hilsenrath, *Washington Strips New York Fed's Power*, WALL ST. J. (Mar. 4, 2015). For an extended discussion of the Federal Reserve Board and its independent status, *see generally* PETER CONTI-BROWN, THE POWER AND INDEPENDENCE OF THE FEDERAL RESERVE (Princeton Univ. Press 2016). What kind of empirical evidence, if any, would move this debate in one direction or the other? Should normative arguments based on democratic values operate as trump cards in this debate, or are considerations of central bank effectiveness equally—or more—important? Internationally, in the aftermath of the Financial Crisis, the European Central Bank has now taken on a new role beyond monetary policy similar to the role of the Federal Reserve Board: responsibility for the supervision of the largest European financial institutions.

3. ***Interagency Coordination in the Dodd-Frank Act.*** "Interagency coordination is one of the central challenges of modern governance" because of the congressional tendency towards "fragmented and overlapping delegations of power to administrative agencies." Jody Freeman & Jim Rossi, *Agency Coordination in Shared Regulatory Space*, 125 HARV. L. REV. 1131, 1134 (2012). For instance, prudential banking supervision is divided among the Federal Reserve Board, the OCC, and the FDIC, while investor protection authority is divided between the SEC and the CFTC. To be sure, a lack of coordination has its benefits: fragmented delegations may prevent the executive branch from controlling the direction of a given policy and redundant delegations may "provid[e] a form of insurance against a single agency's failure." *Id.* at 1138, 1140. Interagency coordination may, however, still be desirable in order to avoid agency gridlock and inefficiency. *See id.* at 1135; *see also* Jason Marisam, *Duplicative Delegations*, 63 ADMIN. L. REV. 181, 184 (2011) ("Duplication would drain government coffers, interagency conflict would undermine regulatory goals, and overlapping oversight would burden regulated entities.").

The Dodd-Frank Act included numerous provisions designed to improve interagency coordination, including requirements for joint rulemaking in many of its provisions and "interagency consultation prior to rule promulgation in several others." Freeman & Rossi, *Agency Coordination in Shared Regulatory Space,* at 1168. These requirements are designed to "minimize potentially inconsistent regulations and manage numerous overlaps." *Id.* Another example of a coordination effort made by the Dodd-Frank Act is its amendment of Section 23A of the Federal Reserve Act, which imposes restrictions on transactions between banks and their affiliates. 12 U.S.C. § 371c (2010); *see also* Saule T. Omarova, *From Gramm-Leach-Bliley to Dodd-Frank: The Unfufilled Promise of § 23A of the Federal Reserve Act*, 89 N.C. L. REV. 1683, 1686–88 (2011). The Dodd-Frank Act granted the OCC and the FDIC the power to block the Federal Reserve Board from granting exemptions to Section 23A's requirements for institutions under their respective supervision. *See id.* at 1760.

Moreover, the Federal Reserve Board, the OCC, and the FDIC are prohibited "from exempting any transaction or relationship . . . if the FDIC determines that such exemption presents an unacceptable risk to the federal deposit insurance fund." *Id.* Section 23A's requirements will be discussed in more detail in Chapter 2.3. Perhaps chief among the Act's coordination efforts is the creation of the FSOC, an agency that, as we saw in the excerpt from the GAO earlier in this Chapter, is charged with identifying and ameliorating risks to the financial stability of the United States and is composed of the heads of the nation's financial regulators. The FSOC also has limited powers, in some instances limited to recommendations, to revisit or supersede decisions of other financial authorities. *See* U.S. GOV'T ACCOUNTABILITY OFF., GAO 13-180, FINANCIAL REGULATORY REFORM 8–9 (Jan. 2013). The Dodd-Frank Act, however, did not substantially reduce or consolidate existing federal regulators, despite, for example, calls to merge the SEC and the CFTC, as we saw earlier in the Treasury's 2008 proposal earlier in the chapter. *See* U.S. DEP'T OF THE TREAS., BLUEPRINT FOR A MODERNIZED FINANCIAL REGULATORY STRUCTURE (Mar. 2008). In fact, the only consolidation, the merger of the OTS into the OCC, see 12 U.S.C. § 5412(b)(2)(B) (2014), was arguably offset by the additions of the FSOC and the CFPB. As a result, "information sharing and coordination remain significant challenges to the effective operation of the fragmented regime." Freeman & Rossi, *Agency Coordination in Shared Regulatory Space*, at 1148. For further discussion of regulatory coordination problems and solutions arising from the Dodd-Frank Act, see generally Jacob E. Gersen, *Administrative Law Goes to Wall Street: The New Administrative Process*, 65 ADMIN. L. REV. 689 (2013). Can interagency coordination be successful without agency consolidation? Are there additional reasons why we would want to promote interagency coordination, or to instead preserve or even increase fragmentation and duplication?

4. ***External Perspectives on the Organizational Structure of U.S. Financial Regulation.*** Around the turn of the millennium, the International Monetary Fund (IMF) started to prepare periodic reports on the financial stability of developed countries such as the United States, going beyond its traditional focus on the developing world. In its 2010 and 2015 reports on the United States, the IMF, among other things, critically discussed the nation's organizational structure of financial regulation. In its 2015 report, the IMF

recommended that the FSOC "should be strengthened with member agencies being given an explicit financial stability mandate" and that "comprehensive data" on "systemic risks and interconnections must be collected." INT'L MONETARY FUND, UNITED STATES: FINANCIAL SYSTEM STABILITY ASSESSMENT 7 (July 2015). The IMF made these recommendations in light of the perceived weaknesses of the FSOC, including the disparate mandates of its various member agencies, which could "complicate their input to the FSOC" and "undermine [their] response to FSOC recommendations." *Id.* at 23. In addition, the IMF recommended the creation of an "independent insurance regulatory body with nationwide responsibilities and authority." *Id.* at 8. Motivating this recommendation was what the IMF perceived as "important gaps in compliance with international [insurance] standards," as well as the inability of any existing regulatory body, including the NAIC and the FSOC, either to enforce convergence on such standards or to "provide for sector-wide coverage" through its membership. *Id.* at 28. Interestingly, the IMF's 2010 report, which was published around the same time as the passage of the Dodd-Frank Act, recommended that the Federal Reserve Board be defined as "the lead executor" of the FSOC, based on the Federal Reserve Board's "existing expertise, broad understanding of the financial sector, role as lender of last resort, the synergies with monetary policy, and its statutory mandate." INT'L MONETARY FUND, UNITED STATES: FINANCIAL SYSTEM STABILITY ASSESSMENT 34 (July 2010). Contrast this recommendation with the Act's designation of the Secretary of the Treasury as the Chairperson of the FSOC. The 2010 report also called for Federal Reserve Board "oversight authority over systemically important payment, clearing, and settlement infrastructure," strengthened channels for coordination between federal banking agencies, market regulators, and the states, and improved cooperation between the CFTC and the SEC. *Id.* at 9. The Financial Stability Board (FSB) also issued a report on the financial stability of the United States and focused its recommendations on the FSOC's coordinating role and uniform insurance supervision. *See* FINANCIAL STABILITY BOARD, PEER REVIEW OF THE UNITED STATES 11–12 (Aug. 2013). To what extent should we pay attention to external recommendations such as those by the IMF and the FSB? Do such recommendations carry greater or lesser weight due to their foreign origin?

5. ***The Volcker Alliance Report.*** The Volcker Alliance, a non-partisan group created in 2013 by former Federal Reserve Board Chairman Paul A. Volcker, released in 2015 a report offering recommendations for financial regulation reform in the United States. Much like the IMF and the FSB as discussed above, the Volcker Alliance has paid close attention to potential improvements to the FSOC. Unlike the two former organizations, however, the Volcker Alliance recommended reducing the role of the Secretary of the Treasury by removing the Secretary's ability to vote on FSOC decisions. *See* THE VOLCKER ALLIANCE, RESHAPING THE FINANCIAL REGULATORY SYSTEM: LONG DELAYED, NOW CRUCIAL 30 (2015). This recommendation stems from the concern that allowing the Treasury, and therefore the presidential administration, a voting role in FSOC decisions may create "the appearance of injecting short-term, politically expedient considerations when long-term, often politically difficult decision-making may be required." *Id.* Since only the chairman or the director of the financial agencies, always a member of President's party, sits on the FSOC, is it

tilted towards presidential power? The Volcker Alliance also offered several proposals for organizational consolidation. For example, in a spirit similar to that of the IMF and FSB, the Volcker Alliance has proposed a systemic issues committee, established by the FSOC and "composed of the chairman of the Federal Reserve [Board], the chairman of the FDIC, the director of the FHFA, the director of the CFPB, the chair of a new SEC-CFTC, the director of the OFR, and a state insurance commissioner designated by the state insurance commissioners." *Id.* The motivating rationale of this proposal is to eliminate the voting members who either do not have a financial stability mandate, such as the NCUA, or pose a threat of short-term political perceptions, such as the Treasury, and to include members who possess "invaluable expertise and regulatory insight," such as the state insurance regulator. *Id.* at 31. The Volcker Alliance also proposed the creation of a prudential supervisory authority, which would encompass the prudential supervisory functions of the Federal Reserve Board, the OCC, the FDIC, the SEC, and the CFTC with respect to certain entities. *See id.* at 34. The motivating rationale for this proposal is to increase prudential expertise and efficiency, as well as to reduce coordination problems that plague U.S. prudential supervision. *See id.* at 35–36. Lastly, the Volcker Alliance proposed the combination of the SEC and CFTC, also to reduce coordination problems and regulatory asymmetry. *See id.* at 36–37. What do you think of the Volcker Alliance's recommendation to reduce the influence of the Treasury on the FSOC in particular? Might it be argued that the Secretary of the Treasury, due to his or her direct political link to the President, represents the public, or at least the public fisc? That the Secretary of the Treasury therefore injects a vital element of political accountability into the FSOC? The Volcker Alliance proposal is only the last in a line of dozens of reports and other proposals, stretching back at least to the 1950s, many of them presented by the Treasury, Congress, or regulatory agencies, to reform the architecture of U.S. financial regulation. Why has it been so difficult to achieve a consensus for change?

IV. THE INTERNATIONAL FINANCIAL ARCHITECTURE

In the last section of this Chapter, we will discuss the structure of financial regulation at the international level. We begin with an overview of the international financial architecture, as described by Professor Pierre-Hugues Verdier and several other commentators. We then briefly consider the post-financial crisis trend towards greater political involvement in financial regulation across the globe.

A. THE BUILDING BLOCKS

The following excerpt traces the historical development of the system of international financial regulation, culminating in several general observations about this system and how the Financial Crisis has affected it. As you read, pay attention to how the history of the system's development relates to these later conclusions.

Pierre-Hugues Verdier, The Political Economy of International Financial Regulation

88 INDIANA L.J. 1405 (2013)

The worldwide impact of the [Financial Crisis] has revealed fundamental weaknesses in the system of international financial regulation (IFR) that has emerged since the 1970s. At the same time, diagnosing and repairing these weaknesses has proven difficult because the system and its functions are poorly understood. In sharp contrast with other international regimes like trade or environmental law, IFR relies not on treaties and formal international organizations but on "soft law" standards designed by informal networks of national regulators—so-called "transnational regulatory networks" (TRNs). The development of these standards is highly uneven; detailed rules like the Basel accords on bank capital adequacy long cohabited with negligible progress in areas like insurance, hedge funds, and credit rating agencies. Scholars, for their part, differ sharply in their assessments of IFR. The conventional wisdom is that the current, informal system of IFR allows regulators to respond effectively and flexibly to new market and technological challenges. In light of the financial crisis, however, skepticism is growing. Some prominent legal and economic commentators have even called for a World Financial Authority—a formal, treaty-based organization to regulate international finance. . . .

To understand the origins of the current, decentralized system of IFR, one must go back to the post-World War II settlement that created the modern international economic order. As early as 1941, the Allies expressed in the Atlantic Charter their desire to "bring about the fullest collaboration between all nations in the economic field with the object of securing, for all, improved labor standards, economic advancement and social security." The new system would be a multilateral alternative to the chaotic economic competition of the 1930s—what U.S. Treasury Secretary Morgenthau called the "desperate tactics of the past—competitive currency depreciation, excessive tariff barriers, uneconomic barter deals, multiple currency practices and unnecessary exchange restrictions." These practices, the postwar planners believed, had deepened the Great Depression and ultimately contributed to the war. In their place, they sought "to recreate a liberal world economy in which stable exchange rates and free trade were the norm."

The cornerstone of the postwar economic order would be a new international monetary system to replace the gold standard that had disintegrated in the 1930s. A stable monetary system would, in turn, provide the foundation for reviving international trade by abolishing discriminatory preferences and reducing tariffs and other barriers to trade. In both areas—monetary affairs and trade—the postwar planners envisioned a highly legalized regime based on formal treaty obligations and intergovernmental organizations. In crafting the treaties, they strived to balance multilateral obligations with domestic economic and social policy autonomy. The most ambitious manifestation of this vision was the IMF Articles of Agreement, which established an elaborate code of conduct for international monetary relations. . . . The crucial point is that while they prohibited restrictions on current transactions, the IMF Articles of Agreement did not prohibit—and indeed encouraged—capital controls. . . . Thus, the Bretton Woods system, [the system of monetary management in the mid-20th century that established the rules for commercial financial relations among major industrial countries] "strongly encouraged closed national financial markets, with limited capital flows, and open markets for trade in goods." . . .

The collapse of Bretton Woods [in the 1970s and 1980s] and the dramatic increase in international capital flows immediately caused problems for economic policymakers. In the 1960s and early 1970s, the ministers of finance and central bank governors of the "Group of 10" [the G-10 refers to the group of 11 countries that meet to consult, debate, and cooperate on international financial matters that includes Belgium, Canada, France, Germany, Italy, Japan, the Netherlands, Sweden, Switzerland, the [UK], and the United States] met on a regular basis to coordinate exchange rate management and consider adjustments to the Bretton Woods system. At the same time, banking and securities regulators faced their own set of challenges. The world of self-contained domestic financial systems to which they were accustomed was rapidly changing. While banks had been expanding internationally since the 1950s, the trend accelerated, making it ever more difficult for national authorities to regulate and supervise their worldwide activities. Banks also found a major new source of revenue—and risk—in the massive new foreign exchange markets. In 1974, the collapse of several banks—notably Bankhaus Herstatt in Germany and Franklin National Bank in the United States—disrupted interbank lending and drew attention to the cross-border impact of bank failures and the lack of regulatory coordination. The oil crisis was also straining financial markets and causing worries about the international banking system.

In response, the governors of the G-10 central banks formed the Basel Committee on Banking Supervision. As was the case for macroeconomic coordination, the prevailing ethos of IFR was informality. The committee would be a forum for regulators "not . . . to make far-fetched attempts to harmonise the twelve countries' individual systems of supervision, but . . . to learn from each other and to apply the knowledge so acquired to improving their own systems of supervision, so indirectly enhancing the likelihood of overall stability in the international banking system." It was the first major TRN in financial regulation. TRNs usually share several characteristics: their members are not states but specialized regulatory agencies; they are not created by treaty and have no international legal personality; they lack formal assemblies or voting procedures; the instruments they promulgate are not internationally binding; and, at least until recently, they do not systematically monitor or enforce compliance with those instruments. Over the following decades, TRNs became the backbone of IFR, with formal organizations like the IMF, World Bank, and [Bank for International Settlements (BIS)] playing only a supporting role.

The evolution of IFR prior to the [Financial Crisis] can be divided into three major phases. The first, between 1974 and the Asian financial crisis in 1997–98, saw the creation of the principal TRNs—the Basel Committee, [International Organization of Securities Commissions (IOSCO)], and the International Association of Insurance Supervisors (IAIS)—and the development of the first generation of international standards. In response to the bank collapses of the 1970s, the Basel Committee adopted the Concordat, an informal agreement on the supervision of international banks that placed primary responsibility on a bank's home country for supervising the solvency of a bank and its foreign branches. While the Concordat allocated supervisory responsibility among national regulators, it stopped short of allocating corresponding financial responsibility. In other words, the Concordat designated which country should take the lead on various aspects of supervision, but expressly refrained from designating which country should act as lender of last resort or deposit insurer for a given bank or its foreign offices. It also did not allocate authority over resolution of failed banks—individual countries remained free to set up competing proceedings and prioritize local creditors.

The Basel Committee's most important achievement during that period was undoubtedly the 1988 Basel Accord on bank capital adequacy. The Latin American debt crisis of the 1980s had left international banks, especially in the United States and the [UK], severely undercapitalized. While regulators in those countries wished to adopt more stringent capital adequacy requirements, they were hampered by concerns that they would undermine the international competitiveness of their banks. There was also concern that the growing off-balance-sheet activities of banks created risks that existing standards did not adequately reflect. Under pressure from the United States and the [UK], the other G-10 authorities agreed to a detailed framework for determining mandatory capital levels for banks. Basel I defined regulatory capital, established rules for weighting assets and off-balance-sheet liabilities based on their risk, and prescribed a minimum capital ratio of

8%. Over the course of the 1990s, the Accord was adopted by many countries outside the G-10, becoming a de facto worldwide standard.

IOSCO developed in a somewhat different way from the Basel Committee. Its membership was larger and its structure closer to that of a traditional international organization, with an assembly, an executive committee, and a secretary general. Its formation was prompted not by an identifiable crisis, but rather by a sense that securities regulators increasingly faced common problems, particularly in respect to cross-border transactions. For instance, an early concern was that firms could avoid U.S. securities fraud or insider trading laws by operating from countries whose authorities were unable or unwilling to cooperate with the SEC. To address this problem, the SEC entered into memoranda of understanding (MOUs) with other securities regulators and led an IOSCO effort to promote greater uniformity among MOUs, encourage more regulators to sign them, and help them secure domestic legal authority to provide assistance. IOSCO also initiated efforts to harmonize regulation in some areas, for instance by preparing a model form for nonfinancial disclosure in securities offerings. IOSCO failed, however, in its efforts to create capital standards for securities firms. The last major TRN, the IAIS, was formed only in 1994 and its activities have been much more limited; for instance, it did not agree on solvency standards for insurance firms until the 2000s.

During these years, some of the fastest-growing economies of Asia—Indonesia, Thailand, South Korea, and Malaysia—faced major banking and currency crises, and the first three resorted to IMF and World Bank assistance to face massive currency outflows. These crises, along with the early 1990s Mexican crisis, shared several features: macroeconomic imbalances, asset bubbles, lax financial sector regulation, and tenor and currency mismatches (*i.e.*, banks borrowing short-term in foreign currencies to make long-term local currency loans). After the crisis, a consensus developed among the international financial institutions (IFIs) and the G-7 [the 7 most industrialized world economies, Canada, France, Germany, Italy, Japan, the [UK], and the United States, that meet to discuss international economic and monetary issues] that weak financial regulation in those countries had been a major cause of the crisis. In response, they placed a high priority on improving regulation in developing countries to reduce the risk of future crises. The head of the IMF declared that the "world community . . . look[ed] forward for the definition of international standards and codes of good practices, which would be progressively disseminated by the IMF through its surveillance."

The G-7 took on a more active and detailed priority-setting role for IFR. It created a new body, the Financial Stability Forum (FSF), to coordinate the activities of the various TRNs and develop a compendium of standards whose implementation would be encouraged by the IFIs. The FSF did not develop its own standards, but relied on the TRNs to provide substantive content. The Basel Committee issued its "Core Principles for Effective Banking Supervision;" IOSCO, its "Objectives and Principles of Securities Regulation;" and the IAIS, its "Insurance Core Principles." These principles established basic requirements across a range of issues, often referencing existing standards such as the Basel Accord. Many of the recommendations were structural, steering developing countries towards creating regulatory systems based on Western models. For example, all three sets of principles required that they set up independent regulatory agencies and give them adequate enforcement powers and resources. The G-20 [a forum of 19 major world economies, plus representation by the European Union, to discuss key global economic issues] was also created at that time to give a voice to leading developing countries, although its influence was limited. Finally, the IMF encouraged reforms by linking them to its lending programs and conducting audits of national regulation under two programs, ROSC [Reports on the Observance of Standards and Codes] and FSAP [Financial Sector Assessment Program].

The third phase runs from 2001 to the subprime crisis. During that period, the IFIs' work on implementing financial standards continued, but regulators and TRNs turned their attention to various other problems. After September 11, 2001, a major effort was made to step up the fight against money laundering and terrorist financing. Led by the United States, the Financial Action Task Force (FATF) coordinated a campaign to compel offshore financial centers (OFCs) to improve their cooperation with onshore jurisdictions under threat of "blacklisting" and sanctions, with reluctant assistance from the IMF. IOSCO strove to strengthen cross-border assistance by adopting the 2002 Multilateral Memorandum of Understanding (MMOU). All IOSCO members were expected to sign the MMOU, which required prior screening to ensure they had the necessary domestic authority to comply with assistance requests. IOSCO has also been engaged in a multitude of projects to develop recommendations on credit rating agencies, mutual funds, hedge funds, securities analysts, and others. More importantly, the [International Accounting Standards Board] made great strides in developing a comprehensive set of international accounting standards. The European Union decided to adopt them in 2002, followed by several other countries. The SEC recently decided to permit foreign issuers to report under [International Financial Reporting Standards] and is considering adopting them for U.S. issuers as well.

The most emblematic development of the 2000s was the decade-long effort to develop the Basel II Accord. Over the 1990s, the original Accord came under increasing criticism, mainly on the grounds that its risk-weighting formulas were outdated relative to the internal risk measurement systems developed by the largest banks. In 1999, the Basel Committee released a major revision that uses parameters generated by banks to calculate the risk of each exposure. The development of Basel II was long and controversial, and the committee engaged in an elaborate notice-and-comment process. The debate did not stop with the adoption of the final international document in 2004; U.S. implementation proved intensely contentious, and Basel II is not yet fully implemented there [the U.S. has since implemented Basel III, which effectively superseded Basel II]. Throughout the 2000s, the Basel Committee's attention was dominated, if not monopolized, by Basel II—perhaps to the detriment of other important issues like liquidity management or cross-border resolution. The IAIS, for its part, finally published a common framework for assessing insurer solvency in 2007, albeit one much less prescriptive and detailed than the Basel Committee's. Like Basel II, the IAIS framework provides insurers considerable flexibility to use their own risk management models.

This brief overview supports some general observations on the origins of IFR. First, unlike in many other areas of international cooperation, national regulators rather than governments played the leading role. Without a formal organization to coordinate their action, they stepped beyond their traditional domestic role to pursue common objectives, limiting themselves at each step to the problems immediately facing them. Second, the outcome was the creation of a system based, not on binding rules and institutions, but on informal networks and soft law arrangements. Even after the Asian crisis, the role of IFIs was limited to overseeing implementation of basic standards by developing countries, and they almost always relied on TRNs to develop their content. Third, the usual preference was to develop very general standards that outlined the essential desiderata of a sound domestic regulatory system, rather than detailed prescriptions. Looking through the FSF's compendium of standards, the few detailed prescriptive ones like the Basel Accord stand out against numerous general, sometimes hortatory, statements. Finally, several pivotal areas of financial regulation with cross-border implications, like bank resolution, deposit insurance, the lender of last resort function, bank liquidity, and capital adequacy for securities and insurance firms, remained essentially untouched....

The financial crisis has had two major implications for IFR. First, prudential regulation, systemic risk, and moral hazard concerns have taken center stage. The failure of several major institutions and the struggle by governments to manage the consequences drew attention to critical weaknesses in financial markets. These included high leverage, widespread liquidity vulnerabilities, lack of transparency of positions, inadequate risk analysis, and interconnected exposures among market participants. The sum of these weaknesses is "systemic risk," the risk that the failure of one or more financial institutions can cause a cascading failure that leads to the collapse of the financial system. Financial institutions can be systemically significant for several reasons: some are so large that their failure affects many other market participants, others are extensively interconnected with others through financial contracts, and clusters of institutions with highly correlated exposures can be systemically significant in aggregate. Because the failure of such institutions could cause extensive economic damage, governments come under pressure to rescue them. Since these institutions know this, they have ex ante incentives to take excessive risks, a phenomenon known as moral hazard. Other market participants also expect that these institutions will not be allowed to fail and deal with them on favorable terms, exacerbating their systemic importance.

As a result, controlling systemic risk and moral hazard has become the central concern of post-crisis financial reform. Numerous approaches have been proposed: identifying systemically significant financial institutions (SSFIs) and subjecting them to enhanced prudential regulation and supervision; limiting their size or activities; establishing a credible resolution procedure for SSFIs; prohibiting government bailouts to SSFIs; and regulating financial contracts that may create systemic risk, such as [over-the-counter (OTC)] derivatives. Other post-crisis measures aim at improving prudential regulation more generally, such as raising bank capital requirements and expanding the regulatory net to the shadow banking system. Each of these approaches is complex, and their relative effectiveness is debated. However, they share one fundamental objective: to force systemic institutions and market participants to internalize costs that would otherwise be borne by governments and taxpayers. In other words, they are precisely the type of stricter prudential regulation that IFR has historically failed to deliver consistently.

Second, the crisis has led to a major effort to update the architecture of IFR and develop new substantive international standards. The G-20, which had been created after the Asian financial crisis but played a marginal role, supplanted the G-7 as the principal forum for international economic cooperation. It has taken a more direct role in setting priorities for regulatory reform and coordinating the work of TRNs, IFIs, and other actors. It reorganized the Financial Stability Forum as the Financial Stability Board, with a broader mandate and membership, including all G-20 members. The FSB's mission is to coordinate and oversee the work of other standard-setting bodies, and in some cases to develop new standards itself in areas that cut across the mandate of individual TRNs. The Basel Committee and IOSCO's Technical Committee also expanded their membership. The G-20 has adopted a detailed action plan for reforming IFR, including initiatives on capital adequacy, cross-border resolution, regulation of rating agencies, hedge funds and OTC derivatives, global accounting standards, executive compensation, and many others. One feature of many of these initiatives is the decline in reliance on private standards and self-regulation in favor of mandatory rules. The actual standard-setting work, however, typically remains in the hands of national regulators and TRNs.

Thus, the post-crisis reforms do not fundamentally replace TRNs and soft law, but rather attempt to expand, rationalize, and strengthen the existing system in various ways. Nevertheless, the assumption by the G-20 of authority over IFR is an important structural development. The G-20 is not a TRN; it is a political body made up of the national leaders (or ministers) of the member states. However, it is not a formal international organization either. Like TRNs, the G-20 does not have international legal personality, its decisions are made by consensus, and they are not legally binding. In theory, it has no formal authority to set goals for IFIs and TRNs. In practice, however, the G-20 members collectively control a large majority of votes in the IFIs, their financial regulators dominate the principal TRNs, and they comprise about 85% of the world's

GDP. Thus, the G-20 has the capacity to exercise enormous influence on IFR and potentially overcome the constraints that have hindered progress in the past. It could play a leadership role, compelling TRNs to undertake reforms that they would not initiate on their own because of resistance by national regulators or the financial industry. With its broader membership, it could also balance the influence of the great powers. It could facilitate trade-offs across issues, overcoming distributive roadblocks that specialized TRNs cannot handle, and better handle issues that cut across the functional jurisdiction of individual TRNs, like OTC derivatives and shadow banking. The new system could also provide more effective monitoring and enforcement.

---

1. ***Should We Be Optimistic?*** Verdier paints an international picture of national regulators and informal agreements that created gaps in coverage and foresight that proved critical during the Financial Crisis. He strikes, however, a somewhat optimistic note near the end of the excerpt, arguing that, while "post-crisis reforms do not fundamentally replace TRNs and soft law," developments such as the G-20's increased authority may "potentially overcome the constraints that have hindered progress in the past." Does his cautious optimism resonate with you, or do you find the history of international financial regulation, especially the failures during the Financial Crisis, to contain more pessimistic lessons moving forward? What might set international financial regulation apart from other areas of international cooperation, where, as Verdier observes, governments rather than national regulators have taken center stage?

2. ***Who's in Charge on the International Stage?*** In a 2014 article, Professor Michael Barr also reflects on the shortcomings of international financial regulation:

> The 2008 crisis exposed fundamental weaknesses—both procedural and substantive—in the international financial regulatory architecture. The Bretton Woods institutions (the [IMF], World Bank, and World Trade Organization) were never really equipped to deal with the growing complexity, breadth, and size of the global financial system, and instead left rulemaking and supervision largely to the domestic arena.

Michael S. Barr, *Who's in Charge of Global Finance?*, 45 GEO. J. INT'L L. 971, 972 (2014). Barr further explores the question of how best to design an international system of financial regulation with "more than one architect," echoing the concern identified by Verdier that national regulators, rather than a single institution, generally governed the space of international financial regulation. Looking ahead, Barr, like Verdier, notices the "hardening of rulemaking at the global level" due to the "dominant role of the G-20 political leadership" as well as the rise of the FSB. *Id.* at 1016. Barr, however, goes on to sound a more pessimistic note, observing that "this political involvement facilitates national variation that in some instances, as with Basel III implementation, may lead to global races to the top, and in others, as with derivatives implementation, may well provoke cross-border tension and complicate regulatory oversight unless further coordination is pursued." *Id.* Barr concludes on a cautionary note, claiming that "conceptually 'easy' answers—a treaty-based World Financial Organization, centralized adjudication, a global financial supervisor . . . are neither politically feasible nor normatively desirable." *Id.* at 1027. *But see* Eric J. Pan, *Challenge of International Cooperation and Institutional Design in Financial Supervision: Beyond Transgovernmental Networks*, 11 CHI. J. INT'L L. 243, 246–47 (2010) (arguing for the "creation of an international body that has the power and resources to supervise cross-border financial institutions, demand action by national supervisors, promulgate supervisory standards, conduct inspections, and initiate enforcement proceedings."). Which view on the prospects for international financial regulation resonates more with you, Verdier's cautiously optimistic view or Barr's cautiously pessimistic one? What kind of empirical evidence, if any, would help support one view over the other?

3. ***Monitoring and Information Sharing Solutions.*** Also recognizing the impediments to "conceptually easy answers," such as a global financial supervisor and the necessity of building on the patchwork of national regulators and informal agreements, Professor Chris Brummer has proposed a solution to the disciplinary limits of international soft law. By implementing "surveillance of compliance with international rules" through, for example, mandatory conditions on membership in the IMF and improving "information sharing between surveillance institutions and market participants," Brummer believes that financial centers would be forced to "internalize the costs of their regulatory decision making." Chris Brummer, *How International Financial Law Works (and How it Doesn't)*, 99 GEO. L.J. 257, 327 (2011). Consider whether increased monitoring and information sharing can overcome the previously identified lack of a central enforcement authority in the international financial regulatory space, or whether such solutions fall short for other reasons. What other solutions can you think of?

B. REFORM AFTER THE FINANCIAL CRISIS

While the United States adopted substantial changes in financial legislation in the aftermath of the Financial Crisis, other countries also adjusted their regulatory structure. In the following excerpt, Professor Stavros Gadinis offers one perspective on these changes:

Stavros Gadinis, From Independence to Politics in Financial Regulation

101 CALIF. L. REV. 327 (2013)

Since the early 1990s, most Western democracies have followed the United States' lead and strengthened the independence of their financial regulators. Influential international organizations, such as the Basel Committee and the [IMF], encouraged countries to bolster the independence of their financial supervisors. Leading academic commentators support agency independence in the financial regulatory sphere and track countries' progress toward more independent institutional mechanisms. In scholarly circles and in the field of policy action alike, agency independence has long been the hallmark of financial regulation.

[T]he agency independence paradigm is [, however,] under attack. The [Financial Crisis] prompted policy makers worldwide to establish new regulatory mechanisms designed to monitor financial institutions more thoroughly and to facilitate intervention in case of emergency. That new regulations followed a major crisis is hardly surprising; what is surprising are the government bodies chosen to wield these new powers. Instead of independent banking regulators, postcrisis reformers assigned the new powers to politically controlled officials, typically high-ranking executive officers such as treasury secretaries and finance ministers. These cabinet appointees sit very close to the chief executive, president, or prime minister, who can typically remove them at will. As a result, there is now a direct link between the top elected officer and banking supervision.

The degree of politicians' newly found influence over banking supervision is evident in three distinct institutional features of their new powers. First, politicians now have authority not only over financial emergencies, but also over some regular issues arising during times of smooth business operation. Politicians cast the decisive vote on the decision to sustain or terminate an ailing institution, including whether to declare it bankrupt, liquidate it, take it over, or sell it. In addition to emergency situations, politicians now also have a say over some key aspects of a financial institution's regular operation, such as licensing its establishment, requiring stricter prudential supervision, or approving its managers' appointment. Second, politicians' new powers represent direct grants of authority. Rather than relying on appointment powers to select bureaucrats with whom they share a regulatory philosophy, politicians can now explicitly undertake or authorize specific actions against individual financial institutions. A third feature of postcrisis reforms is politicians' newly acquired status as the leaders of administrative coordination mechanisms that encompass preexisting agencies. To address the obvious need for exchange of information and coordination of regulatory action in light of systemic threats, reformers put in place institutional arrangements that bring all financial regulators around the same table under the leadership of politicians.

These institutional arrangements . . . define a new balance of power between agencies and politicians. Agencies, as the primary experts in financial markets, collect information, assess alternatives, and formulate proposals for action. Ultimately, however, the decision over whether to intervene in the market belongs to politicians. This nuanced relationship between agencies and politicians emerged with striking similarity in reforms that occurred in multiple countries within months of one another.

---

1. ***Do Post-Financial Crisis Reforms in the United States Align with Gadinis's Diagnosis?*** Perhaps in response to the trend identified by Gadinis, the Volcker Alliance, as discussed above, has proposed reducing the power of the Secretary of the Treasury in financial regulation by removing the Secretary's vote on FSOC decisions. Also discussed above, the Federal Reserve Board has remained politically independent despite various opponents arguing for greater democratic accountability. What should we make of the trend towards political involvement in financial regulation? Is this trend prevalent only in certain areas of financial regulation? As a matter of policy, is it desirable to inject political involvement in certain areas rather than others? What factors might help us determine which areas are appropriate for such involvement? Such efforts to increase the political accountability of financial regulators are just the latest in a long line that stretches back to the powerful Representative Wright Patman, who, as Chairman of the House Financial Services Committee from the mid-1950s through the late 1960s, made it his life mission to limit the independence of the Federal Reserve Board. Although Patman was largely unsuccessful, the political impulse he represented still exists.

CHAPTER 1.4

THE REGULATORY PERIMETER

CONTENTS

I. INTRODUCTION

In Chapter 1.3, we explored the organizational structure of financial supervision in the United States and some of the ways in which those supervisory bodies coordinate with their counterparts around the world. We now turn to the issue of jurisdiction and look at what kinds of financial activities are subject to each regulatory regime. For every financial regulator and each financial regulatory question, there exists a set of definitions that define the regulatory perimeter. Activities falling within that regulatory perimeter are subject to that regulatory regime and activities outside the perimeter are not subject to that regulatory regime or that regulator. Being experts in issues of jurisdiction, lawyers play a major role in drafting these jurisdictional lines and overseeing their enforcement.

In this Chapter, we first examine several cases that illustrate the difficulty of drawing the regulatory perimeter in different areas of financial regulation. We then present a conceptual taxonomy for organizing these and other materials. Finally, we discuss a particularly important regulatory perimeter problem arising in the law of usury.

II. SETTING JURISDICTIONAL BOUNDARIES

The following four readings illustrate the interpretation of a regulatory perimeter in different areas of financial regulation. As you read over these materials, pay particular attention to the content of the legal standards that define the regulatory perimeter. These standards define the kinds of financial activities that are subject to special legal protections beyond those that govern ordinary economic exchanges.

A. THE TEXAS ATTORNEY GENERAL'S LETTER

Office of the Attorney General, State of Texas

Texas Att'y Gen. Op. No. DM-329 (Mar. 9, 1995)

Dear Commissioner Ghiglieri:

On behalf of the Texas Department of Banking (the "department"), you ask about state and private university "debit card" programs. You generally describe such programs as follows: "[A] university accepts money from students (and sometimes from faculty and staff) and, in turn, issues a card to each . . . to be used for drawing against this account to obtain goods and services on campus." You state that the department is aware of at least three state universities [and at least one private university] that have established a debit card program. . . .

. . . As we read your request, we understand that you are only interested in those debit card programs with the following features: A student, faculty member or staff person deposits a certain amount in an account with the university, and receives a card (or perhaps encoded information on a preexisting identification card) that identifies the account. The cardholder presents the card when making a purchase from a university vendor or, in some cases, third-party vendors operating concessions on campus pursuant to a contract with the university. When a purchase is made, the cashier uses the card to identify the account and determine whether the account balance is sufficient. After the purchase is made, the amount of the purchase is automatically deducted from the account. Because the purchase may not be made with the card if the account balance is insufficient, it is impossible to overdraw the account. We limit our discussion to the foregoing type of debit card program. . . .

You . . . suggest that universities which issue debit cards are engaged in the unauthorized business of banking. We are not aware of a Texas statute which defines the term "bank" or "banking." You suggest that accepting deposits is the primary indicia of a bank. It is clear from Texas case law, however, that no one feature defines a bank.

Historically a bank merely served as a place for the safekeeping of the depositors' money and even now that is the primary function of a bank. 9 C.J.S., Banks and Banking, § 3, page 31. The term "bank" now by reason of the development and expansion of the banking business does not lend itself to an exact definition. 7 Am. Jur., Banks, § 2. . . .

Furthermore, authority from other jurisdictions suggests that an entity is not necessarily a bank just because it engages in certain acts that are typical of banks; rather one must look at the activities of the entity as a whole. *See, e.g.*, 9 C.J.S. Banks and Banking § 1, at 30 (1938) ("Banking is the business of receiving deposits payable on demand, discounting commercial paper, banking loans on collateral security, issuing notes payable on . . . collecting notes or drafts, buying and selling bills of exchange, negotiating loans, and dealing in negotiable securities. Exercise of all these functions is not necessary, nor does exercise of certain of them necessarily render a corporation a bank."). . . . We do not believe that a court would conclude that a university that offers a debit card program such as the one you describe among its many and various activities engages in banking.

You have submitted to this office an opinion issued by the Comptroller of Florida regarding whether the card program of a public university in that state constituted a banking activity. The cards in that program could be used to pay for goods and services and to make cash withdrawals from automated teller machines (ATMs) on and off campus operated by a private bank. Relying in part on a federal appeals court decision holding that the payment of a cash withdrawal from an ATM constitutes payment of a check, *Illinois ex rel. Lignoul v. Continental Illinois Nat'l Bank & Trust Co.*, 536 F.2d 176 (7th Cir.), *cert. denied*, 429 U.S. 871 (1976), the Comptroller of Florida concluded that the university paid checks by allowing cash withdrawals with its card at ATMs operated by a private bank.

We do not believe that this opinion supports your position that the kind of debit card program at issue here involves a sale of checks under the act or unauthorized banking. First, *Illinois ex rel. Lignoul* dealt with whether a cash withdrawal from an ATM constituted "branch banking" within the meaning of the National Bank Act, 12 U.S.C. § 36(f). We do not read that case to hold that an ATM withdrawal, or the use of any other card, necessarily constitutes payment of a check for purposes of § 3-104(3) of the Uniform Commercial Code. Indeed, the primary case upon which *Illinois ex rel. Lignoul* relies clearly points out the difference between the Uniform Commercial Code's narrow definition of a check and the expansive definition of a branch bank in Section 36(f) of the National Bank Act. Thus, although a cash withdrawal from an ATM may constitute payment of a check for purposes of the National Bank Act, it does not necessarily constitute a check for purposes of the Uniform Commercial Code or the common commercial understanding of the term. Therefore, the Florida comptroller's opinion does not convince us that the debit card programs at issue here involve the sale of "checks" as that term is defined by the act. We also believe that the Florida opinion is inapposite with respect to the question whether Texas universities that offer debit card programs engage in banking. The type of debit card program you ask about does not permit cardholders to make cash withdrawals from their accounts much less allow them to make cash withdrawals from ATMs operated by a private bank. . . .

---

1. ***Implications of Engaging in the Business of Banking.*** Most states, like Texas, require that the business of banking—as that term is used in this context—be conducted only by appropriately chartered depository institutions, such as banks, thrifts, and credit unions. Almost invariably, these authorized institutions are subject to extensive regulation and protected by some form of deposit insurance. The determination that an activity constitutes the business of banking, therefore, has substantial legal and financial consequences, while the benefits of offering functionally comparable services outside of this regulatory perimeter are substantial as well. As a result, commercial firms and their lawyers expend considerable effort keeping activities outside the regulatory perimeter, and regulatory authorities must be constantly mindful of the possibility that private parties are evading their oversight. Difficult questions arise when such evasion is driven by market and technological changes that disturb vested interests. You will learn more about the business of banking in Chapter 2.2.

2. ***Do Stored-Value Card Holders Require Regulatory Protection?*** The definition of the regulatory perimeter is intricately connected to the purposes for which an underlying regulatory regime is established. Why, exactly, have Texas and other jurisdictions established mandatory regulatory requirements for the business of banking? Do students holding stored-value cards at the University of Texas need these protections? What about other kinds of stored-value cards or gift cards or prepaid cards? To the extent that banking regulations or other

specialized legal regimes do not extend to these financial products, what legal requirements will govern their terms?

3. ***Regulatory Perimeters Built on Functional Foundations.*** The business of banking test employed in the Texas Attorney General's letter reflects a functional definition of banking. If an entity engages in sufficient activities identified in that definition, then the entity must bring itself into compliance with the regulatory system designed for banks and other depository institutions. A functional definition thus forces banking activities into a regulatory regime organized around financial sectors.

B. *KOCH V. FIRST UNION CORP.*

In this next decision, a Pennsylvania court explores the application of a variety of legal regimes to an extension of credit designed to finance home improvements. Note the combination of federal and state laws at issue in this case. Note also the absence of a traditional bank or thrift lender in this litigation.

Koch v. First Union Corp.

Pennsylvania Court of Common Pleas, 2002 WL 372939 (Jan. 10, 2002)

■ Herron, J.

Defendants. . . . First Union National Bank of Delaware ("FUNBD"), Pennsylvania Resource Corporation ("PRC"), and First Liberty Financial Services, Inc. ("First Liberty") filed these Preliminary Objections to the Amended Complaint of Plaintiffs Harry W. Koch, et al. . . .

BACKGROUND

The plaintiffs in the present action are homeowners. PRC is a contractor who provides home repairs and home improvement financing, through its broker First Liberty. The plaintiffs, through PRC and First Liberty, obtained home equity loans from FUNBD. . . .

The present action arises from allegations that all the defendants worked in concert to secure home equity loans on the basis of misleading "good faith cost estimates." The plaintiffs allege that these estimates were misleading in several ways. First, the same good faith estimates were given to all borrowers regardless of their financial status or creditworthiness. Second, the good faith estimates only identified closing costs totaling $470. However, the plaintiffs allege that these totals were far less than what they eventually paid. Third, the loan origination fee, listed in the estimate, was explained as "N/A" and therefore misleading. Further, the mortgage broker fee of 4-7% did not reveal what these percentages were based upon. Finally, the settlement charges that the plaintiffs actually paid far exceeded the amounts specifically disclosed in the estimates. . . .

DISCUSSION . . .

A. Violations of the UTPCPL Based Upon RESPA Violations

The plaintiffs contend that the defendants did not comply with the requirements of [the Federal Real Estate Settlement Procedures Act of 1974] (RESPA), since the defendants failed to provide them with a "good faith estimate" of the charges they would incur when settling their mortgages. Conversely, the defendants argue that since RESPA contains no private right of action for the plaintiffs' claim, the plaintiffs have failed "to explain how an alleged RESPA violation gives rise to a claim under the [Unfair Trade Practices and Consumer Protection Law (UTPCPL)]."...

Here, although the plaintiffs concede in their Amended Complaint that "[§ 2604 (c)] of RESPA has been held not to provide a private cause of action in and of itself," the plaintiffs argue that the good faith estimates provided to them by the defendants were not only inadequate, but were in fact intentionally misleading, thereby violating 12 U.S.C.A. § 2604(c) of RESPA and the relevant regulation, Regulation X, 24 C.F.R. § 3500.7(c). However, this court finds that the plaintiffs do not have a private cause of action based upon § 2604(c) of RESPA. Not only does the statute explicitly not provide for one, but there is significant support in extensive legislative history for not allowing a private cause of action based on § 2604(c) of RESPA. . . . Since RESPA specifically contains no private cause of action for alleged violations of "good faith estimates" provisions, this court will not construe the UTPCPL to provide relief for these alleged RESPA violations. However, this does not preclude the plaintiffs from finding a private cause of action from the UTPCPL. Therefore, the court sustains this preliminary objection.

B. Violations of UTPCPL

The defendants argue that since the plaintiffs have not adequately alleged all the elements of fraud, they cannot recover under any of the provisions of the UTPCPL. . . .

Here, however, the plaintiffs have [pled] all the elements of fraud. In their Amended Complaint, the plaintiffs allege, inter alia, that defendants engaged in fraudulent and deceptive conduct which created a likelihood of confusion or misunderstanding. Specifically, the plaintiffs have argued that they "detrimentally rel[ied]" upon the defendants' alleged misrepresentations. Moreover, the plaintiffs specifically allege that they justifiably relied upon misrepresentations and non-disclosures [with regards to, *e.g.*, the closing costs]. . . .

Finally, the plaintiffs also argue that "as a result of defendants' violations of the UTPCPL, plaintiff and members of the class have suffered an ascertainable loss of property." Having determined that the plaintiffs have sufficiently alleged the elements of fraud in support of an alleged violation of the Catchall Provision of the UTPCPL, this court overrules all the preliminary objections to this count.

C. Breach of Fiduciary Duty

The defendants argue that since the Pennsylvania Mortgage Bankers and Brokers Act, 63 P.S. 456.01, et seq, imposes no fiduciary duty on mortgage brokers, the plaintiffs cannot allege that the defendants breached a fiduciary duty. The plaintiffs disagree and argue that, here, a confidential relationship gave rise to a fiduciary duty which the defendants allegedly breached.

. . . "[A confidential relationship] appears when the circumstances make it certain the parties do not deal on equal terms, but, on the one side there is an overmastering influence, or, on the other, weakness, dependence or trust, justifiably reposed[.]" *Frowen v. Blank*, 493 Pa. 137, 425 A.2d 412, 416-17 (1981).

As a result of this confidential relationship . . . "the party in whom the trust and confidence are reposed must act with scrupulous fairness and good faith in his dealings with the other and refrain from using his position to the other's detriment and his own advantage." *Young v.. Kaye*, 443 Pa. 335, 279 A.2d 759, 763 (1971). Furthermore, the resulting fiduciary duty may attach "wherever one occupies toward another such a position of advisor or counselor as reasonably to inspire confidence that he will act in good faith for the other's interest." *Basile*, 777 A.2d at 102. . . .

Here, the plaintiffs have sufficiently alleged the existence of a legally cognizable fiduciary duty of PRC and First Liberty. Specifically, the plaintiffs argue that a confidential relationship arose when the PRC and First Liberty acted as "the position of financial advisor and actively [sought] to inspire confidence that they will act in good faith for" the plaintiffs' interests. Furthermore, the plaintiffs argue the following:

> Defendants entered the plaintiffs' homes armed with vastly superior knowledge of financing and home equity loans; sought extremely personal information from plaintiffs, including sources and debt factors; and promised to help take care of plaintiffs financial needs and desires.

Finally, the plaintiffs allege that PRC and First Liberty breached their fiduciary duties by materially misrepresenting the closing costs associated with the home equity loans. Since the plaintiffs have sufficiently alleged that a fiduciary duty has arisen from the confidential relationship between PRC, First Liberty and the plaintiffs and that this duty was allegedly breached, this court overrules the preliminary objection as to PRC and First Liberty.

However, the plaintiffs have not sufficiently alleged a fiduciary duty owed to them by FUNBD. "Under Pennsylvania law, the lender-borrower relationship ordinarily does not create a fiduciary duty . . . unless a creditor gains substantial control over the debtor's business affairs." Although the plaintiffs do argue that there was a "frequent presence of a First Union loan officer at PRC's place of business," nowhere in the Amended Complaint, do the plaintiffs allege that FUNBD was involved in the actual "day-to-day management and operations" of their affairs. Unlike the plaintiffs' contact and reliance upon the financial advice and counsel of PRC and First Liberty, there is no such evidence of a similar relationship with FUNBD. Instead, FUNBD was merely the lender in this matter. Since the plaintiffs have not alleged a confidential relationship between them and FUNBD, there is no resulting fiduciary duty. Therefore, all the preliminary objections to the breach of fiduciary duty claim as to FUNBD are sustained.

---

1. ***Overlapping Regulatory Authority.*** Take note of the existence of numerous overlapping regulatory structures in *Koch*. The misleading Good Faith Estimates on which the plaintiffs' claims were based was required by RESPA, a federal statute that regulates real estate closings, but does not provide a private right of action for the misconduct alleged to have taken place here. Pennsylvania also had a regulatory regime in place at the time for the licensing of mortgages brokers, but that law apparently did not impose fiduciary duties on those mortgage brokers. Still, the court ruled in favor of the plaintiffs on several preliminary objections. What was the legal basis for the court's ruling and how was that ruling reconciled with the limitations on remedies under RESPA and Pennsylvania laws regulating mortgage brokers?

2. ***Jurisdictional Perimeter of RESPA.*** Passed in 1974, RESPA provides for a transaction-based regulatory regime focused on eliciting disclosure of mortgage settlement-related information to consumers in a clear, effective package. As *Koch* discussed, RESPA includes a Good Faith Estimate requirement designed to allow consumers to determine whether their settlement costs were comparable to market rates. *See* 12 U.S.C. § 2604(c). RESPA's requirements apply to highly regulated entities, such as banks and thrifts, but can also extend to other lenders, such as mortgage brokers, which are not engaged in the business of banking per se, as defined under state laws like the one at issue in the Texas Attorney General decision discussed earlier in this Chapter. *See, e.g.*, Mary S. Robertson, *The "New and Improved" Real Estate Settlement Procedures Act and*

Regulation X, 47 CONSUMER FIN. L.Q. REP. 273, 282 (1993) ("No longer an isolated piece of consumer protection legislation, RESPA's coverage now extends to virtually every loan made by a covered lender which is secured by residential real property. . . . Lenders, mortgage brokers, and settlement agents should carefully scrutinize their business practices to ensure compliance with the expanded coverage of [RESPA]."). While HUD had been responsible for RESPA's implementation since the statute's inception, the Dodd-Frank Act transferred this responsibility to the CFPB in 2011. Before the Dodd-Frank Act, the Department of Housing and Urban Development (HUD) administered RESPA disclosures while the Federal Reserve Board administered disclosures under the Truth in Lending Act (TILA). Transferring RESPA and TILA responsibility to the CFPB was thus intended to unify the administration of mortgage disclosures under one agency. *See, e.g.*, Jonathan W. Cannon & Christine Acree, *Survey of RESPA and TILA Developments—2014*, 70 BUS. LAW. 553, 553 (2014).

3. ***Judicial Regulation of Finance.*** Long before the creation of the first administrative agency, the courts were policing financial transactions at both common law and equity. As we will see later, in some areas of regulation, notably in insurance regulation, special rules involving the interpretation of contract continue to play an important regulatory role. The law of fiduciary duties, however, is perhaps the most pervasive example of judicial oversight of finance. What is the regulatory perimeter of fiduciary duties and how does that perimeter interact with statutory structures, such as the ones present in *Koch*? When fiduciary duties exist, what is the content of those duties? To what extent should the scope of fiduciary duties that evolved as regulatory standards, such as those established under RESPA, emerge?

C. *UNITED STATES V. HOM*

The creation of the internet has posed numerous challenges to regulatory boundaries, as consumers can interact through cyberspace with financial services providers anywhere around the globe. The next case is illustrative of these challenges.

United States v. Hom

45 F. Supp. 3d 1175 (N.D. Cal. 2014)

■ WILLIAM H. ALSUP, Magistrate Judge.

During 2006, pro se defendant John Hom gambled online through internet accounts with PokerStars.com and PartyPoker.com. . . . In 2007, defendant continued to gamble online through his PokerStars account. . . . Both poker websites allowed defendant to deposit money or make withdrawals.

Defendant used his account at FirePay.com, an online financial organization that receives, holds, and pays funds on behalf of its customers, to fund his online PokerStars and PartyPoker accounts. He deposited money into his FirePay account via his domestic Wells Fargo bank account or other online financial institutions, such as Western Union. In 2006, FirePay ceased allowing United States customers to transfer funds from their FirePay accounts to offshore internet gambling sites, so defendant used Western Union and other online financial institutions to transfer money from his Wells Fargo bank account to his online poker accounts. . . . Defendant admits that at some points in both 2006 and 2007, the aggregate amount of funds in his FirePay, PokerStars, and PartyPoker accounts exceeded $10,000 in United States currency. . . .

After the Internal Revenue Service detected discrepancies in defendant's federal income tax returns for 2006 and 2007, it opened a Foreign Bank and Financial Accounts Report ("FBAR") examination. . . . Individuals must file an FBAR with respect to foreign financial accounts exceeding $10,000 maintained during the previous year by June 30. 31 C.F.R. 103.27(c). Defendant did not file his 2006 or 2007 FBARs until June 26, 2010. . . . Moreover, his submitted FBAR for 2006 did not include his FirePay account. . . .

On September 20, 2011, the [Internal Revenue Service] assessed defendant with civil penalties under 31 U.S.C. 5321(a)(5) for his non-willful failure to submit FBARs, as required by 31 U.S.C. 5314, regarding his interest in his FirePay, PokerStars, and PartyPoker accounts. . . . The Court has tried to appoint a free lawyer for defendant—but no one would take the case.

ANALYSIS

The Bank Secrecy Act of 1970 [(BSA)] was enacted "to require certain reports or records where they have a high degree of usefulness in criminal, tax, or regulatory investigations or proceedings." *United States v. Clines*, 958 F.2d 578, 581 (4th Cir. 1992) (citations omitted), *cert. denied*, 505 U.S. 1205 (1992). To accomplish this end, the Act established reporting requirements for transactions involving foreign financial agencies. 31 U.S.C. 5314. The provisions of the Act relating to foreign financial transactions resulted from the concern of Congress that foreign financial institutions located in jurisdictions having laws of secrecy with respect to bank activity were being used extensively to violate or evade domestic criminal, tax, and regulatory requirements. . . .

In sum, an individual must file an FBAR for a reporting year if: (1) he or she is a United States person; (2) he or she has a financial interest in, or signature or other authority over, a bank, securities, or other financial account; (3) the bank, securities, or other financial account is in a foreign country; and (4) the aggregate amount in the accounts exceeds $10,000 in U.S. currency at any time during the year. . . .

2. INTEREST IN "A BANK, SECURITIES, OR OTHER FINANCIAL ACCOUNT."

The second element is whether defendant had a financial interest in, or authority over, a bank, securities, or other financial account in 2006 or 2007. Defendant does not contest in his opposition that he had a financial interest in his online FirePay, PokerStars, and PartyPoker accounts in 2006 and his online PokerStars account in 2007. Rather, defendant argues that those accounts are not a "bank or other financial accounts" for purposes of the applicable statute and regulations.

While our court of appeals has not yet answered what constitutes "other financial account[s]" under 31 C.F.R. 103.24, the Court of Appeals for the Fourth Circuit found that an account with a financial agency is a financial account under Section 5314. *Clines*, 958 F.2d at 582. Under Section 5312(a)(1), a "person acting for a person" as a "financial institution" or a person who is "acting in a similar way related to money" is considered a "financial agency." Section 5312(a)(2) lists 26 different types of entities that may qualify as a "financial institution." Based on the breadth of the definition, our court of appeals has held that "the term 'financial institution' is to be given a broad definition." *United States v. Dela Espriella*, 781 F.2d 1432, 1436 (9th Cir. 1986). The government claims that FirePay, PokerStars, and PartyPoker are all financial institutions because they function as "commercial bank[s]." Section 5312(a)(2)(B). The Fourth Circuit in *Clines* found that "[b]y holding funds for third parties and disbursing them at their direction, [the organization at issue] functioned as a bank [under Section 5314]." *Clines*, 958 F.2d at 582. . . .

3. THE FINANCIAL ACCOUNT IS IN A FOREIGN COUNTRY.

The third element is whether defendant's three financial accounts are located in foreign countries. The government argues that "located in" refers to where the financial institution that created and managed the account is located, whereas defendant argues that "located in" refers to the geographic location of the funds. As defendant has provided some evidence to suggest that PokerStars has several dozen bank accounts located in the United States, he asserts that "there is a real possibility that Defendant's funds are in an American bank". . . .

This order agrees with the government. It is irrelevant where PokerStars, FirePay, or PartyPoker opened their bank accounts. Those accounts belong to them, not defendant. Rather, his accounts are digital constructs that these financial institutions, all located outside of the United States, created and maintained on his behalf. . . .

The Financial Crimes Enforcement Network of the Department of the Treasury has recently provided more guidance in its response to comments on its notice of proposed 2011 amendments to [BSA], stating, "an account is not a foreign account under the FBAR if it is maintained with a financial institution located in the United States." Final Regulations, 76 Fed. Reg. 10,235 (Feb. 24, 2011) (to be codified at 31 C.F.R. pt. 1010) (emphasis added). . . .

As defendant concedes, PokerStars, FirePay, and PartyPoker are all licensed and operated in foreign countries. . . . These foreign countries are where the companies created and maintained defendant's online accounts. Accordingly, this order finds that defendant's accounts are all located in foreign countries. . . .

[The court also found that the first and fourth elements were met, and granted the government's motion for summary judgment.]

---

1. **Hom's *Regulatory Perimeter*.** How is the regulatory perimeter defined in *Hom*? Are we still in the realm of finance or does this case extend beyond it?

2. ***Bank Secrecy and Anti-Money Laundering (AML) Measures.*** As alluded to in *Hom*, BSA requires financial institutions to assist U.S. government agencies with the detection and prevention of money laundering and terrorist financing. *See* 31 U.S.C. § 5311 ("It is the purpose of this subchapter . . . to require certain reports or records where they have a high degree of usefulness in criminal, tax, or regulatory investigations or proceedings, or in the conduct of intelligence or counterintelligence activities, including analysis, to protect against international terrorism."). Note the contrast between the BSA's anti-crime purpose and more traditional goals of financial regulation, such as safety, soundness, consumer protection, and the elimination of systemic risks. After the BSA came the passage of the Money Laundering Control Act of 1986, which created criminal penalties for and expanded the reach of AML laws. *See, e.g.*, Ernest L. Simons IV, *Anti-Money Laundering Compliance: Only Mega Banks Need Apply*, 17 N.C. BANKING INSTITUTE 249, 252 (2013). In the 2000s, federal emphasis on AML and counterterrorism increased substantially, in large part due to the globalization of the financial sector, advances in financial technology, and, of course, the 9/11 terrorist attacks. *See id.* at 249–51. Both the Uniting and Strengthening America by Providing Appropriate Tools Required to Intercept and Obstruct Terrorism Act of 2001 (USA PATRIOT Act) and further amendments to the BSA strengthened the anti-money laundering regime. *See id.* at 253. Note that the BSA grants the Treasury primary responsibility for

promulgating regulations under its anti-money laundering provisions, even though the vast majority of transactions subject to these provisions are filtered through financial institutions regulated by a variety of federal agencies. *See id.* at 252. We will return to this topic in Part VII, where we take up the regulation of payments.

3. ***Extraterritorial Application.*** Note the offshore reach of this regulatory regime and the complexities of enforcement without cooperation of foreign regulatory bodies. To what extent are foreign sovereigns likely to cooperate with the Treasury in such cases? How might that cooperation be encouraged? For a discussion of how international financial regulatory networks have been used to combat offshore financial centers catering to terrorists and other criminals, see, *e.g.*, Stavros Gadinis, *Three Pathways to Global Standards: Private, Regulator, and Ministry Networks*, 109 AM. J. INT'L L. 1, 28–32 (2015). For a discussion of how the United States has leveraged the international financial system to isolate North Korea and Iran, *see, e.g.*, Rachel L. Loeffler, *Bank Shots: How the Financial System Can Isolate Rogues*, 88 FOREIGN AFF. 101, 103–07 (2009).

D. *MORRISON V. NATIONAL AUSTRALIA BANK*

Before the Supreme Court's landmark securities case, *Morrison v. National Australia Bank*, 561 U.S. 247 (2010), federal courts applied the Second Circuit conduct-and-effects test to determine when § 10(b) of the Securities and Exchange Act of 1934 (1934 Act) could apply extraterritorially. Such a test was important because it defined the scope of liability for suits brought under Rule 10b-5, which has been interpreted to create an expansive private right of action for securities fraud and a civil remedy much broader than those generally available in other jurisdictions. *See* Joshua L. Boehm, *Private Securities Fraud Litigation after* Morrison v. National Australia Bank: *Reconsidering a Reliance-Based Approach to Extraterritoriality*, 53 HARV. INT'L L.J. 249, 252 (2012). The test was actually comprised of two separate but related tests. The first, the conduct test, considers "whether the wrongful conduct occurred in the United States." *Morrison*, 561 U.S. at 257 (citations omitted). The second test, the effects test, evaluates "whether the wrongful conduct had a substantial effect in the United States or upon United States citizens." *Morrison*, 561 U.S. at 257 (citations omitted).

The Second Circuit clarified in a 1975 case that the effects test required "injury to purchasers or sellers of those securities in whom the United States has an interest, not where acts simply have an adverse effect on the American economy or American investors generally." Bersch v. Drexel Firestone, Inc., 519 F.2d 974, 989 (2d. Cir. 1975); *see also* Boehm, *Private Securities Fraud Litigation after* Morrison, at 254. *Bersch* also clarified the limits of the conduct test, rejecting activity that is "merely preparatory," such as partial drafting of a misleading securities prospectus. *See Bersch*, 519 F.2d at 987; *see also* Boehm, *Private Securities Fraud Litigation after* Morrison, at 255. Interestingly, activity that would not satisfy either test independently nonetheless can trigger § 10(b)'s extraterritorial reach when the two tests are combined. *See, e.g.*, Itoba Ltd. v. Lep Group P.L.C., 54 F.3d 118 (2d Cir. 1995); *see also* Boehm, *Private Securities Fraud Litigation after* Morrison, at 255–56. The fact-intensive and unpredictable nature of the case law generated by the conduct-and-effects test led to both scholarly criticism and marketplace uncertainty. *See, e.g.*, Stephen J. Choi & Linda J. Silberman, *The Continuing Evolution of Securities Class Actions Symposium: Transnational Litigation and Global Securities Class-Action Lawsuits*, 2009 WIS. L. REV. 465, 466–68 (2009); John C. Coffee, Jr., *Foreign Issuers Fear Global Class Actions*, NAT'L L.J. (June 14, 2007); *see also* Boehm, *Private Securities Fraud Litigation after* Morrison, at 251.

Morrison, as authored in 2010 by Justice Scalia, rejected the conduct-and-effects test outright, surprising many experts who had expected the Supreme Court to refine the test's limits. The Court first clarified that its own decision as well as the conduct-and-effects test had nothing to do with jurisdiction in the technical sense, reasoning that "to ask what conduct § 10(b) reaches is to ask what conduct § 10(b) prohibits, which is a merits question," and not a question of subject-matter jurisdiction. *Morrison*, 561 U.S. at 254. The Court then established a presumption against extraterritorial application of all federal laws, including the 1934 Act, and adopted a bright-line rule for when § 10(b) would have extraterritorial application. Specifically, the Court held that, in the absence of express congressional authorization,

> the focus of the [1934] Act is not upon the place where the deception originated, but upon purchases and sales of securities in the United States. Section 10(b) does not punish deceptive conduct, but only deceptive conduct "in connection with the purchase or sale of any security registered on a national securities exchange or any security not so registered." 15 U.S.C. § 78j(b). . . . Those purchase-and-sale transactions are the objects of the statute's solicitude. . . . And it is in our view only transactions in securities listed on domestic exchanges, and domestic transactions in other securities, to which § 10(b) applies.

Morrison, 561 U.S. at 266–67. The Court thus rejected the previous case law's concern with the location of the fraudulent activity, instead focusing on the location of the transactions themselves. While the Court's holding easily resolved the facts underlying *Morrison* itself, which involved purchases in foreign locations of an Australian company's securities that were not listed on any U.S. stock exchange, interpretive difficulties have persisted, especially with respect to the second prong of the *Morrison* rule regarding "domestic transactions in other securities."

Transactions in securities traded over-the-counter, with all their diverse forms, have proved particularly vexing for lower courts in applying *Morrison's* second prong. Despite the demise of its conduct-and-effects test, the Second Circuit has once again assumed a leading interpretive role in this area. In *Absolute Activist Value Master Fund Ltd. v. Ficeto*, 677 F.3d 60 (2d Cir. 2012), the Second Circuit had to "determine under what circumstances the purchase or sale of a security that is not listed on a domestic exchange should be considered 'domestic' within the meaning of *Morrison*." *Id.* at 66–67. At issue in *Absolute Activist* was the direct purchase of over-the-counter (OTC) shares from U.S. companies by foreign hedge funds. The Second Circuit held that, "to sufficiently allege the existence of a 'domestic transaction in other securities,' plaintiffs must allege facts indicating that irrevocable liability was incurred or that title was transferred within the United States." *Id.* at 62. Because the plaintiff hedge funds' complaint contained only conclusory allegations as to where irrevocable liability was incurred or where title was transferred, the Second Circuit remanded the case for further consideration.

Transactions in exchange-traded securities have proved to be less problematic for lower courts in applying *Morrison*, largely because the first prong of the *Morrison* rule regarding "transactions in securities listed on domestic exchanges," presents a more straightforward inquiry as to whether the security being purchased is indeed listed and purchased on an official U.S. stock exchange. *See, e.g.*, United States v. Martoma, No. 12 CR 973 PGG, 2013 WL 6632676, at *2 (S.D.N.Y. Dec. 17, 2013) (finding that *Morrison's* first prong applies to purchases of American Depository Receipts made on the New York Stock Exchange (NYSE), even though these securities were "derivatives that simply repackaged [a foreign company's] stock, which is traded abroad"). Drawing on *Morrison's* emphasis on the locus of the transaction, the Second Circuit has confirmed that *Morrison's* first prong requires not just that the relevant security was listed on an official U.S. stock exchange, but also that the transaction in said security occurred in the United States. In so doing, the Second Circuit thus rejected, as many district courts have done, the "listing theory" that mere listing on an official U.S. stock exchange is sufficient to satisfy *Morrison's* first prong. *See* City of Pontiac Policemen's & Firemen's Ret. Sys. v. UBS AG, 752 F.3d 173, 180 (2d Cir. 2014) ("*Morrison's* emphasis on '*transactions* in securities listed on domestic exchanges', makes clear that the focus of both prongs was domestic transactions of any kind, with the domestic listing acting as a proxy for a domestic transaction." (footnote omitted)); *see also* Michael Flynn & Craig Bergman, *With City of Pontiac, 2nd Circ. Shifts Morrison Focus*, LAW360, May 2014. Based on this reasoning, the *City of Pontiac* court imposed a limit on "foreign-cubed" claims involving the mere domestic cross-listing of a foreign security purchased abroad. *See City of Pontiac*, 752 F.3d at 179 ("*Morrison* does not support the application of § 10(b) of the Exchange Act to claims by a foreign purchaser of foreign-issued shares on a foreign exchange simply because those shares are also listed on a domestic exchange.").

Notably, with regard to both prongs of *Morrison*, the Second Circuit has created an additional limit on transactions involving "unusual" securities that satisfy *Morrison's* rule but whose coverage by § 10(b) would nonetheless "constitute an impermissibly extraterritorial extension of the statute." Parkcentral Glob. Hub Ltd. v. Porsche Auto. Holdings SE, 763 F.3d 198, 201 (2d Cir. 2014). In *Parkcentral*, the plaintiff hedge funds had incurred losses in "securities-based swap agreements based on the price movements of foreign securities." *Id.* Although the Second Circuit found that the second prong of *Morrison* was satisfied by these agreements, which had been executed in the United States, it nonetheless rejected the plaintiffs' § 10(b) claim, holding that,

> while [*Morrison*] unmistakably made a domestic securities transaction (or transaction in a domestically listed security) *necessary* to a properly domestic invocation of § 10(b), such a transaction is not alone *sufficient* to state a properly domestic claim under the statute.

Id. at 215 (emphasis added).

Crucial to the Second Circuit's reasoning was the interest in not allowing "the plaintiffs, by virtue of an agreement independent from the reference securities, to hale the European participants in the market for German stocks into U.S. courts and subject them to U.S. securities laws." *Id.* at 216. Coupled with *Absolute Activist* and, arguably, *City of Pontiac*, the Second Circuit has thus added a fair amount of fact-intensive inquiry to Justice Scalia's bright-line *Morrison* rule.

---

1. ***Applying* Morrison *and* Absolute Activist.** While the court in *Morrison* attempted to create an easily administrable bright-line rule, *Absolute Activist* interpreted *Morrison* less rigidly, moving toward a more fact-intensive inquiry in order to prevent abuse of securities laws. A comparison of a couple of cases decided in the aftermath of *Morrison* and *Absolute Activist* illustrates the continuing difficulty of this area of the law. In *S.E.C. v. Benger*, No. 09 C 676, 2013 WL 593952, at *1, 13 (N.D. Ill. Feb. 15, 2013), the defendants had engaged in an "international boiler room scheme" to sell "shares in a foreign company to foreign investors." Although the defendants had employed escrow agents as intermediaries in the United States, the Share Purchase Agreement signed by the investors apparently did not grant the escrow agents any power to transfer or accept title, and all acceptances of purchase offers and receipts of stock purchases allegedly occurred outside the United States. Given that the scheme's only domestic connection was the use of the escrow agents, how do you think the *Benger* court should have ruled? In *Liberty Media Corp. v. Vivendi Universal, S.A.*, 861 F. Supp. 2d 262 (S.D.N.Y. 2012), the defendants had signed and announced a Merger Agreement in the United States that ultimately resulted in the exchange of foreign shares in foreign companies in France. Given that the only domestic connection was the signing and announcement of the Merger Agreement, how do you think the *Liberty Media* court should have ruled? In fact, the *Liberty Media* court held that the shares swap was covered by § 10(b) under *Morrison*, while the *Benger* court held that the shares sales were *not* so covered. Do you find this difference in results sensible, based on the purposes underlying § 10(b)? Are you convinced that the use of escrow agents in the United States implicates less domestic concern than the signing and announcement of a contract in the United States? How might *Parkcentral*, also discussed above, apply to change the result in *Liberty Media*?

2. ***Conduct-and-Effects Test versus* Morrison's *Bright Line Rule.*** As discussed above, the *Benger* court held that, under *Morrison*, § 10(b) could not reach the defendants' fraudulent conduct because the transactions themselves did not take place in the United States. Is it possible to reach the opposite result without effectively resurrecting the pre-*Morrison* conduct test? Would the pre-*Morrison* conduct-and-effects test have led to a different result in this case? The *Bersch* case, discussed earlier, sheds some light on how the test might be applied. Given the lack of injury to any U.S. purchaser or seller, the effects test is almost certainly not satisfied. The conduct test, however, presents a more difficult question. *Bersch* excluded conduct that is "merely preparatory," such as partial drafting of a misleading securities prospectus. *See Bersch*, 519 F.2d at 987. Are the U.S. intermediaries' actions, such as entering into distribution agreements, hiring foreign "boiler room" agents, and transmitting certificates, akin to "merely

preparatory" partial drafting of prospectuses, or do they rise to the level of "significant conduct"? Is it not a strength of the conduct-and-effects test that it has the flexibility to facilitate such an extension?

3. ***Post-*Morrison *Regulatory Developments.*** Enacted just a month after the *Morrison* decision, § 929P of the Dodd-Frank Act appeared to revive the conduct-and-effects test for actions brought by the SEC or the United States. *See* 15 U.S.C. § 78aa(b). In light of this fact, why did the *Benger* court apply *Morrison* in what was clearly an SEC enforcement action? For an exploration of various interpretations of § 929P and its impact on the *Morrison* decision, see Richard W. Painter, *The Dodd-Frank Extraterritorial Jurisdiction Provision: Was It Effective, Needed, or Sufficient?*, 1 HARV. BUS. L. REV. 195, 195 (2011). More generally, what explains the discrepancy in congressional treatment of enforcement actions and private rights of action? Is the need for compensation and punishment greater in the public enforcement context, or is it greater when private litigants, who may be relatively modest investors, are subject to fraudulent international securities schemes? Section 929Y of the Dodd-Frank Act also directed the SEC "to solicit comments and conduct a study on the extent to which the conduct[-and]-effects test should be restored for private anti-fraud actions under the [1934] Act." Boehm, *Private Securities Fraud Litigation after* Morrison, at 262. The SEC released its study two years later, but did not offer any firm policy recommendations, instead limiting itself to "identify[ing] the relevant policy considerations that Congress might want to consider as part of a process for determining whether to enact legislation regarding the cross-border scope of § 10(b) private actions." SEC. & EXCH. COMM'N, STUDY ON THE CROSS-BORDER SCOPE OF THE PRIVATE RIGHT OF ACTION UNDER § 10(B) OF THE SECURITIES EXCHANGE ACT OF 1934, at 69 (Apr. 2012).

4. ***Balancing Domestic and Foreign Interests.*** In later chapters, we will explore the extraterritorial application of many key provisions of the Dodd-Frank Act, including the Volcker Rule, the new regulatory regime governing OTC derivatives, and the application of European solvency requirements for insurance companies to U.S. insurers doing business overseas. In this area, Congress has rebutted the *Morrison* presumption against extraterritorial application of U.S. financial laws by expressly providing that these provisions would extend to offshore activities. For instance, the Act empowers the CFTC and the SEC to prohibit foreign entities from participating in U.S.-based swap activities if either agency determines that swap regulation in a foreign country "undermines the stability of the United States." 15 U.S.C. § 8304. As a result of these congressional modifications, U.S. regulatory authorities have broader reach in deciding how to coordinate various rules with overlapping and sometimes inconsistent requirements regarding foreign application.

III. THE CLASSIFICATION PROBLEM

A. FORMAL VERSUS FUNCTIONAL DEFINITIONS

The four cases presented above offer a few examples of jurisdictional disputes in the field of financial regulation. We will see many more cases of this sort in later Chapters as we define the regulatory perimeter in each area of substantive regulation. The next excerpt, which alludes to some of the materials you have already seen and anticipates a number of themes that recur throughout later chapters, offers a taxonomy for organizing these materials.

Howell E. Jackson, Regulation in a Multisectored Financial Services Industry: An Exploratory Essay

77 WASH. U. L. REV. 319 (1999)

A. Classifications of Financial Arrangements

In the United States, the rules governing bilateral contract constitute the default regulatory structure for financial arrangements. Unless another regulatory structure applies, the presumption is that our lowest cost, least intrusive method of risk regulation applies. In my view, we use two basic classifications systems to assign financial arrangements to regulatory structures: formal definitions and functional definitions, of which the latter category (functional definitions) is the more prevalent. Though useful, functional definitions suffer from the serious problems of indeterminacy and overinclusion. As a result, functional definitions of financial activities are typically bounded by a series of exceptions or exclusions, which are discussed separately below.

1. Formal Definitions of Financial Activities

Perhaps the simplest way to classify financial arrangements is through a formal definition. In certain regulatory contexts, this is the approach we use. A formal definition creates a regulatory category and typically applies a regulatory standard on an entity that falls within the category. Often times, the category involves the chartering statute under which the entity is organized (*e.g.*, all banks organized under the National Bank Act). Formal definitions, however, can also turn on other legal characteristics (*e.g.*, all depository institutions with FDIC insurance or all banks that are members of the Federal Reserve [Board]). The hallmark of formal definitions is that they depend on relatively unambiguous legal requirements, and not the sort of precedential or analogical reasoning that characterizes functional definitions.

Formal definitions of the business of banking are typically used in two different contexts. First, they are sometimes used to limit access to some governmental franchise or business privilege. For example, FDIC insurance is statutorily limited to institutions that meet what is primarily a formal definition of banking. Similarly, access to the Federal Reserve Board's payments system is restricted to entities meeting another formal definition of banking. . . .

The second common use of formal definitions of banking is to impose statutory obligations on categories of institutions that meet formal statutory requirements. For example, a category of institutions known as "insured depository institutions"—that is, banks with FDIC insurance—are subject to numerous regulatory obligations. Such entities must, among other things, meet reserve requirements established under the Federal Reserve Act; they must also conform with Community Reinvestment Act of 1977 obligations with respect to the provision of credit to low-and middle-income borrowers. A separate, but similarly formal definition of the term "depository institution" describes entities subject to the federal Management Interlocks Act. Outside of the banking field, formal definitions are used to determine which entities must join [FINRA] or an SEC-registered securities exchange: any broker-dealer registered with the SEC.

The problem with formal definitions is that they are subject to a high degree of manipulation. Functionally-equivalent products can be developed with different appellations. This problem is particularly acute when the definition is used as a predicate for imposing a regulatory burden, as opposed to a prerequisite for obtaining a valuable franchise. For example, in the early 1980's, a number of securities firms developed money-market mutual funds with check-writing privileges. Functionally, these products were quite similar to bank deposits, but formally they were specialized investment companies with contractual links with commercial banks that had access to check clearing systems. As long as these entities were not formed as state or nationally chartered banks, they were free from a wide range of regulatory structures (and associated costs) that are imposed only on entities formally chartered as banks. . . .

2. Functional Definitions

More sophisticated and flexible than formal definitions are functional approaches to defining regulatory jurisdiction. A good example of a functional definition is one used to define the jurisdictional boundaries of the federal securities laws, which potentially apply to any transaction involving a "security." In addition to a few dozen illustrative examples, the statutory definition of the term includes "investment contracts," which the courts have interpreted to mean "a contract, transaction or scheme whereby a person invests his money in a common enterprise and is led to expect profits solely from the efforts of the promoter or a third party." Over the years, this definition has been interpreted to embrace a wide variety of multi-party investment relationships. In disputes arising under this definition, the creator of the disputed transaction is typically arguing that the arrangement should be treated as a simple contract (where anti-fraud rules are more lenient) as opposed to a security (where rule 10b-5 and the duty to be truthful in all material respects apply). Sometimes the party that initiated the transaction is already regulated under one regulatory regime, and the question is whether federal securities laws should also extend to the transaction in question.

Functional definitions are used to establish the jurisdictional boundaries of most of the regulatory systems discussed in this essay. For example, under § 3(a) of the Investment Company Act of 1940 [(1940 Act)], any entity that invests or proposes to invest more than 40 percent of its total assets in securities is presumptively subject to 1940 Act regulation. The definition extends not just to entities operating in corporate form, but includes partnerships, trusts, and other less formal legal structures. Most insurance company statutes have a similar structure. A typical insurance statute would govern all transactions in which "one party . . . is obliged to confer benefit of pecuniary value upon another party . . . dependent upon the happening of a fortuitous event in which the [second party] has a material interest which will be adversely affected." Another illustration of a functional approach to jurisdiction is the manner in which the Employee Retirement Income Security Act of 1974 [(ERISA)] defines who should be regulated as a plan fiduciary: any one that "controls" plan assets, renders paid investment advice to a plan, or has "discretionary authority" over plan administration.

Another prominent example of functional definitions can be found in the foundational elements of American banking law: state prohibitions on unauthorized banking. These statutes typically prohibit unregulated entities from engaging in the business of banking. . . .

The premise underlying these provisions is that an entity should not be allowed to engage in the business of banking unless the entity complies with the regulatory safeguards designed to restrain the risks associated with depository institutions and also presumably complies with the social obligations and political constraints imposed on the banking industry.

While the policies motivating such statutes are clear, the scope of their application often is not. It is not uncommon for an individual or organization to resist the assertion that it is engaged in the business of banking, and in response to such disputes, courts and regulatory agencies have developed an intensive set of precedents in this area. While there is considerable variation in the manner in which the business of banking is defined from jurisdiction to jurisdiction, the courts and agencies generally identify a set of "core" banking activities and then inquire whether the entity in question is sufficiently engaged in those core activities to be deemed in the business of banking.

The great advantage of functional definitions, as compared for formal ones, is that they allow jurisdictional lines to track more closely the policies that motivate our regulatory structures. So, for instance, the purpose of the 1940 Act is to protect investors who place their financial resources in investment pools, and the § 3(a) definition reviewed above provides a fairly simple definition of an investment pool-a legal entity with a substantial percentage of its assets allocated to investment securities. Similarly, the goal of insurance regulation is to police the issuance of contingent promises, and the jurisdictional provision excerpted above embodies that concept. In addition, the basic definitions of broker and dealer under the [1934 Act] are designed to extend our federal system of regulating brokers and dealers to all those engaged in the regular business of buying and selling securities, either for their own account or for the account of customers.

In practice, however, an important problem of functional definitions is that they are overinclusive and indeterminate. Let me begin with over-inclusion: Take the basic 1940 Act definition of investment company. Though at first blush a perfectly reasonable definition of an investment pool, it turns out that it picks up a wide variety of economic relationships to which we most likely would not want to apply 1940 Act restrictions. Examples include corporate holding companies (like GM or IBM), start-up entities holding investments securities for a short period of time until they can be invested in plant and equipment, or banks, insurance companies and pensions, all of which regularly invest more than 40 percent of their assets in securities of one sort or another.

Section 3(a)'s definition presumptively brings all these entities under control of the 1940 Act. Functional definitions of insurance have similar problems. It turns out that in many transactions one party makes a pecuniary commitment to another party based on fortuitous events that cause harm. Express warranties in standard contracts often have precisely this function, and there is a long line of definition-of-insurance cases in which the courts attempt to distinguish between real warranties and disguised insurance contracts.

. . . the courts have been inundated in the past few decades with litigation in which one party claimed an activity constitute a certain type of financial arrangement while the other side asserted it was another. So, for example, when a national bank wanted to get into the life insurance business a few years ago, it offered its customers loans with "debt cancellation" provisions under which the bank would forgive the loan in the event the borrowed died while the loan was outstanding. In ensuing litigation, the local insurance commissioner took the view that these arrangements constituted insurance transactions, whereas federal banking regulators sanctioned the activity as reasonably incidental to banking. Faced with such disputes, courts typically attempt to determine to determine the predominant characteristic of the transactions in question–*e.g.*, whether the activity had more in common with the business of banking or more in common with insurance–and then classify it accordingly. But this sort of balancing test is notoriously subjective, and susceptible to manipulation.

As a result of these problems of over-inclusion and indeterminacy, almost wherever functional definitions of financial activities are employed, the definitions also include (either directly or through judicial and administrative interpretations) a series of exceptions and exclusions to prevent confusion and over-broad applications.

3. Solutions to Over-Inclusion and Indeterminacy

There are four basic ways in which courts and legislative drafters impose limitations on functional definitions of financial activities: *de minimis* exceptions, sophisticated investor exclusions, institutional carve-outs, and extra-territorial exemptions.

a. *De Minimis* Exceptions

Many definitions of banking include *de minimis* exceptions for entities that potentially fall within the scope of a definition but do not engage in sufficiently substantial activities to warrant the exertion of regulatory supervision. *De minimis* exceptions are implicit in threshold business of banking tests in that they typically specify that to qualify as the conduct of the business of banking, an entity must engage in core banking functions. The conduct of incidental or secondary banking activities, being *de minimis*, will not trigger most threshold business of banking tests.

Similarly, the statutory definition of bank written into the current version of the Bank Holding Company Act [(BHCA)] first encompasses a broad range of institutions but then provides a series of *de minimis* exemptions for entities whose banking activities are limited to non-commercial and/or non-transactional services, including certain qualifying trust companies and industrial banks. *De minimis* exceptions are also common elsewhere in the field of financial regulation. In a sense, the decision of most insurance commissions not to exert authority over commercial firms offering standard warranties is an example of this tendency. More common, however, are numerical exclusions. If an investment pool has fewer than one hundred investors, it is exempted from regulation under the 1940 Act under the "private investment company" exemption. Similarly, securities authorities typically exclude from regulation under the broker-dealer statutes individuals who participate in only a small number of transactions, usually fewer than a handful a year.

De minimis exceptions reflect a sensible balancing of the costs and benefits of regulation. Beneath a certain level of activity, the costs associated with regulatory compliance are just not worth the candle. *De minimis* exceptions are, however, also susceptible to abuse and manipulation. There is considerable incentive for private parties to avoid regulation by keeping their activities beneath the de minimis level. (Hedge funds, for example, were originally all designed to fall within the private investment company exception.) Often, what emerges is a series of parallel *de minimis* exceptions which if aggregated would cross jurisdictional lines. As a result, regulatory official must expend some effort policing for abuses of these exceptions. Typically, *de minimis* exceptions are bounded by a functional rules of integration used to determine when formally distinct *de minimis* activities should be aggregated into a unitary, fully regulated structure.

b. Sophisticated Investor Exclusions

A related, but distinctive limitation on functional definitions is the sophisticated investor exclusion. Under this exclusion, an entity is exempt from some sort of regulatory structure provided the entity limits to business activities to transactions with counter-parties that satisfy some minimum standard of expertise or wealth. The classic illustration of such an exemption is the private placement exemption under the Securities [1933 Act], and its regulatory extensions. . . . In 1996, [the 1940 Act] was amended to allow an analogous exception for investment pools that limit themselves to "qualified purchasers," defined to include individuals with more than $5 million of investments.

Sophisticated investor exclusions are less common where the regulatory structures involve more complex intermediaries, such as depository institutions and insurance companies. . . . Regulation in both of these areas is not solely designed to align informational disparities between investors and intermediaries. The control of externalities and the enforcement of both redistributive norms and considerations of policy economy are reflected in these regulatory regimes. Accordingly, where one does observe sophisticated-investor exclusions in these fields–such as the [BHCA]'s exclusion for credit card banks or the proposed. . . .

c. Institutional Carveouts

A third exemption from functional definitions, I term an institutional carveout. This exemption might be thought of as the already-regulated-elsewhere exclusion. Such exclusions are commonly built into functional definitions in recognition that it would be redundant and costly to impose a second system of regulation on an institution that is already subject to a comprehensive system of regulations. . . .

[I]llustrations of institutional exclusions abound. The 1940 Act (with its broad functional definition of investment pools) excludes from its coverage insurance companies, depository institutions, and pension plans. Another institutional exclusion can be found in ERISA. In connection with its broad functional definition of regulated plan fiduciaries described above, ERISA provides a series of institutional exemptions for plan assets that are placed under the control of regulated entities. Thus, for example, if plan assets are placed in an investment pool regulated under the 1940 Act, the investment company in control of those asset is expressly excluded from ERISA's definition of plan fiduciary. . . .

The merits of institutional exclusions are self-evident. Once an entity is already subject to one set of regulations, it is costly and wasteful to require the firm to comply with another set of rules and accept oversight from another group of supervisory authorities. To the extent that the justifications for regulatory intervention across sectors of the financial services industry are congruent, one set of regulatory safeguards is an appropriate substitute for another regime. In addition, where institutional carveouts are not available, there are often substantial administrative difficulties present if a single legal entity is required to comply with two completing sets of requirements. For example, the current SEC net-capital requirements for broker-dealers, if applied without adjustment to commercial banks, would impose prohibitively high capital requirements on commercial loans, which lack readily verifiable market values. Similar conflicts exist when entities must comply with both insurance underwriting and depository institution regulations.

The drawbacks of institutional carveouts are more subtle. The chief problem with institutional exclusions is that the regulatory goals and strategies of the regulation governing the excluded institution may differ in important respects from the goals and strategies of the regime that acquiesces as a result of the exclusion. To make this point more concrete, consider the regulatory strategies of broker-dealer regulation in the United States: heavily emphasis on fiduciary duties, considerable scrutiny on individual qualifications, and lots of disclosure obligations. In granting an exclusion for banks from the definition of broker-dealers, the [original] 1934 Act acquiesce[d] to a regulatory regime that proceeds on quite different operating principles: mostly portfolio-shaping rules and mandatory bonding arrangements, most of which offer little protection for investors who rely on banks for assistance with securities transactions. . . .

d. Extraterritorial Exemptions

A fourth and similarly spirited exception is for financial intermediaries, including banking organizations, chartered and primarily conducting operations in foreign jurisdictions. Many definitional statutes include exemption for banking organizations chartered under foreign laws or for special purposes entities principally organized to do business in foreign markets. . . .

Other interesting illustration of extraterritorial exemptions involve transactions by U.S. citizens or residents who enter into economic relations outside of our borders, either by traveling to foreign locations or employing agents in remote locations. . . . And, of course, the rising of electronic commerce over the Internet raises analogous questions regarding the application of U.S. regulatory structures when U.S. residents access Internet sites located in other jurisdictions.

Like other limitations on functional definitions of financial activities, extraterritorial exclusions present conflicting considerations. Exercising jurisdiction over foreign transactions is costly and difficult; moreover, in many jurisdictions it will be redundant if foreign regulatory structures also govern the transactions and are effectively enforced.

On the other hand, open-ended extra-territorial exclusions invite manipulation, and potentially undermine domestic regulatory goals. Without some attention to policing extraterritorial exclusions, a domestic regulatory structure can become eviscerated.

---

1. ***Functional Regulation or Entity-Based Regulation.*** In Chapter 1.3, we explored different approaches to the organization of financial regulation. Functional regulation, as you may recall, contemplates a supervisory system that determines regulatory requirements based on economic functions. All entities that engage in the same economic function are subject to the same financial regulations. Entity-based regulation determines regulation requirements based on the kind of legal entity involved. Entities chartered as banks are subject to bank regulation, entities licensed as insurance companies are covered by insurance regulations, and so on. Based on the materials you have read so far, which approach more accurately describes the organization of financial regulation in the United States?

2. ***The Prevalence of Regulatory Carveouts.*** The excerpt above noted the existence of a number of regulatory carveouts, for example for *de minimis* transactions, for sophisticated customers, for otherwise regulated institutions, and for certain extraterritorial transactions. Do these carveouts strike you as sound regulatory policy? Can you think of other categories of transactions that should also enjoy regulatory carveouts? For example, what if the provider of a financial service is a government entity? Or a non-profit entity?

B. CLASSIFICATION CHOICES UNDER THE DODD-FRANK ACT

As you saw in the previous section, the field of financial regulation is rife with jurisdictional disputes and choices between function and entity-based supervision. The Dodd-Frank Act features a number of such choices, chief among them the creation of the Financial Stability Oversight Council (FSOC) and the CFPB.

The FSOC, which will be discussed in greater detail in later chapters, is a macro-prudential regulatory body composed of the heads of the major financial regulators, such as the Federal Reserve Board, the SEC, and the CFTC, and chaired by the Secretary of the Treasury. Among the FSOC's various supervisory and coordinating responsibilities, its power to designate non-bank entities as systemically important is the most significant, and most controversial. *See, e.g.*, Stavros Gadinis, *From Independence to Politics in Financial Regulation*, 101 CAL. L. REV. 327, 369 (2013) ("By far, the FSOC's most important substantive function consists in its power to decide whether to subject a non-bank financial company to prudential supervision by the Federal Reserve [Board]."); Arthur E. Wilmarth, Jr., *Turning a Blind Eye: Why Washington Keeps Giving in to Wall Street*, 81 U. CIN. L. REV. 1283, 1297 (2013) (pointing to the "heavy industry resistance" encountered by the FSOC in exercising its designation power, among other powers). An examination of the authorizing text in Title I of the Dodd-Frank Act shows that the FSOC has been given a functional definition of "systemic risk" that has a fair amount of flexibility, thus granting the FSOC considerable discretion in which entities it chooses to designate as systemically important. *See* 12 U.S.C. § 5323(a)(1) (providing that the FSOC can designate an entity as systemically important, subject to a two-thirds vote by its members, if it "determines that material financial distress at the U.S. non-bank financial company, or the nature, scope, size, scale, concentration, interconnectedness, or mix of the activities of the U.S. non-bank financial company, could pose a threat to the financial stability of the United States."). Upon designation as systemically important, an entity faces a number of enhanced prudential requirements from the Federal Reserve Board, including risk-based capital requirements and liquidity requirements. *See* 12 U.S.C. § 5325(b). In Chapters 6.2 and 10.1, we will discuss the application of the FSOC's designation power over insurance companies and asset managers, as well as the FSOC's parallel power under Title VIII to designate financial market utilities as systemically important. *See* 12 U.S.C. § 5463.

The CFPB, which will also be discussed in greater detail in Part V, is a market conduct regulator led by a unitary executive. Four areas of the CFPB's authority are worth mentioning here.

First, the CFPB gained rulemaking authority over a number of existing consumer protection statutes, such as TILA, RESPA, the Electronic Fund Transfer Act, and the Equal Credit Opportunity Act of 1974 (ECOA). *See* 12 U.S.C. § 5481(12). Notably, given the scope of some of these statutes, the CFPB's authority extends to some entities that do not provide consumer financial products or services. *See* Adam Levitin, *The Consumer Financial Protection Bureau: An Introduction*, 32 REV. BANKING & FIN. L. 321, 347 (2013).

Second, the CFPB took on a significant role in mortgage regulation under Title XIV of the Dodd-Frank Act. Among other things, the CFPB was given rulemaking authority over residential mortgage loan origination standards and mortgage servicing requirements. *See* 15 U.S.C. §§ 1638, 1639b.

Third, the CFPB received expansive general powers over consumer financial products, subject to rather functional statutory definitions. *See* 12 U.S.C. §§ 5512(a), (c)(1) ("The Bureau is authorized to exercise its authorities under federal consumer financial law to administer, enforce, and otherwise implement the provisions of federal consumer financial law."; "In order to support its rulemaking and other functions, the Bureau shall monitor for risks to consumers in the offering or provision of consumer financial products or services, including developments in markets for such products or services."). Specifically, the CFPB received, *inter alia*, the power to designate a sector act or practice as "unfair, deceptive, or abusive," the power to mandate consumer-friendly disclosures from sector actors, and the power to require registration of non-bank entities. *See* 12 U.S.C. §§ 5531(d), 5536(a)(1)(B), 5532(a), 5512(c)(7); *see also* Levitin, *The Consumer Financial Protection Bureau*, at 344. Interestingly, these powers are subject to a number of institutional carveouts, including securities and insurance, as well as an exemption for auto dealers. *See* 12 U.S.C. §§ 5517(f), (h)-(i), 5519; *see also* Levitin, *The Consumer Financial Protection Bureau*, at 360–61.

Lastly, the CFPB supervises large depository institutions, which are major players in consumer finance that are not traditionally regulated as such. *See* 12

U.S.C. § 5515(a)-(b) (providing that the CFPB "shall have exclusive authority to require reports and conduct examinations on a periodic basis" of insured depository institutions with greater than $10 billion in assets). These powers are effectively subject to a community bank carveout for depository institutions with less than $10 billion in assets, which remain under the supervision of their primary regulators, typically the FDIC or the OCC. The CFPB was also given direct supervisory powers over a number of different entities that provide important consumer financial services, including payday lenders, private student lenders, and mortgage originators, brokers, and servicers. *See* 12 U.S.C. § 5514(a)(1). The Bureau has adopted a series of "large participant" regulations that define the scope of the agency's supervisory oversight. In contrast to carveouts for what Congress deemed to be community bank-sized institutions, these regulations impose CFPB oversight on entities that represent major participants in certain lines of business. Businesses that fall short of these thresholds must still comply with substantive federal requirements, like TILA and the ECOA, but are not subject to periodic CFPB examination and other forms of direct supervision.

IV. OVERLAPPING REGULATORY PERIMETERS

This section deals with regulatory perimeters that overlap and sometimes conflict due to the U.S. federal structure. The law of usury, which is the legal limits on the permissible rate of interest charged on loans, provides a prominent example of this overlap, and will be the central focus of this section.

A. THE REGULATION OF USURY

Traditionally, in the United States, usury restrictions were imposed at the state level and varied considerably from state to state. The following case explores the application of state usury rules to a national bank doing business across state lines.

Marquette Nat'l Bank v. First Omaha Serv. Corp.

439 U.S. 299 (1978)

MR. JUSTICE BRENNAN delivered the opinion of the Court.

The question for decision is whether the National Bank Act, Rev. Stat. § 5197, as amended, 12 U. S. C. § 85, authorizes a national bank based in one State to charge its out-of-state credit-card customers an interest rate on unpaid balances allowed by its home State, when that rate is greater than that permitted by the State of the bank's nonresident customers. The Minnesota Supreme Court held that the bank is allowed by § 85 to charge the higher rate. 262 N. W. 2d 358 (1977). We affirm.

The First National Bank of Omaha (Omaha Bank) is a national banking association with its charter address in Omaha, Neb. Omaha Bank is a card-issuing member in the BankAmericard plan. This plan enables cardholders to purchase goods and services from participating merchants and to obtain cash advances from participating banks throughout the United States and the world. Omaha Bank has systematically sought to enroll in its BankAmericard program the residents, merchants, and banks of the nearby State of Minnesota. The solicitation of Minnesota merchants and banks is carried on by respondent First of Omaha Service Corp. (Omaha Service Corp.), a wholly owned subsidiary of Omaha Bank.

Minnesota residents are obligated to pay Omaha Bank interest on the outstanding balances of their BankAmericards. Nebraska law permits Omaha Bank to charge interest on the unpaid balances of cardholder accounts at a rate of 18% per year on the first $999.99, and 12% per year on amounts of $1,000 and over. Minnesota law, however, fixes the permissible annual interest on such accounts at 12%. To compensate for the reduced interest, Minnesota law permits banks to charge annual fees of up to $15 for the privilege of using a bank credit card.

The instant case began when petitioner Marquette National Bank of Minneapolis (Marquette), itself a national banking association enrolled in the BankAmericard plan, brought suit . . . to enjoin Omaha Bank and Omaha Service Corp. from soliciting in Minnesota for Omaha Bank's BankAmericard program until such time as that program complied with Minnesota law. Marquette claimed to be losing customers to Omaha Bank because, unlike the Nebraska bank, Marquette was forced by the low rate of interest permissible under Minnesota law to charge a $10 annual fee for the use of its credit cards. . . .

Marquette named as defendants Omaha Bank [and] Omaha Service Corp., which is organized under the laws of Nebraska but qualified to do business and doing business in Minnesota. . . . Omaha Service Corp. participates in Omaha Bank's BankAmericard program by entering into agreements with banks and merchants necessary to the operation of the BankAmericard scheme. . . . At the time Marquette filed its complaint, Omaha Service Corp. had not yet entered into any such agreements in Minnesota, although it intended to do so. . . . For its services, Omaha Service Corp. receives a fee from Omaha Bank, but it does not itself extend credit or receive interest. . . .

II

The federal question presented for decision is the application of 12 U.S.C. § 85 to the operation of Omaha Bank's BankAmericard program. . . .

Omaha Bank is a national bank; it is an "instrumentalit[y] of the Federal government, created for a public purpose, and as such necessarily subject to the paramount authority of the United States." *Davis v. Elmira Savings Bank*, 161 U. S. 275, 283 (1896). The interest rate that Omaha Bank may charge in its BankAmericard program is thus governed by federal law. *See Farmers' & Mechanics' Nat. Bank v. Dearing*, 91 U. S. 29, 34 (1875). The provision of § 85 called into question states:

> "Any association may take, receive, reserve, and charge on any loan or discount made, or upon any notes, bills of exchange, or other evidences of debt, interest at the rate allowed by the laws of the State, Territory, or District *where the bank is located*, . . . and no more, except that where by the laws of any State a different rate is limited for banks organized under State laws, the rate so limited shall be allowed for associations organized or existing in any such State under this chapter." (Emphasis supplied.)

Section 85 thus plainly provides that a national bank may charge interest "on any loan" at the rate allowed by the laws of the State in which the bank is "located." The question before us is therefore narrowed to whether Omaha Bank and its BankAmericard program are "located" in Nebraska and for that reason entitled to charge its Minnesota customers the rate of interest authorized by Nebraska law.

There is no question but that Omaha Bank itself, apart from its BankAmericard program, is located in Nebraska. Petitioners concede as much. . . . The National Bank Act requires a national bank to state in its organization certificate "[t]he place where its operations of discount and deposit are to be carried on, designating the State, Territory, or district, and the particular county and city, town, or village." Rev. Stat. § 5134, 12 U. S. C. § 22. The charter address of Omaha Bank is in Omaha, Douglas County, Neb. The bank operates no branch banks in Minnesota . . . nor apparently could it under federal law. *See* 12 U.S.C. § 36 (c).

The State of Minnesota, however, contends that this conclusion must be altered if Omaha Bank's BankAmericard program is considered. . . .

We disagree. Section 85 was originally enacted as § 30 of the National Bank Act of 1864, 13 Stat. 108. The congressional debates surrounding the enactment of § 30 were conducted on the assumption that a national bank was "located" for purposes of the section in the State named in its organization certificate. *See* Cong. Globe, 38th Cong., 1st Sess., 2123-2127 (1864). Omaha Bank cannot be deprived of this location merely because it is extending credit to residents of a foreign State. Minnesota residents were always free to visit Nebraska and receive loans in that State. It has not been suggested that Minnesota usury laws would apply to such transactions. Although the convenience of modern mail permits Minnesota residents holding Omaha Bank's BankAmericards to receive loans without visiting Nebraska, credit on the use of their cards is nevertheless similarly extended by Omaha Bank in Nebraska by the bank's honoring of the sales drafts of participating Minnesota merchants and banks. Finance charges on the unpaid balances of cardholders are assessed by the bank in Omaha, Neb., and all payments on unpaid balances are remitted to the bank in Omaha, Neb. Furthermore, the bank issues its BankAmericards in Omaha, Neb., after credit assessments made by the bank in that city. . . .

Nor can the fact that Omaha Bank's BankAmericards are used "in transactions with Minnesota merchants" be determinative of the bank's location for purposes of § 85. The bank's BankAmericards enables its holder "to purchase goods and services from participating merchants and obtain cash advances from participating banks throughout the United States and the world." . . . Minnesota residents can thus use their Omaha Bank BankAmericards to purchase services in the State of New York or mail-order goods from the State of Michigan. If the location of the bank were to depend on the whereabouts of each credit-card transaction, the meaning of the term "located" would be so stretched as to throw into confusion the complex system of modern interstate banking. A national bank could never be certain whether its contacts with residents of foreign States were sufficient to alter its location for purposes of § 85. We do not choose to invite these difficulties by rendering so elastic the term "located." The mere fact that Omaha Bank has enrolled Minnesota residents, merchants, and banks in its BankAmericard program thus does not suffice to "locate" that bank in Minnesota for purposes of 12 U.S.C. § 85. *See Second Nat. Bank of Leavenworth v. Smoot*, 9 D.C. 371, 373 (1876).

III

Since Omaha Bank and its BankAmericard program are "located" in Nebraska, the plain language of § 85 provides that the bank may charge "on any loan" the rate "allowed" by the State of Nebraska. Petitioners contend, however, that this reading of the statute violates the basic legislative intent of the National Bank Act. *See Train v. Colorado Public Interest Research Group*, 426 U. S. 1, 9-10 (1976). At the time Congress enacted § 30 of the National Bank Act of 1864, 13 Stat. 108, so petitioners' argument runs, it intended "to insure competitive equality between state and national banks in the charging of interest." . . . This policy could best be effectuated by limiting national banks to the rate of interest allowed by the States in which the banks were located. Since Congress in 1864 was addressing a financial system in which incorporated banks were "local institutions," it did not "contemplate a national bank soliciting customers and entering loan agreements outside of the state in which it was established." . . . Therefore to interpret § 85 to apply to interstate loans such as those involved in this case would not only enlarge impermissibly the original intent of Congress, but would also undercut the basic policy foundations of the statute by upsetting the competitive equality now existing between state and national banks.

We cannot accept petitioners' argument. Whatever policy of "competitive equality" has been discerned in other sections of the National Bank Act, see *e.g.*, *First Nat. Bank v. Dickinson*, 396 U. S. 122, 131 (1969); *First Nat. Bank of Logan v. Walker Bank & Trust Co.*, 385 U. S. 252, 261-262 (1966), § 30 and its descendants have been interpreted for over a century to give "advantages to National banks over their State competitors." *Tiffany v. National Bank of Missouri*, 18 Wall. 409. 413 (1874). "National banks," it was said in *Tiffany*, "have been National favorites." The policy of competitive equality between state and national banks, however, is not truly at the core of this case. Instead we are confronted by the inequalities that occur when a national bank applies the interest rates of its home State in its dealing with residents of a foreign State. These inequalities affect both national and state banks in the foreign State. Indeed, in the instant case Marquette is a national bank claiming to be injured by the unequal interest rates charged by another national bank. Whether the inequalities which thus occur when the interest rates of one State are "exported" into another violate the intent of Congress in enacting § 30 in part depends on whether Congress in 1864 was aware of the existence of a system of interstate banking in which such inequalities would seem a necessary part.

Close examination of the National Bank Act of 1864, its legislative history, and its historical context makes clear that, contrary to the suggestion of petitioners, Congress intended [315] to facilitate what Representative Hooper termed a "national banking system." Cong. Globe, 38th Cong., 1st Sess., 1451 (1864). . . . Section 31 of the Act, for example, fully recognized the interstate nature of American banking by providing that three-fifths of the 15% of the aggregate amount of their notes in circulation that national banks were required to "have on hand, in lawful money" could

> "consist of balances due to an association available for the redemption of its circulating notes from associations approved by the comptroller of the currency, organized under this act, in the cities of Saint Louis, Louisville, Chicago, Detroit, Milwaukie [*sic*], New Orleans, Cincinnati, Cleveland, Pittsburg, Baltimore, Philadelphia, Boston, New York, Albany, Leavenworth, San Francisco, and Washington City." 13 Stat. 108, 109.

The debates surrounding the enactment of this section portray a banking system of great regional interdependence. . . .

Although in the debates surrounding the enactment of § 30 there is no specific discussion of the impact of interstate loans, these debates occurred in the context of a developed interstate loan market. . . . Evidence of this market is to be found in the numerous judicial decisions in cases arising out of interstate loan transactions. . . .

We cannot assume that Congress was oblivious to the existence of such common commercial transactions. We find it implausible to conclude, therefore, that Congress meant through its silence to exempt interstate loans from the reach of § 30. We would certainly be exceedingly reluctant to read such a hiatus into the regulatory scheme of § 30 in the absence of evidence of specific congressional intent. Petitioners have adduced no such evidence.

Petitioners' final argument is that the "exportation" of interest rates, such as occurred in this case, will significantly impair the ability of States to enact effective usury laws. This impairment, however, has always been implicit in the structure of the National Bank Act, since citizens of one State were free to visit a neighboring State to receive credit at foreign interest rates. . . . This impairment may in fact be accentuated by the ease with which interstate credit is available by mail through the use of modern credit cards. But the protection of state usury laws is an issue of legislative policy, and any plea to alter § 85 to further that end is better addressed to the wisdom of Congress than to the judgment of this Court.

Affirmed.

---

1. ***Competitive Equality versus National Favorites.*** *Marquette* spotlights the tension between two competing policies with respect to national banks: competitive equality and national favorites. Competitive equality is the idea that banks with one type of charter should not be at a material competitive disadvantage to banks with the other type of charter. National favorites is the idea that national banks should be entitled to preferential treatment. Pertinent to *Marquette*, interest rates historically were governed solely by state law. Along with the National Bank Act came 12 U.S.C. § 85 (1980), which authorizes a national bank to charge interest at the rate allowed by the laws of the state where that bank is located (except that, if a state provides a different rate for state banks, then that rate is allowed for national banks), or at 1% above the discount rate of its district Federal Reserve Bank, whichever is higher. 12 U.S.C. § 85 has been the source of extensive litigation for over 100 years. While the text of the provision suggests competitive equality, the regulatory elaboration of the provision contains an important additional facet, the concept of most favored lender, which allows a national bank to charge the same rate as any competing lender in the state for a specified class of loans. *See* 12 C.F.R. § 7.4001(c). Given the various differences between national and state charters, can the policies of competitive equality and national favorites coexist, or must one necessarily dominate the other? Ultimately, do the policies serve any purpose today? As for *Marquette* itself, which policy does the Court advance? Is your answer affected by the fact that *Marquette* involves not a suit between a national and a state bank, but rather "a national bank claiming to be injured by the unequal interest rates charged by another national bank"?

2. ***Marquette's Implications for State Banks.*** *Marquette* held that a national bank chartered in one state could export that state's interest rates to its dealings in another state. Given *Marquette's* rationale, does its holding extend to state banks? Can a state bank chartered in Nebraska export Nebraskan interest rates to its dealings in Minnesota? How do the policies of competitive equality and national favorites play out differently when the actors involved are all state banks?

B. *MARQUETTE* AND RESPONSES TO IT

1. Legal Developments

The Supreme Court's decision in *Marquette* spurred significant developments in usury and related areas of law. The first significant post-*Marquette* reaction was the move by some states, such as South Dakota, toward lenient usury laws in an effort to attract national banks. Indeed, South Dakota itself removed "usury ceilings on consumer loan receivables." *In re* Citibank (South Dakota), N.A., 67 FED. RES. BULL. 181 (1981). As a result of geographic restrictions in place at the time, banks such as Citibank had to set up banking affiliates in order to take advantage of South Dakota's favorable laws. *See id.*

("South Dakota amended its banking laws to permit an out-of-state bank holding company to acquire a single new bank located in the state."). Such acquisitions required approval by the Federal Reserve Board, which approved of Citigroup's move into South Dakota, observing that,

> [Citigroup's affiliate] will not solicit or encourage personal or commercial deposits or loans from customers in South Dakota . . . [t]he proposal is thus essentially an internal reorganization that will not alter the number of firms or the structure of the national market for bank credit card services. . . . Accordingly, the overall competitive effects of the proposal are consistent with approval.

Id. While the response to *Marquette* by states like Delaware could be viewed as an example of innovative federalism, this kind of maneuvering by states and banks might arguably be characterized as a race to the bottom in usury standards. It might also lead one to ask whether Congress intended for the National Bank Act to empower a bank's home state to overrule interest rate regulation in a credit card borrower's state? Did Congress authorize the law of all other states to be overruled by South Dakota or Delaware?

In response to the high interest rates of the 1970s and early 1980s, which increasingly burdened state chartered banks, as well as the growing trend of interest rate exportation by national banks, Congress passed § 521 of the Depository Institutions Deregulation and Monetary Control Act of 1980 (DIDMCA) in 1980. Section 521 provided state chartered, federally insured banks with the power to charge "interest at a rate of not more than 1 per centum in excess of the discount rate on ninety-day commercial paper in effect at the Federal Reserve Bank in the Federal Reserve district where such State bank . . . is located or at the rate allowed by the laws of the State, territory, or district where the bank is located, whichever may be greater." 12 U.S.C. 1831d(a) (1989). In effect, § 521 functions as the equivalent of a § 85 for state banks, allowing them to engage in interest rate exportation, too. This interpretation was confirmed by *Greenwood Trust Co. v. Commonwealth of Massachusetts*, 971 F.2d 818 (1st Cir. 1992), *cert. denied*, 506 U.S. 1052 (1993), where the state of Massachusetts challenged the exportation of late fees by a Delaware-chartered bank to Massachusetts residents. At the time, Massachusetts law prohibited the imposition of exported late fees, while Delaware law permitted it. The *Greenwood Trust* court held in favor of exportation, reasoning that § 521, like its "direct lineal ancestor," § 85, extends to a "wide variety of fees and charges" and thus preempts state laws that limit exportation. *Id.* at 830. Furthermore, the Supreme Court in *Smiley v. Citibank (South Dakota), N.A.*, 517 U.S. 735 (1996) agreed with and extended *Greenwood Trust*, holding that a *national* bank could export late fees as part of the interest rate law of the state where it is located.

As *Greenwood Trust* and *Smiley* demonstrate, the federal exportation statutes have been interpreted to encompass not just what one might traditionally think of as interest rates, but also late fees and other charges. The OCC and the FDIC have also leaned toward generous interpretations of these statutes. *See, e.g.*, 12 C.F.R. § 7.4001 (implementing a broad definition of interest under § 85); FDIC, General Counsel's Opinion No. 10; Interest Charges Under § 27 of the Federal Deposit Insurance Act, 63 Fed. Reg. 19258 (Apr. 17,

1998) ("While neither § 85 nor § 27 defines what charges constitute 'interest', court decisions have not limited the scope of the term solely to a state's numerical percentage rate, but have broadly construed the term to include various other types of credit charges."). In light of the judicial and agency interpretations in this area, it is a fair question to ask whether the credit card borrower's jurisdiction retains any meaningful control over the credit terms charged by out-of-state lenders.

The Riegle-Neal Interstate Banking and Branching Efficiency Act of 1994 (Riegle-Neal Act), allowed national banks to branch across state lines, thus altering a "basic assumption" of *Marquette* that the national bank headquartered in Nebraska "did not, and *legally could not*, have a branch in Minnesota." Elizabeth R. Schiltz, *The Amazing, Elastic, Ever-Expanding Exportation Doctrine and Its Effect on Predatory Lending Regulation*, 88 MINN. L. REV. 518, 548 (2004). The passage of the Riegle-Neal Act thus raised the question whether national banks such as Citibank still needed to set up banking affiliates to export interest rates from states such as South Dakota, or whether branches would suffice for exportation purposes. The OCC, as the primary regulator of national banks, answered this question a few years later, interpreting the Act to mean that "a bank can be 'located' in either its home state or any of its host states [*i.e.*, states where the bank has branches]," and that "a bank [can] export rates from either location, depending on where the loan is 'made'." *Id.* at 556; *see also* OFFICE OF THE COMPTROLLER OF THE CURRENCY, Interpretive Letter No. 822, 1997-1998 Transfer Binder, FED. BANKING L. REP. (CCH) P 81,265 (Feb. 17, 1998). The test for determining where a loan is made has in turn been interpreted generously by the OCC: if at least one of three lending functions—the decision to extend credit, the extension of credit itself, and the disbursal of loan proceeds—is not performed in a state, then the loan is not deemed to have been made in that state. *See* Schiltz, *The Amazing, Elastic, Ever-Expanding Exportation Doctrine*, at 554–55. In this scenario, it is then possible that either the home or host state rates may be applied.

Another issue worth briefly considering is how long a loan needs to stay on the books of a lending institution for an exported interest rate to travel with the loan if the loan is then later sold. A closely related issue is whether a bank, which clearly enjoys the ability to export interest rates under either § 85 or § 512, can assign exported interest rates along with a loan to a non-bank entity. Put another way, can a non-bank entity, as assignee of a bank, charge interest at the rate the bank itself could have charged? The prevailing position in the courts, which is also the prevailing assumption in financial services, had been that exportation by non-bank assignees is perfectly acceptable. *See, e.g.*, Krispin v. May Dep't Stores Co., 218 F.3d 919 (8th Cir. 2000). A nationwide business of loan sales and securitization has relied upon this view. At least one court, however, has challenged this position, thus creating a circuit split. *See* Madden v. Midland Funding LLC, 768 F.3d 246 (2015) (holding that the National Bank Act did not preempt the claims of a credit card customer against a non-bank debt collector who had purchased the customer's debt from a national bank and attempted to charge and collect on higher, exported interest rates).

2. Developments in Credit Card Markets

Marquette and its progeny also spurred significant developments in consumer lending in the United States. Since *Marquette*, the market for credit card loans has become a national market, exhibiting both substantial concentration and economies of scale. As Figure 1.4-1 demonstrates, in 2015, the six largest credit card issuers accounted for 66.5% of the total market share.

Figure 1.4-1 Concentration of Total Market Share among Credit Card Issuers

JPMorgan Chase & Co.
Capital One Financial Corporation
Discover Financial Inc.

15.8 | 14.1 | 13.2 | 10.6 | 7.2 | 5.6 | 33.5

American Express Company
Bank of America Corporation
Citigroup Inc.
Other

Source: IBISWorld, Industry Report 52221: Credit Card Issuing in the US (Mar. 2015).

These issuers have acquired and maintained their dominant positions due in part to the high barriers to entry in the credit card issuing sector, including "tight regulations, high firm concentration, large capital requirements[,] and loyal customer bases due to reward programs." IBISWORLD, INDUSTRY REPORT 52221: CREDIT CARD ISSUING IN THE US 23 (Mar. 2015). Moreover, all six of these issuers issue credit cards internationally, further cementing their competitive edge. *See id.* Looking at the sector as a whole, despite *Marquette's* permissiveness with regard to interest rate exportation, issuers face at least some pressures to focus on lowering interest rates and improving card reward programs, in large part due to increased external and internal competition, as well as "the increased responsiveness of credit card interest rates to issuers' costs of funds in recent years as more issuers have tied their interest rates directly to one of several indexes that move with market rates." *Id.* at 22. The processing side of the sector exhibits somewhat lower but still significant levels of concentration. In 2015, for example, the four largest credit card processers (Visa, KKR & Co., American Express, and MasterCard) accounted for 40.3% of total market share. IBISWORLD, INDUSTRY REPORT 52232: CREDIT CARD PROCESSING & MONEY TRANSFERRING IN THE US 27 (Jan. 2015). As compared to the credit card issuing sector, levels of concentration are lower because the credit card processing sector "comprises a wide variety of companies with different specialties," including "check processing, automated clearinghouse (ACH) payments, wire transfers, debit card servicing[,] and credit card purchases." *Id.* at 22. Significant levels of concentration, however, are still possible due in part to barriers to entry in this sector, such as "capital requirements needed to stay up to date with [processing] technology." *Id.*

The Financial Crisis spurred the passage of legislation designed to protect credit card borrowers, signaling the federal government's newfound willingness to become more directly involved in credit card oversight. The Credit Card Responsibility and Disclosure Act of 2009 (CARD Act) imposes restrictions on rate increases and calls for greater transparency and accountability on the part of card issuers. *See* IBISWORLD, INDUSTRY REPORT 52221, at 27. The Act, however, does not set usury limits, and the CFPB is specifically precluded from doing so by the Dodd-Frank Act. *See* 12 U.S.C. § 5517(o) ("No provision of this title shall be construed as conferring authority on the Bureau to establish a usury limit applicable to an extension of credit offered or made by a covered person to a consumer, unless explicitly authorized by law."). For an empirical assessment of the Act's effects on credit card pricing, *see, e.g.*, Oren Bar-Gill & Ryan Bubb, *Credit Card Pricing: The CARD Act and Beyond*, 97 CORNELL L. REV. 967 (2012); Sumit Agarwal et al., *Regulating Consumer Financial Products: Evidence from Credit Cards*, 130 Q. J. ECON. 111 (2015).

The purpose these first four chapters has been to provide an introduction to the financial sector and its regulatory frameworks. One excellent post-Financial Crisis theoretical analysis suggests that there was a "serious failure of prevailing wisdom" in financial regulation, because the financial sector changed more comprehensively than the regulatory frameworks. JOHN ARMOUR ET AL., PRINCIPLES OF FINANCIAL REGULATION (Oxford Univ. Press, forthcoming 2016). The co-authors point to the structural separation of U.S. financial regulation into banking and securities spheres in the wake of the New Deal. The co-authors suggest that "the resulting intellectual partition has continued to frame debates in US law schools and policy circles ever since" and that "the idea of the partition was exported to frame the structure of financial regulation in the EU and elsewhere, and continues to do so even post-crisis." *Id.*

CHAPTER 1.5

A TOUR OF THE BALANCE SHEET

CONTENTS

I. INTRODUCTION

In Chapter 1.1, you were introduced to the different types of financial intermediaries that serve a wide variety of roles in the financial system. Some of these functions are advisory, such as when a securities firm makes recommendations to a customer about stock purchases or an insurance company offers advice about how much a couple should set aside in savings for retirement. In many other contexts, however, financial institutions themselves participate in financial transactions by obtaining funds from customers, depositors, or investors, which together constitute the public, and reinvesting those funds by making loans to consumers or businesses, or by making investments in government or businesses, all of which goes back to that same public. The financial institution is an intermediary between those members of the public with excess funds, called savers, and those members of the public in need of additional funding, or borrowers.

Financial intermediaries can be broadly grouped into two types: depository institutions and non-depository institutions. In short hand, they are often referred to as banks and non-banks. Broadly speaking, depository institutions are funded by deposits. Examples of depository institutions include commercial banks, thrifts, and credit unions. Non-depository institutions may include bank holding companies (BHCs), insurance companies, securities firms, mutual funds, payday lenders, private equity funds, hedge funds, and pension plans. Financial intermediaries may be hybrid in form, and the trend has been towards institutions that perform multiple functions within one consolidated group, often referred to as a financial conglomerate. There is also a tendency for financial intermediary functions to overlap among different types of institutions. This overlap poses a particular challenge for regulators, since, as you saw in Chapters 1.3 and 1.4, the United States has a fragmented system of regulators overseeing different types of institutions on a functional basis.

In this book, we will also explore instances of disintermediation, such as the rise of the commercial paper market, where large commercial borrowers sought funding from the capital markets, as well as reintermediation, such as money market funds and securitization, where new kinds of intermediaries rose up and took business away from traditional forms. We will also consider new forms of direct finance, such as crowdfunding and peer-to-peer lending, where small businesses, non-profits, individuals, and startups have begun to turn directly to individual investors to provide their financing needs. *See, e.g.*, Moorad Choudhry, *Why We All Need Banks*, CNBC (July 7, 2014).

In order to gain a deeper understanding of many of the concepts you will encounter throughout the course of this book, it is important to have an understanding of some of the key principles of accounting. The regulation of financial institutions does not exist in a vacuum. Rather, it is deeply informed by and intertwined with how financial institutions and the financial system operate as a business and the accounting principles that apply to them. To get through this chapter, you do not need any prior knowledge of accounting.

II. AN INTRODUCTION TO FINANCIAL STATEMENTS

In this Chapter, we first examine basic accounting concepts that are integral to understanding the financial system and its regulation. We then turn our discussion to financial institutions' financial statements. Typically, there are four financial statements: (1) the Balance Sheet, (2) the Income Statement, (3) the Cash Flow Statement, and (4) the Statement of Changes in Shareholders' Equity. We first examine the balance sheet, which provides insight into how various financial intermediaries are structured and how they interact with one another. We then look at the income statement that describes the revenue and expenses of the firm, which together determine a firm's profitability.

A. THE BALANCE SHEET

The balance sheet gives a snapshot of an entity's financial position at a particular point in time, for example, the end of the fiscal period, which is often, but not always, December 31. Typically, balance sheets of two or more prior periods are juxtaposed so as to show the changes between these snapshots. A balance sheet is composed of three components: assets, liabilities, and equity, also known as shareholders' equity, which we will refer to as equity for the sake of convenience. The balance sheet's foundation equation is shown in Figure 1.5-1.

Figure 1.5-1 The Accounting Equation of Balance Sheets

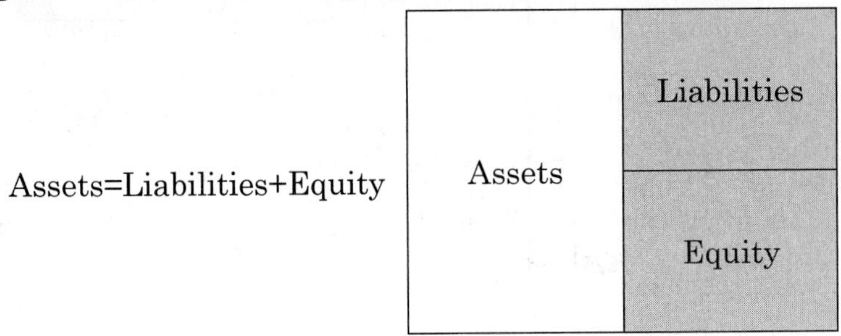

The balance sheet must balance, that is, assets must always be equal to liabilities plus equity. This equation will always hold true. One can see from the equation that assets minus liabilities equals equity, hence equity is the difference between assets and liabilities. If liabilities exceed assets, which can happen when a firm becomes insolvent, the firm is said to have negative equity.

1. Assets

The asset side of the balance sheet—the left hand side—is a list of a firm's economic resources at a particular time. It is expressed as showing asset values "as of" a date, such as "as of December 31, 2015." Under established accounting principles, assets are resources with "probable future economic benefits obtained or controlled by an entity resulting from past transactions or events." *See* Howell E. Jackson et al., *Analytical Methods for Lawyers* 113 (Foundation Press 2d ed. 2011). Assets therefore have to arise from past transactions or events, meaning that economic benefits emanating from future or even imminent transactions are not assets.

To make these concepts a bit more concrete, we present below in Figure 1.5-2 General Motors's balance sheets for the fiscal years ending 12/31/2012 and 12/31/2013.

Figure 1.5-2 General Motors Balance Sheets

General Motors Balance Sheet as of Year-End 2013 and 2012 (*$ millions*)					
Assets			**Liabilities**		
	12/31/13	**12/31/12**		**12/31/13**	**12/31/12**
Cash and Cash Equivalents	$ 21,268	$ 19,108	Accounts Payable	$ 48,254	$ 48,474
Short-Term Investments	8,972	8,988	Short-Term Debt	14,158	1,748
Net Receivables	33,162	23,868			
Inventory	14,039	14,714			
Other Current Assets	4,060	3,318	Other Current Liabilities		3,770
Total Current Assets	**81,501**	**69,996**	**Total Current Liabilities**	**62,412**	**53,992**
			Long-Term Debt	22,025	3,424
Long-Term Investments	22,448	13,837	Other Liabilities	39,300	55,762
Property Plant and Equipment	29,250	25,845	**Total Liabilities**	**$ 123,737**	**$ 113,178**
			Equity		
Goodwill	1,560	1,973	Stock (Common and Preferred); Additional Paid-in Capital	$ 28,791	$ 26,187
Intangible Assets	5,668	6,809	Retained Earnings	13,816	10,057
Other Assets	25,917	30,962	**Total Equity**	**42,607**	**36,244**
Total Assets	**$ 166,344**	**$ 149,422**	**Total Liabilities and Equity**	**$ 166,344**	**$ 149,422**

Focus on the asset side of these balances sheets. By convention, assets are listed in the United States from the most liquid, such as *cash and cash equivalents*, to the least liquid. As its name suggests, cash equivalents are non-cash assets that are as liquid as cash, such as checks yet to be deposited, checking and savings accounts, and short-term highly-liquid investments with maturity less than three months, such as U.S. treasury bills or commercial paper. The upper left part of the balance sheet includes the *current assets*, which are assets expected to be turned into cash within one year. After *cash and cash equivalents* are *short-term investments*, which are expected to be sold or liquidated within one year, followed typically by the *receivables*, which are payments due and owed to the company by customers. Next is the inventory line, which accounts for products in stock available for sale, like cars and trucks. All these are expected to be turned into cash within one year. At the lower left part of the balance sheet is the long-term, less liquid assets, such as *long-term investments*, which are expected to be held for more than one year, and *property plant and equipment*, such as buildings and equipment. These long-term assets are not expected to be turned into cash by sale within one year. Note that *intangible assets* fall last on the balance sheet because they are the least liquid.

By comparing the two year ends, you can learn about the change in the entity's assets. In our example, you can see that GM's *total assets* grew around $17 billion between the two dates. You can also see that *cash and cash equivalents* grew around $2 billion. Total assets increased by some $17 billion. How did GM fund its growth in assets during 2013? By looking only at the asset side of the balance sheet, you cannot learn where the funds needed to make these changes came from. To understand changes in funding, you need to look at the other side of balance sheet. The $17 billion increase in total assets could be attributed to three sources: (1) an increase in liabilities, which would mean that the firm has taken more debt, (2) an increase in equity accounts that could happen if the firm sold more of it shares to existing or new shareholders, or (3) an increase in retained earnings, if the firm accumulated profits over the past year. These three sources are shown on the liabilities and equity side of the balance sheet—the right hand side. We now turn to these accounts, starting first with liabilities.

2. Liabilities (including Debt)

Like assets, liabilities are divided into current and non-current liabilities, where non-current liabilities are obligations that are payable after one year. Liabilities are defined as "probable future sacrifices of economic benefits arising from present obligations to transfer assets or render services in the future as a result of past transactions or events." Jackson et al., *Analytical Methods for Lawyers*, at 116. A liability, therefore, is a claim on assets or future services of the firm. A lawsuit, for example, especially if at an early stage, is not a liability if it is not yet probable that liability will be found or damages awards.

Like assets, liabilities are generally listed in the United States from the closest to maturity to the least mature. *Accounts payable* is an account that shows how much money the company owes to its creditors, such as suppliers and vendors. *Short-term debt*, as opposed to *long-term debt*, is debt expected to be paid within one year. As can be seen in Figure 1.5-2, GM's *accounts payable* did not change a lot in 2013, whereas short-term debt increased by around $12.4 billion. Long-term debt also increased nearly $19 billion, and, all in all, total liabilities increased around $10.6 billion. Therefore, over $10 billion in the GM's growth in total assets in 2013 was funded through additional liabilities.

3. Equity

Equity in a typical corporation consists of capital that has been contributed by shareholders in the form of *stock* (*common* or *preferred*) plus accumulated profits, commonly known as retained earnings. Another item under equity called *additional paid-in capital* is money contributed in excess of the par value of stock. There are more accounts under equity and there is a whole financial statement called Statement of Changes in Shareholders' Equity that depicts the changes of the different items, but we will mainly focus on overall changes in GM's equity accounts and additions to *retained earnings*. Retained earnings are a measure of the firm's accumulated profits, chiefly a product of the firm's past undistributed income. When the firm distributes a dividend, on the other hand, it is subtracted from retained earnings. Other than for dividends, retained earnings could be used to fund firm activities, such as increases in total assets, and or to reduce (that is, repay) liabilities. We will revisit retained earnings after learning about the income statement.

4. Elaborations

Keep in mind that each section of the balance sheet is divided into many accounts and every transaction usually affects two accounts. For example:

- When a company takes a $100 loan from a bank or another creditor, its liabilities increase by $100 and its assets (cash) increase by a $100. When the company pays back its debt, its assets (cash) decrease by $100 and so do its liabilities, because the company has paid back its debt.

- When a company buys securities with cash it has on hand, only the asset side is affected, as the company turns cash (assets) into securities (assets), whether they are short- or long-term.
- When the company raises money by selling stock, its equity increases and so do its assets (cash).
- When a company distributes dividends to its shareholders, its cash decreases, and its retained earnings, or equity, decreases.

B. INCOME STATEMENT

Unlike the balance sheet, the income statement provides a summary of the entity's business activity over the time of the fiscal period (not a snapshot, but rather occurrences that took place during that period). It is expressed as showing income for a period, such as "for the period ending December 31, 2016" which means, in the case of fiscal year, from January 1, 2015 to December 31, 2016. The income statement focuses on revenues and expenses. Profit is generated when revenues exceed expenses. If expenses exceed revenues, the firm incurs a loss. Income statements usually begin with a measure of *total revenue*, also known as *sales*. *Total revenue* is then reduced by a cascade of expenses as follows:

1. The *cost of sales*, also known as *cost of goods*, is deducted from total revenue to get *gross income*, which is a measure of profitability. *Gross income* is also known as net revenue or net sales because it is revenue/sales after netting out the cost of sales.
2. Operating expenses, such as overhead costs, salaries, and administrative expenses, including research expenses, are deducted from gross income. The result is *operating income*. Outside of financial intermediaries, *operating income* is often referred to as EBITDA, which stands for earnings before (deducting) interest, tax, depreciation, and amortization. This is an important term for corporate valuation and investments and is frequently used by managers, investment bankers, and business consultants. Note that many firms use EBIT instead of EBITDA, which stands for earnings before interest and tax. In this case, depreciation and amortization are already deducted.
3. After deducting all the above from the *operating income*, the firm will be left with *net income*, or profits. Net income is then "poured into" *retained earnings* on the balance sheet, forming the link between the income statement and the balance sheet. The net income of a firm is thus ultimately reflected in the equity on its balance sheet. These earnings are either left in the company, and thus become a source of funding, in the form of one of the three funding sources mentioned earlier, or could be distributed to the shareholders as dividends or in some other way, such as a stock repurchase.

Take a look at General Motors's Income Statement in Figure 1.5-3. To facilitate analysis, we have simplified the statement and included columns reporting percentage. These columns would not appear in actual income statements.

Figure 1.5-3 General Motors Income Statement

General Motors Income Statement for 2013 (*$ millions)*			
		12/31/13	**% of Total Revenue**
Total Revenue	$	155,427	11.6%
Cost of Revenue (to deduct)		(137,373)	
Gross Profit		**18,054**	
Operating Expenses (to deduct):			
Selling, General and Administrative		(12,382)	
Other Expenses		(541)	
Operating Income		**5,131**	**3.3%**
Interest Expense (to deduct)		(334)	
Total Other Income (to add)		2,676	
Income Before Tax		**7,473**	
Tax Expense (to deduct)		(2,127)	
Net Income	**$**	**5,346**	**3.4%**

The largest number on this income statement is the company's *total revenue* (over $155 billion) offset by $137 billion in *cost of revenue*, generating a *gross profit* of $18 billion. Though GM now has many lines of business, you can conceptualize this as the firm's total car sales in the course of the year minus its cost of producing those cars. For ease of analysis, we have included to the right of the income statement a calculation of each figure as a percentage of *total revenue*. The cost of revenue was 88% of *total revenue*, leaving a gross margin of 12%. Using percentages of this sort makes it easier to make comparisons across different firms and over time.

If you work your way further down GM's income statement, you'll see that the firm also had substantial expenses ($12 billion or 8% of total revenue) for various kinds of overhead, such as the expense category denominated as *selling, general and administrative*. Typically, such a category would include lots of marketing and research costs, as well as expenses associated with senior management. Deducting these and other operating expenses leaves GM with operating income of $5 billion or 3% of total revenue. Next is an additional deduction for *interest expense*, which is the cost of debt, offset by other income, possibly including income on its auto financing activities, as well as taxes. This deduction leads to a bottom line, called *net income*, of $5.3 billion for 2013. This figure is 3% of *total revenue*. Notice that GM's profit for 2013 was only a small fraction of its total sales for the year.

Let's review the connection between the income statement and the balance sheet. *Net income* from the income statement is directly linked to the *equity* account in the balance sheet. As previously mentioned, *retained earnings*, a component under the equity, is the accumulated profits of the corporation. Every year, the *net income* a corporation makes is poured into this bucket called *retained earnings*. If, assuming all other variables are held constant, the number is positive, resulting in a profit, *retained earnings* will go up, and as will *equity*. Likewise, if the number is negative, resulting in a loss, *retained earnings* will go down and so will *equity*. Let us go back to the two figures above. *Net income* for

2013 was $5,346 billion. This amount is poured into the *retained earnings* according to this simplified formula:

Retained Earnings (RE) = RE from last year + Net Income – Dividends

Hence, RE (2013)=RE (2012)+Net Income (2013)–Dividends (2013). Plug in the values: 13,816=10,057+5,346–Dividends. GM therefore distributed $1,587 million in dividends in 2013.

Of course, this is a simplified formula that assumes there were no other income into or expenses out of the retained earnings account. This formula, with all its components, is contained in what is called the Statement of Changes in Shareholders' Equity, but we will not delve into it in this book. For our purposes, suffice it to know that *net income* from the income statement goes into the *retained earnings* on the balance sheet.

C. FINANCIAL RATIOS

Financial ratios offer valuable tools to analyze financial statements. This field of analysis is an important component of business school curricula and a significant part of what financial analysts at investment banks and consulting firms do. For corporate lawyers, literacy in the subject is required as financial ratios are drivers of the business deal and are routinely incorporated into legal documents. A firm's financial ratios are typically compared to the financial ratios of its peer group of competitors in the sector, thus giving the analyst a better idea of the company's performance relative to its peers at hand. While there are many financial ratios, we will focus on three categories of ratios: liquidity, solvency, and profitability.

1. Liquidity

Liquidity is the ability of a firm to meet its short-term financial obligations. Jackson et al., *Analytical Methods for Lawyers*, at 160. Liquidity describes the ease with which a firm's asset can be turned into cash, if required. For example, a one-year maturity receivable is more liquid than a five-year maturity one. Cash is the most liquid asset, but, as you will recall, all current assets are, by definition, convertible into cash within a year's time. Focused as it is on the conversion of assets to cash, liquidity analysis is centrally concerned with the asset side of the balance sheet. One way to assess liquidity is to determine how much cash, cash reserves, or current assets the firm has on hand at a given time. Another common measure is the *current ratio*, which is the ratio of current assets to current liabilities, where current means less than one year maturity.

$$\textit{Current Ratio} = \frac{\textit{Current Assets}}{\textit{Current Liabilities}}$$

As a rule of thumb, the current ratio should be greater than 1.5 to 2.0, that is, current assets should be at least 1.5 to two times as large as current liabilities. What was GM's current ratio at the end of 2012 and how did it change over the course of 2013?

2. Solvency

Solvency is the firm's ability to meet its long-term obligations. Financial analysts typically measure solvency by the *leverage ratio*, which is debt (liabilities) divided by equity. As leverage increases, a greater and greater share of the firm's assets are funded by debt as opposed to equity. A similar solvency measure is the *capital ratio*, which is equity over total assets, or, thanks to balance sheet equation, equity over liabilities plus equity. As a firm's leverage ratio increases, its capital ratio necessarily declines. Increased leverage and decreased capital ratios are associated with greater financial risk. Capital ratios in particular help detect a decline in the quality of a firm's assets, which can lead to a firm's becoming insolvent.

$$\textit{Leverage Ratio} = \frac{\textit{Debt}}{\textit{Equity}} \qquad \textit{Capital Ratio} = \frac{\textit{Equity}}{\textit{Total Assets}}$$

Take a look at GM's balance sheets. Notice that its leverage ratio declined from 3.1 to 2.8 between year-end 2012 and year-end 2013. Similarly, its capital ratio improved from 24.3% to 25.6% during the same period. As you will see shortly, compared to industrial companies like GM, banks and financial institutions are more highly levered and less well capitalized. Why should that be?

3. Profitability

Other financial measures focus on a firm's profitability. These are particularly important ratios for corporate valuations before investment decisions are made. One commonly used ratio outside of the financial sector is the firm's operating earnings (EBITDA or EBIT) to its sales revenue, referred to as the firm's operational margin. In our discussion of GM's income statement earlier, we were essentially performing a margin analysis when we noted how large the company's operating margin was as a percentage of total revenues.

Another approach to profitability analysis is to compare net income—that is a firm's bottom line—to its overall size. Return on total assets (ROA) describes the amount of profit that a firm earned on each dollar of assets. Return on equity (ROE) is measured by net income divided by equity, which is basically a measurement of shareholders' return on their investment. ROE increases if net income increases or equity decreases. We will revisit these ratios shortly.

$$\textit{Operational Margin} = \frac{\textit{Operating Income}}{\textit{Total Revenue}}$$

$$\textit{ROA} = \frac{\textit{Net Income}}{\textit{Total Assets}} \qquad \textit{ROE} = \frac{\textit{Net Income}}{\textit{Equity}}$$

In 2013, GM had a ROA of 3.21%, which means that, for every dollar of its \$166 billion in total assets, it made 3.21 cents of profit from its \$5.4 billion in net income. (Here and below, we use the amount of total assets at the end of the period to calculate ROA; in practice, it is more common to use average total assets during the period.) Meanwhile, GM's ROE that year was 12.5%, equaling the total return, \$5.4 billion, which its shareholders earned on the balance sheet value of the total equity account at year-end, \$42.6 billion. As long as a firm has some leverage and is not fully funded by equity, the ROE in years with positive net income will always be higher than the firm's ROA. Do you see why?

III. FINANCIAL STATEMENTS OF FINANCIAL INSTITUTIONS

We now will turn to the financial statements of the principal categories of financial institutions that we will be exploring throughout the chapters that follow. In addition to reviewing the basic contours of these statements, we will also focus on how different kinds of financial institutions generate a profit.

A. DEPOSITORY INSTITUTIONS

Depository institutions embrace a range of firms from commercial banks to thrifts to credit unions. The shared characteristic of these firms is their reliance on various forms of deposits to fund loans. When depository institutions take in deposits, they pay the depositors interest on the deposits, which is typically a low rate because liabilities are very liquid so the deposits can be withdrawn any time on demand. From the institution's point of view, these deposits are liabilities, or debt, to be paid back to the depositors whenever they demand it. The firms then use these funds to make loans to borrowers who need financial resources while charging them an interest rate higher than what the firms pay their demand depositors, thus profiting from the margin. This spread is one of the chief ways that depository institutions make money. The firm's net interest income is the difference between what it makes on loans and what it pays out on deposits. From the institution's point of view, these loans are assets because they are rights to receive money from borrowers at a later date. Unlike the deposits, however, these loans are illiquid because the bank cannot demand them back before the payment date. The firm has taken liquid cash from the depositors and turned it into an illiquid asset with a longer maturity. This intermediation is called maturity transformation or asset transformation. As discussed earlier, liquidity has a value in itself, and this explains why a depositor receives a lower interest rate on a demand deposit than on a fixed-term deposit.

Recording deposits as liabilities and loans as assets can be confusing and counterintuitive because a depository institution's balance sheet is in some sense opposite of that of most corporations, such as the GM example above. In terms of financial structure, when a depository institution takes in a deposit, its debt increases, and it becomes more levered. In terms of liquidity, a new deposit has the immediate effect of increasing a depository institution's liquid assets (cash). Typically, however, depository institutions use most of the funds they raise through deposit-taking to make loans to other customers, thereby decreasing cash and increasing long-term assets (loans) increase.

Using deposits to fund loans is inherently risky. One risk is the risk of asset-liability mismatch or maturity mismatch from possessing short-term liabilities (deposits) matched by longer-term assets (loans). Since deposits are typically payable on demand, they are short-term, and a firm cannot predict when customers might decide to withdraw their money in large amounts and demand more cash than what the firm has on hand because the firm has lent out this cash to borrowers in the form of longer-term loans. Many events can trigger the public's demand for their deposits, such as a holiday season or bank runs.

See Chapter 2.4 for more information on bank runs. If this happens, the bank could develop serious liquidity problems. To mitigate this and other systemic risks, regulators developed the fractional reserve system, where banks are required to hold a fraction of their highly-liquid deposits as reserves, say 10% for example, and the rest can be loaned out. These reserves are safety cushions for times when depositors withdraw above-average amounts of money. A bank that holds enough reserves to meet all depositor requests is considered to be very safe, but then has little excess funds to originate new loans, which is the key mode of profit generation for a bank and the key way that banks are able to support economic growth in the economy and fulfill their function as financial intermediaries.

Another risk that depository institutions may find themselves exposed to is the risk of insolvency that occurs when the loans that the firm has made go bad. This is a risk because high levels of loan losses deplete retained earnings and equity just as profits increase those accounts. A sudden decline in the value of a firm's assets can even lead to sudden insolvency. For example, if a commercial bank holds many loans to oil and gas companies and the price of oil drops precipitously, the loans can become uncollectible and wipe out the bank's capital reserves.

Liquidity crises, such as bank runs, can also lead to solvency concerns. Bank runs occur when a large number of depositors suddenly and simultaneously try to withdraw their deposits. A deposit run forces a bank to draw down its cash and sell its highly liquid investments in order to pay off depositors. Suppose an institution facing liquidity pressure runs out of cash and highly liquid investments to pay its depositors and now needs to sell off its less liquid assets, such as loans, quickly in order to obtain cash to pay its depositors. This panic, or fire sale, as it is often called, in turn causes the value of loans and other less liquid assets—reflected on the asset side of the balance sheet—to decline. This decline in the value of assets can deplete a firm's equity, hence affecting the firm's solvency, or ability to pay its creditors. Declines in general asset values, even if short lived, might trigger further bank runs in other institutions by signaling that other firms may have become more risky or even insolvent, thus inciting widespread panic. This is why there is no clear line between illiquidity and insolvency risk, especially in times of financial crisis.

1. Savings Bank

Having worked through this theoretical overview of the funding structure and attendant risk of depository institutions, let's take a look at some actual financial statements, starting with the Cambridge Savings Bank, a form of thrift institution based in Harvard Square. On the next page, you will find this firm's balance sheet as of year-end 2007, followed by its income statement for that fiscal year. All of the upcoming balance sheets and income statements in this Chapter are based on financial statements from 2007, right before the Financial Crisis when interest rates were at more normal levels than has been true in the years following the Financial Crisis. Note that, in 2007, the Federal Funds rate ranged between 4.25% and 4.75% and 10-year Treasuries yield ranged from 4.1% to 5.1%. To facilitate analysis, we have simplified the statements and included columns reporting percentage. These columns would not appear in actual financial statements.

Figure 1.5-4 Cambridge Savings Bank Balance Sheet

Cambridge Savings Bank Balance Sheet as of Year-End 2007 (*$ millions)*					
Assets		**% of Assets**	**Liabilities**		**% of Liabilities and Equity**
Cash and Due from Banks	$ 30.7	1.5%	Deposits	$ 1,600.5	77.6%
Investment Securities and Other Short-Term Holdings	496.7	24.1%	Other Liabilities	281.4	13.6%
Loans Secured by Real Estate	1,410.4	68.4			
Other Loans	48.2	2.3			
(Allowance for Possible Loan Losses)	(8.5)	(0.4%)			
Total Loans Net of Allowances	1,450.1	70.3%	**Total Liabilities**	**1,882.0**	91.3%
Premises and Equipment	18.4	0.9%			
Other Assets	66.5	3.2%	Equity	180.4	8.7%
Total Assets	**$ 2,062.4**	**100.0%**	**Total Liabilities and Equity**	**$ 2,062.4**	**100.0%**

Figure 1.5-5 Cambridge Savings Bank Income Statement

Cambridge Savings Bank Income Statement for 2007 (*$ millions)*			
		2007	**% of Total Interest Income**
Interest on Investment Securities and Other Short-Term Holdings	$	27.1	
Interest on Loans Secured by Real Estate		83.8	
Interest on Other Loans		3.6	
Total Interest Income		**114.5**	**100.0%**
Interest Expense on Deposits		(51.9)	
Interest Expense on Other Liabilities		(12.1)	
Total Interest Expense		**(64.0)**	**(55.9%)**
Provision for Possible Loan Losses		(0.0)	
Net Interest Income	$	**50.5**	**44.1%**
Non-Interest Income (to add)		6.5	
Salaries and Benefits (to deduct)		(27.9)	
Office Occupancy and Equipment (to deduct)		(6.5)	
Other Expenses (to deduct)		(11.8)	
Total Non-Interest Expense		**(46.2)**	**(40.3%)**
Net Non-Interest Income		**(39.7)**	**(34.7%)**
Income Before Taxes		**10.8**	**9.4%**
Taxes (to deduct)		(3.6)	
Net Income	**$**	**7.3**	**6.4%**

For assets, as you can see in Figure 1.5-4, *cash and due from bank* is the equivalent of *cash and cash equivalents* for real economy corporations. Below that is *investment securities* and *other short-term holdings*, which are comparable to *short-term investments* on the GM balance sheet. All of these are current assets. Collectively, these current assets account for over one-quarter of the Cambridge Savings Bank's total assets (1.5% plus 24.1%). The next asset listed, *loans secured by real estate* are long-term assets, similar to *long-term investments*, and account for some 68.4% of total assets. The firm has a smaller amount of *other loans* plus relatively modest holdings of *premises and equipment,* which is equivalent of *property plant and equipment* on the GM balance sheet, plus a limited number of *other assets.* The liabilities and equity section of the Cambridge Savings Bank balance sheet is relatively straightforward. Deposits and other liabilities is the only category under liabilities, while the lion's share of the firm's assets (77.6%) are funded by deposits. Together, these liabilities fund 91.3% of *total assets*, implying, as a result of the fundamental balance sheet equation, that equity backs only 8.7% of *total assets.*

Having worked our way around the Cambridge Savings Bank balance sheet, consider for a moment how it compares to the GM balance sheet we explored earlier. For one thing, Cambridge Savings Bank is a good deal smaller than GM, with only $2 billion in total assets as compared with GM's total assets of over $166 billion. While GM has a reasonable amount of cash and net receivables, its assets are dominated by inventory, long-term investments, and property in the form of plants and equipment. The assets of Cambridge Savings Bank are overwhelmingly dedicated to loans. This heavy investment in loans means that the Cambridge Bank's current ratio, current assets divided by current liabilities, is much lower than GM's. Also, Cambridge Savings Bank is much more highly leveraged than GM, with a capital ratio of only 8.7% compared with GM's 25.6%. Do these differences mean that Cambridge Savings Bank is risker than GM?

Let us turn now to the income statement of Cambridge Savings Bank, Figure 1.5-5. The structure of this statement is quite different from GM's income statement. The top of the Cambridge Savings Bank income statement is focused on interest income, which is collected from investments and loans. Interest expenses on deposits and other liabilities are subtracted from interest income, and a further adjustment is made for loan loss revenues (a subject you will explore in Chapter 2.5, but left largely to the side for now), leading to *net interest income.* This line, with a total of $50.5 million, represents the contribution to income from Cambridge Savings Bank's financial intermediation, raising funds primarily through deposits and allocating those funds to investments and loans. Even though industrial companies like GM have both liabilities and investments, net interest income is not typically a major component of their income statements. For depository institutions by contrast, net interest income is of central importance.

The bottom half of the Cambridge Savings Bank income statement reports on non-interest items, including *non-interest income*, such as fees earned on safe deposit boxes, credit card fees, and overdraft charges, and non-interest expenses, like salaries, office space, and taxes. In the case of Cambridge Savings Bank, its non-interest income and expenses yield a negative $39.7 million in *net non-interest income*, and so the firm's total *income before taxes* is only $10.8 million. Its *net income*, or income after taxes, is $7.3 million.

If one were to evaluate the profitability of Cambridge Savings Bank, it is clear that most of its income comes from financial intermediation. With a bit of effort, one can deconstruct the components of that contribution. On the asset side, its investment securities and short-term holdings seem to yield about 5.5% (interest of $27.1 million divided by year-end holdings of $496.7). By similar calculations, its real estate loans yield 5.9% and its other loans 7.5%. In terms of funding costs, Cambridge Savings Bank's deposits cost about 3.2% in 2007 ($51.9 million divided by $1,600.5 million) and its other liabilities cost about 4.3%. Earning higher rates of interest on its loans than it pays on its liabilities is what makes intermediation profitable for Cambridge Savings Bank and most other depository institutions. A depository institution's interest margin, the amount by which its interest income exceeds interest expense, is roughly analogous to the operating margin of an industrial company like GM.

As previously discussed, another approach to profitability is ROA, or return on assets, which reflects the net income made for each dollar of assets. The Cambridge Saving Bank's ROA in 2007 was equal to 0.35% ($7.3 million divided by $2,062.4 million). Depository institutions typically have a low ROA relative to industrial firms like GM. Comparing their ROA to that of non-financial firms, however, can be misleading. According to FDIC data at the end of 2007, the average ROA for a savings bank was 0.91% and for commercial banks was 1.20%.

Another measure of profitability is ROE, the ratio of a firm's net income to total equity. Cambridge Savings Bank's ROE in 2007 was 4.05% (that is, $7.3 million divided by $180.4 million). By comparison, FDIC data indicates that the average ROE for a savings bank in the fourth quarter of 2007 was 7.72%, while the average ROE for commercial banks was 12.18%. Notice that this average ROE for commercial banks was fairly close to GM's ROE in 2013 (12.5%), even though average ROA for commercial banks was at 1.20% was much lower than GM's 3.21%. How would you explain that result?

---

1. ***Problem.*** Assume that you work for a management consultant that the Board of Directors has brought in to review the operations and, most importantly, the profitability of Cambridge Savings Bank. You've been charged with devising a plan to bring the Cambridge Savings Bank up to a level of above-average ROE for a savings bank. The Board would like a menu of at least a half a dozen options for how it might go about achieving this goal. What would you recommend?

---

2. Commercial Bank

Let's turn now to another set of financial statements, this time for a commercial bank, the Fifth Third Bancorp, which is a regional BHC headquartered in Cincinnati, Ohio, whose principal operating subsidiary is the Fifth Third National Bank. Once again, we have chosen to use financial statements from 2007 as they reflect a more normal interest rate environment. In this example, you are looking at the consolidated balance sheet of the holding company, which includes the bank as its subsidiary.

Start by taking a look at the Fifth Third Bancorp balance sheet, Figure 1.5-6. How is it similar to or different from the balance sheet of Cambridge Savings Bank? To begin with, Fifth Third Bancorp is dramatically larger with $111 billion in total assets versus just over $2 billion in total assets for Cambridge Savings Bank. Scale aside, however, there are important structural similarities between the two balance sheets. Like Cambridge Savings Bank, Fifth Third Bancorp allocates the lion's share of its assets to loans, and receives most of its funding from deposits, although the commercial bank has both domestic and foreign deposits, so it is international in a way that Cambridge Savings Bank is not. See Chapter 6.3 for more on cross border banking. Fifth Third Bancorp is also somewhat less reliant on deposits than Cambridge Savings Bank and makes greater use of other sources of funding, like long-term debt and shorter-term funding, including repurchase agreements or repos. Larger commercial banks, such as Fifth Third Bancorp and other financial intermediaries, have another source of liquidity known as the repo market, an area we will discuss in some detail in Chapter 12.4. Under repurchase agreements, banks sell low-risk, liquid securities to institutional and governmental buyers who pay cash and hold the securities for a short period of time, ranging from overnight to a month. Then, the bank buys the securities back. Because this period is very short, the purchase and sale looks more like borrowing and lending, and it provides banks with liquidity at a low cost. When these institutional or governmental entities sell the securities back to the bank, they make a small margin, akin to an interest payment, and the transaction usually involves low risk because the securities are very liquid and usually almost riskless.

Now that you have oriented yourself with the Fifth Third Bancorp balance sheet, take your own hand to comparing Fifth Third Bancorp's profitability to that of Cambridge Savings Bank. How do its cost of funds and yield on loans compare? Does it have the same business model as Cambridge Savings Bank? If not, how does its business model differ? Is it more or less profitable? Is it more or less safe?

Figure 1.5-6 Fifth Third Bancorp Balance Sheet

Fifth Third Bancorp Balance Sheet as of Year-End 2007
($ millions)

Assets		% of Assets	Liabilities		% of Liabilities and Equity
Cash and Demand Balances Due from Bank	$ 2,687	2.4%	Deposits in Domestic Offices	$ 69,992	63.1%
Portfolio Securities and Other Short-Term Holdings	11,796	10.6%	Deposits in Foreign Offices	5,453	4.9%
			Total Deposits	75,445	68.0%
Loans and Leases Net of Allowances	83,645	75.4%	Repos and other Short-Term Borrowings	9,174	8.3%
Premises and Equipment	2,576	2.3%	Accrued Taxes, Interest and Expenses	2,427	2.2%
			Long-Term Debt	12,857	11.6%
			Other Liabilities	1,898	1.7%
			Total Liabilities	**101,801**	91.7%
Other Assets	10,258	9.2%	Equity	9,161	8.3%
Total Assets	**$ 110,962**	**100.0%**	**Total Liabilities and Equity**	**$ 110,962**	**100.0%**

Figure 1.5-7 Fifth Third Bancorp Income Statement

Fifth Third Bancorp Income Statement for 2007
($ millions)

	2007	% of Total Interest Income
Interest on Loans Including Fees	$ 5,418	
Interest on Portfolio Securities and Other Short-Term Holdings	609	
Total Interest Income	**6,027**	
Interest Expense on Deposits	(2,007)	
Interest on Other Short-Term Borrowings	(324)	
Interest on Long-Term Debt	(687)	
Total Interest Expense	**(3,018)**	**50.1%**
Provision for Loan and Lease Losses	(628)	
Net Interest After Provision for Loan and Lease Losses	2,381	2.15%
Electronic Payment Processing Revenue	826	
Trading Revenue and Service charges on Deposit Accounts	579	
Other Noninterest Income	1,062	
Total Other Revenues	**2,467**	**40.9%**
Salaries, Benefits & Other Compensation	(1,517)	
Net Occupancy and Equipment	(269)	
Other Expense	(1,525)	
Total Non-Interest Expenses	**(3,311)**	**54.9%**
Income Before Taxes	**1,537**	**25.5%**
Taxes	(461)	
Net Income	**$ 1,076**	**17.8%**

B. INSURANCE COMPANIES

We next turn to a Massachusetts-based property and casualty insurance company, the Plymouth Rock Company, which underwrites auto insurance.

Take a look at Plymouth Rock's balance sheet, Figure 1.5-8, and see how it compares to the two depository institutions we already discussed. While

Plymouth Rock's balance sheet does not show any assets in the form of loans, the firm does have a substantial amount of *investment securities*, which represent nearly 60% of total assets. Plymouth Rock is therefore a financial institution in the sense that it holds a large amount of financial assets. It also has another 8.82% of total assets in *cash and cash equivalents*, a larger liquidity reserve than the two institutions you saw earlier. It may be hard to decipher Plymouth Rock's other assets, but many of them clearly relate to the business of insurance. For example, premiums receivable represent insurance premiums, such as monthly payments on an automobile insurance policy, which are due to be paid to Plymouth Rock fairly promptly. Notwithstanding some unfamiliar entries on the asset side of the Plymouth Rock Balance Sheet, the general structure of its assets is not too different from the depository institutions you have seen.

Where insurance companies really differ from banks and thrifts is evident on the liability side of the balance sheet. The largest source of funding for Plymouth Rock is *Claim and Claim Adjustment Expense Reserves,* which equal 34.5% of total assets. This figure represents the insurance claims that Plymouth Rock expects to pay out on outstanding policies. A fair amount of additional funding comes from premiums and fee income that Plymouth Rock has already received but that it has not yet recognized as income, for example, when people pay for a full year of auto insurance in advance. Critically, for current purposes, Plymouth Rock does not fund itself with deposits or repos or other short-debt instruments. Its financial intermediation involves the collecting and reinvesting of premiums and other service fee income over a period of time until insurance claims are paid off or other services are rendered. That is a very different business model than that of Cambridge Savings Bank and Fifth Third Bancorp. Note also the contrast between Plymouth Rock's lack of short-debt instruments and the sizable short-term obligations of large insurance organizations such as AIG in 2008.

The Plymouth Rock business model is also clearly apparent from its income statement. Its revenues consist primarily of premiums and service fees received, plus some investment income. Plymouth Rock's primary expenses are associated with claims and services. Notice how large Plymouth Rock's total revenues are compared to its total assets: 65.1% ($457.1 million divided by $702.1 million). In contrast, Cambridge Savings Bank's comparable ratio is only 5.8% (the sum of $114.5 million in total interest income plus $6.5 million in non-interest income, divided by $2,062.4 million in total assets). That is because Cambridge Savings Bank earns almost all of its income from return on its loans and other investments and that income is a direct function of total assets. In contrast, Plymouth Rock primarily earns income from the flow of premiums, which is related to but not a direct function of its total assets. When we get to our discussion of insurance companies in Part III, you will see that size is often measured in terms of premium flows rather than total assets, especially for property and casualty firms like Plymouth Rock.

As a final exercise here, consider how Plymouth Rock compares to the other firms we have considered in terms of leverage and profitability.

Figure 1.5-8 Plymouth Rock Balance Sheet

Plymouth Rock Balance Sheet for Year-End 2007 ***($ millions)***					
Assets		**% of Assets**	**Liabilities**		**% of Liabilities and Equity**
Cash and Cash Equivalents	$ 61.9	8.8%	Claim and Claim Adjustment Expense Reserves	$ 145.9	34.3%
Investment Securities	400.1	57.0%	Unearned Premium Reserve	113.4	26.7%
Accrued Investment Income	3.4	0.5%	Advance Premiums	7.3	1.7%
Premiums Receivable	95.9	13.7%	Commissions Payable and Accrued Liabilities	79.9	18.8%
Deferred Acquisition Costs	9.5	1.4%			
Receivable from Reinsurers	37.1	5.3%	Payable to Reinsurers	35.1	8.3%
Amounts Due from Service Clients	13.3	1.9%	Unearned Service Fees	33.9	8.0%
Prepaid Expenses, Agent Loans and Deposits	7.2	1.0%	Amounts Due to Service Clients	5.4	1.3%
Real Estate	23.0	3.3%	Deferred Income Taxes	1.7	0.4%
Fixed Assets	45.1	6.4%	Income Tax Payable	2.3	0.5%
Goodwill and Intangible Assets	3.2	0.5%	Other Liabilities	0.0	0.01%
			Total Liabilities	**425.0**	**60.5%**
Other Assets	2.4	0.3%	Equity	**277.2**	**39.5%**
Total Assets	**$ 702.1**	**100.0%**	**Total Liabilities and Equity**	**$ 702.1**	**100.0%**

Figure 1.5-9 Plymouth Rock Income Statement

Plymouth Rock Income Statement for 2007 ***($ millions)***		
	2007	**% of Total Revenue**
Revenues		
Premiums Earned in Underwriting Activities	$ 241.2	
Fees Earned from Service Activities	181.6	
Investment Income and Capital Gains	34.3	
Total Revenues	**457.1**	
Expenses:		
Claims and Claim Adjustment Expenses	(179.5)	
Policy Acquisition, Underwriting and General Expenses	(72.2)	
Service Activity Expenses	(148.2)	
Total Expenses	**(399.9)**	**87.5%**
Income Before Taxes	57.1	
Taxes	(20.8)	
Net Income	**$ 36.3**	**7.9%**

C. MUTUAL FUNDS

Our next example is for a mutual fund, the American Balanced Fund, a California-based investment company pursuing what is known a balanced growth and income strategy. With American Balanced Fund's balance sheet, Figure 1.5-10, the first thing to notice about the Fund is its size; with over $60 billion in total assets, it is much bigger than both Cambridge Savings Bank and Plymouth Rock Company, and a little over half the size of Fifth Third Bancorp. The fund's holdings at year-end 2007 are almost entirely investments in securities, largely *common stocks* (63.1% of total assets) and Bonds & Notes (29.2% of total assets). The fund's cash reserves are minimal, a tiny fraction of *total assets*. Moreover, if you look closely, you will see that the fund has no real estate or property and equity. Mutual funds typically do not have any property of their own, or even employees. Rather, they constitute investment vehicles that are managed and serviced by affiliated firms in a highly regulated environment that we will take up in Part X.

The liabilities and equity side of American Balanced Fund's balance sheet is also interesting. Liabilities fund less than 1% of its assets. The entity has practically no leverage and a capital ratio of 99.4%. Still, the American Balanced Fund is a financial intermediary. Rather than getting its funding through liabilities, such as deposits or insurance reserves, it is funded through equity. Shareholders of American Balanced Fund purchase those shares to participate in returns on fund investments. These shareholders bear the risk of loss and enjoy the benefits of expert management of the fund, as well as diversification across many investments. The mutual fund therefore provides financial intermediation, but of a different sort than you have seen before. The shares in a mutual fund are, however, redeemable, which allows for the possibility of runs on funds, similar to how short-term deposits allow for the possibility of runs on depository institutions.

Now, take a look at the fund's income statement, Figure 1.5-11, starting with its operating cases, labeled *fees and expenses*. The most significant charges are investment advisory fees paid to the fund's adviser plus distribution costs, payments made to promote the sale of fund shares. Adding together these and all other expenses, the sum is $473.3 million, which is 0.78% of the fund's *total assets*. The total costs of operating this fund, therefore, was equal to roughly 78 cents for every $100 of assets. How does this compare to the costs of operating Cambridge Savings Bank or Fifth Third Bancorp? Does that differential in operating expenses give mutual funds some sort of competitive advantage?

The income sources of mutual funds are also interesting. They consist of *dividends* (on stock) and *interest* (on bonds and notes) shown at the top of the income statement, which generate sufficient return to cover all of the fund's fees and expenses and leave over enough to generate $1,475.3 million of net investment income. The income statement then adds in additional types of realized gains and unreleased appreciation to generate a total return measure for the fund in 2007, labelled *net increase in net assets resulting from operations*, and totaling $3,607.8 billion. This is a common measure of mutual fund performance and suggests a ROA of 5.92% and a ROE of 6.0% using year-end total assets and total equity. How does this level of return compare to similar figures for

Cambridge Savings Bank and Fifth Third Bancorp? What measures are comparable?

Figure 1.5-10 American Balanced Fund Balance Sheet

American Balanced Fund Balance Sheet as of Year-End 2007
($ millions)

Assets		% of Assets
Cash	$ 7.7	0.01%
Receivables	473.8	0.78%
Investments in Securities:		
Common Stocks	38,449.7	63.08%
Preferred Stock and Convertibles	339.9	0.56%
Bonds & Notes	17,788.2	29.18%
Short-Term Investments	3,893.1	6.39%
Total Securities Investments	6,0470.9	99.21%
Total Assets	**$ 60,952.3**	**100.0%**

Liabilities		% of Liabilities and Equity
Payables:		
Purchases of Investments	$ 110.8	0.18%
Repurchases of Fund's Shares	208.0	0.34%
Other Deferred Expenses	44.5	0.07%
Total Liabilities	**363.3**	**0.60%**
Equity		
Capital Paid in on Shares of Capital Stock	52,195.8	85.6%
Undistributed Net Investment Income and Realized Gain	581.6	0.95%
Net Unrealized Appreciation	7,811.6	12.8%
Equity (Net Asset Value)	**60,589.0**	**99.4%**
Total Liabilities and Equity	**$ 60,952.3**	**100.0%**

Figure 1.5-11 American Balanced Fund Income Statement

American Balanced Fund Income Statement for 2007
($ millions)

	2007	% of Total Investment Income
Investment Income		
Dividends	$ 798.0	
Interest	1,136.6	
Total Investment Income	**1,934.6**	
Fees and expenses:		
Investment Advisory Services	(140.7)	
Distribution Services	(253.4)	
Transfer Agent Services	(41.1)	
Administrative Services	(28.6)	
Other Expenses	(9.5)	
Total Fees and Expenses Before Reimbursements	**(473.4)**	**24.5%**
Investment Advisory Services Reimbursement (to add)	14.1	
Net Investment Income	**1,475.3**	**76.3%**
Net Realized Gain and Unrealized Appreciation on Investments and Currency		
Net Realized Gain on:		
Investments	1,907.3	
Currency Transactions	0.4	
Total Realized Gain	**1,907.7**	
Net Unrealized Appreciation on:		
Investments	224.8	
Currency Translations	(0.1)	
Total Unrealized Appreciation	**224.8**	
Net Realized Gain and Unrealized Appreciation	**2,132.5**	
Net Increase in Net Assets Resulting from Operations	**$ 3,607.8**	

D. BROKER-DEALERS

Our next set of financial statements are for Charles Schwab Corporation, a financial holding company (FHC). Charles Schwab was founded in 1986 as an early discount brokerage firm and has since grown substantially. Once again, we use 2007 as a reference. While its principal operating subsidiary is still a broker-dealer, a type of securities firm, the holding company also owns a federally chartered thrift, Charles Schwab Bank, located in Reno, Nevada, as well as an investment adviser that manages mutual funds affiliated with the Charles Schwab organization. While Charles Schwab is a financial conglomerate in structure, it is essentially a large broker-dealer with relatively simple operations. What appears in Figures 1.5-12 and 1.5-13 are consolidated financial statements that combine all of the group's operations.

Take a look at Charles Schwab's balance sheet. You can see that some components are similar to those you saw on the previous balance sheets for depository institutions: *loans* (here, 8.2% of total assets) and *deposits from banking clients* (36% of total assets). These items reflect the activities of Charles Schwab's thrift subsidiary. The remainder of the asset side of Charles Schwab's balance sheet consists of financial assets of the sort you have seen before. *Receivables from brokerage clients* (30.8% of total assets) are margin loans, typically used by customers to purchase securities. On the liabilities side, however, there are some new sources of funding. In particular, Charles Schwab has a very large liability denominated *payables to brokerage clients and various intermediaries* (57.6% of total assets). The lion's share of this account represents cash balances from Charles Schwab's retail customers' money those clients hold with Charles Schwab in anticipation of making investments in the future or as a result of proceeds received on past investments. These payables are functionally akin to bank deposits, though not insured by the FDIC, and allow Charles Schwab to engage in additional financial intermediation. According to notes in its financial statements, these funds are used to fund Charles Schwab's margin loans to other clients. A recurring question in this text will be whether deposit-like instruments, such as cash balances held at Charles Schwab's broker-dealer subsidiary, should be regulated differently than the deposits held at its bank subsidiary. Many broker-dealers including Charles Schwab offer brokerage customers the ability to sweep cash balances at the broker into a deposit account at an affiliated depository institution or into a money market fund.

Another point of interest on the liability side of Charles Schwab's balance sheet is the extent to which the firm gets some of its funding from other financial intermediaries. A relatively small fraction of the payables mentioned above fall into this category. In addition, Charles Schwab maintains an $800 million line of credit, or option to obtain credit, from a consortium of 18 commercial banks. This line of credit is designed to provide the firm with additional liquidity if the need arises. When might that happen? Can we rely on commercial banks to offer this support in times of true financial stress?

Turning, finally, to Charles Schwab's income statement, you can see that its revenue sources are diversified across three primary sources, including interest, asset management (much of it likely coming from its investment adviser subsidiary), and trading revenue, which is revenue from dealing in securities as a principal. How would you compare Charles Schwab's overall business model to that of the depository institutions we considered earlier? What about its profitability?

Figure 1.5-12 Charles Schwab Balance Sheet

Charles Schwab Balance Sheet as of Year-End 2007 (*$ millions*)					
Assets		**% of Assets**	**Liabilities**		**% of Liabilities and Equity**
Cash and Cash Equivalent	$ 6,764	16.0%	Deposits from Banking Clients	$ 13,882	36.0%
			Payables to Brokerage Clients and Various Intermediaries	22,212	57.6%
U.S. Government and Agency Cash and Investments	8,803	20.8%	Accrued Expenses and Other Liabilities	1,621	4.2%
Equity Securities	8,201	19.4%	Long-Term Borrowing	899	2.3%
Loans	3,487	8.2%			
Receivables from Brokerage Customers	13,039	30.8%	**Total Liabilities**	**38,554**	**91.2%**
Other Assets, including Intangibles	1,992	4.7%	Equity	3,732	8.8%
Total Assets	**$ 42,286**	**100.0%**	**Total Liabilities and Equity**	**$ 42,286**	**100.0%**

Figure 1.5-13 Charles Schwab Income Statement

Charles Schwab Income Statement for 2007 (*$ millions*)		
	2007	**% of Total Revenues**
Revenues:		
Interest Income	$ 2,270	
Asset Management	2,358	
Trading Revenue	860	
Other	129	
Total Revenues	**5,617**	
Interest Expense	(623)	11.1%
Revenues, Net of Interest Expense	**4,994**	
Non-Interest Expenses:		
Compensation and Employee Related	(1,781)	
Other Non-Interest Expense	(1,360)	
Total Non-Interest Expense	**(3,141)**	**55.9%**
Income from Continuing Operations	1,853	
Income Tax Expense	(733)	
Income from Discontinued Operations	1,287	
Net Income	**$ 2,407**	**42.8%**

E. ALTERNATIVE LENDERS

So far, we have focused our attention on traditional financial intermediaries: banks, insurance companies, mutual funds, and broker-dealers. These are firms subject to familiar and long-standing systems of financial regulation. There are many other firms that engage in financial transactions and operate outside of these principal regulatory regimes. While these firms are subject to a host of legal requirements, including many anti-money laundering rules of the sort discussed in the *Hom* case in Chapter 1.4, and are now regulated by the CFPB, as we will see in Part V, they have not traditionally been subject to the kind of comprehensive regulatory oversight applied to FDIC-insured banks or SEC-regulated securities firms. Still, these firms play a major role in the lives of many Americans and offer competition to more traditionally regulated financial intermediaries.

An example of an alternative lender is Cash America, a leading operator of pawn shops and a major provider of payday loans, which are short-term credit structured to be repaid within a few weeks on the borrower's next payday. Cash America's financial statements appear in Figure 1.5-14 and 1.5-15. How does the Cash America balance sheet compare to intermediaries we've already discussed? Start on the liabilities and equity side of the balance sheet. One feature that distinguishes Cash America's funding from all the other balance sheets we've considered is the absence of substantial resources provided by individuals. Aside from the very modest amount of *customer deposits*, which total a mere 0.9% of total assets, there is nothing on Cash America's balance sheet that is equivalent to the deposits at Cambridge Savings Bank, the cash balances held at Charles Schwab, the prepaid premiums and claims reserves at Plymouth Rock, or shareholder's equity in the American Balanced Fund. Indeed, Cash America's most substantial liability is a block of long-term debt totaling 31.0% of total assets. This debt represents senior unsecured note offerings through which Cash America has accessed the capital markets. Whereas the depository institutions we considered earlier were engaging in the transformation of short-term liabilities into long-term loans, Cash America transforms long-term debt into short-term lending. Note the differing liquidity implications for an alternative lender such as Cash America. Unlike traditional lenders, Cash America holds relatively little cash, instead relying on other financial institutions for liquidity. Note also that all of Cash America's assets are denominated as current assets, meaning that they are expected to have maturities of less than one year. How does that compare to the maturity structure of the assets of Cambridge Savings Bank?

Finally, consider Cash America's business model. Did the firm make money in 2007 and, if so, how does its profitability compare to that of the other firms we have seen? What about its ROA and ROE? Finally, examine the size of the expense-denominated *cash advance loss provision*, the amount the firm set aside in 2007 to cover anticipated loss on loans. How does that compare to the loss reserves in the income statements of Cambridge Savings Bank or Fifth Third Bancorp? What are the implications of any differences here? Finally, and in anticipation of a discussion we will take up in Part V, does the success of Cash America and similar firms imply that these alternative lenders supply an important economic function that regulated firms fail to offer, or do they do something else?

Figure 1.5-14 Cash America International Balance Sheet

Cash America Balance Sheet as of Year-End 2007 (*$ millions*)						
Assets		**% of Assets**	**Liabilities**			**% of Liabilities and Equity**
Cash and Cash Equivalents	$ 22.7	2.5%	Accounts Payable and Accrued Expenses	$ 87.4		9.7%
Pawn Loans	137.3	15.2%	Customer Deposits	7.9		0.9%
Cash Advances, net	88.1	9.7%	Income Taxes Currently Payable	3.8		0.4%
Merchandise Held for Disposition, net	98.1	10.8%	Short-Term Debt	8.5		0.9%
Finance and Service Charges Receivable	27.0	3.0%	**Total Current Liabilities**	**107.5**		**11.9%**
Other Receivables and Prepaid Expenses	16.3	1.8%	Deferred Tax Liabilities	18.6		2.1%
Deferred Tax Assets	20.2	2.2%	Other Liabilities	1.7		0.2%
Total Current Assets	**409.8**	**45.3%**	Long-Term Debt	280.3		31.0%
Property and Equipment, net	161.7	17.9%	**Total Liabilities**	**408.0**		**45.1%**
Goodwill	306.2	33.8%				
Intangible Assets, net	23.5	2.6%				
Other Assets	3.5	0.4%	Equity	496.6		54.9%
Total Assets	**$ 904.6**	**100.0%**	**Total Liabilities and Equity**	**$ 904.6**		**100.0%**

Figure 1.5-15 Cash America International Income Statement

Cash America Income Statement for 2007 (*$ millions*)		
	2007	**% of Total Revenue**
Revenue		
Finance and Service Charges	$ 161.0	
Proceeds from Disposition of Merchandise	396.3	
Cash Advance Fees	355.2	
Check Cashing Fees, Royalties and Other	16.4	
Total Revenue	**929.4**	
Cost of Revenue	(246.8)	26.5%
Net Revenue	**682.6**	
Expenses:		
Operations	(304.5)	
Cash Advance Loss Provision	(155.2)	
Administration	(57.3)	
Depreciation and Amortization	(32.1)	
Total Expenses	**(549.1)**	**59.1%**
Operational Income	**133.5**	**14.3%**
Interest Expense	(16.0)	
Interest Income	1.0	
Foreign Currency Transaction	–	
Gain on Sale of Foreign Notes	6.3	
Income from Continuing Operations Before Taxes	124.8	
Provision for Income Taxes (to add)	45.4	
Net Income	**$ 170.2**	**18.3%**

F. FINANCIAL RATIO SUMMARY

As a final exercise, compare the various solvency and profitability ratios of the six intermediaries we have explored as summaries in Figure 1.5-16. What do these figure tell us about these firms? Are some firms more analogous than others and, if so, which ones?

Figure 1.5-16 Financial Ratios Summary

Cambridge Savings Bank
Capital Ratio = 8.7%
ROA = 0.35%; ROE = 4.03%

Fifth Third Bancorp
Capital Ratio = 8.3%
ROA = 0.97%; ROE = 11.75%

Charles Schwab
Capital Ratio = 8.8%
ROA = 5.69 %; ROE = 64.50%

American Balanced Fund
Capital Ratio = 99.4%
ROA = 5.92%; ROE = 5.95%

Plymouth Rock
Capital Ratio = 39.5%
ROA = 5.17%; ROE = 13.10%

Cash America
Capital Ratio = 54.9%
ROA = 18.81%; ROE = 34.27%

IV. CONCLUDING THOUGHTS

The financial system is complex, multifaceted, and interconnected. While we have focused on a handful of relatively simple financial statements in this Chapter, even in this small sample you can see many areas of overlap and connection. Consumers have many choices for where to put their money, from deposit accounts in depository institutions, such as Cambridge Saving Bank or Fifth Third Bancorp, to cash balances with Schwab's securities affiliate, to investments in the American Balanced Fund or other mutual funds. Consumers can also use excess cash reserves to prepay their auto insurance premiums with Plymouth Rock, likely enjoying a discount, akin to interest on deposits, on the cost of paying premiums on a quarterly or monthly basis. Corporations and businesses have a variety of choices for how they wish to fund growth and other productive activities.

As an example, suppose General Motors needs funds to open a new plant. Fifth Third Bancorp could extend GM a loan, which would show up on GM's balance sheet as a debt and on Fifth Third Bancorp's balance sheet as an asset. Alternatively, GM could choose to raise debt, as Cash America does, through the issuance of unsecured notes, perhaps underwriting by the investment banking affiliate of an FHC like Fifth Third Bancorp. GM's debt might end up being held by the American Balanced Fund as part of its debt portfolio, which incidentally might also include some of Cash America's debt instruments.

Lending markets are also interconnected. An individual needing credit, for example for a new car loan, could go to a local bank such as Cambridge Savings Bank. As it turns out, in 2007, the customer could also have gone to GM, which had a major financial subsidiary set up to finance car loans for GM dealerships. Alternatively, if none of these sources was willing to extend a new car loan to the consumer on acceptable terms, that person could, in many parts of the country, turn to an alternative lender like Cash America to get a few hundred dollars, albeit at fairly high interest rates, to repair the muffler on her old car.

Understanding these relationships, as well as the basics of financial statements and business models of different types of financial intermediaries, will be critical for the materials that follow. In many instances, the regulatory structures we will discuss throughout the book are designed to constrain profit-maximizing incentives that market forces encourage. In essence, regulation is intended to take certain business models, or at least extreme versions of those business models, off the table. In addition, while we will tend to explore regulatory regimes in one sector at a time, starting with banks in Part II, you should keep in mind that the sectors are interrelated. Limitations on the activities of commercial banks may force financial activities to alternative lenders, such as Cash America, or shadow banking activities, which we will explore in Part XII. Market forces tend to move activity to less regulated sectors, if regulations are not imposed uniformly on similar financial functions. As we saw in Chapter 1.3, however, our regulatory perimeters are not currently built upon functional definitions, at least not completely.

In short, the world of financial regulation is challenging but, as we hope you will find in the chapters that follow, also fascinating.

PART II

INSURED DEPOSITORY INSTITUTIONS

CHAPTER 2.1

THE IMPACT OF CHARTER CHOICE

CONTENTS

I. THE BANK CHARTER

A bank needs a charter issued by a government authority before it can start taking deposits and making loans. The chartering process for a bank and a corporation are radically different. Anyone with access to the Internet and a credit card can fill out a few forms to incorporate a general purpose corporation and begin business almost overnight. No state authority examines the moral character, the qualifications and experience of the investors, or whether the community needs the product offered by the new company. On the contrary, it is considered a virtue of the American capitalist system that two guys in a dorm room or a garage with no experience and an idea about a novel product can start a company.

The process could not be more different for those seeking to charter a new bank and there is no guarantee that the application will be approved. The Federal Reserve Board's website describes the process:

> Starting a bank involves a long organization process that could take a year or more, and permission from at least two regulatory authorities. Extensive information about the organizer(s), the business plan, senior management team, finances, capital adequacy, risk management infrastructure, and other relevant factors must be provided to the appropriate authorities.

See How Can I Start a Bank?, FEDERAL RESERVE BOARD (Aug. 2, 2013).

Why is it that Steve Jobs did not need to first prove his moral fitness or that the world needed Apple products before starting a company making products that no one had ever imagined they needed, but those who start a bank need to do so? The answer lies in the special role of the chartered bank in the economy.

E. Gerald Corrigan, *Are Banks Special?*, *in* FEDERAL RESERVE BANK OF MINNEAPOLIS, ANNUAL REPORT 2 (1982).

Bank charters of all types have long been closely controlled by the sovereign. The tight control over who can own and operate a bank relates to the fact that only banks can take deposits from the public, which puts the chartered bank in a special position of trust and confidence, especially in light of the fractional reserve system. The need for trust and confidence, still important today, carried even more importance in the many centuries between the creation of the chartered bank, and the creation of deposit insurance in the early 20th Century.

Another reason for the tight control is the connection between the chartered bank and government debt. In England, the king was originally the sole source of charters for banks, reflecting the sovereign's need to finance its European wars. CHARLES W. CALOMIRIS & STEPHEN H. HABER, FRAGILE BY DESIGN 88–89 (2014). Early state banks were required to invest in the bonds issued by their chartering states and national banks were created in the midst of the Civil War with a requirement that they invest in debt issued by the federal government to finance the Civil War. In much of the 20th Century, the consequences of the requirement that the chartered bank invest in government debt was forgotten by many academics and policymakers. The crisis in the Eurozone, especially in Cyprus and Greece, has been a good reminder of this link.

In the United States, state legislatures took up the role of the king, and during the early 19th Century after the end of the Second Bank of the United States, only states could grant bank charters. At that time, new bank charters were, in most states, only granted by special bills passed by acts of the legislatures, with the predictable result that friends, family and those connected to or willing to make backroom promises to state politicians often got their special bills passed while others struggled. Over time, the granting of special charters by legislative act came to be seen for what it was: a system that invited corruption. The counterreaction, referred to as the Free Banking Era, was a move away from the requirement of a special act of the state legislature into a chartering process with review by a state banking authority. The name "Free Banking Era" is somewhat misleading in that bank charters were still tightly controlled at the state level.

Since 1863 when the national bank charter was created, the United States has had a dual bank chartering and regulatory system, with both the federal and state governments involved in chartering and regulation of commercial banks and the other types of depository institutions that will be discussed in this Chapter.

In this chapter, we examine trends in bank chartering in the United States and then look at the history of national bank chartering standards, as a case study. We then review the various types of depository institution charters most widely available in the United States today and discuss the differences between state and federal law as they apply to charter choice. We also discuss the "rent-a-charter" trend among non-bank Internet-based lenders. Finally, we ask about what constitutes a bank in today's financial system.

The United States has historically been a country with a phenomenal number of banks. Severe limits on intrastate branching, which encouraged the proliferation of small, one-branch banks, known as unit banks, as well as interstate limits on branching, are the historical reason for the unusually high number of banks in the United States. In 1920, the United States had 30,000 banks, many of them small rural and one-branch banks. In 1934, after many bank failures during the Great Depression, there were 14,146 commercial banks in the United States. This number decreased slightly, hovering between 13,000 and 14,000, until the mid-1970s, and decreased to around 6,000 by 2013.

For many years after the Great Depression, the number of bank charter additions (conversions and *de novo* charters) roughly equaled the number of bank charter deletions (mergers and failures). This equilibrium was disrupted beginning with the bank and thrift failures of the 1980s and never recovered. Bank and thrift failures (stemming from the Savings & Loan Crisis), along with unassisted mergers (*i.e.*, mergers in which the FDIC played no part), were the prime causes of the decrease in total number of charters in the 1980s; unassisted mergers explain most of the decreases in bank charters during this period. With very few bank failures in the 1990s and a moderate number of additions, the large number of unassisted mergers substantially reduced the number of bank charters. The failure of approximately 440 banks during the Financial Crisis only continued this trend of falling numbers of banks. Figure 2.1-1 illustrates the gradual decline in the number of bank charters.

Figure 2.1-1 Number of Independent Banks in the United States

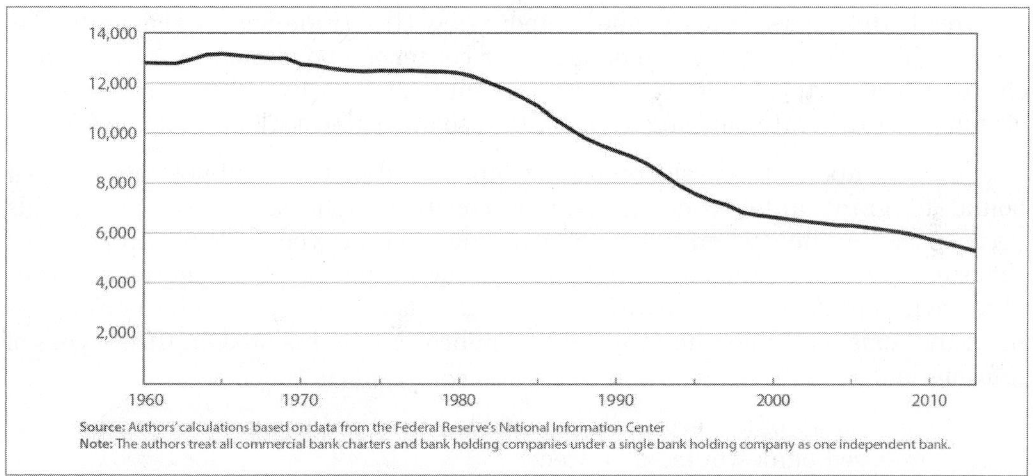

From Roisin McCord, Edward Simpson Prescott, & Tim Sablik, Fed. Reserve Bank of Richmond, Explaining the Decline in the Number of Banks since the Great Recession (Mar. 2015).

Since the Financial Crisis, very few new bank charters have been granted. More than 800 commercial banks disappeared due to mergers and failures between 2007 and 2013, while the OCC granted only six bank charters in that period. Since 2010, the number of *de novo* banks has markedly declined; there were no newly formed banks in 2012 and only one in 2013. Roisin McCord, Edward Simpson Prescott & Tim Sablik, *Explaining the Decline in the Number of Banks since the Great Recession*, FED. RESERVE BANK OF RICHMOND 1, Mar. 2015. Figure 2.1-2 illustrates the almost unprecedented collapse in the granting of new national bank charters.

Figure 2.1-2 Numbers of Newly Created Banks (De Novos)

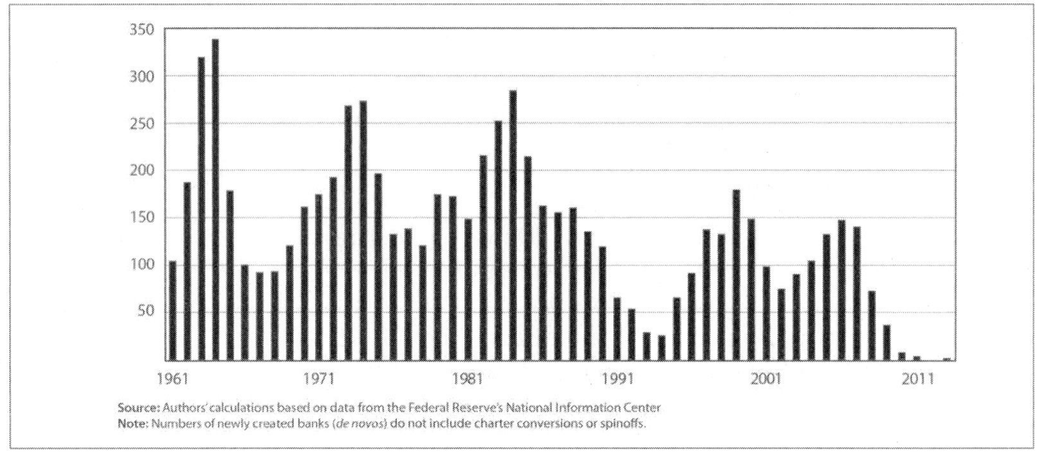

From Roisin McCord, Edward Simpson Prescott, & Tim Sablik, Fed. Reserve Bank of Richmond, Explaining the Decline in the Number of Banks since the Great Recession (Mar. 2015).

The dearth of new bank charters is also echoed at the state level, and is understandable in light of the Financial Crisis but is likely to have impacts on the banking sector and its non-bank competitors in the years to come.

As a case study, we now consider the different standards for the grant or denial of national bank charters used by different Comptrollers since 1863. As you read this case study, reflect upon how the Financial Crisis, and its aftermath, have changed some of the older concerns about the granting of bank charters from a topic of purely historical interest into live concerns. You can assume that the state banking authorities also struggled with similar concerns.

Mr. McCulloch, the first Comptroller appointed in 1863, did not view himself bound to grant automatic approval of charter applications. He made his decisions at a time when the U.S. banking system was largely composed of thousands of small unit banks with just a few larger banks in the major cities and when neither a central bank with lender of last resort capability nor deposit insurance existed. When he received an application, he insisted on three types of information:

- a summary of the economic potential of the local community in which the proposed bank would be located;
- satisfactory references about the character and responsibility of the organizers; and
- data on the existing banks in the city of the proposed bank and in nearby communities.

Mr. McCulloch exercised what he believed to be his wide discretionary power in granting or denying the charter. John Knox, the fourth Comptroller, who served from 1872 to 1884, believed that he had no discretionary power but must instead grant a charter if the applicants had conformed to the legal requirements (proper application, sufficient capital, etc.). Mr. Knox's view prevailed throughout the remainder of the 19th Century. Does a plain reading of 12 U.S.C. § 27 suggest that if the charter applicant meets all the statutory requirements stated, the Comptroller must grant the charter?

Approximately 1,000 national banks failed between 1890 and 1900, and, in 1908, Lawrence O. Murray, the Comptroller newly appointed after the Panic of 1907, concluded that he had to change the automatic approval philosophy to avoid further "over-banking." Mr. Murray believed that, even though particular applicants had complied with the letter of the law, he had the discretion to deny them a charter because of his responsibility for the stability of the overall banking system.

Since 1908, few have seriously challenged the proposition that the Comptroller has the discretion to consider the impact of the proposed bank on the stability of the banking system in deciding whether to grant a charter. A Supreme Court decision, decided in the pre-*Chevron* era, affirmed the extraordinary deference that the Comptroller enjoys in charter grants and denials. *See* Camp v. Pitts, 411 U.S. 138, 141–43 (1973). Overall, there have been periods in which this discretion has been used to grant charters, and other periods when it has been used to deny charters so that the national banking system was effectively a closed club.

The automatic approval policy of the post-Civil War era has never completely returned, although the position of James Saxon, who served as Comptroller from 1961 to 1966, outlined below, still has some force.

Statement of James Saxon, Comptroller of the Currency

Hearing Before the H. Comm. on Banking & Currency on the Conflict of Federal and State Banking Law, 88th Cong. 274 (1963)

I believe that it is fair to say, within the spirit of our private enterprise system, that a great deal of weight must be attached to decisions by our citizens to risk their capital in new enterprises.

Banking is a regulated industry, and there are sound considerations of the public interest which underlie our policy of restricting entry into this industry, and regulating the operating practices of banks. But we should not interpret the regulation of entry as a bar to entry. Controls over the formation of new banking institutions, and over the expansion of existing institutions, were not designed for the purpose of erecting an impenetrable barrier to new initiative in this industry. They were designed, instead, to provide a basis for judicious limitations conceived in terms of the public interest.

What are the standards by which the public interest in the expansion of banking facilities may properly be judged? There are two basic criteria which should be applied. Recognition must be accorded to the fact that our economy is a living and growing instrument, and that for its progress it requires the adequate provision of banking facilities. Our needs are ever changing, and our banking facilities must be attuned to these changing needs.

There is also a second consideration of coordinate importance, by which we must appraise private efforts to expand banking facilities. In the vast unregulated sector of our economy, we rely entirely upon private initiative to determine the desirability of undertaking new ventures. Indeed, through our anti-trust statutes, we endeavor to maintain conditions in which full freedom of entry will be sustained. There are some who believe that we could safely apply this policy to the industry of banking.

For a number of years after Mr. Saxon's tenure, the three most frequently cited factors that played a significant role in the decision to grant or deny a charter were (1) the prevention of bank failures—that is, the financial strength of the proposed bank; (2) the attainment of a competitive market in that local community; and (3) the convenience and needs of the public. The full list of factors was laid out at 12 U.S.C. § 816 (1964) and 12 C.F.R. § 4.2(b) (1967). The most generous characterization of the "convenience and needs" test is to describe it as a catch-all that grants the Comptroller wide discretion in the chartering decision. This discretion is seldom successfully challenged. Kenneth Scott, *In Quest of Reason: The Licensing Decisions of the Federal Banking Agencies*, 42 U. CHI. L. REV. 235, 257–68, 294–95 (1975). That wide discretion has been upheld by the Supreme Court. *Camp,* 411 U.S. at 141–43.

Under the Comptroller's 1997 policy for chartering banks, which is still in effect today, there is an emphasis on whether the proposed bank has organizers that are familiar with the national banking laws or regulations, competent management with relevant experience, and sufficient capital to support the projected volume and type of business. 12 C.F.R. §§ 5.20(f)(2)(i)(A)-(C). Under this policy, the OCC will also evaluate both whether the bank "can reasonably be expected to achieve and maintain profitability" and whether it will be operated in a "safe and sound manner." *Id.* §§ 5.20(f)(2)(i)(D)-(E). Additionally, in the post-9/11 environment, the required background checks of the board of directors and senior management include not only financial and criminal background checks, but also checks by other unnamed government agencies. The process is well described in the OCC's Licensing Manual.

---

1. ***Comparison of Standards.*** Do you prefer the old emphasis on the convenience and needs of the market where the proposed bank is to operate, the new emphasis on the experience and moral character of the people filing the application, the capital they bring to the enterprise, and their business plans for the bank, or something else? Should it be enough in our free enterprise system if the organizers are willing to risk their own capital or have raised enough capital? Or, are responsibilities to the overall banking system and depositors also relevant, because banks have access to the federal safety net and occupy a special place in the economic system? How appropriate is the Comptroller's near complete discretion?

2. ***Comparison to UK.*** The UK government has expressed concerns because no new retail banks have been chartered in the UK for over one hundred years. While there are other types of institutions in the UK, such as building societies, a type of thrift, the lack of entry by new retail banks has led to concerns about competition, especially in consumer banking. Competition & Mkts. Auth., *Retail Banking Market Investigation: Metro Bank Case Study* 3 (2015). What features of the U.S. system mitigate this concern?

3. ***Competition in Banking Markets.*** In a world of bank runs and crises, is there renewed validity to the older concerns about limiting competition in commercial banking? Is that possible in the era of nationwide Internet banking and global competition?

II. DIFFERENT CHARTER TYPES

Historically, there were many different types of charters, but today only a very few types of insured depository institutions (IDIs) remain relevant. Moreover, as we shall see, the historical differences among the powers granted in the different types of charters or their business models have narrowed considerably but not disappeared. The dominant form of bank charter was historically referred to as the commercial bank because, in its 19th Century and early 20th Century business models, it focused on short-term lending to manufacturers, farmers, and others in commerce. Today, commercial bank charters are the basic national bank or state-chartered bank, and during the latter half of the 20th Century, commercial banks also moved into long-term corporate lending, mortgages, and consumer lending. The next most common form of charter is that of the thrift, originally conceived in the mid-19th Century as a way for the urban working class to place long-term funds (that is, no demand deposits) and use the savings to purchase a home. As we will see, this focus on home mortgages and other real estate loans led to massive failures during the Great Depression and proved to be ill-fated in the Savings & Loan Crisis of the late 1980s. A third type of charter is that of the credit union, a member-owned institution originally conceived in the first decades of the 20th Century as a way for the emerging urban working class to get personal and consumer loans of the type that commercial banks of the time would not touch. The final major charter type we will discuss is the industrial loan company, a charter type originally conceived in the first decade of the 20th Century to serve the financing needs of industrial workers, hence the word "industrial" in its name. As we shall see, industrial loan companies, often also referred to as ILCs, underwent a substantial transformation and became a way for commercial and other non-bank companies to own an IDI. The commercial bank, thrift, and credit union charters are creatures of the dual banking system and charters can be granted at either the federal or state level. The ILC exists only in a state-chartered form.

There are several types of traditional charters that we will not discuss, including mutual savings banks (because of their declining importance), limited purpose trust companies, and credit card banks. For those who want a deeper understanding of the latter two charter types, *see* Saule T. Omarova & Margaret E. Tahyar, *That Which We Call a Bank: Revisiting the History of Bank Holding Company Regulation in the United States*, 31 REV. BANKING & FIN. L. 113, 169–74 (2011). We will also not discuss private banks, which were, historically, unincorporated deposit-taking institutions run as partnerships. Although private banks were of major importance in the 18th, 19th and early 20th Centuries, they are rare to virtually nonexistent today; we know of only one example in the United States.

A. NATIONAL BANK VS. STATE BANK

The choice of chartering authority is also a choice of primary regulator for the chartered commercial bank. For most of the 20th Century, the powers contained within the charter differed substantially enough between state and national banks to make that decision a very significant one and there was a long pattern of states being generous with their powers to attract charters. As you will see in Chapter 2.2, in which we will examine commercial bank powers in detail, the powers contained in a commercial bank charter are limited by the concept of the "business of banking." By the late 20th Century, the powers of state and national banks were largely, but not perfectly, aligned.

Still, the primary regulator remains different: it is the OCC for the national bank and the relevant state banking authority for the state-chartered bank. A national bank is required to become a member of the Federal Reserve System but a state bank may choose to remain a nonmember. For much of the 20th Century, beginning with the creation of the Federal Reserve Board in 1913, there were substantial differences between the regulation of member banks (all national banks and those state-chartered banks who voluntarily choose to become members of the Federal Reserve System) and state-chartered member banks. During the last half of the 20th Century and accelerating in its final quarter, the differences in regulatory treatment of member and nonmember banks has narrowed, but is not perfectly identical. Federal law requires that all national banks be FDIC-insured and all state laws require that a state-chartered commercial bank obtain FDIC insurance. The vast majority of national and state banks are wholly owned by holding companies that are regulated by the Federal Reserve Board as bank holding companies (BHCs). You will learn more about BHCs in Chapter 6.1.

Since all national banks are both member banks and insured, the Federal Reserve Board, as the supervisor of member banks, and the FDIC, as the deposit insurer, also regulate the national bank. The primary regulator of a state-chartered bank is its state banking authority. If it is a member bank, the Federal Reserve Board is also a supervisor and the FDIC as deposit insurer also has a supervisory role. Nonmember state banks, all of whom are insured, therefore have the FDIC as their primary federal regulator. Since the creation of the CFPB in the Dodd-Frank Act, all banks are also subject to the federal CFPB's regulations on consumer financial protection, although only banks with $10 billion or more in assets are subject to direct examination by the CFPB; those that are smaller are generally examined by their primary federal supervisor instead.

As a structural matter, in the U.S. banking system today, the largest banks with nationwide consumer retail operations tend to be national banks and regional or smaller banks tend to be state-chartered banks. As a result, as of the second quarter of 2014, the vast majority of commercial banking assets were held in national banks (68.7% for 1,109 institutions) while the remaining 31.3%, were held by 4,648 state-chartered banks. Figure 2.1-3 illustrates that structure.

Figure 2.1-3 Commercial Bank Charters as of Second Quarter of 2014

Data as of Q2 (2014)	**Number of Institutions**	**Percentage of Total**	**Total Consolidated Assets (in $b)**	**Percentage of Total**
All commercial banks	5,757	—	14,106	—
Federal charter	1,109	19.3%	9,696	68.7%
State charter	4,648	80.7%	4,410	31.3%

Source: FDIC.

The OCC and Federal Reserve Board are often seen as the federal regulators most attuned to the needs of the larger banking institutions. State-chartered nonmember banks, with just a few exceptions, are heavily weighted towards smaller community banks and so the FDIC is often seen as the protector of the smaller state-chartered banks.

---

1. ***Regulatory Architecture***. What is the purpose of having three different federal agencies supervise banks (the Federal Reserve Board for state-chartered member banks, the OCC for national banks, and the FDIC for state-chartered nonmember banks)? Multiple studies and bills introduced in Congress, almost too countless to name, have suggested combining and streamlining federal bank regulatory authorities. The first such bill was introduced in 1919 and the most recent one in 2009. Major studies began in 1937 and have been put forth by regulators, Presidential commissions, or others at roughly five-year intervals ever since. *See* J. L. Robertson, *Federal Regulation of Banking: A Plea for Unification*, 31 LAW & CONTEMP. PROBS. 673 (1966); Raymond H. Lopez & Surendra S. Kaushik, *Consolidation in the Commercial Banking Industry* (Pace Univ., Lubin Sch. Bus., Working Paper No. 216, 2005); Elizabeth F. Brown, *Prior Proposals to Consolidate Federal Financial Regulators* (Apr. 20, 2015). What institutional imperatives have prevented consolidation of this authority?

B. THRIFTS AND SAVINGS AND LOAN ASSOCIATIONS

We will now turn to an examination of the thrift or savings and loan charter, as described in the excerpt below.

Saule T. Omarova & Margaret E. Tahyar, That Which We Call A Bank: Revisiting the History of Bank Holding Company Regulations in the United States

31 REV. BANKING & FIN. L. 113, 179–187 (2011)

The first savings associations, or 'thrifts,' emerged in the United States before the Civil War. Thrifts began as state-chartered institutions whose purpose was to encourage savings and help "persons belonging to a deserving class, whose earnings [were] small, and with whom the slowness of accumulation discourage[d] the effort . . . to become . . . owners of homesteads."[1] During the Great Depression, a sizable fraction of these institutions failed, spurring the creation of a new regulatory regime for savings institutions under the Home Owners' Loan Act of 1933 ("HOLA"). Administered by the newly created Federal Home Loan Bank Board ("FHLBB"), this separate regulatory regime ran parallel to the regulatory regime created for banks because of the functional distinction that Congress had drawn between commercial banks and thrifts, which focused on home mortgage lending and did not engage in the general business of banking. The original HOLA prohibited thrifts from accepting deposits or issuing certificates of indebtedness and allowed them to "raise their capital only in the form of payments on such shares as are authorized in their charter." The lending capacity of thrifts was also restricted primarily to secured residential mortgages. . . .

---

[1] LISSA L. BROOME & JERRY W. MARKHAM, REGULATION OF BANK FINANCIAL SERVICE ACTIVITIES 73 (4th ed. 2011) (quoting *Wash. Nat'l Bldg., Loan & Inv. Ass'n v. Stanley*, 63 P. 489, 491-92 (Ore. 1901)).

Only in 1980, when federal regulators started loosening traditional constraints on thrifts' business activities in an ill-fated attempt to boost the sector's profitability, were thrifts permitted to make commercial loans, issue credit cards and offer [Negotiable Order of Withdrawal] accounts. In 1982, the Garn-St Germain Act permitted thrift institutions to "raise capital in the form of such savings deposits, shares, or other accounts, for fixed, minimum, or indefinite periods of time . . . or in the form of such demand accounts of those persons or organizations that have a business, corporate, commercial, or agricultural loan relationship with the association" and to issue "passbooks, time certificates of deposit, or other evidence of accounts as are so authorized." Thus, while thrift institutions could not accept demand deposits in the same way that commercial banks could, they could accept them from commercial entities if they were in connection with a commercial loan relationship.

Both the Depository Institutions Deregulation and Monetary Control Act of 1980 ("DIDMCA") and the Garn-St Germain Act were part of concerted legislative and regulatory efforts in the 1980s to reverse the declining profitability of thrifts in the highly competitive and volatile market environment. These deregulatory measures, however, encouraged excessive risk-taking that ultimately resulted in massive losses and failures of savings institutions during the [Savings & Loan] crisis of the 1980s. In 1987, in response to the ongoing crisis, Congress enacted [the Competitive Equality Banking Act of 1987 (CEBA)], which authorized a $10.8 billion recapitalization of the [Federal Savings and Loan Insurance Corporation] and prescribed forbearance measures to prevent or postpone closures of thrifts. . . .

Historically, Congress has treated savings associations differently from banks, distinguishing between the traditional savings associations' focus on home mortgage lending and the more expansive business-oriented services provided by banks. . . . Legislation targeting thrift holding companies has traditionally been aimed at "reinforcing the residential and consumer lending mission of their subsidiary associations" instead of "curbing the unrelated business activities of thrift holding companies," which further highlights the distinction Congress has drawn between savings associations and banks. . . .

In the period between the enactment of the [Gramm-Leach-Bliley Act (GLBA)] and the financial crisis of 2007-09, thrifts experienced a period of growth. In 2005, there were 484 thrift holding companies under [the Office of Thrift Supervision (OTS)] supervision with $7.2 trillion in total U.S. assets, controlling 451 thrifts with total assets of $1.2 trillion.[2] The recent crisis, however, significantly weakened the industry.[3] As a result, by 2010, there were 437 thrift holding companies under OTS supervision with $4.2 trillion in total U.S. assets, controlling 399 thrifts with total assets of $723 billion.

The Dodd-Frank Act significantly reformed the structure of thrift regulation by eliminating the OTS and transferring its authority to regulate thrifts and thrift holding companies to the OCC and the [Federal Reserve Board], respectively, and by taking other steps to effectively erase regulatory differences between thrifts and banks.

---

[2] OFFICE OF THRIFT SUPERVISION, 2010 FACT BOOK: A STATISTICAL PROFILE OF THE THRIFT INDUSTRY 80 (2011).

[3] The failure of Washington Mutual, the country's largest savings association based in Seattle, was a critical blow to the thrift industry. In September 2008, the federal government seized Washington Mutual, which was heavily exposed to risky mortgage-backed assets and suffered from a creditor run, and struck a controversial deal to sell its assets to J.P. Morgan. *See* Robin Sidel et al., *WaMu is Seized, Sold Off to J.P. Morgan, In Largest Failure in U.S. Banking History*, WALL ST. J., Sept. 26, 2008, at A1; *see also* Dain C. Donelson & David Zaring, *Requiem for a Regulator: The Office of Thrift Supervision's Performance During the Financial Crisis*, 89 N.C. L. REV. 1777, 1779 (2011) (discussing the impact the failure of Washington Mutual had on the U.S. economy as part of the larger financial crisis).

Some have suggested that, in the aftermath of the Financial Crisis and the Dodd-Frank Act, the advantages of the thrift charter, which at the federal level at least enjoyed a friendly and many would say lax regulator in the OTS, are now disappearing. The original constraints on thrift powers, through the Qualified Thrift Lender or QTL test, have been loosened in the last quarter of the 20th Century. Today, the QTL test requires that only 65% of assets be within the categories of home mortgage loans, home equity loans, mortgage-backed securities, credit cards, small business loans, and student loans. 12 U.S.C. §§ 1467a(m)(1), (m)(4)(C). Some of these categories are far afield from the original home mortgage mission of thrifts. One additional advantage of the federal thrift charter made it easier to branch interstate, but that too was cut back by the Dodd-Frank Act. Although the Dodd-Frank Act maintained the federal thrift charter, it eliminated the most important advantages of the thrift charter and imposed new penalties for failure to comply with the QTL test. As a result, thrifts increasingly find themselves in a world where they must continue to meet the constraints of the admittedly much loosened QTL test and yet without many of the previous advantages. Since 2010, federal and state thrift assets have declined.

C. CREDIT UNIONS

We now turn to an examination of the credit union charter, as described in the excerpt below.

Saule T. Omarova & Margaret E. Tahyar, That Which We Call A Bank: Revisiting the History of Bank Holding Company Regulations in the United States

31 REV. BANKING & FIN. L. 113 (2011)

Credit unions are not-for-profit financial cooperatives owned by their member-customers. Their principal purpose is to provide deposit-taking and lending services exclusively for their members rather than the general public. Credit unions engage in a limited set of financial activities tailored to consumer credit needs of their members. Credit unions can be federally or state chartered, and their deposits are insured. Federal credit unions are regulated by the [NCUA] and insured by the National Credit Union Share Insurance Fund ("NCUSIF").

Similar to ILCs and thrifts, credit unions were originally formed to serve the credit needs of the working class. Membership criteria for credit unions began with the use of the "common bond" requirement, which first arose in 1914. In 1934, the Federal Credit Union Act (the "FCUA") stated that credit union membership was to be limited to groups having a "common bond of occupation or association, or to groups within a well-defined neighborhood, community, or rural district."[4] The idea behind the common bond requirement is that "credit worthiness is evaluated on the basis of knowledge that the members have of each other."[5] In 1982, the NCUA loosened the common bond requirement to "broaden credit union access to groups that were too small to support a

---

[4] Federal Credit Union Act, Pub. L. No. 105-219, § 9, 48 Stat. 1216, 1219 (1934).

[5] Nicholas Ryder & Clare Chambers, *The Credit Crunch: Are Credit Unions Able to Ride Out the Storm?*, 11 J. BANKING REGULATION 76, 80 (2009).

viable credit union."[6] By the late 1990s, "the demographic characteristics of credit-union members have become more like the median American."[7]

Congress has consistently treated credit unions and banks as different categories of institutions. The enactment of the FCUA in 1934 was based on Congress's belief that credit unions were "mutual or cooperative organizations operated entirely by and for their members," and thus meaningfully different from banks. In 1937, Congress' decision to make credit unions tax exempt was also based on the view that credit unions were not the same as commercial banks. In 1998, Congress reiterated its belief in the distinction between credit unions and commercial banks in the Credit Union Membership Access Act.[8] . . .

Credit unions continue to be restricted in their lending authority. Credit unions may only lend to credit union members, other credit unions and credit union organizations. Credit unions are allowed to make commercial loans to members, but the net loan balance is limited to the lesser of 1.75 times the credit union's actual net worth or 12.25% of the credit union's total assets. In the wake of the recent financial crisis, some credit unions started to grow their commercial lending business. Credit unions also offer checking and savings accounts and credit card services.

The total number of credit unions has decreased in the last few decades, falling from a peak of 23,687 credit unions in 1970 to 7,605 credit unions at the end of 2010. At the same time, the number of credit union members has steadily increased each year since 1950; by the end of 2010, there were over 92 million credit union members. Total assets of credit unions have also steadily increased, from $17.8 billion in 1970 to over $934 billion as of December 2010. In terms of the relative size of the industry, at the end of 2010, credit union assets made up three-quarters of total FDIC-insured savings institution assets and approximately eight percent of total FDIC-insured commercial bank assets.

In general, consumer-owned credit unions emerged relatively unscathed from the recent financial crisis. Both total assets and membership levels increased during the crisis. However, so-called corporate credit unions were "in imminent danger of insolvency" due to an "over-concentration in what were once highly rated mortgage-backed securities" and required government rescue.

Since the passage excerpted above was written, the fight between the commercial banking sector and the credit unions over the common bond requirement, which is really a fight over the credit unions' exemption from taxation as they move more into commercial bank territory, especially business lending, has intensified.

---

[6] *See id.* at 81.

[7] William R. Emmons & Frank A. Schmid, *Credit Unions and the Common Bond*, 81 FED. RESERVE BANK OF ST. LOUIS REV. 43, 43 (1999).

[8] Congress explained the key differences between credit unions and commercial banks:

> Credit unions, unlike many other participants in the financial services market, are exempt from Federal and most state taxes because they are member-owned, democratically operated, not-for-profit organizations generally managed by volunteer boards of directors and because they have the specified mission of meeting the credit and savings needs of consumers, especially persons of modest means.

Credit Union Membership Access Act, Pub. L. No. 105-219, § 2(4), 112 Stat. 914, 914 (1998).

A primary area of litigation between banks and credit unions in recent years has been the NCUA's liberal interpretation of the common bond requirement for credit union charters, which historically has been restricted to occupational or associational groups. One liberalization has been to allow multiple unrelated occupational groups to join together in a single credit union. A second liberalization has been to allow senior citizen organizations to charter a credit union, resulting in the American Association of Retired Persons operating a credit union for a few years before the members voted to cease operations. In 1998, the Supreme Court struck down the NCUA's interpretation of the common bond requirement. *See* Nat'l Credit Union Admin. v. First Nat'l Bank & Trust Co., 522 U.S. 479, 499–503 (1998). Shortly thereafter, however, Congress enacted legislation largely reversing the Court's ruling. *See* Credit Union Membership Access Act, Pub. L. No. 105-219, 112 Stat. 913 (1998). In 2004, the NCUA proposed a rule that limits the common bond requirement by requiring that an association "not be formed primarily for expanding the federal credit union's membership," while at the same time making it easier to get approved if the NCUA has previously allowed a particular association category. NCUA, ASSOCIATIONAL COMMON BOND PROPOSED RULE CUTS RED TAPE, INCREASES CLARITY (2014).

Wholesale or corporate credit unions, which are also regulated by the NCUA, provide retail credit unions with short- and long-term investment and settlement services, but do not provide retail services directly to consumers. Although traditionally viewed as financially conservative, some corporate credit unions invested in mortgage-backed securities before the Financial Crisis and suffered heavy losses. In fact, five wholesale credit unions, including the two largest by asset size, experienced losses of roughly $15 billion and were seized by federal regulators in 2009–2010. Mark Maremont & Victoria McGrane, *Credit Unions Bailed Out*, WALL ST. J., Sept. 25, 2010.

The largest credit unions these days are the credit unions for military personnel, and they are now large enough that some have begun to suggest that some individual credit unions might be systemic. The largest credit union today, ranked both by total assets and by membership, is the Navy Federal Credit Union, based in Vienna, VA. As of June 2015, the Navy Federal Credit Union had nearly $70 billion in assets and almost 5.7 million members. In the last few years, credit unions have begun to expand their operations to participate in business lending, and they are doing so with increased frequency. Credit unions are becoming important participants in the commercial lending market.

D. INDUSTRIAL LOAN COMPANIES

We now turn to an examination of ILCs, a type of charter that has changed substantially from its original purpose, as described in the excerpt below.

Saule T. Omarova & Margaret E. Tahyar, That Which We Call A Bank: Revisiting the History of Bank Holding Company Regulations in the United States

31 REV. BANKING & FIN. L. 113, 158–169 (2011)

Industrial banks and industrial loan corporations (collectively referred to as "ILCs") began in the early twentieth century as "small, state-chartered loan companies that primarily served the borrowing needs of industrial workers unable to obtain non-collateralized loans from banks." At the time, commercial banks focused primarily on serving the financial needs of businesses and were largely unwilling to provide loans to low- and moderate-income individuals, typically industrial workers. ILCs emerged as a new type of financial institution catering to this growing but underserved market, functioning as a new form of financial self-help for working-class borrowers with stable jobs but no access to credit.[9] Initially, many ILCs did not accept any deposits and funded themselves instead by issuing investment certificates.

As commercial banks expanded their consumer lending business and gradually took over that segment of the market, they forced ILCs and industrial banks to redefine their business focus. One hundred years after its birth, an ILC effectively "reemerged as a way for commercial and financial firms to offer banking services without being subject to the ownership restrictions and parent company supervision that typically apply to other companies owning depository institutions." As a result of this transformation, by the mid-2000s, the ILC industry has evolved from a collection of "small niche lenders" into a distinct sector comprising some of "the nation's largest and more complex financial institutions." The key factor driving this functional transformation was the special exempt status that ILCs—and, accordingly, business entities that control them—received under the [Bank Holding Company Act (BHCA)].

The first prong of the CEBA exemption effectively grandfathered the exempt status for ILCs existing at the time of its enactment but froze their permissible activities on a going-forward basis. The second prong of the statutory test exempts any FDIC-insured ILC, as long as it meets one of the three requirements. These three requirements were presumably designed to exempt ILCs that did not function as commercial banks (in that they did not take demand deposits); ILCs that were not economically significant (with assets less than $100 million); or ILCs that could not provide commercial or financial companies a means to acquire a nonbank bank (by forbidding changes in ownership after the date of the CEBA's enactment). Thus, the most important practical effect of the statutory language, as added by the CEBA, was to allow ILCs with FDIC-insured retail deposits to remain outside the definition of a bank, as long as none of their deposits qualified technically as "demand deposits." Since 1987, this exemption has not been amended. . . .

As of 2010, only six states had active ILC charters, with most ILCs chartered in Utah.[10]

At the time of CEBA's enactment, congressional understanding was such that ILCs would not be used by large commercial companies to offer banking services to their commercial customers. By and large, ILCs were still small, state-chartered financial institutions that had limited deposit-taking powers and engaged primarily in making consumer loans to low- and middle-income individuals. Total ILC assets in 1987 were $4.2 billion, and the largest ILC had assets of only $420 million. Compared to commercial banks and trust companies, which at the time held $3.5 trillion in assets, ILCs were a minor player in the U.S. financial system.

In more than three decades since the passage of the CEBA, the ILC industry has undergone considerable changes. To enhance the value of their ILC charters, state authorities gradually increased ILC powers to the extent where ILCs can essentially function like FDIC-insured state-chartered banks, offering a full range of banking services. An explicit exemption from the BHCA definition of a bank made ILCs a

---

[9] *See* JAMES R. BARTH & TONG LI, MILKEN INSTITUTE, INDUSTRIAL LOAN COMPANIES: SUPPORTING AMERICA'S FINANCIAL SYSTEM 11 (2011) (explaining that instead of relying on collateral, these new financial institutions extended loans on the basis of "recommendations from creditworthy individuals who knew the [borrower]").

[10] *Id.* at 14.

particularly attractive option for securities firms and other non-bank financial institutions, as well as commercial companies that sought access to lending and deposit-taking.[11] Notably, General Motors was the first commercial company to acquire an ILC charter in 1988, shortly after the enactment of CEBA that closed the nonbank bank loophole. In many respects, ILCs have become a post-CEBA version of a nonbank bank.[12]

Although ILCs continued to be dwarfed by commercial banks and other depository institutions in terms of the sheer numbers and size,[13] the ILC industry experienced rapid growth in its total asset base and increased concentration.[14] This trend has become especially pronounced in the decade preceding the financial crisis of 2007-09. Thus, in 1998, there were roughly ninety ILCs controlling $28.6 billion in total assets. Total assets tripled in the span of two years to $92.6 billion in 2000. From 2000 to 2005, total assets steadily increased by approximately $10 billion each year, reaching $160.9 billion in 2005, spread over approximately ninety-six ILCs. From 2005 to 2007, the ILC industry experienced tremendous growth: while the number of ILCs did not change dramatically, total assets shot up from $160.9 billion in 2005 to $219.9 billion in 2006, and then to a staggering all-time high of $270.3 billion in 2007.[15]

Most of this growth was the result of a small number of "securities firms converting the cash management accounts held by their clients into insured ILC deposits."[16] . . .

Thus, before the latest crisis, the largest ILC was Merrill Lynch Bank USA with assets of $78.1 billion in 2007.[17] Merrill Lynch Bank USA was first established in 1988 and became inactive in 2009 following Bank of America's takeover of Merrill Lynch.[18] During the run-up to the crisis, Merrill Lynch Bank USA's total assets steadily increased. From 2000 to 2007, its total assets grew from $43.2 billion to $78.1 billion. The second largest ILC before the [F]inancial [C]risis was Morgan Stanley Bank. Morgan Stanley Bank was established in 1990, and became inactive in 2008 when it converted to a bank charter. Its total assets in 2000 were $1.9 billion, which grew to $8.7 billion in 2005, then jumped to $21 billion in 2006, and finally reached $35.1 billion before the crisis.[19]

---

[11] While many ILCs originated as small, community-based stand-alone institutions, the majority of currently active ILCs are owned and operated by a corporate parent—either a financial institution or a commercial enterprise. *See id.* at 16.

[12] Financially-owned ILCs continue to dominate commercially-owned ILCs with respect to both the number of ILCs and total assets. In 2010, financially-owned ILCs accounted for eighty-six percent of total assets and roughly three quarters of all ILCs between 2000 and 2010. *Id.* at 18. As of 2010, the two largest financially-owned ILCs—American Express Centurion Bank (owned by American Express) and UBS Bank USA (owned by UBS AG)—controlled about $30 billion in total assets each, while the largest commercially-owned ILC—BMW Bank of North America, owned by BMW AG—had only $8.2 billion in total assets. *Id.* at 20-24.

[13] As of 2010, ILCs accounted for approximately 0.5% of total insured institutions, and one percent of total insured deposits and total assets of insured institutions. *Id.* at 14.

[14] *See id.* at 11–15.

[15] *Id.* at 78 (Appendix 4).

[16] Kenneth Spong & Eric Robbins, *Industrial Loan Companies: A Growing Industry Sparks a Public Policy Debate*, 2007 FED. RESERVE BANK OF KAN. CITY ECON. REV. 41, 46 (2007).

[17] As an ILC, Merrill Lynch Bank USA offered a variety of deposit accounts, including money market deposit accounts, certificates of deposit, individual retirement accounts and market participation certificates. *Id.* at 48 (concluding that the rapid growth of Merrill Lynch Bank can be attributable to its decision to "[sweep] balances out of cash management accounts at the brokerage subsidiary and into MLB, thereby providing brokerage customers with deposits insured up to $100,000 at rates competitive with, or even exceeding, money market mutual funds. This practice is typical of ILCs owned by securities firms.").

[18] BARTH & LI, *supra* note 9, at 81. Following the takeover, it converted to a commercial bank charter. *Id.* at 45.

[19] *Id.* at 51.

The third largest ILC before the crisis was Ally Bank (formerly GMAC Automotive Bank), owned by General Motors. Ally Bank was established in 2004 and converted into a commercial bank charter in 2009. Ally Bank reported total assets of $1.2 billion in 2004, a number that jumped to $20 billion in 2006 and then to $28.4 billion in 2007. It exemplified a typical commercially-owned ILC, which served primarily to finance purchases of the commercial parent's products.[20] In 2006-07, however, the bulk of Ally Bank's assets were residential mortgages and related assets.[21] This shift in the business profile of Ally Bank reflected a larger trend toward financialization of the U.S. economy in the pre-crisis era, when large manufacturing and other commercial companies derived an increasingly high share of their profits from providing various financial services, often through their ILC subsidiaries.[22]

Interestingly, the greatest political controversy over commercial ownership of ILCs was not related to the transformation of household names like General Motors or General Electric into financial service providers. It arose in 2005, when the retail giant Walmart attempted to form a Utah-chartered ILC.[23] The primary activity of Walmart's proposed ILC was to "act as a sponsor for the processing and settlement of credit card payments, debit card payments, and check payments made by customers at Walmart stores."[24] Yet, the public outcry that resulted was unprecedented.[25] In response to widespread opposition from community bankers, the [Federal Reserve Board], labor unions, retail stores and members of Congress,[26] the FDIC placed a six-month moratorium on

---

[20] Thus, Ally Bank provided financing for consumers purchasing GM cars from the dealers, as well as so-called floor financing for GM dealerships. Other automotive companies, such as Toyota, BMW, and Harley-Davidson, also used their ILCs in a similar fashion. *See* Spong & Robbins, *supra* note 16, at 52.

[21] *See id.* (stating that, in 2007, $13.4 billion out of $16.4 billion in Ally Bank's total loans consisted of residential mortgages).

[22] GMAC's aggressive move into residential mortgage lending and trading of mortgage-backed securities was one of the causes that led it to the brink of failure and the federal bailout of GM and GMAC in 2009. *See* CONG. OVERSIGHT PANEL, THE UNIQUE TREATMENT OF GMAC UNDER THE TARP 39-41 (2010).

[23] This was not the first time that Wal-Mart had attempted to enter the banking industry. On June 29, 1999, Wal-Mart applied to acquire an Oklahoma federal savings association. This attempt was later blocked by the GLBA, which closed the unitary thrift holding company possibility that Wal-Mart had sought to use. *See* Zachariah J. Lloyd, *Waging War with Wal-Mart: A Cry for Change Threatens the Future of Industrial Loan Corporations*, 14 FORDHAM J. CORP. & FIN. L. 211, 223-24 (2008) ("Wal-Mart commenced its quest to own a bank in June 1999 when it applied to purchase a small thrift in Broken Arrow, Oklahoma named the Federal Bank Center."); Kevin Nolan, *Wal-Mart's Industrial Loan Company: The Risk to Community Banks*, 10 N.C. BANKING INST. 187, 191 (2006) ("Wal-Mart's first attempt to enter banking was an effort to purchase a small thrift institution named Federal BankCenter in Broken Arrow, Oklahoma."). On September 10, 2001, Wal-Mart entered into an agreement with TD Bank, by which TD Bank would offer banking products and services in Wal-Mart stores. This plan was eventually blocked by the OTS, which objected to Wal-Mart's plan to share the profits with TD Bank and to have its retail store employees perform banking transactions for TD Bank in its Wal-Mart stores. *Id.* In April 2002, Wal-Mart tried to purchase a $2.5 million California-chartered industrial bank named Franklin Bank. The California legislature quickly responded to this by enacting a law prohibiting non-financial institutions from acquiring state-chartered industrial banks, with certain exceptions. *Id.* at 192; Riva D. Atlas, *Wal-Mart is Seeking Approval to Buy a California Bank*, N.Y. TIMES, May 16, 2002, at C9.

[24] Arthur E. Wilmarth, Jr., *Wal-Mart and the Separation of Banking and Commerce*, 39 CONN. L. REV. 1539, 1541–42, 1544 (2007).

[25] In response to its invitation for public comments on Wal-Mart's application, the FDIC received approximately 13,800 comment letters, most of which vehemently opposed the idea. Lloyd, *supra* note 23, at 229.

[26] The widespread fear at the time was that Wal-Mart would eventually expand its banking services after the initial three-year period. ILCs are bound to its original business plan for the first three years. Afterwards, an ILC may seek permission to amend its charter and expand its business into full-service banking. Thus, it was conceivable that Wal-Mart, if permitted to acquire an ILC, could engage in full-service banking and establish additional branches in other states in a matter of years. *See* Lloyd, *supra* note 23, at 225-26.

Walmart's application and all other pending applications to obtain federal deposit insurance for ILCs. This moratorium was later extended for an additional year, but only with respect to applications by commercial firms for ILC ownership. Ultimately, on March 16, 2007, Walmart withdrew its application for an ILC bank charter.[27]

Even before the Walmart ILC controversy, members of Congress had attempted to pass legislation to block commercial companies from owning depository institutions. The financial crisis of 2007-09 pushed that issue to the background of the political debate. The crisis also fundamentally altered the landscape of the ILC industry, as many ILCs, including the three largest ones, closed or converted to commercial banks.[28] Nevertheless, commercial ownership of ILCs remains a potentially controversial matter.[29]

The controversy around Walmart and the use of the ILC structure by many investment banks led the Obama Administration to attempt to eliminate the ILC charter. That attempt was not successful and, in 2010, Congress only imposed a three-year moratorium on the granting of any new FDIC insurance for ILCs, essentially preventing any new charters. That moratorium ended on July 21, 2013 but the FDIC has not lifted its informal moratorium policy and it is widely understood that no new ILCs will be granted federal deposit insurance, a situation that has made the few remaining ILC charters even more valuable.

Also, in 2012, the Government Accountability Office (GAO) issued a congressionally mandated report on ILCs that found that, even with the BHCA ILC exemption in place, ILCs make up a very small percentage of the assets of the overall banking system and that there has been a consistent decline in the number of ILCs since 2006. The report found that subjecting ILCs to direct supervision under the BHCA would likely lead to a divestment or change in the business model for many holding companies with ILCs, which would lead to an even further decline in ILCs. GAO, BANK HOLDING COMPANY ACT: CHARACTERISTICS AND REGULATION OF EXEMPT INSTITUTIONS AND THE IMPLICATIONS OF REMOVING THE EXEMPTIONS 33–35 (2012).

---

1. ***Walmart Bank.*** Was the controversy of Walmart about the purity of the line between banking and commerce or concerns about the social and political power of Walmart? How is the situation different from the UK where a major grocery chain (Tesco) also runs a bank? After Walmart gave up on forming its own bank, it was not, in fact, deterred from placing banking services in its stores. Instead, it entered into partnerships and other prepaid card arrangements with some smaller banks. What, if anything, was achieved by keeping Walmart from

---

[27] Wal-Mart appears to have found other methods of engaging in banking activities. On June 20, 2007, Wal-Mart unveiled its plan to open "MoneyCenters" in its stores, which are financial services centers that allow customers to cash checks, pay bills and obtain prepaid Visa cards. *See generally* Jonathan Birchall, *Walmart Extends its Banking Interests*, FIN. TIMES (June 16, 2010); Charles Kabugo-Musoke, *Consumer Focus: A Walmart Owned ILC: Why Congress Should Give the Green Light*, 15 N.C. BANKING INST. 393 (2011) (examining in detail Wal-Mart's efforts to offer financial services).

[28] BARTH & LI, *supra* note 9, at 45. In 2007, the total assets of the five largest ILCs stood at \$192.7 billion; in 2010, the figure was \$90.4 billion. *Id.* at 51.

[29] Today, many commercially owned ILCs are in the automotive industry, with parents companies like Toyota, BMW and Harley-Davidson. Other commercial companies with ILCs include GE, Target and Fry's Electronics. *Id.* at 67.

owning a bank while permitting its competitor, Target, to do so? For an interesting argument by one academic on how the motivations behind "Sam's Bank" were actually related to Walmart's goal to decrease its payments processing costs by issuing its own credit cards, see Ronald Mann, *A Requiem for Sam's Bank*, 83 CHI.-KENT L. REV. 953 (2008). For an argument that the acquisition of ILCs by commercial companies will lead to systemic risk, see Arthur E. Wilmarth Jr., *Wal-Mart and the Separation of Banking and Commerce*, 39 CONN. L. REV. 1539 (2007). For another example of the fight between the banking sector and big box retailers, see the discussion of the Durbin Amendment in Chapter 7.2.

III. COMPETITIVE EQUALITY—FEDERAL AND STATE LAW

The interplay between state and federal law historically cast a long shadow over the choice between a state or federal charter for a commercial bank. Understanding how this interplay has evolved over time is important for understanding why the banking system and its regulatory architecture look as they do today. Early struggles between the federal and state banking systems were intense battles, sometimes to the point of one system trying to destroy the other. The famous case of *McCulloch v. Maryland* was triggered by Maryland's attempt to tax the branches of the Second Bank of the United States. 17 U.S. 316, 317 (1819). Additionally, Treasury Secretary Chase unsuccessfully attempted to drive state-chartered banks out of business after the Civil War by a punitive tax on bank-issued notes. By the mid to late 20th Century, the competition between the two systems had devolved into the much less intense and poorly defined concept of competitive equality. Regulatory competition is the idea that the presence of two potential primary regulators reduces the likelihood of unimaginative and unresponsive regulation of the banking system that could occur where there is a monopoly of regulation. This competition was an important element of the dual banking system during much of the 20th Century. The main functional way regulators competed for influence was through the powers they afforded to banks. Duality and competition, especially among charters and their powers, it was thought, would force both state and federal regulators to respond to a changing market and technological forces. At least one academic has suggested that the dual banking system is a pale shadow of its past. Carl Felsenfeld & Genci Bilali, *Is There a Dual Banking System?*, 2 J. BUS., ENTREPRENEURSHIP & L. 30, 64–75 (2008).

Arthur Burns, a former chairman of the Federal Reserve Board, once called the dual banking system "competition in laxity." Because it is possible for an existing bank to convert its charter from national to state, or vice versa, during the 20th Century, state and federal bank regulators tried to dissuade banks under their jurisdiction from converting to the other system through interpretation or amendment of existing law. For conversions, see 12 U.S.C. §§ 214–214c. History has shown more than one instance of a regulator offering greater powers or more friendly regulation and supervision in order to encourage banks to convert from one form of charter to the other. For example, in order to forestall conversions from state to national charter, a majority of state legislatures enacted "wild card" statutes, under which powers granted to national banks automatically extend to their state-chartered banks. During the latter half of the 20th Century, there was a trend by some states to provide the state-chartered banks with powers not available to national banks, especially in the arena of insurance underwriting, real estate, and corporate debt/equity underwriting, at a time when the value of the bank charter was declining from competitive incursions from other parts of the financial sector.

The Comptroller, the Federal Reserve Board, and the FDIC have one weapon that is not available to the states due to federal preemption. If a federal regulator can convince Congress to enact a law that is binding, not only on national banks and member banks but also on all IDIs, the national system need not adjust to the state law to remain attractive as a chartering authority; state banks would be subject to the federal law regardless of their charter. The structure of the "wild card" statutes means that even state-chartered banks can preempt state law with respect to powers.

During the course of the 20th Century, the federal government gained increasing power over the banking system and over state-chartered banks. Under the Federal Reserve Act of 1913, the Federal Reserve Board gained direct supervisory authority over state banks that chose to join the Federal Reserve System, as an increasing number, but not all of them, did. Gradually, many federal-level constraints on national banks, which are required to be members in the Federal Reserve System, were also imposed upon state member banks. The federal government gained additional authority over state nonmember banks when it offered them deposit insurance from the FDIC. Insurance has been available to state nonmember banks since 1933, and today it is obligatory for state-chartered and national banks, thrifts, ILCs, and federal credit unions to carry federal insurance on their deposits. For several years, the Federal Reserve Board lobbied for Congressional approval of identical reserve requirements for most deposits, whether for member or nonmember banks. The legislation was finally enacted in 1980. As a result, state-chartered nonmember banks lost most of the competitive advantage of differing state-law reserve requirements. In the period between the development of a national market in banking and the Dodd-Frank Act, the OCC also took an aggressive view on the preemption of other state financial consumer laws. As a result, during the late 20th Century, many state-chartered banks found it advantageous to convert to national bank charters as their operations became multi-state to take advantage of the strong preemption regulations issued by the OCC. You will learn more about consumer protection and the Dodd-Frank Act cutbacks to national bank preemption of consumer financial protection laws in Part V.

Preemption has also played out in the courts. You will recall the *Marquette* case in Chapter 1.4 in which the Supreme Court permitted national banks to export the interest rates in one state to another. 439 U.S. 299, 313–19 (1978). The Exportation Doctrine, as it is called, was so powerful that only two years after the *Marquette* decision, Congress also applied the same principles to state-chartered banks. DIDMCA of 1980, Pub. L. No. 96-221, § 521, 94 Stat. 132 (1980) (adding 12 U.S.C. § 1831d(a)). *See also* Elizabeth R. Schiltz, *The Amazing, Elastic, Ever-Expanding Exportation Doctrine and Its Effect on Predatory Lending Regulation*, 88 MINN. L. REV. 518, 567 (2004).

The long-standing competition over powers was limited by the Federal Deposit Insurance Corporation Improvement Act (FDICIA) in 1991, which added § 24 to the Federal Deposit Insurance Act of 1950 (FDIA) in response to the Savings & Loan Crisis. Section 24, as implemented by the FDIC's regulations at 12 C.F.R. § 362, restricts state-chartered banks from engaging in activities or making investments, as principal, not permitted to national banks, absent FDIC approval. 12 U.S.C. § 1831a. These restrictions only apply to activities undertaken as principal rather than on an agency basis. "For example, this [restriction] does not cover acting solely as agent for the sale of insurance, securities, real estate, or travel services; nor does it cover acting as trustee, providing personal financial planning advice, or safekeeping services." 12 C.F.R. § 362.1(b)(1). Additionally, the restrictions have certain exceptions for even principal-based activities, such as underwriting certain agricultural insurance products, and grandfathered the insurance underwriting activities of approximately six state banks. Richard M. Whiting, *Key Issues Unresolved as Banks, Insurance Firms Keep Fighting over Turf*, BANKING POL'Y REP. 1, May 15, 1995.

From the above discussion, one might conclude that state and national banks, after many years of variances, are essentially equal under state or federal law. Certainly, we are now far from the original dual banking system, with independent federal and state regulators and independent state and national banking systems. Felsenfeld & Bilali, *Is There a Dual Banking System?*, at 64–75. Thrifts, credit unions, and ILCs, moreover, all continue to have power limitations in their charters. Federal law may be more or less generous than state law in governing traditional banking activity, and that calculation will change as federal or state law changes.

In addition, § 24 of the FDIA may not have put to rest the fight between state banks and national banks, as the section grants the FDIC power to approve activities for state banks that are impermissible for national banks, if the activities do not threaten the Deposit Insurance Fund (DIF). *See* Robyn Meredith, *FDIC Lets State Banks Do What National Banks Can't*, AM. BANKER, August 18, 1994. In its regulations, the FDIC has stated that certain activities can be engaged in by state banks or their subsidiaries that are impermissible for national banks without any application or notice to the FDIC, such as holding stock in IDIs or investing up to 15% of tier one capital in money market preferred stock. For certain real estate investments and activities, the FDIC has provided a quick-turnaround notice procedure. Other activities require more fulsome applications, in which the FDIC will likely consider the condition of the state bank and the risk of the proposed activities, and will likely attach various conditions to the state bank's permission to engage in the activities. Some of these applications and approvals are listed on the FDIC's website, and include, for example, engaging in travel agency activities as principal, engaging in auto rental activities, and creating a joint venture to construct mausoleums. *See* 12 C.F.R. § 362; FDIC, DECISIONS ON BANK APPLICATIONS: INVESTMENTS & ACTIVITIES (2012).

Despite convergence in the rules governing bank powers, a bank's experience will almost certainly be different at the level of supervision, enforcement, and intensity of regulatory attitude. An adviser to incorporators should be prepared to identify and investigate the factors that may make one charter more desirable than the other depending upon the size and business model of the bank. There has been one study that posited, for example, that since 2003, smaller banks have preferred the state charter because of lower supervisory costs and higher lending limits while larger banks have preferred the national bank charter to take advantage of the preemption of state consumer loans. Gary W. Whalen, *Why do De Novo Banks Choose a National Charter?* (OCC Economics Working Paper No. 2010-2). The increasingly strict attitude of the NYDFS, and its propensity to enter into enforcement proceedings with high fines (discussed further in Chapter 8.1), has led many to shy away from the New York State bank charter in the post-Financial Crisis era even though, traditionally, the New York State charter has been viewed as an attractive one.

An important regulatory consideration for those banks with a nationwide consumer business model is the extent to which the states may regulate the activities of federally chartered institutions. We will discuss preemption and consumer protection in Chapter 5.2.

---

1. ***Lottery-Linked Savings.*** A client comes to you with an idea for a lottery-linked savings account. The concept is to encourage banking clients in poorer urban areas where lottery tickets are often sold to put the same amount into a savings account. Every week, every person who puts money into that account will be entered into a bank-run lottery and might get a large cash prize. The difference between a state-run lottery and the bank-run lottery is that the customer still has their savings after the lottery. The savings accounts would pay little or no interest, other than the cash prizes. Why would a bank want to enter into such a scheme? Could a national bank do it? *See* 12 U.S.C. § 25a; *see also* 18 U.S.C. § 1306. What about a federal thrift? 12 U.S.C. § 1463(e). What about a federal credit union? *Id.* § 1757. What about a state member bank? *See id.* § 339. Is the situation the same for a nonmember state bank or a state-chartered credit union? *Id.* § 1829a; MICH. COMP. LAWS § 490.411 (2004). Are state laws likely to permit lottery-linked savings? *See* VA. CODE ANN. § 6.2-603.1 (2015); ILL. PUB. ACT 099-0149 (2015); ARK. CODE ANN. § 23-47-209 (2015). Would states that run and rely upon the revenue from their own lotteries be more or less likely to support lottery-linked savings?

2. ***Marijuana Banking.*** How can or should a legal marijuana business operating in a state that has made medical or recreational use of marijuana legal obtain banking services? The sale and distribution of marijuana remains a crime at the federal level, as does aiding and abetting, which would include banking services. 21 U.S.C. § 841(a)(1) (making it unlawful "to manufacture, distribute, or dispense . . . a controlled substance"); § 802(6) (defining controlled substances to include drugs in "schedule I"); § 812(c) (classifying marijuana as a schedule I drug). Does a Department of Justice (DOJ) policy of non-prosecution change the law enough for a national bank or a state-chartered bank to open a business bank account or make loans to such a business? Could a state pass a law creating a type of financial institution that escaped all federal control? *See* COLO. REV. STAT. §§ 11-33-101 to 128 (2014) (authorizing financial cooperatives to provide banking services to marijuana businesses). How would such an

institution function without deposit insurance and how would it gain access to the federally run payments system? *See* Julie A. Hill, *Banks, Marijuana, and Federalism*, 65 CASE W. RES. L. REV. 597 (2015). In July 2015, Denver-based Fourth Corner Credit Union filed suit against the Federal Reserve Board alleging it was unfairly denied access to the financial system after the Federal Reserve Board denied its application for a master account. The master account would have allowed Fourth Corner to interact with other financial institutions and engage in business with state-licensed marijuana businesses in Colorado. In its decision, the Federal Reserve Board cited its discretion in granting or denying applications. Nathaniel Popper, *Banking for Pot Industry Hits a Roadblock*, N.Y. TIMES, July 30, 2015.

IV. RENT-A-CHARTER

The development of the Internet, as well as the creation of sophisticated computer algorithms for analyzing the creditworthiness of borrowers, has led to the rapid growth of online lending platforms operating on a national scale without a bank charter. Large banks have noticed, with the Chairman and CEO of JPMorgan remarking that:

> Silicon Valley is coming. There are hundreds of startups with a lot of brains and money working on various alternatives to traditional banking. The ones you read about most are in the lending business, whereby the firms can lend to individuals and small businesses very quickly and—these entities believe—effectively by using Big Data to enhance credit underwriting.

Letter from Jamie Dimon, Chairman & CEO, JPMorgan Chase, to JPMorgan Chase Shareholders (Apr. 8, 2015).

Most of the online peer-to-peer lenders are fulfilling a need for consumer and small business loans which most banks, other than the smallest community banks, have cut back on post-Financial Crisis. Online lenders can be more attractive than community banks, or other non-bank sources of financing, because their loan applications are typically granted or denied within a few hours as a result of the computer algorithms used to gauge creditworthiness. Online lenders also compete for credit card customers by offering lower-rate installment loans.

The absence of a bank charter means, of course, that the online lenders cannot take deposits from the public. It also means that the online lender cannot avail itself of the preemption powers, discussed in section III above. Unlike chartered banks, these online lenders would need to comply with the laws of each state in which they originate loans. For example, many states have requirements that a lender be licensed if it wants to lend to borrowers in that state. Some states do not have a licensing requirement or the requirement may only apply to certain kinds of loans, such as consumer loans, or up to a certain level of loan, say $5,000. An online lender needs to be attentive to the requirements of each state and pay attention to any changes in the regulations. A chartered bank, however, may make loans in most states without a separate state-by-state license and need only concern itself with the licensing requirements of its chartering authority. Moreover, a chartered bank benefits from the Usury Exportation Doctrine from *Marquette*.

As a result, the most common business model for online lenders has been to enter into a partnership with a relatively small chartered bank. This bank partnership, also known as the rent-a-charter model, enables the online lender to operate on a much wider scale without the added burden of state-by-state compliance. In the typical rent-a-charter arrangement, the online lender markets the loans and runs its proprietary computer algorithms, but the actual loan is granted and funded by the bank. The bank holds the loan for a few days, typically three days, and then sells it to the online lender or a third party. The originating bank might retain a portion of the loan, usually 5%, on its books.

---

1. ***Different Charters in Bank Partners.*** It is common for an Internet marketplace lender to have partnerships with more than one bank. Utah ILCs are a common choice in combination with either a national bank or a state-chartered bank from another state. Why would Internet lenders choose to enter into a partnership with banks that have different chartering authorities?

2. ***Technology-driven Change.*** As a matter of policy, should the banking regulators permit non-banks to take advantage of a bank charter? Consider how technological change has an impact on an existing marketplace with licensed incumbents. Does anything about the rent-a-charter model remind you of Uber, smartphone technology, and taxi drivers who have had to purchase highly controlled and limited licenses (read charters) from a governmental authority? How much has technology driven the online lenders and how much is driven by the dearth of new bank charters since the Financial Crisis?

3. ***Small Business Lending.*** It is often said that small businesses are the engine of job growth in the United States and yet banks have cut back their lending in that area post-Financial Crisis. As a matter of social and economic policy, who benefits and who is hurt by the online lenders? What happens when the business cycle turns and the loan default rate goes up? What about protections for small business owners? They are generally not covered by most consumer protection laws. Should they be?

4. ***A Fintech Regime?*** The UK has decided to regulate online lenders by instituting a regulatory regime, overseen by the Financial Conduct Authority, that licenses online lenders and requires them to abide by certain regulations including capital requirements. Why haven't the U.S. regulators chosen this route? Why are the banking regulators choosing to let this new competitor to the chartered bank operate? What benefits and risks do you see? Ryan Tracy & Peter Rudegeair, *U.S. Treasury Looks into Online Marketplace Lending Industry*, WALL ST. J., July 16, 2015. Should bank regulators set up a new regulatory system under which bank partners of online lenders using the rent-a-charter model have to comply with a set of fintech-tailored prudential and consumer protection requirements to facilitate responsible online lending? Or should they stand back and let innovation take place?

5. ***Exportation Doctrine.*** Online lenders, as purchasers from a national or state-chartered bank, benefit from the Exportation Doctrine, which is necessary

since many of the loans have high interest rates. There is now a split in the circuits as to whether third-party non-bank buyers of debt from banks should benefit from the Exportation Doctrine. *See* Madden v. Midland Funding, LLC, 786 F.3d 246, 249–53 (2d Cir. 2015), *petition for cert. filed*, (U.S. Nov. 10, 2015) (No. 15-610) (holding that federal preemption did not extend to a non-bank purchaser of debt from a bank under a substantial interference test); Krispin v. May Dep't Stores Co., 218 F.3d 919, 924 (8th Cir. 2000) (finding that federal preemption applied to credit card accounts purchased from a national bank because "it makes sense to look to the originating entity (the bank), and not the ongoing assignee (the store), in determining whether the [National Bank Act] applies"). At least one state, West Virginia, has reached the conclusion that a bank should have a predominant economic interest in the loan in order to apply the Exportation Doctrine. CashCall, Inc. v. Morrisey, No. 12-1274, 2014 WL 2404300 (W. Va. May 30, 2014). Aside from the uncertainty these court decisions create for the rent-a-charter model, can you think of other consequences for the business of banking if more courts were to follow *Madden* and/or *CashCall*?

V. WHAT IS A BANK?

The traditional bank and other depository institution charter permits firms to take deposits and make loans. Chartered depository institutions have exclusive rights to take insured deposits. Many non-banks, however, make or arrange loans or their functional equivalents, from consumer finance companies and peer-to-peer platforms to broker-dealers underwriting bonds or placing commercial paper in the capital markets. Moreover, many institutions without a bank charter provide deposit-like facilities that are functionally similar to deposit taking. Shadow banking activities involve engaging in maturity transformation and using deposit-substitutes to make loan-substitutes. Money Market Funds offer instant liquidity to investors and use the funds they raise to lend to broker-dealers and other financial intermediaries. In the lead up to the Financial Crisis, for example, large broker-dealers funded themselves, and the mortgage-backed securitizations that they sponsored, with overnight repo, which investors treated as cash; when the crisis hit, these repo depositors ran, just as in prior days when retail depositors ran on banks. *See* Gary Gorton, *Slapped in the Face by the Invisible Hand: Banking and the Panic of 2007* (2009); MORGAN RICKS, THE MONEY PROBLEM: RETHINKING FINANCIAL REGULATION (2016). Yet shadow banking activities were subject to a much different set of rules. Is securitization backed by repo, banking? How should shadow banking activities be regulated? Should there be the equivalent of deposit insurance, Federal Reserve liquidity provision and prudential regulation for shadow banking? Or conversely, should the government consider shadow banking activities to be market-based financing that should be governed by different rules? Eugene Ludwig, former Comptroller of the Currency, has suggested a regulatory principle of "like kind, like size, like regulation." Eugene Ludwig, *Unregulated Shadow Banks Are a Ticking Time Bomb*, AM. BANKER (Mar. 15, 2016). If the government regulates some shadow banking institutions or activities more heavily than in the past, where will risk go next? These are central questions that will be raised throughout the remainder of the book as you explore different aspects of financial markets.

CHAPTER 2.2

ACTIVITIES RESTRICTIONS AND THE BUSINESS OF BANKING

CONTENTS

I. INTRODUCTION

A. THE BUSINESS OF BANKING

The chartered commercial bank is an institution with limited powers that does not enjoy the general powers of the modern business corporation. The model of fractional reserve banking with maturity mismatch and its penchant for panics and runs, especially in the era before deposit insurance, brought about an early and intense governmental interest in limiting the powers of the chartered commercial bank. In this chapter, we consider the powers designated as the "business of banking," a concept that applies solely to the chartered commercial bank. It should not be confused with the broader yet separate concepts of "closely related to banking," "financial in nature," and "complementary," all of which apply to limit the activities of affiliates of banks within a financial conglomerate and which will be covered in Chapter 6.1. Because bank affiliates are broader than the "business of banking," any activity within "the business of banking" is logically part of the activities deemed to be "closely related to banking," or "financial in nature." The reverse is not true.

A core principle used to define the "business of banking" is the separation of banking and commerce and English banking history has had a major influence on banking in the United States. The proposal to establish the Bank of England in 1694 made the existing merchant bankers, who were also commercial traders, apprehensive that the Bank of England might be a formidable competitor in the field of commercial trade. To put the fears of the merchants to rest, a clause was added to the bill forbidding the Bank of England to trade in "goods, wares or merchandise." The limit on the power of a bank to enter directly into trade or commerce remains the dominant philosophy used to define the business of banking. The first incorporated bank in the United States was The Bank of North America, and the bank's charter, issued by the Pennsylvania Assembly on April 1, 1782, expressly forbade the bank from engaging in commercial activities like trading goods and holding real estate; most 19th Century commercial bank charters were similar. There are, however, a few scattered counterexamples, such as the Manhattan Company, which ran both a waterworks and a bank in 19th Century New York City, and the erstwhile Chemical Bank, which began as a chemical manufacturer. For more information on this era in U.S. banking, see HOWARD BODENHORN, STATE BANKING IN EARLY AMERICA 134–35 (2002) and BRAY HAMMOND, BANKS AND POLITICS IN AMERICA: FROM THE REVOLUTION TO THE CIVIL WAR 151–57, 569 (2003). Limitations on commercial investors in IDIs and in the treatment of ILCs, were discussed in Chapter 2.1. Commercial investments by non-bank affiliates of financial conglomerates present a more complex and porous situation and are discussed in Chapter 6.2.

In the long period during which deposit-taking banks in the United States participated in a fractional reserve system but there was no lender of last resort or stable system of federal deposit insurance, portfolio shaping rules were a key way that the states, and later the OCC, tried to limit risk. The asset side of the balance sheets of classic 19th Century or early 20th Century banks would be barely recognizable to us now. During that time, commercial banks engaged largely in short-term business loans, the discounting of receivables, and bills of exchange, the "real bills" of farmers, manufacturers and which matured within 60 to 90 days. The other major asset of commercial banks was government bonds: either U.S. Treasuries (keeping in mind that the main purpose of the national banking system was to finance the Civil War) or bonds issued by the state in which a state bank was chartered. Long-term loans extended to finance commercial industry or secured by real estate (mortgages) were not seen as part of the core business of a commercial bank and were discouraged by the real bills orthodoxy, although much recent historical research shows that such longer-term loans were happening more often than a strict real bills theory would permit. BODENHORN, STATE BANKING IN EARLY AMERICA, 52–56. Most long-term corporate lending took place in the form of bonds (initially railroad bonds) underwritten by investment banks, which we would today call broker-dealers.

In essence, 19th Century commercial banks were narrow banks that focused on short-term lending in order to control the risks of the maturity mismatch as compared to today's commercial banks, which engage in a wider variety of business. One highly liquid banking system forgotten to history was the Forstall System put in place by the Louisiana Banking Act of 1842. The core of the Forstall System was that banks were required to maintain specie reserves (gold in their vault or a reserve city vault) equal to one-third of bank notes issued plus deposit liabilities. The other two-thirds were required to be invested in 90-day short-term paper. The Forstall System was the forerunner to the National Banking Act, and it grew out of the financial panic of 1837. The U.S. Postal Savings System was also a narrow bank from 1911 to 1967 and, at the time of the Banking Panic of 1933, was the only depository institution whose deposits were backed by the full faith and credit of the United States. Its deposits were invested solely in U.S. Treasuries. Both of these systems might be called either limited fractional reserve systems or narrow banks.

Economic historians have noted that the concept of long-term corporate lending commitments by banks was developed after the Great Depression and that lending on real estate (what we would call mortgages) was perceived by many of the 19th and early 20th Century bankers as inherently risky, albeit a practice that clearly grew as a proportion of commercial bank balance sheets in the 1920s even before deposit insurance was introduced. Loans collateralized by home mortgages or agricultural land were seen as very risky and either severely limited or, in the case of early national banks, prohibited.

Investors in chartered banks have always preferred to have a broader range of powers and a significant factor underlying the desire and support for broadening banking powers has long been competition from other financial intermediaries. In the late 19th and early 20th Centuries, national banks, unlike state banks, were prohibited from making any loans secured by real estate; naturally, national banks fought to gradually increase their ability to make loans where real estate was the collateral. For a long time, national banks did not have trust powers and so, in the early 20th Century, a competing system of trust companies developed while national banks were gradually given trust powers. The question of whether national banks could broker or underwrite property and life insurance has been ongoing since the early part of the 20th Century. The late 20th Century battle around the erosion of the Glass-Steagall Act limits—which played out only in small part in the business of banking in the chartered bank itself and more significantly in the "closely related to banking activities" of bank affiliates that will be discussed in Chapter 6.1—should be seen as one small and very recent subchapter in a centuries-old debate about the scope of the powers of the chartered commercial bank.

As you explore the limits on the "business of banking," *i.e.*, the powers of what can be done within the actual insured depository institution (IDI) itself, remember that the limits on the business of banking have not been shaped in a pure environment of disinterested public policy experts concerned solely with the safety and soundness of bank depositors. The expansion of or limits on bank powers have involved a mix of legislative and regulatory battles, sometimes including court decisions in the United States, and have been shaped by the rough and tumble scrum of competing stakeholders. Whether it was English merchant bankers wanting to keep the Bank of England out of trade 300 years ago, the insurance agents wanting to keep national banks out of insurance agency beginning in the early 20th Century, travel agents and data processors 30 years ago, or the mutual fund and securities sector 25 years ago, each expansion or limitation on the powers of the chartered commercial bank reflects past battles between various stakeholders in financial services as much as it reflects concerns about bank safety and soundness and the stability of the banking system overall. It also reflects the nature of the banking and financial system of that economic and social time, and what happens to those systems as markets, technology, and social norms change.

It is ironic that the most major expansion of commercial bank powers in the 20th Century—the ability to make long-term mortgage loans on real estate collateral, a major contributor to the last two major banking crises in this country (the Savings & Loan Crisis and the Financial Crisis), which also played a major role in the Great Depression—is rarely focused on in banking law courses because, unlike other expansions of bank powers, it came about gradually during the 20th Century, was expanded and not contracted during the New Deal, and did not generate any court decisions from competing financial sector stakeholders. The expansion is also an integral part of promoting the American Dream of owning one's own home.

B. INCIDENTAL POWERS

The core starting point for the business of banking is defining the scope of permissible bank activities. The fact that the powers of the chartered commercial bank are limited is well understood; the precise nature of the limitation is not. The confusion is due in part to the fact that bank powers are typically defined circularly to include "the business of banking"—a phrase that can be found in banking statutes or charters since the earliest days of the United States and in the National Bank Act since the initial statute was enacted in 1863. The critical statutory phrasing in 12 U.S.C. § 24(Seventh) has changed little since then:

> [A] national banking association . . . shall have power . . . [t]o exercise . . . all such incidental powers as shall be necessary to carry on *the business of banking*; by discounting and negotiating promissory notes, drafts, bills of exchange, and other evidences of debt; by receiving deposits; by buying and selling exchange, coin, and bullion; by loaning money on personal security; and by obtaining, issuing, and circulating notes according to the provisions of [this Chapter]. (emphasis added)

Exactly what this clause means has been a matter of considerable debate and litigation. Under a narrow view, permissible banking activity is limited to the enumerated five powers. The broad view sees the business of banking as a separate grant of power that is flexible and open to interpretation under the "incidental thereto" language.

The issues of interpretation around the broad and narrow views are explored in the following case and the comments and questions that follow:

Arnold Tours, Inc. v. Camp

472 F.2d 427 (1st Cir. 1972)

HAMLEY, Circuit Judge.

This class action involves the authority of national banks to engage in the travel agency business. The plaintiffs are Arnold Tours, Inc., and forty-one other independent travel agents of Massachusetts engaged in the travel agency business.

One of the defendants is William B. Camp, Comptroller of the Currency (Comptroller), whose office has issued rulings and regulations to the effect that national banks may engage in that business. The other defendant is South Shore National Bank (South Shore), a national banking association chartered by the United States Government, with a principal place of business in Quincy, Massachusetts, and with twenty-seven branch offices throughout Massachusetts. South Shore has been engaged in the travel agency business, operating it as a department of the bank, since November, 1966, after having bought out the fourth largest travel bureau in New England. Plaintiffs asked for declaratory and injunctive relief, the effect of which would be to force South Shore out of the travel business. . . .

The parties are in agreement that if there is any statutory authority for national banks to engage in the travel agency business, it is to be found in the following language contained in 12 U.S.C. § 24, Seventh, a provision of the National Bank Act (Act): "Seventh. To exercise . . . all such incidental powers as shall be necessary to carry on the business of banking. . . ."

The Comptroller relied upon the quoted statutory words in his 1963 ruling that national banks could engage in the travel agency business. Thus, paragraph 7475 of the Comptroller's Manual for National Banks (1963), which is now codified as 12 C.F.R. § 7.7475, reads:

> § 7.7475 National banks acting as travel agents
>
> Incident to those powers vested in them under 12 U.S.C. 24, national banks may provide travel services for their customers and receive compensation therefor. Such services may include the sale of trip insurance and the rental of automobiles as agent for a local rental service. In connection therewith, national banks may advertise, develop, and extend such travel services for the purpose of attracting customers to the bank.

In holding that 12 U.S.C. § 24, Seventh, did not authorize national banks to engage in the travel agency business the district court, in its opinion, first focused attention on the nature of South Shore's travel agency operation. . . .

The district court then observed that "To say that conduct of a [travel agency business] is a sine qua non to the successful operation of a national bank is a self-refuting proposition, especially in view of the fact that on the defendants' own claim only 122 national banks out of the many hundreds if not thousands in existence were providing travel agency services in 1967." 338 F. Supp. at 723.

The Comptroller argues that the district court applied an erroneous legal standard in reviewing the Comptroller's construction of the "incidental powers" clause of the National Bank Act (12 U. S.C. § 24, Seventh), as indicated by the court's above-quoted use of the term sine qua non.

We are in agreement with the Comptroller that a sine qua non standard would be an inappropriate measure of a national bank's incidental powers under 12 U.S.C. § 24, Seventh. While the pertinent language of that section refers to all such incidental powers "as shall be necessary to carry on the business of banking," we do not believe "necessary" was there used to connote that which is indispensable.

But we believe that, read in context with its entire opinion, the district court's reference to the concept of sine qua non was not intended to state the test for determining whether a particular bank activity is authorized as an incidental power. What seems to us to be a more reliable gauge of the district court's rationale is its discussion immediately following the sine qua non statement quoted in the margin.[6]

The district court therein indicated that its chief concern was whether a travel agency business primarily involves the performance of financial transactions pertaining to money or substitutes therefor. If not, the court in effect ruled, that business was not within the normal and traditional range of the monetary activities of a national bank, and thus not encompassed by the "incidental powers" provision of 12 U.S.C. § 24, Seventh. It was on this basis that the district court distinguished the travel agency business from such approved "incidental powers" of national banks as those employed in selling travelers' checks or foreign currency, issuing letters of credit, or making travel loans.

But the Comptroller and South Shore do not agree that the "incidental powers" of national banks should even be restricted to the performance of financial transactions pertaining to money or substitutes therefor or that only such transactions lie within the normal traditional range of the activities of a national bank. The Comptroller and South Shore, for example, refer to *McCulloch v. Maryland*, 17 U.S. (4 Wheat.) 316, 4 L. Ed. 579 (1819), which upheld the constitutionality of the first Bank of the United States, as laying down the broad principle that the word "necessary" may include that which is convenient, or useful. . . .

The Comptroller and South Shore refer to the fact that the New York free banking law, enacted in 1838, contained an "incidental powers" provision almost identical with that contained in the National Bank Act, enacted in 1863; that, in 1857, a New York Court of Appeals in *Curtis v. Leavitt*, 15 N.Y. 9 (1857), gave the quoted words of the New York Act an expansive reading; and that those who sponsored the National Bank Act in Congress made it clear that the federal legislation was copied, almost word for word, from the earlier New York Act.

The essence of the New York decision in *Curtis* is distilled in these words in the opinion of the court:

> But necessity is a word of flexible meaning. There may be an absolute necessity, and a small necessity; and between these degrees there may be others depending on the ever varying exigencies of human affairs. It is plain that corporations, in executing their express powers, are not confined to means of such indispensable necessity that without them there could be no execution at all. . . .

15 N.Y. at 64.

We are in accord with these views and we are willing to assume that Congress entertained these views when it enacted the National Bank Act. But we do not find these views particularly helpful in determining whether the district court erred in holding that a national bank's incidental powers under 12 U.S.C. § 24, Seventh, are limited to the

---

[6] Immediately after its sine qua non references, the district court said:

> I find that defendants' argument that because the bank may engage in selling letters of credit, travelers' checks and foreign currency, or make travel loans, it therefore should also be allowed to engage in the travel business, is a complete non sequitur. Selling travelers' checks or foreign currency, issuing letters of credit or making loans, are all financial transactions as they involve money or substitutes therefor, and all are obviously within the normal traditional range of monetary activities of a national bank. The difference between these activities and conducting a travel agency is just as great as the difference between these activities and running a mill, which was proscribed many many years ago in Cockrill v. Abeles, 86 F.2d 505 (8 Cir. 1898). 338 F. Supp. at 723.

performance of financial transactions pertaining to money or substitutes therefor, and that the travel agency business falls outside the scope of such powers because it is not within the normal traditional range of the monetary activities of a national bank. It may be convenient and useful for a national bank to carry on any number of activities. But one of the critical questions here is whether a convenient and useful activity be within the incidental powers of a bank if it is not directly related to what 12 U.S.C. § 24, Seventh, refers to as "the business of banking."

The most reliable guides as to what is encompassed in the term "the business of banking" are the express powers of national banks as set out in the National Bank Act. And when one looks at past decisions it becomes apparent that the activities of national banks which have been held to be permissible under the "incidental powers" provision have been those which are directly related to one or another of a national bank's express powers.

Thus, in *Merchants' Bank v. State Bank*, 77 U.S. (10 Wall.) 604, 19 L. Ed. 1008 (1870), the Supreme Court held that national banks may, as an incidental power, engage in the practice of certifying checks. The Court there recognized the great similarity between the activity of certifying checks and the express power granted by the National Bank Act to discount and negotiate bills of exchange.

In *First National Bank v. National Exchange Bank*, 92 U.S. 122, 127, 23 L. Ed. 679 (1875), the Court held that the power to acquire stock in settlement of a claim arising out of a legitimate banking transaction is an incidental power of national banks. In *Wyman v. Wallace*, 201 U.S. 230, 243 (1906), the Court held that national banks may, as an incidental power, borrow money. The Court referred to a line of cases which trace back to *Auten v. United States Nat. Bank*, 174 U.S. 125, 141, 142 (1899), in which the Court had noted that a greater part of banking practice was "in strict sense borrowing" and that several of the express powers granted to banks created a debtor-creditor relationship.

In *Miller v. King*, 223 U.S. 505, 510-511 (1912), the Court held that national banks may, as an incidental power, collect a judgment on behalf of a depositor. Similarly, in *Clement National Bank v. Vermont*, 231 U.S. 120, 139-140 (1913), the Supreme Court held that national banks may, as an incidental power, pay taxes on behalf of depositors. As the Court there indicated, this activity is directly related to the express power of national banks to receive deposits.

In *First National Bank v. Hartford*, 273 U.S. 548, 559-560 (1927), the Court found that the sale of mortgages and other evidences of debt, acquired in the exercise of the express power to loan money and to discount and negotiate other evidences of debt, was permissible under the bank's incidental powers. In *Colorado Nat. Bank v. Bedford*, 310 U.S. 41, 49 (1940), the Court held that the operation of a safe deposit business was embraced within the bank's incidental powers because the operation of a safe deposit business is virtually identical to the express statutory authority of national banks to accept special deposits. 12 U.S.C. § 133.

Finally, in *Franklin Nat. Bank v. New York*, 347 U.S. 373, 375-377 (1957), the Court held that national banks were entitled to advertise the word "savings" because such advertising was incidental to the express power of such banks to receive time and savings deposits and to pay interest thereon.

In our opinion, these decisions amply demonstrate that a national bank's activity is authorized as an incidental power, "necessary to carry on the business of banking," within the meaning of 12 U.S.C. § 24, Seventh, if it is convenient or useful in connection with the performance of one of the bank's established activities pursuant to its express powers under the National Bank Act. If this connection between an incidental activity and an express power does not exist, the activity is not authorized as an incidental power.

This brings us to a consideration of the question of whether the operation of a travel agency business, such as that conducted by South Shore, may reasonably be said to be convenient or useful in connection with the performance of one of the bank's established activities in the exercise of its express powers.

While the Comptroller and South Shore do not concede that such a relationship between an incidental and an express power must exist, they suggest ways in which they believe a travel agency business is directly related to a national bank's normal banking operations. In presenting this view, they pursue two lines of argument. One of these is an effort to equate the basic functions performed by travel agencies with functions which have historically been performed by banks. The other is based on the premise that a substantial number of banks have, for a long time, been providing travel agency services.

With regard to the first of these contentions, defendants assert that the basic functions performed by travel agencies consist of: (1) procuring carrier passage and other travel accommodations by acting as agent for passengers and carriers, and (2) providing various informational services to the traveler. Defendants then assert that both of these "basic" travel agency functions are only particular applications of the broad agency and informational services which banks traditionally offer among their "congeries of services."

In our view this analysis unrealistically minimizes the basic functions of a travel agency business and unjustifiably exalts the agency and informational functions of national banks.

The operation of a travel agency in the United States today is a highly complex activity. . . . It is true that a travel agent acts as an agent for the traveler, but it also acts as an agent for carriers. A travel agency provides informational service for the traveler, but it also solicits travel business, advertises and in general promotes the interests of its carrier principals. More importantly, the agency and informational services a bank travel agency renders are pursuant to its own interest in making its travel department profitable, wholly apart from the bank's normal banking operations.

On the other hand, while national banks provide certain agency and informational services they are normally of a kind which are germane to the financial operations of the bank in the exercise of its express powers. There are, of course, instances in which banks have, as a convenience to their regular customers, and without additional compensation, obtained railroad, steamship or airline tickets for such customers, or provided information helpful to such customers in connection with their travels. But incidental good will service of this kind cannot reasonably be equated with the operation of a modern travel agency for profit. In short, there is a difference between supplying customers with financial and informational services helpful to their travel plans and developing a clientele which looks to the bank not as a source of general financial advice and support but as a travel management center.

The Comptroller asserts that one of the central purposes of the National Bank Act, enacted during the Civil War, was to serve as a unifying force to the nation and that the draftsmen of the Act contemplated that the Act would fulfill its unifying purpose by, among other things, facilitating interstate commerce and "facilitating travel."

As a reading of these documents demonstrates, the objective of establishing a "unifying force" and "facilitating travel" were viewed in those early years, not as being attainable through the operation of a banking travel service, but as being attainable through the establishment and circulation of a national currency. Prior to the National Currency Act of 1863, now also known as the National Bank Act, there was no national currency and financial transactions were largely conducted through the medium of bank notes issued by state banks. The establishment of a national currency provided a form of legal specie acceptable throughout the country, and it was this which provided the desired "unifying force" and assisted in "facilitating travel."

South Shore asserts that banks in the United States have been offering travel services to their customers since at least 1865, when the Security National Bank in Sheboygan, Wisconsin, formally established its bank travel department. According to South Shore, in the ensuing years of the nineteenth century and the period preceding World War I, numerous other banks began to offer travel services largely to accommodate the great number of immigrants arriving in this country. The travel service then rendered by banks involved assisting immigrants in remitting money to families in their native lands, obtaining steamship tickets for relatives, and transmitting these prepaid tickets to foreign addresses. Immigrants during this period made periodic trips "home" and needed travelers' checks, letters of credit, foreign currency and other banking assistance.

The limited and largely uncompensated services of this kind, rendered by banks during this period, bear very little resemblance to the functioning of a modern travel agency. Moreover, it was not until 1959 that the Comptroller of the Currency ruled that national banks could engage in a regular travel agency business. . .

Despite the Comptroller's sanction, since 1959, of the operation of travel agency businesses by national banks, only one hundred twenty-two out of about four thousand seven hundred national banks were engaged in that business in 1967, when this action was brought. This is far from persuasive evidence that the operation of travel service departments is useful and convenient to the functioning of normal banking services under the express powers granted by the National Bank Act.

The Comptroller and South Shore urge us, on the authority of *Inland Waterways Corp. v. Young*, 309 U.S. 517, 524-525 (1940), and *Investment Co. Inst. v. Camp*, 401 U.S. 617, 626-627 (1971), and other cases, to accord great weight to the Comptroller's construction, in 12 C.F.R. § 7.7475, of the "incidental powers" provision, 12 U.S.C. § 24, Seventh.

We fully recognize the principle to which defendants refer. But, as the Supreme Court said in *Zuber v. Allen*, 396 U.S. 168, at 192-193 (1969):

> While this Court has announced that it will accord great weight to a departmental construction of its own enabling legislation, especially a contemporaneous construction . . . it is only one input in the interpretational equation. . . .
>
> "The Court may not, however, abdicate its ultimate responsibility to construe the language employed by Congress."

In view of the many considerations which lead to a contrary conclusion, as reviewed above, the lack of essential articulation supporting the Comptroller's 1963 ruling, issued without opinion or accompanying statement, and in the light of the lack of uniformity in the Comptroller's own interpretation of the statute, we conclude that the Comptroller's current interpretation, as embodied in 12 C.F.R. § 7.7475, is not entitled to dispositive deference. . . .

In our view the divestiture should be reasonably expeditious, but a limit should not be set which would be oppressive or inequitable. Our approval of the divestiture feature of the judgment is given with the qualification that the district court entertain and seriously consider any factual presentation South Shore wishes to make in the direction of lengthening the time for divestiture.

Subject to the qualification just stated, the judgment is affirmed.

---

1. ***Necessary for the Business of Banking.*** Is it fair to summarize *Arnold Tours* as follows: an activity is considered to be necessary to the business of banking if it is "convenient or useful" in the performance of a § 24(Seventh)

express power. The activity must, therefore, be convenient or useful to credit granting, deposit taking, or credit exchange. If an activity is not convenient or useful to a § 24(Seventh) power, or is not granted as an express power by another statutory provision, then the activity cannot be permitted. How does this compare to the Supreme Court's interpretation of the necessary and proper clause in *McCulloch v. Maryland*, 17 U.S. 316, 411–24 (1819)?

2. ***Chevron Deference.*** More than a decade after the First Circuit's decision in *Arnold Tours*, the Supreme Court decided *Chevron v. NRDC*, 467 U.S. 837 (1984). The importance of *Chevron* to bank permissible activities was evident in *NationsBank of North Carolina, N.A. v. Variable Annuity Life Insurance Co.*, 513 U.S. 251 (1995), where the Supreme Court held that the Comptroller's view that national banks may serve as agents in the sale of insurance company annuities was reasonable. A crucial footnote stated "We expressly hold that the 'business of banking' is not limited to the enumerated powers in § 24 Seventh and that the Comptroller therefore has discretion to authorize activities beyond those specifically enumerated." *Id.* at 258 n.2. The Court went on to say that, "[t]he exercise of the Comptroller's discretion, however, must be kept within reasonable bounds. Ventures distant from dealing in financial investment instruments—for example, operating a general travel agency—may exceed those bounds." *Id.* Thereafter, the OCC used a three-part test to determine if an activity was within the scope of the National Bank Act. The OCC would determine if the activity was functionally equivalent to or a logical outgrowth of a traditional banking activity. If so, the activity would need to respond to customer needs or otherwise benefit the bank or its customers. Finally, the activity could not involve risks to which the bank was not already exposed. Julie L. Williams & Mark P. Jacobsen, *The Business of Banking: Looking to the Future,* 50 BUS. LAWYER 783, 810–14 (1995). The test followed logically from the OCC's post-1970s interpretations and it is fair to say that the broad view now predominates.

II. CORE BANKING POWERS

In the United States, the definition of the "business of banking" has a long history of being changed through legislation, regulatory interpretation, and—in the 20th Century—court challenges by stakeholders in other parts of the financial sector seeking to keep chartered banks from competing on their protected turf. The section that follows describes many of the activities that have become part of the "business of banking" and includes a description of some of the legislative, regulatory, and court battles around them. It is critical to understand that the court cases represent only a small slice of the activities contained within the "business of banking" and may be more reflective of the fact that there was a well-heeled competitor who could sue, rather than the true riskiness of the activity. Today, the Comptroller's Manual of Activities permissible for a national bank is over a 126 pages long and can be found on the OCC's website.

While some of the powers described below were granted to national banks to ensure competitive parity with state-charted banks, the long history of competition between national and state banks over bank powers has largely been blunted by § 24 of the Federal Deposit Insurance Corporation

Improvement Act of 1991 (FDICIA), which limits state-chartered banks, as discussed in Chapter 2.1.

A. DISCOUNTING—CREDIT EXCHANGE

The discounting of bills and promissory notes issued by manufacturers, farmers, and others in commerce was the major function of commercial banks in the 19th and early 20th Centuries and this credit exchange function is explicitly in the text of 12 U.S.C. § 24(Seventh). In a world of sparse communications, long travel times, and shortages of notes and specie—a world we can hardly imagine—the ability of merchants, manufacturers, and farmers to take promissory notes (a real bill) from their customers to the local bank for discounting (*i.e.*, for an immediate credit into their bank account at an amount less than the face amount of the note (the discount) while the bank, rather than the merchant, manufacturer or farmer waited for the original customer to pay) was a key function of banks as intermediaries.

That process has today been replaced by highly liquid secondary markets, commercial paper, factoring, and the financing of receivables, just to name a few. Only some of today's credit exchange functions happen in chartered commercial banks.

B. GOVERNMENT AND CORPORATE DEBT

Both national and state banks have always had the power to invest in sovereign debt. The link between chartered banks and sovereign debt has been most recently analyzed in Charles W. Calomiris & Stephen H. Haber, FRAGILE BY DESIGN 69–71 (2014), and its importance shown recently in the EU sovereign debt crisis. Indeed, it is fair to say that, historically, U.S. banks were required to invest in government debt. Recall that 19th Century state-chartered banks were required to invest in state bonds, and that the primary purpose of creating national banks was to finance the Civil War by requiring them to invest in Union government debt. Such requirements remain common in emerging markets today.

The very first regulations issued by the Comptroller limited the types and amounts of government and corporate debt securities, called investment securities, in which national banks were permitted to invest. 12 C.F.R. § 1. Similarly, these regulations specify in which securities national banks can deal (*i.e.*, when a bank buys and sells to customers for its own account) and underwrite (*i.e.*, when a bank purchases from the issuer of the securities in order to sell to investors). Securities that a bank can invest in or underwrite are known colloquially as "bank-eligible securities" and others are "bank-ineligible securities." MELANIE L. FEIN, BANKING AND FINANCIAL SERVICE: BANKING, SECURITIES AND INSURANCE REGULATORY GUIDE, Vol. 2 § 14.02[B] (2006).

The OCC's regulations set out five types of investment securities with various corresponding limitations on investment by national banks based on the risk profile of the securities. There are no limitations on a bank's investment in obligations issued by the United States or by a U.S. department or agency provided that repayment is backed by the full faith and credit of the United States, as well as general obligations of the states or their political subdivisions.

Banks are limited to investing 10% of their capital and surplus in corporate bonds and municipal bonds, among other instruments.

Chartered commercial banks have long been permitted to underwrite U.S. government debt, although in today's market, that function, for business reasons, is typically carried out by an affiliated broker-dealer known as a primary dealer. Whether it is U.S. Treasuries, agency securities, or state or municipal bonds, underwriting, dealing in, and investing in sovereign debt is and historically has been a core function of commercial chartered banks—a fact that some find surprising in light of the Glass-Steagall Act's separation of commercial and investment banking activities. These authorities are common to commercial banks in virtually all countries.

C. MAKING LOANS

While the power to make long- and short-term loans is core to the business of banking, the ability of banks to make certain types of loans has been limited in the past. For example, commercial banks have not always had the power to make long-term loans or loans secured by real estate as collateral—a business dominated by the savings and loan sector for much of the 20th Century. During the 19th Century and first decades of the 20th Century, state-chartered banks gradually gained the power to make such loans. While national banks were first granted limited power to make such loans during the New Deal, it was not until the Garn-St Germain Act of 1982 that national banks obtained the same power as most state-chartered banks to engage in a full range of real estate lending activities.

Banks' power to make loans has also required reassessment and redefinition to align to innovations in banking. Large syndicated corporate long-term loans, which dominated bank balance sheets in the late 1950s and 1960s, are a post-WWII invention. Similarly, credit cards and many consumer lending products, including auto and student loans, are relatively recent innovations. While these innovations present business opportunities for banks, the chartered commercial bank has competitors in each of its core lending areas: corporate loans (capital markets and commercial paper), mortgages (non-bank lenders), autos (finance affiliates of major auto companies), consumer lending (consumer finance companies), and small business loans (online lending platforms).

In addition to direct limitations on the power of banks to make certain loans, banks have, at times, been constrained in their ability to lend by other government policies, including allocations of credit by the U.S. government to favored sectors and industries (and away from consumers and small businesses) during and immediately after WWII. Further, certain monetary policy decisions and price controls on the interest rates that could be paid to depositors (Regulation Q) have had the effect of causing credit crunches in the 1960s and, at times, have made it impossible for banks to extend credit even to creditworthy borrowers.

D. TRUST FIDUCIARY POWERS AND FINANCIAL ADVICE

Trust and fiduciary powers originally grew from the business of being an executor or trustee of an estate and, in the 19th and early 20th Centuries, a separate system of trust companies developed. To compete with these trust companies, many states granted state-chartered banks trust and fiduciary powers, and national banks were given the power to act in a trustee or fiduciary capacity in 1913. Today the power of both state and national banks to act as trustee or fiduciary is well-established and extends beyond management of personal estates. 12 C.F.R. § 9. Banks act as indenture trustees for bond issues, serve as the Employee Retirement Income Security Act and pension plan trustees, run collective investment funds, and manage family offices, family trusts, and other wealth vehicles. Certain banks also act as custodians of securities owned by their customers.

Under these authorities, national and state banks may provide investment and transactional advice. They may serve as investment advisors to real estate investment trusts, mutual funds, and other funds (known as investment companies). They may provide consumer financial advice, advice to pension plans, Medicare and other benefits counseling, and a wide-range of other financial advisory services. Additionally, banks may provide transactional advice in mergers and acquisitions, joint ventures, syndicated loans and capital markets.

E. REPO AND SECURITIES LENDING

A bank may borrow and lend securities on its balance sheet for a fee, engage in agreements to repurchase securities (known as repos), and act as an agent for the buyers and sellers of repos who often have placed their securities in the custody of the bank. These activities are a major business for many of the largest banks, particularly those engaged in the provision of custody services, but they have not been the subject of any case law. When two financial institutions engage in these transactions with each other without relying on a third-party bank to hold custody of the securities for both of the entities, the transactions are referred to as "bilateral." An alternative approach is known as "tri-party" repo, in which certain banks act as a clearing agent between the two counterparties. These types of transactions are described in Chapter 12.4.

F. PAYMENTS PROCESSING

The role of the chartered bank in processing payments is essential to the functioning of the financial system. Banks not only transfer funds or exchange currencies for individual clients (where there is significant competition from money transmitters such as Western Union and Internet-based services) but many of the larger banks run payments and transaction processing operations within their chartered bank and their global branch network. These operations permit the treasurers of large multinational companies to manage cash and liquidity and to transfer dollars and any other currency around the globe. To date, the power of banks to provide payment processing services, which can be traced to the origins of the chartered bank, has not been the subject of court cases or interpretive battles. With advancements in Internet payment platforms, however, it is not difficult to imagine that payment processing activities, which compose a significant source of revenue for certain large banks, could be the source of future stakeholder conflicts. *See* Part VII for a broader discussion of payment systems.

G. GUARANTEES AND LETTERS OF CREDIT

A manufacturer who reaches an agreement to deliver goods to a buyer in several months' time might be more comfortable if a well-capitalized bank guarantees that the manufacturer will be paid, even if the buyer defaults. Banks have always been allowed to issue such guarantees, as long as they were in the form of letters of credit or independent undertakings. When a bank issues a letter of credit to its customer, it is guaranteeing that the customer's counterparty can present the letter and certain documents (*i.e.*, a bill of lading) and receive payment from the bank. Letters of credit have been used for hundreds of years, primarily to facilitate international trade. The OCC's current regulations on letters of credit can be found at 12 C.F.R. § 7.1016.

At the same time, however, banks have often been prohibited from offering general guarantees under the theory that such guarantees are not within the business of banking. *See* Note, *Power of Banks to Guarantee the Liabilities of Other Banks*, 46 YALE L.J. 528, 528 (1937). Today, guarantees are permitted under conditions as codified in the OCC's regulations at 12 C.F.R. § 7.1017. Under these regulations, a national bank may make a guarantee if it has a substantial interest in the transaction and the customer provides certain high-quality collateral, which the bank holds in a segregated account, and in which the bank has perfected its security interest. Banks are also permitted to issue a guarantee for a customer, subsidiary, or affiliate if the guarantee is financial in character and the amount of the bank's financial obligation is reasonably ascertainable, among other requirements.

H. DERIVATIVES AND COMMODITIES

For many centuries, banks kept gold and silver as reserves in their vaults or in the vaults of the central bank. The issuance of futures and forwards on bullion is therefore a very old bank power. With the advent of floating interest rate loans and the increase in international transactions during the latter half of the 20th Century, banks began to engage in interest rate and foreign currency derivatives transactions, which are central to many aspects of risk management activities of banks. These "plain vanilla" derivatives are in fact over 93% of the notional value of the derivatives market among insured U.S. banks. OCC's Quarterly Report on Bank Trading and Derivatives Activities, 10–11 (Q3 2015).

During the 1980s and 1990s, the OCC gradually, through a series of interpretive orders, began to increase the power of national banks to engage in a wider range of derivatives transactions, including those referencing commodities and equities, by (1) looking through the derivative to see if investment in the reference asset is permitted, (2) considering whether the derivative was functionally equivalent to a permissible activity such as lending and deposit-taking, and (3) expanding the business of banking to cover any modern form of financial intermediation. That history is described in Saule T. Omarova, *The Quiet Metamorphosis: How Derivatives Changed the "Business of Banking,"* 63 MIAMI L. REV. 1041 (2009). The OCC has generally recognized that such derivatives activities are permissible, subject to certain stated conditions both for the purpose of providing bank customers with the ability to hedge their own risks as part of a customer-driven transactions, as well as for the purpose of allowing the bank to directly hedge the risks from its permissible banking activities. A "customer-driven" transaction is one entered into for a customer's valid and independent business purpose. *See* OCC, Interpretive Letter No. 892 (Sept. 13, 2000).

In addition to derivatives activities referencing commodities and equities, the OCC has permitted national banks and federally licensed branches to make and take physical delivery of certain commodities and equities in limited circumstances in order to hedge exposure arising from otherwise permissible banking activities. In the case of physically settled commodity transactions, this authority is narrowly confined to transactions undertaken for hedging purposes and the OCC has explicitly required that a national bank submit a detailed plan to the OCC to obtain written authorization before engaging in such transactions. *See, e.g.*, OCC, Interpretive Letter No. 632 (June 30, 1993).

During the legislative activity around the bill that eventually became the Dodd-Frank Act, Senator Blanche Lincoln, who was facing a tough primary battle, placed into the bill what became known as the "Swaps Pushout Rule." As originally conceived, the rule would prevent a chartered bank from entering into any derivatives, thereby forcing financial conglomerates to conduct such transactions through a non-bank affiliate. Neither the Obama Administration nor any federal banking regulator supported this version of the Swaps Pushout Rule. Indeed, both Chairman Ben Bernanke of the Federal Reserve Board and Chairman Sheila Bair of the FDIC testified against it, and former Chairman Volcker opposed it as originally drafted. There was significant concern that this version of the rule would adversely influence banks' ability to manage their risks by entering into derivative instruments that reference interest and foreign exchange rates. As passed in the Dodd-Frank Act, after last minute changes in a midnight conference, the rule was written only to prevent banks from engaging in uncleared credit default swaps and derivatives on non-investment-grade debt, equities and commodities, that were not used to hedge or mitigate risk related to the activities of the bank. Under the provision that became law, banks retained their authority to engage in derivatives that reference "bank eligible" rates or assets, including those that reference interest and foreign exchange rates.

When Senator Lincoln lost her primary battle, support for the Swaps Pushout Rule, which had always been resisted by the prudential regulators, faded. Several extensions of its application were granted and, in late 2014, an amendment to the Swaps Pushout Rule was attached to an appropriations bill. That amendment significantly narrowed the scope of the rule, which currently only prevents banks from entering into derivatives on asset-backed securities if such transactions are undertaken for purposes other than to hedge or mitigate risk. National banks may thus enter into any type of derivative that has previously been deemed bank-permissible by the OCC, unless that derivative is a prohibited asset-backed security swap. Senator Elizabeth Warren spoke out against the changes to the Swaps Pushout Rule, arguing that the elimination of the pushout allows "derivatives traders on Wall Street [to] gamble with taxpayer money and, when it all blows up, require the government to bail them out." Press Release, Warren and Cummings Ask Banks about Swaps Trading Practices After Key Sections of Dodd-Frank Gutted (Jan. 29, 2015). Leading up to the vote on the provision, the American Bankers Association argued that:

> The majority of banks, including community banks, that use swaps do so in order to hedge or mitigate risk from their ordinary business activities, including lending. Hedging and mitigating risk are not only good business practices, but are important tools that banks use to help borrowing customers hedge their own business risks. The push-out requirement to move some swaps into separate affiliates makes one-stop shopping impossible for businesses ranging from family farms to energy companies that want to hedge against commodity price changes.

ABA Statement on Swaps Push-Out Provision in Omnibus Bill (Dec. 10, 2014).

---

1. ***Competing Views on Derivatives in the Business of Banking***. Six years after the passage of Dodd-Frank Act, the Swaps Pushout Rule remains an area of great tension between legislators and policy-makers in opposing camps. Why is that so? Is there a basis by which a clear understanding of the facts and the history might be agreed upon or is that impossible? Recall the discussion of the differing points of view around the causes of the Financial Crisis in Chapter 1.2 and the differences of opinions about the role that derivatives played in the Financial Crisis.

I. MUTUAL FUNDS

Mutual funds, which have existed since the early 20th Century, were not offered by banks until the mid-1960s when the OCC issued a regulation that effectively permitted national banks to offer shares in certain types of mutual funds to retail customers. Under this regulation, national banks could offer their customers open-end mutual fund shares, which—unlike closed-end mutual funds—national banks can continuously issue to and buy back fund shares from investors. In *Investment Co. Inst. v. Camp*, 401 U.S. 617 (1971), a trade association for the securities sector challenged the OCC's regulation and the Supreme Court confronted the question of whether the OCC's regulation violated §§ 16 and 21 of the Glass-Steagall Act, both of which are still in force today. These provisions limit a national bank's ability to underwrite and deal in corporate debt and equity securities, although they have never been read to limit a national bank's ability to underwrite or deal in U.S. government debt or state and municipal securities. In the decision below, the Court finds that §§ 16 and 21 also prohibit national banks from underwriting or dealing in open-end mutual fund shares.

Investment Co. Inst. v. Camp

401 U.S. 617 (1971)

MR. JUSTICE STEWART delivered the opinion of the Court.

The issue before us is whether the Comptroller of the Currency may, consistently with the banking laws, authorize a national bank to offer its customers the opportunity to invest in a stock fund created and maintained by the bank.

. . . The petitioners contend that a purchase of stock by a bank's investment fund is a purchase of stock by a bank for its own account in violation of [sections 16 and 21 of the Glass-Steagall Act and] that the creation and operation of an investment fund by a bank which offers to its customers the opportunity to purchase an interest in the fund's assets constitutes the issuing, underwriting, selling, or distributing of securities or stocks in violation of these sections. . . .

IV

The Glass-Steagall Act confirmed that national banks could not engage in investment banking directly, and in addition made affiliation with an organization so engaged illegal. One effect of the Act was to abolish the security affiliates of commercial banks.

It is apparent from the legislative history of the Act why Congress felt that this drastic step was necessary. The failure of the Bank of United States in 1930 was widely attributed to that bank's activities with respect to its numerous securities affiliates. Moreover, Congress was concerned that commercial banks in general and member banks of the Federal Reserve System in particular had both aggravated and been damaged by stock market decline partly because of their direct and indirect involvement in the trading and ownership of speculative securities.

. . . Congress acted to keep commercial banks out of the investment banking business largely because it believed that the promotional incentives of investment banking and the investment banker's pecuniary stake in the success of particular investment opportunities was destructive of prudent and disinterested commercial banking and of public confidence in the commercial banking system. . . .

V

The language that Congress chose to achieve this purpose includes the prohibitions of § 16 that a national bank "shall not underwrite any issue of securities or stock" and shall not purchase "for its own account . . . any shares of stock of any corporation," and the prohibition of § 21 against engaging in "the business of issuing, underwriting, selling, or distributing . . . stocks, bonds, debentures, notes, or other securities." In this litigation the Comptroller takes the position that the operation of a bank investment fund is consistent with these provisions, because participating interests in such a fund are not "securities" within the meaning of the Act.

. . . But there is nothing in the phrasing of either § 16 or § 21 that suggests a narrow reading of the word "securities." To the contrary, the breadth of the term is implicit in the fact that the antecedent statutory language encompasses not only equity securities but also securities representing debt. And certainly there is nothing in the language of these provisions to suggest that the sale of an interest in the business of buying, holding, and selling stocks for investment is to be distinguished from the sale of an interest in a commercial or industrial enterprise.

Indeed, there is direct evidence that Congress specifically contemplated that the word "security" includes an interest in an investment fund. . . .

But in any event, we are persuaded that the purposes for which Congress enacted the Glass-Steagall Act leave no room for the conclusion that a participation in a bank investment fund is not a "security" within the meaning of the Act. From the perspective of competition, convenience, and expertise, there are arguments to be made in support of allowing commercial banks to enter the investment banking business. But Congress determined that the hazards outlined above made it necessary to prohibit this activity to commercial banks. Those same hazards are clearly present when a bank undertakes to operate an investment fund.

A bank that operates an investment fund has a particular investment to sell. It is not a matter of indifference to the bank whether the customer buys an interest in the fund or makes some other investment. If its customers cannot be persuaded to invest in the bank's investment fund, the bank will lose their investment business and the fee which that business would have brought in.

Promotional incentives might also be created by the circumstance that the bank's fund would be in direct competition with mutual funds that, from the point of view of the investor, offered an investment opportunity comparable to that offered by the bank. The bank would want to be in a position to show to the prospective customer that its fund was more attractive than the mutual funds offered by others. The bank would have a salesman's stake in the performance of the fund, for if the fund were less successful than the competition the bank would lose business and the resulting fees.

A bank that operated an investment fund would necessarily put its reputation and facilities squarely behind that fund and the investment opportunity that the fund offered. . . . Imprudent or unsuccessful management of the bank's investment fund could bring about a perhaps unjustified loss of public confidence in the bank itself. If imprudent management should place the fund in distress, a bank might find itself under pressure to rescue the fund through measures inconsistent with sound banking.

The promotional and other pressures incidental to the operation of an investment fund, in other words, involve the same kinds of potential abuses that Congress intended to guard against when it legislated against bank security affiliates.

And there are other potential hazards of the kind of Congress sought to eliminate with the passage of the Glass-Steagall Act. The bank's stake in the investment fund might distort its credit decisions or lead to unsound loans to the companies in which the fund had invested. The bank might exploit its confidential relationship with its commercial and industrial creditors for the benefit of the fund. The bank might undertake, directly or indirectly, to make its credit facilities available to the fund or to render other aid to the fund inconsistent with the best interests of the bank's depositors. The bank might make loans to facilitate the purchase of interests in the fund. The bank might divert talent and resources from its commercial banking operation to the promotion of the fund. Moreover, because the bank would have a stake in a customer's making a particular investment decision—the decision to invest in the bank's investment fund—the customer might doubt the motivation behind the bank's recommendation that he make such an investment. If the fund investment should turn out badly there would be a danger that the bank would lose the good-will of those customers who had invested in the fund. It might be unlikely that disenchantment would go so far as to threaten the solvency of the bank. But because banks are dependent on the confidence of their customers, the risk would not be unreal. . .

VI

. . . Because the potential hazards and abuses that flow from a bank's entry into the mutual investment business are the same basic hazards and abuses that Congress intended to eliminate almost 40 years ago, we cannot but apply the terms of the federal statute as they were written. We conclude that the operation of an investment fund of the kind approved by the Comptroller involves a bank in the underwriting, issuing, selling, and distributing of securities in violation of §§ 16 and 21 of the Glass-Steagall Act. . . .

In 1972, following the Supreme Court's decision in *Investment Co. Inst. v. Camp*, the Federal Reserve Board promulgated a regulation and interpretive ruling that permitted non-banking subsidiaries of bank holding companies (BHCs) to engage in the services of an investment adviser to closed-end investment companies. The Board's interpretive ruling carefully distinguished between open-end and closed-end mutual funds, expressing the opinion that a

BHC may not lawfully sponsor, organize, or control an open-end investment company, but expressing no objection to sponsorship of a closed-end investment company, provided that a bank acting as investment adviser may not underwrite or otherwise participate in the sale or distribution of the investment company's securities and may not have an ownership interest in the investment company.

In *Bd. of Governors of Fed. Res. Sys. v. Investment Co. Inst.*, 450 U.S. 46 (1981), the Supreme Court upheld the Federal Reserve Board's interpretation, finding the activity to be permissible under both §§ 16 and 21 of the Glass-Steagall Act. With respect to § 16, the Court distinguished this case from *Investment Co. Inst. v. Camp* by focusing on the nature of the activity:

> Section 16 expressly prohibits a bank from "underwriting" any issue of a security or purchasing any security for its own account. The Board's interpretive ruling here expressly prohibits a [BHC] or its subsidiaries from participating in the "sale or distribution" of securities of any investment company for which it acts as investment adviser. [12 C.F.R. § 225.125(h) (1980).] The ruling also prohibits [BHCs] and their subsidiaries from purchasing securities of the investment company for which it acts as investment adviser. [§ 225.125(g).] Therefore, if the restrictions imposed by the [Federal Reserve] Board's interpretive ruling are followed, investment advisory services—even if performed by a bank—would not violate the requirements of § 16.
>
> . . . In contrast to the bank's activities in issuing, underwriting, selling, and redeeming the units of participation in the *Camp* case, in this case the [Federal Reserve] Board's interpretive ruling expressly prohibits such activity.

In addition to distinguishing between the legal permissibility of the activities involved in these two cases, the Supreme Court also found that the activity of acting as an investment adviser to a closed-end fund implicated none of the subtle hazards discussed in the *Investment Co. Inst. v. Camp* decision.

Both of these cases remain good law today as applied to a bank or a mere BHC. In the post-Gramm-Leach-Bliley Act (GLBA) era, closed-end and open-end mutual funds may be sponsored and offered by financial holding companies (FHCs) through non-bank affiliates under the expanded powers we will discuss in Chapter 6.1.

J. COMMERCIAL PAPER

The next stakeholder battle around the securities activities of the chartered bank revolved around whether the underwriting of commercial paper was the underwriting of a "security" under § 16 of the Glass-Steagall Act. In the late 1960s and early 1970s, large blue chip corporates began to issue short-term commercial paper in the capital markets, rather than pursuing loans from commercial banks at higher interest rates. As a result, commercial banks were losing out on the corporate lending business, while investment banks benefited from their role in commercial paper issuances.

In 1979, the Securities Industry Association, a trade association for the investment banks, petitioned the Federal Reserve Board to bring an enforcement action against Bankers Trust, a state-member bank that was placing the commercial paper of their corporate customers, on the grounds that such activity violated § 16 of the Glass-Steagall Act. The Federal Reserve Board, applying a functional analysis, determined that the activity was similar to traditional commercial banking operations and, therefore, the commercial paper instrument should not be viewed as a "security" for purposes of § 16 of the Glass-Steagall Act. The Securities Industry Association appealed the Federal Reserve Board's decision, and in *Sec. Indus. Ass'n v. Bd. of Governors of the Fed. Reserve*, 468 U.S. 137 (1984) [hereinafter "Bankers Trust I"], the Supreme Court agreed with the petitioners that commercial paper is a "security" under the Glass-Steagall Act and, thus, banks could not underwrite or deal in such instruments.

The case was then remanded to the Federal Reserve Board to determine whether or not the placement activity conducted by Bankers Trust with respect to the commercial paper "securities" was, in fact, prohibited underwriting or dealing activity. The Board determined that Bankers Trust's placement of the commercial paper was permissible under § 16 of the Glass-Steagall Act as the "'selling' of a security without recourse and solely upon the order and for the account of customers, a practice permitted by [§ 16] of the Act." Sec. Indus. Ass'n v. Bd. of Governors of the Fed. Reserve, 807 F.2d 1052, 1055 (D.C. Cir. 1986) [hereinafter "Bankers Trust II"]. The Securities Association sued again and this time the appeals court agreed with the banking regulator stating that a private placement of commercial paper was permitted. *Id.*

A key difference between Bankers Trust I and Bankers Trust II, and indeed with the earlier cases on the underwriting of open and closed-end funds, is that by the time Bankers Trust II had been decided, *Chevron* deference was in effect. In Bankers Trust II, the D.C. Circuit concluded that the Federal Reserve Board's interpretation of § 16 with respect to commercial paper issuances was "reasonable" and therefore entitled to deference. *Id.* at 1059. Further, even though the D.C. Circuit opined that one of the *Investment Co. Inst. v. Camp* "subtle hazards" was present, it found that "the 'subtle hazards' analysis as a whole is a specific instance of the *Chevron* principle that requires our deference to an agency's reasonable construction of its statute's ambiguities." *Id.* at 1069.

K. MORTGAGE SECURITIZATION

The issue of whether or not certain activity by commercial banks is underwriting or dealing of "securities" in violation of §§ 16 and 21 of the Glass-Steagall Act arose again in the late 1980s in relation to the securitization of financial assets, *i.e.*, the process by which a group of financial assets (typically loans) are placed in a separate legal entity, typically a special-purpose vehicle, and then interests in that entity are sold into the capital markets. Under federal securities laws, interests in securitized loan pools are generally considered to be securities, and asset securitizations are routinely registered under the 1933 Act. The Comptroller of the Currency, however, reached the opposite conclusion when examining the issuance of "mortgage pass-through certificates" (known commonly today as "mortgage-backed securities") by a national bank in relation to a 1987 offering. The case below includes excerpts from the Comptroller's decision, which was appealed by the Securities Industry Association in a classic stakeholder battle.

Sec. Indus. Ass'n v. Clarke

885 F.2d 1034 (2d Cir. 1989), *cert. denied*, 493 U.S. 1070 (1990)

MESKILL, Circuit Judge:

BACKGROUND

A. Mortgage Pass-Through Certificates

Mortgage pass-through certificates are used by banks as a mechanism for selling mortgage loans. A number of mortgage loans previously originated by a bank are placed in a pool. The bank then transfers the pool to a trust. In exchange for the pool, the trustee transfers to the bank pass-through certificates. These certificates represent fractional undivided interests in the pool of mortgage loans. The certificates may then be sold publicly or privately.

After sale of the certificates, the mortgage loans are often serviced by the originator-bank. In such a case, the bank collects the loan payments and "passes through" the principal and interest on a pro rata basis to the certificate holders. In doing so, the bank may deduct service or other fees.

Use of this mechanism has important benefits for banks, benefits that have resulted in its increasing popularity and use. Because residential mortgage loans typically are of long duration, banks traditionally have bought and sold the loans to facilitate management of their assets and liabilities. Use of the pass-through certificate mechanism makes the sale of these loans easier. Individual loans do not have to be sold separately, and buyers may find it more efficient and less risky to purchase interests in a pool of mortgages instead of single mortgages.

DISCUSSION . . .

D. The Comptroller's Decision

As it is the decision of the Comptroller that is at issue here, we review that decision in some detail.

1. Sale of Mortgages Is Permitted

In considering the legality of the [Bank] transaction under federal banking laws, the Comptroller began his analysis by examining the national bank's authority to sell its mortgage loans generally. In concluding that national banks have such authority, the Comptroller relied on three bases. First, since the enactment of the National Bank Act in 1864, national banks have had the express power to "carry on the business of banking . . . by . . . negotiating promissory notes . . . and other evidences of debt." 12 U.S.C. § 24 (Seventh). Second, the Supreme Court long ago concluded that the sale of mortgages is within the incidental powers of national banks. *See First National Bank v. City of Hartford*, 273 U.S. 548, 560 (1927). Finally, under 12 U.S.C. § 371(a), national banks are permitted to "make, arrange, purchase or sell loans or extensions of credit secured by liens on interests in real estate." The Comptroller concluded that "it is clearly established that national banks may sell their mortgage assets under the express authority of 12 U.S.C. §§ 24 (Seventh) and 371(a)."

2. Use of the Pass-Through Certificate Mechanism To Sell Mortgages Is Either an Express or an Incidental Banking Power

Having determined that [Bank] had the express power to sell its mortgage loans, the Comptroller concluded "[t]he fact that the negotiation and sale may be accomplished through the creation and sale by a bank of participation certificates, an activity which [the OCC] long has approved, does not alter in any respect the substance of the transaction, nor its permissibility under the national banking laws."

The Comptroller justified permitting use of the pass-through certificate mechanism on two grounds. First, he considered use of the mechanism as simply a new way of performing the old job of selling bank assets. He cited the Ninth Circuit's admonition that "the powers of national banks must be construed so as to permit the use of new ways of conducting the very old business of banking." *M & M Leasing Corp. v. Seattle First Nat'l Bank*, 563 F.2d 1377, 1382 (9th Cir.1977), cert. denied, 436 U.S. 956 (1978). He concluded that the transaction at issue here "represents nothing more than the negotiation of evidences of debt and the sale of real estate loans, which is expressly authorized under 12 U.S.C. §§ 24 (Seventh) and 371(a)."

Alternatively, the Comptroller concluded that use of the pass-through certificate mechanism to sell mortgages is an "incidental power[ ]" of [Bank]. *See* 12 U.S.C. § 24 (Seventh). . .

3. The Prohibitions and Concerns of the Glass-Steagall Act Are Not Implicated

The Comptroller then stated that "[b]ecause the sale of bank assets through this medium is authorized under the national banking laws, the prohibitions of the Glass-Steagall Act are inapplicable to this transaction." Nevertheless, the Comptroller went on to argue that, even if the Glass-Steagall prohibitions were to be applied, they would not forbid this transaction.

First, the Comptroller found that [Bank]'s program did not involve "securities" within the meaning of the Glass-Steagall Act. The Comptroller noted that [Bank]'s registration of the offering with the [SEC] did not mean that the certificates were "securities" for purposes of the Glass-Steagall Act. *See Investment Co. Inst. v. Clarke*, 630 F.Supp. 593, 594 n. 2 (D.Conn.), *aff'd*, 789 F.2d 175 (2d Cir.) (per curiam), *cert. denied*, 479 U.S. 940 (1986); *see also Conover*, 790 F.2d at 933. The Comptroller wrote:

> Th[e OCC] has previously considered pass-through certificates representing undivided interests in pooled bank assets to be legally transparent for purposes of the Glass-Steagall analysis. In other words, because the certificateholders have essentially the same rights, liabilities, and risks as if they were the owners of the underlying assets, the certificates are considered to be substantially the same as those assets. . . . To the extent that the participation certificates represent "investment opportunities", the opportunity being offered is, in substance, no different than the opportunity of investment in the underlying loans which banks are clearly authorized to sell.

The means used to pool and package the sale of the mortgages was thus thought not to transform the transaction into a sale of "securities." Finally, the Comptroller reinforced his interpretation of the term "securities" by referring to his finding that the "subtle hazards" identified by the Supreme Court as motivating the Glass-Steagall Act were not implicated by this transaction. *See infra.*

The Comptroller next concluded that even if the mortgage pass-through certificates are considered "securities" for purposes of the Glass-Steagall Act, the Act was still not violated here because [Bank]'s activities did not fall within the meaning of "dealing" or "underwriting" securities, as prohibited by section 16. In concluding that [Bank] was not "dealing" or "underwriting" here, the Comptroller said:

> An issuer that merely participates in the initial placement of its own securities with investors, and does not subsequently engage in the business of repurchasing those securities, does not thereby enter into the "business of underwriting" nor does it become involved in the "business of dealing." In this regard, we underscore the point that the activity in question is, in substance, a sale of [Bank]'s assets. [Bank] is not in this transaction purchasing and selling securities of other issuers but, rather, is participating in the placement of certificates representing interests in its own assets.
>
> (footnotes omitted).

. . . The Comptroller concluded by considering the purposes of the Glass-Steagall Act, finding that they were not implicated here. He first noted that the most obvious risks associated with banks participating in the securities business, *see Camp*, 401 U.S. at 630, were not present here because "[a]t no time will [Bank]'s resources be committed to any securities investment whatsoever, since the program involves only the sale of bank assets."

Turning to the "subtle hazards" identified by the Supreme Court, *see Bankers Trust I*, 468 U.S. at 145–47; *Camp*, 401 U.S. at 630–34, the Comptroller first noted that [Bank]'s program "does not involve the marketing of bank customers' securities." Under these circumstances, he found, "the conflicts of interest identified by the Supreme Court . . . are simply not at issue." Because the bank has no "promotional interest" in customers' securities, it will not be tempted to make unsound loans to improve the success of the securities offerings. "Similarly, there is no possibility that the Bank might improperly advise its customers on how and when to issue securities in order to profit from the distribution process or to use the proceeds in obtaining repayment on outstanding loans."

The Comptroller next turned to the possibility that [Bank] would offer limited credit support for the offering. He noted that the Prospectus provided that such credit support could only be, at a maximum, ten percent of the aggregate principal balance. He noted that in the absence of the sale of the mortgage loans, [Bank] would retain 100 percent of the associated credit risk. In light of this, he found it "difficult to conceive how a decision to provide credit support for no more than 10% of the initial aggregate principal balance of a pool comprised of these same assets could be the product of 'unsound' lending practices."

The Comptroller rejected the argument that permitting use of the pass-through certificate mechanism would affect the soundness of [Bank]'s mortgage lending practices. He concluded:

> We think it extremely unlikely that a bank would engage in unsafe mortgage lending practices simply because of the possibility that the resulting mortgage loans might thereafter be placed in a pool and sold in certificate form. In this regard, at the time of origination, it will generally not be possible for the Bank to know whether a particular loan will be suitable for subsequent inclusion in a public offering. In addition, the Bank would have difficulty marketing the Certificates if the underlying mortgages were themselves unsound investments because the federal securities laws require full disclosure of all material facts concerning the Certificates and the offering. In short, the Bank does not stand to profit by making unsound loans with the intent of remarketing them to uninformed purchasers.

Finally, the Comptroller found that [Bank]'s program would not likely result in its making unsound loans to its own depositors so as to finance sale of the certificates. "[S]ince [Bank]'s objective is to sell the mortgage loans, it would hardly make economic sense for it to replace these assets with unsound loans acquired in the process." The Comptroller found such a scenario equally irrational from the point of view of the depositor. Because service charges would be deducted from the "pass-through" payments, it would not make sense, the Comptroller thought, for the depositor to obtain a loan at a higher commercial rate so as to invest in the certificates.

E. The Comptroller Correctly Determined That [Bank]'s Sale of the Certificates Was Within the "Business of Banking" and Therefore Did Not Violate the Glass-Steagall Act

As our review of the Comptroller's decision indicates, under his interpretation of the Glass-Steagall Act, the conclusion that [Bank]'s activity was authorized by the banking laws was sufficient to resolve the dispute. That is, once the Comptroller concluded that [Bank]'s activity was encompassed by its power "to carry on the business of banking," 12 U.S.C. § 24 (Seventh), he found it unnecessary to consider the application of the Glass-Steagall prohibition on national banks' "underwrit[ing] securities," *id.* . . .

We find support for the Comptroller's interpretation of section 16 in *Bankers Trust I*, 468 U.S. at 158 n. 11. . . . The Court's reading of section 16 of the Glass-Steagall Act establishes the threshold question as whether the challenged activity of [Bank] constitutes "the business of banking" or, instead, the "business of dealing in securities and stock." *See* 12 U.S.C. § 24 (Seventh). Activity that falls within the "business of banking" is not subject to the restrictions the latter part of section 16 places on a bank's "business of dealing in securities and stock." Thus, the issues concerning the definitions of "securities" and "underwriting" only become relevant if the activity constitutes the "business of dealing in securities and stock." If the activity constitutes the "business of banking," then the Glass-Steagall Act prohibitions SIA claims are violated here do not apply.

The Comptroller correctly concluded that [Bank] has the express power under the national banking laws to sell its mortgage loans. . . . The Comptroller properly recognized that once he determined that SPN Bank's activity was authorized under section 16, he did not need to analyze the transaction under section 21. "[S]ection 21 cannot be read to prohibit what section 16 permits. . . . Therefore, if we find that the [Comptroller] acted reasonably in concluding that section 16 permits [SPN Bank's] activities, that is the end of our analysis." *See Securities Industry Ass'n v. Board of Governors*, 807 F.2d 1052, 1057 (D.C.Cir.1986), *cert. denied*, 483 U.S. 1005 (1987) (*Bankers Trust II*). . . . That is to say, even if SPN Bank's activity here were to be considered "underwriting . . . securities," section 21 would not prohibit such activity if it were permitted under section 16, as we have found it to be. . . .

---

1. ***Subtle Hazards?*** Recall the discussion of the contending visions of the Financial Crisis in Chapter 1.2. Of the many debated causes of the Financial Crisis, it is apparent that the offering and sponsoring of mutual funds by bank affiliates was not one of them. Instead, the epicenter of the Financial Crisis was a loosening of credit combined with the growth of short-term funding, *i.e.*, the hot money of repos in investment banks. Yet, many of the subtle hazards that *Investment Co. Inst. v. Camp* discusses were apparent in the originate-to-distribute model where banks (and many non-banks as well) originated mortgage loans secure in the knowledge that they would not stay on their balance sheet. Is it possible that *Investment Co. Inst. v. Camp* was correct in its subtle hazards

analysis but for the wrong reason and on the wrong products? What does this say about the limits of judge made law that arises out of stakeholder battles?

L. BROKERAGE

Because the agency business of brokerage did not involve the bank putting its own balance sheet at risk, banks had long engaged in the business of securities brokerage for their customers. Traditionally, those services were bundled with investment advice, also a traditional bank power. The following excerpt is from a Supreme Court decision upholding the Federal Reserve Board's approval of Bank of America's acquisition of 100% of Charles Schwab, which operated a discount brokerage subsidiary that did not offer investment analysis or advice to its customers. Notice that this case was also brought by the trade associations representing the investment banks, which, at that time, operated full-service brokerage firms.

> . . . Banks long have arranged the purchase and sale of securities as an accommodation to their customers. Congress expressly endorsed this traditional banking service in 1933. Section 16 of the Glass-Steagall Act authorizes banks to continue the practice of "purchasing and selling . . . securities and stock without recourse, solely upon the order, and for the account of, customers, and in no case for [their] own account[s]." 12 U.S.C. § 24 Seventh. The [Federal Reserve] Board found that in substance the brokerage services that Schwab performs for its customers are not significantly different from those that banks, under the authority of § 16, have been performing for their own customers for years. See 69 Fed.Res.Bull., at 107–109. Moreover, the amendment to Regulation Y, added by the Board in 1983 to reflect its decision in this case, expressly limits the securities brokerage services in which a bank may engage "to buying and selling securities solely as agent for the account of customers" and does not authorize "securities underwriting or dealing or investment advice or research services." 48 Fed. Reg. 37006 (1983).
>
> . . . § 16 of the Glass-Steagall Act allows banks to engage directly in the kind of brokerage services at issue here, to accommodate its customers. . . .

Sec. Indus. Ass'n v. Bd. of Governors of the Fed. Reserve, 468 U.S. 207, 215, 221 (1984) (citations omitted).

---

1. ***Broker-Dealer Pushout***. This decision affirmed the idea that the operation of a brokerage business is a banking activity and thus falls under the business of banking. In 1999, fifteen years after this case was decided, Congress passed GLBA, which contained a broker-dealer pushout clause, designed to even the competitive playing field between the chartered bank and broker-dealers. The GLBA broker-dealer pushout required that banks either register as broker-dealers subject to the SEC's regulations or refrain from any brokerage activities

outside of identified banking products, including deposit accounts, bankers acceptance, loans, debit accounts from a credit card, loan participations, and swaps. Not on the list, of course, are corporate debt and equity, municipal bonds, and U.S. government debt. Of course, in the post-GLBA era, most banks are affiliated with a broker-dealer, so the question is which subsidiary of the financial conglomerate can conduct the activity, not whether it can take place at all within the conglomerate.

M. EQUITY INVESTMENTS

National banks are largely prohibited from owning the stock of corporations with very limited exceptions. In fact, for a long period of time, the prohibition was interpreted so strictly, that there were questions about whether a national bank could own the stock of a subsidiary bank. Agreement and Edge Act corporations, discussed in Chapter 6.3, were created to permit national banks to invest in a subsidiary corporation that engaged in international activities.

Many state-chartered banks had extensive powers to invest in the stock of companies before the New Deal, with variances from state to state. Today, both national and state banks have only limited equity investment powers. Section 24(Seventh) generally prohibits national banks from owning stock, "except as hereinafter provided or otherwise permitted by law." They may take "equity kickers" in loan transactions, 12 C.F.R. § 7.1006, or may end up taking possession of equity posted as collateral for a debt previously contracted in good faith. *See* OCC Interpretive Letter 643 (July 1, 1992). National banks also have the authority to buy convertible securities—securities that are convertible into stock—provided that they are not convertible at the option of the issuer. 12 U.S.C. § 1.6.

N. INSURANCE

The insurance sector (both life and property/casualty) and its affiliated and independent agents have been extreme in their opposition to the entry of banking institutions into insurance activities. While there are some exceptions, the entry of banks into the highly lucrative insurance business has been very controlled in the United States. Since insurance powers do not involve securities, the Glass-Steagall Act did not prevent bank entry to insurance activities. Instead, the line of argument has been that insurance is part of commerce, a rhetorical move that would be surprising to the Europeans who have long had a concept of bank assurance. From the early 20th Century, it was merely an accepted view that national banks do not have the power to sell or underwrite insurance. Emeric Fischer, *Banking and Insurance—Should Ever the Twain Meet?*, 71 NEB. L. REV. 726, 747 n.118 (1992).

In 1916, Congress passed § 92 of the National Bank Act which gave national banks the power to be the agent for the selling of fire, life, or other insurance in towns of less than 5,000. At that time, many Americans were covered by that exception. The passage of § 92 began a century-long battle between the insurance sector and banks—banks wanted insurance powers and insurance companies did not want to lose their own business to banks. In *NationsBank of*

North Carolina, N.A. v. Variable Annuity Life Insurance Co., referred to earlier in this Chapter for its wide ruling on the incidental powers of national banks, the Supreme Court upheld a decision by the Comptroller of the Currency that national banks could underwrite annuities, on the grounds that annuities are similar to other investments typically sold by banks.

With the passage of GLBA in 1999, there came many changes in the rules governing bank insurance activities. Though the Act permitted underwriting of insurance within an FHC, it was only permitted for the non-bank subsidiaries of FHCs—not national banks or bank subsidiaries. Under GLBA § 302, national banks are expressly forbidden from underwriting insurance products, unless the insurance product had been previously approved by the Comptroller for national banks as of January 1, 1999. Such insurance products include the limited categories of safe deposit box insurance, private mortgage insurance, self-insurance of business risk insurance, municipal bond insurance, and credit-related insurance. Further, under 12 U.S.C. § 24(Seventh), national banks or their subsidiaries may sell credit-related insurance products, including credit life insurance, involuntary unemployment insurance, vendors single interest insurance and double interest insurance, mechanical breakdown insurance, and vehicle service contracts. These products, however, account for a small portion of the insurance market.

Banks also cannot engage in underwriting or sale of title insurance, except national banks may sell title insurance in states which specifically authorized such sales for state banks, or where they conducted such activities before the date of enactment of the law. GLBA § 303, 15 U.S.C. § 6713. Both banks and their subsidiaries may, however, offer insurance as an agent. GLBA § 104(d)(2), 15 U.S.C. § 6701(d)(2).

Although GLBA afforded banks some insurance powers, most permissions were given to the non-bank affiliates of FHCs. Banks still remain unable to underwrite property and life and casualty insurance, which is the most significant portion of the insurance market. After the long 20th Century battle between the insurance sector and the banking sector, the insurance agents and insurance companies, unlike the former stand-alone investment banks, have largely succeeded in keeping the two sectors separate. It is ironic, as you will see in Chapter 6.1, that it was Citigroup's decision to acquire Travelers Insurance Company that was used to force Congress's hand to finally pass what became GLBA. Yet, within seven years, and before the Financial Crisis, Citigroup had sold Travelers. You will learn in Chapters 3.1–3.3 about the insurance sector and it may be worthwhile reflecting on whether the separateness is caused by market conditions, different regulatory structures or other factors.

---

1. ***Successes and Failures in Stakeholder Battles.*** A review of the 20th Century stakeholder battles over the "business of banking" and its companions for non-bank affiliates that you will study in Chapter 6.1, "closely related to banking," "financial in nature," "incidental thereto," and "complementary" reveal that travel agents, and real estate agents have been very successful in defining the regulatory perimeter so that banks and their affiliates may not enter that

market. The insurance agents were successful for a long time and, in practice the sectors remain separate. By contrast, the investment banks were, ultimately, not successful in keeping commercial banks and their affiliates out of their protected sector. What accounts for this difference, even taking into account that the underwriting of corporate debt and equity is done within the bank affiliated broker-dealer?

O. STATE BANK POWERS

This Chapter has largely concentrated on the powers of national banks. In the long history of stakeholder battles around bank powers in the last quarter of the 20th Century, many states attempted to make their state charter more attractive by expanding the powers of their state-chartered banks. By 1999, on the eve of GLBA, 30 states had authorized general insurance brokerage; eight states had authorized insurance underwriting; 17 states had authorized general securities underwriting; 17 states had authorized general real estate brokerage; 26 states had authorized real estate development; a not-quite-identical list of 26 states had authorized real estate equity participation; and a few have authorized travel agencies. HOWELL E. JACKSON & EDWARD L. SYMONS, JR., REGULATION OF FINANCIAL INSTITUTIONS 140–41 (1999). Many of the statutes have conditions, such as that the activity must be conducted through a subsidiary, or is subject to individual regulatory approval, or is subject to a limited amount of investment. As discussed in Chapter 2.1, however, § 24 of FDICIA, placed a brake on these expanded state level "business of banking" powers by requiring that no insured state bank (and all of them are) could engage as a principal in any activity not permitted for national banks unless the FDIC approved the activity and made a determination that the activity posed no danger to the deposit insurance fund.

III. NARROW BANKING REPRISED SINCE THE FINANCIAL CRISIS

The 20th Century history of financial sector stakeholder battles, with its headlines and court cases, has obscured the fact that many of the expansions of commercial bank powers during the 20th Century were noncontroversial, happened without any stakeholder battles and, yet, were prime drivers of bank failures. The key examples are real estate lending, long-term corporate lending and lending to foreign sovereigns, all of which have contributed to banking failures during the last half of the 20th Century. As a result, since the Financial Crisis, the concept of narrow banking has been a frequent topic of discussion. Traditionally a narrow bank has meant a super safe bank that is only permitted to invest in a few types of very liquid short-term assets.

Professor Laurence Kotlikoff, in his book *Jimmy Stewart is Dead* (2010) suggests turning all banks and most financial intermediaries into super safe mutual funds. He suggests that "trust me banking" (the fractional reserve system) is "unsafe at any speed." Kotlikoff would create "cash mutual funds" that would be prohibited from borrowing, would be used for payments and would be the only financial intermediary backed by the full faith and credit of the

United States. All other risk would be mediated through closed-end mutual funds. This narrow bank proposal is quite different from an alternative proposal, made before GLBA by Professor Robert Litan and after the Financial Crisis by Professor Arthur Wilmarth. They both propose that any financial conglomerate with expanded powers to engage in underwriting and trading of corporate debt and equity could only affiliate with an IDI that is limited to making short-term, very safe loans. *See* ROBERT E. LITAN, WHAT SHOULD BANKS DO? (1987); THE CHANGING LANDSCAPE OF GLOBAL FINANCIAL GOVERNANCE AND THE ROLE OF SOFT LAW 160–61 (Friedl Weiss & Armin J. Kammel eds., 2015).

In essence, what some are now describing is a variant of the Forstall system or the Postal Bank. The proponents of the real bills doctrine, who also mistakenly saw it as a way to control the money supply, developed their thinking in an era before deposit insurance and at a time when the United States did not have a lender of last resort. Some post-Financial Crisis proposals for narrow or any public utility banks thus sometimes embed a concept of deposit insurance and sometimes do not. Essentially, a narrow bank is a bank that does not engage, or engages in a very limited extent in the maturity transformation that is the essence of post-New Deal 20th and 21st Century commercial banking. It issues liabilities that customers can call on demand and its assets are very short-term with low credit risk.

One post-Financial Crisis narrow banking proposal, however, is quite different than the proposals just described. Instead, it involves structural solutions that would separate or ring fence the "narrow" bank with access to retail deposits, the discount window, and the payments system from the non-ring fenced bank. The narrow bank would have a monopoly on taking deposits from the public and access to the deposit system. Such narrow banks could engage in consumer lending, lend on mortgage, and lend to businesses, but would not enjoy a monopoly of these functions. The idea was first mooted by Mervyn King, then governor of the Bank of England, and expanded upon in a paper by John Kay. John Kay, *Narrow Banking: The Reform of Banking Regulation* (2009). As actually adopted in the UK, the ring-fence proposal became quite different from the first narrow bank discussed by King and Kay. We will discuss the new UK law in Chapter 6.1.

---

1. ***Should Banks be Public-Owned or a Public Utility?*** The recurring debate about narrow banking is also related to another debate about whether banks should, in fact be profit-making institutions with private profit-seeking shareholders. Many countries, other than the United States, have decided at one phase or another to nationalize their banks and treat them as part of the public purse. French banks were nationalized by President Mittterand in 1981 but the experiment was not successful and the banks were later resold to public shareholders. Many countries, with very different social and economic systems from the United States, such as India and China, currently have state-owned banks; in the recent past, state-owned banks were also common in continental Europe. Most of these state-owned banks are not narrow banks, however, and nothing stops a fractional reserve state-owned bank from getting into trouble with its loans. Indeed, politically motivated lending may increase the risk. The

public utility argument is slightly different from public ownership. Utilities are granted a monopoly by the state (as the king did with the Bank of England), other entrants are limited, and policy is state-controlled. Is a capitalist economy and society willing to take such steps with banking and credit?

2. ***Postal Banks***. Even in the United States, the most capitalist of countries, there was for many years a Postal Bank which functioned as a narrow bank and, recently, the Office of the Inspector General of the U.S. Postal Service suggested that the creation of a new Postal Bank could serve as a lifeline account to the underbanked. France still has a government-owned postal bank while Germany and Japan have privatized their postal banks. Is there any natural advantage in a post office running a simple savings bank that takes deposits from lower income consumers? For an argument in favor, see Mehrsa Baradaran, *It's Time for Postal Banking*, 127 HARV. L. REV. F. 165 (2014).

CHAPTER 2.3

PORTFOLIO DIVERSIFICATION AND RESTRICTIONS ON TRANSACTIONS WITH AFFILIATES

CONTENTS

I. INTRODUCTION

A look at a typical bank balance sheet will reveal that the great majority of its assets are either different types of loans or different types of fixed-income securities, such as U.S. Treasuries, agency securities, municipal bonds, foreign government bonds, or investment grade corporate bonds, commonly referred to as "investment securities" after the term in 12 U.S.C. § 24(Seventh). These loans and investment securities belong on the asset side of a bank's balance sheet, and the bank generates interest income on the principal amounts. To fund its lending and asset purchases, a bank use its customers' time and demand deposits, as well as other short- and long-term borrowings. As discussed in Chapter 1.5, because banks tend to borrow at short-term maturities and lend at longer-term maturities, the typical bank balance sheet is highly leveraged, meaning the bank has significantly more debt, especially demand deposits (its liabilities to its customers) than equity (shareholder contributions and retained earnings). Because banks are both highly leveraged and have a mismatch of the maturity profile on the balance sheet, prudential regulators not only have placed controls on the business of banking, as we saw in Chapter 2.2, but also have placed limits by law and through supervisory guidance on how a bank can lend. The classic limits are those that control how much a bank can lend to one borrower or group of borrowers, credit concentrations, social goals in lending, how it can lend to insiders, and how and under what conditions the bank can lend money or enter into transactions with its affiliates. In this chapter, we explore these portfolio-shaping laws and regulations.

II. LENDING AND COUNTERPARTY LIMITS

One of the oldest and most widespread concepts in banking law is that a bank is limited in how much it may lend to one borrower or a group of affiliated borrowers. Particularly when a bank has relatively few creditworthy customers (a common situation in an earlier era of geographic limits and smaller banks), it will be incentivized to lend predominantly to those customers. The goal of lending limits is to reduce the risk that the bank might fail because of lending too much to one borrower. In essence, lending limits capture the wisdom of the old adage: "Don't put all your eggs in one basket." By limiting the bank's exposure to any one risk, lending limits safeguard the assets of the bank, and thus the bank's depositors.

Under current law, and subject to numerous exceptions, a national bank may lend no more than 15% of its unimpaired capital stock and surplus to any one person. 12 U.S.C. § 84. The amount rises by another 10% if the loan is fully secured. *Id.* The term "person" is broadly defined in § 84(b)(2) to include any individual, business organization, trust, estate, government, or similar entity or organization. State-chartered banks have their own lending limits, which vary by state; many states have lending limits that are more generous than the limit for national banks. We will focus on the lending limits imposed on national banks as a case study.

The basic rule is contained in § 84 and has been so central to banking law that, from 1906 to the Dodd-Frank Act, the section was amended 19 times, with the last amendment before the Dodd-Frank Act being in 1983. Section 84 is not a particularly long statute, but the OCC—tasked with implementing it—has enlarged its scope. *See* 12 C.F.R. § 32. Therefore, it is important to understand not only the plain language of the statute, but also how the OCC has interpreted and defined what a loan is, which loans fall outside of the statute's scope, and how the statute and regulations have changed to address new risks.

Section 84 applies to both loans and extensions of credit. Loans and extensions of credit are "all direct or indirect advances of funds to a person made on the basis of any obligation of that person to repay the funds or repayable from specific property pledged by or on behalf of that person." 12 U.S.C. § 84(b)(1). When determining if a loan or extension of credit has been made, the principal inquiry is whether funds have been advanced in exchange for an obligation to repay the lending bank. Loans and extensions of credit that the OCC has recognized as falling within the scope of § 84 include repurchase agreements, personal property leases, discount commercial paper, bank overdrafts, renewals of existing loans, standby letters of credit, guarantees and other arrangements, and a binding written commitment to lend. If a bank discharges a loan obligation—through bankruptcy or because the loan becomes unenforceable by law—the loan no longer falls within the scope of the lending limits statute. The most recent amendment to § 84 occurred in the wake of the Financial Crisis through § 610 of the Dodd-Frank Act, which expanded the definition of "loans and credit" to include "any credit exposure to a person arising from a derivative transaction, repurchase agreement, reverse repurchase agreement, securities lending transaction, or securities borrowing transaction between the national banking association and the person." *Id.* § 84.

Not all engagements by a bank to extend credit will be considered loans or extensions of credit for the purpose of § 84. Some credit risk does not fall within the scope of the statute because it is too contingent, such as documentary letters of credit based on transactions in goods, and direct commitments to lend in the future that are not considered contractual commitments to advance funds. *Id.*

Another important distinction lies between "loans and extensions of credit" and the purchase of assets. While the purchase of assets will be subject to other regulatory limitations, most of them are not subject to those contained in § 84. There is a simple way to distinguish between a purchase and a loan. If the other party in the transaction has an obligation of repayment to the bank, the transaction is a loan. If the bank and the other party exchanged money for assets and there was no promise made to repay the money, then the transaction is an asset purchase. Banks both purchase assets and make loans for long-term and short-term periods. A purchased asset can be loans from other banks, federal and state government securities, or goods and services.

In addition, some loans are excepted by statute. Despite involving an extension of credit, §§ 84(c)(1)–(10) exclude some loans because they are not thought to pose substantial risk to the lending institution. Several of these exceptions are ones you will come to find familiar in banking regulation, and others reflect the concerns of a bygone era.

- **Loans secured by U.S. obligations and loans guaranteed by a federal agency or corporation.** A bank may give unlimited loans and extensions of credit secured by U.S. obligations, an exception that should not be surprising in light of the tight link between the chartered bank and sovereign debt.

- **Loans secured by segregated deposit amounts.** If a bank makes a loan that is secured by a segregated cash deposit—a deposit the bank will have ready access to in order to receive payment if warranted—the lending limits do not apply.

- **Loans approved by the OCC.** Loans made to a financial institution, receiver, conservator, bank superintendent, or other financial institution agent that is approved by the OCC are exempt from the lending limits. *Id.* § 84(c)(7). For purposes of the rule, a financial institution includes any commercial bank, savings bank, trust company, savings association, or credit union. 12 C.F.R. § 32.3(c)(7). You will see that this traditional indifference towards financial institution interconnections has changed in other areas since the Financial Crisis when we study capital (Chapters 2.5–2.7), liquidity (Chapter 2.7), and total loss-absorbing capacity (Chapter 9.3). Why should loans to other financial institutions be exempted in a world of financial interconnections?

- **Loans secured by certain favored collateral categories.** Some of the loans exempted from lending limits reflect that the statute was originally designed for a much more rural country; loans secured by dairy cattle or livestock are exempted, loans secured by readily marketable staples such as items of agriculture, commerce, and industry (including basic metals, wheat, cotton, and wool) are exempted, as is the discounting of commercial or business paper used to finance commodities, which echoes the real bills doctrine.

A further problem that lending limit rules have had to grapple with is the concern that a borrower—or, more likely, a bank and a borrower working together—could avoid the lending limit by funneling a loan through a different legal entity while capturing the benefit of the loan for the borrower. To counter this problem, § 84(d)(2) grants the OCC the authority to determine when a loan is supposedly made to one person but is actually to be attributed to another person for the purpose of calculating the bank's lending limit. The rules for determining whether loans to seemingly separate borrowers should be aggregated are found in 12 C.F.R. § 32.5. The general rule, found at § 32.5(a) is comprised of two tests; it reads:

> Loans or extensions of credit to one borrower will be attributed to another person and each person will be deemed a borrower (1) [w]hen proceeds of a loan or extension of credit are to be used for the direct benefit of the other person . . . or (2) [w]hen a common enterprise is deemed to exist between the persons.

The first prong of this subsection is known as the direct benefit test. The second prong is known as the common enterprise test.

The direct benefit test is the more straightforward of the two tests. Under it, the OCC will aggregate loans if either the direct proceeds or the assets purchased with the proceeds of a loan are transferred to another person in a non-*bona fide* arm's-length transaction. This is a fact-specific determination that turns not on the stated beneficiary of the loan, but on the actual beneficiary of the loan.

In situations where the connection between the borrowers is less direct, the common enterprise test is used. This test is more complicated because it contains three per se tests and one catch-all test within it. The first test is if "the expected source of repayment for each loan or extension of credit is the same for each borrower," as it would be if two corporations have loans from the same bank and their incomes are derived entirely from each other, the OCC will aggregate the loans. 12 C.F.R. § 32.5(c)(1). Under the second test, the loans are aggregated when "borrowers . . . are related directly or indirectly through common control . . . and [s]ubstantial financial interdependence exists between or among the borrowers." *Id.* § 32.5(c)(2). Interdependence occurs, for example, when a corporation and its owner have loans from the same bank and 50% or more of the owner's gross receipts come from the corporation. The OCC aggregates loans under the third test when "separate persons borrow from a national bank or savings association to acquire a business enterprise of which those borrowers will own more than 50% of the voting securities or voting interests, in which case a common enterprise is deemed to exist between the borrowers." *Id.* § 32.5(c)(3). If four individual buyers obtain loans to then collectively purchase 100% of membership interest in a company, the loans will be attributed to the company.

Lastly, the common enterprise test contains a catch-all test. This test allows the OCC to determine if there is a common enterprise "based upon an evaluation of the facts and circumstances of particular transactions." *Id.* § 32.5(c)(4). National banks may request an interpretative letter from the OCC in order to determine if they will aggregate certain loans under this broad test. The OCC has left itself much discretion under this test, and the only guidance it has provided is a list of 13 factors that it considers relevant to a common enterprise determination. OCC, Interpretive Letter No. 925 (Apr. 12, 2001). The OCC has determined that a common enterprise exists under this catch-all test when borrowers have supporting lines of business; an interchange of goods and services; common ownership of assets; common management; use of common facilities; commingling of assets and liabilities; closely related business activities; similarity in structure, financing and holding; use of same business address; centralized cash management program; a likelihood that a financially troubled member of the group would receive financial aid from other members of the group; family relationships among the borrowers; and pledging of assets to support another's loans. *See id.*; *see also* Kenneth C. Rojc, *National Bank Lending Limits—A New Framework*, 40 BUS. LAWYER 903, 923–24 (1985). The OCC has provided no instruction regarding how many factors are needed to warrant attribution or how they are weighed against one another.

The attribution and aggregation rules mean that the OCC has a wide degree of discretion in determining whether a loan violates a lending limit. For an exhaustive treatment of the lending limits and their exceptions, see Donald E. Frechette, *National Bank Lending Limits and the Attribution Rules of 12 U.S.C. § 84, Congress and the Comptroller Cover the Bases*, 2 U. MIAMI BUS. L. REV. 1 (1991), which, despite its age, is still largely up to date.

In reality, it is rare that a bank will deliberately make extensions of credit at or near its lending limits. Problems usually arise when a loan has become troubled or needs restructuring and participating the loan is not an option. Lending limits, as a practical matter, work differently at a small bank and a large bank. A small bank will find that watching its lending limits is important when lending to larger businesses in its area while a large bank will rarely breach its lending limits. Earlier generations of young lawyers routinely cut their teeth on the calculation of lending limits, especially those which involved the potential application of the attribution rule.

---

1. ***Syndicated Credits, Loan Sales and Loan Participations.*** The development of the syndicated credit agreement in the 1960s has made the lending limits less of a binding constraint. In a syndicated credit agreement, an agent bank gathers together a number of other banks and each bank takes only a portion of the lending obligation. In this way, large corporations can receive large loans while banks spread their risk. Most syndicated credit agreements also contain loan participation and assignment provisions, which has led to an active market in loan sales. While loan participations have both loan and asset purchase qualities, they are treated as an asset purchase under the lending limits rules and so are not covered. Does this treatment make sense given the policy rationales underpinning lending limits? Does the presence of an active secondary trading market make a difference to the policy rationale?

2. ***Single Counterparty Credit Limits Among Financial Institutions.*** Loans by a bank to other banks or financial institutions have traditionally been exempt from lending limits regulations. In light of the financial contagion experienced during the Financial Crisis, Congress enacted a provision in the

Dodd-Frank Act that directs the Federal Reserve Board to limit the risks that the failure of any one individual firm could pose to a bank holding company (BHC) with $50 billion or more in assets or a non-bank designated as systemically important by the Financial Stability Oversight Council (FSOC) (*see* Chapter 6.2) by establishing single counterparty credit limits of no greater than 25% of capital stock and surplus. 12 U.S.C. § 5365(e). The Federal Reserve Board proposed a regulation in 2011 that faced fierce opposition from the banking sector and was not finalized. In March 2016, the Federal Reserve Board reproposed the rule, which limits credit exposures to unaffiliated counterparties to 25% of capital stock and surplus for any BHC with $50 billion or more in assets were proposed. The reproposal imposes a stricter limit of 25% of Tier 1 capital on BHCs with $250 billion or more in total consolidated assets or $10 billion or more in on-balance sheet foreign exposures. Further, the reproposal replaced the previously proposed 10% threshold with a single counterparty credit limit of 15% of Tier 1 capital for Global Systemically Important Banks (G-SIBs) with respect to their exposures to large counterparties, including other G-SIBs and FSOC-designated non-banks. The reproposal does not apply directly to FSOC-designated non-banks, which will, according to the Federal Reserve Board, be subject to similar requirements through future regulations. For more information about tiered regulation applying to G-SIBs and FSOC-designated non-banks, see Chapter 6.2.

III. CREDIT CONCENTRATIONS AND SOCIAL GOALS IN LENDING

Lending limits are an imperfect tool of prudential regulation. The U.S. banking system has seen many examples of lawful loan transactions, well within the lending limits, that resulted in bank failure. Consider for example the problems of Detroit banks leading up to the Banking Crisis of 1933 and the extent to which they were related to Depression-era collapses in the purchase of new cars in a one-industry town, the impact of the lowering of oil prices on the concentration of thrift and bank failures in Texas in the Savings & Loan Crisis of the late 1980s, and, more recently, the impact of sharp declines in housing markets on banks in Nevada, Florida and Georgia during the Financial Crisis. Depository institutions have suffered extensive losses in their credit relationships because of geographic concentration, mortgage loans, real estate investment trusts, foreign country loans, energy loans, highly leveraged corporate buyout transactions, and real estate loans. In addition, depository institutions, which are subject to similar risks in off-balance-sheet activities, would assert that concentrations of credit in certain economic sectors or geographic areas has been the most important risk for portfolio diversification on the asset side of a bank's balance sheet that, as much as lending limits, reflects the way that prudential regulators evaluate the concentration of risk on a bank balance sheet. To better evaluate these effects, consider this excerpt from the Comptroller's manual on credit concentration.

OCC, Comptroller's Handbook: Concentrations of Credit

14, 67, 910, 1415 (2011)

Introduction

[C]redit risk management does not conclude with the supervision of individual transactions. It also encompasses the management of concentrations, or pools of exposures, whose collective performance has the potential to affect a bank negatively *even if each individual transaction within a pool is soundly underwritten.* When exposures in a pool are sensitive to the same economic, financial, or business development, that sensitivity, if triggered, may cause the sum of the transactions to perform as if it were a single, large exposure.

Excessive concentrations of credit have been key factors in banking crises and failures. . . . A central lesson learned from past financial crises is that concentrations can accumulate across products, business lines, countries, and legal entities within a banking company. Products containing the same types of risks under different labels and in different booking units, such as structured products and off-balance-sheet funding structures, can mask some exposures and risks. . . .

[C]redit risk concentrations are often the most material concentration risk in a bank because lending is the primary activity for most banks.

Definition

[I]ndividual transactions rarely cause material losses or bank failures. Rather, *pools of individual transactions that may perform <u>similarly</u> because of a common characteristic or common sensitivity to economic, financial, or business developments* have been the primary cause of credit-related distress. If the common characteristic becomes a common source of weakness, loans in the pool could pose considerable risk to earnings and capital. This statement is true *even when each transaction within a pool is soundly underwritten.*

Because a concentration of credit tends to perform like a single large exposure, concentrations have the potential to pose risk to earnings and capital. Depending on how broadly a bank defines its common pools of credit exposures, nearly all banks will have concentrations in their credit portfolios. Historically, concentrations of commercial real estate loans, energy loans, leveraged loans, collateralized debt obligations, counterparty credit, loans to emerging market countries, loan participations, and agricultural loans have played major roles in the failure or material weaknesses of a large number of banks. Other credit concentrations, such as loans secured by first liens on residential real estate, have historically posed fewer problems. However, during the recession of 2007–2009, the banking industry experienced significant losses in these exposures when the national housing market suffered broad declines in home values. This experience indicates that although a concentration has not proven problematic in the past does not mean that it is precluded from becoming a problem in the future. For this reason, bank management needs to monitor and assess the potential risk arising from all of the bank's credit concentrations.

In most instances, concentrated exposures were booked during periods of rapid economic expansion that were typically fueled in part by bank credit and frequently included a weakening of underwriting standards. At many institutions, bank management didn't fully understand how these exposures would perform under stressed economic conditions and therefore did not implement risk mitigation strategies prior to the recent mortgage crisis. During the economic downturn, many correlated exposures deteriorated, resulting in a significant number of banking problems, including failures.

Governance

[T]he OCC expects banks with significant credit concentrations to maintain capital levels substantially above regulatory minimums to help mitigate the risk such concentrations can pose. There also may be cases in which the potential risk to capital is so severe that reduction of the concentration will be the most effective risk mitigation action. On the concentration's page in the report of examination (ROE), examiners should note concentrations or pools of transactions that either pose a challenge to management or present unusual or significant risk to the bank. Examiners should require management to take corrective action when concentration risk management is weak or the quantity of concentration risk is too high. . . .

Identifying Concentrations

Existing regulatory guidance defines a "concentration" to include direct, indirect, or contingent obligations *exceeding 25 percent of the bank's capital structure.* Obligations include the firm-wide aggregate (across all lines of business) of all types of loans and discounts; overdrafts; cash items; securities purchases outright or under resale agreements; sale of federal funds; suspense assets; leases; acceptances; letters of credit; placements; loans endorsed, guaranteed, or subject to repurchase agreements; credit exposure from derivatives transactions; and any other actual or contingent liabilities. The "obligation" (i.e., the amount of exposure) is defined as the committed or outstanding amount, depending on the concentration's characteristics. For example, using outstanding amounts may make more sense for a credit card portfolio, but commitments might better capture the risk of a portfolio of home equity lines of credit or agricultural production loans. For derivative contracts with a counterparty, the credit exposure would be the net current market value of the portfolio of contracts, plus a conservative measure of the potential future exposure of that portfolio . . .

Correlation of Pools

Transactions that may perform similarly because of a common characteristic or common sensitivity to economic, financial, or business developments may be formed into pools, some of which an institution may subsequently designate as concentrations because of their size or risk profile. However, that is not necessarily the end of the concentration identification and risk management process.

Once an institution separates exposures that may behave similarly into pools, the next issue to consider is whether some of those individual pools might behave similarly. The identification of correlated pools of exposure is an extremely important, but difficult, part of managing credit concentration risk. Two pools that do not exhibit strong performance correlation (i.e., similar credit performance metrics) in a benign economic environment may show very strong correlation in a deteriorating environment. For example, many banks assumed that individual pools of residential mortgages, each representing a different geographic area, would not be highly correlated. While this was a reliable assumption during a benign economic environment, the performance of these pools became highly correlated when home prices declined broadly throughout the country. Accordingly, experience and judgment play important roles in helping banks identify pools that might perform similarly in the future.

Banks should review all of their relatively larger and riskier pools—both those designated as concentrations and those not—to determine if there might be an additional level of performance correlation between two or more pools. While the list of all such combinations is potentially long, it is appropriate to focus on the relatively larger or riskier pools to determine if such a correlation exists.

Suppose, for example, that exposure in each of two industry pools, air transportation and hotels, was equal to 15 percent of capital. Although neither might be designated a concentration initially, if there were a downturn in the demand for passenger air service for any reason, the hotel business probably would suffer as well. Both pools would exhibit common performance characteristics and, at 30 percent of capital, may warrant scrutiny.

Depending on the industry groups defined by an institution, there may also be a positive correlation between industries in the same supply chain. An institution may distinctly identify Auto Manufacturing and Fabricated Metal Product Manufacturing within its industry structure. To the extent that borrowers within the Fabricated Metal Product Manufacturing industry sell to auto manufacturers, a downturn in auto sales would negatively affect the performance of both industries.

Conclusion

All banks have credit concentrations. In some cases, this is by choice as the institution seeks to develop expertise in a particular segment. In other cases, it may be the result of mergers or acquisitions. Alternatively, credit concentrations may be unavoidable due to a lender's limited geographic footprint combined with its market's dependence on a relatively few employers or industries. Whatever the reason, it is incumbent on management and the board of directors to ensure that the bank has an effective process in place to identify, measure, monitor, and control concentration risk. The board of directors also needs to ensure that the bank maintains adequate capital relative to concentration risks.

Although each individual transaction within a concentration may be prudently underwritten, collectively the transactions are sensitive to the same economic, financial, or business development events. If something triggers a negative development, the risk is that the sum of the transactions may perform as if it were a single, large exposure.

The size of a concentration, however, does not necessarily determine the risk. Different pools of the same size may represent very different levels of risk. Although 25 percent of capital remains the threshold for capturing concentrations for regulatory purposes, the OCC expects that institutions will build their concentration management process *based on the risk that a pool of loans represents.* The extent of risk mitigation undertaken by each bank should relate to the level of risk posed by the particular credit concentration.

Identifying, measuring, and appropriately mitigating concentration risk is ultimately dependent on the accurate and timely receipt and analysis of data. The absence of a sufficiently robust set of data elements will hinder an institution's ability to identify and monitor concentration risk, regardless of the data's accuracy and timeliness. Similarly, a comprehensive data set is of little use if inaccurate, untimely, or unexamined. The OCC expects that each bank's concentration risk management systems and [management information systems] will be accurate and timely, and that the scope of the data elements collected and analyzed will be proportional to the size and complexity of the bank's portfolio. Examiners should note pools that pose a challenge to management or that present unusual or significant risk to the bank in the [report of examination]. When concentration risk management is weak, examiners should require management to take corrective action.

---

1. ***Leveraged Lending Guidelines.*** In 2013, the OCC, the FDIC and the Federal Reserve Board issued guidelines on leveraged lending by financial institutions. Interagency Guidance on Leveraged Lending, 78 Fed. Reg. 17,776 (Mar. 22, 2013). Leveraged lending is defined in relation to the borrower. Specifically, it includes lending to companies that are highly indebted as measured by a high debt-to-net-worth ratio, are in a management buyout, are unable to access capital markets, or are otherwise recognized as leveraged borrowers. In order to reduce risk, the guidelines outline regulator expectations on what these financial institutions' risk management programs should entail, including a recommendation that the financial institutions consider the effects of a financial crisis on their credit portfolio.

The policy has been explained as a means to prevent another asset bubble by reining in fast growth, reflecting the agencies' broader willingness to use monetary policy to contain risk. Indeed, Federal Reserve Board Governor Daniel Tarullo has said that, "monetary policy action cannot be taken off the table as a response to the build-up of broad and sustained systemic risk." Daniel K. Tarullo, Governor of the Federal Reserve Board, Address at the National Association for Business Economics, Economic Policy Conference: Monetary Policy and Financial Stability (Feb. 25, 2014). In rare on-the-record press statements, senior banking regulators made it clear that they mean to discourage these loans by non-regulated unlevered entities; Federal Reserve Board Governor Jeremy Stein said that, in addition to keeping an eye on measures of leverage in banking and shadow-banking, "the rapid growth of fixed-income funds—as well as other, similar vehicles—bears careful watching" and that "it would be a mistake to be complacent about this phenomenon." Jeremy C. Stein, Governor of the Federal Reserve Board, Comments on "Market Tantrums and Monetary Policy" at the U.S. Monetary Policy Forum (Feb. 28, 2014). In a post-Financial Crisis era, is this type of proactive portfolio shaping a good idea? Does it matter that it happens via regulatory guidance and not through notice and comment rulemaking? How do the banking regulators achieve their jurisdictional authority over the non-regulated lenders, such as private equity funds?

2. ***Operation Choke Point.*** The DOJ's Operation Choke Point, which was aimed at cutting off certain "high-risk" businesses from access to the payments system, became public beginning in 2013. It imposed a duty on banks to conduct due diligence and undergo other risk controls on these high-risk companies that borrow from them, making it more costly to lend to these businesses. Banks already have "know your customer" duties that require them to detect and report suspicious activities that may be illegal or involve persons on government terrorist watch lists. The additional burdens imposed by Operation Choke Point decreased incentives for banks to lend to businesses that have been deemed to be high-risk for other reasons.

William Isaac, former FDIC Chairman, argued that the real goal of Operation Choke Point was "to target entire industries deemed undesirable by putting regulatory pressure on the banks that serve them." William Isaac, Op-Ed., *Don't Like an Industry? Send a Message to Its Bankers*, WALL ST. J., Nov. 21, 2014. The FDIC had previously published a list of "high-risk" businesses in a Financial Institutions letter, which included payday lenders, coin dealers, firearms dealers, escort services, and other businesses. Notably absent from the list were legal marijuana businesses, which, while still criminal on a federal level, have been subject to a DOJ policy of prosecutorial forbearance. Conservative groups noted that legal gun sales were labeled high risk, while legal abortion clinics were not. The FDIC removed the "high-risk" merchant categories from previously issued materials in 2014, and instead in 2015 issued risk-based guidance for banks.

Whatever the good intentions of its start in anti-money laundering and anti-terrorist enforcement, the FDIC staff's foray into a morality-based portfolio-shaping rule drew controversy both in the press and in Congress. Should portfolio-shaping rules be concerned with reputational and moral risk or should they be confined to credit risk? What happens to these rules when the political winds change and banks are subject to different informal rules?

3. ***Social Goals in Portfolio Shaping.*** The Community Reinvestment Act of 1977 (CRA) encourages banks to lend to low- and moderate-income neighborhoods in the community in which a bank is chartered. This social or targeted lending requirement is also a portfolio-shaping tool influenced by social policy choices rather than by goals of credit risk reduction. Federal bank regulators evaluate banks for their compliance with the CRA based on a set of criteria by rating them under the CRA. The ratings, along with a written report, become a part of the banks' supervisory record and can influence regulator decisions on new branch applications or merger and acquisition (M&A) applications. The CRA will be discussed in more depth in Chapter 5.4. Some have suggested that CRA policies led to the lowering of underwriting standards in mortgages in the run-up to the Financial Crisis, see *Reviewing the Financial Crisis Inquiry Commission's Final Report: Hearing Before the S. Comm. on Banking, Hous. & Urban Affairs*, 112th Cong. 32–42 (2011) (statement of Peter J. Wallison, Arthur F. Burns Fellow in Financial Policy Studies, American Enterprise Institute), while others have hotly contested that point, see David Min, *Why Wallison Is Wrong About the Genesis of the U.S. Housing Crisis*, CENTER FOR AMERICAN PROGRESS (July 2011). For another defense of the CRA, see Michael S. Barr, *Credit Where It Counts: The Community Reinvestment Act and Its Critics*, 75 N.Y.U. L. REV. 101 (2005). It is worth noting that the United States is not the only country with social or targeted lending rules. Indeed, such laws are very common elsewhere in the world, especially in emerging markets. India, for example, requires that domestic commercial banks and foreign banks with 20 or more branches direct 40% of their adjusted net bank credit to underserved rural areas. How does a bank balance a required social goal in portfolio shaping with credit risk?

IV. TRANSACTIONS WITH AFFILIATES

For most of the 20th Century, the vast majority of the larger banks have existed within the holding company form of organization. Only the rare larger bank and many of the very smallest banks, of which there are many in number, exist in a bank-only or bank-at-the-top-level company structure. Most have acquired or created additional banks and non-bank affiliates engaged in such activities as mortgage banking, consumer finance, leasing, and securities activities. As a consequence, most banks are part of a financial group, with a parent BHC owning them and their non-bank affiliates. *See* Chapter 6.1. Community and midsize banking groups can have relatively simple structures, while large banking organizations can be highly complex.

Transactions between insured depository institutions (IDIs) and their non-bank affiliates, including their holding companies, first became a policy concern in the wake of the Banking Crisis of 1933. At that time, there was no direct regulation of BHCs. A limited version of Section 23A of the Federal Reserve Act was enacted as part of the Banking Act of 1933. As substantially expanded and revised in 1982, Section 23A became one of the key ways that the Federal Reserve Board regulates the relationships between an IDI and its affiliates. 12 U.S.C. § 371c. Section 23A places both quantitative and qualitative restrictions on transactions between an IDI and its affiliates. Section 23B was enacted in

1987 and requires that transactions between an IDI and its affiliates be at arm's length. *Id.* § 371c-1. Both Sections 23A and 23B apply to national banks, state member banks, and state non-member banks, as well as to federal and state thrifts and industrial loan companies. *Id.* § 1828(j)(1). The implementing regulation for Sections 23A and 23B, Regulation W, was not put into place until 2002. Before that time, the Federal Reserve Board relied upon a series of informal and sometimes nonpublic interpretations.

Neither Section 23A nor Section 23B prevent or limit dividends from a bank to its holding company, and it is worth recalling that, in its normal operations, a healthy and profitable bank will send dividends to its parent holding company on a regular basis. The ability of healthy national banks to declare dividends is regulated by 12 U.S.C. § 60 and is subject to its own set of quantitative limits based upon retained earnings and surplus. If a bank is undercapitalized or would become undercapitalized in the event of a dividend payout, the bank is generally prohibited from paying a dividend by statute. *Id.* § 1831o(d)(1)(A). State-chartered banks are subject to similar restrictions that vary according to state law.

According to the Federal Reserve Board, "Sections 23A and 23B and Regulation W limit the risks to a bank from transactions between the bank and its affiliates and limit the ability of a bank to transfer **to** its affiliates the subsidy arising from the bank's access to the Federal safety net." Federal Reserve Board, Supervisory Letter, SR 03-2: Adoption of Regulation W Implementing Sections 23A and 23B of the Federal Reserve Act (2003) (emphasis added). One key way to understand the restrictions is to remember that they focus on cash, credit risk or other value **from** the IDI **to** non-bank affiliates. There is no Section 23A restriction on value flowing the other way from the non-bank affiliate to the IDI. The restrictions and limits of Section 23A apply to "covered transactions" with most "affiliates," terms the meaning of which will be explored more deeply in the following paragraphs. Section 23B applies to almost any interaction between the bank and its "affiliates." The terms "affiliate" and "covered transaction" are best introduced by reference to a simplified organizational chart in Figure 2.3-1.

Figure 2.3-1 Application of Sections 23A and 23B to Bank Affiliates

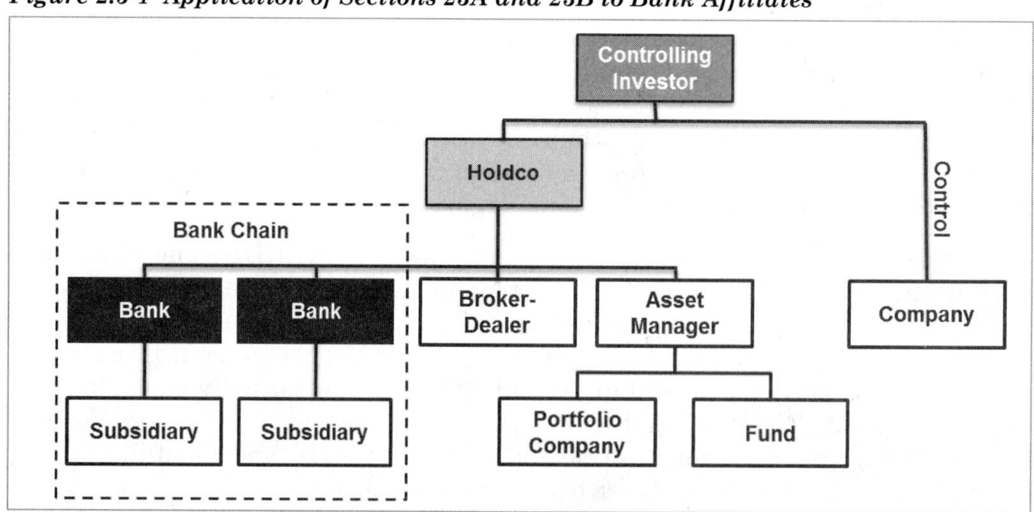

The definition of affiliate is a key building block to understanding Sections 23A and 23B. "Affiliate" includes the parent holding company, a foreign bank that controls a U.S. bank, domestic and foreign bank subsidiaries of the holding company or controlling foreign bank, non-bank subsidiaries of the holding company, bank subsidiaries of the bank, any company controlled by the shareholders who control the bank, any company (such as a real estate investment trust) that is sponsored and advised by the bank, and any other company that the Federal Reserve Board determines has such relationship with the bank, or any subsidiary or affiliate, that may affect the relationship and make a transaction other than at arm's length. The meaning of control was introduced in Chapter 2.1 and will be discussed further in Chapter 6.1. For this Chapter and the current discussion, it will be assumed that control exists. It is common to speak of the "bank chain" of ownership and the "non-bank chain" when analyzing transactions under Sections 23A and 23B. Generally, though not always, transactions between members of the bank chain are less regulated under Sections 23A and 23B.

Section 371c(d) also contains the sister bank exemption, which removes most of the Section 23A restrictions between banks controlled by the same company so long as the parent holding company owns at least 80% of each bank. *See* Figure 2.3-2. In effect, the section treats separate bank subsidiaries like a branch banking system, allowing unlimited transactions among the bank subsidiaries (except for the purchase of low-quality assets) while still requiring that every transaction be consistent with safe and sound banking practices. Consequently, it is possible to raise funds (*e.g.*, attract deposits) in the most creditworthy bank subsidiary of a holding company to fund loans in another bank subsidiary. Similarly, under § 371c(b)(2)(A), a non-bank subsidiary of a bank is generally not an affiliate.

Figure 2.3-2 Sister Bank Exemption to Sections 23A and 23B

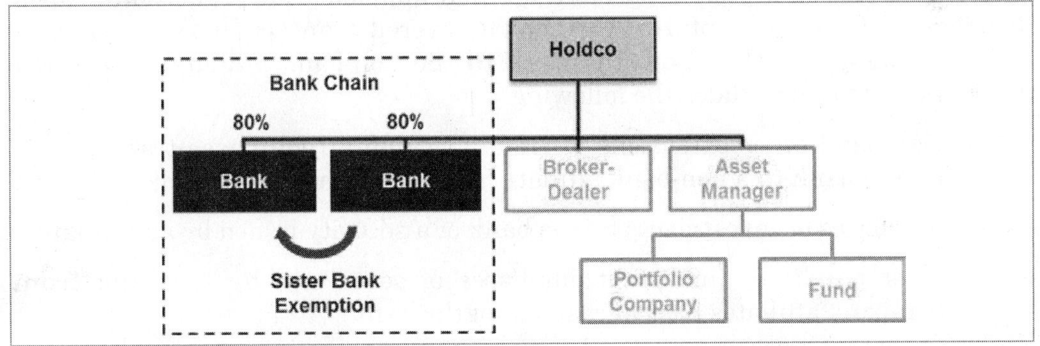

In contrast, although financial subsidiaries are in the bank chain, transactions between IDIs and financial subsidiaries are not exempt from Section 23A limitations. Financial subsidiaries, which were first introduced in GLBA, are separately-incorporated subsidiaries in the bank chain that are permitted to conduct certain activities in which their parent banks may not engage, including corporate debt and equity securities dealing and underwriting. Under the Gramm-Leach-Bliley Act (GLBA) framework, financial subsidiaries were subject to most, but not all, of the Section 23A restrictions. Following Dodd-Frank Act amendments to the Federal Reserve Act, however, all Section 23A limitations apply to limit transactions between IDIs and financial subsidiaries. There are other measures banks must meet to ensure safety and soundness with a financial subsidiary. For example, a bank that establishes financial subsidiaries must deduct the aggregate amount of its outstanding equity investment in the financial subsidiaries from its capital and from total assets for calculating its total risk-based capital. 12 U.S.C. § 24a(c). Although at the time of GLBA it was expected that many banks would create financial subsidiaries, the combined impact of the capital deduction and the Section 23A limits have made the form unattractive, and they have been rarely used.

Figure 2.3-3 Application of Section 23A to Financial Subsidiaries

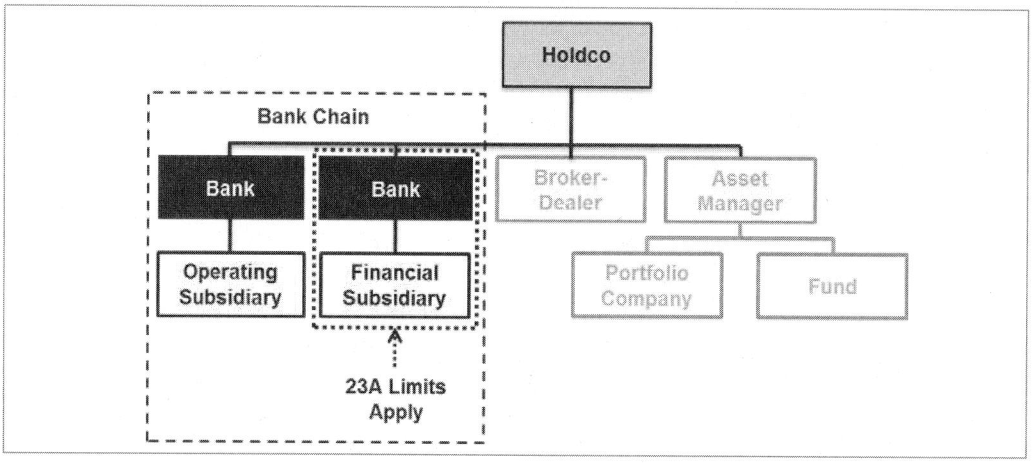

A. SECTION 23A

For purposes of Section 23A, any "covered transaction," as defined in the statute, between a bank and any "affiliate" is subject to the qualitative and quantitative limits in Section 23A and its final implementing regulations, called Regulation W. It is helpful to think of a covered transaction as involving a transfer of cash or value **from** the bank **to** the non-bank affiliate. A covered transaction broadly includes the following:

- loans and other extensions of credit, including repurchase transactions, **by** the bank **to** a non-bank affiliate (risk of cash out of the bank);
- purchases or investments by the bank of a security issued by an affiliate;
- asset purchases (including purchases of securities) **by** the bank **from** non-bank affiliates (risk of cash out of the bank);
- acceptance as collateral of securities issued by or other debt obligations of non-bank affiliates (risk on the value of the affiliate's securities after making a loan and cash out of the bank);
- derivatives transactions, securities lending and borrowing transactions to the extent that these activities cause the bank to have a credit exposure to the non-bank affiliate, and repurchase transactions (risk of loss due to exposure); and
- guarantees **on behalf** of affiliates (risk of cash out of the bank).

Section 23A and Regulation W generally do not prohibit transactions between a bank and its non-bank affiliates but rather limit and control them. The exception to this general rule is an absolute prohibition on purchases of low-quality assets. The general limits of Section 23A include a quantitative limit that a bank's credit transactions with a single non-bank affiliate may not exceed 10% of the bank's capital and surplus, and the bank's transactions with all non-bank affiliates may not in the aggregate exceed 20% of capital and surplus. "Capital stock and surplus" is the capital of the entire bank as calculated under applicable capital standards, which will be discussed in Chapters 2.5–2.6.

Other key provisions of Sections 23A include:

- a quantitative requirement that credit transactions with affiliates must be fully secured by specified types of collateral. The requirement applies to derivatives transactions between banks and affiliates that increase the bank's credit exposure. Under the Dodd-Frank Act, the transaction must be secured by a statutorily mandated level of collateral for the duration of the transaction and not just at its inception;
- a qualitative requirement that transactions with affiliates be carried out on terms and conditions consistent with safe and sound banking practices; and
- a qualitative requirement that banks not purchase or accept as collateral low-quality assets from affiliates.

Similar to the lending limit context, attribution rules apply to loans between a bank and third parties to prevent a circumvention of these quantitative and qualitative restrictions. In particular, a loan made to a third party that benefits an affiliate will be deemed a loan to an affiliate that may be subject to the restrictions of Section 23A and Regulation W.

One of the most important exemptions, in practice, to Section 23A is the market quotation exemption, which provides a complete exemption for any transactions with any affiliate that can be objectively priced at arm's length. For example, purchases from any affiliate of any asset "having a readily identifiable and publicly available market quotation and purchased at or below the asset's current market quotation" are exempted from the quantitative and qualitative restrictions under Regulation W. In a world with large and highly liquid financial markets with massive secondary trading of securities, the market quotation exemption is highly significant. 12 C.F.R. § 223.42. It will cover virtually all government, investment-grade, corporate, and asset-backed debt that is traded in the secondary market. Another important exemption, which is similar to principles that apply in the lending limit context, involves transactions with affiliates that are otherwise lower-risk because of the quality of the collateral pledged against the transaction. Transactions that are fully secured by government obligations or guaranteed by the United States or its agencies are similarly exempted from the quantitative limits of Section 23A, as are transactions secured by a segregated cash collateral deposit (once again, also similar to principles that apply in the lending limit context).

B. SECTION 23B

Congress adopted Section 23B in 1987, possibly based on the assumption that commercial banks would soon become affiliated with securities firms. Although Section 23B, in essence, applies to almost any interaction between the bank and its affiliates, not just covered transactions, its core requirement is that the transaction be on market terms. The section deals with conflicts of interest between a bank and non-bank affiliate and covers a much broader range of transactions than Section 23A, including the sale of securities or other assets to an affiliate, the payment of money and the furnishing of services to an affiliate. It also includes transactions in which an affiliate acts as an agent or broker or receives a fee for its services to the bank. Transactions with covered affiliates may be made only on terms and under circumstances that are substantially the same as those prevailing for comparable transactions involving non-affiliated enterprises.

C. WAIVERS

Until the Financial Crisis and the passage of the Dodd-Frank Act, the Federal Reserve Board had the sole ability to create waivers from the requirements of Section 23A. The scope of transactions permissible under Section 23A because of existing statutory exemptions was even further expanded under the Federal Reserve Board's long history of using its exemptive authority. Specifically, before the Financial Crisis, if the Federal Reserve Board determined that a transaction that was limited by Section 23A was "in the public interest and consistent with the purposes of Section 23A," it had the sole authority to exempt that transaction from the rule. Because no regulations were issued under Section 23A until Regulation W was promulgated in 2002, there was an exceedingly long history of informal interpretation and exemptions with the two concepts sometimes blending into one another.

During the Financial Crisis, the Federal Reserve Board aggressively used its exemptive authority under Section 23A to provide liquidity to frozen markets, often in conjunction with its emergency secured lending programs, and it also granted waivers in connection with the emergency acquisitions and conversions to BHC status. While highly successful in helping to contain the systemic emergency, this suspension of "peacetime regulations" raised concerns at the FDIC and among members of Congress. Saule T. Omarova, *From Gramm-Leach-Bliley to Dodd-Frank*, 89 N.C. L. REV. 1683, 1762 (2011). As a result, the Dodd-Frank Act made it more difficult for the Federal Reserve Board to grant waivers. Section 608 now requires the Federal Reserve Board to act in coordination with the FDIC (for state member banks) and the OCC (for national banks) in issuing any such exemptions.

It has been argued that, in the wake of the passage of GLBA, Sections 23A and 23B were accorded a new and more important status. "After the enactment of [GLBA] . . . which removed the Glass-Steagall [Act] era prohibition on affiliation between commercial banks and investment banks, [S]ection 23A effectively became the principal statutory firewall protecting the depository system from subsidizing potentially risky activities of non-depository financial institutions and, in a broader sense, safeguarding the foundational U.S. principle of separation of banking and commerce." *Id.* at 1687. Indeed, GLBA was drafted under the assumption that Sections 23A and 23B, rather than the stricter limits that had previously applied to transactions with securities affiliates, would effectively protect the depository system. In a Supervisory Letter, the Federal Reserve Board stated, "A key premise of GLBA was that [S]ections 23A and 23B would limit the risk to depository institutions from these broader affiliations." Federal Reserve Board, Supervisory Letter, SR 03-2: Adoption of Regulation W Implementing Sections 23A and 23B of the Federal Reserve Act (2003). It is an open question, shrouded in the mists of confidential supervisory information, as to the extent of securities affiliate transactions during the Financial Crisis.

The Volcker Rule, enacted as part of the Dodd-Frank Act following the Financial Crisis, applies a stronger version of Section 23A and 23B to more subsidiaries of a financial conglomerate, but for a more limited pool of transactions. These stronger versions have been dubbed Super 23A and Super 23B to distinguish them from the regular versions discussed in this Chapter. You will learn more about the Volcker Rule, including Super 23A and Super 23B, in Chapter 6.1.

---

1. ***Purchases from a Broker-Dealer in a Liquidity Crunch.*** In the depths of the Financial Crisis, a large affiliated broker-dealer is experiencing a severe liquidity drain. The management of the broker-dealer approaches the affiliated bank, a national bank, with a request that the bank buy from it Treasury securities, municipal bonds, corporate debt, and stocks listed on the S&P 500. Can the bank purchase these securities? *See* 12 U.S.C. §§ 371c(a)(3), 371c(d)(6). Does the bank need a waiver to do so? Do the quantitative limits apply? *See* 12 C.F.R. § 223.16.

2. ***Segregated Cash Deposit.*** A bank client comes to you with an idea designed to simplify its Section 23A compliance. The bank is engaged in a number of transactions with affiliates every day, keeping track of the collateral requirements is becoming burdensome, and, of more concern, mistakes are made in the daily rush. The idea is that the holding company would place a large segregated cash deposit with the bank. Is the holding company permitted to do so under Section 23A? The bank will then use that segregated cash deposit as a collective pool for the collateral required in any transactions subject to Section 23A with other affiliates. *See* 12 U.S.C. § 371c(d)(4)(C) and its implementing regulation 12 C.F.R. § 223.42(c). *See also* 12 U.S.C. § 371c(a)(2) and its implementing regulation 12 C.F.R. § 223.16. Is this permissible?

V. LOANS TO INSIDERS

One of the traditional fringe benefits of working for a bank has been the ability of employees to get loans at a better interest rate. Banks, like airlines and retail stores, which provide employee discounts on tickets and store products, often have extensive employee lending programs at preferential rates. These company-wide benefit programs are permitted as long as they are available to all employees equally as part of benefits and compensation. *See* 12 C.F.R. § 215.4(a)(2). Section 402 of the Sarbanes-Oxley Act of 2002 (Sarbanes-

Oxley Act), in reaction to sweetheart loans given to CEOs and other top executives, also prohibits loans to employees of public corporations, unless the loans are available to the public and on market terms. 15 U.S.C. § 78m(k).

A special category of loans—those to insiders—are subject to stricter regulation than company work programs. As the OCC has noted, "Studies of bank failures have found that insider abuse—such as poor-quality loans made and unjustified fees paid to directors, and officers—often contributes to the failure." Insider Activities, OCC Bulletin 2013-31 (Nov. 6, 2013). There are three classifications of insiders: executive officers, directors and principal shareholders. 12 U.S.C. § 375b(8). A principal shareholder is one who, together with family members, has the power, directly or indirectly, to vote 10% or more of any class of voting securities of the bank. A director includes not only directors of the bank but also directors of the BHC and any of its affiliates. Finally, an executive officer includes the chairman of the board, the president, vice presidents, the cashier, the secretary, the treasury, and every other officer who has the power to engage in major policymaking decisions, unless excluded by resolution or bylaws to participate in policymaking. 12 C.F.R. § 215.2(e)(1).

The general objective of these regulations is to limit the size of loans to insiders and to require that the board of directors approve such loans above a certain level. Loans to insiders are governed by §§ 375a and 375b and are elaborated on in 12 C.F.R. § 215, more commonly known as Regulation O. While §§ 375a and 375b, by their terms, apply only to member banks, § 1828(j)(2) provides that §§ 375a and 375b apply to all insured banks. Section 375a applies only to executive officers of banks. The lending restrictions of § 375b apply to insiders and their related interests whether affiliated with a bank, a BHC or any subsidiary of either. Exceptions can be made, however, for officers and directors of subsidiaries who do not participate in the bank's policymaking functions. As a result, under § 375b, insiders are, in effect, treated as having the same position with the bank as they actually have with the affiliated company. Companies, as well as political or campaign committees affiliated with an insider, are typically considered to be "related interests."

The regulation requires prior approval by the board of directors for loans to any insider aggregating more than the greater of $25,000 or 5% of bank capital and surplus, but not more than $500,000. 12 C.F.R. § 215.4(b)(1)(i). The effect of these limits is that there is always a lower limit of $25,000 for banks having total assets of approximately $500,000 or less and an upper limit of $500,000 for banks having approximate total assets exceeding $10 million. For banks in between those two limits, the amount would be 5% of capital and surplus. Prior approval by the bank's directors is required for all loans to insiders exceeding $500,000 in the aggregate. *Id.* § 215.4(b)(2).

Loans to executive officers of banks are even more strictly regulated under § 375a and 12 C.F.R. § 215.5. Executive officers can receive loans in any otherwise permissible amount for the purposes of residential mortgages or education, and in any otherwise permissible amount for any other purpose if secured by a perfected security interest in government obligations or bank deposit accounts. Otherwise, loans to executive officers can be made only to the higher of $25,000 or 2.5% of bank capital and surplus, but not more than $100,000. The general purpose of these regulations is to control loans to individuals who have particular influence within a bank, and especially to control loans to those who have the power to obtain preferential or excessive credit that could threaten the financial stability of the bank. Exactly who is an executive officer? *See* 12 C.F.R. § 215.2(e)(1) and the accompanying footnote.

One easy way around §§ 375a and 375b would be for banks to engage in reciprocal lending practices to each other's insiders. To some extent, this may be possible. This type of activity, however, is limited by 12 U.S.C. § 1972(2) for banks with correspondent relationships. Banks with correspondent relationships may extend credit to officers of correspondent banks only on terms no more favorable than those prevailing for other customers. Nevertheless, correspondent banks are not limited by the more severe restrictions in §§ 375a and 375b applicable to their own insiders. In addition, there are no special limits on loans to insiders of another bank if there is no correspondent banking relationship. For an excellent treatment of the topic of insider loans, see Patrick B. Augustine, *Loans to Insiders after FIRREA and FDICIA*, 110 BANKING L.J. 216 (1993) and Patricia A. Murphy, *Insider Loans: How Restricted is the Banker*, 9 FORDHAM URB. L.J. 431 (1980).

CHAPTER 2.4
BANK DEPOSITS

CONTENTS

I. INTRODUCTION

When Franklin D. Roosevelt took office as the thirty-second President of the United States on March 4, 1933, the banking system was in the throes of widespread financial panic. Fearful of losing their savings, citizens had been withdrawing their deposits *en masse* throughout the preceding month. To prevent further withdrawals of cash, the governors of all 48 states had already declared bank holidays, a term for mandated restrictions on banking transactions. These inconsistent, haphazardly-announced state measures failed to reassure a nervous public. One of Roosevelt's first actions as President was to declare a nation-wide banking holiday to provide his administration enough time to plan, announce, and execute a coordinated national response.

On the evening of Sunday, March 12, 1933, with numerous bank holidays set to expire, Roosevelt gave his first fireside chat, a 15-minute radio address to the American public. He explained that the root of the crisis was the public's loss of confidence in the banking system and outlined the actions the government planned to take to restore their confidence:

> Confidence and courage are the essentials of success in carrying out our plan. You people must have faith; you must not be stampeded by rumors or guesses. Let us unite in banishing fear. We have provided the machinery to restore our financial system, and it is up to you to support and make it work.

Franklin D. Roosevelt, President of the United States, *Fireside Chat*: On the Banking Crisis (Mar. 12, 1933).

The Administration's efforts to restore confidence and halt the financial panic were surprisingly successful. By the end of March, two-thirds of the cash withdrawn from banks during the panic was returned. The success of these efforts has been attributed to the power of Roosevelt's rhetoric and the widespread belief that, by enacting the Emergency Banking Act of 1933 three days before the fireside chat, Roosevelt's administration had implicitly guaranteed 100% of deposits in re-opened banks.

Policy-makers in Congress did not intend to pin their hopes for financial stability on the force of Roosevelt's personality or an amorphous, possibly unlimited, guarantee deriving from an Act that few of them had even had the chance to read before voting to pass it. Instead, policymakers settled on what they hoped would be a more durable solution: explicit deposit insurance. Roughly three months after his fireside chat, Roosevelt signed legislation establishing the nation's first federal deposit insurance system. It was a controversial experiment. Opponents of deposit insurance—a group including most large banks, many congressmen, and, for a while, even Roosevelt himself—pointed out the number of disastrous and now defunct state-level deposit insurance schemes. They also argued that deposit insurance would encourage widespread bank mismanagement. *See* HELEN M. BURNS, THE AMERICAN BANKING COMMUNITY AND NEW DEAL BANKING REFORMS, 1933-1935 (Greenwood Press, 1974); FED. DEPOSIT INS. CORP., THE FIRST FIFTY YEARS: A HISTORY OF THE FDIC 1933-1983 24–29 (1984).

Despite these fears, deposit insurance maintained public confidence and largely eliminated bank runs. Bank failures dropped from over 4,000 in 1933 to only nine in 1934. Bank runs have remained virtually nonexistent in the United States since the 1930s, even during periods with high levels of bank failure. *See* Charles W. Calomiris & Gary Gorton, *The Origins of Banking Panics: Models, Facts, and Bank Regulation*, *in* FINANCIAL MARKETS AND FINANCIAL CRISES 109 (1991). Of course, the Financial Crisis re-introduced a new generation to the fact that bank runs can happen, this time largely through the shadow banking system, including money market funds and repo. You will learn about that development in Chapters 12.3 (discussing money market funds) and 12.4 (discussing wholesale funding).

In this Chapter, we discuss U.S. deposit insurance, including the objectives, design, and criticisms of the program. We also briefly outline other government guarantees in the financial system. We conclude this Chapter with a discussion of the role of deposit insurance internationally. We discuss the mechanics of bank resolution in Chapter 9.1.

II. THE ROLE OF DEPOSIT INSURANCE IN FINANCIAL STABILITY

A. THE BANK BALANCE SHEET REVISITED

To understand the role that deposit insurance plays in preventing runs and maintaining financial stability, it makes sense to examine the banking balance sheet. Consider the following balance sheet for a simple commercial bank, which we will call Bank ABC.

Figure 2.4-1 Bank ABC Balance Sheet as of Year-End 2014

Bank ABC Balance Sheet as of Year-End 2014
($ millions)

Assets		% of Assets	Liabilities		% of Liabilities and Equity
Cash and Due from Banks	$ 17	1%	Deposits	$ 1,154	85%
Short Term Investments	22	2%	Other Liabilities	106	8%
Investment Securities	308	23%	**Total Liabilities**	**$ 1,260**	**93%**
Loans					
Mortgage / Commercial Real Estate Loans	939	69%			
Commercial and Industrial Loans	28	2%	**Total Equity**	**$ 101**	**7%**
Other Loans	9	1%			
Allowance for Possible Loan Losses	(11)	(1)%			
Total Loans	**$ 962**	**71%**			
Premises and Equipment	18	1%			
Other Assets	31	2%			
Total Assets	**$ 1,361**	**100%**	**Total Liabilities and Equity**	**$ 1,361**	**100%**

Bank ABC's primary source of funding is deposits, which account for 85% of its funding. Bank ABC pools these deposits from numerous small depositors and transforms those funds into assets, primarily long-term, illiquid loans. As you can see, these loans, on which banks earn interest, make up 71% of Bank ABC's assets. On a bank balance sheet, loans are assets and deposits are liabilities. Demand deposits, such as checking and savings accounts, may be withdrawn at any time. Bank ABC will make as many loans as it can to maximize profits, allowing its reserves to fall to a level that is only a fraction of the total amount of deposits outstanding. These reserves consist of cash on hand at the bank, commonly known as vault cash, as well as a bank's *own* deposits held at a central bank. In the United States, banks keep their reserves at the Federal Reserve bank in their district. Here, Bank ABC only has $17 million in immediately available cash to satisfy withdrawals on over $1 billion in deposits. A system in which a bank's reserves are only a fraction of its outstanding deposits is known as fractional reserve banking. If banks had to hold all of their deposits as cash, the bank could not make any loans. Banks and their regulators assume that depositors will behave in predictable ways; not all depositors will demand their funds back at the same time. Generally, this assumption is justified.

The problem is that sometimes, in periods of economic or financial stress, banks are unable to honor withdrawal requests if depositors withdraw their funds *en masse* in a short time frame. This phenomenon is commonly known as a bank run. Bank ABC customers, for example, would only need to pull out 1.5% of their deposits before the bank's reserves were depleted and it could no longer honor cash requests. Bank ABC would have numerous options to stave off failure, but all of them would have adverse side effects that would restrict economic activity or further damage the bank, and oftentimes those options in fact accelerate the bank run. For example, Bank ABC could quickly try to sell other assets to raise cash, impose controls that limit the amount of deposits that could be withdrawn each day, like Greece did in 2015, or it could suspend all withdrawals and other banking transactions indefinitely.

In many cases, banks will try to sell assets to survive. In the first instance Bank ABC could convert its short-term investments ($22 million) and investment securities ($308 million), most of which are highly liquid marketable assets, into cash. The sales, however, may have to made at a discount. The bank could also attempt to sell its loans to raise more cash, but, because loans are illiquid and hard to value, potential buyers can capitalize on this forced sale to purchase the assets at a deep discount, often called a fire sale. By selling at a discount, the bank collects significantly less cash than it would have collected from interest and principal payments over the life of the loan. The forced asset sale, in turn, exacerbates liquidity problems, because the bank is then worth less than expected, so it will have fewer resources than expected to satisfy its liabilities. The bank's depositors and other lenders will, therefore, be likely to demand more of their funds at a faster pace, because they fear they will not be paid in full. To meet the lenders' demands, the bank is then forced to sell still more assets.

During a full-blown banking panic, in which multiple banks experience runs at the same time, institutions may all try to sell their assets simultaneously, which reinforces falling sale prices for bank assets. In extreme cases, persistent depositor withdrawals and resulting asset sales can lead to bank failures, even if the banks were completely healthy before the run. Runs and failures also lead to sharp monetary contractions and disrupt the flow of credit, which hampers overall activity in the real economy, decreasing output, raising unemployment, and making further bank failures more likely. *See, e.g.*, Douglas W. Diamond & Philip H. Dybvig, *Bank Runs, Deposit Insurance, and Liquidity*, 91 J. POL. ECON. 401, 401–02 (1983).

B. CAUSES OF BANK RUNS

The dominant explanation for bank runs and panics is the asymmetric information theory. Runs occur when depositors perceive a significant increase in the riskiness of bank portfolios in response to adverse economic news. *See* Calomiris & Gorton, *The Origins of Banking Panics: Models, Facts, and Bank Regulation,* at 111. Depositors generally have a limited capacity to assess the strength of any individual bank and cannot determine how *their own* bank will withstand an economic shock.

Fearful depositors then rush to withdraw their deposits, rather than risk losing everything if the bank fails. Withdrawing deposits, however, makes it even more likely that a bank will fail. Why don't depositors just leave their deposits in the bank if it increases the chances of their bank's survival? The answer can be found by examining the problem of the prisoner's dilemma. In this classic formulation, two individuals are held captive with no opportunity to communicate with each other. Each prisoner much choose between two options: betraying the other prisoner by revealing damaging information, or remaining silent at the risk of receiving a harsher sentence. If both prisoners opt for betrayal, they are each sentenced to two years in prison. If both remain silent, they each serve only one year in prison. In the event that one prisoner chooses betrayal but the other chooses silence, the one who opts for betrayal goes free while the other is sentenced to three years in prison. *See, e.g.*, JOHN CASSIDY, HOW MARKETS FAIL 139–50 (2009).

The prisoner's dilemma illustrates that the choices made by individuals, each acting rationally in their own best interest, lead to a sub-optimal outcome. If the prisoners have the opportunity to communicate with each other and they trust each other, basic tenets of game theory dictate that they will minimize the total length of their sentences by negotiating an agreement to remain silent. The problem, however, stipulates that the prisoners cannot communicate with each other. For each prisoner, the optimal choice is clear: remaining silent could lead to either one year in prison or three years, whereas betraying the other leads to either immediate release or a two year sentence at most. Between these two choices, a coldly calculating rational actor will always opt for betrayal.

Without deposit insurance, a banking crisis presents the same dilemma. Each depositor is presented with two choices. She can run to the bank to withdraw her money, knowing that it will undermine the bank's soundness and have potentially disastrous consequences for the bank's remaining depositors. Or, she can choose to leave her money in the bank and hope that other depositors will do the same, forestalling the need for the bank to liquidate its assets at depressed values, thereby preserving its soundness. Depositors understand that deposits are redeemed on a first-come, first-serve basis, known as a sequential service constraint. Depositors who choose to get to the bank first are more likely to be paid in full than those who make withdrawals later. In a world where depositors are not certain they will receive their money back on demand, making a run on the bank is an individually rational choice that leads to a collectively irrational outcome.

C. THE ROLE OF DEPOSIT INSURANCE

A fundamental purpose of deposit insurance is to correct this misalignment between individual incentives and systemic effects. Under federal deposit insurance, which is administered by the FDIC, the government guarantees that depositors will be reimbursed for deposit losses caused by a bank's failure up to a fixed amount. By placing the full faith and credit of the United States behind insured depositor balances, deposit insurance eliminates insured depositors' incentives to run on the bank. Insurance eliminates the damaging collective action problem for insured depositors. The problem of runs, however, still exists for large uninsured depositors and other uninsured short-term creditors.

In the U.S. commercial banking sector, the proportion of liabilities on a bank's balance sheet that are insured deposits varies by size and business model. Virtually all of the deposits in smaller banks will be insured because they rarely have deposits that are above the insurance limit. By contrast, a large global bank with many large corporate clients and foreign branches may have as little as one-third of its deposits protected by U.S. deposit insurance. On an aggregate basis, as of year-end 2014, approximately 40% of deposits in the commercial banking system were insured. Commercial banks also issue other forms of liabilities. Working in tandem with central bank liquidity, which we discuss in Chapter 9.1, deposit insurance has effectively ended the phenomenon of bank runs in the United States.

During the 19th Century, the U.S. experienced numerous bank runs, including major panics in 1837, 1857, 1873, and 1893. *See* Michael D. Bordo et al., *Why Didn't Canada Have a Banking Crisis in 2008 (or in 1930, or 1907, or...)?*, 68 THE ECON. HIST. REV. 218 (2014). The Panic of 1907 and the Banking Crisis of 1933 also led to major bank runs. After U.S. deposit insurance was established, the United States has seen very few runs, even during periods marked by a large number of bank failures, like the Savings & Loan Crisis in the 1980s, as well as the Financial Crisis. It is not that runs never occur. In 1984, Continental Illinois suffered a bank run by uninsured depositors and, in 2008, IndyMac bank of California collapsed after a massive bank run. See Chapter 9.2 for a further discussion of Continental Illinois. Moreover, "bank" runs can occur in the financial system through other forms of short-term borrowing, like the runs on money market mutual funds (MMFs) and repos during the Financial Crisis, which we explore further in Chapter 12.3 and 12.4.

Figure 2.4-2 Commercial Bank Liabilities

Aggregate U.S. Commercial Bank Liabilities as of YE 2014 *(millions of dollars)*	
Estimated Uninsured Deposits	4,205
Estimated Insured Deposits	6,204
Other Liabilities	2,875

Source: FDIC 2014 Annual Report; Fed. Reserve Bd.

D. RESERVE REQUIREMENTS

Reserve requirements are used to guard against bank runs and can play a role in monetary policy. *See* Chapter 9.1. Regulation D is the primary rule promulgated by the Federal Reserve for regulating bank reserves. 12 C.F.R.

§ 204. As you have seen, reserves consist primarily of vault cash and deposits with the Federal Reserve. Since the passage of the Depository Institutions Deregulation and Monetary Control Act in 1980, all banks, thrifts, and credit unions are subject to the requirements of Regulation D. 12 C.F.R. § 204.2(m)(1).

Regulation D prescribes the amount of reserves a bank needs to hold against its outstanding deposits. The reserve requirement, expressed as a percentage of total deposits outstanding, is known as the reserve ratio. It is assessed against demand deposits (and equivalent transaction accounts). 12 C.F.R. § 204.4. For most banks, reserve requirements are 10% of demand deposits (with some minor adjustments).

The decline in the importance of required reserves as a regulatory tool is unmistakable. One study found that reserve requirements are not binding upon the vast majority of institutions subject to the requirements. *See* Paul Bennett & Stavros Peristiani, *Are U.S. Reserve Requirements Binding?*, ECON. POL'Y REV. 8 (2002). Those banks, therefore, voluntarily hold reserves that exceed requirements under Regulation D. By 2011, central banks in Australia, Canada, Denmark, Mexico, New Zealand, Norway, Sweden, Timor-Leste, and the UK had eliminated reserve requirements entirely. SIMON GRAY, INTERNATIONAL MONETARY FUND, CENTRAL BANK BALANCES AND RESERVE REQUIREMENTS (2011). Effective beginning in 2008, the Federal Reserve pays interest on both required and excess reserves, which helps the Federal Reserve to effectuate monetary policy by adjusting the interest rate it will pay. 12 C.F.R. § 204.10. Following the Financial Crisis, regulators established liquidity requirements, which are much higher than reserve requirements and bind the financial conglomerate as a whole. We will discuss liquidity requirements in Chapter 2.7.

---

1. ***Chartered Depository Monopoly on Deposits as Funding.*** In the United States, institutions other than regulated depositories are legally prohibited from using deposits as a source of funding. 12 U.S.C. § 378. Why might this be?

2. ***Deposit Insurance and Shadow Banking.*** In Chapter 12.3, we discuss how money has shifted out of the highly regulated chartered banks and into shadow banking, including money market funds that are not insured by the FDIC. Why has that occurred? Should money market funds be insured or regulated as banks?

III. FEDERAL DEPOSIT INSURANCE

A. THE BASICS

The United States introduced the world's first effective deposit insurance system in 1933 when it established the predecessor to today's Deposit Insurance Fund (DIF). Asli Demirgüç-Kunt & Enrica Detragiache, *Does Deposit Insurance Increase Banking System Stability?: An Empirical Investigation*, 49 J. MONETARY ECON. 1373, 1373 (2002) [hereinafter *Banking System Stability*]. The FDIC, which began operations the same year, administers the DIF. The FDIC is governed by a five-member Board of Directors. Three of the directors are appointed for six-year terms by the President, subject to Senate confirmation. The other two directors are the Comptroller of the Currency and the Director of the CFPB. The President appoints one director as the chairman, also subject to Senate approval.

As of year-end 2014, 6,509 institutions, excluding the seven grandfathered insured branches of foreign banks, were covered by deposit insurance. FDIC 2014 ANNUAL REPORT 67. We will discuss foreign branches in Chapter 6.3

Confidence in the DIF's ability to protect depositors from loss has contributed significantly to the virtual elimination of bank runs in the United States. The confidence seems well-founded. As the FDIC's website brags, "[n]o depositor has lost a penny of FDIC insured funds." *Understanding Deposit Insurance*, FDIC (Oct. 9, 2015).

B. DEFINING A DEPOSIT

You have already seen how insuring deposits helps to prevent bank runs, but up to this point we have ignored a more fundamental question: What *is* a deposit? Most of us store money in banks and withdraw money at a teller or an ATM. The money you store at the bank is a deposit. Why? Is it a deposit *because* you store it at the bank? Or is it a deposit because you can withdraw it immediately? You can put jewelry in a safe deposit box at a bank and withdraw that immediately, but that is not a deposit. FDIC, YOUR INSURED DEPOSITS (2014). Do policy considerations determine what a deposit is?

Consider the FDIC website's list of what the fund covers, along with some basic descriptions to help you understand what these items are:

- **Checking accounts**, also known as demand deposit accounts, permit immediate withdrawal of funds. From 1933–2010, the payment of interest on these accounts was prohibited by law. That restriction was lifted by the Dodd-Frank Act. *See* Dodd-Frank Act § 627.

- **Negotiable Order of Withdrawal (NOW) accounts** are like regular checking accounts but they pay interest. NOW accounts are not demand deposits because the bank has the right to require seven days advance notice before withdrawals, although in practice that is rarely done. These accounts were structured to bear interest at a time when checking accounts were not permitted to offer interest.

- **Savings accounts** are deposit accounts that may pay higher interest but provide depositors with less flexibility to make withdrawals or transfer funds. For example, a bank reserves the right to require seven days advance notice from the depositor before she before withdraws deposits from a savings account, and may limit the number of withdrawals.

- **Money market deposit accounts** pay higher interest rates but typically require higher balances than savings accounts. They also limit check writing. Despite having a similar name to money market funds and a similar function, the two are not regulated in the same way. Money market funds will be discussed in Chapter 12.3.

- **Time deposits, such as certificates of deposit**, are savings accounts that allow withdrawal only after a specified time period. Penalties are imposed for early withdrawal. Time deposits typically offer a higher interest rate than other savings accounts, but they are structured so that funds are tied up for a longer period of time.
- **Cashier's checks, money orders, and other official items issued by a bank** are documents that create a claim on the bank's own funds. A cashier's check is a check written on the bank's own funds. A money order allows a named payee to receive cash on demand.

The list here is not exclusive. A comprehensive list of what constitutes a deposit can be found in the Federal Deposit Insurance Act of 1950 (FDIA), 28 U.S.C. § 1811.

Consider the following Supreme Court decision, *FDIC v. Philadelphia Gear Corp.*, 476 U.S. 426 (1986). In the case, the Court accepts the argument that although a letter of credit falls within the plain text of the statutory definition of a "deposit," it is *not* a deposit for insurance purposes.

In this case, Penn Square Bank, a depository institution insured by the FDIC, issued a "standby" letter of credit obliging it to pay Philadelphia Gear $145,200 in the event that one of Philadelphia Gear's customers, Orion, failed to make timely payment to Philadelphia Gear for a sale of goods. Orion also executed a $145,000 promissory note payable to Philadelphia Gear as a "Back Up Letter Of Credit."

In 1982, Penn Square Bank was declared insolvent and the FDIC became its receiver. Philadelphia Gear tried to obtain payment from the FDIC on the Letter of Credit, arguing that it was an insured "deposit" under the FDIA and that they were entitled to the $100,000 maximum payout for depositors at a failed institution. The FDIC refused to make the payment, and Philadelphia Gear brought suit in federal court to recover.

Standby letters of credit are guarantees in which a financial institution promises to pay a seller a specified sum of money if a buyer fails to make payment on a sales contract. Such letters of credit facilitate sales transactions by overcoming a seller's hesitance to contract with a buyer that is unknown, operates in a different legal system, or otherwise gives the seller a reason to fear they will not be paid.

The District Court for the Western District of Oklahoma held for Philadelphia Gear, finding that its letter of credit was a "deposit" under federal law. The Court of Appeals for the Tenth Circuit affirmed. The Supreme Court granted certiorari and reversed.

Fed. Deposit Ins. Corp. v. Philadelphia Gear Corp.

476 U.S. 426 (1986)

JUSTICE O'CONNOR delivered the opinion of the Court. . . .

II

Title 12 U.S.C. § 1813(l)(1) provides:

"The term 'deposit' means-

> (1) the unpaid balance of money or its equivalent received or held by a bank in the usual course of business and for which it has given or is obligated to give credit, either conditionally or unconditionally, to a commercial . . . account, or which is evidenced by . . . a letter of credit or a traveler's check on which the bank is primarily liable: *Provided*, That, without limiting the generality of the term 'money or its equivalent,' any such account or instrument must be regarded as evidencing the receipt of the equivalent of money when credited or issued in exchange for checks or drafts or for a promissory note upon which the person obtaining any such credit or instrument is primarily or secondarily liable. . . ."

Philadelphia Gear successfully argued before the Court of Appeals that the standby letter of credit backed by a contingent promissory note constituted a "deposit" under 12 U.S.C. § 1813(*l*)(1) because that letter was one on which the bank was primarily liable, and evidenced the receipt by the bank of "money or its equivalent" in the form of a promissory note upon which the person obtaining the credit was primarily or secondarily liable. The FDIC does not here dispute that the bank was primarily liable on the letter of credit. Nor does the FDIC contest the fact that the backup note executed by Orion is, at least in some sense, a "promissory note." The FDIC argues rather that it has consistently interpreted § 1813(*l*)(1) not to include standby letters of credit backed only by a contingent promissory note because such a note represents no hard assets and thus does not constitute "money or its equivalent." Because the alleged "deposit" consists only of a *contingent* liability, asserts the FDIC, a standby letter of credit backed by a contingent promissory note does not give rise to a "deposit" that Congress intended the FDIC to insure. . . .

[A]s the FDIC points out, the terms "letter of credit" and "promissory note" as used in the statute have a federal definition, and the FDIC has developed and interpreted those definitions for many years within the framework of the complex statutory scheme that the FDIC administers. The FDIC's interpretation of whether a standby letter of credit backed by a contingent promissory note constitutes a "deposit" is consistent with Congress' desire to protect the hard earnings of individuals by providing for federal deposit insurance. . . . [I]ndeed, Congress in 1960 adopted the FDIC's regulatory definition as the statutory language. When we weigh all these factors together, we are constrained to conclude that the term "deposit" does not include a standby letter of credit backed by a contingent promissory note.

A

Congress' purpose in creating the FDIC was clear. Faced with virtual panic, Congress attempted to safeguard the hard earnings of individuals against the possibility that bank failures would deprive them of their savings. . . . The focus of Congress was [to ensure] that a deposit of "hard earnings" entrusted by individuals to a bank would not lead to a tangible loss in the event of a bank failure. As the chairman of the relevant Committee in the House of Representatives explained on the floor:

"[T]he purpose of this legislation is to protect the people of the United States in the right to have banks in which their deposits will be safe. They have a right to expect of Congress the establishment and maintenance of a system of banks in the United States where citizens may place their hard earnings with reasonable expectation of being able to get them out again upon demand." . . . (remarks of Rep. Steagall) . . .

To prevent bank failure that resulted in the tangible loss of hard assets was therefore the focus of Congress' effort in creating deposit insurance. . . .

[The Court then discussed amendments to the deposit insurance statute since its initial enactment, but concluded that those amendments contained nothing that would alter the proper understanding of what constituted a deposit.]

Congress' focus in providing for a system of deposit insurance—a system that has been continued to the present without modification to the basic definition of deposits that are "money or its equivalent"—was clearly a focus upon safeguarding the assets and "hard earnings" that businesses and individuals have entrusted to banks. Congress wanted to ensure that someone who put tangible assets into a bank could always get those assets back. The purpose behind the insurance of deposits in general, and especially in the section defining deposits as "money or its equivalent," therefore, is the protection of assets and hard earnings entrusted to a bank.

This purpose is not furthered by extending deposit insurance to cover a standby letter of credit backed by a contingent promissory note, which involves no such surrender of assets or hard earnings to the custody of the bank. Philadelphia Gear, which now seeks to collect deposit insurance, surrendered absolutely nothing to the bank. The letter of credit is for Philadelphia Gear's benefit, but the bank relied upon Orion to meet the obligations of the letter of credit and made no demands upon Philadelphia Gear. Nor, more importantly, did Orion surrender any assets unconditionally to the bank. The bank did not credit any account of Orion's in exchange for the promissory note, and did not treat its own assets as increased by its acceptance of the note. The bank could not have collected on the note from Orion unless Philadelphia Gear presented the unpaid invoices and a draft on the letter of credit. In the absence of a presentation by Philadelphia Gear of the unpaid invoices, the promissory note was a wholly contingent promise, and when Penn Square went into receivership, neither Orion nor Philadelphia Gear had lost anything except the ability to use Penn Square to reduce Philadelphia Gear's risk that Philadelphia Gear would go unpaid for a delivery of goods to Orion.

III

Philadelphia Gear essentially seeks to have the FDIC guarantee the contingent credit extended to Orion, not assets entrusted *440 to the bank by Philadelphia Gear or by Orion on Philadelphia Gear's behalf. With a standard "commercial" letter of credit, Orion would typically have unconditionally entrusted Penn Square with funds before Penn Square would have written the letter of credit, and thus Orion would have lost something if Penn Square became unable to honor its obligations. As the FDIC concedes, deposit insurance extends to such a letter of credit backed by an uncontingent promissory note. . . . But here, with a standby letter of credit backed by a contingent promissory note, Penn Square was not in possession of any of Orion's or Philadelphia Gear's assets when it went into receivership. Nothing was ventured, and therefore no insurable deposit was lost. We believe that, whatever the relevant State's definition of "letter of credit" or "promissory note," Congress did not by using those phrases in 12 U.S.C. § 1813(*l*)(1) intend to protect with deposit insurance a standby letter of credit backed only by a contingent promissory note. We thus hold that such an arrangement does not give rise to a "deposit" under 12 U.S.C. § 1813(*l*)(1).

Accordingly, the judgment of the court below is reversed.

---

1. ***Defining a Deposit.*** As discussed above, only insured depository institutions can offer deposits. Now that you have read *Philadelphia Gear*, is it obvious what a deposit is? As we will discuss more fully in Chapter 12.4, this question has serious implications for regulation of the shadow banking system.

C. COVERAGE

Figuring out whether you have made a deposit at the bank is only the first step in determining how much protection you receive from the DIF. The DIF does not provide unlimited insurance against deposit losses. The exact extent of insurance protection is governed by a series of complex provisions. After the enactment of the Dodd-Frank Act, the standard maximum deposit insurance amount is set at $250,000 per ownership account category, per depositor, per institution. Ownership account categories include single accounts, certain retirement accounts, joint accounts, revocable trust accounts, irrevocable trust accounts, employee benefit plan accounts, corporation/partnership/unincorporated association accounts, and government accounts.

If a depositor holds up to $250,000 in deposits in a single ownership category at one bank, the full balance is insured if the bank fails. All deposits in that ownership category at that bank above $250,000 would not be insured. A depositor could hold more than $250,000 in *total* funds in a depository institution and still be insured for the full amount if she held $250,000 or less within any ownership category.

Coverage is extended on a per depositor, per type of account, per institution basis. Therefore, if an individual holds up to $250,000 in a single account at one bank and up to $250,000 in a single account at a different insured bank, the full amount of each deposit is insured. Depositors can split up their deposits among many different banks through a marketplace of brokered deposits. FDIC, YOUR INSURED DEPOSITS.

If a bank account owner can get essentially unlimited deposit insurance by splitting up her accounts among different banks, what is the rationale for the $250,000 (or any) cap?

D. FUNDING

The DIF is funded through assessments on insured institutions. Like most insurance plans, the DIF collects premiums on an *ex-ante* basis. Contrast this system with an *ex-post* assessment, in which premiums to replenish the fund are collected from surviving institutions when an insured institution fails. Asli Demirgüç-Kunt et al., *Deposit Insurance Database*, 37–38 (IMF, Working Paper No. 14/118, 2014). The FDIC calculates each bank's premium by multiplying its assessment base by its assessment rate.

Figure 2.4-3 DIF Funding

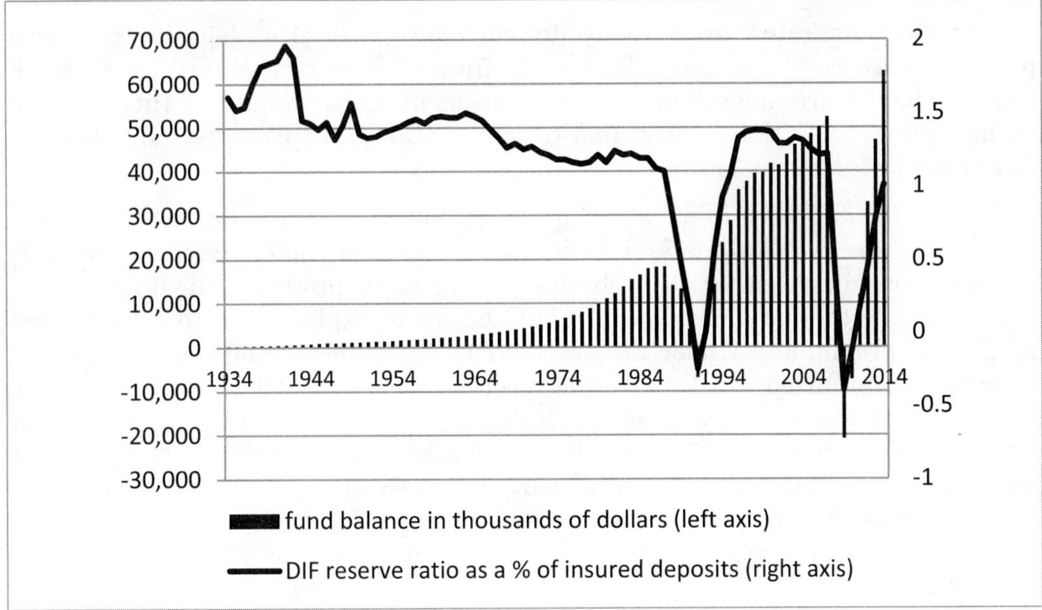

Source: FDIC 2014 Annual Report at 116-18.

As you can see from Figure 2.4-3, the DIF has run out of funds twice: first during the 1980s Savings & Loan Crisis, and again during the Financial Crisis. By year-end 2014, the balance of the DIF had grown to approximately $62.8 billion and the DIF reserve ratio, which measures the ratio between the amount of money in the deposit insurance fund and estimated insured deposits, had reached 1.01%. FDIC 2014 Annual Report at 116-18.

1. The Assessment Base

Before the Dodd-Frank Act, DIF premiums were assessed on a bank's total domestic deposits. Demirgüç-Kunt et al., *Deposit Insurance Database*, at 8. After the Dodd-Frank Act, the assessment base shifted to a bank's average total consolidated assets minus average tangible equity, which essentially ties the assessment base to total liabilities. Total liabilities are much bigger than demand deposits, providing a larger assessment base. Dodd-Frank Act § 331; 12 C.F.R. § 327.5.

Since 1933, the deposit assessment base has been set so that the larger banks—whose failure would be most destabilizing for the financial system and whose failure could cause the greatest loss to the DIF—pay proportionally more in deposit insurance than smaller banks. The higher rates were one of the reasons larger banks objected to deposit insurance in 1933.

The Dodd Frank Act's revision of the assessment base weights premium payments even more heavily towards the larger banks because, as you will recall from our discussion of bank balance sheets in Chapter 1.3, the largest banks use a great deal of non-deposit liabilities for funding. As of 2016, the country's 20 largest banks make up approximately 60% of the total assessment base. They made up only 50% of the base before the Dodd-Frank Act.

2. Assessment Rates

Assessment rates used today to calculate a bank's deposit insurance premiums are risk adjusted. To benefit from DIF protection, riskier or more complex banks are subject to higher assessment rates, requiring them to pay higher premiums, than safer institutions. Demirgüç-Kunt et al., *Deposit Insurance Database*, at 37–38.

Risk-adjusted premiums were first established in 1991, but for years the relevant statutory language and FDIC policies limited the effectiveness of risk-adjusted premiums either to curb risk taking or to protect against the DIF's depletion. In the early 1990s, the FDIC began to explore how to set effective risk-based premiums. Under the old system, premiums would not be collected from "well capitalized" banks once the reserve ratio reached 1.25%. *See* Chapter 2.5 for what constitutes a "well capitalized" bank. From 1996 to 2006, the reserve ratio exceeded 1.25%, and 90% of banks—with nearly all the system's assets—were considered well capitalized. As a result, none of these banks paid into the DIF, but they all received deposit insurance protection. In 2006, Congress enacted some reforms. The 1.25% target was repealed and replaced by a reserve ratio range of 1.15%-1.50%. Despite the increase in the reserve ratio, however, DIF growth was slowed by a requirement that the DIF rebate half of the premiums it collected once the reserve ratio hit 1.35%. *See* Viral V. Acharya, Joao C. Santos & Tanju Yorulmazer, *Systemic Risk and Deposit Insurance Premiums,* Fed. Reserve Bank N.Y. ECON. POL'Y REV. 91. Because of these rules and other problems, at the end of 2007 the reserve ratio sat at only 1.22%, a level insufficient to absorb losses stemming from the Financial Crisis. FDIC 2014 ANNUAL REPORT 116.

The Dodd-Frank Act put in a place a new system for risk-adjusted premiums. Understanding the process for calculating a bank's risk adjusted premiums requires a basic knowledge of CAMELS scores, described more thoroughly in Chapter 8.2. CAMELS scores are supervisory ratings that measure various dimensions of a bank's health. These scores are blended to create a composite CAMELS score, which provides an overall picture of a bank's health.

The first step in the process to calculate a bank's risk adjusted premium is determining the bank's annual base assessment rate. For smaller banks, the rates are based on which of four risk categories that bank falls into. Dodd-Frank Act § 332. Banks are slotted into these categories based on their composite CAMELS score and their underlying capital position. *Glossary, Quarterly Banking Profile*, FDIC (Oct. 6, 2015) (defining "Risk Categories and Assessment Rate Schedule").

Large and highly complex banks are assigned an initial annual base assessment rate using a scorecard. Large banks are depository institutions with at least $10 billion in assets. Highly complex banks are generally defined as depository institutions that have more than $50 billion in assets and are owned by a parent company with more than $500 billion in assets. The scorecard measures a bank's riskiness, the magnitude of losses it could inflict on the DIF, and any other aggravating or mitigating factors that are not otherwise captured. 12 C.F.R. §§ 327.8, 327.9, 327 Subpt. A, App. D. The scorecard numbers are converted to an initial annual base assessment rate. After the rate is calculated, adjustments are made based on the riskiness of the composition of a bank's liabilities. The assessment rate for banks that fund their operations through less-risky unsecured debt is adjusted down. *Glossary*, *Quarterly Banking Profile*, FDIC. The assessment rate for banks that use brokered deposits, which may run faster than other deposits, is adjusted up. 12 C.F.R. pt. 327.

3. Premium Payments and the Reserve Ratio

Premium payments are a function of the assessment base and assessment rate, in combination with other rules. Under the Dodd-Frank Act, a set of reforms should bolster the DIF and make risk-based premiums more effective. As discussed, a change in the assessment base will cause the largest banks to pay significantly more in premiums, and the assessment rates vary significantly by the size, complexity, and riskiness of the bank, at least as measured by the FDIC, although query whether that risk measurement is accurate. Moreover, well-capitalized banks are no longer exempt from paying deposit insurance premiums. The minimum reserve ratio has been increased to 1.35%. The 1.5% upper limit on the reserve ratio, as well as the rebate requirements, have been removed, and the FDIC has discretion to set higher minimum reserve targets. Dodd-Frank Act §§ 332, 334. The FDIC has used that authority to target a 2% reserve ratio.

---

1. ***Deposit Insurance Premiums and CAMELS Ratings.*** The deposit insurance premiums and CAMELS ratings of banks are never released to the public. Why that might be true? Should they be released?

2. ***Community Banks.*** The Dodd-Frank Act protects banks under $10 billion in assets from the cost of increasing the minimum reserve ratio from 1.15 to 1.35%. Dodd-Frank Act § 334(e). Why would Congress have so provided?

IV. DEPOSIT INSURANCE AND MORAL HAZARD

While deposit insurance has practically eliminated bank runs in the United States and is deeply supported by the public, it is not a cost-free policy choice. Deposit insurance increases moral hazard and poorly designed or unreliable systems can *decrease* financial stability. Moral hazard refers to situations where one actor is incentivized to take on risk because another party is set up to absorb the costs of the first actor's bad behavior. *See, e.g.*, CHARLES W. CALOMIRIS & STEPHEN H. HABER, FRAGILE BY DESIGN 461–62 (2014). Even risk-based deposit insurance premiums may not cover the risk posed by a firm, and in a worst case scenario, the DIF might be insufficient to resolve a large bank whose excessive risk-taking has brought it to the brink of insolvency. The problem is even more acute when the whole system is at risk. Even with explicit limits on deposit insurance and explicit insurance premiums, there is a risk—borne out by history—that taxpayer funds will be used to bailout a bank or replenish the DIF. We begin by discussing how deposit insurance can increase moral hazard and then outline features of deposit insurance that aim to mitigate the moral hazard problem. We conclude by examining the problem of implicit deposit insurance guarantees, systemwide risk, and "too big to fail."

A. THE PROBLEM OF MORAL HAZARD

In any business organization, monitoring and pressure from stakeholders—such as creditors and shareholders—may check the firm management's risk-taking or self-dealing. The phenomenon is popularly known as market discipline. In the banking context, depositors could impose market discipline by pulling their funds from a bank whose activities are seen as too risky. The adverse consequences would, in principle, incentivize bank managers to act prudently.

Deposit insurance dampens depositors' incentives to monitor their banks' performance because the depositors are indemnified against loss even if risky activities lead to failure. Some empirical evidence suggests that overly generous deposit insurance schemes are related to more frequent banking crises. *See, e.g.*, *Banking System Stability*. Of course, that concern may be overstated. It is unclear whether depositors have the expertise, resources, or sufficient incentive to monitor banks even without deposit insurance. Depositors may also be unable to band together to overcome collective action problems or gain sufficient bargaining power to make a difference. Financial Stability Forum's Working Group on Deposit Insurance Systems, Subgroup on Moral Hazard, Options for Addressing Moral Hazard (Mar. 15, 2010) (unpublished manuscript) (on file with author). Moreover, even large *uninsured* depositors have little incentive to monitor bank performance because their deposits are typically acquired by a healthy bank post failure rather than lost completely. For more information on how FDIC resolutions of failed banks work, see Chapter 9.2. *See also* Lawrence J. White, *The Reform of Federal Deposit Insurance*, 3 J. ECON. PERSP. 11, 13 (1989).

Regardless, the ability of banks to raise funds from depositors means that a very large class of its creditors will be unlikely to monitor or enforce sound risk management. Other creditors, as you will see, can impose such discipline. At the same time, bank managers often face pressure from shareholders who often encourage managers to take on greater risk. *See, e.g.*, Jonathan R. Macey & Maureen O'Hara, *Solving the Corporate Governance Problem of Banks: A Proposal*, 120 BANKING L.J. 326, 327 (2003). When a firm is experiencing financial difficulty, shareholders will increase that pressure to pursue riskier investment strategies to return the firm to health. If the investments succeed, shareholders reap the benefits. If the investments fail, shareholder losses are capped at the value of their initial investment. Any additional losses are absorbed by the DIF. We will discuss this corporate governance conundrum in financial institutions in Chapter 8.1

Some critics argue that privately run deposit insurance would be preferable to government insurance. White, *The Reform of Federal Deposit Insurance*, at 25. Would private deposit insurance be workable? Perhaps it would, but the resulting regime would look very different from the deposit insurance we know. Consider the following comments on possible reforms in federal deposit insurance from former Federal Reserve chairman Alan Greenspan.

Testimony of Alan Greenspan

United States Senate Committee on Banking, Housing, and Urban Affairs Oversight Hearing on "The Federal Deposit Insurance System and Recommendations for Reform." (Apr. 23, 2002)

To eliminate the subsidy in deposit insurance—to make deposit insurance a real *insurance* system—the FDIC average insurance premium would have to be set high enough to cover fully the very small probabilities of very large losses, such as during the Great Depression, and thus the perceived costs of systemic risk. In contrast to life or automobile casualty insurance, each individual insured loss in banking is not independent of other losses. Banking is subject to deposit run contagion, creating a far larger extreme loss tail on the probability distributions from which real insurance premiums would have to be calculated. Indeed, pricing deposit insurance risks to fully fund potential losses—pricing to eliminate subsidies—would require premiums that would discourage most depository institutions from offering broad coverage. Since the Congress has determined that there should be broad coverage, the subsidy in deposit insurance cannot be *fully* eliminated, although we can and should eliminate as much of the subsidy as we can.

Parenthetically, the difficulties of raising risk-based premiums explain why there is no private insurer substitute for deposit insurance from the government. No private insurer would ever be able to match the actual FDIC premium *and* cover its risks. A private insurer confronted with the possibility, remote as it may be, of losses that could bankrupt the insuring entity would need to set especially high premiums to protect itself, premiums that few, if any, depository institutions would find attractive.

Many countries have some private-sector involvement in deposit insurance. Roughly 20% of high-income countries have schemes administered privately by covered banks, while 35% rely on schemes that are handled jointly by the private and public sectors. Demirgüç-Kunt et al., *Deposit Insurance Database*, at 13. The United States used to have some state and private coverage plans for banks and thrifts, but they were abolished following the failure of many such funds in the 1980s. While most credit unions today are federally insured, some credit unions still use state funded and even private insurance plans. Should they be able to? What would happen if those insurance plans failed?

B. DEPOSIT INSURANCE DESIGN FEATURES

Moral hazard is a persistent problem in insurance, and insurers use a variety of techniques to mitigate insured parties' risk-taking. Chances are you are acquainted with efforts by insurers to curb *your* moral hazard risk. Your automobile insurance plan might require you to pay a fixed amount of repair costs, called a deductible, before insurance coverage kicks in, or disqualify you from coverage if you incur costs while engaging in certain prohibited activities, like driving drunk. Your health insurance plan might use coinsurance, requiring you to pay a share of the healthcare costs that you incur. These tools encourage you to exercise caution even though you are insured against loss.

Designing a deposit insurance scheme that effectively eliminates the risk of bank runs, while exposing depositors and banks to a level of risk sufficient to encourage good behavior, is a difficult task. Important design features include the following:

- **Liability caps** fix an insurer's maximum liability to an insured party. Deposit insurance funds employ liability caps to limit the amount they have to pay to depositors if a bank fails. Since most depositors fall well under the U.S. caps at a single bank, the biggest impact of liability caps is to force large depositors to diversify by placing their funds in more than one bank to be fully insured. *See* Asli Demirgüç-Kunt & Harry Huizinga, *Market Discipline & Deposit Insurance*, 51 J. MONETARY ECON. 375 (2004).

- **Risk-adjusted premiums** are used to curb risk-taking activity. Institutions that are riskier or more complex are required to pay more, with the goal of incentivizing them to reduce their risk-taking activity. Demirgüç-Kunt et al., *Deposit Insurance Database* at 8.

- **Coinsurance** refers to contractual arrangements in which an insured party pays a portion of the cost for activities covered by his insurance policy. In the deposit insurance context, coinsurance agreements operate so that depositors recoup only a portion of their insured deposits in the event of a failure. For example, a deposit insurance system might set its liability cap at $100,000 but also impose a 10% coinsurance requirement. If a depositor has $100,000 in deposits at a failed bank, she would only be entitled to a $90,000 payout. The exposure to loss incentivizes a depositor to monitor a bank's activities more closely. *See* FINANCIAL STABILITY FORUM'S WORKING GROUP ON DEPOSIT INSURANCE SYSTEMS, SUBGROUP ON MORAL HAZARD, OPTIONS FOR ADDRESSING MORAL HAZARD. Almost no country with explicit deposit insurance, including the United States, uses coinsurance because coinsurance harms depositors and exacerbates bank runs. Although the number of countries using coinsurance was never large, it decreased even further after the Financial Crisis. During the Financial Crisis, to save small depositors from losses, countries with coinsurance rules did not enforce them. With no expectation that coinsurance agreements would be enforced in future crises, their credibility was destroyed. They were not reintroduced. Demirgüç-Kunt et al., *Deposit Insurance Database*, at 13, 37–38.

- **Portfolio Constraints and Prudential Regulation.** Limitations on what assets a bank may generate, requirements to hold a minimum amount of capital, liquidity provisions, and other prudential regulation and supervision that you will learn about in this book, can all be thought of as elements of deposit insurance design, in the sense that the deposit insurer uses these techniques to minimize its risk of loss.

C. THE PROBLEM OF IMPLICIT GUARANTEES

Thus far, we have focused on moral hazard problems associated with explicit deposit insurance, but even worse moral hazard problems occur when the government is perceived to be offering implicit guarantees, without charging for them. A government offering an implicit guarantee stands ready to indemnify creditors against losses even in the absence of any formal authority confirming that creditors are insured or formal rules governing the extent of coverage. As with explicit guarantees, implicit guarantees can slacken market discipline.

1. Uninsured Deposits

In financial crises, countries often issue new blanket deposit guarantees to halt banking crises. The guarantees often exceed previously announced statutory coverage limits. A notable example of this phenomenon is the UK government's blanket guarantee of the deposits of Northern Rock Bank in 2007. While this approach can calm an immediate financial panic, it decreases depositors' perceptions that their funds will be at risk in the future. *See, e.g.*, Richard Blackden & Katie Franklin, *Government Guarantees Northern Rock Funds*, TELEGRAPH, Sept. 17, 2007; Ash Demirgüç -Kunt, Edward Kane & Luc Laeven, *Deposit Insurance Around the World* 16–17. Even if explicit deposit insurance coverage is scaled back after a crisis, the expectation that the government is implicitly guaranteeing all deposits can be difficult to shake. Demirgüç-Kunt et al., *Deposit Insurance Database*, at 3.

During the Financial Crisis, U.S. policymakers greatly expanded deposit insurance guarantees on top of statutory limits through the first-ever use of the FDIA's systemic risk exception. The systemic risk exception allows the FDIC to take extraordinary action to resolve institutions without adhering to a typical least cost requirement if "compliance with [the least cost requirement] with respect to an insured depository institution would have serious adverse effects on economic conditions or financial stability" and "action or assistance [under this power] would avoid or mitigate such adverse effects." 12 U.S.C. §§ 1823(c)(4)(G)(i)(I)-(II). In order to use these emergency powers, the FDIC must receive approval from two-thirds of the FDIC Board of Directors, two-thirds of the Federal Reserve Board, and the Secretary of the Treasury, after consultation with the President. 12 U.S.C. § 1823(c)(4)(G)(i). We will discuss this provision more in Chapter 9.2.

The FDIC's expansive emergency guarantees were collectively known as the Temporary Liquidity Guarantee Program and consisted of two parts. First, the Debt Guarantee Program aimed to shore-up interbank lending and promote stability in unsecured funding markets by guaranteeing the principal and interest payments of banks and their holding companies issuing senior unsecured debt. Second, under the Transaction Account Guarantee Program, the FDIC gave a blanket guarantee for the full value of all non-interest bearing transaction accounts, typically checking accounts. The program reassured business depositors that certain transaction accounts, such as those used to meet payroll and those used to conduct business transactions, would be completely insured in the event of bank failure. FDIC, TEMPORARY LIQUIDITY GUARANTEE PROGRAM (Feb. 27, 2013).

Despite the fact that these extraordinary measures were highly successful in averting bank runs during the Financial Crisis, Congress's discomfort with this extraordinary assistance led to numerous reforms under the Dodd-Frank Act. Under the Dodd-Frank Act, FDIC broad-based guarantees like those used during the Financial Crisis are substantially limited. Dodd Frank Act, Title XI, §§ 1105–1106.

2. Problems with Wholesale Funding

Broker-dealers, other financial intermediaries, and large, complex financial institutions fund themselves with a wide variety of liabilities other than deposits. These liabilities are not insured. During the Financial Crisis, however, the equivalent of bank runs occurred on these liabilities, which nearly crushed the financial system and led the government to provide widespread taxpayer support. Consider the moral hazard problems associated with wholesale funding guarantees as compared to deposit guarantees. How are they the same, and how are they different? You will learn more about Financial Crisis programs in Chapters 9.1 and 9.2 and about the wholesale funding system in Chapter 12.4.

---

1. ***Interbank Deposits.*** Interbank deposits are rarely insured. Why might that be? What incentives does this create? Why might policymakers seek to create these kinds of incentives?

2. ***Limits on FDIC Guarantees.*** Do you find limitations on the FDIC's guarantees after the Financial Crisis wise? Why or why not?

V. OTHER GOVERNMENT GUARANTEE PROGRAMS

Deposit insurance is not the only instance where the federal government guarantees private-firm liabilities. In fact, the federal government guarantees a vast amount of housing, student, agricultural, small business, and other debt. For details, see Analytic Perspectives, Budget of the United States Government, Fiscal Year 2016, Chapter 20 (pp. 301-327). In this section, we outline two government guarantee programs, the Securities Investor Protection Corporation (SIPC) and the Pension Benefit Guaranty Corporation (PBGC), for comparison with the FDIC and federal deposit insurance.

A. SECURITIES INVESTOR PROTECTION CORPORATION

In the late 1960s, broker-dealers had a paperwork problem. Firms were experiencing significant increases in trade volume, and they were not equipped to handle the paperwork those trades entailed. The paperwork crunch coincided with a wave of broker-dealer failures in which investors' cash and securities were either lost or tied up in lengthy bankruptcy proceedings. The New York Stock Exchange (NYSE) stepped in by providing $140 million of assistance to the customers of failed broker-dealers. *See* NYSE, *Crisis in the Securities Industry, A Chronology: 1967-1970.*

In response, Congress enacted the Securities Investor Protection Act of 1970, 15 U.S.C. § 78aaa, *et seq.*, which created SIPC to protect a broker-dealer's customers from the loss of cash and securities if the broker-dealer has to be liquidated. SIPC's guarantee applies only to the broker-dealer's custody function —that is, SIPC restores to customers cash and securities that are in their brokerage accounts when the firm enters liquidation. SIPC does not protect customers from fluctuations in the value of their securities. It also does not protect against losses stemming from fraud, misrepresentations, or inappropriate investment strategies. SIPC's guarantee is subject to a statutory maximum of $500,000 in cash and securities per customer, with a maximum of $250,000 in cash.

When a broker-dealer fails, the SEC or FINRA refers the firm to SIPC, which initiates the liquidation of the firm in federal bankruptcy court. SIPC typically petitions the court to appoint a trustee, who oversees the liquidation of the firm. If the broker-dealer's records are accurate, SIPC and the trustee may transfer customer accounts to another broker-dealer. The trustee then solicits claims from each of the broker-dealer's customers for unrecovered cash and securities. When a broker-dealer's available assets are insufficient to cover customer claims, the trustee reimburses customers through an advance from the SIPC fund, which is funded by assessments on SIPC member broker-dealers. The trustee seeks to replenish the SIPC fund by recovering assets from the broker-dealer during the liquidation process.

SIPC has conducted several high-profile liquidations since the Financial Crisis, including Bernard L. Madoff Investment Securities LLC and MF Global Inc.. Perhaps most notably, Lehman Brothers's failure triggered the largest liquidation in SIPC history. SIPC was charged with liquidating Lehman Brothers Inc., the broker-dealer subsidiary of Lehman Brothers Holdings Inc.. By the end of 2014, SIPC's trustee, James W. Giddens, had resolved 13,000 customer claims totaling $123 billion and had recovered more than $560 million from Lehman Brothers Inc.'s affiliates, repaying in full all SIPC advances.

---

1. ***SIPC compared to FDIC***. Although SIPC and the FDIC both protect consumers by insuring against losses, SIPC plays a much narrower role than the FDIC in the broader financial system. The advent of deposit insurance during the New Deal had a significant stabilizing effect on the banking sector. Indeed, deposit insurance largely put an end to bank runs because customers were assured that their deposits were protected. SIPC, in contrast, does not reduce run risk for broker-dealers. As you will learn in Chapter 12.4, broker-dealers fund themselves largely through wholesale funding, including repo and other securities financing transactions. SIPC does not protect these market-based financing arrangements and, thus, SIPC does not deter the types of wholesale funding runs that broker-dealers experienced during the Financial Crisis.

2. ***The Resolution of Lehman Brothers.*** The bankruptcy of Lehman Brothers presented many complex issues regarding cross-border resolution. The firm's failure triggered the application of insolvency laws in more than 80 jurisdictions in which it operated. U.S. authorities experienced difficulties in getting Lehman Brothers's assets into the United States as a result of these dueling insolvency regimes. *See, e.g.*, Michael J. Fleming & Asani Sarkar, *The Failure Resolution of Lehman Brothers*, ECON. POL'Y REV., Dec. 2014. We discuss the problem of resolving non-bank systemically important financial institutions and cross-border resolution in Chapter 9.3.

B. PENSION BENEFIT GUARANTY CORPORATION

Congress created the PBGC in 1974 to encourage the continuation of privately sponsored defined benefit plans. Defined benefit plans are pension plans in which beneficiaries receive a stream of predetermined, fixed-dollar payments at retirement. In contrast, in a defined contribution plan, beneficiaries pay a defined amount into a pension fund and receive compensation at retirement that varies depending on the success of the pension fund's investments. The PBGC guarantees defined benefit plan beneficiaries that they will be paid, up to a statutory cap, if the fund is unable to meet its obligations. In 2014, the PBGC paid monthly retirement benefits to approximately 813,000 retirees under 4,600 insolvent pension plans. *Who We Are*, PBGC (last visited Jan. 26, 2016). The PBGC is an independent agency within the Executive Branch, headed by a Senate-confirmed Director. The PBGC Director reports to a Board of Directors composed of the Secretaries of Labor, Commerce, and the Treasury.

The PBGC typically begins paying benefits at the request of a sponsor that is ending its pension program under a distressed termination. PBGC payments are funded by assessments on firms with covered pension plans, investments, assets from firms for whom it serves as a trustee, and recoveries in bankruptcy from former plan sponsors. It is not funded by tax dollars, although the perpetual underfunding of the PBGC puts taxpayers at risk. The PBGC uses a risk-based premium approach when making assessments on some of its covered plan sponsors. For example, firms with single employer plans—in which a single firm is running a plan solely for the benefit of its own employees—initially pay a flat-rate premium for each employee participating in its plan. A pension plan is underfunded when it does not have sufficient assets and income to meet its obligations to beneficiaries. When pension plans are underfunded, firms pay an additional variable-rate premium that increases as the level of unfunded liabilities increases. *Pension Insurance Premiums Fact Sheet*, PBGC (last visited Jan. 26, 2016). In practice, Congress has capped the premiums that PBGC may charge at a level that makes it impossible for the PBGC to fully cover its current and potential liabilities. Why would Congress cap PBGC fees at such a level?

---

1. ***State Insurance Guarantee Funds:* Ex Post *Assessments*.** You will learn in Chapter 3.1 that insurance liabilities are protected by a system of state-wide guarantee funds. In contrast to the DIF's *ex ante* assessments on insured banks, most insurance guarantee funds are funded by *ex post* assessments on surviving member firms. When an insurer fails and is unable to meet the obligations of its policyholders, the state guarantee fund assesses remaining firms in the policyholders' state to satisfy covered claims. What do you think are the pros and cons of *ex ante* versus *ex post* assessments? Which approach do you think is better in what context?

2. ***State Insurance Guarantee Funds: Prohibition on Advertising.*** Most states prohibit insurers from advertising the existence of guarantee funds to prospective customers. Why might this be so? Banks, by contrast, prominently advertise that depositors are protected by FDIC insurance—indeed, the FDIC requires them to do so. Which approach do you think is better? *See* Daniel

Schwarcz, *Transparently Opaque: Understanding the Lack of Transparency in Insurance Consumer Protection*, 61 UCLA L. REV. 394, 441–42 (2014).

VI. INTERNATIONAL PERSPECTIVES

Countries around the world use deposit insurance to prevent and mitigate the impact of bank runs. In the past, explicit deposit insurance guarantees were not honored in three instances: twice in Argentina, in 1989 and 2001, and in Iceland in 2008. Demirgüç-Kunt et al., *Deposit Insurance Database*, at 9. This section explores the expansion of deposit insurance and the difficulties of administering deposit insurance in a global financial system.

A. THE SPREAD OF DEPOSIT INSURANCE

Explicit deposit insurance has spread dramatically. Today, 113 countries have explicit deposit insurance protection. Demirgüç-Kunt et al., *Deposit Insurance Database*, at 11; Daniel Ren, *China Issues Rule on Bank Deposit Insurance Scheme*, S. CHINA MORNING POST, Apr. 1, 2015. In 1980, only 20 countries had deposit insurance protection. All countries offer at least some implicit protection of deposits because of heavy political pressure to rescue bank stakeholders during a crisis. A variety of factors have influenced the surge in deposit insurance. First, many developing countries adopt deposit insurance to encourage the flow of funds into the formal banking system and increase the flow of credit. Second, deposit insurance has been effective in stopping bank runs in developed countries, leading other countries to adopt similar measures. Third, deposit insurance is developing due to efforts to harmonize international financial markets. For example, numerous Central and Eastern European countries seeking EU membership adopted insurance in response to the European Commission Directive on Deposit Insurance, which set a minimum amount of deposit insurance coverage that EU member states must provide. Some countries adopted explicit deposit insurance during the Financial Crisis to stave off a panic. Demirgüç-Kunt et al., *Deposit Insurance Database*, at 9.

China has adopted a final rule for deposit insurance, making it G-20's last adopter of deposit insurance. Daniel Ren, *China Issues Rule on Bank Deposit Insurance Scheme*, S. CHINA MORNING POST, Apr. 1, 2015. China's explicit deposit insurance, administered by the People's Bank of China, replaces the Chinese government's system of implicit insurance guarantees for its approximately $19.7 trillion in deposits. Lingling Wei, *China to Begin Deposit Insurance in May*, WALL ST. J., Mar. 31, 2015. China is adopting deposit insurance to signal strongly to its population that there is no longer an implicit guarantee of 100% of deposits in the state-owned Chinese banks, but only a guarantee up to 500,000 renminbi, worth roughly $80,000 at the time of adoption. The New York Times reported:

> The reality in China was that the deposits of the proletariat have always been de facto backed up by the central government,' said Jim Antos, a banking analyst in Hong Kong at Mizuho Securities Asia. Formal deposit insurance is 'the first step in a process where maybe we can have some way to deal with the resolution of financial problems in banks in China, something like a bank failure.'

Neil Gough, *China Rethinks Safety Net for Its Banking System*, N.Y. TIMES, Apr. 30, 2015.

B. CROSS-BORDER DEPOSIT TAKING: WHO PAYS?

Banks operate across borders, collecting funds from depositors outside of their home jurisdiction. If these institutions fail, questions can arise as to who is responsible for protecting depositors from loss. Consequently, deposit insurance funds often prescribe differences in coverage applicable to domestic and foreign banks operating in the same country.

In the United States, whether a foreign firm can offer insured deposits depends on if it uses the subsidiary or branch form to do business in the United States. U.S. chartered bank subsidiaries of foreign banks are eligible for deposit insurance, and they are subject to domestic capital requirements. They pay premiums into the deposit insurance fund for protection. By contrast, since the enactment of the Foreign Bank Supervision Enhancement Act in 1991, foreign branches and agencies are effectively prohibited from taking retail deposits and receiving deposit insurance. As a result, they are limited to taking large uninsured deposits of more than $250,000 from corporate customers. The requirements, which shield U.S. retail depositors from the failure of poorly managed foreign banks, was largely a response to the dramatic collapse of the multinational firm Bank of Credit and Commerce International (BCCI). Although its central offices were in London and Karachi, BCCI was headquartered in Luxembourg and deliberately structured to avoid regulatory oversight. BCCI habitually engaged in money laundering and other forms of financial crime. When BCCI was denied access to the U.S. market by wary regulators, it covertly purchased U.S. banks in Georgia, California, and Washington D.C. Each of those banks benefitted from deposit insurance. When regulators in five countries simultaneously shut down the operations of the failing BCCI in 1991, almost one million depositors were affected, including some with insured deposits in BCCI's improperly purchased U.S. banks. JOHN C. DUGAN ET AL., U.S. REGULATION OF FOREIGN BANKS & AFFILIATES 610, 612 (2012). For a more in-depth discussion of BCCI, see Chapter 6.3.

The U.S. approach to deposit insurance for foreign bank branches has not been universally adopted, and the situation in other countries is far more complicated. For example, the European Economic Area (EEA), which includes all 28 member states of the EU, Iceland, Lichtenstein, and Norway, is governed by the EU's Directive on Deposit Insurance. Countries in the EEA are required to establish deposit insurance with minimum coverage. While EEA countries generally insure domestic banks' deposits, their deposit insurance protection for locally chartered subsidiaries and branches of foreign banks varies significantly. Directive 94/19/EC of the European Parliament and of the Council of 30 May 1994 on Deposit-Guarantee Schemes, 1994 O.J. (L 135) 5.

When a country fails to honor deposit guarantee obligations in the EEA, other countries may incur obligations far exceeding what they would otherwise expect. The Icelandic Bank Landasbanki illustrates this problem. Before the Financial Crisis, Landasbanki maintained branches in London and Amsterdam that collected funds from local depositors through an online portal called Icesave. In 2008, all three of Iceland's major commercial banks, including Landasbanki, collapsed. Icesave customers attempting to withdraw funds found the portal blocked. Under the EU Deposit Insurance Directive, Iceland was required to insure English and Dutch depositors up to the minimum amount. Icelandic authorities demurred, however, largely due to the Icelandic deposit insurance fund's insolvency following the collapse of its major banks. Consequently, British and Dutch depositors suffered a total loss. Iceland's failure to pay the depositors, combined with its decision to pass a law guaranteeing the domestic deposits of Icelandic customers in Icelandic banks, led to recriminations and outright retaliation from British and Dutch authorities. The British and Dutch governments repaid local Icesave depositors in full, at levels exceeding the liability offered by their own national deposit guarantees.

Europe's disjointed response to the Financial Crisis has led to reforms aimed at creating a safer, more integrated European financial regulatory system. A 2015 report from the heads of the European Commission, European Central Bank, and others called for the creation of European Deposit Insurance. Proponents of a pan-European deposit insurance system argue it would be more efficient and effective than the fragmented national deposit insurance schemes, enhance customer confidence, and produce administrative savings. Thierry Bosly & Diane Verhaegen, *Deposit Guarantee Schemes in the Banking Union*, WHITE & CASE, Mar. 2014. Critics argue that a unified deposit insurance plan is unlikely to succeed without a unified fiscal authority to serve as a backstop. Adam Posen & Nicolas Véron, *Europe's Half a Banking Union*, BRUEGEL, June 20, 2014. European Deposit Insurance will likely face tough opposition from powerful forces in the EU, like Germany. Andreas Rinke et al., *Germany opposes EU's propose deposit insurance plan—sources*, REUTERS, June 24, 2015.

---

1. ***Treatment of Foreign Branches.*** Do you agree with the decision in the United States to prevent foreign branches from taking small retail deposits from the general public and limiting them to large uninsured deposits? Are these large uninsured deposits more or less likely to run? Foreign subsidiaries can take retail deposits and are covered by deposit insurance. Should they be covered? Why might other countries make different choices?

2. ***Unified Deposit Insurance in the EU.*** In what ways does the absence of a unified deposit insurance plan harm or help financial stability in the EU? Do you agree that a credible European-wide fiscal backstop is needed before the deposit insurance plan can be established?

CHAPTER 2.5

CAPITAL REGULATION: AN INTRODUCTION

CONTENTS

I. WHAT IS CAPITAL?

Capital regulation is arguably the most important component of financial regulation. All of the major categories of financial intermediaries, including depository institutions, insurance companies, and securities firms, are subject to extensive capital regulation, although the content of those regulations and the terminology used differ widely from sector to sector. The next three chapters introduce the subject of capital regulation for banks and their holding companies. In this Chapter, we start with the basic building blocks of capital regulation, offer a thumbnail sketch of the evolution of bank and bank holding company (BHC) capital requirements in the 20th Century, and set the stage for the more sophisticated discussion of capital requirements that follow in the next two chapters.

One word of warning: the term capital, as used in this context, is based on accounting principles. To understand how capital regulations work, and why they sometimes do not work so well, you need to understand how capital is reported on the balance sheet of a financial institution and some of the factors that can affect the valuation of an institution's assets. You also need to appreciate that capital is, itself, a defined term, and over time accountants and regulators have adjusted that definition to reflect changes in financial sector practices and experience. As you will see, today's capital regulations include a number of different definitions of capital, each with its own set of requirements. The system of capital regulation is quite complicated but is built on a number of fairly straightforward principles, to which we now turn.

A. THE DEFINITION OF CAPITAL

In functional and slightly idealized terms, capital measures the amount of losses that an institution can suffer without impairing its obligations to creditors and other claimants. An institution that is funded entirely with capital, meaning it has no creditors or other claimants, could lose 100% of its assets imposing any losses on creditors or other claimants. Similarly, an institution with half of its funding from capital and half from creditors could suffer losses of 50% of its assets without impairing those obligations.

An institution with a greater reliance on capital will have a larger cushion against losses, and the suppliers, typically shareholders, of its capital will have stronger incentives to monitor carefully the activities of the firm. These two factors explain why financial regulation is so attuned to capital levels; capital protects bank creditors, most notably uninsured depositors (or for deposits that are insured, the Deposit Insurance Fund (DIF)), and also creates incentives for shareholders to monitor excessive risk-taking by their firm.

As we explored in Chapter 1.5, the balance sheets of financial institutions are well-designed to highlight the amount of capital for a particular institution. Consider, for a moment, the simplified bank balance sheet presented in Figure 2.5-1. The left hand side of the balance reports $100 million of total assets, matched against $90 million of liabilities and $10 million of equity on the right. Although the balance sheet reflects the assets and liabilities of a bank, the analysis would be very similar at the consolidated BHC level, which will also include the assets, liabilities, and capital of non-bank affiliates. Keep in mind that capital requirements apply at both levels.

Figure 2.5-1 Simple Balance Sheet

Simple Balance Sheet ***($ millions)***			
Assets		**Liabilities**	
Cash and Due from Banks	$ 10	Deposits	$ 70
Investment Securities	20	Bonds	20
Mortgage Loans	10	**Total Liabilities**	**90**
Other Consumer Loans	15	Preferred Stock	2
Commercial Loans	40	Common Stock:	
Other Assets	5	Paid-in Capital	3
		Retained Earnings	5
		Total Equity	**10**
Total Assets	**$ 100**	**Total Equity and Liabilities**	**$ 100**

So how much capital does this bank have? At first blush, the question might seem fairly straightforward: $10 million is the total equity shown in the lower right hand corner of the balance sheet, and $10 million is also the difference between the firm's total assets and total liabilities. Is that really the amount of loss the bank could absorb before any creditor or other claimant would also have to share the loss? Might the holders of preferred stock be considered claimants that should absorb losses? Should that kind of equity count as capital in the same way that paid-in capital from common stock and retained earnings are considered capital? Furthermore, even if we are not concerned about protecting preferred stockholders from losses, what about other claimants whose interests are important but are not reflected on this balance sheet (sometimes referred to as off-balance sheet liabilities)? A guarantee would be one example of such a contingent liability. Should some capital be set aside for these potential obligations?

Additionally, what about the portion of liabilities represented by bonds as opposed to deposits? To the extent that bank regulators are focused on protecting depositors from losses, should they also be concerned with protecting bondholders from losses? Put another way, should funding from bondholders be considered a form of capital available to absorb losses or not? What factors would bear on that decision? Recall that in the Financial Crisis, the practical impact of the taxpayer bailouts was to protect bondholders while shareholders were either wiped out, in the case of failures, or diluted, in some cases massively. *See* Chapter 9.3; DAVID A. SKEEL, THE NEW FINANCIAL DEAL: UNDERSTANDING THE DODD-FRANK ACT AND ITS (UNINTENDED) CONSEQUENCES 147 (2010).

We will discuss these and many other related issues in the following pages. Throughout the discussion keep in mind the underlying function of capital and consider how regulators have altered their approach to capital regulation in order to accommodate an increasingly complex and interconnected financial services sector.

B. THE FALL AND RISE OF CAPITAL LEVELS

Concern over bank capital adequacy as a way to protect both depositors and the banking system has a long history. Early legal requirements often established minimum capital requirements in absolute terms, such as $50,000 of paid-in capital. At the start of the 20th Century, state regulators developed a more generalized capital adequacy standard, which required a capital to total deposits ratio of one to ten. This ratio of capital to deposits was subsequently used by the Comptroller of the Currency as well. Notwithstanding these capital regulations, in the years preceding the establishment of federal deposit insurance in the 1930s, regulatory capital requirements tended not to be a binding regulatory constraint for depository institutions because market forces, particularly the concerns of the then uninsured depositors and other potential claimants, forced banks and thrifts to maintain capital well above legal requirements. For example, for national banks in the 1890s, a recent study estimated average net worth (*i.e.*, capital) to total assets ratios in excess of 30%. *See* Charles W. Calomiris & Mark Carlson, *Corporate Governance and Risk Management at Unprotected Banks: National Banks in the 1890s*, 119 J. FIN. ECON. 512 (2016).

With the New Deal reforms, capital requirements evolved. In the late 1930s, banking regulators began to use a capital to assets ratio rather than a capital to deposits ratio for the determination of capital adequacy. The change reflected the fact that banks tended to sustain losses on their assets rather than on their deposits, and so it became common practice to link capital requirements to asset levels. During the mid-20th Century, the establishment of capital adequacy levels also shifted to a qualitative analysis of asset risk, based on *ad hoc* determinations by bank examiners and other supervisors with respect to the risk profiles of individual institutions.

Capital standards also varied considerably across different federal banking agencies within their specialized jurisdictions. Without specific quantitative standards, the stringency of capital requirements diminished in the years following the Great Depression, and aggregate bank capital levels as a percentage of assets in the banking industry declined more than 50% from the inception of federal deposit insurance through the early 1980s. A combination of public confidence stemming from the existence of federal deposit insurance and a prolonged period of sustained economic growth in the post-World War II era contributed to this secular decline in bank capital levels.

Using a capital to total assets ratio, Figure 2.5-2 shows how capital levels have generally changed since the 19th Century.

Figure 2.5-2 Capital to Total Assets Ratio of U.S. Banks, 1834–2014

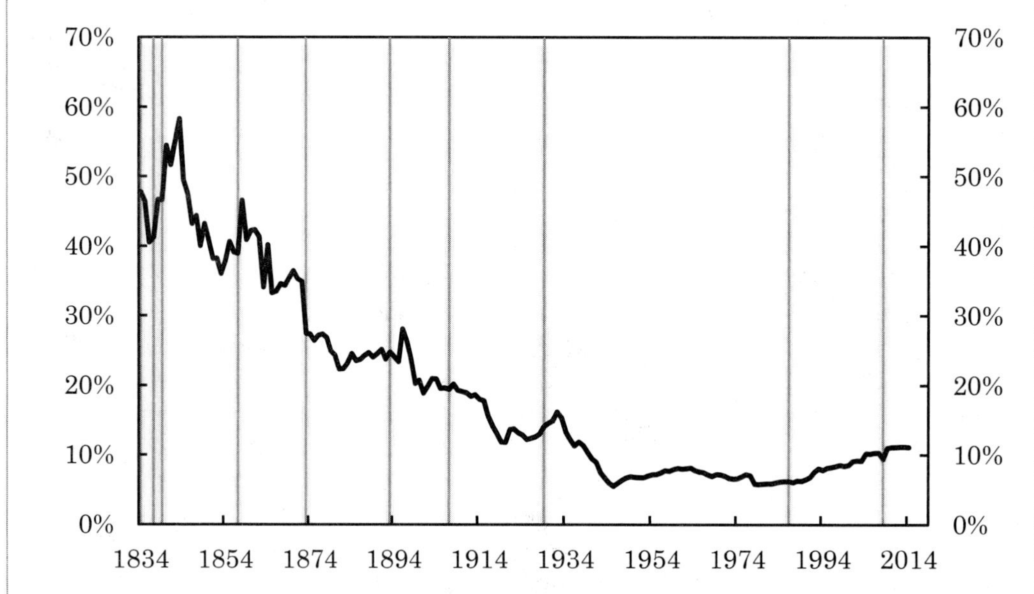

Sources: Susan B. Carter, Scott Sigmund Gartner, Michael R. Haines, & Alan L. Olmstead, eds., Historical Statistics of the United States, Earliest Times to the Present (2006); FDIC Historical Statistics on Banking; Andrew J. Jalil, A New History of Banking Panics in the United States, 1825–1929: Construction and Implications, 7 Am. Econ. J.: Macroeconomics 295 (2015).

By the early 1980s, concern over declining capital levels emerged. Amid the economic challenges of the late 1970s, bank activities were perceived to be increasingly complex, diverse, and risky, and demands for higher capital increased. Losses on major money center bank loans to Latin American borrowers precipitated the passage of the International Lending Supervision Act of 1983. The Act required federal bank regulatory agencies to cooperate on establishing minimum levels of capital for banks and BHCs and empowered regulators to issue capital directives to individual banks and BHCs, which are enforceable in federal district court in the same manner that final, administrative agency cease and desist orders can be enforced. The Act also provided a specific grant of authority to establish levels of capital both for categories of institutions and for individual institutions. While the legislative history suggests that Congress did not expect all banking agencies to have a single uniform capital ratio for all banks and BHCs under all circumstances, the practice since 1983 has been for these agencies to work towards common capital standards for all federally insured depository institutions and holding companies.

The following case presented a legal challenge to one feature of the International Lending Supervision Act of 1983: the new power granted to federal banking agencies to issue capital directives.

FDIC v. Bank of Coushatta

930 F.2d 1122 (5th Cir.), *cert. denied*, 502 U.S. 857 (1991)

The [FDIC] issued a capital directive to the Bank of Coushatta and its directors (Board). After they failed to comply, the FDIC obtained an ex parte order from the district court to enforce the directive. The Bank and Board appeal from the order. . . .

Chartered by Louisiana, the Bank is federally insured, subject to the Federal Deposit Insurance Act [(FDIA)], 12 U.S.C. § 1811, et seq., and FDIC rules and regulations. In July, 1989, it was operating under the FDIC capital forbearance program in an attempt to bring its capital to a minimum level. Under its second capital forbearance plan, the Bank had agreed to bring its primary capital ratio to 5.49% by year end. The FDIC determined that the Bank could not comply with the plan, because its loss classifications exceeded amounts projected for all of 1989. As a result, in July 1989, the FDIC issued a notice of intent, with preliminary findings of fact and conclusions of law, stating that the Bank's primary capital was lower than required by regulation and that the FDIC proposed to issue a capital directive requiring the Bank by December 31, 1989, to increase that capital by not less than $725,000 and to achieve ratios of primary and total capital to total assets of not less than 5.5% and 6.0% respectively.

Accompanying the notice was a letter to the Board, which discussed the financial condition of the Bank, the reasons for its deteriorating status, and the intent of a capital directive action. Also enclosed was the report on the examination of the Bank conducted as of April 1989 by the FDIC and a state examiner.

Any response to the notice was due within 14 days after receipt and was to: "state any basis for relief from the proposed CAPITAL DIRECTIVE, and may seek modification of its terms, or seek other appropriate relief. Such response shall include any information, mitigating circumstances, documentation, or other relevant evidence which supports the Bank's position, and may include a plan for attaining the minimum capital requirement."

By only a 1 1/2 page letter in August 1989, the Board responded; it noted its efforts to find additional capital, its lack of financial capacity, and the weakened nature of the Louisiana economy, stating that "[t]he main reason for failure to achieve the goals in the Capital Forbearance Plan is loan losses and the deterioration of the parcels held as Other Real Estate." The Board did not dispute any of the FDIC's classifications of assets or its calculations. Nor did it submit any proposal for meeting the FDIC requirements, stating only that "[t]he Board believes it will have sufficient earning[s] to have a capital ratio in excess of 4% by year end, and will continue its efforts to find additional capital." The Board acknowledged the "capital deficiency" and requested modification of the capital forbearance plan in lieu of a capital directive.

The FDIC issued the directive in September 1989, with supporting findings of fact and conclusions of law and a cover letter to the Board. The Bank was directed (1) by December 31, 1989, to restore its ratio of primary capital to total assets to at least 5.5% and enhance that capital by at least $725,000; and (2) within 30 days, to submit a plan for achieving the capital level. The directive stated that it was binding upon "the Bank [and] its directors," among others.

Because the Bank failed to comply, the FDIC filed a letter in May 1990, in the United States District Court in Louisiana, pursuant to 12 U.S.C. § 1818(i), requesting an order enforcing the directive against the Bank and Board. Attached to the letter was a Petition for Enforcement of Administrative Order, stamped filed on June 14, 1990. On July 13, 1990, the district court issued the requested ex parte order. The Bank, its officers and directors were ordered to comply with the directive and to submit a report within 30 days "setting forth in detail the manner and form in which Respondent has complied with the provisions of this Order. This Court shall retain jurisdiction . . . for the purpose of entertaining any petition which . . . [the FDIC] may make and entering further orders as may be necessary to enforce compliance with the terms of this Order." The Bank and Board filed an appeal from that order and a motion for stay pending appeal; the district court and this court denied the stay.

II.

The FDIC's authority to issue capital directives is one of its regulatory tools for dealing with troubled banks. Most of these methods are set forth in 12 U.S.C. § 1818; however, authority for a directive is found in the International Lending Supervision Act of 1983 (ILSA), 12 U.S.C. § 3907, which provides in part: (a)(1) Each appropriate Federal banking agency shall cause banking institutions to achieve and maintain adequate capital by establishing minimum levels of capital for such banking institutions and by using such other methods as the appropriate Federal banking agency *deems* appropriate. (2) Each appropriate Federal banking agency shall have the authority to establish such minimum level of capital for a banking institution as the appropriate Federal banking agency, *in its discretion, deems* to be necessary or appropriate in light of the particular circumstances of the banking institution. (Emphasis added.) Moreover, failure to maintain the requisite capital "may be *deemed* by the appropriate Federal banking agency, *in its discretion*, to constitute an unsafe and unsound practice. . . ." 12 U.S.C. § 3907(b)(1) (emphasis added).

If a bank fails to maintain the required capital, the agency may issue a directive: (B)(i) Such directive may require the banking institution to submit and adhere to a plan acceptable to the appropriate Federal banking agency describing the means and timing by which the banking institution shall achieve its required capital level. (ii) Any such directive issued pursuant to this paragraph . . . shall be enforceable under the provisions of Section 1818(i) . . . to the same extent as an effective and outstanding order issued pursuant to Section 1818(b) . . . which has become final. 12 U.S.C. §§ 3907(b)(2)(B)(i) and (ii).

The above referenced § 1818(b) governs cease-and-desist proceedings. Cease-and-desist orders are issued only after an agency hearing, §§ 1818(b)(1) and (h)(1), and "become effective at the expiration of thirty days after the service of such order . . . and shall remain effective and enforceable . . ., except to such extent as it is stayed, modified, terminated, or set aside by action of the agency or a reviewing court." 12 U.S.C. § 1818(b)(2). Such orders may be reviewed in a court of appeals within thirty days after service of the order. § 1818(h)(2). . . .

Accordingly, a capital directive may be enforced in the district court under § 1818(i). But, as also referenced above, the district court's jurisdiction is limited. "[S]ection 1818(i) . . . evinces a clear intention that [the] regulatory process is not to be disturbed by untimely judicial intervention, at least where there is no 'clear departure from statutory authority.'" Groos Nat'l Bank v. Comptroller of Currency, 573 F.2d 889, 895 (5th Cir. 1978) (citation omitted). Furthermore, the hearing requirements for cease-and-desist orders are not incorporated in the procedures for capital directives.

Section 3907 was enacted to provide "a stronger, unambiguous statutory directive to the regulators to strengthen banks' capital positions." H.R. Rep. No. 98-175, 98th Cong., 1st Sess. 45[:]

> The [Senate Banking and Finance] Committee's amendment explicitly makes failure to maintain established capital levels an "unsafe and unsound practice. . . ." The amendment requires regulators to demand that institutions below the required capital levels submit and adhere to an acceptable plan to achieve prescribed levels.

Id. at 1929.

Another congressional purpose behind § 3907 was in response to this court's decision in *First Nat'l Bank of Bellaire v. Comptroller of Currency*, 697 F.2d 674 (5th Cir. 1983), where the portion of a cease-and-desist order requiring a capital ratio was set aside as not being supported by substantial evidence. *Id.* at 684–87. Congress was concerned that Bellaire "clouded the authority of the bank regulatory agencies to exercise their *independent discretion* in establishing and requiring the maintenance of appropriate levels of capital." S. Rep. No. 98-122, 98th Cong., 1st Sess. 16 (emphasis added). "The Committee believes that establishing adequate levels of capital is properly left to the *expertise* and *discretion* of the agencies. Therefore, in order to clarify the authority of the banking agencies to establish adequate levels of capital requirements, to require the maintenance of those levels, and *to prevent the courts from disturbing such capital,* the Committee has provided a specific grant of authority to the banking agencies to establish levels of capital. . . ." *Id.* (emphasis added). . . .

The examination may lead to a capital directive being issued. But, the regulations require the FDIC to first issue a notice of its intention to issue the directive; and the notice must include detailed data, such as the current total capital ratio and the basis upon which the ratio is calculated. 12 C.F.R. § 325.6(c)(1). The bank has 14 days to respond, including explaining why the directive should not issue and seeking modification of its terms.

After the bank responds, the FDIC issues a decision, explaining its determination whether to issue a directive. The directive may order the bank to achieve the minimum capital requirement by a certain date; to submit a plan for achieving the minimum capital requirement; or to take other action necessary to achieve the minimum capital requirement; or a combination of the above. § 325.6(c)(3). If a directive is to be issued, it may be served upon the bank with the final determination. *Id.*

The regulations then allow enforcement, as described above, in the same manner as for a final cease-and-desist order. Moreover, "[i]n addition to enforcement of the directive, the FDIC may seek . . . penalties for violation of the directive against any bank, any officer, *director*, employee, agent, or other person participating in the conduct of the affairs of the bank, pursuant to 12 U.S.C. § 3909(d)." § 325.6(d)(1) (emphasis added). . . .

In response to the contention that the district court ex parte proceedings deprived the Bank and Board of a right to judicial review under the [Administrative Procedure Act (APA)], the FDIC asserts that the decision to issue a capital directive is not reviewable, because it is committed to agency discretion by law. Likewise, in denying a stay pending appeal, the district court held that "whether . . . to issue a capital directive is committed to the sole discretion of the FDIC and is, therefore, unreviewable under the [APA]. 5 U.S.C. § 701(a)(2)."

There is a presumption of reviewability. "[J]udicial review of a final agency action by an aggrieved person will not be cut off unless there is persuasive reason to believe that such was the purpose of Congress." Abbott Laboratories v. Gardner, 387 U.S. 136, 140 (1967); *see also Bowen v. Michigan Academy of Family Physicians*, 476 U.S. 667, 671 (1986) ("'Very rarely do statutes withhold judicial review.'") (quoting legislative history of APA).

The APA's provisions for judicial review of final agency actions are contained in 5 U.S.C. §§ 701–706. Section 702 provides: "A person suffering legal wrong because of agency action, or adversely affected or aggrieved by agency action within the meaning of a relevant statute, is entitled to judicial review thereof." Section 702, however, is limited by § 701(a). "[B]efore any review . . . may be had, a party must first clear the hurdle of § 701(a)." Heckler v. Chaney, 470 U.S. 821, 828 (1985). That section provides for judicial review, "except to the extent that (1) statutes preclude judicial review; or (2) agency action is committed to agency discretion by law." 5 U.S.C. § 701(a). The distinction between subparts (1) and (2) in § 701(a) is that, "[t]he former applies when Congress has expressed an intent to preclude judicial review. The latter applies in different circumstances; even where Congress has not affirmatively precluded review, review is not to be had if the statute is drawn so that a court would have no meaningful standard against which to judge the agency's exercise of discretion. In such a case, the statute ("law") can be taken to have "committed" the decision-making to the agency's judgment absolutely." Heckler, 470 U.S. at 830.

In looking first to determine whether review is precluded under § 701(a)(1), we note that there is no statutory prohibition against it; but neither is there any procedure for it—unlike final cease-and-desist orders. Furthermore, no review is allowed in the district court enforcement proceeding; as discussed above, its jurisdiction is limited to the "power to order and require compliance." § 1818(i)(1).

As noted, § 3907 was enacted, in part, in response to judicial interference with capital requirements, as in Bellaire. Examination of the statutory scheme and its legislative history supports a congressional intention to preclude review. However, in the absence of an express prohibition, there is a "strong presumption that Congress did not mean to prohibit all judicial review of [the] decision." *Dunlop v. Bachowski*, 421 U.S. 560, 567 (1975). "[O]nly upon a showing of 'clear and convincing evidence' of a contrary legislative intent should the courts restrict access to judicial review." *Id.* (quoting Abbott Labs, 387 U.S. at 141). Because the standard for finding preclusion of review under § 701(a)(1) is a difficult hurdle to cross, we turn instead to the applicability, vel non, of § 701(a)(2) (agency action committed to its discretion). . . .

The FDIC contends that the legislative history and language of ILSA demonstrate that Congress . . . intended capital directives to be unreviewable. . . . [I]t asserts that the repeated use of the word "deem" in the statute evidences deference and forecloses review. Section 3907 uses the terms "deem" or "discretion" in almost every provision: the FDIC may cause institutions to maintain adequate levels of capital by such methods as it "deems appropriate," § 3907(a)(1); it can establish minimum levels of capital which it "in its discretion, deems to be necessary or appropriate in light of the particular circumstances of the banking institution," § 3907(a)(2); the failure of a banking institution to maintain its capital "may be deemed by the appropriate Federal banking agency, in its discretion, to constitute an unsafe and unsound practice," § 3907(b)(1). And, the legislative history, discussed supra, also supports such a construction. . . .

The legislative history and language of the statute do not leave a court with a meaningful standard against which to judge the agency's exercise of its discretion. . . .

Accordingly, the order of the district court is AFFIRMED.

---

1. ***Capital Requirements Circa 1989.*** The capital requirements at issue in the *Bank of Coushatta* case were fairly straightforward; FDIC-insured banks had to have primary capital of at least 5.5% of total assets and banks' total capital—a more capacious measure of capital—needed to be above 6.0% of total assets. These capital requirements, which we today call a leverage ratio, were the first uniform capital requirements established by federal banking agencies after the passage of the International Lending Supervision Act of 1983. At roughly the

time this case was being litigated, federal authorities were in the midst of devising the more elaborate system of risk-based capital requirements that distinguish among different levels of risk posed by different types of assets or counterparties described later in this Chapter.

2. ***The Role of Loss Classifications.*** The enforcement action at issue in this case arose out of an FDIC determination that the bank's loss classifications exceeded projections. The amount of loss reserves that the bank had set aside to cover projected losses on its loan portfolio were, therefore, determined to be inadequate. Establishing higher reserves would reduce the bank's income and thereby decrease its capital levels relative to those levels to which the bank and its board had committed themselves. A deterioration in the quality of a bank's loan portfolio often leads to a reduction in capital levels. How did the FDIC become aware of this problem with the bank's loan loss reserves? Who is in the best position to determine the quality of a bank's assets, its managers, a bank examiner, or someone else?

The next case offers another perspective on capital regulation arising out of the thrift crisis of the 1980s. The excerpt recounts the practice of federal thrift regulators once known as the Federal Home Loan Bank Board and later renamed the Office of Thrift Supervision (OTS) in 1989 only to be merged into the OCC under the Dodd Frank Act.

Winstar Corp. v. United States

64 F.3d 1531 (Fed. Cir. 1995)

In its Winstar decisions, the Court of Federal Claims found that an implied-in-fact contract existed between the government and Winstar and that the government breached this contract when Congress enacted the Financial Institutions Reform, Recovery, and Enforcement Act of 1989 (FIRREA), Pub.L. No. 101–73, 103 Stat. 183 (codified in relevant part at 12 U.S.C. § 1464). Similarly, in the Statesman decision the Court of Federal Claims found that plaintiffs Statesman Savings Holding Corporation, the Statesman Group Incorporated and the American Life and Casualty Insurance Company (together "Statesman") and plaintiff Glendale Federal Bank ("Glendale") had express contracts with the government and citing its Winstar decision, found that these contracts were breached by the enactment of FIRREA. . . .

II

A.

During the Great Depression of the 1930s, 40 percent of the nation's $20 billion in home mortgages went into default, 1700 of the approximately 12,000 thrift institutions failed, and depositors in these thrifts lost $200 million. H.R.Rep. No. 54(I), 101st Cong., 1st Sess. 292 (1989), reprinted in 1989 U.S.C.C.A.N. 86, 88–89 (House Report). Congress took several measures in response. First, Congress created the Federal Home Loan Bank Board (Bank Board) to channel funds to thrifts in order to prevent foreclosures and to allow thrifts to make loans on residences. House Report at 292, 1989 U.S.C.C.A.N. at 88; *see* Federal Home Loan Bank Act, Pub.L. No. 72–304, 47 Stat. 725 (1932) (codified as amended at 12 U.S.C. §§ 1421–1449 (1988)). Next, Congress added the Home Owners' Loan Act, which authorized the Bank Board to charter and regulate federal savings and loan associations. Pub.L. No. 73–43, 48 Stat. 128 (1933) (codified as amended at 12 U.S.C. §§ 1461–1468 (1988)). Then, to further restore public confidence in thrift institutions,

Congress in the National Housing Act of 1934 provided federal deposit insurance for depositors. Pub.L. No. 73–479, 48 Stat. 1246 (1934) (codified as amended at 12 U.S.C. §§ 1701–1750g (1988)). This act also established the Federal Savings and Loan Insurance Corporation (FSLIC), an agency under the Bank Board's authority that regulated all federally insured thrifts.

Among the regulatory requirements promulgated and enforced by the agencies were capital requirements, which were minimum reserves of capital that a thrift had to maintain. Failure to comply with minimum regulatory capital requirements had severe repercussions for a thrift. The agencies had a variety of measures that could be taken against noncomplying thrifts. In the most serious cases, the government could seize the thrift and place it into receivership where it might later be sold or liquidated. This drastic remedy was rarely necessary, however, because of the relative health of the thrift industry until the thrift crisis of the late 1970s and early 1980s.

In the late 1970s and early 1980s high interest rates resulted in sharply higher costs of funds for thrifts. The thrifts' main assets were long-term, fixed-rate mortgages taken during times of lower interest rates. As a result, the revenues produced by these mortgages were exceeded by the rapidly rising costs of attracting short-term deposits. Thrifts that were locked into long-term low interest rate loans simply could not meet their deposit obligations. This interest rate mismatch was one of the principal causes of numerous thrift failures. Eighty-one thrifts failed in 1981, 252 in 1982, and 102 in 1983. House Report at 296, 1989 U.S.C.C.A.N. at 92.

With all of these bank failures and the likelihood of more occurring, the FSLIC faced deposit insurance liabilities that threatened to exhaust its insurance fund. *See Olympic Fed. Sav. & Loan Ass'n v. Director*, OTS, 732 F.Supp. 1183, 1185 (D.D.C. 1990). As an alternative to liquidating failing thrifts and expending the FSLIC's insurance funds, the Bank Board and FSLIC encouraged healthy thrifts to merge with the failing ones. In these supervisory mergers, the regulators provided direct assistance and other incentives necessary for the healthy thrifts to maintain their financial well-being after the mergers and in this way the regulators tried to avoid paying off the failing thrifts' deposits out of the FSLIC's insurance fund. Among the incentives offered by the FSLIC and the Bank Board was the use of the purchase method of accounting under which "supervisory goodwill" resulting from the merger would be treated as satisfying part of the merged thrift's regulatory capital requirements. *See* Bank Board Memorandum R-31b (1981).

The purchase method of accounting is a generally accepted accounting practice (GAAP) for mergers, which accounts for the surplus of the purchase price over the fair market value of the acquired organization as goodwill, an intangible asset. As explained by the Court of Federal Claims:

> Under [the purchase method of accounting,] . . . the book value of the acquired thrift's assets and liabilities was adjusted to fair market value at the time of the acquisition. Any excess in the cost of the acquisition (which included liabilities assumed by the acquirer) over the fair market value of the acquired assets was separately recorded on the acquirer's books as "goodwill." . . . Goodwill was considered an intangible asset that could be amortized on a straight-line basis over a number of years.

Winstar I, 21 Cl.Ct. at 113. In the context of a supervisory merger, the difference between the fair market value of the failing thrift's liabilities assumed by an acquirer and the fair market value of the failing thrift's assets was considered "supervisory goodwill." The Bank Board and the FSLIC allowed the merged thrifts to count this supervisory goodwill toward the minimum regulatory capital requirements and to amortize this goodwill over periods of up to 40 years. This permitted the healthy thrift to assume the deposit liabilities of the failing thrift and to maintain capital compliance without having to put up large amounts of its own money and without requiring large amounts of monetary assistance from the government. . . .

Allowing acquirers of failing thrifts to treat supervisory goodwill and . . . as regulatory capital stimulated many acquisitions that would otherwise not have taken place because of the difficulty of meeting the minimum capital requirements. Indeed this was the precise intention of the Bank Board and FSLIC—supervisory mergers could not have occurred without the approval by the regulatory agencies of these accounting treatments. As former Bank Board Chairman Richard Pratt stated in testimony before Congress:

> The Bank Board was caught between a rock and a hard place. While it did not have sufficient resources to close all insolvent institutions, at the same time, it had to consolidate the industry, move weaker institutions into stronger hands and do everything possible to minimize losses during the transition period. Goodwill was an indispensable tool in performing this task. The GAAP approach to purchase method accounting mergers provided a bridge which allowed the Bank Board to encourage the necessary consolidation of the industry, while at the same time husbanding the financial resources which were then available to it.

Savings and Loan Policies in the Late 1970s and 1980s: Hearings Before the House Comm. on Banking, Finance and Urban Affairs, 101st Cong., 2d Sess., No. 176, at 227 (1990).

B.

Winstar [and] Statesman acquired insolvent, failing thrifts under this policy of encouraging thrift mergers. In each case, they received the government's approval and assistance. In each case, the government saved millions of dollars that it would have had to pay to the insured depositors if the failing thrifts had been liquidated instead of being acquired. . . .

In 1987 Statesman approached the FSLIC about acquiring a subsidiary of an insolvent state-chartered FSLIC insured savings and loan in Florida, First Federated Savings Bank (First Federated). The FSLIC responded to the inquiry by indicating that Statesman would have to acquire all of First Federated if the government was to assist. Further, it would require that Statesman's acquisition of First Federated be combined with the acquisition of three other financially troubled thrifts in Iowa. After a year of negotiating the FSLIC and Statesman agreed on the terms of a complex plan whereby Statesman would acquire the four thrifts.

. . . [S]tatesman's merger plan called for the use of the purchase method of accounting. The Statesman plan called for an investment by Statesman and its co-investor American Life and Casualty Company of $21 million into Statesman's Savings Holding Company, which in turn would purchase $21 million of stock in a newly-formed federal stock savings bank named Statesman Bank for Savings. The Statesman Bank for Savings would then merge with the four failing thrifts.

As part of the transactions, the FSLIC and Statesman entered into an Assistance Agreement calling for the FSLIC to provide a $60 million cash contribution to the Statesman Bank for Savings. Under the Assistance Agreement and the Bank Board Resolution approving the merger, $26 million of this cash contribution (including $5 million represented by a debenture that Statesman was required to pay back) was to be permanently credited to Statesman's regulatory capital . . .

The Bank Board resolution permitted use of the purchase method of accounting. Supervisory goodwill arising from the merger acquisitions in the amount of $25.8 million was recognized as a capital asset for purposes of meeting regulatory capital requirements and Statesman was allowed to amortize that goodwill over 25 years. The Bank Board granted authority to the FSLIC to enter into the Assistance Agreement with Statesman and required Statesman to provide an opinion letter from its independent accountants to justify its use of the purchase method of accounting and supervisory goodwill. Statesman provided the opinion letter to the agency's satisfaction. By the government's estimates, the cost of the Statesman merger to the government was $50 million less than the cost of liquidating the four thrifts. . . .

In 1983 a Minnesota-based thrift, Windom Federal Savings and Loan Association (Windom), was in danger of failing. The board of directors of Windom determined that its failure could not be avoided without assistance from the FSLIC. The FSLIC estimated that liquidating the federally insured thrift could cost $12 million dollars and it pursued an alternative to paying this money out of its insurance fund. It chose to solicit bids for the acquisition of Windom.

Winstar Corporation was a holding company formed by investors for the purpose of acquiring Windom. Winstar in turn formed a new wholly-owned, federal stock savings bank, United Federal Savings Bank, to merge with Windom. Winstar's plan contemplated financing the merger by cash contributions by both the investors and the FSLIC. The plan also called for use of the purchase method of accounting and recording supervisory goodwill as an intangible asset which initially was to amortized over a period of 40 years (later changed to 35 years). After negotiating the terms with Winstar Corporation and its investors, the FSLIC recommended to the Bank Board that it approve the merger plan. The Bank Board approved the merger again subject to Winstar providing an opinion letter from its independent accountants justifying the use of the purchase method of accounting and detailing the resulting supervisory goodwill. As a part of the transaction, FSLIC signed an Assistance Agreement with Winstar Corporation and the Bank Board issued a forbearance letter. The forbearance letter stated that intangible assets resulting from use of the purchase method of accounting "may be amortized . . . over a period not to exceed 35 years by the straight-line method." By the government's estimates, the Winstar-Windom merger saved the government $7 million over what liquidation of Windom would have cost.

C.

In spite of these and similar actions taken by the Bank Board and the FSLIC, thrifts continued to fail and the public confidence in the thrift industry continued to erode during the late 1980s. In response to this crisis in the savings and loan industry, Congress in 1989 passed FIRREA. FIRREA substantially modified the overall thrift regulatory scheme. As pertinent here, it (1) abolished the FSLIC and transferred its functions to other agencies; (2) created a new thrift deposit insurance fund under the [FDIC]; (3) eliminated the Bank Board and replaced it with the [OTS], an office within the Department of Treasury, and made the OTS Director responsible for the regulation of all federally insured savings associations and the chartering of federal thrifts; and (4) established the Resolution Trust Corporation (RTC), which was charged with closing certain thrifts. *See* 12 U.S.C. §§ 1437 note, 1441a, 1821.

Among the legislative reforms of FIRREA was the requirement that the OTS "prescribe and maintain uniformly applicable capital standards for savings associations." 12 U.S.C. § 1464(t)(1)(a). In addition, Congress expressly restricted the continued use of supervisory goodwill to satisfy regulatory capital requirements.

FIRREA required federally insured thrifts to satisfy three new minimum capital standards: "tangible" capital, "core" capital, and "risk-based" capital. 12 U.S.C. § 1464(t). Under FIRREA supervisory goodwill could not be included at all in satisfying minimum tangible capital. The amount of supervisory goodwill that could be included in satisfying "core" capital decreased each year after FIRREA's enactment and was entirely phased out on December 31, 1994. Finally, thrifts were required to maintain "risk-based" capital in an amount substantially comparable to that required by the Comptroller of the Currency for national banks. 12 U.S.C. § 1464(t)(2)(C). Although supervisory goodwill could be used for this purpose, FIRREA limited its amortization to a period of no more than 20 years. 12 U.S.C. § 1464(t)(9)(B). . . .

After FIRREA, Statesman immediately fell below the three new capital standards established by the Act. As a result, the OTS appointed the RTC as receiver for Statesman in July of 1990. Winstar also fell into noncompliance as soon as the FIRREA capital requirements became effective. Winstar was placed in receivership by the OTS in May of 1990.

D.

The plaintiffs filed suit in the Court of Federal Claims alleging that under FIRREA the preclusion or limited availability to them of supervisory goodwill . . . for satisfying regulatory capital constituted a breach of contract or, in the alternative, a taking of their contract rights without compensation in violation of the Fifth Amendment. The plaintiffs claimed that the government was contractually obligated to recognize supervisory goodwill generated by the mergers (and capital credits) as an intangible capital asset for purposes of their compliance with minimum regulatory capital standards. The plaintiffs also claimed that they were entitled to amortize that supervisory goodwill for the agreed periods established at the time of their acquisitions of failing thrifts. Under their contract claims, plaintiffs asserted that FIRREA, and the regulations thereunder, as applied to them, breached those contract obligations. All of the plaintiffs filed summary judgment motions on the issue of liability.

The government defended on the grounds that there were no contractual rights as alleged and that in any event the alleged agreements were subject to statutory and regulatory changes. Relying principally on Bowen v. Public Agencies Opposed to Social Security Entrapment (POSSE), 477 U.S. 41, 106 S.Ct. 2390, 91 L.Ed.2d 35 (1986), the government argued that the thrifts impermissibly sought to enjoin Congress' power to legislate and the agencies' power to regulate. The government further argued that the sovereign acts doctrine, as stated in Horowitz v. United States, 267 U.S. 458, 461, 45 S.Ct. 344, 344–45, 69 L.Ed. 736 (1925), precluded recovery for any contractual rights breached by FIRREA . . .

---

1. ***Regulatory Forbearance.*** As the *Winstar* decision recounts, federal authorities made a number of accommodations, known as regulatory forbearance, whereby regulatory capital requirements were waived so as to avoid shutting down thrifts facing insolvency. In addition to preventing the federal DIF from incurring losses on thrift failures, these practices allowed large segments of the thrift sector to survive a period of high interest rates and declining real estate prices in certain markets. Recall the discussion in Chapter 1.2. The acceptance of "supervisory goodwill" as regulatory capital in certain transactions was just one example of forbearance during this era. For a more general treatment of the thrift crisis, *see* LAWRENCE J. WHITE, THE S&L DEBACLE: PUBLIC POLICY LESSONS FOR BANK AND THRIFT REGULATION (1992). Under what circumstances, if any, is it appropriate for financial regulators to relax regulatory standards in the face of financial stress?

2. ***Thrift Capital Requirements Under FIRREA.*** The *Winstar* case offers a window into the emergence of multiple capital requirements in the late 1980s, including two leverage requirements, specifying that tangible capital and core capital be a certain percentage of total assets, as well as a risk-based capital requirement. Notice that supervisory goodwill was treated differently under each approach. With multiple capital requirements, which became increasingly

common in later years, regulated entities must comply with all applicable capital requirements, they cannot just pick one requirement to meet. Why do we need so many different capital requirements? Can each of these requirements impose binding constraints on financial institutions?

3. ***Should Supervisory Commitments Bind Future Legislative Actions?*** The key legal question posed in the *Winstar* litigation was whether Congress was free to override the Federal Home Loan Bank Board's agreements with respect to supervisory goodwill. That issue was ultimately decided by the Supreme Court in *United States v. Winstar Corp.*, 518 U.S. 839 (1996) (finding that congressional action breached plaintiffs' agreements). The legislated change in the regulatory capital treatment of supervisory goodwill in 1989 clearly disrupted the investment expectations of the plaintiffs in *Winstar*. Do you agree that institutions with supervisory goodwill on their balance sheets should not have had to bear the risk of legal change? Does your view depend on there being a contract between the government and the institutions? Could Congress have achieved a similar result by changing the manner in which regulators supervised these institutions, perhaps by requiring them to raise more capital, or would that also have constituted a breach of contract?

4. ***Regulatory Refinements and Bilateral Treaties.*** A recurring question of regulatory policy concerns the question of how frequently and extensively legislative bodies or regulators should change the content of regulatory requirements. At what point do changes disrupt the reasonable expectations of private parties and potentially discourage future investment? Regulatory changes with adverse consequences for foreign investors can also sometimes be challenged under bilateral investment treaties. *See, e.g.*, Anthea Roberts, *Clash of Paradigms: Actors and Analogies Shaping the Investment Treaty System*, 107 AM. J. INT'L L. 45, 45 (2013) ("Investors are increasingly challenging specific regulatory actions . . . or general regulatory measures . . . that adversely affect them."). Are treaty protections necessary to protect foreign investors from adverse changes in domestic laws or do ordinary political processes provide adequate safeguards for foreign as well as domestic investors?

C. U.S. CAPITAL REQUIREMENTS IN THE BASEL I ERA

In the late 1980s, federal banking agencies began to transition towards a new system of capital requirements that encompassed both simple leverage rules, that is capital to asset requirements, similar to the capital requirements at issue in the *Bank of Coushatta* case, and a new type of risk-based capital to asset requirement of the sort that Congress imposed on thrifts in FIRREA and mentioned in the *Winstar* decision. Capital requirements of this era are often associated with the work of the Basel Committee, described as follows:

> [The Basel Committee is] an institution that meets under the auspices of the Bank for International Settlements in Basel, Switzerland. The [Basel] Committee is composed of representatives of the central banks and supervisory authorities of the G-10 countries (Belgium, Canada, France, Germany, Italy, Japan, Netherlands, Spain, Sweden, Switzerland, the United Kingdom, and

> the United States) and Luxembourg. Launched to coordinate responses to an international banking crisis in 1974 stemming from the failure of Herstatt Bank in Germany, the [Basel] Committee evolved into a forum for harmonizing national supervision and capital standards for banks. Over the [next] two decades, the Basel Committee has developed progressively more sophisticated guidelines for capital adequacy in depository institutions. The [Basel] Committee's 1988 Accord ('Basel I') was initially intended to govern only internationally active banks in the G-10 and Luxembourg. It is fair to say that Basel I is one of the most successful international regulatory initiatives ever attempted. It was adopted as domestic law by the G-10 nations, applied by them to all of their banks, and then promulgated by over 100 countries around the world although implementation varies widely from country to country.

Michael S. Barr & Geoffrey P. Miller, *Global Administrative Law: The View from Basel*, 17 EUR. J. INT'L L. 15, 17 (2006). As discussed in Chapter 2.6, the Basel Committee expanded its membership considerably, beginning in 2009.

The initial impetus for Basel I was concern among regulatory authorities that differences in capital requirements across industrialized nations were leading to an uneven playing field for internationally active banks. Japanese banks, in particular, were thought to be unfairly advantaged by lenient home-country capital requirements. Basel I was designed to address this problem. While not formally binding on national authorities, Basel I was adopted, with some modifications, by all participating countries. Within a decade, Basel I was also incorporated into the Basel Committee's Core Principles for Effective Banking Supervision (Sept. 1997), at least for internationally active banks. As a result, Basel I became a near-universal standard for risk-based capital requirements throughout the developed world and variants of it were more slowly adopted in the developing world, even though most countries did not participate in the Basel Committee's deliberations and had no say in the content of the rules. Does this process reflect a democracy deficit or the healthy operation of regulatory networks? For a discussion of global regulatory networks, *see* ANNE-MARIE SLAUGHTER, A NEW WORLD ORDER (2004).

Though regulatory harmonization of capital requirements across national boundaries was the basis for Basel I, the establishment of genuinely comparable capital requirements in multiple countries proved a complicated task from the start. As we have seen, capital requirements are based on accounting standards for the recognition of assets on the balance sheet or the treatment of exposures as off-balance sheet exposures, and those standards have traditionally varied from country to country. Enforcement policies, tax rules, business practices, and contract law also have substantial national differences. For a combination of these reasons, according to one study, the Japanese implementation of Basel I differed in material respects from its implementation in other countries. *See* Hal S. Scott & Shinsaku Iwahara, *In Search of a Level Playing Field: The Implementation of the Basel Accord in Japan and the United States* (Group of Thirty Occasional Paper No. 46, 1994). Even though regulatory officials in the United States were among the earliest and strongest proponents of Basel I, the

United States also deviated in its implementation, adding a leverage requirement not included in Basel I itself and also applying Basel I to BHCs and not just banks.

We now turn to the U.S. implementation of Basel I, circa the mid-1990s. While the Basel I rules may initially strike you as ancient history, this system of rules remains the foundation of today's capital requirements.

D. BASIC LEVERAGE AND SIMPLE RISK-BASED CAPITAL REQUIREMENTS

The U.S. implementation of Basel I included both a leverage standard, in the form of a simple ratio of capital to average total assets over a quarterly period, as well as risk-based capital standards.

The leverage standard is a ratio of balance sheet capital to assets—it specifies that a certain minimum amount of tier 1 capital, essentially common and most preferred stock, be held against the average assets shown on the balance sheet. Leverage ratio requirements varied for both banks depending on their examination ratings and other factors.

$$\textit{Leverage Ratio} = \frac{\textit{Tier 1 Capital}}{\textit{Average Assets}}$$

The original leverage requirement depended on the regulator's overall risk assessment of a bank. To measure overall risk, regulators used supervisory ratings that measure various dimensions of a bank's health, known as CAMELS ratings, which range from one to five. CAMELS ratings are described more thoroughly in Chapter 8.2. Banks that had a CAMELS rating of one had to have a minimum leverage ratio of at least 3%. This high rating applied only to banks in very sound condition. Banks with a CAMELS rating of less than one had to have a leverage ratio of at least 4%.

Under earlier leverage requirements, of the sort discussed in the *Bank of Coushatta* case, primary capital ratios included certain loan- and lease-loss reserves, but the definition of tier 1 capital for Basel I purposes excluded such loss reserves. As a result, when failing banks increased their loss reserves, as is typically needed for growing expected losses, tier 1 capital was reduced because the reduction in equity capital was not offset by the inclusion of the correlative increase in loan loss reserves.

The risk-based capital standard of Basel I were more complex. These rules incorporated both equity and other forms of capital in the numerator of the ratios and measured both balance sheet assets and off-balance sheet exposures (contingencies such as loan commitments, letters of credit, and swaps) on a risk-adjusted basis in the denominator of the ratios.

$$\textit{Tier 1 Risk-Based Capital Ratio} = \frac{\textit{Tier 1 Capital}}{\textit{Risk-Weighted Assets}}$$

$$\textit{Total Risk-Based Capital Ratio} = \frac{\textit{Tier 1 Capital + Tier 2 Capital}}{\textit{Risk-Weighted Assets}}$$

With the Basel I risk-based standard, risk weights were assigned to different categories of assets and counterparties. There were four main categories of risk-weights: 0%, 20%, 50%, and 100%. A fifth category is discussed in Chapter 2.6. Cash and U.S. government securities were given a zero risk weight because they are considered to have no default risk; municipal securities, federal agency securities, and exposures to banks and certain broker-dealers were given a 20% risk weight; loans secured by first liens on residential real estate were assigned a 50% risk weight; and other assets, including most consumer and corporate loans, were given a risk weight of 100%. In addition, credit equivalencies were assigned to off-balance sheet exposures, which were risk weighted and added to the risk-adjusted assets on the balance sheet to arrive at total risk-weighted assets against which certain levels of capital must be held. The more complex the on- and off-balance sheet activities of a bank, the more complex the computation of its risk-based capital.

Under the U.S. implementation of the Basel I risk-based standard, all banks and BHCs were required to maintain tier 1 capital of at least 4% of risk-weighted assets. There was also a broader measure of capital, total capital, which combined tier 1 and tier 2 capital. Tier 2 capital primarily included subordinated debt, certain hybrid debt-equity capital instruments, and loss reserves of not more than 1.25% of risk-weighted assets. Banks and BHCs had to maintain total capital of at least 8% of risk-weighted assets.

The risk weights are applied to the exposure amounts for the purpose of calculating the amount of risk-weighted assets. For example, a bank holding $100 million of U.S. Treasury securities, which are risk-weighted at 0%, would recognize zero risk-weighted assets for that exposure and no capital would have to be held against that exposure. A bank holding $100 million of unsecured senior debt securities issued by Microsoft, which are risk-weighted at 100%, would recognize $100 million of risk-weighted assets for that exposure. In order to meet a minimum of 8% total risk-based capital requirement under Basel I, the bank would have to hold at least $8 million of total capital against the Microsoft exposure.

Let us try an exercise. Suppose Bank A has a CAMELS rating of one and the following assets: $200 million in cash and U.S. government securities, $400 million in net residential mortgages, and $800 million in net business and consumer loans. Bank A's capital accounts consist solely of $65 million in paid-in capital for common stock and earned surplus. Does the bank meet the leverage ratio capital requirements? If Bank A's balance sheet also included $15 million in the loan loss reserve account, does Bank A meet the risk-based capital requirements?

If Bank A sold off $200 million of commercial loans in participations, what effect would that transaction have on Bank A's capital requirements? What if Bank A agreed to buy back any of the loans that experience credit problems? What if Bank A agreed to buy back up to 50% of the loans sold? How about 5%? What if Bank A offers the purchasers of the loans standard representations and warranties as to the quality of the loans?

---

1. ***Why a 50% Risk Weighting for Mortgages?*** Residential mortgages were generally assigned a 50% risk weighting under Basel I. As a result, mortgages are required to be backed by only half of the capital under the Basel I risk-based capital requirements as compared to commercial and other consumer loans. Does that differential make sense? In answering this question, is it relevant that the representatives of the United States were pushing vigorously for a reduced risk-weighting for mortgages, recognizing the importance of home mortgages in various domestic constituencies?

2. ***Basel I and Agency Discretion.*** Other countries also brought domestic considerations to Basel I negotiations. For example, many countries pushed for the inclusion in the definition of capital forms of capital that had previously been accepted under their domestic laws. *See* DANIEL K. TARULLO, BANKING ON BASEL: THE FUTURE OF INTERNATIONAL FINANCIAL REGULATION 51–52 (2008). Many of the compromises negotiated in Basel I were then incorporated in U.S. regulations, promulgated under the APA. Under the terms of the International Supervision Lending Act of 1983, bank regulators were and are authorized to adopt minimum capital standards using such "methods as the appropriate banking agency deems appropriate." 12 U.S.C. § 3907. Elsewhere, the International Supervision Lending Act of 1983 specifies that the "Federal banking agencies shall consult with the banking supervisory authorities of other countries to reach understandings aimed at achieving the adoption of effective and consistent supervisory policies and practices with respect to international lending." *Id.* § 3901(b). Did this statutory language provide federal authorities the authority to incorporate elements of the Basel I requirements that the agencies themselves would not have deemed appropriate in the absence of international horse-trading at the Basel Committee?

3. ***Fluctuating Asset Values and Mark-to-Market Accounting.*** Remember that capital is not an asset or the market value of a bank or BHC's outstanding shares of stock. Rather, it is a regulatory concept designed to measure a bank's loss-absorbing capacity. It includes equity, which is, generally speaking, the difference between a bank or BHC's total assets and total liabilities, but also includes certain forms of subordinated debt, which is itself a liability on the balance sheet. A bank or BHC's capital level, as well as its capital ratios, will therefore fluctuate with the value of its assets, and one of the major challenges of measuring capital levels is accounting for these fluctuations. In some instances, a bank or BHC's financial assets are routinely traded in public markets and the market prices of these assets could be used to adjust asset values. This practice is known as mark-to-market accounting, or sometimes fair value accounting. There is a presumption under financial accounting standards in favor of using mark-to-market valuations when appropriate market valuations are available, although the accounting treatment of bank assets differs based on the type of asset and its intended use. For example, loans and leases that are held for investment, as opposed to for sale, are subject to historical cost accounting, under which the asset is generally valued at its original cost. In contrast, trading assets are subject to mark-to-market accounting. The advantage of mark-to-market accounting is that it incorporates market information into accounting valuations and financial statements. Critics have argued that mark-to-market valuation can be procyclical in times of financial stress, like during the Financial

Crisis, reducing capital levels of banks or BHCs in downturns, thereby constraining the availability of credit at just the wrong time. Others contend "that the claim that fair-value accounting exacerbated the [Financial Crisis] is largely unfounded . . . imply[ing] that the case for loosening the existing fair-value accounting rules is weak." Christian Laux & Christian Leuz, *Did Fair-Value Accounting Contribute to the Financial Crisis?*, 24 J. ECON. PERSPS. 93 (2010). Should financial regulators resist mark-to-market accounting in general or at least waive its application in times of financial distress?

4. ***Monitoring Market Valuations of Capital Instruments Issued by Financial Institutions.*** The use of mark-to-market valuations has not been limited to the realm of accounting. For example, in 2001, the Shadow Financial Regulatory Committee, an independent committee sponsored by the American Enterprise Institute, advocated for a market-based approach to capital regulation by requiring banks to "back their assets with a certain minimum percentage of long-term uninsured subordinated debt." Shadow Fin. Reg. Comm., *Statement of the Shadow Financial Regulatory Committee on The Basel Committee's Revised Capital Accord Proposal* 6 (Feb. 26, 2001). The motivating idea behind this requirement was that "[t]he yields on such debt would signal to banks how much risk the market is willing to tolerate, and to regulators when to intervene and prevent banks from taking additional risks." *Id.* More recently, Professors Oliver Hart and Luigi Zingales have documented the use of mark-to-market valuations to assess the financial viability of credit default swaps. *See* Oliver Hart & Luigi Zingales, *A New Capital Regulation for Large Financial Institutions*, 13 AM. L. ECON. REV. 453, 456 (2011) ("In our mechanism, when the [credit default swap] price rises above a critical threshold the [large financial institution] can issue equity to bring it down. If this effort fails . . . the regulator intervenes."). As mentioned above, the use of mark-to-market valuations is subject to the criticism that it is procyclical and may lead to lower capital in times of financial distress. Will market signals in capital instruments help regulators assess the strength of a financial institution? We will take up this issue again when we discuss bail in bonds in Chapter 9.3.

5. ***Allowance for Loan and Lease Losses (ALLL) Reserves.*** Market values are not readily available for the bulk of a bank or BHC's assets, including many commercial and consumer loans. The primary accounting mechanism for valuation adjustments of these assets is the creation of ALLL reserves, a contra-asset that reduces the total value of loans and leases on a bank or BHC's balance sheet by estimated losses. Traditionally, bank regulators have preferred that ALLLs reflect expected loan losses based on forecasted future events to safeguard bank and BHC solvency, while the SEC has preferred ALLL to reflect loan losses probably incurred based on events up to the present to safeguard transparency to investors. Accounting standards in the United States have long been based upon an incurred loss principle. The SEC's primary concern has been the potential for ALLL to be manipulated to smooth earnings and mislead investors. In 1998, in order to move forward with an acquisition, Suntrust voluntarily restated its earnings, driven by a reduction in ALLL, for three years at the behest of the SEC, which prompted other financial institutions to limit their ALLLs in line with the incurred-cost approach. Academic commentators have expressed concern that this approach may have allowed financial institutions to defer the

recognition of losses on some loans during the Financial Crisis. *See, e.g.*, Paul J. Beck & Ganapathi S. Narayanamoorthy, *Did the SEC Impact Banks' Loan Loss Reserve Policies and Their Informativeness?*, 56 J. ACCT. & ECON. 42, 42 (2013); Vicki Been, Howell Jackson & Mark Willis, *Sticky Seconds—The Problems Second Liens Pose to the Resolution of Distressed Mortgages*, 9 N.Y.U. J. L. & BUS. 71, 102–04 (2012). Reform of U.S. accounting standards to change ALLL an expected-loss approach is expected to be put into place by the Financial Accounting Standards Board (FASB) during 2016. *FASB Now Expects Final CECL Rule in 2016*, ALLL SAGEWORKS, Oct. 14, 2015. Are the two approaches to ALLL mutually exclusive or could ALLL be used to promote both bank solvency and transparency?

II. PROMPT CORRECTIVE ACTION

There was a trend towards imposing higher capital requirements on depository institutions and financial conglomerates during the 1980s. At the same time, there was a trend towards linking supervisory standards to capital levels. The Federal Deposit Insurance Corporation Improvement Act of 1991 (FDICIA) was the apotheosis of these trends with its creation of capital-based prompt corrective action. As explained by Professor Richard Carnell, a key Senate staffer at the time FDICIA was enacted, the reforms established a new system of supervision based, in the first instance, on capital levels:

> FDICIA established a system of capital-based prompt corrective action (also known as "early intervention"), codified in section 38 of the [FDIA]. . . . This system classifies insured depository institutions into five categories according to their capital: well-capitalized; adequately capitalized; under-capitalized; significantly undercapitalized; and critically undercapitalized.
>
> An institution falling below minimum capital standards faces progressively more stringent regulatory restrictions and requirements. The goal is to correct problems before they metastasize, and in any event before they cause losses to the [DIF]. Thus, for example, no institution can pay a dividend that would render it undercapitalized. An undercapitalized institution faces limits on asset growth and must submit a plan for restoring its capital. A significantly undercapitalized institution must normally recapitalize by selling stock or subordinated debt. A critically undercapitalized institution faces conservatorship or receivership.

Richard Scott Carnell, *A Partial Antidote to Perverse Incentives: The FDIC Improvement Act of 1991*, 12 ANN. REV. BANKING 317, 327–28 (1993).

The capital-based approach of the FDICIA era is best known for the interventions that prompt corrective action authorized and, in certain cases, strongly encouraged regulatory authorities to impose on financial institutions that fell beneath required capital levels. The system also included regulatory carrots for firms that met or exceeded capital requirements. For example, an FDIC-insured bank is not permitted to accept brokered deposits unless the bank is well-capitalized. *See* 12 U.S.C. § 1831f. In addition, the ability of a state-chartered bank to engage as principal in activities beyond those permitted to national banks is constrained, among other things, by a requirement that the bank comply with applicable capital standards. *Id.* Both of these provisions were adopted by the FDICIA. Later in the decade, when Congress substantially expanded the list of authorized activities for BHCs, the liberalization was limited to firms that were both well-capitalized—that is, exceeded capital requirements by a specified amount—and well-managed. *See* 12 U.S.C. § 1843(l)(1). The rules governing holding company powers are explored in Chapter 6.1.

Prompt corrective action was thought, at the time of FDICIA's adoption, to represent an important regulatory innovation. The following two excerpts are from Government Accountability Office (GAO) reports from 2007 and 2011, which offer retrospective reviews of the efficacy of prompt corrective action in the United States.

GAO, Deposit Insurance: Assessment of Regulators' Use of Prompt Corrective Action Provisions

GAO-07-242 (Feb. 2007)

With the failure of more than 2,900 federally insured banks and thrifts in the 1980s and early 1990s, federal regulators were criticized for failing to take timely and forceful action to address the causes of these failures and prevent losses to the [DIF] and taxpayers. In response to the federal banking regulators' failure to take appropriate action, Congress passed the [FDICIA], implementing significant changes to the way banking regulators supervise the nation's depository institutions. FDICIA created two new sections in the [FDIA]—sections 38 and 39—that required the federal banking regulators to create a two-part framework to supplement their existing supervisory authority to address capital deficiencies and unsafe or unsound conduct, practices, or conditions. The addition of sections 38 and 39 to FDIA were intended to improve the ability of regulators to identify and promptly address deficiencies at an institution to better safeguard the [DIF]. Specifically, section 38 requires regulators to classify depository institutions into one of five capital categories based on their level of capital—well capitalized, adequately capitalized, undercapitalized, significantly undercapitalized, and critically undercapitalized—and take increasingly severe actions, known as [prompt corrective action], as an institution's capital deteriorates. Section 38 primarily focuses on capital as an indicator of trouble, thus the supervisory actions authorized under it are almost exclusively designed to address an institution's deteriorating capital level (for example, requiring undercapitalized institutions to implement capital restoration plans). However, section 38 also authorizes noncapital supervisory actions (for example, removing officers and directors or downgrading an institution's capital level). Section 39 required the banking regulators to prescribe safety and soundness standards related to noncapital criteria, including operations and management; compensation; and asset quality, earnings, and stock valuation, and allows the regulators to take action if an institution fails to meet one or more of these standards. . . .

Since the enactment of FDICIA, the financial condition of federally insured depository institutions generally has been strong and regulators have increased their presence at banks and thrifts. Net income and total assets exceeded $133 billion and $10 trillion, respectively, in 2005, and the industry's two primary indicators of profitability—returns on assets and equity—remained near highs at the end of 2005. In this strong economic environment, the percentage of well-capitalized institutions steadily has increased from 94 percent in 1992, the year regulators implemented FDICIA, to just over 99 percent in 2005, while the percentage of well-capitalized institutions with capital in excess of the well-capitalized minimum increased from 84 percent in 1992 to 94 percent in 2005. Over the period, the number of institutions in undercapitalized and lower capital categories experienced a corresponding decline from 1,235 in 1992 to 14 in 2005, and the number of failed institutions also fell dramatically. In addition to requiring regulators to take prompt corrective action against institutions that fail to meet minimum capital requirements, FDICIA also required examiners to conduct annual, on-site examinations at all federally insured banks and thrifts to improve their ability to identify and address problems in a more timely manner. Although we did not evaluate the regulators' timeliness in conducting examinations, regulatory data show that the average time between examinations fell from a high of 609 days in 1986 to 373 in 1992. Based on information we obtained from all four regulators, the average interval between examinations for all institutions generally has remained from 12 to 18 months since 1993 (the year after FDICIA requirements were implemented) and in many instances, has been even shorter, especially for problem institutions (those with composite CAMELS ratings of 4 or 5).[1]

For the sample of 18 banks and thrifts that were subject to [prompt corrective action], we found that regulators generally implemented [prompt corrective action] in accordance with section 38, consistent with findings in our 1996 report. For example, regulators identified when each of the institutions failed to meet minimum capital requirements, required these institutions to implement capital restoration plans or corrective actions outlined in enforcement orders, and took steps to close or require the sale or merger of those institutions that were unable to adequately recapitalize. Fifteen of the 18 institutions in our sample remain open or were merged into other institutions or closed without causing losses to the [DIF], and 3 failed causing losses, one of which was a material loss (that is, a loss exceeding $25 million or 2 percent of an institution's assets, whichever is greater). Although regulators appeared to have used [prompt corrective action] appropriately, capital is a lagging indicator and thus not necessarily a timely predictor of problems at banks and thrifts. All four regulators generally agreed that by design, [prompt corrective action] is not a tool that can be used upon early recognition of a bank or thrift's troubled status. In most cases we reviewed, regulators had responded to safety and soundness problems in advance of a bank or thrift's decline in [prompt corrective action] capital category. For example, each of the 18 institutions subject to [prompt corrective action] appeared on one or more regulatory watch lists prior to or concurrent with experiencing a decline in its capital category, and a majority of the 18 institutions had at least one enforcement action in place prior to becoming undercapitalized. Finally, the inspectors general [] of the federal banking agencies found that in 12 of 14 cases where regulators used [prompt corrective action] to resolve capital problems at an institution that failed with material losses, the regulators' use of [prompt corrective action] was appropriate. In two cases, the [inspectors general] found that the regulator could have used [prompt corrective action] sooner than it did. . . .

Based on a sample of cases, we found that regulators generally acted appropriately to address problems at institutions that failed to meet minimum capital requirements by taking increasingly severe enforcement actions as these institutions' capital deteriorated, as required by section 38.

---

[1] At each examination, examiners assign a supervisory CAMELS rating, which assesses six components of an institution's financial health: capital, asset quality, management, earnings, liquidity, and sensitivity to market risk. An institution's CAMELS rating is known directly only by the institution's senior management and appropriate regulatory staff. Regulators never publicly release CAMELS ratings, even on a lagged basis.

GAO, Bank Regulation: Modified Prompt Corrective Action Framework Would Improve Effectiveness

GAO-11-612 (June 2011)

After the savings and loan crisis, federal regulators were criticized for failing to take timely and forceful action to address the causes of bank failures and prevent losses to taxpayers and the [DIF]. In response, Congress passed the [FDICIA], which made significant changes to the [FDIA]. In particular, FDICIA created sections 38 and 39 of FDIA to improve the ability of regulators to identify and promptly address deficiencies at depository institutions—banks and thrifts—and better safeguard and minimize losses to the DIF. . . .

Before 2007, [prompt corrective action] was largely untested by a financial crisis that resulted in a large number of bank failures. After the passage of FDICIA, sustained growth in the U.S. economy meant that the financial condition of banks was generally strong. For instance, as a result of positive economic conditions, the number of bank failures declined from 180 in 1992 to 4 in 2004. And from June 2004 through January 2007, no banks failed.

Since 2007, failures have increased significantly. In 2010, 157 banks failed, the most in a single year since the savings and loan crisis of the 1980s and 1990s. The 157 banks had combined assets of approximately $93 billion, costing the DIF an estimated $24 billion. Overall, more than 300 banks have failed since the current financial crisis began in 2007, at an estimated cost of almost $60 billion to the DIF to cover losses to insured depositors. During this time, the balance of the DIF has declined dramatically, becoming negative in 2009. As of December 31, 2010, the DIF had a negative balance of $7.4 billion. . . .

The number and size of failures during the recent financial crisis have raised questions about the ability of [prompt corrective action] to help turn around troubled banks and minimize losses to the DIF. Section 202(g) of the [Dodd-Frank Act] requires GAO to study the federal regulators' use of [prompt corrective action] and report our findings to the Financial Stability Oversight Council [(FSOC)]. . . .

To examine the extent to which various regulatory activities and enforcement actions, including [prompt corrective action], detected and addressed troubled banks, we examined the type and timing of regulatory actions across the oversight cycle. This work encompassed analyzing the extent to which existing regulatory steps provided warning of likely bank deterioration or failure. Specifically, we reviewed off-site monitoring tools and examined if these tools provided effective warnings of bank distress. For all bank failures that occurred from the first quarter of 2006 through the third quarter of 2010, we also reviewed formal and informal enforcement actions in the 2-year period before a bank failed to identify the earliest enforcement action taken in relation to other regulatory milestones associated with financial deterioration. We also reviewed the timing and nature of [prompt corrective action] enforcement actions in relation to bank failure. . . .

As the recent financial turmoil unfolded, the number of banks that fell below one of the three lowest [prompt corrective action] capital thresholds—undercapitalized, significantly undercapitalized, or critically undercapitalized—increased dramatically. All four regulators told us that [prompt corrective action] was not designed for the type of precipitous economic decline that occurred in 2007 and 2008. . . . [T]he total number of banks in undercapitalized and lower capital categories averaged fewer than 10 per quarter in 2006 and 2007, whereas the total averaged approximately 132 from 2008 through the third quarter of 2010.

The number of banks that entered the [prompt corrective action] process for the first time each quarter also increased dramatically. In 2006 and 2007, the number of banks newly entering undercapitalized or lower capital categories averaged fewer than 5 per quarter, compared with an average of 48 from 2008 through the third quarter of 2010. . . .

The vast majority of banks that underwent the [prompt corrective action] process from 2006 through the third quarter of 2010 had not returned to a condition of financial stability by the end of this period. As shown in figure 8, of the 569 banks that fell into the undercapitalized or lower capital categories of [prompt corrective action], 270 failed. Another 25 banks failed without first being identified as falling into the undercapitalized or lower capital categories of [prompt corrective action], bringing total bank failures to 295 during this period. Banking regulators told us that because of the sharp economic downturn in 2008, banks could deteriorate more rapidly than [prompt corrective action] was designed to handle. For example, nearly half failed after being undercapitalized for two or fewer quarters. In addition, three regulators told us that early in the economic turmoil, banks that encountered sudden liquidity problems often did not trigger the [prompt corrective action] process before failure.

Figure 8. Failures and Nonfailures of Banks That Underwent the Prompt Corrective Action Process, First Quarter 2006–Third Quarter 2010

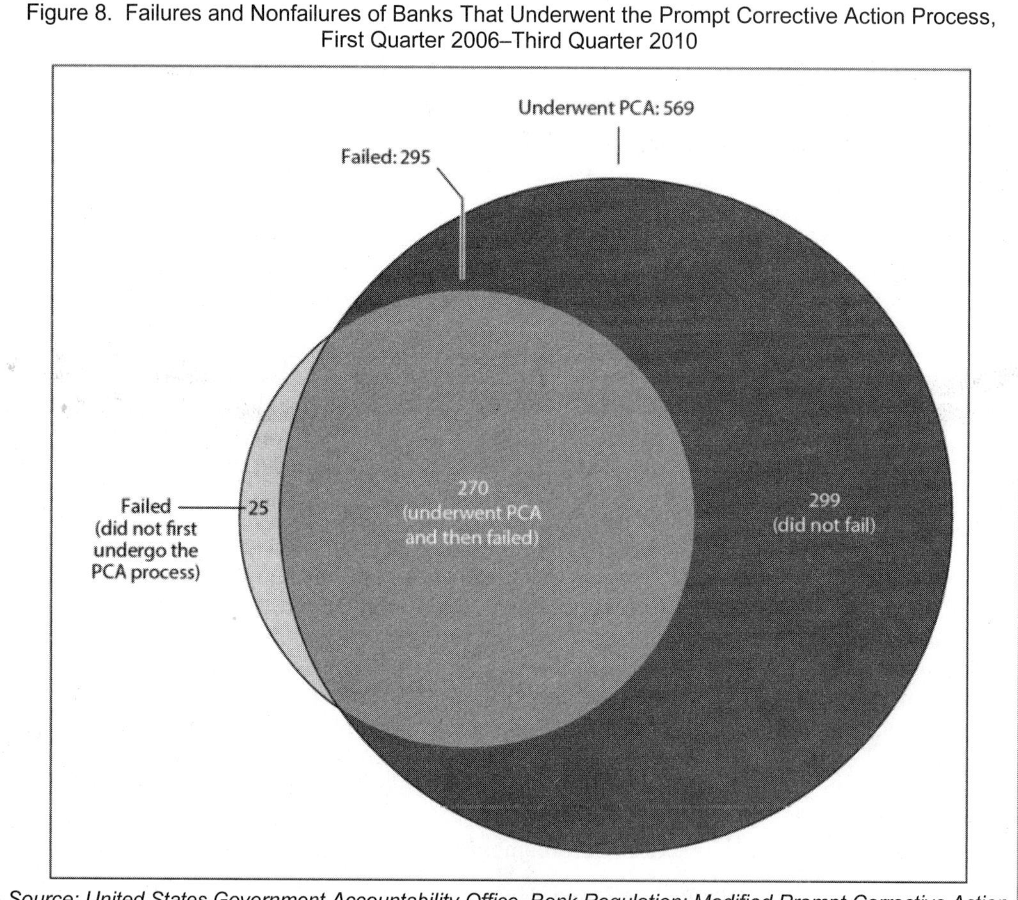

Source: United States Government Accountability Office, Bank Regulation: Modified Prompt Corrective Action Framework Would Improve Effectiveness, GAO-11-612, 18 (June 2011).

Although the remaining banks that underwent the [prompt corrective action] process did not fail, most of them continue to struggle financially. Specifically, 299 of the 569 banks that underwent the [prompt corrective action] process did not fail during the period of analysis. Of these 299 banks, 223 remained undercapitalized or on the problem bank list through the third quarter of 2010. . . . According to regulators and industry representatives, the large number of troubled banks may be due to sustained economic weakness during the period of analysis, which likely has hindered the ability of these banks to raise additional capital. Another 46 of the 299 undercapitalized banks were dissolved with minimal or no losses to the DIF. And the remaining 30 banks remained open and were neither undercapitalized nor on the problem bank list at the end of the period. . . .

Weaknesses in the current [prompt corrective action] framework stem primarily from tying mandatory corrective actions to only capital-based indicators. We and others have argued since 1991 that capital-based indicators have weaknesses, particularly because they do not provide timely warnings of bank distress. A number of alternative indicators exist or could be developed, and their advantages derive primarily from the early warnings of distress they could provide. In particular, a composite indicator can integrate information from a number of noncapital indicators in a single number. Regulators have stressed that the effectiveness of the [prompt corrective action] framework depended on making early and forceful use of other enforcement tools. However, while regulators have their own authorities and [prompt corrective action] also authorizes other discretionary actions, the regulators have not used these enforcement tools consistently. Tying mandatory corrective actions to additional indicators could mitigate these current weaknesses of [prompt corrective action] and increase the consistency with which distressed banks would be treated. And, enhancing the [prompt corrective action] framework in such a way would allow both regulators and banks more time to address deteriorating conditions. More important, banks facing such corrective actions likely would not be in as weakened a condition as typically is the case when current capital thresholds are triggered. Thus, the banks might have more options available to them to bolster their safety and soundness and avoid failure. Moreover, without an additional [prompt corrective action] trigger, the regulators risk not acting soon enough to address a bank's deteriorating condition, thereby limiting their ability to minimize losses to the DIF.

Expert stakeholders we surveyed also called for modifications to the [prompt corrective action] framework and identified several options for doing so. The top three options they identified include (1) adding a measure of risk to the capital category thresholds; (2) increasing the capital ratios that place banks into [prompt corrective action] capital categories and (3) adding an additional trigger. As the expert stakeholders noted and we also recognize, making any changes to the [prompt corrective action] framework would entail some trade-offs. Specifically, regulators would have to strike a balance between more corrective actions and unnecessary intervention in healthy banks. The [FSOC] could provide a forum for vetting changes to the [prompt corrective action] framework and proposing these changes to Congress. Building consensus for potential changes, including working through the details of the changes and the associated trade-offs, will not be easy. But, in light of significant losses to the DIF in recent years, including at banks that underwent the [prompt corrective action] process, changes to the [prompt corrective action] framework are warranted.

---

1. ***The GAO's Shift in Perspective.*** In its 2007 report, the GAO expressed optimism about the effectiveness of prompt corrective action, finding that "regulators generally acted appropriately to address problems at institutions that failed to meet minimum capital requirements by taking increasingly severe enforcement actions as these institutions' capital deteriorated." Post-Financial Crisis, the GAO sounded a more pessimistic note in its 2011 report, observing that "[t]he number and size of failures during the recent financial crisis have raised questions about the ability of [prompt corrective action] to help turn around troubled banks." The GAO also noted, however, that "[w]e and others have argued since 1991 that capital-based indicators have weaknesses, particularly because they do not provide timely warnings of bank distress." Is the GAO only covering its bases, or did its earlier report foresee the problems

with prompt corrective action? The GAO did state, however, in its 2007 report that "[a]lthough regulators appeared to have used [prompt corrective action] appropriately, capital is a lagging indicator and thus not necessarily a timely predictor of problems at banks and thrifts." This cautionary statement was embedded in a larger success story about the effective use of prompt corrective action by regulators.

The timing of the GAO's shift in perspective also raises another question: how much time do regulators and policymakers need to assess the effectiveness of capital regulation? According to the GAO, it had spotted potential issues with prompt corrective action since at least 1991, 17 years before the Financial Crisis. If nearly two decades is not a sufficient time frame on which to evaluate a capital regulatory scheme such as prompt corrective action, what would be a sufficient time frame? Might one argue that, due to the cyclical but occasional nature of financial crises, a longer time frame for evaluation is needed?

2. ***Basel Core Principles and the International Monetary Fund's (IMF) Financial Sector Stability Assessment of Japan.*** Although the efficacy of prompt corrective action has been called into question in the United States, the regulatory strategy was incorporated into the Basel Committee's Core Principles for Effective Banking Supervision in 1997:

> Principle 22: Banking supervisors must have at their disposal adequate supervisory measures to bring about timely corrective action when banks fail to meet prudential requirements (such as minimum capital adequacy ratios), when there are regulatory violations, or where depositors are threatened in any other way. In extreme circumstances, this should include the ability to revoke the banking licence or recommend its revocation.

BASEL COMM., CORE PRINCIPLES FOR EFFECTIVE BANKING SUPERVISION 38 (Sept. 1997). These Core Principles are used to assess the quality of financial supervision of other countries around the world. For example, Japan's Financial Supervisory Authority was criticized by the IMF in its 2012 Financial Sector Stability Assessment of Japan. According to the IMF, Japan's Financial Supervisory Authority had set its prompt corrective action triggers "too low" and insufficiently deployed more direct and aggressive supervisory tools, such as prudential limits. *See* INT'L MONETARY FUND, FINANCIAL SECTOR ASSESSMENT PROGRAM: JAPAN 97 (Aug. 2012) ("[Prompt corrective action] triggers are currently set too low . . . Intervention efforts of [Japan's Financial Supervisory Authority] could be further enhanced through the greater use of more direct supervisory tools such as its powers to directly impose prudential limits, thresholds on banks or across the banking sector, which were seldom or never used."). Prompt corrective action was incorporated into the Basel Committee's Core Principles largely as a result of the FDICIA reforms of the United States in 1991. Is it appropriate for the IMF to criticize other jurisdictions for failing to maintain effective prompt corrective action standards now that the approach's efficacy has been called into question in the United States? Or does prompt corrective action remain an appropriate standard for supervisory authorities around the world?

CHAPTER 2.6

CAPITAL REGULATION: PRE-FINANCIAL CRISIS TO BASEL II

CONTENTS

I. INTRODUCTION

The introduction of standardized capital requirements in Basel I was the first major success for international regulatory cooperation. Basel I established a widely followed set of minimum guidelines that in many ways are still used today. By the late 1990s, however, Basel I had attracted a fair amount of criticism, and regulators and the banking sector soon started meeting again to revise Basel I, eventually paving the way for a revised capital accord known as Basel II, the guidelines for which were published by the Basel Committee in 2004. Basel II was never fully implemented in the United States, although in April 2008, 12 of the largest banking organizations began the transition process to Basel II. That transition was later replaced by Basel III.

In this Chapter, we begin by discussing why Basel I's shortcomings prompted Basel II. We then explore the process by which Basel II was developed, its characteristics, and how and why it was only partly implemented in the United States. We conclude this Chapter by describing the criticisms of Basel II and capital regulation generally that emerged as a result of the Financial Crisis, all of which led to the development of Basel III, which is discussed in Chapter 2.7.

II. BASEL I AND ITS SHORTCOMINGS

Basel I helped reduce the risk of an international regulatory race to the bottom in capital standards and it succeeded in raising capital levels globally from the then very low levels. Commentators, however, soon began to point out weaknesses in Basel I's methodology, arguing that Basel I's approach to risk weights was overly simplistic and could lead to regulatory arbitrage. Banks and bank holding companies (BHCs) argued that Basel I's risk-weighting was crude as compared to the more advanced models of risk that were developed by the banking sector by the mid-1990s as a result of the increasing sophistication of computer models. It is almost impossible to overstate the then widespread sense that the newly developed quantitative risk management and developments of value-at-risk models were major advances. To understand the critiques of Basel I at the time, it is necessary to regain that frame of mind. The Government Accountability Office (GAO) report below describes why Basel I's shortcomings prompted calls for a revised approach under Basel II.

GAO, Risk-Based Capital: Bank Regulators Need to Improve Transparency and Overcome Impediments to Finalizing the Proposed Basel II Framework

GAO-07-253 (Feb. 2007)

Basel I Is a Simple Framework with Broad Risk Categories That Is Inadequate for Large Banking Organizations

When established internationally in 1988, Basel I represented a major step forward in linking capital to risks taken by banking organizations, strengthening banks' capital positions, and reducing competitive inequality among international banks. Regulatory officials have noted that Basel I continues to be an adequate capital framework for most banks, but its limitations make it increasingly inadequate for the largest and most internationally active banks. As implemented in the United States, Basel I consists of five broad credit risk categories, or risk weights. Banks must hold total capital equal to at least 8 percent of the total value of their risk-weighted assets and tier 1 capital of at least 4 percent. All assets are assigned a risk weight according to the credit risk of the obligor and the nature of any qualifying collateral or guarantee, where relevant. Off-balance sheet items, such as credit derivatives and loan commitments, are converted into credit equivalent amounts and also assigned risk weights. The risk categories are broadly intended to assign higher risk weights to—and require banks to hold more capital for—higher risk assets.

U.S. Basel I Credit Risk Categories	
Risk Weight	**Major Assets**
0%	Cash; claims on or guaranteed by central banks of Organization for Economic Cooperation and Development [(OECD)] countries; claims on or guaranteed by [OECD] central governments and U.S. government agencies. The zero weight reflects the lack of credit risk associated with such positions.
20%	Claims on banks in [OECD] countries, obligations of government-sponsored enterprises, or cash items in the process of collection.
50%	Most one-to-four family residential mortgages; certain privately issued mortgage-backed securities and municipal revenue bonds.
100%	Represents the presumed bulk of the assets of commercial banks. It includes commercial loans, claims on non-[OECD] central governments, real assets, certain one-to-four family residential mortgages not meeting prudent underwriting standards, and some multifamily residential mortgages.
200%	Asset-backed and mortgage-backed securities and other on-balance sheet positions in asset securitizations that are rated one category below investment grade.

However, Basel I's risk-weighting approach does not measure an asset's level of risk with a high degree of accuracy, and the few broad categories available do not adequately distinguish among assets within a category that have varying levels of risk. For example, although commercial loans can vary widely in their levels of credit risk, Basel I assigns the same 100 percent risk weight to all these loans. Such limitations create incentives for banks to engage in regulatory capital arbitrage—behavior in which banks structure their activities to take advantage of limitations in the regulatory capital framework. By doing so, banks may be able to increase their risk exposure without making a commensurate increase in their capital requirements. For example, because Basel I does not recognize differences in credit quality among assets in the same category, banks may have incentives to take on high-risk, low-quality assets within each broad risk category. As a result, the Basel I regulatory capital measures may not accurately reflect banks' risk profiles, which erodes the principle of risk-based capital adequacy that the Basel Accord was designed to promote.

In addition, Basel I recognizes the important role of credit risk mitigation activities only to a limited extent. By reducing the credit risk of banks' exposures, techniques, such as the use of collateral, guarantees, and credit derivatives, play a significant role in sound risk management. However, many of these techniques are not recognized for regulatory capital purposes. For example, the U.S. Basel I framework recognizes collateral and guarantees in only a limited range of cases. It does not recognize many other forms of collateral and guarantees, such as investment grade corporate debt securities as collateral or guarantees by externally rated corporate entities. In addition, the Basel Committee acknowledged that Basel I may have discouraged the development of specific forms of credit risk mitigation by placing restrictions on both the type of hedges acceptable for achieving capital reduction and the amount of capital relief . . .

Furthermore, Basel I does not address all major risks faced by banking organizations, resulting in required capital that may not fully address the entirety of banks' risk profiles. Basel I originally focused on credit risk, a major source of risk for most banks, and was amended in 1996 to include market risk from trading activity. However, banks face many other significant risks—including interest rate, operational, liquidity, reputational, and strategic risks—which could cause unexpected losses for which banks should hold capital. For example, many banks have assumed increased operational risk profiles in recent years, and at some banks operational risk is the dominant risk.[1] Because minimum required capital under Basel I does not depend directly on these other types of risks, U.S. regulators use the supervisory review process to ensure that each bank holds capital above these minimums, at a level that is commensurate with its entire risk profile.

Basel I Does Not Reflect Financial Innovations and Risk Management Practices at Large Banking Organizations

The rapid rate of innovation in financial markets and the growing complexity of financial transactions have reduced the relevance of the Basel I risk framework, especially for large banking organizations. Banks are developing new types of financial transactions that do not fit well into the risk weights and credit conversion factors in the current standards. For example, there has been significant growth in securitization activity, which banks engaged in partly as regulatory arbitrage opportunities.[2] In order to respond to emerging risks associated with the growth in derivatives, securitization, and other off-balance sheet transactions, federal regulators have amended the risk-based capital framework numerous times since implementing Basel I in 1992. Some of these revisions have been international

[1] The Basel Committee defines operational risk as the risk of loss resulting from inadequate or failed internal processes, people, and systems or from external events, including legal risks, but excluding strategic and reputational risk. Examples of operational risks include fraud, legal settlements, systems failures, and business disruptions.

[2] Securitization is the process of pooling debt obligations and dividing that pool into portions (called tranches) that can be sold as securities in the secondary market. Banks can use securitization for regulatory arbitrage purposes by, for example, selling high-quality tranches of pooled credit exposures to third-party investors, while retaining a disproportionate amount of the lower-quality tranches and therefore, the underlying credit risk.

efforts, while others are specific to the United States. For example, in 1996, the United States and other Basel Committee members adopted the Market Risk Amendment, which requires capital for market risk exposures arising from banks' trading activities. By contrast, federal regulators amended the U.S. framework in 2001 to better address risk for asset securitizations. . .

Despite these amendments to the current framework, the simple risk-weighting approach of Basel I has not kept pace with more advanced risk measurement approaches at large banking organizations. By the late 1990s, some large banking organizations had begun developing economic capital models, which use quantitative methods to estimate the amount of capital required to support various elements of an organization's risks. Banks use economic capital models as tools to inform their management activities, including measuring risk-adjusted performance, setting pricing and limits on loans and other products, and allocating capital among various business lines and risks. Economic capital models measure risks by estimating the probability of potential losses over a specified period and up to a defined confidence level using historical loss data. This method has the potential for more meaningful risk measurement than the current regulatory framework, which differentiates risk only to a limited extent, mostly based on asset type rather than on an asset's underlying risk characteristics.

---

1. ***Regulatory Arbitrage and Increased Risk Taking.*** Because Basel I required the same amount of capital for all loans to borrowers within a specific risk-weight category, banks and BHCs could maximize profits and still comply with capital rules by selecting the riskiest borrowers within each category. By the same token, the banks and BHCs that lent predominantly to lower-risk borrowers within each category were not rewarded for their prudence in credit underwriting standards, and were required to hold as much capital as their riskier counterparts. Both the commentators who felt that Basel I incentivized banks and BHCs to invest in relatively riskier assets and the banks and BHCs that felt that they were required to hold an inordinate amount of capital pushed for a more sophisticated approach to the risk weightings of assets.

2. ***Portfolio Concentration.*** Critics also pointed out that Basel I failed to link a bank or BHC's capital requirements to its portfolio of loans as a whole. Recall the OCC excerpt on credit concentrations in Chapter 2.3. In principle, portfolio diversification, or lending to a wide variety of borrowers in different locales with different risk profiles, reduces the risk to the bank or BHC and should be reflected in lower capital requirement levels. Similarly, portfolio concentration ought to increase capital requirement levels. Basel I, however, did not take portfolio concentration or diversification into account.

3. ***Large Banking Organizations and Internal Models.*** The GAO report stated that Basel I may not be appropriate for large banking organizations in particular because they had developed increasingly sophisticated methods for assessing assets' risks since 1988. The late 1990s saw the influence of quantitative computer models, created and run by economics PhDs, in many elements of risk management at larger banking organizations. In the trading and markets area, value-at-risk models became the norm within large sophisticated banks and disclosure of them was required by the SEC in its Market Risk Disclosure Rule as of 1998. *See* 17 C.F.R. § 229.305. Of course, only the largest banking organizations, and the Federal Reserve Board, could afford to hire the necessary talent and to make the necessary investments in technology.

Remember the critique of Basel I with respect to larger and more sophisticated banking organizations as you read about Basel II and its implementation in the United States in the next section.

4. ***Market Risk Amendment.*** In 1996, the Basel Committee published a revision to Basel I, known as the Market Risk Amendment, which introduced a market risk capital charge. Under the Market Risk Amendment, banks and BHCs with significant trading assets were required to also measure market risk, the risk of loss from changes in market prices such as interest rates and stock prices, arising from their trading activities using internal models and reflect these risk exposures in their risk-weighted asset calculations. As a practical matter, only the largest BHCs, what we would today call global systemically important banks, had significant trading assets. Then-Professor Daniel Tarullo writes,

> the 1996 amendment to incorporate market risk reflected an important departure in the committee's substantive approach to capital regulation, one that emerged from a process unlike that which had produced the original accord. In both respects, the market risk amendment foreshadowed Basel II. As to substance, in addressing market risk, the committee extended its reach beyond credit risk for the first time. Moreover, the amendment provided for the calculation of capital charges for market risk using the internal value-at-risk models employed by financial institutions, though only within certain parameters set by the supervisors. As to process, the committee engaged in a multi-year exercise that involved significant interaction with internationally active banks.

DANIEL K. TARULLO, BANKING ON BASEL: THE FUTURE OF FINANCIAL REGULATION 61 (2008). The practical impact of the Market Risk Amendment was to lower risk-weights for high-rated and liquid trading assets.

5. ***200% Risk Weight.*** You may have noticed that Chapter 2.5 stated that there were four main credit risk categories under Basel I, but the figure in the GAO excerpt above shows five U.S. Basel I credit risk categories. In 2001, U.S. banking regulators added a 200% risk weight category for asset-backed or mortgage-backed securities that had a credit rating of BB in an attempt to address regulatory arbitrage via securitization. Through securitization, a bank or BHC could retain most of a pool of assets' credit risk by retaining a securitization vehicle's riskiest tranches, but reduce the capital it must hold against this risk by selling the higher quality tranches to investors. With the added risk category, banks and BHCs that retained BB-rated tranches of a securitization vehicle were required to hold more capital against the retained securities than previously required. Although the issue of regulatory arbitrage via securitization would persist, the use of credit rating agency assessments foreshadowed elements of Basel II.

III. BASEL II OVERVIEW

The process of moving from Basel I to Basel II was long and involved multi-layered negotiations. Beginning in the mid-1990s, banking regulators in the developed financial centers and the banking sector began calling for significant improvements to Basel I. At the Conference on Capital Regulation in the 21st Century in February 1998, Federal Reserve Board Chairman Alan Greenspan captured the mood of the times when he warned,

> we must . . . take note that observers both within the regulatory agencies and the banking industry itself are raising warning flags about the current standard. These concerns pertain to the rapid technological, financial, and institutional changes that are rendering the regulatory capital framework less effectual, if not on the verge of becoming outmoded, with respect to our largest, most complex banking organizations. In particular, it is argued that the heightened complexity of these large banks' risk-taking activities, along with the expanding scope of regulatory capital arbitrage, may cause capital ratios as calculated under the existing rules to become increasingly misleading.

Alan Greenspan, The Role of Capital in Optimal Banking Supervision and Regulation, Remarks before the Conference on Capital Regulation in the 21st Century (Feb. 26, 1998).

Federal Reserve Bank of New York President William McDonough became chair of the Basel Committee soon after Greenspan's remarks, and, in September 1998, McDonough announced, with the backing of the EU financial regulators and the Federal Reserve Board, that the Basel Committee would revise Basel I, spurring the Basel II process. The Basel Committee did not release final Basel II guidance until 2004, however. Unlike many lengthy international negotiations, the Basel II process was not drawn out because of the inactivity of the Basel Committee or its member countries' regulators. The Basel II process included multiple consultations, many regulatory working groups, numerous studies, and hundreds of comment letters. It is safe to say that many economics and math PhDs, both within the banking organizations and within the regulators, spent nearly a decade tinkering with the models.

The negotiations among the many different national regulators were also more complex than they had been in the 1980s. After the Basel Committee released Basel II, but before it had been implemented in the United States, Federal Reserve Governor Susan Bies commented that,

> [s]ome might bemoan [Basel II's] long formative period, but we must all remember that an international undertaking of this magnitude takes substantial time to complete. Part of the reason for the long gestation period is that we have been purposely transparent about the proposals, taken substantial time to listen to industry and other public comments, and worked diligently to make the framework better in response to those comments. In addition, this is an international agreement for which a certain 'common denominator' had to be found to accommodate the variety of banking and financial systems involved.

Susan Bies, Basel II Developments in the United States, Remarks before the Institute of International Bankers (Sept. 26, 2005).

The Basel Committee released its first consultation in 1999 and received over 200 comments in response, primarily from the banking sector. The first consultation's innovation to measuring credit risk was to use external credit ratings, such as those from Moody's or Standard & Poor's, in assigning assets' risk weights. The first consultation's proposal was criticized for being too simplistic, however, and large banks and BHCs, in particular, advocated for being allowed to use their own internal models to determine assets' risk weights. In response, the Basel Committee

> expanded the number of working groups, task forces, and subgroups to address some of the concerns that had been expressed during the initial comment periods. At one time or another, there [were] no fewer than 20 of these sub-committees, conducting studies and writing papers on one aspect or another of [Basel II].

John D. Hawke, Jr., Remarks Before the Risk Management Association's Capital Management Conference: The Road to Basel II: Good Intentions and Imposing Challenges (June 6, 2002). The Basel Committee released its second consultation, which, together with supporting documents, was 541 pages long, in 2001. Although the more complex second consultation embraced the use of internal risk models to assign risk weights, it also prompted criticism, resulting in 259 comments; the Basel Committee received an additional 187 comments on a third consultation released in 2003. Each stage of the process resulted in major substantive changes to Basel II.

The Basel II process was long not only because the Basel Committee had to determine the right rules (*i.e.*, those rules that would most successfully promote banking sector safety and soundness and international regulatory harmony), but it also had to navigate the domestic and international political waters. The United States was represented on the Basel Committee by regulators, not elected officials, raising questions of democratic accountability. In fact, as is the case for Federal Reserve Bank of New York officials, some of the U.S. Basel Committee representatives may not even be members of the executive branch. Nonetheless, members of Congress did not idly stand by while the Basel Committee debated Basel II and later while U.S. regulators proposed and adopted rules implementing Basel II in the United States. Indeed, members of Congress put pressure on U.S. regulators over the Basel Committee's deliberations. For example, at a House Committee on Financial Services hearing in 2003 featuring testimony from Federal Reserve Board, OCC, and FDIC officials on Basel II, members of Congress expressed concerns over Basel II's complexity, potential unintended consequences, and impact on competitive equality.

In addition, there were disagreements amongst the U.S. regulators during the long Basel II gestation. In particular, the FDIC worried that Basel II would leave large U.S. banking organizations with too little capital. The Basel Committee overcame these pressures and disagreements and agreed on a final Basel II capital accord in June 2004. It was an unwelcome surprise to many EU regulators, who relatively promptly implemented Basel II in their own countries, when the U.S. banking regulators, especially the Federal Reserve Board, which had led many of the consultations at the Basel level, then decided to slow walk the implementation of Basel II in the United States and to apply Basel II only to a very small group of internationally active banks and BHCs. As the United

States slowly began the process of implementing Basel II between 2004 and 2008, it applied only to 12 internationally active banking organizations that started their transition process in April 2008. It did not apply to the vast majority of U.S. banks and BHCs.

The following excerpts provide an overview of Basel II. First, European Central Bank President Jean-Claude Tritchet's remarks upon Basel II's release show what a major accomplishment it was. In particular, the use of internal models was a significant change to capital regulation. As you read about Basel II, it is important to remember that this approach to capital regulation was influenced by a genuine desire to work with the private sector to design more creative and effective policies, which included delegating regulation to private parties under certain circumstances. *See* IAN AYRES & JOHN BRAITHWAITE, RESPONSIVE REGULATION: TRANSCENDING THE DEREGULATION DEBATE (1992).

Second, the GAO report and notes below discuss the different facets of Basel II, especially its implementation in the United States, which differed from its implementation elsewhere in meaningful ways, in more depth. To foreshadow this Chapter's next section, note the date of the GAO report.

President Jean-Claude Tritchet, European Central Bank, Announcement of Basel II

June 2004

This work, which was conducted by the [Basel Committee], represents a landmark achievement. In particular, its comprehensive approach to risk management and bank supervision ensures that capital regulation will remain a cornerstone of safety and soundness for banking in the twenty-first century. In the same vein, Basel II will enhance banks' safety and soundness, thereby strengthening the stability of the financial system as a whole. That, in turn, will improve the ability of the financial sector to serve as a source of sustainable growth for the broader economy. I am pleased to offer this revised framework to the international community.

Today marks the culmination of nearly six years of challenging work. During those years, the Basel Committee sought to develop significantly more risk-sensitive capital requirements that are conceptually sound. At the same time, the [Basel] Committee wanted to be sensitive to the characteristics of markets and supervisory systems in numerous countries. For such an effort to be successful, the [Basel] Committee undertook a careful review of the existing rules and of the recent advances achieved in the industry. It consulted widely and publicly with industry representatives, other public authorities, and outside observers. The governors and heads of supervision believe that the [Basel] Committee's efforts and dedication have been fruitful and invaluable, and we appreciate the dedication that all [Basel] Committee members demonstrated.

Basel II builds on the solid foundation set out by [Basel I]. Indeed, the new framework will preserve key elements of the existing capital rules. This includes retaining the definition of eligible capital components; maintaining the general requirement that banks should hold total capital equivalent to at least 8% of their risk-weighted assets; and continuing the basic structure of the capital requirements for market risk that are outlined in the [Basel] Committee's 1996 Market Risk Amendment.

The new framework marks a substantial step forward in creating incentives for banks to improve the quality of their risk management. One of the most significant innovations of the new framework is that it will allow banks to make greater use of their own assessments of risk as inputs to capital calculations. In that vein, Basel II will provide banks with a range of options for determining their capital requirements for credit and operational risk. This will allow both banks and supervisors to select approaches that are most appropriate for banks' operations and local financial markets.

National authorities in the G10 countries will now continue their focus on adopting and implementing the new framework through domestic rule-making processes. Consistent implementation of the new framework across borders through enhanced supervisory co-operation will become a critical and challenging task in the years ahead.

GAO, Risk-Based Capital: New Basel II Rules Reduced Certain Competitive Concerns, but Bank Regulators Should Address Remaining Uncertainties

GAO-08-953 (Sept. 2008)

Basel II rests on the New Basel Accord, which established a more risk-sensitive regulatory framework that was intended to be sufficiently consistent internationally but that also took into account individual countries' existing regulatory and accounting systems. The U.S. bank regulators have been adapting the New Basel Accord for use by U.S. banks.

The New Basel Accord

The New Basel Accord sets forth minimum requirements, which regulators may complement with additional capital requirements, such as a leverage ratio. The New Basel Accord also identifies a number of areas for national discretion, thus requiring regulators from different countries to work together to understand how each country is implementing the New Basel Accord and to ensure broad consistency in the application of the regulatory framework across jurisdictions. The New Basel Accord consists of three pillars: (1) minimum capital requirements, (2) supervisory review of an institution's internal assessment process and capital adequacy, and (3) effective use of disclosure to strengthen market discipline as a complement to supervisory efforts. As shown in [the figure below], Pillar 1 establishes several approaches (of increasing complexity) to measuring credit and operational risks. The advanced approach for credit risk (also known as the advanced internal ratings-based approach) uses risk parameters determined by a bank's internal systems as inputs into a formula developed by supervisors for calculating minimum regulatory capital. In addition, banks with significant trading assets—assets banks use to hedge risks or to speculate on price changes in markets for themselves or their customers—must calculate capital requirements for market risk under Pillar 1. Pillar 2 explicitly recognizes the role of supervisory review, which includes assessments of capital adequacy relative to a bank's overall risk profile and early supervisory intervention that are already part of U.S. regulatory practices. Pillar 3 establishes disclosure requirements that aim to inform market participants about banks' capital adequacy in a consistent framework that enhances comparability. . . .

The Three Pillars of Basel III

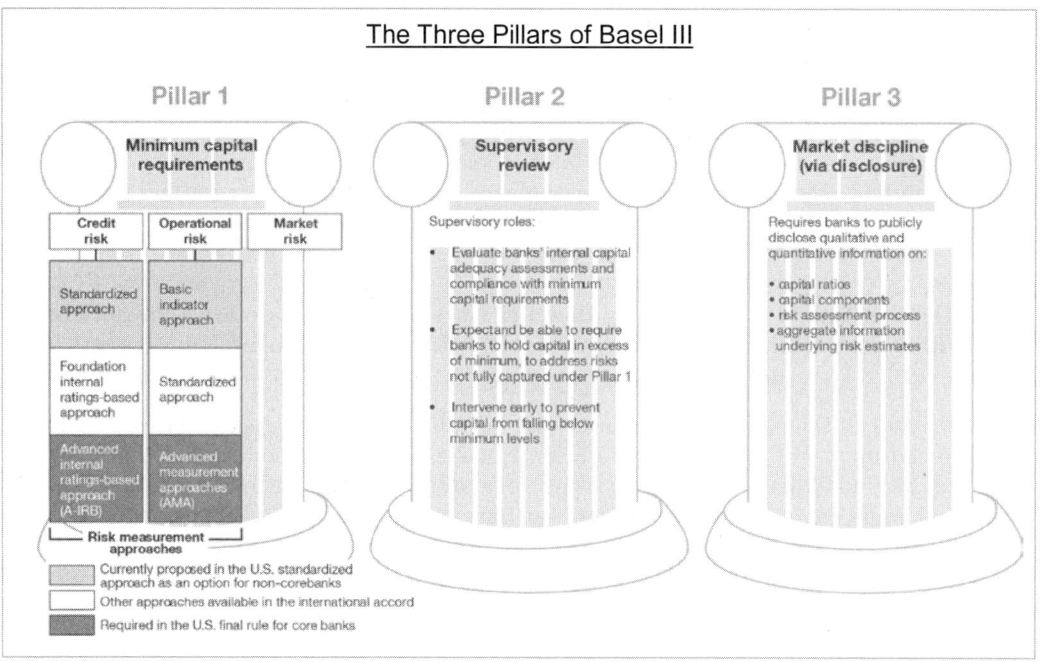

After extensive discussions and consultation that included issuing an advanced notice of proposed rulemaking in 2003 and a [notice of proposed rulemaking] in 2006, the U.S. banking regulators issued a final rule on the advanced approaches that became effective on April 1, 2008. Under the rule, only certain banks—core banks—will be required to adopt the advanced approaches for credit and operational risk. Core banks are those with consolidated total assets (excluding assets held by an insurance underwriting subsidiary of a [BHC]) of $250 billion or more or with consolidated total on-balance sheet foreign exposure of $10 billion or more. Publicly available information shows that, as of July 2008, 12 banks met the rule's basic criteria for being a core bank. A depository institution also is a core bank if it is a subsidiary of another bank that uses the advanced approaches. Under the rule, a core bank's primary federal regulator may determine that application of the advanced approaches is not appropriate in light of a core bank's asset size, level of complexity, risk profile, or scope of operations. In addition, banks that are not required to adopt the advanced approaches, but meet certain qualifications, may voluntarily choose to comply with the advanced approaches. Generally, core banks had or will have from April 2008 until April 2010 to begin the four phases that lead to the full implementation of Basel II.[3] As a result, core banks could be ready for full implementation between April 2012 and April 2014. By January 1, 2008, banks in the European Union, Canada, and Japan had moved off of Basel I and begun implementing some version of the New Basel Accord's advanced approaches or standardized approach for all of their banks. Banks located in the

[3] The four phases are (1) the parallel run—four consecutive quarters in which a bank meets the qualification requirements and is subject to the Basel I rules but simultaneously calculates its risk-based capital ratios under the advanced approaches; (2) the first transitional period—a period of at least four consecutive quarters in which the bank computes its risk-based capital ratios using the Basel I rule and the advanced approaches rule, and required risk-based capital must be at least 95 percent of the Basel I requirement; (3) the second transitional period—a period of at least four consecutive quarters in which the bank computes its risk-based capital ratios using the Basel I rule and the advanced approaches rule, and required risk-based capital must be at least 90 percent of the Basel I requirement; and (4) the third transitional period—a period of at least four consecutive quarters in which the bank computes its risk-based capital ratios using the Basel I rule and the advanced approaches rule, and required risk-based capital must be at least 85 percent of the Basel I requirement.

European Union, Canada, and Japan expect to have fully implemented Basel II sometime in 2010.

Non-core banks—those that do not meet the definition of a core bank—will have the option of adopting the advanced approaches, a standardized approach when finalized, or remaining on Basel I. The proposed standardized approach rule, published in July 2008, provides for a more risk-sensitive approach than Basel I by classifying banks' assets into more risk categories and assessing different capital requirements according to the riskiness of the category. While Basel I has 5 risk categories, the proposed standardized approach rule includes 16 categories. In contrast to the advanced approaches, the standardized approach relies more on external risk assessments—conducted by rating agencies—than on a bank's own assessments of a certain product's or borrower's risk. The proposed U.S. standardized approach generally is consistent with the standardized approach outlined in the New Basel Accord, but diverges from the New Basel Accord to incorporate more risk sensitive treatment, most notably in the approaches for residential mortgages and equities held by banks.

Additional U.S. Capital Requirements

The U.S. regulatory capital framework also includes minimum leverage capital requirements. Banks, thrifts, and [BHCs] are subject to minimum leverage standards, measured as a ratio of Tier 1 capital to total assets. The minimum leverage requirement is either 3 or 4 percent, depending on the type of institution and a regulatory assessment of the strength of its management and controls. Leverage ratios are a commonly used financial measure of risk. Greater financial leverage, as measured by lower proportions of capital relative to assets, increases the riskiness of a firm, all other things being equal. If the leverage capital requirement is greater than the risk-based level required then the leverage requirement would be the binding overall minimum requirement on an institution. Depository institutions also are subject to the Federal Deposit Insurance Corporation Improvement Act of 1991, which created a new supervisory framework known as [prompt corrective action] that links supervisory actions closely to these banks' capital ratios. [Prompt corrective action], which applies only to depository institutions and not [BHCs], requires regulators to take increasingly stringent forms of corrective action against banks as their leverage and risk-based capital ratios decline. Under this rule, regulators also can require banks to hold more than minimum levels of capital to engage in certain activities. In addition, under the Bank Holding Company Act, the Federal Reserve [Board] can require that [BHCs] hold additional capital to engage in certain activities.

---

1. ***Internal Ratings-Based Approaches.*** Basel II provided three approaches for determining a borrower's credit risk for purposes of calculating an asset's risk weight: the advanced internal ratings-based approach, the foundation internal ratings-based approach, and the standardized approach. Under the advanced internal ratings-based approach, which was the only Basel II approach implemented in the United States, the largest and most internationally active banks and BHCs, which are called core banks in the GAO report but are better known as advanced approaches banks and BHCs, were to be permitted to use their own internal models, validated by regulators, for estimating risk parameters, such as probability of default and loss given default. Risk weights are then calculated by inputting these risk parameter estimates into a formula provided by regulators. Under the foundation internal ratings-based approach, some of these risk parameters are instead provided by regulators. More important than the technical details, the advanced and foundation internal ratings-based approaches rely, to at least some degree, on proprietary internal models developed by each large bank or BHC to calculate risk weights. Although

the advanced internal ratings-based approach did not allow a bank or BHC to calculate capital requirements by any estimation method it chose, it did leave them with a material amount of discretion when determining the risk of their borrowers and therefore the amount of capital they had to hold. Recall that two of Basel II's main objectives were to encourage risk management practice improvements and to better align assets' risk weights with their underlying credit risk. Does the adoption of an internal ratings-based approach help achieve these goals? How? What are some potential drawbacks to using internal models to calculate risk weights?

2. ***Standardized Approach.*** Basel II's standardized approach used a two-step system to determine a given asset's risk weight. First, the asset was sorted into one of 12 broad categories dependent on the type of borrower. This categorization, premised on broad categories of borrower type, resembles that used under Basel I. In the standardized approach's second step, these borrowers are further subdivided by their credit risk rating, as provided by an external credit rating agency (*e.g.*, Standard & Poor's, Moody's, Fitch), resulting in a finer categorization of borrowers than under Basel I. For example, a loan to a corporation had a 100% risk weight under Basel I, but a loan to a corporation with an AAA credit rating had a 20% risk weight under Basel II's standardized approach. Instead of relying on internal models, the standardized approach relied on an external credit rating agency's risk ratings. What are the benefits to relying on external credit ratings instead of internal models? What are the possible problems with this approach? More importantly, although U.S. banking regulators proposed a rule implementing Basel II's standardized approach, they never promulgated a final rule for non-advanced approaches banks and BHCs, therefore most U.S. banks and BHCs remained under Basel I.

3. ***Advantages of Basel I?*** Recall that Basel I's risk-weighting was criticized as simplistic, causing risk-based capital ratios to be potentially misleading. What are some potential benefits of Basel I's simpler approach?

4. ***Barings Bank's Failure and Operational Risk.*** Basel II also introduced a measurement and capital charge for operational risk. The inclusion of operational risk in Basel II was driven in part by Barings Bank's failure in 1995. Barings Bank, originally founded in 1762, collapsed after discovering that one of its Singapore branch traders, Nick Leeson, lost $1.3 billion in unauthorized derivatives trades made through the bank's error accounts. Leeson's fraudulent trading was exposed when the Kobe earthquake on January 17, 1995 caused financial turmoil in Asia, resulting in losses that Leeson could no longer conceal. One of the lessons from the failure of Barings Bank is that a bank's capital could be depleted through rogue traders and other operational events, not just credit or market losses.

In many ways mirroring its approach to credit risk, Basel II provided multiple methods of increasing sophistication for measuring operational risk. Under the advanced measurement approaches framework, U.S. advanced approaches banks and BHCs quantified operational risk using internal models. Federal Reserve Governor Randall Kroszner elaborated on the advanced measurement approaches' goals in a 2008 speech, noting that,

> [w]ith regard to credit risk, the advanced approaches of Basel II improve regulatory capital measures by requiring banks to distinguish among the credit quality of individual borrowers. Generally speaking, banks holding riskier credit exposures are required to hold more capital. Similarly, the [advanced measurement approaches] framework requires a more systematic approach for assessing the operational risk to which a bank is exposed and ties an explicit regulatory risk-based capital requirement to these exposures. Under Basel I, this charge was indirect and embedded in credit and market risk measures. In contrast, under the [advanced measurement approaches], banks with higher levels of operational risk—such as those more heavily involved than others in activities that have elevated loss potential from fraud, business disruption, or systems failure—generally should have higher capital requirements. By establishing a much more refined approach that requires banks to hold capital commensurate with the actual risks of their exposures and activities, Basel II should lead institutions to make better decisions about assuming, retaining, and mitigating risks.

Randall Kroszner, Risk Management and Basel II, Speech at the Federal Reserve Bank of Boston AMA Conference (May 14, 2008). Furthermore, speaking to the Basel Committee's goal of maintaining Basel I capital levels while improving risk management practices, Professor Richard Herring writes that the Basel Committee "calibrated the Basel II capital charge for operational risk to offset, on average, the potentially reduced charges for credit risk." Richard J. Herring, *The Rocky Road to Implementation of Basel II in the United States*, 35 ATL. ECON. J. 411–29 (Dec. 2007).

5. ***The U.S. Implementation of Basel II and Competitive Equality.*** Although one of Basel II's goals was to promote competitive equality, its implementation varied across banks and countries. Indeed, the U.S. implementation of Basel II raised competitive equality concerns with respect to U.S. and foreign banks as well as advanced approaches and non-advanced approaches banks and BHCs. In 2007, an international banking association representative, referring to the U.S. implementation, commented, "[w]e are concerned today about the slow pace in which a consistent, global regulatory capital regime is being put in place. . . There is not much progress made on further convergence. . . It's a real threat to the global implementation of the Basel II accord." *Bankers Concerned About Slow Basel Implementation*, REUTERS (May 31, 2007). Why do you think the United States only required advanced approaches banks and BHCs to implement Basel II's advanced internal ratings-based approach and advanced measurement approaches? What would your concerns be about the U.S. implementation of Basel II if you were a community or regional banker?

6. ***U.S. Transitional Arrangements.*** U.S. banking regulators' implementation plan for Basel II was cautious and involved four separate phases for each advanced approaches bank and BHC, as described in footnote three of the GAO report. The transitional arrangements allowed U.S. banking regulators to maintain Basel I-linked capital floors and monitor the effect of Basel II on

capital levels. The timing of U.S. implementation also meant that advanced approaches banks and BHCs were in the early stages of beginning their parallel runs under Basel II when the Financial Crisis hit in 2008. As a result, no U.S. bank or BHC had yet actually applied the internal ratings models in calculating its reported capital ratios. In the pre-Financial Crisis era it was widely assumed that, when applied, such internal models would result in lower capital ratios for the banks and BHCs that were able to use them. There is some empirical evidence from the experience of European banks that implemented Basel II, which shows a correlation between that greater use of internal ratings-based approaches and lower risk-weights. *See, e.g.*, Brunella Bruno et al., *The Credibility of European Banks' Risk-Weighted Capital: Structural Differences of National Segmentations?* (BAFFI CAREFIN Centre Research Paper Series No. 2015-9, 2015). Since the U.S. banks and BHCs had only started their parallel runs, the performance of these models in the United States during and after the Financial Crisis is not publicly known. It is unclear whether the internal models would have indeed led to lower capital ratios, and the results of the parallel runs in a Financial Crisis and post-Financial Crisis era remain outside of the public realm.

7. ***Additional Capital Requirements in the United States.*** Like Basel I, Basel II did not include a leverage ratio. Concerned that implementation of Basel II would result in a significant drop in capital levels if the United States abandoned its leverage ratio requirement, the FDIC insisted that the United States keep it, as well as the prompt corrective action regime discussed in more depth in Chapter 2.5. Specifically, the FDIC conducted a quantitative study in 2005 that concluded that, if Basel II risk-based capital standards were applied to 26 banking organizations and each targeted a 6% Tier 1 capital ratio (*i.e.*, they were well-capitalized with respect to this ratio), 17 of them would be undercapitalized with respect to the leverage ratio. *See Statement on the Development of the New Basel Capital Accords*, 109th Cong. 50 (2005) (statement of Donald E. Powell, Chairman, FDIC). FDIC Chairman Shelia Bair later commented,

> [t]o be honest and frank, we don't yet know whether Basel II's advanced approaches will work. We don't know whether, or when, the risk inputs will become reliable. We don't know whether the level of minimum capital requirements will be sufficient. . . Given this uncertainty, regulators must proceed with caution.

Sheila Bair, FDIC Chairman, Speech at the 2007 Risk Management and Allocation Conference (June 25, 2007). The FDIC's reluctance stalled the U.S. implementation of Basel II, and, unlike virtually all other countries, the United States maintained a parallel leverage ratio requirement. The Additional U.S. Capital Requirements section of the GAO report therefore serves as an important reminder that other forms of capital regulation in the United States did not disappear with the implementation of Basel II. Some have argued that the leverage ratio requirement, as well as the transitional arrangements, operated as a capital backstop for U.S. banks leading up to the Financial Crisis, putting them in a somewhat better position than other banks and prompting calls for the adoption of an international leverage ratio standard. It is certainly true that the EU, in particular, was strongly against a leverage ratio then, with the result that, at the time of the Financial Crisis, the largest global EU banks were much more highly leveraged than the U.S. advanced approaches banks.

8. ***Pillar 2 and Pillar 3.*** The discussion of Basel II has focused on Pillar 1 so far, but Basel II's three pillars were intertwined. Pillar 2 and Pillar 3 subjected a bank or BHC's capital levels and processes to supervisory oversight and market disclosure and might require or, in the case of market disclosure, cause a bank or BHC to hold more capital than would be required under Pillar 1. For instance, under Pillar 2, a bank's supervisors would assess risks not captured under Pillar 1 and could require the bank to hold more capital accordingly. Federal Reserve Chairman Ben Bernanke described the purpose of Pillar 2 and Pillar 3 as follows:

> Besides making regulatory capital ratios more risk-sensitive, Basel II provides a consistent framework for improving supervisory assessments of capital adequacy and risk management. Under Pillar 2, a bank would be required to maintain a capital cushion above the regulatory minimums to capture the full set of risks to which the bank is exposed. These include liquidity risk, interest rate risk, and concentration risk, none of which is reflected in Pillar 1. Currently, the U.S. banking agencies assess a bank's overall capital adequacy as a normal part of the examination process. But the overall quality of both the supervisors' and each bank's assessments of capital adequacy should improve greatly under Basel II because of the expanded information that will be available from Pillar 1, from supervisory reviews of a bank's systems for implementing Pillar 1 and Pillar 2, and from the bank's own analyses. Under Pillar 3, banks will be required to disclose to the public the new risk-based capital ratios and more extensive information about the credit quality of their portfolios and their practices in measuring and managing risk. Such disclosures should make banks more transparent to financial markets, thereby improving market discipline.

Benjamin Bernanke, Basel II: Its Promise and Challenges, Speech at the Federal Reserve Bank of Chicago's 42nd Annual Conference on Bank Structure and Competition (May 18, 2006). Does Basel II's Pillar 2 and Pillar 3 resolve concerns you may have had with Pillar 1? Why or why not?

9. ***Developing Countries and Basel II.*** With respect to Basel Committee member country implementation of Basel II, officials from developing countries took issue with the standardized approach's reliance on external ratings agencies because many borrowers in these countries were not rated. Moreover, the intensive investment in computers and PhD-level quantitative talent to build internal models was as beyond the budgets of many developing country banks as it was community and regional banks and BHCs in the United States. As with Basel I, Basel Committee member countries were not the only ones to implement elements of Basel II. Developing countries implemented elements of Basel II as well despite the fact that they did not play a major role in formulating Basel II. For example, although China and India chose to not apply the Basel II capital standards to their banks, due in part to the complexity of the internal ratings-based approaches, high investment costs for the computer models, and the decision by the United States to only apply these approaches to 12 of its largest

banking organizations, they signaled they would implement Pillar 2 and Pillar 3. Other countries, like South Africa, planned to implement Basel II more quickly. The South Africa Reserve Bank stated that, "Basel II is suitable for application in both G-10 and non-G-10 countries, since it provides a menu of approaches suitable for both sophisticated and the least sophisticated banks." SOUTH AFRICA RESERVE BANK, BANK SUPERVISION DEPARTMENT, ANNUAL REPORT 28 (2003). What challenges might developing countries face in implementing international capital standards, in general, and Basel II, in particular, compared to the United States and European countries? The Basel Committee, which only included the G-10 countries at the time of Basel II, expanded its membership in 2009 and 2014, and several developing countries, including Argentina, China, India, Indonesia, and Mexico, are now members.

IV. CAPITAL REGULATION AND THE FINANCIAL CRISIS

One of the few areas of policy consensus after the Financial Crisis is that financial institutions did not hold enough capital to withstand the sharp decline in asset values from the plunge in housing price. Governor Daniel Tarullo provides an overview of capital regulation failures during the Financial Crisis in the speech below. These failures led to Basel III, the subject of Chapter 2.7.

Governor Daniel Tarullo, Fed. Reserve Bd. of Governors: The Evolution of Capital Regulation

Speech at the Clearing House Business Meeting and Conference (Nov. 2011)

Although they had long used bank capital ratios as a supervisory instrument, U.S. bank regulators did not impose explicit minimum capital requirements until the 1980s. The proximate reason for this change was regulatory concern over the decline in capital ratios of the largest banks—a concern reinforced by Congress, as it saw some of those large banks facing enormous losses on their loans to foreign sovereigns. Within a few years this U.S. regulatory innovation was effectively internationalized by [Basel I].

At the same time, regulators came to regard capital requirements as a supple prudential tool. As activity and affiliation restrictions were loosened in the United States, capital requirements seemed a promising way to protect the public's interest in the stability of financial institutions that had access to the Federal Reserve's discount window and [FDIC] insurance. Capital requirements promised to provide a buffer against bank losses from any activities in which the bank or its affiliates might engage, a consideration of equal or greater relevance in countries with universal banking models. Some support also developed for the proposition that minimum capital levels could, by maintaining a material equity value for the bank, serve as a disincentive for excessive risk-taking by management and shareholders.

In the ensuing quarter century, banking regulators around the world focused considerable attention toward elaborating capital requirements to reflect more precisely the particular risks faced by a financial institution. Capital requirements had, to a considerable extent, become the dominant prudential regulatory tool.

The financial crisis showed that this concentrated, almost all-consuming regulatory focus on refining bank capital requirements in Basel II had come at the expense of attention to other risks in the financial system. In particular, banking regulators failed to appreciate fully the implications of the growth—in size, leverage, and maturity transformation levels—of the shadow banking system for the balance sheets of commercial banks and for overall financial stability. The crisis showed that liquidity problems can be an independent source of severe stress, perhaps even for firms that might otherwise have remained solvent.

But it was also evident that the specifics of pre-crisis capital regulation fell far short of what this prudential instrument can achieve. The Basel I and Basel II capital requirements relied almost exclusively on capital ratios that were essentially snapshots of balance sheets and thus all too often a lagging indicator of a bank's condition. Declines in asset values—particularly of non-traded assets—were often not reflected in capital calculations for some time. Though already well-known before the crisis, this phenomenon was particularly problematic as asset values declined rapidly, causing both markets and supervisors alike to regard regulatory capital ratios as providing only limited information about a firm's current financial condition.

In addition, minimum capital levels had simply been set too low, in general and with respect to particular assets. One of the most obvious examples was the capital requirement for asset-backed securities in the trading books of banks. The requirement was based on returns over a 10-day holding period, used a one-year observation period that had been characterized by unusually low price volatility, and did not adequately account for the credit risks inherent in these traded instruments.

Furthermore, at least some of the instruments that qualified as "Tier 1 capital" for regulatory purposes were not reliable buffers against losses, at least not on a going concern basis. It is instructive that during the height of the crisis, counterparties and other market actors looked almost exclusively to the amount of tangible common equity held by financial institutions in evaluating the creditworthiness and overall stability of those institutions. They essentially ignored the Tier 1 and total risk-based capital ratios in regulatory requirements. In the fall of 2008, there was widespread doubt in markets that the common equity of some of our largest institutions was sufficient to withstand the losses that those firms appeared to be facing. This doubt made investors and counterparties increasingly reluctant to deal with those firms, contributing to the severe liquidity strains that characterized financial markets at the time.

Finally, the crisis validated the concerns expressed by some academics and by policy staff at the Bank for International Settlements that the effectiveness of capital regulation was limited by its exclusively microprudential focus. Capital requirements had been set with reference solely to the balance sheet of a specific firm. The risk weights assigned to the firm's assets were calculated with reference to ordinary times, whether through a supervisory determination or a combination of supervisory formulas and a firm's own modeling. This microprudential focus did not take into account the potential impact of a shock to the value of widely-held assets—whether exogenous, caused by the distress sales of such assets by a large firm suffering particularly severe problems, or, as in the financial crisis, a lethal interaction between these two factors.

The limits of the microprudential approach were particularly evident with respect to very large, interconnected firms. There would be very substantial negative externalities associated with the disorderly failure of any such firm, distinct from the costs incurred by the firm and its stakeholders. The failure of one large firm, especially in a period of stress, significantly increases the chances that other financial firms will fail, for two reasons. First, direct counterparty impacts can lead to a classic domino effect. Second, because losses in a tail event are much more likely to be correlated for firms deeply engaged in trading, structured products, and other capital market instruments, all such firms are vulnerable to accelerating losses as troubled firms sell their assets into a declining market.

---

1. ***Use of Internal Models and Opacity of Capital Positions.*** Some Basel II shortcomings were identified before the Financial Crisis. For example, one concern was the opacity of capital positions, especially those of advanced

approaches banks and BHCs, despite Pillar 2 and Pillar 3. Before he was a Governor at the Federal Reserve Board, Tarullo outlined this concern before Congress:

> [O]versight of this process presents a new kind of supervisory challenge. The complexity of, and differences among, bank models will require a highly specialized expertise within the banking agencies in order to oversee compliance of advanced internal ratings-based banks with their capital requirements. . . . Questions about the ability of our banking agencies to supervise the use of internal credit models for regulatory capital calculations naturally raise the question of who can monitor the supervisors. The difficulties raised by the complexity of the bank models are compounded by the fact that much of the information contained in the models will be proprietary to the bank. Congress, academics, and other interested observers will thus not be in a position to assess how good a job the bank agencies are doing. Nor will creditors of banks be able to make their own informed assessment of the bank's risk and capital position, thereby limiting a source of market discipline that might contribute to bank safety and soundness. Finally, the opaque nature of the supervisory process for internal credit risk models means it is not clear whether and how U.S. banking agencies will be able to determine if their foreign counterparts are effectively supervising their own advanced internal ratings-based banks.

Development of the New Basel Accords: Testimony at Hearing Before the S. Comm. On Banking, Hous. & Urban Affairs, 109th Cong. 11 (2005) (testimony of Daniel K. Tarullo). Tarullo later raised further concerns over whether supervisors could monitor and adequately challenge advanced approaches banks and BHCs' internal models:

> With risk ratings generated by banks' internal models poised to play a central role in capital regulation, supervisory oversight of the construction and adoption of the models becomes central to the regulatory system. Prior to the reorientation of the Basel II process following the scrapping of the 1999 proposals, banking supervisory agencies in the United States and elsewhere had relatively little expertise with credit risk models. It is fair to say that only a small proportion of banking examiners are trained to evaluate credit risk models. Supervisory agencies have, of course, acquired financial model expertise in the course of working on Basel II. But a modest number of financial economists in the research or policy groups of the agencies will hardly be adequate for the task of supervising [advanced approaches] banks once Basel II takes effect.

DANIEL K. TARULLO, BANKING ON BASEL: THE FUTURE OF FINANCIAL REGULATION 170 (2008). The importance of supervisory expertise with respect to model oversight is especially important given the incentives that banks and BHCs face when constructing their internal models, keeping in mind that the key goal was to use these more precise models to lower risk weights on higher credit-quality assets.

2. ***Capital Regulation as a Lagging Indicator.*** Many institutions that were rescued or failed during the Financial Crisis were in full compliance with their minimum capital requirements at the time of their bailout or failure. For example, as of September 30, 2008, Citigroup's Tier 1 risk-based capital ratio was 8.19% and its total risk-based capital ratio was 11.68%, each of which greatly exceeded the minimum requirements. Nonetheless, Citigroup went on to receive $45 billion in capital injections from the U.S. government starting in October 2008. Citigroup's experience during the Financial Crisis reveals one of the limitations of the capital regulation, that quarterly capital ratios will not reveal much about an institution's health during a fast-paced crisis, which is not limited to the technical details of a particular Basel regime. Given Citigroup's and others' experience during the Financial Crisis, do you think the emphasis on capital regulation is misplaced? Why or why not?

3. ***Not Enough High Quality Capital.*** Capital quantities and qualities proved insufficient to absorb the losses during the Financial Crisis. In a study of 26 large U.S. financial institutions by the Federal Reserve Bank of Boston, half of the institutions had over a two percentage point decrease in their Tier 1 common equity capital ratios at some point during the Financial Crisis and eight institutions had over a five percentage point drop, revealing a dramatic erosion in capital levels. Those with the biggest drops, like Washington Mutual, Countrywide Financial, and Merrill Lynch, either failed or merged with other institutions during the Financial Crisis. SCOTT STRAH, JENNIFER HYNES & SANDERS SHAFFER, THE IMPACT OF THE RECENT FINANCIAL CRISIS ON THE CAPITAL POSITIONS OF LARGE U.S. FINANCIAL INSTITUTIONS: AN EMPIRICAL ANALYSIS, FEDERAL RESERVE BOARD OF BOSTON (2013). Furthermore, a study by McKinsey & Company showed that banks with larger proportions of Tier 2 capital in relation to Tier 1 capital were more likely to experience incidents of distress including bankruptcy, government takeover or receivership, merger under duress, or receipt of a substantial government bailout. KEVIN BUEHLER, HAMID SAMANDARI, AND CHRISTOPHER MANZINGO, MCKINSEY AND CO., CAPITAL RATIOS AND FINANCIAL DISTRESS: LESSONS FROM THE CRISIS 10 (Dec. 2009). In addition, as noted by Tarullo, investors and counterparties often only considered a bank's or BHC's tangible common equity, or common stock, when assessing its capital position during the Financial Crisis. Certain intangible assets that were not fully deducted from Tier 1 capital, such as mortgage servicing rights and deferred tax assets, were deemed by the market during the Financial Crisis not to be reliable enough to absorb losses. It was particularly understandable that external parties viewed mortgage servicing rights during the Financial Crisis as being of questionable value, because mortgage servicing fees are fixed and servicing expenses increased substantially during the housing downturn.

4. ***Microprudential Focus.*** Basel I and Basel II's capital requirements did not look outside of a given bank's or BHC's balance sheet or off-balance sheet exposures to prescribe capital levels to account for systemic risk in the financial system as a whole. The Financial Crisis revealed Basel I and Basel II's focus on individual institutions, rather than the financial system as a whole, had serious shortcomings. One of the most important lessons of the Financial Crisis was the need for regulation to be concerned about the financial system's interconnectedness and strength as a whole.

5. ***Treatment of Securitization Exposures and Reliance on External Credit Ratings.*** The U.S. implementation of Basel II's advanced approaches generally assigned risk weights for securitization exposures based on their external credit ratings, giving advanced approaches banks and BHCs a strong preference for higher ratings. In addition, recall that the risk weights of asset-backed and mortgage-backed securities depended on their external credit ratings under the U.S. implementation of Basel I. The Financial Crisis called any reliance on external credit ratings into question, however. The Financial Crisis Inquiry Commission (FCIC) was particularly scathing in its criticism of credit rating agencies' role in the Financial Crisis:

> The three credit rating agencies were key enablers of the financial meltdown. The mortgage-related securities at the heart of the crisis could not have been marketed and sold without their seal of approval. Investors relied on them, often blindly. In some cases, they were obligated to use them, or regulatory capital standards were hinged on them. This crisis could not have happened without the rating agencies. Their ratings helped the market soar and their downgrades through 2007 and 2008 wreaked havoc across markets and firms. . . From 2000 to 2007, Moody's rated nearly 45,000 mortgage-related securities as AAA. This compares with six private-sector companies in the United States that carried this coveted rating in early 2010. In 2006 alone, Moody's put its AAA stamp of approval on 30 mortgage-related securities every working day. The results were disastrous: 83% of the mortgage securities rated AAA that year ultimately were downgraded.

FINANCIAL CRISIS INQUIRY COMMISSION, THE FINANCIAL CRISIS INQUIRY REPORT xxv (2011). The FCIC located credit rating agencies' errors in faulty computer models, pressure from firms that paid for the ratings, inadequate resources, and a lack of public oversight. The Dodd-Frank Act required that references to external credit ratings in banking regulations, including capital rules, be removed and replaced with alternative standards of creditworthiness.

6. ***Lack of Liquidity Standards.*** Basel I and Basel II did not contain quantitative liquidity requirements. Rather, liquidity risk was treated as a supervisory matter under Pillar II of Basel II. The Financial Crisis sharply revealed the importance of liquidity regulation across the financial sector, however, as

> [t]he financial turbulence of 2008 was largely defined by the dangers of runs—realized, incipient, and feared. Facing deep uncertainty about the condition of counterparties and the value of assets serving as collateral, many funding markets ground to a halt, as investors refused to offer new short-term lending or even to roll over existing repos and similar extensions of credit. In the first instance, at least, this was a liquidity crisis.

Daniel Tarullo, Liquidity Regulation, Speech at the Clearing House 2014 Annual Conference (Nov. 20, 2014).

7. ***Differential Treatment of Savings and Loan Holding Companies (SLHCs).*** The U.S. implementation of Basel I and Basel II did not apply to

SLHCs, although some SLHCs were subject to supervisory capital maintenance and support agreements imposed by their regulators. Therefore, even a fully implemented Basel II would not have applied to AIG, Indymac, or Washington Mutual, SLHCs which experienced failure or near failure during the Financial Crisis. SLHCs are subject to the U.S. implementation of Basel III.

8. ***Capital Regulation of Broker-Dealers and Other Non-Bank Financial Intermediaries.*** We will discuss the pre- and post-Financial Crisis capital regulation in the then standalone broker-dealers, such as Lehman Brothers, Bear Stearns, Morgan Stanley, and Goldman Sachs, in Chapter 4.1. In addition, other standalone financial intermediaries, such as insurance companies and asset managers, were not subject to capital regulation under one of the Basel frameworks at the time of the Financial Crisis, prompting regulators to later contemplate whether different non-bank financial intermediaries should be subject to comparable capital regulation. *See* Daniel Tarullo, Capital Regulation Across Financial Intermediaries, Speech at the Banque de France Conference: Financial Regulation—Stability versus Uniformity (Sept. 28, 2015).

CHAPTER 2.7

CAPITAL REGULATION: BASEL III AND BEYOND

CONTENTS

I. INTRODUCTION

It is widely acknowledged that both the absolute level of capital and capital regulation proved to be inadequate during the Financial Crisis. Banks and bank holding companies (BHCs), regardless of whether they were subject to Basel I or Basel II, held too little high-quality capital. It also became apparent that capital regulation, which focused on the last quarter's credit and market risk, was a lagging indicator and needed to be supplemented with liquidity regulation. Finally, there were concerns about the microprudential focus of capital regulation. The largest investment banks and insurance conglomerates, including Lehman Brothers and AIG, had even weaker capital regulation and oversight. Basel I and Basel II's flaws, which were apparent to some in advance and which became apparent to most in hindsight, led to a major reform of capital and liquidity regulation in the United States and elsewhere through a new Basel framework known as Basel III.

In this Chapter, we discuss the U.S. response to the Financial Crisis, specifically stress testing and the Collins Amendment, and provide an overview of Basel III's capital and liquidity requirements. We conclude by discussing the complexity of Basel III and the debate between those who think that Basel III still does not require banks and BHCs to hold enough capital and those who think it has gone too far.

II. U.S. RESPONSE TO THE FINANCIAL CRISIS

A. STRESS TESTING AND CAPITAL PLANNING

Capital stress tests were introduced by Secretary Timothy Geithner's Treasury Department early in 2009 with the Supervisory Capital Assessment Program (SCAP, pronounced *ess-cap*), the purpose of which was to determine whether the largest BHCs in the United States needed additional capital injections from the U.S. taxpayer. The importance that Geithner accords to the impact of the initial round of stress testing on stabilizing the financial system is reflected in the title of his memoir, *Stress Test*. TIMOTHY F. GEITHNER, STRESS TEST: REFLECTIONS ON FINANCIAL CRISES (2014). The success of SCAP led to the permanent establishment of stress testing under the Dodd-Frank Act and the introduction of capital planning requirements, each of which have become important supervisory tools.

Governor Daniel Tarullo, Fed. Reserve Bd.
The Evolution of Capital Regulation

Speech at the Fed. Reserve Bank of Chicago Annual Risk Conference (Apr. 10, 2012)

The importance of robust capital requirements for financial stability and the serious shortcomings of the pre-crisis capital regulatory regime have been well documented. In the last few years, domestic and international initiatives have strengthened standards for the quantity and quality of capital held by banking organizations. Implementation of these new standards should significantly increase the safety and soundness of the financial system.

But there are at least four reasons why simple compliance with the stricter standards will not achieve this goal. First, as has long been recognized, a capital ratio—even a much higher one—is essentially a snapshot of a bank's balance sheet and, thus, often a lagging indicator of the bank's actual condition. Second, the ability of a bank to remain a viable financial intermediary in times of stress depends not only on the losses likely to affect the value of current assets, but also the impact on revenues and, thus, the capacity to replenish capital during the stress period. Third, if capital requirements are set solely with reference to more ordinary economic circumstances, they will not capture the potential impact of a shock to the value of widely held assets to the financial system as a whole. Fourth, the capacity of both bank management and regulators to understand a firm's capital position depends on its having good information and quantitative risk-management systems.

Thus, stronger capital standards must be complemented with supervisory tools that incorporate dynamic, macroprudential elements. Two important such tools that have been adopted by the Federal Reserve [Board] since the onset of the financial crisis are stress testing and firm-specific capital planning. . .

Tools for Dynamic Capital Supervision

The potential utility of comprehensive stress testing had been much discussed among academics, analysts, and regulators in the years preceding the financial crisis, but it was only during the crisis that this tool was used across large firms at the same time. In February 2009, the federal banking agencies—led by the Federal Reserve [Board]—created a stress test and required the nation's 19 largest [BHCs] to apply it as part of [SCAP]. The test involved two scenarios—one based on the consensus forecast of professional forecasters, and the other based on a severe, but plausible, economic situation—with specified macroeconomic variables such as GDP growth, employment, and house prices. Each participating institution was asked to supply, in a standardized format, detailed information on portfolio risk factors and revenue drivers that supervisors could use to estimate losses and revenues over a two-year period. These data allowed supervisors to make consistent estimates across all 19 firms.

The immediate motivation for the 2009 stress test was to determine how much additional capital a [BHC] would need to ensure that it would remain a viable financial intermediary even in the adverse scenario. The Treasury Department stood ready to provide capital to any bank that could not raise the required amount from private sources. But the Federal [Reserve Board's] decision to disclose the results of the test on a firm-specific basis served a second purpose—to provide investors, and markets more generally, with information that would help them form their own judgments on the condition of U.S. banking institutions. This decision proved to be an important step in establishing market and public confidence that the U.S. financial system would weather the crisis.

Though conceived and developed in the midst of the financial crisis, SCAP will be remembered as a watershed for supervisory policies applicable to large institutions. Congress drew on the lessons of the 2009 exercise by including a requirement for stress testing in the [Dodd-Frank Act]. But well before Congress passed the Dodd-Frank Act, the SCAP experience had already profoundly affected attitudes toward supervision within the Federal Reserve [Board]. It demonstrated in practice, not just in theory, the value of a simultaneous, forward-looking projection of potential losses and revenue effects based on each bank's own portfolio and circumstances. The forward-looking feature overcame the limitations of static capital ratios. The simultaneity, along with stress test features such as an assumed instantaneous market shock, introduced a critical macroprudential dimension that offered insights into the condition of the entire financial system, including whether banks were sufficiently resilient to continue to provide their critical intermediation functions even under such adverse conditions.

Regular and rigorous stress testing thus provides regulators with knowledge that can be applied to both microprudential and macroprudential supervision efforts. Disclosure of the methodology and firm-specific results of our stress testing has additional regulatory benefits. First, the release of details about assumptions, methods, and conclusions exposes the supervisory approach to greater outside scrutiny and discussion. Such discussions will almost surely help us improve our assumptions and methodology over time. Second, because bank portfolios are difficult to value without a great deal of detailed information, the test results should be very useful to investors in and counterparties of the largest institutions. The market discipline promoted by means such as resolution mechanisms will be most effective if market participants have adequate information with which to make informed judgments about the banks.

But stress testing is no more a panacea for the supervision of large financial institutions than capital requirements themselves, or any other regulatory device. By design, the stress tests to date have not covered other sources of stress, such as funding and interest rate risks, which are the subjects of other supervisory exercises. But just as strengthened capital requirements remain at the center of a better financial regulatory system, so stress testing is now recognized as a critical, forward-looking tool for ensuring that minimum capital requirements can be maintained. Indeed, stress testing has already come to epitomize the horizontal, interdisciplinary approach to supervising our largest [BHCs] that the Federal Reserve System has instituted over the past few years.

Firm-specific capital planning has also become an important supervisory tool. In November 2011, the Federal Reserve [Board] issued a new regulation requiring large banking organizations to submit an annual capital plan. This tool serves multiple purposes. First, it provides a regular, structured, and comparative way to promote and assess the capacity of large [BHCs] to understand and manage their capital positions, with particular emphasis on risk-measurement practices. Second, it provides supervisors with an opportunity to evaluate any capital distribution plans against the backdrop of the firm's overall capital position, a matter of considerable importance given the significant distributions that some firms made in 2007 even as the [F]inancial [C]risis gathered momentum. Third, at least for the next few years, it will provide a regular assessment of whether large holding companies will readily and comfortably meet the new capital requirements related to various Basel agreements as they take effect in the United States.

A stress test is a critical part of the annual capital review. But, as these different purposes indicate, the capital review is about more than using a stress test to determine whether a firm's capital distribution plans are consistent with remaining a viable financial intermediary even in an adverse scenario. As indicated during our capital reviews in both 2011 and 2012, the Federal Reserve [Board] may object to a capital plan because of significant deficiencies in the capital planning process, as well as because one or more relevant capital ratios would fall below required levels under the assumptions of stress and planned capital distributions. Likewise, the stress test is relevant not only for its role in the capital planning process. As noted earlier, it also serves other important purposes, not least of which is increased transparency of both [BHC] balance sheets and the supervisory process of the Federal Reserve [Board].

---

1. ***SCAP.*** On February 10, 2009, Geithner unveiled the Obama Administration's Financial Stability Plan. Critics quickly panned Geithner's speech as vague and the S&P 500 dropped nearly 5% that day. With admirable humor, Geithner later self-deprecatingly wrote in his memoir:

> It's fair to say the speech did not go well. I swayed back and forth, like an unhappy passenger on an unsteady ship. I kept peering around the teleprompter to look directly at the audience, which apparently made me look shifty; one commentator said I looked like a shoplifter. My voice wavered. I tried to sound forceful, but I just sounded like someone trying to sound forceful.

TIMOTHY F. GEITHNER, STRESS TEST: REFLECTIONS ON FINANCIAL CRISES 12 (2014). In Saturday Night Live's parody of the speech, Geithner, played by Bill Hader, offered $420 million to the first caller to come up with a solution to the Financial Crisis. One aspect of the plan outlined in Geithner's speech that did not receive much attention at the time was the announcement that BHCs would undergo "a carefully designed comprehensive stress test," which later became SCAP. Three months later, the Treasury Department, the Federal Reserve Board, the FDIC, and the OCC announced that ten of the 19 largest U.S. BHCs needed to raise more capital to withstand SCAP's most adverse scenario. Chairman of the Federal Reserve Board Ben Bernanke later stated that,

> in retrospect, the SCAP stands out for me as one of the critical turning points in the financial crisis. It provided anxious investors with something they craved: credible information about prospective losses at banks. Supervisors' public disclosure of the stress test

> results helped restore confidence in the banking system and enabled its successful recapitalization.

Ben Bernanke, Chairman, Fed. Reserve Bd., Speech at "Maintaining Financial Stability: Holding a Tiger by the Tail" Financial Markets Conference: Stress Testing Banks: What Have We Learned? (Apr. 8, 2013).

2. ***Stress Testing in Europe***. In 2010, the Committee of European Banking Supervisors oversaw the first stress testing of European banks. In contrast to SCAP, these stress tests failed to restore market confidence because they included assumptions that the market did not believe were realistic, such as no sovereign defaults, and were not seen as sufficiently transparent. In fact, Bank of Ireland and Allied Irish Bank passed the stress tests only to be bailed out months later. *See* Larry D. Wall, *The Adoption of Stress Testing: Why the Basel Capital Measures Were Not Enough* 8 (Fed. Reserve Bank of Atlanta, Working Paper Series 2013-14, Dec. 2013).

3. ***Comprehensive Capital Analysis and Review (CCAR) and Dodd-Frank Act Stress Testing***. U.S. BHCs with over $50 billion in total consolidated assets are required to undergo two related capital assessments. First, CCAR (pronounced *see-car*)

> evaluates a BHC's capital adequacy, capital adequacy process and planned capital distributions, such as dividend payments and common stock repurchases. . . . If the Federal Reserve [Board] objects to a BHC's capital plan, the BHC may not make any capital distribution unless the Federal Reserve [Board] indicates in writing that it does not object to the distribution.

FED. RESERVE BD., *Comprehensive Capital Analysis and Review 2015: Assessment Framework and Results* iii (Mar. 2015). In essence, a BHC may not pay dividends or buy back shares unless it passes an annual stress test of its capital. Second, Dodd-Frank Act stress testing

> is a forward-looking quantitative evaluation of the impact of stressful economic and financial market conditions on BHC capital. . . . In addition to the annual supervisory stress test conducted by the Federal Reserve [Board], each BHC is required to conduct annual company-run stress tests under the same supervisory scenarios and conduct a mid-cycle stress test under company-developed scenarios.

FED. RESERVE BD., *Dodd-Frank Act Stress Test 2015: Supervisory Stress Test Methodology and Results* vii (Mar. 2015). BHCs with more than $10 billion but less than $50 billion in total consolidated assets must conduct company-run stress tests annually.

4. ***Past CCAR Results.*** The 2015 CCAR results show the importance of stress testing and capital planning to overall supervision. CCAR includes a quantitative assessment and a qualitative assessment. First, CCAR's quantitative assessment, like Dodd-Frank Act stress testing, analyzes BHCs' capital ratios under baseline, adverse and severely adverse economic scenarios, except that it incorporates each BHC's planned capital actions. The severely adverse economic scenario consists of a deep recession and a steep drop in asset

prices. Figure 2.7-1 shows the 2015 results of the eight U.S. Global Systemically Important Banks (G-SIBs) under the severely adverse economic scenario.

Figure 2.7-1 G-SIBs' Projected Minimum Regulatory Capital Ratios and Tier 1 Common Ratio in the Severely Adverse Scenario (2015–2016)

Bank Holding Company	Common Equity Tier 1 Ratio (%)	Tier 1 Risk-Based Capital Ratio (%)	Total Risk-Based Capital Ratio (%)	Tier 1 Leverage Ratio (%)
2015–16 Minimum Requirements	**4.5**	**6.0**	**8.0**	**4.0**
Bank of America Corporation	6.6	7.7	10.7	5.0
The Bank of New York Mellon Corporation	11.1	12.9	13.3	4.8
Citigroup Inc.	6.4	6.6	9.4	4.4
The Goldman Sachs Group, Inc.	5.4	6.4	8.1	4.8
JPMorgan Chase & Co.	5.3	6.5	8.8	4.1
Morgan Stanley	5.9	6.2	8.2	4.2
State Street Corporation	6.5	8.7	10.6	4.3
Wells Fargo & Company	5.5	7.1	10.5	5.6

Source: Fed. Reserve Bd., Comprehensive Capital Analysis and Review 2015: Assessment Framework and Results 15 (Mar. 2015).

The BHCs' projected ratios under the severely adverse scenario in Figure 2.7-1 are considerably lower than the BHCs' actual capital ratios at the time of the 2015 CCAR, reflecting the severity of the severely adverse scenario. For example, Bank of America Corporation's third quarter of 2014 common equity Tier 1 was 12.0%, Tier 1 risk-based capital ratio was 12.8%, total risk-based capital ratio was 8.0% and Tier 1 leverage ratio was 7.9%. Because a BHC will not know the Federal Reserve Board's models, the Federal Reserve Board provides an opportunity for the BHC to adjust its capital plan if the Federal Reserve Board's models have the BHC under a quantitative minimum. Taking this opportunity has been dubbed taking a mulligan, and it is not unusual for BHCs to take a mulligan. In 2015, Goldman Sachs, JPMorgan Chase & Co., and Morgan Stanley took mulligans.

Second, CCAR's qualitative assessment focuses on each BHC's internal processes for determining capital needs during a period of severe stress. The Federal Reserve Board has objected to BHCs' capital plans on qualitative grounds as well. For example, in 2015, Federal Reserve Board deemed that Deutsche Bank Trust Corporation and Santander Holdings USA, Inc. may not pay dividends or buy back shares without the Federal Reserve Board's permission until they correct qualitative deficiencies in their capital plans. In addition, although the Federal Reserve Board did not object to Bank of America's plan, it instructed Bank of America to revise and resubmit its plan in September 2016.

It is likely that different BHCs than the ones named in 2015 will be deemed to have deficiencies or have to resubmit their capital plans in the future.

5. ***Benefits of Stress Tests.*** Recall the criticisms of Basel II, and capital regulation generally, discussed in Chapter 2.6. Do stress tests help resolve these

shortcomings? If so, how? Bernanke highlighted three benefits of stress tests in a 2013 speech:

> First, stress tests complement standard capital ratios by adding a more forward-looking perspective and by being more oriented toward protection against so-called tail risks; by design, stress tests help ensure that banks will have enough capital to keep lending even under highly adverse circumstances. Second, as applied by the Federal Reserve, the stress tests look horizontally across banks rather than at a single bank in isolation. This comparative approach promotes more-consistent supervisory standards. It also provides valuable systemic information by revealing how significant economic or financial shocks would affect the largest banks collectively as well as individually. Third, the disclosures of stress test results promote transparency by providing the public consistent and comparable information about banks' financial conditions.

Ben Bernanke, Chairman, Fed. Reserve Bd., Speech at "Maintaining Financial Stability: Holding a Tiger by the Tail" Financial Markets Conference: Stress Testing Banks: What Have We Learned? (Apr. 8, 2013). How do these benefits relate to criticisms of traditional capital regulation?

6. ***Opacity of Stress Tests.*** One criticism that the financial sector has levied against the Federal Reserve Board is that it keeps its own models confidential:

> Notwithstanding the demonstrated benefits of comprehensive stress testing, this evolving tool also presents challenges. For example, even as we continue to explore ways to enhance the transparency of the models we use to estimate banks' projected revenues and losses, we have chosen not to publish the full specification of these models. As a result, we hear criticism from bankers that our models are a 'black box,' which frustrates their efforts to anticipate our supervisory findings. We agree that banks should understand in general terms how the supervisory models work, and, even more importantly, they need to be confident that our models are empirically validated and sound. . . . Over time, we expect banks to better understand the basic elements of the supervisory models, rendering them at least somewhat less opaque.

Ben Bernanke, Chairman, Fed. Reserve Bd., Speech at "Maintaining Financial Stability: Holding a Tiger by the Tail" Financial Markets Conference: Stress Testing Banks: What Have We Learned? (Apr. 8, 2013). At other times, Federal Reserve governors and staff have remarked that they are keeping their models opaque so that BHCs do not learn to manage to the models. In essence, the Federal Reserve Board, by changing the assumptions and keeping its models cloaked, is determined that its stress tests cannot be gamed by the financial sector. Do you feel differently about the internal models developed by banks and BHCs and vetted by Federal Reserve staff under the advanced approaches and models developed by Federal Reserve staff and not shared with the banks and BHCs? Do the different incentives at play make a difference? Should the Federal Reserve Board be more transparent about how it stress tests BHCs?

B. COLLINS AMENDMENT

As discussed in Chapter 2.6, the FDIC was a critic of Basel II's reliance on internal models even before the Financial Crisis. FDIC Chairman Sheila Bair reiterated the agency's disapproval of Basel II's advanced internal ratings-based approach in a January 2010 statement, even suggesting that the U.S. leverage ratio may not sufficiently constrain advanced approaches banks and BHCs, which are generally banks and BHCs with $250 billion in total consolidated assets or $10 billion or more in on-balance sheet foreign exposures, from reducing their capital levels as they implement Basel II.

Sheila C. Bair, Chairman, FDIC, Statement on the Causes and Current State of the Financial Crisis

Financial Crisis Inquiry Commission (Jan. 14, 2010)

In 2004, the Basel Committee published a new international capital standard, the Basel II advanced internal ratings-based approach (as implemented in the United States, the Advanced Approaches), that allows banks to use their own internal risk assessments to compute their risk-based capital requirements. The overwhelming preponderance of evidence is that the Advanced Approaches will lower capital requirements significantly, to levels well below current requirements that are widely regarded as too low.

Thus, despite widespread discussion of strengthening capital requirements, including recent proposals by the Basel Committee, banks around the world continue to implement Advanced Approaches designed to lower those requirements. The basic engine of capital calculation in the Advanced Approaches, its so-called "supervisory formulas," and the use of banks' own risk estimates as inputs to those formulas, remain in place even though there is growing evidence that these formulas are seriously flawed.

These critical elements of the Advanced Approach will produce capital requirements that are both too low and too subjective. Large reductions in risk-based capital requirements under the Advanced Approach could effectively swamp the beneficial effects of other reforms the Basel Committee has proposed. Unrestricted use of the Advanced Approach risks a situation in which these capital reforms ultimately are little more than mitigating factors that turn a large drop in capital requirements into a somewhat smaller drop, resulting in a failure to address the excessive leverage that preceded the crisis.

These considerations strongly support the use of a simple and straightforward international leverage constraint as a complement to the risk-based capital rules. The FDIC has advocated a minimum leverage requirement for many years and we are gratified that this proposal is included in the recent Basel Committee consultative package.

Even with a simple leverage constraint, however, we believe that allowing the Advanced Approach to be used to effect an ongoing reduction in risk-based capital requirements during a multi-year project to strengthen requirements is unwise. I am and continue to be, a strong advocate of the view that the Advanced Approaches should not be used to reduce capital requirements.

The FDIC's concerns were addressed in the Dodd-Frank Act's Collins Amendment, which was originally drafted by FDIC staff. The Collins Amendment set a risk-based capital floor by requiring advanced approaches banks and BHCs to calculate their risk-based capital under the generally applicable standardized approach in addition to the advanced approaches and to determine their compliance with minimum capital requirements by applying the higher of the two standards, establishing a one-way ratchet. In essence, an advanced approaches bank or BHC no longer has the benefit of any lower capital requirements under internal models. There is no equivalent to the Collins Amendment in the EU.

III. BASEL 2.5

The Basel Committee began revising Basel II soon after the Financial Crisis, beginning with the release of amendments to the Market Risk Amendment, commonly referred to as Basel 2.5 or II.5, in 2009:

> Basel II.5 is designed to better capture credit risk in the "trading book" of a bank. The trading book refers to securities that a bank would not hold to maturity and would also be accounted for at current market value. A security held to maturity is accounted for in the "banking book" at its original book value, unless the bank decides to sell it; if so, it then moves over to the trading book where it is given fair market value accounting treatment. Distinguishing between assets that should be held in the trading and banking books is not always easy, thus making it difficult to determine the proper accounting and risk weighting treatment. Nonetheless, Basel II.5 is intended to prevent strategic but inappropriate placement of securities in the book that would provide the most favorable accounting treatment at a particular point in time, potentially resulting in a bank having an insufficient capital buffer to mitigate lending risks. The U.S. federal banking regulators issued proposed rules on the adoption of Basel II.5 revisions in the United States on January 11, 2011; these were amended and re-proposed on December 7, 2011. The final rule on the adoption of Basel II.5, also known as the market capital risk rule, was issued by the U.S. federal banking regulators on June 7, 2012.

DARRYL E. GETTER, CONG. RESEARCH SERV., R42744, U.S. IMPLEMENTATION OF THE BASEL CAPITAL REGULATORY FRAMEWORK 3 (2014). Basel 2.5 generally raised the capital requirements for the trading book.

IV. BASEL III

In sharp contrast to Basel II, Basel III was approved by the members of the Basel Committee in September 2010, less than two years after the beginning of negotiations. Basel III maintained Basel II's general approach to capital regulation, that is, advanced and standardized risk adjusted capital requirements and the three pillars of minimum capital requirements, supervisory review, and market discipline, but it also established much stricter measures of capital and risk-weighted assets, instituted new and higher capital requirements, and introduced liquidity requirements.

U.S. regulators finalized rules on Basel III's key capital requirements and the liquidity coverage ratio in October 2013 and September 2014, respectively. Like under Basel II, these requirements were not immediately imposed on U.S. banks and BHCs. Rather, under the Basel III transitional arrangements in the

United States, the liquidity coverage ratio and capital conservation buffer, for example, will not be fully implemented until 2017 and 2019, respectively. Unlike Basel II, Basel III was applied to virtually all banks and BHCs, with the exception of BHCs with less than $1 billion in total consolidated assets, although the requirements vary by asset size. Consider the advantages and disadvantages of transitional arrangements and other approaches to introducing new financial regulations as you read about Basel III and its critiques.

A. CAPITAL REQUIREMENTS

The U.S. implementation of Basel III changed existing capital requirements for U.S. banks and BHCs and introduced new ones. Importantly, Basel III made technical changes which tightened risk-based capital ratios' numerators, that is, the definition of different capital measures, and denominator, that is, the measurement of risk-weighted assets.

With respect to changes to risk-based capital ratio numerators under the U.S. implementation of Basel III, Basel III introduced a new tier of tangible Tier 1 capital known as common equity Tier 1, and disqualified certain instruments, such as trust preferred securities, which are shares of special purpose vehicles that hold long-term subordinated debt issued by BHCs, as Tier 1 capital. In addition, mortgage servicing rights, certain deferred tax assets, and significant investments in unconsolidated financial institutions that exceed 10% of common equity Tier 1 capital per category or 15% of common equity Tier 1 capital in the aggregate must be deducted from common equity Tier 1 capital.

With respect to changes to the risk-based capital ratio denominator, or risk-weighted assets, the standardized risk weights of certain assets, such as past due exposures and high volatility commercial real estate loans, increased with the U.S. implementation of Basel III. Basel III also includes a new framework for derivatives, under which centrally cleared derivatives receive preferential capital treatment. The new derivatives framework was part of a post-Financial Crisis effort to promote central clearing of derivatives, which is discussed in more depth in Chapter 11.2. In addition, rather than relying on external credit ratings to determine the standardized risk weights of securitization exposures, a new supervisory formula was introduced and generally subjects these exposures to higher risk weights. The formula takes into account the exposure's position in the securitization structure and measures delinquencies and loss of the underlying assets, among other things. There is a 20% risk weight floor, and certain junior securitization exposures could even receive a risk weight of 1,250%, which requires capital to be held dollar for dollar against such an exposure at a total risk-based capital ratio requirement of 8% and more capital than the exposure amount if the bank manages itself to a higher total capital ratio.

Relatedly, the Financial Accounting Standards Board sought to improve financial reporting transparency with respect to securitization exposures soon after the Financial Crisis. Financial Accounting Standards 166 and 167, which became effective in 2010, required banks and BHCs to consolidate certain special purpose vehicles generally involved in securitizing assets, many of which were previously treated as separate from the sponsoring bank or BHC, or off balance sheet. Consolidating these entities meant that the banks and BHCs were required to recognize the related assets and liabilities as belonging to the bank or BHC, or on balance sheet, both for financial accounting and regulatory capital purposes. As a result, affected banks and BHCs were required to maintain capital to support the full amount of credit risks posed by these assets, effectively subjecting them to higher capital requirements for certain securitization exposures even before Basel III was implemented.

Remember that risk-based capital ratio inputs have become stricter under Basel III as you read about how the requirements have changed. Also recall that changes to standardized risk weights affect advanced approaches banks and BHCs because of the Collins Amendment. Nonetheless, advanced approaches banks and BHCs continue to calculate their risk-based capital requirements using internal models under Basel III, in addition to the standardized approach, and non-U.S. banks are not subject to the Collins Amendment.

The following sections provide an overview of changes to capital requirements under Basel III. Figure 2.7-2 provides a graphical representation of these changes and shows that Basel III requires U.S. banks and BHCs, especially the largest ones, to calculate and meet many more capital requirements and hold significantly more capital. Each of these requirements, as well as those imposed under stress testing and the Collins Amendment, could serve as a bank's or BHC's binding constraint, and the binding constraint for a bank or BHC could change over time. One can think of capital regulation after the Financial Crisis as the implementation of multiple potential backstops.

Figure 2.7-2 Risk-Based Capital Requirements under the U.S. Implementation of Basel III

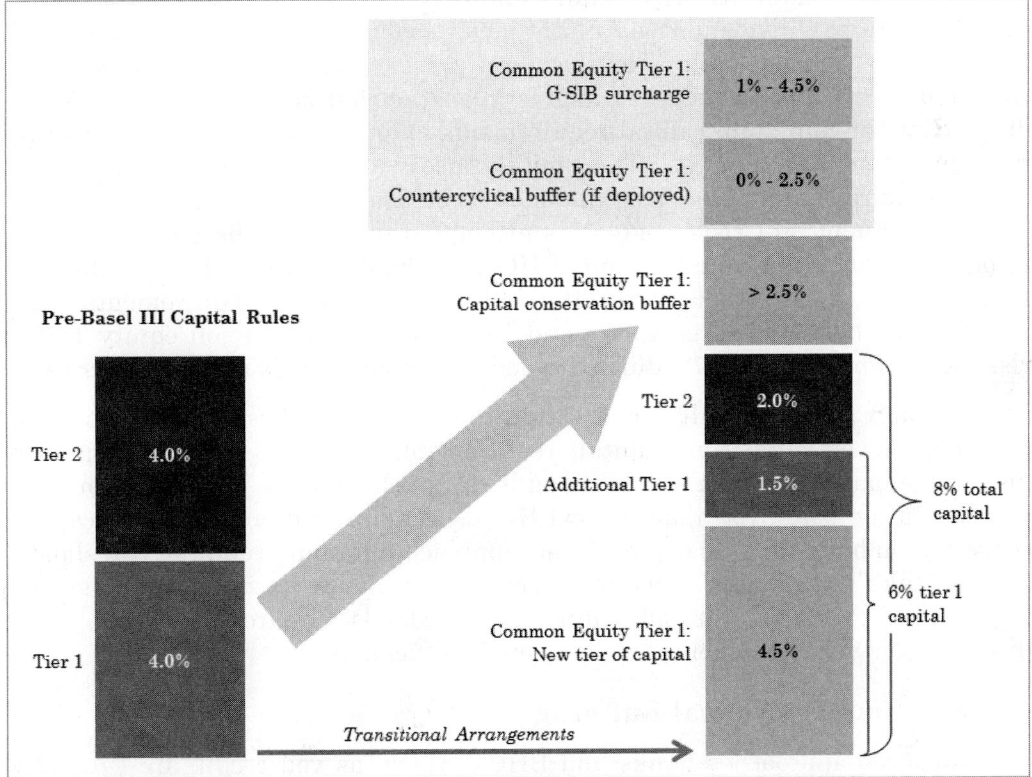

Source: Davis Polk & Wardwell LLP.

1. Minimum Regulatory Capital Ratios

The U.S. implementation of Basel III introduced a new minimum regulatory capital ratio for common equity Tier 1 capital in order to improve the quality of capital held by banks and BHCs. Remember that common shares and retained earnings proved most able to absorb losses during the Financial Crisis. To prioritize these forms of capital, Basel III subdivided Tier 1 capital into two subcategories: common equity Tier 1 capital, which consists of common shares and retained earnings, and additional Tier 1 capital, which consists of certain perpetual preferred shares. Basel III in turn requires that banks and BHCs maintain a minimum common equity Tier 1 risk-based capital ratio of 4.5%. Tier 1 capital, or both common equity Tier 1 capital and additional Tier 1 capital combined, must be at least 6% of a bank or BHC's risk-weighted assets, and total capital must be at least 8% of a bank or BHC's risk-weighted assets. The changes to the minimum regulatory capital ratios therefore change the composition of the minimum regulatory capital ratios, requiring banks and BHCs to hold more high-quality capital than previously required. Basel III also provides for more deductions from capital than before, including for certain levels of mortgage servicing rights, certain deferred tax assets, and certain levels of both non-significant and significant investments in unconsolidated financial institutions. Basel III provides more deductions for mortgage servicing rights, for example, because the value of these rights decrease when mortgage defaults increase. These deductions are made from common equity Tier 1 capital.

2. Capital Conservation Buffer

During the Financial Crisis, banks and BHCs reduced their capital levels by continuing to pay dividends and discretionary bonuses. In response, Basel III introduced a common equity Tier 1 capital conservation buffer of 2.5% of risk-weighted assets, the purpose of which is to ensure that banks and BHCs do not drop below the minimum capital requirements by providing a buffer that can be used during periods of stress. The capital conservation buffer is not a minimum capital requirement; rather, it is intended to be drawn down when appropriate. Before the Financial Crisis, regulators attempted to achieve the buffer's goal by strongly encouraging banks and BHCs to hold capital above minimum requirements. Together with the minimum capital requirements, the conservation buffer requires banks and BHCs to have a common equity Tier 1 risk-based capital ratio of 7% during periods in which there is no financial stress.

Although the capital conservation buffer exists to be used for the preservation of minimum capital requirements, it has been designed to discourage banks and BHCs from using it too much or being too slow to build it back up after use. As a bank or BHC uses more and more of the capital conservation buffer and its capital levels approach minimum required thresholds, it must take increasingly greater action to reestablish its capital position by conserving earnings through limiting dividends, share buybacks, and discretionary bonus payments to management officials.

3. Countercyclical Buffer

Advanced approaches banks and BHCs, which, as you recall, are generally banks and BHCs with over $250 billion in assets, may also be subject to a common equity Tier 1 capital countercyclical buffer, if and when deployed by the U.S. banking regulators, of up to 2.5% of their risk-weighted assets under the U.S. implementation of Basel III. Because the countercyclical buffer is meant to address systemic risk, its implementation in the United States only applies to advanced approaches banks. The countercyclical buffer serves two purposes. First, regulators may use it to limit excessive asset price appreciation during economic expansion. Second, it may serve as an additional loss absorbing capacity during economic downturns. The countercyclical buffer operates similarly to the capital conservation buffer in that an advanced approaches bank or BHC may dip into its countercyclical buffer, but doing so would trigger a requirement to conserve earnings.

4. G-SIB Surcharge

Basel III introduced a G-SIB surcharge, which requires G-SIBs to hold additional common equity Tier 1 capital. This additional capital requirement, known as the G-SIB surcharge, is not uniform for all G-SIBs. The common equity Tier 1 capital surcharge for G-SIBs ranges from 1% to 4.5% of risk-based assets, depending on the systemic importance of the G-SIB.

As of the end of 2015, eight U.S. BHCs are G-SIBs under the U.S. implementation of the G-SIB surcharge: Bank of America, Bank of New York Mellon, Citigroup, Goldman Sachs, JPMorgan Chase & Co., Morgan Stanley, State Street, and Wells Fargo & Company. U.S. G-SIBs are required to calculate their surcharge under two methods. Under the first method, based on the Basel Committee's methodology, the G-SIB surcharge is based on the G-SIB's size, interconnectedness, cross-jurisdictional activity, substitutability, and complexity. Substitutability refers to the degree to which a BHC provides important customer services that would be difficult to replace if it failed. The second method uses similar inputs, but replaces substitutability with the extent to which a G-SIB relies on short-term wholesale funding. Thus, the second method requires G-SIBs with greater liquidity risks to hold more capital.

G-SIBs will be required to meet a minimum Total Loss-Absorbing Capacity (TLAC) requirement. TLAC (pronounced *tee-lack*) consists of long-term unsecured debt and other liabilities in a form that could be expected to incur losses without triggering a contagious run and is discussed in more detail in Chapter 9.3. Essentially, the purpose of the capital requirements discussed here is to prevent a bank or BHC from becoming insolvent; in contrast, the TLAC requirement's purpose is to ensure that a BHC has enough long-term unsecured debt and other liabilities that can be used to recapitalize a BHC or its subsidiaries in the event it experiences material financial distress and has to be resolved.

5. Supplementary Leverage Ratio

Unlike Basel I and Basel II, Basel III has a leverage ratio requirement. The United States implemented the Basel III leverage ratio, which is known as the supplementary leverage ratio, for advanced approaches banks and BHCs and maintained its pre-existing leverage ratio requirement for all banks and BHCs. Unlike the U.S. leverage ratio, the supplementary leverage ratio's denominator takes into account both on- and off-balance sheet exposures. Therefore, an advanced approaches bank or BHC with substantial off-balance sheet exposures will have a larger denominator under the supplementary leverage ratio than under the U.S. leverage ratio, potentially subjecting it to a higher capital requirement. The numerator for both leverage ratios is Tier 1 capital. The minimum supplementary leverage ratio for advanced approaches banks and BHCs is 3%, as opposed to 4% for the U.S. leverage ratio. Advanced approaches banks must have a 5% U.S. leverage ratio to be considered well-capitalized.

In addition, the eight U.S. G-SIBs are subject to an enhanced supplementary leverage ratio, requiring them to maintain a supplementary leverage ratio of at least 5% at the BHC level. U.S. G-SIBs' banks must maintain a supplementary leverage ratio of 6% to be considered well-capitalized.

B. LIQUIDITY REQUIREMENTS

The Financial Crisis revealed the limits of capital as a regulatory tool. The inability of many banks to meet their short-term financing obligations during the Financial Crisis caused massive disruptions, and Basel I and Basel II's capital requirements did not account for liquidity risk. Historically, short-term liquidity strains have generally been resolved by central banks lending to solvent banks against collateral as a lender of last resort. The lender of last resort function of central banks is discussed in Chapter 9.1. There are tradeoffs, however, between relying largely on central banks to act as lenders of last resort to resolve liquidity strains versus requiring banks to internalize the risk of a liquidity crisis by making them hold a certain level of highly liquid assets. For example, strict liquidity requirements may cause liquidity to be restricted during ordinary conditions or cause banks to hoard liquid assets like cash and Treasury bills instead of making loans or acquiring other longer-term or higher-risk assets during a crisis as they try to ensure they fulfill the requirements. On the other side, it may be difficult for a central bank to determine whether a bank is solvent and whether its collateral is capable of valuation during a financial crisis. Liquidity requirements may also provide regulators with time to evaluate the condition of a bank under liquidity stress:

> When a firm faces a run on its funding, it is likely either insolvent or in a condition that makes an assessment of its solvency difficult for counterparties, investors, and regulators. That is, by this point the capital position of the firm is perceived as sufficiently uncertain so as to call into question its continued viability. Liquidity regulation can ensure that, even in these circumstances, officials have at least a bit of time to assess liquidity troubles and the underlying condition of the firm, as well as the degree to which the troubles are idiosyncratic or systemic. With appropriate insolvency mechanisms available, authorities can then decide whether the firm will recover or needs to be placed into a resolution or liquidation regime.

Daniel K. Tarullo, Governor, Fed. Reserve Bd., Speech at the Clearing House 2014 Annual Conference: Liquidity Regulation (Nov. 20, 2014).

Basel III introduced two new liquidity standards, which require banks and BHCs to greater internalized liquidity risk and are intended to complement the lender of last resort function of the Federal Reserve Board and other central banks. Only the liquidity coverage ratio has been implemented in the United States thus far.

1. Liquidity Coverage Ratio

The liquidity coverage ratio seeks to ensure that banks and BHCs have enough assets that are both easy to sell and maintain their value to meet banks' obligations over 30 days of financial stress. The U.S. liquidity coverage ratio applies to advanced approaches banks and BHCs, and a modified version applies to other BHCs with over $50 billion in total consolidated assets.

As a formula, the liquidity coverage ratio can be written as follows:

$$\frac{\textit{High-Quality Liquid Assets}}{\textit{Total Net Cash Outflows}} \geq \textit{100\%}$$

The liquidity coverage ratio has two central components: high-quality liquid assets, the numerator, and net cash outflows during a thirty-day period of financial stress, the denominator. The numerator must always be equal to or greater than the denominator. High-quality liquid assets must be unencumbered, or not pledged to secure any transaction, easy to value, and enjoy a large and robust market such that, even in times of financial stress, there are purchasers willing to buy them. In addition to being easily sold, high-quality liquid assets must also be value preserving.

Figure 2.7-3 and Figure 2.7-4 provide more details on the numerator and the denominator.

Figure 2.7-3 The Liquidity Coverage Ratio Numerator: High-Quality Liquid Assets

<table>
<tr><th colspan="2">The U.S. liquidity coverage ratio divides high quality liquid assets into Level 1, Level 2A and Level 2B asset categories.</th></tr>
<tr><td rowspan="2">Level 1 Assets
(not subject to haircut)
• Excess reserves held at a Federal Reserve Bank;
• Withdrawable reserves held at a foreign central bank;
• Securities issued or guaranteed by the Treasury;
• Securities issued or guaranteed by a U.S. government agency whose obligations are explicitly guaranteed by the full faith and credit of the U.S. government; and
• Certain securities that are claims on or guaranteed by a sovereign entity, a central bank, and other international entities that are assigned a 0% risk weight under the U.S. Basel III standardized approach capital rules.
  o This category general includes all Organization for Economic Cooperation and Development sovereign debt unless it has defaulted or was restructured in the previous 5 years.</td>
<td>Level 2A Assets
(subject to 15% haircut)
• Claims in or guaranteed by a U.S. government-sponsored enterprise such as Fannie Mae and Freddie Mac; and
• Claims on or guaranteed by a sovereign entity or a multilateral development bank that is assigned a 20% risk weight under the U.S. Basel III standardized approach capital rules.</td></tr>
<tr><td>Level 2B Assets
(subject to 50% haircut)
• Certain corporate debt securities issued by non-financial companies; and
• Certain publicly-traded common equities issued by non-financial companies that are included in the Russell 1000 index or a foreign equivalent index for shares held in foreign jurisdictions.</td></tr>
</table>

Source: Davis Polk & Wardwell LLP.

Figure 2.7-4 The Liquidity Coverage Ratio Denominator: Total Net Cash Flows

The total net cash outflow amount, the liquidity coverage ratio denominator, uses prescribed cash outflow and inflow rates. Underlying these rates are standardized assumptions applicable to all subject banking organizations, including the following:	
Loss of funding sources	• A partial loss of unsecured wholesale funding capacity; • A partial loss of secured, short-term financing with certain collateral and counterparties; and • a partial loss of retail deposits and brokered deposits from retail customers.
Increased funding needs	• Losses from derivative positions and the collateral supporting those positions; • Unscheduled draws on committed credit and liquidity facilities that a banking organization has provided to its clients; • The potential need for a banking organization to buy back debt or to honor non-contractual obligations in order to mitigate reputation and other risks; and • Other shocks that affect outflows linked to structured financing transactions, mortgages, central bank borrowings, and customer short positions.

Source: Davis Polk & Wardwell LLP.

2. Net Stable Funding Ratio

Basel III's net stable funding ratio is intended to ensure that banks and BHCs hold a minimum amount of stable funding, given their on-balance sheet assets and off-balance sheet activities, over a one year time period. The net stable funding ratio is intended to discourage and limit reliance on short-term wholesale funding, like repo and commercial paper. The United States has not yet implemented the net stable funding ratio.

V. CRITIQUES OF AND ALTERNATIVES TO BASEL III

Like Basel I and Basel II before it, Basel III soon attracted criticism. One critique, as elaborated by Andrew Haldane below, is that capital regulation has grown too complex under Basel II and Basel III. Another critique, for which Professor Anat Admati is particularly known, is that capital requirements should be much, much higher than those in place under Basel III.

Andrew G. Haldane, Executive Director, Bank of England,
The Dog and the Frisbee

Speech at the Fed. Reserve Bank of Kansas City's 366th Economic Policy Symposium (Aug. 31, 2012)

Catching a frisbee is difficult. Doing so successfully requires the catcher to weigh a complex array of physical and atmospheric factors, among them wind speed and frisbee rotation. Were a physicist to write down frisbee-catching as an optimal control problem, they would need to understand and apply Newton's Law of Gravity.

Yet despite this complexity, catching a frisbee is remarkably common. Casual empiricism reveals that it is not an activity only undertaken by those with a Doctorate in physics. It is a task that an average dog can master. Indeed some, such as border collies, are better at frisbee-catching than humans.

So what is the secret of the dog's success? The answer, as in many other areas of complex decision-making, is simple. Or rather, it is to keep it simple. For studies have shown that the frisbee-catching dog follows the simplest of rules of thumb: run at a speed so that the angle of gaze to the frisbee remains roughly constant. Humans follow an identical rule of thumb.

Catching a crisis, like catching a frisbee, is difficult. Doing so requires the regulator to weigh a complex array of financial and psychological factors, among them innovation and risk appetite. Were an economist to write down crisis-catching as an optimal control problem, they would probably have to ask a physicist for help.

Yet despite this complexity, efforts to catch the crisis frisbee have continued to escalate. Casual empiricism reveals an ever-growing number of regulators, some with a Doctorate in physics. Ever-larger litters have not, however, obviously improved watchdogs' Frisbee-catching abilities. No regulator had the foresight to predict the financial crisis, although some have since exhibited supernatural powers of hindsight.

So what is the secret of the watchdogs' failure? The answer is simple. Or rather, it is complexity. For what this paper explores is why the type of complex regulation developed over recent decades might not just be costly and cumbersome but sub-optimal for crisis control. In financial regulation, less may be more. . .

The foundations for today's financial regulatory framework were laid in the 1980s. [Basel I] was a landmark. It was the first-ever genuinely international prudential regulatory agreement. For the first time in financial history, a minimum standard had been established for all internationally-active banks. Yet despite its breadth, the Basel I agreement was only 30 pages long.

This brevity came courtesy of focussing on a limited set of credit risks measured at a broad asset class, rather than individual exposure, level. Only five different risk weights were defined under Basel I, varying from zero to 100%. Calculating regulatory capital ratios was possible using pad and pen.

In taking this simplified approach, the Basel Committee fully recognised its limitations. It was recognised that the role of regulatory rules was not to capture every raindrop. Rather, they served as a backstop to banks' own risk assessments. Basel rules were there to support, not supplant, commercial risk decisions.

During the 1990s, the bluntness of the risk judgements embodied in Basel I came increasingly to be questioned—and arbitraged. Basel I was perceived as lacking risk-sensitivity, at least by comparison with the new wave of credit and market risk models emerging at the time. Change came in 1996 with the Market Risk Amendment. This introduced the concept of the regulatory trading book and, for the first time, allowed banks to use internal models to calculate regulatory capital against market risk.

With hindsight, a regulatory rubicon had been crossed. This was not so much the use of risk models as the blurring of the distinction between commercial and regulatory risk judgements. The acceptance of banks' own models meant the baton had been passed. The regulatory backstop had been lifted, replaced by a complex, commercial judgement. The Basel regime became, if not self-regulating, then self-calibrating.

A revised [Basel I], Basel II, was agreed in 2004. It followed closely in the footsteps of the trading book amendment. Internal risk models were allowed as a means of calibrating credit risk. Indeed, not so much permitted as actively encouraged, with internal models designed to deliver lower capital charges. By design, Basel II served as an incentive device for banks to upgrade their risk management technology.

As a by-product, there was a step change in the granularity of the Basel framework. Risk exposures were no longer captured at a broad asset class level. And risk weights on these exposures were no longer confined to five buckets. That meant greater detail and complexity. Reflecting these changes, Basel II came in at 347 pages—an order of magnitude longer than its predecessor.

The ink was barely dry on Basel II when the financial crisis struck. This exposed gaping holes in the agreement. In the period since, the response has been to fill the largest of these gaps, with large upwards revisions to the calibration of the Basel framework. Agreement on this revised framework, Basel III, was reached in 2010. In line with historical trends the documents making up Basel III added up to 616 pages, almost double Basel II.

The length of the Basel rulebook, if anything, understates its complexity. The move to internal models, and from broad asset classes to individual loan exposures, has resulted in a ballooning in the number of estimated risk weights. For a large, complex bank, this has meant a rise in the number of calculations required from single figures a generation ago to several million today.

That increases opacity. It also raises questions about regulatory robustness since it places reliance on a large number of estimated parameters. Across the banking book, a large bank might need to estimate several thousand default probability and loss-given-default parameters. To turn these into regulatory capital requirements, the number of parameters increases by another order of magnitude.

It is close to impossible to determine with complete precision the size of the parameter space for a large international bank's banking book. That, by itself, is revealing. But a rough guess would put it at thousands, perhaps tens of thousands, of estimated and calibrated parameters. That is three, perhaps four, orders of magnitude greater than Basel I.

If that sounds large, the parameter set for the trading book is almost certainly larger still. To give some sense of scale, consider model-based estimates of portfolio Value at Risk (VaR), a commonly-used technique for measuring risk and regulatory capital in the trading book. A large firm would typically have several thousand risk factors in its VaR model. Estimating the covariance matrix for all of the risk factors means estimating several million individual risk parameters. Multiple pricing models are then typically used to map from these risk factors to the valuation of individual instruments, each with several estimated pricing parameters.

Taking all of this together, the parameter space of a large bank's banking and trading books could easily run to several millions. These parameters are typically estimated from limited past samples. For example, a typical credit risk model might comprise 20-30 years of sample data—barely a crisis cycle. A market risk model might comprise less than five years of data—far less than a crisis cycle.

Regulatory complexity has also found its way into the numerator of the capital ratio—the definition of capital. Under Basel I, the focus was on common equity capital, with restrictions on non-equity instruments. Progressively, a complex undergrowth of new non-equity capital instruments began to emerge. Additional "tiers" of regulatory capital, and tiers within tiers, were added.

In the end, it did all end in tears. During the crisis, investors lost confidence in non-equity capital instruments. Basel III simplified the definition of core regulatory capital, basing it around a common equity Tier 1 definition. Yet measuring capital remains a complex task. The numerator of the capital ratio adds dozens, perhaps hundreds, of parameters to the complexity quotient.

This degree of complexity complicates greatly the task for investors pricing banks' financial instruments. For example, serious concerns have been expressed about the opacity of the

Basel risk weights and their consistency across firms. Their granularity makes it close to impossible to account for differences across banks. It also provides near-limitless scope for arbitrage.

This degree of complexity also raises serious questions about the robustness of the regulatory framework given its degree of over-parameterisation. This million-dimension parameter set is based on the in-sample statistical fit of models drawn from short historical samples. If previous studies tell us it may take 250 years of data for a complex asset pricing model to beat a simple one, it is difficult to imagine how long a sample would be needed to justify a million-digit parameter set. . .

The quest for risk-sensitivity in the Basel framework, while sensible in principle, has generated problems in practice. It has spawned startling degrees of complexity and an over-reliance on probably unreliable models. The Tower of Basel is at risk of over-fitting—and over-balancing. It may be time to rethink its architecture.

A useful starting point might be to take a more sceptical view of the role and robustness of internal risk models in the regulatory framework. These are the main source of opacity and complexity. With thousands of parameters calibrated from short samples, these models are unlikely to be robust for many decades, perhaps centuries, to come. It is close to impossible to tell whether results from them are prudent.

One simple response to that concern may be to impose strict limits, or floors, on model outputs. These would provide a binding regulatory backstop. There are precedents for such an approach. At the introduction of Basel II, temporary floors were introduced into aggregate capital requirements, set at 80% of Basel I requirements. And under the Collins amendment to the Dodd-Frank Act, banks using internal models will be subject to a 100% floor based on the simpler standardised approach.

But these measures only take us so far. Regulatory-imposed floors do little by themselves to simplify the underlying regulatory architecture. Only by removing internal models from the regulatory framework can this be achieved. As an alternative foundation stone, simplified, standardised approaches to measuring credit and market risk, on a broad asset class basis, could be used. . . .

Modern finance is complex, perhaps too complex. Regulation of modern finance is complex, almost certainly too complex. That configuration spells trouble. As you do not fight fire with fire, you do not fight complexity with complexity. Because complexity generates uncertainty, not risk, it requires a regulatory response grounded in simplicity, not complexity.

Delivering that would require an about-turn from the regulatory community from the path followed for the better part of the past 50 years. If a once-in-a-lifetime crisis is not able to deliver that change, it is not clear what will. To ask today's regulators to save us from tomorrow's crisis using yesterday's toolbox is to ask a border collie to catch a frisbee by first applying Newton's Law of Gravity.

Statement of Anat R. Admati, Professor, Stanford University, Examining the Impact of the Proposed Rules to Implement Basel III Capital Standards

Hearing before the H. Comm. on Fin. Servs., 112th Cong. (2012)

Basel III is an international agreement, but it is specified as a minimum requirement. Any nation can go beyond the minimum. As you will hear, in my view and that of my colleagues, Basel III is insufficient to protect the public from risks in the financial system. The claim that we cannot go beyond Basel and design our own regulation because this might disadvantage our banks in global competition is invalid. . .

In banking, the term "capital" refers essentially to funding that is obtained not by borrowing. Elsewhere, unborrowed funding is called equity, and the word "capital" is not used in this way. When banks are said "hold capital" or "set aside capital," or indeed when the term "capital reserves" is used, the impression is created that capital and reserves are the same. But this is false. We do not say, for example, that Apple "holds 100% capital." Apple's equity is not sitting idle in reserves, and it is not actually "held" by Apple. Rather, Apple's shareholders hold Apple stock and Apple invests and generates profits for its shareholders. The same is true for bank equity or capital. Shareholders hold bank shares, banks also borrow from depositors and others and their shareholders are entitled to profits as long as debts are paid. Banks do not actually "hold" their capital.

Capital is analogous to a down payment when buying the house, which later becomes the homeowner's equity. A homeowner's equity is not sitting idle in reserve; it is invested in the house. Similarly, the banks' capital is put into loans and investments. Having more capital does not prevent banks from making loans.

Are banks well capitalized? In my view, US financial institutions are very poorly capitalized. They might be in better shape relative to many European banks, but this statement does not speak to where the banks should be and can be. In answering this question one important issue, which indeed the regulation struggles with, is how we measure the capital and relative to what it should be viewed. Capital regulation is generally based on accounting measures, but these are not always good indicators of financial health. Balance sheets are created in this country according to so-called Generally Accepted Accounting Principles or GAAP. Companies report a "book value" for their assets and liabilities or debts, and shareholder equity is the difference between them.

Because accounting rules often use historical values and allow significant discretion, there is frequently a discrepancy, at times substantial, between the book value of equity and its market value. Market values reflect how much investors would pay for the shares, which in turn is based on the views investors have about the strength of the company. The market value is often significantly above the book value for healthy non-financial companies. For example, October 31, 2012, the book value of Wal-Mart equity was about \$73 billion, whereas the total market value of its shares was almost \$253 billion, higher than the total book value of the company's assets. Whereas Wal-Mart has over \$40 billion in long-term debt, it can obviously absorb significant losses without becoming distressed.

Banks' market values are currently low relative to their book values. For example, JPMorgan Chase reported almost \$200 billion in shareholder equity on September 30, 2012, but the value of all its shares was only about \$154 billion at that time. Its total assets were reported at \$2.32 billion. . . . Bank of America reported over \$238 billion in shareholder equity, but the market value of all its shares at that time was barely over \$95 billion, significantly less than a half of the book value. The total assets of the bank were reported as \$2.26 trillion, and would again be much larger by international accounting standards.

Banks were considered to be in good shape before the crisis. Even Bear Stearns was considered strong months before it collapsed. As it turned out, an enormous amount of risk built up in the system. Investors and regulators did not realize it or did not want to recognize it. The consequences were disastrous. In the crisis, market values plunged, credit froze, and the government and Fed intervened massively to support the banks and the system. Yet, throughout the crisis, banks' accounting-based capital ratios did not change very much. You would not know there was a crisis looking at them. The market values told a different story, being high prior to the crisis and then plunging. . . .

Banks do not need to borrow as much as they do. No healthy corporation in the economy has anywhere near the level of indebtedness that banks maintain, even though we do not regulate how much most companies borrow. Nothing that banks do necessitate that they are so highly indebted. Banks can do everything better if they had more equity.

Yet, banks fight to continue to live on the edge. Regulators and others seem to accept that the equity levels that we have gotten used to are somehow appropriate or that there is a cost to increasing them significantly. Basel III requires 4.5% equity to so-called "risk weighted assets," (plus 2.5% "conservation buffer," also relative to these risk weighted assets). Only some banks are subject to a simple leverage ratio requirement and that is set at somewhere between 3% and 4% depending on what is included in the denominator. . . . I still find the levels outrageously low. There is actually no scientific basis for these numbers, and there is no relevant cost to society from increasing them dramatically.

Instead of taking clue from recent history, let's go further in time. In the middle of the 19th century, banks had 40% or 50% equity; back at the start of the 20th century, banks routinely had 25% equity, without any regulation. This did not necessarily make them safe, but the reasons were different. The increased reliance on borrowing matches the expansion of safety nets for the banking system, such as the creation of the Federal Reserve, and deposit insurance.

If anything, banks today have more access to investors who might provide them with equity funding than in the past. If they have profitable investments, they should be able to fund them with equity like other companies do, even at levels of 15% or 20% or even 25% of assets.

Why do banks hate equity so much and claim such regulations are so costly for them? There are four reasons.

1. Debt overhang—because banks are already indebted, they (meaning their managers and shareholders) prefer debt over equity as a form of funding. This phenomenon is true for every borrower. In a sense, borrowing can be "addictive."

2. The tax code encourages borrowing because of the tax deductibility of interest payments.

3. Flawed fixation on return-on-equity (ROE) or similar measures for compensation. Such compensation encourages excessive risk taking, which does not create value unless someone else bears the downside.

4. The government safety net—implicit and explicit guarantees—makes it possible and attractive to borrow at subsidized rates.

Importantly, none of these reasons represents a cost to society of imposing high equity requirements given that high indebtedness harms the public. . . .

Basel III continues the quest to find proper "scientific" risk calibration. It tries to address some of the obvious weaknesses that were seen in the crisis. What it fails to recognize is that the entire approach of risk weights is highly problematic. The attempt to fix the regulation with ever more complex rules is based on the illusion that this can be done properly. Regulators should realize the limitations of models and data to capture complex systems.

In fact, while the approach tries hard to be "scientific" in measuring some risks, it entirely ignores some. For example, it does not quite take into account interest rate risk. And there is no way that the models will be based on enough information about the counterparties to be able to predict the dynamics of liquidity breakdowns or what the next crisis might bring. Banks continue to be allowed to use their risk models, and regulators are burdened with having to approve these models, all of which does not quite give confidence that the system can be trusted to protect us. The approach neglects "black swans" or "unknown unknowns."

The risk weights of Basel II actually allowed banks to "innovate" to hide risks from investors and regulators and they made the system more interconnected and more fragile. Concentrating enormous credit risk on AIG did not make the risk go away; it only transfers it to AIG. When the government bailed AIG out, banks did not [factor in] the risk they took by counting on AIG to be able to pay them. Regulators, meanwhile, also ignored the risks building up at AIG.

Basel III uses narrow lessons from the previous crisis by changing some of the ways risk weights are calculated but it continues to trust the models and the approach and it continues to ignore or be unable to treat some risks. If credit rating agencies are not used, do we know that the alternative models would perform better?

A good analogy for capital regulation is speed limits. Think of banks as trucks with different amounts of dangerous cargo. (The most systemic banks are like trucks carrying explosives.) The truck companies might say that there should be no tight speed limit because they have good drivers and fancy risk models. They might argue that low speed limit, or mandated rest breaks, would increase their costs and increase prices for delivery and thus harm the economy. Would we allow them to drive at 80 miles per hours on the basis of their models and assertions? If we try, there will be much outcry after the first major disaster.

The financial system was allowed to operate with excessive leverage and a major disaster did occur. Striving for a fancy model should not detract us from the objective of a safe system, particularly when safety can be achieved at little relevant cost. The equivalent of driving at 35 mph and taking reasonable rest break is that banks do not take excessive debt-fueled gambles that endanger the economy. There is absolutely no cost associated with that for society, only benefits. . .

The most systemic institutions should have much higher capital requirements, particularly if nothing else is done to control their risk and complexity. Their equity levels should be maintained between 20%-30% equity to total assets. If they are unable to reach these levels in a managed transition, their solvency and viability should be called into question. Note that this does not mean that they should stay at this size. Their current size may well be inefficiently large, and if subsidies are reduced, they might shrink naturally.

---

1. ***Complexity and Capital Regulation.*** After Chapter 2.5, Chapter 2.6, and this Chapter, you may share Haldane's criticism: capital regulation is far too complex. But if banks seek new and complex ways to engage in risk taking not fully captured by capital regulation, how should regulators respond? Furthermore, banks must measure and manage risk on their own for business purposes. Should regulators not work to understand or supervise how banks do this if it is complex?

2. ***Compliance Costs.*** One of the consequences of complexity is compliance costs. Haldane further writes that,

> The costs of constructing and maintaining [the Basel III] regulatory skyscraper are not trivial. A recent study by McKinsey estimates the compliance costs of Basel III. For a midsize European bank, these are put at up to 200 full-time jobs. Given that Europe has around 350 banks with total assets over €1 billion, this translates into over 70,000 new full time jobs to comply with Basel III requirements.

Andrew G. Haldane, Exec. Dir., Fin. Stability, Bank of England, The Dog and the Frisbee, Speech at Fed. Reserve Bank of Kansas City's 366th Economic Policy Symposium (Aug. 31, 2012).

3. ***Modigliani and Miller.*** Professors Frank Modigliani and Merton Miller have theorized that a firm's capital structure, or the mixture of debt and equity

that it chooses, is irrelevant to its value. As a firm becomes increasingly levered and takes on more debt, as opposed to equity, to finance its activities, it may experience greater returns, but these returns are offset by the greater risk that the equity has taken on, making the equity less valuable. If a bank or BHC is indifferent to how it finances itself, increased capital requirements, like those suggested by Admati, would not impose costs on society. Would increasing capital requirements, however, have no costs? Professor Charles Calomiris cautions that:

> [t]he costs of higher capital requirements come primarily in the form of reduced banking activity—especially reduced lending (in other words, a 'credit crunch') that can result from a large, sudden increase in capital requirements. After all, a capital requirement is a ratio of capital to assets, which means that a higher ratio can be achieved both by increasing the amount of capital in the numerator of the ratio and by *reducing* the quantity of assets in the denominator—that is, by reducing lending. . . . Equity finance is relatively disadvantaged by the fact that it is difficult for investors to properly assess the value of a bank, so it tends to be harder for banks to sell equity than to raise debt finance. An important consequence of this reality is that banks tend to respond to higher required capital ratios mainly by curtailing their lending rather than by raising new capital. Thus, despite the benefits of banking-system stability that may accompany higher capital requirements, there are significant downsides in the associated contraction in the supply of bank credit.

Charles Calomiris, *How to Regulate Bank Capital*, 10 NAT'L AFFAIRS 41, 48–49 (Winter 2012). Furthermore, Modigliani and Miller have emphasized that their theorem made a number of simplifying assumptions that do not hold true in reality. For example, the theorem assumes that there are no taxes, individuals and corporations have perfect information, choice of funding does not affect productivity, and consumers and corporations can borrow at the same rate. In reality, however, corporate tax rules encourage debt over equity, financial balance sheets are relatively opaque, financial firms may get subsidies from borrowing because of deposit insurance or the perception among bondholders that they are too big to fail, some of the cost of firm failure can be externalized to society at large, and managers' interests may not fully align with the interests of shareholders or creditors. Because Modigliani and Miller's simplifying assumptions may not hold and there may be other unintentional consequences, such as driving activity to the shadow banking sector, substantially increasing capital requirements may have trade-offs, rather than be costless. Douglas J. Elliott, *Higher Bank Capital Requirements Would Come at a Price*, BROOKINGS INSTITUTE (2013). For more on Modigliani and Miller, Admati, and capital regulation generally, see Chapter 14 of JOHN ARMOUR ET AL, PRINCIPLES OF FINANCIAL REGULATION (Oxford Univ. Press, forthcoming 2016).

4. ***Bank of International Settlements Study on the Long-Term Economic Impact of Basel III's Capital and Liquidity Reforms.*** The Bank of International Settlements released a study in 2010 which concluded that there are long-run expected net benefits from imposing a range of higher capital requirements. According to the study, increasing the minimum total common

equity to risk-weighted assets ratio to as high as 17% would have a positive impact on economic growth in the long run because higher capital levels would reduce the chances of a crisis. Figure 2.7-5 summarizes the study's results.

Figure 2.7-5 Long-run Expected Annual Net Economic Benefits of Increases in Capital and Liquidity

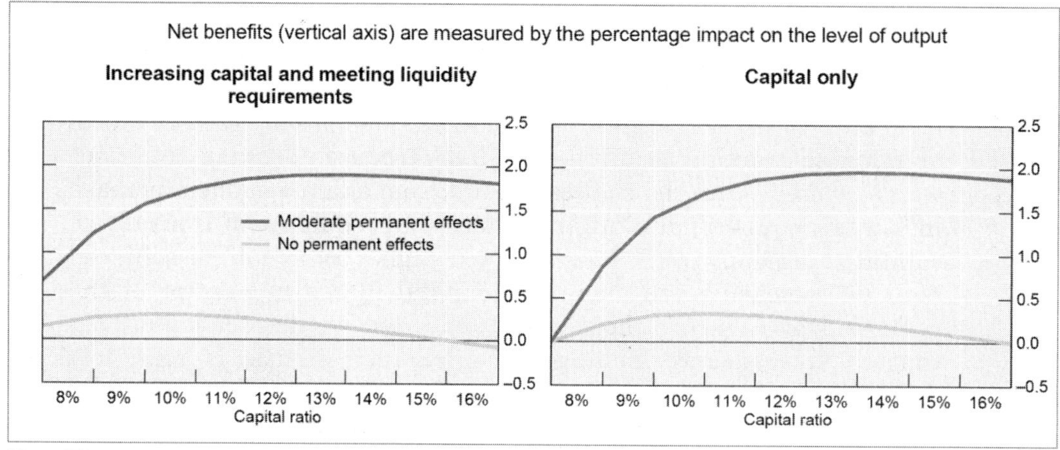

Note: The capital ratio is defined as total common equity over risk-weighted assets. The origin corresponds to the pre-reform steady state, approximated by historical averages for total capital ratios (7%) and the average probability of banking crises. Net benefits are measured by the difference between expected benefits and expected costs. Expected benefits equal the reduction in the probability of crises times the corresponding output losses. The black and gray lines refer to different estimates of net benefits, assuming that the effects of crises on output are permanent but moderate (which also corresponds to the median estimate across all comparable studies) or only transitory.

Source: Bank for Int'l Settlements, An Assessment of the Long-Term Economic Impact of Stronger Capital and Liquidity Requirements 2 (Aug. 2010).

In contrast to the Bank of International Settlements study, JPMorgan Chase & Co. CEO Jamie Dimon, reflecting the view of many in the banking sector, stated that capital requirements under Basel III are excessive and warned that they will stifle economic growth. Andrew Ackerman, *Jamie Dimon Says Regulations Will 'Stifle' Economic Growth*, WALL ST. J. (Apr. 5, 2011).

5. ***Extra-Basel Surcharges in Europe.*** The United States is not the only country that has considered or imposed capital regulation that goes beyond the Basel framework. For example, in 2011, the Independent Commission on Banking, a UK government commission tasked with recommending banking sector reforms and chaired by Sir John Vickers, advocated requiring systemic UK banks to hold more capital than they would be required to under the standards set forth by the Basel Committee, specifically recommending an additional common equity buffer of 3% of risk-weighted assets for these banks. A 2016 Bank of England proposal, however, revealed that the required buffer is expected to be considerably lower than 3%. Vickers believes that,

> the Bank of England is getting the balance wrong, in particular by watering down his recommendations on the amount of equity capital the biggest banks should hold as a percentage of risk-weighted assets. It is also setting a lower equity capital requirement for the system as a whole than previous estimates suggested. His criticism will renew questions over the resilience of the British banking

> system, and cast doubt on the [Bank of England's] claim that the system is already within sight of the amount of capital it needs to raise by the end of the decade.

Simplicity is the key to a resilient banking regime, FIN. TIMES (Feb. 16, 2016). In fact, Vickers cited Admati and Professor Martin Hellwig's work in his criticism of the Bank of England's approach. *See* John Vickers, *The Bank of England must think again on systemic risk*, FIN. TIMES (Feb. 14, 2016).

Elsewhere in Europe, Switzerland has imposed capital requirements on its largest banks, Credit Suisse and UBS, that go beyond those established by the Basel Committee. Under these requirements, known as Swiss Finish, Credit Suisse and UBS may be required to hold up to 19% of their risk-weighted assets in capital and hybrid debt instruments that can absorb losses by converting to equity, including 10% of their risk-weighted assets in the form of common equity Tier 1 capital.

VI. CAPITAL AND LIQUIDITY LEVELS TODAY

This Chapter's discussion of changes to capital and liquidity regulation after the Financial Crisis invites the question of whether bank and BHC capital and liquidity positions have increased since the Financial Crisis and, if so, how much. As noted by Chair Janet Yellen, U.S. G-SIBs have dramatically increased their capital and liquidity since the Financial Crisis:

> From early 2009 through 2014, capital held by the eight most systemically important U.S. [BHCs] more than doubled, reflecting an increase of almost $500 billion in the strongest form of capital held by these companies. Likewise, the Federal [Reserve Board's] increased focus on liquidity has contributed to significant increases in firms' liquidity. The high-quality liquid assets held by these eight firms has increased by roughly one-third since 2012, and their reliance on short-term wholesale funding has dropped considerably.

Janet Yellen, Chair, Fed. Reserve Bd., Speech at the Citizens Budget Commission: Improving the Oversight of Large Financial Institutions (Mar. 3, 2015). Figure 2.7-6 further shows how much U.S. BHCs have increased the quantity and quality of capital since the Financial Crisis.

Figure 2.7-6 Aggregate Ratio of Common Equity Capital to Risk-Weighted Assets of 2015 Comprehensive Capital Analysis and Review BHCs

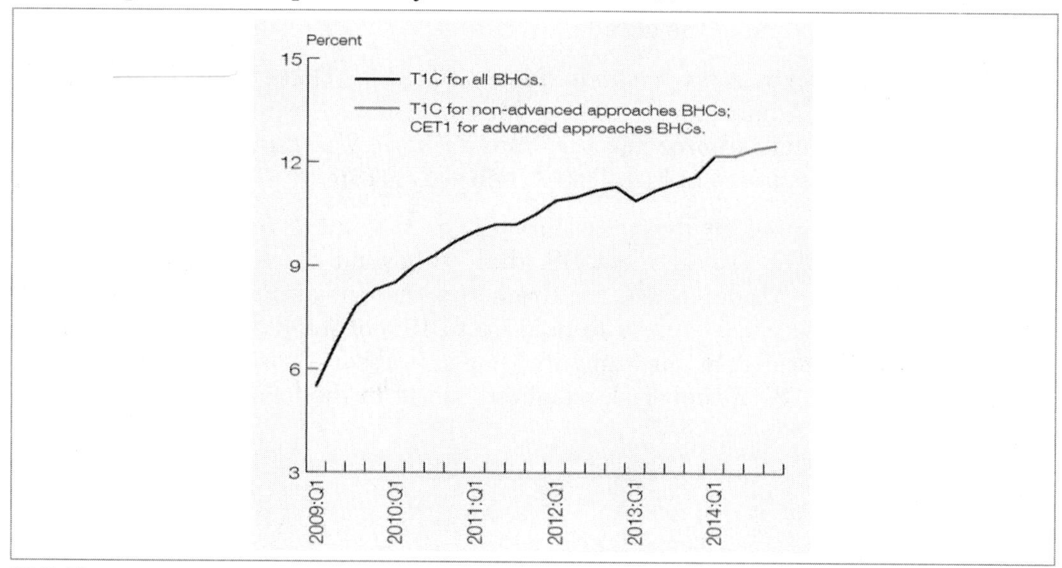

T1C Tier 1 common.

CET1 Common equity tier 1.

Source: FR Y-9C. From 2009 through 2013, tier 1 common was used to measure common equity capital for all BHCs. In 2014, both tier 1 common capital (for non-advanced approaches BHCs) and common equity tier 1 capital (for advanced approaches BHCs) were used.

From Fed. Reserve Bd., Comprehensive Capital Analysis and Review 2015: Assessment Framework and Results 2 (Mar. 2015).

Whether capital and liquidity levels are now set at appropriate levels remains the subject of intense debate.

PART III

INSURANCE

CHAPTER 3.1

INTRODUCTION TO INSURANCE REGULATION

CONTENTS

I. INTRODUCTION

With this Chapter, we turn our attention to the regulation of insurance. We begin with an overview of insurance regulation in the United States, including a brief summary of the history of insurance regulation and an introduction to the responsibilities of state and federal governments in the supervision of insurance companies. We then explore how the regulatory perimeter of insurance regulation is articulated. Finally, we consider a few instances where the line between insurance and other financial products has produced legal controversy.

Before turning to these materials, consider the economic function of insurance: to spread the risk of an adverse event across a group of individuals or firms. In exchange for payments from insurance policyholders, typically known as premiums, insurance companies commit themselves to make contingent payments back to those policyholders in the event that some specified adverse event happens in the future, such as when an automobile is damaged, a house burns down, or a person dies. An insurance company's commitments are probabilistic. Not all policyholders will suffer the event against which they purchase insurance; indeed, the business model of insurance companies typically requires that the vast majority of policyholders do not make claims on their policy. With the help of actuaries, the amount of an insurance company's commitments can be predicted, often with considerable accuracy, but the obligations are not fixed in the same way that a bank deposit is fixed. The distinguishing characteristic of an insurance company's balance sheet is the presence of policy reserves as the firm's principal liabilities. These reserves reflect the value of an insurance company's collective commitments to make payments to its policyholders.

The contingent nature of insurance contracts poses many challenges for the insurance sector and its regulators. To give a flavor of these complexities, consider the following transactions:

- Suppose you were an insurance executive hoping to offer bicycle insurance in Cambridge, Massachusetts, an urban center with many student riders. According to police reports for the Boston metropolitan market, where Cambridge is located, one in five bicycles is stolen each year. What annual premium should an insurance company charge for a $100 bicycle owned by a student living in Cambridge?
- What considerations are relevant to your pricing decision? For example, are those who purchase insurance policies likely to face average risks? Will the purchase of insurance policies have an impact on the amount of care that a policyholder takes with respect to her bike? How might an insurance company structure the terms of the insurance policy to address these issues?
- Should different considerations apply to pricing decisions for fire insurance on a $100,000 property if your actuaries told you that there was a one in 300 chance that the property would be destroyed by fire in any particular year? To what extent do the considerations related to the bicycle insurance policy discussed above differ with respect to homeowners insurance?

How should an insurance company's commitments to insure a bicycle from theft or a home from fire be valued on that balance sheet? Should the reserves be based on the expected value of the insurance company's obligations or some other measure? Is the role of capital on an insurance company's balance sheet the same as its role on a bank's balance sheet?

II. AN OVERVIEW OF INSURANCE REGULATION

A. SECTOR STRUCTURE

The following thumbnail sketch of the insurance sector is instructive on many levels.

> By any measure, insurance is a significant sector of the U.S. economy. Insurance premiums in the life and health (L/H) and property and casualty (P/C) insurance sectors totaled more than $1.1 trillion in 2012, or approximately 7 percent of gross domestic product. In the United States, insurers directly employ approximately 2.3 million people, or 1.7 percent of nonfarm payrolls. More than 2.3 million licensed insurance agents and brokers hold more than 6 million licenses. Moreover, as of year-end 2012, the L/H and P/C sectors reported $7.3 trillion in total assets—roughly half the size of total assets held by insured depository institutions. . . .

FED. INS. OFFICE, HOW TO MODERNIZE AND IMPROVE THE SYSTEM OF INSURANCE REGULATION IN THE UNITED STATES 1 (2013).

To begin with, this quote highlights the importance of product lines in the organization of insurance firms. The two major categories of insurance companies are life and health insurance and property and casualty insurance, each specializing in different types of insurance and subject to different regulatory requirements. There are many other types of insurance firms, such as title insurance companies, and within the general category of property and casualty firms, there are many different lines of business, such as automobile insurance, workers' compensation, and homeowners insurance. Figure 3.1-1 reports on property and casualty premiums by line of business in 2012 and 2013.

As the figure suggests, premium flows are a common measure of insurance sector size, and property and casualty companies had more than $542 billion in premiums in 2013 or roughly 29% of total sector premiums of $1.87 trillion that year. *See* NAIC REPORT CARD FOR 2013 (Aug. 14, 2014). Life and health insurance accumulated the largest amounts of premiums in 2013 with $729 billion and $571 billion in premiums, respectively. *Id.* Insurance companies can also be measured in terms of balance sheet measure, as we saw in Chapter 1.1. On this dimension, life insurance companies have the largest holdings, as many of their policies include asset accumulation features as well as risk pooling. Insurance regulation imposes different kinds of portfolio restrictions on various categories of insurance companies, so the financial holdings of firms differ considerably by line of business.

The insurance sector is also highly fragmented. According to 2014 figures, there were 6,118 domestic insurance companies, or insurance companies domiciled in a state in which business is written, in the United States, with 582 in New York, the largest concentration of any state. *See* NAIC, 2014 INSURANCE DEPARTMENT RESOURCES, Vol. 1, at 35–37 (2015). Property and casualty firms represent the largest number of these domestic insurance companies with 2,583 firms, followed by life insurance companies with 895 firms, and health insurers with 857 firms. *Id.* Many of these firms are also authorized to do business in other jurisdictions, where they are known as foreign insurance companies. In 2014, there were 72,232 licensed foreign insurance companies in the United States. *Id.*

Figure 3.1-1 U.S. Property & Casualty Premium by Line of Business

U.S. Property & Casualty Premium by Line of Business

Line of Business	2013	2014
Accident & Health	5,943,310,369	5,601,767,251
Allied lines	13,349,691,960	12,995,129,881
Federal flood	3,078,500,389	3,028,609,117
Crop		967,755,975
Farm	15,084,480,622	13,666,645,811
Homeowners multiple peril	82,660,181,703	86,303,533,486
Commercial multi peril	37,721,168,598	38,961,757,164
Mortgage guaranty	4,546,543,732	4,534,832,939
Ocean & Inland Marine	19,947,274,865	21,586,864,497
Financial guaranty	608,444,024	477,564,807
Fire	13,098,155,584	12,670,360,838
Earthquake	2,280,047,235	2,301,676,840
Workers' compensation	55,708,292,405	59,444,975,584
Products liability	3,321,275,989	3,358,246,777
Automobile	207,309,338,508	218,409,045,763
Aircraft (all perils)	1,550,680,659	1,502,705,778
Fidelity	1,171,257,946	1,211,389,569
Surety	5,214,468,817	5,459,383,404
Burglary and theft	246,775,411	265,462,287
Boiler and machinery	1,466,336,006	1,492,824,809
Credit	1,695,022,129	1,714,424,883
Other	57,058,714,233	61,491,956,150
Medical professional liability	9,784,635,293	9,658,127,504
Total	**542,844,596,029**	**567,105,040,780**

Source: National Association of Insurance Commissioners

(Premiums from Property Annual Statements plus State Funds)

Source: Nat'l Ass'n of Ins. Commissioners, State Insurance Regulation: Key Facts and Market Trends (2015).

Notwithstanding the large number of firms, there are numerous insurance groups in the United States, *i.e.*, conglomerates with controlling interests in many affiliated insurance companies. Measured by premiums, the largest of these is Metropolitan Life and its affiliated firms with total direct written premiums in 2013 of nearly $94 billion or roughly 5.4% of total insurance sector premiums that year. *See* NAIC REPORT CARD FOR 2013 (Aug. 14, 2014). The top five insurance groups accounted for nearly $341 billion in premiums in 2013, or roughly 18.3% of total premiums. *Id.* While these market shares are significant, they do not approach the degrees of concentration we discussed earlier with respect to major bank holding companies (BHCs).

A final point on the structure of the insurance sector noted in the Federal Insurance Office (FIO) excerpt previously quoted is the existence of a large number, 2.3 million, of independent brokers and agents that distribute insurance products. These individuals are a part of the 7.8 million individuals and entities licensed to provide some sort of insurance service in the United States in 2014, including adjusters, third-party administrators, and ratings/advisory organizations that help process insurance sector data. *See* NAIC, 2014 INSURANCE DEPARTMENT RESOURCES, Vol. 1, at 51 (2015).

B. A BRIEF HISTORY OF U.S. INSURANCE REGULATION

Chapter 1.2 offered a general overview of the history of financial regulation in the United States, with a slight bias in the direction of banks and other depository institutions. We now present a deeper perspective, oriented towards insurance and insurance regulation.

1. Colonial Times Through the Civil War: 1776–1865

Marine insurance was the predominant line of insurance during the colonial period, meeting the demand from New England merchants to insure their ships and cargo. Not a single building in the colonies was insured until 1752. The colonists' insurance policies were often bought from British insurance companies. This was due, in part, to the Act of Parliament of 1719, explicitly extended to the American colonies in 1741, which made the organization of stock insurance companies illegal in the British colonies. The development of a domestic American insurance sector proceeded slowly. The earliest known advertisement for an opening of an insurance office was in 1721 in Philadelphia, followed by another insurance office in Massachusetts in 1728.

The emergence of the corporate form was a key factor in the development of the insurance sector. Individual underwriting, which was the bulk of colonial domestic insurance activity, was limited in scope. The corporate form enabled insurers to raise enough capital to issue a large number of insurance policies and diversify risk. Additionally, the indefinite life of a corporation allowed insurers to credibly enter into the long-term contractual obligations that insurance policies often require. The first known domestic insurance company, the Corporation for the Relief of Poor and Distressed Presbyterian Ministers, was based in Philadelphia and issued its first policy in 1761.

The use of the corporate form offered states the opportunity to impose restrictions on the insurance corporation. Incorporation was usually granted by special enactment by the state legislature, often conditioned on various restrictions. Accordingly, the early insurance sector was regulated by a diverse collection of restrictions rather than by generally applicable statutes. After the panic of 1837, general incorporation laws became the norm at approximately the same time that free banking laws were enacted for banks.

The insurance sector did not experience its first period of rapid growth until roughly the 1830s. Before this period, insurance was of marginal importance in the economy. The number of insurance companies then increased dramatically, from nine in 1830, to 15 in 1840, and to 43 in 1860. A large portion of the growth in the 1840s was in life insurance. While economic growth no doubt contributed to the rise of the insurance sector in the mid-19th Century, some experts also attribute a portion of the sector's expansion to the introduction of the mutual form, an incorporated entity owned and controlled by policyholders, not shareholders. Nearly all the special charters granted in New York City in the 1840s were for mutuals, such as Mutual Life in 1843.

During the pre-Civil War period, the predominant regulatory tool was the use of public and periodical reports at the state level. As early as 1807 Massachusetts required that the president and directors of domestic insurance companies provide a statement describing the financial status of the company to the legislature. Other popular regulatory features included requiring the publication in a newspaper of various financial data and the filing of a financial statement in a local public office where citizens could inspect it. New York developed a regulatory structure similar to that of Massachusetts. In 1824, New York imposed certain filing requirements on foreign companies and shortly thereafter enacted a statute requiring domestic corporations to file annually a form specifying certain financial information, such as debts owed by the corporation, which had to be submitted to the comptroller of the state. If the comptroller believed something was amiss, then a report was supposed to be filed with the legislature.

Some states also enacted more substantive regulation. Massachusetts, at the early date of 1817, limited the risks of fire companies to one-tenth of their capital and forbade insurance companies from engaging in other types of businesses. New York, in 1851, required a $100,000 deposit for corporations, whether foreign or domestic, requesting to underwrite insurance in the state. This concern with ensuring the financial health of insurance companies became a major focus of regulatory attention over time.

There were several motivations in enacting insurance regulation at this early date. One of the most important was the desire for revenue. Much of the early insurance legislation was located in taxation statutes. The earliest officials in charge of insurance regulation were fiscal officials. Massachusetts and Pennsylvania, in 1827, named the state treasurer as the official in charge of the insurance filings, while New York named the state comptroller. Imposing a requirement of filing financial information with state officials aided in the collection of revenue. Many states collected revenue from licensing fees. Some of the motivation was protectionist or retaliatory in nature. Massachusetts required agents of foreign companies to post bonds. Pennsylvania, in 1829, imposed a 20% tax on all premiums collected by agents of foreign companies.

In the 1850s, independent agencies emerged whose sole responsibility was to regulate the insurance sector. The first board was established in 1851 by New Hampshire. Massachusetts established a board in 1852. The Massachusetts board's duties included examining the annual reports of the insurance companies and ensuring that the insurance laws were enforced. In 1854, and again in 1855, the power of the board was expanded. Massachusetts provided an annual salary to the members of the board. Soon, other states followed. In 1859, New York established a single superintendent of insurance with fairly extensive powers. The establishment of an independent administrative agency responsible for insurance regulation made possible more extensive regulation than was possible when the responsible official had other duties. The independent board also allowed for specialization in insurance regulation, a necessary perquisite to administrating statutes more complex than the ones that existed up to that point.

2. Post-Civil War Developments: 1865–1944

After the passage of the National Bank Act of 1864, the insurance sector sought relief from state regulation by attempting to convince Congress to pass a federal insurance law. One of the focuses of the second meeting of the National Board of Fire Underwriters, held in 1868, was the passage of a federal insurance law. Although bills were introduced in Congress, these efforts never succeeded. The insurance sector turned towards the courts for relief. The landmark case of *Paul v. Virginia*, 75 U.S. 168 (1869), was the result.

Decided in 1869, *Paul v. Virginia* had a fundamental impact on the course of insurance regulation. The dispute involved Virginia statutes that required the licensing of foreign (that is, out of state) insurance companies and their agents. Paul applied for a Virginia license to represent unadmitted New York insurance companies as an agent, but refused to comply with a licensing condition that securities be deposited with the state. The litigation was financed by an insurance group that the Virginia licensing rules would be declared unconstitutional, thereby prompting congressional adoption of a national insurance law modeled on the National Bank Act.

The insurance sector's strategy was thwarted when the Court held that insurance companies did not operate in interstate commerce. Justice Johnson Field explained that "[insurance contracts] are not subjects of trade and barter offered in the market as something having an existence and value independent of the parties to them. They are not commodities to be shipped or forwarded from one State to another, and then put up for sale. . . . Such contracts are not interstate transactions, though the parties may be domiciled in different states." In later cases, the Supreme Court repeatedly endorsed and expanded the *Paul* doctrine, effectively granting state authorities unbridled authority to develop insurance regulations and taxes, including provisions that discriminated between local and out-of-state companies, and denying the federal government power to regulate insurance.

After the Civil War, the country experienced rapid growth and increasing financial and economic concentration; the insurance sector participated in this growth. In 1860, there was $205 million of life insurance in force. By 1900, the figure was over $7.6 billion. Many lines of insurance developed for the first time in this period. Casualty insurance experienced growth of 318% in assets and 275.5% in income between 1894 and 1904. Before this period the size of the casualty insurance sector was insignificant. Personal accident insurance, introduced only in 1863, also experienced significant growth. Rapid growth in the health insurance sector, whose formation can be located in the 1890s, occurred at the turn of the century.

With the expansion of the insurance sector and the intensity of insurance regulation by the states after the Civil War, the need for regulatory uniformity increased. In 1871, a group of state insurance commissioners began to hold meetings to discuss issues such as establishing standardized annual forms and uniform methods of valuing the assets of insurance firms. Over time, these meetings evolved into an organization known as the National Association of Insurance Commissioners (NAIC), which has played an important role over the years in coordinating insurance regulation across state lines and facilitating periodic reform efforts, as will be discussed in more detail below.

Throughout the post-Civil War era, there was a widespread belief that the investments of insurance companies should be geographically limited so that they might serve local interests. One of the first laws that attempted to force local investment was passed by Wisconsin in 1865, but it was repealed in less than a year. In 1907, Texas passed the Robertson Law, which required that 75% of the Texas reserves be invested in Texas securities to receive a license to sell insurance there. Many life insurance companies initially withdrew from Texas after the passage of this law, but they eventually returned.

Towards the latter half of the 19th Century, a recurrent problem in the fire insurance sector was the cyclical nature of fire insurance losses. New insurers were tempted to enter the market when losses were low and profits were high and insurers, whether new or old, had an incentive to charge rates that were too low to sustain long-term profitability. This problem was particularly acute during the 19th Century because of the primitive state of actuarial science. When a major fire occurred, many of the insurers who had engaged in over-confident predictions of future losses became insolvent. Of course, there were other important sources of insolvency, including mismanagement, fraud, and a weak economy. Responding to this cycle of booms and busts, the president of the Fire Underwriter's Association of the Northwest in 1877 estimated that about 4,000 insurance companies had come into existence at one point or another, and that only 1,000 remained. An insurance sector committee in 1850 estimated that the fire insurance suffered a net loss from 1791 to 1850.

Destructive rate cutting was especially difficult to stop. Even if an insurer was able to resist the temptation to cut rates, it was difficult, sometimes impossible, for an insurer to prevent its agents from selling the insurance at below cost. The agent had a powerful incentive to sell as much insurance as possible since the more insurance sold the larger the agent's commissions. The downside, or the liability of potential future losses, was borne by the insurer and not the agent. This problem was exacerbated because insurers were anxious not to upset their agents for fear of the agents switching, along with their business, to another company.

The first systematic attempt to prevent destructive rate cutting was the establishment of local boards that attempted to maintain minimum rates. One of the first boards, the Salamander Society, was established in 1819, though informal agreements between companies existed as early as 1806. The boards were usually dominated by local agents and generally proved to be ineffective. The incentive to cheat during profitable times proved too powerful. The rates established by the boards were often inadequate, as well.

In 1864 and 1865, the insurance sector suffered from heavy losses and rate cutting. In response, the National Board of Fire Underwriters was established in 1866. The first two planks in the National Board platform stated the goal of establishing a uniform system of rates and a uniform rate of compensation to agents. The National Board relied on local boards of agents to establish rates. Despite some initial success, in the years following the establishment of the National Board, as after previous attempts at concerted action, the incentive for insurers to rate cut undermined its effectiveness. In 1871, two devastating fires occurred: the Chicago fire and a fire that destroyed the small city of Peshtigo, Wisconsin. The Chicago fire alone caused approximately $200 million in property damage, approximately half of which was insured. As a result, one-third of the companies that incurred liability as a result of the fire went out of business. The following year, fires ravaged Boston. These fires, and the resulting insolvencies, revealed the pressing need for some system of rate maintenance.

A system more decentralized than had previously existed emerged. The National Board focused its attention on fire prevention and insurance statistics. Numerous regional organizations were established in an attempt to maintain adequate rates. These associations were usually dominated by the insurance companies, not their agents. The associations used the technique of the compact and the stamping office to maintain discipline. One of the first was the St. Louis Compact in 1879. Under this arrangement, a compact manager usually had the authority to establish rates and maintain discipline according to the terms of the compact. With the stamping office, agents had to send in information concerning the policies they sold. This information would be reviewed in order to ensure that the proper rates were charged. Despite the elaborate methods used, the regional associations were not successful. Some companies refused to join the association or compact; others joined and then cheated.

The attempt to maintain rate adequacy was given a further blow when many states in the late 1800s passed anti-compact legislation, reflecting strong public feeling against monopolies and price fixing. This antitrust feeling manifested itself at the federal level with the Sherman Antitrust Act of 1890. On the state level, one of its manifestations was laws forbidding price fixing among insurers. The first anti-compact legislation was enacted by Ohio and New Hampshire in 1885. By 1913, 23 states had enacted anti-compact legislation, although insurers vigorously opposed this legislation.

In an attempt to circumvent the anti-compact legislation, some companies resorted to private rating services, which would publish advisory rates, with which firms were supposed to comply, but these efforts also failed to prevent wide-spread rate cutting. Insurance company failures following the San Francisco fires of 1906 highlighted the need for more robust measures to sustain adequate insurance rates. The anti-compact laws, in many states, were gradually replaced by laws that regulated rates themselves.

The first rate laws banned differential pricing for insuring the same risk. These laws were generally ineffective because of the inability to classify risks. In 1909, Kansas required insurers to file their rates with the commissioner. Once filed, insurers could not charge different rates. Most importantly, the commissioner had the authority to change the rates if the commissioner found them to be either too high or too low. This legislation was held to be constitutional by the Supreme Court in *German Alliance Insurance Co. v. Lewis*, 233 U.S. 389 (1914). Other states, sometimes as a result of their own investigations into insurance rates, followed Kansas's lead in permitting cooperative rate fixing with state supervision. The Joint Legislative Committee of New York, commonly known as the Merritt Committee, investigated fire insurance rates after the San Francisco fire of 1906. The Merritt Committee investigation resulted in legislation that made rate filings with the superintendent mandatory and cooperative price fixing legal. The superintendent had the authority to adjust rates so as to remove any discrimination. In the 1920s, legislation was enacted that permitted insurers, with the superintendent's approval, to deviate from bureau rates. More importantly, the superintendent, like the Kansas commissioner, was given power to change any rates he found to be either too high or too low. The NAIC, in 1914, drafted model bills that allowed for cooperative price fixing. Several states adopted the NAIC model bills when formulating their own insurance laws governing rate regulation.

At the turn of the 20th Century, there were several state investigations which uncovered abuses within the sector. The most famous and influential was the New York Legislative Insurance Investigation Committee of 1905, commonly referred to as the Armstrong Investigation. As a result of this investigation, and the abuses it uncovered, New York passed a number of laws which became a model and a catalyst for other states. The results of the Armstrong Investigation were especially influential because, at the time, more than half of the insurance sector's assets were held by New York insurance companies.

One of the Armstrong Committee's lines of investigation concerned the ties between industrial interests and life insurance companies. Powerful railroad firms had purportedly used these ties to pressure life insurance companies to purchase excessive quantities of railroad securities. While scholars have come to question aspects of the Armstrong Committee's analysis, public outrage at the time prompted the Armstrong Committee to recommend, and the New York legislature to enact, a statute prohibiting life insurance companies from purchasing stock unless secured by collateral in which the company could have directly invested. Other states quickly emulated New York's restrictions on insurance investments in equity securities. While these restrictions have been liberalized over time, they remain an important element of insurance regulation.

The Armstrong Committee made a number of other influential recommendations. These recommendations included encouraging the formation of mutual companies, standard policies for all companies, annual distribution of dividends, and limitations on agents' commissions. Many changes were made by the New York legislature in response to the hearings and the report. Companies had to advance loans to their policyholders in sums not exceeding the legal reserve required on the policy upon the security of the policy. Standard policy forms were also required by law.

Among the more significant reforms was legislation governing mutualization. New laws made it possible to organize mutual companies in New York, something that had been impossible during the previous 50 years. The Armstrong Commission concluded that, "while both stock and mutual corporations have exhibited the abuses incident to management without a becoming sense of responsibility, the latter are more amenable to the demands of public sentiment." In 1922, New York extended this policy of favoring mutual companies by prohibiting demutualization, the conversion of mutual companies into stock form. The NAIC followed New York by proposing a model law prohibiting demutualization in 1923.

3. The McCarran-Ferguson Act

Due to the *Paul* case and its progeny, insurance regulation remained the province of states. Though the insurance sector had initially resisted state supervisory authority when the *Paul* case was litigated, by the mid-20th Century, it had grown accustomed to local oversight and particularly state-sponsored rate bureaus. The 1940s threatened the stability of this arrangement.

In response to complaints about price fixing among fire insurance companies, the Department of Justice initiated an investigation of the South-Eastern Underwriters Association (SEUA) which resulted in criminal indictments in 1944 of the Association, 198 member companies, and 27 of its officers for violations of the federal antitrust laws The Association and its member companies were charged with organizing an illegal boycott of agents that dealt with insurance companies that were not members of SEUA. Invoking the *Paul* doctrine, the defendants persuaded the district court to dismiss the indictment on the grounds that the business of insurance was not commerce, and, therefore, the federal antitrust laws did not apply.

In *United States v. South-Eastern Underwriters Association (SEUA),* 322 U.S. 533 (1944), the Supreme Court reversed. The Court held that fire insurance transactions across state lines were interstate commerce. The Court explained:

> No commercial enterprise of any kind which conducts its activities across state lines has been held to be wholly beyond the regulatory power of Congress under the Commerce Clause. We cannot make an exception of the business of insurance.

Though the court attempted to distinguish *Paul,* the *SEUA* decision clearly marked a dramatic change in the Court's approach to whether the business of insurance was interstate commerce. Both the insurance sector and the state regulatory structure immediately perceived the *SEUA* decision as a serious threat. Application of the federal antitrust laws could hamper the operation of many sector rate-setting mechanisms, and the Court's reinterpretation of the Commerce Clause threatened to invalidate many aspects of state insurance regulations and taxes that differentiated between domestic and foreign insurance companies.

Reaction to the *SEUA* litigation was strong and prompt. Even while the case was pending before the Supreme Court, there were efforts to pass federal legislation, which would exempt the insurance sector from the federal antitrust laws. The property and casualty companies in particular wished to preserve the pre-*SEUA* regime. Early efforts to obtain legislative relief were hampered by political resistance to granting insurance companies too broad an exemption from federal antitrust laws. Eventually the NAIC, along with representatives of the insurance sector, offered a compromise approach that provided for only partial exemption from federal antitrust law. Under the NAIC bill, the insurance sector, after a phase-in period, would be subject to the federal antitrust law, with an exemption for state-approved cooperative rates, forms, and underwriting plans. Senators Pat McCarran and Homer Ferguson introduced a bill modeled on the NAIC bill. That bill was swiftly passed by Congress and was signed into law by President Truman on March 9, 1945, less than a year after the Court handed down the SEAU decision.

The McCarran-Ferguson Act, although a very short statute, has had a major impact on the structure of insurance regulation in the United States. It states that the silence of Congress is not to be construed as a barrier to the enactment of state laws governing the business of insurance. The statute affirmatively provides that the business of insurance "shall be subject to the laws of the several states which relate to the regulation or taxation of such business." Besides the antitrust laws, no federal law should be construed to invalidate, impair, or supersede any state law regulating the "business of insurance" or imposing a tax on such business unless the law specifically relates to the business of insurance. The business of insurance is subjected to the Sherman Antitrust Act, Clayton Act, and the Federal Trade Commission Act to the extent to which it is not regulated by state law. This provision was a compromise between a group that wanted complete exemption from the federal antitrust laws and those desiring more federal involvement. The Sherman Antitrust Act exemption is, however, inapplicable to "any agreement to boycott, coerce, or intimidate, or act of boycott, coercion or intimidation."

As a result of the passage of the McCarran-Ferguson Act, it became important for states wishing to avoid application of the federal antitrust statutes to pass laws regulating insurance. Model bills governing rate making, labeled the All-Industry bills, were drafted by the NAIC and insurance representatives. These model bills were widely adopted. By March 1951, every state had adopted a fire and casualty insurance rating law. Most states eventually also passed an Unfair Trade Practices Act to block application of the Federal Trade Commission Act. The effectiveness of these laws varied as a result of a number of factors.

The McCarran-Ferguson Act, and the policy of leaving the states primarily responsible for insurance regulation, has come under attack in recent decades. During the 1980s, insurance costs skyrocketed and several large insurance companies failed. Some commentators blamed these problems on inadequate state regulation. Repeal of the McCarran-Ferguson Act and the establishment of federal oversight were proposed. Several powerful stakeholder groups, including the commercial banking sector, favored repeal of the McCarran-Ferguson Act. The insurance sector has opposed its repeal, and all efforts to repeal the Act have failed.

We will turn shortly to the system of state insurance regulation that evolved in the years after the passage of the McCarran-Ferguson Act, but first it is worth highlighting a few important themes from the foregoing historical overview.

---

1. **Paul v. Virginia *Contrasted with* McCulloch v. Maryland.** The Supreme Court's decision in *Paul v. Virginia* had a profound impact on the evolution of insurance regulation in the United States. By ruling that insurance lay outside of the Commerce Clause powers of Congress, the Court gave states free rein to develop a state-based system of insurance regulation in the latter half of the 19th Century at the same time that the national bank system was rivalling state-charter banks for supremacy. While *Paul v. Virginia* was ultimately reversed in *U.S. v. SEAU* in 1944, the passage of nearly 80 years had allowed the states to establish a strong regulatory structure and powerful constituency that has important implications for U.S. insurance regulation today.

The scope of the Commerce Clause's reach over the insurance sector remains a matter of debate. In *National Federation of Independent Business v. Sebelius*, 132 S. Ct. 2566 (2012), Chief Justice John Roberts, speaking for the Court, concluded that the Affordable Care Act's individual mandate did not fall within Congress's powers under the Commerce Clause, though the statutory structure was upheld as a permissible application of Congress's taxing powers. *See* Chapter 3.3.

2. ***Rate Regulation as a Perennial Challenge.*** Another recurring theme is the complexity of setting rates for insurance products, the issue with which we began this Chapter in the problem on pricing bicycle insurance. The boom-bust cycles of the past are one example of inadequate insurance policy pricing, while the boycotts that gave rise the government antitrust enforcement action in *U.S. v. SEAU* is arguably a case of excessive, or at least anti-competitive, pricing practices. As we will see in Chapter 3.2, the regulation of insurance company rates, to prevent both inadequate and excessive pricing, remains a major area of insurance regulation and an important plank of market conduct, namely consumer protection, regulation.

3. ***The Armstrong Investigation.*** The Armstrong Investigation is an important landmark in financial regulation in the United States. While the investigation focused on a familiar problem of financial intermediation, the alleged misuse of assets to benefit insiders to the detriment of policyholders, the investigation was one of the first public examinations of the money trusts of Wall Street and provided an important spring board for the Pujo Committee's investigation in Congress in 1912 and 1913, which itself provided essential background for Justice Louis Brandeis's famous tract, OTHER PEOPLE'S MONEY AND HOW BANKERS USE IT (1914), which is often cited as the intellectual fountainhead of President Franklin D. Roosevelt's New Deal reforms of the securities sector. On a more technical level, the Armstrong Investigation led to important reforms in insurance regulation. The first was tighter restrictions on portfolio investments, a regulatory strategy we already discussed in Chapter 2.2 with respect to depository institutions. The second was encouraging the use of the mutual form of ownership, a regulatory strategy explored later in this Chapter.

4. ***The McCarran-Ferguson Act.*** Some have labeled the McCarran-Ferguson Act quasi-constitutional because it allocates regulatory authority between the states and the federal government and establishes a presumption against preemption; few, if any, other federal statutes so clearly assign states such a prominent jurisdictional role. The McCarran-Ferguson Act leaves open several interpretive questions, however, that frequently have gone to the Supreme Court. A concept central under the McCarran-Ferguson Act is the "business of insurance." The Supreme Court has on numerous occasions decided cases interpreting these words. Many of the most important of these decision have involved private suits challenging insurance sector practices alleged to fall outside the bounds of the "business of insurance" and therefore subject to liability under federal antitrust laws. In *Union Labor Life Insurance Co. v. Pireno*, 458 U.S. 119 (1982), the Supreme Court articulated a three-part test designed to clarify the concept, considering (1) whether the activity involves underwriting or a spreading of risk, (2) whether it involves a relationship between the insurer

and the policyholder, and (3) whether the activity involves entities with the insurance sector. In *U.S. Dep't of the Treasury v. Fabe*, 508 U.S. 491 (1993), the Court clarified that the broad category of laws enacted for the purpose of regulating the "business of insurance" consist of laws that possess the "end, intention or aim" of "adjusting, managing, or controlling the business of insurance," concluding that the federal bankruptcy laws did not preempt a state statute giving priority in bankruptcy to policyholders.

---

4. Mutualization and Demutualization

The mutual form is an organizational structure that is owned and controlled by policyholders rather than shareholders, who retain ownership and control in the more familiar corporate structure. The mutual form was recommended by early insurance reformers like the Armstrong Committee on the assumption shareholders tended to favor excessive risk-taking to the potential detriment of policyholders, whereas the mutual form better aligned the incentives of insurers and policyholders. Following the Committee's recommendations, an era of mutualizations occurred in the early 20th Century. For a look at the effects of mutual ownership on management incentives, see Ryan Bubb & Alex Kaufman, *Consumer Biases and Mutual Ownership*, 105 J. PUB. ECON. 39 (2013). In practice, policyholders have little control over the business and management operates without fear of policyholder intervention. The mutual form can also make it more difficult for insurance companies to raise capital and to acquire or be acquired by other firms. For these reasons, a number of insurance companies in more recent years have preferred to convert back into a stock form of ownership where the company is owned by its shareholders. The conversion, known as demutualization, can also make management respond more quickly to market fluctuations and competitive pressures. Due to a host of factors, including a removal of tax incentives for mutuals, demutualization swept through the insurance sector in the 1990s. In the wake of this movement, there is some evidence that the insurance firms involved grew faster and were more profitable after demutualizing. For a more detailed discussion of the effects of the demutualization wave, see Lal C. Chugh & Joseph W. Meador, *Demutualization in the Life Insurance Industry: A Study of Effectiveness*, 27 REV. BUS. 10 (2006). As mentioned in Chapter 2.1, the mutual form was also popular for savings banks but has declined in that sector as well. The mutual form can be considered a form of regulation through corporate structure. Should mutualization stay part of our modern regulatory toolkit? If so, when should it be employed?

C. THE NAIC AND STATE INSURANCE REGULATION

One of the distinguishing characteristics of insurance regulation is the dominant role of state supervisory authorities and the coordinating function of the NAIC. The following excerpt, taken from the leading casebook on insurance law, offers an overview.

Kenneth Abraham & Daniel Schwarcz, Insurance Law and Regulation

(Foundation Press 6th ed. 2015)

In the wake of the McCarran-Ferguson Act, every state enacted rate regulation legislation intended to ensure that insurance was "regulated by the State law" under Section 2(b) of the Act, thus triggering the antitrust exemption. *See* Robert H. Jerry II & Douglas S. Richmond, Understanding Insurance Law 69 (4th ed. 2007). These statutes required state insurance departments to assure that insurance rates were not "excessive, inadequate, or unfairly discriminatory." Although these laws still persist and play an important role in many states' insurance regulation, the substance of modern state insurance regulation has grown substantially in its scope and complexity in the last eighty years. *See* The Future of Insurance Regulation in the United States (Martin F. Grace & Robert W. Klein eds., 2009).

Every state (as well as the District of Columbia and the five U.S. territories) has an office that is charged with regulating the business of insurance. These departments are headed by a "commissioner" or "director," who is either elected or appointed by the Governor. Either way, state insurance departments are subject to a variety of political pressures. Total staff in these departments varies from fewer than 100 in small states like Delaware to over 1,000 in large states like New York. *See* National Association of Insurance Commissioners, Insurance Department Resources Report (2013). All state insurance departments are subject to their state's administrative law rules. These rules track federal administrative law in their basics. For instance, states' administrative law generally (i) requires notice and comment procedures to promulgate rules, (ii) permits affected parties to challenge regulators' actions in court in some cases, and (iii) requires deferential judicial review of certain agency decisions. *See* Michael Asimow & Ronald M. Levin, State and Federal Administrative Law (3d ed. 2009).

By far the most important single player in state insurance regulation is the National Association of Insurance Commissioners. *See generally* Susan Randall, Insurance Regulation in the United States: Regulatory Federalism and the National Association of Insurance Commissioners, 26 Fla. St. U.L. Rev. 625 (1999). The NAIC is not a regulator or even a public entity; it is a non-profit corporation with over 450 employees and an annual budget of approximately $80 million. Its Board of Directors is comprised of several state insurance commissioners, who are themselves elected by the commissioners of every jurisdiction. Broadly conceived, the NAIC has three major functions: it promotes uniformity in state insurance law, it facilitates coordination and cooperation among the states, and it directly provides services to state regulators and consumers.

Promoting Uniformity. Perhaps the primary goal of the NAIC is to promote uniform insurance law and regulation. For insurers who operate on a multi-state basis, differences in state insurance laws can create substantial administrative costs, even when those differences are not substantively significant. Insurance agents and brokers also have some interest in uniformity across states. Varying requirements for obtaining a state license can result in duplicative licensing fees and application standards in order to sell products across state lines. Even consumers have a direct interest in uniformity of state insurance regulations. For instance, regulatory uniformity may increase consumers' ability to learn about different coverage options using non-state specific resources. At the same time, uniformity is not without its downsides. Uniform laws limit the capacity of jurisdictions to develop rules that match the particular views of their population, and covered risks in certain lines of insurance—such as property/casualty and health—can vary significantly across different regions of the country.

The most important strategy that the NAIC uses to promote uniformity is drafting model insurance statutes and regulations. Like the Uniform Commercial Code, NAIC model laws do not themselves have the force of law. Rather they serve as a template for state legislatures and regulators who are interested in harmonizing their insurance law with other jurisdictions. Although the model law process promotes consistency, it is imperfect. Some state legislatures and regulators do not enact model laws and regulations while others enact model laws or regulations that deviate slightly from the national model. When researching state insurance statutes and regulations, it is often helpful to first determine whether an NAIC model law exists on the relevant issue. All model laws are available for free online at the NAIC's website. For each model law, the NAIC maintains an up to date list indicating which jurisdictions have enacted that model law or a substantially similar version of that law.

Facilitating Coordination and Cooperation. The efficiency and effectiveness of many regulatory activities can be enhanced when state regulators work collaboratively. In some cases, this may simply amount to states dividing up overlapping regulatory responsibilities so as to limit duplicative efforts. In other cases, state collaboration may be more active, allowing states to identify and respond to national regulatory issues, to learn from their varying experiences and perspectives, or to double-check each other's work in a form of "peer review." Therese M. Vaughan, The Implications of Solvency II for U.S. Insurance Regulation (Networks Fin. Inst., Policy Brief No. 3, 2009). The NAIC organizes individual state regulators into numerous working groups and committees to explore a wide range of regulatory issues. These committees collaborate during tri-annual NAIC meetings and regular conference calls to evaluate individual companies and produce white papers, bulletins, model laws, regulatory manuals, accounting forms, educational materials, and various other forms of regulatory work product. *See, e.g.*, Timothy Stoltzfus Jost, Reflections on the National Association of Insurance Commissioners and Implementation of the Patient Protection and Affordable Care Act, 159 U. Penn. L. Rev. 2043 (2011) (discussing the NAIC's substantial role in fostering collaboration among the states and other stakeholders in the implementation of the Affordable Care Act).

Services for Insurance Regulators and Consumers. A third substantial role of the NAIC is to provide services to both state regulators and insurance consumers. State regulators rely extensively on the NAIC in performing their basic regulatory functions. For instance, the NAIC helps individual departments collect and analyze data, particularly in the solvency sphere. It also provides centralized research and logistical support for states. The NAIC offers some consumer services as well, such as the production of buyers' guides and the aggregation of relevant information, like consumer complaint data.

Reprinted with permission of Foundation Press.

In general, the top priority of state insurance regulation is to ensure that carriers have the financial capacity to pay claims when they come due. State insurance regulation, however, also devotes substantial resources to a number of additional functions, including preventing excessive or unfairly discriminatory rates, regulating the content of insurance policy forms, policing against market conduct abuses in claims payments, marketing, and sales, and operating residual markets that provide coverage to individuals who cannot secure insurance from private carriers.

---

1. ***Perspectives on the Regulatory Structure for the Supervision of Insurance Companies.*** In terms of organization design, state insurance authorities are responsible for safeguarding insurance company solvency, as well as otherwise protecting the interests of consumers. The regulatory structure, therefore, does not reflect a twin peaks model of the sort discussed in Chapter

1.3, but is built around a system of consolidated supervision. What is distinctive about insurance regulation is the existence and importance of the NAIC as a coordinating body. The role the NAIC plays for state insurance regulation is somewhat analogous to the role the Basel Committee and other elements of the international financial architecture play for national authorities seeking to coordinate on an international basis. As we explore the challenges the NAIC has faced in providing effective coordination of state insurance regulators, consider whether similar problems are likely to hamper the work of international regulatory networks in the field of finance.

2. ***Guaranty Funds.*** The insurance sector is also protected by a system of guaranty funds that function somewhat similarly to FDIC deposit insurance from the FDIC. As with so much else in the field of insurance, these funds are operated on a state level and provide separate coverage for property/casualty lines as opposed to health and life lines. There also exist separate coordinating bodies to support these guaranty funds, a role that is especially important when insolvent insurance firms have been doing business in multiple states. For information on the National Organization of Life & Health Insurance Guaranty Associations and the National Conference of Insurance Guaranty Funds, see their websites.

3. ***Insurance Materials.*** In addition to the Abraham and Schwarcz book previously excerpted, for another leading text on insurance regulation, see TOM BAKER AND KYLE LOGUE, INSURANCE LAW AND POLICY: CASES, MATERIALS AND PROBLEMS (2013).

D. INSURANCE REGULATION UNDER THE DODD-FRANK ACT

While the States have traditionally dominated insurance regulation in the United States, the Dodd-Frank Act departed from this tradition by creating the FIO. One of the FIO's first tasks was to produce a report on how to modernize and improve insurance regulation. The following excerpt is from that report and emphasizes some of the short-comings of state supervision.

FIO, How To Modernize and Improve the System of Insurance Regulation in the United States

Dec. 2013

The business of insurance in the United States is primarily regulated at the state level. Insurance laws are enacted by state legislators and governors and are implemented and enforced by state regulators. Broadly speaking, state regulation is divided into prudential regulation (frequently referred to as "solvency" regulation) and marketplace regulation. Prudential regulation consists of oversight of an insurer's financial condition and its ability to satisfy policyholder claims. Marketplace regulation governs an insurer's business conduct, such as the pricing of premiums, advertising, minimum standards governing the terms of insurance policies, licensing of insurance agents and brokers (producers), together with general issues of consumer protection and access to insurance.

Although reforms to solvency and marketplace regulation are continually discussed, for over a century a centerpiece of the debate among policymakers and [insurance sector] leaders over modernizing insurance regulation has been the extent to which the federal government should be involved in insurance regulation. These conversations have generally focused on the question of whether a state-based system can answer the regulatory demands of a national, and increasingly global, insurance market. Proponents of modernizing insurance regulation through federal involvement have noted that the current state-based system does not impose the uniformity necessary for the U.S. insurance market to function efficiently. They explain that state regulation is often duplicative or inconsistent, that the multiplicity of jurisdictions makes state regulators more prone to "capture," and that differences in standards between the states provide opportunities for arbitrage, if not a race to the bottom. Moreover, proponents of federal involvement contend that limitations on the jurisdictional reach of states' legal authority impede effective regulation of entities whose businesses span multiple jurisdictions and sectors.

Those who favor continuation of the current regime of state regulation counter that much of the business of insurance is local in nature and generally does not lend itself to uniform national regulation, and that states are better positioned to respond to consumer complaints. They add that mechanisms for cooperation and achieving uniformity already exist among the states, and that a state-based system provides better opportunities for experimentation so that the best ideas developed in one jurisdiction can be adopted and replicated in others. They also assert that, by and large, state regulation works well. . . .

The Crises of Insurer Insolvencies, Congressional Reaction, and State Regulatory Responses

A wave of insolvencies among auto insurers in the 1960s rekindled the debate over the adequacy of state regulation and the inadequate level of uniformity in insurance regulation among the states. In the absence of guaranty funds, failure of these auto insurers left policyholders without adequate recourse against the assets of the insolvent insurer. The crisis attracted Congressional attention and, in 1966, prompted a proposal to create a federal guaranty system for insurers, modeled on federal bank deposit insurance. A decade later, in 1976, Senator Edward Brooke introduced the Federal Insurance Act, which would have authorized the federal government to offer optional federal insurance charters, preempting state law, and would also have created a federal guaranty fund. In a parallel effort a few years earlier, in 1969, state regulators, through the NAIC, developed a model guaranty fund act for property and liability insurance and, in 1970, a similar model for life and health insurance. Guaranty funds aimed to improve policyholder protection with an [insurance sector]-funded, ex post claims payment system whereby consumers would receive some contractual benefit despite an insurer's failure. Many states adopted versions of this model legislation.

After another series of insurer insolvencies, this time involving over 50 insurers in the 1980s and 1990s, including the largest life insurer in California at the time, Congress began a more extensive investigation into the adequacy of insurer solvency regulation. The House Committee on Energy and Commerce's Subcommittee on Oversight and Investigations, chaired by Congressman John Dingell, issued a report in 1990 entitled Failed Promises: Insurance Company Insolvencies. The report found that, "the present system for regulating the solvency of insurers is seriously deficient" due to rapid and unbridled expansion, underpricing, inadequate oversight, inadequate loss reserves, poor reinsurance transactions, and fraud. In 1992, Chairman Dingell introduced a bill that, if enacted, would have instituted federal regulation of insurer solvency. In 1994, the same subcommittee issued a second report on insurer solvency regimes, entitled Wishful Thinking: A World View of Insurance Solvency Regulation. The report stated that, notwithstanding state regulatory efforts to address solvency reform, regulation remained insufficient because state regulators lacked adequate national and international authority. A minority report released by the subcommittee, however, disagreed and stated that it favored "strengthening, not dismantling, the current State regulatory system."

In the aftermath of the Failed Promises and Wishful Thinking reports, in the 1990s, state regulators, through the NAIC, developed and adopted risk-based capital (RBC) formulae for life, property/casualty and health insurers. At the same time, states developed and adopted a self-accreditation program now known as the Financial Standards and Accreditation Program, a peer review process intended to improve consistency of financial regulation across the state system. Later, in 2001, after several years of development, state regulators codified statutory accounting principles (SAP) in an effort to further policyholder protection.

Recent Proposals for Federal Regulation of Insurance to Promote Uniformity

A number of proposals have been set forth more recently to enact federal legislation to address the inconsistency and absence of uniformity in the state-based system of insurance regulation. An important initial effort occurred in 1999, when Congress passed the [Gramm-Leach-Bliley Act (GLBA)]. Although GLBA allowed banks to affiliate with insurers through a federally regulated financial holding company, it preserved the states' authorities to regulate insurance company affiliates. GLBA introduced the possibility of addressing the absence of uniformity in one key area of state regulation, however, when it included the requirement for the creation of [National Association of Registered Agents and Brokers (NARAB)] to implement national insurance agent licensing requirements if a majority of the states and territories did not meet a 2002 deadline for reciprocity in producer licensing. In 2002, the state regulators certified that 35 states and territories had satisfied the GLBA requirement, enough to constitute a majority and thereby avoiding the creation of NARAB.

GLBA was the beginning of a series of efforts over the ensuing decade to bring a federal regulatory presence to insurance. Between 2001 and 2006, the House Financial Services Committee held more than a dozen hearings at both the subcommittee and full committee levels on insurance matters at which witnesses discussed issues such as the increasing globalization of the insurance sector and inefficiencies attendant to the lack of uniformity in the state-based system of regulation. Members of Congress also offered legislative solutions. Congressman Michael Oxley and Congressman Richard Baker, for example, released a discussion draft called the State Modernization and Regulatory Transparency Act (SMART Act) in 2004, which proposed that states comply with uniform standards for licensing, market conduct regulation, reinsurance practices, and receivership rules. It also proposed expediting the process of introducing new insurance products to the market and shifting toward a system of market- based rates.

Although the SMART Act would have required significant increases in the degree of uniformity, state regulators' authorities would have been preserved. Other proposals, however, have prescribed more extensive federal regulatory involvement to promote uniform national insurance regulation. For example, a number of bills have called for the creation of an optional federal charter, such as the National Insurance Act of 2007, co-sponsored in the Senate by Senators Tim Johnson and John Sununu, and in the House by Representatives Melissa Bean and Edward Royce. This proposed legislation would have created an optional federal charter for property/casualty and life insurance.

The Executive Branch presented a similar proposal in a 2008 report by the Treasury entitled Blueprint for a Modernized Financial Regulatory Structure. Noting that the insurance regulatory system suffered from duplicative, inconsistent, and non-uniform regulation, the report proposed the creation of an optional federal insurance charter as an interim step toward a unified national chartering system. The Blueprint also included proposals for federal licensing for insurance producers and the creation of an Office of Insurance Oversight at Treasury. In April 2009, The National Insurance Consumer Protection Act was introduced in the House by Representatives Bean and Royce with the stated purpose of improving uniformity in insurance regulation. The bill proposed a single, optional federal charter for the insurance industry, including insurers, reinsurers, and insurance producers. . . .

---

1. ***The NAIC Accreditation Program.*** Congress's critique of state regulation of insurance company solvency in the 1980s included the lack of coordination between state insurance regulators with respect to multi-state insurers. The NAIC had a program to facilitate multistate solvency evaluations, but was powerless to force states to participate and, as a result, states rarely participated. Some state regulators were concerned that, if other states learn about a problem insurer, they might suspend the insurer's license, making the situation public and increasing the chances of insolvency. In response to threats of congressional intervention, the NAIC established the Financial Regulation Standards Accreditation Program (Accreditation Program) for state insurance departments. A state insurance department could become accredited after passing an NAIC evaluation, which included an on-site evaluation and a determination as to whether the state had the required laws and regulations in place. Once accredited, their decisions on domestic insurers can be deferred to by other states.

A series of scathing Government Accountability Office (GAO) reports criticizing the Accreditation Program followed. The Accreditation Program's weakness stemmed from three flaws: the program requirements were general and interpreted permissively, were not sufficiently documented, and focused primarily on the passage of laws and the existence of certain regulatory authorities instead of the actual implementation. The actual effectiveness of a state insurance department was therefore largely untested by the accreditation process. In 1993, the GAO again expressed concern, this time stating that the level of broad discretion in the accreditation process allowed for "inconsistent and inadequate regulation." The 1993 GAO report also highlighted the significant resistance from the states to the NAIC's limited ability to adapt accreditation requirements over time due to the difficulty of gaining support for new measures in every state. By 2001, perhaps due to increased federal pressure, the Accreditation Program had improved, though the GAO noted that there were still gaps in the accreditation review.

The actions of state insurance commissioners are not the only explanation for the slow implementation of the Accreditation Program. Holdout issues are endemic to state insurance regulation insofar as it depends on the passage of legislation by state governments. The Accreditation Program works, in part, by requiring the passage of certain model acts as a condition of accreditation. Depending on the legislature in addition to the insurance departments creates an extra layer of potential discord. New York, for example, was one of the first states to be accredited, but that accreditation was suspended when the New York legislature failed to pass required legislation.

While these issues were eventually overcome and all 50 states are currently accredited, there is debate over the Accreditation Program's effectiveness at bringing uniformity to solvency regulation. The FIO Report argues that the risk-based capital standards that lay at the heart of the Accreditation Program are not being applied uniformly by states.

2. ***The Coordination of Licensing Standards***. The FIO Report touches on the struggle between state and federal authorities over insurance agent licensing in its discussion of GLBA, but it is worth fleshing this out as it illustrates the potential shortcomings of state regulation. An insurance producer is a person "who markets, distributes, or sells an insurance product to consumer." Until recently, a producer had to be licensed by a state in order to sell insurance there, and a producer who wished to sell in a new state had to go through that state's separate licensing procedure and pay separate fees. This requirement cost extra time and money for the many producers operating in multiple states, while providing no recognizable benefit to consumers. When Congress reevaluated state solvency regimes in the 1980s, it also pressured states to use standardized licensing procedures. The first iteration of NARAB was introduced in 1993 as part of the Insurance Solvency Act. This bill did not pass, but the NARAB concept resurfaced in 1999 as part of GLBA. In order to avoid the creation of NARAB, the NAIC developed the Producer Licensing Model Act (PLMA), which provided basic licensing standards and licensing reciprocity between states. PLMA was successful enough to avoid the creation of NARAB, with 38 states passing the model act by the deadline set out in GLBA.

While the NAIC was eager to promote uniform licensing standards so as to avoid the establishment of NARAB, it was not able to garner enough support for and compliance with PLMA to permanently fend off federal intervention. First, while a majority of states passed PLMA by the 2002 deadline and 47 states were in compliance by 2009, the holdouts included three of the four largest insurance markets: New York, California, and Florida. One barrier preventing those states from complying was that they were unwilling to eliminate criminal background checks using fingerprint identification as a requirement for licensing, while many other states did not even have access to the necessary databases to perform a nationwide background check on applicants. Second, PLMA provided for incomplete reciprocity even between states that were in compliance. PLMA's reciprocity requirements do not apply in all situations, leading to licensing redundancy even between states that have both passed PLMA. States continue to have varying criteria for the licensing of business entities that sell insurance, including "entity appointment requirements, licensing for branch locations, affiliation requirements, and filing of organizational documents." In addition, PLMA did not cover post-licensing requirements, which can vary from state to state. Still unsatisfied with licensing reciprocity, Congress passed the National Association of Registered Agents and Brokers Reform Act of 2015 (NARAB II) in 2015. NARAB II ends this 22-year-long struggle by transferring licensing authority to a federal entity charged with developing and implementing licensing standards.

Critics of state insurance regulation, including many in Congress, have long voiced concern with the ability of state authorities to provide effective and efficient oversight of the insurance sector. The Financial Crisis added fuel to the fire, particularly as a result of the very prominent difficulties that AIG encountered in the fall of 2008, which raised the possibility that insurance companies might be systemically important. The following excerpt summarizes these developments.

Daniel Schwarcz & Steven L. Schwarcz, Regulating System Risk in Insurance

81 U. CHI L. REV. 1569 (2014)

The financial crisis of 2008 poses obvious difficulties for the view that insurance is not systemically risky. This is most visible with respect to the dramatic and massive failure of AIG, a holding company with numerous subsidiaries engaging in a wide range of financial-services operations. Although many of these subsidiaries were indeed traditional insurance companies, AIG's problems resulted in large part from the activities of a company that was not licensed as an insurance company: AIG Financial Products (AIGFP).

This AIG subsidiary issued an immense number of [credit default swaps (CDSs)] to numerous financial companies. From an economic perspective, CDSs act much like insurance: in exchange for a premium payment, the protection seller promises to pay the purchaser in the event of a default or other credit event on an underlying instrument. If, during the term of the CDS, a credit event or default becomes more likely to occur, then the protection seller is typically required to post additional collateral. Unlike traditional insurance, however, there is no need for the purchaser of a CDS to have an insurable interest in the underlying risk: a company can purchase a CDS on an underlying instrument even if it does not own that instrument.

In the years leading up to 2008, AIGFP wrote a tremendous number of CDSs on mortgage-backed securities and similar financial instruments that were ultimately linked to homeowners' mortgage payments. For years, this subsidiary produced massive profits for AIG. But in the financial crisis, as markets started to indicate an increased risk of default on mortgage-backed securities and related financial instruments, AIG was forced to post increasing amounts of collateral and ultimately amassed staggering debts to its various counterparties. Concerned that AIG's failure to pay these debts to its counterparties could cause those counterparties to fail and trigger larger financial panic, the US government bailed out AIG by infusing capital that was used to pay off AIG's CDS counterparties in full.

Although AIG's largest problems stemmed from its CDS business, it also experienced major stresses related to its securities lending program, which more directly involved its insurance entities. Coordinating through a noninsurer AIG affiliate, AIG's insurers lent their securities to other firms on a short-term basis in exchange for fees. Borrowers of those securities were required to post cash collateral, but they were entitled to have that collateral returned to them if they returned the borrowed securities.

As AIG began to experience financial turmoil, borrowers of the firm's securities availed themselves of this substitution option en masse, worried about their cash collateral not being returned by AIG. This, in turn, created dramatic and unanticipated liquidity needs for AIG, which had invested about 60 percent of the cash collateral it had received from securities borrowers in the very mortgage-backed securities whose value was precipitously declining.

AIG's bailout was not the only way in which insurers contributed to the 2008 financial crisis. In fact, financial-guarantee insurers also played a substantial role in the financial crisis. Financial-guarantee insurers are one type of monoline insurer: their business is in a single (that is, mono) line of insurance precisely because it is different in kind, and riskier, than other types of insurance. Originally, monoline financial-guarantee insurance covered the risk that municipal bonds would default.

But in recent decades, financial-guarantee insurers expanded this coverage to the then-rapidly growing securitization markets, which offered numerous transactions to insure. Such coverage was generally purchased by the issuer of a covered security, which helped increase investor appetite for these instruments by limiting the financial consequences of default to the investor. In fact, financial-guarantee insurance supported much of the $330 billion market for auction-rate securities (ARSs), which are long-term debt securities with short-term resetting interest rates issued by municipalities, museums, schools, and similar entities. In February 2008, the ARS market came to a halt because investors feared that monolines could not be counted on to pay their insurance. As the fear became contagious, investors started avoiding all ARSs, even those of strong issuers.

Like AIG, then, financial-guarantee insurers "insured" policyholders against the risk that financial instruments linked to the housing market would default. Unlike AIG, however, the companies that issued these products were explicitly regulated as insurers. At the same time, one of the primary reasons that financial-guarantee insurers are required to be monolines is that state regulators have long understood that this type of insurance is inherently riskier than other forms of insurance. By forcing insurers that sold this type of coverage to refrain from expanding into more traditional forms of insurance, state regulators may have limited the exposure of most of the insurance industry to this risk.

Additionally, many traditional insurers—particularly life insurers—did indeed experience substantial capital deterioration during the financial crisis. This resulted from both sharp decreases in net income and dramatic increases in unrealized losses on investment assets in 2008. These capital shortfalls led insurers to apply for federal bailout funds, to seek changes to accounting rules in order to provide capital relief, to sell insurance policies for less than their actual economic cost, and to receive capital infusions from their affiliate noninsurance companies. Life insurers with large portfolios of variable annuities with guaranteed lifetime benefits were particularly hard-hit, because they had to increase their reserves in response to declines in equity markets.

Ultimately, as emphasized by a recent GAO report, both life insurers' capital cushions and their income rebounded quickly. By 2009 their capital levels and income had improved significantly, and by 2011 their investment portfolios had also largely rebounded. Moreover, throughout the financial crisis, very few life insurers failed: in 2008, consistent with historical trends, six life insurers were placed into receivership and three insurers were liquidated. Although 2009 saw increases in these numbers, rates of insurer failures fell below historical trends in 2010, when only four were placed into receivership and three were liquidated.

---

1. ***The Saga of AIG***. The financial distress that AIG faced in the fall of 2008 is a signature event that had profound influence on the structure of the Dodd-Frank Act. While AIG had many regulated subsidiaries, including a number of regulated insurance companies and thrift subsidiaries supervised by the now-defunct federal Office of Thrift Supervision (OTS), its losses and liquidity requirements during the Financial Crisis occurred primarily in an affiliate, AIGFP, whose major operations, including extensive CDS activities, were based out of London. As financial markets roiled in the summer of 2008, there was considerable uncertainty as to who was responsible for AIGFP's problems. EU authorities had been led to believe that the OTS was providing consolidated oversight for the entire firm, but a thrift supervisor was hardly equipped to supervise complex derivatives transactions. Perplexingly, in post-Financial Crisis investigations, senior OTS personnel purported to have been uncertain as to their authority over AIGFP even though just a few years earlier the organization had made representations to EU as to its supervisory capabilities all AIG affiliates. *See* THE FINANCIAL CRISIS INQUIRY REPORT 350-52 (2011). As the Financial Crisis deepened, AIG attempted to persuade New York State insurance regulators to allow the firm to gain access from insurance subsidiaries

to $20 billion in securities which were then to have been pledged to provide emergency funding to AIGFP, but New York State insurance authorities, concerned that the regulated insurance subsidiaries would not have "sufficient capital to protect policyholders after the asset swap occurred," initially declined to approve the request, later indicated a willingness to do so, but ultimately failed to give formal approval of the transaction. U.S. GOV'T ACCOUNTABILITY OFFICE, GAO-09-358, FINANCIAL CRISIS: REVIEW OF FEDERAL RESERVE SYSTEM FINANCIAL ASSISTANCE TO AMERICAN INTERNATIONAL GROUP, INC. (2011); *see also* Governor David Paterson, Remarks at the Press Conference on AIG (Sept. 15, 2008). Finally, at the eleventh hour, as the amounts needed grew larger, and in the wake of the Lehman failure, the Federal Reserve Board intervened, invoking its powers under § 13(3) of the Federal Reserve Act to provide AIG with an $85 billion cash infusion in exchange for a loan and the receipt of preferred stock in a transaction that was later refinanced, in part, through Troubled Asset Relief Program funds, which raised the government's total financial commitment to AIG to the vicinity of $180 billion. Even though the government ultimately earned a positive return, estimated at $22.7 billion on its bail-out of AIG, the transaction survives as the poster-child of too big to fail, and many have criticized the government's decision to insulate many AIG customers, claimants, and shareholders from suffering losses in the fall of 2008. The shareholders of AIG, who were substantially diluted by the firm's losses in the Financial Crisis and the terms of the government's investments in AIG, later sued the government, arguing among other things that the Federal Reserve Board's use of preferred stock exceeded its authority under § 13(3). In the first stage of litigation, shareholders lost in the Southern District of New York on the argument that the Federal Reserve exceeded its power under § 13(3). *See* Starr Int'l Co. v. Fed. Reserve Bank of N.Y., 906 F. Supp.2d 202 (S.D.N.Y. 2012). Later the shareholders prevailed on this argument in the U.S. Court of Federal Claims ruling issued in the summer of 2015, but were denied any damages on the grounds that they had suffered no economic loss. *See* Starr Int'l Co. v. United States, 121 Fed. Cl. 429 (Fed. Cl. 2015). That case is currently pending on appeal.

2. ***AIG versus Monoline Insurers.*** One interpretation of AIG's financial difficulties is that the root of the company's problem was that it used its London affiliate to specialize in insurance-like products, credit default swaps, but without the solvency oversight that insurance regulation would have provided. As the Schwarcz and Schwarcz excerpt notes, however, there was also a class of companies that specialized in financial guarantees functionally similar to the positions AIG took in its CDSs. These mono-line carriers also fared poorly in the Financial Crisis:

> Financial guaranty insurers are organized as "monoline" insurers because state insurance regulations generally prohibit these firms from writing other types of insurance. The financial crisis showed that the monoline nature of the business, together with the performance of het assets underlying the guaranties, contributed to insolvencies of financial guaranty issuers.
>
> For many years, the assets guaranteed by most financial guaranty insurers, such as mortgages and municipal bonds, were generally

> considered low-risk because of historically low default rates. As a result, financial guarantors held low levels of capital with the consent of regulators. On the same rationale, financial guarantors received top ratings from [Credit Rating Agencies] notwithstanding low capital levels and the eventual movement from the core business model to provide guaranties on assets such as riskier structured products, including collateralized debt obligations consisting of mortgage backed securities.
>
> During the crisis, as the number of defaults on the underlying assets increased, the mortgage-backed securities were downgraded and dropped in value. Financial guaranty insurers were forced to recognized losses which eroded already thin layers of capital. The loss recognition in turn caused [Credit Rating Agencies] to downgrade the insurers, thereby subjecting the insurers to a vicious cycle of collateral calls and additional market pressures, which further accelerated loss recognition. The losses for financial guaranty insurers contributed to temporary dislocation in the municipal bond market, and limited the access of municipal issuers to the market. Since the crisis, much of the municipal bond market has moved ahead without the wrap of a financial guaranty.

FIO, HOW TO MODERNIZE AND IMPROVE THE SYSTEM OF INSURANCE REGULATION IN THE UNITED STATES 50 (2013).

The failure of AIG and many monoline carriers in the Financial Crisis contributed to the creation of the FIO under the Dodd-Frank Act. The following excerpt summarizes its function, as well as its relation to other Dodd-Frank Act reforms related to insurance.

FIO, How To Modernize and Improve the System of Insurance Regulation in the United States

Dec. 2013

The Dodd-Frank Act introduced reforms to remedy the weaknesses in supervision of the financial system that were exposed through the financial crisis, including those that touched the insurance industry. For example, Title I of the Dodd-Frank Act established a new supervisory structure for the oversight of the U.S. financial system through the creation of the Council, which is charged with identifying and responding to threats to the stability of the U.S. financial system. The Council is authorized to determine that a nonbank financial company shall be supervised by the Federal Reserve [Board] and be subject to prudential standards if the Council determines that the nonbank financial company's material financial distress or activities could pose a threat to the financial stability of the United States. The Federal Reserve [Board] must establish and enforce prudential standards for the largest [BHCs] and for nonbank financial companies supervised by the Federal Reserve [Board].

The Dodd-Frank Act also addresses insurance more directly by creating FIO and by assigning to it an important financial stability role. FIO has the authority and responsibility to monitor all aspects of the insurance industry and to identify issues or regulatory gaps that could threaten the stability of the insurance industry or, more broadly, the U.S. financial system. FIO may also recommend to the Council that it designate an insurer as an entity subject to regulation as a nonbank financial company supervised by the Federal Reserve [Board]. FIO's financial stability mission also includes playing a role in the context of Title II's Orderly Liquidation Authority. Title II confers "key turning" responsibilities upon FIO, whereby the affirmative approval of the FIO Director and two-thirds of the Governors of the Federal Reserve [Board] are required before the Secretary may make a determination on whether to seek the appointment of the FDIC as receiver of an insurance company.

Under the FIO Act, FIO's mission also extends to international matters, where FIO is responsible for coordinating federal efforts and developing federal policy on prudential aspects of international insurance matters, including representing the United States, as appropriate, in the [International Association of Insurance Supervisors (IAIS)]. Until the creation of FIO, a single federal entity had not been specifically designated to represent the United States in discussions about the global insurance regulatory framework and international regulatory standard-setting.

FIO's current efforts on prudential aspects of international insurance matters, primarily coordinated through the IAIS, complement the reforms of the Dodd-Frank Act and include: (1) the identification of global systemically important insurers (G-SIIs) to be subject to heightened supervision and regulation; (2) the development of a common framework for the supervision of internationally active groups, including a quantitative capital standard; and (3) the integration of resolution measures into international standards applicable to insurers operating in multiple countries.

---

1. ***The FIO and Other Insurance Sector Representatives on the Financial Stability Oversight Council (FSOC)***. One of the responsibilities of the director of the FIO is to serve on the FSOC as a non-voting member. The FSOC also includes a voting member with insurance expertise, appointed by the President and confirmed by the Senate, plus another non-voting member designated by state insurance commissioners. One of the FSOC's most important roles with respect to the insurance sector is determining which of these firms are systemically important and therefore should be subject to enhanced prudential oversight by the Federal Reserve Board. To date, the FSOC has designated three insurance groups as systemically important: AIG, Prudential, and MetLife, although MetLife is challenging that designation in a litigation that we will take up in Part VI. The voting member of the FSOC with expertise in insurance matters dissented from the Metropolitan Life designation.

III. DEFINING INSURANCE

A. THE REGULATORY PERIMETER

We complete our introduction to insurance regulation with a review of a series of cases and decisions that attempt to define insurance for regulatory purposes. What kinds of financial transactions are subject to insurance regulations and which are treated as mere commercial contracts or transactions subject to some other system of financial regulation? As you review these cases, consider the policies underlying each of the decisions. What is it about the underlying transactions that warrants a special regulatory regime? What is special about insurance?

State *ex rel.* Duffy v. Western Auto Supply Co.

134 Ohio St. 163 (Ohio 1938)

[In this case, the attorney general of Ohio brought an action in *quo warranto* against a corporation that had been offering certain guarantees as part of its retail business in automobile equipment and supplies. The attorney general, as relator, sought a judgment of ouster to prevent the respondent company from "enjoying the franchise and privilege of engaging in the business of insurance."]

[The corporation's sale of pneumatic rubber tires came with two printed forms of guarantees.] One form was a specific guarantee for the period stated therein "against blowouts, cuts, bruises, rim-cuts, under-inflation, wheels out of alignment, faulty brakes or other road hazards that may render the tire unfit for further service (except fire and theft)." It then provided that "In the event that the tire becomes unserviceable from the above conditions, we will (at our option) repair it free of charge, or replace it with a new tire of the same make at any of our stores, charging . . . th[e average] of our current price for each month which has elapsed since the date of purchase. The new tire will be fully covered by our regular guarantee in effect at time of adjustment. Furthermore: every tire is guaranteed against defects in material or workmanship without limit as to time, mileage or service." In the blank spaces were inserted the trade name of the tire, the period covered by the guarantee and the fractional part thereof represented by a single month's wear.

[The other form provided for a guarantee against wear for the length of a specified replacement period.]

It was further stipulated as follows: "All pneumatic tires, regardless of the quality of material and workmanship, are subject to failure in varying degrees by cuts, bruises, breaks, blow-outs, rimcuts, under-inflation, wheels out of alignment, faulty brakes and collision, as well as other road hazards not herein specifically enumerated."

The sole question presented by the record is whether these oral or written agreements or statements or either of them as employed by the respondent in connection with its sale of automobile tires constitutes insurance. It is contended by the relator that in the respect complained of the respondent is engaged in the business of insurance in violation of Section 665, General Code. Its provisions are as follows:

> "No company, corporation, or association, whether organized in this state or elsewhere, shall engage either directly or indirectly in this state in the business of insurance, or enter into any contracts substantially amounting to insurance, or in any manner aid therein, or engage in the business of guaranteeing against liability, loss or damage, unless it is expressly authorized by the laws of this state, and the laws regulating it and applicable thereto, have been complied with. . . . ."

[The attorney general conceded that a warranty against defects is not insurance, but argued that an agreement that goes further would violate state insurance law and that this warranty does so because tires are subject to general wear and road hazards and that the general guarantee for injuries within the replacement period, with no limitation as to cause, shifts the risk of accidental damage or loss unrelated to the quality of material or workmanship from the buyer to the seller. The corporation argued that its forms of guarantee are intended as a method of carrying out and performing on its guarantee that promotes good will, and that, in the absence of such a pre-determined method, disputes as to the cause of the failure of a tire would be constant and annoying because ascertaining the cause of a tire failure is difficult. The corporation also argued that the guarantees represent a limited undertaking that only has to do with the product sold, and does not promise a financial return to the purchaser in any event.]

Are such agreements of guarantee permissible as incidental to the sale of automobile tires; or do they constitute "the business of insurance" or "the business of guaranteeing against liability, loss or damage" or are these agreements of guarantee "contracts substantially amounting to insurance" within the purview of Section 665, General Code, and therefore inhibited?

What is insurance? "Broadly defined, insurance is a contract by which one party, for a compensation called the premium, assumes particular risks of the other party and promises to pay to him or his nominee a certain or ascertainable sum of money on a specified contingency. As regards property and liability insurance, it is a contract by which one party promises on a consideration to compensate or reimburse the other if he shall suffer loss from a specified cause, or to guarantee or indemnify or secure him against loss from that cause." It is a contract "to indemnify the insured against loss or damage to a certain property named in the policy by reason of certain perils to which it is exposed."

It seems well settled that to constitute insurance the promise need not be one for the payment of money, but may be its equivalent or some act of value to the insured upon the injury or destruction of the specified property. It is well settled, also, that the business of insurance is impressed with a public use and consequently its regulation, supervision and control are authorized and required to protect the general public and safeguard the interests of all concerned. We are in accord with the suggestion that business and enterprise should not be unduly restricted or interfered with but should be permitted as great freedom in the conduct and management of their affairs as is consistent with the public interest and welfare. However, our conclusion of the issue presented in this case must be determined from the provisions of our own statutes and our especial inquiry is whether the guarantees in question constitute insurance or are contracts substantially amounting to insurance.

Numerous decisions have been cited which deal with conditions and transactions so at variance with those involved in this case that they are of little assistance in reaching a conclusion of the legal question before us. It is essential that the distinction between warranty and insurance be clearly stated. Section 8392, General Code, defines an express warranty as follows: "Any affirmation of fact or any promise by the seller relating to the goods is an express warranty if the natural tendency of such affirmation or promise is to induce the buyer to purchase the goods, and if the buyer purchases the goods relying thereon." A warranty promises indemnity against defects in the article sold, while insurance indemnifies against loss or damage resulting from perils outside of and unrelated to defects in the article itself.

The respondent, in one of its forms of contract, specifically guarantees "against defects in material and workmanship without limit as to time, mileage or service"; but it goes further and undertakes to indemnify the owner of such tires against all road hazards (except fire and theft) which may render his tire unfit for service. The terms employed in the guarantee are sufficiently broad to include not only damage from blow-outs, cuts and bruises, whether resulting from under-inflation, faulty brakes or misalignment, but any and every hazard, including collisions, whether resulting from negligence of the owner or another. It clearly embraces insurance upon the property of the owner, such as is authorized by the provisions of Section 9556, General Code, to be written by companies required to comply with the insurance laws of the state.

The ultimate force and effect of the contract of indemnity embraced in this guarantee may be appreciated if extended to cover not only the automobile tire but the automobile itself. Surely no one would contend that an undertaking by an automobile manufacturer to replace an automobile damaged or destroyed (excepting only by fire and theft) within a specified period after its purchase is not a contract to reimburse one if he suffers loss from a specified cause, or to indemnify him against such loss.

The fact that such contract of indemnity is made only with the purchaser of the indemnitor's product does not relieve the transaction of its insurance character. When the sale is complete, title passes and the property which is the subject of insurance or indemnity belongs to the purchaser. If the contracts of indemnity involved here are not violative of the insurance laws, then every company may, in consideration of the purchase price paid therefor, furnish its product and also undertake to insure it against all hazards for a specified period. Even if such contract is an incident in the sale of merchandise and its use therein does not constitute the business of insurance, it in effect is a contract "substantially amounting to insurance" within the restrictive provisions of Section 665, General Code. . . .

It follows that a judgment of ouster should issue in all respects as prayed for.

---

1. ***Warranties versus Insurance***. How does the court distinguish between permissible guarantees and unauthorized insurance contracts? Is this a sensible distinction? Will this legal rule have a desirable effect on the way goods and services are produced? What is the public's interest in policing arrangements of this sort?

B. INSURANCE VS. OTHER FINANCIAL PRODUCTS

Jurisdictional boundary questions also arise when other regulated financial intermediaries incorporate insurance-like features into other products. For example, in the case that follows, a state insurance commissioner sought to enjoin a national bank from engaging in an activity that the commissioner concluded was insurance underwriting. Before reading this case, you may find it helpful to recall our discussion of the business of banking in Chapter 2.2. You should also consider that national banks have only limited express authority to engage in insurance activities. *See* 12 U.S.C. § 92 (national banks "located and doing business in any place the population of which does not exceed five thousand . . . may . . . act as the agent for any fire, life, or other insurance company authorized by the authorities of the State in which said bank is located"). This limited authority was understood to establish an outer bound on the permissible insurance activities of national banks. *See, e.g.*, Saxon v. Georgia Association of Independent Insurance Agents, 399 F.2d 1010 (5th Cir. 1968). In later years, however, the courts allowed national banks to make greater inroads into the insurance business, provided the Comptroller of the Currency ratifies the incursions in reasoned interpretation of statutory authority. *See* NationsBank, N.A. v. VALIC, 513 U.S. 251 (1995) (approving the authority of national banks to sell variable annuity products).

First Nat'l Bank of Eastern Arkansas v. Taylor

907 F.2d 775 (8th Cir. 1990)

In July, 1987, First National Bank of Eastern Arkansas (FNB) began offering debt cancellation contracts as additional-cost options to customers borrowing $10,000 or less. These contracts obligated FNB to cancel the unpaid loan balance remaining at the borrower's death, regardless of the cause of death. FNB offered the debt cancellation contracts at rates that did not vary with a borrower's age or medical condition. A regulation promulgated by the United States Comptroller of Currency (Comptroller) authorizes national banks to enter into debt cancellation contracts. *See* 12 C.F.R. 7.7495 (1990).

I

In September, 1987, the Arkansas Insurance Department notified FNB that debt cancellation contracts were the equivalent of credit life insurance policies, and thus subject to state insurance laws. The Department requested that FNB stop offering the contracts. FNB complied, but then brought a suit in federal district court seeking a declaration that the Department's action was preempted by the National Bank Act. . . .

Our inquiry in this case is limited to the question whether the Arkansas Insurance Commissioner may prohibit FNB from entering into debt cancellation contracts. The Commissioner initially urges that such a prohibition does not conflict with federal law because the National Bank Act does not grant national banks the power to offer debt cancellation contracts. The Commissioner argues that in authorizing the contracts, the Comptroller has exceeded his authority. We disagree.

In addition to enumerating specific powers, including the lending of money, the National Bank Act grants national banks the power to exercise "all such incidental powers as shall be necessary to carry on the business of banking." 12 U.S.C. § 24 (Seventh). The Comptroller, through 12 C.F.R. § 7.7495, has interpreted "incidental powers" to include the offering of debt cancellation contracts. . . .

[Asking whether the activity is closely related to an express power and is useful in carrying out the business of banking, the district court here found that the debt cancellation contracts are directly related to FNB's express-authorized lending power as they are sold only in connection with loans made by FNB, and involve only FNB and its borrowing customers.] . . . . The contracts provide borrowers with a convenient method of extinguishing debt in case of death, and enable FNB to avoid the time, expense, and risk associated with attempting to collect the balance of the loan from a borrower's estate. Because we agree with the district court that the debt cancellation contracts are directly connected to FNB's lending activities, we deem the Comptroller's authorization of this activity as reasonable and within the incidental powers granted by the National Bank Act.

II

[Under the principle of federal preemption, the court found in favor of FNB, arguing that national banks are considered federal instrumentalities.] . . . Thus, the National Bank Act preempts the Commissioner's authority to prohibit FNB from offering debt cancellation contracts.

The Commissioner argues, however, that section 2 of the McCarran-Ferguson Act limits the preemptive power of the National Bank Act in this case because it forbids courts to construe the National Bank Act in a manner that impairs a state's authority to regulate the "business of insurance." 15 U.S.C. § 1012(b). The Commissioner urges that because debt cancellation contracts have the same effect as credit life insurance contracts, they are subject to the exclusive regulatory authority of the state under the McCarran-Ferguson Act. We reject this argument. We hold that because the debt cancellation contracts offered by FNB fall within the incidental powers granted by the National Bank Act, they do not constitute the "business of insurance" under the McCarran-Ferguson Act.

We reach this holding for two reasons. The primary reason is that the McCarran-Ferguson Act was not directed at the activities of national banks. The McCarran-Ferguson Act was passed by Congress in response to the Supreme court's decision in *United States v. South-Eastern Underwriters Ass'n*, 322 U.S. 533 (1944), which held that the insurance industry was subject to regulation by Congress under the Commerce Clause, and that insurance company activities were subject to federal antitrust laws. *Id.* at 553. The McCarran-Ferguson Act was designed to preserve traditional state regulation and taxation of insurance companies, and to provide insurance companies with a partial exemption from federal antitrust laws. . . .

The McCarran-Ferguson Act was not intended to give states power to regulate beyond that which they had been thought to possess prior to the South-Eastern Underwriters decision. . . . Yet, well before the South-Eastern Underwriters decision, regulation of national banks was within the exclusive domain of the federal government. *E.g., First Nat'l Bank v. California*, 262 U.S. 366, 369 (1923). This strongly indicates that Congress did not intend the "business of insurance" to encompass lawful activities of national banks.

[The court also found that the debt cancellation contracts do no not require the bank to take an investment risk, obviating the primary and traditional concern behind state insurance regulation, the prevention of insolvency.]

---

1. ***Retirement CDs Distinguished.*** Contrast the *Taylor* decision with *Blackfeet Nat'l Bank v. Nelson*, 171 F.3d 1237 (11th Cir. 1999), where another federal appellate court concluded that an OCC-authorized retirement certificate of deposit was not incidental to the business of banking and also subject to substantive standards of state insurance law. The product included a commitment on the part of the bank to make certain payments until the depositor died, thereby passing "mortality risk" to the issuing bank. The court explained:

> The primary purpose of state regulation of insurance—at least arguably—is the prevention of insolvency. . . . Underlying this concern over insolvency is the understanding that, for many reasons, the nature of insurance lends itself to the possibility of substantial abuse. As a result, we have acknowledged the push for special regulation of the insurance industry, with the fundamental goal being " 'the protection of solvency of the insurance industry, and the prevention of coercion, which in turn protects all potential, present and future policyholders.'" . . . It is exactly the risk shifting and use of actuarial tables present here—in other words, the underwriting—that necessitates the exclusion of the Retirement [certificate of deposit] from the business of banking and its inclusion in the business of insurance. . . .
>
> Our conclusion that the Comptroller unreasonably expanded the powers of a national bank through its "no objection" letter to Blackfeet is a sufficient ground on which to affirm the district court, despite the fact that the district court did not rely on this ground. . . . There is, however, an alternative reason for affirming the district court's decision. Assuming arguendo that the Bank Act permits national banks to market the Retirement [certificate of deposit], we conclude that the McCarran-Ferguson Act nonetheless enables the State of Florida to regulate the issuance of the Retirement [certificate of deposit] in Florida. McCarran-Ferguson reverses the doctrine of preemption in cases involving state insurance laws, such that a state law specifically regulating the business of insurance shall preempt a conflicting federal law unless that federal law specifically relates to the business of insurance. . . .

Did the debt cancellation contracts at issue in the *Taylor* case not also have an element of mortality risk shifting? If so, can the holdings of *Taylor* and *Blackfeet* be reconciled?

2. ***Legislated Détente.*** In the face of a growing body of cases challenging the line between the business of banking and the business of insurance, Congress in § 104 of the Gramm-Leach-Bliley Act attempted to draw boundaries around the extent to which state insurance regulations would apply to bank insurance activities. *See* Karol K. Sparks, Insurance Activities of Banks (2d ed. 2014). The legislation established expedited judicial review "in the case of a regulatory conflict between a State insurance regulator and a federal regulator regarding insurance issues, including whether a State law . . . is preempted under Federal law." The section goes on to specify that a court reviewing such conflicts should base its ruling "on its review on the merits of all questions presented under State and Federal law, including the nature of the product or activity and the history and purpose of its regulation under State and Federal law, without unequal deference." *See* 15 U.S.C. § 6714. Would either the *Taylor* or *Blackfeet* case be decided differently under this standard of review?

3. ***Credit Default Swaps as Insurance or Not?*** In 2000, the Office of the General Counsel of the New York Insurance Department issued an opinion stating that a CDS in which the protection seller was obligated to pay the protection buyer upon the occurrence of a negative credit event was not insurance because the seller must pay the buyer upon the occurrence of a negative credit event regardless of whether the buyer suffered a loss. Eight years later, in the midst of the Financial Crisis, the New York Insurance Department apparently changed its mind:

> With today's Circular Letter, the Department clarifies that to the extent that the making of the CDS itself may constitute "the doing of an insurance business" within the meaning of Insurance Law § 1101, then the protection seller should consider seeking an opinion from the Department's Office of General Counsel to assess whether the protection seller should be licensed as an insurer pursuant to Insurance Law § 1102. Although [Office of General Counsel's] June 16, 2000 opinion suggests that a CDS is not an insurance contract if the payment by the protection buyer is not conditioned upon an actual pecuniary loss, that opinion did not grapple with whether, under Insurance Law § 1101, a CDS is an insurance contract when it is purchased by a party who, at the time at which the agreement is entered into, holds, or reasonably expects to hold, a "material interest" in the referenced obligation. That omission will be rectified and addressed in a forthcoming opinion to be prepared by [Office of General Counsel].

See N.Y. DEP'T OF FIN. SERVICES, Circular Letter No. 19 (Sept. 22, 2008). Later still, the New York Insurance Department suspended its plan to regulate covered CDSs because of federal progress towards regulation. These developments are nicely summarized in Andrea S. Kramer et al., The New York State Insurance Department and Credit Default Swaps: Good Intentions, Bad Idea, J. Taxation & Regulation of Financial Institutions, Jan./Feb. 2009, at 22. For an overview of a similarly spirited debate over whether derivatives should be classified as insurance, see Robert F. Schwartz, *Risk Distribution in Capital Markets: Credit Default Swaps, Insurance and a Theory of Demarcation*, 12 FORDHAM J. CORP. & FIN. L. 167, 183–88 (2007). For more on CDSs, see Chapter 11.2.

CHAPTER 3.2

THE PROTECTION OF CONSUMERS IN INSURANCE REGULATION

CONTENTS

I. INTRODUCTION

This Chapter introduces the consumer protection side of insurance regulation. We begin with a discussion of insurance contracts, focusing on several prominent examples of specialized rules that have evolved from courts' interpretation of these agreements. We also look briefly at the role of state insurance commissions in reviewing and determining the content of insurance contracts. We look next at the regulation of insurance rates, starting with the familiar example of automobile rates and then digging into the specialized topic of risk classifications. Over the years, insurance regulators have played a much more active role in setting prices for insurance products than in other areas of the financial sector. As you work your way through these materials, you should consider why price controls have been so prevalent in insurance. Are similar safeguards appropriate for other financial services? The Chapter concludes with a short section on the mutual form.

II. THE INTERPRETATION OF INSURANCE CONTRACTS

Once a transaction is deemed to be insurance, the party issuing the contract, the insurance underwriter, becomes subject to comprehensive regulatory oversight. A large part of that regulatory structure concerns the content and interpretation of insurance contracts themselves. Though the field offers many fascinating issues, we devote only a few pages to the subject, providing two short cases to give a flavor of the subject. Why do we regulate insurance contracts but leave the content of bank loans and deposit relationships largely to private negotiation? Should we be more concerned about lending transactions and depository instruments?

A. *CONTRA PREFERENTEM*

One norm in the interpretation of insurance contracts is that ambiguous provisions should be interpreted in favor of the insured. As you read the case below, consider why this doctrine may have been adopted and whether it provides meaningful protection to policyholders.

State Farm Mutual Autom. Ins. Co. v. Moore

544 A.2d 1017 (Pa. Super. Ct. 1988), *appeal denied*, 557 A.2d 725 (Pa. 1989)

Johnson, Judge.

The accident underlying this action occurred in 1980, while Brian Stuck was driving a 1961 Pontiac owned by Charles Royer and insured by Ohio Casualty [Insurance Company]. Although owned by Charles Royer the Pontiac was paid for and primarily used by his daughter Leigh Ann Royer. On the night of the accident Leigh Ann, Brian Stuck and some friends visited several bars. Initially, Leigh Ann drove the Pontiac. Later in the evening, when she wished to ride in her friends' car she gave Brian Stuck the keys to the Pontiac so that he could drive her car to the agreed upon destination. Brian Stuck did not have a driver's license. On the way to the destination an accident occurred.

Personal injury actions were brought naming Brian Stuck as defendant. Ohio Casualty denied coverage claiming, in part, that because Stuck was not licensed to drive he was excluded from coverage under the policy. At the time of the accident Stuck resided with his parents who had a no-fault insurance policy with State Farm Mutual Automobile Insurance Company. State Farm undertook the defense of claims asserted against Stuck. State Farm maintains that its policy provides only excess coverage. State Farm commenced the instant declaratory judgment action seeking a determination that primary liability coverage should be furnished by Ohio Casualty.

Following trial the jury returned a verdict specifically finding that Brian Stuck had a reasonable belief that he was entitled to use the vehicle in question. Accordingly, the trial court found Ohio Casualty's exclusion was avoided and that Brian Stuck was entitled to liability coverage under the Ohio Casualty policy. . . .

Ohio Casualty contends that the trial court misconstrued the policy provision in question. This clause, contained in Ohio Casualty's policy, stated:

We do not provide Liability Coverage: . . .

> 11. For any person using a vehicle without a reasonable belief that the person is entitled to do so.

Ohio Casualty argues that "entitled" encompasses not only permission of the owner but also possession of a driver's license.

The trial court instructed the jury that they were to decide the narrow issue of whether or not Mr. Stuck had a reasonable belief that he was entitled to operate the vehicle. . . . [T]he court charged that:

> The term "entitled" as used in the Ohio Casualty policy means "permitted by the owner or person in lawful possession of the vehicle" . . . .

Ohio Casualty argues that this additional charge was erroneous. It argues that the term "entitled" is not ambiguous and that it includes not only permission but also possession of a license.

The question of the meaning of "entitled" in the Ohio Casualty policy is a question of interpretation. The often-quoted principles applicable to interpretation of insurance contracts provide that:

> The task of interpreting a contract is generally performed by a court rather than by a jury. The goal of that task is, of course, to ascertain the intent of the parties as manifested by the language of the written instrument. Where a provision of a policy is ambiguous, the policy provision is to be construed in favor of the insured and against the insurer, the drafter of the agreement. Where, however, the language of the contract is clear and unambiguous, a court is required to give effect to that language.

Standard Venetian Blind Co. v. American Empire Insurance Co., 503 Pa. 300, 304-05, 469 A.2d 563, 566 (1983) (citations omitted). As applied to the case at hand what is essential is the determination of whether the policy provision is ambiguous. In determining this we have stated that:

> A provision of a contract of insurance is ambiguous if reasonably intelligent persons, considering it in the context of the whole policy, would differ regarding its meaning.

Musisko v. Equitable Life Assurance Society, 344 Pa.Super. 101, 106, 496 A.2d 28, 31 (1985) (citations omitted).

Considering the clause in the context of the whole policy, we believe reasonably intelligent persons would differ regarding its meaning. Certainly one interpretation is that advanced by Ohio Casualty. That is, for a person to reasonably believe that he is entitled to use a car a person must have the owner's permission and a valid driver's license. However, the clause could also be interpreted to mean that a person can reasonably believe he is entitled to use a car once he has obtained the owner's permission. The mere use of the word "entitled" in the policy language does not require that one interpretation be accepted to the exclusion of the other. If Ohio Casualty had wanted to specifically exclude from coverage unlicensed drivers it could have defined the word "entitled" in its policy. We note that it has a section entitled "Definitions" in its policy and "entitled" is not one of the words it chose to define. Ohio Casualty could also have listed persons without a driver's license as an additional exclusion. The clause we are now interpreting is number 11 of 12 separate exclusions. Unlicensed drivers could have been specifically set forth as exclusion number 13. This was not done.

Accordingly we find that "entitled" as it is used in the clause at issue is ambiguous. As such, the provision is to be construed against the insurer, who was the drafter of the agreement. Standard Venetian Blind Co., supra. As applied to these facts we then agree with the trial court that it is "sufficient to avoid Ohio Casualty's exclusion that Brian Stuck have had a reasonable belief that he had the permission of the owner or a person in lawful possession of the Royer vehicle." The trial court's charge was not in error. We find no merit to appellant's first argument. . . .

MONTEMURO, Judge, concurring and dissenting:

. . . [T]his contract of automobile insurance does not contemplate coverage for the deliberate perpetration of an illegality, as is clear from the reasonableness requirement. Had appellant's policy merely referred to the insurability of permissive users . . . , there would be no difficulty in finding coverage for Stuck. . . . However, the clause here under examination speaks of reasonable belief, a phrase which implies the exercise of sound judgment. Insofar as the test for such a belief is concerned, it "takes into account a variety of circumstances, including the borrower's age, personality, and social milieu, and the effect of such attendant influences on his judgment and mind as may be credibly discerned from the proofs." *Miller v. U.S.F. & G. Co.*, 28 D. & C.3d 389 (1983).

At the time of the accident Brian Stuck was 23 years old and a high school graduate. He admitted, both in deposition and at trial, to knowledge that it was illegal to operate a motor vehicle without a license, and that his prior driving experience had been limited. Although, given all these factors, it is remotely possible that Stuck thought himself "entitled," that is, empowered by permission of the owner to operate the car simply by virtue of having been handed the keys, that conclusion involves more wishful thinking than reasonableness. Such judgment as it demonstrates is neither sound nor rational since it endows the (putative) teenage owner of an automobile with the authority to permit an activity, driving without a license, which the state clearly and specifically forbids.

---

1. ***Litigation Between Insurance Companies.*** This case involved a contest between State Farm, which had issued a policy to the parents of the unlicensed driver who caused the accident, and Ohio Casualty, which had a policy covering the vehicle itself. State Farm contended that Ohio Casualty's primary coverage should cover the accident, whereas Ohio Casualty attempted, unsuccessfully, to invoke an exclusion in its policy and thereby push liability onto excess coverage of State Farm's policy. Determining which insurance company is liable when two or more policies arguably cover an accident is a common subject of insurance litigation.

2. ***Reasonableness and the Entitlement Exclusion.*** Both the opinions in this case focus on the reasonableness of the driver's understanding that he had permission to drive the vehicle. Which opinion do you find more persuasive? If, as the facts suggest, it was demonstrated that the driver was intoxicated when he got behind the wheel, would that be dispositive? Should the fact that automobile insurance is mandatory in most jurisdictions affect a court's interpretation of such clauses? For an analysis of conflicting authority interpreting this exclusion, see Davla L. Keen, *The Entitlement Exclusion in the Personal Auto Policy*, 84 KY. L.J. 349 (1995).

3. ***Other Types of Policy Exclusions.*** Interpreting policy exclusions presents difficulties in many areas of insurance. Particularly contentious in recent years has been the scope of exclusions for environmental damage in commercial liability policies, as well as exclusions for experimental medical procedures in health insurance policies. For an introduction to these lines of authority, see Melody A. Hamel, *The 1970 Pollution Exclusion in Comprehensive General Liability Policies: Reasons for Interpretations in Favor of Coverage in 1996 and Beyond*, 34 DUQ. L. REV. 1083 (1996), and Peter J. Thill, Note, *Insurers' and Courts' Response to High Dose Chemotherapy with Autologous Bone Marrow Transplants in the Treatment of Breast Cancer*, 43 DRAKE L. REV. 863 (1995). For an interesting overview of doctrines governing the interpretation of insurance contracts, see Kenneth S. Abraham, *A Theory of Insurance Policy Interpretation*, 95 MICH. L. REV. 531 (1996).

4. ***Standardized Insurance Contracts.*** One distinctive feature of the insurance contracts is the prevalence of standardized forms used, with some variations to reflect proprietary language, by a large number of insurance

companies or, in some cases, an entire sector. *See* Daniel Schwarcz, *Reevaluating Standardized Insurance Policies*, 78 U. CHI. L. REV. 1263 (2011). Many pragmatic considerations explain this prevalence of standardized contracts. First, in many contexts, state insurance authorities must approve the form of insurance contracts. Standardized contracts simplify this approval process. Standardized contracts also facilitate the development of a body of judicial authority with considerable precedential value. Furthermore, standardized contracts allow sector trade groups to develop loss data for standardized policies, which many members of the sector can then use for pricing decisions. Are there drawbacks in allowing different companies to employ standardized contracts? What might they be?

B. THE INSURABLE INTEREST DOCTRINE

The insurable interest doctrine dictates that a policyholder cannot insure against an event that would not cause them financial loss. As you read the following case, consider the policy justifications for this doctrine.

Johnson v. Allstate Ins. Co.

870 P.2d 792 (Okla. Civ. App. 1993)

Garrett, Judge.

Appellant, Sherry A. Murdock Johnson (Sherry) sued Allstate Insurance Company (Allstate), Union National Bank of Arkansas (Bank), and Jack D. Murdock (Jack). The purpose of the action was to collect the proceeds of an insurance policy covering her former home in Tulsa, Oklahoma, after it had been destroyed by fire. The trial court overruled Sherry's motion for summary judgment. . . . Sherry appeals.

Jack and Sherry were divorced on May 8, 1991. The Divorce Decree, in its division of property, vested title to the home of the parties in Jack, subject to the balance due on a note, secured by a mortgage on the home in favor of Bank, which he was ordered to pay. Jack was also ordered to pay various other debts of the parties, and to hold Sherry harmless as to them. She was ordered to execute and deliver to Jack a quit claim deed to the home, and she did so. The deed contained a recital that it was executed pursuant to the order in the Divorce Decree. She was not given any lien or claim against the home as security in the event Jack failed to pay the debts of the parties, as ordered by the Court. The quit claim deed did not reserve any such security interest.

In October, 1991, Jack filed for Chapter 7 Bankruptcy. In the Federal Court, by objections filed October 24, 1991, Sherry contested Jack's right to a discharge of his obligation to her to pay the debts assigned to him by the Divorce Decree, and to hold her harmless. However, the Bankruptcy Court held Jack's obligations in that respect were subject to discharge.

Sherry applied for insurance on the home, apparently to protect herself from possible liability on the note and mortgage to Bank. Allstate issued an insurance policy on the home to Sherry, in her name, on October 26, 1991. The policy covered the usual hazards, including fire, and contained a standard loss payable clause, as its interest appears, to Bank as mortgagee. The policy contained a provision limiting Allstate's liability to Sherry's insurable interest. It is consistent with Oklahoma's statutes, and is as follows:

> . . . Allstate . . . , to an amount not exceeding the limit of liability specified, does insure the Insured named in the Declarations and legal

> representatives, to the extent of the actual cash value of the property at the time of loss, but not exceeding . . . , *nor in any event for more than the interest of the Insured*, . . .(emphasis supplied [in original])

On December 1, 1991, the home was destroyed by fire. Allstate furnished Proof of Loss forms to Sherry. About January 20, 1992, she returned the Proof of Loss to Allstate. She claimed a loss for the value of the structure, but not for its contents. Allstate took her sworn examination and also the sworn examination of Jack. For reasons not readily apparent in this appeal, Allstate thought the circumstances of the fire were suspicious and caused an investigation to be made.

On April 2, 1992, Allstate advised Sherry, through her attorney, that it would pay Bank in full for all principal and interest due on its note and mortgage, but would not pay Sherry any additional sum of money because . . . Sherry's insurable interest was limited to the amount required to pay the balance due on the note and mortgage to Bank, and the payment to Bank satisfied [Allstates'] liability in full. Sherry contended she had the right to collect the balance of the policy because Jack's discharge in bankruptcy and his failure to hold her harmless on various debts (as listed in the Divorce Decree) caused her to be required to expend several thousand dollars in paying debts that Jack had been ordered to pay.

Sherry contends the [trial court] erred in holding her insurable interest in the home was limited to the amount due Bank on its note and mortgage. In effect, she contends Jack's failure to pay various debts, as ordered by the divorce court, gave her a security interest in the home. Applicable authority to support this contention has not been cited. In making her argument in support of her contentions, the holding of the Bankruptcy Court that Jack's obligation to her was dischargeable is not considered. If Jack received a discharge in bankruptcy, he would have no obligation to Sherry to pay debts. At the time of the hearing, in this case, the automatic stay, under bankruptcy laws, was in effect.

Sherry contends she executed and delivered a quit claim deed to Jack, which put the title to the home in his name, with the oral understanding that he would sell the home and pay their joint debts. This contention ignores the provision in the Divorce Decree ordering her to execute and deliver the deed, the provision in the Decree that it would constitute such a conveyance if she failed to do so, and the provision in the decree restraining her from claiming any interest in the home. In addition, the deed does not contain any reservation of any security interest. In addition, this contention does not consider the effect of [Oklahoma real estate law] which requires a deed, mortgage, or conveyance of real estate or any interest in real estate . . . to be in writing and subscribed by the grantors.

Sherry contends Allstate is estopped from denying her payment of the full proceeds of the insurance policy (less the amount paid to Bank). Before estoppel may apply, the insurance policy must constitute a lawful contract. Contracts of insurance are valid and enforceable insofar as authorized by statute. Such contracts, not authorized by statute, have generally been held illegal and not enforceable because of public policy considerations and laws prohibiting gambling. Oklahoma statutes, as a prerequisite to validity of an insurance contract, require the beneficiary to have an insurable interest.

As pointed out in Allstate's brief, [Oklahoma insurance law] provides:

> A. No insurance contract on property or of any interest therein or arising therefrom shall be enforceable as to the insurance except for the benefit of persons having an insurable interest in the things insured.
>
> B. "Insurable interest" as used in this section means any actual, lawful, and substantial economic interest in the safety or preservation of the subject of

> the insurance free from loss, destruction, or pecuniary damage or impairment.
>
> C. The measure of an insurable interest in property is the extent to which the insured might be damnified by loss, injury, or impairment thereof.

In *Snethen v. Oklahoma State Union of the Farmers Educational And Co-operative Union of America*, 664 P.2d 377 (Okl.1983), the Court . . . discussed the requirement of an "insurable interest". The Court said:

> It is well settled that both the validity and enforceability of an insurance contract depend upon the presence of insurable interest in the person who purchased the policy. Considerations underlying the insurable interest concept are generally articulated in terms of policy (1) against allowing wagering contracts under the guise of insurance, (2) against fostering temptation to destroy the insured property in an effort to profit from it and (3) favoring limitation upon the sweep of indemnity contracts. . . .

While American jurisdictions generally agree with the public policy considerations that underl[ie] the necessity for an insurable interest, they stand divided on what constitutes an insurable interest. Two basic theories were evolved for measuring the nexus which must be present between the property and its insured for an insurable interest to attach. The literature refers to one of these as the "legal interest" and to the other as the "factual expectation" theory.

Sherry had no title, ownership, insurable interest, or other [legal] interest in the real property (the home) involved here. She had no factual expectation of an actual, lawful, substantial economic interest in Jack's general assets from which she would ever be satisfied.

The trial court correctly held that Sherry's "insurable interest" in the home was limited to the amount due to Bank on its note and mortgage. . . .

---

1. ***Responsibilities of the Insurer.*** Did the court let Allstate off too easily? Should an insurance company have a responsibility to determine whether a party has an appropriate insurable interest before accepting premiums for the full face amount of the insurance policy? Or was it reasonable to make Shelly bear the risk that she would not be found to possess a fully insurable interest once the property was destroyed? How does the court's approach square with the *contra proferentem* principle invoked in the preceding *State Farm* decision?

2. ***Justifications for the Insurable Interest Doctrine.*** The insurable interest doctrine was initially based on a moral judgment that individuals should not enter into insurance contacts for speculative purposes, as well as on pragmatic considerations that such contracts present an acute moral hazard in that an insured party may be tempted to destroy the insured property in order to recover on the party's policy. Are these considerations still valid today? After all, in our modern economy, investors are permitted to speculate in futures and options contracts without having any underlying economic interests in these insurance-like contracts. *See* Chapter 11.1. Indeed, economists generally regard this sort of speculation as a valuable source of liquidity. Should we therefore allow insurance companies to underwrite traditionally uninsurable interests in order to broaden insurance pools and expand business opportunities?

3. ***Moral Hazard.*** The insurable interest doctrine limits one type of moral hazard that insurers face, but there are others. Because insurance removes some of the risk of financial loss, people may engage in riskier behavior once they have insurance. Insurers use a host of tools to minimize this moral hazard, including risk-based pricing, contract provisions such as coverage limits, and educating their policyholders about how they can avoid loss. To learn more about the steps insurers take to limit moral hazard amongst their policyholders, see Tom Baker & Rick Swedloff, *Regulation by Liability Insurance: From Auto to Lawyers Professional Liability*, 61 UCLA L. REV. 1413 (2013).

4. ***Changes in Value and Insurable Interest.*** The Joneses live in an economically depressed region of Pennsylvania. In 2007, they bought their current home for $100,000 and have ever since been insuring the property for its fair market value. Over the past few years, the home prices in their neighborhood have declined substantially, and now the Joneses estimate that their home's market value is less than $70,000, whereas it would cost them at least $125,000 to rebuild the house if it were destroyed. Can the Joneses insure the property up to its replacement cost? Should they be able to? Does the amount of outstanding balance due on the Joneses' mortgage matter?

C. SUPERVISORY OVERSIGHT OF POLICY TERMS

As the preceding cases illustrate, the courts play an important role in interpreting insurance contracts. Insurance contracts are also subject to oversight by insurance regulators, who must pre-approve the content of insurance contracts in many contexts. In addition, state laws establish mandatory contractual terms that constrain parties in negotiating insurance contracts. The excerpt below describes these mandatory rules.

Tom Baker & Kyle D. Logue, Mandatory Rules and Default Rules in Insurance Contracts

Research Handbook on the Economics of Insurance Law (2015)

As with contract law generally, the overwhelming majority of the law that governs the actions of parties' to an insurance contract is found in the language of the contracts themselves. Although the vast majority of insurance policies are standard form contracts, which policyholders (rationally) never bother to read until a loss occurs, there are good reasons why the rights and responsibilities of insurers and insureds are governed primarily by the plain language of the policies. There are, however, ways in which the parties to insurance contracts are not free to choose whatever terms they wish. The common law of insurance or a particular state's insurance code (or the regulations promulgated by the insurance regulatory authority under the authority of that state's insurance code) may impose limitations on what terms may be inserted into an insurance policy, how those terms will be interpreted by courts, or what background duties will be imposed on insurers and insureds.

Such mandatory rules generally fall into three categories: (1) insurance policy terms that are expressly required by state legislatures or by state insurance regulators to be included into certain types of insurance policies; (2) common law contract and insurance law duties; and (3) the rules of contract interpretation and enforcement (including rules that expressly forbid certain terms in insurance contracts). . . .

Over the years, states have begun to require specific terms in many different policies. For example, some states now require insurers to insert in all of their policies a term explicitly excluding coverage for losses caused 'willfully' or 'intentionally' by the insured (*see, e.g.*, Cal. Ins. Code § 533). A somewhat controversial example of a mandatory insurance contract term involves the issue of multiple concurrent causes.

Insurance companies sometimes wish to exclude from coverage particular causes of a loss, either for moral hazard reasons (as with the intentional harm exclusion already mentioned), for market segmentation reasons (a particular risk is better insured through a different type of policy), or for other reasons (perhaps the risk in question is entirely uninsurable). The interesting question is what should be done when a given loss has more than one cause, one that is covered and one that is specifically excluded. Some insurers have drafted and redrafted their policies to make clear that coverage is not owed if an excluded cause—earth movement or flood, for example has any causal connection whatsoever to the loss, no matter how remote. The courts have tended to apply such language literally, which tends to favor insurers. In some states, however, legislatures have been unwilling to permit insurers to draft such exclusions and have instead enacted laws requiring that causal exclusions apply only if the excluded cause was the 'dominant' or 'primary' or 'efficient proximate' cause of the loss in question. . . . In those states, the dominant cause requirement has in effect been made a mandatory term in every insurance policy. In other states, the efficient proximate cause rule is merely a default rule, which insurers have successfully contracted around. . . .

Certain duties developed in the common law of contracts can also be understood as mandatory terms in every insurance policy. For example, it is hornbook law that every contract, including every insurance contract, contains an implied duty on the part of all parties to the contract to act in good faith, or to refrain from acting in bad faith, when enforcing their contractual rights or carrying out their contractual obligations or both (*see, e.g.*, U.C.C. § 1-102(3) (stating that the obligation of contracting parties to act in good faith may not be disclaimed by agreement of the parties)). This general duty has a number of special applications in the insurance context. One example involves the insurer's duty to pay benefits owed. In most if not all jurisdictions, an insurer who relies on a patently unreasonable interpretation of the language in the policy to refuse payment to a deserving insured may later be found by a court to have breached the duty of good faith and fair dealing . . .

The duty to defend and the duty to settle in liability insurance policies are examples of what might be called 'quasi-mandatory' or 'sticky' implied contract terms. The concepts of 'quasi-mandatory default rules' and 'sticky defaults' have been discussed in the law and economics contracts literature. The basic idea is that there is a continuum between regular default rules, which are relatively easy for contracting parties to alter, and mandatory rules, which by definition are impossible to contract around. Quasi-mandatory rules fall somewhere in between. Thus, quasi-mandatory rules provide courts and policymakers with another policy instrument, beyond normal default rules and mandatory rules, for responding to information asymmetry and externality concerns in contract settings.

The duty to defend and the duty to settle are 'quasi' rather than fully mandatory rules because, although insurers can eliminate the duties contractually, they can do so only by redrafting their policies in ways that substantially alter the allocation of rights and responsibilities between the insurer and insured. . . .

The basic rules of interpretation developed in the common law of contract are generally considered mandatory, and this is true in the insurance context as well. For example, the doctrine of *contra proferentem*, under which ambiguous terms are construed against the party who supplied the term, is routinely applied in insurance cases (typically to the benefit of insureds against insurers), irrespective of whether there is language in the policy seeking to eliminate that rule. . . .

Some common law decisions refusing to enforce provisions in insurance policies can also be understood as creating a kind of mandatory rule. The refusal to enforce a term in an insurance policy substitutes silence for that term, potentially making the inverse of that term a mandatory rule. In some jurisdictions, for example, courts have held that insurance for intentionally caused losses is against public policy, on the theory that permitting such insurance would increase incentives for insureds to cause losses intentionally, the classic moral hazard concern. . . . In such jurisdictions, therefore, insurance policies contain an implied, mandatory exclusion for intentionally caused losses. Likewise, the insurable interest requirement says that, if (or to the extent that) an insured has no insurable interest in the thing being insured against (that is, she stands to lose nothing if the insured event happens), the insurance policy in question will typically be found unenforceable, again on moral hazard/public policy grounds. In such jurisdictions all insurance policies can be understood to contain a mandatory insurable interest requirement.

---

1. ***Constraining Contractual Choice as a Regulatory Tool.*** What are the pros and cons of policing the terms of insurance contracts in the way described in this excerpt? As you explore other areas of consumer protection in this book, consider whether similar requirements exist or should exist for other financial services.

2. ***Mandatory Provisions.*** State or federal law often requires that insurance policies cover certain contingencies or provide some minimum level of coverage. For example, in *Prepaid Dental Services, Inc. v. Day*, 615 P.2d 1271 (Utah 1980) (available in the Annex), an HMO-style dental plan would have had to cover emergency care had it been deemed an insurance plan. For more on mandatory rules, see Tom Baker & Kyle D. Logue, *Mandatory Rules and Default Rules in Insurance Contracts, in* RESEARCH HANDBOOK ON THE ECONOMICS OF INSURANCE LAW (Daniel Schwarcz & Peter Siegelman ed., 2015).

3. ***Duty to Settle.*** Liability insurance policies typically empower the insurer to settle claims against its policyholders. Discretion to insurers is generally optimal given an insurer's informational advantages plus perverse incentives for insureds to settle up to the amount of policy limits. If the settlement is large relative to the policy's coverage limit, however, the insurer is incentivized to litigate even when it is not in the policyholder's best interest since the cost of an award in excess of the coverage limit would be borne by the policyholder. To mitigate this conflict of interest, courts require insurers to make reasonable settlement decisions when defending claims against their policyholders. This duty takes a wide array of forms, and varies by state. To learn more about the different flavors of the duty to settle, see Scott G. Ball et al., *The Right and Duty to Settle Third-Party Liability Claims: A 50 State Survey* (2015).

III. THE REGULATION OF AUTOMOBILE RATES

A. OVERVIEW OF STATE APPROACHES

One of the most publicized aspects of insurance regulation is the government's role in approving or, in some circumstances, setting the prices that insurance companies charge their consumers. The regulation of insurance rates, which is typically confined to the property / casualty side of the sector, is largely a post-World War II development. Until the 1940s, insurance companies in most jurisdictions had considerable freedom to establish whatever rates they chose, and often collaborated with each other through the use of rate bureaus to pool loss data and establish uniform prices. With the Supreme Court's decision in *United States v. South-Eastern Underwriters Ass'n*, 322 U.S. 533 (1944), however, these practices became vulnerable to challenge under the federal anti-trust laws. In 1945, the McCarran-Ferguson Act granted the sector a limited exemption to federal antitrust law, but only to the extent that the sector was subject to state regulation. The National Association of Insurance Commissioners (NAIC) promptly developed model laws for rate regulation, which all of the states eventually adopted with various modifications. The following excerpt introduces the rate regulation process as it has evolved during the second half of the 20th Century.

Kenneth S. Abraham, Insurance Law and Regulation

106–12 (2d ed. 1995)

In contrast to regulation for solvency, where financial data regarding an insurer's assets and liabilities is used to assess the economic health of the company, in ratemaking statistical data on claims and losses takes center stage. Insurance premiums, like prices for most products in imperfectly competitive markets, tend to be set with one eye on cost and profitability, and the other on market share. Unlike most products, however, the lion's share of an insurer's costs are unknown at the time it must set a price for coverage. Admittedly, this difference between insurance and other products is sometimes exaggerated. Companies in other lines of business also must make decisions in the face of uncertainty about the future. For example, General Motors must decide whether to build a new plant, open a new assembly line, hire more employees, or design a new model vehicle before it knows what all of its costs will be and how future economic forces will affect demand for its product. But insurers probably know with certainty a smaller proportion of the costs they will ultimately incur when they set their prices than most businesses that operate in other sectors of the economy.

Operating Profit: Underwriting Results and Investment Income

Both the process of insurance ratemaking and the regulation of that process are somewhat uncertain undertakings. If an insurer is to earn an operating profit, then the sum of its underwriting and investment profit and loss must be positive. The underwriting side of the insurance business is the sale of insurance and the payment of claims. Generally, underwriting profit and loss are expressed as the ratio of claim payouts and expenses to premiums earned. If this combined ratio is below 100 (or 1.00, depending on the scale used) then the insurer has earned an underwriting profit. If the combined ratio exceeds 100, the insurer has incurred an underwriting loss. For example, an insurer might find that its payouts ("losses") for a given year in a particular line were \$.88 for every dollar of premium earned, and that its expenses (for marketing, administration, claim processing, etc.) per dollar of premium were \$.22. Its combined ratio would then be 110. Notice that the combined ratio is the result of a comparison (like any ratio) of two numbers: losses-plus-expenses as compared to premiums. Consequently, this ratio will rise either when losses-plus-expenses increase, or when premiums decline similarly, the combined ratio will fall either when losses-plus-expenses fall or when premiums rise.

The underwriting experience measured by the combined ratio, however, is only half the story. Because the insurer holds premiums for a period of time before it must pay claims against its policies, it can earn income on those premiums by investing them prior to payout. Positive investment income at least partially offsets underwriting losses, and sometimes more than offsets these losses. The longer the insurer holds premiums, the greater the income it can earn by investing them. In a long-tail line (one in which the claims against a single year's policies are issued) such as medical malpractice or products liability, investment income may be able to offset sizeable underwriting losses. As a consequence, premiums should be lower than they would be for coverage of the same aggregate expected loss with a shorter tail. In contrast, in short-tail lines such as automobile collision or fire insurance, most claims are made and paid shortly after the expiration of the policy period, and investment income constitutes a smaller percentage of profit or loss. Thus, in a world where insurance companies compete for business, premiums are inevitably set with potential investment income taken into account. Similarly, once all the results are in, a complete picture of an insurer's profitability cannot be obtained without taking its investment income into account.

Ratemaking

Unfortunately, it is a fact of insurance life that at the time an insurer sets rates—and at the time a regulator scrutinizes them—neither can know for certain whether the level at which rates are set will produce profit or loss. In the absence of certainty about the future, past underwriting results are some evidence of what the future may bring. For two reasons, however, even past underwriting results must be adjusted to take account of the future. First, some differences between past and future results may already be known. Comparative negligence may have been adopted, or a statute requiring the installation of sprinkler systems in all public buildings may have been enacted. Second, unless the past underwriting results used as a ratemaking building block are complete, they may be an inaccurate predictor of the future; and to the extent that these results are complete, they may be older than would be ideal for use as predictors. For example, suppose that in 1995 an insurer wanted to set a rate for products liability insurance in 1996. If it looked at data regarding losses paid under 1995 policies, there would be very little data, because claims would only just be coming in. Data on losses paid under 1989 policies would be much more complete; but that data would also be less relevant, because of changes in the social, economic, and legal environments in the interim.

Consequently, when insurers project the future based on underwriting experience in recent years, the validity of their projections depends heavily on the completeness of the data used. When that data is incomplete, insurers follow accounting conventions for projecting the ultimate magnitude of claims and payouts against a particular year's policies, and then draw conclusions regarding the profitability of that year based on these projections. As a result, conclusions about the profitability of long-tail lines of coverage sold in a recent year are partly historic statements, but these conclusions also are partly predictions.

For example, in 1995 an insurer may attempt to determine how profitable its 1994 products liability insurance was, or (what amounts to almost the same thing) how profitable it ultimately will be. The insurer may know that it has paid $500,000 in claims against 1994 policies, and that claims likely to result in payouts of an additional $1,000,000 have already been reported. It will therefore reserve $1,000,000 for these reported claims. Then, on the basis of past experience, the insurer may also project that claims payouts in the first year after a given year's products liability policies have been issued plus sums reserved for claims already-reported-but-not-yet-paid usually have turned out to constitute only 20 percent of ultimate payouts against that year's policies. The insurer will therefore estimate, based on this past pattern of loss development, that it will ultimately incur an additional $6,000,000 in losses against 1995 policies for claims incurred but not reported (IBNR). It may also note, however, that each year for the past several years its loss development estimates of this sort have turned out to be low; an additional loss development factor may therefore be added. In addition, the insurer will employ a trend factor to revise this figure upward, based on the pattern of increases in loss rates that it has observed over the past years.

Notice that this entire exercise involves prediction of the future by projecting past results. On top of these projections of past experience, the insurer may also include a factor to take account of the economic and legal inflation that it predicts for the period during which these 1995 policies still will be exposed to claims. In the aggregate, these estimates of the total losses that ultimately will be paid by 1995 policies produce a projection of ultimate underwriting experience that may be used as part of the bases for setting 1996 rates. As long as everyone involved understands what is going on, statements about the underwriting profitability of recent policy years for particular insurance lines can be understood for what they are: the best estimates that may be available, but estimates nonetheless.

If there were no regulation of insurance rates, all this would merely be a description of some of the factors insurers take into account in setting rates. Any insurer that overestimated its future losses—deliberately or in error—might fool its shareholders for a short time, but ultimately other insurers would make more accurate projections and increase their market shares by underpricing the first insurer. To a great extent that kind of competition can and does occur in the existing insurance markets. . . . [H]owever, in at least some lines of property/casualty insurance a somewhat more collective process of ratemaking is the norm, arguably because of the inability of even the largest companies to make rates based on the limited loss data available to them individually.

Partly for this reason, and partly out of independent concern that certain segments of the insurance market are not completely competitive, insurance rates are subject to regulatory scrutiny. Ostensibly, such regulation has been motivated by the tripartite concern that rates not be "excessive, inadequate, or unfairly discriminatory," to quote the standard provision in almost every state's regulatory legislation. In practice, however, most regulatory scrutiny of rates is not focused on whether they are inadequate (a solvency concern) or unfairly discriminatory, though the latter is receiving increasing emphasis. Rather, the typical Insurance Commissioner in a rate hearing, or in deciding whether to have a hearing, is concerned to assure that rates are not excessive.

At an administrative hearing considering the proposed rate increase, both parties (and/or others, depending on the nature of the proceeding and those granted standing) would present evidence in support of their contentions. . . . Normally this testimony will be from experts who have examined the insurer's claims experience, and who have made projections based in part on this experience (or the total claims experience of the companies represented by a rate service bureau such as [the Insurance Service Office]) and in part on judgments about future trends that are not subject to objective proof. The Commissioner would then rule depending on the nature of his authority under the state's insurance code or statutes. . . .

Whatever the form of regulation, a Commissioner's scrutiny of a rate involves consideration of roughly the same issues. Few really informed observers believe that all segments of the insurance market are always fully competitive, and few believe that there is always widespread parallel action by insurers, let alone outright conspiracy. The basic philosophical difference between proponents of regulation and proponents of open competition, therefore, turns on their level of confidence (or lack of it) in the capacity of insurance regulators to make the kinds of pricing decisions that would otherwise be made by market forces.

Private automobile insurance is one area in which state insurance regulators have been particularly active in policing rates. A variety of factors explain the more extensive regulation of automobile insurance. To begin with, private automobile insurance is a significant expenditure for many individuals. In 1993, for example, consumers spent more than $93.4 billion on automobile insurance (or more than $500 for every licensed driver). While some of this expenditure is voluntary, much is not. Almost all U.S. jurisdictions have some form of mandatory automobile insurance law requiring automobiles to be covered by certain minimum amounts of insurance, typically to provide coverage for personal injuries and property damage caused to third parties.

While the methods Insurance Commissioners use to regulate insurance rates varies across states and across lines of insurance, current methods of rate regulation fall into the following six categories. A seventh form of rate regulation is state prescription of rates, which is exceptionally rare today (although it was the regulatory method used in Massachusetts until 2008). Under this method, states Commissioners dictate insurance rates relying on information provided by insurance companies.

Prior approval. Insurers file proposed rates with the Insurance Commissioner that go into effect either when a specified waiting period lapses or when the state regulator approves the filing.

Modified prior approval. Under this approach, rate changes based on a change in expense ratio or rate classifications are subject to the stricter prior approval method. However, rate revisions based on a change in loss experience are subject to the more lenient file and use regulation.

Flex rating. The file and use or use and file provisions apply to increases or decreases in rates within a certain range. If a rate change falls outside of the determined band, prior approval provisions apply.

File and use. Insurance rates become effective immediately upon being filed with the Commissioner, but they can be disapproved at a future time.

Use and file. Rates go into effect upon use but must be filed with the Commissioner within a certain period of time after their first use.

No file. Rates become effective when used and do not need to be filed with the state regulator.

J. W. Wilson & Associates: A HYPOTHETICAL RATE CASE
(dollars in thousands)

		As Seen By:	
		Insurer	**Consumer**
1.	Earned Premium (Current Rates)	$1,597,265	$1,597,265
2.	Incurred Losses (Current Year)	$1,287,416	$1,287,416
3.	Trend Factor	1.100	1.060
4.	Loss Development Factor	1.150	—
5.	Composite Factor (3 x 4)	1.265	1.060
6.	Ultimate Losses (2 x 5)	$1,628,581	$1,364,661
7.	Loss Adjustment Expense Factor	1.120	1.110
8.	Ultimate Losses & LAE (6 x 7)	$1,824,010	$1,514,774
9.	Current Loss & LAE Ratio (8/1)	1.142	0.948
10.	Commission & Expense Factor	1.250	1.10 + $159,727
11.	Profit & Contingency Factor	1.050	0.90
12.	Indicated Rate Change Factor (9 x 10 x 11)	1.499	0.939 + $143,754
13.	Required Rate Increase	$797,035	$46,321
14.	Percentage Increase (13/1)	+ 49.9%	+ 2.9%

Notes

1. Both parties agree on total premiums earned last year.

2. Both accept the insurer's stated "losses"—which includes those paid and those incurred but not paid.

3.-5. The consumer advocate wants to combine development and trend factors into a single number; more importantly, the consumer's projection of development plus trend is .205 lower than the insurer's. In effect, the consumer advocate argues that the insurer's prediction of future increases in loss payouts is excessive.

6. The result is a substantial difference in future projected costs.

7.-8. Differences between the parties as to the projected increase in loss adjustment expenses (in liability insurance, mainly counsel fees) further separates their estimates.

9. Summarizes this difference in the form of a projected combined ratio for this year.

10. The parties also differ about how to project other expense increases—the consumer advocate uses actual expenses plus a factor for future increases, while the insurer simply uses an increase factor.

11. Because the insurer projects an underwriting loss, *see* item 9 above, it counts on its investment income to offset it, while the consumer advocate projects an underwriting profit, and wants 10 percent of the insurer's investment income used to reduce premiums.

12.-13. This difference between the parties results in different total rate change factors, and a different dollar increase in rates requested.

14. Because of the differences noted, the percentage increase in rates suggested by the parties are radically different.

B. ILLUSTRATIVE CASES: MASSACHUSETTS AND CALIFORNIA

Because states require such large personal expenditures on private automobile insurance, regulatory authorities often feel an obligation to ensure that the product is available to all drivers at a fair price. As of 2008, 15 states subjected automobile insurance to prior approval procedures, and 24 other states had file and use or some variant thereof.

Before deregulating in 2008, for example, Massachusetts maintained the most elaborate rate regulation structure, an administratively developed pricing system applicable to all private auto insurance sold in the state. Each year, the Massachusetts Commissioner of Insurance would establish a fee structure, based on an administrative proceeding where the Commissioner would evaluate insurers' rate proposals and typically find them excessive and set the rates at a lower level. OFFICE OF THE MASS. ATT'Y GEN., AUTOMOBILE INSURANCE: THE ROAD AHEAD 8 (2009). In many years that this was done, the insurance sector would challenge the Commissioner's rate schedule, and the courts would have to decide whether the rates were appropriate. As you review the following cases, consider the factors the Commissioner must take into account in this rate-setting process. How likely is it that the Commissioner will evaluate these factors accurately? Would a private insurance company likely evaluate these factors better? Can courts provide meaningful review?

Mass. Auto Rating & Acc. Prevention Bureau v. Comm'r of Ins.

453 N.E.2d 381 (Mass. 1983)

Lynch, Justice.

[In 1982, Massachusetts enacted a law increasing penalties for driving under the influence of alcohol increased insurance surcharges for repeat offenders. The Commissioner of Insurance, relying on predictions by the State Ratings Board (SRB), lowered rates on the premise that the new law would decrease costs to insurers by deterring drunk driving. A group of insurers filed suit, arguing that the Commissioner overstated the effects of the new law.]

As a means of determining the likely effect of these changes, the SRB reviewed the results of two analogous programs designed to decrease the incidence of drunk driving. The SRB's first source was the experience of the Alcohol Safety Action Programs (ASAP) conducted in several locations in the United States during the past decade. The data on the effect of these programs were varied, but many programs showed a decrease in offenses ranging from 15% to 25%. From these results, the SRB concluded that an effectively implemented program directed at deterring drunk driving could produce a similar decrease in such offenses.

The SRB also studied the effects of the recent enactment by the State of Maine of a drunk driving law which requires a mandatory jail sentence of one year for first offenders convicted of driving under the influence of alcohol. The study revealed that during approximately the first year, the number of fatal alcohol related accidents in Maine declined by 35%. . . .

The plaintiffs disagree with the major premise of the SRB's analysis that the new law and increased merit rating surcharges will have a deterrent effect. They assert that the Massachusetts law is not sufficiently similar to the law in Maine or the ASAP's results to justify extrapolating future Massachusetts results from this evidence. The plaintiffs claim that, unlike these programs, the Massachusetts law does not provide for increased enforcement of the law, and they assert that this fact lessens any supposed deterrent impact. In sum, the plaintiffs conclude that the anticipated change in frequency claims due to these measures is too speculative to warrant use in this year's rates.

After reviewing the evidence and the arguments of both the plaintiffs and the SRB, the Commissioner concluded that the increased sanctions against drunk driving will have some impact on the problem. Although the use of evidence gleaned from other jurisdictions' programs, which are admittedly different in degree and kind from the changes made in Massachusetts, is not completely satisfactory, we cannot say that the Commissioner's assumption does not have reasonable support in the evidence. The plaintiffs' criticism, renewed here, of the SRB's methodology and evidence were considered by the Commissioner and rejected by him. As we noted above, we do not substitute our judgment for that of the Commissioner.

Mass. Auto. Rating & Acc. Prevention Bureau v. Comm'r of Ins.

411 N.E.2d 762 (Mass. 1980)

Braucher, Justice.

a. Appraisals. Effective September 1, 1978, the Division promulgated Regulation 1-78, a set of rules designed to reduce losses by improving practices in the appraisal and repair of motor vehicles. In most respects the Commissioner accepted the Bureau's estimates of resulting loss savings, but the Bureau objects to savings attributed to the provisions of the Regulation relating to licensing and supervision of appraisers. In his decision on 1979 rates, the Commissioner rejected the Bureau's contention that those provisions would produce no savings, but accepted the Bureau's argument that the benefits would take time; hence he projected savings of .5% in place of 4% recommended by the Division for collision coverages and assumed no savings at all for comprehensive coverage. In the hearings on the 1980 rates the Bureau introduced evidence that some of the major companies, accounting for more than 50% of the market, had long had internal standards similar to the requirements of the Regulation; it now argues that there was no evidence of improved qualifications of appraisers or of action to enforce higher standards. The Division pointed to an increase from 1978 to 1979 in the difference between body shop estimates and company appraisals, attributing the increase to improvement in the quality of appraisals. . . .

c. The drinking age. Effective April 16, 1979, the Legislature raised the legal age for purchasing and selling alcoholic beverages from eighteen to twenty years. St.1979, c. 15. The Commissioner accepted an analysis by the Division indicating that the lowering of the drinking age in 1973 had increased accident frequencies and that raising the age would have an opposite effect. He found that the Division estimate overstated the effect and should be adjusted to take account, first, of the number of vehicles involved in an accident, and, second, of the difference between lowering the age from twenty-one to eighteen in 1973 and raising it from eighteen to twenty in 1979. But he made an offsetting adjustment because the Division data, counting only accidents where an alcohol-related citation was issued, understated the number of alcohol-related accidents. He made a 1% frequency reduction for all coverages except comprehensive, a result close to that recommended by the Division.

The Bureau attacks the result as optimistic and speculative. It says that in the past the Commissioner has required "compelling evidence" to support a frequency adjustment, citing Attorney Gen. v. Commissioner of Ins., 370 Mass. 791, 800, 353 N.E.2d 745 (1976). We agree, as did the Commissioner, that the evidence is not completely satisfactory, particularly with respect to the severity of alcohol-related claims. But we think his conclusion has reasonable support in the evidence. Our conclusion on this point would not be changed if we took into account the Registry statistics and the Probation study included in the plaintiffs' supplementary affidavit. . . .

d. The tort threshold. In many cases an accident victim can recover damages for pain and suffering only if his medical expenses exceed $500. G.L. c. 231, s 6D. This threshold has been steadily eroded by inflation of medical expenses, and the erosion increases claim frequencies for bodily-injury liability. Hence the Commissioner allowed a 1% upward adjustment for this coverage. The Bureau argues that the adjustment is too small. Claims data for 1977 and 1978 would support a larger adjustment, but there was testimony that a reporting problem rendered those data unreliable. We hold that the Commissioner's decision to omit the unreliable data had reasonable support in the evidence.

Massachusetts's rate setting system was controversial. Opponents argued that it increased the number of people seeking insurance in the residual markets and suppressed premiums. The number of companies offering passenger auto insurance in Massachusetts dropped from 35 to 19 between the 1990s and 2008, with many blaming the rate setting regime for the departures. Faced with more insurance companies threatening to leave and concerns that competition was being suffocated, Massachusetts switched to a file and use system in 2008. As a part of the change, insurers were allowed to use non-driving factors to determine rates and decline to insure any individual they choose. Nine insurance companies reentered Massachusetts the year after the new law was passed, and the state claimed that consumers saved $270 million in the first year under file and use.

Price deregulation may not have had the same effect for all. While rates appear to have gone down overall, rates appear to have gone up for certain populations. A report by the Office of the Attorney General of Massachusetts stated that Hispanics and low-income consumers were more likely to experience rate increases than other demographics under the new system. While the new system did prohibit the use of income and homeownership as criteria when setting rates, it allowed the use of factors like coverage, payment history, and the purchase of homeowner's insurance, which can act as proxies for the forbidden factors. In addition, insurance companies declined to make rate calculations public, making it difficult to evaluate fairness. OFFICE OF THE MASS. ATT'Y GEN., AUTOMOBILE INSURANCE: THE ROAD AHEAD 8 (2009).

Whereas Massachusetts has traditionally heavily regulated automobile insurance rates, California has historically been a low-regulation jurisdiction, relying primarily on competitive forces to control costs. In the 1980s, however, rising insurance rates, particularly in automobile lines, caused California to reconsider its system of rate regulation. Initially, reform efforts focused on the legal liability system. The insurance sector supported various efforts to move away from traditional tort liability rules, with their relatively high administrative costs and potentially excessive jury awards, to a presumably less costly no-fault liability system. For an empirical analysis of the relative costs of no-fault and traditional tort liability, see Jeffrey O'Connell et al., *The Comparative Costs of Allowing Consumer Choice for Auto Insurance in All Fifty States*, 55 MD. L. REV. 160 (1996). When these efforts failed, consumer advocates invoked the state's referendum procedures to address the problem more directly.

In 1988, California voters passed Proposition 103. Instead of adopting tort reform, Proposition 103 forced insurers to cut rates across the board by 20%, using the rates in place on November 8, 1987 as a baseline. In order to increase rates, insurers would need to seek the prior approval of the Insurance Commissioner, whom Proposition 103 turned into an elected official. Even further, rates were to be based on the following factors, in descending order of importance: "(1) The insured's driving safety record, (2) The number of miles he or she drives annually, (3) The number of years of driving experience the insured has had," and "(4) Those other factors that the commissioner may adopt by regulation and that have a substantial relationship to the risk of loss." CAL. INS. CODE § 1861.02(a). The legacy of Proposition 103 has been heavily debated. Consumer advocates argue that the new regime has saved consumers billions, while others argue that the rate decline should be attributed to several court decisions from the same period that limited frivolous claims. Compared to Massachusetts, California's rate regulation scheme provides more robust protections for low-income and minority drivers. California's scheme accomplishes this in part by emphasizing the factors listed above over factors that can act as proxies for income. In addition, California guarantees a discount to drivers who meet certain good driver criteria. CAL. INS. CODE § 1861.02(b).

IV. THE REGULATION OF RISK CLASSIFICATIONS

A. THE FUNCTION OF RISK CLASSIFICATIONS

The classification of risks is one of the most important and potentially controversial aspects of insurance regulation. In the following article, a leading academic expert sketches out the basic trade-off between efficiency and fairness that characterizes this area of the law.

Kenneth S. Abraham, *Efficiency and Fairness in Insurance Risk Classification*

71 VA. L. REV. 403 (1985)

Insurance operates best in the face of a very special sort of uncertainty. The tension between risk assessment and risk distribution is so characteristic of the operation of insurance that risksharing schemes from which the tension is missing seem only to resemble what we think of as insurance. For example, if we knew precisely how many losses of a certain sort would occur, but nothing about who would suffer them, then insurance against such losses would be feasible. It would be insurance embodying only the distribution of risk among those insured, however, with no assessment of the extent of each individual's risk: each insured would pay the same premium. Similarly, if we knew who was at risk of suffering a loss if it occurred, but nothing about how many of those at risk would suffer losses, insurance would also be feasible: insureds would be charged retroactively for their proportionate share of whatever losses ultimately occurred. Again, this arrangement would embody risk distribution, but no individualized risk assessment. Although both of these schemes involve risk sharing, each is simpler than the standard insurance arrangement because neither involves any individual risk assessment.

Typically, however, insurers know something about individual risks. Because in such instances it is usually possible both to assess and to distribute risk, the tension between assessment and distribution is inevitable. Risk assessment through classification of insureds into groups posing similar risks necessarily limits the amount of risk distribution achieved by an insurance arrangement, because it uses knowledge about risk expectancies to set different prices for members of different groups. No risk classification system, however, can classify and price individual risks with anything near complete accuracy; the future is too uncertain for that. Nevertheless, when reasonably accurate risk assessment is feasible, insurance classification can promote economically efficient behavior by encouraging insureds to compare the cost of insurance with the cost of investment in loss prevention that would reduce the sum of these two costs. In contrast, when risk assessment is inaccurate but insurance is still available, inefficient behavior is a likely result. This is the 'moral hazard' of insurance.

Often a classification scheme can be made more efficient. [H]owever, promoting efficiency through risk classification sometimes requires sacrificing other values. The burdens of inaccuracy may be unevenly distributed; risk classes may be based on variables not within the control of insureds; and certain variables may have unacceptable social or moral connotations. . . . Although these concerns are similar in that each sometimes demands inefficient forms of risk classification, risk-distributional fairness itself is not a monolithic notion. Without attention to the differences among these concerns, proposed remedies will be overbroad, undereffective, or both.

A variety of legal tools is available for addressing these issues and regulating the combination of efficiency and risk distribution reflected in the insurance market's classification practices. Legislatures can exercise control through statutes governing insurance classification or through general prohibitions against various forms of discrimination. Legislation in almost every state also delegates considerable authority to insurance commissioners to regulate risk classification and premium rates. Often these commissioners are required to assure that premium rates are not 'excessive, inadequate, or unfairly discriminatory.' This mandate affords commissioners broad discretion to fashion compromises between the twin goals of efficiency and risk-distributional fairness. Finally, the courts also play a role through judicial enforcement of statutory standards and through oversight of administrative action. In short, the inevitable tensions between risk assessment and risk distribution create the context in which the institutions that make law governing risk classification operate. . . .

The Nature of Insurance Classification and Pricing

The starting point for any analysis of insurance classification is an obvious but fundamental fact: insurance is only one of a number of ways of satisfying the demand for protection against risk. With few exceptions, insurance need not be purchased; people can forgo it if insurance is too expensive. Indeed, as the price of coverage rises, the amount purchased and the number of people purchasing will decline. Instead of buying insurance, people will self-insure by accumulating savings to serve as a cushion in the event of loss, self-protect by spending more on loss prevention, or simply use the money not spent on insurance to purchase other goods and services. An insurer must compete against these alternatives, even in the absence of competition from other insurers.

One method of competing for protection dollars is to classify potential purchasers into groups according to their probability of loss and the potential magnitude of losses if they occur. Different risk classes may then be charged different premiums, depending on this expected loss. Were it not for the need to compete for protection dollars, an insurer could simply charge each individual a premium based on the average expected loss of all its insureds (plus a margin for profit and expenses), without incurring classification costs.

An insurer can capture protection dollars by classifying because, through classification, it can offer low-risk individuals lower prices. Classification, however, involves two costs. First, the process of classification is costly. Insurers must gather data and perform statistical operations on it; marketing may also be more costly when prices are not uniform. Second, classification necessarily raises premiums for poor risks, who purchase less coverage as a result. In the aggregate, classification is thus worthwhile to an insurer only when the gains produced from extra sales and fewer pay-outs outweigh classification costs plus the costs of lost sales. Even in the absence of competition from other insurers, an insurer who engages in at least some classification is likely to capture more protection dollars than it loses.

When there is not only competition for available protection dollars, but competition among insurers for premium dollars, the value of risk classification to insurers becomes even clearer. The more refined (and accurate) an insurer's risk classifications, the more capable it is of 'skimming' good risks away from insurers whose classifications are less refined. If other insurers do not respond, either by refining their own classifications or by raising prices and catering mainly to high risks, their 'book' of risks will contain a higher mixture of poor risks who are still being charged premiums calculated for average risks. These insurers will attract additional poor risks, and this resulting adverse selection will further disadvantage their competitive positions. . . .

Risk Assessment and Economic Efficiency

Other things equal, insurers strive to charge insureds in accord with expected costs, which equal their expected losses plus a portion of the other costs of providing coverage. To the extent that risk classes and prices conform to this standard, a number of results follow. The first effect is that individual insureds pay premiums based on expected losses and thereby share the risk of random losses. The members of each class are charged in accord with their expected costs, so that total premiums cover the aggregate losses of the class. No subsidies run from one risk class to another. The only subsidy under this ideal flows from the lucky members of the class to the unlucky.

Even efficiently classified insurance coverage, therefore, has elements of both risk assessment and risk distribution, but the scope of each is distinct. Individual insureds are assessed the risk of suffering expected losses and are charged on that basis. The risk of suffering random losses is distributed among all insureds.

The second effect of an efficient classification system is that it does not discourage insureds from allocating an optimal amount of resources to loss prevention. Because insurance is priced in accord with expected cost, insureds have the incentive to compare the cost of protecting against risk through insurance with the cost of reducing risk through loss prevention. Efficient classification discourages insureds from purchasing insurance when they can more cheaply protect against risk by investing in loss prevention. In contrast, inefficient classification may produce suboptimal loss prevention incentives. When coverage is priced below expected cost, for example, insureds may not take safety precautions that would otherwise be worthwhile. In this situation, they can obtain equivalent protection against risk by purchasing insurance at a lesser cost than the precautions.

Finally—and this is a vital point—an efficient classification system does not strive to make its prices equal expected cost when improvement in accuracy is not worth the cost of achieving it. Information about expected cost is accumulated and risk classes are thereby refined only so long as the competitive benefits of refinement are worth their cost. Consequently, efficient classification does not recognize all individual differences. When an insurer can no longer attract or make enough profit from additional low-risk insureds to justify discovering and classifying them, an equilibrium is reached and no further refinement occurs. Some groups may then seem to 'subsidize' or be 'subsidized' by others.

For example, suppose that people raised on farms are especially poor drivers or that obstetricians born in Ohio are unusually immune to malpractice suits. Because classification systems are unlikely to have the information necessary to make these variables the basis of risk classes, neither farm-born drivers nor Ohio-born obstetricians will be charged exactly in accord with their true expected costs. Thus, the former may seem to be subsidized by other drivers, and the latter may seem to subsidize other insured physicians. It is a bit misleading, however, to say that a situation involves a subsidy even when it would be inefficient to make the investment necessary to discover and eliminate the 'subsidy.'

This example makes it plain that there is nothing special or preordained about the classifications that turn out to be efficient. Had insurers begun decades ago to maintain data about farm-born drivers or the birth places of obstetricians, it might now be efficient to use these variables for classification. In many cases, however, a new approach cannot be taken without sacrificing real economies. Even if restructuring a classification system would otherwise be efficient, probably no individual insurer would have an incentive to restructure. Competitors would take advantage of the classifications introduced by the innovating insurer and compete on an equal basis for the newly-discovered low-risk insureds, but without having made the investment required of the innovator. Some form of collective action would therefore be required for the innovation to occur. . . .

To sum up the implications of the discussion thus far, insurance relies on group rather than individual estimates of expected loss. With few exceptions (such as large enterprises with detailed loss histories and frequent current losses), estimating expected loss 'individually' is impossible. Most individual loss experience is not statistically credible enough to warrant individual rating, though a few insurers occasionally gamble on unique risks—the well-being of [a top ranked tennis player's] left arm, for example. Group probabilities provide the credibility necessary to the predictions that are at the heart of the insurance system. Until an individual insured is treated as a member of a group, it is impossible to known his expected loss, because for practical purposes that concept is a statistical one based on group probabilities. Without relying on such probabilities, it would be impossible to set a price for insurance coverage at all. In this sense there is risk sharing even within the risk assessment component of insurance classification. For practical purposes, no individual can have a 'true' expected loss. Rather, insureds share the risk that characteristics of those in their risk class, not considered in the classification, render the class's expected loss higher than it would be were those characteristics considered in setting premium rates.

Risk-Distributional Fairness

In addition to asking how well a classification system assesses risk to produce efficient results, we may also raise a series of different questions regarding how insurance classification and pricing systems distribute risk. Because these questions are not always clearly formulated, they need both explication and evaluation. Moreover, because the questions are not all of the same order, it is important to consider the different solutions that are available for the different kinds of unfairness that these questions highlight. Certain solutions may appropriately be fashioned within the insurance system, but for other risk-distributional problems, noninsurance approaches are more suitable. This part begins the analysis of such solutions by examining the distributional objections to the drive for efficiency in classification.

Criticisms of risk classification schemes seem to fall into three general categories. The first cluster of criticisms is composed of accuracy-equity concerns: demands that classification and pricing closely reflect expected cost, so that low-risk insureds are not forced to subsidize high-risk insureds and so that the burdens of inaccuracy are equitably distributed. Accuracy concerns obviously have much in common with the efficiency notions discussed in the preceding section. Efficiency, however is a characteristic of an entire system; risk-distributional fairness is a notion that also pertains to the treatment of individuals within that system and touches on more than economic considerations alone. The second category of criticisms is composed of control-causality concerns. These involve the contention that risk classes should be based on variables that are within the control of or at least caused by the insured. The third set of criticisms is directed at the use of suspect variables. These criticisms are occasioned by the use of variables that are 'suspect,' even apart from accuracy-equity or control-causality issues. A fourth consideration, different from these criticisms, is one in favor of redistributional policies. This consideration does not necessarily raise fairness questions in the same way as the first three; rather, it involves separate objectives of public policy.

B. ANTI-DISCRIMINATION NORMS IN STATE LAWS

The following excerpts show how states have dealt with the conflict between efficiency and fairness discussed in Professor Abraham's article.

1. Gender Classifications

This case explores one area that has been particularly controversial.

Dep't of Ins. v. Ins. Servs. Office

434 So. 2d 908 (Fla. Dist. Ct. App. 1983)

Larry G. Smith, Judge.

The [Florida Insurance] Department appeals the final order of a hearing officer of the Division of Administrative Hearings, in a rule challenge proceeding, declaring its Rule 4-43.03 to be an invalid exercise of delegated legislative authority.[1]. . .

In January, 1978, Dade County petitioned the Department to adopt two rules, one prohibiting the continued use of age,[2] sex, marital status, and scholastic achievement as automobile insurance rating factors and the other prohibiting the use of arbitrary territorial boundaries as a factor. . . .

The insurance companies (whose premium rates are formulated using sex, marital status or scholastic achievement, or some combination thereof) challenged the validity of the rule on the [grounds that] the rule extends, modifies, conflicts with or enlarges upon the requirements of the Florida Insurance Code and thus exceeds the Department's rule-making authority. . . .

At the heart of this controversy is section 626.9541(15)(h), Florida Statutes (1979), one of the laws being implemented by Rule 4-43.03, which provides as follows:

> (h) No insurer shall, with respect to premiums charged for automobile insurance, unfairly discriminate solely on the basis of age, sex, marital status, or scholastic achievement.

In enacting this statute the legislature obviously intended to permit discrimination based on sex, marital status, and scholastic achievement so long as this discrimination is not unfair or based solely on these factors. Yet the Department, by promulgating Rule 4-43.03, imposed a total prohibition against the use of sex, marital status or scholastic achievement in the formulation of premiums or rate classifications. The legislative history of Section 626.9541(15)(h) irrefutably shows that the legislature expressly considered, but rejected, provisions which would prohibit the use of these factors as unfairly discriminatory. This provides strong evidence that the legislature did not intend, by enactment of Section 626.9541(15)(h), to completely prohibit the use of these factors. This history provides strong support for the hearing officer's determination that the Department's contrary construction of the statute in Rule 4-43.03 is unauthorized. . ..

Nevertheless, the Department urges that the rule does not conflict with the statute because the use of sex, marital status, and scholastic achievement in the formulation of premium rates necessarily unfairly discriminates solely on the basis of those criteria. Hence, the Department contends that in promulgating Rule 4-43.03, it implemented Section 627.031(1)(a), Florida Statutes (1979), which provides that it is the purpose of the Insurance Code to " . . . promote the public welfare by regulating insurance rates . . . to the end that they shall not be . . . unfairly discriminatory. . . ." The Department also

---

[1] Rule 4-43.03 Unfair Discrimination in Private Passenger Motor Vehicle Insurance Rates—Based on Sex, Marital Status and Scholastic Achievement ("No insurer authorized to engage in the business of insurance in the State of Florida shall establish classifications or premium rates for any policy, contract or certificate of private passenger motor vehicle insurance based upon the sex, marital status or scholastic achievement of the person or persons insured.").

[2] Noticeably, the use of age as a rating factor was not prohibited in Rule 4-43.03, as the Department found a strong correlation between age classifications and loss experience resulting from vehicle accidents. Further, no workable alternative to age as a primary risk assessment factor was suggested, and without that, it was concluded that elimination of age as a rating variable would lead only to greater inequities. Interestingly, the Department has also not come forth with verified alternatives to sex, marital status and scholastic achievement, although these have proven reliability as rating factors. Yet use of these factors seems to have been forbidden in large part because they are "socially unacceptable.". . .

maintains that it implemented Section 627.062(1), Florida Statutes (1979), which provides: "The rates for all classes of insurance to which the provisions of this part are applicable shall not be . . . unfairly discriminatory."

"Unfairly discriminatory" is not defined in the Code. However, Section 627.0651, Florida Statutes (1979) (also implemented, according to the Department, in its promulgation of Rule 4-43.03), provides several standards to be applied by the Department in making a determination as to whether a rate is unfairly discriminatory. In particular, Section 627.0651(6) provides:

> (6) One rate shall be deemed unfairly discriminatory in relation to another in the same class if it clearly fails to reflect equitably the difference in expected losses and expenses. (emphasis supplied)

It is the Department's contention that "unfairly discriminatory" and "equitably" are not technical terms of art and should be given their common ordinary meaning. Giving these words their common ordinary meaning, the Department urges, a rating factor will be deemed unfairly discriminatory and inequitable unless it has a causal connection to expected losses. Thus the Department reasons that since sex, marital status and scholastic achievement have no direct or indirect causal connection to a person's driving habits they are necessarily unfairly discriminatory and inequitable rating factors. The Department further reasons that these rating factors are always unfairly discriminatory because their use results in the misclassification of a large number of individuals who share the distinguishing feature of the group (*e.g.*, male sex) but do not share the "average" driving characteristics of the group.

On the other hand, the insurance companies contend that "unfairly discriminatory" and "equitable" are technical words, with a particular meaning in the insurance industry, and that Section 626.9541(15)(h) must be construed with this meaning in mind. *United States v. Cuomo*, 525 F.2d 1285, 1291 (5th Cir.1976). Reading Section 627.0651(6) in pari materia with the other standards contained in Section 627.0651(3) through (8), the insurance companies urge that the word "equitably" (used in Section 627.0651(6)), means "accurately" in the actuarial sense. The hearing officer agreed, finding that the most equitable classification factors are those that are the most actuarially sound. In making this finding, the hearing officer relied upon the testimony of the Department's own Chief Actuary and Director of the Division of Rating. The hearing officer further found that the classification factors of sex, marital status and scholastic achievement, in light of the present state of the art in the industry, enhanced the actuarial soundness of a rate classification for automobile insurance.[8] Thus, as the hearing officer concluded, the Department has not established that the use of the criteria prohibited by Rule 4-43.03 necessarily results in unfair discrimination.

We find it highly significant that in presenting its argument on this point the Department has changed its own interpretation of the word "equitably," as used in Section 627.0651(6), as well as its interpretation of the phrase "unfairly discriminatory," relevant to this proceeding. Historically, the Department has measured the equitableness of a rating factor by its predictive accuracy. Further, until the enactment of the challenged rule, the Department interpreted the insurance code and Section 626.9541(15)(h) as permitting rate classification plans using sex, marital status and scholastic achievement criteria in their formulation.

---

[8] The Department does not dispute this finding and has in fact admitted that within some groups (all policyholders 25 years of age . . .) the subgroup consisting of all females has a lower actual or expected loss experience than the subgroup consisting of all males, and that a subgroup consisting of all married policyholders also has a lower actual or expected loss experience than the subgroup consisting of all unmarried policyholders. . . .

We also attach great significance to the finding of the hearing officer that the Department did not offer evidence or testimony sufficient to establish that factual changes of any nature have occurred, or that the Department has become aware of new factual information, which would support a deviation from their historic interpretation of the Florida Insurance Code. . . .

Turning again to the statutes, we note that when the legislature enacted Section 626.9541(15)(h), it also reenacted Section 627.0651(3) through (8), which correspond with the Department's settled interpretation that rates "reflect equitably the difference in expected losses" if the rates reflect those differences as accurately as possible. Thus, by implication, the legislature approved the interpretation that rates based upon sex, marital status or scholastic achievement are unfair only if those rating factors are found to be actuarially unsound. As previously stated, the evidence below overwhelmingly shows these factors are actuarially sound. We conclude, therefore, that even under the alternate theory advanced by the Department, the statutes do not authorize a blanket prohibition against use of these factors.

---

1. ***Is Regulatory Action Necessary to Limit Discrimination by Insurers?*** In the order overturned by the court in this case, the Florida Insurance Department offered the following justification:

> Charging more or less to policyholders on the basis of race, religion, or economic status would be socially unacceptable regardless of any statistical justification a company might offer. Several witnesses at the hearings argued that it is socially unacceptable to continue the use of sex and marital status to justify lower premiums to women and married couples. . . . . [However], it was apparent from the hearings that the insurance industry does not have such reservations with respect to any existing rate classifications. . . . [T]here were indications from the testimony that fears of being placed at a competitive disadvantage might in part be responsible for a lack of industry introspection as to the social acceptability of current rating factors.
>
> Therefore, it is clear that the power and responsibility to make public policy in this area must rest with the regulator. The private sector has neither the incentive nor the will to make such judgments. To leave the determination of social acceptability to the private sector would serve only to further retard the already slow movement in the direction of ending discrimination based on certain classifications which the Supreme Court has found to be invidious.

Dep't of Ins., 434 So. 2d at 935 (appendix to dissenting opinion). Is the Department correct in suspecting that the private sector is incapable of assuming responsibility in this area?

2. ***Gender as a Factor in Risk Classifications.*** The use of gender as a classification factor in automobile insurance was a deeply contested issue in the 1980s. A number of jurisdictions prohibited the practice. *See, e.g.*, Hartford Accident & Indem. Co. v. Ins. Comm'r, 482 A.2d 542 (Pa. 1984) (affirming Pennsylvania Insurance Commissioner's decision to ban gender-based automobile rates). A number of states have adopted similar restrictions, and one

state, Montana, has banned the use of gender in all insurance classifications, including life insurance. The equitable case against gender-based or similar classifications is summarized in a 1978 Report of Rates and Rating Procedures of the NAIC Task Force of the Automobile Insurance Subcommittee:

> In terms of simplicity and consistency (*i.e.*, stability and ease of verification), age, sex and marital status receive high marks as rating factors. This is not the case from the viewpoint of causality. Causality refers to the actual or implied behavioral relationship between a particular rating factor and loss potential. The longer a vehicle is on the road, for example, the more likely it is that the vehicle may be involved in a random traffic accident; thus, daily or annual total mileage may be viewed as a causal rating factor. To the extent that sex and marital status classifications may be defended on causal grounds, the implied behavioral relationships rely largely on questionable social stereotypes. . . . Given the significant changes in traditional sex roles and social attitudes which have occurred in recent years, justifications for rating plans on the grounds of such implied assumptions are unacceptable.

How strong of a causal link should we require before accepting a ban on a risk classification? Are there costs, in terms of economic efficiency or some other values, in requiring causality as opposed to mere correlation with loss experience?

3. ***Should Credit History be a Permitted Factor?*** Another risk classification practice that has attracted controversy concerns the use of credit histories. As one sector executive admitted in a recent press account:

> [My] insurance company uses credit reports . . . "to help us identify where not to renew business". . . . Poor credit histories "seem to correlate directly to greater exposure to arson cases or situations where jewelry and other valuables items 'disappear.' When people need money because of credit problems, it just seems that those types of claims are more likely to occur."

Credit Reports Aid Underwriters, Best's Review—Life-Health Edition, July 1, 1995, at 36. Do you think this is an appropriate classification system? Would your views change if it turned out that minorities were substantially more likely to have poor credit histories than other members of the population? *See* Darcy Steeg Morris, Daniel Schwarcz & Joshua C. Teitelbaum, *Do Credit-Based Insurance Scores Proxy for Policyholder Income in Predicting Auto Claim Risk?* J. EMPIRICAL LEGAL STUD. (forthcoming, 2016).

---

2. Cross-State Variation Today

The following excerpt explores variations in state anti-discrimination laws.

Ronen Avraham, Kyle L. Logue, & Daniel Schwarcz, Understanding Insurance Antidiscrimination Laws

87 S. CAL. L. REV. 195 (2014)

Although there has been considerable theorizing about the extent to which insurance companies should be allowed to discriminate among insureds in the underwriting process . . . there has been almost no research on the question of what the law actually permits. It is a surprisingly complex and difficult issue. Because the governing law in this area is primarily state law, we first had to identify and analyze the relevant state statutes and regulations in all fifty states as well as the District of Columbia, as of 2012. To make the project manageable, we focused specifically on how states have regulated insurers' use of nine characteristics—race, religion, national origin, gender, age, genetic testing, credit score, sexual orientation, and geographic location—and we focused on the five largest lines of insurance—life, health, disability, auto, and property/casualty. This exercise revealed statutes at all levels of generality: statutes that limited or prohibited all "unfair discrimination" in all lines of insurance with no mention of particular traits; statutes that limited or prohibited "unfair discrimination" generally within a particular line of insurance; and statutes that limited or prohibited the use of one or more specific characteristics either for all lines or for a specific line of insurance. . . .

1. Race, Religion, National Origin (The "Big Three")

. . . Perhaps the most surprising finding was the fact that states do not uniformly prohibit insurers from using race, religion, and national origin . . . . [O]nly ten states have forbidden the use of race, national origin, and religion across all lines of insurance. Those states are California, Delaware, Illinois, New Jersey, New Mexico, New York, Tennessee, Texas, Washington, and Wisconsin. Two additional states—Georgia and North Carolina—prohibit the use by insurers of race and national origin, but do not apply the same prohibition to religion. . . .

2. Gender

[T]he average level of regulation for gender risk classification is . . . less strict than for race, religion, and national origin but more strict than for age. This difference is statistically significant. . . .

[M]any states permit the usage of gender, especially in life and health insurance. Indeed, with respect to life insurance in particular, every jurisdiction but one in the country expressly permits insurers to take gender into account . . .

Outside of the life insurance contexts, . . . [there is] a large degree of variation across states with respect to gender discrimination in auto, disability, and health insurance, with some states clustering around strong limitations and others around no limitations or specific permissions. . . . Life insurance is . . . significantly less regulated than health insurance, but auto insurance is more regulated on average. . . .

3. Sexual Orientation

For life/health insurance, we [find] a moderate level of average regulation for insurer usage of sexual orientation: less strict than for the big three but stricter than for age. . . . The difference is statistically significant. . . . [S]ix states have outright bans on the use of sexual orientation across all lines of insurance. Sexual orientation is the only characteristic other than the big three and gender where states have enacted bans across all lines of insurance...

Nevertheless, most states have no specific regulation on sexual orientation at all. . . . With respect to health insurance, for example, eighteen states either prohibit or strongly limit the use of sexual orientation and all the other states have no specific regulation on sexual orientation, but have only general unfair discrimination laws.

4. Age

. . . [A]ge [is] the least regulated [classification] on average. . . . Thirty-nine states specifically permit the use of age in life insurance; and the remaining states merely impose a general unfair discrimination limitation. Health insurance is similar, but with less uniformity: thirty-seven states permit the use of age in health insurance; and the rest impose specific regulations. . . .

5. Credit Score and Zip Code

We predicted regulation of credit score and zip code would on average be more restrictive than for age, but less than for the big three, and that prediction was borne out. . . . The data are also largely consistent with our prediction of variation across states, with some states limiting (though probably not prohibiting) and others either not mentioning or expressly permitting the use of credit score and zip code . . . . For health, life, and disability insurance, there is a great deal of variation among the states about how they treat both zip code and credit score, with no discernible pattern. And again, there are very few states with absolute prohibitions. Somewhat surprisingly, for health insurance, substantial numbers of jurisdictions explicitly permit the use of zip codes; and the same can be said of health, life, and disability insurance with respect to credit scores.

6. Genetics

. . . [T]here are sixteen states that have statutes specifically permitting the use of genetic testing by life insurers . . . . There were also a few (five) states with specific limitations, and only two states had prohibitions on the use of genetic testing by life insurers. The most common type of result was a general restriction on unfair discrimination . . . . All but three jurisdictions prohibit the use of genetic testing in health insurance. . . . For disability insurance, we predicted more variation than with health insurance, because of the greater moral hazard concern than there is with health insurance. The result in fact shows variation, although there are more states (twenty) expressly permitting the use of genetics in disability insurance than we expected. . . .

---

1. ***The Genetic Information Nondiscrimination Act.*** In 2008, the federal government passed the Genetic Information Nondiscrimination Act (GINA), which prevents health insurers from acquiring or using genetic information to determine eligibility, premiums, or other coverage terms. The act also governs employers' hiring decisions. In an era of rapidly declining costs of DNA screening, GINA addressed concerns of fairness posed by insurance companies potentially charging more for health insurance policies sold to individuals with a genetic pre-disposition for serious disease, like cancer, GINA does not, however, prevent individuals from purchasing their own DNA tests and then deciding how much health insurance to acquire. Should that be a concern for federal authorities? *See generally*, Jessica L. Roberts, *Preempting Discrimination: Lessons from the Genetic Information Nondiscrimination Act*, 63 VAND. L. REV. 439 (2010) (exploring the fact that GINA prohibited genetic testing before the practice had become widespread). As noted in the previous excerpt, many states allow health insurance rates to vary by zip code, implicitly allowing environmental factors to affect pricing. Should GINA be amended to prohibit such classifications as well? *See* Recent Legislation, 122 HARV. L. REV. 1038 (2009). Note that GINA was preceded by two years the passage of the much more far-reaching Affordable Care Act, which we take up in the next chapter.

CHAPTER 3.3

THE EXPANDING FEDERAL ROLE IN INSURANCE REGULATION

CONTENTS

I. INTRODUCTION

In this Chapter, we explore the increasing role of the federal government in the regulation of insurance. As discussed in Chapter 3.1, the McCarran-Ferguson Act has long subjected certain aspects of the business of insurance to regulation under federal antitrust laws. Since 2010, the FSOC has had authority under the Dodd-Frank Act to designate major insurance groups as systemically important, and has done so with respect to three firms, AIG, Prudential, and MetLife, though MetLife's designation remains in litigation as we will explore in some detail in Chapter 6.2. Dodd-Frank also established a new Federal Insurance Office (FIO) within the Treasury, which slightly expanded the federal role in insurance oversight. The McCarran-Ferguson Act and the new provisions of the Dodd-Frank Act, however, are by no means the only, or even the most important, sources of federal authority over insurance markets. We will now take a look at three other areas of insurance where federal laws are dominant: social insurance, such as Social Security and Medicare; oversight of employer-sponsored fringe benefits plans under the Employer Retirement Income Security Act of 1974 (ERISA); and the Patient Protection and Affordable Care Act of 2010 (ACA). We then turn to emerging areas of insurance regulation where the federal government may play a more important role in the years to come, with a focus on the potentially expanding role of the FIO and other federal agencies in coordinating insurance regulation on a global basis.

II. AREAS OF FEDERAL DOMINANCE

A. SOCIAL INSURANCE: SOCIAL SECURITY AND MEDICARE

In 2002, Peter Fisher, then Under Secretary of the Treasury, characterized the financial posture of the United States as follows: "Think of the federal government as a gigantic insurance company (with a side line business in national defense and homeland security)." *See* Remarks of Under Secretary of the Treasury Peter R. Fisher to the Columbus Council on World Affairs Columbus, Ohio Beyond Borrowing: Meeting the Government's Financial Challenges in the 21st Century (Nov. 14, 2002). Fisher's characterization is apt. The federal government operates the country's two most substantial insurance programs: Social Security, which offers a retirement income program, as well as disability and limited life insurance coverage, for most Americans, and Medicare, which provides retirement health benefits for most Americans over 65 years of age, as well as some segments of the disabled community.

The role of these two programs cannot be overstated. Twenty-four percent of Americans 65 years of age or older rely solely on Social Security for retirement benefits. In the same age bracket, 65% of individuals rely on such benefits for half or more than their income. *See* SSA, "Income of the Population 55 or Older," 2012, Table 9.A1 (2014). Put another way, "[w]ithout Social Security benefits, 44.4 percent of elderly Americans would have incomes below the official poverty line, all else being equal; with Social Security benefits, only 9.1 percent do." Paul N. Van De Water, Arloc Sherman & Kathy Ruffing, Social Security Keeps 22 Million Americans Out of Poverty: A State-by-State Analysis, Center on Budget and Policy Priorities (Oct. 25, 2013). As currently structured, Social Security is funded primarily through payroll taxes, supplemented by interest paid on government securities held in the Social Security trust funds as well as a limited allocation of income tax revenues.

Medicare is similarly important to both eligible disabled and the elderly, as it is one of the principal sources of health insurance for those populations. As of the end of 2015, Medicare covered more than 55 million Americans. *See* Press Release, Centers for Medicare & Medicaid Services. Measured in terms of total health care expenses, Medicare accounted for $619 billion in health expenditures in 2014, or 20.4% of total health expenditures countrywide. *See* National Health Expenditure Fact Sheet, Table 03 Nation Health Expenditures, by Source of Funds, Center for Medicare & Medicaid Services. Medicare coverage is available to those reaching 65, regardless of their health condition or wealth, provided they meet employment eligibility requirements. Medicare is funded through a combination of payroll taxes, general revenue funds, and income-based premiums paid by retirees.

Medicaid is another important government health insurance program that provides health care for low-income families and individuals. In 2014, Medicaid paid for $495 billion in healthcare expenditures, the equivalent of 16.4% of national health expenditures. *Id.* Unlike Medicare, Medicaid is jointly funded by federal and state governments but is administered solely by the state governments, which have leeway to determine eligibility. Though federal law does not mandate that states participate in Medicaid, all states currently do.

Adding together Medicare, Medicaid, and other federal health insurance programs, such as the Children's Health Insurance Programs and Veterans Administration benefits, the federal government's health insurance programs cover over 40% of national health care expenditures.

Most public discussions of the financial aspects of federal social insurance focus on cash flows in and out of federal trust funds, highlighting the date on which those trust funds will be depleted. According to the 2015 Annual Report of the Social Security Trust Funds, the funds will be depleted in 2034. It is, however, also possible to estimate the current value of the federal government's implicit liabilities to pay Social Security and Medicare benefits to current workers and retirees. *See* Howell E. Jackson, *Counting the Ways, in* FISCAL CHALLENGES: AN INTERDISCIPLINARY APPROACH TO BUDGET POLICY 185, 206–09 (Elizabeth Garrett et al. eds., 2008). As of year-end 2014, the implicit liabilities of the federal government to current workers and current retirees are estimated to equal $29.2 trillion dollars and the comparable figure for Medicare is an additional $29.0 trillion dollars for a total of $58.2 trillion. *See* DEP'T OF THE TREASURY, FINANCIAL REPORT OF THE U.S. GOVERNMENT: FISCAL YEAR 2015 62-64 (2016). These financial obligations dwarf the kinds of numbers discussed elsewhere in this book, and even exceed by more than four times the $13.1 trillion of federal debt outstanding to public holders as of year-end 2015.

---

1. ***Are the Government's Implicit Obligations the Equivalent of Wealth?*** In 2015 op-ed, Professor Martin Feldstein, Chairman of the Council of Economic Advisers under President Ronald Reagan, drew on similar estimates to make a different point. Responding to a number of recent studies decrying the growth of wealth inequality in the United States, Feldstein argued that these studies fail to include the actuarial value of future benefits of social insurance programs such as Social Security and Medicare. By omitting this Social Security and Medicare wealth, Feldstein asserted, claims of growing inequality in recent decades are overstated. Specifically, Feldstein noted that, for the bottom 90% of households, the addition of social insurance wealth would increase the net worth of those cohorts by approximately $75 trillion and substantially diminish other estimates of the growth in wealth inequality in the United States. *See* Martin Feldstein, Op-Ed, *The Uncounted Trillions in the Inequality Debate: Wealth isn't so highly concentrated if you take into account Medicare and Social Security benefits*, WALL ST. J. (Dec. 13, 2015). Is Feldstein correct? Should this view of social insurance as future assets make us less concerned about the distribution, and inequality, of wealth across the country? Does it matter that Congress has reserved the right to adjust benefit levels under federal social insurance programs? *See* Fleming v. Nestor, 363 U.S. 603 (1960). Is it relevant that the political barriers to cutting back federal entitlements, especially for Social Security, are formidable, nigh unto insurmountable?

While today's political discourse proceeds on the assumption that Social Security and Medicare are uncontroversial functions of the federal government, that was not the case when these programs were established. In the 1930s when the Social Security Act was initially enacted, *Paul v. Virginia* was still good law and so the business of insurance was understood to be outside of Congress's power under the Commerce Clause. *See* Chapter 3.1. As a result, in the early years of the New Deal, although Congress did not have the authority to promulgate Social Security under the Commerce Clause, Congress justified the Social Security Act under its Article I powers. The legal basis of the Social Security Act was nevertheless challenged in a series of cases decided ultimately by the Supreme Court.

The first case, *Steward Machine Co. v. Davis*, 301 U.S. 548 (1937), considered Title IX of the Social Security Act, which imposed a payroll tax on employers with eight or more employees. Steward Machine asserted that these taxes unconstitutionally coerced states and were beyond Congress's enumerated powers under Article I of the U.S. Constitution. In rejecting these claims, the Court reasoned that the Act's tax was insufficiently coercive and was sufficiently related to the general welfare of the American people to fall within Congress's Article I powers. *Id.* at 588–93.

Decided on the same day as *Steward Machine*, the next case adjudicating the Social Security Act's constitutionality was *Helvering v. Davis*, 301 U.S. 619 (1937). In addition to challenging other aspects of Social Security's tax titles, the plaintiff in *Helvering,* Edison Electric Illuminating Company, known as Consolidated Edison, or ConEd, challenged the authority of Congress to create an account in the Treasury from which social security benefits were to be paid. Similar to the challenges presented in *Stewart Machine,* Edison Electric claimed that the provisions interfered with states' rights and were beyond Congress's enumerated powers. The following is an excerpt from the Court's decision in *Helvering.*

Helvering v. Davis

301 U.S. 619 (1937)

Cardozo, J.

[Congress] may spend money in aid of the 'general welfare.' . . . The line must still be drawn between one welfare and another, between particular and general. Where this shall be placed cannot be known through a formula in advance of the event. There is a middle ground or certainly a penumbra in which discretion is at large. The discretion, however, is not confided to the courts. The discretion belongs to Congress, unless the choice is clearly wrong, a display of arbitrary power, not an exercise of judgment. This is now familiar law. . . .

The problem [of poverty among the elderly] is plainly national in area and dimensions. Moreover, laws of the separate states cannot deal with it effectively. Congress, at least, had a basis for that belief. States and local governments are often lacking in the resources that are necessary to finance an adequate program of security for the aged. This is brought out with a wealth of illustration in recent studies of the problem. Apart from the failure of resources, states and local governments are at times reluctant to increase so heavily the burden of taxation to be borne by their residents for fear of placing themselves in a position of economic disadvantage as compared with neighbors or competitors. We have seen this in our study of the problem of unemployment compensation. . . . A system of old age pensions has special dangers of its own if put in force in one state and rejected in another. The existence of such a system is a bait to the needy and dependent elsewhere, encouraging them to migrate and seek a haven of repose. Only a power that is national can serve the interests of all.

Congress did not improvise a judgment when it found that the award of old age benefits would be conducive to the general welfare. . . . A great mass of evidence was brought together supporting the policy which finds expression in the act. Among the relevant facts are these: The number of persons in the United States 65 years of age or over is increasing proportionately as well as absolutely. What is even more important the number of such persons unable to take care of themselves is growing at a threatening pace. . . . In times of retrenchment the older are commonly the first to go, and even if retained, their wages are likely to be lowered. The plight of men and women at so low an age as 40 is hard, almost hopeless, when they are driven to seek for reemployment. . . . With the loss of savings inevitable in periods of idleness, the fate of workers over 65, when thrown out of work, is little less than desperate. A recent study of the Social Security Board informs us that 'one-fifth of the aged in the United States were receiving old-age assistance, emergency relief, institutional care, employment under the works program, or some other form of aid from public or private funds; two-fifths to one-half were dependent on friends and relatives, one-eighth had some income from earnings; and possibly one-sixth had some savings or property. Approximately three out of four persons 65 or over were probably dependent wholly or partially on others for support.' . . . [O]ther studies by state and national commissions . . . point the same way. . . .

When money is spent to promote the general welfare, the concept of welfare or the opposite is shaped by Congress, not the states. So the concept be not arbitrary, the locality must yield.

---

1. ***Foreshadowing Recent Challenges to the ACA***. From the perspective of the 21st Century, one of the striking features of the legal challenges to Social Security that dates back to the 1930s is the eerily familiar uncertainty over congressional authority to adopt the Social Security Act. Rather than justifying the Act as a whole, combining its tax provisions with its benefit formulae, the New Deal attorneys asserted separate sources of congressional authority for the various titles of the Act and were successful in persuading the Supreme Court to accept the legislation on those grounds. Flash forward nearly eight decades and we continue to see government attorneys attempt, albeit unsuccessfully, to defend individual mandate provisions of the ACA as a legitimate exercise of congressional power under the Commerce Clause, but then falling back on a defense of the legislation's key provision, the individual mandate, as also defensible under Congress's taxing powers. *See* NFIB v. Sebelius, 132 S. Ct. 2566 (2012), which is excerpted later in this Chapter. Why does Congress have so much trouble getting courts to accept its authority to adopt legislation affecting social insurance and so much latitude in regulating banking and securities?

2. ***Separate Sources of Constitutional Authority But a Unified Political Vision***. While judicial acceptance of the Social Security Act proceeded title by title, the political support for the program has always been based on a unified view of the program. This public understanding is something that President Franklin D. Roosevelt foresaw. Consider the following account by Mr. Luther Gluck, an expert on public administration who met with President Roosevelt in the summer of 1941 to discuss the on-going study of fiscal matters:

> In the course of this discussion I raised the question of the ultimate abandonment the [Social Security] payroll taxes in connection with old age security . . . in the event of another period of depression. I suggested that it had been a mistake to levy these taxes in the 1930's when the social security program was originally adopted. [Roosevelt] said, "I guess you're right on the economics. They are politics all the way through. We put those payroll contributions there so as to give the contributors a legal, moral, and political right to collect their pensions. . . . With those taxes in there, no damn politician can ever scrap my social security program. Those taxes aren't a matter of economics, they're straight politics."

Larry DeWitt, *Research Note #23: Luther Gulick Memorandum re: Famous FDR Quote*, SSA HISTORIAN'S OFFICE (Jul. 21, 2005). Was Roosevelt right?

B. THE POLICIES UNDERLYING SOCIAL INSURANCE

The following excerpt from a chapter by Professor James Kwak explores the many different policies underlying our chief social insurance programs.

James Kwak, 'Social Insurance,' Risk Spreading, and Redistribution

in Research Handbook on the Economics of Insurance Law
(Daniel Schwarcz & Peter Siegelman ed., 2015)

The core function of any insurance program is spreading risk among a pool of participants. In theory, insurance works because human beings are risk averse. If premiums are set equal to expected losses, risk-averse purchasers benefit (in utility terms) and sellers break even; even if premiums include transaction costs and a return on the capital invested in insurers, purchasers will often be made better off because of risk aversion. A private product or a government program provides insurance to the extent that it spreads the risk of uncertain future events across the people who face that risk. It is also insurance to the extent that it allows a participant to shift her resources among different future states of the world (that is, from states in which a loss does not occur to states in which it does occur).

Insurance necessarily involves redistribution in the relatively trivial sense that, seen retrospectively, cash is transferred from people who do not suffer losses to those who do. At the time people purchase insurance, however, this is not redistribution, assuming that each individual pays for her expected losses in the form of premiums. In practice, insurance also redistributes resources in another, more substantive sense. Among any group of insureds, even those whom the insurer identifies as equivalent risks, some will have a higher than average risk of loss and others will have a lower than average risk. The fact that they pay the same premiums means that, *ex ante*, there is redistribution from low-risk participants to high-risk participants. . . . One objective of insurance underwriting is to identify and price degrees of risk accurately in order to avoid undercharging high-risk people and overcharging low-risk people. . . .

In unregulated private markets, some people will buy insurance and others will not. People decline to buy insurance for several reasons. The best reason is that they simply do not need it: even risk-averse people are effectively risk-neutral with respect to small changes in wealth and thus should not insure themselves against small losses. . . . But there are many other, more worrisome reasons for underinsurance. Insurers may not offer needed insurance because of some market failure. Individuals may underestimate their own risk of loss. They may recognize the risk they face, but may not be aware that insurance exists. They may not be able to find insurance at a fair price—one that only moderately exceeds their expected losses. Or, even given a fair price, they may not be able to afford it. As a result, people face significant risks against which they have no protection. The programs generally thought of as social insurance attempt to make insurance available to these people for one or more reasons of public policy. . . .

Social Security, Medicare, and unemployment insurance, which in the United States are typically thought of as canonical examples of social insurance. These programs typically use one or more mechanisms to provide insurance that is considered socially beneficial but that, in the opinion of policymakers, would not be sufficiently provided or purchased in a purely private market. . . .

First, compulsory participation is a requirement that a program cover all people in a certain class. In the United States, Medicare Part A (hospital insurance) and unemployment insurance are mandatory for virtually all workers, as is Social Security with a few narrow exceptions. This means that contributions must be paid by or on behalf of workers, who thereby gain a right to benefits. Compulsory participation overcomes potential adverse selection problems because low-risk individuals cannot opt out of insurance, which would drive up premiums for everyone else. Not all programs commonly thought of as social insurance are mandatory, however; Medicare Parts B (medical insurance) . . . [is] not paid for by or on behalf of workers until they become beneficiaries, and participation is voluntary.

Second, government insurance programs often place constraints on underwriting, which limit the ability of insurers to decide whom they want to insure and at what price. In a theoretical free market, insurers can use any factors to differentiate between high-risk and low-risk insureds. With social insurance—especially if it is compulsory—some limits on risk underwriting may be necessary either to make insurance affordable to everyone or because of fairness concerns. Medicare does not differentiate among participants according to their health status, either during their working years or when collecting benefits; if it did charge premiums based on existing medical conditions, many people would probably not be able to afford [coverage]. . . .

Third, government programs often incorporate explicit subsidies either from 'outside' or from within the pool of insureds. These subsidies are in addition to the implicit subsidy created by underwriting constraints. For example, the lack of medical underwriting in Medicare Part B is an implicit subsidy from healthy people to people with chronic illnesses that helps reduce the cost of insurance for the latter. That is not enough to make Medicare Part B affordable, however: if every beneficiary were charged the average expected losses for the entire pool, Part B would likely be too expensive for most, largely because the elderly incur high health care costs on average. Therefore, approximately 75 percent of the costs of Part B are an explicit subsidy paid out of general revenues collected from income and other taxes.

Social Security, too, provides explicit subsidies from within the pool of participants. The program's founders recognized that some degree of redistribution was necessary to provide meaningful insurance to all. Social Security accomplishes this goal by using a progressive benefit formula: low earners receive a higher percentage of their contributions as benefits than do high earners. This formula compensates for the fact that high earners make higher contributions while working. On balance, the program transfers income from high earners to low earners, at least on an expected basis. . . .

---

1. ***Private Insurance versus Social Insurance.*** Many of the problems in private insurance markets that Kwak identifies are issues that we explored in

Chapter 3.2. How were those problems addressed in the areas of insurance that we addressed in that chapter? Should social insurance programs be extended into other areas? What is the appropriate domain of social insurance as opposed to private insurance markets?

2. ***Social Insurance versus Means-Tested Programs.*** As the preceding excerpt explores, the major social insurance programs in the United States include a certain element of redistribution in addition to risk sharing. As Kwak explains elsewhere, "some progressives . . . object to the insurance features of these programs, which sometimes mandate that high-income participants receive benefits that they seem not to need. These critics prefer means-tested public assistance to social insurance because it more effectively transfers resources to those who need them most." Do you agree? When might means-tested assistance be preferable to social insurance?

C. ERISA AND EMPLOYEE BENEFIT PLANS

ERISA, as amended, is another important piece of federal legislation that has a major influence on financial functions that would traditionally have been the subject of insurance regulation at the state level. Though initially motivated over concerns about the solvency of old-fashioned defined benefit pension plans, ERISA also extends to defined contribution pension plans, like 401(k)s, and employer-sponsored plans providing "medical, surgical, or hospital care or benefits, or benefits in the event of sickness, accident, disability, death or unemployment, or vacation benefits, apprenticeship or other training services, or day care centers, scholarship funds, or prepaid legal services." 29 U.S.C. § 1002(1)(A) (2012). Therefore, whenever a private employer offers a fringe benefit that insures employees against risks, ERISA's regulatory requirements potentially come into play. In many instances, those requirements supersede otherwise applicable state insurance laws.

ERISA's substantive requirements are generally beyond the scope of this casebook. For an excellent introduction to the subject, see JOHN H. LANGBEIN, DAVID A. PRATT & SUSAN J. STABILE, PENSION AND EMPLOYEE BENEFIT LAW (5th ed. 2010). The basic structure of these requirements will, however, be familiar to students acquainted with other forms of financial institution regulation. For example, ERISA plans must file periodic financial reports with the federal agencies charged with enforcing the statute, the Department of Labor, the Internal Revenue Service, and, for some plans, the Pension Benefit Guaranty Corporation (PBGC). Plan participants must also receive summary plan descriptions on a regular basis. Financial resources committed to ERISA plans must generally be held in trust, and federal fiduciary standards govern the management of these assets, requiring, among other things, that the resources be prudently invested and used for the exclusive benefit of plan participants and beneficiaries. In addition, ERISA imposes strict prohibited transaction rules designed to prevent plan fiduciaries and sponsors from doing business with affiliated ERISA plans.

For pension plans governed by ERISA, an additional layer of rules applies. To begin with, ERISA imposes funding requirements, similar to capital requirements for the depository institution or reserve requirements in the insurance field, to ensure that pension plans have sufficient resources to meet their obligations to plan participants and beneficiaries. Participants in ERISA pension plans are also protected by mandatory vesting and accrual rules, designed to prevent employers from revoking pension promises or otherwise frustrating the expectations of beneficiaries and participants. Some ERISA-regulated pension plans, the defined benefit ones, are further protected by PBGC insurance, similar to FDIC coverage for bank and thrift deposits or state guaranty fund coverage for many insurance policies. Finally, ERISA imposes an elaborate system of anti-discrimination rules on pension plans intended to ensure that employers provide lower-paid workers with pension benefits comparable to those offered to higher-paid workers. The anti-discrimination rules and many other ERISA provisions are largely enforced by the Internal Revenue Code, which conditions favorable tax treatment on a plan's meeting a host of ERISA requirements. *See* I.R.C. § 401(a). Among other things, these Internal Revenue Code rules put a cap on the amount of contributions employers and employees are permitted to make to their pension plans each year and also limits the terms on which participants can make withdrawals from pensions or assign interests in plan assets.

While even a cursory review of ERISA is beyond the scope of this book, readers should appreciate the very substantial impact of ERISA on the financial services sector. Figure 3.3-1 summarizes the distribution of U.S. retirement assets at the end of 2014. The lion's share of these assets are Individual Retirement Arrangements, defined contribution plans, and private sector defined benefit plans, which are subject to extensive regulation under ERISA. Note also the very limited amount of unfunded pension liability for private-sector defined benefit plans, in contrast to the unfunded pension liabilities of government defined benefit plans that are not subject to ERISA regulation. Another area where ERISA's coverage has been important is in the area of employer-provided health insurance. According to the Kaiser Family Foundation's 2015 Employer Health Benefits Survey, released in September 2015, "employer-sponsored [health] insurance covers over half of the non-elderly population, 147 million people in total."

Figure 3.3-1 U.S. Retirement Assets

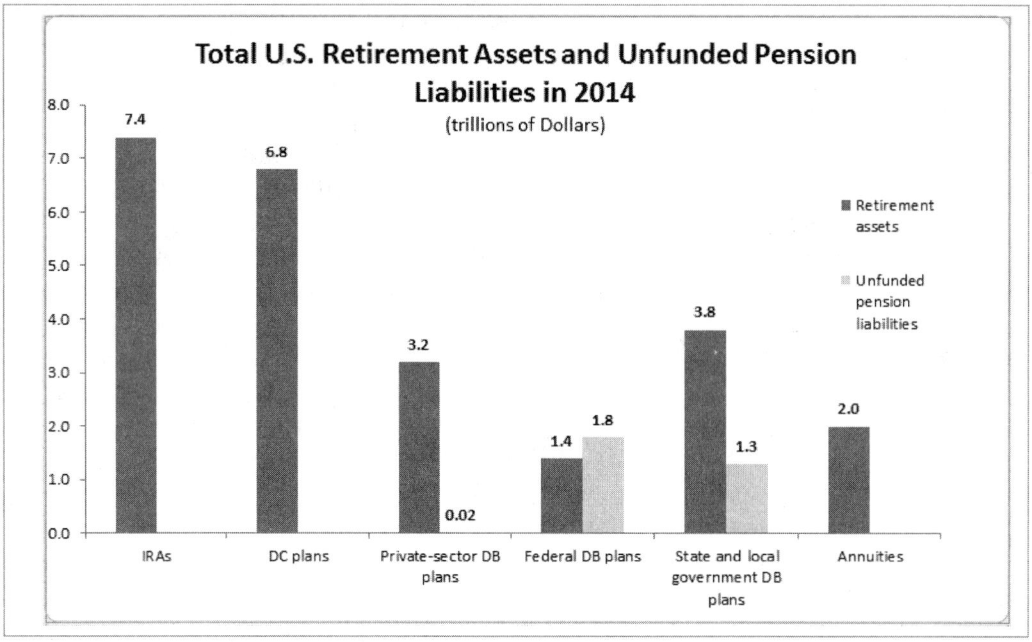

Sources: Inv. Co. Inst., Fed. Reserve Bd., Nat'l Ass'n of Gov't Defined Contribution Admin., Am. Council of Life Insurers, Internal Revenue Service Statistics of Income Division, and Gov't Accountability Office. See Inv. Co. Inst., "The U.S. Retirement Market, Fourth Quarter 2014."

1. ERISA's Preemption Provision

In terms of the structure of financial regulation in the United States, one of the most interesting aspects of ERISA is its relationship to state insurance law. That relationship is defined by § 514 of ERISA, which states in relevant part that:

> (a) Except as provided in subsection (b) of this section, the provisions of [ERISA] supersede any and all State laws insofar as they may now or hereafter relate to any employee benefit plan . . .
>
> (b) . . . .(2)
>
> (A) Except as provided in subparagraph (B), nothing in this subchapter shall be construed to exempt or relieve any person from any law of any State which regulates insurance, banking, or securities.
>
> (B) Neither an employee benefit plan . . . nor any trust established under such a plan, shall be deemed to be an insurance company or other insurer, bank, trust company, or investment company or to be engaged in the business of insurance or banking for purposes of any law of any State purporting to regulate insurance companies, insurance contracts, banks, trust companies, or investment companies.

ERISA's preemption provision is essentially the inverse of the McCarran-Ferguson Act. Rather than establishing a presumption of state authority, ERISA expressly trumps state law. The scope of the preemption is also unusually broad, displacing not just conflicting state rules, but all state laws that relate to employee benefit plans. The preemption provision does, however, have limits. Section 514(b)(2)(A), known as the "savings clause," carves out an exception for state insurance, banking, and securities regulation. The savings clause is limited by § 514(b)(2)(B), the "deemer clause," which stipulates that ERISA plans shall not be deemed to be financial institutions for purposes of state regulation.

A combination of reasons explains ERISA's strong bias for federal law in the field of employee benefit plans. In part, the Congress that enacted ERISA was concerned that large national corporations could be burdened by conflicting and opportunistic local regulations if the states retained concurrent jurisdiction over ERISA plans. In part, too, the premise of ERISA was that the statute would establish a regulatory framework in which employers and employees would have considerable freedom to bargain over appropriate fringe benefit packages. While ERISA thus sets various parameters on fringe benefits, much is left to private negotiation. The mandatory nature of state insurance and other local rules, it was thought, might conflict with this contractual model, see Daniel M. Fox & Daniel Schaffer, *Semi-Preemption in ERISA*, 7 AM. J. TAX POL'Y 47 (1988), and so a strong preemption provision was added to the final version of the statute. In addition, the political climate at the time of ERISA's enactment during the summer of 1974 was a high-water mark for national and congressional power in the United States. In this environment, it seemed entirely reasonable to make federal authority exclusive.

Whatever policies underlay its enactment, the ERISA preemption provision has been one of the most litigated sections of the United State Code. Since 1974, the Supreme Court has decided more than a dozen cases interpreting this provision. The following decision gives a flavor of the kinds of the disputes that have arisen in this area. Is there a better way to divide jurisdiction between federal and state authorities in this field?

FMC Corp. v. Holliday

498 U.S. 52 (1990)

Justice O'CONNOR delivered the opinion of the Court.

This case calls upon the Court to decide whether [ERISA] pre-empts a Pennsylvania law precluding employee welfare benefit plans from exercising subrogation rights on a claimant's tort recovery. . . .

Petitioner, FMC Corporation (FMC), operates the FMC Salaried Health Care Plan (Plan), an employee welfare benefit plan within the meaning of ERISA, § 3(1), that provides health benefits to FMC employees and their dependents. The Plan is self-funded; it does not purchase an insurance policy from any insurance company in order to satisfy its obligations to its participants. Among its provisions is a subrogation clause under which a Plan member agrees to reimburse the Plan for benefits paid if the member recovers on a claim in a liability action against a third party.

Respondent, Cynthia Ann Holliday, is the daughter of FMC employee and Plan member Gerald Holliday. In 1987, she was seriously injured in an automobile accident. The Plan paid a portion of her medical expenses. Gerald Holliday brought a negligence action on behalf of his daughter in Pennsylvania state court against the driver of the automobile in which she was injured. The parties settled the claim. While the action was pending,

FMC notified the Hollidays that it would seek reimbursement for the amounts it had paid for respondent's medical expenses. The Hollidays replied that they would not reimburse the Plan, asserting that § 1720 of Pennsylvania's Motor Vehicle Financial Responsibility Law, 75 Pa.Cons.Stat. § 1720 (1987), precludes subrogation by FMC. Section 1720 states that "[i]n actions arising out of the maintenance or use of a motor vehicle, there shall be no right of subrogation or reimbursement from a claimant's tort recovery with respect to . . . benefits . . . payable under section 1719." Section 1719 refers to benefit payments by "[a]ny program, group contract or other arrangement." . . .

We indicated in Metropolitan Life Ins. Co. v. Massachusetts, 471 U.S. 724 (1985), that the[ERISA preemption] provisions "are not a model of legislative drafting." Id., at 739. Their operation is nevertheless discernible. The pre-emption clause is conspicuous for its breadth. It establishes as an area of exclusive federal concern the subject of every state law that "relate[s] to" an employee benefit plan governed by ERISA. The saving clause returns to the States the power to enforce those state laws that "regulat[e] insurance," except as provided in the deemer clause. Under the deemer clause, an employee benefit plan governed by ERISA shall not be "deemed" an insurance company, an insurer, or engaged in the business of insurance for purposes of state laws "purporting to regulate" insurance companies or insurance contracts. . . .

Pennsylvania's antisubrogation law "relate[s] to" an employee benefit plan. We made clear in Shaw v. Delta Air Lines, [463 U.S. 85, 95 (1983)] that a law relates to an employee welfare plan if it has "a connection with or reference to such a plan." Id., 463 U.S., at 96-97 (footnote omitted). We based our reading in part on the plain language of the statute. Congress used the words "'relate to' in § 514(a) [the pre-emption clause] in their broad sense." Id., at 98. It did not mean to pre-empt only state laws specifically designed to affect employee benefit plans. That interpretation would have made it unnecessary for Congress to enact ERISA § 514(b)(4), which exempts from pre-emption "generally" applicable criminal laws of a State. We also emphasized that to interpret the pre-emption clause to apply only to state laws dealing with the subject matters covered by ERISA, such as reporting, disclosure, and fiduciary duties, would be incompatible with the provision's legislative history because the House and Senate versions of the bill that became ERISA contained limited pre-emption clauses, applicable only to state laws relating to specific subjects covered by ERISA. These were rejected in favor of the present language in the Act, "indicat[ing] that the section's pre-emptive scope was as broad as its language." Shaw v. Delta Air Lines, 463 U.S., at 98.

Pennsylvania's antisubrogation law has a "reference" to benefit plans governed by ERISA. The statute states that "[i]n actions arising out of the maintenance or use of a motor vehicle, there shall be no right of subrogation or reimbursement from a claimant's tort recovery with respect to . . . benefits . . . paid or payable under section 1719." 75 Pa.Cons.Stat. § 1720 (1987). Section 1719 refers to "[a]ny program, group contract or other arrangement for payment of benefits." These terms "includ[e], but [are] not limited to, benefits payable by a hospital plan corporation or a professional health service corporation." § 1719.

The Pennsylvania statute also has a "connection" to ERISA benefit plans. In the past, we have not hesitated to apply ERISA's pre-emption clause to state laws that risk subjecting plan administrators to conflicting state regulations. *See, e.g.*, Shaw v. Delta Air Lines, supra, at 95-100 (state laws making unlawful plan provisions that discriminate on the basis of pregnancy and requiring plans to provide specific benefits "relate to" benefit plans). . . . Pennsylvania's antisubrogation law prohibits plans from being structured in a manner requiring reimbursement in the event of recovery from a third party. It requires plan providers to calculate benefit levels in Pennsylvania based on expected liability conditions that differ from those in States that have not enacted similar antisubrogation legislation. Application of differing state subrogation laws to plans would therefore frustrate plan administrators' continuing obligation to calculate uniform benefit levels nationwide. . . .

There is no dispute that the Pennsylvania law falls within ERISA's insurance saving clause, which provides, "[e]xcept as provided in [the deemer clause], nothing in this subchapter shall be construed to exempt or relieve any person from any law of any State which regulates insurance," § 514(b)(2)(A). Section 1720 directly controls the terms of insurance contracts by invalidating any subrogation provisions that they contain. *See* Metropolitan Life Ins. Co. v. Massachusetts, 471 U.S., at 740-741. It does not merely have an impact on the insurance industry; it is aimed at it. *See* Pilot Life Ins. Co. v. Dedeaux, 481 U.S. 41, 50 (1987). This returns the matter of subrogation to state law. Unless the statute is excluded from the reach of the saving clause by virtue of the deemer clause, therefore, it is not pre-empted.

We read the deemer clause to exempt self-funded ERISA plans from state laws that "regulat[e] insurance" within the meaning of the saving clause. By forbidding States to deem employee benefit plans "to be an insurance company or other insurer . . . or to be engaged in the business of insurance," the deemer clause relieves plans from state laws "purporting to regulate insurance." As a result, self-funded ERISA plans are exempt from state regulation insofar as that regulation "relate[s] to" the plans. State laws directed toward the plans are pre-empted because they relate to an employee benefit plan but are not "saved" because they do not regulate insurance. State laws that directly regulate insurance are "saved" but do not reach self-funded employee benefit plans because the plans may not be deemed to be insurance companies, other insurers, or engaged in the business of insurance for purposes of such state laws. On the other hand, employee benefit plans that are insured are subject to indirect state insurance regulation. An insurance company that insures a plan remains an insurer for purposes of state laws "purporting to regulate insurance" after application of the deemer clause. The insurance company is therefore not relieved from state insurance regulation. The ERISA plan is consequently bound by state insurance regulations insofar as they apply to the plan's insurer. . . . Our interpretation of the deemer clause makes clear that if a plan is insured, a State may regulate it indirectly through regulation of its insurer and its insurer's insurance contracts; if the plan is uninsured, the State may not regulate it. . . .

Justice STEVENS, dissenting.

The Court's construction of the statute draws a broad and illogical distinction between benefit plans that are funded by the employer (self-insured plans) and those that are insured by regulated insurance companies (insured plans). . . . From the standpoint of the beneficiaries of ERISA plans—who after all are the primary beneficiaries of the entire statutory program—there is no apparent reason for treating self-insured plans differently from insured plans. Why should a self-insured plan have a right to enforce a subrogation clause against an injured employee while an insured plan may not? The notion that this disparate treatment of similarly situated beneficiaries is somehow supported by an interest in uniformity is singularly unpersuasive. If Congress had intended such an irrational result, surely it would have expressed it in straightforward English. At least one would expect that the reasons for drawing such an apparently irrational distinction would be discernible in the legislative history or in the literature discussing the legislation. The Court's anomalous result would be avoided by a correct and narrower reading of either the basic pre-emption clause or the deemer clause.

---

1. ***The Advantages of Self-Insured Plans.*** Opinions such as the *FMC* decision confirmed the advantages of self-insured plans for employers, and over the past few years, self-insured plans have become increasingly prevalent in the United States. While only six million Americans were covered through self-

insured plans when ERISA was enacted in 1974, some 55 million people and 40% of all group coverage was through self-insured plans by the late 1980s. *See* Gail A. Jensen & Kevin D. Cotter, *State Insurance Regulation and the Decision to Self-Insure*, 62 J. RISK & INS. 185 (1995). To qualify as self-insured for purposes of ERISA's preemption provision, a plan need not sever all ties with the insurance sector. Most self-insured plans contract with insurance companies to process claims and provide other administrative services for self-insured plans. Suppose an employer was concerned about incurring unexpectedly large medical claims from its self-insured plan. Suppose further that the employer purchased stop-loss coverage from an insurance company to recover losses incurred if its medical plan experienced more than $1 million in claims in any calendar year. How would ERISA's preemption provision apply to this arrangement? *See* Thompson v. Talquin Bldg. Prods. Co., 928 F.2d 649 (4th Cir. 1991).

2. ***Who Decides on Subrogation.*** The Pennsylvania legislature presumably made a considered choice that subrogation clauses should not be permitted with respect to injuries arising out of car accidents. Who decided the appropriate scope of subrogation in the *FMC* case? Who is best positioned to make such decisions?

3. ***ERISA Preemption as a Barrier to Health Care Reform.*** One of the unanticipated consequences of the Supreme Court's broad interpretation of ERISA's preemption provisions was the barrier it imposed on state efforts to reform health insurance programs. To the extent that large segments of the population were covered by self-insured, employer-sponsored plans, states had relatively little latitude to require large employers to provide health insurance coverage or limit the acceptable terms of that coverage, for example by placing restrictions on the ability of self-insured plans to limit coverage for pre-existing conditions. While the states did retain the ability to regulate the practice of medicine and the operation of hospitals, even that authority was limited when self-insured employers provide coverage through health maintenance organizations. These restrictions were one of the reasons that the Affordable Care Act, discussed later in this Chapter, had to be adopted at the federal level. *Compare* Aetna Health Inc. v. Davila, 542 U.S. 200 (2004) (finding that state law claims against an ERISA plan administrator for wrongful denial of benefit coverage are preempted), *with* Pegram v. Herdrich, 530 U.S. 211 (2000) (permitting state law claims that involve mixed decisions of treatment and coverage but are held to not involve fiduciary functions under ERISA). For a critical view of the Supreme Court's jurisprudence in this area, see John Langbein, *What ERISA Means by "Equitable": The Supreme Court's Trail of Error in Russell, Mertens, and Great-West*, 103 COLUM. L. REV. 1317, 1365 (2003).

2. Fiduciary Duties Under ERISA

Another distinctive feature of ERISA is its imposition of fiduciary duties on a variety of parties and how they manage ERISA plans. The application of these fiduciary duties to traditional pension plans is relatively straightforward, as a trustee is typically required to hold those assets in a structure quite similar to a traditional trust. As the following case demonstrates, the application of fiduciary duties to other sorts of employee benefit plans is less straightforward.

Firestone Tire & Rubber Co. v. Bruch

489 U.S. 101 (1989)

Justice O'CONNOR delivered the opinion of the Court.

[This case involved a dispute arising out of the sale of Firestone's Plastics Division. At the time of the sale, Firestone maintained a severance plan, covered by ERISA, which would have provided the plaintiffs severance benefits in the event of a "reduction in workforce." Payment of those severance benefits would have imposed additional costs on Firestone because the plan was not required to have advanced funding. Firestone concluded, however, that the sale of the division did not constitute a "reduction in service" for purposes of the plan. The question before the Supreme Court was the standard of review that should be applied to Firestone's interpretation of plan terms. The courts below had split over whether Firestone's decision should be reviewed under a deferential "arbitrary and capricious standard" or a more taxing "de novo" review.]

ERISA provides "a panoply of remedial devices" for participants and beneficiaries of benefit plans. Massachusetts Mutual Life Ins. Co. v. Russell, 473 U.S. 134, 146 (1985). Respondents' action asserting that they were entitled to benefits because the sale of Firestone's Plastics Division constituted a "reduction in work force" within the meaning of the termination pay plan was based on the authority of § 502(a)(1)(B). That provision allows a suit to recover benefits due under the plan, to enforce rights under the terms of the plan, and to obtain a declaratory judgment of future entitlement to benefits under the provisions of the plan contract. . . .

ERISA abounds with the language and terminology of trust law. *See, e.g.*, ERISA § 3(7) ("participant"), 1002(8) ("beneficiary"), 3(21)(A) ("fiduciary"), 403(a) ("trustee"), 404 ("fiduciary duties"). ERISA's legislative history confirms that the Act's fiduciary responsibility provisions, ERISA §§ 401-414, "codif[y] and mak[e] applicable to [ERISA] fiduciaries certain principles developed in the evolution of the law of trusts." H.R.Rep. No. 93-533, p. 11 (1973), U.S.Code Cong. & Admin.News 1974, pp. 4639, 4649. Given this language and history, we have held that courts are to develop a "federal common law of rights and obligations under ERISA-regulated plans." . . .

Trust principles make a deferential standard of review appropriate when a trustee exercises discretionary powers. *See* Restatement (Second) of Trusts § 187 (1959) ("[w]here discretion is conferred upon the trustee with respect to the exercise of a power, its exercise is not subject to control by the court except to prevent an abuse by the trustee of his discretion"). A trustee may be given power to construe disputed or doubtful terms, and in such circumstances the trustee's interpretation will not be disturbed if reasonable. Whether "the exercise of a power is permissive or mandatory depends upon the terms of the trust." 3 W. Fratcher, Scott on Trusts § 187, p. 14 (4th ed. 1988). Hence, over a century ago we remarked that "[w]hen trustees are in existence, and capable of acting, a court of equity will not interfere to control them in the exercise of a discretion vested in them by the instrument under which they act." Nichols v. Eaton, 91 U.S. 716, 724-725, 23 L.Ed. 254 (1875). . . . Firestone can seek no shelter in these principles of trust law, however, for there is no evidence that under Firestone's termination pay plan the administrator has the power to construe uncertain terms or that eligibility determinations are to be given deference. . . .

Finding no support in the language of its termination pay plan for the arbitrary and capricious standard, Firestone argues that as a matter of trust law the interpretation of the terms of a plan is an inherently discretionary function. But other settled principles of trust law, which point to de novo review of benefit eligibility determinations based on plan interpretations, belie this contention. As they do with contractual provisions, courts construe terms in trust agreements without deferring to either party's interpretation. "The extent of the duties and powers of a trustee is determined by the rules of law that are applicable to the situation, and not the rules that the trustee or his attorney believes to be applicable, and by the terms of the trust *as the court may interpret them*, and not as they may be interpreted by the trustee himself or by his attorney." 3 W. Fratcher, Scott on Trusts § 201, at 221 (emphasis added). A trustee who is in doubt as to the interpretation of the instrument can protect himself by obtaining instructions from the court. . . . The terms of trusts created by written instruments are "determined by the provisions of the instrument as interpreted in light of all the circumstances and such other evidence of the intention of the settlor with respect to the trust as is not inadmissible." Restatement (Second) of Trusts § 4, Comment d (1959).

The trust law de novo standard of review is consistent with the judicial interpretation of employee benefit plans prior to the enactment of ERISA. Actions challenging an employer's denial of benefits before the enactment of ERISA were governed by principles of contract law. If the plan did not give the employer or administrator discretionary or final authority to construe uncertain terms, the court reviewed the employee's claim as it would have any other contract claim—by looking to the terms of the plan and other manifestations of the parties' intent. . . .

As this case aptly demonstrates, the validity of a claim to benefits under an ERISA plan is likely to turn on the interpretation of terms in the plan at issue. Consistent with established principles of trust law, we hold that a denial of benefits challenged under § 502(a)(1)(B) is to be reviewed under a de novo standard unless the benefit plan gives the administrator or fiduciary discretionary authority to determine eligibility for benefits or to construe the terms of the plan. . . .

Because we do not rest our decision on the concern for impartiality that guided the Court of Appeals . . . , we need not distinguish between types of plans or focus on the motivations of plan administrators and fiduciaries. Thus, for purposes of actions under § 502(a)(1)(B), the de novo standard of review applies regardless of whether the plan at issue is funded or unfunded and regardless of whether the administrator or fiduciary is operating under a possible or actual conflict of interest. Of course, if a benefit plan gives discretion to an administrator or fiduciary who is operating under a conflict of interest, that conflict must be weighed as a "facto[r] in determining whether there is an abuse of discretion." Restatement (Second) of Trusts § 187, Comment d (1959). . . .

---

1. ***Contracting Out of* Bruch.** What is the significance of the *Bruch* decision? How would you expect employers to respond to the decision? Suppose, for example, employers amended their plans to grant a plan administrator discretion to deny benefits. To what sort of judicial review would such a provision be subject? *See* John H. Langbein, *The Supreme Court Flunks Trusts*, 1990 SUP. CT. REV. 207.

2. ***ERISA as Illustrative of the Fourth Stage of Capitalism.*** Just seven years after ERISA was enacted, Professor Robert Clark characterized the legislation as heralding the arrival of a new stage of economic and legal development:

> Today, decisions about whether and how much to save are increasingly being made by group representatives on behalf of a large number of group members, rather than by each individual whose present consumption is being deferred in favor of future consumption. The objective signs of this change are the steadily increasing predominance of group over individual health and life insurance policies, and the rapid growth since World War II of

> employee pension plans, especially as compared to the relative stagnancy of the individual annuities business. Today, the decision to save is only indirectly controlled by many of the workers who are to benefit from these plans (which can no longer accurately be described as "fringe" benefits), just as the decision to invest in particular financial claims is only rarely controlled by public suppliers of capital to financial intermediaries. And those new professional savings planners—for example, the sponsors and administrators of large corporate pension plans—rarely perform the active investment function. Most pension plan sponsors and administrators contract with outside bank trust departments, insurance companies, and investment advisory firms for investment management services.

Robert C. Clark, *The Four Stages of Capitalism*, 94 HARV. L. REV. 561, 566–67 (1981). Against this framework, should we regard the *Bruch* decision as creating appropriate space for savings planners to devise appropriate savings plans for group members? Should ERISA's preemption provision, previously discussed, be understood to serve a similar function? Should the more rigid restrictions of traditional insurance regulation discussed in Chapter 3.2 be considered obsolete and anachronistic in this brave new world, or perhaps not?

D. THE AFFORDABLE CARE ACT OF 2010

Further federal involvement in insurance regulation came with the passage of ACA in March of 2010. Colloquially known as Obamacare, ACA sought to implement a broad overhaul of the healthcare system with the goal of ensuring that all Americans have access to affordable, quality health care. Before its passage, health insurers were generally free, absent contrary state laws, to deny coverage based on preexisting medical conditions and to set insurance premiums as they desired. Insurance companies confronting the prospect of higher costs due to sickly individuals often chose to charge those individuals more, instead of raising rates for everyone and potentially losing customers. As a result, many Americans found themselves either denied coverage or priced out of it when they needed it most. Moreover, the young and healthy frequently chose to forego insurance altogether, and insurance risk pools were often slanted towards higher risk and higher rates. Higher rates made it even less likely for these groups to buy coverage and more difficult for low-income families to do so, further exacerbating the problem. Individuals without insurance could also delay seeking medical treatment until absolutely necessary, whereupon they would go to the local emergency room. Hospitals were required by law to treat the emergency needs of these patients and would pass on a lot of the associated costs to insurers by raising their fees in turn. The net effect was that those buying insurance were in no small part subsidizing the cost of those who were not.

ACA undertook to address these problems through a series of complementary measures. First, under the guaranteed issue provision, it requires health insurers to accept anyone who seeks coverage regardless of health status. Second, it seeks to make health insurance affordable by prohibiting premium variation based on health using a community rating, by implementing tax subsidies for persons with qualifying incomes, and by expanding Medicaid coverage. Third, it requires most individuals to maintain health insurance or pay a penalty pursuant to the individual mandate. These measures were broadly modeled on a similar system that Massachusetts adopted successfully in 2006. The following excerpt from the Supreme Court's opinion in *King v. Burwell*, describes how these measures were intended to work:

> [ACA] adopts a version of the three key reforms that made the Massachusetts system successful. First, the Act adopts the guaranteed issue and community rating requirements. The Act provides that "each health insurance issuer that offers health insurance coverage in the individual . . . market in a State must accept every . . . individual in the State that applies for such coverage." 42 U. S. C. §300gg-1(a). The Act also bars insurers from charging higher premiums on the basis of a person's health. §300gg.
>
> Second, the Act generally requires individuals to maintain health insurance coverage or make a payment to the IRS. 26 U. S. C. §5000A. Congress recognized that, without an incentive, "many individuals would wait to purchase health insurance until they needed care." 42 U. S. C. §18091(2)(I). So Congress adopted a coverage requirement to "minimize this adverse selection and broaden the health insurance risk pool to include healthy individuals, which will lower health insurance premiums." *Ibid.* In Congress's view, that coverage requirement was "essential to creating effective health insurance markets." *Ibid.* Congress also provided an exemption from the coverage requirement for anyone who has to spend more than eight percent of his income on health insurance. 26 U. S. C. §§5000A(e)(1)(A), (e)(1)(B)(ii).
>
> Third, the Act seeks to make insurance more affordable by giving refundable tax credits to individuals with household incomes between 100 percent and 400 percent of the federal poverty line. §36B. Individuals who meet the Act's requirements may purchase insurance with the tax credits, which are provided in advance directly to the individual's insurer. 42 U. S. C. §§18081, 18082.
>
> These three reforms are closely intertwined. As noted, Congress found that the guaranteed issue and community rating requirements would not work without the coverage requirement. §18091(2)(I). And the coverage requirement would not work without the tax credits. The reason is that, without the tax credits, the cost of buying insurance would exceed eight percent of income for a large number of individuals, which would exempt them from the coverage requirement.

135 S. Ct. 2480, 2486–87 (2015). A significant portion of Americans receive health insurance from a large employer, and this large-group market was perceived as generally effective. The Act's reforms were targeted primarily towards the individual and small-group health insurance markets. As of March 2016, the Department of Health and Human Services reported that some 20 million people gained insurance due to the passage of the Act, representing an

overall decline from about 15% of uninsured Americans, or approximately 48 million people, to about 9% uninsured. This includes 6.1 million young adults whom, pursuant to the Act, insurers must allow to remain on parental plans until age 26. The Department also reported over 14 million new enrollees in Medicaid programs, including 12 million in states that expanded Medicaid coverage and 2 million in states that did not. In addition, as of the close of the last enrollment period on January 31, 2016, 12.7 million people enrolled in individual insurance plans through the new government health insurance marketplaces, 9.6 million on HealthCare.gov and 3.1 million through state marketplaces. It should be noted, however, that the Medicaid and marketplace numbers do not accurately represent previously uninsured individuals as some of these people had alternative prior coverage. OFFICE OF THE ASSISTANT SECRETARY FOR PLANNING AND EVALUATION, DEPARTMENT OF HEALTH AND HUMAN SERVICES, HEALTH INSURANCE COVERAGE AND THE AFFORDABLE CARE ACT, 2010–2016 (March, 2016).

The passage of ACA proved politically contentious, engendering strong opposition from the Republican Party and polarized views on its merits among Americans. Numerous lawsuits were filed in federal courts, and the Supreme Court has heard two prominent cases challenging elements of the Act and its implementation. In particular, many saw the mandate to purchase insurance as encroaching on individual freedom. The Act also authorized the withdrawal of current Medicaid funding from states that refused to expand their Medicaid programs, and many states did not take well to what they saw as federal coercion. These two issues were addressed by the Court in the following case, *NFIB v. Sebelius*, 132 S. Ct. 2566 (2012).

1. *National Federation of Independent Business v. Sebelius*

In *NFIB v. Sebelius*, the Court heard the argument that the individual mandate and the accompanying penalty of ACA are unconstitutional, as no enumerated power authorized Congress to mandate a purchase by an individual. *NFIB* also challenged the validity of the Medicaid expansion as violating the principles of state sovereignty embedded in the Tenth Amendment by coercing state decision making through the threat of lost funding. Writing for the Court, Chief Justice John Roberts found that the individual mandate was an unconstitutional extension of the Commerce power, but upheld the accompanying penalty as a legitimate use of Congress's Taxing power. The Court's holding did not rely on the *Paul v. Virginia* theory that insurance was not a form of commerce, but on the theory that Congress could not compel an individual's activity under the Commerce power. The Court explained that:

> The individual mandate . . . does not regulate existing commercial activity. It instead compels individuals to *become* active in commerce by purchasing a product, on the ground that their failure to do so affects interstate commerce. Construing the Commerce Clause to permit Congress to regulate individuals precisely *because* they are doing nothing would open a new and potentially vast domain to congressional authority.

Id. at 2587. Given that the Act never envisioned any sanctions other than a modest penalty, as Congress had assumed that four million people would just opt to pay the penalty, the Court's holding functionally left the individual mandate in place while generally restricting congressional authority under the Commerce power.

The Court also held that the Medicaid expansion was an unconstitutional coercion of the States under the Tenth Amendment. This holding left the states with the option to refuse to expand their Medicaid programs without losing their current government funding. As of January 2016, only 31 states adopted the Medicaid expansion, despite the availability of federal funding for at least 90% of the additional Medicaid insurance costs.

2. *King v. Burwell*

Three years later, the Court entertained another major challenge to the Affordable Care Act in *King v. Burwell.* 135 S. Ct. 2480 (2015). To understand the nature of this challenge, some background is necessary. As noted earlier, the individual mandate was a critical feature of the Act. Without it, healthy individuals could elect not to purchase insurance, knowing that the guaranteed issue and community rating requirements assured them the right to purchase insurance in the future at a similar price to those with insurance. The prospect of sick individuals buying insurance in the future at the common price meant that insurers would have to raise rates on everyone to accommodate tomorrow's more costly risk pool. Higher rates would mean that more people would choose to forego insurance and only purchase it when necessary, leading in turn to an even riskier pool and even higher rates in a process known as adverse selection. ACA's mandate solved these problems by pushing everyone into the risk pool. The lower costs of healthy individuals would offset the higher costs of those who became ill. The mandate only applied, however, if the cost of insurance was not more than 8% of income, and for many Americans it was more.

To account for this, the Act introduced tax subsidies to reduce insurance costs for Americans with an income between 100% and 400% of the federal poverty level. The subsidies were calculated to reduce insurance costs below the 8% threshold such that virtually everyone would be subject to the mandate. The Act also called for each state to establish a health insurance exchange, a central marketplace for health insurance in the state, with federal grant money, and authorized the federal government to create the exchange for the state if it failed to do so. As of 2016, some 27 states have exchanges run entirely by the federal government while only 16 exchanges are regarded as state-run. The essence of the challenge in *King v. Burwell* was that the language of the Act only authorized the provision of these subsidies for plans purchased on exchanges "established by the State," and not those established by the federal government on behalf of a state. The Court ultimately held that, in context, the term "established by the State" was ambiguous and that the structure and purpose of the Act "lead[] us to conclude that . . . tax credits [are allowed] for insurance purchased on any Exchange created under the Act." *Id.* at 2496.

---

1. ***Rate Regulation under ACA.*** A primary goal of ACA was to ensure affordable health insurance rates for everyone. To this end, the Act implements a community rating measure which limits the use of health status in determining

rates. Under this measure, insurers in the individual and small-group health insurance markets may take only four variables into account in determining differences in premiums between individuals: age, tobacco use, geographic area, and whether the plan is for an individual or a family.

The use of each of these factors is further limited. For age, unless a state places additional restrictions, insurers *may* vary rates by a maximum factor of 3:1 for adults over 21. In the regulatory scheme adopted by the Department of Health and Human Services, adults age 21 are assigned a factor of 1. This factor increases minimally every year following an age rating curve set by the state or the Department until it reaches the full 3:1 ratio at age 64. Rates for children under 21 are to be set based on actuarially justified proportions to adult rates, which under the Department's default age rating curve results in a ratio of 0.635:1. For tobacco use, defined as the use of any tobacco an average of four times per week over the last six months, insurers may vary rates up to a ratio of 1.5:1. For families, total premiums may vary based on the number of family members but, to limit the effects on large families, only three children under 21 may be counted towards the total number of family members. Finally, for the geographic area variable, states may establish rating areas between which rates may vary, based on counties, the first three digits in a standard five-digit zip code, or metropolitan and non-metropolitan statistical areas. These divisions must be adequate in size and reflect real differences in health care costs. There is no specified factor for inter-area variation, but the factors used must be actuarially justified.

In Chapter 3.2, we saw the surprising degree of variation among states as to what factors insurers may use in setting rates in different insurance markets, even when it comes to such controversial factors as race, religion, gender, and sexual orientation. ACA is notable for both the uniformity it establishes as to permissible rating factors, and for its strong limitations on which factors may be used and to what degree. These restrictions go well beyond those of the vast majority of individual states, and the motivation for this was the attempt to enable everyone to purchase health insurance on an equal footing. Working together, these limitations go a long way to ensuring similar rates from person to person regardless of health status.

In Chapter 3.2, we also explored how many states subject insurers to some form of rate review process, particularly in the auto insurance sector. ACA establishes such a review process for health insurers as well, requiring insurers to submit justifications for unreasonable rate increases and to post them on their websites. As implemented, rate increases of 10% or more are subject to unreasonable increase review by the Department of Health and Human Services, which reviews the insurer's justification and then issues a determination as to whether the rate increase is adequately justified. Unlike similar state processes, the Act does not empower the Department to revise or reject rates. If a determination is made that a rate is not justified, the insurer is free to revise the rate or to keep it, in which case the insurer must file a final justification, which is then posted online as well.

2. ***ACA and the Role of the States.*** While ACA is quite comprehensive, it preserves, and relies upon, a limited role for state regulation, in addition to the option to oversee implementation of the Act through the creation of state-run

exchanges. This limited role generally takes the form of a minimum set of federal requirements upon which states may add, such as we previously saw for the permitted rating factors. A state may also add to the basket of essential health benefits that must be covered by insurance plans under the law. If a state chooses to run its own exchange, it may set the requirements for how many plans an insurer on the exchange must offer, other than the Gold- and Silver-tier plans required by the Act, or conversely, may control the complexity of the marketplace by restricting plans-per-tier or limiting variation between plans. Whereas the federal standard for an adequate health network for exchange plans is very general and the network must be able to provide all services without unreasonable delay, a state may set more concrete requirements or even mandate that insurers cover out-of-network benefits in some or all circumstances. In this vein, some states set a maximum travel time or distance that an insurer may require an individual to see a primary care provider, or set a minimum ratio of in-network physicians to plan enrollees. Many states require insurers to contract with any medical provider that will accept their preset terms and rates, or even to allow subscribers to choose freely between in- or out-of-network providers without variation in coverage. Other states, however, rely on the general federal standard and leave its policing to the federal government. The resultant national legal framework is thus a hybrid of an elaborate federal regulatory system with a patchwork overlay of varied state regulation.

3. ***Large-group Plans, the Employer Mandate, and the Cadillac Tax.*** Although the individual and small-group markets were the primary targets of the Act, a number of its important measures cover large-group plans, plans covering groups of 100 or more employees, as well. These plans must also, for instance, cover dependents until age 26, cover preventive services with no cost-sharing, and eliminate annual and lifetime limits on benefits. Participants in group plans in general do not receive direct tax subsidies, although a number of old and new tax subsidies are available at the employer level. The Act also mandates that any employer with 50 or more employees must offer insurance to its employees, and that this insurance must be affordable, or not more than 9.5% of annual household income, provide a minimum actuarial value of 60% of expected costs, and have limited cost sharing. If it does not comply and if its employees receive subsidies on the individual exchanges, the employer is subject to a yearly penalty of $2,000 per employee. Finally, the Act implements a Cadillac tax, a 40% excise tax on expensive employer-provided health plans, on amounts exceeding $10,200 for an individual and $27,500 for a family. This measure was intended to discourage waste and to cover some of the costs of ACA, but has proven controversial and Congress continues to delay its implementation.

4. ***The Long-term Viability of the Individual Health Insurance Market.*** As previously described, the guaranteed availability and community rating pricing measures on their own would have sent the individual health insurance market into a death spiral by allowing individuals to delay enrollment until they were ill. The Act attempted to solve this perennial problem by requiring that everyone buy insurance to effectively distribute costs evenly between the healthy and the ill. The critical assumption was that enough young and healthy people would indeed buy new insurance plans through the health insurance exchanges

in the individual market, leading to a balanced risk pool. Under political pressure, however, the Obama Administration has allowed people to remain on their old grandfathered insurance plans not subject to the Act's community pricing restrictions, incentivizing those with more expensive plans, generally less healthy individuals, to move into the exchanges, while healthier people remain behind. This drives up costs in the individual market, further discouraging this crucial segment from participating. While it is still too soon to ascertain how these market interactions will play out, it is at least possible that not enough young and healthy people will participate in the exchanges and that large insurers will therefore sustain losses in the individual market and eventually leave it, threatening the viability of the individual health insurance market. *See* Anna Wilde Mathews & Stephanie Armour, *Biggest Insurer Threatens to Abandon Health Law*, WALL ST. J., Nov. 19, 2015. For a pessimistic perspective on the future of the Affordable Care Act, see Professor Seth Chandler's blog ACA Death Spiral.

III. THE FUTURE OF FEDERAL INTERVENTION

In the final part of this Chapter, we will explore the future of federal interventions in insurance regulations. As noted earlier, one significant new power of the federal government in this area is the capacity of the Financial Stability Oversight Council (FSOC) to designate certain insurance groups as systemically important financial institutions (SIFIs). This is a power that the FSOC has already exercised with respect to several major insurance companies, and its most recent designation of MetLife is currently under challenge in court. We will explore that litigation and the legal issues it raises in detail in Chapter 6.2, but for now we will focus on another area where federal authority over insurance could be expanded in the future.

One of the greatest challenges for U.S. authorities in the field of insurance has been coordinating the regulation of capital requirements under state insurance regulations with other systems of capital regulation, which are based on different principles and call for different levels of capital. The Federal Reserve Board has encountered this problem with respect to insurance firms subject to the Bank Holding Company Act (BHCA). As will be explained in greater detail in Part VI, many insurance groups included insured banks or insured thrifts, and so these firms are subject to regulation under the BHCA even for insurance companies that have not been designated systemically important. In its implementation of Basel III, the Federal Reserve Board staff has struggled with the application of modern capital requirements to insurance groups, as the Basel III rules were not designed to assess the risks of insurance companies. In one of the few legislative amendments to the Dodd-Frank Act that has made its way through Congress, the Insurance Capital Standard Clarifications Act of 2014 gives the Federal Reserve Board greater latitude in how to apply Basel III rules or modified capital requirements to insurance groups. Sector sources suggest that the Federal Reserve Board may allow insurance companies to rely heavily on the current system of state-based capital regulation, but the matter is still pending at this time. *See Fed Talks with Insurers Proceed on New Capital Rules*, REUTERS, June 16, 2015.

Another area of conflict concerns the coordination of state-based insurance capital requirements in the United States and standards imposed on insurance companies in other countries. The following excerpt explores this issue.

Elizabeth F. Brown & Robert W. Klein,
Insurance Solvency Regulation: A New World Order

Research Handbook on the Economics of Insurance Law (2015)

Insurance solvency regulation seeks to reduce the risk that an insurer will be unable to meet its financial obligations due to financial distress or bankruptcy and to promote confidence in the financial stability of the insurance sector. It is based on a societal judgment of the optimal risk-return trade-off involved with insurance transactions, in which solvency regulations that allow for greater flexibility for insurers lead to a wider range of possible product/price options but expose consumers to greater risk in return for these benefits. Solvency standards for insurance companies vary around the globe in accordance with different assessments of the optimal risk-return trade-off as well as different regulatory philosophies. . . .

II. [The Political Economy of Solvency Regulation]

. . . While the 2008 financial crisis led to the creation of the [FIO] in 2010, it has no independent regulatory authority. Its powers are limited mainly to advising other federal agencies and Congress on insurance issues. In order to obtain the information it needs to fulfill its advisory duties, the FIO may subpoena information from insurers and their affiliates but only after it has attempted to obtain the required information from existing federal and state regulatory agencies or from publically available sources. The [Dodd-Frank Act] did give the US Treasury Secretary and the US Trade Representative the power to negotiate bilateral or multilateral agreements covering prudential standards for insurance or reinsurance. The Dodd-Frank Act refers to such agreements as 'covered agreements'. The FIO may advise the US Treasury Secretary and the US Trade Representative during such negotiations but it is not authorized to carry on such negotiations. Following the entry into force of such an agreement, the FIO may determine if existing state laws conflict with the provisions in the covered agreement and therefore are preempted as a result.

[T]he US Treasury Secretary and the US Trade Representative have not negotiated any covered agreements. While the FIO recommended that the US Treasury Secretary and the US Trade Representative should negotiate a covered agreement on reinsurance collateral requirements, neither the US Treasury Secretary nor the US Trade Representative have shown much interest in beginning negotiations for a covered agreement on reinsurance collateral requirements. . . .

[P]art of the explanation for the differences in insurance solvency standards among nations can be attributed to the differences between national and state-level politics and their interactions with economic concerns. For example, US state governments tend to be less concerned with the international implications of insurance solvency regulation than the national governments of other countries because, unlike national governments, the states are not responsible for conducting foreign affairs or engaging in international economic cooperation.

III. Important Developments and Initiatives

. . . [E]conomic trends have prompted the US, EU, and the IAIS to undertake several significant initiatives aimed at addressing the solvency issues that such trends have raised. These initiatives include the [National Association of Insurance Commissioners' (NAIC)] [Solvency Modernization Initiative (SMI)], the EU's Solvency II, and the

[International Association of Insurance Supervisors' (IAIS)] ComFrame and related programs.

The US, EU, and the IAIS represent the three most important entities for developing insurance regulatory norms. The US and the EU are important because over two-thirds of the world's insurance premiums are written by insurance firms from these two areas. The IAIS is the most important international body for the development of insurance regulatory norms. The IAIS's membership is broader than comparable international bodies for banking or securities. It has almost 140 nations who are members while the Basel Committee on Banking Supervision, which establishes international guidelines for banking, has fewer than 30 nations who are members. While the US and the EU establish legally binding requirements for insurers operating within their borders, the IAIS influences insurance standards globally by promulgating non-binding principles and norms that attempt to influence and shape the content of the domestic insurance laws of its member nations over time.

1. Solvency Modernization Initiative

The NAIC's SMI constitutes a fairly ambitious effort by US state regulators to examine and reform several key elements of their system for insurance solvency regulation. As described by the NAIC, 'The SMI is a critical self-examination of the United States' insurance solvency regulatory framework and includes a review of international developments regarding insurance supervision, banking supervision, and international accounting standards and their potential use in US insurance regulation' (NAIC 2012). The SMI, which began in 2008, has six major components: 1) capital requirements; 2) risk management; 3) corporate governance; 4) group supervision; 5) reinsurance; and 6) statutory accounting and financial reporting. A significant number of NAIC committees, task forces, and working groups have been involved in developing specific recommendations in each of these areas, which can take various forms including model laws, model regulations, and guidelines, among others.

The individual states, however, must ultimately support any NAIC recommendations in order for them to become law and be enforced. In the past, the states generally have adopted the NAIC recommendations regarding solvency regulations, although they have not applied them uniformly to all insurers nor have they enforced them uniformly. . . .

Unlike the slate of solvency regulatory reforms that the NAIC adopted in the late 1980s and early 1990s, the SMI is not motivated by a dramatic rise in insurer insolvencies or some other crisis, although the recent financial crisis has added a new wrinkle to the NAIC's reform agenda. Arguably, at least two of the principal motivators behind the SMI are Solvency II and the development of international regulatory standards in the context of the growing globalization of the insurance business. Gone are the days when US regulators could operate in relative isolation without concern to how their policies conformed to those employed in other countries. Now US regulators must bring their policies up to a level consistent with international standards and generally accepted notions of what constitutes best practices in insurance solvency regulation.

This observation is not meant to imply that US regulators would not want to employ best practices for their own reasons. The issue is whether the policies US regulators believe make the most sense in an American context are acceptable to regulators in other countries. Their hope is that the US version of solvency regulatory reform will be deemed sufficient by other regulators so that there will be no conflicts over regulatory equivalency. It would be surprising if international acceptance of the policy reforms being developed under the SMI did not weigh on the minds of the NAIC's leadership; how this may be affecting the decisions being made is a matter of speculation for outsiders. US regulators also must deal with federal officials' assessment of the adequacy of SMI reforms as well as lobbying by the insurance industry. Hence, there are several forces pulling on US insurance regulators as they proceed down the path of reform . . . .

2. Solvency II

The EU began considering replacing Solvency I over ten years ago because it only set minimum prudential standards, while several national regulators within the EU imposed more stringent capital standards. As a result, insurers operating within the EU were subject to different solvency standards depending on which national regulator supervised them, creating an uneven playing field.

Solvency II aims to establish a harmonized regime for solvency regulation organized around three pillars. Pillar I defines quantitative financial requirements, including capital adequacy rules, for insurance firms (European Union 2009). Pillar II defines the supervisory activities of each national authority. Pillar III defines the reporting and public disclosure requirements for insurance firms and supervisory authorities. The European Insurance and Occupational Pensions Authority (EIOPA) has set January 1, 2016 as the deadline for the delivery of the regulatory and supervisory framework for the technical implementation and application of Solvency II.

In addition, Solvency II would require that non-EU insurance companies be regulated both at the entity and group levels by a supervisory authority equivalent to the national authorities within the EU in order for their capital held outside of the EU to count towards their capital requirements. It is unclear at this time if US state regulation would be deemed equivalent under this standard, or to what extent the states would have to change their laws and regulations to be deemed equivalent. In the long run, Solvency II may pressure US regulators to adopt the same or similar standards for regulating insurance so that US insurance companies with international operations are not handicapped when they try to compete in the EU. It remains to be seen how this interplay between the US and the EU over regulatory equivalency will ultimately influence US regulatory standards.

For now, the EU has unilaterally resolved the matter by allowing the European Commission and EIOPA jointly to classify a non-EU country, like the US, as having solvency standards that are 'provisionally equivalent' to those required under Solvency II as long as they meet certain standards. . . . The non-EU nation does not need to apply to the European Commission and EIOPA in order to be deemed by them as provisionally equivalent. Provisional equivalence may be granted for an initial ten-year period and may be renewed for an unlimited number of additional ten-year periods . . . . Under the Omnibus II Directive, the European Commission and EIOPA could classify the US state insurance regulatory regimes as provisionally equivalent without the states having to apply or make any commitments to change their solvency standards.

The EU felt pressured to enact this compromise after lobbying from many large EU insurers with US operations. Prudential, one of the UK's largest insurance companies, even warned that it was considering relocating its operations out of London because of the Solvency II equivalence requirements and the questions raised about whether the US would meet them.

3. International Standards and Programs

For over a decade the IAIS has promoted the convergence of market conduct and prudential requirements around the world by encouraging nations to adopt regulations that conform to its Insurance Core Principles (ICPs), which are non-binding principles and norms (IAIS 2011). IAIS members consider the ICPs as roughly equivalent to the standards set for banks under the Basel Accords. Unlike the Basel Accords for banks, however, the ICPs do not establish clear, uniform capital standards for insurers. . . .

The IAIS envisions the insurer's responsibility as managing risk and the insurance regulator's responsibility as guaranteeing that the insurer meets this obligation. Thus, the IAIS encourages supervisors to require that an insurer 'translate its risk exposure as far as practicable into quantitative measures which provide a sound and consistent basis for the setting of premium levels, determining technical provisions and deciding on the economic capital it finds optimal from its risk management perspective'. IAIS standards would allow supervisors to give individual insurers a great deal of latitude in terms of assessing and reserving for the risks they face. In fact, the IAIS believes that such risk-sensitive regulatory requirements are preferable to fixed ratios or limits because they provide insurers with better incentives for managing risk, discourage regulatory arbitrage, and enable the better use of resources. . . .

V. [Capital Regulation]

1. Capital Standards in the US

In the US, insurers are subject to fixed capital requirements set by each state as well as uniform risk-based capital (RBC) standards based on complex formulas developed by the NAIC that have been adopted by every state. Different formulas are required for property-casualty, health, and life insurance companies. In each of these RBC formulas, selected factors (*e.g.*, 10 percent) are multiplied by various accounting values (*e.g.*, assets, reserves, or premiums) to produce RBC charges for each item. . . .

An insurer's RBC is compared to its actual total adjusted capital (TAC) to determine whether any company or regulatory action is required. Certain company and regulatory actions are prescribed if a company's TAC falls below its RBC. Four RBC levels for company and regulatory action have been established, with more strict action required for companies as they reach lower ratios of RBC to TAC. . . .

Arguably, the US approach to determining RBC requirements reflects both the heights and the limits to what can be achieved with a formula based method. When first adopted, the US system was considered relatively advanced compared with regulatory capital requirements in other countries, and was seen as a significant improvement over fixed capital requirements. However, over time, regulators' use of static formulas to determine insurers' capital requirements has come to be seen by many academics as increasingly outmoded in view of the improvements that have occurred in dynamic financial analysis (DFA) and the use of models to assess and manage insurers' financial risk.

2. Capital Standards in the EU

The capital standards being developed under Solvency II in the EU under the oversight of the EIOPA have also received considerable attention. When the EU began working on a common set of capital standards, it was able to take advantage of the advances in risk analysis and modeling that have occurred since the NAIC initially developed its RBC standards in the early 1990s. . . .

Based on the Solvency II directives that have been adopted to date, there will be two levels of regulatory capital requirements. The first level is the [solvency capital requirement (SCR)], also known as 'target capital', that is intended to represent the economic capital an insurer needs to hold that will allow it meet its claims obligations within a prescribed safety level. The economic capital for a given insurer will be derived by using a value at risk (VaR) calibration at a 99.5 percent confidence level over a one-year time horizon. The SCR will encompass all risk categories that are viewed as significant by regulators, including underwriting, market, credit, and operational risk as well as risk mitigation techniques employed by insurers (*e.g.*, reinsurance and securitization). The second level is the minimum capital requirement (MCR) which is the minimum amount of capital that an insurer would be required to hold and below which policyholders would be subject to an 'unacceptable' level of risk (in the view of regulators). The MCR would be calibrated at an 85 percent VaR confidence level and bounded between 25 and 45 percent of an insurer's SCR. An insurer that fails to meet its MCR would be subject to immediate regulatory intervention. An insurer that falls between its MCR and SCR may be subject to regulatory action based on regulators' determination of whether corrective steps are warranted. . . .

VI. Summary and Concluding Remarks

Whither solvency regulation? The IAIS and the EU have embraced an [enterprise risk management] approach to capital standards within an integrated solvency framework that welcomes the use of both standard and internal models. Having committed themselves to this course, it is unlikely that they will deviate from it. NAIC and state insurance regulators seem equally wedded to their RBC standards and probably will not budge significantly absent the threat of action by the federal government to impose uniform prudential standards on them. The Dodd-Frank Act gave the US Treasury and the [U.S. Trade Representative] the authority to negotiate international agreements establishing prudential insurance standards. If the EU changes its mind and refuses to declare the US state regulatory system as at least provisionally equivalent (which seems highly unlikely), then the major US insurers that operate internationally will likely begin to lobby the federal government heavily to take action to correct this problem. In addition, international bodies like the [Financial Stability Board] may increase their pressure on the federal government to create a national insurance regulator, particularly if they feel the states are not doing enough to address systemic risks.

More likely, the EU will classify the US system as provisionally equivalent without requiring any material changes on the part of the US regulators other than those already adopted or contemplated under the NAIC's SMI. If this occurs, as is likely, then two different solvency regimes will continue to operate in the EU and the US until the next financial crisis reveals the flaws in one or both systems.

As for the rest of the world, developed nations like Japan probably will move closer to adopting a system similar to Solvency II, while developing and emerging nations continue to use traditional fixed capital requirement systems or some form of RBC standards. Developing and emerging nations lack the economic resources and the personnel to administer a system like Solvency II. While these different solvency systems generally have not proven problematic when insurance was still mostly comprised of separate, national markets, it is unclear if it will continue to work as the insurance market becomes more global and interconnected with other financial services.

Against the backdrop of EU equivalency determination, the absence of a clear and unified voice representing U.S. insurance regulators becomes especially problematic.

Justin Schardin, How FSOC Undermined, and the Fed May Save, U.S. Case for Insurance Regulatory Equivalence

Bipartisan Policy Ctr. (July 30, 2015)

In 2008, the NAIC began its Solvency Modernization Initiative (SMI) to address group capitalization and supervision, among other issues. The NAIC has adopted model legislation to improve group supervision, including the Insurance Holding Company System Model Act, which gives state regulators the authority to supervise insurance groups. The NAIC has argued that its "windows and walls" approach can effectively give regulators "windows" to look at group activity and the ability to "wall" off insurance capital from the rest of any non-insurance activities of a group.

In 2014, the State of New Jersey went further, passing legislation that authorizes the New Jersey Commissioner of Banking and Insurance to be the group-wide supervisor for internationally active insurance groups (IAIGs) headquartered in that state. It even gives the commissioner the authority to act as a group supervisor for IAIGs with substantial operations in New Jersey but headquartered in other states, under certain conditions. However, it is unclear exactly how New Jersey could actually regulate the behavior of subsidiaries in other states or how insurance regulators in other states would respond to New Jersey attempting to exert its authority.

The 2015 International Monetary Fund's (IMF) assessment of U.S. insurance regulation reported that states were making progress under SMI but that changes are "a work in progress" that still face obstacles. EU officials will need to determine whether progress by states so far will be enough to grant equivalence to the United States on group supervision. The [FIO] and the U.S. Trade Representative have the authority to negotiate a "covered agreement" with the EU on certain insurance matters, which may include group supervision.

FSOC Rebuts State Regulators

The context for these negotiations will likely be informed in part by the case FSOC has made against the ability of states to engage in adequate group supervision.

In its December 2014 designation of MetLife as a SIFI, FSOC explicitly said that the company "is currently not subject to consolidated supervision," and that state insurance regulators lack the authority to require insurance holding companies or other subsidiaries of holding companies to take or not take actions to preserve the safety and soundness of insurers or to avoid risks that would threaten U.S. financial stability. Further, FSOC said that state regulators' authorities, "have never been tested by the material financial distress of an insurance company of the size, scope, and complexity of MetLife's insurance subsidiaries."

FSOC's arguments, perhaps inadvertently, effectively undermine the NAIC's case that its "windows and walls" approach is sufficient. Since FSOC's designation represents the views of all U.S. federal financial regulators, this makes it more difficult for the U.S. government to argue on behalf of a temporary or permanent granting of equivalence.

Enter the [Federal Reserve Board]

Dodd-Frank gave FSOC the authority to designate nonbank financial companies as SIFIs and subject them to oversight by the [Federal Reserve Board]. Three of FSOC's four designations have been insurers: AIG, Prudential, and MetLife. In addition, Dodd-Frank gave the [Federal Reserve Board] oversight of savings and loan holding companies, which includes 14 holding companies that operate significant insurance companies. A major question remains: How much will the [Federal Reserve Board] exercise its new authority?

Last month, Federal Reserve Board Senior Advisor Thomas Sullivan, who has been identified as the [Federal Reserve Board's] point person on insurance matters, said at an Institute of International Finance conference that the agency sees its role as complementary to state oversight, not duplicative. He also said the [Federal Reserve Board] would focus on group supervision and financial stability rather than on the kind of supervision and regulation of individual insurers that states have been doing for decades. Indeed, the [Federal Reserve Board's] roughly 70 employees who work to one degree or another on insurance could not duplicate the supervisory and regulatory activities of about 12,000 employees of state insurance regulators and the NAIC.

Taken together, FSOC and the [Federal Reserve Board] are in effect saying that states are either unable or ill-suited to deal with supervision of insurance groups and the risks they might pose to U.S. financial stability, but that the [Federal Reserve Board] can and will fill these gaps. Since foreign regulators generally view the [Federal Reserve Board's] increased role in group supervision as a positive—the IMF's 2015 assessment said that the [Federal Reserve Board's] new group supervisory role "has strengthened supervision"—this amounts to an argument for U.S. equivalence on group supervision. Ironically, if the EU accepts this line of argument, it would likely cement the new federal role in insurance oversight in the long run.

---

1. ***Further Developments.*** In June 2015, the EU announced that it was adopting a provisional equivalence decision for the United States with respect to its capital standards, referred to as a Solvency Calculation. This decision appears to be a significant benefit for EU insurers operating in the United States, but does not address the other two areas necessary for a full equivalence determination: group supervision and reinsurance. The EU stated that it expects to make more determinations soon, but there is still a great deal of uncertainty for insurers operating in both markets. The previous excerpt discusses a potential weakness in the states' ability to regulate large insurance companies, but points out that the regulation provided by the Federal Reserve Board could fill the void. Is federal regulation an adequate response to the purported shortcomings in group supervision? Might SIFI designations supplemented by Federal Reserve Board oversight of insurance companies with bank and thrift affiliates prove a credible mechanism for bringing U.S. insurance oversight up to international standards over the long haul? Does it matter that the Federal Reserve Board may end up relying on state-based capital rules and guaranty funds? Does it matter that the Federal Reserve Board apparently assigns only 70 individuals to this task?

2. ***Coordination Going Forward.*** It remains unclear whether the U.S. insurance regulatory system can meaningfully coordinate with international entities. This difficulty has significant implications for Solvency II and the implementation of IAIS guidelines. One barrier to international coordination is the NAIC's inability to create binding international agreements. Since state insurance commissioners cannot create binding international agreements under the Constitution, and the Tenth Amendment limits the federal government's ability to force states into compliance, there is no clear mechanism for the United States to enter into binding international agreements regarding insurance regulation. The fragmented nature of insurance regulation in the United States has made it difficult to turn soft law standards promulgated by the IAIS into binding law. The Dodd-Frank Act sought to remedy this by creating the FIO and granting some powers to the Treasury. Could regulation by the Federal Reserve Board provide a solution to the coordination difficulties presented by the current system of insurance regulation? What would be the shortcomings of such a system? The Dodd-Frank Act provides that the Secretary of the Treasury (with the assistance of the FIO) and the U.S. Trade Representative are jointly authorized to negotiate certain international "covered agreements" dealing with prudential matters in insurance. See § 502 of the Dodd-Frank Act. Following a determination by the FIO, these covered agreements may preempt contrary state laws under certain circumstances. Treasury has indicated its intent to negotiate such a treaty with the EU. A covered agreement might address issues of insurance collateral, group supervision, or other matters, and potentially overrule conflicting state requirements.

PART IV

SECURITIES FIRMS AND CAPITAL MARKETS

CHAPTER 4.1

INTRODUCTION TO THE REGULATION OF SECURITIES FIRMS

CONTENTS

I. OVERVIEW

With this Chapter, we begin our study of the securities sector. As with the regulation of depository institutions and insurance companies, the supervision of securities firms has evolved in a distinctive manner that has left its mark on our modern regulatory structure. There are two main types of securities firms, broker-dealers and investment advisers. We focus principally on broker-dealers, but also discuss investment advisers at various points. In the first few decades of the 20th Century, when the sector first became the subject of serious regulatory attention, the states were the exclusive regulators of securities firms. As you saw in Chapter 1.2, while the Securities Act of 1933 (1933 Act) focused primarily on corporate issuers and public offerings, it was only with the passage of the Securities Exchange Act of 1934 (1934 Act) that the federal government began to regulate securities firms in earnest. Furthermore, with the Investment Advisers Act of 1940, the federal government brought investment advisers under supervisory control. Today, virtually all broker-dealers are regulated at both the state and federal level. Therefore, like depository institutions, broker-dealers operate under a dual system of regulation. Most large investment advisers, meanwhile, are supervised only at the federal level.

Another distinguishing characteristic of U.S. securities firm regulation is the prominence of private organizations, known as self-regulatory organizations (SROs), that perform quasi-governmental functions. Most importantly, FINRA, like its predecessor the National Association of Securities Dealers (NASD), plays a major role in supervising broker-dealers. As you read through these chapters, pay attention to the role of private organizations in this field and consider whether similar systems of self-regulation should be encouraged in other financial fields.

Finally and most significantly, the regulation of securities firms is not just based on the sort of mandatory rules—such as restrictions on activities and formal rate-making procedures—that characterize oversight of the depository institution and insurance fields. Rather, disclosure obligations and fiduciary norms (fashioned as suitability obligations) form the core of broker-dealer regulation in this country. How does this mixture of regulatory controls compare with regulatory structures you have already studied? Is there something about the activities of broker-dealers that make it necessary to employ a different regulatory strategy in this field? Or would it be preferable to move away from such open-ended standards of conduct in this area?

II. A BRIEF HISTORY OF SECURITIES REGULATION

In the second half of the 19th century, when the basic forms of depository institutions and insurance companies were already well-established, a separate class of institutions specializing in the underwriting of corporate securities emerged as a new and significant economic force. These precursors of today's securities sector included J.P. Morgan & Co., Kidder, Peabody, and Brown Brothers. The firms were primarily located in the eastern financial centers of New York, Boston, and Philadelphia, and many of the larger firms were affiliated with firms in Europe. As a group, these investment banks played a major role in the industrialization of the U.S. economy, helping railroads and industrial firms like U.S. Steel raise large amounts of capital. Until the end of the century, securities underwritten through private banks were primarily debt instruments, which were largely sold to institutional holders or wealthy clients. With the turn of the century, however, the securities business underwent several profound changes, transforming the sector and our regulatory structure.

Jonathan R. Macey & Geoffrey P. Miller, Origins of the Blue Sky Laws

70 TEX. L. REV. 347, 352–54 (1991)

A number of factors coalesced to create active public securities markets during [the last years of the nineteenth century. The growth of large industries such as railroads and heavy manufacturing stimulated unprecedented demands for capital. At the same time, increases in wealth among the middle classes created a new source of capital that could be tapped effectively by means of public securities issuance. Developments in transportation and communication technology made widespread promotion and distribution of securities practicable. Realizing the potential purchasing power of the rising middle class, bond issuers began to offer securities in denominations of $100 instead of the traditional denominations of $1,000 or even $10,000. A surge of new investment followed.

Most securities sold to investors during this period were reputable and safe—the classic examples being railroad and municipal bonds. Interest rates on these securities were low, however. For the investor with a taste for risk, plenty of speculative issues were available in the market. . . . [T]he speculative securities in the early 1900s were typically equity securities issued by mining and petroleum companies, land development schemes (such as irrigation and tract housing projects), and patent development promotions. . . .

Sales of speculative securities surged in the period from 1910 to 1911. The relatively high inflation prevailing during this period spurred investors to seek high-yielding investments such as bonds of smaller railroads, public utilities, and industrial firms. These investments, while still relatively safe, paid as much as 6 percent as compared with blue chip bonds at 4 to 4½ percent. Equity securities offered even greater potential yields—albeit coupled with greater risk—while hedging against inflation. Meanwhile a strong agricultural economy from 1910 to 1912 placed disposable income in the hands of the American farmer, who sometimes invested in securities that were as alluring as they were ultimately unwise.

The First World War, and more particularly the government's efforts to finance the war through the sale of Liberty Bonds to the general public, accelerated the expansion of the securities sector:

> Financial institutions were expected to assist the government in widely distributing the large war loans. They were encouraged to lend investors the purchase price of government bonds on liberal repayment terms. By the end of the war, every large urban bank throughout the country was involved in the creation of an atmosphere favorable to security investment that ultimately reached over 14 million Americans.
>
> . . . After 1919, corporations of all types, not just railroads and heavy industries, discovered an American public, now committed to the investing habit, very receptive to new security issues of an unprecedented frequency and dollar volume. As a consequence of this new access to the supply of long-term capital, many companies found they were far less reliant on banks to provide short-term, seasonal financing. In addition, high profits gave many corporations such a large cash flow that outside borrowing was unnecessary. This decline in loan demand threatened the earning power of commercial banks and encouraged them to seek other opportunities for profit.

> An expansion of investment banking functions to offset the reduction in loan revenues was a course chosen by [many] large urban institutions.

Edwin J. Perkins, *The Divorce of Commercial and Investment Banking: A History*, 88 BANKING L.J. 483, 491–93 (1970).

The forays of commercial banks into investment banking in the 1920s were halted in 1933 with the passage of the Glass-Steagall Act, as discussed in Chapter 1.2 and which we will consider more in Chapter 6.1. For now, however, we focus on the problems that the expanding securities sector created in the first few decades of the 20th century, and how the states and then the federal government first responded to those problems.

A. EARLY REGULATION AND STATE BLUE SKY LAWS

Perhaps not surprisingly in light of their primacy in other forms of financial regulation at the time, the states were the first to develop a supervisory structure for the emerging securities sector. Kansas's adoption of legislation in 1911 is generally considered to be the first state securities regulation statute, and forty-six other jurisdictions followed suit before any action was taken at the federal level. The following excerpt provides a brief overview of these early state regulatory initiatives and the problems they faced:

Elisabeth Keller & Gregory A. Gehlmann, A Historical Introduction to the Securities Act of 1933 and the Securities Exchange Act of 1934

49 OHIO ST. L.J. 329, 331–33 (1988)

State securities statutes were known as 'blue sky' laws, because some lawmakers believed that 'if securities legislation was not passed, financial pirates would sell citizens everything in [the] state but the blue sky.' Legislators were reacting to both genuine and spurious complaints . . . regarding fraudulent securities deals. . . .

Blue sky laws varied from state to state but can be classified into two broad categories: antifraud laws and licensing laws. Antifraud laws did not take effect until evidence appeared that fraud had been or was about to be committed in the sale of securities. State authorities were empowered by statute to investigate suspected fraud and could enjoin such fraudulent activities and in some cases undertake criminal proceedings. Licensing laws gave state officials control over traffic in securities by prohibiting sales until an application was filed and permission granted by the state. Officials of the state agency, charged with enforcement of this type of blue sky law, usually reviewed detailed information supplied by the issuer regarding the issuer's financial history and present status and passed judgment on the soundness of the securities offering. If the securities appeared to meet the statutory requirements, the issuer was permitted to sell the securities within the state. . . .

Many states boasted of great success. . . . In reality, the laws proved quite ineffective for several reasons. First, responsibility for the enforcement of these laws was delegated to 'unspecialized attorneys working for state officials as disparate as the railroad commission or the state auditor. When political administrations changed, responsibility for blue sky law enforcement frequently also was reassigned.' In addition to the lack of expertise among the enforcers, state funding was generally inadequate to support the fulltime manpower needed to investigate the securities and to take remedial or prosecutional action. Also, many states were deliberately lax in the regulation of securities traffic in order to attract outside industry and to prevent the exodus of industry to more lenient states. . . .

In 1917, the Supreme Court clearly established the constitutionality of blue sky laws. [*See Hall v. Geiger-Jones Co.*, 242 U.S. 539 (1917).] By that time the laws had already been analyzed by the securities industry, in particular, the Investment Banker's Association (IBA), an organization interested in resisting regulation. In 1915, the IBA informed its members that the blue sky laws could be evaded easily by operating across state lines. Promoters could sell their securities through the mails in other states, as long as the sale was finalized through an acceptance from the seller's office by mail or telegram. Since a sale consists of an offer and acceptance, until the buyer accepts an offer there is no sale. Under the law of contracts, the sale is legally made at the place where the acceptance is given. Sellers took great care to avoid the jurisdiction of states that had effective statutes. Even with offers that were strictly intrastate, effective lobbying, principally by the IBA, riddled the statutes with exemptions. . . .

The blue sky laws were not much of an obstacle for the fraudulent promoter. According to contemporary reports, promoters used the devices noted above to continue their dealings. They selected ventures, such as mining, oil, or real estate, and set up companies with no legitimate prospects, in order to sell stock. In 1922, a movement was begun to draft uniform blue sky legislation directed at eliminating some of the inherent problems that permitted evasion of the laws. At the time of the enactment of the federal securities laws, no state had adopted the uniform act that had been drafted between 1922 and 1930 by the National Conference of Commissioners on Uniform State Laws.

B. SECURITIES REGULATION AND THE NEW DEAL

Though federal legislation was not adopted until the 1930s, a number of congressional investigations foreshadowed that development. For example, following the lead of the Armstrong Commission's study of corruption in the New York life insurance sector, a congressional investigation popularly known as the Pujo Committee instituted its own investigation of J.P. Morgan and other members of the Money Trust in 1912. Many of the committee's findings, which concerned excessive compensation and favoritism of investment bankers, found their way into Louis Brandeis's celebrated Other People's Money (1914). Brandeis recommended mandatory disclosure as the appropriate response to the excesses of Wall Street, commenting that, "[p]ublicity is justly commended as a remedy for social and industrial diseases. Sunlight is said to be the best of disinfectants; electric light the most efficient policeman."

Despite the early support for federal intervention and the increasingly obvious deficiencies of state blue sky laws, no significant federal legislation was adopted in the 1920s. The Republican administrations of the post-World War I era were reluctant to interfere with the business world, and the not-yet overturned *Paul v. Virginia* decision cast doubt on the constitutionality of federal regulation over securities transactions. These concerns, however, were not entirely resolved until the Supreme Court implicitly endorsed the constitutionality of the federal securities laws in *Jones v. SEC.*, 298 U.S. 1 (1936). The Republicans' laissez-faire attitude came to an end with the Crash of 1929, which you learned about in Chapter 1.2.

The Crash and the depression that followed transformed U.S. financial services. In the presidential elections of 1932, New York Governor Franklin Roosevelt defeated Herbert Hoover and brought to Washington a new team of economic advisers intent on imposing vigorous federal authority to oversee the country's financial markets. Their offensive began with a congressional investigation into stock exchange practices. Under the leadership of Ferdinand Pecora, counsel of the Senate Banking Committee and former New York prosecutor, the hearings explored charges of corruption and shady practices.

Many witnesses alleged that underwriters had marketed securities to the general public without revealing critical information about the purpose of the offering or the prospects of the issuer. Others claimed securities firms were also manipulating market prices. In a typical scheme, called a bear raid, securities firms would collude to depress the price of a particular stock, either through short sales or even illusory wash sales, with the intention of prompting other investors to sell their shares in a panic and then later buying the securities back at a lower price. Witnesses also repeatedly charged securities firms with favoritism in their treatment of customers. Hearings uncovered many instances in which either officers of the securities firms or else colleagues and acquaintances were given investment opportunities that were not shared with the general public.

By bringing these charges and other evidence of corruption to light, the Pecora hearings awakened the public to the need for federal regulation. Precisely what form this federal regulation should take remained a subject of considerable debate for the first few years of the first Roosevelt Administration. Some of the more diehard New Dealers argued that the government had to take an active role in conducting merit reviews of the quality and appropriateness of publicly-traded securities, a role the government had in fact played to a limited degree during the First World War. In fact, a number of state blue sky laws in place at the time operated in this way. The alternative view opposed such intrusive government involvement and advanced a Brandeisian vision of a disclosure-based regulation.

1. The Securities Act of 1933: Oversight of Public Offerings

The first of the New Deal securities statutes, the 1933 Act, established a federal system for the registration of new issues of securities. The direct subjects of the 1933 Act's regulation were corporations making public offerings. From the perspective of the securities sector, the primary importance of this legislation was its imposition of federal authority over the underwriting process. Under the federal securities laws, underwriting is a term of art. *See* § 2(11) of the 1933 Act (entailing the distribution of securities to the general public). Among other things, the 1933 Act established elaborate procedural and disclosure requirements for public offerings of securities. The 1933 Act required the registration statement to contain specified information about the security, the issuer, and the underwriters. The 1933 Act also established a stringent system of civil, administrative, and criminal sanctions designed to ensure compliance with the 1933 Act's procedural and disclosure requirements.

While it had a profound effect on capital formation, the 1933 Act was recognized from the start as the first phase of federal regulation over the securities sector. The 1933 Act, for example, had little impact on the secondary securities markets—that is, the trading markets where many of the abuses uncovered in the Pecora hearings had occurred—nor did the 1933 Act directly regulate securities firms themselves. Indeed, as far as the securities sector was concerned, the 1933 Act was arguably not even the most important piece of federal legislation passed that year. From a structural perspective, the Banking Act of 1933, which included the Glass-Steagall Act provisions mandating the separation of commercial and investment banking, was more important because it separated a large portion of the sector from commercial banking affiliates.

2. The Securities Exchange Act of 1934: Regulation of Exchanges

The 1934 Act addressed the more complex problem of establishing federal oversight in the country's trading markets. Because the 1934 Act is a multi-faceted statute, it is more difficult to summarize than the 1933 Act. As a preliminary matter, it is important to recognize that the political climate had changed a considerable degree between 1933 and 1934. Worsening economic conditions caused some in Congress and many in the business world to question the wisdom of the stringent new requirements of the 1933 Act. Accordingly, the Roosevelt Administration was more inclined to seek compromises in 1934, and the legislation enacted that year, which somewhat weakened the liability rules of the 1933 Act, reflects that attitude.

The central compromise of the 1934 Act was its acceptance of the continued importance of the major stock exchanges, most notably the NYSE, which was then, as it is now, the largest and more prominent trading market in the United States. Rather than impose direct federal control over the trading markets, the 1934 Act required all stock exchanges to register with the federal government and become, along with their member firms, subject to SEC oversight. This process transformed exchanges from private enterprises to quasi-public SROs. In turn, the registered exchanges regulated all companies with securities listed on these exchanges, namely by imposing periodic disclosure requirements similar to the 1933 Act's requirements for public offerings.

The 1934 Act also created a new federal agency, the SEC, and charged it with overseeing the exchanges and also administering the requirements of the 1933 Act, which had previously been under the jurisdiction of the Federal Trade Commission. The initial staffing of the SEC reflected the pragmatism of the time. While a number of prominent New Dealers were appointed as members of the SEC, Roosevelt picked former market manipulator Joseph P. Kennedy to be the SEC's first chair. According to one witness to the decision, "[t]he President has great confidence in him because he has made his pile . . . and knows all the tricks of the trade." While Kennedy was SEC chair for only one year, he played a major role in launching the agency by attracting an expert staff and developing a reputation for effective and pragmatic oversight.

The 1934 Act also gave the SEC a number of tools to improve the integrity of the nation's markets. For example, the 1934 Act included several substantive rules designed to curb market manipulation, including the specific practices identified in the Pecora hearings. The 1934 Act also granted the SEC open-ended rulemaking authority with which to address other manipulation and fraudulent activities. The most prominent example of this power is §10(b), under which the SEC promulgated the now familiar Rule 10b-5 in 1942. Section 15(c) of the 1934 Act includes a similarly broad mandate for the SEC to develop specialized anti-fraud rules for the broker-dealer sector. In an effort to restrain speculation, the 1934 Act also authorized the Federal Reserve Board to regulate credit used to finance stock purchases.

3. The 1938 Amendments and the Creation of the NASD

Perhaps not surprisingly in light of the many compromises written into the 1934 Act, the years immediately following the 1934 Act's enactment were characterized by low-level warfare between the existing exchanges, primarily the NYSE, and the SEC over dominance in the securities sector. Politically, the exchange—and its President, Richard Whitney—were well-connected and maintained close ties with both the Roosevelt Administration and Congress. Although the federal securities laws were a centerpiece of the New Deal, experts remained divided over how much authority the SEC should exercise over the NYSE in its dealings with its members. Defenders of the NYSE argued that the new federal securities laws were contributing to the continuing economic problems of the Great Depression and asserted that further regulation would only worsen the situation.

In 1938, the tide moved against the exchanges. There was internal division within the NYSE's membership as the old guard—the elite private banking houses represented by Whitney—increasingly opposed governmental intrusions into their enclave, while rank and file members, who had extensive retail networks and depended on consumer confidence for their livelihood, favored reform efforts to improve their situation. The final blow fell when it was discovered that Whitney was embezzling client funds and was convicted of grand larceny. In the wake of the Whitney scandal, the NYSE revised its internal operations to ensure a more rigorous review of its members. In addition, the position of the retail-broker members of the exchange was generally enhanced at the expense of the old guard.

When William O. Douglas became chair of the SEC in 1937, one of his primary goals was to bring the over-the-counter markets under commission control. As Douglas recognized, the 1934 Act left an asymmetry of regulation between exchanges and OTC markets; securities listed on the exchanges were subject to a more extensive system of regulation than those traded on the OTC markets and securities firms that were members of exchanges came under indirect SEC oversight, whereas broker-dealers that limited themselves to OTC markets were, effectively, free from federal regulation, aside from several general and inadequately enforced anti-fraud rules. The OTC markets were, moreover, a difficult environment to supervise. Unlike the exchanges, these markets had no physical location; rather, they typically consisted of a loose network of dealers connected through telegraph lines or the circulation of quotation sheets. In addition, unlike the exchanges, the OTC markets had no formal organizational structure onto which federal supervision could be superimposed. Under the original 1934 Act, the only way for the SEC to reach the over-the-counter markets was through direct federal oversight, and the size and complexity of the market made that approach a daunting prospect.

Douglas found the solution to this dilemma on another plank of the New Deal platform. At roughly the same time that the federal securities laws were enacted, Congress adopted the National Industrial Recovery Act, under which industries were encouraged to form themselves into trade associations and adopt binding codes of fair trade practices to alleviate perceived problems of excessive competition. In *Schechter Poultry Corp. v. United States*, 295 U.S. 495 (1935), the Supreme Court struck down the National Industrial Recovery Act as an unconstitutional delegation of power, but before the National Industrial Recovery Act's demise, the Investment Banker's Association began to fashion a Code Committee to oversee OTC market activities. The SEC, hesitant to cede too much of its enforcement power, urged the creation of a cooperative system:

> In December 1937, Douglas invited leaders of the investment banking community to discuss means of better coordinating enforcement activities. At the meeting several bankers agreed with an SEC proposal to amend the [1934 Act] to give voluntary associations like the Investment Bankers Conference an official status similar to that of the organized exchanges "in order to enable the associations to undertake effective programs of enforcement." Douglas soon emphasized to a congressional committee that if effective self-regulation of the securities exchanges were to succeed, the SEC could not compromise its enforcement role, but should play a residual role: "Government would keep the shotgun, so to speak, behind the door, loaded, well oiled, cleaned, ready for use but with the hope it would never have to be used."

SELIGMAN, THE TRANSFORMATION OF WALL STREET, at 185.

With the passage of the Maloney Act of 1938, Congress accepted Douglas's recommendation and created a self-regulatory system for the OTC market based on the principle of cooperative regulation. Modeled after the 1934 Act's treatment of exchanges, the Maloney Act provided for the formation of national securities associations that would, under the supervision of the SEC, have the power to promulgate rules governing voluntary membership of non-exchange broker-dealers. The NASD is the only such association ever formed, and survives as a lineal descendent of the National Industrial Recovery Act.

C. FURTHER REFINEMENTS OF THE MODERN ERA

In the years following the Maloney Act, the SEC's authority over the broker-dealer sector and the trading market gradually expanded and solidified. Between 1945 and 1962, the number of salespersons registered with the NASD increased from 25,000 to 95,000 and the number of broker-dealer branch offices increased from 790 to 4,713. The professionalism of many of the new entrants, however, was inconsistent, and a number of registered representatives were inadequately trained and poorly supervised. In response to these and other concerns, the SEC undertook a Special Study of the Securities Markets, which resulted in the Securities Act Amendments of 1964. These amendments expanded the substantive authority of the SEC over broker-dealer affairs and mandated additional standards regarding broker-dealer competence and capital. In addition, before 1964, the SEC could only suspend or revoke a firm's registration; the amendments extended this power to include the authority to censure and placed limitations on the activities, functions, or operations of a broker-dealer. The 1964 amendments also closed the last major loophole in OTC regulation: the disclosure obligations of issuers of securities trading in that market. As mentioned earlier, the original 1934 Act had imposed mandatory disclosure obligations only on issuers with securities listed on registered exchanges. Not until the 1964 amendments did Congress expand the 1934 Act to establish similar periodic disclosure requirements for public companies with securities traded in OTC markets.

The next important amendment to the federal securities laws was enacted in 1970, when Congress passed a series of changes designed, among other things, to respond to the back office crisis of the 1960s. During this crisis, a number of broker-dealers fell into insolvency and many customer securities were lost or misapplied, leaving customers unable to recover their assets from a bankruptcy trustee or receivership. In addition to tightening financial standards for the sector, the 1970 amendments created the Securities Investor Protection Corporation (SIPC) to guarantee the safekeeping of customer securities and cash balances held by registered broker-dealers and to oversee broker-dealer liquidations. As discussed in Chapter 2.4, SIPC provides coverage for up to $500,000 in losses for an individual account, of which not more than $100,000 may be in cash balances. SIPC coverage does not extend to losses on securities from market fluctuations or to losses from fraudulent or manipulative activities by broker-dealers. Analogous to the FDIC, SIPC is financed by an annual assessment of members, supported by a residual and as-yet-unused billion-dollar line of credit from U.S. Treasury.

In 1975, Congress again adopted major amendments to the 1934 Act. Most of the 1975 amendments were designed to increase competition in trading markets and to develop a more unified national market system. Chapter 4.4 of this book discusses these aspects of the amendments in some detail. The 1975 reforms also expanded the scope of SEC authority over pockets of the securities sector that were previously exempted from federal oversight. Most significantly, the 1975 amendments expanded SEC authority over municipal securities broker-dealers, and established a new SRO—the Municipal Securities Rulemaking Board—to develop uniform guidelines for this segment of the sector. Eleven years later, in 1986, Congress made a comparable extension of broker-dealer coverage when it enacted yet another registration requirement for broker-dealers that limited their business to U.S. government securities.

The final decades of the 20th century saw numerous additional refinements of SEC authority over the broker-dealer sector. For example, in 1984 and 1988, Congress enacted a series of technical amendments aimed at reducing insider trading and imposing new supervisory obligations on the broker-dealer sector. In 1990, Congress further amended the 1934 Act to expand the array of the SEC's supervisory powers, making them roughly comparable to the enhanced powers granted to federal bank and thrift regulators in the post-thrift crisis reforms of 1989. The 1990 reforms also included a new statutory directive for the regulation of penny stock fraud, and enhanced SEC powers for dealing with sudden market drops, such as the market break of October 1987.

1. Realignment of Federal-State Authority Over Broker-Dealers

The enactment of the National Securities Market Improvements Act of 1996 (NSMIA) was the last amendment to the 1934 Act before the Dodd-Frank Act and signals a realignment of supervisory authority over the securities sector. The original federal securities statutes enacted in the 1930s were intended to supplement, not supersede, existing state blue sky laws. Both the 1933 Act and the 1934 Act had savings clauses that expressly preserved state law unless they were in direct conflict with federal requirements. Out of concern that overlapping state and federal regimes impose unnecessary costs, NSMIA partially repealed the traditional joint federal-state oversight. In particular, NSMIA added §15(h) to the 1934 Act, which invalidates all state or local laws that "establish capital, custody, margin, financial responsibility, [record-keeping], bonding, or financial or operational reporting requirements for brokers, dealers, municipal securities dealers, government securities brokers, or government securities dealers that differ from, or are in addition to the requirements" of the 1934 Act. Left unaffected by this new provision were state anti-fraud rules and other common law rights and remedies. NSMIA also reconfigured the oversight of investment advisers, leaving the responsibility of smaller firms largely to state authorities and focusing SEC oversight on larger investment advisers. For a review of the impact of the 1996 legislation, see Howard M. Friedman, *The Impact of NSMIA on State Regulation of Broker-Dealers and Investment Advisers*, 53 BUS. LAW. 511 (1998).

2. The Emergence of FINRA

Another important regulatory change of the past two decades has been the emergence of FINRA as a consolidated self-regulatory organization for securities firms, combining functions that were previously the responsibility of the NASD and stock exchange personnel.

a. The National Association of Securities Dealers

As mentioned earlier, the NASD was established as the self-regulatory organization for OTC dealers in 1939, and the NASD founded what is now known as the NASDAQ in 1971, a trading venue for major OTC stocks.

In 1994, the DOJ announced that it was investigating potentially anticompetitive practices in the OTC stock market based, in part, on an academic study detecting pricing anomalies in the NASDAQ market suggesting collusive behavior on the part of securities firms. *See* Joel Seligman, *Cautious Evolution or Perennial Irresolution: Stock Market Self-Regulation During the First Seventy Years of the Securities and Exchange Commission*, 59 BUS. LAW. 1347, 1354, 1368 (2004). The SEC launched a parallel investigation of NASDAQ's trading practices that year. As a result of these investigations, the NASD appointed former Senator Warren Rudman to head a review of NASDAQ's structure and governance. Rudman's study found that the NASD's governance structure blurred the distinction between regulating the broker-dealer profession and overseeing the NASDAQ stock market and recommended reconstituting the NASD into a parent company with two subsidiaries: NASDAQ and NASD Regulation Inc., as the entity responsible for regulating broker-dealers. The Board of Governors of the NASD adopted these recommendations, which were approved by the SEC on July 11, 1996. The NASD later divested itself of NASDAQ, which later became a private for-profit exchange and later became part of the NASDAQ OMX Group of exchanges.

b. NYSE Regulation

In 1999, the NYSE announced its intent to demutualize and become a for-profit corporation. Following this announcement, Arthur Levitt, then-Chairman of the SEC, expressed concerns that a for-profit NYSE could conflict with its role as an SRO. For this reason, as well as several others, the NYSE delayed its demutualization plan. When NYSE eventually merged with Archipelago Holdings in 2006 to become a publicly traded company, NYSE Regulation was transferred to a separate entity that was not part of the for-profit corporation. This change was necessary in order to obtain the SEC's approval of the merger.

c. Consolidation into FINRA

In November 2006, the NASD and NYSE Regulation announced their plan to consolidate their member regulation operations into a single SRO, and on March 19, 2007, the NASD filed a proposed rule change to amend the bylaws of the NASD to implement the governance changes necessary to effect the consolidation. After reviewing extensive public comments on the matter, the SEC approved the consolidation of the NASD and the member regulation, arbitration and enforcement functions of NYSE Regulation on July 26, 2007.

Pursuant to the consolidation, the regulation, arbitration, and enforcement functions of NYSE Regulation, as well as its employees, were transferred to the NASD, and the NASD changed its name to FINRA. As a result of the consolidation, FINRA has responsibility for regulatory oversight of all securities firms; training, testing and licensing of registered persons; arbitration and mediation of disputes; market regulation by contract for certain exchanges; and providing trade reporting and other utilities.

In March 2008, FINRA published an information notice that set forth the process for consolidating the NASD and NYSE Regulation regulations into a new consolidated rulebook. The consolidation process is still underway. To facilitate the transition to the FINRA Rulebook, conversion charts demonstrating how the FINRA rules relate to the NASD rules or Incorporated NYSE Rules that they replace are available on FINRA's website. A number of the materials presented in this section of the book make reference to earlier versions of NASD and NYSE rules. You can find the FINRA versions of these rules on the FINRA website.

III. OVERVIEW OF THE SECURITIES SECTOR TODAY

A. SECTOR PARTICIPANTS AND LINES OF BUSINESS

As we have done with other sectors of the field, we begin our introduction to the securities sector with a brief summary of the business, distinguishing between broker-dealers and investment advisors.

1. Broker-Dealers

The broker-dealer segment of the securities sector encompasses a diverse set of institutions that fulfill several important functions, such as raising capital for companies, supplying liquidity to markets, and providing investment advice to customers. The following excerpt describes the segment's general composition:

> The securities industry includes a large number of firms and individuals. Brokerage firms range from national companies employing tens of thousands of brokers to sole proprietorships located in remote towns. The Securities Industry and Financial Markets Association ("SIFMA"), the securities [sector's] trade and research group, divides the industry into four principal categories: (1) major firms consisting of national full-line firms and large investment banks; (2) the largest full-line regional firms (outside New York City); (3) the largest full-line regional firms of the New York City area; and (4) discount brokerage firms that are NYSE members. In 2012, approximately 4,358 broker-dealers did a public business. The most important segment of the securities industry consists of the 190 member firms of the NYSE (as of the end of 2012) that do business directly with the public. Although these firms comprised approximately 4% of all broker-dealers, they accounted for 63% of all revenues and 87% of all assets of the securities industry. At the end of 2012, securities firms employed approximately 819,900 persons in the United States, about 21% of whom worked in New York City, the financial center of the United States. The New York City employment number has been steadily declining over the years. The broker-dealers had approximately 630,000 registered representatives. As a result of the recent financial crisis, employment in the securities industry, particularly in New York City and State, declined. . . .

NORMAN S. POSNER & JAMES A FANTO, BROKER-DEALER LAW AND REGULATION 1-8 to 1-10 (2015) (reproduced with the permission of publisher).

In certain respects, the structure of the securities sector is similar to the structure of other sectors of financial services. There are a very large number of firms engaged in the securities business, though the number has been declining in recent years. Of this group, a relatively small number of firms based in New York City play a dominant role, especially in the high-profile and high-profit field of investment banking, which we will consider in more detail in Chapter 4.3.

Within the broker-dealer sector, there is a small group of securities firms known as primary dealers that trade directly with the Federal Reserve System and play a crucial role in U.S. monetary policy. The Federal Reserve Bank of New York describes these dealers' role in the monetary system as follows:

> Primary dealers serve as trading counterparties of the [Federal Reserve Bank of New York] in its implementation of monetary policy. This role includes the obligations to: (i) participate consistently in open market operations to carry out U.S. monetary policy pursuant to the direction of the Federal Open Market Committee (FOMC); and (ii) provide the [Federal Reserve Bank of New York's] trading desk with market information and analysis helpful in the formulation and implementation of monetary policy. Primary dealers are also required to participate in all auctions of U.S. government debt and to make reasonable markets for the [Federal Reserve Bank of New York] when it transacts on behalf of its foreign official account-holders.

FED. RESERVE BANK OF NEW YORK, PRIMARY DEALERS LIST. Notable primary dealers include Barclays Capital, Inc., Goldman, Sachs & Co., J.P. Morgan Securities LLC, and Morgan Stanley & Co. LLC. For a complete list of the twenty-two primary dealers in the United States, see *id.*

2. Investment Advisers

Investment advisers also play an integral role in the broker-dealer sector, aptly described by the following excerpt:

> Over 11,000 investment advisers are registered with the [SEC]. As of September 30, 2010, [SEC]-registered advisers managed more than $38 trillion for more than 14 million clients. In addition, there are more than 275,000 state-registered investment adviser representatives and more than 15,000 state-registered investment advisers. Approximately 5% of [SEC]-registered investment advisers are also registered as broker-dealers, and 22% have a related person that is a broker-dealer. Additionally, approximately 88% of investment adviser representatives are registered representatives of broker-dealers. A majority of [SEC]-registered investment advisers reported that over half of their assets under management related to the accounts of individual clients. Most investment advisers charge their clients fees based on the percentage of assets under management, while others may charge hourly or fixed rates.

SEC, STUDY ON INVESTMENT ADVISERS AND BROKER-DEALERS iii (Jan. 2011).

Note the very large number of investment advisers that are denominated state-registered and thus largely outside of SEC supervision. This dominant role of state supervision over smaller firms contrasts with the operation of the dual banking system with respect to smaller state-chartered banks and thrifts, all of which are subject to substantial and direct federal oversight, typically through the FDIC. Does it make sense for the federal government to impose such a light touch on small investment advisers, given its practices with respect to smaller banks and thrifts? Before answering this question, consider the following statistics concerning the recent growth of small investment advisors:

> In the very first Moss Adams study, published in 2002, revenue for the average participating firm was $600,000. Today, the average revenue for firms in the study is $3.5 million. That's an annualized growth rate of 19.3% for the last 10 years, which means the average advisory firm doubles in size in just under four years . . . . The InvestmentNews/Moss Adams study highlights the evolutionary stages of an advisory firm, breaking the industry into three distinct types of practices. . . . The first is the "solo," a firm with a single, client-facing professional. The next is the "ensemble," a firm with more than one adviser and with less than $5 million in annual revenue. The third is the "superensemble," a multiprofessional firm with $5 million or more in annual revenue. . . . The average financial advisory firm in the study has a staff of seven, and the most common job description is "employee adviser." More than 80% of the participants were ensemble firms. In addition, there were 61 firms with more than $5 million in revenue and/or $1 billion in assets under management.

Bruce Kelly, *Financial Advice Firms Soar*, INVESTMENTNEWS, Oct. 6, 2013.

As with broker-dealers, there is substantial segmentation of the investment advisory business, with firms operating on different scales and pursuing disparate business models. How should regulators respond to this diversity?

B. STATE-FEDERAL ALLOCATIONS OF AUTHORITY AND SELF-REGULATORY ORGANIZATION

The following excerpt, drawn from a recent SEC study, offers a succinct overview of the allocation of regulatory authority over securities firms in the United States. In Chapter 4.2, we will turn to this study's focus, which was a congressionally-mandated inquiry into the question of whether broker-dealers and investment advisers should be subject to harmonized regulatory standards, at least with respect to fiduciary duties to advisory clients.

SEC, Regulation of Investment Advisers and Broker-Dealers

Study on Investment Advisers and Broker-Dealers, iii-v (Jan. 2011)

The regulatory schemes for investment advisers and broker-dealers are designed to protect investors through different approaches. Investment advisers are fiduciaries to their clients, and the regulation under the [Investment] Advisers Act generally is principles-based. The regulation of broker-dealers governs how broker-dealers operate, for the most part, through the Commission's antifraud authority in the [1933 Act] and the [1934 Act], specific [1934 Act] rules, and SRO rules based on [1934 Act] principles, including (among others) principles of fairness and transparency. Certain differences in the regulation of broker-dealers and advisers reflect differences, current and historical, in their functions, while others may reflect differences in the regulatory regime, particularly when investment advisers and broker-dealers are engaging in the same or substantially similar activity. . . .

Investment Advisers: An investment adviser is a fiduciary whose duty is to serve the best interests of its clients, including an obligation not to subordinate clients' interests to its own. Included in the fiduciary standard are the duties of loyalty and care. An adviser that has a material conflict of interest must either eliminate that conflict or fully disclose to its clients all material facts relating to the conflict.

In addition, the Advisers Act expressly prohibits an adviser, acting as principal for its own account, from effecting any sale or purchase of any security for the account of a client, without disclosing certain information to the client in writing before the completion of the transaction and obtaining the client's consent.

The states also regulate the activities of many investment advisers. Most smaller investment advisers are registered and regulated at the state level. Investment adviser representatives of state- and federally-registered advisers commonly are subject to state registration, licensing or qualification requirements.

Broker-Dealers: Broker-dealers that do business with the public generally must become members of FINRA. Under the antifraud provisions of the federal securities laws and SRO rules, including SRO rules relating to just and equitable principles of trade and high standards of commercial honor, broker-dealers are required to deal fairly with their customers. While broker-dealers are generally not subject to a fiduciary duty under the federal securities laws, courts have found broker-dealers to have a fiduciary duty under certain circumstances. Moreover, broker-dealers are subject to statutory, [SEC] and SRO requirements that are designed to promote business conduct that protects customers from abusive practices, including practices that may be unethical but may not necessarily be fraudulent. The federal securities laws and rules and SRO rules address broker-dealer conflicts in one of three ways: express prohibition; mitigation; or disclosure.

An important aspect of a broker-dealer's duty of fair dealing is the suitability obligation, which generally requires a broker-dealer to make recommendations that are consistent with the interests of its customer. Broker-dealers also are required under certain circumstances, such as when making a recommendation, to disclose material conflicts of interest to their customers, in some cases at the time of the completion of the transaction. The federal securities laws and FINRA rules restrict broker-dealers from participating in certain transactions that may present particularly acute potential conflicts of interest. At the state level, broker-dealers and their agents must register with or be licensed by the states in which they conduct their business.

Examination and Enforcement Resources

The [SEC]'s Office of Compliance Inspections and Examinations ("OCIE") examines [SEC]-registered investment advisers using a risk-based approach. Due, among other things, to an increase in the number of [SEC]-registered advisers, a decrease in the number of OCIE staff, and a greater focus on more complex examinations, the number and frequency of examinations of these advisers [has] decreased in recent years . . . .

FINRA has primary responsibility for examining broker-dealers. The [SEC] staff also examines broker-dealers, particularly when a risk has been identified or when evaluating the examination work of an SRO, including FINRA, but generally does not examine broker-dealers . . . . The states are responsible for examining state-registered investment advisers, and they work with FINRA and the [SEC] on examinations.

The [SEC] has broad statutory authority under the federal securities laws to investigate violations of the federal securities laws and SRO rules. The [SEC's] Division of Enforcement investigates potential securities law violations, recommends that the [SEC] bring civil actions or institute administrative proceedings, and prosecutes these cases on behalf of the [SEC]. Examples of enforcement actions involving investment advisers include failures to disclose material conflicts of interest, misrepresentations, and other frauds. For broker-dealers, examples include abusive sales practices, failures to disclose material conflicts of interest, misrepresentations, failures to have a reasonable basis for recommending securities, other frauds, failures to reasonably supervise representatives.

---

1. ***The Relationship Between State and Federal Oversight.*** One of the interesting features of U.S. securities regulation is the overlapping roles of state and federal authorities. A leading expert on the topic summarizes the relationship as follows:

> What is the proper relationship between the federal securities laws and state blue sky laws? The federal securities acts expressly allow for concurrent state regulation under the blue sky laws. The state securities acts have traditionally been limited to disclosure and qualification with regard to securities distributions. Typically, the state securities acts have general antifraud provisions to further these ends—especially since, beginning in the 1980s, many states have become involved in the regulation of tender offers . . . which have been federally preempted. . . . NSMIA preempts regulatory provisions but does not preempt state law fraud actions. In contrast, the Securities Litigation Uniform Standards Act of 1998 preempts certain securities fraud class actions involving publicly traded securities.
>
> Other areas where the state and federal laws intersect is with respect to broker-dealer and investment adviser regulation. The states have significant influence over broker-dealer activities both in terms of registration requirements . . . and with respect to enforcement of the antifraud provisions of state law.
>
> In 1996, the Investment Advisers Act was amended to provide for exclusive federal jurisdiction over larger investment advisers and those advising registered investment companies, while reserving regulation of smaller advisers to the states. Investment advisers managing more than $25 million in assets, and advisers to registered investment companies fall under the exclusive jurisdiction of the SEC. All other advisers are subject to the exclusive jurisdiction of the states.

Thomas Lee Hazen, *Treatise on the Law of Securities Regulation*, 2 LAW SEC. REG. § 8.1[2] (Jul. 2015), reprinted with permission of Thomson Reuters. The Dodd-Frank Act raised the asset threshold for SEC oversight of investment advisers to $100 million. Investment advisors managing between $25 million and $100 million in assets generally need not register with the SEC and are subject instead to state registration. 15 U.S.C. § 80b-3a (2011). Note, however, that Wyoming does not have any formal registration requirements for investment advisers. Consequently, an investment adviser whose principal place of business is located in Wyoming must register with the SEC regardless of the amount of assets it has under management. *See, e.g., In re* New Line Capital, LLC, Investment Advisers Act Release No. 4017, Administrative Proceeding No. 3-16371 (Feb. 4, 2015) (sanctioning an investment adviser for maintaining dummy offices in Wyoming so that it could register with the SEC despite having less than $100 million under management).

2. ***The States' Criticism of the SEC's SRO Proposal.*** In 2011, the North American Securities Administrators Association, Inc. testified before Congress on

the SEC's push to establish a self-regulatory organization for investment advisers. Steven Irwin, the Pennsylvania Securities Commissioner and Chairman of the North American Securities Administrators Association's Federal Legislation Committee at the time, first spoke positively about the important role of states in securities regulation:

> State securities regulators have protected Main Street investors from fraud for the past 100 years, longer than any other securities regulator. State securities regulators have continued, more than any other regulators, to focus on protecting retail investors. Our primary goal is to act for the protection of investors, especially those who lack the expertise, experience, and resources to protect their own interests. . . . Traditionally, state securities regulators have pursued perpetrators at the local level who are trying to defraud "mom and pop" investors in your states, leaving the SEC to focus on larger, more complex fraudulent activities involving the securities market at a national level. States have investigated violations on a national level such as the successful state effort to expose and force Wall Street to correct rampant conflicts of interest among stock analysts. We led all regulators on late trading and market timing in mutual funds. And state securities regulators continue to lead the nationwide effort to address problems related to the offer and sale of auction rate securities, an effort that has resulted in the largest return of funds to investors in history; more than $61 billion.

Steven D. Irwin, Pennsylvania Securities Commissioner and Chairman, Federal Legislation Committee, North American Securities Administrators Association, Inc., Testimony Before the House Subcommittee on Capital Markets and Government Sponsored Enterprises, "Ensuring Appropriate Regulatory Oversight of Broker-Dealers and Legislative Proposals to Improve Investment Adviser Oversight" (Sept. 13, 2011).

Building further on these themes, Irwin then criticized the SEC's proposal to create a self-regulatory organization for investment advisers as a hindrance to coordinated federal and state regulation:

> [Investment adviser regulation] should continue to be the responsibility of state and federal governments . . . [G]overnment regulators bring to the table decades of experience unmatched by any entity in existence. We see little benefit in constructing a new layer of bureaucracy, with its incumbent expense. If the goal is strengthening investor protection through improvements to the oversight of SEC regulated investment advisers, then the shortest distance to the goal is to ensure that federal regulators are adequately funded and have the resources to properly oversee investment advisers for the protection of Main Street investors. Most importantly, government regulators are answerable to our constituents, and not to a Board of Directors. . . .
>
> We appreciate the Chairman's desire to enhance regulation for investment advisers, but as we read the Chairman's discussion draft, it would require the small and mid-sized firms to register with the

> new investment adviser SRO. Small and mid-size investment advisers are primarily located in one state and shifting the regulation of these advisers to a SRO headquartered in Washington, DC would increase costs without substantially enhancing investor protection. This would subject these small businesses to duplicative regulation and add new and unnecessary costs . . . Securities regulators are the local "cops on the beat" and best positioned to be the primary regulator for these small and midsize firms.

Id. What do you think of Irwin and North American Securities Administrators Association's position? How might you defend the SEC's proposal? Or would an alternative route, such as requiring investment advisers to hire third-parties to conduct annual audits and examinations, be a better option?

IV. THE REGULATORY PERIMETER

As we have seen in earlier chapters of the book, the regulatory framework for securities firms depends on certain foundational definitions that establish the regulatory perimeter. Key here is the definition of a security itself, a topic that we explore in our discussion of the *Banco Espanol* case, which considered whether loan participations should be securities for purposes of federal securities laws. We will revisit the definition-of-securities question later in the book. After *Banco Espanol*, we will consider the separate question of whether a person or business participates in transactions in securities in such a manner as to be subject to the regulatory requirements that federal securities laws impose on brokers and dealers and investment advisers. Later, in Chapter 4.4, we will take up the analogous question of when trading activities in securities is sufficiently extensive to warrant regulation as a securities exchange.

A. WHAT IS A SECURITY?

Both broker-dealers and investment advisors are defined with reference to activities involving securities. With some minor differences, the term "security" is defined in both the 1933 Act and the 1934 Act, and there is a wide body of case law that has developed to interpret this definition. A detailed discussion of these cases would be more suited for a course on securities regulation. We will focus here on the *Banco Espanol* case, which illustrates the definitional problem by exploring the boundaries of securities regulation and banking regulation:

Banco Espanol de Credito v. Security Pacific National Bank

973 F.2d 51 (2d Cir. 1992)

ALTIMARI, Circuit Judge:

Plaintiffs-appellants, purchasers of various "loan participations" sold by defendants-appellees Security Pacific National Bank and Security Pacific Merchant Bank (collectively "Security Pacific"), appeal from a judgment entered in the United States District Court for the Southern District of New York (Milton Pollack, Judge), granting summary judgment for Security Pacific and dismissing plaintiffs' complaints. In the two underlying actions, which were consolidated for appeal, plaintiffs charged that Security Pacific had withheld material information on the financial solvency of Integrated Resources, Inc.

("Integrated") when Security Pacific sold plaintiffs portions of loan notes owed by Integrated to Security Pacific. Plaintiffs sought to rescind their purchase agreements based on an alleged violation of Section 12(2) of the [1933 Act] and sought damages for Security Pacific's alleged breach of various common law duties.

[The district court granted the defendants' motion for summary judgment, holding that the loan participations were not "securities" within the meaning of the 1933 Act and therefore were not governed by the federal securities laws. The court also held that Security Pacific had no duty to disclose information on Integrated's financial condition].

On appeal, plaintiffs contend that the district court erred in: (1) determining that loan participations sold by Security Pacific were not securities; and (2) determining that Security Pacific owed no duty to disclose negative financial information about Integrated.

BACKGROUND

In 1988, Security Pacific extended a line of credit to Integrated permitting Integrated to obtain short-term unsecured loans from Security Pacific. Security Pacific subsequently made a series of short-term loans to Integrated. Security Pacific sold these loans, in whole or in part, to various institutional investors at differing interest rates. Resales of these loans were prohibited without Security Pacific's express written consent. The practice of selling loans to other institutions is known as "loan participation." Short-term loan participation permits a primary lender such as Security Pacific to spread its risk, while at the same time allowing a purchaser with excess cash to earn a higher return than that available on comparable money market instruments. Security Pacific, as manager of the loans, earned a fee equal to the difference between the interest paid by the debtor and the lower interest paid to the purchaser.

Security Pacific assumed no responsibility for the ability of Integrated to repay its loans. Indeed, each purchaser of loan participations was required to enter into a Master Participation Agreement ("MPA"), which contained a general disclaimer providing, in relevant part, that the purchaser "acknowledges that it has independently and without reliance upon Security [Pacific] and based upon such documents and information as the participant has deemed appropriate, made its own credit analysis."

In late 1988, Integrated began to encounter financial difficulties. In April 1989, Security Pacific refused a request by Integrated to extend further credit. Despite this refusal, Security Pacific continued to sell loan participations on Integrated's debt. Indeed, from mid-April through June 9, 1989, Security Pacific sold seventeen different loan participations to plaintiffs-appellants. Unable to obtain enough working capital, Integrated began defaulting on its loans on June 12, 1989. Integrated subsequently declared bankruptcy.

As a result of Integrated's default, two sets of investors, who had purchased the seventeen loan participations, initiated separate actions against Security Pacific in the United States District Court for the Southern District of New York. Contending that the loan participations were "securities" within the meaning of the [1933 Act], plaintiffs sought to rescind their purchase agreements by alleging that Security Pacific had failed to disclose to them material facts about Integrated's financial condition in violation of § 12(2) of the 1933 Act. 15 U.S.C. § 77l (2). Plaintiffs in each of the two actions moved for partial summary judgment on the securities claim. Security Pacific cross-moved for summary judgment on all claims. The cases were consolidated for argument.

[T]he district court concluded that the loan participations were not "securities" within the meaning of the [1933 Act], and that, therefore, plaintiffs could not assert a violation under § 12(2) of this Act. . . . Accordingly, the district court granted summary judgment to Security Pacific and dismissed the complaints. *See Banco Espanol de Credito v. Security Pacific National Bank*, 763 F.Supp. 36 (S.D.N.Y.1991). Plaintiffs now appeal.

DISCUSSION

Section 2(1) of the 1933 Act provides in pertinent part:

> [U]nless the context otherwise requires—(1) the term "security" means any note . . . evidence of indebtedness, . . . investment contract, . . . or any certificate of interest or participation in . . . any of the foregoing.

15 U.S.C. § 77b(1). It is well-settled that certificates evidencing loans by commercial banks to their customers for use in the customers' current operations are not securities. *See, e.g., Reves v. Ernst & Young*, 494 U.S. 56, 65, 110 S.Ct. 945, 951, 108 L.Ed.2d 47 (1990) (citing *Chemical Bank v. Arthur Andersen & Co.*, 726 F.2d 930, 939 (2d Cir.), *cert. denied*, 469 U.S. 884, 105 S.Ct. 253, 83 L.Ed.2d 190 (1984)). However, as the district court noted, a participation in an instrument might in some circumstances be considered a security even where the instrument itself is not. *See Banco Espanol de Credito*, 763 F.Supp. at 41.

With respect to loan participations, the district court reasoned that "because the plaintiffs . . . did not receive an undivided interest in a pool of loans, but rather purchased participation in a specific, identifiable short-term Integrated loan, the loan participation did not have an identity separate from the underlying loan." *Id.* at 42. Thus, Judge Pollack reasoned, because under Chemical Bank the loans to Integrated were not securities, the plaintiffs' purchase of discrete portions of these loans could not be considered securities.

On appeal, plaintiffs concede that traditional loan participations do not qualify as securities. Instead, plaintiffs contend that the peculiar nature of Security Pacific's loan participation program—which aimed at the sale of 100% of its loans through high speed telephonic sales and often prepaid transactions—qualified these loan participations as securities. Specifically, plaintiffs argue that the loan participations sold by Security Pacific are more properly characterized as securities—in the nature of "notes"—as enumerated in § 2(1) of the 1933 Act.

In examining whether the loan participations could be considered "notes" which are also securities, the district court applied the "family resemblance" test set forth by the Supreme Court in *Reves*, 494 U.S. at 63-67, 110 S.Ct. at 950-952. Under the family resemblance test, a note is presumed to be a security unless an examination of the note, based on four factors, reveals a strong resemblance between the note and one of a judicially-enumerated list of instruments that are not securities. *Id.* at 65, 110 S.Ct. at 951. If the note in question is not sufficiently similar to one of these instruments, a court must then consider, using the same four factors, whether another category of non-security instruments should be added to the list. *Id.* at 67, 110 S.Ct. at 951. The four *Reves* factors to be considered in this examination are: (1) the motivations that would prompt a reasonable buyer and seller to enter into the transaction; (2) the plan of distribution of the instrument; (3) the reasonable expectations of the investing public; and (4) whether some factor, such as the existence of another regulatory scheme, significantly reduces the risk of the instrument, thereby rendering application of the securities laws unnecessary. *Id.* at 66-67, 110 S.Ct. at 951-952.

In addressing the first *Reves* factor, the district court found that Security Pacific was motivated by a desire to increase lines of credit to Integrated while diversifying Security Pacific's risk, that Integrated was motivated by a need for short-term credit at competitive rates to finance its current operations, and that the purchasers of the loan participations sought a short-term return on excess cash. Based on these findings, the district court concluded that "the overall motivation of the parties was the promotion of commercial purposes" rather than an investment in a business enterprise. *Banco Espanol de Credito*, 763 F.Supp. at 42-43.

Weighing the second *Reves* factor—the plan of distribution of the instrument—the district court observed that only institutional and corporate entities were solicited and that detailed individualized presentations were made by Security Pacific's sales personnel. The district court therefore concluded that the plan of distribution was "a limited solicitation to sophisticated financial or commercial institutions and not to the general public." *Id.* at 43. We agree.

The plan of distribution specifically prohibited resales of the loan participations without the express written permission of Security Pacific. This limitation worked to prevent the loan participations from being sold to the general public, thus limiting eligible buyers to those with the capacity to acquire information about the debtor. This limitation also distinguishes *Gary Plastic Packaging v. Merrill Lynch, Pierce, Fenner & Smith, Inc.*, 756 F.2d 230 (2d Cir. 1985), which involved a secondary market for the instruments traded in that case.

With regard to the third factor—the reasonable perception of the instrument by the investing public—the district court considered the expectations of the sophisticated purchasers who signed MPA's and determined that these institutions were given ample notice that the instruments were participations in loans and not investments in a business enterprise. *Id.*

Finally, the district court noted that the [OCC] has issued specific policy guidelines addressing the sale of loan participations. Thus, the fourth factor—the existence of another regulatory scheme—indicated that application of the securities laws was unnecessary. *Id.*

Thus, under the *Reves* family resemblance analysis, as properly applied by the district court, we hold that the loan participations in the instant case are analogous to the enumerated category of loans issued by banks for commercial purposes and therefore do not satisfy the statutory definition of "notes" which are "securities." Since the loan participations do not meet the statutory definition of securities, plaintiffs may not maintain their action for relief under § 12(2) of the 1933 Act. . . .

OAKES, Chief Judge, dissenting:

For reasons that I will explain in detail, I agree with the [SEC], which submitted a brief amicus curiae, a brief which is not mentioned in the majority opinion, that these so-called loan notes were purchased in investment transactions and are securities accordingly, and that the loan note program engaged in by Security Pacific, while bearing a superficial resemblance to traditional loan participations, differs from those traditional participations in several important respects, including (1) who the participants are; (2) what the purposes of the purchasers or participants are; and (3) what the promotional basis used in marketing the loan notes is. The participants, rather than being commercial lenders who engage in traditional loan participations, were instead in many cases non-financial entities not acting as commercial lenders but making an investment, and even though there were some banks that purchased the so-called loan notes, they generally did so not through their lending departments but through their investment and trading departments. These participants were motivated not by the commercial purpose of operating a lending business in which participations are taken as an adjunct to direct lending operations, but were motivated by an investment purpose. The promotional literature put out by Security Pacific advertised the so-called loan notes as competitive with commercial paper, a well-recognized security under the [1933 Act], and on the basis of the return that they offered over that of other investments.

Beyond that, . . . these loan notes differ from traditional loan participations in the scope of information available to the purchasers. In the traditional loan participation, participants generally engage in one-to-one negotiation with the lead lender, and at times with the borrower, and can inspect all information, public and non-public, that is relevant, and consequently are able to do their own credit analysis. Here, Security Pacific did not provide the participants with non-public information it had, . . . and the purchasers were not in a position [to] conduct their own examinations.

---

1. ***Overlapping Regulatory Perimeters.*** The *Banco Espanol* decision presents a case of overlapping regulatory perimeters. Security Pacific was a national bank, chartered by the OCC, performing the characteristic banking function of extending commercial loans. The case asked whether federal securities laws should also govern the bank when it sold loan participations to other institutional investors. Why did the plaintiffs in this case seek application of federal securities laws? Would the result have been the same if the loans had been originated by a less regulated entity, such as a commercial firm?

2. ***Relevance that Purchasers Were Institutional Investors.*** One of the points on which the majority and dissent in *Banco Espanol* differed was whether the characteristics of the purchasers were relevant. Why did it matter that the purchasers were all institutional investors? To what extent should institutional investors be allowed to operate outside the regulatory perimeter?

3. ***Marketplace Lending.*** Marketplace lending describes internet-based lending companies that connect borrowers seeking credit with prospective lenders with capital to deploy. Potential borrowers fill out online loan applications, which the online lending company then uses to evaluate the potential borrower's credit risk. Prospective lenders may view this information for each loan request on a website and determine whether they wish to fund the loan or any portion of it. A loan will usually fund if lenders subscribe for the full amount of the loan before the funding deadline stated in the loan request. Meanwhile, the lending company maintains a segregated deposit account on behalf of the lenders with a bank. Each lender must have deposited in this account, at the time a loan is issued, an amount sufficient to provide the requested funding. The bank where the account is located will then issue the loan to the borrower. After the loan is dispersed to the borrower, the lending company will (1) purchase the loan from the bank using funds of the applicable lenders on deposit in the bank account, and (2) issue to each such lender a note of the lending company representing the right to receive a proportionate share of all principal and interest payments received by the lending company from the borrower on the applicable loan. Based on the *Banco Espanol* opinions, would you consider these notes to be securities? Should they be? *See In re* Prosper Marketplace, Inc., Securities Act Release No. 8984, Administrative Proceeding No. 3-13296 (2008).

B. BROKER-DEALERS AND INVESTMENT ADVISORS

Under the Exchange Act, a broker is defined as "any person engaged in the business of effecting transactions in securities for others." Securities and Exchange Act of 1934 § 3(a)(4). There are thus two defining characteristics of a broker. The first is that the person is "engaged in the business" of securities transactions. The most important factor of whether someone is "engaged in the business" is whether there is "regularity of participation." Massachusetts

Financial Services, Inc. v. Securities Investor Protection Corp., 411 F. Supp. 411 (D. Mass. 1976). The second characteristic is that the person effects transactions. The SEC has interpreted "effecting transactions" to include any participation "at the key points in the chain of distribution," which consists of any part in structuring the transaction, finding potential purchases, soliciting investors, and assisting in taking or routing the order. MuniAuction, Inc., SEC No-Action Letter, 2000 WL 291007 (Mar. 13, 2000).

Over time, the courts and the SEC have developed multi-factor tests to determine the existence of a broker. The most widely-cited factors were first developed in *SEC v. Hansen* and include whether a person: (1) works as an employee of the issuer, (2) receives a commission rather than a salary, (3) sells or earlier sold the securities of another issuer, (4) participates in negotiations between the issuer and an investor, (5) provides either advice or a valuation as to the merit of an investment, and (6) actively, rather than passively, finds investors. 1984 WL 2413, at *10 (S.D.N.Y. 1984) (noting that few courts had conducted in-depth legal analysis on question of what defines a broker); *see also In re* Joseph Kemprowski and the Cambridge Consulting Co., Exchange Act Release No. 35058, 1994 WL 684628 (Dec. 8, 1994) (listing SEC factors, which included whether a person actively solicited investors, advised investors as to the merits of the investment, and received commissions or other transaction-based compensation).

While the definition of broker may seem relatively straightforward, its application in practice can be uncertain. For example, in *SEC v. Kramer*, 778 F. Supp. 2d 1320 (M.D. Fla. 2011), the two defendants, Kramer and Baker, were business partners. Baker had facilitated a reverse merger on behalf of a company called Skyway Communication and continued to be compensated for his promotional efforts pursuant to his agreement with Skyway. Kramer helped promote Skyway, and Skyway agreed to compensate him directly if he introduced potential investors who ultimately invested in the company. Kramer informed his family, close friends, and businesses acquaintances of Skyway, telling them it was a good investment and encouraging them to read Skyway press releases. The SEC argued that Kramer was a broker because he received transaction-based compensation, solicited investors by distributing promotional material and directing people to Skyway's web site, and used a network of associates to promote the company, among other things. The District Court, however, concluded that Kramer was not a broker for purposes of the Exchange Act because there was no evidence that Kramer had sold any shares of Skyway, performed any transaction-related work, or advertised for Skyway.

In contrast, in *Salamon v. Teleplus Enterprises, Inc.*, No. CIV. 05-2058, 2008 WL 2277094 (D.N.J. June 2, 2008), the firm Teleplus had hired Howard Salamon as a consultant to find sources of financing for the company. Salamon introduced Teleplus to an investor, Cornell, and Cornell agreed to purchase up to $10 million of Teleplus's stock. Salamon argued that he did not participate in the negotiations between the two parties while Teleplus argued that he set up and participated in conference calls and advised Teleplus on the financing. Teleplus later refused to pay Salamon after mistaking Salamon and his firm Salamon Brothers for the former investment bank Salomon Brothers. In denying the defendant's motion for summary judgment, the Court implied that if Salamon had set up the calls, provided Teleplus financing advice, and negotiated with Cornell on the financing terms, then he would be considered a broker.

A separate line of legal authority concerns the term dealer, which is defined under federal securities laws to encompass "any person engaged in the business of buying and selling securities (not including security-based swaps, other than security-based swaps with or for persons that are not eligible contract participants) for such person's own account through a broker or otherwise." Securities and Exchange Act of 1934 § 3(a)(5).

Back in the 1980s, when commercial banks were first finding their way around the Glass-Steagall Act's prohibitions, the question arose whether banks that offered securities services to their customers should be regulated as brokers or dealers under the 1934 Act. The original 1934 Act had explicitly exempted banks from the definitions of broker and dealer, apparently under the assumption that the Glass-Steagall Act—adopted the year before—had barred commercial banks from engaging in such activities. In the 1980s, when some banks were beginning to offer their customers various forms of retail brokerage services, the SEC attempted to revise its regulations to subject those banks to SEC oversight as broker-dealers. The courts, however, struck down the SEC's regulation on the grounds that it was inconsistent with the statutory definitions that Congress created in the 1930s. *See* ABA v. SEC, 804 F.2d 739 (D.C. Cir. 1986). In 1999, when Congress adopted the Gramm-Leach-Bliley Act, it revised the definition of broker and dealer, still retaining an exemption for banks but limiting that exemption to a relatively narrow range of bank securities activities. *See* Securities and Exchange Act of 1934 §§ 3(a)(4)(B), 3(a)(5)(C). Given the difficulty for a single entity to comply with both bank regulation and broker-dealer regulation, under these reforms, commercial banks must push out full service brokerage activities into separate affiliates where they are subject to the same rules as other broker-dealers. As mentioned in the discussion of the Swaps Pushout Rule in Chapter 2.2, if a bank limits its activities to the specific functions Congress enumerates, its business can be conducted without direct SEC oversight.

As mentioned earlier, the Investment Advisers Act established a separate set of regulatory requirements for investment advisers. The following case concerns an SEC regulation designed to clarify when registered broker-dealers must also comply with the requirements of the Investment Advisers Act.

Financial Planning Ass'n v. SEC

482 F.3d 481 (D.C. Cir. 2007)

ROGERS, CIRCUIT JUDGE.

Brokers and dealers are not subject to the requirements of the Investment Advisers Act ("IAA") where their investment advice is (1) "solely incidental to the conduct of [their] business as a broker or dealer," and (2) the broker or dealer "receives no special compensation therefor." 15 U.S.C. § 80b-2(a)(11)(C) (2000). The [SEC], acting pursuant to § 202(a)(11)(F) and § 211(a) of the IAA, 15 U.S.C. §§ 80b-2(a)(11)(F)1, 80b-11(a), promulgated a final rule exempting broker-dealers from the IAA when they receive "special compensation therefor." The Financial Planning Association ("FPA") petitions for review of the final rule on the ground that the SEC has exceeded its authority. We agree, and we therefore grant the petition and vacate the final rule.

I.

The IAA was enacted by Congress as one title of a bill "to provide for the registration and regulation of investment companies and investment advisers." The other title was the Investment Company Act ("ICA"). These were the last in a series of congressional enactments designed to eliminate certain abuses in the securities industry that contributed to the stock market crash of 1929 and the depression of the 1930s. . . .

Under the IAA, investment advisers are required, among other things, to register and to maintain records; to limit the type of contracts they enter; and not to engage in certain types of deceptive and fraudulent transactions. Congress has amended the IAA on several occasions, see VII Louis Loss & Joel Seligman, Securities Regulation 3314–15 (3d ed. 2003), but the provisions at issue in this appeal have remained, in relevant part, unchanged.

In § 202(a)(11) of the IAA, Congress broadly defined "investment adviser" as

> "any person who, for compensation, engages in the business of advising others, either directly or through publications or writings, as to the value of securities or as to the advisability of investing in, purchasing, or selling securities, or who, for compensation and as part of a regular business, issues or promulgates analyses or reports concerning securities. . . ."

Carving out six exemptions from this broad definition, Congress determined that an "investment adviser" did not include:

> (A) a bank, or any bank holding company [(BHC)] as defined in the Bank Holding Company Act of 1956 [(BHCA)] which is not an investment company, except that the term "investment adviser" includes any bank or [BHC] to the extent that such bank or [BHC] serves or acts as an investment adviser to a registered investment company, but if, in the case of a bank, such services or actions are performed through a separately identifiable department or division, the department or division, and not the bank itself, shall be deemed to be the investment adviser;
>
> (B) any lawyer, accountant, engineer, or teacher whose performance of such services is solely incidental to the practice of his profession;
>
> **(C) any broker or dealer [1] whose performance of such services is solely incidental to the conduct of his business as a broker or dealer and [2] who receives no special compensation therefor;**
>
> (D) the publisher of any bona fide newspaper, news magazine or business or financial publication of general and regular circulation;
>
> (E) any person whose advice, analyses, or reports relate to no securities other than securities which are direct obligations of or obligations guaranteed as to principal or interest by the United States . . . ; or
>
> **(F) such other persons not within the intent of this paragraph, as the Commission may designate by rules and regulations or order.**

(Emphasis added). Subsections (C) and (F) are at issue in this appeal.

Before enactment of the IAA, broker-dealers and others who offered investment advice received two general forms of compensation. Some charged only traditional commissions (earning a certain amount for each securities transaction completed). Others charged a separate advice fee (often a certain percentage of the customer's assets under advisement or supervision). See 11 Fed. Reg. 10,996 (Sept. 27, 1946). The Committee Reports recognized that the statutory exemption for broker-dealers reflected this distinction; the Reports explained that the term "investment adviser" was "so defined as specifically to exclude . . . brokers (insofar as their advice is merely incidental to brokerage transactions for which they receive only brokerage commissions)." S. Rep. No. 76–1775, at 22 [HA 164]; H.R. Rep. No. 76–2639, at 28 [HA 168].

The final rule took a different approach. After determining in 1999 that certain new forms of fee-contracting adopted by broker-dealers were "not . . . fundamentally different from traditional brokerage programs," the SEC proposed a rule very similar to the final rule, see Notice of Proposed Rulemaking, 64 Fed. Reg. 61,228 (Nov. 10, 1999) ("1999 NOPR"), stating it would act as if it had already issued the rule, id. at 61,227. In adopting the temporary rule, pursuant to subsection (F) and its general rulemaking authority under IAA § 211(a), the SEC exempted a new group of broker-dealers from the IAA. 64 Fed. Reg. 61,226 (Nov. 10, 1999). After re-proposing the rule in January 2005, again pursuant to its authority under subsection (F) and § 211(a), the SEC adopted a slightly modified final rule on April 12, 2005, codified at 17 C.F.R. § 275.202(a)(11)–1. 70 Fed. Reg. 20,424, 453–54.

The final rule provides, generally, in Paragraph (a)(1), on "fee-based programs," that a broker-dealer who (1) receives special compensation will not be deemed an investment adviser if (2) any advice provided is solely incidental to brokerage services provided on a customer's account and (3) specific disclosure is made to the customer. In Paragraph (a)(2), on discount brokerage programs, a broker-dealer will not be deemed to have received special compensation merely because it charges one customer more or less for brokerage services than it charges another customer. Paragraph (b) lists three non-exclusive circumstances in which advisory services, for which special compensation is received under paragraph (a)(1), would not be performed "solely incidental to" brokerage: when (1) a separate fee or contract exists for advice; (2) a customer receives certain financial planning services; and, (3) generally, a broker-dealer has investment discretion over a client's account. Paragraph (c) states a "special rule" that broker-dealers registered under the [1934 Act] are investment advisers only for those accounts for which they receive compensation that subjects them to the IAA. Paragraph (d) defines the term "investment discretion," which appears in paragraphs (a)(1) and (b)(3), to have the same meaning as § 3(a)(35) of the Exchange Act, 15 U.S.C. § 78c(a)(35), except for "discretion granted by a customer on a temporary or limited basis."

The FPA petitions for review, challenging the SEC's authority to promulgate the final rule. . . . [Analysis of standing omitted.]

III.

The FPA contends that when Congress enacted the IAA, Congress identified in subsection (C) the group of broker-dealers it intended to exempt, and that subsection (F) was only intended to allow the SEC to exempt new groups from the IAA, not to expand the groups that Congress specifically addressed. The resolution of the FPA's challenge thus turns on whether the SEC is authorized under § 202(a)(11)(F) or § 211(a) to except from IAA coverage an additional group of broker-dealers beyond the broker-dealers exempted by Congress in subsection (C). Subsection (F) of § 202(a)(11) authorizes the SEC to except from the IAA "such other persons not within the intent of this paragraph, as the Commission may designate by rules and regulations or order." As such, we review the SEC's exercise of its authority pursuant to subsection (F) under the familiar two-step analysis of *Chevron, U.S.A., Inc. v. Natural Res. Def. Council, Inc.*, 467 U.S. 837, 842–43 (1984). Under step one, the court must determine whether Congress has directly spoken to the precise question at issue. . . . Under step two, "if the statute is silent or ambiguous with respect to the specific issue, the question for the court is whether the agency's answer is based on a permissible construction of the statute." *Id.* at 843. In reviewing an agency's interpretation of its authority under a statute it administers, the court will uphold that interpretation as long as it is a reasonable interpretation of the statute. . . .

Applying the "traditional tools of statutory construction," see *Chevron*, 467 U.S. at 843 n. 9, 104 S.Ct. 2778, the court looks to the text, structure, and the overall statutory scheme, as well as the problem Congress sought to solve. [Citations Omitted]. All four elements demonstrate that the SEC has exceeded its authority in promulgating the rule under § 202(a)(11)(F) because Congress has addressed the precise issue at hand.

Section 202(a)(11) lists exemptions (A)-(E) from the broad definition of "investment adviser" for several classes of persons—including, for example, lawyers, accountants, and others whose advice is "solely incidental" to their regular business; and publishers of newsletters that circulate widely and do not give individually-tailored financial advice. [S]ubsection (C)'s exemption [is] for "*any* broker or dealer whose performance of such [investment advisory] services is solely incidental to the conduct of his business as a broker or dealer and who receives no special compensation therefor." (Emphasis added). Beyond the listed exemptions, subsection (F) authorizes the SEC to exempt from the IAA "such *other* persons not within the intent of this paragraph, as the Commission may designate by rules and regulations or order." (Emphasis added).

In the final rule, the SEC purports to use its authority under subsection (F) to broaden the exemption for broker-dealers provided under subsection (C). The rule is inconsistent with the IAA, however, because it fails to meet either of the two requirements for an exemption under subsection (F). First, the legislative "intent" does not support an exemption for broker-dealers broader than the exemption set forth in the text of subsection (C); therefore, the final rule does not meet the statutory requirement that exemptions under subsection (F) be consistent with the "intent" of paragraph 11 of section 202(a). Second, because broker-dealers are already expressly addressed in subsection (C), they are not "other persons" under subsection (F). . . .

Just as the text and structure of paragraph of 202(a)(11) make it evident that Congress intended to define "investment adviser" broadly and create only a precise exemption for broker-dealers, so does a consideration of the problems Congress sought to address in enacting the IAA. [The Court discussed the "flagrant abuses and grossest violations of fiduciary duty" identified during the floor debate on the IAA, claiming the discussion evidenced an intention to protect investors and bona fide investment advisors].

The overall statutory scheme of the IAA addresses the problems identified to Congress in two principal ways: First, by establishing a federal fiduciary standard to govern the conduct of investment advisers, broadly defined, see *Transamerica Mortgage Advisors v. Lewis*, 444 U.S. 11, 17 (1979), and second, by requiring full disclosure of all conflicts of interest. As the Supreme Court noted, Congress's "broad proscription against 'any . . . practice . . . which operates . . . as a fraud or deceit upon any client or prospective client' remained in the bill from beginning to end." *Capital Gains*, 375 U.S. at 191. . . . This statutory scheme is inconsistent with a construction of the SEC's authority under subsection (F) that would enable persons Congress determined should be subject to the IAA to escape its restrictions.

Accordingly, we grant the petition and vacate the final rule. . . .

GARLAND, CIRCUIT JUDGE, DISSENTING.

The Investment Advisers Act contains five specific exceptions, and further authorizes the SEC to exempt "such other persons not within the intent of this paragraph, as the Commission may designate by rules." 15 U.S.C. § 80b-2(a)(11). Unlike my colleagues, I cannot derive an unambiguous meaning from the terms "such other persons" and "within the intent of this paragraph." As required by *Chevron*, I would therefore defer to the SEC's reasonable interpretation of the statute . . . and uphold the [rule].

---

1. ***Ramifications of the* Financial Planning Ass'n *Decision.*** In adopting a rule that narrowed the "special compensation" prong of Section 202(a)(11), the SEC hoped to shift regulatory focus away from the type of compensation received to the type of services provided. Brokers have traditionally received compensation in the form of a per-transaction commission, but competition among broker-dealers led many of these firms to experiment with different forms of compensation, including asset-based fee structures. The SEC viewed these new fees as beneficial, at least to the extent that they eliminated incentives for brokers to engage in aggressive sales practices. Nonetheless, the D.C. Circuit's ruling effectively ended brokers' practice of providing fee-based accounts. For a critical analysis of the decision, *see* Arthur Labby, *Reforming the Regulation of Broker-Dealers and Investment Advisers*, 65 BUS. LAW 395, 410-18 (2010).

2. ***Applying the* Chevron *Doctrine.*** The Financial Planning Association case presents a rather conventional application of the *Chevron* doctrine. As you read the decision, does the majority or the dissent have the better view?

3. ***Standing.*** The previous excerpt omitted the discussion of standing, but clearly there was a question of where the plaintiff, Financial Planning Association, was authorized to bring the case. Why do you think the organization wanted to spend the time and resources to mount this kind of challenge to the SEC rulemaking, which after all did not apply to most Association members who were already registered as investment advisers and not eligible for the exemptive relief the SEC was proposing?

4. ***Investment Advisor Exemptions.*** Finally, note the several exemptions that Congress wrote into the definition of an investment adviser. What approach (or approaches) to regulatory boundaries do these exemptions reflect?

C. APPLICATION OF U.S. REQUIREMENTS TO FOREIGN ENTITIES

As a general matter, foreign securities firms that enter the United States and market their services to U.S. investors are required to comply with U.S. regulatory requirements for broker-dealers. There are, however, a few important exceptions, and in the past, the SEC contemplated a fairly substantial change in the SEC's approach to foreign broker-dealers and foreign exchange.

Rule 15a-6 promulgated under the 1934 Act contains one long-standing exception to U.S. broker-dealer registration requirements and is described, along with a proposed amendment, in the following excerpt:

Howell E. Jackson, Substituted Compliance: The Emergence, Challenges, and Evolution of a New Regulatory Paradigm

1 J. FIN. REG. 169, 181–82 (2015)

This complicated rule, first adopted in 1989, exempts from the 1934 Act registration of foreign brokers that have only a limited amount of contact with US institutional investors, and offers somewhat more lenient treatment for transactions involving US institutional investors with more than $100 million of assets under management. The regulation, which is highly technical and often requires foreign broker-dealers to obtain chaperoning services from US registered firms, has long been the source of criticism from practitioners and the [SEC] has long been under pressure to liberalize the rule. In June of 2008, the [SEC] proposed such a change. ([T]he proposal was never adopted.) Under the [SEC's] proposal, foreign broker-dealers would have much wider latitude to do business with US investor, both relaxing many of the technical requirements of the prior rule and also lowering the level of favoured institutions to those with less than $25 million under management and for the first time also granting relief for contacts with natural persons managing portfolios of similar size. The [SEC's] proposed reform of rule 15a-6 is best understood as a continuation of the Commissioner's older modified national treatment approach [whereby foreign issuers are entitled to more lenient treatment as compared to domestic issuers]; it narrowed the scope of domestic regulation for foreign firms that constrain their US activity within clearly defined boundaries and did so without consideration of the quality of supervision in the firm's home jurisdictions. The proposal would thus have been available for broker-dealers based in any jurisdiction around the world, and not just dominant financial centres. . . .

A critical issue was the rule 15a-6 proposal's treatment of retail investors. Especially among traditionalists at the [SEC] there was concern that the proposed rule could expose qualifying retail investors—that is, those with more than $25 million in investable assets—to unregulated and possibly also unscrupulous securities firms. While a number of SEC exemptions turn on the net worth of individual investors and often employ much lower thresholds than the new $25 million level proposed for rule 15a-6, those exemptions traditionally have involved domestic transactions that take place against an institutional setting where federal anti-fraud rules clearly apply and dispute resolution through judicial venues or arbitration is readily available. Under the SEC's proposal, retail investors with sufficient assets would have been able to engage in largely unregulated interactions with foreign brokerage houses, even those located in unsavory jurisdictions or without good reputations in their home markets. By eliminating any element of SEC pre-approval, the proposed 15a-6 reform relied almost exclusively on principles of caveat emptor, requiring simply that US investors be informed that domestic regulatory safeguards do not apply.

An alternative approach for the treatment of foreign broker-dealers, as well as foreign exchanges, was proposed by two senior SEC staffers in Ethiopis Tafara & Robert J. Peterson, *A Blueprint for Cross-Border Access to U.S. Investors: A New International Framework*, 48 HARV. INT'L L.J. 31 (2007). Under the proposal, the SEC would first determine whether the regulatory regime of a foreign jurisdiction was sufficiently equivalent to U.S. regulatory standards. If such a finding were made, securities firms from that jurisdiction could apply to enter the United States without complying with U.S. broker-dealer registration requirements, although U.S. anti-fraud rules would continue to apply. Critically—and in contrast to Rule 15a-6—qualifying foreign entities could do business with any U.S. customer, including retail investors; they would not be limited to institutional investors or individuals with a sufficient amount of assets. The case for and against substituted compliance was debated extensively in the journal cited above where the proposal first appeared. In 2008, the SEC moved forward with pilot programs of substituted compliance with Canada and Australia, although both efforts were tabled due to the onslaught of the Financial Crisis. *See* Pierre-Hugues Verdier, *Mutual Recognition in International Finance*, 52 HARV. INT'L L.J. 55 (2011).

The concept of substituted compliance has reemerged in the post-Financial Crisis era as a means to address the extra-territorial application of new U.S.

rules regulating OTC derivatives markets, a topic we will take up in Chapter 11.3. The following excerpt distinguishes between the first generation substituted compliance approach proposed in 2007 and the current SEC-CFTC experimentations with second-generation substituted compliance:

> Most importantly, second-generation substituted compliance is applied in an out-bound context. That is, its application is not premised on offshore firms seeking access to new customers—whether retail or wholesale—in the USA. Rather the second-generation regime is primarily designed to provide exemptive relief to foreign entities and activities that are being subject to the extraterritorial application of new statutory provisions adopted in the Dodd-Frank Act of 2010. In other words, second-generation substituted compliance offers regulatory relief from the out-bound application of new regulatory requirements. This distinction between in-bound and out-bound explains why substituted compliance today has a quite different feel to foreign jurisdictions. With the original Tafara-Peterson version, foreign jurisdictions and firms would voluntarily apply for comparability determinations in order to gain access to US markets. . . . With second-generation substituted compliance, regulatory relief is still being granted, but it is in the form of an exemption to the mandatory extraterritorial application of US laws. Foreign entities can escape the requirements of US law but only by reorganizing business activities so as to avoid US jurisdictional triggers.

Jackson, *Substituted Compliance*, at 200.

V. CONSOLIDATED OVERSIGHT OF MAJOR SECURITIES FIRMS

The notion that a country should distinguish regulatory standards applicable to foreign firms based on the quality of home country regulation—the logic underlying substituted compliance—is hardly novel. In our discussion of the Federal Insurance Office's (FIO) response to the EU's Solvency II directive, we saw a situation where the European supervisory posture with respect to U.S. insurance companies depended on an EU assessment whether certain features of U.S. insurance regulation were substantially equivalent to EU regulatory requirements. A decade earlier, U.S. firms faced a similar problem with another EU directive, one policing financial conglomerates. U.S. securities firms operating in the EU faced the prospects of potential redundant and conflicting EU regulation at the holding company level unless these firms could demonstrate that the U.S. imposed substantially equivalent oversight. The following materials recount the U.S. response.

A. LEADING UP TO THE FINANCIAL CRISIS

In 2004, the SEC adopted a Consolidated Supervised Entity (CSE) Program for certain large U.S. broker-dealers and investment BHCs. The CSE Program was designed to respond to regulatory gaps in investment banking oversight by establishing a program of comprehensive, consolidated supervision at the holding company level—in addition to regulation at the broker-dealer subsidiary—that included holding company capital and liquidity reporting requirements, documentation of risk management practices, and examination of formerly unregulated affiliates and the holding company itself. The SEC sought to model its program on the type of consolidated supervision conducted by the banking regulators, but on a significantly more modest scale. Only five investment BHCs were ultimately approved for the CSE Program.

The CSE Program was voluntary, but the largest, most globally active U.S. broker-dealers found participation to be an attractive alternative because it permitted them to use internally-developed and SEC approved statistical models for computing certain market risk and credit risk charges under the broker-dealer net capital rule, much in the same way that Basel II was moving towards internal models at the time. The CSE Program was based on the SEC's authority under the 1934 Act to determine net capital rules for broker-dealers. It provided an alternative net capital program at the broker-dealer entity level, in exchange for conditions at the affiliated holding company, including consent to group-wide supervision. Another reason for voluntary participation by broker-dealers, and an articulated justification for the establishment of the CSE Program by the SEC, was the implications of the EU's Financial Conglomerates Directive. The Directive required consolidated supervision of investment banks doing business in the EU, either internationally or at the European level, unless the investment bank was subject to comparable consolidated supervision in its home country. In the absence of participation in the CSE Program, the largest investment banks would have been required to establish and separately capitalize intermediate holding companies in the EU, which at the time was seen as a costly proposition with negative competitive impacts for internationally active U.S. broker-dealers.

The CSE Program was designed to provide consolidated oversight only to those holding companies affiliated with a large and well-capitalized broker-dealer. The holding company oversight was layered on top of the regulatory regime that applied to the broker-dealer subsidiary, including the financial responsibility and net capital requirements at the broker-dealer level. The CSE Program was limited to firms whose broker-dealer met certain minimum requirements for tentative net capital (regulatory capital less deductions of illiquid assets) and subjected these broker-dealers to an early warning requirement of $5 billion, essentially establishing a capital floor of $5 billion.

CSEs were required to compute a capital adequacy measure at the holding company that was consistent with the Basel Standard (at that time, Basel II), applicable to commercial banks, but without any independent leverage requirement of the sort imposed under U.S. bank capital rules. CSEs were expected to maintain an overall Basel capital ratio at the consolidated level of not less that the Federal Reserve's 10% "well-capitalized" standard (based on risk-weighted assets) for BHCs. CSEs provided monthly capital computations to the SEC, applying Basel II. They also were required to file early warning notice with the SEC if certain thresholds were breached, or likely to be breached, such as the 10% capital ratio or the $5 billion capital floor.

As alluded to in Chapter 1.2, during the Financial Crisis many of these CSEs lacked sufficient liquidity to operate effectively. Mortgage-related assets began to decrease in value, and these institutions, who had significant amounts of these assets on their books or held off-balance sheet in ways that became the firms' liabilities in the Financial Crisis, were forced to recognize billions of dollars of losses. Investment banks became increasingly reliant on short-term funding to continue their operations as investors, concerned with the financial health of these institutions, demanded shorter loan terms to limit their exposure. Eventually, these investors started refusing to lend altogether, creating conditions akin to a bank run, but in the wholesale markets. Efforts by the Federal Reserve to inject additional liquidity into the system by lowering interest rates proved too little, too late. As the full effects of the crisis began to be felt in late 2008, many CSEs either failed, were acquired, or converted to BHCs in order to access government support.

These events led to strong criticism of the CSE Program. Consider, for example, the following assessment:

The Financial Crisis Inquiry Commission, The Financial Crisis Inquiry Report

153–54 (2011)

The CSE program was based on the bank supervision model, but the SEC did not try to do exactly what bank examiners did. For one thing, unlike supervisors of large banks, the SEC never assigned on-site examiners under the CSE program; by comparison, the OCC alone assigned more than 60 examiners full-time at Citibank. According to Erik Sirri, the SEC's former director of trading and markets, the CSE program was intended to focus mainly on liquidity because, unlike a commercial bank, a securities firm traditionally had no access to a lender of last resort. (Of course, that would change during the crisis.) The investment banks were subject to annual examinations, during which staff reviewed the firms' systems and records and verified that the firms had instituted control processes.

The CSE program was troubled from the start. The SEC conducted an exam for each investment bank when it entered the program. The result of Bear Stearns's entrance exam, in 2005, showed several deficiencies. For example, examiners were concerned that there were no firmwide VaR limits and that contingency funding plans relied on overly optimistic stress scenarios. In addition, the SEC was aware of the firm's concentration of mortgage securities and its high leverage. Nonetheless, the SEC did not ask Bear to change its asset balance, decrease its leverage, or increase its cash liquidity pool—all actions well within its prerogative, according to SEC officials. Then, because the CSE program was preoccupied with its own staff reorganization, Bear did not have its next annual exam, during which the SEC was supposed to be on-site. The SEC did meet monthly with all CSE firms, including Bear, and it did conduct occasional targeted examinations across firms. In 2006, the SEC worried that Bear was too reliant on unsecured commercial paper funding, and Bear reduced its exposure to unsecured commercial paper and increased its reliance on secured repo lending. Unfortunately, tens of billions of dollars of that repo lending was overnight funding that could disappear with no warning. Ironically, in the second week of March 2008, when the firm went into its four-day death spiral, the SEC was on-site conducting its first CSE exam since Bear's entrance exam more than two years earlier.

See also Stephen Labaton, *Agency's '04 Rule Let Banks Pile Up New Debt*, N.Y. TIMES, Oct. 2, 2008. ("The SEC assigned seven people to examine the [CSE] parent companies—which last year controlled financial empires with combined assets of more than $4 trillion. Since March 2007, the office has not had a director, and as of last month, the office had not completed [an] inspection . . .").

As with much of the history of the Financial Crisis, these issues remain the subject of intense debate. *See* Chapter 1.2. Whether the large U.S. securities firms would have fared differently had they been free to establish intermediate holding companies in the EU under direct EU supervision before the Financial Crisis is, of course, a matter of speculation. One element of the CSE Program is indisputable, however. The SEC had no authority to provide access to the discount window or emergency funding like the Federal Reserve Board or equity infusions like the Treasury under the Troubled Asset Relief Program. The CSE Program, like the entities it regulated, therefore had no direct access to the federal safety net when the music stopped in 2008. After the Lehman Brothers failure, virtually all of the major U.S. BHCs as well as the entities that had been previously regulated as CSEs, received substantial assistance from the Federal Reserve Board and the Treasury. The Dodd-Frank Act continued the concept of a voluntary opt in to Federal Reserve consolidated supervision for those few remaining investment banks that had not converted to BHCs during the Financial Crisis, but transferred the CSE authority from the SEC to the Federal Reserve Board. *See* Michael S. Barr, *The Financial Crisis and the Path of Reform*, YALE J. ON REG. 91, 98-9 (2012).

B. UNDER THE DODD-FRANK ACT

The inability of the SEC to provide effective consolidated oversight of major securities firms, as well as the near failure of several banking entities during the Financial Crisis, was very much on the minds of government officials as proposals leading to up to the Dodd-Frank Act were debated. Among other things, the Dodd-Frank Act established new resolution powers (to be discussed in Chapter 9.3) to provide a better mechanism for resolving distressed financial conglomerates. In addition, the Financial Stability Oversight Council (FSOC) was given the authority to designate any major securities firm as systemically important and thus subject to consolidated oversight by the Federal Reserve Board even if the entity does not own a commercial bank, which is ordinarily a prerequisite for Federal Reserve Board supervision. To date, however, the FSOC has not exercised that power with respect to a securities firm. As mentioned above, the major securities firms that survived the crisis were forced to come within Federal Reserve Board oversight. Lehman Brothers and Bear Stearns failed. Currently, Lazard is the largest securities firm operating without consolidated supervision from the Federal Reserve Board, though some of the major private equity firms likely now rival Lazard in terms of economic significance. To the extent that new securities firms grow into greater financial significance, the FSOC could still use its Dodd-Frank Act authority to designate such entities as systemically important. Conceivably, the CSE Program itself might be revitalized under Federal Reserve Board oversight. Though not directly related to issues of consolidated supervision, the Dodd-Frank Act also included a number of reforms to the various SEC powers, dealing with, among other things, enforcement options, corporate issuers, credit rating agencies, and hedge funds. These areas of expanded SEC authority will be covered in later chapters.

CHAPTER 4.2

SECURITIES FIRMS AND THE RETAIL INVESTOR

CONTENTS

I. INTRODUCTION

This Chapter focuses on the duties of securities firms to their customers. As you will see, the courts have played an important role in defining these duties, and judicial opinions have greatly influenced the requirements that the SEC and self-regulatory organizations have imposed through rulemaking and enforcement actions. Many times these duties are denominated as fiduciary, though the precise meaning of that term varies depending upon the context. Another recurring and important issue to consider is the interplay between the open-ended fiduciary duties articulated in judicial opinions on the one hand and the increasingly detailed and prescriptive disclosure requirements and market conduct rules that regulators have articulated on the other. When should compliance with the these requirements provide a defense to alleged violations of fiduciary duties?

II. DEFINING THE DUTIES OF BROKER-DEALERS

In addition to registering with the SEC and state securities commissions, broker-dealers and their employees are required to abide by a number of substantive provisions of federal securities laws, as well as the codes of conduct of the various self-regulatory organizations. These restrictions greatly influence the manner in which broker-dealers participate in the distribution of new security issues and in the trading of outstanding securities in the U.S. secondary markets.

The following materials suggest the tenor and complexity of these regulations, as well as the role that self-regulatory organizations play in the supervision of broker-dealers. A distinctive feature of broker-dealer regulation is its focus on individual accountability. Whereas individually imposed penalties were, until recently, unusual in the insurance sector and depository institution fields, such penalties have been the norm in securities enforcement for many years. Individual suspensions and fines are also common punishments for errant broker-dealers. Why do the enforcement mechanisms in this field focus on individuals as well as institutions? Should a similar system of individual-based penalties be imposed in other areas of financial institution regulation?

Another distinguishing characteristic of broker-dealer regulation is its emphasis on protection through disclosure. Often times, broker-dealers are subject to sanctions not because of the substance of transactions they have engaged in, but rather because of their failure to make adequate disclosures to their customers. Is this a model of regulation that could be adopted more extensively in other fields? Under what conditions are disclosure-based regulations sufficient? Under what conditions are substantive requirements preferable? Does it matter that not all individuals will be able to understand and act upon disclosures?

A. EARLY CASES

We begin with two cases handed down in the 1940s when federal securities laws were still new statutes and our modern regulatory structure had yet to develop. The principles developed in these cases have been of enduring importance and are reflected in many later judicial decisions and regulatory enactments. As you read through these cases and the materials that follow, consider the extent to which the law in this area draws upon traditional fiduciary principles. To what extent has the jurisprudence in this field expanded upon its equitable foundations? Should we continue to rely upon open-ended legal principles enforced through case-by-case adjudication to police the securities sector? Or should we move towards more detailed regulations tailored to address specific legal problems?

Charles Hughes & Co. v. SEC

139 F.2d 434 (2d Cir. 1943)

CLARK, CIRCUIT JUDGE.

This is a petition, pursuant to § 25(a) of the Securities Exchange Act of 1934 [(1934 Act)], to review an order of the [SEC], entered July 19, 1943, under § 15(b) of that Act, in which petitioner's registration as a broker and dealer was revoked. The order [stems from a proceeding] instituted by the [SEC] to determine whether or not petitioner had willfully violated § 17(a) of the Securities Act of 1933 [(1933 Act)], and § 15(c)(1) of the [1934 Act]. . . .

Petitioner . . . engaged in over-the-counter trading in securities as a broker and dealer, being registered as such with the [SEC] under the 1934 statute cited above. The dealings which resulted in the revocation were continued sales of securities to customers at prices very substantially over those prevailing in the over-the-counter market, without disclosure of the mark-up to the customers. The [SEC] concluded that such practices constituted fraud and deceit upon the customers in violation of § 17(a) of the Securities Act, § 15(c)(1) of the [1934 Act], and its own Rule 15c1-2. . . .

. . . The customers were almost entirely single women or widows who knew little or nothing about securities or the devices of Wall Street. An outline of the sales plan used with Mrs. Stella Furbeck gives a representative picture of how petitioner worked. Stillman, a Hughes & Co. agent, having her name as a prospect, called Mrs. Furbeck on the telephone and told her of a "wonderful" stock that she should buy. She replied that she was not interested. [Stillman continued to call until Mrs. Furbeck relented and made a purchase. He and a co-employee eventually gained her complete confidence, and she placed virtually complete control of her securities portfolio in their hands.] Every few days one or the other would have another "marvelous" buy—one that was definitely "beyond the usual"—and she would add it to her collection, selling a more reputable security in order to finance the transaction.

The prices which Mrs. Furbeck and other customers paid for the securities purchased in this manner ranged from 16.1 to 40.9 percent over market value. In addition, most of the transactions involved little or no risk for petitioner, because an order was usually confirmed before it bought the securities that it was selling. There is conflict in the record as to whether Stillman and Armstrong made any direct representations to Mrs. Furbeck of the relation of the price paid to market value. She claims that every time she made a purchase it was directly induced by the statement that the price would be under that current in the over-the-counter market, while they deny such statements completely. It is unchallenged, however, that at no time did either Stillman or Armstrong reveal the true market price of any security to Mrs. Furbeck or the fact that petitioner's profits averaged around 25 percent. [Based on this and other similar evidence, the court concluded that there was "substantial evidence" the petitioners engaged in a course of business to sell securities at excessive mark-up prices without disclosing their market values to customers.]

There is evidence in the record to show a threefold violation of § 17(a) of the [1933 Act] viz., the obtaining of money "by means of any untrue statement of a material fact"; the "omission to state a material fact" necessary to make statements actually made not misleading; and the engaging in a course of business which operates "as a fraud or deceit upon the purchaser." It is true that the only specific evidence of false statements of a material fact is that of Mrs. Furbeck that the sales price was under the market price, and, as we have noted, these statements were denied by the salesmen. Although the [SEC] has neglected to make any finding of fact on this point, we need not remand for a specific finding resolving this conflict, for we feel that petitioner's mark-up policy operated as a fraud and deceit upon the purchasers, as well as constituting an omission to state a material fact.

An over-the-counter firm which actively solicits customers and then sells them securities at prices as far above the market as were those which petitioner charged here must be deemed to commit a fraud. It holds itself out as competent to advise in the premises, and it should disclose the market price if sales are to be made substantially above that level. Even considering petitioner as a principal in a simple vendor purchaser transaction (and there is doubt whether, in several instances at least, petitioner was actually not acting as broker-agent for the purchasers, in which case all undisclosed profits would be forfeited), it was still under a special duty, in view of its expert knowledge and proffered advice, not to take advantage of its customers' ignorance of market conditions. . . . [T]he failure to reveal the mark-up pocketed by the firm was both an omission to state a material fact and a fraudulent device. When nothing was said about market price, the natural implication in the untutored minds of the purchasers was that the price asked was close to the market. The law of fraud knows no difference between express representation on the one hand and implied misrepresentation or concealment on the other.

We need not stop to decide, however, how far common-law fraud was shown. For the business of selling investment securities has been considered one peculiarly in need of regulation for the protection of the investor. "The business of trading in securities is one in which opportunities for dishonesty are of constant recurrence and ever present. It engages acute, active minds, trained to quick apprehension, decision and action." Archer v. Securities and Exchange Commission, 133 F.2d 795, 803 (8th Cir., cert. denied, 319 U.S. 767 (1943). . . . We think the [SEC] has correctly interpreted its responsibilities to stop such abusive practices in the sale of securities.

---

1. ***Securities Firms as Broker-Dealers?*** What was the relationship between the securities firm and its customers in this case? Was the firm an agent/broker or a principal/dealer? Do merchants selling other products and services operate under similar obligations? Should they? Within the securities bar, the theory articulated in this decision—sometimes called *Hughes I* to distinguish it from the following decision, *Hughes II*—has come to be known as the shingle theory, and is derived from a notion that when a securities firm hangs out its shingle to do business it implicitly represents that it will deal fairly with the general public. For a discussion of how this theory and the underlying concept of fair dealing has evolved over the years, see Roberta S. Karmel, *Is the Shingle Theory Dead?*, 52 WASH. & LEE L. REV. 1271 (1995).

2. ***Obligations of Broker-Dealers, Depository Institutions and Insurance Firms.*** How do the obligations imposed in this decision compare to the responsibilities of depository institutions or insurance companies? What obligations do we impose on these firms to ensure that they charge a fair price to their customers? Should standards of fair dealing as imposed on broker-dealers be expanded to other areas of financial regulation? Why or why not?

Hughes v. SEC

174 F.2d 969 (D.C. Cir. 1949)

CLARK, CIRCUIT JUDGE.

The case is before this court on petition of Arleen W. Hughes, doing business as E.W. Hughes & Company, to review and set aside an order of respondent [SEC] revoking her registration as a broker and dealer.

[Petitioner, referred to below as the registrant or petitioner, was a registered broker-dealer and a registered investment adviser. At the time of the SEC action against her, Mrs. Hughes' firm had approximately 175 clients. Each client had signed a "Memorandum of Agreement" with the firm which included two key provisions. The first was a schedule for per-transaction fees, showing that the price for a transaction in which the firm was acting as an investment adviser was slightly higher than the price for a transaction where the firm was acting merely as a dealer. The SEC took no issue with this form of compensation.

The second key provision in the "Memorandum," however, stated that the firm "when acting as investment adviser, shall act as Principal in every such transaction, except as otherwise agreed." Mrs. Hughes testified that her clients followed her investment advice when asked for "in almost every instance." The firm would fill a client's order for the purchase of a security either by selling it out of its own inventory or by buying it for the firm's own account on the open market and then selling it as principal to the client. The

SEC took issue with this latter conduct, believing that it was illegal absent stronger disclosure to the clients.]

. . . After [an administrative hearing], the [SEC] issued an opinion dated February 18, 1948, in which the [SEC] found that petitioner was a fiduciary, that as such she was under a duty to make full disclosure of her adverse interest, that no such complete disclosure was made, and that her clients had not given their "informed consent" to her taking a position adverse to their interests. The [SEC] also found that the proceedings were properly based in part upon alleged violations of the [1933 Act] and the [1934 Act], and that the violations were wilful. Accordingly, and we think properly, the [SEC] concluded that the "revocation of the registrant's broker-dealer registration is compelled in the public interest."

[On petition for judicial review, t]here was filed in this court, prior to oral argument of the case and pursuant to order of this court, a brief on behalf of 120 of petitioner's 175 clients, who call themselves amici curiae. . . . It argues that the clients have at all times had full knowledge and understanding of the Memorandum of Agreement and the capacity in which petitioner dealt with her clients and that the action of the [SEC] deprives the clients "of the right to continue to do business with Petitioner under a contractual relationship which they fully understand, and which has afforded them a high degree of investment protection, financial gain and security and financial peace of mind." Therefore, amici urge reversal of the order of revocation. Assuming arguendo the truth of the unverified statements in the amici brief, many of which are based on matters outside the record in the instant case, such statements do not constitute grounds for overturning the decision of the [SEC] in this case. If the [SEC]'s decision that petitioner had wilfully violated specified anti-fraud sections of pertinent statutes and regulations is legally correct . . . it is immaterial whether or not a majority, or even all, of petitioner's clients understood completely the nature of their dealings with petitioner and were satisfied with, and had profited by, petitioner's method of doing business with them. . . . [T]he revocation is proper even if one, or none, of the particular clients here involved has been misled or has suffered injury. . . .

In the vast majority of transactions between this petitioner and her clients, petitioner concededly acted as a fiduciary. The record shows clearly that, except for a few isolated instances, petitioner acted simultaneously in the dual capacity of investment adviser and of broker and dealer. In such capacity, conflicting interests must necessarily arise. When they arise, the law has consistently stepped in to provide safeguards in the form of prescribed and stringent standards of conduct on the part of the fiduciary. More than 100 years ago the Supreme Court set forth this principle as follows:

> "In this conflict of interest, the law wisely interposes. It acts not on the possibility, that, in some cases, the sense of that duty may prevail over the motives of self-interest, but it provides against the probability in many cases, and the danger in all cases, that the dictates of self-interest will exercise a predominant influence, and supersede that of duty."

But the [SEC] in this case did not, and we in turn do not, base the validity of the revocation order upon common law principles of fraud or deceit. Section 17(a) of the [1933 Act], Sections 10(b) and 15(c)(1) of the [1934 Act], and [SEC]-made rules thereunder, all quoted supra, in prohibitory language, set out the statutory prescription as to the conduct of the business of a broker and dealer in securities. If any one of these statutes or rules has been wilfully violated by petitioner and revocation is found to be in the public interest, the respondent, by virtue of § 15(b), supra, has authority to revoke.

It cannot now be doubted that, as respondent points out, the securities field . . . requires specialized and unique legal treatment. This is recognized by the very statutes and regulations here under consideration as well as by recent federal and state court decisions. . . .

> "The business of trading in securities is one in which opportunities for dishonesty are of constant recurrence and ever present. It engages acute, active minds, trained to quick apprehension, decision and action. The Congress has seen fit to regulate this business. Though such regulation must be done in strict subordination to constitutional and lawful safeguards of individual rights, it is to be enforced notwithstanding the frauds to be suppressed may take on more subtle and involved forms than those in which dishonesty manifests itself in cruder and less specialized activities."[14]

The acts of petitioner which constitute violations of the antifraud sections of statutes and of regulations thereunder are acts of omission in that petitioner failed to fully disclose the nature and extent of her adverse interest. The [SEC] found that petitioner failed to disclose to her clients (1) the best price at which the securities could be purchased for the clients in the open market in the exercise of due diligence and (2) the cost to petitioner of the securities sold by her to her clients. In no less than three places in the above-quoted statutes and regulations we find that, "any omission to state a material fact necessary in order to make the statements made, in the light of the circumstances under which they were made, not misleading," is expressly made unlawful. These quoted words as they appear in the statute can only mean that Congress forbid not only the telling of purposeful falsity but also the telling of half-truths and the failure to tell the "whole truth." These statutory words were obviously designed to protect the investing public as a whole whether the individual investors be suspicious or unsuspecting. The best price currently obtainable in the open market and the cost to registrant are both material facts within the meaning of the above-quoted language and they are both factors without which informed consent to a fiduciary's acting in a dual and conflicting role is impossible.

Petitioner strongly urges that she has fully and completely fulfilled any disclosure requirement by the insertion in the Memorandum of Agreement (entered into with each of her clients since 1943) of the clause that the "Company, when acting as investment adviser, shall act as Principal in every such transaction, except as otherwise agreed," and that, in any event, petitioner has always stood ready to provide any further information which her clients desired. The clause inserted in the Memorandum of Agreement does not even approach the minimum disclosure requirements. In the first place, it is certainly doubtful whether petitioner's clients either knew of or understood the legal effect of this technical language inserted in fine print in the printed document which each client signed when he or she first became a client of petitioner. Secondly, even assuming, as urged by amici, that all of petitioner's clients are persons of more than average experience and intelligence with regard to the conceded intricacies of securities transactions, an assumption which is at best dubious in view of the present record, their full knowledge that petitioner either sold them securities she then owned or bought securities in her own name and then resold them to the clients cannot be considered sufficient knowledge to enable the clients to give their informed consent. When Mrs. Hughes took the witness stand in the proceedings below she categorically denied that she ever disclosed to her clients either the price she paid for a security, its market price, or any bid and ask prices for the security. She thereafter stated: "If at any time one of my clients wants to ask anything, why, of course, I will answer them and they all know that." Based upon petitioner's own testimony then, the [SEC]'s finding that her disclosure was inadequate was reasonable and correct and supported by substantial evidence of record. It is not enough that one who acts as an admitted fiduciary proclaim that he or she stands ever ready to divulge material facts to the ones whose interests she is being paid to protect. Some knowledge is prerequisite to intelligent questioning. This is particularly true in the securities field. Readiness and willingness to disclose are not equivalent to disclosure. The statutes and rules discussed above make it unlawful to omit to state material facts

[14] *Archer v. SEC*, 133 F.2d 795, 803 (8th Cir. 1943).

irrespective of alleged (or proven) willingness or readiness to supply that which has been omitted.

---

1. **Hughes I *versus* Hughes II.** How does the holding in this *Hughes II* decision compare with the holding of *Hughes I*? Are the securities firms in both cases offering the same service? Are their pricing strategies equivalent?

2. ***The Role of Customers in Securities Regulation Enforcement.*** An interesting and unusual aspect of the Hughes II decision is the intervention of a large number of the petitioner's customers. Were the SEC and the court unduly dismissive of these customers' assertion that revocation of the petitioner's registration was unwarranted? Is it really "immaterial whether . . . all . . . of petitioner's clients understood completely the nature of their dealings with petitioner and were satisfied with . . . petitioner's method of doing business?" Might the court have considered the customer's execution of the Memorandum of Agreement as a waiver of their rights to receive additional information about contemporaneous costs and alternative sources of supply? Would such a waiver be permissible under federal securities laws? *See* Section 29(a) of the 1934 Act.

B. THE ADVISORY RELATIONSHIP

As *Hughes I* and *Hughes II* suggest, broker-dealers often provide not just access to the securities market but investment advice on which securities to buy and sell. In this section, we consider a number of ways in which federal securities laws police the investment advice given by broker-dealers and other regulated entities. A number of broker-dealer obligations are designed to ensure the appropriateness of investment advice. The following case is illustrative.

Mihara v. Dean Witter & Co.

619 F.2d 814 (9th Cir. 1980)

WILLIAM J. CAMPBELL, SENIOR DISTRICT JUDGE.

On April 26, 1974, Samuel Mihara filed this action in United States District Court for the Central District of California. He alleged both federal statutory and California common law fiduciary duty claims arising from the handling of Mihara's securities accounts by defendants. Specifically, plaintiff alleges that the defendants, Dean Witter & Company and its account executive, George Gracis, engaged in excessive trading or "churning" in plaintiff's securities account, and purchased "unsuitable" securities which did not conform to Mihara's stated investment objectives. Plaintiff sought relief under Section 10(b) of the [1934 Act] and Rule 10b-5 promulgated thereunder, as well as for breach of fiduciary duties. [After the trial, a verdict was entered against the defendants on both claims and was awarded $24,600 in compensatory damages. Dean Witter & Company and Gracis were assessed punitive damages awards of $66,666 and $2,000, respectively.]

[Mihara was a 38-year-old engineer who had some money saved. In 1971, he approached an investment advisory firm, Dean Witter, and opened an account with $30,000. Gracis was the Dean Witter investment adviser assigned to handle Mihara's account. Gracis and Mihara initially met to discuss Mihara's investment objectives, where Mihara said he told Gracis that he knew nothing about money and investing and wanted to ensure his family's financial security. Gracis, on the other hand, contends that Mihara told him that he was a relatively sophisticated investor who wanted to pursue a fairly risky investment strategy.

In any case, Gracis began to pursue a risky strategy with Mihara's account, and it lost $46,464 during the period of January 1971 to May 1973 (Mihara added money to the account several times). During this period, Mihara complained numerous times to various members of Dean Witter, starting with Gracis himself and proceeding up the hierarchy to eventually take a meeting with Dean Witter's National Compliance Director. Mihara, dissatisfied with the handling of his account, ultimately filed this lawsuit in 1973.]

At trial plaintiff gave his recollection of the initial meeting with Gracis. He testified that Gracis recommended securities which did not appear to conform to those objectives. He also related the dismal record of the account, and how attempts to remedy the situation through meetings with Gracis' superiors proved fruitless. Plaintiff also introduced the Dean Witter Account Executive Manual which stated that Dean Witter account executives had a "sacred trust to protect" their customers, that Dean Witter customers have confidence in the firm, and "under no circumstances should we violate this confidence.". . .

Plaintiff's expert, Mr. White, a former attorney with the [SEC], testified at trial that the pattern of trading in the Mihara account reflected a pattern of churning. Plaintiff's [evidence] indicated the following holding periods for Mihara's securities. In 1971, 50% of the securities were held for 15 days or less, 61% for 30 days or less, and approximately 76% were held for 60 days or less. Through June of 1973, 81.6% of the securities in the Mihara account were held for a period of 180 days or less. White also relied on the "turnover rate" in Mihara's account in reaching his conclusion. The turnover rate for a given period is arrived at by dividing the total dollar amount of stock purchases for a given period by the average monthly capital investment in the account. Plaintiff's [evidence also] indicates that between January 1971 and July 1973, Mihara's average monthly investment of $36,653 was turned over approximately 14 times. On an annualized basis, Mihara's average capital monthly investment in 1971 of approximately $40,000 was turned over 9.3 times. His average capital investment in 1972 was $39,800 and that was turned over approximately 3.36 times. His average monthly capital investment for the first half of 1973 was $23,588 and that was turned over approximately .288 times. White testified that a substantial turnover in the early stages of the account followed by a significant decline in the turnover rate was typical of a churned account. . . .

The defendant Gracis testified that Mihara was more interested in riskier growth potential investments. He stated he recommended such stocks, but also noted the drawbacks of such investments. Gracis testified that he also warned of the dangers of utilizing a margin account. Gracis also confirmed Mihara's testimony concerning complaints about losses.

. . . When a securities broker engages in excessive trading in disregard of his customer's investment objectives for the purpose of generating commission business, the customer may hold the broker liable for churning in violation of Rule 10b-5. *Hecht v. Harris Upham & Company*, 430 F.2d 1202 (9th Cir. 1970). In order to establish a claim of churning, a plaintiff must show (1) that the trading in his account was excessive in light of his investment objectives; (2) that the broker in question exercised control over the trading in the account; and (3) that the broker acted with the intent to defraud or with the wilful and reckless disregard for the interests of his client.

Whether trading is excessive is a question which must be examined in light of the investment objectives of the customer. While there is no clear line of demarcation, courts and commentators have suggested that an annual turnover rate of six reflects excessive trading. . . . In *Hecht v. Harris Upham & Company*, 283 F.Supp. 417 (N.D. Cal., 1968), aff'd at 430 F.2d 1202, 1210 (9th Cir., 1970), this Court affirmed a finding of churning where an account had been turned over 8 to 11.5 times during a six-year ten-month period. In that case, 45% of the securities were held for less than six months, 67% were held for less than nine months, and 82% were held for less than a year. Under this Court's holding in *Hecht*, the evidence in the present case clearly supports a finding of excessive trading.

With regard to the second prerequisite, we believe that Gracis exercised sufficient control over Mihara's account in the present case to support a finding of churning. The account need not be a discretionary account whereby the broker executes each trade without the consent of the client. As the *Hecht* case indicates, the requisite degree of control is met when the client routinely follows the recommendations of the broker. The present case, as in *Hecht*, reflects a pattern of de facto control by the broker.

The third requisite element of a 10b-5 violation scienter has also been established. The manner in which Mihara's account was handled reflects, at best, a reckless disregard for the client's investment concerns, and, at worst, an outright scheme to defraud plaintiff. Perhaps in recognition of this, appellants have constructed a curious argument as to the scienter element. They suggest that plaintiff must establish an intent to defraud as to each trade executed by the broker. This assertion is entirely without merit. The churning of a client's account is, in itself, a scheme or artifice to defraud within the meaning of Rule 10b-5. With regard to the definition of scienter, this circuit has held that reckless conduct constitutes scienter within the meaning of *Ernst & Ernst v. Hochfelder*, 425 U.S. 185 (1976).

. . . As in the present case, the plaintiff in Hecht received confirmation slips stating exactly what had been purchased and indicating the amount paid. The Court in Hecht went on to find, however, that while the plaintiff was barred from complaining about specific purchases of stock, she was not estopped from maintaining a claim for excessive trading. The Court concluded that while confirmation slips were sufficient to inform plaintiff of the specific transactions made, they were "not sufficient to put her on notice that the trading of her account was excessive." *Hecht v. Harris Upham*, 430 F.2d, at 1210. Thus, the defenses raised by appellants apply only to plaintiff's claims regarding the suitability of the stocks purchased, and not to the claim of churning.

---

1. ***Measuring Damages.*** The measure of damages in churning cases is often a contested issue. Traditionally, damages were limited to the amount of excess commissions, though more recent decisions have also allowed recovery for losses suffered. *See, e.g.*, Miley v. Oppenheimer & Co., 637 F.2d 318 (5th Cir. 1981). Which is the more appropriate measure? Suppose a brokerage firm churned an account, but the account still earned substantial profits. Could the client still recover excessive commissions? *See* Nesbit v. McNeil, 896 F.2d 380 (9th Cir. 1990).

2. ***The Special Study of Securities Markets and the Suitability Doctrine.*** Historically, broker-dealers, like investment advisers today, were subject to a fiduciary obligation to their clients based on common law. In 1963, however, the SEC submitted its Report of Special Study of Securities Markets (the Special Study) to Congress, which shifted the standard of care that broker-dealers were subject to from one of fiduciary to one of suitability. Concerned that broker-dealers were frequently recommending low price, speculative securities to unknown customers, the Special Study recommended "[g]reater emphasis" be given to the "concept of 'suitability' of particular securities for particular customers" instead of applying broad fiduciary standards. The Special Study further called for the National Association of Securities Dealers (NASD) to

provide more guidance and context for its suitability doctrine, such as information on practices that are incompatible with a suitability standard and approved practices for the handling of discretionary accounts. *See* Robert H. Mundheim, *Professional Responsibilities of Broker-Dealers: The Suitability Doctrine*, 1965 DUKE L.J. 445 (1965).

3. ***The Suitability Doctrine and Institutional Investors.*** The suitability doctrine requires that broker-dealers ensure that the recommendations provided to their clients are suitable based on the clients' needs and goals. FINRA Rule 2111 implements this doctrine, requiring broker-dealers to understand the products they recommend to customers and, before making specific recommendations, to consider customer-specific factors such as their age, other investments, financial situation, tax status, investment objectives, investment experience, liquidity needs, and risk tolerance. The doctrine also applies to the servicing of institutional investors, who are typically larger and more sophisticated than individual retail investors. Professor Colombo summarizes this application:

> [FINRA] Rule 2111 is frequently, and advisably, read in conjunction with FINRA Rule 2090—FINRA's 'know your customer' rule. [Reading these two rules together], suitability requires a broker to comprehend his or her client's financial situation . . . via the use of 'reasonable diligence.' Further, the broker must restrict his or her investment suggestions to those that are 'suitable' to the client in light of the client's situation. Observe that what may or may not be suitable is not wholly determined by the client's own wishes, but rather takes into account certain objective factors ('the customer's age, other investments, financial situation and needs, [and so on]'). . . . Further, the suitability requirement does not automatically vanish when a broker's client happens to be an institutional investor. As Rule 2111(b) explains, even in this situation the broker has important suitability obligations. More specifically, the broker must be satisfied that the institutional investor is capable of adequately evaluating the transaction in question, and the institutional investor must affirmative declare that it is indeed exercising independent judgment with regard to the transaction.

Ronald J. Colombo, *Merit Regulation via the Suitability Rules*, 12 J. INT'L BUS. & L. 1, 10–11 (2013). Given the characteristics of institutional investors, do you think that FINRA's suitability rules should apply to the servicing of such investors? What obligations should be imposed on a broker-dealer if an institutional investor affirmatively declares its intention to exercise independent judgment with respect to a transaction?

4. ***Historical Scope of Securities Laws.*** Several years before the *Mihara* case was decided, the Supreme Court handed down a series of cases cutting back on the scope of federal securities laws. In *Santa Fe Industries v. Green*, 430 U.S. 462 (1977), the Court ruled that anti-fraud claims under Rule 10b-5 must be based on the withholding of material information, called deception, rather than simple unfairness or breach of fiduciary duty. In a similar spirit, *Ernst & Ernst v. Hochfelder*, 425 U.S. 185 (1976), held that violations of Rule 10b-5 must entail

intentional misconduct, not mere negligence. Many proceedings against broker-dealers include claims arising under Rule 10b-5. Should the restrictions of the *Ernst & Ernst* and *Santa Fe* cases be read into these actions? Do the specialized anti-fraud provisions for broker-dealers authorize a broader scope of liability in this area? *See* Section 15(c) of the 1934 Act; Rule 15c1-2. *Compare* Donald C. Langevoort, *Fraud and Deception by Securities Professionals*, 61 TEX. L. REV. 147 (1983) (arguing against a strict application of *Santa Fe*'s deception requirement in this context), *with* Karmel, *Is the Shingle Theory Dead?* (arguing that intervening Supreme Court decisions have vitiated the shingle theory).

5. ***Applying the Suitability Doctrine to Robo-Advisers.*** Automated investment services, commonly referred to as robo-advisers, are trading platforms that use algorithms to manage customer investment portfolios. Similar to a human adviser, the robo-advisers rely on customer information such as age, income, and risk tolerance to determine appropriate investments. While used for many years by financial professionals to develop a customer's trading portfolio, robo-advisers can now be accessed directly by customers through platforms, provided by securities firms like Betterment and SigFig. The use of robo-advisers, however, raises questions as to the extent and appropriateness of an automated application providing investment advice directly to customers without the guidance of a human adviser. As noted in a by the joint European Supervisory Authorities: "The potential risks [of customers interacting directly with robo-advisers] include the possibility that consumers could misunderstand advice provided to them without the benefit of a human adviser to support the advice process, and the potential for limitations or errors in automated tools that may not be easily identifiable for customers of financial institutions." What are the advantages and disadvantages of receiving investment advice from a human adviser versus a robo-adviser? What types of suitability concerns are raised by the use of a robo-adviser? *See* SEC Investor Alert, Automated Investor Tools (May 8, 2015); Caroline Binham, *European Watchdogs to Scrutinize Robo-advice Industry*, FINANCIAL TIMES (Dec. 4, 2015).

Part of broker-dealers' suitability obligation includes the duty to become educated about the securities recommended to customers. That issue is taken up in the following case:

Hanly v. SEC

415 F. 2d 589 (2d Cir. 1969)

TIMBERS, DISTRICT JUDGE.

Five securities salesmen petition to review an order of the Securities and Exchange Commission which barred them from further association with any broker or dealer. The [SEC] found that petitioners, in the offer and sale of the stock of U.S. Sonics Corporation (Sonics) between September 1962 and August 1963, willfully violated the antifraud provisions of Section 17(a) of the Securities Act of 1933, Sections 10(b) and 15(c)(1) of the [1934 Act], and Rule 10b-5. Specifically, the [SEC] held that "the fraud in this case consisted of the optimistic representations or the recommendations . . . without disclosure of known or reasonably ascertainable adverse information which rendered them materially misleading. . . . It is clear that a salesman must not merely avoid affirmative misstatements when he recommends the stock to a customer; he must also disclose material adverse facts of which he is or should be aware." Petitioners individually argue that their violations of the federal securities laws were not willful but involved at most good faith optimistic predictions concerning a speculative security . . . .

Violations

[The facts are as follows. Five securities salesmen, named Gladstone, Paras, Hanly, Stutzmann, and Fehr worked for a New York securities broker named Richard J. Buck & Co. In 1962, they learned of a publicly-traded company called Sonics, which manufactured high-tech radio components. Sonics had never turned a profit and was actually insolvent during the time the salesmen pushed it to their clients. While the salesmen knew of the firm's insolvency, they did not relay this information to their clients. To varying degrees, the five salesmen asserted to their customers that Sonics was an excellent buy and omitted information that would have caused their clients to think otherwise. Take, for instance, the Court's summary of assertions and omissions offered by salesman Gladstone:

> Evidence of affirmative misrepresentations by Gladstone to his customers regarding Sonics stock included the following: Sonics was a winner and would make money. It had a fabulous potential and would double or triple. It would make Xerox look like a standstill and would revolutionize the space age industry. Gladstone himself had purchased the stock for his own account and he would be able to retire and get rich on it. It had possibilities of skyrocketing and would probably double in price within six months to a year. Although it had not earned money in the past, prospects were good for earnings of $1 in a year. Sonics had signed a contract with General Instrument. The stock would go from 6 to 12 in two weeks and to 15 in the near future. The 14 page report had been written by Value Line. The company was not going bankrupt. Its products were perfected and it was already earning $1 per share. It was about to have a breakthrough on a new product that was fantastic and would revolutionize automobile and home radios.
>
> In addition to these affirmative misrepresentations, the testimony disclosed that adverse information about Sonics' financial difficulties was not disclosed by Gladstone; that some customers had received confirmations for orders they had not placed; and that literature about the company was not provided. Most of the customer-witnesses testified that they had purchased in reliance upon the recommendations of Gladstone.

The salesmen's information about the company derived from two main sources—an anonymous 14-page report (referenced above) and a conversation with its CEO. The report was a glowing appraisal of Sonics' future as a company but contained no financial information that could be used to assess the company's health. The salesmen never knew who published the report and it was unattributed as-written. In a subsequent conversation, Sonics' CEO corroborated most of the assertions made in the report, but also relayed that the company was insolvent and had never turned a profit. The salesmen apparently made no further efforts to investigate the prospects of Sonics, other than to receive information from one Mr. Roach that Sonics was attempting various measures to stave off bankruptcy. In 1963, the company was declared bankrupt and this suit followed.]

Law Applicable to Violations

In its opinion the [SEC] quoted from the record in attributing the representations discussed above respectively to each of the petitioners. It concluded that their optimistic representations or recommendations were materially false and misleading. Fraud was found both in affirmative falsehoods and in recommendations made without disclosure of known or reasonably ascertainable adverse information, such as Sonics' deteriorating financial condition, its inability to manufacture the filter, the lack of knowledge regarding the filter's commercial feasibility, and the negative results of pending negotiations.

The [SEC] found that the sophistication of the customers or prior relationships which many of them had enjoyed with the respective petitioners were irrelevant. It held that the absence of a boiler room did not justify affirmative misrepresentations or a failure to disclose adverse financial information. The relevance of a customer's nonloss of money or a salesman's speculation in the stock likewise was discounted. . . .

When a securities salesman fraudulently violates the high standards with which he is charged, he subjects himself to a variety of punitive, compensatory and remedial sanctions. In the instant proceedings petitioners have not been criminally charged, nor have they been sued for damages by their customers arising from the alleged misrepresentations. Instead, in private proceedings initiated by the [SEC], each petitioner's privilege of being employed in the securities industry has been revoked. It is in this context that the issues before the Court must be considered. More particularly, we are here concerned with the expertise of the [SEC] in its assessment of how the public interest best may be protected from various kinds of intentional fraud and reckless misconduct which often threaten securities transactions, especially, as here, in the over the counter market.

Brokers and salesmen are "under a duty to investigate, and their violation of that duty brings them within the term 'willful' in the [1934] Act." Thus, a salesman cannot deliberately ignore that which he has a duty to know and recklessly state facts about matters of which he is ignorant. He must analyze sales literature and must not blindly accept recommendations made therein. The fact that his customers may be sophisticated and knowledgeable does not warrant a less stringent standard. Even where the purchaser follows the market activity of the stock and does not rely upon the salesman's statements, remedial sanctions may be imposed since reliance is not an element of fraudulent misrepresentation in this context.

A securities dealer occupies a special relationship to a buyer of securities in that by his position he implicitly represents he has an adequate basis for the opinions he renders. While this implied warranty may not be as rigidly enforced in a civil action where an investor seeks damages for losses allegedly caused by reliance upon his unfounded representations, its applicability in the instant proceedings cannot be questioned.

Sonics was an over the counter stock. Those who purchased through petitioners could not readily confirm the information given them. In *Charles Hughes & Co., Inc. v. SEC*, 139 F.2d 434 (2 Cir. 1943), cert. denied, 321 U.S. 786 (1944), this Court recognized the difficulties involved in over the counter stocks and the special duty imposed upon those who sell such stocks not to take advantage of customers in whom confidence has been instilled.

In summary, the standards by which the actions of each petitioner must be judged are strict. He cannot recommend a security unless there is an adequate and reasonable basis for such recommendation. He must disclose facts which he knows and those which are reasonably ascertainable. By his recommendation he implies that a reasonable investigation has been made and that his recommendation rests on the conclusions based on such investigation. Where the salesman lacks essential information about a security, he should disclose this as well as the risks which arise from his lack of information. . . .

Sanctions

The [SEC] is authorized by Section 15(b)(7) of the [1934] Act, to bar any person from association with a broker or dealer "if the [SEC] finds that such . . . barring . . . is in the public interest . . . ," and that such person has willfully violated the [1933] Act or the [1934] Act.

Acting pursuant to this statutory authority and upon a finding that it was in the public interest to do so, the [SEC], having found that each petitioner had violated the antifraud provisions of the securities laws, ordered that each be barred from further association with any broker or dealer, except that Fehr was barred for only 60 days, after which he may return to the securities business in a non-supervisory capacity and upon an appropriate showing that he will be adequately supervised.

The courts, including ours, uniformly have recognized the fundamental principle that imposition of sanctions necessarily must be entrusted to the expertise of a regulatory commission such as the SEC; and only upon a showing of abuse of discretion—such as the imposition of a sanction unwarranted in law or without justification in fact—will a reviewing court intervene in the matter of sanctions.

For the most part, petitioners' attacks upon the sanctions here imposed do not merit discussion. Their arguments were fully considered by the [SEC] which, in accordance with its undoubted authority, gave different weight to such arguments than petitioners would like. . . . [T]he obvious disparity in culpability between petitioners, reflected in our summary above of the evidence of violations by each, is not a proper basis for challenging the [SEC's] sanctions; nor is the fact that in the case of one or more petitioners only one investor witness testified against him. And of course even the permanent bar order which the [SEC] in its discretion has imposed as to four of the petitioners is not necessarily an irrevocable sanction; upon application, the [SEC], if it finds that the public interest no longer requires the applicant's exclusion from the securities business, may permit his return—usually subject to appropriate safeguards.

There is one aspect of the sanction issue in the instant case which does merit brief mention: the [SEC's] imposition of greater sanctions upon four of the petitioners than ordered by the hearing examiner. This appears to be a matter of first impression, at least in this Court. The [SEC] clearly has the authority to modify, including the authority to increase, sanctions ordered by a hearing examiner in his initial decision, and we so hold.

---

1. ***Defining the Responsibilities and Requirements of Broker-Dealers.*** The *Hanly* decision extends the *Hughes I* and *Hughes II* line of cases in that it defines the responsibilities of broker-dealers when recommending securities to clients. The SEC has also adopted a variety of rules that serve a similar purpose as the *Hughes I*, *Hughes II*, and *Hanly* cases. For example, Rule 15c2-11 specifies the financial information that a broker-dealer must possess before it can set a price by publishing a quotation for a security. Under this rule, publishing a quotation without the requisite information is a fraudulent and manipulative act for purposes of § 15(c)(1) of the 1934 Act. Is it inherently fraudulent and manipulative to quote prices without information of the sort specified in Rule 15c2-11? Would it be better to impose a more open-ended standard of reasonableness in this area?

2. **Hanly *in Civil Actions.*** An interesting and controversial aspect of the *Hanly* decision is its suggestion that the implied warranty in this case "may not be as rigidly enforced in a civil action." The court is, therefore, suggesting that, while the SEC can bring an enforcement action in this case, one of the customers who suffered a loss as a result of the brokers' recommendations might not be able to recover. What is the statutory basis of this distinction? Is it sound policy?

3. ***Sanctions on Individual Violators.*** A critical issue in cases such as the *Hanly* enforcement action is the sanction imposed on individual violators. In this case, several individuals were barred from the securities sector for life. Is this an

appropriate penalty? In *Steadman v. SEC*, 450 U.S. 91 (1981), the Supreme Court ruled that administrative sanctions of this sort need only be supported by "the preponderance of the evidence." We will consider the topic of enforcement strategies in greater detail in Chapter 8.2.

4. ***SEC's 1977 Investigation of Merrill Lynch.*** Shortly after the *Hanly* decision was handed down, the SEC began an enforcement action against Merrill Lynch, one of the nation's largest brokerage firms. An SEC investigation revealed problems similar to those underlying the *Hanly* case: members of the Merrill Lynch sales force had allegedly made false and misleading statements about a company's securities and the firm's research department failed to adequately investigate the company's past performance and future prospects. The SEC eventually settled the matter on the following basis:

> [A]fter consideration of the offer of settlement of Merrill Lynch wherein the firm offers: to accept the imposition of a censure; to pay a sum of up to $1,600,000 pursuant to the terms of its offer to compensate customers of Merrill Lynch who suffered losses resulting from transactions in Scientific; to undertake to review, and, where appropriate, adopt new or modified guidelines relating to its research and sales activities; and, to undertake to review and, where necessary, strengthen its Account Executive Training Programs, the [SEC] accepts Merrill Lynch's offer of settlement.
>
> In deciding to accept this offer, the [SEC] has given weight to the fact that the violations occurring herein, although serious in nature, related to a small portion of Merrill Lynch's total business and a relatively small number of the firm's total employees. The [SEC] recognizes that since the occurrence of the violations found herein Merrill Lynch has improved the quality of its research capability by increasing the number of security analysts the firm employs in its research department and by reducing the number of securities each analyst is assigned to follow. The [SEC] also recognizes that the violations took place in the somewhat speculative climate of the late 1960s when high technology companies were in vogue, however, the [SEC] warns that a speculative climate, no matter how rampant, will not attenuate duties imposed by the securities laws.

Merrill Lynch, Pierce, Fenner & Smith, Inc., Exchange Act Release No. 14,149 (Nov. 9, 1977). How does this penalty compare to the one imposed in the *Hanly* case? Is it appropriate for large firms to be treated differently? *See* Stavros Gadinis, *The SEC and the Financial Industry: Evidence from Enforcement Against Broker-Dealers,* 67 BUS. LAW. 679 (2012) (reporting evidence that SEC enforcement actions may have a tendency to be more lenient with respect to larger broker-dealers as compared with smaller firms).

C. BROKER-DEALERS AS MARKET-MAKERS

We now turn our attention to the responsibilities of broker-dealers in contexts where they perform functions other than giving advice or executing orders for retail investors. Often times, these additional functions present real or potential conflicts of interest. Back in the 1930s, some reformers were so concerned with these conflicts that they recommended the brokerage side of the securities business be completely segregated from the rest of the securities business, just as the Glass-Steagall Act separated commercial banking from investment banking. The idea behind this proposal was that the only effective way to protect consumers from market manipulation and overly aggressive underwriting was to prohibit those sectors from dealing with customers directly. Practical considerations and a sluggish economy ultimately persuaded New Deal legislators not to subdivide the securities sector in this way. Instead, the courts and the SEC have developed a complex system of rules and standards to ameliorate potential problems. As you read through the following materials, consider whether complete segregation would have been a better solution.

Chasins v. Smith, Barney & Co.

438 F.2d 1167 (2d Cir. 1971)

JOSEPH SMITH, CIRCUIT JUDGE.

This is an appeal by Smith, Barney & Co., Inc., a stock brokerage firm (hereinafter "Smith, Barney") from a judgment for damages on a determination by Judge Dudley B. Bonsal in the United States District Court for the Southern District of New York that Smith, Barney had violated Rules 10b-5 and 15c1-4, in not disclosing to appellee (Chasins) that it was making a market in the securities it sold Chasins in the over-the-counter market. . . .

This action brought by Chasins in the district court under the [1933 Act], and the [1934 Act], for damages resulting from Smith, Barney's alleged violations of the Acts . . . in handling Chasins' securities brokerage account was tried to the court without a jury. [Chasins was the musical director of a radio station and the commentator on a musical program sponsored by Smith, Barney. According to Chasins, he opened a brokerage account with Smith, Barney because of this relationship. In the four transactions at issue on appeal, Smith, Barney acted both as a stockbroker and as a principal, i.e. the owner of the security being sold to Chasins. Although Smith, Barney revealed in the confirmation slips that it was acting as principal, it did not reveal it was "making a market" in the securities as well. Nor did Smith, Barney disclose how much it had paid for the securities sold as principal to Chasins or that it had acted as an "underwriter" in connection with the distribution of securities of Welch Scientific Company and Howard Johnson Company, two of the companies whose securities Smith, Barney sold to Chasins.]

Preceding the four sales of July and August, 1961, Smith, Barney sent Chasins a written analysis of his then current security holdings and its recommendations in regard to his objective of aggressive growth of his holdings. The recommendations included strong purchase recommendations for securities of Welch Scientific, Tex-Star Oil and Gas Corp., and Howard Johnson Company. Chasins and Thomas N. Delaney, Jr., an authorized agent of Smith, Barney had various telephone conversations prior to the transactions in question. [Delaney testified that Smith, Barney was "making a market" in these securities, i.e., it was maintaining a position in the stocks on its own account by participating in over-the-counter trading in them. Smith, Barney's records indicated that it had been trading in those stocks and had held positions in them during the times Chasins purchased the securities from it.][4] There was no testimony that Chasins had any

---

[4] Market maker has been defined by SEC Rule 17a-9(f)(1). . . as follows: (1) The term 'market-maker' shall mean a dealer who, with respect to a particular security, holds himself out (by entering indications of interest in purchasing and selling in an inter-dealer quotations system or otherwise) as being willing to buy and sell for his own account on a continuous basis otherwise than on a national securities exchange.

knowledge or notice that Smith, Barney was "making a market" in the securities of the three companies.

The decision of the district court was based on conflicting evidence as to whether Chasins had a "discretionary account" with Smith, Barney and on the four transactions above. Although the court ruled that Smith, Barney had not violated any common law fiduciary duty to Chasins, Smith, Barney was found to have violated Rules 10b-5 and 15c1-4 (the latter in a supplemental opinion) in not disclosing its market making (or dealer) status in the securities that it recommended Chasins purchase, when Chasins followed that advice and purchased the securities and Smith, Barney was the other principal in the sales. Damages were awarded to Chasins in the amount of $18,616.64, with interest, which constituted the difference between the price at which Chasins purchased the securities from Smith, Barney and the price at which he later sold them (prior to discovering Smith, Barney's market making in the securities). . . .

Smith, Barney's major contention . . . is that failure to disclose its "market making" role in the securities exchanged over the counter was not failure to disclose a material fact. Appellant contends that the district court's holding went farther than any other decision in this area and that no court had ever found failure to disclose a "market making" role by a stock brokerage firm to a client-purchaser to be a violation of Rule 10b-5. Smith, Barney also asserts that all brokerage firms had followed the same practice and had never thought such disclosure was required; moreover, the SEC had never prosecuted any firm for this violation. However, even where a defendant is successful in showing that it has followed a customary course in the industry, the first litigation of such a practice is a proper occasion for its outlawry if it is in fact in violation. . . . In any event, it cannot fairly be said that no one in the trade had ever considered such nondisclosure to be significant. . . .

Appellant also points to the fact that in over-the-counter trading, a market maker with an inventory in a stock is considered the best source of the security (the best available market); thus, the SEC has even punished a brokerage firm for not going directly to a firm with an inventory in a stock, i.e., interposing another firm between them. . . . However, the fact that dealing with a market maker should be considered by some desirable for some purposes does not mean that the failure to disclose Smith, Barney's market-making role is not under the circumstances of this case a failure to disclose a material fact. The question here is not whether Smith, Barney sold to Chasins at a fair price but whether disclosure of Smith, Barney's being a market maker . . . might have influenced Chasins' decision to buy the stock. . . . The test of materiality "is whether a reasonable man would attach importance in determining his choice of action in the transaction in question." . . . [T]he question of materiality becomes whether a reasonable man in Chasins' position might well have acted otherwise than to purchase if he had been informed of Smith, Barney's market making role in the three stocks in addition to the fact that Smith, Barney was the other principal in the transaction. The broker-dealer, Smith, Barney, had undertaken to make a written evaluation of Chasins' securities holdings and had strongly recommended sales of some of his holdings and purchases of these three stocks in which Smith, Barney was dealing as a principal.

Knowledge of the additional fact of market making by Smith, Barney in the three securities recommended could well influence the decision of a client in Chasins' position, depending on the broker-dealer's undertaking to analyze and advise, whether to follow its recommendation to buy the securities; disclosure of the fact would indicate the possibility of adverse interests which might be reflected in Smith, Barney's recommendations. Smith, Barney could well be caught in either a "short" position or a "long" position in a security, because of erroneous judgment of supply and demand at given levels. If over supplied, it may be to the interest of a market maker to attempt to unload the securities on his retail clients. Here, Smith, Barney's strong recommendations of the three securities Chasins purchased could have been motivated by its own market position rather than the intrinsic desirability of the securities for Chasins. An investor who is at least informed of the possibility of such adverse interests, due to his broker's market making in the securities recommended, can question the reasons for the recommendations. The investor, such as Chasins, must be permitted to evaluate overlapping motivations through appropriate disclosures, especially where one motivation is economic self-interest. *See* SEC v. Capital Gains Research Bureau, Inc., 375 U.S. 180 at 196 (1963).

[T]he broker-dealer had undertaken at its customer's request to make a written evaluation of his securities holdings and recommendations for further purchases and sales knowing that the customer, who was, as pointed out above, musical director of a radio station and commentator on a musical program sponsored by Smith, Barney, would rely on its report to him. In this situation failure to inform the customer fully of its possible conflict of interest, in that it was a market maker in the securities which it strongly recommended for purchase by him, was an omission of material fact in violation of Rule 10b-5. . . .

FRIENDLY, CIRCUIT JUDGE (DISSENTING FROM DENIAL OF REHEARING EN BANC).

. . . The district court initially found that the confirmations here, which disclosed that Smith Barney was selling "as principal for our own account," were in full compliance with the rule. Although Rule 17a-9(f) defines "market-maker," this is in a reporting requirement; it is conceded that in 1961 no rule of the SEC (other than, allegedly, the inevitable Rule 10b-5), the NASD or the New York Stock Exchange required disclosure of that fact to a customer.

The complaint nowhere asserted that Smith Barney was under a duty to tell Mr. Chasins it was a "market-maker" in the three over-the-counter stocks that he bought. It alleged rather that defendant did not disclose the "best price" at which these and other securities could have been bought or sold in the open market, or the prices it had paid or received, and that plaintiff was deceived by Smith Barney's failure to disclose "the material fact of its adverse interest, the extent of which is today still unknown to and not determinable by plaintiff." The plaintiff, a noted musicologist, said nothing about market-making in his testimony. The closest he came to making the claim now sustained was that, despite his alleged inability to comprehend financial matters, he would have understood if told that the stock reflected by the confirmations was owned by the defendant, since "if you have a great picture, for example, and you know that the picture is going to be worth a lot more the next year or five years or ten, I don't think you would be anxious to dispose of it." Although this is hardly convincing, since great pictures are constantly being sold and bought under exactly such circumstances, Mr. Chasins had been plainly told of defendant's ownership by the confirmation slips. In addition, the Smith Barney research report he had received on Tex-Star contained the legend in common use at the time: "We point out that in the course of our regular business we may be long or short of any of the above securities at any time," and the prospectus he received of Welch Scientific Company disclosed that Smith Barney was one of the underwriters of that stock, which had only recently been placed on the market. All that the trial record contained about non-disclosure of market making was a statement by Delaney, a registered representative of Smith Barney, that he normally would bring this fact to the attention of clients if he knew it; that he did know Smith Barney was making a market in the three stocks; and that he couldn't recall whether or not he had brought this to Mr. Chasins' attention. . . .

The conclusions on the materiality of disclosure of market making by the district court and in this court's opinion are predicated on an essential misconception of the role of the market maker in over-the-counter transactions. When a reputable house like Smith Barney acts as one of several market makers, as was the case here, it serves a highly desirable purpose in reducing the spreads characteristic of over-the-counter trading. It has been widely recognized that the "best price" can be obtained by dealing directly with market makers, for one reason because a commission to an intermediary is avoided. . . . The district judge's fears concerning the ability of a market maker to set an arbitrary price are inapplicable when as here there were several market makers, as Smith Barney pointed out in its post-trial motion and the SEC now confirms in its letter to us as amicus curiae. Moreover Smith Barney offered to prove that in fact Mr. Chasins bought at the lowest available price. So far as concerns the fears of ulterior motives voiced by the district judge and now by the court, the market maker, who buys as well as sells, is less likely to be interested in palming off a stock than a dealer with only a long position. Yet the confirmation here would plainly have been adequate for such a dealer, and we held only recently, in a case curiously not cited, that a dealer need not make the additional disclosure that it had originally acquired the stock for investment and not with a view towards distribution, something considerably more material than being one of several market makers, *SEC. v. R.A. Holman & Co.*, 366 F.2d 456, 457 (2 Cir., 1966). At the very least the materiality of market making to an investment decision was an issue on which Smith Barney was entitled to submit proofs. It never had a fair opportunity to do this, although we read the court's opinion as leaving this open to defendants in future cases.

---

1. ***Broker-Dealers' Obligation to Disclose.*** The *Chasins* case illustrates the problem of defining the scope of the broker-dealer's obligation to disclose material information to customers. As is true in many cases of this sort, the transaction took place in a highly regulated environment. The SEC had adopted fairly detailed rules regarding the kinds of information broker-dealers must include in the confirmation slips issued in connection with every securities transaction. These requirements are codified in Rule 10b-10 under the 1934 Act. When the transactions at issues in the *Chasins* case were executed, SEC confirmation rules did not require disclosure of Smith Barney's market-maker status. Should the absence of such government-mandated disclosures have been a complete defense for the firm?

2. ***FINRA Mark-Up Rule.*** FINRA Rule 2121 requires broker-dealers to buy or sell securities at prices which are fair after taking into account all relevant circumstances, including market conditions. Under the rule, one factor that broker-dealers should consider is whether they disclosed their commission rates or mark-up fees to the client. Broker-dealers, therefore, can at least partly justify higher commission rates or mark-up fees by disclosing these figures to clients before effecting a transaction. Regardless, FINRA has taken the general position that in most customer transactions markups of 5% or less are fair and reasonable. Has FINRA achieved the correct balance between disclosure and fairness? If yes, what should the disclosure include?

3. ***Customers' Right to Information.*** Hansen Ltd., a brokerage firm, wants to develop its reputation for expertise in small, over-the-counter stocks. To align its sales force with this corporate objective, Hansen would like to establish a sales incentive program under which registered representatives receive additional compensation for transactions involving over-the-counter securities as opposed to New York Stock Exchange (NYSE) listed shares. Should the terms of the program be revealed to customers? Note that the customers would pay the same commission regardless of where the securities were traded. *See* Shivangi v. Dean Witter, 825 F.2d 885 (5th Cir. 1987).

III. BROKER-DEALERS VERSUS INVESTMENT ADVISERS

A. ILLUSTRATING THE DIFFERENCES

As noted in the previous section, securities laws have developed such that investment advisers remain subject to more stringent common law fiduciary duties than broker-dealers, whose duties are constrained by the suitability doctrine. *See, e.g.*, SEC v. Capital Gains Research Bureau, 375 U.S. 180 (1963) (interpreting the Advisers Act to impose a fiduciary duty on investment advisers.) This difference in duties has caused confusion among relatively unsophisticated retail investors, who may not realize that the broker-dealer giving them advice is not held to the same legal standard as an investment adviser. Recall from Chapter 4.1 that broker-dealers can offer investment advice to customers under an exception in the Investment Advisers Act of 1940, so long as their compensation arrangements do not include an additional charge for advisory services.

The following is an excerpt from a report commissioned by the SEC and prepared by the RAND Institute that attempts to clarify the distinction between broker-dealers and investment advisers. It first describes the duties of broker-dealers, then investment advisers, and ends with a direct comparison of the two.

RAND Institute for Civil Justice, Investor and Industry Perspectives on Investment Advisors and Broker-Dealers

2008

Regulation of Broker-Dealers

. . . Both the SEC and FINRA have several rules that govern the conduct of broker-dealers. The "regulatory-conduct" duties for broker-dealers are significant. We begin with discussion of registration requirements for broker-dealers. We then list some of the more important regulatory requirements in the sections that follow. We conclude the section on regulation of broker-dealers with discussion of the extension of fiduciary duties to broker-dealers handling discretionary (or "discretionary-like") accounts. . . .

Broker-Dealers and Fiduciary Duties

An important factor in the legal obligations of financial service providers (and the rights of their clients) is the extent to which such financial professionals owe fiduciary duties to their clients. Unlike a contractual duty (which allows a party relatively broad discretion to pursue its own self-interest, subject to a loose good-faith constraint), fiduciary duties require a heightened duty to act on another's behalf, in good faith, with honesty, with trust, with care, and with candor. Nearly 80 years ago, U.S. Supreme Court Justice Benjamin N. Cardozo famously described the distinct nature of the fiduciary duty:

> Many forms of conduct permissible in a workaday world for those acting at arm's length are forbidden to those bound by fiduciary ties. A trustee is held to something stricter than the morals of the market place. Not honesty alone, but the punctilio of an honor the most sensitive is then the standard of behavior.

Unlike the case of investment advisers, broker-dealers are not categorically bound—by statute, regulation, or precedent—to a per se rule imposing fiduciary obligations toward clients. Instead, the existence of fiduciary obligations within a broker-client relationship has historically been significantly more contingent, turning ultimately on the factual nature of the relationship (usually as interpreted by courts and arbitrators).

Perhaps the most critical distinction along these lines is that between nondiscretionary accounts (for which the broker-dealer simply carries out specific market or limit orders on behalf of its client) and discretionary accounts (for which the client has given consent for the broker-dealer to purchase and sell securities on his or her behalf without consent for each transaction—often with restrictions on the categorical domain of such securities). By both title and description, discretionary accounts give a broker-dealer significantly more freedom to exercise judgment for the client. Instead of merely executing the client's transactional instructions, a broker for a discretionary account will tend to make trades on his or her own accord, on an ongoing basis, on the client's behalf. It is not surprising, then, that such freedom comes at additional potential risk that the broker may abuse that discretion or otherwise run afoul of the client's best interests. Accordingly, brokers who handle discretionary accounts are generally thought to owe fiduciary obligations to their clients. Not only do such duties transcend the basic regulatory constraints placed on the broker, but they also give rise to individual enforcement rights by the client.

In contrast, brokers handling nondiscretionary accounts are generally thought to owe a much more limited and shallow pool of duties to the customer, principally concerning many of the rules that apply to all registrants, including prompt order execution, knowing one's security, knowing one's customer, disclosing conflicts of interest, and refraining from engaging in securities fraud. Significantly, this set of duties is generally perceived not to rise to the level of a fiduciary relationship.

At least two additional factors further cloud this landscape. First, some brokerage accounts may possess some characteristics of both discretionary and nondiscretionary accounts. For example, a broker handling a putatively nondiscretionary account may simply begin to make decisions on behalf of his or her client, effectively exercising de facto control over not only executions of client orders but also over the contents of those orders themselves. Even when the client is continuously apprised of such orders, courts have, on occasion, found that the broker's course of performance in exercising control created a fiduciary obligation.

Second, for nearly two decades, the jurisprudential tests for divining the existence and extent of fiduciary obligations among brokers have remained in a form of doctrinal stasis, with little or no evolutionary development of legal precedents. The reason for this hiatus is that virtually all disputes in this period involving brokers' allegedly breached duties to their clients have been adjudicated through arbitration, a process that does not generate published, written opinions. . . .

Regulation of Investment Advisers

The federal Investment Advisers Act of 1940 regulates the collection of financial professions that typically includes financial planners, money managers, and investment consultants. The act defines an investment adviser as any person who, for compensation, is engaged in a business of providing advice to others or issuing reports or analyses regarding securities. This test is conjunctive (and thus both parts must be satisfied for a party to be deemed an investment adviser under the act). However, the SEC—which is authorized under statute to administer the act—has interpreted its ambit relatively broadly. . . .

Fiduciary Duties [for Investment Advisers]

In addition to registration requirements, and unlike broker-dealers, federally registered investment advisers owe fiduciary obligations to their clients as a categorical matter. As noted already, such obligations require the adviser to act solely with the client's investment goals and interests in mind, free from any direct or indirect conflicts of interest that would tempt the adviser to make recommendations that would also benefit him or her. Although the specific standards for fiduciary obligations are not laid out clearly in the statute, they are unambiguously a centerpiece of the [Investment Company Act of 1940's (1940 Act)] differential treatment of investment advisers, and their categorical application has since been upheld in numerous specific circumstances (see, e.g., *Lowe v SEC*, 472 U.S. 181, 1985, p. 210). Some of these requirements are similar to those that apply to nonfiduciary broker-dealers, including a suitability requirement, a requirement that the adviser have a reasonable basis for his or her recommendations, and a best-execution requirement. However, the universal duties imposed on investment advisers differ in number, degree, and mechanism of enforcement. As noted, the kernel of the fiduciary obligations that investment advisers owe to clients is to refrain from any undisclosed conflicts of interest, a requirement that constrains only some broker-dealers. In addition, even for those requirements that appear similar to those for broker-dealers, violation may be viewed as much more significant.

The fiduciary duties imposed on investment advisers require any adviser either to refrain from acting with a conflict of interest or to fully disclose the conflict and receive specific consent from the client to so act. Examples of such conflicts include various practices in which an adviser may have pecuniary interest (through, e.g., fees or profits generated in another commercial relationship, finder's fees, outside commissions or bonuses) in recommending a transaction to a client. Moreover, these duties have been held to apply both to current and to prospective clients, and thus even deceptive advertising falls under the act's proscriptions. . . .

The Dividing Line Between Investment Advisers and Broker-Dealers

Because of the distinct regulatory structures of registration, disclosure, and legal duties placed on investment advisers and broker-dealers, the dividing line between these two categories has always been an important (though also an elusive) one. Under the 1940 [A]ct, registered brokers and dealers are excluded from the terms of the 1940 [A]ct so long as the following are true:

- Any advice that the broker-dealer gives to clients is "solely incidental" to its business as a broker-dealer.
- The broker-dealer does not receive any "special compensation" for rendering such advice.

The proscription on special compensation has traditionally meant that broker-dealers receive compensation from their brokerage clients in the form of commissions, markups, and markdowns on specific trades. In essence, then, investment advisers' business practice of charging a general fee, rather than broker-dealers' practice of charging transaction-specific fees, has evolved into one of the hallmark distinctions between investment advisers and broker-dealers. Although a broker-dealer could, in theory, charge a management fee and avoid being deemed an investment adviser by giving solely incidental investment advice, the judicial interpretation of solely incidental is fraught with ambiguity, and thus the mechanism by which broker-dealers and investment advisers charge clients for services has become a significant issue from a regulatory perspective. Consequently, over the past two decades, broker-dealers have begun to drift subtly into a domain of activities that (at least under the regulatory regime) have historically been the province of investment advisers. Simultaneously, investment advisers have also begun to enhance the scope of advisory activities they offer in a way that has not been part of the traditional norm. Some investment advisers, for example, may offer services that employ computerized trading programs and may take an active, discretionary management role over customer accounts. From the retail investor's prospective, these activities may not be obviously distinct from those in which brokers typically engage. Adding further ambiguity to the mix is the emergence, also during the past 20 years, of a category of financial service provider known as financial planners. This field is itself highly professionalized, with a certification program that involves rigorous training and testing. Moreover, the financial planner is sometimes identified as an entity independent of either the broker-dealer or the investment adviser, offering generalized advice about a general financial plan for a client and not handling client accounts or executing transactions.

However, it is widely acknowledged that financial planners typically offer a range of services, which need not correspond with this description.

In the 1990s, a number of other types of brokerage accounts, including "discount" brokerage accounts and "fee-based" accounts, further blurred the distinction between broker-dealers and investment advisers. The popularity of discount brokerage programs grew in the 1990s because they were attractive to brokerage customers who wanted to trade securities at a lower commission rate and who did not want assistance from a registered representative. Full-service broker-dealers began to introduce discount brokerage accounts to compete with discount broker-dealers. However, they continued to offer full-service brokerage accounts that still included assistance from registered representatives, for a higher commission rate than that charged for discount brokerage accounts. There was concern that offering both discount and full-service brokerage accounts would require full-service accounts to come under the proscription of the 1940 [A]ct. This concern arose because, with a two-tiered commission structure, the difference in commission rates between full-service and discount brokerage accounts could be viewed as special compensation . . . .

During this same period, fee-based brokerage programs were gaining popularity as well . . . In 1994, at the request of then-SEC chair Arthur Levitt, a committee was formed to identify conflicts of interest in the retail brokerage industry and to identify best practices to reduce these conflicts. Formation of the Committee on Compensation Practices was, in part, motivated by concerns that commission-based compensation may encourage registered representatives to churn accounts or make unsuitable recommendations. The chair of the committee was Daniel Tully, and the resulting report came to be known as the Tully report. In terms of compensation policies, the Tully report defined best practices as those "designed to align the interest of all three parties in the relationship—the client, the registered representative, and the brokerage firm." Among the best practices that the committee found was "paying a portion of [registered-representative] compensation based on client assets in an account, regardless of transaction activity, so the [registered representatives] received some compensation even if they advise a client to 'do nothing'" In further discussion of compensation based on client assets, the report specifically mentions fee-based accounts as potentially being "particularly appropriate for investors who prefer a consistent and explicit monthly or annual charge for services received, and whose level of trading activity is moderate."

Fee-based brokerage accounts typically provide customers with a bundle of brokerage services for either a flat fee or a fee based on assets in the account. As with discount brokerage accounts, there was concern that the introduction of fee-based accounts would trigger the 1940 [A]ct, due to violation of the special-compensation exemption.

The burgeoning size, scale, and intertwined scope of activities among various financial service providers likely enhanced a general sense of uncertainty about the regulatory categorization of such providers. This sense of uncertainty, in turn, contributed to additional rulemaking activity by the SEC.

B. HARMONIZATION OF FIDUCIARY DUTIES

The previous section juxtaposed the differing fiduciary duties of broker-dealers and investment advisers. While there may be some reasons to believe that some such distinction is justified, such as the relative sophistication of retail investors or the ongoing nature of advisory relationships as opposed to the transaction-based nature of broker-dealer relationships, one can also argue for the harmonization of securities firms' duties. Indeed, in 2011, the SEC released a report pursuant to § 913 of the Dodd-Frank Act, which mandated that the SEC conduct a study to evaluate, among other things, the efficacy of current legal standards in retail investing, potential confusion among retail investors regarding the broker-dealer and investment adviser distinction, and the potential impact of holding broker-dealers to the standard of care applicable to investment advisers. *See* Dodd-Frank Act § 913(b)–(c). In fact, the RAND Institute's 2008 report that you read in the previous section informed this 2011 SEC report. Read the following excerpts of the report and ask yourself if the SEC's position is persuasive, and why.

SEC, Study on Investment Advisers and Broker-Dealers

Jan. 2011

[This is a study by the Staff of the SEC. The SEC has expressed no view regarding the analysis, findings, or conclusions contained herein.]

Broker-dealers and investment advisers are regulated extensively, but the regulatory regimes differ, and broker-dealers and investment advisers are subject to different standards under federal law when providing investment advice about securities. Retail investors generally are not aware of these differences or their legal implications. Many investors are also confused by the different standards of care that apply to investment advisers and broker-dealers. That investor confusion has been a source of concern for regulators and Congress. . . .

Uniform Fiduciary Standard: Consistent with Congress's grant of authority in Section 913, the Staff recommends the consideration of rulemakings that would apply expressly and uniformly to both broker-dealers and investment advisers, when providing personalized investment advice about securities to retail customers, a fiduciary standard no less stringent than currently applied to investment advisers under [Investment] Advisers Act Sections 206(1) and (2). . . .

The Staff notes that Section 913 explicitly provides that the receipt of commission-based compensation, or other standard compensation, for the sale of securities does not, in and of itself, violate the uniform fiduciary standard of conduct applied to a broker-dealer. Section 913 also provides that the uniform fiduciary standard does not necessarily require broker-dealers to have a continuing duty of care or loyalty to a retail customer after providing personalized investment advice.

The following recommendations suggest a path toward implementing a uniform fiduciary standard for investment advisers and broker-dealers when providing personalized investment advice about securities to retail customers:

- *Standard of Conduct*: The [SEC] should exercise its rulemaking authority to implement the uniform fiduciary standard of conduct for broker-dealers and investment advisers when providing personalized investment advice about securities to retail customers. Specifically, the Staff recommends that the uniform fiduciary standard of conduct established by the [SEC] should provide that: "the standard of conduct for all brokers, dealers, and investment advisers, when providing personalized investment advice about securities to retail customers (and such other customers as the [SEC] may by rule provide), shall be to act in the best interest of the customer without regard to the financial or other interest of the broker, dealer, or investment adviser providing the advice."

- *Implementing the Uniform Fiduciary Standard*: The [SEC] should engage in rulemaking and/or issue interpretive guidance addressing the components of the uniform fiduciary standard: the duties of loyalty and care. . . .
- *Duty of Loyalty*: A uniform standard of conduct will obligate both investment advisers and broker-dealers to eliminate or disclose conflicts of interest. The [SEC] should prohibit certain conflicts and facilitate the provision of uniform, simple and clear disclosures to retail investors about the terms of their relationships with broker-dealers and investment advisers, including any material conflicts of interest. . . .
- *Duty of Care*: The [SEC] should consider specifying uniform standards for the duty of care owed to retail investors, through rulemaking and/or interpretive guidance. Minimum baseline professionalism standards could include, for example, specifying what basis a broker-dealer or investment adviser should have in making a recommendation to an investor. . . .

The Staff believes that the uniform fiduciary standard and related disclosure requirements may offer several benefits, including the following:

- Heightened investor protection;
- Heightened investor awareness;
- It is flexible and can accommodate different existing business models and fee structures;
- It would preserve investor choice;
- It should not decrease investors' access to existing products or services or service providers;
- Both investment advisers and broker-dealers would continue to be subject to all of their existing duties under applicable law; and
- Most importantly, it would require that investors receive investment advice that is given in their best interest, under a uniform standard, regardless of the regulatory label (broker-dealer or investment adviser) of the professional providing the advice.

---

1. ***Relevance of Business Models.*** Broker-dealers and affiliated trade associations have criticized the SEC's proposal for a uniform fiduciary duty, pointing to the compliance costs generated by the difference in business models between broker-dealers and advisers. *See, e.g.*, Letter from Ira D. Hammerman, Senior Managing Director and General Counsel, SIFMA, to Elizabeth M. Murphy, Secretary, SEC, (July 5, 2013), at 10; *see also* Ryan K. Bakhtiari, Katrina Boice, and Jeffrey S. Majors, *The Time for a Uniform Fiduciary Duty is Now*, 87 ST. JOHNS L. REV. 313, 329–30 (2013). For example, because broker-dealers operate on a transaction-by-transaction basis with their customers, the Investment Advisers Act of 1940, which characterizes an adviser's duty as continuous and ongoing, may be inapt and confusing when applied to broker-dealers. *See* Hammerman, SIFMA Letter at 11–12. FINRA, a prominent self-regulatory organization, has also criticized the staff study on similar grounds, arguing instead for a more nuanced uniform fiduciary duty for broker-dealers and investment advisers based on common law agency principles and focused on disclosure of conflicts. *See* Letter from Mark Menchel, Executive Vice President and General Counsel, Financial Industry Regulatory Authority to Elizabeth M.

Murphy, Secretary, SEC, at 2 (Aug. 25, 2010) ("[T]he [SEC] should not merely export to broker-dealers the regulatory scheme applied to advisers under the Advisers Act . . . [because this would] fail to acknowledge the specialized role of broker dealers . . . . Instead, the [SEC] should . . . incorporate common law agency principles and require cogent, plain English disclosure at the time of account opening of permissible conflicts . . . .") However, note that certain broker-dealers are dually-registered, providing both broker-dealer and advisory services to their customers. Such firms currently face two compliance regimes, requiring extensive procedures and employee training. Arguably, a uniform fiduciary duty would help reduce the cost of compliance for such dually registered firms by reducing or eliminating one of the compliance regimes altogether. *See, e.g.*, Stephen Wink, Stefan Paulovic & Michael Shaw, *Dually Registered Brokers and Advisers*, 46 REV. SEC. & COMMODITIES REG. 191, 197 (2013) ("A harmonized fiduciary standard for Advisers and Brokers would further simplify the compliance structure of dually registered entities.").

2. ***Impact on Investor Access to Brokerage Services.*** In addition to the concern about the disproportionate impact on broker-dealers due to their transaction-based business models, there is also the concern that a uniform fiduciary duty would increase brokerage costs to investors and even eliminate whole areas of brokerage services, including middle and lower income investment products. *See, e.g.*, Letter from Susan B. Waters, Chief Executive Officer, National Association of Insurance and Financial Advisors to Elizabeth M. Murphy, SEC, at 11 (Aug. 30, 2011). Putting aside potential concerns about the desirability of such middle and lower income products when provided by broker-dealers under the lower suitability standard, should such economic arguments nonetheless hold as much sway as their proponents say they should? Or do investor expectations, and confusion when such expectations are not met, overcome such economic arguments? For further discussion, *see* Arthur B. Laby, *Selling Advice and Creating Expectations: Why Brokers Should Be Fiduciaries*, 87 WASH. L. REV. 707 (2012) (arguing that the better justification for a uniform fiduciary duty is the importance of reasonable investor expectations).

3. ***Potential Dilution of Adviser Standards.*** Other critics, such as investment advisers and affiliated trade associations, argue that a uniform fiduciary duty may dilute protections for investors overall because the duty's stringency would be decreased in order to accommodate broker dealers. *See, e.g.*, Letter from A. Heath Abshure, President, North American Securities Administrators Association, et al. to the Honorable Mary Jo White, Chairman, SEC, at 2 (June 4, 2013) ("[W]e fear that [the staff's study proposal for harmonization] would significantly weaken the fiduciary standard for SEC-registered investment advisers while adding few protections for investors who rely on broker-dealers for investment advice."); *see also* Kristina A. Fausti, *A Fiduciary Duty for All?*, 12 DUQUESNE BUS. L.J. 183, 193 (2010) ("[M]elding the fair dealing and fiduciary standards together will only serve to dilute fiduciary principles, which currently place the burden on the professional to act in the investor's best interest."). Notice how this criticism stands in contrast to the worry that a uniform fiduciary duty would be too onerous for broker-dealers. How do you think the duty should be adjusted in practice? What kinds of empirical evidence would be helpful in determining which possibility is more

likely? For an example of empirical research done in this area, see Sendhil Mullainathan, Markus Noeth & Antoinette Schoar, *The Market for Financial Advice: An Audit Study* 9-19, (Nat'l Bureau of Econ. Research, Working Paper No. 17929, 2012) (sending "mystery shoppers" to financial advisers and brokers posing as regular customers seeking advice on how to invest their retirement savings, each representing different levels of bias or misinformation about financial markets, cataloging the general content of advice received and whether the shoppers misconceptions about the market were corrected). For a more general overview of the economics of fiduciary duties, *see* Robert H. Sitkoff, *An Economic Theory of Fiduciary Law, in* PHILOSOPHICAL FOUNDATIONS OF FIDUCIARY LAW 197 (Andrew S. Gold & Paul B. Miller eds., 2014).

4. ***The Department of Labor's Proposed Fiduciary Duty Rule under ERISA.*** While the SEC has not made significant strides toward implementing a fiduciary duty for broker-dealers, the Department of Labor has promulgated a proposed rulemaking that would expand the applicability of a fiduciary best interest standard to any person providing "investment advice or recommendations to an employee benefit plan, plan fiduciary, plan participant or beneficiary, [Individual Retirement Arrangement], or [Individual Retirement Arrangement] owner as fiduciaries" under the Employee Retirement Income Securities Act of 1974 (ERISA) or the Internal Revenue Code. DEP'T OF LABOR, Definition of the Term "Fiduciary"; Conflict of Interest Rule—Retirement Investment Advice, 80 FED. REG. 21928, 21928 (2015). This rulemaking has not only been criticized by securities firms, but also has encountered subtle opposition from SEC Chair Mary Jo White. *See* Dave Michaels, *SEC Joins Battle on Broker Bias That Could Remake Industry*, BLOOMBERG, Mar. 17, 2015. Going forward, the harmonization of duties in this area may feature interagency cooperation or conflict, beyond the securities sector perspectives discussed above.

5. ***Suitability in the EU.*** In 2004, the EU passed the Markets in Financial Instruments Directive (MiFID) to harmonize regulation of investment services across the EU member states and Iceland, Norway, and Liechtenstein. MiFID subjected investment advice to a suitability requirement that was enhanced by MiFID II in 2007. Under MiFID II, a suitability determination takes two forms: (1) an assessment of suitability for firms providing investment advice or portfolio management services; and (2) an assessment of appropriateness for all other services provided. The MiFID's suitability requirement requires firms to gather "necessary information" about their clients including a client's risk tolerance and ability to bear losses. Securities firms must also provide customers with a suitability statement specifying the basis on which the investment recommendations made are suitable for the client. *See* NIAMH MOLONEY, EU SECURITIES AND FINANCIAL MARKETS REGULATION ch. 9 (Oxford Univ. Press 2014); Directive 2004/39/EC of the European Parliament and of the Council on Markets in Financial Instruments, 2004 O.J. L 145, 30.4.2004 (MiFID I); Directive 2014/65/EU of the European Parliament and of the Council on Markets in Financial Instruments, 2014 O.J. L 173/349 (MiFID II).

IV. THE RISE OF SECURITIES ARBITRATION

We now turn our attention to a Supreme Court decision that revolutionized the way in which customer disputes are resolved in the securities sector.

Shearson/American Express Inc. v. McMahon

482 U.S. 220 (1987)

JUSTICE O'CONNOR DELIVERED THE OPINION OF THE COURT.

This case presents two questions regarding the enforceability of predispute arbitration agreements between brokerage firms and their customers. The first is whether a claim brought under § 10(b) of the [1934 Act], must be sent to arbitration in accordance with the terms of an arbitration agreement. . . .

I

Between 1980 and 1982, respondents Eugene and Julia McMahon, individually and as trustees for various pension and profit-sharing plans, were customers of petitioner Shearson/American Express Inc. (Shearson), a brokerage firm registered with the [SEC]. Two customer agreements signed by Julia McMahon provided for arbitration of any controversy relating to the accounts the McMahons maintained with Shearson. The arbitration provision provided in relevant part as follows:

> "Unless unenforceable due to federal or state law, any controversy arising out of or relating to my accounts, to transactions with you for me or to this agreement or the breach thereof, shall be settled by arbitration in accordance with the rules, then in effect, of the National Association of Securities Dealers, Inc. or the Boards of Directors of the New York Stock Exchange, Inc. and/or the American Stock Exchange, Inc. as I may elect." 618 F.Supp. 384, 385 (1985).

In October 1984, the McMahons filed an amended complaint against Shearson and petitioner Mary Ann McNulty, the registered representative who handled their accounts, in the United States District Court for the Southern District of New York. The complaint alleged McNulty, with Shearson's knowledge, had violated § 10(b) of the Exchange Act and Rule by engaging in fraudulent, excessive trading on respondents' accounts and by making false statements and omitting material facts from the advice given to respondents. . . .

II

The Federal Arbitration Act, 9 U.S.C. § 1 et seq., provides the starting point for answering the questions raised in this case. The Act was intended to "revers[e] centuries of judicial hostility to arbitration agreements," *Scherk v. Alberto-Culver Co.*, 417 U.S. 506, 510 (1974), by "plac[ing] arbitration agreements 'upon the same footing as other contracts.'" 417 U.S., at 511, quoting H.R. Rep. No. 96, 68th Cong., 1st Sess., 1, 2 (1924). The Arbitration Act accomplishes this purpose by providing that arbitration agreements "shall be valid, irrevocable, and enforceable, save upon such grounds as exist at law or in equity for the revocation of any contract." 9 U.S.C. § 2. The Act also provides that a court must stay its proceedings if it is satisfied that an issue before it is arbitrable under the agreement, § 3; and it authorizes a federal district court to issue an order compelling arbitration if there has been a "failure, neglect, or refusal" to comply with the arbitration agreement, § 4.

The Arbitration Act thus establishes a "federal policy favoring arbitration," *Moses H. Cone Memorial Hospital v. Mercury Construction Corp.*, 460 U.S. 1, 24 (1983), requiring that "we rigorously enforce agreements to arbitrate." *Dean Witter Reynolds Inc. v. Byrd,* 470 U.S. 213, 221 (1985). This duty to enforce arbitration agreements is not diminished when a party bound by an agreement raises a claim founded on statutory rights. As we observed in *Mitsubishi Motors Corp. v. Soler Chrysler-Plymouth, Inc.*, "we are well past the time when judicial suspicion of the desirability of arbitration and of the competence of arbitral tribunals" should inhibit enforcement of the Act "'in controversies based on statutes.'" 473 U.S. 614, 626–27 (1985), quoting *Wilko v. Swan*, 346 U.S. 427, 432 (1953). Absent a well-founded claim that an arbitration agreement resulted from the sort of fraud or excessive economic power that "would provide grounds 'for the revocation of any contract,'" 473 U.S., at 627, the Arbitration Act "provides no basis for disfavoring agreements to arbitrate statutory claims by skewing the otherwise hospitable inquiry into arbitrability." Ibid.

The Arbitration Act, standing alone, therefore mandates enforcement of agreements to arbitrate statutory claims. Like any statutory directive, the Arbitration Act's mandate may be overridden by a contrary congressional command. The burden is on the party opposing arbitration, however, to show that Congress intended to preclude a waiver of judicial remedies for the statutory rights at issue. See id., at 628. If Congress did intend to limit or prohibit waiver of a judicial forum for a particular claim, such an intent "will be deducible from [the statute's] text or legislative history," ibid., or from an inherent conflict between arbitration and the statute's underlying purposes. See Id., at 632–37; *Dean Witter Reynolds Inc. v. Byrd*, 470 U.S., at 217.

To defeat application of the Arbitration Act in this case, therefore, the McMahons must demonstrate that Congress intended to make an exception to the Arbitration Act for claims arising under . . . the Exchange Act, an intention discernible from the text, history, or purposes of the statute. . . .

III

To carry their argument that Congress intended for § 10(b) [1934] Act claims to be excluded from the Arbitration Act, the McMahon's raised three main arguments.

First, they argued that § 29 of the [1934] Act, which they contended forbade the waiver of any provision of the Act—including the provision that gave exclusive jurisdiction of [1934] Act violations to the U.S. courts, § 27. The Court rejected this argument, finding that § 29 didn't forbid the waiver of *any* section of the Exchange Act, only those sections that included substantive obligations. Because § 27 wasn't a substantive obligation, the Court reasoned, it could be waived by contract.

Second, the McMahons argued that the arbitration agreement [was] an unenforceable attempt to waive compliance with a substantive provision of the [1934] Act. According to the McMahons, § 29(a) created an obligation for covered entities to not force customers to sign arbitration agreements using superior bargaining power. Again the Court disagreed with the McMahon's interpretation. Although the Court conceded that § 29(a) created a substantive obligation that could not be waived, that obligation was not the one described by the McMahons. According to the Court, § 29(a) barred any agreement that would weaken a customer's ability to recover under the [1934] Act.

Whether an arbitration agreement weakened a customer's ability to recover under the [1934] Act was at the heart of the McMahon's final argument. To the McMahons, an arbitral proceeding would not be an adequate forum for § 10(b) complaints because such claims were inherently subjective, because judgments could be issued without complete explanation, and because arbitral proceedings lacked sufficient judicial review.

The Court rejected this final argument, finding that the McMahons were ignoring decades of pro-arbitration legislation and jurisprudence. This finding was consistent with Justice Felix Frankfurter's famous dissent in *Wilko v. Swan*, 346 U.S. 427, 432 (1953), a case from 1953 that the McMahons had relied on heavily in their argument, and extended further the Supreme Court's decision in *Scherk v. Alberto-Culver Co.*, 417 U.S. 506, 510 (1974) and numerous other subsequent decisions that upheld arbitration clauses. The

Court recounted how these previous decisions had found that arbitration proceedings were readily capable of handling many complex disputes, and that the streamlined procedures of an arbitral tribunal presented no consequential restriction on substantive rights to a fair trial.

Thus, the mistrust of arbitration that formed the basis for the *Wilko* opinion in 1953 is difficult to square with the assessment of arbitration that has prevailed since that time. This is especially so in light of the intervening changes in the regulatory structure of the securities laws. Even if *Wilko*'s assumptions regarding arbitration were valid at the time *Wilko* was decided, most certainly they do not hold true today for arbitration procedures subject to the SEC's oversight authority.

In 1953, when *Wilko* was decided, the [SEC] had only limited authority over the rules governing self-regulatory organizations (SROs)—the national securities exchanges and registered securities associations—and this authority appears not to have included any authority at all over their arbitration rules. Since the 1975 amendments to § 19 of the Exchange Act, however, the [SEC] has had expansive power to ensure the adequacy of the arbitration procedures employed by the SROs. No proposed rule change may take effect unless the SEC finds that the proposed rule is consistent with the requirements of the Exchange Act, section 19(b)(2) of the 1934 Act; and the [SEC] has the power, on its own initiative, to "abrogate, add to, and delete from" any SRO rule if it finds such changes necessary or appropriate to further the objectives of the Act, section 19(c) of the 1934 Act. In short, the [SEC] has broad authority to oversee and to regulate the rules adopted by the SROs relating to customer disputes, including the power to mandate the adoption of any rules it deems necessary to ensure that arbitration procedures adequately protect statutory rights.

In the exercise of its regulatory authority, the SEC has specifically approved the arbitration procedures of the [NYSE], the American Stock Exchange, and the NASD, the organizations mentioned in the arbitration agreement at issue in this case. We conclude that where, as in this case, the prescribed procedures are subject to the [SEC's] § 19 authority, an arbitration agreement does not effect a waiver of the protections of the Act. While stare decisis concerns may counsel against upsetting *Wilko*'s contrary conclusion under the [1933] Act, we refuse to extend *Wilko*'s reasoning to the [1934] Act in light of these intervening regulatory developments. The McMahons' agreement to submit to arbitration therefore is not tantamount to an impermissible waiver of the McMahons' rights under § 10(b), and the agreement is not void on that basis under § 29(a). . . .

We conclude, therefore, that Congress did not intend for § 29(a) to bar enforcement of all predispute arbitration agreements. . . .[W]here the SEC has sufficient statutory authority to ensure that arbitration is adequate to vindicate [1934] Act rights, enforcement does not effect a waiver of "compliance with any provision" of the Exchange Act . . . .

---

1. ***Predispute Arbitration Agreements.*** Two years after the *McMahon* decision, the Supreme Court extended its reasoning and ruled that predispute arbitration agreements would also govern claims arising under the 1933 Act. *See* Rodriguez de Luijas v. Shearson/American Express, Inc., 490 U.S. 477 (1989). As a result of these decisions, individuals who have signed predispute arbitration agreements are generally unable to obtain judicial resolution of federal securities law claims arising out of brokerage transactions. The principal exceptions to this rule are class actions, which under FINRA rules are generally not subject to arbitration, and situations in which the arbitration agreement was fraudulently induced. *See* Joel Seligman, *The Quiet Revolution: Securities Arbitration Confronts the Hard Questions*, 33 HOUSTON L. REV. 327, 338, 341–42 (1996); *see also* Matthias Rieker, *Finra Wins Appeal in Schwab Class-Action Dispute*, WALL

ST. J. (Apr. 24, 2014) (detailing brokerage firm Charles Schwab's failed challenge to FINRA rules prohibiting firms from placing judicial class action waivers in their customer account agreements). See also Michael S. Barr, *Mandatory Arbitration in Consumer Finance and Investor Contracts*, N.Y.U. J. L. & BUS. 11, no. 4, 793-817 (2015) (analyzing problems with class action waivers).

2. ***Why Arbitration?*** Historical evidence suggests that arbitration systems originated as a primary means of promoting investor protection and, similarly, maintaining the securities sector's good reputation. For instance, NYSE established one of the earliest arbitration systems in the early 1800s. NYSE organized arbitrators to hear disputes from any aggrieved party so that it could ensure its own rules, customs, and practices would be enforced even if they were unlawful or unenforceable in court. Have these historical motivations changed over time? *See* Jill Gross, *The Historical Basis of Securities Arbitration as an Investor Protection Mechanism*, 2016 J. DISP. RESOL. (forthcoming 2016).

2. ***Mandatory Predispute Arbitration Agreement.*** After arbitration agreements were held enforceable, the question arose whether securities firms could make such agreements a mandatory condition of all customer accounts. Massachusetts attempted to prohibit the mandatory arbitration agreements, but its effort was ruled preempted by the Federal Arbitration Act. *See* Sec. Indus. Ass'n v. Connolly, 883 F.2d 1114 (1st Cir. 1989), *cert. denied*, 495 U.S. 956 (1990). Are mandatory arbitration agreements consistent with the FINRA standards of fair practice? Should the SEC intervene to ensure customers have the option of resolving disputes in court?

3. ***The Fairness of Securities Arbitration.*** Underlying much of the debate over securities arbitration is the question of whether arbitration procedures are fair to investors. In the *McMahon* decision, the Supreme Court accepted the sector's view that advances in SRO and SEC oversight elevated the quality of arbitration procedures. Members of the plaintiffs' bar have, however, remained skeptical about the fairness of arbitration proceedings, particularly when those proceedings are conducted under the rules of the securities sector's SROs, such as the FINRA and NYSE, as opposed to the more independent American Arbitration Association. *But see* U.S. GENERAL ACCOUNTING OFFICE, SECURITIES ARBITRATION: HOW INVESTORS FARE (May 1992) (finding SRO arbitration results generally comparable to those of the AAA).

4. ***Does Arbitration Favor Defendants?*** Implicit in most of the opposition to arbitration is an assumption that plaintiffs do better in court than before an arbitration panel. Not everyone accepts this assumption:

> [Consider] the suitability rule that requires the broker to make only recommendations that are appropriate for the customer and to disclose the investment risks. . . . If a court hears a suitability dispute, the court will see the dispute as a disclosure issue under old familiar Rule 10b-5, and the court will look to see whether appropriate disclosures were made. . . . As the law presently stands, if the requisite disclosures are in the documents, the court is required to dismiss the case. . . . [I]n arbitration, the decisionmaker behaves quite differently. Inherently, arbitrators look at the reasonableness of the investment advice . . . . Even with disclosure of

> investment risks in the documents, the question is going to be, "how could you, Prudential, Merrill Lynch, or whoever, have let this person put half his or her portfolio in these risky securities? We do not care what the disclosure says."

John C. Coffee, *Commentary on Seligman*, 33 HOUSTON L. REV. 376, 380 (1996). Does this ring true?

5. ***Arbitration and Securities Case Law.*** One advantage of arbitration is that it offers a cheaper forum for resolving disputes. One may think that, over the long run, this cost advantage will benefit both the securities sector and its customers. As more disputes are channeled through arbitration and other alternative dispute resolution mechanisms, none of which typically generate written opinions, legal precedents in the field become less common. Since federal securities laws were enacted in the 1930s, the judiciary has played a major role in developing the law governing broker-dealers. Should we be concerned that the expansion of arbitration will lock us in to a future that will have to rely primarily upon pre-*McMahon* precedents? *See* David A. Lipton, *Generating Precedent in Securities Industry Arbitration*, 19 SEC. REG. L.J. 26 (1991).

6. ***Fine-Tuning the Securities Sector Arbitration Process.*** Since 1990, there have been many changes to the securities sector arbitration process, in part due to several reports issued by the GAO analyzing the arbitration process. In 1992, the GAO issued its first report, addressing such topics as whether a bias towards the securities sector existed in the arbitration process. In 2000, the GAO released a second report with a third in 2003, focusing on the number of unpaid arbitration awards to customers. *See* U.S. GENERAL ACCOUNTING OFFICE, SECURITIES ARBITRATION: HOW INVESTORS FARE (1992); U.S. GENERAL ACCOUNTING OFFICE, SECURITIES ARBITRATION: ACTIONS NEEDED TO ADDRESS PROBLEM OF UNPAID AWARDS (2000); U.S. GENERAL ACCOUNTING OFFICE, FOLLOW-UP REPORT ON MATTERS RELATING TO SECURITIES ARBITRATION (2003). FINRA, as well as its predecessor the NASD, has made efforts to improve the arbitration process in response to such studies. In 1994, the NASD appointed a task force, chaired by former SEC Chairman David Ruder, which made a series of recommendations to improve NASD arbitration proceedings. Among other things, the Ruder Task Force proposals concerned the training and selection of arbitrators, discovery rules for arbitration, and the scope of permissible remedies in arbitration, defining in particular the availability of punitive damage awards. *See* Arbitration Policy Task Force, NASD Securities Arbitration Reform (1996). Might the Ruder task force have gone too far? Since 2008, FINRA has filed over 40 proposed rule changes relating to the arbitration process to be approved by the SEC, and more changes may be in the works. In 2015, the FINRA Dispute Resolution Task Force issued a report making 51 recommendations to improve the arbitration process, including recommendations relating to arbitrators, whether awards should be explained in detail, and the use of mediation in lieu of arbitration. *See* FINRA Dispute Resolution Task Force, Final Report and Recommendations (2015). Section 921 of the Dodd-Frank Act provides the SEC with rulemaking authority to prohibit or restrict the use of arbitration agreements by securities firms if such a rulemaking would be in the interest of the public. To date, the SEC has not used this rulemaking authority. See Chapter 5.4.

CHAPTER 4.3

SECURITIES FIRMS IN CORPORATE TRANSACTIONS

CONTENTS

I. INTRODUCTION

Investment banking is one of the most visible segments of the securities sector and encompasses both the glamorous work associated with underwriting initial public offerings for new companies as well as the very lucrative business of advising corporate clients on mergers and acquisitions. The business is dominated by a relatively small number of firms based out of New York City. According to data collected by the Securities Industry and Financial Markets Association (SIFMA), a trade association, total revenues from investment banking activities have fluctuated from roughly $25 to $45 billion a year in recent times, divided between mergers and acquisitions, debt capital markets, equity capital markets, and loan work. Although the former two categories have historically generated the bulk of investment banking fees, all four categories generated approximately equal fee amounts in 2014. In this Chapter, we explore some of the legal issues that arise in this segment of the securities sector, covering transactions involving both prominent Wall Street firms as well as less savory elements of the securities world.

II. THE ROLE OF THE UNDERWRITER

As an underwriter, securities firms arrange for corporations to sell their securities, either equity or debt, to investors. Underwriting is thus to be contrasted with ordinary, and much more voluminous, secondary market transactions in securities, where securities firms may also act as principals, or dealers. The difference is that, with secondary market transactions, the securities firms will be purchasing and selling securities from other investors and not working in privity with corporate issuers. The regulation of public offerings of securities and other forms of capital raising is the central focus of many courses on Securities Regulation and entails a detailed study of the Securities Act of 1933 (1933 Act) and regulations promulgated thereunder. We will not attempt such a comprehensive analysis of the field here, but we do focus in on aspects of the underwriting process that establish important duties for securities firms working in this space. We begin with the due diligence obligations that the 1933 Act establishes for underwriters of public offerings.

A. DUE DILIGENCE UNDER THE SECURITIES ACT OF 1933

In re Software Toolworks, Inc.

38 F.3d 1078 (9th Cir. 1994)

Cynthia Holcomb Hall, Circuit Judge.

In this case, we again consider the securities-fraud claims raised by disappointed investors in Software Toolworks, Inc., who appeal the district court's summary judgment in favor of auditors Deloitte & Touche and underwriters Montgomery Securities and PaineWebber, Inc. We affirm in part, reverse in part, and remand.

I.

In July 1990, Software Toolworks, Inc., a producer of software for personal computers and Nintendo game systems, conducted a secondary public offering of common stock at $18.50 a share, raising more than $71 million. After the offering, the market price of Toolworks' shares declined steadily until, on October 11, 1990, the stock was trading at $5.40 a share. At that time, Toolworks issued a press release announcing substantial losses and the share price dropped another fifty-six percent to $2.375.

The next day, several investors ("the plaintiffs") filed a class action alleging that Toolworks, auditor Deloitte & Touche ("Deloitte"), and underwriters Montgomery Securities and PaineWebber, Inc. ("the Underwriters") had issued a false and misleading prospectus and registration statement in violation of sections 11 and 12(2) of the [1933 Act] and had knowingly defrauded and assisted in defrauding investors in violation of section 10(b) and Rule 10b-5 of the [Securities Exchange Act of 1934 (1934 Act)]. Specifically, the plaintiffs claimed that the defendants had (1) falsified audited financial statements for fiscal 1990 by reporting as revenue sales to original equipment manufacturers ("OEMs") with whom Toolworks had no binding agreements, (2) fabricated large consignment sales in order for Toolworks to meet financial projections for the first quarter of fiscal 1991 ("the June quarter"), and (3) lied to the [SEC] in response to inquiries made before the registration statement became effective.

Toolworks and its officers quickly settled with the plaintiffs for $26.5 million. After the completion of discovery, the district court granted summary judgment in favor of the Underwriters on all claims and in favor of Deloitte on all claims other than one cause of action under section 11. See *In re Software Toolworks, Inc. Sec. Litig.*, 789 F. Supp. 1489 (N.D. Cal. 1992) [*Toolworks I*]. The district court held that (1) the Underwriters had established a "due diligence" defense under sections 11 and 12(2) as a matter of law, *id.* at 1494–98, [and] (2) Deloitte had made no material misrepresentations or omissions, other than the OEM revenue statements, on which liability under sections 11 and 12(2) could attach. . . .

II.

We first address the plaintiffs' claims against the Underwriters under sections 11 and 12(2) of the 1933 Act. Section 11 imposes liability "[i]n case any part of [a] registration statement . . . contain[s] an untrue statement of a material fact or omit[s] to state a material fact required to be stated therein or necessary to make the statements therein not misleading." 15 U.S.C. § 77k(a). Similarly, section 12(2) imposes liability for using a prospectus "which includes an untrue statement of a material fact or omits to state a material fact necessary in order to make the statements, in light of the circumstances under which they were made, not misleading." Id. § 77l(2).

Liability under sections 11 and 12(2) properly may fall on the underwriters of a public offering. See id. §§ 77k(a)(5), 77l(2). Underwriters, however, may absolve themselves from liability by establishing a "due diligence" defense. Under section 11, underwriters must prove that they "had, after reasonable investigation, reasonable ground to believe and did believe . . . that the statements therein were true and that there was no omission to state a material fact required to be stated therein or necessary to make the statements therein not misleading." Id. § 77k(b)(3). Similarly, under section 12(2), underwriters must show that they "did not know, and in the exercise of reasonable care, could not have known, of [the] untruth or omission." Id. § 77l (2). . . .

The plaintiffs next assert that . . . the district court erred [in granting summary judgment] in this case because three "hotly disputed" issues of material fact preclude summary judgment on the question of the Underwriters' due diligence. . . .

1.

The plaintiffs first argue that the Underwriters failed to investigate properly Toolworks' Nintendo business. Specifically, the plaintiffs assert that the Underwriters should have discovered that, in contravention of statements in the prospectus, Toolworks had lowered prices on its Nintendo games and had "sold" significant inventory on a consignment basis, giving buyers an unqualified right to return unsold merchandise. See [*Miller v. Pezzani (In re Worlds of Wonder Sec. Litig.)*, 35 F.3d 1407, 1418 (9th Cir.1994),] [*WOW II*] ("a company that substantially overstates its revenues by reporting consignment transactions as sales makes false or misleading statements of material fact") (quotations omitted).

The district court disagreed, noting that the Underwriters had obtained written representations from Toolworks and Deloitte that the prospectus was accurate, had confirmed with Toolworks' customers that the company did not accept returns of non-defective cartridges, and had surveyed retailers to ensure that the company had not lowered its prices. *Toolworks I*, 789 F. Supp. at 1497. Thus, the court concluded that the Underwriters had, as a matter of law, "performed a thorough and reasonable investigation of Toolworks' Nintendo business." Id. For the following reasons, we agree.

a.

The plaintiffs argue that the prospectus was false and misleading because it stated that Toolworks' "Nintendo software products have not been subject to price reductions," when, in fact, Toolworks had begun a price-cutting promotion days before the offering. The plaintiffs, however, presented no direct evidence that the Underwriters knew of this promotion. Indeed, the record illustrates that Toolworks' management consistently assured the Underwriters that the company would not reduce prices. The plaintiffs nevertheless assert that summary judgment was inappropriate because a jury might infer that the Underwriters knew about the price cuts because Toolworks' management discussed the promotion while on a private plane with the Underwriters. All personnel who were on the plane, however, testified that no conversations regarding price cutting reached the Underwriters. As such, any inference that the Underwriters knew about the sales would not be based in fact and would be unreasonable. See *Weinberger*, ¶ 95,693 at 98,255. The district court properly granted summary judgment in favor of the Underwriters on this issue.

b.

The plaintiffs also claim that the prospectus was false and misleading because it stated that Toolworks "does not currently provide any product return rights to its retail Nintendo customers," when, in fact, the company had booked several consignment sales prior to the offering. Again, however, the plaintiffs offered no direct evidence that the Underwriters knew about the sales, which represented a significant departure from prior Toolworks' policy. In fact, the record illustrates that the Underwriters made a substantial effort to ascertain Toolworks' return policy, both before and after the consignment sales occurred. The plaintiffs nevertheless assert that circumstantial evidence permits an inference that the Underwriters knowingly "watered down" the prospectus' risk-disclosure statement about merchandise returns and ignored a memorandum from one Toolworks customer ("Walmart") describing an unlimited right-of-return. This argument, however, misconstrues the full record.

In the process of drafting the prospectus, the Underwriters did change the risk-disclosure statement. An original draft stated that, "[i]n light of increased competition among the [Nintendo] entertainment titles on the market, it may be necessary for [Toolworks] to modify its return policy." The final version stated only that "[t]here can be no assurance that [Toolworks] will not be subject to product returns in the future." This change, however, is not sufficient to permit a reasonable inference that the Underwriters knew or should have known that Toolworks actually had changed its return policy. In fact, the Underwriters changed the disclosure statement in direct response to assertions by Toolworks' management that the company would never offer return rights and that the prospectus as originally written could prompt customers to seek such concessions in the future.

Moreover, although the Underwriters did receive a memorandum from Walmart describing an unqualified right to return nondefective merchandise, the record illustrates that Walmart never actually had such rights. Upon receiving the Walmart memorandum, the Underwriters called the retailer and confirmed that the statement regarding returns was erroneous (it should have said that Walmart had an unqualified right to return defective merchandise). Thus, in light of this correction, the fact that the actual contract between Toolworks and Walmart provided only for the return of defective items, and the fact that Walmart never returned any undamaged products, an inference that the Underwriters attempted to conceal Toolworks' return policy would be unreasonable. The district court properly granted summary judgment in favor of the Underwriters on this issue.

2.

The plaintiffs next assert that a material issue of fact exists regarding whether the Underwriters diligently investigated, or needed to investigate, Toolworks' recognition of OEM revenue on its financial statements. The plaintiffs claim that the Underwriters "blindly rel[ied]" on Deloitte in spite of numerous "red flags" indicating that the OEM entries were incorrect and that, as a result, the district court erred in granting summary judgment.

An underwriter need not conduct due diligence into the "expertised" parts of a prospectus, such as certified financial statements. Rather, the underwriter need only show that it "had no reasonable ground to believe, and did not believe . . . that the statements therein were untrue or that there was an omission to state a material fact required to be stated therein or necessary to make the statements therein not misleading." 15 U.S.C. § 77k(b)(3)(C); see *WOW II*, 35 F.3d at 1421. The issue on appeal, therefore, is whether the Underwriters' reliance on the expertised financial statements was reasonable as a matter of law.

a.

As the first "red flag," the plaintiffs point to Toolworks' "backdated" contract with Hyosung, a Korean manufacturer. During the fourth quarter of fiscal 1990, Toolworks recognized $1.7 million in revenue from an OEM contract with Hyosung. In due diligence, the

Underwriters discovered a memorandum from Hyosung to Toolworks stating that Hyosung had "backdated" the agreement to permit Toolworks to recognize revenue in fiscal 1990. The plaintiffs claim that, after discovering this memorandum, the Underwriters could no longer rely on Deloitte because the accountants had approved revenue recognition for the transaction.

If the Underwriters had done nothing more, the plaintiffs' contention might be correct. The plaintiffs, however, ignore the significant steps taken by the Underwriters after discovery of the Hyosung memorandum to ensure the accuracy of Deloitte's revenue recognition. The Underwriters first confronted Deloitte, which explained that it was proper for Toolworks to book revenue in fiscal 1990 because the company had contracted with Hyosung in March, even though the firms did not document the agreement until April. The Underwriters then insisted that Deloitte reconfirm, in writing, the Hyosung agreement and Toolworks' other OEM contracts. Finally, the Underwriters contacted other accounting firms to verify Deloitte's OEM revenue accounting methods.

Thus, with regard to the Hyosung agreement, the Underwriters did not "blindly rely" on Deloitte. The district court correctly held that, as a matter of law, the Underwriters' "investigation of the OEM business was reasonable." *Toolworks I*, 789 F. Supp. at 1498.

b.

The plaintiffs next assert that the Underwriters could not reasonably rely on Deloitte's financial statements because Toolworks' counsel, Riordan & McKinzie, refused to issue an opinion letter stating that the OEM agreements were binding contracts. This contention has no merit because, contrary to the plaintiffs' assertions, Toolworks had never requested the law firm to render such an opinion. The plaintiffs attempt to infer wrongdoing in such circumstances is patently unreasonable. The district court correctly granted summary judgment in favor of the Underwriters on this issue.

c.

Finally, the plaintiffs assert that, by reading the agreements, the Underwriters should have realized that Toolworks had improperly recognized revenue. Specifically, the plaintiffs claim that several of the contracts were contingent and that it was facially apparent that Toolworks might not receive any revenue under them. As the Underwriters explain, this contention misconstrues the nature of a due diligence investigation:

> [The Underwriters] reviewed the contracts to verify that there was a written agreement for each OEM contract mentioned in the Prospectus—not to analyze the propriety of revenue recognition, which was the responsibility of [Deloitte]. Given the complexity surrounding software licensing revenue recognition, it is absurd to suggest that, in perusing Toolworks' contracts, [the Underwriters] should have concluded that [Deloitte] w[as] wrong, particularly when the OEM's provided written confirmation.

We recently confirmed precisely this point in a case involving analogous facts: "[T]he defendants relied on Deloitte's accounting decisions (to recognize revenue) about the sales. Those expert decisions, which underlie the plaintiffs' attack on the financial statements, represent precisely the type of 'certified' information on which section 11 permits nonexperts to rely." *WOW II*, 35 F.3d at 1421; see also *In re Worlds of Wonder Sec. Litig.*, 814 F. Supp. 850, 864–65 (N.D. Cal. 1993) ("It is absurd in these circumstances for Plaintiffs to suggest that the other defendants, who are not accountants, possibly could have known of any mistakes by Deloitte. Therefore, even if there are errors in the financial statements, no defendant except Deloitte can be liable under Section 11 on that basis.") [*WOW I*], aff'd in relevant part by *WOW II*, 35 F.3d at 1421.

Thus, because the Underwriters' reliance on Deloitte was reasonable under the circumstances, the district court correctly granted summary judgment on this issue. See

Toolworks I, 789 F. Supp. at 1498 ("Given the complexity of the accounting issues, the Underwriters were entitled to rely on Deloitte's expertise.")

---

1. ***Section II Gatekeepers.*** The *Software Toolworks* case offers a window into the underwriting process for public offerings. Under § 11 of the 1933 Act, underwriters are liable for material misstatements or omissions in registration statements filed with the SEC unless the underwriters can establish a due diligence defense. While the preparatory work leading up to a public offering fulfills many different functions, one of the purposes is to establish due diligence defenses for underwriters and others should problems arise down the road. This aspect of § 11 creates what is sometimes described as a gatekeeper liability regime. In order to gain access to the public markets, issuers hire investment bankers with strong reputations in the marketplace. Section 11 imposes liability on these gatekeepers if they fail to investigate the offering in a reasonable manner. There is extensive academic literature on the merits and limitations of gatekeeper regimes. *See, e.g.*, JOHN C. COFFEE, GATEKEEPERS: THE PROFESSIONS AND CORPORATE GOVERNANCE (2006); Reiner H. Kraakman, *Gatekeepers: The Anatomy of a Third-Party Enforcement Strategy*, 2 J.L. ECON. & ORG. 53 (1986). As the *Software Toolworks* case also illustrates, multiple firms often engage in gatekeeping functions simultaneously, for example, accountants as well as underwriters. For an exploration of the special problems that arise with more than one gatekeeper, see Andrew Tuch, *Multiple Gatekeepers*, 96 VA. L. REV. 1583 (2010).

2. ***Rule 10b-5 Compared to § 11.*** Section 11 of the 1933 Act applies only to misstatements in registration statements filed with the SEC in public offerings. Rule 10b-5 under the 1934 Act establishes a more general prohibition against fraud and material misstatements in connection with the purchase and sale of securities. As you have seen in Chapter 4.2, Rule 10b-5 also creates a private right of action and can be used by investors in corporate offerings that are exempt from 1933 Act registration requirements, such as private placements, or for fraudulent behavior in connection with public offerings that take place outside of a registration statement. Rule 10b-5 is also available for fraudulent conduct in connection with secondary market transactions. While broader in scope than § 11 of the 1933 Act, Rule 10b-5 has more stringent requirements as to a defendant's state of mind, and generally requires demonstration of scienter, that is, a form of intentionality, or at least a high degree of recklessness. As a result, when securities firms assist in capital raising transactions that are not publicly registered and thus not subject to § 11 liability, the firms still can be sued under Rule 10b-5, and therefore engage in a modified form of due diligence so as to be able to demonstrate an absence of recklessness or intentionality.

B. DECEPTIVE UNDERWRITERS AND OTHER FORMS OF MANIPULATION

The *Software Toolworks* case concerned a fairly typical sort of public offering in a familiar context involving well-known securities firms and accountants. The following case explores another segment of the securities world.

Pagel, Inc. v. SEC

803 F.2d 942 (9th Cir. 1986)

Wollman, Circuit Judge.

Pagel, Inc., a Minneapolis registered broker-dealer in securities, its president and sole stockholder, Jack W. Pagel, and its executive vice president, Duane A. Markus, petition for review of a final order of the [SEC] revoking the broker-dealer registration of Pagel, Inc., and barring Pagel and Markus from association with any broker or dealer. . . .

Pagel, Inc., served as the principal underwriter for the first public offering of the securities of FilmTec Corporation in March 1979. Pursuant to the underwriting agreement, the firm was to underwrite the sale of 320,000 shares of FilmTec stock at $3.25 per share, with an option to purchase an additional 32,000 shares should customer allocations exceed the original number of shares. Retaining the balance for itself, the firm allotted only 34,800 shares of the issue to other dealers. On March 26, 1979, Pagel, Inc., began offering FilmTec at 3¼. The offering was ostensibly completed on March 29, 1979, when the firm exercised its over-allotment option, increasing its share of the offering to 317,200 shares, or over 90% of the total issue.

On March 30, 1979, aftermarket trading began, with the firm's opening prices for FilmTec stock set at 4⅜ bid and 4⅝ offered, increases of 35% and 42%, respectively, over the offering price of 3¼. At this time, Pagel, Inc., began to maintain a "long" position in FilmTec, or an excess of purchases from its customers over sales to them, which would continue until March 1980. The firm's FilmTec trading activities were all at the direction of Pagel and Markus. Within the first fifteen minutes of trading, the firm's customers sold 49,300 shares of FilmTec to the firm and purchased 39,205 shares, including 7,650 shares purchased by Markus through nominees, and the firm raised the price of FilmTec to 5¾ bid and 7 offered. By the day's closing, Pagel, Inc., had purchased a total of 70,455 shares from its customers and sold a total of 56,830 shares, charging as much as 7¾.

During the next seven trading days, April 2–10, 1979, the firm's customers sold 88,987 shares and purchased 66,680 shares, a 33% excess of sales over purchases. By April 10, 1979, the firm's long position had increased to 48,607 shares, but seven other dealers were short FilmTec stock in the amount of 4,750 shares. Pagel, Inc., and its customers cumulatively owned 329,875 shares, or 93.7% of the 352,000-share public offering. Despite the lack of customer demand, evidenced by the excess of customers' sales over purchases, Pagel, Inc., was offering FilmTec at a high of 10½, an increase of more than 300% above the offering price of 3¼.

Between April 11, 1979, and the end of February 1980, Pagel, Inc., continued to dominate the FilmTec market, and the stock remained at a fairly constant price level. Throughout March 1980, however, the firm steadily lowered its prices for FilmTec, this despite the fact that customers' purchases exceeded customers' sales for the month. The firm's prices for FilmTec declined from 14 bid and 15½ offered on March 3, to 7 bid and 8½ offered on March 31, a 50% drop in price in one month. On March 21, 1980, with a bonus the firm gave to him, Pagel purchased 32,000 shares of FilmTec from the firm, apparently its entire inventory, at a price of 7½. The sale enabled Pagel, Inc., to realize a $180,000 tax loss at the close of its fiscal year on March 31, offsetting the firm's trading profits. Furthermore, Pagel acquired stock with a potential for realizing long-term capital gains.

On June 9, 1982, the [SEC] ordered a public proceeding to determine whether petitioners had violated provisions of the securities laws and to determine what remedial action, if any, would be appropriate. An evidentiary hearing was held before an Administrative Law Judge (ALJ) on December 13–21, 1982. On August 29, 1983, the ALJ found that Pagel, Inc., Pagel, and Markus had violated the fraud, manipulation, and record keeping provisions of the securities laws by: (1) manipulating the price of FilmTec stock in the initial eight days of public trading; (2) manipulating the price of FilmTec stock in March 1980 to secure significant tax and investment benefits; (3) purchasing FilmTec stock within the period of distribution; and (4) failing to maintain records identifying the beneficial ownership of nominee accounts through which Pagel and Markus traded. The ALJ recommended the revocation of the firm's broker-dealer registration and the barring of Pagel and Markus from association with any broker or dealer.

Petitioners appealed the ALJ's decision to the [SEC], which held that petitioners had violated the prohibitions of fraud and manipulation in securities dealings contained in section 17(a) of the [1933 Act], and section 10(b) of the [1934 Act], and Rule 10b-5 thereunder. The [SEC] also found that petitioners had violated the provisions of Rule 10b-6, prohibiting the purchase of securities by an underwriter participating in a distribution of the securities. Additionally, the [SEC] found that Pagel, Inc., had violated, and Pagel and Markus aided and abetted its violations of, the record keeping provisions of section 17(a) of the [1934 Act], and Rule 17a-3(a)(9) thereunder.

Petitioners challenge the sufficiency of the evidence supporting the [SEC's] findings with respect to the violations of section 17(a) of the [1933 Act], section 10(b) of the [1934 Act], and Rule 10b-5. They also argue that the [SEC] erred in drawing an adverse inference from the individual petitioners' invocation of their fifth amendment privilege against self-incrimination and in approving the ALJ's exclusion of expert testimony. Petitioners argue further that the [SEC] imposed excessive sanctions.

First, petitioners argue that the evidence does not support the [SEC's] finding of manipulation of the market in FilmTec stock. They contend that "regardless of how much prominence [Pagel, Inc.] had in the making of the FilmTec market during the periods in question and the effect its trades had on price, there was no unlawful purpose, intent to induce others to act, artificial prices, or prices based on factors other than legitimate ones.". . .

In connection with the securities markets, manipulation is a "term of art connot[ing] intentional or willful conduct designed to deceive or defraud investors by controlling or artificially affecting the price of securities." *Ernst & Ernst v. Hochfelder*, 425 U.S. 185 (1976). As this case illustrates, there is room for considerable disagreement whether manipulation may be present on a given set of facts. The [SEC], however, did not find petitioners liable solely because of their dominant position in the FilmTec market. Rather, it determined that petitioners had manipulated the market by abusing their position both during the first eight days of aftermarket trading and in March 1980. The [SEC] stated:

> When individuals occupying a dominant market position engage in a scheme to distort the price of a security for their own benefit, they violate the securities laws by perpetrating a fraud on all public investors. In addition, their failure to disclose that market prices are being manipulated not only constitutes an element of a scheme to defraud, but is also a material omission of fact in the offer and sale of securities.

The [SEC] primarily relied on evidence of the price movements of FilmTec stock and the trading activities of petitioners during the periods at issue to conclude that manipulation had occurred. We agree that "rapidly rising prices in the absence of any demand are well-known symptoms of unlawful market operations." *Dlugash v. Securities & Exchange Commission*, 373 F.2d 107, 109 (2d Cir.1967). Moreover, the [SEC] also considered other factors, such as the use of nominee accounts and the timing of the bulk sale to Pagel near the end of the Pagel, Inc., tax year, in reaching its conclusions. . . .

Petitioners argue further, however, that the [SEC] failed to establish the requisite element of intent, or "scienter." The [SEC] noted its finding of scienter in a footnote to its opinion. Scienter is the "mental state embracing intent to deceive, manipulate, or defraud." *Ernst & Ernst*, 425 U.S. at 193 n. 12. In *Aaron v. Securities & Exchange Commission*, 446 U.S.

680, 689–91 (1980), the Supreme Court held that the [SEC] must prove scienter in actions under sections 10(b) and 17(a)(1), but that it need only prove negligence in actions under sections 17(a)(2) or (3). Although the [SEC] could have been more explicit in its findings here, we cannot say that its conclusion on this issue is without substantial support in the evidence. Proof of scienter need not be direct but may be "a matter of inference from circumstantial evidence." *Herman & MacLean v. Huddleston*, 459 U.S. 375, 390 n. 30 (1983). We believe the [SEC] could reasonably have inferred from the evidence of price movement, trading activity, and other factors that the manipulation was undertaken for the purpose of securing financial and tax benefits for petitioners and thus was intentional.

Second, petitioners argue that the [SEC] impermissibly drew an adverse inference against Pagel and Markus based on their invocation of the fifth amendment privilege against self-incrimination. Although they concede that an adverse inference may be drawn against a party in a civil proceeding, they assert that in this case it was impermissible because there was insufficient evidence independent of their silence to support the [SEC's] findings.

In determining whether an inference may be drawn from invocation of the fifth amendment, a distinction is made between civil and criminal cases. *Rosebud Sioux Tribe v. A & P Steel, Inc.*, 733 F.2d 509, 521 (8th Cir.), cert. denied, 469 U.S. 1072 (1984). In *Baxter v. Palmigiano*, 425 U.S. 308, 318–20 (1976), the Supreme Court held that the fifth amendment privilege against self-incrimination did not forbid drawing adverse inferences from an inmate's failure to testify at his own disciplinary proceedings. The Court noted that the fifth amendment " 'does not preclude the inference where the privilege is claimed by a party to a civil cause.' " *Id.* at 318 (quoting 8 J. Wigmore, Evidence 439 (McNaughton rev. 1961)) (emphasis in original). The Baxter Court also found, however, that silence alone would be insufficient to support an adverse decision against one who refuses to testify. Id. at 317. This principle was reiterated in *Lefkowitz v. Cunningham*, 431 U.S. 801, 809 n. 5 (1977): "Respondent's silence in Baxter was only one of a number of factors to be considered by the finder of fact in assessing a penalty, and was given no more probative value than the facts of the case warranted." It is clear that the [SEC] did not rely solely on Pagel's and Markus' refusal to testify but also, as we have stated above, on the evidence of FilmTec price movements, petitioners' trading activities, and other relevant facts. Furthermore, in earlier proceedings the ALJ chose not to draw an adverse inference against petitioners and still found violations. Consequently, the [SEC's] inference served only to support already established findings. . . .

Finally, petitioners argue that the sanctions imposed are excessive. The [SEC's] choice of sanctions is not to be overturned unless we find them "unwarranted in law or without justification in fact." *Brickner v. Federal Deposit Insurance Corp.*, 747 F.2d 1198, 1203 (8th Cir. 1984). In imposing these sanctions, the [SEC] considered the overpayments customers made for purchases of FilmTec stock during the first eight days of trading and the lower prices they received on sales in March 1980. The [SEC] also considered the fact that petitioners previously had been sanctioned, pursuant to an offer of settlement, for violations of customer protection, credit extension, record keeping, and reporting provisions. The [SEC] could reasonably have concluded that protection of the public interest required the sanctions it imposed, see *Berdahl v. Securities & Exchange Commission,* 572 F.2d 643, 649 (8th Cir. 1978). Accordingly, we find no abuse of discretion in the imposition of these sanctions.

---

1. ***Protecting the Investing Public.*** How did the petitioners' actions injure the investing public in this case? What substantial risks were the petitioners taking by pursuing the trading strategy outlined in *Pagel*? Consider the role of customers in the *Pagel* case. Customers were submitting buy and sell orders at

the quoted prices, which Pagel then fulfilled. What are the responsibilities of the investing public when engaging in trading?

2. ***Policing Manipulative Practices.*** A number of provisions of the 1934 Act are designed to prevent market manipulating schemes of the sort described in the *Pagel* decision. *See, e.g.*, Section 9 of the 1934 Act (outlawing specific manipulative practices for securities traded on exchanges). In addition, the SEC has promulgated numerous rules implementing general prohibitions against manipulative practices. For example, Regulation M prohibits certain trading practices while an underwriting is in progress. Within the securities bar, there is an ongoing debate over whether manipulative practices must entail an element of nondisclosure, or whether the prohibitions should also extend to activities that are either substantively unfair or otherwise disruptive of trading markets. For an introduction to this debate, see Daniel R. Fischel & David J. Ross, *Should The Law Prohibit "Manipulation" in Financial Markets?*, 105 HARV. L. REV. 503 (1991). Would you characterize the *Pagel* decision as a case of non-disclosure? What would full disclosure accomplish in these situations?

3. ***The Development of Securities Laws Against Market Manipulation.*** If you think back to the history behind the enactment of federal securities laws in the 1930s, many of the behaviors that gave rise to public outrage involved different forms of market manipulation—conspiracies to drive up or down securities prices were believed to have been rampant in the 1920s. Over the years, many SEC and state enforcement actions, including against boiler rooms, have included elements of market manipulation. *See, e.g.*, United States v. Santoro, 302 F.3d 76, 78–79 (2d Cir. 2002) (stock promoters conspired to artificially inflate prices by giving brokers extraordinary compensation to recommend certain stocks). *See also* SEC v. Pearson, 426 F.2d 1339 (10th Cir. 1970) (round-robin trading activity to give a false appearance of trading volume can constitute manipulation). As many of the 1934 Act's statutory prohibitions against manipulation are limited to securities traded on exchanges, the more general antifraud prohibition of Rule 10b-5 is typically used as a basis for policing manipulative practices in securities traded in over-the-counter markets.

4. ***The Criminality of SEC Violations.*** As the *Pagel* decision suggests, targets of SEC enforcement actions may also face parallel criminal prosecutions. *See* § 32 of the 1934 Act (establishing criminal penalties for willful violations of the 1934 Act). The coordination of civil and criminal proceedings presents numerous complex tactical and legal issues. Note, for example, the use the SEC made in this case of Pagel's invocation of the Fifth Amendment privilege against self-incrimination.

C. PENNY STOCKS VERSUS EMERGING GROWTH COMPANIES

The *Pagel* case illustrates a recurring problem in the broker-dealer sector. Firms obtain control over the market for shares of small, thinly traded companies and then promote those shares to unsophisticated customers at prices that bear little relation to underlying values. Often times, these practices violated numerous legal standards, including suitability rules, markup regulations, and more general fiduciary standards. Difficulties of proof and limitations in regulatory resources, however, have made it difficult for the government to police these practices effectively. The SEC responded in 1989 with the adoption of new penny stock regulations, which were later supplemented with specific statutory authorization.

1. Penny Stock Rules

The term penny stock generally refers to a security issued by a very small company that trades at less than $5 per share. Penny stocks are generally quoted over-the-counter, such as on the OTC Bulletin Board, which is a facility of FINRA or OTC Link LLC, which is owned by OTC Markets Group, Inc., formerly known as Pink OTC Markets Inc. Penny stocks may, however, also trade on securities exchanges, including foreign securities exchanges. In addition, the definition of penny stock can include the securities of certain private companies with no active trading market.

Penny stocks may not be traded frequently, which means that it may be difficult to sell penny stock shares once you own them. Moreover, because it may be difficult to find quotations for certain penny stocks, they may be difficult, or even impossible, to accurately price. For these and other reasons, penny stocks are generally considered speculative investments. Consequently, investors in penny stocks should be prepared for the possibility that they may lose their whole investment or an amount in excess of their investment if they purchased penny stocks on margin.

Because of the speculative nature of penny stocks, Congress prohibited broker-dealers from effecting transactions in penny stocks unless they comply with the requirements of § 15(h) of the 1934 Act and the rules thereunder. These SEC rules provide, among other things, that a broker-dealer must: (1) approve the customer for the specific penny stock transaction and receive from the customer a written agreement to the transaction; (2) furnish the customer with a disclosure document describing the risks of investing in penny stocks; (3) disclose to the customer the current market quotation, if any, for the penny stock; and (4) disclose to the customer the amount of compensation the firm and its broker will receive for the trade. In addition, after executing the sale, a broker-dealer must send to its customer monthly account statements showing the market value of each penny stock held in the customer's account.

The SEC's approach to penny stocks represents an interesting regulatory strategy. Often times, regulations and disclosures standards are designed to make transactions more efficient. The SEC's penny stock rules, however, are intended to slow transactions down, forcing the exchange of information and written agreements, which make it more difficult for securities firms to engage in high-pressured sales tactics encouraging less sophisticated clients to agree to ill-considered investments. The rules, however, apply only to penny stocks, defined to be those with a share price of less than $5. Why would the SEC limit the rules' protections to this class of securities? Is it acceptable for securities firms to exploit their customers with high-pressure tactics as long as they limit their sales pitches to stocks that cost more than $5.01? Is a rule with such bright line limitations too easy to evade?

2. The Jumpstart Our Business Startups Act of 2012

In contrast to the SEC's traditional skepticism with respect to low-priced securities, consider the Jumpstart Our Business Startups Act of 2012 (JOBS Act), which made a number of changes to the federal securities laws to increase the ability of small companies to raise capital without having to engage in a public offering or otherwise comply with SEC registration requirements for public firms. The JOBS Act relaxed the disclosure burdens of a new category of firms called emerging growth companies, which are firms that have recently made public offerings but do not yet have gross revenue in excess of $1 billion per year. The JOBS Act was supported by a diverse array of interests, including Silicon Valley entrepreneurs, free-market Republicans, and the Obama Administration. All saw the JOBS Act as a potential engine for creating new employment opportunities. The SEC and much of the academic community working in the field have been more skeptical. *See, e.g.*, Robert B. Thompson & Donald C. Langevoort, *Redrawing the Private-Public Boundaries in Entrepreneurial Capital-Raising*, 98 CORNELL L. REV. 1573 (2013); Donald C. Langevoort & Robert B. Thompson, *"Publicness" in Contemporary Securities Regulation after the JOBS Act*, 101 GEORGETOWN L.J. 337 (2013).

The JOBS Act also includes a new regulatory regime intended to promote crowdfunding for new companies. Crowdfunding is the process of funding a project or a venture by raising monetary contributions from large numbers of investors, typically done through the Internet. The exemption contained in Title III of the JOBS Act allows crowdfunding to be used to offer and sell securities. In 2015, the SEC adopted this regulation, which provides a limited exemption from registration requirements under the 1933 Act to issue up to $1 million during a 12-month period in crowdfunding transactions, subject to certain limitations. The new crowdfunding regulation has the effect of enabling a large number of investors to make relatively small investments to private issuers raising investment capital through the Internet. Such offerings and investments must be transacted through an intermediary—either an SEC-registered broker-dealer or a funding portal, a new SEC-registrant created under the regulation. Issuers using crowdfunding are subject to significant reporting requirements under the SEC's regulatory regime, including updates for material changes in disclosure and annual reports. Despite graduated reporting requirements for financial statements based on the size of the offering, the regulatory burden may outweigh the benefits of a public offering for some issuers. *See* Commissioner Michael S. Piwowar, SEC, Dissenting Statement at Open Meeting on Crowdfunding and Small Business Capital Formation (Oct. 30, 2015) (stating that, "[the fears] that many traps for the unwary are hidden in the regulations, creating potential nightmares for small business owners that fail to place regulatory compliance at the top of their business plans. Such burdens will spook many small businesses from pursuing crowdfunding as a viable path to raising capital."). Why might an issuer choose to crowdfund an offering rather than register the issuance with the SEC? What are the advantages and disadvantages of crowdfunding in the securities space? *See* Crowdfunding, 60 Fed. Reg. 71,388 (Nov. 16, 2015).

Exactly how much capital raising the JOBS Act will actually promote is an empirical question that may take some time to calculate. *See* Telis Demos & Josh Zumbrun, *How Many Jobs Did 2012 IPO Act Create? Hard to Tell*, WALL

ST. J., Apr. 2, 2015. Even if the JOBS Act does promote capital formation, to what degree should a public policy analyst discount that effect by the possibility that the JOBS Act will also facilitate a new generation of boiler room operations?

D. THE DUTY TO SUPERVISE

Another distinguishing feature of broker-dealer regulation is its attention to the supervisory responsibilities of management. Under the federal securities laws, controlling persons are potentially liable for violations committed by their subordinates. *See, e.g.*, § 20(a) of the 1934 Act. Special oversight responsibilities govern the liability of controlling persons for civil penalties imposed on insider trading. *See* § 21A(b) of the 1934 Act. The following reading explores the contours of oversight responsibilities imposed on broker-dealer supervisors under § 15(b)(4)(E) of the 1934 Act. Interestingly, the underlying violations in this case involve one of the most prominent examples of market manipulation of the past several decades, a form of behavior that prefigured many of the scandals of the early 2000s, such as the London Interbank Offered Rate price-fixing and exchange rate manipulation, discussed in Chapter 11.3. The duties articulated in this decision apply much more broadly.

In re John H. Gutfreund

Exch. Act Release No. 31,554, 52 SEC Docket 2849 (Dec. 3, 1992)

[This proceeding arises out of a series of false bids that Paul Mozer, head of the Salomon Brothers, Inc. ("Salomon") Government Trading Desk, submitted in the first half of 1991 in an effort to corner the trading markets of certain issues of government securities. In late April of 1991, three members of the senior management of Salomon—Chief Executive Officer John Gutfreund, President Thomas Strauss, and Vice Chairman John Meriwether—became aware of Moser's activities. They discussed the matter with Donald Feuerstein, the firm's chief legal officer, who informed them that Mozer's actions appeared to be criminal and recommended that the matter be reported to the government. Despite Feuerstein's advice, senior management failed to intervene effectively, and Mozer continued to submit false bids until the summer of 1991 when the practice became public and SEC investigation ensued.]

1. Legal Principles

Section 15(b)(4)(E) of the [1934 Act] authorizes the [SEC] to impose sanctions against a broker-dealer if the firm has:

> failed reasonably to supervise, with a view to preventing violations [of federal securities laws], another person who commits such a violation, if such person is subject to his supervision.

Section 15(b)(6) of the [1934 Act] incorporates Section 15(b)(4)(E) by reference and authorizes the [SEC] to impose sanctions for deficient supervision on individuals associated with broker-dealers.

The principles which govern this proceeding are well-established by the [SEC's] cases involving failure to supervise. The [SEC] has long emphasized that the responsibility of broker-dealers to supervise their employees is a critical component of the federal regulatory scheme. As the [SEC] stated in Wedbush Securities, Inc.:

> In large organizations it is especially imperative that those in authority exercise particular vigilance when indications of irregularity reach their attention.

The supervisory obligations imposed by the federal securities laws require a vigorous response even to indications of wrongdoing. Many of the [SEC's] cases involving a failure to supervise arise from situations where supervisors were aware only of "red flags" or "suggestions" of irregularity, rather than situations where, as here, supervisors were explicitly informed of an illegal act.

Even where the knowledge of supervisors is limited to "red flags" or "suggestions" of irregularity, they cannot discharge their supervisory obligations simply by relying on the unverified representations of employees. Instead, as the [SEC] has repeatedly emphasized, "[t]here must be adequate follow-up and review when a firm's own procedures detect irregularities or unusual trading activity. . . ." Moreover, if more than one supervisor is involved in considering the actions to be taken in response to possible misconduct, there must be a clear definition of the efforts to be taken and a clear assignment of those responsibilities to specific individuals within the firm.

2. The Failure to Supervise

As described above, in late April of 1991 three supervisors of Paul Mozer—John Meriwether, Thomas Strauss, and John Gutfreund—learned that Mozer had submitted a false bid in the amount of $3.15 billion in an auction of U.S. Treasury securities. Those supervisors learned that Mozer had said that the bid had been submitted to obtain additional securities for another trading area of the firm. They also learned that Mozer had contacted an employee of the customer whose name was used on the bid and falsely told that individual that the bid was an error. The supervisors also learned that the bid had been the subject of a letter from the Treasury Department to the customer and that Mozer had attempted to persuade the customer not to inform the Treasury Department that the bid had not been authorized. The supervisors were also informed by Salomon's chief legal officer that the submission of the false bid appeared to be a criminal act.

The information learned by the supervisors indicated that a high level employee of the firm with significant trading discretion had engaged in extremely serious misconduct. As the cases described above make clear, this information required, at a minimum, that the supervisors take action to investigate what had occurred and whether there had been other instances of unreported misconduct. While they could look to counsel for guidance, they had an affirmative obligation to undertake an appropriate inquiry. If they were unable to conduct the inquiry themselves or believed it was more appropriate that the inquiry be conducted by others, they were required to take prompt action to ensure that others in fact undertook those efforts. Such an inquiry could have been conducted by the legal or compliance departments of the firm, outside counsel, or others who had the ability to investigate the matter adequately. The supervisors were also required, pending the outcome of such an investigation, to increase supervision of Mozer and to place appropriate limitations on his activities.

The failure to recognize the need to take action to limit the activities of Mozer in light of his admitted misconduct is particularly troubling because Gutfreund and Strauss did place limitations on Mozer's conduct in connection with the June two-year U.S. Treasury note auction at a time when they thought the firm had not engaged in misconduct, but press reports had raised questions about the firm's activities. Although they had previously been informed that a serious violation had in fact been committed by Mozer, they failed for over three months to take any action to place limitations on his activities to deal with that misconduct.

The need to take prompt action was all the more critical in view of the fact that the potential unlawful conduct had taken place in the market for U.S. Treasury securities. The integrity of that market is of vital importance to the capital markets of the United States, as well as to capital markets worldwide, and Salomon occupied a privileged role as a government-designated primary dealer. The failure of the supervisors to take vigorous action to address known misconduct by the head of the firm's Government Trading Desk caused unnecessary risks to the integrity of this important market.

To discharge their obligations, the supervisors should at least have taken steps to ensure that someone within the firm questioned other employees on the Government Trading Desk, such as the desk's clerk or the other managing director on the Desk. Since the supervisors were informed that Mozer had said that he submitted the false bid to obtain additional securities for another trading desk of the firm, they should also have specifically investigated any involvement of that area of the firm in the matter. The supervisors should also have reviewed, or ensured that others reviewed, documentation concerning the February 21, 1991 auction. Such a review would have revealed, at a minimum, that a second false bid had been submitted in the auction and that false trade tickets and customer confirmations had been created in connection with both false bids. Those facts would have raised serious questions about the operations of the Government Trading Desk, and inquiries arising from those questions might well have led to discovery of the additional false bids described above. . . .

Each of the three supervisors apparently believed that someone else would take the supervisory action necessary to respond to Mozer's misconduct. There was no discussion, however, among any of the supervisors about what action should be taken or about who would be responsible for taking action. Instead, each of the supervisors assumed that another would act. In situations where supervisors are aware of wrongdoing, it is imperative that they take prompt and unequivocal action to define the responsibilities of those who are to respond to the wrongdoing. The supervisors here failed to do that. As a result, although there may be varying degrees of responsibility, each of the supervisors bears some measure of responsibility for the collective failure of the group to take action.

After the disclosure of one unauthorized bid to Meriwether, Mozer committed additional violations in connection with the submission of two subsequent unauthorized customer bids. Had limits been placed on his activities after the one unauthorized bid was disclosed, these violations might have been prevented. While Mozer was told by Meriwether that his conduct was career-threatening and that it would be reported to senior management and to the government, these efforts were not a sufficient supervisory response under the circumstances. The supervisors were required to take action reasonably designed to prevent a repetition of the misconduct that had been disclosed to them. They could, for instance, have temporarily limited Mozer's activities so that he was not involved in the submission of customer bids pending an adequate review of what had occurred in the February 21, 1991 auction, or they could have instituted procedures to require verification of customer bids.

Under the circumstances of this case, the failure of the supervisors to take action to discipline Mozer or to limit his activities constituted a serious breach of their supervisory obligations. Gutfreund, Strauss and Meriwether thus each failed reasonably to supervise Mozer with a view to preventing violations of the federal securities laws. . . .

Donald Feuerstein, Salomon's chief legal officer, was informed of the submission of the false bid by Paul Mozer in late April of 1991, at the same time other senior executives of Salomon learned of that act. Feuerstein was present at the meetings in late April at which the supervisors named as respondents in this proceeding discussed the matter. In his capacity as a legal adviser, Feuerstein did advise Strauss and Gutfreund that the submission of the bid was a criminal act and should be reported to the government, and he urged them on several occasions to proceed with disclosure when he learned that the report had not been made. However, Feuerstein did not direct that an inquiry be undertaken, and he did not recommend that appropriate procedures, reasonably designed to prevent and detect future misconduct, be instituted, or that other limitations be placed on Mozer's activities. Feuerstein also did not inform the Compliance Department, for which he was responsible as Salomon's chief legal officer, of the false bid.

Unlike Gutfreund, Strauss and Meriwether, however, Feuerstein was not a direct supervisor of Mozer at the time he first learned of the false bid. Because we believe this is an appropriate opportunity to amplify our views on the supervisory responsibilities of legal and compliance officers in Feuerstein's position, we have not named him as a respondent in this proceeding. Instead, we are issuing this report of investigation concerning the responsibilities imposed by Section 15(b)(4)(E) of the Exchange Act under the circumstances of this case.

Employees of brokerage firms who have legal or compliance responsibilities do not become "supervisors" for purposes of Sections 15(b)(4)(E) and 15(b)(6) solely because they occupy those positions. Rather, determining if a particular person is a "supervisor" depends on whether, under the facts and circumstances of a particular case, that person has a requisite degree of responsibility, ability or authority to affect the conduct of the employee whose behavior is at issue. Thus, persons occupying positions in the legal or compliance departments of broker-dealers have been found by the [SEC] to be "supervisors" for purposes of Sections 15(b)(4)(E) and 15(b)(6) under certain circumstances.

In this case, serious misconduct involving a senior official of a brokerage firm was brought to the attention of the firm's chief legal officer. That individual was informed of the misconduct by other members of senior management in order to obtain his advice and guidance, and to involve him as part of management's collective response to the problem. Moreover, in other instances of misconduct, that individual had directed the firm's response and had made recommendations concerning appropriate disciplinary action, and management had relied on him to perform those tasks.

Given the role and influence within the firm of a person in a position such as Feuerstein's and the factual circumstances of this case, such a person shares in the responsibility to take appropriate action to respond to the misconduct. Under those circumstances, we believe that such a person becomes a "supervisor" for purposes of Sections 15(b)(4)(E) and 15(b)(6). As a result, that person is responsible, along with the other supervisors, for taking reasonable and appropriate action. It is not sufficient for one in such a position to be a mere bystander to the events that occurred.

Once a person in Feuerstein's position becomes involved in formulating management's response to the problem, he or she is obligated to take affirmative steps to ensure that appropriate action is taken to address the misconduct. For example, such a person could direct or monitor an investigation of the conduct at issue, make appropriate recommendations for limiting the activities of the employee or for the institution of appropriate procedures, reasonably designed to prevent and detect future misconduct, and verify that his or her recommendations, or acceptable alternatives, are implemented. If such a person takes appropriate steps but management fails to act and that person knows or has reason to know of that failure, he or she should consider what additional steps are appropriate to address the matter. These steps may include disclosure of the matter to the entity's board of directors, resignation from the firm, or disclosure to regulatory authorities.

These responsibilities cannot be avoided simply because the person did not previously have direct supervisory responsibility for any of the activities of the employee. Once such a person has supervisory obligations by virtue of the circumstances of a particular situation, he must either discharge those responsibilities or know that others are taking appropriate action. . . .

In view of the foregoing, the [SEC] deems it appropriate and in the public interest to impose the sanctions specified in the Offers of Settlement submitted by John H. Gutfreund, Thomas W. Strauss, and John W. Meriwether.

Accordingly, IT IS HEREBY ORDERED that:

A. John H. Gutfreund be, and he hereby is:

(i) ordered to comply with his undertaking not to associate in the future in the capacity of Chairman or Chief Executive Officer with any broker, dealer, municipal securities dealer, investment company or investment adviser regulated by the Commission; and

(ii) ordered to pay to the United States Treasury a civil penalty aggregating $100,000 pursuant to Section 21B(a)(4) of the Exchange Act;

B. Thomas W. Strauss be, and he hereby is:

(i) suspended from associating with any broker, dealer, municipal securities dealer, investment company or investment adviser for a period of six (6) months; and

(ii) ordered to pay to the United States Treasury a civil penalty aggregating $75,000 pursuant to Section 21B(a)(4) of the Exchange Act;

C. John W. Meriwether be, and he hereby is:

(i) suspended from associating with any broker, dealer, municipal securities dealer, investment company or investment adviser for a period of three (3) months; and

(ii) ordered to pay to the United States Treasury a civil penalty aggregating $50,000 pursuant to Section 21B(a)(4) of the Exchange Act.

---

1. ***Who does 15(b)(4)(E) and 15(b)(6) Apply to?*** Within the legal community, one of the most interesting aspects of the *Gutfreund* decision is its discussion of the responsibilities of Donald Feuerstein, who was the firm's legal officer but did not have direct supervisory authority over Mozer. The decision suggests that liability can attach to anyone with "a requisite degree of responsibility, ability or authority to affect the conduct of the employee." Since then, the SEC appears to have backed away from this expansive definition somewhat, suggesting that supervisory liability accrues strongly to those possessing the power to "hire, fire, and punish, to reassign, [or] affect very strongly the working conditions of an individual." *See* James Fanto, *The Vanishing Supervisor*, 41 J.C.L. 117 (2015) (reviewing the liability of compliance officers and the SEC's current and historical positions on the topic). Even under this new definition, those in Feuerstein's position may still face sanctions if they fail to prevent violations of this sort. Is this an appropriate scope of responsibility?

2. ***Attorneys and the Rules of Professional Responsibility.*** In the final footnote of the decision, the SEC acknowledges that attorneys may also be bound by rules of professional responsibility, stating that "in the case of an attorney, the applicable Code of Professional Responsibility and the Canons of Ethics may bear upon what course of conduct that individual may properly pursue." *In re* Gutfreund, Exchange Act Release No. 31,554 at n.26. For someone in Feuerstein's position, what effect would these rules have?

3. ***What are the Appropriate Sanctions for a Failure to Supervise?*** Compared to the monetary penalties, the suspension or expulsion from the securities sector is certainly the real censure in *Gutfreund*. Consider the case of

John Gutfreund, who lost his job as CEO at one of Wall Street's once most illustrious investment banks. Is this too far? Not far enough? *See* Peter Truell, *A Fallen King in Search of a Lesser Throne*, N.Y. TIMES, May 3, 1998 ("Before his precipitous fall from grace in 1991, amid a scandal over Treasury bond auctions, Mr. Gutfreund was like a monarch, ruling Salomon Brothers for almost a decade . . . he then suffered one of the steepest falls of any financial giant in the modern era.").

4. ***The Liability of Chief Compliance Officers.*** Broadly speaking, the Compliance department provides advice, training, and education regarding a securities firm's regulatory requirements to business units and senior management on an ongoing basis. Compliance also monitors and reviews business activities with respect to both external regulations and internal policies and procedures. Chief Compliance Officers head these departments, and are responsible for maintaining the effectiveness of the compliance function. Senior management, however, is ultimately responsible for a firm's overall supervisory and compliance obligations. When should sanctions be imposed on Chief Compliance Officers for misconduct by other employees at the firm? The SEC has taken the position that Chief Compliance Officers are not supervisors of business personnel solely by virtue of their position. *See* Frequently Asked Questions About Liability of Compliance and Legal Personnel at Broker-Dealers Under §§ 15(b)(4) and 15(b)(6) of the Exchange Act, SEC, Sept. 30, 2013. The SEC has stated its intention, however, to bring actions where legal or compliance personnel have affirmatively participated in the misconduct, helped mislead regulators, or failed to carry out a clear responsibility to implement compliance programs. *See* Andrew Ceresney, SEC, Keynote Address at Compliance Week 2014 (May 20, 2014). Nonetheless, will the possibility of being held liable for others misconduct dissuade otherwise qualified people from becoming Chief Compliance Officers? Or might these employees become more hesitant to involve themselves in the day-to-day operations of a firm lest they be considered an affirmative participant in another employee's misconduct?

III. CONFLICTS OF INTEREST WITH CORPORATE CLIENTS

A. *EL PASO* AND INFORMATION BARRIERS

We begin this section with a Delaware Chancery Court decision involving an oil merger and conflicted Goldman Sachs bankers. Here, the court explores—though ultimately does not resolve—the duties of investment bankers to their corporate clients. The court nonetheless is trenchant in its criticism of the bankers' conduct exhibited in the case. As you read the following excerpt, consider what conduct you find egregious, if any, and whether such conduct should be regulated, and how.

_In re_ El Paso Corp. Shareholder Litig.

41 A.3d 432 (Del. Ch. 2012)

Strine, Chancellor.

Stockholder plaintiffs seek a preliminary injunction to enjoin a merger between El Paso Corporation and Kinder Morgan, Inc. (the "Merger").

The chief executive officer of El Paso, a public company, undertook sole responsibility for negotiating the sale of El Paso to Kinder Morgan in the Merger. Kinder Morgan intended to keep El Paso's pipeline business and sell off El Paso's exploration and production, or "E & P," business to finance the purchase. The CEO did not disclose to the El Paso board of directors (the "Board") his interest in working with other El Paso managers in making a bid to buy the E & P business from Kinder Morgan. He kept that motive secret, negotiated the Merger, and then approached Kinder Morgan's CEO on two occasions to try to interest him in the idea. In other words, when El Paso's CEO was supposed to be getting the maximum price from Kinder Morgan, he actually had an interest in not doing that.

This undisclosed conflict of interest compounded the reality that the Board and management of El Paso relied in part on advice given by a financial advisor, Goldman, Sachs & Co., which owned 19% of Kinder Morgan (a $4 billion investment) and controlled two Kinder Morgan board seats. Although Goldman's conflict was known, inadequate efforts to cabin its role were made. When a second investment bank was brought in to address Goldman's economic incentive for a deal with, and on terms that favored, Kinder Morgan, Goldman continued to intervene and advise El Paso on strategic alternatives, and with its friends in El Paso management, was able to achieve a remarkable feat: giving the new investment bank an incentive to favor the Merger by making sure that this bank only got paid if El Paso adopted the strategic option of selling to Kinder Morgan. In other words, the conflict-cleansing bank only got paid if the option Goldman's financial incentives gave it a reason to prefer was the one chosen. On top of this, the lead Goldman banker advising El Paso did not disclose that he personally owned approximately $340,000 of stock in Kinder Morgan. . . .

Although a reasonable mind might debate the tactical choices made by the El Paso Board, these choices would provide little basis for enjoining a third-party merger approved by a board overwhelmingly comprised of independent directors, many of whom have substantial industry experience. The *Revlon* doctrine, after all, does not exist as a license for courts to second-guess reasonable, but arguable, questions of business judgment in the change of control context, but to ensure that the directors take reasonable steps to obtain the highest value reasonably attainable and that their actions are not compromised by impermissible considerations, such as self-interest. . . .

Regrettably for the defendants, the record . . . belies their argument that there is no reason to question the motives behind the decisions made by El Paso in negotiating the Merger Agreement. Although it is true that measures were taken to cabin Goldman's conflict (for example, Goldman formally set up an internal "Chinese wall" between the Goldman advisors to El Paso and the Goldman representatives responsible for the firm's Kinder Morgan investment) . . . efforts were not effective. Goldman still played an important role in advising the Board by suggesting that the Board should avoid causing Kinder Morgan to go hostile and by presenting information about the value of pursuing the spin-off instead of the Kinder Morgan deal. Indeed, Goldman's advice to placate Kinder Morgan by entering into due diligence "raised [El Paso] management's concerns" that the Goldman team was "receiving pressure from other parts of Goldman Sachs to avoid a strategy that might result in [Kinder Morgan] going public and making a hostile approach on [El Paso]," prompting El Paso to exclude Goldman from internal tactical discussions about how to respond to Kinder Morgan. . . .

Even then, though, Goldman was not out of the picture entirely, as El Paso management only thought it was necessary to limit Goldman's involvement in the Kinder Morgan side of the advisory work. Goldman continued its role as primary financial advisor to El Paso for the spin-off. . . .

The fact that Goldman continued to have its hands in the dough of the spin-off is important, because the Board was assessing the attractiveness of the Merger relative to the attractiveness of the spin-off.

That was critical because the Board, at the recommendation of Foshee [the El Paso CEO], Goldman, and Morgan Stanley, decided not to risk Kinder Morgan going hostile and not to do any test of the market with other possible buyers of El Paso. . . . Thus, the Board was down to two strategic options: the spin-off or a sale to Kinder Morgan. Therefore, because Goldman stayed involved as the lead advisor on the spin-off, it was in a position to continue to exert influence over the Merger. . . .

Heightening these suspicions is the fact that Goldman's lead banker failed to disclose his own personal ownership of approximately $340,000 in Kinder Morgan stock. . . .

Even worse, Goldman tainted the cleansing effect of Morgan Stanley. Goldman clung to its previously obtained contract to make it the exclusive advisor on the spin-off and which promised Goldman $25 million in fees if the spin-off was completed. . . . Goldman refused to concede that Morgan Stanley should be paid anything if the spin-off, rather than the Merger, was consummated. Goldman's friends in El Paso management—and that is what they seem to have been—easily gave in to Goldman. . . .

. . . Then, despite saying that it did not advise on the Merger—a claim that the record does not bear out in large measure—Goldman asked for a $20 million fee for its work on the Merger. Of course, by the same logic it used to shut out Morgan Stanley from receiving any fee for the spin-off, Goldman should have been foreclosed from getting fees for working on the Merger when it supposedly was walled off from advising on that deal. . . .

Worst of all was that the supposedly well-motivated and expert CEO entrusted with all the key price negotiations kept from the Board his interest in pursuing a management buy-out of the Company's E & P business. . . . [T]he reality is that Foshee was interested in being a buyer of a key part of El Paso at the same time he was charged with getting the highest possible price as a seller of that same asset. At no time did Foshee come clean to his board about his self-interest, and he never sought permission from the Board before twice going to the CEO of the company's negotiating adversary. . . .

The concealed motives of Foshee, the concealed financial interest of Goldman's lead banker in Kinder Morgan, Goldman's continued influence over the Board's assessment of the spin-off, and the distortion of Morgan Stanley's incentives that arose as a result of El Paso management's acquiescence to its Goldman friends' demands leave me persuaded that the plaintiffs have a reasonable probability of success on a claim that the Merger is tainted by breaches of fiduciary duty. . . .

[However, g]iven that the El Paso stockholders are well positioned to turn down the Kinder Morgan price if they do not like it, I am not persuaded that I should deprive them of the chance to make that decision for themselves. Although an after-the-fact monetary damages claim against the defendants is not a perfect tool, it has some value as a remedial instrument, and the likely prospect of a damages trial is no doubt unpleasant to Foshee, other El Paso managers who might be added as defendants, and to Goldman. And, of course, the defendants themselves should be mindful . . . [that a]fter full discovery, it would hardly be unprecedented for additional troubling information to emerge, given the suspicious instances of non-disclosure that have already been surfaced.

For now, however, I reluctantly deny the plaintiffs' motion for a preliminary injunction, concluding that the El Paso stockholders should not be deprived of the chance to decide for themselves about the Merger, despite the disturbing nature of some of the behavior leading to its terms.

---

1. ***Duties of Investment Bankers.*** In *El Paso*, the court was heavily critical of Goldman Sachs's conduct, even concluding that "the plaintiffs have a reasonable probability of success on a claim that the Merger is tainted by breaches of fiduciary duty." Having read the decision, do you think Goldman Sachs's conduct in

particular was sufficiently egregious as to merit a finding of breach of fiduciary duty? Are you persuaded at all by the argument that the seriousness of Goldman Sachs's conduct ought to be mitigated in light of an experienced El Paso board, which apparently found further conflict-of-interest controls to be unnecessary, and a conflicted El Paso CEO who seems to have played a critical role in failing to seek the highest price? More generally, what do you think the scope of investment bankers' duties to their corporate clients should be? Professor Andrew Tuch has argued for a robust duty of loyalty:

> Powerful reasons exist for a client . . . to reasonably expect loyalty from the investment bank providing it with [M&A] advice. First, . . . change-of-control transactions are matters of great strategic significance to a company and its management. . . . [S]ince these transactions often pit a client against an adversary (or at least against a party or parties with divergent interests), a notion of partisanship prevails among each party and its advisers. . . . Second, the [duty] is supported by the close analogy between the counselling role of a law firm and the financial advisory role of an investment bank . . . During a transaction the client will divulge to its advisers confidential and sensitive information about its strategic direction, vulnerabilities and other matters for the purpose of receiving advice and thereby be vulnerable to the misuse of this information. . . . Third, the advice itself—regarding the structure, terms and timing of the proposed transaction, price and form of any consideration offered and proposed uses of funds—are matters of central importance to the success or otherwise of [the proposed transaction]. . . . Finally, . . . [p]ermitting investment banks to have interests conflicting with that of their clients would likely erode community confidence in the integrity and utility of the relationship and in the financial markets generally.

Andrew F. Tuch, *Obligations of Financial Advisers in Change-of-Control Transactions: Fiduciary and Other Questions*, 24 CO. & SEC. L.J. 488, 508–09 (2006); *see also* Andrew F. Tuch, Banker Loyalty in Mergers and Acquisitions, 94 TEX. L. REV. __ (forthcoming 2016). (This article was first published by Thomson Reuters in the Company and Securities Law Journal.)

2. ***Information Barriers.*** Goldman Sachs attempted to address its conflict of interest by erecting an internal communication barrier between the Goldman Sachs advisers to El Paso and the Goldman Sachs employees responsible for managing the firm's investment in Kinder Morgan. In the court's view, however, this internal control proved to be ineffective, perhaps because it was not fully implemented or too porous to prevent the passage of critical information. Beyond this particular case, what are some potential problems associated with information barriers more generally? Consider the following criticisms of information barriers: (1) they excel at preventing the accidental transmission of information across walled-off groups but do little to stop deliberate efforts to communicate; (2) they may inadvertently prevent the flow of important but non-restricted information to a walled-off group within the firm that owes a fiduciary duty to the firm's client, thus resulting in suboptimal advising and possibly a breach of a fiduciary duty; and (3) they decrease the efficiency and synergies of a firm. *See, e.g.*, Christopher M. Gorman, *Are Chinese Walls the Best Solution to the Problems of Insider Trading*

and Conflicts of Interest in Broker-Dealers?, 9 FORDHAM J. CORP. & FIN. L. 475, 490–93 (2004). Which of these criticisms are the most worrisome? Can you think of any additional problems with information barriers, or ways of improving their effectiveness?

3. **El Paso *Follow-on Cases: The* Rural/Metro *Litigation.*** In the Rural/Metro Stockholders Litigation, a Delaware Chancery Court judge held that RBC Capital Markets' conflicts of interest tainted a $438 million buyout of Rural/Metro, a national ambulance service company, and issued a decision awarding nearly $76 million in damages against RBC. The judge found that the bankers at RBC Capital Markets misled Rural/Metro directors regarding the company's value to encourage the board to quickly sell to buyout firm Warburg Pincus LLC and failed to disclose their attempts to use their financial-adviser work on the deal to secure financing work on another acquisition. *In re* Rural Metro Corp., 88 A.3d 54 (Del. Ch. 2014). One year after the Chancery Court decision, the Delaware Supreme Court affirmed the lower court ruling, reaffirming the importance of financial advisor independence. RBC Capital Markets, LLC v. Jervis, No. 140, 2015, 2015 WL 7721882 (Del. Nov. 30, 2015) (stating that, "[p]ropelled by its own improper motives, RBC misled the Rural directors into breaching their duty of care, thereby aiding and abetting the Board's breach of its fiduciary obligations."). What do decisions such as El Paso and Rural/Metro indicate with respect to the court's scrutiny of conflicts of interest?

B. ABACUS LITIGATION

We now turn to a prominent example of conflicts of interests in the subprime mortgage context. In the aftermath of the Financial Crisis, the SEC brought enforcement actions against investment banks for their role in the sale of collateral debt organizations (CDOs). Because many of these enforcement actions resulted in out-of-court settlements, the following description of the ABACUS transaction is drawn from a law review article. As you read, try to ascertain the nature and extent of the conflict of interest.

Scott Bell, Clarity and Predictability at the SEC: ABACUS, Citigroup, and the Political Economy of Securities Fraud Settlements

2012 COLUM. BUS. L. REV. 865 (2012)

In 2006, John Paulson began purchasing CDSs on debt securities referencing mortgage loans via his fund, Paulson & Co. ("Paulson"). During the winter of 2006–07, Paulson approached representatives at [Goldman Sachs] to ask them to help it buy protection on "various bonds it expected to experience credit events." Allegedly, GS&Co. and Fabrice Tourre, a [Goldman Sachs]. representative who was working with Paulson, believed that it would be difficult "to place the liabilities of a synthetic CDO if they disclosed to investors that a short investor . . . played a significant role in the collateral selection process." As a result, [Goldman Sachs] sought to engage a collateral manager for the transaction, but realized that "not every collateral manager would 'agree to the type of names [of RMBS] Paulson want[ed] to use' and put its 'name at risk . . . on a weak quality portfolio.'"

ACA Management LLC ("ACA"), a company that had previously sponsored twenty-two transactions, ultimately agreed to serve as collateral manager, in large part, the SEC alleges, because "[Goldman Sachs was] responsible for ACA's misimpression that Paulson had a long position, rather than a short position, with respect to the CDO." There is some contrary evidence here, however: Paolo Pellegrini, a former employee of Paulson, has stated that he informed ACA that Paulson "wanted to buy protection on traunches [sic] of a synthetic RMBS portfolio." . . . Finally, after an involved bargaining process between Paulson and ACA, the two parties settled on a reference portfolio of ninety RMBS for the deal.

As noted above, the marketing materials for the deal did not include any mention of Paulson's involvement, and in marketing to outside investors such as IKB Deutsche Industriebank AG ("IKB"), [Goldman Sachs] emphasized that the portfolio was selected by ACA. IKB invested $150 million in Classes A-1 and A-2, most of which was paid to Paulson. The SEC alleges that IKB would not have invested in the transaction without the presence of an "independent third party with knowledge of the U.S. housing market and expertise in analyzing RMBS," or, in short, ACA. Similarly, ACA Capital Holdings, Inc. ("ACA Capital"), ACA's parent, sold protection on the $909 million super senior (unfunded) tranche, a substantial portion of which was eventually guaranteed by ABN AMRO Bank N.V. ("ABN"). ABN ultimately paid approximately $840.9 million to unwind its position in the trade, most of which went to Paulson. Finally, it is worth noting that GS&Co. also had a net long position in the trade of $90 million, which it lost.

As a result of this trade, the SEC sued [Goldman Sachs] and Fabrice Tourre on April 16, 2010 for violations of Section 17(a)(1), (2), and (3), as well as Section 10(b) and Rule 10b- 5. Each claim, however, was tied to two actions: first, that GS&Co. had misled investors—such as IKB—through the use of misleading materials, and second, that [Goldman Sachs] had misled ACA by not correcting ACA's "misimpression" of Paulson's economic interests. As a result of the SEC's suit, GS&Co.'s share price closed $23.57 below its previous day close, meaning that the firm's market capitalization fell by more than $10 billion. [Goldman Sachs] later settled with the SEC on July 14, 2010, and paid $15 million in disgorgement of profits and $535 million in civil penalties. Although [Goldman Sachs] neither admitted nor denied the allegations of the complaint, it agrees that "it was a mistake for the Goldman marketing materials to state that the reference portfolio was 'selected by' ACA Management LLC without disclosing the role of Paulson & Co. Inc. . . . Goldman regrets that the marketing materials did not contain that disclosure."

---

1. ***Investment Bankers' Duties.*** What duties, if any, did Goldman Sachs violate in its handling of the ABACUS transaction? Due to the no-admit settlement reached by the SEC and Goldman Sachs, we can only speculate as to Goldman Sachs's potential liability had the case proceeded through the usual stages of litigation. That being said, Scott Bell provides a useful discussion of why the SEC may have found it difficult to prosecute Goldman Sachs under existing fiduciary duty standards:

> First, it is not entirely clear that, on the facts provided, the use of anti-fraud provisions . . . to regulate the alleged behavior is conceptually appropriate. . . . [It is arguable] whether non-disclosure of Paulson's involvement could be held to be actionable. There is some authority indicating that [Goldman Sachs] had a duty to Paulson *not* to disclose his role in the transaction, not least since the theory under which the SEC had sued [Goldman Sachs] was based on enforcement of misstatements, rather than nondisclosure. [Second, an inference of scienter and materiality would also have been difficult to establish because Goldman Sachs] statements that each portfolio was selected

> by one party (and omission of a second, adverse party) do not necessarily lead to the conclusion that [Goldman Sachs was] trying to hide the presence of that adverse party from potential investors. . . . [As for materiality, the question is] whether telling the investors [about Paulson] . . . would have significantly altered the total mix of information available, or whether a reasonable investor would have considered it important in evaluating the transaction. . . . Given the nature of this type of transaction, it is far from certain that such a position can be maintained. [For example], it does not appear that Paulson had superior information to ACA or IKB, since every party had full access to the portfolio of reference securities and other information in the prospectus.

Bell, *Clarity and Predictability at the SEC*, at 902–07.

2. ***Fabrice Tourre's Liability.*** Consider also the role of Fabrice Tourre, the young banker at Goldman Sachs who was principally responsible for structuring the ABACUS CDO, and the SEC's related enforcement action. Goldman Sachs's settlement did not cover Fabrice Tourre, who was ultimately ordered to pay the SEC $650,000 in penalties and approximately $175,000 more as a disgorgement of related bonuses. *See* SEC. v. Tourre, 4 F. Supp. 3d 579 (S.D.N.Y. 2014). The case was an important victory for the SEC, which has had a mixed track record in enforcements arising from the Financial Crisis. *See* Ben Protess, *For S.E.C., A Much Needed Win*, N.Y. TIMES, Mar. 12, 2014. Does the imposition of penalties on the particular individuals provide a more appropriate deterrent for misconduct than firm-level penalties? Who are the appropriate targets for such enforcement—the individuals most closely involved in the misconduct, their supervisors, or someone else? Consider as well the steps taken by the leadership of Goldman Sachs to revise its culture and business standards in the wake of the Financial Crisis. On May 7, 2010, Goldman Sachs announced the creation of a Business Standards Committee under the oversight of its Board of Directors, which reviewed among others, standards for dealing with conflicts of interest. See Goldman Sachs, Report of the Business Standards Committee (Jan. 2011). What role does corporate governance play in addressing conflicts of interest and other ethical issues? We will revisit this topic in Chapter 8.1.

3. ***The Continuing Importance of ABACUS.*** Although the SEC settled with Goldman Sachs over the ABACUS transaction, this case has had lasting significance due to its role in generating support for the Volcker Rule and in certain respects rekindling public support for the legislation that became the Dodd-Frank Act. As discussed in Andrew Tuch's *Conflicted Gatekeepers: The Volcker Rule and Goldman Sachs*, one purpose behind the Volcker Rule was "to impose conflicts of interests rules on underwriters selling securities to investors, including sophisticated investors." *See* Andrew Tuch, *Conflicted Gatekeepers: The Volcker Rule and Goldman Sachs*, 7 VA. L. & BUS. REV. 365, 366 (2012). We will discuss the Volcker Rule in detail in Chapter 6.1.

IV. THE EFFICIENT MARKETS HYPOTHESIS

Turning to the macro level, the efficient markets hypothesis is a theory describing the relationship between the disclosure of financially significant information and changes in securities market prices. Under this theory, markets price in all available information about a given firm, and competition will drive investors to discover relevant and material information. These actions drive the market to become efficient. STEPHEN A. ROSS, RANDOLPH W. WESTERFIELD & BRADFORD D. JORDAN, FUNDAMENTALS OF CORPORATE FINANCE 391–93 (2009). Put differently, in a perfectly efficient market, there will be no opportunities for arbitrage because the price of the asset will reflect its true value.

The efficient market hypothesis comes in three forms: weak, semi-strong, and strong. The weak version, universally accepted, states that security prices are determined by currently available information rather than historical market trends. The highly controversial strong version states that even non-public information is impounded into security prices through mechanisms like insider trading. The semi-strong version, meanwhile, states that information is impounded into the stock price quickly, but only once it becomes public.

To the extent the efficient markets hypothesis is accepted, it could have significant political, regulatory, and judicial implications. Donald C. Langevoort, *Theories, Assumptions, and Securities Regulation: Market Efficiency Revisited*, 140 U. PA. L. REV. 851, 886 (1992). Most fundamentally, the theory's tenants as to the processing of public information have been relied on to streamline procedural requirements as to corporate disclosures. As the SEC states on its website:

> The laws and rules that govern the securities industry in the United States derive from a simple and straightforward concept: all investors, whether large institutions or private individuals, should have access to certain basic facts about an investment prior to buying it. To achieve this, the SEC requires public companies to disclose meaningful financial and other information to the public, which provides a common pool of knowledge for all investors to use to judge for themselves if a company's securities are a good investment. Only through the steady flow of timely, comprehensive and accurate information can people make sound investment decisions.

Securities and Exchange Commission, *The SEC: Who We Are, What We Do*.

Another implication has been seen in litigation under the SEC's anti-fraud provisions, including Rule 10b-5. One of the elements to satisfying a Rule 10b-5 claim is showing that there was reliance on a fraudulent statement. The fraud-on-the-market theory allows a presumption of reliance to be shown from the fact that there was misinformation incorporated in the market prices, and that the investor relied on that misinformation by paying the market price. Basic v. Levinson, 108 U.S. 978 (1988). The Supreme Court recently re-affirmed this approach, with some procedural modifications, in *Erica P. John Fund v. Halliburton Co.*, 563 U.S. 804 (2011). More controversially, the Supreme Court also reaffirmed the theory's implications regarding the assessment of damages in private securities class action lawsuits. *See* Halliburton Co. v. Erica P. John Fund, Inc., 134 S. Ct. 2398 (2014).

Think back on the *Pagel*, *El Paso*, and ABACUS litigation discussed earlier in this chapter. To what degree is the efficient market hypothesis relevant to the topics discussed within those cases? While thinking about this question, consider the assumptions underlying the efficient markets hypothesis. For example, while dissenting in the *Basic* case, Justice White argued that that many investors purchase or sell stock because they believe the price *inaccurately* reflects a corporation's worth, the paradigmatic example being a short-seller who predicts that the price of a security will fall. Similarly, the efficient markets hypothesis also assumes that increased efficiency benefits all investors, a belief seen in many other areas of securities regulation. But does faith in informational efficiency obscure other concerns? Take, for example, an unsophisticated investor looking to purchase a single stock. In order to make a truly informed investment decision, this investor cannot just rely on the stock's price—they must also consider other factors such as transaction costs and the stock's impact on the diversification of their existing portfolio. *See* Howell E. Jackson, *To What Extent Should Individual Investors Rely on Mechanisms of Market Efficiency: A Preliminary Investigation of Dispersion in Investor Returns*, 28 J. CORP. L. 671 (2003).

Also consider that at the very least some markets may not be efficient at all, or at least not fundamentally efficient. Markets, for instance may be informationally efficient, meaning share prices will react quickly to new information, but they will only be fundamentally efficient if those price reactions reflect the true value of those shares. While markets may become more efficient as trading by sophisticated investors increases, some thinly traded markets may by consequence be fundamentally inefficient. *See* Ronald J. Gilson & Reiner H. Kraakman, *The Mechanisms of Market Efficiency*, 70 VA. L. REV. 549 (1984). Given this possibility, are initial public offering markets efficient? If not, how, if at all, should the current regulatory structure be altered?

Empirical evidence has also called efficient markets hypothesis into question more generally. *See, e.g.* Robert Shiller, *Do Stock Prices Move too Much to be Justified by Subsequent Changes in Dividends?* 71 AM. ECON. REV. 421 (1981). These studies formed the basis for theories of "noise trading." In contrast to the efficient markets hypothesis, noise theory states that some investors are not fully rational; that is, their demand for assets is affected by beliefs or sentiments that are not entirely justified by news that would be expected to impact the price of that asset. Because arbitrage strategies are often risky, rational investor activity will not fully counter these sentiment-driven changes, affecting security returns. Put differently, while the fraud-on-the-market theory may accurately predict that markets are informationally efficient, markets may nonetheless not be efficient from an allocative standpoint. That is arguably how and why bubbles occur. Further empirical support is provided through what has been identified as the low-risk anomaly, which suggests that *low risks* were often correlated with higher returns. Malcom Baker, Brendan Bradley, & Ryan Taliaferro, *The Low Risk Anomaly: A Decomposition into Macro and Micro Effects*, 70 FIN. ANALYSTS' J. 43 (2014). Based on these critiques, what role should the efficient market hypothesis play in securities regulation writ large?

CHAPTER 4.4

EXCHANGES AND TRADING

CONTENTS

I. INTRODUCTION

In this Chapter, we turn our consideration to the regulation of exchanges and trading markets. The materials build on the readings in the preceding chapters of Part IV, especially our exploration of the fiduciary duties of securities firms in Chapters 4.2 and 4.3. As you will see, establishing efficient trading markets requires coordination among many parties that must agree in advance how trading markets are to be organized and information shared. In certain respects, trading markets produce public goods, including information on the value of securities and liquidity in times of financial distress. As discussed in the pages that follow, these features pose many regulatory challenges.

II. EXCHANGES AND OTHER TRADING MARKETS

A. ENDING FIXED COMMISSIONS ON THE NYSE

We begin our discussion of trading markets with a piece of what might now seem ancient history. In the pre-1975 era, most equity trading in the United States was located on the New York Stock Exchange (NYSE), an organization that had functioned as a trading market since the late 18th Century and where member firms abided by a number of operating constraints, including an agreement to charge the same prices—known as fixed commissions—to all customers. Investors challenged the practice in a litigation that ultimately reached the Supreme Court:

Gordon v. N.Y. Stock Exch.

422 U.S. 659 (1975)

JUSTICE BLACKMUN DELIVERED THE OPINION OF THE COURT.

This case presents the problem of reconciliation of the antitrust laws with a federal regulatory scheme in the particular context of the practice of the securities exchanges and their members of using fixed rates of commission.

In early 1971 petitioner Richard A. Gordon, individually and on behalf of an asserted class of small investors, filed this suit against the [NYSE], the American Stock Exchange, Inc. (Amex), and two member firms of the Exchanges. The complaint challenged a variety of exchange rules and practices and, in particular, claimed that the system of fixed commission rates, utilized by the Exchanges at that time for transactions less than $500,000, violated §§1 and 2 of the Sherman Act. . . .

Commission rates for transactions on the stock exchanges have been set by agreement since the establishment of the first exchange in this country. The [NYSE] was formed with the Buttonwood Tree Agreement of 1792, and from the beginning minimum fees were set and observed by the members. . . .

These fixed rate policies were not unnoticed by responsible congressional bodies. For example, the House Committee on Banking and Currency, in a general review of the stock exchanges undertaken in 1913, reported that the fixed commission rate rules were "rigidly enforced" in order "to prevent competition amongst the members." H.R. Rep. No. 1593, 62d Cong., 3d Sess., 39 (1913). . . .

Despite the monopoly power of the few exchanges, exhibited not only in the area of commission rates but in a wide variety of other aspects, the exchanges remained essentially self-regulating and without significant supervision until the adoption of the Securities Exchange Act of 1934 [(1934 Act)], as amended. At the lengthy hearings before adoption of that Act, some attention was given to the fixed commission rate practice and to its anticompetitive features. . . .

As finally enacted, the [1934 Act] apparently reflected [debate from the legislative history], for it gave the SEC the power to fix and insure 'reasonable' rates. Section 19(b) provided:

> *The [SEC] is further authorized*, if after making appropriate request in writing to a national securities exchange that such exchange effect on its own behalf specified changes in its rules and practices, and after appropriate notice and opportunity for hearing, *the [SEC] determines* that such exchange has not made the changes so requested, and that *such changes are necessary or appropriate for the protection of investors or to insure fair dealing in securities traded* in upon such exchange or to insure fair administration of such exchange, by rules or regulations or by order *to alter or supplement the rules of such exchange* (insofar as necessary or appropriate to effect such changes) in respect of such matters as . . . (9) *the fixing of reasonable rates of commission*, interest, listing, and other charges.

This provision conformed to the [1934 Act]'s general policy of self-regulation by the exchanges coupled with oversight by the SEC. . . .

With this legislative history in mind, we turn to the actual post-1934 experience of commission rates on the NYSE and Amex. . . . [An extensive review of the SEC's study of fixed commissions on the NYSE and its eventual decision to end the practice is omitted.]

This lengthy history can be summarized briefly: In enacting the [1934 Act], Congress gave clear authority to the SEC to supervise exchange self-regulation with respect to the "fixing of reasonable rates of commission." Upon SEC determination that exchange rules or practices regarding commission rates required change in order to protect investors or to insure fair dealing, the SEC was authorized to require adoption of such changes as were deemed necessary or appropriate. . . . Since the [1934 Act]'s adoption, and primarily in the last 15 years, the SEC has been engaged in thorough review of exchange commission rate practices. The committees of the Congress, while recently expressing some dissatisfaction with the progress of the SEC in implementing competitive rates, have generally been content to allow the SEC to proceed without new legislation. As of May 1, 1975, the SEC, by order, has abolished fixed rates. And new legislation, enacted into law June 5, 1975, codifies this result, although still permitting the SEC some discretion to reimpose fixed rates if warranted.

This Court has considered the issue of implied repeal of the antitrust laws in the context of a variety of regulatory schemes and procedures. Certain axioms of construction are now clearly established. Repeal of the antitrust laws by implication is not favored and not casually to be allowed. Only where there is a "plain repugnancy between the antitrust and regulatory provisions" will repeal be implied. *United States v. Philadelphia National Bank*, 374 U.S. 321, 350-51 (1963). . . .

The starting point for our consideration of the particular issue presented by this case, *viz.*, whether the antitrust laws are impliedly repealed or replaced as a result of the statutory provisions and administrative and congressional experience concerning fixed commission rates, of course, is our decision in *Silver v. New York Stock Exchange*, 373 U.S. 341 (1963). There the Court considered the relationship between the antitrust laws and the [1934 Act], and did so specifically with respect to the action of an exchange in ordering its members to remove private direct telephone connections with the offices of nonmembers. Such action, absent any immunity derived from the regulatory laws, would be a per se violation of § 1 of the Sherman Act. 373 U.S., at 347, 83 S.Ct. at 1251. Concluding that the proper approach to the problem was to reconcile the operation of the antitrust laws with a regulatory scheme, the Court established a "guiding principle" for the achievement of this reconciliation. Under this principle, "[r]epeal is to be regarded as implied only if necessary to make the [1934 Act] work, and even then only to the minimum extent necessary." *Id.*, at 357, 83 S.Ct. at 1257.

In *Silver*, the Court concluded that there was no implied repeal of the antitrust laws in that factual context because the [1934 Act] did not provide for SEC jurisdiction or review of particular applications of rules enacted by the exchanges. It noted:

> Although the Act gives to the [SEC] the power to request exchanges to make changes in their rules, § 19(b), and impliedly, therefore, to disapprove any rules adopted by an exchange, see also § 6(a)(4), it does not give the [SEC] jurisdiction to review particular instances of enforcement of exchange rules. *Ibid.*

At the time *Silver* was decided, both the rules and constitution of the NYSE provided that the [SEC] could require discontinuance of wire service between the office of a member and a nonmember at any time. There was no provision for notice or statement of reasons. While these rules were permissible under the general power of the exchanges to adopt rules regulating relationships between members and nonmembers, and the SEC could disapprove the rules, the SEC could not forbid or regulate any particular application of the rules. Hence, the regulatory agency could not prevent application of the rules that would have undesirable anticompetitive effects; there was no governmental oversight of the exchange's self-regulatory action, and no method of insuring that some attention at least was given to the public interest in competition.

The Court, therefore, concluded that the absence in *Silver* of regulatory supervision over the application of the exchange rules prevented any conflict arising between the regulatory scheme and the antitrust laws. . . . The Court in *Silver* cautioned, however, that "[s]hould review of exchange self-regulation be provided through a vehicle other than the antitrust laws, a different case as to antitrust exemption would be presented." 373 U.S., at 360, 83 S.Ct. at 1258. It amplified this statement in a footnote:

> Were there [SEC] jurisdiction and ensuing judicial review for scrutiny of a particular exchange ruling . . . a different case would arise concerning exemption from the operation of laws designed to prevent anticompetitive activity, an issue we do not decide today. *Id.*, at 358, n. 12, 83 S.Ct. at 1257.

It is patent that the case presently at bar is, indeed, that "different case" to which the Court in *Silver* referred. In contrast to the circumstances of *Silver*, § 19(b) gave the SEC direct regulatory power over exchange rules and practices with respect to "the fixing of reasonable rates of commission." Not only was the SEC authorized to disapprove rules and practices concerning commission rates, but the agency also was permitted to require alteration or supplementation of the rules and practices when "necessary or appropriate for the protection of investors or to insure fair dealings in securities traded in upon such exchange." Since 1934 all rate changes have been brought to the attention of the SEC, and it has taken an active role in review of proposed rate changes during the last 15 years. Thus, rather than presenting a case of SEC impotence to affect application of exchange rules in particular circumstances, this case involves explicit statutory authorization for SEC review of all exchange rules and practices dealing with rates of commission and resultant SEC continuing activity.

Having determined that this case is, in fact, the "different case," we must then make inquiry as to the proper reconciliation of the regulatory and antitrust statutes involved here, keeping in mind the principle that repeal of the antitrust laws will be "implied only if necessary to make the [1934 Act] work, and even then only to the minimum extent necessary." 373 U.S., at 357, 83 S.Ct., at 1257. We hold that these requirements for implied repeal are clearly satisfied here. To permit operation of the antitrust laws with respect to commission rates, as urged by petitioner Gordon and the United States as amicus curiae, would unduly interfere, in our view, with the operation of the [1934 Act]. . . .

---

1. ***Anti-Trust and Financial Services.*** How does the application of anti-trust laws to the practices of securities exchanges and their members compare with what we have seen elsewhere in financial services? In particular, how does the application of anti-trust laws in this instance compare to the federal regulation of competitive practices in the insurance sector?

2. ***Justifying Price Restrictions.*** Given our legal system's general aversion to price fixing, why did it take so long for the era of NYSE-fixed commissions to end? A close reading of the *Gordon* case reveals several plausible justifications for restricting price competition among exchange members. What were those justifications? Are they plausible? Could such arguments ever offer a credible basis for restraining competition in capital markets?

3. ***Competition for Issuers.*** One of the traditional functions of established trading markets, such as the NYSE, has been to develop listing standards for the issuers of securities. As the number of registered exchanges grows, these exchanges now compete for issuer business. Is this competition between exchanges for issuer business an example of a healthy market? Or, is it a race to the bottom? Clearly concerned that competition between exchanges would lead to a race to the bottom, the SEC adopted 1934 Act Rule 19c-4 in 1988, which barred self-regulatory organizations from listing the stock of a corporation that takes any corporate action "with the effect of nullifying, restricting or disparately reducing the per share voting rights of [existing common stockholders]." The

purpose of this language in Rule 19c-4 was to prevent disparate voting rights plans due to recapitalizations or stock dividends. The D.C. Circuit Court vacated Rule 19c-4, finding that the rule exceeded the SEC's authority under § 19 of the 1934 Act. *Bus. Roundtable v. SEC*, 905 F.2d 406, 411 (D.C. Cir. 1990) (stating that "[w]ith its step beyond control of voting procedure and into the distribution of voting power, the [SEC] would assume an authority that the [1934 Act]'s proponents disclaimed any intent to grant."); *see also* Voting Rights Listing Standards; Disenfranchisement Rule, 53 Fed. Reg. 26,376 (Jul. 12, 1988) (adopting Rule 19c-4).

B. THE RISE OF THE NATIONAL MARKET SYSTEM

As the *Gordon* case illustrates, 1975 marked the end of fixed commissions on the NYSE. After this, something of a revolution in the securities sector ensued. A new breed of discount brokerage houses emerged, which opened the door for depository institutions to enter the securities business, as we saw in Chapter 2.2. The 1975 legislation discussed in the *Gordon* decision also gave the SEC a new mandate: to develop a national market system (NMS) for trading in securities. The following excerpt reports on the SEC's progress with that task over the first two decades of the NMS.

Polly Nyquist, Failure to Engage: The Regulation of Proprietary Trading Systems

13 YALE L. & POL'Y REV. 281 (1995)

I. Background

[Along with the controversy over fixed commissions on the NYSE, a] "back room" crisis in the 1960s, caused by the paper-driven market's inability to deal with an increasing trade volume, led to the enactment of the 1975 Amendments to the [1934 Act], the first major structural reform effort since 1934. The primary focus of the 1975 Amendments was adoption of section 11A of the 1934 Act, which gave the SEC the mandate to establish a [NMS]. This term was not defined, as Congress wanted to give the SEC and market forces the ability to create the best system. However, Congress outlined the goals it had for this system: (1) create a level playing field for competition among various market participants; (2) increase the dissemination of price quotes; (3) increase the efficiency of the market; and (4) ensure "best execution."

The debate over the meaning of the congressional mandate with respect to the development of the NMS illustrates the underlying theoretical tension in the regulation of the securities markets. As with the original drafting of the securities regulation laws, the current debate vacillates between the desire for centralized trading, which enhances price discovery, liquidity, and best execution, and the desire for competition among the markets that will improve the entire system through the "survival of the fittest." With the 1975 Amendments, Congress and the SEC, in its rule-making activities, seem to have sought both to encourage centralization through greater transparency and to encourage intermarket competition. The NMS legislation did not resolve this tension and thus leaves the SEC with an unclear mandate as to how to deal with an issue such as the regulation of [proprietary trading systems (PTSs)] which implicates both goals.

The SEC and the markets have undertaken several projects designed to implement the 1975 Amendments. The first, and perhaps the most successful to date, was the establishment of the Consolidated Tape for real-time reporting of trading in "eligible" securities, and the Consolidated Quotation System (CQS), which collects firm quotes from the various exchanges and [over-the-counter (OTC)] dealers. The second major project, the Intermarket Trading System (ITS), electronically links eight national exchanges and the NASD. The ITS provides brokers on the floor of any participating exchange with a means of executing a trade in any of the other markets, thus allowing the broker or specialist to execute their transaction at the best displayed price. The ITS also allows all participants to enter pre-opening interest in securities that will be executed when the market opens. The participants in the ITS have developed a set of uniform trading rules in order to enhance the effectiveness of the system in actually linking the markets.

[Since 1975, t]he U.S. securities markets have seen several dramatic changes since the enactment of the 1975 Amendments, which may question the continuing viability of these reforms. The purpose of the SEC's "Market 2000" study, announced in 1992 and released in January 1994, was to analyze these market changes and determine what, if any, regulatory response was needed.

1. Changes in Volume

The first important change is the increase in the total volume and dollar amount of equity securities traded in the United States. In 1975, the total market value of U.S. equities was $85 billion. By 1992, the total market value reached $5 trillion. More individuals participate in the markets today than ever before, either as individual investors or as members of the increasingly large and popular mutual funds and pension plans. More businesses are turning to the markets for their capital needs. Technological advances have allowed the markets and the market professionals to handle the increasing demand for access to the markets. Arguably, this huge growth means that the SEC, now more than ever, needs to take an active role to protect the increasing percentage of U.S. savings that are at risk in the markets.

2. Changes in Investors

One of the most important changes is the so-called "institutionalization" of the ownership of equity securities in the U.S. In 1975, institutional investors owned 30% of U.S. equity securities, but by 1992, they owned slightly over 50% of the market. Thus, individual investors now account for less than 50% of the market. A 1990 survey by the NYSE indicated that 51 million individuals in the U.S., or about 21% of the population, own corporate stock. This is compared to the approximately 25 million individuals that owned equity issues in 1975. Individuals do not trade directly on the markets or with each other. Rather, individual investors trade through a professional intermediary, such as a broker-dealer. . . .

Institutional investors are professional money managers or financial institutions who execute large numbers of transactions and manage large sums of money. The largest of these are the private pension plans, which in 1992 owned about 20% of U.S. equities, an increase from the less than 13% the pension funds owned in 1975. The second largest are the mutual funds, whose market share has more than doubled since 1975, jumping from 4% to 9.1% in 1992. Other types of institutional investors are hedge funds (typically involving less than 100 individual investors), insurance companies, and public pension funds. . . .

3. Changes in the Markets

The markets themselves have also been changing in response to the changing demands of the investors. The most striking changes are the shift in the distribution of volume between the various exchanges and the increased use of technology by both existing and emerging markets. Although the NYSE is and always has been the largest of the equity markets, it is currently losing market share to the regionals, NASDAQ, and other markets. This shift is due in part to the activities of the institutional investors who like to route their block trades through the regionals, where the specialists are less likely to interfere with the crosses or force them to be exposed to the limit order book. For the same reason, the PTSs often favor the regionals for execution of their trades, which are often matched within the system before transfer to the floor. The potential for increased market fragmentation that results has been met with concern by both academics and the regulators.

As the dominance of the NYSE has been challenged by other markets, the NYSE has moved to preserve itself in several ways. First, it has vigorously defended its remaining anti-competitive rules, such as restrictions on member off-board trading activity. Second, the NYSE has made several adaptations to match the services offered by its competitor markets. These efforts include development of the "upstairs" or "off-board" market where institutional investors can negotiate large block trades without exposing them to the market, and the addition of two after-hours crossing sessions to stem the flow of after-hours transactions to the international markets or PTSs.

Perhaps the NYSE's most fundamental change has been the partial automation of its functions through the addition of its Designated Order Turnaround (DOT) system that offers members the ability to execute or route orders to the specialist posts without the time-consuming process of using slips of paper carried by their floor brokers. The DOT experienced a significant operational failure during the 1987 Market Break, after which members were asked to curtail use of the system for program trading. Since that time, the NYSE has enhanced and strengthened it. . . .

II. Proprietary Trading Systems

The rising popularity of PTSs is dramatic evidence of the invasion of computer technology. Although these systems currently account for a relatively small percentage of the total markets, 1.4% of NYSE and 13% of NASDAQ/NMS trading volume in 1993, their recent explosive growth, and their future potential, make them a real issue for both market users and regulators. In 1991, 2.9 billion shares traded though PTSs, but in only the first six months of 1993, that number had jumped to 4.7 billion shares. A vast majority of that trading, 87%, is in NASDAQ-listed issues where use of PTSs avoids paying dealer spreads and may allow users to take advantage of the interquote prices currently unavailable on NASDAQ. [Institutional i]nvestor participation in PTSs is particularly high, with TIAA-CREF, for example, recently reporting that it routes almost 75% of its orders through these systems. Institutional investors are drawn to these systems because they offer both anonymity and lower commission costs without the technical hassle of fourth market trading. They are particularly attractive to passive investors, such as funds managed by indexing, who do not need the continuous trading offered by the traditional exchanges. Investors trading in NASDAQ stocks may also be able to use the systems to avoid paying the dealer spreads. [In later analysis, the SEC has estimated that alternative trading systems in 1997 accounted for roughly 20 percent of orders for NASDAQ securities and almost 4 percent of NYSE orders.]

---

1. ***Emerging Trading Systems.*** As the above excerpt indicates, one of the principal developments in our trading markets over the first twenty years of the NMS was the emergence of new trading systems. By the mid-1990s, the NYSE was no longer the dominant force it once was, and the 1975 Amendments' goal of increasing competition across markets was realized, at least in part. Questions remain, however, over whether the fragmentation of markets is necessarily a good thing, as noted in the excerpt below:

> Market centers compete to offer innovative services and reduced trading costs to attract order flow from other market centers. . . At the same time, the existence of multiple market centers competing for order flow in the same security may isolate orders and hence reduce the opportunity for interaction of all buying and selling

> interest in that security. This may reduce competition on price, which is one of the most important benefits of greater interaction of buying and selling interest in an individual security.

Commission Request for Comment on Issues Relating to Market Fragmentation, Securities Exchange Act Release No. 42450 (February 3, 2000).

Some of the new markets, such as the proprietary trading systems, are only available to large institutional investors and cannot be accessed by retail investors. Should the SEC be concerned with this trend? Is it consistent with the SEC's over-arching goal of protecting investors? Are there other costs associated with market fragmentation? Keep these questions in mind when we discuss high-frequency traders and their use of these proprietary systems.

2. ***Regulation NMS.*** In Shirking at the SEC: The Failure of the National Market System, Jonathan Macey and David Haddock critiqued the NMS, focusing on the SEC's response to the 1975 legislation in which Congress mandated that the SEC implement a competitive market for securities by developing a NMS. The article examines the SEC's failure to deregulate—beyond the abolition of fixed-rate commissions—thereby keeping in place competitive restrictions such as rules against exchange delisting and restrictions on off-board trading, which is trading that does not take place on an exchange. Macey and Haddock ultimately rejected the SEC's arguments against deregulation, arguing that the SEC is not motivated by public interest but rather by political pressure applied by special interest groups. Macey and Haddock argued that, without deregulation, there is little promise of a truly competitive NMS and that if the SEC relaxed restrictions against off-board trading, then market forces would develop the necessary reporting and communications systems to guarantee the success of a NMS. How does deregulation make a stronger, more competitive NMS? What concerns does deregulation of the securities markets raise? In 2005, the SEC adopted Regulation NMS, which addressed many of the issues raised in the Macey and Haddock article. Regulation NMS modernized the rules applicable to securities markets to take into account the profound changes brought about by technological changes. *See* Jonathan R. Macey & David D. Haddock, *Shirking at the SEC: The Failure of the National Market System*, 1985 U. ILL. L. REV. 315 (1985); *see also* Regulation NMS, 70 Fed. Reg. 37,496, 37,497 (Jun. 29, 2005).

3. ***Private versus Public Trading Markets.*** One result of the SEC's measured approach to deregulation is the increase in private trading markets for certain securities. For example, Rule 144A provides a safe harbor from the registration requirements of § 5 of the Securities Act of 1933, allowing for certain qualifying securities to be sold among qualified institutional buyers. The rise of private trading markets and legislative and regulatory actions, such as the Jumpstart Our Business Startups Act (JOBS Act) and regulation crowdfunding, both discussed in Chapter 4.3, are evidence of the SEC's continuing effort to appropriately balance investor protection and capital formation. For a discussion of factors influencing the SEC's regulation of securities offering and public companies, see Donald C. Langevoort & Robert B. Thompson, *"Publicness" in Contemporary Securities Regulation After the JOBS Act*, 101 GEO. L.J. 337, 372–73 (2013) (stating that "[t]he orthodox account is that . . . we seek an optimal balance of the costs and benefits of disclosure. . . . But, there are

externalities to disclosure. . . . Issuer-specific information and the integrity of stock prices generate benefits for society. . . . Although the externalities issue is well-known and widely discussed, our claim . . . is that the extent to which—purely as a descriptive matter—securities regulation is about social, political, and economic interests, in addition to investor protection and capital formation, has been seriously underestimated.").

C. THE DEFINITION OF EXCHANGE

An interesting development noted in the Nyquist excerpt is the emergence of new trading markets, described as proprietary trading systems in that piece. These new trading systems represent a significant form of innovation in U.S. trading markets, but also pose definitional challenges for the SEC as the following decision illustrates:

Bd. of Trade v. SEC

923 F.2d 1270 (7th Cir. 1991)

POSNER, CIRCUIT JUDGE.

. . . The question we must answer this time is whether a system for trading options on federal government securities that has been put together by RMJ, a broker; Delta, a clearing agency; and SPNTCO, a bank (the last playing an essentially custodial role unnecessary to discuss further) is an "exchange" within the meaning of section 3(a)(1) of the [1934 Act], 15 U.S.C. § 78c(a)(1), in which event it must register with the [SEC]. . . . The [SEC] held that it was not an exchange. . . . The Board of Trade and the Chicago Mercantile Exchange again petition for review. They are concerned about competition from the Delta system. . . .

An ingenious device for facilitating the purchase and sale of securities, the Delta system works roughly as follows. . . . The system specifies the form of option contract that shall be the security traded. Some of the terms of the contract are fixed, such as the maximum term of the option and the day of the month on which it expires. Others are left open to be negotiated by the parties, such as the premium, the exercise price, and the month of expiration. The traders, who consist not only of securities dealers but also of banks, pension funds, and other institutional investors, communicate their buy or sell offers to RMJ, which enters the offers in the system's computer. Delta, the clearing agency, monitors the computer and when it sees a matching buy and sell offer it notifies the traders that they have a deal (but doesn't tell them with whom) and it takes the necessary steps to effectuate the completed transaction. The interposition of Delta between the traders protects the anonymity of each from the other as well as guaranteeing to each that the other will honor the terms of the option traded.

The fixing of some standardized terms so that one trader is not offering to buy apples and the other offering to sell oranges; the guarantees of anonymity and performance; the pooling of buy and sell offers in a single (electronic) place—these essential features of the Delta system are methods for creating a market that will bring together enough buy and sell offers to enable transacting at prices that will approximate the true market values of the things traded. Does this make the Delta system an exchange, that is, "any organization, association, or group of persons . . . which constitutes, maintains, or provides a market place or facilities for bringing together purchasers and sellers of securities or for otherwise performing with respect to securities the functions commonly performed by a stock exchange as that term is generally understood"? There is no doubt that the Delta system creates an electronic marketplace for securities traders, and the petitioners say that no more is required to establish that the system must register as an exchange. The [SEC's] reply emphasizes the words "generally understood." The Delta system is not—not quite, anyway—what is generally understood by the term "stock exchange." It lacks a trading floor. It lacks specialists, who enhance the liquidity of an exchange by using their own capital to trade against the market when the trading is light, in order to buffer price swings due to the fewness of offers rather than to changes in underlying market values. Not all conventional exchanges have specialists, but those that do not have brokers who trade for their own account as well as for their customers' accounts, and the additional trading enhances the market's liquidity. It is fitting that such brokers are called "market makers." . . . RMJ does not trade for its own account in the Delta system.

The petitioners reply that the words "generally understood" apply only to functions other than the central one of "provid[ing] a market place or facilities for bringing together purchasers and sellers of securities." In other words they want us to put a comma after "sellers of securities." This done, they argue as follows: the statute defines exchange as any entity that provides a facility for bringing together purchasers and sellers of securities, whether or not in providing that facility it is performing an exchange function as the term exchange is generally understood; the Delta system provides a facility for bringing together purchasers and sellers of securities; therefore Delta is an exchange.

Unless the petitioners can be permitted to add their own punctuation to the statute, we do not think that their reading is any more persuasive, even at the literal level, than the [SEC's] reading, which places the provision of a market place or of other facilities for bringing securities traders together among those functions performed by a stock exchange as the term is generally understood, and thus subjects "provid[ing] a market place or facilities" to the qualifying force of "generally understood." Moreover, if the petitioners are to be consistent in advancing a "literal" reading of the statute, they should read "bring together" literally too. But even an admitted exchange does not literally "bring together" purchasers and sellers of securities, except when the floor brokers are trading for their own account. It does not bring them into physical propinquity. And a broker's waiting room, which does bring purchasers and sellers of securities into physical propinquity, is not an exchange. We therefore question whether the petitioners have a coherent approach to the interpretation of the statute.

The consequence of their interpretation must also give us pause. The Delta system cannot register as an exchange, because the statute requires that an exchange be controlled by its participants, who must in turn be registered brokers or individuals associated with such brokers. . . . So all the financial institutions that trade through the Delta system would have to register as brokers, and RMJ, Delta, and the bank would have to turn over the ownership and control of the system to the institutions. The system would be kaput. One must question an interpretation of the definitional provision that would automatically prevent competition for the exchanges from an entity that the exchanges are unable to show poses a threat to the safety of investors by virtue of not being forced to register and assume the prescribed exchange format. As the [SEC] stresses, each of the three firms that constitute the Delta system is comprehensively regulated; no regulatory gaps are created by declining to place the system itself in the exchange pigeonhole; the only thing that such classification would do would be to destroy the system.

What is true is that the Delta system differs only in degree and detail from an exchange. Its trading floor is a computer's memory. Its structure is designed to encourage liquidity, though not to the same extent as the structure of an exchange is. Section 3(a)(1) is broadly worded. No doubt (considering the time when and circumstances in which it was enacted) this was to give the [SEC] maximum control over the securities industry. So the [SEC] could have interpreted the section to embrace the Delta system. But we do not think it was compelled to do so. The statute is not crystal clear; on the contrary, even when read literally, which is to say without regard to context and consequence, it does not support the petitioners' argument without repunctuation of the statute and without overlooking the impossibility of a consistently literal reading. An administrative agency has discretion to interpret a statute that is not crystal clear. *Chevron v. Natural Resources Defense Council*, 467 U.S. 837, 844–45 (1984). The [SEC] can determine better than we generalist judges whether the protection of investor and other interests within the range of the statute is advanced, or retarded, by placing the Delta system in a classification that will destroy a promising competitive innovation in the trading of securities. Of course, if the statute were unambiguous, the [SEC] would have to bow. . . . It has not been given the power of statutory revision. But in this case there is enough play in the statutory joints that its decision must be AFFIRMED.

FLAUM, CIRCUIT JUDGE, DISSENTING.

No doubt there is some ambiguity in the statutory definition of "exchange." The ambiguity lies in the broad formula Congress adopted: "as that term is generally understood." On one point, however, the statute is not ambiguous. An organization that "constitutes, maintains, or provides a market place or facilities for bringing together purchasers and sellers of securities" is an exchange. The statute makes it unnecessary to speculate whether bringing together buyers and sellers is one of the "generally understood" functions of an exchange; it makes that function a determinative characteristic, sufficient unto itself to confer exchange status. . . . Since—as the majority acknowledges—we cannot ignore an unequivocal statutory mandate, I respectfully dissent from the court's decision to defer to an SEC interpretation that does. . . .

Exchanges are required to impose rules on their participants "designed . . . in general to protect investors and the public interest." Securities Exchange Act § 6(b)(5); see also Securities Exchange Act § 6(f) (to maintain fair and orderly markets, [the SEC] may require those trading on an exchange to comply with exchange rules). Exempting the System from exchange registration will create, in effect, another futures market in government securities (hence the opposition of the [Chicago Board of Trade] and the Merc), one subject to even less regulation than the futures exchanges. Exempting the System may, therefore, exacerbate the problems inherent in the uneasy coexistence of primary and derivative markets under different regulatory regimes. . . . The [SEC] has wide discretion to interpret the securities laws. But it is not free to disregard an unambiguous provision, and Congress was crystal clear that an organization "bringing together purchasers and sellers of securities" constitutes an exchange. Until Congress concludes that its definition of exchange is antiquated and superfluous, I am not prepared to disregard it.

---

1. ***Regulatory Perimeters Revisited.*** The *Board of Trade* case is another example of what you should now recognize as a problem involving the regulatory perimeter, in this case with respect to the definition of the term exchange under the 1934 Act. In this context, of course, the failure to find the enterprise to be an exchange does not imply that the activity occurs totally outside the oversight of the SEC. Given the nature of the activities, other statutory provisions are likely to be applicable. Typically, proprietary trading systems are operated by a registered broker-dealer and the SEC has adopted a rather extensive body of law articulating a special set of rules applicable to such activities.

2. ***Regulation of Alternative Trading Systems (ATSs).*** In 1998, the SEC adopted Regulation ATS and accompanying Rule 3b-16 to update the regulation of exchanges that had originally been devised to address trading conducted on the physical exchange floors. *See* Regulation of Exchanges and Alternative Trading Systems, 63 Fed. Reg. 70,844 (Dec. 22, 1998). Rule 3b-16 defines which automated trading systems are exchanges, while Regulation ATS exempts certain ATSs from registration as an exchange. In order to qualify for the

exemption, an ATS (1) must be registered as a broker-dealer or be operated by a registered broker-dealer, (2) cannot exercise self-regulatory powers, (3) cannot use the word exchange or similar terms in its name, and (4) cannot dominate the market. Though not required to register as an exchange, an ATS must register with the SEC by filing Form ATS. A registered ATS is also subject to ongoing notice and reporting obligations. In 2015, the SEC proposed amendments to Regulation ATS. The amendments, driven by concerns that significant trading activity had migrated to off-exchange venues, would require an extensive level of disclosure by an ATS and heightened oversight, including approval, of the design and operations of an ATS by the SEC. If adopted, the amendments will dramatically increase the regulatory burdens associated with operating an ATS facilitating transactions in equity stocks. *See* Regulation of NMS Stock Alternative Trading Systems, 80 Fed. Reg. 80,998 (proposed Dec. 28, 2015).

III. DUTIES OF BROKER-DEALERS IN TRADING MARKETS

As the NMS evolved, and more and more trading venues emerged, a number of disputes arose over the obligations of broker-dealers with respect to customers seeking to effect trades in this new market environment. We now explore two contexts in which the SEC and the courts applied the fiduciary duties we explored in Chapters 4.2 and 4.3 in novel contexts.

A. DUTIES WITH RESPECT TO LIMIT ORDERS

When a broker-dealer buys and sells securities in its capacity as a market-maker while also buying and selling the same securities on behalf of its customers, how should such orders be prioritized? Our first case study concerns the potential for conflicts of interest when a customer places limit orders with a broker-dealer that is also a market maker in the security to be traded.

In re E.F. Hutton & Co.

Exch. Act Release No. 34-25887, 41 S.E.C. Docket 413 (July 6, 1988)

E.F. Hutton & Company Inc., now known as Shearson Lehman Hutton Inc. ("Hutton"), a member of the National Association of Securities Dealers ("NASD"), appeals from NASD disciplinary action. . . .

[On] January 11, 1984, William Manning placed an open limit order with Hutton's Rochester, New York branch office to sell 5,000 shares of Genex Corporation stock in his account at 17⅛.[2] Hutton accepted Manning's order and a ticket was prepared and sent to Hutton's [OTC] trading department.

When Manning gave his order, Hutton was a registered NASDAQ market maker in Genex. The inside Genex quotation on NASDAQ was 17 bid, 17⅛ asked,[3] and Hutton's quotation was 17 bid, 17½ asked. While Hutton was holding Manning's order, it sold 4,755 shares of Genex from its own inventory at prices of 17¼ and 17½, higher than the 17⅛ sought by

---

[2] A limit order for the sale of stock allows the customer to set a specific price at or above which he will sell securities. An open limit order stays in effect until such time as it is executed or cancelled by the customer. . . .

[3] The inside quotation is the highest bid and the lowest asked prices from the dealers entering quotations into the NASDAQ system. . . .

Manning.[4] Subsequently, the price of Genex declined substantially. Although Manning's order did not call for "all-or-none" execution, no part of the order was ever executed.

The NASD concluded that, by accepting Manning's limit order, Hutton had an obligation to give that order priority over its own proprietary position unless it had previously arrived at a different understanding with Manning. Since the NASD found that no such understanding had been reached, it concluded, among other things, that Hutton did not fulfill its fiduciary duty to Manning. The NASD accordingly found that Hutton had violated Article III, Section 1 of the NASD's Rules of Fair Practice.[5]

Hutton contends that it had no obligation to execute Manning's limit order. It points out that, as Manning knew, Hutton was making a market in Genex. It accordingly argues that, because the inside bid never reached the price set by Manning, it had no obligation to buy his stock. It also contends that it had no obligation to step aside and allow Manning's order to take preference in filling incoming buy orders that Hutton received as a market maker.

Both Hutton and the Securities Industry Association ("SIA") further assert that it is contrary to industry practice for OTC market makers to grant priority to customer limit orders over the market makers' proprietary trades. They maintain that, generally, such orders are executed only if a quotation reflecting "contra-side interest" (in this case a bid) reaches the limit order price. They argue that the concept of limit order priority (although applicable to exchanges where customer orders are centrally held, matched and given priority over specialists' proprietary trading) is fundamentally inconsistent with the dispersed nature of the OTC market and would, if adopted, entail serious adverse consequences. Finally, they contend that the obligation imposed on Hutton by the NASD cannot reasonably or fairly be implied from existing law and that, if the NASD wishes to impose such an obligation, it must do so by adopting a rule.

At the outset, it should be emphasized that the NASD's decision does not impose a "limit order priority rule" on the OTC market. Market makers and other broker-dealers do not have to accept limit orders if they choose not to do so. Moreover, if they do accept such orders, they are free to specify the terms governing the orders' execution provided that those terms are fully and clearly disclosed to the customer, and the customer agrees to them, at the time that any such order is placed. The only questions presented by this appeal are: (1) whether under the NASD's rules a broker-dealer that accepts a customer's limit order may trade for its own proprietary account ahead of that order without having informed the customer that this is the practice it intends to follow, and (2) whether a determination that the type of conduct in which Hutton engaged was improper can be reached through adjudication or only through rulemaking.

When Manning entrusted his limit order to Hutton, and Hutton agreed to accept that order and act on Manning's behalf in obtaining execution, Hutton assumed certain fiduciary obligations. Those obligations were not extinguished even though Hutton could have acted in a principal capacity in executing Manning's order. A broker-dealer's determination to execute an order as principal or agent cannot be "a means by which the broker may elect whether or not the law will impose fiduciary standards upon him in the actual circumstances of any given relationship or transaction."

Our aim is to give effect to the reasonable expectations of the parties to the relationship. Where there is no explicit agreement to the contrary and the relationship is a fiduciary one, the law governing fiduciary duties provides presumptive definition for such expectations. We need not consider whether in some circumstances an industry practice might be so universal and overt that investor expectations inconsistent with that practice are

[4] The bid and asked prices quoted by a market maker are the prices at which it is willing to buy stock from or sell it to other dealers. . . .

[5] That provision requires NASD members to "observe high standards of commercial honor and just and equitable principles of trade." . . .

unreasonable, since we are not persuaded that such is the situation here. Thus Manning was entitled to expect that industry practice would comport with fiduciary principles and that conflicts of interest would be disclosed. It is hornbook law that, absent disclosure and a contrary agreement, a fiduciary cannot compete with his beneficiary with respect to the subject matter of their relationship. Thus, far from being a "technical matter" that only involves the manner of executing a limit order, the practice at issue affects the fundamentals of the broker-dealer-customer relationship.

Hutton's willingness to sell Genex stock for its own account at prices equal to or higher than the price of Manning's limit order created a conflict between the interests of Hutton and Manning that affected the task Hutton had undertaken on Manning's behalf. Hutton was, in effect, competing with Manning with respect to the subject matter of their relationship—the execution of Manning's order. As the facts in this case illustrate, this can result in a broker-dealer seizing a customer's only opportunity for execution at his limit order price. Thus, as the NASD concluded, Hutton was required to disclose the priorities that would govern its handling of Manning's order unless it was willing to refrain from competing with him.

If Manning had known that Hutton would execute its own transactions ahead of his, he would have had an opportunity to decide whether to leave his order with Hutton and have it executed on Hutton's terms, attempt to negotiate better terms with Hutton, or look for another broker willing to give his limit order priority in filling incoming buy orders.[14] However, Hutton deprived Manning of that opportunity.

Absent a conflict of interest, the only affirmative obligation Hutton assumed by accepting Manning's limit order was to execute the order when the inside bid reached the limit order price. Here, however, there was such a conflict. And Hutton traded for its own account ahead of Manning without having made any disclosure of that conflict. We think it clear that, by doing so, it violated "high standards of commercial honor and just and equitable principles of trade." We accordingly affirm the NASD's finding of violation. . . .

COMMISSIONER GRUNDFEST, DISSENTING:

. . . I write . . . to emphasize that: (1) a broker-dealer's obligation to a customer depends on the facts and circumstances of the relationship; (2) Mr. Manning was a sophisticated customer; (3) the record indicates that Hutton disclosed its "inside bid" policy to Manning; and (4) the NASD's own general counsel provided evidence that industry practice regarding limit orders is not uniform.

. . . When Hutton agreed to accept Mr. Manning's limit order, Hutton assumed certain fiduciary obligations. To call Hutton a fiduciary, however, "only begins the analysis."[2] Fiduciary duties are not all created equal, and "the nature of fiduciary duty owed will vary, depending on the relationship between the broker and the investor." Accordingly, the nature and extent of Hutton's disclosure obligations with respect to Mr. Manning's limit order "depends on all the circumstances, including the degree of sophistication and the course of conduct between them." In this regard, the obligations owed to an unsophisticated customer will not necessarily be the same as those owed to a customer who is knowledgeable about the securities market and can bargain effectively to protect his own interests.

---

[14] Hutton argues that disclosure to Manning was unnecessary because Manning knew that his limit order would not be filled until the inside bid reached the limit order price. Manning acknowledges that he understood that trades by other firms might occur at prices above his limit price and that, on previous occasions when he complained to Hutton that a limit order had not been executed, Hutton informed him that it was because the inside bid never reached his price. He states, however, that he was never aware until the present situation arose that Hutton would prefer its own proprietary position to his. Hutton's branch manager conceded that neither he nor his salesmen told customers that Hutton would trade for its own account ahead of them. . . ."

[2] *SEC v. Chenery Corp.*, 318 U.S. 80, 85–86 (1943).

Industry practice is also relevant in determining the nature and extent of Hutton's fiduciary obligation to Mr. Manning. In the absence of regulations governing the practice at issue, courts consider whether the conduct deviates from an industry norm. An indication that an industry engages in a widespread practice tends to negate an inference that clients expect to be treated differently. Of course, the fact that a practice is endemic within an industry does not, in and of itself, require that the practice be condoned.

Finally, we must keep in mind the rationale for the creation of fiduciary duties. In this case, where there are sophisticated parties on both sides of the transaction, a "fiduciary duty is a standby or off-the-rack guess about what parties would agree to if they dickered about the subject explicitly." The law imposes fiduciary duties "on a case-by-case basis by fashioning obligations that approximate what the parties would have contracted ex ante had they anticipated the particular events," and requires a "careful analysis . . . to determine what is the particular duty of a fiduciary under specific circumstances." As the majority puts it, the aim is to "give effect to the reasonable expectations of the parties to the relationship." . . .

---

1. ***Aftermath: The Display and Quote Rules.*** The *E.F. Hutton* decision prompted a reexamination of the treatment of limit orders and related issues. After an extensive rulemaking procedure, the SEC adopted a rule requiring market makers to display the price and size of customer limit orders when those orders represent buying and selling interest that is a better price than the market maker's public quote. *See* Order Execution Obligations, 61 Fed. Reg. 48,290 (Sept. 12, 1996) (adopting new Rule 11Ac1-4 and amending Rule 11Ac1-1). Rule 11Ac1-4, known as the Display Rule, requires customer limit orders priced better than a specialists or an over-the-counter market maker's quote to be displayed. Rule 11Ac1-1, known as the Quote Rule, requires a market maker to publish quotations for any listed security when it is responsible for more than 1% of the aggregate trading volume for that security. The Quote Rule also requires the market maker to make publicly available any superior prices quoted privately through certain electronic communication networks.

B. PAYMENT FOR ORDER FLOW AND BEST EXECUTION

Our second case study concerns another controversial practice that combines both fiduciary obligations and issues of market structure: payments-for-order flow. We begin with a brief overview of the practice and potential public policy concerns before turning to a court decision ruling on a related legal challenge.

Note, The Perils of Payment for Order Flow

107 HARV. L. REV. 1675 (1994)

A number of familiar problems in the securities broker-customer context have been adequately addressed by enforcement initiatives and by structural changes that properly align broker incentives. In recent years, however, problems associated with the relatively new practice of "payment for order flow" (POF) have caused critics to call for regulation of that practice. More specifically, critics contend that "hidden kickbacks"—payment for orders—to brokers by market-makers and regional specialists distort broker incentives so that their choices diverge from what would best serve customers. Critics also claim that these distortions do more than disserve individual investors—they damage the market structure itself.

Stock markets in the United States come in two basic types. First are the centralized exchange markets, in which a restricted group of dealers trade listed securities. The exchanges are agency-auction markets. In this type of market, customers trade with one another through commission brokers, who search for other brokers whose clients want to buy or sell at the price that their own clients are seeking. Second is the [OTC] market, in which customers trade directly with broker-dealers, who use a computerized network that allows them to trade in any stock. The OTC market is a dealer market, not an agency-auction market. Unlike the exchanges, "the OTC market [does] not depend on centralizing order flow activity in one physical location." Customers buy and sell from an OTC dealer who maintains his own portfolio in certain stocks.

A "third market" straddles these two basic markets. It consists of approximately fifty OTC market-makers who trade certain stocks listed on the [NYSE] or the American Stock Exchange (AMEX). The existence of this additional market means that a broker can choose to execute a customer order for a stock listed on the NYSE or AMEX either on the primary exchanges or on the third market. The stream of customer orders from a broker either to an exchange or to the third market is referred to as "order flow."

Market-makers profit from orders by capturing the "spread" on each trade—the dealer buys a security at the lower "bid" price, sells a stock at the higher "offer" price, and captures the difference with every trade. Payment for Order Flow (POF) is the practice whereby OTC market-makers and regional specialists pay brokers one to two cents per share for sending them order flow. This practice originated with similar payments made by wholesale firms to their regional correspondents. Because retail brokers—particularly discount brokers—are likely to engage in POF, the practice has its greatest impact on small investors.

POF has become particularly controversial in the past several years as regional specialists and OTC market-makers have extended their order flow payments beyond transactions in OTC stocks to transactions in exchange-listed stocks. According to the most recent SEC estimates, fifteen to twenty percent of order flow in listed stocks is directed pursuant to payment-for-order-flow arrangements—arrangements that divert trades from the exchanges to the OTC market. This development is one of the major causes of the recent decrease in trading on the NYSE—a drop from 79% of the total number of trades of NYSE-listed stocks in 1982 to 65% in 1992. . . .

I. BENEFITS OF THE PRACTICE

Supporters of POF argue that the practice contributes to efficient competition among markets, which ultimately improves capital allocation and maximizes investor returns. On this view, the payors behind POF are market-makers who can execute customer orders more efficiently than other dealers. The benefits of the competition that these payors provide, proponents maintain, will be "indirectly passed through to customers in the form of lower commission rates, more expeditious executions, and enhanced services." POF is thus said to lead to reduced per-trade execution costs. Moreover, payments compensate order-routing firms for efficient aggregation of orders. Loss of business by markets that do not efficiently compete for order flow through improved execution facilities, order-routing mechanisms, and technology is thus a "natural phenomenon of competition and not one to be interfered with lightly by regulation."

II. DANGERS ASSOCIATED WITH PAYMENTS FOR ORDER FLOW

A. Best Execution

Under SEC guidelines, "[b]roker-dealers are under a duty to seek to ensure that their customers obtain the 'best execution' of their orders." Despite the assertions of POF proponents that brokers who take part in payment-for-order-flow arrangements do fulfill their duty of best execution by obtaining for customers the benefit of the quick, price-guaranteed executions that characterize their market, structural incentives and the weight of the evidence both indicate otherwise. Moreover, the problem of skewed incentives is exacerbated because customers are handicapped by information deficiencies.

POF causes brokers to conduct their business in ways that, were they known to the customers, might not meet with the customers' approval. For example, customers may prefer to wait fifteen seconds or even half an hour and have the opportunity to price-improve on the primary exchange rather than execute quickly at the best posted price; but customers are not given the opportunity to choose, because the broker—who benefits from the payment—exercises virtually invisible and therefore unchecked discretion. Moreover, because the mechanics of order-flow-payment arrangements require execution in a predetermined market, the customer loses the benefit of trade-by-trade assessment of execution quality. . . .

For customers, however, the most significant disadvantage of POF is that diversion of order flow from the NYSE floor destroys the opportunity for customers to execute their orders in between the spread or, if the spread is only ⅛, to obtain a price cheaper by one-eighth. A "market order" routed to the NYSE floor is not necessarily executed immediately at the best displayed quote. Instead, the specialist exposes it to the market and allows other investors to interact with the order at a price superior to the posted bid or offer; the specialist cannot trade as long as there are other investors willing to better his price. By contrast, most OTC market-makers who pay for order flow tend to execute orders immediately at the "prevailing displayed best bid or offer." . . .

B. Market Structure

In addition to endangering best execution for customers, POF threatens the structure of the equity-trading market. POF-related fragmentation may erode crucial aspects of a healthy capital market, such as liquidity, price discovery, pricing efficiency, public confidence, competitiveness, and price stability. Proponents of the practice concede that POF may result in some fragmentation, but they argue that this is the natural result of an unregulated market and claim that fragmentation actually improves market structure by multiplying the number of market-makers, thereby increasing liquidity. In addition, proponents contend that the OTC participants contribute to the creation of public goods such as price discovery.

Primary exchanges provide liquidity, which is a necessary element of a healthy capital market. Liquidity is available in a centralized exchange because the probability of linking customers increases with the flow that comes to the floor. Because POF diverts order flow away from the exchanges, it erodes the exchanges' ability to provide liquidity. The fragmentation that POF causes will lead buyers and sellers to arrive at the market at different times, and may result in "transaction induced volatility."

POF also impairs the price-discovery function of the centralized exchanges. In a centralized exchange, accurate price discovery is achievable because posted prices reflect valuation by many traders instead of only a few, and are therefore more likely to reflect the true value of a security. POF-related fragmentation may thus hide from the economy "significant messages concerning the most efficient allocation of resources." Failure to reveal the payments for order flow to the public further contributes to the distortion of pricing by hiding part of the trade price. The resulting inaccurate securities prices may also lead to "fundamental volatility."

Even as POF impairs price discovery by fragmenting the market, it also exacerbates the problem of "free riding" on the price information produced by the NYSE. The NYSE provides a forum for determining the price of a NYSE-listed security. This price is then used by other traders, like OTC market-makers, who do not contribute to the investment made to produce it. If payors for order flow continue to free-ride on the public goods of liquidity and price discovery, not only will they erode these elements of the market, but the exchanges may not generate enough revenue to stay profitable. Impairing the primary exchanges may endanger the supply of these public goods, and potentially endanger the trading markets themselves.

As a result of the diversion of profitable stocks and trades from the NYSE, POF may result in wider spreads. Many payors for order flow cherry-pick safer stocks, leaving NYSE specialists to trade riskier ones. The evidence also suggests that payors for order flow divert small retail orders from the floor—orders that do not threaten a specialist because they are unlikely to be based on information that the specialist does not have. This means that the specialist is left to trade the larger and riskier orders—the very ones that may be based on information that the specialist does not have. The combination of POF diversion of both profitable stocks and small orders ultimately forces a specialist to widen spreads in order to gain enough profits to subsidize his riskier role.

POF may also foster oligopolistic concentration within the broker-dealer market, because brokers will tend to direct their orders to "large dealers to assure for themselves the maximum and most efficient payment of rebates." By the same token, dealers have an incentive to give larger payments to large brokers, thereby securing the maximum order flow at the minimum operational expense. This increased concentration of both market-makers and brokers will ultimately hurt public investors by decreasing competitive pressures on price.

POF may harm the market in other ways as well. Because POF involves secret payments, it may diminish public confidence in the market and lead to decreased investment. Payments for order flow divert trading away from primary exchanges, and so hurt the public investors who are favored by the rigid regulation in these markets. Finally, because payors for order flow receive a guaranteed quantity of orders from brokers, they may have less incentive to attract customers by posting competitive quotes with a narrow spread.

Newton v. Merrill, Lynch, Pierce, Fenner & Smith

135 F.3d 266 (3d Cir. 1998) (en banc)

STAPLETON, CIRCUIT JUDGE.

Plaintiff-Appellants are investors who purchased and sold securities on the NASDAQ market, the major electronic market for "over-the-counter" securities, during the two year period from November 4, 1992 to November 4, 1994 ("the class period"). The defendants are NASDAQ market makers. NASDAQ is a self-regulating market owned by the [NASD], subject to oversight by the [SEC].

An "over-the-counter" market like NASDAQ differs in important respects from the more familiar auction markets, like the New York and American Stock Exchanges. The NYSE and AMEX markets are distinguished by a physical exchange floor where buy and sell orders actually "meet," with prices set by the interaction of those orders under the supervision of a market "specialist." In a dealer market like NASDAQ, the market exists electronically, in the form of a communications system which constantly receives and reports the prices at which geographically dispersed market makers are willing to buy and sell different securities. These market makers compete with one another to buy and sell the same securities using the electronic system; NASDAQ is, then, an electronic inter-dealer quotation system.

In a dealer market, market makers create liquidity by being continuously willing to buy and sell the security in which they are making a market. In this way, an individual who wishes to buy or sell a security does not have to wait until someone is found who wishes to take the opposite side in the desired transaction. To account for the effort and risk required to maintain liquidity, market makers are allowed to set the prices at which they are prepared to buy and sell a particular security; the difference between the listed "ask" and "bid" prices is the "spread" that market makers capture as compensation.

The electronic quotation system ties together the numerous market makers for all over-the-counter securities available on NASDAQ. All NASDAQ market makers are required to input their bid and offer prices to the NASD computer, which collects the information and transmits, for each security, the highest bid price and lowest ask price currently available. These prices are called the "National Best Bid and Offer," or NBBO. The NASD computer, publicly available to all NASDAQ market makers, brokers and dealers, displays and continuously updates the NBBO for each offered security.

Plaintiffs allege that technological advances made it feasible during the class period for the defendant market makers to execute orders at prices quoted on private on-line services like SelectNet and Instinet and that those prices were frequently more favorable to their investor clients than the NBBO price. According to plaintiffs, the defendants regularly used these services and knew that prices better than NBBO were often available through them. Even though they knew that their investor clients expected them to secure the best reasonably available price, plaintiffs say, the defendants executed plaintiffs' orders at the NBBO price when they knew that price was inferior and when they, at the same time, were trading at the more favorable price for their own accounts. In this way, they were able to inflate their profit margins at the expense of their investor clients. This practice is alleged to violate section 10 of the [1934 Act], and Rule 10b-5 promulgated thereunder.

The plaintiffs also charge defendants with two other violations of section 10 and Rule 10b-5. Market makers who simultaneously hold a market order for both sides of a transaction may obtain more favorable prices than the NBBO by "crossing" these in-house orders. Transactions handled in this way are executed within the spread, giving both the purchaser and seller a better price. . . . Plaintiffs allege that the failure of the defendants to execute orders of their clients in these ways when feasible constitutes a fraudulent practice because, by executing at the NBBO rather than matching customer orders, the defendants capture the full market "spread" as a fee for their services without incurring any actual risk in the transaction. . . .

The parties agree that a broker-dealer owes to the client a duty of best execution. They further agree that a broker-dealer, by accepting an order without price instructions, impliedly represents that the order will be executed in a manner consistent with the duty of best execution and that a broker-dealer who accepts such an order while intending to breach that duty makes a misrepresentation that is material to the purchase or sale. The parties differ, however, on whether a trier of fact could conclude from this record that the implied representation made by the defendants included a representation that they would not execute at the NBBO price when prices more favorable to the client were available from sources like SelectNet and Instinet.

As we explain hereafter, this difference can be resolved only by determining whether, during the class period or some portion thereof, it was feasible for the defendants to execute trades through SelectNet and Instinet when prices more favorable than the NBBO were being quoted there. This is a matter concerning which the record reflects a material dispute of fact. If such prices were reasonably available and the defendants, at the time of accepting plaintiffs' orders, intended to execute them solely by reference to the NBBO, they made a material misrepresentation in connection with the purchase or sale of the securities involved. If a finder of fact could infer, in addition, that the defendants' implied representation was knowingly false or made with reckless indifference, it would follow that summary judgment for the defendants was inappropriate.

The duty of best execution, which predates the federal securities laws, has its roots in the common law agency obligations of undivided loyalty and reasonable care that an agent owes to his principal. Since it is understood by all that the client-principal seeks his own economic gain and the purpose of the agency is to help the client-principal achieve that objective, the broker-dealer, absent instructions to the contrary, is expected to use reasonable efforts to maximize the economic benefit to the client in each transaction.

The duty of best execution thus requires that a broker-dealer seek to obtain for its customer orders the most favorable terms reasonably available under the circumstances. *See, e.g.*, *Sinclair v. SEC*, 444 F.2d 399, 400 (2d Cir. 1971) (fiduciary duty requires broker-dealer "to obtain the best available price" for customers' orders); Arleen W. Hughes, 27 S.E.C. 629, 636 (1948) ("A corollary of the fiduciary's duty of loyalty to his principal is his duty to obtain . . . the best price discoverable in the exercise of reasonable diligence."), aff'd sub nom. . . . That is, the duty of best execution requires the defendants to execute the plaintiffs' trades at the best reasonably available price. While ascertaining what prices are reasonably available in any particular situation may require a factual inquiry into all of the surrounding circumstances, the existence of a broker-dealer's duty to execute at the best of those prices that are reasonably available is well-established and is not so vague as to be without ascertainable content in the context of a particular trade or trades. . . .

We believe the evidence is sufficient to allow a reasonable trier of fact to conclude that, by the time of the class period, both technology and over-the-counter markets had developed to a point where it was feasible to maximize the economic benefit to the client by taking advantage of better prices than the NBBO. Summary judgment for defendants on this element of plaintiffs' claim was therefore not appropriate. . . .

---

1. ***International Perspectives on Trading Requirements.*** What is the relationship between fiduciary duties and the elaborate trading requirements of the SEC? As the *Newton* case illustrates, in the United States, fiduciary duties may be imposed on top of the SEC's mandatory rules. In the UK, however, compliance with trading rules offers what is effectively a safe harbor, where compliance with the regulatory rule could be deemed to satisfy fiduciary duties. *See, e.g.*, U.K. LAW COMM'N, FIDUCIARY DUTIES AND REGULATORY RULES (Consultation Paper 236, 1995) (stating that, "in situations where a regulatory rule permits a lower level of disclosure than that required of a fiduciary by common law and equity, the court might be willing to hold that it is an implied term of the contract that the customer is entitled only to the level of disclosure permitted by the relevant rule, provided that it incorporates adequate protection for the customer."). Which approach do you believe is more appropriate?

2. ***Disclosing Execution Practices.*** How can investors police the quality of the execution of their trades? For any individual case, it is difficult to determine whether an investor may have received price improvement in a different market. The SEC adopted two rules to improve public disclosure of order execution and routing practices. Rule 11Ac1-5 requires market centers that trade equity securities to make available to the public monthly reports that include uniform statistical measures of execution quality. Rule 11Ac1-6 requires broker-dealers to make publicly available quarterly reports that identify the venues that they route orders for execution. Additionally, if a customer submits a request, the broker-dealer must disclose the venue to which their orders were routed. *See* Disclosure of Order Execution and Routing Practices, 65 Fed. Reg. 75,414 (Dec. 1, 2000) (adopting Rules 11Ac1-5 and 11Ac1-6); *see also*, Ekkehart Boehmer et al., *Public Disclosure and Private Decisions: Equity Market Execution Quality and Order Routing*, 20 R. FIN. STUD. 315 (2007) (noting that execution costs and execution speed increased after the promulgation of these rules). For its part, FINRA also has various order execution rules which, among other things, forbid

broker-dealers from engaging in order routing practices aimed at maximizing their monetary gain through credits, commissions, and rebates at the expense of their best execution duties. *See, e.g.*, Order Approving Proposed Rule Change to Adopt Rule 5290 (Order Entry and Execution Practices), 74 Fed. Reg. 64,109 (Dec. 7, 2009).

C. DEMUTUALIZATION AND DECIMALIZATION

In the late 1990s and early 2000s, substantial changes in the structure of the securities market, such as demutualization and decimalization, revolutionized the securities sector. In the late 1990s, the major exchanges demutualized to raise capital and support investments in new technology. Shortly thereafter, in April 2001, the trading markets completed the conversion from a fractional to a decimal pricing system, which allowed for bid-ask spreads to narrow and made price fixing more difficult. The following excerpts discuss both developments in turn.

Stavros Gadinis & Howell E. Jackson, Markets as Regulators: A Survey

80 S. CAL. L. REV. 1239 (2007)

Changes in the ownership structure of stock exchanges have compelled regulators around the world to reexamine the allocation of regulatory authority. Traditionally run as mutual membership organizations, stock exchanges had developed rules for their members, listed companies, and trading processes. Most states had established systems of public oversight that took advantage of the benefits of self-regulation while mitigating the inherent conflicts of interest. In the last decade, most stock exchanges "demutualized": they abandoned their traditional nonprofit mutual membership structure in favor of a for-profit corporate format. Some privatized stock exchanges took the additional step of listing their shares on their own markets. These developments gave rise to new puzzles for regulators. Are institutions that are designed to maximize shareholder value well-suited to regulate their own markets? Does demutualization result in new conflicts of interest that call for greater regulatory intervention? In most leading jurisdictions, policymakers introduced reforms in securities markets supervision to respond to these concerns. . . .

Our research suggests that there are three distinct models for the division of regulatory responsibility over securities markets. . . . [C]ountries in the "Government-led Model" (France, Germany, and Japan) provide central governments with direct channels of influence over securities markets regulation. These jurisdictions reacted to stock exchange demutualization by enhancing the efficiency of government supervision: they reshuffled the organization of their administrative agencies and increased their already strong regulatory powers. The "Flexibility Model" countries (the United Kingdom, Hong Kong, and Australia) traditionally relied more heavily on market participants and granted them significant leeway in regulating many aspects of their activity. "For-profit" stock exchanges pose greater challenges for these jurisdictions. In response to demutualization, Flexibility Model countries curtailed the powers of [self-regulatory organizations (SROs)] and enhanced oversight by administrative agencies. Yet, administrative agencies in these jurisdictions maintain a regulatory philosophy of cooperation with market participants, and typically issue guidance rather than mandatory rules. In the "Cooperation Model" countries (the United States and Canada), the regulatory powers of stock exchanges extend over most issues, but are exercised under close supervision by government agencies. Instead of substantially limiting self-regulation, governments in the Cooperation Model developed mechanisms to insulate stock exchange regulatory activity from the operation of the markets. Thus, under government influence, stock exchanges segregated their regulatory functions in a separate, independently-run subsidiary. . . .

SEC, Report to Congress on Decimalization

2012

Regulatory History of Decimalization

Prior to implementing decimal pricing in April 2001, the U.S. equity market used fractions as pricing increments, and had done so for hundreds of years. The [SEC] started examining the prudence of the fraction pricing structure in the mid 1990s. In the SEC Staff's 1994 report on the equities markets, the Staff expressed concern that 1/8th of a dollar tick sizes were "caus[ing] artificially wide spreads and hinder[ing] quote competition," leading to excessive profits for market makers. The report also expressed concern that 1/8th fraction pricing put U.S. equity markets at a competitive disadvantage to foreign equity markets that used decimal pricing increments. The [SEC] used these findings as part of a public discussion on whether the U.S. equities markets should adopt a lower fraction for minimum tick size or whether to adopt decimal pricing.

In light of this public discussion and even prior to the Staff's report on how tick sizes affected the competitiveness of U.S. equity markets, the exchanges and NASDAQ started implementing lower tick sizes. In 1992, the [SEC] approved an American Stock Exchange (AMEX) rule that lowered its tick size for stocks priced between $0.25 and $5 to 1/16th of a dollar. A subsequent rule in 1997 applied this tick size to all AMEX stocks trading at or above $0.25. Also in 1997, the [NYSE] and NASDAQ promulgated rules to use 1/16th as tick sizes. The [SEC], the exchanges and NASDAQ believed that the reductions would [result in] better pricing and greater liquidity. . . .

In January 2000, the [SEC] ordered the exchanges and NASDAQ to develop a phase-in plan for implementing decimal pricing that would include preparation of necessary rule changes. The [SEC] mandated that the exchanges start implementing decimal pricing in September 2000 and finish implementation by April 2001.

The exchanges and NASDAQ started the phase-in on time and finished implementing decimalization by April 2001. In 2004, the [SEC] proposed, and then reproposed, Rule 612 of Regulation NMS to establish a minimum price variation (MPV) of one penny. Several commenters on the original proposal had recommended an MPV of greater than one penny. In response, the [SEC] noted that proposed Rule 612 would "set a floor for the MPV, not determine an optimal MPV." It further stated that the move to a penny MPV had "reduced spreads, thus resulting in reduced trading costs for investors entering orders—particularly for smaller orders—that are executed at or within the quotations," and that therefore the [SEC] had not initially proposed a higher MPV. It added, however, that "if the SROs in the future believe that an increase in the MPV is necessary or desirable, they may propose rule changes to institute the higher MPV" and that the [SEC] would evaluate them at that time. In 2005, the [SEC] adopted Regulation NMS Rule 612. The one penny MPV specified in Rule 612 essentially applies to all listed stocks at all price levels. This is the pricing structure in place today.

---

1. ***Demutualization and Conflicts of Interest.*** Should demutualized securities exchanges be allowed to trade their own shares? What types of conflicts of interest does such trading raise? In *Stock Exchanges at the Crossroads*, Andreas M. Fleckner explores the conflicts of interest that arise when a stock exchange demutualizes and goes public. Fleckner argues that the main concern of a demutualized stock exchange is that the exchange will be too soft on self-

regulation, while harder on competitors. What other conflicts of interest may arise in such a situation? *See* Andreas M. Fleckner, *Stock Exchanges at the Crossroads*, 74 FORDHAM L. REV. 2541 (2006).

2. ***The Continuing Viability of Decimalization.*** Though popular for providing more transparency and simplicity to the trading markets, decimalization has also been criticized. In the JOBS Act, Congress saw fit to provide the SEC with authority to engage in rulemaking that would allow for securities of emerging growth companies to be quoted and traded in increments greater than $0.01 but less than $0.10. In its Report to Congress on Decimalization, the SEC cites to a number of other reports on the issue including one by the initial public offering (IPO) Task Force, a securities sector group. The IPO Task Force report recognized that decimalization had reduced the incentives to underwrite and make markets in emerging growth companies, but concluded that its benefits outweighed the costs. Should the SEC use its authority to increase the tick size for securities of emerging growth companies? *See* IPO TASK FORCE, REBUILDING THE IPO ON-RAMP: PUTTING EMERGING COMPANIES AND THE JOB MARKET BACK ON THE ROAD TO GROWTH (Oct. 20, 2011).

IV. CHALLENGES IN TRADING MARKETS TODAY

We conclude our discussion with an exploration of the challenges facing trading markets today and how regulators are responding. We begin with a reading from the SEC's Concept Release on Equity Market Structure, which provides an overview of the trading markets, followed by an excerpt discussing how securities markets are changing and the impact of high-frequency traders.

Concept Release on Equity Market Structure

Exch. Act Release No. 61358 (Jan. 14, 2010)

In Section 11A of the [1934 Act], Congress directed the Commission to facilitate the establishment of a national market system in accordance with specified findings and objectives. The initial Congressional findings were that the securities markets are an important national asset that must be preserved and strengthened, and that new data processing and communications techniques create the opportunity for more efficient and effective market operations. Congress then proceeded to mandate a national market system composed of multiple competing markets that are linked through technology. In particular, Congress found that it is in the public interest and appropriate for the protection of investors and the maintenance of fair and orderly markets to assure five objectives:

(1) economically efficient execution of securities transactions;

(2) fair competition among brokers and dealers, among exchange markets, and between exchange markets and markets other than exchange markets;

(3) the availability to brokers, dealers, and investors of information with respect to quotations and transactions in securities;

(4) the practicability of brokers executing investors' orders in the best market; and

(5) an opportunity, consistent with efficiency and best execution, for investors' orders to be executed without the participation of a dealer.

The final Congressional finding was that these five objectives would be fostered by the linking of all markets for qualified securities through communication and data processing facilities. Specifically, Congress found that such linkages would foster efficiency; enhance competition; increase the information available to brokers, dealers, and investors; facilitate the offsetting (matching) of investors' orders; and contribute to the best execution of investors' orders.

Over the years, these findings and objectives have guided the [SEC] as it has sought to keep market structure rules up-to-date with continually changing economic conditions and technology advances. This task has presented certain challenges because, as noted previously by the [SEC], the five objectives set forth in Section 11A can, at times, be difficult to reconcile. In particular, the objective of matching investor orders, or "order interaction," can be difficult to reconcile with the objective of promoting competition among markets. Order interaction promotes a system that "maximizes the opportunities for the most willing seller to meet the most willing buyer." When many trading centers compete for order flow in the same stock, however, such competition can lead to the fragmentation of order flow in that stock. Fragmentation can inhibit the interaction of investor orders and thereby impair certain efficiencies and the best execution of investors' orders. Competition among trading centers to provide specialized services for investors also can lead to practices that may detract from public price transparency. On the other hand, mandating the consolidation of order flow in a single venue would create a monopoly and thereby lose the important benefits of competition among markets. The benefits of such competition include incentives for trading centers to create new products, provide high quality trading services that meet the needs of investors, and keep trading fees low.

The [SEC's] task has been to facilitate an appropriately balanced market structure that promotes competition among markets, while minimizing the potentially adverse effects of fragmentation on efficiency, price transparency, best execution of investor orders, and order interaction. An appropriately balanced market structure also must provide for strong investor protection and enable businesses to raise the capital they need to grow and to benefit the overall economy. Given the complexity of this task, there clearly is room for reasonable disagreement as to whether the market structure at any particular time is, in fact, achieving an appropriate balance of these multiple objectives. Accordingly, the [SEC] believes it is important to monitor these issues and, periodically, give the public, including the full range of investors and other market participants, an opportunity to submit their views on the matter. This concept release is intended to provide such an opportunity.

III. Overview of Current Market Structure

This section provides a brief overview of the current equity market structure. It first describes the various types of trading centers that compete for order flow in NMS stocks and among which liquidity is dispersed. It then describes the primary types of linkages between or involving these trading centers that are designed to enable market participants to trade effectively. . . .

A. Trading Centers

A good place to start in describing the current market structure is by identifying the major types of trading centers and . . . their current share of trading volume in NMS stocks.

[Two types of trading centers display their quotations in the consolidated quotation data feed that widely distributed to the public—registered exchanges and electronic communication networks (ECNs). As of September 2009, these displayed trading centers represented approximately 63.8% and 10.8% of share trading volume, respectively. Two other types of trading centers do not display their quotations—dark pools and broker-dealers that execute trades internally. These trading centers represented approximately 7.9% and 17.5% % of share trading volume, respectively, during the same period. All four trading centers are described below.]

1. Registered Exchanges

Registered exchanges collectively execute approximately 63.8% of share volume in NMS stocks, with no single exchange executing more than 19.4%. Registered exchanges must undertake self-regulatory responsibility for their members and file their proposed rule changes for approval with the [SEC]. These proposed rule changes publicly disclose, among other things, the trading services and fees of exchanges.

The registered exchanges all have adopted highly automated trading systems that can offer extremely high-speed, or "low-latency," order responses and executions. Published average response times at some exchanges, for example, have been reduced to less than 1 millisecond. Many exchanges offer individual data feeds that deliver information concerning their orders and trades directly to customers. To further reduce latency in transmitting market data and order messages, many exchanges also offer co-location services that enable exchange customers to place their servers in close proximity to the exchange's matching engine. . . .

Registered exchanges typically offer a wide range of order types for trading on their automated systems. Some of their order types are displayable in full if they are not executed immediately. Others are undisplayed, in full or in part. For example, a reserve order type will display part of the size of an order at a particular price, while holding the balance of the order in reserve and refreshing the displayed size as needed. In general, displayed orders are given execution priority at any given price over fully undisplayed orders and the undisplayed size of reserve orders.

In addition, many exchanges have adopted a "maker-taker" pricing model in an effort to attract liquidity providers. Under this model, non-marketable, resting orders that offer (make) liquidity at a particular price receive a liquidity rebate if they are executed, while incoming orders that execute against (take) the liquidity of resting orders are charged an access fee. Rule 610(c) of Regulation NMS caps the amount of the access fee for executions against the best displayed prices of an exchange at 0.3 cents per share. Exchanges typically charge a somewhat higher access fee than the amount of their liquidity rebates, and retain the difference as compensation. Sometimes, however, exchanges have offered "inverted" pricing and pay a liquidity rebate that exceeds the access fee.

Highly automated exchange systems and liquidity rebates have helped establish a business model for a new type of professional liquidity provider that is distinct from the more traditional exchange specialist and [OTC] market maker. In particular, proprietary trading firms and the proprietary trading desks of multi-service broker-dealers now take advantage of low-latency systems and liquidity rebates by submitting large numbers of non-marketable orders (often cancelling a very high percentage of them), which provide liquidity to the market electronically. . . . [T]hese proprietary traders often are labeled high-frequency traders, though the term does not have a settled definition and may encompass a variety of strategies in addition to passive market making.

2. ECNs

The five ECNs that actively trade NMS stocks collectively execute approximately 10.8% of share volume. Almost all ECN volume is executed by two ECNs operated by Direct Edge, which has submitted applications for registration of its two trading platforms as exchanges. 27 ECNs are regulated as [ATSs]. Regulation of ATSs is discussed in the next section below in connection with dark pools, which also are ATSs. The key characteristic of an ECN is that it provides its best-priced orders for inclusion in the consolidated quotation data, whether voluntarily or as required by Rule 301(b)(3) of Regulation ATS. In general, ECNs offer trading services (such as displayed and undisplayed order types, maker-taker pricing, and data feeds) that are analogous to those of registered exchanges.

3. Dark Pools

Dark pools are ATSs that, in contrast to ECNs, do not provide their best-priced orders for inclusion in the consolidated quotation data. In general, dark pools offer trading services to institutional investors and others that seek to execute large trading interest in a manner that will minimize the movement of prices against the trading interest and thereby reduce trading costs. There are approximately 32 dark pools that actively trade NMS stocks, and they executed approximately 7.9% of share volume in NMS stocks in the third quarter of 2009. ATSs, both dark pools and ECNs, fall within the statutory definition of an exchange, but are exempted if they comply with Regulation ATS. Regulation ATS requires ATSs to be registered as broker-dealers with the Commission, which entails becoming a member of the [FINRA] and fully complying with the broker-dealer regulatory regime. Unlike a registered exchange, an ATS is not required to file proposed rule changes with the Commission or otherwise publicly disclose its trading services and fees. ATSs also do not have any self-regulatory responsibilities, such as market surveillance. . . .

Dark pools can vary quite widely in the services they offer their customers. For example, some dark pools, such as block crossing networks, offer specialized size discovery mechanisms that attempt to bring large buyers and sellers in the same NMS stock together anonymously and to facilitate a trade between them. The average trade size of these block crossing networks can be as high as 50,000 shares. Most dark pools, though they may handle large orders, primarily execute trades with small sizes that are more comparable to the average size of trades in the public markets, which was less than 300 shares in July 2009. These dark pools that primarily match smaller orders (though the matched orders may be "child" orders of much larger "parent" orders) execute more than 90% of dark pool trading volume. The majority of this volume is executed by dark pools that are sponsored by multi-service broker-dealers. These broker-dealers also offer order routing services, trade as principal in the sponsored ATS, or both.

4. Broker-Dealer Internalization

The other type of undisplayed trading center is a non-ATS broker-dealer that internally executes trades, whether as agent or principal. Notably, many broker-dealers may submit orders to exchanges or ECNs, which then are included in the consolidated quotation data. The internalized executions of broker-dealers, however, primarily reflect liquidity that is not included in the consolidated quotation data. Broker-dealer internalization accordingly should be classified as undisplayed liquidity. There are a large number of broker-dealers that execute trades internally in NMS stocks—more than 200 publish execution quality statistics under Rule 605 of Regulation NMS. Broker-dealer internalization accounts for approximately 17.5% of share volume in NMS stocks.

Broker-dealers that internalize executions generally fall into two categories—OTC market makers and block positioners. An OTC market maker is defined in Rule 600(b)(52) of Regulation NMS as "any dealer that holds itself out as being willing to buy and sell to its customers, or others, in the United States, an NMS stock for its own account on a regular or continuous basis otherwise than on a national securities exchange in amounts of less than block size." "Block size" is defined in Rule 600(b)(9) as an order of at least 10,000 shares or for a quantity of stock having a market value of at least $200,000. A block positioner generally means any broker-dealer in the business of executing, as principal or agent, block size trades for its customers. . . . [B]lock positioners often commit their own capital to trade as principal with at least some part of the customer's block order.

Broker-dealers that act as OTC market makers and block positioners conduct their business primarily by directly negotiating with customers or with other broker-dealers representing customer orders. OTC market makers, for example, appear to handle a very large percentage of marketable (immediately executable) order flow of individual investors that is routed by retail brokerage firms. A review of the order routing disclosures required by Rule 606 of Regulation NMS of eight broker-dealers with significant retail customer accounts reveals that nearly 100% of their customer market orders are routed to OTC market makers. The review also indicates that most of these retail brokers either receive payment for order flow in connection with the routing of orders or are affiliated with an OTC market maker that executes the orders. The Rule 606 Reports disclose that the amount of payment for order flow generally is 0.1 cent per share or less. . . .

Jennifer Victoria Cristine Dean, Paradigm Shifts & Unintended Consequences: The Death of the Specialist, the Rise of High Frequency Trading, & the Problem of Duty-Free Liquidity in Equity Markets

8 FLA. INT'L U. L. REV. 217 (2012)

As both trading volume and regulatory control have drifted away from the NYSE (and other exchanges), the reign of the specialist has ended. In its place, a new type of market participant has emerged as victor. This new reigning champion of Wall Street is the high-frequency trader. During the last quarter of the twentieth century, various regulations and congressional actions (generally designed to help create more efficient markets through competition and transparency) came together and gave birth to a new breed of equity trading venue. These new venues (alternately referred to as alternative trading systems, automated trading systems, electronic communications networks, and proprietary trading systems), in turn, gave rise to high-frequency trading. Computers have changed nearly every aspect of our world, and the stock market is certainly no exception. Where once upon a time stocks were traded in a physical marketplace and routed through brokers-human beings with a pulse-with the rise of alternative trading systems (and more specifically high-frequency trading), the trading volume that once flowed through the exchanges has been re-routed to these new order-matching venues. . . .

High-frequency trading is conducted at a blindingly fast pace. Trades are executed in increasingly smaller fractions of a second. Huge volume is transacted, and almost none of it is initiated by human beings—except insofar as a human being is needed to execute a run command for the computer's trading algorithm. The emergence of the high-frequency trader is the direct result of the proliferation of alternative trading systems. These hybrid trading systems are alternative venues for the purchase and sale of stock; they are venues that are by design, not classified as "exchanges" by the SEC. In order to be able to register with the SEC as a "national exchange," a trading venue must meet extremely high standards, including the ability to self-regulate. The standards for participating in the equity marketplace as an alternative trading system do not include this requirement. As alternative-trading systems entered the market and began competing for (and successfully capturing) ever-larger percentages of the trading volume, a serious problem emerged.

For most of trading history, human beings (acting in the role of market-makers) have served as market liquidity providers. This is no longer the case. As blindingly fast technology and computer algorithms have acquired an increasingly large percentage of equity trading volume, the liquidity provision post that specialists once occupied, has been left vacant. If this were where the story ended, it would be yet another sad tale of a class of workers being made obsolete by technology-but this is not where the story ends. The NYSE specialists were not just men doing their jobs; they served a crucial function in the maintenance of a healthy financial marketplace. As the specialists were forced out of the business of market-making; they were resultantly also forced out of their role as the U.S. equity markets' primary trading liquidity providers. Their role as market liquidity providers was not voluntary. Specialists were required to provide market liquidity in accordance with the NYSE Byelaws and SEC Rules and Regulations.

When the SEC was created, the rule regarding market-makers was fairly simple and straightforward; the SEC would not tell market-makers how to make a market. The SEC simply required that exchanges choosing to use specialists disclose that usage to the SEC;

but because ninety-five percent of the volume went through the NYSE, the NYSE specialists were, as a result, the largest single group of market-makers in the industry. The NYSE specialists were, by default, responsible for providing trading liquidity to the equity market as a whole.

With the exchange-based specialists forced out by changes in monetary policy, high-frequency traders ostensibly filled the void and became the new (albeit unofficial) market-makers. High-frequency traders have become the new liquidity providers. The problem with this new paradigm is that the high-frequency traders—who have taken over the incredibly important role of providing liquidity to one of the most important marketplaces in the world—have no obligation to provide market liquidity. NYSE specialists and other exchange based market-makers ensured liquidity because they were subject to both SEC and exchange-imposed obligations. . . . Voluntary market-makers can withdraw their capital from the market whenever they choose to do so, and history has shown that when the market takes a downturn, they often do.

This new category of market participant—the high-frequency trader—claims to provide market liquidity and yet is not bound by the same rules and regulations that the specialists once were. Because there are no SEC rules for how one must "make a market," there is, at present, no way to fill the void that was left by the departure of the affirmatively obligated specialists. This void must be filled. The role of the specialist evolved over more than a hundred years." It evolved to meet the needs of the market, but now, that role has been all but obliterated, and the market needs that the specialists once filled are not being met. Market liquidity is central to a healthy market. It dampens volatility, and it promotes consumer confidence. There are no longer enough active obligated market participants to ensure sufficient market liquidity. Since the early 1990s, as the number of [ATSs] has risen, so has the level of volatility in the stock market. This is not a coincidence. The trading paradigm changed, and equity market regulation has not kept pace.

If the SEC wants to protect long-term investors (both individual and institutional) from the inherent dangers in this new paradigm, then the SEC needs to refine the definition of a market-maker and adopt a system of market-wide affirmative obligations. Taking this sort of action will make de facto markets (like high-frequency traders) into de jure market-makers. This process should begin with a re-evaluation of the extremely outdated definition of a market-maker and the implementation of market-wide affirmative obligations for those market participants who act as market-makers. The new definition should include market participants with daily transactions above a certain intraday position threshold. Furthermore, the SEC needs to impose uniform affirmative obligations on these newly re-defined market-makers regardless of any other potential monikers they may hold. This will, in turn, level the playing field and create uniform standards for both official market-makers and de facto liquidity providers who hold themselves out as market-makers.

---

1. ***The Pros and Cons of High-Frequency Trading.*** As the above excerpt illustrates, one of the most cited benefits of high-frequency trading is added liquidity, which reduces bid-ask spreads, trade execution time, and price volatility. These benefits can also be valuable to the economy at large because investors will require less compensation for liquidity risk, resulting in a lowered cost of raising capital. High-frequency trading, however, could in fact cause points of extreme volatility due to the unexpected interactions of trading algorithms, such as the Flash Crash of May 6, 2010, in which the Dow Jones Industrial Average fell by 36% in less than four minutes then recovered almost completely within one minute. High-frequency traders could also engage in structural or directional trading strategies to the detriment of other investors.

Structural strategies use superior speeds, measured in milliseconds, to take advantage of slower market participants accepting trades at stale prices. Directional strategies include front-running and spoofing. A high-frequency trader can front-run a trader submitting a large buy order by buying the securities ahead of that trader then re-selling them to that trader. High-frequency traders can also spoof other traders by creating the impression of a large-trade interest and taking advantage of the responses of other traders to the faked interest. Are the benefits of high-frequency trading worth the associated risks? Directional strategies like spoofing are examples of market manipulation and have been banned since 1934. More generally, some argue that high frequency trading undermines efficient capital allocation because it severs the relationship between informational and allocative efficiency. *See* Yesha Yadev, *How Algorithmic Trading Undermines Efficiency in Capital Markets*, 68 VAND. L. REV. 1607 (2015). Could these concerns be addressed with new regulation or through interpretation of existing regulation? *See* Charles R. Korsmo, *High Frequency Trading: A Regulatory Strategy*, 48 U. RICH. L. REV. 523 (2014).

2. ***The Philosophy of High Frequency Trading.*** Has the act of trading improperly become an end in itself, operating to separate itself from the goods-and-services producing part of the economy? At the end of World War II, a U.S. stock was held, on average, for four years. In 2008, that average time had fallen to 2 months. By 2011–22 seconds. Tor Brunzell, *High-Frequency Trading—To Regulate or Not to Regulate—That is the Question*, 2 J. BUS. & FIN. AFFAIRS 1 (2013). Is this what we want our markets to be like? Also of concern are the vast amounts of resources that high-frequency trading firms spend upgrading their trading systems every year. *See* Eric Budish, Peter Cramton & John Shim, *The High-Frequency Arms Race: Frequent Batch Auctions as a Market Design Response*, 130 QUART. J. ECON. 1547 (2015). Is this an efficient use of resources?

3. ***Regulating High Frequency Trading.*** Different regulatory solutions have been proposed to address problems posed by high-frequency trading. The SEC is developing recommendations for a new anti-disruptive trading rule and is considering whether high-frequency traders should be subject to SEC regulation as dealers. Would these proposals address the concerns posed by high-frequency trading? *See* Mary Jo White, Chair, Sec. & Exch. Comm'n, Enhancing Our Equity Market Structure (Jun. 5, 2014). A different approach would be the imposition of a financial transaction tax, comprising a miniscule fee per transaction such that trading strategies relying on large volumes of trades would be discouraged. *See, e.g.*, Council Directive COM(2011)594 (proposed Sept. 28, 2011). Could such a tax have unintended consequences? Could trading be slowed by imposing batch auctions every few seconds as done in Europe? Still another approach would focus on the high frequency traders themselves, subjecting them to various registration and disclosure requirements. *See* Exemption for Certain Exchange Members, 80 Fed. Reg. 18,306 (Apr. 2, 2015) (proposing an amendment to Rule 15b9-1 that would require many HFT firms to register with FINRA). Alternatively, consider the impact of rolling back some of the reforms of the past two decades, such as a move back to a fractional pricing system or consolidating trading into a single exchange like the NYSE. What are the costs and benefits of these different approaches? For a critical analysis of proposed reforms, *see* Merritt B. Fox, Lawrence R. Glosten, &

Gabriel V. Rauterberg, *The New Stock Market: Sense and Nonsense*, 65 DUKE L.J. 191 (2015).

4. ***Private Market Solutions.*** Another solution would be to rely instead on private market actors. Exchanges often sell co-location services under which traders can pay to set up stations closer to the exchange, reducing their latency for the purposes of high-frequency trading. High-frequency traders also tend to take advantage of rebates offered by exchanges for traders who submit a large volume of trades to the exchange. In his highly publicized book on high-frequency trading, FLASH BOYS: A WALL STREET REVOLT, author Michael Lewis criticized these kinds of practices and brought them to public attention. In 2015, IEX, the ATS that is the subject of the book, filed to register as an exchange with the SEC. In particular, IEX does not offer any rebates and also imposes a lag of 350 milliseconds on all participants by using a 38-mile coil of fiber optic cable. Does IEX represent a market solution to the problems posed by high-frequency trading? Is such a solution sufficient, or do regulators still have a role to play in curbing high-frequency trading? *See, e.g.*, Matt Levine, *The 'Flash Boys' Exchange is Still Controversial*, BLOOMBERG VIEW, Dec. 22, 2015.

5. ***Transfer Agents.*** A related, but often overlooked, area of modern securities markets is the transfer agency sector. Transfer agents act as agents for securities issuers and play an important role in the clearance and settlement of almost all U.S. securities transactions. They track, and maintain records of ownership in securities, facilitate communications between issuers and shareholders, and distribute dividends, principal, and interest payments to shareholders. Transfer agents may also play a gatekeeper function, at least in the sense that they can detect and prevent frauds, particularly with respect to unregistered securities. The rules governing transfer agents, however, have largely remained unchanged since they were first released. In December 2015, the SEC, believing these rules were out-of-sync with current industry practices, issued an advanced notice of proposed rulemaking for new requirements for transfer agents along with a concept release requesting comment on the SEC's broader review of transfer agent regulation. *See* Transfer Agent Regulations, 80 Fed. Reg. 81,948 (Dec. 31, 2015). Among other things, the SEC proposed specific rules that would require transfer agents to register with the SEC, enhance their obligations with respect to the safeguarding of customer assets, revise their recordkeeping requirements, and apply an anti-fraud provision to certain of their activities. The concept release also indicates that the SEC is considering new rules governing, among other things, transfer agents' processing of securities transactions and their involvement in crowdfunding offerings.

PART V

CONSUMER PROTECTION AND THE CFPB

CHAPTER 5.1

THE CONSUMER FINANCIAL PROTECTION BUREAU

CONTENTS

I. INTRODUCTION

Consumers and households need the financial sector to conduct their daily lives. Receiving income, storing it in a safe place, and paying bills are a critical part of everyday life. Consumers often use debit or credit cards to purchase goods or services, and access to credit permits them to buy a car or a home. Many students and their families rely on credit, particularly when it comes to post-high school technical training, college, or graduate and professional school. Recent history has shown that consumers often do not fully understand the financial products they use, and sometimes these financial products can end up harming households instead of helping them. Problems in consumer markets can lead to higher costs, diminished capacity to weather income and expense shocks, decreases in household wealth, lowered credit scores, and even bankruptcy and foreclosure. Widespread financial harms from abusive practices can contribute to financial crises and stall economic growth, as seen in the aftermath of the Financial Crisis.

As Professor Michael Barr argued before Congress, the regulation of consumer financial products before the Financial Crisis was seriously flawed:

> The present system of consumer protection regulation is not designed to be independent or accountable, effective or balanced. It is designed to fail. It is simply incapable of earning and keeping the trust of responsible consumers and providers. . . .
>
> The system fragments jurisdiction and authority for consumer protection among many Federal regulators, most of which have higher priorities than protecting consumers. Nonbanks avoid Federal supervision and banks can choose the least restrictive supervisor among several different banking agencies. Fragmentation of rulewriting, supervision, and enforcement among several agencies lead to finger-pointing in place of action and make actions taken less effective.
>
> The structure is a welcome mat for bad actors and irresponsible practices. Responsible providers are forced to choose between keeping market share and treating consumers fairly. The least common denominator sets the standard, standards inevitably erode, and consumers pay the price.

Creating a Consumer Financial Protection Agency: A Cornerstone of America's New Economic Foundation: Hearing Before the S. Comm. on Banking, Hous., & Urban Affairs, 111th Cong. (2009) (statement of Michael S. Barr, Assistant Sec'y for Fin. Institutions, Dep't of the Treasury).

To address weaknesses in consumer financial regulation, the Dodd-Frank Act created the CFPB. This new agency has a focused consumer protection mission; comprehensive jurisdiction over nearly all consumer financial services providers, both banks and non-banks; and the full range of regulatory, supervision, and enforcement authorities, with some exclusions. The CFPB is mandated to ensure high and consistent standards and a level playing field across nearly the whole marketplace without regard to the form of a product or the type of its provider. The CFPB, however, remains controversial.

This Chapter focuses on the mandate of the CFPB and identifies regulatory approaches employed historically and currently to govern the interaction between consumers and financial intermediaries. We first explore the variety of state and federal regulatory approaches to consumer protection before the creation of the CFPB, and we compare the neoclassical view of consumer protection that informed many of these regulatory approaches with the behavioral view of consumer protection. We then look at proposals for a consumer protection agency to address the need for greater consumer protection. We next examine the structure of the CFPB and its rulemaking, supervision, and enforcement authorities, and discuss exclusions from the CFPB's regulatory authority. We explore the balance of consumer protection regulation between the CFPB and the states after the Dodd-Frank Act, as well as ongoing policy debates surrounding the CFPB. Finally, we conclude with a comparison of consumer and investor protection in the United States and in the EU.

II. HISTORY OF CONSUMER FINANCIAL PROTECTION

Historically, states took a primary role in enacting and enforcing consumer protection laws as part of their general police power. Before the New Deal, state tort and contract laws were the key tools to protect against fraud, misrepresentation, and other forms of unfair dealing. States enacted usury laws that set caps on the interest rate that could be charged on loans. Beginning in the 1960s, the federal government assumed an increasingly important role in consumer financial protection. Over the decades, Congress and federal regulators gradually preempted state usury and consumer protection laws applicable to banks, while non-depository providers remained subject to myriad state laws. Federal consumer protection law generally adopted an approach more rooted in disclosure than in usury or other substantive protections, with a few notable exceptions.

A. STATE USURY LAWS

The United States has a state-specific system of usury laws, dating back to the colonial era. These laws prohibit lenders from charging more than a specified amount of interest. Lenders that exceed the usury rate cannot enforce the debt in court because the loan is deemed illegal. Caps on interest rates vary widely by state, with some states permitting relatively high usury rates, while others do not set any caps at all. States often have different usury caps for different types of loans. Usury laws have been justified on religious grounds, as a means of protecting creditors from exposure to high-risk loans, and as a method to counteract consumer behavioral biases that might induce over-borrowing, among other factors. *See* Paul G. Hayeck, *An Economic Analysis of the Justifications for Usury Laws*, 15 ANN. REV. BANKING L. 253, 255–58 (1996); *see also* Eric A. Posner, *Contract Law in the Welfare State: A Defense of the Unconscionability Doctrine, Usury Laws, and Related Limitations on the Freedom to Contract*, 24 J. LEGAL STUD. 283, 301–04 (1995).

While the federal government has traditionally disfavored usury laws, Congress adopted a federal interest rate cap for military personnel and their dependents in 2006. The Military Lending Act, 10 U.S.C. § 987, establishes a 36% interest rate cap and other restrictions for products such as credit cards, installment loans, student loans, and payday loans. Among its substantive provisions, the Military Lending Act also restricts lenders from linking the issuance of a loan to an allotment for repayment from the service person's paycheck.

Critics of usury laws argue that there are tradeoffs when states impose firm caps on interest rates. *See, e.g.*, Todd J. Zywicki, *The Economics of Credit Cards*, 3 CHAP. L. REV. 79, 146–66 (2000). Consumers might be protected from high rates but might also find that less credit is actually available to them. Small loan lenders might find lending at the permitted rate to be unprofitable, particularly given the risk profile of lower income borrowers. Usury laws, according to some, might actually harm consumers, since credit might become overly restricted.

As you learned in Chapter 1.4, the Supreme Court's decision in *Marquette National Bank v. First Omaha Service Corp.*, 439 U.S. 299 (1978), established the

Exportation Doctrine, allowing national banks to export interest rates from one state to another. Congress applied the same exportation principles to state-chartered banks in § 521 of the Depository Institutions Deregulation and Monetary Control Act of 1980 (DIDMCA). In the 1980s, many banks flocked to states such as South Dakota, which established lenient usury laws. The Riegle-Neal Act's liberalized interstate branching provisions made it even easier for banks to locate in states that permitted high interest rates. Recall further, from Chapter 2.1, that many online lenders have adopted the rent-a-charter model, which allows them to enter into a partnership with a chartered bank and thereby take advantage of the Exportation Doctrine. Consider the continued practical significance of state usury laws in light of these developments and the development of a nationwide banking system.

B. FEDERAL CONSUMER PROTECTION LAWS

A traditional theme of much of federal consumer financial regulation is disclosure. To promote the informed use of consumer credit, Congress enacted the Truth in Lending Act (TILA), 15 U.S.C. §§ 1601–1667f, in 1968. TILA envisions a system of uniform credit cost disclosure so that consumers are presented with comparable information about the loan. To this end, TILA requires the standardized disclosure of key terms and costs of a loan to consumers so that the costs of borrowing are fully disclosed before the consumer enters into the loan. TILA also requires that consumer lenders calculate interest in the same way, using the annual percentage rate, and disclose the total of all loan payments.

Disclosure-based regulations aim to provide comprehensive information about financial products so that consumers can make better decisions on borrowing. In theory, when armed with better information about loans, consumers can compare loans across institutions. Disclosure-based regulations also encourage price competition among lenders. To some extent, TILA and other disclosure-based regulations have resulted in getting better information to borrowers. Disclosure policy, however, often assumes rational consumer behavior in borrowing practices. Consumers are often unable to perfectly compare loans and are fallible in ways that the lender may exploit, even with disclosure.

Beyond disclosures to consumers, federal law imposes obligations on banks and thrifts engaging in retail lending. The Community Reinvestment Act (CRA), 12 U.S.C. §§ 2901–2908, enacted in 1977, requires insured depository institutions (IDIs) such as banks and thrifts to meet the credit needs of their communities, including low- and moderate-income communities. The CRA requires an IDI to report the boundaries of its community, list the types of credit it is prepared to extend, and describe the credit needs of the community and its efforts to meet those needs. Routine examinations assess the institution's success in meeting the community's credit needs. Regulators then use this assessment to evaluate any application from the IDI for a deposit facility. Some scholars have argued that CRA encourages IDIs to make bad loans. *See, e.g.*, Charles W. Calomiris et al., *Housing-Finance Intervention and Private Incentives: Helping Minorities and the Poor*, 26 J. MONEY, CREDIT & BANKING 634, 654 (1994). Others contend that the loans made under CRA expand access without undermining safety. *See, e.g.*,

Michael S. Barr, *Credit Where It Counts: The Community Reinvestment Act and Its Critics*, 80 N.Y.U. L. REV. 513 (2005).

Other laws aim to protect against discriminatory practices against consumers in the credit market. The Fair Housing Act, 42 U.S.C. §§ 3601–3619, enacted in 1968, prohibits discrimination in all aspects of "residential real-estate related transactions" because of race, color, religion, sex, national origin, familial status, or disability. The Equal Credit Opportunity Act (ECOA), 15 U.S.C. §§ 1691–1691f, enacted in 1974, prohibits discrimination in any extension of credit on the basis of race, color, religion, national origin, sex, marital status, age, because an individual receives income from a public assistance program, or because an applicant has in good faith exercised any right under the Consumer Credit Protection Act. To comply with fair lending laws, IDIs are subject to routine examination to ensure adequate training, supervision, and internal compliance measures, including monitoring and self-testing.

Mortgage lending is subject to further public disclosure requirements. The Real Estate Settlement Procedures Act (RESPA), 12 U.S.C. §§ 2601–17, enacted in 1974, requires IDIs, non-depository mortgage lenders, and mortgage brokers to disclose information to consumers of real estate settlement services. For example, RESPA requires disclosures that delineate the costs associated with the settlement, outline lender servicing and escrow account practices, and describe business relationships between settlement service providers. RESPA also bars certain kick-backs. The Home Mortgage Disclosure Act of 1975 (HMDA), 12 U.S.C. §§ 2801–2810, requires IDIs and non-depository mortgage lenders to disclose information to the public about loan applications, rejections, and approvals. HMDA data can be used to identify housing discrimination. For example, if a bank has a disproportionately low percentage of approvals from certain areas, the bank may be engaging in redlining, although other factors, such as low demand from qualified applicants, may also be in play. HMDA data could also alert regulators to price-based discrimination, where certain classes of consumers are provided higher-interest loans, if such data is combined with information on the credit-worthiness of borrowers.

III. COMPARING THE NEOCLASSICAL AND BEHAVIORAL VIEWS OF CONSUMER PROTECTION

Lawmakers' approaches to consumer and investor protection are guided by their philosophical, political, and economic beliefs, as well as the influence of stakeholder battles at the time the policy choice is made. One factor that influences policy choices is the policy-maker's theoretical framework of consumer behavior. Two schools of economic thought, neoclassical and behavioral economics, often have different implications for how consumer and investor protection regulations should be structured. This Section explores that debate.

A. THE NEOCLASSICAL VIEW OF CONSUMER PROTECTION

The neoclassical view informed many of the federal regulatory approaches described in the previous Section. The term "neoclassical economics" describes the school of thought that dominated law and economics, essentially unchallenged, in the 1970s and 1980s. *See* Richard A. Epstein, *The Neoclassical*

Economics of Consumer Contracts, 92 MINN. L. REV. 803 (2008). According to neoclassical economics, competitive markets will generate a mix of financial products and services that is superior to those that can be generated by government intervention. Under this view, government regulation, including in the consumer and investor protection context, is justified only in non-competitive, monopolized markets, or in markets characterized by information asymmetries.

In a non-competitive market, consumers and investors are disadvantaged because monopolistic institutions can use that power to take advantage of consumers and investors. In such cases, neoclassical economics prescribes regulation in two main forms. First, as in the case of antitrust law, regulators can seek to prevent the creation or to require the divestment of monopoly power. Under this framework, by preventing or destroying monopoly power, competitive equilibrium is restored to the market and consumers and investors are, once again, able to make utility maximizing choices. Alternatively, direct product regulation can be used to protect investors and consumers by requiring terms and prices for financial products and services that would be present in a competitive market. Although the market remains non-competitive under the product regulation framework, the monopolistic institution is prevented from exerting that power to the detriment of consumers and investors.

In a market with information asymmetries, consumers and investors are disadvantaged relative to financial institutions because they do not have the perfect information with which to make utility maximizing decisions. According to neoclassical economics, the regulatory remedy to this problem is mandatory disclosure of the terms of the financial product or service. This disclosure then restores informational symmetry to the market, allowing consumers and investors to make utility maximizing decisions and eliminating the ability of financial institutions to take advantage of the consumers and investors.

B. THE BEHAVIORAL VIEW OF CONSUMER PROTECTION

The behavioral view of consumer protection began to gain support in the early 2000s. Behavioral economics, grounded in both economics and psychology, studies actual human decision-making and behavior. Repeated studies have shown that human beings deviate from the neoclassical rational actor model in important ways. Behavioral economics views these human failings as resulting not only from non-competitive markets and information asymmetries, but also from the fact that consumers and investors have imperfect rationality and do not always make utility maximizing decisions. As a result, even if mandatory disclosure restores informational symmetry to a market, consumers and investors may still fail to make utility maximizing decisions. Some scholars have argued that the large social welfare costs from markets taking advantage of these human failings can justify regulatory intervention in certain circumstances. *See, e.g.*, Oren Bar-Gill, *The Behavioral Economics of Consumer Contracts*, 92 MINN. L. REV. 749 (2008).

In the following excerpt, Professors John Campbell, Howell Jackson, Brigitte Madrian, and Peter Tufano present their views on some of the reasons why consumers fail to make utility maximizing decisions in selecting financial products and services.

John Y. Campbell et al., Consumer Financial Protection

25 J. ECON. PERSPS. 91, 91–92 (2011)

Over the past 65 years, financial innovation has presented U.S. households with an ever widening set of financial options from an expanding set of firms and accompanied by a sometimes dizzying amount of information. At the same time, consumer finance has increasingly become a "do-it-yourself" activity. Households are expected to make decisions about pension plan contributions and payouts, to choose from a wide array of credit instruments to fund everything from home purchase to short-term cash needs, and more generally to assume a greater level of responsibility for their financial well-being.

This greater consumer autonomy with respect to more, and more important, financial decisions poses special public policy concerns in light of the mounting evidence that consumers do not always behave as time-consistent, rational utility maximizers. For example, many consumers appear to have present-biased preferences, which lead them to favor present consumption, although they would display greater patience if they could commit to a plan of savings and future consumption. Some consumers may lack the cognitive capacity to optimize their financial situation even if presented with all the information that in principle is required to do so.

Such biases and cognitive limitations may be particularly important in the financial context because learning from experience in major financial decisions is difficult. Many financial decisions like choosing a mortgage or investing in a retirement account are undertaken only infrequently. Moreover, the outcomes of these decisions are delayed, perhaps for decades, and are subject to large random shocks, so that personal experience is slow to accumulate and is contaminated by noise. It can also be difficult to learn about financial decisions from the experiences of others. Financial shocks are often correlated across individuals, so that averaging the experience of neighbors or acquaintances may not eliminate noise. The rapid pace of financial innovation reduces the relevance of older cohorts' experiences. Social taboos on discussing personal finances further reduce the effectiveness of social learning.

In the following excerpt, published at the height of the Financial Crisis, Professors Michael Barr, Sendhil Mullainathan, and Eldar Shafir argue that taking into account advances in behavioral research when formulating financial regulations can improve the consequences for household well-being.

Michael S. Barr et al., Behaviorally Informed Financial Services Regulation

NEW AM. FOUND., 17–18 (2008)

[B]ehaviorally informed regulation would take account of the importance of framing and defaults, of the gap between information and understanding, and between intention and action, as well as of other psychological factors affecting how people behave. At the same time, we argue, behaviorally informed regulation should take into account not only behavioral insights about individuals, but also economic insights about markets. Markets can be shown to systematically favor overcoming behavioral biases in some contexts, and to systematically favor exploiting those biases in other contexts. A central illustration of this distinction is the contrast between the market for saving and the market for borrowing—in which the same human failing in understanding and acting upon the concept of compound interest leads to opposite market reactions.

Rather than relying on the classic model of rational agents and maximizing firms, . . . we understand outcomes as an equilibrium interaction between individuals with specific psychologies and firms that respond to those psychologies within specific markets. As we have seen rather dramatically in the case of subprime mortgages, for example, market outcomes may not be socially optimal. To the extent that the interaction produces real harms, regulation could potentially be usefully addressed to the social welfare failures, if any, in this equilibrium. Taking both individuals and industrial organization seriously suggests the need for policy makers to consider a range of market-context specific policy options, including both changing the "rules" of the game, as well as changing its "scoring.". .

It is noteworthy that our current framework largely retains the classical perspective of consumers interacting in competitive markets. The difference is that consumers are now shown to be fallible in systematic and important ways, and firms are now understood to have incentives either to overcome such fallibility, or to exacerbate it, in different specific market contexts. Recognition of the serious social failures that can result from the interaction between individual psychology and industrial organization ought to lead to a range of behaviorally informed regulation of the types that we have described here, in order to restore fair and healthy competition.

---

1. ***Comparing the Neoclassical and Behavioral Views.*** Do you find the behavioral view of consumer protection more persuasive than the neoclassical view? If the application of neoclassical economics to consumer and investor protection is incorrect, why do you think that the regulatory models based upon it persisted, largely unchallenged, for so long?

2. ***Critics of the Behavioral View.*** Some critics argue that the preference of behavioral law and economics for neoclassical regulatory approaches that preserve "freedom of choice" has led to incomplete policy analysis and ineffective or counterproductive policy recommendations. For example, behavioral economics may wrongly exclude "traditional regulatory tools . . . from its analysis of policy options." Ryan Bubb & Richard H. Pildes, *How Behavioral Economics Trims Its Sails and Why*, 127 HARV. L. REV. 1593, 1597 (2014). Others examine the role of behavioral law and economics in the creation of the CFPB and its regulations, arguing that the regulations are often inconsistent with the purpose of improving consumer choices. These critics argue "that the selective modeling of behavioral bias in the [behavioral law and economics] framework causes an overestimation of the ability of regulators, who in actuality use inefficient, heavy-handed rules based upon little if any real empirical findings of 'consumer irrationality.'" Adam C. Smith & Todd Zywicki, *Behavior, Paternalism, and Policy: Evaluating Consumer Financial Protection*, 9 N.Y.U. J. L. & LIBR. 201, 205 (2015).

IV. EARLY CALLS FOR A CONSUMER PROTECTION AGENCY

The rise of behavioral economics coincided with calls for stronger consumer protections. Before the creation of the CFPB, responsibility for consumer financial protection was divided among a number of federal regulatory agencies, each with different jurisdictions and missions. For example, the OCC regulated national banks; the Federal Housing Finance Agency regulated the Federal Home Loan Banks, Fannie Mae, and Freddie Mac; the U.S. Department of Housing and Urban Development regulated real estate settlement procedures and Federal Housing Administration-insured mortgage loans; the Federal Trade Commission (FTC) regulated non-banks but had no supervisory authority; the

Federal Reserve Board had authority to prescribe rules under TILA and certain other consumer protection statutes; and the DOJ governed anti-fraud authority and fair lending enforcement; among others. Professor Adam Levitin characterized the federal regulatory landscape before the Dodd-Frank Act as a "poorly coordinated . . . mélange [that] co-existed uneasily with state regulation and enforcement by state attorneys general and state bank regulators, as well as private litigation." Levitin also noted that states "were increasingly excluded from consumer financial services regulation because of federal preemption, with the preempted state protections rarely replaced with equivalent federal protections." *The Consumer Financial Protection Bureau: An Introduction*, 32 REV. BANKING & FIN. L. 321, 328 (2013). Furthermore, federal regulators responsible for monitoring lenders did not prioritize consumer protection. For example, between 2000 and 2006, the OCC brought 495 enforcement actions against national banks, yet only 13 were consumer-related and only one addressed subprime mortgage lending.

In 2007, then-Professor Elizabeth Warren brought these issues to the forefront and sparked a nationwide debate on the regulation of financial products. In the following excerpt, Warren argues that a new agency, the Financial Product Safety Commission, should be created to address the greater need for consumer protection.

Elizabeth Warren, Unsafe at Any Rate

Democracy, Summer 2007, at 8, 8–10, 16–19

It is impossible to buy a toaster that has a one-in-five chance of bursting into flames and burning down your house. But it is possible to refinance an existing home with a mortgage that has the same one-in-five chance of putting the family out on the street—and the mortgage won't even carry a disclosure of that fact to the homeowner. . . . Why are consumers safe when they purchase tangible consumer products with cash, but when they sign up for routine financial products like mortgages and credit cards they are left at the mercy of their creditors?

The difference between the two markets is regulation. . . . Nearly every product sold in America has passed basic safety regulations. . . . Credit products, by comparison, are regulated by a tattered patchwork of federal and state laws that have failed to adapt to changing markets. . . .

[I]t is time for a new model of financial regulation . . . focused primarily on consumer safety. . . . [W]hy not create a Financial Product Safety Commission (FPSC)? . . . [T]his agency would be charged with responsibility to establish guidelines for consumer disclosure, . . . review new financial products for safety, and require modification of dangerous products before they can be marketed to the public. . . . [T]he FPSC would evaluate these products to eliminate the hidden tricks and traps that make some of them far more dangerous than others.

Warren expanded on her proposal for a new consumer financial regulator in the following article, which she co-authored with Professor Oren Bar-Gill.

Oren Bar-Gill & Elizabeth Warren, Making Credit Safer

157 U. PA. L. REV. 1, 98–100 (2008)

We propose the creation of a single federal regulator—a new Financial Product Safety Commission or a new consumer credit division within an existing agency (most likely the [Federal Reserve Board] or FTC)—that will be put in charge of consumer credit products. Our proposed regulatory framework has three critical elements: (1) *ex ante* regulation, rather than *ex post* judicial scrutiny; (2) regulation by an administrative agency with a broad mandate, rather than by specifically targeted piecemeal legislation; and (3) entrusting the authority over consumer credit products to a single, highly motivated federal regulator, such that the same regulation applies to all similar products, regardless of the identity of the lender.

First, the proposed solution adopts an *ex ante* approach. The regulation of consumer credit markets is not amenable to *ex post* judicial review. While extreme practices may be policed using the unconscionability doctrine or other common law doctrines, these tools are too blunt to provide a comprehensive regulatory response to unsafe consumer credit products. The proposed regulator will develop expertise that will enable it to promulgate nuanced regulations that account for product innovation.

Second, we propose that the *ex ante* regulations be promulgated and enforced by an administrative agency with broad rulemaking and enforcement authority over consumer credit products. Legislation targeted to specific practices, with narrowly defined authority delegated to administrative agencies, is incapable of effectively responding to the high rate of innovation in consumer credit markets and the subtle ways in which creditors can exploit consumer misunderstanding. An administrative agency with a broad mandate could develop more institutional expertise and quicker responses to new products and practices.

Third, we propose to regulate consumer financial products, much in the same way that manufactured products—meat, agricultural products, drugs, cosmetics, and a host of other physical products—are regulated: regulation follows the product, not the manufacturer. Regardless of who issues the product, a single federal regulator will oversee the design and dissemination of the product. This approach will eliminate regulatory gaps and contradictions, and it will halt the state and federal regulatory competition that undercuts consumer safety. In this respect our proposal has much in common with the Conduct of Business Regulatory Agency (CBRA) envisioned in Secretary [Henry] Paulson's "Blueprint for a Modernized Financial Regulatory Structure." Paulson proposes the establishment of a single federal regulator that will "be responsible for business conduct regulation across all types of financial firms."

We recognize that concentrated, broad authority in itself will not guarantee adequate protection for consumers. To be effective, authority must be coupled with motivation to exercise that authority. An agency that views its core mission as ensuring the safety and soundness of banks might not dedicate sufficient resources to consumer protection even if it has complete authority to regulate the safety of consumer credit products. In implementing our proposal, a central challenge will be the design of enabling legislation that provides this crucial combination of authority and motivation.

As the excesses of the pre-Financial Crisis credit market became clear to the public, dissatisfaction with the existing regulatory regime increased. As discussed earlier in this Chapter, Barr, Mullainathan, and Shafir argued for a system of financial regulation that takes into account the realities of consumer behavior in the credit market. *See also* Michael S. Barr et al., *The Case for*

Behaviorally Informed Regulation, in NEW PERSPECTIVES ON REGULATION 25 (David A. Moss & John A. Cisternino eds., 2009).

In June 2009, the Department of the Treasury proposed a new agency exclusively tasked with the responsibility of protecting consumers.

Dep't of the Treasury, Protect Consumers and Investors from Financial Abuse

Fin. Regulatory Reform:
A New Foundation: Rebuilding Financial Supervision and Regulation 55–57 (2009)

Prior to the current financial crisis, a number of federal and state regulations were in place to protect consumers against fraud and to promote understanding of financial products like credit cards and mortgages. But as abusive practices spread, particularly in the market for subprime and nontraditional mortgages, our regulatory framework proved inadequate in important ways. Multiple agencies have authority over consumer protection in financial products, but for historical reasons, the supervisory framework for enforcing those regulations had significant gaps and weaknesses. Banking regulators at the state and federal level had a potentially conflicting mission to promote safe and sound banking practices, while other agencies had a clear mission but limited tools and jurisdiction. Most critically in the run-up to the financial crisis, mortgage companies and other firms outside of the purview of bank regulation exploited that lack of clear accountability by selling mortgages and other products that were overly complicated and unsuited to borrowers' financial situation. Banks and thrifts followed suit, with disastrous results for consumers and the financial system.

This year, Congress, the Administration, and financial regulators have taken significant measures to address some of the most obvious inadequacies in our consumer protection framework. But these steps have focused on just two, albeit very important, product markets—credit cards and mortgages. We need comprehensive reform.

For that reason, we propose the creation of a single regulatory agency, a Consumer Financial Protection Agency (CFPA), with the authority and accountability to make sure that consumer protection regulations are written fairly and enforced vigorously. The CFPA should reduce gaps in federal supervision and enforcement; improve coordination with the states; set higher standards for financial intermediaries; and promote consistent regulation of similar products.

Consumer protection is a critical foundation for our financial system. It gives the public confidence that financial markets are fair and enables policy makers and regulators to maintain stability in regulation. Stable regulation, in turn, promotes growth, efficiency, and innovation over the long term. We propose legislative, regulatory, and administrative reforms to promote transparency, simplicity, fairness, accountability, and access in the market for consumer financial products and services. . . .

Create a New Consumer Financial Protection Agency

We propose the creation of a single federal agency, the Consumer Financial Protection Agency, dedicated to protecting consumers in the financial products and services markets, except for investment products and services already regulated by the SEC or CFTC. We recommend that the CFPA be granted consolidated authority over the closely related functions of writing rules, supervising and examining institutions' compliance, and administratively enforcing violations. The CFPA should reduce gaps in federal supervision; improve coordination among the states; set higher standards for financial intermediaries; and promote consistent regulation of similar products. Nothing in this proposal is intended to constrain the Attorney General's current authorities to enforce the law or direct litigation on behalf of the United States.

The CFPA should give consumer protection an independent seat at the table in our financial regulatory system. Consumer protection is a critical foundation for our financial system. It gives the public confidence that financial markets are fair and enables policy makers and regulators to maintain stability in regulation. Stable regulation, in turn, promotes growth, efficiency, and innovation over the long term. Consumer protection cannot live up to this role, however, unless the financial system develops and sustains a culture that places a high value on helping responsible consumers thrive and treating all consumers fairly.

The spread of unsustainable subprime mortgages and abusive credit card contracts highlighted a serious shortcoming of our present regulatory infrastructure. It too easily allows consumer protection values to be overwhelmed by other imperatives—whether short-term gain, innovation for its own sake, or keeping up with the competition. To instill a genuine culture of consumer protection and not merely of legal compliance in our financial institutions, we need first to instill that culture in the federal regulatory structure. For the public to have confidence that consumer protection is important to regulators, there must be clear accountability in government for this task.

The current system of regulation does not meet these needs. Oversight of federally supervised institutions for compliance with consumer protection, fair lending, and community reinvestment laws is fragmented among four agencies. This makes coordination of supervisory policies difficult, slows responses to emerging consumer protection threats, and creates opportunities for regulatory arbitrage, where firms choose their regulator according to which entity will be least restrictive.

The [FTC] has a clear mission to protect consumers but generally lacks jurisdiction over the banking sector and has limited tools and resources to promote robust compliance of nonbank institutions. Mortgage companies not owned by banks fall into a regulatory "no man's land" where no regulator exercises leadership and state attorneys general are left to try to fill the gap. State and federal bank supervisory agencies' primary mission is to ensure that financial institutions act prudently, a mission that, in appearance if not always in practice, often conflicts with their consumer protection responsibilities.

In addition, the systems, expertise, and culture necessary for the federal banking agencies to perform their core missions and functions are not conducive to sustaining over the long term a federal consumer protection program that is vigorous, balanced, and creative. These agencies are designed, and their professional staff is trained, to see the world through the lenses of institutions and markets, not consumers. Recent Federal Reserve [Board] regulations have been strong, but quite late in coming. Moreover, they do not ensure that the federal banking agencies will remain committed to consumer protection.

We do not propose a new regulatory agency because we seek more regulation, but because we seek better regulation. The very existence of an agency devoted to consumer protection in financial services will be a strong incentive for institutions to develop strong cultures of consumer protection. The core of such an agency can be assembled reasonably quickly from discrete operations of other agencies. Most rule writing authority is concentrated in a single division of the Federal Reserve [Board], and three of the four federal banking agencies have mostly or entirely separated consumer compliance supervision from prudential supervision. Combining staff from different agencies is not simple, to be sure, but it will bring significant benefits for responsible consumers and institutions, as well as for the market for consumer financial services and products.

The 15-page proposal, later fleshed out in detailed legislative language, encountered strong opposition within Congress. In a hearing before the Senate Committee on Banking, Housing, and Urban Affairs on July 14, 2009, Senator Richard Shelby (R-Ala.) criticized the proposal for a Consumer Financial Protection Agency as denying consumers the right to make their own decisions about financial products.

Statement of Sen. Richard C. Shelby

Creating a Consumer Financial Protection Agency: A Cornerstone of America's New Economic Foundation: Hearing Before the S. Comm. on Banking, Housing, and Urban Affairs, 111th Cong. (2009)

Beyond the practical issues regarding the program, I want to highlight some conceptual issues that I believe we must recognize as we consider financial consumer protection reform.

First, I believe that we must clearly acknowledge and accept that risk cannot be eliminated from our financial markets[.] It is risk taking that generates return. It would be both false and irresponsible to lead the American people to believe that an enhanced regulator can provide them with risk-free opportunities.

Second, I believe that we must also acknowledge that the risk associated with financial products are largely depending on the circumstances surrounding a particular transaction and the consumer. Some have tried to make oversimplistic analogies comparing defective consumer products to certain financial products. This is inaccurate, and I believe it is highly inappropriate.

For example, a defective electrical device is dangerous under every circumstance where it is used. We know that. But that is not the case for financial products. A plain-vanilla 30-year fixed mortgage is not inherently safer, some argue, than a shorter adjustable rate product[.] In fact, a 30-year fixed mortgage could involve high costs and provide less value to the consumer. We have to look at the circumstances.

Consumers need the relevant information and the means to understand it so they can purchase products and engage in the transactions that best fit their needs and circumstances. This point bears on what I believe is finally the most important issue associated with consumer protection reform. Who is best able to decide about the value and the necessity of any particular financial product or service?

Some, including those in the Administration, have decided that consumers will not act in their own best interests and, therefore, it is necessary that we remove or greatly restrict products that in some situations might cause financial harm. Implied in this belief is the notion that some people, such as the Government bureaucrats, can make informed decisions about the value of products and services while others, such as the American consumer, cannot. In other words, "Yes, we can," has become "No, you can't."

While I can accept the view that in some cases consumers do not have the necessary information or understanding to make sound financial decisions, I do not accept the premise that the remedy is to deny consumers decision-making power altogether. I think this would be a very significant and paternalistic departure from the notions of liberty and personal responsibility that have previously guided all our regulatory efforts. Quite frankly, I find it a bit disturbing and somewhat offensive that the concept of the "intellectually deficient consumer" as now found a voice in our legislative process.

To the extent that there is any merit to this theory, I believe it would be better to provide those with deficiencies the means to address them rather than seizing from them their right to make free and informed choices. . . .

Barr, then Assistant Secretary for Financial Institutions at the Department of the Treasury, responded to criticisms of the proposed consumer agency in the following statement.

Prepared Statement of Michael S. Barr, Assistant Secretary for Financial Institutions, Department of the Treasury

Creating a Consumer Financial Protection Agency: A Cornerstone of America's New Economic Foundation: Hearing Before the Sen. Comm. on Banking, Housing, and Urban Affairs, 111th Cong. (2009)

The need could not be clearer. Today's consumer protection regime just experienced massive failure. It could not stem a plague of abusive and unaffordable mortgages and exploitative credit cards despite clear warning signs. It cost millions of responsible consumers their homes, their savings, and their dignity. And it contributed to the near collapse of our financial system. We did not have just a financial crisis; we had a consumer crisis. Americans are still paying the price, and those forced into foreclosure or bankruptcy or put through other wrenching dislocations will pay for years.

There are voices saying that the status quo is fine or good enough. That we should keep the bank regulators in charge of protecting consumers. That we just need some patches. They even claim consumers are better off with the current approach.

It is not surprising we are hearing these voices. As Secretary [of the Treasury Timothy] Geithner observed last week, [President Barack Obama's] proposals would reduce the ability of financial institutions to choose their regulator, to shape the content of future regulation, and to continue financial practices that were lucrative for a time, but that ultimately proved so damaging. Entrenched interests always resist change. Major reform always brings out fear mongering. But responsible financial institutions and providers have nothing to fear.

We all aspire to the same objectives for consumer protection regulation: independence, accountability, effectiveness, and balance. The question is how to achieve them. A successful regulatory structure for consumer protection requires mission focus, marketwide coverage, and consolidated authority.

Today's system has none of these qualities. It fragments jurisdiction and authority for consumer protection over many Federal regulators, most of which have higher priorities than protecting consumers. Nonbanks avoid Federal supervision; no Federal consumer compliance examiner lands at their doorsteps. Banks can choose the least restrictive supervisor among several different banking agencies. Fragmentation of rule writing, supervision, and enforcement leads to finger-pointing in place of action and makes actions taken less effective.

The President's proposal for one agency for one marketplace with one mission—protecting consumers—will resolve these problems. The Consumer Financial Protection Agency will create a level playing field for all providers, regardless of their charter or corporate form. It will ensure high and uniform standards across the market. It will end profits based on misleading sales pitches and hidden traps, but there will be profits made on a level playing field where banks and nonbanks can compete on the basis of price and quality.

If we create one Federal regulator with consolidated authority, we will be able to leave behind regulatory arbitrage and interagency finger-pointing. And we will be assured of accountability.

Our proposal ensures, not limits, consumer choice; preserves, not stifles, innovation; strengthens, not weakens, depository institutions; reduces, not increases, regulatory costs; and increases, not reduces, national regulatory uniformity.

---

1. ***A Supernanny Agency?*** David Evans and Joshua Wright argued that the proposed Consumer Financial Protection Agency would "create a 'supernanny agency' . . . designed to substitute the choice of bureaucrats for those of consumers." David S. Evans & Joshua D. Wright, *The Effect of the Consumer Financial Protection Agency Act of 2009 on Consumer Credit*, 22 LOY. CONSUMER L. REV. 277, 280 (2010). Do you agree with this assessment? Or do you think that a single agency for consumer protection would promote free and informed decisions by consumers?

2. ***Financial Sector Opposition to CFPB.*** The proposed Consumer Financial Protection Agency "startled the entire conservative banking industry." ROBERT G. KAISER, ACT OF CONGRESS: HOW AMERICA'S ESSENTIAL INSTITUTION WORKS, AND HOW IT DOESN'T 134 (2013). Edward L. Yingling, President and CEO of the American Bankers Association criticized the breadth of the proposal in the same July 2009 hearing:

> I would . . . ask you to look at this issue from an additional point of view. While banks of all sizes would be negatively impacted, think of your local community banks and credit unions, for that matter. These banks never made one subprime loan, yet these community banks have found the Administration proposing a potentially massive new regulatory burden. While the shadow banking industry, which includes those most responsible for the crisis, is covered by the new agency, their regulatory and enforcement burden is, based on history, likely to be much less. . . .
>
> All this cost, regulation, conflicting requirements, and uncertainty would be placed on community banks that in no way contributed to the crisis.

Yingling further argued that "[t]he fundamental flaw in the proposal is that consumer regulation and safety and soundness regulation are two sides of the same coin. You cannot separate a business from its products." *Id.*

V. THE CONSUMER FINANCIAL PROTECTION BUREAU

A. STRUCTURE AND POWERS OF THE CFPB

Created by the Dodd-Frank Act, the CFPB's primary mission is "to implement and, where applicable, enforce Federal consumer financial law consistently for the purpose of ensuring that all consumers have access to markets for consumer financial products and services and that markets for consumer financial products and services are fair, transparent, and competitive." 12 U.S.C. § 5511(a). The CFPB is an independent agency established in the Federal Reserve System that regulates the offering and provision of consumer financial products or services under federal consumer financial laws, specifically (1) the CFPB's authority under the Consumer Financial Protection Act (Title X of the Dodd-Frank Act), and (2) preexisting laws that have been transferred to the CFPB's authority, such as TILA, the Fair Housing Act, and ECOA, among others. *See* 12 U.S.C. § 5481(12) for a complete list of "enumerated consumer laws" transferred to the CFPB's authority.

Where previous regulators had other priorities, such as the safety and soundness of financial institutions, the CFPB's sole focus is consumer protection. The CFPB is authorized to exercise its authorities with the following objectives in mind with respect to consumer financial products and services:

- consumers are provided with timely and understandable information to make responsible decisions about financial transactions;
- consumers are protected from unfair, deceptive, or abusive acts and practices and from discrimination;
- outdated, unnecessary, or unduly burdensome regulations are regularly identified and addressed in order to reduce unwarranted regulatory burdens;
- federal consumer financial laws are enforced consistently, without regard to the status of an institution as an IDI, in order to promote fair competition; and
- markets for consumer financial products and services operate transparently and efficiently to facilitate access and innovation.

Meanwhile, the primary functions of the CFPB are:

- conducting financial education programs;
- collecting, investigating, and responding to consumer complaints;
- collecting, researching, monitoring, and publishing information relevant to the functioning of markets for consumer financial products and services to identify risks to consumers and the proper functioning of such markets;
- supervising covered persons for compliance with federal consumer financial laws, and taking appropriate enforcement action to address violations of these laws;
- issuing rules, orders, and guidance implementing federal consumer financial laws; and
- performing such support activities as may be necessary or useful to facilitate the other functions of the CFPB.

1. Structure of the CFPB

Although originally conceived as a freestanding agency, the CFPB was established in the Federal Reserve System as a political compromise between consumer advocates and the financial sector. *See, e.g.*, Adam J. Levitin, *The Consumer Financial Protection Bureau: An Introduction,* 32 REV. BANKING & FIN. L. 321 (2013); *see also* Rachel E. Barkow, *Insulating Agencies: Avoiding Capture Through Institutional Design*, 89 TEX. L. REV. 15, 73 (2010). Despite the placement of the CFPB within the Federal Reserve System, however, the CFPB is completely autonomous in its leadership, budget, policy, rulemaking, supervision, and enforcement.

The Director, appointed by the President with the advice and consent of the Senate, heads the CFPB and serves a five-year term. The President may remove the Director for cause, such as "inefficiency, neglect of duty, or malfeasance in office." 12 U.S.C. § 5491(c)(3). The Director must appear semi-annually before committees in both houses of Congress to discuss the CFPB's budget, rules, and public supervision and enforcement actions.

The Dodd-Frank Act provides for the establishment of functional units within the CFPB that focus on research, community affairs, and collecting and tracking complaints. The following divisions are also established within the CFPB: the Office of Fair Lending and Equal Opportunity, the Office of Financial Education, the Office of Service Member Affairs, and the Office of Financial Protection for Older Americans. The Consumer Advisory Board, established by the Director, advises the CFPB in the exercise of its functions, and provides information on emerging practices in the consumer financial products or services sector.

Like the Federal Reserve Board, the FDIC, and the OCC, the CFPB is not funded by annual Congressional appropriations. Instead, the CFPB is funded "from the combined earnings of the Federal Reserve System." 12 U.S.C. § 5497(a)(1). The CFPB Director shall determine the amount reasonably necessary to carry out the authorities of the CFPB under federal consumer financial laws. The amount is capped at 12% of the total operating expenses of the Federal Reserve System in 2010, subject to an upward adjustment for inflation and based on the costs of hiring new federal employees. The funds derived from the Federal Reserve System are not subject to Congressional appropriations. The Government Accountability Office conducts an annual audit of the CFPB's financial statements in accordance with generally accepted government auditing standards. See Figure 5.1-1 for a comparison of the budgets of financial regulatory agencies for Fiscal Year 2014.

Figure 5.1-1 Budgets for the Financial Regulatory Agencies

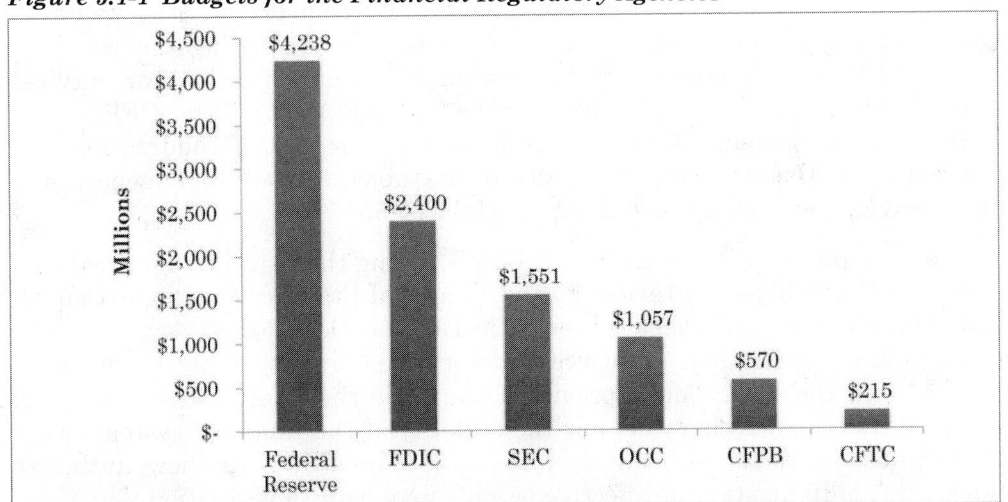

Sources: Fed. Reserve Bd., 101st Annual Report 402 (2015); FDIC, 2014 Annual Report 70 (2015); SEC, Agency Financial Report 48 (2014); OCC, Annual Report 42 (2014); CFPB, Financial Report of the Consumer Financial Protection Bureau 48 (2014); CFTC, Summary of Performance and Financial Information 18 (2015).

---

1. ***Structural Independence.*** Professors Kirti Datla and Richard Revesz analyzed several indicia of independence in independent and executive agencies that inform the ongoing debate over the structural [independence] of the CFPB. For example, the Director's for-cause removal protection increases the political costs of a decision to remove the Director since invoking the provision will make the removal more politically salient and susceptible to judicial challenge. The five-year tenure protection also insulates the Director from political influence since the need to secure re-nomination is less frequent. Additionally, automatic funding through earnings of the Federal Reserve System, rather than through Congressional appropriations, reduces pressure from Congress on rulemaking and enforcement actions that can result from annual budget battles. *See* Kirti Datla & Richard L. Revesz, *Deconstructing Independent Agencies (and Executive Agencies)*, 98 CORNELL L.J. 769 (2013).

---

2. Rulemaking Authority

The CFPB is authorized to administer, enforce, and otherwise implement the provisions of federal consumer financial laws. The Director may prescribe rules and issue orders and guidance, as may be necessary or appropriate, to enable the CFPB to administer and carry out the purposes and objectives of these laws, and to prevent evasions of these laws. The CFPB's rulemaking authority is subject to required notice and comment procedures under the Administrative Procedure Act (APA), see 5 U.S.C. § 553, and judicial review under administrative law jurisprudence.

The CFPB must follow standards for its rulemaking authority. For example, the CFPB must consult with "appropriate prudential regulators or other Federal agencies" before proposing rules. 12 U.S.C. § 5512(b)(2)(B). The CFPB shall address any written objections during this consultation process when issuing final regulations. Notably, in prescribing a rule, the CFPB, like some other agencies, must engage in cost-benefit analysis by considering "the potential benefits and costs to consumers and covered persons, including the potential reduction of access by consumers to consumer financial products or services resulting from such rule. . . ." 12 U.S.C. § 5512(b)(2)(A)(i). The CFPB shall "conduct an assessment of each significant rule or order," addressing the effectiveness of the rule with respect to the objectives of the agency, and reflecting available evidence and data. 12 U.S.C. § 5512(d).

As a compromise with critics of the CFPB during the legislative process, the CFPB's rules are subject to review by the Financial Stability Oversight Council (FSOC), which was established under Title I of the Dodd-Frank Act. If, upon petition by a member agency, the FSOC determines, by a two-thirds vote of its members, that "the regulation or provision would put the safety and soundness of the United States banking system or the stability of the financial system of the United States at risk." 12 U.S.C. § 5513(a). The FSOC's review authority includes the ability to stay the effectiveness of or set aside a regulation.

In addition to its authorities to implement existing consumer financial protection laws and to promulgate regulations under such laws, the CFPB has the authority to write rules under new provisions of the Dodd-Frank Act, including rules on mortgages, which we discuss in Chapter 5.2. The Dodd-Frank

Act also provides for specific additional rulemaking authorities of the CFPB. The CFPB may, for example, prescribe rules that prohibit unfair, deceptive, or abusive acts or practices (UDAAP). The statute further defines what the CFPB can reasonably consider unfair or abusive. The CFPB may also prescribe rules on disclosures "to ensure that the features of any consumer financial product or service, both initially and over the term of the product or service, are fully, accurately, and effectively disclosed to consumers in a manner that permits consumers to understand the costs, benefits, and risks associated with the product or service, in light of the facts and circumstances." 12 U.S.C. § 5532. The CFPB may also restrict mandatory pre-dispute arbitration provisions, among other measures. *See* Michael S. Barr, *Mandatory Arbitration in Consumer Finance and Investor Contracts*, 11 N.Y.U. J. L. & BUS. 793 (2015).

---

1. ***Cost-Benefit Analysis.*** Professor Jeffrey Gordon argues that cost-benefit analysis "as it has come to be used in the modern administrative state is virtually useless in the setting of optimal financial regulation and simply gets in the way of the genuinely hard work to be done." Jeffrey N. Gordon, *The Empty Call for Benefit-Cost Analysis in Financial Regulation*, 43 J. LEGAL STUD. S351, S353 (2014). Gordon argues that, because the modern financial system is created through a system of rules and adaptation to those rules, the costs and benefits of rule adoption are "impossible to quantify in a meaningful way." *Id.* at S360. Professor John Coates conducted case studies of six non-CFPB rules and concluded that precise, reliable, quantified cost-benefit analysis is unfeasible and can be no more than "guesstimated." Coates argues that, until cost-benefit analysis passes its own test, "no new legal mandates should be adopted to require such review and more serious attention should be given to how to improve the capacities of the agencies to improve the reliability and precision of [cost-benefit analysis] in practice." John C. Coates IV, *Cost-Benefit Analysis of Financial Regulation: Case Studies and Implications*, 124 YALE L.J. 882, 1011 (2015). By contrast, Professors Eric Posner and Glen Weyl argue that cost-benefit analysis is well suited to financial regulation and advocate for further development of institutional support for cost-benefit analysis in the executive branch. *See, e.g.*, Eric A. Posner & E. Glen Weyl, *Benefit-Cost Paradigms in Financial Regulation*, 43 J. LEGAL STUD. S1 (2014).

2. ***Judicial Scrutiny of Cost-Benefit Analysis.*** How should courts interpret the requirement imposed on the CFPB to conduct cost-benefit analysis? In *Business Roundtable v. SEC*, 647 F.3d 1144 (D.C. Cir. 2011), the D.C. Circuit analyzed the SEC's proxy access rule and held that the agency neglected its statutory obligation to assess the economic consequences of the rule it adopted. The D.C. Circuit signaled that, in applying the APA, federal courts may demand fairly detailed financial cost-benefit analysis for new regulations from the SEC and perhaps other financial regulatory agencies, including the CFPB. Critics argued that the D.C. Circuit had imposed a severe new standard on the SEC. *See, e.g.*, James D. Cox & Benjamin J.C. Baucom, *The Emperor Has No Clothes: Confronting the D.C. Circuit's Usurpation of SEC Rulemaking Authority*, 90 TEX. L. REV. 1811, 1813 (2012). Meanwhile, the SEC and other financial regulatory agencies, including the prudential regulators, responded to *Business Roundtable* by instituting internal reforms to improve their cost-benefit analysis procedures.

3. ***UDAAP.*** The CFPB's ability to prohibit UDAAP is an expansion from earlier similar mandates that allow federal and state regulators to regulate "unfair or deceptive acts or practices". The Dodd-Frank Act adds "abusive" acts or practices, which it defines as acts or practices that "materially interfere[] with the ability of a consumer to understand a term or condition of a consumer financial product or service" or "take[] unreasonable advantage of" a consumer's lack of understanding of a product, inability to protect his or her interests in selecting or using the product, or the consumer's reasonable reliance on the offeror to act in the consumer's interests. Dodd-Frank Act § 1031(d). CFPB Director Richard Cordray has stated that the CFPB does not yet intend to engage in rulemaking to further define "abusive" practices, suggesting that the CFPB's authority could instead be defined incrementally through enforcement actions, which are not subject to notice and comment procedures but permit the agency to develop law on a case-by-case basis, as applied to particular facts. Cordray noted, however, that "[f]or something to be an abusive practice it would have to be a pretty outrageous practice." Dave Clarke, *US abusive lending bar likely set high—Cordray*, REUTERS, Jan. 24, 2012.

Although the CFPB's enforcement actions to date have drawn upon existing interpretations of "unfair or deceptive acts or practices" law, critics argue that the CFPB could establish a sweeping definition of "abusive" practices through future rulemakings or enforcement adjudications, which could "pose substantial compliance challenges for financial institutions and other creditors." Jeffrey P. Naimon & Kirk D. Jensen, *The UDAP-ification of Consumer Financial Services Law*, 128 BANKING L.J. 22, 32 (2011). Nina Mendelson argues that when an agency chooses to engage in policymaking through avenues other than notice-and-comment rulemaking, such as issuing guidance documents, "this choice interferes with critical tools that regulatory beneficiaries can use to hold agencies accountable for the policy choices they make. Regulatory beneficiaries lose significant access both to the courts and to their ability to participate in agency decision making." *See* Nina A. Mendelson, *Regulatory Beneficiaries and Informal Agency Policymaking*, 92 CORNELL L. REV. 397, 420 (2007). Is it appropriate for the CFPB to use its enforcement authority to signal, on a case-by-case basis, which practices it believes to be unfair, deceptive, or abusive? What challenges might this approach pose for the financial sector? Do you think that the CFPB should instead conduct notice-and-comment rulemaking? What approach is best for consumers?

4. ***Rulemaking Authority and States.*** In an unusual procedure, the CFPB must issue a notice of proposed rulemaking whenever a majority of states enacts a resolution in support of the CFPB's establishment or modification of a consumer protection regulation. Before issuing a final regulation based on this notice, the CFPB must take into account whether (1) "the proposed regulation would afford greater protection to consumers than any existing regulation;" (2) "the intended benefits of the proposed regulation for consumers would outweigh any increased costs or inconveniences for consumers, and would not discriminate unfairly against any category or class of consumers; and" (3) "a Federal banking agency has advised that the proposed regulation is likely to present an unacceptable safety and soundness risk to [IDIs]." 12 U.S.C. § 5551(c)(2). The

relationship between federal and state financial regulation after the Dodd-Frank Act is discussed in greater detail later in this Chapter.

---

3. Supervision Authority

The Dodd-Frank Act authorizes the CFPB to supervise and examine large depository institutions and their affiliates and certain non-depository consumer financial services companies, including debt collectors and credit reporting companies. The CFPB requires reports and conducts examinations on a periodic basis to assess if an entity is in compliance with the requirements of federal consumer financial laws, to obtain information about the entity's activities and its compliance systems and procedures, and to determine whether the entity poses risks to consumers and to markets for consumer financial products and services. In its Supervision and Examination Manual, the CFPB explains that three main principles guide the supervision process: (1) its focus on risks to consumers when it evaluates the policies and practices of a financial institution; (2) its reliance on available data about the activities of entities it supervises, the markets in which they operate, and risks to consumers posed by activities in these markets; and (3) consistent standards in its supervision of entities, to the extent possible. CFPB SUPERVISION AND EXAMINATION MANUAL 4 (2012).

The CFPB has supervision authority over IDIs and insured credit unions with total assets of more than $10 billion. It must coordinate examinations and supervisory activities with the prudential regulators and state bank regulatory authorities of these institutions, including consultation with regard to their respective examination schedules and reporting requirements from covered entities. The CFPB, for example, entered into an agreement with prudential regulators to align related supervisory activities and decrease the risk of conflicting supervisory directives. *See* Memorandum of Understanding on Supervisory Coordination (May 16, 2012). It is further mandated to pursue similar arrangements with state bank supervisors. The prudential regulators generally retain supervisory authority for consumer financial protection with respect to smaller IDIs and insured credit unions. The CFPB coordinates some activities with the prudential regulators of these institutions and may, in limited circumstances, directly supervise such institutions.

The CFPB also supervises a range of non-depository institutions, including entities that offer or provide origination, brokerage, or servicing of loans secured by residential real estate, or loan modification or foreclosure relief services in connection with such loans; larger participants of a market for other consumer financial products or services; entities that the CFPB has reasonable cause to determine have engaged in conduct that poses risks to consumers; private education lenders; and payday lenders. The CFPB has defined larger participants in the consumer reporting market and the debt collection market, for example, as entities with annual receipts of more than $7 million and $10 million, respectively. *See* 12 C.F.R. §§ 1090.104(b), 1090.105(b).

The CFPB regularly shares key findings with the public in order to help financial services limit risks to consumers and comply with federal consumer financial laws. In the following excerpt, the CFPB shares supervisory observations from Summer 2015 in the areas of consumer reporting, debt collection, student loan servicing, mortgage origination, mortgage servicing, and fair lending. When supervision and examination procedures demonstrate that a violation has occurred, the CFPB may direct a supervised entity to resolve the issue through non-public remediation or may initiate an enforcement action against the entity.

CFPB, Supervisory Observations

Supervisory Highlights 9–10, 22–23 (8th ed. 2015)

Student loan servicing

The Supervision program covers certain Federal and private student loan servicers. The Bureau's recent examinations identified deceptive practices and a [Fair Credit Reporting Act (FCRA)] violation.

Deceptive statements about the deductibility of student loan interest

During one or more examinations, examiners determined that student loan servicers included language on periodic statements suggesting that borrowers could not deduct on tax filings interest paid on qualified student loans unless they paid more than $600 in interest. Examiners found this practice to be deceptive because there is no minimum amount of qualified student loan interest that borrowers must pay before taking a deduction.

At the time of the examination, one or more student loan servicers had already removed the language suggesting a $600 threshold for deducting student loan interest. In addition, the relevant servicers offered free tax advice and re-filing assistance for borrowers negatively affected by the misleading language.

Deficient FCRA adverse action notices

The FCRA requires that every adverse action notice contain the name, address, and telephone number of the [credit reporting agency] that furnished the report, and a statement that the [credit reporting agency] did not make the decision to take the adverse action and is unable to provide the consumer the specific reasons why the adverse action was taken. The FCRA further provides that if any person takes an adverse action with respect to any consumer that is based in whole or in part on any information contained in a consumer report, the person must, if they use a credit score, provide to the consumer the credit score, the range of possible credit scores, a maximum of four key factors that adversely affected the credit score, the date on which the credit score was created, and the name of the entity that provided the credit score.

Lenders sometimes require borrowers to have a cosigner in order to take out a private student loan. In many instances, a borrower may later request the release of a cosigner from the loan obligation provided that some conditions are met. These conditions often include satisfying certain credit criteria. If a student loan servicer uses a consumer report to deny a cosigner release request, the servicer must provide a FCRA adverse action notice. During one or more examinations, Supervision determined that a student loan servicer did not include all required information in FCRA adverse action notices when denying cosigner release requests.

In response to a citation, one or more student loan servicers conducted a root cause analysis to determine why the adverse action notices were deficient, and have undertaken remedial and corrective actions regarding this violation, which is under review by Supervision.

---

4. Enforcement Authority

The CFPB may bring a civil action "to impose a civil penalty or to seek all appropriate legal and equitable relief including a permanent or temporary injunction" against any person who violates a federal consumer financial law. 12 U.S.C. § 5564. The CFPB's enforcement authority covers violations under the Consumer Financial Protection Act and related rulemakings, the Dodd-Frank Act more generally, and the enumerated consumer laws transferred to the CFPB's authority and related rulemakings.

The CFPB may bring enforcement actions against entities under its jurisdiction. It has primary, but non-exclusive, enforcement authority over large IDIs, along with prudential regulators. The CFPB also has back-up enforcement authority over other depository institutions and shares enforcement authority with the FTC over non-depository institutions. As discussed later in this Chapter, state enforcement agencies also retain significant enforcement authority.

Once the CFPB determines that a violation has occurred, it may conduct hearings and adjudication proceedings under the APA or bring a civil action in a federal district court. The party to a civil action may appeal a decision of the proceeding to a federal court of appeals. The CFPB may obtain the following relief: rescission or reformation of contracts; refund of moneys or return of real property; restitution, disgorgement or compensation for unjust enrichment; payment of damages or other monetary relief; public notification with regard to the violation, including the costs of notification; limits on the activities or functions of the institution or person; and civil money penalties. Punitive damages may generally not be imposed.

---

1. ***Potential Conflicts Between Supervision and Enforcement.*** The Bipartisan Policy Center's Consumer Protection Task Force has argued that inconsistencies may arise between the CFPB's supervision and enforcement activities. *See* BIPARTISAN POLICY CTR., THE CONSUMER FINANCIAL PROTECTION BUREAU: MEASURING THE PROGRESS OF A NEW AGENCY 26–27 (2013). The CFPB initially included enforcement staff in its examination process and supervisory meetings on the ground that participating in examinations enabled enforcement staff to better understand the institutions and practices that the CFPB regulates. The Task Force countered, however, that the inclusion of enforcement staff has "a chilling effect on the sharing of information with the CFPB."

Do you agree with the assessment of the Task Force? Or do you think that coordinating supervision and enforcement activities is an efficient means to curb activities that harm consumers? Why have none of the banking regulators, which have performed examinations for many years, followed this practice? A short time after the Bipartisan Policy Center issued its report, the CFPB announced that it would end its practice of including enforcement staff in regular examinations. *See* Alan Zibel, *Consumer Regulator to Stop Bringing Lawyers to Firm Exams*, WALL ST. J., Oct. 9, 2013.

2. ***Consumer Complaints.*** Another primary function of the CFPB is to collect, investigate, and respond to consumer complaints. It has been accepting

and publishing complaints and companies' responses through its Consumer Complaint Database since July 2011. In May 2015, the CFPB began giving consumers and companies the option to publish narratives, as well. The strategy of engaging the public through crowdsourcing data in the form of consumer complaints allows the CFPB to analyze and prioritize issues for supervisory, enforcement, and regulatory action. Some scholars have argued that the database provides a tool for the agency and the public to hold financial institutions accountable. *See, e.g.*, Michael S. Barr, *Comment: Accountability and Independence in Financial Regulation: Checks and Balances, Public Engagement, and Other Innovations*, 78 LAW & CONTEMP. PROBS. 119, 127 (2015). Others, however, have taken the view that the CFPB's complaint mechanism is unlikely to improve the overall level of consumer protection and, in fact, may hinder the agency's enforcement, rulemaking, or financial education initiatives. *See, e.g.*, Katherine Porter, *The Complaint Conundrum: Thoughts on the CFPB's Complaint Mechanism*, 7 BROOK. J. CORP. FIN. & COM. L. 57, 82–85 (2012).

---

5. Exclusions from the CFPB's Authority

The Dodd-Frank Act provides for exclusions of a number of entities from the CFPB's rulemaking, supervision, enforcement, and other authorities. Each of the exclusions is subject to certain limitations that place the respective entity back within the jurisdiction of the CFPB if the relevant conditions are met.

Broker-dealers, asset managers, and other entities regulated by the SEC, CFTC, or state securities commissions are generally excluded from the CFPB's authority. Insurance companies that are regulated by state insurance regulators are also excluded. The CFPB may not exercise its authorities over merchants, retailers, or sellers of nonfinancial goods or services, "except to the extent that such person is engaged in offering or providing any consumer financial product or service, or is otherwise subject to" enumerated consumer laws. 12 U.S.C. § 5517(a)(1). The CFPB, however, does have jurisdiction to the extent that such entity (1) "assigns, sells or otherwise conveys to another person [non-delinquent] debt owed by a consumer," (2) extends credit that "significantly exceeds the market value of the nonfinancial good or service provided," (3) "regularly extends credit and the credit is subject to a finance charge," or (4) "engage[s] significantly in offering or providing consumer financial products or services." 12 U.S.C. §§ 5517(a)(2)(B)–(C). The CFPB's authorities require special procedures with respect to rules affecting small businesses.

Auto dealers are also excluded from the CFPB's jurisdiction. The CFPB may, however, exercise jurisdiction if such auto dealer (1) "provides consumers with any services related to residential or commercial mortgages or self-financing transactions involving real property[,]" (2) extends directly to consumers retail credit or retail leases involving motor vehicles that are "not routinely assigned to an unaffiliated third party finance or leasing source[,]" or (3) "offers or provides a consumer financial product or service not involving or related to the sale, financing, leasing, rental, repair, refurbishment, maintenance, or other servicing of motor vehicles, motor vehicle parts, or any related or ancillary product or service." 12 U.S.C. §§ 5519(b)(1)–(3). The FTC retains jurisdiction over auto dealers and has the authority to prescribe rules with regard to unfair or deceptive, but not abusive, trade practices against such dealers.

The CFPB may generally not exercise its authorities over real estate brokers, real estate agents, retailers of manufactured homes, accountants, income tax preparers, and attorneys, unless they offer a consumer financial product or service. Other entities and activities that generally fall outside of the CFPB's jurisdiction include employee benefit and compensation plans, and entities regulated by the Farm Credit Administration, unless they offer a consumer financial product or service. Read these exclusions carefully. Why would Congress have provided for elaborate carve-outs from CFPB oversight, only to provide for CFPB jurisdiction whenever such entities provide a consumer financial product or service?

---

1. ***Auto Financing.*** In a classic political stakeholder battle, the exclusion for auto dealers was the result of substantial lobbying from the auto dealers. The CFPB, nonetheless, has considered indirect methods to reach auto dealers. For example, the CFPB has warned that it will enforce the ECOA against "indirect auto lenders," or institutions that purchase consumer auto loans from auto dealers to finance auto loans for consumers, if such institutions engage in discriminatory lending. *See* CONSUMER FIN. PROT. BUREAU, CFPB BULL. NO. 2013-02, INDIRECT AUTO LENDING AND COMPLIANCE WITH THE EQUAL CREDIT OPPORTUNITY ACT (2013). As we will discuss in Chapter 5.3, the CFPB has used this authority several times. *See, e.g.*, Press Release, CFPB and DOJ Order Ally to Pay $80 Million to Consumers Harmed by Discriminatory Auto Loan Pricing (Dec. 20, 2013). The Bipartisan Policy Center has argued that the current system for auto financing "is opaque and may not give consumers the benefit of market competition." It further argued that the CFPB "should be able to regulate auto financing directly, rather than being forced to indirectly attempt to regulate the car's financing terms through the interactions of auto-dealers with financial services providers." BIPARTISAN POLICY CTR., THE CONSUMER FINANCIAL PROTECTION BUREAU: MEASURING THE PROGRESS OF A NEW AGENCY 37–38 (2013). The CFPB contends that it has clear jurisdiction over auto finance. *See* Videotape: Hearing on the CFPB's Semi-Annual Report to Congress before the Sen. Comm. on Banking, Housing, and Urban Affairs (July 15, 2015) (testimony of CFPB Director Richard Cordray) ("[T]he law has spoken clearly that [the CFPB has a] responsibility to address any sort of issues of discrimination or any other violations of law by [auto] lenders, but not by dealers."). Is it appropriate for the CFPB to indirectly regulate what it is explicitly prohibited from regulating directly?

B. BALANCE OF FEDERAL AND STATE AUTHORITY AFTER THE DODD-FRANK ACT

As you have learned, the Dodd-Frank Act strengthens and centralizes federal consumer protection regulation. At the same time, the Dodd-Frank Act also preserves an active role for state governments in protecting consumers. For instance, the Dodd-Frank Act expressly provides that states may continue to enact their own consumer protection regulations. The Dodd-Frank Act thus makes it clear that the CFPB's rules operate as a floor for consumer protections, not as a ceiling.

The Dodd-Frank Act authorizes state attorneys general to enforce federal consumer protection laws and CFPB regulations, subject to some limitations. This provision significantly enhances the enforcement power behind federal consumer protections. For example, the Illinois Attorney General has used this authority to bring an action against a payday lender for allegedly charging borrowers an account protection fee that offered no benefit, in violation of the Dodd-Frank Act's prohibition on UDAAP. *See* Illinois ex rel. Madigan v. CMK Investments, Inc., No. 14-C-2783, 2014 WL 6910519 (N.D. Ill. 2014). Additionally, the CFPB has partnered with state attorneys general to bring joint enforcement actions. *See, e.g.,* CFPB v. Wells Fargo Bank, N.A., No. 1:15-cv-00179 (D. Md. filed Jan. 22, 2015).

While the Dodd-Frank Act contemplates an active consumer protection role for the states, it also contains some limitations on state power. Federal preemption of state consumer protection laws as they relate to national banks is discussed in Chapter 5.2 in the context of mortgage regulation.

C. ONGOING POLICY DEBATES

As one of the most controversial parts of the Dodd-Frank Act, the CFPB continues to attract strong opposition from many in the financial services sector and some members of Congress. Critics have submitted a number of bills to amend the Consumer Financial Protection Act. At a hearing before the House Committee on Financial Services on November 19, 2013, Representative Jeb Hensarling (R-Tex.) regarded the CFPB as "the single most powerful and least accountable federal agency in the history of our nation." Hensarling and others have argued that the CFPB lacks accountability and transparency because it is exempted from the Congressional appropriations process, among other structural concerns. Other critics have attacked regulation over consumer financial products and services more broadly. Professor Todd Zywicki argues that the CFPB's "punitive and ill-advised regulation" has produced results that "have been both predictable and tragic: systematically driving consumers out of the mainstream financial system, withdrawing high-quality products, and increasingly forcing consumers to resort to inferior substitutes such as payday lending, overdraft protection, and prepaid cards." Todd J. Zywicki, *The Consumer Financial Protection Bureau: Savior or Menace?*, 81 GEO. WASH. L. REV. 856, 927 (2013); *see also* THOMAS A. DURKIN ET AL., CONSUMER CREDIT AND THE AMERICAN ECONOMY (2014).

---

1. ***Constitutionality of the CFPB.*** Recall the discussion in Chapter 1.3 in which some critics have challenged the constitutionality of the CFPB. In *State National Bank of Big Spring v. Lew*, 795 F.3d 48 (2015), the U.S. Court of Appeals for the D.C. Circuit held that Big Spring had standing to challenge the constitutionality of the CFPB. The bank argued that the CFPB is unconstitutional because independent agencies must be headed by multiple members rather than a single person, and Congress's broad delegation authority to the CFPB allegedly violates the non-delegation doctrine, among other reasons.

Hensarling has also argued that "the CFPB is uniquely unaccountable to the courts. Section 1022 of Dodd-Frank provides that where the Bureau disagrees with any other agency about the meaning of a provision of Federal consumer financial law, a reviewing court must give deference to the Bureau's views under the *Chevron* Doctrine." Do you agree with critics that argue that the CFPB is unconstitutional? Do you think that a five-member commission of three members of the President's party and two members from the other party, as is the case with the SEC and the CFTC, would provide balance or introduce partisanship? Do you think that the CFPB lacks sufficient Presidential control or Congressional oversight? The Dodd-Frank Act requires the Director of the CFPB to testify before Senate and House committees at least twice per year, and the CFPB must submit semi-annual reports to Congress and the President. *See* Dodd-Frank Act § 1016(a).

2. ***Director Richard Cordray's Recess Appointment.*** In *Big Spring*, the plaintiff also contested the constitutionality of President Barack Obama's recess appointment of Director Richard Cordray. On July 18, 2011, President Obama nominated Cordray as Director of the CFPB. On January 4, 2012, President Obama used his recess appointment power to appoint Cordray during a three-day intra-session Senate recess. After a lengthy delay, on July 16, 2013, the Senate confirmed Cordray's appointment on a bipartisan basis. Big Spring argued that Cordray's recess appointment, as well as the rulemakings and enforcement actions that he took before he was confirmed, was unconstitutional because the appointment occurred during an intra-session recess of insufficient length. In light of the Supreme Court's decision in *NLRB v. Noel Canning*, 134 S.Ct. 2550 (2014) (holding that President Obama's three appointments to the NLRB on January 4, 2012 were unconstitutional), the D.C. Circuit held that the bank had standing to challenge the issue and remanded to the district court for consideration of its merits. Cordray was later confirmed by the full Senate, rendering the issue moot.

CHAPTER 5.2

MORTGAGES

CONTENTS

I. INTRODUCTION

As Professor John Campbell describes, mortgages play a central role in the financial lives of individual consumers and in the broader financial system and economy:

> Residential mortgages are of first-order importance for households, for financial institutions, and for macroeconomic stability. The typical household in a developed economy has one dominant asset—a house—and one dominant liability—a mortgage. Mortgages are a major fraction of bank assets. . . . And the financial crisis that began in 2007 has made it abundantly clear that problems in mortgage lending have the potential to destabilize the financial system and the economy.

John Y. Campbell, *Mortgage Market Design*, 17 REV. FIN. 1, 1 (2013). As a result, the regulation of residential mortgages has implications not only for individual borrowers and lenders, but also for broader economic stability. This Chapter focuses on the regulation of residential mortgages from the perspective of consumer protection, while Chapters 12.1 and 12.2 focus on macroeconomic implications of securitization of mortgage loans and the roles of Fannie Mae and Freddie Mac.

This Chapter begins with a brief introduction to mortgages and the major players in a mortgage transaction, as well as a summary of some of the changes made by the Dodd-Frank Act in this area. We then examine some of the key federal laws and regulations governing the origination and terms of residential mortgages, as well as federal preemption of state regulations governing mortgage lending. Throughout the Chapter, we pay particular attention to regulations enacted in the aftermath of the Financial Crisis. Many of these regulations use innovative regulatory approaches, which may be applied to other consumer financial products and services in the future.

II. MORTGAGE BASICS

A. MORTGAGE OVERVIEW

A mortgage loan is a loan secured by real property. The borrower agrees that, if she fails to repay the loan, the lender can foreclose on, or seize, her home. Consumers typically use mortgages to buy houses, access equity in their houses, and finance home improvements. Borrowers may also refinance mortgages to obtain a lower interest rate or monthly payment.

Mortgages have different terms, rates, and features. In the United States, and unlike most other countries, 30-year, fixed-rate mortgages are most common. As of June 2015, 30-year, fixed-rate mortgages made up 84.9% of the total. Lenders also offer adjustable rate mortgages—mortgages with interest rates that adjust based on changes to a reference rate. In the run-up to the Financial Crisis, adjustable rate mortgages grew to as much as 29% of originations. Adjustable rate mortgages are no longer as widely used. They fell to 1% of all originations in 2009 and, as of March 2015, they account for only 4.6% of total originations. Adjustable rate mortgages often have fixed interest rates for the first two or three years of the mortgage and then become adjustable. These types of adjustable rate mortgages are known as 2–28 or 3–27 adjustable rate mortgages for the years they have fixed interest rates versus adjustable rates. *See* HOUSING FIN. POL'Y CTR., URBAN INST., HOUSING FINANCE AT A GLANCE: A MONTHLY CHARTBOOK 9 (June 2015). Figure 5.2-1 describes several other key mortgage types and features.

Figure 5.2-1 Key Terms

Adjustable-Rate Mortgage	The loan's interest rate adjusts over the life of the loan based on an interest rate index, which could increase a borrower's monthly payment. Many adjustable rate mortgages have a fixed rate for a few years at the beginning of the loan and then become adjustable.
Balloon Payment	A lump sum payment of the loan's outstanding balance, placed at the end of some mortgages.
Fixed-Rate Mortgage	The loan's interest rate remains the same over the life of the loan.
Home Equity Loan	A loan that allows homeowners to borrow against the equity in their home. Homeowners usually receive a lump sum payment, which they agree to pay back over a fixed term, with a fixed interest rate.
Prepayment Penalty	An amount the borrower is required to pay if they refinance or otherwise pay off the loan early.
Interest-only	A mortgage on which the borrower makes only interest payments for a fixed term and then must make higher monthly payments or a balloon payment to pay off the loan.
Reverse Mortgage	A home equity loan available to older homeowners, which allows homeowners to convert their home equity to cash. The loan must be repaid if the house is sold or when the borrower dies.

Before the Great Depression, adjustable rate mortgages were the most common in the U.S. mortgage market. Mortgages were available only for 5- to 10-year terms and with loan-to-value ratios of 50% or less. During the Great Depression, there were widespread foreclosures as borrowers could neither refinance nor pay off their balloon payments when due. As part of the New Deal, President Franklin D. Roosevelt's housing initiatives, including the precursor to Fannie Mae, encouraged the development of fixed-rate, longer-term loans. During this era, borrowers typically obtained mortgages from commercial banks and thrifts, which relied on deposits to fund the loans. The bank or thrift would hold the mortgage on its balance sheet and collect the borrower's principal and interest payments for the life of the loan. The development of the secondary mortgage market in the decades after World War II, however, changed the way how most residential mortgages are funded and, as a result, how mortgages are originated and serviced.

Today, borrowers can still obtain a mortgage from banks and thrifts, but they can also obtain mortgages from non-bank mortgage companies or through mortgage brokers, which act as intermediaries between borrowers and lenders. Most lenders immediately sell the mortgages they originate to investment banks or one of the government-sponsored entities (GSEs)—Fannie Mae, Freddie Mac, or, if it is an Federal Housing Administration (FHA) insured loan, to a government securitizer known as Ginnie Mae. These entities then package hundreds of loans together into mortgage-backed securities (MBSs), which they then sell to investors. Investors receive a stream of income from borrowers' principal and interest payments. Mortgage servicers collect payments, administer escrow accounts, work with borrowers who fall behind, and, if necessary, foreclose.

The process of packaging loans into MBSs and selling interests to investors is known as securitization. We discuss the U.S. mortgage market, securitization, and the role of the GSEs in Part XII.

B. DODD-FRANK ACT MORTGAGE REFORMS

Problems with the mortgage market were seen as a large factor contributing to the Financial Crisis. Professor Michael Barr examined the collapse of the U.S. housing market in Congressional testimony in 2008:

> The U.S. economy is caught in a vicious downward spiral of declining home prices, escalating foreclosures, rising losses on [MBSs], and disappearing liquidity. . . .
>
> Lax regulation, supervisory neglect, lack of transparency, and conflicts of interest all undermined the foundations of our financial system. Financial innovations . . . brought increased liquidity, but also broadened the wedge between the incentives facing brokers, lenders, borrowers, rating agencies, securitizers, loan servicers, and investors. The lack of transparency and oversight, coupled with rising home prices, hid the problems for some time. When home prices and other assets imploded, credit woes cascaded through the financial system, and the lack of trust in the system meant that even sound financial institutions faced contagion from the crisis.

Is Treasury Using Bailout Funds to Increase Foreclosure Prevention, as Congress Intended? Hearing Before the Subcomm. on Domestic Pol'y of the H. Comm. on Oversight & Gov't Reform, 110th Cong. 60 (2008) (statement of Michael S. Barr, University of Michigan Law School).

In response to the housing market collapse, the passage of the Dodd-Frank Act brought about many changes. Mike Calhoun, the president of the Center for Responsible Lending, summarized some of the key mortgage-related provisions of the Dodd-Frank Act as follows:

Mike Calhoun, Center for Responsible Lending, Dodd-Frank Measures Fundamentally Reform the Mortgage Market

Americans for Financial Reform & the Roosevelt Institute, An Unfinished Mission: Making Wall Street Work for Us 30, 33, 36–37, 39 (2013)

Qualified Mortgage/Ability to Repay Requirement

The most significant and prominent of the Dodd-Frank Act mortgage provisions is its requirement that [a] lender[]. . . . determine the borrower's ability to repay the loan. Lenders must also verify and document the borrower's income and expenses that establish that ability. This new duty to determine ability to repay carries liabilities if it is violated, including penalties and damages, and it can be raised as a defense if the loan is foreclosed. The statute directs the CFPB to define a class of safe loans that, in exchange for meeting certain clear standards, will be assumed to meet ability to repay rules, and where lenders will be partially shielded from liability. These [are] so-called "Qualified Mortgages." . . .

High-Cost and Subprime Loan Protections

The Dodd-Frank Act also specifically targeted high-cost and subprime loans, including enacting long overdue updates to the Home Ownership and Equity Protection Act (HOEPA). The HOEPA . . . provided strong protections for loans defined as "high cost.". . . High-cost loans were defined as those with very high fees—8 percent or more. . . .

The Dodd-Frank Act revisions of the HOEPA lowered this fee threshold to five points, and more important, included key fees such as payments to mortgage brokers and prepayment penalties that had previously been excluded. . . .

The Dodd-Frank Act also added to the protections that apply to the broader set of subprime mortgages that do have fees or interest rates high enough to trigger the new revised HOEPA protections. It required that subprime loans have escrow for taxes and insurance, so that borrowers would not be hit with payment shocks when those bills come due. . . .

Anti-Steering Provisions

The Dodd-Frank Act also sought to deal with mortgage abuses by preventing the financial incentives that encouraged brokers and lenders to steer borrowers to more expensive and riskier loans than they qualified for, which had ultimately harmed both individual consumers and the market as a whole. . . .

The Dodd-Frank Act reined in these steering practices in several ways. First, it created a general prohibition against steering, and provided remedies for borrowers. Financial incentives for steering were also reduced. The Dodd-Frank Act prohibited mortgage broker and loan officer compensation from being tied to loan structures, such as negative amortizing or no interest loans, or to the interest rate of the loan. . . .

Mortgage Servicing Reforms . . .

The Dodd-Frank Act added new servicing protections and empowered the CFPB to oversee and regulate the servicing industry. The CFPB in turn issued regulations that created new standards for servicers, including the correct credit of borrower payments, limitations on fees, and enhanced duties to modify loans. . . .

Additional Protections

Other Dodd-Frank Act provisions enhance the safety and transparency of the mortgage market. These include new appraisal standards that were needed because in the lead up to the [Financial Crisis], appraisals often far overvalued properties. Also included were simplified standard disclosure forms to help borrowers better understand loans and enriched Home Mortgage Disclosure Act Data, which will allow the public to better understand who is getting what kind of mortgages.

This Chapter will not go into detail on all of these topics, but rather we have selected a few mortgage lending provisions to give you a sense of some of the key changes the Dodd-Frank Act brought about in these areas.

III. MORTGAGE LENDING

This section examines several key federal laws and regulations governing the origination and terms of mortgages.

A. ABILITY-TO-REPAY REQUIREMENTS

1. Background

For decades, sound underwriting played a key role in managing risk in the mortgage market. When a borrower applied for a loan, the lender assessed the likelihood that the borrower would be able to repay the loan by looking at factors such as the borrower's income, assets, debts, credit history, down payment, and the value of the home to be purchased. This process helped lenders calculate a borrower's risk of default, which could be used to determine the interest charged on the loan and help the lender manage the risk in its portfolio. Lenders occasionally waived underwriting requirements, but usually only for borrowers "with fluctuating or hard-to-verify incomes, such as the self-employed, or to serve longtime customers with strong credit." FCIC, THE FIN. CRISIS INQUIRY REPORT 110 (Jan. 2011).

In the mid-2000s, however, underwriting standards began to deteriorate rapidly. Lenders were willing to extend loans to borrowers with little or no proof of the borrower's income or assets. From 2000 to 2007, these low- and no-documentation loans grew from "less than 2% to roughly 9% of all outstanding loans." *Id.* The Federal Reserve Board described the factors contributing to this decline in underwriting standards in the following excerpt.

Bd. of Governors of the Fed. Reserve Sys., Truth in Lending

73 Fed. Reg. 44,522, 44,540-41 (July 30, 2008) (codified at 12 C.F.R. § 226)

Evidence of a recent widespread disregard of repayment ability. . . .

Payment increases on 2–28 and 3–27 [adjustable rate mortgages] have not been a major cause of the increase in delinquencies and foreclosures because most delinquencies occurred before the payments were adjusted. Rather, a major contributor to these delinquencies was lenders' extension of credit on the basis of income stated on applications without verification. Originators had strong incentives to make these "stated income" loans, and consumers had incentives to accept them. Because the loans could be originated more quickly, originators, who were paid based on volume, could increase their earnings by originating more of them. The share of "low doc" and "no doc" loan originations in the securitized subprime market rose from 20 percent in 2000, to 30 percent in 2004, to 40 percent in 2006. The prevalence of stated income lending left wide room for the loan officer, mortgage broker, or consumer to overstate the consumer's income so the consumer could qualify for a larger loan and the loan officer or broker could receive a larger commission. There is substantial anecdotal evidence that borrower incomes were commonly inflated.

Lenders relying on overstated incomes to make loans could not accurately assess consumers' repayment ability. Evidence of this failure is found in the somewhat steeper increase in the rate of default for low/no doc loans originated when underwriting standards were declining in 2005 and 2006 relative to full documentation loans. . . .

[T]here is reason to believe that creditors did not underwrite [adjustable rate mortgages] to a rate and payment that would take into account the risk to consumers of a payment shock. Creditors also may not have factored in the consumer's obligation for the expected property taxes and insurance, or the increasingly common "piggyback" second-lien loan or line of credit a consumer would use to finance part or all of the down payment.

By frequently basing lending decisions on overstated incomes and understated obligations, creditors were in effect often extending credit based on the value of the collateral, that is, the consumer's house. Moreover, by coupling these practices with a practice of extending credit to borrowers with very limited equity, creditors were often extending credit based on an expectation that the house's value would appreciate rapidly. Creditors may have felt that rapid house price appreciation justified loosening their lending standards, but in some locations house price appreciation was fed by loosened standards, which permitted consumers to take out larger loans and bid up house prices. Loosened lending standards therefore made it more likely that the inevitable readjustment of house prices in these locations would be severe.

In the following testimony before a U.S. Senate subcommittee, Professor Patricia A. McCoy described the role that private-label securitization played in the deterioration of underwriting standards.

Prepared Statement of Patricia A. McCoy, Professor of Law, Univ. of Conn. School of Law

Securitization of Assets: Problems and Solutions: Hearing Before the Subcomm. on Sec., Ins., & Inv. of the Sen. Comm. on Banking, Hous., & Urban Affairs, 111th Cong. 31–32 (2009)

II. The Role of Securitization in the Financial Crisis

A. How Private-Label Securitization Increased the Risk of Mortgage Lending

Before securitization, lenders usually did it all: they solicited loan applicants, underwrote and funded the loans, serviced the loans, and held the loans in portfolio. Lenders earned profits on loans from interest payments as well as from upfront fees. If the loans went into default, the lenders bore the losses. Default was such a serious financial event that lenders took care when underwriting loans.

All that changed with private-label securitization. Securitization allowed lenders to offload most of the default risk associated with nonprime loans. Under the "originate-to-distribute" model, lenders could make loans intending to sell them to investors, knowing that investors would bear the financial brunt if the loans went bellyup. Similarly, securitization altered the compensation structure of nonprime lenders. Lenders made their money on upfront fees collected from borrowers and the cash proceeds from securitization offerings, not on the interest payments on loans.

Lenders liked the security of being paid in advance, instead of having to wait for uncertain monthly payments over the life of loans. And, because they could pass the lion's share of the default risk onto faceless investors, lenders had less reason to care about how well their loans performed. In my examinations of internal records of major nonprime lenders, including [f]ederal thrift institutions and national banks, too often I found two sets of underwriting standards: high standards for the loans they kept on their books and lax standards for the loans that they securitized.

At their peak, investment grade, nonprime residential [MBSs] were considered excellent investments because they supposedly posed minimal default risk while offering high returns. Investors clamored for these bonds, creating demand for ever-riskier loans.

Lenders were not the only players in the chain between borrowers and investors. Investment banks played significant roles as underwriters of nonprime securitizations. Lehman Brothers, Bear Stearns, Merrill Lynch, JP Morgan, Morgan Stanley, Citigroup, and Goldman Sachs underwrote numerous private-label nonprime securitizations. From 2000 through 2002, when [initial public] offerings dried up during the 3-year bear market, [residential] MBS and [collateralized debt obligation] deals stepped into the breach and became one of the hottest profit centers for investment banks.

Investment banks profited from nonprime underwriting by collecting a percentage of the sales proceeds, either in the form of discounts, concessions, or commissions. Once an offering was fully distributed, the underwriter collected its fee in full. This compensation system for the underwriters of subprime offerings caused Donna Tanoue, the former Chairman of the [FDIC], to warn: "[T]he underwriter's motivation appears to be to receive the highest price . . . on behalf of the issuer—not to help curb predatory loans."

Tanoue's warning proved prophetic. In February 2008, Fitch Ratings projected that fully 48 percent of the subprime loans securitized by Wall Street in 2006 would go into default. Despite that dismal performance, 2006 produced record net earnings for Goldman Sachs, Morgan Stanley, Merrill Lynch, Lehman Brothers, and Bear Stearns. That year, manager pay reflected the bottom-line importance that investment banks placed on private-label [residential] MBS, with managing directors in the mortgage divisions of investment banks earning more on average in 2006 than their counterparts in other divisions.

As underwriting standards fell and mortgage defaults increased, academics and consumer advocates proposed a number of policy changes aimed at promoting sounder lending practices. Some argued for applying a suitability standard, which had long been used in securities regulation, to mortgage lending. Such a standard would impose a duty on lenders to recommend or make loans that are suitable for, or in the best interest of, borrowers. *See, e.g.*, Letter from the Nat'l Cmty. Reinvestment Coal. to the Office of Thrift Supervision (Apr. 30, 2007). Barr proposed requiring lenders to offer borrowers a standard set of mortgages, such as a 30-year, fixed-rate mortgage, or a standard five-year adjustable rate mortgage, with reasonable underwriting standards. *See* Michael S. Barr et al., *Behaviorally Informed Financial Services Regulation*, NEW AM. FOUND., 9 (Oct. 2008). Lenders could offer borrowers other, more exotic mortgages alongside this plain vanilla option, but these more exotic mortgages would be subject to heighted regulation and lenders would face greater liability if the mortgage did not work out. *See id.* Receiving a plain vanilla option would make it easier for borrowers to compare loan offers and make it more likely that borrowers would get a straightforward loan they could understand. Congress and regulators took little action in the lead up to the Financial Crisis to rein in weak lending standards.

2. Ability-To-Repay

In the aftermath of the Financial Crisis, Congress addressed declining underwriting standards in the Dodd-Frank Act. One of the ways it sought to improve lending standards was by imposing an ability-to-repay requirement on all residential mortgage lenders. Under the requirement, lenders must make "a reasonable and good faith determination, based on verified and documented information, that the consumer has a reasonable ability to repay the combined payments of all loans on the same dwelling according to the terms of those loans and all applicable taxes, insurance (including mortgage guarantee insurance), and assessments." Dodd-Frank Act, Pub. L. No. 111-203, § 1411(a)(2), 124 Stat. 1376, 2143 (2010). Congress set forth the minimum underwriting standards lenders must follow when determining a borrower's ability to repay.

Minimum Standards for Residential Mortgage Loans

15 U.S.C. § 1639c

(a) ABILITY TO REPAY.—

(1) IN GENERAL.—In accordance with regulations prescribed by the [CFPB], no creditor may make a residential mortgage loan unless the creditor makes a reasonable and good faith determination based on verified and documented information that, at the time the loan is consummated, the consumer has a reasonable ability to repay the loan, according to its terms, and all applicable taxes, insurance (including mortgage guarantee insurance), and assessments. . . .

(3) BASIS FOR DETERMINATION.—A determination under this subsection of a consumer's ability to repay a residential mortgage loan shall include consideration of the consumer's credit history, current income, expected income the consumer is reasonably assured of receiving, current obligations, debt-to-income ratio or the residual income the consumer will have after paying non-mortgage debt and mortgage-related obligations, employment status, and other financial resources other than the consumer's equity in the dwelling or real property that secures repayment of the loan. A creditor shall determine the ability of the consumer to repay using a payment schedule that fully amortizes the loan over the term of the loan.

(4) INCOME VERIFICATION.—A creditor making a residential mortgage loan shall verify amounts of income or assets that such creditor relies on to determine repayment ability, including expected income or assets, by reviewing the consumer's Internal Revenue Service Form W–2, tax returns, payroll receipts, financial institution records, or other third-party documents that provide reasonably reliable evidence of the consumer's income or assets. In order to safeguard against fraudulent reporting, any consideration of a consumer's income history in making a determination under this subsection shall include the verification of such income by the use of—

(A) Internal Revenue Service transcripts of tax returns; or

(B) a method that quickly and effectively verifies income documentation by a third party subject to rules prescribed by the [CFPB]. . . .

Both borrowers and regulators can bring suit against lenders if they fail to comply with the ability-to-repay requirement. A borrower can raise a violation as a defense to foreclosure and is entitled to actual and statutory damages, attorney fees, and, if the violation is material, damages equal to the sum of all finance charges and fees paid by the borrower. *See* 15 U.S.C. § 1640(a), (k). The CFPB and state attorneys general can bring enforcement actions seeking civil monetary penalties and equitable relief. *See* 12 U.S.C. §§ 5514-16; *see also* 15 U.S.C. § 1640(e).

3. Qualified Mortgages

To provide certainty to lenders and future assignees, the Dodd-Frank Act included a presumption that certain qualified mortgages (QMs) would satisfy the ability-to-repay requirement. 15 U.S.C. § 1639c(b). The CFPB rule implementing the provision lays out the minimum requirements for QMs.

Qualified Mortgage Defined

12 C.F.R. § 1026.43(e)(2)

(2) [QM] defined—general. . . . [A QM] is a covered transaction:

(i) That provides for regular periodic payments that are substantially equal, except for the effect that any interest rate change after consummation has on the payment in the case of an adjustable-rate or step-rate mortgage . . . ;

(ii) For which the loan term does not exceed 30 years . . . ;

(iv) For which the creditor underwrites the loan, taking into account the monthly payment for mortgage-related obligations, using:

(A) The maximum interest rate that may apply during the first five years after the date on which the first regular periodic payment will be due; and

(B) Periodic payments of principal and interest that will repay either:

(*1*) The outstanding principal balance over the remaining term of the loan as of the date the interest rate adjusts to the maximum interest rate set forth in paragraph (e)(2)(iv)(A) of this section, assuming the consumer will have made all required payments as due prior to that date; or

(*2*) The loan amount over the loan term;

(v) For which the creditor considers and verifies at or before consummation the following:

(A) The consumer's current or reasonably expected income or assets other than the value of the dwelling . . . that secures the loan . . . ; and

(B) The consumer's current debt obligations, alimony, and child support . . . ; and

(vi) For which the ratio of the consumer's total monthly debt to total monthly income at the time of consummation does not exceed 43 percent. . . .

In addition, QMs generally must have total points and fees equal to 3% or less of the total loan amount. 12 C.F.R. § 1026.43(e)(3). Loans eligible for purchase, guarantee, or insurance by a GSE, FHA, the Department of Veterans Affairs, or the Department of Agriculture are also deemed QMs, and there are special rules in place for small lenders that continue to hold their mortgages after origination. *Id.* at §§ 1026.43(e)(4)(ii)(1), (e)(5).

During the CFPB's rulemaking process on QMs, there was considerable debate over the scope of the presumption that QMs satisfied the ability-to-repay requirement. Consumer advocates pushed for a rebuttable presumption, arguing, among other things, that an absolute safe harbor would allow lenders to "focus on only the letter but not the spirit of the rule," creating an opportunity for lenders to make loans that meet the QM requirements but are not truly affordable for a borrower. *See* Comment from Nat'l Consumer Law Ctr. & Nat'l

Ass'n of Consumer Advocates to the CFPB 7 (July 9, 2012). The financial sector countered that the uncertainty of opportunity for litigation created by a rebuttable presumption would "force lenders to retreat to far more conservative lending standards" and "markedly lessen the availability and affordability of sustainable mortgages to consumers." Letter from Am. Bankers Ass'n et al., to Richard Cordray, Director, CFPB (Apr. 27, 2012).

The CFPB's final rule was a compromise between the two positions. The final rule creates a rebuttable presumption for higher-priced QMs, defined as QMs with an annual percentage rate of 1.5 percentage points or more above the average prime offer rate for first mortgages and 3.5 percentage points or more above the average prime offer rate for second mortgages, first mortgages with balloon payments, or mortgages made under the exclusion for small creditors. *See* 12 C.F.R. § 1026.43(b)(4). It created an irrebuttable safe harbor for all other QMs. *See id.* at § 1026.43(e)(1).

4. Qualified Residential Mortgages and Risk Retention

In addition to seeking to strengthen consumer protections through the ability-to-pay rule, the Dodd-Frank Act also sought to strengthen prudential regulation to correct the misaligned incentives in the securitization process that contributed to the deterioration in underwriting standards. The Dodd-Frank Act directed the banking regulators, the SEC, the U.S. Department of Housing and Urban Development (HUD), and the Federal Housing Finance Agency to develop regulations to require any securitizer to retain at least 5% of the credit risk of any residential mortgage asset it securitizes. Congress created a safe harbor for securitizers issuing securities composed of mortgages that meet certain standards, or qualified residential mortgages (QRMs). *See* Dodd-Frank Act, Pub. L. No. 111-203, § 941, 124 Stat. 1376, 1891–92 (2010). As you will learn in Chapter 12.1, the agencies defined a QRM to have the same meaning as a QM. *See* 12 C.F.R. § 373.13(a).

---

1. ***Ability-to-Repay Requirement and Access to Credit.*** During the congressional debate over the ability-to-repay requirement and the CFPB's rule writing process, financial sector representatives argued that the requirement could harm consumers' access to credit. *See, e.g., Examining How the Dodd-Frank Act Hampers Home Ownership: Hearing Before the H. Subcomm. on Fin. Insts. & Consumer Credit*, 113th Cong. 11–12 (2013) (statement of James Gardill on behalf of the American Bankers Association). One question that emerged during rule-writing was whether the CFPB should include a strong loan-to-value cap and down payment requirements. Did the CFPB get the balance between access, protection, and safety right?

2. ***QM as a Plain Vanilla Mortgage Requirement?*** In its financial reform plan, the Obama Administration initially proposed that mortgage lenders be required to offer plain vanilla mortgages, to be defined by the CFPB. *See* U.S. DEP'T OF THE TREASURY, FINANCIAL REGULATORY REFORM, A NEW FOUNDATION: REBUILDING FINANCIAL SUPERVISION AND REGULATION 66 (June 17, 2009). Confronted with strong opposition, the House of Representatives removed the plain vanilla mortgage proposal before marking up the financial reform

legislation. *See, e.g.*, *Community and Consumer Advocates' Perspectives on the Obama Administration's Financial Regulatory Reform Proposals*, 111th Cong. 21–22 (2009) (statement of Rep. Jeb Hensarling opposing plain vanilla mortgage proposal). Later, however, Congress added the QM exception to the ability-to-repay requirement and the QRM exemption to the risk-retention requirement. Consider whether the QM and QRM exceptions operate like a plain vanilla mortgage requirement by providing a strong incentive for lenders to offer safer, more standardized mortgages, while permitting lenders to offer other products subject to heightened liability. Some commentators have estimated that virtually all mortgages fall within the QM and QRM exceptions. *See, e.g.*, CTR. FOR RESPONSIBLE LENDING, CFPB REGULATIONS ESTABLISH A BROAD QUALIFIED MORTGAGE EXEMPTION (Jan. 3, 2014) (estimating that 95% of the current mortgage market is covered by the QM safe harbor).

B. INTEGRATED DISCLOSURE

For decades, federal law required lenders to provide borrowers with two overlapping, inconsistent disclosure forms, one when the borrower applied for a loan and another at closing. One set of forms was mandated by the Truth in Lending Act (TILA) and designed by the Federal Reserve Board. The other was mandated by the Real Estate Settlement Procedures Act (RESPA) and designed by HUD.

In mandating the forms, Congress sought to ensure that consumers received accurate and meaningful disclosures of the cost of their loans, to make it easier for consumers to compare loan products, and to ensure that home buyers had advance notice of settlement costs, the costs borrowers pay at closing. *See* 15 U.S.C. §1601(a) (1976); *see also* 12 U.S.C. § 2601(b)(1) (1974). The forms, however, were universally disliked; borrowers often found the forms confusing and lenders considered the forms "burdensome to provide and explain." Integrated Mortgage Disclosures Under [RESPA] (Regulation X) and [TILA] (Regulation Z), 78 Fed. Reg. 79,730, 79,730 (Dec. 31, 2013) (codified at 12 C.F.R. §§ 1024, 1026). Moreover, multiple studies found that the disclosures did little to improve consumer understanding or the quality of loans consumers received. *See, e.g.,* Omri Ben-Shahar & Carl E. Schneider, *The Failure of Mandated Disclosure*, 159 U. PA. L. REV. 647, 665–67 (2011).

To increase the likelihood of consumer comprehension, the Dodd-Frank Act directed the CFPB to develop a new "single, integrated" disclosure form for mortgages. 12 U.S.C. § 2603(a); *see also* 15 U.S.C. § 1604(b). The Dodd-Frank Act also directed the CFPB to use new testing procedures when developing model disclosures, including the integrated TILA-RESPA disclosure, and provided for an innovative new procedure to allow market participants to test disclosures in the market place with waivers from existing requirements for piloting new approaches. *See* Dodd-Frank Act §§ 1032(b)(3), (e).

The following excerpt from a report by a consultant that worked with the CFPB to create the integrated TILA-RESPA disclosure describes how the CFPB used consumer testing when developing the form.

Kleimann Communication Group, "Know Before You Owe: Quantitative Study of the Current and Integrated TILA-RESPA Disclosures"

Know Before You Owe: Quantitative Study of the Current and Integrated TILA-RESPA Disclosures, xv–xvi (Nov. 20, 2013)

Importance of Consumer Testing

The Mortgage Disclosure Project shows the advantages and benefits of two types of consumer testing: Qualitative Testing and Quantitative Testing.

Qualitative Testing

The Qualitative Study ensured that consumers could comprehend the basic facts about a loan, could compare two initial loan disclosures, and could state their reasons for making that choice. The study also allowed the CFPB to design the proposed disclosures on an iterative basis, using the qualitative testing results of one round to refine the designs of the integrated disclosures for the next round. Further, it allowed the development of the Closing Disclosure with the Loan Estimate to enable better comparison between the initial and final disclosures. In addition, the inclusion of industry representatives in the qualitative testing allowed the CFPB to ensure that industry personnel could understand the disclosures and explain them to consumers. The CFPB understands that consumers do not obtain or close loans in isolation and often discuss the disclosures with loan officers and settlement agents. . . .

Quantitative Testing

The Quantitative Study looked at both the current and the proposed disclosures used at application and at closing. Thus, the study allowed the CFPB to compare the performance of the proposed disclosure to the current disclosure to ensure that the proposed disclosure showed significant improved performance. The CFPB wanted to ensure that it was not merely changing the disclosures, but improving and streamlining the mortgage disclosures for consumers.

The Quantitative Study confirmed that the proposed disclosures indeed performed better and we can extrapolate that the disclosures then provided benefits in ease of use and understanding for consumers. Importantly, the differences between the current and proposed disclosures were statistically significant whether considering all respondents, experienced versus inexperienced respondents, easier versus more challenging loans, or fixed versus adjustable rate loans.

The results also provided an added advantage to the CFPB by allowing it to identify areas in which the proposed disclosures did not perform well before issuing the Final Rule. For only 4 questions did the current disclosures perform better and only one [question, regarding closing costs,] was statistically significant. . . . Based on these results, the CFPB examined the answers [to the closing costs question], identified why respondents answered incorrectly, further improved the disclosure, and tested the change with consumers in an additional round of qualitative testing. . . . Thus, the results of the quantitative testing helped to ensure even better performance on the disclosures before issuing the Final Rule. . . .

The thoroughness of the qualitative testing ensured that the disclosures resulted in improved consumer comprehension, comparison, and more knowledgeable choices. The quantitative testing documents the benefits of the new disclosures. . . .

Figure 5.2-2 shows the new, integrated loan estimate and closing disclosure form.

Figure 5.2-2 TILA-RESPA Integrated Disclosure

FICUS BANK
4321 Random Boulevard • Somecity, ST 12340

Save this Loan Estimate to compare with your Closing Disclosure.

Loan Estimate

DATE ISSUED	2/15/2013
APPLICANTS	Michael Jones and Mary Stone 123 Anywhere Street Anytown, ST 12345
PROPERTY	456 Somewhere Avenue Anytown, ST 12345
SALE PRICE	$180,000

LOAN TERM	30 years
PURPOSE	Purchase
PRODUCT	Fixed Rate
LOAN TYPE	☒ Conventional ☐ FHA ☐ VA ☐ ______
LOAN ID #	123456789
RATE LOCK	☐ NO ☒ YES, until 4/16/2013 at 5:00 p.m. EDT *Before closing, your interest rate, points, and lender credits can change unless you lock the interest rate. All other estimated closing costs expire on* ***3/4/2013*** *at 5:00 p.m. EDT*

Loan Terms		Can this amount increase after closing?
Loan Amount	$162,000	**NO**
Interest Rate	3.875%	**NO**
Monthly Principal & Interest *See Projected Payments below for your Estimated Total Monthly Payment*	$761.78	**NO**
		Does the loan have these features?
Prepayment Penalty		**YES** • **As high as $3,240** if you pay off the loan during the first 2 years
Balloon Payment		**NO**

Projected Payments		
Payment Calculation	**Years 1-7**	**Years 8-30**
Principal & Interest	$761.78	$761.78
Mortgage Insurance	+ 82	+ —
Estimated Escrow *Amount can increase over time*	+ 206	+ 206
Estimated Total Monthly Payment	$1,050	$968

		This estimate includes	In escrow?
Estimated Taxes, Insurance & Assessments *Amount can increase over time*	$206 a month	☒ Property Taxes	YES
		☒ Homeowner's Insurance	YES
		☐ Other:	
		See Section G on page 2 for escrowed property costs. You must pay for other property costs separately.	

Costs at Closing		
Estimated Closing Costs	$8,054	Includes $5,672 in Loan Costs + $2,382 in Other Costs – $0 in Lender Credits. *See page 2 for details.*
Estimated Cash to Close	$16,054	Includes Closing Costs. *See Calculating Cash to Close on page 2 for details.*

Visit **www.consumerfinance.gov/mortgage-estimate** for general information and tools.

LOAN ESTIMATE PAGE 1 OF 3 • LOAN ID # 123456789

Source: CFPB, Loan Estimate 1 (2013).

---

1. ***Disclosure as a Regulatory Approach.*** Do you think disclosures like the integrated loan estimate and closing disclosure form will help consumers make better, more informed choices? We will consider the pros and cons of mandatory disclosure in detail in Chapter 5.4.

C. HOME OWNERSHIP AND EQUITY PROTECTION ACT

In 1994, Congress passed the HOEPA, Subtitle B of Title I of the Riegle-Neal Cmty. Dev. and Regulatory Improvement Act, Pub. L. No. 103-325, 108 Stat.

2190 (1994) (codified in scattered sections of 15 U.S.C.). The legislation, which was designed to "shine a bright spotlight on high-cost subprime loans," was prompted by increasing reports of abusive home lending in disadvantaged communities. EDWARD M. GRAMLICH, SUBPRIME MORTGAGES: AMERICA'S LATEST BOOM AND BUST 27 (Urban Inst. Press, 2007).

Rather than imposing an outright ban on loans with high interest rates and fees, HOEPA subjected loans with rates or fees that exceed a certain threshold to increased disclosure requirements, substantive restrictions, and enhanced liability. For high-cost loans—that is, loans that exceeded the prescribed thresholds—HOEPA prohibited certain loan terms and practices, including balloon payments, prepayment penalty periods longer than five years, and lending without first verifying a borrower's ability to repay the loan. *See* 15 U.S.C. § 1639. It also imposed heightened statutory damages for violations of these provisions and increased liability on assignees, or purchasers, of covered loans. *See id.* §§ 1640(e), 1641.

Despite these protections, HOEPA largely failed to provide meaningful protections against subprime and predatory lending in the lead up to the Financial Crisis. For one, HOEPA covered only refinances and closed-end home equity loans, not mortgages that borrowers used to purchase houses. Moreover, lenders could easily evade HOEPA's restrictions by structuring loans to fall just below HOEPA's bright line, high thresholds. As a result, between 2004 and 2011, HOEPA's restrictions covered less than one half of 1% of all refinance or home-improvement loans. High-Cost Mortgage and Homeownership Counseling Amendments to the Truth in Lending Act (Regulation Z) and Homeownership Counseling Amendments to the Real Estate Settlement Procedures Act (Regulation X), 78 Fed. Reg. 6,856, 6,858 (Jan. 31, 2013) (codified at 12 C.F.R. §§ 1024, 1026).

As subprime and predatory lending grew in the late 1990s, both consumer advocates, other government agencies, and even Federal Reserve Board Governors themselves repeatedly called for the Federal Reserve Board to use its broad regulatory authority under HOEPA to strengthen and expand HOEPA's protections. *See, e.g.,* EDWARD M. GRAMLICH, SUBPRIME MORTGAGES: AMERICA'S LATEST BOOM AND BUST 86–91 (Urban Inst. Press, 2007); *see also* HUD & U.S. DEP'T OF THE TREASURY, CURBING PREDATORY HOME MORTGAGE LENDING 111–12 (June 20, 2000). HOEPA specifically directed the Federal Reserve Board to "prohibit acts or practices in connection with . . . mortgage loans that the [Federal Reserve Board] finds to be unfair, deceptive, or designed to evade the provision of [HOEPA]." 15 U.S.C. § 1639(p)(2)(a). The Federal Reserve Board, however, resisted. Chairman Alan Greenspan was explicit that he was not interested in further mortgage regulation. *See* FCIC, THE FINANCIAL CRISIS INQUIRY REPORT 79, 95 (Jan. 2011). The Federal Reserve Board only issued new rules under HOEPA in 2008, a year after the subprime mortgage market's implosion. Truth in Lending (Regulation Z), 73 Fed. Reg. 44,522 (July 30, 2008) (codified at 12 C.F.R. § 226).

In 2010, Congress expanded HOEPA's coverage and protections in the Dodd-Frank Act. First, the Dodd-Frank Act expands the scope of HOEPA to include purchase-money mortgages and open-ended home equity loans. *See* Dodd-Frank Act, Pub. L. No. 111–203, § 1431, 124 Stat. 1376, 2157–60 (2010). Second, it revises the triggers for HOEPA coverage by lowering the fee trigger from 8% to 5% and expanding the charges that must be included in the fee calculation. *See id.* The Dodd-Frank Act also adds a new prepayment penalty trigger. Loans with prepayment penalties after 36 months or with prepayment penalties exceeding 2% prepaid are deemed high-cost. *See id.* Finally, it strengthens and expands the restrictions that apply to high-cost mortgages to include, among other things, bans on balloon payments, caps on late fees, and restrictions on fees and pre-payment penalties. *See id.* at § 1433. The Dodd-Frank Act also requires lenders to confirm that borrowers have received counseling from a federally-approved housing counselor before extending them a high-cost loan. *See id.*

---

1. ***The Lessons of HOEPA.*** What lessons do you take away from HOEPA's failure to stem predatory and subprime lending in the lead up to the Financial Crisis? Was it a failure of regulatory design? Or regulator inaction? Consider that in 2014, out of six million loan originations nationwide, only 1,263 were covered by HOEPA. *See* Press Release, Federal Financial Institutions Examination Council Announces Availability of 2014 Data on Mortgage Lending (Sept. 22, 2015). Is it desirable for lenders to structure loans so that they are not covered by HOEPA?

D. YIELD SPREAD PREMIUMS

Many of the abusive practices in mortgage origination that arose before the Financial Crisis occurred, in part, because of the imbalance of knowledge and experience between the typical borrower and the mortgage broker or loan officer. These brokers and loan officers often had incentives that were not aligned with borrowers' interests. A particularly serious principal-agent problem arose because of a common compensation structure under which the broker would receive payment from both the borrower and the lender. The lender would pay the mortgage broker a commission for originating the loan, while the borrower would pay the mortgage broker an origination fee as compensation for the "time and expense of working with the [borrower] to submit the loan application." Loan Originator Compensation Requirements Under the Truth in Lending Act (Regulation Z), 78 Fed. Reg. 11,280, 11,286 (Feb. 15, 2013) (codified at 12 C.F.R. § 1026). This compensation structure was problematic because the borrower would often pay these fees to the broker without knowing it was not the broker's sole source of revenue from the transaction. Moreover, some commentators have observed that "[b]orrowers whose brokers are paid both directly by the borrower and by the lender, as most were, pay more in closing costs than borrowers who pay the broker directly." Comment from Nat'l Consumer Law Ctr. et al. to the CFPB 7 (Oct. 16, 2012).

An especially controversial aspect of mortgage broker compensation was the yield spread premium—a commission paid to the broker by the lender that varied with the interest rate of the loan. Because loans with higher interest rates resulted in higher commissions, the use of yield spread premiums led to a steering problem whereby brokers had a lucrative incentive to steer borrowers to higher cost loans. *See, e.g.*, Loan Originator Compensation Requirements Under the Truth in Lending Act (Regulation Z), 78 Fed. Reg. at 11,286 (Feb. 15, 2013).

Moreover, this practice was not well-known among borrowers. *See, e.g.*, Howell E. Jackson & Laurie Burlingame, *Kickbacks or Compensation: The Case of Yield Spread Premiums*, 12 STAN. J.L. BUS. & FIN. 289, 291 (2007).

Borrowers brought class actions under RESPA in an attempt to rein in the use of yield spread premiums. Borrowers were initially successful in arguing for a favorable interpretation of RESPA and obtaining class certification. *See, e.g.*, Culpepper v. Inland Mortg. Corp., 132 F.3d 692 (11th Cir. 1998) (setting forth a two-pronged test under RESPA's kickback provisions requiring the factfinder to determine whether the yield spread premium was related to a good or service rendered and, if so, whether the premium was reasonable); *see also* Glover v. Standard Fed. Bank, 283 F.3d 953 (D. Minn. 2000) (adopting the *Culpepper* test and granting class certification). Just a year after the borrower-friendly *Culpepper* decision, however, HUD issued a policy statement that accepted a more broker-friendly interpretation of RESPA, permitting yield spread premiums as long as they were reasonable. *See* Real Estate Settlement Procedures Act (RESPA) Statement of Policy 1999-1 Regarding Lender Payments to Mortgage Brokers, 64 Fed. Reg. 10,080 (Mar. 1, 1999) (codified at 12 C.F.R. § 3500).

While class action litigation tapered off after the promulgation of HUD's policy statement, the controversy did not. The following excerpt discusses the costs of yield spread premiums incurred by borrowers.

Howell E. Jackson & Laurie Burlingame, Kickbacks or Compensation: The Case of Yield Spread Premiums

12 STAN. J.L. BUS. & FIN. 289, 295–96 (2007)

[This paper] presents an empirical study of approximately 3,000 mortgage financings of a major lending institution operating on a nationwide basis through both a network of independent mortgage brokers and some direct lending. The data for this study was obtained through discovery in litigation that has subsequently been settled and for which one of the authors served as an expert witness on behalf of the plaintiff class. . . . [T]he study suggests that for transactions involving yield spread premiums, mortgage brokers received substantially more compensation than they did in transactions without yield spread premiums. Depending on the method of comparison, the estimated difference in mortgage broker compensation range from $600 to $1200 per transaction, and our best guess of the average cost impact is approximately $800 to $900 per loan. This difference in mortgage broker compensation is statistically significant and robust to a variety of formulations, which include controls for type of loan, creditworthiness of transactions, neighborhood characteristics and geographic regions.

Industry representatives have long argued that yield spread premiums are not harmful to consumers because these payments are recouped through lower direct payments to mortgage brokers. However, our analysis suggests that this claim is baseless, at least with respect to samples included in our database. With a high degree of statistical confidence and using multiple formulations, we can reject the proposition that consumers fully recoup the cost of yield spread premiums. Our best estimate is the consumers get less than thirty-five cents of value for every dollar of yield spread premiums, a very bad deal for consumers.

Our study also provides evidence that the payment of yield spread premiums may allow mortgage brokers to engage in price discrimination among borrowers. In transactions where yield spread premiums are not present—that is, where mortgages receive only direct cash compensation—brokers seldom receive total compensation of more than 1.5% of loan value, and the largest group (on the order of 40 to 45%) pay mortgage brokers compensation in the range of 1.0 to 1.5% of loan values. In other words, when borrowers can easily monitor mortgage broker compensation, there is a pretty clear market price for mortgage broker services. But when yield spread premiums are present, consumers have a harder time telling how much they are paying their brokers. Many borrowers pay more than 1.5% of loan value; more than a third pay more than 2.0% of loan value; and roughly ten percent pay more than 3.5 percent of loan value. This price dispersion strongly suggests that yield spread premiums are not simply another form of mortgage broker compensation, but rather a unique form of compensation that allows mortgage brokers to extract excessive payments from many consumers. Our study suggests that the least sophisticated borrowers, including Hispanics and African Americans, may be particularly susceptible to these abusive pricing practices. . . .

---

1. ***The Financial Sector's Views.*** The Mortgage Bankers Association argued that "yield spread premiums can be an important financing option" that "clearly is a borrower choice issue when used properly, based upon a borrower's individual financial goals, desires, and circumstances." *Predatory Mortgage Lending Practices: Abusive Uses of Yield Spread Premiums: Hearing Before the S. Comm. On Banking, Hous., & Urban Affairs*, 107th Cong. 18 (2002) (statement of John Courson, Chairman-Elect, Mortgage Bankers Ass'n). The National Association of Mortgage Brokers sounded a similar theme, emphasizing the need for flexible indirect compensation methods and less class action litigation in light of "record homeownership rates" and robust demand for brokers' services. *Id.* at 20–21 (statement of Joseph L. Falk, President, National Association of Mortgage Brokers).

2. ***HUD's Attempted Disclosure Reform.*** In 2002, HUD attempted to improve disclosure of yield spread premiums by proposing a rule that would require brokers to disclose any compensation they received from lenders as such, including any portions of yield spread premiums. *See* Real Estate Settlement Procedures Act (RESPA); Simplifying and Improving the Process of Obtaining Mortgages to Reduce Settlement Costs to Consumers, 67 Fed. Reg. 49,134 (proposed July 29, 2002) (to be codified at 24 C.F.R. § 3500). Opposition to the proposed rule was fierce; HUD received more than 45,000 comment letters. Moreover, the Federal Trade Commission (FTC) released a study in 2004 showing that, upon testing, the proposed disclosures have the opposite of the intended effect. The FTC study found that the disclosures "reduce significantly the proportion of respondents correctly identifying the less expensive loan and the proportion stating they would choose that loan if they were shopping for a mortgage." JAMES M. LACKO & JANIS K. PAPPALARDO, FED. TRADE COMM'N, BUREAU OF ECON., THE EFFECTS OF MORTGAGE BROKER COMPENSATION DISCLOSURES ON CONSUMERS AND COMPETITION: A CONTROLLED EXPERIMENT 57 (Feb. 2004); *see also* MACRO INT'L INC., CONSUMER TESTING OF MORTGAGE BROKER DISCLOSURES 26-27 (July 2008) (report prepared at the request of the Federal Reserve Board). The combined weight of this opposition led HUD to withdraw its proposal in March 2004. For further discussion of HUD's failed attempt at disclosure reform, see Jackson & Burlingame, *Kickbacks or Compensation*, at 306–07; *see also* Michael S. Barr et al., *The Case for*

Behaviorally Informed Regulation, *in* NEW PERSPECTIVES ON REGULATION 25 (David A. Moss & John A. Cisternino eds., 2009).

3. ***Post-Financial Crisis Reforms.*** In August 2009, the Federal Reserve Board proposed to amend Regulation Z to ban yield spread premiums. *See* Truth in Lending; Proposed Rule, 74 Fed. Reg. 43,232 (Aug. 26, 2009). Before the Federal Reserve Board finalized its proposal, Congress adopted a statutory prohibition on yield spread premiums paid to a mortgage originator in the Dodd-Frank Act. 15 U.S.C. § 1639b. The Dodd-Frank Act also prohibits mortgage originators from receiving double compensation, *i.e.* compensation from both the borrower and another party, subject to certain exceptions. *See* 15 U.S.C. § 1639b. In 2013, the CFPB adopted a final rule that refines the Dodd-Frank Act's requirements. *See* Loan Originator Compensation Requirements Under the Truth in Lending Act (Regulation Z), 78 Fed. Reg. 11,280 (Feb. 15, 2013) (codified at 12 C.F.R. § 1026).

The bans on yield spread premiums and double compensation are examples of another regulatory tool—a duty that imposes a negative prohibition—that we will discuss in Chapter 5.4. Do you think that the negative prohibition against yield spread premiums is a better approach than the disclosure model HUD proposed in 2002? What are the potential costs and benefits of the alternative approaches?

4. ***Discrimination in Mortgage Lending.*** In the previous excerpt, Professors Howell Jackson and Laurie Burlingame noted that yield spread premiums disproportionately affected Hispanics and African Americans. Discriminatory practices have long been prevalent in mortgage lending. Although redlining, the practice of denying or limiting credit to certain geographic areas based on racial or ethnic demographics, has been illegal since the passage of the Fair Housing Act in 1968, disparities in credit denials and the pricing of credit have remained a persistent and troubling practice. *See* Michael S. Barr, *Credit Where It Counts: The Community Reinvestment Act and Its Critics*, 75 N.Y.U. L. Rev. 513, 544–54 (2005). As you saw in Chapter 5.1, several federal laws—including the Equal Credit Opportunity Act (ECOA) and Fair Housing Act—aim to prohibit discrimination in credit transactions on the basis of race, color, religion, sex, and other characteristics. Lenders can be liable under the ECOA for either disparate treatment, in which they discriminate between borrowers on a prohibited basis, or disparate impact, in which their facially neutral lending policies result in adverse effects on a protected class of individuals. *See* CFPB, CFPB CONSUMER LAWS AND REGULATIONS: EQUAL CREDIT OPPORTUNITY ACT (2013). In 2015, the Supreme Court held that disparate impact claims are also cognizable under the Fair Housing Act, in addition to disparate treatment claims. *See* Tex. Dep't of Hous. & Cmty. Affairs v. The Inclusive Cmtys. Project, Inc., 135 S. Ct. 2507 (2015). What do you think a plaintiff should have to show to establish a disparate impact claim under the ECOA or Fair Housing Act? Are limitations on disparate impact claims necessary to protect potential defendants? For further discussion of the use of disparate impact analysis under ECOA, see, *e.g.*, David Skanderson & Dubravka Ritter, *Fair Lending Analysis of Credit Cards* (Fed. Reserve Bank of Philadelphia, Discussion Paper, Aug. 2014). For a more general treatment, see, for example, Ian Ayres, *Market Power and Inequality: A Competitive Conduct*

Standard for Assessing When Disparate Impacts Are Unjustified, 95 CAL. L. REV. 669 (2007). For a critique of the use of disparate impact in this area, see, for example, Andrew L. Sandler & Kirk D. Jensen, *Disparate Impact in Fair Lending: A Theory Without a Basis and the Law of Unintended Consequences*, BANKING & FIN. SERV. (Aug. 2014).

5. ***The Trilateral Dilemma in Financial Services.*** The manner in which some mortgage brokers abused borrowers through the use of yield spread premiums is just one example of financial services providers increasing their profits by exploiting their discretionary authority. This more general phenomenon has been labeled the trilateral dilemma, whereby consumers' decisions are steered by financial services providers towards a "financial product or service that produces a collateral benefit" for the provider, which is hard for consumers to detect and is made possible by the increasing complexity and quantity of consumers' financial decisions. Howell E. Jackson, *The Trilateral Dilemma in Financial Regulation*, in OVERCOMING THE SAVING SLUMP: HOW TO INCREASE THE EFFECTIVENESS OF FINANCIAL EDUCATION AND SAVING PROGRAMS 82 (Annamaria Lusardi, ed., 2009). We have seen examples of the trilateral dilemma in several other contexts, such as payment for order flow in Chapter 4.4. Does the pervasive nature of this dilemma suggest that it is a widespread problem in consumer finance?

IV. FEDERAL PREEMPTION AND STATE MORTGAGE REGULATION

Recall from Chapter 1.4 that the Supreme Court's decision in *Marquette Nat'l Bank v. First Omaha Service Corp.*, 439 U.S. 299 (1978), allowed a national bank chartered in one state to export that state's interest rates to its dealings in another state. The *Marquette* decision turned on the Supreme Court's interpretation of the National Bank Act, 12 U.S.C. § 85. The Court held, in effect, that the National Bank Act trumped the usury laws of all states other than those of a national bank's home state. Under this authority, national banks came to offer unified national pricing of credit cards, as well as other products, by locating their activities in a state, such as South Dakota, without usury caps. In this section, we explore federal preemption of state consumer protection law in greater detail, with a focus on state mortgage regulation.

A. PREEMPTION BEFORE THE DODD-FRANK ACT

In the late 1990s, in response to growing subprime and predatory lending, and the weakness of federal rules, states began enacting legislation to regulate mortgage lending, especially high-cost mortgage lending. *See* Raphael W. Bostic et al., *State and Local Anti-Predatory Lending Laws: The Effect of Legal Enforcement Mechanisms*, 60 J. ECON. & BUS. 47, 49 (2008). Many states modeled their legislation after the HOEPA but often set lower triggers for their statute's protections and prohibited more abusive terms and practices. *Id.* By the eve of the Financial Crisis in 2007, more than half of the states had adopted anti-predatory lending legislation. *Id.* at 48.

Commercial banks argued that these state laws made it difficult for them to operate nationwide. The state laws forced commercial banks to "craft different products or services (with associated procedures and policies, and their attendant additional costs) for each state in which it does business, or elect not to provide all of its products or services (to the detriment of consumers) in one or more states." Bank Activities and Operations; Real Estate Lending and Appraisals, 69 Fed. Reg. 1,904, 1,907 (Jan. 13, 2004) (codified at 12 C.F.R. §§ 7, 34). Commercial banks argued that the state laws should be preempted by the National Bank Act.

In 2004, the OCC adopted broad regulations preempting the application of state anti-predatory laws to national banks under the National Bank Act. 12 C.F.R. § 34.4(a). The regulation provided that "state laws that obstruct, impair, or condition a national bank's ability to fully exercise its Federally authorized real estate lending powers do not apply to national banks." *Id.* It also provided that "a national bank may make real estate loans . . . without regard to state law limitations concerning" interest rates, mortgage origination and servicing, disclosures, and loan terms. *Id.* The Office of Thrift Supervision also broadly preempted state anti-predatory lending laws' application to federally chartered thrifts.

Shortly thereafter, the question arose whether federal preemption also applied to a bank's operating subsidiary. In *Watters v. Wachovia Bank, N.A.*, 550 U.S. 1 (2007), Wachovia Bank insisted that the National Bank Act preempted Michigan's financial regulatory agency from registering and examining its operating subsidiary, a state-chartered mortgage company. The Supreme Court sided with Wachovia, reiterating the federal preemption standard it established in *Barnett Bank of Marion County, N.A. v. Nelson*, 517 U.S. 25 (1996):

> States are permitted to regulate the activities of national banks where doing so does not prevent or significantly interfere with the national bank's or the national bank regulator's exercise of its powers. But when state prescriptions significantly impair the exercise of authority, enumerated or incidental under the [National Bank Act], the State's regulations must give way. *Barnett Bank*, 517 U.S. at 32-34. . . .
>
> [R]eal estate lending, when conducted by a national bank, is immune from state visitorial control: The [National Bank Act] specifically vests exclusive authority to examine and inspect in OCC. 12 U.S.C. § 484(a) ("No national bank shall be subject to any visitorial powers except as authorized by Federal law."). . . .
>
> Michigan, therefore, cannot confer on its commissioner examination and enforcement authority over mortgage lending, or any other banking business done by national banks. . . .
>
> [Michigan] argues that the State's regulatory regime survives preemption with respect to national banks' operating subsidiaries. Because such subsidiaries are separately chartered under some State's law, [Michigan] characterizes them simply as "affiliates" of national banks, and contends that even though they are subject to

> OCC's superintendence, they are also subject to multistate control. We disagree. . . .
>
> [J]ust as duplicative state examination, supervision, and regulation would significantly burden mortgage lending when engaged in by national banks, so too would those state controls interfere with that same activity when engaged in by an operating subsidiary.

Watters, 550 U.S. at 12–13, 15–18.

There has been extensive debate over what role the preemption of state anti-predatory lending laws played in the Financial Crisis. Raymond Natter, the Deputy Chief Counsel at the OCC from 1995 to 2004, and Katie Wechsler argued that preemption played little role in the Financial Crisis because national banks and their subsidiaries accounted for only a small share of the subprime mortgage originations. *See* Raymond Natter & Katie Wechsler, *Dodd-Frank Act and National Bank Preemption: Much Ado About Nothing*, 7 VA. L. & BUS. REV. 301, 329–34 (2012). By contrast, in testimony before the Financial Crisis Inquiry Commission (FCIC), Illinois Attorney General Lisa Madigan argued that national banks' contribution was not insignificant—in 2006 "national banks, federal thrifts, and their operating subsidiaries were responsible for 31.5 percent of subprime mortgage loans. . . ." Lisa Madigan, Ill. Att'y Gen., Testimony before the FCIC 10 (Jan. 14, 2010). Moreover, Madigan argued that federal preemption and the lack of federal action on predatory practices made it difficult to enforce state laws that remained on the books. Madigan asserted that "states found it extremely difficult to enact underwriting standards and other lending reforms for state-licensed entities" because state licenses demanded "that they should be subject to the same lax standards as federal charters." Madigan further argued that "states struggled to make the argument that the predatory practices and products which fueled the oncoming [Financial Crisis] were unfair and deceptive, because the federal regulators' refusal to reform those practices and products served as an implicit endorsement of their legality." *Id.* at 11. Similarly, some scholars have argued that federal preemption "effectively gut[ted] states' ability to legislate against predatory lending practices and set[ ] federal law as a de facto ceiling for borrower protection from abusive lending." Nicholas Bagley, *The Unwarranted Regulatory Preemption of Predatory Lending Laws,* 79 N.Y.U. L. REV. 2274, 2275 (2004).

Just two years after *Watters*, the Supreme Court again addressed the issue of National Bank Act preclusion of state laws in *Cuomo v. Clearing House Ass'n, L.L.C.*, 557 U.S. 519 (2009). The Attorney General for the State of New York, in an enforcement action of the state's fair lending laws, sought non-public information from national banks regarding their lending practices. The OCC filed suit, claiming that enforcement of the fair lending laws was preempted by its regulation, which interpreted the National Bank Act. Despite the similarity between New York's conduct and the visitorial powers exercised by Michigan in *Watters*, the Court declined to find preemption. Instead, the Court invoked the "well established distinction between supervision and law enforcement" and argued that New York's conduct fell under the latter. *Id.* at 528 ("*Watters* held that a State may not exercise 'general supervision and control' over a subsidiary of a national bank, because 'multiple audits and surveillance under rival oversight regimes' would cause uncertainty. '[G]eneral supervision and control' and 'oversight' are worlds apart from law enforcement.") (citations omitted). Moving beyond legal distinctions, note the Financial Crisis context of *Cuomo.* Perhaps the greater scrutiny of consumer protection violations, which were arguably fueled by blanket preemption of more stringent state visitorial powers, nudged the Court away from applying *Watters*. *See, e.g.*, Arthur E. Wilmarth, Jr., Cuomo v. Clearing House: *The Supreme Court Responds to the Subprime Financial Crisis and Delivers a Major Victory for the Dual Banking System and Consumer Protection, in* THE PANIC OF 2008: CAUSES, CONSEQUENCES, AND IMPLICATIONS FOR REFORM 19 (Lawrence E. Mitchell & Arthur E. Wilmarth, Jr., eds., 2010) ("The most plausible explanation for the three Justices' change in perspective [in *Cuomo*] is that they were influenced by the outbreak of the subprime financial crisis in August 2007 and by subsequent federal bailouts of several major national banks that were deeply involved in nonprime lending.").

B. PREEMPTION AFTER THE DODD-FRANK ACT

In the Dodd-Frank Act, Congress codified *Cuomo*, overruled the holding of *Watters,* and established a statutory preemption standard that was arguably narrower than the OCC's "obstruct, impair, or condition" standard. The Dodd-Frank Act provides that "state consumer financial laws" are preempted only if: (a) application of such a law "would have a discriminatory effect on national banks"; (b) either the OCC "on a case-by-case basis" or a court determines, "in accordance with the legal standard for preemption" described in *Barnett Bank of Marion Cnty., N.A. v. Nelson*, 517 U.S. 25 (1996), that the law "prevents or significantly interferes with the exercise by the national bank of its powers"; or (c) the law is preempted by a federal law other than the National Bank Act. 12 U.S.C. § 25b(b)(1).

The requirement that the OCC make case-by-case preemption determinations is notable for several reasons. First, the OCC's case-by-case determinations are not entitled to *Chevron* deference. A reviewing court is required to go beyond assessing whether the OCC's interpretation of the state law's effect on the National Bank Act is a reasonable one. Rather, the court must evaluate the "thoroughness" and validity of the OCC's reasoning, the "consistency with other valid determinations" made by the OCC, and "any other factors which the court finds persuasive and relevant to its decision." 12 U.S.C. § 25b(b)(5)(A). Second, the OCC's case-by-case determination must be supported by substantial evidence. *See id.* at § 25b(c). Third, the Dodd-Frank Act requires the OCC to publish a quarterly listing of its preemption determinations and to conduct a review of its determinations every five years. *See id.* at § 25b(d), (g). Finally, the OCC's determination must be made in consultation with the CFPB. *See id.* at § 25b(b)(3)(B).

Scholars and practitioners are divided on whether the Dodd-Frank Act's preemption standard is actually significantly narrower than the analogous OCC standard that came before it. *Compare* Kathleen C. Engel & Patricia A. McCoy, *Federal Preemption and Consumer Financial Protection: Past and Future*, 3 BANKING & FIN. SERVICES POL'Y REP. 25 (2012), *with* Raymond Natter & Katie Wechsler, *Dodd-Frank Act and National Bank Preemption: Much Ado about Nothing*, 7 VA. L. & BUS. REV. 301 (2012). Based on the language of the two standards, do you think that the Dodd-Frank Act has made preemption more difficult?

Perhaps not surprisingly, the OCC itself concluded that "the Dodd-Frank Act does not create a new, stand-alone "prevents or significantly interferes" preemption standard, but, rather, incorporates the conflict preemption legal standard and the reasoning that supports it in the Supreme Court's *Barnett* decision." Office of Thrift Supervision Integration; Dodd-Frank Act Implementation, 76 Fed. Reg. 43,549, 43,555 (July 21, 2011) (codified at 12 C.F.R §§ 5, 7, 34). The OCC reasoned that, because other provisions of the Dodd-Frank Act referred to *Barnett* but did not include the "prevent or significantly interferes" phrase, Congress could not have intended for different preemption standards to apply to similar provisions referring to *Barnett*. *See id.* The OCC therefore read the statutory preemption standard as one that codified *Barnett*.

The OCC reaffirmed all of its pre-Dodd-Frank Act preemption decisions. *See id.* It did so without making a case-by-case determination or consulting with the CFPB (which did not yet exist). The OCC's amended preemption rules sparked considerable debate. In an unprecedented move, less than one week after the OCC issued its proposed rules, the U.S. Department of Treasury's General Counsel, George W. Madison, sent a letter to the Comptroller of Currency, expressing the Treasury Department's concerns with the rules. As you read the letter, bear in mind that the OCC is an independent bureau of the Treasury.

Letter from George W. Madison, Chief Law Officer, U.S. Dep't of the Treasury, to John Walsh, Acting Comptroller of the Currency

June 27, 2011

Dear Acting Comptroller Walsh:

On behalf of the Treasury Department, I am writing to comment on the [OCC's] proposed rule relating to the federal preemption of state consumer financial law.

The OCC's proposed rule raises three principal concerns for Treasury: (1) it is not centered on the key language of the Dodd-Frank Act's preemption standard, and instead seeks to broaden the standard; (2) even though the proposed rule deletes the OCC's current "obstruct, impair, or condition" standard, the rule asserts that preemption determinations based on that eliminated standard would continue to be valid; and (3) the rule could be read to preempt *categories* of state laws in the future, even though Dodd-Frank requires that preemption determinations be made on a "case-by-case" basis, and after consultation with the [CFPB] where appropriate.

1. The OCC's proposed rule is not centered on the key language of Dodd-Frank's preemption standard and seeks to broaden the standard.

Although Congress adopted a specific preemption standard in Dodd-Frank, the OCC's rule articulates a preemption standard that is broader than the language of the Dodd-Frank standard.

One of the most strenuously debated provisions of Dodd-Frank was the scope and extent of the preemption standard for national banks. In the end, Congress chose to enact a specific preemption standard. In particular, Dodd-Frank states that a state consumer financial law may be preempted "only if . . . in accordance with the legal standard for preemption in the decision of the Supreme Court . . . in *Barnett Bank of Marion County, N.A. v. Nelson* . . . , the State consumer financial law *prevents or significantly interferes* with the exercise by the national bank of its powers."

The OCC rule, however, essentially reads the "prevents or significantly interferes" language out of the statute. Specifically, the rule takes the position that Congress sought to codify the Barnett opinion, but not any particular formulation in the opinion. This avoidance of the specific standard is inconsistent with the plain language of the statute and its legislative history.

We believe that, as provided by the plain language of the statute, Congress intended that a state consumer financial law may be preempted only if the law "prevents or significantly interferes" with the exercise of a national bank's powers, as those terms are used in the *Barnett* opinion. While it is proper to look to the *Barnett* opinion to interpret the "prevents or significantly interferes" standard, we believe that Congress intended "prevents or significantly interferes" (as used in *Barnett*) to be the relevant test, not some broader test encompassing the entirety of the *Barnett* opinion.

2. The proposed rule validates all prior preemption determinations, including those based on its deleted "obstruct, impair, or condition" standard.

The OCC rule asserts that all prior preemption determinations continue to be valid, including those that were based on the OCC's previous "obstruct, impair, or condition" standard. In our view, this position is not in accordance with Dodd-Frank. The proposed rule acknowledges that the "obstruct, impair, or condition" standard was not drawn directly from the *Barnett* opinion, and it proposes the deletion of that standard. Nonetheless, the rule maintains that this deleted standard was "an amalgam of prior precedents relied upon in [*Barnett*]" and, therefore, argues that determinations based on it are consistent with the new Dodd-Frank standard. According to the preamble of the rule: "To the extent any existing precedent cited those terms in our regulations, that precedent remains valid, since the regulations were premised on principles drawn from the *Barnett* case."

In our view, this position is contrary to Dodd-Frank. As discussed above, Congress chose a specific preemption standard—"prevents or significantly interferes"—from the *Barnett* opinion. To the extent that a prior preemption determination was based on the "obstruct, impair, or condition" standard—and is not congruent with the "prevents or significantly interferes" standard—such prior determination does not satisfy the preemption standard enacted in Dodd-Frank.

The rule seems to take the position that the Dodd-Frank standard has no effect: the proposed rule expressly argues that the new Dodd-Frank standard would not change the outcome of any previous determination, and the same logic would apply to any future determination. The notion that the new standard does not have any effect runs afoul of basic canons of statutory construction; it is also contrary to the legislative history, which states that Congress sought to "*revis[e]* the standard the OCC will use to preempt state consumer protection laws."

3. The OCC's proposed rule may not comport with the "case-by-case" requirement.

Dodd-Frank requires that each preemption determination be made on a "case-by-case" basis and after consultation with the CFPB where appropriate. Despite this case-by-case requirement, the OCC's proposal could be read to preempt broad *categories* of state consumer financial laws going forward.

The OCC's intent on this issue is unclear: the proposed rule addresses the case-by-case requirement in the preamble (i.e., acknowledging the requirement), but not in the text of the proposed rule; as a result, it is unclear how the OCC intends to apply the case-by-case requirement going forward. Nonetheless, the language of the proposed rule could be read to preempt categories of state laws in the future. To the extent that the OCC seeks to preempt categories of state consumer financial laws going forward, rather than through a case-by-case approach (and after consulting with the CFPB in appropriate instances), that would not comply with Dodd-Frank. Thus, we recommend that you clarify the rule to state that any future determination will be made only on a case-by-case basis, and after consultation with the CFPB to the extent required by Dodd-Frank.

On behalf of the Treasury Department, thank you for your careful consideration of these comments.

Very truly yours,
George W. Madison

---

1. ***Reaction to the OCC Preemption Rule and Treasury's Response.*** What do you make of the OCC's amended preemption rule and Madison's response to it? Do you find the OCC's reliance on other, non-preemption provisions of the Dodd-Frank Act to be problematic as a matter of statutory interpretation? Note that judicial decisions have been reluctant to interpret the Dodd-Frank Act as creating a narrower preemption standard, instead maintaining the OCC's 2004 standard. *See, e.g.*, Baptista v. JPMorgan Chase Bank, N.A., 640 F.3d 1194 (11th Cir. 2011); *see also* U.S. Bank Nat'l Ass'n v. Schipper, 812 F. Supp. 2d 963 (S.D. Iowa 2011).

2. ***Federal vs. State Regulation of Mortgage Lending.*** What do you think is the right balance of federal and state regulation and oversight of mortgage lending? Should the balance depend on the type of lender (*e.g.*, national bank, state bank, or mortgage company)? Are there reasons why states might be in a better position to regulate mortgage lending in their jurisdictions? Or, with national banks and online lenders creating a national mortgage market, are uniform federal regulations preferable?

CHAPTER 5.3

CONSUMER FINANCIAL PRODUCTS AND SERVICES

CONTENTS

I. INTRODUCTION

Millions of U.S. households rely on consumer financial products and services every day. Students take out student loans to finance their educations; car buyers obtain auto loans to pay for their vehicles; and consumers use credit cards to pay for their groceries and gym memberships. Some households over-draw their bank accounts and rely on a variety of bank products to manage their balances. A number of households use alternative financial products, such as payday loans, for what, at least at the outset, is intended to be short-term borrowing of small amounts to help make ends meet.

While access to credit has helped many households, some consumers have been harmed by their use of such products. For some households, over-reliance on credit cards or payday loans has created a downward spiral of borrowing. For other consumers, challenges with student loan servicers or credit card billing practices have led to costly fees and late charges. These issues can cause a consumer's account to be placed into collection or for a delinquency or default to show up on the consumer's credit report. Some households that over-borrow or are subject to abusive practices wind up in bankruptcy.

Rather than an exhaustive presentation of these issues, this Chapter explores a number of consumer financial products and services commonly used by U.S. households to illustrate the types of consumer protection problems that arise and regulatory techniques for dealing with them. In particular, this Chapter focuses on student loans, auto loans, credit cards, and payday loans, as well as overdrafts, debt collection, credit reporting, and financial privacy.

II. STUDENT LOANS

College students in the United States have been financing their educations with federally-sponsored student loans since the Cold War. In 1957, the Soviet Union successfully launched the first-ever satellite, Sputnik, and the United States began to fear that it was falling behind the Soviets in science and technology. In response, Congress passed the National Defense Education Act of 1958, which offered federal loans for students earning engineering, science, and education degrees. Seven years later, Congress expanded government-backed student loans to other areas of study.

At first, the federal student loan program was a public-private partnership. Private lenders processed applications, funded loans, and collected payments. Meanwhile, the federal government established interest rates, set eligibility criteria, and backed loans with a 100% government guarantee. The government guarantee was a crucial feature of the federal student loan program because students typically do not have significant income or collateral. Private lenders would therefore have been unlikely to fulfill demand for student loans absent the guarantee. *See* Susan M. Dynarski, *An Economist's Perspective on Student Loans in the United States* (Brookings Inst., ES Working Paper Series, 2014).

The federal government changed its practice in 2010. That year, Congress passed the Health Care and Education Reconciliation Act, Pub. L. No. 111-152, 124 Stat. 1029, which ended the federal government's student loan guarantees, and replaced it with direct student loans. Private lenders still offer student loans without a government guarantee, but private loans account for less than 15% of total student debt outstanding. *See* CFPB, PRIVATE STUDENT LOANS 9 (2012).

Most students typically use federal loans first and only turn to private loans to bridge the funding gap if they do not have enough other funding, through grants or family, to cover their costs. Federal direct loans offer many student-friendly features such as flexible repayment options, deferment or forbearance periods when a student experiences economic hardship, and loan forgiveness for students who pursue careers in public service. In addition, some federal loans are subsidized by the government, and the government issues loans without regard to the borrower's credit history. Many critics argue, however, that the Congressionally-mandated fixed interest rate of 6.8% on federal student loans is too high in the current interest-rate environment. *See, e.g.,* Matthew M.

Chingos, *End Government Profits on Student Loans: Shift Risk and Lower Interest Rates*, THE BROOKINGS INST. (Apr. 30, 2015). Ironically, in the current interest-rate environment, private student loans may carry a lower interest rate for creditworthy borrowers. Since the vast majority of private student loans require a co-signor, typically the parents of the student, a credit worthy co-signor can receive lower interest rates. Private student loans, unlike direct loans, however, have variable interest rates and, depending upon the lender, may lack all of the deferral and forbearance options available for federal loans. *See* U.S. DEP'T OF EDUC., STRENGTHENING THE STUDENT LOAN SYSTEM TO BETTER PROTECT ALL BORROWERS (2015).

Student loans are now the largest source of unsecured consumer debt in the United States and second only to mortgages in total household debt. Since 2007, federal student loan debt has more than doubled from $516 billion to $1.2 trillion. *See* U.S. DEP'T OF EDUC., FEDERAL STUDENT AID PORTFOLIO SUMMARY (2015). More than 40 million Americans owe federal student loan debt, with an average outstanding balance of close to $30,000.

A. STUDENT LOAN DELINQUENCIES AND DEFAULTS

As the volume of student loan debt has risen, so too have student loan delinquencies and defaults. Seven million Americans have gone at least one year without making a payment on their federal student loans. *See* Susan Dynarski, *Why Small Student Debt Can Mean Big Problems*, N.Y. TIMES, Sept. 1, 2015. Student loans now have the highest delinquency rate out of all the major types of household debt. In fact, student loan delinquencies have risen since 2010, while delinquencies in other types of debt have fallen during the same time period:

Figure 5.3-1 Percent of Balance 90+ Days Delinquent by Loan Type

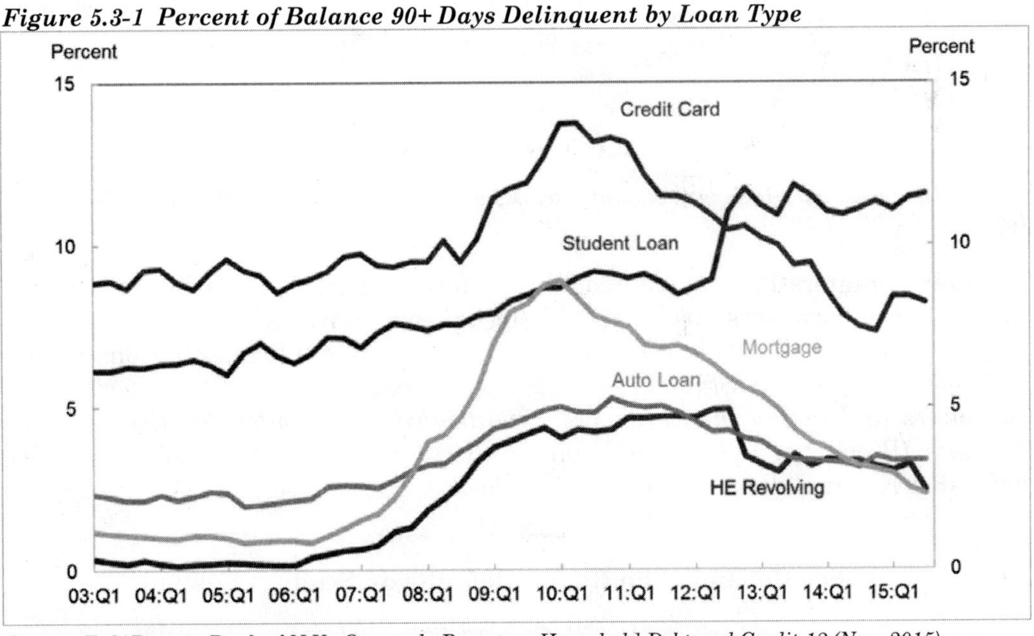

Source: Fed. Reserve Bank of N.Y., Quarterly Report on Household Debt and Credit 12 (Nov. 2015).

Furthermore, as the Federal Reserve Bank of New York has noted, reported delinquency rates for student loans likely *understate* effective delinquency rates because roughly half of federal student loans are in deferment, grace periods, or forbearance. Among loans that are currently in the repayment cycle, 90-day delinquency rates may exceed 20%. *See* Press Release, Fed. Reserve Bank of N.Y.: New York Fed Report Finds Advances in Auto Loans, Mortgage Originations (Nov. 19, 2015).

You might expect that the student loan default rate is positively correlated with the dollar amount of loans a student has taken out. The reality, however, is the opposite—students who borrow the *least* are *most* likely to default. For instance, consider the cohort of students who obtained federal student loans in 2009. By the end of 2014, 34% of the students who borrowed less than $5,000 had defaulted. In contrast, the default rate for students who borrowed more than $100,000 was nearly 50% lower. *See* Figure 5.3-2.

Figure 5.3-2 2009 Cohort: Default Rates by School-Leaving Balance

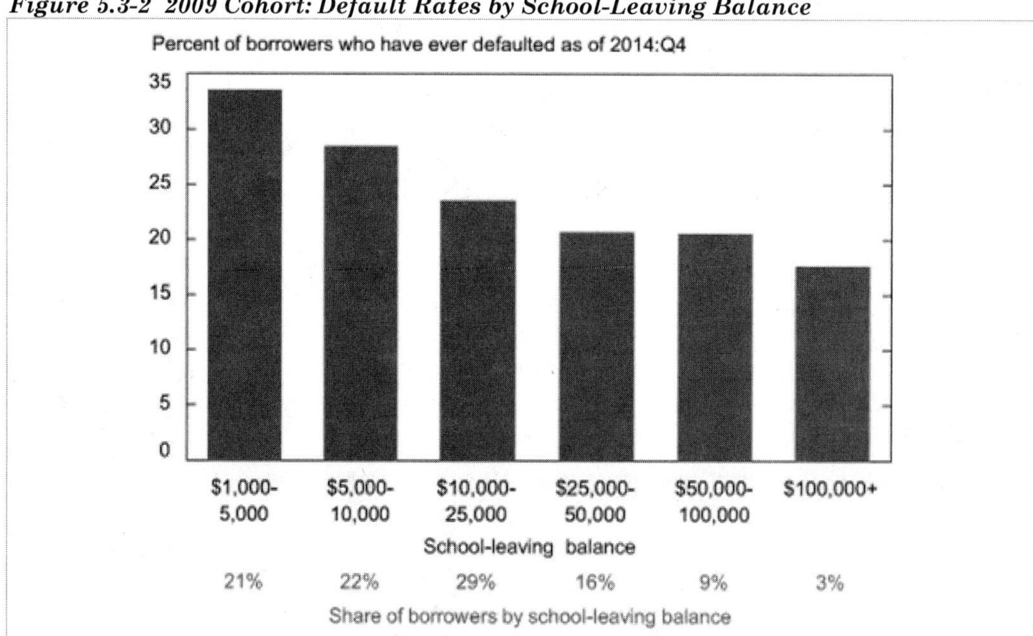

Source: Meta Brown et al., Looking at Student Loan Defaults Through a Larger Window, Fed. Reserve Bank of N.Y. (Feb. 19, 2015).

Commentators have explained this pattern in default rates by noting that high-balance borrowers are more likely to earn advanced degrees and get lucrative jobs than low-balance borrowers. *See, e.g.*, Adam Looney & Constantine Yannelis, *A Crisis in Student Loans? How Changes in the Characteristics of Borrowers and in the Institutions They Attended Contributed to Risking Loan Defaults* (Brookings Papers on Econ. Activity, Sept. 10–11, 2015). Consider journalist Kelley Holland's explanation below.

Kelley Holland, Who Really Defaults on Student Loans

CNBC, Oct. 2, 2015

Overwhelmingly, the people borrowing the largest amounts are attending graduate school, often in preparation for lucrative careers in law, medicine or business. . . . These heavily indebted people may live on ramen noodles for a few years after graduation, but they are highly likely to be on track to soon earn more than enough to pay off their loans. . . .

Community college students tend to be a rather different group. . . . [T]hey are older than typical students at four-year colleges and universities, and about one-third are part of the first generation in their family to attend college. They are also more likely to attend part time. . . .

Older students are more likely to be working while attending college, and almost two-thirds of full-time community college students have jobs, as do 73 percent of part-time students. In addition, 17 percent are single parents. All of those attributes can make it much harder for community college students to complete a degree in a linear progression. . . .

Perhaps most important, community college students' finances are more fragile. . . . And when these students stop going to college before completing their degrees, as many do, they are contending with their loans on income from jobs that probably pay far less than those for graduates.

B. DISCHARGE IN BANKRUPTCY

In contrast to most consumer loans, student loans are generally not dischargeable in bankruptcy. In 2005, Congress amended the Bankruptcy Code, codifying that all student loans are exempt from discharge in bankruptcy absent "undue hardship." 11 U.S.C. § 523. Under one test commonly used by courts, in order to establish undue hardship, the borrower must show: "(1) that [she] cannot maintain, based on current income and expenses, a 'minimal' standard of living for herself and [any] dependents if forced to repay the loa[n]; (2) that additional circumstances exist indicating that this state of affairs is likely to persist for a significant portion of the repayment period. . . .; and (3) that [she] has made good faith efforts to repay. . . ." *See* Brunner v. New York Higher Educ. Servs. Corp., 831 F.2d 395, 396 (2d Cir. 1987).

In practice, the undue hardship standard is extremely difficult to meet. Some have stated that the standard requires the borrower to prove a "certainty of hopelessness." *See, e.g., In re* O'Hearn, 339 F.3d 559, 564 (7th Cir. 2003). One study found that, in 2008, only 29 of 72,000 student loan borrowers in bankruptcy succeeded in having their loans discharged. *See* Brendan Baker, *Deeper Debt, Denial of Discharge: The Harsh Treatment of Student Loan Debt in Bankruptcy, Recent Developments, and Proposed Reforms*, 14 U. PA. J. BUS. L. 1213, 1214 (2012). Another study, by contrast, found that very few student loan debtors who filed for bankruptcy (0.1%) attempt to discharge their student loans but that those who do seek discharge were successful almost 40% of the time. *See* Jason Iuliano, *An Empirical Assessment of Student Loan Discharges and the Undue Hardship Standard*, 86 AM. BANKR. L.J. 495 (2012). The Department of Education has supported strict application of the undue hardship standard. *See* Brief for United States of America as Amicus Curiae Supporting Appellee, Murphy v. U.S. Dep't of Educ. et al., No. 14-1691 (1st Cir. filed Oct. 29, 2015).

Congress included the non-dischargeability rule in part out of a desire to prevent strategic defaults:

> The initial decision to make federal student loans virtually immune to bankruptcy discharge was based, in part, upon the perceived moral hazard inherent in encouraging a student to use credit to purchase a valuable intellectual asset which cannot be repossessed.

> Supporters of special bankruptcy protection claimed that students could discharge the financial obligation through bankruptcy after graduation, while reaping the financial benefits of the intellectual asset for a lifetime. . . .

CFPB, PRIVATE STUDENT LOANS (2012).

Professors Rafael Pardo and Michelle Lacey, however, argue that preventing moral hazard is an insufficient justification for the non-dischargeability of student loan debt:

> Two reasons occur to us why moral hazard should be deemed an inappropriate justification for the conditionally dischargeable status of educational debt. First, past empirical evidence did not indicate systemic manipulation by debtors of the legal opportunity to discharge their student loans when bankruptcy law allowed for their automatic discharge. Second, and above all else, the Code has already created safeguards against such abusive and opportunistic behavior on a general basis. These safeguards can adequately respond to moral hazard in the educational debt context. . . .

Rafael I. Pardo & Michelle R. Lacey, *Undue Hardship in the Bankruptcy Courts: An Empirical Assessment of the Discharge of Educational Debt*, 74 U. CIN. L. REV. 405, 430–31 (2005).

The Obama Administration proposed amending the Bankruptcy Code to make private student loans dischargeable in bankruptcy, unless the loans include flexible income-based repayment plans, similar to federal student loans. *See* U.S. DEP'T OF EDUC., STRENGTHENING THE STUDENT LOAN SYSTEM TO BETTER PROTECT ALL BORROWERS 17 (2015). For borrowers with federal student loans, the burden to establish undue hardship is somewhat mitigated by the income-based repayment, forebearance, and deferral options described above. Bills have been introduced in Congress that would ease discharge in bankruptcy for both private and federal student loans. Consider the advantages and disadvantages of such a discharge. How would the taxpayer's fiscal interest be balanced against the fresh start that bankruptcy permits? Many banks have been exiting the private student loan market. *See, e.g.*, Dan Fitzpatrick & Robin Sidel, *J.P. Morgan to End Student-Loan Business*, WALL ST. J., Sept. 5, 2013. Why do you think that is occurring?

C. STUDENT LOAN SERVICING

Servicers, or companies that collect payments and administer loans, are a primary focus the CFPB and the key interface with many student borrowers. In some cases, student borrowers face payment processing delays that lead to additional interest accumulation. In other cases, servicers divide up a borrower's partial payment and apply it evenly across all of the borrower's student loans so that the borrower incurs a late fee on all of her outstanding loans. *See* Press Release, CFPB: Factsheet: Borrower Experiences with Student Debt Distress (May 14, 2015).

CFPB Director Richard Cordray summarized some consumer complaints about student loan servicers in the following speech.

Prepared Remarks of CFPB Director Richard Cordray at the Field Hearing on Student Loans

May 14, 2015

Borrowers who finance a home, a car, or an education often find that a company they never heard of acts as their loan servicer, with the responsibility to collect and allocate the loan payments. For young people finishing college, student loan servicers will be their primary point of contact on their outstanding loans. These companies are responsible for collecting payments and sending the payments to the loan holders. Borrowers rely on them to process payments accurately, to provide billing information, and to answer questions about their accounts, including ways to help prevent default. The servicer is often different from the lender. This means consumers often have no control or choice over the company they are dealing with to manage their loans.

As a growing share of student loan borrowers reach out to their servicers for help, the problems they encounter bear an uncanny resemblance to the situation where struggling homeowners reached out to their mortgage servicers before, during, and after the financial crisis. . . . At every stage of the process of paying back their student loans, borrowers have told us they are wrapped in mounds of red tape, particularly for private student loans. From the beginning, when they first graduate and start making their initial payments, consumers can experience problems with payment posting, problems with attempted prepayments, and problems with partial rather than full payments. For example, some former students have told us they find it takes a few days for servicers to process their payments, which can cause them to have to pay additional interest. We have also heard from borrowers who complain about inconsistency, noting that they often get widely different information, protections, and rights depending on what type of loan they have.

When borrowers do seek any sort of help, the range and severity of their problems can quickly snowball. They have told us about lost paperwork, unanswered inquiries, and no clear path to get answers. They also find that when errors are made, they may not be fixed very quickly. They may encounter limited access to basic account information, including their payment history over the years. One borrower told us, for example, that she made her payment on-time and in-full each month through an automatic payment system established by the lender but still faced problems with unexpected fees. Once again, these kinds of problems are not new to loan servicing in general, and in particular they have happened repeatedly in the mortgage servicing market over the past decade.

The stress can get even worse when loans change hands from one servicer to another. . . . These loan transfers can produce real headaches and confusion for consumers. Some borrowers have complained that they are charged late fees because they mailed their payments to their old servicers without being aware that this was now an error. Other types of problems can arise as well. We heard from one person who said he made full payments each month for six years. But when he informed the new company handling his loan that he wished to enroll in an alternative payment plan that had been available from his original servicer, he was told that was no longer an option.

In 2015, the CFPB, Department of Education, and the Department of Treasury launched a joint effort to improve student loan servicing. *See* Request for Information Regarding Student Loan Servicing, 80 Fed. Reg. 29,302 (May 21, 2015). What approaches would you suggest that the agencies take?

1. ***Income-Based Repayment.*** Congress and the Obama Administration first created an income-based repayment program for federal student loans in 2009. Three years later, the Obama Administration established another flexible repayment option, the Pay-as-You-Earn plan. Under both the income-based repayment program and the Pay-as-You-Earn plan, as in effect at the end of 2015, new borrowers pay up to 10% of their discretionary income towards their student loans, but never more than they would be obligated to pay under the standard ten-year repayment plan. Any remaining loan balance is forgiven if the borrower's federal student loans are not fully repaid at the end of 20 years. Despite the favorable terms, few student borrowers—only 19% as of 2014—are enrolled in income-based repayment options. *See* Press Release, Government Accountability Office: Federal Student Loans: Education Could Do More to Help Ensure Borrowers are Aware of Repayment and Forgiveness Options (Aug. 2015). Why are participation rates not higher? Some experts speculate that borrowers may not be aware of income-driven repayment options, may not understand them, or may have difficulty applying or meeting annual income certification requirements. *See id.* at 15–16. Those borrowers who would likely benefit the most from these repayment options are the same people who have trouble navigating the complexity of the process. As a result, a mechanism that is supposed to help students avoid default often does not reach the most vulnerable people it was designed to help.

2. ***Student Loans and For-Profit Colleges.*** Student loan delinquencies and defaults are particularly prevalent among borrowers who attend for-profit colleges. These schools—such as the University of Phoenix and Corinthian Colleges—typically cater to older students who take online classes part-time and rely heavily on student loans. Critics argue that these colleges mislead potential students about job placements and leave students with few job prospects and heavy debt loads after graduation:

> Dependence on student loans was not incidental to the for-profit boom—it was the business model. The schools may have been meeting a genuine market need, but, in most cases, their profits came not from building a better mousetrap but from gaming the taxpayer-funded financial-aid system. Since the schools weren't lending money themselves, they didn't have to worry about whether it would be paid back. So they had every incentive to encourage students to take out as much financial aid as possible, often by giving them a distorted picture of what they could expect in the future. Corinthian, for instance, was found to have lied about job-placement rates nearly a thousand times. And a 2010 undercover government investigation of fifteen for-profit colleges found that all fifteen "made deceptive or otherwise questionable statements." One told an applicant that barbers could earn up to two hundred and fifty thousand dollars a year. Schools also jacked up prices to take advantage of the system. A 2012 study found that increases in tuition closely tracked increases in financial aid. . . .

James Surowiecki, *The Rise and Fall of For-Profit Schools*, NEW YORKER, Nov. 2, 2015. The Department of Education, DOJ, and CFPB have investigated several for-profit colleges, including Corinthian Colleges, for making unsubstantiated claims about their job placement rates. In April 2015, Corinthian Colleges ceased operations amidst the government scrutiny. After student protests and Congressional pressure, the Department of Education has forgiven the federal student loans of more than 85,000 students who attended Corinthian Colleges. *See* Stephanie Saul, *Government to Expand Program to Forgive Student Loan Debt*, N.Y. TIMES, Nov. 17, 2015. In addition, a CFPB enforcement action resulted in more than $480 million in debt relief for students who obtained high-cost private student loans from Corinthian.

In October 2014, the Obama Administration adopted new regulations requiring for-profit colleges to prepare students for "gainful employment in a recognized occupation." Under the regulations, a program is considered to lead to gainful employment if the estimated annual loan payment of a typical graduate does not exceed 20% of her discretionary income or 8% of her total earnings. For-profit colleges that exceed these levels risk losing the ability to participate in federal student aid programs. *See* 34 C.F.R. §§ 600.1 and 668.1. What are the pros and cons of the gainful employment rule? Should it be applied more widely than just for-profit schools?

III. AUTO LOANS

Imagine that you are in the market for a new car. You spend weeks researching makes and models, comparing prices, and deciding on colors and features. You take a few cars for test drives. Once you finally decide which car you want, you may haggle with the dealer over price and add-on products, such as an extended warranty, rustproofing, roadside protection, or a service plan. At this point, you are probably growing impatient to finish the process and drive the car off the lot. The car purchase, however, is not yet complete. Unless you plan to pay for the car in cash, which few consumers do, you must still arrange financing—*i.e.*, an auto loan. Financing is a critical aspect of the car-buying process, and one that could matter more than the purchase price when determining how much you will ultimately pay for the car.

Your imaginary car-buying experience is a reality for thousands of car buyers each day. In fact, auto loans are the third largest source of household debt in the United States, after mortgages and student loans, and auto loan origination has been growing steadily in recent years. By 2015, U.S. households owed approximately $1.05 trillion in outstanding auto loans. *See* Fed. Reserve Bank of N.Y., *Quarterly Report on Household Debt and Credit* (Nov. 2015).

A. TYPES OF AUTO LOANS

Car buyers have a choice between two general types of auto loans. In the first type, called a direct auto loan, the car buyer obtains a loan directly from a lender, such as a bank or a credit union. Oftentimes, a lender will pre-approve a car buyer for a direct auto loan, so the buyer knows the amount of the loan for which she is eligible before selecting a car. Despite this advantage, only 20% of cars financed in the United States are financed through direct loans. *See* Delvin Davis, *Auto Loans, in* THE STATE OF LENDING IN AMERICA & ITS IMPACT ON U.S. HOUSEHOLDS 66 (2012).

In the second type of auto financing, an indirect auto loan, the dealership enters into a retail installment sales contract with the car buyer. The dealer then sells the contract to a third party—such as an auto finance company, bank, or credit union—after the deal is closed. Dealers arrange indirect auto loans as follows:

> [T]he salesperson will often collect the information needed to determine financing terms before the consumer actually talks to the [finance and insurance] office. While the consumer is negotiating with the salesperson, the [finance and insurance] employee communicates with lenders who may be interested in buying the loan. When a consumer applies for credit with the dealer, the dealer sends the consumer's financial information to one or several potential lenders. Interested lenders then respond to the dealer with offers to purchase the contract, specifying the minimum interest rate and the specific conditions and terms that the lender will require to purchase the loan.

Id. at 65. Dealers sell the majority of indirect auto loans to captive finance companies, which are subsidiaries of automobile manufacturers, such as Ford Motor Credit Company or Honda Financial Services. *See id.* at 66.

B. CRITICISM OF AUTO LENDING PRACTICES

Consumer advocates argue that auto lending is plagued by predatory or abusive practices that cost consumers billions of dollars and put them at risk of losing their cars. *See, e.g.*, Written Testimony of Lisa Stifler, Policy Counsel, CTR. FOR RESPONSIBLE LENDING, Apr. 23, 2015, at 6. Auto dealers and lenders, by contrast, defend their practices and argue that they expand access to vehicle ownership. *See* Press Release, Consumer Bankers Association: Statement of Richard Hunt, President and CEO of the Consumer Bankers Association in Response to the CFPB Auto Lending Bulletin (March 21, 2013).

The controversy over auto loan markups is particularly contentious. As noted above, in an indirect auto loan, a third-party lender quotes the dealer an interest rate at which it is willing to purchase the loan. This interest rate is known as the buy rate. The buy rate is based on the consumer's credit risk, so dealers will be quoted different buy rates for car buyers with different credit profiles. A dealer markup occurs when the dealer charges the car buyer an interest rate that exceeds the buy rate. Third-party lenders generally give the dealer some discretion to add a dealer markup. Depending on the dealer's agreement with the third-party lender, the dealer could pocket the dealer markup as profit, or the dealer could split the mark-up with the third-party lender to whom it sold the auto loan. The total interest rate charged to the consumer—*i.e.*, the buy rate plus the dealer markup—is known as the contract rate.

Consumer advocates argue that dealer markups are costly for car buyers. The CFPB alleged, for instance, that American Honda Finance Corporation permitted dealers to add dealer markups of 2.25% for contracts with terms of five years or less, and 2% for longer-term contracts. *See* Press Release, CFPB: CFPB and DOJ Reach Resolution with Honda to Address Discriminatory Auto Loan

Pricing (July 14, 2015); *see also* Abbye Atkinson, *Modifying Mortgage Discrimination in Consumer Bankruptcy*, 57 ARIZ. L. REV. 1041, 1066–67 (describing other auto loan discrimination settlements). One study found that consumers who financed cars through dealerships in 2009 will pay more than $25.8 billion in interest rate markups over the lives of their loans. *See* DELVIN DAVIS & JOSHUA M. FRANK, UNDER THE HOOD: AUTO LOAN INTEREST RATE HIKES INFLATE CONSUMER COSTS AND LOAN LOSSES (2011).

Critics argue that dealers do not disclose markups to their customers, who may assume that the contract rate is based solely on their risk profile. *See id.* Some counter, however, that markups are an important source of compensation for auto dealers and, thus, auto lenders cannot eliminate dealers' discretion to charge markups without "committing corporate suicide." REPUBLICAN STAFF OF H. COMM. ON FIN. SERVS., 114TH CONG., UNSAFE AT ANY BUREAUCRACY: CFPB JUNK SCIENCE AND INDIRECT AUTO LENDING (Comm. Print 2015).

Critics also allege other abuses by auto dealers. In one practice, called a yo-yo scam, a dealer allows a buyer to drive a vehicle off the lot thinking that financing has been finalized but later calls the buyer and says that the sale cannot be made as originally made because financing has fallen through. The dealer then forces the buyer to return the car or renegotiate financing on more expensive terms. *See* Don Oldenburg, *Yo-Yo Deals: Stringing Car Buyers Along*, WASH. POST, Oct. 19, 2004, at C09. Critics also allege that dealers engage in loan packing—selling buyers add-on products, such as plastic door edge guards, car alarms, floor mats, and extended service contracts—without making clear that the add-on products are optional. *See* Karen Lundegaard, *Did You Overpay for Your Car?*, WALL ST. J., June 20, 2002, at D1. Finally, consumer advocates criticize Buy Here Pay Here dealers, which cater to consumers with seriously impaired credit who are unable to obtain financing from traditional lenders. Buy Here Pay Here dealers usually sell older used cars at high prices, oftentimes at double the wholesale price. Approximately one in every five Buy Here Pay Here borrowers default, and Buy Here Pay Here dealers are notoriously quick to repossess vehicles following a default. *See* Written Testimony of Lisa Stifler, Policy Counsel, Ctr. for Responsible Lending, Apr. 23, 2015, at 6; *see also* Jeff Bailey, *'Buy-Here, Pay-Here' Car Lots: Basic and Gritty Loan Businesses*, WALL ST. J., July 8, 2003, at B9.

Critics have long argued that auto dealers and finance companies use the practices identified above in a racially-discriminatory fashion. *See, e.g.*, Mark A. Cohen, *Imperfect Competition in Auto Lending: Subjective Markup, Racial Disparity, and Class Action Litigation*, 8 REV. OF L. & ECON. 21 (2012); *see also* Ian Ayres, *Fair Driving: Gender and Race Discrimination in Retail Car Negotiations*, 10 HARV. L. REV. 817 (1991). In the following excerpt, Mr. Delvin Davis summarizes some of the academic research on racial disparities in auto lending.

Delvin Davis, Non-Negotiable: Negotiation Doesn't Help African Americans and Latinos on Dealer-Financed Car Loans

Ctr. for Responsible Lending, Jan. 2014, at 5–6

Mark Cohen of Vanderbilt University (2006) found that borrowers of color are more likely to receive an interest rate markup when financing a car through the dealer, and that the rate is typically increased at larger amounts, than for similarly-situated white borrowers. His loan-level analysis of five major auto finance companies indicated that 54.6% of African Americans received an interest rate markup, compared to 30.6% of whites. Moreover, African Americans on average paid over twice the amount of rate markup ($742) compared with the average markup paid by whites ($315). Latinos also paid higher rate markups than whites, although not as high as those paid by African Americans. . . .

Other research also found disparate impact in car loan interest rates. Using data from the Survey of Consumer Finances, researchers Charles, Hurst, and Stephens (2008) find that for car loans with higher interest rates (at the 75th percentile), African Americans paid 168 basis points more than whites with similar credit profiles financing through a finance company. In contrast, the rates African Americans paid on car loans originated directly by a bank or credit union did not have a statistically significant difference from whites.

Likewise, Edelberg (2007) found that interest rate data prior to 1995 showed racially disparate impact for several types of loan products, including car loans. . . . For car loans specifically, minorities paid rates 80 basis points higher than whites on a statistically significant level.

Davis' own research found that, for minority car buyers, negotiation tactics and comparison shopping do not result in better rate pricing outcomes. Davis determined that African Americans and Latinos try more frequently than white consumers to negotiate their interest rates, but they still experience pricing disparities. In fact, Davis found that African Americans and Latinos who try to negotiate obtain higher interest rates on average than white borrowers who did not try to negotiate at all. *See id.* at 10.

C. SUPERVISION AND ENFORCEMENT

As we discussed in Chapter 5.1, auto dealers successfully lobbied Congress for an exclusion from CFPB oversight in the Dodd-Frank Act. Instead, the Federal Trade Commission (FTC) retains primary regulatory and enforcement authority over auto dealers. The FTC proscribes regulations pursuant to various consumer protection laws—*e.g.*, the FTC Act, the Consumer Leasing Act, and the Truth in Lending Act—that are applicable to auto dealers. The FTC also brings enforcement actions under these authorities. For instance, in March 2015, the FTC charged two dealers with failing to disclose fees associated with various add-on products and services. *See* Press Release, FTC: FTC, Multiple Law Enforcement Partners Announce Crackdown on Deception, Fraud in Auto Sales, Financing and Leasing (Mar. 26, 2015).

The CFPB supervises auto lending by banks with more than $10 billion in assets. The Dodd-Frank Act also grants the CFPB authority to bring certain non-bank auto lenders, or "larger participants," under its supervisory authority, and the CFPB has exercised this authority. *See* 12 C.F.R. §§ 1001.1, 1090.100.

Under this rule, a lender is a larger participant if it originates at least 10,000 auto loans annually. The CFPB estimates that the larger participant rule extends its supervision to 34 of the largest non-bank auto finance companies that account for approximately 90% of non-bank auto loans. *See* Press Release, CFPB: CFPB to Oversee Nonbank Auto Finance Companies (June 10, 2015).

The CFPB has used its authority under the Equal Credit Opportunity Act—which makes it illegal for a creditor to discriminate in any aspect of a credit transaction because of race, color, religion, or other factors—to take enforcement actions with respect to alleged discriminatory auto loan pricing. The CFPB has used its supervisory authorities over indirect auto lenders to address dealer markups. In March 2013, the CFPB issued a bulletin cautioning that an indirect auto lender that permits dealer markups and compensates dealers on that basis may be liable for its policies and practices if they result in disparate pricing on a prohibited basis. *See* CFPB Bulletin 2013-02, *Indirect Auto Lending and Compliance with the Equal Credit Opportunity Act*, Mar. 21, 2013. Later that year, the CFPB alleged that Ally Bank, one of the country's largest indirect auto lenders, charged African American, Hispanic, and Asian/Pacific Islander borrowers approximately $200–$300 more in dealer markups than similarly-situated white borrowers. The CFPB and DOJ entered into a consent order with Ally Bank requiring Ally Bank to pay $80 million in damages. *See* Press Release, CFPB: CFPB and DOJ Order Ally to Pay $80 Million to Consumers Harmed by Discriminatory Auto Loan Pricing (Dec. 20, 2013). Since then, the CFPB and DOJ have entered into similar consent orders with Fifth Third Bank, American Honda Finance Corporation, and Toyota Motor Credit Corporation. The consent orders contain the facts as alleged by the CFPB and do not involve admissions of wrongdoing. The consent orders require the auto lenders to change their policies to reduce auto dealer discretion to mark up interest rates. While the consent orders are with indirect auto lenders, which are subject to CFPB jurisdiction, the orders require the indirect lenders to alter their contracts with auto dealers, which are not subject to CFPB jurisdiction.

---

1. ***Dealer Markups.*** You probably notice some similarities between dealer markups for auto loans and yield spread premiums for mortgages, which we discussed in Chapter 5.2. As you will recall, the Dodd-Frank Act banned yield spread premiums based on any factor other than the amount of credit extended. Should Congress have banned dealer markups as well? Or should the CFPB stay out of dealer pricing altogether and let competition determine markup prices?

2. ***CFPB Enforcement Actions and Proxy Data.*** In the enforcement actions discussed above, the CFPB and DOJ analyzed the dealers' retail installment sales contracts, which are not permitted to contain information on the race or national origin of borrowers. How did the agencies evaluate differences in dealer markups across races? The agencies used a methodology known as Bayesian Improved Surname Geocoding, a proxy that combines geography-based and name-based probabilities to form joint race and national origin probabilities for each retail installment sales contract. The agencies' use of the Bayesian Improved Surname Geocoding model sparked a contentious debate over the model's reliability. The American Financial Services Association, for instance, commissioned a study of retail installment sales contracts and argued that the

Bayesian Improved Surname Geocoding model correctly identified African Americans less than 25% of the time. *See* AFSA, FAIR LENDING: IMPLICATIONS FOR THE INDIRECT AUTO FINANCE MARKET (2014). After the consent order, a report prepared by the Republican staff of the House Financial Services Committee heavily criticized the CFPB's assertion of jurisdiction and argued that the CFPB's enforcement actions were themselves "misguided and deceptive." REPUBLICAN STAFF OF H. COMM. ON FIN. SERVS., 114TH CONG., UNSAFE AT ANY BUREAUCRACY: CFPB JUNK SCIENCE AND INDIRECT AUTO LENDING (Comm. Print 2015). Do you agree with the CFPB's approach? When should policy-makers mandate the collection of race and ethnicity data (*e.g.*, as is currently done under the Home Mortgage Disclosure Act for mortgages), and when should policy-makers use proxies? When using proxies, how should policy-makers reduce the risk that people who were not subject to discrimination might get restitution?

IV. CREDIT CARDS

Credit card debt in the United States totaled $929 billion in November 2015. *See* FED. RESERVE BD., CONSUMER CREDIT: NOVEMBER 2015 (2016). Revolving credit enables consumers to smooth consumption, and credit cards can help households weather temporary income shocks like unemployment or expense shocks such as a medical emergency. Sarah Wolff, *Credit Cards, in* THE STATE OF LENDING IN AMERICA AND ITS IMPACT ON U.S. HOUSEHOLDS 88 (2013). Despite these benefits, many critics argue that credit cards can also lead to large and costly debt burdens for consumers.

A. THE NEED FOR CONSUMER PROTECTION

Regulators and consumer groups are concerned about credit cards in part because consumers appear to have difficulty understanding credit card terms and pricing. Credit card contracts are often printed in legalese and in fine print. Credit card issuers, moreover, have specialized information that the average consumer does not, including the probability of delinquency, the true cost of credit, which includes complex fee structures and conditional, variable rates, and details of their competitors' offerings. This asymmetric information is worsened by the fact that Americans on average have low financial literacy, and this literacy is correlated with socioeconomic status. *See, e.g.*, Annamaria Lusardi & Olivia S. Mitchell, *The Economic Importance of Financial Literacy: Theory and Evidence*, 52 J. ECON. LIT. 5 (2014).

Consumer behavior also demonstrates limitations in understanding and acting on information, known as cognitive biases—such as myopia, a limited attention span, or excessive optimism about one's financial future—that cause consumers to systematically underestimate the true cost of credit. Lenders may exploit these cognitive biases profitably by offering consumers a deferred-cost contract with cheap baseline repayment terms in the short-term, but large penalties in the long-term. *See* Paul Heidhues & Botond Kőszegi, *Exploiting Naïvete About Self-Control in the Credit Market*, 100 AM. ECON. REV. 2279, 2279 (2010). An unsophisticated consumer can get caught in a debt cycle by being lured into a contract with a low teaser interest rate, then over borrow and incur penalties. *See* Ronald J. Mann, *Bankruptcy Reform and the "Sweat Box" of Credit Card Debt*, 2007 U. ILL. L. REV. 375, 385 (2007).

In the mid–2000s, policy-makers and consumer advocates became particularly worried about unfair billing practices used by credit card companies. One common practice was double-cycle billing, where a card issuer charged interest on an account "during the interest-free 'float' period between the time of purchase and the due date of the payment." Jonathan Slowik, *Credit CARD Act II: Expanding Credit Card Reform by Targeting Behavioral Biases*, 59 UCLA L. REV. 1292, 1301 (2012); *see* 15 U.S.C. § 1637(j)(1). Card issuers also increased the interest rates or fees on accounts and then applied the new rates and fees retroactively to existing balances. *See* Adam J. Levitin, *Rate Jacking: Risk-Based & Opportunistic Pricing in Credit Cards*, 2011 UTAH L. REV. 339, 339 (2011). One study found that 77% of card issuers reserved the right to increase a cardholder's interest rate both prospectively and retroactively under "any time, any reason" clauses. S. REP. NO. 111-16, at 4 (2009). The U.S. Senate concluded that the credit card market was filled with "unfair, misleading and deceptive practices." *Id.* at 1.

B. THE CARD ACT OF 2009

Congress and the Obama Administration intended that the Credit Card Responsibility and Disclosure Act of 2009 (CARD Act) would restrict deceptive credit card billing practices and thereby uphold "basic standards of fairness, transparency, and accountability" in consumer lending. *See* CFPB, CARD ACT FACTSHEET (2011). According to the CFPB, the CARD Act has promoted greater transparency and upfront pricing by limiting back-end fees, such as overlimit and late fees, and restricting an issuer's ability to raise interest rates retroactively. *See* CFPB, CARD ACT REPORT (2013).

The CARD Act has largely eliminated overlimit fees. Although the CARD Act does not expressly prohibit overlimit fees, it requires consumers to opt-in to overlimit fees before they are permitted to exceed their credit limit. The CARD Act also requires that overlimit fees be "reasonable and proportional" to the violation of the consumer's credit limit. 15 U.S.C. § 1661d(a). The CFPB found that overlimit fees have dropped precipitously since these restrictions went into effect. Since 2014, only 0.0008% of active accounts have been charged an overlimit fee per quarter, saving consumers more than $9 billion. The CFPB concluded that "[o]verlimit fees . . . are all but extinct." CFPB, THE CONSUMER CREDIT CARD MARKET 66 (2015).

The CARD Act also requires late fees to be "reasonable and proportional," and it restricts setting payment cut-off times and unpredictable due dates. Among the restrictions, the CARD Act prohibits issuers from charging late payments exceeding $25, except if the borrower has also been late on one of her previous six payments, in which case the late fee is capped at $35. Since 2012, late fees have stabilized at $27 on average, down from $35 before the Act's passage. *Id.* at 68. The CFPB estimated that consumers have saved more than $7 billion in late fees for the period from 2011 to 2014. *Id.*

Before the CARD Act, cardholder agreements permitted issuers to increase the interest rates applied to the consumer's account at any time for virtually any reason. If a cardholder was delinquent in one account, the card issuer could apply a significantly higher penalty APR to all of the cardholder's accounts. The CARD Act limits the circumstances under which issuers could increase interest rates for existing balances and requires heightened disclosure to consumers before an increase can be applied to new transactions.

The CARD Act also mandates new disclosure requirements for credit card statements, intended to affect consumer behavior by better informing them of the consequences of their financial decisions. *See* Christine Jolls & Cass R. Sunstein, *Debiasing Through Law*, 35 J. LEGAL STUD. 199 (2006); *see also* Michael S. Barr et al., *The Case for Behaviorally Informed Regulation*, *in* NEW PERSPECTIVES ON REGULATION 25 (David A. Moss & John A. Cisternino eds., 2009). For example, the CARD Act requires card issuers to give cardholders a "minimum payment warning" on their monthly statement. This warning prominently states the total principal and interest amount that the consumer would owe on the payment due date if the consumer were to make only the minimum payment for that monthly billing statement. These requirements have led to a modest increase in the percentage of cardholders who repay their credit card balances within 36 months. Sumit Agarwal et al., *Regulating Consumer Financial Products: Evidence from Credit Cards*, 130 Q.J. ECON. 111, 114 (2014).

The CARD Act drew criticism from many who believed that the Act would raise rates and reduce access. For example, Professor Todd Zywicki argued that, by making it more difficult to raise interest rates when a borrower's risk profile changes, the CARD Act would lead to the card issuers raising everyone's interest rates at the front end. Zywicki also argued that card issuers would reduce their risk exposure by either refusing to lend to high-risk borrowers or lending less to existing consumers by reducing available credit lines. Todd Zywicki, *Economic Uncertainty, the Courts, and the Rule of Law*, 35 HARV. J.L. & PUB. POL'Y 195, 198 (2012).

Despite these concerns, early evidence suggests that the CARD Act has reduced the use and incidence of particular pricing structures and has resulted in increased consumer welfare. One study found that the CARD Act has saved consumers $11.9 billion per year with no offsetting reduction in access to credit. *See* Sumit Agarwal et al., *Regulating Consumer Financial Products: Evidence from Credit Cards*, 130 Q.J. ECON. 111, 114 (2014). The CFPB determined in late 2015 that the total cost of credit was nearly two percentage points lower than before the CARD Act and that available credit had increased 10% since 2012, with the caveat that the CFPB's data did not establish a direct causal link to the CARD Act. *See* CFPB, THE CONSUMER CREDIT CARD MARKET 77, 108 (2015).

There remain, however, a few areas of concern for consumers. Deferred interest products, which create back-end fees that disproportionately affect consumers with low credit scores, remain commonplace. Subprime specialist credit card issuers offer more expensive products than mass market issuers, and subprime specialist credit card issuers frequently target less educated consumers. Most credit cards, moreover, have variable interest rates; consumers may accumulate or roll-over credit card balances without comprehending that their interest rates may increase in the future. *See id.* at 10–11.

---

1. ***Pre-Dispute Arbitration Clauses.*** Arbitration clauses are prevalent in credit card and other financial services agreements. According to a CFPB study, as of December 31, 2013, 15.8% of card issuers used arbitration clauses, covering 53.0% of outstanding credit card loans. CFPB, ARBITRATION STUDY 9–10 (2015). Although there are many benefits to arbitration in other contexts, in credit card agreements, consumers are generally presented with these contracts on a "take it or leave it" basis. Michael S. Barr, *Mandatory Arbitration in Consumer Finance and Investor Contracts*, 11 N.Y.U. J.L. & BUS. 793, 795 (2015). Arbitration clauses are frequently not clearly disclosed or, even when they are disclosed, consumers may not realize the implications of arbitrating a dispute or may miscalculate the likelihood of a dispute. *Id.* Most of these provisions also state that arbitration may not proceed on a class basis. *Id.* The CFPB has released an outline of proposals, pursuant to its authority under the Dodd-Frank Act, for a regulation to prohibit pre-dispute agreements that purport to bar class actions and to take other measures. SMALL BUS. ADVISORY REV. PANEL FOR POTENTIAL RULEMAKING ON ARBITRATION AGREEMENTS, OUTLINE OF PROPOSALS UNDER CONSIDERATION AND ALTERNATIVES CONSIDERED 13–23 (2015). Do you think this proposal will help or hurt consumers?

V. PAYDAY LOANS

Cash-strapped borrowers often turn to a payday loan—a high-interest lump-sum loan with a due date timed to coincide with the borrower's next receipt of income. Operating out of storefront locations, or online, payday lenders generally do not consider a borrower's credit score or the ability of borrowers to repay the loan. The borrower typically provides the payday lender with a personal check for the loan principal or information that enables the lender to debit the borrower's bank account for that same amount. In return, the borrower receives cash minus the lender's fees. Payday loans typically have terms of two weeks, and they can be expensive. Fees average $15 per $100 loan, with variations reflecting the maximum fees set by state laws. *See* CFPB, PAYDAY LOANS AND DEPOSIT ADVANCE PRODUCTS 9 (2013). This yields an annual percentage rate (APR) of 391%. *Id.*

Between 2000 and 2004, the amount of payday lending outlets grew from 10,000 to 22,000. Mark Flannery & Katherine Samolyk, *Payday Lending: Do the Costs Justify the Price?* 2 (FDIC, Working Paper No. 2005-09). By 2003, payday loan volume was estimated at $40 billion, and by 2005, payday storefronts outnumbered both McDonald's and Starbuck's locations combined. *See* Alex Kaufman, *Payday Lending Regulation* 4 (Fed. Res., Divs. of Research & Statistics and Monetary Affairs, Fin. & Econ. Discussion Series, Working Paper No. 2013-62). Approximately 4.7% of all U.S. households have used payday lending at some time. *Id.*

Payday lenders allow borrowers to defer, or roll over, their loan payment due date for an extra fee. MICHAEL S. BARR, NO SLACK: THE FINANCIAL LIVES OF LOW-INCOME AMERICANS 136–39 (Brookings Inst. Press 2012). A CFPB study found that more than 80% of payday loans are rolled over or followed by another loan in 14 days, and that few borrowers actually have reductions in principal amounts between the first and last loan in a loan sequence. CFPB, DATA POINT: PAYDAY LENDING 4 (2014). As a result, payday loans are often described as "debt traps" for trapping consumers in long-term debt through unaffordable short-term loans. *See* CFPB, SMALL BUS. ADVISORY REV. PANEL FOR POTENTIAL RULEMAKINGS FOR PAYDAY, VEHICLE TITLE, AND SIMILAR LOANS 12 (2015). Payday lenders are criticized for preying on overburdened people with loans that can be difficult to pay off and for using aggressive collection practices. THE PEW CHARITABLE TR., PARTY LENDING IN AMERICA: WHO BORROWS, WHERE THEY BORROW, AND WHY 2 (2012).

Concerns about high fees and frequent rollovers of payday loans have motivated some states to regulate payday loans through consumer protection laws, while other states have put in place more permissive systems. Recall our discussions from Chapters 1.4 and 5.1 of state usury laws that set interest rate caps. By the early 1900s, an illegal underground market had grown for short-term loans at extremely high interest rates. To curtail this practice and fill the consumer need for short-term loans, many states relaxed their usury laws. By the middle of the 20th Century, national lenders became prevalent, and state usury laws waned with deregulation. State-licensed payday lending flourished, and the sector began growing dramatically in the early 1990s. *Id.*

Since then, controversy surrounding payday lending has intensified. Payday lenders proliferated through the rent-a-charter arrangement you learned about in Chapter 2.1. Payday lenders contracted with banks in states without usury caps and—under their authority—were able to avoid application of state interest rate caps in the borrower's state. *See* OFFICE OF INSPECTOR GEN., FDIC, THE FDIC'S ROLE IN OPERATION CHOKE POINT AND SUPERVISORY APPROACH TO INSTITUTIONS THAT CONDUCTED BUSINESS WITH MERCHANTS ASSOCIATED WITH HIGH-RISK ACTIVITIES 53 (2015). In June 2000, the Chairman of the FDIC expressed concern over these rent-a-charter agreements and, by 2003, the FDIC issued guidance criticizing payday loans as raising consumer protection issues. *Id.* at 10–11. At the same time, a number of states began cracking down on payday loan practices. Some states, like New Mexico, began prohibiting the renewal, or rollover, of payday loans above a certain amount. *See* N.M. STAT. ANN. § 58-15-34 (2009). Others, like New York, set APR caps too low for payday business models to operate profitably. *See* N.Y. PENAL LAW § 190.40 (2009) (making it a violation of New York criminal law to exceed a 25% usury cap).

The federal government has only recently become involved in consumer protection issues surrounding payday loans. The Dodd-Frank Act gave the CFPB the authority to write rules prohibiting "unfair, deceptive, or abusive acts or practices" and establishing requirements designed to prevent such practices. 12 U.S.C. § 5531. With this authority, the CFPB, in 2015, released an outline of proposals under consideration for regulating payday loan practices. The CFPB is considering proposals that require payday lenders to make a good-faith, reasonable determination that the borrower is able to repay the loan. The proposal would require lenders to verify and consider the borrower's income, major financial obligations, and borrowing history before making a payday loan. If adopted, these CFPB proposals will be the most significant federal regulations on payday loans to date. *See* CFPB, SMALL BUS. ADVISORY REV. PANEL FOR

POTENTIAL RULEMAKINGS FOR PAYDAY, VEHICLE TITLE, AND SIMILAR LOANS 7–8 (2015).

---

1. ***Bans on Payday Loans.*** Professor Paige Marta Skiba argues against bans on payday loans on the basis that payday loans can enhance the utility of consumers and, in particular, the welfare of low-income individuals. *Regulation of Payday Loans: Misguided?*, 69 WASH. & LEE L. REV. 1023–46 (2012). Skiba suggests that a better policy would be to help consumers avoid using payday loans for long-term financing, and to regulate the loans such that they preserve the ability of payday loans to improve the welfare of consumers. *Id.* at 1030, 1041. Skiba argues that payday loans help otherwise credit-constrained individuals manage their income stream and avoid the financial consequences of overdraft fees or utility shutoffs, which can have greater net costs. According to Skiba, an outright ban on these credit-constrained groups could force them to turn to even riskier, or less legitimate, methods of financing, including approaching loan sharks or other private moneylenders. What do you think?

2. ***Deposit Advance Products.*** To ensure consistent standards for banks and non-banks, the CFPB's proposals for payday loans would also apply to deposit advance products—*i.e.*, low-value, short-term loans or lines of credit offered by banks to customers whose deposit accounts reflect recurring direct deposits. Are there other potential substitutes for payday loans that the CFPB should regulate?

3. ***Car-Title Loans.*** Car-title loans are transactions where lenders take, or purport to take, the title of a borrower's vehicle as collateral for a short-term loan. Like payday loans, car-title loans require no borrower credit check and have high interest rates—usually $25 for every $100 borrowed, with a typical term of 30 days, for a resulting APR of 300%. One study found that one in six car-title borrowers faced vehicle repossession, with the average borrower renewing her loan eight times and paying an average of $2,141 in interest on a $951 loan. JEAN ANN FOX ET AL., DRIVEN TO DISASTER: CAR-TITLE LENDING AND ITS IMPACT ON CONSUMERS, CTR. FOR RESPONSIBLE LENDING 3 (2013).

Consumer advocates argue that car-title loans are "more damaging than payday loans because borrowers who cannot pay the required fees lose their transportation to and from work." JEFF PETERSON, ARIZ. RURAL POL'Y INST., PREDATORY LENDING: PROFILE AND ANALYSIS 5 (2007). Some, therefore, have called for bans on car-title loans. *See, e.g.*, *Payday and Title Loans, Hearing Before the Ill. Senate Fin. Comm.* (statement of Daniel A. Edelman on behalf of the Ill. Consumer Just. Council). Professor Jim Hawkins, by contrast, contends that actual repossession rates are much lower than reported and that borrowers who lose their vehicles typically have other means of transportation. Hawkins argues, therefore, that bans on car-title loans would prevent beneficial uses of car-title loans for borrowers with emergency needs. *Credit on Wheels: The Law and Business of Auto-Title Lending* 69 WASH. & LEE L. REV. 535, 589 (2012). Should the state or federal government restrict car-title loans? Note that the CFPB's payday lending proposals would apply to car-title loans.

VI. DEPOSIT AND TRANSACTION SERVICES

Consumers use deposit and transaction services daily. In the course of this usage, consumers face issues concerning the availability of funds, whether their funds are covered by deposit insurance (as discussed in Chapter 2.4), and the potential for overdrafts. Moreover, many households are excluded from the banking system altogether. In 2009, one-quarter of low-income households and 13% of moderate-income households were unbanked, meaning they had neither a checking account nor a savings account. MICHAEL S. BARR, NO SLACK: THE FINANCIAL LIVES OF LOW-INCOME AMERICANS 3 (Brookings Inst. Press 2012). Many consumers turn to alternate forms of transaction services, including the use of prepaid cards, and face high fees for routine transactions, such as check cashing. The problem of the unbanked raises broader questions concerning financial access in the U.S. *See id.* at 3–7. In this section, we focus on two issues in deposit and transaction services, prepaid cards and overdrafts. We will return to a discussion of debit transactions and payment systems in Chapter 7.1.

A. PREPAID ACCOUNTS

Prepaid accounts can allow consumers to make payments, store money, retrieve cash from ATMs, receive direct deposits, and send money. A common type of prepaid card is a general purpose prepaid card. They come in many forms, including reloadable or single-use. Other common forms of prepaid accounts include payroll cards, student financial disbursement cards, tax refund cards, and government benefit cards, including those used to distribute Social Security, unemployment benefits, and child support. Prepaid cards may or may not offer FDIC deposit insurance protection depending on how they are structured; most do not. FED. RESERVE BANK OF ST. LOUIS, CARDS, CARDS AND MORE CARDS: THE EVOLUTION TO PREPAID CARDS (2011).

Prepaid accounts serve as a convenient financial tool to consumers unable or unwilling to open conventional banking accounts. The popularity of prepaid accounts has grown significantly in recent years. According to the CFPB, the amount stored in prepaid accounts has grown from $1 billion in 2003 to nearly $65 billion in 2013, and the figure is expected to continue to grow. Press Release, CFPB Proposes Strong Federal Protections for Prepaid Products (Nov. 13, 2014). Their popularity is mainly due to the fact that prepaid accounts do not require credit checks or stringent bank approval processes. FED. RESERVE BANK OF ST. LOUIS, CARDS, CARDS AND MORE CARDS: THE EVOLUTION TO PREPAID CARDS (2011).

Despite their benefits, prepaid accounts can be costly to consumers. For example, prepaid account service providers may assess fees on consumers for reloading funds into their accounts or for customer service. These fees, combined with limited access to account balance information, make it difficult for consumers to determine the exact costs of a prepaid account. Additionally, prepaid accounts provide little liability protection. Unlike credit or debit cards, prepaid accounts are exempt from mandatory consumer fraud protection laws. Prepaid account service providers therefore have discretion to refund a consumer who has suffered losses due to theft or fraud. Prepaid account service providers may also offer overdraft coverage or advances on direct deposit, which extend a line of credit to prepaid account consumers who have overdrafted. With annual percentage rates as high as 200%, these additional lines of credit can effectively trap consumers in long-term debt cycles. Martha C. White, *4 Reasons a Prepaid Debit Card Can Cost You Big*, TIME, Aug. 8, 2011.

The CFPB, in November 2014, proposed a rule to regulate this area. Among other provisions, the CFPB proposes to impose "Know Before You Owe" disclosure requirements on prepaid account service providers. The CFPB also proposes to extend the federal credit card consumer protection laws to cover prepaid accounts with credit functions. Prepaid card trade groups generally supported the CFPB's disclosure proposals, but they argued that the CFPB's proposal to extend credit card protections to the prepaid market would increase the cost of delivering prepaid accounts and thereby reduce consumers' options for financial services. *See, e.g.*, Network Branded Prepaid Card Association, Comment Letter in Response to Notice of Proposed Rulemaking on Prepaid Accounts; Docket Not. CFPB–2014–0031 (March 23, 2015).

---

1. ***Effectiveness.*** Is expanding credit card consumer protection laws to cover prepaid accounts a sound way of ensuring consumer protection? Are there any unique aspects of prepaid accounts that may make this approach ineffective?

B. OVERDRAFT PROTECTION

A bank may dishonor items that would create an account deficit, known as an overdraft, unless it has contracted with the account holder to pay the overdraft. U.C.C. § 4-402(a). If the bank agrees to pay the overdraft, which is the standard checking arrangement, an account holder incurs overdraft fees when his account is overdrawn. An overdraft fee is different from the charge for "non-sufficient funds," which penalizes bounced checks. Combined, these fees account for more than 40% of checking-related fees. CFPB, DATA POINT: CHECKING ACCOUNT OVERDRAFT 9 (2014). Thirty percent of consumer accounts incur at least one overdraft or non-sufficient funds fee per year. The CFPB found that 8% of consumers overdraft more than ten times a year, incurring an average of $380 in fees annually, and these consumers account for about 75% of total overdraft fees. *Id.* at 11–12.

In many cases, account holders incur these fees by overdrawing by a small amount. When an account faces multiple withdrawal requests but contains insufficient funds to pay all of those items, the payor bank may choose to honor the checks or debits in any order, thereby dishonoring any combination or size of checks or debits. U.C.C. § 4-303(b); *see also* U.C.C. § 4-303 cmt. 7 (noting that there is no priority rule). The policy of many banks is to pay items in descending order by amount, paying the largest checks first. Some account holders prefer this arrangement because it first pays important checks, such as rent, but it also tends to maximize overdraft and non-sufficient funds fees, which are incurred per item. For this reason, and because individual account holders lack bargaining power to negotiate fee schedules, banks have faced criticism that overdraft fees are excessive and lack transparency. Indeed, some courts have found that excessive fees are unconscionable or violate a bank's implied duty of good faith towards its customers. This is particularly true if such charges substantially exceed the cost of processing bad checks. *See, e.g.*, Best v. United States Nat'l Bank, 739 P.2d 554, 558 (Or. 1987) (highlighting that such charges are not in line with the "reasonable contractual expectations of the parties"). Other courts, however, have rejected such claims. *See, e.g.*, McGuire v. Bank One, La., N.A., 744 So. 2d 714 (La. App. 1999). Much overdraft litigation has focused on debit card overdraws, which we discuss in Part VII.

U.C.C. Article 4 is the governing framework for bank deposits and collections. Banks and customers, however, can contract out of the standard U.C.C. Article 4 arrangement. *See* Paul S. Turner, *Contracting out of the UCC: Variation by Agreement under Articles 3, 4, and 4A*, 40 LOY. L.A. L. REV. 443, 444–45 (2006). Circumventing U.C.C. Article 4 provides benefits to banks, as fees from overdraft protection more than offset losses suffered from customer nonpayment and fraud. In 2011, the principal balances of customers' unpaid charged-off accounts, triggered by overdraft protection programs, represented 14.4% of net overdraft fees, not including non-sufficient funds fees. CFPB, CFPB STUDY OF OVERDRAFT PROGRAMS 17 (2013). CFPB Director Cordray has publicly stated that "[o]verdrafts can provide consumers with access to funds, but the growing costs of overdraft practices have the capacity to inflict serious economic harm." Remarks at the CFPB Roundtable on Overdraft Practices (Feb. 22, 2012).

A 2010 amendment to Regulation E requires banks to obtain affirmative accountholder opt-in before charging overdraft fees on ATM and one-time debit-card transactions. 12 C.F.R. § 205.17. The drafters were motivated to amend Regulation E based on consumer behavioral studies. These studies revealed that, when faced with a choice, most consumers would not switch from the default framework. Lauren E. Willis, *When Nudges Fail: Slippery Defaults*, 80 U. CHI. L. REV. 1155, 1179 (2013). The banks, however, have since managed to achieve high opt-in rates, especially among consumers with a history of overdrafts and new accountholders. *Id.* at 1184. For banks with the highest number of opt-ins, 66% of heavy overdraft users had opted in by 2010. Meanwhile, 15% of the large banks achieved opt-in rates of 15% by the end of 2010, but by 2012, this increased to over 50% for all new accounts. *Id.* Banks have achieved this opt-in rate by making opting in as costless as possible, such as by providing pre-addressed stamped cards or engaging in one-on-one marketing, particularly for consumers with a history of overdrafts. *Id.* at 1186. Some consumers mistakenly believe that a failure to opt in will be costly. *Id.* at 1187. This experience suggests that regulators need to be sensitive to market context when using behavioral techniques for regulation. In market contexts in which firms have a strong incentive to reinforce consumers' behavioral biases, as in borrowing, defaults are unlikely to be sufficiently robust to alter market outcomes. *See* Michael S. Barr et al., *Behaviorally Informed Financial Services Regulation*, NEW AM. FOUND. 1–5 (2008).

Recall our discussion of credit card overlimit fees earlier in this Chapter. The CFPB found that opt-in rules were extremely effective in reducing those fees. Why do you think the opt-in method worked better in that context?

---

1. ***Overdraft Fees and Profitability.*** First Choice Bank is in a bind. Part of its mission is to serve low- and moderate-income consumers, and its management is determined to keep its branches open in lower-income neighborhoods. Its data shows, however, that those branches are unprofitable due to the high volume of overdrafts. First Choice has come up with two possible ways to turn these branches around. On the one hand, it can increase the overdraft fee from $28 to $50. On the other hand, it can begin charging a monthly checking account fee of $15 (as of 2016, branch checking accounts are free). Are these changes permitted under the U.C.C.? *See* U.C.C. §§ 4-401 cmt. 3, 4-403 cmt. 1.

2. ***Insufficient Funds.*** First Choice Bank approaches you with another problem. One of its accountholders, Carrie Consumer, drew a $1,800 check payable to Plumber's Payday, dating it April 20. The check was presented to First Choice Bank for payment on April 8, when Carrie's account held just $1,500. First Choice Bank, whose automated system is unable to catch post-dated checks, dishonored the check on April 11 and charged Carrie a $35 non-sufficient funds fee. Carrie's account lacks overdraft protection. Carrie deposited a $500 check on April 17, which would have pushed her account balance above $1,800. Were the bank's actions proper? Should Carrie have acted any differently? *See* U.C.C. §§ 3-113(a), 4-401(c), 4-401 cmt. 3, 4-403(b).

3. ***Overdrafts and Credit.*** Should overdrafts be regulated as a credit product rather than a deposit product? *See* Todd J. Zywicki, *The Economics and Regulation of Bank Overdraft Protection*, 69 WASH. & LEE L. REV. 1141, 1169 (2012) (noting that overdraft protection "can be used functionally like a credit card").

VII. DEBT COLLECTION AND CREDIT REPORTING

A. DEBT COLLECTION

Debt collection refers to the process by which creditors collect debts owed when they are past due. *See* U.S. Gov., *Dealing with Debt*. Debt collection is an omnipresent issue in the United States; approximately 35% of adults have debts in collection. CFPB, FAIR DEBT COLLECTION PRACTICES ACT: CFPB ANNUAL REPORT 2015 7 (2015) [hereinafter CFPB ANNUAL REPORT].

When a borrower fails to pay a debt, the creditor may attempt to collect in a number of ways. For instance, the creditor may attempt to collect the debt directly, by sending the borrower collection notices. Alternatively, the creditor may contract with a third party, called a debt collector, to seek payment of the debt. The creditor could also sell the debt to a third party, who would then attempt to collect from the borrower. Debt may be sold multiple times, making it difficult to trace the true ownership of debt. CFPB ANNUAL REPORT 8–9.

Debt collection can place consumers in a vulnerable position in which they may face loss of employment, a financial squeeze, as well as stress and anxiety. In some cases, collectors have been found to use illegal means to coerce consumers into paying their debt, including intimidation, speaking to third parties about a consumer's debt without their permission, and harassment. *Id.* at 12–13. Consumers also face the issue of phantom debt collection, in which debt collectors use unfair, deceptive, or abusive practices to collect debts that do not exist or are not owed to that collector. *Id.* at 34. The prevalence of consumer dismay in the debt collection process is highlighted by the 88,300 debt collection complaints the CFPB handled in 2014 alone. *Id.* at 12.

In 1978, Congress enacted the Fair Debt Collection Practices Act. The Act prohibits debt collectors from using false statements, such as claiming that they are a government representative, or stating that a consumer committed a crime, when trying to collect a debt. FTC, *Debt Collection* (2015). The Act also prevents debt collectors from collecting extra fees or interest, unless it is a term of the contract that created the debt. FTC, *Debt Collection* (2015). Additionally, the Act prohibits debt collectors from calling before 8:00 a.m. and after 9:00 p.m., telling third parties that a debt is owed, using harassing language, or making misrepresentations of fact. *See* 15 U.S.C. § 1692c(a)–(d).

Under the Dodd-Frank Act, the CFPB has the authority to supervise non-bank entities such as debt collectors. *See* 12 U.S.C. § 5514(a)(1)(C). Both the CFPB and the FTC can bring enforcement actions. CFPB ANNUAL REPORT 6. In recent years, the FTC and CFPB have focused on bringing more cases against debt collectors. CFPB ANNUAL REPORT 3; *see also id.* at 53, Appendix A (noting the agencies' increased efforts). For instance, in 2016, Citibank agreed to pay more than $19 million in fines and consumer relief and forego collecting $34 million from consumers to settle CFPB allegations that it caused debt collectors to overstate the interest rate of Citibank accounts in collection and used law firms to alter court documents. *See* Press Release, CFPB Orders Citibank to Provide Relief to Consumers for Illegal Debt Sales and Collection Practices (Feb. 23, 2016). The FTC and CFPB have also focused on educating the public about unfair and deceptive practices and the availability of consumer redress. Consumers have judicial recourse if they believe a debt collector has used an illegal means of collecting debt. Violations can also be reported to the FTC, CFPB, or a state attorney general's office.

B. CREDIT REPORTING

Credit reporting is the dissemination of a consumer's borrowing history and other financial information to a third party, such as a lender, to help the third party decide whether to lend to the consumer and, if so, what interest rate to charge. Employers also frequently request credit reports for potential employees. There are three primary credit reporting agencies in the United States: Experian, Equifax, and TransUnion. The credit reporting agencies are privately owned and operated. In addition to providing credit history in a credit report, credit reporting agencies calculate a credit score for each consumer.

Since credit reports contain sensitive information, particular importance is placed on the accuracy of information in the report and access to the report. Incorrect negative information on a credit report can cause a consumer to be denied employment, turned down for a loan, or harassed by debt collectors. *See* Nat'l Ass'n of Consumer Advocates, *Credit Reporting.* In addition to problems relating to errors in credit reports, consumers may be subject to identity thefts and delays in public record reporting, which negatively affect consumers' credit reports. CFPB, MONTHLY COMPLAINT REPORT, VOL. 2, 12 (2015). The CFPB, since its inception, has handled 105,500 complaints with respect to credit reporting, noting incorrect information as the biggest problem. *Id.* at 11.

The Fair Credit Reporting Act, originally passed in 1970, aims to promote fair credit reporting practices by focusing compliance efforts on credit reporting agencies, consumer report users, and information sources. It is enforced by the FTC, CFPB, and private parties engaged in litigation. The Fair Credit Reporting Act gives consumers the right to know if information in their credit report was used against them, know what information is contained in their file, request a credit score, dispute inaccurate information and have that information corrected, and be protected from outdated negative information. Additionally, consumers must give consent for reports to be provided to employers. FTC, A SUMMARY OF YOUR RIGHTS UNDER THE FAIR CREDIT REPORTING ACT 1–2.

The Dodd-Frank Act gave the CFPB the authority to supervise the credit reporting bureaus and transferred rulemaking authority for the Fair Credit Reporting Act to the CFPB. Dodd-Frank Act §§ 1024, 1088(a)(1)–(9) (2010). Section 615(h) of the Fair Credit Reporting Act was amended to require disclosure of a consumer's credit score if that score is used to make a decision regarding the consumer's creditworthiness. CFPB, CFPB CONSUMER LAWS AND REGULATIONS: FAIR CREDIT REPORTING ACT 29 (2012). It requires creditors to provide consumers with a risk-based pricing notice or an adverse action notice. These disclosures will give consumers more information about any factors that adversely affect their credit, allowing them to make informed decisions to improve their credit history. Consumers can file complaints with the FTC and CFPB, or pursue private litigation, to recover damages for violations of the Fair Credit Reporting Act. If consumers find inaccuracies or incomplete information in a credit report, the credit rating agency and the information provider have a duty to correct this information. FTC, FREE CREDIT REPORTS (2013). Upon correction, the credit rating agency must provide a consumer with written results and a new copy of the report. A consumer also has a right to a free copy of his or her credit report annually. *See* 15 U.S.C. § 1681j.

VIII. FINANCIAL PRIVACY

Financial institutions collect large quantities of confidential and personal information from consumers through their spending behavior, which financial institutions can assemble for internal use or to sell to other businesses. Retailers and manufacturers value this information for marketing purposes, which allows them to tailor products to consumers' preferences. Contemporary business incentives to use consumer information as a marketable commodity increasingly conflict with consumer expectations that their information remains private to those outside the financial institution. Such practices could lead to harms arising from information sharing, which can include fraud through the unauthorized collection, use, or transfer of information—including monitoring personal habits, profiling, identity theft, telemarketing, and denying benefits based on inaccurate information. Victoria Boyd, *Financial Privacy in the United States and the European Union: A Path to Transatlantic Regulatory Harmonization*, 24 BERKELEY J. INT'L LAW 939, 943 (2006).

The United States protects consumer privacy through a combination of market and self-regulatory mechanisms, as well as federal and state legislative systems. Title V of the Gramm-Leach-Bliley Act (GLBA), 15 U.S.C. §§ 6801–6805, for instance, requires financial institutions to develop policies, standards, and internal procedures to safeguard consumers. The GLBA requires financial institutions to disclose their privacy policies and provide an opt-out notice to consumers, which warns consumers that their information will be shared with non-affiliates unless they opt out.

In addition to the GLBA, other federal statutes that govern financial privacy include the Fair Credit Reporting Act of 1970, 15 U.S.C. §§ 1681–1681u, which governs disclosures of credit information by credit reporting agencies in consumer reports. The Bank Secrecy Act, as amended by the USA PATRIOT Act, regulates certain information sharing between financial institutions.

Great volumes of consumer data cross national borders daily. Yet, diverging philosophies on the appropriate levels of privacy protection between nations can lead to conflicting standards of data protection. The EU and United States are fighting over a wide range of such issues. *See, e.g.*, Virginia Boyd, *Financial Privacy of in the United States and European Union: A Path to Transatlantic Regulatory Harmonization*, 24 BERKELEY J. INT'L L. 939 (2006).

CHAPTER 5.4

COMPARING CONSUMER PROTECTION MODELS ACROSS SECTORS

CONTENTS

I. INTRODUCTION

The preceding Chapters of Part V introduced you to the consumer protection framework in the United States and focused on the technical aspects of that framework. This Chapter takes a different approach. Rather than concentrating on the detailed rules to which financial institutions are subject, this Chapter explores different regulatory models of consumer protection employed across different sectors of U.S. financial services and the schools of economic thought that animate those regulatory models. The Chapter is intended to highlight consistencies and inconsistencies across models and sectors. Coming as it does in the middle of the book, the Chapter looks back to earlier materials on banking, securities, and insurance, and anticipates materials to come, such as the regulation of mutual funds. While there are a number of approaches one might take to the material, this Chapter categorizes consumer protection laws as disclosure, behaviorally informed regulation, duties that impose affirmative obligations or negative prohibitions, product regulation of terms and price, and subsidy or tax. For various formulations of consumer protection typologies, see, *e.g.*, Michael S. Barr, *Modes of Credit Market Regulation*, *in* BUILDING ASSETS, BUILDING CREDIT: CREATING WEALTH IN LOW-INCOME COMMUNITIES 206–36 (N. Retsinas & E. Belsky ed., 2005); *see also* John Y. Campbell et al., *Consumer Financial Protection*, 25 J. ECON. PERSP. 91 (2011)

As we get started, consider the following matrix, Figure 5.4-1, which depicts each of these five regulatory models and examples of how they have been used in key financial services sectors.

Figure 5.4-1 Examples of Regulatory Models Across Key Financial Services Sectors

	Banking	**Insurance**	**Securities**
Disclosure	Creditors' obligation to disclose loan cost to borrowers. *See* Truth in Lending Act (TILA), 15 U.S.C. § 1631(a).	Insurers' requirement to disclose premium reductions and surcharges on auto insurance. *See, e.g.*, N.Y. Insurance Law § 2345.	Quarterly reporting requirements for publicly traded companies. *See* Securities Exchange Act of 1934 (1934 Act), 15 U.S.C. 78m(a).
Behavioral Regulation	De-biasing through minimum payment disclosures under the Credit Card Responsibility and Disclosure Act of 2009 (CARD Act), 15 U.S.C. §§ 1637(b)(11), (12); *see also* 12 C.F.R. §§ 1026.7(b)(11)–(13).	Safe harbors and other measures to encourage automatic enrollment and escalator plans. *See* Pension Protection Act of 2006, Pub. L. No. 109–280, 120 Stat. 780.	Harmonizing the fiduciary duty for brokers and advisers providing individualized investment advice. Dodd-Frank Act § 913(b).
Duties	Prohibition of credit discrimination on the basis of race, color, religion, national origin, sex, marital status, age, or receipt of public assistance. *See* Equal Credit Opportunity Act (ECOA), 15 U.S.C. § 1691(a)(1).	Duty to settle. *See* SCOTT BALL ET AL., THE RIGHT AND DUTY TO SETTLE THIRD PARTY LIABILITY CLAIMS: A 50-STATE SURVEY (2015).	Prohibition on the use of deceit, misrepresentations, and other fraud in the sale of securities. *See* Securities Act of 1933 (1933 Act), 15 U.S.C. 77q(a).
Product Regulation	Regulation of terms in home equity loans. *See* Home Ownership and Equity Protection Act (15 U.S.C. § 1637a).	Regulation of rates on auto insurance. *See, e.g.*, N.Y. Ins. Law § 2303.	Risk-limiting requirements for money market mutual funds. *See* 17 C.F.R. § 270.2a-7.
Subsidy or Tax	Federal Housing Administration insurance on home loans. *See* National Housing Act of 1934, 12 U.S.C. § 1709.	National Flood Insurance Program. *See* 42 U.S.C. § 4011.	Tax benefits of qualified retirement savings plans. *See, e.g.*, 26 U.S.C. § 401(k).

II. DISCLOSURE

Disclosure is arguably the most commonly employed regulatory model in the United States, extending everywhere from online shopping to criminal procedure. *See, e.g.*, Miranda v. Arizona, 384 U.S. 436 (1966). Professors Omri Ben-Shahar and Carl E. Schneider describe disclosure-based regulation as follows: "It aspires to help people making unfamiliar and complex decisions while dealing with specialists by requiring the latter (disclosers) to give the former (disclosees) information so that disclosees choose sensibly and disclosers do not abuse their position." OMRI BEN-SHAHAR & CARL E. SCHNEIDER, MORE THAN YOU WANTED TO KNOW: THE FAILURE OF MANDATED DISCLOSURE 3 (2014). While ubiquitous across many regulatory fields, disclosure is particularly important for consumer finance, insurance, and investor protection. One might think of disclosure as falling into three types: generalized disclosure that describes a product for all consumers, individualized disclosure that describes how a product applies to a particular consumer, and aggregated disclosure that describes the market performance for a particular product, service, or firm.

In the consumer finance context, regulations that require both generalized and individualized disclosures can be found, for example, in TILA, 15 U.S.C. § 1601. TILA "[relies] on providing information to consumers to ensure a well-functioning market[.]" Michael S. Barr, *Modes of Credit Market Regulation in* BUILDING ASSETS, BUILDING WEALTH: CREATING WEALTH IN LOW-INCOME COMMUNITIES 9 (N. Restsinas & E. Belsky, ed., 2005). It requires lenders to disclose loan cost information to protect consumers from unfair credit practices, and to allow consumers to comparison shop for loans more efficiently and effectively based on standard information. OCC, TRUTH IN LENDING. While mandated disclosures can help consumers comparison shop, TILA disclosures also have limitations in their ability to protect consumers, as Judge Richard Posner of the Seventh Circuit explores in the following case.

Emery v. American General Finance, Inc.

71 F.3d 1343 (7th Cir. 1996)

This is a suit for damages under the [Racketeer Influenced and Corrupt Organizations] statute. 18 U.S.C. §§ 1961 et seq. The plaintiff, Verna Emery, charges the defendant, American General Finance, a maker of small loans, with engaging in the practice of 'loan flipping,' a practice that the plaintiff claims is 'racketeering activity' within the meaning of [Racketeer Influenced and Corrupt Organizations]. § 1962(c). To be such, it must involve one or more of the crimes listed in section 1961(1), among which (see § 1961(1)(B)), and the only one alleged by the complaint, is mail fraud, prohibited by 18 U.S.C. § 1341. The district judge dismissed the complaint under Fed.R.Civ.P. 12(b)(6) on the ground that the facts alleged do not violate section 1341.

Here is what is alleged. On July 14, 1992, Emery borrowed $1,983.81 from American General Finance, the loan being secured by miscellaneous personal property, including a typewriter and a television set. The finance charge, based on the 36 percent annual rate of interest charged for the loan, was $1,327.08, and the loan was for three years. Six months later, American General Finance wrote a letter to Emery. The letter, signed by a branch manager, reads as follows:

> Dear Verna:
>
> I have extra spending money for you.
>
> Does your car need a tune-up? Want to take a trip? Or, do you just want to pay off some of your bills? We can lend you money for whatever you need or want.
>
> You're a good customer. To thank you for your business, I've set aside $750.00 * in your name.
>
> Just bring the coupon below into my office and if you qualify, we could write your check on the spot. Or, call ahead and I'll have the check waiting for you
>
> Make this month great with extra cash. Call me today—I have money to loan.
>
> * Subject to our normal credit policies.

At the bottom of the letter is a coupon captioned '$750.00 Cash Coupon' made out to Verna M. Emery at her address. Her name and address are preceded by the words '$750.00 cash for:' Small print explains at the bottom, 'This is not a check.'

Emery wanted a loan, so she responded to the letter. When she showed up in the branch manager's office, he gave her forms for a refinancing of her existing loan with additional funds advanced. The new note which she signed was for an amount financed of $2,399.83 and a finance charge (computed at the same 36 percent interest rate) of $1,641.28, payable over three years. The monthly payment, which had been $89.47 under the original loan, jumped to $108.20 (more for the first payment) for the new loan. Had she not refinanced she would have had to pay $89.47 a month for another 30 months or so (for the refinancing took place approximately six months after the original loan was made), while with the refinancing she had to pay $108.20 for the next 36 months—and this to receive $200. The increment in cost to her came to about $1,200, paid over three years, and this is for the right to get only $200 now. The cost to her of borrowing $200 in this way was roughly three times as great as it would have been had she borrowed that amount for three years in a separate loan at the annual interest rate of 36 percent. By our calculation, the implicit interest rate that she paid for the $200 loan exceeded 110 percent per annum. This was not disclosed on the [TILA] form that Emery received because the Act treats the transaction as a reborrowing of the original amount of the loan plus $200. So much for the [TILA] as a protection for borrowers. . . .

We do not of course know the state of mind of the employees of American General Finance who drafted the letter to Emery and its other customers; nor can the plaintiff have more than an inkling until she has an opportunity to conduct pretrial discovery. But assume, as the complaint adequately invites us to do, that these employees, desiring to exploit the financial naiveté of working-class borrowers, realizing that these borrowers do not read [TILA] disclosure forms intelligently, and hoping to trick them into overpaying disastrously for credit, drafted a letter that they believed would be effective in concealing the costs of refinancing. Read against this background of nefarious purpose, the letter is seen to be replete with falsehoods and half truths. 'Dear Verna . . . You're a good customer. To thank you for your business, I've set aside $750.00* in your name.' She is no 'Dear Verna' to them; she has not been selected to receive the letter because she is a good customer, but because she belongs to a class of probably gullible customers for credit; the purpose of offering her more money is not to thank her for her business but to rip her off; nothing has been 'set aside' for her. 'We could write your check on the spot. Or, call ahead and I'll have the check waiting for you.' Yes—along with a few forms to sign whereby for only $1,200 payable over three years at an even higher monthly rate than your present loan (and than your present loan plus a separate loan for $200, which we could have made you), you can have a meager $200 now. We were not reassured when at the oral argument American General Finance's lawyer was unable to tell us what it cost Verna Emery to obtain the $200 through a refinancing compared to what it would have cost her had the company simply made her a separate loan for that amount.

The district court thought the scheme saved from illegality by the plaintiff's failure to allege either a violation of [TILA] or a fiduciary relationship between the finance company and her. The points turn out to be related. A careful reader, comparing the [TILA] disclosure forms for the original loan to Emery and the refinancing-plus-additional-advance loan, would notice that the monthly payment was almost $20 a month higher under the second loan and by comparing the dates of the two forms would also realize that the second loan would require six more months of payments. But not all persons are capable of being careful readers. Suppose Emery were blind. . . . Would anyone argue that shoving a [TILA] disclosure form in front of her face would be a defense to fraud? The allegation is that she belongs to a class of borrowers who are not competent interpreters of such forms and that the defendant knows this and sought to take advantage of it. Taking advantage of the vulnerable is a leitmotif of fraud. *United States v. Newman*, 965 F.2d 206, 211 (7th Cir.1992). Competent people can protect themselves well enough against most forms of fraud. The incompetent are for that reason a frequent target of con men and other defrauders, and such targeting is, of course, unlawful, and indeed earns the criminal a longer sentence. *Id.* at 211; *United States v.*

Sutherland, 955 F.2d 25, 26 (7th Cir.1992); *United States v. Leonard*, 61 F.3d 1181, 1188 (5th Cir.1995).

---

1. ***Disclosure versus Duties.*** Are disclosure requirements a way of policing underlying substantive duties owed to consumers, or is compliance with disclosure rules the goal in itself?

2. ***Purposes of Disclosure: Coordinating or Information Forcing?*** In competitive markets, firms should have incentives to disclose information about their products. Mandated disclosure might help firms coordinate so that disclosures are comparable. If markets are not fully competitive, or if consumers are not modeled as fully rational, mandated disclosure can help to force firms to reveal shrouded information. *Compare* Alan Schwartz & Louis L. Wilde, *Intervening in Markets on the Basis of Imperfect Information: A Legal and Economic Analysis*, 127 U. PA. L. REV. 630, 632–35 (1979), *with* Michael S. Barr et al., *Behaviorally Informed Regulation, in* THE BEHAVIORAL FOUNDATIONS OF POLICY 440–65 (Eldar Shafir ed., 2013), *and* Xavier Gabaix & David Laibson, *Shrouded Attributes, Consumer Myopia, and Information Suppression in Competitive Markets*, 121 Q. J. ECON. 505 (2006).

3. ***Consumer-Facing Disclosure Compared with Aggregated Market Disclosure.*** TILA is focused on improving decision-making by individual consumers to improve market competition. The Home Mortgage Disclosure Act (HMDA), by contrast, which requires mortgage lenders to disclose aggregated information to the public about the mortgage loans they issue, purchase, and deny is an example of a disclosure law that "assist[s] in the enforcement of other legal rules or social norms. . . ." Michael S. Barr, *Modes of Credit Market Regulation, in* BUILDING ASSETS, BUILDING WEALTH: CREATING WEALTH IN LOW-INCOME COMMUNITIES 9 (N. Restsinas & E. Belsky, ed., 2005); *see also* 12 U.S.C. §§ 2801, 2803. It seeks to improve the mortgage market by requiring the disclosure of loan data that can be used to "[determine] whether financial institutions are serving the housing needs of their communities; [assist] public officials in distributing public-sector investments so as to attract private investment to areas where it is needed; and [identify] possible discriminatory lending patterns." FFIEC, HOME MORTGAGE DISCLOSURE ACT: BACKGROUND & PURPOSE (2015).

In the investor protection context, disclosure is the foundation of both the 1933 Act and the 1934 Act. The 1933 Act's main goals are to provide investors with adequate information regarding securities offered for sale in primary markets (that is, sales by the securities' issuers directly to investors), and to protect investors from fraud and misrepresentations in the sale of those securities. *See* SEC, THE LAWS THAT GOVERN THE SECURITIES INDUSTRY (2013). It strives to accomplish these goals by mandating that issuers disclose important financial information about both their business and the securities being offered for sale, and by imposing liability on issuers for inaccuracies in the disclosures. *See id.* The 1934 Act seeks to achieve the same investor protection goals as the 1933 Act, but it focuses on secondary market transactions, or sales of securities between investors. In addition to the 1933 Act's registration requirements at the time securities are initially sold, the 1934 Act imposes ongoing reporting requirements on those issuers. The 1934 Act mandates that issuers put out both periodic reports disclosing financial information and *ad hoc* reports upon the occurrence of certain significant events, and attaches liability to material misstatements or omissions in those reports.

Professors Michael Greenstone, Paul Oyer, and Annette Vissing-Jorgensen summarized some aspects of the debate over whether mandated securities disclosures are justified:

> One traditional view of securities market regulation, often attributed to Stigler [1964] and Coase [1960], is that government intervention is at best ineffective and, at worst, damaging. The basis of this view is that private contracts, combined with the possibility of litigation, between shareholders on the one side and managers, underwriters, auditors, and analysts on the other, is a cost-effective way to achieve efficient disclosure. This private enforcement will be especially successful in settings with repeated interactions where agents with superior information are concerned about their reputations. These views imply that a firm's failure to provide some information must be due to the high costs of provision, lack of value relevance, or valid concerns that competitors may benefit from its release. In this setting, mandatory disclosure regulations are either inconsequential or cause firms to release an inefficiently large amount of information.
>
> An alternative view posits that prohibitively high costs of writing and enforcing complete contracts make mandatory disclosure regulations welfare enhancing. There are at least three reasons that regulations may be preferable to an exclusive reliance on private contracts. First, the costs of filing a lawsuit may introduce a free-rider problem among shareholders. In contrast, a regulator does not face these coordination problems. Second, regulations that mandate increased provision of information may be less vulnerable to subversion of justice than litigation (see Glaeser and Shleifer [2003]). Third, regulators' exclusive focus on securities cases may make them more effective than judges or juries at detecting fraud.

Michael Greenstone et al., *Mandated Disclosure, Stock Returns, and the 1964 Securities Acts Amendments*, 121 Q.J. ECON. 399, 404–05 (2006)

In general, there are two reasons why policymakers might compel firms to disclose information. First, disclosure can solve a coordination problem. Under this theory, firms want to disclose information to the market, but they need to coordinate their disclosures in order for that information to be useful to consumers or investors. Alternatively, mandated disclosures may be necessary if firms do not want to disclose. Under this theory, firms have an incentive to withhold or falsify information, and the market functions inefficiently based on consumers' and investors' imperfect information. In their article *Intervening in Markets on the Basis of Imperfect Information: A Legal and Economic Analysis*, Professors Alan Schwartz and Louis L. Wilde explain the economic justifications for disclosure-based regulations when firms otherwise would not disclose and contrast disclosure with product regulation.

Alan Schwartz & Louis L. Wilde, Intervening in Markets on the Basis of Imperfect Information: A Legal and Economic Analysis

127 U. PA. L. REV. 630, 632–35 (1979)

The existence of imperfect information is thought to justify legal intervention, according to conventional understanding, because consumers cannot contract in their own best interests without the data to rank the purchase choices that markets offer. This understanding implies that in determining whether to intervene in a given market decisionmakers should ask whether each (i.e., an idealized) consumer is sufficiently informed to make purchase choices that maximize his own utility. For example, assume three firms sell a homogeneous product for $2, $3, and $4, respectively. A consumer pays $4 because he is unaware of the existence of lower prices. Imperfect information prevented this consumer from making the utility maximizing contract choice—a purchase at the lowest price. Legal intervention in this or any other market should be designed to enable each individual consumer to make the optimal choice, or otherwise to protect him from the consequences of making uninformed choices.

The most common methods of protecting consumers in such situations are to have the state impose standards for purchase terms or take action to reduce information acquisition costs. Courts determine purchase terms by refusing to enforce particular contract clauses; legislatures determine purchase terms by statutorily prohibiting some clauses and requiring others. Two justifications for such a determination of purchase terms follow from the conventional analysis. First, if all consumers have identical preference rankings and a court or legislature is in a better position than market participants to ascertain which purchase choices are consistent with this ranking, state determination of the terms will maximize each person's utility. Assume, for example, that all consumers prefer insurance against injuries caused by the products they purchase, but are unable to understand the language of warranty disclaimers imposing the risk of these injuries on buyers. A state prohibition of such disclaimers is then optimal.

Second, a standard objection to such state intervention in consumer markets is that individuals know their preferences better than public decisionmakers do. This assumption becomes untenable, however, when individuals are imperfectly informed. Consequently, when a condition of imperfect information exists, decisionmakers should feel less constrained in substituting their view of what constitutes a fair exchange for the outcomes reached by private agreements. As an illustration, some consumers, unaware of the legal and personal consequences of giving security, may mistakenly agree to contracts granting broad security interests to the sellers of goods they purchase; these consumers actually may prefer to pay higher interest rates for financing installment purchases rather than bear the risk of harsh repossessions. In these circumstances, the contracts will not reflect consumer preferences. Thus, a court or legislature that believes it to be fair to limit the scope of security interests that consumers can grant or to prevent repossessions without judicial process should simply direct such outcomes, for the argument that the contracts to which consumers have agreed demonstrate contrary consumer preferences is factually incorrect.

According to conventional wisdom, however, reduction of information acquisition costs, other things being equal, is preferable to legislative or judicial determination of contract terms, because reducing information costs enables individuals to make informed choices to maximize their own utility. Because consumers seldom have identical preference rankings, external determination of terms rarely is optimal. Also, if one accepts the notion that decisionmakers should intervene to regulate contract terms only if consumers are uninformed, then it is incumbent upon the state to attempt to create conditions under which informed contract choices can be made. Because more consumers will become informed if information acquisition costs are decreased, reducing these costs is thought to be the preferable response to the problem of imperfect information. Regulating terms is therefore a second best solution, to be used primarily by the judiciary, because courts cannot create and police disclosure schemes. In keeping with this conventional analysis, many of the recently enacted consumer protection laws require firms to disclose information rather than to contract on state-supplied terms.

Ben-Shahar and Schneider are skeptical of disclosure's efficacy. In the following excerpt, Ben-Shahar and Schneider summarize the results of studies on the failures of disclosure laws across all regulatory fields.

> [I]n field after field there is good evidence that mandated disclosure does not achieve disclosurites' goals. The evidence comes from numerous studies, many conducted by researchers truly committed to making disclosure work, many pouring impractically generous resources into disclosure. The evidence does *not* say that no disclosure ever improves any disclosees' understanding. *Many* studies show some improvements. But repeatedly even strenuous efforts to educate disclosees do not bring them near the level of understanding needed to make good decisions. If you take a multiple-choice test covering basic information about a choice and can answer only half the questions, you don't know or are wrong about too many things to evaluate your choices the way disclosurites want.

OMRI BEN-SHAHAR & CARL E. SCHNEIDER, MORE THAN YOU WANTED TO KNOW: THE FAILURE OF MANDATED DISCLOSURE 47 (2014).

Professor Margaret Jane Radin offers some reasons for the failures of disclosure described above:

> [W]hy don't we read these things? Here are seven answers: (1) We wouldn't understand the terms if we did read them, so it isn't worth our time. (2) We need the product or service and have no access to a supplier that does not impose onerous clauses, so reading the terms wouldn't make any difference. (3) We are not even aware that we are becoming subject to these terms, so we don't know that there is anything to read. (4) We trust the company not to have included anything harmful. (5) We suppose that anything harmful would be unenforceable. (6) We think that the company has power over us, so that we are simply stuck with what it imposes on us. (7) Yet another reason, and an important one: we don't believe that we will ever need to exercise our background legal rights. We don't expect misfortune to befall us. As psychological research has shown, we are not able to make accurate assessments of risks.

MARGARET JANE RADIN, BOILERPLATE 12 (2013).

In the following excerpt, Professor Lauren E. Willis advocates that the CFPB should supplement mandatory disclosure requirements with a performance-based approach.

Lauren E. Willis, The Consumer Financial Protection Bureau and the Quest for Consumer Comprehension

2 RSF J. OF THE SOCIAL SCIENCES 5, (Michael S. Barr, ed., forthcoming 2016)

[The] Dodd-Frank [Act] tasked the [CFPB] with ensuring that "consumers . . . understand the costs, benefits, and risks associated with" financial products and services. Despite this ambitious mandate, the [CFPB]'s pursuit of consumer comprehension has thus far focused on the same twentieth century tool that has already proven ineffective at regulating consumer finance: required disclosures. No matter how well the [CFPB]'s "Know Before You Owe" disclosures perform in the lab, or even in field trials, firms will run circles around disclosures when the experiments end, misleading consumers and defying consumers' expectations. Even without any intent to deceive, firms not only will but *must* leverage consumer confusion to compete with other firms that do so. While firms are not always responsible for their customers' confusion, firms today take advantage of this confusion to sell products. . . .

To meet its mandate to ensure that consumers understand the financial transactions in which they engage, the [CFPB] needs to summon the innovative data-driven twenty-first century spirit that otherwise pervades the [CFPB's] approach to consumer protection. Specifically, the [CFPB] must induce firms themselves to promote consumer comprehension, whether by helping their customers understand transactions and/or by conforming transactions to their customers' understanding. To generate this change in firm behavior, the [CFPB] should require firms to regularly demonstrate, through third-party testing of random samples of their customers, that a good proportion of their customers know, at the time they can use this knowledge, the key pertinent "costs, benefits, and risks" of the products they have bought.

For example, the [CFPB] should require firms to prove that their customers are aware of the costs the customers will incur at the moment when they are deciding whether to take an action that will trigger those costs, whether that be taking out a mortgage, overdrawing a checking account, or calling customer service to inquire about a prepaid debit card balance. Where consumers are confused about benefits, such as the benefit of signing up for a credit repair service, enrolling in a credit card rewards program, or paying a debt that is beyond limitations, firms should show that their customers understand the actual benefits the firm is offering.

Demonstrating sufficient customer comprehension could be a precondition firms must meet before enforcing a term or charging a fee or firms could be sanctioned (or rewarded) for demonstrating low (or high) comprehension levels. In effect, rather than prescriptively regulating the marketing and sales process with mandated disclosures or pursuing firms on an ad hoc ex post basis for unfair, deceptive, and abusive marketing and sales practices, the [CFPB] would monitor and incentivize firm performance in achieving customer comprehension as the marketing and sales process unfolds over time.

Performance-based regulation is widely used in other fields and its use has been expanding in the consumer arena. Environmental and building code regulations have long employed it. Rather than the law dictating the scrubber a factory smokestack must use or the material a builder must use, the law sets emissions limits or imposes strength and durability requirements, and the factory owner or builder can decide how to meet those limits or requirements. . . .

Making firms responsible for effectively informing their own customers would capitalize on firms' greater knowledge of and access to their customers and greater ability to experiment and innovate. Comprehension rules would incentivize firms to educate rather than obfuscate and to develop product designs that align with rather than defy consumer expectations.

Financial education is sometimes posited as a complement to disclosure. Professor Howell Jackson and his co-authors have written that efforts to improve consumers' financial literacy are some of the simplest forms of government intervention. Jackson and his co-authors argue that "there is growing evidence that consumers make avoidable financial mistakes with non-trivial financial consequences. Moreover, these mistakes are more common among consumers with lower levels of education and income and who are less financially literate. If consumers cannot maximize their own welfare, there is no reason to believe that competitive markets will be efficient." John Y. Campbell et al., *The Regulation of Consumer Financial Products: An Introductory Essay with Four Case Studies* 10 (2010 Draft version).

Willis argues that the benefits of effective financial education are not worth the costs due to the substantial intrusion into individual autonomy. In order to be effective,

> financial education would reduce consumer control over how to spend time and effort, as well as over when, whether, and with whom to share private financial and psychological information. Because only mandatory financial education would be effective, it would force those who would not have autonomously chosen to participate to do so. Because only personally tailored content and debiasing measures would be effective, consumers would be required to reveal the details of their financial and emotional lives. These impositions on people's lives would be significant, given the extensiveness and frequency of the education that would be required.

Lauren E. Willis, *The Financial Education Fallacy*, 101 AM. ECON. REV. 429, 431 (2011).

---

1. ***Popularity of Disclosure as a Regulatory Tool.*** If disclosure is an ineffective regulatory model, why is it so popular? Why might firms welcome disclosure requirements?

2. ***Consumer Comprehension Standard.*** What is your reaction to Willis' proposed consumer comprehension standard? How would such a standard be implemented? Even if comprehension is achieved, will it necessarily lead to better decisions by consumers? *See* Michael S. Barr et al., *Behaviorally Informed Regulation, in* THE BEHAVIORAL FOUNDATIONS OF POLICY 440 (Eldar Shafir ed., 2013). For an extended discussion in the context of mutual fund disclosures, see Chapter 10.3. *See also* Talia B. Gillis, *Putting Disclosure to the Test: Toward Better Evidence Based Policy*, 27 LOY. CONSUMER L. REV. (forthcoming 2016).

3. ***Do Consumers Actually Read Disclosures?*** Think about how you interact with disclosure-based regulations on a daily basis; do you actually take the time to read them? For an exaggerated take on the potential consequences of not reading the disclosures in an end-user license agreement, see *South Park: HUMANCENTiPAD* (Comedy Cent. television broadcast Apr. 27, 2011).

4. ***Structure of Disclosures.*** There are, undoubtedly, some merits to disclosure. Could the problem be not with disclosure itself, but with the way that

disclosures have traditionally been structured? What do you think regulators could do to make disclosures more effective? As you learned in Chapter 5.2, the Dodd-Frank Act now requires the CFPB to validate model forms through consumer testing and permits private-sector pilots of alternative disclosures. *See* Dodd-Frank Act §§ 1032(b)(3), (e).

5. ***Disclosure and Duties, Redux.*** When should disclosure substitute for duties or product regulation? Think back to Chapter 4.2. When can duties of securities firms to avoid conflicts of interest be met by disclosing the potential conflict? When is disclosure a substitute for mandatory contract terms? Why?

III. BEHAVIORALLY INFORMED FINANCIAL REGULATION

Mandated disclosure may have limitations in part because the neoclassical economic model on which disclosure is based is itself subject to limitations. As you learned in Chapter 5.1, research in psychology suggests that the "availability and dissemination of data do not always lead to effective communication and knowledge; understanding and intention do not necessarily lead to the desired action; and purportedly inconsequential contextual nuances, whether intentional or not, can shape behavior and alter choices, often in ways that people themselves agree diminish their well-being in unintended ways." Michael S. Barr et al., *Behaviorally Informed Regulation*, *in* NO SLACK: THE FINANCIAL LIVES OF LOW-INCOME AMERICANS 247 (Michael S. Barr ed. 2012). Professors Michael Barr, Sendhil Mullainathan, and Eldar Shafir argue that firms' incentives in many contexts to exacerbate, rather than overcome, behavioral biases mean that the form of regulation deployed may need to be aimed not only at behavioral change for consumers, but also at market structural change. *Id.* at 256. Thus, policies might range from nudges to encourage welfare-enhancing consumer behavior, to default rules changing the starting point for decisions, to "sticky" defaults that change the starting point and alter liability rules, to more prescriptive product or service regulation prohibiting certain products or conduct.

Recall from Chapter 5.3 the range of approaches taken in the CARD Act. For instance, Congress mandated improved disclosures in credit card agreements, required credit card companies to notify consumers 45 days in advance of major changes in card terms, and compels companies to publish a "minimum payment warning" on the consumers' monthly statements. Congress also required that consumers opt-in to over-limit transactions, severely restricted late fees, and prohibited retroactive rate increases on existing balances. Professors Barr, Mullainathan, and Shafir examined the behavioral basis for the CARD Act:

> The CARD Act of 2009 enacted a number of key changes to the credit card market that take seriously the behavioral insights and the incentives of firms to exploit consumer failings. . . . These practices have in common that consumers cannot readily shape their behavior to avoid the charges; the fees or changes in question are not readily shopped for in choosing a credit card, and disclosures are of little help. Since consumers generally do not understand how payments are allocated across account balances even after improved

> disclosures, the act requires a consumer's first payments above the minimum required to be applied first toward higher-cost balances. In addition . . . recognizing that consumers do not shop for penalty fees and that they often mis-forecast their own behavior, [the act] requires that late fees and other penalty fees be "reasonable and proportionate," as determined by implementing rules; that in any event the fees not be larger than the amount charged that is over the limit or late; and that a late fee or other penalty fee cannot be assessed more than once for the same transaction or event. Furthermore, the act takes steps to make it easier for the market to develop mechanisms for consumer comparison shopping by requiring the public posting to the Federal Reserve of credit card contracts in machine-readable format. Private firms or nonprofits can then develop tools for experts and consumers to use to evaluate these various contracts. . . .

Michael S. Barr et al., *Behaviorally Informed Regulation, in* THE BEHAVIORAL FOUNDATIONS OF PUBLIC POLICY 454–55 (Eldar Shafir ed., 2013).

As you learned in Chapter 5.2, one way of thinking about the qualified mortgage/qualified residential mortgage exemptions to the risk retention and ability-to-pay rules is as a form of "plain vanilla" mortgage, or a "sticky default" designed to anchor the market by incentivizing providers to offer consumer-friendly mortgages with straightforward terms. *See id.* at 449–51. In Chapter 5.3, you saw that the CARD Act's over-limit opt-in provision had significant effects, while the opt-in requirements for overdrafts pursuant to Federal Reserve Board rules were not that effective.

Behavioral approaches have been used in a wide variety of other areas as well. *See* RICHARD THALER & CASS SUNSTEIN, NUDGE: IMPROVING DECISIONS ABOUT HEALTH, WEALTH, AND HAPPINESS (2008); *see also* Cass Sunstein, *Empirically Informed Regulation*, 78 U. CHI. L. REV. 1349 (2011). One important area is in asset management, particularly for retirement plans. For example, setting a default rule that workers will be enrolled in a retirement plan at work unless they opt out increases retirement plan enrollment. Tweaks to the plans that automatically increase savings, for example, as income rises, unless the worker opts out, further increase savings. *See* Brigitte C. Madrian & Dennis F. Shea, *The Power of Suggestion: An Analysis of 401(k) Participation and Saving Behavior* 116 Q. J. ECON. 1149 (2001); *see also* Richard H. Thaler & Shlomo Benartzi, *Save More Tomorrow: Using Behavioral Economics to Increase Employee Saving*, 112 J. POL. ECON. 164 (2004). These insights were incorporated into the Pension Protection Act of 2006, Pub. L. No. 109–280, 120 Stat. 780, which encourages such automatic enrollment and escalator plans; these have had their intended effects, although further refinements are possible. *See* Shlomo Benartzi et al., *Choice Architecture and Retirement Savings Plans, in* THE BEHAVIORAL FOUNDATIONS OF PUBLIC POLICY 245 (Eldar Shafir ed., 2013).

Behavioral economics informed the Dodd-Frank Act's requirement for the harmonization of fiduciary duties for brokers and advisers providing individualized investment advice. Dodd-Frank Act § 913(b). The Treasury Department described the proposal behind this provision in the following excerpt.

Dep't of the Treasury, Protect Consumers and Investors from Financial Abuse

Financial Regulatory Reform:
A New Foundation: Rebuilding Financial Supervision and Regulation 70–71 (2009)

Establish a fiduciary duty for broker-dealers offering investment advice and harmonize the regulation of investment advisers and broker-dealers.

Retail investors face a large array of investment products and often turn to financial intermediaries—whether investment advisors or brokers-dealers—to help them manage their investments. However, investment advisers and broker-dealers are regulated under different statutory and regulatory frameworks, even though the services they provide often are virtually identical from a retail investor's perspective.

Retail investors are often confused about the differences between investment advisers and broker-dealers. Meanwhile, the distinction is no longer meaningful between a disinterested investment advisor and a broker who acts as an agent for an investor; the current laws and regulations are based on antiquated distinctions between the two types of financial professionals that date back to the early 20th century. Brokers are allowed to give "incidental advice" in the course of their business, and yet retail investors rely on a trusted relationship that is often not matched by the legal responsibility of the securities broker. In general, a broker-dealer's relationship with a customer is not legally a fiduciary relationship, while an investment adviser is legally its customer's fiduciary.

From the vantage point of the retail customer, however, an investment adviser and a broker-dealer providing "incidental advice" appear in all respects identical. In the retail context, the legal distinction between the two is no longer meaningful. Retail customers repose the same degree of trust in their brokers as they do in investment advisers, but the legal responsibilities of the intermediaries may not be the same.

The SEC should be permitted to align duties for intermediaries across financial products. Standards of care for all broker-dealers when providing investment advice about securities to retail investors should be raised to the fiduciary standard to align the legal framework with investment advisers. In addition, the SEC should be empowered to examine and ban forms of compensation that encourage intermediaries to put investors into products that are profitable to the intermediary, but are not in the investors' best interest.

New legislation should bolster investor protections and bring important consistency to the regulation of these two types of financial professionals by:

- requiring that broker-dealers who provide investment advice about securities to investors have the same fiduciary obligations as registered investment advisers;
- providing simple and clear disclosure to investors regarding the scope of the terms of their relationships with investment professionals; and
- prohibiting certain conflict of interests and sales practices that are contrary to the interests of investors.

See also Polina Demina, *Broker-Dealers and Investment Advisers: A Behaviorial-Economics Analysis of Competing Suggestions for Reform*, 113 MICH. L. REV. 429 (2014).

Scholars have long suggested that behavioral economics could improve insurance markets. For example, there is a good deal of evidence that consumers do not optimize in Medicare prescription drug insurance plans. *See, e.g.*, Florian Heiss et al., *Plan Selection in Medicare Part D: Evidence from Administrative Data*, 32 J. OF HEALTH ECON. 1325–44 (2013). Better choice architecture might improve outcomes and a variety of such techniques were included in the Affordable Care Act of 2010. *See generally*, Katherine Baicker et al., *Health Insurance Coverage and Take-Up: Lessons from Behavioral Economics*, 90 MILBANK Q. 107 (2012); Howard C. Kunreuther et al., INSURANCE & BEHAVIORAL ECONOMICS (2013); Brigitte C. Madrian, *Applying Insights from Behavioral Economics to Policy Design* (Nat'l Bureau Econ. Research, Working Paper No. 20318, 2014); Thomas Rice, *The Behavioral Economics of Health and Health Care*, 34 ANN. REV. OF PUB. HEALTH 431 (2013).

The requirement of certain mandatory terms in insurance contracts could be understood as reflecting behavioral economic concerns. For example, the requirement that health insurance include emergency room care coverage (discussed in Chapter 3.2) reflects in part a concern that individuals rarely foresee their need for emergency services. Similarly, prohibitions against subrogation of claims arising out of auto accidents (mentioned in Chapter 3.3) arguably addresses excessive consumer discounting of low probability events plus basic cognitive problems arising out of reading fine print.

---

1. ***Libertarian Paternalism?*** Are nudges libertarian because they do not impose mandatory terms, paternalistic because they convey normative values, some combination of the two (if that is not an oxymoron), or something else entirely? *See* Richard Thaler & Cass Sunstein, *Libertarian Paternalism*, 93 AM. ECON. REV. 175 (2003); *see also* Cass Sunstein & Richard Thaler, *Libertarian Paternalism is Not an Oxymoron*, 70 U. CHI. L. REV. 1159 (2003); *see also* Colin Camerer et al., *Regulation for Conservatives: Behavioral Economics and the Case for 'Asymmetric Paternalism'*, 151 U. PA. L. REV. 1211 (2003).

2. ***Behaviorally Informed Regulation?*** Barr, Mullainathan and Shafir argue that behavioral economics should not naively assume that nudges and default rules will work when firms have strong incentives to overcome them. In what contexts that you have studied do you think these approaches might work best?

IV. DUTIES

Duties imposing affirmative obligations and negative prohibitions match a colloquial understanding of what the law does: it tells people what they must do and what they may not do. Because any affirmative obligation can be recast as a negative prohibition—for example, the affirmative obligation to obey a speed limit can be reformulated as a negative prohibition from violating a speed limit—we discuss both in this section. There may, however, be significant differences in the way that affirmative obligations and negative prohibitions operate, and in their relative effectiveness in achieving objectives. Duties are used in banking, securities, and insurance regulation in a variety of contexts.

The Community Reinvestment Act (CRA), 12 U.S.C. §§ 2901–08, which was enacted against a history of redlining in low-income and minority communities, is an example of an affirmative obligation imposed on banks and thrifts. It requires depository institutions to meet the credit needs of the community, including low-income neighborhoods, consistent with safe and sound banking practices. Regulators enforce those obligations by evaluating CRA compliance in determining whether to approve an institution's application to expand its deposit facilities, including expansion by mergers with and acquisitions of other depository institutions. BOARD OF GOVERNORS OF THE FED. RES. SYSTEM, COMMUNITY REINVESTMENT ACT (CRA) (2014). In his article *Credit Where it Counts: The Community Reinvestment Act and Its Critics*, Barr outlines some criticisms of the CRA's regulatory approach, before going on to refute them.

Michael S. Barr, Credit Where it Counts: The Community Reinvestment Act and Its Critics

80 N.Y.U. L. REV. 513, 527–29, 533–34 (2005)

Critics contend that CRA has provided little benefit at a very high cost because it is the wrong answer to a nonexistent problem. The benefits are insignificant, they argue, because economic growth, bank deregulation, technological innovation, and competition would have driven banks to lend in low-income areas even without CRA. Loan commitments that make headlines are a public relations boon but simply represent what the banks would do anyway. Others contend that city renewal policies and community development financial institutions were responsible for increased lending. Critics contend that lending not covered by CRA and lending by banks and thrifts outside their CRA assessment areas spurred the lending increases in low-income areas, so CRA could not have been responsible for any increased lending in these communities.

At the same time, critics have argued that CRA imposes high costs in a number of ways, and recent scholarship has suggested that the 1995 regulatory reform did not reduce compliance costs or enhance shareholder value. First, critics argue that CRA conflicts with bank safety and soundness regulation. CRA expects banks not only to expand credit to households to whom they would not otherwise lend but also to maintain safety and soundness. Critics deride these aims as mutually inconsistent. Because, in their view, market failures and discrimination are not significant factors justifying CRA, they argue that CRA forces banks to engage in unprofitable, risky lending. To the extent that CRA forces banks to lend to less creditworthy borrowers, CRA increases the bank's risk and reduces its profitability. To the extent that CRA forces banks to lend locally, CRA undermines the ability of banks to diversify their lending geographically, thereby undermining the soundness of their portfolio. Moreover, critics charge that during economic downturns, when banks must necessarily reduce their risk profiles, CRA examiners would give banks bad ratings for what are in fact only prudent reductions in risk. . . .

I will discuss how the theoretical support for CRA derives from three bases. First, CRA addresses market failures caused by imperfect information, collective action problems, agency costs, and neighborhood externalities that are more acute in low-income neighborhoods and for low-income borrowers than in credit markets generally. Contrary to the views of CRA's critics, I will argue that the market failures are significant, and that CRA is an appropriate response to them. Second, I will argue that CRA helps to reduce discrimination against minority borrowers and communities. CRA was not designed to address racial discrimination against individual borrowers directly, but it was aimed, in part, at addressing 'redlining' discrimination and its legacy in segregated, low-income neighborhoods. Moreover, the significant correlation between race and income, and between race of homeowner and racial composition and income of neighborhood, gives CRA leverage to overcome barriers to credit faced by minority households. In some contexts, this leverage is greater than that of fair lending laws. Thus, I will explain why CRA is an important part of a broader regulatory strategy to overcome the legacy of discrimination in order to expand access to credit to minority households. Third, I will contend that CRA has largely not done enough to break down inefficient barriers between the bifurcated prime and subprime lenders in [low- and moderate-income (LMI)] neighborhoods. Over time, along with market changes, CRA can help make the subprime and prime markets more efficient by completing the market. In addition, CRA could play a strong role in reducing discrimination that results from, and occurs in, bifurcated credit markets.

Negative prohibitions, such as ECOA, 15 U.S.C. § 1691, require regulated financial institutions to refrain from certain actions. ECOA prohibits lenders from discriminating between borrowers "on the basis of race, color, religion, national origin, sex, marital status, age, or because [a borrower] get[s] public assistance." FED. TRADE COMM'N, YOUR EQUAL CREDIT OPPORTUNITY RIGHTS (2013). ECOA provides for enforcement of its negative prohibitions by subjecting a violating lender "to civil liability for actual and punitive damages." 12 C.F.R. § 1002.16. Recall from Chapter 5.2 that lenders can be liable under ECOA for either disparate treatment or disparate impact. CFPB, CFPB CONSUMER LAWS AND REGULATIONS: EQUAL CREDIT OPPORTUNITY ACT (ECOA) (2013). Returning to *Credit Where it Counts: The Community Reinvestment Act and Its Critics*, Barr compares the CRA's affirmative obligations to the negative prohibitions in ECOA, and their respective success in preventing discriminatory lending practices.

Michael S. Barr, Credit Where it Counts: The Community Reinvestment Act and Its Critics

80 N.Y.U. L. REV. 513, 625–28 (2005)

Critics of CRA contend that, if CRA is aimed at redressing racial discrimination, the government simply should enforce ECOA instead. ECOA prohibits creditors from discriminating in the provision of credit on the basis of 'race, color, religion, national origin, sex or marital status, or age.' For home mortgage lending, that prohibition also is reinforced by the Fair Housing Act of 1968. As with other antidiscrimination laws, ECOA prohibits both animus-based discrimination and statistical discrimination, as measured by the disparate treatment and disparate impact tests. ECOA's rule that statistical discrimination is prohibited, as opposed to a rule that subsidized creditors for deciding not to engage in such discrimination, is based on our deeply rooted sense that distinctions based on race, even if 'rational' in the short run, are wrong. Thus the law prohibits the conduct rather than subsidizing adherence to the rule. Empirical evidence suggests that ECOA seems to help increase lending to minorities. For example, the share of bank and thrift lending to [LMI] borrowers and areas that went to minority borrowers increased from twenty-one percent to twenty-eight percent from 1993 to 1999. Most of the increase occurred during a period of intense Justice Department focus on enforcing fair lending laws from 1993 to 1995. HMDA data also show improvements in lending to minority and low-income borrowers.

Yet, relying on ECOA lawsuits alone to advance antidiscrimination norms has its own limitations. Few ECOA lawsuits have been brought. Developing proof of lending discrimination is costly and difficult. When credit scoring is not the sole basis for a lending decision, lenders have a high degree of discretion, particularly in the case of applicants who are neither highly qualified nor unqualified. Even when credit scoring is the sole basis, disparate treatment might arise when creditors subjectively evaluate data before entering it into the credit system, provide different levels of assistance to borrowers in completing credit applications, or permit overrides of credit scoring in close cases. Given the complex and proprietary nature of credit scoring systems, and the difficulty of proving that any two applicants are similarly situated except for race, disparate treatment on the basis of race is hard to prove.

Disparate impact analysis is often no easier. Creditors have essential information about their loan portfolio and proprietary credit evaluation systems and the weights placed on all the variables in their system. Plaintiffs do not have such information, and creditors resist revealing their methodology because of competitive concerns. ECOA's disparate impact test as currently formulated cannot easily detect discriminatory overages, yield spread premiums, or risk-based pricing because of the difficulty of identifying the factor causing the discriminatory effect, as opposed to factors appropriately based on objective measures not related to race. Moreover, because ECOA focuses on the policies of each lender, ECOA has difficulty addressing the different experience of minority borrowers relying on different lenders than white borrowers in highly segmented subprime, as compared to prime, markets, even though the market-wide effect on minorities could be significant. . . .

ECOA itself sets out important antidiscrimination norms, and should be strengthened. Banking regulators could pay greater attention to rooting out problems arising from disparate impact. The [Federal Trade Commission (FTC)] and the [DOJ] could be given greater resources to investigate fair lending abuses, together with investigatory authority. Building on the strength of HMDA, a disclosure law requiring creditors to disclose the borrower's credit score and the creditor's rate sheet could help address price discrimination. A new law on product regulation could bar the payment of yield spread premiums, which disproportionately fall on minority borrowers.

Still, each of these new measures would have their own costs, and CRA plays an important role in reinforcing the antidiscrimination principles underlying ECOA and in expanding access to credit for minority borrowers. CRA may help uncover and remedy some practices with discriminatory effects that both disparate treatment analysis and disparate impact analysis, as they are currently formulated, have difficulty detecting or remedying. Moreover, minority households are disproportionately represented among low- and moderate-income households and in low- and moderate-income communities. CRA has encouraged banks and thrifts to increase their lending in such communities significantly, and minority households now constitute a larger share of such lending than they did a decade ago. CRA's focus on low-income neighborhoods may address structural inequalities facing African Americans and other minorities more effectively than ECOA's disparate impact standard, which is hemmed in, on one side, by equal protection jurisprudence limiting consideration of race to assist minorities and, on the other, by the business necessity defense permitting the use of factors that have an adverse effect on minorities if such factors are justified by business necessity.

CRA can help to overcome the legacy of decades of official and private-sector discrimination reflected in segregated, low-income neighborhoods, while ECOA is only addressed to discrimination by current market participants. In addition, by encouraging banks and thrifts to get to know these communities, CRA may help to overcome cultural barriers to equality. Moreover, CRA goes beyond ECOA's focus on credit discrimination to address broader market failures affecting low-income borrowers and communities, from collective action problems, information externalities, information asymmetries, and neighborhood externalities. Overcoming these market failures not only improves the functioning of the market, but also furthers antidiscrimination goals. While CRA helps to reinforce ECOA, fair lending laws are no substitute for CRA.

In the mutual fund context, as you will see in Part X, the investment advisers that run the funds owe their investors broad fiduciary duties, simultaneously imposing both affirmative obligations and negative prohibitions. These fiduciary duties spring out of the Investment Advisers Act of 1940, 15

U.S.C. §§ 80b-1–80b-21, and the Investment Company Act of 1940 (the 1940 Act), 15 U.S.C. §§ 80a-1–80a-64, and later case law interpreting those acts. An investment adviser that violates those fiduciary duties risks lawsuits by both the funds' investors and the SEC. The fiduciary duties have been described as "affirmative dut[ies] of 'utmost good faith, and full and fair disclosure of all material facts,' as well as an affirmative obligation 'to employ reasonable care to avoid misleading' . . . clients." SEC v. Capital Gains Research Bureau, 375 U.S. 180, 194 (1963). Encompassed in these duties are both the affirmative obligation to perform all tasks in good faith in the interests of the client and to disclose any conflicts of interest, and the negative prohibition on defrauding investors and taking self-interested actions. *See generally* Arthur B. Laby, *Current Issues in Fiduciary Law:* SEC v. Capital Gains Research Bureau *and the Investment Advisers Act of 1940*, 91 B.U. L. REV. 1051 (2011); *see also* Investment Advisers Act § 206. In the following case, focused on the mutual fund context, the Supreme Court discusses the fiduciary duties owed by investment advisers, how the standards-based approach of fiduciary duties differs from a rules-based approach, and how to determine the proper balance between market forces based on disclosure and product regulation in setting investment advisers' fees. We explore these issues in further detail in Chapter 10.2; for now, consider how fiduciary duties work as a regulatory tool compared with other approaches explored in this Chapter.

Jones v. Harris Associates L.P.

559 U.S. 335, 338–43 (2010)

The [1940 Act], 54 Stat. 789, 15 U.S.C. § 80a–1 *et seq.*, regulates investment companies, including mutual funds. "A mutual fund is a pool of assets, consisting primarily of [a] portfolio [of] securities, and belonging to the individual investors holding shares in the fund." Burks v. Lasker, 441 U.S. 471, 480 (1979). The following arrangements are typical. A separate entity called an investment adviser creates the mutual fund, which may have no employees of its own. *See* Kamen v. Kemper Financial Services, Inc., 500 U.S. 90, 93 (1991); Daily Income Fund, Inc. v. Fox, 464 U.S. 523, 536 (1984); Burks, 441 U.S., at 480–481. The adviser selects the fund's directors, manages the fund's investments, and provides other services. *See id.*, at 481. Because of the relationship between a mutual fund and its investment adviser, the fund often "cannot, as a practical matter sever its relationship with the adviser. Therefore, the forces of arm's-length bargaining do not work in the mutual fund industry in the same manner as they do in other sectors of the American economy." *Ibid.* (quoting S. Rep. No. 91–184, p. 5 (1969) (hereinafter S. Rep.)).

"Congress adopted the [1940 Act] because of its concern with the potential for abuse inherent in the structure of investment companies." Daily Income Fund, 464 U.S., at 536 (internal quotation marks omitted). Recognizing that the relationship between a fund and its investment adviser was "fraught with potential conflicts of interest," the [1940] Act created protections for mutual fund shareholders. *Id.*, at 536–538 (internal quotation marks omitted); *Burks, supra*, at 482–483. Among other things, the [1940] Act required that no more than 60 percent of a fund's directors could be affiliated with the adviser and that fees for investment advisers be approved by the directors and the shareholders of the fund. *See* §§ 10, 15(c), 54 Stat. 806, 813.

The growth of mutual funds in the 1950's and 1960's prompted studies of the 1940 Act's effectiveness in protecting investors. *See* Daily Income Fund, 464 U.S., at 537–538. Studies commissioned or authored by the [SEC] identified problems relating to the independence of investment company boards and the compensation received by investment advisers. *See ibid.* In response to such concerns, Congress amended the [1940] Act in 1970 and bolstered shareholder protection in two primary ways.

First, the amendments strengthened the "cornerstone" of the [1940] Act's efforts to check conflicts of interest, the independence of mutual fund boards of directors, which negotiate and scrutinize adviser compensation. *Burks, supra,* at 482. The amendments required that no more than 60 percent of a fund's directors be "persons who are interested persons," *e.g.*, that they have no interest in or affiliation with the investment adviser. 15 U.S.C. § 80a–10(a); § 80a–2(a)(19); *see also* Daily Income Fund, supra, at 538. These board members are given "a host of special responsibilities." *Burks*, 441 U.S., at 482–483. In particular, they must "review and approve the contracts of the investment adviser" annually, *id.*, at 483, and a majority of these directors must approve an adviser's compensation, 15 U.S.C. § 80a–15(c). Second, § 36(b), 84 Stat. 1429, of the [1940] Act imposed upon investment advisers a "fiduciary duty" with respect to compensation received from a mutual fund, 15 U.S.C. § 80a–35(b), and granted individual investors a private right of action for breach of that duty, *ibid.*

The "fiduciary duty" standard contained in § 36(b) represented a delicate compromise. Prior to the adoption of the 1970 amendments, shareholders challenging investment adviser fees under state law were required to meet "common-law standards of corporate waste, under which an unreasonable or unfair fee might be approved unless the court deemed it 'unconscionable' or 'shocking,'" and "security holders challenging adviser fees under the [1940 Act] itself had been required to prove gross abuse of trust." Daily Income Fund, 464 U.S., at 540, n. 12. Aiming to give shareholders a stronger remedy, the SEC proposed a provision that would have empowered the [SEC] to bring actions to challenge a fee that was not "reasonable" and to intervene in any similar action brought by or on behalf of an investment company. *Id.*, at 538. This approach was included in a bill that passed the House. H.R. 9510, 90th Cong., 1st Sess., § 8(d) (1967); *see also* S. 1659, 90th Cong., 1st Sess., § 8(d) (as introduced May 1, 1967). [Financial sector] representatives, however, objected to this proposal, fearing that it "might in essence provide the [SEC] with ratemaking authority." Daily Income Fund, 464 U.S., at 538.

The provision that was ultimately enacted adopted "a different method of testing management compensation," *id.*, at 539 (quoting S.Rep., at 5 (internal quotation marks omitted)), that was more favorable to shareholders than the previously available remedies but that did not permit a compensation agreement to be reviewed in court for "reasonableness." This is the fiduciary duty standard in § 36(b).

Petitioners are shareholders in three different mutual funds managed by respondent Harris Associates L.P., an investment adviser. Petitioners filed this action in the Northern District of Illinois pursuant to § 36(b) seeking damages, an injunction, and rescission of advisory agreements between Harris Associates and the mutual funds. The complaint alleged that Harris Associates had violated § 36(b) by charging fees that were "disproportionate to the services rendered" and "not within the range of what would have been negotiated at arm's length in light of all the surrounding circumstances." App. 52.

The District Court granted summary judgment for Harris Associates. Applying the standard adopted in *Gartenberg v. Merrill Lynch Asset Management, Inc.*, 694 F.2d 923 (C.A.2 1982), the court concluded that petitioners had failed to raise a triable issue of fact as to 'whether the fees charged . . . were so disproportionately large that they could not have been the result of arm's-length bargaining.' App. to Pet. for Cert. 29a. The District Court assumed that it was relevant to compare the challenged fees with those that Harris Associates charged its other clients. *Id.*, at 30a. But in light of those comparisons as well as comparisons with fees charged by other investment advisers to similar mutual funds, the Court held that it could not reasonably be found that the challenged fees were outside the range that could have been the product of arm's-length bargaining. *Id.*, at 29a–32a.

A panel of the Seventh Circuit affirmed based on different reasoning, explicitly "disapprov[ing] the *Gartenberg* approach." 527 F.3d 627, 632 (2008). Looking to trust law, the panel noted that, while a trustee "owes an obligation of candor in negotiation," a trustee, at the time of the creation of a trust, "may negotiate in his own interest and accept what the settlor or governance institution agrees to pay." *Ibid.* (citing Restatement (Second) of Trusts § 242, and Comment f). The panel thus reasoned that "[a] fiduciary duty differs from rate regulation. A fiduciary must make full disclosure and play no tricks but is not subject to a cap on compensation." 527 F.3d, at 632. In the panel's view, the amount of an adviser's compensation would be relevant only if the compensation were "so unusual" as to give rise to an inference "that deceit must have occurred, or that the persons responsible for decision have abdicated." *Ibid.*

The panel argued that this understanding of § 36(b) is consistent with the forces operating in the contemporary mutual fund market. Noting that "[t]oday thousands of mutual funds compete" the panel concluded that "sophisticated investors" shop for the funds that produce the best overall results, "mov[e] their money elsewhere" when fees are "excessive in relation to the results," and thus "create a competitive pressure" that generally keeps fees low. *Id.*, at 633–634. The panel faulted *Gartenberg* on the ground that it "relies too little on markets." 527 F.3d, at 632. And the panel firmly rejected a comparison between the fees that Harris Associates charged to the funds and the fees that Harris Associates charged other types of clients, observing that "[d]ifferent clients call for different commitments of time' and that costs, such as research, that may benefit several categories of clients 'make it hard to draw inferences from fee levels." *Id.*, at 634.

---

1. ***Affirmative Obligations Compared to Negative Prohibitions.*** Are the differences between affirmative obligations and negative prohibitions meaningful?

2. ***Duties Compared to Rate Regulation.*** In *Jones*, the Court draws an explicit distinction between the affirmative obligations and negative prohibitions encompassed in fiduciary duties and "rate regulation." We discuss rate regulation later in this Chapter. How do you think investment advisers' fees would change if subjected to rate regulation rather than fiduciary duties?

3. ***Standards vs. Rules.*** When structuring duties, is it better to use a flexible, standards-based approach, similar to investment advisers' fiduciary duties, or is it better to have a harder, rules-based approach? A rules-based approach reduces the costs of regulatory compliance and the risks of lawsuits or enforcement by establishing, *ex ante*, a bright line that must be followed by the regulated financial institution. By declaring exactly what must be done and not done, however, regulators also provide a roadmap for firms to work around the rules, creating loopholes. Standards, by contrast, permit *ex post* adjustment to the wide variety of factual situations that might arise. In what circumstances might a standards-based approach be better than a bright line rule or vice versa?

4. ***The Suitability Requirement.*** As we saw in Chapter 4.2, securities firms operate under a broad range of fiduciary duties. The suitability requirement is one noteworthy aspect of the duties that broker-dealers owe their clients. Under this requirement, a broker or adviser must "determine that the investment advice it gives to a client is suitable for the client, taking into consideration the client's financial situation, investment experience, and investment objectives." DIV. OF INV. MGMT., SEC, GENERAL INFORMATION ON THE REGULATION OF INVESTMENT ADVISERS (2011). The suitability requirement obligates brokers and

advisors to consider their clients' interests when giving investment advice. No such suitability requirement has traditionally existed for mortgage brokers, *but see* 12 C.F.R. § 1026.43, and some commentators have argued that the "subprime mortgage and credit crisis would have been avoided, or at least greatly mitigated, if [a suitability requirement] had been properly applied to subprime mortgage brokers and originators." Jonathan R. Macey et al., *Helping Catch Up to Markets: Applying Broker-Dealer Law to Subprime Mortgages*, 34 J. CORP. L. 789, 790 (2009). Do you agree that a suitability requirement could have helped prevent, or at least mitigate, the Financial Crisis? Why do you think securities brokers are subject to a suitability requirement, but mortgage brokers are not?

5. ***The Duties of Insurance Agents.*** The decision in *Murphy v. Kuhn*, 682 N.E.2d 972 (N.Y. 1997), is characteristic of a long line of judicial decisions revealing a reluctance on the part of courts to impose on insurance agents an ongoing, general disclosure obligation regarding opportunities to obtain additional insurance coverage. The question in that case was whether an insurance agent should be liable to a former customer for the alleged failure of the insurance agent to advise the plaintiff as to possible additional coverage needs. The opinion noted that "the law is reasonably settled on initial principles that insurance agents have a common-law duty to obtain requested coverage for their clients within a reasonable time or inform the client of the inability to do so; however, they have no continuing duty to advise, guide or direct a client to obtain additional coverage." *Id.* at 974. Some have argued that "mortgage brokers occupy a somewhat undefined space in the commercial world, being positioned between lenders and borrowers while usually maintaining that they represent neither." *See* Andrea Lee Negroni & Joya K. Raha, *Mortgage Brokers—What Fiduciary Duties Exist*, 68 MORTGAGE BANKING 1, 2 (2007). Judges have been more willing to craft detailed obligations for brokers, dealers, and advisers. As you may recall from Chapter 4.2, in addition to the open-ended fiduciary duties articulated in judicial opinions, securities firms owe duties to their customers in the form of detailed disclosure requirements and compliance with market conduct rules. Why are insurance agents and mortgage brokers held to a lower standard of care? Are insurance and mortgages less important than securities investments? Are individuals who buy insurance and take out mortgages more sophisticated than individuals who buy securities? Are insurance agents or mortgage brokers less prone to ignore the best interest of their customers?

6. ***Anti-Discrimination Duties.*** As explained in Chapter 5.1, ECOA prohibits discrimination on the basis of race, religion, national origin, sex, marital status, and age. As you learned in Chapter 3.2, however, state insurance laws vary widely in their approaches to such duties, with a number of states permitting, for example, price to vary based on age and gender. In a number of states, racial discrimination in insurance is not explicitly prohibited. Are these different approaches to anti-discrimination duties justified?

V. PRODUCT REGULATION

Under product regulations, regulators directly control the attributes of the financial products and services provided to consumers, insureds, and investors, rather than regulating the process by which those products and services are provided. In a sense, product regulation is a form of affirmative obligation and negative prohibition, directing financial institutions to structure or refrain from structuring financial products and services in certain ways. Product regulation differs from affirmative obligation and negative prohibition regulation, however, as it directly controls the terms of financial institutions' products and services rather than their actions. Product regulation might involve regulation of terms or price. To illustrate, Mr. Donald C. Lampe describes some of the differences between and implications of product and practice regulation in the context of North Carolina.

Donald C. Lampe, Wrong from the Start? North Carolina's "Predatory Lending" Law and the Practice vs. Product Debate

7 CHAP. L. REV. 135, 135–36 (2004)

Lawmakers seeking to protect consumers from 'predatory' lenders face an initial, critical decision: should the state regulate specific loan products or specific loan practices? North Carolina lawmakers have tried both.

The North Carolina high-cost home loan ('predatory lending') statute, enacted in 1999, was the first state statute of its kind. The basic design of the law has been emulated and followed in nearly forty states, municipalities, and counties. As such, the law has become the de facto model for state and municipal 'predatory lending' legislation, regulation, and ordinances throughout the country. This initial law emerged from a nearly unregulated setting for mortgage loan originations in North Carolina. It was 'threshold-based,' meaning it imposed severe restrictions and regulations on loans carrying interest rates and terms above a certain numerical threshold. As observers have noted and experience has shown, threshold-based loan regulation ultimately impacts the basic availability of certain loan products.

Laws directed toward mortgage originators and their sales practices regulate the process by which consumers obtain those products-without necessarily impairing availability of credit. Despite the attention given the original 1999 statute, the evidence shows that the state's consumer protection objectives were better realized by the enactment of a second law, known as the Mortgage Lending Act. It provided for comprehensive mortgage broker licensure and oversight. The recent upsurge in enactment of residential mortgage lending laws has given rise to a lively debate on whether threshold-based ('product') regulations are appropriate in light of more market-friendly options that reach the sales process and practice.

---

1. ***Product Regulation and Credit Availability.*** Lampe draws a distinction between the impact of product and practice regulation on the availability of credit. Is product regulation less market-friendly than process and disclosure regulation? How do different forms of regulation affect access? For a nuanced perspective on state anti-predatory lending laws, written in the midst of the Financial Crisis, see Raphael W. Bostic et al., *The Impact of State Anti-Predatory Lending Laws: Policy Implications and Insights* (Joint Ctr. for Hous. Stud., Harvard Univ. Working Paper No. UCC08–09, 2008).

2. ***Standards vs. Rules, Revisited.*** Compare rules-based product regulation to the fiduciary duties we discussed previously. If you were advising a regulated financial institution, which laws would you rather your client fall under?

Product regulation comes in two basic forms: regulation of prices (or price controls) and regulation of non-price provisions (such as penalties and term of loan) of financial products and services. The Military Lending Act, 10 U.S.C. § 987, contains price controls. Under the Military Lending Act, no member of the military may be charged an interest rate higher than 36% on some types of consumer loans. 10 U.S.C. § 987(b). It is intended to protect military personnel from predatory payday lending and other rates by implementing a ceiling on the rate that can be charged on such loans. CTR. FOR RESPONSIBLE LENDING, SUMMARY OF THE MILITARY LENDING ACT OF 2007 (2010).

State insurance laws commonly use product regulation in the form of both price controls and the regulation of non-price terms of insurance contracts. As you learned in Chapter 3.2, rate making is a central feature of state insurance regulation. Recall our discussion of the Massachusetts auto insurance rate setting practices, for example. Product term and price regulation in insurance are further discussed in the following excerpt.

Federal Insurance Office, How to Modernize and Improve the System of Insurance Regulation in the United States

48–49, 54 (2013)

Product Approval

State regulators use product approval, or 'form regulation,' to assess whether insurance products comply with state consumer protection laws, such as those governing insurance policy or contract design, pricing, and coverage terms. The process for product review and approval varies by state, as do the standards with which the insurer must comply. For example, some states require approval before a product is offered in the market, but others permit introduction to the market without prior approval, while still other states reserve the option for later review. The duration of review and substantive standards for review also vary, depending on factors ranging from regulatory processes to state resource constraints.

The absence of a uniform national standard and protocol for product approval is a continuing complaint for insurers that argue the lack of uniformity creates inefficiencies and compromises the ability to offer the same products simultaneously and in the same manner on a nationwide basis. Insurers assert further that both speed-to-market and innovation are harmed by product approval delays in many jurisdictions. Consumer advocates note that the lack of uniformity creates opportunities for regulatory arbitrage, both with respect to personal and commercial lines insurance.

Rate Regulation

An insurance rate determines the price at which an insurance policy or contract is sold. Insurers use rates to determine the premium due on a particular insurance policy: premium equals the rate multiplied by the number of units of insurance purchased. The rate typically reflects the risk characteristics of the purchaser of insurance.

The evolving views on the manner of setting rates is reflected in the variety of processes through which states now permit insurers to file rates with the state regulator. However, many empirical studies suggest rate regulation, particularly in auto and homeowner insurance, may adversely impact market supply resulting in higher prices and an increase in the market share of the residual market.

---

1. ***Regulating Price and Non-Price Terms.*** Is the distinction between regulating the price and non-price terms of a financial product or service

meaningful? A neoclassical economist would say that rational individuals take into account all of the terms of a product or service in determining its price. As such, regulating a non-price term just increases its price. For example, on this view prohibiting firms from moving around the due date on credit card bills every month would increase interest rates and other fees. By contrast, a behavioral economist would say that consumers translate information into understanding, and understanding into action, and may mis-forecast their own behavior; thus, changes in the non-price terms may not necessarily affect price terms. For example, regulating a term that is non-salient or shrouded (*e.g.*, late fees or prepayment penalties) may, in this view, increase consumer welfare.

2. ***Rate Regulation Through Enforcement.*** Recall our discussion of CFPB enforcement actions against auto lenders from Chapter 5.3. These actions have resulted in consent orders that limit auto dealer markups to fixed percentages. *See, e.g.*, Press Release, CFPB: CFPB and DOJ Reach Resolution with Toyota Motor Credit to Address Loan Pricing Policies with Discriminatory Effects (Feb. 2, 2016).

3. ***Rate Regulation in Interchange.*** As you will learn in Chapter 7.2, the Federal Reserve Board was charged with the task of setting interchange rates for debit card transactions in the Durbin Amendment to the Dodd-Frank Act.

4. ***Rate Regulation in Securities.*** Rate regulations are used in a variety of contexts in the securities markets. For example, consider again the case of *Jones v. Harris,* 559 U.S. 335 (2010), in which the Court considered the effect of the requirement in 36(b) of the 1940 Act that fees not be excessive. Recall from Chapter 4.2 FINRA's "5% policy" under Rule 2121 regarding fair prices and commissions.

VI. SUBSIDY AND TAX

Like affirmative obligations and negative prohibitions, subsidies and taxes are two sides of the same coin: they both seek to affect regulatees' behavior by changing the marginal costs of certain actions. Subsidies seek to make the subsidized, desirable actions cheaper and, thus, more likely to be taken, while taxes make the taxed, less desirable actions more costly and, thus, less likely to be taken. Alan O. Sykes, *The Questionable Case for Subsidies Regulation: A Comparative Perspective*, 2 J. LEGAL ANALYSIS 473, 473 (2010). Unlike liability rules for violations of disclosure, duties, or product regulation, the disfavored action is not deemed unlawful, nor is the favored action required.

The Government Sponsored Enterprises (GSEs) that support the residential mortgage market, including Fannie Mae and Freddie Mac, are examples of entities that receive subsidies from taxpayers, and some of these subsidies may be passed on to borrowers, although whether and how much that has occurred is subject to extensive debate. As you will learn in Chapter 12.2, Fannie Mae and Freddie Mac purchase loans in the secondary market from the mortgage lenders that originate the loans. The GSEs package the loans into securities and sell those securities to investors. This securitization is intended to benefit consumers by providing liquidity to the mortgage market, thereby expanding consumers' access to credit. In addition, the GSEs can fill a consumer protection role by purchasing standardized mortgages with terms that are more borrower-friendly than those in non-subsidized loans. As you will learn in Chapter 12.2, the GSEs' standards deteriorated in the lead up to the Financial Crisis, with disastrous results. The benefits that consumers may derive from the ways in which subsidies provided to Fannie Mae and Freddie Mac may flow through to consumers when the GSEs adhere to standard mortgage terms are described in the following excerpt.

Julia Patterson Forrester, Fannie Mae/Freddie Mac Uniform Mortgage Instruments: The Forgotten Benefit to Homeowners

72 MO. L. REV. 1077, 1087–1102 (2007)

Because of their widespread use and their exceptionally fair terms, Fannie Mae/Freddie Mac uniform instruments provide a significant benefit to homeowners. Because the GSEs require the use of their forms for single-family loans that they buy and because they will not accept loans with modifications or additions to the uniform instruments, borrowers actually receive the benefits that consumer advocates negotiated when the uniform instruments were drafted. The benefits to homeowners are the result of both the financial and legal terms of the loans. . . .

In addition to the financial terms of loans that Fannie Mae and Freddie Mac purchase, their uniform mortgage instruments contain many other terms that are beneficial to homeowners. Most striking are the borrower's rights upon default. Other terms of the instruments protect borrowers during the term of the loan prior to default. . . .

Perhaps more important than the terms included in the uniform mortgage instrument are the terms not included. Many onerous or unfair provisions that often appear in other mortgage documents are not in the Fannie Mae/Freddie Mac uniform instruments. . . .

Because most lenders use the Fannie Mae/Freddie Mac uniform mortgage instruments . . . consumers do not need to shop for their loan based on the legal terms of the documents. The documents are usually identical to those used by other lenders, and in fact are more favorable to the borrower than consumers would probably expect. . . .

Because so many residential mortgage lenders use the uniform instruments, whether the loans are to be sold to the GSEs or not, the number of attributes that a consumer must choose from is greatly reduced. With fewer attributes to choose from, the consumer is less likely to experience information overload. In addition, because the only choice of loan documents is a good choice, consumers only need to focus on financial terms. . . .

Finally, because consumers tend to underestimate the likelihood of their default on a loan, the foreclosure of their home, or the occurrence of a casualty loss, they are likely to underestimate the importance of legal terms relating to default, foreclosure, and casualty loss. Empirical studies show that people tend to underestimate the occurrence of certain low-probability, high-loss events. Default on a home mortgage loan, loss of a home to foreclosure, and loss of a home by fire, flood, or other casualty are low-probability events that involve a major loss.

Thus, the Fannie Mae/Freddie Mac uniform mortgage instruments are particularly beneficial to consumers because mortgage loan documents are typically not negotiable, because consumers do not have adequate information or the ability to choose between lenders based on the legal terms of their loan documents, because consumers either would experience information overload when faced with choosing based on legal terms or would ignore those terms altogether, and because consumers are unlikely to be concerned with important document provisions relating to default and casualty loss.

---

1. ***Standardization and Market Liquidity.*** The GSEs theoretically benefit consumers by increasing the number of loans that have their standardized, borrower-friendly terms. The GSEs only purchase loans that have standard terms. Lenders are able to sell loans with standard terms more easily, allowing them to access additional liquidity. Secondary market mortgage purchases by the GSEs thus reduce the costs of lending using standard mortgages.

2. ***Criticism of GSEs.*** As you will discover in Chapter 12.2, the GSEs faced criticism even before their spectacular failure during the Financial Crisis. Because lenders are able to shift the default risks of borrowers to the GSEs, the subsidies "reduce the incentive for mortgage originators to avoid making risky loans in the first place." CONGRESSIONAL BUDGET OFFICE, FANNIE MAE, FREDDIE MAC, AND THE FEDERAL ROLE IN THE SECONDARY MORTGAGE MARKET ix (2010). The federal government's sponsorship of the GSEs "expose[s] taxpayers to the risk of potentially large losses when the cost of honoring guarantees exceeds the value of guarantee fees collected. . . ." *Id.* Because homeowners are also taxpayers, the benefits derived from the GSE subsidies must be weighed against the costs to the government when they go astray, which are ultimately borne by those same individuals.

Subsidization and taxation are flip sides of a coin. Either could be used to incentivize consumer-friendly products. For example, the ability-to-repay and risk retention requirements and the qualified mortgage (QM) and qualified residential mortgage (QRM) exception to those rules in the Dodd-Frank Act are examples of regulations intended to protect consumers by changing the relative costs to financial institutions of making different types of mortgages by increasing the liability and loss risks to firms for making non-QM and non-QRM loans. *See* 15 U.S.C. § 1639c; *see also* 15 U.S.C. § 78o-11. These liability and loss rules make lower quality loans more expensive to financial institutions, relative to high quality loans and are thus a form of tax.

Under the ability-to-repay requirement, mortgage lenders must make good faith determinations as to borrowers' ability to repay the mortgages. Under the risk retention requirement, securitizers of mortgage loans are required to retain 5% of the credit risk of those loans. The QM and QRM rules create exemptions from the ability-to-repay and risk retention requirements of the Dodd-Frank Act for loans deemed high quality. The loans that satisfy the requirements of the QM and QRM rules, which are aligned, are generally thought of as lower credit risk loans that do not have predatory or abusive features. Additional requirements are placed on loans that are viewed as less consumer-friendly, making those loans less likely to be originated by lenders. The QM and QRM rules can also be considered a form of behaviorally informed regulation—a "sticky default" in which the starting point of safer mortgages is reinforced with liability and risk-retention rules that apply to mortgages not included in the starting position.

Subsidy and tax are also widely used in insurance and in specialized areas of securities law. For example, as you learned in Chapter 3.3, employer-sponsored retirement plans provide significant tax benefits but require compliance with detailed rules designed to ensure that the plans broadly benefit workers. *See, e.g.*, 26 U.S.C. § 401(a). States commonly create insurance pools to provide auto insurance for high-risk or otherwise uninsurable drivers, and many states offer tax credits to insurance companies to offset the costs of accidents involving uninsured motorists.

---

1. ***Consumer and Investor Protection and Financial Stability.*** In addition to using direct regulatory means to achieve consumer and investor protection ends, policy-makers achieve those goals indirectly through prudential regulation. There may sometimes be tension between how prudential regulators and consumer and investor protection regulators seek to achieve their goals, but, when done properly, the two may be mutually reinforcing. *See* Erik F. Gerding, *The Subprime Crisis and the Link between Consumer Financial Protection and Systemic Risk*, 4 FIU L. REV. 435, 437 (2009); *see also* David Min, *How Government Guarantees Promote Housing Finance Stability*, 50 HARV. J. ON LEGIS. 437 (2013). The lapses in prudential regulation that led to the Financial Crisis ultimately hurt consumers and investors. Lapses in consumer and investor protection permitted the origination and securitization of low-quality mortgages that generated huge systemic risk. From this perspective, greater consumer and investor protection can sometimes mitigate systemic risk, and greater prudential regulation can be used to protect investors and consumers. *See* Anita I. Anand, *Is Systemic Risk Relevant to Securities Regulation?*, 60 U. TORONTO L.J. 941 (2010). In what circumstances do consumer and investor protection help financial stability, and in what circumstances do they undermine it? How does prudential regulation support consumer and investor protection, and how does it weaken them? Consider, for example, the 30-year fixed-rate mortgage, which has historically been subsidized by the U.S. government for the benefit of consumers but is "observed in few other countries." ANDREAS FUSTER & JAMES VICKERY, FED. RES. BANK OF N.Y. STAFF REPORTS, NO. 594, SECURITIZATION AND THE FIXED-RATE MORTGAGE 1 (2014). For discussions of the systemic risks that can be posed by such mortgages, see Michael Lea & Anthony B. Sanders, *Government Policy and the Fixed-Rate Mortgage*, 3 ANN. REV. FIN. ECON. 223 (2011), and Amir E. Khandani et al., *Systemic Risk and the Refinancing Ratchet Effect*, 108 J. FIN. ECON. 29 (2013). For the counterargument, see David Min, *How Government Guarantees Promote Housing Finance Stability*, 50 HARV. J. ON LEGIS. 437 (2013).

2. ***Twin Peaks: Prudential Regulation and Consumer Protection.*** Is it better to have specialized agencies that regulate based on an institution's legal status, as in the United States, or a single agency tasked with regulating across the entire financial sector, as in the UK pre-Financial Crisis? Arguably, neither model performed as well in the Financial Crisis. Recall our discussion of the Twin Peaks model from Chapter 1.3, in which one agency is responsible for all prudential regulation and another is responsible for regulating all market conduct, including consumer and investor protection. Should the United States move to this model, similar to Australia and the UK post-Financial Crisis? *See* Elizabeth F. Brown, *A Comparison of the Handling of the Financial Crisis in the United States, the United Kingdom, and Australia*, 55 VILL. L. REV. 509 (2010).

3. ***Prudential Justification for Consumer Protection.*** As the Financial Crisis began, the OCC, the Federal Reserve Board, the FDIC, the OTS, and the NCUA belatedly issued guidance noting that borrowers may not fully understand

the risks of products that can cause payment shock, and that lenders would face liquidity risks when these borrowers started to default. The regulators urged lenders to use teaser rates only for those who could likely withstand the payment shock. *See* Statement on Subprime Lending, 72 Fed. Reg. 37,573 (2007).

4. ***Comparing U.S. and EU Consumer and Investor Protection Laws.*** The consumer and investor protection laws of the United States and the EU have many similarities. For instance, as with the securities regulation system in the United States, disclosure has traditionally been the hallmark of the EU's retail investor protection framework. NIAMH MOLONEY, EU SECURITIES AND FINANCIAL MARKETS REGULATION 820 (3d ed. 2014). There are, however, key differences between the two sides of the Atlantic. While the explicit differences between the regulatory norms in the United States and the EU are the easiest to spot, there are also more subtle differences that should not be ignored. In the following excerpt, Professor Niamh Moloney teases out some of those subtleties:

> [T]here are two ways of characterising the individual who accesses the investment markets for household welfare provision and asset accumulation: the 'retail investor' and the 'consumer of financial products and services'. . . . [T]he 'consumer' of financial services and products suggests a more interventionist approach to regulation than that associated with the 'retail investor' . . . .
>
> There is some evidence of this distinction in recent policy discussions. In the US, discussions related to the establishment of the [CFPB] point to a distinction between the SEC's treatment of retail investment products and the [CFPB's] contested and more interventionist approach to the most common household finance products, notably credit products. . . .
>
> A more precautionary and interventionist approach to the retail or household markets [in the EU] is now evident across a number of fronts. . . . The introduction of labelling requirements for independent investment advice and a prohibition on commissions is an attempt to bolster what is currently a very small segment of the EU distribution market by clarifying the nature of these services through controls on how the service is delivered, rather than through the traditional disclosure controls which dominate in this area. The obligation to consider a wide range of investments is in part a response to entrenched conflict of interest risk. . . . In each case, the autonomy of the investor is being limited in a manner which can be associated more closely with, for example, the regulation of potentially toxic or dangerous consumer products generally.

Niamh Moloney, *The Investor Model Underlying the EU's Investor Protection Regime: Consumers or Investors?*, 13 EUR. BUS. ORG. L. REV. 169, 172–75, 180 (2012).

Part VI

Financial Conglomerates

CHAPTER 6.1

REGULATION OF HOLDING COMPANIES

CONTENTS

I. INTRODUCTION

In this Chapter, we explore the evolution of U.S. banking institutions' organizational structure into the modern financial conglomerate and how the regulatory framework that governs banking organizations changed over time as a result of stakeholder battles, market forces, and technological change. First, we discuss the most common form of financial conglomerate in the United States: the bank holding company (BHC) parent with a lead commercial bank subsidiary. Next, we discuss the Bank Holding Company Act (BHCA), including its core concepts of a "company," a "bank," and the exercise of "control" or "controlling influence." We then explore the activities that are permissible for non-bank subsidiaries of BHCs, typically referred to as non-bank affiliates, through the lens of stakeholder battles that drew the historic lines between banking and commerce, banking and insurance, and banking and investment banking. You will recall from Chapter 2.2 that the "business of banking" is a concept used to capture the activities that may take place within a chartered commercial bank, but it does not apply to limit the activities of the financial conglomerate as a whole, which may include, among other types of subsidiaries, broker-dealers (*see* Part IV), insurance companies (*see* Part III), and pooled investments or funds (*see* Part X). We also look at more recent legal developments that are affecting the structure of banking organizations, including the introduction of financial holding companies (FHCs), a new category of BHC created in 1999 under the Gramm-Leach Bliley Act (GLBA), as well as the passage of the Volcker Rule, a major structural reform, as part of the Dodd-Frank Act of 2010. Finally, we compare recent policy choices made in the United States to the structural reforms underway in the UK.

II. TYPICAL HOLDING COMPANY STRUCTURES

In the United States, large complex banking organizations and midsize regional banking organizations typically operate in corporate groups, with a holding company at the top and a lead bank or other insured depository institution (IDI) as a subsidiary of the holding company. *See* Figure 6.1-1. When such organizations are publicly traded, as is the case for all of the large financial conglomerates, the holding company is listed on a stock exchange, while the IDI subsidiary is 100% owned by the holding company and not directly owned by investors. Although some community banks have only an IDI, or have an IDI as the top-level company, U.S. banking organizations of significant size rarely take that form.

Figure 6.1-1 Simplified Depiction of U.S. Holding Company-IDI Structure

Holding Company

Insured Depository Institution

Branches

The near ubiquity of the BHC structure, with a lead bank as a subsidiary, is a direct result of the evolution of the U.S. regulatory framework. Historically, chartered banks and their subsidiaries in the bank chain of ownership have been limited to "the business of banking." *See* Chapter 2.2. Meanwhile, non-bank subsidiaries of the holding company have long been granted more latitude to engage in activities that are "closely related to banking," a concept that has been the subject of legislative and regulatory change since its introduction of the BHCA of 1956. Starting in 1999, certain BHCs have also been able to engage in a broader range of activities deemed to be "financial in nature," "incidental thereto", or "complementary" to financial activities.

These distinct categories of activities within the financial conglomerate were created iteratively and grounded in two cornerstones of U.S. banking regulation: (1) the separation of banking and commerce, and (2) the Glass-Steagall Act separation of investment banking (*i.e.*, the underwriting of corporate debt and equity securities and merchant banking) and commercial banking. As we will see, the walls that separate banking from commerce and commercial banking from investment banking have been and remain more porous than many believe.

Under the current statutory framework and regulations, a holding company is regulated because of its controlling investment in an IDI. Where the IDI takes the form of a bank, the holding company is a BHC and is subject to prudential regulation by the Federal Reserve Board under the BHCA. Where the IDI is a thrift, the holding company is a savings and loan holding company (SLHC) and is, as of 2010, regulated by the Federal Reserve Board under the Home Owners' Loan Act (HOLA). SLHCs had been separately supervised by now defunct regulators, first the Federal Home Loan Bank Board and then by the Office of Thrift Supervision (OTS), which was eliminated under the Dodd-Frank Act.

In 1999, when GLBA repealed much of the remaining portion of the Glass-Steagall Act prohibition on affiliation between commercial and investment banking, Congress created FHCs, a new category of BHC. The flexibility of the FHC structure has enabled the development of financial conglomerates with affiliates involved in a diverse array of financially related businesses. *See* Figure 6.1-2. These organizations are often referred to as financial conglomerates, although this is a loosely defined concept that may also encompass the universal banking structures common in other parts of the world, especially Europe, where the chartered bank is the top listed company.

Figure 6.1-2 Simplified Depiction of the U.S. FHC Structure Commonly Adopted by Financial Conglomerates

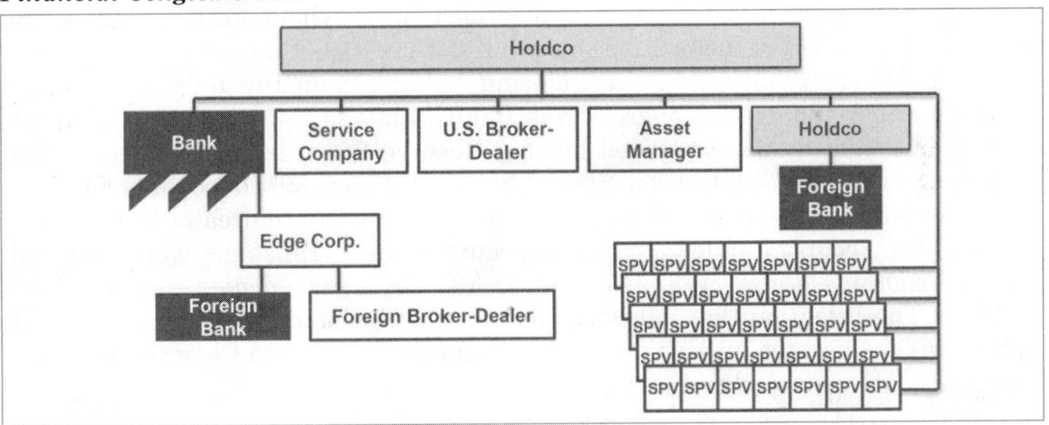

Until recently, the holding company-IDI subsidiary structure was an American anomaly driven by the unique American policy priority of separating commercial banking from other financial business lines. In other countries with developed financial sectors, banking organizations have traditionally taken a comparatively unitary form, often consisting of only one main corporate entity. In the aftermath of the Financial Crisis, however, EU regulators motivated by concerns regarding the resolvability of large complex banking organizations are potentially nudging some EU banking institutions towards a holding company-IDI subsidiary structure. As we will see later in this Chapter, UK regulators are also imposing structural organizational changes on UK-headquartered banks that will result in a form similar to U.S. structure of affiliated companies.

III. THE BANK HOLDING COMPANY ACT

The BHCA grants the Federal Reserve Board the authority to regulate and supervise BHCs, a term defined to include "companies" that are in "control" or have a "controlling influence" over a "bank." 12 U.S.C. §§ 1841(a)(1)-(2). Through authority granted by the statute, the Federal Reserve Board has jurisdiction over not only BHCs and FHCs but also the activities of holding company subsidiaries and the relationships between entities within the corporate group. Traditionally, these building block terms defined the regulatory perimeter of which holding companies are regulated as BHCs, which holding companies are regulated under one of the many other statutory schemes analyzed in this book, and which holding companies are not regulated at all. As we saw in Chapter 1.1 and will explore more closely in this Chapter, the development of financial conglomerates has meant that many activities and subsidiaries of a BHC will be subject to multiple regulatory regimes. The Federal Reserve Board is often referred to as the umbrella supervisor of financial conglomerates, but each separate unit of the group (including banks, broker-dealers, insurance companies, and asset managers) remains subject to functional regulation by its primary federal or state regulator. *See* Roger Ferguson Jr., Vice Chairman, Fed. Reserve Bd., Remarks Before the National Association of Urban Bankers, Urban Financial Services Coalition: Umbrella Supervision: Emerging Approaches (May 26, 2000).

Before the passage of the BHCA in 1956, the Federal Reserve Board of the Marriner Eccles era had long urged Congress to provide it with the authority necessary to regulate banking organizations as a whole, rather than being limited to oversight of the member bank only. FED. RESERVE, THIRTIETH ANNUAL REPORT 34–37 (1943). After considering holding company bills many times between 1938 and 1956, Congress was finally spurred to action after antitrust charges brought by the Eccles-led Federal Reserve Board against Transamerica, which controlled 41% of the commercial banking offices, 39% of commercial bank deposits, and 50% of commercial bank loans in a five-state area of the Western region of the country, failed after a long court battle. Transamerica Corp. v. Bd. of Governors, 206 F.2d 163, 167, 170–71 (3d Cir.), *cert. denied*, 346 U.S. 901 (1953). The litigation that followed, combined with the lobbying efforts of small unit banks, animated anticompetitive concerns and prompted Congress to finally pass legislation squarely addressing BHCs.

The BHCA was enacted with the dual goals of restricting the geographic expansion of large banking groups and preventing excessive concentration in the banking sector. S. REP. No. 84-1095, at 2 (1955); Saule T. Omarova & Margaret E. Tahyar, *That Which We Call a Bank: Revisiting the History of Bank Holding Company Regulations in the United States*, 31 REV. BANKING & FIN. L. 113, 120 (2011-2012). In service of these goals, the BHCA explicitly prohibited BHCs from acquiring banks in other states, unless the applicable state law authorized such an acquisition which, at the time, no state permitted. BHCA, Pub. L. No. 84-511, § 3(d), 70 Stat. 134, 135 (1956) [hereinafter *Original BHCA*]. The Act restricted the activities of BHCs and their subsidiaries to activities that were "so closely related to the business of banking or of managing or controlling banks as to be a proper incident thereto." Original BHCA § 4(c)(6).

The original version of the BHCA did not apply to holding companies that controlled only one bank. Original BHCA § 2(a). The one-bank exception permitted the owners of small banks, who were opposed to interstate branching and whose support was essential for the passage of the BHCA, to continue to hold their banking and commercial interests under a holding company without being subject to Federal Reserve Board regulation at the holding company level. In the late 1960s, as part of the ongoing 160-year-old battle over interstate branching, and owing to intense competitive pressures, big BHCs, then referred to as money-center banks, began to convert to a one-bank model in order to escape the requirements of the BHCA. In 1970, Congress amended the BHCA to apply to all "companies" that control a "bank," thereby forcing investors in small banks to hold their non-bank commercial interests through a separate holding company.

In the decades following its enactment, the amendments to the BHCA were primarily the result of oppositional stakeholder battles among financial sector participants competing in different subsectors of the financial markets. *See* Adam J. Levitin, *The Politics of Financial Regulation and the Regulation of Financial Politics: A Review Essay*, 127 HARV. L. REV. 1991 (2014) (book review). These battles, which were largely driven by a desire to limit or expand the areas in which BHCs and commercial banks could compete, were often nominally over the appropriate construction of the definitional building blocks of the BHCA: the concepts of company, bank, and control or controlling influence. As a result, these terms must be understood not just for their legal or technical meaning, but also as products of long-fought and, in some cases, now-forgotten, political battles concerning the regulatory perimeter of the BHCA and the scope of the Federal Reserve Board's power. Remnants of these battles are seen in today's debate about the scope of systemic regulation, which we will discuss in Chapter 6.2 and the regulation of shadow banking activities, which we will discuss in Part XII.

A. COMPANY UNDER THE BHCA

The BHCA definition of "company" includes any corporation, partnership, business trust, association, or similar organization. It does not, however, apply to individuals who control a bank. 12 U.S.C. § 1841(b). The more difficult questions arise when determining what types of relationships among individuals or business organizations might be deemed to be a company. For example, a group of linked partnerships (where linked means that some individuals are in more than one of the partnerships), with each partnership owning less than 5% of the same bank, may or may not constitute a company. Generally, the Federal Reserve Board is looking for relationships that have indications of a "formalized structure" or "unifying force." *See* Order Approving Formation of WISCUB, Inc., a Bank Holding Company, 65 Fed. Res. Bull. 773, 777 (1979).

---

1. ***Foreign Governments.*** The U.S. government and its instrumentalities are excluded from the definition of "company" but the BHCA is silent with respect to foreign governments. By Federal Reserve Board interpretation, foreign governments are not considered "companies" under the BHCA. Foreign banks, however, are often instrumentalities of their home country's sovereign

government. These banks could be a part of the foreign government, such as a central bank, or the government may directly or indirectly own shares through a government-controlled entity. *See* Letter from the Federal Reserve Board to Patricia S. Skigen and John B. Cairns (Aug. 19, 1988). If a foreign bank or BHC is an instrumentality of a foreign government, would it be considered a "company" under the BHCA, or would it be excluded because it is controlled by a foreign government? What type of effects might such a designation have on the extraterritorial activities of the foreign bank? How should a sovereign wealth fund owned by a foreign government be treated? *See* China Inv. Corp., Order Approving Acquisition of an Interest in a Bank Holding Company, 96 Fed. Res. Bull. B31 (2010).

B. THAT WHICH WE CALL A BANK

The ordinary man or woman on the street has little trouble identifying a bank. Under the BHCA, however, there have been a series of complex definitions and exceptions created as part of the ongoing dance of stakeholders trying to avoid, or impose upon emerging competitors, the full weight of BHCA regulation. *See* Omarova & Tahyar, *That Which We Call a Bank*, at 138–88. When the BHCA was passed in 1956, a "bank" was sensibly defined according to its charter as "any national banking institution or any state bank, savings bank, or trust company." The 1956 definition was later found to be overbroad because the term "savings bank" covered a few companies that controlled two or more industrial loan companies (ILCs), institutions not thought to be within the scope or purpose of the BHCA. *See* Chapter 2.1. In 1966, the definition was narrowed based on activities to include only "any institution that accepts deposits that the depositor has a legal right to withdrawal on demand," because it was then believed that the objective of the BHCA could be achieved without applying it to certain institutions that did not take demand deposits including, at that time, ILCs.

In 1970, the definition of "bank" under the BHCA was narrowed again to require that a bank engage in commercial lending and taking demand deposits. This definition permitted the creation of non-bank banks, which are institutions with national or state bank charters that took demand deposits or made commercial loans, but did not do both. The deposits of non-bank banks were federally-insured as a consequence of the 1970 Amendments to the BHCA and a number of commercial companies, such as Sears Roebuck, sought to acquire IDIs without becoming subject to the BHCA by creating a non-bank bank. Commercial companies primarily adopted the non-bank bank form to carry out consumer finance activities.

The Federal Reserve Board tried to control the growth of non-bank banks by regulation but lost the argument in *Board of Governors v. Dimension Financial Corp.*, 474 U.S. 361 (1986). The Federal Reserve Board had tried to establish a broad definition of both demand deposit and commercial loan, on the basis that the BHCA's plain purpose was to regulate institutions functionally equivalent to banks. The Federal Reserve Board believed that non-bank banks posed three dangers to the banking system: (1) by being outside the reach of many banking regulations, non-bank banks had a significant competitive advantage; (2) the proliferation of non-bank banks threatened the structure established by

Congress for limiting the affiliation of banking and commercial enterprises; and (3) the interstate acquisition of multiple non-bank banks undermined the then extant statutory proscriptions on interstate banking absent specific state legislative authority. The Court held that the plain language of the BHCA did not support the Federal Reserve Board's regulations and concluded that "[i]f the [BHCA] falls short of providing safeguards desirable or necessary to protect the public interest, that is a problem for Congress, and not the [Federal Reserve] Board or the courts, to address." *Id.* at 374.

To address this concern, Congress passed the Competitive Equality Banking Act of 1987 (CEBA), amending again the definition of "bank" to include nearly all FDIC-insured institutions, including non-bank banks. The few remaining exceptions are ILCs, credit card banks, and limited-purpose trust banks. Thrifts and credit unions are also exempt from the "bank" definition under the BHCA, but are subject instead to an alternative statutory scheme. *See* Chapter 2.1. The ownership of the non-bank banks by approximately 160 commercial enterprises was grandfathered, with a few restrictions placed on their activities, including restrictions on acquiring another bank or insured institution and permitting overdrafts. 12 U.S.C. § 1843(f)(2).

---

1. ***What is a bank?*** Why has it been so hard to define the term "bank" under the BHCA and why has the term changed so much? What influence have changing technology and the changing policy goals of various players had on the definitions? What do the changing definitions tell us about the scope of the regulatory perimeter of the Federal Reserve Board? Consider how and why the term "bank" under the BHCA differs from the charter types of IDIs we discussed in Chapter 2.1.

C. CONTROL AND CONTROLLING INFLUENCE

Under the BHCA, a relationship of "control" must exist between a "company" and a "bank" in order for the company to be subject to regulation as a BHC. 12 U.S.C. § 1841(a)(1). The definition of control in the bank regulatory context differs greatly from common corporate, tax, and accounting conceptions of control. As originally passed in 1956, control was an objective test, whereby a company that owned more than 25% of any class of voting securities in a bank or which is capable of electing a majority of its board of directors controlled the bank. *Id.* § 1841(a)(2)(A)-(B). The 1970 Amendments to the BHCA added a subjective test, which has given broad discretion to the Federal Reserve Board to find a relationship of "control" where a third party is able to exercise a "controlling influence" over the management or policies of a banking organization. *Id.* § 1841(a)(2)(C). This subjective test does not require absolute control, but required solely the ability for a party to exercise significant influence due to ownership of voting or non-voting securities, director representation, consultations with management, or business relationships. Under the regulations promulgated by the Federal Reserve Board, a controlling influence will presumptively not be found if an investor owns less than 5% of voting securities. 12 C.F.R. § 225.31(e). The presumption can be rebutted, however, where business relationships and other indicators of control exist.

The discretion associated with the subjective test has been known to give would-be investors pause before investing in a bank or BHC. After all, if an investment causes a relationship of control to be found between, for example, a private equity fund and a bank or BHC, the fund will be itself be considered a BHC and will be subject to supervision and regulation by the Federal Reserve Board.

The attachment of the BHC regulatory framework, of course, includes limitations on the commercial activities that may be performed by non-bank companies in the private equity fund's investment portfolio. To encourage private equity funds and other investors to provide much needed capital to banks during the Financial Crisis, the Federal Reserve Board issued a policy statement in 2008 intended to provide certain limited safe harbors to investors acquiring less than 25% of the voting securities of a bank or BHC. A few weeks after issuing this statement, and under "unusual and exigent circumstances" at the height of the Financial Crisis, the Federal Reserve Board approved the application of Mitsubishi UFJ (MUFJ) to acquire up to 24.9% of the voting shares of Morgan Stanley. MUFJ Financial Group, Inc., 95 Fed. Res. Bull. B35 (2009) (order dated Oct. 6, 2008). The Federal Reserve Board determined that the acquisition would not cause MUFJ to control Morgan Stanley, because it would be a "passive" investment. As part of its application, MUFJ warranted that it would not "exercise or attempt to exercise a controlling influence over the management or policies of [Morgan Stanley] or any of its subsidiaries and [would] not to have more than one representative serve on the board of directors of [Morgan Stanley] or its subsidiaries." *Id.* at B36. In a later order, the Federal Reserve Board approved MUFJ's proposal to appoint two representatives to the Morgan Stanley board of directors, relying on the fact that the MUFJ representatives would represent less than 15% of the board members, and that they would only be able to cast one vote on any committee or subcommittee of the board. MUFJ Financial Group, Inc., Order Approving Acquisition of Interests in a Bank Holding Company and Certain Nonbanking Subsidiaries, 97 Fed. Res. Bull. 10 (2011).

---

1. ***Foreign Bank Minority Investment in Another Foreign Bank.*** You have been hired by an EU bank that has a wholesale uninsured branch licensed in New York through which it does dollar clearing. The EU bank has a 20% investment in a Chinese bank that has a small uninsured branch in San Francisco. The EU bank also has two directors on the Chinese bank's board of directors and significant business ties with the Chinese bank's head office. The other 80% of the Chinese bank is owned by the Chinese government. The Chinese bank has just entered into a cease-and-desist order with the Federal Reserve Board for money laundering violations out of its San Francisco branch. The New York examiner-in-chief has just informed your client that its examination ratings will be lowered because its controlled financial subsidiary did not have adequate compliance to address anti-money laundering regulations. When the New York branch calls you for help, how do you respond?

2. ***Private Equity Investments in Banks.*** While the Federal Reserve Board's 2008 policy statement was designed to encourage investments in financial institutions in distress, concerns soon arose about the risks that the Deposit Insurance Fund may face if private equity funds that structure their investments as non-controlling because their business model is not amenable to BHCA regulation, invested in a failing bank but were not a source of strength and remained exempt from other safety and soundness requirements. In 2009, in response to Congressional and other pressures, the FDIC issued a policy statement requiring private investors that acquire interests in a failed bank through the bidding process of an FDIC receivership to comply with affiliate transactions restrictions and meet other criteria. In addition, higher capital requirements were imposed on the new bank that emerged from receivership. Final Statement of Policy on Qualifications for Failed Bank Acquisitions, 74 Fed. Reg. 45,440 (Sept. 2, 2009). It is an open question whether the FDIC's policy statement limited private equity bids on failed banks, the vast majority of which were in the community bank sector. Which do you prefer: the Federal Reserve's loosening of its controlling influence standards during the Financial Crisis to encourage private capital, or the FDIC's more cautious attitude? Does the FDIC policy disfavor community banks? We will discuss failed banks more in Part IX.

IV. ACTIVITIES OF BANK HOLDING COMPANIES: CLOSELY RELATED TO BANKING

Under the original 1956 version of the BHCA, a BHC and its non-bank affiliates were limited to engaging in those activities that are "so closely related to the business of banking or of managing or controlling banks as to be a proper incident thereto." Original BHCA § 4(c)(6); compare with BHCA § 4(c)(8); 12 U.S.C. § 1843(c)(8). The Federal Reserve Board's interpretation of the "closely related" concept was narrow; it required that the banks in the holding company structure to actually be engaged in the activity as "the business of banking" in order for non-bank subsidiaries to conduct the activity. At the urging of the banking sector, Congress, in the 1970 Amendments, struck the words "business of" and broadened the concept to "closely related to banking"—meaning that there existed a range of activities not permitted in the chartered bank that could be conducted by non-bank affiliates.

The Federal Reserve Board's screening of proposed activities under the "so closely related to banking . . . as to be proper incident thereto" standard grew to involve two separate determinations: (1) whether a given activity is "closely related" to banking, and (2) whether allowance of an activity in a particular instance constitutes a "proper incident thereto." The Federal Reserve Board must find that both prongs of this test are satisfied before allowing a BHC to engage in a non-banking activity under BHCA § 4(c)(8). The "proper incident" determination is case-specific and is used to evaluate the merits of a particular BHC engaging in a particular non-banking activity. The "closely related" determination was articulated both in the form of regulations applicable to all BHCs and by individual orders. A full list of activities deemed "closely related to banking" by the Federal Reserve Board can be found in Regulation Y at 12 C.F.R.

§ 225.28. For reasons shrouded in the mists of history, this list has long been referred to by Federal Reserve Board staff and bank regulatory lawyers as the laundry list.

There is no technical legal analysis that would make sense of the laundry list of activities designated by the Federal Reserve Board as "closely related to banking." Instead, it is best understood as the outcome of a number of extrinsic forces that intensified competitive pressures on banks and BHCs, filtered through the usual stakeholder battles among different participants in the financial sector trying to protect or expand the competitive turf. Most critically, the value of the bank charter was in steep decline during the 1980s and 1990s as money market mutual funds eroded the core banking deposit base, the commercial paper market became a desirable alternative to prime corporate loans and short-term working capital loans, and blue chip corporates turned increasingly to bond markets as a substitute for corporate loans. In addition, competition in the consumer finance space from non-banks, and in corporate lending from foreign banks, increased. Technological advances, including the development of computing power, the lowering of telecommunications costs, globalization, and inflation, all also played a role in the declining value of the commercial bank charter. To remain competitive, BHCs in the United States began to diversify their offerings and increasingly expanded into a variety of financial activities.

As new financial activities came into being or old financial activities were transformed to compete with the traditional "business of banking," BHCs were increasingly successful in convincing the Federal Reserve Board, typically over the objections of preexisting competitors in that space, that such activities satisfied the "closely related to banking" test and could be added to the laundry list. Jerry W. Markham, *Banking Regulation: Its History and Future*, 4 N.C. BANKING INST. 221 (2000). There was no shortage of formidable opponents from other parts of the financial services sector protesting the gradual liberalization of the "closely related to banking" definition. The Federal Reserve Board, however, tended to authorize the loosening of restrictions on BHCs. BHC-favorable interpretations by the Federal Reserve Board often resulted in symmetric litigation between the Federal Reserve Board, representing an interest supported by the commercial banking sector, and the non-bank competitors of BHCs, such as insurance companies, broker-dealers and mutual funds. Symmetric litigation is part of a broader arena of what Professor Adam Levitin terms "symmetrical policy contestations" between the commercial banks, investment banks, and insurance companies that competed as rivals. *See* Levitin, *The Politics of Financial Regulation and the Regulation of Financial Politics: A Review Essay*, at 2060–61.

In the course of this litigation, the courts set forth a test for determining whether a Federal Reserve Board interpretation of "closely related to banking" would be upheld:

> The Federal Reserve [Board] must, we think, articulate the ways in which banking activities and the proposed activities are assuredly connected, and must determine, not arbitrarily or capriciously, that the connections are close. As to what kinds of connections may qualify, at least the following seem to us within the statutory intent:

1. Banks generally have in fact provided the proposed services.
2. Banks generally provide services that are operationally or functionally so similar to the proposed services as to equip them particularly well to provide the proposed service.
3. Banks generally provide services that are so integrally related to the proposed services as to require their provision in a specialized form.

National Courier Ass'n v. Bd. of Gov. of Fed. Reserve Sys., 516 F.2d 1229, 1237 (D.C. Cir. 1975).

Ultimately, these cases were often resolved by the courts' application of deference, both before, and even more so after, *Chevron v. NRDC*. Because deference to the Federal Reserve Board's interpretation was often determinative, the aggregate result of these cases was a strong trend of permitting BHCs to expand their range of activities from the late 1970s onward. This line of cases ultimately yielded the "laundry list" of permissible activities for non-bank subsidiaries of BHCs.

In 1999, Congress passed GLBA, which created FHCs, expanded the powers of these new entities dramatically, and eliminated the Federal Reserve Board's power to designate new activities as "closely related to banking." GLBA thus froze the laundry list as it existed on November 10, 1999, the day before GLBA was enacted, and shifted stakeholder battles to the definitional boundaries of the new statutory terms of "financial in nature" and "complementary."

---

1. ***Freezing the Laundry List.*** Why would Congress choose to freeze the laundry list of "closely related to banking" activities in GLBA—an Act that otherwise expanded the permissible activities for BHCs that qualified for the broader FHC status? In 1999, what would have been the concern about continuing to add to the laundry list? Was it an attempt to control Federal Reserve Board's discretion, to put a stop to the long and painful process of rent-seeking stakeholder battles among different parts of the financial sector? Was the Federal Reserve Board motivated by concerns about the declining competitiveness of the banking sector or was it cognitively captured by that sector? Or was it an attempt to push all BHCs that sought expanded powers into the more difficult to achieve FHC status?

2. ***Scope of the Laundry List.*** Review the Regulation Y laundry list at 12 C.F.R. § 225.28. Are mere BHCs permitted to engage in travel agency or real estate brokerage activities? Can a BHC engage in management consulting? Can it engage in data processing activities for third parties, today often called fintech? Are there any limits on its data processing or management consulting? Can a mere BHC underwrite property and casualty insurance, auto insurance, or life insurance? Is there a financial stability, safety and soundness or consumer protection rationale for what is on or off the laundry list? Or is it instead a reflection of history and long past stakeholder battles?

3. ***Obsolescence of Statutes.*** Should financial regulatory statutes, which are typically the result of stakeholder battles and destined for regulatory arbitrage

as markets and technology change, have a predefined sunset period? Roberta Romano, *Regulating in the Dark*, *in* REGULATORY BREAKDOWN: THE CRISIS OF CONFIDENCE IN U.S. REGULATION 86 (Cary Coglianese ed., 2012); Donald C. Langevoort, *Statutory Obsolescence and the Judicial Process: The Revisionist Role of the Courts in Federal Banking Regulation*, 85 MICH. L. REV. 672 (1987).

V. EROSION OF THE GLASS-STEAGALL ACT

While it is sometimes thought that the passage of GLBA resulted in the complete tear-down of the Glass-Steagall Act wall between investment banking and commercial banking, the reality is more complicated. The Glass-Steagall Act barriers, initially put in place as part of the Banking Act of 1933, eroded slowly in the 1980s and 1990s in the same way that the scope of activities within the "closely related to banking" definition gradually expanded: through changing regulatory interpretations made at the behest of the U.S. commercial banking sector that were contested at each step, often in court, by the then-separate U.S. investment banking sector, seeking to protect its turf, or at least delay the inevitable. These stakeholder battles did not take place in the EU, where, under the universal banking model, chartered deposit-taking banks had always been permitted to underwrite corporate debt and equity and possessed broad powers with respect to investing in commercial companies.

Section 20 of the Glass-Steagall Act prohibited affiliations between banks and firms "engaged principally in the issue, flotation, underwriting, public sale, or distribution at wholesale or retail or through syndicate participation of stocks, bonds, debentures, notes, or other securities." *See* 12 U.S.C. § 377 (repealed 2000). Section 20 essentially prohibited BHCs from controlling non-bank subsidiaries "engaged principally" in corporate debt and equity underwriting activities. For many decades following the enactment of the Glass-Steagall Act as part of the Banking Act of 1933, the "engaged principally" language of § 20 lay dormant. During this time, neither market nor technological forces pushed commercial banks to leave what was then their protected competitive space. U.S. commercial banks began to experience competition from investment banks, however, as the capital markets, through investment banking services, began to take away some of the best and most reliable large corporate customers of the money-center banks. As a result, commercial banks began to make efforts to loosen the interpretation of the long-dormant "engaged principally" restriction in § 20 of the Glass-Steagall Act.

Beginning in the late 1980s and throughout the mid-1990s, as the value of the bank charter declined in tandem with the growth of the capital markets, which displaced commercial lending, the Federal Reserve Board took a view of § 20 of the Glass-Steagall Act that was increasingly favorable to the commercial banking sector. The Federal Reserve Board's BHC-favorable interpretations were matched by the OCC's bank-favorable interpretation of the "business of banking" language under § 16 of the Glass-Steagall Act, as discussed in Chapter 2.2.

In 1987, the Federal Reserve Board began to expand the scope of BHC-permissible activities under § 20 by finding that certain forms of securities underwriting were permissible for BHCs and not proscribed corporate debt and equity underwriting activity. *See* Citicorp, J.P. Morgan & Co. Inc., Bankers Trust New York Corp., Order Approving Applications to Engage in Limited Underwriting and Dealing in Certain Securities, 73 Fed. Res. Bull. 473, 485–86 (1987). By the time GLBA was passed in 1999, the Federal Reserve Board had, through interpretation, already approved BHCs and their subsidiaries to engage in the underwriting of instruments, such as municipal bonds, commercial paper, mortgage-backed securities, and consumer-receivable related securities. James R. Barth et al., *The Repeal of Glass-Steagall and the Advent of Broad Banking* 8 (OCC, Working Paper No. 2000-5).

In addition to classifying certain underwriting activities as permissible for BHCs, the Federal Reserve Board also gradually raised the amount of revenue that a § 20 BHC subsidiary could derive from corporate debt and equity underwriting to not be considered "engaged principally" in the activity. In 1987, the Federal Reserve Board opined that § 20 subsidiaries could receive no more than 5% of gross revenues from corporate debt and equity underwriting activity. *Id.* These revenue limits were later raised from 5% to 10% in 1989, then to 25% in 1996. *Id.* By the time that the GLBA was passed, discussions were underway about a possible increase in the revenue limit to 50%.

In 1999, GLBA repealed §§ 20 and 32 of the Glass-Steagall Act, which, respectively, prohibited affiliations between banks and firms "engaged principally" in the underwriting and dealing of corporate debt and equity, and prohibited banks from having overlapping boards and officers with firms "primarily engaged" in investment banking. *See* 12 U.S.C. §§ 78, 377 (repealed 2000). By the time of their repeal, because of the interpretations described above, existing law functioned mostly to prohibit BHCs from making private equity investments in commercial companies, either directly or through private equity funds affiliated with or sponsored by the BHC. As a result, many would date the true fall of the Glass-Steagall Act barriers to corporate debt and equity underwriting to the early 1990s rather than to 1999. As discussed in Chapter 2.2, §§ 16 and 21 of the Glass-Steagall Act, however, are still law today.

VI. SEPARATION OF INSURANCE AND BANKING ACTIVITIES

Stakeholder battles over the inclusion of insurance activities as "closely related to banking" were another important impetus for the GLBA changes, even though insurance is completely unrelated to the Glass-Steagall Act and the underwriting of corporate debt and equity securities. Since the beginning of the 20th Century, the insurance sector had resisted efforts by the commercial banking sector to enter the insurance business. *See* Right of a National Bank to Write Insurance Through Its Officers, 2 Fed. Res. Bull. 73, 73–74 (1916); Emeric Fischer, *Banking and Insurance—Should Ever the Twain Meet?*, 71 NEB. L. REV. 726, 747 n.118 (1992). In the 1966 Amendments to the BHCA, insurance companies were able to convince Congress to cut back express authority given to BHCs under the original 1956 version of the BHCA to own subsidiaries "all the activities of which are of [an] . . . insurance nature." Original BHCA § 4(c)(6).

The stakeholder battles continued in the 1980s. The fact that most insurance activity, with some explicit exceptions, was not closely related to banking was made explicit in § 601 of the Garn-St Germain Act of 1982, stating that "but for purposes of this subsection it is not closely related to banking or managing or controlling banks for a BHC to provide insurance as a principal, agent, or broker . . . ." By 1996, at least some in the insurance sector had joined the commercial banking sector in its efforts to create financial conglomerates. The 1998 announcement of an agreement to merge between Citicorp, a large BHC, and Travelers, a larger insurance company, was a stark challenge to the existing regulatory landscape. Under the BHCA, Travelers had to apply for BHC status in order to acquire Citigroup and the merger had to be approved by the Federal Reserve Board. In what some view as an aggressive move to put pressure on Congress to finally make the changes in the law which it had considered nearly a dozen times, the Federal Reserve Board, led by Chairman Alan Greenspan, gave its conditional approval for the acquisition, but required that the activities of the merged firm that were not in conformance with the BHCA represent less than 15% of the combined company's total assets and less than 20% of its revenues. Federal Reserve Board, Travelers Group Inc., Citicorp, Order Approving Formation of a Bank Holding Company and Notice to Engage in Nonbanking Activities (Sept. 23, 1998). Because the merged firm had a limited time period of two to five years to terminate or spin off nonconforming activities that exceeded this threshold, intense pressure was applied on lawmakers to pass legislation that would allow for the unified entity to remain intact without conforming activities as required by the Federal Reserve Board approval.

In essence, Citicorp and Travelers, with the approval of the Federal Reserve Board, were putting pressure on Congress to change the law within a two to five year time period. In the aftermath of the Financial Crisis, many have found this game of legislative chicken shocking. At the time, however, it was understood against a backdrop in which Congress had considered and almost passed repeals of the Glass-Steagall Act and expansions of insurance activities on a bipartisan and White House-backed basis over a dozen times during that decade. The gambit worked and, in 1999, Congress passed GLBA, creating the FHC form to allow eligible BHCs to engage in an expanded list of activities, including insurance.

VII. ACTIVITIES OF FINANCIAL HOLDING COMPANIES

Despite the gradual expansion of permissible activities under the "closely related to banking" test and the gradual erosion of the Glass-Steagall Act barriers, it is still fair to say that the passage of GLBA fundamentally changed the nature of financial services in the United States. First, GLBA eliminated the division between insurance and banking, which was so hard-fought for so many years. This elimination, in turn, permitted the Citibank/Travelers acquisition to remain in place without divestitures. At the time, it was widely believed that a new bank/insurance model, similar to the EU bank assurance model might develop. In reality, this development was short-lived and, in 2005, before the Financial Crisis, Citigroup sold Travelers. Second, GLBA permitted affiliates of BHCs to make equity investments in commercial companies for a ten-year period via the merchant banking rule described below. Third, GLBA changed the dominant culture of many large banking organizations from a commercial banker mindset to an investment banker and trader mindset. Finally, GLBA put an end to the intra-financial sector stakeholder battles that had defined the U.S. financial sector since the beginning of the 20th Century vis-a-vis the insurance sector, and since the mid-1970s vis-à-vis the investment banking sector.

These changes were achieved through several technical legal mechanisms. First, in addition to repealing the Glass-Steagall Act restrictions on affiliations between commercial and investment banks, GLBA also created a new category of BHC: the FHC. An FHC can be understood as a BHC with expanded powers as long as it maintains its status as "well-managed" and "well-capitalized." As of May 15, 2015, approximately 432 U.S. BHCs and 56 foreign banking organizations (FBOs) successfully elected to be FHCs. These 488 registered FHCs vary greatly in size and complexity. Nearly all BHCs with more than $50 billion in assets have elected to become FHCs, demonstrating the attractiveness of FHC status to the larger BHCs. In addition, many small BHCs, such as the Young Americans Education Foundation, which is the holding company for the Young Americans Bank of Denver with a $16 million in assets, have elected FHC status. Today, mere BHC status is rare among all but the smallest U.S. BHCs and, as a practical matter, it is typically limited to foreign banks with a limited U.S. footprint.

A. BECOMING AN FHC

Because FHC status offers more freedom and flexibility, Congress set eligibility criteria to restrict FHC status to qualifying BHCs. To successfully elect to become an FHC, a BHC must first demonstrate that the holding company and all of its IDI subsidiaries are well-capitalized and well-managed. 12 U.S.C. §§ 1843(l)(1)(A)-(C). Additionally, at the time it becomes an FHC, the BHC must not be subject to any written agreement, order, capital directive, or prompt corrective action directive issued by the Federal Reserve Board to meet and maintain a specific capital level for any capital measure. 12 C.F.R. § 225.2(r)(1)(iii). With respect to an IDI, "well-capitalized" means that the institution has and maintains at least the capital levels required to be well capitalized under the capital adequacy regulations or guidelines applicable to the institution that have been adopted by the appropriate federal banking agency. *Id.* § 225.2(r)(2). The Federal Reserve Board has also promulgated regulations that designate a company or IDI as "well managed" if, at the time of its last inspection or examination, it received at least a satisfactory composite rating and at least a satisfactory rating for management, if such rating is given. *Id.* § 225.2(s). Finally, to engage in any of the FHC-specific activities, the FHC and its IDIs must have received at least a "satisfactory" rating under the Community Reinvestment Act. 12 U.S.C. § 1843(l)(2).

If the Federal Reserve Board finds that an FHC is not in compliance with these requirements but is acting on authority granted to FHCs only (and not to mere BHCs under BHCA § 4(c)(8)), the Federal Reserve Board must provide notice to the FHC of its violation, and the FHC must agree within 45 days to be in compliance with the relevant conditions in what is commonly referred to as a "4(m) agreement," so named after § 4(m) of the BHCA, which contains the provision. *Id.* §§ 1843(m)(1)-(2). The existence and content of these 4(m) agreements is confidential supervisory information. The Federal Reserve Board may place limitations on the FHC's activities and may even require an FHC to divest control of any subsidiary depository institution if it fails to come into compliance within 180 days. *Id.* §§ 1843(m)(3)-(4)(A). To avoid divestiture, the FHC may elect to terminate the activities that are not permissible for BHCs under § 4(c)(8) of the BHCA. *Id.* § 1843(m)(4)(B). As a practical matter, this draconian authority has not yet been used. Instead, the Federal Reserve Board has widely used its authority, under § 4(m) of the BHCA, to restrict any new non-banking activities of FHCs and to limit their acquisitions of non-banking affiliates.

B. ACTIVITIES THAT ARE FINANCIAL IN NATURE

The BHCA provides a list of activities deemed by Congress to be "financial in nature" and, thus, permissible activities for FHCs that are in compliance with applicable regulations. As previously mentioned, Congress ordained all of the activities previously determined to be "closely related to banking" under the BHCA as "financial in nature" and permissible for FHCs. *Id.* § 1843(k)(4)(F). In addition, Congress specified that underwriting and dealing in corporate debt and equity was a permissible activity and clarified that FHCs may engage in insurance brokerage or underwriting activities. *Id.* §§ 1843(k)(4)(B), (E). As discussed in more detail below, Congress also granted FHCs the authority to engage in merchant banking activities, such as investments in commercial companies, under certain conditions.

GLBA also added a provision to the BHCA that vests authority in the Federal Reserve Board to determine if additional activities are (1) financial in nature, (2) incidental to financial activity, or (3) complementary to financial activity without posing a substantial risk to the safety and soundness of depository institutions or the financial system generally. *Id.* § 1843(k)(1). The statute also provides the Federal Reserve Board with a list of factors to be considered in determining whether an activity is financial in nature or incidental to a financial activity, including the purposes of GLBA, changes in technology or in the marketplace in which FHCs compete, and whether such activity is necessary or appropriate to allow an FHC and its affiliates to compete effectively within the United States. *Id.* § 1843(k)(3).

To determine whether an activity is "financial in nature" or "incidental to financial activity," the Federal Reserve Board must consult with the Secretary of the Treasury, who is vested with the authority to prevent such a determination. *Id.* § 1843(k)(2). To date, most of the Federal Reserve Board's determinations regarding activities that are "complementary" relate to FHC physical commodities activities. The Federal Reserve Board did, however, use its authority to determine that "disease management and mail-order pharmacy activities" are complementary to underwriting and selling health insurance, which is considered a financial activity. Order Determining that Certain Activities Are Complementary to the Financial Activity of Underwriting and Selling Health Insurance, 93 Fed. Res. Bull. C133 (2007).

C. MERCHANT BANKING

Before GLBA, BHCs were only permitted to make very small equity investments, not to exceed 5% or more of any class of voting securities, in any commercial company. 12 U.S.C. §§ 1843(c)(6)-(7). This restriction under the

BHCA was meant to enforce what had become an increasingly strict separation between banking and commerce in the United States, first introduced in Chapter 2.2 in the context of the charter of the Bank of England. This policy choice is quite different from many in continental European and Asian countries where banks and their affiliates have long been permitted to own major stakes in commercial companies. The growth of private equity funds and their long-term equity investments in growth companies, along with competition from banking organizations headquartered in universal banking countries, put pressure on the strict U.S. BHCA rules on equity investments by non-bank affiliates. As a result, GLBA authorized FHCs to directly or indirectly acquire or control up to 100% of the ownership interest in any commercial entity, subject to certain conditions. *Id.* § 1843(k)(4)(H).

These conditions were interpreted by the Federal Reserve Board and the Treasury Department in a 2001 joint rulemaking that restricted these investments in commercial companies to those investments (1) that last for no more than ten years unless the Federal Reserve Board approves an extension, (2) that are a part of a bona fide underwriting, merchant, or investment banking activity, and (3) where the FHC does not routinely manage or operate the company. 12 C.F.R. §§ 225.170-172. Additionally, the FHC must hold the assets in a distinct portfolio company, which should separate management and the FHC and should maintain books and records apart from those of the FHC. *Id.* § 225.170. The purpose of these restrictions is to keep FHCs from engaging in the routine day-to-day management of a portfolio company, while allowing them to access often lucrative private equity investments. The Federal Reserve Board provided a list of activities that an FHC may engage in with respect to a portfolio company, including providing financial, investment, and management consulting advice to a portfolio company, meeting with the officers or employees of a portfolio company to monitor or provide advice with respect to the company's performance or activities, or adding restrictive covenants that require the portfolio company to consult with the FHC before taking actions outside of the ordinary course of business. *Id.* §§ 225.171(d)(2)-(3).

---

1. ***Different Policy Choice in Europe.*** The line between banking and commerce has been drawn very differently in other countries where banks and commercial companies invest in each other. Consider the situation of continental European banks, such as the Germans and the French. Deutsche Bank has long owned a big stake in Mercedes Benz and French banks have, at various times, owned large stakes in the French electricity company GDF Suez and the French nuclear power company, Areva. Do the different systems of capitalism between continental Europe and the United States and UK world explain these differences in treatment? Consider the perspective of Professor Mark Roe, who argues that the governance structures of U.S. firms are the result of political and social choices, not just economics. Roe writes: "American democracy affected American finance, which in turn affected the structure of American's large public firms. . . . American politics deliberately weakened and shattered financial intermediaries, thereby making managers more powerful than they otherwise had to be." Mark ROE, STRONG MANAGERS WEAK OWNERS, at ix-x (1994).

Furthermore, does it matter that Germany and France have long had a system more weighted towards the government ownership of companies and union representation on boards, as opposed to the U.S. system of dispersed ownership of public companies? Is the concern one of concentrations of economic power over the economy and social system or of the distribution of power between the state and the private sector? Is the view expressed by Roe in 1994 describing the 19th and early 20th Century history of the banking sector in the United States still valid today as seen from a post-Financial Crisis perspective?

2. ***How Solid Is the Line?*** The separation of banking and commerce has not been as solid in the United States as many believe. Rather, banking and commerce "has long followed a non-linear and complex pattern," creating a murky distinction between the two. Saule T. Omarova, *The Merchants of Wall Street: Banking, Commerce, and Commodities*, 98 MINN. L. REV. 265, 277 (2013). Remember the single-bank BHCs, which owned both commercial companies and banks but were exempted from registration with the Federal Reserve Board under the BHCA until the law was changed in 1970. As of December 31, 1968, there were 783 existing or proposed one-bank BHCs in the U.S., most of which were personal one-bank BHCs owned by families or individuals. CARL ARLT, THE ONE BANK HOLDING COMPANY 68–69 (Herbert V. Prochnow ed., 1969). Why was it considered appropriate for one family to own both a small bank and the major company in its town through the same holding company? Were the 1970 Amendments driven by the need to control possible abuses in that arrangement at a time when most banks were geographically segmented or to protect smaller banks from bigger banks entering their protected markets across state lines? If that were the problem, did forcing the family to have two separate holding companies solve the potential for abuse? One historian of the Detroit automobile industry has suggested that the Ford family's control of banking in the state of Michigan led to the downfall of many independent auto companies and privileged the "Big Three" auto manufacturers. *See* DARWYN H. LUMLEY, BREAKING THE BANKS IN MOTOR CITY (2009).

3. ***Policy Reasons for Separation.*** The quote below proffers some reasons for the separation of banking and commerce:

> This policy reflects a concern that a bank that controls industrial enterprises would be economically too powerful. There is also a concern that commercial or industrial activities of banks may endanger the safety of deposits: bankers may be bad industrialists; they may extend credit to the bank's commercial affiliates on preferential terms, and once a commercial affiliate of a bank incurs losses, the bank may be under great pressure to extend unsound credit. The policy of separation also reflects a concern that a bank that engages in a commercial activity may refuse to extend credit to competitors of its subsidiaries.

Michael Gruson, *Foreign Banks and the Regulation of Financial Holding Companies* 1 n.1 (Johann Wolfgang Goethe-Universität Frankfurt am Main, Working Paper No. 92).

How convincing do you find these arguments? Are there instances in which such concerns might not pose as much of an issue as the quote suggests? How have equity investments under the merchant banking rule played out in practice?

4. ***Indonesian Banking.*** Consider the situation of the Liem family in Indonesia. Born in China in 1916, Liem Sioe Liong arrived in Indonesia in his early twenties and became close to Suharto, the eventual Indonesian president. When Suharto rose to the presidency, Liem received a number of monopoly rights over businesses, such as banking, commodities, food processing, cement, steel, and real estate. At one point in time, 60% of loans from Liem's Bank Central Asia went to related affiliates, compared to a legal limit of 20%. Indonesia's largest private bank, Bank Central Asia, eventually collapsed in 1998 during the Asian Financial Crisis. JOE STUDWELL, ASIAN GODFATHERS: MONEY AND POWER IN HONG KONG AND SOUTH EAST ASIA 60, 251 (2008). Consider also the situation in post-Communist Europe. Before the fall of the U.S.S.R., banks in Communist Europe countries were largely state-owned. The wave of privatization that followed the collapse of Communism led to a messy and often unclear divide between what was ultimately private and public in the banking sector. Would a stricter line between banking and commerce, as exists in the United States, have helped curb these abuses?

VIII. SAVINGS AND LOAN HOLDING COMPANIES

Investors forming an IDI may elect to charter as a savings and loan association, often called a thrift, instead of as a bank. As we saw in Chapter 2.1, while the powers granted by a thrift charter are more limited than those granted by a bank charter, a thrift institution is still an IDI with access to the federal safety net. The same concerns that motivated passage of the BHCA thus drove the regulation of SLHCs, initially through the National Housing Act, which was amended to include SLHC provisions in the CEBA, and eventually through § 10 of HOLA (amended to include SLHC provisions in the Financial Institutions Reform, Recovery, and Enforcement Act).

Though the relevant definitions and restrictions vary from those outlined in the BHCA, the regulatory framework governing SLHCs is largely similar to the regulatory architecture for BHCs. For example, an entity is considered an SLHC if it is a "company" that directly or indirectly "controls" a "savings association" or another SLHC. 12 U.S.C. § 1467a(a)(1)(D). Similarly, an SLHC and its subsidiaries are subject to activities restrictions, including "commenc[ing] any business activity" outside of an approved list. *Id.* § 1467a(c)(1)(B). SLHCs may, however, engage in a defined set of exempt activities, including those which the Federal Reserve Board, "by regulation, has determined to be permissible" for BHCs under the BHCA. *Id.* § 1467a(c)(2)(F)(i).

In order to register as an SLHC rather than a BHC, the holding company's controlled savings association must be a "qualified thrift lender." *Id.* § 1467a(m)(3)(C). This requirement forces the holding company's thrift to maintain at least 65% of its portfolio assets in qualifying thrift instruments, including home mortgage loans, home equity loans, mortgage-backed securities, educational loans, small business loans, and credit card loans. *Id.*

§§ 1467a(m)(1), (4)(C). The regulation of SLHCs departs significantly from the BHCA framework in its distinction between unitary SLHCs (SLHCs with only one thrift) and multiple SLHCs (SLHCs with more than one thrift). *Id.* §§ 1467a(a)(1)(E), (c)(3). While most SLHCs are subject to activities restrictions on their non-thrift affiliates, unitary SLHCs are exempt from such restrictions. *Id.* § 1467a(c)(3). Unitary SLHCs that existed before May 4, 1999, referred to as "grandfathered unitary thrift holding companies," are exempt from affiliation restrictions otherwise placed on SLHCs, provided that certain requirements are met. *Id.* § 1467a(c)(9)(C). This favorable regulatory treatment has made the grandfathered unitary thrift holding company particularly desirable, even after the FHC was introduced by GLBA.

The Office of Thrift Supervision (OTS), which regulated thrifts and SLHCs from 1989 to 2011, was generally viewed as a more friendly regulator and was known for adopting views with a deregulatory bent and being aggressive in preempting state laws. Binyamin Appelbaum & Ellen Nakashima, *Banking Regulator Played Advocate Over Enforcer*, WASH. POST, Nov. 23, 2008, at A1. Further, as a matter of policy, OTS chose to focus its efforts on regulating thrifts, rather than taking an umbrella supervisor approach to regulating SLHCs and their non-thrift subsidiaries. As a result, in a working display of regulatory arbitrage, numerous firms sought to register as SLHCs to avail themselves of more favorable regulation and lower supervisory standards. Notably, AIG, IndyMac, and Washington Mutual, all of which experienced failure or near failure during the Financial Crisis, were registered and regulated as SLHCs. MARC JARSULIC, ANATOMY OF A FINANCIAL CRISIS 79, 82–84 (2012). The trouble experienced by these firms during the Financial Crisis prompted Congress to eliminate the OTS in the Dodd-Frank Act and to reallocate SLHC supervisory power to the Federal Reserve Board. Just as thrifts have survived as a viable organizational structure and are regulated next to banks by the OCC, the SLHC structure has also endured, under new supervision by the Federal Reserve Board.

Section 626 of the Dodd-Frank Act also strengthened the Federal Reserve Board's ability to regulate grandfathered unitary thrift SLHCs. 12 U.S.C. § 1467b. Specifically, the Federal Reserve Board may require a grandfathered unitary SLHC that engages in nonfinancial activities to establish an IHC and conduct its financial activities only through the Intermediate Holding Company (IHC). *Id.* § 1467b(b)(1). The new IHC would then be regulated as an SLHC, while the grandfathered unitary thrift holding company would be subject only to source-of-strength obligations, limited reporting requirements, and limited enforcement authority. *Id.* §§ 1467b(b)(3)-(5). The Federal Reserve Board has the authority, similar to the authority granted in Federal Reserve Act Sections 23A and 23B with respect to BHCs, to restrict transactions between the IHC and the grandfathered unitary thrift holding company and its affiliates. *Id.* § 1467b(c). This firewall approach was presumably designed in an attempt to maintain some separation between the FHC-like aspects of a grandfathered unitary SLHC and entirely commercial enterprises.

---

1. ***Grandfathering as a Technique.*** Most unitary grandfathered thrift holding companies are insurance companies which used the format as a way to own an IDI but avoid regulation as a BHC or the full activities regulation of a regular SLHC. Why were unitary thrift holding companies grandfathered in GLBA but BHCs were not in the 1970 BHCA amendments? Is grandfathering a beneficial or a harmful legislative tool? Consider the following arguments for or against grandfathering: (1) by privileging certain industries or firms over others, grandfathering is nothing more than a sop to special interests and further evidence that Congress is captured by such interests; (2) grandfathering is valuable and necessary because it acknowledges the reliance existing companies have on the present regulatory structure and rules; (3) grandfathering is politically valuable because, without such provisions, Congress may not be able to make significant changes to regulatory rules and structure. Which of these arguments do you find most persuasive? Grandfather status can be lost if there is a change in the control or ownership of a company or bank. What if, instead of grandfathering and making exceptions for certain firms or industries, you instead gave firms a certain amount of time to adjust or conform to new regulations? As we shall see later in this Chapter, this was the approach taken by the Volcker Rule.

2. ***Insurance and Banking***. Recall that stakeholder battles, beginning in the first decade of the 20th Century in which a separation of insurance and banking was hard fought by the insurance sector. Does it affect your views on the stakeholder battles to know that, during much of that period, insurance companies had, under an exemption, acquired IDIs?

3. ***Commerce and Banking***. Either through a unitary grandfathered thrift holding company or through an ILC, or the now defunct but partially grandfathered non-bank banks, commercial companies have purchased IDIs. Some of these companies include: GE, Sears, GM, Target, and John Deere. As discussed in Chapter 2.1, Walmart was treated differently.

IX. THE VOLCKER RULE

The most significant structural change to come in the Dodd-Frank Act amendments to the BHCA is the introduction of the Volcker Rule—a term used to refer both to the statutory text in § 619 of the Dodd Frank Act and the implementing regulations promulgated by the five Volcker Rule agencies: the Federal Reserve Board, OCC, FDIC, SEC, and CFTC. BHCA § 13; 12 U.S.C. 1851; 12 C.F.R. pt. 248. The introduction of the Volcker Rule shifted the paradigm for banks and BHCs that are considering questions of permissibility and legal authorities. Even if the activity is permitted under older legal authorities (*e.g.*, "business of banking," "closely related to banking," "financial in nature," "incidental thereto," or "complementary"), if an activity is not permitted under the Volcker Rule, it cannot happen within any part of the BHC. The Volcker Rule is layered on top of and cuts across all the powers and activities of banks and BHCs described in this Chapter and in Chapter 2.2.

A. LEGISLATIVE HISTORY

Named by President Obama after Paul Volcker, the highly-respected former Chairman of the Federal Reserve Board, the Volcker Rule was a late addition to the bill that became the Dodd-Frank Act. The Administration announced the proposal in January 2010 and, despite a firestorm of opposition, convinced Senator Chris Dodd to include the proposal in his bill, which passed out of the Banking Committee in March and passed the full Senate in May of that year. Volcker's proposal was designed to exclude speculative activities from the banking safety net and to close off related conflicts of interest. Volcker stated the policy purpose for the Volcker Rule as follows:

> The need to restrict proprietary trading is not only, or perhaps most importantly, a matter of the immediate market risks involved. It is the seemingly inevitable implication for the culture of the commercial banking institutions involved, manifested in the huge incentives to take risk inherent in the compensation practices for the traders. Can one group of employees be so richly rewarded, the traders, for essentially speculative, impersonal, short-term trading activities while professional commercial bankers providing essential commercial banking services to customers, and properly imbued with fiduciary values, be confined to a much more modest structure of compensation?

Paul A. Volcker, *Commentary on the Restrictions on Proprietary Trading by Insured Depository Institutions* (Feb. 13, 2012). Senators Jeff Merkley and Carl Levin, who sponsored the version of the Volcker Rule that was ultimately added to the Dodd-Frank Act in the conference committee in June 2010, supported the enactment of the legislation, stating:

> The inclusion of a ban on proprietary trading is a victory. If implemented effectively, it will significantly reduce systemic risk to our financial system and protect American taxpayers and businesses from Wall Street's risky bets. This is an important step forward from the current system that has placed few limits on speculative trading by either banks or other financial firms. Now banks will be prohibited from doing these trades and other financial giants will have to put aside the capital to back up their bets.

Press Release, Merkley & Levin: Ban on High Risk Trades Victory for Workers and Businesses (June 25, 2010).

Volcker himself acknowledged that the proposed provisions bearing his name would not have prevented the Financial Crisis: "It certainly would not have solved the problem at AIG or solved the problem with Lehman Brothers, alone. It was not designed to solve those particular problems." *Prohibiting Certain High-Risk Investment Activities by Banks and Bank Holding Companies: Hearing Before the S. Comm. on Banking, Hous., & Urban Affairs*, 111th Cong. 28 (2010) (statement of Paul A. Volcker, Chairman, President's Economic Recovery Advisory Bd.). His view was that the Volcker Rule would be part of an effort to address the problems that might contribute to the next crisis. In Volcker's own words during a congressional hearing on the proposed legislation, "I tell you, sure as I am sitting here, that if banking institutions are protected by the taxpayer and they are given free rein to speculate, I may not live long enough to come back to see the next crisis, but my soul is going to come back and haunt you." *Id.* Some commentators have argued, however, that the speculative activities targeted by the Volcker Rule were indeed among the causes of the Financial Crisis. Professor Charles Whitehead, for example, has asserted that investment banks facing competition from commercial banks post-GLBA turned to riskier activities, including principal investments, to seek yield, and that such activities contributed to the meltdown. *See* Charles K. Whitehead, *Size Matters: Commercial Banks and the Capital Markets*, 76 OHIO ST. L.J. 765, 765–69 (2011).

While Volcker's original proposal was fairly simple in proscribing speculative activities through an "I know it when I see it" test, the Administration's legislative language included in Dodd's Senate bill was much more detailed, and the final version of the statutory text that emerged out of the conference committee—after stakeholder battles involving interests on all sides—was far more complex. The statute imposes two basic prohibitions on "banking entities": (1) a ban on "proprietary trading" and (2) restrictions on investments in, and certain relationships with, hedge funds or private equity funds. 12 U.S.C. § 1851(a)(1). The statute includes multiple exceptions to these general prohibitions.

There are several unusual features of the Volcker Rule. Unlike most banking legislation, there is no provision to grandfather existing activities or investments, but instead a very extended transition period to allow banking entities to conform to the regulations and markets to adjust. Although it was passed as part of the Dodd-Frank Act on July 21, 2010, the provisions of the Volcker Rule officially went into effect on July 21, 2015, with an additional two-year extension period for certain fund activities and investments, and a potential seven-year extension period for the divestment of nonconforming interests in illiquid funds. Additionally, unlike most other provisions in the Dodd-Frank Act, the regulators were given limited interpretive flexibility. 12 U.S.C. § 1851(d)(1)(J). Finally, in a very unusual statutory delegation, five separate agencies—the Federal Reserve Board, OCC, FDIC, CFTC, and SEC—were given co-equal rule-making and implementation authority over a provision in the BHCA. The difficulty of inter-agency rulemaking meant that the Volcker Rule was not finalized until December 2013.

B. APPLICATION TO BANKING ENTITIES

The Volcker Rule was drafted to apply to all "banking entities," a brand new and very broad term that includes *all* banking institutions and *all* affiliates of banking institutions, as opposed to just banks or BHCs. As defined, all IDIs, including chartered banks, thrifts, and ILCs, are "banking entities." Further, all parent companies, including BHCs, FHCs, and FBOs, that control these IDIs, as well as the affiliates and subsidiaries of the IDIs or their parent companies, are themselves considered "banking entities." Because the terms "affiliate" and "subsidiary" incorporate the expansive "control" definition discussed earlier in this Chapter, even far-flung affiliates with no direct U.S. nexus are caught under the "banking entity" definition, although such affiliates may find that their activities conducted "solely outside the United States" qualify for an exemption from the Volcker Rule's prohibitions.

Because of the expansive "banking entity" definition, the Volcker Rule applies beyond BHCs and is significantly broader than many in the financial sector anticipated. Moreover, the extraterritorial application of the Volcker Rule is also broader than many observers anticipated. While proprietary trading activities by foreign banks that take place "solely outside of the United States" are largely exempt from the Volcker Rule restrictions, U.S.-headquartered BHCs are not eligible for this exemption even in their foreign subsidiaries. Further, FBOs with any U.S. presence must undertake efforts to conform their activities or ensure that their activities are in fact conducted "solely outside the United States." Jai Massari, *Foreign Bank Cross-Border Trading under the Volcker Rule: the "Trading Outside the United States" Exemption's Incongruous Consequences*, 10 CAP. MARKETS L.J. 523 (2015). The recordkeeping and compliance requirements associated with properly documenting activities as "solely outside the United States" can themselves amount to a significant regulatory burden for FBOs.

While the general approach is that the Volcker Rule applies to affiliates of IDIs, the definition of banking entity sweeps in one type of entity that is not affiliated with an IDI and sweeps out another type of entity that is affiliated with an IDI. First, foreign banks with uninsured branches in the United States, the dominant model as we will see in Chapter 6.3, are treated as banking entities for their worldwide operations, even if they have no access to insured deposits in the United States. Second, limited-purpose trust companies with insured deposits, which fall under one of the exceptions to the "bank" definition in the BHCA and are an important corporate form to the Boston-based fund sector, are also excluded from the Volcker Rule's definition of banking entity. Is there a unifying policy reason behind these two seemingly contradictory approaches, one of which brings an uninsured entity into the regulatory perimeter and one of which excludes a financial group with an IDI? Or, do these exceptions just represent stakeholder wins and losses?

C. PROPRIETARY TRADING

The Volcker Rule prohibition on proprietary trading prevents banking entities from:

> engaging as principal for the trading account of the banking entity . . . in any transaction to purchase or sell, or otherwise acquire or dispose of, any security, any derivative, any contract of sale of a commodity for future delivery, any option on any such security, derivative, or contract, or any other security or financial instrument that the appropriate [federal agencies] may . . . determine.

12 U.S.C. § 1851(h)(4). The first and most important of the entities affected by the Volcker Rule were the internal hedge funds and the walled-off speculative proprietary trading desks of financial conglomerates which had arisen in the early 2000s. Most major financial conglomerates announced that they had sold or pushed out these purely speculative trading activities well before the final regulations were passed in anticipation of the final regulations.

While the statutory language of the Volcker Rule operates to prohibit banking entities from engaging in proprietary trading activities, it also provides major exemptions and exclusions from this prohibition to allow active trading of certain instruments and for certain purposes. For example, in what should not be a surprise to those familiar with the preferential treatment typically applied to activities involving U.S. Treasuries under U.S. banking law, banking entities are permitted by statute to trade freely U.S. government securities. Other important exemptions and exclusions permit banking entities to engage in trading activities in connection with underwriting or market making, to hedge risks through trading activities, and to trade on behalf of their customers. *Id.* § 1851(d)(1).

These statutory exceptions are subject to broadly worded backstop provisions preventing banking entities from engaging in activity that would (1) "involve or result in a material conflict of interest," (2) "result, directly or indirectly, in a material exposure by the banking entity to high-risk assets or high-risk trading strategies," (3) "pose a threat to the safety and soundness of such banking entity," or (4) "pose a threat to the financial stability of the United States." *Id.* § 1851(d)(2)(A).

D. COVERED FUNDS

One of the policy goals of the Volcker Rule was to prevent banking entities from sponsoring or investing in private equity funds and hedge funds, except under very limited circumstances. While most hedge funds are independent and not affiliated with banks or BHCs, there was a concern that banking entities would continue to engage in proprietary trading through affiliated fund structures without these provisions. This was not an unrealistic concern, given the long U.S. regulatory history of treating disparate legal entities within the financial conglomerate differently. These restrictions on sponsorship of, or investments in, funds were also meant to address the reputational and market pressures experienced by financial conglomerates during the Financial Crisis to make investors whole or to add more capital to funds and other off-balance-sheet vehicles that they had sponsored and which bore their brand names. This pressure was evident when Bear Stearns faced questions about the health of the entire conglomerate after letting two of its hedge funds fail in Summer 2007. Dealbook, *Bear Stearns: A Tale of Two Reckless Hedge Funds?*, N.Y. TIMES, Oct. 12, 2007. After the failure of the Bear Stearns funds, HSBC was the first financial conglomerate to bailout its structured investment vehicles and take troubled assets onto its balance sheet. Carrick Mollenkamp, *HSBC Becomes First Bank to Bail Out Troubled SIVs*, WALL ST. J., Nov. 27, 2007. Société Générale followed suit a few weeks later and Citigroup also bailed out seven troubled structured investment vehicles that dealt in subprime mortgage securities, even though it had no contractual obligation to do so. Paul J. Davies, *SocGen Joins Other Banks to Bail Out its SIV*, FIN. TIMES, Dec. 10, 2007; Robin Sidel, David Reilly & David Enrich, *Citigroup Alters Course, Bails out Affiliated Funds*, WALL ST. J., Dec. 14, 2007.

As previously described, the proponents of the Volcker Rule had clear reasons for restricting banking entity sponsorship of, or investments in, hedge funds and private equity funds. The technical mechanism used in the statute to define hedge funds and private equity funds, however, turned out to be imperfect. The Volcker Rule defines funds that are the subject of the restrictions as those that rely on one of two particular exemptions, §§ 3(c)(1) and 3(c)(7), from the definition of "investment company" under the Investment Company Act of 1940 (1940 Act). While most hedge funds and private equity funds indeed rely on these exemptions, this cross-reference inadvertently picked up many more fund vehicles, including a broad swath of foreign funds and some U.S.-based trusts that also relied on those exemptions from registration under the 1940 Act. *See* Erik F. Gerding, *Volcker's Covered Funds Rule and Trans-statutory Cross References: Securities Regulation in the Service of Banking Law*, 10 CAP. MARKETS L.J. 488 (2015). The cross-reference technique combined with the Federal Reserve Board's broad interpretations of "controlling influence", which is included in a prong of the "sponsorship" definition, have given the funds provisions a broader application than may have been intended.

Similar to the prohibition on proprietary trading, there are exceptions to the funds prohibitions of the Volcker Rule if banking entities are acting in a fiduciary capacity, underwriting or market-making in the fund interests, or if banking entities are managing the funds within the confines of the Volcker Rule's asset management exemption. Further, banking entities are not prohibited from maintaining relationships with, or owning interests in, funds that are explicitly prohibited from being offered to U.S. investors, or funds that fall within the "solely outside the United States" exemption. 12 U.S.C. § 1851(d)(1). Activities that qualify under these exceptions, however, are subject to the backstop prohibitions described above.

---

1. ***Coordination and Organizational Imperatives.*** What were the causes of the delay in writing the final regulations? Consider the extent to which stakeholder politics, including the competing interests of the financial sector, government agencies, politicians, and interest groups, influenced the pace at which the Volcker Rule was implemented. What positions would these respective stakeholders have likely taken? Consider also the extent to which the lack of a statutorily defined leader in the agency rule-making process may have contributed to delays in implementation. For example, the SEC and the FDIC now have the ability to enforce, a part of the BHCA since the Volcker Rule is a component of that Act.

2. ***The Line Between Proprietary Trading and Market Making.*** The statutory text of the Volcker Rule both explicitly prohibits "proprietary trading" as a principal for short-term gain and also explicitly permits "market-making" if it meets the "reasonably expected near-term demand" of clients and counterparties. Since market-making is a short-term principal trade by a banking entity, what is the difference between proprietary trading and market making? Is there a difference to be found in the requirement that there be near term demand by clients? *Id.* § 1851(d)(1)(B). What about the requirement, set forth in the regulation, that the banking entity routinely stands ready to make purchases on both sides of the market? 12 C.F.R. § 248.4(b)(2)(i). Is one activity more speculative and dangerous to financial stability than the other? Consider

the alternative definition of proprietary trading that, three years after the Volcker Rule, was proffered in a EU directive:

> "proprietary trading" means using own capital or borrowed money to take positions in any type of transaction to purchase, sell or otherwise acquire or dispose of any financial instrument or commodities for the sole purpose of making a profit for own account, and without any connection to actual or anticipated client activity or for the purpose of hedging the entity's risk as result of actual or anticipated client activity, through the use of desks, units, divisions or individual traders specifically dedicated to such position taking and profit making, including through dedicated web-based proprietary trading platforms.

Proposal for a Regulation of the European Parliament and of the Council on Structural Measures Improving the Resilience of EU Credit Institutions, at 24, COM (2014) 043 final (Jan. 20, 2014). What advantages and disadvantages do you see in this alternative definition?

3. ***Long-Term Investments.*** A banking entity that is also an FHC desires to invest in a wind farm and wants to own at least 50% of the wind farm. Can the entity do so under the Merchant Banking Rule? 12 C.F.R. §§ 225.170-177. What if, instead of investing directly, the banking entity decides to sponsor and create a private equity fund and bring in other investors to also invest, via the private equity fund; can it do so? Under what conditions? 12 C.F.R. § 248.11(a). What if the banking entity were a foreign bank that was also an FHC? Could it invest in the fund? *Id.* § 248.13(b). Would it matter if the wind farm were in the United States?

4. ***Movement to Hedge Funds.*** Professor Charles Whitehead argues that the Volcker Rule prohibitions on proprietary trading will lead more trading into the lightly regulated sector of hedge funds and that, due to financial interconnections, "even if proprietary trading is no longer located *in* banks, it may now be conducted by less-regulated entities that *affect* banks and banking activities." Charles K. Whitehead, *The Volcker Rule and Evolving Financial Markets*, 1 HARV. BUS. L. REV. 39, 46 (2011).

5. ***Super 23A.*** As discussed in Chapter 2.3, Section 23A of the Federal Reserve Act restricts the ability of an IDI to engage in "covered transactions," such as lending or extending credit, with an affiliate, whereby there is a transfer of value **from** the IDI **to** the affiliate. The covered funds portion of the Volcker Rule builds on this concept by limiting the ability of a banking entity and its affiliates to engage in covered transactions with covered funds that result in a transfer of value **from** any affiliate of the banking entity **to** the covered fund, if the banking entity has a triggering relationship with the covered fund. 12 U.S.C. § 1851(f)(1); 12 C.F.R. § 248.14(a). This provision, which is widely known as "Super 23A," is in some ways broader in scope than Section 23A, because it restricts not only an IDI but also all of its non-bank affiliates (*i.e.*, the entire financial conglomerate) from engaging in covered transactions with a related covered fund. Super 23A can, however, also be seen as narrower than Section 23A, because it restricts transactions only where a banking entity (or its affiliate) has a "triggering relationship" with the covered fund, which includes acting as an investment

adviser, investment manager, commodity trading advisor, or sponsor to the covered fund. *Id.* These triggering relationships are much narrower than the covered transaction concept under Section 23A. Further, Super 23A regulates only transactions by a banking entity directly with a covered fund; it does not restrict transactions with other affiliated or non-affiliated parties, even where a benefit to the covered fund results.

The general purpose of Super 23A was to prohibit banking entities from bailing out covered funds that they manage, advise, sponsor, or in which they invest. Its focus is not solely on the protection of the IDI, like Section 23A, but on pushing the relationships outside of the financial conglomerate altogether.

6. ***The Volcker Rule as Structural Law.*** Professor John Coates has suggested that the Volcker Rule is a structural law rather than a mere activities prohibition that is designed to change the organizational culture of banks and, in so doing, "reduce the interconnectedness of banks from other, riskier components of the capital markets[,] . . . dampen the incentives of individual bankers to take risk, . . . reduce the power of traders within banks, . . . reduc[e] the power and influence of banks generally, and . . . reduce moral hazard implicit in . . . government support." John Coates, *The Volcker Rule as Structural Law: Implications for Cost-Benefit Analysis and Administrative Law*, 10 CAP. MARKETS L.J. 447, 454 (2015). Coates argues that, as a structural law with such non-quantifiable goals, the Volcker Rule should not be subject to cost-benefit analysis because such analysis would require the agencies "to anticipate, in advance of relevant data, the private market behavior in response to novel structural constraints on banking activity." *Id.* at 468.

X. UK RING-FENCING

The BHC structure that developed in the United States, which consists of separate IDIs, broker-dealers, and other non-banking subsidiaries under a single holding company, is unique. In the UK, for example, all activities that could be conducted within a U.S. BHC (*i.e.,* those activities that are considered "the business of banking," "closely related to banking," or "financial in nature") could be conducted within a single depository institution. Banking conglomerates in the UK have, therefore, historically largely taken the form of a single entity that conducts commercial banking, investment banking, and other financial activities.

In response to the Financial Crisis, the UK implemented a structural law with the goal of protecting the UK economy and taxpayers from the risk of another crisis. The UK Financial Services (Banking Reform) Act of 2013 ring-fences activities and core services that are considered vital to the operation of the UK economy within a single entity, and requires the conglomerate's other activities to be conducted outside of the ring-fenced entity in a separately capitalized and independently governed entity. The ring-fenced bank is essentially a protected UK high street bank, somewhat similar to a large U.S. regional bank, with a portfolio of consumer, small and medium-sized enterprises, and basic corporate deposits and loans in the European Economic Area (EEA), along with some simple derivatives. All investment banking, trading activities, and non-EEA activity sits within the non-ring-fenced bank. The policy rationale behind the geographical distinction is that it allows the UK government to allow the non-ring-fenced bank, which has the non-EEA deposits, to fail and instead use UK taxpayer money to protect only the UK ring-fenced bank.

While the Volcker Rule and the UK Financial Services (Banking Reform) Act are both structural reforms seeking to protect against the failure of IDIs and resulting taxpayer losses, the reforms are quite different. In contrast to the Volcker Rule, which, subject to many exceptions, pushes certain activities (proprietary trading and direct investment in hedge funds and private equity funds) *entirely* outside of financial conglomerates, the UK Financial Services (Banking Reform) Act allows these activities to continue within the conglomerate in a separately capitalized and independently governed subsidiary.

The Volcker Rule and the UK Financial Services (Banking Reform) Act are both part of a larger body of structural reform proposals seeking to change the fundamental structure of banking entities in order to promote market-wide financial stability. Structural reform can have the effect of clarifying lines of accountability and supervision within institutions and simplifying the organizational structures of complex financial institutions to enhance resolvability. Additionally, structural reforms can bolster horizontal buffers, such as restrictions on transactions between banks and affiliates or caps on counterparty credit exposures, to help stop crises from spreading and minimize contagion. Michael S. Barr & John Vickers, Banks Need Far More Structural Reform to be Safe, Fin. Times, July 21, 2013.

---

1. ***Ring-Fencing vs. Full Push Out***. Instead of a partial separation of mandated and prohibited activities into ring-fenced and non-ring-fenced entities, the UK could have considered full separation of such activities into entirely different corporate entities. What are some reasons that such a proposal might have been rejected?

2. ***Volcker, Vickers, and Too Big To Fail.*** Randall D. Guynn and Patrick S. Kenadjian argue that structural solutions. such as Volcker and the UK Financial Services (Banking Reform) Act, to the "too big to fail" problem are fundamentally misguided. In particular, the authors see structural reforms as complements to, rather than substitutes for, policies that they see as doing the real work of addressing "too big to fail," such as capital and liquidity requirements and ex-post resolution regimes. Are these two sets of solutions at odds with each other? Will an emphasis on structural solutions detract from other, possibly better alternatives? Randall D. Guynn & Patrick S. Kenadjian, *Structural Solutions: Blinded by Volcker, Vickers, Liikanen, Glass-Steagall and Narrow Banking, in* TOO BIG TO FAIL III: STRUCTURAL REFORM PROPOSALS—SHOULD WE BREAK UP THE BANKS? 125 (Patrik S. Kenadjian & Andreas Dombret ed., 2015). Compare this to the viewpoint espoused by the ICB Final Report, which justifies a structural solution on three grounds: (1) it would make it easier to resolve banks without taxpayer support; (2) it would insulate vital banking services from problems in the global financial system; and (3) it would reduce implicit government guarantees. ICB FINAL REPORT 24–25 (Sept. 2011).

4. ***Affiliate Transactions and Ring Fencing.*** Consider how the implementation of the UK Financial Services (Banking Reform) Act in the UK will require the introduction of a rule similar to that of Sections 23A and 23B of the Federal Reserve Act, which we discussed in Chapter 2.3. Section 23A limits the ability of insured banks to enter into certain transactions with their affiliates to the extent that such transactions would pose risks to the insured banks. Section 23B mandates that all transactions between an insured bank and its affiliates be on market terms.

CHAPTER 6.2

SYSTEMICALLY IMPORTANT FINANCIAL INSTITUTIONS

CONTENTS

I. INTRODUCTION

In this Chapter, we discuss the regulation of systemically important financial institutions (SIFIs), a new designation for certain large complex financial organizations that was created in the aftermath of the Financial Crisis and has been integrated into both international and domestic regulatory frameworks. We trace the recent development of financial conglomerates in the United States, discuss the designation of SIFIs, global systemically important banks (G-SIBs), and domestic systemically important banks (D-SIBs) globally and in the United States, and then explore some of the heightened standards that apply to these organizations outside of the areas of capital and liquidity, which we discussed in Part II. Finally, we discuss the debate in the United States and UK around breaking up the largest financial institutions, drawing a distinction between hard and soft breakup.

II. CONSOLIDATION IN THE 1980S AND 1990S

Until the mid-1980s, the United States, with its restrictions on interstate banking, had always been one of the more fragmented banking markets in the world. As described in detail in Chapter 1.2, the gradual erosion of barriers to interstate banking and Glass-Steagall Act affiliation restrictions set off a wave of banking mergers and acquisitions in the 1980s and 1990s, and the Financial Crisis precipitated another wave of consolidation. The U.S. BHC market is tiered and concentrated at the top, with the four largest firms holding approximately 45% of holding company assets and the top 10 firms holding over 60% of such assets as of 2014. At the same time, the United States has a thriving regional and super-regional banking market, a diverse range of specialty and foreign institutions, a total of more than 100 firms with over $10 billion in assets, over 6,000 community banks and thrifts with under $10 billion in assets, and another 6,000 credit unions (most of which are quite small). *See* FED. RESERVE SYS., NAT'L INFO. CTR. Of course, these BHCs do not only contain commercial banking assets, which have been in decline as a share of total financial assets, but also contain non-bank assets of broker-dealers and other affiliates in the holding company.

It may be surprising to many Americans that the U.S. banking market is not as heavily concentrated as the banking markets in other countries. Indeed, the ratio of consolidated assets of the four largest commercial banks to total banking assets in the United States is comparatively low, as Figure 6.2-1 shows.

Figure 6.2-1 Assets as a Percentage of Home Country Gross Domestic Product for Four Largest Banking Organizations in Country (as of Q4 2014)

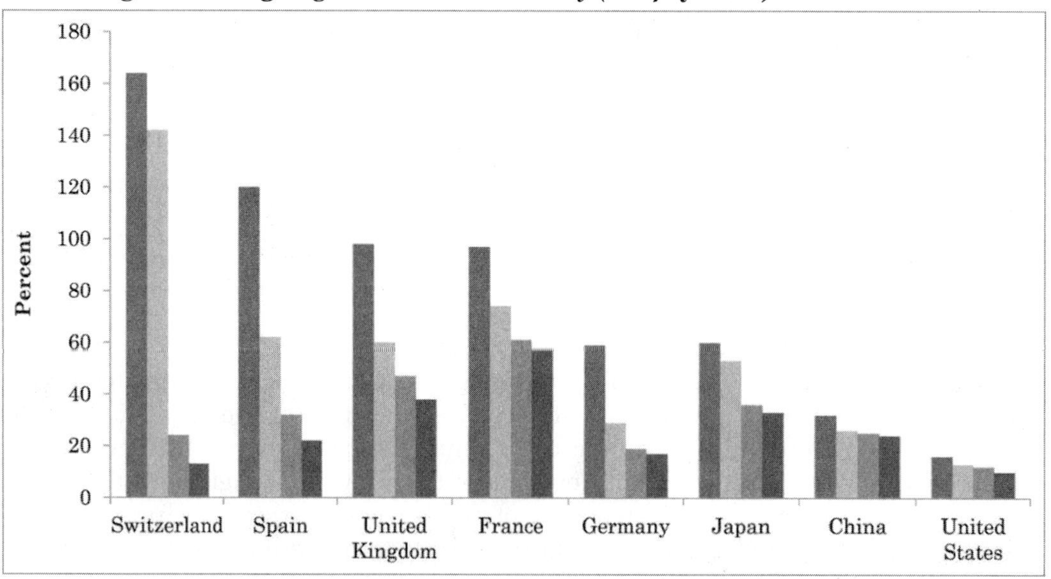

Sources: See Figure 1.1-3.

The mismatch between perception and reality is a side effect of the rapid pace of change over the short 18 years after interstate banking was introduced in a country that had for its entire history mistrusted large concentrated financial institutions. No international comparisons can take into account the unique and peculiar history of banking in the United States, going back to the arguments over the First Bank of the United States and the debate between Jefferson and Hamilton. Concerns about the concentration of economic power and the political dominance of large banking groups remain a major theme in U.S. history. A curious tension has been created by the rapid pace of change: the U.S. banking market is more concentrated among its largest banks than it has ever been, but it nevertheless remains one of the least concentrated markets in the world.

III. REGULATORY LIMITS ON CONCENTRATION

With the removal of the barriers to interstate branching and banking and the gradual erosion of Glass-Steagall Act restraints on affiliation, the main legal limits placed on the size of banks and financial conglomerates were deposit caps, antitrust market analysis, and acquisition restrictions.

A. DEPOSIT CAPS

The Riegle-Neal Act of 1994 preempted existing state banking regulations that dealt with branching and established a nationwide regime governing interstate branching by state and national banks. While the primary effect of the Riegle-Neal Act was to allow bank holding companies (BHCs) to acquire or open new branches in states other than their home state without regard to local branching laws, it also established concentration limits that governed the maximum share of deposits that a bank could acquire both nationwide and in a particular state. Under the Bank Holding Company Act (BHCA) as amended by the Riegle-Neal Act, the Federal Reserve Board may not approve a merger application if the merging bank and its affiliates would control more than 10% of the total amount of insured deposits nationwide, or more than 30% in any given state. 12 U.S.C. § 1842(d). The amended BHCA provides states the opportunity to opt out of or modify the 30% limit, but only to the extent that they do not discriminate against out-of-state participants. The deposit cap applies only to merger approvals and does not limit organic growth. Further, in approving the 2008 mergers of Bank of America and Merrill Lynch, and Bank of America and Countrywide, the Federal Reserve Board found that the deposit cap should not be read to limit the acquisition of thrifts by BHCs, even if the 10% deposit cap is exceeded by the resulting entity. Bank of America Corporation, Order Approving the Acquisition of a Savings Association and an Industrial Loan Company, 95 Fed. Res. Bull. B13, B14 n.6 (2009); Bank of America Corporation, Order Approving the Acquisition of a Savings Association and Other Nonbanking Activities, 94 Fed. Res. Bull. C81, C83 n.13 (2008). Congress effectively overturned this interpretation in § 623 of the Dodd-Frank Act, providing that the deposit caps apply equally to commercial banks and thrifts.

B. ANTITRUST MARKET ANALYSIS

One of the many factors considered by regulatory agencies in the merger context is an antitrust market analysis, which is designed to evaluate the likely impact of a proposed acquisition on competition. Classic antitrust analysis was not a practical barrier in the consolidation waves described above. Market concentration analysis in this context is based on analyzing the concentration of the relevant product market in the various geographic areas in which the merging entities are currently doing business, using the classic Herfindahl-Hirshman Index (HHI) factors. "The HHI is calculated by squaring the market share of each firm competing in the market and then summing the resulting numbers. . . . The HHI increases both as the number of firms in the market decreases and as the disparity in size between those firms increases." DEP'T OF JUSTICE, HERFINDAHL-HIRSCHMAN INDEX (2015). The HHI for a single market can range from close to zero in a market with thousands of competing firms, to 10,000 in a market served by just one firm. An HHI of over 1,800 is considered concentrated, with the typical solution being branch divestitures in the affected market. While regulators will generally not subject mergers that fall within the market concentration safe harbor to enhanced antitrust scrutiny, they do have the ability to object to such a transaction on antitrust grounds if other factors indicating anticompetitive effects are present. Regulators also have the ability to approve a merger even in the face of anticompetitive effects, either on the basis of the convenience and needs of the community or, more rarely, by using what is known as the failing company defense. As implied by its name, this defense is often used in the context of rescuing a distressed bank and requires that the anticompetitive effects of a transaction be "clearly outweighed in the public interest by the probable effect of the transaction in meeting the convenience and needs of the community to be served." FDIC Statement of Policy on Bank Merger Transactions, 63 Fed. Reg. 44,762 (Aug. 20, 1998). There is a rich volume of literature in this area. *See, e.g.*, Allen N. Berger & David B. Humphrey, *Megamergers in Banking and the Use of Cost Efficiency as an Antitrust Defense*, 37 ANTITRUST BULL. 541 (1992); Katerina Simons & Joanna Stavins, *Has Antitrust Policy in Banking Become Obsolete?* NEW ENG. ECON. REV. 13 (Mar./Apr. 1998); Gregory J. Werden, *Perceptions of the Future of Bank Merger Antitrust: Local Areas Will Remain Relevant Markets*, 13 FORDHAM J. CORP. & FIN. L. 581 (2008). For a critique of the banking regulators' antitrust analysis during the consolidation waves, see, *e.g.*, Donald I. Baker, *Searching for an Antitrust Beacon in the Bank Merger Fog*, 37 ANTITRUST BULL. 651 (1992); Robert P. Zora, *Bank Failure Crisis: Challenges in Enforcing Antitrust Regulation*, 55 WAYNE L. REV. 1175 (2009).

C. ACQUISITION RESTRICTIONS

The concentration limits imposed by the Riegle-Neal Act were further refined by § 622 of the Dodd-Frank Act, which amended the BHCA by adding a provision to prevent acquisitions where the resulting entity would have consolidated liabilities of more than 10% of the aggregate consolidated liabilities of all financial companies at the end of the calendar year preceding the transaction. 12 U.S.C. § 1852(b). For purposes of this calculation, non-deposit liabilities and off-balance sheet liabilities are taken into account. The provision applies not only to BHCs but also to SLHCs and non-bank SIFIs. A Financial Stability Oversight Council (FSOC) study at the end of 2011 determined that only the four largest U.S. Financial Holding Companies (FHCs) would be affected: Bank of America, Citigroup, JPMorgan, and Wells Fargo. *See* FSOC, STUDY & RECOMMENDATIONS REGARDING CONCENTRATION LIMITS ON LARGE FINANCIAL COMPANIES 8 (2011).

In addition, the Dodd-Frank Act modified §§ 3 and 4 of the BHCA, requiring the Federal Reserve Board to consider the "extent to which a proposed acquisition, merger, or consolidation would result in greater or more concentrated risks to the stability of the United States banking or financial system." *See* 12 U.S.C. § 1842(c)(7). The Federal Reserve Board analyzed the financial stability factor for the first time when the PNC Financial Services Group, Inc. acquired RBC Bank (USA) from the Royal Bank of Canada. The relevant portion of an analogous Federal Reserve Board order, authorizing the acquisition of ING Bank by Capital One Financial Corporation, is excerpted below:

Order Approving the Acquisition of a Savings Association and Nonbanking Subsidiaries Financial Stability Standard

98 Fed. Res. Bull. 7 (2012)

In reviewing applications and notices under sections 3 and 4 of the BHC Act, the [Federal Reserve] Board expects that it will generally find a significant adverse effect if the failure of the resulting firm, or its inability to conduct regular-course-of-business transactions, would likely impair financial intermediation or financial market functioning so as to inflict material damage on the broader economy. This kind of damage could occur in a number of ways, including seriously compromising the ability of other financial institutions to conduct regular-course-of-business transactions or seriously disrupting the provision of credit or other financial services.

To assess the likelihood that failure of the resulting firm may inflict material damage on the broader economy, the [Federal Reserve] Board will consider a variety of metrics. These would include measures of the size of the resulting firm; availability of substitute providers for any critical products and services offered by the resulting firm; interconnectedness of the resulting firm with the banking or financial system; extent to which the resulting firm contributes to the complexity of the financial system; and extent of the cross-border activities of the resulting firm. . . . These metrics are useful in evaluating the extent to which an institution's creditors, counterparties, investors, or other market participants may have financial exposure to the institution and thus may experience strain when the firm does not meet its financial obligations to them; the extent to which the institution holds assets that, if liquidated quickly, would significantly disrupt trading or funding in key markets or cause significant losses or funding problems for other firms with similar holdings due to falling asset prices; the extent to which financial distress in the resulting institution may cause other institutions that hold similar assets or are engaged in similar activities or are perceived to be dependent in important ways upon the distressed institution to experience a loss of market confidence; and the extent to which an institution in financial distress may no longer be able to provide a service that market participants rely upon and for which there are limited readily available substitutes.

In addition to these quantitative measures, the [Federal Reserve] Board will consider qualitative factors, such as the opaqueness and complexity of an institution's internal organization, that are indicative of the relative degree of difficulty of resolving the resulting firm. . . .

[T]he [Federal Reserve] Board will consider the systemic footprint of the resulting firm relative to the [U.S. financial system]. . . . [U]nder the [Federal Reserve] Board's approach, it is possible that if even a single category of metrics indicates that a resulting firm would pose a significant risk to the stability of the U.S. banking or financial system, the [Federal Reserve] Board may determine that there is an adverse effect of the proposal on the stability of the U.S. banking or financial system. This methodology will help identify not only the more obvious risks associated with significant expansion proposals by [G-SIBs], but also transactions involving other firms that could pose a risk to the stability of the U.S. banking or financial system, even if the resulting firm is not a [G-SIB].

On the other hand, certain types of transactions likely would have only a *de minimis* impact on an institution's systemic footprint and, therefore, are not likely to raise concerns about financial stability. . . .

Size. An organization's size is one important indicator of the risk that the organization poses to the financial system. Congress has imposed a specific 10 percent nationwide deposit limit and a 10 percent nationwide liabilities limit on potential combinations by banking organizations. *See* 12 U.S.C. §§ 1843(i)(8) and 1852. Other provisions of the Dodd-Frank Act impose special or enhanced supervisory requirements on large banking organizations. These measures are helpful indicators of potential systemic risk; however, the fact that Congress also requires the [Federal Reserve] Board to review the potential systemic impact of a transaction that does not reach these limits likely indicates they were not meant to substitute for an analysis of size as part of the systemic risk factor.

The [Federal Reserve] Board has considered measures of Capital One's size relative to the [U.S. financial system], including Capital One's consolidated assets, its consolidated liabilities, its total leverage exposures, and its U.S. deposits. As a result of the proposed acquisition of [ING Bank, FSB] and the HSBC assets, Capital One would become between the 14th and 20th largest [U.S. financial institution] based on assets, liabilities, and leverage exposures with between 1.1 percent and 1.6 percent of the [U.S. financial system] total. Based on deposits, Capital One would become the fifth largest [U.S. financial institution], with 2.3 percent of the total. These measures suggest that, although the combined organization would be large on an absolute basis, its shares of [U.S. financial system] assets, liabilities, leverage exposures, and deposits would remain modest, and its shares of national deposits and liabilities would fall well below the 10 percent limitations set by Congress.

Measures of a financial institution's size on a pro forma basis could either understate or overstate risks to financial stability posed by the financial institution. For instance, a relatively small institution that operates in a critical market for which there is no substitute provider, or that could transmit its financial distress to other financial organizations through multiple channels, could present significant risks to the stability of the [U.S. financial system]. . . .

Substitutability. . . . Capital One accepts retail deposits and engages in mortgage lending, mortgage and credit card servicing, commercial real estate financing, small business lending, credit card and other consumer lending, and securities brokerage services. [ING Bank, FSB] offers savings accounts, certificates of deposit, residential mortgage loans, and retail securities brokerage services. In most of these activities, Capital One has, and as a result of the proposals, would continue to have a small share on a nationwide basis, and numerous competitors would remain for each of the activities in which Capital One and [ING Bank, FSB] engage.

Capital One is currently the fifth largest provider of credit cards in the United States. Assuming the acquisition of the HSBC credit card assets . . . Capital One would increase its share of outstanding credit card balances in the United States from 7.7 percent to 11.8 percent and thereby become the fourth largest provider of credit cards in the United States. . . . [T]he [Federal Reserve] Board also has considered that three competing credit card lenders would each have outstanding credit card balances that are between one-third and two-thirds larger than those of Capital One, and two other lenders would each have balances approximately half the size of the outstanding credit card balances of Capital One. In addition, there are numerous other credit card lenders that operate on a national or regional basis. Capital One's share of credit card loans does not appear to be substantial enough to cause significant disruptions in the supply of credit card loans if

Capital One were to experience distress, due to the availability of substitute providers that could assume Capital One's business.

Interconnectedness. . . . Capital One does not engage currently and as a result of this transaction would not engage in business activities or participate in markets to a degree that would pose significant risk to other institutions, in the event of financial distress of the combined entity. The combined entity's use of wholesale funding, as a share of [U.S. financial system] wholesale funding usage, is less than 1 percent and is well below its corresponding share of [U.S. financial system] consolidated assets. The combined entity's shares of [U.S. financial system] intra-financial system assets and liabilities also are less than 1 percent. The transaction under review in this case also would not increase exposure to any single counterparty that is among the top three counterparties of either Capital One or [ING Bank, FSB] before the merger.

Complexity. . . . The combined entity's complex assets and trading book and available-for-sale securities represent a significantly lower share in the [U.S. financial system] than its corresponding share of consolidated assets. The [Federal Reserve] Board also has considered whether the complexity of the combined entity's assets and liabilities would hinder its timely and efficient resolution in the event it were to experience financial distress. Capital One and [ING Bank, FSB] do not engage in complex activities, such as being a core clearing and settlement organization for critical financial markets, that might complicate the resolution process by increasing the complexity, costs, or time frames involved in a resolution. . . .

Cross-Border Activity. . . . Capital One has credit card operations in the United Kingdom and Canada that total approximately $8.7 billion. These businesses are similar to Capital One's operations in the United States and do not add any substantial complexity to its operations. Although [ING Bank, FSB] currently is owned by ING Groep, a Dutch financial institution, [ING Bank, FSB] operates only in the United States. The combined organization is not expected to engage in any additional activities outside the United States as a result of the proposed transaction. In addition, the combined organization would not engage in the provision of critical services whose disruption would impact the macroeconomic condition of the United States by disrupting trade or resulting in increased resolution difficulties.

Financial Stability Factors in Combination. . . . As discussed above, the combined entity would not be highly interconnected. Furthermore, the organizational structure and operations of the combined organization would be centered on a commercial banking business, and in the event of distress, the resolution process would be handled in a predictable manner by relevant authorities. The [Federal Reserve] Board also has considered other measures that are suggestive of the degree of difficulty with which Capital One could be resolved in the event of a failure, such as the organizational and legal complexity and cross-border activities of the resulting firm. These measures suggest that Capital One would be significantly less complicated to resolve than the largest U.S. universal banks and investment banks.

Based on these and all the other facts of record, the [Federal Reserve] Board has determined that considerations relating to financial stability are consistent with approval.

---

1. ***Presumption Against Acquisitions.*** Since the emergency acquisitions of the Financial Crisis, none of the largest U.S. financial conglomerates, including both G-SIBs and D-SIBs, have made a major acquisition. Some regional BHCs have created larger regional BHCs, but most mergers and acquisitions have been among BHCs in the $6 to $7 billion range. In an important speech, Governor Daniel Tarullo expressed his view that there should be a "strong, though not

irrebuttable, presumption of denial for any acquisition by any firm that falls in the higher end of the list of G-SIBs developed by the Basel Committee for purposes of assessing capital surcharges." Daniel K. Tarullo, *Financial Stability Regulation*.

2. ***Political Economy of Mergers.*** In their book, *Fragile by Design*, Charles Calomiris and Stephen Haber argue that the megamergers of the last 25 years were backed both by regional banks that wanted to grow across state lines and Community Reinvestment Act (CRA) activists who sought pledges of financial support and increased lending to underserved communities during the merger process. Specifically, Calomiris and Haber argue that the "good-citizenship" merger criterion of the CRA became a powerful lever for "activist groups seeking to direct credit to their membership and constituencies." *See* CHARLES CALOMIRIS & STEPHEN HABER, FRAGILE BY DESIGN 208 (2014). According to Haber and Calomiris, "As part of that merger process, [bankers and activists] contractually committed more than $850 billion in credit to be channeled from the banks through the activists groups between 1992 and 2007." *Id.* Do you agree with this characterization? For a different view, see Michael S. Barr, *Credit Where it Counts: The Community Reinvestment Act and Its Critics*, 80 NYU L. REV. 513 (2005). For further discussion of the CRA, see Part V.

IV. DESIGNATIONS OF SYSTEMIC IMPORTANCE

It became evident during the Financial Crisis that a number of financial institutions were systemically important, meaning that their failure, or even their potential failure, could cause negative externalities to radiate through the economy. The gravity of these externalities prompted a sweeping suite of domestic and international reform efforts that aimed both to reduce the systemic risk posed by such institutions and to insulate the rest of the economy from shocks in the financial sector. Professor Steven Schwarcz has suggested that regulation of systemic risk is necessary because, "like a tragedy of the commons, no individual market participant has sufficient incentive, absent regulation, to limit its risk taking in order to reduce the systemic danger to other participants and third parties." Steven L. Schwarcz, *Systemic Risk*, 97 Geo. L. J. 193, 198 (2008).

Post-Financial Crisis analysis often attributed the systemic consequences of such institutions' failure or near-failure to the dual financial phenomena of interconnectedness and contagion. *See* Hal S. Scott, *Interconnectedness and Contagion: Financial Panics and the Crisis of 2008* (Comm. on Capital Mkts. Regulation, Working Paper, 2014). In this context, interconnectedness refers to a SIFI's vulnerabilities arising from exposure to competitor institutions. Contagion describes the perception that infirmities at one SIFI will be mirrored at similarly situated institutions owing to the fact that these institutions often have similar risk profiles and engage in similar activities. The international and domestic reform efforts that followed the Financial Crisis focused on reducing these effects through a combination of prophylactic regulation, aimed at decreasing the likelihood of failure, such as enhanced capital standards, and the development of tools that regulators could use in the event of a future crisis, such as resolution planning. The next few sections will focus on prophylactic regulation, discussing the designation of institutions as SIFIs on both a global and domestic basis, as well as the enhanced prudential regulatory standards that apply to such entities. Part IX will address the development of new tools to help regulators react to future crises.

While efforts to coordinate financial regulatory reform efforts across borders were ongoing for years, the Financial Crisis pushed international cooperation into overdrive. Discussions traditionally limited in participation to central bankers and finance ministers from the G-8 countries were expanded to include political leaders, central bankers, and finance ministers from all members of the G-20, thereby increasing the number of jurisdictions coordinating on crisis reactions and reform matters, as well as the national legitimacy of the reform agenda. *See* Michael S. Barr, *Who's In Charge of Global Finance?*, 45 GEO. J. INT'L L. 971, 1001 (2014). In 2009, the nine-member-country Financial Stability Forum was converted into the G-20's Financial Stability Board (FSB), an organization charged with coordinating domestic post-Financial Crisis reforms across member nations. The FSB's broad mandate to "address vulnerabilities affecting financial systems in the interest of global financial stability" significantly expanded the purview of international coordination efforts, which had formerly been limited to silos of regulation. See, for example, the discussion of the Basel Committee in Chapters 2.5, 2.6 and 2.7.

The G-20 met three times between November 2008 and September 2009 to discuss the unfolding Financial Crisis and the path forward. The third set of meetings, known as the Pittsburgh Summit, built on broad agreement by member countries that regulatory reform efforts must be coordinated to prevent regulatory arbitrage, conflicting regulatory requirements, and the fragmentation of markets. One of the key understandings to come out of the international regulatory agreements was that SIFIs would be identified on a global basis by the FSB as G-SIBs and global SIFIs, and a domestic basis by national regulators as D-SIBs and non-bank SIFIs, and that institutions identified as systemically important would be subjected to enhanced supervision and regulation, including through the imposition of higher capital requirements, higher loss absorbency requirements, requirements for group-wide resolution planning, and higher supervisory expectations for risk management functions.

On an annual basis since 2011, the FSB has identified G-SIBs using 12 indicators that measure a banking conglomerate's size, interconnectedness, substitutability, complexity, and cross-jurisdictional activity. The list of G-SIBs published by the FSB in 2015, shown in Figure 6.2-2, includes 30 global banking organizations, including eight U.S. BHCs.

Figure 6.2-2 G-SIBs Designated by the FSB in 2015

- Agricultural Bank of China
- **Bank of America**
- Bank of China
- **Bank of New York Mellon**
- Barclays
- BNP Paribas
- China Construction Bank
- **Citigroup**
- Credit Suisse
- Deutsche Bank
- **Goldman Sachs**
- Group BPCE
- Group Crédit Agricole
- HSBC
- Industrial and Commercial Bank of China Limited
- ING Bank
- **JP Morgan Chase**
- Mitsubishi UFJ FG
- Mizuho FG
- **Morgan Stanley**
- Nordea
- Royal Bank of Scotland
- Santander
- Société Générale
- Standard Chartered
- **State Street**
- Sumitomo Mitsui FG
- UBS
- Unicredit Group
- **Wells Fargo**

Note: Bolded G-SIBs are U.S.-based.
Source: Fin. Stability Bd., 2015 Update of List of G-SIBs (Nov. 3, 2015).

In addition to designating banking organizations as G-SIBs, the FSB also annually designates insurance conglomerates as global systemically important insurers (G-SIIs). In 2015, nine insurers were identified by the FSB as G-SIIs, including three U.S.-based institutions: AIG, MetLife, and Prudential. Finally, the FSB is evaluating whether or not to designate certain non-bank, non-insurer SIFIs (NBNI G-SIFIs) and has published a methodology for evaluating asset managers, finance companies, market intermediaries, such as securities broker-dealers, and investment funds. FIN. STABILITY BD., ASSESSMENT METHODOLOGIES FOR IDENTIFYING NBNI G-SIFIS (2015). More recently, the FSB has turned its attention to the regulation of activities, rather than managers and funds. The FSB's proposed methodology would focus on the mismatch between the liquidity of fund investments and redemption terms and conditions for fund units, borrowings by funds, operational risk, and challenges in transferring investment mandates in a stressed condition, and securities lending activities.

V. TIERED REGULATION OF BHCS AND NON-BANK FINANCIAL ENTITIES

Following the Pittsburgh Summit, G-20 members worked in parallel to implement domestic regulatory reforms that would align with the FSB's global standards. Whereas in the past, international regulatory competition at times resulted in a race to the bottom and cross-border regulatory arbitrage opportunities, in the post-Financial Crisis era, some commentators have observed a global race to the top between national regulators. *See* Michael S. Barr, *Who's In Charge of Global Finance?*, at 1001. The United States arguably led the charge among national regulators, becoming the first major country to implement financial reforms in accordance with the G-20 agenda less than one year after the Pittsburgh Summit. This was no coincidence. The United States was the primary advocate for global reform, having proposed both the creation of the FSB and the Pittsburgh Summit's heightened prudential standards. *See, e.g.*, TIMOTHY F. GEITHNER, STRESS TEST: REFLECTIONS ON FINANCIAL CRISES 409–10 (2014).

The Dodd-Frank Act contemplates a graduated approach to supervision for banks and BHCs based on asset size and other risk characteristics, beginning with community banks and working up to the largest, systemically important firms. The Act permits the FSOC to expand the regulatory perimeter for prudential supervision by providing the FSOC with the authority to designate non-bank financial institutions to be subject to Federal Reserve Board supervision on the basis of their systemic importance, risk, and other factors. The Act delegates authority to the Federal Reserve Board, on its own accord and upon recommendations from the newly-created FSOC, to create a new regulatory system through supervision and rulemaking. In this Chapter we discuss the application of tiered regulation to banks, BHCs and non-bank firms designated under Title I of the Dodd-Frank Act. The designation and regulation of systemically important financial market utilities is discussed in Chapter 7.2 and Chapter 11.2.

A. GRADUATED SUPERVISION AND PRUDENTIAL STANDARDS

Under Title I of the Dodd-Frank Act, BHCs are subject to a graduated application of enhanced supervision and prudential standards based on asset size and other factors. Specifically, the statute orders the Federal Reserve Board to establish standards that "increase in stringency" based on its consideration of identified risk factors. 12 U.S.C. § 5365(a)(1)(B). These enhanced prudential measures include risk-based capital requirements and leverage limits, liquidity requirements, risk management, resolution planning, credit exposure reporting, concentration limits, and annual stress tests. Congress gave the Federal Reserve Board the authority, pursuant to a recommendation by the FSOC, to establish a higher asset threshold for application of certain enhanced prudential standards. *Id.* § 5365(a)(2)(B). Additionally, the Federal Reserve Board is permitted to take size and other risk factors into account when tailoring the application of the enhanced prudential standards for a single company or a category of companies. *Id.* § 5365(a)(2)(A). Citing the "risks to the financial stability of the United States that could arise from the material distress or failure . . . of large, interconnected financial institutions," Congress delegated to the Federal Reserve Board the authority to design prudential standards, mandating that the resulting requirements be "more stringent" than the requirements imposed upon companies that "do not present similar risks to the financial stability of the United States." 12 U.S.C. § 5365(a)(1). Congress specifically required the Federal Reserve Board to promulgate such heightened regulations pertaining to risk-based capital, leverage limits, liquidity, overall risk management, resolution planning, credit exposure reporting, and concentration limits. *Id.* § 5365(b)(1)(A). In addition, Congress delegated to the Federal Reserve Board the authority, at its discretion, to issue contingent capital requirements, enhanced public disclosures, short-term debt-limits, and "such other prudential standards" that the Federal Reserve Board may find appropriate. *Id.* § 5365(b)(1)(B). While the authority to promulgate such regulations lies solely with the Federal Reserve Board, Congress authorized the FSOC to "make recommendations" regarding the establishment and refinement of these standards. *Id.*

This graduated regulatory system for BHCs means that, as a BHC moves up in asset size, it becomes subject to more requirements. Figure 6.2-3 illustrates this progression.

Figure 6.2-3 BHC Regulatory Requirements by Asset Size Category

Regulation	Less than $10bn assets	$10-$50bn	$50-$250bn	>$250 (not G-SIBs)	U.S. G-SIBs
Recovery Plans					✓
TLAC Requirement					✓
G-SIB Capital Surcharges					✓
Supplementary Leverage Ratio (5% / 6% requirement)[1]					✓
AOCI included in Basel 3 capital				✓	✓
Full Liquidity Coverage Ratio				✓	✓
Supplementary Leverage Ratio (3% requirement)				✓	✓
Advanced Approach RWA				✓	✓
Resolution Plans			✓	✓	✓
Early Remediation Tools			✓	✓	✓
Modified Liquidity Coverage Ratio			✓	✓	✓
Annual Fed-run Capital Plan and Stress Test			✓	✓	✓
Annual Company-run Stress Test		✓	✓	✓	✓
Durbin (interchange) Amendment		✓	✓	✓	✓
Subject to Regulation by CFPB	Certain Products	✓	✓	✓	✓
Prompt Corrective Action Tools	✓	✓	✓	✓	✓
Volcker Rule	✓	✓	✓	✓	✓

[1] 5% requirement at the holding company, 6% at insured depository institutions

Source: Davis Polk & Wardwell LLP.

1. BHCs with Assets Under $10 Billion

No enhanced measures apply to about 95% of banks, the category commonly described as community banks, those under $10 billion in assets—more than 6,000 banks in across the country. The Volcker Rule, however, does apply. Some of these banks use a BHC structure, although many of the smallest do not.

2. BHCs with Assets Over $10 Billion

BHCs with assets over $10 billion must conduct annual company-run stress tests and, if the BHC is publicly traded, establish a risk committee. 12 U.S.C. §§ 5365(h)(2)(B), (i)(2)(A); 12 C.F.R. § 252.132.

3. BHCs with Assets Over $50 Billion

In addition to those standards that apply to BHCs with assets over $10 billion, Title I of the Dodd-Frank Act subjects BHCs with more than $50 billion in assets to Federal Reserve Board-run stress tests, enhanced supervision and prudential standards under 12 U.S.C. § 5365, early remediation requirements under § 5366, and certain merger and acquisition restrictions under § 5363.

As of September 2015, there were 38 U.S. BHCs with more than $50 billion in assets. Under § 116(a) of the Dodd-Frank Act, the FSOC can require a BHC with total consolidated assets of $50 billion or more to "keep the [FSOC] informed" regarding the financial condition, controls, inter-affiliate transactions, and activities and operations of a BHC and its subsidiaries. *Id.* § 5326(a). Further, BHCs with total consolidated assets of $50 billion or more are required to, among other things, establish an enterprise-wide risk committee and appoint a chief risk officer. For more details, see Enhanced Prudential Standards (Regulation YY), 12 C.F.R. pt. 252.

To forestall potential regulatory arbitrage given the attachment of these heightened standards to only a certain category of institutions, Congress included in the Dodd-Frank Act a provision that prevents BHC recipients of Troubled Asset Relief Program (TARP) from selling their bank to escape the heightened regulatory requirements. Section 117 of the Dodd-Frank Act, commonly referred to as the "Hotel California" provision (as the Eagles sang, "You can check out any time you like, but you can never leave"), prevents an entity that was a BHC with greater than $50 billion in assets as of January 1, 2010 from exiting the heightened regulatory system by debanking its subsidiary insured depository institution (IDI), *if* it received financial assistance under TARP. 12 U.S.C. § 5327. Upon debanking, such companies are automatically designated non-bank SIFIs and are subject to enhanced supervision and prudential regulation restrictions. There is no similar provision that applies these heightened standards to a BHC that drops below the $50 billion asset threshold.

The $50 billion asset threshold has been the subject of intense debate, with many contending that the threshold is too low, while others contend that the graduated approach is appropriate. Federal Reserve Board Governor Tarullo has indicated that $100 billion in assets, which would capture 29 U.S. BHCs, may be a more appropriate threshold. *See* Daniel K. Tarullo, Governor of the Federal Reserve Board, Speech at the Federal Reserve Bank of Chicago Bank Structure Conference: Rethinking the Aims of Prudential Regulation (May 8, 2014). Other commentators, including one of the co-authors, see the $50 billion threshold as one rung in the graduated application of regulatory standards designed to increase the resiliency of the financial system as a whole, and not as equivalent to a SIFI or D-SIB designation. *Measuring the Systemic Importance of U.S. Bank Holding Companies: Hearing Before the S. Comm. on Banking, Hous. & Urban Affairs*, 114th Cong. 1–3 (2015) (statement of Michael S. Barr, Professor at University of Michigan School of Law). Another co-author believes that not only should the threshold be raised, but that for the system of tailored regulation to work properly, community banks should be exempt from the Volcker Rule and the tailoring should be less subject to supervisory discretion. For a discussion of how the benchmark applies to foreign banks in the United States, see Chapter 6.3.

4. BHCs with Assets Over $250 Billion

Congress gave the Federal Reserve Board the authority, pursuant to a recommendation by the FSOC, to establish a higher asset threshold for application of certain enhanced prudential standards. *Id.* § 5365(a)(2)(B). Additionally, the Federal Reserve Board is permitted to take size and other risk factors into account when tailoring the application of the enhanced prudential standards for a single company or a category of companies. *Id.* § 5365(a)(2)(A). So far, the primary way that the Federal Reserve Board has engaged in the tailoring of enhanced prudential standards above $50 billion in asset size is through the calibration of capital and liquidity regulations, many of which apply with increasing stringency after a BHC reaches $250 billion in assets. The Federal Reserve Board, for example, imposes a supplementary leverage ratio, a counter-cyclical capital buffer, and detailed liquidity coverage rules only on the 14 firms with over $250 billion in assets. In December 2015, the Federal Reserve Board announced that it would also be tailoring BHC stress tests to ensure that these 14 firms with greater than $250 billion in assets are scrutinized most carefully in the stress tests to reflect their systemic risk profile. Federal Reserve Guidance on Supervisory Assessment of Capital Planning and Positions for LISCC Firms and Large and Complex Firms, Supervisory Letter SR 15-18 (Dec. 18, 2015).

5. G-SIBs

The very largest U.S. BHCs on a global basis, only eight BHCs at the end of 2015, are subjected by the Federal Reserve Board to even tougher standards, including a capital surcharge that increases with their size, risk, complexity, and use of short-term funding, a much more stringent supplemental leverage ratio, as well as detailed resolution planning under the living wills process and significant long-term debt (total loss absorbing capacity, or TLAC) requirements designed to counter "too big to fail". These eight BHCs correspond to the BHCs that have designated by the FSB as G-SIBs. The capital surcharge and leverage ratio were discussed in Chapter 2.7, and the resolution planning and total loss absorbing capacity will be discussed in Chapter 9.3.

B. NON-BANK DESIGNATIONS

In alignment with the FSB's designation of G-SIIs and NBNI G-SIFIs, U.S. non-bank institutions, *i.e.*, U.S. institutions that are not chartered as banks or BHCs, may be designated as SIFIs by the FSOC, a regulator created under Title I of the Dodd-Frank Act. The FSOC is headed by the Secretary of the Treasury and is comprised of ten voting members and five non-voting members. The Comptroller of the Currency, Chairpersons of the Federal Reserve Board, FDIC, SEC, and CFTC, and Director of the CFPB are all voting members of the FSOC, which was created to "identify risks to the financial stability of the United States," "promote market discipline," and "respond to emerging threats to the stability of the United States financial system." 12 U.S.C. § 5322(a)(1). Perhaps because a majority of the voting members of the FSOC are members of the President's political party, it has been the subject of political controversy and there have been attempts to pass legislation that would reduce the FSOC's authority and/or increase its political accountability. *See, e.g.*, FSOC Transparency and Accountability Act, H.R. 4387, 113th Cong. (2014). Some commentators, however, have argued in favor of restructuring the FSOC in order to *increase* its authority to obtain information and other support from the various federal financial regulators that it is supposed to coordinate. *See, e.g.*, Hilary J. Allen, *Putting the "Financial Stability" in Financial Stability Oversight Council*, 76 OHIO ST. L.J. 1087 (2015). Others have expressed disappointment that the FSOC was not granted broader authority to address the underlying flaws of financial regulation in the United States. Donald Kohn, former Vice Chairman, Fed. Reserve. Bd., Remarks to the Federal Reserve Board's Boston Conference: Implementing Macroprudential and Monetary Policies: The Case for Two Committees (Oct. 2, 2015).

Title I of the Dodd-Frank Act delegates to the FSOC the authority to designate as systemically important non-bank institutions that are "predominantly engaged in financial activities." 12 U.S.C. §§ 5311, 5323(a)(1). Designated non-bank SIFIs are then subject to Federal Reserve Board supervision and tailored enhanced prudential standards, similar to those that apply to BHCs with over $50 billion in assets, but tailored in application to suit the business model of the non-bank SIFI. Such a designation requires determination by a two-thirds vote, including an affirmative vote of the Secretary of the Treasury, that material financial distress at the institution—or the nature, scope, size, scale, concentration, interconnectedness, or a mix of activities at the institution—could pose a threat to the financial stability of the United States. *Id.* § 5323(a)(1). In making such a determination, Congress ordered the FSOC to consider several enumerated factors relating to the risks posed by the institution, including the extent of the leverage of the company, the extent and nature of the company's off-balance sheet exposures, and the extent and nature of the transactions and relationships of the company with other significant non-bank financial companies and significant BHCs. *Id.* § 5323(a)(2); 12 C.F.R. § 1310.11. Congress also gave the FSOC the authority to designate foreign non-bank financial companies as systemically important through a similar process. 12 U.S.C. § 5323(b).

The FSOC issued its first three proposed designations in June 2013 and finalized two of those determinations for GE Capital and AIG without contest one month later. The GE Capital and AIG designations, which were the result of unanimous votes of FSOC, were surprising to no one. GE Capital, a grandfathered unitary thrift holding company already subject to prudential regulation by the Federal Reserve Board under Home Owners' Loan Act, see Chapter 6.1, had consolidated assets of $539 billion, making it one of the larger financial conglomerates. AIG, also a grandfathered unitary thrift holding company whose bailout had become one of the most controversial events of the Financial Crisis, was destined for designation due to its eminently apparent systemic importance during the Financial Crisis. Prudential Financial, also in the first round of proposed designees, contested the proposed designation and requested a hearing. The FSOC granted an oral hearing, but voted 7-2 to designate Prudential Financial as the third non-bank SIFI in September 2013. In all instances, the FSOC's formal determinations focused on the runnable nature of key financial instruments and the potential that a fire sale resulting from a run could have on the broader markets.

Below are excerpts from the FSOC's public announcement of its designation of Prudential Financial as a non-bank SIFI, as well as excerpts of dissents filed by one voting member and one nonvoting member of the FSOC. Pay special attention to how the FSOC focuses on the business and product lines that it thinks may become transmission channels of risk during times of material financial distress at the institution. How do the dissenting members respond to the FSOC's analysis of transmission risk?

U.S. Dep't of Treasury, Basis for the FSOC's Final Determination Regarding Prudential Financial, Inc. (2013)

* * *

Analysis of Potential Effects of Material Financial Distress at Prudential

Consideration of Transmission Channels

[T]he Council evaluated the extent to which material financial distress at Prudential could be transmitted to other financial firms and markets and thereby pose a threat to U.S. financial stability through the following three transmission channels: (1) the exposures of counterparties, creditors, investors, and other market participants to Prudential; (2) the liquidation of assets by Prudential, which could trigger a fall in asset prices and thereby could significantly disrupt trading or funding in key markets or cause significant losses or funding problems for other firms with similar holdings; and (3) the inability or unwillingness of Prudential to provide a critical function or service relied upon by market participants and for which there are no ready substitutes. . . .

Exposure Channel

A nonbank financial company's creditors, counterparties, investors, or other market participants have exposure to the company that is significant enough to materially impair those creditors, counterparties, investors, or other market participants and thereby pose a threat to U.S. financial stability. . . .

Through its domestic and international subsidiaries, Prudential provides a wide mix of financial services including individual and group life insurance, annuities, asset management, commercial mortgage lending, mortgage servicing, trust, and other retirement-related services. As of December 31, 2012, Prudential has $424 billion of assets in its general account investment portfolio and $253 billion in separate accounts. Prudential's annuity offerings through its insurance subsidiaries make the company a leader in the domestic individual variable annuity market.

Certain of Prudential's activities have a high degree of interconnectedness. The financial system is exposed to Prudential through the capital markets, including as derivatives counterparties, creditors, debt and equity investors, and securities lending and repurchase agreement counterparties. Material financial distress at Prudential could affect third parties that hold Prudential's debt, including other insurance companies that hold a significant portion of the company's long-term debt. In addition, large corporate and financial entities have significant exposures to Prudential through the company's retirement and pension products, corporate-owned and bank-owned life insurance, and other group insurance products. Prudential also uses derivatives to hedge various risks related to its assets and liabilities. Prudential's derivatives counterparties include several large financial firms, which are significant participants in the global debt and derivatives markets. In the aggregate, these exposures could serve to spread material financial distress at Prudential to counterparties and financial markets more broadly.

Prudential's off-balance sheet exposures could serve as a mechanism by which material financial distress at Prudential could be transmitted to banks and to financial markets more broadly. For example, Prudential's total off-balance sheet exposure due to derivatives counterparty and credit facilities commitments with large global banks is significant.

By allowing for the potential reduction of the total amount of available capital, Prudential's use of captive reinsurance could increase the potential losses of policyholders and creditors.

Prudential's liabilities include debt securities, insurance contracts, annuity contracts, separate account obligations, securities lending and repurchase agreements, and reinsurance, among others. Although Prudential does not substantially depend on short-term funding, and its life insurance and annuity products are generally considered to be relatively long-term liabilities, a substantial portion of the liabilities in the U.S. general account are available for discretionary withdrawal with little or no penalty and therefore could, in practice, have characteristics of short-term liabilities. Policyholders in Prudential's separate account and international insurance business are also able to surrender policies for significant cash values on short notice.

The Council has considered potential mitigants that could reduce the potential for material financial distress at Prudential to be transmitted to other financial firms and markets through the exposure channel. For institutional and retail policyholders, losses could be mitigated by Prudential's assets and the activity of state receivers and the GA System. In addition, individual exposures to Prudential may be small relative to the capital of its individual counterparties. In the aggregate, however, the exposures across multiple markets and financial products are significant enough that material financial distress at Prudential could aggravate losses to large, leveraged financial firms, which could contribute to a material impairment in the functioning of key financial markets or the provision of financial services by Prudential's counterparties. The correlations across asset classes and the similar exposures and holdings by many of Prudential's key counterparties and peers could spread the financial contagion triggered by material financial distress at Prudential.

Asset Liquidation Channel

A nonbank financial company holds assets that, if liquidated quickly, would cause a fall in asset prices and thereby significantly disrupt trading or funding in key markets or cause significant losses or funding problems for other firms with similar holdings.

Although Prudential's life insurance and annuity products are generally considered to be long-term liabilities, a substantial portion of these liabilities are available for immediate discretionary withdrawal with little or no penalty and therefore could, in practice, have characteristics of short-term liabilities. A large number of withdrawal and surrender requests within a short period of time could strain Prudential's liquidity resources and compel the company to sell assets in order to meet its obligations to policyholders. A liquidation resulting from withdrawal requests of Prudential's policyholders also could be exacerbated by its derivative and short-term funding counterparties, which could, under existing agreements, require Prudential to either post additional collateral or to raise cash to close out certain funding transactions. Material financial distress at Prudential in the context of overall stress in the financial services industry could lead to the liquidation of certain of the company's separate account assets and have significant effects on the broader financial markets. While some of these assets may be transferable to other asset managers, certain of the company's businesses could be difficult to sell in a stressed market.

The Council has considered the potential effects on other large financial firms of Prudential's asset fire sales based on the size, leverage, asset composition, and liquidity of Prudential's assets. A forced liquidation of a significant portion of Prudential's assets, possibly including separate account assets, could cause significant disruptions to key markets including corporate debt and asset-backed securities markets, particularly during a period of overall stress in the financial services industry and in a weak macroeconomic environment when liquidity dries up and price swings can be magnified. Such a liquidation could be exacerbated by Prudential's asset leverage.

The severity of the disruption caused by a forced liquidation of Prudential's assets could be amplified by the fact that the investment portfolios of many large insurance companies are composed of similar assets, which could cause significant reductions in asset valuations and losses for those firms. The erosion of capital and potential de-leveraging could result in asset fire sales that cause significant damage to the broader economy.

This rapid liquidation of assets could also depress the value of similar assets held broadly in the economy, including those held by other large financial firms. Holders of these assets could be subject to financial stress as they recognize lower asset values or sell such assets at fire-sale prices.

The Council has considered mitigants that could reduce the potential for material financial distress at Prudential to be transmitted to other financial firms and markets through the asset liquidation channel. For example, the company has the right to defer payouts on a significant portion of policies with immediately payable cash surrender value of surrendered policies; however, the company could have strong disincentives to invoke this option because of the negative signal invoking such a deferral could provide to counterparties, investors, and policyholders. Other mitigants include the authority of state courts to impose stays on policyholder withdrawals and surrenders; and the sale of certain subsidiaries or lines of business to third parties. While these factors and others could mitigate the potential for material financial distress at Prudential to be transmitted to other firms and markets, attempts to invoke these mitigation tools, especially during a period of overall stress in the financial services industry and in a weak macroeconomic environment, could cause concern about similar products offered by other large insurance companies and spread contagion throughout the system.

Critical Function or Service Channel

A nonbank financial company is no longer able or willing to provide a critical function or service that is relied upon by market participants and for which there are no ready substitutes.

Prudential is a leader in several of its key markets and products, including life insurance, annuity, retirement, asset management, and commercial mortgage servicing. While certain factors could aggravate the transmission of stress in this transmission channel, Prudential's share in these generally fragmented and competitive markets does not appear large enough to cause a significant disruption in the provision of services if the company experiences material financial distress and is unable or unwilling to provide services. Nevertheless, general market conditions could aggravate the transmission of stress through this transmission channel, particularly if accompanied by a period of economic stress and broader pullbacks across the industry in certain of Prudential's core insurance and non-insurance businesses. . . .

Prudential is an important source of credit for both businesses and households. While Prudential is among the top commercial and multifamily mortgage servicers, its commercial and multifamily mortgage servicing operations represent a small percentage of the overall market. Prudential is also an important investor in corporate bonds. Prudential's holdings of state and local government obligations are small relative to the size of the overall market. At this time, Prudential does not appear to be an important source of short-term liquidity for the U.S. financial system via wholesale or short-term funding arrangements. . . .

Existing Supervision and Regulation

Prudential's insurance company subsidiaries are subject to supervision by regulators in all 50 U.S. states, the District of Columbia, the five U.S. territories, and numerous foreign countries. Prudential's major foreign subsidiaries are regulated by applicable financial services regulatory authorities in their host countries, particularly those in Japan. In the United States, Prudential's insurance company subsidiaries are separately subject to a state-based regulatory regime, the purposes of which are to protect policyholders and to ensure competitive insurance markets. State insurance regulators' approach to group supervision is indirect, conducted through the regulation of one or more licensed insurance companies. . . .

Resolvability

Prudential is a complex and interconnected organization operating in all 50 states and numerous foreign countries, which could increase the obstacles to its rapid and orderly resolution. There is no precedent for the resolution of an insurance company the size and scale of Prudential. Coordinated resolution of Prudential would require accommodations with each of its local supervisory authorities, as well as cooperation among a number of home and host jurisdiction supervisory authorities and courts. This could delay and complicate steps to resolve Prudential in an orderly fashion that would minimize disruption to financial stability. If Prudential were to become insolvent, separate and possibly conflicting judicial proceedings in multiple countries could also lead to a disruption of the critical services necessary to ensure the continuity of its businesses.

Views of the Acting Director of the Federal Housing Finance Agency

[M]y dissenting vote is based on placing greater weight on mitigants . . . an alternative view of the significance of certain factors, the availability of other tools or methods to address identified risks, and concerns about the consequences of designation, including market impacts. . . .

The analysis of Prudential's balance sheet leverage does not fully take account of the stability of Prudential's liabilities, the quality of its assets, or the strength of its equity capital. Prudential has limited market-based funding, its assets are generally high-quality government debt and senior corporate securities, and it lacks the intangible assets that have been a key component of many past failures in the financial services industry. The above characteristics, as well as the company's limited amount of debt outstanding and a lack of analysis of Prudential's leverage compared to noninsurance companies, leads to this factor being less significant.

The analysis of risk to Prudential's derivatives counterparties could be stronger. The analysis does not adequately consider the unique risks and characteristics of Prudential's derivatives activities—for example, the largest component of Prudential's derivatives portfolio is interest rate swaps, which (as the analysis acknowledges) lack the same principal and jump-to-default risk as some other derivatives such as credit default swaps. In addition, to fully consider the risks posed by Prudential's derivatives activities (which are almost entirely hedges) the collateral and the instruments being hedged should be more fully evaluated. . . .

I am also concerned that without a better understanding of how enhanced supervision will be implemented the designation of Prudential could distort market equilibrium and competition. The effects are unknown at this point but could be magnified by the fact that with the designation of Prudential, only one insurer will be operating under a materially different capital and regulatory regime than all other participants in the market.

Views of the Council's Independent Member Having Insurance Expertise

As the [FSOC's] Independent Member having insurance expertise, I dissent . . .

Transmission Channels

The Council identified three transmission channels as avenues by which a nonbank financial company could transmit risk of instability to the financial system: (1) exposure; (2) asset liquidation; and (3) critical function or service. The Council has determined that Prudential's material financial distress could pose a threat to financial stability focusing on two of the channels: exposure and asset liquidation.

(1) Exposure Transmission Channel

The Council's Interpretive Guidance explains that its consideration of the exposure channel would involve exposures "significant enough to materially impair" creditors, counterparties, investors, or other market participants.

Neither the Basis nor the administrative record supports the conclusion that the exposure of Prudential's creditors, counterparties, investors, and other market participants to Prudential are significant enough that Prudential's material financial distress could *materially impair* those entities and thereby could pose a threat to U.S. financial stability. No specific adverse effect on the financial condition of those other entities is presented to support any conclusion of material impairment. . . .

The Basis does not establish that any individual counterparty would be materially impaired because of losses resulting from exposure to Prudential. Instead, the Basis relies on broader market effects and aggregates the relatively small individual exposures to conclude that exposures across multiple markets and financial products are significant enough that material financial distress at Prudential could contribute to a material impairment in the functioning of key financial markets. Although aggregate exposures are large, individual losses may be able to be absorbed by counterparties or policyholders without materially impairing financial condition, financial services or economic activity. . . .

[The Basis's] line of reasoning would inevitably lead to a conclusion that any nonbank financial company above a certain size is a threat—contradicting pronouncements that "size alone" is not the test for determination. . . .

(2) Asset Liquidation Transmission Channel

The Council's asset liquidation channel hinges on an assumed run by *millions* of life insurance policyholders, who would collectively surrender or withdraw a significant portion of life insurance cash values. In addition to alleging that such withdrawal and surrender requests could strain Prudential's liquidity resources to meet such a run with all of its insurance subsidiaries being rendered insolvent, put into receivership, and liquidated, the Basis postulates that such a run could cause liquidity runs on other life insurers. In addition to a run by life insurance policyholders, the Basis appears to assume that separate account holders, like variable annuity and other contract holders, would also run *en masse*, causing asset liquidations, and that these consequences would lead to financial instability.

The Council's analysis is flawed in several significant respects. . . .

- The asset liquidation analysis appears to assume a contemporaneous run against the general and separate accounts by *millions* of life insurance policyholders and a significant number of annuity and other contract holders of products with cash surrender value—a scale for which there is no precedent, and for which the likelihood is believed by most experts to be extraordinarily low. . . .
- The run behavior assumed in the Basis is a homogenous view of Prudential's policy and contract holders in disregard of important distinctions in behaviors of institutional versus retail customers; customer demographics and domicile; an insured's health; economic, market risk, penalty, tax and substitution disincentives; and product type and design (i.e., terms and conditions). There also appears to be a false perception, contradicted by facts and experience, that policyholders value life insurance only or primarily as cash instruments.
- The First Determination Standard requires that the Council consider Prudential, as the parent holding company, to be in material financial distress, but such distress does not necessarily include the material financial distress of all of its major insurance subsidiaries. . . . [The Basis's] approach . . . is dependent upon its misplaced assumptions of the simultaneous failure of all of Prudential's

insurance subsidiaries and a massive and unprecedented, lightning, bank-style run by a significant number of its cash value policyholders and separate account holders, which apparently is the only circumstance in which the Basis concludes that Prudential could pose a threat to financial stability. . . .

- One of the key bases underpinning the Basis is the proposition that a significant portion of U.S. general account cash surrender values would be payable within a very short period of time and that Prudential would be unable to accommodate such a large cash outflow, thereby incentivizing other "runners" from Prudential's life insurance companies as well as other non-affiliated life insurance companies. The existing built-in fail-safes of insurance and annuity product terms and conditions, and Federal and State regulatory and judicial stay authorities—all combine to impede the transmission and slow the potential asset liquidation to a point that it could be managed by Prudential. . . . The Basis contends though that these tools could affect market confidence in the life insurance sector as a whole, and possibly trigger surrenders and withdrawals at other insurers. Even assuming arguendo that such fail-safes might perhaps lead to other negative effects, the alleged threat to financial stability from a feared rapid asset liquidation can be countered.
- Runs from separate accounts and asset management accounts are indistinguishable from a market perspective. Therefore, it is difficult to reconcile the Basis's analysis of assumed runs and forced asset liquidation tied to separate account products and its skepticism as to the sale or transfer of whole companies or blocks of such business, with its different conclusions as to a possible reputational run, asset liquidation, and transfers of Prudential's asset management business.
- The Basis does not give enough weight to mitigants and appears to question both the professional judgments of regulators to intervene and the effectiveness of stays to stop runs. . . . In fact, not only the U.S. State insurance regulators, but also the [SEC], and Japan's Financial Services Agency, all have the authority to impose early stays. . . .
- Having already contemplated Prudential and its insurance subsidiaries to be in material financial distress, insolvent, and in liquidation, the Basis's analysis becomes distracted by certain solvency issues, such as captive reinsurance. The Basis's reliance on the lack of a precedent for a failure of an insurance company the size and scale of Prudential begs the question. . . . That there is "no precedent" is, in large part, a testament to the proven results of State insurance regulators, individually and collectively working through the National Association of Insurance Commissioners ("NAIC"), in strengthening the quality, depth and sophistication of the State regulatory framework for its legal entity supervision, particularly over the last two decades.
- The Basis also does not give sufficient credence to the ability of the state resolution and guaranty systems to serve as a mitigant.

Significant Damage to the Broader Economy

The Basis and the administrative record lack any analysis as to how Prudential's material financial distress would lead to a threat where "there would be an impairment of financial intermediation or financial market functioning that would be sufficiently severe to inflict *significant damage on the broader economy*." The Basis does not contain any analysis that presents any findings as to severe impairment of financial intermediation; severe impairment of the functioning of U.S. and global financial markets; or resulting significant damage to the economy. . . .

* * *

[Three dissents were filed in opposition to the Prudential determination. The third dissent has been omitted from this excerpt. *See* John Huff, *View of Director John Huff, the State Insurance Commissioner Representative* (Sept. 18, 2013).]

In the year following Prudential's designation, MetLife, Inc. was also designated by the FSOC as a non-bank SIFI after a hearing contesting the proposed designation. The final determination was issued on December 18, 2014, after a 9-1 vote, in which the FSOC's "independent member with insurance expertise" was the lone dissenter. MetLife brought suit to challenge the designation, claiming that the FSOC made "numerous critical errors that fatally undermined the reasoning" in its designation and that the FSOC's conclusion that MetLife's "material financial distress could lead to an impairment of financial intermediation" was arbitrary and capricious. Complaint at 2, MetLife Inc. v. Fin. Stability Oversight Council, No. 15-45 (D.D.C. filed Jan. 13, 2015). On March 30, 2016, the trial court held for MetLife and ordered their de-designation on the grounds that the FSOC determination, based on the record before it, was arbitrary and capricious. The opinion was not available as this book went to print and an appeal is likely.

GE Capital, which did not contest its FSOC designation, is also looking to shed its non-bank SIFI designation. In April 2015, General Electric announced plans to sell or spin off its financial services businesses and related assets, including through a spin-off in its retail lending business, Synchrony Financial, and the sale of its real estate business. Nick Carey & Lewis Krauskopf, *GE to Sell Bulk of Finance Unit, Return up to $90 Billion to Investors*, REUTERS, Apr. 11, 2015. General Electric has also announced publicly that it will make an application to reverse its SIFI designation in 2016. *Id.*

Following the designation of Metlife, the FSOC appeared to have shifted its focus from consideration of insurance companies to the potential designation of asset managers as systemically important. At the request of the FSOC, the Office of Financial Research (OFR) wrote a widely criticized report identifying the potential ways that problems in the asset management sector could be channeled to the financial markets more broadly. OFR, ASSET MANAGEMENT AND FINANCIAL STABILITY (2013). In July 2014, however, FSOC stated that it had determined to shift its focus to products and activities in the asset management sector to assess systemic risk, rather than seeking to designate individual firms as systemic. The OFR report and responses to it are covered in depth in Chapter 10.1.

VI. BREAKING UP THE BANKS

A. HARD BREAKUP AND THE POST-FINANCIAL CRISIS DEBATE

The wave of consolidation during the Financial Crisis caused many to question the size and scale of the largest G-SIBs, especially in light of the renewed understanding of the risk that taxpayer funds could be used to the benefit of the creditors and managers of such institutions. The debate about breaking up the banks took place almost solely in the United States and the UK. Other countries, such as Canada, China, Germany, Japan, and France support the size, scope, and scale of their national champion global banks in a world of global competition. The view from the financial sector is that large complex financial organizations are necessary to serve large global corporations in a world of global competition, as expressed in the following report commissioned by The Clearing House, a trade association for the largest banks.

The Clearing House, Identifying the Right Question

10–11 (Clearing House, Working Paper No. 1, 2013)

Large banks are necessary in the modern bank ecosystem, providing particular and important financial services not provided by smaller banks. While banks of varying sizes are necessary and play different roles in the modern banking system, large banks uniquely provide three types of financial services that are critical to the U.S. economy:

- Payments and clearing services to move cash, settle financial transactions, and record and transfer ownership of securities.
- Commercial banking services for cash management, lending, and trade finance, particularly for middlemarket and larger companies.
- Investment banking services for underwriting the debt and equity offerings of corporations and governments and providing liquidity to financial markets—both directly by acting as dealers in securities and indirectly by providing financing and other prime brokerage services to institutional investors.

In order to provide these services to customers in an efficient manner, banks have grown in size to achieve economies of scale and scope. Moreover, in addition to providing the critical financial infrastructure to serve the needs of the business community as well as to support the activities of community banks, large banks have better met the needs of retail and commercial customers as a direct result of their size and scope. This is especially true for large banks that compete with international institutions in the global marketplace. Large customers in the U.S. or any customer needing international services are particularly well-served by large banks, and U.S. institutions can and should be able to safely and soundly compete in these international markets in order to service these customers.

The Bipartisan Policy Center has observed that both businesses and individuals continue to flock to bigger banks.

Martin N. Baily, Douglas J. Elliott & Phillip L. Swagel, The Big Bank Theory: Breaking Down the Breakup Arguments

Bipartisan Policy Ctr., 23–26 (2014) [hereinafter Bipartisan Policy Center Report]

BUSINESSES. . . . One set of customers that rely on large U.S. banks are globally active U.S. businesses. These firms face different economic and legal conditions across the variety of locations in which they operate. Large banks with a presence in multiple jurisdictions are often vital for these businesses. In addition to providing valuable cross-border payments and capital markets services, they can help U.S. businesses navigate local laws and business practices and facilitate relationship-building with local business partners.

A 2013 survey commissioned by the U.S. Chamber of Commerce of public and private companies with at least $75 million in annual revenue found that among companies that issue debt, 84 percent use a financial company with global operations. For comparison, 34 percent use national institutions and 21 percent used regional or local institutions. Another 2013 survey of 212 CEOs by the Business Roundtable highlighted the importance of large banks for U.S. multinational businesses. Specifically, majorities of the CEOs surveyed cited large U.S. banks' cash management, foreign exchange, and cross-border payments services as essential to their businesses, as well as the debt and equity offerings provided by large banks. The CEOs also felt that large U.S. banks were either essential or useful in providing mergers and acquisitions advice, large loans, swaps, and derivatives products. . . .

INDIVIDUALS. There is no question that big banks suffered substantial reputational damage as a result of the financial crisis. . . . [O]ne might have expected a substantial number of customers to vote with their feet and move their deposit holdings to smaller financial institutions. The empirical evidence does not, however, show this.

The data show instead that the five largest retail banks—Bank of America, J.P. Morgan Chase, Citibank, Wells Fargo, and U.S. Bank—added nearly 25 million new deposit accounts between 2010 and 2014. This is particularly interesting, because the 2010 to 2014 time period is the only one in recent history in which large financial institutions were not growing by merger and acquisition, as large institutions have been prohibited from doing so after the financial crisis under Section 622 of the Dodd-Frank Act.

It could be argued that customers thought that larger banks were safer as a result of being [too big to fail]. This would represent one avenue of the implicit subsidy of government action flowing through as a benefit to large financial institutions. Accounts with up to $250,000 in deposits are guaranteed, however, at any FDIC member institution, so concerns over [too big to fail] would not be expected to drive the relationship decision for people with such accounts (which includes most people). The data show that the overwhelming bulk of new accounts were. . . accounts with less than $250,000 held in them, implying that individual consumers were using the services of large financial institutions for reasons other than the perceived safety benefits of being [too big to fail] . . . .

The Bipartisan Policy Center Report also suggested that the biggest banks were more responsible for the dissemination of financial innovations, but nonetheless acknowledged that one of the lessons of the Financial Crisis was that innovation comes with both benefits and costs.

Others have taken a sharply more critical view of large complex financial organizations. Senators Elizabeth Warren (D-MA) and 2016 presidential candidate Bernie Sanders (D-VT) have become two of the most well-known advocates for breaking up the biggest banks. The break-up-the-banks view was prominently outlined in Simon Johnson and James Kwak's highly influential book, *13 Bankers*.

> The right solution is obvious; do not allow financial institutions to be too big to fail; break up the ones that are. This is a controversial idea. It is a virtually unquestioned assumption in the American business world that bigger is better. Banking executives have spent the last twenty years making their banks as big as possible by entering new businesses, expanding into new geographic regions, and above all by acquiring other banks. The idea that the United States, as the world's largest economy, should also have its largest banks seems self-evident to most people.

SIMON JOHNSON & JAMES KWAK, 13 BANKERS: THE WALL STREET TAKEOVER AND THE NEXT FINANCIAL MELTDOWN 208 (2010).

Professors Johnson and Kwak proposed a hard cap on bank size of 4% of GDP, or approximately $750 billion in the year of their book's publication, and pointed out that, in 2010, it would affect six financial conglomerates: Bank of America, JPMorgan Chase, Citigroup, Wells Fargo, Goldman Sachs, and Morgan Stanley. They acknowledged the widespread concern about international competition, quoting Harvard professor Hal Scott: "If we break up our banks and Europe doesn't break up theirs and the Chinese don't break up theirs, this is going to have an immense impact on who are the players in the international banking system." *Id.* at 217. Johnson and Kwak's response to this argument was that other countries, possibly through the World Trade Organization, should also break up their banks.

The call to break up the banks is often animated by concerns regarding competitive distortions. Specifically, many commentators believe that the largest G-SIBs enjoy an implicit subsidy, in the form of less expensive average cost of funding from the bond markets as a result of creditors understanding that the government will, in a time of crisis, protect the creditors by bailing out the "too big to fail" firm. Richard W. Fisher, formerly a President and Chief Executive Officer of the Federal Reserve Bank of Dallas, has emphasized the procompetitive benefits of breakup:

> While there may be *some* economic benefits to size and scope, numerous studies suggest that the benefits of size are limited. In fact, simple logic would dictate that if you are "too big to fail," you're also "too big to manage." If a large multinational corporation needs a huge bridge loan to close a deal or expand services, a group of lenders could share the risk. From lending data, we know that smaller banks serve the smaller businesses that drive job growth. A healthy and competitive banking model that serves the needs of job creators will help get the economy back on the path to stronger growth.
>
> Restructured, refocused and *unsubsidized* financial conglomerates will still provide a full range of financial services. They will operate with a clarified understanding of the boundaries of FDIC protection and access to the Federal Reserve [Board]'s discount window—only traditional commercial banking operations should benefit from the safety net. . . .
>
> Viable business models should be given the opportunity to compete and prosper on their own merits, while unattractive strategies should be allowed to fail. Subverting the ability to fail, on the taxpayers' dime, is a perversion of American capitalism.

FED. RESERVE BANK OF DALL., 2012 ANNUAL REPORT 11, 13 (2012). The same report suggested that 12 institutions were worthy of being broken up but did not name them. The 12 institutions were selected for their complexity and presumed "Too Big To Fail" subsidy, and at the time held more than two-thirds of banking assets. *See id.* at 43–45.

Professor Paul Krugman has countered the call to break up the banks not by defending large complex financial organizations, but by arguing that the break up process would not yield the desired results.

> One argument I don't buy, however, is that we should try to shrink financial institutions down to the point where nobody is too big to fail. Basically, it's just not possible. The point is that finance is deeply interconnected, so that even a moderately large player can take down the system if it implodes. Remember, it was Lehman—not Citi or [Bank of America]—that brought the world to the brink.

Paul Krugman, *Too big to fail FAIL*, N.Y. TIMES, June 18, 2009.

Another portion of the debate has centered around whether there are, in fact, economies of scale and scope in financial conglomerates or whether the one-stop shopping of the financial conglomerate makes sense. Since the creation of FHCs in the Gramm-Leach-Bliley Act (GLBA) in 1999, scant empirical analysis has been done to examine the threshold at which financial conglomerates maximize economies of scale and scope. Governor Tarullo has appealed to academics to engage in this research, but has acknowledged that the small sample size, fast-paced growth of financial conglomerates in the early 21st Century, and the difficulty of obtaining helpful data or isolating costs for particular banking activities may continue to hinder the empirical analysis. Daniel K. Tarullo, Governor, Fed. Reserve. Bd., Speech at the Brookings Institution Conference on Structuring the Financial Industry to Enhance Economic Growth and Stability: Industry Structure and Systemic Risk Regulation (Dec. 4, 2012). The Bipartisan Policy Center Report describes the state of play and lists existing research in the debate regarding economies of scale and scope.

In addition to the size-based break-up proposals, there are also proposals to break up the largest U.S. BHCs based on the mix of activities in which BHCs engage. Thomas Hoenig, Vice Chairman of the FDIC, would permit banking organizations to engage in traditional commercial banking (including taking deposits and making loans), provide payment services and credit intermediation, give merger advice, engage in trust activities and wealth management, and underwrite corporate debt and equity—all of which are activities that had been previously prohibited in the Glass-Steagall Act era. Hoenig would, however, prohibit banking organizations from dealing securities or derivatives for either their own account or for customers—a move that would be stricter than the Volcker Rule, sponsoring private equity and hedge funds, and engaging in prime brokerage. *See* Thomas M. Hoenig & Charles S. Morris, *Restructuring the Banking System to Improve Safety and Soundness* (Working Paper, 2012). Another example is a bill proposed by Senators John McCain (R-AZ) and Elizabeth Warren, which has not moved legislatively. It would not only fully restore the Glass-Steagall Act but would also institute a type of narrow banking by rolling back the definition of the business of banking. 21st Century Glass-Steagall Act of 2015, S. 1709, 114th Cong. § 2 (2015). Others have suggested a twist on the reinstatement of the Glass-Steagall Act, which would include the creation of a banking public utility for simple retail banking and the separation of wholesale banking activities. *See* James Fanto, *"Breaking Up Is Hard to Do": Should Financial Conglomerates Be Dismantled*, 79 U. CIN. L. REV. 553, 584–85

(2011). Support for activities-based separation has come from unlikely corners, including from Sandy Weill, the former CEO of Citigroup who engineered the merger of Citigroup and Travellers that pressured Congress to pass GLBA. *See* Chapter 6.1; *see also* Donal Griffin & Christine Harper, *Former Citigroup CEO Weill Says Banks Should Be Broken Up*, BLOOMBERG, July 25, 2012.

By the time the bill that eventually became the Dodd-Frank Act was under consideration, a number of breakup proposals were on the table, some of them with a bipartisan flavor. The Safe Banking Act, introduced by Senators Sherrod Brown (D-OH) and Ted Kaufman (D-DE), would have imposed additional limits on deposits, while restricting nondeposit liabilities to 2% of GDP for banks and 3% for non-bank financial firms and bank assets to 10% of GDP. It garnered 33 votes in the Senate, illustrating the deep distrust that remains in the United States for large concentrated power in banking groups. Such proposals continue to attract attention. *See, e.g.*, Too Big to Fail, Too Big to Exist Act, S. ____, 114th Cong. (1st Sess. 2015); Heidi Przybyla, *Bernie Sanders Proposes Bill to Break Up Big Banks and Pressure Hillary Clinton*, BLOOMBERG, May 6, 2015.

B. BREAKUP OPTIONS UNDER THE DODD-FRANK ACT

The Dodd-Frank Act contains two provisions that explicitly authorize regulators to break up large financial conglomerates. The first provision, § 121 of the Dodd-Frank Act, known as the Kanjorski Amendment, grants the Federal Reserve Board the power to limit the activities of any BHC with total consolidated assets over $50 billion or any non-bank financial company supervised by the Federal Reserve Board upon a finding that the entity in question "poses a grave threat to the financial stability of the United States." 12 U.S.C. § 5331(a). No definition of grave threat was discussed or given and the concept was not one that existed previously in banking law. In addition to requiring an affirmative vote of no fewer than two-thirds of the voting members of the FSOC, § 121 requires that the Federal Reserve Board provide notice and the opportunity for a hearing to any company that might be subject to actions under § 121.

The factors to be considered by the Federal Reserve Board and FSOC in making a determination under the Kanjorski Amendment are the same as those considered by the FSOC in deciding whether to subject a non-bank financial company to the Federal Reserve Board's supervision under § 113 of the Dodd-Frank Act. In the event that the Federal Reserve Board, with the FSOC's affirmation, determines that a company poses a "grave threat," it can (1) limit the company's ability to acquire, merge, or affiliate with another company; (2) restrict the company's ability to offer financial products; (3) require the company to terminate activities; and (4) impose conditions on how activities are conducted. Lastly, the Federal Reserve Board can require the company to sell or transfer assets or other items to unaffiliated entities, but only if it determines that actions (1) through (4) are insufficient to mitigate the threat to financial stability. *Id.*

Another provision of the Dodd-Frank Act, which garnered much less attention at the time, also contains a path to requiring that large complex banking organizations sell assets or divest parts of their business but with many fewer procedural protections. Section 165(d) of the Dodd-Frank Act mandated that BHCs with total consolidated assets over $50 billion and non-bank financial companies supervised by the Federal Reserve Board prepare resolution plans (or living wills), which are plans for rapid and orderly resolution of the company in the event of material financial distress or failure. This will be discussed in further detail in Part IX. As part of the living will mandate, the Federal Reserve Board and the FDIC have the power to make a joint determination that the submitted living will is not credible or would not facilitate an orderly resolution of the company under the Bankruptcy Code. In the event that a company fails to resubmit a credible plan, the Federal Reserve Board and the FDIC may jointly impose certain restrictions on the company, including more stringent capital, leverage, or liquidity requirements, or restrictions on the growth, activities, or operations of the company until the company submits a plan that remedies the deficiencies. As a final option, the Federal Reserve Board and the FDIC may, in consultation with the FSOC, order a company to divest certain assets or operations as identified by the Federal Reserve Board and FDIC in order to facilitate an orderly resolution of such company under the Bankruptcy Code. This measure may only be taken if a company has not submitted a credible living will within two years of a finding of noncredibility and the Federal Reserve Board and the FDIC have already taken restrictive measures against the company. On December 17, 2014, the FDIC made public its new guidelines for the required strategies for the living wills to be filed under the FDIC's solo rule for IDIs of over $50 billion in assets. The strategy includes a required breakup scenario.

---

1. ***Judicial Review.*** What is the standard of judicial review under §§ 121 and 165(d) of the Dodd-Frank Act? Dodd-Frank Act § 113(h), which addresses designations of systemic importance, contains an explicit subsection on judicial review of such determinations that operates to limit a court's review to whether the decision was "arbitrary and capricious." 12 U.S.C. § 5323(h). Does the fact that §§ 121 and 165(d) do not explicitly include a subsection on judicial review mean that none exists?

C. SOFT BREAKUP

Another way to manage the size of the largest financial institutions is soft breakup, or taxing size and complexity "in order to encourage [the largest banks] to break up." BIPARTISAN POLICY CENTER REPORT, at 38.

> An example of this approach is a piece of legislation . . . proposed in 2013, known as the Terminating Bailouts for Taxpayer Fairness [] Act. The proposal would require institutions with more than $500 billion in assets to fund themselves with high-quality, Tier 1 capital equal to at least 15 percent of their assets. One estimate suggests that the [Terminating Bailouts for Taxpayer Fairness] Act would require the largest banks to raise another $600 billion in Tier 1 capital funding in addition to the $400 billion they raised in 2013. These costs would provide incentives to the firm's owners and management to divest assets or break up their operations.

Id. at 39.

The Obama Administration has repeatedly proposed a tax on the liabilities of the largest firms, but Congress has not taken up the idea. Another example of a soft breakup proposal is Cornelius Hurley's subsidy reserve plan, which would require each of the largest banks to "establish a 'subsidy reserve' line item on its balance sheet and add to it each year the estimated subsidy it receives from taxpayers in the form of reduced funding costs." Cornelius Hurley, *End 'Too Big to Fail' by Making It Shareholders' Problem*, AMERICAN BANKER, Jan. 23, 2013. Soft break-up could also be encouraged through use of the Federal Reserve Board's supervisory authority, which can be deployed to restrict activities, require divestiture of assets, or "take such other action as the banking agency determines to be appropriate" in light of safety and soundness concerns. 12 U.S.C. §§ 1818(b)(6)-(7).

In the post-Financial Crisis era, a number of soft breakup measures are being put in place. They include the leverage ratio, which is a tax on size, higher risk-based capital surcharges on larger financial institutions, higher liquidity requirements, limits on short-term funding, larger risk-based FDIC deposit insurance premiums for larger banks, more intense prudential regulations tailored for larger banks, activities restrictions through the Volcker Rule, large fines and penalties in enforcement proceedings, and informal limits on certain activities, such as leveraged lending or commodities activities. Combined with limits on acquisitions, these and other supervisory actions seem designed to encourage the largest and most complex U.S. financial institutions not only to de-risk and deleverage, but also to divest certain activities or lines of business. Pressures by activist and other shareholders, who are increasingly impatient with low returns since the Financial Crisis, have led some large complex financial conglomerates, including some designated by the FSOC, to publicly acknowledge that they are considering sales of major business units. Other conglomerates have made it clear that they believe there are synergies in their current structure and that their size is necessary for U.S. financial conglomerates to compete in a global economy. Whether soft breakup measures driven by investors or regulators will fundamentally change the structure of the largest financial conglomerates and the U.S. financial sector as a whole remains to be seen.

Although framed in 21st Century terms like too big to fail and financial stability, the debate about breaking up the biggest banking organizations has deep roots in American history. Recall the quotes from Hamilton, Jefferson and Jackson at the very beginning of the book. To what extent does the debate in America today continue to reflect the contrasting views of Hamilton, Jefferson and Jackson?

CHAPTER 6.3

FOREIGN BANKS IN THE UNITED STATES AND U.S. BANKS ABROAD

CONTENTS

I. INTRODUCTION

There are myriad types of cross-border and global banking operations and transactions, many of which can be done from a head office or through foreign correspondent banks, such as letters of credit, funds transfers, and loans. For much of the 19th Century and early 20th Century, commercial and investment banks worked with foreign correspondents or agents, and the opening of offices or direct investment in a bank or broker-dealer in another country was rare. All of that changed in the mid-20th Century. The post-World War II era was driven by increasing trade, the lifting of wartime exchange controls, a return to the international movement of capital, and the rise of the large multinational corporation with both production and sales in many countries. In essence, globalization happened, and banks followed their customers abroad at a time when the dollar replaced the British pound as both reserve currency and the dominant trading currency. As former Governor of the Bank of England Mervyn King said, "Banks live globally but die locally." The stark lessons of the Financial Crisis have thus led to a period of pause and reflection on the growth and forms of cross-border banking. Certainly, there has been a change in the U.S. regulation of large foreign banking organizations (FBOs) with the imposition of intermediate holding companies, as well as increased political and enforcement risk. It is unclear whether we are entering a phase of regionalization of cross-border banking or a slowing of its growth.

Opening an office in another country brings to bear the laws, regulations, and supervision of that country. In this Chapter, we discuss how foreign banks that decide to open an office in the United States are regulated by U.S. banking regulators and how U.S. regulators have approached the supervision of U.S. banks that expand abroad. You might think of foreign banks opening offices in the United States as inward-bound regulation and U.S. banks opening offices or making investments abroad as outward-bound regulation. Of course, the foreign bank opening an office in the United States remains subject to the laws of its home country, and the U.S. bank opening an office in a host country becomes subject to the laws of the host country.

II. FOREIGN BANKS IN THE UNITED STATES

A. OVERVIEW

In the 19th Century, the physical presence of foreign banks in the United States was largely driven by home country trade or remittances, and there was a strong protectionist bent against branches of foreign banks. Most states prohibited, or severely limited, foreign banks from opening branches that could take deposits from the public. These restrictions continued well into the 20th Century and, as of 1940, 35 states still prohibited foreign banks from conducting business entirely, and only five states expressly allowed foreign banks to accept deposits. Even New York, the center of international banking activities, prohibited foreign bank branches from taking deposits. Foreign banks were largely absent from New York commercial banking at the time because, among other limits, the National Bank Act required that all directors of a national bank be U.S. citizens and New York State law had similar restrictions. New York did permit foreign banks to operate agencies. These banks were licensed annually to take limited deposits, which became major providers of trade finance to U.S. companies at a time when U.S. national banks were barred from opening foreign branches themselves.

Furthermore, as noted in Chapter 4.1, European banking houses played a significant role in providing the United States with long-term capital by underwriting and distributing U.S. securities. In California, the Hongkong and Shanghai Banking Corporation (now known as HSBC) opened in San Francisco in 1875, focusing on foreign exchange and helping the city's Chinese immigrant community send remittances back home. Yokohama Specie Bank's San Francisco branch served the Japanese-American community in a similar way starting in 1899, although California later took a more restrictive stance on foreign banking, forcing the bank to separately incorporate the branch. Remittances remain an important part of international cash flows today but often take place outside the branch networks of banks. For additional discussion of remittances, see Chapter 7.1. For more on the history of foreign banking in the United States before World War II, *see generally* CLYDE WILLIAM PHELPS, THE FOREIGN EXPANSION OF AMERICAN BANKS (1976), MIRA WILKINS, THE HISTORY OF FOREIGN INVESTMENT IN THE UNITED STATES TO 1914 453–90

(1989), Joseph L. Abraham, *State Regulation of Foreign Banks*, 9 FORDHAM L. REV. 343 (1940).

Federal and state laws are not nearly as restrictive now and foreign banks are no longer limited to trade finance and remittance services. In fact, the U.S. market has been relatively open to foreign bank entry since the late 1960s. Today, foreign banks, which employ a variety of business models and strategies, are an important part of the U.S. financial sector, especially the wholesale markets. There are 135 foreign bank branches in New York City, located there because of the city's status as a global financial center and the dollar's continuing prominent international currency role. Foreign banks open U.S. branches if for no other reason than to clear dollars and to have an account with the Federal Reserve Bank of New York. The largest FBOs operating in the United States do so as financial holding companies (FHCs) and have large wholesale branches and subsidiary broker-dealers, such as Deutsche Bank, Barclays, Credit Suisse. Other FBOs are more invested in their commercial bank subsidiaries, which are largely run under their familiar U.S. brand names, or engage in a combination of wholesale banking and a commercial banking activity. As of September 2015, FBOs held about 22% of the banking assets in the United States, which does not account for the fact that the ten largest FBOs hold half their assets outside of their banks in broker-dealer subsidiaries. Figure 6.3-1 reveals the banking assets held by FBOs in the United States by form of organization as of September 30, 2015.

Figure 6.3-1 FBOs Operating in the United States (Sept. 30, 2015)

Forms of Organization	**Number of Institutions**	**Assets ($ billions)**
Branches and agencies	223	2,502
Subsidiaries	44	1,324
Edge and agreement corporations	10	11
Representative offices	142	0
Others	11	0
Total	430	3,837

Source: Fed. Reserve Bd., Structure Data for the U.S. Offices of FBOs.

Not shown in Figure 6.3-1 above are the affiliated broker-dealers of FBOs, which, especially in the larger FBOs, can be a significant portion of their operations. Figure 6.3-2 shows the size of the largest FBOs including broker-dealer operations, revealing the variety of FBO business models.

Figure 6.3-2 Largest FBOs Operating in the United States (2014)

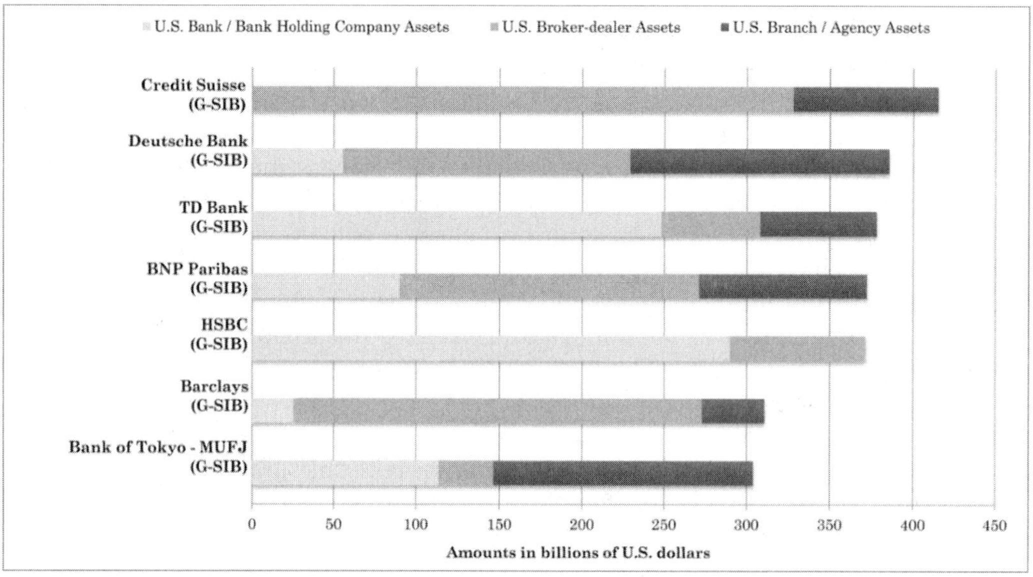

U.S. Bank / Bank Holding Company Assets
U.S. Broker-dealer Assets
U.S. Branch / Agency Assets

Credit Suisse (G-SIB)
Deutsche Bank (G-SIB)
TD Bank (G-SIB)
BNP Paribas (G-SIB)
HSBC (G-SIB)
Barclays (G-SIB)
Bank of Tokyo - MUFJ (G-SIB)

0 50 100 150 200 250 300 350 400 450

Amounts in billions of U.S. dollars

Note: Asset-size of certain entities may change materially from quarter to quarter.
Source: Davis Polk & Wardwell LLP; Based on publicly available data regarding U.S. branch/agency, U.S. broker-dealer and U.S. bank.

B. FORMS OF ENTRY

Cross-border banking can happen without establishing an office and, unlike securities firms which, as we learned in Chapter 4.1, cannot engage in broker-dealer activities in the United States without a license or a chaperone, banks may make cross-border loans and transfer funds without a local office or license. The taking of deposits, however, requires a license. Once a decision is made to establish an office, foreign banks can enter the United States, and U.S. banks can commonly enter foreign countries, through a number of different legal forms, the most common of which are described in the following U.S. Government Accountability Office (GAO) report excerpt.

GAO, Foreign Banks: Assessing Their Role in the U.S. Banking System

GAO/GGD-96-26 (1996)

Like their U.S. counterparts, foreign branches and agencies are legal and operational extensions of their parent banks. Their assets and liabilities are consolidated into the accounts of their parent banks, and they operate on the consolidated equity of those banks. For example, their lending limits are based on the capital of their parent banks. Regulators in both the United States and their home country oversee their operations. . . .

Foreign branches and agencies may conduct a wide range of banking activities, including lending, money market services, trade financing, and other activities related to the service of home-country and U.S. clients. They can also access the U.S. payments system through the [Federal Reserve Board] and obtain other [Federal Reserve Board] services. However, they are banned from certain activities. Foreign branches have been prohibited from accepting insured deposits since the end of 1991. In addition, federally licensed agencies and most state-licensed agencies cannot accept deposits.

Foreign banks can charter or acquire a full-service U.S. bank subsidiary. Foreign banks have exercised this option when state law prohibited them from establishing branches or when a foreign bank wanted to offer retail banking services. Foreign-owned subsidiary banks have all the powers of U.S.-owned banks, are insured by the [FDIC], and are subject to all the rules and regulations governing U.S.-owned banks. However, subsidiary banks have some disadvantages compared with branches and agencies. They are more costly to operate, requiring not only separate boards of directors and managers but also their own capital base. They are also subject to the collateralization requirements and lending limits of the [Federal Reserve Board's] section 23A and 23B restrictions, which limit banks' extension of credit to their affiliates.

Foreign banks also offer services to U.S. customers through offices located outside the U.S. (offshore offices). Some offshore offices have practically no office or staff and are referred to as shell branches. Much of their management—including funding decisions and setting lending policies—is handled elsewhere, in many instances by branches or agencies located in the United States. In these cases, banking products—such as commercial and industrial [] loans or deposits—are marketed to U.S. customers from U.S. offices but are held by the shell branch. Although the shell branches of U.S. banks, including foreign-owned U.S.-chartered banks, are subject to all U.S. laws and regulations, the shell branches of foreign banks are subject to U.S. regulation only for those activities that are managed within the United States.

Foreign banks can also serve U.S. customers through International Banking Facilities (IBF). Like shell branches, IBFs represent a separate set of accounts rather than an operating entity of the bank. For this reason, IBFs are sometimes referred to as onshore shell branches. The [Federal Reserve Board] authorized U.S. banks and the offices of foreign banks to establish IBFs to engage in Eurocurrency lending in 1981 in response to the growth of shell branches. The activities of IBFs are restricted. They can be used to take deposits from the non-U.S. offices of U.S. and foreign banks, other IBFs, IBF parent banks, and foreign governments. They can also make loans to those cited above, plus non-U.S. residents, and the foreign offices of a domestic corporation. They are free from reserve requirements, federal deposit insurance premiums, and some state income taxes. An IBF may not engage in domestic banking activities.

C. THE BRANCH AND THE SEPARATE ENTITY DOCTRINE

The branch office has long been seen by bank management as the most flexible way to operate across borders, whether they be interstate or international. The branch does not require separate capital, is not subject to separate lending limits and is not legally separate from the head office bank itself. Not surprisingly, the most common form of entry by foreign banks into the United States is the branch office. As of September 2015, more than 65% of foreign banking assets were held by branches or agencies. FEDERAL RESERVE BOARD, STRUCTURE DATA FOR U.S. BANKING OFFICES OF FOREIGN ENTITIES (2015). Because the vast majority of foreign branches cannot accept retail deposits (since seven are insured and no new insured branches are permitted), foreign bank branches focus on wholesale banking activities. As discussed later in this Chapter, the branch is also the most common way that U.S. banks have expanded abroad.

The branch is an unusual legal concept. It is not legally separate from the home country bank, yet it requires a separate license from the host country to operate. In the United States, that license can come either from the state banking authority or the OCC. It is not separately capitalized, but the host country supervisor may require asset maintenance pledges or limit the amount that the branch can lend to its home office. In New York, which has, at least since the mid-20th Century and until quite recently, worked to make its laws friendly to foreign banks to encourage the tax and revenues accrued by New York State and City as a global financial center, there has been much litigation on the extent to which a branch is liable for the debts of a branch in another country. New York has thus been at the forefront in developing much of the law in this area and has developed a common law doctrine called the separate entity doctrine. *See* CLEARY GOTTLIEB STEEN & HAMILTON LLP, DAVIS POLK & WARDWELL LLP, AND SULLIVAN & CROMWELL LLP, WHITE PAPER ON THE SEPARATE ENTITY DOCTRINE AS APPLIED TO THE U.S. BRANCHES OF FOREIGN HEADQUARTERED (NON-U.S.) BANKS (2012). Consider the following case, which lays out the debate.

Motorola Credit Corp. v. Standard Chartered Bank

21 N.E.3d 223 (N.Y. 2014)

GRAFFEO, J.:

In this case, the United States Court of Appeals for the Second Circuit asks us whether the "separate entity" rule prevents a judgment creditor from ordering a garnishee bank operating branches in New York to restrain a judgment debtor's assets held in foreign branches of the bank. We conclude that it does.

I.

Between April 1998 and September 2000, several members of the Uzan family (the Uzans) induced plaintiff Motorola Credit Corporation (Motorola) to loan over $2 billion to a Turkish telecommunications company they controlled, purportedly to finance a major expansion of the company's operations. Unbeknownst to Motorola, the Uzans diverted a substantial portion of these funds to themselves and other entities they controlled. In 2003, after discovering that the Uzans had "perpetrated a huge fraud" and concealed "their scheme through an almost endless series of lies, threats, and chicanery," the United States District Court for the Southern District of New York entered a judgment in Motorola's favor for compensatory damages of about $2.1 billion. Three years later, the District Court awarded Motorola an additional $1 billion in punitive damages.

The Uzans have gone to great lengths to avoid satisfying the judgments and remain in contempt for failure to comply with the District Court's orders, subjecting them to arrest if they enter the United States. As a result of enforcement obstacles, Motorola has pursued collection of the judgments through third-party discovery and the District Court has conducted postjudgment proceedings ex parte and under seal. In February 2013, the District Court entered an order pursuant to Federal Rules of Civil Procedure 65 and 69 and CPLR 5222 restraining the Uzans and anyone with notice of the order from selling, assigning or transferring their property.

Motorola served the restraining order on the New York branch of defendant Standard Chartered Bank (SCB), a foreign bank incorporated and headquartered in the United Kingdom. SCB, which had no connection to Motorola's loan to the Uzans or the underlying litigation, did not locate any Uzan property at its New York branch. Two months later, a global search of its branches revealed Uzan-related assets valued at roughly $30 million in its branches in the United Arab Emirates (U.A.E.). SCB froze those assets in accordance with the restraining order, but regulatory authorities in the U.A.E. and Jordan quickly intervened. The Central Bank of Jordan sent a bank examiner to seize documents at SCB's Jordan branch, while the U.A.E. Central Bank unilaterally debited about $30 million from SCB's account with the bank.

In May 2013, SCB sought relief from the restraining order, claiming in the District Court that the restraint of the $30 million in assets violated U.A.E. law and subjected it to double liability. SCB also contended that, under New York's separate entity rule, service of the restraining order on SCB's New York branch was effective only as to assets located in accounts at that branch and could not freeze funds situated in foreign branches. . . .

The Second Circuit, recognizing that we have never explicitly addressed the separate entity doctrine . . . , certified the following question to us:

> [W]hether the separate entity rule precludes a judgment creditor from ordering a garnishee bank operating branches in New York to restrain a debtor's assets held in foreign branches of the bank.

II.

Motorola, as the judgment creditor, argues that the service of a [Civil Practice Law and Rules (CPLR)] 5222 restraining notice on the New York branch of a foreign bank garnishee is sufficient to freeze the funds of the judgment debtor in any branch account with the bank, regardless of where the assets are located. . . . Motorola asks us to disavow the separate entity doctrine as outmoded and unnecessary.

As the garnishee bank, SCB responds that the separate entity rule is deeply rooted in New York banking law and that foreign banks have reasonably relied on it over the years when deciding whether to open branches and conduct business in New York. . . .

The separate entity rule, as it has been employed by lower New York courts and federal courts applying New York law, provides that even when a bank garnishee with a New York branch is subject to personal jurisdiction, its other branches are to be treated as separate entities for certain purposes, particularly with respect to CPLR article 62 prejudgment attachments and article 52 postjudgment restraining notices and turnover orders . . . In other words, a restraining notice or turnover order served on a New York branch will be effective for assets held in accounts at that branch but will have no impact on assets in other branches.

Courts and commentators traditionally have ascribed three basic rationales for the separate entity doctrine. First, courts applying the rule have emphasized the importance of international comity and the fact that "any banking operation in a foreign country is necessarily subject to the foreign sovereign's own laws and regulations." Second, it was viewed as necessary to protect banks from being "subject . . . to competing claims" and the possibility of double liability. . . . And third, the rule has been justified based on the "intolerable burden" that would otherwise be placed on banks to monitor and ascertain the status of bank accounts in numerous other branches.

The existence of the separate entity rule as a component of New York's common law can be traced back to a 1916 decision. It was first applied in the postjudgment context a few decades later in *Walsh v Bustos*, where the court concluded that a restraining order served on a New York branch of the bank garnishee did not "extend to the deposits of the judgment debtor in the Mexican branch of this foreign bank" (46 NYS2d 240, 241 [NY City Ct 1943]). By the 1950s and 1960s, the separate entity rule was described by state and federal courts as "well established" (*Cronan*, 100 NYS2d at 476) and supported by "a consistent line of authority" (*Det Bergenske Dampskibsselskab v Sabre Shipping Corp.*, 341 F2d 50, 53 (2d Cir 1965)). And its endurance continues into the 21st century in the postjudgment context. Although we have not expounded on the separate entity rule, contrary to Motorola's suggestion, it is a firmly established principle of New York law, with a history of application both before and after the 1962 adoption of the CPLR. . . .

Motorola and the dissent further submit that the separate entity rule is incompatible with CPLR article 52 because nothing in CPLR 5222, governing postjudgment restraining notices, expressly embraces the rule. Motorola cites *Commonwealth of the N. Mariana Is. v Canadian Imperial Bank of Commerce*, where we stated, in determining the expanse of CPLR article 52, that the "starting point is the language itself, giving effect to the plain meaning thereof" (21 NY3d 55, 60 (2013). But Motorola's reliance on *Canadian Imperial Bank* is misplaced because the separate entity rule predates the CPLR by several decades and the issue is not one of statutory construction but, rather, whether to retain a common-law principle.

Finally, we decline Motorola's invitation to cast aside the separate entity rule. As discussed, the doctrine has been a part of the common law of New York for nearly a century. Courts have repeatedly used it to prevent the postjudgment restraint of assets situated in foreign branch accounts based solely on the service of a foreign bank's New York branch. Undoubtedly, international banks have considered the doctrine's benefits when deciding to open branches in New York, which in turn has played a role in shaping New York's "status as the preeminent commercial and financial nerve center of the Nation and the world" (*Ehrlich-Bober & Co. v University of Houston*, 49 NY2d 574, 581 (1980)).

In large measure, the underlying reasons that led to the adoption of the separate entity rule still ring true today. The risk of competing claims and the possibility of double liability in separate jurisdictions remain significant concerns, as does the reality that foreign branches are subject to a multitude of legal and regulatory regimes. By limiting the reach of a CPLR 5222 restraining notice in the foreign banking context, the separate entity rule promotes international comity and serves to avoid conflicts among competing legal systems. And although Motorola suggests that technological advancements and centralized banking have ameliorated the need for the doctrine, courts have continued to recognize the practical constraints and costs associated with conducting a worldwide search for a judgment debtor's assets. . . .

Indeed, as the District Court observed, the facts of this case aptly demonstrate that the policies implicated by the separate entity rule run deeper than the ability of a bank to communicate across branches. In seeking to comply with the restraining order, SCB faced regulatory and financial repercussions abroad. Representatives of the Central Bank of Jordan compelled SCB to disclose records and directed SCB to immediately unfreeze the assets. The U.A.E. Central Bank, which possesses regulatory oversight in that nation, would not allow SCB's Uzan-related payment obligation to remain unsatisfied. As a result, the U.A.E. Central Bank debited SCB's account with that bank for an amount equivalent to the frozen funds—approximately $30 million. In essence, SCB was placed in the difficult position of attempting to comply with the contradictory directives of multiple sovereign nations. Consequently, in contrast to the dissent, we believe that abolition of the separate entity rule would result in serious consequences in the realm of international banking to the detriment of New York's preeminence in global financial affairs. For all of these reasons, we conclude that a judgment creditor's service of a restraining notice on a garnishee bank's New York branch is ineffective under the separate entity rule to freeze assets held in the bank's foreign branches.

ABDUS-SALAAM, J. (dissenting):

Today, in the year 2014, the majority for the first time expressly adopts the separate entity rule for post-judgment enforcement proceedings under CPLR article 52. The rule has no statutory basis and was initially formulated by the lower courts nearly a century ago based on a rationale that has no application to these modern times. . . .

The majority has, in this particular case, permitted the judgment debtors, individuals who owe plaintiff over $2 billion in consequential damages and $1 billion in punitive damages, who are subject to arrest orders from the United States District Court for the

Southern District of New York and The English High Court of Justice, and who have been convicted of multibillion dollar bank frauds in Turkey, to evade enforcement proceedings in New York. . . . Standard Chartered Bank, by persuading the majority of this Court to adopt the obsolete separate entity rule, has aided its fugitive customers by erecting a monumental roadblock to plaintiff's enforcement of the staggering judgment.

In broader terms, today's holding permits banks doing business in New York to shield customer accounts held in branches outside of this country, thwarts efforts by judgment creditors to collect judgments, and allows even the most egregious and flagrant judgment debtors to make a mockery of our courts' duly entered judgments. In an age where banks are being held more accountable than ever for their actions vis-à-vis their customers, today's holding is a deviation from current public policy regarding the responsibilities of banks and a step in the wrong direction.

---

1. ***The Act-of-State Doctrine.*** U.S. banks likewise have branches operating in countries outside the United States. 20th Century case law is littered with examples of depositors in communist countries, such as Russia, Cuba, and Vietnam, arriving in the United States and claiming that deposits expropriated by the communist government from the host country branch should be paid by the bank's U.S. home office, similarly testing the extent to which a foreign branch should be treated as being part of the same legal entity as the home country bank and other branches. The courts developed a doctrine of comity, called the act-of-state doctrine, under which they would defer to acts of a foreign state even though expropriation was contrary to U.S. public policy. The result, however, was often confused case law. *Compare* Perez v. Chase Manhattan Bank, N.A., 463 N.E.2d 5 (N.Y. 1984), *cert. denied*, 469 U.S. 966 (1984) *and* Garcia v. Chase Manhattan Bank, N.A., 735 F.2d 645 (2d Cir. 1984), in which the foreign branches were open when the deposits were expropriated, *with* Vishipco Line v. Chase Manhattan Bank, 660 F.2d 854 (2d Cir. 1981), *cert. denied*, 459 U.S. 976 (1982), in which the bank closed down the branch before assets were expropriated. Sovereign risk can also arise between sophisticated players arguing about which party took the risk of sovereign action in the sudden imposition of exchange controls. Wells Fargo placed Eurodollars at the Philippines branch of Citibank earning a higher interest rate. When the Philippines imposed exchange controls, Wells Fargo sought repayment from Citibank's head office in New York and won its case in the Supreme Court. *See* Citibank v. Wells Fargo Asia, Ltd., 495 U.S. 660 (1990). New York state law was reformed in 1984 so that any bank located in the state of New York with foreign branches is liable for foreign branch deposits only to the extent that a bank in that country would be liable. *See* N.Y. BANKING LAW § 138 (McKinney 2011). After the *Wells Fargo* decision, the Federal Reserve Act was amended to similarly protect a member bank from liability for repayments of deposits made at a foreign branch if the branch is unable to repay because of "(1) an act of war, insurrection, or civil strife; or (2) an action by a foreign government," such as expropriation, unless the member bank has expressly agreed to repay the foreign branch deposits in writing. 12 U.S.C. § 633. The issue of the home office liability for deposits at a foreign branch that is closed, expropriated, or suddenly subject to exchange controls is one that is likely to resurface in trouble spots around the world. The changes to the Federal Reserve Act have resolved nearly a century of litigation for U.S. banks. Or have they?

2. ***Branches of Foreign Banks in the U.S.*** After the International Banking Act of 1978 (IBA), which we will discuss in more detail later in this chapter, foreign bank branches can, like domestic banks, choose to be state or federally licensed. Although most foreign branches are state licensed, owing to states like New York and California that have long histories of regulating foreign bank branches, Georgia does not allow foreign bank branches, a prohibition that extends to federally licensed branches, but does allow foreign bank agencies. GA. CODE ANN. §§ 7-1-710, 7-1-716(e) (LEXIS through 2015 Sess.). Why would a state prohibit foreign bank branches? Is it possible to imagine California, Florida, or New York passing such a law?

3. ***Resolution and Insolvency.*** Are the act-of-state type issues different if the home country proceeding is an insolvency proceeding? What would happen if, under home country law, a bank bails in uninsured depositors in a host country branch by writing them down or turning them into equity holders under of the new post-Financial Crisis resolution regimes. *See* Chapter 9.3. Will the host country law recognize that? Should it? Imagine that a German bank with a large wholesale New York branch has entered into a German resolution proceeding and all uninsured deposits have been haircut by 30%, including deposits in the New York branch. *See* Council Directive 2014/59, 2014 O.J. (L 173) (permitting bail-in of uninsured deposits). How should the New York courts view U.S. public policy with respect to the bail-in of deposits? Does it matter if there has been an explicit contractual consent?

4. ***Ring-Fencing Under New York Law.*** Foreign branches are treated as separate from their parent banks in other ways under state and federal law. For example, foreign branches are typically liquidated separately from their head office under state bank receivership laws. A New York State court upheld the Superintendent of Banks of the State of New York's seizure of all of the assets of a foreign bank's state agency and disbursement of these assets to the agency's creditors. *In re* Liquidation of the N.Y. Agency & Other Assets of the Bank of Credit & Commerce International, S.A. (BCCI), 587 N.Y.S.2d 524 (N.Y. Sup. Ct. 1992). This ring-fencing approach resulted in the agency's New York creditors receiving more than other international creditors, and the plaintiff failed to convince the court that N.Y. Banking Law § 606 unconstitutionally favored some creditors over others. The BCCI scandal is discussed in more detail later in the chapter and you will learn more about resolution and bail-in of debt in Part IX.

5. ***Long-Term Debt Issued by Branches.*** Securities issued or guaranteed by a bank are exempt under the Securities Act of 1933 (1933 Act), as well as the SEC, by a series of no-action letters and an interpretive statement issued in 1986, determined that securities issued or guaranteed by the branches of foreign banks are also exempt. As a result, foreign bank branches issue what are called § 3(a)(2) securities. *See* Securities Issued or Guaranteed by United States Branches or Agencies of Foreign Banks, Securities Act Interpretive Release No. 33-6661, 51 Fed. Reg. 34,460 (Sept. 29, 1986) (to be codified at 17 C.F.R. pts. 231 and 261). The OCC has explicitly limited the sale of such securities by federal branches to accredited investors. No such limit exists for state-licensed branches. 12 C.F.R. pt. 16.

D. NATIONAL TREATMENT AND THE INTERNATIONAL BANKING ACT

It was not until 1978 that there was any federal regulation of foreign bank representative offices, agencies, or branches. The International Banking Act of 1978 (IBA) was enacted after a period of intense expansion by foreign banks in the early 1970s and was, as statutes always are, a political compromise reflecting the competitive tensions of the time, many of which the prohibitions on interstate banking and corporate debt and equity underwriting have since disappeared. The following excerpt from the GAO report below describes its main provisions.

GAO, Foreign Banks: Assessing Their Role in the U.S. Banking System

GAO/GGD-96-26 (1996)

The IBA of 1978 stands as the landmark federal legislation affecting foreign bank operations in the United States. In passing the IBA, the United States adopted a policy of national treatment governing the activities of foreign banks. The goal of national treatment is to allow foreign banks to operate in the United States without incurring either significant advantage or disadvantage compared with U.S. banks. To implement this policy, the IBA brought U.S. branches and agencies of foreign banks under federal banking laws and regulations. The [Federal Reserve Board] was given regulatory authority for all U.S. international banking laws, which it administers through regulation K.

Before passage of the IBA, foreign branches and agencies operating in the United States enjoyed many regulatory advantages compared with U.S. banks. They were not subject to reserve requirements or deposit interest-rate ceilings, they could operate full-service branches in any state that allowed them to enter, and they could offer both commercial and investment banking services. The 1978 Act was designed to eliminate these advantages and to place foreign banks on an equal footing with U.S. banks. The act required foreign banks to choose a home state and prohibited them from establishing full-service branches in states outside the home state. The IBA also limited foreign bank involvement in U.S. securities and other nonbanking markets by restricting them to those activities that could be done by U.S. [BHCs].

The act also expanded the options of foreign banks. Prior to the IBA, only states could license foreign branches and agencies. Foreign banks were subject to the laws of the states in which they were licensed, and, in some cases, these laws were more restrictive than federal law for national banks. The act made federal licenses available to foreign banks. It also allowed foreign branches to obtain federal deposit insurance, requiring it for any branch with a significant amount of retail deposits. The act permitted foreign banks to establish Edge Act Corporations and it granted foreign branches and agencies access to the [Federal Reserve Board]'s discount window.

Although the IBA eliminated many of the advantages that foreign branches and agencies had over U.S. banks, those foreign branches and agencies that were already engaged in interstate branching or securities activities were allowed to continue these activities under the grandfathering provisions of the act. Restrictions, however, were applied to their growth. Foreign banks with interstate branches were only allowed to establish new full-service branches in their home state. They could not establish full-service branches in other states, even in those states where they were already located. Similarly, foreign banks with grandfathered securities activities were limited to those activities in which they were engaged (or had applied to engage) on the grandfather date. In addition, securities firms owned by foreign banks could only expand by internal growth—they were restricted from acquiring or merging with other securities firms or from expanding by hiring significant numbers of employees from other securities firms. Foreign banks that acquire U.S. banks lose their grandfathered securities rights.

With the exception of the grandfathered activities, the IBA and subsequent laws and regulations brought foreign banks under the same restrictions as those governing U.S. banks with some adaptations. The application of U.S. laws and regulations to foreign banks reflects the fact that structural and organizational differences exist between foreign and U.S. banks. For example, foreign banks are not generally organized under the holding company structure, as are most U.S. banks.

Because of these differences, subjecting foreign banks with branches and agencies in the United States to all U.S. laws and regulations without adaptation would likely violate the policy of national treatment. While this policy tries to ensure equal treatment of U.S. and foreign banks in the United States, it recognizes that equal treatment does not necessarily mean the same treatment. Similarly, the United States seeks to have the policy of national treatment applied to U.S. banks operating abroad.

---

1. ***Reciprocity.*** Congress could have embraced a different principle for regulating foreign banks: reciprocity. Instead of treating foreign banks the same as domestic banks, legislation based on reciprocity would restrict foreign bank activities to the extent that their home country restricts U.S. bank activities there, perhaps providing, at that time, an incentive for other countries to liberalize their regulation of foreign banks. One reason reciprocity was not embraced to the extent that national treatment was in the IBA, however, was that in 1978, foreign countries often imposed fewer restraints on U.S. banks than the United States itself did.

2. ***Passporting.*** The concept of national treatment is different from the EU's passporting model of the mid-1990s, a period in which the regional bloc started to create a single banking market among its member states. The Second Banking Directive, which entered into force in 1993, established single licensing for credit institution operations and mutual recognition of regulatory regimes. The Second Banking Directive allowed regulated credit institutions authorized to operate in one member state to expand to other member states, either physically or just through the provision of services, after notifying its home member state regulator, which will take primary responsibility for the credit institution. Host member state authorization is not required for the credit institution to branch throughout the EU, and it is not allowed to institute any barriers to entry. The initiative greatly benefited non-EU banks because they only needed to establish an entity in a single member state before expanding across the EU. *See* Council Directive 89/646, 1989 O.J. (L 386). What are the advantages and disadvantages of the passporting model?

3. ***Mutual Recognition/Substituted Compliance.*** In 2007, Ethiopis Tafara and Robert Peterson, both SEC attorneys at the time, published an article putting forward a mutual recognition proposal for foreign stock exchanges and broker-dealers. Under the proposal, the SEC would grant registration exemptions "based on . . . compliance with substantively comparable foreign securities regulations and laws and supervision by a foreign securities regulator with oversight powers and a regulatory and enforcement philosophy substantively similar to the SEC's." *See* Ethiopis Tafara & Robert J. Peterson, *A*

Blueprint for Cross-Border Access to U.S. Investors: A New International Framework, 48 HARV. INT'L L.J. 31, 32 (2007). Although the SEC and Australian Securities and Investments Commission's mutual recognition arrangement stalled during the Financial Crisis, the CFTC has incorporated substituted compliance into its approach to cross-border swap regulation. *See* Interpretive Guidance and Policy Statement Regarding Compliance with Certain Swap Regulations, 78 Fed. Reg. 45,292 (July 26, 2013); *see also* Part XI.

4. ***Regulation K.*** The Federal Reserve Board's regulations implementing the legislation discussed in this chapter and governing foreign bank operations in the United States are contained in Subpart B of Regulation K, 12 C.F.R. § 211. Section 211.23(f)(1) states that an FBO that is organized in a foreign country and that has more than half of its revenues and assets from overseas sources, known as a Qualifying Foreign Banking Organization (QFBO) may "engage in activities of any kind outside of the United States." Why is it necessary for the Federal Reserve Board to explicitly state that a Chinese bank, or any other foreign bank, can engage in any activities in China or elsewhere in Asia? *See* 12 U.S.C. § 3106(a).

Germany, unlike the United States, does not separate commerce and banking. Deutsche Bank has long owned a significant percentage of the Daimler Benz car company. Does the minority ownership by Deutsche Bank prohibit Daimler Benz from setting up a U.S. subsidiary that will manufacture cars in the United States? *See* 12 C.F.R. § 211.23(f)(5).

5. ***Gramm-Leach-Bliley Act (GLBA).*** The IBA's focus on national treatment and the establishment of competitive equality between domestic and foreign banks put foreign banks on equal footing when it came to the then-active political struggles over interstate branching and non-banking activities. The Riegle-Neal Act eased interstate restrictions for both domestic and foreign banks, allowing foreign banks to similarly grow beyond their home state via branch and bank acquisitions and mergers. *See* Chapter 2.1. Previously uninsured foreign bank branches were not subject to the Community Reinvestment Act (CRA), but the Riegle-Neal Act required newly acquired branches to remain subject to the CRA. GLBA relaxation of restrictions on non-banking activities similarly had an impact on both domestic and foreign banks. Foreign banks are thus allowed to form FHCs, even if they do not operate through a federally insured bank subsidiary. *See* Chapter 6.2. Before GLBA, certain foreign banks, namely QFBOs, were allowed to engage in then impermissible activities indirectly inside the United States by regulation. Over half of a QFBO's business must be banking and over half of a QFBO's banking business must be outside the United States. 12 C.F.R. § 211.23(a). This regulatory relief is still relevant after GLBA because it applies not only to non-banking activities, but also to nonfinancial activities broadly.

6. ***Investments in Commercial Companies.*** A bank from a universal banking country that relies heavily on tourism for its GDP owns 60% of its country's largest tourist and hotel company. The bank has a small uninsured branch in New York City. The tourist and hotel company has just acquired one of the largest U.S. hotel chains. Can the U.S. hotel subsidiary arrange air, car, or plane reservations for its U.S. customers? *See* 12 C.F.R. § 211.23(f)(5)(iii).

7. ***Grandfathering Provision.*** Foreign banks did not necessarily have to abruptly make changes to their U.S. operations after Congress passed the IBA, because the legislation contained grandfather provisions, including ones for the new interstate branching and non-banking activity restrictions. Similarly, the Federal Deposit Insurance Corporation Improvement Act of 1991 (FDICIA) attached a grandfather provision to its prohibition on foreign bank branches accepting retail deposits and receiving federal deposit insurance. Seven foreign banks retained insured branches as of 2014. Consider the different impacts of the policy choice to engage in grandfathering as opposed to a transition period. For example, both the new Basel III capital standards as discussed in Chapter 2.7, and the Volcker Rule as discussed in Chapter 6.1, have long transition periods. Other changes, such as insured branches under the IBA and unitary thrifts as discussed in Chapter 6.1, have created grandfather status for certain institutions. When might a policymaker choose one option over the other?

E. THE BCCI SCANDAL AND CONGRESSIONAL REACTION

The BCCI failure led to the Foreign Bank Supervision Enhancement Act of 1991 (FBSEA) which resulted in increased Federal Reserve Board control and approval over the opening of branches and a requirement, also endorsed by the Basel Committee, that a host country should require that a foreign bank be subject to comprehensive and consolidated supervision, known as CCS, in its home country before it can open a branch or acquire control of a commercial bank subsidiary in the host country. CCS has now been enacted in a number of countries.

BCCI was a clandestine private bank with a unique criminal structure. Unlike any ordinary bank, BCCI deliberately layered the corporate structure and fractured the record keeping, regulatory review, and audits to evade control or regulation by any government. This Karachi-based bank even infiltrated the U.S. market by secretly purchasing U.S. banks while opening branch offices of BCCI throughout the U.S., and eventually merging the institutions. Despite regulatory barriers, which delayed BCCI's entry, BCCI was ultimately successful in acquiring control of four banks, operating in seven states and the District of Colombia, with no jurisdiction successfully preventing BCCI's infiltration. To cover its operation, BCCI leveraged the reputation of several prominent U.S. politicians and well-connected former bank regulators. *See* JOHN KERRY & HANK BROWN, THE BCCI AFFAIR: A REPORT TO THE COMMITTEE ON FOREIGN RELATIONS 4–6 (1992). When BCCI finally collapsed in 1991, it was the largest corporate criminal enterprise and the biggest Ponzi scheme to date. Jonathan Beaty & S.C. Gwynne, *B.C.C.I.: The Dirtiest Bank of All*, TIME, July 29, 1991.

In response to the BCCI Scandal, Chairman Alan Greenspan of the Federal Reserve Board recommended several legislative changes in the letter excerpted below.

Letter to Chairman Donald W. Riegle, Jr., Senate Committee on Banking, Housing, and Urban Affairs from Alan Greenspan

1991

The [Federal Reserve Board]'s first recommendation would require federal approval for foreign banks seeking to establish state licensed branches and agencies or commercial lending subsidiaries in this country. Under the IBA, the [Federal Reserve Board] is given certain responsibilities for the supervision of foreign banks in the United States, but no federal agency has a voice in the decision as to whether individual institutions seeking to enter U.S. markets through state branches and agencies, commercial lending companies, or representative offices meet the standards generally applicable to banking organizations in this country. . . .

The [Federal Reserve Board] believes that it is desirable to have clear and definite standards governing the entry of foreign banks into the United States. These would include consideration of whether a foreign bank has the financial and managerial resources and banking expertise to operate in the United States and whether the bank is subject to comprehensive supervision on a consolidated basis by home country authorities. We believe this latter standard is of particular importance when dealing with a financial institution that operates internationally because only if the institution is reviewed on a consolidated basis can there be any certainty as to its condition and the extent and lawfulness of its operations. . . .

In addition to new authority to govern the entry of foreign banks into the United States, the [Federal Reserve Board] recommends that the activities of a foreign bank through a branch, agency, commercial lending subsidiary or representative office in the United States be subject to termination by federal authorities for a violation of law or for an unsafe or unsound banking practice where the continued operation of the office or subsidiary would not be consistent with the public interest or relevant statutory standards. . . .

Given the [Federal Reserve Board's] responsibility under the statute for the supervision of a foreign bank's overall operations in the United States, the [Federal Reserve Board] believes that the IBA should be amended to remove the requirement that the [Federal Reserve Board] defer to other regulators in exercising its examination authority. If the proposed provision is adopted, the [Federal Reserve Board] would consult with state and other authorities regarding the frequency and type of examination program for foreign bank offices, in the same fashion it does currently in the case of examinations of state member banks.

Following the BCCI affair, Congress swiftly passed the FBSEA in 1991. The FBSEA bars the entry of a foreign bank into the U.S., unless it is subject to consolidated home country supervision and agrees to permit supervisory access to any information regarding it that U.S. regulators request. It also extends to foreign banks the same financial, managerial, and operational standards governing U.S. banks. Finally, the FBSEA grants the Federal Reserve Board the authority to examine any office of a foreign bank and to terminate the activities of any foreign bank that is engaging in illegal, unsafe, or unsound practices. JOHN KERRY & HANK BROWN, THE BCCI AFFAIR: A REPORT TO THE COMMITTEE ON FOREIGN RELATIONS 338.

---

1. ***Federal Reserve Board Prior Approval.*** FBOs must receive Federal Reserve Board prior approval opening a state or federally licensed U.S. branch or acquire control of a subsidiary bank or a BHC. 12 U.S.C. §§ 3105, 1842. The Federal Reserve Board must find that the FBO is subject to CCS in its home country, a standard comparable to that required by the Basel Committee. *Id.* § 1842(c)(3). To determine whether an FBO is subject to CCS, the Federal Reserve Board assesses, among other things, whether the home country supervisor ensures that the FBO has proper policies and procedures in place and monitors the FBO's prudential standards. 12 C.F.R. § 211.24(c). For example, in 2012, the Federal Reserve Board conferred CCS status to three state-owned Chinese institutions and approved their request to acquire control of the Bank of East Asia, a U.S. national bank, finding that,

> authorities in China have continued to enhance the standards of consolidated supervision to which banks in China are subject, including through additional or refined statutory authority, regulations, and guidance; adoption of international standards and best practices; enhancements to the supervisory system arising out of supervisory experiences; upgrades to the [China Banking Regulatory Commission] in the areas of organization, technological capacity, staffing, and training; and increased coordination between the [China Banking Regulatory Commission] and other financial supervisory authorities in China.

Indus. & Commercial Bank of China Ltd., China Inv. Corp., Ctr. Huijin Inv. Ltd., Order Approving Acquisition of Shares of a Bank, 98 Fed. Res. Bull. 1, 6–7 (2012).

2. ***Ability to Terminate.*** The FBSEA authorizes the Federal Reserve Board to terminate a foreign bank's U.S. presence, if the bank is not subject to CCS and the home country is not making progress in CCS or if the foreign bank's U.S. operations are reasonably believed to be unsafe and unsound or in violation of law. 12 U.S.C. § 3105(e)(1). The Federal Reserve Board has used this authority only once, when it terminated the New York branch of Daiwa Bank after a senior official at the branch confessed to losing $1.1 billion on secret trades, losses that he accumulated and covered up for 11 years. Daiwa consented to the Federal Reserve Board's termination order. *See* In the Matter of Daiwa Bank, Ltd. Osaka, Japan and Daiwa Bank, Ltd. New, Docket No. 95-028-B-FB (1995). The Dodd-Frank Act, in § 173, expanded the termination power when a foreign bank presents a risk to U.S. financial stability. 12 U.S.C. § 3105(e)(1)(C).

3. ***Examinations.*** Bank regulators, coordinated by the Federal Reserve Board, examine foreign bank branches for risk management, operational controls, compliance, and asset quality. Regulators assign an overall rating as well as a rating for each component. The Federal Reserve Board also assign foreign banks a Strength of Support Assessment rating, reflecting the overall condition. Weak examination outcomes can slow down or halt a foreign bank's expansion in the United States and result in increased regulatory scrutiny.

F. FOREIGN BANKS AND THE FINANCIAL CRISIS

After the Financial Crisis, the Federal Reserve Board began another re-examination of the role of the branches of foreign banks in the United States, driven in part by the high usage by certain foreign banks of the Federal Reserve Board's discount window, concerns about the liquidity and stability of some foreign banks, and the need to develop an effective international resolution framework, as discussed in Part IX. As Lawrence Broz notes,

> During the financial crisis of 2007-2010, the [Federal Reserve Board] served as a global lender of last resort providing dollar liquidity to foreign banks with significant dollar-denominated exposures. Through bilateral agreements known as "Central Bank Liquidity Swap Lines," the [Federal Reserve Board] channeled over half a trillion dollars to foreign central banks, which then used the dollars to provide liquidity to private financial institutions in their jurisdictions. As the only central bank capable of providing an unlimited supply of dollars, the [Federal Reserve Board] became the world's *de facto* lender of last resort.

The Politics of Rescuing the World's Financial System: The Federal Reserve as a Global Lender of Last Resort, 13 KOR. J. OF INT'L STUD. 323, 324 (2015).

In 2011, Bloomberg News acquired data on the Federal Reserve Board's emergency lending programs during the Financial Crisis. The data revealed that foreign banks were active borrowers. For example, foreign banks accounted for approximately 70% of the $110 billion borrowed at the discount window during the first week of October 2008. Bradley Keoun & Craig Torres, *Foreign Banks Used Fed Secret Lifeline Most at Crisis Peak*, BLOOMBERG, Apr. 1, 2011. Indeed, the Federal Reserve Board came under criticism for the its role as a lender of last resort to foreign banks, likely contributing to the U.S. House of Representatives passing the Federal Reserve Transparency Act both in 2012 and 2014, although this piece of legislation stalled in the Senate.

Moreover, the Dodd-Frank Act's Collins Amendment essentially imposed new capital requirements on foreign banks' U.S. intermediate holding companies, which are holding companies for an FBO's bank subsidiaries, by no longer allowing them to rely on home country capital. In response, some large FBOs moved to restructure their U.S. banking operations to avoid the new requirements, which provoked a supervisory reaction. The following speech by Tarullo was the beginning of this period of restructuring.

Daniel Tarullo, Governor, Fed. Reserve Bd.,
Regulation of Foreign Banking Organizations

Speech at Yale School of Management Leaders Forum, New Haven, CT (Nov. 28, 2012)

Although foreign banks expanded steadily in the United States during the 1970s, 1980s, and 1990s, their activities here posed limited risks to overall U.S. financial stability. Throughout this period, the U.S. operations of foreign banks were largely net recipients of funding from their parents and generally engaged in traditional lending to home-country and U.S. clients. U.S. branches and agencies of foreign banks held large amounts of cash during the 1980s and '90s, in part to meet asset-maintenance and asset-pledge requirements put in place by regulators. Their cash-to-third-party liability ratio from the mid-1980s through the late 1990s generally ranged between 25 percent and 30 percent.

The U.S. branches and agencies of foreign banks that borrowed from their parents and lent those funds in the United States ("lending branches") held roughly 60 percent of all foreign bank branch and agency assets in the United States during the 1980s and '90s. Commercial and industrial lending continued to account for a large part of foreign bank branch and agency balance sheets through the 1990s.

This profile of foreign bank operations in the United States changed in the run-up to the financial crisis. Reliance on less stable, short-term wholesale funding increased significantly. Many foreign banks shifted from the "lending branch" model to a "funding branch" model, in which U.S. branches of foreign banks were borrowing large amounts of U.S. dollars to upstream to their parents. These "funding branches" went from holding 40 percent of foreign bank branch assets in the mid-1990s to holding 75 percent of foreign bank branch assets by 2009. Foreign banks as a group moved from a position of receiving funding from their parents on a net basis in 1999 to providing significant funding to non-U.S. affiliates by the mid-2000s—more than $700 billion on a net basis by 2008.

A good bit of this short-term funding was used to finance long-term, U.S. dollar-denominated project and trade finance around the world. There is also evidence that a significant portion of the dollars raised by European banks in the pre-crisis period ultimately returned to the United States in the form of investments in U.S. securities. Indeed, the amount of U.S. dollar-denominated asset-backed securities and other securities held by Europeans increased significantly between 2003 and 2007, much of it financed by the short-term, dollar-denominated liabilities of European banks. Meanwhile, commercial and industrial lending originated by U.S. branches and agencies as a share of their third-party liabilities fell significantly after 2003. In contrast, U.S. broker-dealer assets of the top-10 foreign banks increased rapidly during the past 15 years, rising from 13 percent of all foreign bank third-party assets in 1995 to 50 percent in 2011.

G. THE INTERMEDIATE HOLDING COMPANY REQUIREMENT

As a result of its experience in the Financial Crisis and its views about the need for a stronger base of capital, liquidity, risk governance, and stress testing at the largest FBOs with more than $50 billion in assets at their combined broker-dealer and commercial bank subsidiaries, the Federal Reserve Board passed new regulations imposing enhanced, prudential standards on FBOs in 2014. The new rule requires a dozen or so of the very largest FBOs in the United States to form intermediate holding companies, which would then be subject to various capital, liquidity and other regulatory requirements. Figures 6.3-3 and 6.3-4 show how an FBO's U.S. structure has to change under the Enhanced Prudential Standards rule.

Figure 6.3-3 U.S. Operations Before Establishing an Intermediate Holding Company

Foreign Bank
U.S. Branch
Non-U.S. Commercial Company
Other holding companies omitted for simplification
DPC Branch Subsidiary
U.S. Funding Vehicle
U.S. Commercial Company (Section 2(n)(2) Company)
U.S. Bank Holding Company
U.S. Bank
U.S. Broker-Dealer
U.S. Financial Company
U.S. Commercial Company (Merchant Banking Authority)
U.S. Operating Subsidiary
Edge Act Subsidiary
Non-U.S. Company
Non-U.S. Company
Non-U.S. Company
U.S. legal entity
Subject to U.S. Basel III and Dodd-Frank stress testing requirements. If ≥ $50 billion in assets, also subject to capital planning, liquidity, risk management and other EPS on a consolidated basis
Non-U.S. legal entity
"Control" relationship under Federal Reserve's definition of "control"

Source: Davis Polk & Wardwell LLP, U.S. Intermediate Holding Company: Structuring and Regulatory Considerations for Foreign Banks (Apr. 2, 2014).

Figure 6.3-4 U.S. Operations After Establishing an Intermediate Holding Company

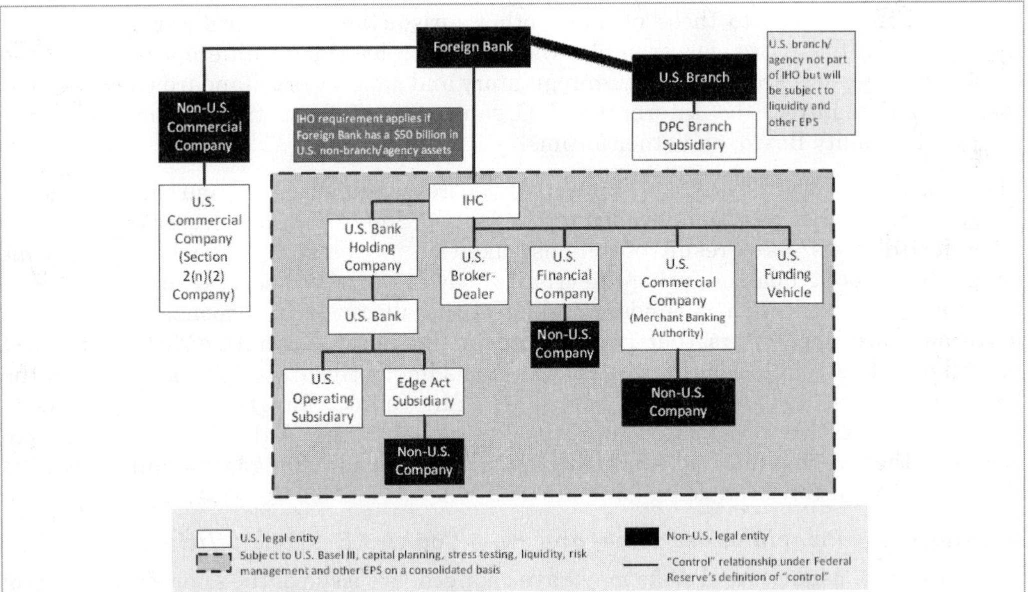

Source: Davis Polk & Wardwell LLP.

Tarullo defended the intermediate holding company policy at a dinner gathering of international bankers in the following excerpt.

Daniel Tarullo, Governor, Fed. Reserve Bd., An Agenda for Europe and the United States: Regulating Large Foreign Banking Organizations

Speech at Harvard Law School Symposium on Building the Financial System of the Twenty-First Century (Mar. 27, 2014)

The financial crisis exposed, in painful and dramatic fashion, the shortcomings of existing regulatory and supervisory regimes. In both the United States and the [EU], the crisis also revealed some particular vulnerabilities created by foreign banking operations. This evening I would like to focus on these vulnerabilities and on how best we should address them.

Let me note at the outset the now commonplace observation that we have a quite integrated international financial system, with many large, globally active firms operating within a system of national government and regulation or, in the case of the EU, a hybrid of regional and national regulation. I add the equally commonplace observation that there is no realistic prospect for having a global banking regulator and, consequently, the responsibility and authority for financial stability will continue to rest with national or regional authorities. The question, then, is how responsibility for oversight of these large firms can be most effectively shared among regulators. This, of course, is the important issue underlying the perennial challenge of home-host supervisory relations.

Another introductory observation is that—at least in a world of nations with substantially different economic circumstances, different currencies, and banking and capital markets of quite different levels of depth and development—there will be good reason to vary at least some forms of regulation across countries. Presumptively, at least, nations should be able to adjust their regulatory systems based on local circumstances and their relative level of risk aversion as it pertains to the potential for financial instability. Although the financial systems and economies of the United States and the EU are more similar to one another than they are to those of many other jurisdictions, they are hardly identical. Even between these two, for example, there may be legitimate differences within the broader convergence around minimum regulatory and supervisory standards developed at the Basel Committee, the International Organization of Securities Commissions, the Financial Stability Board, and other forums.

These opening observations are important in responding to the curious charge of "Balkanization" that has been levelled at the United States and, to a lesser extent, some other jurisdictions, as a result of actions taken or proposed in response to problems presented by foreign banks during the crisis. I say "curious" for several reasons. One is that the charge reflects a misunderstanding of the allocation of responsibility between home and host supervisors that has evolved in the Basel Committee during the past several decades. Another is that the charge seems implicitly, and oddly, premised on the notion that what we had in 2007 was a well-functioning, integrated global financial system with effective consolidated supervision of global banks. A third is that the charge overlooks the fact that much of what the United States is now doing is matching what the EU has quite sensibly been doing for years. . . .

International Principles on Home- and Host-Country Responsibilities

While the circumstances and risks may have changed, the issue of the appropriate roles of home and host countries is not a new one. Indeed, it was a key motivation for creation of the Basel Committee in 1975 following the failures of the Herstatt and Franklin National banks. Many of the Basel Committee's early activities were focused on the challenges created by gaps in the supervision of internationally active banks, as evidenced by the fact that Basel "Concordats" on supervision preceded Basel "Accords" and "Frameworks" on capital and other subjects. This task has, of necessity, been ongoing, as experience revealed gaps in supervisory coverage and as the scale and scope of internationally active banks grew. The principle of consolidated supervision emerged in the early 1980s to ensure that some specific banking authority—generally the home-country regulator—had a complete view of the assets and liabilities of the bank. This principle was reinforced and elaborated following the [BCCI] episode in the early 1990s.

It is important to note that each Basel Committee declaration on the importance of home-country consolidated oversight has also included a statement of the obligations and prerogatives of host states in which significant foreign bank operations are located. This feature of the Basel Committee's approach makes sense as a reflection both of the host authority's responsibility for stability of its financial system and of the practical point that a host authority will be more familiar with the characteristics and risks in its market. In accordance with this history, the current version of the "Core Principles for Effective Banking Supervision" sets out as one of its "essential criteria" for home-host relationships that "[t]he host supervisor's national laws or regulations require that the cross-border operations of foreign banks are subject to prudential, inspection and regulatory reporting requirements similar to those for domestic banks."

It is clear, then, that consolidated supervision is not intended to displace host-country supervision. Instead, as the Basel Committee has regularly noted, the two are intended to be complementary, so as to assure effective oversight of large, internationally active banks. Similarly, the stated purpose of the Basel Committee in requiring consolidated capital requirements is not to remove from host countries any responsibility or discretion to apply regulatory capital requirements, but to "preserve the integrity of capital in banks with subsidiaries by eliminating double gearing." Likewise, and contrary to suggestions that are sometimes made, the capital accords and frameworks developed by the Basel Committee have always been explicitly *minimum* requirements. They are floors, not ceilings.

Finally, it is worth noting that, in establishing a post-crisis framework for domestic systemically important banks (D-SIBs), the Basel Committee made clear that a host country may in appropriate circumstances designate domestic operations of a foreign bank as systemically important for that country, even if the parent foreign bank has already been designated a global systemically important bank (G-SIB). . . . I cite this feature of the D-SIB framework that permits designation of the domestic operations of foreign G-SIBs because it reflects rather clearly the principle that the specific characteristics of domestic markets may call for regulation of foreign banks in the host country, not just at a consolidated level.

In short, the work of the Basel Committee over the years has not been directed at restraining host-country authorities from supervising and regulating foreign banking operations in their country. On the contrary, the committee has repeatedly asserted the complementary responsibilities of both home and host countries to oversee large, internationally active banking groups, in the interests of both national and international financial stability. And the committee has frequently returned to this set of issues in responding to developments that pose a threat to the safety and soundness of the international financial system. . . .

The Regulatory Response

In a sense, the major strengthening during the past few years of capital and liquidity requirements for internationally active banks—including the capital surcharge for banks of global systemic importance—has to date been the most important international regulatory response to the revealed vulnerabilities associated with large foreign banking operations. Building capital and improving the liquidity positions of banks on a consolidated basis is surely a key step toward assuring the stability of major FBOs in host countries. . . .

The EU has not, since the crisis, specifically adjusted the structure of regulation of foreign banks by its member states in their role as host supervisors. For more than a decade before the crisis, EU member states had prudently required that not only commercial banking, but also investment banking subsidiaries of foreign (non-EU-based) banking organizations, be subject to Basel capital requirements in the same way as EU-based firms. With the adoption of CRD IV, the directive implementing the new EU capital requirements, Basel III will now be applied to all EU firms, including EU bank and investment bank subsidiaries of non-EU banking organizations. Branches of non-EU banks are generally not subject to local requirements.

Before the crisis and the subsequent development of Basel III, there was no leverage ratio requirement in EU capital directives. Insofar as a new leverage ratio is part of the Basel III package agreed upon internationally, one would anticipate that it will be applied to commercial banking and investment banking firms in the EU, again including local subsidiaries of non-EU firms. Likewise, one would anticipate that the Basel III liquidity requirements will be implemented in the EU in accordance with the internationally agreed timeline and, again, that it will apply to EU subsidiaries of FBOs.

A greater challenge for the EU has been dealing with banks headquartered in one EU country but doing business in other EU countries under the "single passport," which basically allows for full access in the rest of the EU, with supervision provided only by the home country. During the crisis, there were some notable instances of banking stresses and failures involving such institutions, with consequent negative effects on depositors, counterparties, and economies in other parts of the EU. Much of the ongoing post-crisis reform agenda in Europe seems directed at ensuring the safety and soundness of EU-based institutions. The most important of these changes may be the assumption by the European Central Bank of supervisory responsibility for larger euro area banks. And, as we saw just last week, work continues on the long process of creating a credible resolution mechanism for those banks.

As a member state of the EU, the United Kingdom of course implements the EU policies I have just described. But that country has applied an additional set of requirements on the local operations of foreign banks, particularly with respect to liquidity. The Prudential Regulation Authority of the Bank of England applies local liquidity requirements to commercial and investment banking subsidiaries of non-U.K. banks, requiring them to hold local buffers as determined by internal stress tests with both 14- and 90-day components. The assumptions on which the stress tests are premised are quite strict. For example, the U.K. subsidiary generally must assume zero inflows from non-U.K. affiliates—even for claims on non-U.K. affiliates with short terms that mature within the stress test period—and 100 percent outflows to non-U.K. affiliates. The requirements generated by the test are subject to a supervisory review and add-on that for some firms has resulted in a significant increase in the buffer requirement. Branches of foreign commercial banks may in some circumstances be subject to local liquidity requirements as well.

The U.K. initiative in applying local liquidity requirements is wholly understandable in light of the difficulties encountered because of stress on foreign institutions, including the Lehman bankruptcy, during the crisis. Because London is one of the world's two largest financial center hosts, the United Kingdom is the only country other than the United States hosting numerous, very large broker-dealers that are owned by foreign banks and also a broad array of commercial bank subsidiaries and branches that are owned by foreign banks. In fact, the six institutions headquartered outside the United States and the United Kingdom that are in the top three tiers of G-SIBs hold roughly 40 percent of their worldwide assets in those two jurisdictions. Thus the U.K. initiative on liquidity and its internal debates on matters such as structural supervision, the Vickers proposals, and stress testing have all been very instructive for the Federal Reserve Board. Even where we have eventually adopted somewhat different approaches, we respect the motivation and scrupulousness of the U.K. banking authorities in addressing the systemic vulnerabilities posed by FBOs and in fulfilling their responsibility to the rest of the world to assure the stability of one of the world's two most important financial centers.

Unlike the EU, the United States did not—prior to the financial crisis—require that all broker-dealers and investment banks meet Basel capital standards. The legacy of the Glass-Steagall Act, which had separated investment banking from commercial banking, meant that only commercial banks were subject to the prudential regulation of the federal banking agencies. In Europe, the dominance of universal banking, or variants thereon, led more naturally to application of capital and other prudential standards to all forms of banking activity. Even after the [GLBA] removed the remaining barriers to affiliation between investment banks and commercial banks in the United States, Basel capital requirements applied at a consolidated level to the activities of an investment bank or broker-dealer only if it did affiliate with a commercial bank. Thus, the five large "free-standing" U.S. investment banks were generally not subject to full application of Basel capital standards.

During the crisis, the ill-advised nature of this regulatory state of affairs became apparent. The decline in value of many mortgage-backed securities and the consequent market uncertainty as to the true value of that entire class of securities raised questions about the solvency of major broker-dealers. Because the dealers were so highly leveraged and dependent on short-term financing, the uncertainty also led to serious liquidity strains, first at Bear Stearns and Lehman Brothers and eventually at most dealers—domestic and foreign owned. Bear Stearns and Merrill Lynch were acquired by existing [BHCs] after coming close to failure. Lehman Brothers went bankrupt. Goldman Sachs and Morgan Stanley became [BHCs].

Through its Primary Dealer Credit Facility, the [Federal Reserve Board] provided substantial liquidity to the broker-dealer affiliates of the [BHCs], as well as to the primary dealer subsidiaries of foreign banks. At the same time, the shift in strategy of many foreign banks toward using their U.S. branches to raise dollars in short-term markets for lending around the world created another set of vulnerabilities that resulted in substantial and, relative to total assets, disproportionate use of the [Federal Reserve Board]'s discount window by foreign bank branches. . . .

Congress also required the [Federal Reserve Board] to apply special prudential standards to large FBOs. As I have already implied, much of what we have done is simply to catch up to EU and U.K. practice. Under our recently finalized Section 165 enhanced prudential standards regulation, an FBO with U.S. non-branch assets of $50 billion or more must hold its U.S. subsidiaries under an intermediate holding company (IHC), which must meet the risk-based and leverage capital standards generally applicable to [BHCs] under U.S. law. Such an FBO must also certify that it meets consolidated capital adequacy standards established by its home-country supervisor that are consistent with the Basel Capital Framework. FBOs with combined U.S. assets of $50 billion or more must also meet liquidity risk-management standards and conduct internal liquidity stress tests. The IHC must maintain a liquidity buffer in the United States for a 30-day liquidity stress test. The U.S. branches and agencies of an FBO must maintain a liquidity buffer in the United States equal to the liquidity needs for 14 days, as determined by a 30-day liquidity stress test. The IHCs of FBOs must also conform to certain risk-management and supervisory requirements at the IHC level.

Structurally, the U.S. capital requirements for FBOs are similar to those that apply to foreign banks in the EU. That is, generally applicable Basel capital requirements are applied to the U.S. operations of FBOs that own local banking subsidiaries, investment banks, and broker-dealers. In fact, the new U.S. rules are somewhat more favorable to foreign institutions, in that they only apply once the non-branch U.S. assets of an FBO exceed $50 billion. That dollar amount, incidentally, is the same as the Dodd-Frank threshold for more stringent prudential measures, though note that this statutory threshold applies if the *total* assets of any U.S. banking organization—foreign, as well as domestic—exceed that level. As in the EU, the capital requirements do not apply to U.S. branches of foreign banks, even though the crisis experience provides some credible arguments for doing so.

The leverage ratio requirement has received particular attention. One complaint is that the foreign operations of U.S. banks are not subject to leverage ratios for their local operations. It is true that many foreign countries—including the EU member states—do not currently have leverage ratio standards for their banks. As noted earlier, however, one may reasonably expect that those countries will be implementing the Basel III leverage ratio in a timely fashion. Also, I would note in passing that the U.S. leverage ratio requirement for foreign firms will be phased in more slowly than originally proposed, so as to align it more closely with the effective date of the Basel III leverage ratio requirement.

A second complaint is that there is something unfair about the United States requiring an FBO to meet the international leverage ratio in its U.S. operations, because its operations may be heavily weighted toward broker-dealer activities, which generally have higher leverage, whereas the leverage ratio for U.S. firms is based on their global operations. Again, one suspects that the foreign operations of U.S. firms could be subject to a similar ratio requirement abroad as countries implement their Basel III commitments. However, quite apart from what may happen in the future, there are two U.S.-based firms—Goldman Sachs and Morgan Stanley—whose global business mix resembles that of the U.S. subsidiaries of FBOs that are predominantly engaged in broker-dealer activities in the United States. In fact, under the enhanced supplementary leverage ratio the [Federal Reserve Board] proposed during the summer, these and other U.S. G-SIBs would be subject to a higher Basel III leverage ratio requirement (5 percent) than would apply to FBO IHCs (3 percent).

The applicable liquidity requirements, while somewhat differently defined, are roughly comparable to those already applicable to FBOs in the United Kingdom. The similar positions of our two nations as host countries for foreign bank operations heavily involved in trading and significantly reliant on potentially runnable short-term wholesale funding explain this rough parallelism.

The most notable departure of the new U.S. FBO standards from existing EU and U.K. practice lies in the IHC requirement for foreign banks with large domestic operations. Given the structure of U.S. financial regulation that is a legacy of Glass-Steagall, as well as the efforts by a small number of very large foreign banks to evade the intent of Congress that capital standards apply to their U.S. operations, we needed to create this structural requirement. It is unclear how much difference this makes for the capital requirements of FBOs in the United States as opposed, say, to those of U.S. operations in the EU. That would depend on the existence and size of financial affiliates owned by the U.S. firm that are not subject to Basel standards directly. In any case, it seems sound prudential practice—and consistent with the various Basel Committee principles to which I earlier referred—that large domestic operations of foreign banks meet capital standards on the basis of all exposures in the host jurisdiction and, indeed, that they manage their risks in that country across all their affiliates.

"Balkanization" and Home-Host Responsibilities

To return to the issue of Balkanization, three things should now be apparent. First, in its new capital regulations applicable to FBOs, the United States is more a follower of the pattern set by the EU than it is an initiator of new kinds of requirements. Of course, a few foreign banks would prefer the old system under which they held relatively little capital in their very extensive U.S. operations. But that was neither safe for the financial system nor particularly fair to their competitors—U.S. and foreign—that hold significant amounts of capital here. Indeed, a firm that is genuinely well capitalized, including holding the G-SIB surcharge at its global consolidated level, should require only moderate adjustment efforts during the transition period established in the FBO rule.

Second, there is considerable scope for a foreign bank to integrate its U.S. operations with its global activities within the rule the [Federal Reserve Board] adopted last month. For example, while foreign firms with more than $10 billion in non-branch assets have some additional reporting requirements, only when U.S. non-branch assets rise above $50 billion do the quantitative Basel capital requirements become applicable to the U.S. subsidiaries. Moreover, no capital requirements apply to branches so long as their parent is subject to home-country consolidated capital rules consistent with Basel standards. The U.S. operations of FBO branches and subsidiaries will not be subject to "due from" restrictions. They remain free to lend money to their worldwide affiliates; they must simply do so with a more stable funding base. Finally, I note that many FBOs, like many U.S.-based banks, have made considerable progress in reducing dependence on short-term wholesale funding and in building capital. To some extent, the new requirements are intended to preserve this progress.

Third, the capital and liquidity requirements that do apply are wholly consistent with the responsibility of host-country supervisors to assure financial stability in their own markets. Collectively, foreign banks with a large presence in the United States conduct activities of a scope, and at a scale, that could lead to problems for the U.S. financial system should they come under stress. Realistically, exposures and vulnerabilities in a large host-country market are much more difficult for home-country supervisors to assess. Indeed, U.S. regulators count on the expertise and proximity of U.K. regulators in overseeing the London operations of large U.S. financial institutions to enhance the effective consolidated supervision and regulation for which we are responsible.

On the issue of home-host-country coordination in regulating large, globally active banking organizations . . . . we—by which I mean both home and major host banking regulators—need to find better ways of fostering genuine regulatory and supervisory cooperation. Particularly at the most senior levels of the agencies that actually supervise globally active banks, our interactions with our counterparts from other countries have become almost exclusively focused on developing international standards or reviewing compliance with existing ones. These discussions are usually conducted with numerous colleagues who are not themselves responsible for banking regulation in their own jurisdictions. As important as these efforts have been, and continue to be, following the crisis, there is a risk that by not having opportunities for senior officials of the various national agencies that have direct supervisory responsibility for banking organizations to meet and discuss shared challenges, we give short shrift to the collective interest of bank regulators in effective supervision of *all* globally active firms. Proposals to include prudential requirements or, more precisely, to include limitations on prudential requirements in trade agreements would lead us farther away from the aforementioned goal of emphasizing shared financial stability interests, in favor of an approach to prudential matters informed principally by considerations of commercial advantage.

Conclusion

The job of regulating and supervising large, globally active banking organizations is a tough one. Issues of moral hazard, negative externalities, and asymmetric information are, if not pervasive, then at least significant and recurring. The job is made only harder by the fact that these firms cross borders in ways their regulators do not. But we cannot ignore this fact and pretend that we have global oversight. International standards for prudential regulation are not the same as global regulations, and consolidated supervision is not the same as comprehensive supervision. The jurisdictions represented on the Basel Committee not only have the right to regulate their financial markets—including large FBOs participating in those markets—they have a responsibility to their home jurisdictions, and to the rest of the world, to do so. The most important contribution the United States can make to global financial stability is to ensure the stability of our own financial system.

There must be some assurance beyond mere words from parent banks or home-country supervisors that a large FBO will remain strong or supported in periods of stress. After all, as we saw in the crisis, while a parent bank or home-country authorities may have offered those words with total good faith in calm times, they may be unable to carry through on them in more financially turbulent periods. None of this means that we need be at odds with one another. On the contrary, these very circumstances call not only for more tangible safeguards in host countries, but also for more genuine cooperation among supervisory authorities. Indeed, as I hope will continue to be the case with the international agenda on resolution, total loss absorbency, and related matters, we should aspire to converge around the kinds of protections that we can expect at both consolidated and local levels.

---

1. ***Following, Not Leading.*** Why did Tarullo feel that it was wise or necessary to assert that the United States was following the lead of the EU and the UK by imposing new requirements of capital and liquidity and the new requirement that an IHC be formed?

2. ***Balkanization.*** What is behind the criticism of Balkanization? While there are reasons to support consolidated regulation, Balkanization can ensure "that an array of viewpoints temper regulatory decision-making so that financial regulation decisions, given their far-reaching consequences, are not mistakenly applied or abused." *See* Sabrina Pellerin et al., *The Consolidation of Financial Market Regulation: Pros, Cons, and Implications for the United States* 3 (Federal Reserve Bank of Richmond, Working Paper No. 09-08, 2009).

III. U.S. BANKS ABROAD

A. OVERVIEW

American banks came to international banking quite late compared to European banks, which had been international in scope even before the age of their colonial empires, which created powerful trading and banking routes. During the 19th Century, UK banks, riding the power of the British Empire, were much more important to international trade, while U.S. banks, with their strong domestic focus, were heavily dependent upon the more powerful UK banks in almost all things international. The United States was not an economic powerhouse until the late 19th Century, and the dollar was unimportant in international trade during the Gilded Age.

It was not until World War I that U.S. banks and the dollar became important internationally. The laws and regulations, developed in an era of unit banking and very limited interstate branching, were slow to permit foreign branches. Although not strictly true, the National Monetary Commission commented in 1910 that "[w]e have no American banking institutions in foreign countries. The organization of such banks is necessary for the development of our foreign trade." National banks were only permitted to open foreign branches, with Federal Reserve Board approval, after the Federal Reserve Act in 1913 and were not permitted to own the stock of foreign banks directly. At that time, not a single U.S. bank was on the list of the world's top ten banks as measured by deposits. MIRA WILKINS, THE HISTORY OF FOREIGN INVESTMENT IN THE UNITED STATES TO 1914 454. The Edge Act corporation, discussed later in this Chapter, was created by statute in 1919 to permit national banks to engage more in international trade and to invest in foreign banks. While there were extensive international capital flows between World War I and the Great Depression and a number of the larger U.S. banks, typically New York banks, began to open branches during this time, large U.S. banks did not begin to extensively open overseas branches or invest in foreign banks until the mid-20th Century, riding the same wave of trade growth and the dollar as the reserve currency that brought foreign banks to the United States. For more on the early history of U.S. banks abroad, see CLYDE WILLIAM PHELPS, THE FOREIGN EXPANSION OF AMERICAN BANKS (1976).

The development of the Eurodollar and the Eurobond markets brought about major changes in the international orientation of the large money center U.S. commercial and investment banking groups. During the 1980s and 1990s, large New York money center banking organizations expanded in Europe, largely through London branches and by taking advantage, through foreign broker-dealer affiliates, of the greater scope for debt and equity underwriting that the Federal Reserve Board had determined to be usual in connection with the business of banking abroad. The large U.S. investment banks also expanded into London during this period. By sharp contrast, virtually all regional and community BHCs remained very domestic in their business models. In the international arena, the largest U.S. BHCs were hampered in their ability to compete against banks from the universal banking model countries, and there were fears in the late 1980s and early 1990s that U.S. BHCs were not among the world's largest. As the Glass-Steagall Act barriers slowly eroded during the 1990s, culminating in GLBA, some U.S. BHCs and investment banks grew quite large and those fears faded somewhat, although U.S. banking organizations are now smaller on a global scale.

The early 2000s saw growth in Asia and Latin America, although large U.S. BHCs remained quite concentrated in London. Indeed, the FDIC conducted a heat map exercise of five U.S. systemically important financial institutions that showed that 88% of reported foreign activity, assets, and some off-balance sheet items of those institutions' foreign subsidiaries and branches were in the UK. FDIC, INTERNATIONAL RESOLUTION COORDINATION OVERVIEW 4 (Jan. 25, 2012).

B. THE GROWTH OF U.S. BANKS' INTERNATIONAL ACTIVITIES AND EDGE ACT CORPORATIONS

The restrictions on bank powers explains in large part why U.S. banks were slow to expand abroad. The following excerpt considers the legal forms available to a U.S. bank seeking to enter a foreign market. While the excerpt is from 1999, it nicely captures the state of play even today.

James Houpt, International Activities of U.S. Banks and in U.S. Banking Markets

85 Fed. Res. Bull. 599 (1999)

For U.S. banks, the 1960s and 1970s were years of rapid growth in international banking. The few truly global ones, which had long before ventured abroad, refined their networks and penetrated foreign markets more deeply. Other large regional and money center banks also expanded their operations, though they largely confined their activities to foreign financial centers and to commercial lending and wholesale financial business.

Meanwhile (mostly in the 1970s), many smaller U.S. regional institutions began to recognize the benefits of a foreign presence, principally to accommodate and retain domestic customers whose activities were beginning to extend beyond U.S. borders. Some of these banks established full-service branches, typically in European cities, but most of them sought only "shell branches" in Caribbean centers as a means of gaining access to Eurodollar markets. . . .

By the early 1980s, strains from the rapid growth of international banking were beginning to show. Borrowers in many emerging economies were having difficulty servicing their debt, and the specter of losses loomed. By the end of the decade, despite efforts by creditor banks worldwide to postpone or avoid them, many of those losses were realized, requiring significant charge-offs and additional loss reserves. The threat of still further large losses on loans to developing countries did not disappear until the early 1990s, when improving domestic economic conditions and strong earnings enabled U.S. banks to charge off additional foreign loans and to put those problems behind them. . . .

Structural Framework for International Banking

The institutional structure for international banking by U.S. banks is in large part a reflection of efforts to restrain banking power. Throughout this country's history, government policy has sought to restrain concentration in banking and other financial activities. . . .

Although such restrictions helped diffuse financial power, they also, some observers argued, hindered U.S. banks from providing international banking services to U.S. customers and from competing effectively in foreign markets with institutions that offered a greater range of financial services. As early as 1919 these concerns led to enactment of section 25(a) of the Federal Reserve Act (the portion known as the "Edge Act") and, through limited-purpose Edge corporations, to meaningful relief from restrictions on branching interstate and investing abroad. Although some of the structures that developed over the years to facilitate international banking by U.S. banks are unique to U.S. banking, the main types of offices used by U.S. banks and [BHCs] to engage in international banking are also used by foreign banks. . . .

Foreign Offices

Foreign branch offices are the most important, and in most instances the preferred, vehicle through which U.S. banks provide international banking services, for several reasons. First, they are, legally, integral parts of the corporate bank and have the full authority to represent and commit the bank—an advantage in many commercial and interbank situations. For example, the lending limits imposed by a host country on the local branches of a foreign bank are ordinarily based on the bank's worldwide capital not on some lower level of capital imputed from an individual branch's own balance sheet. Also, the activities of branches are typically more easily integrated into the internal reporting and control procedures of the bank than are the activities of other types of offices, and branches accommodate a more streamlined organizational structure.

Many U.S. banks also find it necessary to operate abroad through separately incorporated, separately capitalized *foreign subsidiaries*. Most of the subsidiaries are wholly owned by the U.S. banking parent; all are at least majority owned and controlled by the parent. Although a subsidiary's financial strength and reputation, and in many cases its operations, are closely tied to its parent's, in the legal sense a subsidiary could survive on its own. Banks (or [BHCs]) establish or acquire foreign subsidiaries for any of several reasons:

- U.S. or foreign tax or banking laws favor operations through subsidiaries
- The host government does not permit foreign banks to have local branches
- The parent bank seeks consumer business in the foreign market or a local image, or it has other specialized business that is facilitated by separate incorporation
- U.S. laws prohibit branches from engaging in certain activities that subsidiaries may perform . . .
- Acquiring an established institution helps the purchaser gain an immediate, and perhaps sizable presence in the market.

Limited liability is another reason for establishing separately incorporated subsidiaries. Although that is sometimes a consideration for banking organizations—for example, in the case of specialized leasing company subsidiaries—it is generally not an important factor in planning banking networks. Financial institutions depend on raising large sums daily, and they recognize that a good reputation is essential for long-term viability. The incentive to support ailing subsidiaries is strong, limited liability notwithstanding.

Banks also engage in international banking through *foreign joint ventures.* These foreign companies, in which the U.S. bank or [BHC] has a noncontrolling 20 percent to 50 percent investment offer several advantages and serve the needs of certain banks. Investing banks can combine their expertise and resources while sharing the risks in what may be for them a relatively new business. Also, U.S. regulations allow banks to invest in a broader range of foreign activities if the investments do not represent controlling interests. . . . Since the 1970s, joint ventures have been of little interest to U.S. banks, and they are not discussed further.

Some banks engage in international banking in some locales through simple *representative offices.* The principal role of the bank "representatives" that staff these offices is to promote the bank's interest in the local market—generating business, dealing with local authorities and customers, and providing information about local business conditions to the bank's other offices. Representative offices are not licensed or chartered and may not accept deposits or make loans. Indeed, they have no financial statements of their own, and they direct any business they generate to other offices or affiliates of the bank.

U.S. Offices

Although U.S. banking organizations conduct most of their international activities through foreign branches and subsidiaries, they also handle much international banking directly from domestic offices—the bank's head office, an Edge corporation, or an international banking facility. Banks need no foreign office to issue and process letters of credit, for example, or to purchase international loans, trade foreign exchange, take deposits from foreign sources, or place funds in foreign banks. For these transactions, banks can typically accommodate customers through their head offices and with the assistance of foreign correspondent banks.

Edge (and *agreement*) *corporations* are subsidiaries that enable banks to conduct international banking business outside their home states and to invest abroad in a wider range of activities than is otherwise permissible for U.S. banks. Banking and investing functions are almost always conducted by separate Edge corporations. Banking Edges are essentially limited-purpose banks; they may accept deposits and offer a full range of banking services, but the business must be linked to a foreign or international transaction. Nonbanking (or "investment") Edge corporations are U.S. subsidiaries through which banks hold most of their foreign subsidiaries and other foreign investments.

International banking facilities (IBFs), which have existed only since 1981, have no separate organizational identity but are merely separate sets of accounts maintained by their establishing (or "host") banking offices. IBFs are attractive to banks for several reasons. First, their deposits are exempt from any reserve requirements and are not assessed for (nor are they covered by) federal deposit insurance. Also, in some states the earnings derived from balances booked in IBFs receive favorable state tax treatment. To qualify for placement in an IBF, a banking transaction must meet several tests to ensure that it is international and does not directly affect domestic financial markets. IBFs have been described as effectively being shell branches, similar to those in the Caribbean. The only difference is that IBF balances are assets or obligations of offices located in the United States rather than abroad.

---

1. ***Edge Act Corporations.*** The Edge Act corporation form continues to be surprisingly relevant today. Some of the largest U.S. G-SIBs still hold their foreign bank and broker-dealer investments through an Edge Act corporation underneath their main bank, reflecting the traces of history when that was the only structure possible.

2. ***Continuous Linked Settlement (CLS) Bank.*** CLS Bank, a financial market utility that specializes in foreign exchange settlement, was chartered as an Edge Act corporation by the Federal Reserve Board in 2002. Because CLS Bank settles many currencies and maintains accounts with these currencies' corresponding central banks, the Federal Reserve Board and other central banks have organized a cooperative oversight arrangement of the institution. *See* FEDERAL RESERVE BOARD, PROTOCOL FOR THE COOPERATIVE OVERSIGHT ARRANGEMENT OF CLS (Nov. 25, 2008). *See* Chapter 11.1 for more information on the regulation of CLS Bank.

3. ***Incidental to International or Foreign.*** An Edge Act corporation may only engage in international banking activities and U.S. banking activities that are "incidental to international or foreign business." For example, an Edge Act corporation may accept deposits from foreign persons, and it may also accept deposits from U.S. persons if the deposits are transmitted abroad or are otherwise connected to the Edge Act corporation's international or foreign business. *See* 12 C.F.R. § 211.6.

PART VII

PAYMENT SYSTEMS

CHAPTER 7.1

INTRODUCTION TO PAYMENT SYSTEMS

CONTENTS

I. INTRODUCTION

Imagine that John goes to Walmart to buy a new toothbrush. As John approaches the cashier, he pulls out his wallet. Inside his wallet are a $20 bill, a check from John's checkbook, a credit card, and a debit card. Each of these are payment instruments—tools that initiate the transfer of monetary value.

You might imagine that the payment instrument John chooses is of little significance. Not so. Although John may not realize it, his choice of payment instrument has meaningful consequences. It could determine whether he may rescind the transaction, whether his money is at risk if his account is compromised, and whether he is exposed to overdraft or overlimit fees. John's choice of payment instrument has consequences for Walmart, too. The payment instrument determines when Walmart will receive value in exchange for the purchase and whether Walmart will have to pay transaction fees and in what amount. John's payment instrument also affect John's bank and Walmart's bank by determining the steps they have to go through to process the transaction.

Behind each payment instrument that John may choose is a different payment system with its own procedures and rules that transfers value from John's financial intermediary to Walmart's financial intermediary. Part VII examines the United States' payment systems and explores the different legal frameworks applicable to each one. In this Chapter, we focus on settlement and risk allocation in various payment systems, including cash, checking, credit cards, debit cards, and prepaid cards. We also examine problems facing unbanked and underbanked households. We conclude with a look at interbank funds transfers, the transfers of value between banks.

To begin our discussion of payment systems, consider the following selection from an essay by Professor Ronald Mann.

Ronald J. Mann, Making Sense of Payments Policy in the Information Age

93 GEO. L.J. 633, 634 (2005)

Although I had been mulling over the ideas in this Essay for quite some time, I finally was driven to put the ideas on paper by a call from a colleague one Friday afternoon. He recently had purchased something on the Internet. Regrettably, the Internet merchant had never shipped the goods; apparently the merchant had failed. My colleague had given the merchant the number from his Visa card to pay for the transaction. Being well educated, my colleague assumed that he could have the charge removed from his credit card statement.

When he called the toll-free service line for the bank that issued his card, however, he was surprised to hear that he could not rescind the charge because it had been processed as a debit card transaction, rather than a credit card transaction. He called me, hoping that I would tell him his bank was incorrect. Unfortunately, because the Visa card was a debit card rather than a credit card, I was forced to tell him no, that his bank was acting within its rights.

That anecdote crystallizes something that is deeply wrong with the current framework of our payments policy. The portion of that policy reflected in the Truth in Lending Act (TILA) grants consumers a variety of generous rights in credit card transactions. By contrast, the Electronic Fund Transfer Act (EFTA), which governs debit card transactions, is relatively chary in its protections. Today, however, with the debit card market increasingly dominated by the [personal identification number (PIN)]-less debit cards marketed by Visa and MasterCard, the distinction between the credit card and the debit card is almost invisible to all but the most sophisticated consumers. . . .

The cause of the problem is easy to see: technology has altered the landscape of private payment institutions, and Congress has not updated the statutes that regulate those transactions. The solution, however, seems sufficiently difficult to warrant detailed consideration. . . .

As you read this Chapter, ask yourself: Why do consumer protections differ among seemingly similar payment instruments? Who bears the risks of a payment system in a consumer transaction? Who should? Who gains and who loses from different forms of payment regulation? For further exploration of these issues, see RONALD J. MANN, CHARGING AHEAD: THE GROWTH AND REGULATION OF PAYMENT CARD MARKETS (2007).

A. TRACING THE HISTORY OF PAYMENT SYSTEMS

It is worth pausing to reflect for a moment that the familiar green paper in John's wallet today did not exist until 1913. Before that, the United States was a "monetary [tower of] Babel." Roger Lowenstein, AMERICA'S BANK: THE EPIC STRUGGLE TO CREATE THE FEDERAL RESERVE 12 (2015) (quoting Paul Warburg). As we discussed in Chapters 1.2 and 2.1, in the early days of the American republic, banks were chartered by the states, and each state-chartered bank issued its own notes under the rules of the state that had granted its charter. These banknotes were paper money and functioned as the currency of the day, but they were supposed to be asset-backed, meaning that a person with a banknote in his wallet could, in theory, show up at the bank and demand either gold or government bonds from the bank vault. Variation in banknotes and the quality of the many small and faraway banks (recall the wildcat banks from Chapter 1.2), impeded long-distance transactions. Counterfeiting was rampant and, despite banknotes' common denomination in U.S. dollars, they were not exchanged at par. Instead, each merchant kept a book that set forth the discount applicable to each banknote based upon the market's views of the strength of the issuing bank, and distance or other difficulty in redeeming notes for gold or bonds. The National Banking Act of 1864 was intended to eliminate this cacophony of values. It imposed a punitive tax on banknotes issued by state banks, with the intent of driving state-chartered banks and their banknotes out of existence. The attempt to thwart state-chartered banks failed when state banks switched to the checking account, an example of innovation and regulatory arbitrage. The National Banking Act also established strict standards under which notes could be issued by national banks, resulting in national banknotes being largely traded at par. The standards, however, limited the amount of national bank notes issued to a portion of the government bonds and gold in the vault of the national bank, leading to chronic shortages of paper currency.

Throughout the late 19th Century and up to the creation of the Federal Reserve System, discount rates on banknotes and checks changed constantly. Meanwhile, banks often routed checks through other banks to minimize discounts, causing protracted delays. Roger Lowenstein has captured a typical story of one check in his book, AMERICA'S BANK.

> A check for $43.56, drawn by Woodward Brothers, a general store in Sag Harbor, New York, on eastern Long Island, on its account at the local Peconic Bank and paid to Berry, Lohman & Rasch, a wholesale grocer in Hoboken, New Jersey. The check was deposited in the Second National Bank of Hoboken, which sent it along to a New York bank, which-not having a regular correspondent in Sag Harbor-bundled it with other checks to their Boston correspondent. The latter, inexplicably, transferred the nomadic debit to the First National Bank of Tonawanda, New York, near Niagara Falls. The Tonawanda bank, realizing the check had wandered off course, shipped it to a bank in Albany, which endeavored to get it nearer to home and relayed it to the First National Bank of Port Jefferson, only sixty miles from its point of issue. Alas the check took another detour, to the Far Rockaway Bank, thence to the Chase National, the weary check's second visit to New York City. After two more stops, it was returned to the Peconic and duly laid to rest.

Id. at 40.

By the dawn of the 20th Century, this disjointed system was not a good fit for the developing national, industrial economy. The Federal Reserve System, discussed in more detail in Chapter 9.1 with respect to its role as lender of last resort, was also charged with issuing and distributing uniform national banknotes, backed by gold in the reserves of the federal government, and collecting and processing checks. One of the Federal Reserve's first actions was to force as many state banks as possible to clear checks at par. The Federal Reserve System played a crucial role in developing a national system of check clearance, and it continues to play a crucial role in the payments system, including as an intermediary in interbank payments. *See The Federal Reserve in the U.S. Payments System, in* THE FEDERAL RESERVE SYSTEM: PURPOSE AND FUNCTIONS 83–101 (2005).

Not surprisingly, during the 20th Century, both payment instruments and payment systems shifted from paper-based to electronic. Among the first impacts of data processing on the banking system was the clearing of checks. In another example, credit cards, dating back to the Diners Club charge card introduced in 1950 and really taking off in the 1960s, have transformed the consumer payment environment. Debit cards arrived in the 1970s. Stored-value cards, mostly in the form of prepaid gift cards, appeared around the same time and later evolved to encompass a range of products, from prepaid, reloadable cards to telephone cards to toll-road transponders. Figure 7.1-1 depicts the shift of non-cash payments from checking towards greater reliance on payment cards and Automated Clearing House (ACH) transfers, discussed later in this Chapter.

Figure 7.1-1 Non-Cash Payment Transactions by Payment Type

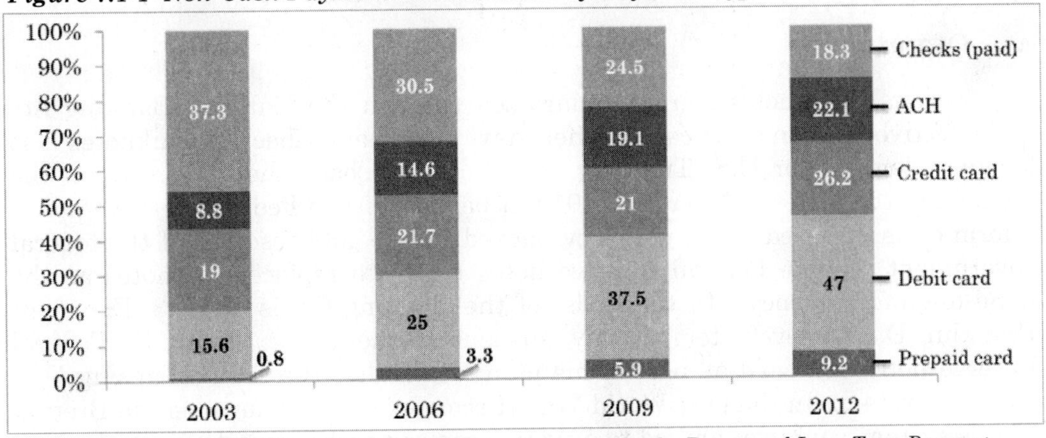

Source: Fed. Reserve Sys., The 2013 Federal Reserve Payments Study: Recent and Long-Term Payment Trends in the United States (2003–2012)—Summary Report and Initial Data Release 8 (2013).

Payment systems in the United States have been the subject of increased attention by the banking sector and have piqued the interest of potential new entrants in the fintech sector. Reforming the payment system, and designing and implementing a cohesive regulatory approach that not only keeps pace with innovation but also encourages its evolution, is challenging. With the emergence of alternative payment instruments, which we discuss in Chapter 7.2, consumers enjoy unprecedented options. How should the goals of consumer protection and financial stability be balanced against the need for competition and innovation? Although new payment systems enhance convenience and increase access, they also produce new risks. Should new entrants be permitted to operate in a less regulated space as they innovate and lower costs? Are the regulations themselves a barrier to entry protecting the status quo and current incumbents?

B. LEGAL LANDSCAPE

The fundamental purpose of all payment systems is to facilitate settlement, or to discharge obligations between two or more parties. Legal frameworks are crucial for effective settlement. This Chapter focuses on the laws, regulations, and private contractual arrangements that form these frameworks. We examine how these frameworks function, and we ask how the frameworks allocate risk and liability between users of the payment system and entities such as banks that facilitate their operation.

Payments regulation has grown in spurts and often lags technological and market-driven changes. As a result, the relevant law is unwieldy and tensions exist between functional and jurisdictional regulatory approaches. For historical reasons and because state and federal authorities coexist, parts of the Uniform Commercial Code (U.C.C.) sometimes apply alongside or as a substitute for one or more federal statutory regimes. The wide array of payment system business models also contributes to regulatory variations.

II. CASH

A. OVERVIEW

National banknotes were standardized through the National Banking Act and effectively became the cash of their day. These asset-backed banknotes also led to a demand for U.S. Treasury bonds, used to back the notes. Upon the creation of the Federal Reserve in 1913, it began to issue Federal Reserve notes, a form of asset-based paper currency backed by the gold reserves of the federal government. These Federal Reserve notes began to replace banknotes as the hand-to-hand currency. In the midst of the Banking Crisis of 1933, President Franklin D. Roosevelt temporarily suspended the convertibility of Federal Reserve notes into gold as part of his plan to stabilize the then-collapsing U.S. banking system. In the post-World War II economic order known as the Bretton Woods system, countries agreed to a system of fixed exchange rates with the U.S. dollar convertible to gold, but President Richard Nixon formally ended dollar convertibility to gold in 1971. Ever since, the United States, and every other country in the world, has had a fiat currency.

Fiat currency is not backed by any promise to deliver an asset like gold or a government bond. Instead, U.S. bills and coins are pieces of paper declared by the U.S. government to be "legal tender for all debts, public charges, taxes, and dues." 31 U.S.C. § 5103. It is a trust-based system that works so long as the public has confidence in it. While the government must accept such currency, no federal statute mandates that private individuals or businesses accept currency or coins as payment for goods or services. U.S. DEP'T OF THE TREASURY, RESOURCE CENTER FAQS: LEGAL TENDER STATUS (2011). Absent state law to the contrary, subway systems may adopt non-currency fare arrangements, airlines may require credit cards for in-flight services, and gas stations may refuse currency in large denominations. Nevertheless, paper currency, known as Federal Reserve notes (take a look at the familiar green paper in your wallet) and what we all call "cash," underlies the basic functioning of the economy.

B. WHY CASH?

Cash is easy, simple, and convenient. It requires no access device and is nearly universally accepted. Merchants sometimes prefer cash because it is immediate, does not involve intermediaries or transaction fees, and because its contemporaneousness eliminates the risk of nonpayment, although the cost of managing cash is not trivial. Recipients bear the risk of counterfeit, but that risk is actually lower with cash than with many other forms of payment. Federal Reserve notes are difficult to counterfeit, and extensive resources are devoted to prosecution. *See* 18 U.S.C. § 471 ("Whoever, with intent to defraud, falsely makes, forges, counterfeits, or alters any obligation or other security of the United States, shall be fined . . . or imprisoned not more than 20 years, or both.").

Cash is the dominant instrument for low-value payments. In 2014, cash accounted for 66% of transactions valued between $0 and $9.99 and 45% of transactions between $10 and $24.99. Cash is among the common payment methods for low-income consumers who do not have an account at an insured depository institution. *See* BARBARA BENNETT ET AL., CASH PRODUCT OFFICE OF THE FEDERAL RESERVE SYSTEM, CASH CONTINUES TO PLAY A KEY ROLE IN

CONSUMER SPENDING: EVIDENCE FROM THE DIARY OF CONSUMER PAYMENT CHOICE 3 (2014). Cash's finality, however, leaves consumers no way to cancel or stop payment and is not a favored method for large purchases. In 2014, cash accounted for less than 15% of consumer transactions of $100 or more. *See id.*

Until the invention of decentralized payment systems such as Bitcoin, which we will discuss in Chapter 7.2, cash had long been the only form of payment neither requiring nor recording in any way the identity of end users. Anonymity has many implications. For one, cash harbors the inherent risk of theft or loss, the entire burden of which rests on its rightful owner. Loss is limited, however, to the amount the owner actually carries or hides under the proverbial mattress. By contrast, the potential consequences of altered checks or card-related identity theft can be quite large. In addition, cash's anonymity can make it an appealing payment instrument in connection with illegal activities and the informal economy. Moreover, in a world in which privacy is harder and harder to come by, cash ensures a measure of privacy.

III. CHECKS

A. OVERVIEW

Although declining in use, checks remain a common payment instrument, particularly among older populations. Ronald J. Mann, *Adopting, Using, and Discarding Paper and Electronic Payment Instruments: Variation by Age and Race* 19 (Fed. Reserve Bank of Boston, Pub. Policy Discussion Paper No. 11-2, 2011). Checking, like most forms of non-cash payments, achieves settlement by ultimately moving funds from the payor's bank (John, the person writing the check) to the payee's bank (Walmart) by decreasing the payor's account balance and increasing that of the payee. Settlement becomes final upon the receipt of acceptable funds by Walmart's bank, which irrevocably extinguishes the obligation of John's bank, and thus John's payment obligation to Walmart. Figure 7.1-2 depicts the movement of funds in a checking transaction.

Figure 7.1-2 Overview of a Checking Transaction

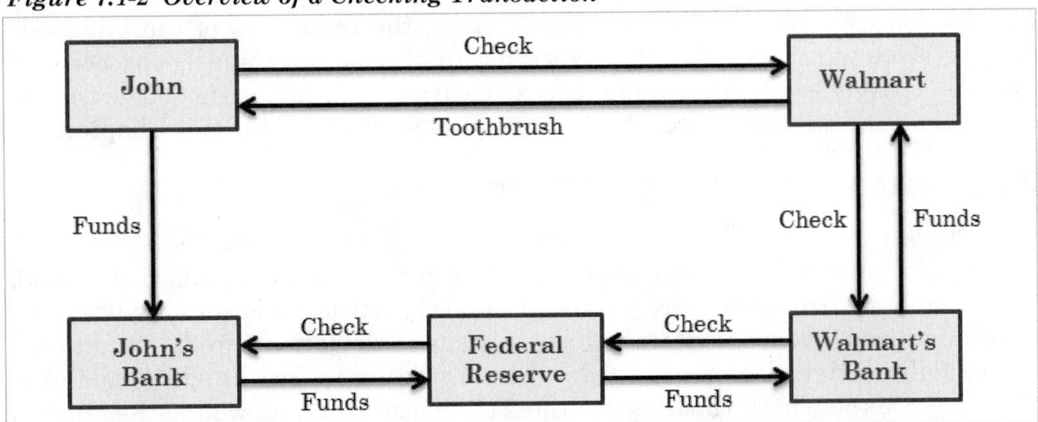

When Walmart deposits John's check, Walmart's bank credits Walmart's account. Walmart's bank in turn presents the check to its regional Federal Reserve Bank, which credits Walmart's bank's account and passes the obligation on to John's bank. The Federal Reserve Bank then debits the account that John's bank maintains at the Federal Reserve Bank. Finally, John's bank satisfies the claim by debiting the amount from John's account.

Achieving settlement through the movement of claims (in this case, the check) and funds to satisfy the claim (in this case, adjustments in account balances) is common to all non-cash payment systems. Understanding how the claims pass among the financial intermediaries in a payment system, how they are satisfied, and if, when and how those claims can be reversed, is critical. Settlement is nothing more than a trusted system to update ledgers at different financial intermediaries to adjust deposit balances. Adjusting account balances reflects the transfer and settlement of claims among the financial intermediaries as they move along the chain from payor to payee accounts.

B. HISTORY

Checking is the oldest non-cash payment system in the United States. Recall Lowenstein's vignette of the inefficiencies in early checking because of banks' refusal to honor or insistence on discounting checks from other banks. Par check clearing finally appeared in the early 20th Century. *See* Fed. Reserve Bank of N.Y., *Fiftieth Anniversary Problems of the Federal Reserve System—Early Problems of Check Clearing and Collection*, 9 MONTHLY REV. 182 (1964).

Checking has grown increasingly automated since the introduction of check sorters and magnetic ink character recognition in the late 1950s and early 1960s. The development of electronic imaging technology in the 1990s provided another opportunity to expedite checking transactions and reduce costs for banks, which until then had to pay for storing paper checks, trucking them around the country, and returning the originals to their writers with monthly statements. Banks gradually began exchanging images rather than physical checks, but the law still required presentation of each original paper check to the payor bank when requesting payment. Finally, in 2004, the Check Clearing for the 21st Century Act acknowledged substitute checks, or printed copies or images of original paper checks, as their legal equivalent. Today, although a checking transaction usually begins with a paper check, the remainder of the process is largely electronic, which in turn expedites the transaction and keeps per-unit costs relatively low. Electronic check clearing is similar in operation to interbank fund transfer systems, which we discuss at the end of this Chapter.

C. LEGAL AND REGULATORY FRAMEWORKS

Checking is governed by both state and federal law. At the state level, checks are negotiable instruments subject to some provisions of U.C.C. Article 3, "Negotiable Instruments." *See* § 3-104(f). U.C.C. Article 4 focuses specifically on checking and accommodates that system's deviation from traditional negotiability principles. At the federal level, the Expedited Funds Availability Act of 1987, the Check Clearing for the 21st Century Act, as well as Regulation CC and other rules promulgated by the Federal Reserve Board, where applicable, supersede U.C.C. provisions governing funds availability and check return deadlines. The Expedited Funds Availability Act, for example, requires banks to make funds available to accountholders within specified timeframes and to disclose their policies on funds availability. Good funds availability can have important consequences for consumers, affecting, for example, whether they inadvertently overdraft on their account. Moreover, the fact that funds may not be immediately available upon deposit causes many low-income households to use check cashers, to turn to alternative short-term credit such as payday loans, or to stay out of the banking system altogether. We discuss problems of the unbanked and underbanked later in this Chapter. What considerations should regulators and banks take into account in setting funds availability policies? What risks and rewards are entailed with immediate funds availability?

D. RISK ALLOCATION

Checking is subject to various risks. Compared to cash, it is a time-delayed process and exposes depository institutions to the risks of nonpayment and fraud. The post-1990 U.C.C. framework seeks to allocate losses based on comparative negligence and the best loss avoider principle. *See, e.g.*, Menichini v. Grant, 995 F.2d 1224, 1232 (3d Cir. 1993). Banks bear the responsibility for losses that would be difficult for another party to avoid, but these losses may be shared with or even shifted completely to other parties whose negligence contributed to the loss. *See, e.g.*, Melissa Waite, *Check Fraud and the Common Law: At the Intersection of Negligence and the Uniform Commercial Code*, 54 B.C. L. REV. 2205 (2013). Some of the risks in checking are as follows:

Insufficient Funds. The payor bank may dishonor a check if the payor's account contains insufficient funds or if the payor gives the bank adequate notice to stop payment. *See* U.C.C. § 4-403 and cmt. 7. Recall our discussion of checking overdraft in Chapter 5.3. Banks and customers may agree that if the payor's funds are insufficient, the payor bank will nevertheless transmit funds to the payee bank, but will charge overdraft fees and impose interest on the amount overdrawn. If the payor (John) bank dishonors the check, the payee (Walmart) can enforce the check against only the payor (John), who may bring a case against his bank for wrongful dishonor. A check does not create a direct legal relationship between payor bank and payee, and even if the payor bank wrongfully dishonors the check, the payee has no direct right against the bank to force it to pay the check.

Forgery. The payor bank may charge a customer's account only when presented with a properly payable check. Accordingly, the payor bank bears the loss if it improperly honors a forged check, unless it can locate the forger and recover from him (an unlikely event). If the payor bank can show that other parties were negligent and substantially contributed to a forgery, then the loss may be shared based upon each party's comparative negligence. If the payor bank dishonors a forged check, then the loss shifts back through the collection chain because each bank, when transferring it to another, warrants that the check is valid—the "presentment warranty"—and thus must re-credit prior transferors after forgery is discovered. Once the check returns to the depository bank, that bank can shift its loss to the payee if it accepted the check in good faith and for value. The rule is justified as embodying a best-cost avoider principle: as the only party to have had direct contact with the forger, the payee is in the best position to prevent risk of forgery.

Unauthorized Issuance. Unauthorized issuance occurs when a wrongdoer writes a check without the payor's permission. Unauthorized issuance can occur, for example, in the context of employee embezzlement. In general, an employer cannot externalize the costs of employee embezzlement under the U.C.C. framework, which reflects that the employer is best positioned to detect and prevent such loss. *See, e.g.*, Mackin Eng'g Co. v. Am. Express Co., 437 Fed. Appx. 100, 102 (3d Cir. 2011). Applying this rationale, courts have rejected employers' attempts to hold payor banks liable for accepting unauthorized checks. *See, e.g.*, Dean v. Commonwealth Bank & Tr. Co., 434 S.W.3d 489, 510 (Ky. 2014). Indeed, a major thrust of the U.C.C. provisions is to encourage *all* account holders to monitor their own accounts. Banks usually provide their customers with monthly statements containing a comprehensive list of transactions, triggering a customer duty to read the statements and report unauthorized transactions.

IV. CREDIT CARDS

Since the 1970s, one of the most common forms of payment has become the credit card. Credit cards and debit cards, discussed later in this Chapter, have the same basic, electronic payment structure. The general structure of the credit card payment system is depicted in Figure 7.1-3. It is commonly referred to as the four corner payments model. The consumer (payor), who initiates the need to settle the payment by using her card, is depicted in the top left of the figure. The merchant (payee) is in the top right, and in the lower half of the chart is the payments settlement transaction between financial institutions facilitated by the card network, such as Visa or MasterCard in the credit and debit card markets.

Figure 7.1-3 Overview of a Credit Card Transaction

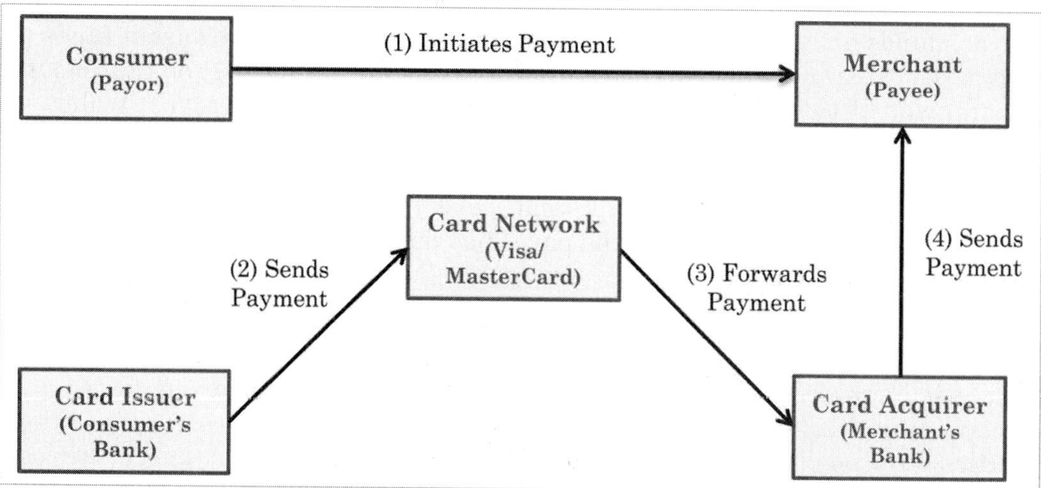

Although most traditional electronic payment systems use a four-corners payment model, the flow of information and funds differs for each payment instrument. Even more importantly, networks for various payment instruments follow different rules of the road, like rules that establish protection for consumers and merchants, transaction fees, and settlement procedures.

A. OVERVIEW

A precursor to credit cards first appeared in the mid-20th Century, but the first modern card, Diners Club, launched in 1950, allowed customers to charge meals at restaurants in and around New York City. In the 1950s, banks introduced general-use credit cards, which eliminated the need for multiple cards designed for specific purchases like restaurant meals or gas. The first general-use credit card nationally licensed to banks appeared in the 1960s, known as BankAmericard, was also the first card to offer revolving credit, allowing customers to pay down their balances over time in exchange for the payment of interest. The credit card sector took off in the 1970s, with the rise of the Visa and MasterCard networks. These two companies still dominate the sector: in 2014, they together accounted for about 84% of the global 196 billion card transactions. *See* THE NILSON REPORT, *Purchase Transactions Worldwide* (2014). Visa was the product of the 1976 merger between National BankAmericard Inc., the domestic association of BankAmericard-licensing banks, and another multinational member corporation. The new entity was named Visa to signify universal acceptance across borders. MasterCard stemmed from a competing group of California banks. Originally structured as not-for-profit associations of member financial institutions, both Visa and MasterCard went public in the late 2000s. We will explore antitrust and other structural issues in card networks in Chapter 7.2.

The average American consumer today has more than three credit cards. Mitch Lipka, *Can You Have Too Many Credit Cards?*, REUTERS, Apr. 18, 2012. Credit cards' popularity owes much to their unique features. For one, they increase flexibility in spending decisions. Credit cards enable consumers to smoothen their consumption over time despite inconsistent income, and they are convenient and nearly universally accepted. Ancillary benefits include loyalty points redeemable for goods, services, or cash. Both federal statutes and internal credit-card policies limit consumers' fraud liability.

Visa and MasterCard serve as intermediaries in what is known as an open-loop exchange system: a hub-and-spoke model that enables consumers, merchants, and intermediaries to transact without direct relationships. In contrast, American Express and Discover operate as both intermediaries and card-issuing creditors. When intermediary banks join a card network, their customers immediately gain payment access to other member institutions—fostering a high degree of interoperability, even internationally. In addition, card networks exert significant control over member institutions, which must adhere to network rules, discussed more fully in Chapter 7.2.

Two primary regulatory regimes govern credit card transactions: card network rules and federal laws. We discuss card network rules in Chapter 7.2. We discussed federal consumer protection regulations for credit cards, including the TILA and the Credit Card Responsibility and Disclosure Act (CARD Act), in Chapter 5.3. As a practical matter, state usury laws no longer constrain credit cards because credit card banks have long since relocated their operations to states with no usury limit, relying on the exportation doctrine as blessed by federal statutes and by the Supreme Court in *Marquette National Bank of Minneapolis v. First of Omaha Service Corp.*, 439 U.S. 299 (1978) (recall the discussion in Chapter 1.4), and *Smiley v. Citibank,* 517 U.S. 735 (1996), which limited the state's ability to regulate credit card and interest fees.

B. HOW CREDIT CARDS WORK

When a cardholder swipes her card at a merchant terminal, information is transmitted to the issuer bank to determine the validity of the card and the availability of credit sufficient to effect the transaction, a process that is virtually instantaneous. If authorized, the transaction data will be captured or acquired by the merchant's bank, often referred to as the acquiring bank or merchant acquirer. The data is then passed through the card association, then to the bank that issued the card. Payments are settled, on a net basis, among these participants quite rapidly. The issuer bank will then bill the cardholder, who will repay the bank as required under the card agreement.

Issuers earn interest on monthly balances, profiting from consumers who carry month-to-month balances, exceed their spending limits, pay late, or incur other fees. Issuers also offer higher-end cards to more creditworthy consumers, who are less likely to produce profit from interest and late fees. These cards charge annual fees to offset costs of usage and rewards programs. Issuers also earn interchange fees from the use of credit cards in the payment system, as discussed in Chapter 7.2.

An entire infrastructure has grown around the credit card payment framework. Many companies act as intermediaries between the merchant's bank and the merchant. These companies, such as Global Payments, Paymentech, and Elavon, often provide and service merchant terminals, capture transaction data, route information, confirm the collection of funds from the card association, and assure that funds are credited to the merchant's bank account.

C. RISK ALLOCATION

In general, losses from unauthorized card-present transactions—when the consumer uses the physical credit card at the point-of-sale to complete a purchase—fall on issuers. Merchants bear the losses from fraudulent card-not-present transactions—when the consumer uses the credit card number, but not the actual credit card, for the purchase, as in Internet or mobile transactions. Does this difference in risk allocation make sense?

Credit card issuers and networks have long striven to counter fraud. The introduction of card verification value (CVV) data in the 1990s reduced unauthorized card-present transactions because CVV data, encoded in a card's magnetic strip, is difficult to counterfeit. Another fraud control measure is CVV2, a three- or four-digit number printed on either the front or the back of the card, which must be supplied in card-not-present transactions in an effort to ensure the purchaser's physical possession of the card. These may be familiar to you from your online shopping experiences. Chip cards, with embedded microchips that encrypt transaction data, are quickly replacing magnetic-strip cards in many countries because they tend to lower the rates of forged card transactions. Europe is far ahead of the United States in this field, but chip technology has been rapidly deployed in the United States in recent years.

Consumers have the right to stop payment on certain credit card transactions. Pursuant to TILA § 170(a), a cardholder can withhold payment from an issuer based on any contract or equity claim or defense that could be asserted against the merchant. The right to cancel, however, disappears with repayment of the relevant card balance. TILA § 170(b) (limiting the right to "the amount of credit outstanding with respect to the transaction"); *see* Regulation Z § 226.12(c). Additionally, in order to withhold payment, the cardholder must "ma[k]e a good-faith attempt to obtain satisfactory resolution of [the] disagreement . . . from the [merchant] honoring the credit card." 15 U.S.C. § 166i(a). TILA does not grant cardholders the right to withhold payment on transactions occurring outside the cardholder's state of residence nor a transaction more than 100 miles from the cardholder's billing address.

TILA establishes a dispute resolution procedure for billing errors on credit-card statements. The cardholder must notify his issuer of such errors in writing within 60 days from the day the relevant statement is sent. The issuer must acknowledge such notice in writing within 30 days from receipt and resolve the claim within two billing cycles. The issuer cannot close or restrict the cardholder's account for failure to pay the disputed amount before its resolution. If the issuer fails to comply with these requirements, it may be liable to the cardholder for actual damages, twice the amount of the finance charge, in addition to the cardholder's costs and attorney's fees. *See* Lau v. Credit Concepts, Inc., 2007 U.S. Dist. LEXIS 12417, *5 (N.D. Okla. Feb. 20, 2007) (*citing* Am. Express Co. v. Koerner, 452 U.S. 233, 235 (1981)).

TILA also sets forth the conditions and limits on cardholder liability in unauthorized transactions. 15 U.S.C. § 1643. In many cases, cardholder liability is capped at $50, and no liability is incurred if the issuer is notified of loss or theft before a card is used for unauthorized transactions. MasterCard and Visa have adopted more generous policies, exempting cardholders from liability for unauthorized charges if a lost card is reported within two business days from date of loss. The $50 cap is not absolute. Cardholder negligence may move courts to allocate up to $500, and in some instances an unlimited amount in liability. With respect to corporate credit cards, the issuer and the business can contract out of TILA's statutory loss regime, provided that the business does not pass liability to individual employees. 15 U.S.C. § 1645.

---

1. ***Data Breaches.*** Several retailers, including Target and Home Depot, have experienced data breaches that compromised millions of customers' credit card accounts. A variety of private contracts—including contracts among retailers, issuer banks and banks that acquire and handle payments, credit card companies such as Visa and MasterCard, and third party payments processors authorized by the acquirer—determine liability for a data breach. These contracts generally require the issuing financial institution to pay for the costs of card reissuance and for fraudulent charges on compromised cards. Depending on state cybersecurity and notification laws, these financial institutions can sue retailers for failure to meet the requisite standards, and recover damages for the costs arising from the breach. Judicial decisions have allocated losses from data breaches, like Target's in 2013 and Home Depot's in 2014, on a case-by-case basis, and under a variety of state laws, leading to a lack of uniformity in outcomes. *See* N. ERIC WEISS, CONG. RESEARCH SERV., R43496, THE TARGET AND OTHER FINANCIAL DATA BREACHES: FREQUENTLY ASKED QUESTIONS 19-20 (2015).

2. ***Merchant Restraints.*** Professor Adam Levitin has written extensively on merchant restraints, credit card network rules that "prohibit merchants from accepting certain credit cards selectively and from pricing goods and services according to cost of payment." Adam J. Levitin, *Priceless? The Economic Costs of Credit Card Merchant Restraints*, 55 UCLA L. REV. 1321, 1321 (2008). We examine the payments ecosystem effects of credit card network rules in Chapter 7.2. For now, consider the consumer distributive effects in credit card markets. Levitin argues that, because of merchant restraints, non-credit card users subsidize credit card users, especially those who use premium rewards cards:

> Merchant restraint rules impose the externality of rewards program costs on merchants and prevent merchants from making rewards card users pay their own way. Merchants are able, however, to pass on the costs of credit card rewards to all consumers, and empirical evidence shows that they do so by raising prices across the board. This creates a cross-subsidy of credit card consumers by non-credit-card consumers, and of rewards card consumers by all consumers not using rewards cards.
>
> The cross-subsidy is highly regressive. The poorest Americans do not have access to credit cards, much less super-premium rewards and corporate cards. In its worst form, food stamp consumers are subsidizing first-class frequent flier upgrades.

Id. at 1356. Is Levitin correct that the distributive effects of merchant restraints are problematic? If so, what should be done about it? Or is the fight over network rules and pricing a stakeholder battle between merchants and banks, with little to do with helping consumers? *See* DAVID S. EVANS & RICHARD SCHMALENSEE, PAYING WITH PLASTIC: THE DIGITAL REVOLUTION IN BUYING AND BORROWING (2005). We explore these issues in Chapter 7.2.

V. DEBIT CARDS

A. OVERVIEW

Debit cards were initially introduced in the 1970s but did not become more widely distributed in the United States until the late 1980s and early 1990s. Since then, debit-card usage has grown dramatically, while checks have been in steady decline. By 2009, debit card transactions accounted for 35% of non-cash retail payments by number, making debit cards the most popular non-cash retail payment instrument in the United States. *See* Fumiko Hayashi, *The New Debit Card Regulations: Initial Effects on Networks and Banks*, FED. RES. BANK OF KANSAS CITY ECON. REV., Fourth Quarter 2012, at 82–85.

At first, the debit card emerged as a means of accessing cash through ATMs, replacing, believe it or not, the paper punch cards that were used in early machines. ATM networks began regionally. After a long series of mergers and acquisitions, several large national networks, such as Interlink (now owned by Visa), Maestro (now owned by MasterCard), Pulse (now owned by Discover), STAR (now owned by First Data), and NYCE (now owned by FIS) emerged, along with a number of smaller networks operating regionally. These networks allow customers to debit their bank accounts instantaneously. PIN debit cards operated by ATM networks work by having customers enter a code, while signature debit cards sponsored by credit card networks use signature verification. For more on market structure, see Chapter 7.2.

B. RISK ALLOCATION

Debit card transactions are regulated by the EFTA and Regulation E, generally now under the supervision of the CFPB, as discussed in Chapter 5.3. The EFTA defines an electronic fund transfer as "any transfer of funds, other than a transaction originated by check, . . . which is initiated through an electronic terminal, telephonic instrument, or computer so as to order, instruct, or authorize a financial institution to debit or credit an account. The term includes, but is not limited to, point-of-sale transfers, automated teller machine transactions, direct deposits or withdrawals of funds, and transfers initiated by telephone. . . ." 15 U.S.C. § 1693a.

The EFTA and Regulation E establish rights and liabilities for consumers and banks including debit card transactions. Regulation E's 60-day deadline for disputing transactions incentivizes consumers to read their account statements, but to hold them liable, the cardholder's bank must first have fulfilled certain conditions. For debit-card transactions, the cardholder's bank must disclose in writing to the consumer the terms and conditions of electronic fund transfer services. The access device—such as a card, code, or other means of account access—used to initiate the electronic fund transfer must be accepted by the consumer, meaning the consumer himself must have requested either the device itself or its validation. The mandatory authorization prevents cardholder liability for unauthorized transactions involving cards intercepted in the mail. The cardholder's bank must provide a means to identify the consumer to whom the access device was issued, typically by a signature or PIN.

Consumer liability then turns on whether the unauthorized electronic fund transfer involved loss or theft and the promptness with which the consumer notified his cardholder's bank. Figure 7.1-4 is a summary of consumer liability under Regulation E, but many card issuers provide greater protection by contract for their cardholders than what is outlined below as a matter of federal law.

Regulation E has been amended to strengthen consumer protections. Recall, for instance, our discussion of overdrafts in Chapter 5.3. Regulation E was amended in the Dodd-Frank Act to provide that consumers must opt in, or affirmatively consent, to their bank's overdraft policies in order for those banks to charge overdraft fees for ATM and debit card transactions. As you will recall, the opt-in rule has not significantly affected overdraft usage or fees.

Figure 7.1-4 Consumer Liability for Unauthorized Transfers

Event	Timing of Consumer Notice to Cardholder's Bank	Maximum Liability
Loss or theft of access device[1]	Within two business days after learning of loss or theft	Lesser of $50 or total amount of unauthorized transfer
Loss or theft of access device	More than two business days after learning of loss or theft up to 60 calendar days after transmittal of statement showing first unauthorized transfer made with access device	Lesser of $500 or the sum of: (a) $50 or the total amount of unauthorized transfers occurring in the first two business days, whichever is less, and (b) The amount of unauthorized transfers occurring after two business days and before notice to the cardholder's bank.[2]
Loss or theft of access device	More than 60 calendar days after transmittal of statement showing first unauthorized transfer made with access device	For transfers occurring within the 60-day period, the lesser of $500 or the sum of (a) Lesser of $50 or the amount of unauthorized transfers in first two business days, and (b) The amount of unauthorized transfers occurring after two business days. For transfers occurring after the 60-day period, unlimited liability (until the cardholder's bank is notified).[3]
Unauthorized transfer(s) not involving loss or theft of an access device	Within 60 calendar days after transmittal of the periodic statement on which the unauthorized transfer first appears	No liability.
Unauthorized transfer(s) not involving loss or theft of an access device	More than 60 calendar days after transmittal of the periodic statement on which the unauthorized transfer first appears	Unlimited liability for unauthorized transfers occurring 60 calendar days after the periodic statement and before notice to the cardholder's bank.

(1) Includes a PIN if used without a card in a telephone transaction, for example.

(2) Provided the cardholder's bank demonstrates that these transfers would not have occurred had notice been given within the two-business-day period.

(3) Provided the cardholder's bank demonstrates that these transfers would not have occurred had notice been given within a 60-day period.

Source: Fed. Reserve Sys., Consumer Compliance Handbook, Regulation E: Electronic Fund Transfer Act 13 (2013).

VI. THE UNBANKED AND UNDERBANKED

By now, you have probably realized the pivotal role that the banking system plays in all of the non-cash payment systems we discussed so far. More than 25 million Americans, however, are unbanked, or lack an account at an insured depository institution. Another 67.5 million people are underbanked, meaning that although they have bank accounts, they also obtain financial services from non-bank, alternative-financial-services providers such as check cashers or payday lenders. *See* FDIC, 2013 FDIC NATIONAL SURVEY OF UNBANKED AND UNDERBANKED HOUSEHOLDS 4 (2014). Being unbanked or underbanked presents significant challenges for participating in many payment systems.

Consequently, unbanked and underbanked consumers often pay high fees to cash checks, use cash more frequently and for a wider variety of transactions than other consumers, and spend more time and pay more to pay bills, either in person or by using money orders. Unbanked and underbanked persons are often unable to save easily or invest due to the high costs and risks of financial products and services, and they use high-interest loans from nontraditional lenders, as you saw in our discussions of payday lenders and loan sharks in Chapter 5.3. Low-income individuals are sometimes excluded from mainstream lending due to low, incorrect, or even nonexistent credit scores, which are calculated in part from transactions involving bank accounts. *See id.*

Professor Michael Barr examined the consequences of being unbanked, based on a large-scale survey of low- and moderate-income neighborhoods in Detroit, Michigan. Barr found that being unbanked can be costly:

> [U]nbanked households do not . . . escape the need to use financial services. Rather, they piece together strategies to use formal and informal mechanisms to achieve their financial needs. In doing so, they often seek to optimize their financial behavior within external constraints that impose serious financial costs, but they often lack the time or resources to take a step back and determine whether it would be possible to expand their choice sets. For example, while check cashers offer essential services, the fees involved in converting paper checks into cash are high relative both to income and to analogous services that middle- and upper-income families use, such as depositing a check into a bank account or using electronic direct deposit. Pawnshops, check cashers, rent-to-own stores, tax-refund lenders, and other [alternative financial services] providers are often the dominant means for [low- and moderate-income] households to access financial services in their neighborhoods, but such services come at a high cost and leave these households with little opportunity to save.

See MICHAEL S. BARR, NO SLACK: THE FINANCIAL LIVES OF LOW-INCOME AMERICANS 24 (2012) [hereinafter BARR, NO SLACK].

What alternative payment options are available? This section explores several methods used by low-income households.

A. PREPAID CARDS

Prepaid cards are "a type of debit card, but also a distinct category of non-cash payments that are considered separately." FED. RESERVE SYS., 2013 FEDERAL RESERVE PAYMENTS STUDY 8 (2014). Unlike ordinary debit cards, they are not linked to an individually owned bank account. To be used to make payments, they must be purchased and loaded with funds. With each purchase or cash withdrawal, the amount is subtracted from the card's balance. Some prepaid cards can be reloaded with additional funds, while others must be discarded once they reach a zero balance. The funds are generally held in a bank account maintained by the card issuer, and most prepaid cards offer deposit insurance to the cardholder on a pass-through basis. Some scholars have argued that prepaid cards can promote financial inclusion. *See, e.g.*, Liran Haim & Ronald J. Mann, *Putting Stored-Value Cards in Their Place*, 18 LEWIS & CLARK L. REV. 989 (2015).

Several developments have boosted prepaid card use. First, general purpose prepaid cards, by using the Visa and MasterCard network, have become useful because of near universal acceptance. Second, many employers have found prepaid cards to be an important tool for managing business expenses. Some employers use a special type of prepaid card, a payroll card, to pay employees who do not use direct deposit into a bank account. Finally, many federal and state government assistance programs issue benefits through prepaid cards.

Even though to most consumers the plastic in their wallet is indistinguishable, prepaid cards, debit cards, payroll cards, and credit cards differ from one another, sometimes significantly, in consumer protections, risk allocation, settlement, deposit insurance coverage, and error resolution. For example, since rule changes in 2006, payroll cards are subject to EFTA and Regulation E, but other prepaid cards are not subject to most sections of the EFTA or Regulation E. The CARD Act did, however, amend the EFTA in 2009 to generally prohibit the imposition of dormancy fees, inactivity fees, or service fees on prepaid cards absent 12 or more months of inactivity. It also prohibited the issuance of prepaid cards with expiration dates occurring under five years after date of issuance. The CFPB proposed in 2014 to amend Regulation E under EFTA and Regulation Z under TILA to provide "comprehensive consumer protections for prepaid financial products." The CFPB proposal, for example, would generally apply Regulation E's disclosure, limited liability, and error resolution coverage to prepaid cards, and would subject prepaid cards with a credit feature to certain obligations under Regulation Z, including requiring that consumers affirmatively opt-in to the credit feature. CFPB, Proposed Rule, Prepaid Accounts under the Electronic Funds Transfer Act (Regulation E) and the Truth in Lending Act (Regulation Z). These issues were brought to the forefront when, in fall 2015, the RushCard, a popular prepaid card, suddenly stopped working, apparently because of a botched transfer to a new processing agent, leaving many cardholders unable to access their funds for extended periods. *See* CFPB, STATEMENT BY CFPB DIRECTOR RICHARD CORDRAY ON RUSHCARD PREPAID CARD INCIDENT (Oct. 23, 2015).

B. MONEY TRANSMITTERS

Retail remittance transfer providers, such as Western Union, have long provided small-scale money transfer services. Indeed, Western Union first came into being with the telegraph in the 19th Century and, as we discussed in Chapter 6.3, much of the early entry of foreign banks into the West Coast of the United States was driven by remittances of immigrant labor back to the home country. Therefore, it should be no surprise that non-bank money transmitters today remain a primary mechanism that serves the unbanked, notably foreigners and new immigrants, many of whom send money home regularly. What is different in today's world of global migration is the massive overall size of remittance transfers even if, on an individual basis, each transfer remains quite small. Remittance transfer providers often maintain agency relationships with businesses around the world, permitting secure, fairly speedy transfers. Just a handful of U.S.-based providers conduct the vast majority of worldwide consumer money transfer services, working with hundreds of thousands of independently owned businesses known as "send-and-receive agents." U.S. non-bank providers transfer an estimated $50 billion annually. CFPB, CFPB PROPOSES RULE TO OVERSEE LARGER NONBANK INTERNATIONAL MONEY TRANSFER PROVIDERS (Jan. 23, 2014). Estimates of global remittances, including through informal channels, put the total dollar volume at close to $600 billion. Bonnie McGeer, *A Plan to Help the Poor with Cheaper Remittances*, AM. BANKER, Jan. 1, 2016.

Fees charged for these remittances remain stubbornly high. It is estimated that the cost of global remittances is about 10% of the transaction and can reach 15% to 20% for some destinations. Dilip Ratha, *Remittances: Funds for the Folks Back Home*, INT'L MONETARY FUND, Mar. 28, 2012. In the last decade, G20 leaders have committed to reducing the costs of remittances to 5% through various initiatives, though little progress has been made so far. THE WORLD BANK, REPORT ON THE REMITTANCE AGENDA OF THE G20 5 (2014). Mobile banking and other new payments technologies hold out the promise of reducing the costs of remittances, but that promise has of yet not been realized. Why not?

In 2013, the CFPB amended Regulation E to regulate remittances under provisions added by the Dodd-Frank Act. Among other things, the CFPB's amendments require providers to disclose clearly and conspicuously to consumers information such as relevant exchange rates, fees and taxes to be charged by both the remittance provider itself and its agents abroad, the amount of money expected to be delivered, and, if appropriate, a statement that foreign taxes or fees may be charged to the recipient. Providers must also disclose when the money will become available and must provide instructions on cancellation and error resolution. 12 C.F.R. § 1005.31(b). If applicable, the disclosures must be available in any foreign languages that the remittance provider principally uses to advertise, solicit, or market its services. 12 C.F.R. § 1005.31(g). Remittance transfer providers must adhere to various error-resolution requirements, but they will not bear the loss if funds are deposited into the wrong account due to the sender's mistake and if certain conditions are satisfied. The provisions are complex, and many providers have been concerned, for example, about their ability to comply with respect to their overseas agents.

These regulations are intended to provide consumer protection and transparency on the theory that competition will drive down prices; however, high prices remain, in part because of concerns regarding regulatory scrutiny over money laundering. For example, in 2015, Merchants Bank of California announced that it was suspending its remittance service to Somalia due to money laundering concerns, even though it was one of the few services that was still facilitating transfers to the country. Ryan Tracy, *Bank to Close Accounts Related to Somalia*, WALL ST. J., Feb. 4, 2015. How likely is it that terrorists and drug money launderers are financing their operations through monthly transfers in the range of $200 or twice yearly transfers of $1,500? THE WORLD BANK, REPORT ON THE REMITTANCE AGENDA OF THE G20 5 (2014); *see also* NOEL

MAURER, MOBILE MONEY | GLOBAL MONEY: AN IN-DEPTH LOOK AT MODERN DAY MONEY TRANSFERS (2015). What is the appropriate balance?

C. MOBILE PHONE FINANCIAL SERVICES

The growth of smartphone technology and expanded access has resulted in an opportunity to provide low-income households with a range of financial services and financial management tools. The full potential of mobile payment to facilitate economic inclusion, however, is constrained by the fact that mobile banking is often designed to work together with online banking. Some mobile operators overseas deliver payments services to the unbanked without linking to a bank account. Safaricom, for instance, offers a mobile-phone based money transfer service in Africa that allows users to deposit money into an account stored on their cell phones, to send balances using SMS technology to other users (including sellers of goods and services), and to redeem deposits for currency. *See* William Jack & Tavneet Suri, *The Economics of M-PESA* (NBER, Working Paper No. 16721, 2011). Adapting these solutions to the United States, however, is fraught with challenges. U.S. banking laws are much more rigid, and mobile payments solutions could face heavy scrutiny. Mobile payments in the United States might end up looking different than it does in Africa, perhaps involving partnerships among wireless carriers, hardware companies, and banks. *See* Dayo Olopade, *Africa's Tech Edge*, ATLANTIC, May 9, 2014. Should policy-makers in the United States ease payment regulations that constrain the development of non-bank mobile phone financial services for the unbanked and underbanked? Or would such steps jeopardize the integrity and safety of the payments system and undermine consumer protection?

---

1. ***What Other Solutions are There for the Unbanked?*** What more can be done to address the needs of the unbanked? Some experts have suggested reviving the postal bank. *See* MEHRSA BARADARAN, HOW THE OTHER HALF BANKS (Harvard Univ. Press, 2015). Recall our discussion in Chapter 2.2. Barr has called for regulatory changes, such as speeding up good funds availability, as well as an expansion of a Social Security benefits prepaid card that could be used more broadly for low-income households. For example, prepaid cards could be used to send tax refunds to low-income households, many of whom receive significant refunds under the Earned Income Tax Credit, and often spend significant sums to get their refund check. *See* BARR, NO SLACK, at 84. Can you think of other ideas? What regulatory changes might help bank the unbanked? Or is that the wrong goal?

VII. INTERBANK FUNDS TRANSFERS

Most payments involve the transfer of funds between the payor's bank and the payee's bank. How are these transfers accomplished? An interbank funds transfer system is an arrangement between banks, built on private contract or statute with common rules and standardized procedures, that facilitates the transmission and settlement of obligations arising between the members, either for their own account or on behalf of their customers. *See* BANK OF INT'L SETTLEMENTS, *A Glossary of Terms Used in Payments and Settlement Systems*

(2003). There are two types of interbank funds transfer systems. Retail systems such as ACH handle a large volume of payments of relatively low value. Wholesale systems such as Fedwire or the Clearing House Interbank Payments System (CHIPS) handle large-value payments in connection with financial market transactions.

Interbank funds transfers involve two key elements. The first of these is the transfer of information between payer and payee banks. A funds transfer is initiated by the transmission of a payment message requesting the transfer of funds to the payee. The payment messages are processed according to rules and operating procedures. Processing may include procedures such as identification, reconciliation and confirmation of payment messages. The second key element is settlement, the actual transfer of funds between the payer's bank and the payee's bank. Settlement is operationally a matter of updating the ledgers of the financial institutions involved to reflect changes in deposit balances resulting from a payment. Settlement can occur on a gross basis, in which each transfer is settled individually, or periodically on a net basis, in which credits and debits can offset each other. Settlement is final upon the receipt of acceptable funds by the payee's bank, which irrevocably extinguishes the obligation of the payer's bank, and thus the payer's payment obligation to the payee. *See* OCC, COMPTROLLER'S HANDBOOK: PAYMENTS SYSTEMS AND FUNDS TRANSFER ACTIVITIES 1 (1990). In this section, we discuss the two major interbank funds transfer systems, ACH and FedWire.

A. RETAIL FUNDS TRANSFERS: THE AUTOMATED CLEARING HOUSE

1. Overview

ACH electronically clears and settles low-value retail payments between participating banks and other depository institutions, including thrifts and the branches of foreign banks. For the sake of simplicity, we will use the term bank to mean all of these depository institutions in this section. The ACH exchanges batched debit and credit payments between businesses, consumers, and government accounts. The system processes pre-authorized recurring payments, such as payroll, Social Security, mortgage and utility payments, and non-recurring payments such as telephone-initiated payments and checks converted into ACH payments at lockboxes and points of sale. ACH moves more than $40 trillion in electronic transactions per year. NACHA, WHAT IS ACH?: QUICK FACTS ABOUT THE AUTOMATED CLEARING HOUSE (ACH) NETWORK (2015).

In an ACH transaction, the initial instruction to transfer funds, known as an entry, can originate with either the payor or the payee. Settlement can create either a credit or a debit entry. In a credit entry, the originator, the payor, asks its bank to credit the recipient's account. In a debit entry, an originator-payee asks its bank to debit the recipient's account. Between its origination and disbursement, the payment instruction moves from the originating bank to one or two regional ACH operators, usually regional Federal Reserve Banks, which transmit data and funds to the recipient's bank. An originating bank's act of forwarding binds it to pay the originating ACH operator all requested credits. Settlement, which is the transfer of funds between banks, is completed quickly, usually the same day or within two business days of the transaction.

There are two main ACH operators in the United States: FedACH, operated by the Federal Reserve Banks, and Electronic Payments Network, privately operated by the Clearing House Payments Company. A key element of the ACH network is the possibility for intraday credit by either a regional Federal Reserve Bank or a correspondent bank. As the settlements take place in batches, during the course of a day, any particular bank may be in either a credit or a debit position to its regional Reserve Bank or its correspondent bank. Banks typically have a net debit cap available in the network with the intraday credit risk taken by the regional Reserve Bank or the correspondent bank. When an individual bank is not in sound financial condition, it may be required to pre-fund, have its net debit capture reduced, or be monitored in real time.

2. Legal and Regulatory Frameworks

ACH payments are regulated by the EFTA and Regulation E. EFTA defines an electronic fund transfer as

> any transfer of funds, other than a transaction originated by check, . . . which is initiated through an electronic terminal, telephonic instrument, or computer or magnetic tape so as to order, instruct, or authorize a financial institution to debit or credit an account. The term includes, but is not limited to, point-of-sale transfers automated teller machine transactions, direct deposits or withdrawals of funds, and transfers initiated by telephone. . . .

EFTA § 903(7).

In addition, the Operating Rules of NACHA, formerly known as the National Automated Clearing House Association, contractually govern the rights and obligations of banks that use the ACH network. Those banks, also by contract, transfer parts of these requirements to their corporate customers who receive and begin ACH transactions. NACHA is a private, self-governing, not-for-profit group of 13 regional payments associations and financial institutions. Transactions via FedACH are also governed by Federal Reserve Operating Circulars. Meanwhile, a Treasury Department document known as the "Green Book" governs ACH payments between financial institutions and the federal government. The Green Book generally follows the NACHA Operating Rules.

3. Risk Allocation

Under the EFTA, implemented by Regulation E, if an unauthorized transfer occurs—that is, if a person other than the consumer without actual authority initiates a fund transfer from the consumer's account with no benefit on the consumer—then the consumer will not be liable absent certain conditions. 12 C.F.R. § 1005.2(m). For ACH transactions, the consumer's financial institution must disclose in writing to the consumer the terms and conditions of electronic funds transfer services. Consumer liability turns on the promptness of the consumer's notification of his or her financial institution. The consumer bears full liability for ACH losses occurring more than 60 days after bank statement transmission but before the consumer notifies the bank. He is also liable for such *post-notification* losses if the bank can show that the unauthorized transactions would not have occurred if the consumer had notified the bank within 60 days. This arrangement also applies to debit-card transactions. How does it compare to the U.C.C. Article 4 provisions for stopping check payment?

On an ACH credit entry, except for a narrow error exception, neither the originator nor the originating depository institution may retract the entry once the originating ACH operator has received it. NACHA Rule 8.1. Meanwhile, the receiving depository institution may reject an ACH credit entry "for any reason," NACHA Rule 6.1.1, so long as that return occurs in time for the originating depository institution to receive it by opening of business on the second banking day after the settlement date. NACHA Rule 6.1.2. Unlike credit-card law, the NACHA Rules do not permit later rejection of a credit entry for reasons such as the originator's unsatisfactory performance of an underlying contractual obligation. On a debit entry, the recipient's right to stop payment turns on whether the recipient is a corporate entity or a natural person. A corporate recipient can stop payment by notifying the receiving depository institution "at such time and in such manner as to allow the receiving depository institution a reasonable opportunity to act upon the stop-payment order before acting on the debit entry." NACHA Rule 8.5. A natural-person recipient of a debit entry must notify the receiving depository institution at least three banking days before the scheduled settlement date. NACHA Rule 8.4. This rule typically applies to consumers who have previously agreed to receive a recurring ACH debit, for example, a monthly bill payment.

When a debit entry is sent without recipient authorization, the NACHA Rules grant a recipient the right to be re-credited. To trigger this right, the recipient must provide, within 15 days, an affidavit stating that the entry was unauthorized. NACHA Rules 8.6.1, 8.6.2. The receiving depository institution must then promptly re-credit the recipient's account. NACHA Rules 8.6.1, 8.6.2, 8.6.3. These rules can be murky, however. *See, e.g.*, Sec. First Network Bank v. C.A.P.S., Inc., 47 U.C.C. Rep. Serv. 2d 670 (N.D. Ill. 2002) (declining to address the effect of NACHA Rule 14.1.30, which expressly incorporates U.C.C. Article 4). The NACHA Rules recognize the possibility of accidental duplicate ACH entries. The originating depository institution may reverse a duplicate entry batch within 24 hours after discovery and within five banking days of the relevant settlement date. NACHA Rule 2.4.2. To reverse a single duplicate entry, the originator must notify the recipient no later than the settlement date. NACHA Rule 2.5.1. In each case, the party seeking reversal must indemnify participating ACH operators and financial institutions for related losses. NACHA Rules 2.4.5, 2.5.2.

---

1. ***Access to the ACH.*** Only depository institutions may directly access the ACH system. In some cases, a non-bank company may contract with a depository institution, which allows the non-bank to initiate ACH transactions using the depository's routing number. Under this arrangement, the depository institution warrants the non-bank's transactions. *See* Terri Bradford et al., *Nonbanks in the Payments System* (World Bank Working Paper No. WP02-02, 2003). Should the ACH allow non-banks to originate and terminate transactions directly? What are the pros and cons of this approach? As you will see in Chapter 7.2, depository institutions continue to play a gatekeeper function for many payment systems, even as new technologies evolve.

B. WHOLESALE FUNDS TRANSFERS

1. Overview

The two major wholesale payment systems in the United States are FedWire and CHIPS. Depository institutions use these large-dollar payments mechanisms both to transfer funds related to their own operations, for example, federal funds transactions, and to transfer funds on behalf of their customers.

FedWire, operated by the Federal Reserve System, allows any depository institution with a Federal Reserve account to transfer funds from that account to the Federal Reserve account of any other depository institution. Each transfer is final and irrevocable when a receiving depository institution is notified of it. A depository institution receiving a FedWire transfer is thus not exposed to any credit risk from the sending depository institution, nor does it normally bear any credit risk in making the proceeds of the transfer immediately available to a customer. The Federal Reserve Banks provide intraday credit by allowing depository institutions to initiate FedWire transfers that may exceed, at a given moment, the balance in their reserve or clearing accounts. These intraday overdrafts of accounts are referred to as daylight overdrafts. The Reserve Bank, not the receiving depository institution, is exposed to the risk that the sending institution will be unable to deposit sufficient funds in its account to cover the transfers. The operation of the FedWire system is thus based on the provision of liquidity and the absorption of the resulting risk by the public sector. The other major payments mechanism is CHIPS, operated by the New York Clearing House Association. In this system, information about individual transfers is exchanged by the participating depository institutions throughout the day. At the end of the day, the value of all transfers sent and received by each of the participants is totaled and netted to determine a net credit or debit position for each participant. Settlement is accomplished through a settlement account on the books of the Federal Reserve Bank of New York. *See* OCC, COMPTROLLER'S HANDBOOK: PAYMENTS SYSTEMS AND FUNDS TRANSFER ACTIVITIES 2-3 (1990).

2. Legal and Regulatory Frameworks

Payment transactions over Fedwire are governed by the Federal Reserve Board's Regulation J, which incorporates the requirements of Article 4A of the U.C.C. Regulation J, in particular subpart B, defines the rights and responsibilities of financial institutions that use Fedwire, as well as the rights and responsibilities of the Federal Reserve Banks. Federal Reserve Board Regulation CC regulates the time within which a depository institution receiving a Fedwire or CHIPS funds transfer on behalf of a customer must make those funds available to their customer. In addition, Federal Reserve Operating Circular 6 covers items such as Fedwire operating hours, security, authentication, and fees. Bank of International Settlements, *Payment Systems in the United States*, at 434, CPSS Red Book (2003). Funds transfers made through CHIPS are subject to CHIPS rules and procedures. The CHIPS rules stipulate that the laws of the state of New York, which include Article 4A of the U.C.C., apply to CHIPS transactions. *Id.*

CHAPTER 7.2

EXAMINING CRITICAL ISSUES IN PAYMENT SYSTEMS

CONTENTS

I. INTRODUCTION

In Chapter 7.1, we explored the legal frameworks that govern different payment systems. In this Chapter, we take a step back and broaden our focus from individual payment systems to the payments ecosystem as a whole. We explore a number of the critical issues that policy-makers face in designing and implementing a cohesive regulatory approach given the existing hodgepodge of regulatory authorities. We first examine the multi-decade effort to mitigate systemic risks in cross-border, interbank clearing and settlement to prevent the type of calamitous consequences that occurred when Germany's Herstatt Bank failed in 1974. We also analyze the new authorities provided under the Dodd-Frank Act's Title VIII for the Federal Reserve Board to supervise and regulate systemic financial activities. We next discuss the contentious stakeholder battles over credit and debit card interchange fees and network rules and the judicial, legislative, and regulatory arenas in which those battles are being fought. We then turn to initiatives to combat money laundering, terrorist financing, and other illicit uses of payment systems. Finally, we examine emerging payment innovations coming out of the fintech world. These include consumer-facing innovations such as Venmo and Apple Pay, which create new user experiences but use existing payment systems, as well as Bitcoin and related innovations in encryption, validation, and decentralized ledgers, which, in at least some forms, attempt to supplant existing payment systems.

II. MANAGING RISK IN INTERBANK CLEARING AND SETTLEMENT

In Chapter 7.1, we briefly examined how interbank clearing and settlement plays a crucial role in almost all payment systems. Given how crucial interbank clearing and settlement systems are for the payments ecosystem, risk management is a major focus of regulators, banks, and operators alike. In this section, we identify some of the major risks that arise in interbank clearing and settlement and we consider several approaches to controlling such risk. The following remarks from former Federal Reserve Board Governor Edward Kelley provide a good overview of the risks inherent in interbank clearing and settlement. Kelley also raises public policy issues about risk management, given the wide variety of transaction types, users, and systems that rely on them.

Edward W. Kelley, Jr., Governor, Fed. Reserve Bd., Clearinghouses and Risk Management

Remarks at the 1996 Payments Sys. Risk Conference, Washington, D.C. (Dec. 3, 1996)

One key type of risk is interbank credit risk . . . [which] is the financial risk that a bank or other participant will default on its payment or settlement obligations to the clearing group when they are due, causing losses to other participants. There is also liquidity risk. If settlement payments are delayed or otherwise not completed on time, one or more banks in a clearinghouse, for example, might be short of cash, which would prevent the completion of other transactions. . . . Further, there are legal risks. . . . There are also operational and security risks. Concerns about these risks are often greatest in the wholesale payments area, where the dollar flows are largest. However, operational and security breakdowns could pose very significant problems for retail payment systems, especially if large numbers of payment items were involved. You are no doubt aware of publicity surrounding these risks in connection with the development of emerging payment technologies, such as stored-value cards, Internet-based payment systems, and new retail banking technologies generally. . . .

A fundamental concern of central banks, of course, is systemic risk. This can involve risks that one bank's problem will spill over onto others, risks that whole clearing systems may cease to operate effectively, and even more broadly, risks that unexpected events will destabilize the banking system as a whole. It is this type of concern that has motivated a sustained effort by the international central banking community in a number of areas. In the payment field, concerns about systemic risk have led central banks to call for reductions in settlement risk, in general, and stronger clearing and settlement arrangements, in particular.

The usual focus of concern is on payment systems that are explicitly designed to handle large-value payments. But the same types of risk—credit, liquidity, legal, operational, and systemic—are often present in clearing systems for smaller-value payments; only the scale of risk is different. It is also important to recognize that although the average dollar value of daily clearings and settlements may be relatively low, the number of checks or other items in the daily clearings may be very high. These payments may include paychecks, corporate payments to suppliers and securities holders, and other routine but very important payments whose completion we take for granted as part of the normal functioning of the economy. Thus, a settlement failure in a check clearinghouse, for example, could be extremely disruptive to the banking system, and even to segments of the economy more broadly, if many thousands of payments were returned or not completed on time.

Let me turn now to a variety of techniques for risk control commonly used by clearinghouses in the wholesale financial markets to control interbank credit, liquidity, and systemic risks. . . . Their risk control techniques often encompass membership standards relating to operational expertise and creditworthiness. Most clearinghouses also designate a risk manager along with a risk management committee. Further, the clearing rules and operational systems typically implement some type of credit and liquidity risk limits, such as caps on net debit positions. . . . To ensure that settlement can occur even if a member defaults, clearinghouses typically employ backstop liquidity resources, such as margin or collateral deposits, participants' funds, and lines of credit. Loss sharing rules are intended to allocate credit losses unambiguously to surviving members, in the event that a participant's default would not be covered by its collateral or other funds at the clearinghouse.

For what we traditionally think of as "small-value" payments, however, the clearinghouse has often been treated simply as a convenient way to exchange bundles of checks and other items and to administer settlements. Although a handful of check and [Automated Clearing House (ACH)] clearinghouses use some more advanced risk controls, the vast majority seem to take the approach that if anything goes wrong, clearinghouse participants will take two aspirin and return payments in the morning. While this point of view is not necessarily wrong, and may be quite cost-effective when amounts at risk are low, it also should not be defended simply because we have always done things this way.

Instead, we need to ask ourselves some basic questions about the reasons why risks and risk controls have been viewed differently for different clearinghouses.... In addition, since many institutions participate in more than one clearinghouse, do we get too limited a picture of risk and risk management if we analyze clearinghouses individually? Finally, are there minimum risk standards that all [clearinghouses] should meet . . . ?

As Kelley suggests, an initial disruption in settlement can activate a chain of risks and transmit them through multiple payment systems, propagating systemic risk. Various stakeholders in the global payments ecosystem have taken different approaches to addressing systemic risk. Typically, risk management has involved coordinated efforts between financial sector participants, legislators, central banks, regulatory agencies, and multinational organizations. We will examine two such approaches to systemic risk management: the creation of the Continuous Linked Settlement (CLS) Bank and reforms instituted under Title VIII of the Dodd-Frank Act.

A. CLS BANK

Payments that settle in foreign currencies involve risk that could become systemic. Foreign exchange (FX) settlement typically takes place in the country of issue of each currency, so that the separate legs of a foreign exchange transaction are settled independently and in many cases at different times. The following excerpt about the failure of Germany's Herstatt Bank illustrates how foreign exchange settlement risk led to systemic disruption across multiple payment systems:

> On 26 June 1974, at 15:30 CET, the German authorities closed Bankhaus Herstatt, a medium-sized bank that was very active in foreign exchange markets. On that day, some of Herstatt's counterparties had irrevocably paid large amounts of Deutsche marks to the bank but not yet received dollars in exchange, as the US financial markets had just opened for the day. Herstatt's closure started a chain reaction that disrupted payment and settlement systems. . . .
>
> The risk that one party in a foreign exchange trade pays out the currency it sold but does not receive the currency it bought is called foreign exchange settlement risk or "Herstatt" risk. . . . ["Herstatt"] risk . . . is likely to have systemic implications for several reasons. First, foreign exchange activity has an international dimension, since currencies are cleared in their home country. Since the working hours of payment systems in the biggest foreign exchange cent[er]s . . . do not overlap completely, a large proportion of foreign exchange activity is settled outside the business hours of one of the counterparties. Second, trading in foreign exchange markets has grown very rapidly and is very large compared to activity in other financial markets. . . . Third, trading between banks accounts for the largest share of foreign exchange market activity. . . . Finally, activity in foreign exchange markets is increasingly concentrated in the hands of relatively few banks.

Gabriele Galati, *Settlement Risk in Foreign Exchange Markets and CLS Bank*, BIS Q. REV. 55, 55, 57–58 (2002).

Herstatt Bank's failure caused $620 million in cross-default losses on its open FX positions. Although Herstatt Bank's closure was the first and most dramatic case of a bank failure where incomplete settlement of FX transactions caused severe problems in payment and settlement systems, it was not the last. Several other episodes occurred in the 1990s. These disruptions eventually spurred a coordinated response by the Federal Reserve Bank of New York and the private sector to address FX settlement as a major source of systemic risk. These efforts culminated in 2002 with the creation of CLS Bank, a limited-purpose bank chartered and supervised by the Federal Reserve System. Through CLS Bank, counterparties to FX transactions exchange payments simultaneously in a process known as payment-versus-payment. CLS Bank requires its members to hold a positive account balance, and it applies haircuts to the exchange rates used to compute each member's account balance. CLS Bank also maintains private-sector liquidity facilities that it can use to swap one currency for another. These measures help mitigate settlement and liquidity risk in FX transactions. As of the end of 2015, CLS Bank has more than 60 members and settles FX transactions in 18 currencies. *See id.* at 62–64.

What additional risks does CLS Bank create, despite its benefits? How should the Federal Reserve Board or other supervisors oversee CLS Bank to address these risks? What is the difference between settlement provision and serving as a central counterparty? We will return to these types of issues in Part XI when we discuss the regulation of derivatives.

B. TITLE VIII OF THE DODD-FRANK ACT

Title VIII of the Dodd-Frank Act created a mechanism for the Federal Reserve Board to supervise and regulate systemically important payment, clearing, and settlement (PCS) systems—such as CLS Bank—and to regulate any systemically important PCS activities. PCS activities are defined quite broadly, including, for example, foreign exchange contracts, clearing transactions for derivatives trading and securities settlement, as well as repo agreements and other securities financing transactions. The following excerpt describes Title VIII's approach to overseeing systemic risks related to PCS systems and activities.

Marc Labonte, Supervision of U.S. Payment, Clearing, and Settlement Systems: Designation of Financial Market Utilities (FMUs)

Cong. Research Serv., Supervision of U.S. Payment, Clearing, and Settlement Systems: Designation of Financial Market Utilities 1-2 (2012)

Prior to the Dodd-Frank Act, various federal regulatory authorities had oversight responsibilities for certain systems or entities engaged in processing those financial transactions. Title VIII reflects recommendations by the previous and current administrations to give the Federal Reserve [Board] explicit statutory oversight authority with respect to elements of the financial infrastructure in the United States, while also giving similar authority to the [SEC] and [CFTC] for certain parts of the infrastructure. Title VIII introduces the term "financial market utility" (FMU or utility) for those multilateral systems that transfer, clear, or settle payments, securities, or other financial transactions among financial institutions . . . or between a FMU and a financial institution.

Title VIII regulatory powers apply specifically to those financial market utilities and PCS activities (of financial institutions) that are designated as systemically important by the Financial Stability Oversight Council (FSOC). . . . On July 18, 2012, FSOC voted unanimously to designate eight FMUs as systemically important. [These are: The Clearing House Payments Company LLC, CLS Bank International, Chicago Mercantile Exchange, Inc., The Depository Trust Company, Fixed Income Clearing Corporation, ICE Clear Credit LLC, National Securities Clearing Corporation, and The Options Clearing Corporation]. . . .

Some Representatives opposed Title VIII and struck the title governing PCS supervision from the financial reform bill that the House of Representatives passed in December 2009. Concerns held by some opponents of the title may have included a sense that the U.S. financial infrastructure was adequately supervised, or that the title might have given too much discretionary authority to the Federal Reserve. Other reservations may have included the view that Title VIII was unnecessary in light of the Federal Reserve's efforts to encourage firms to voluntarily strengthen infrastructure procedures in various markets, and the absence of a PCS-related breakdown in September 2008.

FMUs, institutions designated as systematically important under Title VIII, are subject to risk management standards prescribed by the Federal Reserve Board, as well as the SEC and the CFTC if they are otherwise subject to their supervision. FMUs are subject to annual examinations and potential enforcement actions by the relevant supervising regulators, and reporting and record-keeping requirements. 12 U.S.C. §§ 5464(a)(1), 5467(a)–(b), 5468(b). The Federal Reserve Board promulgated final rules addressing the risk-management standards for FMUs in 2012. *See* Designated Financial Market Utilities (Regulation HH), 12 C.F.R. § 234. As noted above, activities may also be designated as systemic by the FSOC, in which case the Federal Reserve Board may prescribe rules governing the activities, and such rules apply broadly across the entire financial market, not simply to FMUs or bank holding companies.

III. REGULATING PAYMENT CARD INTERCHANGE FEES

A. WHO BEARS THE COST OF CREDIT AND DEBIT CARD TRANSACTIONS?

Payments systems are not free; someone has to bear their costs. Where and how those costs are allocated are critical questions. We now turn to credit and debit card payments as a case study. As we discussed in Chapter 7.1, a consumer's choice of payment method determines the speed with which the transaction will be settled and which party bears the risks. The consumer's choice of payment method has two other important consequences: it determines both how much the retailer is charged for processing the transaction and the set of card network rules by which the parties are bound. When a cardholder swipes her card at a merchant terminal, the cardholder's bank (the issuer) debits her account, and sends the transaction to the card network, which then forwards the transaction information to the merchant's bank (the acquirer). The acquirer then credits the merchant's account. The acquirer does not credit the merchant the full amount of the retail transaction because the issuer charges the acquirer an interchange fee, and the acquirer deducts those fees, along with the acquirer's own fees, from the amount credited to the merchant. That amount is known as the merchant discount. Interchange fees are costs to merchants and revenue to card issuers. Issuers and acquirers also pay a switch fee to the network.

Figure 7.2-1 Overview of Interchange Fees

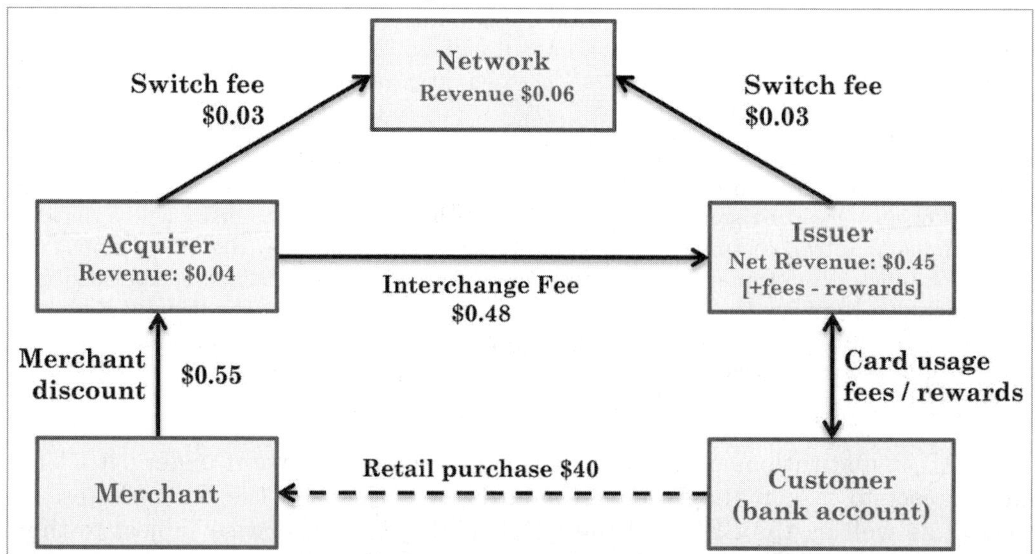

Source: Benjamin S. Kay et al., Bank Profitability and Debit Card Interchange Regulation: Bank Responses to the Durbin Amendment, Divisions of Research & Statistics and Monetary Affairs, Fed. Reserve Bd. Fin. and Econ. Discussion Series 7 (2014).

Interchange income for banks from credit and debit cards constituted $41 billion in 2010, before the introduction of Federal Reserve Board regulations issued under the Durbin Amendment to the Dodd-Frank Act, which we will discuss later in this Chapter. Benjamin S. Kay et al., *Bank Profitability and Debit Card Interchange Regulation: Bank Responses to the Durbin Amendment* 3, (Divisions of Research & Statistics and Monetary Affairs, Fed. Reserve Bd. Fin and Econ. Discussion Series No. 2014-77, 2014).

Interchange fees, although they accrue to the benefit of issuing banks, are set on a network-wide basis by the card networks. Interchange may be a flat fee per transaction, a percentage of the transaction amount, or some combination of the two. Interchange fees are set for both debit and credit cards, although credit card fees tend to be higher than debit card fees. In 2009, interchange fees for credit card transactions averaged from 1.5% to 2% of the transaction value, while fees for debit cards averaged 1.15%. *See* Robin A. Prager et al., *Interchange Fees and Payment Card Networks: Economics, Industry Developments, and Policy Issues*, FED. RESERVE BD., 2009; *see also* FED. RESERVE SYS., *2009 Interchange Revenue, Covered Issuer Cost, and Covered Issuer Merchant Fraud Loss Related to Debit Card Transactions*, June 2011. For a discussion of the economic rationale for networks setting interchange fees, see William F. Baxter, *Bank Exchange of Transactional Paper: Legal and Economic Perspectives*, 26 J.L. & Econ. 541 (1983); *see also* Alan S. Frankel, *Monopoly and Competition in the Supply and Exchange of Money*, 66 ANTITRUST L. J. 313 (1998); *see also* David S. Evans & Richard Schmalensee, *The Economics of Interchange Fees and Their Regulation: An Overview*, *in* INTERCHANGE FEES: THE ECONOMICS AND REGULATION OF WHAT MERCHANTS PAY FOR CARDS 1–33 (2011).

Merchants and issuers have frequently clashed over interchange fees in the United States and in other countries, and a battle has emerged over the allocation of costs among merchants, issuers, and consumers. Merchants argue that interchange fees increase the cost of processing transactions and instead are used by banks to cover their own costs of marketing and rewards programs. Merchants complain that the existing system leaves them trapped: they cannot reject the network's cards because customers rely on these commonly used methods of payment. Robin A. Prager et al., *Interchange Fees and Payment Card Networks: Economics, Industry Developments, and Policy Issues*, FED. RESERVE BD., 2009. In addition to the networks setting interchange fees, the networks set operating rules that merchants must follow. These rules include a requirement that a merchant agree to accept all types of a given payment card, such as Visa or MasterCard, regardless of the higher interchange fee that may be associated with a card's rewards program or other features (the honor-all-cards rule), and a prohibition on adding a surcharge even if a customer pays with a credit or debit card that is more expensive to the merchant (the no-surcharge rule). *See id.* at 12–13. Merchants argue that network rules limit competition and increase interchange fees.

Issuers counter that interchange fees and card network rules are necessary to coordinate across the network and to cover costs related to authorization, clearance, and settlement of transactions; fees paid to card networks; costs of card production and delivery, cardholder inquiries, rewards, and other incentives; and fraud losses and fraud prevention costs. *See, e.g.*, Debit Card

Interchange Fees and Routing, 76 Fed. Reg. 43394 (July 20, 2011). Issuers highlight the costs embedded in developing and managing the system, which requires innovation to support its use by consumers, especially during an era of high growth in use, technological change, and increased risks. Networks and issuers, who have developed and managed the system, can cover these costs themselves, shift them to consumers, or push them on to merchants. The networks argue that they are restrained in pushing on too much in costs to merchants because merchants may reject cards altogether.

Credit and debit card networks are highly concentrated. Visa, followed by Mastercard and American Express, account for approximately 95% of the credit card network market, with Discover accounting for the remaining 5% share. United States v. Am. Express Co., No. 10-4496, slip op. at 67 (E.D.N.Y. Feb. 19, 2015). In the debit card market, Visa has about a 60% market share overall. In the signature debit market, Visa has a 75-80% share, with most of the rest of the market dominated by MasterCard, and a small slice by Discover. PIN debit has about a dozen competitors, including networks owned by Visa, MasterCard, and Discover; the top five firms have 95% market share. Fumiko Hayashi, *The New Debit Card Regulations: Initial Effects on Networks and Banks*, FED. RES. BANK OF KANSAS CITY ECON. REV., Fourth Quarter 2012, at 84.

B. ANTITRUST LITIGATION

A number of different stakeholder battles over interchange fees have ensued. We begin with antitrust litigation. In 2005, a group of merchants brought a class action lawsuit against Visa, MasterCard, and issuing and acquiring banks alleging price-fixing in violation of the Sherman Act. The lawsuit also challenged the card network's honor-all-cards and no-surcharging rules. The parties agreed to settle the case for more than $7 billion and certain changes in Visa and MasterCard's network rules, including the elimination of the no-surcharge rule. The district court approved the settlement in 2013, despite opposition from big box retailers such as Target, Walmart, and Home Depot, as well as the National Association of Convenience Stores and National Restaurant Association. *See In re* Payment Card Interchange Fee and Merchant Discount Antitrust Litigation, 986 F. Supp. 2d 207 (E.D.N.Y. 2013). The district court's settlement order, which has been challenged on appeal, is excerpted below.

In re Payment Card Interchange Fee & Merch. Disc. Antitrust Litig.

986 F. Supp. 2d 207 (E.D.N.Y. 2013)

[T]he vitriol and poor behavior and feigned hysteria mask complex and difficult issues on which reasonable merchants can and do disagree. Some of those issues stem from the fact that a lawsuit is an imperfect vehicle for addressing the wrongs the plaintiffs allege in their complaint. For example, there are forms of relief many objectors seek, such as the regulation of interchange fees, that this Court could not order even if the plaintiffs obtained a complete victory on the merits. In addition, there are features of the industry landscape, such as other credit card issuers with whom the defendants compete, and laws in some states that prohibit merchants from surcharging the use of credit cards, that are beyond the reach of this case but will undermine (at least in the near term) the efficacy of the agreed-upon relief.

I conclude that the proposed settlement secures both a significant damage award and meaningful injunctive relief for a class of merchants that would face a substantial likelihood of securing no relief at all if this case were to proceed.

Specifically, although the settlement either obtains or locks in place an array of rules changes, at its heart is an important step forward: a rules change that will permit merchants to surcharge credit cards at both the brand level (*i.e.*, Visa or MasterCard) and at the product level (*i.e.*, different kinds of cards, such as consumer cards, commercial cards, premium cards, etc.), subject to acceptance cost and limits imposed by other networks' cards. For the first time, merchants will be empowered to expose hidden bank fees to their customers, educate them about those fees, and use that information to influence their customers' choices of payment methods. In short, the settlement gives merchants an opportunity at the point of sale to stimulate the sort of network price competition that can exert the downward pressure on interchange fees they seek.

The DOJ and a number of state attorneys general also brought suit in 2010 against American Express, Visa, and MasterCard for antitrust violations in credit card networks. In a settlement approved in 2011, Visa and MasterCard agreed to remove their no-discounting provisions from their network agreements. American Express did not settle. After a lengthy trial, the district court ruled in the DOJ's favor in 2015. After the district court entered an injunction in this case, merchants were able, for example, to offer consumers a discount for using PIN debit, with its lower interchange fees, instead of signature debit, or for using Visa instead of American Express. *See* Order re: Plaintiffs' Motion to Enforce Permanent Injunction, United States v. Am. Express Co., No. 10-4496 (E.D.N.Y. Dec. 15, 2015). The defendants appealed to the Second Circuit, which stayed the injunction on December 18, 2015.

Scholars have questioned the suitability of addressing interchange fees and network rules through litigation. In the excerpt below, written before these settlements and the Dodd-Frank Act's debit card interchange amendment, Professor Adam Levitin identifies the complex interests at stake:

Adam J. Levitin, Priceless? The Social Costs of Credit Card Merchant Restraints

45 HARV. J. ON LEGIS. 1, 57–58 (2008).

In the United States, it is litigation, rather than regulation, that is driving possible credit card reform. Merchants have filed what has been described by a former [Federal Trade Commission] Chairman as "the largest private antitrust litigation in the hundred-plus year history of the Sherman Act" against the credit card networks and their leading member banks These suits allege that a variety of practices, including merchant restraints, constitute antitrust violations. Already, Discover has dropped its no-surcharge rule as part of a settlement agreement. Merchants, however, have different concerns and incentives than do consumers. Merchants are not aiming to eliminate cross-subsidizations and social externalities, but only to limit their payment expenses. Merchants also have different settlement incentives than consumers. While consumers might benefit from a merchant victory, it might not produce optimal results for consumers. . . . Ultimately, only Congress can solve the problem of merchant restraints. Even if merchants win their antitrust suits, the most they can hope for is damages and an injunction against the credit card networks. Such an injunction will block private merchant restraints, but it will not affect state no-surcharge rules, including Florida's criminal statute. Merchants with interstate operations will be very hesitant to engage in price discrimination so long as state no-surcharge rules exist in states (most notably California, Florida, New York, and Texas) that collectively contain approximately 40% of the United States population. While it may be possible to repeal state no-surcharge rules, and state legislation has even been proposed to do so, only Congress can solve the merchant restraint problem cleanly, neatly, and completely by passing legislation that guarantees merchants the right to decide which payment products within a brand they wish to accept and the right to choose the prices they charge for payment acceptance. The problem, though, is that Congress is unlikely to act absent a merchant victory in the courts because of the tremendous political power of the credit card lobby.

Other scholars argue that the criticism of merchant restraints is misguided, contending that the rules were originally put in place to protect consumers from merchants steering them to higher-priced merchant credit, and that merchant restraints are part of a system of rules designed to expand card networks, to the benefit of both consumers and merchants. *See* DAVID S. EVANS & RICHARD SCHMALENSEE, PAYING THE PLASTIC: THE DIGITAL REVOLUTION IN BUYING AND BORROWING (2015); *see also* David S. Evans, *The Antitrust Economics of Multi-Sided Platform Markets,* 20 YALE J. ON REG. 325 (2003). The legislative history of these issues is tortured: Congress permitted cash discounts under Truth in Lending Act (TILA) amendments in 1974, Pub. L. No. 93–495, 88 Stat. 1500, and then barred merchant surcharges in 1976 amendments, Pub. L. No. 94–222, 90 Stat. 197. Congress debated the merchant surcharge provision for many years before first loosening it and then allowing it to expire in 1984. *See, e.g.,* Sen. Christopher Dodd, *Credit Card Surcharges: Let the Gouger Beware*, N.Y. TIMES, March 12, 1984; *see also* Adam J. Levitin, *Priceless? The Economic Costs of Credit Card Merchant Restraints*, 55 UCLA L. Rev. 1321, 1381 (2008). A number of states prohibit merchant surcharges, while permitting cash discounts. *See* NAT'L CONFERENCE OF STATE LEGISLATORS, CREDIT OR DEBIT CARD SURCHARGE STATE STATUTES (2015). Are surcharges and discounts flip sides of the same coin, or does the frame matter to consumer behavior? Why did credit card firms lobby for TILA to prohibit merchant surcharging? *See* Amos Tversky & Daniel Kahneman, *Rational Choice and the Framing of Decisions*, 59 J. BUS. 251, 261 (1986). Which of these approaches, if any, best protects consumers and fosters a strong payments system?

The battle between stakeholder interests and the difficulty of finding an appropriate balance is illustrated by Australia's experience. In 2003, the Reserve Bank of Australia reduced interchange fees on credit cards by approximately 50% and prohibited no-surcharge rules. The Reserve Bank of Australia expressed its view a decade later that its reforms benefited consumers:

> This reform was important in allowing merchants to signal to consumers that some payment methods are more expensive for merchants to accept than others so that consumers could consider whether to pay with a less costly method. Directly charging users of higher-cost payment methods also meant that merchants did not need to build card acceptance costs into the prices of all their goods

> and services. In other words, it was no longer necessary for users of less costly payment methods to cross-subsidies users of more expensive payment methods.
>
> Since the implementation of the [Federal] Reserve Bank's reforms, average merchant service fees (the percentage fee that the merchant pays on each card payment) have fallen. . . . The ability of merchants to surcharge has made more apparent the cost of particular payment methods to consumers and enabled merchants to encourage the use of lower-cost payment methods. The Bank's 2010 Consumer Payments Use Study found that around half of consumers that hold a credit card would seek to avoid paying a surcharge by using a different payment method that does not typically attract a surcharge (debit card or cash). The effect of the Reserve Bank's reforms and the reduction in costs to merchants will have applied downward pressure on prices in a range of industries, to the benefit of all consumers.

RESERVE BANK OF AUSTRALIA, REFORMS TO PAYMENT CARD SURCHARGING, (2013).

Professor Steven Semerano, however, argues that Australia's approach to surcharging created some risks:

> The experience with surcharging in Australia illustrates the danger of relying on merchant customer-steering efforts. Although Australian merchant card-acceptance fees dropped when the merchants' obtained the power to surcharge, cardholders paid a price. Annual cardholder fees increased; credit card rewards were reduced; and banks required cardholders to pay their bills faster. The potentially beneficial effect of surcharging on card acceptance fees must be balanced against these costs. In addition to the costs that surcharging would shift to cardholders, merchants would bear the costs of determining the appropriate surcharge or discount given market conditions, training sales staff, and educating consumers about the purpose of the practice. Merchants would need to recoup these costs from consumers, limiting the potential efficiency gains.
>
> The benefits of surcharging to consumers, again even under the best of circumstances, are highly uncertain because a merchant's economic interests would lead it to undervalue the utility that its customers derive from using credit cards when they would still make a purchase without them. As a result, at least some merchants would surcharge at excessive levels. The experience in Australia again appears to confirm that this risk is real. Nine years after Australian regulators permitted surcharging, they determined that some merchants were abusing the practice to the detriment of consumers.

Steven Semerano, *Settlement Without Consent: Assessing the Credit Card Merchant Fee Class Action*, 2105 COLUM. BUS. L. REV. 186, 246–48 (2015). *See also* Howard H. Chang et al., *An Assessment of the Reserve Bank of Australia's Interchange Fee Regulation*, 4 REV. OF NETWORK ECON. 329 (2005). Semerano highlights the real possibility that, while merchants and issuers battle over these issues, consumers might be the ones caught in the middle, with costs passed on to them by banks or merchants to make up the difference.

C. THE DURBIN AMENDMENT

As of the end of 2015, the antitrust litigation was still ongoing 11 years after it began. During that time, the card payment system also experienced other developments. The second avenue through which interchange fees were addressed was through legislative action. The conflict between merchants and issuers came to the forefront when Congress responded by stepping in to regulate fees that card issuers were able to charge. Illinois Senator Richard Durbin, taking the side of the big box retailers and merchants against the banks and card networks, put considerable effort into sponsoring a provision of the Dodd-Frank Act, known as the Durbin Amendment, which directs the Federal Reserve Board to cap debit card interchange fees. *See* Dodd-Frank Act § 1075, codified at 15 U.S.C. § 1693. The Durbin Amendment requires the Federal Reserve Board to issue rules requiring that "[t]he amount of any interchange transaction fee that an issuer may receive or charge with respect to an electronic debit transaction shall be reasonable and proportional to the cost incurred by the issuer with respect to the transaction." In a political compromise designed to lessen opposition from community banks, the Durbin Amendment exempts banks with under $10 billion in assets from these rules.

In addition to the provision setting a price cap, the Durbin Amendment also includes provisions designed to increase competition in debit card payment networks. The Durbin Amendment opens up competition by barring networks and issuers from using network exclusivity or priority-routing rules to restrict merchants to a single network for payment processing. The Durbin Amendment also bars networks or issuers from prohibiting merchants from offering discounts for use of different types of payments systems. *Id.* The theory of these parts of the Durbin Amendment is that merchants will be able to increase competition among networks, first by having a choice themselves among competing networks, and second by offering consumers choices among payment processing options and by reflecting those choices in the prices consumers pay for goods or services. These provisions are designed to provide incentives for networks to compete not only for bank issuers, as in the past, but also for merchants, and potentially, for consumers.

The Durbin Amendment was widely promoted as consumer friendly during the legislative process. Merchants argued that they were subject to unreasonable fees and inflexible rules and were passing on these costs to consumers through increased prices. Retail industry titans such as Walmart and Target led the charge to regulate interchange fees, as had been the case with the antitrust litigation. The Retail Industry Leaders Association played a role in the development and passage of the Durbin Amendment. These big box retailers lobbied Congress and rallied consumer and small business organizations around their cause. Recall the discussion of Sam's Bank in Chapter 2.1 and the suggestion of Professor Ronald Mann that Walmart's attempt to enter banking in the 1990s was primarily an attempt to lower its massive card processing costs. *See* Ronald Mann, *A Requiem for Sam's Bank*, 83 CHI.-KENT L. REV. 953 (2008). With public anger towards the banking sector at a high point in the aftermath of the Financial Crisis, the Dodd-Frank Act was the ideal time politically for merchants to lobby to bring about change in the interchange fees system.

Once the Durbin Amendment passed, the battle among the stakeholder interests continued at the regulatory level. There was disagreement on how to set the fee caps. The Federal Reserve Board initially proposed to cap debit interchange fees at 12 cents per transaction, down from the then average fee of 50 cents. *See* 75 Fed. Reg. 81,722 (Dec. 28, 2010). Both sides of the stakeholder interests attacked the Federal Reserve Board's proposed rule. Merchants argued that the Federal Reserve Board overestimated card issuers' costs and that the 12-cent cap was too high. *See, e.g.*, Dell Inc., Comment Letter on Proposed Rule 12 C.F.R. Part 235 (Feb. 22, 2011). Bank issuers insisted that the Federal Reserve Board had failed to take into account all of their costs and that the cap was thus too low. *See, e.g.*, JPMorgan Chase, Comment Letter on Proposed Regulation II, Docket No. R-1404 (Feb. 22, 2011). Merchants and issuers also clashed over what it meant for a fee to be "reasonable and proportional" to costs incurred by the issuer. *See id.*; *see also* Network Branded Prepaid Card Association, Comment Letter on Proposed Rule Docket No. R-1404 (Feb. 17, 2011).

Ultimately, the Federal Reserve Board adopted a 21-cent interchange cap, significantly higher than the proposed amount but, with adjustments, about 45% of the then average fee of 50 cents. The final rule provided that a card issuer may charge a base fee of 21 cents per transaction to cover processing costs, plus .05% of the transaction amount to cover potential fraud losses and an additional 1 cent per transaction for fraud prevention costs. The rule went into effect on October 1, 2011 and was met with disappointment on both sides of the issue.

The first legal challenge was made by merchants. The National Association of Convenience Stores and National Restaurant Association, involved in the antitrust litigation, brought suit against the Federal Reserve Board. The merchant groups claimed that the Federal Reserve Board had exceeded its Congressional authority by including certain costs in its calculations that were allegedly not contemplated by the statute, and claimed that *Chevron* deference was not appropriate. In a spirited opinion, U.S. District Court Judge Leon ruled in favor of the merchants and agreed that the Federal Reserve Board had not complied with the Durbin Amendment, thus ordering a stay and remanding the issue to the Board.

Nat'l Ass'n of Convenience Stores v. Bd. of Governors of Fed. Reserve Sys.

958 F. Supp. 2d 85, 94-95 (D.D.C. 2013)

The [Federal Reserve] Board increased the allowable interchange fee (from twelve cents in Alternative 2 to twenty-one cents in the Final Rule) after concluding that the language and purpose of the Durbin Amendment allow the [Federal Reserve] Board to consider additional costs not explicitly excluded from consideration by the statute. According to the [Federal Reserve] Board, [the Durbin Amendment] on the one hand requires the [Federal Reserve] Board to consider incremental [authorization, clearance, and settlement of a transactions (ACS)] costs incurred by issuers, and on the other hand prohibits consideration of any issuer costs that are not specific to a particular transaction; but it is silent with respect to costs that fall into neither category (*e.g.*, costs specific to a particular transaction but are not incremental ACS costs). The [Federal Reserve] Board concluded that it had discretion to consider costs on which the statute is silent. . . .

As individual retailers that accept debit cards and trade associations comprised of merchants, plaintiffs contend that the Final Rule is an unreasonable interpretation of the Durbin Amendment because it ignores Congress's directives regarding interchange fees and network exclusivity. As to the former, plaintiffs assert that the Durbin Amendment limits the [Federal Reserve] Board's consideration of allowable costs to the "incremental cost" of "authorization, clearance and settlement of a particular electronic debit transaction," and that, by including other costs in the fee standard, the [Federal Reserve] Board acted unreasonably and in excess of its statutory authority. Regarding the latter, plaintiffs argue that the [Federal Reserve] Board disregarded the plain meaning of the Durbin Amendment and misconstrued the statute by adopting a network non-exclusivity rule requiring all debit cards be interoperable with at least two unaffiliated payment networks, rather than requiring that all debit transactions be able to run over at least two unaffiliated networks.

[T]he interchange transaction fee and network non-exclusivity regulations are fundamentally deficient. It appears that the [Federal Reserve] Board completely misunderstood the Durbin Amendment's statutory directive and interpreted the law in ways that were clearly foreclosed by Congress. Because the Court cannot be sure that the agency will interpret the statute in the same way and arrive at the same conclusion after further review, let alone whether, on further judicial review, this or a similar Final Rule will withstand challenge under the [Administrative Procedure Act], this factor weighs heavily in favor of vacatur.

The Federal Reserve Board appealed and the case was then heard by the D.C. Circuit Court of Appeals, which reversed the lower court decision and upheld the Federal Reserve Board's regulation in its entirety. The court recognized the difficulty with the structure and language of the Durbin Amendment and the administrative gymnastics required to implement it:

> [W]e think it worth emphasizing that Congress put the [Federal Reserve] Board, the district court, and us in a real bind. Perhaps unsurprising given that the Durbin Amendment was crafted in conference committee at the eleventh hour, its language is confusing and its structure convoluted. But because neither agencies nor courts have authority to disregard the demands of even poorly drafted legislation, we must do our best to discern Congress's intent and to determine whether the [Federal Reserve] Board's regulations are faithful to it.

NACS v. Bd. of Governors of Fed. Reserve Sys., 746 F.3d 474, 483 (D.C. Cir. 2014).

D. WHO ENDS UP PAYING?

The interchange cap in the Federal Reserve Board's rule struck an unhappy balance for both sides. In the wake of the rule, debit card interchange fees have decreased significantly. Indeed, the average card interchange fee charged by issuers with $10 billion or more in assets has fallen from 50 cents to 24 cents per transaction. *See* Hayashi, *The New Debit Card Regulations: Initial Effects on*

Networks and Banks, at 90–91. When interchange fees drop, who pays for the decrease?

Answering that question is not straightforward as an empirical matter, and studies are often sponsored or contested by one or the other side in the debate. While the distributive effects of the Durbin Amendment are not yet entirely clear, several studies suggest that most of the benefit of the Durbin Amendment has flowed to merchants at the expense of large banks, and that merchants have not passed along substantial cost savings to consumers. One Federal Reserve Bank of Richmond study found that merchants generally have not reduced prices in response to lower interchange fees. *See* Zhu Wang et al., *The Economic Impact of the Durbin Amendment on Merchants: A Survey Study*, 100 ECON. Q. 183 (2014). Another study, funded by Visa, found that consumers were worse off because card issuers raised fees more than merchants reduced prices. David S. Evans et al., *The Impact of the U.S. Debit Card Interchange Fee Regulation on Consumer Welfare: An Event Study Analysis* (Coase-Sandor Inst. for Law and Econ., Working Paper No. 658 (2d Series), 2013). A study, funded in part by MasterCard and described in the following excerpt, found that issuers tried to recoup their interchange fee income in ways that caused disproportionate harm to low-income consumers by, for example, discontinuing fee-free checking accounts and increasing monthly fees. *See* Todd J. Zywicki et al., *Price Controls on Payment Card Interchange Fees: The U.S. Experience* (George Mason Law & Econ. Research Paper No. 14-18, 2014).

> Bank consumers have borne the brunt of the Durbin Amendment, especially low-income consumers. Running a secure, instantaneous, globally-connected payment card system takes money and forcibly reducing the freight paid by merchants by an estimated $6.6 to $8.5 billion per year didn't magically make the costs of the payment card system disappear. Instead, it simply transferred those costs to card issuers and, in turn, forced banks to reallocate those costs onto their customers. . . . [T]he percentage of bank accounts eligible for free checking plummeted from 76% in 2009 to 38% last year. The minimum average balance necessary to qualify for free checking has doubled during that same period as has the monthly maintenance fees required for those who fail to meet the steeper eligibility requirements for free checking. . . .
>
> And what have Wal-Mart, Amazon, and ExxonMobil done with their windfall? Pocketed it. . . . [W]e estimate that because banks pass-through their increased costs to consumer[s] faster and more completely than retailers do their cost savings, lower-income households will transfer roughly $1 to $3 billion per year to large retailers as a result of the Durbin Amendment.

Todd Zywicki et al., *How to Help the Unbanked? Repeal the Durbin Amendment*, FORBES, Aug. 4, 2014.

Another scholar suggests that the Durbin Amendment dis-incentivizes investment in new technologies, such as mobile payments. *See* Jonathon Reinisch, *Swipe Freeze: How the "Durbin Amendment" is Preventing Your Mobile Phone from Replacing Your Wallet*, 63 DEPAUL L. REV. 123 (2013).

A study by Federal Reserve Bank of Boston staff, however, suggests that banks were not able to offset most of the lost interchange income by increasing other fees on consumers. The study suggests that banks increased fees somewhat, but took a large hit as a result of the Durbin Amendment by an estimated reduction in bank income of $14 billion per year. *See* Benjamin S. Kay et al., *Bank Profitability and Debit Card Interchange Regulation: Bank Responses to the Durbin Amendment*, FED. RES. BANK OF BOSTON, Mar. 2014. A study sponsored by the Merchant Payments Coalition argues that the Durbin Amendment saved merchants $8.5 billion in 2012, and that merchants passed on savings to consumers of $5.87 billion, retaining $2.64 billion of the benefit. Robert J. Shapiro, *The Costs and Benefits of Half a Loaf: The Economic Effects of Recent Regulation of Debit Card Interchange Fees* (Sonecon, LLC, 2013).

The Durbin Amendment—and the battle over interchange fees in general—illustrates some of the themes we have been exploring. First, it was a classic stakeholder fight, with battles fought in the courts and legislative and regulatory arenas. Second, public interest goals were not the sole aims of those fighting against or seeking to protect the status quo. Finally, the battle played out over a long time, with collateral economic consequences, both foreseen and unforeseen, and the battle is not yet over.

IV. PREVENTING ILLICIT USE OF PAYMENT SYSTEMS

Payments systems are the essential plumbing of the financial system and, like other parts of finance, can be used for good or ill. The United States attempts to police the financial system to avoid its use for money laundering or terrorist financing. Money laundering is the process of making illegal proceeds appear legal. A money launderer places illegal monies in the legitimate financial system, may transfer them through numerous accounts or shell companies to create confusion, and integrates these funds into the financial system until they appear legitimate. Financial institutions are a money-laundering target because they can rapidly transfer funds from entity to entity and from one jurisdiction to another. Terrorist financing might involve either legitimately or illegitimately obtained funds used to support terrorism. *See generally* PETER REUTER AND EDWIN M. TRUMAN, CHASING DIRTY MONEY: THE FIGHT AGAINST MONEY LAUNDERING (2004). The United States also polices the financial system for its use in violation of sanctions regimes. In this section, we first provide a brief overview of anti-money laundering (AML), anti-terrorist financing, and economic sanctions laws. We then explore some of the tradeoffs in compliance.

A. ANTI-MONEY LAUNDERING AND RELATED LAWS

The Bank Secrecy Act of 1970 (BSA) established a broad AML structure requiring, among other things, that financial institutions report cash transactions of $10,000 or more. The legislation has since been amended and strengthened, notably by the Money Laundering Control Act of 1986, which established money laundering as a federal crime, and by the USA PATRIOT Act of 2001, which expanded reporting requirements to combat terrorist financing in response to the September 11, 2001 terrorist attacks. New requirements arising from Title III of the USA PATRIOT Act, known as the International Money Laundering Abatement and Anti-Terrorist Financing Act, are particularly significant. The post-9/11 political climate also heightened the rigor with which regulators and the Justice Department enforced existing BSA requirements.

Know-Your-Customer (KYC) rules are perhaps the USA PATRIOT Act's most substantial AML development. For banks, KYC comprises two parts. First, pursuant to USA PATRIOT Act § 326 and related regulations, banks must collect specific customer data and verify their identities with prescribed procedures. *See* 31 C.F.R. § 103.121. Second, bank regulators have required banks to conduct "customer due diligence." *See* FED. FIN. INST. EXAMINATION COUNCIL BANK SECRECY ACT/ANTI-MONEY LAUNDERING EXAMINATION MANUAL 56–59 (2014). The KYC regulatory regime varies based on a risk rating of each customer account. *See id.* at 18–27. Regulators recommend that financial institutions analyze the frequency of currency exchanges, wire transfers, and international transactions in connection with offshore financial centers. *See id.* at 164-293. High risk ratings trigger more extensive due diligence at an account's opening, as well as closer ongoing monitoring for suspicious activity, which must be reported to the Treasury. *See id.*; *see also* 31 C.F.R. § 103.18. Each bank performs these tasks pursuant to its own written Customer Identification Program, 31 C.F.R. § 103.121(b)(1), in order to "enable the bank to form a reasonable belief that it knows the true identity of each customer," 31 C.F.R. § 103.121(b)(2). Customer Due Diligence is an outgrowth of post-9/11 bank supervision, arising from the requirement that that banks file "suspicious activity" reports whenever they "know[], suspect[], or *ha[ve] reason to suspect*" such activity. 31 C.F.R. § 103.18(a)(2) (emphasis added). This objective standard means that a bank's failure to report suspicious activity can create liability absent the bank's actual knowledge or suspicion, thereby incentivizing banks to assess expected activity in customer accounts to monitor them for unusual activity.

Its name notwithstanding, the BSA now applies sweepingly to all financial institutions, as defined in 31 U.S.C. §§ 5312(a)(2), (c)(1), including banks, broker-dealers, and money service businesses, which include check cashers, currency exchanges, money transmitters, the U.S. Postal Service, and casinos, among others. The BSA also reaches "person[s] subject to supervision by any state or federal bank supervisory authority." 31 C.F.R. § 103.11(n).

Financial institutions are also subject to supervision and enforcement with respect to the Trading with the Enemy Act and the International Economic Emergency Powers Act and various sanctions regimes, such as against Iran, under regulations issued by the Office of Foreign Assets Control (OFAC), a bureau within the Treasury. Regulators, OFAC, the Department of Justice, and state supervisory and enforcement officials have brought a range of civil and criminal actions against foreign and domestic financial institutions, resulting in significant fines, for allegedly violating these sanctions rules. *See, e.g.,* Paul L. Lee, *Compliance Lessons from OFAC Case Studies—Part II,* 131 BANKING L.J. 717 (2014).

B. ISSUES IN COMPLIANCE

Community banks argue that the costs of compliance are onerous for them and disproportionate to the risks they pose. *See* INDEPENDENT COMMUNITY BANKERS OF AMERICA, ICBA POLICY RESOLUTIONS FOR 2015: BANK SECRECY ACT

AND ENFORCEMENT (2015). Others argue that suspicious activity reporting is an inefficient way to catch money launderers and terrorists. Many agree that AML compliance is ripe for reform. *See* Aaron Klein & Kristofer Readling, *Acceleration in Suspicious Activity Reporting Warrants Another Look*, BIPARTISAN POL'Y CTR. BLOG (Sept. 15, 2015); *see also* Kristofer Readling, *Casting a Wide Net: The Expanding Reach of Anti-Money Laundering Laws*, BIPARTISAN POL'Y CTR. BLOG (Sept. 11, 2015).

Faced with increasingly stringent AML requirements, financial institutions, including money services businesses, are sometimes incentivized to terminate high-risk clients. Challenges remain, for example, as to how to incentivize financial institutions to manage AML requirements without unnecessarily dropping underbanked customers or turning away the unbanked. *See, e.g.*, David S. Cohen, Under Secretary for Terrorism and Financial Intelligence, U.S. Dep't of the Treasury, Opening Remarks at the Treasury Roundtable on Financial Access for Money Services Businesses (Jan. 13, 2015). *See also* G-20, Global Partnership for Financial Inclusion, Global Standard Setting Bodies and Financial Inclusion—The Evolving Landscape, Consultation Document, Nov. 2015 (calling for better risk-based approaches to AML and counter terrorist-financing regulations).

AML enforcement has resulted in large fines for foreign and domestic banks on the basis of consent orders reciting facts alleged by the regulators and generally neither admitted nor denied by the institutions. For example, in 2014, French bank BNP Paribas was fined $8.97 billion for concealing client transactions in Sudan, Iran, and Cuba. In 2012, an HSBC case involving laundering funds for Latin American drug cartels resulted in a $1.92 billion deferred prosecution agreement. The $1.92 billion includes $665 million in civil penalties. Other major AML fines include ING's $619 million fine in 2012 for money laundering Cuban and Iranian client funds and threatening to fire employees who failed to conceal the money's origin, and Credit Suisse's $2.6 billion fine in 2014 for conspiracy to help U.S. citizens evade taxes. In total, more than $12 billion in AML fines were imposed on major banks between 2012 and 2014. *See* Paul L. Lee, *Compliance Lessons from OFAC Case Studies—Part II*, 131 Banking L.J. 717 (2014). Regulators have also imposed hefty fines on banks for weaknesses in internal controls for money laundering even without identifying instances of actual crimes. Is that problematic? *See* Lanier Saperstein et al., *The Failure of Anti-Money Laundering Regulation: Where is the Cost Benefit Analysis?*, 91 NOTRE DAME L. REV. 1, 2–3 (2015).

In the following excerpt, Mr. Paul Lee argues that there are significant issues and lessons learned regarding sanctions enforcement.

Compliance Lessons from OFAC Case Studies—Part II

131 Banking L. J. 717 (2014) (emphasis in original)

Differences in political, cultural and legal norms even among nominally allied countries have been highlighted in the economic sanctions area. . . .

The U.S. authorities maintain that they are not applying U.S. sanctions rules extraterritorially but instead simply applying the U.S. rules to transactions that *are being cleared within the United States*. Certain foreign authorities nonetheless perceive an extraterritorial element to U.S. sanctions rules because the rules apply to U.S. dollar transactions that have no connection to the United States other than the fact that they *are being cleared within the United States*. . . . Additional factors are at work at the level of the individual financial institutions. In a recent speech, Thomas C. Baxter, Executive Vice President and General Counsel of the Federal Reserve Bank of New York, shared his personal observations on the failure of foreign banks to comply with U.S. sanctions regimes. . . .

[Foreign] institutions looked at [U.S.] economic sanctions very differently [than U.S. institutions]. They looked at economic sanctions as technical "American" rules that were not seen as consistent with the organization's and the home country's larger value system. In Europe, they found no similar sanctions, and there it was perfectly legal at the time to do business with these sanctioned jurisdictions. Some European bankers almost naturally adopted the view that there was no value system underlying the technical American legal rule.

The . . . proclivity of foreign institutions to regard the U.S. sanctions as "technical" rules may have been unwittingly reinforced by the approach taken by U.S. counsel in rendering legal advice, which in some instances may have been too technical and not sufficiently policy oriented. In the early stages of analysis of OFAC sanctions, could one safely draw a distinction between the deletion of information in a payment message relating to an Iranian entity by the foreign bank and the omission of information in a payment message by the Iranian entity at the request of the foreign bank? Could one appropriately draw a distinction between sending payment messages for sanctioned entities to an unaffiliated financial institution and sending such messages to a branch or affiliated financial institution? From a policy perspective, the answer should have been "no" then—as it clearly is now. Yet in some instances these distinctions were drawn. . . .

Other lessons [include the] . . . need for a stronger "voice" for the compliance function[,] . . . for real independence of the compliance function [, and for] . . . an effective enterprise-wide compliance risk management program. . . . Despite the recurring discussion of the need for a stronger compliance culture, prominent enforcement actions against banking institutions by the U.S., the U.K. and the E.U. authorities across a range of issues have recently confirmed that there is substantial room for improvement in the compliance culture of the banking sector. . . .

Reprinted from The Banking Law Journal with permission.

V. RESPONDING TO INNOVATION

Technological advances in mobile and web-based applications can make payment systems more consumer-friendly, efficient, secure, fast, and accessible; however, they also pose challenges to regulators who must try to apply frameworks that might be outdated. *See* John Douglas, *Old Wine into Old Bottles: Fintech Meets the Bank Regulatory World*, N.C. BANKING INST. (forthcoming 2016). We briefly survey the regulatory and public policy issues surrounding some important innovations in the payments ecosystem. First, we discuss innovative consumer-facing mobile and Internet applications such as Venmo, Paypal, Apple Pay and GooglePay, that have been built on top of existing settlement infrastructures such as ACH and credit card networks. Then, we discuss the virtual currency Bitcoin and other new payments systems, which have given rise to fundamentally new conceptual models of settlement and units of value, but which do not seem to fit into existing regulatory frameworks.

A. NEW TECHNOLOGIES RUNNING ON OLD RAILS

The near-ubiquity of smartphones and the advancements in mobile payment systems have made visits to brick and mortar branches almost obsolete for many individuals. In a move that links one of the oldest payments systems to one of the newest, remote check capture lets individuals take a photo of their paper check on their mobile phone and deposit it through an app. New technologies, such as Venmo, Paypal, and Apple Pay, allow for the transfer of money between parties and between consumers and merchants without the need to carry or present a credit or debit card. On the merchant side, innovations like Square allow small merchants to accept cards without relying on traditional point-of-sale terminals. Additionally, the growth of online portals at banks and payment systems, such as PayPal and Google Wallet, allow for online payment without requiring consumers to be physically present at a merchant or bank to engage in transactions.

These new consumer-facing technologies all run on old rails, including the networks put in place by Visa, MasterCard, ACH, and the Federal Reserve System. In part due to existing laws, regulations, and network rules that channel electronic transactions through depository institutions, these new systems often rely on the prevailing framework that has been developed by card issuers and wholesale payment systems. For instance, Venmo is a mobile payment system that allows users to link their personal accounts and easily transfer money. Interestingly, the founders credit a forgotten wallet as the impetus for the idea (think back to Chapter 7.1 and how the Diners Club began). ANDREW KORTINA, ORIGINS OF VENMO (2014). Underlying Venmo is the existing ACH network. PayPal and its subsidiary, Venmo, use ACH transactions to fund their customers' e-commerce purchases and peer-to-peer payments. Google, Apple Pay, and the other systems rely on existing credit and debit card networks. Professor Tom Lin points out how Apple Pay has layered itself on top of the existing system:

> Apple Pay, for instance, has made credit card payments easier by allowing individuals to make payments with a simple tap of their phone, using their fingerprints as authentication. While the outward-facing technology of Apple Pay appears incredibly simple and convenient, it has not simplified the credit card transaction process. Instead of eliminating a link in that highly intermediated process, Apple Pay has added another layer of intermediation—Apple—into that process. Apple Pay may have disintermediated the steps it takes to find and use a credit card, but it has not simplified the overall credit card transaction process. As such, Apple Pay may have ironically created the mirage of disintermediation by adding another layer of intermediation.

Tom C.W. Lin, *Infinite Financial Intermediation*, 50 WAKE FOREST L. REV. 643, 656 (2015).

These technologies have helped to deal with many problems with older systems. Delays and inconveniences of using checks, the costs associated with merchant terminals, transaction costs, and inaccessibility have been reduced by these new systems. For a survey of the positive and negative effects of mobile payment on merchants, see Fumiko Hayashi & Terri Bradford, *Mobile Payments: Merchants' Perspectives*, FED. RESERVE BANK OF KANSAS CITY ECON. REV., Second Quarter 2014.

As new technologies contend with the existing regulatory framework, classic stakeholder battles are emerging. Some trade groups have highlighted the risks of newer payment technologies, calling for increased regulation with respect to data integrity, privacy, and consumer protection. *See, e.g.*, ISACA, MOBILE PAYMENTS: RISK, SECURITY AND ASSURANCE ISSUES (2011). Visa and MasterCard are fighting to maintain their position as intermediaries. For example, in Europe, Visa recently developed the capability to expand Apple Pay to European consumers as a way to retain its position. In other regions, such as in Asia, net banking has bypassed the card networks, allowing for the direct transfer of money from bank accounts through mobile platforms. Financial institutions have the most to lose or gain from these new technologies. In some situations, they are fighting for emerging systems to be subjected to more regulation, while in others, they are becoming big investors in and business partners with emerging payment technologies. Why would financial institutions be investing heavily in disruptive technologies? *See* Sunil Gupta, *The Mobile Banking and Payment Revolution*, EURO. FIN. REV. (2013). How should regulators approach the regulation of emerging payment systems?

B. DECENTRALIZED PAYMENT SYSTEMS: FAD OR REVOLUTION?

Although the innovations discussed above are built on existing payment infrastructures, virtual currencies, such as Bitcoin, and other new technologies have introduced a fundamentally new paradigm—the decentralized payment system. We highlight some of the public policy issues related to such systems. First, what place should these decentralized systems have in the payments ecosystem? Second, how should policy-makers regulate them? These payment systems pose challenges to regulators because they do not fit neatly into any existing regulatory framework. *See* Marcel T. Rosner & Andrew Kang, Note, *Understanding and Regulating Twenty-First Century Payments Systems: The Ripple Case Study,* 114 MICH. L. REV. 649 (2016).

What is this all about? Here's how a recent Brookings post put it:

Brookings Institution, The Hutchins Center Explains: How Blockchain Could Change the Financial System (Part 1)

Jan. 11, 2016

Any payments system needs trust. People won't accept payments if they can't count on the payments being of value; a loss of trust in a currency or in other intermediary institutions can trigger a destabilizing run. The question is how to generate that trust if banks aren't at the center of the system. A problem with any electronic payment system is ensuring that two people can't claim the same money. With coins or dollar bills, the physical act of possession means one can't spend the same money twice. A payment system that relies on digital records must have a way of preventing "double spending" because we all know that digital records can be edited, altered or copied. That is at odds with the key feature of money. Once you trade it away, you no longer have it. Modern banks maintain ledgers that are the definitive record of an individual's balances. . . .

Bitcoin and its many look-a-likes do away with that centralized ledger. Instead, there's a decentralized ledger distributed among all participants and a process in which all the users agree on changes to the ledger. Most such ledgers are built with a blockchain, a database that consists of chronologically arranged bundles of transactions known as blocks. . . . A distributed ledger allows people to exchange electronic money with someone else without necessarily having the transactions settled centrally through a bank. Members of the system police transactions. The technical details are complicated, but essentially a network of computers uses cryptography to secure, update and maintain the integrity of the ledger. It is, as The Chain Blog puts it, "a collection of mathematical, recordkeeping and communications procedures that makes it possible to trade digital assets securely.". . .

As a Bank of England report argues,

> the key innovation of digital currencies is the 'distributed ledger' which allows a payment system to operate in an entirely decentralized way, without intermediaries such as banks. This innovation draws on advances from a range of disciplines including cryptography (secure communication), game theory (strategic decision-making) and peer-to-peer networking (networks of connections formed without central co-ordination). When payment systems were first computerised, the underlying processes were not significantly changed. Distributed ledger technology represents a fundamental change in how payment systems could work. . . .

Robleh Ali et al., *Innovations in Payment Technologies and the Emergence of Digital Currencies*, BANK OF ENGLAND Q. BULL. Q3 2014.

1. The Value of Decentralized Payment Systems

Decentralized payment systems like Bitcoin offer an interesting dilemma. On the one hand, Bitcoin as a unit of value or form of money is deeply flawed. On the other hand, the underlying encryption technology and the system of distributed ledgers are ingenious and efficient methods of settling transactions.

Economists define money as having three functions: a medium of exchange, a unit of account, and a store of value. As the following excerpt suggests, virtual currencies like Bitcoin have qualities that make them very poor forms of money.

David Yurmack, Is Bitcoin a Real Currency? An Economic Appraisal

Nat'l Bureau of Econ. Research, Working Paper No. 19747, 2013

Bitcoin somewhat [functions as a medium of exchange], because a growing number of merchants, especially in online markets, appear willing to accept it as a form of payment. However, the worldwide commercial use of bitcoin remains minuscule, indicating that few people use it widely as a medium of exchange.

[B]itcoin performs poorly as a unit of account . . . Bitcoin requires merchants to quote the prices of common retail goods out to four or five decimal places with leading zeros, a practice rarely seen in consumer marketing and likely to confuse both sellers and buyers in the marketplace. Bitcoin exhibits very high time series volatility and trades for different prices on different exchanges without the possibility of arbitrage. All of these characteristics tend to undermine bitcoin's usefulness as a unit of account.

As a store of value, bitcoin faces great challenges due to rampant hacking attacks, thefts, and other security-related problems. Bitcoin's daily exchange rate with the U.S. dollar exhibits virtually zero correlation with the dollar's exchange rates against other prominent currencies such as the euro, yen, Swiss franc, or British pound, and also against gold. Therefore bitcoin's value is almost completely untethered to that of other currencies, which makes its risk nearly impossible to hedge for businesses and customers and renders it more or less useless as a tool for risk management.

These deficiencies are compounded by the fact that virtual currencies like Bitcoin suffer from low velocity because Bitcoin owners have an incentive to hold on to the currency as an investment asset and exploit its price volatility. According to one study, less than 50% of all bitcoins in circulation are used in transactions. About half of these transactions are for less than $100. Even though Bitcoin is being more frequently used for purchases, many bitcoins lie dormant, traded as an asset rather than used for transactions, which contributes to its volatility and weakens its attractiveness as a currency or payment system. ANTON BADEV & MATTHEW CHEN, BITCOIN: TECHNICAL BACKGROUND AND DATA ANALYSIS 21–22 (2014).

Professor Michael Barr argues that even setting aside the deficiencies of the underlying virtual currency, public ledger systems can offer upsides to our existing payments ecosystem. While the most obvious upsides are improved speed and lower transaction costs for settlement, new technologies might serve broader social policy goals. First, they can provide a viable payment alternative for the unbanked, for example by making it faster and cheaper to send remittances, such as for migrant workers. Second, real time, straight-through settlement can prevent the incidence of overdraft, fees from which cost consumers nearly $32 billion each year. Similarly, low-cost payments might change the fundamental economics of the internet, giving consumers more control of over their privacy and the information they usually have to relinquish in exchange for using the internet. Third, distributed ledgers could be used to track financial transactions, allowing regulators and market participants to overcome the difficulty of ascertaining who is owed what to whom and when, what collateral is where, and what transactions have been engaged in. For corporate governance, open ledgers might be used to significantly improve the ability of investors to see what is actually going on in the balance sheet of firms and to reduce fraud. *See* Michael S. Barr, Remarks at Brookings Institute conference "Beyond Bitcoin: the Future of Blockchain and Disruptive Financial Technologies" (Jan. 14, 2016); *see also,* David Yermack, Corporate Governance and Blockchains, New York University Stern School of Business and NBER, Working Paper, Nov. 29, 2015.

Can the blockchain be used while avoiding the underlying virtual currency altogether? The simple answer is yes—in fact, fintech startups, financial institutions, and exchanges have already looked into building private blockchains, including for cross-border bank payments, securities settlement, and other uses. *See* Brookings Institution, The Hutchins Center Explains: How blockchain could change the financial system, part 2, Feb. 25, 2016.

Some, like private equity investor Glenn Hutchins, however, believe that Bitcoin is essential to make the system work:

> Regulators think about Bitcoin as a currency [like gold]. But I think a better analogy is copper. Copper is a metal that people mine, people spectate in it, it is traded in exchanges . . . but its fundamental use is to move either electricity or voice messages around. It carries something that we use. The Bitcoin currency unit is a means . . . to transfer value. And so you can't have the system work without the Bitcoin token moving around. . . . [Y]ou can't have one without the other. . . .

Glenn Hutchins, Remarks at Brookings Institute roundtable "Beyond Bitcoin: the Future of Blockchain and Disruptive Financial Technologies" (Jan. 14, 2016). The more difficult question is, can the upside power of the blockchain be harnessed without the downsides of Bitcoin? Here, there is a deep divide. Part of the debate over Bitcoin relates to deeper questions about individual autonomy, the role of government, and attempts to create self-governing, open networks. *See* JOHN H. CLIPPINGER & DAVID BOLLIER, FROM BITCOIN TO BURNING MAN AND BEYOND: THE QUEST FOR IDENTITY AND AUTONOMY IN A DIGITAL SOCIETY (2014).

2. Approaches to Regulation

Decentralized payment systems pose significant problems for regulators, who are accustomed to dealing with bank-based payment systems. None of the federal statutes or regulations for traditional payment systems contains explicit language about their applicability, or non-applicability, to decentralized payment systems. There is a question of jurisdiction as various regulatory agencies scramble for control. As the following excerpt illustrates, the legal landscape for decentralized payment systems and digital currencies is hazy and unclear.

Edward V. Murphy et al.,
Bitcoin: Questions, Answers, and Analysis of Legal Issues

Cong. Research Serv. (2015)

[Legal and Regulatory Framework]

[Congressional Activity]

In Congress, interest in virtual currencies is at the exploratory stage. The Senate Finance Committee directed the Government Accountability Office (GAO) to review any tax requirements and compliance risks implicated. . . . The Senate Homeland Security and Governmental Affairs Committee has begun to look into how federal agencies are confronting the rise of virtual currencies. . . .

[Federal Regulatory Activity]

Federal regulators are increasingly scrutinizing how virtual currency and Bitcoin relate to their mandates. Law enforcement agencies have had to confront criminal hacking of Bitcoin wallets and kidnappers requiring ransom payment in Bitcoins. Moreover, the Department of the Treasury stated that terrorists are embracing Bitcoin. . . . Some federal agencies, including the CFPB, are contemplating further action. After issuing a consumer advisory on the pitfalls associated with Bitcoin, the CFPB began accepting consumer complaints on virtual currency and Bitcoin issues. Other federal regulatory activity includes guidance issued by Treasury's Financial Crimes Enforcement Network (FINCEN) and a Winkelvoss Bitcoin Trust registration statement filed with the SEC. In addition, the SEC published advisories for investors . . . on the threat of virtual currency scams on the Internet; filed a criminal fraud complaint charging a Bitcoin exchange with engaging in a Ponzi scheme; and successfully convinced a federal district court that Bitcoins are money. . . . [T]he Department of Homeland Security charged Mt. Gox, which is the Japanese-based largest Bitcoin exchange in the United States, with operating an unlicensed money services business in violation of 18 U.S.C. Section 1960 and seized its bank account. . . . The federal banking regulators have yet to issue guidance or regulations governing how banks are to deal with Bitcoin, outside of the anti-money laundering framework. . . .

[State Regulatory Activity]

State authorities moving in the direction of regulating virtual currencies sometimes discover problems in applying existing laws to technological currencies. Three states—New York, California, and Connecticut—have taken steps to devise a regulatory framework that could usher in increased use of digital currencies, provided adequate consumer protections and regulatory safeguards can be developed. . . .

[Salient laws and regulations]

[Federal Tax Law]

Digital currencies have characteristics of traditional tax haven jurisdictions: earnings are not reported to the [Internal Revenue Service] and users are provided some level of anonymity. Unlike traditional tax havens, however, digital currencies are able to operate without involving a financial institution. . . . [T]he [Internal Revenue Service] posted [a] . . . guidance [that] advises U.S. taxpayers that virtual currency is treated as property for federal tax purposes. . . .

[Federal Anti-Money Laundering Laws]

[T]he [BSA] imposes various recordkeeping requirements on banks and other financial institutions . . . All of these requirements apply to *money services businesses* (MSBs), a category of financial institution that must register with the Department of the Treasury. . . . Treasury's Financial Crimes Enforcement Network (FINCEN) issued interpretative guidance requiring Bitcoin exchanges—individuals and businesses that change Bitcoins into U.S. or foreign currency—to register as MSBs pursuant to the BSA. . . .

Federal Securities Regulation

Securities regulation focuses on two different legal issues involving Bitcoins—investments purchased with Bitcoins and investing in Bitcoins. The SEC has been active in investigating issues related to Bitcoins and has published an investor alert on Bitcoin and other virtual currency-related investments.

Commodity Futures Trading Commission Regulation

[O]n September 17, 2015, the CFTC issued an order against an online platform for facilitating the trading of Bitcoin options contracts. . . . In the order . . . [t]he CFTC quoted the definition of *commodity* from Section 1a(9) of the [Commodity Exchange Act] and noted that, because the definition is very broad, "Bitcoin and other virtual currencies are encompassed in the definition and properly defined as commodities."

As policy-makers consider whether and how to establish or adapt regulatory frameworks for decentralized payment systems, there is a risk that regulators might draw too much from the past and lock in old methods that block off innovation and prevent the payments ecosystem from evolving in positive directions. The challenge for regulators is thus to work together to focus on the severe downside risk cases—money laundering, terrorist financing, systemic risk, and abusive practices that harm consumers and investors—without deciding all the regulatory answers to the questions about other applications of the technologies that neither they nor market participants yet fully understand.

Part VIII

Corporate Governance, Supervision, and Enforcement

CHAPTER 8.1

CORPORATE GOVERNANCE

CONTENTS

I. INTRODUCTION

The concept of corporate governance began when the ownership and management of a corporation became separate and the problem of the agent (directors and senior management) having an agenda different from the principal (shareholders) developed. In the United States, the dispersed ownership of public companies led to an early interest in corporate governance as a means of aligning managers' and shareholders' incentives. Professors Adolf A. Berle, Jr. and Gardiner C. Means famously illustrated this problem in *The Modern Corporation and Private Property* (1932). It is widely understood that the principal-agency corporate governance problem plays out differently in a bank-centric organization than in, for example, a manufacturing or technology company. Complicating the traditional principal-agency problem is the misalignment of the interests of bank holding company (BHC) shareholders and the interests of the public. Rational BHC shareholders prefer a corporate strategy with the highest risk-adjusted return, even if it engenders a low probability risk that the insured depository institution (IDI) or BHC will face serious troubles or fail. Andreas Kokkinis, *A Primer on Corporate Governance in Banks and Financial Institutions: Are Banks Special?*, *in* IRIS H-Y CHIU, THE LAW ON CORPORATE GOVERNANCE IN BANKS 9-18 (Michael McKee, ed., 2015).

In this Chapter, we explore the special issues that surround the corporate governance of IDIs and BHCs. Next, we focus on director liability and responsibilities, including some changes in the corporate governance of large national banks and financial conglomerates since the Financial Crisis. We then look to the extension of liability and responsibility beyond directors to shareholders and gatekeepers, and will end with a discussion of how executive compensation at financial institutions can modify risk-taking incentives.

This Chapter is not a general introduction to corporate governance in the United States or how it has changed in the last 20 years. Students who do not have a basic grounding in corporate governance might read Sean J. Griffith, *Good Faith Business Judgment: A Theory of Rhetoric in Corporate Law Jurisprudence*, 55 DUKE L.J. 1 (2005). You will also want to keep in mind as you read this Chapter that sometimes we discuss the chartered commercial bank and sometimes we discuss the BHC or financial conglomerate. Their histories and rules differ.

II. POST-FINANCIAL CRISIS CORPORATE GOVERNANCE

The Financial Crisis revealed key weaknesses in the corporate governance of many of the largest financial institutions. In the aftermath of the Financial Crisis, rational and probing questions were raised about whether boards of directors had been too weak or too inattentive and how executive compensation had played a role in the blindness of many to risk management and the developing asset bubble in the housing markets. Brian R. Cheffins, *The Corporate Governance Movement, Banks and the Financial Crisis* (European Corp. Governance Inst. (EGCI), Law Working Paper No. 232/2014). Among the many regulatory fixes was a renewed focus on the strength of financial institution corporate governance, along with a number of very specific fixes that may or may not have any lasting impact. *See, e.g.*, Roberta Romano, *The Sarbanes-Oxley Act and the Making of Quack Corporate Governance*, 114 YALE L.J. 1521 (2005).

The excerpt from Federal Reserve Board Governor Daniel Tarullo's speech below, given to a group of corporate law professors, is a good summary of the corporate governance debate since the Financial Crisis.

Daniel K. Tarullo, Corporate Governance and Prudential Regulation

Speech at Ass'n of American Law Schools 2014 Midyear Meeting (June 9, 2014)

Legislatures and courts have a long history of debating, and sometimes adopting, special corporate law and governance rules for financial institutions. In my remarks this afternoon I will try to further the collaboration between corporate and financial law scholarship by suggesting how the nature of finance and financial regulation affects corporate governance and why, in turn, special corporate governance measures are needed as part of an effective prudential regulatory system. In making the latter argument, I will review some of the measures, both longstanding and more recent, that illustrate the point and then suggest some additional steps that might complement existing prudential regulations. Finally, I will offer some more tentative thoughts on the possible implication of this analysis for corporate law fiduciary duties. A theme running through these remarks will be the centrality of risk—its assessment, assumption, and allocation—in understanding the relationship between corporate governance and financial regulation. . . .

Financial Firms and Corporate Governance

There are at least three significant ways in which the nature of financial activities and regulation affect the operation of key mechanisms of corporate governance.[1]

First, it has long been recognized that the unique features of deposit-taking financial institutions raise the question whether generally applicable corporate law and governance principles are adequate. Because banks are financial intermediaries that use deposits to provide much, if not most, of the funding for their lending, an insolvent bank may well be unable to satisfy all its deposit liabilities. The fear of this possibility lies at the heart of banking runs and panics. In the days before federal deposit insurance, the impracticality of contractual solutions to reduce the vulnerability of depositors led to a variant of normally applicable limited liability rules. Many states enacted so-called double liability rules, whereby shareholders could be liable for the losses of a failed bank in an amount equal, and in addition, to their investment in the bank. Presumably, these rules were intended to change the calculus of shareholders as to the risks they wished their banks to assume and, perhaps, the degree to which they monitored management.

Following the creation of federal deposit insurance, a series of constraints on normal corporate prerogatives has been applied to insured institutions, justified in large part by the need to counteract the resulting moral hazard and to protect the Federal Deposit Insurance Fund (DIF). Bank charters have always differed from general corporate charters insofar as they grant special privileges and forbid certain activities by the chartered institutions. In addition, special prudential requirements have always applied to chartered banks. Perhaps the most important of these today is the imposition of minimum capital requirements on all [IDIs] and [BHCs].

Second, there is a variety of ways in which the attributes of financial markets and financial regulation affect the capital market discipline assumed in much corporate governance theory and corporate law. The prior point about the moral hazard associated with insured deposits implies that—at least in traditional, deposit-reliant banks—the kind of market discipline associated with the price of funding and creditor monitoring will be attenuated. More generally, to the degree uninsured depositors or other bank creditors expect that they will be protected by the government in the event the bank encounters serious difficulties, those same features of market discipline will again be weakened. This, of course, is the problem of moral hazard associated with too-big-to-fail perceptions, whereby investors or counterparties are willing to extend credit at prices that do not fully reflect the risk associated with the bank.[2]

The market discipline traditionally associated with the market for corporate control is also affected by banking regulation and supervision. Mergers and acquisitions involving banking organizations are subject to review, and possible disapproval, on a broad range of grounds beyond the antitrust considerations relevant in all industries. These include an assessment of the adequacy of the financial resources of the firms, the "competence, experience, and integrity" of the officers and directors, and the impact of the acquisition on systemic risk. Moreover, of course, any firm that acquires a commercial bank must be a

---

[1] For a basic description of corporate governance mechanisms, *see* Mark J. Roe (2004), "The Institutions of Corporate Governance," in Claude Menard and Mary M. Shirley, eds., Handbook for New Institutional Economics (The Netherlands: Springer). Useful reviews of corporate governance in financial institutions, reflecting lessons learned from the Financial Crisis, include Hamid Mehran and Lindsay Mollineaux (2012), "Corporate Governance of Financial Institutions," Federal Reserve Bank of New York Staff Report No. 539 (New York: Federal Reserve Bank of New York, February); Moonrad Choudhry (2010), "Effective Bank Corporate Governance: Observations from the Market Crash and Recommendations for Policy," Journal of Applied Finance & Banking, vol. 1 (1), pp. 179-211.

[2] For an argument that shareholders who might otherwise press for breakups of financial conglomerates are disincentivized from doing so for too-big-to-fail institutions, *see* Mark J. Roe (2014), "Structural Corporate Degradation Due to Too-Big-to-Fail Finance," University of Pennsylvania Law Review, vol. 162, pp. 1419–64.

BHC, thereby subject to a range of activity restrictions and other regulatory requirements. There are very good prudential reasons for these constraints upon acquisitions of, and by, banking organizations. But, by screening out transactions that would result in unacceptable increases in risk, either to an institution or to the financial system as a whole, these provisions may in some cases unintentionally limit the salutary disciplining effect on boards and management of the market for corporate control.

The third way in which the nature of financial activities and regulation affect the operation of key mechanisms of corporate governance is that the risks associated with financial intermediaries—especially those that are significantly leveraged and that engage in substantial maturity transformation—pose a particular challenge for corporate governance. All firms bear the risk that problems may unexpectedly arise because of, say, product flaws that were unknown to boards of directors and perhaps even senior management. But in the case of financial intermediaries, these problems can be incredibly fast-moving; including runs on funding that can quickly place the very survival of the firm in doubt. These risks have increased during the past 25 years, as many institutions have combined traditional lending activities with capital markets businesses that rely on other funding models. Accordingly, judgments about risk appetite and control systems to manage risk must be effectively executed by senior management and overseen by the board. This imperative, in turn, means that the information and monitoring processes and systems established for, or available to, boards of financial institutions may need to be more extensive than those in large, nonfinancial firms.

Financial Regulation and Corporate Governance

In the wake of the Financial Crisis, the public interest in regulation of banks and other financial firms is, I think it fair to say, both self-evident and substantial. . . .

Why should prudential regulation need to involve itself with corporate governance? . . .

The answer, I think, lies at least in part with the centrality and nature of risk in the activities of financial intermediaries. Risk-taking—whether well- or ill-considered—is perhaps the central activity of all financial intermediaries. Where those intermediaries are significantly leveraged and engaged in maturity transformation, the risk-taking carries substantial potential societal consequences beyond the possible losses to investors, counterparties, and employees of the financial firm. Microprudential and macroprudential regulation each respond to this divergence between the private and social balances of costs and benefits associated with a given level of risk-taking by financial intermediaries. . . .

Aligning Corporate Governance and Financial Regulation

With no claim to comprehensiveness, let me suggest three kinds of regulatory and supervisory measures that can better align corporate governance of financial firms with regulatory objectives.

First, regulatory requirements can be directed at changing the incentives of those making decisions within a financial firm. One good example is incentive compensation for senior managers and other bank employees with substantial decision-making authority. Compensation arrangements that create high-powered incentives using stock options or other forms of reward dominantly based on equity have their origins in efforts better to align management and shareholder interests. Otherwise, managers who stand to suffer reputational or job loss as their firm declines or fails may have a more conservative risk appetite than diversified shareholders, who value the upside of risk-taking and whose limited liability makes them relatively less concerned with catastrophic downside possibilities. As has been observed by numerous commentators,[3] however, where these

[3] *See*, for example, Lucian Bebchuk and Holger Spamann (2010), "Regulating Bankers' Pay," Georgetown Law Journal, vol. 98 (2), pp. 247–87; and Kenneth R. French, M. N. Baily, J. Y. Campbell, J. H. Cochrane, D. W. Diamond, D. Duffie, A. K. Kashyap, F. S. Mishkin, R. G. Rajan, D. S. Scharfstein, R. J.

kinds of incentive compensation arrangements have succeeded in better aligning the interests of shareholders and employees, they intensify the conflict between shareholder and regulatory interests. Ironically, regulatory objectives match up better with the old-style managers for whom the preservation of the firm is considerably more important than for shareholders.

A second kind of measure to align corporate governance at financial firms more closely to regulatory objectives is a substantive requirement or constraint upon decisions made within the firm. As a practical matter, it would be hard to develop a rule setting a comprehensive risk appetite consonant with regulatory objectives. However, there are regulatory requirements that can serve as partial surrogates for such a rule. A good example, already in place, is a feature of the Federal Reserve [Board's] program of stress testing and capital planning. A firm may not make capital distributions (whether in the form of dividends or capital repurchases) that would, when added to losses under hypothesized adverse scenarios as projected in our annual supervisory stress test, reduce the firm's capital below certain minimum levels.

When we adopted this rule several years ago, we were criticized by some for encroaching on the prerogative of boards of directors of financial firms to decide on capital distribution policies, in accordance with general corporate governance practice. This criticism has always seemed to me misplaced. After all, banking regulators are not only permitted, but obliged, to set minimum capital requirements at banking organizations and other systemically important financial institutions [(SIFIs)]. Limiting capital distributions is, conceptually, no different from requiring a firm to build capital in the first place. A regulation designed to maintain minimum capital levels in large banking organizations in a projected period of stress is consistent with the macroprudential objectives discussed earlier. Indeed, these requirements counteract the practices seen at some banks in the run-up to the Financial Crisis, whereby boards of directors continued to return capital to shareholders even as conditions deteriorated severely. Tying capital levels to corporate governance decisions about capital distributions simply recognizes that capital levels and capital distributions are two sides of the same coin.

A third kind of measure seeks to affect the institutions and processes of corporate governance, rather than directly to change incentive structures or regulate decisions. Many possible actions of this sort would really be efforts to improve the risk assessment and risk management capacities of management and boards, rather than to focus specifically on the divergence between shareholder and regulatory interests with respect to risk appetite. An effective system of controls is important both to shareholders and to regulators. Thus, for instance, the considerable and continuing emphasis we have placed on firms developing and maintaining effective management information systems makes risk assessment work better for shareholders, even as it facilitates supervisory oversight.

With respect to the institutional features of board oversight of risk management, there is also substantial overlap in the interests of shareholders and regulators. For example, both shareholders and supervisors should expect a board to include members with the expertise, experience, and time commitment that are appropriate to risk management of the kinds of activities in which the financial firm engages. Of particular interest are three board positions—the nonexecutive chair or lead director, the head of the risk committee, and the head of the audit committee. More generally, shareholders and supervisors must have confidence that globally active institutions with hundreds of thousands of employees have audit and risk committees with the practical ability to provide effective oversight of risk decisions.[4] I might note in passing that regular discussion between board members and

---

Shiller, H. S. Shin, M. J. Slaughter, J. C. Stein, and R. M. Stulz (2010), The Squam Lake Report: Fixing the Financial System (Princeton: Princeton University Press).

[4] There have also been proposals that boards of large financial firms have a small staff, independent of management, who can help the board sift through the often voluminous materials

supervisors can also serve the interests of shareholders, since supervisors may have an informed perspective on the firm's operations that enables boards better to fulfill their strategic and risk-oversight functions.

Supervisors should also expect a well-conceived process for board review of major firm decisions, which will nearly always carry some implications for risk management and risk appetite. In practical terms, such a process would connect decisions on strategy, risk-appetite setting, and capital planning. Neither we nor shareholders should be comfortable with a process in which strategic decisions are made in one silo, risk-appetite setting in another, and capital planning in yet a third, with the convergence of these efforts coming together only when it is too late for each to affect the other, or for the board to be able to exercise effective oversight. These major decisions need to be made in an integrated manner.

While regulators should have clear expectations for boards, we need to make sure that we are creating expectations that lead to boards spending more time overseeing the risk-management and control functions I have emphasized this afternoon. There are many important regulatory requirements applicable to large financial firms. Boards must of course be aware of those requirements and must help ensure that good corporate compliance systems are in place. But it has perhaps become a little too reflexive a reaction on the part of regulators to jump from the observation that a regulation is important to the conclusion that the board must certify compliance through its own processes. We should probably be somewhat more selective in creating the regulatory checklist for board compliance and regular consideration. One example, drawn from Federal Reserve [Board] practice, is the recent supervisory guidance requiring that every notice of a "Matter Requiring Attention" . . . issued by supervisors must be reviewed, and compliance signed off, by the board of directors. There are some [Matters Requiring Attention] that clearly should come to the board's attention, but the failure to discriminate among them is almost surely distracting from strategic and risk-related analyses and oversight by boards.

One might ask how the strengthening of systems of controls and risk-appetite decision processes can promote achievement of regulatory interests beyond those shared with the owners of firms. One answer is that it clearly improves the supervisory line-of-sight into the safety and soundness of financial firms. The more timely and accurate the information that can be aggregated by supervisors, the more responsive our supervisory and financial stability oversight can be. A well-developed set of risk and control functions also allows an effective point of entry for pursuing certain regulatory objectives.

Regulatory Objectives and Fiduciary Duties

The regulatory focus on risk in corporate governance will produce additional examples of each of the three kinds of measures I have just described. . . Still, particularly with an audience half composed of corporate law professors, it is natural to ask whether corporate law tools might usefully supplement regulatory measures. Specifically, the question arises as to whether the fiduciary duties of the boards of regulated financial firms should be modified to reflect what I have characterized as regulatory objectives. Doing so might make the boards of financial firms responsive to the broader interests implicated by their risk-taking decisions even where regulatory and supervisory measures had not anticipated or addressed a particular issue. And, of course, the courts would thereby be available as another route for managing the divergence between private and social interests in risk-taking.

---

delivered by management to foster informed inquiries of management and decisions on risk appetite. For example, a proposal for a "dedicated secretariat" was offered by a parliamentary committee in the United Kingdom. *See* U.K. House of Commons Treasury Committee (2009), Banking Crisis: Reforming Corporate Governance and Pay in the City, (London: House of Commons, May).

As I noted at the outset, there is a long history of actual or considered measures to alter the duties or liabilities of those with decision-making authority in the corporate governance of banks. A more contemporary variant on these ideas was offered a little over a decade ago by Jon Macey and Maureen O'Hara, who proposed expanded fiduciary duties for directors of [IDIs], including giving bank creditors the right to sue for violations of these duties.[5] In a provocative recent paper, John Armour and Jeff Gordon suggest that the duties of directors of [SIFIs] should be modified precisely because diversified shareholders have a strong interest in avoiding risk decisions by these institutions that increase systemic risk.[6] Their analysis implies that the customary tension between regulatory and diversified shareholders' interests may be considerably mitigated in the case of systemically important firms whose failure could result in financial turbulence and consequent economic loss for the entire economy.

A consideration of the merits of these or other such proposals is beyond the scope of my remarks today. Obviously, any such changes in corporate law are beyond the authority of the Federal Reserve [Board]. I mention them in the hope and anticipation that corporate law scholars will continue to evaluate such ideas, since whatever one's eventual conclusions on their desirability, the analytic process is sure to yield further insights into the key question of how best to respond to the points of divergence between shareholder and regulatory interests in risk-taking by large financial firms.

III. RESPONSIBILITIES AND DUTIES OF DIRECTORS

Boards of financial institutions have overall responsibility for the institution, including approving and overseeing management's implementation of the bank's strategic objectives, governance framework, and corporate culture. BASEL COMMITTEE ON BANKING SUPERVISION, CORPORATE GOVERNANCE PRINCIPLES FOR BANKS 8 (July 2015). In April 2012, the Group of Thirty released a report that stressed the need for stronger corporate governance in financial services firms to maintain global economic stability. The report recommended that directors take a stronger role in overseeing management and monitoring risks at the firm, noting that:

> The board's primary responsibilities vis-à-vis the management of the firm are: (1) reaching agreement with management on a strategy, including the firm's risk appetite and its contours; (2) choosing a CEO capable of executing the strategy; (3) ensuring a high-quality leadership team is in place; (4) assuring appropriate processes, people, and resources are dedicated to compliance with all applicable regulatory, legal, and ethical rules and guidelines and ensuring that appropriate and necessary risk control processes are in place; (5) ensuring all stakeholder interests are appropriately represented and considered (including issues of remuneration); and (6) providing advice and support to management based on experience, expertise, and relationships.

GROUP OF THIRTY, TOWARD EFFECTIVE GOVERNANCE OF FINANCIAL INSTITUTIONS 20 (April 2012).

---

[5] Jonathan R. Macey and Maureen O'Hara (2003), "The Corporate Governance of Banks," Federal Reserve Bank of New York, Economic Policy Review, vol. 9 (April), pp. 91–107.

[6] John Armour and Jeffrey N. Gordon (2013), "Systemic Harms and Shareholder Value," European Corporate Governance Institute Working Paper No. 222 (Brussels: ECGI, August).

Bank directors and officers are also subject to the same duties of loyalty and care that define the core corporate governance responsibilities of company directors and officers generally. *See, e.g.*, FDIC Financial Institution Letter (FIL–87—92) (Dec. 3, 1992). There has long been a belief, however, that bank directors and officers should be held to stricter standards. This belief developed before the United States had a lender of last resort, at a time when bank deposits were uninsured.

The introduction of federal deposit insurance did not eliminate the belief that banks, with their highly leveraged balance sheets and role in the payments system, are special. Rather, it changed the focus from duties to depositors towards liability to the DIF.

A. LIABILITY FOR BANK FAILURE

One way to incentivize bank directors to act in the best interests of the bank's broader constituency, including depositors and the DIF, is by professional liability lawsuit. Directors' and officers' duties of loyalty and care to their institutions arise as a matter of state law, so the applicable standard will depend on which state's law applies. For state-chartered banks, typically, the law of the state of incorporation will apply. A national bank can elect in its bylaws to follow corporate governance rules of the law of the state in which its main office is located, the law of the state in which the national bank's BHC is incorporated, or the Model Business Corporation Act. 12 C.F.R. § 7.2000.

The wave of bank and thrift failures in the 1980s prompted the FDIC, as well as the then-existent Resolution Trust Corporation (RTC), to focus on directors and officers as a way to recover losses from bank failures. As receiver of a failed IDI, the Financial Institutions Reform, Recovery, and Enforcement Act (FIRREA) gave the FDIC standing to bring related professional liability suits as part of its professional liability program. The most common of these claims allege: "(1) dishonest conduct or abusive insider transactions; (2) violations of internal policies, law, or regulations that resulted in a safety or soundness violation; or (3) failure to establish, monitor, or follow proper underwriting procedures, or heed warnings from regulators or advisors." Emily S. May, *Bank Directors Beware: Post-Crisis Bank Director Liability*, 19 N.C. BANKING INST., 31, 33 (2015); Mary C. Gill et al., *Claims Against Bank Directors and Officers Arising From the Financial Crisis*, 26 REV. BANKING & FIN. SERVS. 69, 70 (2010); FDIC Financial Institution Letter (FIL–87—92) (Dec. 3, 1992). The claims above can be sorted into each claim's underlying fiduciary basis: claims brought under (1) are based on a breach of the duty of loyalty; claims brought under (2) and (3) are each based on a claim for a breach of the duty of care. The FDIC views its professional liability program as a success. Between 1985 and 1992, the FDIC brought claims against directors and officers in 24% of bank failures. From 1986 through 2014, the FDIC and former RTC (1989–1995) collected $8.62 billion from professional liability claims. Over that same time, those institutions spent $2.14 billion to fund all professional liability claims and investigations. FDIC, *Professional Liability Lawsuits* (last updated Feb. 19, 2016).

Between 1986 and 1994, approximately 12 states legislated to insulate directors and officers from some claims alleging a breach of the duty of care by requiring conduct that rose to the level of gross negligence or above, although in some cases, liability was permitted only where there was a finding of willful or reckless misconduct. Ronald W. Stevens, *FDIC Lawsuits Against Former Directors and Officers of Banks That Have Failed Since 2008: Is This Déjà Vu All Over Again?*, 97 BNA BANKING REP. 762 (2011); *see also* FDIC, MANAGING THE CRISIS: THE FDIC AND RTC EXPERIENCE, 1980–1994 274–75 (1998). In an effort to prevent this insulation, Congress added a section to FIRREA that established a federal floor of gross negligence as the applicable standard for suit against a director or officer. 12 U.S.C. § 1821(k); Atherton v. FDIC, 519 U.S. 213, 226–28 (1997). In those states where FIRREA acts as a regulatory floor, the FDIC will allege that the IDI's failure was the product of gross negligence. In those few states that require a lower standard, the FDIC will allege the lower standard.

In most states, the business judgment rule protects directors and officers from liability associated with decisions made in the scope of their authority, with due care, and in good faith. Where the rule applies, bank directors and officers are protected from ordinary negligence. Nevertheless, idiosyncrasies in individual state law determine whether the business judgment rule shields officers and directors of failed banks from personal liability in these suits. These differences in state law mean that the standard of care for bank directors and officers remains uncertain in some states.

Many of these uncertainties have been exposed as a result of bank failures in the Financial Crisis. From January 1, 2009, through August 20, 2015, the FDIC filed 108 director and officer lawsuits, naming 826 former directors and officers. Twenty-five of these lawsuits were filed in Georgia alone. FDIC, *Professional Liability Lawsuits*. When those suits were filed, Georgia had not explicitly adopted a business judgment rule by statute or applied a special statutory standard to bank directors and officers. In *FDIC v. Loudermilk*, the Supreme Court of Georgia held that the business judgment rule protected bank directors and officers from ordinary negligence claims. 295 Ga. 579, 588 (2014). It held that the

> reference to ordinary 'diligence, care, and skill' is most reasonably understood to refer to the care required with respect to the process by which a decision is made, most notably the diligence due to ascertain the relevant facts. Understood in this way, the implication of liability means only that an officer or director who acts in bad faith or fails to exercise such ordinary care with respect to the process for making a decision is liable.

Id. at 591.

New York banking law also has a special standard for bank directors, requiring that they "discharge the duties of their respective positions in good faith and with that degree of diligence, care and skill which [an] ordinar[y] and prudent [person] would exercise under similar circumstances in like positions." N.Y. Banking Law § 7015(1). A student of torts will recognize this standard as analogous to the standard of care for ordinary negligence. New York courts have interpreted this statute to mean that the business judgment rule does not entirely shield directors and officers of New York chartered banks from negligence claims. FDIC v. Bober, No. 95 Civ. 9529, 2002 WL 1929486, at *5–7 (S.D.N.Y. July 18, 2002); FDIC v. Ornstein, 73 F. Supp. 2d 277, 281 (E.D.N.Y.

1999); Resolution Trust Corp. v. Gregor, 872 F. Supp. 1140, 1148–50 (E.D.N.Y. 1994). Other state's laws explicitly state that the business judgment rule protects bank directors from any implied duties to depositors. UTAH CODE ANN. § 16-10a-841 (West 2006); Warren v. Robison, 57 P. 287 (Utah 1899).

The New York simple negligence statute also sets forth a number of considerations that a director of a New York chartered bank is entitled to consider when a change of bank control is under consideration. In an environment in which most directors of U.S. public companies confine themselves to considerations of shareholder value, these broader factors for bank directors are different and surprising to many who come to corporate governance from a non-bank perspective. The text of the statute below is a good example:

> In taking action, including, without limitation, action which may involve or relate to a change or potential change in the control of the banking institution, a director shall be entitled to consider, without limitation, (1) both the long-term and the short-term interests of the corporation and its shareholders and (2) the effects that the corporation's actions may have in the short-term or in the long-term upon any of the following: (1) the prospects for potential growth, development, productivity and profitability of the corporation; (2) the corporation's current employees; (3) the corporation's retired employees and other beneficiaries receiving or entitled to receive retirement, welfare or similar benefits from or pursuant to any plan sponsored, or agreement entered into, by the corporation; (4) the corporation's customers and creditors; and (5) the ability of the corporation to provide, as a going concern, goods, services, employment opportunities and employment benefits and otherwise to contribute to the communities in which it does business. Nothing in this subdivision shall create any duties owed by any director to any person or entity to consider or afford any particular weight to any of the foregoing or abrogate any duty of the directors, either statutory or recognized by common law or court decisions.

N.Y. BANKING LAW § 7015.

---

1. ***Are the Duties Different?*** It is widely understood that under Delaware law, a corporation's directors must look to shareholder value as their lodestar. Do some of these state bank statutes create something more akin to stakeholder duties for bank directors? What is the impact on BHCs?

2. ***Finding Good Directors?*** In response to a survey by the American Association of Bank Directors, nearly one quarter of the 80 banks that responded had directors resign, refuse positions, or refuse to serve on the board loan committee out of a fear of personal liability in the past five years. AMERICAN ASSOCIATION OF BANK DIRECTORS, SURVEY RESULTS MEASURING BANK DIRECTOR FEAR OF PERSONAL LIABILITY (Apr. 9, 2014). Is the difficulty more or less troublesome depending upon the size of the bank?

B. HEIGHTENED STANDARDS FOR LARGE NATIONAL BANKS

Soon after the Financial Crisis, the OCC began imposing, as a supervisory matter, "heightened expectations" on the nation's largest national banks and federal thrifts. Comptroller of the Currency Thomas Curry described "achieving excellence in corporate governance" as at the core of the concept. Thomas J. Curry, Comptroller of the Currency, Remarks Before The Clearing House, Second Annual Business Meeting & Conference (Nov. 15, 2012). Curry further stated that the OCC was "no longer willing to accept audit and risk management functions that are simply satisfactory. We are looking for excellence," and stated his expectation that independent directors at large institutions would take a "*strong* hand in ensuring compliance." *Id.* (emphasis in original). The OCC found that its confidential supervisory guidelines were not enough and it decided to adopt enforceable guidelines as an appendix to its regulations.

Thomas J. Curry, Comptroller of the Currency, Remarks before the Prudential Bank Regulation Conference

Washington, D.C. (June 9, 2015)

The guidelines have two major components. The first sets forth the minimum standards for the design and implementation of a covered bank's risk governance framework, stipulating that it should include well-defined risk management roles and responsibilities for what the industry commonly refers to as the three lines of defense: front line units, independent risk management, and internal audit.

The risk governance framework and the three lines of defense are intended to ensure that the bank has an effective system to identify, measure, monitor, and control risk-taking and standards of behavior. Those units must ensure that boards of directors have enough information on their bank's risk profiles and risk management practices, so that the bank operates within the risk appetite statement.

Under the OCC's heightened standards, large banks are required to develop risk appetite statements that define both quantitative and qualitative parameters for safe and sound operating environments. The guidelines require that these statements address the question of how the bank will assess and accept risks, articulating behavioral expectations that shape risk culture. In addition, quantitative limits on risk-taking should incorporate sound stress testing processes and address banks' earnings, capital, and liquidity positions.

The second component of our heightened standards guidelines pertains to the responsibilities of large banks' boards of directors. It provides that bank boards should have at least two independent directors and that all board members should have the information they need for effective oversight, including the ability to pose a credible challenge to management. The guidelines also require each bank to establish and maintain an ongoing training program for all board members and conduct an annual self-assessment of the board's effectiveness in meeting the standards for the board that are articulated in the guidelines.

One important aspect of our guidelines is a requirement that a large bank's compensation and performance management programs complement and support its overall risk governance framework. It's important that these programs prohibit incentive-based payment arrangements that encourage improper risk-taking.

---

1. ***Credible Challenge***. The OCC's "credible challenge" requirement is both an effort to increase director involvement and manage risk. Many directors have struggled with the meaning of this requirement. How is a credible challenge monitored? Does it require a dispute on every issue? Does is set forth a standard by which directors should have independent information or does it refer to a process of questioning management robustly?

2. ***Sanctity of the Charter***. The background section of the OCC's guidelines establishing heightened standards refers to the "sanctity of the national bank or Federal savings association charter." OCC Guidelines Establishing Heightened Standards for Certain Large Insured National Banks, Insured Federal Savings Associations, and Insured Federal Branches; Integration of Regulations, 79 Fed. Reg. 54,518, 54,534 (Sept. 11, 2014). The ordinary meaning of sanctity is of something holy or saintly and we are more used to seeing it in phrases like the "sanctity of life" or the "sanctity of marriage." What signal was the OCC trying to send when it used this phrase, which had, until then, appeared nowhere in the background law or regulations? Consider the question in light of the following description from Curry: "The charter is a special corporate franchise that provides a gateway to federal deposit insurance and access to the discount window, and the highest fiduciary duty of the Board of Directors is to ensure the safety and soundness of the national bank or federal thrift." Thomas J. Curry, Comptroller of the Currency, Remarks Before The Clearing House Second Annual Business Meeting & Conference (Nov. 15, 2012).

C. COMPOSITION OF BHC BOARDS

In this Chapter so far, we have largely considered whether the members of the board of directors of the bank or IDI have special or heightened duties. Of course, as the Tarullo speech at the start of the Chapter assumes, most banks are part of a larger group, including a top-level BHC that is typically publicly listed and incorporated in Delaware. In this section, we will examine the additional requirements that might be placed upon a BHC board.

In the U.S. banking sector, there are two models of how to deal with the two different board levels required for the BHC and the lead bank. Many regional and smaller banks, where the lead bank is typically over 95% of the revenues and assets of the financial group, have identical boards of directors at the BHC and bank levels. The meetings happen at the same time and on the same day, and board committees are often also identical. The situation is different at many, but not all, of the largest U.S. financial conglomerates where there is often limited overlap between the BHC board and the lead bank or broker-dealer board.

The Dodd-Frank Act imposed several new requirements on the boards of BHCs. First, all publicly listed BHCs with more than $10 billion in assets are required to have a risk committee, composed of a majority of independent directors and at least one member who is experienced in risk management. 12 C.F.R. §§ 252.22, 252.33. It seems likely that, by supervisory actions, prudential regulators may also impose this requirement on BHCs that are smaller.

A second change brought about by the Dodd-Frank Act is the codification of the source of strength doctrine as discussed in Chapter 9.3. How that federal duty might affect state law fiduciary duties remains to be seen.

A third change expands a prohibition that formerly meant officers and directors could not simultaneously serve as a management official of an unaffiliated IDI or its BHC company, subject to certain statutory and regulatory exemptions. *See* 12 U.S.C. § 3201. Section 164 of the Dodd-Frank Act expands that prohibition to officers and directors of non-bank firms deemed systemically financially important by the Financial Stability Oversight Council. In addition, like U.S. BHCs with assets of $50 billion or more, a foreign banking organization with combined U.S. assets of $50 billion or more will be required to establish a U.S. risk committee and employ a U.S. chief risk officer to help ensure that the foreign bank manages the risks of its combined U.S. operations. 12 U.S.C. § 5365.

---

1. ***Supervisors and Boards.*** It has long been the case that bank examiners present their findings to the board of directors, often without the presence of management. Since the Financial Crisis, there has been a strengthening of supervisory oversight over boards and a higher degree of frequency in the meetings between supervisors and boards of directors. In some instances, Federal Reserve Board supervisors meet more often with directors than the directors meet formally as a full board. At what point do supervisory initiatives become unduly onerous, either by imposing managerial-type responsibilities on boards or disincentivizing good candidates from serving as directors? As Tarullo recently noted:

> There are many important regulatory requirements applicable to large financial firms. Boards must of course be aware of those requirements and must help ensure that good corporate compliance systems are in place. But it has perhaps become a little too reflexive a reaction on the part of regulators to jump from the observation that a regulation is important to the conclusion that the board must certify compliance through its own processes. We should probably be somewhat more selective in creating the regulatory checklist for board compliance and regular consideration.

Daniel K. Tarullo, Governor, Board of Governors of the Federal Reserve System, Speech at the Association of American Law Schools 2014 Midyear Meeting, Washington, D.C.: Corporate Governance and Prudential Regulation (June 9, 2014).

2. ***Director Interlocks.*** Firms generally want the most experienced directors on their boards. Directors who have had experience in management in similar institutions are often the most equipped to oversee the operations of the firm, manage risk, and make informed business decisions. At what point does that valuable experience become a problem? Consider the following two examples of director interlocks.

- *Same Director at Two Regional Banks.* You represent a private equity firm that makes non-controlling minority investments in regional U.S.

banks with between $10 billion and $20 billion in assets. The firm wants to have its most experienced manager be a member of the boards of two regional banks and their respective BHCs. One is headquartered in Washington state with operations in Washington and Oregon. Its lead subsidiary is a non-member state-chartered bank. The other BHC's bank is a national bank headquartered in Alabama with operations in Alabama and Georgia. Can the manager serve on the board of both banks and both BHCs? Which regulators, if any, have to be approached? 12 U.S.C. § 3202; 12 C.F.R. §§ 26.3, 26.6(a), 212.3, 212.6(a), 348.3, 348.6(a).

- *Former CEO.* A former CEO of an insured non-member regional bank located in Minnesota with operations all around the Midwest and very limited international operations sits on its board. A UK bank with a large broker-dealer subsidiary and a small wholesale insured bank, as well as a large New York branch, has asked him to also sit on the board of its top level company, based in London. May he do so? Must he request a waiver? 12 U.S.C. §§ 3201(3), 3202; 12 C.F.R. § 348.2(f); N.Y. BANKING LAW § 143; N.Y. COMP. CODES R. & REGS. tit. 3, § 70.2.

IV. EXTENDING DUTIES BEYOND DIRECTORS

A. DUAL-LIABILITY OF SHAREHOLDERS

The National Banking Act of 1863 attempted to impose heightened corporate governance standards on banks by imposing double liability on bank shareholders. Shareholders of a failed bank, who were often also the bank's directors, would lose their equity investment and could also be required to pay compensation for the bank's failure. It is worth noting that, during that era, the directors of a bank were expected to directly approve virtually every loan issued or note discounted by a bank. For a thorough treatment of the historical context of bank shareholder double liability, see Jonathan R. Macey & Geoffrey P. Miller, *Double Liability of Bank Shareholders: History and Implications*, 27 WAKE FOREST L. REV. 31 (1991). Others contend that Macey and Miller's article materially understates losses imposed on depositors of national banks during the early part of the Great Depression. *See* Howell E. Jackson, *Losses From National Bank Failures During the Great Depression: A Response to Macey and Miller*, 28 WAKE FOREST L. REV. 919 (1993).

As students of corporate law will quickly recognize, this scheme of double liability runs strongly contrary to the basic concepts of corporate limited liability. Nonetheless, for a critical period in the development of U.S. banking regulation, this deviation from limited liability norms was seen as an appropriate way to address the implicit understanding that banks' special role in the economy called for the application of additional and heightened standards to inform corporate governance and guide the behavior of directors and officers. Although double liability was abandoned in 1933 with the introduction of deposit insurance, two academics have argued that "the nation took a wrong turn when it abandoned double liability for a system of governmentally administered deposit insurance." Macey & Miller, *Double Liability of Bank Shareholders: History and*

Implications, at 32; *see also* the discussion of source of strength and sister bank cross-guarantees in Chapter 9.3, which also run counter to the principle of corporate limited liability. Is the source of strength doctrine an updated version of double liability of shareholders?

Macey and Miller argue that the system of shareholder double liability functioned more effectively to protect depositors than many realized at the time. Historically, it applied solely at the bank level and during an era of small unit banks that were privately held, mostly among a small group of dominant directors and shareholders who were also active in the running of the bank. Would it be possible for a large publicly owned company with a dispersed shareholder base? Is it fair and appropriate to impose double liability on shareholders who may not have full information? Consider this characterization from the Tarullo excerpt at the beginning of the Chapter: "Presumably, these [double liability] rules were intended to change the calculus of shareholders as to the risks they wished their banks to assume and, perhaps, the degree to which they monitored management." Daniel K. Tarullo, Governor, Board of Governors of the Federal Reserve System, Speech at the Association of American Law Schools 2014 Midyear Meeting, Washington, D.C.: Corporate Governance and Prudential Regulation (June 9, 2014). What other mechanisms are in place today to achieve those same goals?

B. GATEKEEPER LIABILITY

Gatekeeper liability, which is based on the premise that professional advisors to financial institutions should have liability for aiding and abetting unsafe and unsound practices, seeks to modify incentive structures. *See* Howell E. Jackson, *Reflections Upon Kaye, Scholer: Enlisting Lawyers to Improve the Regulation of Financial Institutions*, 66 S. CAL. L. REV. 1019, 1033 (1993). This proposal was first controversially asserted in the aftermath of the 1980s Savings & Loan Crisis, when then Chief Counsel to the Office of Thrift Supervision (OTS) Harris Weinstein famously asked "where were the professionals?" Weinstein argued that outside counsel should have the same heightened fiduciary duties as officers and directors of financial institutions. *See* John C. Coffee, Jr., *The Attorney As Gatekeeper: An Agenda for the SEC*, 103 COLUM. L. REV. 1293 (2003).

OTS brought civil actions against several law firms in the aftermath of the Savings & Loan Crisis. The most notorious of these is the Kaye Scholer case. Between 1984 and 1989, law firm Kaye, Scholer, Fierman, Hays & Handler represented Lincoln Savings & Loan Association while the OTS evaluated Lincoln's financial viability and banking practices. Lincoln's chair, Charles Keating, who later served a five-year prison sentence for fraud, was accused of bribing five U.S. Senators, dubbed the Keating Five, to prevent regulators from interfering in Lincoln's affairs. Lincoln remained open as a result. Lincoln's failure cost $3 billion and the life savings of many of its investors. According to Weinstein, Kaye Scholer breached the fiduciary duty it owed to the government by making misstatements and failing to disclose facts that would indicate Lincoln was unsound. Kaye Scholer's duty was based on three theories: (1) the government holds a "negative equity" interest in a financial institution as the holder of the most risk; (2) the government is comparable to a creditor of the financial institution in situations of imminent insolvency; and, (3) the government is insurer of financial institutions and subrogated to the rights of the insured. As part of this fiduciary duty to the government, Weinstein argued that regulatory counsel had an obligation to advance the "whole law," including the underlying principles and goals of financial regulations. Suffering under a governmental freeze of its assets, which made it impossible to fight back, Kaye Scholer buckled under financial pressure and settled for $41 million after just two weeks and agreed to restrict its future banking practice.

Weinstein would not have had the statutory authority to sue Kaye Scholer without FIRREA. By classifying attorneys of financial institutions as "institution affiliated parties" (IAPs), Weinstein attempted to use the FIRREA powers to redefine the relationship between regulatory counsel and their clients. *See* 12 U.S.C. § 1813(u)(4). IAPs had regulatory responsibilities similar to insiders of financial institutions. In addition, under FIRREA, OTS had the authority to initiate proceedings on the basis of probable cause against IAPs for "causing, bringing about, participating in, counseling, or aiding and abetting a violation." *See* 12 U.S.C. § 1467a(i)(2)(E). Rules mandating that lawyers act in a particular way exist in other contexts as well; lawyers practicing in front of the SEC, for example, must report material violations of securities laws up-the-ladder within a company. 17 C.F.R. § 205.

1. Lawyers

There are a number of concerns with gatekeeper regulatory regimes, especially as conceived in *Kaye Scholer*. One of the more obvious questions is, when the interests of a financial institution and those of the regulators clash, to whom does the regulatory lawyer have the greatest duty? Is it fair to regulatory counsel to impose a fiduciary duty to the government, especially one with such excessive monetary consequences? How would this work for in-house counsel, some of whom the SEC has been prosecuting individually for securities violations? While *Kaye Scholer* represents the high water mark for gatekeeper regimes for lawyers, tenets of the Weinstein theory persist. The SEC proposed a "noisy withdrawal" rule as part of its rules setting the minimum standards of professional conduct for attorneys appearing and practicing before the Commission. The "noisy withdrawal" rule would have required an attorney representing a public company who discovered a securities violation or breach of fiduciary duty to report the violation up-the-ladder. If the company did not respond adequately, the attorney would have been required to withdraw from the representation and notify the SEC. When the SEC adopted final professional conduct rules under the Sarbanes-Oxley Act in January 2003, it did not adopt the "noisy withdrawal" rule. In other contexts, aiding and abetting for outside counsel has been limited by the Supreme Court. In the aftermath of Enron and the Sarbanes-Oxley Act, gatekeeper liability was raised again. *See* John C. Coffee, Jr., *Understanding Enron: "It's About the Gatekeepers, Stupid"*, 57 BUS. LAW. 1403 (2002).

2. Consultants

Consultants face a similar challenge to other gatekeepers, but structural differences can make that challenge more acute. One way regulators and financial institutions can deal with resource limitations is by engaging consultants to assist. As former New York Department of Financial Services (NYDFS) Superintendent Benjamin M. Lawsky explains, "consultants are installed at banks and other companies by regulators—usually after an institution has committed serious regulatory violations or broken the law. The intent is that monitors assist companies in improving controls and ensuring that violations do not reoccur. They are supposed to be independent of the bank and working on behalf of the regulator." Benjamin M. Lawsky, N.Y. Superintendent of Fin. Services, Remarks at Regulating Shadow Banking Conference Sponsored by Americans for Financial Reform and the Economic Policy Institute (Nov. 22, 2013).

While head of NYDFS, Mr. Lawsky led the way in regulating consultants and subjecting them to fines and a code of conduct. Although NYDFS has no direct regulatory authority over the consultants, it must approve their access to confidential supervisory information under N.Y. Banking Law § 36(10). If NYDFS refuses access, the consultant cannot effectively work for a New York State-chartered bank or licensed branch of a foreign bank, creating a significant incentive to settle.

In 2015, NYDFS alleged that Promontory Financial Group, LLC, had changed a draft report in ways favorable to the bank it was monitoring after comments from the bank. Promontory settled after NYDFS indicated that it would otherwise deny Promontory access to confidential supervisory information until further notice. Promontory paid NYDFS $15 million and agreed to abstain from new engagements that require access to confidential supervisory information for six months. N.Y. DEP'T. FIN. SERVS., REPORT ON INVESTIGATION OF PROMONTORY FINANCIAL GROUP, LLC (Aug. 2015).

Before Promontory, Deloitte and PricewaterhouseCoopers LLP (PwC) each settled with NYDFS, Deloitte for $10 million in 2013 and PwC for $25 million in 2014. Each was suspended from consulting for New York-regulated banks, Deloitte for one year and PwC for two. NYDFS also required each company to enter into a code of conduct, which requires, among other things:

- monthly meetings between the consultant and NYDFS;
- that the consultant bring to the attention of NYDFS disagreements about material matters between the consultant and the financial institution;
- that the final report produced by the consultant must list all personnel from the financial institution who the consultant knows have substantively reviewed or commented on drafts of the findings; and
- that the consultant maintain recommendations made to the financial institution relating to suspicious activity reports (part of anti-money laundering law) and provide these records to NYDFS on request.

N.Y. Dep't. Fin. Servs., *In re* PricewaterhouseCoopers LLP Settlement Agreement (Aug. 14, 2014); N.Y. Dep't. Fin. Servs., *In re* Deloitte Financial Advisory Services LLP Settlement Agreement (June 18, 2013).

V. MODIFYING INCENTIVES THROUGH COMPENSATION

Instead of regulating the level of executive compensation in the private sector directly, the United States has traditionally regulated executive compensation indirectly through required disclosure in securities filings, tax disincentives, and fiduciary standards under state corporate law. The focus on executive compensation in the financial sector has intensified amid concerns about increasing income inequality and political backlash after taxpayer funds were put at risk in the Financial Crisis. In this section we will discuss the regulation of bank and BHC executive compensation before the Financial Crisis, and then discuss some of the changes that have taken place in the wake of the Financial Crisis both for U.S. financial conglomerates and for all U.S. public companies, such as say on pay. We will then compare the very different approach taken in the EU.

A. THE SITUATION BEFORE THE FINANCIAL CRISIS

Before the Financial Crisis, regulation of executive compensation was largely limited to banks and other IDIs. The key statutory provisions regulating executive compensation in the banking sector were put into place as a response to the Savings & Loan Crisis. The Federal Deposit Insurance Corporation Improvement Act (FDICIA) limited increases in compensation for executive officers of an undercapitalized or critically undercapitalized IDI subject to the prompt corrective action and capital restoration provisions we discussed in Chapter 2.5. The Crime Control Act of 1990 amended the Federal Deposit Insurance Act to give the FDIC authority to limit golden parachutes or indemnification payments from an IDI in a "troubled condition." 12 U.S.C. § 1828(k). The FDIC passed regulations in 1996. 12 C.F.R. § 359.

FDICIA § 132 required the OCC, Federal Reserve Board, FDIC, and OTS to establish standards prohibiting as an unsafe and unsound practice fees, benefits, or compensation to any director, executive officer, employee, or principal shareholder of a bank, BHC, or thrift and its holding company that could lead to material financial loss to an institution. Section 132 also required that the agencies define "excessive compensation," and interagency guidelines prohibiting excessive compensation at financial institutions were published in 1995. 12 C.F.R. pt. 30, Appendix A. The FDIC's implementation of regulations prohibiting golden parachute payments by troubled IDIs did not come into force until 1996. 12 C.F.R. pt. 359. According to the guidelines, "[c]ompensation shall be considered excessive when amounts paid are unreasonable or disproportionate to the services performed by an executive officer, employee, director, or principal shareholder" based on a number of factors. 12 C.F.R. pt. 364, App. A. Factors in the guidelines include total value of the compensation, compensation history of the individual or others with similar skills at the IDI, the financial condition of the IDI, compensation at peer institutions, and "[a]ny connection between the individual and any fraudulent act or omission, breach of trust or fiduciary duty, or insider abuse" at the IDI. *Id.*

As a practical matter, regulatory scrutiny was largely limited to distressed IDIs, which themselves were very rare between the mid-1990s and the Financial Crisis. For a BHC without a troubled bank, executive compensation was treated just as it was for all other U.S. public companies. It is fair to say that, until the Financial Crisis, financial conglomerates answered first and foremost to their shareholders, including their demands to align pay with performance and that top executives align their incentives with shareholder return.

A statute that applied to all U.S. public companies was § 304 of the Sarbanes-Oxley Act, which required the clawback of incentive compensation of the CEO and the CFO within 12 months of a restatement of the public company's financial statements if the restatement was made due to material noncompliance with the securities laws as a result of misconduct. Material restatements of financial statements by a public company are rare in a business-as-usual context, but are a classic indicator that a company is approaching failure.

---

1. ***Incentive Compensation.*** While it can take many forms, the basics of executive compensation involve a package of cash salary plus, if certain performance metrics are met, variable compensation, otherwise known as a bonus. An all-cash bonus, like that given by a law firm, was rare in financial institutions, even before the Financial Crisis. More typically, a bonus would be part cash, some portion of which might be deferred, and part a grant of equity compensation, such as units that track the value of the company's stock or stock options. For a concise discussion, see MERIDIAN COMPENSATION PARTNERS, LLC, THE NEW REALITIES OF EXECUTIVE COMPENSATION IN THE BANKING INDUSTRY: THE IMPACT OF REGULATORY AND SHAREHOLDER INFLUENCE, 2013–2014 (2014).

B. CHANGES AFTER THE FINANCIAL CRISIS

Many have linked the incentives created by the structure and size of executive compensation to a culture of short-term risk-taking that contributed to the Financial Crisis. Lucian A. Bebchuk et al., *The Wages of Failure: Executive Compensation at Bear Stearns and Lehman 2000–2008*, 27 YALE J. ON REG. 257 (2010); *see also* BOARD OF GOVERNORS OF THE FED. RESERVE SYS., INCENTIVE COMPENSATION PRACTICES: A REPORT ON THE HORIZONTAL REVIEW OF PRACTICES AT LARGE BANKING ORGANIZATIONS (2010). Crazy compensation schemes are cited as "villain 7" in the Financial Crisis by Princeton economist and former Vice Chair of the Federal Reserve Board, Alan S. Blinder, who writes:

> to oversimplify a vastly more complicated reality, too many traders earn bonuses that have a 'heads I win a lot, tails I lose a little' character to them. If their bets turn out to be winners, they become fabulously wealthy. If they lose, [other people's money] absorbs almost all the losses; the traders' personal losses are minimal.

ALAN S. BLINDER, AFTER THE MUSIC STOPPED: THE FINANCIAL CRISIS, THE RESPONSE, AND THE WORK AHEAD 283–84 (2013). The Financial Stability Board (FSB) has taken the view that incentive compensation contributed to the Financial Crisis because it was not coordinated with risk management. FINANCIAL STABILITY FORUM: FINANCIAL STABILITY BOARD PRINCIPLES FOR SOUND COMPENSATION PRACTICES (Apr. 2, 2009). In March 2009, the Institute of International Finance, a trade organization for the banking sector, released a survey of member firms with significant wholesale banking businesses in which "98% of survey respondents believe that compensation structures were a factor in the underlying crisis." INSTITUTE OF INTERNATIONAL FINANCE, COMPENSATION IN FINANCIAL SERVICES: INDUSTRY PROGRESS AND THE AGENDA FOR CHANGE (2009).

The first intense regulation of executive compensation came to the United States through Troubled Asset Relief Program (TARP) and its implementing statute, the Emergency Economic Stabilization Act of 2008 (EESA), which was later amended by the American Recovery and Reinvestment Act of 2009. The regime imposed restrictions on any company, including BHCs, AIG, and auto manufacturers, that had received a capital infusion of preferred stock under TARP. The Treasury's implementation of TARP created an Office of the Special Master for TARP Executive Compensation and prohibited severance, tax gross-up and change in control payments; limited incentive compensation; required the clawback of incentive compensation paid on the basis of materially inaccurate financial statements or performance metrics; and required a mandatory but non-binding say on pay vote for shareholders. It is widely understood that the executive compensation restrictions were one of the leading reasons why healthy BHCs exited TARP as quickly as they did.

In June 2010, one month before final votes on the Dodd-Frank Act, the Federal Reserve Board, the OCC, the FDIC, and the OTS jointly issued guidance, inspired by the FSB's Principles, on executive compensation structures that applied to all of the banking organizations supervised by these agencies. The goal of the guidance was to ensure that, post-Financial Crisis, incentive compensation did not encourage imprudent risk-taking that threatened safety and soundness. The interagency guidance set out three high-level principles for executive compensation: (1) incentive compensation programs should balance risk and financial results so that employees do not have incentives to take excessive risks, (2) compensation should be compatible with effective controls and risk management, and (3) organizations should have strong and effective corporate governance structures in place to monitor compensation practices.

Section 956 of the Dodd-Frank Act required the OCC, the Federal Reserve Board, the FDIC, the SEC, the NCUA, and the Federal Housing Finance Agency (FHFA) to jointly prescribe regulations or guidelines on executive compensation for each covered financial institution with assets of $1 billion or more. The definition of covered financial institutions expanded the regulatory perimeter for the regulation of executive compensation and covers banks, credit unions, broker-dealers (whether or not they are affiliated with a bank), investment advisers, Fannie Mae and Freddie Mac, and "any other financial institution" that the regulators jointly determine. 12 U.S.C. § 5641(e)(2)(G). In April 2011, agencies proposed an interagency rule that would subject financial institutions to the following requirements:

- all covered financial institutions with $1 billion of assets or more would be subject to principles-based prohibitions on providing incentive-based compensation that is excessive or that could lead to material financial loss to the institution;
- larger covered financial institutions with $50 billion of assets or more would be required to defer 50% of incentive-based compensation paid to

executive officers and to review and approve incentive-based compensation paid to non-executive officers who individually have the ability to expose the institution to a substantial amount of risk; and

- all covered financial institutions with $1 billion of assets or more would be required to submit annual reports to their appropriate regulators and to establish and maintain policies and procedures governing the award of incentive-based compensation.

Incentive-Based Compensation Arrangements, 76 Fed. Reg. 21,170 (Apr. 14, 2011). The SEC's webpage listing public comments on SEC regulatory initiatives under the Dodd-Frank Act lists more than 100,000 comments on the proposed rule, albeit many submitted by form letter. Another post-Financial Crisis change is the development of "say-on-pay", a non-binding shareholder advisory vote on a public company's executive compensation. As a result, public company engagement with their shareholders has been increasing. *See* MARC GOLDSTEIN, INSTITUTIONAL SHAREHOLDER SERVICES, DEFINING ENGAGEMENT: AN UPDATE ON THE EVOLVING RELATIONSHIP BETWEEN SHAREHOLDERS, DIRECTORS AND EXECUTIVES (Apr. 10, 2014).

In the years since the Financial Crisis, academics have suggested a number of different deferred compensation mechanisms for financial institutions. One suggestion is that incentive compensation be composed solely of stock and stock options which executives cannot sell or exercise for two to four years after their last day in office. Sanjai Bhagat & Brian Bolton, *Financial Crisis and Bank Executive Compensation*, 25 J. CORP. FIN. 313 (2014). As a practical matter, the equity portion of incentive compensation is largely restricted so this proposal largely comes down to eliminating cash. Frederick Tung suggests that incentive compensation be paid in part with subordinated debt. Frederick Tung, *Pay for Banker Performance: Structuring Executive Compensation for Risk Regulation*, 105 NW. U. L. REV. 1205, 1206 (2011). One regulator, William Dudley, President of the Federal Reserve Bank of New York, has suggested that senior managers and material risk-takers' deferred compensation be mostly debt vesting over a long period of time of up to ten years. The deferred compensation could then be used as a performance bond that employees would lose when the financial firm was assessed a fine. In Dudley's proposal, however, there is no link between any fault or involvement of the affected employee and the clawback. William C. Dudley, President and CEO, Fed. Reserve Bank of N.Y., Remarks at the Workshop on Reforming Culture and Behavior in the Financial Services Industry: Enhancing Financial Stability by Improving Culture in the Financial Services Industry (Oct. 20, 2014). There have been initiatives by the private sector to implement such ideas—in 2013, UBS introduced "bonus bonds," whereby bonuses were awarded in the form of debt that would be written down if the bank's regulatory capital fell below seven percent or in the case of a very serious loss. Daniel Schäfer, *UBS Leads Way with Bonuses Shake-Up*, FIN. TIMES, Feb. 5, 2013.

---

1. ***Why Do Rules Take So Long to Finalize?*** One part of the answer might be the presence of multiple federal regulators. In Chapter 2.2, we saw the pre-Financial Crisis example of the broker-dealer pushout rule in Regulation R,

which took eight years of work to finalize as the Federal Reserve Board and the SEC tried to find common ground. In Chapter 6.1, we explored the Volcker Rule, which involved five regulators and took three and a half years plus focused pressure from the White House to enact. The incentive compensation proposed rule involves six regulators. The result of multiple regulators is that each of these regulations changes the regulatory perimeter and raises classic issues of stakeholder interests, not only between the regulated and the regulators but among different subsections within the financial sector. Is it rational for the OCC, the Federal Reserve Board, the FDIC, the SEC, the NCUA, and the FHFA to have an interagency rule on the incentive compensation of their regulated entities? Consider the institutional and profit-generating differences between banks, hedge funds, and broker-dealers. What problems might arise from regulating compensation in these three categories of entities in the same way?

2. ***Expansion of the Scope of Which Financial Sector Players Are Covered.*** The proposed U.S. executive compensation regulations would apply principles-based compensation rules to all banks, branches of foreign banks, credit unions, industrial loan companies, BHCs, savings and loan holding companies, broker-dealers (whether or not affiliated with a bank), and investment advisers. The requirement that 50% of incentive compensation be deferred would apply to larger financial institutions with $50 billion or more in assets. In 2011, the law firm Davis Polk & Wardwell LLP estimated that at least 1,670 financial institutions would be covered, with over 140 qualifying as larger covered financial institutions. DAVIS POLK & WARDWELL LLP, FEDERAL AGENCIES PROPOSE INTERAGENCY RULE ON INCENTIVE-BASED COMPENSATION FOR FINANCIAL INSTITUTIONS, A-3 (Mar. 4, 2011). How does the scope of the institutions covered by the proposed incentive compensation rule compare to the domestic systemically important bank, global systemically important bank, and SIFI designation perimeter discussed in Chapter 2.7 and Chapter 6.2?

3. ***Scope of Individuals Covered.*** The scope of employees covered has been broadened from the CEO and CFO, who were subject to § 304 of the Sarbanes-Oxley Act, and even from the traditional narrow definition of executive officer that we saw in the insider lending rules in Chapter 2.3 and the securities disclosure context. In the proposed regulations, an executive officer:

> means a person who holds the title or, without regard to title, salary, or compensation, performs the function of one or more of the following positions: president, chief executive officer, executive chair, chief operating officer, chief financial officer, chief investment officer, chief legal officer, chief lending officer, chief risk officer, or head of a major business line.

Incentive-Based Compensation Arrangements, 76 Fed. Reg. 21,170, 21,208 (Apr. 14, 2011). Executive officers at larger institutions must have 50% of their incentive compensation deferred over a period of no less than three years. Non-executive officers who individually have the ability to expose the institution to a substantial amount of risk must have their compensation individually reviewed and approved by the board of directors or a committee thereof. *Id.* at 21,209.

4. ***Effectiveness of Proposed Regulations.*** Some of those most critical of existing compensation programs of the larger financial institutions have also

been critical of the proposed interagency rule on incentive compensation under the Dodd-Frank Act. *See, e.g.*, Pay for Performance: Incentive Compensation at the Largest Financial Institutions: Hearing Before the Subcomm. on Fin. Insts. & Consumer Prot. of the S. Comm. on Banking, Hous. and Urban Affairs, 112th Cong. 477 (2012) (statement of Robert J. Jackson, Jr., Professor, Columbia Law School). Professor Jackson contended that the agencies' proposals fall far short of the rigorous oversight of incentive compensation that Congress authorized in § 956. *Id.* He suggested that rules on bonuses apply to all risk-takers, not just executives; that the rules prevent countermeasures, such as hedging, from frustrating the rules' intent; that bonus structures be reviewed by banking regulators rather than boards; and a requirement that regulators be provided with detailed quantitative information to enable them to identify those employees who have incentives to take excessive risk. Is it realistic for financial institution compensation to be regulated in a manner intended to achieve the policy goals of such regulation?

5. ***Constitutional Questions Raised by TARP***. To ensure compliance with TARP restrictions, the Treasury included covenants into stock purchase agreements, which prohibited the companies that received TARP funds from paying certain bonuses and golden parachute payments to top executives. Just as the government prepared to release the second half of TARP funding, Congress passed the American Recovery and Reinvestment Act of 2009, which retroactively applied additional restrictions on executive compensation. In an effort to insulate these restrictions from legal challenge, the Treasury required companies to obtain a waiver from affected executives. The Treasury's form of waiver required an executive to waive "any tort or constitutional claim about the effect of [restrictions imposed by EESA, as amended]." Is there an argument that TARP's restrictions on executive compensation constituted a "taking" under the takings clause of the Fifth Amendment? Could a due process argument under the Fifth Amendment be raised regarding governmental abrogation of a contract's benefits? Would the waivers the Treasury received remain valid despite EESA's subsequent amendments? If there were any tension with state law that would prohibit the clawback of previously paid incentive compensation, would the TARP restrictions preempt state law? *See* Jeremiah Thomas, *TARP's Hard Line on Executive Compensation: Misaligned Incentives and Constitutional Hurdles*, 70 OHIO ST. L.J. 1307 (2009).

6. ***Effect on the War for Talent in the Financial Sector.*** How does the regulation of incentive compensation affect the war for talent within different sub-sectors of the financial sector? Would bankers be more or less likely to go to BHCs, hedge funds, or insurance companies? Is the answer likely to be different for senior and junior bankers? *See, e.g.*, William Alden, *A Mad Scramble for Young Bankers*, N.Y. TIMES, July 5, 2014, at BU1.

C. DIFFERENT APPROACH TAKEN IN EUROPE

The approach taken in the EU in the post-Financial Crisis era has involved many of the same elements in the U.S. proposed regulations with the addition of a wide clawback and an explicit bonus cap. Directive 2013/36/EU of the European Parliament and of the Council of 26 June 2013 on Access to the

Activity of Credit Institutions and the Prudential Supervision of Credit Institutions and Investment Firms, Amending Directive 2002/87/EC and Repealing Directives 2006/48/EC and 2006/49/EC, 2013 O.J. (L 176) [hereinafter Capital Requirements Directive IV]. In essence, under the EU Directive:

- at least 50% of incentive compensation should consist of equity-linked instruments;
- at least 40% of incentive compensation should be deferred over a period of at least three to five years;
- bonus payments must be capped at 100% of total fixed pay or, with a supermajority shareholder approval, 200% of total fixed pay; and
- up to 100% of variable pay will be subject to clawback arrangements or malus, the adjustment of an award of variable remuneration, such as a performance-linked bonus or share award, before it has vested. *Id.* art. 94(l)(1); 94(l)(m); 94(l)(g).

The Capital Requirements Directive IV will apply to all credit institutions and investment firms in the EU, as well as their non-EU subsidiaries and branches, and EU subsidiaries and branches of financial institutions headquartered outside the EU. For example, if a financial institution is headquartered in London or Paris, all covered employees, including employees located in New York or Hong Kong, will be affected and, even if a financial institution is headquartered in New York or Hong Kong, its employees working for an EU subsidiary will be affected. Capital Requirements Directive IV; European Banking Authority, *Consultation Paper, Draft Guidelines on Sound Remuneration Policies Under Article 74(3) and 75(2) of Directive 2013/36/EU and Disclosures Under Article 450 of Regulation (EU) No. 575/2013* (Mar. 4, 2015).

The bonus cap will cover employees whose professional activities have a material effect on the risk profile of the financial institution. Such employees include senior management, defined as "senior management, risk takers, staff engaged in control functions and any employee receiving total remuneration that takes them into the same remuneration bracket as senior management and risk takers." Employees are presumed to be material risk-takers if they meet any of the following quantitative criteria for the preceding financial year: (1) their total pay is €500,000 or more; or (2) they are part of the 0.3% of staff with the highest pay in the institution; or (3) their total pay is equal to or greater than the lowest total pay of a member of senior management or of certain other material risk-takers in the institution. Commission Delegated Regulation (EU) 604/2014, art. 4(1), 2014 O.J. (L 167) 34.

In December 2015, the European Banking Authority extended these compensation restrictions to all mutual fund families that are covered by the Capital Requirements Directive IV, including BlackRock and Fidelity, but not Vanguard and T. Rowe Price. The applicability of EU compensation restrictions has resulted in a division within the U.S. asset management sector, as covered firms are restricted in their ability to recruit and retain talent. European Banking Authority, *Final Report, Guidelines on Sound Remuneration Policies*

Under Articles 74(3) and 75(2) of Directive 2013/36/EU and Disclosures Under Article 450 of Regulation (EU) No. 575/2013 (Dec. 21, 2015).

---

1. ***Caps on Banker Pay.*** Given how much bankers, especially top bankers, make compared to the median salary in the United States, should there be an absolute cap on pay in the financial sector? Does the Capital Requirements Directive IV come close to implementing such a cap indirectly? Will staff at EU banks be more or less likely to leave for financial conglomerates in other countries, or to work for a technology start-up? Is the effect the same on senior and junior bankers? Of those, who are more or less mobile because of family circumstances or language skill sets? It has been suggested that society would be better off if fewer top students from elite schools joined the financial sector. What are the pros and cons of this point of view?

2. ***City of London.*** The UK government was against the compensation rules passed by the EU parliament, although it ultimately abandoned this position in the face of strong European Banking Authority objection. Given that UK taxpayers and the UK government suffered greatly during the Financial Crisis, why would the UK government object to these rules?

CHAPTER 8.2

SUPERVISION AND ENFORCEMENT

CONTENTS

I. INTRODUCTION

Credible supervision and enforcement is required to ensure financial regulation effectively constrains private behavior. *See* Howell E. Jackson & Mark J. Roe, *Public and Private Enforcement of Securities Laws: Resource-Based Evidence*, 93 J. FIN. ECON. 207 (2009). Financial sector regulators supervise and enforce specific legal requirements, as well as financial institutions' broader obligations not to engage in fraudulent activities, to maintain adequate compliance systems, and generally to operate in accordance with principles of "safety and soundness." Active supervision via reporting, onsite examinations and, increasingly, formal and informal enforcement actions is part of what distinguishes the financial sector from other highly regulated sectors.

We have seen a number of examples of supervision and enforcement in earlier chapters. The Chapters in Part IV on securities regulation included illustrations of enforcement actions brought by the SEC against investment advisers, broker dealers, and related parties. Chapter 2.5 featured the FDIC's enforcement of capital directives against the Bank of Coushatta, and several of the jurisdictional perimeter cases in Chapter 1.4 involved various types of enforcement actions.

In this Chapter, we look at the array of supervisory and enforcement tools as a distinct topic of study. We begin with the basic building blocks of supervision, including regulatory examinations and reporting. We then move to the policy and trends of enforcement against banks and financial conglomerates in the United States. We conclude with a discussion of recurring issues in enforcement policies.

Our focus in this Chapter is on supervision and enforcement of financial regulation by federal regulators. Insurance companies are, of course, also regulated. The structure and focuses of insurance regulation often differ from bank regulation, reflecting that insurers are regulated at the state level, with coordination through the National Association of Insurance Commissioners, and face different risks and obligations.

II. BASIC BUILDING BLOCKS OF SUPERVISION AND ENFORCEMENT

In this section we will focus on how the SEC, FINRA, and the four main federal banking regulators with enforcement authority, the Federal Reserve Board, OCC, FDIC, and NCUA supervise financial institutions and those who work in the sector. As you read this section, consider how supervision and enforcement differ between the federal banking regulators and capital markets regulators. How does the focus on disclosure by the SEC and FINRA affect the way they pursue complaints? How are banking regulators' examinations and enforcement actions affected by their focus on financial stability?

As described in Chapter 1.3, the Federal Reserve Board examines bank holding companies (BHCs) and state member banks, the FDIC examines state non-member banks and state thrifts, the OCC examines national banks and federal thrifts, and the NCUA examines credit unions. Additionally, SEC-registered entities are regulated by the SEC's Office of Compliance Inspections and Examinations, while FINRA also regulates broker-dealers.

A. REPORTING, EXAMINATION, AND SUPERVISION BY FEDERAL BANKING REGULATORS

For banks and their BHCs, reporting and examinations are the basic building blocks of the supervisory process. Banks and BHCs must submit a number of reports to regulators. Some of these reports are public and others are treated as confidential supervisory information. Reports are both submitted at regular intervals but can also be triggered by certain events.

Perhaps the most important regularly-submitted report is the publicly-filed Report of Condition and Income (Call Report). The Federal Financial Institutions Examination Council (FFIEC) requires every national bank, state member bank, insured non-member bank, and thrift institution to file a Call Report on Form FFIEC 031 or Form FFIEC 041 as of the close of business on the last day of each calendar quarter. These reports collect basic financial data in the form of a balance sheet, an income statement, and supporting schedules. The Report of Condition schedules provide details on assets, liabilities, and capital accounts. The Report of Income schedules provide details on income and expenses. Regulators use call reports to review the financial condition of an institution without an onsite examination and to prepare for upcoming examinations.

We hope the words "onsite examination" have captured your attention. Onsite examinations permit federal banking regulators to access an organization's books and records and compliance systems without a subpoena. Each "appropriate Federal banking agency" is required to conduct periodic onsite examinations at the insured depository institutions (IDIs) under its jurisdiction. 12 U.S.C. § 1820(d)(1). The NCUA has a similar obligation with respect to credit unions. *Id.* § 1756. The relevant regulator must conduct an examination at least once during each 12-month period. The cycle is longer for certain well-capitalized and well-managed IDIs with total assets of less than $1 billion, in which case examinations are required at least once every 18 months. *Id.* § 1820(d)(4). The asset cap for the 18-month exam cycle increased from $500 million to $1 billion in 2015. *Id.* The Federal Reserve Board and the FDIC examine some state member banks and state non-member banks in alternate examination cycles, sharing responsibility with their state banking counterparts, as allowed by 12 U.S.C. § 1820(d)(3).

Onsite examinations are most relevant for community banks since large, complex banking organizations generally face more intensive supervision on an ongoing basis. In most cases, these larger institutions will have a supervisory team permanently onsite. For regulators, examinations consume enormous resources. For example, the FDIC employed 2,803 bank examiners as of year-end 2014, amounting to 41% of its total workforce. FDIC OFFICE OF MINORITY AND WOMEN INCLUSION, REPORT TO CONGRESS (2014). In 2012, the FDIC estimated that a risk management examination of a community bank with $250 million to $500 million in total assets would involve 710 to 1,500 examiner-hours, depending on the bank's condition. FDIC OFFICE OF INSPECTOR GENERAL, REPORT ON THE FDIC'S EXAMINATION PROCESS FOR SMALL COMMUNITY BANKS (Aug. 2012).

Examinations follow the FFIEC's Uniform Financial Institutions Rating System, better known as CAMELS due to its six aspects of assessment: capital adequacy, asset quality, management, earnings, liquidity, and sensitivity to market risk. Capital adequacy is measured relative to the nature and extent of the institution's risk profile. Examiners may find that a financial institution has deficient capital based on its risk profile even if the institution meets required regulatory minimums. The asset quality rating reflects the credit risk associated with the financial institution's assets and the quality of its credit administration practices. The management rating measures the capability of the institution's board of directors, officers, and other management to manage risks, which vary depending on each institution's nature, size, and sophistication. The earnings rating reflects the quantity, trend, and quality of the institution's earnings. Liquidity is rated based on the institution's current liquidity position, prospective sources of liquidity relative to present and future needs, and the quality of its funds management practices. Sensitivity to market risk, a factor added in 1996, before which the rating system was known as the CAMEL, reflects the degree to which changes in interest and foreign exchange (FX) rates, and commodity and equity prices can adversely affect the institution.

Examiners rate institutions on a one to five scale for each of the six component areas. A rating of one represents the lowest level of concern and five the greatest concern. The ratings for the six CAMELS component areas are combined into a composite score, again on a one to five scale. A composite one rating means an institution is "sound in every respect"; a composite five rating means an institution "exhibit[s] extremely unsafe and unsound practices or conditions." We should note that the composite score is not a mathematical average of the six component ratings; in assigning a composite rating, some components may be given more weight than others depending on the situation at the institution. IDIs with a composite CAMELS rating of four or five are placed on the FDIC's Problem List. While the identity of the IDIs on this list is confidential, the FDIC discloses the total number of problem banks in its Quarterly Banking Profile.

The number of problem banks rose sharply during the Financial Crisis, from 90 at the end of the first quarter of 2008 to a peak of 888 at the end of the first quarter of 2011. The low number of banks with poor composite CAMELS scores before the Financial Crisis is seen by some as a sign of the rating system's failure to reflect long-term risk. A key criticism is that examiners were generally reluctant to assign low management scores for institutions with strong capital and earnings scores, even if the examiners observed long-term risks in management practices. Since the Financial Crisis, the bank regulators have directed their examiners to reflect forward-looking information in the CAMELS ratings, especially the management rating. Regulators have also introduced new systems to track matters requiring attention at individual banks. Examiners use these systems to track corrective progress at individual institutions and to assess whether particular kinds of matters requiring attention are arising across many institutions. *See* U.S. GOV'T ACCOUNTABILITY OFFICE, GAO-15-365, BANK REGULATION: LESSONS LEARNED AND A FRAMEWORK FOR MONITORING EMERGING RISKS AND REGULATORY RESPONSE (June 2015).

Since 1977, each IDI has also been examined as required under the Community Reinvestment Act (CRA), which was enacted to combat discrimination in the provision of banking services, particularly discrimination in neighborhoods based on income and race distinctions, a practice known as redlining. See Chapters 5.1 and 5.4 for additional discussion of CRA.

Pursuant to the Dodd-Frank Act, the CFPB periodically examines IDIs and credit unions with consolidated assets of more than $10 billion and certain non-bank financial companies face periodic examinations for compliance with federal consumer law. *Id.* § 5514–15. For IDIs and credit unions that do not meet the $10 billion threshold, the CFPB may require reports and has discretion to include examiners on a sample of the examinations performed by the institution's prudential regulator. The power to enforce federal consumer financial laws for these smaller institutions remains with the institution's prudential regulator. *Id.* § 2903(a)(1).

With the exception of records prepared in the ordinary course of business and later provided to examiners, the information that financial institutions provide to the FDIC, Federal Reserve Board, OCC, or CFPB is generally confidential. *Id.* §§ 4.31–40, 261.2–23, 309.1–7, 1070.40–48. Information provided to regulators is also subject to the common law bank examination privilege, also known as the governmental deliberative process privilege or the intragovernmental opinion privilege. The privilege applies to "information within the custody or control of a department or agency of the government the disclosure of which is shown to be contrary to the public interest and which consists of . . . intragovernmental opinions or recommendations submitted for consideration in the performance of decisional or policy-making functions." *See In re* Franklin Nat'l Bank Sec. Litig., 478 F. Supp. 577, 580 (E.D.N.Y. 1979) (citing proposed Federal Rule of Evidence 509, which would have codified the intragovernmental opinion privilege). For a discussion of the confidentiality of information collected after the Dodd-Frank Act, see Annette L. Nazareth & Margaret E. Tahyar, *Transparency and Confidentiality in the Post Financial Crisis World—Where to Strike the Balance*?, 1 HARV. BUS. L. REV. 146 (2011).

---

1. ***FFIEC and Financial Stability Oversight Council (FSOC).*** Policymakers' impetus for creating both the FFIEC in 1978 and FSOC in 2010 was to improve coordination among financial regulatory agencies, a priority driven by concerns that regulators were not keeping up with an increasingly complex sector in an adequate and coordinated way. The report to the House Committee on Banking, Finance and Urban Affairs that accompanied the legislation establishing FFIEC stated that FFIEC was intended to remedy the "lack of effective coordination" among financial regulatory agencies, a problem that would only grow more grave "[a]s the holding company movement spreads and as the banking industry becomes more sophisticated and complex." H.R. REP. No. 95-1383, at 23–24 (1978). Similarly, the establishment of an increasing number of large, global, and interconnected financial institutions in the 1990s and 2000s led policymakers to prioritize even greater coordination between financial regulators. The Dodd-Frank Act established FSOC to improve information sharing and coordination among financial regulatory agencies, both generally and specifically with respect to systemically important firms, which may be designated for additional regulation, as described in Chapter 6.2. How far has the goal of coordination advanced in the intervening years from 1978 to present?

2. ***Criticism of Permanent Onsite Examiners at Large Banks.*** The permanent placement of onsite examiners at large banks has one clear advantage: examiners who spend years at the same bank gain unique expertise about the bank's management, activities, and information systems. The risk of onsite examiners is that they get too cozy with the banks they supervise, raising the possibility of regulatory capture. In 2014, a former examiner for the Federal

Reserve Bank of New York released secretly recorded conversations that the leaking examiner asserted illustrated that the examination staff was overly deferential to Goldman Sachs. *See This American Life: The Secret Recordings of Carmen Segarra*, CHICAGO PUB. RADIO (Sept. 26, 2014) (downloaded using iTunes). In a congressional hearing shortly thereafter, Federal Reserve Bank of New York President William Dudley said that supervisory process changes were underway at the Reserve Bank, including "requir[ing] examination teams to spend more time at [the Federal Reserve Bank of New York] headquarters and less time 'in the field.'" *Improving Financial Institution Supervision: Examining and Addressing Regulatory Capture, Hearing Before the Subcomm. on Fin. Insts. & Consumer Prot. of the S. Comm. on Banking, Hous. & Urban Affairs*, 114th Cong. (2014) (statement of William Dudley, President, Fed. Reserve Bank of New York). OCC examiners were also criticized for inadequate oversight leading up to the London Whale trading losses in 2012 at JPMorgan Chase. In 2014, in response to an international peer review of its supervisory practices, the OCC announced that it would establish a formal rotation process for examination staff and that, over time, it would reduce the number of onsite examiners at individual banks. OCC, SUMMARY OF OCC'S RESPONSES TO THE SUPERVISION PEER REVIEW RECOMMENDATIONS (May 28, 2014).

B. SEC AND FINRA EXAMINATIONS

SEC-registered entities, including broker-dealers, investment advisers, clearing agencies, and national securities exchanges, are subject to examination by the SEC. The SEC's Office of Compliance Inspections and Examinations assesses registered entities' compliance with federal securities laws, including the sufficiency of policies and systems designed to ensure continued compliance, and entities' adherence to disclosures made to the public, their clients, and the SEC. The SEC also conducts sweep examinations, which are coordinated reviews of a number of firms relating to a particular subject matter, such as cybersecurity and risks involving alternative mutual funds. SEC examinations have largely focused on investment advisers while FINRA, an independent, not-for-profit organization authorized by Congress to regulate and supervise brokers and brokerage firms, that is, itself, subject to examination by the SEC, conducts the bulk of broker-dealer examinations.

---

1. ***Federal Reserve Board Supervision of SEC-Supervised Affiliates of BHCs.*** The Federal Reserve Board's evolving approach to supervising affiliates of BHCs already subject to SEC supervision is an instructive example of how deregulation and re-regulation affect the compliance framework. Section 111 of the Gramm-Leach-Bliley Act (GLBA) introduced what came to be known as the Fed-lite system of supervision, which intended to streamline supervision by ensuring that "banking activities are regulated by bank regulators [and] securities activities are regulated by securities regulators." H.R. REP. No. 106-434, at 157 (1999). In keeping with such functional regulation, while the Federal Reserve Board was designated the "umbrella supervisor" for financial holding companies, its authority to examine their functionally regulated subsidiaries, like securities

affiliates, was significantly restricted. The authors of the Dodd-Frank Act took the opposite approach, prioritizing full access to information over streamlined supervision. As such, § 604 of the Dodd-Frank Act removed GLBA restrictions on the Federal Reserve Board's supervision of functionally regulated subsidiaries, while still instructing the Federal Reserve Board to use existing reports and other supervisory information provided to other regulators "to the fullest extent possible." 12 U.S.C. § 1844(c).

C. THE PUBLIC ENFORCEMENT ARSENAL

An outgrowth of the New Deal, the public enforcement landscape consists of a largely decentralized system of multiple enforcement authorities with varying, and sometimes overlapping, jurisdictions. Financial regulators are afforded a range of responses to enforce financial regulation on behalf of the public. The SEC investigates and enforces breaches of federal securities laws through civil and administrative proceedings. FINRA works with the SEC to investigate broker-dealers. Both entities can levy fines and bar individuals from the securities sector. Central to bank regulators' missions is to ensure the safety and soundness of the banking system. The Federal Reserve Board, FDIC, OCC, and NCUA each have the authority to impose fines, issue orders, and pursue actions against Institution Affiliated Parties (IAPs), including directors, officers, employees, certain controlling shareholders, and agents. *Id.* §§ 1813(u), 1818.

III. ENFORCEMENT POLICY AND TRENDS

In the aftermath of the Financial Crisis and several ethical and compliance failures at major banking institutions, regulators drastically increased their enforcement activities by assessing higher civil money penalties and more cease-and-desist orders. Perhaps most importantly, these controversies also gave rise to the interagency public enforcement action. For instance, in a rare example of coordinated enforcement by the SEC and a banking regulator, the Federal Reserve Board and the SEC announced enforcement actions against Regions Bank and Regions Financial Corporation, respectively, and against three former senior managers of the bank on the same day in June 2014 for misconduct in 2009 related to the accounting of problem loans.

Most agree that an effective public enforcement regime is necessary to maintain a strong economy. Others point to a question of balance and ask if public enforcement is also influenced by the need of the government to raise revenue. Public enforcement is said to promote investor confidence and participation in financial markets, while reducing the cost of capital and increasing economic growth. As you read the following sections, keep in mind that other jurisdictions set up their public enforcement mechanisms much differently. Why has the U.S. enforcement ethos developed as it has? How can it be made more effective?

A. SEC AND FINRA ENFORCEMENT ACTIONS

In the United States, multiple governmental and quasi-governmental agencies can and do impose substantial sanctions on investment advisers and broker-dealers. Consequently, the overall number of public actions and level of public sanctions each year is quite high. Even so, lawmakers and many investor advocates have criticized securities regulators for not doing enough to hold Wall Street firms and their employees accountable after the Financial Crisis. The SEC and FINRA have borne the brunt of this criticism. In response, both organizations revamped their enforcement divisions, and we outline these substantial efforts below. Nonetheless, questions remain. Have these structural changes altered the actions brought by both organizations in a desirable way? Are these organizations pursuing the right type of cases? Given that the SEC receives its funding from Congress through the appropriations process, and FINRA receives its funding from the financial sector directly, are their enforcement decisions influenced by the goals of those who contribute to their budgets?

1. SEC Enforcement

The SEC's Division of Enforcement was formed in 1972 by consolidating enforcement activities previously handled by various operating divisions. Enforcement staff investigate possible violations of federal securities laws. The Division of Enforcement also pursues the SEC's civil suits and administrative proceedings. The SEC initiates its investigations from many sources, spanning from market surveillance to referrals from other regulators. The Division also works closely with the SEC's Office of Market Intelligence, which collects and analyzes over 15,000 tips, complaints, and referrals each year, and with the Office of Compliance Inspections and Examinations, which conducts regular examinations of registered entities.

The Division of Enforcement underwent a drastic structural and cultural transformation in the wake of the Financial Crisis and the Division's failure to detect Bernie Madoff's $65 billion Ponzi scheme. In 2009, Enforcement Director Robert Khuzami created specialized enforcement units. Since then, SEC enforcement has been decidedly more aggressive. What was once a civil enforcement arm now bears many similarities to a federal prosecutor's office. SEC Chair Mary Jo White, herself a former federal prosecutor, stated upon assuming office that the SEC should punish "even the smallest infractions" while also pursuing the larger violations, to give the impression that "there is a strong cop on the beat." Mary Jo White, Chair, SEC, Remarks to the Securities Enforcement Forum (Oct. 9, 2013). Statistical evidence suggests that the Division has taken White's deterrence-centered strategy to heart. The SEC filed a record 807 actions in 2015, a 7% increase from 2014 and nearly 20% increase from 2013. STEPHEN CHOI *ET AL.*, NYU POLLACK CENTER FOR LAW AND BUSINESS & CORNERSTONE RESEARCH, SEC ENFORCEMENT ACTIVITY AGAINST PUBLIC COMPANY DEFENDANTS, FISCAL YEARS 2010–2015 3 (2016). The SEC's increased case load was accompanied by an increase in staffing; in 2015, the Division of Enforcement employed 1,343 full-time employees, a 7% increase from 2014.

The SEC tends to bring the same types of cases in the same proportions year-over-year. For instance, in 2015, 52% of the actions against public companies involved reporting and disclosure issues while 33% centered on the Foreign Corrupt Practices Act. For the period 2010 to 2014, on average, 57% of these cases involved reporting and disclosure questions while 33% involved the Foreign Corrupt Practices Act. There are, however, some variances. For example, the SEC brought 87 insider trading cases in 2015, a 67% increase from 2014.

The SEC can choose to bring civil proceedings in federal district court or administrative proceedings within the SEC. *See* 15 U.S.C. §§ 78u(d), 78o(b)(4). In either venue, the sanctions available to the SEC to punish violators of the securities laws are similar to those available to federal banking regulators. An administrative cease-and-desist order or a court injunction may bar future violations of the securities laws. The SEC may impose a temporary or permanent ban on individuals' or firms' participation in the broker-dealer sector, while courts may impose injunctions allowing the SEC to initiate separate administrative proceedings to consider such bans. Finally, the SEC or a court may impose monetary penalties. SEC monetary penalties include not only fines, but also orders to disgorge ill-gotten profits. Monetary penalties for public company defendants totaled $1.254 billion in 2014 and $547 million in 2015. STEPHEN CHOI *ET AL.*, SEC ENFORCEMENT ACTIVITY at 9. The SEC uses its disgorgement power frequently, with the aim of making harmed investors whole. *See generally* Stavros Gadinis, *The SEC and the Financial Industry: Evidence from Enforcement Against Broker-Dealers*, 67 BUS. LAW. 679 (2012).

Section 929P(a) of the Dodd-Frank Act granted the SEC authority to impose monetary penalties on unregistered persons in administrative proceedings, something it could previously do only in court. Largely as a result of this change, SEC enforcement actions are overwhelmingly filed as administrative proceedings. Over 80% of actions (many of which were settled) were pursued in this way during 2014, up from less than 50% a decade earlier. The Director of the SEC's Division of Enforcement explained in 2014 that the administrative forum is preferable given its efficiency, its use of specialized factfinders, namely administrative law judges appointed by the SEC, and the non-applicability of the Federal Rules of Evidence in the forum. In hearings before its own judges, the SEC won against 90% of defendants between October 2010 and March 2015, markedly higher than the 69% success rate the agency obtained against defendants in federal court over the same period. In 2014, the SEC's success rate was 100%. The use of administrative proceedings has been the subject of some criticism, most notably by Judge Jed S. Rakoff of the U.S. District Court for the Southern District of New York, as we will see later in this Chapter.

2. FINRA Enforcement

In 1938, the securities sector and the SEC lobbied Congress to add § 15A to the Securities Act of 1933 (1933 Act) to create a national securities association. A sector-funded self-regulatory organization, FINRA emerged from the consolidation of the National Association of Securities Dealers with the member regulation, enforcement, and arbitration operations of the New York Stock Exchange in 2007. FINRA was designed to promote more streamlined and efficient supervision of the broker-dealer sector. It is tasked with preventing fraudulent and manipulative acts and promoting just and equitable trade practices among over-the-counter broker-dealers. FINRA regulates more than 4,100 brokerage firms and more than 600,000 individual brokers. In pursuit of these tasks, FINRA's Enforcement Division investigates a wide range of potential offenses. Particular areas of emphasis include improper communications between companies and research analysts, AML violations, trade reporting violations, and insider trading.

FINRA initiates investigations stemming from examination findings, member filings, customer complaints, anonymous tips, automated surveillance reports, and referrals from other regulators. Working closely with its Market Regulation and Member Regulation departments, FINRA has the authority to fine, suspend, or bar both brokers and member firms. FINRA filed 1,397 disciplinary actions in 2014, reporting $134 million in fines and $32 million in restitution. FINRA may also refer its investigations to other regulators for further actions. In 2012, FINRA referred 692 matters involving potential fraud or insider trading to the SEC and other federal or state law enforcement agencies. After referring slightly fewer cases (660) in 2013, case referrals increased again to over 700 in 2014.

---

1. ***The Appropriations Process.*** Enforcement activities have tended to define the overall mission of the SEC. The agency explicitly states that it is "first and foremost . . . a law enforcement agency." SEC, *The Investor's Advocate: How the SEC Protects Investors, Maintains Market Integrity, and Facilitates Capital Formation* (June 10, 2013). Some commentators have argued that this self-identification as a law enforcement agency is at least partly due to the agency's subjection to the congressional appropriations process, the theory being that Congress primarily evaluates the SEC's yearly performance based on the activity of its Enforcement Division. *See, e.g.*, John Sivolella, *Bureaucratic Decision Making—SEC Enforcement and Federal Courts' Ideology*, MIDWEST POL. SCI. ASS'N (Apr. 12, 2007). The SEC is not an independently funded agency, meaning it must send the fines it collects to the Treasury or, when discernible, to aggrieved investors. The SEC must also submit yearly budget requests to Congress, which are either approved or amended. In these requests, the SEC usually emphasizes two indicators: the number of enforcement actions brought by the agency (both overall and specific offense totals) as well as the total amount of fine money collected. These indicators may not themselves paint an accurate picture of the agency's enforcement activity, nor of the agency's overall performance. *See* Urska Velikonja, *Reporting Agency Performance: Behind the SEC's Enforcement Statistics*, 101 CORNELL L. REV. (forthcoming 2016) (observing that while the SEC ordered more monetary penalties in 2014 than in any previous year, it collected fewer penalties than it did in 2005). If you were designing an indicator that evaluated SEC enforcement activity, what would be included in it? What new information would it provide, or what deficiency would it rectify?

2. ***SEC "Fair Fund" Distributions.*** Despite its varying collection rates, the SEC has become an important source of compensation for defrauded investors since 2002. During that time, the SEC deposited over $14 billion for defrauded investors into 243 distribution funds, usually called fair funds after the statute

that authorizes them. 15 U.S.C. § 7246. The fair fund provision allows the SEC to distribute civil fines and disgorgements collected from defendants. According to various SEC Congressional Budget Justification reports, the SEC used fair funds to distribute more than 75% of all collected monetary penalties between 2003 and 2012. For an in-depth look at the agency's fair fund practices, see Urska Velikonja, *Public Compensation for Private Harm: Evidence from the SEC's Fair Fund Distributions*, 67 STAN. L. REV. 331 (2015).

3. ***FINRA Criticism.*** Several policymakers have criticized FINRA for perceived enforcement deficiencies, namely that the agency does not sanction wrong-doers as heavily as it should. SEC Commissioner Kara Stein, for instance, stated that "I fear the results . . . are too often financial insignificant for the wrongdoers. Your enforcement cases must be impactful, and provide strong motivation for compliance." *See* Jean Eaglesham, *FINRA Weighs Tougher Stance*, WALL ST. J., June 19, 2014. Broker-dealers, however, often complain that FINRA sanctions are too harsh and often overly punitive. *See* FINRA, SANCTION GUIDELINES (2015). Which side do you find more convincing?

B. ENFORCEMENT ACTIVITIES OF FEDERAL BANKING REGULATORS

As we saw earlier in this Chapter, federal banking regulators have a broad range of supervisory and enforcement tools at their disposal. In this section, we will focus on enforcement by the Federal Reserve Board, OCC, and the FDIC. Each of these federal banking regulators can bring public enforcement actions against entities and affiliated individuals within their (sometimes overlapping) jurisdiction. Banking regulators also have the power to bring non-public or informal actions via written agreements and memoranda of understanding.

Much like the SEC and FINRA, federal banking regulators came under intense public scrutiny in the aftermath of the Financial Crisis. In response, these regulators increased their scrutiny of regulatory reports, expanded the scope of their examinations, and aggressively boosted their enforcement activity. While federal banking regulator policies may differ slightly as to whether an enforcement action should be instituted, the general procedures employed by their enforcement personnel bear many similarities. These parallels are partly due to a long-standing policy whereby a federal banking regulator proposing to take a formal enforcement action against a federally regulated financial institution or IAP will notify other federal banking regulators and any appropriate state supervisory authority in writing before taking any action. *See* Revised Policy Statement on Interagency Coordination of Formal Corrective Action by the Federal Bank Regulatory Agencies, 62 Fed. Reg. 7782, 7783 (Feb. 20, 1997).

The reporting and examination regimes sometimes raise supervisory concerns not significant enough to merit formal, public enforcement actions. Banking regulators address these concerns using a variety of informal, confidential enforcement tools. Bank supervisors often communicate relatively minor concerns to an institution's management in a cover letter to their examination report. The letter may also request that the institution's board of directors adopt a resolution stating its intent to address these problems. More structured informal mechanisms of enforcement include commitment letters and memoranda of understanding (MOUs), whereby an institution will agree in writing to take specific steps to correct problems identified by regulators. MOUs tend to be more detailed than commitment letters. Despite the fact that they are treated as confidential supervisory information, banks sometimes choose to seek regulators' permission to disclose the existence of an MOU to the public. While these informal enforcement actions are not legally enforceable, regulators can take formal action if an institution fails to honor its informal commitments.

1. Federal Reserve Board Enforcement Policy and Trends

The Federal Reserve Board pursues formal enforcement actions against institutions for many different types of violations. Areas of focus included violations of the Bank Secrecy Act (BSA), unauthorized distributions of capital under Regulation Y, BHCs' failure to be a "source of strength" due to inadequate levels of capital and insufficient supervision, and various instances of unsafe, unsound, and deceptive practices. In short, the Federal Reserve Board wields its enforcement power as a supervisory tool aimed at correcting significant risk management deficiencies within financial institutions. The Federal Reserve Board has pursued unsafe, unsound, and deceptive practices with particular vigor since the Financial Crisis, exemplifying the continued expansion of its supervision into the day-to-day operations of financial institutional activity.

The Federal Reserve Board's emphasis on using monetary penalties against institutions is also noteworthy. Between 2009 and 2010, the Federal Reserve Board assessed civil penalties totaling approximately $315,000. After 2010, penalty figures jumped. Penalties were approximately $85 million in 2011, $1 billion in 2012, $250 million in 2013 and $817 million in 2014. The number of enforcement actions also increased during this time. The Federal Reserve Board filed 18 enforcement actions that levied a civil monetary penalty in the three-year period between 2008 and 2010. Over the next three years, it filed 37 actions including 19 in 2014.

2. OCC Enforcement Policy and Trends

The OCC's enforcement policy aims to address problems or weaknesses before they develop into more serious issues that adversely affect a bank's financial condition or its responsibilities to customers. The OCC's enforcement actions typically address operating deficiencies, violations of laws and regulations, BSA breaches, and otherwise unsafe or unsound practices. In serious cases like insider abuse and self-dealing, the OCC relies heavily on its ability to impose civil money penalties and prohibit individuals from working in the financial services sector. In less serious cases, the OCC pursues informal enforcement actions.

Like the Federal Reserve Board, the OCC has increased its emphasis on levying comparatively large civil money penalties. Between 2007 and 2009, the OCC assessed approximately $11 million in penalties per year. Since then, the agency has assessed approximately $282 million in penalties per year. The OCC targets institutions almost exclusively. Between 2012 and 2014, 99.9% of civil money penalties collected by the OCC came from institutions, not individuals. Despite the increase in penalties, total enforcement actions, informal and formal, have steadily declined since 2009, decreasing approximately 18% per year through 2014. These data indicate that the OCC, much like the Federal Reserve Board, is pursuing bigger cases and, while civil money penalties per enforcement action averaged approximately $59,721.33 from 2007 to 2011, they averaged over $1.6 million between 2012 and 2014.

3. FDIC Enforcement Policy and Trends

Among federal banking regulators, the combination of the FDIC's responsibilities as insurer, supervisor, and receiver is unique. The FDIC enforcement powers stem from § 8 of the Federal Deposit Insurance Act (FDIA) and are used when corrective action is needed to protect consumers, the banking sector, or a financial institution itself from harm. Like the Federal Reserve Board and the OCC, the FDIC can initiate informal or formal actions when an IDI is found to be in an unsatisfactory condition. Unlike the other two agencies, the FDIC's informal actions represent the final supervisory step before formal enforcement proceedings are initiated.

The FDIC ramped up its enforcement activity in the immediate aftermath of the Financial Crisis. Total enforcement actions more than doubled between 2008 and 2009, and increased another 27% in 2010. Since then, total FDIC enforcement actions have steadily decreased, like those of its regulatory compatriots. The agency filed only 542 actions in 2014, compared with 1,304 four years earlier and far more than the other federal banking regulators.

---

1. ***Formal versus Informal Enforcement Actions.*** From 2005 to 2007, the FDIC, Federal Reserve Board, and OCC issued a total of 740 informal enforcement actions and 391 formal actions, an average of 247 informal actions and 131 formal actions per year. Between 2008 and 2010, those numbers jumped to 2,513 informal actions and 1,871 formal enforcement actions, an average of about 838 informal actions and 624 formal actions per year. Since 2010, both informal and formal actions have steadily declined. What do you think underpins these trends?

2. ***The Distribution of Sanctions.*** The average civil money penalty imposed by the OCC totaled approximately $1.52 million in 2014, compared to only $43,142 in 2007. The Federal Reserve Board saw an even more drastic increase, with average civil money penalty averaging $43 million in 2014 and only $1.8 million in 2007. These high averages are the result of several historically large fines, including a $508 million action taken by the Federal Reserve Board against BNP Paribas S.A. and a $350 million action taken by the OCC against JPMorgan Chase. The FDIC's average civil money penalty was much lower, totaling only $177,783 in 2014. Yet, the FDIC pursued twice as many enforcement actions as the OCC and almost 3.5 times as many as the Federal Reserve Board. Think back to White's discussion of the SEC's enforcement policy. In your opinion, which strategy is more effective, the FDIC's or the OCC and Federal Reserve Board's?

3. ***Corporate Monitors as a Condition of Settlement.*** Authorities increasingly insist on outside monitors as a condition for not pursuing charges

against companies. A monitor is an independent third-party. Although paid by the institution, the monitor does not work for it or for the enforcing authorities. Instead, the monitor's job is to ensure the corporation has a solid compliance program in place and that any wrongful or criminal activity ceases. Corporations to which monitors have been appointed include Credit Suisse Group AG, Standard Chartered PLC, and HSBC Holdings PLC. Using regulator-appointed monitors is controversial. Advocates contend that monitors are a good substitute for regulators who do not have sufficient resources to probe complex problems inside a bank for long periods. Others argue that the monitors are not actually independent and become advocates for the institution. For an in-depth discussion, see BRANDON L. GARRETT, TOO BIG TO JAIL 172 (2014). Recall also our discussion of gatekeeper liability for independent consultants in Chapter 8.1.

4. ***DOJ as a Banking Regulator?*** Since 2013, the DOJ has been eager to prove that no financial institution is "too big to prosecute." The DOJ has entered into several settlements with banking entities involved in the sale of residential mortgage-backed securities. On July 14, 2014, the DOJ entered into a $7 billion settlement with Citigroup to resolve claims that it improperly packaged, securitized, and sold residential mortgage-backed security before January 1, 2009. On August 21, 2014, the DOJ announced that it, along with other federal and state authorities, had entered into a $16.65 billion settlement agreement with Bank of America to resolve similar allegations. Given the presence of other federal regulators, do you feel the DOJ's entry into the fold is necessary, especially when banks are already paying penalties to several other regulators for the same issue? Will the DOJ cause banks to invest in better training and infrastructure, or otherwise behave better? The DOJ has been at the fore of criminal penalties as well. BNP Paribas S.A. pleaded guilty in May 2014 to conspiring to violate the International Emergency Economic Powers Act and the Trading with the Enemy Act by processing financial transactions on behalf of entities subject to U.S. economic sanctions. Credit Suisse AG pleaded guilty in May 2014 to conspiring to aid tax evasion. Citicorp, JPMorgan Chase & Co., Barclays PLC, The Royal Bank of Scotland plc, and UBS AG all pleaded guilty in May 2015 to criminal antitrust violations related to the manipulation of FX markets.

C. ENFORCEMENT ACTIVITIES OF STATE REGULATORS

As discussed in Chapter 1.2, under the dual system of bank regulation, States as well as the federal government may charter, license, register, and/or supervise a dynamic variety of financial institutions, including banks, insurance companies, credit unions, mortgage brokers, and other non-bank financial services providers. Unlike their federal counterparts, state regulators' focus is typically local. Their approach to regulation is shaped by their close geographical proximity and firsthand knowledge of their regulated entities and markets. This specific focus, however, still translates to significant responsibility: state regulators charter and supervise approximately 77% of the nation's insured depository institutions.

In the aftermath of the Financial Crisis, state regulators increasingly pursued significant enforcement actions and penalties against the institutions under their supervision. One of the most active state regulators in this regard was New York's Department of Financial Services (NYDFS). Established in 2011 for the purpose of increasing New York's supervision over emerging financial products and services, NYDFS supervises nearly 3,300 financial institutions operating in New York and elsewhere whose total assets exceed $6.6 trillion.

Despite the relatively short time it has been operational, NYDFS has levied nearly $6 billion in in monetary penalties since its inception, targeting offenses such as tax evasion, subprime lending abuses, and market manipulation. Its greatest area of focus, however, has been AML and sanctions violations. NYDFS has levied ten fines in excess of $100 million, six of which involved deficiencies in AML and sanctions compliance procedures. Included in these is the department's largest penalty of more than $2.2 billion against BNP Paribas in 2014.

NYDFS has also placed significant emphasis on making sure its enforcement actions address individual accountability, a notable contrast to other federal regulators. Although not empowered to bring criminal prosecutions, the department banned multiple senior executives from participating in the operations of NYDFS-regulated institutions for engaging in misconduct. NYDFS has also proposed a new set of regulations that would require banks' chief compliance officers to certify that their institutions maintain robust AML programs, with potential personal criminal consequences to officers for providing false or misleading certifications. NY Dep't of Fin. Services, Superintendent's Regs., Banking Div. Transaction Monitoring And Filtering Program Requirements And Certifications, §§ 504.1–504.6 (Dec. 1, 2015).

---

1. ***State versus Federal Enforcement.*** In what way does aggressive state regulatory enforcement add value to an overall enforcement scheme? Perhaps state regulators serve as a stopgap when federal regulators fail to act, but note how the OCC, Federal Reserve Board, DOJ, and NYDFS all levied monetary penalties against BNP Paribas for alleged violations related to its AML program. Professor Mark Totten argues that state regulators and Attorneys General offer several advantages as compared to federal regulators. State enforcement, he argues, often has distinct informational advantages due to its proximity to regulated entities, facilitating more responsive and swift enforcement to emerging harmful practices. State regulators are also more resistant to capture since it is extremely difficult, on a collective level, to capture regulators in every state across the country. Finally, state regulators are more flexible and can more easily test out and refine new enforcement strategies. Mark Totten, *The Enforcers & the Great Recession*, 36 CARDOZO L. REV. 1611, 1653–61 (2015). Others suggest that state financial regulators may be focused as much on filling state's revenue shortfalls as on supervisory goals, and that aggressive state enforcement risks undermining federal enforcement efforts. *See, e.g.*, Ben McLannahan, *New York's 'Snarling Watchdog' Seeks New Master*, FIN. TIMES (Oct. 30, 2015). Which arguments do you find most persuasive?

D. THE OUTER LIMITS OF BANK REGULATORY ENFORCEMENT

A central rationale for the examination and enforcement regimes described above is bank regulators' imperative to maintain a safe and sound banking system. There is no statutory definition of what constitutes unsafe or unsound conduct, yet such practices serve as the basis for many formal enforcement actions. The following is an excerpt from a memorandum to Congress in connection with the adoption of the Financial Institutions Supervisory Act of 1966 by now-defunct Federal Home Loan Bank Board.

> The concept of "unsafe or unsound practices" is one of general application which touches upon the entire field of the operations of a financial institution. For this reason, it would be virtually impossible to attempt to catalog within a single all-inclusive or rigid definition the broad spectrum of activities which are embraced by the term. The formulation of such a definition would probably operate to exclude those practices not set out in the definition, even though they might be highly injurious to an institution under a given set of facts or circumstances. . . .
>
> Like many other generic terms widely used in the law, such as "fraud," "negligence," "probable cause," or "good faith," the term "unsafe or unsound practices" has a central meaning which can and must be applied to constantly changing factual circumstances. Generally speaking, an "unsafe or unsound practice" embraces any action, or lack of action, which is contrary to generally accepted standards of operation, the possible consequences of which, if continued, would be abnormal risk or loss or damage to an institution, its shareholders, or the agencies administering the insurance funds.

112 CONG. REC. 26,474 (1966) (John Horne, Chair of the Federal Home Loan Bank Board).

Banking agencies have the statutory authority to impose a variety of formal enforcement actions upon a finding of unsafe or unsound practices or other unlawful behavior. The FDIC may terminate an IDI's insured status if (1) the institution, or its directors or trustees, has engaged or is engaging in unsafe or unsound practices, (2) the institution is in an unsafe or unsound condition to continue operations as an IDI, or (3) the institution, or its directors or trustees, has violated any applicable law, regulation, order, condition imposed by the FDIC in connection with the approval of an application or request, or written agreement between the institution and the FDIC. 12 U.S.C. § 1818(a)(2).

1. Liability for Institution-Affiliated Parties

A banking agency may impose a cease-and-desist order if an institution or institution-affiliated party (IAP), defined at *id.* § 1813(u), under its jurisdiction engaged in unsafe or unsound practices or violations of law, or if the agency has reasonable cause to believe that the institution or IAP is about to do so. *Id.* § 1818(b). Such permanent cease-and-desist orders must follow an administrative hearing. In emergency situations, which occur if the agency determines that the unsafe or unsound practice or violation of law is "likely to cause insolvency or significant dissipation of assets or earnings" or is "likely to weaken the condition of the [IDI] or otherwise prejudice the interests of its depositors", an agency may impose a temporary cease-and-desist order. *Id.* § 1818(c).

Another strong deterrent to unsafe and unsound banking practices is banking agencies' authority to remove an individual IAPs from office and/or to prohibit them from further participation in the affairs of any IDI. Such removal or prohibition authority may be exercised upon a determination that (1) the party engaged or participated in any unsafe or unsound practice, or engaged in certain other types of misconduct; (2) such practice had, or probably will have, certain detrimental effects or financial benefit to the IAP; and (3) the practice involved personal dishonesty or willful or continuing disregard for the institution's safety or soundness. *Id.* § 1818(e)(1).

In addition to the enforcement mechanisms described above, the banking agencies have the authority to impose civil monetary penalties upon IDIs and their IAPs. *Id.* § 1818(i). Such civil monetary penalties can fall into three tiers based on the gravity of the punishable conduct, as illustrated in Figure 8.2-1.

Figure 8.2-1 Civil Monetary Penalties

	Tier 1	**Tier 2**	**Tier 3**
Daily penalty may not exceed	$5,000	$25,000	$1,000,000
Applicable to an IDI or institution-affiliated party who	Violates any: • Law; • Regulation; • Order; or • Condition imposed by a federal banking agency.	• Commits a Tier 1 violation; • Recklessly engages in unsafe or unsound practices in conducting the affairs of the IDI; or • Breaches any fiduciary duty, *and, the violation:* • Is part of a pattern of misconduct; • Causes or is likely to cause more than minimal loss to such IDI; or • Results in pecuniary gain or benefit to the party.	• Commits a Tier 1 violation; • Engages in unsafe or unsound practices in conducting the affairs of the IDI; or • Breaches any fiduciary duty, *and, the party knowingly or recklessly causes* • A substantial loss to such IDI, or • A substantial pecuniary gain or other benefit to such party by reason of such violation, practice or breach.

Source: 12 U.S.C. § 1818(i).

In the next case, consider the limits of federal banking regulators to impose liability on IAPs for participating or engaging in an unsafe or unsound practice.

Grant Thornton, LLP v. OCC

514 F.3d 1328 (D.C. Cir. 2008)

WILLIAMS, J.:

Grant Thornton, LLP, an accounting firm, appeals a final decision and order of the Comptroller of the Currency that requires the firm to pay $300,000 in civil penalties for recklessly failing to meet Generally Accepted Auditing Standards (GAAS) in its audit of the First National Bank of Keystone. Grant Thornton also appeals the Comptroller's cease and desist order mandating that the firm comply with a host of conditions whenever it audits depository institutions. We vacate the final decision and both orders, finding that when an accounting firm merely performs an external audit aimed solely at verifying the accuracy of a bank's books, it is not "participat[ing]" or "engaging" in "an unsafe or unsound practice in conducting the business" or "the affairs" of the bank, as those terms are used in 12 U.S.C. §§ 1813(u)(4)(C), 1818(b)(1), and 1818(i)(2)(B)(i)(II).

In 1992 the First National Bank of Keystone, then a small rural bank in West Virginia, sought to increase its revenues, launching an ambitious loan securitization program. . . . By 1999 the bank's assets of approximately $100 million had apparently skyrocketed to about $1 billion.

[In a 1997 report, OCC examiners criticized the accuracy of Keystone's financial statements and its management of the loan securitization program and assigned it low CAMELS scores. Keystone failed to address these concerns so OCC initiated an enforcement action against the bank in May 1998. Keystone agreed to retain a nationally recognized independent accounting firm to conduct an audit, and so it hired Grant Thornton. Grant Thornton's April 1999 audit opinion in effect stated that it found assurance that Keystone's financial statements for 1997 and 1998 had been free of material misstatements.]

In August 1999 OCC examiners uncovered Keystone's fraud. The bank had inflated its interest income by nearly $98 million and its assets by about $450 million. . . . The scheme masked the fact that Keystone had been insolvent since 1996. Several members of Keystone management were convicted of felonies [in connection with the fraud. The OCC] closed the bank. . . .

On December 7, 2006 . . . the Comptroller found that Grant Thornton participated in an unsafe or unsound practice by recklessly failing to comply with GAAS in planning and conducting the Keystone audit. In a cease and desist order, the Comptroller limited Grant Thornton's freedom to accept and conduct audits independently, hire accountants, and handle working papers.

Grant Thornton attacks the Comptroller's decision and orders on multiple grounds. We need address only one. We find that the Comptroller exceeded his statutory authority in characterizing Grant Thornton's external auditing activity as "participat[ing] in . . . [an] unsafe or unsound [banking] practice," *see* § 1813(u)(4), and as "engaging . . . in an unsafe or unsound practice in conducting [Keystone's] business," see § 1818(b)(1), and in "conducting [Keystone's] affairs," see § 1818(i)(2)(B)(i)(II). Those conclusions end the case. . . .

Under 12 U.S.C. § 1818(b)(1), the Comptroller of the Currency may issue a cease-and-desist order if a bank or [IAP, which may include independent contractors such as accounting firms,] "is engaging or has engaged . . . in an unsafe or unsound practice in conducting the business of [an IDI]"; and under § 1818(i)(2)(B)(i)(II) the Comptroller may impose civil monetary penalties when a[n IDI] or IAP "recklessly engages in an unsafe or unsound practice in conducting the affairs of [an IDI]" which causes a more than minimal loss to the bank or meets other aggravating circumstances. . . .

[T]he Comptroller's orders rest on the idea that recklessly conducting a non-GAAS audit of a bank constitutes participation in an unsafe or unsound practice in conducting the business or affairs of the bank. But however incompetently or recklessly the audit may have been performed, conduct of the audit cannot be shoehorned into the controlling statutory language.

First, Grant Thornton didn't participate in an "unsafe or unsound [banking] practice" because an audit of the sort conducted here is not a banking practice. Grant Thornton was fulfilling the classic reporting function of external auditors—examining the company's books from the outside and verifying the accuracy of its records and the adequacy of its internal controls. This sort of outside look into a bank's activity is not a "practice" of a depository institution or bank. . . .

Second, we have some assistance from the Supreme Court on the meaning of a phrase closely parallel to those in question here. In *Reves v. Ernst & Young*, 507 U.S. 170, 113 S. Ct. 1163, 122 L. Ed. 2d 525 (1993), the Court construed the following language from [the Racketeer Influenced and Corrupt Organizations Act]: "to conduct or participate, directly or indirectly, in the conduct of [an enterprise's] affairs." *Id.* at 177–79, 113 S. Ct. 1163 (discussing 18 U.S.C. § 1962(c)). Reasoning that Congress meant something broader than "conduct [the enterprise's] affairs," but narrower than merely "participate in [its] affairs," the Court concluded that a covered party "must have some part in directing [the enterprise's] affairs." *Id.* at 179, 113 S. Ct. 1163. Grant Thornton played no such directive role in Keystone's affairs.

[W]hile Grant Thornton's audit may have been "strikingly incompetent," as described at length by the concurring opinion, it neither proffered advice on nor assumed any directive role in Keystone's conduct of its affairs. The Comptroller nowhere suggests that Grant Thornton was in cahoots with Keystone's fraudulent managers. . .

Finally, we note that Congress has given the Comptroller wide latitude to punish accountants who transgress GAAS in their audits of depository institutions:

In addition to any authority contained in [12 U.S.C. § 1818], the [FDIC] or an appropriate Federal banking agency may remove, suspend, or bar an independent public accountant, upon showing of good cause, from performing audit services required by this section.

12 U.S.C. § 1831m(g)(4)(A). . . . [G]iving the words of [Financial Institutions Reform, Recovery, and Enforcement Act (FIRREA)] their ordinary meaning leaves the banking authorities ample power to sanction delinquent auditors. Here, of course, we need not address the application of § 1831m(g)(4)(A) to Grant Thornton, as the Comptroller has not tried to rest its case on that section.

We vacate the Comptroller's final decision and orders for the reasons stated.

[Concurring opinion of HENDERSON, J. omitted.]

---

1. ***Outer Limits of IAPs.*** What are the reasons for and against Grant Thornton being considered an IAP? How does the rationale underpinning this case compare with that underpinning NYDFS enforcements we discussed in Chapter 8.1?

---

2. Using the Financial Institutions Reform, Recovery, and Enforcement Act of 1989 to Pursue Civil Liability

Congress enacted FIRREA in response to the failure of hundreds of thrifts during the Savings & Loan Crisis. While a number of factors contributed to the failures, commentators suggest that insider abuse and fraud served as a major catalyst, with serious insider misconduct contributing to the insolvencies of at least 75% of all failed institutions on an aggregate level. Filmon M. Sexton IV, *The Financial Institutions Reform, Recovery, and Enforcement Act of 1989: The Effect of the "Self-Affecting" Theory on Financial Institutions*, 19 N.C. BANKING INST. 263, 266 (2015). In response, Congress enacted FIRREA to strengthen criminal and civil penalties for "defrauding or otherwise damaging financial institutions and depositors." FIRREA also sought to help depositors regain confidence in the financial system by deterring fraudulent behavior by individuals and managers. *Id.*

FIRREA authorizes the DOJ to seek civil money penalties for a violation or a conspiracy to violate certain criminal statutes "affecting a federally insured deposit institution." 12 U.S.C. § 1833a. The predicate criminal offenses relate to making false claims or fraudulent statements to the U.S. government, concealing facts from the U.S. Government, fraud on federal receivers and conservators, and mail and wire fraud. 18 U.S.C. §§ 287, 1001, 1032, 1341, 1343. Since the Financial Crisis, the DOJ has employed one particular section of FIRREA in a unique and unexpected way to investigate and prosecute persons suspected of financial fraud. The following case involves the DOJ's prosecution of a financial institution for losses incurred from its own conduct.

United States v. Countrywide Financial Corp.

996 F. Supp. 2d 247 (S.D.N.Y. 2014)

JED S. RAKOFF, District Judge.

[The Court denied a motion for summary judgment by the Bank Defendants[1] and Rebecca Mairone. At trial, the jury found the defendants guilty of fraud. The defendants intentionally induced Fannie Mae and Freddie Mac to purchase thousands of loans that they otherwise would not have purchased by misrepresenting that the loans they were selling were "investment quality" when in fact the defendants knew that their underwriting process was calculated to produce loans that were not of investment quality. In the penalty decision, Judge Rakoff directed Bank of America, N.A., on behalf of the Bank Defendants, to pay the Government $1,267,491,770. Ms. Mairone was ordered to pay the Government $1 million. U.S. *ex rel.* O'Donnell v. Countrywide Home Loans, Inc., 33 F. Supp. 3d 494 (S.D.N.Y. 2014). Separately, Bank of America Corporation settled with the DOJ for $16.65 billion. Settlement Agreement, DOJ et al. and Bank of America Corporation, Bank of America, N.A. and Banc of America Mortgage Securities (Aug. 20, 2014).]

FIRREA imposes civil penalties for substantive violations of, or conspiracies to violate, a number of criminal offenses, including mail and wire fraud, "affecting a federally insured financial institution." *See* 12 U.S.C. § 1833a(c)(2) & (e). As the Court ruled in denying the motions to dismiss, "the key term, 'affect,' is a simple English word, defined in Webster's as 'to have an effect on.' " *Countrywide,* 961 F.Supp.2d at 605, 2013 WL 4437232, at *5. As the Court further noted, the fraud here in question, perpetrated by the Countrywide defendants and Ms. Mairone, had a huge effect on Bank of America defendants, which, as a result of Bank of America's purchase of Countrywide, paid, directly or through affiliates, billions of dollars to settle repurchase claims brought by Fannie Mae and Freddie Mac. *Id.*

At both the summary judgment stage and at trial, defendants argued that this prior conclusion by the Court glossed over the fact that the actual purchase, on July 1, 2008, was

---

[1] Following the convention of the parties, throughout this Opinion the Court refers to defendants Countrywide Financial Corporation, Countrywide Home Loans, Inc., Countrywide Bank, FSB, Bank of America Corporation, and Bank of America, NA, collectively as the "Bank Defendants."

of Countrywide Financial Corporation ("CFC") by Bank of America Corporation ("BAC"), neither of which is a federally insured entity. But it was undisputed at all times that these two entities are, in essence, the parent companies of the federally insured bank defendants, Bank of America, N.A. ("BANA"), Countrywide Home Loans, Inc. ("CHL"), and Countrywide Bank, FSB. Moreover, as part of the accompanying merger of Countrywide Bank into BANA, BANA and its parent company, BAC, signed an indemnification agreement, which caused BAC to indemnify BANA for losses arising from Countrywide's High Speed Swim Lane program. Although defendants argue that, as a result, BANA itself never realized losses, in fact what their argument shows, beyond dispute, is that BANA was hugely affected by Countrywide's fraud in the sense of having huge liabilities resulting therefrom, and that it escaped having to pay for such liabilities only by having its parent bail it out. Indeed, the contractual predicate for indemnity under the agreement between BANA and BAC is that BANA incur "a loss or losses on any asset or assets" transferred to it during the transaction. *See* June 30, 2008, Asset Contribution Indemnification Agreement, at 83.

It is highly improbable that Congress would have intended to place beyond the reach of FIRREA those defendants whose misconduct "affects" federally insured banks that have the great fortune to be fully insured for such losses. Even less so can it be imagined that the device of having BAC indemnify BANA for losses that otherwise would result from Countrywide's fraud immunizes Countrywide from liability under FIRREA. Indeed, defendants' labeling of this theory of liability as the "self-affecting" theory is something of a misnomer; Countrywide's fraud, which culminated before the merger with BANA, directly affected, not just Countrywide, but its merger partner, BANA, as well. While the effect on Countrywide might be "self-affecting," the effect on BANA was not.

Independently of all this, moreover, even if one were to focus only on the effects of Countrywide's fraud on the two Countrywide federally insured defendants (and treat the other defendants as liable only vicariously or as successors in interest), even such "self-inflicting" effects were not only sufficient to satisfy the statutory requirement that a federally insured entity be affected, but also were here sufficient to warrant being found by the Court as a matter of law. This is because the underlying predicates in this case, as found by the jury, were mail fraud and wire fraud. Any federally insured entity that commits these offenses automatically exposes itself to potential civil and criminal liabilities as a matter of law. *See, e.g.*, 18 U.S.C. §§ 1341, 1343, 1344, 1962. Such potential liability is enough to satisfy FIRREA, since even the threat of criminal liability (let alone, as here, the actuality of civil liabilities) is bound to affect any federally insured entity in material fashion.[2] . . .

In short, on each of several alternative grounds, the Court confirms its finding that the "affect" requirement was established in this case as a matter of law.[3]

---

1. ***Using FIRREA.*** What are the advantages for the DOJ in using FIRREA to prosecute financial institutions for losses arising from their own conduct? How does this use fit with FIRREA's original purpose? Critics have argued that the self-affecting theory is inconsistent with FIRREA's legislative purpose. *See* Sexton, *The Effect of the "Self-Affecting" Theory on Financial Institutions*, at 263.

---

[2] This does not render the "affect" language of FIRREA surplusage, since there will be many cases in which the defendant is not itself a federally insured entity.

[3] The Court therefore need not reach the interesting question of whether, in a case in which the facts of "affect" are genuinely disputed, the issue is for the Court (because it is a quasi-jurisdictional issue and because FIRREA sounds at least as much in equity as in law) or for the jury (the presumptive default position).

E. FOREIGN ENFORCEMENT LEVELS CONTRASTED

The number and size of penalties imposed by capital markets regulators in the United States are dramatically higher than in the rest of the world. For example, Australia and the UK are comparable in that they have relatively large and developed capital markets. From 2003 to 2008, however, the UK's primary securities regulator, the Financial Services Authority, imposed an average of £13.4 million in fines per year, which translates to approximately $19 million. The Australian Securities and Investments Commission averaged approximately 144.6 million Australian dollars during the same period, approximately $100 million. SEC civil penalties were noticeably higher during this span, totaling $507 million in 2007 alone. The SEC also averaged far more enforcement actions per year between 2010 and 2014 (716) than either the UK's Financial Services Authority and its successor, the Financial Conduct Authority (FCA), (126) or the Australian Securities and Investments Commission (166).

Numerous factors may help explain these differences. For example, other countries may have different or more modest regulatory goals. Differences in the composition of the financial services sector across jurisdictions and the lawfulness of market participants in those jurisdictions may also explain some of the differences in formal regulatory intensity. We should also note the relationship between public enforcement efforts and private sanctions. As Professor John Coffee notes, private litigation in the United States often follows on the heels of public sanctions, meaning the significance of public enforcement efforts in the United States, as compared with that of the UK or Australia, may be even greater than the raw numbers suggest. *See* John C. Coffee, Jr., *Law and the Market: The Impact of Enforcement*, 156 U. PA. L. REV. 229 (2007). It is also possible that, in some foreign jurisdictions, private monitors do a better job of amplifying public sanctions than do U.S. markets. In London, for example, shareholders are said to have more power in the boardroom and so British investors may respond to FCA sanctions more effectively than their U.S. counterparts respond to SEC sanctions. While the FCA has increased sanctions, most other jurisdictions, especially civil-law jurisdictions, seem to invest fewer resources in regulation and to impose far less in financial penalties. Consider the following theories from Coffee about why the difference in enforcement trends exists.

John C. Coffee, Jr., Law and the Market: The Impact of Enforcement

156 U. PA. L. REV. 229, 292–99 (2007)

First . . . it can be argued that the United States expends more on enforcement than the [UK] because U.S. corporate law gives shareholders fewer control rights than does that of the [UK]—in effect, enforcement might be a substitute for weaker corporate governance.

Second, a political theory can be advanced to the effect that various corporate constituencies-labor in particular-have agreed to acquiesce to the receipt of private control benefits by controlling shareholders in return for the controlling shareholders' tacit agreement to subordinate shareholder wealth maximization to the interests of other constituencies.

. . . Third, the political demand for enforcement may follow from the creation of a deep, retail-oriented securities market. [E]conomics determines politics. Under this view, once a nation achieves dispersed ownership, those individual owners become a potent political force. Following scandals, they demand reforms and retribution. In the United States, the 1929 market crash led directly to the adoption of the federal securities laws in 1933 and 1934, and the 2000-2002 bubble and associated scandals produced [The] Sarbanes-Oxley [Act]. Although the stock market decline in 2000 was just as abrupt in Europe, the economic loss in Europe fell more on institutional investors than individual shareholders (because European markets are dominated by institutions). Hence, the 2000 market decline produced less of a political demand for protection and retribution in Europe.

. . . Potentially, the foregoing theories are complementary. Each could explain to some degree the observed pattern of different levels of enforcement intensity between common law and civil law jurisdictions. That the United States is an outlier is also explained by multiple factors, including (1) the enormous size of its equity markets; (2) the broad retail participation in those markets; (3) the federal structure of the U.S. government, which results in multiple enforcers (and invites competition among them); and (4) the U.S. public's apparent preference for retributive punishment in securities cases.

---

1. ***Why Do U.S. Enforcement Trends Differ from Foreign Trends?*** Which, if any, of Coffee's explanations do you find convincing? Do the substantial differences in regulatory intensity that separate the United States from most other industrialized nations suggest substantial misallocation of regulatory resources and enforcement efforts in some major financial markets?

IV. RECURRING ISSUES IN ENFORCEMENT POLICIES

A. PUBLIC VERSUS PRIVATE ENFORCEMENT

Economists and scholars have long debated whether public regulators are necessary to enforce securities laws, or whether investors can better ensure compliance through private rights of action. As we allude to in Chapter 4.1, private remedies are a longstanding component of the overall design of securities laws. Congressional awareness of the importance of private rights is most evident in the 1933 Act. Section 11 provides a private right of action designed to assure that filed registration statements are accurate, and § 12(a)(1) exposes issuers to liability even where the issuer acted innocently in selling registered securities. Courts have also implied private rights of action under other provisions. *See, e.g.*, Herman & MacLean v. Huddleston, 459 U.S. 375 (1983) (presence of implied cause of action under § 10(b) and Rule 10b-5 "is simply beyond peradventure").

Critics of public enforcement argue that public actors have mixed and often weak incentives to do their jobs effectively. A common claim is that public regulatory bodies, or their officials, may be subject to capture by well-capitalized or politically influential interest groups. *See* Donald C. Langevoort, *The SEC as a Lawmaker: Choices About Investor Protection in the Face of Uncertainty*, 84 WASH. U. L. REV. 1591, 1598 (2006). Public enforcement agencies also suffer from poor information of both general market and specific firm conditions. Critics argue that the best sources of information about private wrongs are the parties themselves. Private enforcement may also provide protections against harm based on the initiative of a few, which counters the problem of agency resources. Private litigation also gives individuals a personal role in regulatory administration and provides an avenue of redress potentially more insulated from capture than public regulatory agencies.

Public enforcement, however, could be run by public-regarding policymakers who invoke sharp criminal and financial penalties that deter egregious wrongdoing. Once wrongdoing is detected, a well-resourced system of public regulation facilitates regulatory investigations, enabling an agency to quickly identify problem areas, bring enforcement actions, and enact reform measures. Bigger budgets and more staff allow a regulatory agency to write, revise, and enforce better and more sophisticated regulatory rules. Public enforcement also complements private enforcement by acting as a signaling device, as enforcement actions also damage a firm's organizational and reputational capital.

Still, a private enforcement system may also be subject to collective action and free rider effects among isolated investors, to slow and inept judiciaries, to lawyers' rent seeking, and to the potential inability of private enforcement to successfully attain severe monetary penalties against wrongdoers. Where wrongdoers are not punished, securities litigation may transfer losses from one innocent group of shareholders to another. It is also unlikely that private enforcement could perform certain regulatory tasks in a cost-efficient manner. Detecting insider trading and market manipulation requires centralized oversight of trading markets, a difficult prospect even for shareholders of a company acting collectively. Private parties are also limited in the sanctions they can impose; private parties cannot revoke licenses or impose criminal penalties. Because no enforcement agent, public or private, will be able to detect every violation, these public enforcement measures act as necessary deterrents.

Several studies examine the public versus private enforcement issue by comparing enforcement across jurisdictions. These studies report that countries whose securities laws provide well-specified, privately enforceable liability standards have larger and more liquid capital markets. The studies also found that public enforcement's role in fostering capital market growth is modest at best. *See* Rafael La Porta et al., *What Works in Securities Laws?*, 61 J. FIN. 1, 14–23 (2006). Other research in banking supervision reached similar conclusions. *See* James R. Barth et al., *Bank Regulation and Supervision: What Works Best?*, 13 J. FIN. INTERMEDIATION 205, 245 (2004). These findings have been criticized for emphasizing the law on the books as opposed to how those laws were applied. Professors Jackson and Roe, using a resource-based measure of enforcement rather than formal legal indices, concluded that public enforcement was consistently associated with several measures of robust capital markets, most notably market capitalization, the number of publicly traded firms, initial public offerings, and overall trading levels. For these measures, the authors claimed that public enforcement performed at least as well as the measures of private enforcement identified as important to capital market development in earlier research. *See* Howell E. Jackson & Mark J. Roe, *Public and Private Enforcement of Securities Laws: Resource-Based Evidence*, 93 J. FIN. ECON. 207 (2009).

Might the better question ask what facets of public enforcement lead to superior capital market outcomes, however defined? For instance, recent evidence suggests that increases in the SEC's budget led to higher levels of regulatory compliance among financial market participants. Similarly, research also demonstrates that market participants quickly alter their activities in response to SEC enforcement actions targeting those activities. More generally, there is also empirical support suggesting that general indicators of public enforcement play a significant role in improving certain features of capital markets, such as the cost of capital and liquidity, but that these benefits do extend to areas such as insider trading and how quickly regulatory measures are adopted by market actors. For a comprehensive discussion of recent empirical research in this area, please see Howell E. Jackson and Jeffery Y. Zhang, *Private and Public Enforcement of Securities Regulation*, *in* OXFORD HANDBOOK OF CORPORATE LAW AND GOVERNANCE (Jeffrey N. Gordon & Wolf Georg-Ringe eds., 2015).

---

1. ***Other Options.*** An intermediate approach to the public versus private debate involves placing the SEC into an oversight role for private suits so that the agency's approval would be a precondition to the suit proceedings. Amanda M. Rose, *Reforming Securities Litigation Reform: Restructuring the Relationship Between Public and Private Enforcement of Rule 10b-5*, 108 COLUM. L. REV. 1301 (2008). Another proposal suggests that there are benefits to combining SEC enforcement with increased enforcement by politically and socially inspired state attorney generals and entrepreneurial class action lawyers. James J. Park, *Rules, Principles, and the Competition to Enforce the Securities Laws*, 100 CALIF. L. REV. 115 (2012). Do either of these options sound reasonable?

B. CONFIDENTIAL SUPERVISORY INFORMATION VERSUS DISCLOSURE

Bank regulators are especially concerned with the stability of the institutions they supervise. Maintaining public confidence in banks is essential to avoid the risk of depositor runs. As a result of this focus, much bank supervision is conducted confidentially so that the public does not have access to information that might undermine public confidence in banks. Conversely, as a capital markets regulator, the SEC is broadly oriented towards disclosure of information to the interested public.

The tension between confidentiality and disclosure is evident when financial institutions issue securities. Securities laws require issuers to disclose all material regulatory risks, but financial institutions cannot disclose confidential supervisory information without specific permission from the relevant regulator. While the existence of informal enforcement actions or exam results may well constitute material regulatory risks, disclosure without consent can lead to civil and criminal penalties. *See, e.g.*, FDIC, FIL-14-2012, Guidelines Regarding the Copying and Removal of Confidential Financial Institution Information (Mar. 19, 2012); *see also* Annette Nazareth & Margaret Tahyar, *Transparency and Confidentiality in the Post Financial Crisis World – Where to Strike the Balance?*, 1 HARV. BUS. L. REV. 146 (2011). As a result, banks' regulatory risk disclosures tend to very broadly discuss relevant rules and their potential consequences.

---

1. ***Issuing Securities from a BHC subject to an MOU.*** You represent a BHC that has entered into an MOU with the Federal Reserve Board on a private and confidential basis. The existence of the MOU is treated as confidential supervisory information. 12 C.F.R. § 261.2(c)(1)(iii). The BHC is contemplating raising equity capital in the markets and the general counsel asks you to evaluate whether the MOU must be disclosed. Would your answer differ under the following two scenarios? Under the first scenario, the MOU deals with the need to enhance compliance around consumer laws and AML. The BHC has determined that the cost to comply is not material. Under the second scenario, the MOU requires the BHC to raise more equity capital and limits its distribution of dividends to shareholders until such time as the regulators are satisfied that capital is strong. Consider the effect of securities laws that might require disclosure as opposed to the banking regulations that prohibit the disclosure. Is there a way out? *See id.* § 261.22(a).

2. ***Disclosure in a Proposed BHC Merger.*** Two BHCs want to merge. The acquiring BHC has a strong composite CAMELS rating of two. The target BHC has a weak composite CAMELS rating of four, driven largely by a low rating in the management category. During merger negotiations, may the two BHCs share their examination reports with one another? *See id.* § 261.20(b). What if capital raising by the acquiring BHC is involved? May the outside auditors and the issuer's counsel review the examination report? What about the underwriter's counsel? *See id.* § 261.20(b). Does the answer change if the parties have signed a non-disclosure agreement?

C. LARGE FIRMS VERSUS SMALL FIRMS

Many claim that effective deterrence requires financial regulators to enforce violations of all kinds across all firms consistently, regardless of size. As we mentioned earlier in this Chapter, Chair White of the SEC is one such proponent. According to her, "[e]ven the smallest infractions have victims, and the smallest infractions are very often just the first step toward bigger ones," which "can foster a culture where laws are increasingly treated as toothless guidelines." Mary Jo White, Chair, SEC, Remarks at the Securities Enforcement Forum (Oct. 9, 2013).

In practice, regulators are constrained by limited resources meaning enforcement actions must be targeted to deter other wrongdoers. Targeted enforcement can stimulate self-policing by alerting the private sector to wrongdoing. The effectiveness of deterrence may be affected by an institution's size. Larger firms usually have more reputational concerns than smaller firms, and enforcement actions of large firms are typically more public, making collateral consequences more acute for a larger firm. Reputational consequences can include lower stock prices, secondary liability, legislative action, and firm closure. In contrast, the consequences of an enforcement action against a smaller firm are typically felt only by its owners.

Empirical evidence, however, suggests that the SEC may give preferential treatment to larger firms. One study found that when large firms and their staff were engaged in misconduct, the SEC often brought actions based exclusively on corporate liability without naming any specific individuals as defendants. The study also found that for the same violation and comparable levels of harm to investors, large firms and their employees were more likely to face administrative, rather than judicial, proceedings, meaning the likelihood of a ban from the broker-dealer sector was lower. Finally, among cases that the SEC assigned to administrative proceedings, large-firm defendants were less likely than small-firm defendants to receive a sector ban, even when controlling for violation type and harm to investors. The study also found that the gap between large and small firms persisted when the analysis was limited to the individual employees of such firms. Stavros Gadinis, *The SEC and the Financial Industry: Evidence from Enforcement Against Broker-Dealers*, 67 BUS. LAW. 679, 728 (2012). Do you think the difference in enforcement is based on the potential collateral consequences for stakeholders of large firms or some other reason?

---

1. ***Middle Ground?*** As described earlier in this Chapter, SEC enforcement sweeps charge multiple companies for certain non-fraud violations. The practice gives the agency an opportunity to send a message about aggressive enforcement of the securities laws while allowing the Division of Enforcement to announce record-breaking case filings without the same resource expenditures as required with individual investigations. Sweeps put defendants in a difficult position: by focusing on strict-liability or negligence-based violations with limited defenses, and setting penalty thresholds that are significant but still lower than typical litigation costs, most defendants have little choice but to accept a settlement. Does this policy disproportionately affect smaller firms with less robust compliance divisions? At least one Commissioner has expressed concern about the strategy, urging the agency to instead focus on higher priority issues. Michael S. Piwowar, Comm'r, SEC, Remarks to the Securities Enforcement Forum 2014 (Oct. 14, 2014). What do you think?

D. CORPORATE VERSUS INDIVIDUAL SANCTIONS

Financial institutions are much more likely to be the subject of an enforcement action than IAPs. The preference for corporate sanctions has often been rationalized as part of an attempt to transform corporate cultures in order to prevent future misconduct. Supporters of corporate enforcement argue the effect on a business of being labelled a wrongdoer results in retribution for those punished and deters prospective wrongdoers. Corporate fines assist in restitution to those wronged, as fines can be distributed among the affected group. Pursuing institutions also makes regulatory action more efficient; institutional targets typically have more assets and greater incentive to settle.

The ability to pursue and prosecute firms is facilitated by vicarious corporate criminal liability, meaning corporations can be tried on the basis of the actions of an employee. Both the SEC and DOJ have published guidelines about the propriety of an enforcement action against a corporation. According to these guidelines, each agency should consider the egregiousness of the misconduct, how widespread it was, whether it posed a risk to the economy, whether the company cooperated and had a strong compliance program, and the damage to innocent employees and shareholders from an enforcement action. In practice, the SEC and DOJ both grant substantial discretion to their lead enforcement officials and prosecutors to determine whether the facts warrant an enforcement action and a substantial corporate penalty. *See* U.S. Attorneys' Manual, title 9-28.000, Principles of Federal Prosecution of Business Organizations; Press Release, SEC, Statement of the Securities and Exchange Commission Concerning Financial Penalties (Jan. 4, 2006).

Critics question whether corporate sanctions actually enhanced compliance and corporate self-monitoring. Professors Richard Biersbach and Alex Stein suggest that the opposite may be true, that, because a corporation is vicariously liable for its agents, it is better not to discover misconduct, thereby disincentivizing internal monitoring. Richard Biersbach & Alex Stein, *Overenforcement*, 93 GEO. L.J. 1743, 1773–74 (2005). Consider the views of Judge Jed S. Rakoff of the Southern District of New York, another prominent skeptic, in an article asking why no high-level executives have been prosecuted since the Financial Crisis.

Jed S. Rakoff, The Financial Crisis:
Why Have No High-Level Executives Been Prosecuted?

N.Y. REV. BOOKS (Jan. 9, 2014)

Companies do not commit crimes; only their agents do. And while a company might get the benefit of some such crimes, prosecuting the company would inevitably punish, directly or indirectly, the many employees and shareholders who were totally innocent. Moreover, under the law of most US jurisdictions, a company cannot be criminally liable unless at least one managerial agent has committed the crime in question; so why not prosecute the agent who actually committed the crime?

. . . Although [prosecuting institutions] is supposedly justified because it prevents future crimes . . . the future deterrent value of successfully prosecuting individuals far outweighs the prophylactic benefits of imposing internal compliance measures that are often little more than window-dressing. Just going after the company is also both technically and morally suspect. It is technically suspect because, under the law, you should not indict or threaten to indict a company unless you can prove beyond a reasonable doubt that some managerial agent of the company committed the alleged crime; and if you can prove that, why not indict the manager? And from a moral standpoint, punishing a company and its many innocent employees and shareholders for the crimes committed by some unprosecuted individuals seems contrary to elementary notions of moral responsibility.

These criticisms take on special relevance, however, in the instance of investigations growing out of the [Financial Crisis], because, as noted, the DOJ's position, until at least recently, is that going after the suspect institutions poses too great a risk to the nation's economic recovery. So you don't go after the companies, at least not criminally, because they are too big to jail; and you don't go after the individuals, because that would involve the kind of years-long investigations that you no longer have the experience or the resources to pursue.

---

1. ***Collateral Damage?*** Pursuing firms rather than individuals can leave shareholders with the burden of sanctions rather than the culpable individuals. Criminal indictments of firms can also cause harm to innocent parties beyond shareholders. One study found that harms include the redirection of management attention away from business, loss of access to financing, and ineligibility for government work. *See* Jonathan M. Karpoff & John R. Lott, Jr., *The Reputational Penalty Firms Bear from Committing Criminal Fraud*, 36 J.L. & ECON. 757, 759, 784 (1993). Others suggest that these actions may harm firm relationships with customers and suppliers while also damaging employee morale. *See* Richard Biersbach & Alex Stein, *Overenforcement*, 93 GEO. L.J. 1743, 1771–72 (2005).

2. ***Parallel Proceedings.*** Special concerns arise for financial institutions and IAPs facing parallel enforcement actions and criminal prosecutions. The D.C. Circuit highlighted such concerns in an opinion confirming that the SEC could bring an enforcement action after a criminal prosecution has been brought for the same conduct. The court noted that "[t]he noncriminal proceeding, if not deferred, might undermine the party's Fifth Amendment privilege against self-incrimination, expand rights of criminal discovery beyond the limits of Federal Rule of Criminal Procedure 16(b), expose the basis of the defense to the prosecution in advance of criminal trial, or otherwise prejudice the case." SEC v. Dresser Indus., 628 F.2d 1368, 1376 (D.C. Cir. 1980).

E. SETTLEMENTS WITHOUT ADMISSION OF WRONGDOING

The vast majority of regulatory enforcement actions end in settlement. Financial regulators have long permitted the subject of an enforcement action to neither admit nor deny wrongdoing. The justification for this policy was the argument that, if required to admit wrongdoing, parties would litigate the matter to avoid collateral estoppel in related private suits. Litigation would prolong resolution and further stretch the resources of regulators. Resolution through neither admit nor deny settlements enables regulators to resolve a matter quickly and with certainty as to the outcome.

Settling an action without an admission of wrongdoing has been criticized, particularly since the Financial Crisis. In a 2009 report, the Government Accountability Office found that the agency's lenient corporate penalty policies compromised the integrity of its enforcement program. U.S. GOV'T ACCOUNTABILITY OFFICE, GAO-09-358, SEC: GREATER ATTENTION NEEDED TO ENHANCE COMMUNICATION AND UTILIZATION OF RESOURCES IN THE DIVISION OF ENFORCEMENT (2009). More recently, SEC Chair Mary Schapiro unchained Enforcement staff from the five-member Commission by allowing them to have formal order authority to investigate defendants without Commission approval. Despite significant reforms, the agency's settlement policies remained under attack, this time from the judiciary.

SEC v. Citigroup Global Markets, Inc.

827 F. Supp. 2d 328 (S.D.N.Y. 2011)

JED S. RAKOFF, District Judge.

[The SEC accused Citigroup Global Markets, Inc. (Citigroup) of a substantial securities fraud.] According to the [SEC]'s Complaint, after Citigroup realized in early 2007 that the market for mortgage-backed securities was beginning to weaken, Citigroup created a billion-dollar Fund (known as Class V Funding III) that allowed it to dump some dubious assets on misinformed investors. This was accomplished by Citigroup's misrepresenting that the Fund's assets were attractive investments rigorously selected by an independent investment adviser, whereas in fact Citigroup had arranged to include in the portfolio a substantial percentage of negatively projected assets and had then taken a short position in those very assets it had helped select. . . . Citigroup realized net profits of around $160 million whereas the investors, as the [SEC] later revealed, lost more than $700 million.

In a parallel Complaint filed the same day against Citigroup employee Brian Stoker, the [SEC] alleged . . . that:

> "Citigroup knew it would be difficult to place the liabilities of [the Fund] if it disclosed to investors its intention to use the vehicle to short a hand-picked set of [poorly rated assets]. . . By contrast, Citigroup knew that representing to investors that an experienced third-party investment adviser had selected the portfolio would facilitate the placement of the [Fund's] liabilities." (emphasis supplied).

Although this would appear to be tantamount to an allegation of knowing and fraudulent intent (scienter, in the lingo of securities law), the [SEC], for reasons of its own, chose to charge Citigroup only with negligence, in violation of Sections 17(a)(2) and (3) of the [1933 Act], 15 U.S.C. § 77q(a)(2) and (3).

Simultaneously with the filing of its Complaint against Citigroup, the [SEC] presented to the Court for its signature [the Consent Judgment and a Consent] that recited that Citigroup consented to the entry of the Consent Judgment "[w]ithout admitting or denying the allegations of the complaint . . ." The Consent Judgment (1) "permanently restrained and enjoined" Citigroup and its agents, employees, etc., from future violations of Sections 17(a)(2) and (3) of the [1933 Act], (2) required Citigroup to disgorge to the [SEC] Citigroup's $160 million in profits, plus $30 million in interest thereon, and to pay to the [SEC] a civil penalty in the amount of $95 million, and (3) required Citigroup to undertake for a period of three years, subject to enforcement by the Court, certain internal measures designed to prevent recurrences of the securities fraud here perpetrated.

. . . [T]he Court has spent long hours trying to determine whether, in view of the substantial deference due the [SEC] in matters of this kind, the Court can somehow approve this problematic Consent Judgment. In the end, the Court concludes that it cannot approve it, because the Court has not been provided with any proven or admitted facts upon which to exercise even a modest degree of independent judgment.

The Court turns first to the standard of review. [The Court concluded that, before a court may employ its injunctive and contempt powers in support of an administrative settlement, the court must, even after giving substantial deference to the views of the administrative agency, be satisfied that it is not being used as a tool to enforce an agreement that is unfair, unreasonable, inadequate, or in contravention of the public interest.]

Applying these standards to the case in hand, the Court concludes, regretfully, that the proposed Consent Judgment is neither fair, nor reasonable, nor adequate, nor in the public interest. Most fundamentally, this is because it does not provide the Court with a sufficient evidentiary basis to know whether the requested relief is justified under any of these standards. . . . [W]hen a public agency asks a court to become its partner in enforcement by imposing wide-ranging injunctive remedies on a defendant, enforced by the formidable judicial power of contempt, the court, and the public, need some knowledge of what the underlying facts are: for otherwise, the court becomes a mere handmaiden to a settlement privately negotiated on the basis of unknown facts, while the public is deprived of ever knowing the truth in a matter of obvious public importance.

Here, the [SEC]'s long-standing policy—hallowed by history, but not by reason—of allowing defendants to enter into Consent Judgments without admitting or denying the underlying allegations, deprives the Court of even the most minimal assurance that the substantial injunctive relief it is being asked to impose has any basis in fact. There is little real doubt that Citigroup contests the factual allegations of the Complaint. In colloquy with the Court, counsel for Citigroup expressly reconfirmed that his client was not admitting the allegations of the Complaint. He also noted, correctly, that he was free—notwithstanding the [SEC's] gag order precluding Citigroup from contesting the [SEC's] allegations in the media[4]—to fully contest the facts in any parallel litigation; and he strongly hinted that Citigroup would do just that.

. . . As a matter of law, an allegation that is neither admitted nor denied is simply that, an allegation. It has no evidentiary value and no collateral estoppel effect. It is precisely for this reason that the Second Circuit held long ago, in *Lipsky v. Commonwealth United Corp.*, 551 F.2d 887 (2d Cir.1976), that "a consent judgment between a federal agency and a private corporation which is not the result of an actual adjudication of any of the issues . . . cannot be used as evidence in subsequent litigation." *Id.* at 893. . . . Indeed the Lipsky court went so far as to hold that "neither [an SEC] complaint nor reference to [such] a complaint which results in a consent judgment may properly be cited in the pleadings" in a parallel private action and must instead be stricken.

As for common experience, a consent judgment that does not involve any admissions and that results in only very modest penalties is just as frequently viewed, particularly in the business community, as a cost of doing business imposed by having to maintain a working relationship with a regulatory agency, rather than as any indication of where the real truth lies. This, indeed, is Citigroup's position in this very case.

. . . If the allegations of the Complaint are true, this is a very good deal for Citigroup; and, even if they are untrue, it is a mild and modest cost of doing business.

. . . By the [SEC's] own account, Citigroup is a recidivist and yet, in terms of deterrence, the $95 million civil penalty that the Consent Judgment proposes is pocket change to any entity as large as Citigroup. . . . [The Consent Judgment] still leaves the defrauded investors substantially short-changed. . . . [T]he combination of charging Citigroup only with negligence and then permitting Citigroup to settle without either admitting or denying the allegations deals a double blow to any assistance the defrauded investors might seek to derive from the [SEC] litigation in attempting to recoup their losses through private litigation, since private investors not only cannot bring securities claims based on negligence, *see, e.g., Ernst & Ernst v. Hochfelder*, 425 U.S. 185, 96 S.Ct. 1375, 47 L.Ed.2d 668 (1976), but also cannot derive any collateral estoppel assistance from Citigroup's non-admission/non-denial of the [SEC]'s allegations. . . .

[The Consent Judgment] is not reasonable, because how can it ever be reasonable to impose substantial relief on the basis of mere allegations? It is not fair, because, despite Citigroup's nominal consent, the potential for abuse in imposing penalties on the basis of facts that are neither proven nor acknowledged is patent. It is not adequate, because, in the absence of any facts, the Court lacks a framework for determining adequacy. And, most obviously, the proposed Consent Judgment does not serve the public interest, because it asks the Court to employ its power and assert its authority when it does not know the facts. . . .

---

[4] On its face, the SEC's no-denial policy raises a potential First Amendment problem. *See* Vitesse, 771 F.Supp.2d at 309 ("[H]ere an agency of the United States is saying, in effect, 'Although we claim that these defendants have done terrible things, they refuse to admit it and we do not propose to prove it, but will simply resort to gagging their right to deny it' ") . . . .

Finally, in any case like this that touches on the transparency of financial markets whose gyrations have so depressed our economy and debilitated our lives, there is an overriding public interest in knowing the truth. . . . [T]he [SEC], of all agencies, has a duty, inherent in its statutory mission, to see that the truth emerges; and if it fails to do so, this Court must not, in the name of deference or convenience, grant judicial enforcement to the agency's contrivances.

Accordingly, the Court refuses to approve the proposed Consent Judgment. . . .

SO ORDERED.

---

1. ***Aftermath***. On appeal, the U.S. Court of Appeals for the Second Circuit held that Rakoff had abused his discretion. According to the Court, an SEC consent judgment must be presumed fair, reasonable, and not contrary to the public interest, unless there exists "a substantial basis in the record for concluding" otherwise. The court chastised Rakoff for "demand[ing] 'cold, hard, solid facts, established either by admissions or by trials,' as to the truth of the allegations in the complaint as a condition for approving a consent decree." Trials "are primarily about the truth. Consent decrees are primarily about pragmatism." SEC v. Citigroup Global Mkts., Inc., 752 F.3d 285, 294–95 (2d Cir. 2014).

2. ***SEC Response***. Despite being overturned on appeal, Rakoff "nevertheless prevailed in changing the [SEC's] policies." Roberta Karmel, *Rakoff revisited: how he changed SEC settlement* policies, INT. FIN. L. REV., July 2014, at 42. In early 2011, SEC Commissioner Luis Aguilar called for an end to the "revisionist history" of corporate press releases "explaining how the conduct was really not that bad or that the regulator over-reacted." Luis A. Aguilar, Comm'r., SEC, Setting Forth Aspirations for 2011: Address to Practising Law Institute's SEC Speaks in 2011 Program (Feb. 4, 2011). Soon after, Khuzami announced the first reform to the SEC's admissions policy in almost 40 years. Pursuant to the new reform, the SEC would require an admission of wrongdoing to settle a parallel action where a defendant had been convicted of or admitted to violations in a criminal prosecution. Robert Khuzami, Dir., SEC Div. Enforcement, Public Statement by SEC Staff: Recent Policy Change (Jan. 7, 2012). In 2013, White announced that in certain cases of "egregious" misconduct, the SEC would seek an admission of wrongdoing from parties before agreeing to settle. White reasoned that the traditional justification for "neither admit nor deny" language does not always hold true, and that the need for public accountability is often great enough that parties in egregious cases must make an admission of wrongdoing as part of their settlement. Admissions for egregious misconduct would "bolster the public's confidence in the strength and credibility of law enforcement, and the safety of [the] markets." *See* Mary Jo White, Chair, SEC, Chairman's Address at SEC Speaks 2014 (Feb. 21, 2014); *but see* Andrew Ceresney, Co-Dir., SEC Div. Enforcement, Speech Before the American Law Institute Continuing Legal Education: Financial Reporting and Accounting Fraud (Sept. 19, 2013) ("[T]he majority of cases w[ould] continue to be resolved on a no admit no deny basis . . ."). Reaction to the policy was mixed. Some lauded the move as successfully holding settling parties accountable. Others questioned whether the policy will disincentivize parties from settling. Marc

Fagel, *The SEC's Troubling New Policy Requiring Admissions*, 45 BNA SEC. REG. & L. REP. 1172 (2013).

3. ***Admissions and Directors & Officers (D&O) Insurance.*** Without an admission of fault, there is also no positive proof of fault by any individual. Companies, therefore, are often left with no recourse against directors and officers, who ultimately may be responsible for the underlying conduct. Companies, however, typically insure against regulatory fines by taking out policies indemnifying them from their own corporate liability exposures. Still, many of these policies have conduct exclusions that preclude coverage for claims involving fraudulent or criminal misconduct. Under the SEC's new policy, a defendant's insurer may argue that an admission of wrongdoing is sufficient to trigger the conduct exclusion and thus bar coverage. Shareholders may thus be harmed in two ways: either the corporation must cover the cost of the fine or the cost of its insurance policy will increase. For a discussion of the SEC's new policy and its ramifications on corporate insurance, see Peter R. Flynn, *Admission of Wrongdoing: Increasing Public Accountability in SEC Settlements*, 8 BROOK. J. CORP. FIN. & COM. L. 538 (2014).

Students interested in an excellent, extended treatment of compliance might consult GEOFFREY P. MILLER, THE LAW OF GOVERNANCE, RISK MANAGEMENT AND COMPLIANCE (Aspen Publ'g 2014).

Part IX

Lender of Last Resort and Resolution

CHAPTER 9.1

LENDER OF LAST RESORT

CONTENTS

I. INTRODUCTION

In this Chapter, we take a closer look at the central bank and its function as the lender of last resort. In the United States, the Federal Reserve System plays this role. Deposit insurance and the lender of last resort are often discussed as complementary since they both protect against runs, but the lender of last resort is a 19th Century idea and older than deposit insurance plans, which only developed in the early 20th Century.

Years of contentious debate accompanied the creation of the Federal Reserve System at the beginning of the 20th Century and, later, the controversy over whether the Federal Reserve used its lender of last resort authority aggressively enough during the 1930s. During the intervening decades of relative financial stability in the United States, however, intellectual and political interest in the function of the lender of last resort waned. As Professor Peter Conti-Brown writes, until roughly the early 1960s, "Central banking was the hinterland; fiscal policy—the stuff of taxes and budgets and spending and deficits—the seat of power." PETER CONTI-BROWN, THE POWER AND INDEPENDENCE OF THE FEDERAL RESERVE ix (2016).

This lack of attention changed abruptly with the Financial Crisis, when many central banks, including the Federal Reserve, made heavy and creative use of their lender of last resort powers to avert a global financial catastrophe. Earlier crises had prompted assertive but incremental action. For example, after Thailand's sharp devaluation of the *baht* in July 1997, central banks established currency swap lines to facilitate foreign exchange and alleviate the market disruption that became known as the Asian financial crisis. The Financial Crisis pushed the Federal Reserve and other lenders of last resort to act far more aggressively. In a highly volatile market, a financial conglomerate might remain solvent while in desperate need of liquidity, but it might already have crossed the brink. Many categorical distinctions—insolvency versus illiquidity; banking versus non-banking activities; systemic versus idiosyncratic risks—collapsed under the weight of overwhelming uncertainty. Clear-eyed theory often gave way to more nuanced and fraught experimentation as the Federal Reserve Board and other policy-makers struggled to understand and respond to the Financial Crisis.

We begin with a history of the lender of last resort, starting with the Bank of England. We then discuss the traditional lender of last resort power in the United States, as well as the extraordinary use of the lender of last resort powers during the Financial Crisis. The Financial Crisis emergency lending sparked a vigorous academic and political debate over the proper role of the lender of last resort, which we will try to capture. The Chapter concludes with an examination of whether the Federal Reserve has become a truly international lender of last resort.

II. HISTORY

A. THE BANK OF ENGLAND

The Bank of England has served as the model for other central bank lenders of last resort. It was granted a corporate charter in 1694 as a private company after a crushing naval defeat and the threat of French invasion required the English crown to rebuild its navy. The English crown had neither funds nor good credit, so it needed another means to get a loan. In order to entice subscribers for the large loan, the crown agreed to grant prospective lenders a bank charter. ANDREAS M. ANDREADÉS, HISTORY OF THE BANK OF ENGLAND 54–59 (4th ed. 2013). The charter granted the Bank of England's private shareholders limited liability protection, which at the time was an innovative idea, especially in banking. *Id.* at 83.

The Bank of England was initially the government's preferred bank, holding its balances and lending it money. CHARLES GOODHART, THE EVOLUTION OF CENTRAL BANKS 5 (3d ed. 1981). It was also empowered to issue banknotes against the government's debt and deal in bills of exchange and gold or silver bullion. ANDREAS M. ANDREADÉS, HISTORY OF THE BANK OF ENGLAND, at 73. Its charter had to be renewed every 20 years and its powers expanded or contracted according to the politics of the time. The 20-year charter, a common feature historically, and private ownership were to be repeated in the earliest, ultimately doomed, attempts to establish a central bank in the United States. (*See* Chapter 1.2). In 1844, the Bank Charter Act granted the Bank of England a monopoly, with certain exceptions, on issuing banknotes, and these notes were declared legal tender. Thomas M. Humphrey & Robert E. Keleher, *The Lender of Last Resort: A Historical Perspective*, 4 CATO J. 275, 289–97 (Spring/Summer 1984). *See also* ANDREADÉS, HISTORY OF THE BANK OF ENGLAND, at 188–89, 200–01, 288–91.

It is unclear when the Bank of England first acted as a lender of last resort. The concept of the lender of last resort was first suggested by Sir Francis Baring in 1797, when he wrote that the Bank of England was the "dernier ressort." SIR FRANCIS BARING, OBSERVATIONS ON THE ESTABLISHMENT OF THE BANK OF ENGLAND AND ON THE PAPER CIRCULATION OF THE COUNTRY 22 (Augustus M. Kelley 1967). *See also* Humphrey & Keleher, *The Lender of Last Resort: A Historical Perspective*, at 282. Baring was not describing a self-conscious role the bank was performing, but rather the brute fact that the Bank of England was the last one left after every other lender had turned down a request for a loan. Richard S. Grossman & Hugh Rockoff, *Fighting the Last War: Economists on the Lender of Last Resort*, *in* CENTRAL BANKS AT A CROSSROADS: WHAT CAN WE LEARN FROM HISTORY? (forthcoming 2016) (manuscript at 9) (on file with authors). The Bank of England did not consistently provide liquidity in times of crisis, nor did it embrace its role as lender of last resort until the mid-19th Century. Humphrey & Keleher, *The Lender of Last Resort: A Historical Perspective*, at 299–300. *See also* ANDREADÉS, HISTORY OF THE BANK OF ENGLAND, at 188–89 (noting the use of Exchequer Bills to provide liquidity in 1797).

In response to the inconsistent policies of the Bank of England when confronting panics during the 19th Century, Walter Bagehot wrote LOMBARD STREET: A DESCRIPTION OF THE MONEY MARKET. Although the Bank of England had sometimes supplied some liquidity to help alleviate panics, it had not developed a consistent policy. Building on the earlier, seminal work of Henry Thornton, Bagehot's book was a landmark, at once sophisticated and accessible, arguing persuasively that the Bank of England's actions during an earlier panic in 1825 defined the exemplary lender of last resort. *See* HENRY THORNTON, AN ENQUIRY INTO THE NATURE AND EFFECTS OF THE PAPER CREDIT OF GREAT BRITAIN (1802); Humphrey & Keleher, *The Lender of Last Resort: A Historical Perspective*, at 297–305.

Walter Bagehot, Lombard Street: A Description of the Money Market

57–60 (1873)

And with the Bank of England, as with other Banks in the same case, these advances, if they are to be made at all, should be made so as if possible to obtain the object for which they are made. The end is to stay the panic; and the advances should, if possible, stay the panic. *And for this purpose there are two rules:*

First, That these loans should only be made at a very high rate of interest. This will operate as a heavy fine on unreasonable timidity, and will prevent the greatest number of applications by persons who do not require it. The rate should be raised early in the panic, so that the fine may be paid early; that no one may borrow out of idle precaution without paying well for it; that the Banking reserve may be protected as far as possible.

Secondly. That at this rate these advances should be made on all good banking securities, and as largely as the public ask for them. The reason is plain. The object is to stay alarm, and nothing therefore should be done to cause alarm. But the way to cause alarm is to refuse someone who has good security to offer. . . . If it is known that the Bank of England is freely advancing on *what in ordinary times is reckoned a good security*—on what is then commonly pledged and easily convertible—the alarm of the *solvent* merchants and bankers will be stayed. But if securities, really good and usually convertible, are refused by the Bank, the alarm will not abate, the other loans made will fail in obtaining their end, and the panic will become worse and worse.

. . . The only safe plan for the Bank is the brave plan, to lend in a panic on every kind of current security, or *every sort on which money is ordinarily and usually lent.* This policy may not save the Bank; but if it do not, nothing will save it.

For an excellent review that places Bagehot's book in context, see Peter Conti-Brown, *Misreading Walter Bagehot: What Lombard Street Really Means for Central Banking*, NEW RAMBLER (Dec. 14, 2015).

Bagehot's dictum, the name by which the modern interpretation of his argument is commonly known, asserts that, in times of panic, the Bank of England should lend freely against what is considered to be good collateral in normal times at very high interest rates. Modern articulations of Bagehot's dictum also include the condition that central banks should lend only to solvent borrowers, a point that would have been implicit when Bagehot wrote but, as we discuss later, has additional relevance today. The actions of the Bank of England reduced the number of 19th Century banking panics in England, especially as compared to the United States, which, after the first and second Banks of the United States' charters lapsed, did not have a central bank to serve as a lender of last resort. *See* Chapter 1.2.

B. THE UNITED STATES WITHOUT A LENDER OF LAST RESORT

At the turn of the 20th Century, the United States was the only developed economy without a lender of last resort. In the absence of a central bank, private clearinghouses stepped in to fill that role. In 1853, certain New York banks joined together to form the New York Clearing House Association. During banking panics, when New York banks became illiquid, the New York Clearing House issued clearinghouse certificates against the banknotes of its members. Member banks paid interest on the certificates and accepted them as payment, relieving other member banks of the need to settle their transactions in greenbacks or specie. This allowed those other banks to use the greenbacks or specie to satisfy deposit withdrawals, making a collapse less likely. The New York Clearing House served as an ad hoc lender of last resort, injecting liquidity into the New York banks by converting banknotes that had ceased to function as money into clearinghouse certificates that were widely accepted as money, and thus avoiding or mitigating a contraction in the supply of money even during a panic. *See* NEW YORK CLEARING HOUSE ASSOCIATION RECORDS, 1868-1950; JOHN H. WOOD, CENTRAL BANKING IN A DEMOCRACY 56–60. Similar systems developed elsewhere, notably in New England under the Suffolk Bank System. The Suffolk

Bank of Boston issued notes in exchange for specie or local banknotes, creating a kind of regional currency between 1824 and 1858. GARY WALTON & HUGH ROCKOFF, HISTORY OF THE AMERICAN ECONOMY 215 (2005); C.J. Maloney, *Life Without the Fed: The Suffolk System*, MISES INSTITUTE (Jan. 5, 2011); *see also* ROGER LOWENSTEIN, AMERICA'S BANK: THE EPIC STRUGGLE TO CREATE THE FEDERAL RESERVE (2015). The weakness of the clearinghouse system was that its solutions were local and the certificates worked only in the city where they were issued. LOWENSTEIN, AMERICA'S BANK, at 41.

As discussed in Chapter 1.2, the severity of the Panic of 1907 was the turning point for the development of a central bank to serve as a lender of last resort in the United States. To address the deficiencies in the banking system that were exposed in that crisis, the Federal Reserve Act was passed in 1913.

C. TODAY'S FEDERAL RESERVE

Today's Federal Reserve System retains 12 Federal Reserve Banks that service financial institutions in 12 Federal Reserve districts. These reserve banks act as banker's banks, providing a wide variety of services such as storing currency and processing checks and electronic payments for both banking institutions and the federal government. The Federal Reserve Banks are overseen by a seven-person Board of Governors based in Washington. Each of these Governors is appointed by the President of the United States and serves a 14-year term. The Chairman of the Board of Governors is appointed from among its members for a four-year term. For a more thorough exploration of the governing structure of the Federal Reserve, see FED. RESERVE BD., THE FEDERAL RESERVE SYSTEM: PURPOSES AND FUNCTIONS 1–13 (2005).

We discussed the Federal Reserve's supervisory authority with respect to bank holding companies (BHCs) and its role in supervising systemic non-bank financial companies in Chapters 6.1 and 6.2, as well as its role in the payments system and check clearing in Chapter 7.2. The Federal Reserve is the primary organ responsible for carrying out U.S. monetary policy and, for many, that is its most crucial role.

III. TRADITIONAL LENDER OF LAST RESORT

As lender of last resort, each of the 12 Federal Reserve Banks can replenish banks' liquidity, on a collateralized basis, when they experience shortfalls and cannot obtain funds elsewhere. *See* Kathryn Judge, *Three Discount Windows*, 99 CORNELL L. REV. 795 (2014). When the banking system is stable, private commercial banks can overcome liquidity shortfalls by borrowing from one another in the interbank lending market. When the banking system is unstable, however, banks may hesitate to lend to one another because they are unable to determine which institutions are solvent or sufficiently liquid to withstand a run by their depositors or other short-term creditors. By standing ready to inject funds into fundamentally solvent banks experiencing temporary liquidity problems, the lender of last resort helps these banks avoid forced asset sales to meet their obligations. It also discourages depositors from running on a bank due to concerns over a bank's liquidity position, which in turn mitigates the risk of bank failure and contagion.

The purpose of the lender of last resort, at least in theory, is *only* to provide temporary fully secured liquidity to solvent banks and *not* to provide capital to rescue banks from insolvency. A collateralized liquidity injection is distinguishable in theory from a bailout, in which insolvent banks receive equity or equity-like infusions of capital, the impact of which is to shield the bank's long- and short-term creditors from losses. Those losses are then redistributed to third parties, like taxpayers, the rationale being that the social costs of the bailout are lower than the social costs of letting the bank fail. *See* Randall D. Guynn, *Are Bailouts Inevitable?*, 29 YALE J. ON REG. 121, 125–29 (2012).

This section focuses on the Federal Reserve's traditional lender of last resort function. It begins with an examination of open market operations. While open market operations are often discussed as a distinct function from the lender of last resort, it makes sense to begin the discussion there for two reasons. First, open market operations are the Federal Reserve's primary tool for regulating liquidity in the banking system. Second, allegations that the Federal Reserve abused its lender of last resort power during the Financial Crisis have sparked efforts to restrain not only the lender of last resort power, but also the Federal Reserve's open market operations function. The Federal Reserve has vigorously resisted these efforts to curb its most powerful monetary policy tool. This section concludes by looking at the Federal Reserve's bilateral lending facility, the discount window, which has historically carried out what most would recognize as the lender of last resort power.

---

1. ***The Federal Reserve's Informational Role.*** Professor Kathryn Judge draws a distinction between a liquidity shortage caused by an exogenous shock, such as the terrorist attacks of September 11, 2001, and a persistent liquidity shortage of the sort that culminated in the Financial Crisis. Persistent liquidity shortages, Judge argues, are symptoms of deeper market dysfunction that the infusion of liquidity alone may be insufficient to alleviate. She proposes a broader understanding of the role of the lender of last resort in today's financial system, in which the Federal Reserve exercises its authority as lender of last resort not only to provide liquidity, but also to collect, synthesize, and disseminate the information necessary to neutralize the crippling uncertainty that may otherwise trigger a contagious panic:

> [C]ontinually pumping new liquidity into a financial system in the midst of a persistent liquidity shortage may increase the fragility of the system and, on its own, is unlikely to resolve the deeper problems causing those liquidity shortages to persist. . . [When] facing persistent liquidity shortages, the [Federal Reserve] should instead use the leverage it enjoys by virtue of controlling access to liquidity to improve its understanding of the ailments causing the market dysfunction to persist. It should also use the information to further policies that can help to counter those underlying issues. This may entail injecting information along with liquidity and working with Congress and other regulators to address problems outside the [Federal Reserve's] domain.

Kathryn Judge, *The First Year: The Role of a Modern Lender of Last Resort*, 116 COLUM. L. REV. (forthcoming 2016) (manuscript at 1) (on file with authors). The traditional prudential view differs in important respects; regulators in the past strove to keep prudential information secret in order to ward off bank runs. The 2009 stress tests began to change that view, as the transparency of the stress tests served to reduce market uncertainty.

A. OPEN MARKET OPERATIONS

The Federal Reserve's primary tool for regulating liquidity in the banking system is the use of open market operations. To expand or contract the money supply, the Federal Reserve purchases or sells U.S. Treasuries on the open market. The broker-dealers that transact directly with the Federal Reserve are known as primary dealers. Dietrich Domanski, Richhild Moessner & William Nelson, *Central Banks as Lenders of Last Resort: Experiences During the 2007–2010 Crisis and Lessons for the Future* 51 (Bank for In'l Settlements, Working Paper No. 79, 2014). You will recall that, even during the Glass-Steagall Act era, commercial banks were affiliated with primary dealers that underwrote and dealt in U.S. government securities. If the Federal Reserve wants to increase liquidity (*i.e.*, the money supply), it will cause one of the Federal Reserve Banks to purchase U.S. Treasuries from a primary dealer. To pay for the purchase, the Federal Reserve Bank credits the account of the primary dealer and debits its own account in an equal amount.

In effect, the U.S. Treasuries purchased by a Federal Reserve Bank conducting open market operations are paid for using newly created money. As a result, the amount of money circulating in the banking system is increased. This expansion in the money supply, in turn, allows banks to lend to one another and to the economy more freely. Interbank lending is measured by reference to the Federal Funds Rate, which is the rate that banks charge one another for overnight loans on balances held at a Federal Reserve Bank. A lower Federal Funds Rate reflects a decrease in the cost of lending to the economy, typically resulting in an expansion of the supply of both money and credit through a mechanism generally known as the money multiplier. JAMES R. KEARL, ECONOMICS AND PUBLIC POLICY: AN ANALYTICAL APPROACH 422–27, 792 (6th ed. 2011). Conversely, the sale of government securities will have the opposite effect of contracting the money supply, as well as the supply of money and credit throughout the banking system. The Federal Reserve's course in open market operations is determined by the Federal Open Market Committee (FOMC), which is composed of all seven members of the Board of Governors, the President of the Federal Reserve Bank of New York, and an annually rotating group of Presidents from four other Federal Reserve Banks. 12 U.S.C. § 263.

The Federal Reserve undertook aggressive open market operations to increase liquidity during and after past crises. For example, aggressive open market operations were key in mitigating broad financial market instability during the 1987 stock market crash. Mark Carlson, *A Brief History of the 1987 Stock Market Crash with a Discussion of the Federal Reserve Response* (Fed. Reserve Bd., Working Paper No. 2007-13). The Federal Funds Rate remained close to 0% for several years until December 2015, meaning that banks could effectively lend to each other interest-free. Federal Reserve Board, Selected Interest Rates (Weekly) (Apr. 6, 2015).

Despite the role that open market operations play in improving bank liquidity, it is important to remember that the primary purpose of open market operations is not to regulate the health of banks, but rather to expand or contract the money supply, adjust interest rates, and either stimulate or tamp down the availability of credit.

B. THE DISCOUNT WINDOW

The fact that a lender of last resort stands ready to exchange cash for illiquid assets during periods of scarce liquidity has many salutary effects. The existence of the lender of last resort discourages depositors from participating in a run. Paul Tucker, *The Lender of Last Resort and Modern Central Banking: Principles and Reconstruction* (Bank for Int'l Settlements, Working Paper No. 79, 2014) [hereinafter Tucker, Lender of Last Resort]. In the event that a run *does* occur, central bank liquidity helps an institution with liquidity difficulties avoid asset fire-sales and insolvency. A central bank is in the best position to act as a lender of last resort for several reasons. Central banks often act as prudential supervisors. This regulatory role positions them to assess banks' health and avoid lending to an insolvent institution. Judge, *Three Discount Windows*, at 808. In a world of fiat currency, central banks possess the ability to print or otherwise create central bank money. *Id.* at 807. Their ability to make emergency loans is not constrained by a lack of money, and they have no incentive to hoard liquid assets in times of financial instability. *Id.* at 808. Central banks with power to expand the money supply are, uniquely, indifferent to liquidity risk.

In normal times, the Federal Reserve provides collateralized loans through its bilateral lending facility, the discount window. The interest rate on discount window loans, known as the discount rate, is set by Federal Reserve Banks in each district, subject to approval by the Board of Governors. Normally, only depository institutions are permitted to access the discount window. 12 C.F.R. § 201.1(b).

Discount window loans contain terms designed to mitigate problems of adverse selection and moral hazard. Banks seeking to tap the discount window must post collateral at the window in exchange for a loan of cash. Judge, *Three Discount Windows*, at 797. A broad range of high-quality collateral is acceptable, including loans and securities. William Nelson, *Lessons from Lender of Last Resort Actions During the Crisis: The Federal Reserve Experience* 78 (Bank for Int'l Settlements, Working Paper No. 79, 2014). If a bank borrower turns out to be insolvent, the Federal Reserve can then sell that collateral for cash to satisfy the bank's secured obligation. Furthermore, discount window loans come with a haircut, meaning that bank borrowers post collateral that has a higher value than the cash they receive in return. This overcollateralization further protects the Federal Reserve against loss. There is no known instance of a Federal Reserve Bank suffering a loss on a secured loan from the discount window.

In addition to these safeguards, all discount window loans carry interest rates higher than those prevailing in the market to discourage banks from using the facility. This above-market rate for federal funds varies depending on the soundness of the banks taking out the loan. Banks in good condition can borrow from the Federal Reserve's standing lending facility at 100 basis points above the targeted Federal Funds Rate. These loans are called primary credit discount loans, and the interest rate on these loans is called the primary rate. Weaker banks that do not qualify for primary discount loans must take a secondary credit discount loan, which usually carries an interest rate 50 basis points higher than the primary rate. The Federal Reserve exercises greater oversight over institutions that take out secondary credit discount loans. *Id.* If a bank is "critically undercapitalized" under the prompt corrective action regime, which we explored in Chapter 2.5, the Federal Reserve can only extend a loan to that institution if it matures in five days or less. 12 C.F.R. § 201.5. Finally, the Federal Reserve offers seasonal credit to small banks that have deposit withdrawals that spike in certain seasons, requiring greater reserves. The interest rates on these loans are typically below the primary rate.

---

1. ***The Monetary Policy Toolkit.*** Open market operations and the discount window are among the most important of the Federal Reserve's tools, but they are not the only instruments of monetary policy. Federal regulations require banks to maintain minimum reserve balances at Federal Reserve Banks and, like commercial banks, Federal Reserve Banks pay interest on these deposits. The power to adjust the interest rates paid to commercial banks on their required and excess Federal Reserve Bank balances is one of the Federal Reserve's conventional monetary policy tools. Lowering interest rates on excess balances incentivizes banks to put these funds to use elsewhere, *i.e.* by making commercial loans instead. Forward guidance is another conventional monetary policy tool; by issuing policy statements that express a commitment to maintaining low interest rates, the Federal Reserve can promote confidence in the availability of credit in the future and thereby encourage economic growth.

2. ***Unconventional Monetary Policy Tools.*** During the period of low interest rates and economic inertia that followed the Financial Crisis, the effectiveness of conventional monetary policy tools was constrained by what is known as the zero lower bound problem; further reduction may be impossible when interest rates are already at or near 0%. In theory, reserves might carry a *negative* interest rate, charging banks for maintaining excess reserves. Some central banks, including the European Central Bank and the Bank of Japan, have ventured into negative interest rate territory. The possibility of the Federal Reserve following the same course remains a subject of academic debate, but the Federal Reserve did begin using other unconventional tools more extensively and creatively after the Financial Crisis to expand the money supply in an effort to stimulate growth. Most prominently, the Federal Reserve launched the first in a series of quantitative easing programs in 2008. Like open market operations, quantitative easing involves the purchase of assets from market participants by Federal Reserve Banks to increase the amount of liquidity in the financial system. It is considered unconventional in that the assets purchased include not

only U.S. Treasuries but also other types of securities, such as mortgage-backed securities issued by government sponsored enterprises. The Federal Reserve has also experimented with the use of overnight reverse repurchase transactions with money market mutual funds (MMFs) as an alternative to purchasing U.S. Treasuries from primary dealers in open market operations to influence the Federal Funds Rate.

C. THE PROBLEM OF STIGMA AND THE EARLY FINANCIAL CRISIS

The discount window was rarely used before the Financial Crisis, primarily due to the problem of stigma. Banks are hesitant to tap the discount window for fear of projecting weakness, and only the most troubled banks would do so. This perceived weakness may invite a bank run, or make it more difficult for a bank to secure cheap financing from nervous investors. Judge, *Three Discount Windows*, at 811. Consequently, discount window loans are made covertly, although news of the loan often reaches the public.

A number of reforms were implemented in 2003 to mitigate the problem of stigma. Before that time, banks were unable to borrow from the discount window unless they demonstrated that private loans were unavailable. *Id.* at 810. This requirement understandably stigmatized banks that did tap the discount window. The 2003 reforms eliminated this requirement. Healthy banks were thereafter allowed to take out primary credit loans with no questions asked and were not subject to increased Federal Reserve oversight as a result. *Id.* Despite these changes, activity at the discount window remained low. Total discount window loans before the Financial Crisis averaged roughly $200 million per day. *Id.* at 810–11. Secondary credit loans were virtually non-existent. Domanski, Moessner & Nelson, *Central Banks as Lenders of Last Resort: Experiences During the 2007–2010 Crisis and Lessons for the Future*, at 51.

Stigma became a particularly problematic issue during the early stages of the Financial Crisis. In early 2007, the interbank lending market began to calcify as fears spread over losses on subprime mortgage portfolios. Despite this hardening, banks were reluctant to borrow from the discount window due to stigma concerns. One study found that these banks were willing to pay roughly 37 basis points more on private loans rather than risk going to the discount window. Olivier Armantier et al., *Discount Window Stigma during the 2007–2008 Financial Crisis* (Fed. Reserve Bank of N.Y., Staff Report No. 483, 2015). The Federal Reserve responded by easing the terms on its discount window loans. Jeffrey Lacker, President, Fed. Reserve Bank of Richmond, Speech at George Washington University: Committing to Financial Stability (Nov. 5, 2014). This easing mirrored the actions of central banks around the world. Many of them, not including the Federal Reserve, broadened the range of counterparties they were willing to deal with and the collateral they were willing to accept for a loan. Domanski, Moessner & Nelson, *Central Banks as Lenders of Last Resort: Experiences During the 2007–2010 Crisis and Lessons for the Future*, at 51. During the summer of 2007, the Federal Reserve lowered the spread between primary credit and the target Federal Funds Rate to 50 basis points. FIN. CRISIS INQUIRY COMM'N, THE FINANCIAL CRISIS INQUIRY REPORT, at 252. In early 2008, following the failure and sale of Bear Stearns, the Federal Reserve further lowered this spread to 25 basis points. Elizabeth Klee, *The First Line of Defense: The Discount Window During the Early Stages of the Financial Crisis* (Fed. Reserve Bd., Working Paper No. 2011-23). By narrowing these spreads, the Federal Reserve decreased the economic disincentive to borrow from the discount window relative to a private lender. The duration of discount window loans was also extended to up to 30 days, renewable at the option of the borrowing bank. Judge, *Three Discount Windows*, at 813. Stigma problems persisted, however, and these measures failed to attract a significant increase in discount window lending. FIN. CRISIS INQUIRY COMM'N, THE FINANCIAL CRISIS INQUIRY REPORT, at 274. Judge, *The First Year: The Role of a Modern Lender of Last Resort*, 116 COLUM. L. REV. (forthcoming 2016) (manuscript at 9).

To work around this problem, the Federal Reserve established the Term Auction Facility (TAF) program under its traditional discount window lending power. Through the TAF, the Federal Reserve auctioned off term loans to depository institutions against a wide range of collateral, with the total amount reaching $50 billion in the final four of ten auctions. Armantier, *Discount Window Stigma during the 2007–2008 Financial Crisis*, at 8. Banks would submit possible interest rates to the Federal Reserve, and the Federal Reserve would make the loans to banks that offered the highest rate. Because banks that were perceived as financially sound participated in this program, and made it known that they were participating, other banks were willing to participate without fear of stigmatization. *See* Tucker, *Lender of Last Resort*, at 21. While the TAF was somewhat successful in providing liquidity, it did so without imposing the typical above-market rates relied upon to discourage discount window borrowing. The final stop-out rate for a TAF loan, meaning the interest rate that all successful bidders in the auction needed to pay, was 4.65%, below the primary discount rate. Press Release, Bd. of Governors of the Fed. Reserve Sys., Fed. Reserve Will Offer $20 Billion in 28-day Credit Through its Term Auction Facility (Dec. 19, 2007). For more information on the TAF, see Federal Reserve, *Term Auction Facility Questions and Answers* (Jan. 12, 2009); *see also* Davis Polk & Wardwell LLP, FINANCIAL CRISIS MANUAL: A GUIDE TO THE LAWS, REGULATIONS AND CONTRACTS OF THE FINANCIAL CRISIS (Margaret E. Tahyar ed., 2009) [hereinafter "DAVIS POLK, FINANCIAL CRISIS MANUAL"].

As liquidity strains intensified both within the banking sector and in the broader financial system, it became increasingly clear that the Federal Reserve's traditional tools were insufficient to increase liquidity and restore financial stability. The increasing intensity of the Financial Crisis would lead the Federal Reserve to unveil an unprecedented array of innovative emergency liquidity programs, which will be examined more thoroughly later in this Chapter.

---

1. ***The Federal Home Loan Banks.*** The Federal Reserve was the largest provider of liquidity to the financial system during the Financial Crisis through its emergency lending power. Yet it was not the only major source of liquidity for U.S. depository institutions, which also sought hundreds of billions of dollars of liquidity from the network of government sponsored enterprises known as the Federal Home Loan Banks (FHLBs). Judge, *Three Discount Windows*, at 814.

Created in 1932, the FHLBs provide cheap, reliable financing to member financial institutions that want to make home loans. During the Financial Crisis, many banks that declined to tap the discount window turned instead to the FHLBs to meet their liquidity needs. Professor Judge argues that banks borrowed more readily from FHLBs because they did not carry the same stigma as the discount window; they offered more flexible terms and were willing to lend against a broader range of potentially riskier collateral. *Id.* at 816. Banks also borrow from FHLBs for reasons other than addressing liquidity shortfalls. By the end of the third quarter of 2008, over $1 trillion in FHLB loans, known as advances, were outstanding to liquidity-starved banks. *Id.* These advances shrank to $418 billion outstanding by year-end 2011, when markets had stabilized. Nonetheless, three of the five banks that borrowed most heavily from the FHLB system during the Financial Crisis had failed by that time; Washington Mutual, Countrywide, and Wachovia either failed or were acquired while in distress to prevent their failure. *Id.* at 815. For a thorough exploration of this history and function of the FHLBs, and the role they played in the Financial Crisis, *see* Judge, *Three Discount Windows*.

2. ***Lender of Last Resort and Financial Market Utilities***. Title VIII of the Dodd-Frank Act has extended discount window access to financial market utilities (FMUs) that have been designated as systemically important. *See* Chapter 6.2. FMU is an expansive term that refers to multilateral platforms that facilitate the transfer, clearing, and settling of payments, securities, and other transactions between financial institutions. FMUs include entities such as clearinghouses and securities and payments settlement systems, many of which are systemically important. In its most recent Financial System Stability Assessment, the International Monetary Fund (IMF) indicated that this expansion should improve overall financial system stability and called for the elimination of technical impediments to FMU discount window borrowing. Still, IMF examiners reiterated that the standard rules of discount window lending, that lending should only be to solvent institutions against good collateral, should apply. INT'L MONETARY FUND, UNITED STATES: FINANCIAL SYSTEM STABILITY ASSESSMENT 34 (2015).

3. ***Reforming the Discount Window.*** Noting that the Federal Reserve's discount window lending during the Financial Crisis did not square with Bagehot's dictum, which we discussed earlier in this Chapter, the IMF has called for reforming the discount window. According to the IMF, the Federal Reserve should renew efforts to reinforce the perception of the discount window as an end-of-day liquidity provider. Specifically, the IMF has suggested that the discount window should *only* provide secondary credit discount loans, and that such loans should carry a *higher* interest rate. *See id.* For a broader discussion of the tradeoffs in lender of last resort policies, see, *e.g.*, Daniel K. Tarullo, *Rules, Discretion and Authority in International Financial Reform*, 4 J. INT'L ECON. LAW 705 (2001) (arguing that tying one's hands in a crisis is not credible). Given the problem of stigma and the performance of the discount window during the Financial Crisis, do you think that such reform is advisable?

IV. FEDERAL RESERVE EMERGENCY LENDING: SECTION 13(3)

As conditions worsened during the early stages of the Financial Crisis, it became clear that the discount window was ill-equipped to ameliorate the severe liquidity shortage plaguing the financial sector. When a lightning-fast liquidity loss pushed investment bank Bear Stearns to the edge of failure, threatening to inflict cataclysmic damage on the U.S. financial system and the broader economy, the Federal Reserve decided to take action. Specifically, the Federal Reserve created and lent money to a special purpose entity that purchased Bear Stearns's toxic assets, clearing the way for Bear's acquisition by JP Morgan.

The source of this power was the then little-known § 13(3) of the Federal Reserve Act, which authorized the Federal Reserve to make emergency loans to individuals, partnerships, or corporations in "unusual and exigent circumstances," and with the approval of at least five members of the Board of Governors. 12 U.S.C. § 343(3), provided that the Federal Reserve Bank was satisfied that the collateral presented was adequate and there was some evidence that such loans were not privately available. As the crisis intensified, especially following the September 2008 collapse of Lehman Brothers, the Federal Reserve invoked § 13(3) repeatedly to create a dizzying array of emergency loan programs. Through these programs, the Federal Reserve engaged in complex and unfamiliar transactions with parties with whom it traditionally had little contact.

Although these programs helped stave off a total collapse of the financial system, they invited bitter recriminations from many, especially in Congress, and led to new restrictions on the Federal Reserve's power. They have also touched off a vigorous debate over the proper role of a modern lender of last resort, the outcome of which may have serious consequences in a future financial crisis.

A. THE HISTORY OF SECTION 13(3)

Section 13(3) was added to the Federal Reserve Act in 1932 by the Hoover Administration. Before March 11, 2008, all secured loans under § 13(3) had been made during the 1932–36 period, with most occurring in 1932 and 1933. Section 13(3) fell into disuse even during the Great Depression principally because of the addition of § 13(b) to the Federal Reserve Act, which authorized the Federal Reserve to make loans to commercial and industrial companies without the emergency condition, and the ability of the Reconstruction Finance Corporation to make loans to non-banking companies on more attractive terms than those offered by the Federal Reserve. The Reconstruction Finance Corporation was liquidated in 1957 and § 13(b) was repealed by the Small Business Investment Act of 1958. *See* Randall D. Guynn, Annette L. Nazareth & Margaret E. Tahyar, *Federal Reserve Emergency Intervention Authority: Old Tools Used in New Ways*, *in* DAVIS POLK, FINANCIAL CRISIS MANUAL 18, 21 n.17.

The Federal Reserve invoked § 13(3) twice more after the 1930s, but no actual loans were made. The first occasion was in 1966 when mutual savings banks and savings and loan associations came under liquidity pressures as a result of substantial withdrawals of deposits over the mid-year interest credit period. The authority to use § 13(3) was effective for about eight months. The second occasion was made in 1969 when it appeared that savings institutions might experience massive deposit losses as individual savers were attracted to higher-yielding investments available in the market. HOWARD HACKLEY, LENDING FUNCTIONS OF THE FEDERAL RESERVE BANKS: A HISTORY 122, 130 (1973).

Further, while the Federal Reserve had not made loans using its § 13(3) authority since the 1930s, the Federal Reserve had been pressured to use its § 13(3) authority several times in recent history. Each time, however, the Federal Reserve refused to lend, such as the Penn Central Railroad failure in 1970, the New York budget crisis in 1975, FDIC Insurance Fund in 1991 and post-September 11th in 2001. *See* Anna J. Schwartz, Senior Research Fellow, Nat'l Bureau of Econ. Research, Speech at the Sixth Annual Homer Jones Memorial Lecture at St. Louis University: The Misuse of the Fed's Discount Window 62–63 (Apr. 9, 1992); David Fettig, *Lender of More than Last Resort: Recalling Section 13(b) and the Years When the Federal Reserve Opened its Discount Window to Businesses*, The REGION 47 (Dec. 2002) (providing a summary of Emergency Programs).

The Federal Reserve's failure to make broader use of its § 13(3) and other lending authorities during the Great Depression has widely come to be considered a mistake. This view was developed in groundbreaking work by Professors Milton Friedman and Anna Schwartz on the effects of contraction in the U.S. money supply during this period and, later, by then Professor Ben Bernanke, whose work illuminated the tight link between the contraction of money and the contraction of credit. Milton Friedman & Anna Jacobson Schwartz, MONETARY HISTORY OF THE UNITED STATES, 1867-1960, Chapter 7 (1963); Ben S. Bernanke, *Nonmonetary Effects of the Financial Crisis in the Propagation of the Great Depression*, 73 AM. ECON. REV. 257 (1983). These cautionary tales about the Federal Reserve's passivity during the Great Depression are widely credited with galvanizing the Federal Reserve to take more aggressive action during the Financial Crisis.

The extraordinary programs employed by the Federal Reserve in the Financial Crisis are an alphabet soup. Rather than parse out these individual programs, we think it will be more useful to classify and summarize the Federal Reserve's emergency programs at a higher level of generality. The actions taken by the Federal Reserve under its § 13(3) power can be summarized as follows:

- **Loans to Save Individual Troubled Firms.** The Federal Reserve lent money to prevent the failure of individual firms seen as systemically critical. To smooth JP Morgan's acquisition of Bear Stearns, the Federal Reserve created and made loans to an entity called Maiden Lane LLC, which in turn purchased assets from Bear Stearns. Board of Governors of the Federal Reserve System, *Support for Specific Institutions*. JP Morgan was resistant to purchase Bear Stearns if it meant taking ownership of these toxic assets. From September through November 2008, the Federal Reserve invoked its emergency power to make loans to insurance giant AIG, its subsidiaries, and its special purpose entities, known as Maiden Lane II and Maiden Lane III, designed to resolve AIG's liquidity problems. *Id.* For a more thorough accounting of the Bear Stearns and the AIG rescue, see FIN. CRISIS INQUIRY COMM'N, THE FINANCIAL CRISIS INQUIRY REPORT 283–91, 344–50, 376–79.

- **Collateral Transformation.** The Term Securities Lending Facility facilitated the swap of low-risk securities held by the Federal Reserve for higher-risk securities held by private entities. Specifically, primary dealers were able to swap their risky, illiquid assets, such as student and car loans, in exchange for safe, liquid collateral, like Treasury bills, notes, and bonds, held by the Federal Reserve. Fed. Reserve Bank of N.Y., *Term Securities Lending Facility: Frequently Asked Questions* (June 25, 2009). The purpose of this practice, known as collateral transformation, merits some explanation. At the time of the Financial Crisis, many financial institutions were overly reliant on short-term collateralized loans to finance their operations. If financial institution counterparties refused to accept collateral offered to secure the loans, or chose to lend fewer funds for the same amount of collateral, this source of funding would dry up. As the crisis took hold, counterparties were increasingly reluctant to accept risky assets like asset-backed securities (ABS) as collateral. Consequently, the Federal Reserve used the Term Securities Lending Facility to exchange relatively more liquid assets for the illiquid assets of securities dealers, who could turn around and use the more liquid assets to obtain cash through secured financing in the private market.

- **Broad-Based Lender of Last Resort Programs for Non-Bank Entities or for Specified Purposes.** The Primary Dealer Credit Facility offered standard liquidity assistance to primary dealers. These entities would not have qualified for these loans under the Federal Reserve's traditional lender of last resort power, and were not able to obtain financing from the FHLBs. Under Term Asset-Backed Securities Loan Facility, the Federal Reserve made large loans to bank and non-bank investors secured by highly rated ABSs, so that those investors could purchase such ABS. The idea was to enable the sellers of those ABS to continue making consumer and small business loans. Similarly, the Asset-Backed Commercial Paper (ABCP) Money Market Mutual Fund Liquidity Facility provided funding secured by high-quality ABCP to banks and BHCs to finance purchases of high-quality ABCP from MMFs, so as to foster liquidity in the ABCP market and assist MMFs in meeting demands for redemption from their investors.

- **Purchaser of Last Resort.** In some instances, the Federal Reserve used its § 13(3) power to act as the purchaser of last resort for certain kinds of assets. Through the Commercial Paper Funding Facility, for example, the Federal Reserve made loans to a special purpose vehicle of its own creation, which would then purchase commercial paper from private entities. Fed. Reserve Bank of N.Y., *Commercial Paper Funding Facility: Frequently Asked Questions* (Oct. 19, 2009). The Federal Reserve's willingness to purchase commercial paper ensured that it would continue to be issued in the private market. The Federal Reserve also participated in the purchase of mortgage-backed securities (MBS), and at one point was purchasing 90% of all new MBS issues in an effort to keep the market functioning. Perry Mehrling, *Why Central Banking Should*

Be Re-imagined 110 (Bank for Int'l Settlements, Working Paper No. 79, 2014). These direct purchases of assets were unusual from a historical perspective. Andrew Hauser, *Lender of Last Resort Operations During the Financial Crisis: Seven Practical Lessons from the United Kingdom* 90 (Bank for Int'l Settlements, Working Paper No. 79, 2014). Commercial paper, and the role that MMFs play in financing these instruments, will be discussed more fully in Chapter 12.4.

All of these emergency lending facilities were closed by early 2010. For more information on the Federal Reserve's emergency lending powers, see generally Federal Reserve Board, Office of Inspector General, *The Federal Reserve's Section 13(3) Lending Facilities to Support Overall Market Liquidity* (Nov. 16, 2010).

---

1. ***Other Government Actors***. The Federal Reserve played a prominent role in determining the course of the U.S. government's response to the Financial Crisis and coordinating with other agencies, but it did not act alone. The U.S. Treasury oversaw the Troubled Asset Relief Program (TARP), which is widely remembered for its bank investment program but also included programs that stabilized the automotive industry and the housing market, as well as numerous measures intended to support small business' continued access to credit. The FDIC also established the Temporary Liquidity Guarantee Program to support banks by guaranteeing deposits and certain debt securities, which we discuss in Chapter 9.2.

B. AFTERMATH AND REFORM

The Federal Reserve's emergency programs unfroze credit markets, prevented the collapse of major financial institutions, and mitigated the economic fallout from the Financial Crisis. All of these programs resulted in positive returns for the U.S. government, including the loans to Bear Stearns and AIG, despite the fact that the programs were developed on the fly in a pressure-cooker environment. Since the Federal Reserve pays remittances to the U.S. Treasury each year, those returns ultimately redounded to the benefit of taxpayers. In 2013, the U.S. Treasury estimated that the Federal Reserve earned approximately $19 billion on its emergency credit and liquidity programs alone. *See* U.S. DEP'T OF TREASURY, THE FINANCIAL CRISIS FIVE YEARS LATER: RESPONSE, REFORM AND PROGRESS 22 (2013). Returns on the Bear Stearns deal were estimated to reach $2 billion, while returns on the AIG bailout, including the portion attributable to the Treasury, were estimated to reach approximately $22.7 billion—a 5.7% annualized rate of return. *Id.* at 21–22. The TARP as a whole also earned a net $12.3 billion; losses on its automotive industry and housing initiatives were more than offset by gains on its investments in banks and other programs designed to support financial markets. *Id.* at 22. The Federal Reserve's crisis-related programs also appear successful in comparison to the efforts of foreign governments to deal with their own troubled financial systems. For example, in March 2015, the UK reported an unrealized loss of £14,708 million on its nationalization of the Royal Bank of Scotland. U.K.

FINANCIAL INVESTMENTS LTD., ANNUAL REPORT AND ACCOUNTS 2014/15 19 (2015).

Despite the success of the Federal Reserve's programs, its actions generated enormous hostility and renewed calls for limits on its power. After the Savings & Loan Crisis in the 1980s, for example, concerns that the Federal Reserve lent to insolvent thrifts, and ultimately increased the hit to the deposit insurance fund (DIF), led to new restrictions on the Federal Reserve's ability to lend to undercapitalized institutions. Judge, *Three Discount Windows*, at 112. Critics after the Financial Crisis had several avenues of attack, many of which will be explored more deeply in the next section. The most potent strand of criticism was that the Federal Reserve provided taxpayer-funded bailouts to insolvent private firms whose poor decisions created the crisis. Not only did this exceed the Federal Reserve's mandate as a liquidity provider, critics argued, but it contrasted uneasily with the economic pain the crisis wrought on millions of Americans. Unemployment rose rapidly during and after the Financial Crisis, with the economy shedding approximately nine million jobs. U.S. DEP'T OF TREASURY, THE FINANCIAL CRISIS FIVE YEARS LATER: RESPONSE, REFORM AND PROGRESS 3. Unemployment peaked at 10% in October 2009, and household net worth fell precipitously, from just under $75 trillion at its peak in 2007, to just under $55 trillion at its nadir in 2008. *Id.* The DIF, ultimately backstopped by taxpayers, sustained an estimated $42.8 billion in losses. GAO, FINANCIAL INSTITUTIONS: CAUSES AND CONSEQUENCES OF RECENT BANK FAILURES (2013).

The backlash led to new restrictions. Since the Dodd-Frank Act was passed, the Federal Reserve's emergency lending authority can no longer be used to aid individual institutions, as it was for Bear Stearns and AIG in 2008. 12 U.S.C. § 343(3)(A). Now, emergency loans may only be made to "participant[s] in any program or facility with broad-based eligibility." *Id.* The Federal Reserve also may not extend credit to an insolvent entity or for the purpose of keeping a specific entity out of insolvency proceedings. *Id.* Reactions to these restrictions have been mixed. In a 2015 interview, Federal Reserve Governor Stanley Fischer expressed strong views against a complete repeal of emergency lending powers but stated that the amended § 13(3) "has been changed in a way we think we can deal with it." Stanley Fischer, Interview at the U.S. Chamber of Commerce (21:00-21:35) (July 17, 2015). Others have been more critical, arguing that the restrictions may unduly hinder the Federal Reserve in times of crisis. The IMF, for example, suggested that legislators should consider allowing for conditional lending to solvent non-banks that have been labeled systemically important. INT'L MONETARY FUND, UNITED STATES: FINANCIAL SYSTEM STABILITY ASSESSMENT, ASSESSMENT 34 (2015).

In November 2015, the Federal Reserve finalized regulations to implement § 13(3) as amended. The final § 13(3) regulations reflect the Federal Reserve's efforts to achieve political compromise by defining "broad-based eligibility" to include programs in which at least five entities can participate, imposing a one-year sunset provision on any programs established thereunder, and extending the prohibition on lending to insolvent entities to borrowing by an entity for the purpose of lending the proceeds of the loan to an insolvent entity. 12 C.F.R. § 201.4(d). The final § 13(3) regulations also require the Federal Reserve to make publicly available a report describing each program within seven days of its establishment. *Id.* By contrast, the Federal Reserve retains some flexibility, albeit less than it previously had, in assessing the value of the collateral securing an emergency loan, setting the interest rate it charges, and determining whether an entity is insolvent, so long as the entity has not yet entered insolvency proceedings or failed to pay undisputed debts within the preceding 90 days. *Id.*

In remarks accompanying the final § 13(3) regulations' release, Federal Reserve Board Chair Janet Yellen alluded to the political and substantive concerns that motivated Congress to narrow the Federal Reserve's emergency lending authority. She also reiterated the importance of this authority, not only to the financial system, but to the United States more broadly: "[e]mergency lending is a critical tool that can be used in times of crisis to help mitigate extraordinary pressures in financial markets that would otherwise have severe adverse consequences for households, businesses, and the U.S. economy." Janet L. Yellen, Chair, Fed. Reserve Bd., Opening Statement on the Draft Final Rule Implementing Amendments Enacted by the Dodd-Frank Act to the Federal Reserve's Emergency Lending Authority under Section 13(3) of the Federal Reserve Act (Nov. 30, 2015). Senator Elizabeth Warren's reaction typifies the views of critics (some on the left and some on the right) who felt that the new restrictions represented a welcome step in the right direction but did not go far enough: "These changes will help promote market discipline and make the financial system safer—but there are still loopholes that the [Federal Reserve] could exploit to provide another back-door bailout to giant financial institutions." Press Release, Elizabeth Warren & David Vitter, Fed's New Bailout Rule is a Step in the Right Direction (Nov. 30, 2015). In an uncommon move, former Federal Reserve Chairman Ben Bernanke, explicitly criticized the bill introduced by Senators Warren and Vitter, calling it "a mistake . . . that would imprudently limit the Fed's ability to protect the economy in a financial crisis." *See* Ben Bernanke, *Warren-Vitter and the Lender of Last Resort*, BROOKINGS INST.: BEN BERNANKE'S BLOG (May 15, 2015).

Other relevant reforms involve forcing banks to hold more liquid assets so that they are less reliant on central banks for liquidity in times of market stress. The two primary regulations used to accomplish this goal are the Liquidity Coverage Ratio, which requires banks to hold enough high-quality, easily salable liquid assets to withstand 30 days of sustained liquidity pressure, and the Net Stable Funding Ratio, which requires banks to use more stable funding sources, like deposits, as the liquidity risk of its portfolio increases. These new liquidity requirements are discussed in Chapter 2.7. To what extent do you think banks should be required to hold liquidity internally, rather than relying on access to a lender of last resort? *See* Andrew W. Hartlage, *The Basel III Liquidity Coverage Ratio and Financial Stability*, 111 MICH. L. REV. 453 (2012).

C. THE LENDER OF LAST RESORT DEBATE

After years of neglect in intellectual and political circles, the lender of last resort power has been thrust back into the spotlight. The Federal Reserve's emergency lending power is the epicenter of a wide-ranging debate, both in the United States and Europe, over the proper role of the lender of last resort in a democracy. Most commentators agree that that the anger engendered by emergency lending around the world during the Financial Crisis shows the need for a regime that is more accountable and responsive to democratic checks. Despite this common ground, participants in the lender of last resort debate differ widely in their policy prescriptions. This discussion has involved a re-examination of many fundamental principles of the lender of last resort.

1. Central Bank Independence

The issue of central bank independence lies at the heart of the debate over the lender of last resort. A credible lender of last resort, one that the public perceives as *only* providing emergency secured liquidity to solvent institutions and *not* capital assistance to insolvent firms, is essential to maintaining the lender of last resort power's legitimacy. As former Deputy Governor of the Bank of England Paul Tucker puts it, "[o]nce central banks are perceived as having overstepped the mark in bailing out bust institutions, critics look for overreach in their more overtly macroeconomic interventions too." *See* Tucker, *Lender of Last Resort*, at 10.

This pattern has manifested itself in the United States, where the Federal Reserve's independent control over monetary policy has come under attack. The justification for this independence rests on the belief that elected officials would be tempted to manipulate monetary policy to enhance their own electoral prospects. For example, legislators who could exert influence over monetary policy might increase the money supply in the run-up to a close election, without regard for the long term economic consequences of that decision. The Federal Reserve is vigorously resisting efforts to dilute its power over monetary policy. Consider the following remarks by Yellen.

Testimony of Janet Yellen, Chair of Fed. Reserve Bd.

Monetary Pol. and the State of the Econ.: Hearing Before the H. Comm. on Fin. Servs. (2015)

[On July 7, 2014, members of the House of Representatives introduced a bill entitled the "Federal Reserve Accountability and Transparency Act of 2014 (FRAT)." The bill contained a provision that laid down a "reference policy rule" for the Federal Reserve to follow in conducting monetary policy. The reference policy would dictate a mechanical response for the Federal Reserve to follow given a particular set of economic inputs. The Federal Reserve could deviate from this rule in setting monetary policy, but would then be required to justify this deviation before Congress. In her testimony, Yellen cautioned against the dangers of increasing legislative input in the monetary policy sphere.]

As this Committee well knows, the Board has for many years delivered an extensive report on monetary policy and economic developments at semi-annual hearings such as this one. And the FOMC has long announced its monetary policy decisions, by issuing statements shortly after its meeting, followed by minutes, with a full account of policy discussion and, with an appropriate lag, complete meeting transcripts. Innovations in recent years have included quarterly press conferences, and the quarterly release of FOMC participants, projections for economic growth, unemployment, inflation, and the appropriate path for the Committee's interest rate target. . . .

Transparency concerning the Federal Reserve's conduct of monetary policy is desirable, because better public understanding enhances the effectiveness of policy. More important, however, is that transparent communications reflect the Federal Reserve's commitment to accountability within our democratic system of government. . . .

> Effective communication is crucial to ensuring that the Federal Reserve remains accountable. But measures that affect the ability of policymakers to make decisions about monetary policy free of short- term political pressure, in the *name* of transparency should be avoided. . . .
>
> Efforts to further increase transparency, no matter how well intentioned, must avoid unintended consequences that could undermine the Federal Reserve's ability to make monetary policy in the long-run interest of American families and businesses. . . .

Later in the hearing, Yellen referred to the imposition of a mechanical rule-based approach to monetary policy as a "grave mistake," noting that adhering to such rules would have made the Financial Crisis even worse. *See, e.g.*, Michael Flaherty & Howard Schneider, *Yellen Defends Fed Independence, Faces House Republican Criticism*, REUTERS, Jul. 16, 2014. Referring to the specifics of the Federal Reserve Accountability and Transparency Act's reference policy rule, Yellen noted that "there is not a single central bank in the world that follows a rule that would rely on two variables [as the Federal Reserve Accountability and Transparency Act's rule does]." Testimony of Janet Yellen, *Monetary Policy and the State of the Economy* (42:30) (2015). The reference policy rule being discussed in the hearing is generally referred to as a "Taylor Rule" after John Taylor, a Stanford economist and former Under Secretary of the Treasury for International Affairs who famously proposed such a rule in 1993. John B. Taylor, *Discretion versus Policy Rules in Practice*, 39 CARNEGIE-ROCHESTER CONF. SERIES ON PUB. POL'Y 195, 195–214 (1993).

2. Criticisms of the Federal Reserve

Criticisms since the Financial Crisis have been many and varied. Some aspects of these criticisms are specific to the Federal Reserve, like those relating to the bailouts of Bear Stearns and AIG. Similar charges, however, have been leveled at other central banks around the world that took extraordinary actions during the crisis to aid their own struggling financial systems.

The most serious charge leveled against the Federal Reserve is that it exceeded its policy mandate by bailing out insolvent institutions. Lenders of last resort are supposed to provide secured liquidity, not solvency support. Of course, whether or not the Federal Reserve actually aided insolvent institutions is controversial. Whether a firm is insolvent or illiquid can be difficult to determine during periods of financial distress.

A distinct but closely related criticism is that the Federal Reserve exercised power that is properly reserved to the fiscal authority. This dimension of the Federal Reserve's actions has been labeled engaging in credit policy. *See Lessons Learned From a Century of Federal Reserve Last Resort Lending: Hearing Before the Subcomm. on Monetary Policy & Trade of the H. Comm. on Fin. Serv.*, 113th Cong. (2013) (statement of Marvin Goodfriend, Professor, Carnegie Mellon University). The substance of this criticism is that the Federal Reserve channeled credit to certain sectors of the economy instead of letting market forces determine where it would be most efficiently allocated, therefore, resulting in a misallocation of credit. Moreover, in allocating this credit, critics charge that the Federal Reserve appeared to pick favorites, making loans to rescue some institutions, such as Bear Stearns and AIG, while letting others, like Lehman Brothers, fail. *Id.* at 5. The public's inability to monitor the rationale behind this selective treatment creates a perception that the beneficiaries of Federal Reserve support are insiders, weakening the public's confidence in government and the rule of law. *Id.*

Another adverse consequence of credit policy is that it exposes taxpayers to losses. Recall that Federal Reserve earnings are remitted to the Treasury each year. *Id.* The Federal Reserve's emergency programs resulted in a dramatic expansion of its balance sheet. Its investments, including the quantitative easing programs undertaken to stimulate the sluggish U.S. economy in the following years, ultimately gained value:

> The [Federal Reserve] sent almost $100 billion to the Treasury in 2014, [a] record, bringing remittances during the six years from 2009 on to nearly $470 billion—more than triple the remittances during the six years before the crisis (2001–2006) and nearly $1,500 for each man, woman and child in the United States.

BEN S. BERNANKE, COURAGE TO ACT 566 (2015). Nevertheless, these gains are a reflection of the Federal Reserve's substantial exposure to risk during this period. There is no data on whether the gains adequately compensated or overcompensated the Federal Reserve for the risk it took, and its success does not guarantee favorable outcomes for similar programs in the future. Indeed, many credit policy actions (at least in the form of unsecured capital injections) taken by other central banks around the world have led to losses. *See* Tucker, *Lender of Last Resort*, at 12.

Finally, there is the familiar problem of moral hazard. Among central bankers, one major approach to curbing moral hazard is to the use of constructive ambiguity, in which central bankers are deliberately vague about whether they will or will not provide extraordinary assistance. Uncertainty over the availability of emergency assistance presumably encourages market participants to curb "excessive" risk-taking behavior. *See, e.g.*, Jeffrey Lacker, President, Fed. Reserve Bank of Richmond, Speech at the Kentucky Economic Association: Reflections on Economics, Policy, and the Financial Crisis (Sept. 24, 2010). According to Jeffrey Lacker, President of the Federal Reserve Bank of Richmond, however, recurrent rescues by the Federal Reserve have effectively eliminated any belief that help will not be forthcoming in future crises.

Lacker is sympathetic to policymakers' impulse to provide liquidity to financial institutions in order to avert a larger catastrophe, especially because regulators often reason that they can impose tougher regulations later on. *See* Jeffrey Lacker, President, Fed. Reserve Bank of Richmond, Speech at Hoover Institution, Stanford University: Comments on "Rules for a Lender of Last Resort" by Michael Bordo (May 30, 2014). In Lacker's view, these regulations tend to push dangerous activity outside the regulated banking sector, while doing little to restrain risk-taking by market participants. *Id.* We will further explore this issue in Chapter 12.4 on wholesale market funding. He therefore suggests that a complete repeal of the emergency lending power might be necessary, supplemented by other market reforms that make the actual failure of a financial institution more feasible. *Id.* at 7.

---

1. ***Political Uses of Federal Reserve Funds.*** In a December 2015 budgetary sleight-of-hand, Congress diverted funding from the Federal Reserve to pay for highway construction. This maneuver helped gather sufficient votes for must-pass budget legislation but, as former chairman Ben Bernanke wrote during the preceding weeks, "it's not good optics or good precedent for Congress to be seen as raiding the supposedly independent central bank to pay for spending." Ben Bernanke, *Budgetary Sleight-of-Hand*, BROOKINGS INST.: BEN BERNANKE'S BLOG (Nov. 9, 2015); *see also* Fixing America's Surface Transportation Act, Pub. L. No. 114-94 (2015). The legislation drew on the Federal Reserve's funds in two ways. First, it capped the Federal Reserve's capital surplus account to $10 billion, which resulted in a transfer of funds from the Federal Reserve to the U.S. Treasury. Second, it lowered the rate of dividends paid by the regional Federal Reserve Banks to member banks, which must purchase stock in their regional Federal Reserve Bank as a condition of membership in the Federal Reserve System. Dividends had previously been fixed by statute at 6%, but for member banks with more than $10 billion in assets will now be tied to the typically much lower interest rate on certain U.S. Treasury securities. What is the justification for diverting central bank capital to highway funding? What factors led Congress to impose this burden only on larger banks? Why do Federal Reserve Banks hold capital? Why do the Federal Reserve Banks pay dividends?

---

3. The Future of Lender of Last Resort

Paul Tucker, former Deputy Governor of the Bank of England for Financial Stability, has provided a comprehensive summary of the broader discussion on the lender of last resort, including on the consequences for policy-setting. Tucker invoked the historical touchstone of the proper role of the lender of last resort, Bagehot's dictum that "central banks should make clear that they stand ready to lend early and freely (*i.e.*, without limit), to sound firms, against good collateral, and at rates higher than those prevailing in normal market conditions." Tucker, *The Lender of Last Resort and Modern Central Banking: Principles and Reconstruction*, at 15.

Tucker summarizes the broad schools of thought concerning the future of the lender of last resort as follows:

- **Free banking**. The federal government, through its central bank, should not act as a lender of last resort. *Id.* at 16. Instead, private clearinghouses should perform the lender of last resort function. *Id.* Advocates of this approach are most concerned with the moral hazard created by the existence of a lender of last resort.

- **Open Market Operations only**. Central banks should only provide liquidity through Open Market Operations. *Id.* at 16, 18. In this view, the central bank only needs to be concerned with the aggregate amount of funds in the economy. *Id.* at 18. Private actors that receive funds through Open Market Operations are best equipped to distribute these funds to sound firms that lack liquidity. *Id.* Moreover, this approach relieves the central bank from picking and choosing which firms should receive funds, which advocates view as inappropriate. *Id.* This view is often associated with Jeffrey Lacker.

- **The classic Bagehot view**. Central banks should lend freely to sound firms, against good collateral, at an above-market rate of interest. *Id.* at 16.
- **Maintain the functioning of the credit system at all costs**. Under this view, lenders of last resort should lend to any parties, regardless of solvency, in order to keep credit markets going. *Id.* These loans can also be made on softer than normal terms if necessary. *Id.*

Dismissing the first two approaches as insufficient for promoting stability, *id.* at 16–19, and the last as unacceptable on moral hazard grounds, among others problems, *see id.* at 19–20, Tucker embraces the classic Bagehot view. *See id.* As Tucker notes, however, Bagehot was primarily concerned with whether or not the central bank would lend at all. *Id.* at 15. According to Tucker, the primary question today is how to stop the central banks in times of crisis from lending too much. *Id.* Do you agree with Tucker?

Paul Tucker, The Lender of Last Resort and Modern Central Banking: Principles and Reconstruction

Bank for Int'l Settlements, Working Paper No. 79b, 2014

Let me put it brutally. Developing a reputation, whether valid or invalid, for being prepared to lend to insolvent firms undermines the purpose and effectiveness of the [lender of last resort]. This is the essence of the stigma problem. . . .

Just as in the 1970s central banks needed to bring about a regime change in the credibility of commitments to achieve low and stable inflation, so in broad analogy they now need to bring about a regime change by credibly committing to lend only to firms that are solvent and viable. . . .

[T]he cardinal principle for independence in providing [lender of last resort] liquidity insurance should be "no lending to insolvent firms". Amongst other things, that means that the central bank cannot be a vehicle for the executive branch of the government to provide solvency support; if it wishes to take that course, government must do so on its own authority and with transparency to the legislature.

The great question is, therefore, *how* to make a credible promise that central banks will lend only to solvent firms. And, moreover, how to do so via a regime that also credibly avoids *over*-supplying liquidity insurance to sound banks. . . .

The technical basis for a solution is, I believe, provided by the current reforms of the regulatory regime; stress testing and resolution.

Systematic, regular, *transparent* stress testing should make it much harder for supervisors and central banks to avoid facing up to a firm's problems being fundamentally of solvency. . . . Stress testing . . . is a disciplining device on supervisors and the [lender of last resort], as well as on firms themselves. Mechanisms are needed to ensure that domestic authorities don't cheat in conducting stress tests. . . .

The incentives for authorities to cheat will, moreover, be significantly reduced if, when faced with insolvency, they have realistic choices other than, first, bankruptcy and systemic distress or, second, going to the fiscal authority to seek taxpayer solvency support. . . .

In the past, central banks faced a dilemma if the condition of an initially insolvent firm deteriorated after [lender of last resort] support had been extended. Faced with that situation in the future galvanized by the knowledge that the firm's plight will be revealed by a forthcoming stress test, central bankers should withdraw support and put the firm into resolution. With termination of liquidity assistance credible, there will be stronger incentives for borrowers to use the time provided by [lender of last resort] to fix their problems.

Conversely, once a fatally wounded firm has gone into resolution, the central bank should be prepared to grant access to its discount window provided it is satisfied that the resolution is delivering a reconstructed business that is sound. Post-resolution provision of liquidity assistance by the central bank can, therefore, be a more powerful signal that solvency and basic viability are being restored. . . .

None of this is to say that judgments on solvency are easy. The future is uncertain. Economic and financial conditions can turn out better or worse than expected. For that reason, a firm judged to be solvent at the point at which a loan is granted, might later become insolvent. Or the supervisors and central bank might have misjudged its initial position. That being so, solvency judgment is inherently probabilistic. It would be sensible for central banks to frame their decisions on solvency based on *forward-looking* probabilities. Plainly, [lender of last resort] assistance should not be extended if the firm is insolvent today or the central expectation is that it will be insolvent tomorrow. Beyond that, society needs to decide what level of probability warrants support. Elected representatives of the people should probably determine that probability threshold. . . .

Such judgments are difficult. But they are not completely foreign territory. . . .

Sometimes those forecasts will turn out to be wrong *ex post* even though they stacked up *ex ante*. There is nothing novel in that. But the pre-conditions for trust in public bodies have evolved. What's needed today is the injection of the kind of formality, analytical rigour and transparency that transformed the practice, and legitimacy, of monetary policy in the 1990s. Central banks should articulate how they will do this. . . .

Many of Tucker's suggestions are reflected in major provisions of the Dodd Frank Act. For more information on the U.S. stress testing regime, see Chapter 2.7. For a deeper discussion of the FDIC's resolution authority, see Chapter 9.2.

The excerpt above is not an all-encompassing view of Tucker's policy prescriptions. With regard to decreasing moral hazard, Tucker believes that disbursed loans should carry above-market rates of interest, a requirement of increased monitoring, and other restrictions, supplemented by measures like higher capital requirements and increased liquidity self-insurance. *Id.* at 23–24. Tucker also argues that some of the major questions surrounding the lender of last resort's role should be resolved by reference to how central banks will inevitably behave in times of crisis. For example, central banks should not suggest that they will only lend against a narrow class of high-quality collateral, because in times of crisis they will inevitably relax this requirement. *Id.* at 26. Instead, central banks should focus more on ensuring that their employees can understand, value, and manage these assets in the event that a borrower fails to repay the loan and the collateral is seized. *Id.* Similarly, central banks should not adopt a per se rule against lending to non-banks. Given the volume of credit these entities provide to the economy, their interconnectedness with the rest of the financial system, and the damaging effects of their failure, it is not credible for central banks to categorically deny that they will provide liquidity to these entities in times of crisis. *Id.* at 27–28.

V. THE FEDERAL RESERVE AS THE INTERNATIONAL LENDER OF LAST RESORT?

Some of the Federal Reserve's emergency facilities have raised questions about whether the Federal Reserve has become an international lender of last resort. During the Financial Crisis, the Federal Reserve made extensive use of currency swap lines to mitigate liquidity shortfalls abroad. Before the crisis, financial and corporate firms had taken out substantial foreign-currency denominated obligations, including in U.S. dollars. *Id.* at 53. When the credit markets froze, these foreign firms suddenly found that they were unable to meet their dollar obligations. The Federal Reserve responded by establishing currency swap lines with the major European central banks, the European Central Bank, the Bank of England, and the Swiss National Bank, as well as central banks in Australia, Brazil, Canada, Denmark, Japan, Korea, Mexico, New Zealand, Norway, Singapore, and Sweden. *Id.* at 54, n.19. The amount of currency lent through these lines peaked at $580 billion in 2008. *Id.* at 54. The Federal Reserve also set up facilities to obtain currencies from the major European banks and the Bank of Japan, but they were never used. *Id.* All of the swap lines were paid in full and terminated on February 1, 2010. *Id.* at 54–55.

Swap lines are now the primary means for providing emergency liquidity assistance in foreign currency, and the Federal Reserve will continue to use them for the foreseeable future. In response to continued dollar scarcity, standing swap lines with the Bank of England, Bank of Japan, European Central Bank, Bank of Canada, and Swiss National bank were reopened. *Id.* at 55. For more information on the Federal Reserve's currency swap line activities, see Domanski, Moessner & Nelson, *Central Banks as Lenders of Last Resort: Experiences During the 2007–2010 Crisis and Lessons for the Future.*

CHAPTER 9.2

TRADITIONAL TOOLKIT FOR BANK FAILURES

CONTENTS

I. INTRODUCTION

In this Chapter, we explore the traditional legal framework that applies when a bank has failed and the FDIC must make good on its deposit insurance guarantee. The FDIC was created and vested with the responsibility for handling bank failures in 1933, when the first nationwide deposit insurance program was implemented to stabilize the U.S. banking system during the Great Depression. The FDIC's resolution authority refers to the powers the agency may exercise under the specialized resolution regime for administering bank failures. The Federal Deposit Insurance Act (FDIA) sets the scope of the FDIC's traditional bank resolution authority.

The Bankruptcy Code governs the failure of virtually all other types of private enterprises and focuses primarily on preserving the rights of creditors and other stakeholders in a failed firm. The goals of the FDIA's traditional bank resolution authority, in sharp contrast, reflect a mandate to protect the safety and soundness of the banking system and to preserve the public's confidence in it by protecting insured deposits. This broader mandate has been interpreted to require swift action outside of a court process. The traditional bank failure resolution authority has three discrete but closely intertwined components: the responsibility to ensure that insured depositors' funds are fully protected; the sole authority to structure the transactions by which a bank is resolved (*i.e.*, its assets disposed of and its liabilities satisfied in accordance with the priority of creditors); and the sole authority to administer the claims of stakeholders in a failed bank, including its depositors, other creditors, counterparties, and shareholders. When a bank fails, the FDIC's duty is to extract as much value as practicable from what remains, to protect and repay any advances made from the deposit insurance fund (DIF), and to distribute the proceeds fairly.

This Chapter begins with a historical overview of bank failures in the United States before proceeding to a discussion of the various types of resolution transactions, the legal framework within which the FDIC administers traditional bank resolution proceedings, and specific features of the FDIC's regulatory authority to take action within this framework.

II. HISTORICAL PERSPECTIVE

In the iconic image of a bank failure, crowds of anxious depositors throng the streets outside the doors of a brick-and-mortar bank, dreading the loss of their hard-earned savings. Before the Financial Crisis, images like this were viewed by some as artifacts of a bygone era. The examples of Northern Rock in the UK and IndyMac in the United States, as well as photographs of distraught depositors lining up at ATM machines in Greece, demonstrate that such images—and the very real concerns that give rise to bank runs and panics—remain very much a part of today's banking system and relevant to an understanding of the current regulatory regime.

In the early 20th Century, the U.S. banking system was highly fragmented for a variety of legal, historical and political reasons. Most bank failures in the United States between 1921 and 1929 were of small, rural banks and considered to be, at the time, the result of poor management, raising little concern about the systemic soundness of the banking system more broadly. Indeed, the prevailing contemporary view was that, with weaker banks culled, the strength of the banking system as a whole had in fact improved. In the aftermath of the October 1929 stock market crash, however, the beginning of the Great Depression was marked by a dramatic increase in the number of bank failures in the later months of 1930 as compared to the preceding years:

> Nine thousand banks—a third of the banking industry in the United States at that time—failed in the four years before [1933]. The failure of one bank set off a chain reaction, bringing about other failures. Sound banks frequently failed when large numbers of depositors panicked and demanded to withdraw their deposits, leading to "runs" on the banks. The behavior of depositors was not irrational. They had learned from hard experience that if they kept their money in a bank, the money might not be available when they needed it, and they might lose a large portion of it if their bank failed.

FDIC, MANAGING THE CRISIS: THE FDIC AND RTC EXPERIENCE 1984–1994 212 (1998). Early attempts to stem the growing tide of bank failures in the early 1930s, initiated at first by a private sector consortium and, later, the Hoover

Administration, proved largely unsuccessful. The Federal Reserve's refusal to provide liquidity to the desiccated banking system—a course of action that, in the following decades, came to be viewed as an egregious policy mistake. Figure 9.2-1 depicts the number of bank suspensions (a term the FDIC used interchangeably with bank failures) from 1921 to 1933:

Figure 9.2-1 Commercial Bank Suspensions, 1921–1933 ($ Thousands)

Year	Number of Suspensions (1)	Deposits (2)	Losses Borne by Depositors (3)	% Loss of Deposits in All Commercial Banks (4)
1921	506	$172,806	$59,967	0.21%
1922	366	91,182	38,223	0.13%
1923	646	149,601	62,142	0.19%
1924	775	210,150	79,381	0.23%
1925	617	166,937	60,799	0.16%
1926	975	260,153	83,066	0.21%
1927	669	199,332	60,681	0.15%
1928	498	142,386	43,813	0.10%
1929	659	230,643	76,659	0.18%
1930	1,350	837,096	237,359	0.57%
1931	2,293	1,690,232	390,476	1.01%
1932	1,453	706,187	168,302	0.57%
1933	4,000	3,596,708	540,396	2.15%

Source: Columns (1), (2), (3), FDIC; Column (4), Milton Friedman & Anna Jacobson Schwartz, Monetary History of the United States, 1867–1970 (1963).
From FDIC, THE FIRST FIFTY YEARS: A HISTORY OF THE FDIC 1933–1983 at 36 (1984).

As the rate of bank failures accelerated, the importance of developing a more effective bank resolution regime became increasingly apparent. The appointment of receivers, the title given to those tasked with supervising the liquidation of failed banks, was haphazard:

> Before the creation of the FDIC, the OCC supervised national bank liquidations. Liquidations of state banks by state regulators were generally handled under the provisions for general business insolvencies. By 1933, most state banking authorities had at least some control over state bank liquidations. However, the increased incidence of national bank failures from 1921 through 1932 created a shortage of experienced receivers. Furthermore, there were concerns that appointments of receivers, both national and state, had been handed out as political favors, with the recipients attempting to make large commissions and to extend the work as long as possible.

FDIC, THE FIRST FIFTY YEARS: A HISTORY OF THE FDIC 1933–1983 24 (1984). The FDIC describes the shortcomings of this regime, and the resulting shift in the appetite for policy reform, as follows:

> In general practice, between 1865 and 1933, depositors of national and state banks were treated in the same way as other creditors—they received funds from the liquidation of the bank's assets after those assets were liquidated. On average, it took about six years at the federal level to liquidate a failed bank's assets, pay the depositors and other creditors, and close the bank's books. Even when

> depositors did ultimately receive their funds, the amounts were significantly less than they had originally deposited into the banks. From 1921 through 1930, more than 1,200 banks failed and were liquidated. From those liquidations, depositors at state chartered banks received, on average, 62 percent of their deposits back. Depositors at banks chartered by the federal government received an average of 58 percent of their deposits back. Given the long delays in receiving any money and the significant risk in getting their deposits back, it was understandable why anxious depositors withdrew their savings at any hint of problems. With the wave of banking failures that began in 1929, it became widely recognized that the lack of liquidity that resulted from the process for resolving bank failures contributed significantly to the economic depression in the United States.

FDIC, RESOLUTIONS HANDBOOK 24–25 (2014), citing C.D. BREMER, AMERICAN BANK FAILURES (1935). By March 1933, the U.S. banking system was in the throes of the worst crisis it had ever faced. *See* Chapter 2.4. At 1:00am on February 14, 1933, Michigan became the first state to declare a bank holiday. The declaration followed a breakdown in the preceding day's negotiations between Henry Ford and Hoover Administration officials dispatched to persuade him not to withdraw the Ford company's deposits from two of Michigan's largest banks, an action that would likely have forced these banks to close and triggered a state-wide bank run. *See* Francis G. Awalt, *Recollections of the Banking Crisis in 1933*, 43 BUS. HIST. REV. 347 (1969).

By March 4, 1933, when President Franklin D. Roosevelt took office, all 48 states had also declared banking holidays, leading Roosevelt to declare a nationwide banking holiday on his first business day in office. The Roosevelt Administration's response to the Banking Crisis of 1933 was far swifter and more effective than the tepid measures implemented in the preceding months by the lame-duck Hoover Administration. In addition to the establishment of a temporary deposit insurance program, which later became permanent, the Roosevelt Administration's reforms included the creation of the FDIC, with new authority over the bank resolution process:

> To manage the crisis, the government of the United States focused on returning the financial system to stability by restoring and maintaining the confidence of depositors in the banking system. When Congress created the FDIC, it addressed that problem by . . . giving the FDIC special powers to resolve failed banks; and by requiring the appointment of the FDIC as receiver for all national banks. Congress believed that the appointment of the FDIC simplified procedures, eliminated duplication of records, and vested responsibility for liquidation in the largest creditor (the FDIC in its corporate capacity, as subrogee for the insured deposits it had paid), whose interest was to obtain the maximum possible recovery.

FDIC, RESOLUTIONS HANDBOOK 35.

Small bank failures often had devastating consequences on the communities they served in the 1920s and 1930s, but in the intervening decades the FDIC has honed the bank resolution process to an art. Today, small and medium-sized banks are resolved in accordance with time-tested, tightly-controlled procedures and their failures typically have little impact on the retail customers whose deposits they hold. A failing bank is typically closed on a Friday evening and reopened the following Monday morning for business as usual, providing the same services from the same location under a new name. Indeed, ATM machines and credit cards typically remain usable throughout the resolution weekend. An episode of the CBS television show *60 Minutes* that aired on May 31, 2009, "Your Bank Has Failed," nicely illustrates the FDIC's handling of a traditional bank failure. As numerous leaders of the FDIC have proudly proclaimed, depositors have "never lost one penny" of their insured deposits. Nevertheless, it would be a mistake to assume that the agency's history has always been one of smooth sailing. In periods of market distress, the FDIC has been forced to make difficult decisions and to innovate by developing new resolution methods in the midst of crises.

III. THE EVOLUTION OF RESOLUTION TRANSACTIONS

In the 1920s and early 1930s, before the creation of the FDIC, receivership of a failed bank meant liquidation. Liquidation means that the bank immediately ceases all operations and is a black-and-white process in that there are only two sides to a balance sheet. A failed bank's liabilities to depositors must be satisfied, and its assets must be sold to do so. As originally conceived, the FDIC's resolution authority was secondary to its role as deposit guarantor. The clear shortcomings of pre-FDIC receivership proceedings created a desire to expedite one part of the receivership process—satisfying liabilities more quickly by paying depositors without requiring rapid liquidation of a failed bank's assets—but otherwise the role of a bank receiver remained unchanged.

Until August 1935, the FDIC had only one procedure for making payments to insured depositors: the creation of a Deposit Insurance National Bank (DINB, pronounced *din-bee*). A DINB is a nationally chartered bank with no capital and a limited lifespan, little more than a vehicle through which depositors could receive payments up to the amounts of their insured deposits. The FDIC advanced funds to the DINB as insured depositors came to collect their funds. In exchange, the FDIC, as insurer, obtained a claim on the assets of the receivership. By virtue of this subrogated claim, the FDIC steps into the shoes of insured depositors and becomes entitled to the proceeds from liquidation of the failed bank's assets that insured depositors would otherwise have received at a later date. Because depositors had already been paid, asset sales could be conducted over a longer period of time in a more orderly fashion to maximize their value.

The use of a DINB, and even cruder methods such as mailing checks to depositors, are known as depositor payoffs and remain part of the FDIC's regulatory toolkit. Today, however, depositor payoffs are the option of last resort, used only when no alternatives are available. Within months of its creation, the FDIC sought to expand the scope of its resolution authority beyond creating DINBs and selling failed banks' assets out of receivership. After the Banking Act of 1935 granted this new authority, nearly three decades passed before the FDIC made use of a DINB again.

Beginning in 1935, the FDIC had the authority to make loans, purchase assets, and provide guarantees to facilitate mergers and acquisitions of failed banks. Making use of these new authorities, the FDIC quickly developed the purchase and assumption (P&A) method. The FDIC sought this authority for two primary reasons. First, there was support for a reduction in the overall number of banks in the banking system at that time and a belief that, by merging weaker banks with their stronger counterparts, the system as a whole would become stronger and less fragmented. Second, and more importantly, the FDIC was concerned that depositor payoffs would quickly become prohibitively expensive. The condition of many banks that had newly benefited from deposit insurance in 1933 remained uncertain. If another wave of bank failures were to occur, there could be a substantial delay during the period between when depositors receive their payments and when the FDIC recovers funds by liquidating a failed bank's assets. The P&A method allowed the FDIC to minimize this period by selling failed banks' assets more quickly, thus reducing the total amount of advances outstanding at any time and enabling more effective use of the DIF's limited resources.

IV. PURCHASE AND ASSUMPTIONS

The P&A remains the standard method for resolving a failed bank today. With the exception of a brief period from 1955 to 1964 during which only 30 banks failed in the United States, a large majority of bank resolutions in the period of relative stability between World War II and the 1980s were conducted through P&A transactions.

A P&A is a transaction with two parts: following one bank's failure, another bank (1) purchases its assets and (2) assumes its liabilities. Payments from a borrower who had taken out a loan from the failed bank would be made to the acquiring institution. Likewise, a depositor whose deposits had been assumed could still write a check from her account, which would then be disbursed from the new bank. The P&A remains the FDIC's default method of bank resolution, and other alternatives are generally pursued only after the FDIC has considered a P&A and determined that the failure of a particular bank would best be handled another way.

From 1935 until 1980, the most common form of P&A transactions were known as clean P&As. *See* FDIC, MANAGING THE CRISIS: THE FDIC AND RTC EXPERIENCE 1984–1994, at 65–67. In a clean P&A, as opposed to a whole bank P&A, the acquiring bank assumes all of the failed bank's insured deposit liabilities (and could assume uninsured deposits and other liabilities as well) but does not purchase all of the failed bank's assets. The assets passed to the acquiring bank were instead limited to clean assets, *i.e.*, cash, cash equivalents such as U.S. Treasuries, highly marketable securities, and, typically some time after resolution, performing loans. Because the value of the liabilities that the acquirer assumes typically exceeds the value of assets purchased, the FDIC makes up the difference by providing a cash payment (or other financial support) to the acquiring bank. To minimize its resolution costs, the FDIC initiates a bidding process—with the greatest possible secrecy to avoid the possibility of a leak that could trigger a run—when a bank's failure appears imminent but before it reaches the point of insolvency. Each bid consists of two parts: the premium the acquiring bank is willing to pay for the assumption of liabilities and the price the acquiring bank is willing to pay for the assets purchased.

The idea that an acquirer would pay for the right to assume liabilities at first appears counterintuitive. Why should an acquirer pay the FDIC to take on a failed bank's debts? The answer lies in the fact that insured deposits, especially stable retail deposits, are among the cheapest sources of funding for a bank, and the chance to acquire more of them in a nearby community permits a bank to grow its assets and market its other banking services to customers with established relationships. By conducting a competitive bidding process, the FDIC can reduce the amount of financial assistance it must provide to make a P&A financially attractive and, accordingly, minimize the costs to the DIF.

Limiting P&As to clean assets also had advantages. First, the fact that a bank had failed was in itself an indication that too high a proportion of its assets were of poor quality, and the FDIC was reluctant to return these assets to the banking system. Second, by restricting purchases to low-risk assets of readily determinable value, acquirers could submit bids with minimal due diligence based on standard procedures that required little negotiation. This was a particularly important consideration before banks' records were digitized, when performing due diligence would have required acquirers to send representatives to a failing bank's premises, raising the likelihood that their presence would rouse suspicion and spark a run—not an implausible event in a small community. Finally, by retaining assets in receivership for a longer period, the FDIC had more time to assess their quality, *e.g.*, by reviewing borrowers' credit files and payment histories, to produce accurate valuations that would maximize the FDIC's long-term recovery. During the long period of relative calm that prevailed in the U.S. banking system from the late 1930s until the 1980s, these processes worked well.

Figure 9.2-2 Depository Institution Failures in the United States, 1934–2015

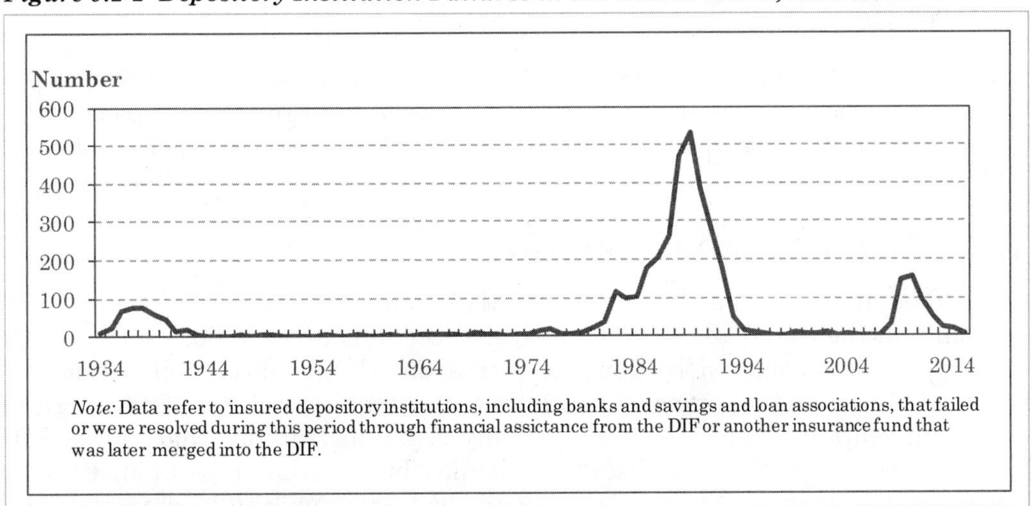

Note: Data refer to insured depository institutions, including banks and savings and loan associations, that failed or were resolved during this period through financial assictance from the DIF or another insurance fund that was later merged into the DIF.

Source: FDIC, Failures and Assistance Transactions Data.

Beginning in the 1940s, the FDIC's confidence in its ability to execute P&A transactions, which at that time were completed without a bank being placed into receivership, grew steadily. Depositor payoffs were chosen only in unusual circumstances, such as where restrictions on branching under state law suppressed interest from potential acquirers or where the FDIC had reason to suspect that fraud or other factors rendered calculation of P&A costs unreliable. The FDIC made incremental refinements to P&A methods in the following decades, but the general structure of P&A transactions remained largely the same. Beginning in the 1960s, rather than conducting P&As of failing banks without closure as it had done in the 1940s, the FDIC begin to conduct P&As after closing banks and placing them into receivership. This change coincided with the appointment of the FDIC as receiver of failing state-chartered banks, which was not required by law as it was for national banks, being adopted as standard nationwide practice and allowed the FDIC to eliminate the inconvenience of obtaining stockholder approval. The FDIC also developed a standard bid package and more formal procedures for calculating the cost of different resolution transactions, soliciting bids, and choosing between them.

The FDIC's use of P&As often amounted to *de facto* insurance coverage for all deposits until the 1980s. In response to Congressional criticism in the 1950s that the FDIC's practice of protecting creditors other than insured depositors exceeded its statutory authority, the FDIC adopted a "cost test," which nominally required calculation of the comparative costs of depositor payoffs and P&As before the FDIC could determine which of these courses to pursue. Yet the FDIC's practice of protecting all of a failed bank's creditors remained in place, in spite of the cost test:

> Since the FDIC made all general creditors whole in a P&A, its share of the likely loss would be increased by the use of a P&A. However, that might be more than offset by the premium bid so that a minimum premium necessary to justify a P&A could be calculated beforehand and compared with the best bid received. In practice, the estimates of likely loss and even the level of insured deposits were not very precise so that there was a considerable margin of error in this calculation.

FDIC, THE FIRST FIFTY YEARS: A HISTORY OF THE FDIC 1933–1983, at 88. During these decades, the FDIC faced little pressure to expedite the pace of the receivership process or to minimize the costs of resolution. This period of calm ended in the 1980s.

V. TURMOIL AND INNOVATION IN THE 1980S

Although the recent experience of the Financial Crisis has pushed the turmoil that the U.S. banking system experienced during the 1980s into the past, these years were marked by genuine fear about the potential collapse of the banking system and a pervasive sense that the stability and growth during the preceding years had come to an end. Many of the institutions that engaged in banking activity at this time were not banks, but another type of institution known as a savings and loan association or thrift. Savings and loan associations were created under a different charter, either state or federal, and their supervision, including savings and loan association resolution, was the responsibility not of the FDIC but of a different federal agency known as the Federal Savings and Loan Insurance Corporation. The scope of permissible activities for savings and loan associations was narrower than for banks; they engaged in the same activities, such as taking retail deposits, but their lending was constrained primarily to residential mortgages. Recall our related discussion of thrifts and the history of the qualified thrift lender test in Chapter 2.1.

The discussion in this Chapter focuses on the FDIC and on bank failures, but it is critical to note that savings and loan associations and their failure *en masse* defined the banking system during this time. The causes of the Savings and Loan Crisis can be summarized briefly. Savings and loan associations were subject to restrictions on the types of assets they could hold, and their balance sheets were comprised mostly of residential mortgages. Mortgages are long-term assets, commonly with 30-year fixed rates. When interest rates rose sharply at the beginning of the 1980s, savings and loan associations, like banks and other financial institutions that engaged in maturity transformation, faced a difficult situation. The spread between the interest income savings and loan associations received on their assets fell below the rate of interest they needed to pay to incentivize customers to deposit their cash. Although the interest rates payable by banks and savings and loan associations on deposit accounts had since 1933 been controlled by law, the deposit interest cap was eliminated by the Depository Institutions Deregulation and Monetary Control Act of 1980. Consequently, many banks and savings and loan associations raised the interest rates paid on deposits in an effort to maintain liquidity. Yet, because the long-term, low-yielding mortgages remained on their balance sheets, many banks and savings and loan associations, with the full approval of regulators who responded by loosening many restrictions, invested in riskier assets with higher yields in an attempt to keep pace with inflation and maintain a positive income spread. Unsurprisingly, these efforts proved largely unsuccessful, resulting in a massive wave of savings and loan association and bank failures.

The following sections describe the important innovations that the FDIC pioneered during the 1980s for resolving large banks with systemic footprints. Given the large numbers of bank failures, the FDIC's past practice of protecting all of the creditors of a failed bank now became prohibitively expensive. As hundreds of banks failed and went into receivership, the FDIC was saddled with billions of dollars in assets of questionable quality. Deliberate review and lengthy sales processes were no longer feasible.

As the FDIC's insurance fund came under increasing strain, the FDIC was forced to develop new resolution transaction structures designed to return assets to the private sector as quickly as possible while allocating losses appropriately. The FDIC developed two strategies to achieve this goal in the 1980s: the whole bank P&A and the P&A with optional loss-sharing. In a whole bank P&A, unlike the clean P&As that prevailed before 1980, offers are solicited for the acquisition of a failed bank's assets and liabilities in their entirety. The FDIC makes a one-time cash payment to make up the difference between the premium offered by the acquirer for assuming the failed bank's liabilities and the price offered to purchase its assets, thereby eliminating any future financial obligation for the FDIC. A P&A with optional loss-sharing is similar to a whole bank P&A except in that, when necessary to incentivize acquirers to purchase assets of indeterminate quality, the FDIC agrees to bear a proportion of any losses on certain assets following the acquisition. Loss-sharing provisions can take a variety of forms, including by changes to the proportions of losses borne by the FDIC and an acquirer at specified thresholds or by allowing an acquirer to put assets back into the receivership under certain circumstances.

VI. OPEN BANK ASSISTANCE AND THE TOO BIG TO FAIL PROBLEM

Until the failure of Washington Mutual in September 2008, the resolution of the Continental Illinois National Bank and Trust Company (Continental Illinois, the national bank subsidiary of the Continental Illinois Corporation, a bank holding company) in 1984, with total assets of more than $45 billion, was the largest bank resolution in U.S. history. FDIC, MANAGING THE CRISIS: THE FDIC AND RTC EXPERIENCE 1984–1994, at 545–46. The failure of Continental Illinois presented a new problem: should the same policies apply to the failure of a bank that, because of its size and its relationships with other banks, threatened to destabilize the banking system as a whole?

In 1981, Continental Illinois was the nation's seventh-largest bank, even though, as required under Illinois law at that time, it had only one branch in Chicago. In the mid-1970s, Continental Illinois's management undertook an aggressive growth strategy that resulted in the massive expansion of the bank's assets. Between 1976 and 1981, its commercial and industrial lending assets grew from $5 billion to $14 billion, an increase of 180%, and Continental Illinois's total assets grew from $21.5 billion to $45 billion, an increase of 110%, making it the largest commercial and industrial lender in the United States at that time. Continental Illinois financed this expansion primarily through wholesale funding, by issuing large-denomination certificates of deposit to institutional investors, including other banks, and soliciting uninsured deposits in large amounts in foreign money markets. At the end of this expansionary period, unlike most small banks, only 20% of its liabilities consisted of core deposits, *i.e.*, deposits from individuals and companies using bank accounts to meet day-to-day cash needs. This reliance on wholesale deposit funding allowed Continental Illinois to quickly raise large amounts of cash to finance its lending, but the providers of this funding were quick to flee as its financial condition deteriorated.

The Federal Reserve Board, OCC, and FDIC monitored Continental Illinois's condition with increasing concern during the early 1980s and, in 1982, advised its board of directors to make changes to its management and lending policies. These suggestions were flatly rejected and regulators were reluctant to take more direct action. In May 1984, however, a prolonged period of deterioration erupted into a full-on run on the bank. By July, only two options remained on the table: closing the bank and conducting a depositor payoff or providing enough financial support to stabilize the bank using, among other measures, the FDIC's little-used authority to provide open bank assistance.

Although the cost test had been applied as a matter of the FDIC's agency policy in earlier years, it became an explicit statutory requirement with the passage of the Garn-St Germain Act in 1982. In most circumstances, the FDIC was obligated to resolve a failed bank either through a depositor payoff or, otherwise, through another means that would be less costly to the insurance fund. There was, however, an alternative. Under legislation enacted in 1950 but rarely used, "when in the opinion of the Board of Directors [of the FDIC] the continued operation of such bank is essential to provide adequate banking service in the community," the FDIC could provide financial assistance to a distressed bank—including through a direct infusion of cash—without placing it into receivership and without regard for the cost to the DIF.

A depositor payoff would result in massive losses to the uninsured depositors and general creditors to whom the vast majority of the Continental Illinois's liabilities were owed. The potential impact of these losses on the banking system was frightening:

> Continental had an extensive network of correspondent banks, almost 2,300 of which had funds invested in Continental; more than 42 percent of those banks had invested funds in excess of $100,000, with a total investment of almost $6 billion. The FDIC determined that 66 of these banks, with total assets of almost $5 billion, had more than 100 percent of their equity capital invested in Continental and that an additional 113 banks with total assets of more than $12 billion had between 50 and 100 percent of their equity capital invested.

FDIC, *Continental Illinois and Too Big to Fail*, *in* AN EXAMINATION OF THE BANKING CRISES OF THE 1980S AND EARLY 1990S 235 (1997). Moreover, allowing Continental Illinois to fail would have threatened the stability of other large banks that were perceived to be in a similarly vulnerable financial condition.

Continental Illinois was ultimately rescued through a financial assistance package through which Continental Illinois's holding company shareholders were heavily diluted and its management replaced, but neither its depositors nor its debt holders bore any losses. The FDIC divested its interest in Continental Illinois's holding company through a series of transactions in the years after the rescue, and the ultimate cost borne by the DIF was roughly $1.1 billion. The permanent assistance package was later described as a nationalization, and is seen as the historical moment at which the question of whether some banks were too big to fail became the subject of public debate, if only among a small cadre of regulators, bankers, academics, and policymakers. The fact that resolution through a depositor payoff or P&A was ruled out for Continental Illinois but remained a possibility for small banks gave rise to "[p]erceptions of inequity in the treatment of banks depending on their size." FDIC, MANAGING THE CRISIS: THE FDIC AND RTC EXPERIENCE 1984–1994, at 545.

VII. BRIDGE BANKS

Based on its experiences in the turbulent 1980s, the FDIC become more acutely aware of the limitations on its traditional bank resolution authority, leading the agency to seek new powers. The FDIC's resolution authority was expanded with the passage of the Competitive Equality Banking Act (CEBA) in August 1987. CEBA "creates a new vehicle, called a 'bridge bank', for dealing with bank failures. This vehicle enables the FDIC to bridge the gap between the failed bank and a satisfactory purchase-and-assumption or other transaction that cannot be accomplished at the time of failure." COMPETITIVE EQUALITY BANKING ACT SENATE CONFERENCE REPORT, S. REP. NO. 100-19, at 550 (1987).

Bridge banks are not intended to serve as permanent solutions for the problems that led to a bank's failure. Rather, as their name implies, the use of a bridge bank is an interim measure to provide the FDIC with more time and more options for arranging a cost-effective resolution. The FDIC sought the authority to use bridge banks to provide an alternative to depositor payoffs when banks fail under circumstances that preclude the arrangement of a cost-effective P&A. The use of a bridge bank provides the FDIC a vehicle through which it can take control of a failed bank's business, stabilize its operations, and preserve its value as a going concern until another resolution transaction can be arranged.

Bridge banks are especially likely to be used in resolutions of larger, more complex banks, both because of the smaller pool of potential acquiring banks and because greater resources are required to plan and execute their resolution. Between 1987 and 1994, bridge banks were used in only 10% of all bank failures but accounted for 45% of all failed bank assets.

Every bridge bank is established as a national bank with a temporary OCC charter. Under the FDIA, a bridge bank's existence is limited to two years, with the possibility of up to three one-year extensions with the approval of the FDIC's Board of Directors. After closing a failed bank and being appointed as its receiver, the FDIC determines which of its assets and liabilities to transfer to the bridge bank. Since the passage of the Federal Deposit Insurance Corporation Improvement Act (FDICIA), the liabilities transferred to a bridge bank generally include insured deposits and secured liabilities. Uninsured deposits would be assumed by a bridge bank only if doing so minimizes losses to the DIF, *e.g.* by increasing the bridge bank's value as a going concern; this requirement generally would not be satisfied if the FDIC's calculations upon the failed bank's entry into receivership project losses to uninsured depositors. Other liabilities are typically left behind in the receivership to be administered as part of the FDIC's claims process. The assets transferred to the bridge bank are typically those of high quality that support the bridge bank's continued operation as a going concern and enhance its marketability to potential acquirers.

Bridge banks may receive financial support from the FDIC through direct capital infusions or through a revolving credit facility as needed to maintain sufficient liquidity for day-to-day operations. Moreover, although bridge banks are not subject to capital requirements, by leaving a failed bank's troubled assets and certain liabilities behind in receivership, the FDIC can restructure a failed bank's balance sheet so as to effect a recapitalization, resulting in a bridge bank of much sounder financial condition than its predecessor.

The FDIC also replaces the failed bank's CEO, appointing a new CEO for the bridge bank, typically from the private sector or senior FDIC staff, and a new board of directors. The failed bank's operations are then stabilized and conducted through the bridge bank under the FDIC's management. The FDIC operates bridge banks conservatively with the intention of preserving the failed bank's franchise value and minimizing disruption to the community it served.

The FDIC made prominent use of bridge banks in Texas during the late 1980s. Many banks in the southwest had significant exposure to the energy sector at that time, and a drop in the price of oil resulted in a wave of bank failures. Early bridge banks—such as First Republic Bank, MCorp and Texas American Bancshares (with 40, 20 and 24 banks, respectively)—each involved multi-bank holding companies in which multiple failed banks were consolidated into a single bridge bank following their entry into receivership, with each bridge bank then sold as a single entity to a single acquirer. By contrast, in the resolution of First City Bancorporation of Texas, Inc., rather than combining all 20 of First City's separate banks into a single bridge bank, the FDIC instead established 20 separate bridge banks, which were ultimately sold to 13 different acquirers. As these examples illustrate, the benefits to the FDIC of greater flexibility and a longer period in which to structure a resolution transaction are of particular importance in circumstances where macroeconomic trends have widespread effects that affect many banks simultaneously.

A prominent, recent example of the FDIC's use of its bridge bank authority was the resolution of IndyMac during the Financial Crisis. IndyMac grew rapidly during the years preceding the collapse of the housing market, tripling its profits between 2001 and 2006 and originating $90 billion in new mortgages in 2006 alone. Many of these loans were known as Alt-A mortgages, which IndyMac provided to borrowers with credit scores in the range between subprime and prime without requiring documentation of their income or assets. Such loans were later dubbed NINJA loans, when it became known that borrowers had no income, no job, and no assets. IndyMac financed this risky lending activity primarily by paying higher interest rates on deposits than any of its competitors, quickly amassing a large deposit base of the most finicky variety—depositors who put their money in IndyMac seeking a high interest rate but who would also be the quickest to leave at any sign of trouble. IndyMac's business model makes its failure seem inevitable in retrospect, but its demise was greatly hastened when concerns about its financial condition were made public in the media, sparking an immediate deposit run. Hundreds of depositors queued on the streets outside IndyMac's offices to seek withdrawals, repeating scenes from the Great Depression, this time with the coverage of a 24-hour media cycle under the sweltering California sun. Two weeks later, on Friday, July 11, 2008, IndyMac, holding $32 billion in assets at the time, was closed and reopened the following Monday as a bridge bank. Its failure cost the FDIC an estimated $13 billion. *See* JOHN F. BOVENZI, INSIDE THE FDIC 1–20 (2015).

VIII. LEGAL REFORMS AND THE LEAST COST REQUIREMENT

From 1934 through 1972, the FDIC's total losses from the resolution of failed banks were only $75 million. In 1988 alone, however, the FDIC suffered losses of roughly $4 billion, depleting the DIF to approximately $14 billion, or about 0.7% of insured deposits, which exceeded $2 trillion at that time. The savings and loan federal insurance system became completely bankrupt. As noted in a June 2015 Government Accountability Office (GAO) Report:

> Between 1980 and 1990, a record 1,020 thrifts failed at an estimated cost of about $100 billion to the Federal Savings and Loan Insurance Corporation (FSLIC) that insured thrift deposits, leading to its demise. During this same period, commercial banks also failed at record rates—a total of 1,315 federally insured banks were closed or

> received financial assistance from the [FDIC]. . . . Estimated losses to the bank insurance fund for resolving these banks was about $26 billion, jeopardizing the fund's solvency for the first time since FDIC's inception. . . .
>
> In response, two laws were enacted. First, the Financial Institution Reform, Recovery, and Enforcement Act of 1989 (FIRREA) authorized the use of taxpayer funds to resolve failed thrifts, replaced the existing thrift regulator, and moved thrift deposit insurance to FDIC. Second, the [FDICIA] made fundamental changes to federal oversight of depository institutions . . .

U.S. GOV'T ACCOUNTABILITY OFFICE, GAO-15-365, BANK REGULATION: LESSONS LEARNED AND A FRAMEWORK FOR MONITORING EMERGING RISKS AND REGULATORY RESPONSE 1 (2015).

FIRREA essentially gave the FDIC the regulatory authority to deal with both bank and savings and loan association failures. FDICIA, the more important of these statutes, enacted reforms to address the insolvency of the bank insurance fund and required the FDIC to select the resolution alternative for failing institutions that results in the lowest cost to the insurance fund. This important provision, known as the "least cost requirement," remains the defining feature of the legal framework governing the FDIC's bank resolution authority today:

> FDIC resolutions were now required to proceed according to a "least cost" test, which would mean that uninsured depositors would often have to bear losses. The FDIC was prohibited from protecting any uninsured deposits or nondeposit bank debts in cases in which such action would increase losses to the insurance fund. One important effect of the least-cost provision was that the FDIC would not be able to grant open-bank assistance unless that course would be less costly than a closed-bank resolution; thus FDICIA limited the discretion the agency had exercised under the old cost test and essentiality provisions of the [FDIA]. These changes have had a significant effect on the protection of uninsured depositors. From 1986 through 1991, 19 percent of bank failure and assistance transactions resulted in the nonprotection of uninsured depositors. From 1992 through 1994, the figure rose to 62 percent. On the basis of total assets, the average percentage of uninsured depositors suffering a loss was 12.3 percent from 1986 through 1991, but from 1992 through 1994 it increased to 65 percent.

FDIC, *Continental Illinois and Too Big to Fail, in* AN EXAMINATION OF THE BANKING CRISES OF THE 1980S AND EARLY 1990S, at 252–53.

The only exception to FDICIA's least cost requirement is the "systemic risk exception" under § 13(c)(1)(G) of the FDIA. Unlike the more flexible "essential . . . to the community" standard for exceptions to the cost test that preceded FDICIA, the systemic risk exception is unavailable except in truly dire circumstances. After the passage of FDICIA, the FDIC did not invoke the systemic risk exception until the Financial Crisis. The Dodd-Frank Act, as discussed below, imposed strict limits on the systemic risk exception and eliminated its use by the FDIC to provide open bank assistance or to issue broad-based guarantees. Other provisions of the Dodd-Frank Act authorize the FDIC to establish a widely available program for guaranteeing the obligations of solvent banks, similar to the Temporary Liquidity Guarantee Program, but the requirement to obtain Congressional approval, albeit under expedited procedures, means that the FDIC could not exercise this authority in a crisis absent Congressional approval. *See* 12 U.S.C. § 5612.

---

1. ***Problem: First National Bank of Sanilac County.*** First National Bank is located in Sanilac County in Michigan, where Michigan's economic woes have weakened tourism on Lake Huron and most of the population is employed in either tourism or sugar beet processing. Seven weeks ago, the sugar beet processing plant caught fire, went out of business, and laid off all of its employees. Unemployment in Sanilac County increased sharply, and house prices are plummeting as residents move to other parts of the state.

As counsel for the FDIC, you receive a letter from the OCC with notification of First National's anticipated failure. Enclosed with the letter are First National's financial statements, which show its balance sheet, current as of the end of the last quarter, eight weeks ago, as follows:

Figure 9.2-3 First National Balance Sheet

First National Balance Sheet as of [ ] *($ millions)*				
Assets			**Liabilities**	
Cash and Due from Banks	$ 10		Deposits	$ 75
Investment Securities	20		Discount Window Loan	20
Loans	70		Capital	5
Total Assets	**$ 100**		**Total Liabilities**	**$ 100**

A team of FDIC resolution specialists is dispatched to First National's headquarters to conduct an asset valuation review. The bulk of First National's assets are residential mortgages, which the bank has classified as performing assets in its books and records. The resolution specialists' report, however, states that many of First National's loans should be reclassified as non-performing—and marked down in value or written off entirely—because the underlying property's value has fallen below the mortgage's outstanding principal amount, leaving borrowers with little incentive to continue making payments. Specifically, the report states that: 10% of First National's loan portfolio should be reclassified as loss or uncollectible and completely charged-off against capital; 20% should be classified as doubtful, of which one-half are projected to be uncollectible and charged-off; and 40% are substandard, for which terms may need to be adjusted and current values are uncertain. Recognizing these reclassifications on First National's balance sheet would render the bank insolvent. The report also states that 80% of First National's deposits are insured.

You can assume that First National's discount window borrowing is secured by its portfolio of investment securities. In the statutory priority of claims under the FDIA, secured claims receive preferential treatment and must be paid in full before any payment can be made to unsecured creditors. In addition, bear in mind that all deposits are unsecured liabilities. Deposit insurance is backed by the full faith and credit of the United States, but insured deposits are nonetheless secured by no collateral. Accordingly, the subrogated claim on the receivership that the FDIC, acting in its corporate capacity, obtains in exchange for making insured depositors whole receives the same statutory treatment as an uninsured deposit liability.

a. How much would it cost the DIF, at a minimum, to resolve First National through a depositor payoff? How much more would it cost if First National's substandard loans are subject to a 25% haircut? Who bears these costs?

b. Lapeer National Bank, located in neighboring Huron County, has submitted two bids to acquire First National through a P&A: (1) $28 million to purchase all of First National's assets and assume only insured liabilities; or (2), to enter into a whole bank P&A in which the FDIC would make a one-time payment to Lapeer of $3 million. If First National's substandard loans are not marked down, would either of these bids be less costly to the DIF than a depositor payoff? Which of the two bids is better for the FDIC? If Lapeer seeks a loss-sharing agreement with the FDIC, how much financial assistance could the FDIC provide before Lapeer's best bid is no longer the least costly resolution?

2. ***JPMorgan Chase—Washington Mutual Litigation.*** Washington Mutual (WaMu), the largest savings and loan association in the United States at the time, "failed in a spectacular way" in September 2008. Deutsche Bank Nat'l Trust Co. v. FDIC, 109 F. Supp. 3d 179 (D.D.C. 2015). Between September 25 and 28, WaMu was placed in receivership, the FDIC marketed its business and solicited bids, and "all of WaMu's assets and substantially all of its liabilities" were acquired by JPMorgan Chase, N.A. *Id.* The P&A was successfully executed, providing a much-needed stabilizing influence during a period of extreme market distress, but related litigation continued for years afterwards. In a June 2015 opinion, a federal district court held that JPMorgan did not assume as part of the P&A certain contingent liabilities related to WaMu's mortgage securitization business. *Id.* "The acquisition of WaMu was governed by a [P&A Agreement], drafted by FDIC, which defined the 'Liabilities Assumed' by [JPMorgan] to mean those 'reflected on the Books and Records' of WaMu." *Id.* The disputed liabilities included, among others, WaMu's obligation to make investors whole after the pools of mortgages underlying the MBS they had purchased fell below contractually stipulated warranties of their quality. These liabilities had not been recognized on WaMu's balance sheet when the P&A was executed but could arguably have been included in a broad interpretation of WaMu's "Records" as they existed at that time. Finding that JPMorgan did not assume these liabilities, the court relied on a plain-language reading of what it means for a liability to be "reflected" on WaMu's balance sheet and interpreted "Records" more narrowly than the FDIC, which argued that "Records" should

include "all 'imaginable' documents, including WaMu's 'Books.'" The case sheds light on the challenges that the FDIC faces when structuring complex transactions with great speed, where slight differences in wording may have consequences that are significant but often hard to foresee, as well as the importance of drafting contracts precisely.

IX. THE FDIC'S BANK RESOLUTION AUTHORITY

A. INITIATION OF RESOLUTION PROCEEDINGS

Under the FDIA, § 1821(c) provides a wide range of potential bases on which the regulatory authorities can determine that a conservator or receiver should be appointed for a depository institution. The most common basis for appointment is that the institution is insolvent. Regulators' discretion in this area is quite broad, and the FDIC may be appointed as the receiver of a bank if any of the following conditions are satisfied:

- an institution's assets are less than its obligations to its creditors and others;
- the bank is in an unsafe or unsound condition to transact business;
- there was willful violation of a cease-and-desist order;
- there was concealment of the institution's books, papers, records, or assets;
- an institution is unable to pay its obligations or meet its depositors' demands in the normal course of business;
- the bank is incurring or is likely to incur losses that will deplete all or substantially all of an institution's capital, with no reasonable prospect for the institution to become adequately capitalized;
- there was a violation of any law or regulation, or any unsafe or unsound practice or condition that is likely to cause insolvency or substantial dissipation of assets or earnings or weaken the institution's condition;
- there was a violation of any law or regulation that is likely to seriously prejudice the interests of the institution's depositors or the DIF;
- an institution's board of directors or its shareholders give consent;
- the bank is critically undercapitalized;
- the bank is found guilty of a federal criminal money-laundering offense.

The grounds for initiating resolution proceedings are in virtually all cases likely to arise long before a bank actually reaches the point of insolvency. In the real world of limited resources and imperfect information, however, many small banks are not resolved until they are balance-sheet insolvent. There are many justifications for the FDIC's broad discretion in this area. It is thought to be necessary for the regulators to be able to act quickly in order to protect the financial interests of depositors and creditors, as well as the welfare of the general public. Bank insolvencies also present difficult questions of evaluation and appraisal of assets and liabilities, which may be more quickly determined by a regulator than by a court. To the extent that judicial review is available, it is based on the arbitrary, capricious, or abuse of discretion standard of the Administrative Procedure Act. Golden Pac. Bancorp v. Clarke, 837 F.2d 509 (D.C. Cir.), *cert. denied*, 488 U.S. 890 (1988).

B. THE CLAIMS PROCESS

Shortly after its appointment as receiver or conservator, the FDIC provides notification to a failed bank's potential claimants. Potential claimants on a failed bank include anyone to whom the failed bank owes a liability not protected by the FDIC's deposit insurance guarantee, such as litigants, bondholders, uninsured depositors, and unpaid suppliers and service providers. All claimants must submit proof of their claims to the FDIC by a deadline within 90 days of the bank's closure, after which the FDIC has 180 days to determine whether the claim has merit. FDIA § 11(d)(3)(B), (d)(5)(A).

Invalid claims are disallowed, and claims on which the FDIC does not act within 180 days are deemed to have been disallowed. The FDIC administers the claims process largely without judicial supervision. Under § 11 of the FDIA, the FDIC's decision to disallow a claim is not subject to judicial review. A creditor may, however, obtain *de novo* judicial review of the validity of a claim by filing suit within 60 days from the date on which a claim is either disallowed or deemed as such. FDIA § 11(d)(6)(b).

Payments on a claim are confusingly referred to as dividends in the FDIC's parlance. Creditors whose claims are deemed valid are paid dividends, typically, less than 100% of the value of their claims, to the extent that funds are available from disposition of the receivership's assets, in accordance with their statutory priority. FDIA § 11(d)(11). Where the value of a failed bank's assets can be readily determined, the FDIC may pay "advance dividends" to claimants before assets are actually sold, allowing claims to be satisfied earlier in the receivership process based on estimated recoveries. Section 11(d)(11) of the FDIA establishes the following order of priority of claims on the receivership of a failed bank:

- administrative expenses of the FDIC as receiver;
- any deposit liabilities, subject to the domestic depositor preference rule;
- any other general or senior liability;
- any obligation subordinated to depositors or general creditors; and,
- any obligation to shareholders or members.

Under the National Depositor Preference Law, enacted in 1993, foreign deposits—*i.e.*, deposits payable solely outside the United States—are subordinate to claims on domestic deposits. FDIA § 11(d).

Notwithstanding the statutory priority of claims, under § 11(i) of the FDIA, the FDIC's maximum liability to any claimant is limited to "the amount such claimant would have received if the Corporation had liquidated the assets and liabilities of such institution without exercising the Corporation's authority" to structure another type of resolution transaction, such as a P&A. The FDIC's liability to any claimant is thus limited to what the claimant would have received in the worst-case scenario of a liquidation and depositor payoff. As a result, the FDIC may discriminate among creditors within the same class, provided that none are paid less than they would have received in a straight deposit payoff. This flexibility to differentiate among similarly situated claimants is particularly significant in light of the FDIC's ability to avoid, set aside, or otherwise limit claims in various manners, as discussed in the following section.

C. FDIC SUPER-POWERS

The FDIC has broad, discretionary authority with respect to the treatment of claimants on a failed bank's receivership. For example, almost any action to which the FDIC is a party is deemed to arise under federal law, and the FDIC may remove a case from state to federal court in virtually all circumstances. 12 U.S.C. § 1819(b)(2)(A)–(B). More importantly, the FDIC has the authority to avoid, set aside or otherwise limit the claims of creditors and other stakeholders in a failed bank, which, as a result of the breadth of the FDIC's discretion, have been termed FDIC super-powers, and are discussed below.

Repudiation of Contracts. Although the FDIC is said to step into the shoes of a failed bank when appointed as its receiver or conservator, § 11(e)(1) of the FDIA grants the FDIC authority to repudiate any contract or lease to which the failed bank was a party if: (1) the FDIC determines that performance would be "burdensome," and (2) that disaffirmance or repudiation "will promote the orderly administration" of receivership proceedings. Other than with respect to qualified financial contracts (QFCs), as discussed below, the FDIC may even cherry-pick among similar contracts or contracts among similar parties. For the counterparty to a repudiated contract, damages are limited to "actual direct compensatory damages" as of the date of the FDIC's appointment, precluding recovery of lost profits and other categories of damages such as punitive damages.

Enforcement and Enforceability of Contracts. Several of the FDIC's super-powers pertain to the enforceability of contracts, favoring the FDIC both as obligor and as obligee.

As obligor, the FDIC has wide latitude to enforce a contract "notwithstanding any provision of the contract providing for termination, default, acceleration, or exercise of rights upon, or solely by reason of, insolvency or the appointment of or the exercise of rights or powers by" the FDIC. FDIA § 11(e)(12)(A). Accordingly, the FDIC can enforce a contract to which a failed bank was a party, even if the contract contains an *ipso facto* clause providing for automatic termination upon the bank's failure. QFCs, as discussed below, are an exception to the FDIC's authority to enforce contracts notwithstanding *ipso facto* clauses.

Favoring the FDIC as obligee, § 13(e) of the FDIA establishes stringent standards regarding the enforceability of a contract by a claimant on the receivership. If an agreement "tends to diminish or defeat" the FDIC's interest in any asset that it acquires "either as security for a loan or by purchase or as receiver" of a failed depository institution, the agreement cannot be enforced unless it:

- is in writing;

- was executed by the depository institution and any person claiming an adverse interest thereunder, including the obligor, contemporaneously with the acquisition of the asset by the depository institution;
- was approved by the board of directors of the depository institution or its loan committee, which approval shall be reflected in the minutes of said board or committee; and
- has been, continuously, from the time of its execution, an official record of the depository institution.

Section 13(e) reaches well beyond the requirements for a contract to be considered enforceable under most state common law and other normally applicable contract law and is among the most heavily litigated provisions of the FDIA. The FDIC's repudiation power is subject to limited exceptions, the most important of which precludes the FDIC from exercising its repudiation power to avoid a legally enforceable and perfected security interest. Through a series of policy statements, the FDIC has also placed limitations on its use of its powers under § 13(e) with respect to securitizations and certain other types of contracts.

Stay of Litigation. The FDIC's super-powers extend to litigation involving the failed bank, which are generally designed to funnel claims into the administrative claims process rather than the judicial system. Ongoing litigation against a failed bank will be stayed, on the request of the FDIC, for 90 days in a receivership and 45 days in a conservatorship. New claims unrelated to litigation that was pending at the time of the bank's closure must be put through the FDIC's administrative claims process before a claimant may commence judicial proceedings. The FDIC may also remove most state court actions to federal court. Finally, the FDIC also benefits from an extended statute of limitations of six years for contract actions and three years for tort actions, or a longer period if provided under applicable state law.

Contingent Claims. Although not derived from specific statutory authority, the FDIC has long taken the position that contingent claims, such as a drawdown on the undrawn portion of a line of credit or a standby letter of credit, are unenforceable.

Special Treatment of Qualified Financial Contracts. Qualified financial contracts, or QFCs, are a class of financial contracts that include, most importantly, derivatives. QFCs receive preferential treatment under the U.S. Bankruptcy Code, under which they are exempted from the automatic stay and other debtor protections that limit creditors' rights upon the filing of a bankruptcy petition. Although QFCs also receive preferential treatment under the FDIA, it is to a lesser extent. For example, notwithstanding the general prohibition on the enforcement of *ipso facto* clauses, counterparties to a failed bank's QFCs may exercise *ipso facto* rights to terminate, liquidate, net or close out their QFCs one business day after the FDIC's appointment. During the one-day cooling-off period, however, the FDIC may choose to transfer the failed bank's QFCs to a third party or to a bridge bank, in which case the counterparty's right to early termination as a result of the failed bank's entry into receivership would be nullified. Alternatively, the FDIC may choose to repudiate the failed bank's QFCs, in which case the counterparty would be entitled to damages. With respect to either transfer or repudiation, although the

FDIC may not cherry-pick from among the QFCs between a failed bank and a specific counterparty, the FDIC need not treat all counterparties in the same manner.

Avoidance of Fraudulent Conveyances. Subject to certain conditions, the FDIC has the authority to deem void and obtain a recovery on any fraudulent transfers or conveyances by an insider of the failed bank or a debtor thereof that took place within five years of its appointment, provided that the transfer was made with intent to hinder, delay, or defraud.

Transfer of Assets and Liabilities. The FDIC may generally transfer the assets or liabilities of a failed bank to a bridge bank or a third party without obtaining consent or approval from any party. The scope of this authority has, however, been challenged by recent cases holding that FDIC may be subject to liability for breach of pre-receivership contracts that were not previously repudiated pursuant to its authority under § 11(e)(1). *See* Bank of Manhattan v. FDIC, 778 F.3d 1133 (9th Cir. 2015). Many, including the dissenting judge, find this case surprising in light of the clear statutory language and contrary precedent in other circuits. How would a prior consent requirement affect bank resolutions?

---

1. ***Bankruptcy versus Bank Failures.*** Because bank failures have broader, potentially systemic implications in ways that the failures of other types of private enterprises do not, the legal framework governing bank failures in the United States differs in many important ways from the Bankruptcy Code. In general terms, bankruptcies are administered in quasi-judicial proceedings under the jurisdiction of a bankruptcy court for the primary purpose of protecting the rights of creditors and other stakeholders in the remaining assets of a failed institution. While bank resolution proceedings likewise respect the rights of creditors and other stakeholders, these rights are also balanced against the public interest in preserving the stability of the banking system and the FDIC's deposit insurance obligations, which are backed by the full faith and credit of the United States. As a result, bankruptcy and bank resolution differ in many important ways, which are cogently described by John Douglas and Randall Guynn.

John L. Douglas & Randall D. Guynn,
Restructuring and Liquidation of US Financial Institutions

Global Financial Crisis: Navigating and Understanding the Legal and Regulatory Aspects 229, 230 (Eugenio A. Bruno ed., 2009)

The overarching issue affecting the rights of creditors and other stakeholders in connection with a failed US bank or thrift is the FDIC's extraordinary powers to administer the receivership process, with little input from creditors or other claimants and virtually no judicial review. . . . Unlike a proceeding under the Bankruptcy Code, there are no creditors' committees and no trustees, and no court oversees the FDIC's activities. Any claims against the failed institution must first be submitted to the FDIC for its own administrative determination, and only after the FDIC considers the claim will a claimant be permitted to assert its claim before a court.

This extraordinary role creates substantial frustrations for creditors and other parties affected by the failure of a bank or thrift. In one sense, everyone other than the FDIC is a passive observer, without direct access or input to the FDIC as it performs its functions. Part of this frustration arises from the FDIC's inherent conflict of interest; it is not only the sale administrator of the receivership process, but also frequently the largest creditor of the receivership estate. The FDIC has a statutory obligation to insure deposits of failed institutions up to certain statutory limits. When it does, it becomes subrogated to the claims of insured depositors and is therefore a creditor against the failed institution.

Although in its role as conservator or receiver of a closed institution the FDIC is supposed to function as the neutral arbiter of the receivership process, its interest as the largest creditor is often pitted against the interests of competing creditors. It has a strong incentive to use its extraordinary powers to deny, avoid or set aside conflicting creditor claims. In addition, the statutory framework gives favourable treatment to the FDIC's subrogated deposit claims priority over the claims of general creditors.

Further, unlike the extensive body of case law, legal commentary and other guidelines that exists with respect to reorganisations and liquidations under the Bankruptcy Code, there is a very limited body of legal guidance supplementing the statute governing depository institution resolutions. The FDIC has not promulgated a comprehensive body of regulations to implement the statute and has issued only a relatively small number of advisory opinions, policy statements and other guidelines to supplement it. The FDIC also takes the position that advisory opinions issued by its staff, including its general counsel, are not binding on it. In addition, the FDIC reserves the right to withdraw any of its policy statements at any time, potentially with retroactive effect. As a result, there is uncertainty surrounding how various issues would be resolved in the conservatorship or receivership of an insured institution.

There is also very little case law and legal commentary because depository institution failures tend to occur in waves with much lower frequency than insolvencies governed by the Bankruptcy Code. For example, it has been nearly 20 years since the US savings and loan crisis, which marked the last wave of US bank and thrift failures. There have been few cases and almost no demand for legal commentaries in the intervening period. As a result, the case law is sparse and there has been little economic incentive to invest time and effort into a body of legal commentary that seems irrelevant for long periods of time.

X. THE FINANCIAL CRISIS AND THE SYSTEMIC RISK EXCEPTION

FDICIA left open one exception to the least cost resolution requirement, known as the systemic risk exception. Under § 13(c)(1)(G) of the FDIA—statutory text that we encourage students to read—should the FDIC's Board of Directors, the Board of Governors of the Federal Reserve System, and the Secretary of the Treasury, in consultation with the President, agree that the closure of an insured depository institution would have a serious effect on economic conditions or the financial stability of the United States, the FDIC may provide financial assistance to an insured depository institution without being required to comply with the least cost requirement. Any loss to the DIF under this exception must be recovered through a special assessment paid by members of that fund.

After the passage of FDICIA, the FDIC did not make use of the systemic risk exception until 2008, when the exception was invoked on several occasions during the Financial Crisis. In the first instance, the FDIC committed to supporting the acquisition of Wachovia by Citigroup, Inc. in September 2008, before ultimately abandoning the proposed transaction when a more favorable proposal was presented by Wells Fargo Bank, with which Wachovia ultimately merged. The FDIC also invoked the systemic risk exception when it took the extraordinary, unprecedented measure of guaranteeing not only insured deposits, but all domestic non-interest bearing transaction deposits and all senior unsecured debt securities issued by certain financial institutions between October 14, 2008 and October 31, 2009 through the implementation of the Temporary Liquidity Guarantee Program.

Through open bank assistance, the FDIC could provide financial support to an insured institution in danger of failing in many forms, including direct loans, contributions, deposits, asset purchases, or the assumption of liabilities. As discussed above, FDICIA's least cost requirement effectively eliminated open bank assistance as an option for resolving a failing financial institution. The passage of the Dodd-Frank Act eliminated the FDIC's open bank assistance authority altogether. After Dodd-Frank, liquidity provided to keep open a large bank such as the FDIC could previously have provided pursuant to the systemic risk exception must now be provided under the Orderly Liquidation Authority (OLA) created under Title II of the Dodd-Frank Act, which requires as a condition of providing such liquidity that an institution be placed into the orderly liquidation process. We will discuss the FDIC's OLA in Chapter 9.3.

---

1. ***FDIC as Owner.*** The FDIC has taken equity positions, through warrants or preferred stock, in closed bank transactions, where the institution is purchased from the FDIC as receiver and continued in business. *See* 12 U.S.C. § 1823(c)(5). Is it appropriate for the FDIC to hold equity interests in banks, acquired through the funding of bank rescues? How does that affect competition and regulation?

CHAPTER 9.3

AFTER THE CRISIS: FROM ORDERLY LIQUIDATION TO BAIL-IN

CONTENTS

I. INTRODUCTION

This Chapter addresses one of the most important areas in financial reform: making it possible for a financial conglomerate to fail without adverse systemic effects. The *ad hoc* and contingent nature of many responses during the Financial Crisis was due to the fact that the United States and other governments lacked the legal toolkit to conduct an orderly resolution of a complex global financial conglomerate.

An effective resolution regime would allow a financial conglomerate to fail and be resolved consistently with the following objectives: sustaining operations critical to the functioning of the financial system; forcing creditors and shareholders, not taxpayers, to bear the costs of failure; minimizing negative externalities; and, finally, providing creditors, counterparties, and shareholders certainty in advance about where they would stand were a financial conglomerate to fail, enabling them to price their risk and to prepare for this contingency. In this Chapter we discuss the measures proposed and implemented since the Financial Crisis to develop more effective resolution tools.

The new post-Financial Crisis tools remain controversial, like the contending visions of the Financial Crisis itself; they are also untested.

The Chapter begins with a summary of the lessons learned in the Financial Crisis, focusing on the failure of Lehman Brothers and the consensus for reform that emerged. We briefly examine the impact of the Financial Crisis on the European financial system before turning back to the most significant changes in the U.S. resolution regime: the Orderly Liquidation Authority (OLA) under Title II of the Dodd-Frank Act. We then discuss the FDIC's single point of entry (SPOE) resolution strategy for resolving a financial conglomerate and regulatory reforms designed to ensure that each one holds sufficient total loss-absorbing capacity (TLAC, pronounced *"TEE-lack"*) to facilitate an orderly resolution. This discussion of OLA, SPOE, and TLAC, all important acronyms with which you will be familiar by the end of this Chapter, segues into a discussion of the focal points in a policy debate on ongoing regulatory reform. In the remaining sections of this Chapter, we turn to a proposal to change the Bankruptcy Code and describe the 2015 International Swaps and Derivatives Association (ISDA) Universal Resolution Stay Protocol and its implementation.

II. LESSONS LEARNED FROM THE FINANCIAL CRISIS

Referring to a financial conglomerate as too big to fail marks the perception that its failure would have such devastating negative externalities that governmental authorities will intervene to prevent its failure under any circumstances. Recall that in a typical government bailout, shareholders are wiped out or drastically diluted. As David Skeel notes, the treatment of bondholders and depositors was quite different: "the bailouts of 2008 were creditor bailouts." DAVID SKEEL, THE NEW FINANCIAL DEAL: UNDERSTANDING THE DODD-FRANK ACT AND ITS (UNINTENDED) CONSEQUENCES (2010). One of the primary goals of the post-Financial Crisis reforms has been to ensure that, next time, long-term bondholders also bear losses while minimizing the risk that short-term creditors like depositors will run.

There has been controversy and public backlash against the treatment of senior management. Insofar as they hold stock in the firms they manage, senior managers suffer the same fate as other shareholders. Some lose their jobs, but some do not; some lose their bonuses, but some do not. Until recently, in the United States, very few senior managers were punished further, and high-profile criminal charges against senior individuals have been dropped. To many, the consequences for those in power at the time of the Financial Crisis appear random. Recall the discussion of executive compensation in Chapter 8.1 and of enforcement in Chapter 8.2.

The reason why some financial conglomerates are perceived as too big to fail is not solely that these firms are too *big*, measured by their size alone, but because they are too *interconnected* to fail without the risk of either triggering a contagious panic or creating negative externalities for the market. Recall our discussion in Chapters 2.4 and 9.2 of the Banking Panic of 1933. Fearful short-term creditors (such as depositors and repurchase transaction counterparties), lacking sufficient information to confidently assess the solvency of each individual firm. Recall the discussion of the prisoner's dilemma in Chapter 2.4;

once a sufficient number of short-term creditors start withdrawing cash from a particular firm, the only rational response of the remaining creditors is to make similar withdrawal requests, even if the firm is indisputably solvent. The concerns of short-term creditors about the *micro*prudential stability of specific firms escalate into concerns about *macro*prudential, systemic stability. As short-term creditors withdrew cash (or refused to roll over short-term credit) from a broad group of firms they feared might be unsound, the individual firms and the financial system as a whole became unsound.

Systemic risk also arises when a firm is so interconnected with others through financial markets, through the payments system, or through counterparty relations with one another, that its failure would not only inflict direct losses on those that have a direct relationship with it (such as its shareholders, depositors and derivatives counterparties) but would also result in uncertainty crippling enough to inflict losses—negative externalities—across the financial system and the economy as a whole. As the Financial Crisis made painfully clear, some financial conglomerates are large and complex enough that microprudential concerns about their stability have macroprudential implications.

A. THE SPREAD OF CONTAGION FROM LEHMAN BROTHERS'S BANKRUPTCY

The petition filed by Lehman Brothers Holdings, Inc. for protection under Chapter 11 of the Bankruptcy Code at around 1 a.m. on Monday, September 15, 2008, in an eerie echo of the timing of the 1933 Franklin D. Roosevelt bank holiday, which also began at 1 a.m. on a Monday after a frantic weekend, began what remains the largest bankruptcy in the history of the United States. Lehman Brothers was not a BHC but the holding company for a broker-dealer, reporting approximately $639 billion in assets on its final SEC quarterly report as of May 31, 2008. Its business consisted of underwriting, making markets in securities, and other investment banking activities, rather than traditional banking activities like taking deposits and making loans. Nevertheless, the destabilizing uncertainty that seized global financial markets in the aftermath of Lehman Brothers's bankruptcy marked the nadir of the Financial Crisis. Minimizing the likelihood that a disorderly bankruptcy like Lehman Brothers's will ever be repeated is the goal of the resolution reforms discussed in this Chapter.

Why was Lehman Brothers's failure so devastating? The direct losses imposed on Lehman Brothers's creditors were not the primary reason. Although the bankruptcy court described the process as "a 'Herculean achievement' five hard-fought years in the making," Lehman Brothers's customers and secured creditors predictably received a 100% recovery on their claims, and potential losses on an estimated $150-250 billion in claims brought by unsecured creditors of Lehman Brothers's parent company and its various subsidiaries "would likely have been perceived as manageable . . . even if these third-party creditors had assumed that they would recover nothing." Hal S. Scott, *Interconnectedness and Contagion* (Comm. on Cap. Mkts. Regs., Working Paper, Nov. 20, 2012). By September 2015, general unsecured creditors of Lehman Brothers's parent company had recovered $5.7 billion, or 27%, of their allowed claims. *See*

Trustee's Twelfth Interim Report, *In re* Lehman Brothers Inc., No. 08-01420 (SCC) SIPA (Bankr. S.D.N.Y. 2015). Rather, Lehman Brothers's failure was so devastating because it sent contagious uncertainty throughout an already fragile financial system.

The first channel of contagion was Lehman Brothers's impact on short-term wholesale funding. Many financial intermediaries, broker-dealers in particular, relied heavily on short-term financing from repurchase transactions and commercial paper sold and rolled over as it matured. We will study changes in wholesale funding markets in Chapter 12.4. On September 18, 2008, the Reserve Primary Fund, a money market mutual fund (MMF) that held $785 million of Lehman Brothers's commercial paper, broke the buck, triggering a run on the $3.8 trillion MMF sector. MMFs began unloading their short-term assets *en masse*, seeking to meet investors' demands to redeem their securities and eschewing risk in a flight to safety. The resulting strain depressed prices for what had, until then, been seen as high-quality short-term assets and sharply curtailed other financial intermediaries' access to liquidity. We will study changes in the regulation of MMFs in Chapter 12.3. A second, closely intertwined channel of contagion was Lehman Brothers's complex derivatives portfolio. Derivatives counterparties became uncertain whether outstanding contracts with Lehman Brothers affiliates would be honored and how much exposure their other counterparties had to Lehman Brothers's failure. Cross-default clauses and operational failures acted as an accelerant. As a result of this uncertainty, financial intermediaries began to demand significantly higher levels of margin and collateral from other counterparties, exacerbating the spread of contagion. This crippling uncertainty and the concomitant evaporation of liquidity threatened to bring financial intermediation in all forms to a grinding halt. We will study changes to the treatment of derivatives in resolution under the 2015 ISDA Universal Resolution Stay Protocol later in this Chapter and, their regulation more generally, in Part XI. After the federal government bailed AIG out on the day after Lehman Brothers's failure, Congressman Barney Frank quipped:

> "The national commitment to the free market lasted one day. . . . It was Monday."

Barney Frank Celebrates Free Market Day, WALL ST. J., Sept. 17, 2008.

Lehman Brothers's highly leveraged business model, its reliance on access to short-term funds that were prone to runs, its overinvestment in what had become hard-to-value mortgage-backed security and the failure of its management to recognize the peril they faced all contributed to its failure. Looking ahead to the next financial crisis, however, the facts most likely to inform critical policy decisions involving the next distressed financial conglomerate will not concern the idiosyncratic failures of Lehman Brothers's management, but the lack of tools that prevented regulators from arranging an orderly resolution.

We will leave to historians the judgment as to why Lehman Brothers was permitted to fail and whether the decision was right or wrong. As stated in the Report prepared by bankruptcy court-appointed Examiner Anton Valukas, Hank Paulson, who was Secretary of the Treasury at the time of Lehman Brothers's failure, "concluded that the Federal Government lacked authority to inject capital into Lehman Brothers, even via an 'exigent circumstances' loan [under § 13(3)] from the Federal Reserve, because Lehman Brothers was not an institution 'perceived to have capital and able to provide a guarantee.'" Anton R. Valukas, *Examiner's Report: Bankruptcy of Lehman Brothers Holdings Inc.*, No. 08-13555 (JMP) at 12 n.45 (Bankr. S.D.N.Y. 2010). Ben Bernanke, then Chairman of the Board of Governors of the Federal Reserve, states this conclusion even more explicitly: "I do not want the notion that Lehman Brothers's failure could have been avoided, and that its failure was consequently a policy choice, to become the received wisdom, for the simple reason that it is not true. We did everything we could think of to avoid it." BEN S. BERNANKE, THE COURAGE TO ACT: A MEMOIR OF A CRISIS AND ITS AFTERMATH 291 (2015). Not everyone agrees, of course. Professor Eric Posner argues that Lehman Brothers's major problem was illiquidity rather than insolvency and that its assets were adequate collateral under § 13(3)'s permissive standard, which required only that emergency loans be "secured to the satisfaction of" the Federal Reserve Board. Eric Posner, *Bernanke's Biggest Blunder*, SLATE, Oct. 29, 2015. For an excellent analysis of the Lehman Brothers bankruptcy, see Emily Kapur, *The Next Lehman Bankruptcy*, *in* MAKING FAILURE FEASIBLE: HOW BANKRUPTCY REFORM CAN END "TOO BIG TO FAIL" 175–242 (Kenneth E. Scott, Thomas H. Jackson & John B. Taylor, eds., 2015).

B. EXPANSION OF THE REGULATORY TOOLKIT

In the words of Timothy Geithner, President of the Federal Reserve Bank of New York when Lehman Brothers failed and, later, Paulson's successor as Secretary of the Treasury during the Obama Administration, crises force public officials to stare "into the abyss." TIMOTHY GEITHNER, STRESS TEST: REFLECTIONS ON FINANCIAL CRISES 208 (2014). They face a Hobson's choice between adherence to the ideal of free market discipline and the real-world imperative to avert the possibility of an unhinged financial meltdown destroying the savings and livelihoods of millions of living, breathing men and women. After the Financial Crisis, broad consensus emerged among the public officials who faced hard decisions in strong support of creating a new resolution system for financial conglomerates. As we shall see, however, not everyone agreed on what the new system should look like.

In June 2009, the Obama Administration released a white paper and draft legislation proposing a broad range of financial reforms. This proposal contained a new resolution authority for most non-bank financial companies—which ultimately became the OLA under Title II of the Dodd-Frank Act at the end of a long and contentious legislative process—and was passed by the House of Representatives in December 2009 with no Republican votes. The changes made in the House to the resolution authority set out in the original Obama Administration proposal presaged disputes that arose later as the new resolution powers were discussed in the Senate. Whereas the Administration's proposal authorized appointment of the FDIC either as conservator or receiver, the House's engrossed bill allowed only for the FDIC to be appointed as receiver due to concerns that a conservator-like appointment would lead to long-term government ownership of a failed institution. Recall that, at the time, Fannie Mae and Freddie Mac had already been placed into conservatorship under a different statute and that they remain in conservatorship. We will discuss them in Chapter 12.2.

As Timothy Geithner was often quoted as saying during the Financial Crisis, "Plan beats no plan." *See* TIMOTHY GEITHNER, STRESS TEST: REFLECTIONS ON FINANCIAL CRISES 292 (2014). Title I of the Dodd-Frank Act also requires any BHC with more than $50 billion in assets and any non-bank company designated as systemic by the Financial Stability Oversight Council (FSOC) to file an annual resolution plan presenting its strategy for rapid and orderly resolution under the U.S. Bankruptcy Code without extraordinary government support. The resolution plans (often called living wills) that these companies must file under Title I of the Dodd-Frank Act are a complement to, rather than a substitute for, the new resolution regime established under Title II. In the political process that shaped Title II, its proponents emphasized its status as an extraordinary authority to be invoked only at the gravest moments of market distress, with the Bankruptcy Code remaining both the conventional touchstone and the sole resolution regime applicable to Title I resolution plans. In light of the panic caused by the Lehman Brothers bankruptcy, why did the proponents of the alternative Title II mechanism emphasize that bankruptcy, not Title II, should be the default mechanism?

The text of the House bill was set aside in favor of the bill passed by the Senate, which was adopted by the House and Senate Conference Committee as its base text and ultimately signed into law. The Senate bill largely retained the core elements of the House bill, with some changes to align the new resolution regime more closely with the Bankruptcy Code. Despite the fact that ultimate passage of the Dodd-Frank Act occurred largely upon party lines in the Senate, with only 3 Republicans joining 57 Democrats, at many points along the way, Chairman Dodd reached out to Republicans to seek bipartisan compromise. One of the most successful of such efforts related to Title II of the bill, containing the resolution authority. Chairman Dodd and Ranking Member Shelby worked together with the Administration on the provisions, and 90 Senators voted for the amendment. Key features of Title II reflect these compromises To get needed votes, the label placed on the new resolution authority was changed from the "Enhanced Resolution Authority," as it was denominated when introduced by Senator Dodd, to the "Orderly Liquidation Authority," or OLA, as Title II is known today. Nothing in the body of the text, however, required immediate liquidation, which traditionally would mean that all operations cease upon the appointment of the receiver. Indeed, the text expressly authorizes the FDIC to transfer all or any portion of a failed company's assets to a bridge financial company before liquidating the failed company. The text also gave the FDIC the authority to operate the bridge financial company as a going concern and either wind it down in an orderly way or convert it into an ordinary company by selling its shares to a third party (including to the market in a public offering), as long as it distributed the residual value of the bridge financial company to the creditors of the failed company in satisfaction of their claims. The OLA raises a number of policy issues that remain the subject of ongoing debate, which we will discuss below.

C. THE EU EXPERIENCE

As in the United States, the Financial Crisis forced national authorities in the EU to provide emergency support to distressed financial conglomerates. Although the actions taken *in extremis* by EU member states and the United States are similar, political and cultural differences can be discerned in the variations that emerged. Unlike the United States, EU member states generally did not have bank-specific insolvency regimes with longstanding historical roots nor such a deeply ingrained aversion to government intervention in financial markets. As a result, the support provided to many EU financial conglomerates during the Financial Crisis was explicitly characterized as nationalization. The UK, for example, lacked a bank resolution regime until February 2009, when the Banking Act was adopted largely in response to the failure of Northern Rock:

> The drawbacks of exclusive reliance on corporate insolvency law were demonstrated as the Northern Rock (NR) crisis unfolded from mid-2007. Without [a special resolution regime], the authorities could not take control of NR away from its shareholders and senior management while the bank was still balance sheet solvent. The result was that an early resolution of NR's problems proved to be impossible. . . Had the authorities been able to have placed NR into [a special resolution regime] at an earlier stage, when more of its value remained, it is possible that part or all of the bank would have been sold to a private sector buyer. This would have avoided the need to impose additional potential losses on the taxpayer by having to nationalise the bank.

Peter Brierly, *The UK Special Resolution Regime for Failing Banks in an International Context* 4 (Bank of England, Financial Stability Paper No. 5, 2009).

The Financial Crisis exposed the need not only for more effective tools but also for more effective coordination among national authorities in a banking system that was, commercially, closely integrated, but, from a regulatory perspective, highly fragmented. As the European Commission stated in 2014:

> The high profile national and cross-border bank failures in the last few years. . . revealed serious shortcomings in the existing tools available to authorities for preventing or tackling failures of systemic banks, those that are intrinsically linked to the wider economy and play a central role in the financial markets. The ability of governments to support banks which are too big to fail with squeezed public finances is becoming increasingly unsustainable. . . .
>
> Until the crisis, many felt that bank failures could be dealt with at a national level. . . . However, the crisis proved that these proceedings would lead to the disorderly failure of some banks with potentially disastrous wider consequences. [A] number of Member States adopted measures to ensure the stability of their financial markets. These measures varied greatly between Member States. [] The crisis also highlighted the lack of arrangements to deal effectively with failing banks that operated in more than one Member State.

European Commission, EU Bank Recovery and Resolution Directive (BRRD): Frequently Asked Questions (April 15, 2014). The Bank Recovery and Resolution Directive (BRRD), discussed later in this Chapter, is the centerpiece of post-Financial Crisis reforms in the EU. In addition to cultural differences, there is an impediment in the United States to the federal government taking an equity interest in any private company without explicit Congressional approval. *See* 31 U.S.C. § 9102; *see also* Youngstown Sheet & Tube Co. v. Sawyer, 343 U.S. 579 (1952). Of course, the EU did impose state aid restrictions as an antitrust matter on the nationalizations.

III. THE ORDERLY LIQUIDATION AUTHORITY

The OLA is loosely based on the traditional bank resolution regime we studied in Chapter 9.2, but could potentially be invoked for any "financial company," a term that is broadly defined but excludes insured depository institutions and certain other companies, under a process initiated by three keys: two-thirds each of the Board of Governors of the Federal Reserve System and the Board of Directors of the FDIC must approve a written recommendation to the Secretary of the Treasury. In consultation with the President, the Secretary may then initiate an OLA proceeding upon reaching a determination that certain statutory criteria of systemic risk are satisfied. Title II's criteria for systemic risk determinations include:

(1) a financial company is in default or in danger of default;

(2) its failure and resolution under otherwise applicable law (*e.g.*, the Bankruptcy Code) would have serious adverse effects on financial stability in the United States;

(3) no viable private sector alternative is available to prevent its default;

(4) any adverse effect on the interests of creditors, counterparties, and shareholders of the financial company and other market participants would be appropriate in light of the benefits to financial stability; and

(5) exercising the OLA would avoid or mitigate potential adverse effects on the financial system, the cost to the U.S. Treasury, and the potential to increase moral hazard.

Unless a financial company's board of directors consents, the Secretary must petition the U.S. District Court for the District of Columbia for an order to appoint the FDIC as its receiver. The legal proceedings that follow would be confidential and highly extraordinary. The financial company must receive notice of the hearing and have an opportunity to oppose the Secretary's systemic risk determination, and the District Court must either rule that the determination was "arbitrary and capricious" or issue the petition, all within 24 hours of filing. It is expected, however, that most boards of directors would consent.

A. THE BRIDGE FINANCIAL COMPANY

As in receivership proceedings for a failed bank, upon appointment the FDIC shall succeed to "all rights, titles, powers, and privileges of the covered financial company and its assets, and of any stockholder, member, officer, or director" of the financial company. 12 U.S.C. § 5390(a)(1)(A)(i). In a notable parallel to the discussion in Chapter 9.2 of how the historical understanding of the role of the receiver evolved during the 20th Century, and despite the denomination of Title II as the Orderly "Liquidation" Authority, it is not expected that the FDIC would immediately adopt a course of action focused on wiping a large, complex financial conglomerate out of existence. Such a course of action would likely repeat the panic and contagion caused by Lehman Brothers's disorderly bankruptcy; it would also be inconsistent with the fifth condition for invoking Title II because it would not "avoid or mitigate" the potential adverse effects of allowing the firm to be resolved under the Bankruptcy Code. The FDIC's immediate focus would instead be to ensure the continuity of operations critical to the economy, such as payments processing and other activities that give rise to interconnectedness. The FDIC has issued notice of its intention to use an SPOE strategy, discussed later in this Chapter. In an SPOE resolution, the failed financial company's operating subsidiaries (such as banks, broker-dealers, and insurance companies) would continue their operations throughout the resolution process, but as subsidiaries of a newly recapitalized bridge company. If one of these operating companies did fail, its resolution would be conducted separately.

The FDIC is required to identify and remove senior executives and directors of the financial company considered responsible for its failure, and would attempt to claw back their compensation, and potentially impose additional restrictions. The FDIC would manage the bridge financial company's operations for a limited period, like a bridge bank created under the Federal Deposit Insurance Act (FDIA), for up to two years with three possible one-year extensions, subject to a statutory duty to maximize the value of the failed financial company and minimize losses for the benefit of its stakeholders, many of whom would at that point be claimants of the receivership. *See* Resolution of Systemically Important Financial Institutions: The Single Point of Entry Strategy, 78 Fed. Reg. 76,614 (Dec. 18, 2013) [hereinafter, FDIC SPOE Notice].

While the bridge financial company is in existence, the FDIC must prepare a restructuring plan (likely based on the failed company's pre-existing living will) so that, when it eventually emerges from the resolution process as a much smaller entity, it is in sound financial condition and resolvable under the Bankruptcy Code without the risk of serious adverse effects on the financial stability of the United States. The restructuring plan must provide for remediation of the deficiencies in management, policies and practices that led to the financial company's failure. It must also set out a value-maximizing business plan, including asset disposition strategies, that meets any capital, funding, liquidity and mandatory repayment requirements imposed by regulatory authorities. It is expected that any financial conglomerate resolved through a Title II process would be at least partially dismantled, so that the organization which emerges would be much smaller and would pursue a different, narrower business model.

To execute an orderly resolution, a bridge financial company must have access to sufficient funding to continue its day-to-day operations. As discussed in Chapter 9.2, when the FDIC establishes a bridge bank under the FDIA, it may provide the bridge bank liquidity from the Deposit Insurance Fund (DIF) to facilitate its resolution, subject to the least cost test under the FDIA. Under Title II, with the failed financial company's troubled assets and loss-absorbing liabilities left behind in a receivership, the FDIC "expects the bridge financial company and its subsidiaries to be in a position to borrow from customary sources in the private markets in order to meet liquidity needs." FDIC SPOE Notice, 78 Fed. Reg. at 76,617. If customary sources of market funding are inaccessible or insufficient, however, Title II gives the FDIC authority to provide guarantees or advances from the Orderly Liquidation Fund for a transitional period until the bridge financial company can be stabilized and its access to market funding restored.

In contrast to earlier proposals, the Orderly Liquidation Fund created by Title II is not a fund so much as a line of credit. The FDIC may obtain financing for resolution costs by issuing debt securities to (*i.e.*, borrowing from) the U.S. Treasury, that is, borrowing from the U.S. taxpayer. Orderly Liquidation Fund borrowing is capped at 90% of the fair value of the financial company's total consolidated assets available for repayment, as determined by the FDIC. Unlike Troubled Asset Relief Program (TARP) funding, for which repayment was not mandatory, all Orderly Liquidation Fund borrowing must be repaid through assessments on, first, claimants on the financial company's receivership to the extent they were paid in excess of what they would have received if the financial company had been liquidated in bankruptcy, or, second, on financial companies with more $50 billion in assets, with assessments to be levied based on a risk matrix that reflects their relative size and riskiness. It is this ability of the FDIC to call upon Treasury funds for liquidity that has led some to view Title II as enshrining bailouts. Those who believe that temporary liquidity that would be repaid by asset sales or by large players in the financial sector is not like a TARP equity or capital infusion disagree. The FDIC has stated that it will only use the Orderly Liquidation Fund to provide liquidity on a fully secured basis, 78 Fed. Reg. at 76,616, but that limitation is not hardwired into the statute. Would it have been better if Title II required that the loans to the bridge financial company be secured like § 13(3)? Should the loans from the Treasury to the FDIC be secured?

---

1. **Ex Ante *Versus* Ex Post *Funding for the Orderly Liquidation Fund*.** The original House proposal called for an Orderly Liquidation Fund, like the DIF, to be funded on an *ex ante* basis by an assessment on financial conglomerates above a certain size. In the Senate, the provision for *ex ante* pre-funding was replaced with a mechanism for funding an OLA resolution through borrowing from the U.S. Treasury to be recouped by assessments on financial conglomerates above certain size thresholds.

Criticizing the decision to strip pre-funding from the final legislation, Professor Jeff Gordon argues:

> Resolution funds will be borrowed from the Treasury and, ultimately, the taxpayers. Politically, this will likely register as a taxpayer "bailout," notwithstanding the strong repayment mandate. The Treasury (read: taxpayer) funding comes up front, when the public is in a politically "hot" state. Repayment comes later. As with TARP, repayment of most of the outlays will not change the public's initial impressions. Regulators will therefore be hesitant to go this route and are likely to delay putting a troubled financial firm into receivership. Instead, they may engage in various forms of regulatory forbearance and nonemergency Fed discount window lending in the hopes of avoiding a firm's insolvency. . . . The lack of pre-funding will therefore have systemic consequences. By the time regulators put a failing firm into receivership, the particular firm will be in a greater loss position, potentially enhancing contagion effects. The pursuit of ultimately unsustainable risk-taking, prolonged in part by regulatory forbearance, may render the entire financial sector less stable.

Jeffrey N. Gordon & Christopher Muller, *Confronting Financial Crisis: Dodd-Frank's Dangers and the Case for a Systemic Emergency Insurance Fund*, 28 YALE J. ON REG. 151, 193–94 (2010).

Other proponents of an *ex ante* arrangement argued that it would also allow the Orderly Liquidation Fund to be funded through assessments levied during the good years preceding a financial conglomerate's failure rather than the downturn likely to follow. This argument has previously been applied to the FDIC's assessments on banks to fund the DIF: "[H]igher premiums can be charged during the good times to avoid large premium increases during the bad times. Bankers will have greater stability in their premium payments. Consumers and businesses will have one less factor contributing to credit booms and busts. Everyone should benefit." JOHN F. BOVENZI, INSIDE THE FDIC 72–77 (2015). The similar fund in the EU is pre-funded. *See* Press Release, Council of the European Union, Single Resolution Fund: Council Agrees on Bank Contributions (Dec. 9, 2014).

The opponents of *ex ante* funding viewed the political price associated with Treasury borrowing as a beneficial measure of public accountability. They feared that establishment of a readily accessible Orderly Liquidation Fund would encourage expectations of government intervention and disrupt the functioning of an efficient market. Opponents also argued that assessments on financial conglomerates to pre-fund the Orderly Liquidation Fund would constitute a tax on all financial conglomerates, conferring disproportionate benefits on the failed financial conglomerate granted access to the Orderly Liquidation Fund to the detriment of its more prudently managed competitors. There was also some concern that the fund could be diverted for unintended purposes. In light of the diversion of funds from the Federal Reserve System's capital surplus account and dividends to fund highway spending in December 2015, that concern may not have been unrealistic.

B. THE ORDERLY LIQUIDATION AUTHORITY RECEIVERSHIP

The Bankruptcy Code governs virtually all insolvencies in the United States and therefore sets the benchmark for expectations regarding the treatment of a failed firm's creditors. Although Title II provides the FDIC many of the super powers it may exercise in bank resolutions under the FDIA, discussed in Chapter 9.2, the OLA seeks to align the rights of claimants in an OLA receivership more closely with those of creditors in a bankruptcy proceeding. Accordingly, the FDIC's role in the administration of the claims of a failed financial company's creditors and other stakeholders under the OLA diverges somewhat from its role under bank resolution provisions of the FDIA.

Most importantly, every creditor of a failed financial company is expressly entitled to recover at least as much under the OLA as it would have received if the company had been liquidated in bankruptcy proceedings, a provision often referred to as the no creditor worse off rule. Among other provisions intended to harmonize the OLA with the Bankruptcy Code, Title II does not include a depositor preference rule, sets a lower bar for the enforceability of agreements, and allows the FDIC to void a legally enforceable or perfected security interest "taken in contemplation of the company's insolvency" under narrower circumstances than the FDIA, only if the security interest would constitute a fraudulent or preferential transfer under the Bankruptcy Code.

Subject to creditors' minimum recovery rights, and in a large departure from the Bankruptcy Code, the FDIC may still treat similarly situated creditors differently, such as by cherry-picking among the liabilities transferred to a bridge financial company. The FDIC may also enforce contracts, even if doing so requires it to override *ipso facto* clauses (*e.g.*, allowing a counterparty to terminate a contract with the financial company as a result of its insolvency) or cross-default provisions (*e.g.*, allowing a counterparty to terminate an agreement with one of the failed financial company's subsidiaries because of the parent's insolvency). The FDIC may also repudiate contracts it determines are "burdensome" within a reasonable period. 12 U.S.C. § 5390(c)(1).

Qualified financial contracts (QFCs), such as derivatives, repurchase transactions, and securities loans, are subject to the same treatment under Title II as under the FDIA. The Bankruptcy Code provides special treatment for QFCs by exempting them from the automatic stay, which would otherwise protect a bankruptcy petitioner from creditors exercising their rights to seize collateral or take similar adverse action. In contrast to the Bankruptcy Code, Title II, like the FDIA, eliminates QFCs' exemption from the FDIC's authority to enforce contracts despite *ipso facto* clauses for one business day. During this period, which is typically understood to include a weekend, the FDIC can transfer QFCs to a bridge financial company or another solvent counterparty, thereby nullifying the QFC counterparty's early termination rights. The FDIC may also cherry-pick among QFCs, but only on a counterparty-by-counterparty basis and not on a contract-by-contract basis, meaning that each of the failed financial company's QFC counterparties will find that the transfer affects either all of their QFCs or none. Some commentators believe that the preferential treatment of QFCs encourages their use; in their view, QFCs should be penalized *ex post* in order to reduce their use. *See* David A. Skeel Jr., *The New Synthesis of*

Bank Regulation and Bankruptcy in the Dodd-Frank Era (U. Pa. L.: Legal Scholarship Repository, Working Paper No. 1564, 2015). Other commentators believe that penalizing QFCs *ex post* would be destabilizing; they propose that QFCs be taxed *ex ante* to reduce their use. *See* Michael S. Barr, *The Financial Crisis and the Path of Reform*, 29 YALE J. ON REG. 91, 106 (2012).

C. LIVING WILLS

The OLA filled one conspicuous gap among the "makeshift tools" in the regulatory toolkit as of 2008 by creating an after-the-failure resolution mechanism. *See* BEN S. BERNANKE, THE COURAGE TO ACT: A MEMOIR OF A CRISIS AND ITS AFTERMATH, at 291. Nevertheless, in the commonly drawn analogy between systemic risk regulation and fire-fighting, both the OLA and the Federal Reserve Board's authority to establish emergency liquidity programs in "unusual and exigent circumstances" represent bigger, better fire hoses. Extending this metaphor, systemic regulation, especially enhanced capital and liquidity requirements, is the fire safety code designed to prevent financial conglomerates from going up in flames in the first place. Under § 165(d) of the Dodd-Frank Act and related regulations jointly promulgated by the FDIC and the Federal Reserve Board, BHCs and non-bank companies designated as systemic by the FSOC (living will filers) must annually prepare and submit resolution plans to these agencies. *See* 12 C.F.R. pts. 243 and 381. Resolution plans, like fire escape plans, seek to minimize the potential for damage if other elements of systemic risk regulation cannot prevent a financial conglomerate's failure.

With some differences based on the size of each living will filer, a resolution plan must provide detailed information on its structure and operations and present strategies for conducting a rapid and orderly resolution of its operations under the Bankruptcy Code in a hypothetical failure scenario. This information must cover any "critical operation" that would pose a threat to the financial stability of the United States if disrupted, any "core business line" that would materially impair the living will filer's revenue, profit, or franchise value if it failed, and any "material entity" that is significant to a critical operation or core business line. 12 C.F.R. §§ 243.4, 381.4. Failure scenarios and resolution strategies must reflect specific assumptions prescribed by the FDIC and Federal Reserve Board, which include a prohibition on relying on "extraordinary support" to prevent the failure of the company or any of its subsidiaries. 12 C.F.R. §§ 243.4(a)(4)(ii), 381.4(a)(4)(ii). Each resolution plan must also provide information of a more practical nature, such as describing a living will filer's organizational structure, critical back-office functions, management information systems, and personnel. 12 C.F.R. §§ 243.4(e), 381.4(e). Although brief, high-level summaries are made publicly available on the Federal Reserve and FDIC websites, the confidential portions of a resolution plan may be thousands of pages long.

The Federal Reserve Board and the FDIC jointly review each resolution plan and determine whether it "is not credible or would not facilitate an orderly resolution." 12 C.F.R. §§ 243.5, 381.5. If a resolution plan does not meet this standard, the Federal Reserve Board and FDIC must provide written notice of the deficiencies they have identified. The living will filer would then have at least 90 days to address these deficiencies and submit a revised resolution plan.

12 C.F.R. §§ 243.5, 381.5. If it fails to do so, or if its revised resolution plan remains deficient, the Federal Reserve Board and FDIC may subject it to more stringent capital, leverage, or liquidity requirements and impose restrictions on its growth, activities, or operations. 12 C.F.R. §§ 243.6, 381.6. If a living will filer fails to remedy identified deficiencies for more than two years after the Federal Reserve Board and FDIC have imposed heightened requirements of this sort, these agencies (after consultation with other FSOC member agencies) may ultimately dismantle it through forced divestitures of its assets or operations. We discussed some of these break-up options in Chapter 6.2.

Separately from § 165(d) of the Dodd-Frank Act, the FDIC requires insured depository institutions with more than $50 billion in assets to submit resolution plans under the FDIA, but many living will filers submit a single resolution plan in response to both sets of requirements. *See* 12 C.F.R. § 360.10; *see also* FDIC, Guidance for Covered Insured Depository Institution Resolution Plan Submissions (Dec 17, 2014). Section 165(d) resolution plans complement Title II by mandating the periodic collection and synthesis of information that enables the FDIC to prepare and, should the occasion arise, to exercise the OLA to resolve a living will filer.

Most importantly, § 165(d)'s resolution planning requirements interlock with the OLA provisions of Title II to advance a common underlying purpose. The submission of a resolution plan is only one component of the broader, iterative endeavor of making complex financial institutions "safe to fail." *See* THOMAS F. HUERTAS, SAFE TO FAIL: HOW RESOLUTION WILL REVOLUTIONISE BANKING (2014). Resolution plans are meant to be more than words on paper; the regulators have issued guidance requiring that resolution planning involve changes to a living will filer's structure and operations to make an orderly resolution more feasible. In 2014, the Federal Reserve Board and FDIC identified shortcomings in the resolution plans filed by eleven financial conglomerates—the eight domestic and three foreign financial conglomerates whose U.S. operations are most extensive—requiring them, *inter alia*, to: establish more rational, less complex organizational structures; adopt measures to ensure the continuity of services supporting their critical operations and core business lines; and demonstrate operational capabilities for resolution preparedness, such as the ability to produce reliable information in a timely manner. Joint Press Release, Federal Reserve and FDIC, Agencies Provide Feedback on Second Round Resolution Plans of "First-Wave" Filers (Aug. 5, 2014). The FDIC went further and deemed all eleven plans not credible. Two Federal Reserve Board supervisory letters also require that certain living wills filers incorporate resolution planning into their business as usual operations. *See* Fed. Reserve Bd., Supervision Letter, Consolidated Supervision Framework for Large Financial Institutions, SR 12-17 (Dec. 17, 2012); Fed. Reserve Bd., Supervision Letter, Heightened Supervisory Expectations for Recovery and Resolution Preparedness for Certain Large Bank Holding Companies—Supplemental Guidance on Consolidated Supervision Framework for Large Financial Institutions, SR 14-1 (Jan. 24, 2014).

In addition to identifying deficiencies in resolution plans, the FDIC and the Federal Reserve Board have also acknowledged that meaningful progress to enhance financial conglomerates' resolvability also depends on the finalization of

TLAC regulations and the broad adoption of the 2015 ISDA Universal Resolution Stay Protocol, both of which are discussed later in this Chapter. In one sign of progress in this area, credit rating agencies have eliminated the uplift previously granted to debt securities issued by the largest financial conglomerates based on an expectation of government support.

IV. SINGLE POINT OF ENTRY

After the passage of the Dodd-Frank Act in the United States and comparable reforms in Europe, policy-makers' focus turned towards the operational aspects of how new resolution authorities and techniques would be employed. Early efforts reflected widespread agreement that an orderly resolution would require international cooperation between the regulators in a financial conglomerate's home country and those in other jurisdictions with authority over segments of its global operations. In October 2011, the Financial Stability Board (FSB) published the "Key Attributes of Effective Resolution Regimes for Financial Institutions" with the goal of establishing international standards to promote consistency across reforms adopted at a national level. FSB, Key Attributes of Effective Resolution Regimes for Financial Institutions (2011). Further collaboration among policy-makers and thinkers in the public and private sectors built on the FSB's Key Attributes, leading to the development of the SPOE resolution strategy, which remains central to ongoing developments in regulatory reform.

A *single* point of entry resolution differs from a *multiple* point of entry resolution in that only one entity, the top level holding company within a financial conglomerate, is placed into resolution proceedings. The FDIC outlined the use of an SPOE strategy to resolve a financial conglomerate in a joint paper published with the Bank of England in 2012, further describing the process of an SPOE resolution under the OLA in a notice and request for comment published in 2013. *See* FDIC & Bank of England, Resolving Globally Active, Systemically Important, Financial Institutions (Dec. 10, 2012); FDIC SPOE Notice. For a step-by-step illustration of how an SPOE resolution would work, see TOO BIG TO FAIL: THE PATH TO A SOLUTION, A REPORT OF THE FAILURE RESOLUTION TASK FORCE OF THE FIN. REGULATORY REFORM INITIATIVE OF THE BIPARTISAN POL'Y CTR. 23-30 (2013).

At the commencement of an SPOE resolution of a U.S. financial company under the OLA, ownership of its operating subsidiaries and other assets are transferred to a newly created bridge financial company. Its liabilities are largely left behind in the receivership, and creditors submit corresponding claims to the FDIC. This transfer of the failed firm's assets to the bridge financial company, while leaving the claims of the failed firm's shareholders and creditors behind in the receivership, effectively recapitalizes the business transferred to the bridge financial company by forcing the failed company's shareholders and creditors to bear any losses. The equity securities of the bridge financial company, once it has been stabilized, would be distributed to such claimants in accordance with the priority of their claims in satisfaction of their claims. This process of distributing equity in the bridge financial company in satisfaction of debt claims against the failed company is known as a bail-in of the debt claims.

In the meantime, the bridge financial company could use its new capital to support the transferred operating subsidiaries, allowing them to remain solvent and maintain operational continuity. The bridge financial company could also access additional funding from the Orderly Liquidation Fund as needed to stabilize its operations. It would develop and execute a restructuring plan, which would include selling some good assets to obtain cash and selling assets of lower quality to improve its financial condition. Ultimately, the bridge financial company would return to the market as a much smaller, healthier entity owned primarily by claimants on the failed company's receivership. The FDIC expects that this process, beginning with the financial company's entry into receivership and concluding with the securities-for-claims exchange, could be completed in six to nine months. *See* FDIC SPOE Notice.

For many, the SPOE strategy presents an elegant solution to two major obstacles that made an orderly resolution of a failed financial conglomerate impossible in 2008. The first is the lack of cross-border cooperation among national authorities in different jurisdictions. When a financial conglomerate with global operations fails, regulators in every jurisdiction where its assets are held have an incentive to ring-fence these assets, protecting the interests of local creditors at the expense of creditors in other jurisdictions, even if doing so disproportionately raises the total costs of the financial conglomerate's failure by resulting in a disorderly resolution. By preventing a failed company's operating subsidiaries from failing along with their corporate parent, an SPOE resolution is designed to negate this incentive.

Second, an SPOE resolution aims to slice the Gordian knot of a financial conglomerate's operational complexity. The resolution process should not disrupt payment processing, custody, or other services integral to the economy. Many clients rely on these services for fundamental needs like meeting payrolls, paying suppliers, and keeping their assets safe; some have complex relationships that would take weeks to reconstruct with another service provider. Simultaneously, settlement procedures for hundreds of thousands of transactions pending in multiple time zones must be completed. Critical data hosted in faraway data centers must be accessed. Paperwork must be processed and organized. Phones and computers must keep working. The lights must stay on. In this multilayered web of functional relationships, preserving the day-to-day continuity of a financial conglomerate's systemically important operations may depend not only on its largest subsidiaries but also on back-office service companies scattered across the globe. An SPOE strategy is designed to minimize the potential threat to orderly resolution posed by a disruption in critical services whose smooth functioning is normally taken for granted. Others have more critical views about an SPOE strategy, which we will discuss later in this Chapter.

---

1. ***The Source of Strength Doctrine***. The source of strength doctrine is a longstanding Federal Reserve Board policy, now codified in § 616 of the Dodd-Frank Act, that requires a BHC to provide support to its insured depository subsidiaries. The doctrine has its roots in supervisory orders issued by the Federal Reserve Board and was more fully articulated in a 1987 policy statement

adopting the view that a BHC's failure to provide financial support to a "troubled or failing subsidiary bank" when the BHC "is in a position to provide the support . . would generally be viewed as an unsafe and unsound banking practice." Policy Statement on the Responsibility of Bank Holding Companies to Act as Sources of Strength to Their Subsidiary Banks, 52 Fed. Reg. 15,707 (Apr. 30, 1987). Does SPOE expand the Federal Reserve Board's source of strength policy from insured depository institutions to all major subsidiaries?

V. TOTAL LOSS-ABSORBING CAPACITY

Among other important concepts, the FSB's Key Attributes included the power for resolution authorities to carry out a "bail-in within resolution." FSB, Key Attributes of Effective Resolution Regimes for Financial Institutions (2011). A bail-*in*, in contrast to a bail*out*, provides a mechanism for allocating the costs of a financial conglomerate's failure by imposing losses on its shareholders and creditors while minimizing or eliminating reliance on public funds. For an SPOE strategy to be feasible, a financial conglomerate must hold sufficient total loss-absorbing capacity at the level of its top-tier corporate parent to recapitalize its operating subsidiaries. This TLAC must consist of long-term unsecured debt and other liabilities in a form that could be expected to incur losses without triggering a contagious run.

In contrast to most European financial conglomerates, the top-tier corporate parent of every large U.S. financial conglomerate is a holding company without material operations of its own. SEC filings and other public financial reports disclose a holding company's balance sheet on a consolidated basis, which means it consolidates the assets and liabilities of a holding company with those of its subsidiaries so that investors can assess the company as a whole by viewing a single balance sheet. What a holding company actually *holds*, however, may be little more than equity in its operating subsidiaries, which are the banks, broker-dealers, and other entities that directly transact with customers and counterparties in the market. In contrast, a holding company does incur substantial liabilities because, as the public face of a financial conglomerate, it is the entity that issues equity and debt securities to obtain funding from capital markets for its subsidiaries' operations.

The use of TLAC in an SPOE resolution strategy takes advantage of structural subordination to mitigate run risk. Let us take a moment to unpack this concept. Run risk is the risk that the providers of funding—the creditors to whom a financial conglomerate's liabilities are owed—will flee, withdrawing liquidity and destroying the financial conglomerate's going-concern value before it can be stabilized. Some liabilities, like deposits, can be withdrawn immediately and therefore carry high run risk. Other liabilities, like long-term bonds, may not mature for years and therefore carry no run risk at all. Subordination refers to the priority of payments to creditors in insolvency proceedings. All of the claims of preferred creditors must be satisfied in full before any payment can be made to subordinated creditors. Stated inversely, subordinated creditors bear losses before preferred creditors. Subordination can be accomplished by contract; one class of creditors might agree to forego payments until preferred creditors are paid, often because they are willing to accept more risk in exchange for higher returns. Subordination can also be accomplished by placing liabilities at different levels within a corporate structure. This structural subordination is based on the principle that the creditors of a failed company have recourse to that company's assets, but not the assets of any other legal entity. In a financial conglomerate, if the holding company fails, its creditors may bear losses, but losses would not reach the creditors of an operating subsidiary until the holding company's creditors have been wiped out entirely. By virtue of this structural subordination, the creditors who are most likely to run (*e.g.*, uninsured depositors of a bank subsidiary) can be insulated by requiring losses to be borne first by creditors who cannot run (*e.g.*, investors holding long-term bonds issued by the holding company).

In October 2015, the Federal Reserve Board proposed regulations that would require the largest financial conglomerates to maintain TLAC above specified thresholds and meet other conditions designed to facilitate an SPOE resolution. Total Loss-Absorbing Capacity, Long-Term Debt, and Clean Holding Company Requirements for Systemically Important U.S. Bank Holding Companies and Intermediate Holding Companies of Systemically Important Foreign Banking Organizations; Regulatory Capital Deduction for Investments in Certain Unsecured Debt of Systemically Important U.S. Bank Holding Companies, 80 Fed Reg. 74926 (proposed Oct. 30, 2015) [hereinafter proposed TLAC rules]. The Federal Reserve Board's proposed TLAC rules are generally consistent with the international TLAC standards set by the FSB, and in some respects more stringent. *See* FSB, *Total Loss-Absorbing Capacity (TLAC) Term Sheet* (Nov. 9, 2015). Like the capital regulations we discussed in Chapters 2.5 to 2.7, under the proposed TLAC rules, the sufficiency of a financial conglomerate's TLAC would be assessed by reference to both its size and its riskiness, with TLAC requirements increasing in proportion to a measure of risk-weighted assets.

The proposed TLAC rules define categories of TLAC-eligible and ineligible liabilities. TLAC-eligible liabilities, which would bear losses in an SPOE resolution, include unsecured debt securities issued by a financial conglomerate's top-tier holding company that are held by unaffiliated investors and have a remaining maturity of at least one year. Ineligible liabilities, which are insulated from losses by TLAC, include deposits, commercial paper, and QFCs. TLAC-eligible liabilities must be structurally subordinate to ineligible liabilities. The proposed rules also establish a clean holding company framework that prohibits certain types of liabilities from being held at the level of a financial conglomerate's top-tier holding company. These restrictions are designed to ensure that, if a financial conglomerate fails, any liabilities that remain within its holding company can be written down or converted into equity in an SPOE resolution without spreading destabilizing contagion.

Like the other reforms discussed in this Chapter, the proposed TLAC rules have been subject to their share of criticism. FDIC Vice Chairman Thomas Hoenig suggests that the proposed TLAC rules encourage financial conglomerates to rely more heavily on long-term debt than on equity capital for funding, and may as a result incentivize financial conglomerates to increase their leverage and expand into riskier, higher-yielding activities. In lieu of TLAC requirements, Hoenig advocates use of the § 165(d) resolution planning process to develop more tailored requirements for individual financial conglomerates, without assuming that SPOE resolution is an ideal "one-size-fits-all" strategy. Thomas M. Hoenig, Vice Chairman, FDIC, The Relative Role of Debt in Bank Resiliency and Resolvability, Remarks Presented to the Peterson Institute for International Economics (Jan. 20, 2016). Mr. Paul Kupiec argues that all of the goals that the FSB has articulated for TLAC reforms could be achieved through higher capital requirements without the proposed TLAC rules' unnecessary complexity. *See* Paul H. Kupiec, *Will TLAC Regulations Fix the G-SIB Too-Big-To-Fail Problem?* (Am. Enter. Inst. Econ. Policy Working Paper 2015-08, Nov. 25, 2015). One central concern about the use of TLAC is that holders of TLAC might themselves undergo stress if their claims are written down, propagating, rather than mitigating, systemic risk. What parties should be permitted to hold TLAC, and how should regulators mitigate the risks facing them, if at all? Does portfolio diversification mitigate this concern? If long-term bondholders cannot be forced to absorb losses, who should?

The proposed TLAC rules would take effect in January 2019, with a transition period lasting until January 2022. Although their antecedents are present in the FDIA's traditional bank resolution regime, TLAC and SPOE resolution are post-crisis innovations. During the Financial Crisis, financial conglomerates were threatened both by liquidity shortages and by potential balance-sheet insolvency. As we discussed in Chapter 2.5 to 2.7, both capital and liquidity were inadequate, and, as a result, many post-Financial Crisis reforms have focused on increasing capital and liquidity levels. If capital and liquidity proved inadequate, at that time, the alternatives were either disorderly failure (Lehman Brothers) or meeting shortfalls with government assistance (AIG). Regulators had no effective mechanism at that time for imposing losses on any class of creditors in an orderly manner, let alone for apportioning losses selectively in a manner that would have been sustainable and consistent with the rule of law. Moreover, the composition of many financial conglomerates' liabilities at that time was weighted far more heavily towards short-term funding than more stable sources of funding that could have absorbed losses.

The Federal Reserve Board's TLAC proposal estimates that the eight largest U.S. financial conglomerates alone had $590 billion in TLAC-eligible long-term debt outstanding as of July 2015, and may need as much as $680 billion to meet the proposed rules' standards. This TLAC-eligible debt is an entirely new layer of loss-absorbing capacity on top of financial conglomerates' Tier 1 capital. As a result of TLAC reforms, liabilities within the financial system have been rearranged on a tectonic scale to, in effect, create new pools within which the costs of a financial conglomerate's failure can be contained. Ongoing TLAC reforms reflect a collaborative process, conceived by practitioners involved with the FSB, developed by financial conglomerates in their § 165(d) resolution plans, and advanced by the Federal Reserve Board in the proposed TLAC rules. Financial markets have also grasped the implications of TLAC reform. The fact that the largest financial conglomerates must now pay higher yields on issuances of TLAC-eligible debt to compensate investors for the increased risk of potential bail-in reflects an implicit vote of confidence in the feasibility of an SPOE resolution.

VI. ONGOING POLICY DEBATES AND PROPOSALS FOR REFORM

A. MORAL HAZARD AND BAILOUTS

Some have criticized the OLA on the grounds that it enshrines bailouts as regulatory policy, increasing moral hazard and preserving the perception among creditors and shareholders that some financial conglomerates are too big to fail. Forms of this critique have been articulated forcefully from both sides of the partisan divide. Conservative critics, including many Republican Congressional representatives, argue that potential use of the OLA sets an expectation of government intervention that inhibits the efficient functioning of market forces. Progressive critics argue that the OLA would be insufficiently punitive to deter cavalier risk-taking.

The OLA is sometimes criticized by analogy to the bailout of AIG. In a report published in July 2014, the Republican-majority House Financial Services Committee stated:

> In fact, had the 'Orderly Liquidation Authority' been in place when AIG failed, under the 'Single Point of Entry' the only thing different would have been the source of funding. Those funds would have come from the U.S. Treasury, by way of the FDIC, rather than the Federal Reserve. Those funds still would have ended up in the pockets of AIG counterparties. . .

H. Fin. Servs. Comm., Failing To End "Too Big To Fail": An Assessment of the Dodd-Frank Act Four Years Later, 113th Cong., 2d Sess. (2014). This criticism mischaracterizes the OLA. Most importantly, while certain classes of AIG's creditors—chiefly its derivatives counterparties—would have been no worse off in a hypothetical resolution under the OLA than in a disorderly bankruptcy, use of the OLA would have forced losses on many AIG creditors, the holders of its unsecured debt, and shareholders who were instead protected by the federal government's *ad hoc* rescue. Second, there is a clear distinction between an equity infusion of the sort that the federal government provided to AIG under TARP, in which the public stood ready to incur losses before any of AIG's creditors, and an extension of credit from the Orderly Liquidation Fund, which makes the taxpayer a temporary (and likely secured) creditor, rather than a shareholder, and must be recouped through assessments on a failed company's creditors and other financial conglomerates. Finally, the OLA would have required the removal of any management or board members responsible for AIG's failure and would have authorized the FDIC to claw back their compensation, hold them personally liable, and impose additional penalties. Recall from Chapter 9.1, moreover, that the federal government's investment in AIG was ultimately repaid at a gain.

Many critiques of SPOE resolution, whether implemented under the OLA or the Bankruptcy Code, focus on the implications of allowing operating subsidiaries to remain open without imposing losses on their creditors. Concerns about the continuity of financial conglomerates' operating subsidiaries reflect three strands of argument pertaining to misuse of public funds and potential market distortions.

First, House Republicans, among others, argue that use of the OLA would allow the FDIC to "funnel liquidity" to an insolvent operating subsidiary through its failed holding company. H. Fin. Servs. Comm., Failing To End "Too Big To Fail," at 72. During periods of severe market distress, the point at which a financial conglomerate crosses from being solvent-but-illiquid to balance-sheet insolvency is difficult to discern. This argument, however, misconstrues temporary liquidity support—a longstanding component of the FDIC's resolution authority used to stabilize operations and preserve going-concern value—as equivalent to equity support, which protects creditors through the public's assumption of their risks. The argument also fails to account for the requirements imposed on financial conglomerates to hold sufficient TLAC to facilitate an orderly resolution. As a result of TLAC requirements, the costs of recapitalizing a financial conglomerate's operating subsidiaries would not be borne by the FDIC but by creditors of the holding company. Moreover, the costs of meeting TLAC requirements will affect financial conglomerates' operating subsidiaries in ways that may be more subtle, but are no less important, than the immediately discernible impact on a holding company. As previously discussed, financial conglomerates must both restructure their balance sheets to hold a higher proportion of their liabilities in TLAC-eligible forms and pay higher yields on their debt securities to compensate investors for the risk that this debt could be bailed in. The customers and counterparties of an operating subsidiary who benefit from expectations of the subsidiary's continued solvency in an SPOE resolution therefore pay for this certainty in the form of lower to no return on their short-term credit exposures to the operating subsidiaries. This transference of costs occurs under normal market conditions.

The second strand of argument focuses on the potential risk of distorted incentives from the market's expectation that a financial conglomerate's operating subsidiaries would remain open and solvent in an SPOE resolution, despite their holding company's failure. Apprehensions about moral hazard are reflected here in two senses. First, to the extent that an SPOE resolution strategy protects a financial conglomerate's operating subsidiaries and preserves its value as a going-concern, the entity that emerges from the resolution process could resemble the one that originally entered. Second, the expectation that an operating subsidiary would remain solvent in an SPOE resolution could dampen the incentive of its customers and counterparties to monitor its financial condition. These concerns pertain to two distinguishable groups of decision-makers—market participants on one hand, and operating subsidiaries' management on the other—but both reflect strands of the same moral hazard critique.

One response to this critique is that the shareholders of a failed financial conglomerate would be wiped out and long-term creditors bailed in. Another response focuses on the FDIC's stated intent, in an SPOE resolution under the OLA, to address the problems that led to a financial conglomerate's failure through measures that "include changes in the company's businesses, shrinking those businesses, breaking them into smaller entities, and/or liquidating certain subsidiaries or business lines or closing certain operations." FDIC SPOE Notice, 78 Fed. Reg. at 76,616. Nevertheless, to mitigate moral hazard, losses should follow risk. The OLA and TLAC requirements seek to internalize the costs of a financial conglomerate's resolution, correcting the misalignment of incentives that leads to excessive risk-taking. For these reforms to function effectively, investors in a financial conglomerate's equity and TLAC-eligible debt must be able to exercise meaningful oversight and impose constraints on the executives whose decision-making may expose them to losses. The TLAC creditors, moreover, must truly believe that, unlike the Financial Crisis and the decades before it, next time, losses will be imposed on creditors. Whether the reforms discussed in this Chapter have successfully inculcated this positive dynamic in financial markets remains to be seen. They will not be tested until the next crisis.

Recall that the Bankruptcy Code treats creditors equally according to their priority or class; secured creditors, senior unsecured creditors, and junior or subordinated creditors are bickered into a class and treated *pari passu*. The key twist in banks' and financial institutions' treatment of creditors in resolution is that some creditors, the class of unsecured creditors, are treated differently according to whether they are short-term runnable debtholders or long-term investors. If the long-term debt is structurally subordinated to the short-term debt in advance of bail-in, the market should properly price the two different classes of debt efficiently, with the long-term debt enjoying a higher return to compensate its holders for their increased risk compared to short-term debt. If, however, the long-term debt is ranked *pari passu* with short-term debt before bail-in, and the FDIC exercises its discretion to bail in the long-term debt but not the short-term debt, the market will not necessarily price long-term and short-term debt efficiently. Professor Arthur Wilmarth argues that the creditors most likely to bear losses in an SPOE resolution are those with long-term investment horizons—which include not only hedge funds and insurance companies but also pension funds and mutual funds with many retail investors—whereas "favored creditors would include uninsured depositors, holders of commercial paper, and counterparties under derivatives and securities repurchase agreements. . . ." Arthur E. Wilmarth, Jr., *The Financial Industry's Plan for Resolving Failed Megabanks Will Ensure Future Bailouts for Wall Street*, 50 GA. L. REV. 43 (2015). Wilmarth suggests that these short-term creditors are Wall Street creditors rather than Main Street creditors and criticizes SPOE for favoring short-term Wall Street creditors over long-term Main Street creditors. Is it true that short-term creditors are Wall Street creditors? If the core idea is to prevent the contagion from the risk that short-term creditors might run, what is the alternative to a system that imposes losses on long-term creditors? Is it possible to determine which creditors are more deserving? How would this determination be made over a weekend and honor the no creditor worse off rule?

B. U.S. BANKRUPTCY CODE

In the years since the passage of the Dodd-Frank Act, a number of bills have been introduced in Congress proposing the addition of a new Chapter 14 to the Bankruptcy Code to facilitate the resolution of financial conglomerates. None of these bills has been enacted. *See, e.g.*, Taxpayer Protection and Responsible Resolution Act, S. 1861, 113th Cong. (2013); Financial Institution Bankruptcy Act of 2014, H.R. 5421, 113th Cong. (2014). Proponents of bankruptcy-based resolution reform stress the more transparent, rules-based nature of proceedings under the Bankruptcy Code in comparison to the administrative, discretionary

FDIC receivership proceedings for traditional bank failures on which the OLA is modeled. Professor Thomas Jackson, one of the architects of the proposal, writes that, "[t]he crucial feature of this new Chapter 14 is to ensure that the covered financial institutions, creditors dealing with them, and other market participants, know in advance, in a clear and predictable way, how losses will be allocated if the institution fails." Thomas H. Jackson, *Bankruptcy Code Chapter 14: A Proposal, in* BANKRUPTCY NOT BAILOUT: A SPECIAL CHAPTER 14 26 (Kenneth E. Scott & John B. Taylor, eds., 2012).

The differences between banks and other types of private enterprises have historically served as justification for the existence of a separate insolvency regime specifically for banks and for broker-dealers. To the question of whether the existence of a separate insolvency regime for banks is desirable, Professor David Skeel answers:

> The conventional answer is yes—that banks need a special, administrative insolvency framework because bank resolution needs to take place extremely quickly to preserve the value of bank assets, to assure that depositors have continuous access to their deposits, and to prevent disruptions to the payment system. Given its ongoing involvement in oversight, the FDIC is well-positioned to intervene quickly, and bank insolvency law gives the FDIC the flexible authority it needs to achieve an effective resolution. By contrast, a bankruptcy judge would have no particular expertise or knowledge about a bank prior to its failure, and the bankruptcy process is too slow, requiring that creditors be notified and given the opportunity to object before a firm's assets could be sold or other major decisions made.

David A. Skeel Jr., *The New Synthesis of Bank Regulation and Bankruptcy in the Dodd-Frank Era* (U. Pa. L.: Legal Scholarship Repository, Working Paper No. 1564, 2015).

Chapter 14 proposes changes to the Bankruptcy Code that would facilitate the orderly resolution of a financial conglomerate in a special type of bankruptcy proceeding. Key provisions of the proposed Chapter 14 include: defining the scope of financial institutions that would be eligible to file petitions thereunder; establishing a designated panel of bankruptcy judges who possess specialized expertise; empowering a financial conglomerate's primary regulator to file an involuntary petition under certain circumstances; granting regulatory authorities standing to be heard as parties or to raise motions in bankruptcy proceedings; clarifying the availability of access to liquidity to the failed financial institution in the form of debtor-in-possession financing; and amending the QFC safe harbor, so that the automatic stay would apply to QFCs for three days. *See* Thomas H. Jackson, *Bankruptcy Code Chapter 14: A Proposal, in* BANKRUPTCY NOT BAILOUT: A SPECIAL CHAPTER 14 25–70 (Kenneth E. Scott & John B. Taylor, eds., 2012); Thomas H. Jackson, *Building on Bankruptcy: A Revised Chapter 14 Proposal for the Recapitalization, Reorganization or Liquidation of Large Financial Institutions, in* MAKING FAILURE FEASIBLE: HOW BANKRUPTCY REFORM CAN END "TOO BIG TO FAIL" 15–58 (Kenneth E. Scott, Thomas H. Jackson & John B. Taylor eds., 2015).

Many support the development of Chapter 14, but there is ongoing debate about the proposal. The focus of ongoing debate is whether it should replace the OLA—a position favored by those who view an OLA resolution as a bailout and would support the repeal of Title II—or whether Chapter 14 would instead best be implemented in addition to the OLA, adding yet another resolution tool to the kit. Mr. Paul Lee articulates a cogent position in support of the continued development of proposals to establish bankruptcy as a viable alternative to the OLA, focused particularly on achieving the international coordination necessary to ensure that U.S. bankruptcy proceedings are accepted by non-U.S. resolution authorities. Paul L. Lee, *Bankruptcy Alternatives to Title II of the Dodd-Frank Act–Part II*, 132 BANK. L. J. 503 (2015).

C. EU BANK RESOLUTION AND RECOVERY DIRECTIVE

The EU has also reached consensus on the need for a new framework to resolve a failing financial conglomerate and to achieve the cross-border cooperation necessary for orderly resolution to be feasible. The BRRD lays out a comprehensive set of rules for each EU member state to implement through national legislation. In 2014, the European Commission described the BRRD as "a necessary step to improve efficiency and cohesion in ensuring that failing banks in the EU single market can be resolved in a way which preserves financial stability and minimises costs for taxpayers across the EU," and stated that the BRRD "largely completes the roadmap of financial sector reforms launched since 2009, in line with G20 agreements" including the FSB's Key Attributes. European Commission, EU Bank Recovery and Resolution Directive (BRRD): Frequently Asked Questions (April 15, 2014).

EU member states have implemented the BRRD in a substantially consistent manner, and the UK provides an illustrative example. After the BRRD was adopted by the European Parliament, the UK adopted legislation to bring the special resolution regime it had previously established under the Banking Act into alignment. *See* Bank of England, The Bank of England's Approach to Resolution (Oct. 2014). The UK special resolution regime defines the types of firms to which it potentially applies and sets triggering requirements for the initiation of resolution proceedings. As the Dodd-Frank Act did in the United States, the Banking Act added stabilisation tools to the UK authorities' regulatory toolkit. These included a private sector purchaser tool (similar to the FDIC's authority to conduct a purchase and assumption), a bridge bank tool and a bail-in tool, as well as a bank insolvency procedure for administering the claims of creditors on failed banks. The Banking Act provides one more tool as an option of last resort: a temporary public ownership tool that allows a financial conglomerate to be stabilized and rehabilitated via equity investments from the public, if deemed necessary by Her Majesty's Treasury, in consultation with the Bank of England, to address a serious threat to the stability of the UK financial system. *Id.*

D. DERIVATIVES AND CROSS-DEFAULTS

In October 2014, ISDA announced the Resolution Stay Protocol, a measure developed to facilitate the resolution of a financial conglomerate by modifying the treatment of certain derivatives in insolvency proceedings. *See Major Banks*

Agree to Sign ISDA Resolution Stay Protocol, REUTERS (Oct. 11, 2014). In November 2015, ISDA announced the Universal Resolution Stay Protocol, which superseded the 2014 Protocol and expanded its scope to include a broader range of financial contracts. 23 of the largest global financial conglomerates, including the eight largest in the United States, have agreed to adhere to the ISDA Resolution Stay Protocol. By adhering to the ISDA Resolution Stay Protocol, each of these financial conglomerates agree to contractually adopt—for certain financial contracts they enter into with one another—the restrictions on early termination and other default rights that would apply under the OLA in the resolution of a U.S. financial conglomerate, or under the BRRD in the resolution of a European financial conglomerate. As a result, these restrictions would apply even if one of these financial conglomerate were resolved under the Bankruptcy Code or analogous, non-extraordinary insolvency regimes.

The ISDA Resolution Stay Protocol is the culmination of a joint effort with support from both the public and private sector. Financial conglomerates recognized that an international, private agreement—that incorporated input from regulatory authorities—could achieve meaningful progress toward the objective of making orderly resolution feasible more easily than any measure that required legislative action.

Regulatory moral suasion, including the imperative to develop credible resolution plans, also influenced the ISDA Resolution Stay Protocol. The Federal Reserve Board and the FDIC strongly encouraged financial conglomerates to participate in its development, which they later applauded as "an important step toward mitigating the financial stability risks associated with the early termination of bilateral, over-the-counter derivatives contracts triggered by the failure of a global banking firm with significant cross-border derivatives activities." Joint Press Release, Federal Reserve Board and FDIC Welcome ISDA Announcement, (Oct. 11, 2014). Although the adoption of the ISDA Resolution Stay Protocol marks a significant milestone, this work remains unfinished. The ISDA Resolution Stay Protocol applies to a financial contract only if both counterparties have adhered. Asset managers have not signed the ISDA Resolution Stay Protocol. In the United States, regulators are expected to expand the scope of the ISDA Resolution Stay Protocol's application through future rulemaking.

---

1. ***Next Time.*** As much as we would like to believe otherwise, periodic financial crises are a feature of our financial system. Once the choice has been made to rely on short-term, runnable debt and to engage in maturity mismatch, there is always going to be a risk of runs. Over 800 years of history tells us that there will be a next time. *See* CARMEN M. REINHART & KENNETH S. ROGOFF, THIS TIME IS DIFFERENT: EIGHT CENTURIES OF FINANCIAL FOLLY (2009). It is also quite likely that the fragility of human cognition means that we will not see it coming.

The Panic of 1907, the Banking Crisis of 1933 and the Financial Crisis led policy-makers to create new tools that they hoped would mitigate the next crisis. The Panic of 1907, despite the ghost of President Andrew Jackson, led finally to the creation of a lender of last resort in the United States. The Banking Crisis of

1933 led to the creation of deposit insurance and a system of bank resolution, both of which have stood the test of time and worked well (though not without tradeoffs) for many years. The Financial Crisis revealed that the regulatory framework for resolving financial conglomerates in a world of global finance had not kept pace with changes in the financial sector. As a result, since the Financial Crisis, policy-makers and the private sector in the United States and around the world have focused on expanding the resolution and regulatory toolkit, all with the hope that these new tools will be fit for their purpose and preserve financial stability next time. We will not know how well they work until they are tested by next time.

PART X

MUTUAL FUNDS AND OTHER INVESTMENT VEHICLES

CHAPTER 10.1

INTRODUCTION TO ASSET MANAGEMENT AND ITS REGULATION

CONTENTS

I. INTRODUCTION TO ASSET MANAGEMENT

In Part X, we explore the asset management sector and its regulation. This chapter first explores the abuses preceding the passage of the Investment Company Act of 1940 (1940 Act) before turning to the substantive protections of the statute. Additionally, we explore the debates about whether asset managers are systemically important to the financial system. Finally, we delve into the role of institutional investors, such as hedge funds, in corporate governance.

The topic of asset management covers a number of different types of legal entities and investment vehicles. While our primary focus will be on investment companies regulated under the 1940 Act, we will also cover a number of different kinds of collective investment vehicles, including hedge funds, private equity, and certain trust products. The common characteristic of all these financial products is that they are based on a pool of financial assets managed on behalf of a group of investors. This is an extraordinarily popular structure as it allows disparate investors to hire an expert investment manager to oversee a pool of assets much larger and more diversified than individual investors could maintain on their own. While the 1940 Act defines the regulatory regime applicable to the largest volume of collective investment vehicles in the United States, many other legal regimes govern other functionally similar products. You should consider whether this proliferation of legal regimes allows for a healthy mix of product offerings or contributes to undesirable regulatory arbitrage.

In 2013, as one of its first major reports, the Treasury's Office of Financial Research (OFR) released a report on asset management. We will return to the report's substantive recommendations later in this Chapter, but for now consider its overview of the asset management sector and its many component parts.

OFR, Asset Management and Financial Stability

Sept. 2013

Asset managers provide investment management services and ancillary services to clients as fiduciary agents. The diversity of clients' needs results in a wide variety of firm structures and business models, ranging from investment boutiques that focus on a single product or clientele to large, complex financial institutions that offer multiple services.

Many asset managers focus their investment strategies on a single asset class, such as equities or fixed income; examples include long-only equity mutual funds and municipal bond funds. Some focus on a style of investing within an asset class, such as large-capitalization growth or dividend-yielding U.S. equities. Other managers cover broad market areas, offering multiple strategies within a fund or family of funds, and provide custom "solution" investment services for clients.

The industry is highly competitive and, in some ways, highly concentrated. Economies of scale in portfolio management and administration, combined with index-based strategies, have increased industry concentration in recent years. The largest asset managers generally offer the most comprehensive, low-cost client solutions. At the end of 2012, the top five mutual fund complexes managed 49 percent ($6.6 trillion) of U.S. mutual fund assets, including 48 percent ($2.8 trillion) of equity funds and 53 percent ($1.7 trillion) of fixed income funds. . . . Higher concentrations could increase the market impact of firm-level risks, such as operational risk and investment risk, or increase the risk of fire sales.

. . . [Asset managers'] diversity suggests that asset management activities should be the analytical building blocks for understanding the industry. . . . Figure 1[, in this excerpt,] illustrates broad categories of sources of investable assets and translates them into various types of investment vehicles through the managers that provide them. It is important to note that there is inherent double-counting in the figure due to cross-investing among managers and to the use of several data sources. . . .

Activities can be divided into functions performed at the client or fund level and those performed at the firm level. Activities at the fund level include asset allocation and security selection, as well as the management of fund liquidity and leverage. Portfolio managers allocate assets and select portfolio holdings according to the guidelines prescribed by a fund's prospectus or a separate account's investment management agreement. . . . Activities undertaken at the firm level include centralized trading (including securities trading, derivatives trading, securities lending, and repo transactions), risk management, market and securities research, and administrative functions. Interconnections between fund- and firm-level activities are extensive; most funds rely on their sponsors for core services, and fund managers are typically employees of the advisory firm.

Risk management practices and structures vary significantly among firms. For example, although all registered investment companies and investment advisers are required by SEC regulation to have chief compliance officers, not all asset managers have chief risk officers. Regardless of the structure used, effective risk management is important for the management of operational limits, counterparty limits, and investment concentrations across funds and accounts.

Figure 1: Asset Management Industry Overview *(as of 12/31/2012)*

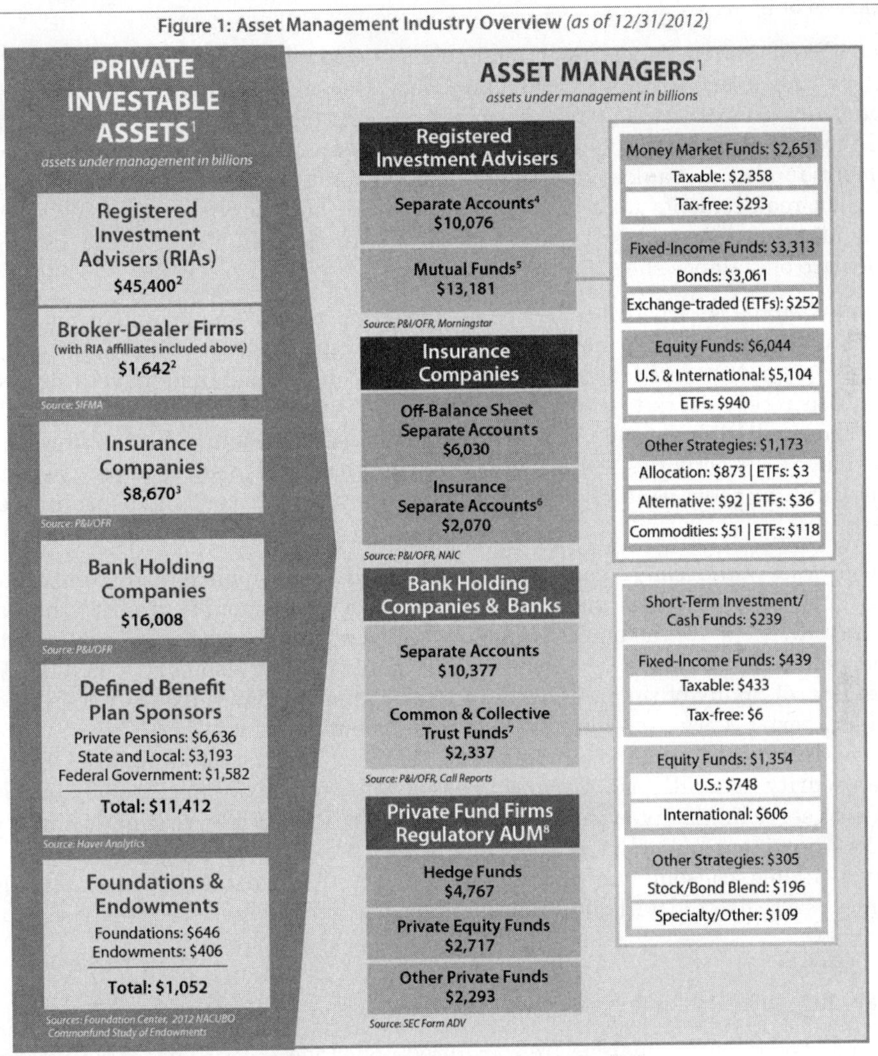

[1] Figures include double-counting due to cross-investing among managers and multi-sourcing of data in construction of table.
[2] Includes all non-exempt registered investment advisers as reported on the SEC's Form ADV.
[3] Some insurance companies reporting data to Pensions & Investments (P&I) classify insurance separate accounts and other on-balance sheet assets as assets under management.
[4] Separate accounts estimated by deducting registered funds from total world-wide assets under management using P&I data.
[5] Mutual funds registered in the United States.
[6] Separate accounts managed by an insurance company, in which the assets are on the insurance company's balance sheet.
[7] Does not include state chartered limited purpose trust companies.
[8] Regulatory AUM refers to gross assets under management, without adjusting for leverage.

Some firms adopt a core investment strategy and implement that strategy across multiple funds and accounts. In addition, firms may offer strategies that seek to hedge risks across asset classes; for example, so-called risk-parity or all-weather funds combine equity and levered, fixed-income portfolios to achieve risk parity across the two asset classes. Such strategies may also be offered through multiple channels. Other activities undertaken at the firm level may either help to manage risk or result in increased risk across the firm's activities, such as taking on leverage through unsecured borrowing, establishing and maintaining redemption lines of credit, and managing proprietary investments. . . .

Firm Types

Figure 1[, above,] displays the major participants in the asset management industry. Three kinds of firms are prominent:

Banks. Banks often have asset management divisions through which they offer depositors and other customers' fiduciary services such as investment funds, wealth management services, trust services, and retirement products. These services may be offered through separate accounts or funds such as bank common trust funds or collective investment funds. A bank's investment management activities are exempt from SEC registration requirements unless the bank provides those services to an SEC-registered investment company, such as a mutual fund. In general, bank asset management activities are off-balance sheet.

Insurance companies. Insurance companies often have asset management divisions that provide investment management and other services, such as retirement plans and guaranteed payments to clients. A number of insurance companies have acquired asset managers in recent years to expand their asset management businesses. For example, Allianz acquired PIMCO and AXA acquired AllianceBernstein. Insurance companies' asset management activities are distinct from their on-balance sheet insurance activities, such as those in their general accounts or associated with certain insurance separate accounts.

Dedicated asset management companies. Dedicated asset management companies have two characteristics: (1) their main business is asset management, and (2) they are not integrated divisions of a bank or insurance company. Although dedicated asset management companies are not regulated as bank holding companies by the [Federal Reserve Board], many of them maintain a trust bank, regulated by the [OCC] or a state bank regulatory agency, to offer collective investment funds to eligible clients or certain individual retirement account products, as required under [the Employee Retirement Income Security Act (ERISA)]. Several are very large organizations involved in disparate businesses, servicing many types of clients and offering services similar to those offered by banks. Some are publicly traded, while others are privately held and do not provide publicly available, consolidated financial statements. Most dedicated asset management companies are registered with, and regulated by, the SEC as investment advisers.

Fund Types

There are four primary fund types in the industry:

Registered investment companies are registered under the. . .1940 Act. They are required to abide by strict rules governing safekeeping and proper valuation of assets. . .and liquidity, among other requirements. Registered investment companies include mutual funds, [exchange-traded funds (ETFs)], closed-end funds, and unit investment trusts.

Private funds, such as hedge funds, private equity funds, and venture capital funds, are excluded from registration under the 1940 Act, but advisers to these funds are generally required to register with the SEC or a state securities regulator.

Bank common and collective investment funds are similarly excluded from rules under the 1940 Act, but, as noted earlier, are often subject to rules established by banking regulators.

Separate accounts are accounts in which an asset manager selects assets on behalf of large institutional investors or high-net-worth individuals under mandates defined in an investment management agreement. Clients retain direct and sole ownership of assets under management. Separate accounts are not specifically regulated under the 1940 Act, the. . .[Securities Act of 1933 (1933 Act)], or bank-specific regulations, although managers of those accounts are often investment advisers required to register with the SEC or a state securities regulator.

II. BACKGROUND ON THE INVESTMENT COMPANY ACT OF 1940

We now turn to the regulation of investment companies, the largest single component of the asset management sector in the United States. Registered investment companies are the most heavily regulated component of asset management, and the 1940 Act establishes the default system of supervision of collective investment vehicles for retail customers in the United States. Many of the other collective investment vehicles discussed in this part, such as hedge funds and private equity firms, are organized so as to qualify for exemptions from the rules applicable to registered investment companies under the 1940 Act.

A. HISTORICAL OVERVIEW

Unlike banks and insurance companies, investment companies are regulated almost exclusively at the federal level. Before the mid-1930s, investment companies only had to comply with state blue sky rules, corporation laws when applicable, and a few state statutes, but federal legislative initiatives soon came to dominate these laws. For many years, investment companies had to comply with both federal and state laws. This dual compliance ceased in 1996 when Congress largely preempted state blue-sky oversight of investment companies.

The first federal moves to regulate investment company practice were the 1933 Act and the Securities Exchange Act of 1934 (1934 Act). These statutes provided an expansive set of issuer disclosure requirements triggered by the offer, sale, and trading of securities and anti-fraud rules, which were designed to protect defrauded investors. They did not, however, address the specific regulatory needs of investment companies.

In 1940, Congress adopted the 1940 Act, which established the first comprehensive federal regulatory framework for investment companies. 15 U.S.C. § 80a-1(b). The 1940 Act's purpose was to protect shareholders of investment companies from a broad array of abuses found in these companies before its enactment. It thus contains broad prohibitions on many activities, requires disclosure of particular information, and forces companies into a corporate governance-style self-regulatory system.

A companion act, the Investment Advisers Act of 1940, placed regulations on those who give investment advice. It set up standards for advisers, established anti-fraud causes of action for defrauded clients, and gave regulatory control over advisers to the SEC. Since then, these companion pieces of legislation have remained relatively unchanged, with only one series of amendments that were enacted in the 1970s. Investment Company Amendments Act of 1970, Pub. L.

No. 91-547, 84 Stat. 1413 (1970) (codified at 15 U.S.C. §§ 80a-1-52(1970)). An appreciation of the abusive practices committed by investment companies before the 1940 Act and the Investment Advisers Act is essential for a clear understanding of the rules and the regulatory structures they put into place.

1. The Origin of Investment Companies

The U.S. investment company structure draws its origins back to Scotland and England in the mid-19th Century, though the concept of investment companies can be traced back even earlier to developments in Amsterdam in 1774 and Brussels in 1822. MATTHEW P. FINK, THE RISE OF MUTUAL FUNDS: AN INSIDER'S VIEW 8 (2011). The development of the investment company was occasioned by two primary social and economic conditions: foreign nations needed capital and a more affluent British public had capital to spare. After the Napoleonic Wars, England became the leading creditor nation, financing foreign governments, colonies, and private industry. Because of the practical difficulties of investing capital abroad, joint investment structures were formed with professional advisers. In fact, many investment companies were set up to invest in the United States, mainly in railroad securities. Mr. Robert Fleming, largely considered to be the father of investment companies, formed the first Scottish association to invest in railway bonds in 1873.

Owing to the English industrial revolution, wealth spread over a larger populace and families and individuals accumulated excess savings available for investment. The combination of the difficulties related to foreign investment, investors' inexperience in making investment decisions, and the lack of financial resources that would be required to hire private investment managers, however, left a gap to be filled by professional investment managers. Companies such as the Foreign and Colonial Government Trust were thus formed to "provide the investor of moderate means the same advantages as the large capitalist, in diminishing the risk of investing in Foreign and Colonial Government Stocks, by spreading the investment over a number of different stocks."

The development of investment companies in the United States was influenced by the examples and experiences of British investment companies. The first wave of investment companies, also known as investment trusts, formed following World War I. Similar to the English experience, at that time the United States had become a creditor nation, exporting capital to help rebuild European economies. In the United States, this was also a time of relative prosperity (combined with inequality). The general public, awakened to the benefits of investments in the stock market in the 1920s, turned to professional managers. In response, a slew of investment companies were formed by bankers, brokers, investment counsel, and industrialists who had experience in the capital markets, or wanted to, either legally or illegally, gain from the investment company funds. Investment companies principally arose in large East Coast and Midwestern cities, such as New York, Chicago, and Boston. In fact, one of the interesting features of the development of the investment company, and in particular the mutual fund, is the relative importance of Boston in the process.

As early as the mid-19th Century, Boston was known for its numerous private trustees managing individual and family wealth. The Boston trustee quickly became associated with the investment company business in the 1920s.

In 1924, what is considered to be the first open-end or mutual fund, Massachusetts Investors Trust, was formed in Boston. The Massachusetts Investors Trust was unique in that it had a share-liquidation feature, that is, it allowed shareholders to redeem their shares with the trust upon demand. It later became the largest investment company for a quarter of a century. State Street Investment Corporation and Incorporated Investors, both considered open-end funds because of their share-redemption features, opened soon thereafter.

Before the 1920s, relatively few investment companies formed. By 1927, however, there were about 160 investment companies with total assets of around $1 billion. In 1928, the flood of new investment companies continued, with 140 new companies formed; in 1929, 186 new companies appeared. By the end of 1929, there were 675 investment companies with total assets close to $7 billion. Of these, 174 were closed-end funds with assets of $2.6 billion, and 19 were open-end funds with $140 million in assets. Closed-end funds have a fixed number of outstanding shares that are traded on an exchange. In contrast, open-end funds continuously offer and redeem their shares. In these early years, the corporate structure of investment companies varied greatly. The majority, however, were corporations of the closed-end variety with a complicated capital structure and were often pyramided, or were owned by, other investment companies.

Despite this rapid growth in investment companies, regulation of the sector was minimal at best. Governing their conduct and development were state blue sky laws, laws related to corporate governance, fraud and private contract, and a few quasi-fiduciary obligations found in the common law. Some states, including Ohio, Minnesota, Michigan, Alabama, Kentucky, and New Hampshire established substantial regulation governing the sale of investment trust securities within those states. Others, such as New York, passed and tried to enforce anti-fraud legislation.

After the stock market crash of 1929, the value of investment company assets declined and most closed-end companies' stocks began trading in the secondary markets at a discount to their net asset values. Some companies failed, while others were swept up in a wave of consolidation that spread through the sector. Management services were up for sale, and many investment companies received new advisers. While from 1927 to 1936 about 1,100 new investment companies were formed, by 1936, after the consolidations, liquidations, and failures, only about 560 remained.

Anxiety over the stock market crash affected the public desire to buy investment company securities, particularly shares of closed-end companies. New public offerings for closed-end companies virtually ceased. In fact, immediately after the crash, the public turned away from all management companies, investing primarily in fixed trusts. Fixed trusts are companies that invest shareholder capital in a fixed set of stocks. This trend was short-lived and, by the mid-1930s, sales of shares in fixed trusts virtually ceased.

The heyday of the open-end company or the mutual fund was just beginning. The 1930s saw the first real increase in the organization of mutual funds. Historians believe that this expansion was driven by the redemption privilege, at net asset value, which protected shareholders from the risk of their shares trading below net asset value and the fact that they did not suffer the negative public reaction that befell the closed-end companies. By 1932, almost all newly organized investment companies adopted the mutual fund form.

The stock market crash precipitated new, strong federal regulation of securities and other markets. The initial wave of New Deal securities legislation did not specifically address investment companies and had little impact on the investment company industry. Possibly of more importance was the Revenue Act of 1936, which allowed highly diversified investment companies to pass income to shareholders without an entity tax. In 1942, the qualifications for diversified status were reduced and remain similar today.

2. Abuses Preceding the Reforms of 1940

Before 1940, federal and state regulation of investment companies was rudimentary at best and investors had little control over investment companies. Furthermore, there were many factors that offered managers and sponsors opportunities to abuse their powers. First, because investment companies developed in order to aid unsophisticated investors, managers were in a position to take advantage of these investors' lack of knowledge. Second, the nature of the discretion given to the managers regarding portfolio investing gave them the freedom to change the nature of their company's investment policies from conservative to speculative, to invest in affiliated companies, or to invest in the securities underwritten by affiliated investment banks. Third, the liquid nature of the investment company's assets facilitated manager embezzlement.

a. Misleading Disclosure

One of the greatest abuses of investment company practice was the rapidity and irresponsibility with which some managements totally changed the nature of their business, which occurred, in most cases, without the knowledge of the shareholders. Stockholders who had invested in self-styled diversified companies could be committed overnight to highly illiquid positions in any other business. Most spectacular was General Investment Company's sudden acquisition of a $70 million subway in Buenos Aires, which tied up practically all of its assets and was later sold for about 10% of its cost. Added to this was the power of managers to sell the investment company or the advisory service to other, sometimes unscrupulous, groups, often without the knowledge or consent of the investors. At best, this meant different investment policies. At worst, the new management looted the fund. In other cases, investors were given inadequate or deceptive reports about the performance of their investment company. Auditor reports of some companies showed misleading accounts of profits. For example, some accounting firms failed to distinguish between income and new capital and included fictitious profits arising out of intercompany transactions among affiliated firms.

b. Self Dealing

Other abusive practices involved management self-dealing whereby investment companies often operated in the interest of their managers and affiliated companies rather than in the interests of the investors. There are examples of insiders and affiliates using investment companies to unload unmarketable securities, loans, and other property in which they had an interest.

One investment company sustained large losses as a consequence of buying the stock of its banking affiliate to support the affiliate's price in a falling market.

Other practices gave preferential treatment, at the expense of other shareholders, to insiders and affiliates who owned stock. These management practices usually resulted in non-insider or affiliate stock being worth less per share, causing shareholder dilution. For example, insiders were frequently permitted to subscribe to newly issued stock at reduced prices and sometimes were able to redeem their stock on a more favorable basis.

Open-end companies similarly engaged in abusive practices resulting in shareholder dilution. For example, many insiders or affiliates were not required to pay sales loads, or distribution fees, upon buying shares of the company. Additionally, some companies engaged in backwards pricing, in which investors bought shares based on the price of the previous day. According to an SEC report, "[i]n a rising market, insiders and favored customers, who did not pay a sales load, could purchase shares based upon the previous day's lower price, turn around and redeem their shares the next day, and be assured of riskless profits, which resulted in dilution of the remaining shareholders' holdings." SEC, *Protecting Investors: A Half Century of Investment Company Regulation* 428-29 (May 1992).

c. Capital Structure

Many commentators also believed that the complicated capital structures of investment companies with high debt loads and many classes of voting and non-voting shares served to harm public investors, or at least create a strong potential for such harm. Leverage, also known as trading on the equity, was thought to dangerously increase the risks of losses to shareholders, who are equity, not debt, claimants on the fund. Many thought the mere existence of senior and junior securities was dangerous. Across the board, commentators attacked the voting structure of companies in which insiders and affiliates normally owned all of the voting stock. The public owned the senior securities, namely preferred stock and debentures. After the crash, the common stock of many companies was worthless, thus prompting these junior holders, who had voting control, to take larger risks. This generally resulted in a sale of the company or management services to other companies or management investing in more speculative ventures.

d. Misappropriation of Funds

Fraud, larceny, and embezzlement by management were not uncommon in the 1920s, and especially in the 1930s. In some cases, individuals bought control of an investment company in order to loot the company, making off with its portfolio of investments. In some cases, the looting was not limited to one investment company. Instead, some of the assets of the company were used to buy control of other companies, which were in turn looted.

One notorious example occurred in 1937 when a group composed mainly of lawyers discovered a way to gain control of investment companies without investing any money of their own. The group carried on its operations through a personal holding company called the Fiscal Management Company. The first victim was a small investment company with assets of $540,000. They gained control of the company by paying the previous management a borrowed $110,000 for the Class A stock that had sole voting power. As collateral for the $110,000 loan, the thieving group took securities with a market value of $152,000 from the portfolio of the victim company. The $42,000 difference was retained by the Fiscal Management group as commission and profit on the deal. Later, most of the remaining portfolio of marketable securities was liquidated. The proceeds were used to buy securities of doubtful value from or make loans to the new management and their associates. Finally, the investment company was taken over for liquidation by the Michigan State Securities Commission. Investors lost almost all they had paid for the securities of this concern.

But this was only the beginning. The next victim was a bank-sponsored investment company with $3 million in assets. Money was again borrowed to pay for 44% of the common stock. Portfolio securities were again sold, with commissions of $114,000 to insiders. After that, the remaining portfolio of securities was liquidated to make personal loans and investments of dubious quality, including an investment in a South American utility project and loans to members of a brokerage firm, management, and other associates, and to purchase other investment companies. In fact, two other trusts were similarly acquired and grossly mismanaged by the same group. As a result of large losses, this investment company filed for reorganization in 1938. Ultimately, the individuals involved were indicted for fraud and larceny. One pled guilty and the others were acquitted. Later, three of those connected to the scams were convicted in federal court for using the mails to defraud the stockholders of the victimized companies.

3. Passage of the Investment Company Act of 1940

By the late 1920s, and particularly in the 1930s, as abuses in the organization and operation of investment companies became more apparent, calls for regulation of the sector increased. When Congress passed the Public Utility Holding Company Act of 1935, it authorized the SEC, which had itself been established only the previous year, to conduct a study of the investment company sector. That study, which was released in numerous volumes over the next seven years, reported substantial abuses and led directly to the 1940 Act and its companion, the Investment Advisers Act. These two Acts, as amended, provide the statutory basis for the regulation of investment companies today.

The original version of the 1940 Act, "a bill to provide for the registration and regulation of investment companies," was drafted by the SEC and introduced in Congress on March 14, 1940. Walter P. North, *Brief History of Federal Investment Company Legislation*, 44 NOTRE DAME L. REV. 677, 680 (1969). While the fund industry agreed that some regulation was necessary and wanted to restore investor confidence in the industry, there were divergent views as to the nature and extent of the regulations—particularly regarding the discretionary power given to the SEC in the original draft. *Id.* at 683. The SEC's draft bill was strongly opposed by the fund industry, but the SEC and the industry collaborated on a revised bill that became the 1940 Act. *Id.* at 684.

In the end, however, the enacted version of the 1940 Act did give significant power to the SEC. *Id.* at 682-83. In general, the SEC has the power to bring actions in federal district courts to enjoin practices constituting violations of the 1940 Act. Under some sections of the 1940 Act, the SEC has the discretion to adopt general rules and regulations. The most controversial power given to the SEC by the Act is the power of exemption, granted in § 6(c) of the Act, which states that, "[t]he [SEC] . . . may conditionally or unconditionally exempt any person, security, or transaction . . . from any provision." 15 U.S.C. § 80a-6(c). The SEC can exercise this power by order with reference to specific persons, securities, or transactions, as well as by general rules and regulations.

Although asset managers initially objected to this SEC authority, they ultimately accepted these discretionary powers as an alternative to strict statutory rules. The SEC's exemptive power did provide greater flexibility for companies in particular cases. Since the passage of the 1940 Act, these powers have been used extensively, particularly the exemptive power.

The stated purpose of the 1940 Act is to remedy certain abuses listed in § 1 of the Act. Though the method of regulation varies with different sections of the 1940 Act, in general, the methods used are: (1) company disclosure, to provide investors with more information; (2) shareholder voting and a watchdog board of directors, to equip the company with the self-regulatory features found in a corporate democracy; and (3) prohibitions on or heavy regulation of certain transactions and interrelationships that may lead to abuses.

a. Registration

All investment companies are required to register with the SEC. The scope of the legislation is thus determined by the definition of an investment company under the 1940 Act. With some exclusions, this definition includes all companies that "are or hold themselves out to be engaged primarily" in the investment business and those companies whose assets are comprised of at least 40% securities. 15 U.S.C. § 80a-3(a)(1)(A)-(C).

Those who fall within the definition of investment companies under the 1940 Act are further sub-classified for different treatment. Registered companies are divided into three categories: face-amount certificate companies, which sell unsecured debentures on an installment plan; unit investment trusts, which sell shares in a fixed or semi-fixed bundle of securities deposited with a trustee; and management companies, which are the focus of the 1940 Act and with which we will be most concerned. 15 U.S.C. § 80a-3. Management companies are further divided in two ways: (1) open-end companies, or mutual funds, and closed-end companies, and (2) diversified and non-diversified companies. *Id.* The 1940 Act's requirements depend on and will vary based on the above classifications.

b. Disclosure

Some of the greatest abusive practices involved the rapid and often fraudulent changes in investment policies that were made without the knowledge or consent of the investors. In the banking and insurance sectors, we saw that federal and state agencies' solution was to restrict the types of activities and investments permitted. This alternative was discussed in Congress as a possible cure for investment company problems. As with the regulation in the broker-dealer sector, however, the 1940 Act as enacted turned to disclosure in the first instance. For example, in § 8 of the 1940 Act, each company is required to disclose its investment policies and those activities it "reserves freedom of action to engage in." *Id.* at § 80a-8(b)(1). This includes any company plans to issue senior securities, to concentrate its portfolio in a certain sector, or to make loans to other persons. Companies must adhere to these policies until a change is authorized by majority vote of the stockholders pursuant to § 13 of the 1940 Act.

Supplementing the specific disclosure requirements of the 1940 Act are the more comprehensive disclosure rules in the 1933 and 1934 Acts, both of which apply to registered investment companies. The 1933 Act mandates disclosure when securities are registered for a public offering and requires that written offers to sell investment company securities be accompanied or preceded by a prospectus meeting certain prescribed standards. *Id.* at § 77j. The prospectus must reflect the policies and activities required by the registration statement under the 1940 Act. The 1934 Act provides for similar public disclosure, such as by proxies and annual reports, of information by issuers whose securities are listed on the exchanges. Over the years, the SEC has developed special forms that tailor the disclosure requirements of the 1933 and 1934 Acts for different types of investment companies.

c. Regulation of Activities and Operations

Many provisions in the 1940 Act were designed to attack the abusive activities found in the SEC's study, and in fact go well beyond mere disclosure.

Self-Dealing. To combat one of the most prolific sources of self-dealing, the 1940 Act prohibited many direct transactions between affiliated persons and investment companies. Section 17 of the Act, with a few exceptions, strictly regulates transactions between an investment company, or its agents, and affiliates and other insiders of that investment company. The SEC has the power to exempt specific transactions that are fair and consistent with the company's policy and the purposes of the 1940 Act. 15 U.S.C. § 80a-17. Under § 21 of the 1940 Act, most loans to affiliated persons are prohibited. *Id.* at § 80a-21. In addition, to prevent an underwriter from dumping unmarketable securities with an affiliated investment company, § 10(f) prohibits an investment company from purchasing securities from an underwriting syndicate if a member of the syndicate is affiliated with the investment company in certain ways. *Id.* at § 80a-10(f). Again, the SEC has the authority to exempt transactions by rule or order.

Investments. The 1940 Act also places limits on portfolio investments available to the company. Section 12(d) attacks the problem of pyramiding, in which one investment company controls other investment companies by owning a large block of their shares. *Id.* at § 80a-12(d). This section requires that no more than 3% of the acquired fund's voting shares be purchased by acquiring fund, no more than 5% of the acquiring fund's assets be invested in the securities of the acquired fund, and no more than 10% of the acquiring fund's assets can be invested in the securities of all acquired funds. *Id.* Additionally, some risky investments are prohibited, such as buying securities on margin and, with some exceptions, various investments in other financial services firms.

Capital Structure. The original draft of the 1940 Act permitted only common stock to be issued by investment companies in the future. The final draft, however, allowed closed-end companies to issue bonds and preferred stock as long as certain asset coverage levels were met. Because of open-end companies' continuous obligation to redeem their stock, the 1940 Act is more restrictive on them and forbids them from issuing senior securities. *Id.* at § 80a-18(f). In addition, all new issues of stock must have full voting rights, and bondholders and preferred stockholders in closed-end companies are given some rights to elect members of the board of directors.

The 1940 Act was also concerned with problems of shareholder dilution arising from self-dealing and complex capital structures. To eliminate some of the most widely used methods of rewarding promoters and other insiders, no securities may be issued by a closed-end company to pay for services or property, and repurchases may only occur on the open market. Section 23 of the 1940 Act prohibits private share repurchases from selective persons. *Id.* at § 80a-23. Open-ended companies or their principal distributors, which made money from the additional sales loads when shareholders exchanged shares for another fund, are prevented from making any offer involving an exchange of securities on any basis other than relative net asset values, unless approved by the SEC as required by § 11 of the 1940 Act. *Id.* at § 80a-11. To protect shareholders from dilution when shares are sold to the public at different prices, as well as negotiation between a dealer and an investor over sales loads, § 22(d) of the 1940 Act prevents any investment company, its principal underwriters, and dealers from selling shares of the investment company except at a current public offering price described in its prospectus. 15 U.S.C. § 80a-22(d).

d. Shareholder Powers

To combat the abuses of the 1920s and 1930s, the 1940 Act did more than prohibit certain transactions and relationships; it adopted the traditional corporate governance mechanisms to make sure advisers would be held accountable for their actions. The 1940 Act thus called for shareholder voting and in most cases, as discussed later in this Chapter, forced investment companies to create independent boards of directors that could act as watchdogs over wayward managers. As one method of increasing the authority of the shareholders over the affairs of their investment companies, § 18 of the 1940 Act requires, with limited exceptions, that all shares of investment company stock "be a voting stock and have equal voting rights with every other outstanding voting stock." *Id.* at § 80a-18(i). Certain voting powers are reserved for shareholders under the 1940 Act. The most important example is the requirement that all changes in investment policy be approved by a shareholder vote, as required by § 13 of the 1940 Act. *Id.* at § 80a-13.

The 1940 Act also calls for shareholder voting with regard to some investment company contracts. *See id.* at § 80a-15. All contracts with an investment adviser and underwriter must be in writing and must be approved by a majority of the voting securities or, in some cases, by the board of directors. *Id.* § 80a-15. To prevent the transfer of an advisory contract without the vote of the shareholders, § 15 of the 1940 Act provides for the automatic termination of these contracts in the event of an assignment. *Id.* at § 80a-15(a)(4).

Additionally, by a majority vote, shareholders can terminate either the advisory contract or auditing contract. Contracts with accountants are also required to have the approval of a majority of the shareholders or board of directors. *Id.* § 80a-31(a).

e. Independent Directors

Another strategy used by the 1940 Act was to force all registered investment companies to create shareholder-elected boards of directors or board of trustees to act as watchdogs over potential management conflicts of interest. Initially, the SEC supported very restrictive rules governing management and affiliate conflicts of interest, such as those prohibiting directors and managers of investment companies from holding similar positions in other investment companies, commercial banks, principal underwriters, or principal brokers of the company. The final draft of the 1940 Act, however, essentially relied on protection by independent directors, a percentage of which must be disinterested. Section 10 of the 1940 Act also provides that no more than 60% of an investment company's board of directors shall be interested persons. *Id.* at § 80a-10. An investment company's board of directors is required to supervise adviser conflicts of interest and approve some contracts. For example, in the absence of shareholder approval, the board must annually approve the company's underwriting and advisory contract. The SEC requires funds to have a majority of independent directors in order to comply with certain exemptions under the 1940 Act. *See* 17 C.F.R. §§ 239, 240, 270, 274.

f. Interaction with the Investment Advisers Act

The Investment Advisers Act of 1940, included in the same legislative package as the 1940 Act, was also designed to deal with some of the abusive practices discovered by the SEC's study. The Investment Advisers Act, however, focused on the regulation of investment advisers. Important provisions include forced registration of investment advisers with the SEC, including investment advisers to registered investment companies. With some limited exceptions, the Investment Advisers Act prohibits performance-based compensation, such as compensation based on the capital gains in a client's account. Like the 1940 Act, the Investment Advisers Act prohibits advisers from assigning their advisory contract to another party without the approval of the advisees and prohibits fraudulent and deceitful transactions between the adviser and the client. The SEC is empowered to discipline violators of the statute and of its rules.

g. SEC's Power to Grant Exemption

Under the 1940 Act, the SEC has the power to exempt any person, security, or transaction from any provision of the Act. As the financial markets have evolved and new products, structures, and sponsors have emerged, investment companies and those wanting to set up or buy investment companies have increasingly turned to the SEC for relief. In 1991, the number of applications for exemption stood at 310.

Some examples of the SEC's use of this power include permitting money market mutual funds (MMFs) to use alternative valuation methods and allowing mutual funds to issue different classes or series of funds. In the past decade,

SEC orders have also permitted new sales and distribution practices in the mutual fund sector. Some of these orders have later been codified as general rules. For example, Rule 12b-1 allows mutual funds to replace or supplement sales loads, or distributions fees paid by buyers of mutual fund shares, with 12b-1 fees, or distribution fees paid by the owners of mutual fund shares based on a percentage of the fund's daily average net assets.

h. Legal Developments Since the 1940s

Since the 1940s, the 1940 Act has remained relatively unchanged. Reforms occurred in the 1970s when several amendments were passed by Congress.

Concern over the quickly rising assets invested in investment company shares prompted three studies in the early to mid-1960s. *See* The Wharton Report, H.R. REP. No. 2274 (1962); Report of the Special Study of Securities Markets, H.R. DOC. No.95, pts. 1 to 4 (1963); Report of the SEC on the Public Policy Implications of Investment Company Growth, H.R. REP. No. 2337 (1966). These reports highlighted a series of concerns about managerial compensation, sales loads, competition among retail sellers, brokerage commissions, the increasing size of some funds, and advertising.

Reforms to the 1940 Act made during the 1970s purported to resolve at least one of these problems: management compensation. The original 1940 Act did not generally impose restrictions on advisory fees but gave managers a large measure of discretion that was subject to shareholder and director review. In practice, adviser compensation was and still is normally based on a percentage of a fund's net asset value. By the 1960s, with substantial increases in fund assets, advisers' compensation increased dramatically. Many argued that this fee was not justified because greater assets meant greater economies of scale, benefits that were not being realized by the investors. According to the Wharton Report's 1960 survey, of 20 of the largest funds, only seven had scaled down advisory fee schedules to reflect the greater economies of size. H.R. REP. No. 2337 at 99.

The 1970 Amendments to the 1940 Act brought about two major changes. First, the amended § 15(c) demanded a stronger role for independent directors in the evaluation and approval of advisory contracts by adding the duty of directors to request and evaluate information relevant to their vote. Second, Congress adopted § 36(b) of the 1940 Act, codified as 15 U.S.C. § 80a-35(b), which imposes a fiduciary duty upon investment advisers with regard to their compensation. Formerly, § 36 only imposed on advisers a prohibition against gross abuse of trust or gross misconduct. Section 36(b), however, gave shareholders a private right of action against their adviser with respect to the adviser's fee. *Id.* For a discussing of the burden of proof for § 36(b) claims, see J. Thomas' concurring opinion in *Jones v. Harris Associates L.P.*, 559 U.S. 335, 354 (2010)

The 1970 Amendments to the 1940 Act also increased the importance of the Investment Advisers Act. These amendments amended the original act to expand its coverage and include many advisers previously exempted from the Act's registration requirements. In addition, the amendments strengthened substantive provisions prohibiting performance fees for investment advisers. In the Securities Act Amendments of 1975, Congress expanded the information necessary for registration under the Investment Advisers Act.

In the National Securities Market Improvements Act of 1996, Congress reformed the regulation of investment companies by, among other things, preempting state registration, qualification, and disclosure requirements for most investment companies. National Securities Markets Improvement Act of 1996, Pub. L. No. 104-290, 110 Stat. 3416 (codified as amended in scattered sections of 15 U.S.C. (2015)). The Act preserved state authority to bring enforcement actions involving fraud and other misconduct on the part of broker-dealers in connection with the sale of investment company shares. In addition, states retained the right to impose filing and registration fees on investment companies. Collectively, the 1996 reforms greatly diminish the role of state regulators in supervising substantive aspects of investment company operations. This is the same legislation that reallocated jurisdiction between investment advisers, establishing, in essence, a bifurcated regulatory system under which state authorities supervise investment advisers with less than $25 million in assets under management, and the SEC oversees those with larger portfolios.

The Dodd-Frank Act made only limited changes to the regulation of investment companies. Most importantly, the Act eliminated an important exemption from the Investment Advisers Act registration for firms advising hedge funds and certain other private funds. We will explore these changes in Chapter 10.4. The Dodd-Frank Act also facilitated the reform of MMFs, which we will take up in Chapter 12.3. Finally, with the creation of the Financial Stability Oversight Council (FSOC), the Dodd-Frank Act brought additional oversight to the entire asset management sector, a topic that we will take up in greater detail later in this chapter.

B. REGULATORY PERIMETERS

Section 3 of the 1940 Act defines the term investment company. Section 3(a) establishes the outer boundary of that definition, creating a presumption that certain kinds of companies should be subject to regulation under the 1940 Act. Sections 3(b) and 3(c) create a number of exemptions from § 3's broad definition. As you look over this statutory structure, consider the jurisdictional line it draws. Business organizations that fall within the definition of investment company are subject to strict and intrusive regulatory requirements. Other entities, including the vast majority of public corporations in the United States, are supervised far less stringently. Are investment companies so different from other types of business organizations as to warrant such different regulation? Consider how the 1940 Act definitions were applied in the following case.

SEC v. Fifth Avenue Coach Lines, Inc.

289 F. Supp. 3 (S.D.N.Y. 1968), aff'd, 435 F.2d 510 (2d Cir. 1970)

[Fifth Ave. Coach Lines ("Fifth") was a New York corporation with almost 900,000 issued shares held by 2,300 stockholders. Fifth had a wholly owned subsidiary called Surface Transit, Inc. ("Surface"), which in turn had a wholly owned subsidiary called Westchester Street Transportation Company, Inc. ("Westchester"). Fifth and Surface operated bus lines in New York City; Westchester operated bus lines in Westchester County. In 1962, the City of New York by condemnation acquired all the bus lines of Fifth and Surface, but not Westchester. After litigation, the City of New York in late 1966 and 1967 paid a total award of over $38 million to Fifth and Surface. Once creditors were paid, $11.5 million of this award actually went to the managers of Fifth. Fifth and its subsidiaries were run by Muscat, Cohn and Krock. From late 1966 onwards, these three men led Fifth into a series of complicated transactions which became the basis of this lawsuit by the SEC.]

Section 3(a)(1)

. . . Section 3(a)(1) says that a company is an investment company if it is engaged primarily in the business of investing, reinvesting or trading in securities, or holds itself out as being engaged primarily in that business, or proposes to engage primarily in that business. "Holding out" and "proposing" imply intent, but "is" does not necessarily imply it. It would seem to be possible for a company to find itself at a given point in time to be actually engaged primarily in this business, even though it originally did not intend to be so engaged. The key word is "primarily." To determine whether a company is engaged primarily in the business of investing, its total activities of all sorts must be considered.

As has been pointed out earlier in this opinion, between March 1962 and October 1966, Fifth itself, as a practical matter, was not engaged in any business. It was merely marking time until it received payment of the condemnation award. Through Westchester, a subsidiary of a subsidiary, it was engaged in operating a bus line in Westchester County. Since that was its only business, it must have been its "primary business" during that period, and although carried on indirectly, the company at that point would seem to have been specifically excluded from investment company status by Section 3(b)(1) of the Act. In any event, no one claims that before October 1966 Fifth was an investment company.

Plaintiff says, however, that Fifth became one in October 1966, at the moment that it received the award. The court does not agree. The mere possession of $11.5 million in cash does not make a company an investment company. It is necessary to examine Fifth's activities thereafter to see what it did with the cash, in other words, to see in what business it became primarily engaged.

In fairness, it should be noted that plaintiff's contention that Fifth became an investment company immediately in October 1966 is based in part on the verbs "holding out" and "proposes," rather than the "is" in Section 3(a)(1). This has reference to the fact that in the President's Letter dated July 28, 1966, in Fifth's annual report for 1965, Muscat stated . . . "as soon as the first monies are received from the City of New York the Surface mortgage bondholders will be paid in full, and the Company intends to make proper and advantageous investments for the benefit of the Company."

These statements are predictions as to what Fifth plans to do in the future. They are too general in nature to justify a finding that they amounted to such a "holding out" or "proposing" that Fifth would engage primarily in the business of investing as to require the conclusion that Fifth became an investment company immediately when the funds were received.

When Fifth first received the $11.5 million, it deposited the cash in a number of different banks. Some of these deposits were time deposits, usually for ninety days, but in some instances longer. Fifth received interest on its time deposits. Plaintiff calls this "investing." The court does not believe that merely putting one's money in the bank, even though one thereby obtains some interest, in and of itself is "investing, reinvesting or trading in securities" within the meaning of Section 3(a)(1). Surely a company which has suddenly come into possession of a substantial amount of cash is entitled to a reasonable time to decide what to do with it without violating the [1940] Act.

[Although Fifth began buying up and accumulating significant amounts of stock with this money, it still possessed a considerable amount of cash on December 31, 1996.] The court believes that up to that time Fifth was still in a period of transition. It still had not fully committed its liquid resources. It had not yet made investing its primary business. Under the 3(a)(1) test, it was not then an investment company.

Defendants say that they were looking around for opportunities for Fifth to buy control of other companies. There is evidence to support that contention. In the fall of 1966 Muscat, Krock and Cohn considered several different proposals for the acquisition of companies by Fifth. All of them fell through for one reason or another. . . . In 1967 Fifth continued to buy stock. It was particularly active in buying bank stocks. . . .

By June 30, 1967 Fifth owned substantially more securities and possessed substantially less cash than it had on December 31, 1966. As of June 30, its immediately available cash was $843,100 which, when added to time deposits of $775,000, made a total of $1,618,100 as compared to the $4,513,594 which it had had on December 31, 1966.

The time must eventually come when a corporation initially possessed of cash and no real business, by spending its cash becomes engaged in a business of some sort. That time had come by June 30, 1967.

What business was Fifth primarily engaged in on June 30? In the court's opinion, the only business that it can fairly be found to be primarily engaged in was the business of investing in securities. That was what it spent its money for. That is where its income came from. It had no other business which could reasonably be called "primary."

Westchester's buses and VIP's limousines were a negligible factor in Fifth's business. According to Fifth's own figures prepared by its new treasurer. . . And it cannot be said, merely because the securities owned by Fifth included stock constituting 26 percent of Mercantile, that Fifth on June 30 was primarily engaged in the banking business.

Defendants argue that Fifth was not engaged primarily in the business of investing in securities on June 30, 1967 or at any other time because its policy was to buy stocks for the purpose of obtaining control of other companies. Although, as previously stated, the evidence indicates that at least at the outset this was Fifth's policy, Fifth has been markedly unsuccessful in carrying out that policy. The only company that it can be said to control is Mercantile.

But regardless of whether the policy was successful or not, the answer to defendants' argument, in the court's opinion, is that it finds no support in the language of the Act and indeed runs counter to the normal meaning of that language and to the fundamental purpose of the Act. The statute does not recognize an exception for the business that defendants claim Fifth is and was engaged in, *i.e.*, the business of acquiring control of other companies. . . . On all the evidence the court finds that on June 30, 1967 Fifth was an investment company within the meaning of Section 3(a)(1). . . .

---

1. ***The Inadvertent Investment Company.*** The Fifth Avenue case is an example of what practitioners refer to as an inadvertent investment company, a problem that arises when a commercial firm inadvertently structures its assets in a way that causes the entity to fall within the definition of an investment company for purposes of § 3 of the 1940 Act. A classic fact pattern involving an operating company risking becoming an inadvertent investment company involves initial public offerings, following which a company is flush with cash and invests much of it. The SEC has adopted a variety of regulations to alleviate this problem in a number of situations, but still the definitional provisions, 15 U.S.C. § 80a-3, constitute a trap for the unwary. The interesting and difficult policy issue underlying these exceptions is the question of when a commercial firm becomes a vehicle for pooled investments such that the firm should be required to

abide by the 1940 Act's restrictions. Was, for example, the *Fifth Avenue* case correctly decided as a matter of regulatory policy? Over the years, the SEC has developed an elaborate set of rules and procedures that start-up ventures and firms winding down operations need to comply with in order to avoid the kinds of problems that the defendants encounter in the *Fifth Avenue* case. For a classic early treatment of the subject, see Edmund H. Kerr, The Inadvertent Investment Company: Section (a)(3) of the Investment Company Act, 12 STAN. L. REV. 29 (1959). Despite its long history, the problem of inadvertent investment companies remains a hardy perennial in the field. *See, e.g.*, SEC v. National Presto Indus., 486 F.3d 305 (7th Cir. 2007) (reversing an SEC enforcement action requiring 1940 Act registration on the grounds that the firm in question was "primarily engaged" in a business other than investing in securities). The Volcker Rule, which we discussed in Chapter 6.2, has meant that becoming an inadvertent investment company also has an impact on whether a banking organization can invest in the company and complicates the underwriting and market-making in such a company's shares.

2. ***1940 Act Exemptions.*** The exemptions from the 1940 Act are instructive. For example, read § 3(c)(3) of the 1940 Act. Why is this exemption necessary? Have we seen similar exemptions elsewhere? Note too § 3(c)(1), which exempts private investment companies, those with fewer than 100 beneficial owners. The existence of this exemption has been critical for the development of certain segments of the financial services sector, most notably hedge funds. *Compare* § 3(c)(1) *with* § 3(c)(7). What is the difference between these two exemptions? Are both exemptions necessary? Recall the transtatutory incorporation of these sections into the Bank Holding Company Act (BHCA), which we discussed in Chapter 6.2.

3. ***Identifying Investment Companies.*** Warren Buffett has been one of the most successful investment managers for many decades. His company, Berkshire Hathaway, holds substantial investments in a number of companies. Most of these investments are held through a Nebraska insurance company that is itself a wholly-owned subsidiary of Berkshire Hathaway. Berkshire Hathaway is a public company with numerous shareholders. Is Berkshire Hathaway subject to the 1940 Act?

The broad definition of investment company contained in the 1940 Act has prompted numerous questions as to when the activities of other financial firms constitute the sort of collective investment pool that must be registered as an investment company under the 1940 Act. One of the most prominent lines of cases here concerns separate accounts of insurance companies. For example, in the 1950s, insurance companies began to develop variable annuity products where the level of annuity payments varied based on the performance of a separately managed pool of assets. The goal of these products was to allow annuitants to participate in the growth of equity markets without imposing investment risk on insurance companies. As the 1940 Act includes an express exemption for insurance companies, the courts eventually concluded that these separate accounts constituted investment companies under what is sometimes referred to as the ectoplasm theory of investment companies. *See* Prudential Ins. Co. v. SEC, 326 F.2d 383 (3rd Cir. 1964). These decisions followed earlier

Supreme Court precedent, concluding that interests in variable annuities could constitute securities notwithstanding similar exceptions for insurance companies under the 1933 and 1934 Acts. *See, e.g.*, SEC v. VALIC, 359 U.S. 65 (1959); SEC v. United Benefit Life Ins. Co., 387 U.S. 202 (1967). Many variable insurance products are thus subject to overlapping regulation under state insurance laws and federal securities law, including the 1940 Act. *See* TAMAR FRANKEL & E. KIRSCH CLIFFORD, INVESTMENT MANAGEMENT REGULATION (Fathom Publishing Co. 2003). Insurance sector representatives also have expended considerable energy attempting to develop variable insurance products that escape SEC oversight, often finding themselves confronted with countervailing efforts from the SEC. *See, e.g.*, American Equity Life Ins. Co. v. SEC, 613 F.3d 166 (D.C. 2010) (striking down SEC regulation intended to limit insurance companies' ability to market annuities linked to the value of a securities index, like the S&P 500, without complying with SEC requirements). With the Harkin Amendment, the Dodd-Frank Act imposed new constraints on the ability of the SEC to adopt new regulation to reach equity-index annuities. *See* 15 U.S.C. § 77(c). As a result, there are certain forms of securities-linked insurance products that insurance companies can distribute outside the federal securities laws.

Another historically important regulatory perimeter is the one between bank trust activities and the distribution of investment company products. As you may recall from Chapter 2.2, one of the early cases defining the scope of the Glass-Steagall Act was the Supreme Court's decision in Investment Co. Inst. v. Camp. 401 U.S. 617 (1971). In that case, the Court concluded that the Comptroller of the Currency erred in authorizing national banks to establish collective managed investment accounts, which were to be registered as investment companies under the 1940 Act. In a majority opinion by Justice Potter Stewart, the Court reasoned that the proposed activity violated § 16 of the Glass-Steagall Act. In dissent, Justice Harry Blackmun argued as follows:

> The Court's opinion and judgments here, it seems to me, are based more on what is deemed to be appropriate and desirable national banking policy than on what is a necessary judicial construction of the Glass-Steagall Act. . .. It is a far different thing to be persuaded that it is wise policy to keep national banks out of the business of operating mutual investment funds, despite the safeguards that the Comptroller of the Currency and the [SEC] have provided, than it is to be persuaded that existing and somewhat ancient legislation requires that result. Policy considerations are for the Congress and not for this Court.
>
> I recognize and am fully aware of the factors and of the economic considerations that led to the enactment of the Glass-Steagall Act. The second and third decades of [the 20th Century] are not the happiest chapter in the history of American banking. Deep national concerns emerged from the distressful experiences of those years and from the sad ends to which certain banking practices of that time had led the industry. But those then-prevailing conditions, the legislative history, and the remedy Congress provided, prompt me to conclude that what was proscribed was the involvement and activity of a national bank in investment, as contrasted with

> commercial, banking, in underwriting and issuing, and in acquiring speculative securities for its own account. These were the banking sins of that time.
>
> The propriety, however, of a national bank's acting, when not in contravention of state or local law, as an inter vivos or testamentary trustee, as an executor or administrator, as a guardian or committee, as a custodian and, indeed, as an agent for the individual customer's securities and funds . . . is not, and could not be, questioned by the petitioners here or by the Court. This being so, there is, for me, an element of illogic in the ready admission by all concerned, on the one hand, that a national bank has the power to manage, by way of a common trust arrangement, those funds that it holds as fiduciary in the technical sense, and to administer separate agency accounts, and in the rejection, on the other hand, of the propriety of the bank's placing agency assets into a mutual investment fund. The Court draws its decisional line between the two. I find it impossible to locate any statutory root for that line drawing. To use the Glass-Steagall Act as a tool for that distinction is, I think, a fundamental misconception of the statute.
>
> Accordingly, I am not convinced that the Congress, by that Act or otherwise, as yet has proscribed the banking endeavors under challenge here by competitors in a highly competitive field. None of the judges of the Court of Appeals was so convinced, and neither was the Comptroller of the Currency whose expertise the Court concedes. I would leave to Congress the privilege of now prohibiting such national bank activity if that is its intent and desire. . . .

Id. at 642 (Blackmun, J., dissenting). How persuasive do you find this dissent?

III. IS ASSET MANAGEMENT SYSTEMICALLY IMPORTANT?

As we explored in Chapter 6.2, the FSOC has the power under Title I of the Dodd-Frank Act to designate financial firms as systemically important and thus subject to prudential oversight by the Federal Reserve Board. To date, the FSOC has exercised that power with respect to two insurance companies and GE Capital. There remains, however, an open question of which other financial firms the FSOC could and should designate as systemically important. The September 2013 Report of the OFR, was understood to explore this question in the context of asset managers. While the report did not recommend the designation of any particular asset management firm, the OFR's analysis was widely understood to be a possible first step in the designation of asset managers as systemically important. The following excerpts give a flavor of the analysis.

OFR, Asset Management and Financial Stability

Sept. 2013

This report provides a brief overview of the asset management industry and an analysis of how asset management firms and the activities in which they engage can introduce vulnerabilities that could pose, amplify, or transmit threats to financial stability.

> The [FSOC] decided to study the activities of asset management firms to better inform its analysis of whether—and how—to consider such firms for enhanced prudential standards and supervision under Section 113 of the Dodd-Frank Act. The [FSOC] asked the [OFR], in collaboration with [FSOC] members, to provide data and analysis to inform this consideration. This study responds to that request by analyzing industry activities, describing the factors that make the industry and individual firms vulnerable to financial shocks, and considering the channels through which the industry could transmit risks across financial markets.
>
> The U.S. asset management industry oversees the allocation of approximately $53 trillion in financial assets. . . . The industry is central to the allocation of financial assets on behalf of investors. By facilitating investment for a broad cross-section of individuals and institutions, discretionary asset management plays a key role in capital formation and credit intermediation, while spreading any gains or losses across a diverse population of market participants. . . . Asset management firms and the funds that they manage transact with other financial institutions to transfer risks, achieve price discovery, and invest capital globally through a variety of activities. Asset management activities include allocating assets and selecting securities, using a variety of investment strategies in registered and non-registered funds; enhancing returns with derivatives or leverage; and creating customized investment solutions for larger clients, primarily through so-called separate accounts.
>
> These activities differ in important ways from commercial banking and insurance activities. Asset managers act primarily as agents: managing assets on behalf of clients as opposed to investing on the managers' behalf. Losses are borne by—and gains accrue to—clients rather than asset management firms. In contrast, commercial banks and insurance companies typically act as principals: accepting deposits with a liability of redemption at par and on demand . . .
>
> However, some types of asset management activities are similar to those provided by banks and other [non-bank] financial companies, and increasingly cut across the financial system in a variety of ways. For example, asset managers may create funds that can be close substitutes for the money-like liabilities created by banks; they engage in various forms of liquidity transformation, primarily, but not exclusively, through collective investment vehicles; and they provide liquidity to clients and to financial markets. . . .
>
> Unfortunately, there are limitations to the data available to measure, analyze, and monitor asset management firms and their diverse activities, and to evaluate their implications for financial stability. These data gaps are not broadly recognized. Indeed, there is a spectrum of data availability among asset management activities. . . . Privately owned asset management firms . . . do not disclose information comparable to the public financial reports filed by asset managers that are public companies or subsidiaries of public companies. Data on some activities—such as involvement in repo transactions and the reinvestment of cash collateral from securities lending—are incomplete, thereby limiting visibility into market practices.

The OFR report, which was written at the request of the FSOC, prompted intense and immediate push back from the financial securities sector. The OFR asserted that asset managers' proclivity to "reach for yield" by purchasing riskier investments in a low interest rate environment, and their tendency to "herd" into these same risky assets, may be a source of systemic risk. The OFR also focused on the runnability of managed funds when the market is stressed, as well as the degree of leverage at asset managers, which may accelerate fire sales in the event of a run. In response to the OFR report, asset managers argued that a managers' size was not indicative of the riskiness of its business and that a focus on the systemic risk of specific activities, rather than firms, would be more appropriate. The following excerpt from a speech by the vice chairman of BlackRock, identified by the OFR report as the top asset manager with $3.7 trillion of assets under management as 2012, illustrates this push back.

Barbara Novick, Vice Chair, BlackRock, Systemic Risk and Asset Management: Improving the Financial Ecosystem for All Market Participants

Harvard Law School EU-US Symposium Concept Paper, Mar. 2014

By now, with the publication in September 2013 of the "Study of Asset Management and Financial Stability" by the OFR and the issuance of the consultation on "Assessment Methodologies for Identifying Non-Bank Non-Insurer Global Systemically Important Financial Institutions" in January 2014 by the [Financial Stability Board (FSB)] and [International Organization of Securities Commissions (IOSCO)], it is apparent that [systemically important financial institution (SIFI)] identification frameworks are not easily applied to asset managers. The asset management business model is an "agency" model which is fundamentally different than that of other financial institutions that act as principals. Asset managers act as agents on behalf of clients rather than managing assets on their own balance sheet. As a result, asset managers are neither the owner of the assets that they manage nor the counterparty to trades or derivatives. In addition, asset managers are much less susceptible to financial distress than banks, making asset managers highly unlikely to "fail" in the sense of a bank failure. Asset managers do not fund their business using the short-term credit markets and therefore, they are not exposed to the type of liquidity squeeze that banks and broker-dealers may encounter. Likewise, asset managers' revenue is generated principally from fees on assets under management and asset managers have the ability to significantly adjust expenses if revenues decline. Larger asset managers are further protected in that their revenues tend to be diversified by some combination of product, client type, and geography making them less susceptible to issues in any one area. Importantly, even if an asset manager does go out of business, the resolution process is straightforward in that clients can reassign their assets to another manager and the remaining assets and liabilities of the manager itself can be resolved easily. Like any other service organization, asset managers go out of business regularly with no systemic implications.

The focus on potential SIFI and/or global SIFI designations on individual asset management firms is misplaced. The issues identified in the OFR paper as well as the issues identified by the FSB involve investment products and investment practices which require industry-wide solutions. . . .

What Distinguishes Asset Managers from Other Types of Financial Institutions?

While part of the financial services sector, asset managers are characterized by a business model that is fundamentally different than that of other financial institutions, such as commercial banks, investment banks, insurance companies and government-sponsored entities. Asset managers are different than most other financial firms in that they act as advisors or agents on behalf of their clients; asset managers are not investing on their own behalf. Asset managers do not act as lenders or otherwise provide credit to individuals or corporations, nor do they perform clearance, custody or related functions. In addition, asset managers do not act as counterparties in derivatives, financing or securities transactions, and they do not cross-hold debt or equity with their funds or other institutions. When a manager transacts in the market, the obligations under the trade (*e.g.*, settlement, posting of margin) belong to the manager's client and are not obligations of the manager itself.

Contrast this with banks, broker-dealers and insurance companies. Although they promise the return of their customers' funds and assets, these entities use customer assets in the ordinary conduct of their businesses. . . .

Because asset management firms are not direct market participants, and do not invest for their own account, they do not assume high levels of balance sheet risk. Conversely, other financial companies engage in activities involving balance sheet risk. For example, investment banks act as principal in trading, market-making and prime brokerage . . . The balance sheet of an asset management firm comprises working capital, an investment portfolio related to seed and co-investment capital, property, premises and equipment; thereby requiring a modest amount of capital. An asset manager's balance sheet is very small compared with that of a bank and its balance sheet is not leveraged. . . . Importantly, end-investors primarily bear the risk of adverse market movements, not the asset manager itself. Investors that hire asset managers or invest in funds understand and accept that they are exposed to the risk of their assets falling in value. While asset managers strive to generate positive performance for clients, asset price deterioration in a given fund or client account has little direct impact on the asset manager. . . .

Improving the Financial Ecosystem

The financial crisis highlighted a number of risks and, in response, over the past several years, many changes to global regulation and to market practices have occurred which reduce systemic risk. These changes range from an increased emphasis on risk management to improvements in liquidity management, enhanced collateral management and counterparty limits, increased transparency, deleveraging of banks and increased capital standards, as well as detailed reporting on private funds, derivatives, and other security transactions. . . . We have identified several areas where regulators can use powers and tools to improve the financial ecosystem: [securities lending, liquidity in fixed income markets, and harmonization of global data reporting.] . . . [Solutions should apply consistently across all regions; otherwise, activity will shift to other market participants] without actually addressing the issue under consideration. . . .

Securities Lending . . .

Securities lending involves a loan of securities to a third party (the borrower), who gives the lender collateral (in the form of cash, shares, or bonds) in an amount equal to the value of the loaned securities plus an additional margin above that amount. The borrower compensates the lender for the securities loan either through a payment or allowing the lender to keep part of the collateral reinvestment return. The lender receives at a minimum the same economic exposure to a security on loan, including any dividends or distributions, as if the loan had not occurred, although the lender must recall shares in order to vote proxies. The market for securities lending is driven by demand from large banks and broker-dealers and their clients, including hedge funds. Investors are, directly or indirectly [through institutional investors such as pension funds and mutual funds], the lenders of securities and they lend securities to achieve enhanced returns on their portfolios. . . . Like any investing activity, securities lending entails risks that must be managed. Key risks include counterparty credit risk, cash collateral reinvestment risk, non-cash collateral risk, and operational risk. During the financial crisis, issues surfaced related to cash collateral reinvestment strategies which have triggered increased scrutiny of securities lending by the SEC, [European Securities and Markets Authority], and others. Each of the potential risks associated with securities lending can and should be addressed and monitored in a well-managed securities lending program. . . . [Nonetheless, a]sset managers act as lending agent for a small subset of the total volume of securities lending transactions; most securities lending activity is conducted by custodial lending agents. As a result, regulating selected market participants, rather than seeking to change practices across all market participants, will not address potential systemic risks associated with securities lending.

Liquidity in Fixed Income Markets

A structural shift is underway in the corporate bond market. The cumulative impacts of regulation, including bank capital rules like Basel III, have reduced banks' appetites for using their balance sheet to take on risk. As a result, . . . primary dealers' inventories of U.S. corporate bonds have plummeted 73% from a high of $235 billion in 2007. This dynamic has been somewhat obscured by record issuance levels and positive price performance. . . . [I]t is important to address this issue as reduced liquidity translates to wider spreads, higher transaction costs, and ultimately diminished returns for investors.

The corporate bond market is highly fragmented as corporations issue various bonds over time with different maturities, different coupons, and other features. Bond investors must sift through thousands of issues even for the top 10 corporate issuers, as [Figure 1 in this excerpt] shows. We believe a more standardized corporate bond market would result in enhanced market liquidity. . . .

Figure 1:
Bonds and Shares Outstanding of Top US Investment Grade Bond Issuers

Issuer	Bonds in Barclays US Corporate Index	Share of Dollar Amount Outstanding	Total Bonds Outstanding	Common Equity Securities	Preferred Equity Securities
GE	44	31.2%	1,014	1	4
J.P. Morgan	32	34.1%	1,645	1	13
Goldman Sachs	25	38.4%	1,242	1	8
Citigroup	39	35.8%	1,965	1	12
Morgan Stanley	29	40.1%	1,316	1	12
Bank of America	30	28.2%	1,544	1	39
AT&T	29	62.6%	74	1	0
Wal-Mart	26	71.6%	50	1	0
Verizon	26	60.8%	71	1	0
Wells Fargo	15	26.2%	274	1	8

Harmonization of Global Data Reporting

Several new regulations require managers to report data on products that they manage. For example, private fund reporting is found in [the Alternative Investment Fund Managers Directive (AIFMD)] and in regulations resulting from the [Dodd-Frank] Act. The data requested on Form PF and Form PQR as well as the data requested for AIFMD is often similar but is requested in a slightly different manner on each form. The result is large amounts of fragmented data. Standardization would enable regulators to aggregate data and analyze data sets, and would facilitate comparisons. Swaps data, threshold reporting, and securities lending are other obvious areas where consistency of data reporting would benefit regulators by providing "information", not just raw data.

---

1. ***Systemically Important Firms versus Activities.*** How would you assess Ms. Barbara Novick's critique of proposals to designate the very largest asset managers as systemically important? Is Novick correct that it would be better for regulatory authorities to focus their attention on potentially problematic activities rather than developing heightened standards for only certain members of the asset management sector? Is it relevant that FSOC's designation authority under Title I of the Dodd-Frank Act is limited to systemically important firms and does not extend to systemically important activities? Or does § 120(a) of Dodd-Frank Act, which empowers the FSOC to "provide for more stringent regulation of a financial activity by issuing recommendations to the primary financial regulatory agencies to apply new or heightened standards and safeguards . . .," provide sufficient regulatory power? Are there other ways in which federal authorities can reach systemically risky activities? Note that Title

VIII of the Dodd-Frank Act gives the FSOC authority to designate payment, clearing and settlement activities as systemically important).

2. ***The FSOC Backs Away from Designating Asset Managers.*** The OFR report generated a firestorm of criticism, including significant resistance from the SEC, the primary regulators of asset managers. The SEC solicited comments on the OFR report, a highly unusual request that was largely understood as a way to include the strong criticism of the report in the public record. In July 2014, FSOC announced that it would shift its focus away from designating individual firms as systemic, and instead focus on products and activities in the asset management sector to assess systemic risk. In January 2015, FSOC issued a notice seeking public comment on whether asset management products and activities may pose potential risks to U.S. financial stability. In response to the controversy following the OFR's report on asset managers, Federal Reserve Governor Daniel Tarullo has made a number of statements on the topic. Consider the following excerpt from a September 2015 speech:

> [L]et me mention asset managers briefly. As they have garnered increasing shares of financial system assets, a trend that accelerated following the financial crisis, the question has arisen whether they too should hold capital buffers. Of course in most cases the asset manager itself does not have much of a balance sheet at all. The funds themselves are often not leveraged, in which case nearly all the liabilities are shares of the fund held by investors, the price of which varies to reflect the value of the assets purchased by the manager of the fund.
>
> While some commentators have suggested that liquidity challenges and consequent fire sale type behavior might develop if the structure of the fund places a premium on exiting first, these kinds of risks would support an argument less for capital buffers than for some form of prudential market regulation, such as rules on liquidity or redemptions. I would note in this regard that last week the SEC issued a proposed rulemaking that would require open-ended funds to have liquidity risk management controls in place for shareholder redemptions, including during times of stress. Likewise, to the degree that certain idiosyncratic risks might exist with respect to the decisions and operations of certain asset managers, their liability structure again suggests that some form of prudential market regulation would be better suited to address these risks.

Daniel K. Tarullo, Governor, Board of Governors of the Fed. Reserve Sys., Remarks at the Banque de France Conference: Financial Regulation—Stability versus Uniformity; A Focus on Non-bank Actors, (Sept. 28. 2015).

In a November 2015 speech to the Brookings Institution, Tarullo suggested some asset managers should be subject to less rigorous regulations than those who pose redemption risks. *See* Daniel K. Tarullo, Governor of the Federal Reserve Board, Speech at the Brookings Institution: Thinking Critically about Nonbank Financial Intermediation 5 (Nov. 17, 2015). He added that "In many instances, and especially where funding vulnerabilities are at the heart of a business model, it is the activity itself that needs to be regulated in some way, whether there are a few large firms involved or many smaller ones." *Id.* at 12. He further noted that "some classes of asset managers, such as bond funds that hold relatively illiquid assets while offering their investors the right to withdraw funds on very short notice, *may* pose redemption risks. Mutual funds and other intermediaries do not, however, pose bank-like risks, because they generally are not leveraged. So, if further analysis supports the conclusion that redemption risks are real, the optimal regulatory response would surely not be one that treats all asset managers as quasi-banks that need to have capital and similar bank regulatory constraints." *Id.* at 5. Has Governor Tarullo adopted Novick's position? What are the implications for FSOC designations going forward?

3. ***SEC Regulatory Efforts.*** In what has been perceived as further response to the OFR study of September 2013, the SEC, in 2015, established a regulatory agenda for investment companies heavily tilted towards initiatives related to systemic risk concerns. Two of the SEC's regulatory efforts are of note. First, in May 2015, the SEC proposed rules to modernize and enhance reporting and disclosure by investment companies and advisers. Press Release, SEC Proposes Rules to Modernize and Enhance Information Reported by Investment Companies and Investment Advisers (May 20, 2015). By requiring such entities to engage in regular but selective and delayed reporting, the SEC appears to address both the OFR's concerns regarding gaps in data availability on the activities of asset management firms, as well as commentators' concerns about competition and information poaching. For example, the Investment Company Institute, the national association of U.S. investment companies, "applaud[ed]" the SEC's decision to withhold from the public "portfolio holdings and certain other data," except for "data for the third month of each quarter." Letter from David Blass, General Counsel, Investment Company Institute to Brent Fields, Secretary, SEC, File No. S7-08-15 (Aug. 11, 2015).

The second regulatory effort, briefly alluded to by Governor Tarullo in the speech previously excerpted, is the SEC's liquidity risk management rules. In September 2015, the SEC proposed rules that would require mutual funds and ETFs to "implement liquidity risk management programs and enhance disclosure regarding fund liquidity and redemption practices." Press Release, SEC Proposes Liquidity Management Rules for Mutual Funds and ETFs (Sep. 22, 2015). The risk management programs are intended to prevent fire sales and the resulting liquidity crunch, while allowing investors to redeem their assets in a timely but orderly manner. While such a proposal addresses the liquidity concerns of Tarullo and the OFR study, it arguably runs counter to Novick's argument that "[a]sset managers do not fund their business using the short-term credit markets and therefore, they are not exposed to the type of liquidity squeeze that banks and broker-dealers may encounter."

The SEC has pursued additional reforms, discussed in Chapter 10.2, Part IV, that address concerns in the OFR report. Assuming the SEC is successful with these initiatives, should the FSOC be satisfied that the systemic risks associated with asset management in the United States have been addressed?

IV. INSTITUTIONAL INVESTORS IN CORPORATE GOVERNANCE

Hedge funds have made headlines in the 21st century for their role in corporate governance. Labeled as activist investors, hedge funds purchase shares in large companies with dispersed and disinterested shareholders and push these companies to make better use of their assets. This role of hedge funds is a significant departure from institutional investors' historical role with respect to corporate governance. As described in Professor Mark Roe's excerpt below, efforts to restrict institutional investors from having too much control over the management of corporations trace back at least to the New Deal. These regulations were characterized as safeguarding Main Street from Wall Street.

In Roe's analysis, banks and life insurers were the main financial institutions that could play a role in corporate governance as stockholder when industrial firms began to go public and ownership diffused at the end of the 19th Century. Banks, confined to state-by-state operations or else to operating from a single location, were too small to own enough stock to play a big role in the large industrial firms emerging at the end of the 19th Century, and were further generally restricted from owning equity. Life insurers were relatively larger than the largest banks in the United States at the beginning of the 20th Century and owned stock and participating in corporate governance, particularly in the large railroads. But by 1906, the largest life insurers were barred from owning stock and participating in corporate governance.

The organization and authority of the largest financial institutions, Roe argues, had an impact on the organization of authority in large industrial firms; if financial institutions could not wield influential blocks of stock, as they could not in the United States, then ownership diffusion and enhancement of executive authority was more likely. In countries that had significant financial institutional involvement in large industrial firms in the latter half of the 20th Century, the institutions were typically large banks and large life insurers, particularly in Germany and Japan. Even in Britain, a nation whose financial system resembles the American in many ways, large life insurers have had a larger corporate governance voice there than they did in the United States. With banks and insurers uninvolved in equity-level corporate governance through much of the 20th Century, mutual funds, pension funds, and hedge funds sometimes sought to fill in parts of that role toward the century's end.

Mark J. Roe, Strong Managers, Weak Owners

21-22, 149 (1994)

. . . Fragmented securities markets are not the only way to move savings from households to the large firm. There is at least one clear contender with the securities markets, namely, the powerful financial intermediary, which would move savings from people to firms and could take big blocks of stock, sit in boardrooms, and balance power with the CEO. Enterprises could have obtained economies of scale and investors could have obtained diversification through large intermediaries that brought small investors and large firms together. But American law and politics deliberately diminished the power of financial institutions in general, and often their power to hold the large equity blocks. . . .

[Institutional investors, such as banks, insurance companies, mutual funds, and pension funds], which hold nearly all of the corporate assets held by U.S. financial intermediaries, clearly could influence big firms. But portfolio rules, antinetworking rules, and other fragmenting rules disable them from systematically having influential blocks. . . . [B]anks, the institution with the most money, have been barred from owning stock or operating nationally. Mutual funds generally cannot own control blocks. Insurers can put only a fragment of their investment portfolios into any one company's stock, and for most of this century the big insurers were banned from owning any stock at all. Pension funds are less restricted, but they are fragmented; securities rules have made it hard for them to operate jointly to assert influence. Private pension funds are under management control; they are not yet ready for a palace revolution in which they would assert control over their managerial bosses.

. . . American politics deliberately fragmented financial institutions so that few institutions could focus their investments into powerful inside blocks of stock. Different ways to develop corporate institutions are imaginable, but American politics cut their development paths off.

Opinion polls show a popular mistrust of large financial institutions with accumulated power, a wariness of Wall Street's controlling industrial America. Politicians responded to that distrust by restricting private accumulations of power by financial institutions. Various interest groups also benefited from fragmentation; Congress and the administrative agencies also responded to them. . . . Legislative history, popular ideology, the power of interest groups, and the views of opinion leaders reveal a consistent political story—and hence one part of the foundation of the [21st Century] American corporation. Politics never allowed financial institutions to become powerful enough to control operating firms; American politics preferred Berle-Means corporations[, those with separate ownership and control,] to the alternative of concentrated institutional ownership, which it precluded. . . .

[We can] look to other economies to see if they have differently organized intermediaries and, consequently, differing corporate forms. . . . Even a superficial glance [at the German and Japanese systems] reveals profound differences, which confirm the political paradigm. After all, if economic evolution best explains how firms are organized, then we would expect the top of the large German or Japanese firm to resemble the top of the large American one. But it does not; the German and Japanese firms have a flatter authority structure at the top. The best explanation seems to lie not in differences of economic task but in differences in the organization of financial intermediaries.

The existence and persistence of the foreign structures casts doubt on the standard paradigm, which tends to see small, liquid holdings in well-developed securities markets as the best and highest, or at least essential, form of financial development and ownership . . .

Despite policymakers' wariness towards institutional investors, many began to see institutional investors as a solution to managerial slack. *See, e.g.*, Ronald J. Gilson & Reinier Kraakman, *Investment Companies as Guardian Shareholders: The Place of the MSIC in the Corporate Governance Debate*, 45 STAN. L. REV. 985 (1993). Initially, this new role of institutional investors manifested itself in proxy voting initiatives, which later raised concerns for investment managers acting as fiduciaries of pension funds' assets. *See* Employee Benefits Security Administration, Interpretive Bulletin Relating to Exercise of Shareholder Rights, 73 Fed. Reg. 61731 (Oct. 17, 2008) (indicating that investment managers that are ERISA plan fiduciaries must vote their proxy shares in a way that enhances the economic value of the plan). An entire sector arose to support institutional investors on how to exercise their proxy voting power in accordance with their fiduciary standards. The most notable of these advisers is Institutional Shareholder Services, which "draws fire for both setting governance standards and helping corporate clients meet them, provoking criticism that it profits handsomely from a possible conflict of interest." Robert D. Hershey, Jr., *A Little Industry With a Lot of Sway on Proxy Votes*, N.Y. TIMES (June 18, 2006). Generally speaking, mutual funds and pension funds do not themselves engage directly with the core of corporate governance—via seats in the boardroom—but they sometimes support others seeking boardroom seats and, because these funds together own some 40% of the American stock market, their votes are important. For a discussion of mutual fund advisers' reluctance to take an active role in corporate governance, see Jennifer S. Taub, *Perhaps Able But Not Willing: The Failure of Mutual Fund Advisers to Advocate for Shareholders' Rights*, 34 J. CORP. L. 843 (2009).

Beyond proxy voting, institutional investors have played an increasing and significant role in shareholder activism. Hedge funds in particular face fewer regulations that would impede them from directly taking large blocks of stock and boardroom seats. *See generally* Edward Rock & Marcel Kahan, "Hedge Funds in Corporate Governance and Corporate Control," *in* INSTITUTIONAL INVESTOR ACTIVISM: HEDGE FUNDS AND PRIVATE EQUITY, ECONOMICS AND REGULATION 151 (William W. Bratton & Joseph A. McCahery, eds., Oxford Univ. Press, 2015). Even without a direct boardroom role, hedge fund activists can benefit companies by initiating new development strategies and, in one view, bringing a voice to the dispersed shareholders. *The Case for and Against Activist Hedge Funds*, VALUEWALK.COM (Oct. 20, 2015). In so doing, activist hedge funds are exploiting a feature of corporate governance law, while assuming that feckless boards must be forced to take action to benefit shareholders. *Id.* Some institutional investors and prominent academics, such as Lucian Bebchuk, have sided with activist hedge funds. *Id.*

Despite their benefits, activist hedge funds investors remain controversial. *Compare* Lucian A. Bebchuk, Alon Brav, & Wei Jiang, *The Long-term Effects of Hedge Fund Activism*, 113 COLUM. L. REV. 1085 (June 2015) (dismissing criticism of shareholder power as not supported by empirical evidence) *with* Martin Lipton, Wachtell, Lipton, Rosen & Katz, *Bite the Apple; Poison the Apple; Paralyze the Company; Wreck the Economy*, HARV. L. SCH. FORUM ON CORP. GOVERNANCE & FIN. REG. (Feb. 26, 2013) (criticizing institutional investors as pushing for short-term profit) *and* Stephen M. Bainbridge, *Investor Activism: Reshaping the Playing Field?* 12 (UCLA School of Law, Law & Econ. Research Paper Series, No. 08-12) (arguing shareholder activism decreases the efficiency benefits of separation of ownership and control). Shareholder activism by institutional investors has also been criticized for antitrust concerns arising from horizontal shareholdings, where "a common set of investors own significant shares in corporations that are horizontal competitors." Einer Elhauge, *Horizontal Shareholding*, 109 HARV. L. REV. (2016) (forthcoming). In the banking sector, for example, where "four institutional investors are among the top 5 shareholders of the nation's five largest [bank holding companies]," common ownership is strongly correlated with higher fees and deposit rate spreads. José Azar, Sahil Raina & Martin C. Schmalz, *Ultimate Ownership and Bank Competition* (Jan. 8, 2016) (unpublished draft).

CHAPTER 10.2

MUTUAL FUNDS: FIDUCIARY DUTIES AND STRUCTURAL RESTRAINTS

CONTENTS

I. INTRODUCTION

This Chapter is the second of three focusing on the regulation of registered investment companies under the Investment Company Act of 1940 (1940 Act). We begin with a brief overview of the growth of investment companies over the past three quarters of a century, introducing the principal kinds of investment companies and also the centrality of the modern mutual fund complex. We then explore the role of independent directors in the oversight of investment companies, an illustration of what is arguably the most developed reliance on external gatekeeper liability in financial regulation. The Chapter concludes with a discussion of the principal structural constraints of the 1940 Act, which also depend on independent director oversight for their implementation.

II. AN OVERVIEW OF INVESTMENT COMPANIES TODAY

A. THE GROWTH OF INVESTMENT COMPANIES AND PRINCIPAL TYPES

Investment companies grew cautiously at first, but by the 1970s, the sector took off. In 1941, total assets invested in the companies registered with the SEC were $2.5 billion. Mutual funds experienced much stronger growth in the years following the passage of the 1940 Act. By 1944, the aggregate assets of mutual funds exceeded those of closed-end companies, which had been the dominant type of fund throughout the 1920s. As we will explore in this Chapter, the distinctive feature of mutual funds is that their shares are continuously offered for sale to and redemption from shareholders at the end of each business day at a price based on the net asset value (NAV) of the shares. Traditionally, the other principal type of investment company was the closed-end company, which is an investment company that does not engage in the continuous offer and redemption of shares. Closed-end investment companies initially sell their shares to the investing public but thereafter shareholders must usually buy and sell their shares in the secondary markets.

By 1970, the aggregate assets of mutual funds were $50 billion, or almost 12 times those of closed-end companies at $4 billion. Over the next 25 years, investment company assets skyrocketed, particularly in the mutual fund side of the sector, aided by flow of assets from 401(k)s. As of November 1997, there were reportedly over 6,700 mutual funds on the market, with $4.5 trillion in assets under management. This represents a large increase even since 1990, when there was only 3,105 mutual funds with $1.1 trillion in assets. The booming stock market of the 1990s attracted many investors to mutual funds for the first time, with many gaining their initial exposure to the asset class as a result of investments through 401(k) retirement plans.

Investment companies have grown significantly since 1997, with mutual funds remaining the largest segment of the sector with some 9,260 separate mutual funds in existence as of year-end 2014 with over $15.8 trillion in assets. There are many fewer closed-end investment companies than mutual funds, and the asset levels have remained flat over the past two decades. Unit investment trusts, another specialized category of investment company, retain a modest market share throughout the period.

In contrast, the greatest growth of investment companies in recent years has been in a category known as exchange-traded funds (ETFs). First sanctioned by the SEC in the early 1990s, ETFs are technically organized as mutual funds (and occasionally as unit investment trusts) but operate under a series of SEC exemptive orders that allow market-makers to trade in ETF shares throughout the day, much like ordinary stocks. The trading is designed to maintain prices at the NAV of ETF shares, so shareholders receive the same kind of pricing associated with traditional mutual funds but can liquidate or purchase shares throughout the business day. Initially, ETFs were tied to widely followed market indices, like the S&P 500, but over time sponsors have expanded into many less well-known indices and even portfolios with some characteristics of active management. For an insightful overview of the rise of ETFs, see Eric D. Roiter, *Exchange Traded Funds: Neither Fish Nor Fowl, in* RESEARCH HANDBOOK ON THE REGULATION OF MUTUAL FUNDS (William A. Birdthistle & John Morley eds., Edward Elgar, forthcoming 2016).

Figure 10.2-1 Institutional and Household Ownership of Mutual Funds (Year-End 2014)

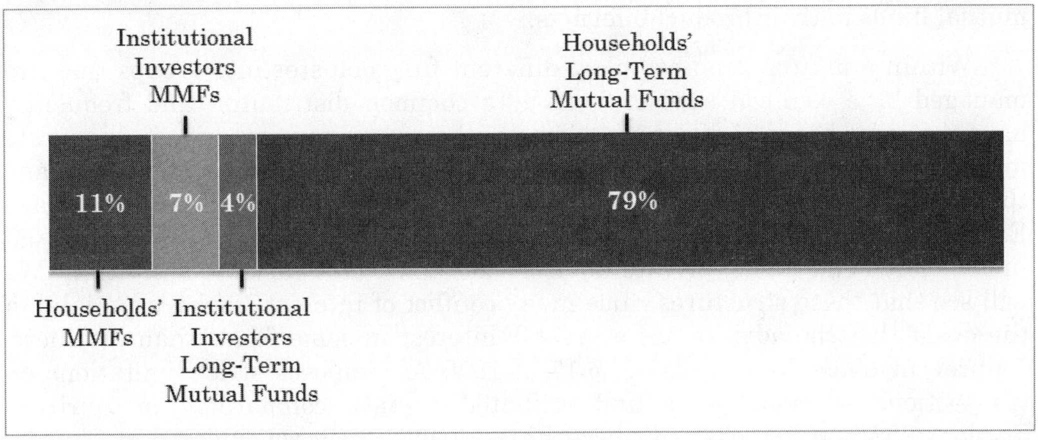

Source: Inv. Co. Inst., 2015 Investment Company Fact Book: A Review of Trends and Activities in the U.S. Investment Company Industry (55th ed. 2015).

Another important category of investment companies is the money market mutual fund, or MMF, which is a specialized form of mutual fund with special pricing and accounting rules and is limited to a well-defined list of short-term, high quality debt instruments. In Chapter 12.3, we will explore the regulation of MMFs in some detail as part of the greater discussion of shadow banking, but for current purposes, consider Figure 10.2-1, which reveals that $2.7 trillion, or 17.2%, of total mutual fund assets as of year-end 2014 were held in MMFs. The majority of the investments were held by individuals ($1.7 trillion or 61.5%) with the balance held by institutional investors ($1.1 trillion or 38.5%).

In this Chapter and the chapters that follow, we will occasionally touch upon closed-end funds and ETFs, but our primary focus will be on mutual funds, as the most important category of investment company, with a detailed detour in Chapter 12.3 into MMFs.

B. PLAN SPONSORS AND MUTUAL FUND COMPLEXES

As the foregoing summary illustrates, there are a large number, close to 17,000 by year-end 2014, of investment companies operating in the United States. These investment companies, however, do not operate as the sort of free standing firm we saw in the *Fifth Avenue* case in Chapter 10.1. Rather, most operate under the umbrella of an investment company complex controlled by a single sponsor. There were 867 fund sponsors operating in the United States as of year-end 2014, yet the top five fund complexes controlled 43% of the market for mutual funds and ETFs, with the top 25 complexes controlling 74% of that market. *See* Inv. Co. Inst., 2015 Investment Company Fact Book, at 16-17.

Another distinctive feature of the investment company sector is the relatively high rate of turnover among investment companies. Unlike other kinds of financial institutions, a reasonably large number of mutual funds are created or disappear each year. For example, in 2014, 654 new mutual funds were opened, 232 were liquidated, and another 130 were merged into other funds. *Id.* at 19. Mergers, for example, can reduce costs by increasing economies of scale or move assets into better-performing funds. The sector is thus more dynamic in terms of market participants than are some of the other sectors we have studied. Many major mutual fund complexes routinely introduce and retire mutual funds in their product offerings.

Within a mutual fund complex, different funds cluster into groups that are managed by a common adviser, sold by a common distributor, and frequently have the same board of directors. Some of the groups are comprised of separate investment companies, while others are organized as one investment company that issues several series of stock, each series representing a different portfolio. Each complex might include a variety of investment media, such as mutual funds, closed-end funds, private advisory accounts, and variable annuities. We will see that these structures raise many conflict of interest issues, especially in the event that the adviser has a greater interest in some funds than in others. To prevent abuse in such cases, § 17 of 1940 Act imposes strict limitations on transactions between funds and affiliated parties, comparable in spirit to Sections 23A and 23B of the Federal Reserve Act, which we explored in Chapter 2.3. As the logic of fund complex requires a good deal of inter-fund transactions, the SEC has adopted a variety of regulations granted exemptive relief for certain inter-affiliate transactions, provided specific safeguards are put in place, commonly including oversight from the funds' board of directors.

Fund complexes also tend to arrange a variety of outside service providers to provide common services for funds within the groups. Typically, these services can include custody of fund services, transfer agency functions for fund shares, fund accounting and administrative functions, legal advice, and even, in some cases, sub-advising of portfolio management. Again, the fund board of directors often is called upon to play a role in overseeing the delegation of these service functions and ensuring that costs are allocated fairly across funds. The following excerpt summarizes the work of fund sponsors and their major service providers:

> Fund sponsors and third-party service providers offer advisory, recordkeeping, administrative, custody, and other services to a growing number of funds and their investors. Fund industry employment in the United States has grown 46 percent since 1997, from 114,000 workers to 166,000 in 2013. . . .
>
> One of the prominent providers of services to funds are fund investment advisers. This group of service providers is responsible for directing funds' investments by undertaking investment research and determining which securities to buy and sell. The adviser will often undertake trading and security settlement for the fund. In March 2013, 34 percent of the industry worked in support of fund management functions . . .
>
> The second-largest group of workers (30 percent) provides services to fund investors and their accounts. Shareholder account servicing encompasses a wide range of activities to help investors monitor and update their accounts. . . .
>
> Fund administration, which includes financial and portfolio accounting and regulatory compliance duties, accounted for 10 percent of industry employment. Employees performing those services are often affiliated with a fund's investment adviser. . . . Distribution and sales force personnel together accounted for 26

> percent of the workforce. Employees in these areas may work in marketing, product development and design, or investor communications, and can include sales support staff, registered representatives, and supermarket representatives.

Inv. Co. Inst., 2015 Investment Company Fact Book: A Review of Trends and Activity in the Investment Company Industry (55th ed. 2015), at 23-24.

Figure 10.2-2 Investment Company Sector Employment by Job Function

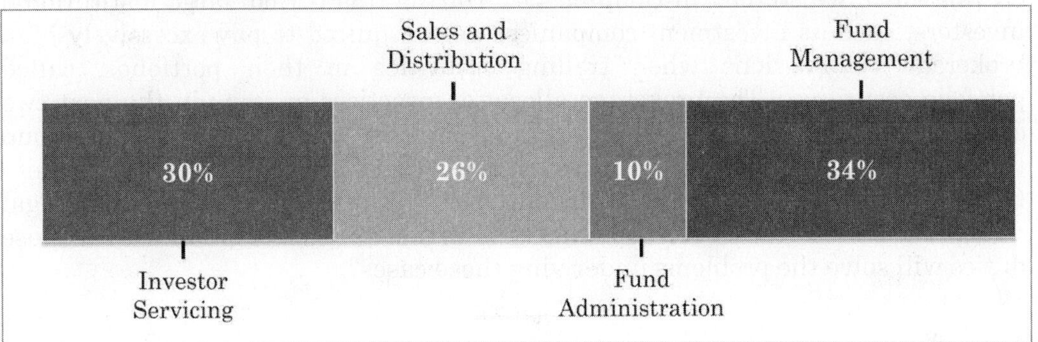

Note: Percentage of Employees of Fund Sponsors and Their Service Providers (Mar. 2013).

Source: Inv. Co. Inst., 2015 Investment Company Fact Book: A Review of Trends and Activities in the U.S. Investment Company Industry (55th ed. 2015).

One of the major ways in which the mutual fund sector has evolved over the years is the manner in which mutual fund shares are distributed. In 1940, most buyers of mutual fund shares also paid a sales load in addition to the price of the shares themselves. This sales load went directly to the sellers, namely the underwriter, dealers, and salespersons, to pay for their expenses and profits. In the 1960s, the sales load was typically 8.5% of the offering price per share. At the time, no-load funds, whose shares are directly marketed to the public without the use of intermediaries, were relatively uncommon. Since the 1960s, however, no-load funds have dramatically increased, with Vanguard, one of the country's largest sponsors of mutual funds, being an early promoter of no-load mutual funds. While sales loads still exist, investment companies have largely replaced these loads with 12b-1 fees, distributions costs paid directly out of mutual fund assets and used to promote distribution under a regulation promulgated by the SEC in 1980 but still in place today. The financing of the costs of mutual funds shares has been and remains a source of controversy and debate.

III. THE CENTRALITY OF FUND DIRECTORS

In the materials that follow, we explore the role directors, particularly independent directors, in overseeing investment companies. Under the 1940 Act, each registered investment company is required to have a board of directors, and independent directors who are unaffiliated with the company's adviser, sponsor, and other key affiliates must constitute at least 40% of directors. Certain board decisions must be made solely by independent directors.

A. BROKERAGE ALLOCATION

We begin our discussion with what many consider to be the most influential line of cases in the investment company sector. These cases involve brokerage allocation practices of investment companies in the 1960s and early 1970s. To understand this cases, you must recall that they took place during the era of fixed commissions on the New York Stock Exchange (NYSE) transactions. These commissions were the focus of *Gordon v. New York Stock Exchange*, 422 U.S. 659 (1975), which we studied in Chapter 4.4. During this period, large institutional investors, such as investment companies, were required to pay excessively high brokerage commissions when trading securities in their portfolios, called portfolio securities. The brokerage allocation practices at issue in the next two cases represented an effort on the part of some investment companies to recoup these commissions. As you read through these cases, try to figure out how these transactions worked and who, if anyone, was injured. Also consider the legal duties these cases establish. How likely is it that future compliance with these duties will solve the problems underlying these cases?

Moses v. Burgin

445 F.2d 369 (1st Cir. 1971)

Aldrich, Chief Judge.

Plaintiff Moses, a shareholder of Fidelity Fund, Inc. (Fund) . . . in December 1967 filed a complaint . . . in this derivative action. Fund is an open-end mutual fund, registered under the [1940 Act]. Defendants, in addition to Fund, are Fidelity Management and Research Company (Management), Fund's investment adviser; The Crosby Corporation (Crosby), a wholly owned subsidiary of Management [and] an underwriter whose sole business is selling shares of Fund to independent broker-dealers; E. C. Johnson 2d, president and director of Fund, and president, director and principal voting stockholder of Management; E. C. Johnson 3d, director of Fund since April 1968, and director and substantial voting stockholder of Management; and [six individuals] who are or were directors of Fund who claim not to be "affiliated" within the meaning of section 10(a) of the [1940] Act, hereinafter the unaffiliated directors. . . .

Fund's shareholders are numbered in five, and its assets in the upper nine, figures. The amount of its assets, apart from changes in the market value of its investments, depends upon the number of shares that it can sell as against the number it must redeem. Both activities are continual. The purchasers of individual participating interests, or shares, pay their net worth in terms of the current value of Fund's assets, plus a 1 1/2% Sales charge to Crosby and a brokerage commission of 6%. In response to advice by Management, Fund is constantly changing its portfolio [through independent broker-dealers trading on the New York and regional stock exchanges] . . .

The exchanges . . . set required commission rates, with no quantity discounts. Because of the size of many mutual fund transactions brokers competing for business were willing to give up a portion of the commissions they received from the fund. "Anti-rebate" rules adopted by every exchange prevented any rebate or discount, direct or indirect, that would bring the net commission paid below the minimum level set by the exchange. . . . [T]he total effect of these rules was in doubt, but they at least prevented direct cash refunds to the customer. On Fund's instructions, at Management's behest, the so-called customer-directed give-ups were paid over to brokers who sold shares of Fund acquired from Crosby to the public, in proportion to their success, in order to stimulate sales. Customer-directed give-ups are to be distinguished from broker-directed give-ups, a long-recognized practice whereby two or more brokers who have shared in the work divide the commission between themselves. Give-ups which are customer-directed (which is what we shall mean by the term "give-up" hereafter) are inherently and necessarily, as the district court found, in the nature of a refund, or rebate to the customer.

First, [plaintiff] complains of Fund's give-up practices because they resulted in the loss of the value of brokerage commissions which could have been recaptured. She claims recapture was possible . . . by creation of a broker affiliate . . . Second, she complains that the give-up practices . . . benefitted Management and Crosby, since stimulating sales of Fund's shares increased Crosby's commissions, and increased Management's advisory fee, which was measured by the size of Fund's portfolio. Accordingly, plaintiff claims that Management and the two Johnsons, who together owned 90% of its voting stock, were using Fund's assets to their own private advantage. More pointedly, she claims in particular that Fund's board never considered these possibilities because relevant information regarding them was improperly withheld from the unaffiliated directors by the Management defendants. . . .

The Duty To Recapture

[The court rejected the plaintiff's first claim, noting that "a change from independent brokerage to an affiliated broker is not a matter to be lightly undertaken," that "the directors had no duty to pursue plaintiff's suggested course of action, and without their doing so, recapture was not freely available," and that because plaintiff knew of Fund's practice, "she could have chosen a fund that did have an affiliated broker".]

NASD Recapture

We turn, accordingly, to plaintiff's second major claim . . . Six of the seven regional exchanges permitted members of the National Association of Securities Dealers (NASD) who were not exchange members . . . to receive customer-directed give-ups. Crosby was a member of NASD. Plaintiff asserts that Crosby . . . was or could have become qualified to receive give-ups on these exchanges, and that Fund could have directed such receipts . . . Management responds that if Fund had so directed, Crosby's crediting Fund would have violated the anti-rebate rules of the exchanges . . . To this plaintiff replies . . . that Management failed to investigate, or even to inform the unaffiliated directors of the possibility of this indirect recapture . . .

Management's Duty of Disclosure

. . . We believe . . . that the [1940 Act] imposes a more fundamental and pervasive requirement where, because of the structure of investment trusts, self-dealing is not the exception but, so far as management is concerned, the order of the day. . . .

Unlike an ordinary trust, or a business, management's normal activities are frequently touched with self-interest, as the example of give-ups, universally used, and benefitting management at least as much as fund shareholders, clearly shows. Management defendants admit that they gained from the give-up practice, while asserting that Fund also benefitted from the resulting growth. To the extent that they . . . imply that their self-interest could not influence the decisions to be made on behalf of Fund, Congress had an answer[:]. . . independent, watchdog directors.

. . . [W]e think the conclusion unavoidable that Management defendants were under a duty of full disclosure of information to these unaffiliated directors in every area where there was even a possible conflict of interest between their interests and the interests of the fund. . . . If management does not keep these directors informed they will not be in a position to exercise the independent judgment that Congress clearly intended. The only question can be whether the matter is one that could be thought to be of possible significance.

Management's Failure To Disclose

. . . In sum, we can only conclude that the Management defendants saw a question, that they knew it to be in an area where there was a conflict between their personal interests and the direct interests of the Fund treasury, and that they did not inform the unaffiliated directors or submit it to their consideration. . . .

Liability

. . . [Management's] failure to disclose the information available to them to the unaffiliated directors was the result of neither inadvertence nor misapprehension of the facts. Among the abuses enumerated in section 1(b) of the [1940] Act . . . is the operation of investment companies in the interest of advisers, underwriters, and other affiliated persons rather than that of the shareholders. By intentionally pursuing a course of non-disclosure these defendants made the effective functioning of the mechanism protecting Fund from their overreaching impossible. We do not believe that Congress intended that the SEC and the federal courts should be powerless to deal with this kind of conduct, or should excuse it on facts such as those disclosed in the case at bar. . . . We therefore conclude that the Management defendants were guilty of gross misconduct within the meaning of the Act in failing to disclose the possibility of NASD recapture to the unaffiliated directors. The two individual management defendants, and the Management corporations, must be held liable for damages under section 36.

---

1. ***The Duty To Recapture.*** The *Moses* decision concerns the roles and responsibilities of mutual funds, investment advisers, and independent (or unaffiliated) directors. The opinion, however, also explores a related structural limitation on mutual funds. In the section of the decision titled "The Duty to Recapture," the court considers whether the practices in question violated a requirement that the fund sell its shares for their "full asset value." What is the source and scope of that requirement? Compare § 22 of the 1940 Act. How does this requirement differ from the fiduciary duties discussed elsewhere in the opinion?

2. ***The New § 36.*** Congress amended § 36 in 1970 to create an express right of action. The content of fiduciary obligations imposed in the newer version of the section differs from the one at issue in the *Moses* case. For one thing, the current version of the section has two subsections, (a) and (b), which impose different standards of conduct and establish different procedures for enforcement. We will explore § 36(b) below.

3. ***Recapturing Excessive Brokerage Commissions.*** In the late 1960s and early 1970s, the courts heard a number of different legal cases challenging the failure of investment companies to return the value of excess brokerage commissions to investors in the fund. *See, e.g.*, Tannenbaum v. Zeller, 552 F.2d 402 (2d Cir. 1977) (finding fault in a mutual funds' proxy statement for not clearly disclosing to shareholders that incumbent directors had failed to recapture excessive brokerage commissions); Fogel v. Chestnutt, 533 F.2d 731 (2d Cir. 1975) (finding breach of fiduciary duty in failure of affiliated directors of the advisor to make full disclosure to the disinterested directors of the possibility to recapture brokerage commissions). *See also* Martin Lipton, *Directors of Mutual Funds: Special Problems*, 31 BUS. LAW. 1259 (1975-1976); James F. Jorden, *Paying Up for Research: A Regulatory and Legislative Analysis*, 1975 DUKE L.J. 1103 (1975); Gavin Miller & Robert E. Carlson, *Recapture of Brokerage Commissions by Mutual Funds*, 46 N.Y.U. L. REV. 35 (1971). At issue in all of these cases was the propriety of investment company advisers making use of fund assets, excess brokerage commissions, for the adviser's own benefit as

opposed to the benefit of investors in the fund. Resolution of this conflict is difficult because some uses, like subsidizing the distribution of fund shares, has benefits for both the adviser and fund investors, though in most cases the benefit to the adviser is more direct and substantial.

With the 1975 amendments to the Securities Exchange Act of 1934 (1934 Act), the era of fixed commissions came to an end, but the conflict animating these cases remains in two contexts that remain controversial (at least in some circles).

The first is Rule 12b-1, adopted by the SEC in 1980, which permits the use of fund assets to promote distribution provided a number of specific conditions are met, including approval of the plan by both shareholders and independent directors. The following excerpt summarizes elements of the rule and its implementation:

John Howat & Linda Reid, Compensation Practices for Retail Sale of Mutual Funds

12 FORDHAM J. CORP. & FIN. L. 685 (2007).

The 1940 Act bans the use of fund assets to pay for the distribution of a fund's shares. However, in the late 1970s, mutual funds experienced a significant and steady outflow of cash from redemptions of shares. This left the remaining shareholders to pay the fixed costs of the funds as the costs were spread over fewer shareholders.

The fund industry lobbied for the use of fund assets to pay for distribution costs and persuaded the SEC to pass Rule 12b-1 in October 1980. The rule permits funds to pay the costs of marketing and distribution of fund shares as long as they are properly disclosed and regulated. The annual fee is included in the fund's reported expense ratio. . . .

Although it was initially meant as a short-term solution to the high level of net redemptions in the 1970s, Rule 12b-1 is largely responsible for the class system of funds used today. A fund will often have various classes of shares that differ in their commission structures. For example, one class might have a high initial sales commission and a small (usually .25%) annual fee paid for by a 12b-1 plan, while another class might have a small initial sales commission and a large (perhaps 1.0%) annual 12b-1 fee. The expense ratio of a fund typically includes three components: an advisory fee, administrative fee (such as legal and accounting costs) and 12b-1 fees. For multiple class shares, the advisory fee is always the same across classes. Administrative fees and 12b-1 fees can vary across classes although the administrative fee is often the same. . . .

There are two important differences between load fees and 12b-1 fees besides the obvious one-time fee versus annual fee. First, they differ in the level of transparency. The load charge is clearly stated in the confirmation statement that the investor receives pays only for his or her costs. 12b-1 fees are charged at the fund level, and investors may pay for other investors' costs. The aggregate amount that investors pay increases as their holding period increases and as the asset level rises. Because the fees are deducted at the fund level, some investors subsidize the costs of other investors. For example, small accounts typically cost more, as a percent of the account size, than large accounts; and yet both investors pay the same percent from the fund or the broker who sold the shares. On the other hand, the investor is never explicitly told the amount of the 12b-1 fees—it is neatly buried in the expense ratio. Second, loads are a fixed amount charged at the account level, and each investor pays only for his or her costs. 12b-1 fees are charged at the fund level, and investors may pay for other investors' costs. . . .

A recent survey by the Investment Company Institute . . . showed that funds use most of the 12b-1 fees to compensate financial advisers for assisting fund investors before and after they purchase fund shares. Only a small fraction of the fees are used for advertising and promotion. Thus, the primary use of revenues raised through 12b-1 fees is to create incentives for advisers to distribute the fund shares, making advisers the main beneficiaries of 12b-1 plans.

The SEC has pursued enforcement action in "distribution in guise" cases against advisers who improperly use mutual fund assets to pay for the marketing and distribution of fund shares. *See* First Eagle Investment Management, LLC, Advisers Act Release No. 4199 (Sept. 21, 2015) (finding that First Eagle unlawfully caused its funds, rather than itself, to pay nearly $25 million for distribution-related services). *See also* SEC, Div. of Inv. Management, "Mutual Fund Distribution and Sub-Accounting Fees," IM Guidance Update, No. 2016-01 (Jan. 2016).

In 1975, when the *Moses* line of cases were still winding their way through the courts, Congress adopted Section 28(e) of the 1934 Act.

Alan C. Porter & Andras P. Teleki, A Hard Look at Soft Dollars

12 INV. LAWYER 1 (July 2005)

Section 28(e) of the [1934 Act] provides a safe harbor against violations of federal and state law, or breach of common law fiduciary duty [for failure to obtain the lowest available commission], for a money manager that directs a client's brokerage in return for research, even if the adviser uses the research to benefit its other accounts. Because Section 28(e) is a safe harbor, failure to adhere to each of its elements does not itself result in a violation of law or breach of fiduciary duty. Rather, it means that the soft dollar arrangement will be subject to regulation under laws that would otherwise apply but for the safe harbor. Section 28(e)(1) provides:

> No person using the mails, or any means or instrumentality of interstate commerce, in the exercise of investment discretion with respect to an account shall be deemed to have acted unlawfully or to have breached a fiduciary duty under State or Federal law unless expressly provided to the contrary by a law enacted by the Congress or any State subsequent to [June 4, 1975], solely by reason of his having caused the account to pay a member of an exchange, broker, or dealer an amount of commission for effecting a securities transaction in excess of the amount of commission another member of an exchange, broker, or dealer would have charged for effecting that transaction, if such person determined in good faith that such amount of commission was reasonable in relation to the value of the brokerage and research services provided by such member, broker, or dealer, viewed in terms of either that particular transaction or his overall responsibilities with respect to the accounts as to which he exercises investment discretion.

This provision is intended to protect money managers that pay more than the lowest available commission rate based on the brokerage services provided, so long as they comply with the requirements of the safe harbor.

What are the implications of § 28(e) for the *Moses* line of cases?

Rule 12b-1 and § 28(e) establish different legal standards for policing the use of fund assets to support different kinds of services. As we will see later in this Chapter, advisory fees are subject to yet another distinctive legal regime. Does it make sense to impose different legal requirements on different kinds of charges imposed on fund shareholders? What incentives do such differences create?

B. SECTION 36(B) AND THE GARTENBERG TEST

One of the most litigated provisions of the 1940 Act is § 36(b), which emerged as a result of a congressional compromise over the appropriate legal regime to govern the level of advisory fees that investment advisers should be permitted to charge registered investment companies. The provisions reads in relevant part:

> For the purposes of this subsection, the investment adviser of a registered investment company shall be deemed to have a fiduciary duty with respect to the receipt of compensation for services, or of payments of a material nature, paid by such registered investment company, or by the security holders thereof, to such investment adviser or any affiliated person of such investment adviser. An action may be brought under this subsection by the [SEC], or by a security holder of such registered investment company on behalf of such company, against such investment adviser, or any affiliated person of such investment adviser, or any other person enumerated in subsection (a) of this section who has a fiduciary duty concerning such compensation or payments, for breach of fiduciary duty in respect of such compensation or payments paid by such registered investment company or by the security holders thereof to such investment adviser or person. With respect to any such action the following provisions shall apply:
>
> (1) It shall not be necessary to allege or prove that any defendant engaged in personal misconduct, and the plaintiff shall have the burden of proving a breach of fiduciary duty.
>
> (2) In any such action approval by the board of directors of such investment company of such compensation or payments, or of contracts or other arrangements providing for such compensation or payments, and ratification or approval of such compensation or payments, or of contracts or other arrangements providing for such compensation or payments, by the shareholders of such investment company, shall be given such consideration by the court as is deemed appropriate under all the circumstances.
>
> (3) No such action shall be brought or maintained against any person other than the recipient of such compensation or payments, and no damages or other relief shall be granted against any person other than the recipient of such compensation or payments. . . .

While the interpretation of many aspects of § 36(b) have been litigated for decades, a few points are clear. First, the provision creates a right of action, similar to a derivative action, that investment company shareholders can bring on behalf of an investment company against investment advisers. It is also clear that the plaintiffs do not need to prove personal misconduct, a standard applicable under earlier law. It is also clear that Congress did not intend to impose a system of rate regulation for advisory fees, an approach which was debated at the time, but ultimately rejected. The legal standard that § 36(b) creates instead is "a fiduciary duty with respect to the receipt of compensation for services." What exactly does that mean?

For many years, the most influential case interpreting § 36(b) was *Gartenberg v. Merrill Lynch Asset Management*, 694 F.2d 923 (2d Cir. 1982), which established a multi-factored test and has been summarized as follows:

> To violate section 36(b), "the adviser-manager must charge a fee that is so disproportionately large that it bears no reasonable relationship to the services rendered." . . . The following factors are to be considered in applying this standard: (a) the nature and quality of services provided to fund shareholders; (b) the profitability of the fund to the adviser-manager; (c) fall-out benefits; (d) economies of scale; (e) comparative fee structures; and (f) the independence and conscientiousness of the trustees.

Krinsk v. Fund Asset Management, 875 F.2d 404, 409 (2d Cir. 1989) (citing *Gartenberg*, 694 F.2d at 928-30).

Over the years, plaintiffs in § 36(b) cases struggled to prove violations of the *Gartenberg* standards, especially as investment advisers have learned to develop substantial records to justify advisory fees in annual advisory contract renewals that investment company boards must undertake pursuant to § 15(c). Proceedings often devolved into battles among experts regarding the level of advisory profitability or the comparability of fees for similar funds. Specifically, with respect to comparing fees of other, similar funds, a recurring question arose over whether fees for funds sold to retail investors should be compared with fees to funds sold to institutional clients, which often occurred with higher average balances but also with more sophisticated purchasers. For a discussion about the usefulness of comparing institutional to retail fees, see *Gallus v. Ameriprise Fin., Inc.*, 675 F.3d 1173 (8th Cir. 2012). The comparability of institutional fund fees was one of the issues raised in litigation involving the Oakmark complex of mutual funds, which led to a series of high profile decisions in the Seventh Circuit and ultimately the Supreme Court.

The first of these decisions was written by Judge Frank Easterbrook in Jones v. Harris Associates, 527 F.3d 627 (7th Cir. 627). After rejecting plaintiff's argument in favor of expanding the *Gartenberg* test to require comparisons with institutional fund fees, the panel reached the unexpected conclusions that the entire *Gartenberg* test should be abandoned and replaced with a reformulated standard of liability under § 36(b):

> Having had another chance to study this question, we now disapprove the *Gartenberg* approach. A fiduciary duty differs from rate regulation. A fiduciary must make full disclosure and play no tricks but is not subject to a cap on compensation. The trustees (and in the end investors, who vote with their feet and dollars), rather than a judge or jury, determine how much advisory services are worth.

Section 36(b) does not say that fees must be "reasonable" in relation to a judicially created standard. It says instead that the adviser has a fiduciary duty. That is a familiar word; to use it is to summon up the law of trusts. . . . And the rule in trust law is straightforward: A trustee owes an obligation of candor in negotiation, and honesty in performance, but may negotiate in his own interest and accept what the settlor or governance institution agrees to pay. . . . When the trust instrument is silent about compensation, the trustee may petition a court for an award, and then the court will ask what is "reasonable"; but when the settlor or the persons charged with the trust's administration make a decision, it is conclusive. John H. Langbein, *The Contractarian Basis of the Law of Trusts,* 105 Yale L.J. 625 (1995). It is possible to imagine compensation so unusual that a court will infer that deceit must have occurred, or that the persons responsible for decision have abdicated—for example, if a university's board of trustees decides to pay the president $50 million a year, when no other president of a comparable institution receives more than $2 million—but no court would inquire whether a salary normal among similar institutions is excessive. . . .

Today thousands of mutual funds compete. . . . People can search for and trade funds over the Internet, with negligible transactions costs. . . . Some mutual funds, such as those that track market indexes, do not have investment advisers and thus avoid all advisory fees. (Total expenses of the Vanguard 500 Index Fund, for example, are under 0.10% of assets; the same figure for the Oakmark Fund in 2007 was 1.01%.) Mutual funds rarely fire their investment advisers, but investors can and do "fire" advisers cheaply and easily by moving their money elsewhere. Investors do this not when the advisers' fees are "too high" in the abstract, but when they are excessive in relation to the results—and what is "excessive" depends on the results available from other investment vehicles, rather than any absolute level of compensation.

New entry is common, and funds can attract money only by offering a combination of service and management that investors value, at a price they are willing to pay. Mutual funds come much closer to the model of atomistic competition than do most other markets. Judges would not dream of regulating the price of automobiles, which are produced by roughly a dozen large firms; why then should 8,000 mutual funds seem "too few" to put competitive pressure on advisory fees? A recent, careful study concludes that thousands of mutual funds are plenty, that investors can and do protect their interests by shopping, and that regulating advisory fees through litigation is unlikely to do more good than harm. *See* John C. Coates & R. Glenn Hubbard, *Competition in the Mutual Fund Industry: Evidence and Implications for Policy,* 33 Iowa J. Corp. L. 151 (2007).

It won't do to reply that most investors are unsophisticated and don't compare prices. The sophisticated investors who do shop create a competitive pressure that protects the rest. *See* Alan Schwartz &

> Louis Wilde, *Imperfect Information in Markets for Contract Terms,* 69 Va. L.Rev. 1387 (1983).... Harris Associates charges a lower percentage of assets to other clients, but this does not imply that it must be charging too much to the Oakmark funds. Different clients call for different commitments of time....
>
> Federal securities laws, of which the [1940 Act] is one component, work largely by requiring disclosure and then allowing price to be set by competition in which investors make their own choices. Plaintiffs do not contend that Harris Associates pulled the wool over the eyes of the disinterested trustees or otherwise hindered their ability to negotiate a favorable price for advisory services. The fees are not hidden from investors—and the Oakmark funds' net return has attracted new investment rather than driving investors away. As § 36(b) does not make the federal judiciary a rate regulator, after the fashion of the Federal Energy Regulatory Commission, the judgment of the district court is affirmed.

Id.

The reaction to Judge Easterbrook's decision was swift and vociferous, starting with his well-known colleague, Judge Richard Posner, who wrote the following in dissenting from the denial of a rehearing petition:

> *Jones* is the only appellate opinion noted in Westlaw as disagreeing with *Gartenberg;* there is a slew of positive citations.... The Coates and Hubbard article that the panel cites . . . expressly approves *Gartenberg* . . .
>
> The panel bases its rejection of *Gartenberg* mainly on an economic analysis that is ripe for reexamination on the basis of growing indications that executive compensation in large publicly traded firms often is excessive because of the feeble incentives of boards of directors to police compensation....
>
> Competition in product and capital markets can't be counted on to solve the problem because the same structure of incentives operates on all large corporations and similar entities, including mutual funds. Mutual funds are a component of the financial services industry, where abuses have been rampant, as is more evident now than it was when Coates and Hubbard wrote their article. A business school professor at Northwestern University recently . . . found "evidence that connections among agents in [the mutual fund industry] foster favoritism, to the detriment of investors. Fund directors and advisory firms that manage the funds hire each other preferentially based on past interactions.... These findings support recent calls for more disclosure regarding the negotiation of advisory contracts by fund boards." . . . The SEC's Office of Economic Analysis (the principal adviser to the SEC on the economic aspects of regulatory issues) believes that mutual fund "boards with a greater proportion of independent directors are more likely to negotiate and approve lower fees, merge poorly performing funds more quickly or provide greater investor protection from late-trading and market

> timing," although "broad cross-sectional analysis reveals little consistent evidence that board composition is related to lower fees and higher returns for fund shareholders.". . .
>
> The *outcome* of this case may be correct. The panel opinion gives some reasons why, though one of them is weak in its unelaborated form: that the funds managed by Harris have grown faster than the industry norm. One would need to know over what period they had grown faster to know whether other than random factors were at work. But the creation of a circuit split, the importance of the issue to the mutual fund industry, and the one-sided character of the panel's analysis warrant our hearing the case en banc.

Jones v. Harris Associates, 537 F.2d 728 (7th Cir. 2008) (Posner, J., dissenting for a denial of a petition for rehearing) (internal citations omitted).

The Oakmark litigation ultimately was resolved by the Supreme Court. After a lively debate in the academic literature as well as amicus brief filings, the Court ultimately issued, without dissent, a decision endorsing the original *Gartenberg* test and vacating the Seventh Circuit ruling.

> By focusing almost entirely on the element of disclosure, the Seventh Circuit panel erred. *See* 527 F.3d, at 632 (An investment adviser "must make full disclosure and play no tricks but is not subject to a cap on compensation"). The *Gartenberg* standard, which the panel rejected, may lack sharp analytical clarity, but we believe that it accurately reflects the compromise that is embodied in § 36(b), and it has provided a workable standard for nearly three decades. The debate between the Seventh Circuit panel and the dissent from the denial of rehearing regarding today's mutual fund market is a matter for Congress, not the courts.

Jones v. Harris Associates, 559 U.S. 335, 353 (2010). In the course of its decision, the Court did, however, timidly enter the debate over the relevance of institutional fund charges in § 36(b) actions involving retail fund fees:

> As noted, the *Gartenberg* court rejected a comparison between the fees that the adviser in that case charged a [MMF] and the fees that it charged a pension fund. 694 F.2d at 930, n. 3 (noting the "[t]he nature and extent of the services required by each type of fund differ sharply"). . . . Since the [1940] Act requires consideration of all relevant factors, we do not think that there can be any categorical rule regarding the comparisons of the fees charged different types of clients. . . . Instead, courts may give such comparisons the weight that they merit in light of the similarities and differences between the services that the clients in question require, but courts must be wary of inapt comparisons. As the panel below noted, there may be significant differences between the services provided by an investment adviser to a mutual fund and those it provides to a pension fund which are attributable to the greater frequency of shareholder redemptions in a mutual fund, the higher turnover of mutual fund assets, the more burdensome regulatory and legal obligations, and higher marketing costs. . . . If the services rendered

> are sufficiently different that a comparison is not probative, then courts must reject such a comparison. Even if the services provided and fees charged to an independent fund are relevant, courts should be mindful that the [1940] Act does not necessarily ensure fee parity between mutual funds and institutional clients contrary to petitioners' contentions.

Id. at 349-350.

The SEC, while generally supportive of the *Gartenberg* test, has not taken an active role in defining the scope of liability under § 36(b). It has, for example, not issued any interpretive rules in the area. The SEC has, however, modified its disclosure requirements to require board of directors to address how each of the *Gartenberg* factors have played into the board's annual approval of advisory fees, and these disclosure are made available to shareholders. *See* Forms N1-A, N-2, N-3; Disclosure Regarding Approval of Investment Advisory Contracts by Directors of Investment Companies, Final Rule, Release No. IC-26,486, n.31 (June 23, 2004) (adopting release).

The *Jones v. Harris Associates* line of cases has led to a modest uptick in the volume of § 36(b) cases, leading to a large number of settlements but no significant court decisions to date. *See, e.g.*, Commonwealth Capital Management, LLC, 1940 Act Release No. 31,678 (SEC, June 17, 2015); Kornitzer Capital Management et al., 1940 Act Release No. 31,560 (SEC, Apr. 21, 2015). In the oral argument for *Jones v. Harris Associates*, in response to questioning by Justice Scalia, the government attorney acknowledged that the SEC had not brought any suits under § 36(b) since 1980. Transcript of Oral Argument at 21, Jones v. Harris Associates, 559 U.S. (No. 08-586). For a discussion of the difficulties of the fee liability doctrine, see Quinn Curtis & John Morley, *The Flawed Mechanics of Mutual Fund Fee Litigation*, 32 YALE J. ON REG. 1 (2015).

---

1. ***Advisory Contract Problem.*** Suppose you were an independent director to a mutual fund about to engage in the fund's annual § 15(c) review of its advisory contract. How would you propose to address the following issues:

> **A.** Typically § 15(c) background materials include detailed information comparing a fund's fees with those of comparable funds to determine, among other things, whether the fund has below or above median pricing. In comparing the funds' fee to other similar funds, should you request information that weights all other funds equally or an asset-weighted comparison that gives more weight? Should you request a comparison with only funds of a similar size? Does it matter whether your fund is relatively small or large? In general, how hard should an independent director push in the annual § 15(c) review to get the best possible fee for fund shareholders? If you were counsel to an independent board, what would your advice be on this score? Why?

> **B.** The *Gartenberg* test includes economies of scale and profitability as two factors. Both of these concepts depend on an allocation of adviser cost to a particular fund when the adviser works

with dozens or even hundreds of funds and also engages in many other lines of business. How much attention should independent directors give to cost allocation principles underlying information presented to the Board on these issues? What would constitute appropriate profitability or a reasonable sharing of economies of scale?

C. A further *Gartenberg* factor includes fall-out benefits, a concept meant to capture additional economic benefits that an adviser earns as a result of its advisory relationship with a fund. How far should an independent director push his or her inquiry here? For example, if an advisory firm runs a profitable 401(k) recordkeeping business on which a fund is featured, should those record-keeping profits be considered in an independent director's negotiation with the advisor as part of annual § 15(c) reviews? What if a fund's exceptionally strong performance, say in winning numerous awards, creates a halo effect for all aspects of an advisor's business. Is that produce fallout benefits?

C. DIRECTOR INDEPENDENCE

As the foregoing materials suggest, directors and particularly independent directors are central to the 1940 Act's regulatory structure. Section 10 of the 1940 Act mandates that at least 40% of investment company directors be independent and then assigns to them the responsibility to oversee a number of operating policies where the interests of management and shareholders are likely to be at odds. The election of directors is assigned to shareholders, and the proxy rules are intended to ensure that those elections are based on materially complete and accurate information. In most cases, however, these directors are not subject to annual shareholder election. Section 16 of the 1940 Act allows fund boards to function without shareholder elections so long as a majority of directors have been elected by shareholders; vacancies can be filled without a shareholder vote as long as thereafter at least two third of directors have been elected by shareholder votes. Unless the law of the state in which an investment company is organized specifies otherwise, and it rarely will, investment company boards, including independent directors, can go for many years without being subject to a shareholder vote. Finally, boards are often initially appointed by the adviser during the wholly-owned, incubation phase for each fund and have limited turnover rates overtime. For these reasons among others, proxy challenges to investment company directors are extremely rare. Notwithstanding this lack of meaningful oversight from shareholders, independent directors sometimes find themselves the focus of both litigation and regulation, as the following materials explore.

Our first reading here is from a case involving the interaction between 1940 Act remedies and Maryland corporate law.

Strougo v. Scudder, Stevens & Clark, Inc.

964 F. Supp. 783 (S.D.N.Y. 1997)

This action arises from the 1995 decision by the board of directors of the Brazil Fund, a closed-end investment company incorporated under Maryland law and traded on the [NYSE], to increase the Fund's capital by offering the Fund's existing shareholders rights to purchase additional shares of newly issued stock (the "Rights Offering"). Strougo [a shareholder] asserts that Scudder[, the fund's investment adviser,] and each of the directors of the Fund breached their respective fiduciary duties of loyalty and due care as a result of the development and implementation of the Rights Offering. [After concluding that the only legal claim on which Strougo could proceed was a derivative action based on § 36(a) of the 1940 Act, which proscribes acts and practices constituting a breach of fiduciary duty involving personal misconduct with respect to any registered investment company, the court then turned to the question of whether Strougo had failed to satisfy the demand requirement for derivative actions required under Maryland corporate law.]

The defendants contend that the derivative claims under Section 36(a) and the common law of Maryland should be dismissed for failure to allege with particularity, as required by Fed.R.Civ.P. 23.1, the reasons he has not made a demand on the Fund's directors and shareholders prior to instituting this action.

As the Fund is a Maryland corporation, Maryland law governs whether demand is required and the conditions that will excuse demand. . . . Under Maryland law, courts ordinarily "will not entertain a derivative suit by a stockholder on behalf of a corporation until it appears that the intra-corporate remedies have been unsuccessfully pursued by the complaining stockholder." *Parish v. Maryland & Virginia Milk Producers Ass'n. Inc.*, 250 Md. 24, 242 A.2d 512, 544 (1968). This means that, in general, the stockholder must make a demand for remedial action on the corporation itself, first by application to the directors, and then by application to the body of the stockholders. . . . However, prior demand on the directors and shareholders is excused when it would be futile. The futility exception is to be applied in a practical, common-sense manner.

[Strougo argues that six of seven directors of the Brazil Fund could not impartially consider demand due to disqualifying financial and professional interests resulting from their paid service on the boards of other Scudder-managed funds.] Under Maryland law, demand is excused where the directors are "dominated and controlled" by persons alleged to be guilty of the misconduct charged in the complaint. . . .

Padegs, Bratt and Villani, who are all employed directly by Scudder, are concededly "interested" in the Rights Offering. However, the defendants contend that the remaining board members, Fiedler, Nolen, Nogueira and Da Costa, are "independent" of Scudder, and therefore are able evaluate a demand and prosecute any action on behalf of the Fund. They contend that the receipt of director's fees and service on the boards of multiple funds managed by Scudder are insufficient to render these defendants "interested" in the transaction.

Ordinarily, allegations that directors receive fees for their services are not sufficient to demonstrate demand futility. *See* Kamen v. Kemper Financial Services, 939 F.2d 458, 460 (7th Cir.1991) (applying Maryland law). If the opposite were true, the futility exception would swallow the demand rule, since most corporate directors receive remuneration for their service. *Id.* [Allegations of business relationships between directors are also insufficient to demonstrate lack of independence.]

Here, however, Strougo has alleged not only that the purportedly independent directors receive remuneration for their service on the Brazil Fund, but that three of the four—Fiedler, Nolen and Nogueira—receive substantial remuneration from their service on the boards of other mutual funds managed by Scudder. He characterizes Fiedler, Nolen and

Nogueira as Scudder's "house directors," essentially as interested in benefitting Scudder (at the potential expense of fund shareholders) as Scudder's own employees. . . .

Here, the fact that all but one of the directors who approved the Rights offering received substantial compensation from funds managed by Scudder, and the allegation that, in approving the rights offering, these directors put the interests of Scudder in increasing their advisor's fees before the interests of the Fund and its shareholders "call into question" whether there was a desire on the part of the directors to benefit Scudder, rather than the Fund, in order to please Scudder to retain their lucrative directorships. In Maryland, two is the minimum number of directors necessary to form a committee to consider a demand. Hanks, Maryland Corporation Law, § 7.21[c] at 269, n. 173 (1994-1 Suppl.). Because only one of the directors does not serve on multiple Scudder boards, the Board could not appoint a committee of sufficiently disinterested directors to consider a demand by a shareholder to institute litigation, and thus demand would be futile.

The defendants contend that imposing a rule that would effectively eliminate multiple directorships in complexes of funds managed by a single advisor is inappropriate for several reasons. First, they contend that such practices are common and provide substantial benefits to investors, such as reduced costs and the ability of directors to use their knowledge gained from one fund in the service of others. Moreover, they contend, the [1940 Act's] definitions of an "interested person" do not include a limitation on directorships of multiple funds in a fund complex. Similarly, the SEC has not prohibited such multiple directorships, but merely required their disclosure in proxy materials. . . .

Although multiple directorships are not *necessarily* determinative of a director's independence, either under the statute or the SEC's interpretations, . . . the receipt of substantial remuneration from a fund complex does call into question the director's independence from the manager of that complex. Moreover, the rule would not eliminate multiple directorships. It would require only that a sufficient number of directors without such multiple directorships serve on a board so that a litigation committee could be convened to consider proposed litigation.

Accordingly, demand on the board of directors is excused as futile.

---

1. ***State Law***. Why did the plaintiff's claims in this 1934 Act case turn on procedural requirements of Maryland corporate law? *See* Kamen v. Kemper Financial Services, 500 U.S. 90, 97-99 (1991); *see also* Burks v. Lasker, 441 U.S. 471 (1979). If you were advising a firm setting up a new mutual fund complex after the *Strougo* decision, would you recommend that the funds be organized under Maryland law?

2. ***Independent Director Requirement***. What is the relationship between the holding of this case and the requirement of § 10(a) of the 1940 Act that no more than 60% of the directors of registered investment companies be interested persons? *See* § 2(a)(19) of the 1940 Act.

3. ***Director Compensation***. As a matter of regulatory policy, what degree of control should directors have over litigation of this sort? To what extent is your response to this question affected by the fact that the SEC also has jurisdiction over cases of this sort? How relevant is it that shareholders can protect themselves by selling their shares? If the amount of compensation to the independent directors is problematic, should the SEC set limits on the amount of compensation that independent directors receive? Would such limitations

enhance shareholder protections, or would they detract from the quality of individuals willing to serve on investment company boards?

A few years after the *Strougo* decision, the SEC chose to revisit a number of its regulations, such as Rule 12b-1, which governs distribution expenses, that impose special conditions involving independent directors. One of those efforts was challenged in the following decision.

Chamber of Commerce v. SEC

412 F.3d 133 (D.C. Cir. 2005)

Early in 2004 the [SEC] proposed to amend ten Exemptive Rules by imposing five new or amended conditions upon any fund wishing to engage in an otherwise prohibited transaction. *See* Investment Company Governance, Proposed Rule, 69 Fed.Reg. 3472 (Jan. 23, 2004).* Although the [SEC] had amended the same ten rules in 2001 to condition exemption upon the fund having a board with a majority of independent directors (that is, directors who are not "interested persons" as defined in § 2(a)(19) of the [1940 Act]), *see* Role of Independent Directors of Investment Companies, Final Rule, 66 Fed.Reg. 3734 (Jan. 16, 2001), by 2004 the [SEC] had come to believe that more was required. "[E]nforcement actions involving late trading, inappropriate market timing activities and misuse of nonpublic information about fund portfolios" had brought to light, in the [SEC's] view, "a serious breakdown in management controls," signaling the need to "revisit the governance of funds." 69 Fed.Reg. at 3472. Accordingly, the [SEC] proposed to condition the ten exemptions upon, among other things, the fund having a board of directors (1) with at least 75% independent directors and (2) an independent chairman . . .

The Chamber maintains the [SEC] did not have authority under the [1940 Act] to condition the exemptive transactions as it did. First the Chamber observes rather generally that "matters of corporate governance are traditionally relegated to state law"; and second, it maintains these particular conditions are inconsistent with the statutory requirement that 40% of the directors on the board of an investment company be independent, *see* 15 U.S.C. § 80a-10(a). The [SEC] points to § 6(c) of the [1940 Act], 15 U.S.C. § 80a-6(c), as the source of its authority.* That provision conspicuously confers upon the [SEC] broad authority to exempt transactions from rules promulgated under the [1940 Act], subject only to the public interest and the purposes of the [1940 Act].

The thrust of the Chamber's first contention is that § 6(c) should not be read to enable the [SEC] to leverage the exemptive authority it clearly does have so as to regulate a matter, namely, corporate governance, over which the states, not the [SEC], have authority. For support the Chamber relies principally upon two cases from this circuit concerning the [SEC's] authority under the [1934 Act]. Neither of those cases, however, arose from an exercise of authority analogous to the rulemaking here under review.

The Chamber's second contention is that the conditions conflict with the intent of the Congress, expressed in § 10(a) of the [1940 Act], that 40% of the directors of an investment company be independent. *See Chevron, U.S.A., Inc. v. NRDC,* 467 U.S. 837, 842–43, . . . (1984) ("If the intent of Congress is clear, that is the end of the matter; for the court, as well as the agency, must give effect to the unambiguously expressed intent of Congress"). Section 10(a), however, states only that a fund may have "no more than" 60% inside directors, 15 U.S.C. § 80a-10(a), which necessarily means at least 40% must be independent and strongly implies a greater percentage may be; it speaks not at all to authority of the

---

*[The exemptive rules include Rule 10f-3; Rule 12b-1; Rule 17a-7; and Rule 17d-1(d)(7). *See* 69 Fed. Reg. 46,378. 46,379 n.9 (Aug. 2, 2004).]

[SEC] to provide an incentive for investment companies to enhance the role of independent directors and, as the [SEC] is keen to point out, the challenged conditions apply only to funds that engage in exemptive transactions.

[Notwithstanding the foregoing analysis of the SEC's legal authority to impose super-majority requirements for independent directors as part of exemptive regulations, the D.C. Circuit panel went on to vacate the SEC regulation in this case on procedural grounds, concluding that the SEC failed to address adequately empirical claims with respect to the value of requiring boards to have an independent chair and also provided insufficient analysis of the costs associated with the regulation's new conditions and the possibility of alternative approaches such as disclosure. One year later, after the SEC attempted to address these considerations in procedures that were accelerated to completion before SEC Chairman William Donaldson, a Clinton appointee, had to hand over leadership of the SEC to Christopher Cox, a Bush appointee, the D.C. Circuit again vacated the regulation. This time, the D.C. Circuit panel concluded that the SEC failed to follow Administrative Procedure Act procedures in considering the costs of, and alternatives to, the two conditions invalided in the Circuit's prior decision. *See Chamber of Commerce of U.S. v. SEC*, 443 F.3d 890, 909 (D.C. Cir. 2006).]

In the aftermath of the two *Chamber of Commerce* rulings, the SEC abandoned efforts to strengthen the board independence requirements on the ten exemptive regulations covered in the invalidated rulemakings. *See* John C. Coates IV, *Cost-Benefit Analysis of Financial Regulation: Case Studies and Implications*, 124 YALE L.J. 882, 950-51, 954-55 (2015). Somewhat curiously, the invalidated rules have never been removed from the Code of Federal Regulation, though practitioners in the field generally regard the invalidated conditions as dead letters. *See* Eric D. Roiter, *Disentangling Mutual Fund Governance from Corporate Governance*, 6 Harv. Bus. L. Rev. 101, ___ n. ___ (2016) ("When a court of final disposition vacates an agency's rule, the rule, of course, has no legal effect. Yet, the Code of Federal Regulations has not been revised to delete the long-vacated 75% independent director supermajority and independent chairman requirement. *See* 17 C.F.R. § 270.0-1(a)(7)(i) & (iv). The SEC apparently has neglected to correct the record or if it has sought to do so, has been unsuccessful.").

Regardless of the legal status of the SEC's rulemaking efforts in this area, sector practice has been to maintain a much higher percentage of independent directors than is specified in the 1940 Act itself (40%) or mandated under the versions of exemptive regulations adopted in 2001 (at least a majority). Figure 10.2-3 tracks the percentage of investment companies with independent directors above the 75% levels. Many fund complexes moved up the representations of independence directors around the time of the SEC's rulemaking efforts and have generally maintained those levels even after the *Chamber of Commerce* decisions.

Figure 10.2-3 Complexes Where 75% or More of Board Seats Are Held by Independent Directors

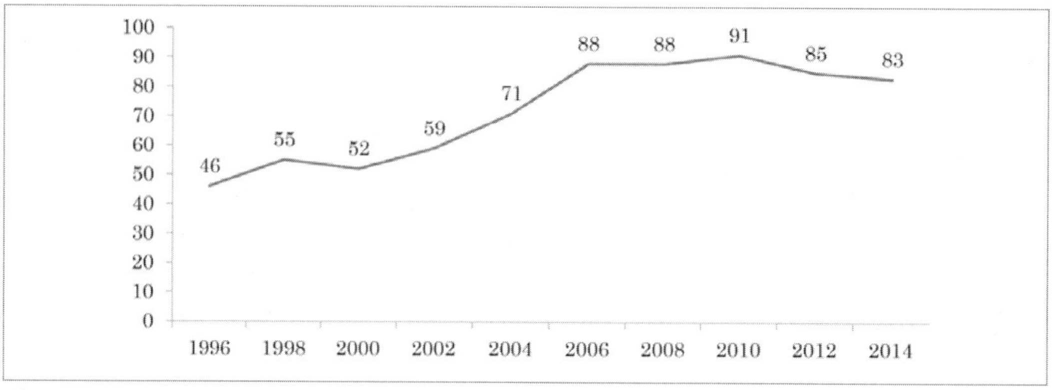

Source: Independent Directors Council and Inv. Co. Inst., Overview of Fund Governance Practices 1994-2014, 6 (2015).

A handful of fund complexes have even adopted fully independent boards. *See* Greg Saitz, *Some Boards are Totally Not Interested and Like it That Way*, BoardIQ (Oct. 8, 2013) ("Although specific data on all-independent boards is elusive, a preliminary review of regulatory filings reveals almost 10 fund families that meet such criteria, and one consulting firm estimates it could be in place at about 10% of the [sector's] 500 to 600 fund boards."). How should we understand these trends in light of the court rulings in the *Chamber of Commerce* cases? Are they reactions to anticipated but ultimately unsuccessful regulation, or do they signify the sector's embrace of the benefits of independent boards?

IV. STRUCTURAL RESTRAINTS UNDER THE INVESTMENT COMPANY ACT OF 1940

For most of this Chapter, we have focused on the duties of independent directors and investment advisors. Much of the analysis has been reminiscent of our discussion of fiduciary duties in Part IV. The 1940 Act also includes, however, formal structural constraints. In the final section of this Chapter, we explore two of these constraints: rules ensuring that fund shareholders redeem and purchase their shares at an appropriate NAV and rules limiting the leverage of mutual funds. While both of these rules represent formal portfolio restrictions, the SEC has turned to directors to ensure that the rules are applied fairly in situations that entail some degree of subjective judgment. Even here, independent directors have an often challenging role to play. Finally, we explore the structural protections for investors in ETFs, a rapidly growing investment company sector that was nonetheless never envisioned by the 1940 Act.

A. NET ASSET VALUE AND FAIR VALUATION

Rule 22c-1 of the 1940 Act requires mutual funds to offer and redeem their shares at the fund's next computed NAV after receipt of an order. 17 C.F.R. 270.22c-1. The NAV must be calculated each business day according to statutory and rule-based guidelines. *See id.*; 15 U.S.C. § 80a-2(a)(41); Accounting for Investment Securities by Registered Investment Companies, Interpretative Release, 35 Fed. Reg. 19986 (1970). The daily reporting and uniform calculation method of the NAV across mutual funds is an important structural safeguard in the 1940 Act for investors, ensuring that investors are able to redeem their shares at their correct value and that remaining investors in the fund do not suffer dilution.

Mutual funds are required to value their portfolio securities at market price when market quotations are readily available or at fair value as determined by the fund's board of directors when market quotations are not readily available. 15 U.S.C. § 80a-2(a)(41)(B). This requirement of fair valuation adjustments to the NAV provides an additional protection for investors. Nonetheless, several mutual fund pricing scandals in the 2000s showed that mutual fund shareholders are still exposed to trading abuses. In 2003, New York Attorney General Elliot Spitzer announced an investigation into the late trading practices of the mutual fund sector, which eventually resulted in over $3 billion in fines to 25 mutual fund families. Todd Houge & Jay Wellman, *Fallout from the Mutual Fund Trading Scandal*, 62 J. BUS. ETHICS 129, 129 (2005). Because most U.S. funds calculate their daily NAV using the closing market price of the securities in the fund at 4:00 p.m., Eastern Standard Time, an order received after 4:00 p.m. must be executed at the next day's NAV. Late trading refers to the illegal practice of allowing fund shares to be sold or purchased after 4:00 p.m. while using the current day's 4:00 p.m. NAV, or what Spitzer described as "betting on a horse race after the horses have crossed the finish line." Houge & Wellman, *Fallout*, at 130 (internal quotations omitted). This timing difference allows such late traders to profit on information regarding market events occurring after 4:00 p.m., thus diluting the value of the other shareholders' shares.

Another issue for mutual fund shareholders is market timing, an arbitrage strategy relying on stale prices that arise from the different closing times of the various international markets. For example,

> [i]f an event affecting the value of the portfolio securities occurs after the foreign market closes but before the [U.S.] fund prices its shares [at the market close of 4:00 p.m.], the foreign market closing price for the portfolio security will not reflect the current value of those securities. Traders may attempt to purchase fund securities with knowledge that the prices are "stale" and do not reflect these intervening events. While not illegal, this short term trading may disadvantage the fund's long-term investors by imposing trading costs, disrupting the management of the fund's portfolio and extracting value from the fund.

Mutual Fund Trading Abuses: Hearing before the U.S. House Subcommittee on Commercial and Administrative Law, 109th Cong. (2005) (prepared statement of Lori A. Richards).

Market timing itself was not illegal, but the SEC charged firms "that secretly allowed select investors to rapidly trade the portfolio despite statements banning the practice in the prospectus. A double standard that favors one investor at the expense of another is illegal . . ." Houge & Wellman, *Fallout*, at 132. Solutions to the late trading and market timing abuses have coalesced around policies to discourage excessive trading, such as redemption fees. *See id.* at 133-37; *see also* Mutual Fund Redemption Fees, Final Rule, 70 Fed. Reg.

13,328 (Mar. 18, 2005) (adopting Rule 22c-2 under the 1940 Act, which allows mutual funds to impose redemption fees on short-term shareholders). More importantly, consistent application of fair value pricing would reduce the ability to profit from market timing. *See* Houge & Wellman, *Fallout*, at 138; *see also* Disclosure Regarding Market Timing and Selective Disclosure of Portfolio Holdings, Final Rule, 69 Fed. Reg. 22,300 (Apr. 23, 2004) (requiring mutual funds to disclose use of fair value pricing). For a discussion of fund abuses, see WILLIAM A. BIRDTHISTLE, EMPIRE OF THE FUND: THE WAY WE SAVE NOW (2016).

Finally, an outstanding issue concerning the fair valuation of mutual fund portfolios is the scope of the directors' duties and their ability to delegate such duties. In the *Morgan Keegan* cease-and-desist proceedings, for example, the SEC alleged that the directors "delegated their responsibility to determine fair value to a valuation committee without providing any meaningful substantive guidance on how those determinations should be made." Kenneth Alderman, 1940 Act Release No. 30,300, at 2 (SEC, Dec. 10, 2012). While the SEC does not require the board to calculate the valuations itself, the board must take steps to review and approve the valuation methodologies. *See* Kenneth Alderman, 1940 Act Release No. 30,557, at 2, 11 (SEC, June 13, 2013).

---

1. ***Difficulties in Valuing Privately Place Securities.*** Mutual funds have also encountered problems in valuing privately place securities in high technology firms that are headed towards initial public offerings. Because fund complexes are using different pricing models to value these shares, the resulting discrepancies in valuation of the same shares affect the funds' NAV. *See* Kirsten Gring, *Mutual Funds Flail at Valuing Hot Startups Like Uber*, WALL ST. J. (Oct. 29, 2015). Is this an appropriate result given the fair valuation procedures previously discussed? How do fair valuation procedures for mutual fund investments compare with practices governing the establishment of loan loss reserves for bank loans discussed in Chapter 2.5?

2. ***Lending by Asset Managers.*** Asset managers have also increased their direct lending to companies. Asset managers' role in this private debt market is seen as part of shadow banking activities. "Direct loans, commercial mortgage lending, social housing, property and infrastructure—lending activities once synonymous with the banking sector—are now a staple for asset managers." *See* David Ricketts, *Asset managers step into the funding frame*, FIN. TIMES (Feb. 9, 2016). This trend is visible in the changes in the investor base of the Lending Club, a company that supports peer-to-peer investment. While 100% of the company's loans were backed by individual investors in 2010, by 2015, only 80% of the loans were backed by institutional investors or individuals investing through investment vehicle or managed accounts. Lending Club, How Has Lending Club's Investor Base Changed? (Dec. 31, 2015).

B. LIMITS ON LEVERAGE AND COMPLEX CAPITAL STRUCTURES

One of the important structural restraints imposed by the 1940 Act is a limit on the amount of leverage an investment company can use. In brief, § 18 limits the ability of closed-end investment companies and mutual funds to issue or sell senior securities. Section 18(f) specifies that mutual funds can issue senior securities, defined broadly to include most forms of indebtedness, only to banks and that such senior securities be subject to an asset coverage ratio of 300%. The purpose of this requirement is to prevent investment companies from taking on excessive amounts of leverage and imposing excessive financial risk on ordinary investors. Section 18(f)'s restrictions are something of a foundational component of the 1940 Act, but one that has been challenged in recent decades through innovations in financial products. With the advent of derivatives in the 1970s, the SEC indicated that, while derivatives such as reverse repos, put options, or forward contracts would generally fall into the definition of senior securities with respect to § 18, the Division of Investment Management would not recommend enforcement against any mutual funds that used such instruments, provided that the fund covers such senior securities with segregated liquid assets, such as cash and U.S. government securities, at least equal in market value to the fund's exposure to derivatives positions. Securities Trading Practices of Registered Investment Companies, General Statement of Policy, 44 Fed. Reg. 25,128, 25,131–32 (Apr. 27, 1979) (Release No. IC-10,666).

Not surprisingly, the SEC's focus on derivatives has ramped up significantly after the Financial Crisis. *See, e.g.*, Inv. Co. Inst., *Board Oversight of Derivatives* (Jul. 2008) (recommending that fund boards obtain reports from advisers regarding a fund's use of derivatives); Use of Derivatives by Investment Companies under the Investment Company Act of 1940, Concept Release, 76 Fed. Reg. 55,237 (Sept. 7, 2011) (requesting comments on issues concerning derivatives by investment companies); Mary Jo White, Chairman, SEC, Statement on Open-End Fund Liquidity Risk Management Programs and Swing Pricing (Sept. 22, 2015) (outlining agenda to examine the risk posed by funds' use of derivatives).

In 2015, the SEC proposed several rules to address the risks arising from registered investment companies' portfolio composition and operations. The SEC first moved to enhance reporting and disclosure requirements of registered investment companies and their advisers, including requiring disclosure of use of derivatives and borrowings. *See* Investment Company Reporting Modernization, Proposed Rule, 80 Fed. Reg. 33,589 (June 12, 2015) (hereinafter Release No. IC-31,610); Amendments to Form ADV and Investment Advisers Act Rules, Proposed Rule, 80 Fed. Reg. 33,717 (June 12, 2015). In order to enhance funds' ability to meet redemption requests, the SEC proposed requiring an internal liquidity risk management program for mutual funds and allowing most funds, but not MMFs or ETFs, to use swing pricing to pass on the costs of redemption activity to the redeeming shareholders, thereby reducing first-mover advantage by internalizing the cost of redemption activity. Open-End Fund Liquidity Risk Management Programs, Proposed Rule, 80 Fed. Reg. 62,273 (Oct. 15, 2015). Under the proposal, a fund's board would have to approve the liquidity risk management program and the swing pricing policies. *Id.* The rulemaking would also require a fund to consider the potential effects of the use of borrowings and derivatives on their liquidity risk. 80 Fed. Reg. 62,308. Finally, the SEC directly addressed limits on leverage with new proposed Rule 18f-4, an exemptive rule that would allow most funds to use derivatives, provided they comply with certain conditions. Use of Derivatives by Registered Investment Companies and Business Development Companies, Proposed Rule, 80 Fed. Reg. 80,883 (Dec. 28, 2015) (hereinafter Release No. IC-31,933). The requirements of the proposed rule include limiting the leverage from senior securities, maintaining certain qualifying coverage assets to cover the extent of its derivatives obligations, and adopting a derivative risk management program subject to board approval and oversight. *Id.* Overall, fund boards have a surprising amount of responsibility in maintaining the integrity of the structural restraints of the 1940 Act.

---

1. ***Directors' Oversight of Derivatives.*** The SEC's proposed rule would require funds who enter into derivative transactions to implement a written derivative risk management program, which must be initially approved by the fund's board of directors and also approved by the board for any material changes thereafter. Release No. IC-31933, at 80,984. To what degree should the SEC issue clear guidelines for fund directors in their oversight of derivative positions? To what extent is ambiguity in this area a more appropriate approach?

C. DEVELOPMENTS IN THE MARKET FOR EXCHANGE-TRADED FUNDS

ETFs have become the fastest growing category of registered investment company, growing from one fund in 1993 to nearly 2,000 funds at year-end 2015. With nearly $3 trillion in assets under management worldwide, ETF assets may soon eclipse MMF assets. ETFs' many benefits that explain their popularity:

> ETFs allow investors to buy and sell throughout the trading day in a liquid, transparent secondary market. ETFs operate with low fees and enable investors to diversify and to gain exposure to asset classes that might often be difficult, if not impossible, to invest in directly. ETF trading fosters stability in a fund's investment portfolio by obviating the need to sell holdings to pay for share redemptions. This, in turn, can lead not only to greater investment efficiency but also greater tax efficiency by limiting the realization of capital gains.

Eric D. Roiter, *Neither Fish Nor Fowl.* ETFs can be passive funds that track a market index by replicating the securities that compose it or, less commonly, active funds that use active investment strategies.

ETFs offer investors a hybrid instrument that combines characteristics of close-ended and open-ended funds, such as mutual funds. Unlike mutual funds, the price of an ETF is determined by the general market demand for the ETF itself. Further, like close-ended fund shareholders, ETF investors do not have redemption rights. Large block holders of ETF shares, however, such as broker-dealers, do hold redemption rights. "Given the grant of redemption rights only to large block holders of ETF shares and the consequent opportunity for arbitrage profits, the issue of investor fairness is intrinsic to ETFs." *See* Roiter, *Neither Fish Nor Fowl.* Disclosure of ETF portfolio holdings has been one of the key requirements the SEC uses to ensure fairness between investors. *Id.* For passive funds, the SEC requires disclosure of the identity of the underlying index and the weightings of the portfolio holdings. *See id.*; *see also* Release No. IC-31,610 (proposed rule would require monthly reporting of portfolio holdings). For active funds, the SEC requires daily disclosure of their complete portfolio holdings. Roiter, *Neither Fish Nor Fowl*.

While ETFs are typically organized as mutual funds, each ETF must receive case-by-case exemptive relief from certain provisions of the 1940 Act, since the structure and operations of an ETF cannot meet a series of 1940 Act provisions applicable to other mutual funds. For example, Rule 22c-1 of the 1940 Act requires shares to be redeemable at the NAV, while ETFs are instead traded at their market price. Exemptive relief is also necessary to limit redemption rights to large holders alone. While the SEC proposed rules to codify the exemptions granted to ETFs in 2008, this initiative has not been completed.

ETFs' rapid growth and their evolution into exotic fund-types, such as synthetic, inverse, and leveraged ETFs, have raised concerns of potential systemic implications for the financial system. *See generally* William A. Birdthistle, *The Fortunes and Foibles of Exchange-Traded Funds: A Positive Market Response to the Problems of Mutual Funds*, 33 DEL. J. CORP. L. 69 (2008). Because the right to redeem in ETFs is limited and most investors trade ETF shares in the secondary market, ETFs should theoretically pose less systemic risk than mutual funds. Nonetheless, the Financial Stability Board, worried by the recent trends in the ETF market, called for increased regulatory attention on ETFs. FSB, POTENTIAL FINANCIAL STABILITY ISSUES ARISING FROM RECENT TRENDS IN EXCHANGE-TRADED FUNDS (Apr. 11, 2011). Further, the Financial Stability Oversight Council drew attention to ETF's potential systemic risks. FSOC, 2015 ANNUAL REPORT 113 (2015).

CHAPTER 10.3

MUTUAL FUNDS: DISCLOSURE AND ITS LIMITATIONS

CONTENTS

I. INTRODUCTION

In this Chapter, we explore disclosure as a regulatory strategy. The SEC is beyond doubt this country's foremost regulator of disclosure and likely holds the world's title in that category as well. Inspired by Justice Louis Brandeis's rallying cry that "[s]unlight is said to be the best of disinfectants; electric light the most efficient policeman," the SEC pioneered the use of mandated disclosures in public capital markets. Since the passage of the Investment Company Act of 1940 (1940 Act), the SEC, working with FINRA and its predecessor, the National Association of Securities Dealers, has developed an elaborate system of specialized disclosure requirements for mutual funds and other investment companies.

First, recall the audience of these disclosures. Mutual funds are overwhelmingly the most important category of investment for retail investors. Approximately 53.2 million households, or some 43.3% of all households, owned mutual funds in 2014. The lion's share of these households held mutual funds through retirement accounts, such as 401(k) plans or Individual Retirement Accounts. In aggregate, these households held a whopping $14.2 trillion in mutual fund investments as of 2014, with some $7.3 trillion in retirement accounts and another $6.9 trillion in other kinds of household accounts. *See* Inv. Co. Inst., 2015 Investment Company Fact Book: A Review of Trends and

Activities in the U.S. Investment Company Industry (55th ed. 2015). The disclosures we explore in this Chapter are intended to reach a wide swath of retail investors, many of whom have very limited, if any, expertise in financial matters. As you read through these materials, consider how well this system of disclosure does and could serve this audience.

We will start by taking a look at several examples of mutual fund disclosures with the goal of giving you a sense of how the current system of disclosure works. We then take up two examples of the kinds of complexities the SEC must negotiate in devising its disclosure requirements for mutual funds. In the final section of this Chapter, we explore some additional constraints on the efficacy of disclosure as a regulatory strategy.

II. AN OVERVIEW OF MUTUAL FUND DISCLOSURES

The basic structure of mutual fund disclosure is built around the registering and reporting requirements of the Securities Act of 1933 (1933 Act) and the Securities Exchange Act of 1934 (1934 Act). Before offering shares for sale to the general public, mutual funds must file a registration statement with the SEC, a portion of which constitutes the fund prospectus. The disclosure requirements applicable to investment companies, however, differ from those that govern public offerings of corporations. For example, whereas SEC Form S-1 is the standard registration statement form for corporate initial public offerings, mutual funds typically must file and keep current SEC Form N-1A. *See* SEC, Div. of Inv. Mgmt., "Guidance regarding mutual fund enhanced disclosure," IM Guidance Update, No. 2014-08 (June 2014). Closed-end investment companies have their own registration form, Form N-2.

Mutual funds also differ from ordinary corporate issuers in that they typically continuously offer shares to the public at the fund net asset value (NAV) at the end of each business day, and so the registration statement must remain continuously effective. In addition, FINRA has specialized rules that govern broker-dealers that sell mutual funds, including requirements regarding disclosure of fees, expenses, and standardized measures of performance, buttressed by pre-clearance procedures for new marketing materials implemented by FINRA's Advertising Regulation Department. *See* FINRA, RULE 2210 (2015).

Similar to other public corporations, mutual funds must make available to their shareholders certain periodic reports. For mutual funds, these reports include audited annual reports, semi-annual reports, and quarterly listings of portfolio holdings. Unlike corporate issuers, mutual funds are also required to produce and make available to investors a Statement of Additional Information, which includes a range of more technical and detailed disclosures. When proxies are solicited from shareholders—a rare event because, as discussed in Chapter 10.2, mutual fund directors are not typically subject to annual election—those proxies must also comply with SEC requirements.

In practice, retail investors rarely review the standard, long-form SEC disclosure documents for mutual funds. Rather, the most common document distributed to prospective shareholders is a slimmed-down summary prospectus. *See* Enhanced Disclosure and New Prospectus Delivery Option for Registered

Open-End Management Investment Companies, Final Rule, 74 Fed. Reg. 4546 (Jan. 26, 2009). This document is designed to convey to the investing public the most salient information about mutual funds. Most major fund complexes also make use of extensive websites, which typically include much of the information required to be placed in summary prospectuses, as well as a link from which other long-form SEC disclosure documents can be downloaded or requested by mail. In the discussion that follows, we will focus on examples drawn from the September 29, 2015 Summary Prospectus of the Fidelity Low-Priced Stock Fund, as downloaded from the Fidelity website on November 9, 2015.

A. ANNOTATED ILLUSTRATIONS OF PERFORMANCE AND FEE DISCLOSURES

We will work our way through a fully annotated illustration of actual mutual fund disclosures, focusing first on disclosures regarding performance and then on disclosures regarding fees and expenses.

1. Performance Disclosures

Financial reporting is, by design, retrospective, typically summarizing financial conditions at a date in the past, like the end of the previous year, or performance over some period of time, like an annual income statement. While mutual funds are routinely required to warn their investors that "past performance does not necessarily predict future results," mutual fund disclosure, including summary prospectuses, highlights past financial returns.

Figure 10.3-1 Past Financial Returns

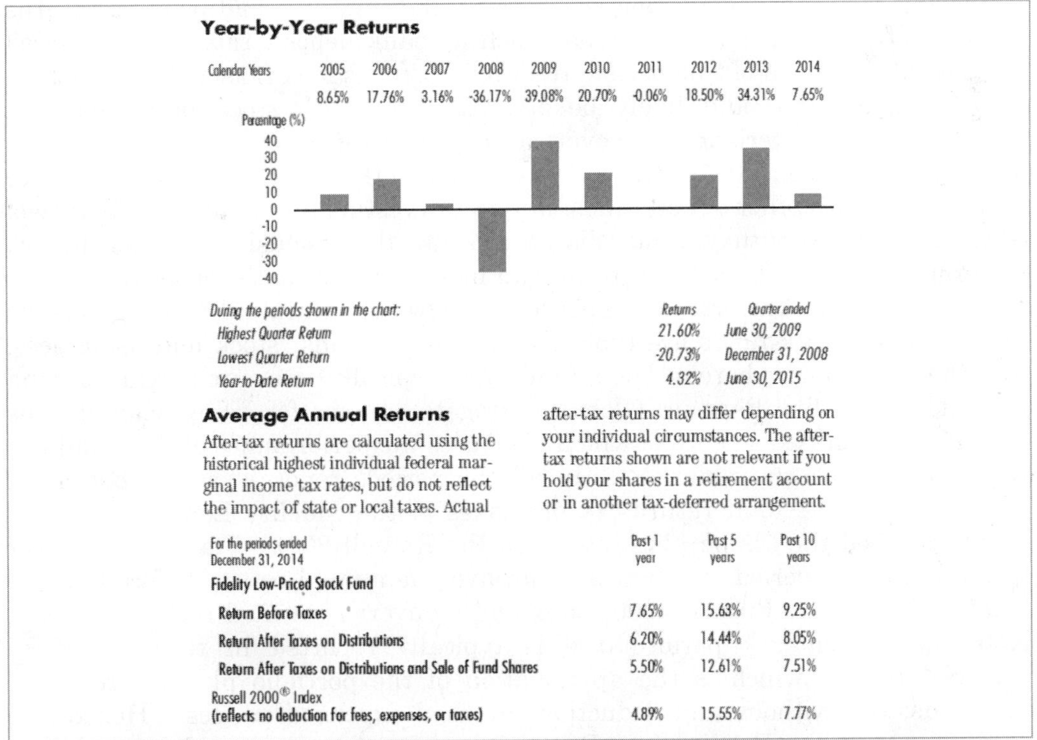

Year-by-Year Returns

Calendar Years	2005	2006	2007	2008	2009	2010	2011	2012	2013	2014
	8.65%	17.76%	3.16%	-36.17%	39.08%	20.70%	-0.06%	18.50%	34.31%	7.65%

During the periods shown in the chart:	*Returns*	*Quarter ended*
Highest Quarter Return	*21.60%*	*June 30, 2009*
Lowest Quarter Return	*-20.73%*	*December 31, 2008*
Year-to-Date Return	*4.32%*	*June 30, 2015*

Average Annual Returns

After-tax returns are calculated using the historical highest individual federal marginal income tax rates, but do not reflect the impact of state or local taxes. Actual after-tax returns may differ depending on your individual circumstances. The after-tax returns shown are not relevant if you hold your shares in a retirement account or in another tax-deferred arrangement.

For the periods ended December 31, 2014	Past 1 year	Past 5 years	Past 10 years
Fidelity Low-Priced Stock Fund			
Return Before Taxes	7.65%	15.63%	9.25%
Return After Taxes on Distributions	6.20%	14.44%	8.05%
Return After Taxes on Distributions and Sale of Fund Shares	5.50%	12.61%	7.51%
Russell 2000® Index **(reflects no deduction for fees, expenses, or taxes)**	4.89%	15.55%	7.77%

Source: Fidelity Low-Priced Stock Fund, Summary Prospectus (Sep. 29, 2015).

Figure 10.3-1 presents a standard presentation of performance of the Fidelity Low-Priced Stock Fund through December 31, 2014.

At the top of the figure, illustrated by a line of numbers and a bar chart below, is the fund's annual performance over the last ten years. If an investor held shares in the fund for all of 2014, reinvesting all distributions, the investor's account would have earned 7.65%. The italicized text below the bar graph highlights the fund's worst quarter, which occurred in the fourth quarter of 2008 in the midst of the Financial Crisis, and its best quarter, which occurred the following year when the stock market rallied.

If you had invested in the Fidelity Low-Priced Stock Fund in 2014, would you really have made 7.65% on your investment? Well, that depends, among other things, on your taxes. As mentioned earlier, while a majority of retail mutual fund investments are held in retirement accounts, which generally do not pay taxes on current earnings and appreciation, funds held in other household accounts may owe taxes at the end of each year, and those taxes will vary from fund to fund depending on the amount of interest and dividends, as well as realized appreciation. The bottom third of Figure 10.3-1 attempts to illustrate hypothetical tax effects for a taxpayer in the top federal marginal tax bracket, state taxes not considered. These numbers show the extent to which federal taxes might diminish the fund's return for some investors. The figure also produces similar estimates for five and ten-year periods, thus conveying a bit of information about longer-term fund performance.

How good was the performance of the Fidelity Low-Priced Stock Fund? To answer this question, you would have to have some idea of what you are comparing the performance against. Clearly the fund has had positive returns for most of the past ten years. Inasmuch as bank deposit rates have hovered beneath 1% for much of this period, the fund's returns look reasonably strong. A better comparison would likely be against funds with stock portfolios with similar risk characteristics, however, as higher returns are generally thought necessary to compensate for higher risks. Later in this Chapter, we will consider comparisons with other actual funds, but an interesting and important feature of SEC mandated mutual fund disclosures is the inclusion of benchmark performance. A benchmark is typically an index of some basket of securities that approximates the universe of securities from which a mutual fund selects its investments. Stock funds are typically compared against stock market indices, like the S&P 500, whereas bond funds are typically measured against bond market indices, like Barclays Global Aggregate. In the foregoing example, the benchmark is the Russell 2000, which measures the performance of the small-cap segment of U.S. equity markets. In all the periods reported at the bottom of Figure 10.3-1, the total returns before taxes of the Fidelity Low-Priced Stock Fund exceeded the comparable return on the Russell 2000. For example, over the full ten-year period, the fund had an average annual return before taxes of 9.25%, whereas the Russell 2000 index had an average annual return of 7.77%. Note that benchmark performance is typically reported in terms of gross financial return, which is the appreciation of the portfolio plus interest and dividends, but without any deduction for fund expenses or fees. Hence, the performance of the Fidelity Low-Priced Stock Fund was arguably even better than the raw numbers reported in Figure 10.3-1 suggest.

2. Disclosures of Fees and Expenses

We now turn to disclosures related to fees and expenses of mutual funds. As a mathematical matter, fees and expenses are factored into the fund performance numbers previously described because these performance figures are the net of fees and expenses. That is, fees and expenses are deducted from gross fund returns in order to calculate total returns for the one-, five- and ten-year periods reported above. Investors have good reasons to want to know how much they are being charged for the management of their mutual funds. For example, empirical investigation suggests that lower fund fees and expenses are associated with better long-term performance. *See, e.g.*, Russel Kinnel, *How Expense Ratios and Star Ratings Predict Success*, 18 MORNINGSTAR FUNDINVESTOR (2010) ("If there's anything in the whole world of mutual funds that you can take to the bank, it's that expense ratios help you make a better decision. In every single time period and data point tested, low cost funds beat high cost funds. Expense ratios are strong predictors of performance. In every asset class over every time period, the cheapest quintile produced higher total returns than the most expensive quintile."). Evidence on the long-term persistence of financial performance of mutual funds is much weaker. *See* Mark M. Carhart, *On Persistence in Mutual Fund Performance*, 52 J. FIN. 57 (1997).

Figure 10.3-2 Fee Disclosure

Shareholder fees **(fees paid directly from your investment)**	
Redemption fee on shares held less than 90 days (as a % of amount redeemed)	1.50%
Annual operating expenses **(expenses that you pay each year as a % of the value of your investment)**	
Management fee (fluctuates based on the fund's performance relative to a securities market index)	0.63%
Distribution and/or Service (12b-1) fees	None
Other expenses	0.16%
Total annual operating expenses	0.79%

Source: Fidelity Low-Priced Stock Fund, Summary Prospectus (Sep. 29, 2015).

Figure 10.3-2 shows a typical disclosure of fund expense ratios and fees, again drawn from the summary prospectus of the Fidelity Low-Priced Stock Fund. The section of the figure labeled annual operating expense shows the fees that are deducted from fund assets each year. The first fee is a 0.63% management fee, also known as a 63 basis point fee, paid to the fund's investment advisor, Fidelity. This is the type of fee that can be the focus of § 36(b) litigation that we explored in Chapter 10.2. If you were to consult the Fidelity Low-Priced Stock Fund's annual report, you would see an SEC mandated disclosure where the board of directors of the fund explains why it concluded that this fee was reasonable under the *Gartenberg* test. The fund also pays 0.16% for other expenses, likely including things like printing and mailing charges, transfer agent costs, and board compensation. Many of these other expenses will be covered by servicing or administrative agreements overseen by the fund's board of directors. The fund is not charged a 12b-1 fee for distribution costs, a charge that we discussed in Chapter 10.2 and that would have to be included in a fee disclosure table for funds that do charge 12b-1 fees. Another fee disclosed in this table is a redemption fee, charged only to investors who hold shares for less than 90 days. Most shareholders will not pay this fee and it is imposed primarily to discourage shareholders from engaging in short-term market timing transactions, which impose costs on other investors and complicate liquidity planning of portfolio managers.

How much does an investor pay to have his or her assets managed in the Fidelity Low-Priced Stock Fund each year? Under the assumption that the investor does not engage in any short-term trading, in which shares are held for less than 90 days, a reasonable fee is 0.79% of invested funds, or $79 on every $10,000 invested. Is that entirely accurate? Consider Figure 10.3-3, showing a Summary Prospectus extract for the fund's Portfolio Turnover. The fund engaged in a certain number of portfolio transactions by buying and selling fund investments. In fact, the turnover rate was 9% of its average portfolio value. Recall our discussion in Chapter 4.2 of portfolio turnover rates in the context of churning allegations against investment advisors and broker dealers.

Figure 10.3-3 Portfolio Turnover

Portfolio Turnover

The fund pays transaction costs, such as commissions, when it buys and sells securities (or "turns over" its portfolio). A higher portfolio turnover rate may indicate higher transaction costs and may result in higher taxes when fund shares are held in a taxable account. These costs, which are not reflected in annual operating expenses or in the example, affect the fund's performance. During the most recent fiscal year, the fund's portfolio turnover rate was 9% of the average value of its portfolio.

Source: Fidelity Low-Priced Stock Fund, Summary Prospectus (Sep. 29, 2015).

In addition to the direct expenses reported above in the expense table, investors in Fidelity's Low-Priced Stock Fund also incurred, indirectly, the costs of commissions on this portfolio turnover. This information is not available in the Summary Prospectus, but is in the fund's Statement of Additional Information, available upon request from Fidelity but seldom accessed by actual investors. The Statement of Additional Information reveals that the Fidelity Low-Priced Stock Fund paid $6.6 million in commissions in the 2015 fiscal year, equal to 0.01% of net average assets. Fidelity maintains a soft dollar program where some of these commissions are allocated to brokerage shops in exchange for research services, and $1.9 million of the fund's commissions in the last year were used to subsidize Fidelity's own research expenses. *See* Fidelity, Statement of Additional Information 27-29 (Sep. 29, 2015).

Should commissions, or at least those allocated to soft dollar expenditures, be reported in a fund's reported expense ratios in Summary Prospectuses? If so, the Low-Priced Stock Fund's expense ratio might have increased as much as 0.01% in 2015. Would it make a difference to you to know that other Fidelity funds, for example, the Fidelity Over-the-Counter Portfolio, whose brokerage activities are reported in the same Statement of Additional Information, had turnover rates in excess of 100% during 2014 with commissions reaching 0.12%

of average net assets, with a quite substantial fraction going to soft dollar services subsidizing the fund's investment advisor? For further discussions of these issues, see John A. Haslem, *Toward Normative Transparency of Disclosure in A Revised Mutual Fund Total Cost Construct*, 18 J. WEALTH MGMT. 73 (2015). Note that Fidelity's SAI disclosures with respect to its soft dollar practices is among the most transparent of major fund complexes.

B. THE ROLE OF THIRD-PARTY ANALYSIS

One of the most distinctive aspects of mutual fund disclosure is the extent to which it facilitates comparisons across funds offered by a particular complex or funds offerings across many different complexes. By standardizing definitions for performance, expense ratios, and reporting time periods, the SEC created a disclosure environment that facilitates inter-firm comparisons in a way that is more effective than what we observe in any other sector of financial services. While this standardized information allows for individual investors to compare one fund to another, the most important mechanism for cross-sector comparison comes from third-party analysts, like Morningstar and others, that specialize in aggregating and analyzing mutual fund performance. Investors have also begun to access these disclosure documents more directly via tools such as Google Finance.

Morningstar is likely the most familiar of these information aggregators and its five-star rating system is widely used and cited. The Morningstar website summarizes the rating system as follows:

> Morningstar rates mutual funds from 1 to 5 stars based on how well they've performed (after adjusting for risk and accounting for sales charges) in comparison to similar funds.
>
> Within each Morningstar Category, the top 10% of funds receive 5 stars . . . and the bottom 10% receive 1 star. Funds are rated for up to three time periods—three-, five-, and 10-years—and these ratings are combined to produce an overall rating. Funds with less than three years of history are not rated.
>
> Ratings are objective, based entirely on a mathematical evaluation of past performance. They're a useful tool for identifying funds worthy of further research, but shouldn't be considered buy or sell signals.

Morningstar, Morningstar Rating for Funds (last visited Feb. 22, 2016).

While the Morningstar excerpt quoted above expressly counsels that its star rating should not be considered simple buy or sell recommendations, it is widely understood in the mutual fund sector that fund flows closely track star ratings, and the lion's share of net fund flows go to mutual funds holding five and sometimes four star Morningstar rankings.

To get a sense of how ubiquitous third-party ratings are, consider Figure 10.3-4, a screenshot pulled from the Fidelity website on November 9, 2015. The website has a screening function that allows users to compare all Fidelity equity funds within the same Morningstar category, which, in Figure 10.3-4, is mid-cap value. This search returns five different Fidelity equity funds, including the Fidelity Low-Priced Stock Fund, which have investment strategies focused on mid-cap value stocks. This search shows the power of the SEC disclosure system for mutual funds, as it allows comparisons of key fund attributes with consistently reported data. It also reveals how Morningstar rankings are incorporated into the marketing materials of fund sponsors. Should we be concerned with how Morningstar is compensated for its services? Should we be concerned with the track record of past ratings, or should there be some mechanism for seeing the accuracy of past ratings?

Figure 10.3-4 Third-Party Ratings

5 Matching Funds — Fidelity Funds Only ✕ U.S. Equity/Mid-Cap Value ✕ — Reset Search — Bookmark Search

Overview | Risk | Management & Fees | Morningstar Rankings | Income Characteristics — Help me read this table

Data as of 10/31/2015 unless otherwise noted — 1

Compare	Name	Morningstar Category	YTD # (Daily)	1 Yr	3 Yr ▾	5 Yr	10 Yr	Expense Ratio Net†	Expense Ratio Gross‡	Morningstar Overall ▾	
Matching Fidelity Funds:										View All Matching Funds	
☐	Fidelity® Mid Cap Value Fund (FSMVX)	Mid-Cap Value	-2.04%	1.81%	18.03%	14.61%	8.50%	0.83%	0.83%	★★★★★ 423 Rated	Buy
☐	Fidelity® Value Fund (FDVLX)	Mid-Cap Value	-2.73%	0.12%	16.04%	13.08%	7.35%	0.76%	0.76%	★★★☆☆ 423 Rated	Buy
☐	Fidelity® Low-Priced Stock Fund (FLPSX)	Mid-Cap Value	1.94%	3.67%	15.33%	13.22%	9.20%	0.79%	0.79%	★★★★☆ 423 Rated	Buy
☐	Fidelity® Leveraged Company Stock Fund	Mid-Cap Value	-1.00%	-0.64%	14.12%	12.83%	8.01%	0.79%	0.79%	★★★☆☆ 423 Rated	Buy
☐	Fidelity® Value Strategies Fund	Mid-Cap Value	0.83%	2.84%	13.79%	12.15%	7.77%	0.69%	0.69%	★★★☆☆ 423 Rated	Buy

Source: Fidelity Inv., Mutual Fund Research (last visited Nov. 9, 2015).

Note that Fidelity has five separate equity funds, likely each run by a different portfolio manager, in the mid-cap value space. Three of the funds have fairly average performance with three-star Morningstar rankings. While the Fidelity Low-Priced Stock Fund did better, earning four stars, and the Fidelity Mid-Cap Value Fund did even better with a five star ranking, should potential investors in these higher rated funds be told that there are several more mid-cap value cousins within the Fidelity complex? Would it make a difference to you in answering this question if the complex had, in the not too distant past, other mid-cap value funds with poor Morningstar ratings that have since been liquidated or merged into other Fidelity funds? Is this additional information something that we should look to third-party services, like Morningstar, to factor into their rating systems? Does Morningstar have the right incentives here?

C. FUND-OF-FUND DISCLOSURES VERSUS WRAP ACCOUNTS

Mutual funds offer a very popular way for retail investors to participate in the capital markets, but there are other ways retail investors can invest in securities, including maintaining brokerage accounts with securities firms of the sort we considered back in Chapter 4.2. Traditionally, the SEC and FINRA have made very little effort to develop a standard set of disclosures for individual securities accounts. For example, brokerage account statements typically do not include standardized measures of performance over one-, three-, and five-year periods or comprehensive presentations of all sources of compensation for the brokerage firm arising out of its account management. Brokerage firms are also under no obligations to report the performance of their retail customers in the aggregate. Academic studies on the subject, however, suggest that retail investors, on average, substantially underperform in the market. *See, e.g.*, Brad M. Barber & Terrance Odean, *The Courage of Misguided Convictions*, 55 FIN. ANALYSTS J. 41, 41 (Nov./Dec. 1999) (highlighting mistakes investors make, such as excessive trading and holding losers while selling winners); *see also* Howell E. Jackson, *To What Extent Should We Rely on the Mechanisms of Market Efficiency: A Preliminary Investigation of Dispersion in Individual Investor Returns*, 28 J. CORP. L. 671 (2003). For a variety of both historical and practical reasons, consistent performance disclosures for brokerage accounts have not been part of our regulatory system.

In certain contexts, however, the lines between mutual funds and brokerage accounts have become sufficiently blurred such that these differences in disclosure obligations might profitably be revisited. For example, mutual funds, like many other investment vehicles, offer fund-of-funds in which the top fund invests in a variety of other funds. One of the most popular examples of this approach are target date funds, where a fund complex will put together groups of stock and bond funds, diversified across investment strategies and geographic markets, that would be appropriate for the retirement savings of a group of investors in their mid-40s and likely to retire around 2035. Such a 2035 target date fund would likely be largely invested in equity funds today but would gradually shift over to more bond funds as 2035 approaches. The SEC has devised a specialized system of disclosures for fund-of-fund mutual funds to make sure that investors in the top-level fund are informed about all the fees and expenses they will be charged, including in the lower-level funds, also known as acquired funds. Accordingly, investors in fund-of-fund mutual funds get a reasonably complete view of their costs and can also make comparisons across different fund-of-funds. For example, with regard to the Fidelity website's screening tool previously discussed, one could compare its two offerings in the 2035 target date space, the first involving actively managed acquired funds and the other involving indexed acquired funds.

Figure 10.3-5 Target Date Funds

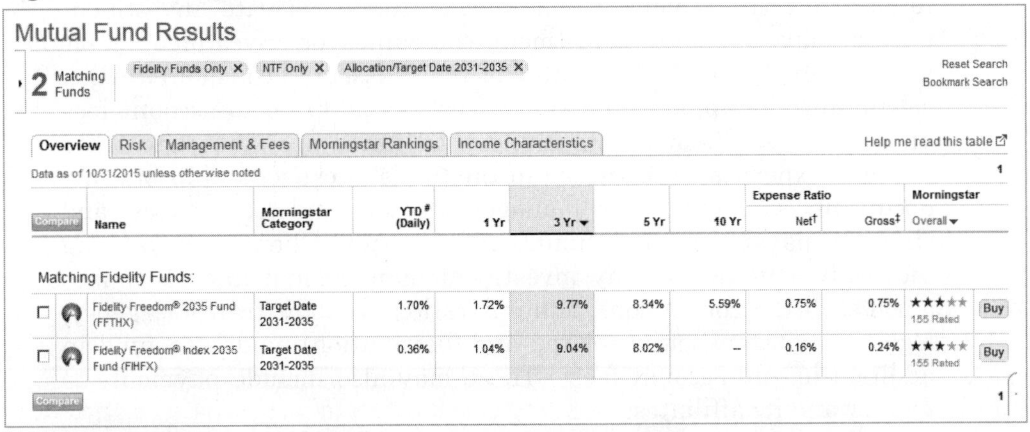

Mutual Fund Results

2 Matching Funds — Fidelity Funds Only ✕ NTF Only ✕ Allocation/Target Date 2031-2035 ✕ — Reset Search / Bookmark Search

Overview | Risk | Management & Fees | Morningstar Rankings | Income Characteristics — Help me read this table

Data as of 10/31/2015 unless otherwise noted

Name	Morningstar Category	YTD# (Daily)	1 Yr	3 Yr	5 Yr	10 Yr	Expense Ratio Net†	Expense Ratio Gross‡	Morningstar Overall
Matching Fidelity Funds:									
Fidelity Freedom® 2035 Fund (FFTHX)	Target Date 2031-2035	1.70%	1.72%	9.77%	8.34%	5.59%	0.75%	0.75%	★★★☆☆ 155 Rated
Fidelity Freedom® Index 2035 Fund (FIHFX)	Target Date 2031-2035	0.36%	1.04%	9.04%	8.02%	--	0.16%	0.24%	★★★☆☆ 155 Rated

Source: Fidelity Inv., Mutual Fund Research (last visited Nov. 9, 2015).

Another, increasingly popular way in which mutual funds are assembled in a retail investor's portfolio is through a wrap account or managed account. A securities firm will then charge an advisory fee and sometimes also receive 12b-1 fees from funds in which the account is invested, as well as, potentially, revenue sharing from the investment advisers of mutual funds. We discussed whether securities firms of this sort were required to register as investment advisers in Chapter 4.2. In Chapter 10.2 we discussed 12b-1 fees and revenue sharing in the context of the financing of mutual fund distribution costs. Wrap accounts and similar products are today the most important distribution channel for many mutual funds selling through independent financial advisers. *See, e.g.*, Thomas Anderson, *Schwab Unveils Wrap Accounts*, KIPLINGER (Nov. 2006) ("Like Ikea furniture, a good portfolio of mutual funds takes some effort to assemble. You find superior funds, buy their shares, monitor performance, and rebalance at least once a year. Too much work? For some people, yes. That explains why $346 billion is invested in mutual fund 'wrap' accounts. Pros make the picks and do the other work for you. But the cost of brokerage-run fund wraps is high, averaging 1.17% annually (not counting the expenses of the underlying funds)—not very attractive to cost-conscious investors.").

From the perspective of the retail investor, the wrap account is quite similar to a fund-of-fund mutual fund. In theory, the wrap account sponsor could put together a different set of underlying funds for each customer, but in practice the portfolios are quite similar across many investors. Wrap account customers do not receive annual reports comparable to the ones that fund-of-fund investors receive, nor can potential investors obtain the sort of historical information about wrap account providers that they can obtain from mutual fund complexes. Rather, wrap account customers receive annual statements about their investments and wrap account advisory fees, though not fees and expenses in the underlying fund. In addition, in many cases, wrap account sponsors give only the most generalized disclosures about the 12b-1 fees and revenue sharing they obtain as a result of funds placed in their wrap accounts. The following disclosure language, taken from the 36-page single-spaced document for Janney Montgomery Scott LLC's Managed Account (Wrap Fee) Program Disclosure Brochure (Aug. 17, 2015), is not unusual:

> [Janney wrap accounts] may include shares of mutual funds (including money market funds), closed-end funds, exchange-traded funds, unit investment trusts, hedge funds, private investment partnerships or other investment companies or investment pools (collectively, "funds"). The value of these assets is considered when calculating the applicable account fees. In addition to account fees and expenses, Client assets invested in funds are subject to other fees and expenses as described in the funds' prospectuses or offering document, including the management fee and other fees and chargers payable by the fund. As a result, Clients are bearing indirectly a portion of any investment management and other fees (such as dealer concessions, administration, custody, transfer agency, legal, audit, transaction-related and distribution) paid by a fund in addition to any account fees. These may also include payments to Janney and its affiliates.

Some wrap account sponsors do, however, either commit to not receiving any 12b-1 fees or to revenue sharing as a result of the mutual fund placements or they agree to credit any such payments to, or deduct those payments from, the wrap account fee they charge for their services.

---

1. ***Fund-of-Fund and Wrap Account Disclosures***. Would you recommend that the SEC attempt to establish uniform disclosures for fund-of-funds and wrap accounts? Are there advantages to maintaining two separate approaches to the creation of fund portfolios with different legal structures, which will work to the advantage of consumers as a result of competitive pressures?

III. TWO CASE STUDIES

We now turn to two case studies involving areas where mutual fund disclosures might be refined or elaborated. The first addresses the SEC's efforts to enhance risk disclosures. The second concerns target date funds.

A. QUANTITATIVE MEASURES OF FINANCIAL RISK

SEC, Improving Descriptions of Risk by Mutual Funds and Other Investment Companies, Concept Release

60 Fed. Reg. 17172 (Apr. 4, 1995)

Today the SEC is continuing its efforts to enhance the information that investors in funds receive to assist them in making an informed investment decision. In recent years, the SEC has taken significant steps designed to improve the understandability and comparability of fund disclosure of performance and expenses. The SEC is now requesting comment on how to improve risk disclosure for investment companies, including ways to increase the comparability of disclosure about funds' risk levels through quantitative measures or other means.

Under existing SEC rules, a fund is required to discuss in its prospectus the principal risk factors associated with investing in the fund. Funds typically describe the risks of investing in the fund by describing the risks of particular investment policies that the fund may use and investments that the fund may make. Lengthy and highly technical descriptions of permissible policies and investments that are often used in meeting existing requirements may make it difficult for investors to understand the total risk level of a fund. The SEC staff has found that funds typically provide only the most general information on the risk level of the fund taken as a whole and has encouraged funds to modify their existing disclosure to enhance investor understanding of risks. The SEC believes that it is now appropriate to explore whether SEC disclosure requirements should be revised in order to improve the communication of fund risks to investors and increase the likelihood that investors will readily grasp the risks of investing in a particular fund before they invest. . . .

Quantitative Measures of Risk

Historical measures of risk and risk-adjusted performance are generally calculated from past portfolio returns and, in some cases, past market returns. There are two broad classes of historical risk measures, . . . total risk measures and market risk measures. In addition, there is a third class of measures, risk-adjusted measures of performance. . . .

Comments are requested on the relative advantages and disadvantages of the three classes of measures and of specific measures within each class.

1. Measures of Total Risk

Total risk measures, including standard deviation and semi-variance, quantify the total variability of a portfolio's returns around, or below, its average return.

> *Standard Deviation of Total Return.* The risk associated with a portfolio can be viewed as the volatility of its returns, measured by the standard deviation of those returns. For example, a fund's historical risk could be measured by computing the standard deviation of its monthly total returns over some prior period, such as the past three years. The larger the standard deviation of monthly total returns, the more volatile, *i.e.*, spread out around the fund's average monthly total return, the fund's monthly total returns have been over the prior period. Standard deviation of total return can be calculated for funds with different objectives, ranging from equity funds to fixed income funds to balanced funds, and can be measured over different time frames. For example, a fund could calculate standard deviation of monthly returns over the prior three years or yearly returns over the prior ten years.
>
> *Semi-variance.* Standard deviation measures both "good" and "bad" outcomes, *i.e.*, the variability of returns both above and below the average return. To the individual investor, however, risk may be synonymous with "bad" outcomes. Semi-variance, which can be used to measure the variability of returns below the average return, reflects this view of risk. A fund with a larger semi-variance has returns that are more spread out below the average return.

2. Measures of Market Risk

Individual securities, and portfolios of securities, are generally subject to two sources of risk: (i) Risk attributable to firm-specific factors, including research and development, marketing, and quality of management; and (ii) risk attributable to general economic conditions, including the inflation rate, interest rates, and exchange rates. . . . [F]irm-specific risk can be reduced or eliminated through portfolio diversification, but the risk attributable to general economic conditions, so-called "market risk," cannot be eliminated through diversification. Unlike standard deviation and variance, which measure portfolio risk from both sources, the measures described in this section are measures of market risk. The SEC requests comment on whether, given that most fund portfolios are diversified, it is appropriate to focus on market risk when measuring fund risks.

> *Beta.* Beta measures the sensitivity of a security's, or portfolio's, return to the market's return. The market's beta is by definition equal to 1. Portfolios with betas greater than 1 are more volatile than the market, and portfolios with betas less than 1 are less volatile than the market. For example, if a portfolio has a beta of 2, a 10% market return would result in a 20% portfolio return, and a 10% market loss would result in a 20% portfolio loss (excluding the effects of any firm-specific risk that has not been eliminated through diversification).

The calculation of a fund's historical beta requires the selection of a benchmark market index, and persons supporting the use of beta are asked to address how the benchmark should be selected and whether a single benchmark should be used for all funds. If a single benchmark should be selected, what should it be? If a single benchmark is not used, how should the lack of comparability of betas for funds using different benchmarks be addressed? . . .

3. Risk-Adjusted Measures of Performance

Risk-adjusted measures of performance were developed in the 1960s to compare the quality of investment management. [Two] widely-used risk-adjusted measures are:

> *Sharpe Ratio.* Also known as the Reward-to-Variability Ratio, this is the ratio of a fund's average return in excess of the risk-free rate of return ("average excess return") to the standard deviation of the fund's excess returns. It measures the returns earned in excess of those that could have been earned on a riskless investment per unit of total risk assumed.
>
> *Jensen's Alpha.* This is the difference between a fund's actual returns and those that could have been earned on a benchmark portfolio with the same amount of market risk, *i.e.*, the same beta, as the portfolio. Jensen's Alpha measures the ability of active management to increase returns above those that are purely a reward for bearing market risk.

Would quantitative risk measures, including risk-adjusted measures of performance, help investors to evaluate historical performance and investment management expertise? The SEC requires that fund prospectuses include standardized return information, even though past returns are not necessarily indicative of future returns. Persons submitting comments are asked to address whether quantitative disclosure of the risk level incurred to produce stated returns may provide investors with a better tool to understand past fund performance and management. Historical data could, for example, help investors distinguish among funds that have achieved comparable rates of return with significantly different levels of risk. . . .

Would quantitative risk measures be useful to investors as indicators or guides to future fund risk levels, enhancing investors' ability to compare risks assumed by investing in different funds? . . .

Historical Measures v. Portfolio-Based Measures v. Risk Objectives

There are three approaches to the use of quantitative risk measures: historical, portfolio-based, and risk objectives or targets.

The simple historical approach to quantitative risk measures is outlined . . . above. This method generally uses actual past returns of a fund to compute a measure of risk for the fund. An alternative is a portfolio-based computation, which calculates a portfolio risk measure based on the particular securities in the portfolio as of a specified measurement date. . . .

There are at least two important limitations of using portfolio-based measures for fund disclosure: first, a fund may be invested in newly introduced financial instruments that have little or no history, and for which historical behavior must be estimated, and, second, portfolio-based measures, which are derived from portfolio composition on one particular date, may be less representative of the risk of a managed portfolio over time than a simple historical measure derived from fund returns over a period of time. . . .

Another approach to risk measures is requiring funds to announce risk objectives or targets. Any of the risk and risk-adjusted performance measures could be used by funds in this manner. For example, a fund could announce its intention to follow a strategy that would yield a standard deviation of 10%-12% per year, a beta of 1.50-1.75 with respect to the S&P 500, or a duration of 7-9 years. Comments are requested regarding the relative merits of this approach as compared to the simple historical and portfolio-based approaches. . . .

---

1. ***Improving Risk Disclosure.*** What approach would you advise the SEC take with respect to quantitative measures? Would any of the measures outlined in the excerpt improve upon graphic presentations of risk of the sort shown in connection with the past performance of the Fidelity Low-Priced Stock Fund?

2. ***Retail Customers' Financial Literacy.*** To what extent should the SEC's approach to risk disclosure take into account the relatively poor financial literacy of retail customers? Consider the following summary of the literature:

> Bernheim (1995, 1998) was among the first to document that many US consumers display low levels of financial literacy. Hilgert et al. (2003) report that most Americans fail to understand basic financial concepts, particularly those relating to bonds, stocks, and mutual funds. Lusardi and Mitchell's (2008, 2011a) module on planning and financial literacy for the 2004 Health and Retirement Study (HRS) provides further evidence of financial illiteracy. They find that many older (50+) individuals cannot do simple interest rate calculations, such as determining how money would grow at an interest rate of 2%, and do not know about the workings of inflation and risk diversification.
>
> Financial literacy is important because it has been linked to saving behavior and portfolio choice. For example, the less financially literate are found to be less likely to plan for retirement (Lusardi and Mitchell, 2007, 2008, 2011a, c), to accumulate wealth (Stango and Zinman, 2009), and to participate in the stock market (Christelis et al., 2010; van Rooij et al., 2011; Yoong, 2011). Moreover, less financially literate individuals are less likely to choose mutual funds with lower fees (Hastings and Tejeda-Ashton, 2008). . . . Moore (2003) reports that respondents with lower levels of financial literacy are more likely to have costly mortgages. Similarly, Campbell (2006) reports that individuals with lower incomes and lower education levels—characteristics that are strongly related to financial literacy—are less likely to refinance their mortgages during a period of falling interest rates.

Annamaria Lusardi & Peter Tufano, *Debt Literacy, Financial Experience, and Overindebtedness*, 14 J. PENSION ECON. & FIN. 332, 333 (2015) (finding low financial literacy correlated with higher debt levels and other indicia of financial distress).

B. TARGET DATE FUNDS

Target date funds, also known as life cycle funds, are popular investment vehicles designed for investors who anticipate retiring at the fund's target date. Life cycle funds hold diversified portfolios of stocks, bonds, and other assets, and this asset mix automatically rebalances to keep the portfolio composition in line with a pre-specified asset allocation pattern, which, as illustrated in Figure 10.3-6, becomes increasingly conservative as the target date approaches. The process by which a fund shifts its assets is known as the glide path.

Figure 10.3-6 Example of a Target Date Fund Glide Path

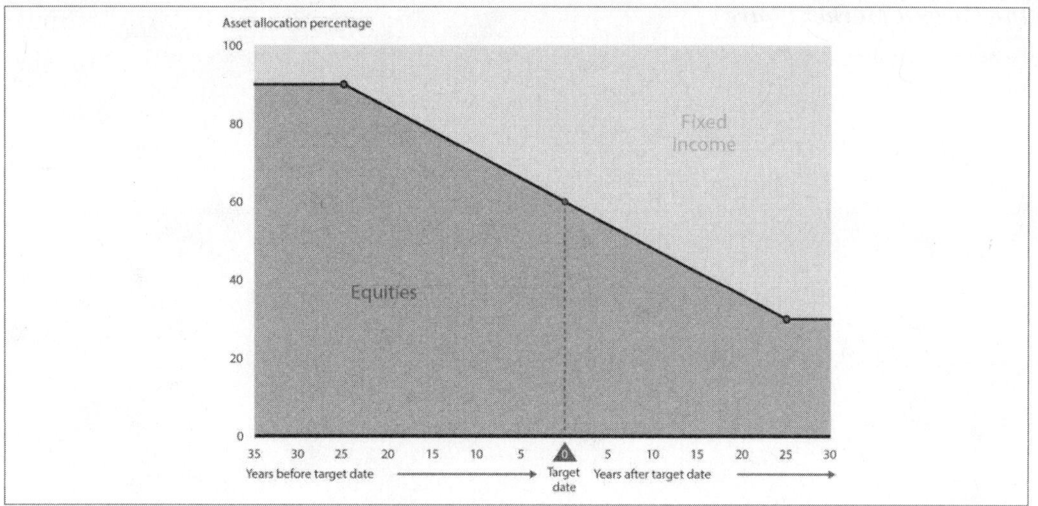

Source: U.S. Gov't Accountability Office, GAO-11-118, Defined Contribution Plans: Key Information on Target Date Funds as Default Investments Should be Provided to Plan Sponsors and Participants, 7 (Jan. 2011).

Although they share these basic characteristics, target date funds differ from one another in a number of significant respects. Different funds, even those sharing the same target date, may vary widely in terms of asset allocation. For example, the equity allocations of funds with a target date of 2010 range from 26% to 72%. The shape of the glide path also varies, as the gradual decrease in equity weightings may maintain a consistent slope, become steeper over time, or follow a stepped pattern. Additionally, target date funds may be categorized as either "to" or "through" funds. Whereas the glide path of a "to" fund generally becomes flat once an investor reaches the target date, the glide path of a "through" fund continues to change past retirement, finally reaching a landing point around ten to 20 years after the target date. *See, e.g.*, Josh Charlson et al., *2009 Industry Survey*, MORNINGSTAR TARGET-DATE SERIES RESEARCH PAPER, Sept. 9, 2009, at 6-8, 10-11.

Target date funds have been available since at least 1988. These funds have grown significantly over the past decade, increasing from $5.5 billion in assets in 2000, to over $150 billion in assets in 2007, to more than $204 billion in assets by May 2008, and over $750 billion in 2015. Gaobo Pang & Mark Warshawsky, *Asset Allocations and Risk-Return Tradeoffs of Target-Date Funds* 1 (Working Paper, Oct. 15, 2009); Janet Yang & Laura P. Lutton, *2014 Industry Survey*, MORNINGSTAR TARGET-DATE SERIES RESEARCH PAPER, July 1, 2014, at 1. In 2007, assets in target date funds made up approximately 7% of total assets in 401(k) plans. Craig Copeland, *Use of Target-Date Funds in 401(k) Plans, 2007*, 327 EBRI ISSUE BRIEF, Mar. 2009, at 4. The increase in popularity is due in part to target date funds' 2007 designation as a Qualified Default Investment Alternative, thereby allowing their use as default investments where a participant does not actively select a different investment option.

Figure 10.3-7 Range of Returns from 2005-2009 for the 2010 Target Date Funds with the Largest Market Share

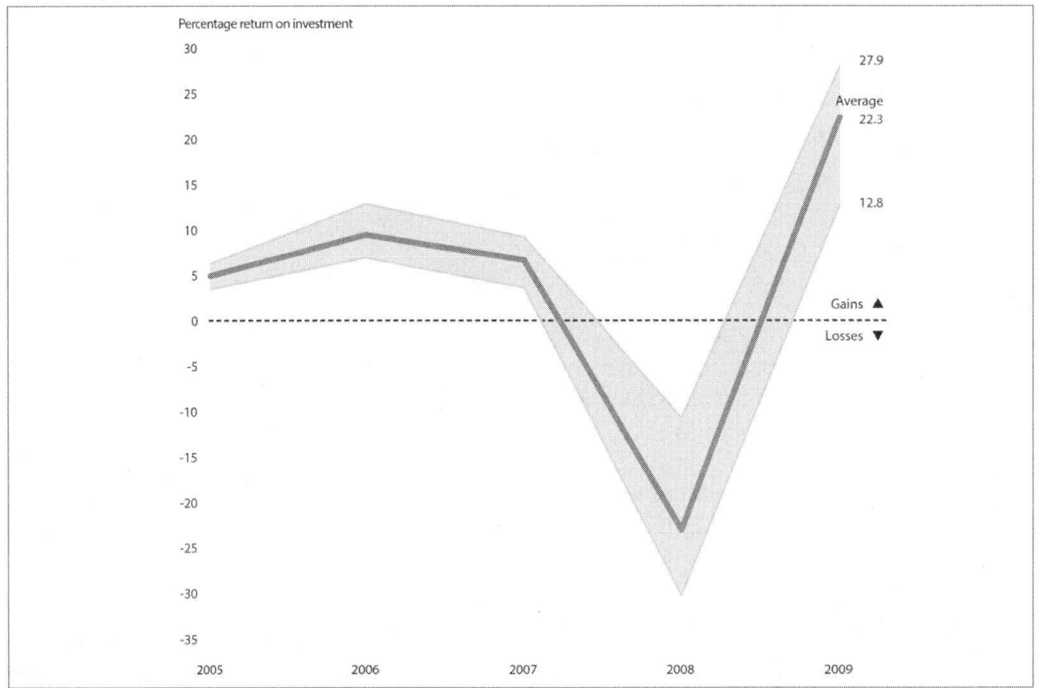

Source: U.S. Gov't Accountability Office, GAO-11-118, Defined Contribution Plans: Key Information on Target Date Funds as Default Investments Should be Provided to Plan Sponsors and Participants, 21 (Jan. 2011).

Most target date funds experienced significant losses during the Financial Crisis. In 2008, short-dated target funds averaged losses of 25% to 30%, while long-dated funds lost an average of nearly 40%, however, performance varied widely from fund to fund. For example, performance for 2010 target date funds ranged from negative 9% to negative 41%. Charlson et al., *2009 Industry Survey*, at 3, 7. These losses have led many to call for increased regulation of these funds, and the SEC and the Department of Labor held a joint public hearing on this issue in June 2009. *See* SEC, DEP'T OF LABOR, Public Hearing on Target Date Funds and Other Similar Investment Options (June 18, 2009). The case study below explores whether the SEC should consider adopting additional regulations for target date funds.

Case Study: Target Date Funds
Considerations related to possible adoption of new target date fund regulations

I. Current Regulatory Framework

The SEC has jurisdiction over target date funds that are organized as mutual funds under the 1933 Act and the 1940 Act. However, the SEC lacks jurisdiction over some investment plans that function as target date funds, such as bank-sponsored collective investment trusts. The SEC also does not regulate 401(k) plans or the use of the Qualified Default Investment Alternative ("QDIA") designation. Under the federal securities laws enforced by the SEC, target date funds, like all mutual funds, must meet certain prospectus disclosure requirements. In its prospectus, each fund must disclose material information concerning its investment objectives, strategies, and risks, and include a table displaying comprehensive information about the costs of investing. Target date funds typically include in their prospectus an illustration of the fund's glide path, information on what occurs when the fund reaches the target date, an explanation of the way that the asset allocation becomes increasingly conservative, and a description of the specific risks related to target date fund investments. Each prospectus must also disclose the costs of the target date fund itself as well as the costs associated with any underlying funds that make up the target date fund's investment portfolio.

The Department of Labor enforces the fiduciary, reporting, and disclosure provisions of ERISA that apply to employee benefit plans. Title I of [Employee Retirement Income Security Act (ERISA)] establishes standards of conduct for plan fiduciaries and makes fiduciaries accountable for making prudent decisions regarding the selection and monitoring of plan providers and investments. In order to encourage 401(k) plan sponsors to adopt automatic enrollment programs, Congress enacted the Pension Protection Act in 2006. In October 2007, the Department of Labor issued final regulations on QDIAs pursuant to the Pension Protection Act. Investments designated as QDIAs are eligible for relief under Section 404(c) of ERISA, which provides liability protection to pension plan fiduciaries for investment results of participant accounts that are placed in default investments. The Department of Labor regulations designated targeted retirement date funds as one of three general categories of funds that can qualify as a long-term QDIA. To meet the definition of a target date fund within the QDIA regulation, a fund must apply generally accepted investment theories, be diversified, and provide varying degrees of long-term appreciation and capital preservation based on the age, retirement date, or life expectancy of participants. The QDIA regulation does not specify the composition of target date funds or the ratio of stocks and bonds.

In 2010, the SEC proposed a rule that "would require marketing materials for target date retirement funds to include a table, chart, or graph depicting the fund's asset allocation over time, together with a statement that would highlight the fund's final asset allocation." SEC, Investment Company Advertising; Target Date Retirement Fund Names and Marketing, Proposed Rule, 75 Fed. Reg. 35920, 35920 (June 23, 2010). The Department of Labor mirrored the SEC's efforts with its own proposed rule on disclosure in the same year. *See* DEP'T OF LABOR, Target Date Disclosure, Proposed Rule, 75 Fed. Reg. 73987 (Nov. 30, 2010). No rules were finalized after four years. In 2014, however, the SEC reopened the comment period for its 2010 proposed rule. *See* SEC, Investment Company Advertising; Target Date Retirement Fund Names and Marketing, Request for Additional Comment, 79 Fed. Reg. 19564 (Apr. 9, 2014). The Department of Labor again mirrored the SEC by also reopening the comment period for its own 2010 rule. *See* DEP'T OF LABOR, Target Date Disclosure, Request for Additional Comment, 79 Fed. Reg. 31893 (June 3, 2014). As of November 2015, no further actions have been published in the Federal Register with regard to either of the agencies' efforts in this area.

II. Concerns

Criticisms of target date funds tend to fall into four general categories: risk and asset allocation, communication and disclosure, fees, and use as a QDIA.

Risk and Asset Allocations. Much of the criticism of target date funds focuses on the contention that funds have assumed too much risk by adopting excessively large equity allocations. Funds have increased equity exposure in two ways: first, by increasing equity allocations along the glide path, and second, by extending the glide path out beyond the target date. Some commentators, speculating on the causes of this phenomenon, have asserted that fund managers have an incentive to use overly aggressive asset allocations in order to increase their own profits and to compete with the short-term performance of other funds, thus fueling an "equity allocation arms race."

Commentators have voiced concern not only that target date funds contain excessive equity allocations, but also that equity exposure differs significantly from fund to fund.

Some critics have expressed great concern with these large variations in equity, as they believe that target date fund investors often make decisions without professional advice and fail to do sufficient research on possible investments, particularly when such funds have been specifically approved as investment options by a retirement plan sponsor. Furthermore, some have asserted that because individuals are led to believe that one target date fund is an appropriate investment until retirement, they tend to stay in only that fund until the target date, despite changes in lifestyle and financial status that may alter their appropriate level of risk.

Communication and Disclosure. A second line of criticism focuses on a perceived lack of adequate communication and disclosure, particularly regarding asset allocation strategies and methodology. Some commentators have argued that more clear and comprehensive disclosure is essential in order to enable individuals and plan fiduciaries to make appropriate investment decisions.

Fees. Fees vary among target date funds. More than fifty percent of target date fund series have asset-weighted expense ratios of more than 1%. Some have expressed concern at the tendency of target date funds to invest only in underlying funds run by the same company, rather than examining many different options to find the best and lowest cost investments.

Use as a QDIA. Some commentators have argued that allowing use as a QDIA conveys government approval, which may lead investors to assume that such funds are appropriate investment vehicles, and have observed that investors who are defaulted into a fund frequently make no further decisions concerning their retirement portfolio.

III. Proposals

Suggestions for improving target date funds have largely fallen into four groups of proposals: limiting risk, increasing disclosure, limiting fees, and modifying QDIA status.

Proposals to Limit Risk. Two main proposals have been suggested to limit the level of risk assumed by target date funds. The first proposal urges government regulators to set specific requirements for fund asset allocations and glide paths. For example, some commentators have called for the SEC, with the help of independent experts, establish industry standards of acceptable ranges of asset allocations for target date funds of different durations.

The second proposal involves requiring funds to take into account characteristics beyond an investor's age, in order to better match the risk tolerance of individual investors with the risk level of their target date fund.

Proposals to Improve Communication and Increase Disclosure Requirements. In order to address concerns about inadequate disclosure, the SEC could consider adopting new disclosure requirements specifically for target date funds. For example, some commentators have advocated for an accessibly written, standardized "fact sheet" that highlights the potential risks of target date funds and illustrates the relationship between the fund's target date benchmark and the fund's glide path.

Proposals to Limit Fees. The SEC could also consider adopting new regulations related to fees charged by target date funds. For example, the SEC could require QDIAs to invest only in low cost index funds or index fund ETFs, in order to limit fees.

Proposals to Ban or Regulate Use of Target Date Funds as QDIAs. Lastly, the SEC and Department of Labor could take steps to increase monitoring and regulation of QDIAs. First, the SEC could provide specific securities registration for funds seeking QDIA status, which might require, for example, that each fund prospectus describe that fund's QDIA capabilities and compliance and prohibit use of funds without this registration as a QDIA. Meanwhile, the Department of Labor could require an annual audit for all QDIA vendors in order to monitor compliance with ERISA regulations and also require vendors to take into account other variables beyond age, such as accumulated wealth, to determine QDIA investment choices.

---

1. ***How Should the SEC and Department of Labor Respond?*** Now that you have gained an understanding of target date funds, their regulatory landscape, the various concerns with these funds as one-stop investment vehicles, and some proposals for reform, how do you think the SEC and Department of Labor should respond? Especially in light of concerns regarding the differing levels of equity exposure from fund to fund, should the SEC impose more stringent requirements on target date funds and attempt to standardize fund offerings, or is it better for the marketplace to offer a diversity of products, even if many customers fail to grasp the full complexity of funds? Is it desirable to increase the amount of responsibility that plan sponsors bear in choosing target date funds, or should sponsors be entitled to safe harbor protection because such investments, despite their associated risks, are probably better retirement options than what individuals are likely to choose on their own? Which of the proposals discussed in this Chapter is most likely to achieve the goals you have identified as important?

IV. THE LIMITS OF DISCLOSURE

In this final part of the Chapter, we explore a small fraction of the growing literature on the quality of investor decisions with respect to mutual fund investments and the larger question of the efficacy of disclosure as a regulatory strategy for retail investors and other consumers of financial products.

A. ACADEMIC STUDIES ON INVESTOR DECISION-MAKING

One way to characterize a mutual fund is by whether it is an actively managed fund or a passive fund. A passive fund seeks to replicate an index and therefore has an investment strategy that remains constant. While the particular holdings of a passive fund may change over time, this will reflect changes in the benchmark it seeks to replicate or perhaps cash inflows or outflows from the investing public. Actively managed funds are funds in which a portfolio manager is appointed to select the fund's investments and constantly monitor and update the investments. The portfolio manager aims to beat the market by selecting investments that they believe will have the highest returns.

The difference between the investment strategies of actively managed funds and passive funds results in significant disparities in the cost of investing in either type of fund. Actively managed funds tend to be more expensive since portfolio managers are paid for their selection and updating of the fund's holdings, resulting in a higher expense ratio. Moreover, actively managed fund investors incur the transaction costs that follow from the constant change in the fund's portfolio.

Given the differences in the costs of the two types of funds, it has been long debated whether actively managed funds justify their costs. A large finance literature has sought to answer whether the selection and constant updating of a portfolio can result in higher market returns to investors than their benchmarks, and if such an advantage exists, whether investors receive higher returns net of the higher fees they pay for this active management. The conclusion of this literature is that, even before accounting for expenses, the actively managed mutual fund sector does not, on average, provide investors with above market returns. *See, e.g.*, Kenneth R. French, *The Cost of Active Investing*, 63 J. FIN. 1537 (2008). Moreover, it is well-documented that, after accounting for fees and expenses, mutual funds typically provide returns lower than passive benchmarks. *See, e.g.*, Martin J. Gruber, *Another Puzzle: The Growth of Actively Managed Mutual Funds*, 51 J. FIN. 783, 787 (1996); *c.f.* Diane Del Guercio & Jonathan Reuter, *Mutual Fund Performance and the Generation of Alpha*, J. OF FIN. (Aug. 14, 2012) (forthcoming) (showing that underperformance of actively managed retail funds might be limited to broker-sold funds, a result perhaps attributable to 12b-1 fees). For the small fraction of funds that earn above market returns, the prevalent view among scholars is that mutual funds do not persistently earn above market returns, see, *e.g.*, Mark M. Carhart, *On Persistence in Mutual Fund Performance*, 51 J. FIN. 57 (1997), and in any event it is attributable to luck and not skill. *See, e.g.*, Eugene F. Fama & Kenneth R. French, *Luck Versus Skill in the Cross-Section of Mutual Fund Returns*, 65 J. FIN. 1915 (2010). For a different perspective on the existence of skill in the mutual fund sector, *see, e.g.*, Jonathan B. Berk & Jules H. van Binsbergen, *Measuring Skill in the Mutual Fund Industry*, 118 J. FIN. ECON. 1 (2015) (using value added data to demonstrate that the average mutual fund is skilled and adds $3.2 million per year in value, and arguing that investors are able to identify this skill and reward it by investing more capital with better funds).

Even if there existed a small subset of skillful fund managers, it is questionable whether retail investors would be able to identify such managers *ex ante*. As expected, the assets managed by passive funds have steadily increased since the inception of the index fund in the 1970s. Actively managed mutual funds, however, continue to dominate the mutual fund sector with 87% of total mutual fund assets. *See* Inv. Co. Inst., 2015 Investment Company Fact Book, at 29, 97. Should policy-makers be concerned about the persistent popularity of actively managed mutual funds, notwithstanding a seemingly strong consensus among financial economists that low-cost passive strategies are superior? Take a look back at the performance records of the Fidelity 2035 target date funds. Does it matter to you that the actively managed fund-of-funds outperformed the passively managed (indexed) fund-of-funds for all relevant periods?

Another relevant and active line of potential relevant academic literature seeks to understand consumer investment behavior, motivated by the puzzling persistence of actively managed funds with high fees and below market returns. The overall conclusion of this literature is that consumers do not select funds to minimize their fees and expenses, and often place weight on fund features that are unlikely to persist, such as the past returns of mutual funds. Erik Sirri & Peter Tufano, *Costly Search and Mutual Fund Flows*, 53 J. FIN. 1589 (1998).

This literature seems to suggest that consumers have difficulty selecting low cost funds since consumers pay attention to salient and accessible fund attributes rather than to fund features that directly affect returns. This explains why consumers avoid funds with salient and easy to calculate fees, and instead select fees with high expense ratios, which are more shrouded. *See, e.g.*, Santosh Anagol & Hugh Hoikwang-Kim, *The Impact of Shrouded Fees: Evidence from a Natural Experiment in the Indian Mutual Funds Market*, 102 AM. ECON. REV. 576 (2012). As mutual funds shift their fee structures to more shrouded fees, consumers will find it difficult to reduce fees and expenses. *See, e.g.*, Brad Barber, Terrance Odean & Lu Zheng, *Out of Sight, Out of Mind: The Effects of Expenses on Mutual Fund Flows*, 78 J. BUS. 2095 (2005). Even when investment skill is irrelevant, such as when selecting amongst funds that track the same index, consumers are unable to select funds with the lowest fees. *See, e.g.*, James Choi, David Laibson & Brigitte Madrian, *Why Does the Law of One Price Fail? An Experiment on Index Mutual Funds*, 23 REV. FIN. STUD. 1405 (2010). Moreover, low levels of financial literacy and the complexity of the information provided by mutual funds, such as the fund prospectus, present challenges even for investors who intend to invest in low cost funds. *See, e.g.*, Annamaria Lusardi & Olivia Mitchelli, *Financial Literacy and Retirement Preparedness: Evidence and Implications for Financial Education*, 42 BUS. ECON. 35 (2007).

Taken as a group, this body of literature poses serious questions as to whether retail investors have the wherewithal to make sensible choices about their investments in mutual funds. In a study that gained prominence in connection with the *Jones v. Harris Associates* litigation we explored in Chapter 10.2, however, Professors John Coates and Glenn Hubbard concluded:

> In this Article, we have attempted to restore some balance to the debate over mutual fund fees, a debate in which the loudest voices have been those of fund industry critics, and the voice of the industry itself (prominently from the [Investment Company Institute]) which is often viewed skeptically as self-interested. Basic economic theory and empirical evidence is enough, we believe, to rebut widespread beliefs dating from the 1960s that the mutual fund industry is not competitive, due to the conflicts of interest faced by mutual fund advisers and directors. Fund critics correctly note that few fund boards put advisory contracts out for bid, but fail to acknowledge the defining legal feature of the mutual fund: that, by contract, fund investors can, and do, rapidly discipline funds and fund advisers by redeeming fund shares at [NAV] and investing the proceeds elsewhere. In addition, basic facts about the fund industry establish a prima facie case that it is competitive: market structure of the industry is conducive to competition; barriers to entry are low; actual entry and expansion of funds has been common and continuous over the past several decades; fees have, if anything, tended to trend down over time; and market shares of funds and fund complexes have shifted significantly over time.
>
> One important factor causing some funds to gain market share (and others to lose market share) over time is lower advisory fees. We provide direct evidence that mutual fund investors are sensitive to fees, as well as evidence of the role of competition in constraining mutual fund advisers from charging excessive fees. Our estimates of the impact of fees on fund and complex market share are large, larger than found in most recent studies, in part because other recent

> studies have focused on fund flows, which bias empirical findings downward, and not (as we do) on fund assets. Our findings are robust to a variety of controls . . .
>
> Based on our economic, empirical and legal analysis, we reject strong claims from fund critics for the SEC to subject funds to heightened additional regulation . . . Put simply, we recommend that fund critics and lawmakers leave the law on fees where it is, but update their beliefs about how effective the law and the market already are in preventing advisers from charging funds excessive fees.

John C. Coates IV & R. Glenn Hubbard, *Competition in the Mutual Fund Industry: Evidence and Implications for Policy*, 33 J. CORP. L. 151, 215-16 (2007). Assuming their evidence is valid, are you reassured, or do you think that there are lingering concerns with retail investors' ability to make prudent choices about where to invest their savings?

B. TESTING THE EFFICACY OF DISCLOSURE

While disclosure is a dominant regulatory strategy in many areas of investor and consumer protection, the efficacy of the approach has come under increasing attack in certain academic circles. *See* OMRI BEN-SHAHAR & CARL E. SCHNEIDER, MORE THAN YOU WANTED TO KNOW: THE FAILURE OF MANDATED DISCLOSURE (2014) (emphasizing the problems of information overload); Lauren Willis, *Decisionmaking and the Limits of Disclosure: The Problem of Predatory Lending: Price*, 65 MARYLAND L. REV. 707 (2006). Studies have shown that, paradoxically, underperforming mutual funds charge higher fees, and that this anomaly can be explained in part by the fact that "funds with worse past performance have a pool of investors that are less sensitive to fund performance." Javier Gil-Bazo & Pablo Ruiz-Verdú, *The Relation between Price and Performance in the Mutual Fund Industry*, 64 J. OF FIN. 2153, 2179 (Oct. 2009). There is also an active and unresolved debate over the ability to improve consumers' ability to make use of mandated disclosures through programs designed to increase financial literacy. *Compare* Annamaria Lusardi & Olivia S. Mitchell, *The Economic Importance of Financial Literacy: Theory and Evidence*, 52 J. ECON. LIT. 5 (2014) (measured but largely optimistic perspective on options to improve financial literacy and consumer choices), *with* Lauren Willis, *Against Financial Literacy Education,* 94 IOWA L. REV. 197 (2008) (a pessimistic perspective) *and* Lauren Willis, *The Financial Education Fallacy*, 101 AMERICAN ECON. REV. 429 (2011) (another pessimistic perspective).

In response to the mounting criticism of disclosure strategies, at least in academic circles, financial regulatory authorities have increasingly taken to testing new forms of disclosure before mandating their use. Just as companies routinely test advertising campaigns and marketing materials through focus groups and surveys, agencies like the SEC and CFPB are now performing similar market research for their own initiatives. What exactly should a government look for in such a testing program? The following excerpt explores this question.

Talia B. Gillis, Putting Disclosure to the Test: Toward Better Evidence Based Policy

28 LOYOLA CONSUMER L. REV. 31, 34–38 (2015)

While consumers face many challenges when making financial decisions, the regulatory structure of consumer finance continues, controversially, to rely heavily on enhancing decision-making by improving disclosures. Opponents of disclosure have argued that disclosure is "ineffective," does not "result in good deliberate decision-making," and that it "has failed time after time, in place after place, in area after area, in method after method, and in decade after decade." Yet disclosure continues to play a central role in many domains including the regulation of consumer finance.

Understanding how regulators decide to require disclosures, despite their potential shortcomings, is crucial to any policy recommendation regarding mandated disclosure. In recent years, the process of adopting disclosures has changed significantly as regulators are required to provide stronger evidence of the benefits and effectiveness of proposed disclosure. Regulators now tend to recognize the need to replace abstract notions about how people process and use disclosures with the empirical study of their impact. Opponents of disclosure have overlooked this change in policy, claiming that the persistence of disclosure is a result of its political appeal and the excessive belief in "disclosurism." In reality, regulators often do not merely assert the benefits of disclosure but try to establish the effectiveness of disclosure by commissioning consumer testing of disclosures. Previous writing on disclosure, however, has failed to engage with the critical issue of the process by which disclosures are adopted by regulators . . .

This article contributes to our understanding of the prevalence of disclosure by analyzing the current testing methodology used to support the adoption of disclosure, showing that it is inadequate and how it might be improved. I evaluate two examples of extensive attempts to test disclosure documents prior to their adoption: the testing of the Integrated Mortgage disclosure by the [CFPB] in the United States, which went into effect on August 1, 2015, and the testing of the Key Investor Information Document by the [EU], which was implemented in 2012. The use of quantitative studies as a means to justify the adoption of disclosures is expected to expand given other disclosures that are currently on the agenda of the [CFPB] and other consumer financial regulators, such as payday lending, credit cards, and insurance.

As empirical testing of financial disclosures is becoming the norm, greater thought must be dedicated to the design and purpose of this testing, if the goal of disclosures is to benefit consumers. First, regulators need to consider the aim of financial disclosures, such as whether disclosures are intended to make consumers fully informed or whether they are meant to influence consumers in a less deliberative manner. I argue that the failure of consumer financial regulators to adequately articulate the mechanism through which disclosures assist consumers creates confusion as to how to judge the effectiveness of disclosures. Second, regulators must analyze whether current testing methodologies coincide with this aim. One concern is that comprehension tests, which are becoming the standard for testing disclosures, may neglect to test the actual effect of disclosures on financial decisions. While regulators assume that improving consumer comprehension in the narrow sense leads to better decisions, improved decision-making may require a number of steps beyond narrow comprehension. Third, regulators need to examine and justify the setting in which they test disclosures given concerns regarding the extent to which experimental settings can provide information on real-life impact of disclosures. This could mean either shifting testing methodologies to real-life testing, such as randomized controlled trials, or designing experiments that attempt to better capture real-life situations. . . .

. . . Current testing has both external and internal validity problems. It lacks external validity because it overlooks the ways in which disclosure may have an effect in real-life and consequently the test results may not be generalizable. It does not test whether consumers will actually read the disclosure when not prompted by test questions. It does not test whether human interaction or other distractions impact the effect of disclosure. Furthermore, it does not test how the financial industry will respond to disclosure requirements, relying instead on the isolated and pro-consumer environment created by regulators testing the disclosure.

Current testing methodologies also raise internal validity concerns. Their current focus on narrow comprehension does not test the stated purpose of disclosure—to improve consumers' decisions. This section provides several reasons to believe that comprehension does not necessarily lead to improved decisions. Current testing efforts, which focus on consumer comprehension, do not therefore establish that disclosures will of themselves improve consumer decisions. For example, relying on disclosures to make financial decisions requires financial literacy beyond the narrow comprehension of the document as well as knowledge of the consumer's financial situation and how it affects the specific transactions being considered. Furthermore, the current testing design does not test additional mechanisms through which disclosure may assist consumers beyond making consumers fully informed, such as increasing financial awareness. . . .

. . . [R]egulators can improve disclosure testing, either by redesigning experimental testing or by using real-life testing through randomized control trials and retrospective analysis. While some of the proposals may be resource-intense, requiring an expansion of testing efforts, many of the proposals require only a refocusing of the current effort levels.

Since regulators rely on empirical evidence in formulating consumer financial regulation, the appropriate focus of scholarly debate should be the nature of that evidence. As quantitative testing becomes the standard for good regulation, there is a greater need to articulate the mechanisms by which they assist consumers, as well as placing greater focus on the content and design of testing. By accurately aligning the testing methodology with the purpose of financial disclosures, as suggested in this article, regulators will then be able to adopt better-informed regulation that benefits consumers.

---

1. ***The Costs of Cost-Benefit Analyses.*** While it is difficult to argue against the desirability of more rigorous empirical validation of new disclosure requirements, should agencies defer promulgating new disclosures for what may turn out to be years until they can obtain convincing evidence that the new disclosures will actually improve individual decision-making? In the context of mutual fund selections, how could the agency determine whether investors were making better choices?

2. ***Adding New Disclosure Requirements.*** Should an agency, contrary to Ms. Talia Gillis's argument, proceed if it can demonstrate that a new disclosure improves investor or consumer comprehension? Would your answer be different if the new disclosure were replacing an old requirement that was never tested?

3. ***Congress and Disclosure***. While the academic community has turned sour on disclosure requirements, it is still an extremely popular regulatory strategy among politicians, especially members of Congress. Why should members of Congress like disclosure more than academics? If you were the head of the SEC or CFPB, would it be appropriate for you to attempt to educate members of Congress about the academic research on disclosure? Would it be wise?

CHAPTER 10.4

THE REGULATION OF HEDGE FUNDS AND OTHER PRIVATE FUNDS

CONTENTS

I. INTRODUCTION

In this Chapter on asset management, we turn to the topic of private funds, which are pooled investment vehicles not subject to regulation under the Investment Company Act of 1940 (1940 Act), and place a particular emphasis on hedge funds. Private funds have been dominated by institutional investors and wealthy individuals. As private funds almost always involve the purchase and sale of securities, certain elements of federal securities laws, such as the anti-fraud rules, apply. Freed from the relatively stringent provisions of the 1940 Act, however, hedge funds and other private funds have traditionally been able to contract with their investors on whatever terms the parties find mutually acceptable. Accordingly, many aspects of the sector have remained shrouded by commitments of confidentiality and knowledge of private fund activities, even amongst policymakers, has often remained quite limited until scandals erupt. One aspect of private fund activities that has been well-publicized is the compensation terms of private fund advisers, which has traditionally been set at 2% of assets under management plus 20% of profits, substantially higher than the levels seen for advisers of registered investment companies.

II. OVERVIEW OF PRIVATE FUNDS POST-DODD-FRANK ACT

Private funds are collective investment vehicles that are not registered as investment companies under the 1940 Act and that do not register their offerings of securities under the Securities Act of 1933 (1933 Act). Like the registered investment companies discussed in Chapter 10.1, these funds pool investments from individual and institutional investors, invest these funds in equities and other financial assets, and issue their own securities to the investors of the fund. The salient feature of private funds is their exemption from registering as investment companies under §§ 3(c)(1) and 3(c)(7) of the 1940 Act. Section 3(c)(1) exempts funds that do not publicly offer their securities and that have no more than 100 beneficial owners of their outstanding securities. Section 3(c)(7) exempts funds that do not publicly offer their securities and that limit the owners of their outstanding securities to qualified purchasers. Qualified purchasers are high-net-worth individuals or institutions; an individual must own no less than $5 million or else manage no less than $25 million to be a qualified purchaser. In addition to exemptions from the 1940 Act, analogous provisions of the Investment Advisers Act exempt certain investment advisers from registration requirements. The Investment Advisers Act exemptions are discussed later in this Chapter. In contrast to private funds, registered investment companies have traditionally been marketed to the broader population but must abide by the stringent regulations of the 1940 Act.

The most widely known examples of private funds are hedge funds, private equity funds, and venture capital funds. Hedge funds are organized and managed by investment advisers and are generally characterized by their fee structure and investment strategies. Their investments are varied and include securities, derivatives, currencies, and other assets. Hedge fund advisers' performance fees are generally calculated by including unrealized gains. Additionally, hedge funds can be distinguished by their investment strategies, which often involve high leverage and short-selling securities in order to hedge risk. *See* SEC, IMPLICATIONS OF THE GROWTH OF HEDGE FUNDS, STAFF REPORT 37-43 (Sep. 2003); SEC, PRIVATE FUNDS STATISTICS, FOURTH CALENDAR QUARTER 2014 39 (Oct. 16, 2015). At the end of 2014, investments in hedge funds totaled over $6 trillion out of nearly $10 trillion invested in all private funds. SEC, PRIVATE FUNDS STATISTICS, FOURTH CALENDAR QUARTER 2014 5 (Oct. 16, 2015). For a comprehensive account of generations of different hedge funds, see SEBASTIAN MALLABY, MORE MONEY THAN GOD: HEDGE FUNDS AND THE MAKING OF A NEW ELITE (2011).

Private equity funds invest in portfolio companies, often with the goal of turning-around an undervalued company. Private equity funds differ from hedge funds in the liquidity of their shares. While hedge fund investors may redeem their shares periodically, such as on a quarterly basis, private equity investors generally commit to contributing money over the life of the fund. Importantly, private equity funds only call in investors' money when there is an identified investment opportunity. *See* SEC, IMPLICATIONS OF THE GROWTH OF HEDGE FUNDS, at 7. Most funds' lifespan ranges from ten to 12 years. Total assets in private equity funds were nearly $2 trillion as of the fourth quarter of 2014. SEC, 2014 PRIVATE FUNDS STATISTICS, at 5.

Venture capital funds are distinguished by their investments in start-up companies. Like private equity funds, venture capital funds often have mandatory capital contributions and are long-term investments without periodic redemption rights for investors. Venture capital funds, however, generally liquidate their investments in a company once they achieve a positive return. SEC, IMPLICATIONS OF THE GROWTH OF HEDGE FUNDS, at 8. Unlike hedge funds, venture capital funds are not leveraged. 17 C.F.R. § 275.203(l)-1(a)(3). Venture capital funds' total assets at end-year 2014 were $39 billion, orders of magnitude less than hedge funds and private equity funds. SEC, 2014 PRIVATE FUNDS STATISTICS, at 5.

III. SIGNATURE EVENTS IN THE RISE OF HEDGE FUNDS

The emergence of hedge funds over the past several decades, at least until the Financial Crisis, has been characterized by both dramatic growth and superior returns, punctuated by episodic but equally dramatic calamities. We now turn to two of these signature events.

A. THE COLLAPSE OF LONG-TERM CAPITAL MANAGEMENT

The first major hedge fund to come to the attention of the general public was Long-Term Capital Management in the late 1990s. Among other things, Long-Term Capital Management represented a then-uncommon collaboration of top flight financial economists and the financial services sector. At the forefront of a trend that would bring to Wall Street hundreds of PhDs trained in econometrics and the hard sciences, several Nobel laureates in economics worked with Long-Term Capital Management to devise complex and, at first, highly lucrative investment strategies. The following materials recount the denouement.

Report of The President's Working Group on Financial Markets, Hedge Funds, Leverage, and the Lessons of Long-Term Capital Management

Apr. 1999

The LTCM Episode

A. Background

Long-Term Capital Management, L.P. ("LTCM") was founded in early 1994. Although LTCM itself is a Delaware limited partnership with its main offices in Connecticut, the fund that it operates, Long-Term Capital Portfolio, L.P., . . is a Cayman Islands partnership. LTCM sought to profit from a variety of trading strategies, including convergence trades and dynamic hedging. LTCM's principals included individuals with substantial reputations in the financial markets and especially in the economic theory of financial markets. From its inception, LTCM had a prominent position in the community of hedge funds, both because of the reputation of its principals, and also because of its large initial capital stake.

The LTCM Fund produced returns, net of fees, of approximately 40 percent in 1995 and 1996, and slightly less than 20 percent in 1997. At the end of 1997, LTCM returned approximately $2.7 billion in capital to its investors, reducing the capital base of the fund by about 36 percent to $4.8 billion. Despite this reduction in its capital base, however, the hedge fund apparently did not reduce the scale of its investment positions. Put another way, the managers of the Fund decided to increase its balance-sheet leverage by reducing its capital base rather than by increasing its positions. . . .

Overall, the distinguishing features of the LTCM were the scale of its activities, the large size of its positions in certain markets, and the extent of its leverage, both in terms of balance-sheet measures and on the basis of more meaningful measures of risk exposure in relation to capital. . . .

The LTCM Fund's size and leverage, as well as the trading strategies that it utilized, made it vulnerable to the extraordinary financial market conditions that emerged following Russia's devaluation of the ruble and declaration of a debt moratorium on August 17 of [1997]. Russia's actions sparked a "flight to quality" in which investors avoided risk and sought out liquidity. As a result, risk spreads and liquidity premiums rose sharply in markets around the world. The size, persistence, and pervasiveness of the widening of risk spreads confounded the risk management models employed by LTCM and other participants. Both LTCM and other market participants suffered losses in individual markets that greatly exceeded what conventional risk models, estimated during more stable periods, suggested were probable. Moreover, the simultaneous shocks to many markets confounded expectations of relatively low correlations between market prices and revealed that global trading portfolios like LTCM's were less well diversified than assumed. Finally, the "flight to quality" resulted in a substantial reduction in the liquidity of many markets, which, contrary to the assumptions implicit in their models, made it difficult to reduce exposures quickly without incurring further losses.

B. LTCM's Near Failure

On July 31, 1998, the LTCM held $4.1 billion in capital, down about fifteen percent from the beginning of the year. During the single month of August, the LTCM suffered additional losses of $1.8 billion, bringing the loss of equity for the year to over fifty percent. The Fund's capital base was now $2.3 billion, and LTCM reported to investors that it was seeking an injection of capital.

During the first two weeks of September 1998, concern about LTCM was a major topic of conversation in the financial markets. The LTCM Fund suffered substantial further losses and found it difficult to reduce its positions because of the large size of those positions. In addition, as its condition deteriorated, previously flexible credit arrangements became more rigid and the daily mark-to-market valuations for collateral calls by counterparties became more contentious. . . .

By Friday, September 18, these liquidity pressures, together with continuing declines in the Fund's capital, were causing serious concerns among [. . .] [LTCM's] principals about the ability of the [LTCM] Fund to continue meeting its cash flow obligations in the event of further shocks to its market value. As LTCM's efforts to raise new capital remained unsuccessful, its condition was also a source of major concern to numerous market participants. These market participants were concerned about the possibility that LTCM could abruptly collapse in the very near term and about the consequences that such a collapse might have on what already were extremely fragile world markets.

By September 21, the LTCM Fund's liquidity situation was bleak. Bear Stearns, LTCM's prime brokerage firm, had required LTCM to collateralize potential settlement exposures, reducing the fund's overall liquidity resources. LTCM's repo and OTC derivatives counterparties were seeking as much collateral as possible through the daily margining process, in many cases by seeking to apply possible liquidation values to mark-to-market valuations. The cash-flow strains were raising the risk that the LTCM Fund would be unable to meet payments due at the end of September. Moreover, in the absence of additional injections of liquidity, further unfavorable market movements could have led to a default as soon as Wednesday, September 23. Thus, a very short period of time remained for the participants to explore resolution alternatives. While LTCM's plight had been known to some market participants to varying degrees, no one had as yet stepped forward to offer an alternative that would avoid a default. . . .

On Tuesday, September 22, a Core Group of four of the most concerned counterparties began seriously exploring the possibility of mutually beneficial alternatives to default. The main alternative the Core Group focused on came to be known as the consortium approach and involved the recapitalization of the LTCM Fund through mutual investments by its major counterparties in a recently set up feeder fund and a relatively small investment in a newly set up limited liability company which became a new general partner of the LTCM. Under this approach, the stake of the original owners would be written down to 10 percent and the consortium would acquire the remaining 90 percent ownership share, as well as operational control of LTCM.

Following lengthy discussions . . . [on] September 23, fourteen firms agreed to participate in the consortium. The Federal Reserve Bank of New York provided the facilities for these discussions and encouraged the firms involved to seek the least disruptive solution that they believed was in their own collective self-interest. . . . The firms participating in the consortium invested about $3.6 billion in new equity in the fund, and in return received a 90 percent equity stake in LTCM's portfolio along with operational control. The responsibility and burden of resolving LTCM's difficulties remained with the counterparties that had allowed the hedge fund to build up its positions in the first place. The principals and investors in LTCM suffered very substantial losses on their equity stakes in the fund when their claim was reduced to 10 percent.

C. The LTCM Fund Achieved Extraordinary Levels of Leverage and Risk

Assessed against the trading practices of hedge funds and other trading institutions discussed above—namely, mark-to-market, leverage, and active trading—and disclosure and monitoring requirements, the LTCM Fund stood out with respect to its opaqueness and low degree of external monitoring, and its high degree of leverage. At the time of its near-failure, the LTCM Fund was the most highly leveraged large hedge fund reporting to the CFTC. The combination of LTCM Fund's large capital base and high degree of leverage allowed it to hold more than $125 billion in total assets, nearly four times the assets of the next largest hedge fund. LTCM then faced severe market liquidity problems when its investments began losing value and the fund attempted to unwind some of its positions. The liquidity problems faced by LTCM were compounded by the large size of its positions in certain markets.

Although its mark-to-market valuations called LTCM's managers' attention to the Fund's problems well before the Fund's net worth was exhausted, individual counterparties—partly because there were so many—were not necessarily aware of the depth of LTCM's liquidity problems. Neither were the balance sheet and income statements that LTCM provided to its counterparties very informative about the Fund's risk profile and concentration of exposures in certain markets. This opaqueness of LTCM's risk profile is an important part of the LTCM story and raises a number of concerns regarding credit-risk management and counterparty trading relationships. . . .

This insufficient monitoring arose, in part, because of LTCM's practice of disclosing only minimal information to these parties, information such as balance sheet and income statements that did not reveal meaningful details about the Fund's risk profile and concentration of exposures in certain markets. In LTCM's case, this minimal level of disclosure was tolerated because of [its impressive principals and track record] . . .

A point whose significance was apparently missed by LTCM and its counterparties and creditors was that, while LTCM was diversified across global markets, it was not very well diversified as to strategy. It was betting in general that liquidity, credit and volatility spreads would narrow from historically high levels. When the spreads widened instead in markets across the world, LTCM found itself at the brink of insolvency. In retrospect, it can be seen that LTCM and others underestimated the likelihood that liquidity, credit and volatility spreads would move in a similar fashion in markets across the world at the same time. . . .

This raises the issue of how events that are assumed to be extreme and very improbable should be incorporated into risk-management and business practice, and how they should be dealt with by public policy. The risk management weaknesses revealed by the LTCM episode were not unique to LTCM and its creditors and counterparties. Financial market participants have made significant progress [since the collapse of LTCM] in strengthening risk-management capabilities. Nevertheless, as new technology has fostered a major expansion in the volume and, in some cases, the leverage of transactions, some existing risk models have underestimated the probability of severe losses. This shows the need for ensuring that decisions about the appropriate level of capital for risky positions become an issue that is explicitly considered; when outlier events are omitted from risk models, such decisions are made by default. . . .

D. Counterparty Losses and Market Disruptions That May Have Resulted from a Default of LTCM

A default by the LTCM Fund would have caused counterparties to move quickly to limit their exposures. These risk-limiting moves may have required the liquidation or replacement of positions and collateral in the many markets where the LTCM Fund held sizable positions at depressed prices. These very actions in a market that, [. . .] [as of] September [1997], was already suffering from a substantial reduction in liquidity could have resulted in significant losses. LTCM itself estimated that its top 17 counterparties would have suffered various substantial losses—potentially between $3 billion and $5 billion in aggregate—and shared this information with the fourteen firms participating in the consortium. The firms in the consortium saw that their losses could be serious, with potential losses to some firms amounting to $300 million to $500 million each. Moreover, if the LTCM had defaulted [. . .] in September [of 1998], the losses, market disruptions, and the pronounced lack of liquidity could have been more severe if not for the use of closeout, netting, and collateral provisions. . . .

Potential market impact of disorderly liquidation

In addition to the credit losses that LTCM's creditors and counterparties would have suffered, a default also could have had broader consequences for the markets in which these firms were active. First, the liquidation and closing out of positions could have generated significant movements in market prices and rates, affecting the market value of positions held by the LTCM's counterparties as well as by other market participants. Second, the resulting rush by the Fund's counterparties and others to reappraise their credit risks, coupled with an increase in uncertainty, could have exacerbated the broader decline in market liquidity . . . Third, those firms with exposures to LTCM could have encountered increased concerns about their own credit standing, with a resulting rise in their cost of obtaining funds.

The LTCM Fund's counterparties and creditors were facing the risk posed by the impact of a default by the LTCM in the unusual market environment prevailing in late September. By that time, worldwide investor confidence had already reached a low ebb. Although markets were already operating in a low interest-rate environment, the flight to safety further reduced the yield on the longest-maturity U.S. Treasury bond to a thirty year low on Friday, September 18. During the previous month, interest rate spreads had widened substantially, while equity markets around the world had suffered significant declines. The level of economic uncertainty as measured by market volatility had risen while liquidity was declining. Finally, most major market participants had already suffered significant trading losses during August and September, and were anxious to avoid further losses.

In the midst of these extraordinary market conditions, a default by the LTCM could have had effects different from a default during less unsettled market conditions. The LTCM Fund's counterparties would have had to manage the effects of the direct credit losses from the default as well as further indirect effects if the default accelerated a flight to safety and liquidity that was already occurring. . . .

III. CONCLUSIONS AND RECOMMENDATIONS

The central public policy issue raised by the LTCM episode is how to constrain excessive leverage more effectively. As events in the summer and fall of 1998 demonstrated, the amount of leverage in the financial system, combined with aggressive risk taking, can greatly magnify the negative effects of any event or series of events. By increasing the chance that problems at one financial institution could be transmitted to other institutions, leverage can increase the likelihood of a general breakdown in the functioning of financial markets.

Although LTCM is a hedge fund, this issue is not limited to hedge funds. Other financial institutions, including some banks and securities firms, are larger, and generally more highly leveraged, than hedge funds. . . . While leverage can play a positive role in [the global] financial system, resulting in greater market liquidity, greater credit availability, and a more efficient allocation of resources in our economy, problems can arise when financial institutions are not disciplined in extending credit to their customers and counterparties. The LTCM episode well illustrates the need for all participants in [the global] financial system, not only hedge funds, to face constraints in the amount of leverage they can assume. . . .

To constrain the leverage of both regulated and unregulated financial entities, [the U.S.] market-based economy relies primarily on the discipline provided by creditors, counterparties and investors. If a firm seeks to achieve greater leverage, its creditors and counterparties ordinarily will respond by increasing the cost or reducing the availability of credit to the firm. History tells us, however, that creditors, counterparties, and investors from time to time misjudge their risks, and that sometimes they become complacent in their risk assessments in an attempt to achieve higher returns. . . . If one looks at the history of financial markets, however, it is also true that market-based constraints can break down in good times as creditors and investors become less concerned about risk, and fail to manage risk appropriately. In the case of LTCM, market discipline seems to have largely broken down. LTCM appears to have received very generous credit terms, even though it took an exceptional degree of risk. The breakdown in market discipline was made possible by risk management weaknesses at LTCM as well as at the large banks and securities firms that were LTCM counterparties. In some cases sound policies were in place, but the pressure to generate profit seems to have caused actual practices to deviate from those policies.

---

1. ***Public–Private Partnerships.*** Consider the following account of the manner in which government authorities responded to the problems at Long-Term Capital Management:

> Upon discovering the potential systemic implications LTCM's problems posed, the Federal Reserve Bank of New York (FRBNY) officials—acting as promoters of financial stability—brought together several LTCM creditors and counterparties [including Goldman Sachs, Merrill Lynch, and J.P. Morgan] to discuss LTCM's problems and possible solutions. . . . FRBNY's role was consistent with that of a central banker. They said it acted as an "honest broker" in facilitating a private-sector resolution of a market event with potential systemic implications. The group of LTCM creditors and counterparties considered various alternatives to avoid a rapid and

> potentially disruptive liquidation of LTCM and ultimately agreed to form a consortium and infuse $3.6 billion into LTCM. FRBNY testified that although FRBNY officials were present at the meeting, they did not participate in discussions about the terms and conditions of the Consortium agreement. Although no federal money was committed to the recapitalization, FRBNY's intervention raised concerns among some market observers that it could create moral hazard by encouraging other large institutions to assume greater risks, in the belief that the Federal Reserve would intervene to avoid potential future market disruptions.

U.S. GEN. ACCOUNTING OFFICE, RESPONSES TO QUESTIONS CONCERNING LONG-TERM CAPITAL MANAGEMENT AND RELATED EVENTS 2 (Feb. 23, 2000). To some observers, the role that private banks played with Long-Term Capital Management was reminiscent of the role J.P. Morgan played in in the Panic of 1907 before the creation of the Federal Reserve System in the next decade. *See* Chapters 1.2 and 9.1. What are the pros and cons of such public-private partnerships?

Before the collapse of Long-Term Capital Management, it was generally assumed that hedge funds were the province of institutional investors and sophisticated individuals who were capable of looking out for themselves without the need of paternalistic government protections. Under this perspective, private contract seems to offer an appropriate legal structure for these funds. What Long-Term Capital Management demonstrated, however, is that the failure of a sufficiently large hedge fund could have negative effects on financial markets and the larger economy. Hedge funds could, therefore, be systemically important. The public response to this insight is recounted in the next excerpt.

B. REGULATORY RESPONSES POST LONG-TERM CAPITAL MANAGEMENT

1. Adviser Regulation and *Goldstein v. SEC*

In one response to the issues posed by the near failure of Long-Term Capital Management, the SEC proposed to change the Investment Adviser Act exemptions for hedge fund advisers in order to extend SEC regulation to most major hedge fund advisers. *Goldstein v. SEC*, excerpted below, illustrates the SEC's efforts.

Goldstein v. SEC

451 F.3d 873 (D.C. Cir. 2006)

RANDOLPH, Circuit Judge.

This is a petition for review of the [SEC's] regulation of "hedge funds" under the Investment Advisers Act of 1940, 15 U.S.C. § 80b–1 et seq. *See* Registration Under the Advisers Act of Certain Hedge Fund Advisers, 69 Fed.Reg. 72,054 (Dec. 10, 2004) (codified at 17 C.F.R. pts. 275, 279) ("Hedge Fund Rule"). Previously exempt because they had "fewer than fifteen clients," 15 U.S.C. § 80b–3(b)(3), most advisers to hedge funds must now register with the [SEC] if the funds they advise have fifteen or more "shareholders, limited partners, members, or beneficiaries." 17 C.F.R. § 275.203(b)(3)–2(a). Petitioners Philip Goldstein, an investment advisory firm Goldstein co-owns (Kimball & Winthrop), and Opportunity Partners L.P., a hedge fund in which Kimball & Winthrop is the general partner and investment adviser (collectively "Goldstein") challenge the regulation's equation of "client" with "investor." . . .

Hedge fund advisers also had been exempt from regulation under the Investment Advisers Act of 1940. . . , a companion statute to the [1940] Act, and the statute which primarily concerns us in this case. Enacted by Congress to "substitute a philosophy of full disclosure for the philosophy of *caveat emptor*" in the investment advisory profession, *SEC v. Capital Gains Research Bureau, Inc.*, 375 U.S. 180, 186, 84 S.Ct. 275, 11 L.Ed.2d 237 (1963), the [Investment] Advisers Act is mainly a registration and anti-fraud statute. Non-exempt "investment advisers" must register with the [SEC], 15 U.S.C. § 80b–3, and all advisers are prohibited from engaging in fraudulent or deceptive practices, id. § 80b–6. By keeping a census of advisers, the [SEC] can better respond to, initiate, and take remedial action on complaints against fraudulent advisers. *See id.* § 80b–4 (authorizing the [SEC] to examine registered advisers' records).

Hedge fund general partners meet the definition of "investment adviser" in the [Investment] Advisers Act. *See* 15 U.S.C. § 80b–2(11) (defining "investment adviser" as one who "for compensation, engages in the business of advising others, either directly or through publications or writings, as to the value of securities or as to the advisability of investing in, purchasing, or selling securities"); Abrahamson v. Fleschner, 568 F.2d 862, 869–71 (2d Cir.1977) (holding that hedge fund general partners are "investment advisers"), overruled in part on other grounds by Transamerica Mortgage Advisors, Inc. v. Lewis, 444 U.S. 11, 100 S.Ct. 242, 62 L.Ed.2d 146 (1979). But they usually satisfy the "private adviser exemption" from registration in § 203(b)(3) of the [Investment Advisers] Act, 15 U.S.C. § 80b–3(b)(3). That section exempts "any investment adviser who during the course of the preceding twelve months has had fewer than fifteen clients and who neither holds himself out generally to the public as an investment adviser nor acts as an investment adviser to any investment company registered under [the 1940 Act]." *Id.* As applied to limited partnerships and other entities, the [SEC] had interpreted this provision to refer to the partnership or entity itself as the adviser's "client." *See* 17 C.F.R. § 275.203(b)(3)–1. Even the largest hedge fund managers usually ran fewer than fifteen hedge funds and were therefore exempt.

Although the [SEC] has a history of interest in hedge funds, . . . the current push for regulation had its origins in the failure of Long-Term Capital Management, a Greenwich, Connecticut-based fund that had more than $125 billion in assets under management at its peak. In late 1998, the fund nearly collapsed. Almost all of the country's major financial institutions were put at risk due to their credit exposure to Long-Term, and the president of the Federal Reserve Bank of New York personally intervened to engineer a bailout of the fund in order to avoid a national financial crisis. . . .

A joint working group of the major federal financial regulators produced a report recommending regulatory changes to the regime governing hedge funds, and the [SEC]'s staff followed with its own report about the state of hedge fund regulation. Drawing on the conclusions in the *Staff Report*, the [SEC]—over the dissent of two of its members—issued the rule under review in December 2004 after notice and comment. The [SEC] cited three. . .shifts in the hedge fund industry to justify the need for increased regulation. First, despite the failure of Long-Term Capital Management, hedge fund assets grew by 260 percent from 1999 to 2004. *Hedge Fund Rule*, 69 Fed.Reg. at 72,055. Second, the [SEC] noticed a trend toward "retailization" of hedge funds that increased the exposure of ordinary investors to such funds. This retailization was driven by hedge funds loosening their investment requirements, the birth of "funds of hedge funds" that offered shares to the public, and increased investment in hedge funds by pension funds, universities, endowments, foundations, and other charitable organizations. *See id.* at

72,057–58. Third, the [SEC] was concerned about an increase in the number of fraud actions brought against hedge funds.... Concluding that its "current regulatory program for hedge fund advisers [was] inadequate," . . . the [SEC] moved to require hedge fund advisers to register under the [Investment] Advisers Act so that it could gather "basic information about hedge fund advisers and the hedge fund industry," "oversee hedge fund advisers," and "deter or detect fraud by unregistered hedge fund advisers," *id.*

The Hedge Fund Rule first defines a "private fund" as an investment company that (a) is exempt from registration under the [1940 Act] by virtue of having fewer than one hundred investors or only qualified investors, *see* 15 U.S.C. § 80a–3(c)(1), (7); (b) permits its investors to redeem their interests within two years of investing; and (c) markets itself on the basis of the "skills, ability or expertise of the investment adviser." 17 C.F.R. § 275.203(b)(3)–1(d)(1). For these private funds, the rule then specifies that "[f]or purposes of section 203(b)(3) of the [Investment Advisers] Act (15 U.S.C. § 80b–3(b)(3)), you must count as clients the shareholders, limited partners, members, or beneficiaries . . . of [the] fund." *Id.* § 275.203(b)(3)–2(a). The rule had the effect of requiring most hedge fund advisers to register by February 1, 2006.

II.

The dissenting Commissioners disputed the factual predicates for the new rule and its wisdom. Goldstein makes some of the same points but the major thrust of his complaint is that the [SEC]'s action misinterpreted § 203(b)(3) of the [Investment] Advisers Act, a charge the [SEC] dissenters also leveled. This provision exempts from registration "any investment adviser who during the course of the preceding [12] months has had fewer than fifteen clients." 15 U.S.C. § 80b–3(b)(3). . . . The Act does not define "client." Relying on *Chevron U.S.A. Inc. v. Natural Resources Defense Council*, 467 U.S. 837, 842–43, 104 S.Ct. 2778, 81 L.Ed.2d 694 (1984), the [SEC] believes this renders the statute "ambiguous as to a method for counting clients." Br. for Resp. 21. There is no such rule of law. The lack of a statutory definition of a word does not necessarily render the meaning of a word ambiguous, just as the presence of a definition does not necessarily make the meaning clear. A definition only pushes the problem back to the meaning of the defining terms. *See Alarm Indus. Commc'ns Comm. v. FCC*, 131 F.3d 1066, 1068–70 (D.C. Cir.1997); *Doris Day Animal League v. Veneman*, 315 F.3d 297, 298–99 (D.C. Cir.2003).

If Congress employs a term susceptible of several meanings, as many terms are, it scarcely follows that Congress has authorized an agency to choose any one of those meanings....

The [SEC] believes that an amendment to § 203(b)(3) suggests the possibility that an investor in a hedge fund could be counted as a client of the fund's adviser. In 1980, Congress added to § 203(b)(3) the following language: "For purposes of determining the number of clients of an investment adviser under this paragraph, no shareholder, partner, or beneficial owner of a business development company . . . shall be deemed to be a client of such investment adviser unless such person is a client of such investment adviser separate and apart from his status as a shareholder, partner, or beneficial owner." Act of Oct. 21, 1980, Pub.L. No. 96–477, § 202, 94 Stat. 2275, 2290 (1980). . . . On the other hand, a 1970 amendment to § 203 appears to reflect Congress's understanding at the time that investment company entities, not their shareholders, were the advisers' clients. In the amendment, Congress eliminated a separate exemption from registration for advisers who advised only investment companies and explicitly made the fewer-than-fifteen-clients exemption unavailable to such advisers. Investment Company Amendments Act of 1970, Pub.L. No. 91–547, § 24, 84 Stat. 1413, 1430 (1970). This latter prohibition would have been unnecessary if the shareholders of investment companies could be counted as "clients." . . . Another section of the [Investment] Advisers Act strongly suggests that Congress did not intend "shareholders, limited partners, members, or beneficiaries" of a hedge fund to be counted as "clients." Although the statute does not define "client," it does define "investment adviser" as "any person who, for compensation, engages in the business of advising others, either *directly* or through publications or writings, as to the value of securities or as to the advisability of investing in, purchasing, or selling securities." 15 U.S.C. § 80b–2(11) (emphasis added). An investor in a private fund may benefit from the adviser's advice (or he may suffer from it) but he does not receive the advice *directly*. . . . If the person or entity controlling the fund is not an "investment adviser" to each individual investor, then *a fortiori* each investor cannot be a "client" of that person or entity. These are just two sides of the same coin.

The [SEC] said much the same in 1985 when it promulgated a rule with respect to investment companies set up as limited partnerships rather than as corporations. The "client" for purposes of the fifteen-client rule of § 203(b)(3) is the limited partnership not the individual partners. *See* 17 C.F.R. § 275.203(b)(3)–1(a)(2). As the [SEC] wrote in proposing the rule, when "an adviser to an investment pool manages the assets of the pool on the basis of the investment objectives of the participants as a group, it appears appropriate to view the pool—rather than each participant—as a client of the adviser." *Safe Harbor Proposed Rule*, 50 Fed.Reg. at 8741. . . .

"The 'reasonableness' of an agency's construction depends," in part, "on the construction's 'fit' with the statutory language, as well as its conformity to statutory purposes." *Abbott Labs. v. Young*, 920 F.2d 984, 988 (D.C. Cir.1990). As described above, the [SEC]'s interpretation of the word "client" comes close to violating the plain language of the statute. At best it is counterintuitive to characterize the investors in a hedge fund as the "clients" of the adviser. *See Am. Bar Ass'n v. FTC*, 430 F.3d 457, 471 (D.C. Cir.2005). The adviser owes fiduciary duties only to the fund, not to the fund's investors. . . .

The *Hedge Fund Rule* might be more understandable if, over the years, the advisory relationship between hedge fund advisers and investors had changed. . . . [But t]he [SEC has not] adequately explained how the relationship between hedge fund investors and advisers justifies treating the former as clients of the latter. *See Shays v. FEC*, 414 F.3d 76, 96–97 (D.C. Cir.2005) (explaining that agency interpretation is not "reasonable" if it is "arbitrary and capricious"). The [SEC] points to its finding that a hedge fund adviser sometimes "may not treat all of its hedge fund investors the same." *Hedge Fund Rule*, 69 Fed.Reg. at 72,069–70 (citing different lock-up periods, greater access to information, lower fees, and "side pocket" arrangements). From this the [SEC] concludes that each account of a hedge fund investor "may bear many of the characteristics of separate investment accounts, which, of course, must be counted as separate clients." *Id.* at 72,070. But the [SEC]'s conclusion does not follow from its premise. It may be that different classes of investors have different rights or privileges with respect to their investments. This reveals little, however, about the relationship between the investor and the adviser. Even if it did, the [SEC] has not justified treating all investors in hedge funds as clients for the purpose of the rule. If there are certain characteristics present in some investor-adviser relationships that mark a "client" relationship, then the [SEC] should have identified those characteristics and tailored its rule accordingly.

---

1. ***Counting Investors.*** How should regulators count the number of investors involved in a transaction or an investment vehicle? How strenuously should regulators look through to ultimate investors as opposed to allowing investor to aggregate in common pools? Many regulatory regimes offers exemptions based on numerical counts, such as the private placement exemption under the 1933 Act, and so the issue is a recurring and important problem. The broader policy question is whether adviser registration is likely to be an effective response to Long-Term Capital Management or the other kinds of investor abuse scandals that prompted the SEC rulemaking efforts here. How likely is it that

registration of advisers under the Investment Advisers Act would have prevented the kinds of problems that occurred with Long-Term Capital Management?

2. ***SEC Dissent.*** Two of five SEC Commissioners dissented to the rule, arguing, among other things, that there was little evidence the SEC-registered advisers of hedge funds had fewer regulatory problems than their unregistered counterparts. Does a court under *Chevron* have more latitude to overturn a regulation adopted by a divided SEC rather than a rule adopted unanimously?

---

2. Sector Best Practices

The President's Working Group on Financial Markets established two private sector committees to research and propose best practices for the hedge fund sector. "The committees were tasked to develop best practices for market participants with a view to enhancing investor protection and mitigating systemic risk." DECHERT LLP, U.S. PRESIDENT'S WORKING GROUP RECOMMENDS BEST PRACTICES FOR HEDGE FUND INDUSTRY (May 2008). The first committee, the Asset Managers' Committee, recommended best practices in five areas: disclosure to investors, valuation, risk management, trading and business operations, and compliance, conflicts, and business practices. *Id.* The second committee, the Investors' Committee's recommendation focused on best practices surrounding due diligence, risk management, legal and regulatory issues, valuation, fees and expenses, reporting, and taxation. *Id.* "The best practice recommendations are not binding and do not have the force of law or regulation. Best practice recommendations such as these, however, may ultimately serve as the basis for a subsequent legal framework." *Id.* Under what circumstances are standards of the sort supported by the President's Working Group likely to be a productive mechanism for regulation?

C. THE MADOFF SCANDAL AND FEEDER FUND LITIGATION

On December 11, 2008, Mr. Bernard L. Madoff was charged with conducting the largest Ponzi scheme in history, with estimated losses of over $17 billion. Press Release, SEC Charges Bernard L. Madoff for Multi-Billion Dollar Ponzi Scheme (Dec. 11, 2008). A majority of the defrauded investors did not invest in Madoff's funds directly, but rather invested their money in feeder funds, separate hedge funds that pooled investors' cash and then invested in Madoff's scheme. Diana Henriques, *Broader Pool of Madoff Victims to Benefit From Fund*, N.Y. TIMES (Nov. 18, 2013). The defrauded investors ran the gamut from small to billionaire investors. *Id.*

1. Excerpts from the Report of the SEC Inspector General

In post-mortems after the Madoff Ponzi scheme collapsed, the SEC faced particular scrutiny because sources had approached SEC staff on several occasions complaining, among other things, that Madoff's returns were too good to be true and that his investment strategy's purported scale was not consistent with publicly reported trading volumes. The SEC Office of Inspector General responded with a massive investigation and report, which is excerpted below.

Investigation of Failure of the SEC To Uncover Bernard Madoff's Ponzi Scheme

SEC Office of Inspector General, Case No. OIG-509 (Aug. 31, 2009)

The [SEC Office of the Inspector General's (OIG)] investigation did not find evidence that any SEC personnel who worked on an SEC examination or investigation of Bernard L. Madoff Investment Securities, LLC (BMIS) had any financial or other inappropriate connection with Bernard Madoff or the Madoff family that influenced the conduct of their examination or investigatory work. The OIG also did not find that former SEC Assistant Director Eric Swanson's romantic relationship with Bernard Madoff's niece, Shana Madoff, influenced the conduct of the SEC examinations of Madoff and his firm. We also did not find that senior officials at the SEC directly attempted to influence examinations or investigations of Madoff or the Madoff firm, nor was there evidence any senior SEC official interfered with the staff's ability to perform its work.

The OIG investigation did find, however, that the SEC received more than ample information in the form of detailed and substantive complaints over the years to warrant a thorough and comprehensive examination and/or investigation of Bernard Madoff and BMIS for operating a Ponzi scheme, and that despite three examinations and two investigations being conducted, a thorough and competent investigation or examination was never performed. The OIG found that between June 1992 and December 2008 when Madoff confessed, the SEC received six substantive complaints that raised significant red flags concerning Madoff's hedge fund operations and should have led to questions about whether Madoff was actually engaged in trading. Finally, the SEC was also aware of two articles regarding Madoff's investment operations that appeared in reputable publications in 2001 and questioned Madoff's unusually consistent returns.

The first complaint, brought to the SEC's attention in 1992, related to allegations that an unregistered investment company was offering "100%" safe investments with high and extremely consistent rates of return over significant periods of time to "special" customers. . . .

The second complaint [from Harry Markopolos] was very specific and different versions were provided to the [SEC's Boston District Office (BDO)] in May 2000, March 2001 and October 2005. The complaint submitted in 2005 was entitled "The World's Largest Hedge Fund is a Fraud" and detailed approximately 30 red flags indicating that Madoff was operating a Ponzi scheme, a scenario it described as "highly likely." The red flags included the impossibility of Madoff's returns, particularly the consistency of those returns and the unrealistic volume of options Madoff represented to have traded.

In May 2003, the SEC received a third complaint from a respected Hedge Fund Manager identifying numerous concerns about Madoff's strategy and purported returns, questioning whether Madoff was actually trading options in the volume he claimed, noting that Madoff's strategy and purported returns were not duplicable by anyone else, and stating Madoff's strategy had no correlation to the overall equity markets in over ten years. . . .

The fourth complaint was part of a series of internal e-mails of another registrant that the SEC discovered in April 2004. The e-mails described the red flags that a registrant's employees had identified while performing due diligence on their own Madoff investment using publicly available information. [. . . One] e-mail clearly explained that Madoff could not be trading on an options exchange because of insufficient volume and could not be trading options over-the-counter because it was inconceivable that he could find a counterparty for the trading. . . .

The fifth complaint was received by the SEC in October 2005 from an anonymous informant and stated, "I know that Madoff . . . [is] running a highly sophisticated scheme on a massive scale."

The sixth complaint was sent to the SEC by a "concerned citizen" in December 2006, advising the SEC to look into Madoff and his firm as follows: "Your attention is directed to a scandal of major proportion which was executed by the investment firm Bernard L. Madoff.". . . [A copy of this report was sent again in March 2008, and included additional information], as follows: "It may be of interest to you to that Mr. Bernard Madoff keeps two (2) sets of records. The most interesting of which is on his computer which is always on his person." . . . The complaints all contained specific information and could not have been fully and adequately resolved without thoroughly examining and investigating Madoff for operating a Ponzi scheme. The journal articles should have reinforced the concerns about how Madoff could have been achieving his returns.

The OIG retained an expert in accordance with its investigation in order to both analyze the information the SEC received regarding Madoff and the examination work conducted. According to the OIG's expert, the most critical step in examining or investigating a potential Ponzi scheme is to verify the subject's trading through an independent third party.

The OIG investigation found the SEC conducted two investigations and three examinations related to Madoff's investment advisory business based upon the detailed and credible complaints that raised the possibility that Madoff was misrepresenting his trading and could have been operating a Ponzi scheme. Yet, at no time did the SEC ever verify Madoff's trading through an independent third-party, and in fact, never actually conducted a Ponzi scheme examination or investigation of Madoff. . . .

Although the [SEC's] Enforcement staff made attempts to seek information from independent third-parties, they failed to follow up on these requests. They reached out to the [National Association of Securities Dealers (NASD)] and asked for information on whether Madoff had options positions on a certain date, but when they received a report that there were in fact no options positions on that date, they did not take any further steps. . . . Had any of these efforts been fully executed, they would have led to Madoff's Ponzi scheme being uncovered. . .

[After Harry Markopolos presented a complaint the SEC's Boston District Office in May 2000,] Markopolos explained his analysis presented in the 2000 complaint at a meeting at the SEC's Boston office and encouraged the SEC to investigate Madoff. After the meeting, both Markopolos and an SEC staff accountant testified that it was clear that the [Boston District Office's] Assistant District Administrator did not understand the information presented. Our investigation found that this was likely the reason that the Boston District Office decided not to pursue Markopolos' complaint or even refer it to the SEC's Northeast Regional Office. . . .

In March 2001, Markopolos provided the [Boston District Office] with a second complaint, which supplemented his previous 2000 complaint with updated information and additional analysis. . . . Although this time the [Boston District Office] did refer Markopolos' complaint, [The SEC's Northeast Regional Office] decided not to investigate the complaint only one day after receiving it. The matter was assigned to an Assistant Regional Director in Enforcement [at the SEC] for initial inquiry, who [inexplicably dismissed the detailed complaint within a day]. . .

In May 2003, [The SEC's Office of Compliance Inspections and Examinations's] investment management group in Washington, D.C. received a detailed complaint from a reputable Hedge Fund Manager, in which he laid out the red flags that his hedge fund had identified about Madoff while performing due diligence on two Madoff feeder funds. . . . The OIG's . . . expert concluded that based upon issues raised in the Hedge Fund Manager's complaint, had the examination been staffed and conducted appropriately and basic steps taken to obtain third-party verifications, Madoff's Ponzi scheme should and would have been uncovered. . . .

During the course of the examination, [which was inexplicably delayed for seven months,] the examination team discovered suspicious information and evidence, but failed to follow up on numerous "red flags." Responses by Madoff to the document requests contradicted the Hedge Fund Manager's complaint and the 2001 articles. For example, Madoff's claim that his firm did not manage or advise hedge funds was contradicted by the articles that reported Madoff was managing billions of dollars in assets. In addition, although known for advanced technology, Madoff claimed not to have e-mail communications with clients. However, the examiners did not follow up on these red flags. . . . Although there were numerous unresolved questions in the examination, in early April 2004, the examiners were abruptly instructed to shift their focus to "mutual funds" projects, placing the Madoff examination on the "backburner." [The OIG] found that it was not unusual at that time to shift attention to high priority projects in [The SEC's Office of Compliance Inspections and Examinations] and leave some projects incomplete. . . .

As the examination of Madoff in Washington, D.C. was shelved, in [The SEC's Northeast Regional Office], a nearly identical examination of Madoff was just beginning. . . . [W]hen the [Northeast Regional Office] examiners pushed Madoff for documents and information about his advisory clients, he rebuffed them, pointing out that he had already provided the information to the Washington, D.C. staff in accordance with their examination. The [Northeast Regional Office's] examiners were taken aback, since they were unaware that the [SEC's Office of Compliance Inspections and Examinations] had been conducting a simultaneous examination of Madoff on the identical issues they were examining. . . . Although the [Northeast Regional Office's] examiners determined Madoff was not engaged in front-running, they were concerned about issues relating to the operation of his hedge fund business, and sought permission to continue the examination and expand its scope. Their Assistant Regional Director denied their request. . . . The examiners' request to visit Madoff feeder funds was denied, and they were informed that the time for the Madoff examination had expired. . . .

Thus, the [SEC's Northeast Regional Office's] cause examination of Madoff was concluded without the examination team ever understanding how Madoff was achieving his returns . . . [After Harry Markopolous sent his third complaint in October 2005, the Boston District Office asked The Northeast Regional Office to investigate.] While the Madoff investigation was assigned within [The SEC's Northeast Regional Office of] Enforcement, it was assigned to a team with little to no experience conducting Ponzi scheme investigations. The majority of the investigatory work was conducted by a staff attorney who recently graduated from law school . . .

The [SEC's Northeast Regional Office of] Enforcement staff also received a skeptical response to Markopolos' complaint from the [Northeast Regional Office] examination team who had just concluded their examination. Even though the [Northeast Regional Office] examination had focused solely on front-running, [the Northeast Regional Office] examination team downplayed the possibility that Madoff was conducting a Ponzi scheme . . . In testimony before the OIG, the examiners acknowledged that their examination "did not refute Markopolos' allegations regarding a Ponzi scheme" and that the examiners' reaction may have given the impression their examination had a greater focus than it did. . . .

On May 19, 2006, Madoff testified voluntarily and without counsel in the SEC investigation. During Madoff's testimony, he provided evasive answers to important questions, provided some answers that contradicted his previous representations, and provided some information that could have been used to discover that he was operating a Ponzi scheme. However, the Enforcement staff did not follow-up with respect to the critical information that was relevant to uncovering Madoff's Ponzi scheme. . . .

During his testimony, Madoff also told the Enforcement investigators that the trades for all of his advisory accounts were cleared through his account at DTC[, the Depository

Trust Company,] . . . Madoff stated that he had thought he was caught after his testimony about the DTC account, noting that when they asked for the DTC account number, "I thought it was the end game, over. Monday morning they'll call DTC and this will be over . . . and it never happened." Madoff further said that when Enforcement did not follow up with DTC, he "was astonished." [The investigation was closed in August 2006 after Madoff agreed to register as an investment adviser.]

This was perhaps the most egregious failure in the Enforcement investigation of Madoff; that they never verified Madoff's purported trading with any independent third parties. As a senior-level SEC examiner noted, "clearly if someone . . . has a Ponzi and, they're stealing money, they're not going to hesitate to lie or create records" and, consequently, the "only way to verify" whether the alleged Ponzi operator is actually trading would be to obtain "some independent third-party verification" like DTC."

A simple inquiry to one of several third parties could have immediately revealed the fact that Madoff was not trading in the volume he was claiming. [As part of this investigation, a review of DTC records by the SEC showed that one 2005 Madoff feeder fund statement indicated it held $2.5 billion in S&P 100 equities, while DTC records on that date showed that Madoff held less than $18 million of these equities.] . . .

As the foregoing demonstrates, despite numerous credible and detailed complaints, the SEC never properly examined or investigated Madoff's trading and never took the necessary, but basic, steps to determine if Madoff was operating a Ponzi scheme. Had these efforts been made with appropriate follow-up at any time beginning in June of 1992 until December 2008, the SEC could have uncovered the Ponzi scheme well before Madoff confessed.

---

1. ***Madoff's Reputation.*** One factor that complicated the SEC's investigation of Bernard L. Madoff Investment Securities LLC was the fact that the firm was an extremely well-known and well-regarded member of the financial services sector, known especially for its innovative electronic trading systems of the sort discussed in Chapter 4.4. Madoff himself was a leading figure in the NASD, served on numerous advisory committees, and was a prominent figure in philanthropic circles.

2. ***Madoff's Strategy.*** A further confounding factor to the SEC's investigation was the SEC staff's confusion as to the most plausible explanation for the usually strong and consistent returns that Madoff reported to his investors. In retrospect, it is now known that Madoff's returns were entirely fictitious since at least the early 1990s. In fact, his computer systems for advisory accounts were not even connected to actual trading platforms. Before his scheme unraveled, SEC investigators primarily focused on the possibility that Madoff used his access to order flow, as all the trading activities that ran through his broker-dealer affiliate as a result of its popular payment-for-order flow arrangements (*see* Chapter 4.4), and the SEC's leading theory seems to have been that Madoff was earning excess returns by front-running those trading platform clients for the benefit of his advisory clients, including the large number of feeder funds that sustained his Ponzi scheme. Indeed, one of the geniuses of the Madoff operation, if one can use that term in this context, is that Madoff led his advisory clients to believe that they were somehow being allowed to share in his access to large volumes of order flow information. This unstated arrangement was seemingly sufficient to keep otherwise sophisticated parties complacent for many

years about what in retrospect seems to be a performance record patently too good to be true. Should supervisory policy attempt to protect such willing dupes?

3. ***Post-Madoff Custody Requirements.*** In response to the Madoff case, the SEC amended its custody rules to prevent repeat Ponzi schemes and similar forms of financial fraud. Before implementation of these rules, investment managers were not prohibited from holding custody over the funds they managed, which presented clear conflicts of interest. The first response to the Madoff scandal came in 2010 when the SEC finalized its investment adviser custody rules. 17 C.F.R. § 275.206(4)-2. These rules do not place an explicit prohibition on an investment adviser maintaining custody of client assets, but they do implement examination and reporting requirements to monitor advisers who also serve as custodians. *Id.* The 2010 SEC rules also expanded the definition custody as defined in the 1940 Act to include situations where a related person holds the relevant securities or funds. *Id.* Once custody is established, various supervisory requirements are triggered under the rule.

Some, however, believed these rules were misguided. According to SEC Commissioner Luis Aguilar, because Madoff was registered as a broker-dealer and not an investment adviser for most of time he conducted his fraudulent activities, the 2010 SEC rules would not have prevented his activities. Luis Aguilar, Commissioner, SEC, Strengthening Oversight of Broker-Dealers by Instituting a Framework to Prevent Another Madoff (Jul. 31, 2013). Commissioner Aguilar also argued that, in practice, investment advisers do not maintain physical custody of the securities and funds, thus making much of the rule impractical. *Id.* In response to these concerns, the SEC issued additional rules in 2013 to further reduce the likelihood of a repeat Madoff by targeting the activity of broker-dealers. Broker-Dealer Reports, 17 C.F.R. §§ 240, 249. Under the new rules, broker-dealers that carry customer assets are required to file a compliance report ensuring safe and appropriate management of customer funds. In addition, broker-dealers must also identify and report areas of weakness and non-compliance with the SEC's financial responsibility rules.

---

2. *Anwar v. Fairfield Greenwich*

We will now explore the role of the financial services sector in facilitating the Madoff scandal. In particular, we will look at the service providers of the Fairfield Greenwich Group, a group of hedge funds that invested in Madoff's scheme (as so called feeder funds), profited hugely therefrom, but ultimately left its investors with large exposures to Madoff's scheme. The investors in four hedge funds operated by Fairfield Greenwich Group brought a class action against the fund advisers, executives, and service providers, including its custodian, administrator, and auditor. The excerpt that follows focuses on the legal claims against Citco, a major service provider to the hedge fund industry. The court ultimately imposed gatekeeper-type liability on the Citco entities, despite their lack of direct contractual relations with investors.

Anwar v. Fairfield Greenwich Ltd.

728 F. Supp.2nd 372 (S.D.N.Y. 2010)

VICTOR MARRERO, District Judge.

Citco . . . contracted with the Funds to perform financial services that included serving as administrator, custodian, bank, and depository. Plaintiffs allege that Citco owed duties to them as fund investors, and wholly failed to fulfill these duties, assisting the Funds in their fraud and breaches in fiduciary duty, and ultimately allowing Madoff to abscond with Plaintiffs' money. . . .

Citco committed to serve a variety of key roles for the Funds. As administrators . . . Citco agreed to reconcile cash and other balances at brokers, independently reconcile the Funds' portfolio holdings, and calculate the Net Asset Value (the "NAV") of the Funds, as well as the NAV per share. The NAV calculations, which Plaintiffs allege were crucial to their decisions to invest and hold investments, determined the number of shares Plaintiffs were entitled for a given investment in addition to their reported profits. Citco also agreed to prepare monthly financial statements in accordance with International Accounting Standards, and reconcile information provided by "the Fund's prime broker and custodian"—Madoff—"with information provided by the Investment Manager." In performing these services, pursuant to the contracts with the Funds, Citco was "permitted only to rely on information it received without making further inquiries if that information demonstrated an 'absence of manifest error.'" . . .

Citco also functioned as the Funds' public liaison. In this role, Citco communicated with Plaintiffs and Plaintiffs communicated with Citco. Contact between Plaintiffs and Citco allegedly included subscription documents and investments sent by Plaintiffs to Citco, and investment confirmations sent by Citco to Plaintiffs in return.

As custodian . . . Citco was responsible for monitoring any subcustodian of the Funds, including, notably, [Bernard L. Madoff Investment Securities LLC]. Citco agreed to record the assets held by them as custodians or by the sub-custodians, and to "'keep the securities in the custody of the Custodian or procure that they are kept in the custody of any sub-custodian.'" . . . In performing these duties, Citco had authority to act without instruction from the Fund if "necessary 'to preserve or safeguard the Securities or other assets of the Fund.'" . . .

Plaintiffs allege that they were aware of the services that Citco provided, and that as investors and shareholders they were relying on Citco to fulfill their obligations to the Funds, and to them as investors and limited partners by extension. The [complaint] alleges that Citco's reputation gave the Funds legitimacy, and "provided potential and current investors with assurance about the quality of financial services provided to the Funds, the security of assets held by the Funds, and the accuracy of the reported values of the Funds and of the investors' individual accounts." This, as Plaintiffs allege, is exactly what Citco intended. But instead of fulfilling its duties as promised, Plaintiffs claim that Citco "utterly failed to take industry-standard steps" in performing its services to the Funds, and that Citco relied on information from Madoff and the Funds "even though that information was manifestly erroneous and should not have been relied on."

The [complaint] alleges Citco should have increased scrutiny and sought independent verification of the information provided by Madoff and the Funds because of the roles consolidated in Madoff, the impossibility of the trade and profit information provided by Madoff, and the warning signs discussed above. Moreover, Plaintiffs claim that Citco did not safeguard the assets entrusted to it, handing over money to Madoff without due diligence, monitoring, or even a good faith basis for its reliance. It further failed, according to Plaintiffs, to record the assets held by the custodians and sub-custodians as it agreed to do. Plaintiffs allege that if Citco had safeguarded investors' assets as required, Plaintiffs could have recovered their investments before December 2008, when Madoff confessed and chaos ensued.

Plaintiffs allege that because of Citco's long history of working with the Funds, as well as its experience in providing hedge fund services, Citco "knew or was willfully blind to the fact that the due diligence and risk controls employed by the Fairfield Defendants were grossly deficient" and that the Funds were misrepresenting to Plaintiffs "that they employed thorough due diligence, monitoring and verification of Fund managers, including Madoff, and strict risk controls." According to Plaintiffs, Citco kept this information from investors and shareholders, and continued to receive investments from Plaintiffs and send investments to Madoff until his fraud was finally revealed . . .

III

. . . The Citco Defendants now move to dismiss the [complaint] based on a variety of purported deficiencies. . . .

Section 10(b) and Rule 10b-5 Claim Against Administrators

The Administrators argue that Plaintiffs fail to state a claim against them under § 10(b) and Rule 10b-5 [of the Securities Exchange Act of 1934 (1934 Act)]. Specifically, they assert that Plaintiffs fail to plead scienter and reliance with sufficient particularity. The Court is not persuaded.

A. Scienter

The Court here applies the scienter standards set forth above. Plaintiffs allege that the Administrators "issued false statements containing inflated NAV calculations and account balance information" and that "[i]n issuing the statements, [the Administrators] acted recklessly because they knew or had access to information suggesting that their public statements were not accurate, including that the values and profits reported to Plaintiffs were not attainable under the circumstances." Further, Plaintiffs allege that the Administrators "acted recklessly by failing to check or verify the information received from [Bernard L. Madoff Investment Securities LLC] despite a duty to scrutinize and verify independently the information relating to the NAV and account balances." They allege that this behavior was reckless because the Administrators were "aware of the red flags surrounding [Bernard L. Madoff Investment Securities LLC], including the consolidation of the roles of investment manager, custodian, and execution agent in Madoff and [Bernard L. Madoff Investment Securities LLC]." . . .

At this stage, the Court finds that the facts alleged by Plaintiffs are sufficient to support a strong inference of scienter that is "cogent and at least as compelling as any opposing inference of nonfraudulent intent.". . . For the purposes of ruling on the instant motion, in the Court's view, the many red flags Plaintiffs point to, taken together, and coupled with the Administrators' familiarity with the Funds and extensive experience in providing financial services to hedge funds, leads to the more compelling inference that the Administrators were "closing [their] eyes to a known danger." . . .

B. Reliance

The Administrators assert that because the [complaint] does not allege that there was an efficient market for shares in the Funds and because Plaintiffs fail to allege actual reliance on the Administrators' misrepresentations in a nonconclusory manner, Plaintiff's § 10(b) and Rule 10b-5 claims should be dismissed for failure to state a claim. The Court disagrees.

In pleading reliance, Plaintiffs need only allege that "but for the claimed representations or omissions, the plaintiff would not have entered into the detrimental securities transactions." . . . Plaintiffs allege that, when investing in the Funds, they "necessarily relied on Citco's NAV calculations.". . . .

Third-Party Beneficiary Breach of Contract

The Citco Defendants argue that Plaintiffs fail to state a third-party beneficiary breach of contract claim. Specifically, the Citco Defendants assert that the language of the agreements at issue evince no clear intent to benefit the Plaintiffs . . .

According to the Citco Defendants, the language of the Citco Agreements clearly evidences an intent to specifically benefit the Funds to the exclusion of Plaintiffs. In support of this argument, the Citco Defendants identify clauses in the Citco Agreements that state that the duties to be performed by the Citco Defendants are on behalf of, and for the benefit of, the Fund. . . . The Citco Defendants also assert that both the Custody and Administration Agreements' nonassignment clauses, and the Administration Agreements' inurement clauses, further demonstrate that the parties never intended to allow third-party enforcement. As the Citco Defendants point out, courts have found nonassignment and inurement clauses to indicate that a contract does not evince an intention to allow third party enforcement. . . .

i. Administration Agreements

The Court is not persuaded by the Citco Defendants' motion to dismiss the third-party beneficiary claim with respect to the Administration Agreements. The Administration Agreements contain language that, when viewed in the light most favorable to Plaintiffs, indicate an intent to benefit a third party. The Fairfield Sentry and Fairfield Sigma Administrative Agreements explicitly state, for example, that the Citco Defendants shall, among other duties, "issue to Shareholders trade confirmations with respect to subscriptions, redemptions and transfers in accordance with the applicable Fund Documents"; "despatch[][sic] to Shareholders notices, proxies, and proxy statements prepared by or on behalf of the Fund in connection with the holding of meetings of shareholders"; "deal[] with and reply[] to all correspondence and other communications addressed to the Fund in relation to the subscription, redemption, transfer (and where relevant, conversion) of Shares"; and "despatch[] to Shareholders and anyone else entitled to receive the same in accordance with the Fund Documents and any applicable law copies of the audited financial statements. . . . Similarly, the Greenwich Sentry and Greenwich Sentry Partners Administration Agreements state that the Citco Defendants "shall, on behalf of the Fund, issue to Limited Partners trade confirmations with respect to subscriptions, redemptions and transfers in accordance with the applicable Fund Documents." . . . . Further, the Greenwich Sentry and Greenwich Sentry Partners Administration Agreements provide that the Citco Defendants are responsible for "communicating with Limited Partners; maintaining the record of accounts; processing subscriptions and withdrawals; preparing and maintaining the Partnership's financial and accounting records and statements; calculating each Limited Partner's capital account balance (on a monthly basis); preparing financial statements; arranging for the provision of accounting, clerical, and administrative services; and maintaining corporate records."

Although the Administration Agreements do not explicitly name Plaintiffs as third-party beneficiaries, the Court is persuaded that Plaintiffs satisfactorily allege intent to permit third-party enforcement evident from within the four corners of the contract—especially given that the Administration Agreements require the Citco Defendants to render certain specific performance directly to Plaintiffs. . . .

ii. Custody Agreements

With respect to the Custody Agreements, the Court finds that Plaintiffs fail to sufficiently allege intent to benefit the Plaintiffs. Whereas the Administration Agreements include language directing the Citco Defendants to render performance directly to Plaintiffs, Plaintiffs can point to no such language in the Custody Agreements. Plaintiffs allege that the Custody Agreements "evince a clear intent to benefit shareholders by affirmatively recognizing Citco's obligation to receive and/or hold shareholder assets and ensure that sub-custodians were qualified to hold the assets." . . . [However], the Custody Agreements never address investors or shareholders, and exclusively lay out the duties among the fund, the depository, and the custodian. From the face of the Custody Agreements it is apparent that any benefit conferred is merely incidental, and that the Custody Agreements do not "clearly evidence[] an intent to permit enforcement by the third party[]." *Consolidated Edison [v. Northeast Utils.]*, 426 F.3d 524, 528 (2d Cir. 2005). Accordingly, the Court grants the Citco Defendants' motion to dismiss with respect to Plaintiffs' thirdparty breach of contract claim as it relates to the Custody Agreements.

Negligence, Gross Negligence, and Negligent Misrepresentation

The Citco Defendants argue that the Court must dismiss Plaintiffs' negligence, gross negligence, and negligent misrepresentation claims because Plaintiffs fail to allege that the Citco Defendants owed them a duty of care. . . . The Court agrees with the Citco Defendants that Plaintiffs do not allege that the Custodians . . . owed them a duty of care, and accordingly that Plaintiffs negligence and gross negligence claims against those defendants must be dismissed. However, the Court denies the Citco Defendants' motion with respect to the Administrators, with regard to whom Plaintiffs plead a plausible negligence, negligent misrepresentation, and gross negligence claim. . . .

Breach of Fiduciary Duty

The Citco Defendants . . . argue that they owed no fiduciary duty to Plaintiffs, and that therefore Plaintiffs' breach of fiduciary duty claims should be dismissed. The Court . . . finds that Plaintiffs sufficiently allege breach of fiduciary duty against the Administrators and the Custodians as the remaining Citco Defendants. . . .

As above, the Citco Defendants argue that they did not owe Plaintiffs any fiduciary duty that was not specified in the Citco Agreements. Further, the Citco Defendants assert that Plaintiffs do not plead that Plaintiffs reposed trust in the Citco Defendants, who thereby gained superiority or influence over Plaintiffs, or that, as purported fiduciaries, the Citco Defendants voluntarily accepted the entrustment of confidence. The Court is not persuaded.

As to the Citco Defendants' protests that the Plaintiffs' attempt to convert a breach of contract claim into a breach of fiduciary duty claim, the Court reiterates that a fiduciary duty can arise from—but remain independent of—a contractual obligation. . . .

With respect to this claim, Plaintiffs allege that the Citco Defendants' significant responsibilities included holding any securities purchased for the Fund, or ensuring that the securities were in the custody of the sub-custodian; maintaining an ongoing, appropriate level of supervision of any sub-custodians, including [Bernard L. Madoff Investment Securities LLC]; and maintaining records of the securities held for the Funds. The Citco Defendants were also charged with independently calculating the "NAV, which was . . . fundamental to Plaintiffs' investment decisions, decisions to invest additional funds, and decisions to maintain the investments over time", . . . preparing monthly financial statements, and preparing records for the external audit. The Citco Defendants "serve[d] as the Funds' agent with the general public, and w[ere] specifically responsible for communications with investors." Finally, the Citco Defendants advertised that they were a "reliable fiduciary."

On this basis, Plaintiffs argue that they sufficiently allege a direct fiduciary relationship in which the Citco Defendants' "superior position or superior access to confidential information [wa]s so great as virtually to require the other party to repose trust and confidence in the first party," and that the Citco Defendants were "under a duty to act for or to give advice for the benefit of another upon matters within the scope of the relation." *Pension Comm.*, 446 F. Supp.2d [163,] 195-96 (S.D.N.Y. 2006). The Court agrees, and finds that Plaintiffs allege sufficient facts to support an inference that the Citco Defendants owed a fiduciary duty to Plaintiffs.

. . . Plaintiffs allege sufficient facts for the Court to infer that the Citco Defendants possessed significant authority over the securities at issue; they were allowed to act independent of the Funds, and in fact, according to Plaintiffs, they were required to take whatever action was necessary to protect the assets. The Citco Defendants agreed to exercise due care in the execution of these duties. According to the [complaint], Plaintiffs had a direct relationship with the Citco Defendants, which included communicating with them before investing in the form of Placement Memos that featured, with permission from the Citco Defendants, their names, duties, and NAV calculations. . . . These factual allegations, among others, support a plausible claim that Plaintiffs reposed their trust in the Citco Defendants and the Citco Defendants accepted this entrustment. . . .

---

1. ***Gatekeeper Liability.*** The legal claims against Citco involve another instance of gatekeeper liability. Unlike underwriters in the traditional public offering context (*see* Chapter 4.3), however, the purported gatekeepers here were providing administrative and custodial services to the Fairfield funds and were not directly involved in the raising of capital. To the extent that the Fairfield fund defendants' primary responsibility was to their investors, does it make sense to impose additional causes of action against service providers with whom the Fairfield funds contracted? Note that the court dismissed some of the third-party beneficiary claims against Citco defendants based on a reading of the intent of parties drafting the underlying agreements. Might it be possible for administrators and custodians of hedge funds in the future to insist on more explicit contractual reservations and escape potential liability in similar situations in the future? Could future investors still bring claims under legal theories grounded in tort or alleged breaches of fiduciary duty?

2. ***Supervisory Failure.*** How relevant to this case is the fact that the SEC's own examiners were unable to detect Madoff's Ponzi scheme? Is the Inspector General's report quoted earlier helpful to the defendants or to the plaintiffs?

3. ***Later Developments.*** The *Anwar* litigation stretched on for at least five years after the District Court opinion with many hearings and appeals on procedural issues, including the question of whether some of the securities law claims at issue in the case were extra-territorial under the Supreme Court's *Morrison* test. *See* Chapter 1.4. In August of 2015, the press reported that Citco Group Ltd. agreed to settle Anwar investor claims for $125 million. This followed a 2013 settlement with Fairfield defendants for $80 million. *See* Patrick Lee, *Citco Reaches $125 Million Settlement With Madoff Victims*, BLOOMBERG BUSINESS (Aug. 13, 2015). Citco remains a major provider of fund services around the world with substantial operations in the United States. To the extent that U.S. regulatory authorities have not yet investigated Citco's role in facilitating funding for the Madoff Ponzi scheme, should the *Anwar* settlement trigger renewed scrutiny? Or would it be more appropriate for authorities to consider the matter closed and accept the monetary settlement of the litigation as a sufficient deterrent?

4. ***Asset Recovery.*** The Securities Investor Protection Corporation appointed a trustee for the liquidation of Bernard L. Madoff Investment Securities LLC. The trustee has recovered over $10 billion, in part by recovering assets, under the clawback powers for preferences and fraudulent transfers in the Bankruptcy

Code and the Securities Investor Protection Act, from investors who made earlier withdrawals and profited from their investments with Madoff.

IV. THE REGULATION OF ALTERNATIVE FUNDS AFTER THE DODD-FRANK ACT

Several portions of the Dodd-Frank Act addressed perceived problems with hedge funds in the pre-Financial Crisis era. These changes include the Volcker Rule's restrictions on banking entities' investments in hedge funds and private equity funds, which have forced major financial conglomerates to spin off their internal hedge fund operations. Further, § 403 the Dodd-Frank Act requires investment advisers to register with the SEC, while § 404 permits the SEC to gather systemic risk data from registered advisers. In addition, the new whistleblower provisions of federal securities law respond, in part, to the SEC staff's failure to take seriously warnings about Madoff. The Dodd-Frank Act's more direct interventions with respect to private funds are summarized below.

A. KEY DODD-FRANK ACT CHANGES

The Dodd-Frank Act authorizes the SEC to require the registration of and heightened disclosure from private fund advisers as a response to the perceived systemic risk implications of private funds. 15 U.S.C. § 80b–4. Title IV amends § 203(b)(3) of the Investment Advisers Act by eliminating the registration exemption for advisers with up to 14 clients. 15 U.S.C. § 80b–3(b). Note that the rule addressed in the *Goldstein* decision, excerpted earlier in this Chapter, was limited to the registration of hedge fund advisers. Nonetheless, limited exemptions from registration as an investment adviser remain for advisers who manage less than $150 million, intrastate advisers, foreign private advisers, family offices, advisers to licensed small business investment companies, and advisers to venture capital funds. 15 § U.S.C. 80b.

Title IV of the Dodd-Frank Act also amended § 204 of the Investment Advisers Act to authorize the SEC to require increased disclosure and record-keeping from registered advisers. The SEC later promulgated rules to amend Form ADV and adopted the new Form PF. The amendments to already-existing Form ADV were the less controversial of the two changes. Form ADV, which is used to register with the SEC as an investment adviser, must be updated annually. The SEC amended Form ADV to require additional disclosures about private funds and further requires registered advisers to deliver brochures to clients with information regarding their business practices and conflicts of interest. Rules Implementing Amendments to the Investment Advisers Act of 1940, 76 Fed. Reg. 42,950, 42,965-68 (July 19, 2011). The SEC chose to make information Form ADV forms publicly available in order to encourage transparency and enable investors' own due diligence. 76 Fed. Reg. 42,981. All private fund advisers with one or more clients and with over $150 million in assets under management must file Form PF yearly, though large advisers must file the form quarterly. Reporting by Investment Advisers to Private Funds and Certain Commodity Pool Operators and Commodity Trading Advisors on Form PF, 76 Fed. Reg. 71,127, 71,132 (Nov. 16, 2011). The information provided through Form PF will not be made public because of the sensitivity of the information collected, including counterparty credit exposure, the amount of assets under management, trading practices, and investment positions. 15 U.S.C. § 80b-4 (2015).

The Dodd-Frank Act also amended the 1934 Act to require the SEC to pay whistleblowers an award of no less than 10% of the total monetary sanctions collected in a judicial or administrative action, a first for the agency. 15 U.S.C. § 78u-6 (2015).

B. PROVISIONAL ASSESSMENTS OF IMPACT

The Dodd-Frank Act's changes to the regulation of private funds and their advisers largely attempted to stem the systemic risk of these funds. In particular, Form PF's expansive and detailed information gathering aimed to support the SEC's and the Financial Stability Oversight Council's (FSOC) efforts to monitor systemic risk. *See* Wulf A. Kaal, *The Systematic Risk of Private Funds After the Dodd-Frank Act*, 4 MICH. BUS. & ENTREPRENEURIAL L. REV. 163, 167 (2015). Preliminary assessments suggest that Form PF may suffer from data insufficiency, thus preventing the SEC and FSOC from making a full assessment of the systemic risk posed by private funds, though too little time has passed for a full assessment of the impact of the new data. *See id.* at 169. The increased regulation of investment advisers is costly, and early assessments suggest that the number of funds managed by an adviser is positively correlated with compliance costs. Wulf A. Kaal, *What Drives Dodd-Frank Act Compliance Cost for Private Funds?* J. OF ALTERNATIVE INV. (2016) (forthcoming). By creating returns to scale, the new regulations may contribute to fund and adviser consolidation and barriers to entry for smaller advisers. *Id.* Some research indicates that the increased compliance costs are being passed on to investors rather than absorbed by advisers. Wulf A. Kaal, *The Post Dodd-Frank-Act Evolution of the Private Fund Industry: Comparative Evidence from 2012 and 2015* 67 (Univ. of St. Thomas (Minnesota), 2015) (unpublished draft) (on file with author). Going forward, what should the FSOC and SEC do with this new information on hedge funds, and what steps should it take to improve the quality of the data?

There are two competing regulatory methods to combat the problems created when the interests of investment managers diverge from those of their investors: mandatory disclosure rules and enforcement actions. Mandatory disclosure rules primarily consist of Form ADV filings, which provide potential investors with information on a firm's disciplinary history and other governance matters. Enforcement actions typically result from SEC examinations of a fund and its manager. Given that these regulatory methods typically occur in tandem, a study by Ms. Colleen Honigsberg sought to compare the effects of mandatory disclosure and SEC enforcement separately. In doing so, Honigsberg found that mandatory disclosure requirements, even in the absence of enforcement actions, drives a reduction in agency costs, concluding that "the marginal benefits of public investments in the development of disclosure rules are likely to exceed the marginal benefits of additional investments in enforcement." Colleen Honigsberg, *Disclosure Versus Enforcement And the Optimal Design of Securities Regulation* 33 (Colum. Bus. Sch., Research Paper 15-58). As lawmakers and practitioners continue to contemplate a regulation scheme that will promote accountability without chilling investment, their focus, to the extent resources are limited, should be on the implementation of disclosure requirements.

The SEC's new examination powers have uncovered several compliance failures after the implementation of the Dodd-Frank Act. Mary Jo White, Chairwoman, SEC, Keynote Address at the Managed Fund Association: Five Years On: Regulation of Private Fund Advisers After Dodd-Frank (Oct. 16, 2015). Such issues include the failure to act in the best interest of clients and to disclose conflicts of interest. For example, the agency's examiner identified advisers who allocated profitable trades to their own proprietary accounts rather than client accounts. Failures have also arisen regarding fee allocation, with some advisers charging fees inappropriately to the fund rather than to the adviser.

C. THE RETAILIZATION OF HEDGE FUNDS

Once the domain of high-net-worth individuals and institutional investors, hedge funds have also begun to reach retail investors, a phenomenon called the retailization of hedge funds. In 2013, the SEC amended two securities registration safe harbors, Rule 506 of Regulation D and Rule 144A of the 1933 Act, to end an 80-year ban on the general solicitation and general advertising of private offerings of securities to investors. Eliminating the Prohibition Against General Solicitation and General Advertising in Rule 506 and Rule 144A Offerings, Final Rule, 78 Fed. Reg. 44,771 (July 24, 2013) (to be codified at 12 C.F.R. §§ 230, 239, 242). The change was mandated by the Jumpstart Our Business Startups Act, often called the JOBS Act, of 2012. While solicitation is not itself restricted, the buyers of these securities must be accredited investors under Rule 506, or qualified institutional borrowers under Rule 144A.

Rule 506 and Rule 144A offerings are widely used by private funds. In 2012, for example, private funds raised $725 billion via Rule 506 offerings and $4 billion via Rule 144A offerings. *Id.* at 44,773. Private funds, and hedge funds in particular, dwarf all other Rule 506 issuers. In fact, "[h]edge funds are the largest fund issuer, and raised almost $1.9 trillion of new capital, . . . of $4.8 trillion total capital raised between 2009-2014]." SEC, CAPITAL RAISING IN THE U.S.: AN ANALYSIS OF THE MARKET FOR UNREGISTERED SECURITIES OFFERINGS, 2009–2014 19 (Oct. 2015). The expansion of offerings to accredited investors, those investors with an annual income of $200,000 or a net worth of $1 million, under Rule 506 alone may significantly increase retail investors' participation in private funds. "[A]t least 8.7 million U.S. households, or 7.4% of all U.S. households, qualified as accredited investors in 2010, based on the net worth standard in the definition of 'accredited investor'." Amendments to Regulation D, Form D and Rule 156, 78 Fed. Reg. 44806, 44,838.

D. EU REGULATION CONTRASTED

The EU has taken drastic measures to regulate hedge and other private funds. The pillar of the EU's regulatory approach to private funds is the EU's Alternative Investment Fund Manager's Directive (AIFMD). Some, but not all, EU member states have implemented this directive to date, although full implementation was legally required by June 2013.

The AIFMD differs from the U.S. approach to the regulation of private funds in several ways. First, the United States does not have an equivalent regulatory scheme in place to oversee private funds. Rather, private funds in the United States are indirectly regulated by complying with the exemptions from the 1940 Act, the Investment Advisers Act, and the 1933 Act. Second, in the EU, alternative investment fund managers are required to register with their home state if they manage funds that reach a certain financial threshold. In the United States, before the Dodd-Frank Act, private funds advisers were exempt from the SEC's registration requirements. As previously discussed in this Chapter, the Dodd-Frank Act eliminated this exemption for most advisers. Third, alternative investment fund managers are required to make periodic public disclosures of information to investors. These disclosures are made to the alternative investment fund manager's home state regulator, and thus may vary, and provide information about an Alternative Investment Fund, including financial statements, activities, and compensation information. In the United States, hedge funds are generally not required to make public disclosures, though fund managers who meet the assets under the management threshold provided by statute are required to make disclosures to the SEC. These disclosures can be released to the public in redacted form. Given these differences, the EU has embraced more stringent regulation of hedge and other private funds, but the Dodd-Frank Act has vastly modified the domestic landscape.

One key issue raised by the adoption of the AIFMD directive is the issue of protectionism, as illustrated by the European Economic Area (EEA) Passport system. Under the AIFMD, European firms are permitted to market their funds throughout the EEA through the use of an EEA passport, akin to the passport available for managers authorized under the Undertakings for Collective Investment in Transferable Securities Directive, but non-EEA firms can only market their funds in the EEA after a registration and approval process. In 2015, the ESMA advised whether it would recommend extending the EEA passport to U.S. managers, but ultimately decided against the extension with the plan to reevaluate the decision at a later date. Some have argued that this decision is the direct result of protectionism, an attempt to limit U.S. investment funds from accessing EU investors while also punishing these funds for their perceived role in the Financial Crisis.

As many U.S.- and other foreign-based hedge funds will inevitably seek to market and operate within the EU, some components of the AIFMD will apply to these foreign funds and their managers. Foreign funds are subject to AIFMD if they either manage or market alternative funds in or from the EU. The AIFMD provides broad definitions for these terms and, as a result, many foreign funds have chosen to withdraw from EU markets instead of attempting compliance. There is, however, an exception that allows foreign funds to effectively operate under the AIFMD without going through this process. Foreign funds are able to operate in the EU without complying with the AFMID registration requirements if they do so under the exception for reverse enquiries, or passive marketing. A reverse enquiry is when an investor contacts an investment manager, without having previous contact with this manager, regarding a potential fund investment and, because the AIFMD only covers active marketing on behalf of the investment manager, that manager would not be subject to the AIFMD.

PART XI

DERIVATIVES AND RATE MARKETS

CHAPTER 11.1

OVERVIEW OF DERIVATIVES

CONTENTS

I. INTRODUCTION

In this Chapter, we describe what derivatives are, why market participants use them, and the origins, size, and scope of the derivatives markets. We explain the regulation of the derivatives markets before the Financial Crisis and the role that over-the-counter (OTC) derivatives played in exacerbating the Financial Crisis. Lastly, in this Chapter, we outline the domestic and international reforms designed to reduce the likelihood that derivatives will pose systemic risks to the global economy in the future.

In Chapter 11.2, we will explore Dodd-Frank Act derivatives reforms in greater detail, with a focus on making the derivatives markets safer and more transparent. We will also discuss cross-border application of such rules. In Chapter 11.3, we will examine business conduct and market integrity. We will explore business conduct regulation under the Dodd-Frank Act, multi-country enforcement actions regarding rate and foreign currency markets, and coordination of business conduct and market integrity oversight across borders.

II. WHAT ARE DERIVATIVES AND WHO USES THEM?

A. OVERVIEW OF DERIVATIVE CONTRACT TYPES

Derivatives are financial contracts between two parties, known as counterparties, with values that are derived from the value of another item, known as the underlying asset. Derivatives allow counterparties to transfer the risks of the underlying asset. A counterparty that holds the underlying asset can use derivatives to decrease exposure to risk (hedge). A counterparty that wishes to gain exposure to risk (speculate) can use derivatives, whether or not it holds the underlying asset. The juxtaposition of these two potential uses of the same derivatives contracts—one use generally viewed as beneficial to society, the other use viewed as potentially harmful—frame an ongoing debate as to whether derivatives should be allowed and, if so, how they should be regulated. This debate raged long before the Financial Crisis. *Compare* Henry T.C. Hu, *Hedging Expectations: "Derivative Reality" and the Law and Finance of the Corporate Objective*, 73 TEX. L. REV. 985 (1995), *with* Frank Partnoy, *Financial Derivatives and the Costs of Regulatory Arbitrage,* 22 J. OF CORP. L. 211 (1997). To give you the tools necessary to think critically about these debates, this section introduces a number of common types of derivatives that are used by market participants to hedge risk or speculate.

1. Forwards

A forward contract is one in which a commercial buyer and seller agree upon the delivery of a specified quality and quantity of goods at a predetermined future date. A forward contract is a derivative because the value of the contract changes as the price of the underlying asset changes. If the price of the underlying asset goes up, the forward is worth more to the person who agreed to buy the underlying asset at a future date for a fixed price, and less to the person who agreed to sell the underlying asset at a future date for a fixed price. Through the contract, the buyer is, therefore, getting a better deal, relative to what the buyer could have paid in the open market, than before the price of the underlying asset increased. Conversely, if the price of the underlying asset goes down, the forward is worth less to the person who agreed to buy the underlying asset for a fixed price and more to the person who agreed to sell it because the seller is getting a better deal relative to what it could have received in the open market at the future date.

Who uses forwards, and why? Consider an airline, which we will call Airline. Airline knows that it will need to purchase vast amounts of jet fuel in a given year, but it cannot accurately predict this future expense because the market price for jet fuel—based at least in part on the price of crude oil—may change. This uncertainty is a problem, however, because in order to set ticket prices, make necessary purchases, pay its workers, and plan for the coming year, Airline needs to know how much money it must set aside for its jet fuel expenses for a given time period. On the other side of the market, imagine a company that produces and refines crude oil into jet fuel, which we will call Refiner, which knows it will have a certain amount of fuel available for purchase in the coming year. Refiner, too, would like certainty on the price of that jet fuel at the time Refiner is ready to sell. Using the current market price of fuel, Airline and Refiner agree on the probable cost of jet fuel for the coming delivery period, and they agree at that moment to exchange jet fuel at that specific price, regardless of what the market price happens to be at the time of delivery. No up-front payment by Airline is required. In this example, depicted in Figure 11.1-1, let's assume Airline and Refiner agree in July that, in October, Refiner will sell and deliver to Airline 100,000 gallons of jet fuel at $2 per gallon, for $200,000 total. If in October the market price of jet fuel has risen to $2.50 per gallon, the contract still allows Airline to buy 100,000 gallons of fuel for $200,000, rather than the current market price for fuel, which would have cost Airline $250,000. Conversely, had the market price of jet fuel dropped from $2 per gallon to $1.50 per gallon, the contract still allows Refiner to sell the fuel for $200,000, or $50,000 more than it would have received if it sold the same amount of fuel at the current market price.

Figure 11.1-1 Diagram of a Basic Forward Contract

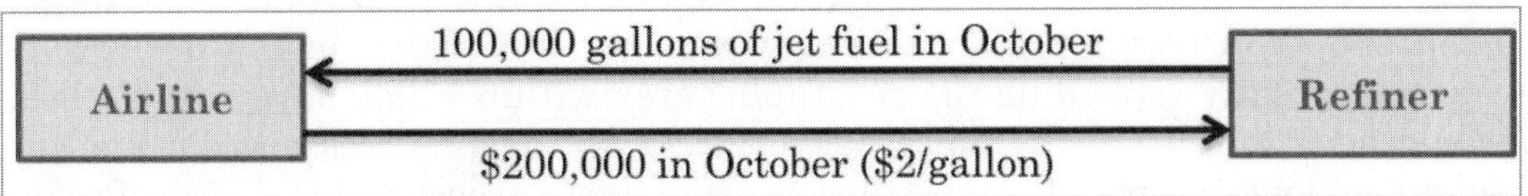

Derivatives are generally a zero-sum contract. From an *ex post* perspective, one party comes out ahead, and the other party comes out behind to the same degree. From an *ex ante* perspective, however, both parties are willing to enter into the contract, and may be better off as a result, because it gives them certainty as to the price of fuel in October.

2. Futures

Like a forward, a futures contract is an agreement to purchase or sell a commodity, or financial instrument, for delivery in the future at a specified price, on a predetermined date. Unlike a forward, however, a future is a standardized, exchange-traded contract. Futures contracts exist for an array of commodities, from fuel to frozen orange juice concentrate. Futures can even reference intangible risks such as the weather. Market participants trade futures on formal exchanges rather than OTC. The largest futures exchange in the United States is the Chicago Mercantile Exchange, which was formed in the 19th Century. The execution of futures through exchanges necessitates standardization and exchanges set standardized contract terms. Futures contracts are standardized in the types and size of the underlying asset and the predetermined dates to which the contracts relate. Standardization allows for more market participants since the contracts based on those commodities are interchangeable—*i.e.*, a contract is not for particular refiner's fuel, but rather for fuel in general. Standardization encourages more hedgers and speculators to enter the market, which in turn promotes liquidity. Liquid futures markets also serve a price discovery function. In some cases, the price at which futures contracts trade constitute a primary means of price discovery for the underlying commodity, which is harder to trade.

Futures contracts that are executed on an exchange are required to be submitted for clearing to a third-party known as a clearinghouse (although the clearinghouse may be associated with the exchange). As discussed in greater detail in Chapter 11.2, when a transaction is submitted for clearing, the clearinghouse is placed between the parties and effectively guarantees the obligations of each party to the transaction for a price. In a forward contract, both parties expose themselves to the risk that the other party will default and will be unable to pay the amount it owes under the contract (commonly known as credit or counterparty risk) whereas for futures contracts, the credit risk is minimized by the clearinghouse's guarantee.

Another significant difference between forwards and futures contracts is that futures sellers usually do not make delivery of the underlying commodity. Instead, the parties to a futures contract can liquidate their positions by entering into an equivalent, but opposite, transaction that offsets the positions and eliminates the delivery obligation. Rather than the seller of the futures contract delivering the underlying commodity to the purchaser, the parties can cash settle the futures contract by paying the difference between the price that was agreed upon and the current price. This was a major innovation in the derivatives markets, greatly expanding the geographic area within which buyers and sellers would be willing to deal. Since delivery was no longer necessary, buyers and sellers no longer worried about transportation costs associated with transferring the underlying commodity.

Figure 11.1-2 Diagram of a Basic Futures Contract

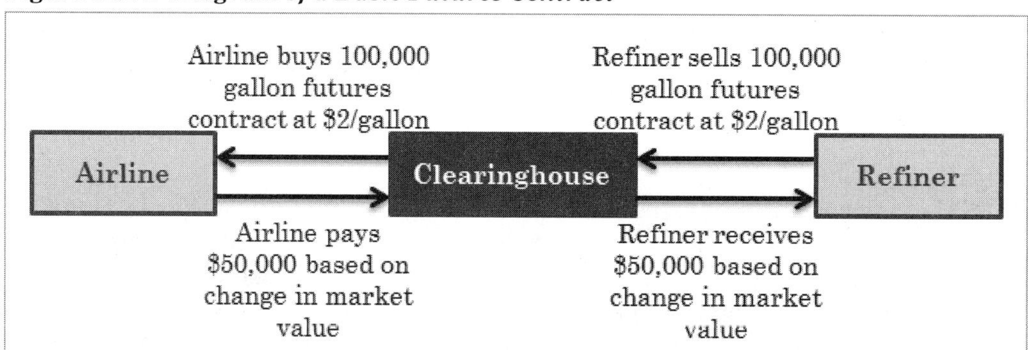

To continue our example, suppose Airline and Refiner buy and sell, respectively, a standardized futures contract for 100,000 gallons of fuel, with cash payments that will be made from Refiner to the exchange's clearinghouse, and from the exchange's clearinghouse to Airline, in October, for a price of $200,000 (the same $2 per gallon price as in the previous example). This exchange is illustrated in Figure 11.1-2. Over the period of time between agreeing to enter into the contract and the October maturity date, the market price for jet fuel drops to $1.50 per gallon. When October arrives, rather than actually requiring Refiner to deliver 100,000 gallons to various airports across the country, the clearinghouse can cash settle the contract between the two parties. In this case, because the market value of the underlying asset went down, Airline would give the clearinghouse $50,000 to account for the difference in price between when it initially entered into the contract and the current market price ((100,000 x $2) – (100,000 x $1.50) = $50,000). The clearinghouse would then give Refiner the $50,000. If Airline still needs the jet fuel, it can purchase the fuel locally at its various airports for the current price of $1.50 per gallon in spot or cash market transactions. Cash settlement is common in the futures markets, as the ultimate goal of entering into a futures contract may not be to receive physical delivery of the asset from the original seller, but rather to secure the agreed upon price, thereby achieving the price certainty both parties were looking for. PHILIP MCBRIDE JOHNSON AND THOMAS LEE HAZEN, DERIVATIVES REGULATION § 1.02[3] (Aspen Publ'g 2004).

3. Options

In an option contract, one party pays the other for the right, but not the obligation, to purchase or sell an underlying asset in the future at an agreed upon price, known as the strike price. An option contract is a derivative because it derives its value from the varying value of the underlying asset, in relation to the strike price. Unlike with forwards and futures, the option is not binding on both parties; the buyer of the option does not have the obligation to exercise it. If the underlying asset's value falls below the strike price in an option contract, the purchaser can choose not to exercise the contract. Since the purchaser is not obligated to exercise the option, the purchaser must account for this uncertainty by paying an upfront premium.

There are two main types of options. A call option gives the option holder the right, but not the obligation, to buy the underlying asset at the strike price. A put option gives the option holder the right to sell the underlying asset at the strike price. A put or call option may come in one of two forms: a European call or put option can be exercised only at the maturity date, while an American call or put option can be exercised on or before that date. *See* RICHARD HECKINGER ET AL., UNDERSTANDING DERIVATIVES: MARKETS & INFRASTRUCTURE 5 (2013). Options are typically traded on exchanges.

While futures and forward contracts have symmetrical payout structures, options payouts are asymmetrical. On the one hand, in a call option, the option holder will profit and the seller will lose money if the market price of the underlying asset's value exceeds the strike price—if the option is "in the money." In this scenario, the buyer could purchase the asset from the option seller at the strike price and turn around and sell that same asset at the market price, profiting from the difference, known as the spread. *Id.* at 4. On the other hand, if the option is "out of the money," the option holder will not exercise the option—why pay more money for an asset that can be purchased for less on the open market? *Id.* at 6. In exchange for the opportunity for up-side gains with no risk of loss, the option buyer must pay a premium. *Id.* In contrast to forwards and futures contracts where the purchaser pays on maturity, with an option, the option buyer pays up front, as a premium for the *right* to purchase or sell in the future, in addition to any transfer of funds from exercising the option at the strike price down the road. While forwards and futures contracts require both parties to perform in the future, an option requires one party, the seller, to perform *only if* its counterparty exercises the option.

Imagine that Airline does not want to spend more than $200,000 for its jet fuel requirements in October. Rather than seeking to enter into a forward or a futures contract for October, Airline decides to enter into a call option for 100,000 gallons at a strike price of $2 per gallon. As a result, if the price of fuel in October is higher than $2 per gallon, say, $2.50, Airline is "in the money" and would exercise its option to buy the 100,000 gallons at $2 per gallon, thereby ensuring that it does not exceed its maximum budget and saving $50,000, minus the premium it had to pay for the option itself. In the alternative, if the price of fuel in October is lower than $2 per gallon, say $1.50, Airline would not exercise its option, would lose the premium it paid, and would purchase fuel in the spot market for $1.50 per gallon. This payoff scale is depicted in Figure 11.1-3.

Figure 11.1-3 Call Option Payoff

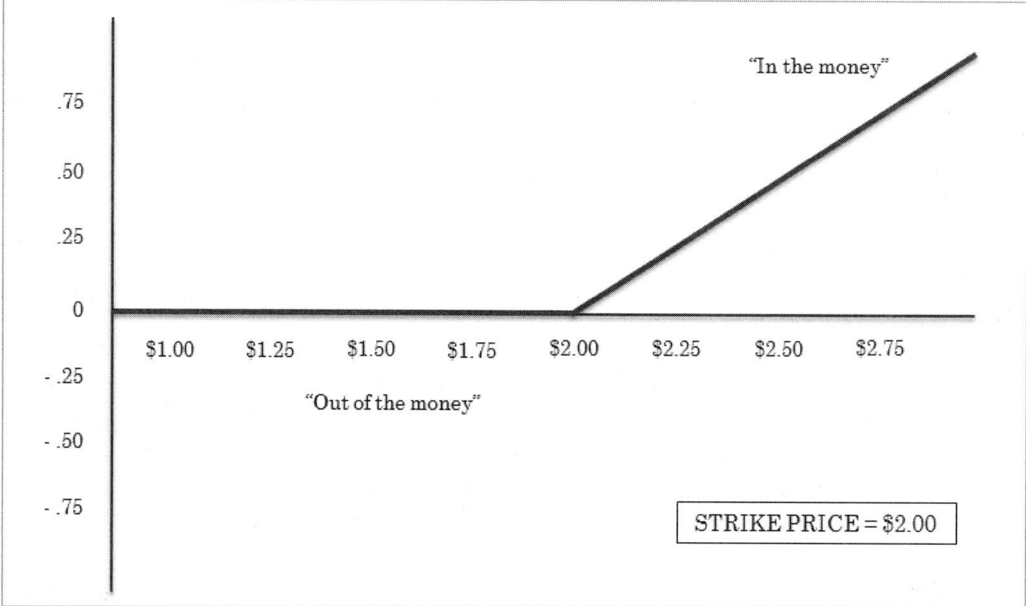

4. Swaps

Swaps are contracts that provide for the exchange of flows of payments. A swap contract is a derivative because the payment flows are based on an underlying asset, instrument, or rate. By exchanging flows of payments, counterparties swap the risk of the underlying obligations that give rise to those payments. There are many different types of swaps, including interest rate, foreign exchange (FX), credit, equity, commodity, and other swaps. In fact, one could imagine a swap that exchanges any two streams of payment. Swaps can be combined with other instruments, for example, an option to enter into a swap is known as a swaption. Swaps have traditionally been traded OTC. Using Airline as an example, below are descriptions of some of the most common types of swaps.

a. Interest Rate Swaps

Interest rate swaps—the most common type of swaps in the market—are contracts to exchange one set of cash flows, based on one interest rate, for another set of cash flows, based on a different rate. Imagine that Airline wishes to take out a loan to finance the purchase of ten new airplanes. Bank offers to finance Airline's purchase, but it does not want to provide Airline with a fixed rate loan because it is concerned that market rates will rise, increasing its own cost of funds and decreasing the value of its loan to Airline in relation to other potential lending opportunities. Bank therefore offers Airline a loan with an interest rate pegged to market interest rates, called a variable-rate loan. Airline, however, does not want to take the risk that market interest rates will rise, because it would like certainty in the repayment amounts it will need to make over the life of the loan. Airline would prefer a fixed-rate loan.

While it seems as though Airline and Bank are at an impasse, the problem can be solved with an interest rate swap, illustrated in Figure 11.1-4. Bank enters into an interest rate swap with a counterparty, typically a large financial institution (Swap Dealer), and pays Swap Dealer fixed rate payments, which correspond with the fixed rate payments it receives from Airline, the borrower. In exchange, Swap Dealer makes floating rate payments back to Bank. Swap Dealer is willing to enter into this transaction because it will charge Bank a fee for the service. As a result of the interest rate swap, Bank is therefore able to hedge its floating rate financing costs, reducing the risks created by interest rate fluctuations, and Airline is able to get the fixed rate payment structure it desires for its loan. In essence, neither Airline nor Bank has to take the risk of changing interest rates— that risk has been passed, or swapped, to Swap Dealer, in exchange for a fee.

Figure 11.1-4 Interest Rate Swap

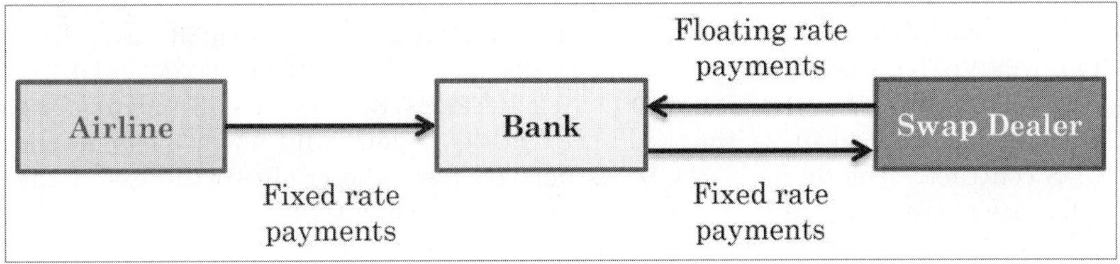

b. Foreign Exchange Swaps

Similar to an interest rate swap, which transfers the risk of changing interest rates, an FX swap is a contract that transfers the risk of FX rates. Through an FX swap, counterparties trade a fixed flow of payments in one currency for a fixed flow of payments, in the corresponding amount, in another currency over a set period of time. A party can use an FX swap to hedge its exposure to changes in the relative value of the two currencies or to gain exposure to those same changes in a speculative manner. *See* Joseph L. Motes III, *A Primer on the Trade and Regulation of Derivative Instruments*, 49 SMU L. REV. 579, 586 (1996).

FX swaps can help firms reduce risk. For example, suppose that Airline, which is based in the United States, has employees who live and work in Europe. Airline needs to pay its European employees in euros each month. Airline could buy euros each month at the current exchange rate in order to pay its employees, but this will expose Airline to changing U.S. dollar to euro exchange rates, that is, FX risk. Instead, Airline can enter into an FX swap to reduce its FX risk because Airline knows it will be able to purchase euros at the agreed rate.

c. Commodity Swaps

Commodity swaps generally shift the risk of a price change in a commodity by requiring one party to pay if the value of the commodity increases, and the other to pay if the value of the commodity decreases. Rather than being standardized products, like futures, commodity swaps are customized. Commodity swaps enable producers and consumers of the commodity to hedge commodity prices. To continue our example, Airline could use a commodity swap to hedge its risk that the price of jet fuel will increase. In that case, Airline could enter into a swap with a counterparty under which Airline would receive payments if the price of jet fuel goes up and would pay the counterparty if the price goes down. Similarly, Refiner could also enter into a commodity swap to hedge its exposure to fluctuations in the price of the jet fuel it produces. Refiner would receive payments if the price of jet fuel decreases and would pay its counterparty if the price increases. Economically, these swaps would function the same as if they were futures contracts.

d. Credit Default Swaps

Credit Default Swaps (CDSs) are transactions that shift credit risk from one party to another. In a CDS, one party, the protection buyer, makes periodic payments to the other party, the protection seller. In return, the protection seller promises to pay the protection buyer if the issuer of the underlying asset (*e.g.*, a bond) defaults, restructures, or files for bankruptcy. ROBERT E. LITAN, THE DERIVATIVES DEALERS' CLUB AND DERIVATIVES MARKETS REFORM: A GUIDE FOR POLICY MAKERS, CITIZENS AND OTHER INTERESTED PARTIES 13 (2010). The relevant issuer, known as the reference entity, is generally not a party to the CDS contract. The value of a CDS is derived from the creditworthiness of the reference entity. Figure 11.1-5 provides an example of a CDS.

Figure 11.1-5 Credit Default Swap

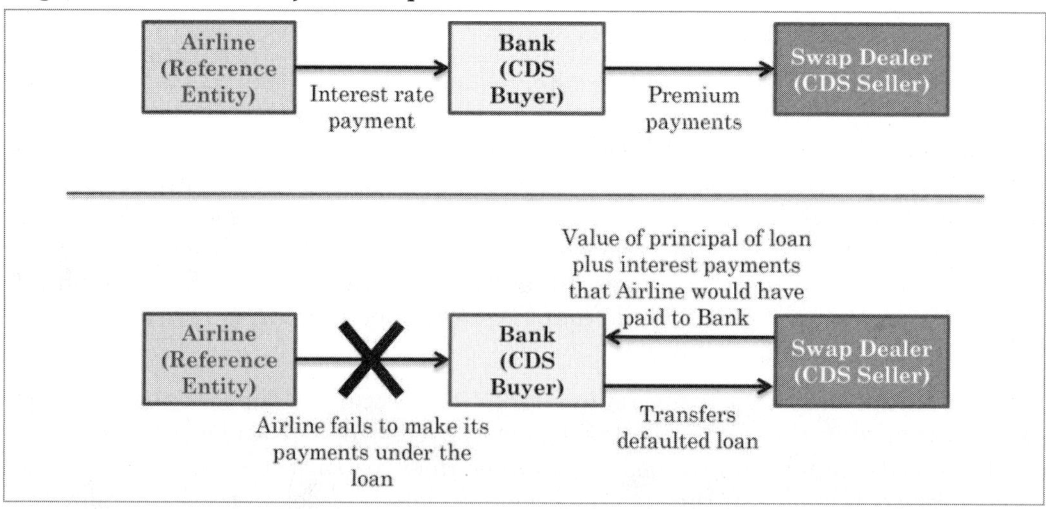

There are generally three categories of CDS: a single name CDS that refers to a single underlying company, sovereign, or debt instrument; a multi-name CDS that refers to more than one underlying issuer; and CDSs that are based on collateralized baskets of agreements and obligations, or on indexes of underlyings. GAO, REGULATORY OVERSIGHT AND RECENT INITIATIVES TO ADDRESS RISK POSED BY CREDIT DEFAULT SWAPS 4 (2009). For example, you may have heard about JPMorgan's positions in an index comprised of 125 CDSs that gained notoriety in 2012 as its large positions became known in the markets, and were colloquially referred to as the London Whale trades owing to their size and the location of the trading desk involved. JPMorgan sustained $6.2 billion in losses by the end of 2012 in connection with its position in the index and was subject to a number of supervisory actions. *See* Arwin Zeissler & Andrew Metrick, *JPMorgan Chase London Whale,* Yale Program on Financial Stability Case Study, 2014-2G-V1, Dec. 1, 2014, Revised Mar. 11, 2015.

As with the other forms of derivatives, CDSs can help companies hedge their risk—in this case, credit risk—by providing institutions a valuable risk management tool. LITAN, at 13. For example, Bank may lend money to Airline to fund Airline's purchase of ten new airplanes, as in the previous examples. Fearing that Airline may go bankrupt or otherwise default on the loan, Bank may buy a single name CDS from a third-party, with the loan to Airline as the reference security. The CDS hedges Bank's risk that Airline defaults on its loan, which would destroy the loan's value. CDSs also allow parties to speculate on the chance that a reference entity will fail to pay or go bankrupt. In the above example, the counterparty to the CDS, the seller of CDS protection, may be a speculator who is hoping to make a profit from the stream of cash payments from Bank by betting that Airline will not default on its loan payments. If Airline does in fact default, however, the speculator will lose a considerable amount of money, because it will have to pay Bank the value of the principal of the loan and the interest payments that the loan would have paid to Bank. If Airline does not default, the speculator receives that steady stream of payments from Bank, the value of which is based on a mutually agreed upon determination between the speculator and Bank of the risk of Airline's default.

Put another (more sinister) way, in a CDS contract, one party is essentially betting that the reference company or other underlying will default. That party need not have any exposure to risk from the reference entity—known as a naked CDS. For this reason, CDSs are perhaps the most controversial major type of swap. Critics have argued that CDSs contributed to several bankruptcies, including the 2009 General Motors Chapter 11 reorganization, because, as George Soros argued, "some bondholders owned CDS and stood to gain more by bankruptcy than by reorganization. It is like buying life insurance on someone else's life and owning a license to kill." George Soros, *The Three Steps to Financial Reform*, FIN. TIMES, June 16, 2009. Moreover, CDSs can be used to create synthetic collateralized debt obligations (CDOs), a form of securitization in which parties can place derivatives bets on the performance of an underlying pool of assets, such as a mortgage-backed security or CDO. *See* FCIC, THE FINANCIAL CRISIS INQUIRY REPORT 142–45 (2011).

1. ***Buy Side versus Sell Side.*** Derivatives counterparties are referred to as being on the buy side or the sell side. Parties on the buy side include investing institutions, hedge funds, regional banks, non-financial corporations, small businesses, and municipalities (which proved especially controversial in Detroit's financial management, for example). On the sell side of derivatives transactions are large broker-dealers. Sell-side firms play different roles in the market—hedging their own risks, creating a market for buy side participants (known as market-making), carrying out underwriting activities on behalf of clients, and speculating in the market.

2. ***Futures versus Swaps.*** Post-Dodd Frank Act, a significant trend known as futurization—the recharacterization of contracts previously transacted as swaps to trade as futures—has occurred. *See* Gabriel D. Rosenberg & Jai R. Massari, *Regulation through Substitution as Policy Tool: Swap Futurization under Dodd-Frank*, 2013 COLUM. BUS. L. REV. 667 (2013). As you learn about the regulation of swaps and futures, consider whether this is a good, bad, or neutral trend.

3. ***Derivatives and the Volcker Rule.*** Recall our discussion of the Volcker Rule in Chapter 6.1. What criteria does the law require be used to determine whether derivatives contracts are used to hedge rather than speculate?

B. VOLUME OF DERIVATIVES CONTRACTS

The derivatives markets are large and global. In June 2015, there existed $553 trillion in total outstanding notional value of OTC derivatives, and $15.5 trillion outstanding in gross market value. THE WORLD BANK, MARKET CAPITALIZATION OF LISTED COMPANIES (2015); BANK FOR INT'L SETTLEMENTS, OTC DERIVATIVES STATISTICS AT END-JUNE 2015 (2015). The notional amount of a derivatives contract represents the nominal or face amount of the contract. Darrell Duffie, *How Should We Regulate Derivatives Markets?* 2–3 (Pew Research Ctr., Briefing Paper No. 5, 2009) [hereinafter Duffie, *How Should We Regulate Derivatives Markets?*]. The gross market value is calculated as the cost of replacing outstanding contracts at current market prices; it helps put a bound on the total cost to market participants if parties defaulted at that moment. Gross market value does not incorporate netting and collateral, which reduce that risk considerably, nor the risk of future price movements, which could increase or reduce that risk. It also does not capture the risk to the financial system as a whole if parties are unable or unwilling to replace the outstanding contracts. *See* BANK FOR INT'L SETTLEMENTS, OTC DERIVATIVES STATISTICS AT END-JUNE 2015, 13 (2015). The gross market value of derivatives markets is comparable in size to the gross domestic product of the United States, which was about $18 trillion in 2014.

As Figure 11.1-6 shows, the greatest share of OTC derivatives contracts are interest rate swaps.

Figure 11.1-6 Global OTC Derivatives Markets

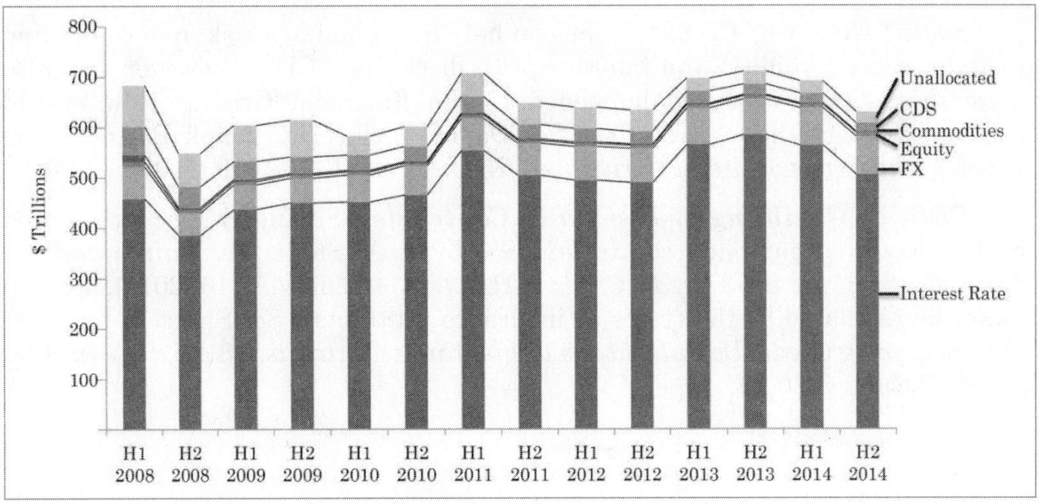

Source: Bank for Int'l Settlements, OTC Derivatives Statistics.

C. DEBATE OVER THE VALUE OF DERIVATIVES

As described above, derivatives are contracts for payments between one party and another based on the value of an underlying asset. Derivatives, however, are not the underlying asset or commodity itself—they are created from nothing. As a result, a derivative's payoff structure is normally zero-sum: one party's gain corresponds to its counterparty's loss, which means that the total value of a class of derivatives held long equals the total value of those same derivatives held short. Duffie, *How Should We Regulate Derivatives Markets?*, at 3. Therefore, the total market value of all derivatives held globally is normally equal to zero if one were to sum up the derivatives on the balance sheets of market participants. *Id.* While derivatives transfer wealth between parties, they do not directly contribute to the total stock of wealth in the economy. *Id.*

Despite the fact that derivatives do not directly add wealth to the economy, proponents and critics alike acknowledge their value. Commercial firms use derivatives primarily to hedge risk or to reduce their exposure to changes in the market. Through derivatives, a firm can pay a counterparty to assume some market risk, providing the firm with a more stable and predictable cash flow because it is better protected from changes in the market. Derivatives serve as a type of insurance that can reduce uncertainty, thus making planning easier and mitigating exposure to risks. Joseph L. Motes III, *A Primer on the Trade and Regulation of Derivative Instruments*, 49 SMU L. REV. 579, 585–86 (1996). While a fund manager can easily diversify her portfolio, a commercial firm without derivatives would have to become a conglomerate to diversify. The firm that uses derivatives to hedge needs a counterparty, and if that counterparty is not a hedger, it will likely be a dealer. While a hedger uses derivatives to protect itself by transferring risk, the dealer provides liquidity to the market in exchange for a small fee on each transaction. By bearing the risks that their counterparties wish to mitigate, dealers provide the liquidity necessary to create a derivatives market, enabling commercial firms to mitigate their operating risks. Speculators also serve a function in the derivatives markets, by providing liquidity, acting as counterparties, and ultimately bearing risks.

---

1. ***Social Utility of CDSs?*** CDSs can help firms manage risk, reduce funding costs, increase liquidity, and improve price discovery. CDSs, however, can also increase systemic risks, as happened in the Financial Crisis. How should regulators weigh these tradeoffs? *See* David A. Skeel & Frank Partnoy, *The Promise and Perils of Credit Derivatives,* 75 U. CIN. L. REV. 1019 (2007).

2. ***CDSs as Gambling or Insurance Contracts?*** Should swaps be regulated by the states as gambling contracts? *See* Lynn A. Stout, *Derivatives and the Legal Origin of the 2008 Credit Crisis,* 1 HARV. BUS. L. REV. 1, 10 (2011). Should swaps be regulated by the states as insurance contracts? *See* Sherri Venokur et al., *Comparing Credit Default Swaps to Insurance Contracts,* 28 J. L. INV. & RISK MGMT. PRODS. 1 (2008).

III. HISTORY OF U.S. DERIVATIVES REGULATION: CRISIS AND REFORM

The history of derivatives trading is in part a story of innovation, utility, and growth, and in part a story of scandal and failure, from 17th Century Europe to the Financial Crisis. While derivatives can provide enormous benefits, the unregulated nature of the OTC derivatives market before the Financial Crisis contributed to the inherent risks in the global financial system. To fully understand the role of derivatives in the Financial Crisis, it is first necessary to understand the history of derivatives and their regulation.

A. HISTORY OF DERIVATIVES REGULATION

The derivatives markets in the United States can be understood most clearly through their development in the agricultural sector as the United States moved towards a developed national economy in the mid-19th Century. Both buyers and sellers of agricultural goods needed a method to establish future price certainty, and derivatives facilitated this purpose. Rather than a refiner making jet fuel and an airline needing jet fuel, imagine a farmer growing wheat and a miller needing wheat. Forwards and other derivative contracts allowed both parties to reduce uncertainty over prices of agricultural products between the growing season and harvest. As these contracts grew in frequency, people began to gravitate towards a central location to facilitate trading. For the Midwest, America's agricultural heartland, Chicago emerged as a natural hub. In 1848, 82 merchants created an organized exchange, the Chicago Board of Trade (CBOT), for buyers and sellers of grain to conduct business. GORDON F. PEERY, WILEY FINANCE: THE POST-REFORM GUIDE TO DERIVATIVES AND FUTURES 300 (Wiley Publ'g 2012). Forward contracts began trading at the CBOT almost immediately. CFTC, HISTORY OF THE CFTC (2016). Soon after, other exchanges were created, including the Kansas City Board of Trade and the Chicago Mercantile Exchange, which traded in cotton, eggs, coffee, and eventually financial futures and options. *Id.*

The example of the farmer illustrates important historical context: forward contracts began as bilateral bespoke contracts negotiated between two individuals, but they were inadequate for the national economy. The bilateral, customized nature of the contracts made high-volume trading difficult, at least in part because the necessity of physical delivery of the underlying agricultural product to the buyer limited the geographic range of potential buyers. After recognizing that traders often had similar needs in terms of quantity and timing of contracts, the exchanges started to create standardized contracts. CARLEY GARNER, A TRADER'S FIRST BOOK ON COMMODITIES 23 (2d ed., 2012). In 1858, the exchanges introduced standardized terms, creating futures contracts for the first time. CFTC, HISTORY OF THE CFTC (2016). In 1865, the CBOT put formal trading rules into place, requiring buyers and sellers to post performance bonds, or margin, to mitigate default risk. CME GRP, TIMELINE OF CME ACHIEVEMENTS (2016). The shift to organized futures trading centralized the ability to liquidate contracts and settle in cash, thereby avoiding the need for delivery of the physical commodity underlying the contract.

While futures trading flourished, it remained marred by frequent corners and manipulations. Between 1880 and 1920, more than 200 bills were introduced in Congress to regulate the futures sector. CFTC, HISTORY OF THE CFTC (2016). In response to grain futures speculation at the end of World War I, Congress passed the Futures Trading Act of 1921, which provided for the regulation of futures trading in grain. PEERY, at 95; *see also* CFTC, HISTORY OF THE CFTC (2016). Pursuant to the Futures Trading Act, the Secretary of Agriculture could designate exchanges that met certain requirements as contract markets. Any trades not executed on one of these Designated Contract Markets (DCMs) would be taxed at 20 cents per bushel. One year later, the Supreme Court invalidated the law in *Hill v. Wallace*, 259 U.S. 44 (1922). In response, Congress passed the Grain Futures Act that same year. The law created the Grain Futures Administration under the Department of Agriculture to administer the act, which barred price manipulation, cornering, and dissemination of false price information. Unlike the Futures Trading Act, the Grain Futures Act banned, rather than taxed, grain futures trading outside of DCMs. CFTC, HISTORY OF THE CFTC (2016). The Supreme Court upheld this legislation in *Board of Trade of City of Chi. v. Olsen*, 262 U.S. 1 (1923).

The Commodity Exchange Act (CEA) was enacted in 1936 as the first comprehensive regulatory framework for the commodities markets. The CEA replaced the Grain Futures Act and extended federal regulation beyond grains to commodities such as cotton, rice, butter, and eggs. *Id.* The CEA prohibited the trading of options on the agricultural commodities it regulated, whether on- or off-exchange, in response to the role of options speculation in the collapse of the wheat market during the Great Depression. Jerry W. Markham & David J. Gilberg, *Stock and Commodity Options—Two Regulatory Approaches and Their Conflicts*, 47 ALB. L. REV. 741, 759–60 (1983) [hereinafter Markham & Gilberg, *Stock and Commodity Options*]. President Franklin D. Roosevelt said of the legislation: "[I]t should be our national policy to restrict, as far as possible, the use of these [futures] exchanges for purely speculative operations." Franklin D. Roosevelt, President, Message to Congress (Feb. 9, 1934). The Commodities Exchange Commission, which replaced the Grain Futures Administration, became responsible for licensing futures exchanges and imposing registration requirements for futures commission merchants and other intermediaries.

PEERY, at 96. The CEA also gave the new agency increased risk-management authority. The agency could set federal positions limits on speculation. The agency could also require that customer funds deposited as margin be segregated and held for the benefit of the customer. CFTC, HISTORY OF THE CFTC (2016). Like the legislation before it, the CEA prohibited futures trading outside of DCMs, effectively giving DCMs a monopoly over futures trading. PEERY, at 302.

Despite initial regulation, abuses of the commodities markets continued, including a scandal involving manipulation of onion futures, and the Great Salad Oil Swindle, in which phony receipts for the warehousing of soybean oil were used as collateral to finance heavy trading in the soybean, soybean oil, and cottonseed oil markets, ultimately causing the collapse of 16 firms. CFTC, HISTORY OF THE CFTC (2016). In addition, options traders sought to take advantage of a loophole in the CEA, which did not prohibit options in certain commodities such as silver, platinum, and coffee. Markham & Gilberg, *Stock and Commodity Options*, at 760. In the early 1970s, a young trader named Harold Goldstein began to exploit this loophole—his firm increased its capitalization from $800 in 1971, to $45 million by the end of 1972. *Id.* His sales of naked options—*i.e.*, options in which the firm did not own the underlying commodity—eventually led to a financial disaster as prices of the underlying commodities increased, resulting in losses of $85 million for Goldstein and millions more for many other firms. *Id.* at 761. As a result of these recurring abuses, Congress sought to create a stronger system of federal regulation of the commodities markets, and in 1974, Congress passed the Commodity Futures Trading Commission Act, which created the CFTC as an independent agency, replacing the Commodities Exchange Commission, and gave the CFTC exclusive jurisdiction over futures and commodity options. CFTC, HISTORY OF THE CFTC (2016). At the same time, the definition of commodity was greatly expanded beyond agricultural products to cover nearly everything with a price. *Id.; see also* Commodity Futures Trading Commission Act of 1974, 7 U.S.C. §§ 4a-22 (1974).

B. THE FIGHT OVER OTC DERIVATIVES REGULATION

A central feature of U.S. derivatives regulation has involved turf wars among federal agencies and between federal and state regulators. Before the creation of the CFTC, the states and the SEC attempted to tackle some of the abuses in the options markets. Markham & Gilberg, *Stock and Commodity Options*, at 769–70. From its inception, the CFTC sought to assert its authority and held that its rules preempted state regulation, and that there was a clear line of authority between CFTC and SEC jurisdiction. *Id.* at 771. In reality, there were significant overlaps and gaps, and as the exchanges began to create markets for futures on securities, a jurisdictional battle developed between the CFTC and SEC. The CFTC's position was that futures on securities were *futures*, separate from the underlying securities, and fell under its remit, while the SEC argued that futures on securities were *securities* and that trading in these instruments should be regulated by the SEC, as such futures trading has an effect on the underlying securities markets. *Id.* at 773–75.

A significant disagreement developed in the 1980s over the trading of options in Ginnie Mae certificates, which represented interests in pools of government-backed home mortgage loans. The CBOT challenged the SEC's jurisdiction to approve trading of these instruments on the Chicago Board Options Exchange, a securities market. Laura M. Homer & Robert P. Lord, Jr., *Observations on the SEC-CFTC Accord Legislation*, 30 FED. B. NEWS & J. 335, 335 (1983). The CBOT argued that the options on Ginnie Mae certificates were not securities, and a divided panel of the Seventh Circuit agreed, finding that Ginnie Mae options were commodities and within the CFTC's exclusive authority. *Id.* at 335–36. The SEC, joined by the Federal Reserve Board as *amicus curiae*, filed a motion for rehearing *en banc*, which was denied. The SEC sought review by the Supreme Court. *Id.* at 336.

In the meantime, SEC Chairman John Shad and CFTC Chairman Philip Johnson negotiated a jurisdictional solution. Todd E. Petzel, *Derivatives: Market and Regulatory Dynamics,* 21 J. CORP. L. 95, 101 (1995). The resulting Shad-Johnson Accord, which was later codified into law by Congress in 1982, granted the CFTC jurisdiction over all futures, options on futures and commodities, and certain futures on broad stock indices and options on futures on broad stock indices, and granted the SEC jurisdiction over options on individual securities, options on certain indices of securities, and exchange-traded options on foreign currencies. *Id.*; Homer & Lord, *Observations on the SEC-CFTC Accord Legislation*, at 336. Under this scheme, responsibility for the vast majority of regulated derivatives fell under the CFTC's remit.

The accord and codifying legislation, however, did not put an end to the tension between the CFTC and the SEC. Further examples of jurisdictional battles arose in the aftermath of the stock market crash in 1987, when a review of regulation across securities and derivatives markets took place in connection with specific instruments such as index participations (cash-settled contracts that operated like futures but were traded on securities exchanges). Jerry W. Markham, *Merging the SEC and CFTC—A Clash of Cultures*, 78 U. CIN. L. REV. 537, 572–74 (2009). While some of the blame for these turf wars can undoubtedly be laid at the feet of the agencies themselves, the divide in their Congressional oversight and funding sources were also partly responsible. Having originated as an agency to regulate agricultural commodities contracts, the CFTC is overseen by the House and Senate agriculture committees, while the House financial services and Senate banking committees supervise the SEC. *See id.* at 597–98. None of the congressional committees wanted to give up any ground or compromise with the other committees on the jurisdiction of their respective agencies, perhaps because each committee believed it had the requisite expertise, thought it best represented the relevant public interests at stake, or wanted to raise campaign contributions from the financial sector.

In effect, OTC derivatives were not regulated by either agency under these arrangements. During the 1990s, the unregulated nature of the OTC market continued despite several scandals and major losses suffered by local governments and both financial and non-financial institutions. For example, Orange County, California declared bankruptcy in 1994 after it lost $1.4 billion because of its use of OTC derivatives. *See* Joseph L. Motes III, *A Primer on the Trade and Regulation of Derivative Instruments,* 49 SMU L. REV. 579, 608–10 (1996). While the Government Accountability Office (GAO) issued a report analyzing the OTC derivatives market stating that a sudden increase in OTC derivatives trading could "pose risks to . . . federally insured banks and the financial system as a whole," further deregulation continued. GAO, FINANCIAL DERIVATIVES: ACTIONS NEEDED TO PROTECT THE FINANCIAL SYSTEM (1994). Recall from Chapter 1.2 that when the CFTC, under Chairperson Brooksley Born, issued a concept release in 1998 calling for regulation of OTC derivatives, Federal Reserve Board Chairman Alan Greenspan, Treasury Secretary Robert Rubin, and SEC Chairman Arthur Levitt "took the unusual step of publicly criticizing the CFTC." FCIC, THE FINANCIAL CRISIS INQUIRY REPORT 47 (2011). They issued a joint statement denouncing potential CFTC regulation of these markets and proposed a moratorium on the CFTC's ability to regulate OTC derivatives. *Id.* Greenspan continued to resist OTC derivatives' regulation even after the Federal Reserve Bank of New York orchestrated a private sector bail-in of Long-Term Capital Management, a hedge fund that had accumulated more than $1 trillion in notional OTC derivatives exposure before failing, apparently without the full understanding of counterparties, investors, or regulators. *Id.* at 47–48.

The debate that ensued between Born and Greenspan in many ways epitomized the fights over both substance and jurisdiction that had come before. Greenspan argued that regulating privately negotiated transactions was unnecessary. He believed that most participants in the OTC derivatives market were "professionals that simply do not require the customer protections that may be needed by the general public." Born, by contrast, asserted that the alignment between CEA exemptions and large financial losses in the OTC derivatives market proved the need for stricter regulation. She warned that the misuse of derivatives could have grave financial consequences for the financial system and for "many Americans—many of us have interests in the corporations, mutual funds, pension funds, insurance companies, municipalities and other entities trading in these instruments." *Financial Derivatives Supervisory Improvement Act of 1998: Hearing on H.R. 4062 Before the H. Comm. of Banking & Fin. Servs.*, 105th Cong. (1998) (testimony of Greenspan & Born).

Despite Born's opposition, in 2000, Congress passed the Commodity Futures Modernization Act (CFMA), which largely exempted OTC swaps from both SEC and CFTC jurisdiction, as long as the swaps were entered into by "eligible contract participants," a newly created category of sophisticated market participants, which included financial institutions, investment companies, and other institutions that met the CFMA requirements. RICHARD HECKINGER ET AL., UNDERSTANDING DERIVATIVES: MARKETS & INFRASTRUCTURE 37 (2013). As a result, between passage of the CFMA and the Financial Crisis, the swap market rapidly expanded, with trillions of dollars being exchanged on a bilateral basis with little transparency or regulatory oversight in the market. FCIC, THE FINANCIAL CRISIS INQUIRY REPORT, 46–47; *see* Annette L. Nazareth & Gabriel D. Rosenberg, *The New Regulation of Swaps: A Lost Opportunity*, 55 COMP. ECON. STUD. 535, 537–38 (2013).

Greenspan later described the growth and expansion of derivatives as "the most significant event in finance" during the 2000s. When the CFMA was passed in 2000, there was $95.2 trillion in notional amount of OTC derivatives outstanding, and $3.2 trillion outstanding in gross market value. FCIC, THE FINANCIAL CRISIS INQUIRY REPORT 48 (2011). In 2007, the notional amount outstanding increased by more than 700% to $672.6 trillion, and the gross amount outstanding increased by more than 630% to $20.3 trillion. *Id.* CDSs, which even Greenspan conceded "create[d] problems" during the Financial Crisis, increased "100 fold between 2000 and 2008 . . . a significant portion [of which] was apparently speculative or naked credit default swaps." *Id.* at 49–50. *See* Figure 11.1-7.

Figure 11.1-7 Notional & Gross Value of Outstanding OTC Derivatives

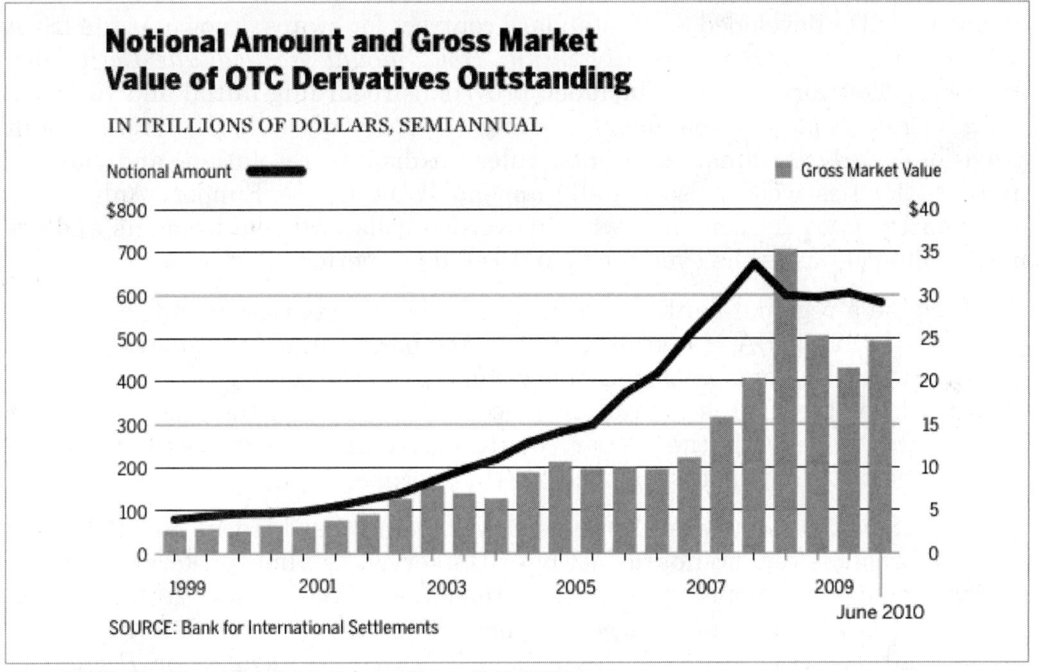

From FCIC, The Financial Crisis Inquiry Report 299 (2011).

Amendments to the Bankruptcy Code further encouraged the use of swaps. Legislation allowed the non-bankrupt counterparty in a swaps transaction to enforce *ipso facto* clauses (clauses that are unenforceable for other agreements in bankruptcy proceedings) in order to terminate the contract, seize and liquidate collateral, and settle amounts owed by closeout netting. Derivatives counterparties could therefore enjoy priority over other creditors. Richard D. Bernstein et al., *Failed Financial Institution Litigation: Remember When*, 5 N.Y.U. J.L. & BUS. 243, 274 (2009). Recall the discussion in Chapter 9.2. The FDIC can delay such actions for one business day during an FDIC receivership, but terminations were permitted thereafter (typically the Monday after a Friday receivership). These policies were designed to reduce market disruptions and cascade effects that could result from a counterparty's failure. *See generally* MICHAEL KRIMMINGER, ADJUSTING THE RULES: WHAT BANKRUPTCY REFORM WILL MEAN FOR FINANCIAL MARKET CONTRACTS 25 (2005).

C. THE PRE-FINANCIAL CRISIS OTC DERIVATIVES INFRASTRUCTURE

As OTC derivatives markets developed, differences in documentation used for similar types of instruments created a "Battle of the Forms." Therefore, broker-dealers were incentivized to work together to create standardized documentation in order to reduce transaction costs, enhance legal certainty, and promote the development of the market. John Biggins, *'Targeted Touchdown' and 'Partial Liftoff': Post-Crisis Dispute Resolution in the OTC Derivatives Markets and the Challenge for ISDA*, 13 GERMAN L.J. 1297, 1310 (2012). This process eventually resulted in the establishment of a trade association, the International Swap Dealers Association, which later changed its name to the International Swaps and Derivatives Association (ISDA), keeping its prior acronym. ISDA developed a full standard contract for swaps, known as the ISDA Master Agreement. *See generally* Duffie, *How Should We Regulate Derivatives Markets?*. This form contract included provisions regarding initial and variation margin requirements, payment netting, events of default, cross-default provisions, early termination events, rules on dispute resolution, and closeout netting. Parties would also usually append ISDA Credit Support Annexes to such master swap agreements, which governed collateral requirements and the parties' obligations in the event one party could not perform. *Id.* at 4.

Imagine a regional bank that wants to hedge its FX risk by entering into a swap. Using the ISDA Master Agreement, the bank can obtain quotes for rates from multiple dealers with the knowledge that the underlying contractual framework for the deal is already in place. The bank can then select a quote, confirm the trade with the dealer counterparty, and proceed with the swap without the need for negotiation of contractual terms.

The ISDA Master Swap Agreement was widely used, so much so, in fact, that the practices and standards set by ISDA served as almost a form of private transnational regulation created by the regulatees. *See* LITAN, at 13; *see also* Michael S. Barr, *Who's in Charge of Global Finance?*, 45 GEO. J. INT'L L. 971, 980–81 (2014). *See generally* David Zaring, *Three Challenges for Regulatory Networks*, 43 INT'L LAW. 211 (2009) (discussing other transnational regulatory networks). ISDA has developed over time to become a powerful institution, playing a key role in pushing for the deregulation of the OTC derivatives markets in the 1990s. Its critics charge it with supplanting public regulation and pushing deregulation towards the interest of large broker-dealers. *See* Biggins, at 1310–12.

That the major dealers behind ISDA created the standards that governed the OTC derivatives market perhaps explains why the Master Swap Agreement focused on counterparty needs but failed to account for negative externalities and systemic risks. As we discuss later in this Chapter, the failure of this transnational private regulatory system contributed significantly to the Financial Crisis. For example, the ISDA Master Agreement did not account for the massive novation that occurred, which posed significant risks to the financial system. Netting only worked bilaterally and between the original counterparties. If a counterparty novated its position in a CDS, the parties would owe the gross amounts due under the contract, not just the netted figure. If unable to net, parties had to post more collateral. Further, the structure disincentivized reducing this exposure, as a party would have to pay an unwind fee to close out its position in a swap contract. Unable to multilaterally net and unwind positions, counterparty risk increased as firms became increasingly interdependent. After novation, performance under the agreement would depend on the gross value of the swap between at least *two* parties, rather than just the net amount. This increased collateral and default exposure for firms. This problem became particularly acute among dealers. *See* Duffie, *How Should We Regulate Derivatives Markets?*. We discussed regulatory intervention in ISDA cross-defaults in Chapter 9.3.

Dealers had little incentive to move trading onto exchanges or to increase transparency. Dealers profited on spreads as market makers, so the lack of price transparency in the swaps market allowed dealers to keep spreads high, increasing their profits. LITAN, at 28. Opacity created inefficiencies in the market because end users received less information about the price of instruments than they would have received in an exchange traded market, permitting dealers to profit on the inefficiency. *Id.* at 28–29; *see also* Duffie, *How Should We Regulate Derivatives Markets?*, at 14. While ISDA privately regulated the OTC derivatives market through standard setting, its interests were not aligned with end users.

Swaps enabled firms to engage in regulatory arbitrage. Because a swap is an off-balance-sheet agreement, it could provide many regulatory and accounting benefits to its users. For example, derivative trades known as negative basis trades would allow a firm to move an item with a large capital charge off of its balance sheet where it would receive a low, if any, capital charge even though the off-balance sheet item was functionally similar to (if not the same as) the on-balance sheet item. This would allow the firm to become more highly leveraged, circumventing regulation designed to provide for its safety and soundness. *See* WILLIAM W. BRATTON, CORPORATE FINANCE 394 (7th ed., 2012). Just as a firm could use a swap to adjust the legal character of its assets to avoid regulatory requirements, swaps could enable a firm to shift and move revenue streams and expenses in order to reduce taxation. *See generally* Michael Patrick Donohoe, *Financial Derivatives in Corporate Tax Avoidance: A Conceptual Perspective*, J. ACCT. & ECON. (forthcoming). Swaps were also used for accounting arbitrage. Because swaps are off-balance sheet transactions, swaps can help a firm make its financial statements appear better than its balance sheet would suggest. This window dressing played a role in various large financial firms, including Lehman Brothers, by making them appear healthier than they would appear if they had not performed these transactions. FCIC, THE FINANCIAL CRISIS INQUIRY REPORT 230 (2011).

The massive growth in derivatives in the years leading up to the Financial Crisis involved incredible innovation. Regulators did not keep up with innovations in the OTC derivatives market, making it difficult to understand the risks associated with the products they were charged with regulating. Market participants also had difficulty keeping up with the growth and innovation in derivative products, which made it difficult for them to understand the risk they had assumed. *Id.* at 51. When things started to unravel in 2007, derivatives' complexity and the interdependence they fostered created major problems.

IV. OTC DERIVATIVES AND THE FINANCIAL CRISIS

A. THE ROLE OF DERIVATIVES IN THE FINANCIAL CRISIS

It is widely acknowledged that, as instruments intended to spread risks throughout the financial markets, OTC derivatives exacerbated the Financial Crisis. *See, e.g.*, FCIC, FINANCIAL CRISIS INQUIRY REPORT 352 (2011); *see also The Role of Derivatives in the Financial Crisis: Hearing Before the Fin. Crisis Inquiry Comm'n*, 111th Cong. 18 (2010) (testimony of Michael Greenberger, Professor, Univ. of Maryland School of Law). For example, in 2008 AIG suffered enormous losses due to its derivatives activities. AIG entered into a huge number of CDS contracts, but rather than entering into CDSs on both sides of the market, AIG only sold CDSs. AIG was on the hook to pay its counterparties if the assets underlying CDSs defaulted, which led to reductions in its credit ratings, requiring it to post even more collateral, which further exacerbated its liquidity needs and credit ratings. *But see* Hal S. Scott, *The Reduction of Systemic Risk in the United States Financial System,* 33 HARV. J.L. & PUB. POL'Y 671 (2010) (arguing that AIG's failure was not systemic).

Before the Financial Crisis, most swaps were traded off-exchange, with little pre- or post-trade price transparency for market participants. Price opacity created inefficiencies in the market because end users and other participants received less information about the price of instruments than they would have received in an exchange-traded market with transparent reporting. The opacity of the pre-Financial Crisis OTC derivatives markets also increased complexity and made it difficult for market participants and regulators to understand the risks in the system and how concentrated those risks had become. LITAN, at 17. As the Financial Crisis unfolded, the lack of data available to regulators drastically stunted their ability to respond. *See* FCIC, FINANCIAL CRISIS INQUIRY REPORT 329 (2011); *see also* Michael S. Barr, *The Financial Crisis and the Path of Reform*, 29 YALE J. ON REG. 91, 103 (2012).

Derivatives caused the largest financial firms to become more interconnected, increasing the risk of contagion. The top five broker-dealers traded 97% of the world's OTC derivatives exposure. FCIC, FINANCIAL CRISIS INQUIRY REPORT 50 (2011). *See* Chapter 9.3 for more discussion on interconnectedness risk. To the extent that counterparties relied on the available means to reduce counterparty risk, such as by requiring a counterparty to post additional collateral for its derivatives as the counterparty's position became more exposed, or as the counterparty's own credit profile weakened, as in the AIG example described above, the counterparty was itself further weakened, and the individual measures to protect individual firms ended up weakening the financial system as a whole. *See id. See generally* Erik F. Gerding, *Credit Derivatives, Leverage, and Financial Regulation's Missing Macroeconomic Dimension*, 8 BERKELEY BUS. L.J. 29 (2011) (describing macroeconomic concerns arising from the use of credit derivatives).

In sum, an opaque web of bilateral OTC derivatives trading was concentrated among the top dealers, who were interconnected to each other. Margin and collateral practices proved weak. Firms, most prominently AIG, sold CDSs with inadequate capital or liquidity to back the trades. Novation undermined the ability to net trades, increasing counterparty risk. Client margin was commingled with dealer assets, exposing end users to dealer risk. Large firms believed that they had reduced their exposure to the mortgage markets or other large firms by using derivatives, but they instead exposed themselves to the risk that their counterparties would fail, and these counterparties were exposed to the same market risks.

B. SUMMARY OF DERIVATIVES REGULATION IN THE DODD-FRANK ACT

1. Overview of Dodd-Frank Act Derivatives Reforms

The Treasury Department called for fundamental reform of derivatives markets to bring transparency to OTC derivatives, to reduce risk, and to promote market integrity. *See* DEP'T OF THE TREASURY, A NEW FOUNDATION: REBUILDING FINANCIAL SUPERVISION AND REGULATION 46–51 (2009); *see also* Michael S. Barr, *The Financial Crisis and the Path of Reform*, 29 YALE J. ON REG. 91, 103–05 (2012). The Dodd-Frank Act closely follows the Treasury's suggested legislative reforms, amending existing law, including the CEA and the federal securities and banking laws, to establish a comprehensive new regulatory framework for swaps. This section outlines the key elements of that framework; Chapters 11.2 and 11.3 explore aspects of them in greater detail.

Title VII of the Dodd-Frank Act was designed to promote four principal objectives: transparency of pricing and trading of derivatives; reduced systemic risk through the use of clearinghouses, as well as capital and margin rules; business conduct regulation of dealers and market participants; and oversight of trading and clearing facilities.

First, Title VII subjects standardized swaps to mandatory clearing and exchange trading. Dodd-Frank Act § 723(a)(3). The Act makes it illegal for a party to trade a swap "unless that person submits such swap for clearing to a derivatives clearing organization . . . if the swap is required to be cleared," subject to an exception for commercial end users. *Id.* The Act requires the SEC and CFTC to regularly review swaps to determine whether they are "required to be cleared." *Id.* This can happen *sua sponte*, or on submissions from clearinghouses. *Id.* Swaps that are required to be cleared must be traded either on a DCM or on a swap execution facility (SEF), unless no DCM or SEF makes the swap "available to trade" or if an end-user exception applies. *Id.*; *see also* Core Principles and Other Requirements for Designated Contract Markets, 77 Fed. Reg. 36,612, 36,613 (June 19, 2012). As not all swaps are required to be cleared, the Dodd-Frank Act provides an incentive for further central clearing, by subjecting non-cleared swaps to higher capital and margin requirements than cleared swaps. Dodd-Frank Act § 731. Basel III also changed capital requirements for derivatives to incentivize central clearing by requiring more capital to be held against non-centrally cleared swaps. *See* BASEL COMM., BASEL III: A GLOBAL REGULATORY FRAMEWORK FOR MORE RESILIENT BANKS & BANKING SYSTEMS 3, 8, 30–31, 34, 44 (2010).

Second, Title VII imposes reporting requirements on swaps trading. The Dodd-Frank Act requires that all swaps, both cleared and non-cleared, be reported to a data repository. Dodd-Frank Act §§ 721(a)(48), 727, 729. This will give regulators the ability to monitor the market in real time, giving insight as to where risk lies in the system no matter where derivatives are traded.

Third, Title VII subjects both clearinghouses and exchanges to extensive regulatory requirements, based on certain core principles. For example, clearinghouses must maintain sufficient resources to meet financial obligations and to cover operating costs for at least one year. *Id.* at § 725(c); 17 C.F.R. § 39.11. Clearinghouses must also have a chief risk officer, impose margin requirements, and are subject to stress tests. *See* 17 C.F.R. § 39.13. Clearinghouses must also regulate their members by establishing and maintaining eligibility standards for members, *id.* at § 39.12, reviewing their risk management practices, *id.* at § 39.13, establishing daily settlement procedures, *id.* at § 39.14, and establishing default procedures. *Id.* at § 39.16.

Fourth, along with regulating the derivatives market infrastructure, the Dodd-Frank Act also regulates the players in the market under Title VII. Swap dealers and major swap participants are subject to supervision by the CFTC and the SEC, as well as business conduct, capital, margin, and other requirements. Dodd-Frank Act § 731.

Title VIII of the Dodd-Frank Act further strengthens the regulatory regime relating to risk management standards for certain financial market utilities (FMUs) and financial institutions that conduct or support multilateral payment, clearing, or settlement activities, when those utilities or activities are designated as systemically important. Title VIII requires the Financial Stability Oversight Council (FSOC) to designate systemically important FMUs. The Federal Reserve Board has the authority to adopt risk management standards for systemically important FMUs. *Id.* at § 805(a)(1). For systemically important derivatives clearing organizations (SIDCOs), the CFTC and SEC, in consultation with the FSOC and the Federal Reserve Board, may issue risk management standards. *Id.* at § 805(a)(2). The FSOC can force the SEC and CFTC to impose higher standards if the FSOC finds existing standards insufficient. *Id.* Of the eight FMUs that FSOC has designated as systemically important, three are SIDCOs. BD. OF GOVERNORS OF THE FED. RES. SYS., DESIGNATED FINANCIAL MARKET UTILITIES (2015).

Figure 11.1-8 Diagram of Players in the Derivatives Market

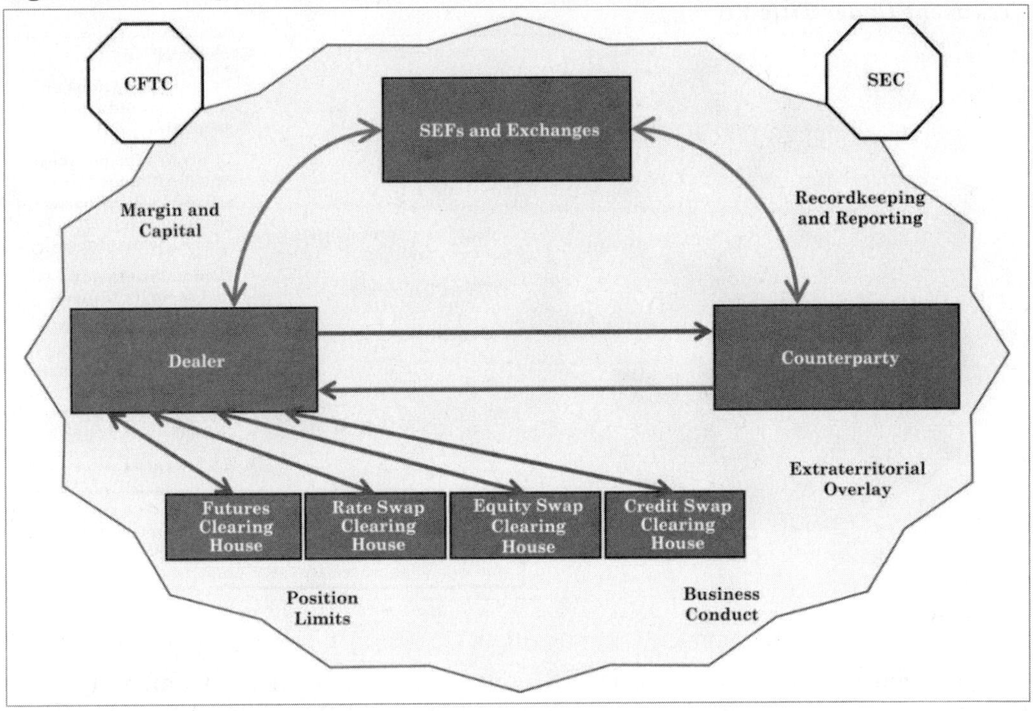

CFTC
SEC
SEFs and Exchanges
Margin and Capital
Recordkeeping and Reporting
Dealer
Counterparty
Extraterritorial Overlay
Futures Clearing House
Rate Swap Clearing House
Equity Swap Clearing House
Credit Swap Clearing House
Position Limits
Business Conduct

Source: Davis Polk & Wardwell LLP.

2. Jurisdiction Over Derivatives Markets Post-Dodd-Frank Act

Notwithstanding the lessons of the turf wars of the 1980s and 1990s, congressional and agency turf battles prevailed, and Title VII perpetuates the split in jurisdiction between the CFTC and the SEC. *See* Figure 11.1-9. The CFTC regulates swaps, which comprise the vast majority of the swap and security-based swap market. Swaps generally include interest rate swaps, options, CDSs, swaps based on broad indices of securities (generally more than nine securities), swaps on government securities, certain non-deliverable forwards, including FX forwards that are non-deliverable, any instrument that combines these, and any other instrument "that is or becomes commonly known as a swap." Further Definition of "Swap," "Security-Based Swap," and "Security-Based Swap Agreement"; Mixed Swaps; Security-Based Swap Agreement Recordkeeping, 77 Fed. Reg. 48,207–48,208 (Aug. 13, 2012).

Figure 11.1-9 Diagram of the Various Types of Derivatives and Their Regulatory Treatment Under Title VII

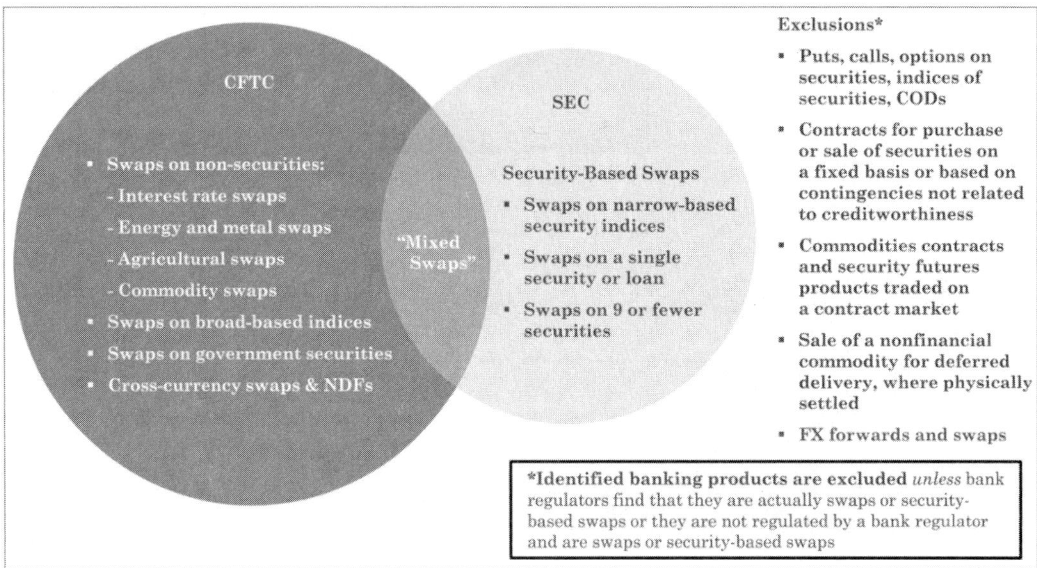

Source: Davis Polk & Wardwell LLP.

A dispute arose over certain FX contracts, which CFTC Chairman Gary Gensler argued should be regulated by the CFTC and the Federal Reserve Bank of New York argued should be outside that framework. *See* Letter from Gary Gensler, CFTC Chairman, to Sens. Tom Harkin & Saxby Chambliss, (Aug. 17, 2009). While deliverable FX forwards and FX swaps were included in the definition of a swap, the Dodd-Frank Act provided that the Secretary of the Treasury could exclude these FX contracts from the definition of swap, if the Treasury determined that deliverable FX swaps and FX forwards "(i) should not be regulated as swaps under the [CEA]; and (ii) are not structured to evade the [Dodd-Frank Act] in violation of any rule promulgated by the [CFTC]." Dodd-Frank Act § 721. The Secretary of the Treasury made such a finding in November 2012, in part because such contracts are generally structured differently from other swaps, are settled through Continuous Linked Settlement Bank, which is supervised by the Federal Reserve Bank of New York, and may be otherwise regulated under Title VIII of Dodd-Frank. Determination of FX Swaps and FX Forwards under the CEA, 77 Fed. Reg. 69,694 (Nov. 16, 2012). *But see* Darrell Duffie, *Replumbing Our Financial System: Uneven Progress*, 9 INT'L J. CENT. BANKING 251 (2013) (arguing that FX should be centrally cleared). *See* Figure 11.1-10.

Figure 11.1-10 Diagram of FX Products Under Title VII

	Product Classification	**Title VII Treatment**
Spot FX	Not a swap	Title VII requirements do not apply
Deliverable FX swap / forward	Not a swap	Limited Title VII requirements apply
Non-deliverable forward / FX options	Swap	All Title VII requirements apply

The SEC regulates "security-based swaps," which are swaps based on a single security or loan, narrow-based security indices, or nine or fewer securities. Dodd-Frank Act § 712. The CFTC and the SEC share jurisdiction over mixed swaps, which are derivatives that materially refer to both swap and security-based swap reference entities. Title VII requires the CFTC and the SEC to "consult and coordinate" with one another in issuing rules. *Id.* The mandated coordination reflects the need to overcome the turf wars between the agencies; however, tensions remain between the CFTC and the SEC over the authority to regulate derivatives. Christopher L. Culp, *OTC-Cleared Derivatives: Benefits, Costs, and Implications of the "Dodd-Frank Wall Street Reform and Consumer Protection Act,"* 2 J. APPLIED FIN. 1, 5 (2010).

C. A COORDINATED INTERNATIONAL RESPONSE

The derivatives market grew exponentially and globally over the last 20 years. Large banks developed trading books that would "follow the sun" and could enter into transactions with clients anywhere in the world. The Financial Crisis made it clear that the markets of the world are interconnected. Former SEC Chairman Elisse Walter noted that, "[t]oday, cross-border derivatives transactions are the norm not the exception." Elisse Walter, Chairman, SEC, Regulation of Cross-Border OTC Derivatives Activities: Finding the Middle Ground (Apr. 6, 2013). Figure 11.1-11 illustrates the global volume of CDS transactions based on the location of the counterparty.

Figure 11.1-11 CDS Transactions by Domicile

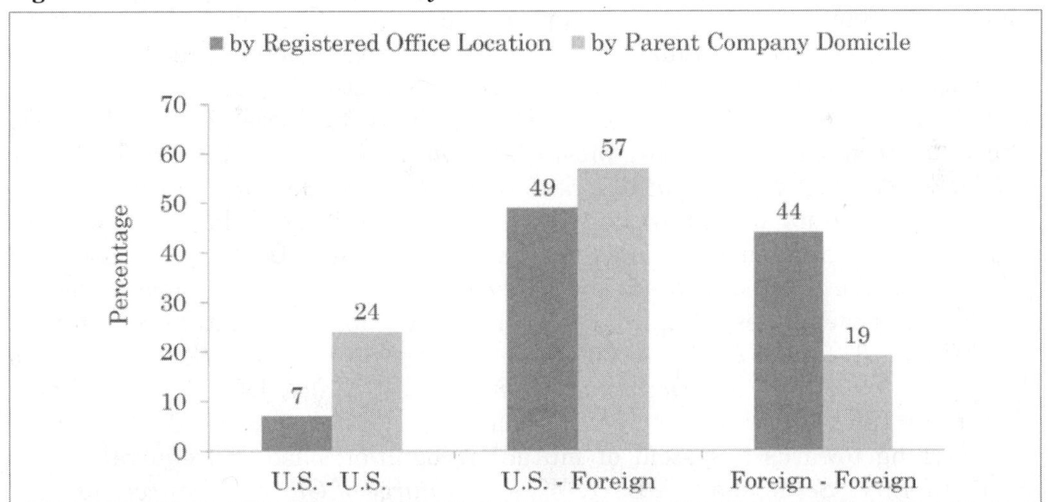

Source: Cross-Border Security-Based Swap Activities; Re-Proposal of Regulation SBSR and Certain Rules and Forms Relating to the Registration of Security-Based Swap Dealers and Major Security-Based Swap Participants, 78 Fed. Reg. 30968, 30976 (May 23, 2013).

As a result of the Financial Crisis, it was clear that a coordinated response would be necessary, not only to increase stability, but to prevent a race to the bottom through regulatory arbitrage. The absence of an internationally coordinated response could allow regulatory evasion that could threaten U.S. and global financial stability. Christian Johnson, *Regulatory Arbitrage, Extraterritorial Jurisdiction, and Dodd-Frank: The Implications of U.S. Global OTC Derivative Regulation*, 14 NEV. L.J. 542 (2014).

While the United States was first out of the gate in regulating derivatives, the Financial Crisis motivated other jurisdictions to act. In 2009, the G-20 heads of state came together and jointly committed to reducing systemic risk by clearing standardized products, facilitating pre- and post-trade transparency through reporting, and increasing capital requirements for non-centrally cleared derivatives. G-20, LEADERS' STATEMENT: THE PITTSBURGH SUMMIT (2009). In 2011, the leaders agreed to add a collateral requirement for uncleared derivatives. We will discuss the cornerstones of the G20 commitment—namely clearing, trading, reporting, and margin requirements—in Chapter 11.2. The G-20 also called for International Monetary Fund surveillance of cross-border activity.

Other key international institutions and groups that have developed include the FSB, the Basel Committee, and the OTC Derivatives Regulators Group. The FSB was established in 2009 to promote stability in the international financial system by bringing together national authorities responsible for financial regulation. The Basel Committee sets supervisory standards for international banking. The OTC Derivatives Regulators Group includes regulatory authorities with responsibility for regulation of OTC derivatives markets and aims to promote consistent policy objectives and coordinate information sharing.

Heterogeneous legal frameworks make implementation of global standards a challenge. The main international policy summits have also struggled to include the voices of developing countries, despite the fact that large-scale economic decisions are being made. Relationships between regulators across borders have long been a source of tension. One approach of cross-border regulation is to have individual jurisdictions implement parallel regulations, allowing each jurisdiction to take into account individualized structural nuances. Regulating OTC derivatives through a parallel framework, however, increases the likelihood of conflict or gaps. *See* Fariborz Moshirian, *The Global Financial Crisis and the Evolution of Markets, Institutions and Regulation*, 35 J. BANKING & FIN. 502 (2011). Regulatory harmonization between countries can help to avoid these problems, but harmonization has its own challenges. Despite the potential challenges, the United States and Europe have taken significant steps in harmonizing their rules. A third approach involves forms of mutual recognition. *See* Ethiopis Tafara & Robert J. Peterson, *A Blueprint for Cross-Border Access to U.S. Investors: A New International Framework*, 48 HARV. INT'L L.J. 31 (2007). Relying on the conceptual principle of home country deference, the CFTC and EU are working towards a system of mutual recognition based on equivalence or comparability. *See* Michael S. Barr, *Who's in Charge of Global Finance?,* 45 GEO. J. INT'L L. 971 (2014).

CHAPTER 11.2

DERIVATIVES: MARKET INFRASTRUCTURE

CONTENTS

I. INTRODUCTION

In Chapter 11.1, we introduced you to various types of derivatives, the parties that trade them, and the reasons they do so. We also introduced you to the role derivatives played in the Financial Crisis and provided a brief overview of the changes brought about by the Dodd-Frank Act in the United States, as well as the coordinated global response. Recall that increasing transparency in the derivatives markets and reducing systemic risk through the use of clearinghouses and capital and margin rules were two of the primary objectives of these reform efforts. *See* DEP'T OF THE TREASURY, A NEW FOUNDATION: REBUILDING FINANCIAL SUPERVISION AND REGULATION 44 (2009). In this Chapter, we delve into greater detail on these aspects of the Dodd-Frank Act's derivatives reforms. We first explore the Dodd-Frank Act's changes to reduce systemic risk through margin and clearing requirements, and then turn to market transparency. We focus on the CFTC's implementation of the Dodd-Frank Act's derivatives reforms, with occasional references to the SEC's approach where important differences or similarities explain a broader theme.

II. MITIGATING CREDIT RISK: MARGIN AND CLEARING

A bilateral over-the-counter (OTC) transaction is an off-exchange transaction between two parties. The two parties negotiate price, quantity, and other relevant terms. In a traditional bilateral swap transaction, depicted in Figure 11.2-1, each counterparty faces two risks. First, market risk is the risk associated with changes in the value of the swap based on changes in the value of the underlying asset. Second, credit risk is the risk that, if the market moves in one party's favor and its counterparty owes amounts under the swap, the counterparty will be unable or unwilling to pay.

Figure 11.2-1 Bilateral Swap Transaction.

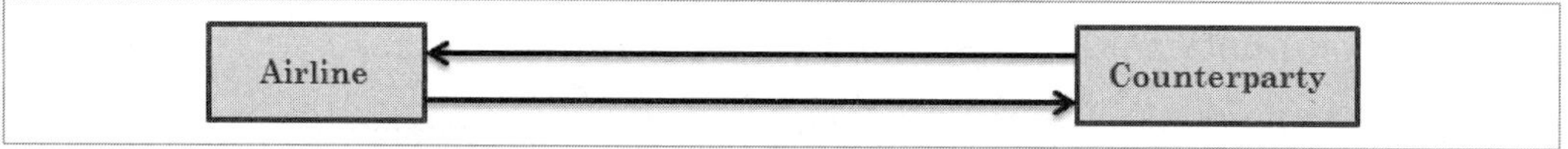

In the jet fuel swap in Chapter 11.1, Airline pays its counterparty if the price of jet fuel goes down and the counterparty pays Airline if the price of jet fuel goes up. In this swap, Airline faces the market risk that the price of jet fuel decreases, and the counterparty faces the market risk that the price of jet fuel increases. If the price of jet fuel goes down, and Airline owes money to its counterparty, it is possible that Airline defaults on its obligation, which is its counterparty's credit risk to Airline. Conversely, if the price of jet fuel goes up, and the counterparty owes money to Airline, the counterparty may nevertheless default. That is Airline's credit risk to the counterparty.

As we discussed in Chapter 11.1, counterparties generally enter into derivatives, including swaps, to gain exposure to, or to hedge, the risk of an underlying asset, which means that they enter into derivatives seeking exposure to market risk, not credit risk. Counterparty credit risk is a harmful byproduct for individual counterparties to a trade. It is also potentially dangerous for the market as a whole. Credit risk increases systemic risk because a default by a significant institution could lead to a domino effect among interrelated market participants, as occurred when Lehman Brothers failed.

Swap market participants may screen their counterparty's credit rating or other indicia of creditworthiness in an effort to minimize counterparty credit risk. In addition, the swap market has developed two primary methods to mitigate counterparty credit risk: the exchange of margin and the central clearing of swaps. Congress made these two methodologies central pillars of the Dodd-Frank Act's swap regulatory system. Margin mitigates credit risk by serving as a buffer to cover potential losses in the case of default (initial margin) and regularly reducing the outstanding exposure under the swap (variation margin). Clearing places a third-party—a central counterparty (CCP) or clearinghouse—between the parties to serve as a well-regulated guarantor of the payments due to each party to the swap, which reduces the likelihood that a default by one institution would affect the market as a whole.

A. INITIAL AND VARIATION MARGIN

Collateral that is posted or collected to protect a counterparty from credit risk is referred to as margin. There are two types of margin: initial margin and variation margin.

1. Initial Margin

Initial margin is collateral posted from one counterparty to a swap to the other counterparty to reflect an estimate of the potential future exposure that the posting counterparty may have to the collecting counterparty. Initial margin is posted at the outset of a transaction as a performance bond to guarantee the posting party's ability to pay amounts owed under the swap. In general, initial margin is designed to serve as a buffer from which the non-defaulting party can be paid amounts that are owed during the swap's close-out period—the time between the counterparty's default and when its swaps can be unwound. To continue our interest rate swap example from Chapter 11.1 between Bank and Swap Dealer (which was entered into to hedge the interest rate risk from the loan Bank made to Airline), Bank and Swap Dealer may agree to exchange an initial amount of collateral to guarantee the respective counterparty's ability to pay future amounts owed should either Bank or Swap Dealer default, as depicted in Figure 11.2-2.

Figure 11.2-2 Exchange of Initial Margin

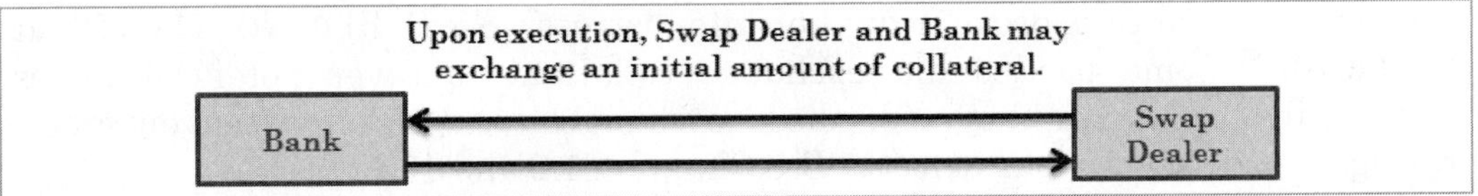

2. Variation Margin

Variation margin is collateral posted from one counterparty to the other to reflect the current exposure that the posting counterparty has to the collecting counterparty. Recall from Chapter 11.1 that a swap is a zero-sum contract. As the market value of the swap changes, its value increases to one counterparty and decreases to the other counterparty. Variation margin is meant to cover a change in the value of a swap over a particular period of time. To continue our interest rate swap example, if the interest rate goes down one day (N) such that the contract is worth $1 more today to Swap Dealer than yesterday, Bank would pay $1 to Swap Dealer to get the value of the swap back to zero. By getting the value of the swap back to zero, Swap Dealer reduces its exposure to Bank's credit risk. Unlike initial margin, which protects in the case that credit risk materializes (*i.e.*, when a counterparty defaults), variation margin decreases Swap Dealer's exposure to Bank's credit risk by bringing the swap's value back to zero during the life of the swap. As you can see in Figure 11.2-3, variation margin can flow both ways, depending on the direction and size of the changes in the swap's market value.

Figure 11.2-3 Exchange of Variation Margin

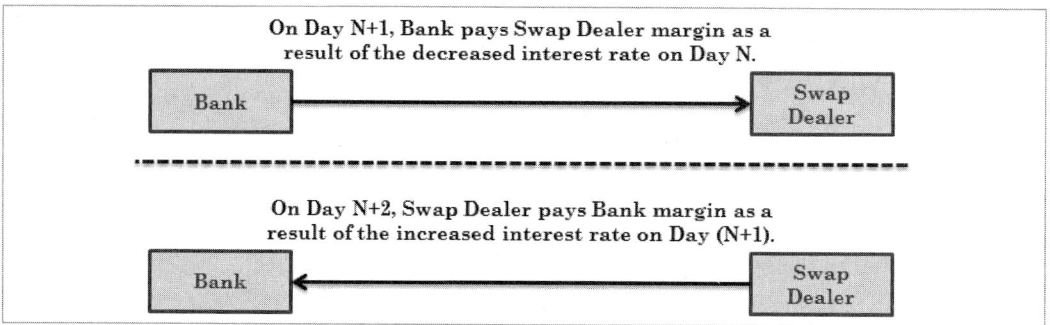

B. USE OF MARGIN FOR SWAPS BEFORE THE DODD-FRANK ACT

Before the Dodd-Frank Act, swap counterparties decided on their own, as a matter of contract, whether to exchange margin. Many market participants chose not to collect margin, viewing their counterparties as safe credits for which no protection was needed. For example, AIG had a high credit rating. As a result, parties facing one of AIG's subsidiaries, AIG Financial Products, required little to no collateral to be posted by AIG Financial Products for swaps, until it was too late. If more information had been available to the market, counterparties may have requested more collateral from AIG Financial Products, and it would have had to post more collateral to cover potential losses, or would not have entered into such positions in the first place. Of course, at the height of the Financial Crisis, AIG's counterparties did demand more collateral, but by then it had disastrous consequences, as AIG was already weakened and the further collateral calls drove it further into distress. *See* S. REP. NO. 111-176, at 30 (2010). Some parties did exchange collateral to cover potential losses voluntarily, but when they did, these exchanges were often based on credit ratings, which had serious defects. *See* Chapters 1.2 and 12.1.

C. THE DODD-FRANK ACT'S MARGIN REQUIREMENTS FOR UNCLEARED SWAPS

In order to mitigate counterparty credit risk and its systemic impact, the Dodd-Frank Act required that the CFTC, SEC, and the banking regulators adopt margin requirements for uncleared swaps. As of December 31, 2015, the CFTC and the banking regulators had finalized their margin rules, while the SEC had proposed, but not yet finalized, margin rules that differ in some respects from the CFTC's and banking regulators' approach. In general, the agencies' margin rules directly apply to swap dealers (SDs) and security-based swap dealers (SBSDs), requiring those regulated market participants to collect and post margin for swaps and security-based swaps. Counterparties of SDs and SBSDs are indirectly affected by these requirements. Given the outcome of the turf wars discussed in Chapter 11.1, the specific margin rules an entity is subject to depends on which regulator's purview the entity falls under.

The U.S. margin rules focus on mitigating credit risk and apply different requirements depending on the estimated credit risk of the counterparty that the dealer is facing. The amount of initial margin to be posted or collected is calculated through use of either a model or a standardized table mandated by the regulators. If calculated by a model, the amount of initial margin is required to be sufficient to cover credit risk over a hypothetical ten-day close-out period, with a statistical confidence level of 99%.

To increase the probability that the swap counterparty receiving the collateral can easily liquidate it—turn it into cash—if needed, the margin rules restrict the types of collateral that may be used to satisfy the margin requirements. Eligible collateral is limited to high-quality liquid assets, such as cash and liquid securities, which generally allow for easy valuation and transfer in the event of a default or termination. For collateral that is not cash, a haircut, which is a percentage deduction from the market value of the collateral, may be applied. Haircuts are used to protect against the possibility that the value of non-cash collateral may decline following a counterparty's default. For example, a U.S. Treasury bill with a maturity between one and five years, valued at $1,000, is subject to a 2% haircut, meaning that it would only satisfy a margin requirement of $980. Equities included in the S&P 500 index are subject to a 15% haircut, which reflects the increased risk of these instruments as compared to the Treasury bill. The margin rules provide a schedule of haircuts to be applied to various types of eligible collateral.

To further protect the collateral, initial margin must be held by one or more custodians unaffiliated with the SD or SBSD and its counterparty. A custodian is an unaffiliated third-party that holds the collateral for safekeeping in order to minimize the risk of the theft or loss of collateral. The largest custodian banks are Bank of New York Mellon, State Street Bank and Trust Company, JPMorgan Chase, and Citigroup. The custodian is prohibited from re-investing or using this collateral as collateral for other transactions, known as rehypothecation. ISDA, STANDARD INITIAL MARGIN MODEL FOR NON-CLEARED DERIVATIVES (2013).

The margin rules also include a complicated framework for inter-affiliate transactions and for application to cross-border transactions. For inter-affiliate transactions, special margin rules apply that waive the initial margin requirements under certain circumstances. For cross-border transactions, some exemptions are provided for foreign banks, but not their U.S. branches, although these exemptions are subject to many limitations. *See, e.g.*, Margin and Capital Requirements for Covered Swap Entities (Regulation KK), 12 C.F.R. Part 237 (2015).

To increase global coordination for the implementation of margin requirements and to limit regulatory arbitrage, the G-20 leaders agreed that counterparties to uncleared swaps should be required to post collateral to their counterparties in the form of initial margin and variation margin. Pursuant to that G-20 commitment, the Basel Committee and the International Organization of Securities Commissions (IOSCO) issued a joint framework that established common principles and guidance for the implementation of the G-20 commitments for margin requirements for uncleared derivatives. *See* BASEL COMM. & IOSCO, MARGIN REQUIREMENTS FOR NON-CENTRALLY CLEARED DERIVATIVES (2013). U.S. regulators were involved in the creation of this framework. The CFTC's and banking regulators' rules are largely consistent with the international framework and how European and other regulators are implementing that framework. The SEC's proposed rules differ from the framework in some respects. We will discuss international implementation of margin rules later in this Chapter.

D. CENTRAL CLEARING

1. What Does it Mean to Clear a Derivative?

In addition to the exchange of margin, the Dodd-Frank Act mandated a second method to reduce systemic risk: the clearing of certain standardized swaps and security-based swaps. Central clearing addresses counterparty credit risk (not market risk) by placing a clearinghouse, or CCP, between the two original swap counterparties. When a swap is submitted for clearing, credit risk is diminished by replacing the trade between the counterparties with two subsequent trades, one between the first counterparty and the clearinghouse and another between the second counterparty and the clearinghouse. Rather than face the credit risk of its original counterparty, each party faces the credit risk of the clearinghouse, which, for reasons described below, is generally better situated to absorb credit risk. Jean S. Chin & David T. McIndoe, *Mandatory Clearing*, *in* OTC DERIVATIVES REGULATION UNDER DODD-FRANK: A GUIDE TO REGISTRATION, REPORTING, BUSINESS CONDUCT, AND CLEARING 335, 337 (William C. Meehan & Gabriel D. Rosenberg eds., 2015). *See* Figure 11.2-4.

Figure 11.2-4 The Use of a Clearinghouse to Clear Swaps

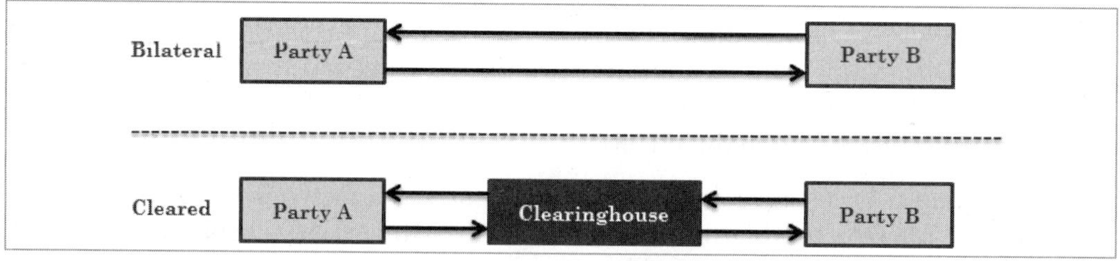

For example, if Airline and Swap Dealer enter into a jet fuel swap so that Airline can hedge against the change in jet fuel, and the counterparties clear the swap at Clearinghouse, Clearinghouse steps in between Airline and Swap Dealer. Once the swap is cleared by Clearinghouse, Airline and Swap Dealer no longer have a relationship with each other, regardless of the change in price of oil. If the price of jet fuel goes up, Airline no longer needs to worry about Swap

Dealer defaulting, because the payments are due to Airline from Clearinghouse, not Swap Dealer. Airline may prefer that its credit risk is to Clearinghouse rather than Swap Dealer because Clearinghouse is highly regulated and uses a number of risk-mitigating tools, described later in this Chapter.

A clearinghouse only accepts swaps for clearing from its members, known as clearing members. To ensure that the clearinghouse can discharge its duties, clearing members must meet significant capital, risk management, and other requirements. As a result, clearing members are typically large financial institutions. A market participant that is not a clearing member of a particular clearinghouse can only access that clearinghouse through an arrangement with a clearing member. Clearing members, in effect, guarantee performance of the party for whom they are submitting the swap for clearing, while the clearinghouse, in effect, guarantees performance of the clearing members. *See* Figure 11.2-5.

Figure 11.2-5 A More Detailed Look at Clearing Relationships

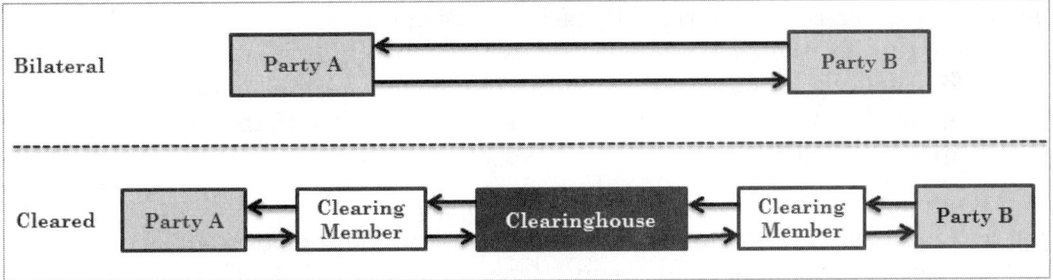

2. How Do Clearinghouses Mitigate Systemic Risk?

The primary function of central clearing is to transfer each counterparty's credit risk exposure to a clearinghouse that stands between the parties and effectively guarantees the obligations of each party. Julia Lees Allen, *Derivatives Clearinghouses and Systemic Risk: A Bankruptcy and Dodd-Frank Analysis*, 64 STAN. L. REV. 1079, 1085 (2012). How does this transfer of credit risk decrease counterparty risk and systemic risk? Just as prudential regulators require minimum bank capital to help ensure safety and soundness, the CFTC requires a clearinghouse that clears swaps to hold enough financial resources that the clearinghouse can "meet its financial obligations to its clearing members notwithstanding a default by the clearing member creating the largest financial exposure for the [clearinghouse] in extreme but plausible market conditions." 17 C.F.R. § 39.11(a). In addition, the clearinghouse must have enough financial resources to cover its operating costs for at least one year, which is calculated on a rolling basis. *Id.* Clearinghouses can use a variety of financial resources to satisfy this requirement. *See id.* at § 39.11(b). These sources include initial and variation margin, a guaranty fund containing deposits collected from clearinghouse members, and other capital contributions from members or the clearinghouse itself (in each case turning to the defaulting member's contributions in the first instance, before the contributions of non-defaulting members). *See* Darrell Duffie et al., *Policy Perspectives on OTC Derivatives Market Infrastructure* 24 (Fed. Reserve Bank of N.Y. Staff Report No. 424, 2010).

We examine these types of buffers in turn, and we then discuss the additional systemic risk reduction achieved through multilateral netting and portability.

a. Initial and Variation Margin for Cleared Swaps

In order to accept a swap or security-based swap for clearing, the clearinghouse requires that the clearing members submitting the swap post collateral in the form of initial margin and variation margin. If the swap counterparty is not a clearing member, the counterparty will generally post the margin to the clearing member, and the clearing member will pass it on to the clearinghouse. Initial margin protects the clearinghouse in the event of counterparty default. Initial margin generally remains on deposit with the clearinghouse throughout the life of the cleared swap unless a counterparty defaults. In addition, clearinghouses require counterparties to post variation margin daily to cover movements in the value of the swap. Since a clearinghouse is always on both sides of a swap, every dollar in variation margin it collects daily from a counterparty to a cleared swap will be owed, and therefore passed on, to the other counterparty. By serving as the conduit for the exchange of variation margin, the clearinghouse helps to ensure that, if a counterparty to a swap does default, the amount owed at that moment represents the change in the value of the swap over a short period of time, rather than from inception of the swap.

If properly calculated and calibrated, margin is a powerful risk mitigant. For example, when Lehman Brothers collapsed in September 2008, many of its derivatives transactions had been cleared through LCH.Clearnet, Ltd., a European clearinghouse. When Lehman Brothers defaulted on its obligations to the clearinghouse, LCH.Clearnet was successfully able to wind down Lehman Brothers's positions using the funds that Lehman Brothers had posted as initial margin to the clearinghouse. By some estimates, LCH.Clearnet only needed to use one-third of the initial margin that Lehman Brothers had posted in order to wind down these transactions. Natasha De Terán, *How LCH.Clearnet got clear of Lehman*, WALL ST. J. EUR., Oct. 14, 2008.

b. Clearinghouse Guaranty Fund and Assessments

If the initial margin and variation margin posted by the defaulting counterparty is not sufficient to meet that counterparty's obligations to the clearinghouse, the clearinghouse may access a guaranty fund to cover the excess. All members are required to contribute to the guaranty fund. Essentially, the guaranty fund serves as a mechanism for the clearinghouse to spread, or mutualize, losses. If the guaranty fund is insufficient to absorb losses, the clearinghouse may be able to make limited assessments on its members. Assessments can help to protect the clearinghouse only if its members are strong enough to support it. As a result, clearing members are required to be well-capitalized before becoming members of a clearinghouse, and the Basel III capital rules we discussed in Chapter 2.7 impose special obligations on clearinghouse members. *See, e.g.*, BANK FOR INT'L SETTLEMENTS, CAPITAL REQUIREMENTS FOR BANK EXPOSURES TO CENTRAL COUNTERPARTIES (2014). The Dodd-Frank Act requires such members to have "sufficient financial resources and operational capacity to meet obligations arising from participation in the [clearinghouse]." Dodd-Frank, § 725(c) If a clearing member does not have sufficient resources, then the clearinghouse may need to access the guaranty fund and require assessments from its clearing members more often, which hurts other clearing members of the clearinghouse. Moreover, requiring assessments of weakened financial institutions would increase systemic risk. A central question is therefore whether clearinghouse risk management and financial resource requirements are sufficiently strong to withstand losses in a financial crisis.

c. Regulation and Governance of Derivatives Clearinghouses

In recognition of their significant role in the Dodd-Frank Act's swaps architecture, clearinghouses are highly regulated in ways that support their ability to absorb risk. A clearinghouse that clears swaps is required to register with the CFTC as a Derivatives Clearing Organization (DCO), and a clearinghouse that clears security-based swaps is required to register with the SEC as a clearing agency. These registered clearinghouses must, among other requirements, maintain sufficient financial resources in the guaranty fund, establish risk management capabilities to oversee the activities of counterparties, and provide the CFTC or SEC with reports on clearinghouse activities. David Gilberg & John Miller et al., *Derivatives Clearing Organization Registration and Regulation, in* OTC DERIVATIVES REGULATION UNDER DODD-FRANK: A GUIDE TO REGISTRATION, REPORTING, BUSINESS CONDUCT, AND CLEARING 631, 635 (William C. Meehan & Gabriel D. Rosenberg eds., 2015); *see also* CFTC, DERIVATIVES CLEARING ORGANIZATIONS (2016).

Similar to the Financial Stability Oversight Council's (FSOC) powers to designate systemically important financial institutions (SIFIs), § 804 of the Dodd-Frank Act requires the FSOC to designate financial market utilities (FMUs) that it determines are, or are likely to become, systemically important. This includes DCOs, which, when designated, are referred to as systemically important derivatives clearing organizations (SIDCOs). *See* Derivatives Clearing Organizations and International Standards, 78 Fed. Reg. 72,476 (Dec. 2, 2013). The parallel SEC proposed rule refers to designated entities as covered clearing agencies. *See* Standards for Covered Clearing Agencies, 79 Fed. Reg. 16,866 (Mar. 26, 2014). Of the eight FMUs that FSOC has designated as systemically important, six are SIDCOs or covered clearing agencies, while the remaining two are entities supervised by the Federal Reserve Board. FED. RES. BD., DESIGNATED FINANCIAL MARKET UTILITIES (2015). SIDCOs and covered clearing agencies are subject to heightened risk management standards and more stringent financial resource requirements. Dodd-Frank § 805(a); *see, e.g.,* 17 C.F.R. § 39.33.

In the event that the financial resources requirements prove insufficient or a SIDCO or covered clearing agency otherwise faces liquidity pressures in a financial crisis, Title VIII of the Dodd-Frank Act gives the Federal Reserve authority to provide discount window access to the clearinghouse under "unusual or exigent circumstances." Dodd-Frank Act § 806(b). This provision—distinct from the Federal Reserve's § 13(3) authority that we discussed in Chapter 9.1—was exceedingly controversial during the Dodd-Frank Act legislative process. Critics argued that it constituted a "back door bailout" of banks, while supporters, including the Treasury Department, argued that it was an essential safety valve in the event of another financial crisis given that risk was being concentrated in clearinghouses under the Dodd-Frank Act. *See, e.g.*, Jeremy C. Kress, *Credit Default Swaps, Clearinghouses, and Systemic Risk: Why Centralized Counterparties Must Have Access to Central Bank Liquidity*, 48 HARV. J. ON LEGIS. 49 (2011).

Derivatives clearinghouses face problems of incentives and potential conflicts of interest. Some have argued that a DCO's incentive to attract clearing business, for instance, could cause it to set margin requirements or guaranty fund assessments too low, thereby increasing systemic risk. *See, e.g.*, *id.* at 74. DCOs owned by large dealers also have contrary incentives to keep clearing fees and clearinghouse minimum capital requirements high to exclude smaller market participants or market participants with riskier customers from membership and thereby preserve their market share. *See* Michael Greenberger, *Diversifying Clearinghouse Ownership in Order to Safeguard Free and Open Access to the Derivatives Clearing Market*, 18 FORDHAM J. CORP. & FIN. L. 245 (2013). Dealer-owners, however, also have a strong and legitimate interest in ensuring the safety of the DCO, through strong prudential rules, because its risk is mutualized and a key line of defense in financial distress would be for dealers to provide more funds or liquidity. The designation of certain DCOs as systemic under Title VIII with enhanced risk management standards, access to the Federal Reserve's discount window, and the treatment of a dealer member in resolution all also raise systemic issues of concern to policy-makers and dealer members. The increased use of derivatives clearinghouses means there is likely to be tradeoffs between open competition and safety and soundness.

Congress recognized the potential for conflicts of interest related to derivatives clearinghouses. It thus required the CFTC to adopt rules "to mitigate conflicts of interests . . . with respect to . . . any [DCO]." Dodd-Frank Act § 726(a). The CFTC proposed a set of rules in 2010. Balancing the tradeoffs discussed above was controversial, and, as of December 2015, the CFTC had not yet finalized the rules. Requirements for Derivatives Clearing Organizations, Designated Contract Markets, and Swap Execution Facilities Regarding the Mitigation of Conflicts of Interest, 75 Fed. Reg. 63,372, 63,733 (Oct. 18, 2010). The rules would include limitations on ownership by dealers and requirements to have independent board members, as well as nomination and risk committees. *Id.; see* Risk Management Requirements for Derivatives Clearing Organizations, 76 Fed. Reg. 3,698, (Jan. 20, 2011); *see also* Ownership Limitations and Governance Requirements for Security-Based Swap Clearing Agencies, Security-Based Swap Execution Facilities, and National Securities Exchanges with Respect to Security-Based Swaps Under Regulation MC, 75 Fed. Reg. 65,882, 65,893 (Oct. 26, 2010). In addition, the CFTC has adopted rules that prohibit a DCO from establishing a potentially restrictive membership requirement if a less restrictive alternative "would not materially increase risk to the DCO or its clearing members." 17 C.F.R. § 39.12(a)(1)(i). The CFTC's rules also require a DCO to accept an entity as a member if it meets the DCO's participation requirements. *Id.* at § 39.12(a)(1)(ii).

In addition, DCOs often own or have business relationships with trading and data aggregation platforms, which leads to concerns that DCOs could force market participants to use these affiliated functions. Thus, a DCO has an incentive to try to force firms to use its affiliated trading services if the firms want to use its clearing services. To overcome that incentive and increase competition among trading platforms, the Dodd-Frank Act amended the CEA to require DCOs to provide "open access" for swaps executed on other, unaffiliated trading exchanges or swap execution facilities. *See* Dodd-Frank Act § 723(a)(3), CEA § 2(h)(1)(B).

---

1. ***Independent Directors and Systemic Risk.*** The CFTC's proposals under the Dodd-Frank Act would impose corporate governance standards on DCOs. The Sarbanes-Oxley Act imposed some independence requirements on the board of public companies; however, commentators criticized these independence requirements, arguing that they would not "reduce the probability of financial statement wrongdoing." Roberta Romano, *The Sarbanes-Oxley Act and the Making of Quack Corporate Governance*, 114 YALE L.J. 1521, 1533 (2004). Do you think requiring DCOs' boards to have independent directors will "reduce the probability" that a DCO will fail or otherwise pose systemic risks, or reduce the potential conflicts of interests that it faces? Should DCOs be non-profit utilities rather than shareholder-owned companies?

2. ***Resolution.*** How should clearinghouses be resolved if they become insolvent? For a discussion of possible resolution procedures for failed clearinghouses, see Darrell Duffie, *Resolution of Failing Central Counterparties*, *in* MAKING FAILURE FEASIBLE: HOW BANKRUPTCY REFORM CAN END "TOO BIG TO FAIL" 87–110 (Kenneth E. Scott et al. eds., 2015). Should a DCO be permitted to terminate the membership of a financial institution in resolution? Consider the context of a single point of entry resolution as discussed in Part IX.

---

d. Multilateral Netting

In a bilateral swap world, Parties A, B, C, and D may each face one another on a swap, as illustrated on the left side of Figure 11.2-6. In this scenario, each party is exposed to the credit risk of its two counterparties. When swaps are centrally cleared, by contrast, the clearinghouse cancels out, or nets, offsetting exposures. Multilateral netting reduces interconnections among market participants, lowers the total amount of collateral in the system, and allows counterparties to make one net payment instead of multiple payments. MICHAEL H. MOSKOW, PUBLIC POLICY AND CENTRAL COUNTERPARTY CLEARING (2006).

Figure 11.2-6 Bilateral versus Multilateral Netting

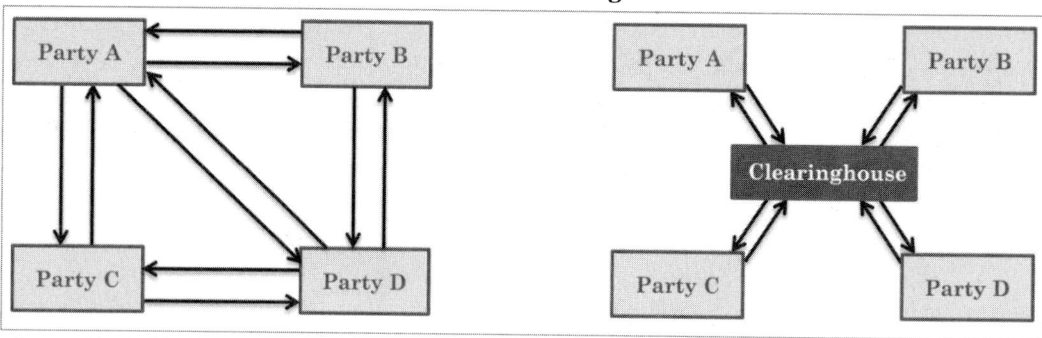

Source: Davis Polk & Wardwell LLP.

e. Portability

The fact that the clearinghouse is the ultimate counterparty to any cleared swap allows for another benefit known as portability. In a bilateral swap, if a counterparty defaults, the non-defaulting counterparty no longer has a swap in place to protect against future movements in the price of the underlying asset. The non-defaulting counterparty may still need the protection of a swap. For example, if our hypothetical Swap Dealer defaults, Airline still needs to hedge its fuel costs. Airline will need to replace its fuel swap, which could be expensive, particularly if general market distress led to the default of its counterparty.

In the cleared context, however, if a market participant's clearing member defaults, the clearinghouse may be able to transfer the positions and assets from a defaulting clearing member's account to a solvent clearing member, which avoids the need to close out positions. *See, e.g.*, General Provisions Applicable to Derivatives Clearing Organizations, 12 C.F.R. § 39.37(c)-(d) (2015). For example, if Airline, as an end user, has a cleared swap held through a clearing member and the clearing member fails, Airline can move its positions to another clearing member, assuming that Airline has all the required documents in place with the new clearing member. *See* COMM. ON PAYMENT AND SETTLEMENT SYS. & TECH. COMM. OF THE INT'L ORG. OF SECURITIES COMMS., PRINCIPLES FOR FINANCIAL MARKET INFRASTRUCTURES (2012); *see also* Figure 11.2-7.

Figure 11.2-7 Diagram of Cleared Transaction Portability

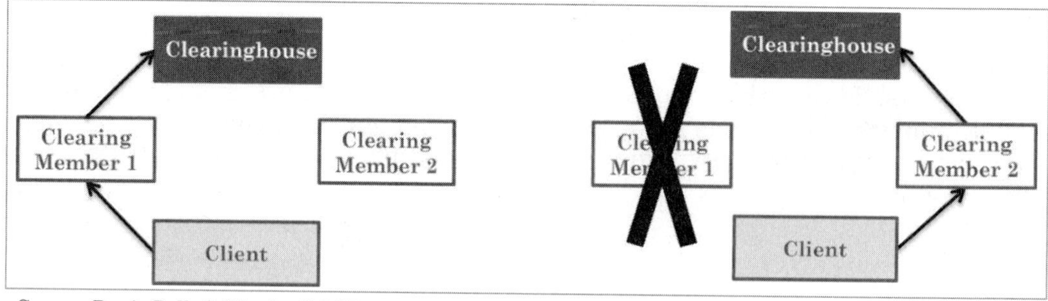

Source: Davis Polk & Wardwell LLP.

3. Mandatory Clearing of Swaps

a. The History of Clearing

As you learned in Chapter 11.1, clearing is not a new concept. It has been used in the futures markets since the 1890s, and the Grain Futures Act of 1922 required some futures contracts to be cleared. Gary Gensler, Chairman, CFTC, Testimony Before the FCIC (July 1, 2010); *see* CFTC, PUBLIC ROUNDTABLE ON THE FUTURIZATION OF SWAPS (2013); *see also* CFTC, HISTORY OF THE CFTC (2016). Before the Dodd-Frank Act, counterparties to swap transactions were not required to clear their transactions, though some recognized the utility in clearing and decided to do so without regulatory mandate. After the Financial Crisis, market participants, under pressure from the Federal Reserve Bank of New York, were beginning to move towards clearing a higher percentage of swaps. In fact, many of the largest financial institutions signed a commitment letter to the Federal Reserve Bank of New York in June 2009 stating that they had "agreed upon a framework for OTC derivative risk management and market structure and [were] working expeditiously to deliver [their] commitments set forth [in the letter, including a commitment to] clearing for OTC standardized derivative products. . . ." Letter from Senior Managements of Alliance Bernstein et al., to The Honorable William C. Dudley, President, Federal Reserve Bank of New York (June 2, 2009). The Dodd-Frank Act then made clearing a regulatory requirement for certain types of swaps and security-based swaps.

b. The Dodd-Frank Act's Mandatory Clearing Requirement

To promote the central clearing of swaps, the Dodd-Frank Act amended the Commodity Exchange Act of 1936 (CEA) and the Securities Exchange Act of 1934 (1934 Act) to mandate the clearing of swaps and security-based swaps, respectively. Not all swaps, however, are subject to this clearing requirement. Market participants must only clear swaps and security-based swaps that the CFTC or SEC, respectively, determines are subject to mandatory clearing. The CFTC, when deciding which swaps should be required to be cleared, has focused on those swaps that constitute a large portion of the market and present unique risks. *See* Clearing Requirement and Related Rules, 12 C.F.R. § 50.

Only swaps that are standardized and have a sufficient level of liquidity are required to be cleared. If swaps are not standardized, clearinghouses may not know how to measure their risk and will not know how much margin to collect. In the futures world, this standardization was inherent in the creation of futures contracts, as compared to forwards, as we discussed in Chapter 11.1. In the swap world, however, there had been less standardization, since swaps were entered into as customized contracts between parties. Despite historical arrangements, swap clearing has increased dramatically since passage of the Dodd-Frank Act. According to CFTC Chairman Timothy Massad, approximately 75% of swap transactions were being cleared in 2015 as compared to only 15% in 2007. *See* Timothy Massad, Chairman, CFTC, Keynote Remarks before the Risk USA Conference (Oct. 22, 2015). As of December 31, 2015, four types of interest rate swaps and two types of credit default index swaps are subject to mandatory clearing. *See, e.g.*, Clearing Requirement Determination Under § 2(h) of the

CEA, 77 Fed. Reg. 74,284 (Dec. 13, 2012). The SEC has not, as of the end of 2015, made any clearing determinations for security-based swaps.

c. Exceptions and Exemptions to Mandatory Clearing

The clearing mandate of the Dodd-Frank Act focused on reducing systemic risk. In drafting the clearing mandate, Congress focused primarily on the risks presented by financial entities. Although Congress wanted to regulate the swap market, it sought to place the burdens of that regulation primarily on SDs and the other largest market participants, and secondarily on financial institutions more generally, rather than on non-financial entities entering into swaps to hedge or mitigate their own commercial risks. For these and other reasons, Congress and the CFTC carved out certain exceptions and exemptions.

First, the Dodd-Frank Act includes an exception from the mandatory clearing requirement for commercial end users that enter into swaps to hedge or mitigate commercial risk and that satisfy other statutory and rule-based requirements. In general, a commercial end user is a non-financial entity that uses swaps to hedge its commercial risk, for example, Airline hedging its exposure to changes in fuel prices or a construction company hedging its exposure to changes in interest rates on an adjustable rate project-finance loan. The commercial end-user exception can be used even if only one counterparty to the swap is a commercial end user. Swaps between a commercial end user and a financial entity, such as an SD, may, therefore, be executed bilaterally and need not be submitted for clearing, provided the conditions of this exception are satisfied. Rules further permit a corporate group's centralized hedging affiliate (its treasury) that collects the risks of the various affiliates of the group and then hedges the net risk to the market, to rely on the commercial end-user exception, subject to conditions, even though treasury affiliates are typically financial entities under the CEA and not commercial end users.

The CFTC carved out an exemption to permit firms to engage in transactions with their affiliates. A large conglomerate will often be composed of multiple legal entities that enter into swaps in order to offset risk exposures within the group. These inter-affiliate swaps reduce the risk that the conglomerate would need to offset through a swap with an outside counterparty. For example, if a subsidiary of a financial institution enters into an interest rate swap, it may enter into an equal and offsetting swap with an affiliate to reduce its interest rate risk. Although there is no statutory exclusion from the clearing requirement for inter-affiliate swaps, the CFTC has provided a rule-based exemption for swaps between qualifying affiliated entities. The inter-affiliate exemption also allows one entity in a corporate group to specialize in aggregating risks within the group and hedging outside the group, on behalf of the company. Exempting affiliates from mandatory clearing allows affiliates to engage in swaps that hedge or mitigate risk within the corporate group more readily, thus reducing the risk that must be hedged with multiple unaffiliated counterparties. In providing the exemption, the CFTC imposed a number of conditions on the affiliates to prevent evasion.

d. Criticisms of the Mandatory Clearing Requirement

Although mandatory clearing was one of the central reforms under the Dodd-Frank Act and one of the key goals of the post-Financial Crisis G-20 commitments, scholars and market participants have raised concerns about the requirement to clear swaps. That is because requiring clearing reduces the credit risk to which each party to a swap is exposed but increases the clearinghouse's exposure to the credit risk of each counterparty to a swap that is submitted to the clearinghouse. If a large market participant defaults and the clearinghouse does not have enough capital to address this default, and does not receive enough additional capital through assessments on clearing members, the clearinghouse itself may default, which would have a significant effect on the market. Mark J. Roe, *Clearinghouse Overconfidence,* 101 CAL. L. REV. 1641, 1697 (2013). These critics argue, in effect, that mandatory clearing does not reduce systemic risk, but transfers it. If the proponents of clearing are wrong that clearinghouses can better manage such risk, the transfer of risk could increase systemic risk.

Moreover, multilateral netting, a key benefit of using a clearinghouse, cannot be fully realized in practice because there are many clearinghouses. Since there are many clearinghouses and each clearinghouse may only net positions that it clears, this results in less multilateral netting than would be available with only one clearinghouse. Additionally, because clearinghouses will tend to focus on particular asset classes, they could feel the effects of asset bubbles more severely. *See* Sean J. Griffith, *Clearinghouse Hope or Hype?: Why Mandatory Clearing May Fail to Contain Systemic Risk*, 3 HARV. BUS. L. REV. ONLINE 160, 163 (2013). Of course, having only one clearinghouse would generate its own problems, concentrating systemic risk in one place.

Market participants also argue that clearing is expensive. As part of the clearing process, parties must provide the DCO with margin, as well as enter into relationships with clearing members, incurring legal costs to do so. Of course, these costs must be weighed against the cost of the former system, including the all-in credit costs of counterparties and the cost to the financial system and the economy when the financial sector nearly collapsed.

E. INTERNATIONAL IMPLEMENTATION

The implementation of margin requirements for uncleared swaps and mandatory clearing of standardized derivatives were two of the goals of the G-20 commitment, and many G-20 members have proposed or finalized mandatory clearing and uncleared swap margin requirements. For example, the EU and Japan have finalized their mandatory clearing requirements and are expected to finalize their uncleared swap margin requirements in early 2016. Though not part of the G-20, Hong Kong also implemented mandatory clearing at certain clearinghouses. HONG KONG MONETARY AUT'Y, OTC DERIVATIVES TRADE REPOSITORY (2014).

Although similarities exist between swaps oversight in the United States and EU, and both the United States and the European Commission were committed in principle to a process of mutual recognition based on comparability or equivalence, a clearing battle emerged between the CFTC and the European

Commission regarding the recognition of foreign clearinghouses in the United States and the EU. *See* Yesha Yadav & Dermot Turing, *The Extra-Territorial Regulation of Clearinghouses*, 2 J. FIN. REG. 1, 29-32 (2016). The CFTC recognizes comparably regulated non-U.S. clearinghouses as exempt from CFTC registration requirements; the CFTC, however, initially took the position not to permit exempt DCOs to clear for U.S. customers. Under European Market Infrastructure Regulation, the recognition of non-EU clearinghouses by the European Securities and Markets Authority (ESMA) depends on, among other things, whether the European Commission considers the non-EU jurisdiction to provide an "effective equivalent" system for the recognition of foreign clearinghouses. Because the CFTC did not permit exempt DCOs to clear for U.S. customers, EU officials asserted that the CFTC did not provide an "effective equivalent" system of recognition for non-U.S. clearinghouses, in effect blocking recognition of U.S. clearinghouses in the EU.

An accord was eventually reached in early 2016, clearing the way for equivalency and comparability determinations, and thus, mutual recognition:

> Following this agreement the European Commission intends to adopt shortly an equivalence decision with respect to CFTC requirements for US CCPs which will allow ESMA to recognise US CCPs as soon as is practicable. Once recognised by ESMA, US CCPs may continue to provide services in the EU whilst complying with CFTC requirements. The CFTC staff will propose a determination of comparability with respect to EU requirements, which will permit EU CCPs to provide services to US clearing members and clients whilst complying with certain corresponding EU requirements. The CFTC staff will also propose to streamline the registration process for EU CCPs wishing to register with them.

THE U.S. COMMODITY FUTURES TRADING COMMISSION AND THE EUROPEAN COMMISSION: COMMON APPROACH FOR TRANSATLANTIC CCPS (2016). The SEC and European Commission are still in dialogue on this issue. For a consideration of substituted compliance by the SEC pre-Dodd-Frank Act, and potential criteria for assessment, see Howell E. Jackson, *Substituted Compliance: The Emergence, Challenges, and Evolution of a New Regulatory Paradigm*, 1 J. FIN. REG. 169 (2015); *see also* John C. Coffee, Jr., *Extraterritorial Financial Regulation: Why E.T. Can't Come Home*, 99 CORNELL L. REV. 1259, 1279 (2014); *see also* Alexey Artamanov, *Cross-border Application of OTC Derivatives Rules: Revisiting the Substituted Compliance Approach*, 1 J. FIN. REG. 206 (2015).

---

1. ***Costs of Not Clearing***. There are significant differences in the amount of initial margin required to be posted for cleared swaps as compared to uncleared swaps. Some estimates have stated that initial margin for cleared swaps may be up to 50% less than for a similar uncleared swap. This may lead to more cleared swaps over time, as contemplated by the Dodd-Frank Act.

III. DEVELOPING A TRANSPARENT MARKETPLACE

A. GOALS OF TRANSPARENCY

Historically, the swap market was not open or transparent. As described in Chapter 11.1, swap contracts were highly customized agreements designed to meet the needs of specific customers, and they carried significant credit risk. Swaps were generally not standardized or fungible, but were entered into on a custom basis between a market participant that needed the protection of a swap or wanted to speculate through it, and a dealer willing to provide that protection. The swap market was not historically characterized by pre-trade transparency—the availability of information regarding the prices and sizes at which market participants are willing to enter into swaps—or post-trade transparency—the availability of information regarding the price or size at which a swap trade was executed in the marketplace. The lack of timely and full information about swaps extended not just to market participants, but also to regulators.

In the Financial Crisis, as we have seen, the opacity of the OTC market increased costs for end-users, exacerbated losses, increased interconnectedness, and fostered uncertainty, contributing to the panic. In the wake of the crisis, the Dodd-Frank Act put in place a new system requiring pre- and post-trade transparency. This section introduces the approaches taken for both types of transparency. While transparency in the swap market is an important reform, it is not as easy as it seems, and it also has downsides costs.

An exchange is a marketplace where buyers and sellers trade financial instruments. The concept of trading financial instruments on an exchange is not new; it has existed in futures and securities markets for centuries. Before the Dodd-Frank Act, market participants could trade swaps on multilateral platforms, but they were not required to do so, and regulators did not closely regulate the activities of these platforms. As part of the Dodd-Frank Act's reforms, and consistent with the G-20 commitments, Congress provided for comprehensive regulation of swap trading.

Before exchange trading requirements, regulators, other market participants, end users, and the public lacked information on the market and the swaps traded on the market because parties were not required to report trade information. Exchange trading is meant both to remove these informational asymmetries and to reduce uncertainty in the swap market. *See* Gary Gensler, Chairman, CFTC, Statement to Open Commission Meeting for Consideration of Rules Implementing the Dodd-Frank Act (May 16, 2013). For example, before the Dodd-Frank Act, dealers had access to transaction and pricing data across their books, but end users generally entered into transactions with minimal market information or comparative terms. *Id.* The lack of transparency of prices allowed the largest U.S. financial institutions to dominate the swap market and keep spreads high for end-users, while keeping smaller institutions from competing with larger dealers on price. S. REP. NO. 111-176, at 29, 34 (2010). As a result of the domination in the market by the largest institutions, there was a concentration of, and increase in, systemic risk in the event that one or more of those large institutions failed. *Id.* at 29. The exchange trading requirement allows buyers to compare multiple offers, which creates competition within the marketplace, reduces spreads to dealers and disperses risk among a wider number of market participants. It also allows regulators greater insight into the financial health of financial institutions and the financial sector as a whole. *See* ROBERT E. LITAN, WHAT SHOULD BANKS DO? 5 (Brookings Inst. Press 1987).

Unlike the exchange-traded securities and futures markets, however, where contracts are generally fungible and most exchange-traded products have significant liquidity, swaps historically were marketed as bespoke products. Market participants have expressed concern that, if contracts with insufficient liquidity are required to be traded on exchanges, market participants may stay away from the contracts in order to avoid providing the market with information about their view of the proper price of the instruments, which would further reduce liquidity. Transparency could also lead other participants to front-run the swap, reducing its usefulness as a hedging tool by making it more costly. Peter Malyshev et al., *SEF Registration and Regulation*, *in* OTC DERIVATIVES REGULATION UNDER DODD-FRANK: A GUIDE TO REGISTRATION, REPORTING, BUSINESS CONDUCT, AND CLEARING 675–676 (William C. Meehan & Gabriel D. Rosenberg eds., 2015). Additionally, opponents have argued that exchange trading would reduce customization in swaps. Exchange trading may inhibit parties from getting the customized terms they desire, forcing them to purchase less efficient instruments. Reed T. Schuster, *Sacrificing Functionality for Transparency? The Regulation of Swap Agreements in the Wake of the Financial Crisis*, 62 SYRACUSE L. REV. 385, 398–99 (2012).

B. PRE-TRADE TRANSPARENCY: MANDATORY EXCHANGE TRADING

The CEA, as amended by the Dodd-Frank Act, requires that all swaps that are subject to mandatory clearing be traded on a Designated Contract Market (DCM) or Swap Execution Facility (SEF) unless no such platform "makes the swap available to trade." Therefore, if a swap is required to be traded on a DCM or SEF, it is a violation of the CEA and CFTC rules to trade that swap bilaterally.

As with mandated clearing, exchange trading is only required for certain standardized and liquid swaps. As of December 31, 2015, of those swaps that were required to be cleared, only a subset, consisting of those swaps that are the most standardized and liquid, are required to be executed on a DCM or SEF. Even if a swap is not required to be exchange traded, a counterparty may, however, wish to enter into the swap on a DCM or SEF because the counterparty may wish to achieve the benefits of transacting on an exchange, including the ability to access liquidity and compare prices. For example, many market participants trade foreign exchange (FX) swaps voluntarily on SEFs or similar platforms, even though FX swaps are not required to be exchange traded, because FX swaps are relatively standardized and the exchanges have the necessary liquidity.

Both DCMs and SEFs are subject to statutory provisions and CFTC regulations, known as "core principles." The core principles for DCMs and SEFs include trading and product requirements, compliance and surveillance obligations, operational capabilities, emergency authority, and financial information and resource requirements.

1. Designated Contract Markets

A DCM is a traditional futures exchange that is required to be registered with, and is regulated by, the CFTC. DCMs pre-date the formation of the CFTC itself, having existed in the United States since the 19th Century. *See* CFTC, HISTORY OF THE CFTC (2016). CFTC regulations require DCMs to have minimum trading functionality for the execution of swaps. Swaps that are made available to trade on a DCM must be executed through an order book. An order book is an electronic list of buy and sell positions for a particular financial product that matches bids and offers, generally through the use of an algorithm. Order books must provide for a delay between a dealer entering an order and crossing that order with its own or another client's order, thus allowing all market participants to observe the quotes and trades in the marketplace. Proponents of the use of order books state that they provide for pre-trade transparency by bringing dealers together for buyers to compare multiple offers at once, which creates competition and disperses risk among a wider number of market participants. *See* DIEGO VALIANTE, SETTING THE INSTITUTIONAL AND REGULATORY FRAMEWORK FOR TRADING PLATFORMS (2012). Gensler noted that the old approach of calling a range of dealers to get a view of the market is not that helpful when a few large banks dominate all the trading. *See* Gary Gensler, Chairman, CFTC, Remarks Before the Int'l Futures Indus. Conference: Implementing the Dodd-Frank Act (Mar. 16, 2011).

2. Swap Execution Facilities

Unlike DCMs, SEFs are a creation of the Dodd-Frank Act. SEFs are distinguished from DCMs in their ability to provide more flexible trading methodologies than DCMs, which is sometimes useful for less-liquid swap markets. Similar to DCMs, SEFs are required to register with the CFTC. If a trading system or platform provides more than one market participant with the ability to execute or trade swaps with more than one other market participant, known as a multiple-to-multiple platform, it must register as an SEF unless it already is registered as a DCM. The SEF registration requirement is also not tied to the trade execution requirement, so any electronic platform that facilitates or has the ability to facilitate the execution of swaps on a multiple-to-multiple basis must register as a SEF, not only those platforms that provide trading of swaps that are required to be executed on an exchange. As of December 31, 2015, there were 23 temporarily registered or pending SEFs.

In contrast to the automated trade matching of an order book, SEFs may also provide a request-for-quote facility, which allows a market participant seeking to enter into a swap to request a direct quote from SDs. To meet the mandatory trading obligation, however, SEFs must provide such a request-for-quote to at least three unaffiliated market participants. Methods of Execution for Required and Permitted Transactions, 17 C.F.R. § 37.9 (2015). In a request-for-quote system, the requestor receives offers from liquidity providers that quote in response to the request, and the system also provides the requester with all resting bids and offers in the same product from the SEF's order book. The quote requester's identity may be known or anonymous.

To illustrate how a market participant might transact on an SEF, imagine that Airline submits a request for quote to the SEF to buy an interest rate swap that must be cleared through a clearinghouse and is subject to the trade execution requirement. Airline, through the SEF, requests quotes from no less than three SDs, including potential Party B. The SEF then receives responses from these SDs, and provides those offers, as well as the resting offers on the SEF's order book, to Airline. Airline then accepts one of the offers—for example, Party B's offer—and the SEF communicates to Party B that the swap is executed.

3. Made Available to Trade

A swap is only required to be traded on a DCM or SEF if the swap is "made available to trade." To make a swap available for trade, DCMs and SEFs must consider various factors relating to liquidity with respect to each swap. The made available-to-trade determination is initiated by a DCM or SEF. A DCM or SEF must submit its determinations to the CFTC, either for approval or self-certification, which allows the DCM or SEF to certify that the determination complies with the CEA and relevant CFTC requirements. When a DCM or SEF uses the self-certification process, the CFTC may only reject the determination by a finding that the determination violates the CEA or CFTC regulations.

---

1. ***Made Available to Trade.*** On a plain reading, what do you think "makes the swap available to trade" means? What might the CFTC have been trying to accomplish by developing a complex "made available to trade" process? How does this provision relate to other provisions in the Dodd-Frank Act, and the Act's history, structure, and purpose?

2. ***Do SEFs and DCMs Engage in Policymaking?*** CFTC Commissioner Mark Wetjen has argued that the "made available to trade" approval process is flawed and that the policy allows DCMs and SEFs to engage in policymaking. *See* Mark Wetjen, Commissioner, CFTC, Remarks before the Cumberland Lodge Fin. Servs. Policy Summit: The Next Opportunity for Trans-Atlantic Collaboration: Shaping a New Era for Swap Execution (Nov. 14, 2014). Since DCMs and SEFs may unilaterally determine if a swap is "made available to trade," Wetjen noted, the process allows "commercial entities that stand to benefit most" to engage in policymaking since the respective trading platform has the authority to determine if a swap is "made available to trade." *Id.* What are some potential issues and conflicts that you see with the SEF or DCM making the "made available to trade" determination, as opposed to the CFTC?

3. ***Dealers' Conflicting Incentives.*** Exchange trading of derivatives raises questions about market participants' incentives and possible conflicts of interest. Dealers, for instance, absent the Dodd-Frank Act's mandatory exchange trading requirement, would face potentially conflicting incentives as to whether to exchange trade derivatives. Exchange trading, when fully functional, may increase liquidity. Dealers, however, have an incentive not to exchange trade because they earn higher spreads in the bilateral, non-exchange-traded market. Dealers may therefore have incentive to encourage commercial end users—which are exempt from the Dodd-Frank Act's mandatory clearing, and therefore mandatory exchange trading, requirements—to make bilateral bespoke trades where their profits would be higher, rather than to use exchange trading. That is

one reason why the Dodd-Frank Act mandates exchange trading for many cleared swaps and requires higher margin requirements for non-cleared trades than for cleared trades. *See* Dodd-Frank Act §§ 723(a), 731; *see also* Sean J. Griffith, *Governing Systemic Risk: Towards A Governance Structure For Derivatives Clearinghouses*, 61 EMORY L. J. 1153, 1207–08 (2012).

C. POST-TRADE TRANSPARENCY: TRADE REPORTING

As noted above, before the Dodd-Frank Act, regulators and market participants had little insight into the terms of swaps that were executed, known as post-trade transparency. Such trade reporting is designed in part to assist regulators in understanding risk exposures for particular firms and across the financial system. In addition to allowing regulators to monitor the swap markets, post-trade transparency allows market participants to look to past swap activity as an indicator of appropriate pricing for future swap activity. In that way, reporting is designed to work alongside exchange trading to improve price discovery, which should reduce dealer spreads and increase efficiency. Such information is also designed to be used by market participants to assess market, counterparty, and systemic risks that they and other participants might face.

The Dodd-Frank Act introduced a new reporting requirement for swaps and security-based swaps. Under the CFTC's and SEC's reporting rules, one of the counterparties to the transaction—the SD when one is a party to the trade—is tasked with reporting the necessary data to a Swap Data Repository (SDR) or security-based SDR. The SDR collects the reported data and provides the CFTC and SEC, upon request, with access to this information. The SDR is also responsible for publicly disseminating a subset of that data to the public in an anonymized way. This public dissemination helps to enable market participants to make better-informed decisions on whether to enter into a particular trade at a particular price. Our hypothetical Airline planning to enter into an interest rate swap, for example, can review the publicly available data to determine whether the price it was quoted from Bank A is consistent with the market price for similar types of interest rate swaps.

Figure 11.2-8 Reporting Under Title VII

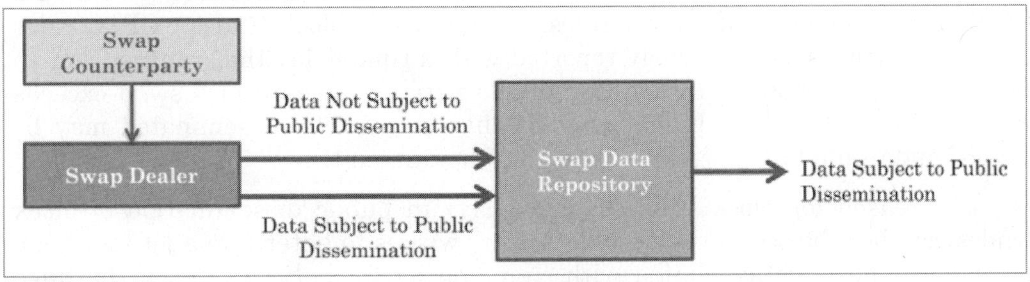

Swap Counterparty
Data Not Subject to Public Dissemination
Swap Dealer
Swap Data Repository
Data Subject to Public Dissemination
Data Subject to Public Dissemination

Source: Davis Polk & Wardwell LLP.

SDRs and security-based SDRs are required to register with the CFTC or SEC, respectively. As of December 31, 2015, there were four SDRs registered with the CFTC. *See* CFTC, CFTC SWAP DATA REPOSITORY ORGANIZATIONS (2016). The first SDRs are expected to register with the SEC in early 2016.

1. Providing the Regulators with Swap Data

Under the new reporting rules for swaps, data for each swap, whether cleared or uncleared, must be reported upon execution and throughout the life of the swap to an SDR. Although FX swaps and FX forwards are excluded from the definition of swap for purposes of Title VII's clearing and trading requirement (as discussed in Chapter 11.1), data relating to these transactions must nonetheless be reported to an SDR. CFTC rules prescribe the standards for regulatory reporting, including the specific data elements that must be reported to, and maintained by, SDRs. These standards vary depending on the particular asset class of a swap transaction, and therefore, market participants must develop different reporting systems for the various asset classes in which they transact. Swaps reported to SDRs must be labeled using unique identifiers that identify the parties to the swap, the product type of the swap and the individual swap. These identifiers can be used by the regulators to aggregate swap data to conduct market and risk surveillance, analyze market data, take enforcement actions, monitor systemic risk, and improve market transparency. *See* Swap Data Recordkeeping and Reporting Requirements, 17 C.F.R. § 45.

2. Providing the Market with Swap Data

Once swap data is reported to an SDR, the SDR must publicly disseminate, in real-time, anonymized swap transaction data, including the type, price, and volume of the transaction. Although the counterparties are required to report swap data for FX swaps and forwards to an SDR, this information is not publicly disseminated. Trades between affiliates also are not publicly disseminated because these transactions may not reflect market prices.

Why is publicly disseminated data anonymized? Congress wanted to protect the identities of counterparties and maintain the confidentiality of business transactions and market positions of the counterparties to swaps.

3. Block Trades

Although the CFTC rules require that swap information and pricing data be publicly reported in real time, there are certain types of swaps for which the trade data is subject to a time delay before it is publicly disseminated. Reportable large swap trades above certain size thresholds that are traded on a DCM or SEF, or pursuant to its rules, are known as block trades. CFTC rules allow block trades to be publicly reported with a time delay that ranges from 15 minutes to a few hours. In addition, if the notional amount of a swap exceeds certain thresholds, the notional amount that is publicly disseminated may be capped and would be reported as exceeding that amount.

The reason for block trading, and delays in public dissemination of block trades, can best be seen by example. Airline wishes to enter into a jet fuel swap to manage the risks associated with changing jet fuel prices. Given the huge quantity of jet fuel that Airline will purchase in a year, Airline will look to purchase a large amount of protection using swaps, likely larger than any one market participant is currently offering for sale. Airline could go to the market and buy small amounts of protection, such as 100 units from Bank A, 50 units from Bank B, and so on, until it obtains the total amount it needs. As Airline aggregates these smaller swaps, however, the market will see increased demand, and the swaps will get more and more expensive. As a result, it may become incredibly expensive, if not impossible, for Airline to hedge its risks this way.

Instead, Airline could ask a single bank, Bank A, to provide Airline with one large fuel swap. Bank A will likely charge Airline a premium over the current market price for this transaction, but this premium may well be cheaper to Airline than buying protection in pieces. The size of the premium that Bank A will charge depends in part on the price at which it can pass on the risk of the swap through hedging its risk in the market. If price and volume data for this jet fuel swap were publicly disseminated in real time, Bank B will know that someone just entered into a large jet fuel swap and this someone will soon need to hedge its position. Bank B will not know that Bank A is the bank that needs to hedge positions, but it does not matter—Bank B will raise its prices for the offsetting trade. Knowing this, Bank A would preemptively raise the premium it charges Airline to compensate for this increased hedging charge. If the public dissemination of information about the block trade between Airline and Bank A is delayed, however, Bank A may have sufficient time to hedge its position before Bank B knows enough to hike the price of its hedge positions.

4. International Implementation

In a global market such as the swap market, laws in one jurisdiction may clash with laws in another jurisdiction. Pursuant to G-20 commitments, many non-U.S. jurisdictions—including Europe, Japan, Australia, Canada, and Hong Kong—have adopted reporting regimes. For the G-20 members, even though the reporting requirements originate from the same international framework, there have been differences in implementation. For instance, some rules do not require public dissemination of swap data, while others only require that a few data fields be reported to a data repository. The European reporting system requires both counterparties to a transaction to report data to a data repository, as contrasted with the U.S. system, which only requires one party to report data.

One of the key goals of the Dodd-Frank Act's reporting requirement was to provide the regulators with access to data about the derivatives market. CFTC rules require that the agency be given access to the data reported to a data repository. There are many data repositories located overseas and many non-U.S. SDs have reporting systems in place to report to such data repositories. Until the CFTC, however, has access to the data held in non-U.S. data repositories, non-U.S. SDs are not permitted to satisfy their CFTC reporting obligations by reporting swap data to these non-U.S. repositories. While the CFTC and EU are still negotiating the appropriate data access standards to data repositories to allow sharing of this information, the CFTC staff has issued no-action relief to non-U.S. SDs when transacting with non-U.S. counterparties.

Additionally, the Dodd-Frank Act required SDRs to provide domestic and foreign regulators with the data the SDRs have collected, upon request. It also required that, before the SDRs share the information, the regulator requesting the information agree to abide by the confidentiality requirements set out in the CEA and to "indemnify the [SDR] and the [CFTC] for any expenses arising from litigation relating to the information" provided by the SDR. Dodd-Frank Act § 728. These provisions created a barrier to sharing swap data across borders because most foreign governmental entities do not have the legal authority to enter into such indemnification agreements. *Swap Data Repository and Clearinghouse Indemnification Correction Act of 2012: Testimony Concerning Indemnification of Security-Based Swap Data Repositories Before the H. Subcomm. on Capital Markets & Govt. Sponsored Enter.*, 112th Cong. (2012) (testimony of Ethiopis Tafara, Director, SEC). In 2015, Congress enacted an unrelated transportation bill that included a provision removing the indemnification provision and replacing it with a requirement that the foreign jurisdiction provide a written agreement to comply with statutory confidentiality requirements.

Another inadvertent conflict arose between U.S. swap reporting rules and the privacy laws of some non-U.S. jurisdictions. The CFTC's reporting rules require a counterparty to report the identities of both parties to a swap to an SDR. Certain non-U.S. jurisdictions, however, require that a counterparty consent to the disclosure of its identity, while others require that the non-U.S. regulator approve such disclosure, and others still prohibit the disclosure of financial- or banking-related information entirely. For example, if a U.S. SD is transacting with a counterparty in Switzerland, it may not be able to report all the information it is required to report to an SDR without violating local privacy laws in that jurisdiction. As it continues to review ways to resolve these issues, the CFTC staff has issued a no-action letter to address trades with counterparties located in various non-U.S. jurisdictions with privacy laws that would conflict with the CFTC's reporting requirements.

---

1. ***Costs and Benefits***. Given the regulatory requirements discussed in this Chapter, what are the costs and benefits for Airline, Bank, and Swap Dealer to continue entering into swaps in the market? Do you think these requirements would become a barrier to entry for smaller entities?

2. ***Clearing and Transparency***. Do you think some of the measures in the Dodd-Frank Act simply shifted or even increased risk? Are there further reforms that would reduce risk and increase transparency?

3. ***Securities vs. Swaps.*** As you review this Chapter and Chapter 11.3, you might compare various other approaches you have learned about, for example, the regulation of securities in such areas as:

- **Dealers.** In the securities markets, brokers and dealers act as intermediaries to connect buyers and sellers and provide liquidity, as discussed in Chapters 4.1 and 4.2. Broker-dealers are subject to registration, capital, and business conduct requirements. In the swap market, newly-created registration categories of SDs and SBSDs serve much the same function, and are regulated in some similar ways, as discussed in Chapter 11.3.

- **End Users.** As outlined in Part IV, the securities markets have various types of end users, including individuals, retirement funds, and corporations. These end users are subject to a different regulatory regime than registered intermediaries. As you have learned, end users in the swap market are exempt from a number of requirements.

- **Trading Platforms and Clearinghouses.** In the securities market, exchanges (such as New York Stock Exchange and NASDAQ) match buyers and sellers of securities in a relatively open and transparent marketplace, and clearing agencies help to ensure that counterparties honor their obligations to each other, as discussed in Chapter 4.4. As you have learned, the securities markets have been rapidly changing and there are many exchanges and alternative venues for trading off-exchange. In the swap market, DCMs and SEFs serve functions similar to securities exchanges, and clearinghouses serve a vital risk protection function.
- **Trade Reporting.** As discussed in Chapters 4.3 and 4.4, the securities markets require transactions to be reported and for price and volume information to be publicly available to market participants. As this Chapter discusses, reporting is required of swap transactions as well.

There are, however, major differences between the implementation of the securities regulatory system and the swap regulatory system. Some of these reflect different policy choices made by Congress or the regulatory agencies at different historical times, while others reflect different market circumstances. The Dodd-Frank Act required reform of the swap market in less than five years, as compared to the decades-long gradual evolution of federal securities regulations from their origins in 1933 and 1934 through legislation, regulation, guidance, no-action letters, and enforcement, to their continued evolution today. Given the speed of implementation and the complexity of regulating swaps markets, the Dodd-Frank Act framework remains a work in progress.

CHAPTER 11.3

DERIVATIVES: BUSINESS CONDUCT AND MARKET INTEGRITY

CONTENTS

I. INTRODUCTION

In 2015, Federal Reserve Bank of New York President William Dudley remarked that,

> [t]wo years ago, I noted that recent scandals in banking evidenced 'deep-seated cultural and ethical failures.' Many of the industry's leaders now agree. According to the Federal Advisory Council of the Federal Reserve System, a group composed of senior representatives from the industry, "as often as not [. . .] the challenges faced in recent years have been behavioral and cultural; post-crisis episodes such as [London Interbank Offered Rates (LIBOR)] and foreign exchange manipulation provide hard evidence that there remains work to be done."

Opening Remarks at Reforming Culture and Behavior in the Financial Services Industry: Workshop on Progress and Challenges (Nov. 5, 2015). While ethics are undoubtedly the responsibility of individuals, ethical cultures and subcultures exist within a specific institutional context, and a key post-Financial Crisis insight is that tone from the top is the responsibility of board of directors and senior managers. Senior managers and employees make choices about their behaviors in part on the basis of their values, the contexts and organizational subcultures in which they operate, and the incentives they face. Long unregulated, at least not directly, there is now a focus on shaping ethical behavior by supervisory, regulatory, and enforcement measures.

In this Chapter, we first examine how the Dodd-Frank Act regulates the conduct of major players who trade derivatives and look at how the Dodd-Frank Act established the regulation of swap dealers and major swap participants. We also explore the business conduct requirements that the Dodd-Frank Act imposes on these institutions to enhance fairness and financial stability in the swaps market. While the securities and commodities markets have long regulated business conduct, *see, e.g.*, 17 C.F.R. § 240.10b-5; Commodity Exchange Act (CEA) § 9(a)(2), the Dodd-Frank Act expands the scope of these requirements by applying business conduct rules to the swaps market. The rules follow a general theme: SDs and MSPs must act fairly towards counterparties and customers. We also introduce the concept of position limits, which are designed to limit the ability of large market participants to manipulate prices.

We then turn to how regulators police business conduct standards and promote market integrity through enforcement actions. We explore the investigations of alleged abuses in the LIBOR and foreign exchange (FX) markets, which involved civil and criminal actions against firms and individuals. We also discuss proposals for reform. We conclude by examining the extraterritorial application of U.S. rules as they apply to SDs and MSPs, and coordination with the EU.

II. REGULATING THE KEY PARTICIPANTS

In this section, we focus on the regulation of key swap market participants through registration with the CFTC and SEC as swap dealers (SDs), security-based swap dealers (SBSDs), major swap participants (MSPs), and major security-based swap participants (MSBSPs), and the related applicable regulations. As discussed in Chapter 1.3 and Part IV, the CFTC and SEC have had, for many years, registration requirements and business conduct obligations for entities that act as futures commission merchants (FCMs) and broker-dealers. Before the Dodd-Frank Act, however, there was no similar registration requirement for key swap market participants. Title VII of the Dodd-Frank Act required these key market participants to register with the CFTC and SEC and to comply with new regulatory obligations. Although FX transactions are exempted from trading and clearing rules, the Dodd-Frank Act includes these transactions for business conduct purposes.

A. SWAP DEALERS AND SECURITY-BASED SWAP DEALERS

Dealers stand ready to purchase or sell a financial instrument at the request of their customers with the goal of buying or selling that instrument to or from other customers. In doing so, and in serving as a central point of contact for participants in the market, a dealer allows its client to buy or sell a financial instrument without looking for another end user who happens to want to take the opposite position.

In many markets, including the securities and futures markets, dealers are subject to registration and heightened regulatory standards. These heightened regulatory standards are generally focused on (1) ensuring the safety and soundness of the dealers; (2) promoting efficient and safe markets; (3) protecting market participants who transact with dealers from unfair, improper, abusive, or fraudulent practices, (4) providing market transparency; and (5) reducing systemic risk.

CEA and the Securities Exchange Act of 1934 (1934 Act), as amended by the Dodd-Frank Act, require the registration of dealers in the swap market as SDs, and dealers in the security-based swap market as SBSDs. An SD or SBSD is any entity that (1) holds itself out as a dealer in swaps or security-based swaps; (2) makes a market in swaps or security-based swaps; (3) regularly enters into swaps or security-based swaps with counterparties in the ordinary course of business; and (4) engages in any activity causing the entity to be commonly known in the trade as a dealer or market maker in swaps or security-based swaps. *See, e.g.*, 7 U.S.C. § 1a(49)(A), CEA § 1a(49)(A); *see also* 15 U.S.C. § 78c(a)(71)(A), 1934 Act § 3a(71)(A).

In recognition of the ambiguity of those terms, the CFTC and SEC jointly published rules that further define activities that would require an entity to register as an SD or SBSD:

- having a reputation in the market for being able to accommodate the demand and need for swaps and security-based swaps and providing advice to investors regarding swaps and security-based swaps;
- providing liquidity to the swap and security-based swap markets by matching buy and sell orders and seeking to profit from providing that liquidity to the market;
- acting as a market maker by quoting bid or offer prices for swaps and security-based swaps on an organized exchange or trading system;

- setting prices for swaps and security-based swaps offered in the market instead of accepting prices (although accepting prices does not foreclose a party from being categorized as a dealer); and
- holding itself out as a dealer by providing marketing materials to investors that describe the types of swaps and security-based swaps that the investor is interested in entering into.

See Alexandra Guest & Jack I. Habert, *Products and Registrants Under Title VII*, *in* OTC DERIVATIVES REGULATION UNDER DODD-FRANK: A GUIDE TO REGISTRATION, REPORTING, BUSINESS CONDUCT, AND CLEARING 23-32 (William C. Meehan & Gabriel D. Rosenberg eds., 2015).

As of December 31, 2015, there were 103 provisionally-registered SDs. Registered SDs include legal entities that are part of the largest global financial institutions, such as JPMorgan, Goldman Sachs, Bank of America, Morgan Stanley, Citigroup, and Credit Suisse. There are no registered SBSDs, as the SEC's rules do not yet require registration.

The 1934 Act and the CEA, as amended by the Dodd-Frank Act, only require an entity to register as an SD or SBSD if it engages in more than a *de minimis* amount of swap dealing activity. In implementing this threshold, the CFTC set the *de minimis* amount for registration as an SD generally at:

- $8 billion in notional amount of swaps in a dealing capacity in the previous 12-month period; and
- $25 million in notional amount of swaps in a dealing capacity in the previous 12-month period with "special entities" (*e.g.*, federal and state agencies, cities, counties, municipalities, and certain employee benefit plans).

If a dealer exceeds either threshold, then it does not qualify for the *de minimis* exemption. 17 C.F.R. § 1.3(ggg)(4), CFTC Rule 1.3(ggg)(4); *see also* 17 C.F.R. § 240.3a71-2, SEC Rule 240.3a71-2 (similar requirements). For further details, see Further Definition of "Swap Dealer," "Security-Based Swap Dealer," "Major Swap Participant," "Major Security-Based Swap Participant," and "Eligible Contract Participant," 77 Fed. Reg. 30,633 (May 23, 2012).

Not all swaps entered into by an entity, however, must be counted towards the *de minimis* threshold; market participants need not count swaps entered into to hedge their own commercial risks, swaps with 100% commonly-owned affiliates, or certain swaps entered into by an insured depository institution in connection with loan activity. For example, a bank entering into interest rate swaps or FX swaps to hedge risks to its own balance sheet is not acting in a dealer capacity, and therefore would not need to count those hedges towards its *de minimis* threshold. In addition, there is a cross-border jurisdictional component to the *de minimis* calculation. Non-U.S. entities must look not only to the type of activity but also to the U.S.-person status of their counterparties to determine whether a particular swap must be counted towards the threshold. If no further action is taken by the CFTC or SEC, the *de minimis* threshold will decrease from $8 billion to $3 billion in 2017, and many smaller market participants will need to register as SDs and SBSDs or leave the market.

B. MAJOR SWAP PARTICIPANTS AND MAJOR SECURITY-BASED SWAP PARTICIPANTS

In addition to requiring registration of dealers in the swaps market, Title VII requires the registration and regulation of market participants that are not dealers but are large enough to pose risks to the marketplace. This concept—not found in broker-dealer or futures regulation—was inspired by the experience of AIG Financial Products during the Financial Crisis, as well as earlier experiences, such as the rise and collapse of Enron. Title VII requires major non-dealer market participants to register as MSPs (for swaps) and MSBSPs (for security-based swaps).

An MSP or MSBSP is any entity that is not an SD or SBSD and that (1) maintains a substantial position in swaps or security-based swaps; (2) holds swaps or security-based swaps that create substantial counterparty exposure that could seriously affect the stability of the U.S. banking system or financial markets; or (3) is a highly leveraged financial entity not subject to capital requirements established by a federal banking agency and that maintains a substantial position in swaps or security-based swaps. 7 U.S.C. § 1a(33), CEA § 1a(33); 15 U.S.C. § 78c(a)(67), 1934 Act § 3(a)(67).

The CFTC and SEC have implemented this relatively open standard through a set of quantitative tests that look to (1) the amount an entity currently owes to its counterparties on swaps; and (2) a calculation of potential future exposure that serves as a proxy for how much an entity may owe in the future on its swaps. Further Definition of "Swap Dealer," "Security-Based Swap Dealer," "Major Swap Participant," "Major Security-Based Swap Participant," and "Eligible Contract Participant," 77 Fed. Reg. 30,751-53 (May 23, 2012). These thresholds are currently set high enough that as of December 31, 2015, there was only one provisionally registered MSP; no MSBSPs yet exist since the SEC's rules requiring MSBSPs registration are not yet effective.

C. REGULATORY OBLIGATIONS OF KEY MARKET PARTICIPANTS

Registration as an SD, SBSD, MSP, or MSBSP comes with significant regulatory obligations. Before the Dodd-Frank Act, over-the-counter (OTC) derivatives dealers were, in effect, self-regulating with respect to swap and security-based swap activity. For example, dealers determined appropriate risk management for swap activity and put into place their own bespoke swap documentation agreements with counterparties, which included limited counterparty representations and due diligence procedures. No body of law, however, regulated these activities. During the Financial Crisis, it became clear that this self-regulation had substantial shortcomings. Swap counterparties were unable to make informed decisions before entering into these transactions due to the lack of transparency and the complexity of the documentation. For example, the SEC alleged that a dealer charged Jefferson County, Alabama higher rates than sophisticated market participants in connection with municipal securities underwriting and interest swap agreements because county officials were less informed than other market participants. *See In the Matter of J.P. Morgan Securities Inc.,* Sec. Exch. Act Release No. 60,928 (Nov. 4, 2009).

To resolve these issues, the swap regulatory regime introduced in Title VII of the Dodd-Frank Act requires SDs, SBSDs, MSPs, and MSBSPs to comply with business conduct standards that require fair dealing and trade disclosures, written trading documentation and swap confirmations that contain all applicable terms of a swap transaction, and portfolio reconciliation to confirm that the terms of their swaps match the terms in the records of their counterparties. These entities are also subject to enhanced capital requirements, robust risk management program requirements, and significant new compliance and regulatory reporting obligations.

1. Fair Dealing

In an attempt to provide swaps customers with the full picture of the risks of entering into these transactions, Congress imposed new business conduct standards on SDs, SBSDs, MSPs, and MSBSPs. The CFTC's external business conduct rules fall into three general categories:

- **Verification of Counterparty Eligibility**. SDs and MSPs must obtain information sufficient to ascertain whether their counterparties are considered sophisticated enough to be permitted to enter into swaps (known as eligible contract participants) or whether they are special entities. They must also obtain know-your-counterparty information, including their counterparty's name, address, and clearing status.
- **Disclosure Requirements**. SDs and MSPs must disclose key information to the counterparties to the trade. In particular, SDs and MSPs must disclose to end-user counterparties the material characteristics and risks of the swap and any conflicts of interest the SD may have. In addition, they must inform counterparties that they have the right to receive a scenario analysis, which is a description of how the swap is expected to perform in various market conditions, and the right to have their swaps cleared by a derivatives clearing organization of their choosing.
- **Suitability and Other Sales Practice Standards.** When recommending a swap, an SD or MSP must ensure that the swap is suitable for its prospective counterparty. SDs and MSPs must communicate with counterparties in a "fair and balanced manner based on principles of fair dealing and good faith." SDs and MSPs are subject to specific anti-fraud and anti-manipulation provisions, as well as restrictions on the use of material confidential counterparty information adverse to their counterparty.

See 17 C.F.R. §§ 23.430–34.

As mentioned above, SDs have heightened regulatory obligations when advising or dealing with special entities. These heightened duties are a direct result of the significant losses incurred by government agencies, municipalities, charitable institution endowments, and beneficiaries of pension and retirement funds during the Financial Crisis because of derivatives exposures. Congress cited to the fact that many financial institutions encouraged governmental entities and retirement and pension plans to enter into sophisticated swap transactions that they knew or should have known were inappropriate or unsuitable for these clients. *Wall Street Reform and Consumer Protection Act—Conference Report*, 111th Cong. 5923 (2010) (statement of Sen. Blanche Lincoln). The heightened rules for transacting with special entities are indicative of Congress's increased awareness that special entities "play an important public interest role by virtue of their responsibility for managing taxpayer funds, the assets of public and private employee pension plans and endowments of charitable institutions." Business Conduct Standards for Swap Dealers and Major Swap Participants with Counterparties, 77 Fed. Reg. 9,817 (Feb. 17, 2012).

2. Swap Trading Relationship Documentation and Confirmations

CFTC regulations require that SDs and MSPs execute written trading documentation with counterparties. The documentation must include all terms governing the trading relationship between the SD and the counterparty. The regulations require the exchange of information between SDs or MSPs and their counterparties through acknowledgments and written confirmations of each swap, which together with the trading documentation memorialize the agreement of the counterparties to all terms of each swap. SDs and MSPs must provide their counterparties with that confirmation "as soon as technologically possible," with certain exceptions.

3. Portfolio Reconciliation and Dispute Resolution

SDs and MSPs must also perform periodic "portfolio reconciliation" and establish dispute resolution procedures with swap counterparties. Portfolio reconciliation is a post-trade execution process and a risk management tool that is designed to: (1) identify and resolve any discrepancies between the records of the counterparties regarding the terms of a swap and the valuation of the swap; and (2) ensure effective confirmation of all terms of the swap. The frequency with which parties must engage in portfolio reconciliation ranges from daily to annually and depends on the number of swaps in the counterparties' portfolio and the parties involved (*e.g.*, whether one party is an end user).

4. Capital Requirements

The CEA, as amended by the Dodd-Frank Act, requires the CFTC to adopt minimum capital requirements for SDs and MSPs that are not prudentially regulated (*e.g.*, an SD that is not a bank). For SDs and MSPs that are prudentially regulated, the Treasury Department, Federal Reserve Board, OCC, FDIC, the Farm Credit Administration, and Federal Housing Finance Agency jointly proposed capital and margin rules. Margin and Capital Requirements for Covered Swap Entities, 79 Fed. Reg. 57,348 (Sept. 24, 2014). As of December 31, 2015, the CFTC has proposed, but not yet finalized, its capital rules for SDs and MSPs, which are based, in part, on concepts set forth under the Basel capital requirements, which we discussed in Chapters 2.5, 2.6 and 2.7. The capital requirements under the proposed rules set forth the minimum levels of capital that SDs and MSPs would be required to maintain, which differs based on whether the SD or MSP is also registered as an FCM or, if not, whether the SD is a non-bank subsidiary of a U.S. bank holding company (BHC). The SEC has also issued proposed rules.

5. Risk Management, Portfolio Compression, and Conflicts Rules

Before the Dodd-Frank Act, financial institutions were not required to have robust risk management practices specifically related to their derivatives businesses. In fact, some have attributed the failure of AIG Financial Products to poor risk management of derivatives products. Some have alleged that AIG Financial Products was able to engage in highly risky behavior without significant oversight because its derivatives activities were unregulated, ultimately leading to the company's near-collapse, averted only by government bailouts. *See* FCIC, THE FINANCIAL CRISIS INQUIRY REPORT 140 (2011).

Congress sought to correct this deficiency by requiring each SD and MSP to establish, document, maintain, and enforce a risk management program designed to monitor and manage the risks associated with its swap activities. Reflecting an integrated approach to risk management at the consolidated entity level, the CFTC's regulation requires an SD or MSP to take into account its own risks and those of its affiliates. The risk management program must monitor risks associated with the entity's swap activities and establish risk tolerance limits. Additionally, the internal business conduct rules require that SDs and MSPs prepare for adverse economic scenarios. Specifically, they must implement a "business continuity and disaster recovery plan," which requires the entity to outline procedures for dealing with a major disruption in business activities. Through this plan, SDs and MSPs must outline mechanisms for (1) resuming operations by the next business day with little disturbance to counterparties and the market; and (2) recovering all required records.

Additionally, SDs must engage in portfolio compression exercises with their swap counterparties, which, like portfolio reconciliation, is a post-trade execution process. Portfolio compression generally involves the swap counterparties terminating or adjusting the notional value of some or all of the swaps between them and replacing those swaps with other swaps that have a lesser combined notional value. The complicated portfolio compression process is designed to reduce the overall notional size and number of swaps between the counterparties without changing the overall swap risk profile or value of the swap portfolio. Portfolio compression is widely used by market participants and effectively allows parties to engage in netting, a concept discussed in Chapter 11.2 with respect to clearing. At its most basic, compression allows SDs to simplify the management of large swap portfolios by aggregating swap positions into fewer overall contracts with reduced outstanding notional values.

SDs and MSPs must also take steps to minimize conflicts of interest by creating firewalls between certain departments within the entity. For example, the trading department cannot interfere with the research department's reports.

6. Risk Exposure and Chief Compliance Officer Reports

SDs must submit quarterly risk exposure reports to their senior management, the SD's board of directors, and the CFTC. These reports include an overview of the SD risk profile and information relating to risk management program implementation and any recommended changes. The SD's chief compliance officer must also prepare and submit an annual compliance report and certification to the SD's board of directors or senior officer and to the CFTC. The report must contain a review of each requirement under the CEA and CFTC regulations that applies to the SD, an assessment regarding the effectiveness of the SD's policies and procedures for each of those requirements, and any necessary or recommended changes to the firm's policies and procedures or compliance program as a result of the chief compliance officer's annual review.

D. POST-DODD-FRANK ACT ISDA PROTOCOLS

Before the Dodd-Frank Act, many counterparties had documentation in place to trade swaps. As you have learned, most used a standard agreement created by the International Swaps and Derivatives Association (ISDA), known as the ISDA Master Agreement. A large bank may have had thousands of ISDA Master Agreements in place with its various counterparties. The new rules adopted by the CFTC under Title VII required changes to this existing documentation. For example, since the external business conduct rules require that certain representations be made before swaps are entered into, the rule effectively requires amended documentation. Given the large numbers of ISDA Master Agreements, however, it would have been impractical for every pair of counterparties to individually negotiate and amend existing documentation as needed to comply with the new requirements.

To solve this problem, ISDA developed two protocols that provided a centralized method for SDs to amend their ISDA Master Agreements. A protocol is a multilateral contractual mechanism that allows for standardized amendments to be made to swap agreements between all adhering parties, rather than requiring every pair of counterparties to negotiate. Put another way, the protocols allowed counterparties to agree once to be bound by the terms of each protocol and, through a web-based platform, to notify counterparties of that agreement. If both counterparties matched terms, the existing trading documentation between them would automatically be amended to include the revised provisions. The protocols, thus, provide a simplified way for swap market participants to amend existing documentation without engaging in tedious and numerous bilateral negotiations.

As of December 31, 2015, ISDA has developed two primary Dodd-Frank Act business conduct protocols: the August 2012 DF Protocol, which relates to compliance with the CFTC's external business conduct rules, and the March 2013 DF Protocol, which addresses the CFTC's rules on (1) swap trading documentation, (2) the end-user exception to the clearing requirement, and (3) portfolio reconciliation. Each of these protocols had close to 17,000 adhering parties.

Figure 11.3-1 Diagram of ISDA Protocol Multilateral Amendment Process

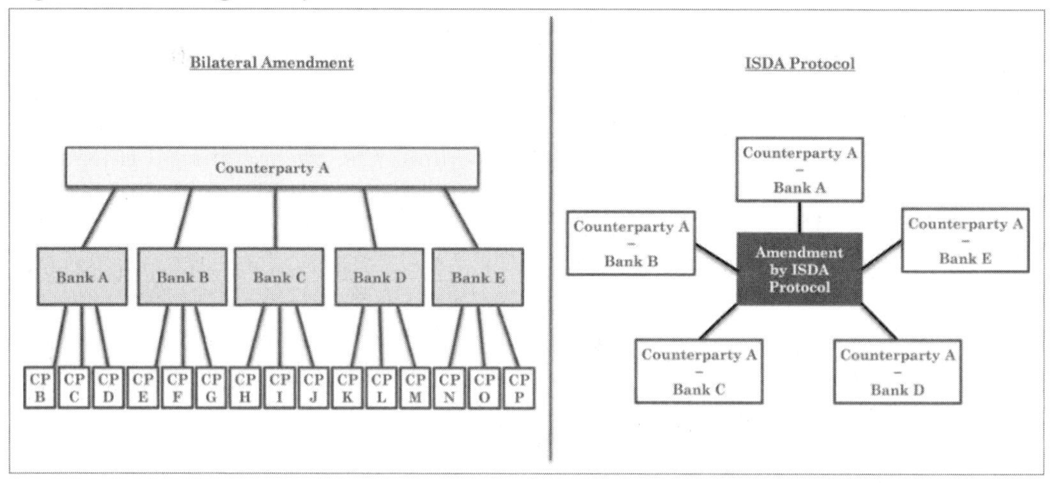

E. POSITION LIMITS

Like other market participants, SDs and MSPs are subject to position limits in swaps. The CEA allows the CFTC to set position limits on commodity derivatives as "necessary to diminish, eliminate, or prevent" excessive speculation. 7 U.S.C. § 6a(a)(1). The Dodd-Frank Act amended the CEA to require the CFTC to "establish limits on the amount of positions . . . that may be held by any person with respect to [commodity derivative] contracts." Dodd-Frank Act § 737. The Dodd-Frank amendment, however, was unclear as to whether the CFTC needed to make a necessity determination before issuing position limits. Market participants argued that, before the Dodd-Frank Act, the CFTC would have had to show that position limits curb excessive speculation before issuing such restraints. Conversely, the CFTC argued that Congress intended the new CEA language to require the CFTC to enact position limits irrespective of any such determination.

In 2011, the CFTC adopted position limit rules without a necessity finding. The position limits restricted the number of contracts a market participant could hold in swaps, futures, and options based on 28 physical commodities. Position Limits for Derivatives, 76 Fed. Reg. 4,752 (Jan. 26, 2011). ISDA and the Securities Industry and Financial Markets Association sued, arguing that the Dodd-Frank Act did not do away with the necessity requirement. Int'l Swaps & Derivatives Ass'n v. Commodity Futures Trading Comm'n, 887 F. Supp. 2d 259 (D.D.C. 2012). The district court noted the CFTC's position in its Final Rule: "Congress did not give the Commission a choice. Congress directed the Commission to impose position limits and to do so expeditiously." 76 Fed. Reg. at 71,628. The district court vacated the CFTC's rule on *Chevron* grounds, holding that "deference to an agency's interpretation of a statute is not appropriate when the agency wrongly believes that interpretation is compelled by Congress." 887 F. Supp. 2d at 280–81 (internal quotations and citation omitted).

The CFTC re-proposed position limits on 28 physical commodities in 2013. Position Limits for Derivatives, 78 Fed. Reg. 75,680 (Dec. 12, 2013). The proposal effectively reinstated the vacated rule but, to comply with the District Court's finding, the CFTC made a necessity determination to avoid future litigation. The CFTC noted that position limits prevent individual traders from speculating on large amounts of derivative commodities. The CFTC concluded that the aggregate effect of restricting individual speculation reduces speculation in the financial system. The proposal caps the number of swaps, futures, and options contracts that a market participant may hold in specified commodities. As of December 31, 2015, the CFTC has not finalized its position limits proposal.

---

1. ***Engaging in Dealing Activities***. Are there other types of activities that may be indicative of dealing in addition to those we already discussed?

2. ***Business Conduct Rules***. If you were writing the business conduct rules, what types of SD activities would you attempt to regulate? Recall our discussion of disclosure as a regulatory tool in Chapter 5.4. Do you think that heightened disclosure would be helpful in reducing the likelihood that a counterparty would enter into an excessively-risky swap transaction? If not, what do you think might prevent a counterparty from entering into a swap transaction with an SD that might not be suitable to that counterparty? Should disclosure and sales practice standards vary by the counterparty, as in the Dodd-Frank Act, or should there be a uniform rule across the market?

3. ***MSP and MSBSP Standards***. Now that you have read about MSPs and MSBSPs and the new regulatory system implemented by the Dodd-Frank Act, how would you have determined which entities meet the MSP and MSBSP standard in order to capture non-dealer entities like AIG Financial Products? Would you have adopted a prescriptive approach, like the CFTC and SEC, to identify these market participants? *See* Jai Massari & Gabriel Rosenberg, *The Perils of a Middle Road to Regulating Systemic Risk: The Volcker Rule's Risk Backstop Provisions*, 104 GEO. L.J. 145 (2015).

III. MARKET INTEGRITY

After the Financial Crisis, enforcement agencies in many different jurisdictions undertook investigations into manipulation in LIBOR rate-setting and in the FX markets. These investigations were broad in scope, involved multiple financial institutions operating in several different jurisdictions, and resulted in billions of dollars in fines. Recall our discussion of market manipulation in Chapter 4.3, involving the submission of false bids for government securities by an individual at Salomon Brothers. In this case, the agencies alleged that traders used a number of similar techniques to manipulate LIBOR and FX rates. Separate from their LIBOR and FX investigations, the CFTC and SEC have also started to enforce their regulations under Title VII of the Dodd-Frank Act. We discuss the CFTC's and SEC's Title VII enforcement actions at the end of this section.

A. LONDON INTERBANK OFFERED RATE MANIPULATION

1. Background

What connects syndicated corporate loans, private college loans, and adjustable rate mortgages to the massive and complex derivatives market? The London Interbank Offered Rate, known as LIBOR. This is the prime example of a benchmark interest rate—a rate used as the basis of derivatives and contract interest rates worldwide. LIBOR is intended to reflect interbank lending in the London money markets, in which financial institutions engage in borrowing and lending money for maturities of up to one year. LIBOR is calculated by taking a trimmed mean average of inputs from the major financial institutions operating in the London money markets. These inputs reflect the subjective rate at which an institution reports it could borrow money at different maturities. LIBOR is used as a reference point for derivatives and other contracts. In 2012, for instance, LIBOR was referenced in derivatives and other transactions worth $360 trillion. DENNIS KUO ET AL., N.Y. FED. RES. BANK, A COMPARISON OF LIBOR TO OTHER MEASURES OF BANK BORROWING COSTS 1 (2012) (unpublished manuscript).

Although the most important, LIBOR is not the only benchmark interest rate. There are similar rates in different markets extending from Europe (EURIBOR) to Japan (Euroyen TIBOR), and even more obscure rates in markets like Mauritius (the Port Louis Interbank Offered Rate, or PLIBOR). Other reference rates are based on averages of swap rates, such as the ISDAFix.

The methodology for setting LIBOR developed in the 1980s, when the OTC derivatives market was in its infancy and the impact of the rate was confined. The British Bankers' Association (BBA) established the rate for the benefit of its members. Having a benchmark reference rate is beneficial to developing a market in which standardization of contracts plays an important role. The utility of LIBOR is underscored by its prevalence and significance. As you have seen, by the time of the Financial Crisis, the derivatives market had expanded to proportions that were inconceivable in the 1980s. The LIBOR rate, a key part of the market infrastructure was, however, still determined by essentially the same methodology and there was no impetus for change.

At the time of the Financial Crisis, LIBOR had several significant structural problems that could lead to its manipulation. First, submitted rates were non-binding, banks were not required to prove the accuracy of their quotes, and the quotes submitted did not have to reflect real transactions. François-Louis Michaud & Christian Upper, *What Drives Interbank Rates? Evidence from the LIBOR Panel*, BANK FOR INT'L SETTLEMENTS Q. REV. 47, 48 (2008). No safeguards existed to prevent a bank from submitting inaccurate rates. Second, because the BBA represented the contributor banks, conflicts of interest existed. HER MAJESTY'S TREASURY, THE WHEATLEY REVIEW OF LIBOR: FINAL REPORT 21 (Sept. 2012) [hereinafter WHEATLEY REVIEW]. Finally, the contributor banks' submissions were made public after the rate was determined. How do you think the knowledge of other banks' recently submitted lending rates could affect LIBOR-submitter behavior?

2. LIBOR Misconduct

On June 27, 2012, Barclays resolved several regulatory and governmental investigations involving misconduct related to LIBOR. Barclays entered into a non-prosecution agreement with the DOJ, which fined the bank $160 million, a settlement with the CFTC, which fined the bank $200 million and required Barclays to agree to various undertakings, and a fine of £59.5 million discounted from £85 million for early settlement from the UK financial services regulator, then the Financial Services Authority (FSA), now the Financial Conduct Authority (FCA). The fines were at that time the largest in the history of the CFTC and FSA. The CFTC and DOJ alleged misconduct relating to Barclays's LIBOR and EURIBOR submissions, including:

- derivatives traders inside the bank requesting that the bank's LIBOR submitters make particular submissions in order to benefit their trading positions;
- requests made to Barclays's submitters by traders outside the bank, including traders who had previously worked at Barclays;
- requests made by Barclays's derivatives traders to LIBOR submitters at other banks; and
- senior management instructions to reduce Barclays's LIBOR submissions owing to negative media and market perceptions that Barclays had a liquidity problem based, in part, on its high LIBOR submissions.

The settlement caused a major market impact—Barclays's share price slid 18% in value the day the settlement was announced—and a strong media response. The settlement also resulted in high-profile resignations (including by Barclays's Chairman, its CEO, and his deputy), hearings in the UK Parliament, the establishment of the UK Parliamentary Commission on Banking Standards, a full-scale review of the LIBOR submission process, and the introduction of new criminal offenses of LIBOR manipulation by UK legislators. The FSA alleged misconduct based in part on communications between traders. For example, the FSA identified the following problematic communications:

- On Monday, 13 March 2006, the following email exchange took place:

  Trader C: "The big day [has] arrived . . . My NYK are screaming at me about an unchanged 3m libor. As always, any help wd be greatly appreciated. What do you think you'll go for 3m?"

  Submitter: "I am going 90 altho 91 is what I should be posting".

  Trader C: ". . . when I retire and write a book about this business your name will be written in golden letters . . . ."

  Submitter: "I would prefer this not be in any book!"

- Trader C requested low one month and three month US dollar LIBOR submissions at 10:52 am on 7 April 2006 (shortly before the submissions were due to be made); "If it's not too late low 1m and 3m would be nice, but please feel free to say "no". . . Coffees will be coming your way either way, just to say thank you for your help in the past few weeks." A Submitter responded "Done . . . for you big boy."

- On 26 October 2006, an external trader made a request for a lower three month US dollar LIBOR submission. The external trader stated in an email to Trader G at Barclays "If it comes in unchanged I'm a dead man." Trader G responded that he would "have a chat." Barclays' submission on that day for three month US dollar LIBOR was half a basis point lower than the day before, rather than being unchanged. The external trader thanked Trader G for Barclays' LIBOR submission later that day: "Dude. I owe you big time! Come over one day after work and I'm opening a bottle of Bollinger".

- On 28 February 2007, Trader B made a request to an external trader in relation to three month US dollar LIBOR "duuuude . . . whats up with ur guys 34.5 3m fix . . . tell him to get it up!!" The external trader responded "ill talk to him right away."

- On 5 February 2008, Trader B (a US dollar Derivatives Trader) stated in a telephone conversation with Manager B that Barclays' Submitter was submitting "the highest LIBOR of anybody . . . He's like, I think this is where it should be. I'm like, dude, you're killing us." Manager B instructed Trader B to: "just tell him to keep it, to put it low." Trader B said that he had "begged" the Submitter to put in a low LIBOR submission and the Submitter had said he would "see what I can do".

FSA FINAL NOTICE TO BARCLAYS BANK PLC ¶¶ 57, 59, 65, 83, 91 (June 27, 2012).

The settlements raised questions about the extent of the misconduct, and other firms' involvement. There were allegations that others in the financial sector knew of the misconduct:

> [A] senior Barclays Treasury manager informed BBA in a telephone call that it had not been reporting accurately, although he noted that Barclays was not the worst offender of the panel bank members. "We're clean, but we're dirty-clean, rather than clean-clean." The BBA representative responded, "no one's clean-clean."

CFTC, Order Instituting Proceedings Pursuant to Sections 6(c) And 6(d) of the Commodity Exchange Act, As Amended, Making Findings and Imposing Remedial Sanctions 23 (June 27, 2012).

The coordinated settlement was an example of increased international cooperation on enforcement regarding alleged manipulation or attempted manipulation in a wide variety of rates and derivatives tied to rates. The Barclays settlement was followed by settlements with other banks and broker-dealers, including UBS, Royal Bank of Scotland, Rabobank, Deutsche Bank, Lloyds, Societe General, JPMorgan, Citigroup, ICAP, and a range of others. These settlements involved multiple authorities: the CFTC, DOJ, UK FSA/FCA, European Commission, Japan Financial Services Agency, Swiss Financial Market Supervisory Authority, and the Dutch Prosecution Service, to name a few. The actions resulted in the imposition of billions of dollars in fines, with the largest fine of approximately $2.5 billion, imposed on Deutsche Bank.

Authorities are also pursuing individuals in criminal prosecutions and regulatory actions. Convictions have been obtained on both sides of the Atlantic. One former UBS trader was sentenced to 14 years in prison after being found guilty of eight charges of conspiracy to defraud in the UK. A former Rabobank employee has been sentenced to two years in prison in the United States; another Rabobank trader has been sentenced to a year and a day. The DOJ is prosecuting a number of other individuals, and three have pleaded guilty. Press Release, DOJ: Deutsche Bank's London Subsidiary Agrees to Plead Guilty in Connection with Long-Running Manipulation of LIBOR (Apr. 23, 2015). Despite the success of the UBS prosecution, some believe that the UK Serious Fraud Office's appetite for individual prosecution is waning because it lost a later LIBOR case and dropped its FX criminal investigation.

3. Reform

Because LIBOR affects trillions of dollars in derivatives and transactions used across the world, legislators and regulators responded with structural reform. WHEATLEY REVIEW, at 3. In July 2012, the UK's Chancellor of the Exchequer commissioned the Wheatley Review to examine and propose changes to LIBOR's framework. Based on the Wheatley Review's recommendations, the UK enacted reforms with the goal of restoring public confidence in LIBOR.

The UK FSA reformed LIBOR's framework in 2013. *See* FSA, THE REG. & SUPERVISION OF BENCHMARKS (2013). Contributor banks must now ensure that submissions are based on objective criteria and relevant information, and banks must also establish procedures to manage conflicts of interest arising from LIBOR submissions. If a bank suspects any person is manipulating LIBOR, it must report the conduct to government authorities. Contributor banks will receive annual audits concerning their LIBOR submission process.

The UK and the BBA also agreed to transfer the administration of LIBOR to Intercontinental Exchange in 2014. Philip Stafford, *IntercontinentalExchange to Take Over Running Libor Benchmark*, FIN. TIMES., Jan. 17, 2014. Intercontinental Exchange is a U.S. public company that operates exchanges and clearinghouses, including the New York Stock Exchange. Reacting to the governance problems associated with the BBA operating LIBOR, regulators believed than an independent LIBOR administrator would ensure "strong and credible governance." WHEATLEY REVIEW, at 21.

---

1. ***Do You Think These Reforms Go Far Enough?*** LIBOR submissions are still based on hypothetical transactions and banks may still have incentives to manipulate LIBOR to profit and protect their reputations. Will these solutions solve the LIBOR problems? *See* Michael S. Barr, *Too LIBOR, Too Late: Time to Move to a Market Rate*, 2 COMPETITION POL'Y INT'L ANTITRUST CHRON. 11 (2012) (arguing for the use of market rates); *see also* Rosa M. Abrantes-Metz & David S. Evans, *Replacing the LIBOR with a Transparent and Reliable Index of Interbank Borrowing: Comments on the Wheatley Review of LIBOR Initial Discussion Paper*, (U. Chicago Working Paper, Nov. 2012) (arguing for "committed" LIBOR). Should policy-makers regulate benchmarks and other indices that could be systemically important? *See* Robert C. Hockett and Saule T. Omarova, *Systemically Significant Prices*, 2 J. FIN. REG. (2016) (forthcoming).

2. ***Alternative Approaches to LIBOR.*** In November 2014, the Federal Reserve Board met with major banks and foreign regulators to discuss replacing LIBOR. Press Release, Federal Reserve Board: Meeting to Consider Alternatives to the Current Libor (Nov. 17, 2014). One option would be to use the overnight-indexed swap rate as a benchmark instead of LIBOR. Overnight-indexed swap relies on real transactions, which means the rate is less susceptible to false submissions compared to LIBOR. The Wheatley Review, however, suggested that the overnight-indexed swap is insufficiently liquid to create a reliable benchmark rate.

Repurchase, or repo, rates could also serve as a substitution for LIBOR. There are multiple published and widely followed repo rates in the market. Repo rates are influenced by the liquidity and credit risk of the underlying collateral, and they reflect factors that the unsecured LIBOR rate excludes. Because the rate reflects the market's view of *both* collateral and the borrower's creditworthiness, commentators suggest it may also be an ineffective benchmark rate. *See* WHEATLEY REVIEW, at 50. Given the pros and cons of each of these possible approaches, which benchmark do you think would be best? Why?

3. ***CFTC Undertakings.*** Each of the banks and broker-dealers fined by the CFTC agreed to comply with a lengthy list of undertakings as part of their settlements. The banks agreed to apply certain specified factors in determining their LIBOR submissions; implement internal controls to prevent conflicts of interest arising between submitters and derivatives traders; document the rationale for their submissions; retain related transactional information and communications data; engage in monitoring and auditing; establish policies, procedures, and controls; conduct training; and make reports to the CFTC on compliance with the undertakings. Is this regulation by the back-door of enforcement? To what extent do you consider it appropriate for these terms to be determined through bilateral settlements?

B. FOREIGN EXCHANGE RATE-RIGGING

1. Background

The FX market is a largely OTC market where traders buy, sell, exchange, hedge, and speculate on currencies. *See generally* MARC LEVINSON, GUIDE TO FINANCIAL MARKETS 15–23 (The Economist 2006). The FX market is the largest and most liquid financial market in the world with an average daily turnover of $5.3 trillion. FED. RESERVE BANK OF N.Y., MANAGING FOREIGN EXCHANGE RISK; *see also* Dagfin Rime & Andreas Schrimpf, *The Anatomy of the Global FX Market Through the Lens of the 2013 Triennial Survey*, 2013 BIS. Q. REV. 27 (2013). Until recently, it has been largely unregulated.

Although the FX market is decentralized, services have emerged to help standardize rates. For example, the WM/Reuters service created benchmark rates in FX. The service produces several rates in a day, but the "WM/R 4 p.m. London fix" is perhaps the most influential. WM/Reuters calculates the 4 p.m. fix by extracting actual FX trades occurring during the fix period (3:59:30 p.m. to 4:00:30 p.m. in London) from an electronic trading system. The benchmark rates are the median prices for each currency pair. *In re* JP Morgan Chase Bank, CFTC Docket No. 15–04, 4 (Nov. 11, 2014).

In 2014, Citigroup, Deutsche Bank, Barclays, UBS, and HSBC accounted, on a combined basis, for more than 60% of FX trading. *Citi Reclaims Top Ranking in Benchmark Euromoney Foreign Exchange Survey*, REUTERS (May 9, 2014). Markets with so few participants may be more susceptible to collusive activity. Because the FX market is decentralized, information is fragmented and opaque, making it difficult for market participants to monitor and compare bid and ask offers. *See* Dagfin Rime & Andreas Schrimpf, *The Anatomy of the Global FX Market Through the Lens of the 2013 Triennial Survey*, 2013 BIS. Q. REV. 27, 27 (Dec. 2013).

2. Alleged Manipulation

The scope of the alleged manipulation in the FX markets was made public through coordinated settlements. The authorities took a different approach to their handling of the FX scandal; rather than taking action against firms one by one, a coordinated regulatory settlement was reached with five firms (Citigroup, HSBC, JPMorgan, RBS, and UBS) on November 12, 2014. The CFTC fined them $1.4 billion collectively, and the UK FCA fined the same firms approximately $1.7 billion. The OCC reached settlements on the same day, levying penalties of $350 million on both Citibank, N.A. and JPMorgan Chase Bank, N.A. Then, on May 20, 2015, the DOJ announced that it had obtained parent-level guilty pleas from Citigroup, JPMorgan, Barclays, and RBS in connection with conspiring to fix bids and offers of euro/U.S. dollar currency pairs in the FX spot market and had fined them $2.5 billion in total. The FX settlement also affected the non-prosecution agreements entered into by UBS and Barclays in relation to LIBOR; UBS and Barclays faced additional penalties and guilty pleas as a result of allegedly violating those agreements. On the same day, the Federal Reserve Board announced it was imposing fines of more than $1.6 billion, and Barclays settled related claims with the New York State Department of Financial Services, the CFTC, and the FCA, with a combined penalty of approximately $1.3 billion. In total, fines for FX manipulation exceeded $10 billion.

According to the DOJ's factual findings, beginning in at least December 2007, FX traders at large firms communicated with each other in an electronic chat room that they referred to as "The Cartel" or "The Mafia" in order to manipulate WM/R rates. Traders coordinated the "trading of the EUR/USD currency pair in connection with European Central Bank and World Markets/Reuters benchmark currency 'fixes' which occurred at 2:15 PM (CET) and 4:00 PM (GMT) each trading day." Additionally, traders would withhold "bids and offers, when one conspirator held an open risk position, so that the price of the currency traded would not move in a direction adverse to the conspirator with an open risk position." Plea Agreement, United States v. Citicorp 3, 5–6, 16–17 (May 20, 2015).

A press account of the alleged manipulation notes:

> One trader with more than a decade of experience said that if he received an order at 3:30 p.m. to sell 1 billion Euros ($1.37 billion) in exchange for Swiss francs at the 4 p.m. fix, he would have two

> objectives: to sell his own euros at the highest price and also to move the rate lower so that at 4 p.m. he could buy the currency from his client at a lower price.
>
> He would profit from the difference between the reference rate and the higher price at which he sold his own euros. A move in the benchmark rate of 2 basis points [0.02 percent], would be worth 200,000 francs ($216,000).

Liam Vaughan et al., Traders Said to Rig Currency Rates to Profit Off Clients, BLOOMBERG, June 12, 2013.

According to press reports, FX traders would, for example, allegedly manipulate prices by flooding a currency with rush orders, or "banging the close," after communicating in chat rooms to move WM/R rates in a desired direction. Roger Aitken, *FX Rate 'Rigging' Scandal Boiling Up After UBS Revelation*, FORBES, Oct. 8, 2014. "Banging the close" occurs when a trader breaks up a large customer order into several smaller orders and processes the many, smaller trades in the moments before and during the 60-second fixing window. Because the WM/R rate is based on the *median* price of transactions, placing a series of smaller trades could have a more significant impact on the WM/R rate than could a large deal. *See* Complaint, *In re* Foreign Exchange Benchmark Rates Antitrust Litigation, No. 1:13-cv-07789-LGS, ¶ 106–107 (Mar. 31, 2014).

Traders would also allegedly "paint the screen." Painting the screen involves traders making fake trades with one another in the fix window to give the illusion that real trades are taking place. They could allegedly move the WM/R benchmark in a particular direction. The traders allegedly then immediately reversed the trades following the fix. *Id.* at ¶ 108.

Owing to the size of the FX market, a bank acting alone could not profit from banging the close or painting the screen. As a former FX trader at Morgan Stanley and Deutsche Bank argued, it would take "collusion of inordinate magnitude for such a strategy to work reliably and consecutively." Roger Aitken, *FX Rate 'Rigging' Scandal Boiling Up After UBS Revelation*, FORBES, Oct. 8, 2014. As in the LIBOR scandal, traders allegedly manipulating the FX markets provided damning (but entertaining) communications, such as "I'd prefer we join forces . . . perfick . . . let's do this . . . lets double team them . . . YESssssss." CFTC, EXAMPLES OF MISCONDUCT IN PRIVATE CHAT ROOMS, TRADERS FROM TWO BANKS "DOUBLE TEAM" TO ATTEMPT TO MANIPULATE FIX 4–5 (2014).

3. Private Litigation

Many firms faced scrutiny from private investors. For example, investors filed a class action lawsuit in 2014 against Bank of America, Barclays, BNP Paribas, Citigroup, Credit Suisse, Deutsche Bank, Goldman Sachs, HSBC, JPMorgan, Morgan Stanley, RBS, and UBS. *See In re* Foreign Exchange Benchmark Rates Antitrust Litigation, No. 1:13-cv-07789-LGS (Mar. 31, 2014). Investors alleged that the banks' joint manipulation of the FX market violated § 1 of the Sherman Antitrust Act by combining to restrain commerce in the United States and abroad. Various institutions have settled with investors, including JPMorgan for $99.5 million, UBS for $135 million, Bank of America for

$180 million, and Citigroup for $394 million. *See* Melissa Lipman, *$5.6B Forex Fines Aren't the End of Rate-Rigging Fallout*, LAW360, May 20, 2015.

4. Reform

In addition to levying penalties, the CFTC forced the settling firms to reform their FX business practices in ways consistent with the settlement agreements following the LIBOR scandal. These institutions agreed to adopt internal controls to detect and deter improper FX conduct. *See, e.g., In re* Citibank, CFTC Docket No. 15–03, at 12–14. The firms will receive annual audits on their FX business' compliance with applicable regulations, and employees involved in FX must receive training on relevant laws. The later Federal Reserve Board and OCC orders also contained significant remediation obligations and audits, creating, in essence, a proto-regulatory regime. While not codified in law, the firms' agreement to change their business practices could reflect the beginning of reform in this area. Remediation efforts began long before the regulatory actions were concluded. Barclays, Citigroup, RBS, JPMorgan, Deutsche Bank, and UBS have either banned their employees from FX chat rooms or severely limited their access. *See, e.g.*, Daniel Schäfer et al., *Banks Ban Traders From Group Chat Rooms*, CNBC (Nov. 22, 2013). All of the settling institutions, and several other firms, terminated or suspended employees involved in the FX manipulation scandal. *See* Complaint, *In re* Foreign Exchange Benchmark Rates Antitrust Litigation, No. 1:13-cv-07789-LGS, ¶ 151–64 (Mar. 31, 2014).

In 2014, the Financial Stability Board (FSB) made recommendations to safeguard the FX market. The FSB proposals included extending the fixing period to five minutes, expanding the number of transactions included in determining the fix, and banning interbank FX communication. FSB, FOREIGN EXCHANGE BENCHMARKS (2014).

---

1. ***Culture or Subcultures?*** Does the bad behavior in LIBOR and FX reflect the overall culture of the institutions or the fact that certain subcultures existed or were permitted to exist by supervisors and managers? What lessons can be drawn more widely for reforming culture? Is the answer to impose criminal liability on compliance officers, as the New York Department of Financial Services proposes, to strengthen compliance and risk management, or to impose executive compensation clawbacks including on senior management (*see* Chapter 8.1)? Will any of this work without swift terminations of culpable, but profitable, traders? Reflect as well on whether the overwhelmingly young male culture of the trading floor and its direct supervisors played a role in the development of some of the subcultures. For research on the impact of gendered subcultures and risk-taking, see JOHN COATES, THE HOUR BETWEEN DOG AND WOLF: HOW RISK TAKING TRANSFORMS US, BODY AND MIND (2013).

2. ***Fabulous Fab***. Recall our discussion in Chapter 4.3 of ABACUS 2007-ACI, the collateralized debt obligation (CDO) that the SEC alleged Goldman Sachs marketed to clients without disclosing that another client, the hedge fund Paulson & Co., had taken the short position on the other side of the deal and therefore wanted the CDO to lose value. This alleged conflict of interest led to a fine of $550 million by the SEC on July 15, 2010. Press Release, SEC: Goldman

Sachs to Pay Record $550 Million to Settle SEC Charges Related to Subprime Mortgage CDO (Jul. 15, 2010). This settlement was followed by a jury verdict against Fabrice Tourre, a junior banker involved in assembling and selling the transaction. *See* Bob Van Voris, *Ex-Goldman's Tourre Ordered to Pay $825,000 in SEC Case*, BLOOMBERG BUSINESS, March 12, 2014. As the article notes, "[i]n one e-mail, Tourre . . . quoted a friend's nickname for him: 'Fabulous Fab.' Tourre referred to the investments he was constructing as 'monstrosities.' In another e-mail, he joked about selling investments in Abacus to 'widows and orphans.'" *Id.*

3. ***Credit Default Swap (CDS) Antitrust Litigation***. Major banks and broker-dealers in the CDS market, and ISDA, have settled claims by investors relating to alleged anti-competitive practices. *See* Nate Raymond, JPMorgan, *Morgan Stanley to pay most in $1.9 billion swaps price-fixing settlement*, REUTERS, Oct. 16, 2015. The settlement also included an agreement by ISDA to certain behavioral remedies, as described by Professor Darrell Duffie, who testified as an expert in the case:

> ISDA owns certain intellectual property, including the rights to the settlement prices generated by CDS auctions administered by ISDA . . . that are necessary for the operation of a viable CDS exchange trading platform. Plaintiffs alleged that ISDA, in collusion with Defendants, refused to grant such licenses to any exchange trading platforms. The changes to its licensing practices that ISDA has now agreed to adopt under the proposed settlement will make it much easier for parties to license ISDA's intellectual property for the exchange trading of CDS.
>
> ISDA has also agreed to a number of measures that will make its licensing process more transparent and inclusive of class members. . . .
>
> I consider these and other terms of the proposed settlement agreement to be important changes that should make the CDS market more transparent, efficient, and competitive. . . .

Decl. Darrell Duffie in support of Pl.s' Motion, Dkt. No. 446, *In re* Credit Default Swaps Antitrust Litigation, 13-md-02476 (DLC), Oct. 16, 2015 (S.D.N.Y.). Is this approach to improving ISDA's procedures appropriate? What does the settlement suggest about the role of self-regulatory organizations?

4. ***Settled Regulatory Outcomes.*** In the early stages of an investigation by an enforcement authority, large financial institutions often conduct their own internal investigations. The common process, when problems of the type discussed in this section are uncovered, is for a firm to self-report and then conduct its own internal investigation run by an independent outside counsel. As a result, the firms cooperate with the investigating authorities by providing the evidence of wrongdoing to the authorities and by taking remedial steps to strengthen relevant systems and controls. Firms and regulatory authorities will negotiate factual allegations, terms, and content of published settlement documents. The strength of a firm's bargaining position might be affected by the relationship of the institution with its regulators and the number of other institutions involved. There is no neutral trier of facts in a settlement and the

content of the factual allegations is also typically a topic of negotiation. Does the knowledge that facts are negotiated change your view about the context of the settlements? What settlement strategy would you recommend to an institutional client involved in a global investigation with a number of other subjects?

5. ***Too Big to Jail, Revisited?*** The DOJ's LIBOR and FX settlements culminated in guilty pleas from parent-level entities. What does this additional punishment achieve? Federal securities laws and SEC regulations restrict persons or institutions with criminal convictions or regulatory orders from engaging in certain types of fiduciary businesses or from taking advantage of certain exemptions under securities laws. *See, e.g.*, 17 C.F.R. § 230.506(d). The SEC issued waivers for each of the settling banks to ensure that they would not be subject to these restrictions. *See* SEC releases 33-9778–87, May 20, 2015. This move proved controversial in some quarters. Consider the following dissenting opinion of SEC Commissioner Kara Stein:

SEC Commissioner Kara M. Stein, Dissenting Statement Regarding Certain Waivers Granted by the Commission for Certain Entities Pleading Guilty to Criminal Charges Involving Manipulation of Foreign Exchange Rates

May 21, 2015

I dissent from the Commission's Orders, issued on May 20, 2015, that granted [UBS, Citigroup, JPMorgan, and RBS] waivers from an array of disqualifications required by federal securities regulations. . . .

The disqualifications were triggered for generally the same behavior: a criminal conspiracy to manipulate exchange rates in the foreign currency exchange spot market. . . . Traders at these firms "entered into and engaged in a combination and conspiracy to fix, stabilize, maintain, increase or decrease the price of, and rig bids and offers for," the euro-dollar foreign currency exchange. . . . To carry out their scheme, the conspirators communicated and coordinated trading almost daily in an exclusive online chat room that the traders referred to as "The Cartel" or "The Mafia." Additionally, salespeople and traders lied to customers in order to collect undisclosed markups in certain transactions. This criminal behavior went on for years, unchecked and undeterred.

There are compelling reasons to reject these requests to waive the automatic disqualifications required by statute or rule. Chief among them, however, is the recidivism of these institutions. . . .

The [SEC] has thus granted at least 23 . . . waivers to these five institutions in the past nine years. The number climbs higher if you include Bad Actor and other waivers. . . .

Allowing these institutions to continue business as usual, after multiple and serious regulatory and criminal violations, poses risks to investors and the American public that are being ignored. . . .

It is troubling enough to consistently grant waivers for criminal misconduct. It is an order of magnitude more troubling to refuse to enforce our own explicit requirements for such waivers. This type of recidivism and repeated criminal misconduct should lead to revocations of prior waivers, not the granting of a whole new set of waivers. We have the tools, and with the tools the responsibility, to empower those at the top of these institutions to create meaningful cultural shifts, yet we refuse to use them.

In conclusion, I am troubled by repeated instances of noncompliance at these global financial institutions, which may be indicative of a continuing culture that does not adequately support legal and ethical behavior. Further, I am concerned that the latest series of actions has effectively rendered criminal convictions of financial institutions largely symbolic. Firms and institutions increasingly rely on the [SEC's] repeated issuance of waivers to remove the consequences of a criminal conviction, consequences that may actually positively contribute to a firm's compliance and conduct going forward.

SEC Commissioner Daniel Gallagher defended the use of waivers on the ground that the SEC has traditionally used waivers as a tool to reduce recidivism, rather than as a part of the sanctioning process. Daniel M. Gallagher, Why is the SEC Wavering on Waivers? Remarks at the 37th Annual Conference on Securities Regulation and Business Law (Feb. 13, 2015). What would have happened to the mutual fund market if the SEC had not issued waivers?

C. THE BEGINNINGS OF ENFORCEMENT UNDER TITLE VII

When a new regulatory regime is built, enforcement by regulators generally does not begin immediately. During the flurry of activity to implement the new swap regulatory regime, the CFTC signaled that market participants must engage in good faith efforts to meet the regulatory requirements applicable to them. *See* Final Exemptive Order Regarding Compliance with Certain Swap Regulations, 78 Fed. Reg. 858 (Jan. 7, 2013). More than two years after the majority of the swap regulations went into effect, the CFTC began to bring public enforcement actions against SDs for failure to comply with these regulations, the first of which was announced in 2015.

As of December 31, 2015, the CFTC had announced four enforcement actions for violations of swap rules under Title VII. Three actions were brought against SDs and one action was brought against an individual employee of one of those SDs. In the individual action, the employee is alleged to have violated CFTC rules that prohibit SDs and their personnel from engaging in fraudulent conduct. The employee allegedly entered into unauthorized swap transactions for two customers' accounts with the intent to recoup losses that had accrued in those accounts because of earlier, authorized swap trading. The employee was fined more than $1 million dollars and banned for life from trading commodities; his employer, a U.S. SD, was fined $200,000 for failing to diligently supervise its traders. The other two CFTC enforcement actions were brought against non-U.S. SDs for failing to comply with technical reporting requirements.

The CFTC has also begun to use anti-manipulation authority provided in § 753 of the Dodd-Frank Act and CFTC Rule 180.1. *See* 17 C.F.R. § 180.1. This framework mirrors the insider trading regime in the Securities Exchange Act and SEC Rule 10b-5. The CFTC may use its authority to pursue traders who use material non-public information. *See, e.g.*, CFTC, In the Matter of Arya Motazedi, Order Instituting Proceedings pursuant to sections 6(c) and 6(d) of the Commodity Exchange Act, Making Findings and Imposing Remedial Sanctions (Dec. 2, 2015); *see also* Yesha Yadav, *Insider Trading in Derivatives Markets*, 103 GEO. L.J. 381 (2015).

In 2015, the SEC brought its first enforcement case for violations of security-based swap requirements under Title VII. This action was against a web-based exchange that allowed members to buy and sell contracts in fantasy stocks based on the potential future value of pre-initial public offering company stocks. The

SEC classified these contracts as security-based swaps, which are required to be traded on an exchange, see Chapter 11.2, unless the customer is an eligible contract participant. The exchange paid a $20,000 civil penalty. *See In the Matter of Sand Hill Exchange, Gerrit Hall & Elaine Ou*, Exch. Act Release No. 75,187, 2015 WL 3777571 (June 17, 2015). This enforcement action is interesting because it demonstrates the SEC's willingness to bring enforcement actions for violations of Title VII even when it has not yet finalized many of its security-based swap regulations and the volume of transactions was relatively small.

More than five years after enactment of the Dodd-Frank Act, the CFTC's Division of Enforcement is still substantially smaller than the SEC's. In 2015, the CFTC had approximately 164 people in its enforcement division and a budget of approximately $49 million compared to the SEC's Division of Enforcement, which employed approximately 1,343 staff and had a budget of $495 million. Ed Beeson, *CFTC Enforcement Earns New Stripe After Besting SEC Haul*, LAW360, Nov. 6, 2015. Even though the SEC has substantially more resources to devote to enforcement than the CFTC, the CFTC has been able to do more with less, and in 2015, the CFTC collected $2.8 billion in monetary sanctions, more than the $2 billion collected by the SEC. Only time will tell whether Congress will provide the CFTC with more resources because of its expanded market coverage, expanded obligations, or recent enforcement success.

IV. THE EXTRATERRITORIAL REACH OF TITLE VII

As you have seen, swap market participants frequently transact across jurisdictions. In fact, more than half of all swap transactions involve a U.S. counterparty on one side and a non-U.S. counterparty on the other side. SDs have trading desks across the world. As the LIBOR and FX actions suggest, regulators and enforcement agencies across multiple jurisdictions may become involved in policing misconduct. The international nature of this market raises critically important issues of the extraterritorial scope of U.S. rules.

A. WHY IS CROSS-BORDER REGULATION NEEDED?

During the Financial Crisis, U.S. markets were significantly affected by derivatives trading overseas. AIG nearly failed because of the risks incurred by the London swap trading operations of its subsidiary AIG Financial Products. Lehman Brothers, at the time of its bankruptcy, guaranteed approximately 130,000 derivatives contracts of its UK subsidiary, Lehman Brothers International (Europe). The relationships between these U.S. corporations and their European subsidiaries are examples of how risk can be transferred across jurisdictional borders when multinational affiliated entities are involved and how these risks can affect the U.S. markets. *See* ROSALIND Z. WIGGINS & ANDREW METRICK, THE LEHMAN BROTHERS BANKRUPTCY G: THE SPECIAL CASE OF DERIVATIVES 14 (2014). As former CFTC Chairman Gary Gensler stated, "[d]uring a default or crisis, the risk that builds up offshore inevitably comes crashing back onto U.S. shores" and thus, without cross-border regulation and coordination, U.S. markets can be significantly affected by overseas activities. *See* Gary Gensler, Chairman, CFTC, Statement of Support (June 29, 2012).

There are, however, several arguments against extending U.S. regulations to non-U.S. participants. Cross-border regulation may interfere with the regulation of similar markets in other jurisdictions and may conflict with the principle of international comity. *See* Scott O'Malia, Comm'r, CFTC, Keynote Address before OpRisk Europe Conference: Taking the Time to Get It Right: The Cross-Border Regulatory Framework (June 12, 2013). Additionally, implementing regulatory regimes for OTC derivatives in various jurisdictions could subject participants to multiple sets of regulation for the same activity. Even in situations where the United States has an interest in regulating activity, other jurisdictions may also, and determining which regulatory regime applies, if not both, is often unclear. Recognizing the desirability of harmonization of global standards, the Dodd-Frank Act requires the regulators to "consult and coordinate with foreign regulatory authorities on the establishment of consistent international standards. . . ." Dodd-Frank Act § 752(a).

B. CROSS-BORDER APPLICATION OF TITLE VII

Title VII includes two provisions to the Dodd-Frank Act that explicitly define its cross-border scope. Section 2(i) of the CEA provides that the provisions of the CEA that relate to swaps (and the rules adopted under the CEA) would not apply to activities outside the United States, unless those activities:

- have a direct and significant connection with activities in, or effect on, commerce of the United States; or
- contravene the rules and regulations as prescribed or promulgated by the CFTC as are necessary to prevent the evasion of any provision of the CEA that was enacted by the Dodd-Frank Act.

Section 30(c) of the 1934 Act addresses the territorial scope of Title VII's security-based swap provisions. It provides that the 1934 Act and any related rule will not apply to any person that transacts in security-based swaps "without the jurisdiction of the United States, unless such person transacts such business in contravention of such rules and regulations as the [SEC] may prescribe as necessary or appropriate to prevent the evasion of any provision. . . ."

These provisions make it clear that a swap or security-based swap between two U.S. entities is subject to Title VII and a swap between two entities with absolutely no nexus to the United States is not subject to Title VII, but is silent on the large number of transactions that fall in between. When will a non-U.S. activity have a nexus to the United States? When will such activity have a "direct and significant connection with, or effect on," U.S. commerce?

1. The CFTC's Cross-Border Approach

To address the scope of the cross-border application of Title VII, the CFTC, after a series of proposals and exemptive orders, adopted guidance commonly referred to as the Cross-Border Guidance. The Cross-Border Guidance generally applies the full set of the CFTC's Title VII requirements if at least one counterparty to the swap is a U.S. person. As a result, the counterparties to an interest rate swap between a U.S. bank and a German swap dealer would generally be subject to the CFTC's requirements. The definition of "U.S. person" in the Cross-Border Guidance is quite expansive and does not mirror definitions used in earlier CFTC or SEC rules. An entity can be a U.S. person under the Cross-Border Guidance, and thus subject to CFTC regulations, while also being a non-U.S. person under SEC rules. In addition, the Cross-Border Guidance applies Title VII requirements in certain situations where neither counterparty is a U.S. person, for example, if the obligations of both counterparties under the swap are guaranteed by a U.S. person.

The Cross-Border Guidance divides CFTC swap regulations into two categories: Entity-Level Requirements and Transaction-Level Requirements. Entity-Level Requirements generally apply to entities that are registered with the CFTC as SDs or MSPs. For example, the risk management requirements discussed in this Chapter are Entity-Level Requirements. Transaction-Level Requirements apply to individual transactions or trading relationships between counterparties. The Transaction-Level Requirements include clearing, documentation, and external business conduct requirements. Whether a CFTC rule will apply to a particular swap transaction between two counterparties depends on whether one or both of the counterparties meet the definition of U.S. person, whether the requirement is an Entity-Level Requirement or a Transaction-Level Requirement, and whether the counterparties are SDs, MSPs, or another category of counterparty, such as affiliates guaranteed by a U.S. entity, or conduit affiliates, those who engage in swaps with non-U.S. third-parties for the purpose of hedging risks faced by its U.S. affiliate. Figure 11.3-2 outlines when some of the CFTC's Transaction-Level Requirements apply.

Figure 11.3-2 Application of CFTC Transaction-Level Requirements

	U.S. Swap Dealer of MSP (including an affiliate of a non-U.S. person)	**Foreign Branch of U.S. Bank that is a Swap Dealer or MSP**	**Non-U.S. Swap Dealer or MSP (including an affiliate of a U.S. person)**
U.S. Person (other than Foreign Branch of U.S. Bank that is a Swap Dealer or MSP)	APPLY	APPLY	APPLY
Foreign Branch of U.S. Bank that is a Swap Dealer or MSP	APPLY	SUBSTITUTED COMPLIANCE	SUBSTITUTED COMPLIANCE
Non-U.S. Person Guaranteed by, or Affiliate Conduit of, a U.S. Person	APPLY	SUBSTITUTED COMPLIANCE	SUBSTITUTED COMPLIANCE
Non-U.S. Person Not Guaranteed by, and Not an Affiliate Conduit of, a U.S. Person	APPLY	SUBSTITUTED COMPLIANCE	DO NOT APPLY

Source: Interpretive Guidance and Policy Statement Regarding Compliance with Certain Swap Regulations, Fed. Reg. 45,292, 45,369 (Jul. 26, 2013).

As its name suggests, the Cross-Border Guidance is guidance from the CFTC and does not have the force of formal rulemaking. The CFTC has argued that, because the cross-border application of its substantive rules is issued in the form of guidance, as opposed to a formal rule, market participants are provided with additional flexibility to interpret and apply the statutory provisions addressing the cross-border application of Title VII. *See id.* at 45,297. Market participants have argued that, notwithstanding its status as guidance, the Cross-Border Guidance is a *de facto* rulemaking that participants are still required to comply with as if it were a final rule. In 2013, three trade associations that represent market participants filed a lawsuit against the CFTC challenging the Cross-Border Guidance. Although the action was dismissed, the excerpt below summarizes the concerns market participants had over the application of the Cross-Border Guidance.

Sec. Indus. & Fin. Markets Ass'n v. CFTC

67 F. Supp. 3d 373 (D.D.C. 2014)

Plaintiffs argue that the Cross-Border Action is a legislative rule because—both on its face and in practice—it is binding upon the CFTC and market participants. Pls.' Mot. at 23–28. The CFTC counters that the Cross-Border Action—as the agency has proclaimed since its promulgation—is a non-binding general statement of policy intended to "communicate its views and intentions" to the regulated community regarding the scope of the Title VII Rules' extraterritorial applications. CFTC Mot. at 31, 24–34. Having considered the parties arguments, the controlling case law, the record before the Court, and—most importantly—the Cross-Border Action itself, the Court agrees with the CFTC that—save for a four-page portion of the Cross-Border Action addressed later in this section—the Cross-Border Action is a policy statement.

For starters, the Cross-Border Action on its face is binding on neither the CFTC nor swaps market participants. The Cross-Border Action, when read in its entirety, does not "purport to carry the force of law." *See Ctr. for Auto Safety v. Nat'l Highway Traffic Safety Admin.,* 452 F.3d 798, 808 (D.C.Cir.2006). It "does not 'command[,]' does not 'require[,]' does not 'order[,]' and does not 'dictate[.]'" *Cement Kiln,* 493 F.3d at 228 (alterations in original) (quoting *Appalachian Power Co. v. EPA,* 208 F.3d 1015, 1023 (D.C.Cir.2000)). Indeed, from its first pages, the Cross-Border Action explicitly distinguishes itself from a "binding rule." 78 Fed.Reg. at 45297. Instead of "stat[ing] with precision when particular requirements do and do not apply to particular situations," it announces the CFTC's "general policy regarding cross-border swap activities and allows for flexibility in application to various situations, including consideration of all relevant facts and circumstances that are not explicitly discussed in the guidance." *Id.* (footnote omitted). Although the Cross-Border Action does convey to market participants "how [the CFTC] ordinarily expects to apply existing law and regulations in the cross-border context," it also makes clear that when determining whether to apply the Title VII Rules extraterritorially, the CFTC "will apply the relevant statutory provisions, including CEA section 2(i), and regulations to the particular facts and circumstances" and parties may "present facts and circumstances that would inform the application of the substantive policy positions set forth in this release." *Id.* The Cross-Border Action further emphasizes that the CFTC's policy positions are tentative and subject to change as "foreign regulatory regimes and the global swaps market continue to evolve." *Id.* This flexible, non-binding approach continues throughout the substantive portions of the Cross-Border Action. Sec. Indus. & Fin. Markets Ass'n v. United States Commodity Futures Trading Comm'n, 67 F. Supp. 3d 373, 417-18 (D.D.C. 2014).

---

2. The SEC's Cross-Border Approach

In contrast to the CFTC, the SEC is implementing the cross-border provisions of Dodd-Frank Act § 722 through formal rulemaking. As of December 31, 2015, the SEC has finalized a handful of rules regarding the cross-border application of its security-based swap requirements. For example, the SEC has finalized its rules on security-based swap counterparty classifications, including the definition of U.S. person. The SEC's U.S. person definition differs from the definition the CFTC outlined in the Cross-Border Guidance. The SEC has also published a proposal that would apply certain requirements to transactions between non-U.S. persons if portions of the conduct occur within the United States. For example, under the proposal, a security-based swap between two non-U.S. counterparties would be subject to the SEC requirements if either counterparty has U.S. personnel involved in negotiating the transaction. For a critique of the SEC's approach, see John C. Coffee, Jr., *Extraterritorial Financial Regulation: Why E.T. Can't Come Home,* 99 CORNELL R. REV. 1259, 1285 (2014) (arguing that the SEC's approach would permit firms to issue implicit guarantees and evade U.S. rules).

C. SUBSTITUTED COMPLIANCE

As discussed above, there are a number of reasons for U.S. regulators to apply U.S. rules to transactions where one or both counterparties is located outside the United States. In a situation where swaps rules exist in the United States and a foreign jurisdiction, and both regimes apply to a single transaction, how should market participants comply with rules that may be duplicative or in conflict? One solution is for regulators to ensure their rules are identical, but this requires significant collaboration and may remain impossible given differences in the underlying legal regimes. *See generally* Ethiopis Tafara & Robert J. Peterson, *A Blueprint for Cross-Border Access to U.S. Investors: A New International Framework*, 48 HARV. INT'L L.J. 31 (2007).

Another solution to the problem of overlapping regulatory regimes is for one jurisdiction to defer to the other. The broadest form of such deference is mutual recognition, under which one country may agree to accept the rules of another country based on mutuality, without regard to whether the substantive rules of the other country are identical, or even harmonized, with its own. Under a narrower form of mutual recognition, one country agrees to accept the rules of another country if the other country's rules are sufficiently harmonized with its own rules that they may be deemed equivalent or comparable. In this vein, the CFTC and the SEC have contemplated a system, known as substituted compliance, where compliance with a comparable local law in a non-U.S. regime may be permissible in lieu of compliance with the relevant U.S. regime. While substituted compliance is a worthwhile goal, its implementation can be quite difficult. For a detailed discussion of approaches to substituted compliance, *see* Howell E. Jackson, *Substituted Compliance: The Emergence, Challenges, and Evolution of a New Regulatory Paradigm*, 1 J. FIN. REG. 169 (2015); *see also* Alexey Artamonov, *Cross-Border Application of OTC Derivatives Rules: Revisiting the Substituted Compliance Approach*, 1 J. FIN. REG. 206 (2015).

In the Cross-Border Guidance, the CFTC describes the steps it intends to take in determining when and where substituted compliance may be permitted. Under the CFTC's regime, a non-U.S. person may submit an application for substituted compliance to the CFTC. In making a substituted compliance determination, the CFTC will consider the non-U.S. jurisdiction's objectives and will base its analysis on a comparison of the specific non-U.S. requirements against the specific CFTC requirements. A substituted compliance determination will be made on a requirement-by-requirement basis, rather than at the level of the non-U.S. regime as a whole. For example, with respect to the portfolio reconciliation and compression requirements discussed in this Chapter, the CFTC has determined that the EU's requirements are comparable to and as comprehensive as the CFTC's requirements. As of December 31, 2015, however, no comparability determinations have been made with respect to the clearing, margin, exchange trading, or reporting requirements discussed in Chapter 11.2. To date, the CFTC has granted requests for comparability determinations for certain requirements that apply to participants in Australia, Canada, the EU, Hong Kong, Japan, and Switzerland. *See* Press Release, CFTC, CFTC Approves Comparability Determinations for Six Jurisdictions for Substituted Compliance Purposes (Dec. 20, 2013).

---

1. ***Cross-Border Regulation***. What alternative solutions could the CFTC and SEC have used to address the cross-border regulatory problem? Do you agree with the CFTC's use of the Cross-Border Guidance as a solution to this problem?

2. ***Comparing Foreign Laws to U.S. Requirements***. What factors should the CFTC and SEC consider when comparing foreign laws to U.S. requirements? Do you think this approach is workable?

PART XII

SHADOW BANKING

CHAPTER 12.1

SECURITIZATION

CONTENTS

I. INTRODUCTION

In this Chapter, we examine the rise of securitization over the past 30 years. The initial readings consist of excerpts from the 1980s and 1990s that describe the logic and benefits of securitization. We then turn to certain flaws of securitization, which were increasingly exposed in the decade leading up to the Financial Crisis.

II. SECURITIZATION'S RISE

A. THE GROWTH OF SECURITIZATION

Securitization is the process of pooling and selling rights to payment and other financial assets in order to better allocate risks to parties able to understand and bear them, increase the amount and reduce the cost of funding available for consumers and businesses, facilitate specialization of functions, leverage economies of scale, and, in the case of securitizing the financial assets of a bank or other regulated financial institution, remove risks from the balance sheet of those institutions. Although any type of financial asset can be securitized, this Chapter focuses primarily on securitizing residential mortgage loans. There are two reasons for this focus. First, most of securitization's flaws are associated with the securitization of those loans. Second, this is the largest sector of securitization, growing from "a non-existent industry in 1970 to $6.6 trillion as of the second quarter of 2003." *Protecting Homeowners: Preventing Abusive Lending While Preserving Access to Credit*, Hearing Before the H. Comm. on Financial Services, 108th Cong. (Nov. 5, 2003) (statement of Cameron L. Cowan, American Securitization Forum). The following excerpt provides further data.

Financial Crisis Inquiry Commission, Securitization and the Mortgage Crisis

Preliminary Staff Report (Apr. 7, 2010)

The 2000s saw a large increase in the market share of non-agency securitization [where the sponsor of the securitization first acquired a set of mortgages, either by originating them or by buying them from an originator]. Figure 4 shows the fraction of total residential mortgage originations in each year that were securitized . . .

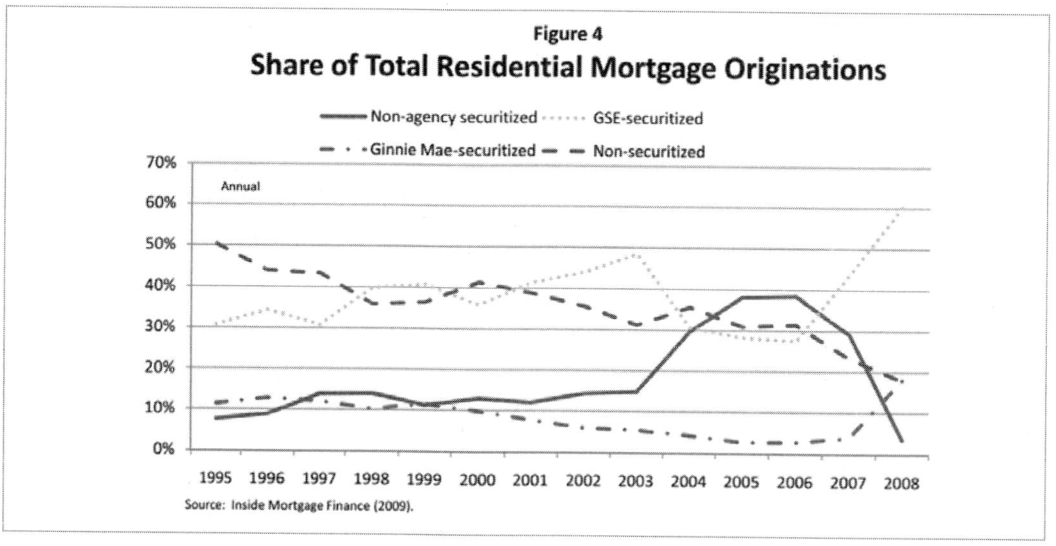

Four trends are notable. Non-securitized mortgage originations declined steadily from half the market in 1995 to under 20 percent in 2008. Non-agency [mortgage-backed security (MBS)] hovered between 8 and 12 percent until 2003; Non-agency MBS then more than trebled in market share to a peak of 38 percent in 2006. During the growth years for non-agency MBS, Ginnie Mae's market share dropped considerably. Finally, both [government sponsored enterprises (GSEs)] and Ginnie Mae rapidly escalated their market share as non- agency securitization dropped in 2008.

Figure 5 plots the volume of prime [(mortgage classification for borrowers with high quality credit history)], subprime [(mortgage classification for borrowers with low quality or limited credit history)], and alt-A [(mortgages with features that increase their risk profile, including higher loan-to-value ratios, greater debt-to-income ratios, or inadequate documentation)] non-agency MBS issued from 1995–2008. Early in the period, the prime non-agency MBS, which contained largely jumbo mortgages, were the biggest of the three types of non-agency MBS. But, by 2006 the subprime and alt-A non-agency MBS had each surpassed prime non-agency MBS in volume. In particular, subprime non-agency MBS showed a dramatic increase from 2003 to 2005. Alt-A non-agency MBS saw its largest jump in volume in 2005. Notably, the non-agency MBS market was nearly nonexistent in 2008.

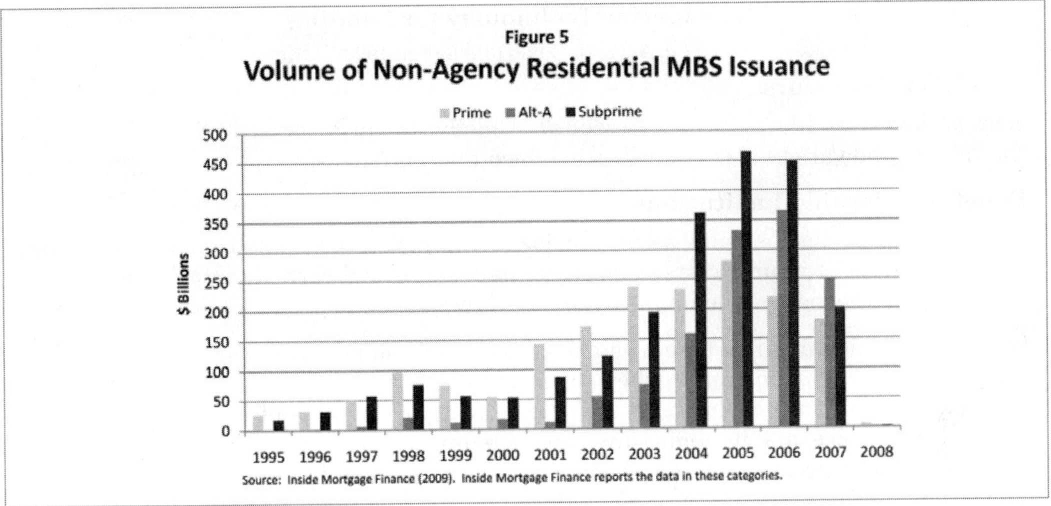

. . . Figure 6 shows the dollar amount of outstanding mortgages that are held in agency MBS and non-agency MBS . . . The amount of all outstanding mortgages held in non-agency MBS rose notably from only $670 billion 2004 to over $2,000 billion in 2006. By 2008, the amount held in non-agency MBS began to decline. With current issuance of non-agency MBS well below pre-crisis levels, the amount of outstanding mortgages held in non-agency MBS will continue to decline as mortgages in these pools either pay off or go into default. . . .

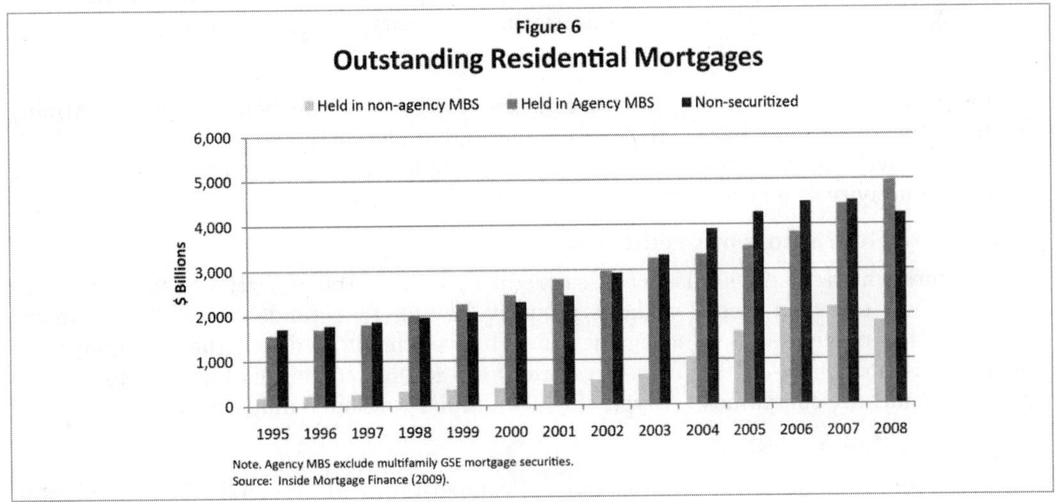

B. BENEFITS AND LOGIC

In the late 1980s, a leading management consultant outlined the benefits that securitization has to offer:

Lowell L. Bryan, Structured Securitized Credit: A Superior Technology for Lending

1 J. APPLIED CORP. FIN. 6 (Fall 1988)

Benefits to Investors

Why do investors like securitized credits? Chiefly, because securitized credit increases the volume and variety of instruments in which they can invest. . . .

Benefits to Issuing Institutions

. . . An intermediary should securitize loans whenever the spread on the securitized transaction (net of issuing costs) is greater than the spread earned (net of funding costs) from keeping the loan on the intermediary's balance sheet. . . .

Securitizing high-quality assets makes sense for almost any intermediary, even institutions of AAA quality, when one considers the full costs of balance sheet intermediation. For a commercial bank these include the costs of its required reserves, its FDIC insurance, and its regulatory capital requirements. In fact, high-quality lenders would reap their greatest savings from securitization in the form of capital cost savings. They would no longer be forced by regulatory capital requirements to hold capital equal to 7 percent of the loan, which is significantly higher than the actual, expected credit losses inherent in many types of high-quality loans. . . .

Of course, the fact that the highest-quality loans can be securitized most cost effectively is of great concern to regulators. They rightly fear that the highest quality loans will go outside the bank and thrift system, leaving the FDIC and the [Federal Savings and Loan Insurance Corporation] guaranteeing the lower-quality loans. But . . . credit securitization can be used by nonbanks to gain a share of high-quality assets, which will have the same effect. . . . It is precisely because credit securitization accelerates the flight of high quality assets that we must address the regulatory issues as soon as possible. . . .

Benefits to Investment Banks

While the issuing intermediaries can capture the bulk of the benefits of securitizing credits, the investment banks that structure and underwrite the securities also have great incentives . . . [*i.e.*,] they can earn underwriting fees and trading profits by financing borrowing activity in which they were not previously involved. . . .

Benefits to Guarantors of Credit Risk

Guarantors who have the skills to assess credit risks have the opportunity to charge fees greater than expected losses without actually having to extend loans. The primary guarantors of credit risk (excluding the federal government, which is the real guarantor behind most mortgage debt that is securitized) are foreign commercial banks and special purpose insurance companies. As yet, this is an underdeveloped industry. . . .

Benefits to Borrowers

. . . [A]s more and more credit is securitized, competition will eventually force lenders to share the savings from securitization with borrowers, and then borrowers will be able to borrow money more cheaply. . . .

Borrowers do benefit today from the increasing availability of credit on terms that lenders would not provide if they were forced to put the loans on their own balance sheets. This effect is most apparent with fixed-rate mortgage debt . . . Through [MBS,] securities lenders can now extend fixed-rate mortgage debt without taking any interest rate risk themselves. As a result, many more borrowers have access to fixed-rate mortgage debt than they would otherwise. . . .

Figure 12.1-1 provides a visual representation of securitization's basic elements. A loan originator, depicted in this figure as a mortgage broker, identifies a group of similar loans to be securitized. A sponsor transfers those loans to a special purpose vehicle, which then is analyzed by a series of gatekeepers, including underwriters, rating agencies, bond insurers, lawyers, accountants, and so on. The sponsor markets the resulting securitized product to investors.

Figure 12.1-1 Elements of Securitization

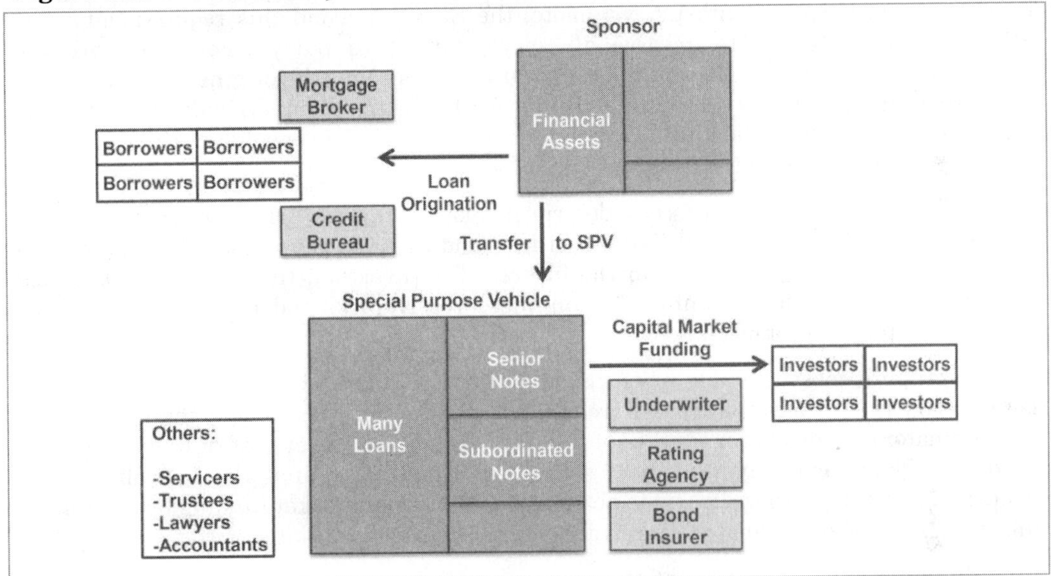

The following excerpt, written a few years after the preceding excerpt, provides an overview of the mechanics of securitization. As you read it, keep in mind Figure 12.1-1.

Steven L. Schwarcz, The Alchemy of Asset Securitization

1 STAN. J.L. BUS. & FIN. 133 (1994)

. . . A company that wants to obtain financing through securitization begins by identifying assets that can be used to raise funds. These assets typically represent rights to payments at future dates and are usually referred to as "receivables." The company that owns the receivables is usually called the "originator." The risk that these payments may not be made on time is an important factor in valuing the receivables. As long as the originator can reasonably predict the aggregate rate of default, however, it can securitize even those receivables that present some risk of uncollectibility. Therefore, a statistically large pool of receivables due from many obligors, for which payment is reasonably predictable, is generally preferable to a pool of a smaller number of receivables due from a few obligors.

After identifying the assets to be used in the securitization, the originator transfers the receivables to a newly formed special purpose corporation, trust, or other legally separate entity-often referred to as a special purpose vehicle, or "SPV." The transfer is intended to separate the receivables from risks associated with the originator. For this reason, the originator will often structure the transfer so that it constitutes a "true sale," a sale that is sufficient under bankruptcy law to remove the receivables from the originator's bankruptcy estate.

To raise funds to purchase these receivables, the SPV issues securities in the capital markets. The SPV, however, must be structured as "bankruptcy remote" to gain acceptance as an issuer of capital market securities. Bankruptcy remote in this context means that the SPV is unlikely to be adversely affected by a bankruptcy of the originator.

To achieve bankruptcy remoteness, the SPV's organizational structure strictly limits its permitted business activities. The goal is to prevent creditors (other than holders of the SPV's securities) from having claims against the SPV that would enable them to file an involuntary bankruptcy petition against the SPV. Furthermore, an SPV that is owned or controlled by the originator is usually required to have one or more independent directors. By structuring itself as bankruptcy remote, the SPV can avoid this requirement. The SPV must also attempt to observe all appropriate third party formalities with the originator. These additional steps help to reduce the risk that the originator, if bankrupt, will either cause the SPV to voluntarily file for bankruptcy or persuade a bankruptcy court, in the exercise of its equitable powers, to substantively consolidate the assets and liabilities of the SPV with those of the originator. . . .

Through the securitization process described above, the SPV raises funds by issuing securities—usually debt or debt-like securities—and uses the receivables purchased from the originator to repay investors in the future. The investors, therefore, are concerned only with the cash flows coming due on these receivables, and care little about the originator's financial condition.

Securitization is most valuable when the cost of funds, reflected in the interest rate that is necessary to entice investors to purchase the SPV's securities, is less than the cost of the originator's other, direct sources of funding. The SPV's lower cost of funds is passed on to the originator through a higher selling price for the originator's receivables. The goal of securitization, therefore, is to obtain low cost capital market funding by separating all or a portion of an originator's receivables from the risks associated with the originator.

The interest rate necessary to entice investors to purchase the SPV's securities is often a function of the "rating" that the SPV's debt securities receive. Such ratings are determined by various independent private companies that have gained widespread investor acceptance as "rating agencies." Given that most investors, except certain institutional investors in private placement transactions . . . have neither the time nor the resources to fully investigate the financial condition of the companies in which they invest, these ratings take on special significance. Investors rely on the assigned ratings to determine the minimum return that they will accept on a given investment.

Companies whose debt securities are rated "investment grade" can usually issue securities in the capital markets at interest rates competitive with, or even lower than, other generally available sources of funds, such as bank loans. The higher the company's rating within the investment grade categories, the lower the company's cost of funds. This reduced cost is a result of the lower interest rate necessary to induce investors to buy the company's securities.

A securitization transaction can provide obvious cost savings by permitting an originator whose debt securities are rated less than investment grade or whose securities are unrated to obtain funding through an SPV whose debt securities have an investment grade rating. Even an originator with an investment grade rating may derive benefit from securitization if the SPV can issue debt securities with a higher investment grade rating and, as a result, significantly decrease the originator's interest costs.

One might expect securitization to be of greatest benefit to riskier companies. This expectation, however, is only partly true. As a company moves toward the extremes of financial instability and towards the brink of bankruptcy, securitization is less of a benefit. At this point, the SPV has a higher than normal risk of being challenged by the originator's trustee in bankruptcy, and risk-averse investors tend to avoid these transactions.

Asset securitization does, however, afford companies with acceptable risk levels the possibility of real cost savings. To determine whether an originator will achieve an overall cost savings from securitization, one must assess the interest savings possible (as discussed above) against the costs of the securitization transaction. A company considering securitization should compare (i) the expected differential between interest payable on non-securitized financing and interest payable on securities issued by an applicable SPV with (ii) the expected difference in transaction costs between the alternative funding options. Whether or not the originator will achieve a cost savings partially depends on the way in which the originator structures the securitization because . . . transaction costs can vary over a wide range. . . .

C. LEGAL PROBLEMS

The emergence of securitization as an economic force in the 1980s and 1990s represented a major innovation in finance and transformed the manner in which mortgages and many other forms of credit, including student loans, auto loans, and credit cards, are financed in the United States. Legal structuring played an important role in this development, and many deal lawyers as well as other lawyers worked through numerous legal challenges.

Initially, the tax laws presented a major impediment because securitization vehicles would not be economically viable unless they were eligible for pass-through treatment for purposes of federal taxation. While tax lawyers found ways to satisfy this requirement with simple securitization structures, eventually legislation was required to make pass-through treatment generally available. In 1986, Congress passed legislation that created the real estate mortgage investment company, which provided a safe haven for securitized pools from corporate level taxation. In order to qualify as such a company, a securitized pool had to meet a number of requirements, including restrictions on what kinds of assets could comprise the pool, limitations on the ability to modify mortgage loans in the pool, and prohibitions on certain transactions, such as receipt of income from non-permitted assets. *See, e.g.*, Michael S. Gambro & Scott Leichtner, *Selected Legal Issues Affecting Securitization*, 1 N.C. BANKING INST. 131, 156 (1997).

Lawyers also had to ensure that the pools were structured in such a way so as to avoid having them regulated as investment companies under the Investment Company Act of 1940 (1940 Act). *See, e.g.*, Steven L. Schwarcz, *Structured Finance: The New Way to Securitize Assets*, 11 CARDOZO L. REV. 607, 627–31 (1990). In addition, considerable attention was spent ensuring that the securitization pools would be bankruptcy remote in the event that the sponsoring entity became insolvent, so as to keep the securitized assets free from any claims by the sponsor's creditors, and would be kept off the sponsor's balance sheet for both accounting and capital regulation purposes. *See id.* at 613–18. For further discussion of the legal issues of securitization in the 1980s and 1990s, see 1

TAMAR FRANKEL, SECURITIZATION: STRUCTURED FINANCING, FINANCIAL ASSETS POOLS, AND ASSET-BACKED SECURITIES (1st ed. 1991).

III. EMERGING PROBLEMS

A. FRAGMENTATION OF FUNCTIONS

As discussed at the end of Part II, the rise of securitization was aided by a considerable amount of sophisticated lawyering, which focused on solving various tax and bankruptcy issues created by securitization pools. The lawyers and everyone else involved, however, underestimated the problems that arose, in part, from the high degree of functional fragmentation that securitization required. Part of the genius of securitization was that it broke up the bank by allocating a range of functions, including origination, credit assessment, pooling risks, and accessing capital markets, to separate legal entities. This structure allowed for specialization and economies of scale. The division of functions can also produce a host of contracting problems. *Cf.* Michael A. Heller, *The Tragedy of the Anticommons: Property in the Transition from Marx to Markets*, 111 HARV. L. REV. 621, 624 (1998) (critiquing the excessive fragmentation of property rights and exploring negative economic consequences).

Besides functional fragmentation, the problems discussed below were also possibly caused, in part, by parties that were unable or unwilling to pay the price for full protection and instead assumed the consistency and completeness of protection provided in the transaction documents. Such protection gaps are multiplied in the context of securitization, which involves many more parties, often with complex interrelationships, and much more complex and novel documentation and structures. *See, e.g.*, Steven L. Schwarcz, *The Roberta Mitchell Lecture: Structuring Responsibility in Securitization Transactions*, 40 CAP. U. L. REV. 803 (2012).

1. Yield Spread Premiums

Fragmentation of functions created many problems, including some in the mortgage lending field that we already discussed in Chapter 5.2. An especially controversial aspect of mortgage broker compensation was the yield spread premium, a commission paid to the broker by the lender that varied with the interest rate of the loan. Because loans with higher interest rates resulted in higher commissions, the use of yield spread premiums led to a steering problem in which brokers had a lucrative incentive to steer borrowers to higher cost loans. *See, e.g.*, Loan Originator Compensation Requirements Under the Truth in Lending Act (Regulation Z), 12 C.F.R. § 1026. Moreover, this practice was not well-known among borrowers, and possibly was used by brokers to discriminate among different categories of borrowers, including by race and gender. *See, e.g.*, Howell E. Jackson & Laurie Burlingame, *Kickbacks or Compensation: The Case of Yield Spread Premiums*, 12 STAN. J. L. BUS. & FIN. 289, 291 (Spring 2007). For further discussion of yield spread premiums, see Chapter 5.2.

2. Multiple Gatekeepers

Another problem associated with securitization is the possibility of negligent or even fraudulent conduct by the various gatekeepers, such as accountants, attorneys, and investment bankers, that facilitate the pooling and selling of similar assets. Professor Andrew Tuch describes the litigation surrounding Commercial Financial Services, Inc., and how gatekeepers arguably failed to stop the fraudulent transactions that led to Commercial Financial Services's demise.

Andrew F. Tuch, Multiple Gatekeepers

96 VA. L. REV. 1583 (2010)

. . . [Commercial Financial Services, Inc. (CFS)] was in the business of collecting delinquent credit card receivables, sums owed by consumers who have defaulted under the terms of their credit cards. CFS bought the receivables from credit card issuers, using funds raised through a financing process similar to mortgage securitization. Using a bankruptcy-remote vehicle, CFS would issue to institutional investors securities "backed" by expected recoveries on the receivables. Since these assets were unsecured (unlike mortgages), the securities' value depended on CFS's collections ability. Under the securitization arrangements, CFS was required to meet minimum monthly collection targets. The securities received an "A" rating, or the equivalent, from credit rating agencies. At the time of its collapse, CFS had issued around $1.6 billion in securities from thirteen transactions.

CFS's collapse came after rating agencies received an anonymous letter insinuating that the company was a Ponzi scheme that had been meeting its collection targets, in part, by selling receivables at inflated prices to a corporate affiliate. . . . Aggrieved investors sued, pointing to alleged misstatements in the offering documents and alleged failures by the gatekeepers to take adequate precautions to prevent the fraud.

The ensuing litigation subjected the gatekeepers—in particular, CFS's law firm, accounting firm, and investment bank—to close scrutiny. They had been integrally involved in structuring each of the relevant transactions. But they had apparently overlooked a golden opportunity to uncover and prevent the alleged fraud. That opportunity occurred when the company's Chief Executive Officer, Mitchell F. Vernick, the first outsider ever admitted to the company's senior management, resigned. . . .

. . . CFS's lawyers had met with Vernick, at the company's request, and with other senior managers of CFS to discuss the resignation. During discussions that took "several hours over the course of two days following his announced intention to resign," Vernick had attempted to convince the lawyers that the CFS model did not work and that the securitizations should stop. He showed them a chart showing transactions apparently designed to make CFS appear (falsely) to be meeting its collection targets.

On the chart, one lawyer wrote, "selling /PUT to meet base?" In his notes, another lawyer wrote, "Mitch [Vernick] showed chart that breaks [cash flow] into components . . . settlements[,] puts and conversion rates." Next to the words "conversion rates," the lawyer wrote, "disguised by sales." . . . [T]he picture that emerges is inconclusive (since the matter settled before discovery . . .), although one plausible and perhaps generous interpretation is confusion, or lack of understanding, on the part of the lawyers. . . .

. . . [T]he accounting firm and investment bank were also aware of Vernick's resignation . . . Vernick discussed his concerns with the audit partner in charge of the CFS account, as well as with the investment bankers. . . . [I]t is unclear whether the auditors and bankers were also shown the chart depicting the sham transactions.

. . . After . . . Vernick's departure, CFS continued financing its activities via securitization transactions and was assisted in doing so by the same gatekeepers. . . .

---

1. ***The Problem of Multiple Gatekeepers.*** As the Commercial Financial Services episode demonstrates, fraudulent conduct can go unnoticed by several different layers of specialized professionals. Why do you think Commercial Financial Services's lawyers failed to take Vernick's comments more seriously? Were Commercial Financial Services's accountants and investment bankers less well-positioned to detect the fraudulent conduct? Tuch suggests three "plausible scenarios in which gatekeepers' precautions might have deterred securities fraud optimally": (1) greater vigilance by one set of gatekeepers alone, here most likely the lawyers, who could have asked Vernick to clarify his remarks and questioned other members of Commercial Financial Services management; (2) simultaneous and combined vigilance by two or more sets of gatekeepers, here the lawyers and the accountants together, combining the lawyers' appreciation for the "need for disclosure of the financial shenanigans" with the accountants' understanding of "the nature of the transactions"; and (3) sequential and combined vigilance by two or more sets of gatekeepers, here the accountants "tak[ing] the lead, probing the alleged sham transactions," followed by the lawyers "hand[ling] disclosure matters." Andrew F. Tuch, *Multiple Gatekeepers*, 96 VIRGINIA L. REV. 1583, 1620–21 (2010). Which of Tuch's scenarios seems most promising?

2. ***Collaborative Gatekeeping.*** The second and third scenarios described above by Tuch point to the deterrence potential of gatekeepers working in tandem and drawing on their respective expertise in order to detect fraudulent conduct. Another form of collaborative gatekeeping that has yielded promising results is the collaboration between enforcement authorities and financial institutions. Professors Stavros Gadinis and Colby Mangels have highlighted the success of the anti-money laundering regime in the United States that relies on communication channels between regulators and financial institutions. By incentivizing these institutions to submit suspicious activity reports by offering reduced liability or even legal immunity, regulators gain an important ally in the fight against financial fraud. *See* Stavros Gadinis & Colby Mangels, *Collaborative Gatekeepers*, WASH. & LEE L. REV. (forthcoming). Can you think of any potential problems with such a regulatory regime? Can this approach easily be exported to other areas of financial regulation?

---

3. Credit Rating Agencies

Besides the increasing importance of, and associated problems with, gatekeepers such as attorneys and accountants, securitization's rise also led to growing reliance on third party information providers to assess the quality of securitized products, like credit rating agencies. From the 1970s to the 1990s, the main policy debate focused on whether the SEC should liberalize its rules to allow for increased competition in the credit rating space. The following excerpt provides a brief overview of the SEC's regulatory role during this time period and then argues for greater liberalization of the SEC's rules.

Amy K. Rhodes, The Role of the SEC in the Regulation of the Rating Agencies: Well-Placed Reliance or Free-Market Interference?

20 SETON HALL LEGIS. J. 293 (1996)

Ratings-dependent regulations rely on ratings issued mostly by [nationally recognized statistical rating organizations (NRSROs)]. NRSROs were first used by the SEC in 1975 to refer to rating agencies whose credit ratings could be used in implementing the net capital requirements for broker-dealers in Rule 15c3-1, under the [Securities Exchange Act of 1934 (1934 Act)]. Rule 15c3-1 was also the first instance in which high ratings by the rating agencies resulted in more favorable regulatory treatment. At the time, the SEC was referring to three agencies, Fitch, Moody's, and Standard and Poor's, which had a national presence in the ratings market. . . .

Any designation process will undoubtedly have the effect of creating a hierarchy of rating agencies, but the SEC should minimize the extent to which designation becomes a stamp of its approval. Instead, designation of NRSROs should focus foremost on internal procedures for handling nonpublic information and structural conflicts of interest . . . Replacing the criterion that NRSROs be indeed "nationally recognized," applicant rating agencies should be required to show empirical studies correlating ratings . . . to interest rates and historical default rates to keep the barrier to entry as low as possible. . . .

. . . [R]atings are publicly available: as such, requiring disclosure of rating processes in the primary market should be predicated on equalizing the playing field among rating agencies to insure that many raters with differing methodologies give their assessment[s] . . . Allowing usage of NRSRO ratings without requiring consent from the NRSRO in the selling effort, but compelling other rating agencies to consent to a higher standard of care in order to publicize their ratings in registration documents confers a competitive advantage upon NRSROs without promoting greater efficiency in the capital market. . . .

The liberalization debate received partial resolution a decade later when Congress passed the Credit Rating Agency Reform Act of 2006 in the wake of highly publicized corporate scandals at Enron and Worldcom, companies that received high credit ratings before collapsing. The Act, designed to foster competition in the credit rating sector, created a streamlined set of registration procedures for rating agencies to follow in order to receive NRSRO status. *See* Credit Rating Agency Reform Act of 2006, Pub. L. No. 109–291, 120 Stat. 1327 (2006); 15 U.S.C. § 78o-7 (2006). Moreover, the Act expressly prohibited the SEC from regulating "the substance of credit ratings or the procedures and methodologies by which any [NRSRO] determines credit ratings." 15 U.S.C. § 78o-7(c)(2) (2006). The SEC still retained, however, significant regulatory authority over credit rating agencies. For example, the Act granted the SEC the power to block the registration of a rating agency that had followed the aforementioned procedures under certain conditions, such as if the SEC determines that the rating agency lacks "adequate financial and managerial resources to consistently produce credit ratings with integrity." 15 U.S.C. § 78o-7(a)(2)(C) (2006). In its rulemaking issued pursuant to the Act a year later, the SEC specified prohibitions on conflicts of interests for NRSROs, such as a prohibition on an NRSRO earning over 10% of annual revenues from a single issuer. *See* 17 C.F.R. § 240.17g-5(c)(1).

Beyond the debate over liberalization, commentators also asked whether credit rating agencies were too stringent or too lax in their ratings. A closely related question was whether additional regulation of rating agencies was warranted. This debate took place in the context of the regulatory incorporation of credit ratings in bank capital requirements, as proposed by the Basel Committee in 1999. *See* BASEL COMM. ON BANKING SUPERVISION, A NEW CAPITAL ADEQUACY FRAMEWORK (June 1999). Some commentators argued that rating agencies already have sufficient incentive to provide accurate ratings because their reputations drive their profitability. On this view, therefore, additional regulation is deemed unnecessary and perhaps even harmful, because such regulation might lead rating agencies to produce overly stringent, or lower, ratings in order to avoid regulatory penalties. *See, e.g.*, Steven L. Schwarcz, *The Role of Rating Agencies in Global Market Regulation, in* REGULATING FINANCIAL SERVICES AND MARKETS IN THE TWENTY FIRST CENTURY 297 (Eilis Ferran & Charles A.E. Goodhart, eds., 2001); Steven L. Schwarcz, *Private Ordering of Public Markets: The Rating Agency Paradox*, 2002 U. ILL. L. REV. 1 (2002). Other commentators responded by pointing out that regulatory incorporation of credit ratings into bank capital requirements puts greater pressure on entities to receive better ratings, and also creates a new set of consumers for ratings, namely the regulators themselves, who will use those ratings to set capital standards for regulated institutions. In this view, therefore, additional regulation would likely be needed to prevent credit rating inflation. *See, e.g.*, Howell E. Jackson, *The Role of Rating Agencies in the Establishment of Capital Standards for Financial Institutions in a Global Economy, in* REGULATING FINANCIAL SERVICES AND MARKETS IN THE TWENTY FIRST CENTURY 311 (Eilis Ferran & Charles A.E. Goodhart, eds., 2001).

As the Financial Crisis developed, commentators observed that the credit rating agencies had, indeed, been too lax in producing their ratings. These inaccurate ratings, in turn, contributed to the troubled mortgage markets that led to the Financial Crisis. Professor John Coffee identified "three distinctive trends" that explain the rating agencies' failure: (1) the agencies' clientele base became increasingly concentrated among "a number of large investment banks that brought deals to them on a continuing basis (and thus could threaten to take a substantial volume of business elsewhere, if dissatisfied)"; (2) Fitch's rise in the ratings sector disrupted the "de facto dual oligopoly" of Moody's and S&P, thus bestowing credibility on major issuers' threats to "go elsewhere if they did not receive the rating they wanted"; and (3) "factual verification and due diligence" by rating agencies reduced significantly after 2000, largely because "investment banks and deal arrangers ceased to pay for such activities, and [ratings agencies] did not insist on their continuation." John C. Coffee, *Ratings Reform: The Good, The Bad, and The Ugly*, 1 HARV. BUS. L. REV. 231, 237–241 (2011). Keep these troubling trends in mind when you read about the Dodd-Frank Act's reforms in the credit ratings space, discussed later in this Chapter.

4. Troubled Mortgage Litigation

Another problem associated with securitization was the troubled mortgage markets, which came to a head in the Financial Crisis. As will be seen later in this Chapter, the Dodd-Frank Act instituted a number of consumer protection reforms in the mortgage servicing area in order to prevent predatory mortgage lending in the first place. Lowered underwriting standards and predatory lending, combined with troubled mortgage markets, led to a growing number of underwater mortgages, which in turn fueled a surge in foreclosure litigation.

Some of these lawsuits were brought not by the original homeowners or lenders, but rather by later assignees who had acquired, or who thought they had acquired, the title in the securitization process. The securitization of mortgage financing thus forced courts to grapple with thorny jurisdictional issues. For example, in *U.S. Bank v. Ibanez*, 941 N.E.2d 40 (Mass. 2011), the Supreme Judicial Court of Massachusetts ruled against a large financial institution, U.S. Bank, that, while acting as a trustee for a securitization vehicle, obtained ownership of the defendants' mortgages through a chain of securitization. The court reasoned that U.S. Bank was not the holder of the mortgages at the time of foreclosure and thus had "failed to demonstrate that [it] acquired fee simple title to these properties by purchasing them at the foreclosure sale." *Id.* at 55. Similarly, *In re Foreclosure Cases*, No. 07CV2532, 2007 WL 3232430, at *2 (N.D. Ohio Oct. 31, 2007), the court dismissed a number of foreclosure cases on jurisdictional grounds, reasoning that none of the plaintiff-lenders were the owners of "the rights, title and interest under the Mortgage at issue as of the date of the Foreclosure Complaint." Interestingly, in a trenchant footnote, the court reflected on the institutional context and its associated difficulties brought about by securitization:

> Plaintiff's, 'Judge, you just don't understand how things work,' argument reveals a condescending mindset and quasi-monopolistic system where financial institutions have traditionally controlled, and still control, the foreclosure process. Typically, the homeowner who finds himself/herself in financial straits, fails to make the required mortgage payments and faces a foreclosure suit, is not interested in testing state or federal jurisdictional requirements . . .
>
> In the meantime, the financial institutions or successors/assignees rush to foreclose, obtain a default judgment and then sit on the deed, avoiding responsibility for maintaining the property while reaping the financial benefits of interest running on a judgment. The financial institutions know the law charges the one with title (still the homeowner) with maintaining the property.
>
> . . . [U]nchallenged by underfinanced opponents, the institutions worry less about jurisdictional requirements and more about maximizing returns. [However,] the federal courts must act as gatekeepers, assuring that only those who meet diversity and standing requirements are allowed to pass through. . . .
>
> The Court will illustrate in simple terms its decision: 'Fluidity of the market'—'X' dollars, 'contractual arrangements between institutions and counsel'—'X' dollars, 'purchasing mortgages in bulk and securitizing'—'X' dollars, 'rush to file, slow to record after judgment'—'X' dollars, 'the jurisdictional integrity of United States District Court'—'Priceless.'

Id. In re Foreclosure Cases, 2007 WL 3232430 at *3 n.3. Recall the earlier discussion of multiple gatekeepers. Can the judiciary also serve as a gatekeeper in mitigating the worst of securitization's consequences?

---

1. ***Mortgage Electronic Registration System (MERS).*** Major participants in the mortgage business created MERS to streamline the paperwork associated with transferring mortgages and interests in mortgages. MERS serves as the mortgagee of record, but its parent maintains a comprehensive database that tracks ownership of the underlying mortgage. The need for such a system became particularly acute with the adoption of the originate and sell business model, the advent of securitization of mortgages, and the separation of servicing from the ownership of the underlying mortgages. According to the MERS website, MERS is "the only national database that provides free public access to servicer information for registered home mortgages, complementing public land recording systems that have their origins in centuries old real property laws." MERS Website, About Us (last visited Nov. 2, 2015). The MERS system is in many ways similar to the way Cede & Co. serves as the nominee owner of record for securities held in trust by Depository Trust and Clearing Corporation, facilitating the transfer of securities through digital entries rather than actual paper transfer of certificates. Commentators have criticized MERS for its "inherent opaqueness" that obfuscates lenders' "shoddy recordkeeping practices," and for the potentially problematic "legal fiction of MERS's status as the 'mortgagee of record'" when assignments are made. *See, e.g.*, Tanya Marsh, *Foreclosures and the Failure of the American Land Title Recording System*, 111 COLUM. L. REV. SIDEBAR 19, 23–24 (2011). The typical legal argument against MERS conducting mortgage assignments is that, because MERS lacks any beneficial interest in the underlying property, any assignment made with MERS serving as mortgagee of record is therefore invalid. *See id.* at 23. Similarly, a number of mostly unsuccessful lawsuits have been filed by both property owners allegedly harmed by mortgage assignments made by MERS, as well as by county recorders allegedly harmed by the corruption of real property records and a loss of recording fee revenues. *See, e.g.*, Harris Cnty. Texas v. MERSCORP Inc., 791 F.3d 545 (5th Cir. 2015); *In re* Mortgage Elec. Registration Sys., Inc., 754 F.3d 772 (9th Cir. 2014). Notwithstanding these colorful characterizations, virtually all of the plentiful litigation involving MERS has been unsuccessful, as MERS has been able to demonstrate that its service as nominee record holder of the mortgage creates no demonstrable injury to the borrowers. Some lenders relying on MERS have had difficulty, however, foreclosing on properties in many states where state property law requires that the holder of the mortgage also hold the note in order to foreclose, as well as in instances where it could not establish clear chain of title for the relevant property prior to foreclosure. For instance, as discussed earlier in this subsection, the Supreme Judicial Court of Massachusetts in *U.S. Bank v. Ibanez* ruled against U.S. Bank, emphasizing the lack of proof showing that U.S. Bank was the mortgage holder at the time of the attempted foreclosure sales of the properties. *See U.S. Bank v. Ibanez*, 458 Mass. 651–52 (2011); *see also* Recent Case, U.S. Bank National Ass'n v. Ibanez, *941 N.E.2d 40 (Mass. 2011)*, 125 HARV. L. REV. 827 (2012). For an extended discussion of these cases and an argument that MERS contributes to "reduced clarity of title" in mortgage transfers, see Adam J. Levitin, *The Paper Chase: Securitization, Foreclosure, and the Uncertainty of Mortgage Title*, 63 DUKE L.J. 637, 637 (2013).

2. ***Robo-Signing.*** Another kind of mortgage servicing practice that attracted controversy in the aftermath of the Financial Crisis was robo-signing, which is

the rapid approval of foreclosures by bank employees without sufficient analysis of the underlying documents. Like MERS, robo-signing initially led to a number of lawsuits, but the most significant ones were brought by government entities such as the DOJ and states' attorney generals. Unlike with MERS, these government lawsuits did not result in widespread legal victories for the involved financial institutions but instead resulted in large no-fault settlements, often amounting to billions of dollars in promised relief to millions of allegedly harmed homeowners. *See, e.g.*, Ronald D. Orol, *U.S. Breaks Down $9.3 Billion Robo-Signing Settlement*, MARKETWATCH (Feb. 28, 2013); Karen Weise, *About That $25 Billion Robo-Signing Settlement*, BLOOMBERGBUSINESS (Nov. 15, 2012). What are some of the advantages and disadvantages of such government-led, settlement-oriented lawsuits, as compared to the largely unsuccessful wave of MERS litigation and appeals?

3. ***The Treasury's Efforts to Encourage Loan Modifications.*** In response to the struggles of homeowners in the aftermath of the Financial Crisis, the Treasury attempted to aid homeowners in renegotiating their mortgage payments to avoid foreclosure. The resulting program, created in 2009, was coined the Home Affordable Modification Program (HAMP). HAMP has faced difficulties and, along with the Treasury Department's other loan modification efforts, has been subject to criticism. *See, e.g.,* SIGTARP, Treasury Should Use HAMP and HHF Together to Help as Many Homeowners as Possible Avoid Foreclosure 1 (July 30, 2014) ("After almost five years, HAMP continues to face considerable challenges, including getting new homeowners into permanent mortgage modifications and keeping homeowners in those modifications from redefaulting."). As of 2015, HAMP had provided 1.6 million permanent mortgage modifications, but nearly 500,000 of them since re-defaulted or were otherwise cancelled. DEP'T OF TREASURY, MAKING HOME AFFORDABLE PROGRAM PERFORMANCE REPORT, THIRD QUARTER 2015. Commentators have pointed to HAMP's "lack of transparency," "its failure to provide for effective enforcement," and, perhaps most importantly, "massive servicer noncompliance" as the main culprits for the program's mixed results. *See, e.g.*, NAT'L CONSUMER L. CTR., AT A CROSSROADS: LESSONS FROM THE HOME AFFORDABLE MODIFICATION PROGRAM (HAMP) 3–4 (Jan. 2013). Despite HAMP's difficulties, it has, in conjunction with other programs created by the Obama Administration, provided significant relief to a large swath of homeowners. Treasury estimates that HAMP permanent modifications have saved borrowers $39 billion thus far. DEP'T OF TREASURY, MAKING HOME AFFORDABLE PROGRAM PERFORMANCE REPORT, THIRD QUARTER 2015. According to the U.S. Department of Housing and Urban Development's (HUD) December 2015 scorecard, "more than 10.1 million mortgage modifications and other forms of mortgage assistance arrangements were completed between April 2009 and the end of November 2015," including HAMP, other programs in Making Home Affordable, and 3 million borrowers helped through the FHA's loss mitigation and early delinquency intervention efforts. Moreover, homeowners' equity rose $6.1 trillion since April 2009, when the Administration's housing stabilization programs were launched, "for a total of nearly $12.4 trillion—the highest level since the fourth quarter of 2006." U.S. DEP'T OF HOUSING & URBAN DEV., THE OBAMA ADMINISTRATION'S EFFORTS TO STABILIZE THE HOUSING MARKET AND HELP AMERICAN HOMEOWNERS 1 (Dec. 2015). HAMP should also be viewed in light of historically successful loan

modification efforts. During the Great Depression, for instance, government officials had greater ability to encourage loan modification because mortgages were typically originated and held by a single financial institution that the government could negotiate with directly. *See, e.g.*, David C. Wheelock, *The Federal Response to Home Mortgage Distress: Lessons from the Great Depression*, FED. RESERVE BANK OF ST. LOUIS REV., May/June 2008. With this advantage and under the auspices of the Home Owners Loan Act of 1933, a key component of President Franklin D. Roosevelt's New Deal, the Home Owners' Loan Corporation was able to acquire and modify an astounding 1,017,827 mortgages. *See, e.g.*, Price V. Fishback et al., *The Influence of the Home Owners' Loan Corporation on Housing Markets During the 1930s* 7 (Nat'l Bureau of Econ. Research, Working Paper, No. 15,824, 2010).

---

5. Eminent Domain Proposals

As the financial system unraveled, one pressing problem facing policy-makers was the valuation of complex financial instruments, such as collateralized debt obligations (CDOs) and asset-backed security (ABS) CDOs, which were based on pools of mortgages. One proposed solution was for the government to purchase these complex financial instruments from investors, thereby reducing uncertainty in the market and preventing the investors from suffering further losses. The Troubled Asset Relief Program (TARP) was actually initially designed to fulfill that function, although, once TARP was enacted, the Treasury Department quickly reversed course and chose to use the funds to provide additional capital to teetering firms, thereby obviating the need to value toxic assets. Another approach to the problem, recommended by some at the time, would have been for the federal government to use its eminent domain powers to purchase mortgages directly from securitization pools, thereby clarifying the value of toxic assets and forcing losses onto the investors who chose to purchase the toxic assets. *See, e.g.*, Robert Hockett, *Paying Paul and Robbing No One: An Eminent Domain Solution for Underwater Mortgage Debt*, 19 CURRENT ISSUES IN ECON. & FIN. 1 (2013); Howell E. Jackson, *Building a Better Bailout*, CHRISTIAN SCIENCE MONITOR (Sept. 25, 2008).

While the idea of having the federal government make use of its eminent domain powers was never realized during the Financial Crisis, a number of municipalities revisited the idea several years later when many borrowers with underwater loans in distressed real estate markets were finding it difficult to obtain loan modifications from mortgage servicers and whole communities were suffering the consequences of multiple years of economic stagnation. Mortgages in danger of default are usually eligible for loan modifications designed to preserve the expected value of repayment. Because foreclosures are costly for borrowers and lenders alike, most creditors are willing to trade a reduction in profit for a reduction in foreclosure risk when a loan exhibits characteristics of imminent default. Mortgages held in privately securitized trusts, however, are subject to restrictions in becoming eligible for loan modifications because their terms often cannot be amended by any single creditor or trustee. For further discussion of these restrictions and legislative efforts to overcome them, *see, e.g.*, MICHAEL S. BARR & JAMES A. FELDMAN, CTR. FOR AM. PROGRESS, ISSUE

BRIEF: OVERCOMING LEGAL BARRIERS TO THE BULK SALE OF AT-RISK MORTGAGES (Apr. 2008).

To surmount this obstacle, the city councils of Richmond, California and other municipalities have considered and, in some cases, passed, eminent domain proposals. *See* Shaila Dewan, *A City Invokes Seizure Laws to Save Homes*, N.Y. TIMES (July 29, 2013). The idea behind these proposals is to use a city's eminent domain power to buy underwater mortgages from homeowners at what the city considers fair market value, then write down the debt and allow the homeowner to refinance, effectively achieving a loan modification through other means. The process occurs as follows:

> In a hypothetical example, a home mortgaged for $400,000 is now worth $200,000. The city plans to buy the loan for $160,000, or about 80 percent of the value of the home, a discount that factors in the risk of default. Then, the city would write down the debt to $190,000 and allow the homeowner to refinance at the new amount, probably through a government program. The $30,000 difference goes to the city, the investors who put up the money to buy the loan, closing costs and [Mortgage Resolution Partners]. The homeowner would go from owing twice what the home is worth to having $10,000 in equity.

Id. Eminent domain proposals have been opposed by the banking and real estate sectors, which argue that the proposals are unconstitutional under the Takings Clause and make for bad policy because they will increase borrowing costs overall. The constitutional question divides into two inquiries: a taking is unconstitutional when a sovereign uses its eminent domain power without (1) demonstrating a clear "public purpose" or (2) providing "just compensation."

The public purpose inquiry likely turns on careful interpretation of the controversial case *Kelo v. City of New London, Connecticut*, 545 U.S. 469 (2005), which held that eminent domain could be used as a vessel to transfer property between private parties if the transfer advanced a public use. In *Kelo* itself, the court held that economic development qualifies as a public use, and that no heightened standard of review would be applied to legislatures using economic development as a justification for exercising eminent domain powers. *See id.* While *Kelo* appears to support the aforementioned set of eminent domain proposals, which also appears to have been justified on economic development grounds, it remains to be seen whether opponents' arguments regarding increased borrowing costs can nonetheless overcome *Kelo's* seemingly deferential stance.

The just compensation inquiry turns on the question of what constitutes "a full and perfect equivalent for the property taken." Monongahela Navigation Co. v. United States, 148 U.S. 312, 326 (1893). In the case of securitized mortgages, it is difficult to ascertain the precise value of the loan itself as opposed to the property that undergirds the loan. For example, the Richmond proposal conflates these two values, effectively taking one in exchange for compensation of the other. The just compensation inquiry may thus prove to be a more promising path for opponents of eminent domain proposals than the public purpose inquiry. For further discussion, *see, e.g.*, Thomas J. Miceli and Katherine A. Pancak,

Using Eminent Domain to Write-Down Underwater Mortgages: An Economic Analysis, 24 J. HOUSING RESEARCH 221 (2015).

The use of eminent domain to take ownership of distressed home mortgages strikes many as a radical proposition. Might it make more sense for the government to require a call option on potentially risky mortgages that would allow for easy government restructuring in the event of another major downturn in real estate prices in the future? *See* Federal Reserve Bank of New York, Liberty Street Economics Blog: Rethinking Mortgage Design (Aug. 24, 2015) (discussing the use of embedded call options to "mitigate legal and other frictions that may prevent efficient [mortgage restructurings] in time of crisis"). If such options were required on an *ex ante* basis, would they be less objectionable than *ex post* takings of the sort discussed above? Would such options be a good idea? Can you think of other viable solutions besides call options? As discussed above, the Home Owners' Loan Corporation played a pivotal role during the Great Depression in refinancing more than one million mortgages. The Corporation had been granted the authority to issue special bonds to purchase non-farm mortgages in danger of foreclosure, and then to refinance those mortgages at more borrower-friendly terms. More than 80% of such refinanced mortgages succeeded in avoiding default. *See, e.g.*, Fishback et al., *The Influence of the Home Owners' Loan Corporation*, at 4.

B. THE CRITIQUE OF ORIGINATE-TO-DISTRIBUTE

Beyond fragmentation of functions, there are more general criticisms that can be made of securitization. Leading up to the Financial Crisis, some commentators anticipated some of the problems associated with securitization. In particular, Professors Kathleen Engel and Patricia McCoy wrote several influential articles in the early 2000s examining the incentive structures in the mortgage markets that contributed to predatory lending. *See, e.g.*, Kathleen C. Engel & Patricia A. McCoy, *A Tale of Three Markets: The Law and Economics of Predatory Lending*, 80 TEX. L. REV. 1255, 1258 (2002) (arguing that "market incentives that historically led lenders to engage in credit rationing have given way to a market where lenders can profit from exploiting new information asymmetries to the detriment of unsophisticated borrowers"); *see also* KATHLEEN C. ENGEL & PATRICIA A. MCCOY, SUBPRIME VIRUS: RECKLESS CREDIT, REGULATORY FAILURE, AND NEXT STEPS (2011).

A decade after the work of Engel and McCoy, Professor Michael Simkovic offered a wholesale critique of the originate-to-distribute model, where lenders make loans not with the intention of holding onto them through maturity, referred to as originate-to-hold, but to distribute or sell them to investors. Simkovic points to excessive competition among securitizers, which purportedly led to a downward spiral in underwriting standards.

Michael Simkovic, Competition and Crisis in Mortgage Securitization

88 IND. L.J. 213 (2013)

U.S. policy makers often assume that market competition is a panacea. . . . However, in the case of mortgage securitization, policy makers' faith in competition is misplaced. Competitive mortgage securitization has been tried three times in U.S. history—during the 1880s, the 1920s, and the 2000s—and every time it has collapsed in a destructive financial and economic crisis. . .

In the mid-2000s, competition between mortgage securitizers for loans led to deteriorating mortgage underwriting standards and a race to the bottom that ended in the late 2000s financial crisis. Underwriting prevents losses at the front end by basing loan approval decisions and lending terms on data-driven predictions of the likelihood of default, or failure to repay, and the severity of losses to lenders in the event of default. Loose underwriting involves making loans that are likely to default.

This Article provides evidence that when competition was less intense and securitizers had more buyer power, securitizers acted to monitor mortgage originators and to maintain prudent underwriting. However, securitizers' ability to monitor originators and maintain high standards was undermined as competition shifted buyer power away from securitizers and consolidation increased originators' supplier power. These changes in market structure and market power match the specific timing of the dramatic deterioration in underwriting standards and vintage loan performance in the mid-2000s that contributed to the crisis. Furthermore, although standards declined across the market, the largest and most powerful of the mortgage securitizers, the [GSEs], remained more successful than other mortgage securitizers at maintaining prudent underwriting.

Competitive pressures exacerbated private financial institutions' strong incentives to take risks. Whereas private investors and managers capture most of the upside of mortgage lending, taxpayers bear much of the downside risk because of the cyclicality of default risk, limited liability, and public safety nets. Because financial institution bailouts are routine, private financial institutions rationally prefer to take more risk than is optimal for taxpayers while government agencies rationally prefer to limit risk. . . .

---

1. ***Critique of the Moral Hazard View of Securitization.*** Simkovic's argument is essentially a variant on the moral hazard view of securitization, which claims that the problem with securitization is the lack of countervailing incentives for market participants, such as underwriters and sponsors of securities, to consider fully the consequences of their actions. For Simkovic, the source of moral hazard was the increased competition between securitizers, which "shifted buying power away from securitizers" and towards loan originators, who could now originate questionable loans that would nonetheless pass the securitizers' relaxed underwriting standards. The moral hazard view has, however, been criticized by Professor Steven Schwarcz:

> Mortgage underwriting standards may have fallen, but there are other explanations. For example, lower standards may well reflect distortions caused by the liquidity glut of that time, in which lenders competed aggressively for business and allowed otherwise defaulting home borrowers to refinance. They also may reflect conflicts of interest between firms and their employees in charge of setting those standards, such as where employees were paid for booking loans regardless of the loans' long-term performance. Blaming the originate-to-distribute model for lower mortgage underwriting standards also does not explain why standards were not similarly lowered for originating non mortgage financial assets used in other types of securitization transactions. Nor does it explain why the ultimate owners of the mortgage loans—the investors in the [MBS]—

> did not govern their investments by the same strict lending standards that they would observe but for the separation of origination and ownership.

Steven L. Schwarcz, *The Future of Securitization*, 41 CONN. L. REV. 1313, 1319–20 (2009).

2. ***The Government's Role in (Inadvertently) Reducing Mortgage Underwriting Standards.*** In his dissent from the Majority Report of the Financial Crisis Inquiry Commission, Peter Wallison argued that Congress pressured HUD to increase home ownership by calling for reduced mortgage underwriting standards, including encouraging greater subprime and other high-risk lending. This reflects a longstanding government desire to increase mortgage lending:

> At least in the United States, the ability of securitization to be used as a multiplier of mortgage-loan money, enabling the country's high amount of mortgage lending, is significantly tied to §3(c)(5)(C) of the [1940 Act] which exempts special purpose entities whose assets consist primarily of mortgage loans from that Act's restrictions. Also, the reduction of lending standards and resulting spike in subprime mortgage lending that preceded the financial crisis were prompted by Congressional pressure on the mortgage-lending sector to make home ownership more egalitarian and widely available. . . . Politics, in other words, inadvertently contributed to mortgage lending becoming a significant source of systemic risk.

Steven L. Schwarcz, *Macroprudential Regulation of Mortgage Lending*, SMU L. REV. (forthcoming).

IV. KEY CHANGES IN THE DODD-FRANK ACT

The previous section examined the rise of securitization and its later fragmentation. This fragmentation led to troubles in the mortgage markets and, eventually, the Financial Crisis. In this section, we discuss the Post-Financial Crisis reforms under the Dodd-Frank Act. We examine here four main types of reforms under the Dodd-Frank Act and its implementing agencies: risk retention, loan-level disclosure, ability-to-repay, and credit rating agency reforms. While these reforms are often focused on correcting abuses in the mortgage markets, it is important to keep in mind that many of the underlying Dodd-Frank Act provisions apply more broadly to other areas of securitization.

A. RISK RETENTION REFORMS

At the heart of the Financial Crisis was the collapse of the housing market, which was driven by the lowering of mortgage underwriting standards, predatory mortgage lending practices, the repackaging of the resulting questionable mortgages into equally questionable MBS, and the later sale of such securities to ignorant or overly optimistic investors. A common reaction to this unsightly chain of lending, repackaging, and selling was the call for a requirement that would require market participants to have some skin in the game, both out of a sense of fairness as well as a desire to force market participants to face the consequences of their actions. In essence, this reaction was based on a moral hazard view of what went wrong with securitization: because "lenders did not have to live with the credit consequences of their loans," underwriting standards fell, "exacerbated by the fact that mortgage lenders could make money on the volume of the loans originated." Steven L. Schwarcz, *The Future of Securitization*, 41 CONN. L. REV. 1313, 1319 (2009). We discussed this moral hazard view earlier in this Chapter.

Congress responded by including risk retention requirements in the Dodd-Frank Act. The intent behind these requirements is that sponsors of securities, if required to retain some level of risk in their products, would be less likely to sell and transfer securities of questionable quality, such as the residential MBS that imploded in 2008. Section 941 of the Dodd-Frank Act attempts to realize this intent by providing that any issuer of an asset-backed security or organizer of an asset-backed securities transaction must retain at least 5% of the credit risk of the asset, subject to a safe harbor for qualified residential mortgages and several other exempt assets. *See* 15 U.S.C. §§ 78o-11(a), (c). The section also provides that issuers and organizers are prohibited from "indirectly hedging or otherwise transferring" the retained credit risk, as such conduct would effectively defeat the purpose of the retention requirements. 15 U.S.C. § 78o-11(c).

Section 941 also directs the OCC, Federal Reserve Board, the FDIC, and the SEC to jointly issue regulations implementing the section and specifying various aspects of the retention requirements, such as "the permissible forms of risk retention," "the minimum duration of the risk retention required," and whether the safe harbor for qualified residential mortgages requires any credit risk retention at all. 15 U.S.C. § 78o-11(c). In 2014, after three years of deliberation, the aforementioned agencies, plus the Federal Housing Finance Agency and HUD, issued a joint final rule implementing the risk retention requirements. *See* Credit Risk Retention, 12 C.F.R. §§ 43, 244, 373, 1234, 17 C.F.R. § 246, 24 C.F.R. § 267. Commentators have observed that the final rule "provides some additional clarity as to the scope and nature of the credit risk retention framework," but "continues to be highly prescriptive and does not give credit for many forms of risk retention or alignment of incentives in securitization transactions that have been commonly been used in the past." *See, e.g.*, SKADDEN, ARPS, SLATE, MEAGHER & FLOM LLP, FINAL RULE TO IMPLEMENT DODD-FRANK RISK RETENTION REQUIREMENT 3 (Dec. 2014). For additional discussion of the risk retention rules and regulations, see Chapter 5.2.

---

1. ***How Effective is Risk Retention in a Housing Bubble?*** The Dodd-Frank Act's risk retention approach has attracted criticism for its reliance on the rational incentive effects it is supposed to have on sophisticated market participants such as sponsors of securities. Professors Ryan Bubb and Prasad Krishnamurthy have argued that such reliance is misguided because, in the context of a housing bubble, market participants irrationally discount the probability that housing prices will fall. Indeed, many large banking organizations held large quantities of MBS in their investment portfolios in the lead up to the Financial Crisis, in essence retaining great chunks of the available

risk. Risk retention requirements thus will fail to deter market participants from sponsoring risky securities, which they irrationally view as not risky, while having the unintended effect of concentrating more risk among those participants. *See* Ryan Bubb & Prasad Krishnamurthy, *Regulating Against Bubbles: How Mortgage Regulation Can Keep Main Street and Wall Street Safe—From Themselves*, 163 U. PENN. L. REV. 1539, 1566–93 (2015). If Bubb and Krishnamurthy's argument is sound, then the Dodd-Frank Act's risk retention approach will actually exacerbate rather than solve the problem. For a critique that focuses on the false investor confidence that might be created by such an approach, see, for example, Steven L. Schwarcz, *Securitisation and Post-Crisis Financial Regulation*, 101 CORNELL L. REV. ONLINE (forthcoming 2016) (manuscript at 13) ("By retaining residual risk portions of certain complex securitisation products they were selling prior to the financial crisis, securities underwriters may actually have fostered false investor confidence, contributing to the crisis.").

2. ***Capital Requirements Under Basel III.*** As discussed in Chapter 2.7, under Basel III, securitization exposures are factored into capital standards. *See* BASEL COMM. ON BANKING SUPERVISION, REVISIONS TO THE SECURITISATION FRAMEWORK (Dec. 2014). The adoption of more stringent or lax securitization reforms thus has a direct effect on the capital requirements that are imposed on banking organizations.

B. LOAN-LEVEL DISCLOSURE REFORMS

A related but distinct area of reform involves the reporting of loan level data, which was unavailable as credit markets collapsed during the Financial Crisis. This information failure was relatively unanticipated, as compared to the concern that predominated about securitization pre-Financial Crisis, which is that securitized pools of assets would not be considered bankruptcy remote and that when the originating financial institution failed, the underlying mortgages would be pulled back into receivership. Instead, when securitized pools failed, regulators and financial institutions did not have a satisfactory way of valuing the underlying assets or performing loan modifications. As you read the following excerpt, consider whether the reforms under the Dodd-Frank Act suffice to address these valuation concerns.

Howell E. Jackson, Loan-Level Disclosure in Securitization Transactions: A Problem with Three Dimensions

Harv. Pub. L. Working Paper No. 10-40 (Jul. 27, 2010)

. . . Limitations on [loan-level information on assets in securitization pools] came to the fore when the financial crisis unfolded in 2007 and 2008 as investors began to question the value of interests in securitization pools and found themselves unable to obtain sufficient information about underlying mortgages to ascertain the current values of their investments. . . . [T]here are at least two [] dimensions . . . on which loan-level information has been found wanting. One is in the area of mortgage renegotiations. While an array of institutional barriers inhibit the renegotiation of under-water mortgages, one aspect of the problem is uncertainty as to the fair market value of loans held in securitized pools and the terms on which comparable loans have been renegotiated or sold in other market transactions. Another dimension on which the value of securitized loans come into play is in disputes over the fairness of the origination of loans that were transferred into securitization pools. The amount by which originators "marked up" mortgages above the price at which those mortgages were sold into securitization pools offers critical evidence as to the presence of unfair origination practices as well as violations of the [ECOA] and other consumer protection statutes. . . .

Reform of loan-level disclosure requirements has now proceeded on four distinct, but related tracks. On the congressional front, legislative proposals in both the House and Senate included securitization reform provisions and these proposals were melded into Subtitle D—Improvements to the Asset-Backed Securitization Process of Title IX of the [Dodd-Frank Act]. Section 942 of the Dodd-Frank Act addresses the issue of loan-level losses in two ways. First, the subsection 942(a) amends section 15(d) of the [1934 Act] to prevent issuers of asset backed securities from discontinuing periodic disclosures relatively soon after a public offering is complete (which is generally permitted for classes of securities with fewer than 300 holders, as is typically the case with securitization offerings) and grants the SEC authority to adopt specific rules for allowing the discontinuation of periodic reporting requirements for asset backed securities. Second, subsection 942(b) instructs the SEC to amend its disclosure requirements for asset-backed securities to mandate additional loan-level data, which would facilitate investor comparisons across different securities and permit investors to perform their own due diligence regarding both the underlying loans and their origination process, including compensation arrangements for originators and risk retention provisions. . . .

. . . [T]he statutory language [of the Act] is still vague, especially with respect to precise loan level disclosure requirements and much is left to the SEC for implementation. Where details are being worked out is the industry level. The American Securitization Forum, [a sector] group . . . has evolved into a multi-faceted effort to addressed weaknesses in securitization practices. . . .

Another somewhat surprising and parallel line of securitization reform is taking place at the [FDIC]. . . . [In 2010,] the FDIC released an advanced notice of proposed rulemaking dealing with the structure of a proposed new safe harbor for future securitizations. Unlike [its] 2000 safe harbor, the FDIC's advance notice contemplated a highly prescriptive set of rules governing many aspects of the structure of securitization transactions, including disclosure requirements. So, under the draft regulatory provision, the FDIC would mandate an extensive list of loan-level information, including all of the information that the SEC Regulation AB requires for public asset backed securities offerings even if the transactions were structured as private placements and thus formally exempt from Regulation AB. . . .

The final participant in the reform of securitization disclosure requirements is the SEC itself, which released on May 3, 2010, its own notice of proposed rulemaking involving extensive revisions of Regulation AB, which governs disclosure requirements for asset-backed securities. The SEC proposal includes elaborate, new requirements for loan-level disclosures both at time of offering and on an on-going basis, and includes a host of ancillary reforms designed to ensure that information is available in machine-readable formats and to slow down shelf offerings so that investors can review disclosures before making investment decisions. . . .

In sum, the debate over loan-level disclosures in securitization transactions is a quadrille with many partners, not all of whom are dancing to the same music. . . . [T]he Dodd-Frank Act contemplates SEC implementation of expanded loan level disclosure standards to be imposed on a periodic reporting basis to at least securitization financings sold to the general public . . . The SEC's May 2010 proposal . . . offers an extensive system of loan level disclosure . . . incorporating the prior work of the [American Securitization Forum] . . . The FDIC initiative covers similar ground, but at this stage seems somewhat out of step with intervening developments. In terms of loan level disclosures, the most striking feature of the FDIC's proposal was the extension of SEC disclosure obligations for public securitization transactions to privately placed offerings sponsored by insured depository institutions. With its May 2010 proposal, the SEC would impose a similar requirement on all privately placed securitization transactions, effectively superseding this aspect of the FDIC's proposal and arguably also going beyond the contours of the relevant provisions of the Dodd-Frank Act, which seem limited to public offerings of ABS. . . .

C. CONSUMER PROTECTION REFORMS

Designed to work in tandem with the risk retention reforms discussed in the previous section, consumer protection reforms focus not on issuers or organizers of residential asset-backed securities, but rather the original mortgage lenders themselves. Ability-to-repay requirements are among the most notable of these consumer protection reforms. The policy intuition behind an ability-to-repay requirement is that lenders, if provided with sufficient incentive to investigate and ensure borrower quality, will reduce the number of problematic loans they make. Section 1411 of the Dodd-Frank Act attempts to realize this intuition by providing generally that:

> In accordance with regulations prescribed by the [CFPB], no creditor may make a residential mortgage loan unless the creditor makes a reasonable and good faith determination based on verified and documented information that, at the time the loan is consummated, the consumer has a reasonable ability to repay the loan, according to its terms . . .

15 U.S.C. § 1639c(a)(1). The basis for such determinations includes "consideration of the consumer's credit history, current income, expected income the consumer is reasonably assured of receiving, current obligations, debt-to-income ratio . . . , employment status, and other financial resources . . ." 15 U.S.C. § 1639c(a)(3). Section 1412 of the Dodd-Frank Act authorizes the CFPB to "prescribe regulations that revise, add to, or subtract from criteria that define a qualified mortgage upon a finding that such regulations are necessary or proper to ensure that responsible, affordable mortgage credit remains available to consumers . . ." 15 U.S.C. § 1639c(b)(3). Similar to the risk retention provisions, Section 1412 also provides a safe harbor for qualified mortgages, which are residential mortgage loans that, *inter alia*, do not contain balloon payment terms or allow the increase of the principal balance, while also meeting certain documentation requirements. *See* 15 U.S.C. § 1639c(b). For additional discussion of the ability-to-pay rules and regulations, see Chapter 5.2 and PRICEWATERHOUSECOOPERS LLP, CFPB "ABILITY-TO-REPAY" STANDARD: AN ANALYSIS OF THE CONSUMER FINANCIAL PROTECTION BUREAU'S ABILITY-TO-REPAY AND "QUALIFIED MORTGAGE" RULE (2013).

In addition to the ability-to-repay requirements previously discussed, there are other mortgage servicing and disclosure requirements also created by the Dodd-Frank Act and implemented by the CFPB. For example, in 2013, the CFPB finalized rules under both the Real Estate Settlement Procedures Act (RESPA) and the Truth in Lending Act (TILA), covering nine areas of mortgage servicing reform, including interest-rate adjustment notices, error resolution and information requests, and early intervention with delinquent borrowers. *See* Mortgage Servicing Rules Under the Real Estate Settlement Procedures Act (Regulation X), 12 C.F.R. § 1024; Mortgage Servicing Rules Under the Truth in Lending Act (Regulation Z), 12 C.F.R. § 1026; *see also* PRICEWATERHOUSECOOPERS, CFPB MORTGAGE SERVICING STANDARDS (Feb. 2013). Also in 2013, the CFPB finalized a mortgage disclosure rule integrating the RESPA and TILA regimes with the "Know Before You Owe" disclosure reforms, which are "intended to help consumers better understand the key terms of a mortgage offered and its associated costs." PRICEWATERHOUSECOOPERS, CFPB MORTGAGE DISCLOSURE REFORMS 1 (Mar. 2014); *see also* Integrated Mortgage Disclosures Under the Real Estate Settlement Procedures Act (Regulation X) and the Truth in Lending Act (Regulation Z), 12 C.F.R. §§ 1024, 1026. For further discussion, see Chapter 5.2.

The Dodd-Frank Act also addresses the use of yield spread premiums through a combination of general prohibitions and delegation of rulemaking and enforcement authority to the CFPB. "For any residential mortgage loan," the Act generally prohibits yield spread premiums, which, as previously discussed, serve as "compensation that varies based on the terms of the loan (other than the amount of the principle)" paid to a mortgage originator. The Act also prohibits mortgage originators from double compensation, from both the borrower and another party, subject to certain exceptions, such as "bona fide third party charges not retained by the creditor, mortgage originator, or an affiliate" of either of those parties. *See* 15 U.S.C. § 1639b.

---

1. ***Incentives, Mandates, or Speedy Recoveries?*** In the area of risk retention and ability-to-repay, the Dodd-Frank Act has focused on providing incentives to financial institutions to create and trade in higher quality securities. Just as we saw with risk retention reforms, Bubb and Krishnamurthy provide a critique of ability-to-repay reforms based on market participants' irrationality in a housing bubble. Their main argument is that, in a housing bubble, lenders will mistakenly believe that rising housing prices will compensate for otherwise risky borrowers' lack of requisite assets, income, or other desired characteristics. Lenders will thus be willing to incur the documentation and verification costs created by an ability-to-repay rule and make the loans anyway. Concluding that the ability-to-repay approach will be ineffective, Bubb and Krishnamurthy call for more direct regulation in the form of mandates, such as banning teaser payment structures. *See* Ryan Bubb & Prasad Krishnamurthy, *Regulating Against Bubbles: How Mortgage Regulation Can Keep Main Street and Wall Street Safe—From Themselves*, 163 U. PENN. L. REV. 1539, 1593–1607 (2015). There is, however, still another kind of solution: to allow securitized products to fail but lower the cost of recovery from such failures. Professor Jason Scott Johnston has argued that such a solution is likely to be superior to others, in large part because it has the beneficial effect of not discouraging mortgage market growth, thus benefiting nontraditional groups of potential homeowners. *See* Jason Scott Johnston, *Do Product Bans Help Consumers? Questioning the Economic Foundations of Dodd-Frank Mortgage Regulation* 5, 58 (Pub. L. & L. Theory Research Paper Series 2015–22, L. & Econ.

Research Paper Series 2015-10, 2015). Assuming Johnston's argument is correct, what kinds of measures might be taken in order to facilitate a "speedy and low cost recovery from failure" of securitized products such as MBS?

D. CREDIT RATING AGENCY REFORMS

A further area of reform under the Dodd-Frank Act focuses not on securitizers or lenders, but rather a particular set of gatekeepers that provide crucial information to purchasers of securities, namely credit rating agencies. The overall thrust of the Dodd-Frank Act's reforms in this area is to decrease the influence of credit ratings while increasing their accessibility and reliance on more reliable sources of information. As aptly put by Professor Nan Ellis and her colleagues, the Dodd-Frank Act

> contains five broad provisions relevant to [credit rating agencies]: 1) It creates an Office of Credit Ratings; 2) It mandates certain disclosures designed to allow investors to evaluate the accuracy of the ratings and to compare performance of [credit rating agencies]; 3) requires [credit rating agencies] to consider relevant independent information; 4) attempts to address the conflicts of interest inherent in the issuer-pays model; [and] 5) removes the statutory reliance on ratings.

Nan S. Ellis, Lisa M. Fairchild, & Frank D'Souza, *Is Imposing Liability on Credit Rating Agencies a Good Idea?: Credit Rating Agency Reform in the Aftermath of the Global Financial Crisis*, 17 STAN. J.L. BUS. & FIN. 175, 208 n.145 (Spring 2012).

In addition, the Dodd-Frank Act contains several provisions that widen existing legal avenues for investors to bring civil suits against credit rating agencies, and give significant oversight and enforcement powers to the SEC to oversee credit rating agencies. *See* 15 U.S.C. §§ 78o-7, 78o-8, 78o-9, 78u-4. Professor Valentin Dimitrov and his colleagues provide a helpful overview of these provisions:

Valentin Dimitrov, Darius Palia, and Leo Tang,
Impact of the Dodd-Frank Act on Credit Ratings

115 J. FIN. ECON. 505 (2015)

Section 933 of [the] Dodd-Frank [Act] explicitly lessens the pleading requirement in private actions under Rule 10b-5 of the [1934 Act], [meaning that] plaintiffs must now only prove that [credit rating agencies] knowingly or recklessly failed to conduct a *reasonable investigation* of the rating security. This change is likely to result in more lawsuits surviving [credit rating agencies'] motion to dismiss . . . Section 939 . . . makes [credit rating agencies] liable as experts under Section 11 of the [1934 Act] for material misstatements and omissions in registration statements filed with the SEC. . . . Section 933 states that the enforcement and penalty provisions of federal securities law apply to statements made by [credit rating agencies] to the same extent as these provisions apply to registered public accounting firms or securities analysts. Section 933 specifically states that [credit rating agencies'] statements are no longer considered forward-looking for the purpose of the safe harbor provisions of the [1934 Act]. These changes make it easier for the SEC to bring claims against [credit rating agencies] for material misstatements and fraud.

The disclosures mandated under Section 932 of [the] Dodd-Frank [Act] further increase the risk of regulatory penalties. According to Section 932, [credit rating agencies] must file annual reports on internal controls with the SEC, disclose their rating methodologies, make third-party due-diligence reports public, and disclose the accuracy of their past credit ratings. Section 932 mandates that the SEC establish an Office of Credit Ratings to better monitor [credit rating agencies'] compliance with the new rules. . . . Section 932 also gives the SEC the authority to revoke or suspend the registration of [an NRSRO] with respect to a particular class of securities if the NRSRO's ratings are deemed inaccurate. . . . Given that [credit rating agencies] are rarely accused of being overly conservative in their ratings, Section 932 can be interpreted as imposing regulatory penalties for issuing upwardly biased (or overly optimistic) ratings.

Pursuant to its authority under the Dodd-Frank Act, the SEC has adopted several rules implementing credit rating agency reforms. Professors Tod Perry and Randle Pollard sample some of the SEC's efforts in this area:

> On January 20, 2011, the SEC adopted rules that required NRSROs to disclose certain information to investors on representations and warranties on the rating of asset-backed securities. The SEC has also proposed rules regarding the remaining requirements of [the] Dodd-Frank [Act] on the regulation of NRSROs on May 18, 2011. These proposed rules are 'designed to improve the practices of credit rating agencies, including rules to limit the conflicts that may arise when NRSROs rely on client payments to drive profits and rules to monitor rating agency employees who move to new positions with rated entities.' On December 27, 2013, the SEC adopted final rules . . . that removed references to credit ratings in certain financial regulations in the [1934 Act] and under the [1940 Act] and the Securities Act of 1933. . . .

Tod Perry and Randle B. Pollard, *"Grade Incomplete": Examining the Securities and Exchange Commission's Attempt to Implement Credit Rating and Certain Corporate Governance Reforms of Dodd-Frank*, 47 INDIANA L. REV. 147, 155–56 (2014). Perry and Pollard go on to argue that the Dodd-Frank Act's mandate for credit rating agency reform has not yet been accomplished and that the proposed SEC rules fail to "reduce the costs associated with becoming an NRSRO, and do not address the inherent conflict of interest existing in the current 'issuer pay' model of the credit rating system." *Id.* at 156.

---

1. ***Reference Removal in Capital Adequacy Regulations.*** As previously mentioned, federal agencies are required to identify and modify regulations containing references to credit ratings. The sheer number of references and the extent of regulatory incorporation of credit ratings means that federal agencies have not completed this task as of the end of 2015. To take one successful example, in the previous chapter, we touched on the debate between commentators who disagreed on whether regulatory incorporation of credit ratings in, for example, capital adequacy regulations, would lead to more

stringent or lax ratings. Following the Dodd-Frank Act's passage in 2013, the Federal Reserve Board and the OCC released a final rule regarding the implementation of Basel III, eliminating all references to credit ratings and replacing them with new measures of creditworthiness, namely the OECD Country Risk Classifications, which measure credit risk in the context of capital adequacy. *See* Regulatory Capital Rules, 12 C.F.R. §§ 3, 5, 6, 165, 167. Are you concerned that the removal of references to credit ratings, in conjunction with their replacement by similar indicators of creditworthiness, might result in the same kind of over-reliance that was on display pre-Financial Crisis? Is there something additionally pernicious about credit ratings themselves, such as the incentives that NRSROs have or have had in the past, that justify this reference removal project?

2. ***Increased Liability for Credit Rating Agencies.*** As discussed above, credit rating agencies face greater potential civil and regulatory liability under the Dodd-Frank Act. Opponents of expanded liability point to increased monitoring and recording costs on the part of rating agencies in order to ensure that they satisfy the lower negligence standard under the Dodd-Frank Act, thus resulting in delayed ratings and more expensive rating services. Proponents of expanded liability respond that the Financial Crisis showed that rating agencies failed to take sufficient time and care in preparing ratings. For further discussion, see, e.g., Ellis et al., *Is Imposing Liability on Credit Rating Agencies a Good Idea?* at 216–17. Interestingly, Dimitrov and his colleagues have examined the impact of the Dodd-Frank Act's civil and regulatory liability provisions on corporate bond ratings. Based on their findings, they argue that such ratings have become less accurate and informative since the passage of the Dodd-Frank Act. Their hypothesis is that the increased legal and regulatory penalties for overly optimistic ratings, combined with an effective lack of such penalties for overly pessimistic ratings, have led to rating agencies artificially downgrading ratings for corporate bonds. *See* Dimitrov et al., *Impact of the Dodd-Frank Act on Credit Ratings.*

V. TRENDS IN SECURITIZATION AFTER THE DODD-FRANK ACT

As we have seen, the reforms discussed in this Chapter have largely split critics into two camps: those that believe such reforms, such as risk retention, are too weak to effect real change, and those that believe such reforms are too punitive and impose an inordinate burden on regulated parties. These reforms were driven, in turn, by serious problems with securitization, arising out of functional fragmentation and other causes. Yet securitization is here to stay. Securitization improves the efficiency of the marketplace and allows otherwise risky borrowers to access liquidity. In light of these considerable benefits, Mark Carney of the Financial Stability Board has argued for the sustainable reform of securitization markets in Europe. *See* Mark Carney, Chair, Fin. Stability Bd., Monetary Authority of Singapore Lecture: The Future of Financial Reform (2014).

What has been the effect of the various reforms in the United States? The following excerpt is from the Financial Stability Oversight Council's 2015 Annual Report, which provides a wealth of data on securitization trends over the past few years.

Financial Stability Oversight Council, 2015 Annual Report

. . . Consistent with strong demand from investors, risk premia for agency MBS, as measured by the spread between 30-year MBS yields and 10-year U.S. Treasury yields, remain depressed (Chart 5.1.10). New issuance of private-label securities backed by residential mortgages remains dormant. Net agency issuance was only slightly positive in 2014 at $87 billion, reinforcing the dynamic of tight supply with increasing demand.

Strong [commercial MBS] issuance continued in 2014, but volumes were still well below 2007 peak levels . . . Spreads remained relatively tight in 2014 . . . and lenders continued to ease underwriting standards by allowing longer amortization schedules and higher loan-to-value ratios. Even so, current underwriting standards are not as weak as they were before the financial crisis. . . .

The housing market recovery continued in 2014, despite some signs of softness early in the year. Home prices rose, and many of the legacy issues from the financial crisis continued to abate, as loan performance improved and negative equity declined. But mortgage origination activity and home sales were generally below 2013 levels. . . .

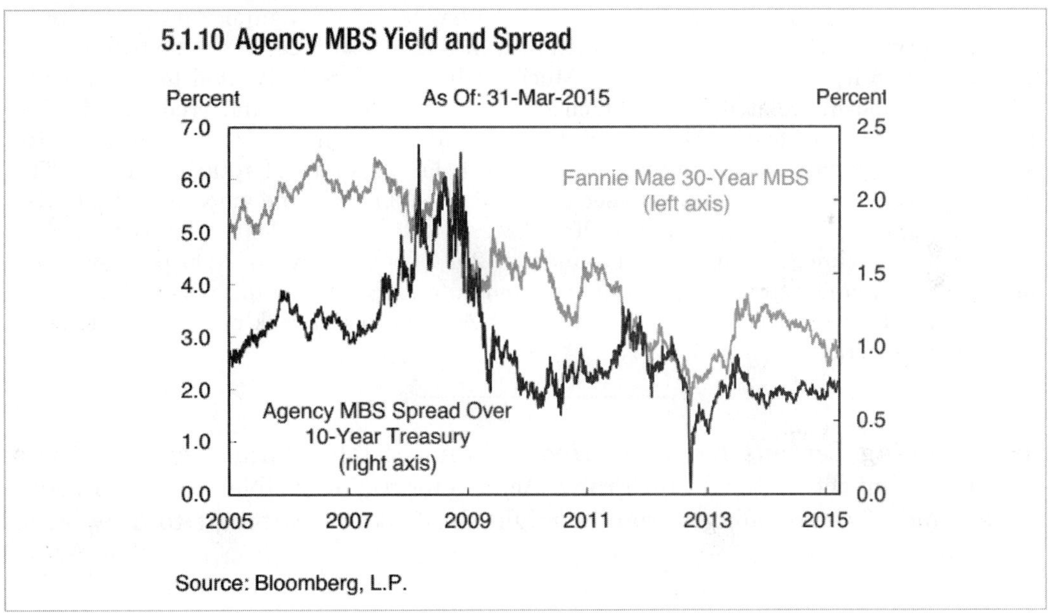

Underwriting standards for new mortgages remained conservative relative to historical norms in 2014. The segment of purchase originations for borrowers with FICO scores below 600, which composed over 10 percent of originations in the early 2000s, is less than 0.5 percent of the market today . . . The private label securitization market, a major source of financing for low-FICO loans in the years before the crisis, remains dormant. . . .

The federal government continues to back the majority of new mortgages, though its market share has declined over the past several years as [banks'] jumbo loans have gained market share . . . Private lending in 2014 was largely concentrated in jumbo loans held in bank portfolios. As has been the case since 2008, the government backed nearly all residential mortgage-backed security (RMBS) issuance in 2014. . . .

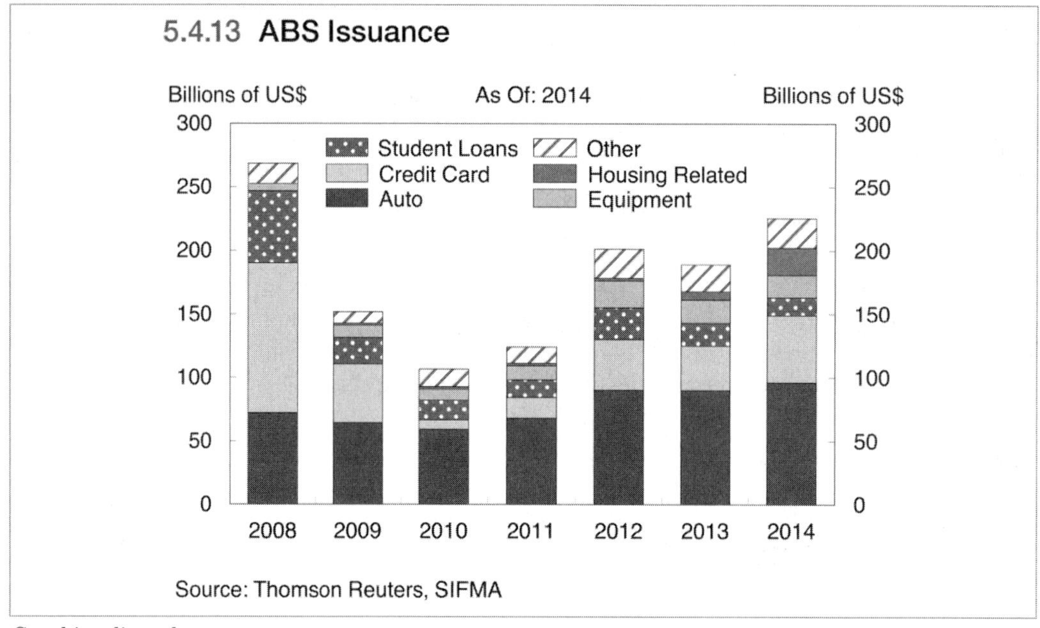

Graphic adjusted.

. . . Given the absence of a deposit base, specialty finance companies rely heavily on securitization. The private securitization market has been highly supportive of growth in the specialty finance company sector, with overall issuance volume increasing 19 percent to $225 billion in 2014 (Chart 5.4.13). Much of the growth is attributed to increases in issuance of housing-related ABS—which does not include MBS—and credit card ABS. Issuance of auto loan ABS increased 7 percent in 2014, as well, with subprime securitizations continuing to compose a larger share of total issuance. The recent growth in subprime auto loan securitizations has brought the amount of these ABS outstanding to levels last observed in 2007. Meanwhile, student loan ABS issuance has continued to decline, reaching $14.1 billion in 2014, well below its 2006 peak of $67.1 billion. Senior credit spreads on credit card and auto ABS relative to Treasury securities have widened since the start of 2014, consistent with the rise in risk premia across credit markets in general. . . .

---

1. ***Drawing Lessons from the Data.*** Is it possible to draw any inferences about the impact of the Dodd-Frank Act's reforms, or is five years too soon? What kind of confounding variables might frustrate the attempt to draw such inferences?

CHAPTER 12.2

MORTGAGE MARKETS AND THE GOVERNMENT-SPONSORED ENTERPRISES

CONTENTS

I. INTRODUCTION

We have discussed different aspects of housing finance many times in earlier parts of this book. In Chapter 1.2, you saw that problems in mortgages and our system of housing finance were a significant contributing factor to the Financial Crisis. In Chapter 2.6, you learned how capital rules for mortgage securitizations were lower than the comparable risk held on the balance sheet of banks. In Chapter 3.1, you learned about the pre-crisis roles of AIG and monoline insurers in providing various forms of support for mortgage securitization. Chapter 4.3 discussed one of the more infamous securities cases involving a synthetic collateral debt obligation based on mortgage securitizations. In Chapter 5.2, you learned about mortgage lending from the vantage point of consumer protection. In Chapter 11.1, you were exposed to the role of derivatives in the Financial Crisis, including through the mortgage securitization channel. In Chapter 12.1, we explained the mechanics of securitization, the rapid growth of private-label mortgage-backed securitization sponsored by large broker-dealers in the run-up to the Financial Crisis.

In this Chapter, we focus on the role of Fannie Mae and Freddie Mac, the private-shareholder-owned, government-sponsored enterprises (GSEs), which have played a central role in U.S. mortgage markets for many decades and which experienced colossal failures in the Financial Crisis. Their failures were driven by woefully low capital for their size and riskiness, inadequate supervision and regulation, concentrated exposure to the risk of mortgages, deteriorating mortgage underwriting standards, accounting practices that did not accurately reflect risk, capital and regulatory arbitrage, mis-aligned incentives for managers whose outsized executive compensation encouraged excessive risk-taking, operating what was in essence huge internal hedge funds and proprietary trading platforms, large-scale use of derivatives linked to mortgage markets, too-big-to-fail subsidies from an implicit, though disclaimed, federal guarantee, and coziness with both sides of the political aisle fed by campaign contributions under the cover of helping the American dream of homeownership. To what extent are these failings similar to, or different from, the failings of large banks, broker-dealers, insurance and other financial conglomerates we have studied elsewhere in the book?

As you saw in Chapter 5.2, the most popular mortgage in the United States has long been the 30-year fixed-rate mortgage. From the perspective of a mortgage originator, a 30-year fixed-rate mortgage poses interest-rate risk in addition to credit risk. The innovative solution of the housing finance system was to transmute that asset into an investable security, which supports the long-term social goals of homeownership for a broad swath of Americans. Credit risk for many mortgages was assumed by Fannie Mae and Freddie Mac, which benefited from an implicit government guarantee. As housing prices rose in the 2000s in a low interest environment in which investors in the United States and abroad were searching for yield, the broadly shared social goals of homeownership, blindness to the housing bubble, and the rise of securitizations contributed to the colossal failure of the GSEs. *See* BETHANY MCLEAN, SHAKY GROUND: THE STRANGE SAGA OF THE U.S. MORTGAGE GIANTS (2015). There is no consensus view on which factors contributed in what combination to their failure.

Homeownership has long been considered central to the American dream. Presidents as ideologically diverse as Franklin D. Roosevelt and Ronald Reagan have expounded the importance of homeownership. The U.S. mortgage market evolved into its current state through a series of federal interventions designed to increase liquidity for housing finance and encourage homeownership. As we have seen in a similar vein throughout this book, these policy goals have intersected with stakeholder and political battles to shape the current system.

The United States created the first government-sponsored housing finance entity, the Federal Home Loan Bank (FHLB) System, and shortly thereafter the precursor to Fannie Mae, in the wake of the Great Depression. Fannie Mae, and a new entity, Freddie Mac, were spun out to the private sector in 1968 and 1970, respectively. The role of GSEs grew as that of the bank and thrift sector declined, during a time when, based on the lessons of the savings and loan crisis, both depository institutions and their regulators viewed the originate-to-distribute model of securitization as critical to reducing risk in the bank and thrift sector. Wall Street securitizations of mortgages by large broker-dealers grew in the late 1990s and then exploded in size in the years leading up to the

Financial Crisis. The GSEs' market share quickly plummeted, and then rebounded sharply upon the collapse of the private sector-sponsored subprime and Alt-A mortgage securitization market. FHLB advances also temporarily filled the gap in bank and thrift financing for subprime and other mortgages in the lead-up to the collapse. During the Financial Crisis, the Federal Housing Administration (FHA) and the taxpayer-backed GSEs in conservatorship backstopped nearly all U.S. mortgages. As of 2015, the GSEs and FHA remain the dominant players, and the GSEs remain in conservatorship.

While the failure of the GSEs in the Financial Crisis brought renewed focus on the need for reform, the inherent problems in their structure were not new, and many from different political backgrounds had called for reform in earlier times, only to be pushed back by the GSEs' political clout, reinforced by a policy consensus in favor of broad-based homeownership. For example, during the Clinton Administration, the Treasury Department released a report critical of the GSEs, but calling for further study. DEP'T OF THE TREASURY, GOVERNMENT SPONSORSHIP OF THE FEDERAL NATIONAL MORTGAGE ASSOCIATION AND THE FEDERAL HOME LOAN MORTGAGE CORPORATION (1996). In 1999, Lawrence Summers, then Treasury Secretary, took on the GSEs in a speech, and the next year, undersecretary Gary Gensler did the same in testimony. According to one account, "All hell broke lose." BETHANY MCLEAN & JOE NOCERA, ALL THE DEVILS ARE HERE 173 (2010). In 2000, the Clinton Administration released a report calling for, among other things, restrictions on the ability of the GSEs to buy subprime, alt-A, and abusive mortgages. *See* DEP'TS OF TREASURY AND HOUS. & URBAN DEV., CURBING PREDATORY HOME MORTGAGE LENDING: A JOINT REPORT 107–10 (2000). Federal Reserve Board Chairman, Alan Greenspan, who otherwise opposed the Treasury report and further Federal Reserve Board regulation of subprime mortgages, argued that the GSEs were creating systemic risk and should be regulated more heavily. *See, e.g., Regulatory Reform of the Government-Sponsored Enterprises Before the S. Comm. on Banking, Hous., and Urban Affairs*, 109th Cong. (2005) (statement of Alan Greenspan, Chairman, Fed. Res. Board). The Bush Administration, with its strong support for homeownership and the "ownership society" more generally, had increased affordable housing goals for the GSEs; despite these goals, the Administration was equally adamant that the GSEs should be reformed and their investment portfolios wound down. According to one account, the Bush White House "engaged in a bitter war" with the GSEs from the beginning of the Administration, and Treasury Secretary Henry Paulson tried to get Congress to enact bi-partisan reform as early as 2006. BETHANY MCLEAN & JOE NOCERA, ALL THE DEVILS ARE HERE 168, 345 (2010). As Secretary Paulson later put it:

> Fannie and Freddie were disasters waiting to happen. They were extreme examples of a broader problem that was soon to become all too evident—very big financial institutions with too much leverage and lax regulation.
>
> But change was hard to come by. The GSEs wielded incredible power on the Hill thanks in no small part to their long history of employing—and enriching—Washington insiders as they cycled in and out of government.

HENRY M. PAULSON, JR., ON THE BRINK 57 (2010).

In this Chapter, we provide a brief history of the GSEs and then analyze key failings and common criticisms of the GSEs in the lead-up to the Financial Crisis. We examine the GSEs' collapse during the Financial Crisis and the government's extraordinary step of placing the GSEs in conservatorship and providing enormous taxpayer-funded capital backstops to them. Finally, we explore options for reforming the U.S. housing finance system and compare it to that of other countries. As you read this Chapter, try to identify inflection points in the development of the U.S. housing finance system. If you think that the system was flawed, when did it go wrong, and what could have been done to change it? To what extent were government policies to blame, and to what extent were private actors? How much of a role does institutional path dependency play? How did stakeholder interests and politics contribute to its development? How should the U.S. housing finance system operate in the future?

II. HISTORY OF THE U.S. MORTGAGE MARKET

In this section, we discuss the history of the GSEs. As was true with respect to the contending visions of the Financial Crisis we presented at the outset of the book, the excerpts below present contending visions of the history and functions of the GSEs, and sometimes even the facts regarding their roles. As you read this section, consider whether the creation and growth of the GSEs was the optimal way for the federal government to promote broad-scale homeownership, including for low- and moderate-income (LMI) households. How else could the government have achieved this goal?

A. THE GSES FROM THE 1930S THROUGH THE FINANCIAL CRISIS

In the following excerpt, Laurie Goodman, Director of the Urban Institute's Housing Finance Policy Center, discusses the history of the GSEs from their establishment until the onset of the Financial Crisis.

Laurie Goodman, A Realistic Assessment of Housing Finance Reform

Urban Inst. 1–6 (2014)

The First Six Decades of GSE History in Six Paragraphs

Before the Great Depression, mortgage finance in the United States was dominated by private entities. The mortgages were short-maturity instruments (10 years or less) with balloon payments at the end. The assumption was that the borrowers would roll over the loans when they matured. The absence of a national housing finance market led to considerable geographical variation in the availability and pricing of credit, and high down payment requirements depressed widespread homeownership.

In the aftermath of the Great Depression, which generated widespread foreclosures (20–25 percent of the mortgage debt was in default) and a falling homeownership rate, the government created the [FHLB] System in 1932. This organization was intended to provide member financial institutions with financial products and services—including on-demand, low-cost funding—to assist and enhance lending for home mortgages as well as small business, rural, agricultural, and economic development. The [FHA] was created in 1934 to offer federally backed insurance for home mortgages made by FHA-approved lenders. Originally a federal government agency, [Fannie Mae] was created in 1938 as a secondary market entity to purchase, hold, and sell FHA-insured loans. Thus, Fannie

Mae was designed to provide liquidity to the mortgage market by buying loans from lenders and allowing them to make new loans with the cash.

In 1954, Fannie Mae was transformed into a public-private mixed ownership corporation exempt from all state and local taxes (except those on real property). In 1968, it was transformed into a for-profit shareholder-owned company and removed from the federal budget. In 1970, Fannie Mae was permitted to buy and sell mortgages not insured by the federal government. [Freddie Mac] was established in 1970, capitalized and owned by the [FHLB], to purchase long-term mortgages from thrift institutions, providing the thrifts with liquidity. The thrifts could use the proceeds from the sale of the mortgages to make more mortgages. The GSEs began to grow rapidly during this period, as shown in figure [12.2-1]. The GSE share of outstanding mortgages increased from 0 percent in early 1968 to 7.2 percent in 1980 and 27.4 percent in 1990.

Figure 12.2-1 Distribution of Outstanding Single-Family Mortgages

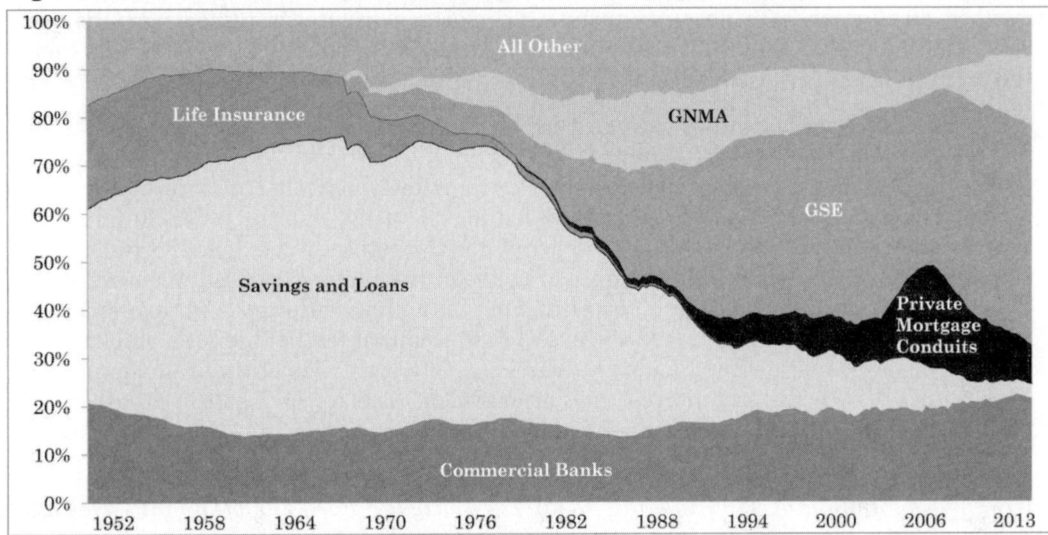

Sources: Fed. Res. Board and Urban Inst. Graphic adjusted.

In the 1970s and 1980s Fannie Mae and Freddie Mac pursued different paths. Fannie Mae primarily retained mortgages on its own balance sheet, leaving the portfolio with a considerable amount of interest-rate risk. Freddie Mac, on the other hand, had a small balance sheet and transferred most of the interest-rate risk of the mortgages it held through securitizations, the first of which was done in 1971. (By contrast, Fannie Mae did not do its first securitization until a decade later.) The market turbulence in the late 1970s and early 1980s thus left Fannie [Mae] but not Freddie [Mac] exposed, with the former requiring government assistance through regulatory forbearance (capital requirements were relaxed) and tax relief.

In 1989, the [FHLB] system was restructured. The [FHLB] Board was abolished, the Federal Housing Finance Board was created as a regulator, and membership in the [FHLBs] was opened to depository institutions that had more than 10 percent of their portfolios in residential mortgage-related assets. Freddie Mac was reorganized into a corporate structure similar to Fannie Mae, a for-profit corporation, owned by private shareholders rather than by the [FHLB].

In 1992, Congress passed the Federal Housing Enterprises Finance Safety and Soundness Act, which created the Office of Federal Housing Enterprise Oversight (OFHEO), within [the Department of Housing and Urban Development (HUD)], as an independent regulator of the GSEs. This act also gave the GSEs an “affirmative obligation to facilitate the financing of affordable housing for low-income and moderate-income families." Beginning in 1995, Fannie [Mae] and Freddie [Mac] were given explicit housing goals.

The GSEs as Businesses: 1990–2008

The GSE share of the outstanding mortgage market continued to increase rapidly, from 27.4 percent at the end of 1990 to 39.7 percent at the end of 2000 to 43.8 percent at the end of 2003 (*see* [Figure 12.1-1]). At the end of 2013, the GSE share stood at 45.7 percent.

Fannie [Mae] and Freddie [Mac] were really in three businesses: (1) a large single-family insurance business, (2) a relatively small multifamily insurance business, and (3) the portfolio management business. This third line of business was an important, if then underappreciated, contributor to their profitability. During the 1990s, the GSE began to grow their retained portfolios rapidly, even more rapidly than their insurance operations. . . . "[I]n 1990 the Fannie [Mae] and Freddie [Mac] retained portfolios equaled 23 percent of their outstanding [mortgage-backed securities (MBSs)], while by 2001, this ratio reached 80 percent." In absolute terms, the mortgage-related retained portfolio grew from $138 billion in 1990 to $1.57 trillion in 2004. This retained portfolio growth fueled the profitability of the organizations:

> The profit potential for the two F&F business lines is substantially different. Revenue on the F&F investor-held MBS line derives primarily from the annual fee received for guaranteeing the timely payment of interest and principal. The average guarantee fee for . . . 2003 was just over 20 basis points . . . for the two firms. Revenue for the retained mortgage portfolios, in contrast, is based on the spread between the interest rate earned on the mortgage assets and the interest cost of the funding liabilities. For example, in 2003, the average spread was 172 [basis points] for Fannie Mae and 186 [basis points] for Freddie Mac. The relatively large size of this rate spread arises from the low interest cost of F&F debt (due to the implicit Treasury guarantee) and the compensation for accepting the interest-rate risk associated with the mortgage securities held in the portfolios.

[Dwight M. Jaffe, *On Limiting the Retained Mortgage Portfolio of Fannie Mae and Freddie Mac* 5 (Wharton Fin. Inst. Ctr., Working Paper No. 05-38, 2005).]

The Seeds of the GSE Difficulties

Both Fannie Mae and Freddie Mac had accounting difficulties in the early 2000s. In 2003, Freddie Mac disclosed it had used improper accounting practices. The new GSE supervisory authority, OFHEO, found this error resulted in a $5 billion misstatement for the years 2000–03; Freddie [Mac] was fined $175 million. OFHEO also investigated Fannie Mae and found that it had used improper accounting to smooth earnings. Fannie [Mae] paid a $400 million penalty. These episodes undermined the credibility of the entities.

Fannie Mae and Freddie Mac have played a critical role in the market. They have reduced mortgage rates for borrowers by bringing transparency and standardization to the housing finance market. They were crucial to securitization of conventional mortgages, which led to the development of national mortgage market. And the GSEs made purposeful efforts to expand access to credit. While Fannie [Mae] and Freddie [Mac] had affordable housing goals, the amount of their activity often exceeded the requirements (*see* . . . figure [12.2-2]).

The government share of total securitizations ranged between 75 and 85 percent from 1995 to 2004, with the GSEs accounting for the bulk of this share. It dropped to 54 percent in 2004 and 44–45 percent in 2005 and 2006 ([Figure 12.2-2]). The GSEs, alarmed at their slipping share, began to follow the private-label market into nontraditional products. Their expansion into these products was aimed at correcting a declining market share, not (as some have claimed) meeting affordable housing goals. The GSEs relaxed their standards for origination, agreeing to provide insurance for more Alt-A loans, more interest-only . . . loans, more adjustable-rate mortgages, and more borrowers with very low FICO scores. . . . Exacerbating the impact of their move into nontraditional lending, the GSEs jumped into that market at the worst time. The private-label securities . . . market was going after increasingly risky loans to feed its voracious appetite for product. Anxious to maintain market share, the GSEs relaxed their standards and chased the [private-label securities] market onto what turned out to be treacherous terrain.

The GSEs' difficulties did not stem solely from the move to nontraditional products. In the early 2000s, subprime [MBSs] were the most profitable item to add to the retained portfolios. . . . Freddie [Mac] and Fannie [Mae] together purchased 3.8 percent of subprime issuance in 2001, 11.9 percent in 2002, 34.7 percent in 2003, 38.9 percent in 2004, and 28.9 percent in 2005, tapering to 23–25 percent in 2006 and 2007. In 2004, when Freddie [Mac] and Fannie [Mae] started reporting their public holdings, nonagency MBS made up 35 percent of Freddie [Mac's] portfolio and 15 percent of Fannie [Mae's] retained portfolio; they remained around that share through the end of 2006. These MBS were often backed by loans that the GSEs would not insure. However, they (like most other investors participating in the market at that time) believed the product they were purchasing had adequate subordination, so they were not taking much risk.

Figure 12.2-2 Agency and Nonagency Shares of Residential MBS Issuance

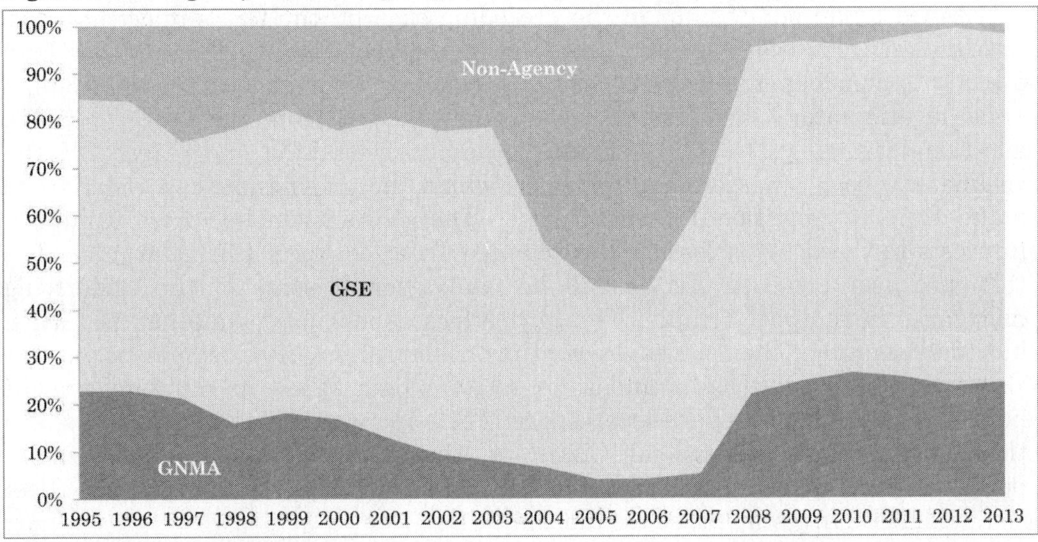

Source: Inside Mortgage Finance. Graphic adjusted.

When Home Prices Stalled, the GSEs Were Vulnerable

When home prices topped out and began to stall, the GSEs were vulnerable in two of their three businesses: the retained portfolio and the single-family insurance operations. The multifamily book of business also experienced losses, but these losses were small and the business recovered quickly.

The problems were first evident on the portfolio side of the business, as markets react in real time. Prices on the MBS in their portfolio began to fall substantially. Though not a perfect proxy for the subprime deals the GSEs had purchased, the ABX, an index of credit default swaps, is at least illustrative. The price of the ABX 06-2, tranches of AAA deals issued in the second half of 2006, plummeted from 100 in late 2006 to around 40 in late 2008 and 20 by March 2009.

By late 2007, the percentage of serious delinquencies in the Fannie [Mae] and Freddie [Mac] single-family guarantee businesses had begun to rise sharply; this rise accelerated further in 2008. . . . The increase in serious delinquencies reflected not only extremely poor performance on the part of the nontraditional products, but also much higher than anticipated delinquents and defaults on Fannie [Mae's] and Freddie [Mac's] traditional products.

The very high delinquencies and defaults on the nontraditional product, especially Alt-A loans, contributed disproportionately to the losses. For example, Fannie [Mae] reports that Alt-A loans were 4.7 percent of its total book of business at the end of 2013 but had contributed 23.7 percent of its 2012 credit losses and 26 percent of its 2013 credit losses. Interest-only loans were 2.9 percent of Fannie [Mac's] total book of business at the end of 2013 but had contributed 21.8 percent of its 2012 credit losses and 18.7 percent of its 2013 credit losses. . . .

The credit performance of loans is determined not only by origination characteristics, but also by the macroeconomic environment, home prices in particular. As home prices continued to crash, the strength of the interaction between home prices and performance was underestimated, as was the magnitude of the feedback effects.

B. THE GSEs AND THE U.S. MORTGAGE MARKET

As Goodman pointed out in the preceding excerpt, the GSEs inject liquidity into the U.S. mortgage market in a variety of ways. The GSEs do not lend directly to homebuyers. Rather, the GSEs purchase mortgages from originators, and the originators then use the funds they receive from the GSEs to make additional loans. The GSEs create liquidity by taking mortgages off the originators' books in exchange for cash, which the originators can redeploy to make loans to additional homebuyers. The GSEs then securitize and sell interests in the pools of loans. In exchange for a fee, the GSEs guarantee that the purchasers of their MBSs will be paid, even if some of the underlying mortgages in the pool default. Guarantee fees generate revenue for the GSEs, but the guarantees themselves are contingent liabilities. As Goodman noted, the GSEs also keep some loans and some of their own MBSs in their investment portfolios, and they purchase interests in MBSs sponsored by broker-dealers,. In the lead up to the Financial Crisis, as Goodman noted, these investment portfolios grew exceedingly large. Just as broker-dealers took on balance-sheet risk with MBS investment, so too did the GSEs.

Professors Viral Acharya, Matthew Richardson, Stijn van Nieuwerburgh, and Lawrence White explain the GSEs' business models in the following excerpt.

Viral Acharya et al., Guaranteed to Fail:
Fannie Mae, Freddie Mac and the Debacle of Mortgage Finance

12–14 (2011)

What exactly do Fannie [Mae] and Freddie [Mac] do? The GSEs are engaged in two somewhat related businesses: residential mortgage securitization (currently about $3.5 trillion) and residential mortgage investment (currently about $1.7 trillion).

In the securitization business, the GSEs buy mortgages from originators (mostly fixed-rate, single-family home mortgages, although they do also buy some adjustable-rate mortgages and some multi-family mortgages); they form pools of these mortgages (so that the "law of large numbers" reduces the variability in outcomes that might arise from a single mortgage); and they issue (sell) "pass-through" [MBS] that are formed from these pools to investors. These MBS represent claims on the interest and principal repayments that are "passed through" from the pool of mortgage borrowers to the securities investors (minus various fees).

Because the investors have no direct knowledge of the creditworthiness of the mortgage borrower, they need to be reassured that they will receive the promised interest and principal repayments. Both Fannie Mae and Freddie Mac provide guarantees to investors in their MBS against the risk of default by borrowers of the underlying mortgages. In return, both charge a "guarantee fee."

Although the GSE guarantee (as long as it can be honored) removes the credit risk from the securities, the MBS investor is still subject to interest-rate risk. Any long-lived fixed-rate debt instrument carries interest-rate risk: When interest rates for new securities are higher than the interest rate on an existing (but otherwise comparable) security, the value of the latter decreases; when interest rates for new securities are lower, the value of the existing security increases. However, for fixed-rate mortgages (and the MBS that are formed from them), the interest-rate risk for the investor is heightened, because mortgage borrowers are usually able to prepay their mortgage (and, in the United States, do so without paying any fee or penalty).

The second business for the GSEs is mortgage investment. They buy and hold residential mortgages (or more often their own MBS). The funding for these investments comes overwhelmingly from issuing debt. They earn net income on the "spread": the difference between the interest yield on the mortgages that they hold and the interest rate on the debt that they have issued. . . By owning these on-balance sheet mortgages, the GSEs are exposed to interest-rate risk as well as credit risk.

III. CRITICISMS OF THE GSES

Fannie Mae and Freddie Mac were the targets of frequent criticism by policy-makers and scholars, as well as by their competitors on Wall Street, and of frequent defense by scholars, as well as by the many different stakeholders who benefited from the existing system. As we noted at the outset, Treasury Secretaries from Summers to Paulson across different Administrations decried the systemic risk posed by the GSEs, but were not able to reform the GSEs before they failed in the Financial Crisis. As you read this section, consider which of the critiques were valid and which missed the mark.

A. TOO BIG TO FAIL SUBSIDY

Perhaps the most trenchant critique of the GSEs was that even though the GSEs were privately owned, the GSEs' quasi-governmental structure created the perception that the federal government guaranteed the GSEs' debts and its guarantees and would make creditors whole if the GSEs were to become insolvent. (This critique, of course, played out fully in the Financial Crisis.) Critics argued that this implicit guarantee had three undesirable consequences.

First, critics argued that implicit guarantees became a self-fulfilling prophecy: because the market expected that the government would back the GSEs' guarantees, taxpayers would be on the hook for billions of dollars if the MBSs, in fact, experienced losses, which they later did. *See, e.g.*, Carrie Stradley

Lavargna, *Government-Sponsored Enterprises Are "Too Big to Fail": Balancing Public and Private Interests*, 44 HASTINGS L.J. 991, 1011 (1993).

Second, critics argued that an implicit government guarantee created moral hazard by incentivizing risk-taking by the GSEs' management and discouraging oversight by the GSEs' creditors. American Enterprise Institute scholar Peter Wallison explains this view in the following excerpt:

> [G]overnment backing eliminates the restrictions—known as market discipline—imposed by wary creditors. . . . Fannie [Mae] and Freddie [Mac] are different . . . : despite the fact that their securities explicitly state that they are not backed by the federal government, their government charter and mission—plus the government's past behavior—have persuaded investors that neither company will be allowed to default. Thus, in a very practical sense, all their debt obligations—not just some limited amount corresponding to a bank's deposits—are seen by U.S. and foreign investors as nearly risk-free, and therefore are not subject to market discipline. In effect, they are given a free pass to take risk. The name for this phenomenon—in which government backing reduces market discipline—is moral hazard, and the GSEs represent moral hazard on steroids.

PETER WALLISON, MORAL HAZARD ON STEROIDS (2006). Reprinted with permission of the American Enterprise Institute.

Third, commenters argued that an implicit government guarantee enabled the GSEs to hold significantly less capital and to borrow more, and more cheaply, from bondholders than they would have without the guarantee, meaning that the guarantee operated as an implicit federal subsidy that distorted competition and exposed taxpayers to risk. Critics also pointed out that the GSEs benefitted from other special treatment; for instance, the GSEs were exempt from state and local income taxes and SEC registration requirements. Critics contended that much of these subsidies accrued to the benefit of the managers, shareholders, and bondholders of the GSEs rather than to borrowers. *See* U.S. DEP'T OF THE TREASURY, GOVERNMENT SPONSORSHIP OF THE FEDERAL NATIONAL MORTGAGE ASSOCIATION AND THE FEDERAL HOME LOAN MORTGAGE CORPORATION (1996).

In 2001, the Congressional Budget Office quantified the federal subsidies from which the GSEs benefitted as summarized in the following excerpt.

Cong. Budget Office, Federal Subsidies and the Housing GSEs

13–14 (2001)

The law treats the GSEs as instrumentalities of the federal government, rather than as fully private entities. They are chartered by federal statute, exempt from state and local income taxes, exempt from the [SEC's] registration requirements and fees, and may use the Federal Reserve as their fiscal agent. In addition, the U.S. Treasury is authorized to lend $2.25 billion to both Fannie Mae and Freddie Mac and $4 billion to the FHLBs. GSE debt is eligible for use as collateral for public deposits, for unlimited investment by federally chartered banks and thrifts, and for purchase by the Federal Reserve in open-market operations. GSE securities are explicitly government securities under the Securities Exchange Act of 1934 and are exempt from the provisions of many state investor protection laws. Those advantages have not been granted to any other shareholder-owned companies. . . .

The special treatment of GSE securities in federal law signals to investors that those securities are relatively safe. Investors might reason, for instance, that if the securities were risky, the government would not have exempted them from the protective safeguards it put in place to prevent losses of public and private funds. This implied assurance appears to outweigh the explicit disavowal of responsibility in every prospectus for GSE securities. The GSEs therefore enjoy lower financing costs than would private financial intermediaries, were they to hold similar levels of capital and take comparable risks.

As a consequence of those provisions, GSE obligations are classified by financial markets as "agency securities" and priced below U.S. Treasuries and above AAA corporate obligations. The super AAA rating reduces borrowing costs for the GSEs, in part by promoting institutional acceptance of the securities. . . General acceptance of the securities increases investors' willingness to buy them and enhances their liquidity. Those characteristics of acceptability and liquidity contribute to the relatively high price investors are willing to pay for GSE securities. . . .

A similar combination of federal regulatory provisions and implied guarantees enhances the credit standing, market acceptance, and liquidity of MBSs guaranteed by Fannie Mae and Freddie Mac. For example, risk-based capital requirements for banks are lower for GSE-guaranteed MBSs than for privately guaranteed MBSs. Federal backing also enables Fannie Mae and Freddie Mac to offer a credit guarantee that the market perceives as more valuable than any similar guarantee by a private company. The enhanced quality of the guarantee reduces the rate of return that investors require on GSE-guaranteed MBSs below the rates required on similar privately guaranteed MBSs. That lower rate permits a mortgage pooler to pay higher prices for mortgages and pass along lower interest rates to borrowers. That competitive advantage on GSE-guaranteed MBSs also enables Fannie Mae and Freddie Mac to charge higher guarantee fees than private guarantors.

The Congressional Budget Office estimated that the GSEs' federal subsidies totaled $13.6 billion in 2000. *See id.* at 24. Federal Reserve Board Senior Adviser Wayne Passmore calculated the gross value of the GSEs' federal subsidies to be around ten times that, or $122–$182 billion. *See* Wayne Passmore, *The GSE Implicit Subsidy and the Value of Government Ambiguity*, 33 REAL EST. ECON. 465, 466 (2005). Under any independent measure, the subsidies were very large.

---

1. ***Distributive Effects of the Implicit Federal Subsidy.*** The Congressional Budget Office found that mortgage borrowers received only about half of the value of pre-Financial Crisis federal subsidies. The remainder was retained by Fannie Mae and Freddie Mac shareholders, creditors, and managers, and by the FHLBs' members. *See* CONGRESSIONAL BUDGET OFFICE, FEDERAL SUBSIDIES AND THE HOUSING GSES 25–28 (2001). Should the government have been concerned that the GSEs (and their shareholders) retained a significant portion of the benefits of the implicit federal subsidy? If so, what should policy-makers have done about it?

B. INVESTMENT PORTFOLIOS AND OTHER PRUDENTIAL CONCERNS

A number of critics argued that the GSEs' sizeable investment portfolios, which reached over $1.65 trillion before the Financial Crisis—in essence, giant hedge funds with high leverage, huge derivatives exposures, and proprietary trading risks—created systemic risks and did not provide offsetting benefits of liquidity to the U.S. mortgage market. For instance, former Federal Reserve Board Chairman Alan Greenspan testified that "[w]e have been unable to find any purpose for the huge balance sheets of the GSEs, other than profit creation through the exploitation of the market-granted subsidy." *Regulatory Reform of the Government-Sponsored Enterprises Before the S. Comm. on Banking, Hous., and Urban Affairs*, 109th Cong. (2005) (statement of Alan Greenspan, Chairman, Fed. Res. Board). Consider the following excerpt, which questions why the GSEs were permitted to build significant investment portfolios.

Viral Acharya et al., Guaranteed to Fail: Fannie Mae, Freddie Mac and the Debacle of Mortgage Finance

136–38 (2011)

[T]he GSEs not only guarantee conforming mortgages held by other investors but also actively invest in a large portfolio of mortgage assets—the so-called retained portfolio. At the end of 2009, Freddie [Mac] and Fannie [Mae] either guaranteed or owned $5.39 trillion dollars in mortgages, fully $1.71 trillion of which (27% of the total) was owned in portfolio. This 27% retained mortgage share is down from 44% in 2002, but is only slightly below the 2008 all-time dollar high of $1.76 trillion.

The rationale for this retained portfolio was to promote liquidity in the secondary mortgage market. Higher liquidity, it was believed, could make secondary mortgage markets more efficient and would ultimately trickle down to homeowners in the form of lower mortgage rates. We believe that this reasoning is obsolete at best and probably false. It is obsolete because the market for conforming [MBSs] is one of the largest and most liquid fixed income markets in the world. By now, markets have had almost 40 years of experience in trading conforming [MBSs]. We believe that they do not need continued liquidity support in the form of proprietary trading purchases from the GSEs. It is potentially false, because there is no evidence for a direct link between the size of the GSE portfolios and the liquidity of secondary mortgage markets.

In reality, the retained portfolio management business became the cash cow of the GSEs. Rather than making markets more liquid, it had as its true objective to make money for the shareholders, traders, and CEOs of the GSEs, just as is true of any other hedge fund. The CEOs gained enormously: Richard Syron of Freddie Mac and Daniel Mudd of Fannie Mae each took home $28 million in 2006 and 2007 alone. Ominously, these were exactly the years that the GSEs ramped up the risk of their portfolios the most. . . .

The nature of the retained portfolio business invites comparison with the hedge fund industry. To put the GSEs' $1.7 trillion retained portfolio into perspective, the total assets under management of the entire hedge fund industry were $2 trillion at the end of 2009. Given aggregate leverage ratios around five, this means that hedge function industry has a balance sheet on the order of $10 trillion. The largest hedge fund in 2009 was Bridgewater Associates with $38 billion. Freddie [Mac's] and Fannie [Mae's] trading operation therefore was around 20% as large as the entire hedge fund industry, and the two GSEs were magnitudes bigger than the largest hedge fund.

The level of sophistication of the GSEs' trading function rivaled that of premier hedge funds. They employed sophisticated quantitative models for predicting the performance of mortgage loans, and they used large derivative positions to manage interest rate and default risk. This trading function generated enormous revenues: about $28 billion in each of 2002, 2003, and 2004. After a dip, the 2009 trading revenue was $31 billion in 2009. . . . Over the past 15 years, trading revenues represented on average 73% of all revenues.

Like many hedge funds, the GSEs increased the riskiness of their mortgage portfolios in the years leading up to the [Financial Crisis]. They purchased $227 billion worth of subprime and Alt-A [MBSs] in 2006 and 2007, in addition to possibly $500 billion more of high-risk mortgages that were not classified as such.

Until the [Financial Crisis], the GSEs appeared to be highly profitable compared to almost any other financial institution including most hedge funds, as witnessed by their return on equity (even though they were losing the race to the bottom . . .). [Freddie Mac's] [return on equity] averaged 23% per year from 1977-2006 and [Fannie Mae's] averaged 17% . . . . Part of this stellar performance is attributable to their ability to borrow at below-market rates because of their implicit government backing . . . and part is due to the GSEs' taking on tail risk, earning consistent spreads in normal times albeit at the risk of significant losses during an economic downturn.

Our first long-term policy recommendation is to discontinue the trading function of the GSEs. . . . The trading function in many respects highlights the worst aspects of a "privatize the gains, socialize the losses" entity. By being able to borrow cheaply, the GSEs invested in a highly levered portfolio of increasingly risky mortgages to boost profits. When the credit risk that they took on materialized, the tax payer was stuck with a huge bill, a significant proportion of which represents the losses of the retained mortgage portfolios.

---

1. ***Investment Portfolios.*** The GSEs' investment portfolios create not only credit risk (*i.e.*, the risk that homeowners would not repay their mortgages) but also interest rate risk regardless of whether rates rose or fell:

> [C]arrying a portfolio of mortgages creates substantial interest rate risk . . . .
>
> A peculiar characteristic of interest rate risk is that it exists whether interest rates rise or fall. Two examples will show why this is true. Assume that a GSE borrows $1 million at 4 percent to buy a portfolio of mortgages that yields 5 percent. As long as it holds this portfolio, the GSE pockets the difference between what it has to pay to its lenders (4 percent) and what it is receiving from the mortgages it is holding (5 percent). . . . However, if interest rates fall to, say, 3 percent, many homeowners will refinance their 5 percent mortgages. The GSE will, of course, get the cash from this refinancing, but the mortgages it will be able to buy with this cash will then only pay 3 percent. Its profitable situation is now reversed; it is paying 4 percent to hold mortgages that are yielding 3 percent, and losing money on every one. . . .
>
> But the GSEs can also lose if interest rates rise. Using the same hypothetical set of facts, what happens if interest rates rise to 6 percent? In that case, homeowners will hold onto their 5 percent mortgages, since refinancing will not pay, and the GSE has to worry about what it will do when its loans mature. If the loans are short-term, and about half of all GSE borrowings are contracted for a year

> or less, the GSE will be compelled to refinance its initial borrowing at 6 percent, and will again suffer a loss as it pays 6 percent to carry a mortgage portfolio that continues to pay only 5 percent. Thus, if its borrowings are short-term, a GSE will suffer a financial loss if interest rates rise, just as it will suffer a loss if interest rates decline while its liabilities are long-term.
>
> To be sure, interest rate risk can be hedged—the risk can be shared with or transferred to others through various kinds of derivatives such as interest rate swaps. But swaps and other hedges are expensive, and to achieve higher levels of profitability, a GSE will not completely hedge its risk.

PETER J. WALLISON, MORAL HAZARD ON STEROIDS (2006).

Why do you think Congress and their regulator allowed the GSEs to develop and then continue expanding their investment portfolios despite these risks?

2. ***Deteriorating Underwriting Standards in Guarantees.*** While the portfolios were the focus of a great deal of criticism before the Financial Crisis and undoubtedly exposed the GSEs to enormous risk, so too did their basic guarantee business. As Goodman noted in the excerpt at the outset of the Chapter, the GSEs increased their exposure to Alt-A and other nontraditional mortgages just as the private-label securitization market for those products was collapsing, and the GSEs' guarantees of such mortgages led to disproportionately high losses as compared to their traditional products; by one measure, Goodman reports Alt-A mortgages were about 5% of their guarantees, but 25% of their losses. As Goodman notes, even their traditional products experienced unusually high default rates as the Financial Crisis led to the Great Recession, massive job losses and concomitant harms to households, making it harder for middle-income families to pay to meet their obligations on traditional mortgages. *See* Manuel Adelino et al., *Loan Originations and Defaults in the Mortgage Crisis: The Role of the Middle Class* (Tuck Sch. of Bus., Working Paper No. 2546427, 2015) (noting that the bulk of defaults occurred among upper- and middle-income borrowers). According to Federal Housing Finance Agency (FHFA), 90% of GSE losses came from their single-family guarantee business rather than their portfolio losses or other sources. CONSERVATOR'S REPORT ON THE ENTERPRISES' FINANCIAL PERFORMANCE 9 (2013).

3. ***Capital.*** The GSEs were operating with enormously high leverage before the Financial Crisis. As the Financial Crisis Inquiry Commission (FCIC) put it, "The kings of leverage were Fannie Mae and Freddie Mac, the two behemoth GSEs. For example, by the end of 2007, Fannie's and Freddie's combined leverage ratio, including loans they owned and guaranteed, stood at 75 to 1." FCIC, FINANCIAL CRISIS INQUIRY REPORT xx (2011). At the end of 2007, the GSEs had combined reported capital of only $71 billion, which (along with another $7 billion in private capital raised by Fannie Mae in 2008) had effectively disappeared by the time they were placed into conservatorship. As of 2015, the GSEs are operating with low levels of nominal capital, and under the terms of the GSEs' agreements with Treasury (discussed below), that nominal capital will gradually drop to zero. Of course, they would be operating with *negative* equity, excluding Treasury support. With the taxpayers' liquidity

preferences of $189.5 billion, the GSEs are actually operating with *negative* $189.5 billion in capital from the perspective of any shareholder recovery in resolution.

4. ***Accounting Scandals.*** The GSEs' actual capital levels were likely much lower than they reported before the Financial Crisis, given their accounting irregularities, which, among other things, dramatically understated the risks that they faced. *Id.* at 314. Their capital reporting problems were part of a broader series of accounting scandals at the GSEs in the years leading up to the Financial Crisis, which resulted in earnings restatements and fines, as well as SEC fraud allegations and other recriminations for their executive leadership. *See, e.g.*, BETHANY MCLEAN, SHAKY GROUND: THE STRANGE SAGA OF THE U.S. MORTGAGE GIANTS (2015).

5. ***Executive Compensation.*** Executives of the GSEs were compensated at high levels before their collapse. For example, the FCIC notes that Fannie Mae CEO Daniel Mudd was paid $65 million from 2000 to 2008. FCIC, FINANCIAL CRISIS INQUIRY REPORT 322 (2011). Critics argue that the compensation was demonstrably unrelated to performance, given both the accounting scandals and the ultimate collapse of the GSEs.

6. ***Political Coziness.*** The GSEs were repeatedly able to stymie efforts to regulate them more seriously. As former HUD Secretary Henry Cisneros explained to the FCIC, the GSEs' regulator "was puny compared to what Fannie Mae and Freddie Mac could muster in their intelligence, their Ivy League educations, their rocket scientists in their place, their lobbyists, their ability to work the Hill." *Id.*

C. AFFORDABLE HOUSING GOALS

Recall that, in 1992, Congress explicitly directed the GSEs to focus on increasing access to mortgage credit for LMI homebuyers. Critics charged that the GSEs' affordable housing goals incentivized risky lending and enabled non-creditworthy borrowers to acquire mortgages. In the aftermath of the Financial Crisis, some scholars point to the affordable housing goals as a primary cause of the housing crash, while other scholars contend that the goals had little or nothing to do with the Financial Crisis. Others argue somewhere in between, that underwriting standards declined for many borrowers, including middle income borrowers, for both GSE and non-GSE loans. Consider Wallison's critique of the affordable housing goals in his dissent to the FCIC report.

FCIC, The Financial Crisis Inquiry Report, Dissenting Views of Peter J. Wallison

452–57 (2011)

In 1992, Congress enacted [the GSE Act], legislation intended to give [LMI] borrowers better access to mortgage credit through Fannie Mae and Freddie Mac. This effort, probably stimulated by a desire to increase home ownership, . . . and its subsequent enforcement by HUD, set in motion a series of changes in the structure of the mortgage market in the U.S. and more particularly the gradual degrading of traditional mortgage underwriting standards. . . .

The GSE Act . . . created a new "mission" for Fannie Mae and Freddie Mac—a responsibility to support affordable housing—and authorized HUD to establish and administer what was in effect a mortgage quota system in which a certain percentage of all Fannie [Mae] and Freddie [Mac] mortgage purchases had to be loans to [LMI] borrowers—defined as persons with income at or below the median income in a particular area or to borrowers living in certain low income communities. . . .

Over the next 15 years, HUD consistently enhanced and enlarged the [affordable housing] goals. . . . By 2008, the main LMI goal was 56 percent, and a special affordable subgoal had been added requiring that 27 percent of the loans acquired by the GSEs be made to borrowers who were at or below 80 percent of area median income. . . . Fannie [Mae] and Freddie [Mac] met the goals in almost every year between 1996 and 2008. . . .

[O]n June 30, 2008, immediately prior to the onset of the [F]inancial [C]risis, the GSEs held or had guaranteed 12 million subprime and Alt-A loans. . . . Fannie [Mae] and Freddie [Mac], accordingly, were by far the dominant players in the U.S. mortgage market before the [F]inancial [C]risis and their underwriting standards largely set the standards for the rest of the mortgage financing industry. . . . To be sure, the government's efforts to increase home ownership through the [affordable housing] goals succeeded. Home ownership rates in the U.S. increased from approximately 64 percent in 1994 (where it had been for 30 years) to over 69 percent in 2004. Almost everyone in and out of government was pleased with this—a long term goal of U.S. housing policy—until the true costs became clear with the collapse of the housing bubble in 2007.

Other scholars counter that the GSEs' affordable housing goals did not cause the Financial Crisis. Scholars point to studies that found that upper- and middle-income borrowers, *not* low-income borrowers, contributed most significantly to the increase in mortgage defaults. *See* Manuel Adelino et al., *Loan Originations and Defaults in the Mortgage Crisis: The Role of the Middle Class* (Tuck Sch. of Bus., Working Paper No. 2546427, 2015). Another study found no evidence that lenders increased subprime originations or altered loan pricing around discrete eligibility cutoffs for the GSEs' affordable housing goals. That study also found that the GSEs' purchases of subprime securities were not directly related to their affordable housing mandates. *See* Ruben Hernandez-Murillo et al., *Did Affordable Housing Legislation Contribute to the Subprime Securities Boom?* (Fed. Res. Bank of St. Louis, Working Paper No. 2012-005D, 2014). Goodman reached a similar conclusion. A REALISTIC ASSESSMENT OF HOUSING FINANCE REFORM 3 (2015) ("Their expansion into these products was aimed at correcting a declining market share, not (as some have claimed) meeting affordable housing goals."); *see also* Michael S. Barr & Gene B. Sperling, *Poor Homeowners, Good Loans*, N.Y. TIMES, Oct. 17, 2008; Adam J. Levitan & Susan Wachter, *Explaining the Housing Bubble,* 100 GEO. L.J. 1177 (2012) (explaining the supply-side factors for the bubble).

In the following excerpt, Professor David Min contends that Wallison's analysis of the GSEs' affordable housing goals is flawed.

David Min, Faulty Conclusions Based on Shoddy Foundations

Ctr. for Am. Progress, 1–3 (2011)

FCIC minority member Peter Wallison . . . concludes federal affordable housing policies were the driving cause behind the [F]inancial [C]risis, causing a decline in underwriting standards that triggered the U.S. housing bubble.

Wallison's conclusion that affordable housing policies were the proximate cause of the [F]inancial [C]risis is integrally based on the claim that "[a]s a result of [U.S. government housing] policies, by the middle of 2007, there were approximately 27 million subprime and Alt-A mortgages in the U.S. financial system—half of all mortgages outstanding—with an aggregate value of over $4.5 trillion.". . .

As Wallison clearly indicates in his FCIC dissent, all of the data on the number of outstanding subprime and Alt-A mortgages outstanding, and their distribution, that he relies on to form his conclusions come from [Edward] Pinto's research. . . .

Unfortunately, Pinto's research findings relied upon so heavily by Wallison and others are false . . . [and are] based on radically revised definitions for the two main categories of high-risk mortgages, subprime loans and so-called Alt-A mortgages, which refer to loans with low documentation of income and wealth. Importantly, these revised definitions are not consistent with how the terms subprime and Alt-A are used for data collection. . . .

As a result of his dramatically expanded new definitions that are not used by other leading scholars, Pinto's findings on the extent of subprime and Alt-A exposure are extreme outliers among mortgage market analysts. Pinto's claim that there were 26.7 million subprime and Alt-A loans outstanding (out of roughly 55 million total) as of June 30, 2008, is exponentially higher than other estimates. In a 2010 report, the nonpartisan Government Accountability Office, the research arm of Congress, found there were only 4.58 million subprime and Alt-A mortgages outstanding at the end of 2009, less than one-fifth of Pinto's estimate. . . .

Pinto also wrongly blames the affordable housing goals of Fannie [Mae] and Freddie [Mac] for the origination of Alt-A loans, which under his analysis account for 65% of the "high risk" mortgages attributable to Fannie [Mae] and Freddie [Mac]. In fact, these Alt-A loans (either according to the normal usage of "Alt-A" or Pinto's newly invented definition of "Alt-A") would not have qualified for the affordable housing goals. . . .

[T]hese and many other similar methodological flaws are fundamentally embedded in Pinto's research, making his conclusions fundamentally unreliable and essentially useless for the purpose of understanding either the causes of the housing bubble or the high rates of delinquencies that have occurred during the housing downturn. Yet based in large part on the inaccurate and misleading data peddled by Pinto, many policymakers are advocating inapt and often counterproductive solutions to the [F]inancial [C]risis.

This material was created by the Center for American Progress.

---

1. ***Did Affordable Housing Goals Cause the Financial Crisis?*** After reading Min's critique, what do you think of Wallison's contention that the GSEs' affordable housing goals contributed to the Financial Crisis? If the GSEs did not have affordable housing goals, would the private label market have nonetheless met investor demand for subprime and Alt-A mortgage-backed securities? Wallison rejoins the debate in his book, HIDDEN IN PLAIN SIGHT (2015).

2. **Affordable Housing Goals and the Investment Portfolios.** While the FCIC found that profit motives rather than the affordable housing goals were the primary factors in the GSEs' purchases of private-label subprime MBSs, the

GSEs did begin in the lead-up to the Financial Crisis to count subprime MBSs held in portfolio towards some of their affordable housing goals. *See* FCIC FINANCIAL CRISIS INQUIRY REPORT 123-125, 183-187 (2011). After the Financial Crisis, the FHFA shut down this practice in a final rule issued in 2010. Consider the following excerpt.

> *Private Label Securities.* [T]he final rule excludes [private label securities] from counting for purposes of the housing goals. . . . [The GSEs] relied on PLS purchases to help them achieve certain affordable housing goals. Freddie Mac met the 2005 and 2006 affordable housing goals and subgoals in part through its purchases of AAA-rated tranches of [private label securities] backed by subprime mortgages that were targeted to satisfy goals and subgoals. As house price appreciation and rising interest rates reduced housing affordability, [private label securities] proliferated as the subprime share of the market grew to more than 20 percent. Fannie Mae and Freddie Mac began to follow suit in response to declining market share and in pursuit of higher profits. The [GSEs] not only modified their own underwriting standards, but also bought hundreds of billions of dollars' worth of AAA-rated tranches of subprime and Alt-A [private label securities] for the yield and, in certain instances, to satisfy specific housing goals and subgoals.
>
> The results of providing large-scale funding for such loans were adverse for borrowers who entered into mortgages that did not sustain homeownership and for the [GSEs] themselves. Although Fannie Mae and Freddie Mac have a combined 57 percent share of mortgages outstanding in their guaranteed portfolio, the mortgages in that portfolio account for only 25 percent of serious delinquencies. However, while [private label securities] account for 12 percent of all mortgages outstanding, [private label securities] account for 34 percent of serious delinquencies. As delinquencies in [private label securities] portfolios triggered downgrades, 90 percent of the [private label securities] holdings of the [GSEs] experienced a downgrade....
>
> In addition to the recent dismal performance of [private label securities], it is reasonable to separate any future growth of the [private label securities] market from the [GSEs'] housing goals. The housing goals reflect Congress' concern that the [GSEs'] charter mission to support the stability, liquidity and affordability of the secondary market not be managed to the detriment or neglect of goal-eligible mortgages. In this way the goals may be seen as a mechanism to ensure that each [GSE] serves all segments of the mortgage market available to it. Accordingly, even to the extent that a non-GSE secondary mortgage market returns, loans backing new or seasoned [private label securities] will not count in either the numerator or the denominator for purposes of the housing goals.

FHFA, 2010–2011 Enterprise Housing Goals; Enterprise Book-entry Procedures; Final Rule, 75 Fed. Reg. 55,892, 55,924–25 (Sept. 14, 2010).

3. ***Other Approaches to Affordable Housing.*** What other approaches could the government have taken to promote affordable housing besides the GSEs' affordable housing goals? Would alternative approaches, such as down payment assistance, or explicit subsidies, have been more effective in providing credit to LMI homebuyers? Would they have been less risky for U.S. taxpayers?

IV. THE GSES IN CRISIS: THE HOUSING AND ECONOMIC RECOVERY ACT AND GOVERNMENT CONSERVATORSHIP

As housing prices began to flatten and then to collapse on the eve of the Financial Crisis, and mortgage defaults and foreclosures began to rise at alarming rates, the GSEs reported troubling financial results. Commentators started to speculate that the GSEs would not be able to survive a prolonged spike in mortgage defaults. Ultimately, as the GSEs' financial position continued to deteriorate, the GSEs were unable to raise the private capital necessary to remain solvent, and investors, creditors, and counterparties began to lose confidence in the GSEs. Congress eventually stepped in during the summer of 2008 to enact the Housing and Economic Recovery Act (HERA), based in large part on legislation that had been pending, but languishing, for many years, and bolstered by proposals put forward by the Paulson Treasury Department. HERA authorized regulators to place the GSEs into conservatorship and created a new regulator, the FHFA, giving it stronger, bank-like supervisory and capital authorities, but it was far too late. In the following excerpt, the FCIC recounts how the government took over the GSEs that fall.

FCIC, Financial Crisis Inquiry Report

309–20 (2011)

September 2008: The Takeover of Fannie Mae and Freddie Mac

From the fall of 2007 until Fannie Mae and Freddie Mac were placed into conservatorship on September 7, 2008, government officials struggled to strike the right balance between the safety and soundness of the two [GSEs] and their mission to support the mortgage market. The task was critical because the mortgage market was quickly weakening—home prices were declining, loan delinquencies were rising, and, as a result, the values of mortgage securities were plummeting. Lenders were more willing to refinance borrowers into affordable mortgages if these [GSEs] would purchase the new loans. If the GSEs bought more loans, that would stabilize the market, but it would also leave the GSEs with more risk on their already-strained balance sheets.

The GSEs were highly leveraged—owning and guaranteeing $5.3 trillion of mortgages with capital of less than 2%. . . . Still, the GSEs kept buying more of the riskier mortgage loans and securities, which by fall 2007 constituted multiples of their reported capital. The GSEs reported billions of dollars of net losses on these loans and securities, beginning in the third quarter of 2007.

But many in Treasury believed the country needed the GSEs to provide liquidity to the mortgage market by purchasing and guaranteeing loans and securities at a time when no one else would. [Treasury Secretary Henry] Paulson told the FCIC that after the housing market dried up in the summer of 2007, the key to getting through the [Financial Crisis] was to limit the decline in housing, prevent foreclosures, and ensure continued mortgage funding, all of which required that the GSEs remain viable. However, there were constraints on how many loans the GSEs could fund; they and their regulators had agreed to portfolio caps—limits on the loans and securities they could hold on their books—and a 30% capital surplus requirement.

So, even as each company reported billions of dollars in losses in 2007 and 2008, their regulator, [OFHEO], loosened those constraints. . . . In mid-September [2007], OFHEO . . . marginally loosened the GSEs' portfolio cap, from about $728 billion to $735 billion[, and OFHEO fully lifted the cap several months later]. . . . As the year progressed, Fannie [Mae] and Freddie [Mac] became increasingly important to the mortgage market. By the fourth quarter of 2007, they were purchasing 75% of new mortgages, nearly twice the 2006 level. With $5 trillion in mortgages resting on razor-thin capital, the GSEs were doomed if the market did not stabilize. . . .

In November [2007], Fannie [Mae] and Freddie [Mac] reported third-quarter losses of $1.5 billion and $2 billion, respectively. At the end of December 2007, Fannie [Mae] reported that it had $44 billion of capital to absorb potential losses on $879 billion of assets and $2.2 trillion of guarantees on [MBSs]; if losses exceeded 1.45%, it would be insolvent. Freddie [Mac] would be insolvent if losses exceeded 1.7%. Moreover, there were serious questions about the validity of their "reported" capital. . . . The government worried that it could not let the $5.3 trillion GSEs fail, because they were the only source of liquidity in the mortgage market and because their failure would cause losses to owners of their debt and their guaranteed mortgage securities. . . .

In July and August 2008, Fannie [Mae] suffered a liquidity squeeze, because it was unable to borrow against its own securities to raise sufficient cash in the repo market. . . . Fannie [Mae] asked the [Federal Reserve Board] for help. . . .

On July 13, the Federal Reserve Board in Washington authorized the [Federal Reserve Bank of New York] to extend emergency loans to the GSEs "should such lending prove necessary . . . to promote the availability of home mortgage credit during a period of stress in financial markets." Fannie [Mae] and Freddie [Mac] would never tap the [Federal Reserve] for that funding.

Also on July 13, Treasury laid out a three-part legislative plan to strengthen the GSEs by temporarily increasing their lines of credit with the Treasury, authorizing Treasury to inject capital into the GSEs, and replacing OFHEO with the new [FHFA], with the power to place the GSEs into receivership. . . .

At the end of July, Congress passed the Housing and Economic Recovery Act . . . of 2008, giving [the Treasury] the ability to extend secured lines of credit to the GSEs, to purchase their mortgage securities, and to inject capital. The 261-page bill also strengthened regulation of the GSEs by creating FHFA, an independent federal agency, as their primary regulator, with expanded authority over [Fannie Mae's] and [Freddie Mac's] portfolios, capital levels, and compensation. . . .

After the Federal Reserve Board consented in mid-July to furnish emergency loans, [Federal Reserve System] staff and representatives of the [OCC] . . . initiated a review of the GSEs. . . . The [Federal Reserve] and the OCC discovered that the problems were worse than their suspicions and reports from FHFA had led them to believe. . . .

Paulson told the FCIC that although he learned of the [Federal Reserve Board] and OCC findings by August 15, it took him three weeks to convince [OFHEO Director James] Lockhart and FHFA that there was a capital shortfall, that the GSEs were not viable, and that they should be placed under government control. . . .

On September 6, FHFA . . . sent separate memos to Lockhart recommending that FHFA be appointed conservator for each GSE. . . .

The boards of both companies voted to accept conservatorship. Both CEOs were ousted . . . .

As promised, the Treasury was prepared to take two direct steps to support solvency. First, it would buy up to $200 billion of senior preferred stock from the GSEs and extend them short-term secured loans. In addition, it pledged to buy GSE [MBSs] from Wall Street firms and others until the end of 2009. Up front, Treasury bought from each GSE $1 billion in preferred stock with a 10% dividend. Each GSE also gave Treasury warrants to purchase common stock representing 79.9% of shares outstanding. Existing common and preferred shareholders were effectively wiped out.

As noted above, the Treasury, the FHFA, and the GSEs entered into these stock agreements in September 2008; they were subsequently amended several times. In early 2009, with the housing crisis worsening significantly, the per-GSE cap was doubled to $200 billion, or $400 billion total. At the end of 2009, the cap was raised again, this time effectively floating up without limit along with any GSE losses that might be incurred until the end of 2012, when it was again capped by operation of the amendment at $445.5 billion. Citing concerns that the GSEs needed to borrow from the Treasury in order to pay Treasury dividends, the parties amended the agreements for a third time in 2012 to replace the fixed 10% dividend and an undetermined commitment fee that Treasury had repeatedly and temporarily waived, with a variable dividend equal to a sweep of the GSEs' profits over a specified capital reserve. Under the terms of the agreements, as amended over time, the Treasury has provided $187.5 billion in funding to the GSEs as of the end of 2015, and the Treasury still maintains an ongoing commitment to fund any losses up to the $445.5 billion cap. As of the end of 2015, the GSEs have paid dividends totaling approximately $230 billion. Under the terms of the agreements, taxpayers still have a liquidation preference of $189.5 billion, an amount that must be paid back to taxpayers before other shareholders can receive any value. Investors in the GSEs sued the government over the 2012 third amendment to the stock agreements, which provides for the profit sweep, arguing that the amendment was a taking and was not lawfully authorized under the Housing and Economic Recovery Act. *See, e.g.*, Perry Capital v. Lew, 70 F.Supp.3d 208 (D.D.C. 2014) (dismissing claims). Now on appeal, this and related litigation is likely to continue for some time.

---

1. ***Taxpayer Bailout.*** Do you think the government was justified in bailing out the GSEs? What real choices did it have?

2. ***Takings Lawsuit.*** Do you think the government was justified in amending the stock agreements to provide for a sweep of the GSEs' profits? What ongoing risks do taxpayers face?

The Congressional Budget Office described the status of the GSEs while in conservatorship, and some of the steps FHFA has taken to reform the GSEs using its administrative powers, in the following excerpt.

Cong. Budget Office, Transitioning to Alternative Structures for Housing Finance

9–10 (2014)

In 2012, the Treasury and the two GSEs revised their agreements: Rather than pay a fixed dividend on the Treasury's preferred shares, Fannie Mae and Freddie Mac began in 2013 to return almost all of their profits to the Treasury. However, those payments do not reduce the amount of preferred stock held by the Treasury, and the GSEs are prohibited from buying back that stock under their agreements with the Treasury and FHFA. Thus, the terms of the agreements and the conservatorship ensure that the federal government effectively retains complete ownership and control of Fannie Mae and Freddie Mac.

FHFA . . . acts as conservator. It oversees the GSEs' operations and sets goals for their performance. In doing so, FHFA pursues several aims: minimizing losses on behalf of taxpayers, supporting a stable and liquid mortgage market, maximizing assistance to homeowners, and minimizing foreclosures. To help struggling borrowers, FHFA has implemented loan modification programs (which generally reduce the interest rates on mortgages rather than the principal) and has streamlined refinancing programs. In addition, the agency has directed the GSEs to limit their portfolio holdings and to experiment with bulk sales of real estate acquired through foreclosures. It has also replaced senior managers at Fannie Mae and Freddie Mac and limited executive compensation.

The two GSEs' share of the housing finance market has expanded since conservatorship began. As of June 30, 2014, Fannie Mae and Freddie Mac owned or guaranteed roughly half of the nearly $10 trillion in outstanding single-family residential mortgages in the United States; they backed about 60 percent of the estimated $1.9 trillion in new mortgages in 2013 and about 50 percent of the mortgages originated in the first half of 2014, whereas in 2006 they backed less than 30 percent of new mortgages. . . In response to past losses, the GSEs have tightened their credit standards.

In the face of the two GSEs' expanding market share, FHFA and lawmakers have begun taking actions to encourage greater involvement by the private sector in the housing finance market. Those actions include reducing the size limit for the mortgages that the GSEs are allowed to purchase in high-cost areas (from $729,750 to $625,500) and raising the GSEs' guarantee fees (which are still lower than those that would be charged by private companies). . . As a result, in January 2014, the GSEs' average guarantee fee for new loans (including both up-front and ongoing fees) was about 55 basis points of a loan's principal, whereas before the [F]inancial [C]risis, it was about 20 basis points.

Under the conservatorship, FHFA has been proceeding with reforms of the GSEs. For example, FHFA has continued to require the GSEs to reduce their investment portfolios, which peaked at a combined total of $1.651 trillion before the Financial Crisis and have been reduced to $692 billion by the end of 2015. The stock agreements require the total to hit $500 billion by the end of 2018. FHFA has been pursuing strategies for the GSEs to reduce the share of credit risk that they take, and increase the role of other private-sector firms, through a variety of insurance, reinsurance, debt issuance, and securitization programs. These covered a total of $417 billion in mortgages in 2015. FHFA has also been pursuing the development of a common securitization platform that could be used by both the GSEs and other securitization sponsors, as well as a common GSE security. *See* FHFA, 2015 SCORECARD PROGRESS REPORT (2016).

V. THE FUTURE OF THE GSEs: PROPOSALS FOR REFORM

The GSEs' roles have changed over many decades, in response to market forces, stakeholder battles, and legislative reforms, including most recently the HERA, enacted in 2008. Despite multiple attempts to reform the GSEs in the years since the Financial Crisis, as of the end of 2015, Congress has yet to determine their future roles. Instead, the enterprises continue to operate under conservatorship with circumscribed powers, while policy-makers debate the future of housing finance. In this section, we discuss some proposals for reforming the GSEs.

A. CONCEPTUAL FRAMEWORKS

Commentators from all sides of the political and intellectual spectrum have created proposals to reform the GSEs. Some commentators believe that the GSEs should operate as a federal agency or corporation, with the explicit backing of the government. Some commentators advocate fully privatizing the GSEs and, in some cases, breaking them up into smaller companies, or eliminating them altogether, with balance sheet lending and private-label securitization filling the gap. Others argue that the GSEs should be regulated as non-profit utilities or as mutuals or cooperatives. A wide variety of bipartisan reform proposals call for a role for an explicit federal government guarantee of MBSs to deal with catastrophic losses, but a stronger private sector role in first-loss mitigation. Still others call for "recap and release," a return to the old, pre-conservatorship GSE structure, but with better regulation and higher capital requirements.

Consider the following remarks by Professor Michael Barr, which he delivered shortly after leaving government service.

Michael S. Barr, A Framework for Housing Finance Reform

Remarks at the N.Y.U. Furman Ctr. (Feb. 4, 2011)

I want to talk today about a framework for housing finance reform. . . . As we consider the next phase of reform, we should keep in mind a set of objectives for a well-functioning, stable housing finance system. . . .

(1) *Widely available mortgage credit.* Mortgage credit should be available and distributed on an efficient basis to a wide range of borrowers, including those with [LMIs], to support the purchase of homes they can afford. . . .

(2) *Housing affordability.* A well-functioning housing market should provide affordable housing options, both ownership and rental, for [LMI] households. . . .

(3) *Consumer protection market-wide.* Consumers should have access to mortgage products that are easily understood, such as the 30-year fixed rate mortgage and conventional variable rate mortgages with straightforward terms and pricing. Effective consumer financial protection should keep unfair, abusive or deceptive practices out of the marketplace and help to ensure that consumers have the information they need about the costs, terms, and conditions of their mortgages. . . .

(4) *Financial stability.* The housing finance system should distribute the credit and interest rate risk that results from mortgage lending in an efficient and transparent manner that minimizes risk to the broader financial and economic system and does not generate excess volatility. . . .

At the same time, history suggests that the government will intervene in the event of a crisis in the housing market of sufficient magnitude. That is because real estate markets are prone to booms and busts; housing is a very large component of the financial sector; and housing assets are a large component of assets held by households. [*See* David Scharfstein & Adi Sunderam, *The Economics of Housing Finance Reform, in* THE FUTURE OF HOUSING FINANCE: RESTRUCTURING THE U.S. RESIDENTIAL MORTGAGE MARKETS (Martin Baily ed., 2011).] Any housing finance system must acknowledge that fact, and provide a realistic mechanism for responding, while protecting taxpayers. That argues in favor of up-front fees for guarantees.

(5) *Alignment of incentives.* A well functioning mortgage finance system should better align incentives for all actors—issuers, originators, brokers, ratings agencies, insurers, borrowers—so that mortgages are originated and held or securitized with the goal of long-term viability rather than short term gains. That means avoidance of privatized gains funded by public losses. . . .

(6) *Standardization.* Standardization of mortgage products improves transparency and efficiency and should provide a sound basis in a reformed system that increases liquidity, helps to keep rates competitive, and promotes financial stability. . . .

(7) *Diversified sources of funding and reduced concentration.* Through securitization and other forms of intermediation, a well functioning mortgage finance system should be able to draw efficiently upon a wide variety of sources of capital and investment both to lower costs and to diversify risk. . . .

(8) *Secondary market liquidity.* Today, the U.S. housing finance market is one of the most liquid markets in the world. . . This liquidity has provided benefits to both borrowers and lenders, including lower borrowing costs. . . .

(9) *Private capital.* [A]ny new housing finance system must draw in private capital, and credit insurers or other system participants must be clearly regulated.

(10) *Stable mortgage products for households.* [W]hile many borrowers appropriately can and should use standard adjustable rate mortgages with straightforward terms, households and the market are benefited by the existence of the 30-year fixed rate mortgage. A fixed rate mortgage does not require households to self-insure against interest rate risk, or against the risk of a change in their financial circumstances that would prevent refinancing. . . .

A central question is whether, beyond FHA-insured mortgages, there will be a role for a government guarantee.

Those who are opposed to such a guarantee focus on moral hazard, on the risk of government mis-pricing the guarantee and putting taxpayers at risk, on the dangers of over-subsidization of housing, and on the political economy of loan limits and the GSE credit box which may increase over time.

Those who favor a role for a government guarantee in the future suggest that the major problem in the past was with the inherent conflict between an implicit guarantee and shareholder ownership, and argue that a government guarantee is required to maintain the availability of the 30 year fixed rate mortgage for most homeowners. Moreover, in the event of a housing crisis, the presence of paid-for guarantees permits the government to be in place as a lender of last resort and to insure against catastrophic loss. Without a government guarantee, the housing finance system will also tend to be concentrated in the banking sector, and given economies of scale, in the top handful of financial institutions. . . .

Fixing our nation's housing finance system is critically important to our economy and to our country's future. . . . A new system must be designed to ensure that our housing finance system is more stable, affordable home ownership and rental options are available, consumers are protected, and sustainable credit is widely accessible.

The Government Accountability Office (GAO) summarized some of the competing ideas for GSE reform in the next excerpt.

GAO, Fannie Mae and Freddie Mac: Analysis of Options for Revising the Housing Enterprises' Long-Term Structures

GAO-09-782, 28–36 (2008)

[R]esearchers and others believe that there is a range of options available to better achieve housing mission objectives (in some cases through other federal entities such as FHA), help ensure safe and sound operations, and minimize risks to financial stability. These options generally fall along a continuum with some overlap among key features and advocate (1) establishing a government corporation or agency, (2) reconstituting the enterprises as for-profit GSEs in some form, or (3) privatizing or terminating them. . . . This section discusses some of the key principles associated with each option and provides details on how each could be designed to support housing objectives.

Government Corporation or Agency

Some proposals advocate that, after the FHFA conservatorships are terminated, consideration should be given to establishing a government corporation or agency to assume responsibility for key enterprise business activities. Supporters of these proposals maintain that the combination of the implied federal guarantee on the enterprises' financial obligations, and their need to respond to shareholder demands to maximize profitability, encouraged excessive risk-taking and ultimately resulted in their failures. Accordingly, they also believe that a government corporation or agency, which would not be concerned about maximizing shareholder value, would be the best way to ensure the availability of mortgage credit for primary lenders, while minimizing the risks associated with a for-profit structure with government sponsorship. Establishing a government corporation or agency also would help ensure transparency in the federal government's efforts through appropriate disclosures of risks and costs in the federal budget. . . . While this proposal advocates the establishment of a government corporation to replace Fannie Mae and Freddie Mac, it states that there are risks associated with doing so. For example, a government corporation might face challenges retaining capable staff or become overly bureaucratic and unreceptive to market developments. . . .

Reconstituted GSEs

While many of the enterprises' critics view the for-profit GSE structure as precipitating the enterprises' financial crises that led to conservatorship, market participants and commenters, trade groups representing the banking and home construction industries, as well as community and housing advocates we contacted, believe that the for-profit GSE structure generally remains superior to the alternatives. They assert that continuing the enterprises as for-profit GSEs would help ensure that they would remain responsive to market developments, continue to produce innovations in mortgage finance, and be less bureaucratic than a government agency or corporation. But, they also generally advocate additional regulations and ownership structures to help offset the financial risks inherent in the for-profit GSE structure. . . .

A variation of this option involves breaking up the enterprises into multiple GSEs. For example, the Congressional Research Service (CRS) has stated that the enterprises could be converted into 10 or so GSEs, which could mitigate safety and soundness risks. That is, rather than having the failure of two large GSEs threaten financial stability, the failure of a smaller GSE likely would have a more limited impact on the financial system.

CRS also has stated that creating multiple GSEs could enhance competition and benefit homebuyers. . . .

It has also been suggested that the enterprises be converted from publicly traded companies into cooperatives owned by lenders similar to the [FHLB] structure. For example, one commenter suggested that, by having lenders assume some of the risks associated with the enterprises' activities, mortgage underwriting standards could be enhanced. . . . However, . . . many smaller banks suffered substantial losses on the preferred stock they held in Fannie Mae and Freddie Mac before their conservatorships and would be very reluctant to make such investments in the future. . . .

Former Treasury Secretary Paulson . . . recommended that the corporations be subject to public utility-type regulation. Specifically, he recommended that a public utility-type commission be established with the authority to set appropriate targets for the enterprises' rate of return and review and approve underwriting decisions and new mortgage products. Paulson also recommended that the enterprises pay a fee to help offset the value of their federal support and thereby also provide incentives for depository institutions to fund mortgages, either as competitors to a newly established government structure or as a substitute for government funding.

Privatization or Termination

Some analysts and financial commenters contend that privatizing, significantly reducing, or eliminating the enterprises' presence in the mortgage markets represents the best public policy option. Advocates of this proposal believe . . . sources of mortgage credit and risk would not be concentrated in two large and complex organizations that might take excessive risks because of the implied federal guarantee on their financial obligations. Instead, mortgage credit and risk would be diversified throughout the financial system. Federal Reserve Chairman Ben S. Bernanke has suggested that privatized entities may be more innovative and efficient than government entities, and operate with less interference from political interests. . . .

Given the substantial financial assistance that Treasury and the Federal Reserve have provided to the enterprises during their conservatorships, it may be very difficult to credibly privatize them as largely intact entities. . . In exploring various options for restructuring the enterprises, Bernanke has noted that some privatization proposals involve breaking the enterprises into smaller units to eliminate the perception of federal guarantees.

Bernanke also has questioned whether fully privatized enterprises would be able to issue MBS during highly stressful economic conditions. He pointed out that, during the [Financial Crisis], private-sector mortgage lending largely stopped functioning. Bernanke cited a study by Federal Reserve economists that advocated the creation of an insurer, similar to the [FDIC], to support mortgage finance under the privatization proposal. . . .

While the Obama Administration did not include reform of the GSEs in its financial reform proposals in 2009, it attempted to advance GSE reform through a report issued two years later. In the report, the Administration did not endorse a particular approach, but described three options for congressional consideration. Option 1 involved a "[p]rivatized system of housing finance with the government insurance role limited to FHA, [Department of Agriculture,] and Department of Veterans' Affairs' assistance for narrowly targeted groups of borrowers." Option 2 called for a "[p]rivatized system of housing finance with assistance from FHA, [Department of Agriculture,] and Department of Veterans' Affairs for narrowly targeted groups of borrowers and a guarantee mechanism to scale up during times of crisis." Option 3 consisted of a "[p]rivatized system of housing finance with FHA, [Department of Agriculture,] and Department of Veterans' Affairs assistance for [LMI] borrowers and catastrophic reinsurance behind significant private capital." The Administration argued that "we are faced with difficult trade-offs. We must decide what we take to be the right balance between providing broad access to mortgages for American families, managing the risk to taxpayers, and maintaining a stable and healthy mortgage market." DEP'TS OF TREASURY AND HUD, REFORMING AMERICA'S HOUSING FINANCE MARKET: A REPORT TO CONGRESS (2011). What constraints was the Administration facing in 2009 that would lead it not to propose GSE reform as part of the Dodd-Frank Act? Why did the Administration find it so difficult to articulate a single approach for reform in its 2011 report?

B. LEGISLATIVE PROPOSALS

Lawmakers from both political parties have introduced proposals to reform U.S. housing finance. For instance, in 2013, the Republican-led House Financial Services Committee passed the Protecting American Taxpayers and Homeowners Act, which called for the GSEs to be liquidated. In addition, the Act would create a non-profit utility that would promote private market competition through the development of MBS disclosure guidelines and by transferring the GSEs' proprietary securitization platforms to an open access domain with access for private securities market participants. There would be no government guarantees of MBSs. By contrast, the Ranking Minority Member of the House Financial Services Committee, Democratic Representative Maxine Waters, introduced the Housing Opportunities Move the Economy Forward Act. The Waters proposal would unwind the GSEs and replace them with a new lender cooperative that would issue government-backed securities. Neither the Protecting American Taxpayers and Homeowners Act nor the Housing Opportunities Move the Economy Forward Act was approved by the full House of Representatives.

A group of senators undertook a serious effort to draft bipartisan legislation to reform the housing finance system. Senators Bob Corker and Mark Warner laid the groundwork with a draft bill, and then in 2014, then-Senate Banking Committee Chairman Tim Johnson and Ranking Member Mike Crapo introduced legislation, called the Johnson-Crapo Bill, to replace the GSEs with a new government guarantor and regulator, the Federal Mortgage Insurance Corporation, modeled after the FDIC. The Federal Mortgage Insurance Corporation would provide an explicit government backstop for eligible MBSs. The private sector would have to hold at least a 10% first loss position on the MBS. The Federal Mortgage Insurance Corporation would regulate issuers, servicers, insurers, and guarantors of eligible MBSs. Affordable housing would be fostered by imposing a charge on guaranteed MBSs, and the charge would vary depending on the institution's record of serving community needs. Smaller lenders would be able to participate in the system through a mutual entity. The Federal Mortgage Insurance Corporation would set underwriting standards for eligible loans. The Johnson-Crapo proposal builds on a variety of plans put forward by scholars at the Bipartisan Policy Center, the Urban Institute, and the Center for American Progress, among others. The proposal died in 2014, weighed down by concerns about the feasibility of the complex proposal, transition costs to the new system, and, most fundamentally, disagreements between those who were most focused on broad access to mortgage credit and those who were most concerned about market-based pricing and taxpayer exposure. As of the end of 2015, the Senate Banking Committee, chaired by Senator Richard Shelby, has not put forward a new proposal.

---

1. ***Options for Reform.*** What do you think the United States should do to reform its housing finance system? Should it have a fully private system without any explicit or implicit guarantee? How should the U.S. mortgage market function if the GSEs were terminated? Should we return to a bank-balance-sheet system or try to encourage a return to private-label securitization? If the GSEs are preserved and exit conservatorship, how could policy-makers limit the perception that the GSEs are implicitly guaranteed by the government? Should the government's guarantee instead be made explicit and the GSEs converted into a government agency or corporation? Or should the implicit government guarantee somehow be eliminated? How? Would that be credible?

2. ***Why is reforming the GSEs so hard?*** What competing public policy concerns are there? What competing stakeholders interests are in play?

3. ***What reform model would you choose?*** How would you balance the policy and political tradeoffs and build a coalition to support your reform?

VI. COMPARATIVE APPROACHES TO HOUSING FINANCE

Mervyn King, the former governor of the Bank of England, reportedly quipped, "Most countries have socialized health care and a free market for mortgages. You in the United States do exactly the opposite." BETHANY MCLEAN, SHAKY GROUND: THE STRANGE SAGA OF THE U.S. MORTGAGE GIANTS 9 (2015). While King may not be quite right about the facts, his observation captures a truth about the importance of firmly embedded social policy choices. The pervasive problems in U.S. housing finance have led some to look abroad for reform ideas. The following excerpt from Professor Min suggests caution in comparative analysis, but also provides evidence regarding underlying commonalities across systems.

Statement of David K. Min, Assistant Professor of Law, U.C. Irvine School of Law, Beyond GSEs: Examples of Successful Housing Finance Models Without Explicit Government Guarantees

Written Testimony Before the H. Comm. on Fin. Services, 113th Cong. (2013)

I want to emphasize a point that may seem obvious, but is not always well understood. And that is that it is extraordinarily difficult to try to compare different models of housing finance, as these are intrinsically and intricately intertwined with the cultural, political, and economic systems with which they co-exist. . . .

With that important caveat in mind, there are seven points I would like to make today:

1. *Government Guarantees Are Universal:* There are three types of funding instruments that collectively account for almost all of the residential mortgage financing in the developed world: bank deposits, [MBS], and covered bonds.

Generally speaking, with only limited exceptions, investors in these instruments enjoy the benefits of either explicit or implicit government guarantees. . . .

2. *European Covered Bonds Are Best Thought of as Government-Sponsored Obligations:* . . . Contrary to the claims of some, European covered bonds are not purely private financial instruments, but rather enjoy a myriad of government guarantees, as well as preferential regulatory and capital treatments that mirror or surpass the benefits provided to Agency obligations in the United States.
3. *Government Guarantees Are Prevalent Because They Address Key Market Failures in Housing Finance:* Government guarantees are so ubiquitous because they address certain market failures that are inherent in financial intermediation—the use of short-term, illiquid liabilities to fund long-term, illiquid loans. . . .
4. *There is No Perfect Housing Finance Model:* . . . While the weaknesses of securitization and deposits as funding vehicles are well recognized in the United States, it is important to recognize that covered bonds come with their own problems. The issuance of covered bonds typically increases the risk to other creditors, including the governmental deposit insurer, and can thus create a moral hazard problem. . . .
5. *The Common Thread in Global Housing Bubbles Was Financial Deregulation:* The United States, Spain, and the United Kingdom were perhaps the countries hardest-hit by housing market issues. All three of these countries underwent significant banking sector liberalization in the decades preceding their housing bubbles. At the same time, Canada, which did not have significant financial deregulation but does have an outsized government role in housing finance, did not experience such housing problems. This suggests that financial deregulation is a primary factor in explaining international problems with housing finance.
6. *Explicit, Ex Ante Guarantees Are Preferable to Implicit, Ex Post Guarantees:* The choice facing policy makers is not whether to adopt a housing finance with explicit guarantees or no guarantees, as the title of this hearing might suggest. Rather, the choice is between explicit, well-defined, *ex ante* guarantees with buffers against taxpayer loss, or implicit, undefined, *ex post* guarantees that have no protections for taxpayers. . . .
7. *Given U.S. Political Priorities, Improving the Status Quo May be Preferable to Importing Other Models:* Housing finance reform efforts should consider the specific characteristics of our polity. . . . [R]ather than trying to adopt radical wholesale changes or import European models of housing finance into our country, we should consider fixing the problems with our current model . . . .

The Global Ubiquity of Government Guarantees in Housing Finance

Critics of the federal government's role in housing finance argue that the United States is unique among developed countries in providing significant levels of government backing for home mortgage financing. . . .

The problem with this analysis is that it focuses myopically on how the United States provides government guarantees for mortgage finance, and ignores how other countries might do so. . . .

Therefore, in comparing the relative level of international governmental support in housing finance, the right question to ask is this: do other countries provide government guarantees on bank deposits and covered bonds?

The answer to this question is unequivocally yes. Bank deposits of course enjoy explicit government guarantees across the world, as 29 of the 30 [Organization for Economic Cooperation and Development (OECD)] countries have governmental deposit insurance programs in place. . . .

When government guarantees on instruments other than MBS are taken into account, it appears fairly clear that the United States is not particularly exceptional in the level of government support it provides to housing finance.

Understanding "Government-Sponsored" Covered Bonds

In the European countries where they account for a significant amount of housing finance, covered bonds benefit from a number of guarantees that are well recognized among investors. . . . [T]hese features of covered bonds are shared with [FHLB] advances. First, and arguably most importantly, covered bonds benefit from the implicit government guarantees that exist for the issuing banks. . . .

Second, covered bonds . . . enjoy a [too big to fail] guarantee, which explains why the European Central Bank felt compelled to announce a major covered bond bailout program in the midst of the [Financial Crisis]. . . .

Third, because covered bonds generally enjoy a first lien on the best assets of the issuer, and continue to replace weak cover pool assets with good assets on a dynamic basis, they effectively benefit from the explicit guarantees behind bank deposits, which help finance the purchases of good bank assets that are then used to collateralize covered bonds. . . .

All three of these types of government guarantees . . . are important factors in the credit quality and liquidity enjoyed by covered bonds in those countries where they have achieved scale . . . It is fair to say that European covered bonds enjoy the same or even greater implicit guarantees as Agency obligations here. . . . [I]t may be most appropriate to describe these instruments as "government-sponsored" covered bonds. . . .

Comparing the Major Housing Finance Models

These problems with covered bonds might be justified, if these instruments brought significantly more systemic stability. But the fact is that covered bond regimes failed just as miserably as bank deposit regimes and MBS did in the [Financial Crisis]. . . .

As the FCIC minority stated in their dissent:

> There were housing bubbles in the United Kingdom, Spain, Australia, France and Ireland, some more pronounced than in the United States. Some nations with housing bubbles relied little on American-style mortgage securitization. A good explanation of the U.S. housing bubble should also take into account its parallels in other nations. This leads us to explanations broader than just U.S. housing policy, regulation, or supervision. It also tells us that while failures in U.S. securitization markets may be an essential cause, we must look for other things that went wrong as well.

---

1. ***Homeownership Around the World.*** According to the Pew Research Center, U.S. homeownership rates (65% in 2013, 69% at their peak before the Financial Crisis) are towards the lower end of the OECD, roughly in line with a diverse mix of countries with quite different housing finance systems from each other and from the United States, including Canada (69%), the UK (68%), Ireland (70%), and Israel (69%). What factors might be at play besides housing finance? What role should housing finance play? *See* Dan Andrews & Aida Caldera Sánchez, "The Evolution of Homeownership Rates in Selected OECD Countries: Demographic and Public Policy Influences," OECD J. Econ. Studies (2011), at 207.

2. ***What's Next?*** The status of the GSEs is one of the major elements of unfinished business since the Financial Crisis. Given your understanding of the experiences in the U.S. and other countries, what do you think U.S. policy-makers should do?

CHAPTER 12.3

MONEY MARKET FUNDS

CONTENTS

I. INTRODUCTION

We discussed mutual funds generally in Part X, and in this Chapter we delve into a specialized form of mutual funds, money market mutual funds (MMFs), that are regulated by the SEC under the Investment Company Act of 1940 (1940 Act) and form an integral part of the shadow banking system. First, we discuss the emergence of MMFs in the 1970s as an alternative to bank deposits, designed to offer similarly low risk while providing substantially higher returns. Next, we discuss the evolution of MMFs into a nearly $3.8 trillion sector by 2008 and their role in the contagious panic of the Financial Crisis. Lastly, we describe the post-crisis reforms of MMFs, concluding with current developments in the market.

II. THE EMERGENCE OF MONEY MARKET MUTUAL FUNDS

A. HISTORICAL CONTEXT

MMFs are a type of mutual fund that emerged as a response to interest rate ceilings imposed on deposits by the Federal Reserve through Regulation Q. Until 1986, Regulation Q imposed a maximum interest rate on bank deposits, with the goals of increasing bank profits by limiting interest rate competition and assisting small banks in retaining market share in local loans. *See* R. Alton Gilbert, *Requiem for Regulation Q: What It Did and Why It Passed Away,* 68 FED. RESERVE BANK OF ST. LOUIS REV. 22 (1986). While Regulation Q's interest rate ceilings had existed since the Banking Act of 1933, the extraordinarily high rates of inflation and interest rates in the 1970s created demand for a new financial instrument that would allow consumers to capture the difference between the interest rate ceilings mandated by Regulation Q and the much higher interest rates available in the wholesale money market. *See* Timothy Q. Cook and Jeremy G. Duffield, *Money Market Mutual Funds: A Reaction to Government Regulations or a Lasting Financial Innovation?,* FED. RESERVE BANK OF RICHMOND, ECON. REV. 15 (July/August 1979). The term money market describes the market in short-term debt instruments, which includes instruments such as commercial paper, Treasuries, repurchase agreements, federal funds, and certificates of deposit. MMFs are mutual funds that are invested in money market instruments. With MMFs, investors purchase shares of the funds and the fund adviser manages their investments through the purchase and sale of money market instruments. As is generally true with mutual funds, each shareholder's return is determined by the rise and fall of the value of the securities held by the fund, as well as interest and dividend payments made on those securities. By investing directly in money market instruments through MMFs, investors could circumvent Regulation Q and obtain higher returns than those offered by bank deposits.

The revolution brought about by MMFs in the 1970s and 1980s arose through a series of accounting innovations and new SEC regulations that created special rules about the ways that shares in these funds could be valued. As we explored in Chapter 10.2, securities in mutual funds are typically valued based on market prices, and these prices are reflected in a net asset value (NAV) per share at the end of each business day. For securities for which there are no active secondary market rates, the boards of registered investment companies may value their holdings "at fair value as determined in good faith." 17 C.F.R. § 270.2a-4 (2015). Because there were no large secondary markets for the money market instruments purchased by MMFs, the boards of MMFs began to use amortized cost accounting as the fair value of their investments. Amortized cost accounting allowed money market instruments to be valued at their acquisition cost while allowing any income (receipt of interest payments) to accrue smoothly over time, or, if the instrument was purchases at a discount, allow a constant increase in value until maturity. *See* Cook and Duffield, *Lasting Financial Innovation?*, at 20.

Amortized cost accounting was a beneficial valuation method for MMFs because it reduced the volatility in pricing of the fund's shares:

> The greater stability, both in principal and in daily yield, that [amortized cost accounting] leads to, relative to the mark-to-market method, is very appealing to certain institutional investors, especially bank trust departments, who have difficulty justifying to their clients yields that vary widely from day to day.

Cook and Duffield, Lasting Financial Innovation?, at 20.

MMFs' use of amortized cost accounting during the 1970s soon caught the attention of regulators. Amortized cost accounting was and is both a cause of MMFs' popularity among investors and a potential source of risk. With this valuation method, redeeming shareholders settle at the amortized cost, rather than at the true market value of their shares. The remaining shareholders then absorb the losses. Amortized cost accounting thus creates a first-mover advantage and can lead to runs on these instruments. When the underlying securities' values drop, shareholders have an incentive to be the first to redeem their shares, essentially transferring wealth from the remaining shareholders to the liquidating shareholders. In 1977, the SEC issued an interpretative guidance that deemed amortized cost valuation inappropriate for securities with maturities over 60 days, but allowed this accounting method for securities with maturities of 60 days or less. *See* Valuation of Debt Instruments by Money Market Funds and Certain Other Open-End Investment Companies, Investment Company Act, Release No. IC-9786, 42 Fed. Reg. 28,999 (June 7, 1977). For instruments with maturities greater than 60 days, the SEC cited concerns that such a valuation method may lead to overvaluation or undervaluation of the fund's assets, and therefore dilution of the value of remaining shares when a fund sells or buys inaccurately valued shares. *Id.*

In the face of continued litigation over the use of amortized cost, the SEC began to offer individual exemptive orders to certain firms to use amortized accounting, and in 1978 allowed MMFs to use penny-rounding, in which funds price their shares to the nearest one penny on a $1.00 share, which was less restrictive than the one-tenth of penny accuracy otherwise required. *See* Cook and Duffield, *Lasting Financial Innovation?*, at 21. Penny-rounding was still inadequate for some bank trust departments, and MMFs continued to litigate for the complete right to use amortized cost accounting. *See id.*

B. THE INTRODUCTION OF RULE 2A-7

In 1983, the SEC adopted Rule 2a-7 to permit MMFs to use amortized cost valuation or penny-rounding to maintain a stable NAV per share. Valuation of Debt Instruments and Computation of Current Price Per Share by Certain Open-End Investment Companies (Money Market Funds), Investment Company Act Release No. 13,380, 48 Fed. Reg. 32,555 (July 11, 1983) (adopting Rule 2a-7) [hereinafter Release 13380]. MMF shares could thus be bought and sold at a stable $1.00 share price. The stable share price had an important tax and administrative convenience for institutional investors, as the purchase or sale of such shares did not count as a capital gain or loss under Internal Revenue Service rules. *See* Jill Fisch, *The Broken Buck Stops Here: Embracing Sponsor Support in Money Market Fund Reform,* 93 N.C. L. REV. 935, 943 (2015). The stable share pricing gave MMF shares the constant pricing of a bank deposit, but with the higher returns of money markets. The stable NAV of MMFs became their distinguishing feature and the subject of intense scrutiny and reform after the Financial Crisis.

In exchange for the ability to maintain a stable share price, Rule 2a-7 imposed strict risk-limiting rules on MMFs, including liquidity, maturity, credit quality, portfolio composition, and other requirements. By limiting permissible investments to short-term, high quality debt instruments with low volatility, Rule 2a-7 sought to ensure that those funds using penny-rounding or the amortized cost valuation would be able to maintain a stable price per share. The rule also imposed obligations on the boards of directors of such funds to monitor and respond to deviations of more than one-half of a cent between the amortized cost valuation and the underlying market price of a share. A fund unable to maintain a market-based share price of $1.00 plus or minus one-half of a cent would no longer be able to use amortized cost valuation or penny-rounding under Rule 2a-7. *See* Release 13,380.

C. EARLY REACTIONS

As the MMF sector quickly expanded, jurisdictional questions arose about whether MMFs were in the business of banking. Specifically, MMFs' daily liquidity, or the ability of shareholders to redeem their shares on a daily basis, allowed MMFs to offer check-writing options to shareholders. First, we look at the controversy surrounding one of the most widely publicized checking accounts tied to MMFs, the Merrill Lynch Cash Management Account program. Next, we will turn to reactions by others to the creation of MMFs, including then-Chairman of the Federal Reserve Board Paul Volcker, the Department of Justice (DOJ), and Congress.

1. Oregon Attorney General's Letter

Opinion of the Attorney General of the State of Oregon

42 Op. Atty Gen. Ore. 273 (Feb. 11, 1981)

QUESTION PRESENTED

Does the Cash Management Account (CMA) program operated by Merrill Lynch, Pierce, Fenner & Smith, Incorporated (Merrill Lynch) constitute "banking business" under ORS 706.005(4)?

DISCUSSION

The Cash Management Account (CMA) program operated by Merrill Lynch, as described in its July 1, 1981, program prospectuses, consists of three parts: a securities margin account, three related [MMFs], and a VISA check/card account maintained by Bank One of Columbus, N.A. (Bank One).

The securities account is a conventional margin account which may be used to purchase and sell securities and options on margin or on a fully paid basis. . . .

Two CMA programs are available. These programs are identical, except that one offers only one [MMF] while the other offers a choice of three money funds. Free credit cash balances in the securities account are automatically invested, not less frequently than weekly, in shares of one of these funds at their current [NAV]. At any time, as with any securities account, free cash balances held in the securities account may be withdrawn by the investor by notifying Merrill Lynch. Dividends are declared daily on money fund shares and are reinvested daily in additional shares. The prospectuses state:

> '. . . Unlike the Securities Account, Money Fund shares are not subject to the protection of the Securities Investor Protection Act or to protection by the [FDIC] or any other governmental insurance agency. . . .'

Money fund shares are redeemed at [NAV] on the customer's request. Shares are automatically redeemed as necessary to satisfy debit balances in the securities account, or amounts owed on the VISA account.

The third component of the CMA program is the VISA account. Bank One issues a VISA card and checks to each customer (with certain minor exceptions). The card may be used to make purchases of merchandise or services at participating VISA establishments, or to obtain cash advances from participating banks. The checks may be used to draw upon the VISA account for any purpose, but neither the card nor the checks may be used to purchase securities in the securities account or money fund shares. . . .

The question presented is whether the CMA program, as described above, constitutes "banking business" under ORS 706.005(4), which provides:

> '(4) 'Banking business' means the business of soliciting, receiving or accepting money or its equivalent on deposit as a regular business whether the deposit is made subject to check or is evidenced by a certificate of deposit, a pass book or other writing, but does not include:
>
> '(a) Depositing money or its equivalent in escrow or with an agent, pending investments in . . . securities for or on account of a principal. . . .'

. . . We do not believe that either the free credit balance in the securities account or the money fund shares represent "deposits" within the meaning of ORS 706.005(4), but even if they did constitute such deposits, they represent "money or its equivalent" deposited "pending investments in . . . securities" and thus are excepted from the definition of "banking business."

Funds deposited with a bank by its customer create a debtor-creditor relationship. *See* Dahl & Penne v. State Bank of Portland, 110 Or 68, 222 P 1090 (1924). The customer has a right to demand an equivalent amount of funds at some time in the future.

Free credit balances are subject to regulation by the SEC under the Securities Exchange Act of 1934. *See* Rule 15co-3 defines "free credit balance" as:

> '. . . [L]iabilities of a broker or dealer to customers which are subject to immediate cash payment to customers on demand, whether resulting from sales of securities, dividends, interest, deposits or otherwise, excluding, however, funds in commodity accounts which are segregated in accordance with the Commodity Exchange Act or in a similar manner.'

In our opinion, the free credit balance does not constitute a "deposit" within the meaning of ORS 706.005(4), although it shares some of the characteristics of such a deposit. Free credit balances are subject to payment to the account holder on demand, but under the CMA program such funds are contractually committed to investment in shares of the money fund, *i.e.*, to investment in a security. Funds in the free credit balance are transitory and in a constantly changing amount resulting from sales of securities, dividends, interest or, in some cases, cash additions to the securities account. The chief characteristic of the free credit balance, however, is that it represents a by-product of securities investment activity.

Free credit balances as described in the SEC rule, supra, are a common element of securities brokerage activity. We are aware of no case in which they have been declared to be "deposits" within the meaning of banking laws similar to ORS 706.005(4). . . .

The CMA prospectuses have gone to great lengths to emphasize the distinctions between the CMA program and bank accounts. The cover of the prospectuses dated July 31, 1981, states in part:

> 'Investors should be aware that the Cash Management Account service is not a bank account. As with any investment in securities, the value of the shareholder's investment in the Funds will fluctuate.'

On page ii this statement appears:

> '. . . Unlike the Securities Account, Money Fund shares are not subject to the protection of the Securities Investor Protection Act or to protection by the Federal Deposit Insurance Corporation or any other governmental insurance agency.'

On page v it is stated:

> 'Investors should be aware that the checking feature of the CMA program is intended to provide customers with easy access to the assets in their account and that the CMA account is not a bank account. As with any investment in securities, the value of a shareholder's investment in the Money Funds may fluctuate.'

These explicit disclaimers make it highly unlikely that a person investing in the CMA program would believe that the investment represented a bank deposit or had the regulatory and insurance protections associated with such a deposit.

We also note that, since our earlier opinion was issued, a number of Attorneys General in other states have considered the question here presented. In no case has the CMA program been found to constitute banking business. . . . We are informed that the CMA program is now offered in some 37 states without challenge. . . .

---

1. ***Regulatory Constituencies.*** Which constituencies would have favored an action of the Oregon Attorney General against Merrill's CMA account? Which would have opposed it?

2. ***Competition and Adaptation.*** What role did Bank One play in the CMA program? Why would a bank participate in an innovation that so clearly threatened the banking sector?

---

2. Other Perspectives

Even in their incipiency, MMFs were the subject of numerous legal controversies. Some commentators contended that MMFs' near equivalency with deposits violated the Glass-Steagall Act division of banking and securities activities.

> The check writing feature offered by most of the major [MMFs] has raised at least in the minds of some observers, the issue of a possible Glass-Steagall violation. It is not always appreciated that Glass-Steagall is a two way street in that it not only restricts the securities

> activities of commercial banks, but circumscribes as well the bank-like activities of securities firms. In particular, Section 21 of the Act prohibits a securities firm, such as a money-market fund, from engaging "at the same time to any extent whatever in the business of receiving deposits subject to check."

James J. Butera, *Money Market Mutual Funds: The Legal and Regulatory Background*, 28 FED. B. NEWS 91, 92 (1981).

Others agreed that MMFs violated the spirit of the Glass-Steagall Act:

> [t]he commercial banking and investment industries cannot be allowed to compete directly in offering the same financial services if the Glass-Steagall distinction between banking and investment is to be preserved. It may be argued that the time has come to remove that distinction, but the fact remains that the existing law recognizes and upholds it.

John A. Adams, *Money Market Mutual Funds: Has Glass-Steagall Been Cracked?*, 99 BANKING L.J. 4, 11 (1982). The DOJ also became involved in MMFs' jurisdictional questions, concluding in 1980 that the funds did not partake in the business of banking. Because the funds given by an investor to MMFs were at risk, the transaction did not create a debtor-creditor relationship as a customer depositing funds in a bank would. Further, using checks to redeem their shares did not change this relationship. *See* Butera, *Money Market Mutual Funds*, at 92. The Justice Department's opinion was not without controversy and was opposed by Independent Bankers Association of America. *Id.*

In post-Financial Crisis discussions of MMFs, Volcker recalled his early concern about the funds' propensity to "break the buck":

> I was at the Federal Reserve [Board] when [MMFs] were born. It was obvious at the time that these products were created to skirt banking regulations—a clear instance of regulatory arbitrage. The first of these Funds to require a bailout by a corporate parent in order to avoid 'breaking the buck' was in 1980. Since then an additional 145 more such bailouts have occurred, several of which directly or indirectly required governmental support.

Paul Volcker, Comment Letter to the SEC 2-3 (Feb. 11, 2011).

In 1980, Congress also considered additional regulation of MMFs, but ultimately declined to pursue it:

> Two members of the House Banking Committee sponsored bills designed to subject the funds to reserve requirements, but these bills did not proceed beyond the point of introduction and committee referral. In January, 1980, the Senate Financial Institutions Subcommittee held two days of oversight hearings on the matter. On behalf of the Federal Reserve Board, Governor J. Charles Partee told the subcommittee that no congressional action concerning [MMFs] was necessary at that time. Subsequently, . . . the 96th Congress

> adjourned without taking any action to restrict the activities of [MMFs].

Butera, *Money Market Mutual Funds*, at 92.

---

1. ***The Choice of Regulatory Structure.*** Should arrangements such as the CMA program be regulated as banks or as investment companies? Which regulatory structure is more appropriate? In addition to Oregon, several other states, including Utah, New Jersey, and Maryland, considered regulation to fold MMFs into the definition of the business of banking. Congress also considered the issue, but was "more inclined toward loosening the competitive restrictions on depository institutions, which includes the possibility of permitting depository institutions to sponsor or operate MMFs, than toward placing regulatory controls on MMFs." Adams, *Has Glass-Steagall Been Cracked?*, at 17.

2. ***Competition Between Banks and MMFs.*** The growth of MMFs such as the ones associated with Merrill Lynch's CMA program has been substantial. By year-end 1997, more than $1 trillion of assets were invested in these funds, up from $498 billion at the end of 1990. Over the same period, deposits in commercial banks and savings associations grew much more slowly. Why? Should we be concerned if MMFs continue to grow at the expense of depository institutions? Should we understand the end of Regulation Q's interest rate ceilings as leading banks to take more risks to compete with MMFs? *See* Jeffrey Gordon, *The Empty Call for Benefit-Cost Analysis in Financial Regulation*, 43 J. LEGAL STUD. S351, S362, note 6 (2014) (arguing that "Regulation Q limited the capacity of banks to compete for deposits, which also limited their need to make risky loans to make a profit").

III. THE GROWTH AND REFINEMENT OF MONEY MARKET MUTUAL FUNDS

A. OVERVIEW OF GROWTH: 1980 TO 2008

By 1980, high interest rates led to a sharp increase in assets in MMFs, which became competitors with banks for investments. At the same time, Congress began the process of phasing out Regulation Q after "realizing that Regulation Q was not yielding the desired results of restraining competition for deposits or increasing the supply of mortgage credit." Gilbert, *Requiem for Regulation Q*, at 30. The elimination of Regulation Q had been under discussion for a number of years, but the rise of MMFs and the pressure they put on banks was another factor that led to its elimination. *See* FDIC, HISTORY OF THE 80S, VOLUME I: AN EXAMINATION OF THE BANKING CRISES OF THE 1980S AND EARLY 1990S 91-92 (1997); Jonathan Macey, *Reducing Systemic Risk: The Role of Money Market Mutual Funds as Substitutes for Federally Insured Bank Deposits*, 17 STAN. J.L. BUS. & FIN. 131 (2011). MMFs, however, remained popular even after Regulation Q ceilings were raised because MMFs remained higher than interest rates on bank deposits. This return advantage led to the exponential increase of MMFs to nearly $3.8 trillion by the Financial Crisis.

There are at least two explanations for the rise of MMFs. Initially, the ability to get higher returns than those possible through Regulation Q was a major factor in the popularity of MMFs, but MMFs also filled a useful role as a financial intermediary. The funds:

> fill a vacuum in the financial system, which previously lacked an intermediary specializing exclusively in short-term assets and liabilities. According to this view, the growth in [MMFs] represents a permanent change in the way many institutional and individual investors manage their liquid assets. This change has occurred because [MMFs] offer these investors the advantages that result from the pooling of large amounts of short-term funds.

Cook and Duffield, *Lasting Financial Innovation?*, at 16.

This later role explains why MMFs continued to flourish even after Regulation Q's interest rate ceilings were lifted in 1986 as illustrated in Figure 12.3-1. In 2015, MMFs were a $2.6 trillion sector. Note also that MMFs' higher yields may stem in part from the fact that MMFs, unlike banks, did not have the costs of any FDIC premia to pass on to their investors.

Figure 12.3-1 The Growth of MMFs as Compared to Deposits

Year	MMFs (total assets, $ billion)	Deposits (total assets, $ billion)	MMFs as a % of Deposits
1978	6	913	1%
1983	197	1,394	14%
1988	342	2,007	17%
1993	554	2,489	22%
1998	1,126	3,123	36%
2003	2,151	4,411	49%
2008	3,383	6,776	50%
2013	2,554	9,301	27%

Source: Fed. Reserve Bank of St. Louis, Federal Reserve Economic Data (series DPSACBM027NBOG and MMFFAQ027S) (last visited Oct. 28, 2015).

---

1. ***Ending Regulation Q.*** Why end Regulation Q, instead of ending MMFs? There is some evidence that Congress supported the role of MMFs, despite the threat they posed to the competitiveness of depository institutions. During the 1980 Senate hearings on MMFs, Senator William Proxmire supported the financial innovation:

> [I]t seems clear to me that [MMFs] are a textbook example of a market response to the need for financial services that were not being offered by other financial intermediaries. They provide small investors with market yields on their investments and high liquidity with very low transactions costs. . . . So I think that the [MMFs] deserve to be commended. They recognized a demand for a service that banks and thrifts could not offer and they have developed a

> product that has been highly successful. I think that as long as interest rates remain relatively high and regulation Q continues to preclude small savers from getting a market rate of interest on their savings, the [MMF] industry will continue to expand and prosper.

Adams, Has Glass-Steagall Been Cracked?, at 7-8.

2. ***The States React to Regulation Q.*** The states tried to deal with the issue of Regulation Q themselves, especially as it became apparent that Regulation Q allowed a wealth transfer from depositors to banks. *See* Gilbert, *Requiem for Regulation Q,* at 34-35. State efforts were largely symbolic because federal interest rate limits were controlling.

> State legislatures are taking two different approaches to control the competition [MMFs] give banking institutions. One would let banks and thrifts offer interest rates competitive with money fund rates. The other would take away checking privileges that make the funds such a threat to financial institutions. There is $95.7 billion currently invested in money funds by consumers and others, many of whom previously kept their funds in depository institutions. Banks and thrifts have been clamoring for relief from Federal legislators and regulators. Since none has been forthcoming from Congress, many have gone to their state legislatures in the hope they can do something. Proponents of banking institutions have already filed bills in the states of Washington, Georgia and Massachusetts, while in Utah a limiting amendment is included in the state's major rewrite of the banking code. . . . And there is strong talk about how to handle the issue in at least the states of Alaska, Florida, North Carolina, Oklahoma and Tennessee. In the case of Washington State, a bill introduced in the legislature would let banks and thrifts offer special savings accounts whose interest would be tied to money market instrument investment of those funds. Even though Federal limits on deposit interest rates would prevent financial institutions in Washington from legally offering these new accounts, and the state knows it, proponents of the legislation feel passage of the bill would send a clear message to the Depository Institutions Deregulation Committee.

AM. BANKER, States Work To Curb Money Funds; Interest Rates, Checking Are Focus Of Lawmakers (Feb. 27, 1981).

B. EVOLUTION OF SEC OVERSIGHT

Since adopting Rule 2a-7 in 1983, the SEC amended it several times to enhance the safety of MMFs by further tightening portfolio maturity, quality, and diversification requirements. In 1986, the SEC adopted reforms to enable the development of tax-exempt MMFs. *See* Acquisition and Valuation of Certain Portfolio Companies Instruments by Registered Investment Companies Investment Company Act Release No. 14,983, 51 Fed. Reg. 9,773 (Mar. 12, 1986).

Rule 2a-7 was further amended in 1991 and 1996 to require all MMFs to comply with a more stringent set of conditions to be able to use amortized cost valuation and penny-rounding. The 1991 final rule release, excerpted below, also formally defined MMFs as 2a-7 compliant mutual funds. *See* Revisions to Rules Regulating Money Market Funds, Investment Company Act Release No. 18,005, 56 Fed. Reg. 8,113 (Feb. 20, 1991); Technical Revisions to the Rules and Forms Regulating Money Market Funds, Investment Company Act Release No. 22921, 65 Fed. Reg. 64,968 (Dec. 9, 1997); Revisions to Rules Regulating Money Market Funds, Investment Company Act Release No. 21,837, 61 Fed. Reg. 42,786 (Mar. 28, 1996) [hereinafter Release 21837]. Note the utilization of ratings by nationally recognized statistical rating organization (NRSROs), otherwise known as credit rating agencies. These organizations, which include Fitch Investors Services, Inc., Moody's Investors Service Inc., and Standard & Poor's Corp., must apply for recognition with the SEC.

SEC, Revisions to Rules Regulating Money Market Funds

56 Fed. Reg. 8113 (Feb. 27, 1991)

The [SEC] is adopting several amendments to rules and forms affecting [MMFs], including rule 2a-7 under the [1940 Act]. . . . Rule 2a-7 is used by most [MMFs] to maintain a stable [NAV] of $1.00 per share.

The [SEC] is adopting amendments to rule 2a-7 to require a [MMF] to: (1) limit its investment in the securities of any one issuer to no more than five percent of fund assets, measured at the time of purchase (five percent diversification test), except for certain investments held for not more than three business days; (2) limit its investment in securities which are "Second Tier Securities" to no more than five percent of fund assets, with investment in the Second Tier Securities of any one issuer being limited to the greater of one percent of fund assets or one million dollars; and (3) limit investments to securities that are determined to have "minimal credit risks" and are "Eligible Securities." "Eligible Securities" are defined as securities rated by the Requisite NRSROs in one of the two highest short-term rating categories and comparable unrated securities. "Second Tier Securities" are Eligible Securities that are not "First Tier Securities." "First Tier Securities" are defined as securities which are rated by at least two nationally [NRSROs] or by the only NRSRO that has rated the security (Requisite NRSROs) in the highest short-term rating category, or comparable unrated securities.

The amendments also (1) limit fund investments to securities with a remaining maturity of not more than thirteen months (except that [MMFs] that do not use the amortized cost method of valuation may invest in U.S. Government securities that have a remaining maturity of not more than twenty-five months); (2) require a fund to maintain a dollar-weighted average portfolio maturity of not more than ninety days; (3) require a fund, in the event that a portfolio security goes into default or the rating of a portfolio security is downgraded so that it is no longer an Eligible Security, and in certain other circumstances, to reassess promptly whether the security presents minimal credit risks, determine whether continuing to hold the security is in the best interest of the fund, and record such actions in fund records; and (4) require a fund to notify the [SEC] if it holds defaulted securities which amount to one-half of one percent or more of fund assets. Finally, the amendments to rule 2a-7 make it unlawful for any registered investment company to use the term "money market" in its name or hold itself out as a "money market fund" unless it meets the risk limiting conditions of the rule. Funds that hold themselves out as distributing income that is exempt from regular federal income tax (tax exempt funds) are exempted from the five percent diversification test for First Tier

Securities, the five percent limit on investments in Second Tier Securities and the one percent limit on investments in the Second Tier Securities of any one issuer.

The [SEC] is also adopting amendments to rule 482 under the Securities Act of 1933 ("1933 Act"), rule 34b-1 under the 1940 Act, and Forms N-1A, N-3, and N-4 under the 1933 and 1940 Acts to: (1) Require the cover page of [MMF] prospectuses, and fund advertisements and sales literature, to disclose prominently that an investment in a [MMF] is neither insured nor guaranteed by the U.S. Government and that there is no assurance that the fund will be able to maintain a stable per share [NAV]; and (2) revise the definition of a "money market fund" for purposes of those funds eligible to quote a seven-day yield in advertisements and sales literature to include only those funds that meet the risk-limiting conditions.

The 1991 MMF reform sought to reduce the likelihood of a MMF breaking the buck by increasing the safety of the funds' assets, and further sought to make clear to investors that [MMFs] were not risk-free deposits. The rule restricted funds' purchase of securities with less than the highest rating from a credit rating agency. Specifically, the reform established a tiered system of securities, based on perceived safety as determined by the credit rating agencies. While the reform relied heavily on ratings from credit rating agencies, it also emphasized that MMF boards are ultimately responsible for determining the creditworthiness of a fund's investments and a high credit rating was a necessary, but not sufficient, condition for investing in a security. The reform required a disclosure on the cover page of a fund's prospectus stating that the funds are not guaranteed by the U.S. government and that the value of their investments is subject to fluctuation.

The 1996 amendments to Rule 2a-7 also emphasized the inherent riskiness embedded in capital market instruments such as [MMFs]:

> The [SEC] acknowledges that none of its rules can eliminate completely the risk that a [MMFs] will break a dollar as a result of a decrease in value of one or more of its portfolio securities. *Thus, in adopting these amendments, the [SEC] is prescribing minimum standards designed not to ensure that a fund will not break a dollar, but rather to require the management of funds in a manner consistent with the investment objective of maintaining a stable [NAV].*

Release 21,837 (Mar. 28, 1996), at 25 (emphasis added).

---

1. ***Tightening the Risk-Limiting Provisions.*** Are the SEC's restrictions on MMFs necessary? How do the limitations on MMFs summarized above compare to the portfolio restrictions imposed on national banks discussed in Part II? Which entity is safer? While the risk-limiting provisions of Rule 2a-7 were intended to make MMFs more liquid than ordinary mutual funds, another perspective is that the SEC requirements actually generated demand for short-term financial instruments, thereby making the financial system as a whole less stable. *See* Jeffrey Gordon, *The Empty Call for Benefit-Cost Analysis*, at S364.

2. ***Operating Cost Differences.*** In addition to the ability to pass on money market rates to consumers, MMFs also have an operational advantage over commercial banks. Operating expenses of MMFs are typically in the neighborhood of 50 basis points or lower. How does that compare to the cost structure of the commercial banks whose balance sheets and income statements we explored in Chapter 1.5? Should differences in operating costs be relevant to policy-makers? If so, what is their relevance? In addition to operating cost differences, MMFs have lower costs than commercial banks both because of their lack of FDIC premia and their lack of capital requirements.

3. ***The Issue of Implicit Government Support.*** Both in the 1990s and after the 2008 run on MMFs, the SEC responded with reforms to make MMFs more secure. Because MMFs have a liquidity mismatch by transferring illiquid instruments like commercial paper to liquid MMFs shares, there will always be a possibility of a run on MMFs. Can portfolio restrictions ever address the fundamental concern of implicit government support of MMFs?

4. ***The Role of NRSROs.*** Who decides whether any particular investment qualifies as a MMF investment? What is the role of the NRSROs defined in the first footnote in the release previously excerpted? Was it appropriate for the SEC to rely on these organizations in this way? Are there risks to such reliance? As part of the post-Financial Crisis reforms, the SEC has removed references to NRSROs in all of its rulemakings. *See* Final Rule, Nationally Recognized Statistical Rating Organizations, Release No. 34-72936, 79 Fed. Reg. 55,077 (Sept. 15, 2014).

C. DEALING WITH INVESTMENT LOSSES

The risk of investment losses was ever-present in MMFs, and the 1991 reforms that strengthened the risk-limiting requirements of Rule 2a-7 were largely a response to market turmoil that caused several funds to lose money:

> Events in the commercial paper market in 1989 and 1990 led the SEC in 1991 to reevaluate the risk-limiting provisions of Rule 2a-7. Prior to 1989, there had been only two major commercial paper defaults in the postwar period. In 1989, however, a major commercial paper issuer defaulted on $213 million of outstanding paper, and two funds held enough of the issuer's paper to jeopardize their ability to maintain a $1 share value. The funds' advisors averted the possibility of a decline in the $1 share value by purchasing the paper in question from the funds. In 1990 two additional issuers defaulted on their commercial paper, which was held by a number of money funds. Once again, the funds' advisors came to the rescue by purchasing the paper in question from the funds.

Timothy Q. Cook and Jeremy G. Duffield, *Chapter 12: Money Market Mutual Funds and other short-term investment pools, in* INSTRUMENTS OF THE MONEY MARKET, 166 (Timothy Q. Cook and Robert K. Laroche eds., Fed. Reserve Bank of Richmond, 1998).

While no government bailouts of MMFs were necessary in the 1980s and 1990s, the distressed MMFs were bailed out by their sponsors. A sponsor of a MMF is the entity that sets up the mutual fund. Examples of MMFs sponsors are mutual fund companies such as Fidelity, Vanguard, and Charles Schwab. Because a MMF's assets are separate from both the assets of the sponsor and the assets of other funds sold by the sponsor, the sponsor can use its assets to capitalize a distressed MMF. *See* Fisch, *The Broken Buck Stops Here*, at 943. Discretionary sponsor support was common both before and during the Financial Crisis, with sponsors supporting their funds, or seeking no-action relief for such support, in 1989, 1990, 1991, 1994, and 1997. Proposed Rule, Money Market Fund Reform; Amendments to Form PF, Release No. 33–9408, 78 Fed. Reg. 36,834, 36,839-40 (June 19, 2013) [hereinafter Release No. 33–9408]. The aftermath of the bankruptcy of Orange County, California in 1994, for example, led to losses in many MMFs that held Orange County bonds. In order to maintain a stable $1.00 share value and avoid breaking the buck, many sponsors of distressed funds purchased securities from these funds, in effect providing capital support. *See, e.g.,* Benham California Tax-Free and Municipal Funds et al., SEC Staff No-Action Letter (June 30, 1995); Lehman Brothers Daily Income Fund, SEC Staff No-Action Letter (July 7, 1995). Sponsors sought exemptive relief from the SEC before they could provide support to their funds because Rule 17(a) of the 1940 Act prohibits affiliates of registered funds from generally giving financial support to the funds. Note that after the Orange County Bankruptcy, Rule 17a-9, passed in 1996, of the 1940 Act permits discretionary sponsor support to MMFs. *See* Release 21,837. Sponsors seeking to provide support beyond the purchase of securities, however, must still seek no-action relief. Pre-Financial Crisis, investment losses in MMFs were thus resolved via an implicit contingency capital requirement, whereupon sponsors of distressed funds recapitalized their funds when necessary. Sponsor support was also common during the Financial Crisis and SEC staff "estimated that during the period from August 2007 to December 31, 2008, almost 20% of all MMFs received some support (or staff no-action assurances concerning support) from their money managers or their affiliates." Release No. 33–9408, at 36,840, note 41. While an estimated 147 MMFs received sponsor support pre-2007, 78 funds received sponsor support during the 2007–2011 period alone. Fisch, *The Broken Buck Stops Here*, at 980. While some have advocated making sponsor support mandatory after the Financial Crisis, the SEC has declined to do so. *See id.*

D. LEHMAN BROTHERS'S FAILURE AND ITS CONSEQUENCES

During the Financial Crisis, MMFs faced heavy redemptions from investors and played a key role in spreading the contagious financial panic that paralyzed credit markets. The first MMF affected was the Reserve Primary Fund. The Reserve Primary Fund was the successor to the very first MMF, created in 1970, and by 2008 was one of the largest MMFs in the United States, holding $785 million of Lehman Brothers commercial paper, which represented 1.25% of the fund's total assets. On September 16, 2008, one day after Lehman Brothers's bankruptcy, the Reserve Primary Fund broke the buck after it received redemption requests totaling nearly $25 billion. An ensuing run on MMFs, including on those funds that had no exposure to Lehman Brothers, lead investors to withdraw 14% of all assets held in prime MMFs. Notably, institutional investors led the run on MMFs, with prime MMFs that invest in commercial paper facing the largest redemptions. Redemptions were particularly problematic for the funds because they occurred in the midst of a fire-sale of assets across the market. In order to meet the redemptions, the funds had to sell their assets at the low fire-sale price, therefore further hurting their ability to keep a stable $1.00 NAV. *See* Jeffrey N. Gordon and Christopher M. Gandia, *Money Market Funds Run Risk: Will Floating Net Asset Value Fix the Problem?,* CO. BUS. L. REV., 314, 314-317 (2014). Many investors shifted from prime funds to government funds, such that total holdings of prime funds decreased in the aftermath of the Reserve Primary Fund's breaking the buck, but holdings of government funds increased. FINANCIAL CRISIS INQUIRY COMMISSION, THE REPORT FINANCIAL CRISIS INQUIRY, 358-59 (2011). Due to investors' and funds' reluctance to invest in commercial paper, the cost of borrowing increased in the period after September 2008 for financial and nonfinancial firms. *Id.*

On September 19, 2008, the U.S. Treasury intervened to halt the run on MMFs by guaranteeing the balances of investors in MMFs against losses of up to $50 billion through the Temporary Guarantee Program. The Federal Reserve also used its emergency powers to create the Asset-Backed Commercial Paper Money Market Mutual Fund Liquidity Facility, a facility that could fund bank purchases of asset-backed commercial paper from MMFs. *See* Gordon and Gandia, *Will Floating Net Asset Value Fix the Problem?,* at 314-317.

IV. MONEY MARKET MUTUAL FUNDS IN THE FINANCIAL CRISIS AND BEYOND

On July 23, 2014, the SEC adopted structural reforms to MMFs to reduce their systemic risk. The MMF reform effort was one of the first regulatory efforts after the 2008 financial crisis to highlight the institutional dynamics between U.S. regulatory agencies, the newly created Financial Stability Oversight Council (FSOC), and the new international institution, the Financial Stability Board (FSB).

A. POLICY DEBATES OVER REFORM

The events of 2008 led to increasing awareness of the systemic risk posed by MMFs. While MMFs were not explicitly backed by the U.S. government, regulators were concerned that their bailout in 2008 created the expectation of government support. MMFs' susceptibility to runs posed systemic concerns because of the important role MMFs play as a cash-management tool for retail, institutional, and sovereign investors. While numerous reform possibilities were proposed by several regulators, the sector, and academics, regulators mainly considered four alternatives: floating MMFs' NAV, imposing liquidity fees, allowing redemption gates, and requiring a loss-absorption capacity of some kind. Lastly, regulators considered whether to differentiate between the three main types of MMFs: institutional prime, retail, and government.

1. Floating the NAV

A floating NAV attempts to address MMF investors' incentive to run on the first sign of financial distress by trying to remove the first mover advantage associated with dilution of the remaining investors that results with runs in a stable NAV context. In addition, by making funds' valuation transparent, the floating NAV is a reminder to investors that MMFs are risky and that losses are not backed by the U.S. government but rather will be absorbed by investors. Nonetheless, floating the NAV will not entirely remove the risk of runs since investors who redeem early in the period of a MMF's financial distress will still receive a higher sum than those redeeming later. One study examined the comparative run rate during the period after the fall of Lehman Brothers among European MMFs, which are issued in both stable and floating NAV, and found that the stable versus floating characteristic did not explain any of the differences in run rates. Gordon and Gandia, *Will Floating Net Asset Value Fix the Problem?*. In addition, a floating NAV would remove one of the primary benefits of MMFs, namely their ability to be used as a cash-like instrument, and transform them into something closer to regular mutual funds. The floating NAV was part of the 2014 final rule on MMF reform.

2. Imposing Liquidity Fees

Liquidity fees are fees imposed on redemptions occurring after the MMFs' liquid asset balance falls below a pre-designated threshold. The fees aim to deter runs on MMFs in times of market distress by making redeeming shareholders internalize some of the costs of their redemption. The liquidity threshold is measured by weekly liquid assets, which include instruments such as cash, U.S. Treasury securities, and other short-term government securities.

3. Allowing Redemption Gates

Redemption gates temporarily block all redemptions from a MMF in order to give time for fund managers to plan how to meet redemptions, for liquidity buffers to increase as portfolio securities mature, and to allow time for a market panic to decrease. The restrictions might also further differentiate MMFs from insured deposits in the minds of investors. Redemption hurdles are imposed on investors by limiting redemption beyond a certain percentage of an investor's investment in a fund. Another possible reform was a redemption hurdle that could take several forms, including mandatory redemption-in-kind, whereby a percentage of an investor's redemption proceed is distributed in the form of less liquid securities and minimum balance at risk, whereby a withdrawal exceeding a certain percentage, for example 97%, of an investor's investment in a MMF must be delayed by 30 days. Critics of these approaches point to the possibility that gates and fees would create an incentive to run by investors who fear that gates or fees might soon be put in place.

4. Requiring a Loss-Absorption Capacity

Another possible reform was requiring that funds maintain a loss-absorption capacity, in the form of capital buffers or redemption hurdles. Capital buffers would require MMFs to maintain a capital buffer of a certain percent of its total assets. Capital buffers were proposed in the President's Working Group on

Financial Markets Report in October 2010, the Federal Reserve Bank of New York's July 2012 report on MMF reform options, the SEC's internal staff proposal in August 2012, and the FSOC's proposed recommendations in November 2012. A small capital buffer would be insufficient in the face of massive redemption requests, such as those that took place in 2008, while larger capital buffers would be costly and would cut into MMFs' already low yields. Lastly, capital buffers may incentivize fund managers to invest in risky assets to make up for lower yields. The SEC did not ultimately adopt capital buffers for MMFs in its 2014 final rule. The EU also considered capital buffers for MMFs after the Financial Crisis. While the European Commission recommended their adoption, capital buffers were nonetheless rejected by the European Parliament. IOSCO, *Peer Review of Regulation of Money Market Funds*, Final Report, The Board of the IOSCO, FR19/2015, 21 (Sept. 2015)

5. Differentiating Between Types of Money Market Mutual Funds

With respect to each of the reforms identified above, regulators also had a choice whether to apply the reforms to all MMFs or just a sub-set of the funds. MMFs can be distinguished both by their investments and investors. Government MMFs invest almost entirely in liquid and safe instruments, such as cash or U.S. government securities, while prime MMFs invest in short-term debt issued by financial and corporate issuers, with financial issuance constituting the overwhelming bulk of issuance. Retail MMFs are those that are beneficially owned by natural persons, while institutional MMFs primarily serve institutional clients. The SEC final rule distinguished between three categories of funds: government, institutional prime, and retail prime. Of the three types, institutional prime MMFs are more prone to runs. In fact, the 2008 run on MMFs was largely limited to institutional prime MMFs. Government MMFs' portfolios are generally thought to be less risky, while retail prime MMFs are generally considered less susceptible to runs. Tailoring rules to different MMFs types was proposed by the President's Working Group on Financial Markets in October 2010, supported by the FSOC's proposed recommendation in November 2012, and ultimately incorporated in the 2014 final rule.

B. SEC PROPOSALS AND FSOC INTERACTIONS

To make MMFs more resilient, the SEC adopted the first MMF reform in January 2010. The 2010 reform, like the 1991 reform previously excerpted, increased the risk-limiting provisions of Rule 2a-7. Specifically, the 2010 reform: imposed constraints on MMF portfolios relating to liquidity, credit quality, and maturity; required stress tests on MMFs' abilities to maintain a stable NAV; permitted funds that are breaking the buck to suspend redemptions and liquidate their portfolios; and imposed constraints on repurchase agreements that are collateralized with private debt instruments. Additionally, the reform required enhanced disclosure of MMFs' portfolio holdings, as well as monthly disclosure of the shadow price, the funds' mark-to-market values on a per-share basis, which previously was only disclosed twice yearly. At the 2010 open meeting, SEC Commissioner Luis Aguilar and SEC Chairman Mary Schapiro suggested that additional legislation might be necessary to address the issues raised by MMFs performance in the 2008 crisis. Additionally, the sole dissenting vote, Commissioner Kathleen Casey, objected to the reform for failing to sufficiently address the risks posed by MMFs and called for a more "fundamental reevaluation" in a second rulemaking. Statement of Commissioner Kathleen L. Casey on Proposing Release, Money Market Fund Reform (January 27, 2010). Not everyone agreed that additional reform was necessary, however, and many groups within the sector, including the Investment Company Institute, vowed to strongly oppose any further reform. *See* Press Release, Investment Company Institute: ICI Comments on SEC's Money Market Fund Reforms (Jan. 27, 2010). The 2010 rule is excerpted below:

Money Market Fund Reform

75 Fed. Reg. 10,060 (Mar. 4, 2010)

Summary

The [SEC] is adopting amendments to certain rules that govern [MMFs] under the [1940 Act]. The amendments will tighten the risk-limiting conditions of rule 2a-7 by, among other things, requiring funds to maintain a portion of their portfolios in instruments that can be readily converted to cash, reducing the maximum weighted average maturity of portfolio holdings, and improving the quality of portfolio securities; require [MMFs] to report their portfolio holdings monthly to the [SEC]; and permit a [MMF] that has "broken the buck" (*i.e.*, re-priced its securities below $1.00 per share), or is at imminent risk of breaking the buck, to suspend redemptions to allow for the orderly liquidation of fund assets. The amendments are designed to make [MMFs] more resilient to certain short-term market risks, and to provide greater protections for investors in a [MMF] that is unable to maintain a stable [NAV] per share. . . .

Discussion

Today we are adopting the amendments we proposed last June to the rules governing [MMFs]. . . . [W]e believe these amendments will make [MMFs] more resilient and less likely to break the buck. They will further limit the risks [MMFs] may assume by, among other things, requiring them to increase the credit quality of fund portfolios and to reduce the maximum weighted average maturity of their portfolios, and by requiring for the first time that all [MMFs] maintain liquidity buffers that will help them withstand sudden demands for redemptions. The rule amendments require fund managers to stress test their portfolios against potential economic shocks such as sudden increases in interest rates, heavy redemptions, and potential defaults. They provide investors with more timely, relevant information about fund portfolios to hold fund managers more accountable for the risks they take. They will improve our ability to oversee [MMFs]. And finally, they provide a means to wind down the operations of a fund that does break the buck or suffers a run, in an orderly way that is fair to the fund's investors and reduces the risk of market losses that could spread to other funds. We believe that these reforms collectively will better protect [MMFs] investors in times of financial market turmoil and lessen the possibility that the [MMF sector] will not be able to withstand stresses similar to those experienced in 2007-08. Thus, we believe that each of the rules and rule amendments we are adopting is necessary or appropriate in the public interest and consistent with the protection of investors and the policies and purposes of [1940 Act]. . . .

After the 2010 reform, there were continual calls from both within and outside the SEC for the agency to implement further reforms to remedy the structural vulnerabilities of MMFs. In October 2010, on the behest of the Treasury, the President's Working Group on Financial Markets, an inter-agency council comprised of the Secretary of the Treasury and the Chairmen of the Federal Reserve Board, the SEC and the CFTC, issued a report arguing that the 2010 reform was not sufficient to prevent a run on MMFs. The report laid out eight policy options and recommended that the SEC "solicit public comments" to help the FSOC review such options. Additionally, the FSOC articulated a similar concern over MMFs' structural vulnerabilities in its 2011 and 2012 annual reports. In particular, the FSOC's 2012 annual report specifically asked the SEC to publish additional structural reform options for MMFs. Various banking regulators, including the Federal Reserve Board Chairman Ben Bernanke and other Federal Reserve representatives, also publicly supported more structural reforms.

International bodies also entered the discussion. In April 2012, the International Organization of Securities Commissions (IOSCO), an international forum for securities regulators, published a preliminary report on the risks associated with MMFs and suggested reforms at the behest of the FSB. The report cited weaknesses in U.S. MMF regulation as an international concern. For example, U.S. MMFs' withdrawal of funding from European banks because of the sovereign debt crisis negatively affected those banks' dollar-denominated funding and operations. Notably, the report was published without the consensus of a majority of the SEC's commissioners. Since neither IOSCO nor the FSB have binding authority and thus rely on national authorities to adopt their recommendations, their actions are usually congruent with the key domestic regulators of the markets being regulated. Given this background, the FSB's and IOSCO's actions regarding MMF reforms were highly unusual.

In October 2012, IOSCO published the final recommendations for MMF reform, which were once again published despite the objection of the majority of the commissioners of the SEC. IOSCO, *Final Recommendations for Money Market Fund Reforms*, Final Report, The Board of the IOSCO, FR07/12 (Oct. 2012). Ultimately, the report concluded that the 2010 SEC reform was a step in the right direction, but did not adequately address the systemic risk of MMFs. The IOSCO report recommended that regulators must ensure that MMFs implement a floating NAV with enhanced measures for those that maintain a stable NAV, hold a minimum amount of liquid assets (*i.e.*, a capital buffer), and institute redemption gates, temporary suspensions, or redemptions-in-kind, in addition to other reforms, such as stress testing and enhanced disclosures, to reduce systemic risk. In a brief, but notable, sentence, the report also highlighted the possibility of a systemically important financial institution (SIFI) designation for MMFs by the FSB. For the FSB, the proposed MMFs reforms are part of its broader push to strengthen oversight of shadow banking.

The SEC, for its part, also began to explore further reform options. Following the President's Working Group report in October 2010, the SEC requested public comments on the structural reform options suggested in the report. Additionally, in May 2011, the SEC hosted a Roundtable on MMFs and Systemic Risk, which was attended by the voting members of the FSOC, as well as financial sector representatives, investors, academics, and foreign regulators. In a hearing before the U.S. House of Representatives Committee on Financial Services on April 25, 2012, Schapiro also stated that the SEC staff was preparing a proposal for structural reforms of MMFs. On August 22, 2012, however,

Schapiro issued a statement announcing that she tabled the proposed rulemaking and made clear that the SEC would not move forward with a reform proposal because a majority of the SEC commissioners did not support the proposal put forth by the SEC staff. In the same statement, Schapiro indirectly urged other regulators to take action on the systemic risk posed by MMFs. She rearticulated this position in a Wall Street Journal opinion piece on September 20, 2012, arguing that the FSOC should address the issue, including by issuing a formal recommendation to the SEC under § 120 of the Dodd-Frank Act. Mary L. Schapiro, *In the Money-Market for More Oversight*, WALL ST. J. (Sep. 20 2012). A week later, on September 27, 2012, the Secretary of Treasury and FSOC Chairman Timothy Geithner also issued a public letter urging other FSOC members to make a § 120 recommendation to the SEC. Geithner also stated that the FSOC and its members "should in parallel, take active steps in the event the SEC is unwilling to act in a timely and effective manner," including using the FSOC's authority under Title I of the Dodd-Frank Act to designate MMFs as systematically important, and thus subject to supervision by the Federal Reserve Board. Timothy Geithner, Letter to Members of the FSOC, U.S. Department of Treasury (Sep. 29, 2012).

The FSOC issued its proposed § 120 recommendation regarding MMF regulation for public comment on November 13, 2012. A regulator receiving a § 120 recommendation should either adopt the FSOC's recommendations or issue a written justification for not applying such standards. Notably, the FSOC proposed recommendation notes that the Council was evaluating alternatives in the case that the SEC failed to act, including exercising its authority to designate MMFs as systemically important. The FSOC proposal contained three non-mutually exclusive options. Option 1 required a floating NAV. In contrast, option 2 allowed a MMF to keep a stable NAV, but required tailored capital buffers of up to 1% of total assets, and a minimum balance at risk of 3% of a shareholder's highest account value during the previous 30 days. Finally, option 3 also maintained a stable NAV, but required risk-based NAV buffers of 3% and other measures such as investment diversification requirements, increased minimum liquidity levels, and more robust disclosure requirements. The FSOC ultimately did not finalize the proposed recommendation after the 60-day comment period ended.

The FSOC's proposal represented its first action citing its § 120 power. Several factors help explain the FSOC's intervention in the SEC's rulemaking in the present case. The issue affected key FSOC member agencies. During the Financial Crisis, the Treasury and the Federal Reserve Board had to respectively guarantee more than $3.8 trillion of MMF shares and introduce liquidity programs to stop the run on the MMFs. Furthermore, MMFs had become one of the biggest buyers of financial institutions' commercial paper and when MMFs stopped buying this debt during the Financial Crisis, the Federal Reserve Board had to lend to these institutions. Therefore, both the Treasury and the Federal Reserve wanted structural vulnerabilities of MMFs to be further addressed, beyond the 2010 SEC reform. Consequently, even though the SEC is the primary regulator of MMFs, other FSOC member agencies also wanted to address their structural vulnerabilities.

The vocal efforts to ensure additional MMF reform in the United States by the FSOC, FSB, and IOSCO, often in conflict with their primary regulator, the SEC, as well as the different roles of the agency head compared to SEC as a whole, illustrate the complex institutional landscape in financial regulation after the Financial Crisis.

C. THE 2014 FINAL RULE

The SEC adopted the final rule regarding MMFs reforms on July 23, 2014. The final rule requires prime institutional MMFs to float their NAVs and gives non-government MMF boards, including institutional prime MMFs and retail MMFs, the ability to impose liquidity fees and redemption gates. Under the floating NAV system that will govern prime institutional funds, sales and redemptions are based on the current market value of the securities in the fund's portfolios. Notably, government MMFs are exempt from the reform. The requirements to qualify as a government MMF were increased, however, and under the rule a government fund is one that invests at least 99.5% of its total assets in cash, government securities, or certain repurchase agreements collateralized by government securities or cash. Money Market Fund Reform; Amendments to Form PF, Release No. 33-9616, 79 Fed. Reg. 47,735 (Aug. 14, 2014). Previously, this threshold was 80%.

The final rule gave the boards of the non-government MMFs discretionary powers to impose liquidity fees or redemption gates if a fund's level of weekly liquid assets falls below 30%, in contrast to the proposed rule's 15% threshold. A liquidity fee would automatically apply if the fund's level of weekly liquid assets falls below 10%, though the fund's boards may still waive the fee. The fund board also has the discretionary power to impose a redemption gate for up to ten days in a rolling 90-day period. As with the proposed rule, the final rule also includes heightened requirements on portfolio diversification, disclosure, and stress testing. The funds are expected to be in compliance with the floating NAV requirement and fees and gates amendments by October 2016.

SEC, Money Market Fund Reform; Amendments to Form PF

79 Fed. Reg. 47,735 (Aug. 14, 2014)

Summary

The [SEC] is adopting amendments to the rules that govern [MMFs] under the [1940 Act]. The amendments are designed to address [MMFs'] susceptibility to heavy redemptions in times of stress, improve their ability to manage and mitigate potential contagion from such redemptions, and increase the transparency of their risks, while preserving, as much as possible, their benefits. The SEC is removing the valuation exemption that permitted institutional non-government [MMFs] (whose investors historically have made the heaviest redemptions in times of stress) to maintain a stable [NAV] per share . . . , and is requiring those funds to sell and redeem shares based on the current market-based value of the securities in their underlying portfolios rounded to the fourth decimal place (*e.g.*, \$1.0000), *i.e.*, transact at a "floating" NAV. The SEC also is adopting amendments that will give the boards of directors of [MMFs] new tools to stem heavy redemptions by giving them discretion to impose a liquidity fee if a fund's weekly liquidity level falls below the required regulatory threshold, and giving them discretion to suspend redemptions temporarily, *i.e.*, to "gate" funds, under the same circumstances. These amendments will require all non-government [MMFs] to impose a liquidity fee if the fund's weekly liquidity level falls below a designated threshold, unless the fund's board determines that imposing such a fee is not in the best interests of the fund. In addition, the SEC is adopting amendments designed to make [MMFs] more resilient by increasing the diversification of their portfolios, enhancing their stress testing, and improving transparency by requiring [MMFs] to report additional information to the SEC and to investors. Finally, the amendments require investment advisers to certain large unregistered liquidity funds, which can have many of the same economic features as [MMFs], to provide additional information about those funds to the SEC. . . .

Introduction

[. . .O]ur historical experience with [stable value MMFs], and the events of the 2007-2009 financial crisis, has led us to re-evaluate the exemptive relief provided under rule 2a-7, including the exemption from the statutory floating NAV for some MMFs. . . . Today, after consideration of the comments received, we are removing the valuation exemption that permits institutional non-government MMFs (whose investors have historically made the heaviest redemptions in times of market stress) to maintain a stable NAV, and are requiring those funds to sell and redeem their shares based on the current market-based value of the securities in their underlying portfolios rounded to the fourth decimal place (*e.g.*,$1.0000), *i.e.*, transact at a "floating" NAV. We also are adopting amendments that will give the boards of directors of MMFs new tools to stem heavy redemptions by giving them discretion to impose a liquidity fee of no more than 2% if a fund's weekly liquidity level falls below the required regulatory amount, and are giving them discretion to suspend redemptions temporarily, *i.e.*, to "gate" funds, under the same circumstances. These amendments will require all non-government MMFs to impose a liquidity fee of 1% if the fund's weekly liquidity level falls below 10% of total assets, unless the fund's board determines that imposing such a fee is not in the best interests of the fund (or that a higher fee up to 2% or a lower fee is in the best interests of the fund). In addition, we are adopting amendments designed to make MMFs more resilient by increasing the diversification of their portfolios, enhancing their stress testing, and increasing transparency by requiring them to report additional information to us and to investors. Finally, the amendments require investment advisers to certain large unregistered liquidity funds, which can have similar economic features as MMFs, to provide additional information about those funds to us. . . .

Background

B. Certain Economic Features of [MMFs]

4. Investors' Misunderstanding About the Actual Risk of Investing in [MMFs]

Lack of investor understanding and lack of complete transparency concerning the risks posed by particular [MMFs] can contribute to heavy redemptions during periods of stress. This lack of investor understanding and complete transparency can come from several different sources.

First, if investors do not know a fund's shadow price and/or its underlying portfolio holdings (or if previous disclosures of this information are no longer accurate), investors may not be able to fully understand the degree of risk in the underlying portfolio. In such an environment, a default of a large-scale commercial paper issuer, such as a bank holding company, could accelerate redemption activity across many funds because investors may not know which funds (if any) hold defaulted securities. Investors may respond by initiating redemptions to avoid potential rather than actual losses in a "flight to transparency." Because many [MMFs] hold securities from the same issuer, investors may respond to a lack of transparency about specific fund holdings by redeeming assets from funds that are believed to be holding the same or highly correlated positions.

Second, [MMFs'] sponsors on a number of occasions have voluntarily chosen to provide financial support for their [MMFs]. The reasons that sponsors have done so include keeping a fund from re-pricing below its stable value, protecting the sponsors' reputations or brands, and increasing a fund's shadow price if its sponsor believes investors avoid funds that have low shadow prices. Prior to the changes that we are adopting today, funds were not required to disclose instances of sponsor support outside of financial statements; as a result, sponsor support has not been fully transparent to investors and this, in turn, may have lessened some investors' understanding of the risk in [MMFs].

Instances of discretionary sponsor support were relatively common during the financial crisis. For example, during the period from September 16, 2008 to October 1, 2008, a number of [MMF] sponsors purchased large amounts of portfolio securities from their [MMFs] or provided capital support to the funds (or received staff no-action assurances in order to provide support). But the financial crisis is not the only instance in which some [MMFs] have come under strain, although it is unique in the number of [MMFs] that requested or received sponsor support. As noted in the Proposing Release, since 1989, 11 other financial events have been sufficiently adverse that certain fund sponsors chose to provide support or to seek staff no-action assurances in order to provide support, potentially affecting 158 different [MMFs].

Finally, the government assistance provided to [MMFs] during the financial crisis may have contributed to investors' perceptions that the risk of loss in [MMFs] is low. If investors perceive that [MMFs] have an implicit government guarantee, they may believe that [MMFs] are safer investments than they in fact are and may underestimate the potential risk of loss.

D. DEVELOPMENTS AFTER THE REFORMS

Since the Financial Crisis, total investments in MMFs have significantly decreased, declining from a peak of nearly $3.8 trillion in 2008 to $2.6 trillion in 2015. In addition to MMFs' plight in 2008, this decline may be in part due to historically low interest rates since 2008, which depress MMF returns. Nonetheless, total MMF assets today are still substantial. Many MMF sponsors are moving away from institutional prime funds that are covered by the 2014 rule, preferring instead the retail and government MMFs that still have a stable NAV. Both Charles Schwab and Fidelity announced they would no longer offer prime institutional MMFs. *See* Daisey Maxey, *Advisers Weigh Impact of New Money Fund Rules*, WALL ST. J. (Aug. 1, 2014); CRANEDATA.COM, *Schwab Going All Retail, Converting Inst Shares; MMP Switches to Govt* (Oct. 13, 2015). Prime-to-government fund conversions have increased as the October 2016 compliance date for MMF reform nears, with about $263 billion of assets already converted or slated to make the change. Beagan Wilcox Volz, *Eight Months to Deadline: More Firms Tweak Money Funds*, IGNITES (Feb. 11, 2016). Another future trend may be private offerings of MMF-like vehicles, thereby avoiding registration with the SEC and compliance with the new floating NAV requirement for prime institutional MMFs. Sabrina Willmer, *Federated, Blackrock Mull Private Money Funds Amid Rules*, BLOOMBERG (Mar. 15, 2015). Will the floating NAV of the 2014 SEC rule bring an end to institutional prime MMFs? Only time will tell.

---

1. ***The Threat of FSOC Intervention.*** Did the threat of FSOC intervention nudge the SEC and the sector towards reform? The FSOC action came at a time when it was unclear whether, and to what extent, the SEC would proceed with reforms beyond those of 2010. Further reform was vehemently opposed by MMF sponsors, with some going so far as to threaten legal action for any reform proposal that included floating NAVs, capital buffers, or redemption restrictions. In fact, by early 2012, vigorous lobbying by the mutual fund sector, led by the Investment Company Institute, seemed to some commentators to have stemmed off further reform indefinitely. Less than two weeks after the FSOC recommendation, Charles Schwab broke ranks with the MMF sector and supported a floating NAV for institutional prime MMFs. Did the threat of FSOC intervention force the sector to support SEC regulation, which was likely seen as more predictable and less costly than being regulated by the Federal Reserve Board as a SIFI?

2. ***The Evolution of MMFs.*** Do MMFs still pose a threat notwithstanding the SEC's substantive reforms? Do restrictions imposed on the Treasury's ability to act to support MMFs in the future and the Federal Reserve Board's now-limited § 13(3) powers to act as lender of last resort (as discussed in Chapter 9.1) mean that federal authorities lack the authority to address future problems with MMFs? How might additional reform, including capital requirements, be implemented? Do the events of the Financial Crisis indicate that the creation of MMFs, as an instrument similar to bank deposits but without the corresponding FDIC insurance, was a mistake from the start? Should the SEC have recognized that the entrance of institutional investors would have made MMFs' stability highly fragile in times of financial distress? Alternatively, should the issues MMFs experienced during the Financial Crisis be considered a bump in the road, during which there were no losses to the federal government, and after which the SEC, with the FSOC's prodding, made appropriate reforms to maintain an instrument that has satisfied the needs of consumers?

CHAPTER 12.4

SHORT-TERM WHOLESALE FUNDING

CONTENTS

I. INTRODUCTION

A. OVERVIEW OF SHORT-TERM WHOLESALE FINANCING

As you have learned, financial institutions fund themselves with a mix of equity and debt. In the corporate finance literature, and making various simplifying assumptions, firms should be indifferent about their financing structures. *See* Franco Modigliani & Merton H. Miller, *The Cost of Capital, Corporation Finance, and the Theory of Investment*, 48 AMER. ECON. REV. 261 (1958). In reality, financial institutions care a great deal about their financing structures, in part because the real world varies from model assumptions, in part because governments subsidize debt over equity, and in part because shareholders and creditors do not internalize significant costs of financial firm failure due to explicit deposit insurance, "too big to fail" subsidies, or the widespread harm caused to the real economy when the financial system fails. These are reasons why, as you have seen, governments regulate the balance sheets of banks and other financial firms. *See* Anat R. Admati et al., *Fallacies, Irrelevant Facts, and Myths in the Discussion of Capital Regulation: Why Bank Equity is Not Socially Expensive* (Working Paper, 2013); *see also* Joseph E. Stiglitz, *Why Financial Structure Matters*, 2 J. ECON. PERSP. 121 (1988).

Even within the category of debt, of course, financial institutions have choices about how to fund themselves. They can borrow at fixed or floating rates, secured or unsecured, long- or short-term. These choices influence the price at which the firm borrows, as well as the risk the firm faces, either from market movements or choices its creditors make regarding whether to fund the firm. Insured depository institutions (IDIs) have a choice of funding that other financial institutions do not. IDIs can raise funds from retail depositors who are willing to lend to depositories at lower rates in exchange for liquidity and transaction services and the backing of explicit federal deposit insurance, which makes the retail deposit a safe asset for depositors. *See* Gary Gorton & George Pennacchi, *Financial Intermediaries and Liquidity Creation*, 45 J. OF FIN. 49 (1990).

Broker-dealers in the United States cannot offer retail, insured deposits, but they still want to be able to borrow in short-term markets to access cheaper funds. They have replicated safe assets for creditors by issuing short-term secured debt in what has come to be known as the money market and other wholesale financing sources. *See, e.g.*, Anna Gelpern & Erik F. Gerding, *Safe Assets*, 33 YALE J. ON REG. (forthcoming 2016). Repurchase agreements (repos), securities lending transactions, commercial paper, prime brokerage deposits, and even derivatives can be and are widely used for funding such firms.

In good times, short-term wholesale funding markets are deep and liquid and provide a ready source of financing that benefits broker-dealers and other financial firms. Short-term wholesale funding also benefits institutional investors by providing them with an income-producing asset that is a substitute for cash and is treated as such by accounting rules on their balance sheet. *See* Gary B. Gorton & Guillermo Ordoñez, *The Supply and Demand for Safe Assets*

(Nat'l Bureau of Econ. Research, Working Paper No. 18732, 2013). Short-term wholesale financing is an integral part of how the financial system operates.

In bad times, however, institutional providers of short-term wholesale funding run, just as in earlier times retail bank deposits ran, because the asset they thought was safe and was just like cash suddenly becomes no longer so. That is what happened in the Financial Crisis. *See* GARY G. GORTON, SLAPPED IN THE FACE BY THE INVISIBLE HAND: BANKING AND THE PANIC OF 2007 (Oxford Univ. Press 2010); *see also* Gary B. Gorton & Andrew Metrick, *Securitized Banking and the Run on Repo,* 104 J. OF FIN. ECON. 425 (2012); Darrell Duffie, *The Failure Mechanics of Dealer Banks*, 24 J. OF ECON. PERSP. 51 (2010). Federal Reserve Board Governor Daniel Tarullo has stated that "the greatest risks to financial stability are the funding runs and asset fire sales associated with reliance on short-term wholesale funding." Address at the Brookings Inst.: Thinking Critically About Nonbank Financial Intermediation (Nov. 17, 2015). Although policy-makers have taken significant steps to reform short-term wholesale funding, progress has been slow. Short-term wholesale funding still accounts for almost half of the liabilities of large broker-dealers, nearly the same level as during the Financial Crisis. *Id.*

In this Chapter, we explore sources of short-term wholesale funding that experienced stress during the Financial Crisis and review efforts to mitigate the risks from these funding sources. We examine the mechanics of short-term wholesale funding runs and the effect of these runs on large broker-dealers during the Financial Crisis. We also explore securities lending transactions and repos, known collectively as securities financing transactions. We then examine commercial paper, prime brokerage accounts, and derivatives. We discuss reforms targeting short-term wholesale funding risks, as well as tools that regulators may use in the future and critiques of the current approach.

B. MECHANICS OF A RUN

Short-term wholesale funding sources vary in form and complexity, but each are short-term liabilities on a firm's balance sheet that investors can pull in a short time frame. If a firm's wholesale investors withdraw their funding simultaneously, the firm will not have enough cash on hand to satisfy those withdrawals, requiring the firm to sell assets. Forced liquidations of assets, or fire sales, can lead to additional asset value declines, more runs, more fire sales, and so on. During the Financial Crisis, this downward spiral helped to push some firms into insolvency and brought others to the brink of collapse. Many more firms would have failed if the government had not intervened. More broadly, the run on repo and similar instruments contributed to a financial panic that caused widespread harm to the financial system and the real economy.

If you think this dynamic sounds like a bank run, you are right. As Professor Darrell Duffie has put it, "[t]he basic economic principles at play in the failure of a large dealer bank are not so different from those of a garden-variety run on a typical retail bank, but the institutional mechanisms and the systemic destructiveness are rather different." DARRELL DUFFIE, HOW BIG BANKS FAIL AND WHAT TO DO ABOUT IT 3 (Princeton Univ. Press 2010). Recall our discussion of the Financial Crisis in Chapter 1.2. At its roots, the Financial Crisis was like the bank panics that came before it, but these were not classic bank runs in which small depositors clamored outside of local banks to convert deposits into cash. Instead, the runs took place at large, complex financial conglomerates, and the creditors who ran were not individuals but large firms seeking to escape financial positions such as repos, which were functionally similar to retail deposits. *See* GARY G. GORTON, SLAPPED IN THE FACE BY THE INVISIBLE HAND: BANKING AND THE PANIC OF 2007 (Oxford Univ. Press 2010); *see also* Gary B. Gorton & Andrew Metrick, *Securitized Banking and the Run on Repo,* 104 J. OF FIN. ECON. 425 (2012); *see also* Markus K. Brunnermeier & Lasse H. Pedersen, *Market Liquidity and Funding Liquidity*, 22 REV. OF FIN. STUD. 2201 (2009).

Recall our discussion of deposit insurance in Chapter 2.4. Retail deposit insurance has largely eliminated traditional bank runs by protecting depositors against their bank's failure. Short-term wholesale creditors, by contrast, have no such protection. Because short-term wholesale creditors are not insured, they bear the losses if borrowers do not pay them back in full and on time. Creditors therefore have all of the traditional incentives to run if they have concerns about a borrower's solvency or liquidity. *See* MORGAN RICKS, THE MONEY PROBLEM: RETHINKING FINANCIAL REGULATION (Univ. of Chicago Press 2015).

C. THE FINANCIAL CRISIS

The problems associated with short-term wholesale funding, so familiar to early 20th Century bankers but forgotten in the long quiet period, were exposed during the Financial Crisis. Short-term wholesale creditors, spooked by Lehman Brothers's collapse, did not know which firm might fail next. Accordingly, they began pulling their money out of large financial institutions, most notably broker-dealers, *en masse*. The sudden loss of liquidity took these firms by surprise, as many short-term wholesale funding sources had been considered reliable. Firms believed they would be able to tap these funds if they had collateral to secure them. They were wrong. Large financial institutions had no plausible contingency plan when short-term wholesale funding dried up.

The following excerpt from the Financial Crisis Inquiry Commission (FCIC) report demonstrates how runs on short-term wholesale funding threatened the global financial system. The excerpt begins on Monday, September 15, 2008, the day that Lehman Brothers filed for bankruptcy and Merrill Lynch sold itself to Bank of America.

FCIC, Morgan Stanley: "Now We're The Next in Line"

The Financial Crisis Inquiry Report 360–62 (2011)

Investors scrutinized the two remaining large, independent investment banks after the failure of Lehman and the announced acquisition of Merrill. Especially Morgan Stanley. . . . "As soon as we come in on Monday, we're in the eye of the storm with Merrill gone and Lehman gone," John Mack, then Morgan Stanley's CEO, said to the FCIC. He later added, "Now we're the next in line."

Morgan Stanley officials had some reason for confidence. On the previous Friday, the company's liquidity pool was more than $130 billion. . . . [I]t had passed the regulators' liquidity stress tests months earlier. But the early market indicators were mixed. David Wong, Morgan Stanley's treasurer, heard early from his London office that several European banks were not accepting Morgan Stanley as a counterparty on derivative trades. He called those banks and they agreed to keep their trades with Morgan Stanley, at least for the time being. . . . Repo lenders, primarily money market funds, likewise did not panic immediately. On Monday, only a few of them requested slightly more collateral.

But the relative stability was fleeting. Morgan Stanley immediately became the target of a hedge fund run. Before the [F]inancial [C]risis, it had typically been prime brokers like Morgan Stanley who were worried about their exposure to hedge fund clients. Now the roles were reversed. The Lehman episode had revealed that because prime brokers were able to reuse clients' assets to raise cash for their own activities, clients' assets could be frozen or lost in bankruptcy proceedings.

To protect themselves, hedge funds pulled billions of dollars in cash and other assets out of Morgan Stanley. . . . On Monday, hedge funds requested about $10 billion from Morgan Stanley. . . . The hedge fund run became a $32 billion torrent on Wednesday. . . .

These developments triggered the event that [Federal Reserve Board] policy-makers had worried about over the summer: an increase in collateral calls by the two tri-party repo clearing banks, JP Morgan and BNY Mellon. . . . [T]he two clearing banks became concerned about their intraday exposures to Morgan Stanley. . . . They would not make [intraday] loans to the three investment banks without requiring bigger haircuts, which translated into requests for more collateral. . . .

Commercial paper markets also seized up for Morgan Stanley. From Friday, September 12, to the end of September, the amount of the firm's outstanding commercial paper had fallen nearly 40% and it had rolled over only $20 million. By comparison, on average Morgan Stanley rolled over about $240 million every day in the last two weeks of August.

In less than two weeks, between September 10 and September 22, 2008, Morgan Stanley lost $85.3 billion of its $176.8 billion in liquidity, an average of approximately $6.6 billion per day. *See* Darrell Duffie, *Replumbing Our Financial System: Uneven Progress*, 9 INT'L J. CENT. BANKING 251, 276 (2013). Similar losses of liquidity occurred at many other large broker-dealers before and after the Lehman Brothers failure, including Bear Stearns, Merrill Lynch, Citigroup, and Goldman Sachs, as well as at AIG.

II. SECURITIES FINANCING TRANSACTIONS

In our exploration of the major sources of short-term wholesale funding, we first turn to repos and securities lending transactions, known collectively as securities financing transactions (SFTs). Repo and securities lending effectuate the same type of financing but are structured differently. SFTs experienced runs during the Financial Crisis, as investors rushed to exit SFTs with suspect financial firms. These two markets were also interrelated, so runs on each type of SFT had procyclical adverse effects on the other.

A. REPURCHASE AGREEMENTS

1. Repo Basics

Before the Financial Crisis, firms assumed that the repo market would always be a reliable source of short-term funding if they had enough high-quality collateral. In part due to this confidence, the repo market grew significantly in the lead-up to the Financial Crisis, as shown in Figure 12.4-1. The repo market dropped precipitously, however, as runs on repo markets accelerated following Lehman Brothers's collapse. While the repo market remains far smaller than its pre-Financial Crisis peak, it still provides more than $3.4 trillion in funding each day to large financial institutions as of 2015, and repos continue to be a critical demand-deposit substitute for institutional investors. *See* OFR ANN. REP. 60 (2015); *see also* Gary B. Gorton & Andrew Metrick, *Regulating the Shadow Banking System*, BROOKINGS PAPERS ON ECON. ACTIVITY, Fall 2010, at 276–79.

Figure 12.4-1 Value of the Repo Market

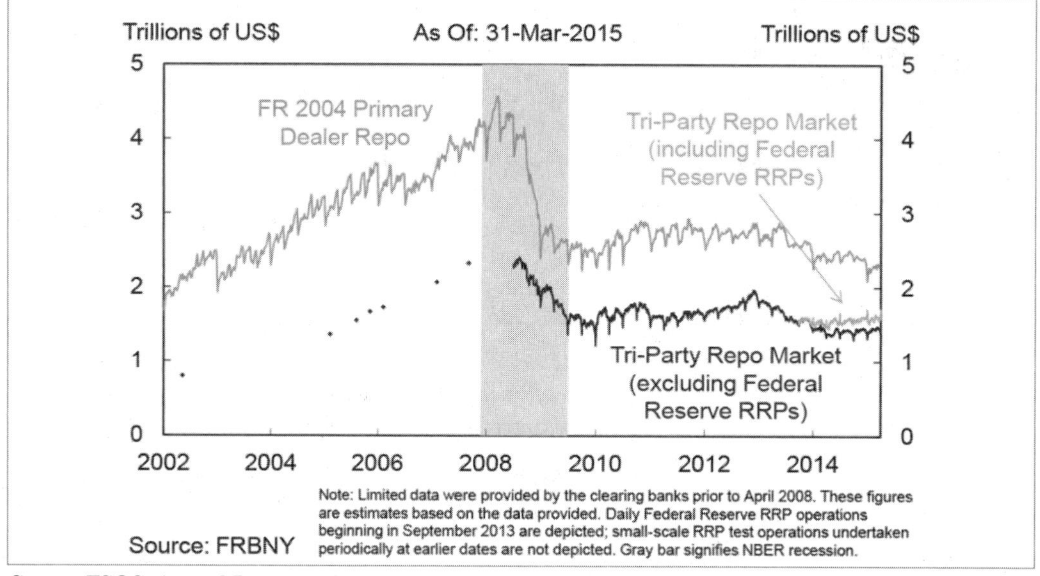

Source: FSOC, Annual Report 54 (2015).

In form, a repo is the sale of a security with a promise to buy it back in the future. In substance, a repo is a collateralized loan. Consider a bilateral repo, diagrammed in Figure 12.4-2. Borrower wants to borrow, while Lender wants to lend. Borrower sells a security to Lender on the understanding that Borrower will repurchase the security from Lender the next day at a premium, which is implicitly an interest payment to Lender for the use of its funds.

Figure 12.4-2 Bilateral Repo

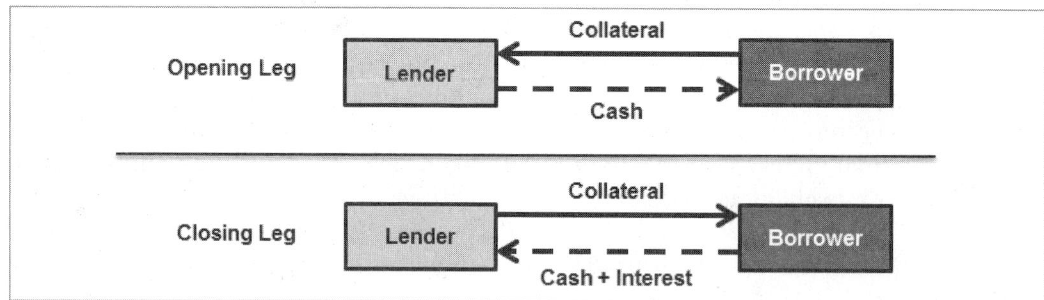

Source: Viktoria Baklanova et al., Reference Guide to U.S. Repo and Securities Lending Markets (Fed. Res. Bank of N.Y. Staff Report No. 740, 2015).

There are different types of repo, with various features, summarized below:

- **Bilateral or Tri-party Repo.** Repo transactions can be either bilateral, in which the borrower and lender transact directly, or tri-party, in which the parties transact through a clearing bank.

- **Maturity Length.** A term repo is a transaction with a specified end date. Term repo maturities were often very short at the time of the Financial Crisis. Financial institutions relied on more than $100 billion in overnight repos, on average, on a daily basis in 2013. Darrell Duffie, *Replumbing Our Financial System: Uneven Progress*, 9 INT'L J. CENT. BANKING 251, 259 (2013). Open or evergreen repos do not have a set maturity date, but can mature at the request of the borrower or lender, also leading to run risk. Since the Financial Crisis, large-broker dealers have generally lengthened the terms of their repo books.
- **Margin Requirements.** The market value of collateral often exceeds the amount of funds lent in a repo transaction. The amount by which the collateral exceeds the funds lent is the margin or haircut.
- **Settlement.** In a bilateral repo, lenders and borrowers deliver cash and securities directly to one another, usually simultaneously. In tri-party settlement, cash and collateral is delivered to a third-party intermediary, which holds the assets in custody for the transacting parties.

2. Bilateral Repo

Bilateral repos, in which parties transact directly with one another, account for roughly half of the repo market. OFR ANN. REP. 60 (2015). The transaction depicted in Figure 12.4-2 is a bilateral term repo. While evidence indicates that the bilateral repo market suffered significant stress during the Financial Crisis, it is impossible to know the extent of that distress because of a lack of publicly reported data.

Since the Financial Crisis, the Office of Financial Research (OFR) and the Federal Reserve Bank of New York have taken steps to enhance transparency in the bilateral repo market. In a study using voluntarily disclosed data, researchers found that the majority of bilateral repo transactions as of 2015 involve Treasuries and agency securities, and overnight maturities remained the most common. Broker-dealers are lenders more frequently than borrowers, the reverse of what is seen in the tri-party repo market. *See* Viktoria Baklanova et al., *The U.S. Bilateral Repo Market: Lessons from a New Survey* (OFR, Brief No. 16-01, 2016). Given the importance, opacity, and risk of the bilateral repo market, many commentators have called for significant further reforms. Professors Gary Gorton and Andrew Metrick, for instance, have proposed that nonbank entities be required to obtain a license to engage in repos, that eligible collateral be significantly restricted, and that minimum haircuts be imposed on all collateral. *See* Gary B. Gorton & Andrew Metrick, *Regulating the Shadow Banking System*, BROOKINGS PAPERS ON ECON. ACTIVITY, Fall 2010, at 287–90; *see also* Paolo Saguato, *The Liquidity Dilemma and the Repo Market: A Two-Step Policy Option to Address the Regulatory Void* (LSE Law Society and Economy Working Paper No. 21, 2015).

3. Tri-Party Repo

In tri-party repo, a third-party intermediary, known as a clearing bank, positions itself between a repo borrower and lender. The clearing bank clears and settles the trade, holding the cash and securities used in the transaction in custody. An overnight tri-party repo transaction is diagrammed in Figure 12.4-3. The first leg of an overnight repo transaction, which typically takes place in the late afternoon, is the initial extension of credit from a tri-party lender to a tri-party borrower in exchange for collateral. The cash and securities used in the transaction are transferred to the clearing bank. The clearing bank then places the collateral given by the borrower in the lender's account, and places the funds furnished by the lender in the borrower's account. If, however, the clearing bank already holds collateral and cash from each of the counterparties, as is typical in most repo transactions, the clearing bank adjusts each of the parties' accounts in its internal recordkeeping and the parties do not transfer additional cash or securities. This process is known as winding the transaction. During the term of the repo transaction, borrowers cannot access the collateral given to the clearing bank, and lenders cannot withdraw their funds.

Figure 12.4-3 Tri-Party Clearing

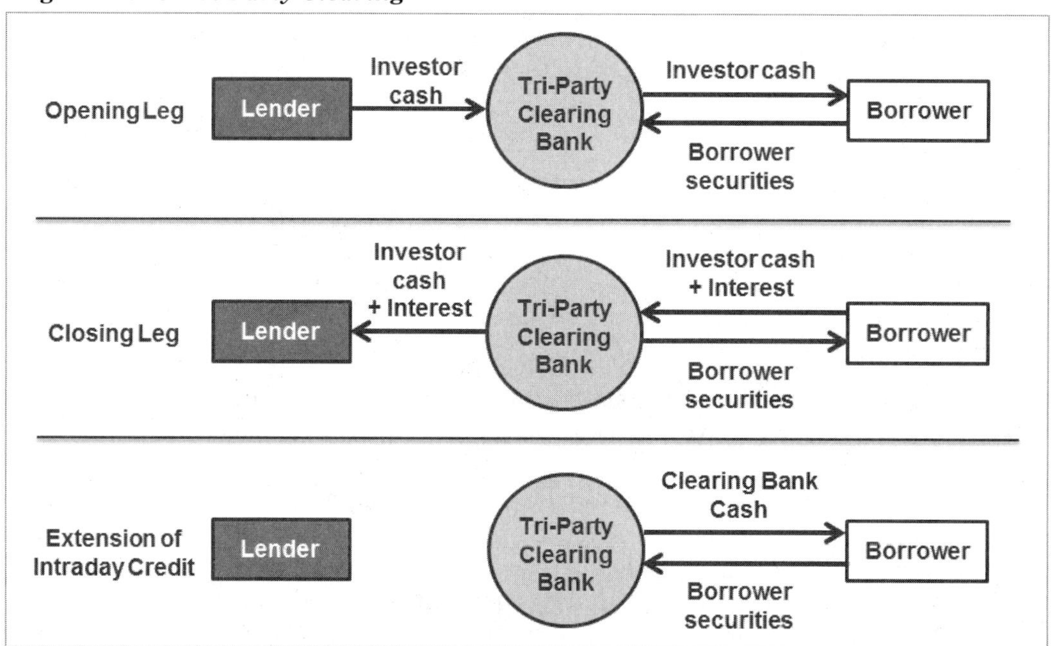

When the repo matures, which usually takes place in the morning, the clearing bank releases the collateral to the borrower and places the lent funds, including a premium, back in the lender's account. This is known as unwinding the repo. Between the unwinding of a repo and the winding of a new one, the clearing bank extends temporary credit to the borrower to allow it to finance its securities inventories. When extending temporary credit, the clearing bank requires the borrower to furnish collateral. The borrower can use the same collateral from the recent transaction or choose to substitute different collateral.

JP Morgan and BNY Mellon are the only two clearing banks in the United States. Borrowers in the tri-party repo market are generally large broker-dealers. Lenders in the tri-party repo market are money market mutual funds (MMFs), mutual funds, insurance companies, and corporate or local government treasurers.

There are advantages to the tri-party system. Tri-party repo lenders typically do not have the operational capability to conduct repos without assistance. Handling the transactions themselves would require these investors to track the collateral they receive, make sure that the collateral is adequate and valued correctly, and ensure that the proper margin has been applied. Clearing banks take over these functions, reducing costs to both borrowers and lenders. Clearing banks protect investors by providing access to their collateral if a repo borrower fails. *See* Adam Copeland et al., *Key Mechanics of the U.S. Tri-Party Repo Market*, FED. RESERVE BANK OF N.Y. ECON. POL'Y REV., Oct. 2012.

The tri-party repo system, however, has vulnerabilities. Many of these shortcomings became painfully evident during the Financial Crisis, when the tri-party repo market experienced significant disruption:

- **Repo Borrower Exposure to Lender Runs.** When a broker-dealer's solvency or liquidity is questioned, lenders or clearing banks may restrict credit by shortening repo maturities, demanding higher effective interest rates and more collateral by increasing haircuts, and stopping lending.

- **Clearing Bank Exposure to Lender Runs.** While a repo transaction is unwound, lender funds are stored at the clearing bank as demand deposits. If a borrower appears weak while the transaction is unwound, lenders can refuse to provide funds to rewind the transaction and pull their deposits. Although lenders generally did not pull their deposits during the Financial Crisis, the possibility of a lender run raised concerns that the clearing banks could be exposed to borrowers' credit risk for longer than expected. *See* FCIC, THE FINANCIAL CRISIS INQUIRY REPORT 295 (2011).

- **Clearing Bank Exposure to Borrower Failure.** Borrower failures can precipitate uncoordinated, disorderly liquidations of the securities held as collateral by repo lenders. Uncoordinated liquidation can drive down the price of securities drastically, which can have spillover effects for other dealers holding the same securities. If a borrower fails while repo transactions are unwound, clearing banks are stuck holding the collateral, leading the clearing bank to engage in a fire sale.

- **Market Dependence on Clearing Banks.** Instability of clearing banks in a crisis would be devastating to the financial system, and the government therefore has a strong incentive to support the two institutions that handle tri-party clearing rather than to let them fail. Repo borrower failure may also cause system risk, requiring government intervention. The possibility of government support weakens market discipline and increases moral hazard.

The distress or failure of a major repo borrower or clearing bank could induce a systemic crisis. During the Financial Crisis, for instance, Lehman Brothers's collapse intensified the run on repo markets and in turn sparked runs on MMFs, which were active repo lenders. These runs, in turn, decreased the amount of repo financing that MMFs provided, further undermining broker-dealers and causing more runs, further destabilizing the market.

In 2009, the Federal Reserve convened a task force to address tri-party repo risks. Among other things, the task force recommended that the clearing banks curtail the extension of intraday credit and that borrowers arrange their repo maturities to ensure that large volumes of repos do not come due simultaneously. The task force called for improving margin practices among all tri-party repo participants to ensure that margins are "risk-based . . . not procyclical, and . . . based on objective/transparent criteria." PAYMENTS RISK COMMITTEE, TASK FORCE ON TRI-PARTY REPO INFRASTRUCTURE: REPORT (2010). The task force encouraged market participants to come up with a coordinated plan in case of a large dealer default, and it called on the clearing banks to supply data to the Federal Reserve so that it could release aggregated statistics on the tri-party repo market each month. The task force concluded its work in 2012. PAYMENTS RISK COMMITTEE, TASK FORCE ON TRI-PARTY REPO INFRASTRUCTURE: FINAL REPORT (2012). The Federal Reserve Bank of New York has increased its oversight of tri-party reform at JP Morgan and BNY Mellon. *See* Press Release, Fed. Reserve Bank of N.Y.: Statement on the Release of the Tri-Party Repo Infrastructure Reform Task Force's Final Report (Feb. 15, 2012). By 2014, the clearing banks were providing $1 trillion less in intraday credit than in 2012. They have eliminated daily unwinds for non-maturing trades, removing the need for the extension of intraday credit by the clearing banks during that time period. Borrowers are making an effort to arrange their repo books so that maturities of repos do not come due simultaneously. Settlement has become increasingly automated. *See* Press Release, Fed. Reserve Bank of N.Y.: Update on Tri-Party Repo Infrastructure Reform (Feb. 13, 2014). At the same time, tri-party repo remains a source of significant risk in the financial system, and many call for further reforms. *See, e.g.*, Jeremy C. Stein, Governor, Fed. Reserve Board, Address at the Fed. Reserve Bank of N.Y. Workshop on Fire Sales as a Driver of Systemic Risk in Tri-Party Repo and Other Secured Funding Markets: The Fire-Sales Problem and Securities Financing Transactions (Oct. 4, 2013).

4. General Collateral Finance Repo

The General Collateral Finance (GCF) repo market was introduced in 1998 to reduce transaction costs and increase liquidity. It is administered by the Fixed Income Clearing Corporation (FICC), a subsidiary of the Depository Trust & Clearing Corporation, in collaboration with the clearing banks. Participants in the GCF market, primarily broker-dealers, must be approved by the FICC. To improve liquidity, only a narrow range of securities can be used as collateral, including Treasuries and agency securities. Unlike with bilateral or tri-party repos, participants in the GCF repo market do not need to locate a counterparty to complete a repo transaction. Instead, borrowers and lenders submit their terms to a third party known as an inter-dealer broker, which brokers the trade and submits the trade details to the FICC. The FICC novates both sides of the transaction, becoming a central counterparty to both sides of the deal. The FICC nets the positions of all borrowers and lenders in the GCF repo market and submits the final positions of each party to the clearing banks. The clearing banks then adjust the accounts of the borrower, lender, and FICC on its books. Finally, settlement is also performed by the FICC on the tri-party platform.

As in the tri-party repo market, there has been a push to decrease the amount of intraday credit in the GCF repo market. Clearing banks still extend significant amounts of intraday credit to both repo dealers and the FICC. Progress has been made in decreasing the amount of intraday credit extended, but significant work remains. *See* Paul Agueci et al., *A Primer on the GCF Repo Service* (Fed. Reserve Bank of N.Y., Staff Report No. 671, 2014).

B. SECURITIES LENDING TRANSACTIONS

Securities lending transactions are arrangements in which one party lends a security to another party. Typical securities lenders include mutual funds, insurance companies, pension plans, and exchange traded funds. Securities lenders earn fees for lending their securities and earn returns from reinvesting collateral. While securities lenders can seek out transactions on their own, they often employ an agent to do so. Agents are usually custodian banks, such as State Street or BNY Mellon. Lending agents get fees for the transactions or for managing the cash collateral reinvestment. Securities borrowers are most often hedge funds, but asset managers, option traders, and others borrow as well. Borrowers are often assisted by prime brokers, which earn interest on balances deposited at the prime broker, or earn fees for serving as the borrower's agent in the securities lending transaction. Broker-dealers participate as both securities borrowers and securities lenders. *See* Frank M. Keane, *Securities Loans Collateralized by Cash: Reinvestment Risk, Run Risk, and Incentive Issues*, 19 CURRENT ISSUES IN ECON. AND FIN. 1, 2 (2013).

Securities lenders earn additional returns, and securities borrowers most commonly use the transactions to conduct a short sale, in which a party borrows and sells securities it does not own. Naked short selling, in which a party sells a security that it neither owns nor borrows, is forbidden by SEC Regulation SHO. *See* 12 C.F.R. § 242.203. The short seller is required to return equivalent securities to its lender at a future date. The short seller hopes to purchase the securities for less than it sold them for and pocket the difference. Securities borrowers also use these transactions to protect against settlement failure. Say Party A promises to sell a security to Party C and plans to purchase that security in the meanwhile from Party B. If B unexpectedly fails to deliver the security, A can borrow an equivalent security and sell it to C to settle the trade. Borrowing allows A to avoid incurring penalties for failure to settle the trade. Securities lending also has the indirect effect of increasing liquidity for securities and therefore generally lowering their bid/ask spreads.

1. Transaction Basics

A securities lending transaction begins when a lender loans securities to a borrower. The borrower can then use the securities to conduct a short sale, hedge a position, or settle a trade. In exchange for the security, the borrower posts collateral with the lender. In the United States, securities lending transactions are usually collateralized by cash, which can be reinvested by the lender or, more commonly, by the lender's agent. Securities lending agents accumulate the cash collateral posted to their clients in cash collateral reinvestment pools. The money is then reinvested in a variety of securities or transactions, including repos, deposits, bank notes, commercial paper, asset-backed commercial paper (ABCP), or other short-term money market debt. Figure 12.4-4 depicts a typical securities lending transaction.

Figure 12.4-4 Securities Lending Transaction

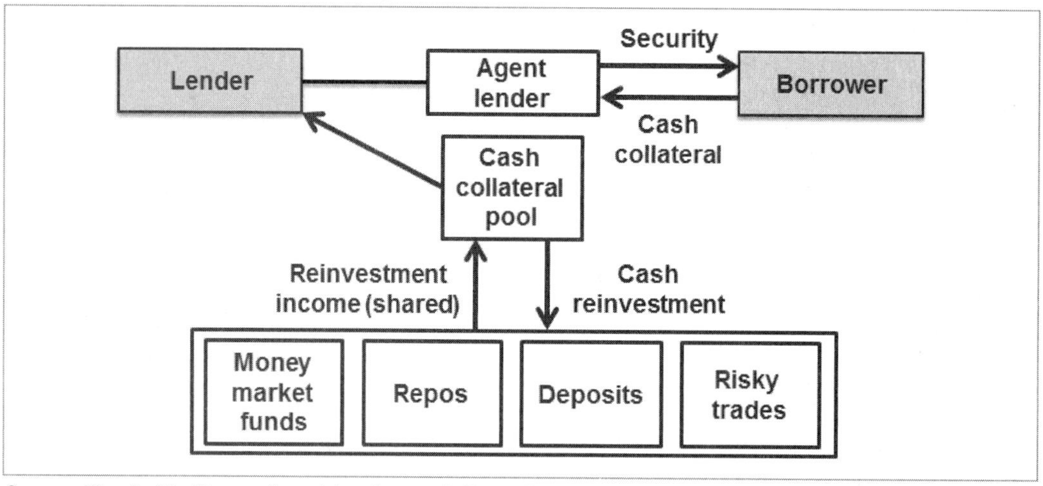

Source: Frank M. Keane, Securities Loans Collateralized by Cash: Reinvestment Risk, Run Risk, and Incentive Issues, 19 Current Issues in Econ. and Fin. 1, 2 (2013).

Securities lending transactions are typically "open," meaning that the trade can be matured by either the borrower or the lender at any time. When a trade is matured, the borrower returns the securities to the lender, and the lender returns the collateral to the borrower. If the collateral is securities or cash that has not been reinvested in some other asset, it can be easily returned. If the lender has reinvested cash collateral, however, as is commonly the case, the lender must find cash from another source. That can cause liquidity problems.

2. Securities Lending During the Financial Crisis

During the Financial Crisis, widespread runs on securities lending drained liquidity and were one of the primary culprits in Lehman Brothers's failure and the near-collapse of AIG and other large financial institutions. Cash collateral reinvestment pools shrank, rendering firms less capable of purchasing short-term financial institution debt or acting as repo lenders. Before the Financial Crisis, securities lending transactions were considered low risk and liquidity enhancing, so the loss of liquidity caught many by surprise. Runs occurred on both sides of securities lending transactions, with lenders and borrowers both seeking to escape their exposures. Lenders unwound transactions to minimize losses on cash collateral pool investments. Some of the pools had invested in Lehman Brothers commercial paper, leading to a total loss. Other investments experienced declines because securities issuers defaulted or structured products became illiquid. When lenders could sell their depreciating reinvestment securities, they often had to do so in a falling market, at fire-sale prices. Many borrowers wanted to recoup cash collateral to deleverage or honor their own short-term liabilities. Hedge funds, for example, needed cash to survive increased quarterly redemptions by their own investors. Some borrowers were forced to unwind to get out of short sales of financial company stock when the SEC temporarily banned such short sales after Lehman Brothers's bankruptcy. *See* Press Release, SEC, SEC Halts Short Selling of Financial Stocks to Protect Investors and Markets (Sept. 19, 2008). Other securities borrowers unwound because of concerns over the solvency of their securities lenders.

The result of these runs was a significant liquidity crunch in cash collateral reinvestment pools, which in turn reinforced the crunch in repo markets. To grasp the significance of this development, consider that cash collateral reinvestment pools provided about 25% of the total funds lent through repurchase agreements. SENIOR SUPERVISORS GRP., RISK MANAGEMENT LESSONS FROM THE GLOBAL BANKING CRISIS OF 2008 12 n.10 (2009). The loss in repo funding from securities lending markets, combined with MMF lending contraction, dramatically limited the tri-party repo market.

The case of AIG demonstrates how unsafe securities lending practices by just a single large institution can have destabilizing effects on the entire financial system. AIG engaged in extensive securities lending operations, borrowing securities from its insurance subsidiaries and lending them out through its securities lending subsidiary. The transactions were driven by a volume strategy in which AIG's primary objective was to lend as many securities as possible to maximize returns on pools of reinvested cash collateral. *See* FCIC, THE FINANCIAL CRISIS INQUIRY REPORT 345 (2011).

AIG had invested a large portion of its collateral reinvestment funds in mortgage-backed securities (MBSs). By June 2008, mortgage investments that AIG had initially valued at $75 billion had declined to $59.5 billion. *See id.* at 272, 345. To make matters worse, securities borrowers demanded that AIG return cash collateral as the value of the securities declined. Collateral returns eventually topped $43 billion. *Id.* at 377. The cash outflows from the securities lending and credit default swap (CDS) business brought AIG to the brink of collapse. As you recall from Chapters 3.1 and 9.1, the Federal Reserve stepped in and provided funds to AIG because it feared cascades throughout the financial system.

3. Post-Financial Crisis Landscape and Reform

After growing dramatically for decades, the global value of securities lending transactions dropped from a peak of approximately $3.9 trillion in May 2008 to approximately $2 trillion by the end of 2008. By 2014, the value of securities lent was about $1.7 trillion. In the United States, the value of securities lent fell from more than $1.5 trillion in 2008 to less than $1 trillion by the end of that year. The total value of securities lent remained under $1 trillion in 2014. Worldwide, reinvested funds declined from approximately $1.8 trillion in 2008 to roughly $600 billion by the end of 2013. FSOC, ANNUAL REPORT 60-61 (2014).

Market participants have taken some steps to mitigate the risks posed by securities lending operations, including:

- **Decreased Use of Cash Collateral.** The number of U.S. securities lending transactions collateralized by cash has fallen since the Financial Crisis. This reduction should make the securities lending market marginally safer by minimizing the dangers associated with reinvestment portfolios. As of 2013, though, 70% of securities lending transactions were still collateralized by cash. Frank M. Keane, *Securities Loans Collateralized by Cash: Reinvestment Risk, Run Risk, and Incentive Issues*, 19 CURRENT ISSUES IN ECON. AND FIN. 1, 3 (2013).

- **More Conservative Investment Strategies.** Collateral reinvestment fund managers are making more conservative investment decisions. Before the Financial Crisis, cash collateral was often invested in illiquid, structured products with lengthy maturities. Fund managers have since returned to investing in shorter-maturity, more liquid assets like commercial paper. Between 2008 and 2014, the weighted average maturity of collateral reinvestment fund assets fell from more than 200 days to less than 100 days. FSOC, ANNUAL REPORT 61 (2014).
- **Greater Segregation of Reinvestment Funds.** During the Financial Crisis, when lenders tried to unwind securities lending transactions, they found that securities purchased with cash collateral could not readily be sold to generate sufficient funds to return the cash collateral. In many cases, lending agents commingled the cash collateral of several securities lenders and made investments out of that pool. Lenders held shares in that commingled fund, which slowed withdrawals. Investors are increasingly requesting that cash collateral be segregated so they can exercise control over where collateral reinvestment funds are invested.

---

1. ***SFTs and the Volcker Rule.*** Recall our discussion of the Volcker Rule's prohibition on proprietary trading in Chapter 6.2. The final implementing regulations under the Volcker Rule exempt SFTs from the definition of proprietary trading on the view that SFTs are the functional equivalent of a loan and loans are excluded under the statutory text. *See* 12 C.F.R. § 248.3(d). Some policy-makers argued against the regulatory exemption for SFTs. *See, e.g.*, Letter from Senators Jeff Merkley and Carl Levin, to the OCC, Federal Reserve Board, FDIC, SEC, and CFTC (Feb. 13, 2013). Do you agree that SFTs are loans and not proprietary trading? Why or why not?

III. COMMERCIAL PAPER, PRIME BROKERAGE, AND DERIVATIVES

A. COMMERCIAL PAPER

1. Basics of Commercial Paper

Commercial paper is a short-term unsecured debt instrument issued by the largest, most creditworthy financial and commercial firms. There was more than $2 trillion in commercial paper outstanding in 2007. By 2014, that figure dropped to just over $1 trillion. FSOC, ANNUAL REPORT 57 (2014). Despite this contraction, commercial paper is still one of the most significant sources of funding in the short-term debt market. Investors, primarily MMFs and other mutual funds, are able to earn a return over and above other short-term debt, like Treasuries, in exchange for taking on what is usually thought of as a small amount of additional risk. Except in a financial crisis.

Commercial paper issuances typically mature in 30 days. For the most part, investors hold commercial paper until maturity, and there is little trading of commercial paper in secondary markets. Once commercial paper matures, purchasers often roll over their investment. In that case, issuers pay interest, but instead of repaying the principal, they replace maturing paper with a new issuance. The process exposes issuers to roll over risk when investors decide they do not want to renew their commercial paper investment. *See* Marcin Kacperczyk & Philipp Schanbl, *When Safe Proved Risky: Commercial Paper During the Financial Crisis of 2007-2009*, 24 J. ECON. PERSP. 29, 31–32 (2010).

There are three types of commercial paper: financial commercial paper (issued by financial firms), corporate commercial paper (issued by non-financial firms), and ABCP (issued by special purpose entities). Nearly all commercial paper is financial or ABCP; a small percentage of commercial paper funds real-economy firms. Firms can use proceeds from commercial paper to pay short-term obligations, like payroll or interest, but they typically cannot use these funds to finance long-term obligations such as equipment purchases. Financial issuers found a way around this restriction in some important contexts, including through ABCP conduits.

2. Asset-Backed Commercial Paper Conduits

ABCP is a form of commercial paper issued by a special purpose entity known as an ABCP conduit. A special purpose entity, also known as a special purpose vehicle, is a catch-all term referring to any legal entity set up to perform a specific purpose. Introduced in the 1980s, ABCP represented 56.8% of the roughly $2 trillion commercial paper market in 2007. *Id.* at 32.

Say that Company X wants to issue an MBS as an investment for its clients, but some of its clients, like MMFs, are barred by law from holding these securities. To avoid this problem, Company X sponsors an independent legal-entity, the ABCP conduit. As sponsor, Company X creates the conduit. The conduit issues commercial paper to its MMF investors and uses the proceeds to purchase the MBS from the sponsor. Interest from the MBS flows into the ABCP conduit, which is then used to make interest payments owed to the commercial paper investors. Company X then keeps any profits over and above the interest payments made to the conduit investors.

ABCP participants benefit in several ways. ABCP conduits allow investors like MMFs to indirectly invest in securities they otherwise could not hold. In addition, investments in ABCP mature quickly, allowing investors to exit their positions swiftly relative to the conduit itself. Financial institution sponsors use ABCP conduits to attract investment capital, obtain cheap financing for structured products, and earn a profit from the conduits' operations. Under the accounting rules before the Financial Crisis, sponsors could usually remove assets held by ABCP conduits from their balance sheet, which reduced their reported leverage and reduced regulatory capital held against those assets.

ABCP conduits, however, also posed significant risks for sponsors. As with other commercial paper, investors could refuse to roll over their investment in ABCP. Pursuant to its legal structure, technically only the conduit was responsible for paying the face value of the paper if the investor refused to roll over the investment. Fearing the conduit would be unable to honor its obligations, investors normally extracted guarantees from the ABCP sponsor to pay off maturing ABCP if the conduit could not. Despite appearing insulated from conduits, sponsors were often exposed to all of their roll over risks.

3. Commercial Paper in the Financial Crisis

Commercial paper markets grew dramatically in the lead up to the Financial Crisis, mainly driven by a steep rise in ABCP. *See* Figure 12.4-5. Runs on both financial commercial paper and ABCP contributed greatly to the severity of the Financial Crisis, and the massive contraction in the commercial paper market choked off credit for real economy firms at the same time.

Figure 12.4-5 The Commercial Paper Market

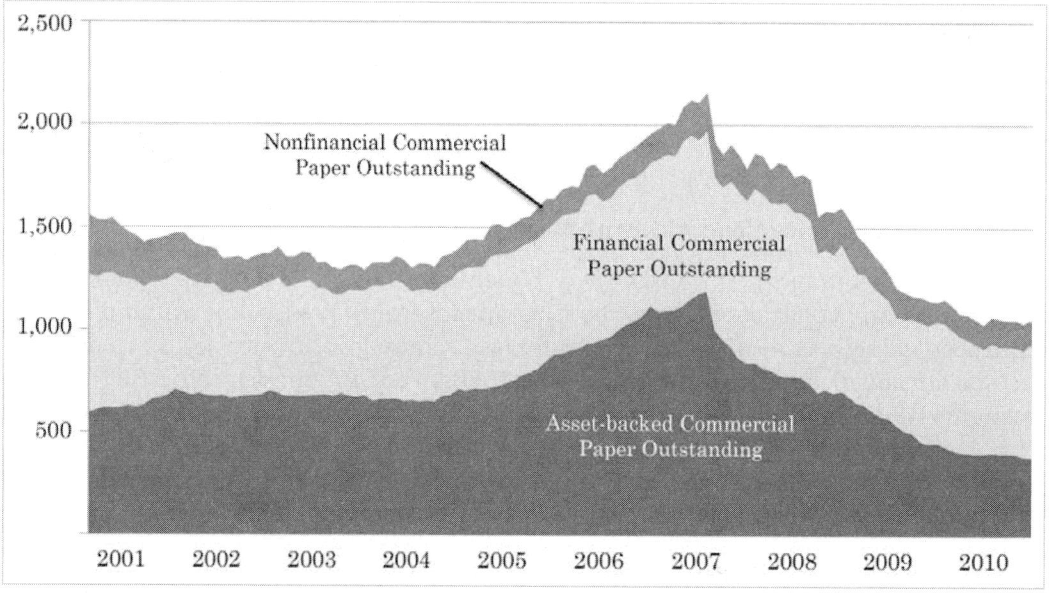

Source: FSOC, 2015 Annual Report 54 (2015).

Commercial paper's involvement in the Financial Crisis can be broken down into two phases. The first phase involved a simultaneous refusal to roll over by a large number of ABCP investors. The run, which began in the summer of 2007, is considered by many to be the beginning of the multifaceted liquidity crisis described in this Chapter. The run on ABCP stemmed from fears about exposure to suddenly suspect MBSs held by ABCP conduits. Fears about exposure were stoked by the failure and deteriorating performance of investment funds backed by major financial institutions that had invested heavily in MBSs. From summer 2007 to August 2008, right before Lehman Brothers's collapse, ABCP outstanding fell from almost $1.25 trillion to approximately $745 billion. Investors were only willing to roll over their positions if maturities were shortened or interest rates were increased. FCIC, THE FINANCIAL CRISIS INQUIRY REPORT 246, 251 (2011).

ABCP investors' refusal to refinance forced conduit sponsors to pay off the full value of these maturing ABCP obligations for which they had offered guarantees. In some cases, to protect relationships with their investors, sponsors paid off maturing paper even without guarantees. *See, e.g.*, Robin Sidel et al., *Citigroup Alters Course, Bails Out Affiliated Funds*, WALL ST. J., Dec. 14, 2007. ABCP payoffs had two additional adverse side effects. First, ABCP payoffs forced financial institutions to recognize on their balance sheets the MBS assets that had been stored in ABCP conduits. Consequently, losses on those assets entered the commercial banking and broker-dealer sectors. Second, large cash payments made by sponsors to pay off maturing paper raised concerns about the solvency and liquidity of those institutions. As a result, rates on interbank loans and other funding sources rose, compounding liquidity problems.

Commercial paper runs intensified in the second phase, precipitated by Lehman Brothers's collapse in September 2008. Lehman Brothers's bankruptcy raised serious questions about the viability of other broker-dealers and led to runs on MMFs. As you learned in Chapter 12.3, a major fund, the Reserve Primary Fund, owned more than $785 billion dollars in Lehman Brothers commercial paper. When Lehman Brothers went bankrupt, those investments became practically worthless. News of the Reserve Primary Fund's exposure to Lehman Brothers started a run that quickly spread to other MMFs exposed to commercial paper. MMFs decreased their holdings in commercial paper to honor customer redemptions and to invest in safer assets like Treasuries, which in turn reduced liquidity for large broker-dealers.

Authorities took aggressive measures to stabilize the commercial paper market. The U.S. Treasury halted the run on MMFs by temporarily guaranteeing MMF assets, and the Federal Reserve Board launched numerous programs to support the commercial paper markets, *see* Chapter 9.1, but financial and asset-backed commercial paper continued to plummet. *See* Marcin Kacperczyk & Philipp Schanbl, *When Safe Proved Risky: Commercial Paper During the Financial Crisis of 2007-2009*, 24 J. ECON. PERSP. 29, 38 (2010).

4. Aftermath and Reforms

Commercial paper has declined as a source of wholesale funding. With roughly $250 billion outstanding at the end of 2014, ABCP has experienced the steepest decrease. FSOC, ANNUAL REPORT 57 (2014). One major factor behind the decrease in ABCP is a change to accounting rules that requires sponsors to consolidate ABCP conduits that formerly would have been off-balance sheet. *See* Statement of Financial Accounting Standards No. 166, *Accounting for Transfers of Financial Assets* and Statement of Financial Accounting Standards No. 167, *Amendments to FASB Interpretation No. 46(R).* Sponsors must now hold capital against assets in ABCP conduits, eliminating one of the greatest incentives for their use. *See* Impact of Modifications to Generally Accepted Accounting Principles; Consolidation of Asset-Backed Commercial Paper Programs, 75 Fed. Reg. 4,636 (Jan. 28, 2010). Other developments include efforts to protect against runs on MMFs through reductions in the maturities of MMF assets, as well as redemption gates, liquidity fees, and requiring floating net asset values for certain institutional funds. *See* Chapter 12.3; *see also* Money Market Fund Reform; Amendments to Form PF, 79 Fed. Reg. 47735 (Aug. 14, 2014). Efforts to protect against runs on commercial paper have also been furthered through enhanced capital and liquidity requirements. *See* Chapter 2.7.

B. PRIME BROKERAGE

1. Basics of Prime Brokerage

Prime brokerage refers to a bundle of services that broker-dealers offer to institutional investors such as hedge funds. The bundle includes trade clearing and settlement, accounting, record keeping, cash and securities lending, and holding clients' cash and securities in custody. Prime brokerage provides benefits for prime brokers and their clients. Clients avoid expensive and time consuming back office aspects of running a fund, allowing them to focus on investments. Clients also obtain loans from their prime broker to finance securities purchases. A prime broker can arrange a loan from one prime brokerage client to another, or use client securities as collateral to obtain a secured loan for the client. Clients also use prime brokers to obtain securities for securities lending purposes. The prime broker earns fees for lending, as well as for clearing and settling trades. A prime broker earns interest on direct loans to clients and on client cash deposits or short balances. Most importantly, a prime broker benefits from its ability to rehypothecate, or reuse, client assets.

2. Rehypothecation

A prime broker's ability to rehypothecate client assets provides a pool of collateral that the prime broker can use to enter into securities financing transactions to finance the prime broker's own securities inventory. A U.S.-based prime broker's ability to rehypothecate assets is limited, however, by SEC Rule 15c3-3, also known as the Customer Protection Rule. 17 C.F.R. § 240.15c3-3. Rule 15c3-3 imposes a lockup requirement on broker-dealers. The requirement prohibits prime brokers from reusing client assets representing more than 140% of the value of loans made to that client, and requires that those assets be deposited in a special account at a reserve bank. More importantly, Rule 15c3-3 prohibits prime brokers from using clients' assets to raise more money than it has lent to those clients. To avoid limits on rehypothecation, prime brokers structure their transactions to take advantage of the UK's less restrictive rules. The UK effectively places no limit on the amount of assets that can be rehypothecated or the amount of funds that can be raised through rehypothecation. Consequently, U.S. prime brokers set up UK-based affiliates and transfer client assets there for rehypothecation. Prime brokers' clients typically acquiesce in these arrangements, known as arranged financing, either because the clients believe that prime brokers' use of their assets facilitates lower-priced services or because the clients are unaware of the arrangements.

3. Prime Brokerage and the Financial Crisis

Runs on prime brokerage occurred during the Financial Crisis because of concerns about the solvency of large broker-dealers. These concerns were likely the primary motivating factor in the prime brokerage runs on Bear Stearns and Lehman Brothers. Lehman Brothers's bankruptcy, and the unexpected consequences for Lehman Brothers's prime brokerage clients, accelerated the run on prime brokerage elsewhere. Clients who failed to withdraw their cash deposits or rehypothecated securities from Lehman Brothers's London-based affiliate before the firm collapsed ended up as unsecured creditors in Lehman

Brothers's bankruptcy proceedings. Recall the complexities of Lehman Brothers's cross-border resolution, which we addressed in Chapters 2.4 and 9.3. Under UK law, title in a security passed from a client to the prime broker as soon as the security was rehypothecated. Once title transferred, the client only had a contractual claim for the return of equivalent securities. Even if clients maintained ownership of assets, they were forced to wait for Lehman Brothers's bankruptcy administrator to determine that no outstanding obligations to Lehman Brothers or its subsidiaries existed. This process was slow.

Following Lehman Brothers's collapse, many investors became worried about their exposure to their prime brokers. Many clients were uncertain about where their assets were custodied, how much of their assets had been rehypothecated, and how easy it would be to recover these assets in a bankruptcy. The uncertainty surrounding the health of broker-dealers sparked a massive system-wide run on prime brokerage accounts. Hedge fund clients, with concerns about their own obligations to their investors, rushed to withdraw their cash deposits and securities.

These runs exacerbated acute liquidity problems for large broker-dealers. The basic procyclical pattern of cash shortfalls and forced deleveraging explored in our discussion of bank runs was present here, too. Prime brokerage business became a drain on liquidity in other ways, including through contraction of the collateral pool available for wholesale funding, reduced ability to roll over wholesale funding, client cash calls that forced prime brokers to pull funds from other business segments to meet their clients' demands, and an increase in demand for uncollateralized loans from prime brokers to their clients, which the prime brokers were required to furnish under their brokerage agreements. Preceding Lehman Brothers's collapse, for example, Morgan Stanley reported $800 billion in prime broker accounts it could pledge as collateral for repo, but it reported only $300 billion after the collapse. Darrell Duffie, *Replumbing Our Financial System: Uneven Progress*, 9 INT'L J. CENT. BANKING 251, 275 (2013). One can think of the massive draw-down of credit lines by borrowers in similar terms as a run. *See* Victoria Ivashina & David Scharfstein, *Bank Lending During the Financial Crisis of 2008*, 97 J. FIN. ECON. 319 (2010).

4. Prime Brokerage Reforms

As you recall from Chapter 2.7, significant regulatory efforts have focused on improving the capital and liquidity positions of financial institutions generally. These requirements lower the risk of runs on prime brokerage and ensure that institutions are more resilient if a run does occur, but essential risks remain. Policy-makers are also taking some steps to address prime brokerage risks specifically. For example, the Financial Stability Board (FSB) commissioned an expert group aimed at developing globally-harmonized standards that increase transparency for prime brokerage clients and limit uncertainties surrounding rehypothecation and bankruptcy. FSB, TRANSFORMING SHADOW BANKING INTO RESILIENT MARKET-BASED FINANCING: AN OVERVIEW OF PROGRESS AND A ROADMAP FOR 2015 7 (2014). Standards of this kind would reduce uncertainty about exposure if the prime broker were to fail, thus making runs less likely. In the interim, the FSB has recommended that financial intermediaries increase disclosures to clients, including whether their assets can be or have been rehypothecated. The FSB has also recommended that only firms subject to heightened liquidity regulations should be able to rehypothecate and that firms be barred from rehypothecating client assets to fund their own investments. *See* FSB, STRENGTHENING OVERSIGHT AND REGULATION OF SHADOW BANKING: POLICY FRAMEWORK FOR ADDRESSING SHADOW BANKING RISKS IN SECURITIES LENDING AND REPOS (2013).

Some changes in prime brokerage practices have taken place as clients seek to limit exposure to their prime brokers. In line with the FSB's recommendations, clients are demanding that prime brokers increase reporting, including disclosures on which assets have been rehypothecated. Clients are also demanding greater segregation of their assets so that they are better protected in bankruptcy. Clients are increasingly requiring use of custodians, relying on multiple prime brokers, and placing limits on rehypothecation. *See* ALARNA CARLSSON-SWEENY, TRENDS IN PRIME BROKERAGE (2010).

C. DERIVATIVES

1. Loss of Derivatives Collateral

Recall from Chapter 11.2 that derivatives counterparties post cash collateral, known as initial margin, and also post additional collateral, known as variation margin, to cover any adverse change in their position under the derivative contract. While both initial and variation margin are meant to protect the broker-dealer against non-payment by its counterparty, margin also serves as a source of rehypothecable wholesale funding that broker-dealers use to finance securities inventories. As of 2009, approximately $2 trillion in derivatives collateral was rehypothecated in this way. *See* Manmohan Singh, *Under-Collateralisation and Rehypothecation in the OTC Derivatives Markets*, 14 FIN. STABILITY REV. 113, 116 (2010). Runs on derivatives contracts—and the concomitant reduction in margin collateral—contributed to the rapid loss of liquidity during the Financial Crisis. Fears about the solvency of broker-dealers encouraged derivative counterparties to refuse to renew expiring derivative contracts. The loss of margin collateral, without new derivatives contracts to replenish it, weakened the liquidity of reeling broker-dealers.

2. Derivatives Runs as a Source of Contagion

Broker-dealers that were perceived as weak were also harmed by a second type of run on their derivatives contracts in the form of counterparties rushing to get out of the other side of their trades. Parties looking to escape a contract would either assign their position to a third-party or bring another party into the transaction through novation. The fact that counterparties wanted to avoid exposure to certain broker-dealers heightened fears that those broker-dealers were insolvent, accelerating runs on other sources of wholesale funding. When a broker-dealer could not step into trades, it further induced fear. Consider the following excerpt from the FCIC's final report.

FCIC, March 2008: The Fall of Bear Stearns

The Financial Crisis Inquiry Report (2011)

Hayman Capital Partners, a hedge fund in Texas wanting to decrease its exposure to subprime mortgages, had decided to close out a relatively small $5 million subprime derivative position with Goldman Sachs. Bear Stearns offered the best bid, so Hayman expected to assign its position to Bear, which would then become Goldman's counterparty in the derivative. Hayman notified Goldman by a routine email on Tuesday, March 11, at 4:06 P.M. The reply 41 minutes later was unexpected: "GS does not consent to this trade."

That startled Kyle Bass, Hayman's managing partner. He told the FCIC he could not recall any counterparty rejecting a routine novation. Pressed for an explanation, Goldman the next morning offered no details: "Our trading desk would prefer to stay facing Hayman. We do not want to face Bear." Adding to the mystery, 16 minutes later Goldman agreed to accept Bear Stearns as the counterparty after all. But the damage was done. The news hit the street that Goldman refused a routine transaction with one of the other big five investment banks. The message: don't rely on Bear Stearns. . . .

[T]he run on Bear accelerated . . . On Wednesday, March 12, the SEC notes that Bear paid . . . $1.1 billion for margin calls from 142 nervous derivative counterparties. . . . Worries about a default quickly mounted.

---

3. Accelerating Margin Calls

The accelerating margin calls on CDS contracts was a third example of run-like behavior on derivatives contracts during the Financial Crisis. Margin calls played a key role in AIG's near-collapse. AIG disputed its counterparties' margin calls, but it eventually posted approximately $35 billion to 16 counterparties to satisfy its obligations. Cash outflows were particularly damaging because AIG had not entered into any offsetting derivative contracts to protect itself from losses on its CDS book, which further strained AIG's already precarious liquidity position and contributed to its eventual bailout. *See* FCIC, THE FINANCIAL CRISIS INQUIRY REPORT 269 (2011).

4. Derivatives Reforms

As discussed in Part XI, several recent reforms under Title VII and VIII of the Dodd-Frank Act and foreign legislation aim to mitigate dangers posed by runs on derivative contracts. Most importantly, the introduction of clearinghouses makes counterparties less likely to run, as they will be less fearful of a clearinghouse default than of a financial firm counterparty default. The migration of an increasing number of derivatives contracts to clearinghouses also minimizes the risk of disputes over the value of reference securities. Uncleared swaps face higher margin requirements. Capital requirements for derivatives dealers also provides a bigger cushion against failure. Data reporting should improve transparency throughout the market, reducing uncertainty.

IV. ASSESSING THE REGULATORY RESPONSE

A. SUMMARY OF REFORMS AFFECTING WHOLESALE FUNDING RISK

In addition to the reforms discussed in this Chapter with respect to particular financing techniques, we have discussed reforms affecting short-term wholesale funding elsewhere in this book. You may want to review those sections now that you have a better understanding of short-term wholesale funding and the mechanics of broker-dealer failure during the Financial Crisis. We summarize some of these other reforms here.

- **Prudential Standards and Affiliation Rules (Chapter 2.3). The** Dodd-Frank Act updates various prudential standards, such as interbank lending limits, limits on loans to one borrower, limits on the exposure of financial institutions to one another, and limits on transactions with affiliates to include securities financing transactions.
- **Deposit Insurance Assessments (Chapter 2.4).** Under the Dodd-Frank Act, deposit insurance assessments are based on total liabilities, which has the effect of taxing wholesale funding for the first time.
- **Capital and Liquidity (Chapter 2.7).** Enhanced capital and liquidity requirements and changes in accounting rules reduce the risk of runs on wholesale funding. Moreover, as implemented in the United States, the systemically important financial institution (SIFI) surcharge increases if the firm relies more heavily on short-term wholesale funding.
- **SIFI Designation (Chapter 6.2).** The Dodd-Frank Act authorizes the Financial Stability Oversight Council (FSOC) to designate systemic non-bank entities to be supervised by the Federal Reserve Board. Designated firms are subject to enhanced capital, liquidity, and other requirements.
- **Resolution (Chapter 9.2).** The Dodd-Frank Act establishes a resolution authority and living wills designed in part to reduce the risk that a run on short-term wholesale funding would destabilize the financial system.
- **Mutual Funds (Chapter 10.2).** The SEC has proposed to allow mutual funds to use derivatives if they meet portfolio exposure limits, asset segregation requirements, and derivative risk management standards.
- **Derivatives (Chapter 11.2).** Derivatives clearinghouses may reduce the risk of a sudden, simultaneous unwind of derivative contracts, as well as the risk of fire sales and attendant loss of liquidity. Exchange and swap execution facility trading may make positions in derivatives contracts easier to value, and thus firms should be able to better manage their risk. Margin rules should increase buffers in the system.
- **Securitization (Chapter 12.1).** The Dodd-Frank Act requires increased transparency, risk-retention, and credit rating agency reforms. Accounting rules have changed to require balance sheet recognition of most common securitization structures, and Basel III requires sponsors to hold capital against potential losses. These reforms are designed to reduce the likelihood that investors would be faced with sudden changes in perceived value from seemingly riskless investments to risky ones, potentially lessening the risk of sudden runs by securitization creditors.
- **MMF Reforms (Chapter 12.3).** MMF reforms are intended to make MMF funds less susceptible to runs. For example, the weighted average life of MMFs has been capped at lower levels to reduce maturity

transformation, portfolio quality requirements have increased, certain institutional MMFs are required to float their net asset values, and certain MMFs are authorized to use redemption gates and fees (although the effects of these measures may be mixed).

Despite these changes, many believe that significant risks remain in wholesale funding markets. There are not yet uniform rules for SFT haircuts or collateral, MMFs continue to be subject to run risks, SEC capital and liquidity requirements for broker-dealers have changed little since the Financial Crisis, and the securitization market and credit rating agencies are still sources of risk despite substantial reforms. Professor Michael Barr has called for further efforts to tax short-term debt, *see SOTU: What Obama Still Needs to Address*, CNBC, Jan. 12, 2016, as have others. *See, e.g.*, Luigi Zingales, *A Tax on Short-Term Debt Would Stabilise the System*, FIN. TIMES, Dec. 16, 2009. Others argue, by contrast, that the upshot of reform is reduced liquidity that makes the system more volatile. *See, e.g.*, Douglas J. Elliott, *Is There a Problem With Liquidity in the Financial Markets?*, BROOKINGS INST., June 16, 2015. The next sections describe further reforms and invite conversation regarding alternative ways of conceptualizing and responding to risks in wholesale funding.

B. DATA COLLECTION

Regulators and private market participants are still quite in the dark about many aspects of short-term wholesale funding markets, but they are making progress towards enhancing transparency in key areas. Regulators are hopeful that enhanced transparency will allow them to map the interconnectedness of firms more easily and track build-ups of systemic risk in the global financial system. Transparency will also improve their ability to weigh the benefits and drawbacks of different policy choices. The FSB has made numerous recommendations to national authorities regarding what kind of data to collect and the form that the data should take. The FSB is also collecting data gathered by national regulators to monitor global trends in wholesale funding markets. *See* FSB, TRANSFORMING SHADOW BANKING INTO RESILIENT MARKET-BASED FINANCE: AN OVERVIEW OF PROGRESS (2015). In the United States, the Federal Reserve System, SEC, and OFR have made strides in data collection. The Federal Reserve System has increased data collection through its supervisory powers. The SEC has proposed a rule to expand repo and securities lending data reporting, in accordance with § 984(b) of the Dodd-Frank Act. *See* Press Release, SEC: SEC Proposes Rule to Modernize and Enhance Information Reported by Investment Companies and Investment Advisers (May 20, 2015). The OFR is undertaking an initiative to create a uniform, global identification code, which will give regulators a clearer picture of which firms are transacting with one another, and the level of their interconnectedness.

C. MANDATORY HAIRCUTS

U.S. and international policy-makers have been working on new haircut standards for SFTs. In 2014, the FSB proposed qualitative standards for market participants to calculate haircuts, as well as a theoretical framework for determining numerical haircut floors on certain SFTs. *See* FSB, STRENGTHENING OVERSIGHT AND REGULATION OF SHADOW BANKING: REGULATORY FRAMEWORK

FOR HAIRCUTS ON NON-CENTRALLY CLEARED SECURITIES FINANCING TRANSACTIONS (2014). Haircuts provide a cushion in the event of deterioration in the value of collateral. Haircut floors seek to increase this cushion. The effect of haircut floors is to tax the transactions, thus reducing their use. *See* Michael S. Barr, *The Financial Crisis and the Path of Reform*, 29 YALE J. ON REG. 91, 106 (2012). The haircut floors would reduce leverage and reduce firms' over-reliance on SFTs to finance their investment portfolios, only to watch that funding disappear through rapidly rising haircuts required by counterparties in times of crisis. Federal Reserve Board Governor Daniel Tarullo has said that the United States plans to implement its own version of the collateral floor framework:

> [The Federal Reserve Board] will be developing a regulation that would establish minimum haircuts for [SFTs] on a market-wide basis, rather than just for specific classes of market participants. . . . A system of numerical haircut floors for SFTs would require any entity that wants to borrow against a security to post a minimum amount of excess margin to its lender, with the amount varying depending on the asset class of the collateral. Like the minimum margin requirements that U.S. regulators have imposed on derivatives contracts, numerical floors for SFT haircuts would serve as a mechanism for limiting the build-up of leverage in the system. They could also mitigate the risk to financial stability posed by pro-cyclical margin calls during times of financial stress, since putting a regulatory floor under SFT haircuts during good times would reduce the amount by which they would increase during periods of stress.

Address at the Brookings Inst.: Thinking Critically About Nonbank Financial Intermediation (Nov. 17, 2015). The Federal Reserve Board might pursue mandatory haircuts under its authority pursuant to the Securities Exchange Act of 1934 or under the Dodd-Frank Act's Title VIII authorities with respect to systemic activities. Some, however, have cautioned that mandatory haircuts would impair financial intermediary's core funding and thereby decrease the efficiency and liquidity of financial markets. *See, e.g.*, EUROPEAN PARLIAMENT, DIRECTORATE GENERAL FOR INTERNAL POLICIES, SHADOW BANKING—MINIMUM HAIRCUTS ON COLLATERAL 45 (2013); *see also* Brian Begalle et al., *Are Higher Haircuts Better? A Paradox*, Liberty St. Econ. (Aug. 19, 2013). Do you think mandatory haircuts are a good idea?

D. TITLE VIII OF THE DODD-FRANK ACT

The Dodd-Frank Act's Title VIII is one tool that regulators might rely on more heavily in the future if current reform efforts prove to be insufficient. As discussed in various sections of Chapters 6.2, 7.2, and 11.2, under Title VIII, the FSOC has authority to designate "financial market utilities or payment clearing or settlement activities that the [FSOC] determines are, or are likely to become systemically important. . . ." 12 U.S.C. § 5463(a)(1).

Designating systemic activities could enable regulators to prescribe rules that apply to short-term wholesale funding or other risks from activities that cross sectors. For example, regulations could mandate the quality of collateral to be used and margin haircuts to be applied for repo and securities lending transactions. Regulations could also govern rehypothecation, segregation of client assets, disclosures, and other clearing and settlement procedures. These rules would apply market-wide because both the relevant activities to be designated and the financial institutions that the rules would cover are broadly defined. *See* 12 U.S.C. §§ 5462(5), (7). Title VIII could be used to reduce risks throughout shadow banking, including risks from systemic activities in MMFs, hedge funds, asset managers, and other sectors. For example, regulators might designate the activity of stable value MMF's purchasing financial commercial paper without a capital buffer as a systemic activity.

E. CRITIQUING THE CURRENT APPROACH TO WHOLESALE FUNDING

Some have proposed that the current approach to regulating short-term wholesale funding, which might be characterized as taxing its use, *see* Barr, *The Financial Crisis and the Path of Reform,* at 106, be abandoned in favor of direct regulation. Professor Morgan Ricks has argued that firms should be forced to obtain a license before using short-term wholesale funding. In exchange, the government would insure short-term wholesale investors. Ricks's plan would effectively recreate deposit insurance for wholesale funding. *See* Morgan Ricks, *Reforming the Short-Term Funding Markets* (Harv. John M. Olin Cen. for L., Econ., & Bus., Discussion Paper No. 713, 2012). Ricks has proposed barring non-bank financial institutions from engaging in maturity transformation and limiting maturity transformation to depository institutions subject to tighter portfolio constraints. Depository institutions would pay risk-based insurance premiums to the FDIC, and all deposits would be fully insured without limit. Ricks argues this approach would be panic-proof. *See* Morgan Ricks, *A Simpler Approach to Financial Reform,* REGULATION (Winter 2013–14). The fundamental point Ricks makes is that short-term wholesale funding is equivalent to the creation of money, and money creation needs to be constrained by government, just as it has done for retail bank deposits. *See* MORGAN RICKS, THE MONEY PROBLEM: RETHINKING FINANCIAL REGULATION (Univ. of Chicago Press 2015). Some market participants, by contrast, contend that any further reforms to short-term wholesale funding should come through market-driven change. *See, e.g.*, BNY MELLON, THE FUTURE OF WHOLESALE FUNDING MARKETS (2015).

Others argue that wholesale funding, rather than being taxed *ex ante*, as proposed by Barr, or insured *ex post*, as proposed by Ricks, should be penalized *ex post* such as by removing exemptions from the automatic stay in bankruptcy and other measures. *See, e.g.*, Stephen J. Lubben, *The Bankruptcy Code Without Safe Harbors*, 84 AM. BANKR. L.J. 123 (2010). We discuss the automatic stay and several other important conceptual issues in the notes below.

---

1. ***Repo in Bankruptcy.*** Repos are exempt from the automatic stay in a bankruptcy. If a repo borrower goes bankrupt, repo lenders are allowed to terminate the repo agreement, liquidate the collateral, and retain the proceeds. Repos were granted this safe harbor to discourage runs. Some academics have called for the elimination of this safe harbor, arguing that it encourages over-extension of credit in the repo market, leads to less monitoring of repo borrowers by repo lenders, and facilitates collateral fire sales in the event of a default. *See id.*; *see also* Darrell Duffie & David A. Skeel, Jr., *A Dialogue on the Costs and*

Benefits of Automatic Stays for Derivatives and Repurchase Agreements (Inst. for L. and Econ. Research Paper No. 12-2, 2012). *But see* Mark D. Scherrill, *In Defense of the Bankruptcy Code's Safe Harbors*, 70 BUS. LAW. 1007 (2015). Recall that under the Federal Deposit Insurance Act and Title II of the Dodd-Frank Act, the FDIC has the power to delay by one business day (essentially the end of the day on Monday) any close-out of repos. *See* Chapters 9.2 and 9.3.

2. ***Repo Resolution Authority.*** Some academics have proposed creating a Repo Resolution Authority that would purchase and resell illiquid collateral from repo lenders in the event of a borrower default. Repo lenders would be unable to sell repo collateral to any entity other than the Repo Resolution Authority. The Repo Resolution Authority would purchase the collateral at a predefined haircut and eventually sell the collateral in an orderly fashion. The FSB notes, however, that creating a Repo Resolution Authority would involve significant practical difficulties. Bankruptcy reform or contractual provisions waiving the right to use the exemption from automatic stay would be required. *See* Viral V. Acharya & T. Sabri Öncü, *A Proposal for the Resolution of Systemically Important Assets and Liabilities: The Case of the Repo Market*, 9 INT'L J. CENT. BANKING 291 (2013).

3. ***Tri-Party Clearing as a Utility.*** Professor Darrell Duffie has proposed replacing clearing banks with a "dedicated tri-party repo utility." Darrell Duffie, *Replumbing Our Financial System: Uneven Progress*, 9 INT'L J. CENT. BANKING 251, 266 (2013). Do you think that the clearing function should remain in the clearing banks, or be moved to a utility, outside of large, complex financial institutions that engage in a variety of risk-taking activities, as Duffie suggests? Would such a move eliminate the risks or merely change their location?

4. ***A Private Solution?*** The FICC submitted a proposal to the SEC in which it would take over some of the clearing functions from the major clearing banks. The FICC argues that it can eliminate the risk of disorderly fire sales though centralized liquidation techniques. *See* Press Release, Depository Tr. and Clearing Corp.: DTCC Proposes Central Clearing for the U.S. $1.6 Trillion Institutional Tri-Party Repo Market (Oct. 15, 2014). What do you think?

5. ***Creating Safe Assets.*** Should the government issue more short-term debt to provide safe assets the financial sector can use instead of securitized financial products such as MBS? Several scholars have advocated this approach. One group, including former Treasury Secretary Lawrence Summers, asserts that "an expansion in T-bill supply would lower the premium on short-term money-like debt and reduce the temptation for private intermediaries to issue short." Robin Greenwood et al., *Government Debt Management at the Zero Lower Bound* 36 (Hutchins Ctr. on Fiscal & Monetary Pol'y, Working Paper No. 5, 2014). *But see* Gary B. Gorton et al., *The Safe Asset Share* 11 (Nat'l Bureau of Econ. Research, Working Paper No. 17,777, 2012). What are the pros and cons of this approach?

GLOSSARY

Term/ Acronym	Meaning
1933 Act	Securities Act of 1933
1934 Act	Securities Exchange Act of 1934
1940 Act	Investment Company Act of 1940
ABCP	asset-backed commercial paper
ABS	asset-backed security
ACA	Patient Protection and Affordable Care Act of 2010
ACH	Automated Clearing House
AIFMD	EU Alternative Investment Fund Managers Directive
ALLL	allowance for loan and lease losses
AML	anti-money laundering
APA	Administrative Procedure Act of 1946
APR	annual percentage rate
ATM	automated teller machine
ATS	alternative trading system
Basel I	Basel Capital Accord
Basel II	The Basel II Framework for Capital Adequacy
Basel III	The Basel III Framework for Capital Adequacy
Basel Committee	The Basel Committee on Banking Supervision
BBA	British Bankers' Association
BCCI	Bank of Credit and Commerce International
BHC	bank holding company
BHCA	Bank Holding Company Act of 1956
BRRD	EU Bank Recovery and Resolution Directive
BSA	Bank Secrecy Act of 1970
Call Report	Report of Condition and Income
CARD Act	Credit Card Responsibility and Disclosure Act of 2009
CBOT	Chicago Board of Trade
CCAR	Comprehensive Capital Analysis and Review
CCS	Comprehensive, consolidated supervision
CDO	collateralized debt obligation
CDS	credit default swap
CEA	Commodity Exchange Act of 1936
CEBA	Competitive Equality Banking Act of 1987
CFMA	Commodity Futures Modernization Act of 2000

Term/ Acronym	Meaning
CFPB	Consumer Financial Protection Bureau
CFTC	Commodity Futures Trading Commission
CHIPS	Clearing House Interbank Payments System
CLS	Continuous Linked Settlement
CRA	Community Reinvestment Act of 1977
CSE	Consolidated Supervised Entity
CVV	card verification value
D-SIB	Domestic Systemically Important Bank
DCM	Designated Contract Market
DCO	Derivatives Clearing Organization
DIDMCA	The Depository Institutions Deregulation and Monetary Control Act of 1980
DIF	Deposit Insurance Fund
DINB	Deposit Insurance National Bank
Dodd-Frank Act	Dodd-Frank Wall Street Reform and Consumer Protection Act of 2010
DOJ	U.S. Department of Justice
EBIT	earnings before interest and tax
EBITDA	earnings before (deducting) interest, tax, depreciation, and amortization
ECN	electronic communication network
ECOA	Equal Credit Opportunity Act of 1974
EEA	The European Economic Area
EESA	Emergency Economic Stabilization Act of 2008
EFTA	Electronic Funds Transfer Act of 1978
EMIR	European Market Infrastructure Regulation
EPS	enhanced prudential standards
ERISA	Employee Retirement Income Security Act of 1974
ESMA	European Securities and Markets Authority
ETF	exchange-traded fund
EU	European Union
Fannie Mae	The Federal National Mortgage Association
FASB	Financial Accounting Standards Board
FATF	Financial Action Task Force
FBO	foreign banking organization
FBSEA	Foreign Bank Supervision Enhancement Act of 1991
FCA	Financial Conduct Authority
FCIC	Financial Crisis Inquiry Commission
FDIA	Federal Deposit Insurance Act of 1950
FDIC	Federal Deposit Insurance Corporation

Term/ Acronym	Meaning
FDICIA	Federal Deposit Insurance Corporation Improvement Act of 1991
Federal Reserve Board	The Board of Governors of the Federal Reserve System
Federal Reserve System	The system comprised of twelve regional Federal Reserve Banks and the Federal Reserve Board
FFIEC	Federal Financial Institutions Examination Council
FHA	Federal Housing Administration
FHC	financial holding company
FHFA	Federal Housing Finance Agency
FHLB	Federal Home Loan Bank
FICC	Fixed Income Clearing Corporation
Financial Crisis	financial crisis of 2007–08
FINRA	Financial Industry Regulatory Authority
FIO	Federal Insurance Office
FIRREA	Financial Institutions Reform, Recovery, and Enforcement Act of 1989
First Bank	First Bank of the United States
FMU	financial market utility
FOMC	Federal Open Market Committee
Freddie Mac	The Federal Home Loan Mortgage Corporation
FSA	Financial Services Authority
FSA	federal savings association
FSB	federal savings bank
FSB	Financial Stability Board
FSOC	Financial Stability Oversight Council
FTC	Federal Trade Commission
FX	foreign exchange
G-8	Canada, France, Germany, Italy, Japan, Russia, the United Kingdom, the United States
G-20	Argentina, Australia, Brazil, Canada, China, France, Germany, India, Indonesia, Italy, Japan, Mexico, Russia, Saudi Arabia, South Africa, South Korea, Turkey, the United Kingdom, the United States, the EU
G-SIB	Global Systemically Important Bank
G-SII	Global Systemically Important Insurer
GAAP	Generally Accepted Accounting Principles
GAO	Government Accountability Office
Garn-St Germain Act	Garn-St Germain Depository Institutions Act of 1982
GCF	General Collateral Finance
Ginnie Mae	The Government National Mortgage Association

Term/ Acronym	Meaning
Glass-Steagall Act	The Glass-Steagall Act provisions of the Banking Act of 1933
GLBA	Gramm-Leach-Bliley Act of 1999
GSE	government sponsored enterprise
HAMP	Home Affordable Modification Program
HHI	Herfindahl-Hirschman Index
HMDA	Home Mortgage Disclosure Act of 1975
HOEPA	Home Ownership and Equity Protection Act of 1994
HOLA	Home Owners' Loan Act of 1933
HUD	U.S. Department of Housing and Urban Development
IAIS	International Association of Insurance Supervisors
IAP	institution-affiliated party
IBA	International Banking Act of 1978
IBF	international banking facility
ICB	Independent Commission on Banking
IDI	insured depository institution
IHC	intermediate holding company
ILC	industrial loan company
IMF	International Monetary Fund
IPO	initial public offering
IOSCO	International Organization of Securities Commissions
ISDA	International Swaps and Derivatives Association
JOBS Act	Jumpstart Our Business Startups Act of 2012
KYC	know your customer
LIBOR	London Interbank Offered Rate
LMI	low-and-moderate income
M&A	merger and acquisition
MBS	mortgage-backed security
Member Bank	A bank that is part of the U.S Federal Reserve System
MERS	Mortgage Electronic Registration Systems
MiFID	EU Markets in Financial Instruments Directive
MMF	money market mutual fund
MOU	memorandum of understanding
MSBSP	major security-based swap participant
MSP	major swap participant
NAIC	National Association of Insurance Commissioners
NARAB	National Association of Registered Agents and Brokers
NASD	National Association of Securities Dealers
NAV	net asset value

Term/ Acronym	Meaning
NBNI G-SIFI	Non-Bank, Non-Insurer Systemically Important Financial Institution
NCUA	National Credit Union Administration
NFA	National Futures Association
NMS	national market system
Non-Member Bank	A bank that is not a member of the U.S Federal Reserve System
NRSRO	nationally recognized statistical rating organization
NSMIA	National Securities Markets Improvement Act of 1996
NYDFS	New York Department of Financial Services
NYSE	New York Stock Exchange
OCC	Office of the Comptroller of the Currency
OECD	Organization for Economic Cooperation and Development
OFAC	Office of Foreign Assets Control
OFHEO	Office of Federal Housing Enterprise Oversight
OFR	Office of Financial Research
OLA	Orderly Liquidation Authority
OTC	over-the-counter
OTS	Office of Thrift Supervision
P&A	purchase and assumption
PBGC	Pension Benefit Guaranty Corporation
PCS	payment, clearing, and settlement
PIN	personal identification number
PLMA	Producer Licensing Model Act
QFBO	Qualifying Foreign Banking Organization
QFC	qualified financial contract
QM	qualified mortgage
QRM	qualified residential mortgage
QTL	Qualified Thrift Lender
Repo	repurchase agreement
RESPA	Real Estate Settlement Procedures Act of 1974
Riegle-Neal Act	The Riegle-Neal Interstate Banking and Branching Efficiency Act of 1994
ROA	return on total assets
ROE	return on equity
RTC	Resolution Trust Corporation
Sarbanes-Oxley Act	The Sarbanes-Oxley Act of 2002
SBSD	security-based swap dealer
SCAP	Supervisory Capital Assessment Program

Term/ Acronym	Meaning
SD	swap dealer
SDR	Swap Data Repository
SEC	Securities and Exchange Commission
Second Bank	Second Bank of the United States
Section 23A	Section 23A of the Federal Reserve Act, 12 U.S.C. § 371(c)
Section 23B	Section 23B of the Federal Reserve Act, 12 U.S.C. § 371(c)-1
SEF	swap execution facility
SEUA	South-Eastern Underwriters Association
SFT	securities financing transaction
SIDCO	systemically important derivatives clearing organization
SIFI	Systemically Important Financial Institution
SIFMA	Securities Industry and Financial Markets Association
SIPC	Securities Investor Protection Corporation
SLHC	Savings and Loan Holding Company
SPOE	single point of entry
SRO	self-regulatory organization
State-chartered bank	A bank that is chartered by a state authority, rather than by the OCC as a national bank
TAF	Term Auction Facility
TARP	Troubled Asset Relief Program
Thrift	A name used to describe savings association and savings bank charters collectively
Tier 1	tier 1 capital
Tier 2	tier 2 capital
TILA	Truth in Lending Act of 1968
TLAC	total loss-absorbing capacity
Treasury	U.S Department of the Treasury
UDAAP	unfair, deceptive, or abusive acts or practices
USA PATRIOT Act	Uniting and Strengthening America by Providing Appropriate Tools Required to Intercept and Obstruct Terrorism Act of 2001
Volcker Rule	Section 619 of the Dodd-Frank Act, codified in Section 13 of the Bank Holding Company Act and its Implementing Regulations

INDEX

References are to Pages